THE NAVARRE BIBLE

NEW TESTAMENT

OTHER VOLUMES IN THIS SERIES

THE NAVARRE BIBLE

NEW TESTAMENT

in the Revised Standard Version and New Vulgate
with a commentary by members of the
Faculty of Theology of the University of Navarre

FOUR COURTS PRESS • DUBLIN
SCEPTER PUBLISHERS • NEW YORK

Nihil obstat: Gerard Deighan, MA, BD, LSS, *censor deputatus*.
Imprimi potest: Diarmuid, Archbishop of Dublin, 21 July 2008

Typeset for
FOUR COURTS PRESS
7 Malpas Street, Dublin 8, Ireland.
www.fourcourtspress.ie
and in North America for
SCEPTER PUBLISHERS, INC.
P.O. Box 211, New York, NY 10018-0004
www.scepterpub.org

A catalogue record for this title
is available from the British Library.

ISBN 978-1-84682-147-9 (Four Courts Press)
ISBN 978-1594170-75-1 (Scepter Publishers)

First edition 2008; reprinted 2011, 2013, 2017.

Library of Congress Cataloging-in-Publication Data [for first volume in this series]

Bible. O.T. English. Revised Standard. 1999.
    The Navarre Bible. – North American ed.
       p.   cm
    "The Books of Genesis, Exodus, Leviticus, Numbers, Deuteronomy in the Revised Standard Version and New Vulgate
      with a commentary by members of the
      Faculty of Theology of the University of Navarre."
    Includes bibliographical references.
    Contents: [1] The Pentateuch.
    ISBN 1–889334–21–9 (hardback: alk. paper)
I. Title.
    BS891.A1   1999.P75   99–23033
    221.7'7—dc21   CIP

ACKNOWLEDGMENTS

Original title: *Sagrada Biblia: Nuevo Testamento*
Quotations from Vatican II documents are based on
the translation in *Vatican Council II:
The Conciliar and Post Conciliar Documents*,
ed. A. Flannery, OP (Dublin 1981).

The New Vulgate, Editio typica altera text of the Bible can be accessed via http://www.vatican.va.archive/bible/index.htm;
it is © Libreria Editrice Vaticana 1906

Printed and bound in Spain by Grafo, S.A.

Contents

Contents

Preface and Preliminary Notes

The Commentary

The distinguishing feature of the *Navarre Bible* is its commentary on the biblical text. Compiled by members of the Theology faculty of the University of Navarre, Pamplona, Spain, this commentary draws on writings of the Fathers, texts of the Magisterium of the Church, and works of spiritual writers, including St Josemaría Escrivá, the founder of Opus Dei; it was he who in the late 1960s entrusted the faculty at Navarre with the project of making a translation of the Bible and adding to it a commentary of the type found here.

The commentary, which is not particularly technical, is designed to explain the biblical text and to identify its main points, the message God wants to get across through the sacred writers. It also deals with doctrinal and practical matters connected with the text.

The first volume of the *Navarre Bible* (the English edition) came out in 1985 — first, twelve volumes covering the New Testament; then seven volumes covering the Old Testament. Many reprints and revised editions have appeared over the past twenty years. All the various volumes are currently in print.

The present volume does not replace the twelve New Testament volumes. Its commentary is different, although it overlaps with theirs to a degree; it often draws on the *Catechism of the Catholic Church* (which they do not); it is also shorter, but it covers the biblical text passage by passage.

The Revised Standard Version

The English translation of the Bible used in the *Navarre Bible* is the Revised Standard Version (RSV) which is, as its preface states, "an authorized revision of the American Standard Version, published in 1901, which was a revision of the King James Version [the "Authorized Version"], published in 1611".

The RSV of the entire Bible was published in 1952; its Catholic edition (RSVCE) appeared in 1966. The differences between the RSV and the RSVCE New Testament texts are listed in the "Explanatory Notes" in the end-matter of this volume. Whereas the Spanish editors of what is called in English the "Navarrre Bible" made a new translation of the Bible, for the English edition the RSV has proved to be a very appropriate choice of translation. The publishers of the *Navarre Bible* wish to thank the Division of Christian Education of the National Council of the Churches of Christ in the USA for permission to use that text.

The Latin Text

This volume also carries the official Latin version of the New Testament in the *editio typica altera* of the New Vulgate (Vatican City, 1986).

PRELIMINARY NOTES

The *headings* within the biblical text have been provided by the editors (they are not taken from the RSV). A full list of these headings, giving an over-view of the New Testament, can be found at the back of the volume.

An asterisk *beside a heading* indicates that the corresponding commentary/note is more general than usual — that is, it explains and discusses the structure or the content of a part or section of the text. A reader may find it helpful to read these asterisked notes before reading the biblical text to which they refer.

An asterisk *inside the biblical text* signals an RSVCE 'Explanatory Note' at the end of the volume.

Marginal references in **bold** type indicate parallel texts in other biblical books; references in *italics* have to do with Old Testament passages being quoted by the New Testament writer. All the marginal references come from the *Navarre Bible* editors, not the RSV.

Abbreviations

1. BOOKS OF HOLY SCRIPTURE

Acts	Acts of the Apostles	1 Kings	1 Kings
Amos	Amos	2 Kings	2 Kings
Bar	Baruch	Lam	Lamentations
1 Chron	1 Chronicles	Lev	Leviticus
2 Chron	2 Chronicles	Lk	Luke
Col	Colossians	1 Mac	1 Maccabees
1 Cor	1 Corinthians	2 Mac	2 Maccabees
2 Cor	2 Corinthians	Mal	Malachi
Dan	Daniel	Mic	Micah
Deut	Deuteronomy	Mk	Mark
Eccles	Ecclesiastes (Qoheleth)	Mt	Matthew
Esther	Esther	Nah	Nahum
Eph	Ephesians	Neh	Nehemiah
Ex	Exodus	Num	Numbers
Ezek	Ezekiel	Obad	Obadiah
Ezra	Ezra	1 Pet	1 Peter
Gal	Galatians	2 Pet	2 Peter
Gen	Genesis	Phil	Philippians
Hab	Habakkuk	Philem	Philemon
Hag	Haggai	Ps	Psalms
Heb	Hebrews	Prov	Proverbs
Hos	Hosea	Rev	Revelation (Apocalypse)
Is	Isaiah	Rom	Romans
Jas	James	Ruth	Ruth
Jer	Jeremiah	1 Sam	1 Samuel
Jn	John	2 Sam	2 Samuel
1 Jn	1 John	Sir	Sirach (Ecclesiasticus)
2 Jn	2 John	Song	Song of Solomon
3 Jn	3 John	1 Thess	1 Thessalonians
Job	Job	2 Thess	2 Thessalonians
Joel	Joel	1 Tim	1 Timothy
Jon	Jonah	2 Tim	2 Timothy
Josh	Joshua	Tit	Titus
Jud	Judith	Wis	Wisdom
Jude	Jude	Zech	Zechariah
Judg	Judges	Zeph	Zephaniah

2. OTHER ABBREVIATIONS

ad loc.	*ad locum*, commentary on this passage
AAS	*Acta Apostolicae Sedis*
Apost.	Apostolic

can.	canon
chap.	chapter
cf.	*confer*, compare
Const.	Constitution
Decl.	Declaration
DS	Denzinger-Schönmetzer, *Enchiridion Biblicum* (4th edition, Naples & Rome, 1961)
Enc.	Encyclical
Exhort.	Exhortation
f	and following (*pl.* ff)
ibid.	*ibidem*, in the same place
in loc.	*in locum,* commentary on this passage
loc.	*locum*, place or passage
par.	parallel passages
Past.	Pastoral
RSV	Revised Standard Version
RSVCE	Revised Standard Version, Catholic Edition
SCDF	Sacred Congregation for the Doctrine of the Faith
sess.	session
v.	verse (*pl.* vv.)

"Sources Quoted in This Volume", which appears at the end of this book, explains other abbreviations used.

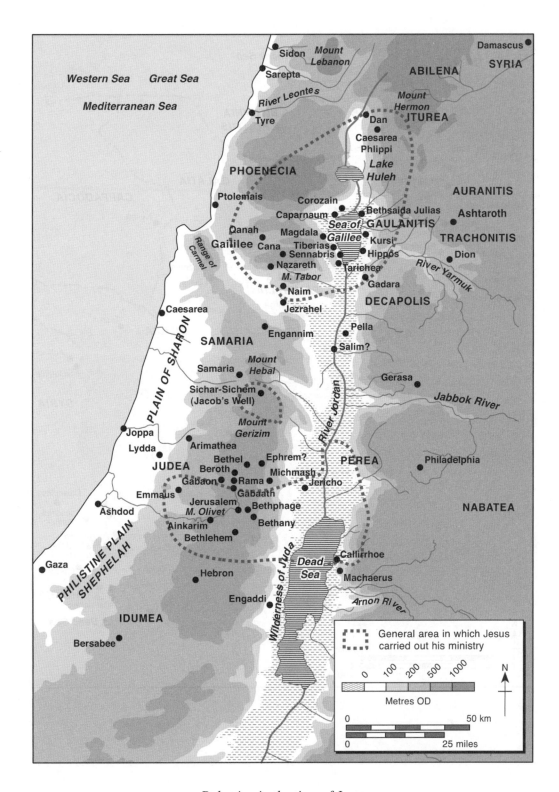

Palestine in the time of Jesus

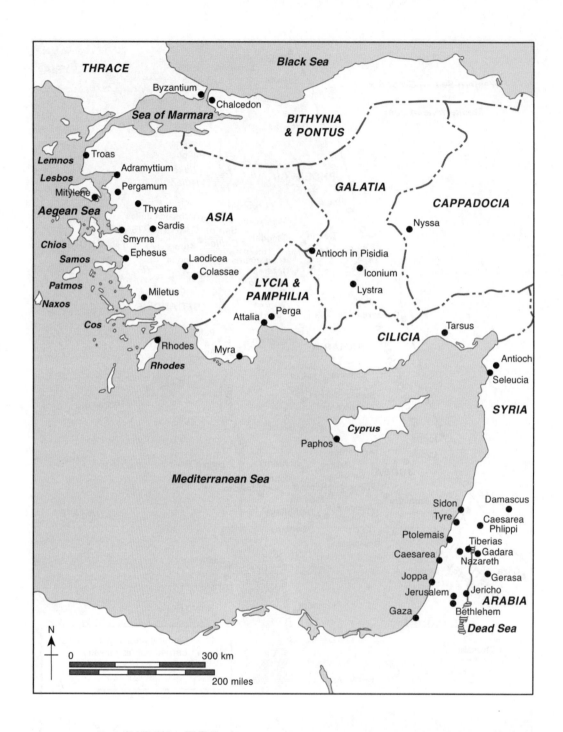

The Eastern Mediterranean Sea in the first century AD

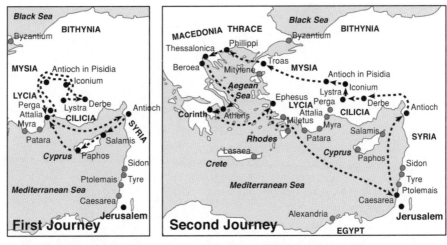

First Journey

Second Journey

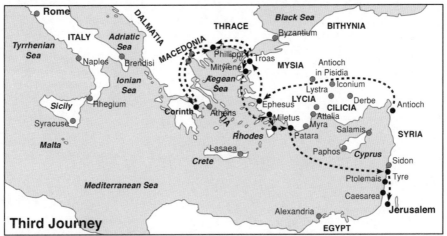

Third Journey

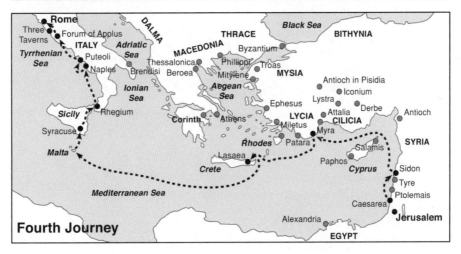

Fourth Journey

Missionary journeys of St Paul

The New Testament's Place in the Bible

1. DIVINE REVELATION REACHES ITS COMPLETION IN JESUS CHRIST

"In many and various ways God spoke of old to our fathers by the prophets; but in these last days he has spoken to us by a Son, whom he appointed the heir of all things, through whom also he created the world" (Heb 1:1–2). Jesus Christ, the Son of God, is the definitive Word spoken by God to humankind, and the New Testament bears witness to that Word. Therefore, the New Testament is the final and concluding part of the Bible, the collection of books which the Church proclaims to be the Word of God and in which we find the revelation made by God to mankind over the course of history. In the light of Christ, the definitive Word of God, whom St John calls "the Word of God" (Rev 19:13; cf. Jn 1:1), we are able to grasp the meaning of the entire Bible and of how God gradually revealed himself.

God reveals himself in creation and in our inner life
Created in the image of God and called to know and love his Creator, man is able to acquire knowledge of God through the natural light of reason. He has a "capacity for God", and God makes himself known through the world around man and in man's own soul. This is usually termed the "natural revelation of God": "starting from movement, becoming, contingency, and the world's order and beauty, one can come to a knowledge of God as the origin and the end of the universe. […] 'For what can be known about God is plain to them [the Gentiles], because God has shown it to them. Ever since the creation of the world his invisible nature, namely, his eternal power and deity, has been clearly perceived in the things that have been made' (Rom 1:19–20)."[1]

Moreover, human beings, by their openness to truth and beauty, by their sense of moral goodness, by their freedom and the voice of their conscience, and by their longings for the infinite and for happiness, are able to see that the seed of eternity that they bear within themselves, irreducible to the merely material, can have its origin only in God.[2]

God can be known through the way he manifests himself in history
"By natural reason man can know God with certainty, on the basis of his works. But there is another order of knowledge, which man cannot possibly arrive at by his own powers: the order of divine Revelation."[3] "Through an utterly free decision, God has revealed himself and given himself to man. This he does by revealing the mystery, his plan of loving goodness, formed from all eternity in Christ, for the benefit of all men. God has fully revealed this plan by sending us his beloved Son, our Lord Jesus Christ, and the Holy Spirit."[4] The entire Bible bears witness to this self-revelation of God.

In the first chapters of Genesis we read that *God made himself known personally to our first parents* and invited them to have intimate communion with himself; we see, too, that after their fall, he encouraged them to hope for salvation by promising them redemption, and he took constant care of the human race, so that all those who sought salvation by persevering in good works might receive eternal life.[5]

---

1 *Catechism of the Catholic Church*, 32.　2 See ibid., 33.　3 Ibid., 50.　4 Ibid., 15　5 See Vatican II, *Dei Verbum*, 3.

After the flood, he made a first pact or covenant with Noah; this was designed to enable all to recognize him as the one true God, and to steer them away from any desire to be like gods themselves. "But, because of sin, both polytheism and the idolatry of the nation and of its rulers constantly threaten this provisional economy with the perversion of paganism."[6]

God's revelation to the people of Israel

The book of Genesis also records that at a certain point in history, to "gather together scattered mankind",[7] God chose Abraham in order to bless, in him, all the nations of the earth. The book of Exodus tells us how, after the era of the patriarchs, God established Israel as his people, rescued it from slavery in Egypt, made a covenant with it at Sinai, and through Moses gave it a Law, "so that they would recognize him and serve him as the one living and true God, the provident Father and just judge, and so that they would look for the promised Saviour".[8]

Through the *prophets* God formed his people "in the hope of salvation, in the expectation of a new and everlasting Covenant intended for all (cf. Is 2:2–4), to be written on their hearts (cf. Jer 31:31–34; Heb 10:16). The prophets proclaim a radical redemption of the People of God, purification from all their infidelities, a salvation which will include all the nations (cf. Ezek 36; Is 49:5–6; 53:11)."[9]

In addition to giving them prophets, God gave his people *wise men* to guide them in their prayer and their meditation on the Law, so that, by contemplating divine wisdom, they would be made ready to receive the "Wisdom of God" made man, Jesus Christ (see 1 Cor 1:23–24). All this revelation was committed to writing in the books of the Old Testament, although the full meaning of what is narrated and taught therein would only become clear in the light of the revelation given us through Jesus Christ.

God's self-revelation in Jesus Christ attains its fullness

"No one has ever seen God; the only Son, who is in the bosom of the Father, he has made him known" (Jn 1:18). It is Jesus Christ who reveals God the Father. With Christ the promises made to the patriarchs are fulfilled, the Law given to Moses is renewed and completed once and for all, the hope preached by the prophets finds fulfilment, and the Wisdom of God rounds off the teaching of the wise men. "God has revealed himself fully by sending his own Son, in whom he has established his covenant for ever. The Son is his Father's definitive Word; so there will be no further Revelation after him."[10] All that God desires to say, he has said through his Word who is Jesus Christ.

2. DIVINE REVELATION IS COMMUNICATED THROUGH THE PROCLAMATION OF THE GOSPEL

The Gospel includes both the Old and the New Covenants

"Christ the Lord, in whom the full revelation of the supreme God is brought to completion, commissioned the Apostles to preach to all men that Gospel which is the source of all saving truth and moral teaching, and to impart to them heavenly gifts. This Gospel had been promised

---

6 *Catechism of the Catholic Church*, 57. 7 Ibid., 59. 8 Ibid., 62; cf. Vatican II, *Dei Verbum*, 3. 9 *Catechism of the Catholic Church*, 64. 10 Ibid., 73.

in former times through the prophets, and Christ himself had fulfilled it and promulgated it with his lips."[11] The Gospel is the good news brought by Jesus Christ and preached by the apostles to the whole world; it includes their belief that Jesus is the Christ and the Son of God. To this Gospel, the fullness of revelation, belong the books of the Old Testament in as much as they contain God's earlier revelations to his people and they announce the coming of Christ and his work.

The apostles teach that events in Jesus' life happened "according to the Scriptures" (1 Cor 15:3), that is, in line with God's design as manifested in the sacred books of Israel. All these books spoke about Christ: "'[E]verything written about me in the law of Moses and the prophets and the psalms [said Jesus after his resurrection] must be fulfilled.' Then he opened their minds to understand the scriptures" (Lk 24:44–45). Enlightened by Jesus, the apostles were able to understand the meaning of the Scriptures of the Jewish people, and they included those Scriptures in their proclamation of the Gospel.

Tradition, Scripture and Magisterium, at the service of the Gospel

The apostles preached the Gospel both orally and in writing. *Orally*, for "by their oral preaching, by example, and by observances, [they] handed on what they had received from the lips of Christ, from living with him, and from what he did, or what they had learned through the prompting of the Holy Spirit".[12] *In writing*, insofar as certain apostles "and apostolic men […] under the inspiration of the same Holy Spirit committed the message of salvation to writing".[13] The books written by the apostles, or by others who recorded their preaching, form the New Testament; whereas the books written during the life and times of the earlier people of Israel and which heralded the coming of Jesus Christ form the Old Testament. Together, the two sets of books make up the Gospel preached by the apostles and passed on to future generations.

This on-going transmission of the Gospel message, which is guided by the Holy Spirit, is called "Tradition" to distinguish it from "Holy Scripture"; but Scripture and Tradition are very closely bound up with one another. The living presence of Tradition and Scripture in the Church is something to which the Fathers of the Church bear witness. This wealth of revelation is entrusted to the Church as a "sacred deposit" whose correct interpretation is something that only the Magisterium, the Church's teaching authority, can provide.[14] The Magisterium, to be sure, "is not above the word of God, but serves it, teaching only what has been handed on, listening to it devoutly, guarding it scrupulously and explaining it faithfully. In accord with a divine commission and with the help of the Holy Spirit, it draws from this one deposit of faith everything which it presents for belief as divinely revealed."[15]

Through these three things—Tradition, Scripture and Magisterium—which are so closely interlinked that none can subsist without the others,[16] divine revelation is transmitted. "The Father's self-communication made through his Word in the Holy Spirit, remains present and active in the Church: 'God, who spoke in the past, continues to converse with the Spouse of his beloved Son; and the Holy Spirit, through whom the living voice of the Gospel rings out in the Church—and through her in the world—leads believers to the full truth, and makes the Word of Christ dwell in them in all its richness' (*Dei Verbum*, 8)."[17]

---

11 Vatican II, *Dei Verbum*, 7.   12 Ibid., 7.   13 Ibid.   14 See *Catechism of the Catholic Church*, 78.   15 Vatican II, *Dei Verbum*, 10; *Catechism of the Catholic Church*, 86.   16 See Vatican II, *Dei Verbum*, 10; see also *Catechism of the Catholic Church*, 95.
17 *Catechism of the Catholic Church*, 79.

Since Jesus Christ and his Gospel are the full and definitive revelation of God, and this revelation is offered to us through Tradition and Scripture, interpreted by the Church's Magisterium,
"each of them makes present and fruitful in the Church the mystery of Christ, who promised to
remain with his own 'always, to the close of the age' (Mt 28:20)",[18] and both of them should be
accepted and honoured with equal devotion and reverence.[19] However, the ways in which revelation is passed on in Scripture and in Tradition are distinct from one another: "'*Sacred Scripture*
is the speech of God as it is put down in writing under the breath of the Holy Spirit' (*Dei Verbum*,
9). 'And [Holy] *Tradition* transmits in its entirety the Word of God which has been entrusted to
the apostles by Christ the Lord and the Holy Spirit. It transmits it to the successors of the apostles so that, enlightened by the Spirit of truth, they may faithfully preserve, expound and spread
it abroad by their preaching' (*Dei Verbum*, 9)."[20]

We shall now focus our attention mainly on Holy Scripture, the nature and purpose of which
can only be seen in the light of the revelation that reached its pinnacle in Jesus Christ.

3. HOLY SCRIPTURE: INSPIRATION, CANON, AND RELIABILITY

Holy Scripture: the Word of God

God's revelation to man reached its climax when "the time had fully come, [and] God sent forth
his Son, born of woman, born under the law, to redeem those who were under the law, so that we
might receive adoption as sons" (Gal 4:4–5). God has made himself known most fully in the
incarnation of his Son. This is a demonstration of the wonderful "condescension" of eternal
Wisdom, whereby we know the ineffable kindness of God, who goes so far as to become truly a
man in order to make himself known to us.[21]

This same condescension is to be found in the revelation that comes through Scripture. In fact,
the nature of Holy Scripture can only be understood by analogy with the Incarnate Word.[22] In
Holy Scripture "the words of God, expressed in human language, have been made like human
discourse, just as the Word of the eternal Father, when he took to himself the flesh of human
weakness, was in every way made like men".[23] Just as we have been given to know the Son of
God in the true human nature of Jesus, so the Word of God reaches us through the human language of Holy Scripture. The incarnation of the Word in the womb of the Blessed Virgin through
the action of the Holy Spirit is foretold and later proclaimed by God himself in the Holy Scriptures which, being formed under the inspiration of the Holy Spirit in the womb of the people of
Israel and of the Church, communicate the Word of God in human language.

Divine inspiration of the Bible

In line with the terminology used by the apostles (see 2 Tim 3:16; 2 Pet 1:21), we describe God's
action in the making of the Holy Scripture as "divine inspiration of Scripture". What this means
is that "in composing the sacred books, God chose men and while employed by him they made
use of their powers and abilities, so that with him acting in them and through them, they, as true
authors, consigned to writing everything and only those things which he wanted". [24] This influence exercised by God on the sacred writers is attributed, by appropriation, to the Holy Spirit.

---

18 Ibid., 80.   **19** Cf. Vatican II, *Dei Verbum*, 9.   **20** *Catechism of the Catholic Church*, 81.   **21** See Vatican II, *Dei Verbum*, 13.
22 See ibid.   **23** See ibid.   **24** Vatican II, *Dei Verbum*, 11.

In the light of the New Testament we can see that, in all the various writings that make up the Bible, God's purpose was to reveal himself and his intentions and plans, and we see, too, that this revelation found its full and definitive expression in Jesus Christ. This means that, in receiving the Gospel of Christ as passed on by the apostles in the living tradition of the Church, we receive also the sacred books as being inspired by God—those of the Old Testament and those of the New.

The Church is very aware that "through all the words of Sacred Scripture, God speaks only one single Word, his one Utterance in whom he expresses himself completely (cf. Heb 1:1–3): 'You recall that one and the same Word of God extends throughout Scripture, that it is one and the same Utterance that resounds in the mouths of all the sacred writers, since he who was in the beginning God with God has no need of separate syllables; for he is not subject to time' (St Augustine, *Enarr.*, 103, 4, 1)."[25] Scripture conveys in human language the plan of God the Father who speaks his Word (*Verbum*), his Son, and he does this through the influence of the Holy Spirit on the sacred writers and on the Church. The Church's grasp of the mystery of the divine inspiration of Holy Scripture is grounded on the mystery of the One and Divine God revealed to us for our salvation.

The canon of the biblical books

Through the Holy Spirit received at Pentecost, the Church has been enabled to discern which books are inspired, and to interpret what they have to tell us in one way or another about Jesus Christ. By following apostolic tradition, the Church was able to establish the "canon of Scripture"—that of both the Old and the New Testaments.[26] By their inclusion in the canon, these books were accepted by the Church as being inspired and thus authoritative as regards faith and Christian life. All these several books form, moreover, a single unit, the Bible, at the centre of which stands Christ, in such a way that the significance of each book becomes clearer because of its inclusion in the corpus of Holy Scripture. In other words, "each individual book only becomes biblical in the light of the canon as a whole".[27]

The reliability of the Bible

The fact that the Holy Scriptures are inspired ensures their *veracity*: they share in the truthfulness of God himself; "since everything asserted by the inspired authors or sacred writers must be held to be asserted by the Holy Spirit, it follows that the books of Scripture must be acknowledged as teaching solidly, faithfully and without error that truth which God wanted put into sacred writings for the sake of salvation".[28] In the Holy Scriptures God's truth is conveyed in a human way and in human language. Human language provides a variety of recourses to convey its meaning (it isn't always formal or didactic), and this applies to Scripture, too. The sacred writers, moreover, express themselves in the cultural contexts of the times in which they lived.

As far as the natural sciences are concerned, the writers often reflect the level of knowledge that people had at the time (for example, they may talk about the sun as if it moved round the earth), but this does not take from the truthfulness of what they wrote.[29]

In writing history, their main purpose was sometimes a pedagogical one—to focus attention on the way God intervened in certain events; here the truthfulness of Scripture lies in its identi-

---

25 *Catechism of the Catholic Church*, 102.   **26** As regards how the different kinds of books came to take shape, see the Introduction to each book.   **27** Pontifical Biblical Commission, *The Interpretation of the Bible in the Church*, I, C, 1.   **28** Vatican II, *Dei Verbum*, 11.   **29** See Leo XIII, *Providentissimus Deus*, 42 (EB 121).

fying the actions of God and the ways in which he expressed his will through historical events. The truth of Scripture consists basically in this—the fact that it enables us to see the true face of God and communicates the Gospel of Jesus Christ from a variety of perspectives.

4. THE INTERPRETATION OF HOLY SCRIPTURE

The various books that make up Holy Scripture, and the way each book took shape and became part of the Bible, are the work of men and, at the same time, the work of God, who inspired those writers and helped them in their task. Therefore, "in order to see clearly what God wanted to communicate to us, we should carefully investigate what meaning the sacred writers really intended, and what God wanted to manifest by means of their words".[30]

The intention of the sacred writers
To discern the intention of the sacred writers we need to study what they wrote, mindful of the literary devices they used to express their teachings. This is the sort of approach one needs to adopt towards any piece of writing. But, given that the biblical books were written in times long past, it should be all the more evident that "the interpreter must investigate what meaning the sacred writer intended to express and actually expressed in particular circumstances by using contemporary literary forms in accordance with the situation of his own time and culture".[31] "For truth is set forth and expressed differently in texts which are variously historical, prophetic, poetic, or of other forms of discourse."[32]

What God wants to say to us
To know what God really wants to tell us through the words of the sacred writers, we need to bear in mind that they wrote under the inspiration of the Holy Spirit, and that their works reach the Church not piecemeal but as part of the Bible, the Book of books through which God addresses his people. This means that in order to grasp the Lord's intention in each book, "Scripture needs to be interpreted in accordance with the Spirit who inspired it."[33] This requires us to be "especially attentive 'to the content and unity of the whole Scripture'. Different as the books which comprise it may be, Scripture is a unity by reason of the unity of God's plan, of which Christ Jesus is the centre and heart, open since his Passover (cf. Lk 24:25–27, 44–46)."[34]

Moreover, given that it is the Tradition of the Church guided by the Holy Spirit himself that has identified which books make up the Bible and has passed on to us its true meaning, Scripture must be read "*within 'the living Tradition of the whole Church'* [...]. The Church carries in her Tradition the living memorial of God's Word, and it is the Holy Spirit who gives her the spiritual interpretation of the Scripture."[35] To interpret Holy Scripture correctly, we need to take account of all the truths of faith professed by the Church. These truths are intrinsically linked with one another, in such a way that when we find one of these truths in the Bible, or some aspect of them, we need to set it in the context of the entire faith proclaimed in the Creed, in which we profess the whole plan of divine revelation.

30 Vatican II, *Dei Verbum*, 12; see also *Catechism of the Catholic Church*, 109. See "The Old Testament and its interpretation" in "The Old Testament in the Context of the Bible" in *The Navarre Bible: The Pentateuch* (Dublin, 1999), pp 13–16. **31** Vatican II, *Dei Verbum*, 12: *Catechism of the Catholic Church*, 110. **32** Ibid. **33** Vatican II, *Dei Verbum*, 12; see also *Catechism of the Catholic Church*, 111. **34** *Catechism of the Catholic Church*, 112. **35** Ibid.

Reading the Bible in the Church

There are a number of different approaches and contexts in which the Church interprets Holy Scripture; but they are really all part of the one interpretation and should all be availed of if we are to read the Bible fruitfully.

There is, for example, *liturgical* reading, where the Bible is proclaimed as the Word of God and throws light on and manifests the meaning of the liturgical celebration. Here the Word accompanies the action of the Lord, as happened when revelation initially occurred: "the economy of Revelation is realized by deeds and words having an inner unity: the deeds wrought by God in the history of salvation manifest and confirm the teaching and realities signified by the words, while the words proclaim the deeds and clarify the mystery contained in them".[36] This liturgical reading takes place especially in the Mass, where the Church, venerating the divine Scripture just as she venerates the Body of the Lord, "never ceases [...] to partake of the bread of life and to offer it to the faithful from the one table of the Word of God and the Body of Christ".[37]

Another setting for the interpretation of Scripture is *spiritual reading* or *lectio divina*. Here each reader of the Bible, listening to what the Lord wants to say to him or her, and guided by the Holy Spirit who ensures that the reader stays in close union with God and the Church, obtains a personal grasp of the Word of God which is helpful to both the reader and to others. In fact, "In Sacred Scripture, the Church constantly finds her nourishment and her strength, for she welcomes it not as a human word, 'but as what it really is, the word of God' (cf. 1 Thess 2:13). 'In the sacred books, the Father who is in heaven comes lovingly to meet his children, and talks with them' (*Dei Verbum*, 21)."[38] The understanding of God and the Christian life obtained by the saints through their reading of and meditation on the Bible has a special place in the Church.

Finally, there is another kind of reading to be mentioned—*critical reading*, which involves analyzing the historical circumstances in which the various books came to be written, their connexion with one another and with the events they narrate, and the special features of each text. This type of reading can enhance our understanding of what the writers of the books are actually saying and what God is saying through them. To be truly biblical, critical reading needs to be done in a spirit of obedience to the Word of God, which is, in the last analysis, Jesus Christ and his Gospel passed on and proclaimed by the Church. Exegetes must therefore bear in mind that, though it is true that by their studies they help the Church to form a firmer judgment, "all that is said about the way of interpreting Scripture is subject finally to the judgment of the Church, which carries out the divine commission and ministry of guarding and interpreting the word of God".[39] "Critical reading" also helps us to be very conscious of the condescension shown by God in his speaking to mankind in truly human language (just as Christ was truly man); it also serves to correct subjective interpretations which have no authority.

When reading Holy Scripture or listening to it being read, it is useful to bear in mind the advice of the Second Vatican Council: "Let them [the faithful] remember that prayer should accompany the reading of Sacred Scripture, so that God and man may talk together; for 'we speak to him when we pray; we hear him when we read the divine saying' (St Ambrose, *De officiis*, 1, 20, 88)."[40]

---

36 Vatican II, *Dei Verbum*, 2. **37** See Vatican II, *Dei Verbum*, 21. Cf. "God speaking to his Church" in the "The Old Testament in the Context of the Bible" in *The Navarre Bible: The Pentateuch*, pp 12–13. **38** *Catechism of the Catholic Church*, 104. **39** Vatican II, *Dei Verbum*, 12. **40** Ibid., 25.

Introduction to the New Testament

1. WHAT IS THE NEW TESTAMENT?

The second part of the Bible, the New Testament, is made up of twenty-seven books, most of them written by apostles or their immediate disciples. It is called "New" to distinguish it from the sacred books of the Jewish people which the Church adopted as the first part of its Bible and which are called the "Old Testament".

The term "testament" comes from the Latin translation of the Greek word *diatheke*, which means "covenant". It refers to the covenant or pact by means of which God makes himself known and shows his favour to man, and through which man promises to acknowledge him as his God and to obey his commandments. Insofar as this covenant is committed to writing, whether in the form of promises and laws given by God or in the form of narrative accounts about how the pact was made, the term "covenant" may be used to describe such texts. The word "testament", however, refers more directly to those same writings in which the covenant is recorded, in the same sort of way that people are said to set down their "last will and testament". That is the sense that St Paul uses when he speaks about reading "the old covenant" (2 Cor 3:14), meaning the books of the Law and the Prophets wherein can be found the covenant that God established with his people through the mediation of Moses, and the promises that he subsequently made to Moses.

The New Testament consists, therefore, in the books that record the New Covenant which God made with mankind through the mediation of our Lord Jesus Christ, to fulfil the earlier promises and to replace the Old Covenant. The writings of the New Testament "hand on the ultimate truth of God's Revelation. Their central object is Jesus Christ, God's incarnate Son: his acts, teachings, Passion and glorification, and his Church's beginnings under the Spirit's guidance."[1]

2. HOW DID THE NEW TESTAMENT TAKE SHAPE?

Its origin

The New Testament comes from Jesus Christ himself. "The covenant he mediates is better [than the old covenant]" (Heb 8:6; cf. 9:15; 12:24). Moreover, "In his gracious goodness, God has seen to it that what he had revealed for the salvation of all nations would abide perpetually in its full integrity and be handed on to all generations. Therefore Christ the Lord, in whom the full revelation of the supreme God is brought to completion (see 2 Cor 1:20; 3:13; 4:6), commissioned the Apostles to preach to all men that Gospel which is the source of all saving truth and moral teaching, and to impart to them heavenly gifts. This Gospel had been promised in former times through the prophets, and Christ himself had fulfilled it and promulgated it with his lips. This commission was faithfully fulfilled by the Apostles who, by their oral preaching, by example, and by observances, handed on what they had received from the lips of Christ, from living with him, and from what he did, or what they had learned through the prompting of the Holy Spirit. The commission was fulfilled, too, by those Apostles and apostolic men who under the inspiration of the same Holy Spirit committed the message of salvation to writing."[2]

1 *Catechism of the Catholic Church*, 124. **2** Vatican II, *Dei Verbum*, 7.

The earliest Christian writings

The "message of salvation" was initially committed to writing in an *ad hoc* way. As early as the years 50–60 AD, St Paul wrote letters to various communities expounding the Gospel he was preaching and its practical implications. Other apostles and apostolic men, too, wrote letters to instruct the communities they had founded (Peter, James, John, Jude). Very early on, too, people must have set down in writing collections of sayings of Jesus that preachers of the Gospel would have carried with them on their travels. One of these collections seems to underlie the gospels of Matthew and Luke, given that these two gospels contain almost word for word the same accounts of many of Jesus' teachings. Scholars refer to this hypothetical collection as the "Q source" ("Q" coming from the German word *Quelle*, meaning "source"). Around the same time, accounts were being written of the main events in our Lord's life (particularly his death and resurrection), which formed the nucleus of the Gospel that was being preached (see 1 Cor 15:3–5); and accounts were also written of the Last Supper, which was commemorated in Christian liturgies (see 1 Cor 11:23–28; Acts 2:42). Other accounts, especially those concerning specific miracles, would have been written for catechetical purposes. Eventually, the same needs led to the writing of the Gospels, accounts of Jesus' life, one of them beginning with his baptism in the Jordan (Mark); and the other three going right back to his incarnation; one evangelist (Luke) even links up the life of Christ with the initial growth of the Church (Gospel of Luke—Acts of the Apostles).

These documents came into being in the second half of the first century and were written for different communities. Some are vouched for by the revelations of the risen Jesus to their authors (see Gal 1:12; Rev 1:10–11); others take the form of testimonies to the tradition handed down from the beginning by eyewitnesses to the life of Jesus (see Jn 20:30–31; 21:24), or by people who, having listened to the apostles, set their teaching down as Gospel truth (see Mk 1:1), or by others who carefully sifted accounts from the beginning to produce an accurate and orderly narrative (see Lk 1:1–4).

For the writers of these texts the words of Jesus had an authority greater than that of any other law (1 Cor 7:10; see Mt 5:21–22; etc.), and they used previous "scriptures" to support the truth of the Gospel preached by the apostles (see 1 Cor 15:3–5). The Person of Jesus Christ, his words, and the Gospel as it was initially preached were the measuring stick or "canon" used by the first generation of Christians, and they saw in these things the fulfilment of the ancient Scriptures. The new writings, therefore, were regarded as having greater authority than those earlier "scriptures", because they carried more fully the message of Jesus Christ.

The formation of collections of apostolic writings

From the early decades of the second century onwards, these Christian writings were used as texts for teaching and preaching in the various churches and were regarded as collections. Very soon there was a collection of the letters of St Paul, and some of the letters may have been amalgamated (2 Corinthians, for example, may be such an amalgam); this collection found acceptance in most of the churches. As early as the middle of the second century, a priest in Rome, Marcion (later to be viewed as a heretic), proposed that the Church should formally acknowledge the letters of St Paul and one gospel (a mutilated version of Luke), and should reject the books of Judaism and other Christian writings which he considered to be influenced by Jewish ideas. However, around the same time, St Justin put it on record that Christians used to meet on Sundays and read the Prophets and the "Recollections of the Apostles".[3] In other words, the writings of the

3 *Apologia*, 1, 67.

apostles were being accorded the same status in liturgical celebrations as the sacred writings that had come down from Judaism.

By "Recollections of the Apostles" St Justin seems to mean the gospels and, although he does not identify them by name, from the way he and other ecclesiastical writers of his time refer to them we are able to see that the gospels of Matthew, Mark, Luke and John were known in most parts of the Church and were held to be part of the authentic apostolic tradition. In or around the year 180, St Irenaeus of Lyons, a man very familiar with churches in both East and West, specified for the first time that there were four, and only four, canonical gospels. He took issue both with those who argued that there should be a single written gospel assembled from the existing gospels (this was the position of Tatian in Syria and Basilides in Alexandria) and with those who favoured other gospel-type writings in circulation among the churches—what are now known as "apocryphal gospels" (see below). These texts either contained doctrine at odds with received Tradition or else could not be traced back to apostolic origin.

Around the year 200, the great Alexandrian teacher Origen seconded St Irenaeus' proposal when he wrote: "The Church has only four gospels, the heretics have very many."[4]

The formation of the New Testament

From this time on, the four Gospels, the book of the Acts of the Apostles (now separate from the Gospel of St Luke), and the collections of letters of St Paul and the other apostles, including the book of Revelation, gradually became established in all the churches as sacred and canonical writings, along with the books received from Judaism; whereas other works—those lacking apostolic authority or containing erroneous teaching—were excluded from that category. Among these excluded books were not only gospels, but also the Acts of various apostles, and letters and revelations of different kinds. The use of the terms "Old Testament" and "New Testament" to designate the collections of writings inherited from Judaism, on the one hand, and the early Christian texts with apostolic authority, on the other, goes back as far as St Irenaeus (c.140–c.202)[5] and the great North African writer Tertullian (c.165–c.235);[6] these terms soon became the common usage of the Church. Other writings, such as Hebrews, James, 2 Peter, 2 and 3 John, Jude and the book of Revelation, took longer to gain general acceptance, either because there was doubt about their apostolic authorship, or because heretics were particularly partial to them, or even (in some cases) because, being very short, they were seldom cited. The church historian Eusebius of Caesarea (in about the year 325) refers to the existence of lists of New Testament books, none of which included the exact number that would later enter the canon. However, he does attest to the mind of the Church (already evident in the thinking of St Irenaeus' assertion that there are only four Gospels) that the canon of the New Testament should be a closed collection of books, written by the apostles or their immediate associates, and containing original testimony regarding Jesus Christ.

The first appearance of the complete list of New Testament books as we have it today comes (although in a different sequence) in the thirty-ninth "Festal Letter", that is, a letter heralding Easter, issued by St Athanasius of Alexandria and written in the year 367. St Augustine, some time later, acknowledged the same list,[7] and it received the approval of the Council of Hippo (393) and the third Council of Carthage (397). In the year 405 it was ratified by Pope Innocent I in a letter to Exuperius, bishop of Toulouse (France), and it was confirmed again later on by various councils held in the East and in the West. Thus was unanimity established on the subject of

---

4 *Homilia in Lucam*, 1, 1.   5 See *Adversus haereses* 2, 35, 4; 4, 15, 2.   6 *Adversus Praxeam*, 15.   7 See *De doctrina christiana*, 2, 8, 18.

which books made up the New Testament, until eventually, in response to Luther and other reformers who downgraded certain books, the Church defined (in 1546, at the Council of Trent) the exact list of the books that make up the canon of the New Testament.

During this long process of identifying the books of the New Testament, the Church, guided by the Holy Spirit, who assisted and continues to assist her pastors, discerned the authentic apostolic tradition and with it her own identity. Only from the vantage point of living tradition, as handed down in the Christian communities from apostolic times, and to which the Fathers of the Church are pre-eminent witnesses, was the Church able to identify the books of the New Testament. "By means of the same Tradition the full canon of the sacred books is known to the Church and the Holy Scriptures themselves are more thoroughly understood and constantly actualized in the Church."[8] Even though the canon of the New Testament is authoritatively set out by the Magisterium of the Church, that does not imply any claim that the Magisterium "is above the word of God"; rather, "it serves it, teaching only what has been handed on, listening to it devoutly, guarding it scrupulously and explaining it faithfully in accord with a divine commission and with the help of the Holy Spirit, it draws from this one deposit of faith everything which it presents for belief as divinely revealed".[9]

Apocryphal books

The apocryphal books of the New Testament (gospels, acts of the apostles and revelations) are books that the Church does not accept as being genuine apostolic tradition, even though such books usually claim an apostle as being the author. Apocryphal gospels, for example, began to circulate very early on, for we find mention of them in the second half of the second century, but unlike the four recognized gospels they never had apostolic credentials, and, besides, many of them contained teachings that were at odds with apostolic teaching. "Apocryphal" originally meant "secret", in the sense that these were writings addressed to a special group of initiates and were kept by them; the word later came to mean "not authentic" and even "heretical". As time went by, the number of apocryphal writings grew considerably—many containing stories about the life of Jesus not found in the canonical gospels (for example, apocryphal accounts of Jesus' infancy and childhood); others using the name of an apostle to spread teaching that was different from that widely held in the Church—for example, the *Gospel of Thomas* (which contains 114 sayings of Jesus presented in a rather esoteric way), or the *Gospel of Judas*, which depicts that apostle as being the only one with a true grasp of the mystery of Christ (it is a full-blown Gnostic text).

3. THE CONTENT OF THE NEW TESTAMENT

The mystery of Christ from a number of different perspectives

"In accordance with the wise design of God, these writings [the New Testament ones other than the Gospels] firmly establish those matters which concern Christ the Lord; his true teaching is more and more fully stated; the saving power of the divine work of Christ is preached; the story is told of the beginnings of the Church and its marvellous growth; and its glorious fulfilment is foretold."[10] The books of the New Testament are "a perpetual and divine witness" to the mystery of Christ, which "had not been manifested to other generations as it was now revealed to his holy

8 Vatican II, *Dei Verbum*, 8. **9** Ibid., 10. **10** Ibid., 20.

Apostles and prophets in the Holy Spirit, so that they might preach the Gospel, stir up faith in Jesus, Christ and Lord, and gather together the Church".[11]

Thus, the various collections of books that make up the New Testament tell us things about the mystery of Christ from several points of view—historical, didactical and prophetical.

The Gospels reveal it from an historical perspective, providing an account of what Jesus did and taught and how he died and rose and ascended into heaven. In general, they keep to the same geographical and chronological framework as was used by the apostles when expounding the life of Christ in their preaching (Acts 10:37–43).

The book of the Acts of the Apostles widens this historical focus to describe how the Church began and developed. It tells us how the Church spread, with the aid of the Holy Spirit sent by Christ after his ascension into heaven (see Acts 2:1–12), until it reached Rome and the limits of the known world. The book of the Acts reveals the mystery of Christ from the perspective of his influence on human affairs through the work of the Holy Spirit and the Church.

The Letters are more didactical in their approach. The apostles and other apostolic men expound the mystery of Christ for the faithful and explain what faith in Christ involves; they teach Christians how to live their lives in union with Christ through faith, and how to live in harmony with their fellow believers; and they try to deal with incorrect interpretations of the Gospel or with behaviour that is at odds with it. The Letters allow us to see the different facets of the mystery of Christ, and the way the Christian communities were organized.

The book of Revelation, the last book in the New Testament, approaches the mystery of Christ from a prophetical stance. It begins with the victory that Christ achieved over sin and death through his resurrection, and goes on to describe, in broad outline, using a great deal of symbolism and imagery (often borrowed from the Old Testament), what the future holds for the Church until eventually Christ's victory becomes fully manifest, the forces of evil are totally destroyed and a new world is brought into being, the heavenly Jerusalem come down from above. In this way, the book of Revelation offers consolation to those suffering persecution on account of their fidelity to Christ, and gives them grounds for hope to help them live in accordance with their faith in the midst of the world.

The New Testament: its variety of content, and its unity

Although the books of the New Testament form a unit, each book contributes in its own way to revealing the mystery of Christ and showing how we should relate to it. All of them reflect faith in the risen Jesus, Christ, God's Son and our Lord.

The first three Gospels (called the Synoptic Gospels, for reasons we will explain later) ground our faith by giving accounts of Christ's miracles and ministry, with special emphasis on his passion. They show that the Christian life consists in following Jesus, being faithful disciples (Mark), obeying his injunctions and abiding in his Church (Matthew) or imitating his goodness and mercy, through genuine conversion (Luke–Acts).

The Gospel of St John and the Letters of this apostle lay special emphasis on the pre-existence of Christ. Jesus is God's Logos who becomes man and, through his words and signs, reveals the Father. The keynote of our faith is that it allows us to know the Father, to live in communion with him and his Son, and to do so by keeping his commandments.

In the Letters of St Paul we see how the Apostle's thinking develops, and the changing circumstances in which he ministered. In the earlier letters (Romans, 1 and 2 Corinthians, Galatians,

11. Ibid., 17.

1 Thessalonians) the emphasis is on inner experience of faith in Christ, his work of sanctification through the Holy Spirit received in Baptism (the sacrament that makes us children of God in Christ), and the implications that this new life brings with it. The next letters written by the Apostle (Philippians, Colossians, Ephesians) also stress the supremacy of Christ over any other authority that might seek to assert its power over man, and how Christ's redemption gathers Jews and Gentiles to form one people, that is, the Church. In the later Pauline letters, the "pastoral" letters (Titus, 1 and 2 Timothy) great emphasis is placed on fidelity to Christ by keeping true to the sound teaching passed on by the apostles, and on obedience to those whom Paul himself commissioned to lead up the communities. The Letter to the Hebrews, which presents Christ as the only High Priest, invites Christians to unite themselves with his sacrifice through faith and the practice of virtue.

Other apostolic writings, in the form of shorter letters, also show their writers' understanding of Jesus Christ and of the Christian life. The Letter of James, using some of Christ's teachings from the Sermon on the Mount, invites people to prove their faith by doing good works, by avoiding quarrels and by meeting the demands of justice. In the First Letter of St Peter, Christians are reminded that they have been redeemed (bought back) by the blood of Christ; it exhorts them to live exemplary lives through the practice of charity, the faithful fulfilment of family, social and church duties, and by being steadfast in adversity. In the Second Letter of St Peter the emphasis is, rather, on being faithful to the teaching handed down, in the face of those who try to undermine it, and patient expectation of the second coming of our Lord. Very similar teaching is found in the Letter of St Jude. In the book of Revelation, which is also framed in letter form, the focus is on contemplation of the victorious Christ in heaven and on Christian living through perseverance in faith, aided by liturgical and personal prayer and, again, a lively hope in the second coming of the Lord.

By authorizing and presenting these books to us as the New Testament, the Church has guaranteed us that the Lord himself speaks through them and that, therefore, there can never be between them any contradiction in teaching. Furthermore, the fact that they all form one single New Testament is a sign of the unity of the Church, granted to her by the Holy Spirit: the Church accommodates a variety of ways of understanding and living the mystery of Christ. The Church's faith is one, and her communion is one, and yet she contains a rich variety. Calm, reflective meditation on the New Testament leads to deeper knowledge of Jesus Christ and to a catholic sense of the Church. "This is the love of Christ that each of us should try to practise in his own life. But to be Christ himself, we must *see ourselves in him*. It's not enough to have a general idea of the spirit of Jesus' life; we have to learn the details of his life and, through them, his attitudes. And, especially, we must contemplate his life, to derive from it strength, light, serenity, peace."[12]

---

12 St Josemaría Escrivá, *Christ Is Passing By*, 107.

Introduction to the Gospels

1. GOSPEL AND GOSPELS

The New Testament opens with four books carrying the same title—"Gospel". These books form the heart of Holy Scripture "because they are our principal source for the life and teaching of the Incarnate Word, our Saviour".[1]

The word "gospel" derives from the Old English translation of a Greek word (*evangélion*) which initially meant "good news". In ancient Greek it was also used to mean the reward given to the bearer of good news. The Romans regarded as "gospels" all the various benefits that the Emperor Augustus bestowed on mankind. In the Greek translation of the Old Testament (the Septuagint) the word *evangélion* was used to mean the proclamation of the arrival of the messianic times, when God would save his people (see Is 52:7–8; 61:1–2).

At the start of his public ministry, Jesus invited people to believe in the gospel of the Kingdom of God, the good news of the coming of the Kingdom that he was proclaiming and which was now coming to pass (see Mk 1:1, 14). This good news was, and is, meant to be heard by the whole world; and so, at the end of his life on earth, Jesus sent out his apostles to preach the Gospel to all creation (cf. Mk 16:15). Apostolic preaching about the life and teachings of Jesus is, then, a "gospel", good news. That preaching does not communicate only Jesus' words; it provides a portrait of him, and of his life and work: the content of the Gospel is Jesus Christ himself, since it is in him that the salvific promises made by God in the Old Testament find fulfilment.

There is, then, really only one Gospel—that preached by the apostles, who received it from Christ and proclaimed it by the power of the Holy Spirit. St Paul wrote, "As we have said before, so now I say again, If anyone is preaching to you a gospel contrary to that which you received, let him be accursed" (Gal 1:9). Later on, when the apostolic proclamation he was referring to was expressed in written form, the same word came to be used for the books containing that very Gospel that had been preached. The first four texts of the New Testament are called "gospels" because they pass on to us the "Gospel" that the apostles received from Christ and preached to others. As the Second Vatican Council says: "[W]hat the Apostles preached in fulfilment of the commission of Christ, afterwards they themselves and apostolic men, under the inspiration of the divine Spirit, handed on to us in writing: the foundation of faith, namely, the fourfold Gospel, according to Matthew, Mark, Luke and John."[2] "The Gospel according to ..." (the way the title is worded even in the ancient manuscripts) shows that the evangelists were not the authors or creators of the Gospel, but rather were writers who bore witness to the Gospel, each in his own way and according to his own talents.

2. THE ORIGIN OF THE GOSPELS

The written Gospels derive from apostolic preaching, or *kérygma*. Jesus did not command his disciples to write things but rather to preach; and they tried to use the resources available to them to

---

1 Vatican II, *Dei Verbum*, 18; cf. *Catechism of the Catholic Church*, 125. **2** *Dei Verbum*, 18.

spread the good news, the news of Jesus Christ. The written Gospels are the product of this apostolic preaching. They are not, then, contemporaneous records of the life of Christ kept by his disciples: no, they are the result of a process that ran from a stage of oral preaching to a later, final, written stage.

The Second Vatican Council, in a paragraph laden with meaning, sums up the process in this way: "Holy Mother Church has firmly and with absolute constancy held, and continues to hold, that the four Gospels just named, whose historical character the Church unhesitatingly asserts, faithfully hand on what Jesus Christ, while living among men, really did and taught for their eternal salvation until the day he was taken up into heaven (cf. Acts 1:1–2). Indeed, after the Ascension of the Lord the Apostles handed on to their hearers what He had said and done. This they did with that clearer understanding which they enjoyed after they had been instructed by the glorious events of Christ's life and taught by the light of the Spirit of truth. The sacred authors wrote the four Gospels, selecting some things from the many which had been handed on by word of mouth or in writing, reducing some of them to a synthesis, explaining some things in view of the situation of their churches and preserving the form of proclamation but always in such fashion that they told us the honest truth about Jesus. For their intention in writing was that either from their own memory and recollections, or from the witness of those who 'themselves from the beginning were eyewitnesses and ministers of the Word' we might know 'the truth' concerning those matters about which we have been instructed" (cf. Luke 1:2–4).[3]

These words help us to understand how the Gospels took shape: we can discern three stages of development. The *first stage* is the *life and teaching of Jesus*, given that these writings tell us about what Jesus did in Palestine in the first three decades of our era.

The *second stage*, running more or less from the year 30 to the year 60, is that of *apostolic preaching*. After our Lord's ascension, the apostles preached about the life and teaching of Christ—but from a new standpoint, for now his resurrection enabled them to understand things better, and they enjoyed the help of the Holy Spirit sent by him: the Gospels themselves bear witness to this greater insight (see Jn 2:22, 12:16). The apostles' preaching involved adapting the message to their audiences: Jesus carried out his ministry in the land of Israel, but the apostles journeyed and worked throughout the Roman empire. This preaching was oral, of course, but it is very likely that some teachings of Jesus were committed to writing very early on, for the purposes of catechesis and liturgy.

Finally, there was a *third stage* (between AD 60 and 90), when the Gospels were composed. Written testimony that has survived from the period tells us that, while the apostles were still living, Christians began to write down their preaching about Jesus, until eventually the canonical Gospels took shape in their original and present form. Inspired by the Holy Spirit, the evangelists put their talents at the service of this task, for the benefit of the Church and their readers. They collected such oral and written material as they could find, and each organized it to suit his purpose. They would have been conscious of writing for their immediate readers in ways accessible to them. Depending on their personal skills and the needs of their readers, they emphasized different features of the life and teaching of our Lord. Sometimes they summarized events; sometimes they grouped together sayings of Jesus on a particular theme or positioned them in a particular setting. They also added words of explanation if they thought their readers might find something puzzling; or they would clarify the meaning of some events or some sayings of Jesus

---

3 Ibid., 19; cf. *Catechism of the Catholic Church*, 126.

by showing how these had been the subject of prophecy in the Old Testament. The evangelists were not, then, simply the arrangers/editors of material given them; they were true authors of their books, each leaving on his text the imprint of his personality.

3. CONTENT AND STRUCTURE OF THE GOSPELS

The names given to these writings in early Christian documents show their close connexion with apostolic preaching: they are meant to be not a complete biography of Jesus but an apostolic witness to him. St Justin refers to them as "recollections of the apostles" or "memoirs of the apostles and their successors".[4] He is also the first to use the name "Gospels",[5] which thereafter was used by St Irenaeus, Clement of Alexandria and others. This title shows that the first thing to know about the four Gospels is their close connexion with apostolic preaching. That connexion can even be seen in the structure of the Gospels. The discourse of Peter in the house of Cornelius the centurion, for example, provides an underlying structure for the four Gospels: Jesus begins his public ministry after being baptized by John in the Jordan; he preaches and works miracles in Galilee and Jerusalem; and his life on earth ends with his passion, death and glorious resurrection.[6] Each evangelist puts flesh on the bones of this structure in a distinctive way. St Mark begins his work with the Baptist's proclamation of the need to undergo a conversion in order to receive the Messiah; his account is a vivid one, a "gospel in action", and he puts Peter's profession of faith at Caesarea Philippi at the centre of his narrative. St Matthew and St Luke each begin their gospel narratives with accounts of the birth, infancy and hidden life of Jesus (Mt 1–2; Lk 1–2), which form a type of prologue to their Gospels. Matthew predominantly presents the sayings of Jesus in the form of lengthy discourses; whereas Luke focuses more on Jesus' preaching as he makes his way from Galilee to the Holy City, on his journey or ascent to Jerusalem. St John begins his account by going right back to the eternity of the Word in the bosom of the Father, leading into the Incarnation of the Son of God and his life among us (cf. Jn 1:1,14); there follows an account of our Lord's public ministry set in the framework of journeys from Galilee to Jerusalem for the various Jewish feasts.

The *four canonical Gospels* do have something very important in common: they are narratives of our Lord's life and they stress the fact that, Son of God though he is, Jesus is also truly man, and truly suffered and died. By contrast, the apocryphal gospels do not do that: some simply record teachings of Jesus; some tone down, or even omit reference to, the sufferings of the Son of God in his passion. These texts were not given a place in the canon of the Church because they were at odds with the rule of faith. From the point of view of historical narrative, the four canonical Gospels, although they form a genre of their own, being as they are vessels of *the* Gospel, share features with certain books of the Old Testament (the accounts of the prophets, for example) and with other writings of antiquity (biographical accounts of important or virtuous figures). Also, each

---

4 See his *Apologia*, 1, 66, 3; 67; and his *Dialogus cum Tryphone*, 100, 4; 103, 8; 106, 1–4. **5** See *Apologia*, 1, 66, 3; *Dialogus cum Tryphone*, 10, 2; 100, 1. **6** "You know [...] the word which was proclaimed throughout all Judea, beginning from Galilee after the baptism which John preached: how God anointed Jesus of Nazareth with the Holy Spirit and with power; how he went about doing good and healing all that were oppressed by the devil, for God was with him. And we are witnesses to all that he did both in the country of the Jews and in Jerusalem. They put him to death by hanging him on a tree; but God raised him on the third day and made him manifest; not to all the people but to us who were chosen by God as witnesses, who ate and drank with him after he rose from the dead. And he commanded us to preach to the people, and to testify that he is the one ordained by God to be judge of the living and the dead. To him all the prophets bear witness that everyone who believes in him receives forgiveness of sins through his name" (Acts 10:36–43).

of the four emphasizes some particular aspect of Christ's life and works: Mark and John seem to want to defend the true humanity and divinity of Jesus, to offset false interpretations; Matthew presents Jesus' actions as being the key to interpret his teachings and a proof that he is the Messiah promised in the Old Testament; Luke in his twin work (Gospel and Acts of the Apostles) shows how the words and actions of our Lord constitute the very basis of Christianity.

The *first three Gospels*—Matthew, Mark and Luke—are in many ways very similar to one another, but there are significant differences. They are known as the "Synoptic Gospels" because when their content is arranged in three parallel columns, one can see at a glance (*synopsis*) where they coincide and where they differ; they are said to share a *concordia discors*, to be in discordant agreement, in the accounts they offer of the actual words of Jesus and the ways they arrange these sayings. Content-wise, the three have some 350 verses in common. Matthew and Luke have, additionally, some 230 verses not found in Mark (these are, mainly, words of our Lord). Matthew and Mark have about 180 verses in common that are not to be found in Luke; and Mark and Luke share about 100 that are not in Matthew. Finally, there are verses unique to each of them, that are not to be found in the other two: about 50 verses in Mark, some 330 in Matthew, and around 500 in Luke. As far as the order goes (where each verse come in the narrative sequence), the Gospels seem to follow the order established in Mark; whereas the passages common to Matthew and Luke but not found in Mark appear in a different order: Matthew has them largely in the Sermon on the Mount, and Luke distributes them here and there throughout his narrative.

Various explanations have been offered for these similarities and differences—particularly the similarities. This whole matter is one of the most complicated in gospel scholarship, and cannot easily be summarized; we will just give a general outline of it here. However, there is no doubt but that the three Gospels derive from *oral* apostolic preaching, and it could be that a need to stay true to apostolic tradition led that preaching to take on very definite forms—those conserved in the Gospels. All four of the evangelists drank from the same sources; some were used by all of them, others were not. Moreover, one should perhaps assume that the evangelists knew each other or at least knew of each other's work; in other words, there is a degree of interdependence among their different writings.

The most time-honoured explanation is the one put forward by St Augustine. Following the order in which the books appear in the canon, Augustine was of the view that Matthew's Gospel came first in order of time; Mark used it to produce his own Gospel, shortening the narrative in the process; and then Luke, with these two Gospels available to him, composed his Gospel for Theophilus.[7] Other authors, following a lead from Clement of Alexandria, who said that the first Gospels to be composed were those that contain genealogies,[8] think that the first Gospel was that of Matthew, who wrote for Jewish Christians; Luke then adapted this for Christians of Gentile background; and finally Mark combined the two earlier texts. However, the theory that has most support among modern scholars is that Mark was the first to write a Gospel. Matthew and Luke, without knowing one another but each having Mark before him, later wrote their gospels quite independently. As well as each having his own sources, both Matthew and Luke drew from Mark and a presumed other text, one unknown to Mark, which contained teachings of our Lord and which scholars call the "Q source". This theory provides a good explanation for the Gospels being as similar as they are—in phrasing, because they use the same sources; and in the order of the text, because they follow the order found in Mark but hardly ever put the sayings of our Lord

---

7 See St Augustine, *De consensus evangelistarum*, 1, 1–2. **8** See Eusebius of Caesarea, *Historia ecclesiastica*, 6, 14, 4.

from the Q source in the order in which they appeared there. However, this theory has one great drawback: it means believing in the existence of a document not a scrap of which remains, and to which there is not one reference in early Christianity. Some scholars have speculated that the Gospel of Matthew in the Hebrew language (attested to by Papias[9]—but that is the only mention) may have been this Q document, and that it later, when translated into Greek and compared with the Gospel of Mark, gave rise to the canonical Gospel of Matthew. When all is said and done, this is nothing more than a clever theory; as far as the "Synoptic Problem" is concerned, the only thing we can say for certain is that no proposed solution has found general acceptance.

4. THE HISTORICAL TRUTH OF THE GOSPELS

The Gospels are by far the most direct and authoritative source we have for information on Jesus of Nazareth. They depict him as a man, the Messiah foretold in the Old Testament, and at the same time as God the Son, the Saviour of the whole human race. Of course, it takes faith to hold that Jesus Christ was both God and man; but that conviction is based on an historical fact—that Jesus truly was born, lived and died. His life is rooted in the history of the real world. Christianity is not only or primarily a set of teachings: it is a testimony to an event that is very precisely set in time and space—the historical reality of Jesus of Nazareth. Therefore, the truth of the evangelical message needs to be approached from the point of view of history. The religious truth of Christianity would be distorted if it were not read in the light of historical truth.

Earlier on we pointed out that "Holy Mother Church has firmly and with absolute constancy held, and continues to hold, that the four Gospels [...] whose historical character the Church unhesitatingly asserts, faithfully hand on what Jesus Christ, while living among men, really did and taught for their eternal salvation."[10] In the early centuries, Christian writers defended the historicity of the Gospels on two fronts: against attacks from enemies of Christianity who rejected miracles, they appealed to the texts as incontrovertible evidence; and where the Gospels seemed to clash with one another, they strove to prove concordance. But they never confined themselves to simple assertion that what the Gospels taught was true: they took pains to show that the events narrated in the Gospels did in fact happen.

For seventeen centuries there was no argument about the historical reliability of the Gospels. Then, during the Enlightenment of the eighteenth century, new theories were put forward that drained the Gospels of any supernatural content. Some writers, clearly with no sympathy for Christianity, said that the authors of the Gospels wove myths around Jesus—myths that are far from being true history. The apostles and others (they claimed) created a legend around Jesus, and in pre-scholarship times their mystique-creating work could not be contradicted. This "rationalistic" approach to the Gospels gave rise to the "Lives of Jesus" that appeared in the nineteenth century which depict Christ as a failed Messiah, a dreamy idealist or, at best, a mere teacher of religion and ethics. However, these views of Jesus could not explain the power that the message of the New Testament had in the very beginning and continues to have. And so we find, in the first half of the twentieth century, other writers who try to dissociate the "Jesus of history" (who, they claim, is unreachable) from the "Christ of faith" preached by the apostles; the Gospels, they argue, have things to tell us about faith in Christ as a way of salvation, but they tell us little about

9 Ibid., 3, 39, 16. **10** Vatican II, *Dei Verbum*, 19.

the Jesus of history, who, being a concrete historical figure, could not have any special relevance as far as faith is concerned. However, even that way of looking at things is at odds with apostolic preaching, which is clearly based on the life and history of the earthly Jesus. The Christ the apostles preached was the very Jesus who lived and died in Palestine. This point has led to the appearance of recent studies on the subject of the historical truth of the Gospels. Although faith is needed to confess Jesus as the Messiah and Son of God (this was true even for the evangelists' contemporaries), no one who brings scholarship to bear on the matter can deny that Jesus was a very remarkable person and did truly unique things; he is both fascinating and mysterious, and the Gospels give an accurate and honest account of him.

It is fair to say that, overall, scholarship has shown that, to understand how the Gospels came to be written, one needs to take account of three things: (1) *the link between* the Old Testament, which contains explicit promises, and the fulfilment of those promises in Jesus of Nazareth; (2) the fact that the Gospel, oral and written, is grounded on the *human existence of Jesus*, that is, the "historical" Jesus; and (3) the *continued relevance* of the Gospel: the risen and glorious Christ is present in it and offers the grace of salvation to those who accept its proclamation. In their efforts to interpret these writings, scholars must take account of these three points of reference, which are interwoven with one another. History, faith and theology, whether in their practical or speculative modes, cannot be separated from one another when it comes to studying the Gospels. These are the main parameters for understanding the Gospel, its historical value, and its religious and theological import.

One also needs to remember that the salvific and theological depiction of Jesus that imbues the Gospels is not a distortion of the truth, making him out to be greater than he was; indeed, given that Jesus is the eternal Son of God, we can say that the image of Jesus that any evangelist or sacred author draws is necessarily incomplete. The fourth evangelist says as much, in a very simple and profound way: "Now Jesus did many other signs in the presence of the disciples, which are not written in this book; but these are written that you may believe that Jesus is the Christ, the Son of God, and that believing you may have life in his name" (Jn 20:30–31).

5. THE GOSPELS IN THE CHURCH

The Christian writers at the end of the first century are already quoting phrases or passages found in the Gospels, though they do not say who wrote them. And among the second-century authors—Irenaeus, Tertullian, Clement of Alexandria, etc.—it is already common to find it said that there are four, and only four, Gospels. The earliest testimony in this regard comes from St Irenaeus: "Given that there are four regions in the world in which we live, and four cardinal winds; given that the Church is spread throughout the world, and the foundation of the Church is the Gospel and the Spirit of life, it is right that the Church should have four pillars, four winds of incorruptibility, which give life to all mankind. Thus, the Word of the whole Universe, who is seated in heaven above the cherubim and who maintains all things in being, has given us the fourfold Gospel, the Gospel of the one Spirit. [...] Since God has created all things in the correct proportions, it is right that his Gospel, too, should be composed and presented to us in a perfect and harmonious way."[11] This goes to show that the early Church held this collection of the four Gospels as its standard.

11 *Adversus haereses*, 3, 11, 8–9.

The early Christians saw these texts as having features similar to those of the holy Scriptures of Israel. St Justin, for example, records that at the Eucharistic celebrations of the early Christians the Gospels were read and commented on like other sacred texts. This is what he says: "In the Gospels, the apostles tell us of the commandment they received when Jesus took the bread and gave thanks and said, 'Do this in memory of me. This is my body'; and when he took the chalice in his hands and gave thanks and said, 'This is my blood', and gave it to them. We have commemorated what Jesus did ever since. [...] On the day named after the sun, all the people gather in one place, those who live in the city and those who live in the countryside, and they read the gospels of the apostles and the writings of the prophets, as time allows. Then, when the reading is finished, the one who presides over the gathering preaches, addressing words of exhortation to his listeners, to encourage them to imitate the wonderful deeds they have read about. Then we stand and pray together; and when the prayers are ended, the bread, wine and water are brought to the one who presides over the gathering, who offers fervent prayers and gives thanks to God for them. The people answer 'Amen' to his prayers, and then the offerings for which God has been thanked are distributed amongst them all; they receive the communion, and the deacons are charged with bringing communion to all the faithful who are not present at the gathering."[12] In this eucharistic context, the Gospels are no mere narrative of the life of our Lord; they recall his passion and make it present in his Church. This is something the Church has done throughout the ages, for the Eucharist and Scripture are treasures she has received from Christ to be bestowed on the faithful: "The Church has always venerated the divine Scriptures just as she venerates the body of the Lord, since, especially in the sacred liturgy, she unceasingly receives and offers to the faithful the bread of life from the table both of God's word and of Christ's body."[13] In the case of the Gospels, even the gestures found in the eucharistic liturgy (incensation, procession, kiss, acclamations) make the rite of reading the Gospel equivalent to a meeting with the living Christ.

Therefore, in the Church the Gospels are not just a witness to the example left us by Christ, nor are they texts to be examined only with the curiosity of a researcher. They are a gift from God to his Church, which the Church causes to bear fruit: in this sense the best interpretations of these writings are to be found in the lives of the saints. The Gospels are not documents to do with the past; they are something current, for in them what is past becomes present. But this can only truly be the case if the reader applies them to the circumstances of his or her own life: "When you open the Holy Gospel, think that what is written there—the words and deeds of Christ—is something that you should not only know, but live. [...] In that holy Writing you will find the Life of Jesus, but you should also find your own life there. You too, like the Apostle, will learn to ask, full of love, 'Lord, what would you have me do?' And in your soul you will hear the conclusive answer, 'The Will of God!'"[14]

---

12 *Apologia*, 1, 66–67.   13 Vatican II, *Dei Verbum*, 21.   14 St Josemaría Escrivá, *The Forge*, 754.

The Dating of the Life of Our Lord Jesus Christ

The year of Jesus' birth

Dionysius Exiguus, a monk who died in 556, had the happy idea of fixing the birth of our Lord Jesus Christ as the centre of the history of humankind, the centre of time; using such historical information as was available to him, he placed our Lord's birth in the year 753 after the foundation of Rome and made the following year AD 1, the first year of the Christian era. This calculation, although it puts the great event of the Incarnation a few years after its actual date, is the one still used in most of the world for dating purposes.

We know from the Gospels that Jesus was born "in the days of Herod the king" (Mt 2:1; cf. Lk 1:5) and that Herod died fairly soon after that (Mt 2:15, 19–20). From information provided by the Jewish historian Flavius Josephus, we know that Herod died thirty-four years after coming to power, not long after a lunar eclipse.[1] Though scholarly opinion on this point is not unanimous, it is very likely that Josephus is referring to the eclipse which, astronomical data tell us, took place on 12/13 March in the year 4 BC, the year 750 after the foundation of Rome. Christ's birth should therefore be dated back to at least four years before the year used by Dionysius Exiguus. Also, Herod's death did not occur immediately after our Lord's birth, for, according to St Matthew, when the magi visited Herod, the king was still in the Holy City and we know from Flavius Josephus that the king was away from Jerusalem for about the last six months of his life, on account of the illness that led to his death.[2] Therefore, Jesus' birth must have taken place at least six months before the death of Herod. But as the Gospel of Matthew tells us, the Child would have been some months old when Herod, while still in Jerusalem (cf. Mt 2:3), ordered the slaughter of the Innocents. His command that all male children under the age of two be killed implies that Herod was confident that his order would be sure to bring about the death of Jesus.

To conclude: the date of Christ's birth should be brought back to about five years before the year assigned by Dionysius (753 from the foundation of Rome)—that is, to the sixth year before the Christian era.[3] It cannot be assigned to a year much earlier than that, for St Luke tells us that Jesus was about thirty years old when he was baptized by John, in the fifteenth year of the reign of Tiberius Caesar (see Lk 3: 1–2, 21–23), which, as we shall see, means sometime within 780–782, that is, AD 27–29.

The beginning of Jesus' public ministry

According to the gospel accounts, Jesus began his public ministry soon after his baptism by John the Baptist (cf. Mt 3:13–17; Mk 1:9–11; Lk 3:21–22). Not much time could have elapsed between the start of the Precursor's preaching and the baptism of Jesus.[4] Therefore the information given by St Luke to indicate when the Baptist started to preach his message can be used to fix the time when Jesus began his public ministry; indeed, many scholars are of the view

---

1 Flavius Josephus mentions Herod's death in two of his works: *The Jewish War*, written between AD 75 and 79, and *Jewish Antiquities*, written in 93 and 94 (see *De bello judaico*, 1, 33, 1 and 5, 6 and 8; 2, 1, 3; *Antiquitates iudaicae*, 17, 6, 1 and 4–5; 8, 1; 9, 3). **2** When he fell ill, Herod went to Jericho. From there he moved to Callirrhoe, for the thermal baths; getting no relief, he returned to Jericho, where he died in the spring of 750. From information in Josephus it can be inferred that it was in November 749, the start of the cold season in Jerusalem, that he moved to Jericho, where the climate was much warmer. **3** As regards the exact date, all we know is that the celebration of our Lord's birth on 25 December is a tradition that arises in the fourth century, for no known historical or chronological reason. **4** See Mt 3:1–13; Mk 1:4–9; Lk 3: 1–22; Acts 1:22; 10:37–38.

that Luke gives these references precisely to tell us when our Lord's baptism took place and when he began his ministry.

St Luke says that John began to preach "in the fifteenth year of Tiberius Caesar, Pontius Pilate being governor of Judea, and Herod being tetrarch of Galilee, and his brother Philip tetrarch of the region of Ituraea and Trachonitis, and Lysanias tetrarch of Abilene, in the high-priesthood of Annas and Caiaphas" (Lk 3:1–2). The reference to Tiberius' reign enables us to establish a more or less exact date. Tiberius was incorporated into the empire by Augustus, to govern the eastern provinces, in the year 765 (AD 12); thus, the fifteenth year of Tiberius' reign was 780 (AD 27). This would be the year of Christ's baptism, when he started his ministry; if we go along with the year of Christ's birth as worked out above, this accords with the approximate age St Luke says Christ was at the time ("about thirty years of age": Lk 3:23).

However, we cannot be sure about this dating, because it is also possible that the fifteenth year of Tiberius' reign is calculated from the death of Augustus, which occurred in Rome in August 767 (AD 14), that is, one year and eight months after Tiberius was formally associated with government of the empire. Moreover, we don't know what type of calendar Luke used. In any event, what we can say is that it is very probable that the baptism of Christ took place between the years 780 and 782 (AD 27–29).

The information that Pontius Pilate was procurator of Judea fits in well with both of the theories under discussion: Pilate took up his appointment in Judea in AD 26 (the year 779); and this date gives us another limit: Jesus could not have begun his public ministry before AD 26.

The dates St Luke mentions for the other rulers do not give us any greater precision, but they do confirm what has already been deduced: Herod Antipas was tetrarch of Galilee from 4 BC to AD 39; Philip held the tetrarchy of Ituraea from 4 BC to AD 33 or 34; of Lysanias all that is known is that he ceased to rule in AD 37. As for Annas, Flavius Josephus states that he was appointed high priest in AD 6; he was deposed by the Roman procurator Valerius Gratus in AD 15, but in spite of this (it was the Romans who deposed him, not the Jewish authorities) Annas continued to enjoy authority (at least moral authority), as is attested by Jewish sources of the period and as can be seen from the part he played in our Lord's trial (see Jn 18:13–14). Caiaphas, Annas' son-in-law, was appointed high priest in AD 18, and held that position until the year 36.

Another piece of information that helps establish when Jesus' public ministry began is to be found in John 2:20, which says, "The Jews then said, 'It has taken forty-six years to build this temple, and will you raise it up in three days?'" According to John 2:13–23, this exchange between Jesus and "the Jews" took place at the Passover in the first year of his public ministry. We know from Flavius Josephus[5] that the rebuilding of the temple began in the year 20–19 BC (the eighteenth year of Herod's reign). If we add forty-six years to that, we come to the year AD 26–27, which corresponds with the dates that Luke gives.

Duration of Jesus' public ministry

None of the evangelists expressly states how long Jesus' public ministry lasted. The Synoptic Gospels each imply that it lasted a little more than a year. But St John clearly refers to three Passovers, corresponding to three different years: the first finds Jesus in Jerusalem (see Jn 2:13–23); the second (see Jn 6:4) occurs shortly after the first multiplication of the loaves; the third is the Passover of Christ's passion and death (see Jn 11:55; 12:1; 13:1; etc.). The public ministry

5 *Antiquitates iudaicae*, 15, 11, 1.

appears to have extended to two full years plus the months that elapsed between Jesus' baptism and that first Passover.

In John 5:1, however, there is a reference to "a feast of the Jews". This expression is somewhat difficult to interpret: the first difficulty is whether it is *the* feast or *a* feast (some of the oldest manuscripts say one thing, some the other). If it is *the* feast, it would seem to refer to the Passover; if it is *a* feast, this does not exclude another Jewish feast (Tabernacles, Pentecost, the Dedication of the Temple, etc.). If it does refer to the Passover, then it is a different Passover from the other three mentioned above, and it means that a year elapsed between the Passovers mentioned in 5:1 and 6:4. However, more than a few scholars think that what is narrated in chapter 5 of John happened chronologically later than what is described in chapter 6. If that is the case, the feast mentioned in 5:1 could be the same feast of Tabernacles referred to in 7:2, or else the same Passover as is mentioned in 6:4. According to this theory, it is not a new, different, Passover. To sum up: from the Passovers mentioned in the Gospel of St John one cannot say for sure whether our Lord's public ministry lasted two years plus a few months, or three years and some months.

The date of Jesus' death

Although we cannot be absolutely certain about the year of Jesus' death, we can arrive at a close approximation of the time by combining data from the Gospels with astronomical computations. The first points to investigate are on what date of what month our Lord was crucified. The evangelists concur in saying that Jesus died in Jerusalem on a Friday,[6] and that his death took place around the time of the Jewish Passover.[7] We also know that, according to the Jewish calendar, the Passover was celebrated on the 15th day of the month of Nisan, a day that falls within the month of April according to our calendar.[8] The information provided in the Gospels, however, does not enable us to say whether that Friday was in fact the day of the Passover (15 Nisan) or the day before (14 Nisan); the Gospel of St John implies that it was 14 Nisan.

What the Synoptics say is that the disciples prepared the Last Supper "on the first day of Unleavened Bread, when they sacrificed the passover lamb".[9] In other words, Jesus' last supper with his disciples was a paschal meal. It should be borne in mind that the Jewish calendar is a lunar one and, since the moon begins to be visible in the evening, the Jewish day begins on what we now refer to as the eve of the day, and lasts until sunset on the day itself. This explains how it is that the Jewish Passover meal was celebrated on the evening prior to the full day. Therefore, according to the Synoptics, Jesus celebrated the Last Supper during the opening hours of the 15th day (Thursday evening), the day of Passover, and died on Friday, during the last hours of that day.

For its part, the Gospel of St John puts our Lord's death on "the day of Preparation" (cf. Jn 18:28; 19:14, 31) for the Passover, that is the day before the Passover, 14 Nisan. The only difficulty about this is that it seems to suggest that Jesus celebrated the Passover meal in the first hours of 14 Nisan, a day ahead of that laid down in the official Jewish calendar.[10] Still, the fourth Gospel seems to offer clearer information than the Synoptics as to the day of Christ's death, and the time-frame it presents makes more understandable some details given by the Synoptics which are difficult to interpret on the premise that our Lord's death did occur on a Passover day.[11]

---

6 See Mt 27:62; Mk 15:42; Lk 23:54; Jn 19:31.   7 See Mt 26:2ff; Mk 14:1ff; Lk 22:1ff; Jn 13:1ff.   8 The date of the Christian Easter is, however, movable. Easter falls on the Sunday after the first full moon following the spring equinox.   9 Mk 14:12; cf. Mt 26:17; Lk 22:7.   10 Exegetes have suggested various reasons why our Lord might have brought forward the celebration of the Passover meal. It is even possible that this was due to discrepancies between the Pharisees and the Sadducees in the fixing of the various feasts. However, up to now, no fully satisfactory explanation has been supplied.   11 For example, it is difficult

As regards the year of his death, we know that it fell during the period when Pilate was in power (AD 26–36). And it is possible to be more precise than that: if, as has been seen, Jesus began his preaching sometime between the years 27 and 29, and his ministry extended over a period of time from one year to three years plus a few months, his death must have occurred between the years 28 and 33.

Further precision may also be possible. Since we know that Jesus died on a Friday, 14 or 15 Nisan, astronomical calculations help us determine in which years (between AD 28 and 33) 14 or 15 Nisan fell on a Friday. However, this procedure cannot give us certainty, because in ancient times the start of the month depended on the *visibility* of the new moon, and sometimes, therefore, it could be delayed.

So, bearing in mind all of the questions and doubts mentioned above, we can say that very probably 14 Nisan fell on a Friday in the years 30 and 33, and 15 Nisan fell on a Friday in the years 27 and 34. Of these, the last two (27 and 34) do not fall within the range of years derived from a reading of Luke and John. However, there are reasonable grounds for settling on the year 30. Thus, if, as we saw earlier, our Lord's public ministry began between the years 27 and 29 and lasted two or three years plus or minus a few months, the year AD 30 would have been the year of his death. Given what St John says (implying that his ministry lasted at least two years and some months), it would seem that the year 29 could not have been the year of Jesus' baptism.

The year 33, although it was also one in which 14 Nisan fell on a Friday, presents additional difficulties. Our Lord's ministry would have begun in AD 29 and it would have gone on for four years, which is not likely.

Therefore, using all the dates at our disposal, we can say that the most likely date of our Lord's death was Friday 14 Nisan in the year 783 from the foundation of Rome, that is, 7 April in AD 30; but other dates cannot be ruled out.

Conclusion

To sum up: most scholars say that Jesus was born around the year 6 BC; that he began his ministry in the year AD 27 or 28; and that after two or three years of active ministry, he died in Jerusalem on Friday 7 April AD 30 at the age of about thirty-five.

---

to explain how Simon of Cyrene could have been coming in from the country on such a solemn feast-day (see Mk 15:21), or how Joseph of Arimathea could have been able to buy a shroud (see Mk 15:46), or how the devout women were able to prepare spices and ointments (see Lk 23:56); etc.

THE GOSPEL ACCORDING TO

MATTHEW

Introduction

The Gospel according to St Matthew is the first book in the New Testament. The Old Testament, which tells the origins and history of the People of God, ends, according to the order in which they are to be found in Christian manuscripts, with the books of the prophets who proclaim events that await future fulfilment. At the start of the New Testament, the first Gospel points out repeatedly that the prophecies and other scriptures come to fulfilment in Jesus and that Jesus and what he does represent the definitive renewal of Israel, the people of the Old Covenant, through the establishment of the Church as the new People of God. The Gospel, in other words, shows that Christianity's roots lie in the Jewish people while at the same time having a universal reference.

The Gospel of St Matthew has always enjoyed great authority. It was already known and referred to by writers of Christian texts that date from the end of the first century—the *Didache*, written between the years 80 and 100; the *Letter to the Corinthians* of Pope St Clement of Rome, between 92 and 101; the so-called *Letter of Barnabas*, between 96 and 98; the Letters of St Ignatius the Martyr, of Antioch, who died around 107–114; the writings of St Polycarp (d. 156); etc. Its influence extended beyond the confines of the Christian West. Eusebius of Caesaria says that Pantaenus (*c*.150–216), who taught Clement of Alexandria, went to India and found that people there were familiar with the Gospel of Matthew, because it had reached them through the apostle Barnabas.[1] The earliest Fathers quote it frequently, and others (Origen, St Hilary of Poitiers, St Jerome etc.) comment on it systematically. St John Chrysostom and St Chromatius of Aquileia each gave a long series of homilies based on the entire text. Also extant are homilies on particular passages, by St Leo the Great, St Maximus of Turin, St Peter Chrysologus, St Gregory the Great, etc. Mention should also be made of treatises on prayer by St Cyprian, Origen and Tertullian, commenting on the Our Father; and of the explanation of that passage given us by St Augustine in his work on the Sermon on the Mount (*De Sermone Domini in monte*). This Gospel was also the subject of commentary by important scholars, such as St Thomas Aquinas; and St Teresa of Avila, too, has a wonderful commentary on the Our Father in her *Way of Perfection*. It is a very rich Gospel, and it is no surprise that it has been called "the catechist's gospel".[2]

Early testimonies assert that St Matthew was the first to write down the Gospel of Jesus Christ. From the second century comes the testimony of Papias, bishop of Hierapolis, who is on record as having said this: "Matthew wrote an ordered account of the discourses [of the Lord] in the language of the Hebrews, and each interpreted these according to his ability."[3] No copy or description of this text mentioned by Papias has survived, so we do not know whether the language he refers to was Hebrew or Aramaic; nor do we know whether by "discourses" he means the whole Gospel or just sayings of the Lord. However, we also know that the Greek text of Matthew's Gospel came to be regarded as canonical very soon.

---

1 See *Historia ecclesiastica*, 5, 10, 3. **2** "Before being written down, the Gospels were the expression of an oral teaching passed on to the Christian communities, and they display with varying degrees of clarity a catechetical structure. St Matthew's account has indeed been called the catechist's gospel, and St Mark's the catechumen's gospel" (John Paul II, *Catechesi tradendae*, 11). **3** Eusebius of Caesarea, *Historia ecclesiastica*, 3, 39, 16.

1. STRUCTURE AND CONTENT

The first Gospel is a carefully written text, of which even the design carries a message. An overview clearly shows that the whole account is structured around five discourses of our Lord. These are interwoven with five sections containing accounts of messianic signs worked by Jesus. Some scholars think that this arrangement of the Gospel reflects Matthew's intention to show that Jesus is the fullness of the Law, which is likewise made up of five books (the Pentateuch).

However, there are other ways of looking at the structure of this Gospel. As in the other two Synoptics, we can see a structure which divides the narrative into two main sections, with the profession of faith by Peter at Caesarea Philippi (Mt 16:13–20) at its pivotal point. Prior to the confession of Peter, the action mostly takes place in Galilee, and Jesus' preaching (covering the Kingdom of heaven, true "justice", the fullness of the Law, etc.) is usually addressed to the multitude. After the confession of Peter, it is mainly his chosen disciples that Jesus addresses, and the focus is on the suffering Messiah and on aspects of the future life of the Church. If we bear in mind these two "sections", it helps us structure the entire narrative: thus, the first part (covering Jesus' activity in Galilee) is preceded by the infancy narrative and the prelude to Jesus' public ministry. In the second section, too, there are two stages—the journey from Galilee to Jerusalem, and events of the life of our Lord in the Holy City. The evangelist also signals this general structure by a stylistic detail: very often (as many as ninety times) he introduces his accounts with a "when" or a "then", but only three times (at the start of Jesus' public ministry; after Peter's confession of faith; and at the time of Judas' betrayal) does he use the expression "from that time" or "from that moment" (4:17; 16:21; 26:16).

The following outline may be a useful guide to reading:

INTRODUCTION (1:1—4:11). This includes the accounts of Jesus' infancy (1:1—2:23), and those of his baptism and the temptations (3:1—4:11). These chapters teach that Jesus is the Son of God, born of the Virgin by the action of the Holy Spirit, and that he is also true man, a descendant of David. He is the long-awaited Messiah (1:1) and Saviour (1:21).

FIRST PART: JESUS' MINISTRY IN GALILEE (4:12—16:20). By his ministry and works, Jesus proclaims that the Kingdom of God has come. He calls his disciples and gathers together the new People of God (4:12–25). As supreme Teacher, Lawgiver and Prophet, he promulgates the New Law of the Kingdom in the "Sermon on the Mount" (5:1—7:29). His teaching is vouched for by "the works of the Messiah"; that is, miracles prove his authority (8:1—9:38). The "Mission Discourse" to the apostles (10:1–42), Jesus' actions and reactions (11:1—12:50), and his teachings in "parables of the kingdom of heaven" (13:1–52) all show him to be more than a Teacher: he is the Messiah of Israel. The religious leaders of the Chosen People (11:16—12:45) stubbornly reject him, but the signs that Jesus works are so clear (14:13—15:39) that St Peter acknowledges him to be truly the Messiah, the Son of God (16:13–20).

SECOND PART: JESUS' MINISTRY ON HIS JOURNEY TO JERUSALEM (16:21—20:34). In this section, the Gospel gives an account of "the journey towards the cross". Jesus' two foretellings of the passion (16:21; 17:22–23) and his explanations of the meaning of the Transfiguration (17:9, 12) indicate the significance of what will later happen: Jesus must accept his mission and hand himself over to its demands and consequences. But he knows, too, that his resurrection and glorification will follow his death. This teaching is complemented by some further instructions on the future life of the Church. The "Discourse on the Church" (18:1–35) stands out among them. Various aspects of the life of the Church—poverty, spirit of service, etc.—are illustrated by incidents that occur during Jesus' journey to Jerusalem (19:1—20:34).

THIRD PART: JESUS' MINISTRY IN JERUSALEM (21:1—28:20). This part begins Christ's self-revelation as the Messiah and his cleansing of the temple (21:1–22), and the resulting controversies with Jewish leaders (21:23—23:39). An underlying theme in these episodes is that Israel has failed to respond to the gift of God, and therefore God is going to establish a new people, one that will yield fruit (21:43). The "Eschatological Discourse" concludes Jesus' teaching to his disciples (24:1—25:46): he calls on them to be vigilant, because fidelity to God must always be shown by deeds. The narrative becomes more concentrated when we reach the last days in Jesus' life—his self-offering to the will of the Father (26:36–46), his arrest, trial and condemnation (26:47—27:31), his death (27:32–66) and his resurrection (28:1–20). We see how Jesus takes on the role of the Suffering Servant of the Lord, and how Israel rejects God's designs. These find their fulfilment in Jesus' death and in his resurrection (see 28:6). With these events and Jesus' mandate to his disciples, a new stage begins: Jesus, the risen Lord, abides with the Church, the gates of heaven are opened, and the message of salvation is to be preached to everyone (28:16–20).

2. CONTEXT

The author and how he came to write his Gospel

All the early documents attribute this first Gospel to Matthew. Moreover, the Gospel itself suggests the name of its author, for it is the only one which names as Matthew the tax collector whom Jesus calls at the start of his public life (Mt 9:9) and which confirms that he is the Matthew named in the list of the Twelve (Mt 10:1–4; cf. Mk 3:13–19; Lk 6:12–16; Acts 1:13). St Luke shows that he was also called Levi, and St Mark refers to him as "Levi the son of Alphaeus" (see Lk 5:27; Mk 2:14).

A reading of the Gospel suggests that both its author and its immediate intended readership were Jewish converts to Christianity. Thus, although the author avoids the use of colloquial language and tries to find suitable Greek words, one finds in his text many turns of phrase that are of Palestinian origin and are not used in the other Gospels—"the kingdom of heaven", "heavenly Father", "holy city", "house of Israel", "flesh and blood", "binding" versus "loosing", etc. And, much more often than in the other Synoptics, reference is made to Jewish customs—the placing of offerings on the altar, priests' forms of sabbath observance, the use of phylacteries, etc. (see Mt 5:23; 12:5; 23:5). All this leads one to think that this Gospel was originally written for Christians of Jewish background, who still observed the Law, although they read it in the light of the New Law of Christ (see 5:18–19). However, none of this takes from the universal reach of the Gospel, as we can see from the commandment at the end of the book that disciples be made of every nation (Mt 28:19), the description of Christians as the salt of the earth and the light of the world (5:13–14), and the clear catechetical thrust of the Gospel. It has sometimes been observed that this evangelist is a man who has taken very much to heart our Lord's counsel that "every scribe who has been trained for the kingdom of heaven is like a householder who brings out of his treasure what is new and what is old" (Mt 12:52).

There are other features, too, that help us identify the community to which the Gospel is addressed. Our Lord warns his disciples that, in carrying out their mission to spread the word, they will meet opposition—from their own families, from Gentiles, from rulers and kings, but, above all, from the Pharisees. It is easy to see that Jesus' controversies with scribes and Pharisees prefigure both the circumstances of the early Christians and the later experience of the Church (see 10:17–21; 23:34). We can see this particularly in the way that the Gospel records words of Hosea twice quoted by our Lord: "I desire mercy and not sacrifice."[4] After the destruction of the temple, these words were often invoked by Palestinian Jews to explain how and why acts of mercy now took the place of acts of liturgical worship. In quoting from the controversies with the scribes, the evangelist seeks to show Pharisees that the meaning of the sacred texts, even of passages to which they themselves appeal, is that given them by Jesus.

Details like this lead us to agree with scholars who think that the Gospel was written in the region of Syrian Antioch, for that was a place where many Jews, and Christians of Jewish background, took refuge after the destruction of Jerusalem. There is general agreement that the "Gospel of St Matthew in the language of the Hebrews" mentioned by Papias should be dated to around the 50s or 60s; the Greek version, which is the canonical one, could have been made as early as two decades later.

Theological and literary features

The didactic Gospel. From what we have seen, the first Gospel has considerable unity to it, including literary unity, in the sense that every paragraph (in terms of what it says, and the circumstances and manner in which it is written) is very focused, very much in line with the author's purpose. The style shows that the evangelist seeks to be precise and clear in his exposition of teaching.

In the accounts of miracles, for example, in contrast to St Mark's vivid writing style, Matthew's narrative is stylized and formal; it omits incidental detail and stresses two things—the majesty of Jesus, and the close connexion between what the questioner asks and how our Lord replies.[5] This approach helps the reader to see the right way in which to behave now, in relation to Jesus Christ. As regards the words of Jesus, the Gospel records many expressions that allow us to catch the tone of the words, the poetic rhythm, in such a way that these sayings may perhaps be easier to learn off by heart and repeat. That is why this Gospel can be called the first book of Christian *catechesis*.

But the Gospel is also catechetical from another point of view: it spells out in an ordered way the rules by which a Christian should live. This is perfectly in line with our Lord's last commandment: "And Jesus came and said to them, 'All authority in heaven and on earth has been given to me. Go therefore and make disciples of all nations, baptizing them in the name of the Father and of the Son and of the Holy Spirit, teaching them to observe all that I have commanded you; and lo, I am with you always, to the close of the age'" (Mt 28:18–20). A quick look through St Matthew's Gospel is enough to show that the discourses of Jesus recorded in it contain the commandments that apostles should teach and that disciples should practise—especially as regards how to pray, fast, teach, exercise ministry in the Church, etc.[6]

The Gospel of the discourses of the Lord. This description has been applied to St Matthew's Gospel because it devotes so much space to long discourses given by our Lord. These enable us to hear our Lord's words and be present when he preaches. Five discourses[7]—the Sermon on the

---

4 "Go and learn what this means, 'I desire mercy, and not sacrifice'" (Mt 9:13); "if you had known what this means, 'I desire mercy, and not sacrifice,' you would not have condemned the guiltless" (Mt 12:7). **5** Thus, very often Jesus replies to petitions by saying, "Be it done to you as you have believed." See, for example, Matthew 8:5–13 as compared to Luke 7:1–10; or Matthew 9:18–26 compared to Mark 5:21–43. **6** See Mt 6:1–18; 23:1–12; 18:1–35; etc. **7** Mt 5:1—7:29; 10:1–42; 13:1–52;

Mount; the Apostolic Discourse; the Parables Discourse; the so-called Discourse on the Church; and the Eschatological Discourse—end in more or less the same terms: "When Jesus finished these sayings ...".[8] The Gospel includes other, shorter, discourses, such as the "Woes" and the controversies with the Pharisees (23:13–36; 12:25–45). In all of them, the Christian can find a clear guide as to how he should live, solid grounds for hope, and encouragement to spread the Gospel and live a life in accordance with the faith in the midst of the world.

The Gospel of fulfilment. Earlier we noted that, although the universal scope of Christianity comes across clearly in St Matthew's Gospel, it must originally have been written in a community made up largely of Christians of Jewish background. Therefore, although the Gospel transcends the particular context in which it was set down in words, one needs to take account of those Jewish Christians for whom it was originally written. St Matthew takes great pains to show that the entire Old Testament found its fulfilment in the Person and work of Jesus, the promised Messiah. His account is replete with references to the Old Testament—as many as 150 in all, including 50 direct quotations from the sacred books. Moreover, he often expressly notes that a particular event "fulfill[ed] what the Lord had spoken by the prophets".[9] But the fulfilment of the Old Testament extends far beyond the fact that Jesus' actions were heralded there. The Law that God gave Israel must still be adhered to, from the greatest to the least commandment (see 5:18–19), and it is retained in spirit (though not always in letter) in the New Law expounded by Jesus Christ. A passage in the Sermon on the Mount sums up this approach: "Think not that I have come to abolish the law and the prophets; I have not come to abolish them but to fulfil them" (5:17).

3. MESSAGE

Clearly, each of the four Gospels is primarily about the person of Jesus Christ and his work. The actions and words of Jesus, and of those who are drawn to him, serve to reveal who he truly is and what he promises for the salvation of man. His teaching reaches us through the apostles, his envoys. But each evangelist has his own points of emphasis. And perhaps the simplest way to summarize the teaching of the Gospel of St Matthew is to say that it has two main points of focus—the Person of Jesus Christ, and the Church founded by him.

Jesus Christ

The aspect of Jesus that comes across most in St Matthew is his majesty or stateliness, much in the same way that we intuitively perceive it in a Byzantine mosaic or in a Pantocrat in medieval churches. He is true man and, at the same time, true God and Lord of all creation. These features are conveyed very well in the titles that are applied to Jesus as the narrative of the Gospel unfolds.

Jesus is, above all, the *Son of God*. Right from his conception by the action of the Holy Spirit, and all the way to the Trinitarian formula of Baptism at the end of the book, St Matthew emphasizes the fact that Jesus, the Christ, is the Son of God (see 1:20; 28:19). Many passages mention the relationship between the Father and the Son. Jesus is the Son of the Father, the Father is God, and the Son is equal to the Father. However, man can know about this filial relationship only with the help of the supernatural gift of faith (see 11:25–27; 16:16–17). In the light of this essential truth all the other messianic titles, as well as those used in the Old Testament prophecies

18:1–35; 24:1—25:46. **8** See Mt 7:28; 11:1; 13:53; 19:1; 26:1. **9** See Mt 1:22–23; 2:15, 17–18, 23; 3:3–4; 4:14–16; 8:17; 12:17–21; 13:35; 21:4–5; 26:56; 27:9–10.

about the Saviour, acquire their fullest meaning—such titles as Son of David, King, Son of Man, Messiah, Lord.

Another way of asserting the divinity of Jesus is to call him *Emmanuel*, "God with us". Jesus is given this title at his very conception (1:23); and he himself uses a paraphrase of this name to describe his presence in the Church: "where two or three [of you] are gathered in my name, there am I in the midst of them" (18:20). Also, at the end of the Gospel, when sending out his disciples, our Lord uses a gloss on this name to confirm that he is present in the midst of the Church until the end of time. Just as God stayed with Israel in the wilderness and with those who guided his people (Moses, Joshua etc.), so too Jesus will stay with the Church: "and lo, I am with you always, to the close of the age" (Mt 28:20; cf. Ex 40:34–38).

But Jesus is not only the Son of God; he is also the *Son of Man*. This is a title he is given (always by himself) thirty times in the Gospel. But, above all, his life on earth shows him to be the humble *Servant of the Lord*, whom Isaiah foretold, who with his words and miracles (see 8:16–17 12:15–21) carries out God's plans for the salvation of the world. One of the features of the Servant of the Lord is the fact that he is rejected by his fellow men. St Matthew's Gospel contains teachings, and describes events, that throw considerable light on the profound and dramatic mystery of the *rejection of Jesus, the promised Messiah*, by Jewish leaders who drew many of the people into their opposition. The evangelist describes in various ways how this happened, by recounting episodes when scribes, Pharisees and leading priests showed hostility towards Jesus, and in his account of our Lord's passion we see that these events did not frustrate the divine plan but, rather, were foreseen and foretold by the prophets and were all part of God's purpose.[10] Hence Christ's warning that God's promise would be given to a new people that would bear fruit for him (see 21:43). That new people is the Church.

The Church

St Matthew's Gospel has been called the "Ecclesiastical Gospel" or the "Gospel of the Church". One reason for this is that it was the Gospel most widely used in the early Church; but there is a more profound reason, too—the fact that the Church figures constantly in the text. The actual word "church" (*ekklesia*), which appears in no other Gospel, appears three times in this one.[11] And even when the Church is not expressly mentioned, it can be seen in the background of the narrative: it is implied in various ways in quite a number of parables; its foundation is announced and explicitly expressed in the promise of the primacy to Peter (and, in a way, is also present in the discourse in chapter 18); we can see it symbolically in some episodes (for example, the calming of the storm); it is cast in the role of the new, fruit-producing, Israel in the parable of the wicked tenants; and its role as the universal vessel of salvation is clearly implied in the apostolic command made by our Lord at the end of the Gospel.

The idea of the Kingdom of God, or *Kingdom of heaven*, which Jesus preached and inaugurated, is closely connected to ecclesiology. St Matthew speaks of the "kingdom" 50 times; St Mark 15; and St Luke 39. But where those other evangelists use the phrase "kingdom *of God*", Matthew (except on two occasions) uses "kingdom *of heaven*". This was a phrase in common use as a circumlocution, a way to avoid (out of respect) saying the name of God. The Kingdom of God is established with the coming of Jesus, and he himself explained the features of that kingdom, especially in his parables. Because the first Gospel highlights them, it is also known as the "Gospel of the Kingdom".

---

10 See Mt 12:17; 13:35; 26:54, 56: 27:9; etc. **11** See Mt 16:18 and 18:17 (in which it appears twice).

Matthew

1. BIRTH AND INFANCY OF JESUS*

The ancestry of Jesus Christ

Lk 3:23–38

1 ¹The book of the genealogy of Jesus Christ, the son of David, the son of Abraham.*

Gen 22:1

[1] ¹Liber generationis Iesu Christi filii David filii Abraham. ²Abraham genuit Isaac, Isaac autem genuit Iacob, Iacob autem genuit Iudam et fratres eius, ³Iudas autem genuit Phares et Zara de Thamar, Phares autem genuit Esrom, Esrom autem genuit Aram, ⁴Aram autem genuit Aminadab, Aminadab autem genuit Naasson, Naasson autem genuit Salmon, ⁵Salmon autem genuit Booz de Rahab, Booz autem genuit Obed ex Ruth, Obed

*1:1—2:23 St Matthew and St Luke begin their Gospels by recounting episodes concerning the birth and infancy of Jesus; they thereby show that the Good News about Jesus Christ also includes—in addition to accounts of his death and resurrection, and of his teachings and public activity—proclamations of his human lineage and of the entirely unique way by which the eternal Son of God became man (cf. Jn 1:14). In his account, especially by its explicit quotations from the Old Testament (1:23; 2:6, 15, 18, 23), St Matthew shows that Jesus is the Messiah, the promised "David", the Saviour in whom are fulfilled the promises made by God to the ancient people of Israel.

From different viewpoints, Matthew and Luke record the same essential facts: the Child is named Jesus, because that is what the angel said his name should be; he was conceived through the action of the Holy Spirit in the womb of the Virgin Mary, who was engaged to Joseph but who did not, as St Luke's Greek has it, "know a man"; he was born in Bethlehem in Judea, but later lived in Nazareth. Matthew focuses especially on the role played by St Joseph; Luke centres his account on the Blessed Virgin. Matthew indicates that it is Joseph who is given the explanation of the virginal conception of the Child; he takes Mary as his wife, and it is he who gives the Child the name of Jesus (1:18–25). After the wise men depart, Joseph is told to take the Child and his mother and to flee to Egypt. After Herod's death, it is Joseph again who is instructed by the angel to return to the land of Israel (2:13–20). It is not surprising that these passages led the Church to cultivate devotion to the Holy Patriarch, who was "a father to our Lord Jesus Christ and a faithful spouse to the Queen of the universe, our Lady of the angels. The eternal Father chose Joseph to be the guardian and protector of his greatest treasures, his Son and his Spouse, and Joseph fulfilled his calling with perfect fidelity. [...] If the Church is indebted to the Blessed Virgin for having given Christ to us, then, after Mary, great gratitude and veneration is also owed to St Joseph" (St Bernadine of Siena, *Sermones*, 2).

1:1–17 By tracing Jesus' ancestry back to Abraham, Matthew wants to show that Jesus belongs to the people of Israel, to whom God made his promises (see Gen 12:2–3), and that the promises of salvation for all, made by God to the patriarch (8:11, see Gen 17:4–5), are fulfilled in Jesus; by mentioning David in the title (v. 1), and calling him "the king" (v. 6), Matthew shows that Jesus is the promised King-Messiah (see 2 Sam 7:14). Luke, for his part, traces the genealogy back to Adam, to emphasize that Jesus belongs to the whole human race (cf. Lk 3:23–38 and note). "Christ is consubstantial with the Father, and he made himself one in substance with his Mother, who alone was free from sin, to take upon himself our human nature [...]. We could not have enjoyed the rewards of his victory if his victory had not been won through our nature. The mystery of the resurrection was opened to us through Christ's human nature, and by the power of the Spirit through whom Christ was conceived, we have been born again in the Spirit" (St Leo the Great, *Letters*, 31).

Gen 21:3, 12; 25:26;
29:32–35; 49:10
Gen 38:29, 30
1 Chron 1:34
1 Chron 2:5, 9
Ruth 4:18–22
Ruth 4:13–17
1 Chron 2: 10–15
2 Sam 12:24
1 Chron 3:10–16
1 Chron 3:17
Ezra 3:2
Lk 1:27

²Abraham was the father of Isaac, and Isaac the father of Jacob, and Jacob the father of Judah and his brothers, ³and Judah the father of Perez and Zerah by Tamar, and Perez the father of Hezron, and Hezron the father of Ram,ᵃ ⁴and Ramᵃ the father of Amminadab, and Amminadab the father of Nahson, and Nahson the father of Salmon, ⁵and Salmon the father of Boaz by Rahab, and Boaz the father of Obed by Ruth, and Obed the father of Jesse, ⁶and Jesse the father of David the king.

And David was the father of Solomon by the wife of Uriah, ⁷and Solomon the father of Rehoboam, and Rehoboam the father of Abijah, and Abijah the father of Asa,ᵇ ⁸and Asaᵇ the father of Jehoshaphat, and Jehoshaphat the father of Joram, and Joram the father of Uzziah, ⁹and Uzziah the father of Jotham, and Jotham the father of Ahaz, and Ahaz the father of Hezekiah, ¹⁰and Hezekiah the father of Manasseh, and Manasseh the father of Amos,ᶜ and Amosᶜ the father of Josiah, ¹¹and Josiah the father of Jechoniah and his brothers, at the time of the deportation to Babylon.

¹²And after the deportation to Babylon: Jechoniah was the father of Shealtiel,ᵈ and Shealtielᵈ the father of Zerubbabel, ¹³and Zerubbabel the father of Abiud, and Abiud the father of Eliakim, and Eliakim the father of Azor, ¹⁴and Azor the father of Zadok, and Zadok the father of Achim, and Achim the father of Eliud, ¹⁵and Eliud the father of Eleazar, and Eleazar the father of Matthan, and Matthan the father of Jacob, ¹⁶and

autem genuit Iesse, ⁶Iesse autem genuit David regem. David autem genuit Salomonem ex ea, quae fuit Uriae, ⁷Salomon autem genuit Roboam, Roboam autem genuit Abiam, Abia autem genuit Asa, ⁸Asa autem genuit Iosaphat, Iosaphat autem genuit Ioram, Ioram autem genuit Oziam, ⁹Ozias autem genuit Ioatham, Ioatham autem genuit Achaz, Achaz autem genuit Ezechiam, ¹⁰Ezechias autem genuit Manassen, Manasses autem genuit Amon, Amon autem genuit Iosiam, ¹¹Iosias autem genuit Iechoniam et fratres eius in transmigratione Babylonis. ¹²Et post transmigrationem Babylonis Iechonias genuit Salathiel, Salathiel autem genuit Zorobabel, ¹³Zorobabel autem genuit Abiud, Abiud autem genuit Eliachim, Eliachim

St Matthew presents the genealogy in a series of three stages of salvation history, attributing fourteen generations to each stage (cf. v. 17) even though the stages are not all of the same length. He is clearly using numbers as part of his argument. In Hebrew, the numerical values of the consonants of the word David (D [= 4] plus V [= 6] plus D [= 4]) is fourteen; thus Matthew is pointing out that Jesus is the true Son of David. Some authors think that, as elsewhere in the Gospel—seven parables (13:1–52), seven "woes" (23:13–36)—the evangelist has in mind here the number seven, which stands for fullness, totality. He lists six generations of seven members each; the birth of Jesus marks the start of the seventh generation, the generation of perfection and abundance.

In the Bible, genealogies have significance beyond that of a simple list of a person's ancestors, a record of his lineage. We know that when the Jews returned from exile in Babylon (cf. Ezra 2:21–62; Neh 7:64), the position of each person, in terms of rights and obligations, depended on his link with a tribe, clan or family. In the genealogies, expressions like "begat" or

"was the son of" can mean direct descent or indirect descent (in the latter case, intermediary links are omitted); also, names can have a collective sense and refer to clans or tribes. In the genealogy of Jesus, the line of the patriarchs (vv. 2–6) agrees with that given in 1 Chronicles 1:34ff; and that of the kings (vv. 6–11) agrees with that of 1 Chronicles 3:1–16; for the other ancestors of Jesus (vv. 12–16), the Old Testament does not provide so clear a list. It is significant that the evangelist uses the same wording ("[was] the father of") to link all the names from Abraham to Joseph; but in v.16 he uses different wording ("of whom Jesus was born"), thereby drawing attention to the action of God in the virginal conception of Jesus. Jesus, God's Son, is Son of David through Joseph.

Apart from Mary, four women are named in the genealogy—Tamar (see Gen 38:1–30); Rahab (see Josh 2:1–21; 6:17); the wife of Uriah, Bathsheba (see 2 Sam 11:2–27; 12:24); and Ruth (see Ruth 1:1—4:22). These were all foreigners who, remarkably, were drawn into the history of Israel, that is, into salvation history, in which men and women equally have a place. In

a Greek *Aram*   b Greek *Asaph*   c Other authorities read *Amon*   d Greek *Salathiel*

Jacob the father of Joseph the husband of Mary, of whom Jesus was born, who is called Christ.*

[17]So all the generations from Abraham to David were fourteen generations, and from David to the deportation to Babylon fourteen generations, and from the deportation to Babylon to the Christ fourteen generations.

The virginal conception of Jesus, and his birth

Lk 1:26–38; 2:1–7

[18]Now the birth of Jesus Christ[f] took place in this way. When his mother Mary had been betrothed to Joseph, before they came together she was found to be with child

autem genuit Azor, [14]Azor autem genuit Sadoc, Sadoc autem genuit Achim, Achim autem genuit Eliud, [15]Eliud autem genuit Eleazar, Eleazar autem genuit Matthan, Matthan autem genuit Iacob, [16]Iacob autem genuit Ioseph virum Mariae, de qua natus est Iesus, qui vocatur Christus. [17]Omnes ergo generationes ab Abraham usque ad David generationes quattuordecim; et a David usque ad transmigrationem Babylonis generationes quattuordecim; et a transmigratione Babylonis usque ad Christum generationes quattuordecim. [18]Iesu Christi autem generatio sic erat. Cum esset desponsata mater eius Maria Ioseph, antequam convenirent inventa est in utero habens de Spiritu Sancto. [19]Ioseph autem vir eius, cum esset iustus et nollet eam traducere, voluit occulte dimittere eam. [20]Haec autem eo cogitante, ecce angelus Domini in somnis apparuit ei dicens: «Ioseph

the Gospel of Matthew these four women are a symbol (one of many) of the fact that divine salvation extends to everyone.

1:18–25 Though not Joseph's son according to the flesh, Jesus is still a descendant of David. This fact is registered in the genealogy, but now the evangelist explains how it was possible: God took the initiative of calling Joseph to be Mary's husband and the Child's father. St Joseph obediently agrees to this, and by God's design exercises the role of father over Jesus, naming him and looking after him and the Blessed Virgin. St John Chrysostom, in words addressed to Joseph, explains this as follows: "Christ's conception was the work of the Holy Spirit, but do not think this divine economy has nothing to do with you. For although it is true that you had no part in the generation of Christ, and that the Virgin remained inviolate, nevertheless, what pertains to a father (not injuring the honour of virginity) that do I give you—the naming of the Child. For 'you shall call his name'. Although you have not generated him, you will act as a father to him. Hence it is that, beginning with giving him his name, I associate you intimately with the one who is to be born" (*In Matthaeum*, 4, 12).

"Mary [was] betrothed to Joseph" (v. 18). Betrothal—*qiddûshîn*, literally "santifications", "consecrations"—was a commitment to marital union, bringing with it the legal and moral effects of true marriage (see Deut 20:7); in fact, a betrothed woman who committed adultery was to be punished by stoning (see Deut 22:23–24).

One year or more after the betrothal, the marriage (*nissûîn*) was celebrated, when the wife was led in procession to her husband's house. As Matthew points out in v. 19, Joseph was certainly an upright man: he had a righteousness that went far beyond fulfilling the letter of the Law's precepts, for what he intended to do was, in effect, to free Mary of her marriage commitment. It is not surprising that many authors (Origen, St Ephrem, St Basil, St Jerome, St Thomas Aquinas etc.) interpreted his intention not as an attitude of suspicion but as a sign that he realized that God was the cause of what had happened: "Joseph considered himself to be an unworthy sinner, unworthy to live with the woman who had astounded him with the greatness of her dignity. Fearful, he saw the unmistakable sign of the divine presence in her, and because he could not understand the mystery, he decided to draw away quietly from her. [...] He marvelled at the greatness of the miracle and the depth of the mystery" (St Bernard, *Laudes Mariae, Sermo*, 2, 14).

"Joseph, Son of David ..." (v. 20). According to Jewish tradition, the action of naming a child meant acknowledgment of parenthood. Joseph does this on God's instruction; so what we see here is Joseph's vocation: "Mary is the Lord's humble servant, prepared from eternity for the task of being the Mother of God. Joseph is the one whom God chose to be the 'overseer of the Lord's birth' (Origen, *Homilia XIII in Lucam*, 7), the one who has the responsibility to look after the Son of God's 'ordained' entry into the world,

f Other ancient authorities read *of the Christ*

of the Holy Spirit; [19]and her husband Joseph, being a just man and unwilling to put her to shame, resolved to send her away quietly. [20]But as he considered this, behold, an angel of the Lord appeared to him in a dream, saying, "Joseph, son of David, do not fear to take Mary your wife, for that which is conceived in her is of the Holy Spirit; [21]she will bear a son, and you shall call his name Jesus, for he will save his people from their sins." [22]All this took place to fulfil what the Lord had spoken by the prophet:

Lk 1:31; 2:21
Acts 4:12

Is 7:14

[23] "Behold, a virgin shall conceive and bear a son,
and his name shall be called Emmanuel"

fili David, noli timere accipere Mariam coniugem tuam. Quod enim in ea natum est, de Spiritu Sancto est; [21]pariet autem filium, et vocabis nomen eius Iesum: ipse enim salvum faciet populum suum a peccatis eorum». [22]Hoc autem totum factum est, ut adimpleretur id, quod dictum est a Domino per prophetam dicentem: [23]*«Ecce, virgo in utero habebit et pariet filium, et vocabunt nomen eius Emmanuel»*, quod est interpretatum *Nobiscum Deus*. [24]Exsurgens autem Ioseph a somno fecit, sicut praecepit ei angelus Domini, et accepit coniugem suam; [25]et non cognoscebat eam,

in accordance with divine dispositions and human laws. All of the so-called 'private' or 'hidden' life of Jesus is entrusted to Joseph's guardianship" (John Paul II, *Redemptoris Custos*, 8).

The Child is to be called Jesus—*Yehosh'a*, "the Lord saves"—"for he will save his people from their sins" (v. 21). In the context of the Old Testament, saving the people meant liberating them from their enemies; after the exile, it also meant the restoration of Israel as the kingdom of God, once its sins had been expiated. As the angel does here, Jesus will assert at the Last Supper (26:28) that through his sacrifice sins will be forgiven: "Jesus is the proper name of the God-man and signifies 'Saviour', a name given him not accidentally, or by the judgment or will of man, but by the counsel and command of God" (*Roman Catechism*, 1, 3, 5). All the names for the Son of God prophesied in the Old Testament can merge in the name Jesus, because "while they partially signified the salvation which he was to bestow on us, this name included the force and meaning of all human salvation" (ibid., 1, 3, 6).

"All this took place to fulfil ..." (v. 22). By pointing out that Isaiah's oracle has now been fulfilled, the evangelist is reaffirming the virginity of Mary and the divinity of Jesus. This astounding event has taken place thanks to the great faith of two admirable people, Mary and Joseph: "I would like," says St Teresa of Avila, "to encourage everyone in their devotion to this glorious Saint because of the great gifts he has obtained for me from God. [...] It is not possible

to contemplate the life of the Queen of angels and all the time she spent with the Child Jesus without giving thanks to St Joseph for how well he took care of them. Whoever has not yet found a master to teach him to pray, turn to this glorious Saint, take him as your master, and you will never stray from the right path" (*Life*, 6, 7–8).

"Emmanuel" (v. 23). Christ is truly God-with-us, not only because he has a divine mission but because he is God made man (see Jn 1:14). Jesus is not normally to be known as or called Emmanuel: that name refers directly to the mystery of his being the Incarnate Word.

"[He] knew her not" (v. 25). The New Vulgate translates it as "Et non cognoscebat eam, donec peperit filium", following the Greek. Literally, *donec* means "until". This participle (in Greek, *heos*) simply points out something that has happened prior to this point in time (in this case, the virginal conception of Jesus); it is not saying anything about a future situation. We find the same word in John 9:18, where we are told that the Pharisees did not believe in the miraculous cure of the man blind from birth "until" they spoke to his parents; however, they did not believe in the miracle after that, either. The Church teaches the perpetual virginity of Mary (see *Catechism of the Catholic Church*, 498), "a virgin before she gave birth, when she gave birth, and after she gave birth; in a unique and unrepeatable way, she is a virgin in mind, soul and body forever" (St John Damascene, *Sermo 6 in nativitatem virginis Mariae*, 5). See also the notes on Lk 1:26–38 and 2:1–7.

(which means God with us). ²⁴When Joseph woke from sleep, he did as the angel of
the Lord commanded him; he took his wife, ²⁵but knew her not until she had borne
a son;* and he called his name Jesus.

The adoration of the Magi

2 ¹Now when Jesus was born in Bethlehem of Judea in the days of Herod the
king, behold, wise men from the East came to Jerusalem, saying, ²"Where is he
who has been born king of the Jews? For we have seen his star in the East, and have
come to worship him." ³When Herod the king heard this, he was troubled, and all
Jerusalem with him; ⁴and assembling all the chief priests and scribes of the people,
he inquired of them where the Christ was to be born. ⁵They told him, "In Bethlehem
of Judea; for so it is written by the prophet:

Lk 2:4–7

Num 24:17

donec peperit filium, et vocavit nomen eius Iesum.   [2] ¹Cum autem natus esset Iesus in Bethlehem Iudaeae in diebus Herodis regis, ecce Magi
ab oriente venerunt Hierosolymam, ²dicentes: «Ubi est, qui natus est, rex Iudaeorum? Vidimus enim stellam eius in oriente et venimus adorare
eum». ³Audiens autem Herodes rex turbatus est et omnis Hierosolyma cum illo; ⁴et congregans omnes principes sacerdotum et scribas populi,
sciscitabatur ab eis ubi Christus nasceretur. ⁵At illi dixerunt ei: «In Bethlehem Iudaeae. Sic enim scriptum est per prophetam: ⁶"*Et tu, Bethlehem*

2:1–12 The first chapter of the Gospel told us
about Jesus' origins; this one deals with his mission, his life's purpose. Jesus is the Messiah, a
king, a new and greater David, in whom the
prophecies found fulfilment—the star heralding
his birth (see Num 24:17), the city of Bethlehem
where he is born (see Mic 5:2), the kings of the
earth submitting to God and offering their gifts
and worship (2 Is 49:23; 60:5–6; Ps 72:10–15).
But Jesus is also the Son of God who accomplishes the work of salvation that Israel (also
called the son of God in the Old Testament: see
Ex 4:22–23; Hos 11:1; etc.) did not succeed in
doing (see 2:15). If Jesus is the one who will
establish the new People of God, these wise
men, since they are not Jews, stand for those first
Gentiles who will receive the call of salvation in
Jesus Christ. The Church interprets the episode
in this way in her celebration of the solemnity of
the Epiphany: "May all the nations come to form
part of the family of the patriarchs. And may the
children of the promise receive the blessing of
the people of Abraham [...]. May all peoples,
represented by the Magi, adore the creator of the
universe, and may God be known not only in
Judea but throughout the whole world, as it is
written, his name shall be great in Israel" (St Leo
the Great, *Sermo 3 in Epiphania Domini*, 2).

"Now when Jesus was born in Bethlehem of
Judea in the days of Herod the King, behold,
wise men ..." (v. 1). The account first gives us
the historical context: Jesus was born in the reign
of Herod the Great. This Herod—father of
Herod Antipas (14:1–12), grandfather of Herod
Agrippa I (Acts 12:1–23) and great-grandfather
of Herod Agrippa II (Acts 25:13—26:32)—was
an Idumean, and therefore was considered only
quasi-Jewish; however, he managed to attain
power with the help of the Roman empire,
whose vassal he was. He was a very active man
politically and, among other projects, rebuilt the
temple of Jerusalem on a lavish scale. He was
also notorious for his cruelty: he put to death
several family members including three of his
sons, and many people of high public standing.

The Gospel tells us little about who these
wise men were. Later traditions specified how
many of them there were and where they came
from. The most famous tradition, from the apocryphal Armenian Gospel, says that the wise men
were three kings from Persia, named Melchior,
Caspar and Balthasar. With the question "Where
is he who has been born king of the Jews?" (v.
2), Matthew, as it were, draws a contrast between
two kings, Herod and Jesus, and two very different ways of exercising authority—Herod's, cruel
and inhuman (vv. 16–18), and Jesus', full of
humility (21:5). This account, quoting the
prophecy of Micah (v. 6) and its fulfilment in the
Child born in Bethlehem, shows that the true
king is Jesus.

"We have seen his star in the East" (v. 2).
Efforts to identify the star as a comet or combination of stars have failed to produce conclusive

2 Sam 5:2
Mic 5:1
Jn 7:42
6 'And you, O Bethlehem, in the land of Judah,
   are by no means least among the rulers of Judah;
   for from you shall come a ruler
   who will govern my people Israel.' "
7Then Herod summoned the wise men secretly and ascertained from them what time the star appeared; 8and he sent them to Bethlehem, saying, "Go and search diligently for the child, and when you have found him bring me word, that I too may come and worship him." 9When they had heard the king they went their way; and lo, the star which they had seen in the East went before them, till it came to rest over the place where the child was. 10When they saw the star, they rejoiced exceedingly with great joy; 11and going into the house they saw the child with Mary his mother, and they fell down and worshipped him. Then, opening their treasures, they offered him gifts, gold and frankincense and myrrh. 12And being warned in a dream not to return to Herod, they departed to their own country by another way.

Ps 72:10–15
Is 49: 23; 60:6

The flight into Egypt. The massacre of the Innocents

Ex 2:15
Deut 23:7
13Now when they had departed, behold, an angel of the Lord appeared to Joseph in a dream and said, "Rise, take the child and his mother, and flee to Egypt, and remain there till I tell you; for Herod is about to search for the child, to destroy him." 14And

terra Iudae, / nequaquam *minima es in principibus Iudae*; / *ex te enim exiet dux,* / *qui reget populum meum Israel*"». 7Tunc Herodes, clam vocatis Magis, diligenter didicit ab eis tempus stellae, quae apparuit eis, 8et mittens illos in Bethlehem dixit: «Ite et interrogate diligenter de puero; et cum inveneritis renuntiate mihi, ut et ego veniens adorem eum». 9Qui cum audissent regem, abierunt. Et ecce stella, quam viderant in oriente, antecedebat eos, usque dum veniens staret supra, ubi erat puer. 10Videntes autem stellam gavisi sunt gaudio magno valde. 11Et intrantes domum viderunt puerum cum Maria matre eius, et procidentes adoraverunt eum; et apertis thesauris suis, obtulerunt ei munera, aurum et tus et myrrham. 12Et responso accepto in somnis, ne redirent ad Herodem, per aliam viam reversi sunt in regionem suam. 13Qui cum recessissent, ecce angelus

results. According to ideas prevalent at the time, the births of important people were thought to be linked to movements of heavenly bodies. Read from this angle, the meaning of the passage is clear: the wise men begin their journey thanks to a divine revelation in nature (in, that is, the stars), but they have to journey by the light of the revelation in the Scriptures of Israel (v. 5) to find the true God: "Christ, our God, who created all things from nothing, was born, made man in the union of soul and body. At the same time, a bright star shines in the East and guides the Wise Men to where the Incarnate Word is laid in a manger; thus, there is a mystical meaning to the Law and the Prophets that leads men to the light of understanding. Read in an allegorical way, the words of the Law and the Prophets are a guiding light, a star, to lead all those called by the power of grace, in accordance with God's plan, to full knowledge of him" (St Maximus the Confessor, *Centuria*, 1, 9).

The gifts mentioned in v. 11 are reminiscent of God's promise (Is 60:1–7) that Israel would be the centre and summit to which all the kings of the earth would flock: the auguries of joy in the Isaian text are even evoked in the superlatives used in v. 10. The gifts mentioned here had great value in the East, and they also have symbolic meaning. St Hilary of Poitiers (*Commentarius in Mattheum*, 1, 5) reads them as a profession of faith in Jesus: he is given gold because he is a king, frankincense because he is God, and myrrh because he is man.

2:13–18 Here the evangelist recounts several mysteries in the life of Christ, showing their deep significance. Jesus' flight into Egypt and return to the land of Israel are a sign that he is like Jacob (Gen 46:1–7), who went down to Egypt, and also that he is like the people of Israel, who came up out of Egypt (Ex 12:37 – 15:20). Jesus is the new Israel, and with him the new People of God, the Church, comes into being. We can also see here a parallel between Jesus and Moses, who was providentially saved from death when he was a baby (Ex 2:1–10) and later became the man called by the Lord to establish his people.

he rose and took the child and his mother by night, and departed to Egypt, [15]and *Hos 11:1*
remained there until the death of Herod. This was to fulfil what the Lord had spoken
by the prophet, "Out of Egypt have I called my son."

[16]Then Herod, when he saw that he had been tricked by the wise men, was in a furi-
ous rage, and he sent and killed all the male children in Bethlehem and in all that region
who were two years old or under, according to the time which he had ascertained from
the wise men. [17]Then was fulfilled what was spoken by the prophet Jeremiah:

[18] "A voice was heard in Ramah,   *Jer 31:15*
        wailing and loud lamentation,   *Gen 35:19*
        Rachel weeping for her children;
        she refused to be consoled,
        because they were no more."

Return to Nazareth   *Lk 2:51–52*

[19]But when Herod died, behold, an angel of the Lord appeared in a dream to Joseph
in Egypt, saying, [20]"Rise, take the child and his mother, and go to the land of Israel,   *Ex 4:19*
for those who sought the child's life are dead." [21]And he rose and took the child and
his mother, and went to the land of Israel. [22]But when he heard that Archelaus

Domini apparet in somnis Ioseph dicens: «Surge et accipe puerum et matrem eius et fuge in Aegyptum et esto ibi, usque dum dicam tibi; futurum
est enim ut Herodes quaerat puerum ad perdendum eum». [14]Qui consurgens accepit puerum et matrem eius nocte et recessit in Aegyptum [15]et erat
ibi usque ad obitum Herodis, ut adimpleretur, quod dictum est a Domino per prophetam dicentem: «*Ex Aegypto vocavi filium meum*». [16]Tunc
Herodes videns quoniam illusus esset a Magis, iratus est valde et mittens occidit omnes pueros, qui erant in Bethlehem et in omnibus finibus eius,
a bimatu et infra, secundum tempus, quod exquisierat a Magis. [17]Tunc adimpletum est, quod dictum est per Ieremiam prophetam dicentem: [18]«*Vox
in Rama audita est, / ploratus et ululatus multus: / Rachel plorans filios suos, / et noluit consolari, quia non sunt*». [19]Defuncto autem Herode, ecce
apparet angelus Domini in somnis Ioseph in Aegypto [20]dicens: «Surge et accipe puerum et matrem eius et vade in terram Israel; defuncti sunt

The episode of the holy innocents is evidence of Herod's brutality. It fits in perfectly with his reputation for cruelty (see Flavius Josephus, *Antiquitates iudaicae*, 15, 202–266; 16, 256–404). The Church venerates these innocent children and martyrs for Christ: "Although they do not know it, the children die for Christ; the children's parents mourn their martyrdom. Christ has made worthy witness to himself of those who could not speak. Thus shall the new king reign and grant freedom, and save his people. [...] What a great gift is grace! What have these children done to merit their glory? Although they cannot speak, they proclaim Christ. Although they cannot take up arms and go into battle, still they win the crown of victory" (St Quodvultdeus, *Sermo 2 de Symbolo*). Just as these innocent victims proclaim the glory of the Lord not by speaking but by their deaths, the Church invites us to "bear witness in our lives to the faith we profess by our words" (*Roman Missal*, Common of Martyrs, Collect Prayer).

Rachel (v. 18) was the more beloved wife of the patriarch Jacob (see Gen 29:30) and the mother of Benjamin and Joseph; the latter, in his turn, was the father of Ephraim and Manasseh. According to the book of Genesis (Gen 35:19; 48:7), Rachel died near Bethlehem and was buried there by Jacob. Jeremiah 31:15, quoted by Matthew, refers to captives from the families of Ephraim and Manasseh who, after the destruction of Jerusalem in 587 BC, were kept in a concentration camp in Ramah (a town near Jerusalem) prior to being sent to their places of exile. But the full text of Jeremiah is an oracle of consolation: it announces that, after the ordeal of the exile, they will find favour with God again; he will restore the people and make a New Covenant with them, a covenant of the heart, one that will endure forever (Jer 31:31). Similarly, behind the misfortune of the Child's persecution and the death of the Innocents, Matthew sees the fulfilment of God's plan to establish a new people through Jesus.

2:19–23 We do not know how long the Holy Family stayed in Egypt. Matthew is the only evangelist to mention this episode, and he does

Judg 13:5, 7
Lk 1:26; 2:39, 51
Jn 1:46
Is 11:1; 53:2

reigned over Judea in place of his father Herod, he was afraid to go there, and being warned in a dream he withdrew to the district of Galilee. ²³And he went and dwelt in a city called Nazareth, that what was spoken by the prophets might be fulfilled, "He shall be called a Nazarene."

2. PRELUDE TO THE PUBLIC MINISTRY OF JESUS*

Mk 1:1–8
Lk 3:1–18
Jn 1:19–34

Mk 4:17

Acts 2:38; 13:24; 19:4

Jn 1:23

John the Baptist preaching in the wilderness

3 ¹In those days came John the Baptist, preaching in the wilderness of Judea, ²"Repent,* for the kingdom of heaven is at hand." ³For this is he who was spoken of by the prophet Isaiah when he said,

enim, qui quaerebant animam pueri». ²¹Qui surgens accepit puerum et matrem eius et venit in terram Israel. ²²Audiens autem quia Archelaus regnaret in Iudaea pro Herode patre suo, timuit illuc ire; et admonitus in somnis, secessit in partes Galilaeae ²³et veniens habitavit in civitate, quae vocatur Nazareth, ut adimpleretur, quod dictum est per Prophetas: «Nazaraeus vocabitur». [3] ¹In diebus autem illis venit Ioannes Baptista praedicans in deserto Iudaeae ²et dicens: «Paenitentiam agite; appropinquavit enim regnum caelorum». ³Hic est enim, qui dictus est per Isaiam prophetam dicentem: «*Vox clamantis in deserto: / "Parate viam Domini, / rectas facite semitas eius!"*». ⁴Ipse autem Ioannes habebat vestimen-

not go into great detail. Herod probably died in March or April of the year 4 BC. His son Archelaus then ruled as ethnarch in Judea, Samaria and Idumea until AD 6, when he was deposed and exiled as a result of protests over his brutality. Therefore, his jurisdiction did not cover Galilee, where Nazareth was situated. We can learn from Joseph's behaviour here: "In the different circumstances of his life, St Joseph never refuses to think, never neglects his responsibilities. On the contrary, he puts his human experience at the service of faith. When he returns from Egypt, learning 'that Archelaus reigned over Judea in place of his father Herod, he was afraid to go there'. In other words, he had learned to work within the divine plan. And to confirm that he was doing the right thing, Joseph received an instruction to return to Galilee" (St Josemaría Escrivá, *Christ Is Passing By*, 42).

Jesus was regarded by everyone as a native of Nazareth—"the Nazarene"—and there was a tendency to be dismissive of him on this account (see Jn 1:46; 7:32). Even in St Paul's time, non-believing Jews tried to humiliate Christians by calling them Nazarenes (cf. Acts 24:5). There is no passage in the Prophets that explicitly says what St Matthew quotes here (v. 23). The most likely explanation is that he is referring to Isaiah 11:1, which announces a descendant of David—a shoot, *neser*, from Jesse—on whom shall rest all the gifts of the Spirit of the Lord.

*3:1—4:11 In this section St Matthew covers the immediate lead-up to Jesus' public ministry. It involves places that were full of salvific significance in the history of the people of Israel—the river Jordan (v. 5), the gateway of the promised land (cf. Josh 3:8), and, more importantly, the wilderness (3:1; 4:1), the place where the people were put to the test and cleansed (Deut 8:2), but also the place where God spoke to the heart of his beloved Israel (Hos 2:16) and where the wonders that the Lord did for his people took place (Is 42:11; 43:19). These are the places where the Kingdom of God will be inaugurated, with the arrival of the Messiah, announced and acknowledged by John the Baptist, the last of the prophets.

3:1–12 John the Baptist is reminiscent of some Old Testament prophets (see 2 Kings 1:8; Zech 13:4–5). The quotation from Isaiah 40 identifies John's prophetic mission—first, to prepare the Jewish people to receive the Kingdom of God; second, to acknowledge Jesus as the Messiah who ushers in that kingdom. In the Baptist's teaching (vv. 8–12), the evangelist subtly underlines the fact that the message of John is the very same as that of Jesus: the Kingdom is about to come (v. 2; cf. 4:17), and the attitude of Pharisees and priests is to be deplored (v. 7; cf. 12:34; 23:33); these people are like barren trees (v. 10; cf. 7:19). Here we have the first instance

"The voice of one crying in the wilderness:
  Prepare the way of the Lord,
    make his paths straight."

Is 40:3

[4]Now John wore a garment of camel's hair, and a leather girdle around his waist; and his food was locusts and wild honey. [5]Then went out to him Jerusalem and all Judea and all the region about the Jordan, [6]and they were baptized by him in the river Jordan, confessing their sins.*

Mt 11:8–9
2 Kings 1:8; 2:8–13

[7]But when he saw many of the Pharisees and Sadducees coming for baptism, he said to them, "You brood of vipers! Who warned you to flee from the wrath to come? [8]Bear fruit that befits repentance, [9]and do not presume to say to yourselves, 'We have Abraham as our father'; for I tell you, God is able from these stones to raise up children to Abraham. [10]Even now the axe is laid to the root of the trees; every tree therefore that does not bear good fruit is cut down and thrown into the fire.

Mt 12:34; 23:33

Jn 8:39
Rom 4:12; 9:7–8

Mt 7:19
Lk 13:7–9
Jn 15:6

[11]"I baptize you with water for repentance, but he who is coming after me is mightier than I, whose sandals I am not worthy to carry; he will baptize you with the Holy Spirit and with fire. [12]His winnowing fork is in his hand, and he will clear his threshing floor and gather his wheat into the granary, but the chaff he will burn with unquenchable fire."

Mk 1:9–11
Lk 3:21–22
Jn 1:15, 19–34
Acts 1:5; 11:16;
13:25

Mt 13:30

Jesus is baptized

Mk 1:9–11
Lk 3:21–22

[13]Then Jesus came from Galilee to the Jordan to John, to be baptized by him. [14]John would have prevented him, saying, "I need to be baptized by you, and do you come to me?" [15]But Jesus answered him, "Let it be so now; for thus it is fitting for us to

tum de pilis cameli et zonam pelliceam circa lumbos suos; esca autem eius erat locustae et mel silvestre. [5]Tunc exibat ad eum Hierosolyma et omnis Iudaea et omnis regio circa Iordanem, [6]et baptizabantur in Iordane flumine ab eo, confitentes peccata sua. [7]Videns autem multos pharisaeorum et sadducaeorum venientes ad baptismum suum, dixit eis: «Progenies viperarum, quis demonstravit vobis fugere a futura ira? [8]Facite ergo fructum dignum paenitentiae [9]et ne velitis dicere intra vos: "Patrem habemus Abraham"; dico enim vobis quoniam potest Deus de lapidibus istis suscitare Abrahae filios. [10]Iam enim securis ad radicem arborum posita est; omnis ergo arbor, quae non facit fructum bonum, exciditur et in ignem mittitur. [11]Ego quidem vos baptizo in aqua in paenitentiam; qui autem post me venturus est, fortior me est, cuius non sum dignus calceamenta portare; ipse vos baptizabit in Spiritu Sancto et igni, [12]cuius ventilabrum in manu sua, et permundabit aream suam et congregabit triticum suum in horreum, paleas autem comburet igni inexstinguibili». [13]Tunc venit Iesus a Galilaea in Iordanem ad Ioannem, ut baptizaretur ab eo. [14]Ioannes

of Christian catechesis, which passes on the truth that Jesus came to teach us.

"The kingdom of heaven is at hand" (v. 1). This is a way of referring to the Kingdom of God. The phrase means that God is intervening powerfully and mercifully in the life of his people. The original plan of creation was shattered by the rebellion of man's sin. To put the plan back into effect, a new intervention by God was called for; this happened through the redemptive work of Jesus Christ, the Messiah and Son of God. This intervention was preceded by a series of preliminary stages—salvation history, recorded in the Old Testament. Jesus is the cornerstone of the Kingdom of God which the Baptist declares to be imminent. But the Kingdom of God that Jesus establishes is a spiritual kingdom, devoid of the nationalistic trap-

pings the Jews of his time expected it to have. To be a descendant of Abraham according to the flesh does not ensure salvation; for that, what is needed is a personal conversion which translates into the deeds of a holy life in the eyes of God: "Repent" (v. 2), "Bear fruit that befits repentance" (v. 8), "good fruit" (v. 10). Citizenship in the Kingdom of God ushered in by the redemptive work of Christ requires radical changes of attitude and behaviour (cf. 9:17; Mk 2:22; Lk 5:37–39).

3:13–17 Why did Jesus have to undergo this baptism if he had no sin to cleanse (cf. Heb 4:15)? The evangelists do not dodge this question. Nor does John the Baptist himself—as can be seen from his reluctance to baptize Jesus (v. 14). But neither the Gospels nor Christian tradi-

fulfil all righteousness." Then he consented.* ¹⁶And when Jesus was baptized, he went up immediately from the water, and behold, the heavens were opened^g and he saw the Spirit of God descending like a dove, and alighting on him; ¹⁷and lo, a voice from heaven, saying, "This is my beloved son,^h with whom I am well pleased."

Jesus fasts and is tempted

4 ¹Then Jesus was led up by the Spirit into the wilderness to be tempted by the devil. ²And he fasted forty days and forty nights, and afterward he was hungry. ³And the tempter came and said to him, "If you are the Son of God, command these stones to become loaves of bread." ⁴But he answered, "It is written,

autem prohibebat eum dicens: «Ego a te debeo baptizari, et tu venis ad me?». ¹⁵Respondens autem Iesus dixit ei: «Sine modo, sic enim decet nos implere omnem iustitiam». Tunc dimittit eum. ¹⁶Baptizatus autem Iesus, confestim ascendit de aqua; et ecce aperti sunt ei caeli, et vidit Spiritum Dei descendentem sicut columbam et venientem super se. ¹⁷Et ecce vox de caelis dicens: «Hic est Filius meus dilectus, in quo mihi complacui». [4] ¹Tunc Iesus ductus est in desertum a Spiritu, ut tentaretur a Diabolo. ²Et cum ieiunasset quadraginta diebus et quadraginta noctibus, postea esuriit. ³Et accedens tentator dixit ei: «Si Filius Dei es, dic, ut lapides isti panes fiant». ⁴Qui respondens dixit: «Scriptum est: / "Non in pane solo vivet homo, / sed in omni verbo, quod procedit de ore Dei"». ⁵Tunc assumit eum Diabolus in sanctam civitatem et statuit eum supra pinnaculum templi ⁶et dicit ei: «Si Filius Dei es, mitte te deorsum. Scriptum est enim: "Angelis suis mandabit de te, / et in manibus tollent te, / ne forte offendas

tion, which produced the Gospels and which follows them, omit this episode. The narrative allows us to deduce that, in going to John for baptism, Jesus is showing that he too supports the plan devised by God to prepare his people by the words and works of his prophets. In this way our Lord fulfils "all righteousness" (v. 15), that is, does everything that God laid down. As the *Catechism of the Catholic Church*, 536 teaches, the baptism of Jesus represents the "acceptance and inauguration of his mission as God's suffering servant". In other words, Jesus is the Servant foretold by the prophet Isaiah; the servant who, as the Lamb brought to the slaughter (cf. Jn 1:29), meekly and humbly accepts the mission his Father gives him. Jesus allows himself to be baptized because this prefigures his baptism of blood, his death on the cross, for the remission of sins. Out of love he submits completely to the Father's will, and the Father is moved and is pleased to accept his Son's offering (v. 17). The very beginning of Christ's mission (to die on account of our sins, in order to enable us to rise to a new life), signalled in this passage, made Christ's baptism a sign of our Baptism. That is how Christian doctrine reads the episode: "Through Baptism the Christian is sacramentally assimilated to Jesus, who in his own baptism anticipates his death and resurrection. The Christian must enter into this mystery of humble self-abasement and repentance, go down into the water with Jesus in order to rise with him, be

reborn of water and the Spirit so as to become the Father's beloved son in the Son and 'walk in newness of life' (Rom 6:4)" (ibid., 537). See the notes on Mk 1:9–11 and Lk 3:21–22.

4:1–11 Before beginning his messianic work and promulgating the New Law in the Sermon on the Mount, Jesus prepares himself by prayer and fasting in the wilderness. Moses acted in a similar way before promulgating, in the name of God, the Old Law at Sinai (Ex 34:28); and Elijah travelled forty days in the wilderness to advance his mission of promoting the Law (1 Kings 19:4–8). The Church, too, encourages us to seek spiritual renewal during the forty days of Lent: "Lord, protect us in our struggle against evil. As we begin the discipline of Lent, make this day holy by our self-denial" (*Roman Missal*, Ash Wednesday, Opening Prayer). See also the note on Lk 4:1–13.

In this episode of the temptations, Matthew portrays Jesus as the new Israel, in contrast to the old. Jesus is tempted, as the Chosen People were during their forty years in the desert. The Israelites succumbed to temptation: they railed against God when they suffered hunger (Ex 16:1ff), demanded a miracle when they were short of water (Ex 17:1–7), and worshipped the golden calf (Ex 32). Jesus, by contrast, overcomes temptation and, in doing so, shows what sort of Messiah he is—not one who seeks personal glory, or political success, but one who humbly does the will of God as it is set out in the Scriptures.

g Other ancient authorities add *to him*   h Or *my Son, my* (or the) *Beloved*

'Man shall not live by bread alone,
   but by every word that proceeds from the mouth of God.'"
[5]Then the devil took him to the holy city, and set him on the pinnacle of the temple, [6]and said to him, "If you are the Son of God, throw yourself down; for it is written,
   'He will give his angels charge of you,'   *Ps 91:11, 12*
and
   'On their hands they will bear you up,
   lest you strike your foot against a stone.'"
[7]Jesus said to him, "Again it is written, 'You shall not tempt the Lord your God.'"   *Deut 6:16*
[8]Again, the devil took him to a very high mountain, and showed him all the king-   *Deut 34:1*
doms of the world and the glory of them; [9]and he said to him, "All these I will give   *Rev 21:10*
you, if you will fall down and worship me." [10]Then Jesus said to him, "Begone,   *Deut 5:9; 6:13*
Satan! for it is written,
   'You shall worship the Lord your God
   and him only shall you serve.'"
[11]Then the devil left him, and behold, the angels came and ministered to him.   *Jn 1:51*
                                                                               Heb 1:6, 14

PART ONE

Jesus' ministry in Galilee*

Jesus begins to preach   *Mk 1:14–15*
                                                                               Lk 4:14–15
[12]Now when he heard that John had been arrested, he withdrew into Galilee; [13]and   *Lk 3:20; 4:14–15*
leaving Nazareth he went and dwelt in Capernaum by the sea, in the territory of   *Jn 3:24*

ad lapidem pedem tuum"». [7]*Ait illi Iesus: «Rursum scriptum est: "Non tentabis Dominum Deum tuum"».* [8]*Iterum assumit eum Diabolus in montem excelsum valde et ostendit ei omnia regna mundi et gloriam eorum* [9]*et dicit illi: «Haec tibi omnia dabo, si cadens adoraveris me».* [10]*Tunc dicit ei Iesus: «Vade, Satanas! Scriptum est enim: / "Dominum Deum tuum adorabis / et illi soli servies"».* [11]*Tunc reliquit eum Diabolus, et ecce*

Jesus' behaviour sets an example for every Christian. When we meet difficulties or temptation, we should not look for easy success or expect God to intervene in some dramatic way; trust in God, prayer, God's grace and our fortitude will lead us, like Christ, to victory: "The Lord allowed the devil to tempt him so that we would have his example as well as the power of his help when we face temptation. [...] He overcame the enemy using the words of the Lord, not with the strength of his arm. [...] He overcame the mortal enemy of men as a man, not as God. He fought in that way to show us how we should fight. He overcame the enemy so that we too may overcome the enemy by following his example" (St Leo the Great, *Sermo 39 de Quadragesima*).

*4:12–16:20 Jesus' ministry in Galilee now begins. In word and deed, he proclaims that the

Kingdom of God has arrived. He starts by calling disciples and gathering to himself the new People of God (4:12–25). Then, as supreme Teacher, Lawgiver and Prophet, he promulgates the New Law of the Kingdom in the Sermon on the Mount (5:1—7:29). His teaching is vouched for by "the works of the Messiah", the miracles he performs (8:1—9:38).

The sending out of the apostles (10:1–42) and the deeds (11:1—12:50) and words (13:1–52) of Jesus show that he is more than a Teacher: he is the Messiah of Israel. The religious leaders of the Chosen People (11:16—12:45) obstinately reject him, but the signs are so evident (14:13—15:39) that St Peter acknowledges Jesus for what he truly is—the Messiah, the Son of God (16:13–20).

4:12–17 Jesus now makes Capernaum the base of his activity (v. 13). This city on the shores of

Jn 2:12; 4:43
Zebulun and Naphtali, ¹⁴that what was spoken by the prophet Isaiah might be fulfilled:

Is 8:23—9:1
Jn 7:52
    ¹⁵ "The land of Zebulun and the land of Naphtali,
       toward the sea, across the Jordan, Galilee of the Gentiles

Lk 1:78f
Jn 1:9
       — ¹⁶ the people who sat in darkness have seen a great light
       and for those who sat in the region and shadow of death light has dawned."

Mt 10:7
¹⁷From that time Jesus began to preach, saying, "Repent, for the kingdom of heaven is at hand."

Mk 1:16–20
Lk 5:1–11
Jn 1:35–51

The first disciples are called

¹⁸As he walked by the Sea of Galilee, he saw two brothers, Simon who is called Peter and Andrew his brother, casting a net into the sea; for they were fishermen.

angeli accesserunt et ministrabant ei. ¹²Cum autem audisset quod Ioannes traditus esset, secessit in Galilaeam. ¹³Et relicta Nazareth, venit et habitavit in Capharnaum maritimam ¹⁴in finibus Zabulon et Nephthali, ut impleretur, quod dictum est per Isaiam prophetam dicentem: ¹⁵«*Terra Zabulon et terra Nephthali, / ad viam maris, trans Iordanem, / Galilaea gentium; / ¹⁶populus, qui sedebat in tenebris, / lucem vidit magnam, / et sedentibus in regione et umbra mortis / lux orta est eis*». ¹⁷Exinde coepit Iesus praedicare et dicere: «Paenitentiam agite; appropinquavit enim regnum caelorum». ¹⁸Ambulans autem iuxta mare Galilaeae, vidit duos fratres, Simonem, qui vocatur Petrus, et Andream fratrem eius, mittentes rete in mare; erant enim piscatores. ¹⁹Et ait illis: «Venite post me, et faciam vos piscatores hominum». ²⁰At illi continuo, relictis retibus, secuti

the Sea of Galilee epitomized the whole region: rich in natural resources and situated at the centre of trade routes, it had a mixed population, of which perhaps a third were Jewish. The episode concerning the centurion (8:5–13) suggests that people of different races and cultures lived in amity here. The region (a number of areas are mentioned: v. 15) was conquered by the Assyrians in the time of Isaiah, in 734 BC; it was laid waste and its people were ill-treated. Some of its Israelite population were deported, and sizeable numbers of foreigners were planted as colonists. That is why in this quotation from Isaiah 9 it is referred to as "Galilee of the Gentiles". This was the region (the evangelist underlines) that was the first to receive the light of salvation and hear the preaching of the Messiah—in fulfilment of the prophecies.

With the Kingdom of heaven so close at hand (cf. the note on 3:1–12), Jesus' preaching is an urgent call to repentance (see v. 17). For "Repent" many translations give "Be converted" or "Do penance". "[Penance] means the inmost change of heart under the influence of the word of God and in the perspective of the kingdom. But penance also means changing one's life in harmony with the change of heart, and in this sense doing penance is completed by bringing forth fruits worthy of penance: it is one's whole existence that becomes penitential, that is to say, directed toward a continuous striving for what is

better. But doing penance is something authentic and effective only if it is translated into deeds and acts of penance. In this sense penance means [...] the concrete daily effort of a person, supported by God's grace, to lose his or her own life for Christ as the only means of gaining it; an effort to put off the old man and put on the new; an effort to overcome in oneself what is of the flesh in order that what is spiritual may prevail; a continual effort to rise from the things of here below to the things of above, where Christ is" (John Paul II, *Reconciliatio et paenitentia*, 4).

4:18–25 Although Jesus' message (4:17) is the very same as John's (3:2), unlike the Baptist, who simply announces that the Kingdom is on its way, our Lord begins to establish that Kingdom in human history by his works and his preaching. Thus, we see him calling his first disciples to follow him and leave everything behind: from these, later, he will pick the Twelve on whom he will found his Church. Paradoxically, Jesus chooses fishermen, uneducated men (see Acts 4:13), lest "anyone should think the faith of believers was attributable not to the action of God, but to eloquence and scholarship" (St Jerome, *Commentarii in Matthaeum*, 5, 19). However, he made them "masters and leaders for the whole world, stewards of the divine mysteries; he commanded them to be like stars, to shine their light not only on the homeland of the Jews but on

¹⁹And he said to them, "Follow me, and I will make you fishers of men." Ezek 47:10
²⁰Immediately they left their nets and followed him. ²¹And going on from there he Mt 19:27
saw two other brothers, James the son of Zebedee and John his brother, in the boat
with Zebedee their father, mending their nets, and he called to them. ²²Immediately Mt 8:21–22
they left the boat and their father, and followed him.

²³And he went about all Galilee, teaching in their synagogues and preaching the Lk 4:14–25, 44;
6:17–19; 9:35
gospel of the kingdom and healing every disease and every infirmity among the Mk 1:39; 3:7–12
Acts 10:38
people. ²⁴So his fame spread throughout all Syria and they brought him all the sick, Mk 6:55–56
those afflicted with various diseases and pains, demoniacs, epileptics, and paralyt-
ics, and he healed them. ²⁵And great crowds followed him from Galilee and the Mk 3:7–8
Lk 6:17–19
Decapolis and Jerusalem and Judea and from beyond the Jordan.

3. THE SERMON ON THE MOUNT*

The Beatitudes   Lk 6:20–26

5 ¹Seeing the crowds, he went up on the mountain, and when he sat down his disciples came to him. ²And he opened his mouth and taught them, saying:

sunt eum. ²¹Et procedens inde vidit alios duos fratres, Iacobum Zebedaei et Ioannem fratrem eius, in navi cum Zebedaeo patre eorum reficientes
retia sua, et vocavit eos. ²²Illi autem statim, relicta navi et patre suo, secuti sunt eum. ²³Et circumibat Iesus totam Galilaeam, docens in synagogis
eorum et praedicans evangelium regni et sanans omnem languorem et omnem infirmitatem in populo. ²⁴Et abiit opinio eius in totam Syriam; et
obtulerunt ei omnes male habentes, variis languoribus et tormentis comprehensos, et qui daemonia habebant, et lunaticos et paralyticos, et curavit
eos. ²⁵Et secutae sunt eum turbae multae de Galilaea et Decapoli et Hierosolymis et Iudaea et de trans Iordanem. [5] ¹Videns autem turbas, ascendit in montem; et cum sedisset, accesserunt ad eum discipuli eius; ²et aperiens os suum docebat eos dicens: ³«Beati pauperes spiritu, quoniam

all men living everywhere in the world" (St Cyril of Alexandria, *Commentarium in Ioannem*, 12, 1).

The evangelist records the immediate and ready response of the apostles to the Lord's call (cf. the note on Mk 1:16–20). St Matthew, from the start, singles out Peter among them (v. 18). "As a person, by his nature, Peter was a man; by grace, a Christian; and by a greater grace, an apostle, the first among all of the apostles" (St Augustine, *In Ioannis Evangelium*, 124, 5).

After his account of the calling of the disciples, the evangelist gives a brief summary of the early ministry of Jesus (v. 23) and its impact in Galilee and the surrounding area (vv. 24–25). Both Jesus' preaching and his miracles are signs that he is establishing the Kingdom of God, signs of the divine grace and mercy that, through Christ, are offered to everyone, as the crowds that flock to him show. "The Lord Jesus inaugurated his Church by preaching the Good News, that is, the coming of the Kingdom of God, promised over the ages in the Scriptures [...]. This Kingdom shone out before men in the world, in the works and in the presence of Christ" (Vatican II, *Lumen gentium*, 5).

*5:1—7:29 The Sermon on the Mount is the first of the five great discourses in which St Matthew brings together Jesus' teachings on the Kingdom of God. By placing our Lord's teaching before his miracles (8:1—9:39), St Matthew may intend to stress the fact that Jesus is truly a Teacher; for that reason, St Matthew's is often called the "didactic Gospel". In this discourse we find a summary of the sorts of people who belong to the Kingdom (5:3–12) and it has much to say about true righteousness (justice)—the kinds of attitudes people should have towards the Law (5:17–48; 6:16–18), towards God (6:25–34), towards one another (6:1–4; 7:1–5), and in the way they pray (6:7–14; 7:7–11).

5:1–12 The Beatitudes form the bedrock of and a prologue to the Sermon on the Mount. Here Jesus recalls the promises made to the Chosen People from the time of Abraham onwards, but he gives them a new character; the promise of possession of a land is transformed into that of belonging to the Kingdom of Heaven: "The Beatitudes depict the countenance of Jesus Christ and portray his charity. They express the

Is 57:15; 61:1
Lk 4:18

Ps 126:6
Is 61:2

Ps 37:11

Rev 7:16f

Mt 18:33
Jas 2:13

Ps 24:3–4; 51:10;
73:1

Sir 4:11
Heb 12:14
Rev 22:4

³"Blessed are the poor in spirit, for theirs is the kingdom of heaven.

⁴"Blessed are those who mourn, for they shall be comforted.

⁵"Blessed are the meek, for they shall inherit the earth.

⁶"Blessed are those who hunger and thirst for righteousness, for they shall be satisfied.

⁷"Blessed are the merciful, for they shall obtain mercy.

⁸"Blessed are the pure in heart, for they shall see God.

⁹"Blessed are the peacemakers, for they shall be called sons of God.

ipsorum est regnum caelorum. ⁴Beati, qui lugent, quoniam ipsi consolabuntur. ⁵Beati mites, quoniam ipsi possidebunt terram. ⁶Beati, qui esuriunt et sitiunt iustitiam, quoniam ipsi saturabuntur. ⁷Beati misericordes, quia ipsi misericordiam consequentur. ⁸Beati mundo corde, quoniam ipsi Deum videbunt. ⁹Beati pacifici, quoniam filii Dei vocabuntur. ¹⁰Beati, qui persecutionem patiuntur propter iustitiam, quoniam ipsorum est regnum caelo-

vocation of the faithful associated with the glory of his Passion and Resurrection; they shed light on the actions and attitudes characteristic of the Christian life; they are the paradoxical promises that sustain hope in the midst of tribulations; they proclaim the blessings and rewards already secured, however dimly, for Christ's disciples; they have begun in the lives of the Virgin Mary and all the saints" (*Catechism of the Catholic Church*, 1717).

The wording of blessing found in the Beatitudes belongs to traditional biblical language: the book of Psalms, for example, begins in the same way: "Blessed is ..." (Ps 1:1). The Beatitudes proclaim how to be fortunate, blessed. In this sense, they are at the heart of human desires, for "we all want to be happy. No one in the whole human race would deny that he wants to be happy, even if he is not sure what to be happy means" (St Augustine, *De moribus ecclesiae*, 1, 3, 4). But Christ gives them an eschatological meaning, that is, one leading to eternal salvation: if people live in the way he describes, they will find the door of heaven open to them. God is not indifferent to us; he is active in our interest: he will console his followers, will meet their needs, will call them his sons and daughters, etc. The Beatitudes are a map of the route to human happiness, and one reason they are such a good one is that they express the dual desire that God has written on the human heart— to attain true happiness on earth and eternal bliss.

St Matthew records nine beatitudes: the first eight deal with the attitudes of the Christian towards the world (vv. 3–10); but the ninth, which begins "Blessed are you", not "Blessed are those", refers to those who suffer on Christ's

account. This last beatitude is followed by a call to joy: suffering for Christ is a sign that a person has chosen the right road. In St Luke's text (see Lk 6:20–26 and note), this aspect is given even more emphasis.

The Beatitudes have been much commented on in the Church's catechesis. The first (v. 3) and the eighth (v. 10) mention the reward of the Kingdom of heaven. The first proclaims the blessedness of "the poor in spirit". In the Old Testament poverty was seen not just as a material condition; it had religious value (cf. Zeph 2:3ff): those are poor who turn to God, not relying on their own merits but realizing that they are sinners in need of God's help. They live temperate and austere lives, not only because of their material circumstances, but because they wish to accept and live in a humble condition, freely and generously. The eighth Beatitude describes as blessed those "who are persecuted for righteousness' sake". In the Bible, righteousness (justice) has a wider, more religious, meaning than it does in a legal-moral context. "In Hebrew a just man means a good and faithful servant of God, someone who fulfils the divine will (cf. Gen 7:1; 18:23–32; Ezek 18:5ff; Prov 12:10), or who is honourable and charitable towards his neighbour (cf. Tob 7:6; 9:6). So a just man is someone who loves God and proves his love by keeping God's commandments and directing his whole life towards the service of his brothers, his fellow men" (St Josemaría Escrivá, *Christ Is Passing By*, 40). This linking of the search for justice to the experience of persecution may imply that this Beatitude "fulfils the other beatitudes in a perfect way: the man who lives according to the beatitudes even when he is persecuted for his

¹⁰"Blessed are those who are persecuted for righteousness' sake, for theirs is the kingdom of heaven.

1 Pet 3:14; 4:14
Acts 5:41

¹¹"Blessed are you when men revile you and persecute you and utter all kinds of evil against you falsely on my account.

¹²"Rejoice and be glad, for your reward is great in heaven, for so men persecuted the prophets who were before you.

Mt 23:30
Heb 11:32–38
Jas 5:10

Salt of the earth and light of the world

¹³"You are the salt of the earth; but if salt has lost its taste, how shall its saltness be restored? It is no longer good for anything except to be thrown out and trodden under foot by men.

Mk 9:50

rum. ¹¹Beati estis cum maledixerint vobis et persecuti vos fuerint et dixerint omne malum adversum vos, mentientes, propter me. ¹²Gaudete et exsultate, quoniam merces vestra copiosa est in caelis; sic enim persecuti sunt prophetas, qui fuerunt ante vos. ¹³Vos estis sal terrae; quod si sal evanuerit, in quo salietur? Ad nihilum valet ultra, nisi ut mittatur foras et conculcetur ab hominibus. ¹⁴Vos estis lux mundi. Non potest civitas

convictions will be blessed" (St Thomas Aquinas, *Super Evangelium Matthaei*, ad loc.).

Two Beatitudes, the second and the fourth (vv. 4, 6), promise the reward in the passive voice: it is God who will comfort and satisfy them. "Those who mourn" are people who suffer some sort of affliction, and especially those who grieve over offences committed against God by themselves or by others. Those who "hunger and thirst" are people who sincerely try to do the will of God, which they can discern from the commandments, from the duties that their state in life involves, and from their inner union with God: they are, in other words, those who seek holiness. Significantly, the reward comes from God, for only he can truly console us and only he can make us saints.

"The meek" (v. 5) are those who, imitating Christ (see 11:25–30 and 12:15–21), remain serene, humble and steadfast in adversity, and do not give in to bitterness or discouragement: "Adopted as true sons of God, we are made in the likeness of our Creator. We do not reflect the power of his image, because that power is his alone; we are like him in innocence, simplicity, meekness, patience, mercy and peace, in the virtues for which our Lord deigned to become one of us and to be like us" (St Peter Chrysologus, *Sermones*, 117). "The merciful" (v. 7) are those who show understanding of the defects and needs of others, overlooking faults and rendering what help they can. The parable of the unforgiving servant (18:23–35), particularly the words of the king (18:32–33), is the best commentary on this Beatitude.

"They shall see God" (v. 8) refers not just to ultimate happiness in heaven. In the language of the Old Testament it means, rather, having a close relationship with God, sharing in his decisions, the way a king's counsellors help him to govern. This is what the virtue of purity enables us to do: "[It] is the precondition of the vision of God. Even now it enables us to see according to God, to accept others as 'neighbours'; it lets us perceive the human body—ours and our neighbour's—as a temple of the Holy Spirit, a manifestation of divine beauty" (*Catechism of the Catholic Church*, 2519).

The "peacemakers" (v. 9) are those who foster peace in themselves and among others, and, as a basis for that, try to be reconciled with God and to help others to be so: "Peace is never attained once and for all, but must be built up ceaselessly. Moreover, since the human will is unsteady and wounded by sin, the achievement of peace requires a constant mastering of passions and the vigilance of lawful authority. But this is not enough. [...] Peace is likewise the fruit of love, which goes beyond what justice can provide" (Vatican II, *Gaudium et spes*, 78).

5:13–16 Salt and light are good images for describing those who practise the Beatitudes, that is, those who are disciples of Jesus, and they show the importance of good works (v. 16). Everyone needs to strive for personal holiness—and for the holiness of others. Jesus uses these two images to illustrate his message.

Mk 4:21
Lk 11:33; 8:16
Jn 8:12
1 Thess 5:5
Rev 21:10f
Eph 5:8–9
1 Pet 2:12

¹⁴"You are the light of the world. A city set on a hill cannot be hid. ¹⁵Nor do men light a lamp and put it under a bushel, but on a stand, and it gives light to all the house. ¹⁶Let your light so shine before men, that they may see your good works and give glory to your Father who is in heaven.

Lk 6:27–36

Lk 4:21

Lk 16:17; 21:33
Rom 3:31; 10:4

Jas 2:10

Jesus and his teaching, the fullness of the Law

¹⁷"Think not that I have come to abolish the law and the prophets; I have come not to abolish them but to fulfil them.* ¹⁸For truly I say to you, till heaven and earth pass away, not an iota, not a dot, will pass from the law until all is accomplished. ¹⁹Whoever then relaxes one of the least of these commandments and teaches men so, shall be called least in the kingdom of heaven; but he who does them and teaches

abscondi supra montem posita; ¹⁵neque accendunt lucernam et ponunt eam sub modio, sed super candelabrum, ut luceat omnibus, qui in domo sunt. ¹⁶Sic luceat lux vestra coram hominibus, ut videant vestra bona opera et glorificent Patrem vestrum, qui in caelis est. ¹⁷Nolite putare quoniam veni solvere Legem aut Prophetas; non veni solvere, sed adimplere. ¹⁸Amen quippe dico vobis: Donec transeat caelum et terra, iota unum aut unus apex non praeteribit a Lege, donec omnia fiant. ¹⁹Qui ergo solverit unum de mandatis istis minimis et docuerit sic homines, minimus

Salt preserves food from corruption. In the sacrifices of the Old Law it symbolized the inviolability and permanence of the Covenant (see Lev 2:13). Our Lord tells his disciples that they are the salt of the earth, that is, they give a divine flavour to human things and help preserve the world from corruption, by keeping the Covenant alive. "As the soul is in the body, so are Christians in the world" (*Epistula ad Diognetum*, 6, 1).

We need light in order to find our way through life. In the Old Testament, this essential light was God (see Ps 27:1) and the word of God (see Ps 119:105). Now Jesus is saying that his disciples should, like him, be a light for those who dwell in darkness (cf. 4:16; Is 8:23–9:1). "It seems to me that this lamp is the symbol of charity; it must shine out not only to fill with joy those we love best, but all in the house" (St Thérèse of Lisieux, *Autobiographical writings*, 9). If the light and leaven of charity are present, all good works are works of Christian apostolate. "Laymen have countless opportunities for exercising the apostolate of evangelization and sanctification. The very witness of a Christian life, and good works done in a supernatural spirit, are effective in drawing men to the faith and to God; and that is what the Lord has said: 'Let your light shine before men, that they may see your good works and give glory to your Father who is in heaven'" (Vatican II, *Apostolicum actuositatem*, 6).

If the disciples lose their sense of Christian identity, they are useless—like salt that loses its flavour. Christians make a nonsense of their belief if their attachment to Christ does not express itself in good works (vv. 14–15). A bushel was a measure of dry goods (about 7.5 litres or 2 gallons); the same word was used for the container which was probably used for putting out oil lamps at night so as to prevent the build-up of fumes in the house. Our Lord does not give us light so that we might then simply put it out.

5:17–48 In the atmosphere of messianic expectancy in the time of Jesus, it was common to attribute to the Messiah the role of authoritative interpreter of the Law. While drawing the parallel with Moses, St Matthew shows that Jesus goes beyond that by putting himself on the same level as God, above the Law. Jesus teaches the true value of the Law given by God to the Jewish people through Moses, and he perfects it by giving it its definitive interpretation; he has divine authority to do so. To the "it was said [by God]", Jesus adds his own teaching. He does not abolish the precepts of the Old Law (v. 18), but he does demonstrate their *personal* significance and brings them to perfection (v. 17), by uncovering their implications, depths that people had not realized. The words of Christ in this Sermon on the Mount are, to use a famous phrase, "the perfect expression of the Christian life" (St Augustine, *De Sermone Domini in monte*, 1, 1, 1).

Having explained the value of the Law in general terms (vv. 17–19), and pointed out that its true practice must go beyond mere formal

them shall be called great in the kingdom of heaven. [20]For I tell you, unless your righteousness exceeds that of the scribes and Pharisees, you will never enter the kingdom of heaven.

[21]"You have heard that it was said to the men of old, 'You shall not kill; and whoever kills shall be liable to judgment.' [22]But I say to you that every one who is angry with his brother[i] shall be liable to judgment; whoever insults[j] his brother shall be liable to the council, and whoever says, 'You fool!' shall be liable to the hell[k] of fire. [23]So if you are offering your gift at the altar, and there remember that your brother has something against you, [24]leave your gift there before the altar and go; first be reconciled to your brother, and then come and offer your gift. [25]Make friends quickly with your accuser, while you are going with him to court, lest your accuser hand you over to the judge, and the judge to the guard, and you be put in prison; [26]truly, I say to you, you will never get out till you have paid the last penny.

Ex 20:13; 21:12
Deut 5:17
Lev 24:17

1 Jn 3:15

Mt 18:35

Lk 12:58–59

vocabitur in regno caelorum; qui autem fecerit et docuerit, hic magnus vocabitur in regno caelorum. [20]Dico enim vobis: Nisi abundaverit iustitia vestra plus quam scribarum et pharisaeorum, non intrabitis in regnum caelorum. [21]Audistis quia dictum est antiquis: *"Non occides*; qui autem occiderit, reus erit iudicio". [22]Ego autem dico vobis: Omnis, qui irascitur fratri suo, reus erit iudicio; qui autem dixerit fratri suo: "Racha", reus erit concilio; qui autem dixerit: "Fatue", reus erit gehennae ignis. [23]Si ergo offeres munus tuum ad altare, et ibi recordatus fueris quia frater tuus habet aliquid adversum te, [24]relinque ibi munus tuum ante altare et vade prius, reconciliare fratri tuo et tunc veniens offer munus tuum. [25]Esto consentiens adversario tuo cito, dum es in via cum eo, ne forte tradat te adversarius iudici, et iudex tradat te ministro, et in carcerem mittaris. [26]Amen dico tibi: Non exies inde, donec reddas novissimum quadrantem. [27]Audistis quia dictum est: *"Non moechaberis"*. [28]Ego autem dico vobis: Omnis,

compliance (v. 20), our Lord now gives a series of examples (vv. 21–47). They don't appear to be in any particular order, though they seem to refer to five of the commandments of the Decalogue—the fifth (vv. 21–26), sixth (vv. 27–32), eighth (vv. 33–37), seventh (vv. 38–42) and tenth (vv. 43–47). Our Lord calls on us to internalize the commandments—by being generous (vv. 40–42) and open-hearted (vv. 44–47), by not using subterfuges or merely giving lip-service (vv. 34–37), etc. But above all, he personalizes his teaching: everyone will appear before God and be called to account.

In v. 22, Jesus points to three faults we can commit against charity. They are listed in ascending order, in terms of their gravity. First comes "anger", or inner irritation, and then comes the sin of uttering insults. As the RSV note mentions, "whoever insults his brother" is a translation of "whoever says Raca to his brother". *Raca* is an Aramaic word not easy to translate; it is the equivalent of calling someone "foolish, empty-headed"; Jews used it to show contempt. Finally, the verse speaks of calling someone "You fool": in the original it is even stronger than *raca*; it implies that a person has lost all moral and religious sense. St Augustine, when commenting on this passage (*De Sermone Domini in monte*, 1, 9, 24), notes that just as

there is a gradation in sin, so there is in punishment. The passage also tells us the seriousness of sins against charity (resentment, hatred etc.) which easily express themselves outwardly (in gossip, backbiting, calumny etc.).

Our Lord shows the full reach of the Old Law precepts about adultery and lust (vv. 27–30). He condemns sinful glances. "Right eye" and "right hand" (vv. 29–30) mean things that we greatly value. He is saying not that we should mutilate ourselves but that we should not give in to ourselves; we should be ready to sacrifice anything that could lead to an offence against God. Our Lord's very graphic words warn us against one of the most common occasions of sin: we need to guard our sight.

The practice of divorce gets special mention. The Law of Moses (see Deut 24:1–4) tolerated it due to the hardness of heart of the Israelites. Jesus re-establishes marriage as God instituted it, giving it back its original indissolubility (cf. 19:4–6; Gen 1:27; 2:24; Eph 5:31; 1 Cor 7:10).

"Except on the ground of unchastity": see the RSVCE note at the end of this volume. This phrase should not be taken as indicating an exception to the principle of the indissolubility of marriage which Jesus has just reinstated. The phrase probably refers to unions that some pagan societies accepted as being true marriages, but

i Other ancient authorities insert *without cause*   j Greek *says Raca to* (an obscure term of abuse)   k Greek *Gehenna*

Ex 20:14
Deut 5:18
Job 31:1

2 Pet 2:14

Mt 18:8–9
Mk 9:43, 47
Col 3:5

27"You have heard that it was said, 'You shall not commit adultery.' 28But I say to you that every one who looks at a woman lustfully has already committed adultery with her in his heart. 29If your right eye causes you to sin, pluck it out and throw it away; it is better that you lose one of your members than that your whole body be thrown into hell.[k]* 30And if your right hand causes you to sin, cut it off and throw it away; it is better that you lose one of your members than that your whole body go into hell.[k]

Mk 10:4–12

Deut 24:1
Mt 19:3–9
Mk 10:3–4, 11–12
Lk 16:18
1 Cor 7:10–11

31"It was also said, 'Whoever divorces his wife, let him give her a certificate of divorce.' 32But I say to you that every one who divorces his wife, except on the ground of unchastity,* makes her an adulteress; and whoever marries a divorced woman commits adultery.

Lev 19:12

Num 30:3
Deut 23:22
Sir 23:9
Mt 23:20–22

Is 66:1; Jas 5:12
Ps 11:4; 48:2
Acts 7:49

Jas 5:12

33"Again you have heard that it was said to the men of old, 'You shall not swear falsely, but shall perform to the Lord what you have sworn.' 34But I say to you, Do not swear at all, either by heaven, for it is the throne of God, 35or by the earth, for it is his footstool, or by Jerusalem, for it is the city of the great King. 36And do not swear by your head, for you cannot make one hair white or black. 37Let what you say be simply 'Yes' or 'No'; anything more than this comes from evil.[l]

Ex 21:24
Lev 24:19, 20

Jn 18:22–23
1 Pet 3:9

Is 50:6
Rom 12:19–21
1 Cor 6:7

Lk 6:30

38"You have heard that it was said, 'An eye for an eye and a tooth for a tooth.' 39But I say to you, Do not resist one who is evil. But if any one strikes you on the right cheek, turn to him the other also; 40and if any one would sue you and take your coat, let him have your cloak as well; 41and if any one forces you to go one mile, go with him two miles. 42Give to him who begs from you, and do not refuse him who would borrow from you.

Lev 19:18
Mt 22:39
Lk 6:27f; 23:34

Sir 4:10
Lk 6:27–36; 23:34
Acts 7:59
Rom 12:14, 20

43"You have heard that it was said, 'You shall love your neighbour and hate your enemy.' 44But I say to you, Love your enemies and pray for those who persecute you, 45so that you may be sons of your Father who is in heaven; for he makes his sun rise on the evil and on the good, and sends rain on the just and on the unjust. 46For

qui viderit mulierem ad concupiscendum eam, iam moechatus est eam in corde suo. 29Quod si oculus tuus dexter scandalizat te, erue eum et proice abs te; expedit enim tibi, ut pereat unum membrorum tuorum, quam totum corpus tuum mittatur in gehennam. 30Et si dextera manus tua scandalizat te, abscide eam et proice abs te; expedit enim tibi, ut pereat unum membrorum tuorum, quam totum corpus tuum abeat in gehennam. 31Dictum est autem: "*Quicumque dimiserit uxorem suam, det illi libellum repudii*". 32Ego autem dico vobis: Omnis, qui dimiserit uxorem suam, excepta fornicationis causa, facit eam moechari; et, qui dimissam duxerit, adulterat. 33Iterum audistis quia dictum est antiquis: "*Non periurabis*; *reddes autem Domino iuramenta tua*". 34Ego autem dico vobis: Non iurare omnino, neque per *caelum*, quia *thronus Dei est*, 35neque per *terram*, quia *scabellum est pedum eius*, neque per Hierosolymam, quia *civitas* est *magni Regis*; 36neque per caput tuum iuraveris, quia non potes unum capillum album facere aut nigrum. 37Sit autem sermo vester: "Est, est", "Non, non"; quod autem his abundantius est, a Malo est. 38Audistis quia dictum est:

which the Mosaic Law (see Lev 18) and rabbinical tradition outlawed because they took place within the forbidden degrees of consanguinity — in other words, unions that were radically invalid due to some impediment.

Verse 48 sums up the teaching of the whole chapter. Inevitably, it is reminiscent of this precept in Leviticus: "therefore you shall be holy, for I am holy" (Lev 11:44). Our Lord amplifies the meaning of the Law by proposing that we take as our model the perfection of our Father in heaven. And the way to do this is to imitate Jesus: "If you want to be like God, in whose image and likeness you were made, follow

[Christ's] example. You are Christians, whose very name is a sign of goodness: imitate the love of Christ" (St Asterius of Amasea, *Homiliae*, 13). The ultimate reason for keeping the Law is to attain the holiness of God. Strictly speaking, it is not possible for a created being to have the perfection that God has. Therefore, what our Lord means here is that divine perfection should be the model towards which the Christian strives, while knowing that there is an infinite distance between us and our Creator. This "universal call to holiness" is not merely a suggestion; it is a requirement laid down by Jesus. "Your duty is to sanctify yourself. Yes, even you. Who thinks that

k Greek *Gehenna*   l Or *the evil one*

if you love those who love you, what reward have you? Do not even the tax collectors do the same? ⁴⁷And if you salute only your brethren, what more are you doing than others? Do not even the Gentiles do the same? ⁴⁸You, therefore, must be perfect, as your heavenly Father is perfect.

Lev 11:44; 19:2
Eph 5:1
Jas 1:4
1 Pet 1:16

An upright intention in almsgiving, prayer and fasting

Lk 11:1–4

6 ¹"Beware of practising your piety before men in order to be seen by them; for then you will have no reward from your Father who is in heaven.

Mt 5:20; 23:5
Lk 16:14–15
Jn 5:44; 12:43

²"Thus, when you give alms, sound no trumpet before you, as the hypocrites do in the synagogues and in the streets, that they may be praised by men. Truly, I say to you, they have their reward. ³But when you give alms, do not let your left hand know what your right hand is doing, ⁴so that your alms may be in secret; and your Father who sees in secret will reward you.

Amos 4:5
Mt 22:18; 23:13–15

Rom 12:8

Ps 139

⁵"And when you pray, you must not be like the hypocrites; for they love to stand and pray in the synagogues and at the street corners, that they may be seen by men. Truly, I say to you, they have their reward. ⁶But when you pray, go into your room and shut the door and pray to your Father who is in secret; and your Father who sees in secret will reward you.*

Jas 4:3

2 Kings 4:33
Is 26:20

"*Oculum pro oculo* et *dentem pro dente*". ³⁹Ego autem dico vobis: Non resistere malo; sed si quis te percusserit in dextera maxilla tua, praebe illi et alteram; ⁴⁰et ei, qui vult tecum iudicio contendere et tunicam tuam tollere, remitte ei et pallium; ⁴¹et quicumque te angariaverit mille passus, vade cum illo duo. ⁴²Qui petit a te, da ei; et volenti mutuari a te, ne avertaris. ⁴³Audistis quia dictum est: "*Diliges proximum tuum* et odio habebis inimicum tuum". ⁴⁴Ego autem dico vobis: Diligite inimicos vestros et orate pro persequentibus vos, ⁴⁵ut sitis filii Patris vestri, qui in caelis est, quia solem suum oriri facit super malos et bonos et pluit super iustos et iniustos. ⁴⁶Si enim dilexeritis eos, qui vos diligunt, quam mercedem habetis? Nonne et publicani hoc faciunt? ⁴⁷Et si salutaveritis fratres vestros tantum, quid amplius facitis? Nonne et ethnici hoc faciunt? ⁴⁸Estote ergo vos perfecti, sicut Pater vester caelestis perfectus est.   [6] ¹Attendite, ne iustitiam vestram faciatis coram hominibus, ut videamini ab eis; alioquin mercedem non habetis apud Patrem vestrum, qui in caelis est.²Cum ergo facies eleemosynam, noli tuba canere ante te, sicut hypocritae faciunt in synagogis et in vicis, ut honorificentur ab hominibus. Amen dico vobis: Receperunt mercedem suam. ³Te autem faciente eleemosynam,

this task is only for priests and religious? To everyone, without exception, our Lord said: 'Be ye perfect, as my heavenly Father is perfect'" (St Josemaría Escrivá, *The Way*, 291). See also the note on 1 Thess 4:1–8.

6:1–18 These verses continue Jesus' teaching about true "righteousness". According to the teachers of the time, almsgiving, prayer and fasting, as essentials of personal piety, were to be seen as practically on a par with the commandments of the Law. Jesus takes issue with mere external fulfilment of these practices, and teaches that true devotion calls for sincerity and a right intention, intimacy with God without parading one's piety. The Church reminds us of these practices at the start of Lent: "Appropriate fasting and almsgiving, together called works of mercy, are praiseworthy and pious actions; in times of inequality of wealth and possessions, the souls of all the faithful may be one and equal in their desire for good" (St Leo the Great, *Sermo 6 in Quadragesima*, 1–2).

But the verses of this text that have been most commented on are those to do with prayer. Our Lord stresses the simplicity and sincerity with which we should approach God. The first injunction comes in a negative form. A Christian's prayer should never be that of someone who is putting on an act (the word "hypocrite" used in v. 5 originally meant an actor, or a person on stage), nor should it be servile or grovelling like that of those pagans who, in their prayers, used to list all the qualities of the god they were addressing, to the point of exhaustion, in case the god should be angered if even one such quality were omitted (v. 7). A Christian's prayer should be sincere: "What we think should conform with what we say" (St Benedict, *Regula*, 19).

Jesus then goes on to teach the Our Father as the distinctive Christian prayer (vv. 9–13). "The Lord's Prayer is truly a summary of the whole Gospel" (Tertullian, *De oratione*, 1). All through Christian tradition this prayer receives commentary that is full of deep feeling and wisdom:

Is 1:15
Sir 7:14

Mt 6:32; 7:11
Lk 12:30

Lk 11:2–4
Ezek 36:23
Jn 17:6

Mt 26:49, 32
Lk 22:42

Jn 6:32–35
Prov 30:8–9

Mt 18:21:35
Eph 4:32
Sir 28:2

Mt 26:41
2 Thess 3:3

Mt 5:7
Mk 11:25–26
Sir 28:1–5
Lk 6:37

Eph 4:32
Jas 2:13

Mt 23:5
Is 58:5–9

[7]"And in praying do not heap up empty phrases as the Gentiles do; for they think that they will be heard for their many words. [8]Do not be like them, for your Father knows what you need before you ask him. [9]Pray then like this:

> Our Father who art in heaven,
> Hallowed be thy name.
> [10] Thy kingdom come,
> Thy will be done,
> On earth as it is in heaven.
> [11]Give us this day our daily bread;[m]
> [12]And forgive us our debts,
> As we also have forgiven our debtors;
> [13]And lead us not into temptation,
> But deliver us from evil.[n]

[14]For if you forgive men their trespasses, your heavenly Father also will forgive you; [15]but if you do not forgive men their trespasses, neither will your Father forgive your trespasses.

[16]"And when you fast, do not look dismal, like the hypocrites, for they disfigure their faces that their fasting may be seen by men. Truly, I say to you, they have their

nesciat sinistra tua quid faciat dextera tua, [4]ut sit eleemosyna tua in abscondito, et Pater tuus, qui videt in abscondito, reddet tibi. [5]Et cum oratis, non eritis sicut hypocritae, qui amant in synagogis et in angulis platearum stantes orare, ut videantur ab hominibus. Amen dico vobis: Receperunt mercedem suam. [6]Tu autem cum orabis, intra in cubiculum tuum et, clauso ostio tuo, ora Patrem tuum, qui est in abscondito; et Pater tuus, qui videt in abscondito, reddet tibi. [7]Orantes autem nolite multum loqui sicut ethnici: putant enim quia in multiloquio suo exaudiantur. [8]Nolite ergo assimilari eis; scit enim Pater vester, quibus opus sit vobis, antequam petatis eum. [9]Sic ergo vos orabitis: Pater noster, qui es in caelis, / sanctificetur nomen tuum, / [10]adveniat regnum tuum, / fiat voluntas tua, / sicut in caelo, et in terra. / [11]Panem nostrum supersubstantialem da nobis hodie; / [12]et dimitte nobis debita nostra, / sicut et nos dimittimus debitoribus nostris; / [13]et ne inducas nos in tentationem, / sed libera nos a Malo. [14]Si enim dimiseritis hominibus peccata eorum, dimittet et vobis Pater vester caelestis; [15]si autem non dimiseritis hominibus, nec Pater vester dimit-

"The Lord's Prayer is the most perfect of prayers […]. In it we ask, not only for all the things we can rightly desire, but also in the sequence that they should be desired. This prayer teaches us not only to ask for things, but also in what order we should desire them" (St Thomas Aquinas, *Summa theologiae*, 2–2, 83, 9). The prayer begins with invoking of the Father; and in the wording recorded by St Matthew its liturgical dimension (prayer in common) is stressed. "The Lord taught us to pray together with and for all our brothers. He did not say: 'My Father, who art in heaven'; he said: 'Our Father'. Our prayer should be the prayer of one heart and one soul, to build up the one body of the Church" (St John Chrysostom, *In Matthaeum*, 19, 41). The invocation is followed by petitions: "After we have placed ourselves in the presence of God our Father to adore and to love and to bless him, the Spirit of adoption stirs up in our hearts seven petitions, seven blessings. The first three, more theological, draw us toward the glory of the Father; the last four, as ways toward him, commend our wretchedness to his grace"

(*Catechism of the Catholic Church*, 2803).

The first petition is for the Name of God to be sanctified (v. 9). In the Bible, a person's "name" often means the person himself. Since God is holiness itself, what is being asked for here is that his holiness be acknowledged and honoured by all those whom he has created. The coming of the Kingdom (v. 10, the second petition) entails the implementing of God's saving plans for the world (see the note on 3:1–12). Therefore, one of the signs of the coming of the Kingdom is loving fulfilment of God's will (third petition).

The final petitions, for daily bread (fourth), forgiveness of debts and offences (fifth), protection from temptation (sixth) and deliverance from evil (seventh)—see the note on Luke 11:1–4—refer to our needs. The first Gospel adds a gloss on the fifth petition (v. 12) consisting of words of our Lord (vv. 14–15) which require us to forgive others if our prayer is to be effective: "We should study this point very carefully, sisters: the Lord's forgiveness of our sins, for which

m Or *our bread for the morrow* n Or *the evil one*. Other authorities, some ancient, add, in some form, *For thine is the kingdom and the power and the glory, for ever. Amen*

reward. [17]But when you fast, anoint your head and wash your face, [18]that your fast- Jud 10:3
ing may not be seen by men but by your Father who is in secret; and your Father Is 58:3
who sees in secret will reward you.

Trust in God's fatherly providence Lk 12:22–34

[19]"Do not lay up for yourselves treasures on earth, where moth and rust° consume Job 22:24–26
Sir 29:10
and where thieves break in and steal, [20]but lay up for yourselves treasures in heaven, Lk 12:33–34; 18:22
where neither moth nor rust° consumes and where thieves do not break in and steal. Mt 19:21
Mk 10:21
[21]For where your treasure is, there will your heart be also. Col 3:1–2
Jas 5:2–3

[22]"The eye is the lamp of the body. So, if your eye is sound, your whole body Lk 11:34–36
will be full of light; [23]but if your eye is not sound, your whole body will be full of Deut 15:9
Sir 14:10
darkness. If then the light in you is darkness, how great is the darkness! Jn 11:9–10

[24]"No one can serve two masters; for either he will hate the one and love the Lk 16:13
other, or he will be devoted to the one and despise the other. You cannot serve God Mt 5:3–4; 19:21–26
and mammon.*

[25]"Therefore I tell you, do not be anxious about your life, what you shall eat or Ps 127
Mt 10:29–31
what you shall drink, nor about your body, what you shall put on. Is not life more Lk 12:6–7, 22–31
than food, and the body more than clothing? [26]Look at the birds of the air; they nei- Mt 10:31

tet peccata vestra. [16]Cum autem ieiunatis, nolite fieri sicut hypocritae tristes; demoliuntur enim facies suas, ut pareant hominibus ieiunantes. Amen dico vobis: Receperunt mercedem suam. [17]Tu autem cum ieiunas, unge caput tuum et faciem tuam lava, [18]ne videaris hominibus ieiunans sed Patri tuo, qui est in abscondito; et Pater tuus, qui videt in abscondito, reddet tibi. [19]Nolite thesaurizare vobis thesauros in terra, ubi aerugo et tinea demolitur, et ubi fures effodiunt et furantur; [20]thesaurizate autem vobis thesauros in caelo, ubi neque aerugo neque tinea demolitur, et ubi fures non effodiunt nec furantur; [21]ubi enim est thesaurus tuus, ibi erit et cor tuum. [22]Lucerna corporis est oculus. Si ergo fuerit oculus tuus simplex, totum corpus tuum lucidum erit; [23]si autem oculus tuus nequam fuerit, totum corpus tuum tenebrosum erit. Si ergo lumen, quod in te est, tenebrae sunt, tenebrae quantae erunt! [24]Nemo potest duobus dominis servire: aut enim unum odio habebit et alterum diliget aut unum sustinebit et alterum contemnet; non potestis Deo servire et mammonae. [25]Ideo dico vobis: Ne solliciti sitis animae vestrae quid manducetis, neque corpori vestro quid

we deserve the fires of hell, the pardon of which we are in such great need, depends on something as small as our forgiving others. I have so little to forgive [others], Lord, that you forgive me for nothing. Such is your great mercy. Blessed are you" (St Teresa of Avila, *Way of Perfection*, 36, 2). "Debts" is the equivalent here of offences or sins. It is not just a matter of acknowledging our past sins: we also need to admit that we are, by our own fallen human nature, sinners.

In the sixth petition (v. 13) we acknowledge our weakness when it comes to fighting temptation if we rely only on our own resources: that is why we pray for God's help (cf. *Roman Catechism*, 4, 15, 14).

"Deliver us from evil" (v. 13b, seventh petition) could also be translated as "Deliver us from the evil one", that is, the devil, who in the last analysis is the author of all the evils to which we succumb.

6:19–34 This series of teachings stresses again the inner, spiritual character of the Law, which

our Lord wants to bring to perfection. The human heart desires a treasure that will provide security and happiness. Jesus teaches that the true treasure trove is made of good works done with an upright intention; these will obtain for us an eternal reward from God in heaven. That is what Christ's disciples should set their hearts on. Once again, the righteousness (holiness) of the Kingdom of God comes across as the only thing that really matters; a person who tries to do the will of the Father in line with Jesus' words will have everything else granted to him or her (see v. 33).

Verses 22–23 are a jewel of Jesus' wisdom teaching. The Master uses the simile of the eye as a lamp that provides the body with light. Christian exegesis has read this "eye" and this "lamp" to mean the motivation behind our actions: "The eye refers to motive. When a person wants to do something, he first forms an intention: thus, if your intention is sound—simple and clear—that is to say, if it is directed towards God, your whole body, that is, all your actions, will be sound, sincerely directed towards

o Or *worm*

ther sow nor reap nor gather into barns, and yet your heavenly Father feeds them. Are you not of more value than they? [27]And which of you by being anxious can add one cubit to his span of life?[p] [28]And why are you anxious about clothing? Consider the lilies of the field, how they grow; they neither toil nor spin; [29]yet I tell you, even Solomon in all his glory was not arrayed like one of these. [30]But if God so clothes the grass of the field, which today is alive and tomorrow is thrown into the oven, will he not much more clothe you, O men of little faith? [31]Therefore do not be anxious, saying, 'What shall we eat?' or 'What shall we drink?' or 'What shall we wear?' [32]For the Gentiles seek all these things; and your heavenly Father knows that you need them all. [33]But seek first his kingdom and his righteousness, and all these things shall be yours as well.

[34]"Therefore do not be anxious about tomorrow, for tomorrow will be anxious for itself. Let the day's own trouble be sufficient for the day.

Various precepts. Do not judge

7 [1]"Judge not, that you be not judged. [2]For with the judgment you pronounce you will be judged, and the measure you give will be the measure you get. [3]Why do you see the speck that is in your brother's eye, but do not notice the log that is in your

1 Kings 10:1–29
2 Chron 9:13–28
Ps 90:5f; 103:15

Phil 4:6
1 Pet 5:7, 1
Tm 6:8
Heb 13:5

Mt 6:8

Rom 14:17
1 Kings 3:13–14
Ps 37:4, 25

Ex 16:19
Wis 7:11
Jas 4:13–14

Mk 4:24
Lk 6:37–42

Rom 2:1
1 Cor 4:5
Jas 4:11f

Jn 8:7

induamini. Nonne anima plus est quam esca, et corpus quam vestimentum? [26]Respicite volatilia caeli, quoniam non serunt neque metunt neque congregant in horrea, et Pater vester caelestis pascit illa. Nonne vos magis pluris estis illis? [27]Quis autem vestrum cogitans potest adicere ad aetatem suam cubitum unum? [28]Et de vestimento quid solliciti estis? Considerate lilia agri quomodo crescunt: non laborant neque nent. [29]Dico autem vobis quoniam nec Salomon in omni gloria sua coopertus est sicut unum ex istis. [30]Si autem fenum agri, quod hodie est et cras in clibanum mittitur, Deus sic vestit, quanto magis vos, modicae fidei? [31]Nolite ergo solliciti esse dicentes: "Quid manducabimus?", aut: "Quid bibemus?", aut: "Quo operiemur?". [32]Haec enim omnia gentes inquirunt; scit enim Pater vester caelestis quia his omnibus indigetis. [33]Quaerite autem primum regnum Dei et iustitiam eius, et haec omnia adicientur vobis. [34]Nolite ergo esse solliciti in crastinum; crastinus enim dies sollicitus erit sibi ipse. Sufficit diei malitia sua. [7] [1]Nolite iudicare, ut non iudicemini; [2]in quo enim iudicio iudicaveritis, iudicabimini, et in qua mensura mensi fueritis, metietur vobis. [3]Quid autem vides festucam in oculo fratris tui, et trabem in oculo tuo non vides? [4]Aut quomodo dices fratri tuo: 'Sine, eiciam

good" (St Thomas Aquinas, *Super Evangelium Matthaei*, ad loc.).

Verses 25–32 tell us more about the attitude we should have when praying the Our Father; in the midst of our ordinary, everyday life, we should put our trust in God. These verses remind us that God is not a stranger to the world in which we live: he feeds the birds of the air (v. 26), gives to the lilies of the field their beauty (v. 29), etc. "If only we could live with more trust in divine Providence, strong in faith, in the certainty of God's daily protection which never fails, how many worries and anxieties we would be spared! Then that fretfulness which, as Jesus said, is typical of pagans, of 'the heathen world', that is, of people who lack a supernatural outlook on life, would disappear. [...] We are, by God's mercy, children of our almighty Father, who is in heaven but who also dwells in the intimacy of our hearts. [...] Since 'your Father well knows what you need', we have every reason to be optimistic on our journey through this life, with our souls completely detached from those earthly

things that seem so very necessary. God will provide" (St Josemaría Escrivá, *Friends of God*, 116). Further on (vv. 33–34), our Lord encourages us to take each day as it comes, avoid unnecessary anxiety, and seek above all the Kingdom of God and his righteousness, that is, give spiritual concerns priority over material ones. "The Lord told us to sow, but not to be anxious; he told us to work, but not to be small-minded or allow ourselves to be overcome by worries. He told us that we should eat, but not to 'be anxious, saying, *What shall we eat?*'" (St John Chrysostom, *In Matthaeum*, 21, 3).

7:1–12 Here St Matthew records more of our Lord's advice about how his disciples should live their lives. We should practise fraternal charity, and not be out to condemn people (vv.1–2). In line with common practice, the passive voice is used to avoid mentioning the name of God. Jesus here uses the passive voice ("you will be judged", "it will be measured out to you") to indicate that God, who knows all our thoughts,

p Or *to his stature*

own eye? [4]Or how can you say to your brother, 'Let me take the speck out of your eye,' when there is the log in your own eye? [5]You hypocrite, first take the log out of your own eye, and then you will see clearly to take the speck out of your brother's eye.

Respect for holy things

[6]"Do not give dogs what is holy; and do not throw your pearls before swine, lest they trample them under foot and turn to attack you.

Ex 29:33
Lev 22:10
Tob 4:17
2 Pet 2:22

Effectiveness of prayer

[7]"Ask, and it will be given you; seek, and you will find; knock, and it will be opened to you. [8]For every one who asks receives, and he who seeks finds, and to him who knocks it will be opened. [9]Or what man of you, if his son asks him for bread, will give him a stone? [10]Or if he asks for a fish, will give him a serpent? [11]If you then, who are evil, know how to give good gifts to your children, how much more will your Father who is in heaven give good things to those who ask him!

Lk 11:5–13

Mk 11:24
Lk 18:1–8
Mt 18:19; 21:22

Jn 14:13; 16:23–24
1 Jn 3:22; 5:14–15

Jas 1:17

The golden rule

[12]So whatever you wish that men would do to you, do so to them; for this is the law and the prophets.

Lk 6:31

Tob 4:15
Mt 22:40
Rom 13:8–10
Gal 5:14

festucam de oculo tuo', et ecce trabes est in oculo tuo? [5]Hypocrita, eice primum trabem de oculo tuo, et tunc videbis eicere festucam de oculo fratris tui. [6]Nolite dare sanctum canibus, neque mittatis margaritas vestras ante porcos, ne forte conculcent eas pedibus suis et conversi dirumpant vos. [7]Petite, et dabitur vobis; quaerite et invenietis; pulsate, et aperietur vobis. [8]Omnis enim qui petit, accipit; et, qui quaerit, invenit; et pulsanti aperietur. [9]Aut quis est ex vobis homo, quem si petierit filius suus panem, numquid lapidem porriget ei? [10]Aut si piscem petierit, numquid serpentem porriget ei? [11]Si ergo vos, cum sitis mali, nostis dona bona dare filiis vestris, quanto magis Pater vester, qui in caelis est, dabit bona petentibus se. [12]Omnia ergo, quaecumque vultis ut faciant vobis homines, ita et vos facite eis; haec est enim Lex et Prophetae. [13]Intrate per angustam portam, quia lata porta et spatiosa via, quae ducit ad perditionem, et multi sunt, qui intrant per eam; [14]quam angusta porta et arta via, quae ducit

will take account of our motives when judging us: "God measures as we measure, and pardons as we pardon, and shows mercy as we show mercy" (St Gregory the Great, *Moralia*, 29). Then (vv. 3–5) he warns us that our sight can become distorted and see things in a bad light, even when they are fine. Recalling this passage, St Augustine advises: "Try to acquire those virtues which you think your brothers lack, and you will no longer see their defects, because you will not have them yourselves" (*Enarrationes in Psalmos*, 30, 2, 2).

We should also respect our Lord's teaching as something holy, as we would a precious pearl (v. 6). "What is holy" brings to mind the offerings made in the temple: these were holy objects and could be handled only by priests; they were not given to strangers, never mind to dogs, which eat anything, not distinguishing pure from impure (cf. Ex 22:30). The Kingdom of heaven is like a precious pearl (13:45–46) and should not be exposed to anyone who, like an unclean animal, will not appreciate its value and will

render it unclean. The early Christians applied this teaching to the Eucharist: "May only those who have been baptized in the name of the Lord eat and drink of your thanksgiving [for the Eucharist], for the Lord said: 'Do not give dogs what is holy'" (*Didache*, 9, 5).

Finally, our Lord encourages us to pray in the confidence that God our Father will listen to us (vv. 7–11; cf. the note on Lk 11:5–13), and to do good to others unconditionally: we then very logically put no limits on what we will dare ask for ourselves (v. 12). This saying of Jesus', called "the golden rule", gives us a standard to apply when practising charity towards others. In the context of the Sermon on the Mount it links up with our Lord's teaching about the fullness of the Law: love for our neighbour sums up all the commandments (see 5:17–48 and note). However, the "golden rule" marks only the minimal limit of the love we should have; Jesus' teaching on this subject will be completed by his "new commandment"—that we are to love others as he himself has loved us (see Jn 13:34).

Lk 13:22–30

Deut 30:15
Sir 21:10
Jn 10:7, 9
Acts 14:22

The narrow gate

13"Enter by the narrow gate; for the gate is wide and the way is easy,[q] that leads to destruction, and those who enter by it are many. 14For the gate is narrow and the way is hard, that leads to life, and those who find it are few.

Lk 6:43–44

Rev 13:11
Mt 24: 11, 24
1 Jn 4:1
2 Pet 2:1–3
Acts 20:29
Gal 5:19–24
Jas 3:12; Sir 27:6
Mt 12:33
Mt 3:10; Lk 3:9
Jn 15:2, 6

False prophets

15"Beware of false prophets, who come to you in sheep's clothing but inwardly are ravenous wolves. 16You will know them by their fruits. Are grapes gathered from thorns, or figs from thistles? 17So, every sound tree bears good fruit, but the bad tree bears evil fruit. 18A sound tree cannot bear evil fruit, nor can a bad tree bear good fruit. 19Every tree that does not bear good fruit is cut down and thrown into the fire. 20Thus you will know them by their fruits.

Lk 13:25–30

Is 29:13; Lk 6:46
Rom 2:13
1 Jn 2:17
Jas 1:22, 25; 2:14
1 Cor 12:3
Jer 14:14; 27:15
Mt 25:11–12

Doing the will of God

21"Not every one who says to me, 'Lord, Lord,' shall enter the kingdom of heaven, but he who does the will of my Father who is in heaven. 22On that day many will say to me, 'Lord, Lord, did we not prophesy in your name, and cast out demons in your name, and do many mighty works in your name?' 23And then will I declare to them, 'I never knew you; depart from me, you evildoers.'

Lk 6:46–49

Prov 10:25
Mt 12:3, 7
1 Jn 2:17

Building on rock

24"Every one then who hears these words of mine and does them will be like a wise man who built his house upon the rock; 25and the rain fell, and the floods came, and the winds blew and beat upon that house, but it did not fall, because it had been

ad vitam, et pauci sunt, qui inveniunt eam! 15Attendite a falsis prophetis, qui veniunt ad vos in vestimentis ovium, intrinsecus autem sunt lupi rapaces. 16A fructibus eorum cognoscetis eos: numquid colligunt de spinis uvas aut de tribulis ficus? 17Sic omnis arbor bona fructus bonos facit, mala autem arbor fructus malos facit: 18non potest arbor bona fructus malos facere, neque arbor mala fructus bonos facere. 19Omnis arbor, quae non facit fructum bonum, exciditur et in ignem mittitur. 20Igitur ex fructibus eorum cognoscetis eos. 21Non omnis, qui dicit mihi: "Domine Domine", intrabit in regnum caelorum, sed qui facit voluntatem Patris mei, qui in caelis est. 22Multi dicent mihi in illa die: "Domine, Domine, nonne in tuo nomine prophetavimus, et in tuo nomine daemonia eiecimus, et in tuo nomine virtutes multas fecimus?". 23Et tunc confitebor illis:

7:13–27 At the end of the discourse, Jesus, looking at things from the perspective of the Last Judgment, outlines the conditions for entering the Kingdom of God. The journey to the Kingdom is a difficult one, but at its end lies everlasting life (vv. 13–14): "The way of Christ 'leads to life'; a contrary way 'leads to destruction.' The Gospel parable of the *two ways* remains ever present in the catechesis of the Church; it shows the importance of moral decisions for our salvation" (*Catechism of the Catholic Church*, 1696).

Our Lord stresses that his disciples will be judged by their works (vv. 15–20); what really matters is whether they did the will of God on earth (vv. 21–23). In the Old Testament (cf. Jer 23:9–40), false prophets were defined as those who, not being God's envoys, led the people astray. Jesus warns his disciples to beware of them; they should not take these people at face value but should focus on their works; and he gives them a yardstick: if these people come from God, they will bear good fruit. Therefore, entry into the Kingdom, belonging to the Church, can be verified from what people do, not just from what they say: to be a good Christian one needs to bear good fruit (v. 19), to do the will of the Father (v. 21) and to put Jesus' words into daily practice (v. 24). Fray Luis de Granada spells it out rather graphically: "Notice that to be a good Christian it is not enough just to pray and fast and hear Mass; God must find you faithful, like another Job or Abraham, in times of tribulation" (*Guide for Sinners*, 1, 2, 21).

The parable of the man building on rock (vv. 24–27) sums up the way people should act if they want to enter the Kingdom of God—which is already present as the Church is present in the world. If we strive to put Jesus' teachings into practice, despite personal trials, and even if error

q Other ancient authorities read *for the way is wide and easy*

founded on the rock. [26]And every one who hears these words of mine and does not do them will be like a foolish man who built his house upon the sand; [27]and the rain fell, and the floods came, and the winds blew and beat against that house, and it fell; and great was the fall of it."

Job 8:15

Jesus teaches with authority

[28]And when Jesus finished these sayings, the crowds were astonished at his teaching, [29]for he taught them as one who had authority, and not as their scribes.

Mk 1:22
Lk 4:32; 7:1
Jn 7:46

4. MIRACLES OF THE MESSIAH*

Curing of a leper

Mk 1:40–45
Lk 5:12–16
Num 12:10–13

8 [1]When he came down from the mountain, great crowds followed him; [2]and behold, a leper came to him and knelt before him, saying, "Lord, if you will,

---

Numquam novi vos; discedite a me, qui operamini iniquitatem. [24]Omnis ergo, qui audit verba mea haec et facit ea, assimilabitur viro sapienti, qui aedificavit domum suam supra petram. [25]Et descendit pluvia, et venerunt flumina, et flaverunt venti et irruerunt in domum illam, et non cecidit; fundata enim erat supra petram. [26]Et omnis, qui audit verba mea haec et non facit ea, similis erit viro stulto, qui aedificavit domum suam supra arenam. [27]Et descendit pluvia, et venerunt flumina, et flaverunt venti et irruerunt in domum illam, et cecidit, et fuit ruina eius magna». [28]Et factum

---

seems to surround us, we will remain firm in the faith, like the wise man who builds his house on rock.

7:28–29 In these two verses following the discourse we can see—from the manner in which he teaches—the messianic nature of Jesus and the reaction of his audience. They also serve as a link with the following section, which reports miracles that confirm Jesus' authority.

Some authors, beginning with Luther, have thought that the ethical demands of the Sermon on the Mount are beyond us, and that Jesus meant them as a sort of charge-sheet serving to shield us against pride, by making us recognize that we are always sinners. This interpretation does not do justice to the Gospel text. Jesus proclaimed these teachings in his discourse because he wanted us to put them into practice—not relying solely on our abilities, but availing ourselves of the help of the grace he won for us. In these teachings Jesus takes account of the natural moral law and brings it to perfection; his aim is to have us share in divine nature itself: "Jesus gradually enlightened human nature so that it may be like God. First came the prescriptions of the Law and the Prophets; then he himself came: the perfect, shining Light" (St Gregory of Nyssa, *In Cantica canticorum commentarius*, 5).

*8:1—9:38 In the previous section (5:1—7:29), Jesus acted in the role of supreme lawgiver and teacher. Now we also see his divine power over disease, death, the elements of nature, and evil spirits. These miracles worked by Jesus vouch for the divine authority of his teaching and for his divinity. "Jesus accompanies his words with many 'mighty works and wonders and signs' (Acts 2:22), which manifest that the kingdom is present in him and attest that he was the promised Messiah (cf. Lk 7:18–23)" (*Catechism of the Catholic Church*, 547).

The section contains three miracles of mercy (8:1–15), followed by a general mention of many more (8:16) and a biblical quotation showing that all these miracles mark the fulfilment of messianic prophecies (8:17): Jesus is the merciful Servant of the Lord. There follow three miracles which reveal the scope of our Lord's power (8:23—9:8), and a further four which show the impact that Jesus' miracles had on those around him (9:18–34). The accounts of miracles in Matthew are not as vivid as those in Mark. But Matthew makes abundantly clear the sovereign authority and majesty of Jesus which the miracles reveal. His account again underlines the need for there to be faith in Jesus (8:13, 26; 9:2, 21, 28) if miracles are to happen.

8:1–4 The Gospel draws attention, for a fourth

Mt 8:15; 9:25; 11:5;
14:36
you can make me clean." ³And he stretched out his hand and touched him, saying,

Mk 1:34; 7:36
Mt 9:30; 12:16
Lk 17:14
Lev 13:49; 14:2–32
"I will; be clean." And immediately his leprosy was cleansed.* ⁴And Jesus said to him, "See that you say nothing to any one; but go, show yourself to the priest, and offer the gift that Moses commanded, for a proof to the people."ʳ

Lk 7:1–10
Jn 4:46–54
The centurion's faith

⁵As he entered Capernaum, a centurion came forward to him, beseeching him ⁶and saying, "Lord, my servant is lying paralyzed at home, in terrible distress." ⁷And he
Lk 5:8
Ps 33:9; 107:20
Bar 3:33–35
said to him, "I will come and heal him." ⁸But the centurion answered him, "Lord, I am not worthy to have you come under my roof; but only say the word, and my servant will be healed. ⁹For I am a man under authority, with soldiers under me; and I say to one, 'Go,' and he goes, and to another, 'Come,' and he comes, and to my slave, 'Do this,' and he does it." ¹⁰When Jesus heard him, he marvelled, and said to those

est cum consummasset Iesus verba haec, admirabantur turbae super doctrinam eius; ²⁹erat enim docens eos sicut potestatem habens et non sicut scribae eorum. [8] ¹Cum autem descendisset de monte, secutae sunt eum turbae multae. ²Et ecce leprosus veniens adorabat eum dicens: «Domine, si vis, potes me mundare». ³Et extendens manum, tetigit eum dicens: «Volo, mundare!»; et confestim mundata est lepra eius. ⁴Et ait illi Iesus: «Vide, nemini dixeris; sed vade, ostende te sacerdoti et offer munus, quod praecepit Moyses, in testimonium illis». ⁵Cum autem introisset Capharnaum, accessit ad eum centurio rogans eum ⁶et dicens: «Domine, puer meus iacet in domo paralyticus et male torquetur». ⁷Et ait illi: «Ego veniam et curabo eum». ⁸Et respondens centurio ait: «Domine, non sum dignus, ut intres sub tectum meum, sed tantum dic verbo, et sanabitur puer meus. ⁹Nam et ego homo sum sub potestate, habens sub me milites, et dico huic: "Vade", et vadit; et alii: "Veni", et venit; et servo meo: "Fac hoc", et facit». ¹⁰Audiens autem Iesus, miratus est et sequentibus se dixit: «Amen dico vobis: Apud nullum inveni tantam fidem in Israel! ¹¹Dico

time (cf. 4:25; 5:1; 7:28), to the huge crowds that flocked to Jesus. There is no denying Jesus' popularity (v. 1). In the cure recounted here, the leper's faith in Jesus' power is evident, as is the fact that Jesus is self-effacing.

The book of Leviticus (Lev 13:45–46) stipulated that a leper should live in isolation and wear torn clothes; he should let his hair hang loose, and cry, "Unclean, unclean" as a warning to people to stay away. If he was cured of his disease, he should go to a priest to have his cure confirmed; only then could he be reintegrated into the civil and religious life of Israel (cf. Lev 14:1ff). These verses (Mt 8:1–4) show Jesus' mercy and his respect for what the Law laid down. But, as so often in Matthew's Gospel, this episode contains lessons for us to learn. "Why did the Lord touch him when the Law forbade any contact with lepers? [...] He touched the leper to give us an example of humility, to show that we must never scorn anyone or despise anyone for the wounds or scars on their body [...]. We may suffer no leprosy of soul, my beloved brothers, or show no marks of sin on our body, but if we did we would immediately prostrate ourselves before the Lord and worship him, saying: 'Lord, if you will, you can make me clean'" (Origen, *Homiliae in Matthaeum*, 2, 2-3).

8:5–13 Any Jew who entered a Gentile's residence contracted legal impurity (cf. Jn 18:28; Acts 11:2–3). This explains the tactfulness and the faith of the centurion in his request to Jesus (vv. 8–9). His faith in Jesus' power is evident: by calling him "Lord" and invoking the parallel of his own military authority, the centurion acknowledges that just as he acts in the name of Caesar and his orders are obeyed because his authority comes from Caesar, Jesus acts on earth with God's authority: whatever he orders will be done. This great profession of faith impresses Jesus (v. 10), who takes the opportunity of this meeting with a Gentile believer to make a solemn prophecy indicating that his Gospel is addressed to the whole world without distinction (vv. 11–12).

The centurion backs up his faith with deeds. As the Gospel of St Matthew shows his doing also on other occasions (cf. 15:28; 17:20; etc.) Jesus asserts that miracles are performed in response to people's faith (v. 13). The exemplary faith of the Roman officer proved effective, for "the servant was healed at that very moment". It is not surprising that the centurion's example resounds over the centuries: "The faith of the centurion prophesies the faith of the Gentiles. His faith was like the grain of mustard seed, small but

r Greek *to them*

who followed him, "Truly, I say to you, not even[s] in Israel have I found such faith. [11]I

Is 49:12; 59:19
Mal 1:11; Ps 107:3
Bar 4:37
Rom 11:11

tell you, many will come from east and west and sit at table with Abraham, Isaac, and
Jacob in the kingdom of heaven, [12]while the sons of the kingdom will be thrown into

Mt 13:42, 50; 22:13;
24:51; 25:30

the outer darkness; there men will weep and gnash their teeth." [13]And to the centurion Jesus said, "Go; be it done for you as you have believed." And the servant was
healed at that very moment.

Curing of Peter's mother-in-law

Mk 1:29–31
Lk 4:38–39

[14]And when Jesus entered Peter's house, he saw his mother-in-law lying sick with a

1 Cor 9:5

fever; [15]he touched her hand, and the fever left her, and she rose and served him.

Mt 9:25
Mk 9:27
Acts 3:7

Other cures

Mk 1:32–34
Lk 4:40–41

[16]That evening they brought to him many who were possessed with demons; and he
cast out the spirits with a word, and healed all who were sick. [17]This was to fulfil what

Is 53:4
Jn 1:29, 36

was spoken by the prophet Isaiah, "He took our infirmities and bore our diseases."

Following Christ is not easy

Lk 9:57–62

[18]Now when Jesus saw great crowds around him, he gave orders to go over to the

Mk 4:35

other side. [19]And a scribe came up and said to him, "Teacher, I will follow you wher-

---

autem vobis quod multi ab oriente et occidente venient et recumbent cum Abraham et Isaac et Iacob in regno caelorum; [12]filii autem regni eicien-
tur in tenebras exteriores: ibi erit fletus et stridor dentium». [13]Et dixit Iesus centurioni: «Vade; sicut credidisti fiat tibi». Et sanatus est puer in hora
illa. [14]Et cum venisset Iesus in domum Petri, vidit socrum eius iacentem et febricitantem; [15]et tetigit manum eius, et dimisit eam febris; et surrexit
et ministrabat ei. [16]Vespere autem facto, obtulerunt ei multos daemonia habentes; et eiciebat spiritus verbo et omnes male habentes curavit, [17]ut
adimpleretur, quod dictum est per Isaiam prophetam dicentem: «*Ipse infirmitates nostras accepit / et aegrotationes portavit*». [18]Videns autem Iesus

---

powerful" (St Augustine, *Sermones*, 6, 1).

At the solemn moment when Christians go to
receive Jesus himself in the Holy Eucharist, the
liturgy of the Church—to stoke their fervour—
puts on their lips and in their hearts the words
used here by the centurion: "Lord, I am not
worthy ...". For, faith should also be accompanied by humility: "What did the Lord praise in
the centurion's faith? His humility: 'Lord, I am
not worthy...', and as a reward for his humility,
the Lord entered under his roof. The centurion's
humility was the door by which the Lord
entered, to take full possession of what he
already possessed" (ibid., 6, 2).

8:14–15 Our Lord recognizes this woman's
ailment, and remedies it: "We all lie sick with
fever. I have a fever, for example, when I lose my
temper and get angry. There are as many fevers as
there are sins. Let us ask the apostles to intercede
for us with the Lord, so that he may come and
take us by the hand; when he touches our hand,
the fever will leave us" (St Jerome, *Commentarium in Marcum*, 3, 5). For her part, the

person cured, Simon's mother-in-law, responds to
Jesus' gift by attending to his needs without delay.
The Fathers of the Church often give a spiritual
interpretation to this passage, stressing the link
between the cure the woman received and the
service that she renders: cured by Jesus, we
should serve God and our neighbours.

8:16–17 St Matthew here provides, in the light
of the prophecy of Isaiah, the true interpretation
of Jesus' miracles: the works done by Jesus are
also a revelation about his Person: "Moved by so
much suffering Christ not only allows himself to
be touched by the sick, but he makes their miseries his own: 'He took our infirmities and bore
our diseases' (Mt 8:17; cf. Is 53:4). But he did
not heal all the sick. His healings were signs of
the coming of the Kingdom of God. They
announced a more radical healing: the victory
over sin and death through his Passover"
(*Catechism of the Catholic Church*, 1505).

8:18–22 Jesus, who acts with authority and
proves this by curing diseases, is at the same

---

s Other ancient authorities read *with no one*

2 Cor 8:9
Ps 8:3; 84:3
1 Kings 19:20
Gen 50:5; Tob 4:3
Jn 1:43; 5:25;
21:19, 22
Mt 4:22; 9:9; 19:21
et par.
Mk 2:14; 8:34; 10:21
Mk 4: 35–41
Lk 8:22–25

Mt 14:22–23

Mt 14:30

Ps 107:25ff
Mt 14:32–33
Mk 6:51

ever you go." [20]And Jesus said to him, "Foxes have holes, and birds of the air have nests; but the Son of man has nowhere to lay his head." [21]Another of the disciples said to him, "Lord let me first go and bury my father." [22]But Jesus said to him, "Follow me, and leave the dead to bury their own dead."

The calming of the storm

[23]And when he got into the boat, his disciples followed him. [24]And behold, there arose a great storm on the sea, so that the boat was being swamped by the waves; but he was asleep. [25]And they went and woke him, saying, "Save us, Lord; we are perishing." [26]And he said to them, "Why are you afraid, O men of little faith?" Then he rose and rebuked the winds and the sea; and there was a great calm. [27]And the men marvelled, saying, "What sort of man is this, that even winds and sea obey him?"

turbas multas circum se, iussit ire trans fretum. [19]Et accedens unus scriba ait illi: «Magister, sequar te quocumque ieris». [20]Et dicit ei Iesus: «Vulpes foveas habent et volucres caeli tabernacula, Filius autem hominis non habet, ubi caput reclinet». [21]Alius autem de discipulis eius ait illi: «Domine, permitte me primum ire et sepelire patrem meum». [22]Iesus autem ait illi: «Sequere me et dimitte mortuos sepelire mortuos suos». [23]Et ascendente eo in naviculam, secuti sunt eum discipuli eius. [24]Et ecce motus magnus factus est in mari, ita ut navicula operiretur fluctibus; ipse vero dormiebat. [25]Et accesserunt et suscitaverunt eum dicentes: «Domine, salva nos, perimus!». [26]Et dicit eis: «Quid timidi estis, modicae fidei?». Tunc surgens increpavit ventis et mari, et facta est tranquillitas magna. [27]Porro homines mirati sunt dicentes: «Qualis est hic, quia et venti et mare oboediunt

time the humble Messiah, rejected by so many of his own people. Anyone who wants to be with him must "follow him". Following Jesus means becoming his disciple (see vv. 19–21). Sometimes crowds "follow him" (4:25; 8:1; 20:29; etc.), but true disciples are those who follow him all the time. A scribe here honours Jesus as a "Teacher" (v. 19), and another disciple calls him "Lord" (v. 21), but Jesus asks both of them to share his lot. He warns the scribe that life at his side is even more unstable than the lives of foxes and birds (who live at the mercy of the elements). The evangelist does not tell us what the scribe eventually decided to do—as if transferring the challenge to the Christian who hears these words. And, in the case of the other disciple, our Lord tells him he must make a radical commitment; that is how we should interpret Jesus' brusque remark (v. 22): "If Jesus forbade him [to first bury his father]," St John Chrysostom comments, "it was not to have us neglect the honour due to our parents, but to make us realize that nothing is more important than the things of heaven and that we ought to cleave to these and not to put them off even for a little while, though our engagements be ever so indispensable and pressing" (*In Matthaeum*, 27).

"Son of man" (v. 20). At the time of Jesus' ministry, the title of "Son of man", as used by Jesus, was not fully understood. It could simply mean "man", but in Daniel 7:13 it has a higher meaning. As a title to explain Jesus' mission, it does not connote Jewish nationalistic aspirations for an earthly Messiah, and probably for that reason was Jesus' preferred way of referring to himself. After his resurrection, the apostles were able to see that, in his case, "Son of man" meant in fact "Son of God".

8:23–27 Jesus has power not only over diseases but also over malign influences and the elements of nature, because he is the Son of God (cf. the note on Mk 4:35–41). The account of this miracle is more a sketched outline than a narrative, but, nevertheless, is very revealing.

In the "ecclesiastical Gospel", as the Gospel of St Matthew is sometimes called, the boat symbolizes the Church: Jesus gets into the boat and his "disciples" follow him (v. 23). Sometimes, the Church, like the boat, gets into difficulties: the waves beat against her, they threaten to swamp her, and she seems to be left on her own, because Christ is asleep. However, the real danger is not from the waves; the disciples' fear comes from their lack of faith (v. 25), their forgetting that Christ is the Lord (v. 26). "The churches who do not keep the word of God alive and alert will be shipwrecked, not because Christ has fallen asleep, but because it [the word] is asleep within us, because we are asleep" (St Hilary of Poitiers, *Commentarius in Matthaeum*, 8, 1). But when his disciple calls for help, Jesus

The demoniacs of Gadara

Mk 5:1–20
Lk 8:26–39

²⁸And when he came to the other side, to the country of the Gadarenes,^t two demoniacs met him, coming out of the tombs, so fierce that no one could pass that way. ²⁹And behold, they cried out, "What have you to do with us, O Son of God? Have you come here to torment us before the time?"* ³⁰Now a herd of many swine was feeding at some distance from them. ³¹And the demons begged him, "If you cast us out, send us away into the herd of swine." ³²And he said to them, "Go." So they came out and went into the swine; and behold, the whole herd rushed down the steep bank into the sea, and perished in the waters. ³³The herdsmen fled, and going into the city they told everything, and what had happened to the demoniacs. ³⁴And behold, all the city came out to meet Jesus; and when they saw him, they begged him to leave their neighbourhood.

Lk 4:34, 41
Jn 2:4
Mk 1:34
2 Pet 2:4

Curing of a paralyzed man

Mk 2:1–12
Lk 5:17–26

9 ¹And getting into a boat he crossed over and came to his own city. ²And behold, they brought to him a paralytic, lying on his bed; and when Jesus saw their faith he said to the paralytic, "Take heart, my son; your sins are forgiven." ³And

Lk 7:48

Mk 2:7

---

ei?». ²⁸Et cum venisset trans fretum in regionem Gadarenorum, occurrerunt ei duo habentes daemonia, de monumentis exeuntes, saevi nimis, ita ut nemo posset transire per viam illam. ²⁹Et ecce clamaverunt dicentes: «Quid nobis et tibi, Fili Dei? Venisti huc ante tempus torquere nos?». ³⁰Erat autem longe ab illis grex porcorum multorum pascens. ³¹Daemones autem rogabant eum dicentes: «Si eicis nos, mitte nos in gregem porcorum». ³²Et ait illis: «Ite». Et illi exeuntes abierunt in porcos; et ecce impetu abiit totus grex per praeceps in mare, et mortui sunt in aquis. ³³Pastores autem fugerunt et venientes in civitatem nuntiaverunt omnia et de his, qui daemonia habuerant. ³⁴Et ecce tota civitas exiit obviam Iesu, et viso eo rogabant, ut transiret a finibus eorum. [9] ¹Et ascendens in naviculam transfretavit et venit in civitatem suam. ²Et ecce offerebant ei paralyticum

---

always answers: the "great storm" (v. 24) becomes a "great calm" (v. 26), and people are amazed to see the Lord's power. The Church, where Christ is always present, is the sure ground of salvation. "The waves beat against her [the Church] but she holds firm, and though the elements of this world often rise up against her, she offers the sure port of salvation to all who are hard-pressed" (St Ambrose, *Epistulae*, 2, 1).

8:28–34 The evangelist places this episode in the country of the "Gaderenes" (v. 28), whereas St Mark and St Luke say "Gerasenes". The two descriptions are compatible; Gerasa and Gadara were only 40km (24 miles) apart; and both towns were to the south-east of the Sea of Galilee. Anyway, the important thing about the passage is how it shows that Jesus' authority extends to pagan areas and is exerted even over demons and diabolical powers. The demons, interestingly, ask Jesus, "Have you come here to torment us before the time?" (v. 29). The question is based on a notion prevalent at that time, according to which devils would have a certain freedom of movement and action until the time of God's final victory. The exorcism in this passage shows

Jesus anticipating that victory (see the note on Lk 8:26–39). Also, for the Jews, pigs were unclean animals (this episode occurs in a Gentile area), whose meat they were not allowed to eat (cf. Lev 11:7; Deut 14:4–8). Both the cure of the demoniacs and the destruction of the swine evidence Jesus' complete victory over the devil.

9:1–8 By curing the paralyzed man simply by giving him an instruction, Jesus shows his critics that he has the power to cure not only the effects of sin (illnesses) but also the cause of illness (sin); in other words, he has divine power. "By forgiving his sins, Jesus cured the man who was paralyzed, and showed in a visible way who he was. If God alone can forgive sins and the Lord forgave and cured men, then he is the Word of God made Son of man, with the power to forgive sins, both as man and as God. As man, he shared our poor nature; as God, he took pity on us and forgave our sins" (St Irenaeus, *Adversus haereses*, 5, 17, 3).

At the end of this passage (v. 8), the evangelist tells of the crowd's wonder and amazement at the fact that this man can forgive sins. Jesus gave a share in this power to forgive sins to his apos-

---

t Other ancient authorities read *Gergesenes*; some, *Gerasenes*

Jn 2:25 behold, some of the scribes said to themselves, "This man is blaspheming." [4]But Jesus, knowing[u] their thoughts, said, "Why do you think evil in your hearts? [5]For Jn 5:8, 24 which is easier, to say, 'Your sins are forgiven,' or to say, 'Rise and walk'? [6]But that you may know that the Son of man has authority on earth to forgive sins"—he then said to the paralytic—"Rise, take up your bed and go home." [7]And he rose and went home. [8]When the crowds saw it, they were afraid, and they glorified God, who had given such authority to men.

Mk 2:13–17
Lk 5:27–32

The call of Matthew

Mt 8:22 [9]As Jesus passed on from there, he saw a man called Matthew sitting at the tax office; and he said to him, "Follow me." And he rose and followed him.

Mt 11:19
Lk 19:7

Lk 15:2   [10]And as he sat at table[v] in the house, behold, many tax collectors and sinners came and sat down with Jesus and his disciples. [11]And when the Pharisees saw this, they said to his disciples, "Why does your teacher eat with tax collectors and sinners?" [12]But when he heard it, he said, "Those who are well have no need of a physi-Hos 6:6
Mt 12:7
Lk 19:10
1 Sam 15:22 cian, but those who are sick. [13]Go and learn what this means, 'I desire mercy, and not sacrifice.' For I came not to call the righteous, but sinners."

iacentem in lecto. Et videns Iesus fidem illorum, dixit paralytico: «Confide, fili; remittuntur peccata tua». [3]Et ecce quidam de scribis dixerunt intra se: «Hic blasphemat». [4]Et cum vidisset Iesus cogitationes eorum, dixit: «Ut quid cogitatis mala in cordibus vestris? [5]Quid enim est facilius, dicere: "Dimittuntur peccata tua", aut dicere: "Surge et ambula"? [6]Ut sciatis autem quoniam Filius hominis habet potestatem in terra dimittendi peccata —tunc ait paralytico—: Surge, tolle lectum tuum et vade in domum tuam». [7]Et surrexit et abiit in domum suam. [8]Videntes autem turbae timuerunt et glorificaverunt Deum, qui dedit potestatem talem hominibus. [9]Et cum transiret inde Iesus, vidit hominem sedentem in teloneo, Matthaeum nomine, et ait illi: «Sequere me». Et surgens secutus est eum. [10]Et factum est, discumbente eo in domo, ecce multi publicani et peccatores venientes simul discumbebant cum Iesu et discipulis eius. [11]Et videntes pharisaei dicebant discipulis eius: «Quare cum publicanis et peccatoribus manducat magister vester?». [12]At ille audiens ait: «Non est opus valentibus medico sed male habentibus. [13]Euntes autem discite quid est: *"Misericordiam volo et non sacrificium"*. Non enim veni vocare iustos, sed peccatores». [14]Tunc accedunt ad eum discipuli Ioannis dicentes:

tles and their successors, that is, the bishops of the Church and their associates, priests (see Jn 20:22–23): "When they forgive sins, men exercise the ministry to which they have been called, they do not exercise the power of forgiveness in their own right; they do not forgive in their own name, but in the name of the Father and the Son and the Holy Spirit. They make the petition and God grants. Men are servants; the generosity of forgiveness is the power of God" (St Ambrose, *De Spiritu Sancto*, 3, 18, 137). See also the note on 18:15–20.

9:9–13 Jesus calls whomever he chooses to call, without reference to the type of distinctions that Pharisees often made. Here he calls a tax collector. (Tax collection was regarded as sinful, because it involved collaboration with the oppressive Roman regime, and often also involved extortion.) Matthew is the same person as the Levi in the Gospels of Mark and Luke (see Mk 2:14; Lk 5:27), and Tradition identifies him as the author of this first Gospel. The fact that

Jesus associated with sinners was a cause of scandal for many people (11:19); but Jesus, quoting Hosea 6:6, explains his mercy towards sinners as a reflection of God's own attitude to them. No one should lose heart on finding that he is full of shortcomings: recognizing ourselves to be sinners is the only proper way to approach God. Jesus has come to seek us all out, but if we think we are already just fine, we thereby close the door against God, for we are all sinners, and all of us stand in need of God.

When God calls us, he does not expect us to have great qualities; he wants us to listen carefully, and to be prompt in our response: "What amazes you seems natural to me: that God has sought you out in the practice of your profession! That is how he sought the first, Peter and Andrew, James and John, beside their nets, and Matthew, sitting in the custom-house. And— wonder of wonders!—Paul, in his eagerness to destroy the seeds of Christianity!" (St Josemaría Escrivá, *The Way*, 799). See also the notes on Mk 2:13–17 and Lk 5:27–32.

u Other ancient authorities read *seeing*   v Greek *reclined*

A discussion on fasting

Mk 2:18–22
Lk 5:33–39
Lk 18:12

¹⁴Then the disciples of John came to him, saying, "Why do we and the Pharisees fast,^w but your disciples do not fast?" ¹⁵And Jesus said to them, "Can the wedding Jn 3:29 guests mourn as long as the bridegroom is with them? The days will come, when the bridegroom is taken away from them, and then they will fast. ¹⁶And no one puts a piece of unshrunk cloth on an old garment, for the patch tears away from the garment, and a worse tear is made. ¹⁷Neither is new wine put into old wineskins; if it is, the skins burst, and the wine is spilled, and the skins are destroyed; but new wine is put into fresh wineskins, and so both are preserved."

The raising of Jairus' daughter and the curing of the woman with a haemorrhage

Mk 5:21–43
Lk 8:40–56

¹⁸While he was thus speaking to them, behold, a ruler came in and knelt before him, saying, "My daughter has just died; but come and lay your hand on her, and she will live." ¹⁹And Jesus rose and followed him, with his disciples.

²⁰And behold, a woman who had suffered from a hemorrhage for twelve years Mt 14:36
Mk 6:56 came up behind him and touched the fringe of his garment; ²¹for she said to herself, "If I only touch his garment, I shall be made well." ²²Jesus turned, and seeing her he Mk 10:52
Lk 7:50; 17:19;
18:42
Acts 14:9 said, "Take heart, daughter; your faith has made you well." And instantly the woman was made well. ²³And when Jesus came to the ruler's house, and saw the flute play-

---

«Quare nos et pharisaei ieiunamus frequenter, discipuli autem tui non ieiunant?». ¹⁵Et ait illis Iesus: «Numquid possunt convivae nuptiarum lugere, quamdiu cum illis est sponsus? Venient autem dies, cum auferetur ab eis sponsus, et tunc ieiunabunt. ¹⁶Nemo autem immittit commissuram panni rudis in vestimentum vetus; tollit enim supplementum eius a vestimento, et peior scissura fit. ¹⁷Neque mittunt vinum novum in utres veteres, alioquin rumpuntur utres, et vinum effunditur, et utres pereunt; sed vinum novum in utres novos mittunt, et ambo conservantur». ¹⁸Haec illo loquente ad eos, ecce princeps unus accessit et adorabat eum dicens: «Filia mea modo defuncta est; sed veni, impone manum tuam super eam, et vivet». ¹⁹Et surgens Iesus sequebatur eum et discipuli eius. ²⁰Et ecce mulier, quae sanguinis fluxum patiebatur duodecim annis, accessit retro et tetigit fimbriam vestimenti eius. ²¹Dicebat enim intra se: «Si tetigero tantum vestimentum eius, salva ero». ²²At Iesus conversus et videns eam dixit:

9:14–17 These verses throw light on Jesus' readiness to call sinners. He enables us to have a new form of relationship with God, one that implies total regeneration. His spirit is too new, too vigorous, to be forced to fit into old moulds, which are ceasing to be the proper ones.

Our Lord did not do away with fasting, but, in contrast to the complicated casuistry of his time, which could only suffocate true piety, he laid stress on simplicity of heart (see 6:1–18 and note). He does state that his disciples "will fast" (v. 15). It will be up to the Church to specify in different circumstances, using the authority given her by God, the forms that fasting should take, to be in accord with the spirit of Christ. St Augustine comments: "This verse explains why we fast in the time before the solemnity of the Passion of our Lord, and why we do not fast for the fifty days that follow it. To fast is to abase one's soul in true faith, crying out in prayer and mortifying the body; to fast is to turn our back on the pleasures of the flesh, to suffer hunger and thirst, our eyes fixed on truth and wisdom.

Jesus was referring to both kinds of fasting when he responded to the accusation 'your disciples do not fast'. […] We cry and fast when the bridegroom is taken away from us; […] and our mourning will be true if our soul burns with the desire to see him again" (*Sermones*, 210, 4).

9:18–26 In this passage, two further miracles show the faith that we need to have if we are to be deemed worthy to receive healing from Jesus (see the notes on Mk 5:21–43 and Lk 8:40–56). However timidly expressed, the faith of the woman with the haemorrhage overcomes the obstacles and achieves what seemed impossible: "Faith cured in a single instant what human medicine could not cure in twelve years. […] The woman touched the hem of his garment and was healed, freed from her long suffering. Woe to us, for we receive the body of the Lord every day and are not cured of our sins. Christ does not fail to cure our infirmity; rather, we lack faith. When he is within us, he can cure much greater infirmities than the one he cured when he passed by

---

w Other ancient authorities add *much* or *often*

Jn 11:11, 14, 25

Mk 1:31; 9:27
ers, and the crowd making a tumult, ²⁴he said, "Depart; for the girl is not dead but sleeping." And they laughed at him. ²⁵But when the crowd had been put outside, he went in and took her by the hand, and the girl arose. ²⁶And the report of this went through all that district.

Lk 11:14–15

Mt 15:22
Curing of two blind men. The dumb devil

²⁷And as Jesus passed on from there, two blind men followed him, crying aloud, "Have mercy on us, Son of David." ²⁸When he entered the house, the blind men came to him; and Jesus said to them, "Do you believe that I am able to do this?" They said to him, "Yes, Lord." ²⁹Then he touched their eyes, saying, "According to your faith be it done to you." ³⁰And their eyes were opened. And Jesus sternly charged them, "See that no one knows it." ³¹But they went away and spread his fame through all that district.

Mt 12:22–24
³²As they were going away, behold, a dumb demoniac was brought to him. ³³And when the demon had been cast out, the dumb man spoke; and the crowds marvelled, saying, "Never was anything like this seen in Israel." ³⁴But the Pharisees said, "He casts out demons by the prince of demons."

Mt 10:25
Mk 3:22

«Confide, filia; fides tua te salvam fecit». Et salva facta est mulier ex illa hora. ²³Et cum venisset Iesus in domum principis et vidisset tibicines et turbam tumultuantem, ²⁴dicebat: «Recedite; non est enim mortua puella, sed dormit». Et deridebant eum. ²⁵At cum eiecta esset turba, intravit et tenuit manum eius, et surrexit puella. ²⁶Et exiit fama haec in universam terram illam. ²⁷Et transeunte inde Iesu, secuti sunt eum duo caeci clamantes et dicentes: «Miserere nostri, fili David!». ²⁸Cum autem venisset domum, accesserunt ad eum caeci, et dicit eis Iesus: «Creditis quia possum hoc facere?». Dicunt ei: «Utique, Domine». ²⁹Tunc tetigit oculos eorum dicens: «Secundum fidem vestram fiat vobis». ³⁰Et aperti sunt oculi illorum. Et comminatus est illis Iesus dicens: «Videte, ne quis sciat». ³¹Illi autem exeuntes diffamaverunt eum in universa terra illa. ³²Egressis autem illis, ecce obtulerunt ei hominem mutum, daemonium habentem. ³³Et eiecto daemone, locutus est mutus. Et miratae sunt turbae dicentes:

and the woman touched his garment" (St Peter Chrysologus, *Sermones*, 33).

The case of the "ruler" is no less edifying. He humbles himself before Jesus for all to see, seeking his help because his daughter has died (v. 18). A miracle on that scale requires great faith: "The man believed, and his daughter was raised from the dead. When Lazarus lay dead in his tomb, the Lord said to Martha: 'Your brother will rise again.' And Martha said: 'I know that he will rise again.' The Lord raised Lazarus to life after he had been dead for four days. Let us grow in the faith that draws forth such power. Faith has raised some to heaven, overcome the waters of the flood, given descendants to the barren, [...] calmed the waves and winds of a storm, cured the sick, cast down the mighty, made walls come tumbling down, stopped the mouths of lions, put out fires, humbled the proud and exalted the humble. Faith has worked all these wonders" (Aphraates, *Demonstrationes*, 1, 17–18).

9:27–34 The two blind men (v. 27) address Jesus as Son of David, in other words, as the long-awaited Messiah. He listens to their appeal and

cures them. The subsequent cure of the man possessed by a devil (v. 33) is a further sign for those present (and for us) that Jesus is indeed the Messiah come among us (cf. 11:3–5). Jesus, then, confirms that he is the Messiah, but he tells them not to spread the word, because the salvation he is bringing is not of the type expected by those who are thinking in terms of a great political leader: his messianism is that of the humble Servant who sacrifices himself on behalf of mankind. We might find the blind men's apparent disobedience somewhat surprising: they paid no heed to what Jesus told them and instead "spread his fame" (v. 31). St John Chrysostom explains that they could not contain their joy, and he comments: "What he wants to teach us is that we should never be boastful or allow others to sing our praises; but because all glory is to God, not only should we not stand in the way of making it known, we should command that it be boasted of and sung" (*In Matthaeum*, 32, 1).

In his account of the cure of the mute demoniac, the evangelist records that opinions about Jesus are divided: there are those who, with simplicity of heart, recognize his unique power, and

The need for good pastors

[35]And Jesus went about all the cities and villages, teaching in their synagogues and

preaching the gospel of the kingdom, and healing every disease and every infirmity.
[36]When he saw the crowds, he had compassion for them, because they were harassed

and helpless, like sheep without a shepherd. [37]Then he said to his disciples, "The

harvest is plentiful, but the labourers are few; [38]pray therefore the Lord of the har-

vest to send out labourers in to his harvest."

5. FROM THE OLD TO THE NEW PEOPLE OF GOD*

The calling of the twelve apostles

10 [1]And he called to him his twelve disciples and gave them authority over
unclean spirits, to cast them out, and to heal every disease and every infir-

«Numquam apparuit sic in Israel!». [34]Pharisaei autem dicebant: «In principe daemoniorum eicit daemones». [35]Et circumibat Iesus civitates omnes et castella, docens in synagogis eorum et praedicans evangelium regni et curans omnem languorem et omnem infirmitatem. [36]Videns autem turbas, misertus est eis quia erant vexati et iacentes sicut oves non habentes pastorem. [37]Tunc dicit discipulis suis: «Messis quidem multa, operarii autem

others whose twisted way of thinking leads them to misinterpret the signs he works.

9:35–38 With his account of the Sermon on the Mount and the miracles worked by Jesus, the evangelist has shown how Jesus put into effect the programme summarized in v. 35 and announced prior to these two sections, in 4:23. It is a programme that will, in time, be extended to the whole world by apostles sent out to work in the field of the Lord.

St Matthew notes that Jesus was moved by the plight of the people of his time. The situation at the time fulfilled the prophecy of Ezekiel 34, where God, through his prophet, berates the evil pastors of Israel, and promises to supplant them by sending the Messiah. So what the evangelist says here gives us an insight into the depth of Christ's feelings: "This Divine Heart is a great abyss which holds all good, and he commands that all his poor people should pour their needs into it. It is an abyss of joy in which we cast away all our burdens; an abyss of humility in which we discard our pride. It is a fount of mercy for the wretched, an abyss of love in which to drown our weakness" (St Margaret Mary Alacoque, *Epistula*, in the *Divine Office*, Office of Readings, 16 October).

Jesus is always conscious of the scale of his mission (vv. 37–38). Now, as in Jesus' time, there is a shortage of labourers, and God counts on our prayer: "There are few workers to reap

such a great harvest. We should feel a deep sorrow, for although many wish to hear the good news, few are willing to preach it to them. [...] Pray for us, so that our work for your good may be very fruitful, so that we may always continue to preach to you in a loud voice" (St Gregory the Great, *Homiliae in Evangelia*, 17, 3).

So far, Jesus has been preaching the Gospel of the Kingdom and demonstrating its arrival by curing diseases and infirmities (v. 35). The evangelist now shows that, in calling them and charging them with their mission, Jesus equips the twelve apostles to do the same; they are his envoys sent to preach the news that the Kingdom is at hand (10:7), and he has enabled them to cure the sick and infirm (10:1).

*10:1–12:50 In this section, the evangelist records a confrontation between Jesus and his disciples on the one hand, and, on the other, unbelieving Jews. The original People of God is being replaced by a new one. This section begins with the second of our Lord's great discourses found in Matthew's Gospel, often called the Mission Discourse (10:5–42). Jesus is training his twelve apostles for their mission, which will be continued by the Church throughout the ages. Jesus is proclaimed the Messiah, but the religious leaders of the Chosen People obstinately reject him (11:6—12:50).

10:1–4 To extend the Kingdom of God, which

Jn 1:40–49
Acts 1:13

mity. ²The names of the twelve apostles are these: first, Simon, who is called Peter, and Andrew his brother; James the son of Zebedee, and John his brother; ³Philip and Bartholomew; Thomas and Matthew the tax collector; James the son of Alphaeus, and Thaddaeus;ˣ ⁴Simon the Cananaean, and Judas Iscariot, who betrayed him.

Mk 6:6–13
Lk 9:1–6

The apostles' first mission

⁵These twelve Jesus sent out, charging them, "Go nowhere among the Gentiles, and

Mt 15:24
Acts 13:46
Jer 50:6
Lk 10:9

enter no town of the Samaritans,* ⁶but go rather to the lost sheep of the house of Israel. ⁷And preach as you go, saying, 'The kingdom of heaven is at hand.' ⁸Heal the

Acts 20:33

Lk 10:4

sick, raise the dead, cleanse lepers, cast out demons. You received without pay, give without pay. ⁹Take no gold, nor silver, nor copper in your belts, ¹⁰no bag for your jour-

1 Tim 5:18
1 Cor 9:5–14
Num 18:31

ney, nor two tunics, nor sandals, nor a staff; for the labourer deserves his food. ¹¹And

pauci; ³⁸rogate ergo Dominum messis, ut mittat operarios in messem suam». [10] ¹Et convocatis Duodecim discipulis suis, dedit illis potestatem spirituum immundorum, ut eicerent eos et curarent omnem languorem et omnem infirmitatem. ²Duodecim autem apostolorum nomina sunt haec: primus Simon, qui dicitur Petrus, et Andreas frater eius, et Iacobus Zebedaei et Ioannes frater eius, ³Philippus et Bartholomaeus, Thomas et Matthaeus publicanus, Iacobus Alphaei et Thaddaeus, ⁴Simon Chananaeus et Iudas Iscariotes, qui et tradidit eum. ⁵Hos Duodecim misit Iesus praecipiens eis et dicens: «In viam gentium ne abieritis et in civitates Samaritanorum ne intraveritis; ⁶sed potius ite ad oves, quae perierunt domus Israel. ⁷Euntes autem praedicate dicentes: «Appropinquavit regnum caelorum. ⁸Infirmos curate, mortuos suscitate, leprosos mundate, daemones eicite; gratis accepistis, gratis date. ⁹Nolite possidere aurum neque argentum neque pecuniam in zonis vestris, ¹⁰non peram in via neque duas tunicas neque calceamenta neque virgam; dignus enim est operarius cibo suo. ¹¹In quamcumque civitatem aut castellum intraveritis, interrogate quis in ea dignus sit; et ibi manete donec exeatis. ¹²Intrantes autem in domum, salutate eam; ¹³et siquidem fuerit domus digna, veniat pax vestra super eam; si autem non fuerit digna, pax vestra ad vos revertatur. ¹⁴Et quicumque non receperit vos neque audierit sermones vestros, exeuntes foras de

he has inaugurated, Jesus will found a new People of God, the Church. To this end, he chooses twelve apostles, whom he empowers and instructs; the successors of the twelve ancient patriarchs of the twelve tribes of Israel, they form the nucleus of the Church. "He sent them first of all to the children of Israel and then to all peoples (cf. Rom 1:16), so that, sharing in his power, they might make all peoples his disciples and sanctify and govern them (cf. Mt 28:16–20; Mk 16:15; Lk 24:45–48; Jn 20:21–23) and thus spread the Church and, administering it under the guidance of the Lord, shepherd it all days until the end of the world (cf. Mt 28:20)" (Vatican II, *Lumen gentium*, 19).

The evangelist makes it quite clear that the ministry of the apostles continues that of Christ, who gave them his own power to "heal every disease and every infirmity" (v. 1; cf. 9:35). Because our Lord told his apostles to go to every nation (28:19), and promised to be with them until the end of the world (28:20), the Church professes her belief that this apostolic power has been passed on to their successors: "For the nurturing and constant growth of the People of God, Christ the Lord instituted in his Church a variety of ministries, which work for the good of the whole body. For those ministers, who are

endowed with sacred power, serve their brethren, so that all who are of the People of God, and therefore enjoy a true Christian dignity, working toward a common goal freely and in an orderly way, may arrive at salvation. [...] Jesus Christ, the eternal Shepherd, established his holy Church, having sent forth the apostles as he himself had been sent by the Father; and he willed that their successors, namely the bishops, should be shepherds in his Church even to the consummation of the world. And in order that the episcopate itself might be one and undivided, he placed Blessed Peter over the other apostles, and instituted in him a permanent and visible source and foundation of unity of faith and communion" (Vatican II, *Lumen gentium*, 18).

10:5–15 These opening verses contain the essence of the discourse. The ministry of the apostles in the Church will be the very same as Christ's ministry: their message that the Kingdom has come (v. 7) is identical with what Jesus said at the start of his ministry (4:17); and their prodigious works (v. 8) are of the same order as those done by Jesus and which have been described in the previous section (8:1 — 9:38): they prove that their mission comes from God (cf. Is 35:5–6; 40:9; 52:7; 61:1).

x Other ancient authorities read *Lebbaeus* or *Lebbaeus called Thaddaeus*

whatever town or village you enter, find out who is worthy in it, and stay with him until you depart. [12]As you enter the house, salute it. [13]And if the house is worthy, let your peace come upon it; but if it is not worthy, let your peace return to you. [14]And if any one will not receive you or listen to your words, shake off the dust from your feet as you leave that house or town. [15]Truly, I say to you, it shall be more tolerable on the day of judgment for the land of Sodom and Gomorrah than for that town.

Lk 10:5, 6
Acts 13:51; 18:6
Lk 10:17
Gen 19:23–29
Mt 11:24

Jesus' instructions to the apostles
[16]"Behold, I send you out as sheep in the midst of wolves; so be wise as serpents and innocent as doves. [17]Beware of men; for they will deliver you up to councils, and flog you in their synagogues, [18]and you will be dragged before governors and kings for my sake, to bear testimony before them and the Gentiles. [19]When they deliver

Mk 13:19–13
Lk 12:1–12, 49–53;
21:12–17
Lk 10:3
Jn 10:12
Eph 5:15
Acts 20:29
Mk 13:9–13
Jn 16:1–4
Lk 21:12–19
Mt 24:9–14; 24:14
Acts 25:23

domo vel de civitate illa, excutite pulverem de pedibus vestris. [15]Amen dico vobis: Tolerabilius erit terrae Sodomorum et Gomorraeorum in die iudicii quam illi civitati. [16]Ecce ego mitto vos sicut oves in medio luporum; estote ergo prudentes sicut serpentes et simplices sicut columbae. [17]Cavete autem ab hominibus; tradent enim vos in conciliis, et in synagogis suis flagellabunt vos; [18]et ad praesides et ad reges ducemini propter me in testimonium illis et gentibus. [19]Cum autem tradent vos, nolite cogitare quomodo aut quid loquamini; dabitur enim vobis in illa hora quid loquamini. [20]Non enim vos estis, qui loquimini, sed Spiritus Patris vestri, qui loquitur in vobis. [21]Tradet autem frater fratrem in mortem, et pater

The apostles are sent first to the "lost sheep of the house of Israel" (v. 6). This is in line with the answer that Jesus will give the Canaanite woman (15:24). This procedure fulfils the divine plan of salvation, according to which the Jewish people received the promises that came with the Covenant and were given, in addition, the Law and were sent the prophets. From this people, according to the flesh, the Messiah would be born. It is easy to see why the Messiah and the Kingdom of God should be announced first to the house of Israel, and only later to the Gentiles, for the people of Israel was the channel through which all other nations would be enabled to find God. A renewed Israel is the seed of the new People of God: "He therefore chose the race of Israel as a people unto himself. With it he set up a covenant. Step by step he taught and prepared this people, making known in its history both himself and the decree of his will and making it holy unto himself. All these things, however, were done by way of preparation and as a figure of that new and perfect covenant which was to be ratified in Christ, and of that fuller revelation which was to be given through the Word of God himself made flesh. [...] Christ instituted this new covenant, the New Testament, that is to say, in his Blood, calling together a people made up of Jew and Gentile, making them one, not according to the flesh but in the Spirit. This was to be the new People of God" (Vatican II, *Lumen gentium*, 9).

The apostles are also to imitate Jesus in his detachment from material things (v. 9), although, in the context of the central message of their mission ("The Kingdom of God is at hand": v. 7), our Lord's intention in giving them these instructions seems to be to inculcate in them a sense of urgency: they need not worry about anything, since the Father will meet their needs (10:29–31). Their treasure is peace (vv. 11–13), which, as Jesus' envoys, they should pour out on those who give them welcome. Peace is the gift that our Lord brought to the world (see Lk 2:14), God's great gift for the life of man on earth: "Peace gives birth to the children of God; peace is the food of love and the source of unity; peace is the reward of the blessed and our heavenly home. The proper end and fruit of peace is that those whom the Lord himself called out of this world are united with God" (St Leo the Great, *Sermo 6 in Nativitate Domini*, 3).

10:16–42 This passage gathers together a series of instructions and counsels about how to spread the Gospel: they form a set of guiding principles. They do not apply only to the twelve apostles: all Christ's disciples will experience contradictions and persecution in the course of their work, just as Christ himself did, for "a disciple is not above his teacher, nor a servant above his master" (v. 24).

The opening verses (vv. 16–25) seem to spell out what is said in the first verse: "I sent you out

you up, do not be anxious how you are to speak or what you are to say; for what you are to say will be given to you in that hour; [20]for it is not you who speak, but the Spirit of your Father speaking through you. [21]Brother will deliver up brother to death, and the father his child, and children will rise against parents and have them put to death; [22]and you will be hated by all for my name's sake. But he who endures to the end will be saved. [23]When they persecute you in one town, flee to the next; for truly, I say to you, you will not have gone through all the towns of Israel, before the Son of man comes.

[24]"A disciple is not above his teacher, nor a servant[y] above his master; [25]it is enough for the disciple to be like his teacher, and the servant[y] like his master. If they have called the master of the house Beelzebul, how much more will they malign those of his household.

[26]"So have no fear of them; for nothing is covered that will not be revealed, or hidden that will not be known. [27]What I tell you in the dark, utter in the light; and what you hear whispered, proclaim upon the housetops. [28] And do not fear those who kill the body but cannot kill the soul; rather fear him who can destroy both soul and body in hell.[z] [29]Are not two sparrows sold for a penny? And not one of them will fall to the ground without your Father's will. [30]But even the hairs of your head are

Jn 14:26
1 Cor 2:4
Mic 7:6
Mt 10: 35

Mt 24:13
Jn 15:21
Mt 16:28; 24:34

Lk 6:40

Jn 13:16; 15:20
Mt 12:24, 27
Mk 3:22
Lk 11:15, 18–19

Lk 12:2–9
Mk 4:22
Lk 8:17

Lk 21:18

filium; et insurgent filii in parentes et morte eos afficient. [22]Et eritis odio omnibus propter nomen meum; qui autem perseveraverit in finem, hic salvus erit. [23]Cum autem persequentur vos in civitate ista, fugite in aliam; amen enim dico vobis: Non consummabitis civitates Israel, donec veniat Filius hominis. [24]Non est discipulus super magistrum nec servus super dominum suum. [25]Sufficit discipulo, ut sit sicut magister eius, et servus sicut dominus eius. Si patrem familias Beelzebul vocaverunt, quanto magis domesticos eius! [26] Ne ergo timueritis eos. Nihil enim est opertum, quod non revelabitur, et occultum, quod non scietur. [27]Quod dico vobis in tenebris, dicite in lumine; et quod in aure auditis, praedicate super tecta. [28]Et nolite timere eos, qui occidunt corpus, animam autem non possunt occidere; sed potius eum timete, qui potest et animam et corpus perdere in gehenna. [29]Nonne duo passeres asse veneunt? Et unus ex illis non cadet super terram sine Patre vestro. [30]Vestri autem et capilli capitis omnes numerati sunt. [31]Nolite ergo timere; multis passeribus meliores estis vos. [32]Omnis ergo qui confitebitur me coram hominibus, confitebor et ego

as sheep in the midst of wolves." Jesus has previously (10:11–15) said that the apostles will be both welcomed and rejected; now he is more explicit: that rejection will take the form of slander (v. 25), persecution (vv. 17–18, 23), hatred (v. 22), betrayal (v. 21). In this respect, the disciples are like their Master (vv. 24–25) and it means they are blessed (5:11). They should not be disconcerted, for it will all be for the best: they will bear witness before all these people to the truth about Jesus (v. 18), and the Holy Spirit will always come to their aid (vv. 19–20). This passage, in effect, summarizes the teaching on martyrdom so familiar to the early Christians, and the Church reminds us that it is still relevant: "The Church considers martyrdom an exceptional gift and the fullest proof of love. By martyrdom a disciple is transformed into an image of his Master [...]. Though few are presented such an opportunity, nevertheless all must be prepared to confess Christ before men. They must be prepared to make this profession of faith even in the midst of persecutions, which will never be lack-

ing to the Church, in following the way of the cross" (Vatican II, *Lumen gentium*, 42).

Verse 23 is one of the most difficult to interpret in the entire New Testament. Here, as in many other places, Jesus refers to himself as the Son of man, indicating that he is the judge who, at the end of the world, will judge all human beings (cf. 25:31). But the "coming" spoken of here does not seem to mean the glorious second coming of Jesus at the end of time. It could mean his resurrection, as the first sign and stage of that future victory in which the final judgment of the whole world is prefigured. In any event, our Lord's words point to two things—the urgent need to preach the Kingdom, and the fact that his preaching will continue until the end of human history.

The exhortations in vv. 26–33 can also be seen in a condensed form in the opening verse: "Have no fear of them" (v. 26). Jesus invites us to trust in the fatherly providence of God, of which he spoke at length in the Sermon on the Mount (see 6:19–34). Now he is speaking in the context of the persecutions that await his disci-

y Or *slave*   z Greek *Gehenna*

all numbered. [31]Fear not, therefore; you are of more value than many sparrows. [32]So every one who acknowledges me before men, I also will acknowledge before my Father who is in heaven; [33]but whoever denies me before men, I also will deny before my Father who is in heaven.

Lk 9:26
Mk 8:38

[34]"Do not think that I have come to bring peace on earth; I have not come to bring peace, but a sword. [35]For I have come to set a man against his father, and a daughter against her mother, and a daughter-in-law against her mother-in-law; [36]and a man's foes will be those of his own household. [37]He who loves father or mother more than me is not worthy of me; and he who loves son or daughter more than me is not worthy of me; [38]and he who does not take his cross and follow me is not worthy of me. [39]He who finds his life will lose it, and he who loses his life for my sake will find it.

Lk 12:51–53

Mic 7:6
Mt 10:21

Deut 33:9
Mt 19:29
Lk 14:26–27

Mt 16:24–25
Mk 8:35
Lk 9:23–24

Lk 17:33
Jn 12:25–26

[40]"He who receives you receives me, and he who receives me receives him who sent me. [41]He who receives a prophet because he is a prophet shall receive a prophet's reward, and he who receives a righteous man because he is a righteous man shall receive a righteous man's reward. [42]And whoever gives to one of these little ones even a cup of cold water because he is a disciple, truly, I say to you, he shall not lose his reward."

Lk 10:16
Jn 12:44; 13:20

Mk 9:41

Messengers from John the Baptist

Lk 7:18–30

11 [1]And when Jesus had finished instructing his twelve disciples, he went on from there to teach and preach in their cities.

eum coram Patre meo, qui est in caelis; [33]qui autem negaverit me coram hominibus, negabo et ego eum coram Patre meo, qui est in caelis. [34]Nolite arbitrari quia venerim mittere pacem in terram; non veni pacem mittere sed gladium. [35]Veni enim separare hominem *adversus patrem suum / et filiam adversus matrem suam / et nurum adversus socrum suam:* / [36]et *inimici hominis domestici eius.* [37]Qui amat patrem aut matrem plus quam me, non est me dignus; et, qui amat filium aut filiam super me, non est me dignus; [38]et, qui non accipit crucem suam et sequitur me, non est me dignus. [39]Qui invenerit animam suam, perdet illam; et, qui perdiderit animam suam propter me, inveniet eam. [40]Qui recipit vos, me recipit; et, qui me recipit, recipit eum, qui me misit. [41]Qui recipit prophetam in nomine prophetae, mercedem prophetae accipiet; et, qui recipit iustum in nomine iusti, mercedem iusti accipiet. [42]Et, quicumque potum dederit uni ex minimis istis calicem aquae frigidae tantum in nomine discipuli, amen dico vobis: Non perdet mercedem suam». [11] [1]Et factum est cum consummasset Iesus praecipiens Duodecim discipulis suis, transiit inde, ut doceret

ples. "If the birds, which are of such little worth, are not abandoned by God's providence and concern, how can you, who in the nature of your souls are eternal, fear that he whom you know as Father will not look after you with special care?" (St Jerome, in *Catena aurea*, ad loc.). But this providence is in the context of a mission: Christians should bear witness to Christ (v. 32), and do so openly (v. 27), in order to have his truth reach every corner of the world: "The Church was founded for the purpose of spreading the kingdom of Christ throughout the earth for the glory of God the Father, to enable all men to share in His saving redemption, and that through them the whole world might enter into a relationship with Christ. All activity of the Mystical Body directed to the attainment of this goal is called the apostolate, which the Church carries on in various ways through all her members" (Vatican II, *Apostolicam actuositatem*, 2).

Finally, the discourse returns to the main theme of the passage: Jesus is a sign of contradiction (vv. 34–35), and his disciple must never forget that. Therefore, two things are asked of Christians—radical commitment, made with the knowledge that it is not easy to follow Christ (vv. 37–39), and identification with the Master (vv. 40–42).

11:1–15 This chapter draws a contrast between those who accept Jesus—John the Baptist (vv. 11–15) and the "babes" (11:25–30)—and those who do not, that is, the people of Christ's generation and the unbelieving cities (11:16–24).

Seeing the "deeds of the Christ" (v. 2), the Baptist sends his disciples to him, and Jesus shows them that his actions are a fulfilment of what the prophets said about the signs that would accompany the Messiah and his Kingdom (see Is 26:19; 29:18–19; 35:5–6; 61:1, etc.). In effect, he

Mt 14:3

Mal 3:1
Jn 1:15–27; 3:31;
11:27
Dan 9:26
Is 26:19; 29:18;
35:5–6; 42:18; *61:1*
Lk 4:18

Lk 1:76

Ex 23:20
Mal 3:1
Mk 1:2
Jn 3:28

Lk 16:16
Jn 6:15

1 Pet 1: 10
Mt 17:10–13

Mk 7:16; 9:13

Mt 13:9, 43
Lk 8:8; 14:35

²Now when John heard in prison about the deeds of the Christ, he sent word by his disciples ³and said to him, "Are you he who is to come, or shall we look for another?"* ⁴And Jesus answered them, "Go and tell John what you hear and see: ⁵the blind receive their sight and the lame walk, lepers are cleansed and the deaf hear, and the dead are raised up, and the poor have good news preached to them. ⁶And blessed is he who takes no offence at me."

⁷As they went away, Jesus began to speak to the crowds concerning John: "What did you go out into the wilderness to behold? A reed shaken by the wind? ⁸Why then did you go out? To see a manᵃ clothed in soft raiment? Behold, those who wear soft raiment are in kings' houses. ⁹Why then did you go out? To see a prophet?ᵇ Yes, I tell you, and more than a prophet. ¹⁰This is he of whom it is written,

'Behold, I send my messenger before thy face,
    who shall prepare thy way before thee.'

¹¹Truly, I say to you, among those born of women there has risen no one greater than John the Baptist; yet he who is least in the kingdom of heaven is greater than he. ¹²From the days of John the Baptist until now the kingdom of heaven has suffered violence,ᶜ and men of violence take it by force. ¹³For all the prophets and the law prophesied until John; ¹⁴and if you are willing to accept it, he is Elijah who is to come. ¹⁵He who has ears to hear,ᵈ let him hear.

et praedicaret in civitatibus eorum. ²Ioannes autem, cum audisset in vinculis opera Christi, mittens per discipulos suos ³ait illi: «Tu es qui venturus es, an alium exspectamus?». ⁴Et respondens Iesus ait illis: «Euntes renuntiate Ioanni, quae auditis et videtis: ⁵*caeci vident* et claudi ambulant, leprosi mundantur et surdi audiunt et mortui resurgunt et *pauperes evangelizantur*; ⁶et beatus est, qui non fuerit scandalizatus in me». ⁷Illis autem abeuntibus, coepit Iesus dicere ad turbas de Ioanne: «Quid existis in desertum videre? Arundinem vento agitatam? ⁸Sed quid existis videre? Hominem mollibus vestitum? Ecce, qui mollibus vestiuntur, in domibus regum sunt. ⁹Sed quid existis videre? Prophetam? Etiam, dico vobis, et plus quam prophetam. ¹⁰Hic est, de quo scriptum est: "*Ecce ego mitto angelum meum ante faciem tuam, / qui praeparabit viam* tuam *ante* te". ¹¹Amen dico vobis: Non surrexit inter natos mulierum maior Ioanne Baptista; qui autem minor est in regno caelorum, maior est illo. ¹²A diebus

tells them that he, Jesus, is the prophet "who is to come" (v. 3).

But the text also tells us about the Baptist (vv. 7–14). Earlier, the Gospel cited an instance of how John's preaching corresponded exactly to that of Jesus (see the note on 3:1–12), and it will later note other similarities: John, like Jesus, met with disbelief from the people (11:16–19), and he, too, suffered a violent death (14:1–12); both of them fulfilled "all righteousness" (3:15). However, what is reported here shows the difference between the two: John, Jesus says, is Elijah (v. 14), the prophet who, according to belief at the time, would come again before the Messiah (17:10–13; Mk 9:11–13); he is a prophet and more than a prophet (v. 9); he is the greatest of those born of woman (v. 11); he is the messenger, or precursor (v. 10); but, on comparing himself with Jesus, John sees himself as a servant and less than a servant (3:11). "Elijah, who was carried up to heaven, is not greater than John; nor Enoch, who was likewise lifted up. Moses was the great lawgiver, and all the prophets holy, but none is greater than John. It is not for me

to compare prophet to prophet: our Lord himself makes the comparison" (St Cyril of Jerusalem, *Catecheses*, 3, 6).

The greatness of John, Jesus also points out, lies in the fact that he belongs to the Kingdom, for "from the days of John the Baptist until now, the kingdom of heaven has suffered violence" (v. 12). From the moment that John announced the presence of Christ, the powers of hell have redoubled their assault, and that persecution will continue over the course of the Church's life (cf. Eph 6:12). That is why effort is needed if one is to attain the Kingdom. The situation described by our Lord seems to have been this: the leaders and a section of the Jewish people saw the future Kingdom of God as being an inheritance to which they had a right, and they rested on their laurels, so to speak, confident in their rights and merits as a race; others, the men of violence (literally, "assaulters"), were taking it by force, as it were, by fighting the enemies of the soul. "This violence is not directed against others. It is a violence used to fight your own weaknesses and miseries, a

a Or *What then did you go out to see? A man …*   b Other ancient authorities read *What then did you go out to see? A prophet?*   c Or *has been coming violently*   d Other ancient authorities omit *to hear*

Jesus reproaches his contemporaries

Lk 7:31–35

[16]"But to what shall I compare this generation? It is like children sitting in the market places and calling to their playmates,

[17] 'We piped to you, and you did not dance;
we wailed, and you did not mourn.'

[18]For John came neither eating nor drinking, and they say, 'He has a demon'; [19]the Son of man came eating and drinking, and they say, 'Behold, a glutton and a drunkard, a friend of tax collectors and sinners!' Yet wisdom is justified by her deeds."[e]

Mt 9:14
Mt 9:10–11
Lk 5:30; 15:1–2; 19:7

Jesus reproaches cities for their unbelief

Lk 10:13–16

[20]Then he began to upbraid the cities where most of his mighty works had been done, because they did not repent. [21]"Woe to you, Chorazin! woe to you, Bethsaida! for if the mighty works done in you had been done in Tyre and Sidon, they would have repented long ago in sackcloth and ashes. [22]But I tell you, it shall be more tolerable on the day of judgment for Tyre and Sidon than for you. [23]And you, Capernaum, will you be exalted to heaven? You shall be brought down to Hades. For if the mighty works done in you had been done in Sodom, it would have remained until this day. [24]But I tell you that it shall be more tolerable on the day of judgment for the land of Sodom than for you."

Is 14:13, 15

Mt 10:15

autem Ioannis Baptistae usque nunc regnum caelorum vim patitur, et violenti rapiunt illud. [13]Omnes enim Prophetae et Lex usque ad Ioannem prophetaverunt; [14]et si vultis recipere, ipse est Elias, qui venturus est. [15]Qui habet aures, audiat. [16]Cui autem similem aestimabo generationem istam? Similis est pueris sedentibus in foro, qui clamantes coaequalibus [17]dicunt: "Cecinimus vobis, et non saltastis; / lamentavimus, et non planxistis". [18]Venit enim Ioannes neque manducans neque bibens, et dicunt: "Daemonium habet"; [19]venit Filius hominis manducans et bibens, et dicunt: "Ecce homo vorax et potator vini, publicanorum amicus et peccatorum!". Et iustificata est sapientia ab operibus suis». [20]Tunc coepit exprobrare civitatibus, in quibus factae sunt plurimae virtutes eius, quia non egissent paenitentiam: [21]Vae tibi, Chorazin! Vae tibi, Bethsaida! Quia si in Tyro et Sidone factae essent virtutes, quae factae sunt in vobis, olim in cilicio et cinere paenitentiam egissent. [22]Verumtamen dico vobis: Tyro et Sidoni

fortitude which prevents you from camouflaging your own infidelities, a boldness to own up to the faith even when the environment is hostile" (St Josemaría Escrivá, *Christ Is Passing By*, 82).

11:16–19 Our Lord's words here follow logically from the previous passage. The Baptist and his disciples have seen that the deeds of Jesus are the works of the Messiah (11:2–6), but the leaders of the people persist in their campaign of criticism of Jesus. Therefore, he once again refers them to his "deeds" (v. 19): these bear clear witness to who he is and what his mission is.

Making reference to a popular song or a child's game of the time (v. 17), our Lord points out to his opponents that they have no grounds for their attitude.

As is also the case in other biblical texts, the stubborn children are depicted not as an illustration of innocence but of a lack of maturity: "Folly is bound up in the heart of a child, but the rod of discipline drives it far from him" (Prov 22:15). In this instance, the reproach is directed

against the leaders of the people who accuse Jesus of being a glutton and a drunkard, a friend of tax collectors and sinners (v. 19; cf. 9:9–17). Our Lord's words are also a warning that *we* run the risk of not appreciating the great gift of fullness of life given us by God in Jesus Christ: "We will be made whole on the day the Father has decided, and cease to be children to become the perfect man. Let us give thanks to the Father of all times and seasons, who has ordained that we lose our childish foolishness so that his gifts may not be squandered" (St Athanasius of Antioch, *Sermones*, 5, 7).

11:20–24 Chorazin and Bethsaida were thriving cities on the northern shore of the lake of Gennesaret, not far from Capernaum. During his public ministry in the north, Jesus often preached in these cities, and he worked many miracles there (v. 20). Tyre and Sidon, in Phoenicia, along with Sodom and Gomorrah (all cities notorious for loose living), were, for Jesus, classical recipients of divine punishment (see Ezek 26–28; Is

e Other ancient authorities read *children* (Luke 7:35)

Lk 10:21–24   **Jesus thanks his Father**

Is 29:14
1 Cor 1:26–29
Sir 51:1
Acts 17:24

Jn 3:35; 10:15; 13:3;
17:2

Phil 2:9
Gal 1:15f

Sir 51:33f
Jer 6:16

1 Kings 12:4
Is 28:12
Ps 2:3

[25]At that time Jesus declared, "I thank thee, Father, Lord of heaven and earth, that thou hast hidden these things from the wise and understanding and revealed them to babes; [26]yea, Father, for such was thy gracious will.[f] [27]All things have been delivered to me by my Father; and no one knows the Son except the Father, and no one knows the Father except the Son and any one to whom the Son chooses to reveal him.* [28]Come to me, all who labour and are heavy laden, and I will give you rest. [29]Take my yoke upon you, and learn from me; for I am gentle and lowly in heart, and you will find rest for your souls. [30]For my yoke is easy, and my burden is light."

remissius erit in die iudicii quam vobis. [23]Et tu, Capharnaum, numquid *usque in caelum exaltaberis? Usque in infernum descendes!* Quia si in Sodomis factae fuissent virtutes, quae factae sunt in te, mansissent usque in hunc diem. [24]Verumtamen dico vobis: Terrae Sodomorum remissius erit in die iudicii quam tibi». [25]In illo tempore respondens Iesus dixit: «Confiteor tibi, Pater, Domine caeli et terrae, quia abscondisti haec a sapientibus et prudentibus et revelasti ea parvulis. [26]Ita, Pater, quoniam sic fuit placitum ante te. [27]Omnia mihi tradita sunt a Patre meo; et nemo novit Filium nisi Pater, neque Patrem quis novit nisi Filius et cui voluerit Filius revelare. [28]Venite ad me, omnes, qui laboratis et onerati estis, et ego reficiam vos. [29]Tollite iugum meum super vos et discite a me, quia mitis sum et humilis corde, et invenietis requiem animabus vestris. [30]Iugum

23). Here Jesus is drawing attention to the ingratitude of people who could have come to know him but who refused to change: on the day of judgment (vv. 22 and 24) they will have a great deal to answer for. St Luke reports our Lord's words here as a lament (see Lk 10:13–16 and note), but St Matthew stresses the tone of reproach (v. 20) in order to show that there is always time and opportunity for repentance, "To fall into sin is not the most serious thing; more serious is to lie stretched out and refuse to struggle to rise again after we have fallen, to give in to apathy and to mask the weakness of our will with thoughts of despair" (St John Chrysostom, *Ad Theodorum lapsum*, 1, 7).

11:25–30 Whereas unbelievers sadden him, Jesus is heartened by those who accept him—simple, humble people who do not trust to their own wisdom, and do not consider themselves to be wise and understanding. This passage is a real jewel because it is the first recorded instance of Jesus addressing God as "Father" in a prayer; because it shows him to know God and to have received everything from Him; and because Jesus declares that he will reveal God to us (v. 27; cf. Lk 10:21–24 and note) if we are humble in heart (v. 25). These words are a beautiful prayer, and they evidence Jesus' deepest feelings: "His exclamation, 'Yes, Father!' expresses the depth of his heart, his adherence to the Father's 'good pleasure,' echoing his mother's *Fiat* at the time of his conception and prefiguring what he will say to the Father in his

agony. The whole prayer of Jesus is contained in this loving adherence of his human heart to the mystery of the will of the Father" (*Catechism of the Catholic Church*, 2603).

The "yoke" (vv. 29–30) was an image of the Law of Moses (see Sir 51:33), which with the passage of time had become weighed down by an endless series of petty regulations (see Acts 15:10) and failed to bring peace of heart. The Lord God had announced that a new time of restoration would come, when he would lead his faithful "with cords of compassion, with the bands of love" (see Hos 11:1–11 and note), and Jesus, with the image of his easy yoke and light burden, portrays himself as the agent of God's initiative: "Any other burden oppresses and crushes you, but Christ's actually takes weight off you. Any other burden weighs down, but Christ's gives you wings. If you take a bird's wings away, you might seem to be taking weight off it, but the more weight you take off, the more you tie it down to the earth. There it is on the ground, and you wanted to relieve it of a weight; give it back the weight of its wings and you will see how it flies" (St Augustine, *Sermones*, 126, 12).

Jesus is also "gentle and lowly in heart" (v. 29). This description (it appears in the Beatitudes: see 5:5) is used in the Old Testament (see Ps 37:11) for the patient person who, refraining from anger, puts his trust in God. By depicting himself in this way, Jesus links to his own Person the wisdom he preaches: "I give you thanks, my Jesus, for your decision to become

f Or *so it was well-pleasing before thee*

The law of the sabbath

Mk 2:23–28
Lk 6:1–5

12 ¹At that time Jesus went through the grainfields on the sabbath; his disciples were hungry, and they began to pluck ears of grain and to eat. ²But when the Pharisees saw it, they said to him, "Look, your disciples are doing what is not lawful to do on the sabbath." ³He said to them, "Have you not read what David did, when he was hungry, and those who were with him: ⁴how he entered the house of God and ate the bread of the Presence, which it was not lawful for him to eat nor for those who were with him, but only for the priests? ⁵Or have you not read in the law how on the sabbath the priests in the temple profane the sabbath, and are guiltless? ⁶I tell you, something greater than the temple is here. ⁷And if you had known what this means, 'I desire mercy, and not sacrifice,' you would not have condemned the guiltless. ⁸For the Son of man is lord of the sabbath."

Ex 20:10
Deut 5:14

1 Sam 21:7

Lev 24:5–9

Num 28:9

Hos 6:6
Mt 9:13

Curing of the man with a withered hand

Mk 3:1–6
Lk 6:6–11

⁹And he went on from there, and entered their synagogue. ¹⁰And behold, there was a man with a withered hand. And they asked him, "Is it lawful to heal on the sab-

Mk 3:1–6, 7–12
Lk 13:11–16; 14:1–6

Jn 5:9–10

enim meum suave et onus meum leve est».   [12] ¹In illo tempore abiit Iesus sabbatis per sata; discipuli autem eius esurierunt et coeperunt vellere spicas et manducare. ²Pharisaei autem videntes dixerunt ei: «Ecce discipuli tui faciunt, quod non licet facere sabbato». ³At ille dixit eis: «Non legistis quid fecerit David, quando esuriit, et qui cum eo erant? ⁴Quomodo intravit in domum Dei et panes propositionis comedit, quod non licebat ei edere neque his, qui cum eo erant, nisi solis sacerdotibus? ⁵Aut non legistis in Lege quia sabbatis sacerdotes in templo sabbatum violant et sine crimine sunt? ⁶Dico autem vobis quia templo maior est hic. ⁷Si autem sciretis quid est: *"Misericordiam volo et non sacrificium"*, numquam

perfect Man, with a Heart which loved and is most loveable; which loved unto death and suffered; which was filled with joy and sorrow; which delighted in the things of men and showed us the way to heaven; which subjected itself heroically to duty and acted with mercy; which watched over the poor and the rich and cared for sinners and the just. I give you thanks, my Jesus. Give us hearts to measure up to yours!" (St Josemaría Escrivá, *Furrow*, 813).

12:1–8 In providing, with divine authority, the true interpretation of the Law, Jesus meets with opposition from some Pharisees who do not accept his teaching even though it is supported by miracles. The point at issue here is the rule of the sabbath. God instituted the sabbath, and commanded that the Jewish people should refrain as much as possible from doing work on that day, to leave them free to give more time to God. Over the years, this divine precept was made so complicated that by Jesus' time there was a list of thirty-nine types of forbidden work. Jesus often taught that sabbath rest was not broken by service to God and one's neighbour; here he rejects the Pharisees' criticism, giving four reasons—the example of David, that of priests, the mercy of God, and Jesus' own lordship of the sabbath.

The words of Hosea in v. 7 (see Hos 6:6) also occur elsewhere in Jesus' controversies with the Pharisees (see 9:13). Here he seems to take it as read that this passage has special relevance for his critics; what is at issue is not really sacrifices in the temple but the need to distinguish between what is important and what is less important. In the episode of the man with the withered hand, Matthew goes on to show how very far away the Pharisees were from mercy and, therefore, from recognizing who Jesus was. A disposition towards mercy makes it much easier to recognize God and his works: "Christian, see the great dignity of your wisdom, how you must behave and the wonderful rewards that have been promised to you. The mercy you have been shown means you must be merciful; justice, that you should be just. The Creator wants to see his likeness in what he has created. God wants to see his image reflected in the human heart as in a mirror through your imitation of his works. The faith of one who acts in this way is always rewarded, your desires will be satisfied, and you will rejoice forever in the object of your love" (St Leo the Great, *Sermones*, 95, 7).

12:9–14 Jesus now works a miracle which bears out his teaching about the sabbath and his

Lk 13:15; 14:5

bath?" so that they might accuse him. [11]He said to them, "What man of you, if he has one sheep and it falls into a pit on the sabbath, will not lay hold of it and lift it out? [12]Of how much more value is a man than a sheep! So it is lawful to do good on the sabbath." [13]Then he said to the man, "Stretch out your hand." And the man stretched

Jn 5:16–18
Mk 11:18
Lk 19:47

it out, and it was restored, whole like the other. [14]But the Pharisees went out and took counsel against him, how to destroy him.*

Jesus, the servant of God

[15]Jesus, aware of this, withdrew from there. And many followed him, and he healed

Is 42:1–4; 41:9

them all, [16]and ordered them not to make him known. [17]This was to fulfil what was spoken by the prophet Isaiah:

[18]"Behold my servant whom I have chosen,
  my beloved with whom my soul is well pleased.
I will put my Spirit upon him,
  and he shall proclaim justice to the Gentiles.
[19]He will not wrangle or cry aloud,
  nor will any one hear his voice in the streets;
[20]he will not break a bruised reed
  or quench a smouldering wick,
  till he brings justice to victory;
[21]and in his name will the Gentiles hope."

condemnassetis innocentes. [8]Dominus est enim Filius hominis sabbati». [9]Et cum inde transisset, venit in synagogam eorum; [10]et ecce homo manum habens aridam. Et interrogabant eum dicentes: «Licet sabbatis curare?», ut accusarent eum. [11]Ipse autem dixit illis: «Quis erit ex vobis homo, qui habeat ovem unam et, si ceciderit haec sabbatis in foveam, nonne tenebit et levabit eam? [12]Quanto igitur melior est homo ove! Itaque licet sabbatis bene facere». [13]Tunc ait homini: «Extende manum tuam». Et extendit, et restituta est sana sicut altera. [14]Exeuntes autem pharisaei consilium faciebant adversus eum, quomodo eum perderent. [15]Iesus autem sciens secessit inde. Et secuti sunt eum multi, et curavit eos omnes [16]et comminatus est eis, ne manifestum eum facerent, [17]ut adimpleretur, quod dictum est per Isaiam prophetam dicentem: [18]«Ecce puer meus, quem elegi, / dilectus meus, in quo bene placuit animae meae; / ponam Spiritum meum super eum, / et iudicium gentibus nuntiabit. / [19]Non contendet neque clamabit, / neque audiet aliquis in plateis vocem eius. / [20]Arundinem quassatam non confringet / et linum fumigans non exstinguet, / donec eiciat ad victoriam iudicium; / [21]et in nomine eius gentes sperabunt». [22]Tunc oblatus est ei daemonium habens, caecus et mutus, et curavit eum, ita ut mutus loqueretur et videret. [23]Et stupebant omnes turbae et dicebant: «Numquid hic est filius David?». [24]Pharisaei autem audientes dixerunt:

authority over it. Reading this passage, we cannot fail to see the dramatic difference between Jesus' generous action and the meanness of those who try to catch him out: "He asked the man with the withered hand to stand in their midst to see if they would be moved by the sight of his suffering to turn their backs on wickedness and cruelty. But those men would have preferred to see Christ's reputation suffer than to see the poor man's suffering healed. Their malice is revealed in two ways: through the open war that they declare on Christ, and in the fact that their opposition is so bitter they do not care if others suffer as a consequence" (St John Chrysostom, *In Matthaeum*, 40, 1).

12:15–21 The episodes so far have shown the authorities' opposition to Jesus, and how Jesus tried to avoid open confrontations (vv. 15–16).

However, he does not cease to work cures. In Jesus' discretion, the evangelist sees the doctrinal key to the mystery of Christ. By quoting Isaiah 42:1–4 (vv. 18–21) he explains the significance of what is recounted in these two chapters (11 and 12), which evidence the hardness of heart of Israel's leaders: the prophecy about the suffering Servant is fulfilled in Jesus—that personage whose gentle, discreet teaching would bring the light of the truth to the world. His mission as the suffering Servant, which began with his baptism in the Jordan (3:17), is shown again by St Matthew in his account of how the Pharisees rejected him; and he will make this plainer still when he writes of the passion and death of Christ (see 27:30). However, the passage from Isaiah (vv. 18–21) ends by asserting that the humble Messiah will achieve victory, for only he can fulfil the hopes of the Gentiles.

Allegations by the Pharisees. The sin against the Holy Spirit

Mk 3:22–30
Lk 6:43–45;
11:14–26v, 22:
Mt 9:32–34

²²Then a blind and dumb demoniac was brought to him, and he healed him, so that the dumb man spoke and saw. ²³And all the people were amazed, and said, "Can this be the Son of David?" ²⁴But when the Pharisees heard it they said, "It is only by Beelzebul,* the prince of demons, that this man casts out demons." ²⁵Knowing their thoughts, he said to them, "Every kingdom divided against itself is laid waste, and no city or house divided against itself will stand; ²⁶and if Satan casts out Satan, he is divided against himself; how then will his kingdom stand? ²⁷And if I cast out demons by Beelzebul, by whom do your sons cast them out? Therefore they shall be your judges. ²⁸But if it is by the Spirit of God that I cast out demons, then the kingdom of God has come upon you. ²⁹Or how can one enter a strong man's house and plunder his goods, unless he first binds the strong man? Then indeed he may plunder his house. ³⁰He who is not with me is against me, and he who does not gather with me scatters. ³¹Therefore I tell you, every sin and blasphemy will be forgiven men, but the blasphemy against the Spirit will not be forgiven.* ³²And whoever says a word against the Son of man will be forgiven; but whoever speaks against the Holy Spirit will not be forgiven, either in this age or in the age to come.

Mt 10:25

1 Jn 3:8
Lk 17:21

Is 49:24
1 Jn 4:4

Mk 9:40

Heb 6:4, 6; 10:26
1 Jn 5:16
Lk 12:10

³³"Either make the tree good, and its fruit good; or make the tree bad, and its fruit bad; for the tree is known by its fruit. ³⁴You brood of vipers! how can you speak good, when you are evil? For out of the abundance of the heart the mouth speaks.

Mt 7:17–18

Jn 8:43
Mt 3:8

«Hic non eicit daemones nisi in Beelzebul, principe daemonum». ²⁵Sciens autem cogitationes eorum dixit eis: «Omne regnum divisum contra se desolatur, et omnis civitas vel domus divisa contra se non stabit. ²⁶Et si Satanas Satanam eicit, adversus se divisus est; quomodo ergo stabit regnum eius? ²⁷Et si ego in Beelzebul eicio daemones, filii vestri in quo eiciunt? Ideo ipsi iudices erunt vestri. ²⁸Si autem in Spiritu Dei ego eicio daemones, igitur pervenit in vos regnum Dei. ²⁹Aut quomodo potest quisquam intrare in domum fortis et vasa eius diripere, nisi prius alligaverit fortem? Et tunc domum illius diripiet. ³⁰Qui non est mecum, contra me est; et, qui non congregat mecum, spargit. ³¹Ideo dico vobis: Omne peccatum et blasphemia remittetur hominibus, Spiritus autem blasphemia non remittetur. ³²Et quicumque dixerit verbum contra Filium hominis, remittetur ei; qui autem dixerit contra Spiritum Sanctum, non remittetur ei neque in hoc saeculo neque in futuro. ³³Aut facite arborem bonam et fructum eius bonum, aut facite arborem malam et fructum eius malum: siquidem ex fructu arbor agnoscitur. ³⁴Progenies viperarum, quomodo potestis bona loqui, cum sitis mali? Ex abundantia enim cordis os loquitur. ³⁵Bonus homo de bono thesauro profert bona, et malus homo de malo thesauro pro-

12:22–37 In vv. 22–24 we find a report that is nearly identical with that of 9:32–34, the only difference being that this one is about a demoniac who is blind as well as mute. (See also Mk 3:22–27 and Lk 11:14–23.) Some malicious Pharisees criticize Jesus (v. 24). Our Lord gives them a very practical answer: there is a struggle between himself and Satan, and Satan is overcome because Jesus is stronger (v. 29). By expelling devils, Jesus demonstrates that the Kingdom of God has begun and that Satan is being ousted from his domain. The words of v. 30 sum up his argument: either one is with him or one is with the devil, a radical claim that can only mean that he himself is divine.

The Pharisees' stubbornness explains what Jesus has to say about the sin against the Holy Spirit being unforgivable. That sin (v. 32) "does not properly consist in offending against the Holy Spirit in words; it consists rather *in the refusal to accept the salvation which God offers to man through the Holy Spirit*, working through the power of the Cross. [...] Blasphemy against the Holy Spirit is the sin committed by the person who claims to have a '*right' to persist in evil*—in any sin at all—and who thus rejects Redemption" (John Paul II, *Dominum et vivificantem*, 46). It is in that sense that the sin is said to be unforgivable.

The final verses (vv. 33–37) contain some very trenchant statements. The Pharisees who criticize Jesus fail to give words their importance; but words are like deeds: they will save us, or cause us to be condemned. "Every offence committed against justice and truth entails the *duty of reparation*, even if its author has been forgiven. When it is impossible publicly to make reparation for a wrong, it must be made secretly. If someone who has suffered harm cannot be directly compensated, he must be given moral satisfaction in the name of charity. This duty of reparation also concerns

Lk 6:45

³⁵The good man out of his good treasure brings forth good, and the evil man out of his evil treasure brings forth evil. ³⁶I tell you, on the day of judgment men will render account for every careless word they utter; ³⁷for by your words you will be justified, and by your words you will be condemned."

Lk 11:24–26, 29–32 **The sign of Jonah**

1 Cor 1:22
Mk 8:11–12

Mt 16:1–4
Jn 6:30

Jon 2:1–2
Mt 27:63

Jon 3:5

1 Kings 10:1–10

Lk 11:24–26

2 Pet 2:20

³⁸Then some of the scribes and Pharisees said to him, "Teacher, we wish to see a sign from you." ³⁹But he answered them, "An evil and adulterous generation seeks for a sign; but no sign shall be given to it except the sign of the prophet Jonah. ⁴⁰For as Jonah was three days and three nights in the belly of the whale, so will the Son of man be three days and three nights in the heart of the earth. ⁴¹The men of Nineveh will arise at the judgment with this generation and condemn it; for they repented at the preaching of Jonah, and behold, something greater than Jonah is here. ⁴²The queen of the South will arise at the judgment with this generation and condemn it; for she came from the ends of the earth to hear the wisdom of Solomon, and behold, something greater than Solomon is here.

⁴³"When the unclean spirit has gone out of a man, he passes through waterless places seeking rest, but he finds none. ⁴⁴Then he says, 'I will return to my house from which I came.' And when he comes he finds it empty, swept, and put in order. ⁴⁵Then he goes and brings with him seven other spirits more evil than himself, and they enter and dwell there; and the last state of that man becomes worse than the first. So shall it be also with this evil generation."

Mk 3:31–35
Lk 8:19–21

Mt 13:55

Lk 2:49

The true kinsmen of Jesus

⁴⁶While he was still speaking to the people, behold, his mother and his brethren* stood outside, asking to speak to him.ᵍ ⁴⁸But he replied to the man who told him,

fert mala. ³⁶Dico autem vobis: Omne verbum otiosum, quod locuti fuerint homines, reddent rationem de eo in die iudicii: ³⁷ex verbis enim tuis iustificaberis, et ex verbis tuis condemnaberis». ³⁸Tunc responderunt ei quidam de scribis et pharisaeis dicentes: «Magister, volumus a te signum videre». ³⁹Qui respondens ait illis: «Generatio mala et adultera signum requirit, et signum non dabitur ei nisi signum Ionae prophetae. ⁴⁰Sicut enim *fuit Ionas in ventre ceti tribus diebus et tribus noctibus*, sic erit Filius hominis in corde terrae tribus diebus et tribus noctibus. ⁴¹Viri Ninevitae surgent in iudicio cum generatione ista et condemnabunt eam, quia paenitentiam egerunt in praedicatione Ionae; et ecce plus quam Iona hic! ⁴²Regina austri surget in iudicio cum generatione ista et condemnabit eam, quia venit a finibus terrae audire sapientiam Salomonis; et ecce plus quam Salomon hic! ⁴³Cum autem immundus spiritus exierit ab homine, ambulat per loca arida quaerens requiem et non invenit. ⁴⁴Tunc dicit: 'Revertar in domum meam unde exivi'; et veniens invenit vacantem, scopis mundatam et ornatam. ⁴⁵Tunc vadit et assumit secum septem alios spiritus

offences against another's reputation. This reparation, moral and sometimes material, must be evaluated in terms of the extent of the damage inflicted. It obliges in conscience" (*Catechism of the Catholic Church*, 2487).

As on other occasions, our Lord reminds people about the last things—in this case, specifically, the fact that there will be a Last Judgment (v. 36). Following the lead of Christ and his apostles, "the Church recognizes that she cannot omit, without serious mutilation of her essential message, a constant catechesis on what the traditional Christian language calls the four last things of man: death, judgment (universal and particular), hell and heaven" (John Paul II, *Reconciliatio et paenitentia*, 26).

12:38–45 In response to a request for a sign, a miracle or some other wondrous action that will confirm his authority, Jesus replies by foretelling his death and resurrection, and by comparing himself with Jonah the prophet. He draws the comparison to show that he himself is the "sign" par excellence. Both the Ninevites and the pagan "queen of the South" will lay charges against the Jews who failed to convert, or even to seek the truth (vv. 41–42). Their rejection of Jesus occasions a grave warning (vv. 43–45): if they continue to reject the light, their last state will be worse than their first.

12:46–50 Those who accept Jesus and do the will of his Father are acknowledged by him to be

g Other ancient authorities insert verse 47, *Some one told him, "Your mother and your brothers are standing outside, asking to speak to you"*

"Who is my mother, and who are my brethren?"* ⁴⁹And stretching out his hand
toward his disciples, he said, "Here are my mother and my brethren! ⁵⁰For whoever
does the will of my Father in heaven is my brother, and sister, and mother."

Rom 8:29
Jn 15:14

6. THE PARABLES OF THE KINGDOM*

Mk 4:1–20
Lk 8:4–15

Parable of the sower. The meaning of parables

13 ¹That same day Jesus went out of the house and sat beside the sea. ²And
great crowds gathered about him, so that he got into a boat and sat there; and

nequiores se, et intrantes habitant ibi; et fiunt novissima hominis illius peiora prioribus. Sic erit et generationi huic pessimae». ⁴⁶Adhuc eo loquente
ad turbas, ecce mater et fratres eius stabant foris quaerentes loqui ei. ⁴⁷Dixit autem ei quidam: «Ecce mater tua et fratres tui foris stant quaerentes
loqui tecum». ⁴⁸At ille respondens dicenti sibi ait: «Quae est mater mea, et qui sunt fratres mei?». ⁴⁹Et extendens manum suam in discipulos suos
dixit: «Ecce mater mea et fratres mei. ⁵⁰Quicumque enim fecerit voluntatem Patris mei, qui in caelis est, ipse meus frater et soror et mater est».
[13] ¹In illo die exiens Iesus de domo sedebat secus mare; ²et congregatae sunt ad eum turbae multae, ita ut in naviculam ascendens sederet, et

members of his own family. Jesus purposely
does not speak of "God", or of "the" Father in
heaven, but of "my" Father in heaven (v. 50).
"Becoming a disciple of Jesus means accepting
the invitation to belong to *God's family*, to live in
conformity with his way of life" (*Catechism of
the Catholic Church*, 2233). Thus, Jesus' words
are to be understood as being praise for Mary's
faithfulness, and not as any kind of put-down:
"She did the will of my Father. That is what the
Lord praises in her: that she did the will of his
Father, not that she bore him in her womb [...].
Our sweet Mother is sweet and holy because of
her obedience to the Word of God, not because
the Word was made flesh in her womb and dwelt
amongst us. She was a faithful guardian of the
Word of God who created her and whom she
bore in her womb" (St Augustine, *In Ioannis
Evangelium*, 10, 3).

The word translated as "brethren" (v. 46)
means Jesus' relatives. In Hebrew, Aramaic,
Arabic and other ancient languages it was
normal for the equivalent term to be used to
mean those belonging to the same family, clan or
even tribe. The Church has consistently professed that Jesus had no brothers or sisters in the
full meaning of the term: it is a dogma that Mary
was ever-Virgin (see the notes on 1:18–25; Mk
3:31–35 and Lk 8:19–21).

*13:1–52 The Parables Discourse, Jesus' third as
presented by St Matthew, is the beginning of a
new section of the Gospel. It records seven

parables about the Kingdom of heaven. All three
Synoptic Gospels (cf. Mk 4:1–34; Lk 8:4–18)
report this discourse, and all three mention these
facts: after the first parable (that of the sower),
the disciples ask Jesus what it means, and he
then explains the "secrets of the kingdom of
heaven" (v. 11; cf. Mk 4:11; Lk 8:10). The
parable of the sower is about how to understand
and appreciate the word of God. That may be
why it comes at the start of this discourse, which
includes the parable of the weeds (not found in
Mark or Luke) and that of the mustard seed; the
latter also appears in Mark (4:30–32) and in
Luke, where it is positioned later (13:18–19).
These are sometimes called the "parables of
growth", because they describe the conditions in
which the seed grows, how small the Kingdom is
to begin with, and the extraordinary growth
produced by the vigour of the seed (cf. the note
on Mk 4:1–34). Matthew also includes here
some complementary parables—those of the
treasure, the pearl and the net.

It is remarkable how often Jesus uses a
parable as a vehicle for his teaching. Teachers of
his time used parables to explain passages in
Scripture, but Jesus uses them more frequently
and in order to reveal the mysteries of the
Kingdom of God: "Jesus' invitation to enter his
kingdom comes in the form of *parables*, a
characteristic feature of his teaching. Through
his parables he invites people to the feast of the
kingdom, but he also asks for a radical choice: to
gain the kingdom, one must give everything.

the whole crowd stood on the beach. ³And he told them many things in parables, saying: "A sower went out to sow. ⁴And as he sowed, some seeds fell along the path, and the birds came and devoured them. ⁵Other seeds fell on rocky ground, where they had not much soil, and immediately they sprang up, since they had no depth of soil, ⁶but when the sun rose they were scorched; and since they had no root they withered away. ⁷Other seeds fell upon thorns, and the thorns grew up and choked them. ⁸Other seeds fell on good soil and brought forth grain, some a hundredfold, some sixty, some thirty. ⁹He who has ears,ʰ let him hear."

¹⁰Then the disciples came and said to him, "Why do you speak to them in parables?" ¹¹And he answered them, "To you it has been given to know the secrets of the kingdom of heaven, but to them it has not been given. ¹²For to him who has will more be given, and he will have abundance; but from him who has not, even what he has will be taken away.* ¹³This is why I speak to them in parables, because seeing they do not see, and hearing they do not hear, nor do they understand. ¹⁴With them indeed is fulfilled the prophecy of Isaiah which says:

'You shall indeed hear but never understand,
     and you shall indeed see but never perceive.
¹⁵ For this people's heart has grown dull,
     and their ears are heavy of hearing,
     and their eyes they have closed,

Marginal references:

Mt 11:15

Lk 8:9–10
Mk 4:10–12

Mk 4:25
Mt 25:29
Lk 8:18; 19:26

Is 6:9–10
Jn 12:40
Acts 28:26–27

---

omnis turba stabat in litore. ³Et locutus est eis multa in parabolis dicens: «Ecce exiit, qui seminat, seminare. ⁴Et dum seminat, quaedam ceciderunt secus viam, et venerunt volucres et comederunt ea. ⁵Alia autem ceciderunt in petrosa, ubi non habebant terram multam, et continuo exorta sunt, quia non habebant altitudinem terrae; ⁶sole autem orto, aestuaverunt et, quia non habebant radicem, aruerunt. ⁷Alia autem ceciderunt in spinas, et creverunt spinae et suffocaverunt ea. ⁸Alia vero ceciderunt in terram bonam et dabant fructum: aliud centesimum, aliud sexagesimum, aliud tricesimum. ⁹Qui habet aures, audiat». ¹⁰Et accedentes discipuli dixerunt ei: «Quare in parabolis loqueris eis?». ¹¹Qui respondens ait illis: «Quia vobis datum est nosse mysteria regni caelorum, illis autem non est datum. ¹²Qui enim habet, dabitur ei, et abundabit; qui autem non habet, et quod habet, auferetur ab eo. ¹³Ideo in parabolis loquor eis, quia videntes non vident et audientes non audiunt neque intellegunt; ¹⁴et adimpletur eis

---

Words are not enough, deeds are required. The parables are like mirrors for man: will he be hard soil or good earth for the word? What use has he made of the talents he has received? Jesus and the presence of the kingdom in this world are secretly at the heart of the parables. One must enter the kingdom, that is, become a disciple of Christ, in order to 'know the secrets of the kingdom of heaven' (Mt 13:11). For those who stay 'outside', everything remains enigmatic (Mk 4:1; cf. Mt 13:10–15)" (*Catechism of the Catholic Church*, 546).

13:1–23 The first parable is the longest in the discourse. Found in all three Synoptics (Mk 4:2–20; Lk 8:4–15), it has the classic form of the Kingdom parable. Its message can be seen as an answer to this question: Why does Jesus' preaching have such diverse effects on his listeners? It is important to remember that we are speculating on the mystery of God's grace and human response. Both aspects need to be safeguarded—

the freedom of God to bestow grace, and the freedom of the recipient to respond positively or not. The disciples, initially, cannot understand the parable. But they make a move from darkness into strong light. The Master shows his patience by taking them through the various stages. The parable becomes clear once the explanation is given (vv. 18–23), and we, the readers of the Gospel, are able to understand it in the context of both the life of Jesus and that of the Church. Jesus' preaching needs to fall on attentive ears. There are those who hear it but do not understand it (v. 19; cf. v. 14): they are deaf to God, like those religious authorities of Israel who were trying to catch Jesus out (see 11:16–12:50) and failed to interpret him correctly. Others are weak or irresolute (v. 21), like the many people who heard his preaching on the mountainside (5:1), or who benefited from his miracles, and yet would leave him on his own when the time of testing came. Others fail to respond, not due to weakness when the time

---

ʰ Other ancient authorities add here and in verse 43 *to hear*

lest they should perceive with their eyes,
and hear with their ears,
and understand with their heart,
and turn for me to heal them.'

[16]But blessed are your eyes, for they see, and your ears, for they hear. [17]Truly, I say to you, many prophets and righteous men longed to see what you see, and did not see it, and to hear what you hear, and did not hear it.

Lk 10:23–24
1 Pet 1:10–12

[18]"Hear then the parable of the sower. [19]When any one hears the word of the kingdom and does not understand it, the evil one comes and snatches away what is sown in his heart; this is what was sown along the path. [20]As for what was sown on rocky ground, this is he who hears the word and immediately receives it with joy; [21]yet he has no root in himself, but endures for a while, and when tribulation or persecution arises on account of the word, immediately he falls away.[i] [22]As for what was sown among thorns, this is he who hears the word, but the cares of the world and the delight in riches choke the word, and it proves unfruitful. [23]As for what was sown on good soil, this is he who hears the word and understands it; he indeed bears fruit, and yields, in one case a hundredfold, in another sixty, and in another thirty."

Mk 4:13–20
Lk 8:11–15

1 Tim 6:9

Jn 15:8, 16

The parable of the weeds

[24]Another parable he put before them, saying, "The kingdom of heaven may be compared to a man who sowed good seed in his field; [25]but while men were sleeping, his

prophetia Isaiae dicens: *"Auditu audietis et non intellegetis / et videntes videbitis et non videbitis. / [15]Incrassatum est enim cor populi huius, / et auribus graviter audierunt / et oculos suos clauserunt, / ne quando oculis videant / et auribus audiant / et corde intellegant et convertantur, / et sanem eos".* [16]Vestri autem beati oculi, quia vident, et aures vestrae, quia audiunt. [17]Amen quippe dico vobis: Multi prophetae et iusti cupierunt videre, quae videtis, et non viderunt, et audire, quae auditis, et non audierunt! [18]Vos ergo audite parabolam seminantis. [19]Omnis, qui audit verbum regni et non intellegit, venit Malus et rapit, quod seminatum est in corde eius; hic est, qui secus viam seminatus est. [20]Qui autem supra petrosa seminatus est, hic est, qui verbum audit et continuo cum gaudio accipit illud, [21]non habet autem in se radicem, sed est temporalis; facta autem tribulatione vel persecutione propter verbum, continuo scandalizatur. [22]Qui autem est seminatus in spinis, hic est, qui verbum audit, et sollicitudo

comes for them to defend the word, but because the Lord's word cannot bear fruit if a person does not lead an upright life (v. 22). But the word of God, when it is sent to earth, is always fruitful (cf. Is 55:10–11); it will always find some fertile ground. The word of Jesus, being the word of God, can produce fruit in varying proportions (v. 23), for human beings are not all the same; but it is always effective: "When this word is proclaimed, the voice of the preacher rings out loud, but the word resounds in the hearts of those who hear it, and can raise the dead to life. The sound of the word gives birth to new sons of Abraham in the faith. The word is alive in the heart of the Father, on the lips of the preacher, in the hearts of those who believe and love; and because it is alive, it is powerful" (Baldwin of Canterbury, *Tractatus*, 6).

13:24–43 The parables take various forms. In these verses, we find all kinds of examples—

from a phrase (v. 33) to a more developed allegory (vv. 24–30; cf. vv. 37–43). Often the parables are somewhat paradoxical: Jesus uses paradox to catch his listeners' attention and excite their curiosity; and almost always the imagination needs to be brought into play: to understand the message, one needs to read more deeply, to get beyond the imagery.

The first evangelist quotes two passages from the Old Testament that are very pertinent to the role of parables in preaching: our Lord uses parables to help him reveal the hidden mystery of the Kingdom (vv. 34–35; cf. 13:11); moreover, to be effective, parables require an active response from the listeners: if they are not interested in understanding the message, they get no further than the surface of the story (13:13–15). However, Jesus' disciples, those who ask him to explain the parables (v. 36), do manage to understand them (13:51), because in the full revelation that comes about in Jesus, God gives them that

i Or *stumbles*

enemy came and sowed weeds among the wheat, and went away. [26]So when the plants came up and bore grain, then the weeds appeared also. [27]And the servants[j] of the householder came and said to him, 'Sir, did you not sow good seed in your field? How then has it weeds?' [28]He said to them, 'An enemy has done this.' The servants [j] said to him, 'Then do you want us to go and gather them?' [29]But he said, 'No; lest in gathering the weeds you root up the wheat along with them. [30]Let both grow together until the harvest; and at harvest time I will tell the reapers, Gather the weeds first and bind them in bundles to be burned, but gather the wheat into my barn.'"

Mk 4:30–34
Lk 13:18–21

The mustard seed; the leaven

Ezek 17:23; 31:6
Ps 104:12

[31]Another parable he put before them saying, "The kingdom of heaven is like a grain of mustard seed which a man took and sowed in his field; [32]it is the smallest of all seeds, but when it has grown it is the greatest of shrubs and becomes a tree, so that the birds of the air come and make nests in its branches."

Lk 13:20–21
1 Cor 5:6
Gal 5:9

[33]He told them another parable. "The kingdom of heaven is like leaven which a woman took and hid in three measures of meal, till it was all leavened."

Mk 4:33–34

[34]All this Jesus said to the crowds in parables; indeed he said nothing to them without a parable. [35]This was to fulfil what was spoken by the prophet:[k]

saeculi et fallacia divitiarum suffocat verbum, et sine fructu efficitur. [23]Qui vero in terra bona seminatus est, hic est, qui audit verbum et intellegit et fructum affert et facit aliud quidem centum, aliud autem sexaginta, porro aliud triginta». [24]Aliam parabolam proposuit illis dicens: «Simile factum est regnum caelorum homini, qui seminavit bonum semen in agro suo. [25]Cum autem dormirent homines, venit inimicus eius et superseminavit zizania in medio tritici et abiit. [26]Cum autem crevisset herba et fructum fecisset, tunc apparuerunt et zizania. [27]Accedentes autem servi patris familias dixerunt ei: "Domine, nonne bonum semen seminasti in agro tuo? Unde ergo habet zizania?". [28]Et ait illis: "Inimicus homo hoc fecit". Servi autem dicunt ei: "Vis, imus et colligimus ea?". [29]Et ait: "Non; ne forte colligentes zizania eradicetis simul cum eis triticum, [30]sinite utraque crescere usque ad messem. Et in tempore messis dicam messoribus: Colligite primum zizania et alligate ea in fasciculos ad comburendum ea, triticum autem congregate in horreum meum"». [31]Aliam parabolam proposuit eis dicens: «Simile est regnum caelorum grano sinapis, quod accipiens homo seminavit in agro suo. [32]Quod minimum quidem est omnibus seminibus; cum autem creverit, maius est holeribus et fit arbor, ita ut volucres caeli veniant et habitent in ramis eius». [33]Aliam parabolam locutus est eis: «Simile est regnum caelorum fermento, quod acceptum mulier abscondit in farinae satis tribus, donec fermentatum est totum». [34]Haec omnia locutus est Iesus in parabolis ad turbas et sine parabola nihil loquebatur eis, [35]ut adimpleretur, quod dictum erat per prophetam dicentem: «*Aperiam in parabolis os meum*, / *eructabo abscondita* a constitu-

gift (13:11) which so many of the just in the Old Testament longed to have (13:16–17). The disciples need to make this gift bear fruit, bringing doctrine to life when they teach others (13:52): "I insist: ask God to grant us, his children, the 'gift of tongues', the gift of making ourselves understood by all. You can find the reason why I want this 'gift of tongues' in the pages of the Gospel, which abounds in parables, in examples which materialize the doctrine and illustrate spiritual truths, without debasing or degrading the word of God. Everyone, both the learned and the less learned, finds it easier to reflect on and understand God's message through these human images" (St Josemaría Escrivá, *The Forge*, 895).

The parable of the weeds complements that of the sower by addressing the presence of evil in the world, which resists the force of God's goodness. Our Lord sows his word, but the devil is also at work (v. 39), sowing bad seed and

drawing some people to himself. This happens during Jesus' lifetime, when his preaching of the Kingdom meets with violent opposition, and it will happen over the course of the Church's life because the children of God live in the world alongside the children of the Evil One (v. 38): good and evil have co-existed and continue to do so over the course of history. Jesus' teaching emphasizes the virtue of patience: just as it is not easy to distinguish wheat from weeds until the grain appears (v. 26), so too it is sometimes difficult to tell the real difference between good and evil. But in the end, Christ—the victorious Son of man—will judge all and give to each person what he or she has earned.

The call to patience and hope is reinforced by the parables of the mustard seed and the leaven (vv. 31–33)—similes drawn from farming and domestic life. In both, we can see the vast disproportion between the final result and the tiny

j Or *slaves*   k Other ancient authorities read *the prophet Isaiah*

"I will open my mouth in parables,   *Ps 78:2*
I will utter what has been hidden
since the foundation of the world."

The parable of the weeds explained

³⁶Then he left the crowds and went into the house. And his disciples came to him,   *Mt 13:24-30*
saying, "Explain to us the parable of the weeds of the field." ³⁷He answered, "He
who sows the good seed is the Son of man; ³⁸the field is the world, and the good   *1 Cor 3:9*
seed means the sons of the kingdom; the weeds are the sons of the evil one, ³⁹and the
enemy who sowed them is the devil; the harvest is the close of the age, and the
reapers are angels. ⁴⁰Just as the weeds are gathered and burned with fire, so will it   *Mt 3:10; 7:19*
be at the close of the age. ⁴¹The Son of man will send his angels, and they will gather *Jn 15:6*
out of his kingdom all causes of sin and all evildoers, ⁴²and throw them into the fur- *Zeph 1:3*
                                                                                        Mt 7:23; 24:31-32;
nace of fire; there men will weep and gnash their teeth. ⁴³Then the righteous will   *25:31-46*
                                                                                        Mt 8:12
shine like the sun in the kingdom of their Father. He who has ears, let him hear.   *Dan 12:3*
                                                                                        Mt 11:15

The hidden treasure; the pearl; the net

⁴⁴"The kingdom of heaven is like treasure hidden in a field, which a man found and   *Lk 14:33*
covered up; then in his joy he goes and sells all that he has and buys that field.   *Phil 3:7*
                                                                                        Prov 2:4

tione mundi». ³⁶Tunc dimissis turbis venit in domum, et accesserunt ad eum discipuli eius dicentes: «Dissere nobis parabolam zizaniorum agri». ³⁷Qui respondens ait: «Qui seminat bonum semen, est Filius hominis; ³⁸ager autem est mundus; bonum vero semen, hi sunt filii regni; zizania autem filii sunt Mali; ³⁹inimicus autem, qui seminavit ea, est Diabolus; messis vero consummatio saeculi est, messores autem angeli sunt. ⁴⁰Sicut ergo colliguntur zizania et igni comburuntur, sic erit in consummatione saeculi. ⁴¹mittet Filius hominis angelos suos, et colligent de regno eius omnia scandala et eos, qui faciunt iniquitatem, ⁴²et mittent eos in caminum ignis; ibi erit fletus et stridor dentium. ⁴³Tunc iusti fulgebunt sicut sol in regno Patris eorum. Qui habet aures, audiat. ⁴⁴Simile est regnum caelorum thesauro abscondito in agro, quem qui invenit homo abscondit et prae gaudio illius vadit et vendit universa, quae habet, et emit agrum illum. ⁴⁵Iterum simile est regnum caelorum homini negotiatori quaerenti

beginning. The mustard seed is proverbial for its smallness (cf. 17:20) but it grows into a leafy tree comparable to the one used by Ezekiel (see Ezek 17:22-24) to foretell the Kingdom of God; a little yeast, in turn, is able to ferment a lot of dough. The leaven is also a metaphor for the Christian. Living in the midst of the world (without losing their character), Christians are able to win souls for Christ by their word and example. This teaching refers in a special way to laypeople: "The images of salt, light and leaven taken from the Gospel, although indiscriminately applicable to all Jesus' disciples, are specifically applied to the lay faithful. They are particularly meaningful images because they speak not only of the deep involvement and the full participation of the lay faithful in the affairs of the earth, the world and the human community, but also and above all, they tell of the radical newness and unique character of an involvement and participation which has as its purpose the spreading of the Gospel that brings salvation" (John Paul II, *Christifideles laici*, 15).

These three parables continue to bolster the hope of Christ's disciples; they will meet with difficulties, but the outcome will always be rewarding: "In the moments of struggle and tribulation, when perhaps the 'good' fill your way with obstacles, lift up your apostolic heart: listen to Jesus as he speaks of the grain of mustard seed and of the leaven, and say to him: *Edissere nobis parabolam*—'Explain the parable to me.' And you'll feel the joy of contemplating the victory to come: the birds of the air under the shelter of your apostolate, now only in its beginnings, and the whole of the meal leavened" (St Josemaría Escrivá, *The Way*, 695).

13:44-52 With the parables of the hidden treasure and the pearl (vv. 44-46) Jesus describes the supreme value of the Kingdom of heaven, and the attitude people need to have if they are to attain it. There are slight differences in the teachings contained in these two parables: the treasure means abundance of gifts; the pearl, the beauty of the Kingdom. The treasure is something stum-

Prov 8:10–11

45"Again, the kingdom of heaven is like a merchant in search of fine pearls, 46who, on finding one pearl of great value, went and sold all that he had and bought it.

47"Again, the kingdom of heaven is like a net which was thrown into the sea and gathered fish of every kind; 48when it was full, men drew it ashore and sat down and sorted the good into vessels but threw away the bad. 49So it will be at the close of the

Mt 8:12

age. The angels will come out and separate the evil from the righteous, 50and throw them into the furnace of fire; there men will weep and gnash their teeth.

51"Have you understood all this?" They said to him, "Yes." 52And he said to them, "Therefore every scribe who has been trained for the kingdom of heaven is like a householder who brings out of his treasure what is new and what is old."*

7. JESUS WITHDRAWS TO THE BORDER COUNTRY*

Mk 6:1–6
Lk 4:16–30

No one is a prophet in his own country

53And when Jesus had finished these parables he went away from there, 54and coming to his own country he taught them in their synagogue, so that they were astonished,

bonas margaritas. 46Inventa autem una pretiosa margarita, abiit et vendidit omnia, quae habuit, et emit eam. 47Iterum simile est regnum caelorum sagenae missae in mare et ex omni genere congreganti; 48quam, cum impleta esset, educentes secus litus et sedentes collegerunt bonos in vasa, malos autem foras miserunt. 49Sic erit in consummatione saeculi: exibunt angeli et separabunt malos de medio iustorum 50et mittent eos in caminum ignis; ibi erit fletus et stridor dentium. 51Intellexistis haec omnia?». Dicunt ei: «Etiam». 52Ait autem illis: «Ideo omnis scriba doctus in regno caelorum similis est homini patri familias, qui profert de thesauro suo nova et vetera». 53Et factum est cum consummasset Iesus parabolas

bled upon; the pearl, the result of a long search. In both cases, the person concerned needs to be generous, because God "never fails to help someone who decides to leave all things for his sake" (St Teresa of Avila, *Way of Perfection*, 1, 2). To live in the Kingdom, to follow Christ, is not easy, but the reward makes the effort worthwhile: "The treasure was hidden because the field must also be bought. The treasure hidden in the field is Christ Incarnate, who is found everywhere. […] But the hidden treasure cannot be possessed without paying for the field: that is, we must sacrifice this world if we are to enjoy the riches of heaven" (St Hilary of Poitiers, *Commentarius in Matthaeum*, 13, 7).

An idea similar to that in the parable of the weeds occurs in the dragnet parable (vv. 47–50). Like the Church, the Kingdom of heaven is open to everyone, even though some will prove unworthy: at the end, the angels will separate the good from the bad. This is the same idea as is found in the parable of the people invited to the marriage feast (22:1–14): all, "both bad and good" (22:10), are invited, but that parable concludes with the lesson that it is not enough to be "called"; one must be "chosen".

The disciples understand what our Lord is

saying (v. 51) and that is why they can become the scribes in the new Israel (v. 52). If they understand Christ, old things (the Law of Moses) and new things (Jesus and the new Law taught by him) will equip them for their evangelizing mission, for Christ "is always new, and constantly renews the soul; he never grows old because he will never fade away" (St Bernard, *In vigilia Nativitatis Domini, Sermo*, 6, 6).

*13:53—16:20 After the Parables Discourse, the evangelist reports some miracles and teachings of Jesus in Galilee and the surrounding area. We are shown that people are forced to take sides regarding Jesus—either with him or against him. Starting with the Parables Discourse, Matthew clearly identifies three groups of people—the disciples (especially Peter), who stay close to Jesus; the crowds, who follow him but fail to understand him; and the religious authorities, who lay traps for him. This section ends with Peter's solemn confession of faith in which he proclaims Jesus to be the Messiah and the Son of God (16:16).

13:53–58 People's amazement at Jesus at the beginning of this passage (v. 54) stands in sharp contrast to their subsequent rejection of him (v.

and said, "Where did this man get this wisdom and these mighty works? ⁵⁵Is not this Jn 6:42 the carpenter's son? Is not his mother called Mary? And are not his brethren James and Joseph and Simon and Judas?* ⁵⁶And are not all his sisters with us? Where then Jn 7:15, 52 did this man get all this?" ⁵⁷And they took offence at him. But Jesus said to them, "A Jn 4:44 prophet is not without honour except in his own country and in his own house." ⁵⁸And he did not do many mighty works there, because of their unbelief.

The martyrdom of John the Baptist

Mk 6:14–29
Lk 3:19–20

14 ¹At that time Herod the tetrarch heard about the fame of Jesus; ²and he said Lk 9:7–9 to his servants, "This is John the Baptist, he has been raised from the dead; that is why these powers are at work in him." ³For Herod had seized John and bound him and put him in prison, for the sake of Herodias, his brother Philip's wife;¹ ⁴because John said to him, "It is not lawful for you to have her." ⁵And though he Lev 18:16; 20:21 wanted to put him to death, he feared the people, because they held him to be a Mt 21:26 prophet. ⁶But when Herod's birthday came, the daughter of Herodias danced before the company, and pleased Herod, ⁷so that he promised with an oath to give her what-

istas, transiit inde. ⁵⁴Et veniens in patriam suam, docebat eos in synagoga eorum, ita ut mirarentur et dicerent: «Unde huic sapientia haec et virtutes? ⁵⁵Nonne hic est fabri filius? Nonne mater eius dicitur Maria, et fratres eius Iacobus et Ioseph et Simon et Iudas? ⁵⁶Et sorores eius nonne omnes apud nos sunt? Unde ergo huic omnia ista?». ⁵⁷Et scandalizabantur in eo. Iesus autem dixit eis: «Non est propheta sine honore nisi in patria et in domo sua». ⁵⁸Et non fecit ibi virtutes multas propter incredulitatem illorum.   [14] ¹In illo tempore audivit Herodes tetrarcha famam Iesu ²et ait pueris suis: «Hic est Ioannes Baptista; ipse surrexit a mortuis, et ideo virtutes operantur in eo». ³Herodes enim tenuit Ioannem et alligavit eum et posuit in carcere propter Herodiadem uxorem Philippi fratris sui. ⁴Dicebat enim illi Ioannes: «Non licet tibi habere eam». ⁵Et volens illum occidere, timuit populum, quia sicut prophetam eum habebant. ⁶Die autem natalis Herodis saltavit filia Herodiadis in medio et placuit Herodi,

57). Jesus' old neighbours in Nazareth did not recognize who he really was; maybe their previous familiarity with him made it difficult for them to see the supernatural nature of his mission. And, if faith is able to work miracles (cf. 8:5–13 and note), unbelief prevents their happening, because "as well as the power of the one who cured them, the faith of those who were cured was essential to the working of the miracle; there can be no miracle if that faith is lacking" (St Gregory Nazianzen, *De theologia*, 30, 10).

"The carpenter's son" (v. 55): this is the only reference in the Gospel to St Joseph's occupation; in Mark 6:3, Jesus himself is described as a "carpenter". The Gospels give us a concordant depiction of Jesus during his hidden life. In terms of social status, the work of Joseph and Jesus as carpenters was not counted among the humblest types of work (that of a day-labourer on the land, for example); nor would it put them on a par with a landowner or someone of high social standing; rather, it would have been on the same sort of social level as that occupied by the apostles—minor officials, fishermen, owners of small businesses, etc. Jesus' work-life is also a part of his revelation to us (cf. the note on Mk

6:1–6), as the early Christians were quick to note: "He was known as the son of Joseph the carpenter [...] and as a carpenter Himself; while he lived among men, he worked as a carpenter, making ploughs and yokes, symbols of salvation, and giving us good example of a life of work" (St Justin, *Dialogus cum Tryphone*, 88, 7).

For an explanation regarding these "brethren" of Jesus (v. 55), see the notes on 12:46–50 and Mk 6:1–6.

14:1–12 This Herod, Herod Antipas, appears later in the account of the Passion (Lk 23:7 ff). A son of Herod the Great (2:1–18), he governed Galilee and Perea. He and Herodias had each divorced their previous spouses to marry each other, and this caused an on-going scandal, because Herodias had been the wife of Herod's half-brother. The historian Flavius Josephus (cf. *Antiquitates iudaicae*, 18, 116–119) provides additional information about this episode; he records, for example, that it took place in the fortress of Makeronte and that Herodias' daughter (Herod's niece) was named Salome.

The evangelist underlines the close connexion between the Baptist and Jesus (vv. 2 and 12).

l Other ancient authorities read *his brother's wife*

ever she might ask. ⁸Prompted by her mother, she said, "Give me the head of John the Baptist here on a platter." ⁹And the king was sorry; but because of his oaths and his guests he commanded it to be given; ¹⁰he sent and had John beheaded in the prison, ¹¹and his head was brought on a platter and given to the girl, and she brought it to her mother. ¹²And his disciples came and took the body and buried it; and they went and told Jesus.

Mk 6:30–44
Lk 9:10–17
Jn 6:1–15

First miracle of the loaves and fish

Mt 9:36

¹³Now when Jesus heard this, he withdrew from there in a boat to a lonely place apart. But when the crowds heard it, they followed him on foot from the towns. ¹⁴As he went ashore he saw a great throng; and he had compassion on them, and healed their sick. ¹⁵When it was evening, the disciples came to him and said, "This is a lonely place, and the day is now over; send the crowds away to go into the villages and buy food for themselves." ¹⁶Jesus said, "They need not go away; you give them something to eat." ¹⁷They said to him, "We have only five loaves here and two fish." ¹⁸And he said, "Bring them here to me." ¹⁹Then he ordered the crowds to sit down on the grass; and taking the five loaves and the two fish he looked up to heaven, and blessed, and broke and gave the loaves to the disciples, and the disciples gave them

2 Kings 4:44

to the crowds. ²⁰And they all ate and were satisfied. And they took up twelve baskets full of the broken pieces left over. ²¹And those who ate were about five thousand men, besides women and children.

⁷unde cum iuramento pollicitus est ei dare, quodcumque postulasset. ⁸At illa, praemonita a matre sua: «Da mihi, inquit, hic in disco caput Ioannis Baptistae». ⁹Et contristatus rex propter iuramentum et eos, qui pariter recumbebant, iussit dari ¹⁰misitque et decollavit Ioannem in carcere; ¹¹et allatum est caput eius in disco et datum est puellae, et tulit matri suae. ¹²Et accedentes discipuli eius tulerunt corpus et sepelierunt illud et venientes nuntiaverunt Iesu. ¹³Quod cum audisset Iesus, secessit inde in navicula in locum desertum seorsum; et cum audissent, turbae secutae sunt eum pedestres de civitatibus. ¹⁴Et exiens vidit turbam multam et misertus est eorum et curavit languidos eorum. ¹⁵Vespere autem facto, accesserunt ad eum discipuli dicentes: «Desertus est locus, et hora iam praeteriit; dimitte turbas, ut euntes in castella emant sibi escas». ¹⁶Iesus autem dixit eis: «Non habent necesse ire; date illis vos manducare». ¹⁷Illi autem dicunt ei: «Non habemus hic nisi quinque panes et duos pisces». ¹⁸Qui ait:

The death of the Baptist heralded, in a way, that of Christ. "The dragon tore off the servant's head, whetting his appetite for the Passion of the Lord" (St Peter Chrysologus, *Sermones*, 174). But from the perspective of hope in Christ, John's death was a victory: "What evil could bring about this just man's death? What could cause his violent death? [...] He did not suffer death, he won victory; it was not the end of his life, but the beginning of a better life. Learn to live as a Christian: nothing will ever harm you and you will be given the great reward" (St John Chrysostom, *De Providentia*, 22, 10).

By contrast, the history of those in authority is one of excess piled on excess, ending with the murder of the Baptist: "The young woman dances; her mother's heart is filled with cruelty; a terrible oath is sworn at the decadent feast, and the terrible oath fulfilled" (St Augustine, *Sermones*, 307, 1). Clearly, Herod is an example of what a ruler should not be. The Church

teaches that oaths should not be taken lightly, for the "The holiness of the divine name demands that we never use it for trivial matters" (*Catechism of the Catholic Church*, 2155). And, of course, immoral oaths and promises should never be made (cf. ibid., 2154), and if they are, they should not be kept: "It was wrong to promise the kingdom as the reward for a dance, cruel to permit the death of the prophet to fulfil an oath" (St Ambrose, *De officiis*, 3, 12, 77).

14:13–21 By this miracle of the multiplication of the loaves, our Lord is symbolically signalling the creation of the new People of God (cf. the note on Mk 6:30–44). St Matthew focuses especially on our Lord's consideration for the needs of the people. That is why, in addition to reporting the miracle of the multiplication, he records that Jesus healed the sick (v. 14).

In the general context of Jesus' doings, this account shows that not only is he meeting the

Jesus walks on the water

Mk 6:45–52
Jn 6:16–21

[22]Then he made the disciples get into the boat and go before him to the other side, while he dismissed the crowds. [23]And after he had dismissed the crowds he went up into the hills by himself to pray. When evening came, he was there alone, [24]but the boat by this time was many furlongs distant from the land,[m] beaten by the waves; for the wind was against them. [25]And in the fourth watch of the night he came to them, walking on the sea. [26]But when the disciples saw him walking on the sea, they were terrified, saying, "It is a ghost!" And they cried out for fear. [27]But immediately he spoke to them, saying, "Take heart, it is I; have no fear."

Lk 6:12; 9:18

Lk 24:37

[28]And Peter answered him, "Lord, if it is you, bid me come to you on the water." [29]He said, "Come." So Peter got out of the boat and walked on the water and came to Jesus; [30]but when he saw the wind,[n] he was afraid, and beginning to sink he cried out, "Lord, save me." [31]Jesus immediately reached out his hand and caught him, saying to him, "O man of little faith, why did you doubt?" [32]And when they got into the boat, the wind ceased. [33]And those in the boat worshipped him, saying, "Truly you are the Son of God."*

Mt 8:26

Mt 16:16; 27:54
Mk 15:39
Jn 1:49; 11:27

«Afferte illos mihi huc». [19]Et cum iussisset turbas discumbere supra fenum, acceptis quinque panibus et duobus piscibus, aspiciens in caelum benedixit et fregit et dedit discipulis panes, discipuli autem turbis. [20]Et manducaverunt omnes et saturati sunt; et tulerunt reliquias fragmentorum duodecim cophinos plenos. [21]Manducantium autem fuit numerus fere quinque milia virorum, exceptis mulieribus et parvulis. [22]Et statim iussit discipulos ascendere in naviculam et praecedere eum trans fretum, donec dimitteret turbas. [23]Et dimissis turbis, ascendit in montem solus orare. Vespere autem facto, solus erat ibi. [24]Navicula autem iam multis stadiis a terra distabat, fluctibus iactata; erat enim contrarius ventus. [25]Quarta autem vigilia noctis venit ad eos ambulans supra mare. [26]Discipuli autem, videntes eum supra mare ambulantem, turbati sunt dicentes: «Phantasma est», et prae timore clamaverunt. [27]Statimque Iesus locutus est eis dicens: «Habete fiduciam, ego sum; nolite timere!». [28]Respondens autem ei Petrus dixit: «Domine, si tu es, iube me venire ad te super aquas». [29]At ipse ait: «Veni!». Et descendens Petrus de navicula ambulavit super aquas et venit ad Iesum. [30]Videns vero ventum validum timuit et, cum coepisset mergi, clamavit dicens: «Domine, salvum me fac!». [31]Continuo autem Iesus extendens manum apprehendit eum et ait illi: «Modicae fidei, quare dubitasti?». [32]Et cum ascendissent in naviculam, cessavit ventus. [33]Qui

immediate and physical needs of the crowd, but by his gestures (which are very like those found at the institution of the Eucharist: v. 19; cf. 26:26) he is also announcing the messianic banquet at which he will be the host. That is why Christian tradition has interpreted this miracle as a symbol that prefigures the instituting of the Eucharist.

To perform this great miracle, Jesus seeks the co-operation of others, and he gets his disciples to distribute the bread and the fish to the people. Something similar happens in the Church, when our Lord offers himself to us in the Eucharistic banquet through his ministers.

14:22–33 Storms are a frequent occurrence on the lake of Gennesaret: they create huge waves, causing great danger to shipping. The episode of Jesus walking on the water (vv. 25–27) is also reported in Mark 6:48–50 and John 6:19–21; but St Matthew is the only one to tell how St Peter walked on the water (vv. 28–31), and he is the only one to record Jesus' solemn promise to Peter (16:17–19) and the episode of the temple

tax (17:24–27). Each of these instances shows the importance that Jesus wanted Peter to have in the Church. In this particular episode, we can see the greatness and weakness of Peter, his faith and the fact that he found it difficult to believe: "Peter said: 'Lord …, bid me come to you on the water.' […] And he said: 'Come.' Peter climbed out of the boat and walked on the water. This is what Peter could do in the Lord. And what could he do on his own? When he saw the wind, he was afraid, and beginning to sink he cried out, 'Lord, save me.' When he trusted in the Lord, he was able to walk on water; but when he trusted in himself, he began to sink, so he cried out to the Lord to save him" (St Augustine, *Sermones*, 76, 8).

The episode has applications for Christian life. The Church, like the apostles' boat, will also have to brave storms, and Jesus, who watches over her, comes to her rescue, after allowing her to wrestle with obstacles and be strengthened in the process. During trials of faith and fidelity, when Christians have to struggle to stay upright despite their weakness, our Lord gives encouragement (v. 27),

m Other ancient authorities read *was out on the sea*   n Other ancient authorities read *strong wind*

Mk 6:53–56

Cures in Gennesaret

34And when they had crossed over, they came to land at Gennesaret. 35And when the men of that place recognized him, they sent round to all that region and brought to him all that were sick, 36and besought him that they might only touch the fringe of his garment; and as many as touched it were made well.

Mt 9:20–22
Lk 6:19

Mk 7:1–23

The tradition of the elders. True cleanness

Deut 4:2
Lk 11:38
Col 2:21–22

15 1Then Pharisees and scribes came to Jesus from Jerusalem and said, 2"Why do your disciples transgress the tradition of the elders? For they do not wash their hands when they eat." 3He answered them, "And why do you transgress the commandment of God for the sake of your tradition? 4For God commanded, 'Honour your father and your mother,' and, 'He who speaks evil of father or mother, let him surely die.' 5But you say, 'If any one tells his father or his mother, What you would have gained from me is given to God,^o he need not honour his father.'* 6So,

Ex 20:12; 21:17
Deut 5:16
Lev 20:9

autem in navicula erant, adoraverunt eum dicentes: «Vere Filius Dei es!». 34Et cum transfretassent, venerunt in terram Gennesaret. 35Et cum cognovissent eum viri loci illius, miserunt in universam regionem illam et obtulerunt ei omnes male habentes, 36et rogabant eum, ut vel fimbriam vestimenti eius tangerent; et, quicumque tetigerunt, salvi facti sunt. [15] 1Tunc accedunt ad Iesum ab Hierosolymis pharisaei et scribae dicentes: 2«Quare discipuli tui transgrediuntur traditionem seniorum? Non enim lavant manus suas, cum panem manducant». 3Ipse autem respondens ait illis: «Quare et vos transgredimini mandatum Dei propter traditionem vestram? 4Nam Deus dixit: *"Honora patrem tuum et matrem"* et: *"Qui maledixerit patri vel matri, morte moriatur"*. 5Vos autem dicitis: "Quicumque dixerit patri vel matri: Munus est, quodcumque ex me profuerit, 6non honorificabit patrem suum"; et irritum fecistis verbum Dei propter traditionem vestram. 7Hypocritae! Bene prophetavit de vobis Isaias dicens:

elicits prayer (v. 30), and stretches out a hand (v. 31). Then, as now, the good disciple makes a confession of faith: "Truly you are the Son of God" (v. 33): "The Lord inspires and sustains our wavering hope. He set Peter's feet firm on the surface of the water when the apostle began to sink. When he sees us drowning in our doubts and worries, he stretches out his hand, which is the Word, and enlightens our mind; if we walk hand in hand with Him, we will know no fear" (St Gregory of Nyssa, *De beatitudinibus*, 6).

14:34–36 Here, by way of contrast with the previous passage, the focus is on the faith of those men who sought help from Jesus and obtained it. They are an example for us: in the adorable humanity of our Saviour we can find relief in all our needs (cf. 11:28).

15:1–20 The first two Gospels (see the note on Mk 7:1–23) report this episode, which had such relevance later in guiding Christians as to how they should respond to the precepts of the scribes and Pharisees. Christ explains that in many instances those traditions have effectively dismissed (v. 6) God's commandment—in which case they should be ignored (v. 14).

Our Lord proclaims the true meaning of

moral precepts. The mistake some scribes made lay in concentrating on external acts and practices and not giving pride of place to purity of heart. For example, they saw prayer as having more to do with exact recitation of set forms of words than with raising the soul to God (cf. 6:5–6). The same thing had happened in the case of other prescriptions: "In the gospel, the Lord recites the commandment of the Law: 'Honour your father and your mother'; we should not pay mere lip service to this commandment in empty flattery that mocks a father or mother's poverty" (St Jerome, *Epistulae*, 123, 5).

In v. 19 Jesus tells us where the true centre of moral agency is to be found—in a person's inner decisions. The two last commandments in the Decalogue touch on this theme: to struggle sincerely against sins of thought (hatred, impure thoughts, etc.), one needs to have an upright conscience; moreover, any faults in this area can lead to external sins. The passage is reminiscent of the sixth beatitude (see 5:8), which says that a clean heart is necessary for seeing God: "'Pure in heart' refers to those who have attuned their intellects and wills to the demands of God's holiness, chiefly in three areas: charity; chastity or sexual rectitude; love of truth and orthodoxy of faith" (*Catechism of the Catholic Church*, 2518).

o Or *an offering*

for the sake of your tradition, you have made void the word[p] of God. [7]You hypocrites! Well did Isaiah prophesy of you, when he said: *Is 29:13*

    [8]'This people honours me with their lips,
        but their heart is far from me;
    [9]in vain do they worship me,
        teaching as doctrines the precepts of men.' "

    [10]And he called the people to him and said to them, "Hear and understand: [11]not   *1 Tim 4:4*
what goes into the mouth defiles a man, but what comes out of the mouth, this
defiles a man." [12]Then the disciples came and said to him, "Do you know that the
Pharisees were offended when they heard this saying?" [13]He answered, "Every plant   *Jn 15:2*
which my heavenly Father has not planted will be rooted up. [14]Let them alone; they   *Lk 6:39*
are blind guides. And if a blind man leads a blind man, both will fall into a pit."   *Mt 23:16, 24*
[15]But Peter said to him, "Explain the parable to us." [16]And he said, "Are you also   *Jn 9:40*
still without understanding? [17]Do you not see that whatever goes into the mouth   *Rom 2:19*
passes into the stomach, and so passes on?[q] [18]But what comes out of the mouth pro-   *Mk 4:13*
ceeds from the heart, and this defiles a man. [19]For out of the heart come evil   *Rom 1:29–31*
thoughts, murder, adultery, fornication, theft, false witness, slander. [20]These are what   *1 Cor 5:10–11*
defile a man; but to eat with unwashed hands does not defile a man."   *Gal 5:19–21*
    Eph 5:3–5
    Col 3:5
    1 Tim 1:9–10
    2 Tim 3:2–4
    1 Pet 4:3

The Canaanite woman

Mk 7:24–30

[21]And Jesus went away from there and withdrew to the district of Tyre and Sidon.
[22]And behold, a Canaanite woman from that region came out and cried, "Have mercy   *Mt 9:27*
on me, O Lord, Son of David; my daughter is severely possessed by a demon." [23]But
he did not answer her a word. And his disciples came and begged him, saying, "Send
her away, for she is crying after us." [24]He answered, "I was sent only to the lost sheep   *Mt 10:16*

[8] "*Populus hic labiis me honorat, / cor autem eorum longe est a me*; / [9] *sine causa autem colunt me, / docentes doctrinas mandata hominum*"». [10]Et convocata ad se turba, dixit eis: «Audite et intellegite: [11]Non quod intrat in os, coinquinat hominem; sed quod procedit ex ore, hoc coinquinat hominem!». [12]Tunc accedentes discipuli dicunt ei: «Scis quia pharisaei, audito verbo, scandalizati sunt?». [13]At ille respondens ait: «Omnis plantatio, quam non plantavit Pater meus caelestis, eradicabitur. [14]Sinite illos: caeci sunt duces caecorum. Caecus autem si caeco ducatum praestet, ambo in foveam cadent». [15]Respondens autem Petrus dixit ei: «Edissere nobis parabolam istam». [16]At ille dixit: «Adhuc et vos sine intellectu estis? [17]Non intellegitis quia omne quod in os intrat, in ventrem vadit et in secessum emittitur? [18]Quae autem procedunt de ore, de corde exeunt, et ea coinquinant hominem. [19]De corde enim exeunt cogitationes malae, homicidia, adulteria, fornicationes, furta, falsa testimonia, blasphemiae. [20]Haec sunt, quae coinquinant hominem; non lotis autem manibus manducare non coinquinat hominem». [21]Et egressus inde Iesus, secessit in partes Tyri et Sidonis. [22]Et ecce mulier Chananaea a finibus illis egressa clamavit dicens: «Miserere mei, Domine, fili David! Filia mea male a daemonio vexatur». [23]Qui non respondit ei verbum. Et accedentes discipuli eius rogabant eum dicentes: «Dimitte eam, quia clamat post nos». [24]Ipse

15:21–28 Tyre and Sidon were Phoenician cities
on the Mediterranean coast, in what is now
Lebanon. They never formed part of Galilee, but
they were not far from its north-western borders.
In the time of Jesus, they fell outside the
domains of Herod Antipas. Our Lord withdrew
there possibly to avoid persecution from Herod
and the Jewish authorities, and to concentrate on
the formation of his apostles. In the region of
Tyre and Sidon, the majority of the population
were pagans. St Matthew calls this woman a
"Canaanite" because according to Genesis 10:15
this area was one of the first to be settled by the
Canaanites. St Mark calls her a "Syrophoenician" (Mk 7:26). Both Gospels refer to the fact

that she was a pagan, a circumstance that makes
her faith in Jesus so remarkable. Her faith leads
her to be persistent and daring: she makes her
request even though the time doesn't seem right
(v. 23), she persists even though she is deemed
unworthy (vv. 24–26), she perseveres despite
obstacles (v. 27), and in the end she gets what
she wants (v. 28). "We often find that our Lord
does not grant us what we ask for immediately;
he delays [meeting our request] so that our desire
might increase in ardour, so that we might better
appreciate the value of what we ask for. It is not
a refusal but a test that prepares us to receive
more abundantly what we desire" (St Jean
Vianney, *Sermon on prayer*).

p Other ancient authorities read *law*   q Or *is evacuated*

of the house of Israel."* [25]But she came and knelt before him, saying, "Lord, help me." [26]And he answered, "It is not fair to take the children's bread and throw it to the dogs." [27]She said, "Yes, Lord, yet even the dogs eat the crumbs that fall from their master's table." [28]Then Jesus answered her, "O woman, great is your faith! Be it done for you as you desire." And her daughter was healed instantly.

Mt 8:10

Curing of many sick people

Mk 7:31–37

[29]And Jesus went on from there and passed along the Sea of Galilee. And he went up into the hills, and sat down there. [30]And great crowds came to him, bringing with them the lame, the maimed, the blind, the dumb, and many others, and they put them at his feet, and he healed them, [31]so that the throng wondered, when they saw the dumb speaking, the maimed whole, the lame walking, and the blind seeing; and they glorified the God of Israel.

Mk 3:10

Mk 7:37

Mk 8:1–10

Second miracle of the loaves and fish

Mt 14:13–21
Mk 6:32–34
Lk 9:10–17
Jn 6:1–13

[32]Then Jesus called his disciples to him and said, "I have compassion on the crowd, because they have been with me now three days, and have nothing to eat; and I am unwilling to send them away hungry, lest they faint on the way." [33]And the disciples said to him, "Where are we to get bread enough in the desert to feed so great a crowd?" [34]And Jesus said to them, "How many loaves have you?" They said, "Seven, and a few small fish." [35]And commanding the crowd to sit down on the ground, [36]he took the seven loaves and the fish, and having given thanks he broke them and gave them to the disciples, and the disciples gave them to the crowds. [37]And they all ate and were satisfied; and they took up seven baskets full of the broken pieces left over. [38]Those who ate were four thousand men, besides women and children. [39]And sending away the crowds, he got into the boat and went to the region of Magadan.

autem respondens ait: «Non sum missus nisi ad oves, quae perierunt domus Israel». [25]At illa venit et adoravit eum dicens: «Domine, adiuva me!». [26]Qui respondens ait: «Non est bonum sumere panem filiorum et mittere catellis». [27]At illa dixit: «Etiam, Domine, nam et catelli edunt de micis, quae cadunt de mensa dominorum suorum». [28]Tunc respondens Iesus ait illi: «O mulier, magna est fides tua! Fiat tibi, sicut vis». Et sanata est filia illius ex illa hora. [29]Et cum transisset inde, Iesus venit secus mare Galilaeae et ascendens in montem sedebat ibi. [30]Et accesserunt ad eum turbae multae habentes secum claudos, caecos, debiles, mutos et alios multos et proiecerunt eos ad pedes eius, et curavit eos, [31]ita ut turba miraretur videntes mutos loquentes, debiles sanos, et claudos ambulantes, et caecos videntes. Et magnificabant Deum Israel. [32]Iesus autem convocatis discipulis suis dixit: «Misereor turbae, quia triduo iam perseverant mecum et non habent, quod manducent; et dimittere eos ieiunos nolo, ne forte deficiant in via». [33]Et dicunt ei discipuli: «Unde nobis in deserto panes tantos, ut saturemus turbam tantam?». [34]Et ait illis Iesus: «Quot panes

15:29–31 On a number of occasions (cf. 11:4–6; Lk 7:21–23) the evangelists give a brief summary of the cures worked by Jesus which fulfilled what the prophet Isaiah had foretold about the messianic times: "Then the eyes of the blind shall be opened, and the ears of the deaf unstopped; then shall the lame man leap like a hart and the tongue of the dumb sing for joy" (Is 35:5–6).

15:32–39 In addition to being actual events, Jesus' miracles were also signs of supernatural realities: "Once we have acknowledged the great power of the miracles, we must also plumb their depths. We must go beyond the striking impression that they make to understand what they

mean, to see and marvel by reading deeply and understanding" (St Augustine, *In Ioannis Evangelium*, 24, 2). In this case (v. 37), the abundance of material food signifies an abundance of divine gifts, particularly that of the Eucharist (cf. Jn 6:1–70). The help lent by the disciples (v. 36) is a sign of the part played by the Church's ministers: "The miracles of the multiplication of the loaves, when the Lord says the blessing, breaks and distributes the loaves through his disciples to feed the multitude, prefigure the superabundance of this unique bread of his Eucharist" (*Catechism of the Catholic Church*, 1335).

For the specific meaning of this second multiplication of leaves, see the note on Mk 8:1–10.

The Pharisees and Sadducees try to test Jesus

Mk 8:11–21
Lk 12:54–56
Lk 11:16, 29–32
Jn 6:30

16 ¹And the Pharisees and Sadducees came, and to test him they asked him to show them a sign from heaven. ²He answered them,ʳ "When it is evening, you say, 'It will be fair weather; for the sky is red.' ³And in the morning, 'It will be stormy today, for the sky is red and threatening.' You know how to interpret the appearance of the sky, but you cannot interpret the signs of the times. ⁴An evil and adulterous generation seeks for a sign, but no sign shall be given to it except the sign of Jonah." So he left them and departed.

Mt 12:39–40
Jn 2:1

⁵When the disciples reached the other side, they had forgotten to bring any bread. ⁶Jesus said to them, "Take heed and beware of the leaven of the Pharisees and Sadducees." ⁷And they discussed it among themselves, saying, "We brought no bread." ⁸But Jesus, aware of this, said, "O men of little faith, why do you discuss among yourselves the fact that you have no bread? ⁹Do you not yet perceive? Do you not remember the five loaves of the five thousand, and how many baskets you gathered? ¹⁰Or the seven loaves of the four thousand, and how many baskets you gathered? ¹¹How is it that you fail to perceive that I did not speak about bread? Beware of the leaven of the Pharisees and Sadducees." ¹²Then they understood that he did not tell them to beware of the leaven of bread, but of the teaching of the Pharisees and Sadducees.

Lk 12:1
Mk 6:52
Mt 14:21
Mk 6:44–45
Mt 15:38
Mk 8:9
Jn 6:27

Peter's profession of faith and his primacy

Mk 8:27–30
Lk 9:18–21

¹³Now when Jesus came into the district of Caesarea Philippi, he asked his disciples, "Who do men say that the Son of man is?" ¹⁴And they said, "Some say John the

Mt 14:2
Mk 6:14–15
Lk 9:7–8

habetis?». At illi dixerunt: «Septem et paucos pisciculos». ³⁵Et praecepit turbae, ut discumberet super terram; ³⁶et accipiens septem panes et pisces et gratias agens fregit et dedit discipulis, discipuli autem turbis. ³⁷Et comederunt omnes et saturati sunt; et, quod superfuit de fragmentis, tulerunt septem sportas plenas. ³⁸Erant autem, qui manducaverant, quattuor milia hominum extra mulieres et parvulos. ³⁹Et dimissis turbis, ascendit in naviculam et venit in fines Magadan.   [16] ¹Et accesserunt ad eum pharisaei et sadducaei tentantes et rogaverunt eum, ut signum de caelo ostenderet eis. ²At ille respondens ait eis: «Facto vespere dicitis: 'Serenum erit, rubicundum est enim caelum'; ³et mane: 'Hodie tempestas, rutilat enim triste caelum'. Faciem quidem caeli diiudicare nostis, signa autem temporum non potestis. ⁴Generatio mala et adultera signum quaerit, et signum non dabitur ei nisi signum Ionae». Et, relictis illis, abiit. ⁵Et cum venissent discipuli trans fretum, obliti sunt panes accipere. ⁶Iesus autem dixit illis: «Intuemini et cavete a fermento pharisaeorum et sadducaeorum». ⁷At illi cogitabant inter se dicentes: «Panes non accepimus!». ⁸Sciens autem Iesus dixit: «Quid cogitatis inter vos, modicae fidei, quia panes non habetis? ⁹Nondum intellegitis neque recordamini quinque panum quinque milium hominum, et quot cophinos sumpsistis? ¹⁰Neque septem panum quattuor milium hominum, et quot sportas sumpsistis? ¹¹Quomodo non intellegitis quia non de panibus dixi vobis? Sed cavete a fermento pharisaeorum et sadducaeorum». ¹²Tunc intellexerunt quia non dixerit cavendum a fermento panum, sed a doctrina pharisaeorum et sadducaeorum. ¹³Venit autem Iesus in partes Caesareae Philippi et interrogabat discipu-

16:1–12 For a second time, the Pharisees ask Jesus for a sign. The two miracles of the loaves which have just taken place (14:13–21; 15:32–39), and the other miracles he worked in between (see 15:29–31 and note), are vividly present in our Lord's mind (and in the minds of the readers of the Gospel). But those men "did not question him to increase their faith, but to put him to the test" (St John Chrysostom, *In Matthaeum*, 53, 2). Therefore, our Lord replies by reproaching them: they have witnessed these marvels but have not been brave enough to ask themselves what they mean.

The discussion between Jesus and his disciples in vv. 5–12 is somewhat puzzling. As on other occasions, the disciples fail to understand a

remark made by Jesus (vv. 5–7). Still, like the true teacher that he is, our Lord explains himself to them privately (vv. 8–12): "It is true that the apostles learnt a lot from Christ by watching him, but they learnt more by listening to him; he spoke to them using ordinary words that they could easily understand, as well as the words he whispered in the depths of their hearts through the power of the Holy Spirit" (St Bonaventure, *Sententiae*, 3, 24, 2).

16:13–20 As recounted by Matthew, this episode refers to two different but closely connected events—Peter's confession of faith, and the promise of his future primacy in the Church.

Unlike all those who failed to discern who

r Other ancient authorities omit the following words to the end of verse 3

Jn 6:69

Gal 1:15–16

Jn 1:42
Eph 2:20
Job 38:17
Is 38:10
Ps 107:17

Baptist, others say Elijah, and others Jeremiah or one of the prophets."* [15]He said to them, "But who do you say that I am?" [16]Simon Peter replied, "You are the Christ, the Son of the living God."* [17]And Jesus answered him, "Blessed are you, Simon Bar-Jona! For flesh and blood has not revealed this to you, but my Father who is in heaven. [18]And I tell you, you are Peter,[s] and on this rock[t] I will build my church, and the powers of death[u] shall not prevail against it.* [19]I will give you the keys of the

los suos dicens: «Quem dicunt homines esse Filium hominis?». [14]At illi dixerunt: «Alii Ioannem Baptistam, alii autem Eliam, alii vero Ieremiam, aut unum ex prophetis». [15]Dicit illis: «Vos autem quem me esse dicitis?». [16]Respondens Simon Petrus dixit: «Tu es Christus, Filius Dei vivi». [17]Respondens autem Iesus dixit ei: «Beatus es, Simon Bariona, quia caro et sanguis non revelavit tibi, sed Pater meus, qui in caelis est. [18]Et ego dico tibi: Tu es Petrus, et super hanc petram aedificabo Ecclesiam meam; et portae inferi non praevalebunt adversum eam. [19]Tibi dabo claves regni caelorum; et quodcumque ligaveris super terram, erit ligatum in caelis, et quodcumque solveris super terram, erit solutum in caelis». [20]Tunc prae-

Jesus was (v. 14; cf. 14:2 and 16:2–4), Peter clearly acknowledges Jesus to be the promised Messiah and the Son of God: "The Lord asked the apostles what men said of him, and their responses reflect the malaise of human ignorance. But when he asked the disciples what they themselves said of him, the first to profess the Lord to be the Messiah is Peter, the first among the apostles" (St Leo the Great, *Sermo 4 in anniversario ordinationis suae*, 2–3). But Peter's confession of faith covers not only Jesus' mission (the fact that he is the Messiah) but also Jesus' inner self: he is the Son of God. This is a full acknowledgment of who Jesus is, and it is one that all Christians affirm. However, our personal experience alone does not allow us to make this profession: we need faith, a gift from God. Hence St Leo's gloss on what Jesus says in v. 17: "Blessed are you, Peter, for my Father in heaven revealed this to you. You have not been led into error by human ignorance; the revelation of heaven has enlightened your mind; it was not revealed to you by anyone of flesh and blood, but by my Father, whose Only-begotten Son I am" (ibid.). And for this reason, too, the *Catechism of the Catholic Church* teaches, the words of Peter's profession of faith must be taken literally (he is not using a metaphor when he says that Jesus is the Son of God); he is able to make his profession of faith because the Father has revealed these things to him (cf. nos. 441 and 442).

St Peter's confession of faith is a gift from God, and what Jesus goes on to promise his apostle (vv. 18–19) is also a grace; he promises to confer on him the power to bind and loose in the Church he founds, and later on he confers on

Peter this authority (cf. Jn 21:15–23 and note). "The Lord adds: 'And I tell you ...' —that is: as my Father revealed my divinity to you, I will reveal your great honour to you. 'You are Peter.' I, the unbreakable stone, the cornerstone that made two peoples one, the foundation of all things, the one without whom nothing can be built, I tell you, Peter, that you too are rock. You will be strengthened with my power; you will share in the power that is mine. On this rock, I will build my Church, and the powers of hell will not prevail against it. That is: on the strong foundation of Peter's faith, I will build the eternal, sublime temple, the Church, which reaches up to heaven" (St Leo the Great, *Sermo 4 in anniversario ordinationis suae*, 2–3).

Elsewhere in the Gospel (18:18), the disciples, too, are promised the power of binding and loosing (v. 19). For this reason, Tradition has seen in Peter a sign of unity in the Church: "The ministry of this power was also granted to the other Apostles and to all the bishops of the Church; but the fact that it is given to one in the name of all is significant: the power is granted to Peter in a special way because Peter is the head of all the pastors of the Church" (ibid.).

From the beginning, this gift to Peter has been interpreted as something that is inherited by his successors, the bishops of Rome. This doctrine of the primacy, together with that of the infallibility of the Pope when he speaks *ex cathedra*, was defined as a dogma of faith in the Dogmatic Constitution *Pastor Aeternus* of the First Vatican Council, and it has been reaffirmed in later documents: "The bishop of Rome, in whom rests the function given in a unique way to Peter, the first of the Apostles, and which he

s Greek *Petros*   t Greek *petra*   u Greek *the gates of Hades*

kingdom of heaven,* and whatever you bind on earth shall be bound in heaven, and whatever you loose on earth shall be loosed in heaven." ²⁰Then he strictly charged the disciples to tell no one that he was the Christ.

PART TWO

Jesus' ministry on the way to Jerusalem*

8. TOWARDS JUDEA AND JERUSALEM*

Jesus foretells his passion and resurrection. The law of Christian renunciation　　Mk 8:31–9:1 / Lk 9:22–27

²¹From that time Jesus began to show his disciples that he must go to Jerusalem and Mk 9:31; 10:32–34 / Lk 9: 44; 18:31–33 / Mt 12:40; 17:22; 20:18–19; 26:2 / Jn 2:19 suffer many things from the elders and chief priests and scribes, and be killed, and on the third day be raised. ²²And Peter took him and began to rebuke him, saying, "God forbid, Lord! This shall never happen to you." ²³But he turned and said to Is 8:14 Peter, "Get behind me, Satan! You are a hindrance^v to me; for you are not on the side of God, but of men."

cepit discipulis, ut nemini dicerent quia ipse esset Christus. ²¹Exinde coepit Iesus ostendere discipulis suis quia oporteret eum ire Hierosolymam et multa pati a senioribus et principibus sacerdotum et scribis et occidi et tertia die resurgere. ²²Et assumens eum Petrus coepit increpare illum dicens: «Absit a te, Domine, non erit tibi hoc». ²³Qui conversus dixit Petro: «Vade post me, Satana! Scandalum es mihi, quia non sapis ea, quae Dei sunt, sed ea quae hominum!». ²⁴Tunc Iesus dixit discipulis suis: «Si quis vult post me venire, abneget semetipsum et tollat crucem suam et

passed on to his successors, is head of the college of bishops, the Vicar of Christ and Pastor of the universal Church on earth; he has, therefore, by virtue of his function, ordinary power which is supreme, full, immediate and universal in the Church, and which he can exercise freely" (*Code of Canon Law*, can. 331; cf. Vatican II, *Lumen gentium*, 18).

The saints have seen love for the Church and the Pope as a true sign of love for Christ: "He who disobeys the Christ on earth [the Pope], who acts for Christ in heaven, will not partake of the fruit of the blood of the Son of God" (St Catherine of Siena, *Epistolae*, 207).

*16:21–20:34 After Peter's confession of faith at Caesarea Philippi (16:13–20), the Gospel takes on a different tone. Jesus now teaches his disciples about his mission as the suffering Saviour and about the life of his Church in the future. In this respect, chapter 18 is especially relevant, so much so that it has been called the "Discourse on the Church". Later, as Jesus makes his way to Jerusalem (19:1–20:34), we

find further episodes that illustrate aspects of church life—poverty, a spirit of service, etc.

*16:21–17:27 By relating Jesus' teaching about his passion, death and resurrection (16:21)—and his reproval of Peter (16:23)—the Gospel clearly signals the "way of the cross". The two announcements of the passion (16:21; 17:22–23) and the explanations of the meaning of the Transfiguration (17:9, 12) prepare the reader for what will take place in the future. Jesus knows that he is going to be sacrificed, and he accepts this destiny. But he also knows that this death is not the end, but will be followed by his resurrection and glorification, and he tells his disciples this.

16:21–28 Jesus is quick to correct Peter when the latter tries to steer him away from the death that is part of his mission as Messiah (cf. the note on Mk 8:31–9:1). In a series of apparently paradoxical phrases our Lord goes on to explain what his disciples' commitment to him entails: "The way of perfection passes by way of the

v Greek *stumbling block*

Mt 10:38–39

Mt 10:39
Lk 17:33
Jn 12:25

Jn 5:29
Rom 2:6
Ps 28:4
Prov 24:12

Mt 24:34; 10:23

²⁴Then Jesus told his disciples, "If any man would come after me, let him deny himself and take up his cross and follow me. ²⁵For whoever would save his life will lose it, and whoever loses his life* for my sake will find it. ²⁶For what will it profit a man, if he gains the whole world and forfeits his life? Or what shall a man give in return for his life? ²⁷For the Son of man is to come with his angels in the glory of his Father, and then he will repay every man for what he has done. ²⁸Truly, I say to you, there are some standing here who will not taste death before they see the Son of man coming in his kingdom."

Mk 9:2–13
Lk 9:28–36

2 Pet 1:16–18

The Transfiguration

17 ¹And after six days Jesus took with him Peter and James and John his brother, and led them up a high mountain apart. ²And he was transfigured before them, and his face shone like the sun, and his garments became white as light. ³And behold, there appeared to them Moses and Elijah, talking with him. ⁴And Peter said to Jesus, "Lord, it is well that we are here; if you wish, I will make three booths here, one for you and one for Moses and one for Elijah."* ⁵He was still speaking, when lo, a bright cloud overshadowed them, and a voice from the cloud said, "This

Deut 18:15
Mt 3:17
Ps 2:7
Is 42:1

sequatur me. ²⁵Qui enim voluerit animam suam salvam facere, perdet eam; qui autem perdiderit animam suam propter me, inveniet eam. ²⁶Quid enim prodest homini, si mundum universum lucretur, animae vero suae detrimentum patiatur? Aut quam dabit homo commutationem pro anima sua? ²⁷Filius enim hominis venturus est in gloria Patris sui cum angelis suis, et tunc reddet unicuique secundum opus eius. ²⁸Amen dico vobis: Sunt quidam de hic stantibus, qui non gustabunt mortem, donec videant Filium hominis venientem in regno suo». [17] ¹Et post dies sex assumit Iesus Petrum et Iacobum et Ioannem fratrem eius et ducit illos in montem excelsum seorsum. ²Et transfiguratus est ante eos; et resplenduit facies eius sicut sol, vestimenta autem eius facta sunt alba sicut lux. ³Et ecce apparuit illis Moyses et Elias cum eo loquentes. ⁴Respondens autem Petrus dixit ad Iesum: «Domine, bonum est nos hic esse. Si vis, faciam hic tria tabernacula: tibi unum et Moysi unum et Eliae unum». ⁵Adhuc eo loquente, ecce nubes lucida obumbravit eos; et ecce vox de nube dicens: «Hic est Filius meus dilectus, in quo mihi bene complacui; ipsum audite».

Cross. There is no holiness without renunciation and spiritual battle. Spiritual progress entails the ascesis and mortification that gradually lead to living in the peace and joy of the Beatitudes" (*Catechism of the Catholic Church*, 2015).

17:1–13 In the Transfiguration, Jesus shows these disciples, in advance, the glory he will merit through his passion (cf. the note on Lk 9:28–36). The linking of this episode with Peter's confession of faith and the first announcement of the passion is not only one of timing (it happened "after six days": v. 1); it also follows logically: from heaven comes confirmation that Jesus is the Son of God (v. 5), just as Peter had confessed (16:16), and revelation that his death and resurrection (16:21) are the fulfilment of the Law and the Prophets, represented here by Moses and Elijah (v. 3). The disciples react with joy (v. 4) and fear (vv. 6–7), though they fail to grasp the full significance of the event (cf. the note on Mk 9:2–13).

Moses and Elijah are the two most prominent representatives of the Old Testament, of the Law

and the Prophets. From the "tableau" of Jesus conversing with them (v. 3), Tradition has drawn two lessons: on the one hand, that Jesus is the centre of revelation for "all of Holy Scripture is one book, and this one book is Christ, for all of Holy Scripture speaks of Christ and is fulfilled in Him" (Hugh of St Victor, *De Arca Noe morali*, 2, 8); on the other, that the books of the Old Testament are necessary for understanding Jesus Christ, for "if, as the apostle Paul says, Christ is the power and wisdom of God, and someone who has not read the Holy Scriptures does not know the power and wisdom of God, it follows that ignorance of the Scriptures is ignorance of Christ" (St Jerome, *Commentarii in Isaiam*, prol. 1).

The episode also tells us important things about of the person of Jesus: he is the Lord (v. 4), the Son of God, with whom the Father is well pleased (v. 5; cf. Is 42:1), and to whom we should listen because he reveals God to us: "He that would now question God, or seek any vision or revelation, would not only be acting foolishly, he would be committing an offence against God by not setting his eyes solely upon Christ, and

is my beloved Son,[w] with whom I am well pleased; listen to him." [6]When the disciples heard this, they fell on their faces, and were filled with awe. [7]But Jesus came and touched them, saying, "Rise, and have no fear." [8]And when they lifted up their eyes, they saw no one but Jesus only.

[9]And as they were coming down the mountain, Jesus commanded them, "Tell no one the vision, until the Son of man is raised from the dead." [10]And the disciples asked him, "Then why do the scribes say that first Elijah must come?" [11]He replied, "Elijah does come, and he is to restore all things; [12]but I tell you that Elijah has already come, and they did not know him, but did to him whatever they pleased. So also the Son of man will suffer at their hands." [13]Then the disciples understood that he was speaking to them of John the Baptist.

Mal 3:23–24

Lk 23:25

Lk 1:17
Lk 9:37–42

Curing of an epileptic boy

Mk 9:14–29
Lk 9:37–43

[14]And when they came to the crowd, a man came up to him and kneeling before him said, [15]"Lord, have mercy on my son, for he is an epileptic and he suffers terribly; for often he falls into the fire, and often into the water. [16]And I brought him to your disciples, and they could not heal him." [17]And Jesus answered, "O faithless and perverse

Deut 32:5
Jn 14:9

[6]Et audientes discipuli ceciderunt in faciem suam et timuerunt valde. [7]Et accessit Iesus et tetigit eos dixitque eis: «Surgite et nolite timere». [8]Levantes autem oculos suos, neminem viderunt nisi solum Iesum. [9]Et descendentibus illis de monte, praecepit eis Iesus dicens: «Nemini dixeritis visionem, donec Filius hominis a mortuis resurgat». [10]Et interrogaverunt eum discipuli dicentes: «Quid ergo scribae dicunt quod Eliam oporteat primum venire?». [11]At ille respondens ait: «Elias quidem venturus est et restituet omnia. [12]Dico autem vobis quia Elias iam venit, et non cognoverunt eum, sed fecerunt in eo, quaecumque voluerunt; sic et Filius hominis passurus est ab eis». [13]Tunc intellexerunt discipuli quia de Ioanne Baptista dixisset eis. [14]Et cum venissent ad turbam, accessit ad eum homo genibus provolutus ante eum [15]et dicens: «Domine, miserere filii mei, quia lunaticus est et male patitur; nam saepe cadit in ignem et crebro in aquam. [16]Et obtuli eum discipulis tuis, et non potuerunt curare eum». [17]Respondens autem Iesus ait: «O generatio incredula et perversa, quousque ero vobiscum? Usquequo patiar vos? Afferte huc illum ad me». [18]Et

seeking no new thing or aught beside. And God might answer him after this manner, saying: If I have spoken all things to you in my Word, which is My Son, and I have no other word, what answer can I now make to you, or what can I reveal to you which is greater than this? Set your eyes on him alone, for in him I have spoken and revealed all things to you, and in him you will find even more than what you ask for and desire [...]. Listen to him, for I have no more faith to reveal, neither have I any more things to declare" (St John of the Cross, *Ascent of Mount Carmel*, 2, 22, 5).

Finally, on coming down from the mountain, in an explanation found in various verses in the first Gospel (cf. the note on 11:1–15), Jesus clarifies for the disciples the relationship between Elijah and John the Baptist.

17:14–20 Through the cure of this boy, Jesus teaches us the important part that faith plays in prayer. The strength of the comparison our Lord makes (v. 20) lies in the fact that a mustard seed is very tiny and yet can grow into a bush over three

metres (ten feet) tall. Similarly, Christians, through their union with Christ, can share in the omnipotence of God. "Moving mountains" was probably a proverbial way of speaking, but it still conveys the idea that sincere prayer is very powerful.

This episode, coming just after the Transfiguration, also teaches us that "on the mountain" (see 17:1–5), when one is able to see the glory of the Lord, it is easy to have faith; but in the comings and goings of everyday life belief can be more difficult (see v. 20). That is why the practice of our faith must be constant. We need to live by faith, and if we have vigorous faith we will be able to go much further than if we rely on our own resources: "Though one in name, faith has two dimensions. One is the faith by which our soul assents to dogmas and teachings and our will attests to specific truths. [...] The other dimension of faith is that which was given by Christ to some as a free gift, [...] a faith capable of performing works beyond any human power. [...] Strive to live the faith that depends on your effort and leads to the Lord who grants that faith

w Or *my Son, my* (or *the*) *Beloved*

generation, how long am I to be with you? How long am I to bear with you? Bring him here to me." [18]And Jesus rebuked him, and the demon came out of him, and the boy was cured instantly. [19]Then the disciples came to Jesus privately and said, "Why could

Lk 17:6
Mk 11:23
Mt 21:21

we not cast it out?" [20]He said to them, "Because of your little faith. For truly, I say to you, if you have faith as a grain of mustard seed, you will say to this mountain, 'Move hence to yonder place,' and it will move; and nothing will be impossible to you."[x]

Mk 9:30–32
Lk 9:43–45

Second announcement of the Passion. The temple tax

Mt 16:21; 20:18–19

[22]As they were gathering[y] in Galilee, Jesus said to them. "The Son of man is to be delivered into the hands of men, [23]and they will kill him, and he will be raised on the third day." And they were greatly distressed.

Ex 30:13

[24]When they came to Capernaum, the collectors of the half-shekel tax went up to Peter and said, "Does not your teacher pay the tax?" [25]He said, "Yes." And when he came home, Jesus spoke to him first, saying, "What do you think, Simon? From whom do kings of the earth take toll or tribute? From their sons or from others?" [26]And when he said, "From others," Jesus said to him, "Then the sons are free. [27]However, not to give offence to them, go to the sea and cast a hook, and take the first fish that comes up, and when you open its mouth you will find a shekel; take that and give it to them for me and for yourself."

increpavit eum Iesus, et exiit ab eo daemonium, et curatus est puer ex illa hora. [19]Tunc accesserunt discipuli ad Iesum secreto et dixerunt: «Quare nos non potuimus eicere illum?». [20]Ille autem dicit illis: «Propter modicam fidem vestram. Amen quippe dico vobis: Si habueritis fidem sicut granum sinapis, dicetis monti huic: "Transi hinc illuc!", et transibit, et nihil impossibile erit vobis». (21) [22]Conversantibus autem eis in Galilaea, dixit illis Iesus: «Filius hominis tradendus est in manus hominum, [23]et occident eum, et tertio die resurget». Et contristati sunt vehementer. [24]Et cum venissent Capharnaum, accesserunt, qui didrachma accipiebant, ad Petrum et dixerunt: «Magister vester non solvit didrachma?». [25]Ait: «Etiam». Et cum intrasset domum, praevenit eum Iesus dicens: «Quid tibi videtur, Simon? Reges terrae a quibus accipiunt tributum vel censum? A filiis suis an ab alienis?». [26]Cum autem ille dixisset: «Ab alienis», dixit illi Iesus: «Ergo liberi sunt filii. [27]Ut autem non scandalizemus eos, vade

to you, so that he may give you the other type of faith beyond any human strength or reckoning" (St Cyril of Jerusalem, *Catecheses*, 5, 10–11). See also the RSV note **x**; this verse is also found in Mark 9:29.

17:22–27 From the time of Peter's confession of faith onwards, our Lord has been teaching his disciples about the salvific events that will take place in Jerusalem (his passion and resurrection) and about the future life of the Church. In these verses the distress they feel when told about the passion (v. 23) is offset by the consolation of Jesus' person and power (vv. 25–27).

The episode of the temple tax contains two clear messages—that Jesus is the Son of God and Lord of the temple, and that Peter is associated with him in the governance of the Church.

The temple tax was quite different from the tax levied by the Roman authorities (22:15–22). The basis for it is to be found in Exodus 30:11–16, which stipulates that everyone who is counted by name in the census and who is twenty or older

should contribute half a shekel towards the temple sacrifices. "Half-shekel" (v. 24) is sometimes translated as "didrachma". We do not know for certain whether in Jesus' time this tax was actually levied or whether it was a contribution that only more observant Jews made. We do know that many people (priests, for example) were exempt from it; and many just did not pay it. Recent episodes covered in the Gospel (the confession of Peter, and the Transfiguration) have made it clear that Jesus is the Son of God and that therefore he cannot be required to pay the tax. However, he tells Peter to pay it, in order not to "give offence" (v. 27). By including a share for Peter in this payment, he is also giving a rule of conduct to Christians—one that is registered elsewhere in the New Testament: "Pay all of them their dues, taxes to whom taxes are due, revenue to whom revenue is due, respect to whom respect is due, honour to whom honour is due" (Rom 13:7; cf. 1 Pet 2:13–17).

A shekel (or "stater", a Greek coin) was worth four denarii. The miracle that he performs

x Other ancient authorities insert verse 21, *But this kind never comes out except by prayer and fasting*   y Other ancient authorities read *abode*

9. THE DISCOURSE ON THE CHURCH*

Mk 9:33–50
Lk 9:46–50;
17:1–3;15:4–7

The "little ones" and the Kingdom. On leading others astray. The lost sheep

18 [1]At that time, the disciples came to Jesus, saying, "Who is the greatest in the kingdom of heaven?" [2]And calling to him a child, he put him in the midst of them, [3]and said, "Truly, I say to you, unless you turn and become like children, you will never enter the kingdom of heaven. [4]Whoever humbles himself like this child, he is the greatest in the kingdom of heaven.

Mk 9:33–47
Lk 9:46–48

Mk 10:15
Lk 18:17
Jn 3:3, 5

[5]"Whoever receives one such child in my name receives me; [6]but whoever causes one of these little ones who believe in me to sin,[z] it would be better for him to have a great millstone fastened round his neck and to be drowned in the depth of the sea.

Jn 13:20
Lk 17:1–2

[7]"Woe to the world for temptations to sin![a] For it is necessary that temptations come, but woe to the man by whom the temptation comes! [8]And if your hand or your foot causes you to sin,[z] cut it off and throw it from you; it is better for you to enter life maimed or lame than with two hands or two feet to be thrown into the eternal fire. [9]And if your eye causes you to sin,[z] pluck it out and throw it from you; it is better for you to enter life with one eye than with two eyes to be thrown into the hell[b]* of fire.

Mt 5:30

Mt 5:29

ad mare et mitte hamum; et eum piscem, qui primus ascenderit, tolle, et aperto ore eius invenies staterem. Illum sumens, da eis pro me et te». [18] [1]In illa hora accesserunt discipuli ad Iesum dicentes: «Quis putas maior est in regno caelorum?». [2]Et advocans parvulum, statuit eum in medio eorum [3]et dixit: «Amen dico vobis: Nisi conversi fueritis et efficiamini sicut parvuli, non intrabitis in regnum caelorum. [4]Quicumque ergo humiliaverit se sicut parvulus iste, hic est maior in regno caelorum. [5]Et qui susceperit unum parvulum talem in nomine meo, me suscipit. [6]Qui autem scandalizaverit unum de pusillis istis, qui in me credunt, expedit ei, ut suspendatur mola asinaria in collo eius et demergatur in profundum maris. [7]Vae mundo ab scandalis! Necesse est enim ut veniant scandala; verumtamen vae homini, per quem scandalum venit! [8]Si autem manus tua vel pes tuus scandalizat te, abscide eum et proice abs te: bonum tibi est ad vitam ingredi debilem vel claudum, quam duas manus vel duos pedes

shows our Lord's kind providence for his disciples.

*18:1—20:34 This section begins with the fourth of our Lord's discourses in St Matthew's Gospel, the "Discourse on the Church" (18:1–35). In it we find a series of instructions and warnings concerning the future administration of the Church—about how Christians should relate to one another, and the roles and responsibilities of those who hold authority.

The section goes on to report Jesus' journey towards Judea and Jerusalem (19:1—20:34). The various episodes contain teachings similar to those in the previous chapter—about the Christian calling, about the order of authority in the Church, etc.

18:1–14 Here we find teachings about the "little ones" in the Church. The passage begins with a question from the disciples about who has most importance in the Church, and Jesus gives a reply that seems paradoxical: "If you ask me

what is the essential thing in the religion and discipline of Jesus Christ, I shall reply: first, humility; second, humility; and third, humility" (St Augustine, *Epistolae*, 118, 22).

Our Lord goes on to warn about the danger of giving scandal: "Scandal is an attitude or behaviour which leads another to do evil" (*Catechism of the Catholic Church*, 2284). To stress how serious a sin scandal is, Jesus uses hyperbole, to great effect. Scandal is at its worst when it is caused in the Lord's most beloved, the most vulnerable—children, for example (v. 14).

At the end comes the parable of the lost sheep. In St Luke this parable is all about the mercy of God, who desires to save all. In the context of the Discourse on the Church, it reflects more on people in a difficult spiritual situation. If people are in danger, they need to be sought out and looked after, even if that means making heroic efforts (vv. 12–14). If the Church in general, and each Christian in particular, desires to spread the faith, then we need to make a special effort to help those who already share our faith, to

z Greek *causes ... to stumble*   a Greek *stumbling blocks*   b Greek *Gehenna*

10"See that you do not despise one of these little ones; for I tell you that in heaven their angels always behold the face of my Father who is in heaven.c 12What do you think? If a man has a hundred sheep, and one of them has gone astray, does he not leave the ninety-nine on the hills and go in search of the one that went astray? 13And if he finds it, truly, I say to you, he rejoices over it more than over the ninety-nine that never went astray. 14So it is not the will of myd Father who is in heaven that one of these little ones should perish.

Fraternal correction. The apostles' authority

Lk 17:3

Lev 19:17
Gal 6:1
Deut 19:15

1 Cor 5:13

Mt 16:19
Jn 20:23

Mk 11:24
Mt 7:7

Jn 14:23
Mt 28:20

15"If your brother sins against you, go and tell him his fault, between you and him alone. If he listens to you, you have gained your brother. 16But if he does not listen, take one or two others along with you, that every word may be confirmed by the evidence of two or three witnesses. 17If he refuses to listen to them, tell it to the church; and if he refuses to listen even to the church, let him be to you as a Gentile and a tax collector. 18Truly, I say to you, whatever you bind on earth shall be bound in heaven, and whatever you loose on earth shall be loosed in heaven.* 19Again I say to you, if two of you agree on earth about anything they ask, it shall be done for them by my Father in heaven. 20For where two or three are gathered in my name, there am I in the midst of them."

habentem mitti in ignem aeternum. 9Et si oculus tuus scandalizat te, erue eum et proice abs te: bonum tibi est unoculum in vitam intrare, quam duos oculos habentem mitti in gehennam ignis. 10Videte, ne contemnatis unum ex his pusillis; dico enim vobis quia angeli eorum in caelis semper vident faciem Patris mei, qui in caelis est. (11) 12Quid vobis videtur? Si fuerint alicui centum oves, et erraverit una ex eis, nonne relinquet nonaginta novem in montibus et vadit quaerere eam, quae erravit? 13Et si contigerit ut inveniat eam, amen dico vobis quia gaudebit super eam magis quam super nonaginta novem, quae non erraverunt. 14Sic non est voluntas ante Patrem vestrum, qui in caelis est, ut pereat unus de pusillis istis. 15Si autem peccaverit in te frater tuus, vade, corripe eum inter te et ipsum solum. Si te audierit, lucratus es fratrem tuum; 16si autem non audierit, adhibe tecum adhuc unum vel duos, *ut in ore duorum testium vel trium stet omne verbum*; 17quod si noluerit audire eos, dic ecclesiae; si autem et ecclesiam noluerit audire, sit tibi sicut ethnicus et publicanus. 18Amen dico vobis: Quaecumque alligaveritis super terram, erunt ligata in caelo, et quaecumque solveritis super terram, erunt soluta in caelo. 19Iterum dico vobis: Si duo ex vobis consenserint super terram de omni re, quamcumque

enable them to overcome their difficulties: "If you wish to be like God, in whose image and likeness you were made, follow his example. You are Christians, whose very name is a sign of goodness: imitate the love of Christ, […] the shepherd of a hundred sheep who did not stay with the ninety-nine that were grazing peacefully but went out in search of the one who had wandered away and was lost. […] Let us consider what these images mean. The sheep means more than any sheep; the shepherd more than any ordinary shepherd: these images reflect supernatural truths. We should never give up on anyone who is lost, nor despair of finding them; we should not abandon them to trials and tribulations, nor fail to help them. Rather, we should try to help them to return to the right path if they wander off, welcome them on their return, and rejoice when all those who live righteous and pious lives are gathered together" (St Asterius of Amasea, *Homiliae*, 13). See also the RSV note c; the addition seems to have come from Luke 19:10.

18:15–20 This passage touches on three aspects of the life of the Church—fraternity, pastoral authority, and prayer in common. Christians, especially pastors, should watch out for one another, following Christ's example, to ensure that none is lost (cf. Jn 17:12). The practice of fraternal correction is one way of helping to save a brother or sister who has strayed from the path of truth (vv. 15–17). The last resort—treating a person as a Gentile or a tax collector (v. 17)—is the equivalent of excommunication, understood as an ultimate step towards saving a person's soul (cf. 1 Cor 5:4–5).

The Tradition of the Church has interpreted our Lord's words in v. 18 as having to do with Christ's action in the remission of sins: "The words 'bind' and 'loose' mean: whomever you exclude from your communion, will be excluded from communion with God; whomever you receive anew into your communion, God will welcome back into his. *Reconciliation with the Church is inseparable from reconciliation with*

c Other ancient authorities add verse 11, *For the Son of man came to save the lost* d Other ancient authorities read *your*

Forgiveness of injuries. Parable of the unforgiving servant   Lk 17:4

²¹Then Peter came up and said to him, "Lord, how often shall my brother sin against me, and I forgive him? As many as seven times?" ²²Jesus said to him, "I do not say to you seven times, but seventy times seven.ᵉ   Lk 17:4 / Gen 4:24

²³"Therefore the kingdom of heaven may be compared to a king who wished to settle accounts with his servants. ²⁴When he began the reckoning, one was brought to him who owed him ten thousand talents;ᶠ ²⁵and as he could not pay, his lord ordered him to be sold, with his wife and children and all that he had, and payment to be made. ²⁶So the servant fell on his knees, imploring him, 'Lord, have patience with me, and I will pay you everything.' ²⁷And out of pity for him the lord of that servant released him and forgave him the debt. ²⁸But that same servant, as he went out, came upon one of his fellow servants who owed him a hundred denarii;ᵍ and seizing him by the throat he said, 'Pay what you owe.' ²⁹So his fellow servant fell   Mt 25:19   Lk 7:42

petierint, fiet illis a Patre meo, qui in caelis est. ²⁰Ubi enim sunt duo vel tres congregati in nomine meo, ibi sum in medio eorum». ²¹Tunc accedens Petrus dixit ei: «Domine, quotiens peccabit in me frater meus, et dimittam ei? Usque septies?». ²²Dicit illi Iesus: «Non dico tibi usque septies sed usque septuagies septies. ²³Ideo assimilatum est regnum caelorum homini regi, qui voluit rationem ponere cum servis suis. ²⁴Et cum coepisset rationem ponere, oblatus est ei unus, qui debebat decem milia talenta. ²⁵Cum autem non haberet, unde redderet, iussit eum dominus venumdari et uxorem et filios et omnia, quae habebat, et reddi. ²⁶Procidens igitur servus ille adorabat eum dicens: "Patientiam habe in me, et omnia reddam tibi". ²⁷Misertus autem dominus servi illius dimisit eum et debitum dimisit ei. ²⁸Egressus autem servus ille invenit unum de conservis suis, qui debebat ei centum denarios, et tenens suffocabat eum dicens: "Redde, quod debes!". ²⁹Procidens igitur conservus eius rogabat eum dicens:

God" (*Catechism of the Catholic Church*, 1445). Over time, the Church, aided by the Holy Spirit, laid down the ways of administering the sacrament of Penance: "The Church has always seen an essential link between the judgment entrusted to the priest in the Sacrament and the need for penitents to name their own sins, except where this is not possible. Since, therefore, the integral confession of serious sins is by divine decree a constitutive part of the Sacrament, it is in no way subject to the discretion of pastors (dispensation, interpretation, local customs, etc.)" (John Paul II, *Misericordia Dei*).

Finally, Jesus stresses the value of prayer in common (vv. 19–20). What he has to say would have underlined his divinity for his disciples, for there was a saying used by teachers of his time that when two men meet to study and consult the words of the Law, God himself is present among them. The Church uses this text to explain the presence of Jesus Christ in the liturgy: "Christ is always present in his Church, especially in her liturgical celebrations. He is present in the sacrifice of the Mass, not only in the person of his minister, 'the same now offering, through the ministry of priests, who formerly offered himself on the cross' (Council of Trent, session 22, chap. 2), but especially under the eucharistic species. By his power he is present in the sacraments, so that

when a man baptizes it is really Christ himself who baptizes. He is present in his word, since it is he himself who speaks when the Holy Scriptures are read in the Church. He is present, lastly, when the Church prays and sings, for he promised: 'Where two or three are gathered together in my name, there am I in the midst of them' (Mt 18:20)" (Vatican II, *Sacrosanctum Concilium*, 7).

18:21–35 To Peter's question about forgiveness, Jesus replies in words that can be translated as "seventy times seven" or "seventy-seven times" (see RSV note e). The response could be read as a counterpoint to Genesis 4:24, in which Lamech expresses his entrenched desire for vengeance by saying, "If Cain is avenged sevenfold, truly Lamech seventy-seven-fold." As against Lamech's determination never to forgive, Jesus says that we should forgive always: "The Lord does not limit forgiveness to a fixed number of times; rather, we must forgive at all times and always" (St John Chrysostom, *In Matthaeum*, 61, 1).

The parable of the unforgiving servant shows the real reason we all need to receive and grant forgiveness—the fact that we are all in God's debt. The force of the parable becomes obvious when we realize the amounts of money involved. A denarius was equivalent to a labourer's

down and besought him, 'Have patience with me, and I will pay you.' ³⁰He refused and went and put him in prison till he should pay his debt. ³¹When his fellow servants saw what had taken place, they were greatly distressed, and they went and reported to their lord all that had taken place. ³²Then his lord summoned him and said to him, 'You wicked servant! I forgave you all that debt because you besought me; ³³and should not you have had mercy on your fellow servant, as I had mercy on you?' ³⁴And in anger his lord delivered him to the jailers,ʰ till he should pay all his debt. ³⁵So also my heavenly Father will do to every one of you, if you do not forgive your brother from your heart."

Mt 6:15

Marriage and virginity

Mk 10:1–12

Mt 7:28; 11:1; 13:53;
26:1
Lk 9:51

19 ¹Now when Jesus had finished these sayings, he went away from Galilee and entered the region of Judea beyond the Jordan; ²and large crowds followed him, and he healed them there.

Gen 1:27

³And Pharisees came up to him and tested him by asking, "Is it lawful to divorce one's wife for any cause?" ⁴He answered, "Have you not read that he who made them from the beginning made them male and female, ⁵and said, 'For this reason a man

daily pay; a talent was worth around six thousand denarii, so the king wrote off a debt of sixty million denarii, an amount so great that the servant could never have paid it off. This exaggeration holds the profound truth that the parable is meant to convey—the revelation of God's infinite mercy towards sinners. If the exaggeration were absent, the whole meaning of the parable would disappear; it is used not to exaggerate the truth but to express it. The servant's hardness of heart after his being released from his huge debt is also very striking; but here, too, lies an insight into human ingratitude towards God and the severity with which we treat others: we find it difficult to forgive even tiny faults: "Force yourself, if necessary, always to forgive those who offend you, from the very first moment. For the greatest injury or offence that you can suffer from them is as nothing compared with what God has pardoned you" (St Josemaría Escrivá, *The Way*, 452).

19:1–12 Jesus uses the trap set by these Pharisees to explain that marriage is indissoluble

(cf. the note on Mk 10:1–12). The "except for unchastity" (v. 9) should not be taken as referring to a justification for divorce (cf. the note on 5:17–48 and the RSVCE notes on Mt 5:32 and 19:9), for the very purpose of marriage (mutual self-giving of the spouses, together with the procreation and education of children) calls for indissolubility: "Thus a man and a woman, who by their compact of conjugal love 'are no longer two, but one flesh' (Mt 19:6), render mutual help and service to each other through an intimate union of their persons and of their actions. Through this union they experience the meaning of their oneness and attain to it with growing perfection day by day. As a mutual gift of two persons, this intimate union and the good of the children impose total fidelity on the spouses and argue for an unbreakable oneness between them" (Vatican II, *Gaudium et spes*, 48).

Then, replying to a question from his disciples, Jesus speaks of the value of celibacy, not in the sense of avoidance of marriage for selfish reasons (v. 10), but celibacy as a gift from God (v. 11). That is how the Church has always seen

h Greek *torturers*

shall leave his father and mother and be joined to his wife, and the two shall become one'?[i] [6]So they are no longer two but one.[i] What therefore God has joined together, let no man put asunder." [7]They said to him, "Why then did Moses command one to give a certificate of divorce, and to put her away?" [8]He said to them, "For your hardness of heart Moses allowed you to divorce your wives, but from the beginning it was not so. [9]And I say to you: whoever divorces his wife, except for unchastity,[j] and marries another, commits adultery; and he who marries a divorced woman commits adultery."[k]*

[10]The disciples said to him, "If such is the case of a man with his wife, it is not expedient to marry." [11]But he said to them, "Not all men can receive this precept, but only those to whom it is given. [12]For there are eunuchs who have been so from birth, and there are eunuchs who have been made eunuchs by men, and there are eunuchs who have made themselves eunuchs for the sake of the kingdom of heaven. He who is able to receive this, let him receive it."*

Jesus blesses the children
[13]Then children were brought to him that he might lay his hands on them and pray. The disciples rebuked the people; [14]but Jesus said, "Let the children come to me, and do not hinder them; for to such belongs the kingdom of heaven." [15]And he laid his hands on them and went away.

Margin references:
Gen 2:24
Eph 5:31
1 Cor 7:10–11

Deut 24:1
Mt 5:31

Lk 16:18
Mt 5:32

1 Cor 7:7, 17

Mk 10:13–16
Lk 18:15–17

Mt 18:3

duo sed una caro. Quod ergo Deus coniunxit, homo non separet». [7]Dicunt illi: «Quid ergo Moyses mandavit *dari libellum repudii et dimittere?*». [8]Ait illis: «Moyses ad duritiam cordis vestri permisit vobis dimittere uxores vestras; ab initio autem non sic fuit. [9]Dico autem vobis quia quicumque dimiserit uxorem suam, nisi ob fornicationem, et aliam duxerit, moechatur». [10]Dicunt ei discipuli eius: «Si ita est causa hominis cum uxore, non expedit nubere». [11]Qui dixit eis: «Non omnes capiunt verbum istud, sed quibus datum est. [12]Sunt enim eunuchi, qui de matris utero sic nati sunt; et sunt eunuchi, qui facti sunt ab hominibus; et sunt eunuchi, qui seipsos castraverunt propter regnum caelorum. Qui potest capere, capiat». [13]Tunc oblati sunt ei parvuli, ut manus eis imponeret et oraret; discipuli autem increpabant eis. [14]Iesus vero ait: «Sinite parvulos et nolite

it: "The Church's holiness is [also] fostered in a special way by the manifold counsels which the Lord proposes to his disciples in the Gospel for them to observe. Towering among these counsels is that precious gift of divine grace given to some by the Father (cf. Mt 19:11; 1 Cor 7:7) to devote themselves to God alone more easily with an undivided heart (cf. 1 Cor 7:32–34) in virginity or celibacy [...]. This perfect continence for love of the Kingdom of heaven has always been held in high esteem by the Church as a sign and stimulus of love, and as a singular source of spiritual fertility in the world" (Vatican II, *Lumen gentium*, 42).

It is interesting that these two subjects—marriage, and virginity for the sake of the Kingdom of heaven—are treated by Jesus in the same context: "Both the sacrament of Matrimony and virginity for the Kingdom of God come from the Lord himself. It is he who gives them meaning and grants them the grace which is indispensable for living them out in conformity with his will. Esteem of virginity for the sake of the kingdom and the Christian understanding of marriage are

inseparable, and they reinforce each other: 'Whoever denigrates marriage also diminishes the glory of virginity. Whoever praises it makes virginity more admirable and resplendent (St John Chrysostom, *Virg.*, 10, 1)' " (*Catechism of the Catholic Church*, 1620).

19:13–15 This incident refers to a Jewish custom: children presented themselves to their father, and pupils to their teacher, to receive a blessing and be remembered in their prayers. In the East, the imposition of hands on a person's head was an act of faith expressed in the sacred character of that gesture. There is no evidence that teachers of the time had any special affection for children; there is no passage in the Talmud (the encyclopedia of Jewish religious tradition) that speaks of affection for children. That seems to be the background to the initial reaction of Jesus' disciples (v. 13). But, as often happens, Jesus does something special, explaining his attitude by saying that the Kingdom of heaven belongs to those who live with childlike simplicity (v. 14).

i Greek *one flesh*   j Other ancient authorities, after *unchastity*, read *makes her commit adultery*   k Other ancient authorities omit *and he who marries a divorced woman commits adultery*

The rich young man. Christian poverty and renunciation

^{Mk 10:17–31}
^{Lk 18:18–30}

¹⁶And behold, one came up to him, saying, "Teacher, what good deed must I do, to

^{Lk 10:26–28}

have eternal life?" ¹⁷And he said to him, "Why do you ask me about what is good?

^{Ex 20:12–16}
^{Deut 5:16–20}

One there is who is good. If you would enter life, keep the commandments." ¹⁸He

said to him, "Which?" And Jesus said, "You shall not kill, You shall not commit

^{Ex 20:12–16}
^{Lev 19:18}
^{Deut 5:16–20}

adultery, You shall not steal, You shall not bear false witness, ¹⁹Honour your father

and mother, and, You shall love your neighbour as yourself." ²⁰The young man said

^{Mt 6:20; 8:22}
^{Lk 12:33}

to him, "All these I have observed; what do I still lack?" ²¹Jesus said to him, "If you

would be perfect, go, sell what you possess and give to the poor, and you will have

^{Ps 62:10}

treasure in heaven; and come, follow me." ²²When the young man heard this he went

away sorrowful; for he had great possessions.

²³And Jesus said to his disciples, "Truly, I say to you, it will be hard for a rich

man to enter the kingdom of heaven. ²⁴Again I tell you, it is easier for a camel to go

through the eye of a needle than for a rich man to enter the kingdom of God."

²⁵When the disciples heard this they were greatly astonished, saying, "Who then can

^{Gen 18:14}
^{Job 42:2}
^{Zech 8:6}
^{Lk 1:37}

be saved?" ²⁶But Jesus looked at them and said to them, "With men this is impossi-

ble, but with God all things are possible." ²⁷Then Peter said in reply, "Lo, we have

^{Lk 5:11}

left everything and followed you. What then shall we have?" ²⁸Jesus said to them,

^{Mt 25:31}
^{Lk 22:30}
^{Rev 3:21}
^{Dan 7:9–18}

"Truly, I say to you, in the new world, when the Son of man shall sit on his glorious

throne, you who have followed me will also sit on twelve thrones, judging the

eos prohibere ad me venire; talium est enim regnum caelorum». ¹⁵Et cum imposuisset eis manus, abiit inde. ¹⁶Et ecce unus accedens ait illi: «Magister, quid boni faciam, ut habeam vitam aeternam?». Qui dixit ei: ¹⁷«Quid me interrogas de bono? Unus est bonus. Si autem vis ad vitam ingredi, serva mandata». ¹⁸Dicit illi: «Quae?». Iesus autem dixit: *«Non homicidium facies, non adulterabis, non facies furtum, non falsum testimonium dices,* ¹⁹*honora patrem et matrem et diliges proximum tuum sicut teipsum»*. ²⁰Dicit illi adulescens: «Omnia haec custodivi. Quid adhuc mihi deest?». ²¹Ait illi Iesus: «Si vis perfectus esse, vade, vende, quae habes, et da pauperibus, et habebis thesaurum in caelo; et veni, sequere me». ²²Cum audisset autem adulescens verbum, abiit tristis; erat enim habens multas possessiones. ²³Iesus autem dixit discipulis suis: «Amen dico vobis: Dives difficile intrabit in regnum caelorum. ²⁴Et iterum dico vobis: Facilius est camelum per foramen acus transire, quam divitem intrare in regnum Dei». ²⁵Auditis autem his, discipuli mirabantur valde dicentes: «Quis ergo poterit salvus esse?». ²⁶Aspiciens autem Iesus dixit illis: «Apud homines hoc impossibile est, apud Deum autem omnia possibilia sunt». ²⁷Tunc respondens Petrus dixit ei: «Ecce nos reliquimus omnia et secuti sumus te. Quid ergo erit nobis?». ²⁸Iesus autem dixit illis: «Amen dico vobis quod vos, qui secuti estis me, in regeneratione, cum sederit

19:16–30 The first three Gospels all report this episode, but Matthew goes into most detail about the conversation between Jesus and the young man. The latter keeps the commandments (vv. 18–20) and he asks Jesus what other "good deed" he should do. Jesus, in his first reply (v. 17), is already preparing him for the challenge he makes at the end (v. 21): "This is not a matter only of disposing oneself to hear a teaching and obediently accepting a commandment. More radically, it involves *holding fast to the very person of Jesus*, partaking of his life and his destiny, sharing in his free and loving obedience to the will of the Father" (John Paul II, *Veritatis splendor*, 19).

In this sense, both this episode and the preceding one about marriage (19:1–12) point to the fullness and perfection of the Law that can be found in those who live in accordance with the lifestyle and teaching of Jesus. Our Lord teaches

the indissolubility of marriage and requires that people keep the commandments; but he also asks some people to follow the way of celibacy and be detached from all things for the sake of the Kingdom of heaven.

The scene ends with the young man going away sad (v. 22). Attachment to his property has won out over Jesus' invitation. His reluctance to respond to our Lord's call for personal self-surrender causes him to feel sorrowful.

After the young man leaves, Jesus teaches his disciples about riches (cf. the note on Mk 10:17–31). Then, in response to a question from Peter, he spells out what awaits those who sincerely follow Christ: to follow Christ is to believe in a "new world" (v. 28), a rebirth, where a new scale of values operates. Those who seem to have lost out will be judges; those who seem not to matter will be the first; whatever a person gives up now will be multiplied one hundredfold.

twelve tribes of Israel. [29]And every one who has left houses or brothers or sisters or father or mother or children or lands, for my name's sake, will receive a hundred-fold,[1] and inherit eternal life. [30]But many that are first will be last, and the last first.

Heb 10:34

Lk 13:30; 20:16

Parable of the labourers in the vineyard

20 [1]"For the kingdom of heaven is like a householder who went out early in the morning to hire labourers for his vineyard. [2]After agreeing with the labourers for a denarius[m] a day, he sent them into his vineyard. [3]And going out about the third hour he saw others standing idle in the market place; [4]and to them he said, 'You go into the vineyard too, and whatever is right I will give you.' So they went. [5]Going out again about the sixth hour and the ninth hour, he did the same. [6]And about the eleventh hour he went out and found others standing; and he said to them, 'Why do you stand here idle all day?' [7]They said to him, 'Because no one has hired us.' He said to them, 'You go into the vineyard too.' [8]And when evening came, the owner of the vineyard said to his steward, 'Call the labourers and pay them their wages, beginning with the last, up to the first.' [9]And when those hired about the eleventh hour came, each of them received a denarius. [10]Now when the first came, they thought they would receive more; but each of them also received a denarius. [11]And on receiving it they grumbled at the householder, [12]saying, 'These last worked only one hour, and you have made them equal to us who have borne the burden of the day

Lev 19:13
Deut 24:15

Filius hominis in throno gloriae suae, sedebitis et vos super thronos duodecim, iudicantes duodecim tribus Israel. [29]Et omnis, qui reliquit domos vel fratres aut sorores aut patrem aut matrem aut filios aut agros propter nomen meum, centuplum accipiet et vitam aeternam possidebit. [30]Multi autem erunt primi novissimi et novissimi primi. [20] [1]Simile est enim regnum caelorum homini patri familias, qui exiit primo mane conducere operarios in vineam suam; [2]conventione autem facta cum operariis ex denario diurno, misit eos in vineam suam. [3]Et egressus circa horam tertiam vidit alios stantes in foro otiosos [4]et illis dixit: "Ite et vos in vineam; et, quod iustum fuerit, dabo vobis". [5]Illi autem abierunt. Iterum autem exiit circa sextam et nonam horam et fecit similiter. [6]Circa undecimam vero exiit et invenit alios stantes et dicit illis: "Quid hic statis tota die otiosi?". [7]Dicunt ei: "Quia nemo nos conduxit". Dicit illis: "Ite et vos in vineam". [8]Cum sero autem factum esset, dicit dominus vineae procuratori suo: "Voca operarios et redde illis mercedem incipiens a novissimis usque ad primos". [9]Et cum venissent, qui circa undecimam horam venerant, acceperunt singuli denarium. [10]Venientes autem primi arbitrati sunt quod plus essent accepturi; acceperunt autem et ipsi singuli denarium. [11]Accipientes autem murmurabant adversus patrem familias [12]dicentes: "Hi novissimi una hora fecerunt, et pares illos nobis fecisti, qui portavimus

20:1–16 This parable is intended to explain what Jesus said in the previous verse (19:30), and it ends with a similar remark (20:16). At the beginning it refers to the Jewish people (God called them at the first hour), but at the end its message extends to Gentiles also.

The parable teaches the goodness and mercy of God, which is to go far beyond human standards of justice. We are all beneficiaries of the largesse of God's goodness, and the invitation to work in his vineyard is a sign of his generosity. There is nothing unjust about God, and we should never presume to judge him. Our natural disposition towards him should be one of gratefulness: "All that we have in soul and body, all that we possess in nature and spirit, come from you and evidence you as our benefactor. [...] Though some may receive more and others less, everything comes from you and without you we have nothing. The one who has more should not

boast as though what he has he has by his own merit, or lord it over others. [...] The one who has less should not be sad or angry or envy the one who has more. [...] You know what is best to give each one" (Thomas à Kempis, *De imitatione Christi*, 3, 22, 2–3).

Another element of the parable's teaching is the need to respond positively to God's call, no matter when it comes. His true disciples are those who appreciate his goodness and prove this by their deeds: "You often ask yourself why souls who have had the great fortune of knowing the true Jesus ever since their childhood hesitate so much in responding with the best they have: their life, their family, their ideals. Look: you are bound to show yourself very grateful to the Lord, precisely because you have received it *all* in one go. Just as it would strike a blind man if he suddenly recovered his sight, while it does not even occur to others to give thanks because

1 Other ancient authorities read *manifold* m The denarius was a day's wage for a labourer

and the scorching heat.' [13]But he replied to one of them, 'Friend, I am doing you no wrong; did you not agree with me for a denarius? [14]Take what belongs to you, and go; I choose to give to this last as I give to you. [15]Am I not allowed to do what I choose with what belongs to me? Or do you begrudge my generosity?'[n] [16]So the last will be first, and the first last."

Rom 9:16, 21

Mt 19:30
Lk 13:30
Lk 22:24–27

Mk 10:32–34
Lk 18:31–34

Third announcement of the Passion

Mt 16:21; 17:22–23

[17]And as Jesus was going up to Jerusalem, he took the twelve disciples aside, and on the way he said to them, [18]"Behold, we are going up to Jerusalem; and the Son of man will be delivered to the chief priests and scribes, and they will condemn him to

Mt 27:63; 28:6
Lk 9:22; 24:7, 46
Acts 10:40
1 Cor 15:4

death, [19]and deliver him to the Gentiles to be mocked and scourged and crucified, and he will be raised on the third day."

Mk 10:35–45

Mt 10:2

Mt 19:28

The mother of the sons of Zebedee makes her request

[20]Then the mother of the sons of Zebedee came up to him, with her sons, and kneeling before him she asked him for something. [21]And he said to her, "What do you want?" She said to him, "Command that these two sons of mine may sit, one at your

Jn 18:11
Mt 26:39

right hand and one at your left, in your kingdom." [22]But Jesus answered, "You do not

pondus diei et aestum!". [13]At ille respondens uni eorum dixit: "Amice, non facio tibi iniuriam; nonne ex denario convenisti mecum? [14]Tolle, quod tuum est, et vade; volo autem et huic novissimo dare sicut et tibi. [15]Aut non licet mihi, quod volo, facere de meis? An oculus tuus nequam est, quia ego bonus sum?". [16]Sic erunt novissimi primi, et primi novissimi». [17]Et ascendens Iesus Hierosolymam assumpsit Duodecim discipulos secreto et ait illis in via: [18]«Ecce ascendimus Hierosolymam, et Filius hominis tradetur principibus sacerdotum et scribis, et condemnabunt eum morte [19]et tradent eum gentibus ad illudendum et flagellandum et crucifigendum, et tertia die resurget». [20]Tunc accessit ad eum mater filiorum Zebedaei cum filiis suis, adorans et petens aliquid ab eo. [21]Qui dixit ei: «Quid vis?». Ait illi: «Dic ut sedeant hi duo filii mei unus ad dexteram tuam et unus ad sinistram in regno tuo». [22]Respondens autem Iesus dixit: «Nescitis quid petatis. Potestis bibere calicem, quem ego bibiturus

they see. But that is not enough. You have to help those around you, daily, to behave with gratitude for their being sons of God. If you don't, don't tell me you are grateful" (St Josemaría Escrivá, *Furrow*, 4).

Finally, by describing the attitude of those who seem to accuse the employer of acting wrongly, Jesus indicates that, rather than judge God, we should accept his gifts and thank him for having chosen to involve us in his plan of salvation.

20:17–19 Making his way up to Jerusalem, to carry out God's plan, Jesus obediently faces into the death that awaits him, and for a third time he predicts it. Moreover, he prepares the apostles so that when the time of testing comes they will call to mind his prophecy and be helped to overcome their sorrow.

The third announcement of the passion is related in more detail by Matthew than by the other two Synoptics, for here Jesus not only speaks about his death but also describes very vividly the degrading way he will be treated.

Maybe he does so to prepare his disciples for the episode that follows, in which he associates James and John with his own destiny. The route to resurrection is long and painful: "But we should not tread this path too hastily, lest we lose sight of a very simple fact which we might easily overlook. We will not be able to share in our Lord's Resurrection unless we unite ourselves with him in his Passion and Death. If we are to accompany Christ in his glory at the end of Holy Week, we must first enter into his holocaust and be truly united to him, as he lies dead on Calvary" (St Josemaría Escrivá, *Christ Is Passing By*, 95).

20:20–28 Jesus corrects the all too human ambitions and desires of the apostles and the mother of the sons of Zebedee (James the Greater and John) by affirming the primacy of the will of God and the need for a spirit of service. Using a language of liturgy/sacrifice that is reminiscent of the suffering Servant of the prophet Isaiah (Is 52:13 — 53:12), our Lord clearly states that his service includes the sacrifice of his life (v. 28).

n Or *is your eye evil because I am good?*

know what you are asking. Are you able to drink the cup that I am to drink?" They said to him, "We are able." ²³He said to them, "You will drink my cup, but to sit at my right hand and at my left is not mine to grant, but it is for those for whom it has been prepared by my Father." ²⁴And when the ten heard it they were indignant at the two brothers. ²⁵But Jesus called them to him and said, "You know that the rulers of the Gentiles lord it over them, and their great men exercise authority over them. ²⁶It shall not be so among you; but whoever would be great among you must be your servant, ²⁷and whoever would be first among you must be your slave; ²⁸even as the Son of man came not to be served but to serve, and to give his life as a ransom for many."

Acts 12:2
Rev 1:9

Lk 22:24–26

Mt 23:11

Mk 9:35; Lk 9:48
Lk 22:27
Is 53:12; Phil 2:7
1 Tim 2:6

Curing of the blind men of Jericho

Mk 10:46–52
Lk 18:35–43
Mt 9:27–30
Mt 15:22

²⁹And as they went out of Jericho, a great crowd followed him. ³⁰And behold, two blind men sitting by the roadside, when they heard that Jesus was passing by, cried out,ᵒ "Have mercy on us, Son of David!" ³¹The crowd rebuked them, telling them to be silent; but they cried out the more, "Lord, have mercy on us, Son of David!" ³²And Jesus stopped and called them, saying, "What do you want me to do for you?" ³³They said to him, "Lord, let our eyes be opened." ³⁴And Jesus in pity touched their eyes, and immediately they received their sight and followed him.

sum?». Dicunt ei: «Possumus». ²³Ait illis: «Calicem quidem meum bibetis, sedere autem ad dexteram meam et sinistram non est meum dare illud, sed quibus paratum est a Patre meo». ²⁴Et audientes decem indignati sunt de duobus fratribus. ²⁵Iesus autem vocavit eos ad se et ait: «Scitis quia principes gentium dominantur eorum et, qui magni sunt, potestatem exercent in eos. ²⁶Non ita erit inter vos, sed quicumque voluerit inter vos magnus fieri, erit vester minister; ²⁷et, quicumque voluerit inter vos primus esse, erit vester servus; ²⁸sicut Filius hominis non venit ministrari sed ministrare et dare animam suam redemptionem pro multis». ²⁹Et egredientibus illis ab Iericho, secuta est eum turba multa. ³⁰Et ecce duo caeci sedentes secus viam audierunt quia Iesus transiret et clamaverunt dicentes: «Domine, miserere nostri, fili David!». ³¹Turba autem increpabat eos, ut tacerent; at illi magis clamabant dicentes: «Domine, miserere nostri, fili David!». ³²Et stetit Iesus et vocavit eos et ait: «Quid vultis, ut faciam

Tradition notes the manner in which Jesus' words would be borne out in the lives of these two brothers: "We may wonder how both the sons of Zebedee, James and John, came to drink from the chalice of martyrdom, since Scripture tells us only that the apostle James was decapitated by Herod. John, on the other hand, died a natural death. But in the history of the Church we are told that he was to be martyred in a vat of boiling oil; an athlete of Christ, he was saved from the oil and banished to the island of Patmos. John too suffered martyrdom; he, like the three young men who stood in the burning fire, drank from the chalice of martyrdom, though his persecutor failed to spill his blood" (St Jerome, *Commentarii in Matthaeum*, 20, 23).

But, going beyond what Zebedee's family learns here, our Lord's words carry a message for all his disciples (vv. 25–28). Jesus depicts himself as an example to be imitated by those who exercise authority in the Church. He, who is God and the Judge who will come to judge the world (see Phil 2:5–11; Jn 5:22–27; Acts 10:42), does not impose his power but, rather, saves us out of

love, to the point of giving his own life (see Jn 15:13); thus, the most humble servant becomes the first and greatest of all. That is the interpretation St Peter later gave when he exhorted priests to shepherd the flock entrusted to them by God (see 1 Pet 5:1–3); and St Paul, while being subject to no one, made himself the servant of all to gain all (see 1 Cor 9:19 ff; 2 Cor 4:5).

The phrase "a ransom for many" (v. 28) should not be interpreted as meaning that God does not want all to be saved. "Many" is not a counterpoint to "all" but to "one": one is he who saves, and to all is salvation offered.

20:29–34 The three Synoptic Gospels report both this miracle worked by Jesus in Jericho and the messianic title ("Son of David") that the blind men, or "man" according to Mark and Luke, gave him immediately prior to his appearance in Jerusalem. Each of the evangelists then gives the episode a particular emphasis. All three note the men's faith, heard in their cries for help (vv. 30–31), and seen in their gratitude, which leads them to follow Jesus (v. 34). St Matthew is

o Other ancient authorities insert *Lord*

PART THREE

Jesus' ministry in Jerusalem*

10. CLEANSING OF THE TEMPLE. CONTROVERSIES*

Mk 11:1–11
Lk 19:28–40
Jn 12:12–19

The Messiah enters the Holy City

21 ¹And when they drew near to Jerusalem and came to Bethphage, to the Mount of Olives, then Jesus sent two disciples, ²saying to them, "Go into the village opposite you, and immediately you will find an ass tied, and a colt with her; untie them and bring them to me. ³If any one says anything to you, you shall say, 'The Lord has need of them,' and he will send them immediately." ⁴This took place to fulfil what was spoken by the prophet, saying,

vobis?». ³³Dicunt illi: «Domine, ut aperiantur oculi nostri». ³⁴Misertus autem Iesus, tetigit oculos eorum; et confestim viderunt et secuti sunt eum. [21] ¹Et cum appropinquassent Hierosolymis et venissent Bethfage, ad montem Oliveti, tunc Iesus misit duos discipulos ²dicens eis: «Ite in castellum, quod contra vos est, et statim invenietis asinam alligatam et pullum cum ea; solvite et adducite mihi. ³Et si quis vobis aliquid dixerit, dicite: "Dominus eos necessarios habet", et confestim dimittet eos». ⁴Hoc autem factum est, ut impleretur, quod dictum est per prophetam dicentem:

the only one to say that it was Jesus' pity that moved him to cure them (v. 34): "Clearly these blind men deserved to be cured: first, because they cried out; and then, because after they received the gift they did not hasten away, the way most people, in their ingratitude, are inclined to do once they have got what they wanted. No, they were not like that: they were both persevering before the gift and grateful after it, for they 'followed him'" (St John Chrysostom, *In Matthaeum*, 66).

*21:1—28:20 The Synoptic Gospels follow the same outline and deal with the same themes in their narrative of the last days of Jesus' life on earth. Matthew begins with an account of the revelation of Jesus as the Messiah and follows it with a description of the cleansing of the temple (21:1–22). Jesus' controversies with the Jewish authorities identify the reasons for which he will be condemned to death (21:23—23:39), and what is called the "Eschatological Discourse" (24:1—25:46) concludes the account of Jesus' teaching. The narrative enters into great detail when it deals with the last hours of Jesus—his self-offering to the Father's will (26:24–46), his arrest, trial and sentencing (26:47—27:31), and his death (27:32–66) and resurrection (28:1–20).

Within this framework, Matthew's account highlights certain aspects of the history of salva-

tion—our Lord's loving acceptance of his role as the suffering Servant, Israel's rejection of God's plans, etc.

*21:1—23:39 Jesus' exchanges with the religious leaders explain what led them to bring about his death. But there is a deeper underlying theme that links the episodes in this section: Israel has failed to respond to the gift of God, and therefore God is going to found a new people that will bear fruit (21:43). Still, our Lord's words also carry a warning for members of that new people, the Church: as he will make plain later (25:1–46), faithfulness to God should always express itself in deeds.

21:1–11 In his triumphant entry into Jerusalem, Jesus reveals himself as the Messiah King. Matthew sees the presence of the ass and its colt (v. 2) as fulfilment of a prophecy of Zechariah (v. 5). The ass, originally a noble mount (cf. Gen 22:3; 49:11; Ex 4:20; Num 22:21; Judg 5:10), was replaced by the horse as a symbol of power in the time of the monarchy (see 1 Kings 10:26–30). Therefore, the prophecy of Zechariah pointed to a peaceful king who gains victory not by force of arms or violence but through humility and weakness (cf. Zech 9:9–10 and note). The Church Fathers read elements of this episode as symbols: the ass, the mother, repre-

> 5"Tell the daughter of Zion,
>   Behold, your king is coming to you,
>   humble, and mounted on an ass,
>   and on a colt, the foal of an ass."

Zech 9:9
Is 62:11

6The disciples went and did as Jesus had directed them; 7they brought the ass and the colt, and put their garments on them, and he sat thereon. 8Most of the crowd spread their garments on the road, and others cut branches from the trees and spread them on the road. 9And the crowds that went before him and that followed him shouted, "Hosanna to the Son of David! Blessed is he who comes in the name of the Lord! Hosanna in the highest!"* 10And when he entered Jerusalem, all the city was stirred, saying, "Who is this?" 11And the crowds said, "This is the prophet Jesus from Nazareth of Galilee."

2 Kings 9:13

Ps 118:25-26
Mt 23:39
Lk 13:35

Jesus in the temple

Mk 11:15-19
Lk 19:45-48
Jn 2:13-25

12And Jesus entered the temple of Godp and drove out all who sold and bought in the temple, and he overturned the tables of the money-changers and the seats of those who sold pigeons. 13He said to them, "It is written, 'My house shall be called a house of prayer'; but you make it a den of robbers."

Is 56:7
Jer 7:11

5«*Dicite filiae Sion*: / *Ecce Rex tuus venit tibi*, / *mansuetus et sedens super asinam* / *et super pullum filium subiugalis*». 6Euntes autem discipuli fecerunt, sicut praecepit illis Iesus, 7et adduxerunt asinam et pullum, et imposuerunt super eis vestimenta sua, et sedit super ea. 8Plurima autem turba straverunt vestimenta sua in via; alii autem caedebant ramos de arboribus et sternebant in via. 9Turbae autem, quae praecedebant eum et quae sequebantur, clamabant dicentes: «*Hosanna* filio David! *Benedictus, qui venit in nomine Domini! Hosanna* in altissimis!». 10Et cum intrasset Hierosolymam, commota est universa civitas dicens: «Quis est hic?». 11Turbae autem dicebant: «Hic est Iesus propheta a Nazareth Galilaeae». 12Et intravit Iesus in templum et eiciebat omnes vendentes et ementes in templo, et mensas nummulariorum evertit et cathedras vendentium columbas, 13et dicit eis: «Scriptum est: "*Domus mea domus orationis vocabitur*". Vos autem facitis eam *speluncam latronum*». 14Et accesserunt ad eum caeci et claudi in templo, et sanavit eos. 15Videntes autem principes sacerdotum et scribae mirabilia, quae fecit, et pueros clamantes in templo et

sents Judaism, subject to the yoke of the Law; the colt represents the Gentiles. Jesus leads both Jews and Gentiles into the Church, the new Jerusalem.

Just as nowadays a red carpet is rolled out in front of a building to greet important arrivals, the disciples and the crowd provide a carpet for Jesus' entry into his city (vv. 7-8). And they acclaim him as Saviour: the Hebrew word *hosanna* (v. 9) originally had that meaning, an appeal addressed to God: "Save us." Later it was used as a cry of enthusiasm to greet someone—similar to "Long live …". So, people of the crowd show their enthusiasm by shouting "Long live the Son of David!" The Church takes up these acclamations in the preface of the Mass, to proclaim the kingship of Christ: "It has long been a common custom to give to Christ the metaphorical title of 'King,' because of the high degree of perfection whereby he excels all creatures. So he is said to reign in 'the hearts of men,' both by the reason of the keenness of his intellect and the extent of his knowledge, and

also because he is the very truth, and it is from him that truth must be obediently received by all mankind. He reigns, too, in the wills of men, for in him the human will was perfectly and entirely obedient to the Holy Will of God, and further by his grace and inspiration he so subjects our free will as to incite us to the most noble endeavours. He is the King of hearts, too, by reason of his 'charity which exceedeth all knowledge.' And his mercy and kindness which draw all men to him, for never has it been known, nor will it ever be, that a man be loved so much and so universally as Jesus Christ" (Pius XI, *Quas primas*, 4).

21:12-17 Matthew records three messianic signs that took place on this first day in Jerusalem—the cleansing of the temple (vv. 12-13; cf. the note on Mk 11:12-25); various cures (v. 14); and praise of God by the humble (vv. 15-16)—in line with Psalm 8:2, which Jesus quotes to show that it has found fulfilment. In these three signs the evangelist gives us a glimpse of the divinity of Jesus Christ.

p Other ancient authorities omit *of God*

Ps 118:25

Ps 8:2

¹⁴And the blind and the lame came to him in the temple, and he healed them. ¹⁵But when the chief priests and the scribes saw the wonderful things that he did, and the children crying out in the temple, "Hosanna to the Son of David!" they were indignant; ¹⁶and they said to him, "Do you hear what these are saying?" And Jesus said to them, "Yes; have you never read,

'Out of the mouth of babes and sucklings
    thou hast brought perfect praise'?"

¹⁷And leaving them, he went out of the city to Bethany and lodged there.

Mk 11:12-14,
20-25

Lk 13:6

Lk 17:6

Mt 7:7

The cursing of the fig tree

¹⁸In the morning, as he was returning to the city, he was hungry. ¹⁹And seeing a fig tree by the wayside he went to it, and found nothing on it but leaves only. And he said to it, "May no fruit ever come from you again!" And the fig tree withered at once. ²⁰When the disciples saw it they marvelled, saying, "How did the fig tree wither at once?" ²¹And Jesus answered them, "Truly, I say to you, if you have faith and never doubt, you will not only do what has been done to the fig tree, but even if you say to this mountain, 'Be taken up and cast into the sea,' it will be done. ²²and whatever you ask in prayer, you will receive, if you have faith."

Mk 11:27-33
Lk 20:1-8

Jn 2:18

The authority of Jesus is questioned

²³And when he entered the temple, the chief priests and the elders of the people came up to him as he was teaching, and said, "By what authority are you doing

dicentes: «Hosanna filio David», indignati sunt ¹⁶et dixerunt ei: «Audis quid isti dicant?». Iesus autem dicit eis: «Utique; numquam legistis: "*Ex ore infantium et lactantium perfecisti laudem*"?». ¹⁷Et relictis illis, abiit foras extra civitatem in Bethaniam ibique mansit. ¹⁸Mane autem revertens in civitatem, esuriit. ¹⁹Et videns fici arborem unam secus viam, venit ad eam; et nihil invenit in ea nisi folia tantum et ait illi: «Numquam ex te fructus nascatur in sempiternum». Et arefacta est continuo ficulnea. ²⁰Et videntes discipuli mirati sunt dicentes: «Quomodo continuo aruit ficulnea?». ²¹Respondens autem Iesus ait eis: «Amen dico vobis: Si habueritis fidem et non haesitaveritis, non solum de ficulnea facietis, sed et si monti huic dixeritis: "Tolle et iacta te in mare", fiet. ²²Et omnia, quaecumque petieritis in oratione credentes, accipietis». ²³Et cum venisset in templum, accesserunt ad eum docentem principes sacerdotum et seniores populi dicentes: «In qua potestate haec facis? Et quis tibi dedit hanc potestatem?».

In the book of Exodus (23:15) the Israelites are instructed not to come to the temple empty-handed, but to bring some victim as an offering. In this connexion a market developed in the temple courtyards, with animals bought and sold for sacrificial purposes. Originally, this may have been a good idea, but the practice later became an abuse, a stain on the character of the temple (v. 13). Moved by zeal for his Father's house (see Jn 2:17), Jesus in holy anger now ejects the traders. His symbolic action (found too in the prophets: see Ezek 5:1-17) was designed to remind people of the respect due to the temple. With even more reason, it is a lesson for us, who have our Lord himself present in the tabernacle. On the subject of Christ's passions and feelings, see the note on Mk 3:1-6.

21:18-22 The cursing of the fig tree is a sort of parable-in-action. It is also an illustration of

God's omnipotence. A person with faith can do anything—even greater things than this. "Christ lays down one condition: we must live by faith; then we will be able to move mountains. And so many things need moving ... in the world, but, first of all, in our own hearts. So many obstacles placed in the way of grace! We have to have faith, therefore: faith and works, faith and sacrifice, faith and humility. For faith makes us all-powerful" (St Josemaría Escrivá, *Friends of God*, 203). Our Lord here tells us one way to apply this spirit of faith: prayer can achieve all ends.

21:23-27 Over the course of two chapters, the Gospel recounts some of the disputes that arose between Jesus and the rulers of the people. His cleansing of the temple may have provoked these people into taking issue with him. Here a number of the chief priests and elders (that is, clerical and lay members of the Sanhedrin) ask

these things, and who gave you this authority?"* [24]Jesus answered them, "I also
will ask you a question; and if you tell me the answer, then I also will tell you by
what authority I do these things. [25]The baptism of John, whence was it? From
heaven or from men?" And they argued with one another, "If we say, 'From
heaven,' he will say to us, 'Why then did you not believe him?' [26]But if we say,
'From men,' we are afraid of the multitude; for all hold that John was a prophet."
[27]So they answered Jesus, "We do not know." And he said to them, "Neither will I
tell you by what authority I do these things.

Jn 1:25

Mt 14:5

Parable of the two sons

[28]"What do you think? A man had two sons; and he went to the first and said, 'Son, go
and work in the vineyard today.' [29]And he answered, 'I will not'; but afterward he
repented and went. [30]And he went to the second and said the same; and he answered, 'I
go, sir,' but did not go. [31]Which of the two did the will of his father?" They said, "The
first." Jesus said to them, "Truly, I say to you, the tax collectors and the harlots go into
the kingdom of God before you. [32]For John came to you in the way of righteousness,
and you did not believe him, but the tax collectors and the harlots believed him; and
even when you saw it, you did not afterward repent and believe him.

Lk 18:14

Lk 7:29–30

[24]Respondens autem Iesus dixit illis: «Interrogabo vos et ego unum sermonem, quem si dixeritis mihi, et ego vobis dicam, in qua potestate haec
facio: [25]Baptismum Ioannis unde erat? A caelo an ex hominibus?». At illi cogitabant inter se dicentes: «Si dixerimus: "E caelo", dicet nobis:
"Quare ergo non credidistis illi?"; [26]si autem dixerimus: "Ex hominibus", timemus turbam; omnes enim habent Ioannem sicut prophetam». [27]Et
respondentes Iesu dixerunt: «Nescimus». Ait illis et ipse: «Nec ego dico vobis in qua potestate haec facio». [28]«Quid autem vobis videtur? Homo
quidam habebat duos filios. Et accedens ad primum dixit: "Fili, vade hodie, operare in vinea". [29]Ille autem respondens ait: "Nolo"; postea autem
paenitentia motus abiit. [30]Accedens autem ad alterum dixit similiter. At ille respondens ait: "Eo, domine"; et non ivit. [31]Quis ex duobus fecit voluntatem patris?». Dicunt: «Primus». Dicit illis Iesus: «Amen dico vobis: Publicani et meretrices praecedunt vos in regnum Dei. [32]Venit enim ad
vos Ioannes in via iustitiae, et non credidistis ei; publicani autem et meretrices crediderunt ei. Vos autem videntes nec paenitentiam habuistis

Jesus to prove to them that he has authority to
act as he does; they challenge him to clearly
admit that he is the Messiah. But Jesus, knowing
their malicious intentions, does not give them a
direct reply; instead, he puts a question to them
about the role of John the Baptist, for John was
the "precursor", the Messiah's herald.

The evangelist puts it on record that these
people did not believe in Jesus (v. 25), but in the
light of what Jesus says in the next passage
(21:32) we know that they made no effort at all
to believe in him. Therefore they deserve the
silence that Jesus gives them (v. 27); nothing that
he might say could move them to repent.

21:28–46 In these two parables our Lord deals
with Israel's rejection of God, and God's resolve
to create a new people (v. 43).

Matthew is the only evangelist to record the
parable of the two sons, which stresses the
importance of conversion (v. 32): Israel is like the
son who said "Yes" but then failed to abide by his
word (v. 30), just like Pharisees who "preach, but

do not practise" (23:3). Notorious sinners, on the
contrary, say "No" to the works of the Law (as
their behaviour shows), but many of them have a
change of heart when they witness God's signs (v.
32); they act as God desires, and they gain entry
to his Kingdom (v. 31). Our Lord points to three
stages on the journey to faith (v. 32)—seeing,
repenting and believing. "When man is in a state
of sin, he cannot see God. But you can be cured
of that state if you want to be: go to the doctor
and he will open the eyes of your soul and your
heart. Who is the doctor? The doctor is God, who
cures us through his Word and his wisdom. [...] If
you understand all this and live a clean, righteous
and holy life, you will be able to see God; but in
order to understand this, faith and fear of the Lord
must be uppermost in your heart" (St Theophilus
of Antioch, *Ad Autolycum*, 1, 7).

The parable of the wicked tenants is a summary of the history of salvation (cf. the note on
Mk 12:1–12). It begins with an allusion to Isaiah
5:1–7, where Israel is compared to a vineyard
which, despite all the care lavished on it by God,

Parable of the wicked tenants

Mk 12:1–12
Lk 20:9–19
Mt 25:14
Is 5:1–2

33"Hear another parable.* There was a householder who planted a vineyard, and set a hedge around it, and dug a wine press in it, and built a tower, and let it out to tenants, and went into another country. 34When the season of fruit drew near, he sent his

Mt 22:6

servants to the tenants, to get his fruit; 35and the tenants took his servants and beat one, killed another, and stoned another. 36Again he sent other servants, more than the first; and they did the same to them. 37Afterward he sent his son to them, saying, 'They will respect my son.' 38But when the tenants saw the son, they said to themselves, 'This is the heir; come, let us kill him and have his inheritance.' 39And they took him and cast him out of the vineyard, and killed him. 40When therefore the owner of the vineyard comes, what will he do to those tenants?" 41They said to him, "He will put those wretches to a miserable death, and let out the vineyard to other tenants who will give him the fruits in their seasons."

Ps 118:22–23
Acts 4:11
Rom 9:33
1 Pet 2:6–8

42Jesus said to them, "Have you never read in the scriptures:

'The very stone which the builders rejected
has become the head of the corner;
this was the Lord's doing,
and it is marvellous in our eyes'?

43Therefore I tell you, the kingdom of God will be taken away from you and given

Dan 2:34–35, 44–45

to a nation producing the fruits of it. 44And he who falls on this stone will be broken to pieces; but when it falls on any one, it will crush him."q

45When the chief priests and the Pharisees heard his parables, they perceived that

Mt 26:4–5

he was speaking about them. 46But when they tried to arrest him, they feared the multitudes, because they held him to be a prophet.

Parable of the marriage feast

Lk 14:15–24

Jn 3:29

22 1And again Jesus spoke to them in parables, saying, 2"The kingdom of heaven may be compared to a king who gave a marriage feast for his son,

postea, ut crederetis ei. 33Aliam parabolam audite. Homo erat pater familias, qui *plantavit vineam et saepem circumdedit ei et fodit in ea torcular et aedificavit turrim* et locavit eam agricolis et peregre profectus est. 34Cum autem tempus fructuum appropinquasset, misit servos suos ad agricolas, ut acciperent fructus eius. 35Et agricolae, apprehensis servis eius, alium ceciderunt, alium occiderunt, alium vero lapidaverunt. 36Iterum misit alios servos plures prioribus, et fecerunt illis similiter. 37Novissime autem misit ad eos filium suum dicens: "Verebuntur filium meum". 38Agricolae autem videntes filium dixerunt intra se: "Hic est heres. Venite, occidamus eum et habebimus hereditatem eius". 39Et apprehensum eum eiecerunt extra vineam et occiderunt. 40Cum ergo venerit dominus vineae, quid faciet agricolis illis?». 41Aiunt illi: «Malos male perdet et vineam locabit aliis agricolis, qui reddant ei fructum temporibus suis». 42Dicit illis Iesus: «Numquam legistis in Scripturis: / *"Lapidem, quem reprobaverunt aedificantes, / hic factus est in caput anguli; / a Domino factum est istud / et est mirabile in oculis nostris"*? 43Ideo dico vobis quia auferetur a vobis regnum Dei et dabitur genti facienti fructus eius. 44Et, qui ceciderit super lapidem istum confringetur; super quem vero ceciderit, conteret eum». 45Et cum audissent principes sacerdotum et pharisaei parabolas eius, cognoverunt quod de ipsis diceret; 46et quaerentes eum tenere, timuerunt turbas, quoniam sicut prophetam eum habebant.   [22] 1Et respondens Iesus dixit iterum in parabolis eis dicens: 2«Simile factum est

produced wild grapes instead of good grapes; that is why God destroys it. In the context in which Jesus spoke the parable, and in the light of future events that the evangelists witnessed, the allegory becomes clear: the tenants symbolize the ruling classes of Israel, those charged by God with looking after his people. On numerous occasions, God sent prophets to them but they found no fruit; instead, they were ill-treated or killed (cf. 2 Chron 24:21). Finally, God has sent his only Son, Jesus. There is an infinite difference: Jesus is the Son, whereas the prophets

were only servants. But the tenants are now prepared to kill the Son, and they will do so outside the vineyard, that is, outside Jerusalem. Thus, the punishment imposed by God makes quite understandable sense. Matthew is the only evangelist who, in his account of the parable, speaks about the vineyard being handed over to "a nation producing the fruits of it" (v. 43)—a reference to the Church, the new People of God.

22:1–14 This parable, which is very like one found in St Luke (see Lk 14:15–24 and note),

q Other ancient authorities omit verse 44

[3]and sent his servants to call those who were invited to the marriage feast; but they would not come. [4]Again he sent other servants, saying, 'Tell those who are invited, Behold, I have made ready my dinner, my oxen and my fat calves are killed, and everything is ready; come to the marriage feast.' [5]But they made light of it and went off, one to his farm, another to his business, [6]while the rest seized his servants, treated them shamefully, and killed them. [7]The king was angry, and he sent his troops and destroyed those murderers and burned their city. [8]Then he said to his servants, 'The wedding is ready, but those invited were not worthy. [9]Go therefore to the thoroughfares, and invite to the marriage feast as many as you find.' [10]And those servants went out into the streets and gathered all whom they found, both bad and good; so the wedding hall was filled with guests.

Mt 21:35

[11]"But when the king came in to look at the guests, he saw there a man who had no wedding garment;* [12]and he said to him, 'Friend, how did you get in here without a wedding garment?' And he was speechless. [13]Then the king said to the attendants, 'Bind him hand and foot, and cast him into the outer darkness; there men will weep and gnash their teeth.' [14]For many are called, but few are chosen."

Mt 8:12

Paying tax to Caesar

Mk 12:13–17
Lk 20:20–26
Jn 8:6
Mk 3:6
Jn 3:2

[15]Then the Pharisees went and took counsel how to entangle him in his talk. [16]And they sent their disciples to him, along with the Herodians, saying, "Teacher, we

regnum caelorum homini regi, qui fecit nuptias filio suo. [3]Et misit servos suos vocare invitatos ad nuptias, et nolebant venire. [4]Iterum misit alios servos dicens: "Dicite invitatis: Ecce prandium meum paravi, tauri mei et altilia occisa, et omnia parata; venite ad nuptias". [5]Illi autem neglexerunt et abierunt, alius in villam suam, alius vero ad negotiationem suam; [6]reliqui vero tenuerunt servos eius et contumelia affectos occiderunt. [7]Rex autem iratus est et, missis exercitibus suis, perdidit homicidas illos et civitatem illorum succendit. [8]Tunc ait servis suis: "Nuptiae quidem paratae sunt, sed qui invitati erant, non fuerunt digni; [9]ite ergo ad exitus viarum et quoscumque inveneritis, vocate ad nuptias". [10]Et egressi servi illi in vias, congregaverunt omnes, quos invenerunt, malos et bonos; et impletae sunt nuptiae discumbentium. [11]Intravit autem rex, ut videret discumbentes, et vidit ibi hominem non vestitum veste nuptiali [12]et ait illi: "Amice, quomodo huc intrasti, non habens vestem nuptialem?". At ille obmutuit. [13]Tunc dixit rex ministris: "Ligate pedes eius et manus et mittite eum in tenebras exteriores: ibi erit fletus et stridor dentium". [14]Multi enim sunt vocati, pauci vero electi». [15]Tunc abeuntes pharisaei consilium inierunt, ut caperent eum in sermone. [16]Et mittunt ei discipulos suos cum hero-

rounds off the message contained in the two previous parables. Israel (represented in the parable by the first people to be invited to the feast) not only refused to partake of the Lord's banquet, his call to salvation, but went so far as to ill-treat and kill the messengers sent her by the Lord; therefore, a dire future awaits her (v. 7). Rejected by Israel, God calls all mankind to join the Church, the new People of God. However, as we have already seen in the parables of the weeds and the dragnet (cf. 13:24–50), "both bad and good" (v. 10) respond to this call, and not all prove worthy, because not all are truly converted and wear their wedding garment to the feast. This episode is a call to vigilance for those who already form part of the Church: Israel's downfall (v. 7) signals our own, if we prove unworthy of our election (v. 13). "What are we to understand by the image of the wedding garment, if not charity? He who enters the wedding feast without the wedding garment is like one who belongs to

the Church, having faith but no love" (St Gregory the Great, *Homiliae in Evangelia*, 2, 18, 9).

22:15–22 Herodians were supporters of the regime of Herod and his dynasty: they were not in favour of direct rule by Rome (and the direct taxation that came with it), exercised by a governor, and they preferred to be governed by a local prince, who was responsible for the payment of part of the Roman taxes. In religious matters, Herodians shared the same kind of pragmatic views that were typical of Sadducees. Pharisees, on the other hand, were zealously observant of the Law, and they regarded both the Romans and the Herodians as usurpers. They were, then, radically different from the Herodians—and yet both parties combined to conspire against Jesus. The question put to Jesus here was a difficult one, and any reply was bound to be controversial. Jesus, however, manages to give an answer that is compatible with everything he has been

know that you are true, and teach the way of God truthfully, and care for no man; for you do not regard the position of men. [17]Tell us, then, what you think. Is it lawful to pay taxes to Caesar, or not?" [18]But Jesus, aware of their malice, said, "Why put me to the test, you hypocrites? [19]Show me the money for the tax." And they brought him a coin.[r] [20]And Jesus said to them, "Whose likeness and inscription is this?" [21]They said, "Caesar's." Then he said to them, "Render therefore to Caesar the things that are Caesar's, and to God the things that are God's." [22]When they heard it, they marvelled; and they left him and went away.

Rom 13:7

Jn 8:9

Mk 12:18–27
Lk 20:27–40

Acts 23:6, 8

Gen 38:8
Deut 25:5–6

The resurrection of the dead

[23]The same day Sadducees came to him, who say that there is no resurrection; and they asked him a question, [24]saying, "Teacher, Moses said, 'If a man dies, having no children, his brother must marry the widow, and raise up children for his brother.' [25]Now there were seven brothers among us; the first married, and died, and having no children left his wife to his brother. [26]So too the second and third, down to the seventh. [27]After them all, the woman died. [28]In the resurrection, therefore, to which of the seven will she be wife? For they all had her."

[29]But Jesus answered them, "You are wrong, because you know neither the scriptures nor the power of God. [30]For in the resurrection they neither marry nor are given in marriage, but are like angels[s] in heaven. [31]And as for the resurrection of the dead,

dianis dicentes: «Magister, scimus quia verax es et viam Dei in veritate doces et non est tibi cura de aliquo; non enim respicis personam hominum. [17]Dic ergo nobis quid tibi videatur: Licet censum dare Caesari an non?». [18]Cognita autem Iesus nequitia eorum, ait: «Quid me tentatis, hypocritae? [19]Ostendite mihi nomisma census». At illi obtulerunt ei denarium. [20]Et ait illis: «Cuius est imago haec et suprascriptio?». [21]Dicunt ei: «Caesaris». Tunc ait illis: «Reddite ergo, quae sunt Caesaris, Caesari et, quae sunt Dei, Deo». [22]Et audientes mirati sunt et relicto eo abierunt. [23]In illo die accesserunt ad eum sadducaei, qui dicunt non esse resurrectionem, et interrogaverunt eum [24]dicentes: «Magister, Moyses dixit, *si quis mortuus fuerit non habens filios, ut ducat frater eius uxorem illius et suscitet semen fratri suo*. [25]Erant autem apud nos septem fratres: et primus, uxore ducta, defunctus est et non habens semen reliquit uxorem suam fratri suo; [26]similiter secundus et tertius usque ad septimum. [27]Novissime autem omnium mulier defuncta est. [28]In resurrectione ergo cuius erit de septem uxor? Omnes enim habuerunt eam». [29]Respondens autem Iesus ait illis: «Erratis nescientes Scripturas neque virtutem Dei; [30]in resurrectione enim neque nubent neque nubentur, sed sunt sicut angeli in caelo. [31]De res-

saying about the Kingdom of God: Give to Caesar what is his, but give to God the things that are God's. These words have been a source used by the Church for her teaching about civil authority (which is responsible for the temporal common good) and church authority (whose province is spiritual welfare). Each of these two authorities is autonomous within its sphere; therefore, if Christians, acting with authentic freedom, choose a particular solution for matters that fall within the temporal sphere, we "ought to remember that in those cases no one is permitted to identify the authority of the Church exclusively with his own opinion" (Vatican II, *Gaudium et spes*, 43). Jesus, in his reply, recognizes the rights of civil authorities (cf. the notes on Rom 13:1–7 and 1 Pet 2:13–17), without compromising the authority of God (cf. Vatican II, *Dignitatis humanae*, 11).

22:23–33 These verses convey the style of

debate typical of teachers in that era. The Sadducees put forward to Jesus a highly theoretical case which may have been inspired by the story of Sarah, the daughter of Raguel, and her seven husbands (Tob 3:8). If the levirate law (see Deut 25:5–10) had to be adhered to, then the case seemed to suggest that there could be no life after death. The Sadducees (Jesus answers) have failed to understand the Scriptures if they believe that the levirate law applies in the afterlife; but, above all, they underestimate the power of God (v. 30): he maintains men in being, even after they have died, and in the resurrection of the body gives them a mode of life similar to that of angels, one in which marriage will no longer be necessary. This teaching, in effect, ratifies that of the resurrection of the dead and that of beatitude in heaven (cf. the note on Lk 20:27–40). At the end of the passage the evangelist delights in recalling the people's amazement at the clarity and depth of this teaching.

r Greek *a denarius*   s Other ancient authorities add *of God*

have you not read what was said to you by God, [32]'I am the God of Abraham, and the God of Isaac, and the God of Jacob'? He is not God of the dead, but of the living." [33]And when the crowd heard it, they were astonished at his teaching.

Ex 3:6

The greatest commandment of all

Mk 12:28–34
Lk 10:25–28

[34]But when the Pharisees heard that he had silenced the Sadducees, they came together. [35]And one of them, a lawyer, asked him a question, to test him. [36]"Teacher, which is the great commandment in the law?" [37]And he said to him, "You shall love the Lord your God with all your heart, and with all your soul, and with all your mind. [38]This is the great and first commandment. [39]And a second is like it, You shall love your neighbour as yourself. [40]On these two commandments depend all the law and the prophets."

Deut 6:5

Lev 19:18
Mt 5:43; 7:12

Rom 13:10
Gal 5:14

The divinity of the Messiah

Mk 12:35–37
Lk 20:41–44

[41]Now while the Pharisees were gathered together, Jesus asked them a question, [42]saying, "What do you think of the Christ? Whose son is he?" They said to him, "The son of David." [43]He said to them, "How is it then that David, inspired by the Spirit,[t] calls him Lord, saying,

Jn 7:42

[44] 'The Lord said to my Lord,
    Sit at my right hand,
    till I put thy enemies under thy feet'?

Ps 110:1
Acts 2:34f

urrectione autem mortuorum non legistis, quod dictum est vobis a Deo dicente: [32]"*Ego sum Deus Abraham et Deus Isaac et Deus Iacob*"? Non est Deus mortuorum sed viventium». [33]Et audientes turbae mirabantur in doctrina eius. [34]Pharisaei autem audientes quod silentium imposuisset sadducaeis, convenerunt in unum. [35]Et interrogavit unus ex eis legis doctor tentans eum: [36]«Magister, quod est mandatum magnum in Lege?». [37]Ait autem illi: «*Diliges Dominum Deum tuum in toto corde tuo et in tota anima tua* et in tota mente tua: [38]hoc est magnum et primum mandatum. [39]Secundum autem simile est huic: *Diliges proximum tuum sicut teipsum*. [40]In his duobus mandatis universa Lex pendet et Prophetae». [41]Congregatis autem pharisaeis, interrogavit eos Iesus [42]dicens: «Quid vobis videtur de Christo? Cuius filius est?». Dicunt ei: «David». [43]Ait illis:

22:34–40 Here Jesus replies to a question put by Pharisees, whose main concern is to ensure full compliance with all the precepts of the Mosaic laws (the list ran to 613 items). He teaches that the entire Law is contained in the two commandments of love (Deut 6:5; Lev 19:18).

Matthew's account of this teaching is distinctive: the scribe asks what is the main commandment of the Law (v. 36), and Jesus replies with a dual commandment or, rather, with two commandments which form a unit; in any event, he makes it clear that this commandment is greater than all the rest: "Neither of these loves is whole if it lacks the other, for you cannot truly love God if you do not love your neighbour, nor truly love your neighbour if you do not love God. [...] This is the only true proof of our love for God: that we love and help and care for our brothers" (St Bede, *Homiliae*, 2, 22). God is to be loved above all things, because love for one's neighbour is a consequence of love for God, and, when man is loved, God is loved, because man is

the image of God (see St Thomas Aquinas, *Sup. Ev. Matt.*, in loc). On the subject of how great our love for God should be, St Bernard wrote: "You ask me for what reason and by what method or means God ought to be loved. My answer is that the reason to love God is God; the method and means are to love him without method or means" (*De diligendo Deo*, 1, 1).

22:41–46 God promised King David that one of his descendants would reign forever (2 Sam 7:12 ff); this was obviously a reference to the Messiah, and it was interpreted as such by all Jewish tradition, which gave the Messiah the title of "Son of David". In Jesus' time this messianic title had come to be understood in a very nationalistic sense: the Jews were expecting an earthly king, a descendant of David, who would free them from Roman rule. Jesus' reply to the Pharisees about the meaning of Psalm 110:1 leaves them at a loss for words. To reply correctly, they would have to accept the pre-exis-

t Or *David in the Spirit*

Mk 12:34
Lk 20:40

⁴⁵If David thus calls him Lord, how is he his son?" ⁴⁶And no one was able to answer him a word, nor from that day did any one dare to ask him any more questions.

Mk 12:38–40
Lk 11:37–54;
20:45–47

Jesus berates the scribes and Pharisees

Deut 17:10
Mal 2:7–8
Mt 11:30

23 ¹ Then said Jesus to the crowds and to his disciples, ²"The scribes and the Pharisees sit on Moses' seat; ³so practise and observe whatever they tell you, but not what they do; for they preach, but do not practise. ⁴They bind heavy burdens, hard to bear,ᵘ and lay them on men's shoulders; but they themselves will not move them with their finger. ⁵They do all their deeds to be seen by men; for they make their phylacteries* broad and their fringes long, ⁶and they love the place of honour at feasts and the best seats in the synagogues, ⁷and salutations in the market places, and being called rabbi by men. ⁸But you are not to be called rabbi, for you have one teacher, and you are all brethren. ⁹And call no man your father on earth, for you have one Father, who is in heaven.* ¹⁰Neither be called masters, for you have one master, the Christ. ¹¹He who is greatest among you shall be your servant; ¹²whoever exalts himself will be humbled, and whoever humbles himself will be exalted.

Num 15:38–39

Lk 14:7
Jn 5:44

Jn 13:13
Prov 29:23

Mt 20:26–27
Mk 9:35; 10:43
Lk 9:48; 22:26
1 Pet 5:5

Lk 14:11; 18:14

«Quomodo ergo David in Spiritu vocat eum Dominum dicens: ⁴⁴"*Dixit Dominus Domino meo: Sede a dextris meis, / donec ponam inimicos tuos sub pedibus tuis*"? ⁴⁵Si ergo David vocat eum Dominum, quomodo filius eius est?». ⁴⁶Et nemo poterat respondere ei verbum, neque ausus fuit quisquam ex illa die eum amplius interrogare.   [23] ¹Tunc Iesus locutus est ad turbas et ad discipulos suos ²dicens: «Super cathedram Moysis sederunt scribae et pharisaei. ³Omnia ergo, quaecumque dixerint vobis, facite et servate; secundum opera vero eorum nolite facere: dicunt enim et non faciunt. ⁴Alligant autem onera gravia et importabilia et imponunt in umeros hominum, ipsi autem digito suo nolunt ea movere. ⁵Omnia vero opera sua faciunt, ut videantur ab hominibus: dilatant enim phylacteria sua et magnificant fimbrias, ⁶amant autem primum recubitum in cenis et primas cathedras in synagogis ⁷et salutationes in foro et vocari ab hominibus Rabbi. ⁸Vos autem nolite vocari Rabbi; unus enim est Magister vester, omnes autem vos fratres estis. ⁹Et Patrem nolite vocare vobis super terram, unus enim est Pater vester, caelestis. ¹⁰Nec vocemini Magistri, quia Magister vester unus est, Christus. ¹¹Qui maior est vestrum, erit minister vester. ¹²Qui autem se exaltaverit, humiliabitur; et, qui se humiliaverit, exaltabitur. ¹³Vae autem vobis, scribae et pharisaei hypocritae, quia clauditis regnum caelorum ante homines! Vos enim non intratis nec

tence and divinity of the Messiah (because he was prior to, and called "Lord" by, David), and at the same time acknowledge that he is truly man (son of David, Messiah). Jesus' answer implies an invitation to believe in him as the Son of God *and* a descendant in the line of David. It is, in effect, a reference to the mystery of there being two natures (divine and human) in the one person of the Word, Jesus Christ: "The two natures are whole and united in one person: majesty took on humility, strength weakness, and eternity mortality. To pay the debt caused by our sinfulness, the perfect divine nature was joined to our changeable human nature: true God and true man in the one Person of our Lord. [...] That was the birth, my beloved brothers, ordained for Christ, the power and wisdom of God. He made himself equal to us in his humanity, and was far superior to us in his divinity. If he had not been truly God, he could not have saved us; and if he had not been truly man, he could not have given us good example" (St Leo the Great, *Sermo 1 in Nativitate Domini*, 2–3).

23:1–36 Here, as in other places in the New Testament, one should not read an unqualified condemnation of scribes and Pharisees. In fact, at the end of the discourse, our Lord speaks of scribes who will undergo the same rigours as himself, and elsewhere (e.g. 13:52) it is taken for granted that there will be Christian scribes who will instruct the disciples about the mysteries of the Kingdom of heaven. However, clearly the passage includes a serious charge against those scribes and Pharisees who were more interested in their public image than in living in accordance with the truth.

The discourse has two main parts: the first (vv. 1–12) is addressed to the people at large and to the disciples; the second (the famous "woes" section: vv. 13–32) is directed to the scribes and Pharisees. Both parts have a common theme: Christ seeks not to abolish the Law as taught by the scribes and Pharisees (see vv. 3 and 23) but to purify that teaching and bring it to perfection.

The early verses (1–12) contrast the practice of scribes and Pharisees with that expected of Christian teachers. The former "preach, but do

u Other ancient authorities omit *hard to bear*

¹³"But woe to you, scribes and Pharisees, hypocrites! because you shut the kingdom of heaven against men; for you neither enter yourselves, nor allow those who would enter to go in.ᵛ ¹⁵Woe to you, scribes and Pharisees, hypocrites! for you traverse sea and land to make a single proselyte, and when he becomes a proselyte, you make him twice as much a child of hellʷ as yourselves.

¹⁶"Woe to you, blind guides, who say, 'If any one swears by the temple, it is nothing; but if any one swears by the gold of the temple, he is bound by his oath.' ¹⁷You blind fools! For which is greater, the gold or the temple that has made the gold sacred? ¹⁸And you say, 'If any one swears by the altar, it is nothing; but if any one swears by the gift that is on the altar, he is bound by his oath.' ¹⁹You blind men! For which is greater, the gift or the altar that makes the gift sacred? ²⁰So he who swears by the altar, swears by it and by everything on it; ²¹and he who swears by the temple, swears by it and by him who dwells in it; ²²and he who swears by heaven, swears by the throne of God and by him who sits upon it.

Ex 29:37

²³"Woe to you, scribes and Pharisees, hypocrites! for you tithe mint and dill and cummin, and have neglected the weightier matters of the law, justice and mercy and

Lev 27:30
Lk 18:12

introeuntes sinitis intrare. ⁽¹⁴⁾ ¹⁵Vae vobis, scribae et pharisaei hypocritae, quia circuitis mare et aridam, ut faciatis unum proselytum, et cum fuerit factus, facitis eum filium gehennae duplo quam vos! ¹⁶Vae vobis, duces caeci, qui dicitis: "Quicumque iuraverit per templum, nihil est; quicumque autem iuraverit in auro templi, debet". ¹⁷Stulti et caeci! Quid enim maius est: aurum an templum, quod sanctificat aurum? ¹⁸Et: "Quicumque iuraverit in altari, nihil est; quicumque autem iuraverit in dono, quod est super illud, debet". ¹⁹Caeci! Quid enim maius est: donum an altare, quod sanctificat donum? ²⁰Qui ergo iuraverit in altari, iurat in eo et in omnibus, quae super illud sunt; ²¹et, qui iuraverit in templo, iurat in illo et in eo, qui inhabitat in ipso; ²²et, qui iuraverit in caelo, iurat in throno Dei et in eo, qui sedet super eum. ²³Vae vobis, scribae et pharisaei hypocritae, quia decimatis mentam et anethum et cyminum et reliquistis, quae graviora sunt legis: iudicium et misericordiam et fidem! Haec oportuit facere et illa non omittere. ²⁴Duces caeci, excolantes culicem, camelum autem glutientes. ²⁵Vae vobis, scribae et pharisaei hypocritae, quia mundatis, quod de

not practise" (v. 3) and they seek the highest positions in the community (v. 6); the latter should be humble servants (vv. 11–12). Jesus gives some specific examples (vv. 7–10): rabbi, father and teacher were titles of honour given to those who taught the Law of Moses. When Jesus tells his disciples not to accept these titles, he is saying that Christians should seek to serve, rather than to be honoured. St Augustine sums this up very well in a well-known sentence: "We are leaders and servants: we lead when we serve" (*Sermones*, 340a).

The "woes" section (vv. 13–32) spells out in detail the sad consequences and the inconsistencies that stem from a purely external practice of the Law. Two descriptions run through the passage as a motif—"hypocrites" (vv. 13, 15, 23, 25, 27, 29) and "blind" (vv. 16, 24, 26). The word "hypocrite" originally meant an on-stage actor (cf. 6:1–18); and a person who is always on a stage runs the risk of becoming a charlatan, because someone who always tries to appear good to others' eyes tends to be ignorant of his true self. Hypocrisy leads to blindness and meaninglessness. Jesus conveys this very graphically

when he talks about straining out a gnat and swallowing a camel: these people are scrupulous about even the tiniest impurity (the gnat, *qamla* in Aramaic, could be technically regarded as unclean: see Lev 11:20–24), and yet they commit grave sins; the camel (*gamla* in Aramaic) is a huge animal, and one expressly declared impure (Lev 11:4).

Our Lord tells us the right road to take (v. 3): we should imitate God in the virtues he proclaims to his people—justice, mercy and faith: "The greatness of our virtue must consist in the triumph of mercy over judgement. It is fitting that the creature, made in his image and likeness, should imitate its Creator. [...] Christian virtue surpasses that of the scribes and the Pharisees not by abolishing the Law but by understanding and applying it in a non-literal way [...]. There is often the appearance of virtue and a deceptive reputation of holiness without regard to the interior disposition of the soul; and what is no more than evil and sin hidden in the heart receives the false praise of men. The soul that truly loves God desires only to please him; the greatest reward we can desire is love itself. Love comes

v Other authorities add here (or after verse 12) verse 14, *Woe to you, scribes and Pharisees, hypocrites! for you devour widows' houses and for a pretence you make long prayers; therefore you will receive the greater condemnation* w Greek *Gehenna*

faith; these you ought to have done, without neglecting the others. ²⁴You blind guides, straining out a gnat and swallowing a camel!

Mk 7:4

Tit 1:15
Jn 9:40

²⁵"Woe to you, scribes and Pharisees, hypocrites! for you cleanse the outside of the cup and of the plate, but inside they are full of extortion and rapacity. ²⁶You blind Pharisee! first cleanse the inside of the cup and of the plate, that the outside also may be clean.

Acts 23:3

Lk 16:15

²⁷"Woe to you, scribes and Pharisees, hypocrites! for you are like whitewashed tombs, which outwardly appear beautiful, but within they are full of dead men's bones and all uncleanness. ²⁸So you also outwardly appear righteous to men, but within you are full of hypocrisy and iniquity.

²⁹"Woe to you, scribes and Pharisees, hypocrites! for you build the tombs of the prophets and adorn the monuments of the righteous, ³⁰saying, 'If we had lived in the days of our fathers, we would not have taken part with them in shedding the blood of

Acts 7:52

Mt 3:7

1 Thess 2:15

the prophets.' ³¹Thus you witness against yourselves, that you are sons of those who murdered the prophets. ³²Fill up, then, the measure of your fathers. ³³You serpents, you brood of vipers, how are you to escape being sentenced to hell?ʷ ³⁴Therefore I send you prophets and wise men and scribes, some of whom you will kill and crucify, and some

Gen 4:8, 10
2 Chron 24:20–21
Mt 27:25

you will scourge in your synagogues and persecute from town to town, ³⁵that upon you may come all the righteous blood shed on earth, from the blood of innocent Abel to the blood of Zechariah the son of Barachiah, whom you murdered between the sanctuary and the altar. ³⁶Truly, I say to you, all this will come upon this generation.

Lk 13:34–35

Jerusalem admonished

Acts 7:59
1 Thess 2:15

³⁷"O Jerusalem, Jerusalem, killing the prophets and stoning those who are sent to you! How often would I have gathered your children together as a hen gathers her

---

foris est calicis et paropsidis, intus autem pleni sunt rapina et immunditia! ²⁶Pharisaee caece, munda prius, quod intus est calicis, ut fiat et id, quod de foris eius est, mundum. ²⁷Vae vobis, scribae et pharisaei hypocritae, quia similes estis sepulcris dealbatis, quae a foris quidem parent speciosa, intus vero plena sunt ossibus mortuorum et omni spurcitia! ²⁸Sic et vos a foris quidem paretis hominibus iusti, intus autem pleni estis hypocrisi et iniquitate. ²⁹Vae vobis, scribae et pharisaei hypocritae, qui aedificatis sepulcra prophetarum et ornatis monumenta iustorum ³⁰et dicitis: "Si fuissemus in diebus patrum nostrorum, non essemus socii eorum in sanguine prophetarum"! ³¹Itaque testimonio estis vobismetipsis quia filii estis eorum, qui prophetas occiderunt. ³²Et vos implete mensuram patrum vestrorum. ³³Serpentes, genimina viperarum, quomodo fugietis a iudicio gehennae? ³⁴Ideo ecce ego mitto ad vos prophetas et sapientes et scribas; ex illis occidetis et crucifigetis et ex eis flagellabitis in synagogis vestris et persequemini de civitate in civitatem, ³⁵ut veniat super vos omnis sanguis iustus, qui effusus est super terram a sanguine Abel iusti usque ad

---

from God; God himself is love. The pious soul seeks his fulfilment in him and hopes for no other reward" (St Leo the Great, *Sermones*, 92, 1–2).

The discourse ends with a prophetic lament (vv. 33–36): just as the prophets suffered (and died) because of their contemporaries' unbelief, so too will the first Christians suffer at the hands of narrow-minded scribes and Pharisees.

Some manuscripts of Matthew's Gospel, apparently influenced by Mark 12:40 and Luke 20:47, add a verse 14: see the RSV note **v**.

23:37–39 The tone of indignation in the previous verses now changes to one of sorrow. In a certain way, Jesus' moving remarks sum up the whole history of salvation, and they are a

testimony to his divinity. Who if not God was the source of all the acts of mercy that mark the stages of Israel's history? The image of protection by wings, which is used often in the Old Testament to describe God's love and protection of his people (cf. Deut 32:11; Ps 17:8; 36:7; 57:1; 61:4; 63:7), is one which Jesus now applies with himself as the protector. By recalling the fate of the prophets sent to Jerusalem (v. 37), he is hinting at what will happen to himself. The Holy City has resisted all the unique graces offered it by God. Jerusalem should serve as a warning to Christians not to harden their hearts against God's calls: Christ has set us free (Gal 5:1), but we have a terrible capacity to reject God's grace.

brood under her wings, and you would not! ³⁸Behold, your house is forsaken and
desolate.ˣ ³⁹For I tell you, you will not see me again, until you say, 'Blessed is he
who comes in the name of the Lord.' ".

Jer 12:7; 22:5
Ps 69:25
1 Kings 9:7–8
Mt 21:9
Ps 118:26

11. THE ESCHATOLOGICAL DISCOURSE*

Announcement of the destruction of the temple

Mk 13:1–2
Lk 21:5–6

24 ¹Jesus left the temple and was going away, when his disciples came to point
out to him the buildings of the temple.* ²But he answered them, "You see
all these, do you not? Truly, I say to you, there will not be left here one stone upon
another, that will not be thrown down."

Lk 19:44

The beginning of tribulations. Persecution on account of the Gospel

Mk 13:3–13
Lk 21:7–19

³As he sat on the Mount of Olives, the disciples came to him privately, saying, "Tell
us, when will this be, and what will be the sign of your coming and of the close of

sanguinem Zachariae filii Barachiae, quem occidistis inter templum et altare. ³⁶Amen dico vobis: Venient haec omnia super generationem istam. ³⁷Ierusalem, Ierusalem, quae occidis prophetas et lapidas eos, qui ad te missi sunt, quotiens volui congregare filios tuos, quemadmodum gallina congregat pullos suos sub alas, et noluisti! ³⁸*Ecce relinquitur vobis domus vestra deserta!* ³⁹Dico enim vobis: Non me videbitis amodo, donec dicatis: "*Benedictus, qui venit in nomine Domini!*"». [24] ¹Et egressus Iesus de templo ibat, et accesserunt discipuli eius, ut ostenderent ei aedificationes templi; ²ipse autem respondens dixit eis: «Non videtis haec omnia? Amen dico vobis: Non relinquetur hic lapis super lapidem, qui non destruetur». ³Sedente autem eo super montem Oliveti, accesserunt ad eum discipuli secreto dicentes: «Dic nobis: Quando haec erunt, et quod signum adventus tui et

*24:1—25:46 Jesus' Eschatological Discourse
(the fifth discourse in St Matthew) appears in all
the Synoptics. Matthew's account is the longest,
and it is brought to a close in the parables of
chapter 25. The theme running through the discourse is an exhortation to watchfulness and
hope, and to making our talents bear fruit.

This discourse marks the end of Jesus' public
ministry and leads into the account of the passion.
Given its position in the narrative, it has a tone of
leavetaking, like the "Farewell Discourse" in St
John's Gospel (Jn 13:1—17:26). As do some apocryphal writings of the time (such as *The Assumption of Moses* and *The Testimony of the Twelve
Patriarchs*), this farewell discourse contains
apocalyptic language, that is to say, symbols and
imagery that are used to speak of what will
happen. Two distinct events are being prophesied
here—the destruction of Jerusalem, and the end of
this present world, with the coming of Christ in
glory. So, the end of Jerusalem operates as a figure
or type of the later event, the end of the world.

Drawing from this shared source, each of the
Synoptics puts greater stress on some themes
rather than others (cf. the notes on Mk 13:1–37
and Lk 21:5–36). Matthew's emphasis is on the
vigilance which Christians ought to have, and
which should manifest itself in service to others;

those who have special responsibility for their
brethren need to be especially watchful (24:45–
51), for they should remember that the trials the
disciples undergo will be very severe (vv. 9–12).
At the same time, we need to have an attitude of
"tense hope", for the Lord will come suddenly
(v. 27), at the time we least suspect (v. 50), without forewarning (vv. 36–41).

24:1–2 The temple of Jerusalem, a truly
magnificent building, was the pride of the Jews.
Its enormous granite blocks produced an
overwhelming impression of permanence, and the
disciples were amazed by it (cf. the note on Lk
21:5–6). The prophecy by Christ that "there will
not be left here one stone upon another" (v. 2) was
fulfilled in the year 70, when the Roman legions
of Titus razed the city to the ground. But that
destruction betokened something more: it was a
consequence and a sign of the fact that the temple
was now redundant. Jesus' words are in line with
what he said earlier when he signalled the three
themes found in this discourse—the persecutions
that would occur in that generation (23:36–37),
the disappearance of the temple (23:38), and the
coming of Christ in glory (23:39).

24:3–14 In v. 3 the disciples, impressed by

x Other ancient authorities omit *and desolate*

Jn 5:43
Acts 5:36–37
1 Jn 2:18

the age?" ⁴And Jesus answered them, "Take heed that no one leads you astray. ⁵For many will come in my name, saying, 'I am the Christ,' and they will lead many astray. ⁶And you will hear of wars and rumours of wars; see that you are not alarmed; for this must take place, but the end is not yet. ⁷For nation will rise against nation, and kingdom against kingdom, and there will be famines and earthquakes in various places: ⁸all this is but the beginning of the sufferings.

Is 19:2
Mt 10:17–22
Jn 16:2–4
Dan 11:41
1 Jn 4:1
Mt 24:23
2 Thess 2:10
2 Tim 3:1–5
Mt 10:22
Rev 13:10
Mt 28:29

⁹"Then they will deliver you up to tribulation, and put you to death; and you will be hated by all nations for my name's sake. ¹⁰And then many will fall away,ʸ and betray one another, and hate one another. ¹¹And many false prophets will arise and lead many astray. ¹²And because wickedness is multiplied, most men's love will grow cold. ¹³But he who endures to the end will be saved. ¹⁴And this gospel of the kingdom will be preached throughout the whole world, as a testimony to all nations; and then the end will come.

Mk 13:14–23
Lk 21:20–24
Dan 9:27; 11:31;
12:11
Mk 13:14–23
1 Mac 1:54

The great tribulation

¹⁵"So when you see the desolating sacrilege spoken of by the prophet Daniel, standing in the holy place (let the reader understand), ¹⁶then let those who are in Judea flee

consummationis saeculi?». ⁴Et respondens Iesus dixit eis: «Videte, ne quis vos seducat. ⁵Multi enim venient in nomine meo dicentes: "Ego sum Christus", et multos seducent. ⁶Audituri enim estis proelia et opiniones proeliorum. Videte, ne turbemini; oportet enim fieri, sed nondum est finis. ⁷Consurget enim gens in gentem, et regnum in regnum, et erunt fames et terrae motus per loca; ⁸haec autem omnia initia sunt dolorum. ⁹Tunc tradent vos in tribulationem et occident vos, et eritis odio omnibus gentibus propter nomen meum. ¹⁰Et tunc scandalizabuntur multi et invicem tradent et odio habebunt invicem; ¹¹et multi pseudoprophetae surgent et seducent multos. ¹²Et, quoniam abundavit iniquitas, refrigescet caritas multorum; ¹³qui autem permanserit usque in finem, hic salvus erit. ¹⁴Et praedicabitur hoc evangelium regni in universo orbe in testimonium omnibus gentibus; et tunc veniet consummatio. ¹⁵Cum ergo videritis *abominationem desolationis*, quae dicta est a Daniele propheta, stantem *in*

Jesus' dramatic pronouncement, ask him when what he said will come about. They are really asking two questions—one about immediate events and the other about what will signal his second coming (literally, his "Parousia", when Christ comes in glory at the end of time) and the end of the world.

Given the way people of the time thought, the disciples probably saw both events as the same one: if the temple disappeared, it could only mean that the Kingdom of God had definitively come. Our Lord tells them that that is not the case: there are two stages. The first (vv. 4–8) will see the arrival of imposters and a series of dire misfortunes which were seen (in apocalyptic literature) as signs that the end of the world was nigh. But Jesus tells them that "the end is not yet" (v. 6), that these events simply signal "the beginning of the sufferings" (v. 8). With hindsight it is obvious that the times referred to were those prior to the destruction of Jerusalem, which were, in turn, a sign of what Christians will experience over the course of history (vv. 9–14): they will encounter external and internal difficulties (vv. 9–11) so severe that their resolve

will be weakened (v. 12). But they must persevere: committed endurance will ensure their salvation (v. 13). The various tribulations are not signs that the end of the world is coming; they are the normal context for the preaching of the Christian message; the Gospel will be preached "throughout the whole world", to all nations (v. 14). And after that the end will indeed come. What Jesus is saying here spells out a hopeful future for Christians: the end of the world will not be a series of catastrophes but a saving event—the Gospel's spread to the whole world. Our Lord's teaching also shows us that we need to press on in the midst of difficulties: "Discouragement is the enemy of your perseverance. If you don't fight against discouragement, you will become pessimistic first and lukewarm afterwards. Be an optimist" (St Josemaría Escrivá, *The Way*, 988).

24:15–28 The discourse now returns to what our Lord was saying earlier (24:5–8). In the first verses of this passage (vv. 15–22) he seems to be referring specifically to the destruction of Jerusalem and all the unimaginable travails that

y Or *stumble*

to the mountains; [17]let him who is on the housetop not go down to take what is in his house; [18]and let him who is in the field not turn back to take his mantle. [19]And alas for those who are with child and for those who give suck in those days! [20]Pray that your flight may not be in winter or on a sabbath. [21]For then there will be great tribulation, such as has not been from the beginning of the world until now, no, and never will be. [22]And if those days had not been shortened, no human being would be saved; but for the sake of the elect those days will be shortened. [23]Then if any one says to you, 'Lo, here is the Christ!' or 'There he is!' do not believe it. [24]For false Christs and false prophets will arise and show great signs and wonders, so as to lead astray, if possible, even the elect. [25]Lo, I have told you beforehand. [26]So, if they say to you, 'Lo, he is in the wilderness,' do not go out; if they say, 'Lo, he is in the inner rooms,' do not believe it. [27]For as the lightning comes from the east and shines as far as the west, so will be the coming of the Son of man. [28]Wherever the body is, there the eagles[z] will be gathered together.

Lk 17:31

Dan 12:1
Joel 2:2

Lk 17:23–242
2 Pet 3:10

Lk 17:37

The coming of the Son of man

[29]"Immediately after the tribulation of those days the sun will be darkened, and the moon will not give its light, and the stars will fall from heaven, and the powers of the heavens will be shaken; [30]then will appear the sign of the Son of man in heaven, and

Mk 13:24–27
Lk 21:25–28

Is 13:10; 34:4
Hag 2:6, 21
Rev 1:7; 19:11
Mt 26:64
Dan 7:13–14
Zech 12:10ff

loco sancto, qui legit, intellegat: [16]tunc qui in Iudaea sunt, fugiant ad montes; [17]qui in tecto, non descendat tollere aliquid de domo sua; [18]et, qui in agro, non revertatur tollere pallium suum. [19]Vae autem praegnantibus et nutrientibus in illis diebus! [20]Orate autem, ut non fiat fuga vestra hieme vel sabbato: [21]erit enim tunc *tribulatio* magna, *qualis non fuit ab initio mundi usque modo* neque fiet. [22]Et nisi breviati fuissent dies illi, non fieret salva omnis caro; sed propter electos breviabuntur dies illi. [23]Tunc si quis vobis dixerit: "Ecce hic Christus" aut: "Hic", nolite credere. [24]Surgent enim pseudochristi et pseudoprophetae et dabunt signa magna et prodigia, ita ut in errorem inducantur, si fieri potest, etiam electi. [25]Ecce praedixi vobis. [26]Si ergo dixerint vobis: "Ecce in deserto est", nolite exire; "Ecce in penetralibus", nolite credere: [27]sicut enim fulgur exit ab oriente et paret usque in occidentem, ita erit adventus Filii hominis. [28]Ubicumque fuerit corpus, illuc congregabuntur aquilae. [29]Statim autem post tribulationem dierum illorum, *sol obscurabitur, et luna non dabit lumen suum, et stellae cadent* de caelo, *et virtutes caelorum* commovebuntur. [30]Et tunc parebit

that will involve (cf. v. 21). To denominate this terrible event, Jesus uses the phrase "the desolating sacrilege", referring to the "abomination of desolation", spoken of in the book of Daniel (9:27; 11:31; 12:11), when the prophet speaks of the idolatrous Antiochus IV Epiphanes, who occupied the temple with his troops and placed images of false gods on the altar of burnt offerings (1 Mac 1:54). Our Lord is applying that episode from the history of Israel to the future destruction of Jerusalem: that is why he calls attention to the passage in Daniel ("let the reader understand"). A new abomination, he says, will occur, ruining the temple to make way for idolatrous worship—as would happen in fact in the year AD 70, when the Roman armies destroyed and profaned the temple, and again later under Hadrian, who ordered the erection of a statue of Jupiter on its ruins.

Our Lord then (vv. 25–28) announces further calamities: amid all these trials, false prophets and messiahs will appear (v. 24), who will perform false signs and wonders. They will try to

pass themselves off as the true Christ who is to come (v. 26). Jesus has a single word of warning for all these eventualities: "Do not believe it" (vv. 23, 26). The Son of man will not come in a hidden way or only for the sake of certain individuals; he will come like lightning that lights up all the earth (v. 27).

24:29–31 In the preceding verses (24:27–28), our Lord has already announced his future return in glory. The sign of the "Son of man" (v. 30) will be his coming; the end of the world will not be a series of calamities, but his definitive coming in triumph. Certainly, it will not be an ordinary event: his light will be so dazzling that the entire cosmos will appear to be in total darkness (v. 29): "Not because the light has failed, but because in comparison to the true Light, everything appears to be in darkness" (St Jerome, *Commentarii in Matthaeum*, 24, 29); his truth will shine so bright that the nations will realize how unworthy of him they are (v. 30), and therefore, "those who think themselves to be

z Or *vultures*

1 Cor 15:52
1 Thess 4:16
Rev 8:1–2
Is 27:13
Zech 2:6
Deut 30:4

then all the tribes of the earth will mourn, and they will see the Son of man coming on the clouds of heaven with power and great glory; [31]and he will send out his angels with a loud trumpet call, and they will gather his elect from the four winds, from one end of heaven to the other.

Mk 13:28–31
Lk 21:29–33

The end will surely come. The lesson of the fig tree

Mt 16:28
Mk 9:1
Lk 9:27

[32]"From the fig tree learn its lesson: as soon as its branch becomes tender and puts forth its leaves, you know that summer is near. [33]So also, when you see all these things, you know that he is near, at the very gates. [34]Truly, I say to you, this generation will not pass away till all these things take place. [35]Heaven and earth will pass away, but my words will not pass away.

Mk 13:32–37
Lk 17:22–37

The time of the second coming of Christ

1 Thess 5:1–2
Gen 6:11–13
Lk 12:39–40
Gen 7:7–13
2 Pet 3:5–6

[36]"But of that day and hour no one knows, not even the angels of heaven, nor the Son,[a] but the Father only. [37]As were the days of Noah, so will be the coming of the Son of man. [38]For as in those days before the flood they were eating and drinking, marrying and giving in marriage, until the day when Noah entered the ark, [39]and they did not know until the flood came and swept them all away, so will be the

Lk 17:35–36

coming of the Son of man. [40]Then two men will be in the field; one is taken and one

---

signum Filii hominis in caelo, et tunc *plangent omnes tribus terrae* et videbunt *Filium hominis venientem in nubibus caeli* cum virtute et gloria multa; [31]et mittet angelos suos cum tuba magna, et congregabunt electos eius a quattuor ventis, a summis caelorum usque ad terminos eorum. [32]Ab arbore autem fici discite parabolam: cum iam ramus eius tener fuerit, et folia nata, scitis quia prope est aestas. [33]Ita et vos, cum videritis haec omnia, scitote quia prope est in ianuis. [34]Amen dico vobis: Non praeteribit haec generatio, donec omnia haec fiant. [35]Caelum et terra transibunt, verba vero mea non praeteribunt. [36]De die autem illa et hora nemo scit, neque angeli caelorum neque Filius, nisi Pater solus. [37]Sicut enim dies Noe, ita erit adventus Filii hominis. [38]Sicut enim erant in diebus ante diluvium comedentes et bibentes, nubentes et nuptum tradentes, usque ad eum diem, quo introivit in arcam Noe, [39]et non cognoverunt, donec venit diluvium et tulit omnes, ita erit et adventus Filii hominis. [40]Tunc duo

---

saints but do not fear the presence of the Judge will be exposed for their pride" (ibid.). But, for his chosen ones, the coming of the Son of man will not cause terror; it will bring consolation: they will be gathered together from all over the world to meet him (v. 31). "The sign of the Son of Man is the cross, so that, as Zechariah and John said, the Jews may see the one whom they have pierced—that is, the standard of triumphant victory" (ibid.).

24:32–35 Now comes the answer to another question: When will all that Christ describes take place? Our Lord tells his listeners that these things will surely come about, that his words will stand (v. 35); just as the fig tree signals the coming of summer, so all that he has been saying should be taken as an exhortation to vigilance, for, as he will go on to say (24:36), "of that day and hour no one knows". When he says that "this generation will not pass away till all these things take place" (v. 34), Jesus may be referring to his resurrection as an anticipation of his glorious

second coming, though the word "generation" could also be read in a broader sense, as meaning the time that elapses between the Lord's first coming and the end of the world.

24:36–51 Our Lord says that people will have no foreknowledge of the End. Jesus' words to his disciples are very clear: they will receive no revelation as to the day or hour of the second coming. They must remain vigilant always.

"Of that day and hour no one knows, not even the angels of heaven, nor the Son, but the Father only" (v. 36). From the early days of Christianity, this famous statement has perplexed many interpreters and theologians. It was one of the texts used by Arius (whose opinions were condemned at the first ecumenical council, held in Nicaea in 325) to deny the divinity of Jesus. St Augustine offered an explanation that has been widely accepted: "Our Lord Jesus Christ, who was sent to us to be our Master, has said that not even the Son of Man knows when the day of judgment will come, because it was not

---

a Other ancient authorities omit *nor the Son*

is left. [41]Two women will be grinding at the mill; one is taken and one is left. [42]Watch therefore, for you do not know on what day your Lord is coming. [43]But know this, that if the householder had known in what part of the night the thief was coming, he would have watched and would not have let his house be broken into. [44]Therefore you also must be ready; for the Son of man is coming at an hour you do not expect.

Mt 25:13

Lk 12:39–46
1 Thess 5:2
2 Pet 3:10

Rev 16:15

Parable of the faithful servant

Lk 12:35–48;
21:34–36

[45]"Who then is the faithful and wise servant, whom his master has set over his household, to give them their food at the proper time? [46]Blessed is that servant whom his master when he comes will find so doing. [47]Truly, I say to you, he will set him over all his possessions. [48]But if that wicked servant says to himself, 'My master is delayed,' [49]and begins to beat his fellow servants, and eats and drinks with the drunken, [50]the master of that servant will come on a day when he does not expect him and at an hour he does not know, [51]and will punish[b] him, and put him with the hypocrites; there men will weep and gnash their teeth.

Mt 25:21, 23

Eccles 8:11

Mt 24:42, 44

Mt 8:12

Parable of the wise and foolish maidens

25 [1]"Then the kingdom of heaven shall be compared to ten maidens who took their lamps and went to meet the bridegroom.[c] [2]Five of them were foolish,

Lk 12:35–36
Rev 19:7

---

erunt in agro: unus assumitur, et unus relinquitur. [41]duae molentes in mola: una assumitur, et una relinquitur. [42]Vigilate ergo, quia nescitis qua die Dominus vester venturus sit. [43]Illud autem scitote quoniam si sciret pater familias qua hora fur venturus esset, vigilaret utique et non sineret perfodi domum suam. [44]Ideo et vos estote parati, quia, qua nescitis hora, Filius hominis venturus est. [45]Quis putas est fidelis servus et prudens, quem constituit dominus supra familiam suam, ut det illis cibum in tempore? [46]Beatus ille servus, quem cum venerit dominus eius invenerit sic facientem. [47]Amen dico vobis quoniam super omnia bona sua constituet eum. [48]Si autem dixerit malus servus ille in corde suo: "Moram facit dominus meus venire", [49]et coeperit percutere conservos suos, manducet autem et bibat cum ebriis, [50]veniet dominus servi illius in die, qua non sperat, et in hora, qua ignorat, [51]et dividet eum partemque eius ponet cum hypocritis; illic erit fletus et stridor dentium.   [25] [1]Tunc simile erit regnum caelo-

---

part of the teaching he was sent to give us" (*Enarrationes in Psalmos*, 36, 1). St Thomas Aquinas' interpretation is along similar lines: "To know neither the day nor the hour means not to want to make it known, for when the Apostles questioned him he did not want to reveal it" (*Summa theologiae*, 3, 10, 2 ad 1). St Athanasius (see the note on Mk 13:28–37) offers another interpretation based on the dual nature of Christ.

Jesus refrains from revealing when the day of judgment will come, in order to help us be vigilant. He reinforces his teaching by the parable about the faithful and unfaithful servants (vv. 45–51) and by what he says in the next chapter. Being vigilant with regard to the second coming of Christ does not mean that one must always be on the look-out for signs; it means living our lives at all times in a Christian way. An essential element of Christian watchfulness is examination of conscience: "You have a court of justice at your disposition. [...] Have your conscience act as judge and reason charge you with your

faults. Examine each fault that you find in your soul and have your soul offer its defence: why did you do this, and this, and this? If your soul will not take responsibility for its faults and seeks to put the blame on someone else, say to it: you will not be judged for another's sins. [...] If you examine your conscience every day, you may go with confidence to the court of justice to which all go in fear and trembling" (St John Chrysostom, *In Matthaeum*, 42, 2–4).

25:1–13 This whole chapter consists of a practical application of the teaching contained in the previous one. The message in its two parables (the wise and foolish virgins; the talents) and in the passage at the end about the Last Judgment concerns the need for vigilance.

The parable of the virgins is an exhortation to watchfulness. Our Lord clearly states that it is a parable about the Kingdom of heaven, and it is one of the rare occasions when he speaks of it in the future tense (v. 1). It has to do, therefore,

---

b Or *cut him in pieces*   c Other ancient authorities add *and the bride*

and five were wise. ³For when the foolish took their lamps, they took no oil with them; ⁴but the wise took flasks of oil with their lamps. ⁵As the bridegroom was delayed, they all slumbered and slept. ⁶But at midnight there was a cry, 'Behold, the bridegroom! Come out to meet him.' ⁷Then all those maidens rose and trimmed their lamps. ⁸And the foolish said to the wise, 'Give us some of your oil, for our lamps are going out.' ⁹But the wise replied, 'Perhaps there will not be enough for us and for you; go rather to the dealers and buy for yourselves.' ¹⁰And while they went to buy, the bridegroom came, and those who were ready went in with him to the marriage feast; and the door was shut. ¹¹Afterward the other maidens came also, saying, 'Lord, lord, open to us.' ¹²But he replied, 'Truly, I say to you, I do not know you.' ¹³Watch therefore, for you know neither the day nor the hour.

Lk 13:25, 27

Mt 7:23

Mt 24:42, 50
Mk 13:35–36

Lk 19:11–27   **Parable of the talents**

Mk 13:24

Rom 12:6   ¹⁴"For it will be as when a man going on a journey called his servants and entrusted to them his property; ¹⁵to one he gave five talents,ᵈ to another two, to another one, to each according to his ability. Then he went away. ¹⁶He who had received the five talents went at once and traded with them; and he made five talents more. ¹⁷So also, he

rum decem virginibus, quae accipientes lampades suas exierunt obviam sponso. ²Quinque autem ex eis erant fatuae et quinque prudentes. ³Fatuae enim, acceptis lampadibus suis, non sumpserunt oleum secum; ⁴prudentes vero acceperunt oleum in vasis cum lampadibus suis. ⁵Moram autem faciente sponso, dormitaverunt omnes et dormierunt. ⁶Media autem nocte clamor factus est: "Ecce sponsus! Exite obviam ei". ⁷Tunc surrexerunt omnes virgines illae et ornaverunt lampades suas. ⁸Fatuae autem sapientibus dixerunt: "Date nobis de oleo vestro, quia lampades nostrae exstinguuntur". ⁹Responderunt prudentes dicentes: "Ne forte non sufficiat nobis et vobis, ite potius ad vendentes et emite vobis". ¹⁰Dum autem irent emere, venit sponsus, et quae paratae erant, intraverunt cum eo ad nuptias; et clausa est ianua. ¹¹Novissime autem veniunt et reliquae virgines dicentes: "Domine, Domine, aperi nobis". ¹²At ille respondens ait: "Amen dico vobis: Nescio vos". ¹³Vigilate itaque, quia nescitis diem neque horam. ¹⁴Sicut enim homo peregre proficiscens vocavit servos suos et tradidit illis bona sua. ¹⁵Et uni dedit quinque talenta, alii autem duo, alii vero unum, unicuique secundum propriam virtutem, et profectus est. Statim ¹⁶abiit, qui quinque talenta acceperat, et operatus est in eis et lucratus est alia quinque; ¹⁷similiter qui duo acceperat, lucratus est alia duo. ¹⁸Qui autem unum acceperat, abiens fodit in terra et abscondit pecuniam domini sui.

with Christians who have been called to the Church and who have responded to that call. But they must not simply wait and hope: they must live out their faith: "Christianity is not an easy way of life. It is not enough just to be in the Church, letting the years roll by. In our life, in the life of Christians, our first conversion—that unique moment which each of us remembers, when we clearly understood everything the Lord was asking of us—is certainly very significant. But the later conversions are even more important, and they are increasingly demanding. To facilitate the work of grace in these conversions, we need to keep our soul young; we have to call upon our Lord, know how to listen to him and, having found out what has gone wrong, know how to ask his pardon" (St Josemaría Escrivá, *Christ Is Passing By*, 57).

What is described here is a big, boisterous wedding typical of the East (cf. Jn 2:1–11). The bride, with her relatives and friends, is awaiting the arrival of the bridegroom and his party, to be escorted to his house. In the allegory we can

readily see that the bridegroom stands for Jesus, and the virgins are those invited to the wedding celebration, that is, to the spousal covenant that God makes with his Church. The teaching is clear: it is not enough to be in the Church, simply biding our time until the big day; we need to practise our faith and do good works: "Watch with the heart, watch with faith, watch with love, watch with charity, watch with good works [...]; make ready the lamps, make sure they do not go out [...], renew them with the inner oil of an upright conscience; then shall the Bridegroom enfold you in the embrace of his love and bring you into his banquet room, where your lamp can never be extinguished" (St Augustine, *Sermones*, 93, 17).

25:14–30 A talent was not strictly speaking a coin but a measure of value worth more or less 34 kilos (75 pounds) of silver (cf. the note on 18:21–35). In this parable our Lord is speaking about the need to respond to grace and to keep the effort up our whole life long. All the gifts of

d A talent was more than fifteen years' wages of a labourer

who had the two talents made two talents more. ¹⁸But he who had received the one talent went and dug in the ground and hid his master's money. ¹⁹Now after a long time the master of those servants came and settled accounts with them. ²⁰And he who received the five talents came forward, bringing five talents more, saying, 'Master, you delivered to me five talents; here I have made five talents more.' ²¹His master said to him, 'Well done, good and faithful servant; you have been faithful over a little, I will set you over much; enter into the joy of your master.' ²²And he also who had the two talents came forward, saying, 'Master, you delivered to me two talents; here I have made two talents more.' ²³His master said to him, 'Well done, good and faithful servant; you have been faithful over a little, I will set you over much; enter into the joy of your master.' ²⁴He also who had received the one talent came forward, saying, 'Master, I knew you to be a hard man, reaping where you did not sow, and gathering where you did not winnow; ²⁵so I was afraid, and I went and hid your talent in the ground. Here you have what is yours.' ²⁶But his master answered him, 'You wicked and slothful servant! You knew that I reap where I have not sowed, and gather where I have not winnowed? ²⁷Then you ought to have invested my money with the bankers, and at my coming I should have received what was my own with interest. ²⁸So take the talent from him, and give it to him who has the ten talents. ²⁹For to every one who has will more be given, and he will have abundance; but from him who has not, even what he has will be taken away.* ³⁰And cast the worthless servant into the outer darkness; there men will weep and gnash their teeth.'

Mt 18:23

Lk 16:10
Mt 24:45–47

Lk 12:44

Mt 13:22
Mk 4:25
Lk 8:18; 19:26

Mt 8:12

¹⁹Post multum vero temporis venit dominus servorum illorum et ponit rationem cum eis. ²⁰Et accedens, qui quinque talenta acceperat, obtulit alia quinque talenta dicens: "Domine, quinque talenta tradidisti mihi; ecce alia quinque superlucratus sum". ²¹Ait illi dominus eius: "Euge, serve bone et fidelis. Super pauca fuisti fidelis; supra multa te constituam: intra in gaudium domini tui". ²²Accessit autem et qui duo talenta acceperat, et ait: "Domine, duo talenta tradidisti mihi; ecce alia duo lucratus sum". ²³Ait illi dominus eius: "Euge, serve bone et fidelis. Super pauca fuisti fidelis; supra multa te constituam: intra in gaudium domini tui". ²⁴Accedens autem et qui unum talentum acceperat, ait: "Domine, novi te quia homo durus es: metis, ubi non seminasti, et congregas, ubi non sparsisti; ²⁵et timens abii et abscondi talentum tuum in terra. Ecce habes, quod tuum est". ²⁶Respondens autem dominus eius dixit ei: "Serve male et piger! Sciebas quia meto, ubi non seminavi, et congrego, ubi non sparsi? ²⁷Oportuit ergo te mittere pecuniam meam nummulariis, et veniens ego recepissem, quod meum est cum usura. ²⁸Tollite itaque ab eo talentum et date ei, qui habet decem talenta: ²⁹omni enim habenti dabitur, et abundabit; ei autem, qui non habet, et quod habet, auferetur ab eo. ³⁰Et inutilem servum eicite in tenebras exteriores: illic erit fletus et stridor dentium". ³¹Cum autem venerit Filius hominis in gloria sua, et omnes angeli cum eo, tunc sedebit super

nature and grace that we have received from God should yield their fruit. It does not matter how many gifts we have received; what matters is our generosity in putting them to good use: "I think it is appropriate here to consider how the man who accepted the one talent behaved. He acted in a way which in my part of the world we'd call 'playing the cuckoo'. His petty mind thinks and wonders, then is made up: 'he went off and made a hole in the ground, and there hid his master's money'. What kind of work can our man undertake henceforth, now that he has given up the very tools of his trade? He has opted irresponsibly for the easy way out. He will simply give back what he has received. [...] How sad not to turn to good account and obtain a real profit from the few or many talents that God has given to each man so that he may dedicate himself to the task of serving other souls and the whole of society! When a Christian kills time on this earth, he is putting himself in danger of 'killing Heaven' for himself, that is, if through selfishness, he backs out of things and hides away and doesn't care. A person who loves God not only hands over to the service of Christ what he has and what he is in life. He gives his very self. [...] You think your life is for yourself? Your life is for God, for the good of all men, through your love for our Lord. Your buried talent, dig it up again! Make it yield, and you will taste the joy of knowing that in this supernatural business it does not matter if in this world the results are not wonders that men can admire. What really matters is to hand over all that we are and all that we have, striving to make our talent yield, and constantly exerting ourselves in order to produce good fruit" (St Josemaría Escrivá, *Friends of God*, 45–47).

The Last Judgment

Zech 14:5
Mt 16:27; 19:28
Deut 33:2
Rev 3:21; 20:11–33
Rom 14:10

Ezek 34:17

Is 58:7

Prov 19:17

Mt 7:23
Rev 20:10, 15

[31]"When the Son of man comes in his glory, and all the angels with him, then he will sit on his glorious throne. [32]Before him will be gathered all the nations, and he will separate them one from another as a shepherd separates the sheep from the goats, [33]and he will place the sheep at his right hand, but the goats at the left. [34]Then the King will say to those at his right hand, 'Come, O blessed of my Father, inherit the kingdom prepared for you from the foundation of the world; [35]for I was hungry and you gave me food, I was thirsty and you gave me drink, I was a stranger and you welcomed me, [36]I was naked and you clothed me, I was sick and you visited me, I was in prison and you came to me.' [37]Then the righteous will answer him, 'Lord, when did we see thee hungry and feed thee, or thirsty and give thee drink? [38]And when did we see thee a stranger and welcome thee, or naked and clothe thee? [39]And when did we see thee sick or in prison and visit thee?' [40]And the King will answer them, 'Truly I say to you, as you did it to one of the least of my brethren, you did it to me.' [41]Then he will say to those at his left hand, 'Depart from me, you cursed, into the eternal fire prepared for the devil and his angels; [42]for I was hungry and you gave me no food; I was thirsty and you gave me no drink, [43]I was a stranger and you did not welcome me, naked and you did not clothe me, sick and in prison and you did not visit me.' [44]Then

thronum gloriae suae. [32]Et congregabuntur ante eum omnes gentes; et separabit eos ab invicem, sicut pastor segregat oves ab haedis, [33]et statuet oves quidem a dextris suis, haedos autem a sinistris. [34]Tunc dicet Rex his, qui a dextris eius erunt: "Venite, benedicti Patris mei; possidete paratum vobis regnum a constitutione mundi. [35]Esurivi enim, et dedistis mihi manducare; sitivi, et dedistis mihi bibere; hospes eram, et collegistis me; [36]nudus, et operuistis me; infirmus, et visitastis me; in carcere eram, et venistis ad me". [37]Tunc respondebunt ei iusti dicentes: "Domine, quando te vidimus esurientem et pavimus, aut sitientem et dedimus tibi potum? [38]Quando autem te vidimus hospitem et collegimus, aut nudum et cooperuimus? [39]Quando autem te vidimus infirmum aut in carcere et venimus ad te?". [40]Et respondens Rex dicet illis: "Amen dico vobis: Quamdiu fecistis uni de his fratribus meis minimis, mihi fecistis". [41]Tunc dicet et his, qui a sinistris erunt: "Discedite a me, maledicti, in ignem aeternum, qui praeparatus est Diabolo et angelis eius. [42]Esurivi enim, et non dedistis mihi manducare; sitivi, et non dedistis mihi potum; [43]hospes eram, et non

25:31–46 The three parables (24:42–51; 25:1–13; 25:14–30) are rounded off by the announcement of a Last Judgment, which Jesus depicts as a solemn and elaborate process that will involve everything relevant to divine justice. Christian Tradition calls it the "Last Judgment" to distinguish it from the "particular judgment" (cf. the note on Rom 2:1–24) which everyone undergoes immediately after death: "Then will the conduct of each one and the secrets of hearts be brought to light. Then will the culpable unbelief that counted the offer of God's grace as nothing be condemned. Our attitude to our neighbour will disclose acceptance or refusal of grace and divine love" (*Catechism of the Catholic Church*, 678).

All the good works listed in vv. 36–46 (feeding the hungry, giving drink to the thirsty, etc.) become acts of Christian love when they are done for the "least of these my brethren" (v. 40), in whom we should see Christ. When we compare this passage to a previous one where our Lord promises that anyone who gave even a glass of cold water to someone "because he is a disciple" (10:42) shall not lose his reward, we will notice that there is no mention of disciples here: any service to a human being is a service to Christ. Hence the importance of the works of mercy (corporal and spiritual) that the Church encourages us to do; hence, too, the gravity of failing to carry them out: such failure deprives Christ of that service. A person's love of God is measured by his or her service to others: "Here the Lord asks only two things of us: love for his Majesty and love for our neighbour. It is for these two virtues that we must strive, and if we attain them perfectly we are doing his will […]. The surest sign that we are keeping these two commandments is, I think, that we should really love our neighbour; for we cannot be sure if we are loving God, although we may have good reasons for believing that we are, but we can know quite well if we are loving our neighbour. And be certain that, the farther advanced you find you are in this, the greater the love you will have for God; for so dearly does his Majesty love us that he will reward our love for our neighbour by increasing the love which we bear to himself, and that in a thousand ways: this I cannot doubt"

they also will answer, 'Lord, when did we see thee hungry or thirsty or a stranger or naked or sick or in prison, and did not minister to thee?' [45]Then he will answer them, 'Truly, I say to you, as you did it not to one of the least of these, you did it not to me.' [46]And they will go away into eternal punishment, but the righteous into eternal life."

Jn 5:29
Dan 12:2
Jn 5:29

12. THE PASSION, DEATH AND RESURRECTION OF JESUS*

Mk 14:1–2
Lk 22:1–2
Jn 11:45–57

Last announcement of the Passion. The conspiracy against Jesus

26 [1]When Jesus had finished all these sayings, he said to his disciples, [2]"You know that after two days the Passover is coming, and the Son of man will be delivered up to be crucified."

Lk 22:1–2
Mt 20:18

collegistis me; nudus, et non operuistis me; infirmus et in carcere, et non visitastis me". [44]Tunc respondebunt et ipsi dicentes: "Domine, quando te vidimus esurientem aut sitientem aut hospitem aut nudum aut infirmum vel in carcere et non ministravimus tibi?". [45]Tunc respondebit illis dicens: "Amen dico vobis: Quamdiu non fecistis uni de minimis his, nec mihi fecistis". [46]Et ibunt hi in supplicium aeternum, iusti autem in vitam aeternam». [26] [1]Et factum est cum consummasset Iesus sermones hos omnes, dixit discipulis suis: [2]«Scitis quia post biduum Pascha fiet, et

(St Teresa of Avila, *Interior Castle*, 5, 3, 7–8).

"Eternal punishment" (v. 46). The eternal punishment of the damned and the eternal reward of the elect are dogmas of faith solemnly defined by the Magisterium of the Church in 1215. "He [Christ] will come at the end of the world; he will judge the living and the dead; and he will reward all, both the lost and the elect, according to their works. And all these will rise with their own bodies which they now have so that they may receive according to their works, whether good or bad; the wicked, a perpetual punishment with the devil; the good, eternal glory with Christ" (Fourth Lateran Council, *De fide catholica*, chap. 1).

*26:1—28:20 The events of the passion of our Lord were deeply etched on the memory of his disciples: this can be seen from the apostles' public addresses recorded in the book of Acts, and from the closely written accounts provided by the evangelists. St Matthew focuses on two things—the majesty of Christ in the face of his accusers, and the reason why he bore all these affronts to his person: he did so because he is the suffering Servant, announced by the prophets, who took upon himself the burden of our sins. God's plans were realized in the death of Jesus, and also in his resurrection. A new stage begins with the resurrection and Christ's mandate to his apostles: the risen Jesus stays on in his Church, the gates of heaven have been opened, and Christians must proclaim this message of salvation to the whole world.

The accounts of the passion in the four Gospels are far more detailed than those of any other event included by them. This is no surprise, for the passion is the climax of Christ's life on earth and of his work of redemption; for it is the atoning sacrifice whereby he offers himself to his Father God for the redemption of our sins. Moreover, the terrible sufferings that our Lord underwent make it plain just how much he loves each and every one of us: "The remedy for all the evil brought about by our sins is to be found in the passion of Christ; but the passion can also be seen as an example or teaching. It shows the perfection of Christian life; he who wishes to be perfect must do no more than scorn what Christ scorned in being nailed to the cross, and desire what he desired on the cross: all the virtues are revealed there. An example of love: no greater love can a man have than he lay down his life for his friends. That is what Christ did on the cross; and if he suffered death on the cross for us, we cannot complain about anything that we may suffer for his sake. [...] An example of humility: look at the One who was crucified. He, God, suffered under Pontius Pilate and died. An example of obedience: he was obedient to the Father unto death. All were made sinners through the disobedience of one man—the disobedience of Adam; and all were redeemed through His obedience—the obedience of Christ" (St Thomas Aquinas, *Expositio in Credum*, 4).

26:1–5 The first three Gospels all describe in the

Mt 21:46

³Then the chief priests and the elders of the people gathered in the palace of the high priest, who was called Caiaphas, ⁴and took counsel together in order to arrest Jesus by stealth and kill him. ⁵But they said, "Not during the feast, lest there be a tumult among the people."

Mk 14:3–11
Lk 22:3–6
Jn 12:1–11

The anointing at Bethany. Judas betrays Jesus

⁶Now when Jesus was at Bethany in the house of Simon the leper, ⁷a woman came up to him with an alabaster jar of very expensive ointment, and she poured it on his head, as he sat at table. ⁸But when the disciples saw it, they were indignant saying, "Why this waste? ⁹For this ointment might have been sold for a large sum, and given to the poor." Lk 11:7 ¹⁰But Jesus, aware of this, said to them, "Why do you trouble the woman? For she has done a beautiful thing to me. Deut 15:11 ¹¹For you always have the poor with you, but you will not always have me. ¹²In pouring this ointment on my body she has done it to prepare me for burial. ¹³Truly, I say to you, wherever this gospel is preached in the whole world, what she has done will be told in memory of her."

Jn 11:57; 13:2 ¹⁴Then one of the twelve, who was called Judas Iscariot, went to the chief priests Zech 11:12 ¹⁵and said, "What will you give me if I deliver him to you?" And they paid him thirty 1 Tim 6:9–10 pieces of silver. ¹⁶And from that moment he sought an opportunity to betray him.

Filius hominis traditur, ut crucifigatur». ³Tunc congregati sunt principes sacerdotum et seniores populi in aulam principis sacerdotum, qui dicebatur Caiphas, ⁴et consilium fecerunt, ut Iesum dolo tenerent et occiderent; ⁵dicebant autem: «Non in die festo, ne tumultus fiat in populo». ⁶Cum autem esset Iesus in Bethania, in domo Simonis leprosi, ⁷accessit ad eum mulier habens alabastrum unguenti pretiosi et effudit super caput ipsius recumbentis. ⁸Videntes autem discipuli, indignati sunt dicentes: «Ut quid perditio haec? ⁹Potuit enim istud venumdari multo et dari pauperibus». ¹⁰Sciens autem Iesus ait illis: «Quid molesti estis mulieri? Opus enim bonum operata est in me; ¹¹nam semper pauperes habetis vobiscum, me autem non semper habetis. ¹²Mittens enim haec unguentum hoc supra corpus meum, ad sepeliendum me fecit. ¹³Amen dico vobis: Ubicumque praedicatum fuerit hoc evangelium in toto mundo, dicetur et quod haec fecit in memoriam eius». ¹⁴Tunc abiit unus de Duodecim, qui dicebatur Iudas Iscariotes, ad principes sacerdotum ¹⁵et ait: «Quid vultis mihi dare, et ego vobis eum tradam?». *At illi constituerunt ei triginta argentos*. ¹⁶Et exinde quaerebat opportunitatem, ut eum traderet. ¹⁷Prima autem Azymorum accesserunt discipuli ad Iesum dicentes: «Ubi vis paremus tibi

same way how the drama begins to unfold: the Jewish authorities are looking for a means to arrest Jesus, and they find an unexpected ally in Judas, "one of the twelve" (26:14). However, each evangelist underlines a different aspect. Matthew highlights the fact that Jesus is in control of all events. Everything that happens is part of God's saving plan: even the thirty pieces of silver paid to Judas for his betrayal (26:15) conform to what the Scriptures said would happen (see 27:9–10).

The fact that the authorities wanted to avoid a public disturbance (v. 5) indicates how popular Jesus was; and their desire to arrest him "by stealth" (v. 4) is itself an insult to Christ. Many other affronts follow—bribing someone to betray him (26:14–16), producing false witnesses (26:59–61), inciting the crowd (27:20), jeering at Christ on the cross (27:39), etc.; and all this "out of envy" (27:18).

26:6–16 Bethany, where Lazarus and his sisters lived (cf. Jn 12:1), was a village to the east of the Mount of Olives, on the route from Jerusalem to Jericho. (There was another town of the same name, close to where John the Baptist baptized people: see Jn 1:28.) The generosity shown by the woman with the ointment is criticized by the disciples on specious grounds (vv. 8–10). They see her action as a waste of money (we read in John 12:5 that the perfume cost over 300 denarii, almost a year's wages for a labourer). They do not realize that the woman is motivated purely by love. "The woman in the house of Simon the leper in Bethany, who anoints the Master's head with precious ointment, reminds us of our duty to be generous in the worship of God. All beauty, richness and majesty seem little to me. And against those who attack the richness of sacred vessels, of vestments and altars, stands the praise given by Jesus: '*opus enim bonum operata est in me*: she has acted well towards me'" (St Josemaría Escrivá, *The Way*, 527).

The woman's gesture is reminiscent of a custom common among wealthier Jews of embalming corpses, using costly ointments and

Preparations for the Last Supper and announcement of Judas' treachery

Mk 14:12–21
Lk 22:7–13
Jn 13:21–32
Ex 12:14–20

[17]Now on the first day of Unleavened Bread the disciples came to Jesus, saying, "Where will you have us prepare for you to eat the passover?"* [18]He said, "Go into the city to such a one, and say to him, 'The Teacher says, My time is at hand; I will keep the passover at your house with my disciples.' " [19]And the disciples did as Jesus had directed them, and they prepared the passover.

[20]When it was evening, he sat at table with the twelve disciples;[e] [21]and as they were eating, he said, "Truly, I say to you, one of you will betray me." [22]And they were very sorrowful, and began to say to him one after another, "Is it I, Lord?" [23]He answered, "He who has dipped his hand in the dish with me, will betray me. [24]The Son of man goes as it is written of him, but woe to that man by whom the Son of man is betrayed! It would have been better for that man if he had not been born." [25]Judas, who betrayed him, said, "Is it I, Master?"[f] He said to him, "You have said so."

Jn 13:18

The institution of the Eucharist

Mk 14:22–25
Lk 22:14–20
1 Cor 11:23–26

[26]Now as they were eating,* Jesus took bread, and blessed, and broke it, and gave it to the disciples and said, "Take, eat; this is my body." [27]And he took a cup, and when he had given thanks he gave it to them, saying, "Drink of it, all of you; [28]for this is

1 Cor 11:23–25

1 Cor 10:16

Ex 24:8
Jer 31:31

comedere Pascha?». [18]Ille autem dixit: «Ite in civitatem ad quendam et dicite ei: "Magister dicit: Tempus meum prope est; apud te facio Pascha cum discipulis meis"». [19]Et fecerunt discipuli, sicut constituit illis Iesus, et paraverunt Pascha. [20]Vespere autem facto, discumbebat cum Duodecim. [21]Et edentibus illis, dixit: «Amen dico vobis: Unus vestrum me traditurus est». [22]Et contristati valde, coeperunt singuli dicere ei: «Numquid ego sum, Domine?». [23]At ipse respondens ait: «Qui intingit mecum manum in paropside, hic me tradet. [24]Filius quidem hominis vadit, sicut scriptum est de illo; vae autem homini illi, per quem Filius hominis traditur! Bonum erat ei, si natus non fuisset homo ille». [25]Respondens autem Iudas, qui tradidit eum, dixit: «Numquid ego sum, Rabbi?». Ait illi: «Tu dixisti». [26]Cenantibus autem eis, accepit Iesus panem et benedixit ac fregit deditque discipulis et ait: «Accipite, comedite: hoc est corpus meum». [27]Et accipiens calicem, gratias egit et dedit illis dicens: «Bibite ex hoc omnes: [28]hic

perfumes, and it anticipates Jesus' death. She saw her action as a generous gesture and a recognition of Jesus' dignity; it proved to be a prophetic sign of his redemptive death (vv. 12–13).

26:17–25 The Passover or feast of Unleavened Bread (v. 17), the most important Jewish feast, commemorates the liberation of the Jews from slavery in Egypt (cf. Ex 12). The rites laid down by Moses involves the offering of an unblemished lamb, none of whose bones should be broken; the entire lamb is then to be eaten in a thanksgiving meal. In our Lord's time the lamb was sacrificed in the temple of Jerusalem, but the meal took place in people's homes, where all the family gathered. The unleavened bread was in the form of "azymes"—loaves that had to be eaten over a seven-day period, in commemoration of the unleavened bread that the Israelites had to take with them in their hurry to leave Egypt (see Ex 12:34). In Jesus' time the Passover supper was held on the first day of the week-long feast of Unleavened Bread.

Mark and Luke go into more detail than Matthew does, to describe the preparations made

for this Passover meal. Matthew records that Jesus knew (v. 25) that Judas would betray him, but did nothing to stop him: "My time is at hand," he tells the owner of the house (v. 18). "The desire to embrace his Father's plan of redeeming love inspired Jesus' whole life, for his redemptive passion was the very reason for his Incarnation" (*Catechism of the Catholic Church*, 607).

26:26–29 Jesus' gestures and words at the Last Supper all carried deep significance. In their account of the institution of the Eucharist, each evangelist emphasizes different facets (cf. the notes on Mk 14:22–25 and Lk 22:7–20). St Matthew is the only one to record what Jesus says explicitly about his death being an expiation for sins (v. 28). Our Lord's words here bring fully into effect God's plan of salvation. "The Scriptures had foretold this divine plan of salvation through the putting to death of 'the righteous one, my Servant' as a mystery of universal redemption, that is, as the ransom that would free men from the slavery of sin [...]. In particular, Jesus' redemptive death fulfils Isaiah's prophecy of the suffering Servant" (*Catechism of the Catholic Church*, 601).

e Other authorities omit *disciples*   f Or *Rabbi*

Heb 7:22; 9:15
Zech 9:11 my blood of the[g] covenant, which is poured out for many for the forgiveness of sins. [29]I tell you I shall not drink again of this fruit of the vine until that day when I drink it new with you in my Father's kingdom."

Mk 14:26–31
Lk 22:31–34
Jn 13:36–38
The disciples' desertion foretold

Ps 113–118

Zech 13:7
Mt 26:56
Jn 16:32
[30]And when they had sung a hymn, they went out to the Mount of Olives. [31]Then Jesus said to them, "You will all fall away because of me this night; for it is written, 'I will

est enim sanguis meus novi testamenti, qui pro multis effunditur in remissionem peccatorum. [29]Dico autem vobis: Non bibam amodo de hoc genimine vitis usque in diem illum, cum illud bibam vobiscum novum in regno Patris mei». [30]Et hymno dicto, exierunt in montem Oliveti. [31]Tunc dicit illis Iesus: «Omnes vos scandalum patiemini in me in ista nocte. Scriptum est enim: *Percutiam pastorem, et dispergentur oves gregis*".

This brief scene contains all the basic truths of faith connected with the mystery of the Eucharist: "At the Last Supper, on the night when he was betrayed, our Saviour instituted the eucharistic sacrifice of his Body and Blood. He did this in order to perpetuate the sacrifice of the Cross throughout the centuries until he should come again, and so to entrust to his beloved spouse, the Church, a memorial of his death and resurrection: a sacrament of love, a sign of unity, a bond of charity, a paschal banquet in which Christ is eaten, the mind is filled with grace, and a pledge of future glory is given to us" (Vatican II, *Sacrosanctum Concilium*, 47).

In the first place, what is described here is the institution of the Sacrament as the real presence of Jesus Christ. Upon the saying of the words "This is my body … , this is my blood", what was merely unleavened bread and wine becomes, by the words and will of Jesus, the true Body and Blood of the Saviour. His words have such a realism about them that they cannot be rightly interpreted as being merely symbolic, nor should they be interpreted in any way that obscures the mysterious fact of the real presence of Christ in the Eucharist. All we can do is humbly subscribe to the belief that the Catholic Church has always held to be true: "The continuous teaching of the Catholic Church, the traditions delivered to catechumens, the perception of the Christian people, the doctrine defined by the Council of Trent, and the very words of Christ as he instituted the most holy Eucharist, all insist that we profess: 'The Eucharist is the flesh of our Saviour Jesus Christ; the flesh which suffered for our sins and which the Father, of his kindness, brought to life.' To these words of St Ignatius of Antioch may be added the statement addressed

to the people by Theodore of Mopsuestia, a faithful witness of the Church's belief on this subject: 'The Lord did not say: "This is the symbol of my body and this the symbol of my blood." He said: "This is my body and my blood" ' " (Paul VI, *Mysterium fidei*, 5). Christian doctrine also holds that this sacrament not only has sanctifying power but actually contains the very Author of Holiness; it was instituted by Jesus Christ to be spiritual nourishment for the soul. It has the effect of forgiving venial sins, and it helps the Christian to avoid mortal sin; it unites us to God and is a pledge of future glory.

Moreover, in instituting the Eucharist, our Lord laid down that the celebrating of it should be repeated until the end of time (cf. Lk 22:19; 1 Cor 11:24–25, and notes), and he made this possible by giving the apostles the power to consecrate bread and wine; this power they passed on to their successors.

Also, at the Last Supper, Christ (in an unbloody way) brought forward his imminent passion and death. Every Mass celebrated from then on renews the sacrifice of our Lord on the cross, for "[The august sacrifice of the altar] is no mere empty commemoration of the passion and death of Jesus Christ, but a true and proper act of sacrifice, whereby the High Priest by an unbloody immolation offers himself as a most acceptable victim to the Eternal Father, as he did upon the cross" (Pius XII, *Mediator Dei*).

The words "which is poured out for many for the forgiveness of sins" (v. 28) mean the same as "which is poured out for all …". Thus, the prophecy of Isaiah 53:1–12 is fulfilled.

26:30–35 Psalms 113–118 are sung at the celebration of the Passover. This is what the refer-

g Other ancient authorities insert *new*

strike the shepherd, and the sheep of the flock will be scattered.' ³²But after I am raised up, I will go before you to Galilee." ³³Peter declared to him, "Though they all fall away because of you, I will never fall away." ³⁴Jesus said to him, "Truly, I say to you, this very night, before the cock crows, you will deny me three times." ³⁵Peter said to him, "Even if I must die with you, I will not deny you." And so did all the disciples.

Mt 28:7, 16

Gethsemane—the agony in the garden

Mk 14:32–42
Lk 22:39–46

³⁶Then Jesus went with them to a place called Gethsemane, and he said to his disciples, "Sit here, while I go yonder and pray." ³⁷And taking with him Peter and the two sons of Zebedee, he began to be sorrowful and troubled. ³⁸Then he said to them, "My soul is very sorrowful, even to death; remain here, and watch[h] with me." ³⁹And going a little farther he fell on his face and prayed, "My Father, if it be possible, let this cup pass from me; nevertheless, not as I will, but as thou wilt." ⁴⁰And he came to the disciples and found them sleeping; and he said to Peter, "So, could you not watch[h] with me one hour? ⁴¹Watch[h] and pray that you may not enter into temptation; the spirit indeed is willing, but the flesh is weak." ⁴²Again, for the second time, he went away and prayed, "My Father, if this cannot pass unless I drink it, thy will be done." ⁴³And again he came and found them sleeping, for their eyes were heavy. ⁴⁴So, leaving them

Heb 5:7

Ps 42:5, 11; 43:5
Jn 12:27

Mt 20:22
Jn 6:38; 18:11
Heb 5:8; 10:9

Heb 2:14; 4:15

2 Cor 12:8

³²Postquam autem resurrexero, praecedam vos in Galilaeam». ³³Respondens autem Petrus ait illi: «Et si omnes scandalizati fuerint in te, ego numquam scandalizabor». ³⁴Ait illi Iesus: «Amen dico tibi: In hac nocte, antequam gallus cantet, ter me negabis». ³⁵Ait illi Petrus: «Etiam si oportuerit me mori tecum, non te negabo». Similiter et omnes discipuli dixerunt. ³⁶Tunc venit Iesus cum illis in praedium, quod dicitur Gethsemani. Et dicit discipulis: «Sedete hic, donec vadam illuc et orem». ³⁷Et assumpto Petro et duobus filiis Zebedaei, coepit contristari et maestus esse. ³⁸Tunc ait illis: «Tristis est anima mea usque ad mortem; sustinete hic et vigilate mecum». ³⁹Et progressus pusillum, procidit in faciem suam orans et dicens: «Pater mi, si possibile est, transeat a me calix iste; veruntamen non sicut ego volo, sed sicut tu». ⁴⁰Et venit ad discipulos et invenit eos dormientes; et dicit Petro: «Sic non potuistis una hora vigilare mecum? ⁴¹Vigilate et orate, ut non intretis in tentationem; spiritus quidem promptus est, caro autem infirma». ⁴²Iterum secundo abiit et oravit dicens: «Pater mi, si non potest hoc transire, nisi bibam illud, fiat voluntas tua». ⁴³Et venit iterum et invenit eos dormientes: erant enim oculi eorum gravati. ⁴⁴Et relictis illis, iterum abiit et oravit tertio, eundem ser-

ence to "a hymn" (v. 30) means. The events that will soon take place are going to be a great test of the disciples' faith, so Jesus now warns them all, and Peter in particular (v. 31). They had professed faith in Jesus as the Messiah (16:13–20), but they failed to realize that he must become the suffering Servant (16:21–23). Events will force that realization on them. But they still find the idea difficult to accept. Peter, generous as ever, assures Jesus that he will never deny him (vv. 33–35); but, being weak, that is what he will in fact do: "Here we learn a great truth: that a man's resolution is not sufficient unless he relies on the help of God" (St John Chrysostom, *In Matthaeum*, 82, 4).

26:36–46 The three Synoptics describe the drama of Christ's prayer in the garden, and the failure of the disciples to keep him faithful company. Mark (see Mk 14:32–42 and note) makes this failure abundantly clear. Matthew puts more emphasis on the fact that by means of this prayer Jesus identified himself with the will of God the

Father, making it truly his own. The opening verses of this passage show what a great effort this was for Jesus: "If it be possible, let this cup pass from me"; further on, his prayer becomes an act of wholehearted abandonment: "My Father, if this cannot pass unless I drink it, thy will be done" (vv. 42 and 44). "Do not forget this, it is important: our intention when we begin to pray is to be determined, to struggle and work to conform our will to God's will" (St Teresa of Avila, *Interior Castle*, 2, 8).

The account of this episode retains the emotion of the tradition from which it derives. The early Christian community must have been vividly aware of how traumatic it was for Christ to accept his destiny (see Heb 5:7): "Theological tradition has not failed to ask how Jesus could possibly experience at one and the same time his profound unity with the Father, by its very nature a source of joy and happiness, and an agony that goes all the way to his final cry of abandonment. The simultaneous presence of these two seemingly irreconcilable aspects is rooted in the

h Or *keep awake*

Jn 2:4; 7:30; 8:20;
12:23; 13:1; 17:1
again, he went away and prayed for the third time, saying the same words. ⁴⁵Then he came to the disciples and said to them, "Are you still sleeping and taking your rest? Behold, the hour is at hand, and the Son of man is betrayed into the hands of sinners.
Jn 14:31
⁴⁶Rise, let us be going; see, my betrayer is at hand."

Mk 14:43–52
Lk 22:47–53
Jn 18:1–12
Arrest of Jesus

⁴⁷While he was still speaking, Judas came, one of the twelve, and with him a great crowd with swords and clubs, from the chief priests and the elders of the people. ⁴⁸Now the betrayer had given them a sign, saying, "The one I shall kiss is the man; seize him." ⁴⁹And he came up to Jesus at once and said, "Hail, Master!"ⁱ And he kissed him. ⁵⁰Jesus said to him, "Friend, why are you here?"ʲ Then they came up and laid hands on Jesus and seized him. ⁵¹And behold, one of those who were with Jesus stretched out his hand and drew his sword, and struck the slave of the high priest,
Gen 9:6
Rev 13:10
Joel 3:11
Lk 2:13
and cut off his ear.* ⁵²Then Jesus said to him, "Put your sword back into its place; for all who take the sword will perish by the sword. ⁵³Do you think that I cannot appeal to my Father, and he will at once send me more than twelve legions of
Lk 19:47
angels? ⁵⁴But how then should the scriptures be fulfilled, that it must be so?" ⁵⁵At that hour Jesus said to the crowds, "Have you come out as against a robber, with swords and clubs to capture me? Day after day I sat in the temple teaching, and you

monem iterum dicens. ⁴⁵Tunc venit ad discipulos et dicit illis: «Dormite iam et requiescite; ecce appropinquavit hora, et Filius hominis traditur in manus peccatorum. ⁴⁶Surgite, eamus; ecce appropinquavit, qui me tradit». ⁴⁷Et adhuc ipso loquente, ecce Iudas, unus de Duodecim, venit et cum eo turba multa cum gladiis et fustibus, missi a principibus sacerdotum et senioribus populi. ⁴⁸Qui autem tradidit eum, dedit illis signum dicens: «Quemcumque osculatus fuero, ipse est; tenete eum!». ⁴⁹Et confestim accedens ad Iesum dixit: «Ave, Rabbi!» et osculatus est eum. ⁵⁰Iesus autem dixit illi: «Amice, ad quod venisti!». Tunc accesserunt et manus iniecerunt in Iesum et tenuerunt eum. ⁵¹Et ecce unus ex his, qui erant cum Iesu, extendens manum exemit gladium suum et percutiens servum principis sacerdotum amputavit auriculam eius. ⁵²Tunc ait illi Iesus: «Converte gladium tuum in locum suum. Omnes enim, qui acceperint gladium, gladio peribunt. ⁵³An putas quia non possum rogare Patrem meum, et exhibebit mihi modo plus quam duodecim legiones angelorum? ⁵⁴Quomodo ergo implebuntur Scripturae quia sic oportet fieri?». ⁵⁵In illa hora dixit Iesus turbis: «Tamquam ad latronem existis cum gladiis et fustibus comprehendere me? Cotidie sedebam docens in templo, et non me tenuis-

fathomless depths of the hypostatic union. Faced with this mystery, we are greatly helped not only by theological investigation but also by that great heritage which is the 'lived theology' of the saints. The saints offer us precious insights which enable us to understand more easily the intuition of faith, thanks to the special enlightenment which some of them have received from the Holy Spirit, or even through their personal experience of those terrible states of trial which the mystical tradition describes as the 'dark night'. Not infrequently the saints have undergone something akin to Jesus' experience on the Cross in the paradoxical blending of bliss and pain. [...] Thérèse of Lisieux lived her agony in communion with the agony of Jesus, 'experiencing' in herself the very paradox of Jesus's own bliss and anguish: 'In the Garden of Olives our Lord was blessed with all the joys of the Trinity, yet his dying was no less harsh. It is a mystery, but I assure you that, on the basis of what I myself am feeling, I can understand something

of it'" (John Paul II, *Novo millennio ineunte*, 26–27).

26:47–56 This scene, rich in contrasts, reveals our Lord's majesty. Judas betrays Jesus with a kiss, a sign of friendship and respect (v. 49); whereas Jesus treats Judas as a friend who does not even realize his true role in the drama (v. 50). Jesus is arrested in the dark, as though he were a fugitive (v. 55), by an armed mob (v. 47). The disciples were ready to come to his aid (cf. 26:35), and one of them (Peter, according to John 18:10) even drew out his sword (v. 51). Although an appeal to his Father could set the mob's plans at nought (v. 53), Jesus offers no resistance; he accepts arrest because he chooses to do so. For his decision to fulfil the Scriptures (vv. 54, 56), is irrevocable, even though it costs him his life (cf. 26:42), "because, being God, he was made man and submitted his will to yours and was obedient to you, God, his Father" (St John Damascene, *Declaratio et expositio fidei*, 1).

i Or *Rabbi*   j Or *do that for which you have come*

did not seize me. ⁵⁶But all this has taken place, that the scriptures of the prophets
might be fulfilled." Then all the disciples forsook him and fled.

Mt 26:31
Jn 16:32

Mk 14:53–65
Lk 22:66–71
Jn 18:13–24

Jesus before the chief priests

⁵⁷Then those who had seized Jesus led him to Caiaphas the high priest, where the
scribes and the elders had gathered. ⁵⁸But Peter followed him at a distance, as far as
the courtyard of the high priest, and going inside he sat with the guards to see the
end. ⁵⁹Now the chief priests and the whole council sought false testimony against
Jesus that they might put him to death,* ⁶⁰but they found none, though many false
witnesses came forward. At last two came forward ⁶¹and said, "This fellow said, 'I
am able to destroy the temple of God, and to build it in three days.' " ⁶²And the high
priest stood up and said, "Have you no answer to make? What is it that these men
testify against you?" ⁶³But Jesus was silent. And the high priest said to him, "I adjure
you by the living God, tell us if you are the Christ, the Son of God." ⁶⁴Jesus said to
him, "You have said so. But I tell you, hereafter you will see the Son of man seated
at the right hand of Power, and coming on the clouds of heaven." ⁶⁵Then the high
priest tore his robes, and said, "He has uttered blasphemy. Why do we still need witnesses? You have now heard his blasphemy.* ⁶⁶What is your judgment?" They
answered, "He deserves death." ⁶⁷Then they spat in his face, and struck him; and
some slapped him, ⁶⁸saying, "Prophesy to us, you Christ! Who is it that struck you?"

Jn 2:19–21
Mt 27:40
Acts 6:14

Mt 16:16
Jn 10:24

Ps 110:1
Mt 16:27; 24:30
Dan 7:13
Acts 7:56
Jn 10:33
Mk 13:26; 16:19
Lk 21:27

Jn 19:7
Lev 24:16

Is 50:6

tis». ⁵⁶Hoc autem totum factum est, ut implerentur scripturae Prophetarum. Tunc discipuli omnes, relicto eo, fugerunt. ⁵⁷Illi autem tenentes Iesum
duxerunt ad Caipham principem sacerdotum, ubi scribae et seniores convenerant. ⁵⁸Petrus autem sequebatur eum a longe usque in aulam principis sacerdotum; et ingressus intro sedebat cum ministris, ut videret finem. ⁵⁹Principes autem sacerdotum et omne concilium quaerebant falsum
testimonium contra Iesum, ut eum morti traderent, ⁶⁰et non invenerunt, cum multi falsi testes accessissent. Novissime autem venientes duo
⁶¹dixerunt: «Hic dixit: "Possum destruere templum Dei et post triduum aedificare illud"». ⁶²Et surgens princeps sacerdotum ait illi: «Nihil respondes? Quid isti adversum te testificantur?». ⁶³Iesus autem tacebat. Et princeps sacerdotum ait illi: «Adiuro te per Deum vivum, ut dicas nobis, si tu
es Christus Filius Dei». ⁶⁴Dicit illi Iesus: «Tu dixisti. Verumtamen dico vobis: Amodo videbitis *Filium hominis sedentem a dextris Virtutis et
venientem in nubibus caeli*». ⁶⁵Tunc princeps sacerdotum scidit vestimenta sua dicens: «Blasphemavit! Quid adhuc egemus testibus? Ecce nunc
audistis blasphemiam. ⁶⁶Quid vobis videtur?». Illi autem respondentes dixerunt: «Reus est mortis!». ⁶⁷Tunc exspuerunt in faciem eius et colaphis
eum ceciderunt; alii autem palmas in faciem ei dederunt ⁶⁸dicentes: «Prophetiza nobis, Christe: Quis est, qui te percussit?». ⁶⁹Petrus vero sedebat

26:57–75 The four Gospels all report this
episode, though with variations (particularly
between the Synoptics and the account of John).
The rulers of the people, later on, will charge
Jesus with being a disturber of the peace, and the
grounds for his condemnation will be that he
called himself the "King of the Jews". The
Synoptics all say that the charge arose from what
he had said in the temple (v. 61): "The words
'Destroy this temple, and in three days I will
raise it up' (Jn 2:19) should be read alongside
those spoken by the false witnesses against Jesus
Christ, recorded by Matthew and Mark at the
end of their gospels; he spoke of the temple of
his body; they took the words to mean the
temple built of stone" (Origen, *Commentaria in
Ioannem*, 10, 37, 251–252).

In this episode we can see the difference
between Jesus' attitude and that of Peter. St
Matthew gives an orderly account of the

offences committed against Jesus. First he is
falsely accused (v. 59) and then he is quoted out
of context (v. 61). In the face of these
accusations, Jesus remains silent (v. 63). Then
his admission that he is the Messiah and the Son
of God (v. 64) is used to charge him with
blasphemy (v. 65), an offence that is grounds for
his execution (v. 66) and that earns him jeers
and insults (vv. 67–68). To cap it all comes
Peter's denial (vv. 70, 72, 74). But Peter weeps
bitter tears of remorse in the end (v. 75). As on
other occasions, what saves Peter is not his
strength, but his contrition: "David did penance
for his terrible crimes and was not cast down
from his throne; Peter wept bitter tears for
having denied the Lord and did not cease to be
an apostle" (St Augustine, *Epistolae*, 185, 10,
45).

However, the Gospel reveals a paradox. The
prediction made by Jesus in v. 64 is evocative of

Mk 14:66–72
Lk 22:54–62
Jn 18:15–18,
25–27

Peter's denials

⁶⁹Now Peter was sitting outside in the courtyard. And a maid came up to him, and said, "You also were with Jesus the Galilean." ⁷⁰But he denied it before them all, saying, "I do not know what you mean." ⁷¹And when he went out to the porch, another maid saw him, and she said to the bystanders, "This man was with Jesus of Nazareth." ⁷²And again he denied it with an oath, "I do not know the man." ⁷³After a little while the bystanders came up and said to Peter, "Certainly you are also one of them, for your accent betrays you." ⁷⁴Then he began to invoke a curse on himself and to swear, "I do not know the man." And immediately the cock crowed. ⁷⁵And Peter remembered the saying of Jesus, "Before the cock crows, you will deny me three times." And he went out and wept bitterly.

Jn 8:55
Mt 26:34

Mk 15:1

Lk 22:66
Jn 18:28

Lk 23:1
Jn 18:31–32

Jesus is brought before Pilate

27 ¹When morning came, all the chief priests and the elders of the people took counsel against Jesus to put him to death; ²and they bound him and led him away and delivered him to Pilate the governor.

Judas' despair and death

Mt 26:15

³When Judas, his betrayer, saw that he was condemned, he repented and brought back the thirty pieces of silver to the chief priests and the elders, ⁴saying, "I have sinned in betraying innocent blood." They said, "What is that to us? See to it yourself." ⁵And throwing down the pieces of silver in the temple, he departed; and he went and hanged himself. ⁶But the chief priests, taking the pieces of silver, said, "It is not lawful to put them into the treasury, since they are blood money." ⁷So they took counsel, and bought with them the potter's field, to bury strangers in.

Acts 1:18–19
2 Sam 17:23
Mk 12:41

foris in atrio; et accessit ad eum una ancilla dicens: «Et tu cum Iesu Galilaeo eras!». ⁷⁰At ille negavit coram omnibus dicens: «Nescio quid dicis!». ⁷¹Exeunte autem illo ad ianuam, vidit eum alia et ait his, qui erant ibi: «Hic erat cum Iesu Nazareno!». ⁷²Et iterum negavit cum iuramento: «Non novi hominem!». ⁷³Post pusillum autem accesserunt, qui stabant et dixerunt Petro: «Vere et tu ex illis es, nam et loquela tua manifestum te facit». ⁷⁴Tunc coepit detestari et iurare: «Non novi hominem!». Et continuo gallus cantavit; ⁷⁵et recordatus est Petrus verbi Iesu, quod dixerat: «Priusquam gallus cantet, ter me negabis». Et egressus foras ploravit amare. [27] ¹Mane autem facto, consilium inierunt omnes principes sacerdotum et seniores populi adversus Iesum, ut eum morti traderent. ²Et vinctum adduxerunt eum et tradiderunt Pilato praesidi. ³Tunc videns Iudas, qui eum tradidit, quod damnatus esset, paenitentia ductus, rettulit triginta argenteos principibus sacerdotum et senioribus ⁴dicens: «Peccavi tradens sanguinem innocentem». At illi dixerunt: «Quid ad nos? Tu videris!». ⁵Et proiectis argenteis in templo, recessit et abiens laqueo se suspendit. ⁶Principes autem sacerdotum, acceptis argenteis, dixerunt: «Non licet mittere eos in corbanam, quia pretium sanguinis est». ⁷Consilio autem inito, emerunt ex illis agrum Figuli in sepulturam peregrinorum. ⁸Propter hoc vocatus est ager ille ager Sanguinis usque in hodiernum diem. ⁹Tunc

the Last Judgment: he who is now being judged will himself be the Judge at the end of time.

27:3–10 We do not know what motivated Judas to betray Jesus; but it is quite clear that he feels remorse when he sees Jesus condemned, and he admits his sin. Unfortunately, he despaired of being forgiven for his action, and he killed himself (see also Acts 1:16–20). "By *despair*, man ceases to hope for his personal salvation from God, for help in attaining it or for the forgiveness of his sins. Despair is contrary to God's goodness, to his justice—for the Lord is faithful to his promises—and to his mercy" (*Catechism of the Catholic Church*, 2091).

The reaction of the chief priests to Judas is equally deplorable. All they worry about is the fulfilment of a precept of the Law, to the last letter; they want to make sure not to give the temple treasury the money obtained by an unconscionable crime, despite the fact that they themselves were the instigators of the crime. Commenting on this passage, St Jerome (*Commentarii in Matthaeum*, 27, 6) observes that they proved by their actions our Lord's charge that they would strain out a gnat and swallow a camel (see 23:24). The evangelist sees in the purchase of the potter's field a further proof that Jesus is the suffering Servant of God in whom the Scriptures find fulfilment.

[8]Therefore that field has been called the Field of Blood to this day. [9]Then was fulfilled what had been spoken by the prophet Jeremiah, saying, "And they took the thirty pieces of silver, the price of him on whom a price had been set by some of the sons of Israel, [10]and they gave them for the potter's field, as the Lord directed me."

Acts 1:19
Zech 11:12–13
Jer 18:2–3; 32:6–9
Ex 9:12

Jesus' trial before Pilate

Mk 15:1–15
Lk 23:1–25
Jn 18:28–19:16

[11]Now Jesus stood before the governor; and the governor asked him, "Are you the King of the Jews?" Jesus said to him, "You have said so." [12]But when he was accused by the chief priests and elders, he made no answer. [13]Then Pilate said to him, "Do you not hear how many things they testify against you?" [14]But he gave him no answer, not even to a single charge; so that the governor wondered greatly.

Mt 26:63
Is 53:7
Mt 2:2; 27:29, 37
Lk 23:37–38
Jn 19:9, 21

[15]Now at the feast the governor was accustomed to release for the crowd any one prisoner whom they wanted. [16]And they had then a notorious prisoner, called Barabbas.[k] [17]So when they had gathered, Pilate said to them, "Whom do you want me to release for you, Barabbas[k] or Jesus who is called Christ?" [18]For he knew that it was out of envy that they had delivered him up. [19]Besides, while he was sitting on the judgment seat, his wife sent word to him, "Have nothing to do with that righteous man, for I have suffered much over him today in a dream." [20]Now the chief priests and the

Mt 21:38
Jn 11:47–48; 12:19
Acts 7:9

impletum est quod dictum est per Ieremiam prophetam dicentem: «*Et acceperunt triginta argenteos, pretium appretiati quem appretiaverunt a filiis Israel*, [10]*et dederunt eos in agrum Figuli, sicut constituit mihi Dominus*». [11]Iesus autem stetit ante praesidem; et interrogavit eum praeses dicens: «Tu es Rex Iudaeorum?». Dixit autem Iesus: «Tu dicis». [12]Et cum accusaretur a principibus sacerdotum et senioribus, nihil respondit. [13]Tunc dicit illi Pilatus: «Non audis quanta adversum te dicant testimonia?». [14]Et non respondit ei ad ullum verbum, ita ut miraretur praeses vehementer. [15]Per diem autem sollemnem consueverat praeses dimittere turbae unum vinctum, quem voluissent. [16]Habebant autem tunc vinctum insignem, qui dicebatur Barabbas. [17]Congregatis ergo illis dixit Pilatus: «Quem vultis dimittam vobis: Barabbam an Iesum, qui dicitur Christus?». [18]Sciebat enim quod per invidiam tradidissent eum. [19]Sedente autem illo pro tribunali, misit ad illum uxor eius dicens: «Nihil tibi et iusto illi. Multa enim passa sum hodie per visum propter eum». [20]Principes autem sacerdotum et seniores persuaserunt turbis, ut peterent Barabbam, Iesum

27:11–26 Matthew puts the emphasis here on Israel's rejection of the Messiah. His account includes a number of scenes which demonstrate Jesus' dignity and the injustice of the charges laid against him.

Jesus is brought "before the governor" (v. 11). Judea at that time was governed by a procurator or prefect. Although he was subordinate to the Roman legate of Syria, he had the *ius gladium*, that is, the authority to condemn a criminal to death. The chief priests bring their charges to the procurator, and Pilate invites Jesus to answer them. But Jesus says nothing (vv. 12, 14); as Isaiah 53:7 had foretold regarding the suffering Servant, he "opened not his mouth; like a lamb that is led to the slaughter and like a sheep that before its shearers is dumb, so he opened not his mouth." And St Ephrem comments on Jesus' eloquent silence: "He spoke in order to teach, and remained silent at his trial before Pilate. [...] The words of the false witnesses and his calumniators were a crown of redemption on his head. His silence was such that the more they jeered and shouted, the more beautiful his crown"

(*Commentarii in Diatessaron*, 20, 16).

Two things now occur that speak for Jesus' innocence—Pilate's attempt to release him (v. 18) and the appeal made by Pilate's wife, who considers Jesus a "righteous man" (v. 19). The governor, an experienced politician, realizes that the whole affair lies outside his competence. Jesus is innocent, but Jesus' enemies are not to be thwarted, so Pilate, coward that he is, tries to negotiate with them and attempts to use the device of the Passover amnesty. His proposed solution unravels. The priests and elders (v. 20) incite the crowd to call for Jesus to be crucified: "It is hard to read that question of Pilate's in the holy Gospel: 'Whom do you wish me to release to you, Barabbas or Jesus, who is called Christ?' But it is more painful to hear the answer: 'Barabbas!' And more terrible still when I realize that very often by going astray I too have said 'Barabbas' and added 'Christ? ... *Crucifige eum!* Crucify him!' " (St Josemaría Escrivá, *The Way*, 296).

This brings us to the central scene. Pilate washes his hands; there is no doubt about what this gesture means (v. 24; cf. Deut 21:6–8): it is

k Other ancient authorities read *Jesus Barabbas*

Acts 3:13, 14
elders persuaded the people to ask for Barabbas and destroy Jesus. [21]The governor again said to them, "Which of the two do you want me to release for you?" And they said, "Barabbas." [22]Pilate said to them, "Then what shall I do with Jesus who is called

Jn 19:14–15
Christ?" They all said, "Let him be crucified." [23]And he said, "Why, what evil has he done?" But they shouted all the more, "Let him be crucified."

Deut 21:6
[24]So when Pilate saw that he was gaining nothing, but rather that a riot was beginning, he took water and washed his hands before the crowd, saying, "I am innocent of

Acts 5:28
Mt 23:35
this righteous man's blood;[1] see to it yourselves." [25]And all the people answered, "His blood be on us and on our children!" [26]Then he released for them Barabbas, and having scourged Jesus, delivered him to be crucified.

Mk 15:16–20
Jn 19:1–3
The crowning with thorns

Mk 15:16–19
Jn 19:2–3
[27]Then the soldiers of the governor took Jesus into the praetorium, and they gathered the whole battalion before him. [28]And they stripped him and put a scarlet robe upon

Lk 23:11
him, [29]and plaiting a crown of thorns they put it on his head, and put a reed in his right hand. And kneeling before him they mocked him, saying, "Hail, King of the

Is 50:6
Jews!" [30]And they spat upon him, and took the reed and struck him on the head. [31]And when they had mocked him, they stripped him of the robe, and put his own clothes on him, and led him away to crucify him.

Mk 15:21–41
Lk 23:26–49
Jn 19:17–30
The crucifixion and death of Jesus

[32]As they were marching out, they came upon a man of Cyrene, Simon by name; this man they compelled to carry his cross. [33]And when they came to a place called

vero perderent. [21]Respondens autem praes ait illis: «Quem vultis vobis de duobus dimittam?». At illi dixerunt: «Barabbam!». [22]Dicit illis Pilatus: «Quid igitur faciam de Iesu, qui dicitur Christus?». Dicunt omnes: «Crucifigatur!». [23]Ait autem: «Quid enim mali fecit?». At illi magis clamabant dicentes: «Crucifigatur!». [24]Videns autem Pilatus quia nihil proficeret, sed magis tumultus fieret, accepta aqua, lavit manus coram turba dicens: «Innocens ego sum a sanguine hoc; vos videritis!». [25]Et respondens universus populus dixit: «Sanguis eius super nos et super filios nostros». [26]Tunc dimisit illis Barabbam; Iesum autem flagellatum tradidit, ut crucifigeretur. [27]Tunc milites praesidis suscipientes Iesum in praetorio congregaverunt ad eum universam cohortem. [28]Et exuentes eum, clamydem coccineam circumdederunt ei [29]et plectentes coronam de spinis posuerunt super caput eius et arundinem in dextera eius et, genu flexo ante eum, illudebant ei dicentes: «Ave, rex Iudaeorum!». [30]Et exspuentes in eum acceperunt arundinem et percutiebant caput eius. [31]Et postquam illuserunt ei, exuerunt eum clamyde et induerunt eum vestimentis eius et duxerunt eum, ut cruci-

a declaration that the people are responsible for the death of Jesus. Their reply has a theological dimension, that is, the rejection of the Messiah, which means that God will give his vineyard to another people who will bear fruit (cf. 21:43): "Neither all Jews indiscriminately at that time, nor Jews today, can be charged with the crimes committed during his passion. [...] The Jews should not be spoken of as rejected or accursed as if this followed from Holy Scripture" (Vatican II, *Nostra aetate*, 4).

Jesus is scourged and handed over for execution (v. 26). The scourging that Jesus underwent was the Roman type, called *flagellatio*, which was inflicted with leather whips that had pieces of bone or metal attached to them. Only slaves and mutinous soldiers were given this treatment. It was so severe that it sometimes caused death.

27:27–31 A Roman cohort, or battalion, was made up of 625 soldiers. In Jesus' time, a cohort was stationed in the Antonia tower, adjoining the temple. The personnel were mercenaries, recruited from outside the region. This explains why they mock him by hailing him as "King of the Jews", and it illustrates how, after being rejected by Jews, Jesus is also rejected by Gentiles. We can see here that Christ's sufferings have redemptive value for everyone, Jew or Gentile: "Look at the spittle on my face that I have endured so as to return the first breath of life to you; contemplate the blows on my cheeks which I have borne in order to remake your deformed image in my image" (an early homily, in the *Divine Office*, office of readings for Holy Saturday).

27:32–56 All four Gospels describe the crucifixion and death of our Lord in great detail.

l Other ancient authorities omit *righteous* or *man's*

Golgotha (which means the place of a skull), [34]they offered him wine to drink, mingled with gall; but when he tasted it, he would not drink it. [35]And when they had crucified him, they divided his garments among them by casting lots; [36]then they sat down and kept watch over him there. [37]And over his head they put the charge against him, which read, "This is Jesus the King of the Jews." [38]Then two robbers were crucified with him, one on the right and one on the left. [39]And those who passed by derided him, wagging their heads [40]and saying, "You who would destroy the temple and build it in three days, save yourself! If you are the Son of God, come down from the cross." [41]So also the chief priests, with the scribes and elders, mocked him, saying, [42]"He saved others; he cannot save himself. He is the King of Israel; let him come down now from the cross, and we will believe in him. [43]He trusts in God, let God deliver him now, if he desires him; for he said, 'I am the Son of God.'" [44]And the robbers who were crucified with him also reviled him in the same way.

[45]Now from the sixth hour there was darkness over all the land[m] until the ninth hour. [46]And about the ninth hour Jesus cried with a loud voice, "Eli, Eli, lama sabachthani?" that is, "My God, my God, why hast thou forsaken me?"* [47]And some of the bystanders hearing it said, "This man is calling Elijah." [48]And one of them at

Ps 69:21
Ps 22:18

Is 53:12

Ps 22:7; 109:25

Mt 26:61
Jn 2:19

Ps 22:8
Wis 2:13, 18–20

Ps 22:1

Ps 69:21

figerent. [32]Exeuntes autem invenerunt hominem Cyrenaeum nomine Simonem; hunc angariaverunt, ut tolleret crucem eius. [33]Et venerunt in locum, qui dicitur Golgotha, quod est Calvariae locus, [34]et *dederunt* ei vinum *bibere* cum *felle* mixtum; et cum gustasset, noluit bibere. [35]Postquam autem crucifixerunt eum, *diviserunt vestimenta* eius *sortem mittentes* [36]et sedentes servabant eum ibi. [37]Et imposuerunt super caput eius causam ipsius scriptam: «Hic est Iesus Rex Iudaeorum». [38]Tunc crucifiguntur cum eo duo latrones: unus a dextris et unus a sinistris. [39]Praetereuntes autem blasphemabant eum *moventes capita sua* [40]et dicentes: «Qui destruis templum et in triduo illud reaedificas, salva temetipsum; si Filius Dei es, descende de cruce!». [41]Similiter et principes sacerdotum illudentes cum scribis et senioribus dicebant: [42]«Alios salvos fecit, seipsum non potest salvum facere. Rex Israel est; descendat nunc de cruce, et credemus in eum. [43]*Confidit in Deo*; *liberet* nunc, *si vult eum*. Dixit enim: "Dei Filius sum"». [44]Idipsum autem et latrones, qui crucifixi erant cum eo, improperabant ei. [45]A sexta autem hora tenebrae factae sunt super universam terram usque ad horam nonam. [46]Et circa horam nonam clamavit Iesus voce magna dicens: «*Eli, Eli, lema sabacthani?*», hoc est: «*Deus meus, Deus meus, ut quid dereliquisti me?*». [47]Quidam autem ex illic stantibus audientes dicebant: «Eliam vocat iste». [48]Et continuo currens unus ex eis acceptam spongiam implevit aceto et imposuit arundini et

Matthew begins with the episode of Simon of Cyrene (v. 32), though he does not mention that he was the father of Alexander and Rufus. Golgotha or Calvary (v. 33) was outside the second wall of Jerusalem. It had been used as a quarry, and thus had been hollowed out roughly to the shape of a human skull.

All four evangelists report that Jesus was stripped of his garments (v. 35). A person condemned to crucifixion lost all his rights as a citizen; he had the status of a slave, so his executioners could do what they wanted with his clothes. The fact that they stripped Jesus has in itself no particular significance. However, early Christian tradition made note of this spoliation because it saw in it the fulfilment of the prophecy in Psalm 22:18, which is quoted at this point in John's Gospel. The placard put on the cross (v. 37)—all the evangelists mention it— was not an innovation of Pilate's specific to this case; it was standard Roman practice to publicly declare in this way the charge for which the person had been sentenced to death.

The jeering of the bystanders (vv. 39–44) and the words spoken by Jesus shortly before he dies (v. 46) are in line with Psalm 22:1ff. Our Lord's words clearly show the degree of his physical and moral suffering. In no sense can they be read as a complaint against God. "Suffering does not consist in not feeling since that is proper to those who have no feelings; nor does it lie in not showing that one feels pain: rather, suffering means that in spite of pain one does not set aside the law or obedience to God. For feeling is natural to the flesh, which is not like bronze; and so reason does not remove it, because reason gives to everything what its nature demands; and our sensitivity is very soft and tender; when it is wounded it of necessity feels, and when it feels it has to cry out" (Fray Luis de León, *Expositio del libro de Job*, 3). In his Agony in the Garden, Jesus experienced in advance the pain and desolation of this moment. He is God as well as Man, but in his human nature (body and soul) he suffers in a way that cannot be alleviated by his divinity.

m Or *earth*

once ran and took a sponge, filled it with vinegar, and put it on a reed, and gave it to him to drink. [49]But the others said, "Wait, let us see whether Elijah will come to save him."[n] [50]And Jesus cried again with a loud voice and yielded up his spirit.

Ex 26:31
Heb 10:19–20

[51]And behold, the curtain of the temple was torn in two, from top to bottom; and the earth shook, and the rocks were split; [52]the tombs also were opened, and many

Acts 26:23
Dan 12:2

bodies of the saints who had fallen asleep were raised, [53]and coming out of the tombs after his resurrection they went into the holy city and appeared to many.

Mt 16:16

[54]When the centurion and those who were with him, keeping watch over Jesus, saw the earthquake and what took place, they were filled with awe, and said, "Truly this was the Son[x] of God!"

dabat ei bibere. [49]Ceteri vero dicebant: «Sine, videamus an veniat Elias liberans eum». [50]Iesus autem iterum clamans voce magna emisit spiritum. [51]Et ecce velum templi scissum est a summo usque deorsum in duas partes, et terra mota est, et petrae scissae sunt, [52]et monumenta aperta sunt et multa corpora sanctorum, qui dormierant, surrexerunt [53]et exeuntes de monumentis post resurrectionem eius venerunt in sanctam civitatem et apparuerunt multis. [54]Centurio autem et, qui cum eo erant custodientes Iesum, viso terrae motu et his, quae fiebant, timuerunt valde dicentes: «Vere Dei Filius erat iste!». [55]Erant autem ibi mulieres multae a longe aspicientes, quae secutae erant Iesum a Galilaea ministrantes ei; [56]inter quas erat Maria Magdalene et Maria

Jesus' words on the cross ("My God, my God, why hast thou forsaken me?": v. 46) must have made his disciples realize later that his crucifixion and death fulfilled everything said about Christ in Scripture (see the note on Mk 15:21–41). This is surely why this passage contains allusions to verses in the Old Testament which describe how the sufferings of a just man will lead all nations to praise God: "Our Saviour's death was a sacrifice of holocaust which he himself offered to his Father for our redemption; for though the pains and sufferings of his passion were so great and violent that anyone else would have died of them, Jesus would not have died of them unless he so chose and unless the fire of his infinite charity had consumed his life. He was, then, himself the sacrificer who offered himself to the Father and immolated himself, dying in love, to love, by love, for love and of love" (St Francis de Sales, *Treatise on the Love of God*, 10, 17).

The rending of the veil in the temple (v. 51) indicates that the way to God the Father has been opened up for all mankind (cf. Heb 9:1–10; 10:20) and that the New Covenant, sealed with the blood of Christ, has come into effect.

The other portents that attend Jesus' death (vv. 45, 51–53) are signs that are interpreted as God's answer to men's actions. It was not a mere man who lost his life; it was the Son of God in his human nature. These events recall Old Testament oracles (Amos 8:9; Is 2:10; Ezek 32:7; Dan 12:2) that proclaim a future day of the Lord, complete with resurrection and a final ret-

ribution. Verses 52–53 are difficult to interpret. The great church writers put forward three possible explanations: (1) it was a matter not of resurrection in the strict sense, but of appearances of these dead people; (2) they were dead people who rose in the way that Lazarus did, and who therefore would die again; (3) their resurrection was definitive, that is, glorious, anticipating the final resurrection. St Jerome, St Augustine and St Thomas Aquinas (see *Summa theologiae*, 3, 53, 3) incline towards the second interpretation. The passage is difficult to understand, but it does carry the message that, by dying, Jesus overcame death itself. The Church says this when it professes faith in Christ's descent into hell: "Scripture calls the abode of the dead, to which the dead Christ went down, 'hell' — *Sheol* in Hebrew or *Hades* in Greek — because those who are there are deprived of the vision of God ... Jesus did not descend into hell to deliver the damned, nor to destroy the hell of damnation, but to free the just who had gone before him" (*Catechism of the Catholic Church*, 633). See also the note on 1 Pet 3:18–22.

The fact that the holy women stayed as close as they could get to Christ on the cross (vv. 55–56) is an object-lesson in fortitude. "Woman is stronger than man, and more faithful, in the hour of suffering: Mary Magdalene and Mary Cleophas and Salome! With a group of valiant women like these, closely united to our Lady of Sorrows, what work for souls could be done in the world!" (St Josemaría Escrivá, *The Way*, 982).

n Other ancient authorities insert *And another took a spear and pierced his side, and out came water and blood*   x Or *a son*

Lk 8:2–3

⁵⁵There were also many women there, looking on from afar, who had followed Jesus from Galilee, ministering to him; ⁵⁶among whom were Mary Magdalene, and Mary the mother of James and Joseph, and the mother of the sons of Zebedee.

Mk 15: 42–47
Lk 23:50–56
Jn 19:31–42

The burial of Jesus

⁵⁷When it was evening, there came a rich man from Arimathea, named Joseph, who also was a disciple of Jesus. ⁵⁸He went to Pilate and asked for the body of Jesus. Then Pilate ordered it to be given to him. ⁵⁹And Joseph took the body, and wrapped it in a clean linen shroud, ⁶⁰and laid it in his own new tomb, which he had hewn in the rock; and he rolled a great stone to the door of the tomb, and departed. ⁶¹Mary Magdalene and the other Mary were there, sitting opposite the sepulchre.

Ex 34:25
Deut 21:22–33

Is 53:9

⁶²Next day, that is, after the day of Preparation, the chief priests and the Pharisees gathered before Pilate ⁶³and said, "Sir, we remember how that imposter said, while he was still alive, 'After three days I will rise again.' ⁶⁴Therefore order the sepulchre to be made secure until the third day, lest his disciples go and steal him away, and tell the people, 'He has risen from the dead,' and the last fraud will be worse than the first." ⁶⁵Pilate said to them, 'You have a guardᵒ of soldiers; go, make it as secure as you can.'ᵖ ⁶⁶So they went and made the sepulchre secure by sealing the stone and setting a guard.*

2 Cor 6:8
Mt 12:40; 20:19
Mt 28:13

Iacobi et Ioseph mater et mater filiorum Zebedaei. ⁵⁷Cum sero autem factum esset, venit homo dives ab Arimathaea nomine Ioseph, qui et ipse discipulus erat Iesu. ⁵⁸Hic accessit ad Pilatum et petiit corpus Iesu. Tunc Pilatus iussit reddi. ⁵⁹Et accepto corpore, Ioseph involvit illud in sindone munda ⁶⁰et posuit illud in monumento suo novo, quod exciderat in petra, et advolvit saxum magnum ad ostium monumenti et abiit. ⁶¹Erat autem ibi Maria Magdalene et altera Maria sedentes contra sepulcrum. ⁶²Altera autem die, quae est post Parascevem, convenerunt principes sacerdotum et pharisaei ad Pilatum ⁶³dicentes: «Domine, recordati sumus quia seductor ille dixit adhuc vivens: 'Post tres dies resurgam'. ⁶⁴Iube ergo custodiri sepulcrum usque in diem tertium, ne forte veniant discipuli eius et furentur eum et dicant plebi: 'Surrexit a mortuis', et erit novissimus error peior priore». ⁶⁵Ait illis Pilatus:

Meditation on the passion of Christ has made many saints over the centuries. Few things are of more benefit to Christians than contemplation (calm, devout, in awe) of the saving events surrounding the death of the Son of God made man.

Saints have asked themselves how Jesus could have borne all his suffering. St Catherine of Siena recorded the following locution from God the Father about how it is possible for sorrow, pain and joy to coexist: "The soul is full of suffering and joy: it suffers for the sins of others, and is filled with joy by the communion and love within itself. Those souls imitate the Immaculate Lamb, my Only-begotten Son, who on the cross was full of suffering and joy" (*Dialogue*, 78).

27:57–66 Jewish law prescribed that the bodies of those executed should be buried before nightfall, for "a hanged man is accursed by God" and his corpse would defile the land (Deut 21:22–23). In Jesus' case there was the additional fact that he had been executed on the eve of the sabbath, which may have been Passover, according

to the Sadducean reckoning. This context explains the haste of the Jewish authorities in making their approach to Pilate. The day of Preparation (the Greek word *parasceve* means "preparation": cf. Lk 23:54) was so called because it was the day on which all the necessary preparations were made for the sabbath (no work could be done on the sabbath because it was a day dedicated to God). The term may also refer to the day prior to a great feast that had sabbath status, such as the Passover (see Jn 19:14).

"In his plan of salvation, God ordained that his Son should not only 'die for our sins' (1 Cor 15:3), but should also 'taste death', experience the condition of death, the separation of his soul from his body, between the time he expired on the cross and the time he was raised from the dead. The state of the dead Christ is the mystery of the tomb and the descent into hell" (*Catechism of the Catholic Church*, 624). St Matthew mentions some details—the new tomb and the huge stone (v. 60), the sealing and the guard (v. 66)—all of which show that Jesus had truly died, and that there were no grounds for the

o Or *take a guard*   p Greek *know*

Mk 16:1–8
Lk 24:1–12
Jn 20:1–10
Mt 27:61

Acts 1:10

Acts 2:36
Mt 12:40; 16:21;
17:23; 20:19; 26:32

Heb 2:11
Gen 45:4; 50:19

Jesus rises from the dead and appears to the women

28 *[1]Now after the sabbath, toward the dawn of the first day of the week, Mary Magdalene and the other Mary went to see the sepulchre. [2]And behold, there was a great earthquake; for an angel of the Lord descended from heaven and came and rolled back the stone, and sat upon it. [3]His appearance was like lightning, and his raiment white as snow. [4]And for fear of him the guards trembled and became like dead men. [5]But the angel said to the women. "Do not be afraid; for I know that you seek Jesus who was crucified. [6]He is not here; for he has risen, as he said. Come, see the place where he^q lay. [7]Then go quickly and tell his disciples that he has risen from the dead, and behold, he is going before you to Galilee; there you will see him. Lo, I have told you." [8]So they departed quickly from the tomb with fear and great joy, and ran to tell his disciples. [9]And behold, Jesus met them and said, "Hail!" And they came up and took hold of his feet and worshipped him. [10]Then Jesus said to them, "Do not be afraid; go and tell my brethren to go to Galilee; and there they will see me."

The soldiers are bribed

[11]While they were going, behold, some of the guard went into the city and told the chief priests all that had taken place. [12]And when they had assembled with the elders

«Habetis custodiam; ite, custodite, sicut scitis». [66]Illi autem abeuntes munierunt sepulcrum, signantes lapidem, cum custodia. [28] [1]Sero autem post sabbatum, cum illucesceret in primam sabbati, venit Maria Magdalene et altera Maria videre sepulcrum. [2]Et ecce terrae motus factus est magnus: angelus enim Domini descendit de caelo et accedens revolvit lapidem et sedebat super eum. [3]Erat autem aspectus eius sicut fulgur, et vestimentum eius candidum sicut nix. [4]Prae timore autem eius exterriti sunt custodes et facti sunt velut mortui. [5]Respondens autem angelus dixit mulieribus: «Nolite timere vos! Scio enim quod Iesum, qui crucifixus est, quaeritis. [6]Non est hic: surrexit enim, sicut dixit. Venite, videte locum, ubi positus erat. [7]Et cito euntes dicite discipulis eius: "Surrexit a mortuis et ecce praecedit vos in Galilaeam; ibi eum videbitis". Ecce dixi vobis». [8]Et exeuntes cito de monumento cum timore et magno gaudio cucurrerunt nuntiare discipulis eius. [9]Et ecce Iesus occurrit illis dicens: «Avete». Illae autem accesserunt et tenuerunt pedes eius et adoraverunt eum. [10]Tunc ait illis Iesus: «Nolite timere; ite, nuntiate fratribus meis, ut eant in Galilaeam et ibi me videbunt». [11]Quae cum abiissent, ecce quidam de custodia venerunt in civitatem et nuntiaverunt principibus sacerdotum omnia, quae facta fuerant. [12]Et congregati cum

misinformation that would be spread soon afterwards (cf. 28:15).

28:1–15 "The Resurrection of Jesus is the crowning truth of our faith in Christ, a faith believed and lived as the central truth by the first Christian community; handed on as fundamental by Tradition; established by the documents of the New Testament; and preached as an essential part of the Paschal mystery along with the cross" (*Catechism of the Catholic Church*, 638). It has two dimensions. In the first place, it is "an event which is historically attested to by the disciples, who really encountered the Risen One. At the same time, this event is mysteriously transcendent insofar as it is the entry of Christ's humanity into the glory of God" (ibid., 656). Secondly, it is of huge importance to mankind, for "Christ, 'the first-born from the dead' (Col 1:18), is the principle of our own resurrection, even now by the justification of our souls (cf. Rom 6:4), and one day by the new life he will impart to our

bodies (cf. Rom 8:11)" (ibid., 658).

The Gospels concur that the first appearances of the Risen Jesus were not to the apostles, but to the "holy women", whose disinterested and generous love, more faithful and valiant than that of the men disciples, was rewarded in this special way. In Jewish society of the time, little weight was given to legal testimony from women; that may be why St Paul makes no mention of these women in his catechetical summary in 1 Corinthians 15:1–9. The fact that they are given such importance in the four Gospels indicates, firstly, that this appearance did happen (which is, of course, a matter of record), and secondly, that God's love goes out first to simple, generous, humble souls.

There are a number of small differences in the Synoptic accounts. Mark's account is typically fresh and spontaneous; Luke's approach is almost clinical in his attention to detail; and Matthew's style is that of a preacher, catechetical and formal (he avoids giving minor details). The

q Other ancient authorities read *the Lord*

Mt 27:64

and taken counsel, they gave a sum of money to the soldiers [13]and said, "Tell people, 'His disciples came by night and stole him away while we were asleep.' [14]And if this comes to the governor's ears, we will satisfy him and keep you out of trouble." [15]So they took the money and did as they were directed; and this story has been spread among the Jews to this day.

Mk 16:14–18
Lk 24:36–49
Jn 20:19–31

Appearance in Galilee. The mission to the world

[16]Now the eleven disciples went to Galilee, to the mountain to which Jesus had directed them. [17]And when they saw him they worshipped him; but some doubted. [18]And Jesus came and said to them, "All authority in heaven and on earth has been given to me. [19]Go therefore and make disciples of all nations, baptizing them in the

Eph 1:20–22
Dan 7:14
Mt 24:14

senioribus, consilio accepto, pecuniam copiosam dederunt militibus [13]dicentes: «Dicite: "Discipuli eius nocte venerunt et furati sunt eum, nobis dormientibus". [14]Et si hoc auditum fuerit a praeside, nos suadebimus ei et securos vos faciemus». [15]At illi, accepta pecunia, fecerunt, sicut erant docti. Et divulgatum est verbum istud apud Iudaeos usque in hodiernum diem. [16]Undecim autem discipuli abierunt in Galilaeam, in montem ubi constituerat illis Iesus, [17]et videntes eum adoraverunt; quidam autem dubitaverunt. [18]Et accedens Iesus locutus est eis dicens: «Data est mihi omnis potestas in caelo

signs he records when describing the announcement of the resurrection (vv. 2–4) imply the sheer scale of the event; like the death of Jesus (27:51–54), the resurrection is an extraordinary event: it makes perfect sense that heaven and earth should proclaim it: "This is the day on which the Lord acted, a day different to every other day since the dawn of time. This day is the dawn of a new creation; as the prophet says, on this day God created a new heaven and a new earth. [...] The true man is created on this day, the one who was made in the image and likeness of God. [...] But we have not yet spoken of the greatest moment in this day of grace: the most important event in this day is that he destroyed the suffering of death and gave birth to the firstborn among the dead. [...] What a beautiful and joyful message! The Only-begotten Son of the Father, who became man to be like us, wants to make us his brothers, to raise his humanity to the Father, drawing with him all those who now belong to his race" (St Gregory of Nyssa, *In Christi Resurrectionis, oratio*, 1).

By registering the lies told about the body having been stolen (vv. 11–15) the evangelist asserts the contrary—that Jesus truly rose from the dead. Even the enemies of the resurrection know that the tomb is empty, and they cannot explain why. St Augustine makes this apt remark: "Wretched craftiness, do you give us witnesses who were asleep? It is you who are really asleep if this is the only kind of explanation you have to offer!" (*Enarrationes in Psalmos*, 63, 15).

28:16–20 All four evangelists record how difficult it was for the apostles to accept the resurrection of Jesus. Mark (see Mk 16:9–20 and note) is more explicit about this than Matthew, who mentions it only once (v. 17): "It is no great thing to believe that Christ died; for this is something that is also believed by pagans and Jews and by all the wicked: everyone believes that he died. The Christians' faith is in Christ's resurrection; this is what we hold to be a great thing—to believe that he rose from the dead" (St Augustine, *Enarrationes in Psalmos*, 120, 6).

"All authority in heaven and on earth has been given to me" (v. 18). Omnipotence, an attribute of God alone, belongs to Jesus Christ. Our Lord's words are reminiscent of a passage in the book of Daniel where it is announced that, after various empires hold sway, there will come "one like a son of man" who is "given dominion and glory and kingdom, that all peoples, nations, and languages should serve him; his dominion is an everlasting dominion, which shall not pass away, and his kingdom one, that shall not be destroyed" (Dan 7:14). Jesus is the Son of man who through his sufferings merited that glory (cf. Dan 7:9–14 and note).

Verses 19–20 record Christ's commission to his apostles. The first mission of the Twelve (10:1–42) was to the house of Israel (10:5–6), and the message they were to bring was that the Kingdom of heaven was at hand (10:7). Now, the Eleven are sent out to the whole world, and they are to baptize in the name of the three divine Persons (v. 19) and

Jn 14:23

name of the Father and of the Son and of the Holy Spirit, [20]teaching them to observe all that I have commanded you; and lo, I am with you always, to the close of the age."

et in terra. [19]*Euntes ergo docete omnes gentes, baptizantes eos in nomine Patris et Filii et Spiritus Sancti,* [20]*docentes eos servare omnia, quaecumque mandavi vobis. Et ecce ego vobiscum sum omnibus diebus usque ad consummationem saeculi».*

teach to all the Lord's commandments (v. 20). Salvation is obtained through belonging to the Church, and the proof that people do belong to it will be their observance of the commandments: "Fulfilment of the commandments earns a great reward. Not only the first and most important commandment [...]: through the other commandments, too, God perfects those who fulfil them, making them beautiful, instructing them, enlightening them, filling them with goodness and joy. You have been created for the glory of God and for your own eternal salvation: this is your goal, your soul's treasure, your heart's desire. If you reach this goal, you will be blessed and holy; if you fail to reach this goal, you will be wretched and full of sorrow" (St Robert Bellarmine, *De ascensione mentis in Deum*, 1).

"I am with you always, to the close of the age" (v. 20). In the Old Testament we are told that God dwelt in the midst of his people (see e.g. Ex 33:15–17) and that he promised his chosen ones that he would remain with them in all their doings and that therefore things would go well for them (see Gen 28:15; Ex 3:12; Josh 1:5; Jer 1:8). The words that close this Gospel indicate that its message is addressed to the entire Church. And in this work of evangelization we are not alone: he is the Emmanuel, the "God-with-us" (1:23), and as God, with his authority and power (v. 18), he stays with us until the end of the world (v. 20). "Although it is not proper to this earthly life, but to eternal life when God will be all in all, the Lord remains at the heart of the temple, the Church, as he promised when he said: 'I am with you always, to the close of the age'. Therefore, not only can everything that the Son of God did and taught for the reconciliation of the world be known through reading about the events in the past, it can be seen and felt in the power of the good works done to this very day" (St Leo the Great, *Sermo in Passione Domini*, 3, 6).

THE GOSPEL ACCORDING TO

MARK

Introduction

In most of the ancient codexes of the New Testament, the Gospel according to St Mark comes second, after Matthew, but very occasionally this position is taken by the Gospel according to St John, probably in order to give precedence to the Gospels written by apostles. Patristic tradition usually has it that Mark was the second Gospel to be written, too, although it has been suggested[1] that the first Gospels to be written were those that contain genealogies, namely, Matthew and Luke.

Patristic tradition, however, is unanimous in saying that the author of this Gospel is Mark, the "disciple and interpreter" of Peter.[2] Some early documents mention that Mark did not know or follow Jesus during his earthly life, but all of them note that his Gospel faithfully reproduces the preaching of Peter. The oldest extant testimony, that of Papias of Hierapolis (second century), has this to say: "Mark was Peter's amanuensis; he wrote down, in no strict order, what Peter remembered the Lord to have said and done. Mark himself did not hear the Lord preach; he was not one of the Lord's followers; rather, as I have said, he was a later follower of Peter's. Peter preached according to the needs and circumstances of the moment; thus, Mark's writing is not a structured exposition of the Lord's teaching. Nevertheless, Mark does not err in any of the things that he records."[3] Papias' reference to a lack of "strict order" is probably meant to explain why the Gospel of Mark does not have many of Christ's teachings that can be found in St Matthew. However, Papias does emphasize that Peter's preaching lies behind Mark's text. All the testimonies from the early Church agree on this point—from Gaul (St Irenaeus)[4] to Egypt (Clement of Alexandria).[5] Later writings repeat this attribution and these distinctive features of the second Gospel.[6] Moreover, Scripture itself vouches for the connexion between Peter and Mark, where Peter calls Mark his son (see 1 Pet 5:13). Mark also had a close connexion with St Paul; although they had a falling-out at first (see Acts 13:1–13), the Apostle of the Gentiles later refers to him as a fellow-worker whom he has found to be a faithful servant of the Gospel.[7]

The last twelve verses of the Gospel (16:9–20), although they show some of the features typical of the second evangelist, have a different style. Moreover, they are absent in some very important codexes, such as the Vatican and the Sinaitic—a fact noted by early authors.[8] However, St Justin and St Irenaeus were familiar with them or at least referred to them.[9] Whether they are by Mark or are a later addition, these verses are considered to be inspired and canonical (according to the spirit of the Council of Trent's decree on sacred books).[10]

Due to its conciseness and its use of more prosaic and less evocative language, St Mark's Gospel has not been as much commented on as the works of Matthew, Luke and John. St Augustine, for example, remarked that the second Gospel seems to follow Matthew's Gospel and be a shorter version of it.[11] That may explain why there are not many commentaries on it by Fathers

---

1 Clement of Alexandria, according to Eusebius of Caesarea, *Historia ecclesiastica*, 6, 14, 5–7. **2** He is called a "disciple" of Peter in Eusebius, ibid., 2, 15, 1; "interpreter", ibid., 3, 39, 14–15; "disciple and interpreter", ibid., 5, 8, 3. **3** Ibid., 3, 39, 14–15. **4** "Mark, the disciple and interpreter of Peter, also handed on to us in writing the preaching of Peter" (St Irenaeus, *Adversus haereses*, 3, 1, 1). **5** "The writing of the Gospel according to Mark came about in the following way: inspired by the Holy Spirit, Peter was preaching the word and teaching the Gospel in Rome. Some in the multitude that had gathered to listen to him urged Mark, who had been one of Peter's followers for a long time and remembered his teachings, to write down all he had said. Mark did as they asked and gave them the written Gospel. When Peter heard of it, he did nothing either to encourage or discourage it" (Eusebius of Caesarea, *Historia ecclesiastica*, 6, 14, 5–7). **6** See e.g. St Jerome, *De viris illustribus*, 8; St Augustine, *De consensu evangelistarum*, 1, 1–2. **7** See Philem 24; Col 4:10; 2 Tim 4:11. **8** See Eusebius of Caesarea, *Historia ecclesiastica*, 3, 10, 6; St Jerome, *Epistulae*, 120, 3. **9** St Justin, *Apologia*, 1, 45; St Irenaeus, *Adversus haereses*, 3, 10, 5. **10** Council of Trent, *Decreta de Sacris Scripturis*, 8 April 1546. **11** *De consensu evangelistarum*, 1, 2, 3–4.

of the Church. We have one by St Jerome, which gives pride of place to the spiritual meaning of the text, and, later on, there was one by St Bede the Venerable. However, in modern times Mark has come to be more appreciated. In particular, his proximity to the sources and the spontaneity with which he writes allow us to find in his Gospel a unique depiction of the Jesus who exerted such a great attraction on the apostles and on the first generation of Christians.

1. STRUCTURE AND CONTENT

The first verse of the Gospel states that Jesus is the Christ, the Son of God. Two dimensions of this fact run throughout the fabric of the text—Jesus' revelation of himself to others as he truly is, and the disciples' realization of Christ's divine nature. In the light of this observation the Gospel of St Mark can be said to consist of two parts, defined and linked by Peter's profession of faith at Caesarea Philippi: (cf. Mk 8:29). Up to that point, Jesus' words and works show him to be the Messiah but neither the crowd nor the disciples manage to see this (cf. 1:27; 2:7, 12; 4:41; 6:2, 14–16). At Caesarea Philippi Peter acknowledges Jesus to be the Messiah and, immediately after this, Jesus begins to explain his messianic mission to his disciples: they should see him not as a political liberator, but as the Son of man who must endure the affronts foretold of the Servant of the Lord—suffering that will lead to his death and which will be followed by his resurrection. Very near the end of the Gospel, a Gentile, the Roman centurion, standing at the foot of the cross, proclaims Jesus to be Son of God. These two testimonies (of Peter and the centurion) corroborate the titles that Mark gives Jesus at the start of his Gospel: Jesus is the Christ and he is the Son of God. There are other things in this Gospel that stress the connexion between who Jesus really is and what people discover and declare him to be. For example, over the course of the narrative, after someone makes a confession of faith, there comes a sign from heaven that confirms and perfects what the person has said: after John's declaration in 1:7 comes, in 1:11, the voice from heaven; after Peter's confession in 8:29 comes the voice at the Transfiguration (9:7); and the words of the centurion in 15:39 are soon followed by those of the young man who announces the Resurrection (16:5–6).

As is also the case in the other Synoptics, the chapters that come after Peter's confession of faith can be divided into two parts—the journey towards Jerusalem, and the events that occur in the city. We could say that the Gospel is structured as follows:

PRELUDE (1:1–13). John the Baptist is introduced as the Precursor announced in the Old Testament, and Jesus is described as the Messiah and Son of God.

FIRST PART: JESUS' MINISTRY IN GALILEE (1:14—8:30). Jesus preaches conversion as the gateway to the Kingdom of God. His teaching and his miracles win the admiration of the crowd (see 1:27–28, 31, 45; 2:2, 12); but he also encounters opposition from scribes and Pharisees (see 2:6, 16, 24; 3:6). He uses parables to teach the large numbers of people who flock to him; but they fail to understand him. However, he imparts special teaching to his chosen disciples. The great things that Jesus does cause the people to wonder who he is (see 1:27; 2:7, 12; 4:41; 6:2, 14–16; 8:27–28). It seems that devils know his identity (see 1:23–25, 34; 3:11–12; 5:7), but Jesus does not accept their testimony: he wants to be acknowledged by men and women, as he is by Peter at the end of this part of the book (8:29).

SECOND PART: JESUS' MINISTRY ON THE WAY TO JERUSALEM (8:31—10:52). After Peter's confession of faith, Jesus concentrates on the formation and training of his disciples, and he shows them that he must undergo his passion in order to enter into glory (8:31—9:13). The three announcements of the passion (8:31; 9:31; 10:33–34) act as a chorus to the chapters in this part of the Gospel. Jesus rounds off his teaching with lessons about the virtues and attitudes that should characterize the lives of his disciples—prayer (9:14–29), humility (9:33–50), poverty (10:17–31), etc.

THIRD PART: JESUS' MINISTRY IN JERUSALEM (11:1—16:20). This narrative of Jesus' doings in the last seven days of his life includes many references to specific times and places. It begins with his triumphant entry into Jerusalem (11:1–19). The Jewish authorities, who have been trying to entrap him almost from the start of his public ministry, now engage in controversy with him (11:27—12:40) and decide that he must die (11:18; 12:12; 14:1–2, 10–11). Jesus is ready to meet his death, seeing in it the fulfilment of his Father's will as revealed in the Scriptures (14:21); but his death is another step on the road to his resurrection. The Gospel ends with Jesus' entry into the glory of heaven.

2. CONTEXT

The author and his sources

We have already noted that tradition unanimously names Mark as the author of the second Gospel; there is also a general consensus that the book came to be written in response to requests to Mark from the Christians of Rome to put on record the preaching of Peter. There are two different traditions about when the book was actually written: Clement of Alexandria says that it dates from before the martyrdom of Peter, and St Irenaeus that it was shortly after that event: "After Peter's death, Mark, his disciple and amanuensis, wrote down what Peter had preached and taught."[12] Peter died in the persecution that took place in the years 64–67; therefore the book must have been written sometime during the 60s.

The New Testament tells us a number of things about Mark. As well as saying that he was a co-worker of Peter and of Paul, it tells us that he was a cousin of Barnabas,[13] and a son of Mary, a woman in whose house the church of Jerusalem used to gather.[14]

A reading of the Gospel itself would tend to confirm the observations that Tradition made about its authorship and place of composition. At no point is the author mentioned as such by name in the text (this is true of all the Gospels). However, the author of this book appears to have received information directly from an eyewitness of the events he records: a close examination of the passages in which Mark gives more anecdotal information than the other Synoptics reveals that Peter is always present.[15] As regards the place of composition and the immediate readership

---

12 *Adversus haereses*, 3, 1, 1. For the Clement of Alexandria reference, see note 5 above. **13** See Col. 4:10. The evangelist is called Mark in Acts 15:39, both John and Mark in Acts 12:12 and 15:37, and John in Acts 13:5–13. It was quite common at the time for Jews to have two different names—here, a Jewish name, John (*Yohannan*) and a Hellenized Latin name, *Marcus* or *Markos*. **14** See Acts 12:12. An early Christian text says that this was the house of the Cenacle, where our Lord celebrated the Last Supper and instituted the Eucharist (cf. *Acta Sanctorum*, 2 [1867] 434). In line with that piece of information, many ecclesiastical writers say that the Garden of Olives also belonged to the mother of Mark. For that reason, they see in Mark 14:51–52 (the episode about the young man who leaves his sheet behind him as he flees from the garden when Jesus is arrested) Mark's own veiled signature to his Gospel. **15** Peter is mentioned 25 times in the Gospel, and we find him acting as the disciples'

of the Gospel, there are many clues that support the idea that it was written in Rome. For example, the narrator explains Jewish customs,[16] and translates Hebrew and Aramaic words used by Jesus,[17] which suggests that he was writing for people who were not familiar with the languages and customs of Palestine; moreover, he uses many Latinisms and various turns of phrase which make more sense if his audience was a Roman one.[18]

Literary and theological features

Most scholars are of the view that, although Mark's writing style has its defects, he is always in command of the story. A cursory examination of his work shows that Greek was not his mother tongue. He is not a polished writer, nor does he always express himself clearly. However, the directness of his style makes his account immediate and vivid. His vocabulary is somewhat limited, and the syntax he uses is unsophisticated: there is a predominance of sentences linked by conjunctions (usually "and" or "then"). Also, he very often uses direct speech in the middle of his narrative, and the reader of the Greek will notice his use of the historical present (such expressions as "he comes", "he says" and "they go" occur some 150 times) and the fact that he often moves unexpectedly from one tense to another within the same passage (this is not reflected in the RSV). A particular feature of his style is the local and exact detail he gives in some episodes which are more soberly treated by Matthew or Luke.[19] Moreover, he often uses the third person plural (meaning Jesus and his disciples) where the other evangelists use the singular ("he", "Jesus").[20] The narrative is so vivid that the reader seems to be listening to the voice of an eyewitness saying, "then we arrived, we came, we went ...". These characteristics are natural elements of a written account based more or less directly on oral teaching: Mark's Gospel, Peter's preaching. At the same time, St Mark, unlike the other evangelists, does not record long discourses. He does say (more than others) that Jesus "taught"; but he tells us relatively little about *what* was taught.[21]

These literary features of the Gospel have a deeper dimension to them, connected with the message that Mark wants to convey. By providing detailed accounts of episodes in the life of Jesus and his disciples, this evangelist helps us to position ourselves in the small towns on the shore of the lake of Gennesaret, to sense the way the people crowded around Jesus, and to see and understand Jesus' gestures: in other words, it is as if we were present, witnessing it all. Certain features of Mark's style (mentioned above) contribute to this: his use of direct speech and the

spokesman (1:36; 9:5; 11:21; 13:3; 14:37). Moreover, this Gospel seems to make a point of mentioning Peter's less praiseworthy interventions. **16** The longest passage where this happens is Mark 7:3–4 ("For the Pharisees, and all the Jews, do not eat unless they wash their hands, observing the tradition of the elders; and when they come from the market place, they do not eat unless they purify themselves, and there are many other traditions which they observe, the washing of cups and pots and vessels of bronze"); but little explanations are also provided elsewhere (Mk 14:12: "on the first day of Unleavened Bread, when they sacrificed the passover lamb"; Mk 15:42: "the day of Preparation, that is, the day before the sabbath"). But Mark assumes his readers are familiar with technical Roman words: "the soldiers led him away inside the palace (that is, the praetorium)" (15:16), and "[she] put in two copper coins, which make a penny [*quadrans*]" (12:42). **17** For example, "Boanerges, that is, sons of thunder" (3:17), "Talitha cumi", which means, "Little girl, I say to you, arise" (5:41). Other examples appear in 7:11; 14:36; 15:22; 15:34. **18** It is possible that Mark's Latin words—denarius, centurion, etc.—were in common use throughout the empire; but there are things in the Gospel that point to specifically Roman customs: for example, Mark uses the Roman method of dividing the night hours (6:48; 13:35). And when mentioning Simon of Cyrene (15:21), he adds that he was the father of Alexander and Rufus, people who were known to the Christians of Rome (see Rom 16:13). **19** See the curing of the paralytic (Mk 2:1–12, as compared with Mt 9:1–8 and Lk 5:17–26), and the curing of the possessed man at Gerasa (Mk 5:1 and 20; Mt 8:28–34 and Lk 8:26–39). And Mark is the only one to give us some other small pieces of information: only he tells us that during the storm on the lake Jesus was asleep on a cushion (4:38); and that Jesus named the sons of Zebedee "sons of thunder" (3:17), and that the blind man of Jericho was named Bartimaeus (10:46), etc. **20** See Mk 1:21, 5:1, 38; 8:22; 9:1–30, 33; 10:32, 46; 11:1, 12, 15, 27; 14:22, 26, 32. **21** Strictly speaking, he records only two major discourses of Jesus—that of the parables (4:1–34) and the eschatological discourse (13:1–37).

historical present helps to draw the reader in, inviting him or her to be involved, just as the disciples were. Similarly, his repeated use of the adverb "immediately" (it appears as many as 40 times), and his reports of the rapid spread of Jesus' fame, convey a sense of urgency about the proclamation of the Gospel and also show the success that the Gospel met with—and will continue to meet with if Christ's disciples follow the example of their Master.

As regards the special features of St Mark's Gospel, the two most significant ones are the idea of "gospel" and what has come to be termed the "mystery of Jesus" or the "messianic secret" in Mark.

The Gospel is for the whole world. Mark is the evangelist who most often (six times) uses the word "Gospel" in its absolute sense: *the* good news. Where other evangelists use phrases such as "gospel of the kingdom", St Mark simply says "gospel". This word is in the very first sentence of Mark's account, and it also appears very near its end.[22] Moreover, the "Gospel" is closely identified with the person of Jesus Christ: Jesus tells his disciples that giving their life for the Gospel is practically the same thing as giving it for him.[23] This makes it quite clear that the Gospel, the good news that has been given to all mankind, is Jesus, who has won our salvation. But the notion of Gospel is also linked to another reality—the fact that it is for the whole world. On a number of occasions Jesus expressly states as much.[24] This universal extension of the Gospel is implied in other ways, too, the most significant being the frequent use of the word "Galilee" in the narrative. Galilee was the place where Jesus began his ministry and where he spent the greater part of it, and it is the place designated for the new stage that begins after the Resurrection (see Mk 14:28; 16:7). From the social point of view, Galilee was also a crossroads of cultures and peoples—the Rome of Palestine, so to speak. Through his work in that region Jesus shows (and St Mark underlines this) that although his earthly ministry is confined to Israel, it encompasses all mankind.

The mystery of Jesus. Certain ideas and observations are repeated throughout the second Gospel. The first is Jesus' instruction not to make it known that he is the Messiah (this has been sometimes called the "messianic secret"); when demons call him the "Holy One" or the "Son" of God, Jesus silences them, because he does not accept their testimony (see 1:25, 34; 3:11–12); he also imposes silence on many of those he has cured (cf. 1:44; 5:43; 7:36; 8:26); finally, he tells Peter and the other disciples to say nothing (for the time being) about the fact that he is the Messiah or about his glorification (cf. 8:30; 9:9).

In addition to these instructions about silence, the narrative also contains frequent reference to the fact that the crowds, and the disciples too, failed to understand Jesus (see 4:1–34; 6:52; 7:14–23; 8:14–21; 9:9–32): hence the term "the mystery of Jesus". However, the Gospel itself makes it quite clear that Jesus is the Messiah and the Son of God, and it also registers that, when they were alone, he explained everything to his disciples because they needed to know who he was and what his teaching meant, for they would have to preach the truth about him.

In all these passages our Lord's teaching method is clear: he explains things gradually because he wants people to respond to him with faith, and not out of short-sighted enthusiasm. He is the Messiah, the Son of God, but this message needs to be preached in the light of the cross and the

---

22 "The beginning of the gospel of Jesus Christ, the Son of God" (1:1); "Go into all the world and preach the gospel to the whole creation" (16:15). **23** "Whoever would save his life will lose it; and whoever loses his life for my sake and the gospel's will save it" (8:35); "Truly, I say to you, there is no one who has left home or brothers or sisters or mother or father or children or lands, for my sake and for the gospel, who will not receive ..." (10:29). **24** "The gospel must first be preached to all nations" (13:10); "Truly, I say to you, wherever the gospel is preached in the whole world, what she has done will be told in memory of her" (14:9); "Go into all the world and preach the gospel to the whole creation" (16:15).

Resurrection. Hearing him speak and seeing his miracles, the crowds asked themselves, "Who is this?" (see 1:27; 2:7, 12; 4:41; 6:2, 14–16), a question that they could not answer. Only with the aid of gradual purification and the Lord's teaching were the disciples able to come to really know him.

3. MESSAGE

Mark's message is as multi-faceted as that of the other evangelists. We have already touched on some aspects of his teaching; other themes very much to the fore in this Gospel are: discipleship, the way to follow Jesus, salvation, faith and prayer. However, the main subject of the Gospel is the same as that of all the other Gospels—Jesus himself.

Jesus, the Messiah

In perfect harmony with the other three Gospels, St Mark's shows that Jesus is the Messiah. The opening words of the Gospel proclaim this, and Jesus' admission of this truth was what caused him to be sentenced to death (see Mk 14:61–64). To reveal his identity as Messiah, however, Jesus followed a special teaching method, in order to avoid misinterpretation—particularly, to prevent people from seeing him as a political liberator, a nationalist leader who would liberate them from Roman rule. An example of his use of this method can be seen in his habit of referring to himself as "the Son of man". The phrase is synonymous with the word "man", but its connexion with the prophecy in Daniel 7:13–14 allowed no grounds for a nationalistic interpretation; it signalled, rather, something on another, higher, religious plane. Other messianic titles, such as "Son of David" or "Messiah", in the circumstances of the time, could have implied that Jesus' mission was largely a matter of earthly power.

By acting in this way, Jesus was able to reveal who he was in a gradual way, training his disciples to see him as the Saviour who would redeem men and reconcile them to God, not by military or political means, but through his sacrifice on Calvary; "for the Son of man also came not to be served but to serve, and to give his life as a ransom for many" (10:45).

Jesus the Son of God

It is no exaggeration to say that the assertion that Jesus is the Son of God, an assertion that St Mark makes in the very first verse, sums up his entire Gospel. It is the key that the reader needs in order to understand everything that follows: if we do not believe that Jesus is the Messiah and the Son of God, we will not be able to understand the rest of the book.

However, at the same time as Mark confesses Christ's divinity, he enables us to see that Jesus is also truly man. The evangelist likes to show that Jesus has truly human feelings: he cannot abide hypocrites; he occasionally gets angry with the apostles; he feels deep compassion; he is happy to have children approach him, and he blesses them, he feels anguish in Gethsemane; etc. (see 3:5; 9:36; 10:13–16; 14:33). But, though he is truly man, Jesus has divine power (see 2:11; 4:41; etc.), and on two occasions, at his baptism and at the Transfiguration, a voice from heaven declares him to be the Son of God (see 1:11; 9:7). The readers of this Gospel cannot but see both things—the true humanity of our Lord, and the power of his deeds which invite us to make our own the words spoken by the centurion at the foot of the cross: "Truly this man was the Son of God" (15:39).

Mark

1. PRELUDE TO THE PUBLIC MINISTRY OF JESUS*

The ministry of John the Baptist

Mt 3:1–12
Lk 3:1–18
Jn 1:19–34

1 ¹The beginning of the gospel of Jesus Christ, the Son of God.ᵃ ²As it is written in Isaiah the prophet,ᵇ

Mal 3:1
Mt 11:10

[1] ¹Initium evangelii Iesu Christi Filii Dei. ²Sicut scriptum est in Isaia propheta: «*Ecce mitto angelum meum ante faciem tuam, | qui praeparabit viam tuam*; | ³*vox clamantis in deserto: | "Parate viam Domini, rectas facite semitas eius"*», ⁴fuit Ioannes Baptista in deserto praedicans bap-

*1:1–13 These verses form a type of prologue. They introduce Jesus in his two natures—as God, whose arrival among his people should be announced by his messenger (vv. 2–3; cf. Mal 3:1; Is 40:3), and as man, subject to temptation and like us in everything except sin (vv. 12–13; cf. Heb 4:15). The baptism of Jesus, the centre of the passage, reveals him to be the Son of God.

The opening verse acts as a gateway to the whole Gospel of St Mark. Jesus of Nazareth is the Messiah ("Jesus Christ") and also "Son of God"; with him the time of salvation has come (the "beginning"), for he himself is the good news of salvation (the "gospel").

The word "gospel" means "good tidings"; in New Testament usage the happy news that God sends to mankind through his Son. Thus, the phrase "gospel of Jesus Christ" (v. 1) refers to the message that Jesus proclaims to mankind on behalf of his Father. The content of the good news is, firstly, Jesus Christ himself, his words and actions. "Jesus himself, the Good News of God (Mk 1:1, Rom 1:1–3), was the very first and the greatest evangelizer: he was so through and through, to perfection and to the point of the sacrifice of his earthly life" (Paul VI, *Evangelii nuntiandi*, 7). The apostles, Christ's envoys, bore witness by means of oral teaching, to Jews and Gentiles, concerning the death and resurrection of Jesus, which fulfilled the prophecies of the Old Testament; and this was his Gospel (see 1 Cor 15:4). The apostles and other apostolic men, inspired by the Holy Spirit, were enabled to write down part of this preaching in their Gospels; in this way, through Holy Scripture and apostolic tradition, the voice of Christ continues to be heard down the ages, reaching all generations and all nations.

1:1–8 With a quotation from the prophets and a mention of his own prophetic actions, John the Baptist is depicted here as the link between the Old and New Testaments: he is the last of the prophets and the first of the witnesses to Christ. The reason why the evangelist mentions Isaiah may be because he was the most important of the prophets to foretell the coming of the Messiah, but the quotation (vv. 2–3) begins with some words from Malachi 3:1, followed by the lines from Isaiah 40:3. In any event, this text points to the fact that the Old Testament, if read in the light of Jesus Christ, is itself Gospel: "The Gospel means, above all, the head of all who have been saved: Jesus Christ. [...] The beginning of the Gospel [...] is all of the Old Testament, of which John is an image, or the link between the New Testament and the Old, which John represents. [...] In light of this, I sometimes wonder why the heretics insist on attributing the two Testaments to two different gods" (Origen, *Commentaria in Ioannem*, 1, 13, 79–82).

The description of the austere lifestyle of the Baptist (vv. 4–6) shows that he practised what he preached: he purified himself to prepare for the coming of the Messiah. John's appreciation of the greatness of the Messiah can be seen from his admission that he is not worthy to untie the straps of his sandals (v. 7). That action was considered so demeaning that it was forbidden to have a Jewish slave perform it: it is an image,

a Other ancient authorities omit *the Son of God* b Other ancient authorities read *in the prophets*

"Behold, I send my messenger before thy face,
who shall prepare the way;
³the voice of one crying in the wilderness:
Prepare the way of the Lord,
make his paths straight—"

Jn 1:23
Is 40:3

⁴John the baptizer appeared^c in the wilderness, preaching a baptism of repentance for the forgiveness of sins. ⁵And there went out to him all the country of Judea, and all the people of Jerusalem; and they were baptized by him in the river Jordan, confessing their sins. ⁶Now John was clothed in camel's hair, and had a leather girdle around his waist, and ate locusts and wild honey. ⁷And he preached, saying, "After me comes he who is mightier than I, the thong of whose sandals I am not worthy to stoop down and untie. ⁸I have baptized you with water, but he will baptize you with the Holy Spirit."

2 Kings 1:8

Acts 13:25

Acts 1:15; 11:16

Mt 3:13–17
Lk 3:21–22
Jesus is baptized

⁹In those days Jesus came from Nazareth of Galilee and was baptized by John in the Jordan. ¹⁰And when he came up out of the water, immediately he saw the heavens opened and the Spirit descending upon him like a dove; ¹¹and a voice came from heaven, "Thou art my beloved Son;^d with thee I am well pleased."

Jn 1:32–34
Mk 9:7

Ps 2:7
Is 42:1

tismum paenitentiae in remissionem peccatorum. ⁵Et egrediebatur ad illum omnis Iudaeae regio et Hierosolymitae universi et baptizabantur ab illo in Iordane flumine confitentes peccata sua. ⁶Et erat Ioannes vestitus pilis cameli, et zona pellicea circa lumbos eius, et locustas et mel silvestre edebat. ⁷Et praedicabat dicens: «Venit fortior me post me, cuius non sum dignus procumbens solvere corrigiam calceamentorum eius. ⁸Ego baptizavi vos aqua; ille vero baptizabit vos in Spiritu Sancto». ⁹Et factum est in diebus illis, venit Iesus a Nazareth Galilaeae et baptizatus est in Iordane ab Ioanne. ¹⁰Et statim ascendens de aqua vidit apertos caelos et Spiritum tamquam columbam descendentem in ipsum; ¹¹et vox facta est de

therefore, that underlines the force of John's proclamation.

The main thing the evangelist emphasizes regarding John is his preaching. The Baptist "preached" (see v. 4) a baptism of repentance, and he "preached" Jesus as someone "mightier than I" (v. 7), who will baptize with "the Holy Spirit". By seeking John's baptism, people showed that they realized they were sinners ("confessing their sins": v. 5), because that was what a baptism of repentance demanded. That confession of sin was not the same thing as the Christian sacrament of Penance. But it was pleasing to God because it was a sign of sincere repentance, and the people who received this baptism bore "fruit that befits repentance" (Mt 3:7–10; see also Lk 3:7–9). "The baptism of John did not effect the forgiveness of sins; rather, it was a baptism of repentance that foreshadowed the remission of sins—that is, the forgiveness that would come afterwards through Christ's work of redemption. […] It was true baptism only in so far as it presaged Christ's death on the cross and his resurrection" (St Jerome, *Contra luciferianos*, 7).

1:9–11 The account of Jesus' baptism records that he went to be baptized by John even though he had no need of a baptism of repentance. The evangelist focuses on the revelation, by the Trinity, that Jesus is the Son and the Messiah. This is shown by the voice of the Father from heaven and by the descent of the Holy Spirit upon Jesus (cf. the notes on Mt 3:13–17 and Lk 3:21–22). Tradition has interpreted the descent of the Spirit in the form of a dove as a sign of peace and reconciliation (see Gen 8:10–11) bestowed by God on mankind in Christ. "Like the dove sent as a sign to Noah of the end of the flood, today the Holy Spirit hovers over the water in the form of a dove as a sign that the world's long drowning has come to an end. But unlike the olive branch that Noah's dove carried in its beak, the Holy Spirit pours out the oil of new chrism to anoint the head of the First-born in the new lineage" (St Peter Chrysologus, *Sermones*, 160).

In keeping with that symbolism, the opening of heaven (v. 10) betokens the fulfilment of the desire for definitive renewal expressed by the people when they prayed to God: "O that thou wouldst rend the heavens and come down" (Is

sc Other ancient authorities omit *John was baptizing*   d Or *my Son, my* (or *the*) *Beloved*

The tempting of Jesus

Mt 4:1–11
Lk 4:1–13

[12]The Spirit immediately drove him out into the wilderness. [13]And he was in the wilderness forty days, tempted by Satan; and he was with the wild beasts; and the angels ministered to him.

PART ONE

Jesus' ministry in Galilee*

2. JESUS BEGINS HIS MINISTRY*

Jesus begins to preach

Mt 4:12–17
Lk 4:14–15
Rom 1:1

[14]Now after John was arrested, Jesus came into Galilee, preaching the gospel of God, [15]and saying, "The time is fulfilled, and the kingdom of God is at hand; repent, and believe in the Gospel."

caelis: «Tu es Filius meus dilectus; in te complacui». [12]Et statim Spiritus expellit eum in desertum. [13]Et erat in deserto quadraginta diebus et tentabatur a Satana; eratque cum bestiis, et angeli ministrabant illi. [14]Postquam autem traditus est Ioannes, venit Iesus in Galilaeam praedicans evangelium Dei [15]et dicens: «Impletum est tempus, et appropinquavit regnum Dei; paenitemini et credite evangelio». [16]Et praeteriens secus mare

64:1). It is not surprising that the earliest Christian writers interpreted the episode in this way, as opening a gate that gave people access to God: "Before, the gates of heaven were closed, and heaven beyond us. We could fall to the lowest depths, but we could not rise to the greatest heights. The Baptism of the Lord was not his baptism alone: at the same time, the old man was wholly renewed. [...] The visible was reconciled with the invisible. All heaven rejoiced, and the illnesses and infirmities of this world were healed; what had been hidden was brought out into the light, and those who were once enemies were reconciled" (St Hippolytus, *De theophania*, 6).

1:12–13 St Matthew and St Luke describe in detail the three temptations that Jesus underwent before embarking on his public ministry, and similar temptations are also recorded in the Gospel of St John (Jn 6:15—7:9). St Mark gives a very brief account, quickly moving on to the public life for which Jesus prepared during his days in the wilderness.

In Holy Scripture, "temptation" usually means an undergoing of some trial, rather than being enticed or tempted. The temptation referred to here tells us something about the true

humanity of Christ: "For we have not a high priest who is unable to sympathize with our weaknesses, but one who in every respect has been tempted as we are, yet without sinning" (Heb 4:15). Jesus' sojourn in the wilderness carries a message we too can profit from: "After he was baptized, Jesus fasted alone for forty days. He teaches us by his example that after our sins have been forgiven in baptism, we should be on our guard through prayer and fasting so that the unclean Spirit that was cast out of our heart does not return when we are newborn in the spirit, weak and slow and vulnerable" (St Bede, *Homiliae*, 11).

"And the angels ministered to him" (v. 13). Throughout the Old Testament we find that angels form part of the court of God in heaven, where they praise him continuously (see e.g. Is 6:1–3; 1 Kings 22:19). The fact that the angels "minister" to Jesus shows that he is greater than they and has lordship over them.

*1:14—8:30 The Gospel of St Mark is similar in structure to the forms the apostles used in their teaching from the start: "You know ... the word which was proclaimed throughout all Judea, beginning from Galilee after the baptism which

Mt 4:18–25
Lk 5:1–11
Jn 1:35–51
Jesus calls his first disciples

[16]And passing along by the Sea of Galilee, he saw Simon and Andrew the brother of Simon casting a net in the sea; for they were fishermen. [17]And Jesus said to them, "Follow me and I will make you become fishers of men." [18]And immediately they

Galilaeae vidit Simonem et Andream fratrem Simonis mittentes in mare; erant enim piscatores. [17]Et dixit eis Iesus: «Venite post me, et faciam vos fieri piscatores hominum». [18]Et protinus, relictis retibus, secuti sunt eum. [19]Et progressus pusillum vidit Iacobum Zebedaei et Ioannem fratrem eius, et ipsos in navi componentes retia, [20]et statim vocavit illos. Et, relicto patre suo Zebedaeo in navi cum mercennariis, abierunt post eum. [21]Et

John preached: how God anointed Jesus of Nazareth with the Holy Spirit and with power; how he went about doing good and healing all that were oppressed by the devil, for God was with him" (Acts 10:36–38). In this first part (1:14–8:30), the evangelist describes Jesus' preaching and the cures he works in Galilee and the surrounding areas, which herald the coming of the Kingdom of God. But what intrigues the people is not so much the Kingdom as Jesus himself; when they see his miracles and hear what he says, they ask themselves, "Who is this?" (see 1:27; 2:7, 12; 4:41; 6:2, 14–16), and they cannot find the answer. St Peter is the first to acknowledge Jesus as the Messiah (see 8:29); but even after that, Jesus asks his disciples not to proclaim it openly; for people to understand what his messianic mission means, he must first undergo his passion.

*1:14–3:35 The account of Jesus' public ministry begins with a summary of his preaching (1:14–15): people must repent if they are to enter the Kingdom of God. The narrative then covers some episodes from Christ's early activity in Capernaum and neighbouring places. Jesus' words and works cause astonishment and admiration in the people at large (see 1:27–28, 37, 45; 2:2, 12), but meet with opposition from scribes and Pharisees (see 2:6, 16, 23–24; 3:6). Also recorded here is Christ's calling of his disciples and, later, of the group of twelve apostles (3:13–19). In this way, the people who appear throughout the Gospel story are introduced.

We are able to see here how Jesus acted and preached during the first stage of his public ministry: St Mark tells us, for example, about a day in the life of the Master (1:21–38), about his exhausting schedule, his feelings of compassion (1:41) and indignation (3:5). These insights enable us to understand the sections that follow—

the description of the Kingdom of God by means of parables (4:1–34) and the manifestation of Jesus' "power" in striking miracles (4:35—6:6).

1:14–15 The fact that Jesus began his ministry after the Baptist was deprived of his freedom indicates that the stage of "promises" is over: with Jesus and his preaching, the Kingdom of God, the time of salvation, has begun. As will become clearer with the martyrdom of the Baptist, the proclamation of the Gospel will not take place unhindered by difficulties.

"The gospel of God" (v. 14). This expression is found in the letters of St Paul (see Rom 1:1; 2 Cor 11:7) where it means the same as "the gospel of Christ" (Phil 1:27; 2 Cor 2:12). It means, above all, the glad tidings that come with Jesus, the news of the Kingdom of God: "As far as I recall, the expression 'the Kingdom of heaven' is not found in the Law, the Prophets or the Psalter; it appears only in the Gospel. The Kingdom of heaven was opened with the coming of the One who said: *the Kingdom of heaven is in your midst*" (St Jerome, *Commentarium in Marcum*, 2).

If people are to have a share in this Kingdom, they must undergo an inner conversion and be ready to accept a new gift from God: "Another mystery of light is the preaching by which Jesus proclaims the coming of the Kingdom of God, calls to conversion (cf. Mk 1:15) and forgives the sins of all who draw near to him in humble trust (cf. Mk 2:3–13; Lk 7:47–48): the inauguration of that ministry of mercy which he continues to exercise until the end of the world, particularly through the Sacrament of Reconciliation which he has entrusted to his Church" (John Paul II, *Rosarium Virginis Mariae*, 13).

1:16–20 In those times, devout young Jews who desired to learn more about the Law of Moses and

left their nets and followed him. ¹⁹And going on a little farther, he saw James the son of Zebedee and John his brother, who were in their boat mending the nets. ²⁰And immediately he called them; and they left their father Zebedee in the boat with the hired servants, and followed him.

Jesus in the synagogue of Capernaum

Lk 4:31–37

²¹And they went into Capernaum; and immediately on the sabbath he entered the synagogue and taught. ²²And they were astonished at his teaching, for he taught

Mt 7:28–29

ingrediuntur Capharnaum. Et statim sabbatis ingressus synagogam docebat. ²²Et stupebant super doctrina eius: erat enim docens eos quasi potestatem habens et non sicut scribae. ²³Et statim erat in synagoga eorum homo in spiritu immundo; et exclamavit ²⁴dicens: «Quid nobis et tibi, Iesu Nazarene? Venisti perdere nos? Scio qui sis: Sanctus Dei». ²⁵Et comminatus est ei Iesus dicens: «Obmutesce et exi de homine!». ²⁶Et discerpens eum spiritus immundus et exclamans voce magna exivit ab eo. ²⁷Et mirati sunt omnes, ita ut conquirerent inter se dicentes: «Quidnam est hoc? Doctrina nova cum potestate; et spiritibus immundis imperat, et oboediunt ei». ²⁸Et processit rumor eius statim ubique in omnem regionem Galilaeae. ²⁹Et protinus egredientes de synagoga venerunt in domum Simonis et Andreae cum Iacobo et Ioanne. ³⁰Socrus autem Simonis decum-

its practice sought to apprentice themselves to a teacher or rabbi: "Seek out a rabbi and your doubts will disappear", as one rabbinical saying had it (*Pirqué Abot*, 1, 16). However, here it is Jesus who does the calling; he calls those "whom he desires" (see 3:13) to be his apostles; his voice is authoritative, and the men he chooses respond to his call. St Jerome, who wrote vivid commentaries on these early chapters of the Gospel, noted the power of Jesus' love (see v. 16 and also 10:21): "If they had not recognized something divine in our Saviour's face, their decision to follow One of whom they had seen no trace would be beyond any reasonable explanation. Would a man leave his father to follow another man who is in every way the same as the father he has left behind?" (*Commentarium in Marcum*, 9).

Those disciples respond to the call "immediately" (v. 18), leaving what they were doing; in fact, leaving everything behind (cf. 10:28). The beckonings of the Gospel still apply today: God passes by us and calls us. If a person fails to respond, Jesus continues on his way and the disciple may lose sight of him and lose his way in life.

Jesus must have known these disciples already (see Jn 1:40–46). St Mark positions this call at the very start of Jesus' ministry in order to show the role of disciples in the proclamation of the Kingdom and to stress the fact that, after the resurrection of Jesus, the apostles' preaching will be an echo of Christ's own.

1:21–28 The account of our Lord's activity begins with a day spent in Capernaum: it begins with a visit to the synagogue (v. 21), which is followed by one to Peter's house (1:29) and by cures in the evening (1:32) when the sabbath rest was over; and it ends with morning prayer (1:35). Already in these verses we see evidence of people's attitudes towards Jesus, which the evangelist will go on to describe—the crowd's astonishment (2:12), the way people flock to him (3:7–10), and the disciples' willingness to follow him (3:13–19).

The first episode reported is the cure of a man possessed by the devil. The evangelist, echoing the words of the crowd (v. 27), notes that Jesus acted and taught "with authority" (v. 22). In these chapters, Jesus shows that his power extends over a wide range of things—diseases and demons (1:29–34), ritual precepts (2:18–28), etc. Here his power is revealed in his preaching and in his ability to command demons. In his preaching, Jesus does not have recourse to the teachers of Israel; nor does he, as the prophets did, introduce his teaching by saying that he is proclaiming the word of God: his word *is* the word of God. And, as if to prove the power of his word, he sets the possessed man free simply by issuing an order. Unlike exorcists, who followed a complicated ritual to discover the demon's name so as to have power over him, Jesus expels the demon by a simple command: "That he cast out devils is not new, for the Hebrew exorcists could do the same. See what the text tells us: *What is this new teaching?* This teaching is new because: *With authority he com-*

them as one who had authority, and not as the scribes. ²³And immediately there was
in their synagogue a man with an unclean spirit; ²⁴and he cried out, "What have you
to do with us, Jesus of Nazareth? Have you come to destroy us? I know who you
are, the Holy One of God." ²⁵But Jesus rebuked him saying, "Be silent, and come
out of him!" ²⁶And the unclean spirit, convulsing him and crying out with a loud
voice, came out of him. ²⁷And they were all amazed, so that they questioned among
themselves, saying, "What is this? A new teaching! With authority he commands
even the unclean spirits, and they obey him." ²⁸And at once his fame spread everywhere throughout all the surrounding region of Galilee.

Mk 5:7

Mk 1:34

Mk 4:41

Curing of Peter's mother-in-law

Mt 8:14–15
Lk 4:38–39

²⁹And immediately he[e] left the synagogue, and entered the house of Simon and
Andrew, with James and John. ³⁰Now Simon's mother-in-law lay sick with a fever,
and immediately they told him of her. ³¹And he came and took her by the hand and
lifted her up, and the fever left her; and she served them.

Mk 5:41; 9:27

Jesus cures many sick people

Mt 8:16–17
Lk 4:40–41

³²That evening, at sundown, they brought to him all who were sick or possessed with
demons. ³³And the whole city was gathered together about the door. ³⁴And he healed
many who were sick with various diseases, and cast out many demons; and he
would not permit the demons to speak, because they knew him.*

Mk 3:12

bebat febricitans; et statim dicunt ei de illa. ³¹Et accedens elevavit eam apprehensa manu; et dimisit eam febris, et ministrabat eis. ³²Vespere autem
facto, cum occidisset sol, afferebant ad eum omnes male habentes et daemonia habentes; ³³et erat omnis civitas congregata ad ianuam. ³⁴Et curavit
multos, qui vexabantur variis languoribus, et daemonia multa eiecit et non sinebat loqui daemonia, quoniam sciebant eum. ³⁵Et diluculo valde

*mands even the unclean spirits, and they obey
him*. He does not invoke another's name; he
commands the spirits in his own name. He does
not command with another's authority but with
his own" (St Jerome, *Commentarium in
Marcum*, 2).

Demons possess knowledge and power superior to man's, but this is of no avail to them
against Jesus' power. And they do not know
everything. For example, they know that Jesus is
the "Holy One of God" (v. 24), but they do not
know that he is also the Servant of the Lord who
will save the world through his death on the
cross. Therefore, remembering what St James
says (Jas 2:19), St Augustine comments: "These
words show that the unclean spirits were possessed of great knowledge and were wholly lacking in love. They fear his punishment and fail to
see and love his justice. He made it known to
them when he wanted to, when it was best, [...]
to fill them with terror" (*De civitate Dei*, 9, 21).

1:29–31 Jesus' power is now shown to cover disease too. As on other occasions (cf. 5:41; 9:27),

Mark reports that, to cure Simon's mother-in-
law, Jesus "took her by the hand and lifted her
up": "He is the true doctor, the doctor beyond
compare. Moses was a doctor, and Isaiah, and all
the saints, but he [Jesus] is the doctor beyond
compare. [...] He is both the doctor and the cure.
Jesus takes her by the hand and the fever leaves
her. May he take us by the hand too, to purify
our life and works; may he enter our house: we
too will be lifted up" (St Jerome, *Commentarium
in Marcum*, 2).

1:32–34 This brief summary of Jesus' activity
makes it clear that Jesus did not work miracles
only occasionally: "No other of the ancients of
whom we read cured so many illnesses and
deformities, so much human suffering, or with
such power" (St Augustine, *In Ioannis Evangelium*, 91, 3). At the end of this passage we find
Jesus forbidding the devils to reveal his identity.
Instructions of this sort are a regular feature of
the early stages of Christ's ministry: he imposes
silence on his disciples (8:30; 9:9), and on
people who have received or witnessed cures

e Other ancient authorities read *they*

Jesus goes to a lonely place to pray

Lk 4:42–44
Mt 14:23

³⁵And in the morning, a great while before day, he rose and went out to a lonely place, and there he prayed. ³⁶And Simon and those who were with him followed him, ³⁷and they found him and said to him, "Every one is searching for you." ³⁸And he said to them, "Let us go on to the next towns, that I may preach there also; for that is why I came out." ³⁹And he went throughout all Galilee, preaching in their synagogues and casting out demons.

Mt 4:23

Curing of a leper

Mt 8:1–4
Lk 5:12–16

⁴⁰And a leper came to him, beseeching him, and kneeling said to him, "If you will, you can make me clean." ⁴¹Moved with pity, he stretched out his hand and touched

mane surgens egressus est et abiit in desertum locum ibique orabat. ³⁶Et persecutus est eum Simon et, qui cum illo erant; ³⁷et cum invenissent eum, dixerunt ei: «Omnes quaerunt te!». ³⁸Et ait illis: «Eamus alibi in proximos vicos, ut et ibi praedicem: ad hoc enim veni». ³⁹Et venit praedicans in synagogis eorum per omnem Galilaeam et daemonia eiciens. ⁴⁰Et venit ad eum leprosus deprecans eum et genu flectens et dicens ei: «Si vis, potes me mundare». ⁴¹Et misertus extendens manum suam tetigit eum et ait illi: «Volo, mundare!»; ⁴²et statim discessit ab eo lepra, et mun-

(1:44; 5:43; 7:36; 8:26), and on devils, too, who know who he is (1:24–25, 34; 3:12) but whose testimony he will not accept. As some Fathers of the Church saw it, Jesus did not want to accept in support of truth the witness of the one who is the father of lies (see Jn 8:44). The Master's instruction to his disciples to be silent was probably designed to counter the idea that most people had of the expected Messiah: Christ wanted them to see and know him in the light of the cross.

1:35–39 After an exhausting day, Jesus gets up very early to pray (v. 35). In many passages in the New Testament we find mention of Jesus praying; in this respect, too, he is a model for Christians. In three places St Mark explicitly tells us that Jesus prayed by himself—here, at the start of his public ministry (v. 35); halfway through it (6:46); and at the end of his life, in Gethsemane (14:32). "When you start out each day to work by Christ's side and to look after all those souls who seek him, remember that there is only one way of doing it—by turning to the Lord. Only in prayer, and through prayer, do we learn to serve others" (St Josemaría Escrivá, *The Forge*, 72).

Contact with Jesus draws many people over to him. Peter and others seem to want to keep him in that region (vv. 36–37). But Jesus has a mission to do (v. 38): he has been sent for that purpose—to preach the Gospel (cf. Lk 4:43). He invites the disciples to accompany him, just as he will send

them out later to evangelize (3:14; 16:15). Preaching is a means chosen by God to effect salvation (1 Cor 1:21; 2 Tim 4:1–2), for faith comes to us through hearing (Rom 10:17; cf. Is 53:1). Jesus "does and teaches" (see Acts 1:1): his preaching is not confined to words; it is proven by deeds. The Church, too, has been sent out to preach salvation and to carry out the saving work that she proclaims. This she does through the sacraments and, particularly, through the renewal of the sacrifice of Calvary in the Mass (see Vatican II, *Sacrosanctum Concilium*, 6).

1:40–45 The horrible disease of leprosy was sometimes seen as a punishment from God (Num 12:1–15; 2 Kings 15:5). The Law declared an infected person to be unclean, and therefore lepers were forced to live away from settlements in order to prevent the transmission of their corruption to other people or to anything they touched (Num 5:2–3). The disappearance of this disease was seen as one of the blessings that messianic times brought (see Is 35:8; Mt 11:5; Lk 7:22).

In the gestures and words of this leper seeking a cure from Jesus, we can see his prayer (which is full of faith), and his delight once he is cured; and Jesus' own gestures and words show his compassion and authority: "This man prostrated himself on the ground, as a sign of humility and shame, to teach each of us to be ashamed of the stains of his life. But shame should not prevent us from confessing: the leper showed his

Mk 5:30

Lev 14:2–32

him, and said to him, "I will; be clean." [42]And immediately the leprosy left him, and he was made clean. [43]And he sternly charged him, and sent him away at once, [44]and said to him, "See that you say nothing to any one; but go, show yourself to the priest, and offer for your cleansing what Moses commanded, for a proof to the people."[f] [45]But he went out and began to talk freely about it, and spread the news, so that Jesus[g] could no longer openly enter a town, but was out in the country; and people came to him from every quarter.

Mt 9:1–8
Lk 5:17–26

Curing of a paralyzed man

Mk 3:20

2 [1]And when he returned to Capernaum after some days, it was reported that he was at home. [2]And many were gathered together, so that there was no longer room for them, not even about the door; and he was preaching the word to them. [3]And they came, bringing to him a paralytic carried by four men. [4]And when they could not get near him because of the crowd, they removed the roof above him; and when they had made an opening, they let down the pallet on which the paralytic lay. [5]And when Jesus saw their faith, he said to the paralytic, "My son, your sins are forgiven." [6]Now some of the scribes were sitting there, questioning in their hearts,

Is 43:25

[7]"Why does this man speak thus? It is blasphemy! Who can forgive sins but God

datus est. [43]Et infremuit in eum statimque eiecit illum [44]et dicit ei: «Vide, nemini quidquam dixeris; sed vade, ostende te sacerdoti et offer pro emundatione tua, quae praecepit Moyses, in testimonium illis». [45]At ille egressus coepit praedicare multum et diffamare sermonem, ita ut iam non posset manifesto in civitatem introire, sed foris in desertis locis erat; et conveniebant ad eum undique.   [2] [1]Et iterum intravit Capharnaum post dies, et auditum est quod in domo esset. [2]Et convenerunt multi, ita ut non amplius caperentur neque ad ianuam, et loquebatur eis verbum. [3]Et veniunt ferentes ad eum paralyticum, qui a quattuor portabatur. [4]Et cum non possent offerre eum illi prae turba, nudaverunt tectum, ubi erat, et perfodientes summittunt grabatum, in quo paralyticus iacebat. [5]Cum vidisset autem Iesus fidem illorum, ait paralytico: «Fili, dimittuntur peccata tua». [6]Erant autem illic quidam de scribis sedentes et cogitantes in cordibus suis: [7]«Quid hic sic loquitur? Blasphemat! Quis potest dimittere pec-

wound and begged for healing. If you will, he says, you can make me clean: that is, he recognized that the Lord had the power to cure him" (St Bede, *In Marci Evangelium*, ad loc.).

2:1–12 Archaeological discoveries at Capernaum bear out St Mark's description of the house in this passage. They reveal small houses, about six metres (twenty feet) square (made of basalt stone, with roofs of thatch and mud), and behind each house a patio of similar size. This helps us to picture the scene of this miracle—the fast-spreading word that Jesus has arrived (v. 1); the crush of the crowd, which makes it impossible to reach Jesus (v. 2); the ingenuity of the bearers, who make a hole in the roof (v. 4). Jesus' words reveal the scope of his salvific action: it cures the body of disease, and the spirit of sin. The passage speaks to us of the divine power of Jesus—he forgives sins, reads the thoughts of the scribes, and cures the paralytic (vv. 8, 11)—and it shows the active faith of the man's friends, who overcome obstacles to bring him to Jesus (vv. 3–5). "The Lord Jesus Christ, physician of

our souls and bodies, who forgave the sins of the paralytic and restored him to bodily health, has willed that his Church continue, in the power of the Holy Spirit, his work of healing and salvation, even among her own members. This is the purpose of the two sacraments of healing: the sacrament of Penance and the sacrament of Anointing of the Sick" (*Catechism of the Catholic Church*, 1421).

In the words "My son, your sins are forgiven" we can see the teaching method used by Jesus. He does not say, "I forgive you your sins"; instead, he uses a circumlocution, common at the time—expressing something in the passive voice to avoid using the proper name of God. People are able to see the power of Jesus, which shows itself visibly in the cure, in the efficacy of his words. "When a punishment is to be meted out, a reward given, sins forgiven, a law interpreted or even more important things done, the Lord never invokes his Father or petitions him: he does these things by his own authority" (St John Chrysostom, *De Christi precibus*, 10, 165–171).

f Greek *to them*   g Greek *he*

alone?" [8]And immediately Jesus, perceiving in his spirit that they thus questioned within themselves, said to them, "Why do you question thus in your hearts? [9]Which is easier, to say to the paralytic, 'Your sins are forgiven,' or to say, 'Rise, take up your pallet and walk'? [10]But that you may know that the Son of man has authority on earth to forgive sins"—he said to the paralytic—[11]"I say to you, rise, take up your pallet and go home." [12]And he rose, and immediately took up the pallet and went out before them all; so that they were all amazed and glorified God, saying, "We never saw anything like this!"

Lk 6:8; 9:47

Jn 5:8

The calling of Matthew

Mt 9:9–13
Lk 5:27–32

[13]He went out again beside the sea; and all the crowd gathered about him, and he taught them. [14]And as he passed on, he saw Levi* the son of Alphaeus sitting at the tax office, and he said to him, "Follow me." And he rose and followed him.

[15]And as he sat at table in his house, many tax collectors and sinners were sitting with Jesus and his disciples; for there were many who followed him. [16]And the scribes of[h] the Pharisees, when they saw that he was eating with sinners and tax collectors, said to his disciples, "Why does he eat[i] with tax collectors and sinners?" [17]And when Jesus heard it, he said to them, "Those who are well have no need of a physician, but those who are sick; I came not to call the righteous, but sinners."

cata nisi solus Deus?». [8]Quo statim cognito Iesus spiritu suo quia sic cogitarent intra se, dicit illis: «Quid ista cogitatis in cordibus vestris? [9]Quid est facilius, dicere paralytico: 'Dimittuntur peccata tua', an dicere: 'Surge et tolle grabatum tuum et ambula'? [10]Ut autem sciatis quia potestatem habet Filius hominis in terra dimittendi peccata—ait paralytico—: [11]Tibi dico: Surge, tolle grabatum tuum et vade in domum tuam». [12]Et surrexit et protinus sublato grabato abiit coram omnibus, ita ut admirarentur omnes et glorificarent Deum dicentes: «Numquam sic vidimus!». [13]Et egressus est rursus ad mare; omnisque turba veniebat ad eum, et docebat eos. [14]Et cum praeteriret, vidit Levin Alphaei sedentem ad teloneum et ait illi: «Sequere me». Et surgens secutus est eum. [15]Et factum est cum accumberet in domo illius, et multi publicani et peccatores simul discumbebant cum Iesu et discipulis eius; erant enim multi et sequebantur eum. [16]Et scribae pharisaeorum, videntes quia manducaret cum peccatoribus et publicanis, dicebant discipulis eius: «Quare cum publicanis et peccatoribus manducat?». [17]Et Iesus hoc audito ait illis: «Non necesse habent sani

2:13–17 In Mark this passage gives a very matter-of-fact account of the calling of "Levi the son of Alphaeus" (v. 14). A parallel passage (Mt 9:9–13) tells us that this was "Matthew", one of the twelve apostles (3:18). Sharing a meal was a clear sign of friendship and mutual respect. The Gospels report Jesus eating meals with Pharisees (Lk 7:36), with friends such as Lazarus and his sisters at Bethany (Jn 12:2), with his disciples (3:20) and, here, with tax collectors and sinners. Moreover, Jesus sometimes described the Kingdom in terms of a banquet (see Mt 22:1–14; Lk 14:16–24). The meaning of the passage is perfectly clear: Jesus excludes no one from his call to salvation: "I am not come for them to continue to be sinners, but to have them change and become better" (St John Chrysostom, *In Matthaeum*, 30, 3).

Our Lord calls everyone; his redemptive mission extends to the whole world. Yet there appears to be a restriction here: Jesus says that he has not come to call the righteous (v. 17). In point of fact, he is not being restrictive; he is reproaching these scribes because they feel superior. They see themselves as saved already, and this complacent attitude, this belief in their own holiness, deafens them to the call to conversion (cf. Jn 9:41). This would explain why Jesus uses the proverb in v. 17; in his preaching he makes it quite clear that "No one is good but God alone" (10:18), and that all of us must have recourse to the mercy of God to obtain the forgiveness we need for salvation, for we are all sinners. Our Lord's words should move us to pray for people who seem bent on a life of sin, just as St Teresa of Avila prayed: "Ah, how hard a thing am I asking of you, my true God! I ask you to love one who loves you not, to open to one who has not called upon you, to give health to one who prefers to be sick and who even goes about in search of sickness. You say, my Lord, that you come to seek sinners; these, Lord, are the true sinners. Look not upon our blindness, my God, but upon all the blood that was shed for us by your Son" (*Exclamations*, 8).

h Other ancient authorities read *and*   i Other ancient authorities add *and drink*

Mt 9:14–17
Lk 5:33–39
A discussion on fasting

[18]Now John's disciples and the Pharisees were fasting; and people came and said to him, "Why do John's disciples and the disciples of the Pharisees fast, but your dis-

Jn 3:29

ciples do not fast?" [19]And Jesus said to them, "Can the wedding guests fast while the bridegroom is with them? As long as they have the bridegroom with them, they

Jn 16:20

cannot fast. [20]The days will come, when the bridegroom is taken away from them, and then they will fast in that day. [21]No one sews a piece of unshrunk cloth on an old garment; if he does, the patch tears away from it, the new from the old, and a worse

Job 32:19

tear is made. [22]And no one puts new wine into old wineskins; if he does, the wine will burst the skins, and the wine is lost, and so are the skins; but new wine is for fresh skins."[j]

Mt 12:1–8
Lk 6:1–5
The law of the sabbath

[23]One sabbath he was going through the grainfields; and as they made their way his disciples began to pluck ears of grain. [24]And the Pharisees said to him, "Look, why

medicum, sed qui male habent; non veni vocare iustos, sed peccatores». [18]Et erant discipuli Ioannis et pharisaei ieiunantes. Et veniunt et dicunt illi: «Cur discipuli Ioannis et discipuli pharisaeorum ieiunant, tui autem discipuli non ieiunant?». [19]Et ait illis Iesus: «Numquid possunt convivae nuptiarum, quamdiu sponsus cum illis est, ieiunare? Quanto tempore habent secum sponsum, non possunt ieiunare; [20]venient autem dies cum auferetur ab eis sponsus, et tunc ieiunabunt in illa die. [21]Nemo assumentum panni rudis assuit vestimento veteri; alioquin supplementum aufert aliquid ab eo, novum a veteri, et peior scissura fit. [22]Et nemo mittit vinum novellum in utres veteres, alioquin dirumpet vinum utres et vinum perit et utres; sed vinum novum in utres novos». [23]Et factum est cum ipse sabbatis ambularet per sata, discipuli eius coeperunt praegredi vellentes

2:18–22 In criticizing Jesus' disciples for not fasting, these people are also criticizing their Master. Our Lord's reply, giving the example of the bridegroom, implies that he is more than a teacher; he is the Messiah (cf. Jn 3:29); because one of the images used in the Old Testament to describe the Messiah was that of a husband (see Hos 2:18–20; Is 54:5f). By using the image of the bridegroom Jesus points to the joy that his arrival implies. He is saying not that there is no need for further penance, but that, given the presence of the Messiah, penance should not be given so much importance. Christ's reply also reveals another connexion between the Old and New Testaments. He shows the difference between the spirit he has brought and that of the Judaism of his time. This new spirit will not be something added on to the old; it will bring to life the perennial teaching contained in the older revelation: "What remained from former times was to be changed, like circumcision, or made whole, like the Law, or fulfilled, like the prophecies, or made perfect, like faith itself. With the coming of the Gospel, the grace of God renewed all flesh in the spirit, purifying everything that had come before" (Tertullian, *De oratione*, 1, 1).

In v. 20, Jesus announces that the bridegroom will be taken away from them: this is the first

reference he makes to his passion and death. The vision of joy and sorrow we see here also helps us understand our human condition during our life on earth.

2:23–28 In Jesus' time, the Pharisees had introduced detailed rules about how the Law should be kept: these, when detached from the spirit of the Law, made a very heavy burden of the Law (see 7:1–13; Acts 15:10). By means of an example (vv. 25–26) and a startling saying (v. 27), Jesus explains that such precepts should yield to the natural law: sabbath observance does not come before the need for basic subsistence. The Second Vatican Council uses this passage to underline the value of the human person: "The social order and its development must constantly yield to the good of the person, since the order of things must be subordinate to the order of persons and not the other way around" (*Gaudium et spes*, 26). But, above all, Jesus describes himself as "lord even of the sabbath" (v. 28); given that sabbath observance is something that God lays down, Jesus' argument implies that he is God.

The bread of the Presence (vv. 25–26) consisted of twelve loaves or cakes placed each week on the temple table as homage to the Lord from the twelve tribes of Israel (see Lev 24:5–9).

j Other ancient authorities omit *but new wine is for fresh skins*

are they doing what is not lawful on the sabbath?" ²⁵And he said to them, "Have you never read what David did, when he was in need and hungry, he and those who were with him: ²⁶how he entered the house of God, when Abiathar was high priest, and ate the bread of the Presence, which it is not lawful for any but the priests to eat, and also gave it to those who were with him?" ²⁷And he said to them, "The sabbath was made for man, not man for the sabbath; ²⁸so the Son of man is lord even of the sabbath."

1 Sam 21:2–7
Lev 24:5–9

Deut 5:14

Curing of the man with a withered hand

Mt 12:9–14
Lk 6:6–11

3 ¹Again he entered the synagogue, and a man was there who had a withered hand. ²And they watched him, to see whether he would heal him on the sabbath, so that they might accuse him. ³And he said to the man who had the withered hand,

spicas. ²⁴Pharisaei autem dicebant ei: «Ecce, quid faciunt sabbatis, quod non licet?». ²⁵Et ait illis: «Numquam legistis quid fecerit David, quando necessitatem habuit et esuriit ipse et qui cum eo erant? ²⁶Quomodo introivit in domum Dei sub Abiathar principe sacerdotum et panes propositionis manducavit, quos non licet manducare nisi sacerdotibus, et dedit etiam eis, qui cum eo erant?». ²⁷Et dicebat eis: «Sabbatum propter hominem factum est, et non homo propter sabbatum; ²⁸itaque dominus est Filius hominis etiam sabbati». [3] ¹Et introivit iterum in synagogam. Et erat ibi homo habens manum aridam; ²et observabant eum, si sabbatis curaret illum, ut accusarent eum. ³Et ait homini habenti manum aridam:

The loaves withdrawn to make room for fresh ones were reserved to the priests performing temple duties. The action of the priest in question (see 1 Sam 21:1–6) was justified by Old Testament practice, which allowed lesser rules to give way to more important ones.

Christ gives back to the sabbath rest its full religious significance (v. 27). Sabbath observance is not a matter of abiding by certain legal rules, or of concern for personal well-being: the sabbath belongs to God; it is one way, in keeping with human nature, of rendering glory and honour to the Almighty. From the time of the apostles onwards, the Church has had the observance of this precept transferred to the following day, Sunday (the Lord's Day), in celebration of the resurrection of Christ (Acts 20:7).

"Son of man" (v. 28). This title is used in the Old Testament (see Dan 7:13–14) for the Messiah Saviour who receives lordship, glory and authority over all peoples and nations. But it is also a synonym for the word "man" (see Ezek 2:1ff). Jesus uses it (as many as 69 times in the Synoptic Gospels) as his preferred way of referring to himself, thereby avoiding the nationalistic overtones associated with other messianic titles such as "Son of David" and "Messiah".

3:1–6 Here we find the culmination of the controversies with scribes and Pharisees that began in 2:5. These controversies show that Jesus and his work encountered resistance not only from

devils but also from men and women. This opposition began when some scribes, "questioning in their hearts", thought that Jesus was guilty of blasphemy; later on, they asked questions to catch him out (2:16), and criticized him and his disciples' behaviour (2:18, 24); now they try to catch him out (v. 2), and, eventually, they decide that his work must be undone (v. 6). This episode also confirms what was said in the previous one: Jesus is "lord of the sabbath". He is the Messiah, endowed with divine power, and he shows this through the miracles he performs. His accusers fail to read the evidence. The hypocrisy of the Pharisees and Herodians (bitter enemies of one another, but now united against Jesus: v. 6; cf. 12:13) is something he reacts to with indignation and sorrow.

The evangelists often mention looks that Jesus gave to people—for example, the rich young man (10:21) and St Peter (Lk 22:61)—but this is the only instance (v. 5) of Jesus looking at people in anger. St Augustine has this to say about our Lord's feelings: "Who would dare describe these feelings, guided and directed by fair judgment, as unruly passions or sins of the soul? The Lord, made man in the form of a servant, unstained by sin, expressed these feelings when he thought that he should do so. In him, true man in body and soul, these feelings were neither failing nor false. What is said of his grief at the hardness of heart of the Jews is true" (*De civitate Dei*, 14, 9, 4).

Lk 14:4

"Come here." [4]And he said to them, "Is it lawful on the sabbath to do good or to do harm, to save life or to kill?" But they were silent. [5]And he looked around at them with anger, grieved at their hardness of heart, and said to the man, "Stretch out your hand." He stretched it out, and his hand was restored. [6]The Pharisees went out, and immediately held counsel with the Herodians against him, how to destroy him.

Mt 22:16
Mk 12:13

Cures beside the Sea of Galilee

Lk 6:17–19
Mt 4:25

[7]Jesus withdrew with his disciples to the sea, and a great multitude from Galilee followed; also from Judea [8]and Jerusalem and Idumea and from beyond the Jordan and from about Tyre and Sidon a great multitude, hearing all that he did, came to him. [9]And he told his disciples to have a boat ready for him because of the crowd, lest they should crush him; [10]for he had healed many, so that all who had diseases pressed upon him to touch him. [11]And whenever the unclean spirits beheld him, they fell down before him and cried out, "You are the Son of God." [12]And he strictly ordered them not to make him known.

Mt 15:30
Mk 5:30
Lk 4:41
Mk 1:34

Mt 10:1–4
Lk 6:12–16

Jesus chooses twelve apostles

Mk 6:7

[13]And he went up into the hills, and called to him those whom he desired; and they came to him. [14]And he appointed twelve,[k] to be with him, and to be sent out to preach [15]and have authority to cast out demons: [16]Simon whom he surnamed Peter;

Acts 1:13
Jn 1:42
Mt 16:18

«Surge in medium». [4]Et dicit eis: «Licet sabbatis bene facere an male? Animam salvam facere an perdere?». At illi tacebant. [5]Et circumspiciens eos cum ira, contristatus super caecitate cordis eorum, dicit homini: «Extende manum». Et extendit, et restituta est manus eius. [6]Et exeuntes pharisaei statim cum herodianis consilium faciebant adversus eum quomodo eum perderent. [7]Et Iesus cum discipulis suis secessit ad mare. Et multa turba a Galilaea secuta est et a Iudaea [8]et ab Hierosolymis et ab Idumaea; et, qui trans Iordanem et circa Tyrum et Sidonem, multitudo magna, audientes, quae faciebat, venerunt ad eum. [9]Et dixit discipulis suis, ut navicula sibi praesto esset propter turbam, ne comprimerent eum. [10]Multos enim sanavit, ita ut irruerent in eum, ut illum tangerent, quotquot habebant plagas. [11]Et spiritus immundi, cum illum videbant, procidebant ei et clamabant dicentes: «Tu es Filius Dei!». [12]Et vehementer comminabatur eis, ne manifestarent illum. [13]Et ascendit in montem et vocat ad se, quos voluit ipse, et venerunt ad eum. [14]Et fecit Duodecim, ut essent cum illo, et ut mitteret eos praedicare [15]habentes potestatem eiciendi daemonia: [16]et

3:7–12 Although there were those who sought to catch Jesus out, and unclean spirits who could do nothing other than submit to him (vv. 11–12), the Master had a huge following. Here we learn that the proclamation of the Gospel, by preaching and miracles, has attracted people not only from Galilee but from all over Palestine (vv. 7–8)—an earnest of its future spread across the world. The crowd press around our Lord (vv. 9–10), as Christians will do in every age, because it is only by contact with the sacred humanity of Christ that we can obtain salvation and be united to God: "Jesus Christ, my beloved brothers, the high priest of our offerings, who helps and sustains us in our weakness, is our path to salvation. Through him, we are able to raise our eyes to heaven; through him, we see, as in a mirror, the glorious and immaculate face of God; through him, the eyes of our heart are opened; through him, our mind, dull and in darkness, is filled with light; the Lord willed that we come to

knowledge of eternity through him" (St Clement of Rome, *Ad Corinthios*, 35–36).

3:13–19 The Gospel will go on to introduce other groups of people—the Twelve, scribes, Pharisees, relatives of Jesus (3:13–35). Each reacts to him in different ways. The evangelist makes special mention of the Twelve (v. 14). The fact that Jesus chose twelve apostles is very significant. This is the same number as that of the patriarchs of Israel, the ancestors of the twelve tribes: the apostles represent the new People of God, the Church founded by Christ (cf. the note on Mt 10:1–4).

The Gospel identifies certain features of these twelve men that have meaning for all Christ's disciples. Firstly, it shows discipleship to be a call from, an initiative of, Christ; and that a person chosen in this way should respond promptly (v. 13; cf. 1:17–20; 2:13–14): "Do not be afraid. Do not be alarmed or surprised. Do not

k Other ancient authorities add *whom also he named apostles*

[17]James the son of Zebedee and John the brother of James, whom he surnamed Boanerges, that is, sons of thunder; [18]Andrew, and Philip, and Bartholomew, and Matthew, and Thomas, and James the son of Alphaeus, and Thaddaeus, and Simon the Cananaean, [19]and Judas Iscariot, who betrayed him.

Jesus' relatives are concerned about him

Then he went home; [20]and the crowd came together again, so that they could not even eat. [21]And when his friends heard it, they went out to seize him, for they said, "He is beside himself."

Mk 6:31
Mk 2:2
Jn 7:5

Allegations of the scribes. Sin against the Holy Spirit

[22]And the scribes who came down from Jerusalem said, "He is possessed by Beelzebul, and by the prince of demons he casts out the demons." [23]And he called them to

Mt 12:22–32
Lk 11:14–26
Mk 7:1
Jn 8:48; 10:20

imposuit Simoni nomen Petrum; [17]et Iacobum Zebedaei et Ioannem fratrem Iacobi, et imposuit eis nomina Boanerges, quod est Filii tonitrui; [18]et Andream et Philippum et Bartholomaeum et Matthaeum et Thomam et Iacobum Alphaei et Thaddaeum et Simonem Chananaeum [19]et Iudam Iscarioth, qui et tradidit illum. [20]Et venit ad domum; et convenit iterum turba, ita ut non possent neque panem manducare. [21]Et cum audissent sui, exierunt tenere eum; dicebant enim: «In furorem versus est». [22]Et scribae, qui ab Hierosolymis descenderant, dicebant: «Beelzebul habet» et: «In

allow yourself to be overcome by false prudence. The call to fulfil God's will—this goes for vocation too—is sudden, as it was for the Apostles: a meeting with Christ and his call is followed. None of them doubted. Meeting Christ and following him was all one" (St Josemaría Escrivá, *The Forge*, 6). Secondly, the call produces a special role in life: the apostle is "appointed" (v. 14), in the same way as God elected priests in the Old Testament (see Num 3:3). Thirdly, the key feature of a disciple is to "be with Jesus" (cf. v. 14) because "'Christ, sent by the Father, is the source of the Church's whole apostolate' (*Apostolicam actuositatem*, 4); thus the fruitfulness of apostolate for ordained ministers as well as for lay people clearly depends on their vital union with Christ" (*Catechism of the Catholic Church*, 864). Fourthly, disciples are called in order to be sent out (v. 14; cf. 1:16–18; 16:20) to repeat what their Master does, that is, "to preach" (v. 14; cf. 1:14, 38, 39; 2:2) with "authority" (v. 15; cf. 1:22, 27; 2:10): "Those holy disciples were the foundation and supporting pillars of the truth. The Lord said that he would send them out as the Father had sent him. In saying so, he not only revealed the dignity of the apostolate and the great power that had been conferred on them, he also implied the way that they should carry out their work. [...] Their mission is to call sinners to repentance and to cure those who are afflicted in body and soul;

the purpose of their ministry is to fulfil the will of the One who sent them; they are to redeem the world through the power of the teaching they received from him" (St Cyril of Alexandria, *Commentarium in Ioannem*, 12, 1).

3:20–21 Some of his relatives regarded Jesus' commitment to his ministry as excessive. This is also mentioned elsewhere (see 6:3 and par.) and it is reminiscent of the kind of reaction that the prophets encountered (see e.g. Jer 12:6). Reading these verses of the Gospel, we cannot but be in awe of the efforts Jesus went to out of love for us. Many saints, followers of Christ's example, have been taken for madmen, but theirs was the madness of love for Jesus Christ.

3:22–30 The assessment that Jesus' relatives make of him pales in comparison with these accusations by scribes arrived from Jerusalem. They realize that Jesus has power over demons, but instead of attributing that power to God, they claim that he acts with the devil's power (v. 22). Jesus makes a series of comparisons (vv. 23–27) to show that their accusation makes no sense: his coming into the world has provoked a conflict between two kingdoms, that of Satan and that of God. Therefore, if Jesus has overcome Satan (cf. 1:24–27, 34, 39; 3:11–12) it is impossible that Jesus should be one of his party (vv. 24–26). Satan is powerful, but Jesus is more powerful (v. 27).

him, and said to them in parables, "How can Satan cast out Satan? [24]If a kingdom is divided against itself, that kingdom cannot stand. [25]And if a house is divided against itself, that house will not be able to stand. [26]And if Satan has risen up against himself and is divided, he cannot stand, but is coming to an end. [27]But no one can enter a strong man's house and plunder his goods, unless he first binds the strong man; then indeed he may plunder his house.

Lk 12:10
1 Jn 5:16

[28]"Truly, I say to you, all sins will be forgiven the sons of men, and whatever blasphemies they utter; [29]but whoever blasphemes against the Holy Spirit never has forgiveness, but is guilty of an eternal sin"—[30]for they had said, "He has an unclean spirit."

Mt 12:46–50
Lk 8:19–21

The true kinsmen of Jesus

[31]And his mother and his brethren* came; and standing outside they went to him and called him. [32]And a crowd was sitting about him: and they said to him, "Your mother and your brethren[1] are outside, asking for you." [33]And he replied, "Who are my mother and my brethren?" [34]And looking around on those who sat about him, he

principe daemonum eicit daemonia». [23]Et convocatis eis, in parabolis dicebat illis: «Quomodo potest Satanas Satanam eicere? [24]Et si regnum in se dividatur, non potest stare regnum illud; [25]et si domus in semetipsam dispertiatur, non poterit domus illa stare. [26]Et si Satanas consurrexit in semetipsum et dispertitus est, non potest stare, sed finem habet. [27]Nemo autem potest in domum fortis ingressus vasa eius diripere, nisi prius fortem alliget; et tunc domum eius diripiet. [28]Amen dico vobis: Omnia dimittentur filiis hominum peccata et blasphemiae, quibus blasphemaverint; [29]qui autem blasphemaverit in Spiritum Sanctum, non habet remissionem in aeternum, sed reus est aeterni delicti». [30]Quoniam dicebant: «Spiritum immundum habet». [31]Et venit mater eius et fratres eius et foris stantes miserunt ad eum vocantes eum. [32]Et sedebat circa eum turba, et dicunt ei: «Ecce mater tua et fratres tui et sorores tuae foris quaerunt te». [33]Et respondens eis ait: «Quae est mater mea et fratres mei?». [34]Et circumspiciens eos, qui in circuitu eius sedebant, ait: «Ecce mater mea et fratres mei. [35]Qui enim fecerit voluntatem Dei, hic frater meus et soror mea et

At the end of the passage (vv. 28–30), Jesus, who has shown his compassion by forgiving sinners and sharing meals with them, points out how difficult it is for people to obtain forgiveness if they close their minds to the truth. That culpable blindness explains the gravity of the sin of blasphemy against the Holy Spirit—attributing to Satan good actions worked by God himself. Anyone who does such a thing is like a sick person who is so distrustful that he rejects the doctor and the medicine that would work his cure. That is why our Lord says that blasphemy against the Holy Spirit will never find forgiveness—not because God cannot forgive every sort of sin, but because the person in question is so blind that he does not appreciate and rejects the graces of the Holy Spirit (cf. the note on Mt 12:22–37).

3:31–35 This passage makes an explicit distinction between two groups of relatives—Jesus' Mother and his "brethren" (v. 31), and those other relatives who thought he was out of his mind (3:21). The episode reported here points to a key truth of Christian life: if someone does the will of God, he or she has a closer connexion to Christ than that afforded by blood relationship. The inclusion of Mary here is very significant, for her response to God's will set the standard for the way Christ's disciples should live: "The Virgin Mary fulfilled the will of the Father; she accepted the divine message, conceived by faith, and was chosen to give birth to the Saviour of us all; she was created by Christ before Christ was made man in her. Mary fulfilled the will of the Father perfectly. Thus, that she is a disciple of Christ is more important than the fact that she is his mother; she is more blessed because she is a disciple of Christ than because she is his mother. Mary is blessed because before she gave birth to the Master she carried him in her soul" (St Augustine, *Sermones*, 25, 7).

Here, as elsewhere, we find a reference to the "brethren" of Jesus (v. 31). The Church holds that Mary is ever-virgin, and therefore it is important to understand who these "brethren" were: "Against this doctrine the objection is sometimes raised that the Bible mentions brothers and sisters of Jesus (cf. Mk 3:31; 6:3; 1 Cor 9:5; Gal 1:19). The Church has always understood these

[1] Other ancient authorities add *and your sisters*

said, "Here are my mother and my brethren! [35]Whoever does the will of God is my brother, and sister, and mother."

3. PARABLES OF THE KINGDOM OF GOD*

Parable of the sower. The meaning of parables

Mt 13:1–23
Lk 8:4–18

4 [1]Again he began to teach beside the sea. And a very large crowd gathered about him, so that he got into a boat and sat in it on the sea; and the whole crowd was beside the sea on the land. [2]And he taught them many things in parables, and in his teachings he said to them: [3]"Listen! A sower went out to sow. [4]And as he sowed, some seed fell along the path, and the birds came and devoured it. [5]Other seed fell

Hos 12:10

mater est». [4] [1]Et iterum coepit docere ad mare. Et congregatur ad eum turba plurima, ita ut in navem ascendens sederet in mari, et omnis turba circa mare super terram erant. [2]Et docebat eos in parabolis multa et dicebat illis in doctrina sua: [3]«Audite. Ecce exiit seminans ad seminandum. [4]Et factum est dum seminat, aliud cecidit circa viam, et venerunt volucres et comederunt illud. [5]Aliud cecidit super petrosa, ubi non habebat terram multam, et statim exortum est, quoniam non habebat altitudinem terrae; [6]et quando exortus est sol, exaestuavit et, eo quod non haberet radicem,

passages as not referring to other children of the Virgin Mary. In fact James and Joseph, 'brothers of Jesus', are the sons of another Mary, a disciple of Christ, whom St Matthew significantly calls 'the other Mary' (Mt 13:55; 28:1; cf. Mt 27:56). They are close relations of Jesus, according to an Old Testament expression (cf. Gen 13:8; 14:16; 29:15; etc.)" (*Catechism of the Catholic Church*, 500).

*4:1–34 Over the course of the Gospel, St Mark often talks about Jesus' teaching (1:21, 39; 2:2, 13; 6:2, 6; etc.). Nevertheless, he records only two important discourses—this one, and that delivered near the temple (13:1–37). Also, at the end of the passage (v. 34) the evangelist says that Jesus always taught in parables—and yet Mark's Gospel contains few parables. In this discourse we find three types of parable—that of the sower (vv. 3–30), that of the lamp and the measure (vv. 21–25), and that of the seed and the mustard seed (vv. 26–32). All of these parables have to do with the Kingdom of God, but they present it from different angles (cf. the note on Mt 13:1–52).

The parables of the Kingdom carry a message of hope. It may happen that Jesus and his enterprise will meet with hostility, or that fruits take time to come, but two things are certain— the intrinsic strength of the Kingdom, and eventual success. These parables help us see how the Kingdom of God will develop. Thus, in the early stages of his preaching, Jesus announces the

coming of the Kingdom of God (1:15). However, as the parable of the sower shows, this kingdom does not carry all before it, contrary to what many of Jesus' contemporaries expected would happen. It begins with Jesus' presence and preaching, but it also depends on man's disposition and response (vv. 14–20). The parable of the measure shows that disciples must be vigilant (vv. 23–25). And, like lamps, they need to bear witness to the word of God (vv. 21–22). Furthermore, we must not judge the Kingdom by the smallness of its beginnings, because, like a little seed, it will grow without our realizing it, and it will bear fruit (vv. 26–29), far exceeding what we might expect (vv. 30–32).

4:1–20 This parable has a connexion with biblical tradition. The prophet Isaiah (Is 55:10–11) had already proclaimed that the word of God is like rain: it falls from the sky but does not return until it bears fruit. Similarly, our Lord scatters his word over the world for it to take root and bear fruit: sometimes it will be spoilt, because it is not well received, but at times too it will bear fruit—though in different measures (cf. the note on Mt 13:1–23).

This is the meaning expressed by all the Synoptic Gospels, but St Mark lays more stress on the difficulties encountered by Jesus' listeners. Jesus' words, like the Kingdom he is preaching, are a mystery: initially, neither the disciples nor the crowd grasp his meaning, but he will explain

on rocky ground, where it had not much soil, and immediately it sprang up, since it had not much soil; [6]and when the sun rose it was scorched, and since it had no root it withered away. [7]Other seed fell among thorns and the thorns grew up and choked it, and it yielded no grain. [8]And other seeds fell into good soil and brought forth grain, growing up and increasing and yielding thirtyfold and sixtyfold and a hundredfold." [9]And he said, "He who has ears to hear, let him hear."

[10]And when he was alone, those who were about him with the twelve asked him concerning the parables. [11]And he said to them, "To you has been given the secret of the kingdom of God, but for those outside everything is in parables; [12]so that* they may indeed see but not perceive, and may indeed hear but not understand; lest they should turn again, and be forgiven." [13]And he said to them, "Do you not understand this parable? How then will you understand all the parables? [14]The sower sows the word. [15]And these are the ones along the path, where the word is sown; when they hear, Satan immediately comes and takes away the word which is sown in them.

Rom 16:25
Col 4:3–5
Is 6:9–10
Mk 8:16
Jn 12:40
Acts 28:26

exaruit. [7]Et aliud cecidit in spinas, et ascenderunt spinae et suffocaverunt illud, et fructum non dedit. [8]Et alia ceciderunt in terram bonam et dabant fructum: ascendebant et crescebant et afferebant unum triginta et unum sexaginta et unum centum». [9]Et dicebat: «Qui habet aures audiendi, audiat». [10]Et cum esset singularis, interrogaverunt eum hi, qui circa eum erant cum Duodecim, parabolas. [11]Et dicebat eis: «Vobis datum est mysterium regni Dei; illis autem, qui foris sunt, in parabolis omnia fiunt, [12]*ut videntes videant et non videant, / et audientes audiant et non intellegant, / ne quando convertantur, / et dimittatur eis*». [13]Et ait illis: «Nescitis parabolam hanc, et quomodo omnes parabolas cognoscetis? [14]Qui seminat, verbum seminat. [15]Hi autem sunt, qui circa viam, ubi seminatur verbum: et cum audierint, confestim venit Satanas et aufert verbum, quod seminatum est in eos. [16]Et hi sunt, qui super petrosa seminantur: qui cum audierint verbum, statim cum gaudio accipiunt illud [17]et non habent radicem

the parable to his disciples later, when he is alone with them (vv. 10–11; 4:34). However, the fact that there is a mystery here does not mean that the teaching is secret or esoteric. As the parable of the lamp will show (4:21–22), our Lord's teaching is not to be kept secret; it must be spread, proclaimed to all. In the background to the whole Gospel, including this passage, lies the idea that we can understand Jesus' preaching only if we know who he truly is and what his mission is: the mystery of the Kingdom of God that he preaches is closely connected with his mission as the Servant of Yahweh who succeeds in establishing the Kingdom by undergoing his passion and death on a cross—a scandalous fate. That is why the evangelist points out that parables were an appropriate method of teaching, explaining that Jesus "spoke the word to them, as they were able to hear it" (4:33). But the disciples were given special instruction, so to speak, because their closeness to Jesus made it easier for them to grasp things that were not immediately clear to all, and because Jesus has chosen them to go out and preach: "What he sometimes appeared to say in veiled terms, at other times he spoke of openly, for he no longer wished his listeners to fall silent at his words, but that they go out to the whole world and preach what he had taught them" (St Augustine, *In Ioannis Evangelium*, 113, 6).

This context may make it easier to understand what is said in vv. 10–12. If the Twelve and the other disciples succeeded in understanding the mystery of the Kingdom of God (cf. Mt 13:51), it was thanks to a gift from God himself (v. 11; cf. Mt 13:11). The disciples were different from "those outside" (v. 11), an expression here meaning not Gentiles, but Jews who failed to understand the significance of Jesus' words and works (cf. Lk 12:54–57). As is often pointed out in the New Testament (see Jn 12:37–40; Acts 28:25–27; Rom 11:7–8), people's lack of receptivity bore out the prophecy of Isaiah 6:9–10. At the start of this discourse, Jesus prefaces his quotation from Isaiah with the words "so that" (v. 12). This might appear disconcerting or shocking, if one were not aware that it is a form of speech found elsewhere in the Old Testament (see Ex 4:21), whereby certain actions performed by human beings are attributed to God. (It is a way of indicating divine foreknowledge: in salvation history both God's grace and man's freedom are at work, in a mysterious manner; but God knows the future.) God opens to the gospel message the hearts of those who seek him in all sincerity (cf. Acts 16:14). See also the note on Rom 9:14–33.

[16]And these in like manner are the ones sown upon rocky ground, who, when they hear the word, immediately receive it with joy; [17]and they have no root in themselves, but endure for a while; then, when tribulation or persecution arises on account of the word, immediately they fall away.[m] [18]And others are the ones sown among thorns; they are those who hear the word, [19]but the cares of the world, and the delight in riches, and the desire for other things, enter in and choke the word, and it proves unfruitful. [20]But those that were sown upon the good soil are the ones who hear the word and accept it and bear fruit, thirtyfold and sixtyfold and a hundredfold."

Jer 4:3–4

Mk 10:23–24

Parables of the lamp and the measure

Mt 7:1–2
Lk 8:16–18
Lk 11:33
Mt 5:15
Mt 10:26
Lk 12:2

[21]And he said to them, "Is a lamp brought in to be put under a bushel, or under a bed, and not on a stand? [22]For there is nothing hid, except to be made manifest; nor is anything secret, except to come to light. [23]If any man has ears to hear, let him hear." [24]And he said to them, "Take heed what you hear; the measure you give will be the measure you get, and still more will be given you. [25]For to him who has will more be given; and from him who has not, even what he has will be taken away."

Lk 6:38

Mt 13:12

Parables of the seed and of the mustard seed

Mt 13:31–33
Lk 13:18–19

[26]And he said, "The kingdom of God is as if a man should scatter seed upon the ground, [27]and should sleep and rise night and day, and the seed should sprout and grow, he knows not how. [28]The earth produces of itself, first the blade, then the ear, then the full grain in the ear. [29]But when the grain is ripe, at once he puts in the sickle, because the harvest has come."

Jas 5:7

Rev 14:15–16

in se, sed temporales sunt; deinde orta tribulatione vel persecutione propter verbum, confestim scandalizantur. [18]Et alii sunt, qui in spinis seminantur: hi sunt, qui verbum audierunt, [19]et aerumnae saeculi et deceptio divitiarum et circa reliqua concupiscentiae introeuntes suffocant verbum, et sine fructu efficitur. [20]Et hi sunt, qui super terram bonam seminati sunt: qui audiunt verbum et suscipiunt et fructificant unum triginta et unum sexaginta et unum centum». [21]Et dicebat illis: «Numquid venit lucerna, ut sub modio ponatur aut sub lecto? Nonne ut super candelabrum ponatur? [22]Non enim est aliquid absconditum, nisi ut manifestetur, nec factum est occultum, nisi ut in palam veniat. [23]Si quis habet aures audiendi, audiat». [24]Et dicebat illis: «Videte quid audiatis. In qua mensura mensi fueritis, remetietur vobis et adicietur vobis. [25]Qui enim habet, dabitur illi; et, qui non habet, etiam quod habet, auferetur ab illo». [26]Et dicebat: «Sic est regnum Dei, quemadmodum si homo iaciat sementem in terram [27]et dormiat et exsurgat nocte ac die, et semen germinet et increscat, dum nescit ille. [28]Ultro terra fructificat primum herbam, deinde spicam, deinde plenum

4:21–25 The parable of the lamp contains two messages. Firstly, it says that Christ's teaching is a light for the whole world and therefore should be passed on (cf. 16:15; Mt 10:27). Secondly, it shows that the Kingdom that Christ proclaims has such ability to penetrate hearts, his light is so strong, that, at the end of time, when Jesus comes again, every single human action, in favour of or against Christ, will become visible to all (cf. Mt 25:31–46).

Our Lord wants his listeners, the seed of the future Church, to pay heed to what he is telling them: they are being given a treasure for which they must render an account. "To him who has will more be given" (v. 25): the person who responds to grace will be given still more grace; but one who does not let grace bear fruit will become poorer and poorer (cf. Mt 25:14–30).

Therefore, the theological virtues admit of no measure: "If you say, Enough, you are already dead" (St Augustine, *Sermones*, 51).

4:26–34 The parables of the seed and the mustard seed are so simple that it is easy to overlook their deep significance. They are based on the idea of growth; that of the seed speaks of the Kingdom's intrinsic effectiveness and gradual development (v. 27); that of the mustard seed has to do with the disproportion between the first stage (when it is the smallest of all seeds: v. 31) and the last (when it has become a huge bush: v. 32). The seed is fruitful, but it must be sown in good ground; if it is, then it will eventually produce the fruit of virtue in the human heart: "Our good desires are the seeds sown in the soil; our first good works are the first shoots they send up;

[m] Or *stumble*

Ezek 17:23; 31:6

³⁰And he said, "With what can we compare the kingdom of God, or what parable shall we use for it? ³¹It is like a grain of mustard seed, which, when sown upon the ground, is the smallest of all the seeds on earth; ³²yet when it is sown it grows up and becomes the greatest of all shrubs, and puts forth large branches, so that the birds of the air can make nests in its shade."

Mt 13:34

The end of the Parables Discourse

³³With many such parables he spoke the word to them, as they were able to hear it; ³⁴he did not speak to them without a parable, but privately to his own disciples he explained everything.

4. MIRACLES AND ACTIVITY IN GALILEE*

Mt 8:23–27
Lk 8:22–25

The calming of the storm

³⁵On that day, when evening had come, he said to them, "Let us go across to the other side." ³⁶And leaving the crowd, they took him with them just as he was, in the boat. And other boats were with him. ³⁷And a great storm of wind arose, and the waves beat into the boat, so that the boat was already filling. ³⁸But he was in the stern, asleep on the cushion; and they woke him and said to him, "Teacher, do you Ps 89:9; 107:23–30
Mk 1:25 not care if we perish?" ³⁹And he awoke and rebuked the wind, and said to the sea,

frumentum in spica. ²⁹Et cum se produxerit fructus, statim mittit falcem, quoniam adest messis». ³⁰Et dicebat: «Quomodo assimilabimus regnum Dei aut in qua parabola ponemus illud? ³¹Sicut granum sinapis, quod cum seminatum fuerit in terra, minus est omnibus seminibus, quae sunt in terra; ³²et cum seminatum fuerit, ascendit et fit maius omnibus holeribus et facit ramos magnos, ita ut possint sub umbra eius aves caeli habitare». ³³Et talibus multis parabolis loquebatur eis verbum, prout poterant audire; ³⁴sine parabola autem non loquebatur eis. Seorsum autem discipulis suis disserebat omnia. ³⁵Et ait illis illa die, cum sero esset factum: «Transeamus contra». ³⁶Et dimittentes turbam, assumunt eum, ut erat in navi; et aliae naves erant cum illo. ³⁷Et exoritur procella magna venti, et fluctus se mittebant in navem, ita ut iam impleretur navis. ³⁸Et erat ipse in puppi supra cervical dormiens; et excitant eum et dicunt ei: «Magister, non ad te pertinet quia perimus?». ³⁹Et exsurgens comminatus est vento et dixit

our perseverance in good works is the coming of the first ears of grain; and our perfection in good works, the mature grain ready for harvest" (St Gregory the Great, *Homiliae in Ezechielem*, 2, 3, 5).

*4:35—6:6 After the Parables Discourse, Mark recounts four miracles. This section opens and closes with verses that pose the central question of the Gospel: "Who then is this?" (4:41; 6:2–3). The disciples are beginning to find out the answer, which will later come from Peter (8:29). Meanwhile, readers grow in their faith in Christ as they witness the increasing admiration shown by the disciples and the people in general (4:41; 5:20, 42; 6:2), the acknowledgment that devils give Jesus (5:7), and the remarkable unbelief that Jesus finds in his own people.

4:35–41 In many instances in the Bible, the sea symbolizes a place of evil forces that only God

can control (cf. Ps 65:7; 89:9–10; 107:23–30). By his domination of the elements, exerted by a giving of the same kind of order that brought demons to heel (v. 39; cf. 1:25), Jesus shows himself to have the power of God: hence the disciples' question (v. 41). The words that Jesus uses here (v. 40; cf. 5:36) teach us a perennial truth: faith conquers fear; if we have faith in Jesus, nothing can disturb our peace: "Christian, Christ is asleep in your boat. Wake him up, and he will calm the storm and your fears. [...] You are afraid because you are asleep; you are tossed about on the stormy desires raised by the breath of those who tempt you to do evil because your faith is asleep. 'Your faith is asleep' means you have forgotten your faith. To wake Christ means to awaken your faith, to recall what you believe. Remember your faith; wake Christ within you. Your faith will immediately still the frightening winds and waves of those who tempt you to do evil" (St Augustine, *Sermones*, 361, 7).

"Peace! Be still!" And the wind ceased, and there was a great calm. [40]He said to them, "Why are you afraid? Have you no faith?" [41]And they were filled with awe, and said to one another, "Who then is this, that even wind and sea obey him?"

Mk 1:27

The Gerasene demoniac

Mt 8:28–34
Lk 8:26–39

5 [1]They came to the other side of the sea, to the country of the Gerasenes.[n] [2]And when he had come out of the boat, there met him out of the tombs a man with an unclean spirit, [3]who lived among the tombs; and no one could bind him any more, even with a chain; [4]for he had often been bound with fetters and chains, but the chains he wrenched apart, and the fetters he broke in pieces; and no one had the strength to subdue him. [5]Night and day among the tombs and on the mountains he was always

mari: «Tace, obmutesce!». Et cessavit ventus, et facta est tranquillitas magna. [40]Et ait illis: «Quid timidi estis? Necdum habetis fidem?». [41]Et timuerunt magno timore et dicebant ad alterutrum: «Quis putas est iste, quia et ventus et mare oboediunt ei?». [5] [1]Et venerunt trans fretum maris in regionem Gerasenorum. [2]Et exeunte eo de navi, statim occurrit ei de monumentis homo in spiritu immundo, [3]qui domicilium habebat in monumentis; et neque catenis iam quisquam eum poterat ligare, [4]quoniam saepe compedibus et catenis vinctus dirupisset catenas et compedes comminuisset, et nemo poterat eum domare; [5]et semper nocte ac die in monumentis et in montibus erat clamans et concidens se lapidibus. [6]Et videns

5:1–20 Gerasa was in the Decapolis, an area inhabited by pagans of Greek and Syrian origin (cf. the note on Mt 8:28–34). That it was inhabited by pagans is clear from the fact that there was a herd of swine in the area; Jews did not raise pigs, since they were forbidden to eat pork (see Lev 11:7; Deut 14:8). But Jesus' mission is not confined to the children of Israel; it extends to the whole world, knowing no boundaries, because Jesus cares for all souls.

Therefore, the words Jesus speaks at the end of the passage explain the main meaning of this episode: he asks the man he has cured to tell all who live in the pagan region that the "mercy" of God is available to them, too (vv. 19–20). "Those who have met Christ must not shut themselves in their own little world: what a sad limitation that would be! They must open out like a fan in order to reach all souls. Each has to create (and widen) a circle of friends, whom he can influence through his professional prestige, his behaviour and his friendship, so that Christ may exercise his influence by means of that prestige, that behaviour and that friendship" (St Josemaría Escrivá, *Furrow*, 193).

St Mark reports this episode very vividly. The possessed man is in a terrible state: he lives like an animal, away from all human settlements and among tombs, which render him unclean (vv. 2–4); the devil has drained him of humanity. But now the devil must face Jesus, who is much stronger than he is (cf. 3:27) and who has been

frustrating him ever since his ministry began (1:21–28). This passage describes an exorcism in which Jesus' exchanges with the devil reveal our Lord's power: a devil capable of controlling two thousand swine is forced to tell Jesus his name (v. 9) and to plead with him, twice (vv. 10–11), to have himself and his cohorts allowed to stay in the swine. Jesus accedes to this, because what interests him is the man, not the devil. So, the man recovers his dignity and we find him "clothed and in his right mind" (v. 15), returning home to be with his people (v. 19). St Jerome explains the exorcism in this way: "It is as if he said: Leave my house. Why are you in my house? I want to go in. *Come out of the man*, this man, this rational animal. Come out of this man, this house prepared for me; the Lord wants to take possession of his home" (*Commentarium in Marcum*, 2).

At the end of the passage, we read of various reactions to the miracle: the man is delighted, but the local inhabitants demand that Jesus leave the area (v. 17), and the demons have begged not to be expelled from the region. Jesus had come among the herdsmen, but they preferred things the way they were; they were selfish. Christ had stood at their side, offering them his grace, but they rejected it. The man freed from the devil, however, wants to stay with Jesus and follow him. Our Lord does not let him do so, but he does give him a task: he is to stay in his own country and tell people "how much the Lord has

n Other ancient authorities read *Gergesenes*; some, *Gadarenes*

Mk 1:24
Jas 2:19

crying out, and bruising himself with stones. [6]And when he saw Jesus from afar, he ran and worshipped him; [7]and crying out with a loud voice, he said, "What have you to do with me, Jesus, Son of the Most High God? I adjure you by God, do not torment me." [8]For he had said to him, "Come out of the man, you unclean spirit!" [9]And Jesus[o] asked him, "What is your name?" He replied, "My name is Legion; for we are many." [10]And he begged him eagerly not to send them out of the country. [11]Now a great herd of swine was feeding there on the hillside; [12]and they begged him, "Send us to the swine, let us enter them." [13]So he gave them leave. And the unclean spirits came out, and entered the swine; and the herd, numbering about two thousand, rushed down the steep bank into the sea, and were drowned in the sea.

[14]The herdsmen fled, and told it in the city and the country. And people came to see what it was that had happened. [15]And they came to Jesus, and saw the demoniac sitting there, clothed and in his right mind, the man who had had the legion; and they were afraid. [16]And those who had seen it told what had happened to the demoniac and to the swine. [17]And they began to beg Jesus[p] to depart from their neighbourhood. [18]And as he was getting into the boat, the man who had been possessed with demons begged him that he might be with him. [19]But he refused, and said to him, "Go home to your friends, and tell them how much the Lord has done for you, and how he has Mk 7:31 had mercy on you." [20]And he went away and began to proclaim in the Decapolis how much Jesus had done for him; and all men marvelled.

Mt 9:18–26
Lk 8:40–56

Jairus' daughter is restored to life. Curing of the woman with a haemorrhage

[21]And when Jesus had crossed again in the boat to the other side, a great crowd gathered about him; and he was beside the sea. [22]Then came one of the rulers of the syn-Mk 7:32agogue, Jairus by name, and seeing him, he fell at his feet, [23]and besought him,

Iesum a longe cucurrit et adoravit eum [7]et clamans voce magna dicit: «Quid mihi et tibi, Iesu, fili Dei Altissimi? Adiuro te per Deum, ne me torqueas». [8]Dicebat enim illi: «Exi, spiritus immunde, ab homine». [9]Et interrogabat eum: «Quod tibi nomen est?». Et dicit ei: «Legio nomen mihi est, quia multi sumus». [10]Et deprecabatur eum multum, ne se expelleret extra regionem. [11]Erat autem ibi circa montem grex porcorum magnus pascens; [12]et deprecati sunt eum dicentes: «Mitte nos in porcos, ut in eos introeamus». [13]Et concessit eis. Et exeuntes spiritus immundi introierunt in porcos. Et magno impetu grex ruit per praecipitium in mare, ad duo milia, et suffocabantur in mari. [14]Qui autem pascebant eos, fugerunt et nuntiaverunt in civitatem et in agros; et egressi sunt videre quid esset facti. [15]Et veniunt ad Iesum; et vident illum, qui a daemonio vexabatur, sedentem, vestitum et sanae mentis, eum qui legionem habuerat, et timuerunt. [16]Et qui viderant, narraverunt illis qualiter factum esset ei, qui daemonium habuerat, et de porcis. [17]Et rogare eum coeperunt, ut discederet a finibus eorum. [18]Cumque ascenderet navem, qui daemonio vexatus fuerat, deprecabatur eum, ut esset cum illo. [19]Et non admisit eum, sed ait illi: «Vade in domum tuam ad tuos, et annuntia illis quanta tibi Dominus fecerit et misertus sit tui». [20]Et abiit et coepit praedicare in Decapoli quanta sibi fecisset Iesus, et omnes mirabantur. [21]Et cum transcendisset Iesus in navi rursus trans fretum, convenit turba multa ad illum, et erat circa mare. [22]Et venit quidam de archisynagogis nomine Iairus et videns eum procidit

done" for him (v. 19). The man begins to proclaim "how much Jesus had done for him" (v. 20). The divinity of Jesus is implied here; he himself is God's mercy.

5:21–43 In his description of these two miracles we can see that St Mark likes to provide small details that bring the story to life. But at the same time, everything he says is designed to carry a message to his readers—about the power of belief in Jesus and how much we can gain from knowing him.

The woman with the haemorrhage had an illness that made her unclean in the eyes of the

Law (see Lev 15:25ff). The evangelist describes how desperate she was and her boldness in going so far as to touch Jesus' garments. After curing her complaint, Jesus engages her in conversation, and makes clear that it was not magic that worked the miracle but rather the woman's faith and the power that came from Jesus: "She touches, the crowd presses. What does 'touched' mean if not 'believed'?" (St Augustine, *In Ioannis Evangelium*, 26, 3).

The story of Jairus shows the faith of this ruler of the synagogue who, encouraged by Jesus, manages to overcome the obstacles that he encounters. Because his daughter is at the point

o Greek *he*   p Green *him*

saying, "My little daughter is at the point of death. Come and lay your hands on her, so that she may be made well, and live." ²⁴And he went with him.

And a great crowd followed him and thronged about him. ²⁵And there was a woman who had a flow of blood for twelve years, ²⁶and who had suffered much under many physicians, and had spent all that she had, and was no better but rather grew worse. ²⁷She had heard the reports about Jesus, and came up behind him in the crowd and touched his garment. ²⁸For she said, "If I touch even his garments, I shall be made well." ²⁹And immediately the hemorrhage ceased; and she felt in her body that she was healed of her disease. ³⁰And Jesus, perceiving in himself that power had gone forth from him, immediately turned about in the crowd, and said, "Who touched my garments?" ³¹And his disciples said to him, "You see the crowd pressing around you, and yet you say, 'Who touched me?'" ³²And he looked around to see who had done it. ³³But the woman, knowing what had been done to her, came in fear and trembling and fell down before him, and told him the whole truth. ³⁴And he said to her, "Daughter, your faith has made you well; go in peace, and be healed of your disease."

³⁵While he was still speaking, there came from the ruler's house some who said, "Your daughter is dead. Why trouble the Teacher any further?" ³⁶But ignoring^q what they said, Jesus said to the ruler of the synagogue, "Do not fear, only believe." ³⁷And he allowed no one to follow him except Peter and James and John the brother of James. ³⁸When they came to the house of the ruler of the synagogue, he saw a tumult, and people weeping and wailing loudly. ³⁹And when he had entered, he said to them, "Why do you make a tumult and weep? The child is not dead but sleeping." ⁴⁰And they laughed at him. But he put them all outside, and took the child's father and mother and those who were with him, and went in where the child was. ⁴¹Taking her by the hand he said to her, "Talitha cumi"; which means, "Little girl, I say to you, arise." ⁴²And immediately the girl got up and walked; for she was twelve years old. And immediately they were overcome with amazement. ⁴³And he strictly charged them that no one should know this,* and told him to give her something to eat.

Margin references:
Mk 3:10; 6:56
Mt 14:36

Lk 6:19

Lk 7:50
Mk 10:52

Jn 11:11
Acts 20:10

Acts 9:40

Lk 7:14

Mk 1:34, 44

ad pedes eius ²³et deprecatur eum multum dicens: «Filiola mea in extremis est; veni, impone manus super eam, ut salva sit et vivat». ²⁴Et abiit cum illo. Et sequebatur eum turba multa et comprimebant illum. ²⁵Et mulier, quae erat in profluvio sanguinis annis duodecim ²⁶et fuerat multa perpessa a compluribus medicis et erogaverat omnia sua nec quidquam profecerat sed magis deterius habebat, ²⁷cum audisset de Iesu, venit in turba retro et tetigit vestimentum eius; ²⁸dicebat enim: «Si vel vestimenta eius tetigero, salva ero». ²⁹Et confestim siccatus est fons sanguinis eius, et sensit corpore quod sanata esset a plaga. ³⁰Et statim Iesus cognoscens in semetipso virtutem, quae exierat de eo, conversus ad turbam aiebat: «Quis tetigit vestimenta mea?». ³¹Et dicebant ei discipuli sui: «Vides turbam comprimentem te et dicis: 'Quis me tetigit?'». ³²Et circumspiciebat videre eam, quae hoc fecerat. ³³Mulier autem timens et tremens, sciens quod factum esset in se, venit et procidit ante eum et dixit ei omnem veritatem. ³⁴Ille autem dixit ei: «Filia, fides tua te salvam fecit. Vade in pace et esto sana a plaga tua». ³⁵Adhuc eo loquente, veniunt ab archisynagogo dicentes: «Filia tua mortua est; quid ultra vexas magistrum?». ³⁶Iesus autem, verbo, quod dicebatur, audito, ait archisynagogo: «Noli timere; tantummodo crede!». ³⁷Et non admisit quemquam sequi se nisi Petrum et Iacobum et Ioannem fratrem Iacobi. ³⁸Et veniunt ad domum archisyn-

of death, he sets aside his social position and begs Jesus to go and cure her (vv. 22–23). Jesus twice (vv. 36, 40) encourages his faith, by words and gestures, despite the report of the child's death and the jeers of the crowd at the ruler's house. In the end, Jairus' faith is rewarded with the raising of his daughter to life. "He who awakes good desires in his children obliges us to ask, seek and call [...]. This might seem strange, if we failed to realize that God our Lord [...] is trying to foster our desires in our prayers and to prepare us to receive what he is about to give us"

(St Augustine, *Epistolae*, 130, 16–17).

The raising of the child from the dead, although it became public knowledge, happened privately, in the presence of her parents and the three disciples that Jesus brought with him. And he "strictly charged them" not to spread word of the miracle. As we have already noticed elsewhere, Jesus apparently wanted to prevent any misinterpretation of what the messianic Saviour was: Christ's work involves not only his miracles but also his death on the cross and his resurrection (cf. the note on 7:31–37).

q Or *overhearing*. Other ancient authorities read *hearing*

Mt 13:53–58
Lk 4:16–30

Jn 7:15

Lk 2:34f
Jn 6:42

Jn 4:44

Mk 7:32

No prophet is honoured in his own country

6 ¹He went away from there and came to his own country; and his disciples followed him. ²And on the sabbath he began to teach in the synagogue; and many who heard him were astonished, saying, "Where did this man get all this? What is the wisdom given to him? What mighty works are wrought by his hands! ³Is not this the carpenter, the son of Mary and brother of James and Joses and Judas and Simon, and are not his sisters here with us?" And they took offence[r] at him. ⁴And Jesus said to them, "A prophet is not without honour, except in his own country, and among his own kin, and in his own house." ⁵And he could do no mighty work there, except that he laid his hands upon a few sick people and healed them. ⁶And he marvelled because of their unbelief.

agogi; et videt tumultum et flentes et eiulantes multum, ³⁹et ingressus ait eis: «Quid turbamini et ploratis? Puella non est mortua, sed dormit». ⁴⁰Et irridebant eum. Ipse vero, eiectis omnibus, assumit patrem puellae et matrem et, qui secum erant, et ingreditur, ubi erat puella; ⁴¹et tenens manum puellae ait illi: «Talitha, qum!» —quod est interpretatum: «Puella, tibi dico: Surge!»—. ⁴²Et confestim surrexit puella et ambulabat; erat enim annorum duodecim. Et obstupuerunt continuo stupore magno. ⁴³Et praecepit illis vehementer, ut nemo id sciret, et dixit dari illi manducare. [6] ¹Et egressus est inde et venit in patriam suam, et sequuntur illum discipuli sui. ²Et facto sabbato, coepit in synagoga docere; et multi audientes admirabantur dicentes: «Unde huic haec, et quae est sapientia, quae data est illi, et virtutes tales, quae per manus eius efficiuntur? ³Nonne iste est faber, filius Mariae et frater Iacobi et Iosetis et Iudae et Simonis? Et nonne sorores eius hic nobiscum sunt?». Et scandalizabantur in illo. ⁴Et dice-

6:1–6 This episode draws to a close a series of passages concerning the power of faith: the faith of Jairus and that of the woman with the issue of blood (5:21–43) stand in marked contrast to the still weak faith of the disciples (4:35–41) and the unbelief of Jesus' own countrymen in Nazareth (v. 6). The evangelist once again shows the difficulty people had in working out who Jesus was: his disciples did not know (4:41), nor did the Gerasenes (5:17), and now his old neighbours actually take offence at his works and deeds (vv. 2–3).

This passage gives us an insight into how Jesus spent most of his life on earth: he lived as a craftsman, with his family, sharing the same lifestyle as his neighbours (v. 3). In this hidden life of Christ we can discover the value of everyday life as a route to holiness: "Your human vocation is a part—and an important part—of your divine vocation. That is the reason why you must strive for holiness, giving a particular character to your human personality, a style to your life; contributing at the same time to the sanctification of others, your fellow men; sanctifying your work and your environment—the profession or job that fills your day ..." (St Josemaría Escrivá, *Christ Is Passing By*, 46).

Jesus is described here as "the son of Mary" (v. 3). We cannot be sure whether we should understand from this that St Joseph had already died, or whether the evangelist reports it as having to do with the virginal conception of Jesus. As regards the "brothers" of Jesus, see the notes on 3:31–35 and on Mt 12:46–50.

*6:6—8:30 Jesus' activity in Galilee is extended by that of his disciples (6:6–13). In the times of Jesus, Galilee was a region with unusual ethnic and economic features. Jews and Gentiles lived side by side in its cities, and employment and trade brought them into contact with neighbouring regions where the population was made up mostly of pagans. By spending time in these border areas (7:24—8:9), as he had already done (5:1–20), Jesus showed that his mission was a universal one, even though it was directed initially to the children of Israel (see 7:27).

During this period people are still asking themselves who Jesus is (cf. 6:14–16; 8:27–28). Earlier, the evangelist showed that the demons knew who he was (cf. 1:24, 34; 5:7), but that Christ did not accept their testimony, because what he cared about was having people acknowledge him as the Messiah. Once that starts happening with Peter's profession of faith (8:29), a new stage in the Gospel begins in which the Teacher instructs his followers as to the redemptive purpose of his role as Messiah.

6:6–13 After spending some time with Jesus, the Twelve are sent out to spread the Gospel. This mission should be seen as an anticipation of the

r Or *stumbled*

5. JESUS JOURNEYS WITH HIS APOSTLES*

And he went about among the villages teaching.

The mission of the Twelve

Mt 10:5–15
Lk 9:1–6

7And he called to him the twelve, and began to send them out two by two, and gave them authority over the unclean spirits. 8He charged them to take nothing for their journey except a staff; no bread, no bag, no money in their belts; 9but to wear sandals and not put on two tunics. 10And he said to them, "Where you enter a house, stay there until you leave the place. 11And if any place will not receive you and they refuse to hear you, when you leave, shake off the dust that is on your feet for a testimony against them." 12So they went out and preached that men should repent. 13And they cast out many demons, and anointed with oil many that were sick and healed them.

Lk 10:4

Lk 10:5–6

Lk 10:11

Jas 5:14–15

Opinions about Jesus

Mt 14:1–2
Lk 9:7–9

14King Herod heard of it; for Jesus's name had become known. Somet said, "John the baptizer has been raised from the dead; that is why these powers are at work with

bat eis Iesus: «Non est propheta sine honore nisi in patria sua et in cognatione sua et in domo sua». 5Et non poterat ibi virtutem ullam facere, nisi paucos infirmos impositis manibus curavit; 6et mirabatur propter incredulitatem eorum. Et circumibat castella in circuitu docens. 7Et convocat Duodecim et coepit eos mittere binos et dabat illis potestatem in spiritus immundos; 8et praecepit eis, ne quid tollerent in via nisi virgam tantum: non panem, non peram neque in zona aes, 9sed ut calcearentur sandaliis et ne induerentur duabus tunicis. 10Et dicebat eis: «Quocumque introieritis in domum, illic manete, donec exeatis inde. 11Et quicumque locus non receperit vos nec audierint vos, exeuntes inde excutite pulverem de pedibus vestris in testimonium illis». 12Et exeuntes praedicaverunt, ut paenitentiam agerent; 13et daemonia multa eiciebant et ungebant oleo multos aegrotos et sanabant. 14Et audivit Herodes rex; manifestum enim factum est nomen eius. Et dicebant: «Ioannes Baptista resurrexit a mortuis, et propterea inoperantur virtutes in illo». 15Alii autem dicebant: «Elias est». Alii vero dicebant: «Propheta est, quasi unus ex prophetis». 16Quo audito,

later mandate to go out into the whole world (16:15–18), and it should be seen, too, as an echo of Christ's own preaching. The three missions have some features in common. Like Jesus, who makes his way through the villages preaching (v. 6), the apostles should not stay in one place but instead move from one to the next (vv. 10–13; cf. 16:5); as in the case of Christ, they will have a mixed reception (vv. 10–11; 16:15). The apostles are also given the power that Jesus has over unclean spirits (v. 7; cf. 16:17). What is particularly noticeable is the emphasis our Lord places on detachment from all things: "However, by these instructions the Lord did not mean that the evangelists should not seek to live in any other way than by depending on what was offered them by those to whom they preached the Gospel; otherwise this very apostle [St Paul] would have acted contrary to this precept when he earned his living by the labours of his own hands" (St Augustine, *De consensu Evangelistarum*, 2, 30, 73).

At the end of the passage, in his summary of how the apostles fared during their journeys, St Mark mentions anointing of the sick (v. 13). The Church sees in this an allusion to the sacrament of Anointing of the Sick, which Christ instituted and which, much later on, was "recommended and proclaimed to the faithful by the Apostle James (cf. Jas 5:14ff)" (Council of Trent, *De Extrema Unctione*, chap. 1; cf. the note on Jas 5:13–18).

6:14–16 At the beginning of the Gospel, Mark declares who Jesus is—the Christ, the Son of God. And the Father, too, proclaimed this at his baptism in the Jordan. However, except for the demons (whose testimony Jesus does not accept), those who have contact with Jesus are amazed by his actions, but they cannot work out who he is (see 1:27; 2:7, 12; 4:41). These verses mark another stage in the process leading to Peter's confession of faith (cf. 8:29); but, even after that, Jesus will continue to help his disciples understand the true nature of his role as Messiah.

s Greek *his*   t Other ancient authorities read *he*

him." [15]But others said, "It is Elijah." And others said, "It is a prophet, like one of the prophets of old." [16]But when Herod heard of it, he said, "John, whom I beheaded, has been raised."

Mt 14:3–12
Lk 3:19–20

The martyrdom of John the Baptist

[17]For Herod had sent and seized John, and bound him in prison for the sake of Hero-

Lev 18:16

dias, his brother Philip's wife; because he had married her. [18]For John said to Herod, "It is not lawful for you to have your brother's wife." [19]And Herodias had a grudge against him, and wanted to kill him. But she could not, [20]for Herod feared John, knowing that he was a righteous and holy man, and kept him safe. When he heard

Esther 1:3; 2:18

him, he was much perplexed; and yet he heard him gladly. [21]But an opportunity came when Herod on his birthday gave a banquet for his courtiers and officers and the leading men of Galilee. [22]For when Herodias' daughter came in and danced, she pleased Herod and his guests; and the king said to the girl, "Ask me for whatever you wish, and I will grant it." [23]And he vowed to her, "Whatever you ask me, I will give you, even half of my kingdom." [24]And she went out, and said to her mother,

Herodes aiebat: «Quem ego decollavi Ioannem, hic resurrexit!». [17]Ipse enim Herodes misit ac tenuit Ioannem et vinxit eum in carcere propter Herodiadem uxorem Philippi fratris sui, quia duxerat eam. [18]Dicebat enim Ioannes Herodi: «Non licet tibi habere uxorem fratris tui». [19]Herodias autem insidiabatur illi et volebat occidere eum nec poterat: [20]Herodes enim metuebat Ioannem, sciens eum virum iustum et sanctum, et custodiebat eum, et audito eo multum haesitabat et libenter eum audiebat. [21]Et cum dies opportunus accidisset, quo Herodes natali suo cenam fecit principibus suis et tribunis et primis Galilaeae, [22]cumque introisset filia ipsius Herodiadis et saltasset, placuit Herodi simulque recumbentibus. Rex ait puellae: «Pete a me, quod vis, et dabo tibi». [23]Et iuravit illi multum: «Quidquid petieris a me, dabo tibi, usque ad dimidium regni mei». [24]Quae cum exisset, dixit matri suae: «Quid petam?». At illa dixit: «Caput Ioannis Baptistae». [25]Cumque introisset statim cum festinatione ad regem,

6:17–29 This account, set in the context of the apostolic mission, shows readers that Christians will often experience these same two realities as John the Baptist and Christ himself did: that many will respond positively to the preaching of the Gospel and that this does not mean that Christians will be free from the influence of worldly powers: "By their eloquent and attractive example of a life completely transfigured by the splendour of moral truth, the martyrs and, in general, all the Church's saints, light up every period of history by reawakening its moral sense" (John Paul II, *Veritatis splendor*, 93).

St John the Baptist has a unique place in salvation history, because he is the Precursor, charged with preparing the way of the Messiah. Even though his Gospel is quite short, St Mark leaves us in no doubt about the Baptist's standing: people regarded him as a prophet (11:32), as the Elijah who would come prior to the Messiah (9:12–13; cf. Mt 17:13), and they travelled great distances to see him (1:5). It is not surprising that Tradition has revered him and gathered as much information about his life as possible: "Josephus tells us that John was imprisoned in the fortress at Makeronte and decapitated there.

Church history tells us that he was buried in Sebaste, a town in Palestine, formerly known as Samaria. During the governorship of Julian, outraged at the Christians who made pious pilgrimage to his tomb, the pagans destroyed the tomb and scattered his bones in the fields; then they gathered the bones together again, burned them and scattered the ashes in the fields" (St Bede, *In Marci Evangelium*, 26, 69).

When commenting on the death of John the Baptist, the Fathers of the Church do not ignore the ascetical lesson to be drawn from the episode. Herod had a certain respect for John and liked to hear him speak (v. 20), and yet ended up beheading him. "We read of three equally wicked, criminal acts: the wild birthday feast; the young woman's seductive dance; and the king's terrible oath. Each should be an example to us of how never to behave. Herod fell and was condemned because he would either have to break his own oath or do something worse. [...] His love for the woman undid him, and he handed over to her a man he knew to be holy and righteous. His lust led him into a worse fault; the greater sin, a consequence of the lesser" (St Bede, *Homiliae*, 2, 23).

"What shall I ask?" And she said, "The head of John the baptizer." 25And she came in immediately with haste to the king, and asked, saying, "I want you to give me at once the head of John the baptizer on a platter." 26And the king was exceedingly sorry; but because of his oath and his guests he did not want to break his word to her. 27And immediately the king sent a soldier of the guard and gave orders to bring his head. He went and beheaded him in the prison, 28and brought his head on a platter, and gave it to the girl; and the girl gave it to her mother. 29When his disciples heard of it, they came and took his body, and laid it in a tomb.

The apostles return. First miracle of the loaves and fish

Mt 14:13–21
Lk 9:10–17
Jn 6:1–15

30The apostles returned to Jesus, and told him all that they had done and taught. 31And he said to them, "Come away by yourselves to a lonely place, and rest a while." For many were coming and going, and they had no leisure even to eat. 32And they went away in the boat to a lonely place by themselves. 33Now many saw them going, and knew them, and they ran there on foot from the towns, and got there ahead of them. 34As he landed he saw a great throng, and he had compassion on them, because they were like sheep without a shepherd; and he began to teach them many things. 35And when it grew late, his disciples came to him and said, "This is a lonely place, and the hour is now late; 36send them away, to go into the country and

Lk 10:17

Mk 2:2; 3:20; 8:1–9

Num 27:17
Ezek 34:5
Mt 9:36
1 Kings 22:17
2 Chron 18:16

petivit dicens: «Volo ut protinus des mihi in disco caput Ioannis Baptistae». 26Et contristatus rex propter iusiurandum et propter recumbentes noluit eam decipere 27et statim misso spiculatore rex praecepit afferri caput eius. Et abiens decollavit eum in carcere 28et attulit caput eius in disco et dedit illud puellae et puella dedit illud matri suae. 29Quo audito discipuli eius venerunt et tulerunt corpus eius et posuerunt illud in monumento. 30Et convenientes apostoli ad Iesum renuntiaverunt illi omnia, quae egerant et docuerant. 31Et ait illis: «Venite vos ipsi seorsum in desertum locum et requiescite pusillum». Erant enim, qui veniebant et redibant multi, et nec manducandi spatium habebant. 32Et abierunt in navi in desertum locum seorsum. 33Et viderunt eos abeuntes et cognoverunt multi, et pedestre de omnibus civitatibus concurrerunt illuc et praevenerunt eos. 34Et exiens vidit multam turbam et misertus est super eos, quia erant sicut oves non habentes pastorem, et coepit docere illos multa. 35Et cum iam hora multa facta esset, accesserunt discipuli eius dicentes: «Desertus est locus hic, et hora iam est multa; 36dimitte illos, ut euntes in villas et vicos in circuitu

6:30–44 This passage gives a very good idea of just how busy a life Jesus led at this time. His dedication to souls was such that Mark again mentions (cf. 3:20) that he did not even have time to eat; the same was true of the apostles. Jesus wants to bring them away to rest, but the crowd is too demanding. "The Lord led the disciples away to rest for a while in order to teach us that those whose task it is to lead the faithful in deed or word cannot work without rest" (St Bede, *In Marci Evangelium*, 2, 5, 31).

Jesus' attitude in the episode of the miracle of the loaves sets an example for Christians. The sight of this leaderless crowd fills him with compassion, so he gives them two kinds of food—spiritual food in the form of teaching, and material nourishment to stay their hunger. Both acts are very significant, because they signal the fulfilment of prophecies which said that God himself was going to shepherd his people, guiding and nourishing them (see Ezek 34:1–31). The miracle is also a symbol of the

new People of God, the Church, which draws sustenance from the word of Christ and the bread of the Eucharist: "The Church has always venerated the divine Scriptures just as she venerates the body of the Lord, since, especially in the sacred liturgy, she unceasingly receives and offers to the faithful the bread of life from the table both of God's word and of Christ's body" (Vatican II, *Dei Verbum*, 21). The sheer scale of this miracle is an example of the largesse associated with the messianic times. Elijah, in one of his miracles, gave a widow just enough for her subsistence (1 Kings 17:13–16), but Jesus gives more than what people simply need. However, he wants the leftovers to be collected (vv. 42–44; cf. Jn 6:12) to teach us not to waste the gifts God gives us. The Fathers recall that Moses distributed the manna for each person to eat as much as he could, and not waste any (Ex 16:16–20). The Eucharist, food of the soul, both is and signifies a gift that God gives us "this day".

2 Kings 4:42–44 villages round about and buy themselves something to eat." [37]But he answered them, "You give them something to eat." And they said to him, "Shall we go and buy two hundred denarii[u] worth of bread, and give it to them to eat?" [38]And he said to them, "How many loaves have you? Go and see." And when they had found out, they said, "Five, and two fish." [39]Then he commanded them all to sit down by companies upon

Mk 7:34; 14:22 the green grass. [40]So they sat down in groups, by hundreds and by fifties. [41]And taking the five loaves and the two fish he looked up to heaven, and blessed, and broke the loaves, and gave them to the disciples to set before the people; and he divided the two fish among them all. [42]And they all ate and were satisfied. [43]And they took up twelve baskets full of broken pieces and of the fish. [44]And those who ate the loaves were five thousand men.

Mt 14:22–33
Jn 6:16–21 **Jesus walks on water**

[45]Immediately he made his disciples get into the boat and go before him to the other
Mk 1:35; 3:13; 9:2 side, to Bethsaida, while he dismissed the crowd. [46]And after he had taken leave of them, he went into the hills to pray. [47]And when evening came, the boat was out on
Job 9:8
Is 43:16 the sea, and he was alone on the land. [48]And he saw that they were distressed in rowing, for the wind was against them. And about the fourth watch of the night he came to them, walking on the sea. He meant to pass by them, [49]but when they saw

emant sibi, quod manducent». [37]Respondens autem ait illis: «Date illis vos manducare». Et dicunt ei: «Euntes emamus denariis ducentis panes et dabimus eis manducare?». [38]Et dicit eis: «Quot panes habetis? Ite, videte». Et cum cognovissent, dicunt: «Quinque et duos pisces». [39]Et praecepit illis, ut accumbere facerent omnes secundum contubernia super viride fenum. [40]Et discubuerunt secundum areas per centenos et per quinquagenos. [41]Et acceptis quinque panibus et duobus piscibus, intuens in caelum benedixit et fregit panes et dabat discipulis suis, ut ponerent ante eos; et duos pisces divisit omnibus. [42]Et manducaverunt omnes et saturati sunt; [43]et sustulerunt fragmenta duodecim cophinos plenos, et de piscibus. [44]Et erant, qui manducaverunt panes, quinque milia virorum. [45]Et statim coegit discipulos suos ascendere navem, ut praecederent trans fretum ad Bethsaidam, dum ipse dimitteret populum. [46]Et cum dimisisset eos, abiit in montem orare. [47]Et cum sero factum esset, erat navis in medio mari, et ipse solus in terra. [48]Et videns eos laborantes in remigando, erat enim ventus contrarius eis, circa quartam vigiliam noctis venit ad eos ambulans super mare et volebat praeterire eos. [49]At illi, ut viderunt eum ambulantem super mare, putaverunt phantasma esse et exclamaverunt; [50]omnes enim eum

6:45–52 Jesus' actions show who he is and what power he has: that is why he works miracles, as the disciples gradually come to see: "His actions spoke louder than his words: Jesus wanted to reveal himself to us above all in his works" (Origen, *Contra Celsum*, 1, 48).

The Romans divided the night into four parts, or watches, each lasting three hours; they began at sunset, and were commonly called evening and night, cockcrow and dawn. Here, our Lord comes to the disciples at dawn. This episode shows us that even when we are under great pressure or can make no sense of what is happening to us, he is with us, to help us; at the same time, he wants us to make an effort, so that our hope will be strengthened and we will become more resilient (cf. the note on Mt 14:22–33): "The Lord allowed his disciples to enter danger to make them suffer, and he did not immediately come to their aid; he left them in peril for the whole night, to teach them to be

patient and not to be accustomed to receiving immediate succour in tribulation" (Theophylact, *Enarratio in Evangelium Marci*, ad loc.).

Once again the Gospel records that the disciples (and we) sometimes fail to appreciate supernatural realities because our hearts are hardened (v. 52). Our Lord will continue to preach and work miracles in order to enlighten our minds, and he will send the Holy Spirit, to remind us of his teaching (see Jn 14:26): "O faithful soul, when your faith is besieged by uncertainty and your weak reason cannot grasp the great mysteries, say without fear, with a desire for deep understanding: 'How can this be?' [...] The great mysteries that Wisdom revealed to his disciples when he was with them in this world will gradually be made clear before your eyes, the mysteries that they themselves could not fathom until they were enlightened by the Spirit of truth who came to reveal the full truth to them" (William of St Thierry, *Speculum fidei*).

u The denarius was a day's wage for a labourer

him walking on the sea they thought it was a ghost, and cried out; ⁵⁰for they all saw
him, and were terrified. But immediately he spoke to them and said, "Take heart, it
is I; have no fear." ⁵¹And he got into the boat with them and the wind ceased. And   Mk 4:39
they were utterly astounded, ⁵²for they did not understand about the loaves, but their   Mk 8:17
hearts were hardened.

Cures at Gennesaret   Mt 14:34–36

⁵³And when they had crossed over, they came to land at Gennesaret, and moored
to the shore. ⁵⁴And when they got out of the boat, immediately the people recognized him, ⁵⁵and ran about the whole neighbourhood and began to bring sick
people on their pallets to any place where they heard he was. ⁵⁶And wherever he   Mk 5:27–28
came, in villages, cities, or country, they laid the sick in the market places, and   Acts 5:15; 19:11s
besought him that they might touch even the fringe of his garment; and as many as
touched it were made well.

The traditions of the elders. What defiles a man   Mt 15:1–20

7 ¹Now when the Pharisees gathered together to him, with some of the scribes, who   Mk 3:22
    had come from Jerusalem, ²they saw that some of his disciples ate with hands   Lk 11:38
defiled, that is, unwashed. ³(For the Pharisees, and all the Jews, do not eat unless they

viderunt et conturbati sunt. Statim autem locutus est cum eis et dicit illis: «Confidite, ego sum; nolite timere!». ⁵¹Et ascendit ad illos in navem, et
cessavit ventus. Et valde nimis intra se stupebant: ⁵²non enim intellexerant de panibus, sed erat cor illorum obcaecatum. ⁵³Et cum transfretassent
in terram, pervenerunt Gennesaret et applicuerunt. ⁵⁴Cumque egressi essent de navi, continuo cognoverunt eum ⁵⁵et percurrentes universam
regionem illam coeperunt in grabatis eos, qui se male habebant, circumferre, ubi audiebant eum esse. ⁵⁶Et quocumque introibat in vicos aut in civitates vel in villas, in plateis ponebant infirmos, et deprecabantur eum ut vel fimbriam vestimenti eius tangerent; et quotquot tangebant eum, salvi
fiebant. [7] ¹Et conveniunt ad eum pharisaei et quidam de scribis venientes ab Hierosolymis; ²et cum vidissent quosdam ex discipulis eius communibus manibus, id est non lotis, manducare panes ³—pharisaei enim et omnes Iudaei, nisi pugillo lavent manus, non manducant, tenentes traditionem seniorum; ⁴et a foro nisi baptizentur, non comedunt; et alia multa sunt, quae acceperunt servanda: baptismata calicum et urceorum et

6:53–56 From 4:35 up to here, everything
recounted in the Gospel has taken place during
journeys around the Sea of Galilee. The summary given here mentions two of the main
themes thus far—Jesus' miracles and the admiration elicited from the crowd.

7:1–23 St Mark here reports Jesus' teaching on
moral conduct as delivered in three contexts—
exchanges with Pharisees who have come from
Jerusalem (vv. 1–13), subsequent teaching given
to the crowd (vv. 14–15), and (as happens very
frequently: see 4:10–20, 34; 9:28–29) private
explanations to his disciples (vv. 17–23).

The scribes from Jerusalem charge Jesus
with being responsible for his disciples' behaviour—their neglect of purification rites (v. 5).
Conscious that some of his readers will not be
familiar with Jewish customs, St Mark explains
why the Pharisees take issue with Jesus on this
point (vv. 3–5). The Old Law (see Ex 30:17ff)
contained certain rules defining the moral purity

expected of people when they approached God;
Jewish tradition extended those rules to other
areas (including diet) in order to give religious
significance to everyday actions. However, in
Jesus' time, in some places (probably including
those lived in by the scribes mentioned here),
rabbinical casuistry had led to the accretion of so
many rules that people lost sight of what true
worship of God meant. Jesus denounces this
trend (he uses Isaiah 29:13 to make his point),
and he gives an instance where human tradition
has become an excuse for shirking a divine command (vv. 8–13).

Jesus then tells the people what true purity
involves. He shows that the source of all defilement is to be found in the human heart: "Some
believe that evil thoughts are inspired wholly by
the devil and that the human will cannot be held
responsible for them. It is true that the devil can
inspire and encourage evil thoughts, but he is not
their origin" (St Bede, *In Marci Evangelium*, 2,
7, 20–21). See also the note on Mt 15:1–20.

wash their hands,[v] observing the tradition of the elders;* [4]and when they come from the market place, they do not eat unless they purify[w] themselves; and there are many other traditions which they observe, the washing of cups and pots and vessels of bronze.[x]) [5]And the Pharisees and the scribes asked him, "Why do your disciples not live[y] according to the tradition of the elders, but eat with hands defiled?" [6]And he said to them, "Well did Isaiah prophesy of you hypocrites, as it is written,

> 'This people honours me with their lips,
>   but their heart is far from me;
> [7]in vain do they worship me,
>   teaching as doctrines the precepts of men.'

[8]You leave the commandment of God, and hold fast the tradition of men."

[9]And he said to them, "You have a fine way of rejecting the commandment of God, in order to keep your tradition! [10]For Moses said, 'Honour your father and your mother'; and 'He who speaks evil of father or mother, let him surely die'; [11]but you say, 'If a man tells his father or his mother, What you would have gained from me is Corban' (that is, given to God)[z]— [12]then you no longer permit him to do anything for his father or mother, [13]thus making void the word of God through your tradition which you hand on. And many such things you do."

[14]And he called the people to meet him, and said to them, "Hear me, all of you, and understand: [15]there is nothing outside a man which by going into him can defile him; but the things that come out of a man are what defile him."[a] [17]And when he had entered the house, and left the people, his disciples asked him about the parable. [18]And he said to them, "Then are you also without understanding? Do you not see that whatever goes into a man from outside cannot defile him, [19]since it enters, not his heart but his stomach, and so passes on?"[b] (Thus he declared all foods clean.) [20]And he said, "What comes out of a man is what defiles a man. [21]For from within, out of the heart of man, come evil thoughts, fornication, theft, murder, adultery, [22]coveting, wickedness, deceit, licentiousness, envy, slander, pride, foolishness. [23]All these evil things come from within, and they defile a man."

Margin references:
Mt 23:25
Is 29:13
Ex 20:12; 21:17
Deut 5:16
Lev 20:9
Acts 10:14–15
Rom 14:14
Mk 4:10; 9:28
Col 2:16, 21–22
Mt 6:23; 20:15

aeramentorum et lectorum— [5]et interrogant eum pharisaei et scribae: «Quare discipuli tui non ambulant iuxta traditionem seniorum, sed communibus manibus manducant panem?». [6]At ille dixit eis: «Bene prophetavit Isaias de vobis hypocritis, sicut scriptum est: *"Populus hic labiis me honorat, / cor autem eorum longe est a me; / [7]in vanum autem me colunt / docentes doctrinas praecepta hominum"*. [8]Relinquentes mandatum Dei tenetis traditionem hominum». [9]Et dicebat illis: «Bene irritum facitis praeceptum Dei, ut traditionem vestram servetis. [10]Moyses enim dixit: *"Honora patrem tuum et matrem tuam"* et: *"Qui maledixerit patri aut matri, morte moriatur"*; [11]vos autem dicitis: "Si dixerit homo patri aut matri: Corban, quod est donum, quodcumque ex me tibi profuerit", [12]ultra non permittitis ei facere quidquam patri aut matri [13]rescindentes verbum Dei per traditionem vestram, quam tradidistis; et similia huiusmodi multa facitis». [14]Et advocata iterum turba, dicebat illis: «Audite me, omnes, et intellegite: [15]Nihil est extra hominem introiens in eum, quod possit eum coinquinare; sed quae de homine procedunt, illa sunt, quae coinquinant hominem!». [17]Et cum introisset in domum a turba, interrogabant eum discipuli eius parabolam. [18]Et ait illis: «Sic et vos imprudentes estis? Non intellegitis quia omne extrinsecus introiens in hominem non potest eum coinquinare, [19]quia non introit in cor eius sed in ventrem et in secessum exit?», purgans omnes escas. [20]Dicebat autem: «Quod de homine exit, illud coinquinat hominem; [21]ab intus enim de corde hominum cogitationes malae procedunt, fornicationes, furta, homicidia, [22]adulteria, avaritiae, nequitiae, dolus, impudicitia, oculus malus, blasphemia, superbia, stultitia: [23]omnia haec mala ab intus procedunt et coinquinant hominem». [24]Inde autem surgens abiit in fines Tyri et Sidonis. Et ingressus domum neminem voluit scire et non potuit latere. [25]Sed statim ut audivit de eo mulier, cuius habebat filia spiritum immundum, veniens procidit ad pedes eius.

His disciples then ask him to explain "the parable" (v. 17). His main point is made now (v. 19): as the true interpreter of the Law, and as its lord (see 2:28), Christ declares all foods to be "clean". There is profound teaching here: the source of evil and sin should not be assigned to created things, for when God made the world, he saw that all things were good (Gen 1:31): it lies in the heart of man which, after original sin, was changed for the worse and became subject to the corruption of the passions. He does not mean that man cannot cope with temptation (see Gen 4:7), but that it is more difficult now for him to do so (see *Catechism of the Catholic Church*, 1707 and also the RSV note **a**).

v One Greek word is of uncertain meaning and is not translated   w Other ancient authorities read *baptize*   x Other ancient authorities add *and beds*   y Greek *walk*   z Or *an offering*   a Other ancient authorities add verse 16, *If any man has ears to hear, let him hear*   b Or *is evacuated*

The Syrophoenician woman

Mt 15:21–28

²⁴And from there he arose and went away to the region of Tyre and Sidon.ᶜ And he entered a house, and would not have any one know it; yet he could not be hid. ²⁵But immediately a woman, whose little daughter was possessed by an unclean spirit, heard of him, and came and fell down at his feet. ²⁶Now the woman was a Greek, a Syrophoenician by birth. And she begged him to cast the demon out of her daughter. ²⁷And he said to her, "Let the children first be fed, for it is not right to take the children's bread and throw it to the dogs." ²⁸But she answered him, "Yes, Lord; yet even the dogs under the table eat the children's crumbs." ²⁹And he said to her, "For this saying you may go your way; the demon has left your daughter." ³⁰And she went home, and found the child lying in bed, and the demon gone.

Curing of a deaf man

Mk 5:20

³¹Then he returned from the region of Tyre, and went through Sidon to the Sea of Galilee, through the region of the Decapolis. ³²And they brought him a man who was deaf and had an impediment in his speech; and they besought him to lay his hand

²⁶Erat autem mulier Graeca, Syrophoenissa genere. Et rogabat eum, ut daemonium eiceret de filia eius. ²⁷Et dicebat illi: «Sine prius saturari filios; non est enim bonum sumere panem filiorum et mittere catellis». ²⁸At illa respondit et dicit ei: «Domine, etiam catelli sub mensa comedunt de micis puerorum». ²⁹Et ait illi: «Propter hunc sermonem vade; exiit daemonium de filia tua». ³⁰Et cum abisset domum suam, invenit puellam iacentem supra lectum et daemonium exisse. ³¹Et iterum exiens de finibus Tyri venit per Sidonem ad mare Galilaeae inter medios fines Decapoleos. ³²Et adducunt ei surdum et mutum et deprecantur eum, ut imponat illi manum. ³³Et apprehendens eum de turba seorsum misit digitos suos in auric-

7:24–30 Once more Jesus moves into a pagan area. A Gentile woman (the evangelist says she was "a Greek, a Syrophoenician by birth": v. 26) asks him to cure her daughter. The detail given here about the words and actions of both Christ and the woman allow us to see that although Jesus preached only to Jews, his salvation is available to everyone, Jew or Gentile. The very forthright conversation that takes place shows that faith in Jesus Christ can overcome all obstacles—even a person's sense of inferiority. "Do not be discouraged. However unworthy a person is, however imperfect his prayer turns out to be, if it is offered with humility and perseverance, God always hears it" (St Josemaría Escrivá, *Furrow*, 468).

Our Lord uses the diminutive ("*little* dogs"), thereby softening a scornful expression used by Jews to refer to Gentiles.

7:31–37 Jesus now works a miracle using gestures that symbolize the saving power of his human nature. At one time the Church used these gestures in the rite of Baptism to show that Christ opens the ears of man to enable him to hear and accept the word of God: "The priest touches your ears to open them to his preaching

and teaching. [...] Open your ears and hear the good news of eternal life given to you through the sacraments. We explained this to you in the celebration of the ceremony of 'opening' when we said: '*Ephphatha*, that is, be opened'" (St Ambrose, *De mysteriis*, 1, 2–3).

This is the third miracle that Mark records Jesus telling people not to say anything about. Jesus imposed this silence when he cured the man with leprosy (1:44), and when he raised a little girl from the dead (5:43); now he does so in the case of the deaf and dumb man (v. 36); and soon he will do so again, when he cures a blind man (see 8:26). These signs are virtually the same ones he referred John's disciples to, to show he was the Messiah (see Mt 11:2–5; Lk 7:18–23 and notes). St Mark mentions these instructions about silence to remind us that Jesus wanted people to come to his mission of Messiah in the light of his death on the cross.

However, the people pay no heed to Jesus' command (v. 36). St Augustine, noticing the apparent contradiction between Jesus' injunction and the people's reaction, says that in this way our Lord "wanted to show the lukewarm and half-hearted with how much zeal and fervour those commanded to proclaim his Name should

c Other ancient authorities omit *and Sidon*

Mk 8:23

Jn 11:41

Mk 1:44; 5:43; 8:26

Is 35:5

upon him. ³³And taking him aside from the multitude privately, he put his fingers into his ears, and he spat and touched his tongue; ³⁴and looking up to heaven, he sighed, and said to him, "Ephphatha," that is, "Be opened." ³⁵And his ears were opened, his tongue was released, and he spoke plainly. ³⁶And he charged them to tell no one; but the more he charged them, the more zealously they proclaimed it. ³⁷And they were astonished beyond measure, saying, "He has done all things well; he even makes the deaf hear and the dumb speak."

Mt 15:32–39

Second miracle of the loaves

Mk 6:30–44

8 ¹In those days, when again a great crowd had gathered, and they had nothing to eat, he called his disciples to him, and said to them, ²"I have compassion on the crowd, because they have been with me now three days, and have nothing to eat; ³and if I send them away hungry to their homes, they will faint on the way; and some of them have come a long way." ⁴And his disciples answered him, "How can

ulas eius et exspuens tetigit linguam eius ³⁴et suspiciens in caelum ingemuit et ait illi: «Effetha», quod est: «Adaperire». ³⁵Et statim apertae sunt aures eius, et solutum est vinculum linguae eius, et loquebatur recte. ³⁶Et praecepit illis, ne cui dicerent; quanto autem eis praecipiebat, tanto magis plus praedicabant. ³⁷Et eo amplius admirabantur dicentes: «Bene omnia fecit, et surdos facit audire et mutos loqui!». [8] ¹In illis diebus iterum cum turba multa esset, nec haberent, quod manducarent, convocatis discipulis, ait illis: ²«Misereor super turbam, quia iam triduo sustinent me, nec habent, quod manducent; ³et si dimisero eos ieiunos in domum suam, deficient in via; et quidam ex eis de longe venerunt». ⁴Et responderunt

act, if those who were forbidden to speak were unable to keep silent" (*De consensu Evangelistarum*, 4, 4, 15).

8:1–10 Both Matthew and Mark report this second miracle of the loaves. In some respects, this miracle is very like the earlier one (see 6:32–44); however, it does have features of its own—the fact that some of those present came from "afar" (v. 3, a literal translation), an expression often used in the New Testament to refer to Gentiles (Acts 2:39; 22:21; Eph 2:13, 17); the seven loaves and the seven baskets of leftovers (vv. 5, 8), as compared to twelve baskets in the previous miracle (see 6:43); etc. Jesus, who previously depicted himself as the Shepherd Messiah of the new people of Israel, now implies that the Gentiles too will have a place in it. This helps to make the meaning of the two miracles clearer: as Jesus implied in his use of the image of bread in his encounter with the Syrophoenician woman (see 7:24–30), salvation, which is offered first to Israel, will in fact be made available to all nations (cf. Acts 2:39; 3:26; 11:18; etc.): "All men are called to this catholic unity [of the People of God] [...]. And in different ways to it belong, or are related, the Catholic faithful, others who believe in Christ, and finally all mankind, called by God's

grace to salvation" (Vatican II, *Lumen gentium*, 13).

The miracle also shows how Jesus rewards those who stay close to him. Those thousands of people were so eager to hear him speak that they forgot everything else; it is easy to see why Christian piety should link this desire to be with Jesus to sacramental Communion, in which he gives himself to us as food: "Give yourself to me, Lord, and fill me; nothing can satisfy me but you. I cannot exist without you, and if you do not come to me, I cannot live. Thus, I go to you often and receive you as a cure for my infirmity. I will not fall by the wayside because I have been given heavenly sustenance. [...] You are sweet food for the soul; those who receive you worthily are made heirs to eternal glory" (Thomas à Kempis, *De imitatione Christi*, 4, 3, 2).

"Dalmanutha" (v. 10). This is the only reference to this place in Scripture. It is difficult to say where it was exactly, but it must have been somewhere near the Sea of Galilee. St Augustine made a note on this subject: "Matthew [...] does not mention Dalmanutha; he refers to Magadan. There can be no doubt but that both names refer to the same place because most of the texts, including the gospel of St Mark, make reference only to Magadan" (*De consensus Evangelistarum*, 2, 51, 106).

one feed these men with bread here in the desert?" [5]And he asked them, "How many loaves have you?" They said, "Seven." [6]And he commanded the crowd to sit down on the ground; and he took the seven loaves, and having given thanks he broke them and gave them to his disciples to set before the people; and they set them before the crowd. [7]And they had a few small fish; and having blessed them, he commanded that these also should be set before them. [8]And they ate, and were satisfied; and they took up the broken pieces left over, seven baskets full. [9]And there were about four thousand people. [10]And he sent them away; and immediately he got into the boat with his disciples, and went to the district of Dalmanutha.[d]

Lk 22:19
2 Kings 4:42–44

The leaven of the Pharisees and Herod

Mt 16:1–12

[11]The Pharisees came and began to argue with him, seeking from him a sign from heaven, to test him. [12]And he sighed deeply in his spirit, and said, "Why does this generation seek a sign? Truly, I say to you, no sign shall be given to this generation." [13]And he left them, and getting into the boat again he departed to the other side.

Lk 11:16, 29
Jn 6:30
1 Cor 1:22

[14]Now they had forgotten to bring bread; and they had only one loaf with them in the boat. [15]And he cautioned them, saying, "Take heed, beware of the leaven of the Pharisees and the leaven of Herod."[e] [16]And they discussed it with one another, saying, "We have no bread." [17]And being aware of it, Jesus said to them, "Why do

Lk 12:1

Mk 6:52; 7:18

ei discipuli sui: «Unde istos poterit quis hic saturare panibus in solitudine?». [5]Et interrogabat eos: «Quot panes habetis?». Qui dixerunt: «Septem». [6]Et praecipit turbae discumbere supra terram; et accipiens septem panes, gratias agens fregit et dabat discipulis suis, ut apponerent; et apposuerunt turbae. [7]Et habebant pisciculos paucos; et benedicens eos, iussit hos quoque apponi. [8]Et manducaverunt et saturati sunt; et sustulerunt, quod super-averat de fragmentis, septem sportas. [9]Erant autem quasi quattuor milia. Et dimisit eos. [10]Et statim ascendens navem cum discipulis suis venit in partes Dalmanutha. [11]Et exierunt pharisaei et coeperunt conquirere cum eo quaerentes ab illo signum de caelo, tentantes eum. [12]Et ingemiscens spiritu suo ait: «Quid generatio ista quaerit signum? Amen dico vobis: Non dabitur generationi isti signum». [13]Et dimittens eos, iterum ascendens, abiit trans fretum. [14]Et obliti sunt sumere panes et nisi unum panem non habebant secum in navi. [15]Et praecipiebat eis dicens: «Videte, cavete a fermento pharisaeorum et fermento Herodis!». [16]Et disputabant ad invicem, quia panes non haberent. [17]Quo cognito ait illis: «Quid disputatis, quia panes non habetis? Nondum cognoscitis nec intellegitis? Caecatum habetis cor vestrum? [18]Oculos habentes non videtis, et aures habentes non

8:11–21 Elsewhere in the Gospels (see Mt 13:33; Lk 13:20–21) Jesus uses the simile of leaven to show the vitality of his teaching. Here "leaven" is used to describe the bad dispositions of Pharisees who do not believe in him and who ask him for a sign, to test him (vv. 11–12); he applies it, too, to the duplicity of Herod, who failed to see the meaning of Jesus' signs (v. 15; cf. 6:14–16; Lk 13:31–32). Our Lord warns his disciples that they need to have a spiritual outlook if they are to understand the things he does, that is, to grasp the true meaning of his saving mission and the full reach of his power. The disciples' failure to understand the significance of the bread (Jesus points it out five times: vv. 17–18, 21) shows that they were still far from attuned to his outlook. This may explain the tone of severity in Jesus' voice: "These were the disciples called by our Lord. Such stuff is what Christ chose. And they remain just like that until they are filled with the Holy Spirit and thus

become pillars of the Church. They are ordinary people, full of defects and shortcomings, more eager to say than to do. Nevertheless, Jesus calls them to be fishers of men, co-redeemers, dispensers of the grace of God" (St Josemaría Escrivá, *Christ Is Passing By*, 2).

The "generation" Jesus refers to (v. 12) is not all the people of his time, but the Pharisees and their followers (cf. 8:38; 9:19; Mt 11:16) who do not want to see his miracles as proof that he is the Messiah. If they refuse to accept the signs offered them, they will be given no further sign, however much they look for it, for "the Kingdom of God is not coming with signs to be observed", as a kind of spectacle (Lk 17:20–21); moreover, even if they were given another sign they would still search for a way to dilute or undo its meaning (Lk 16:31). According to Matthew (12:38–42) and Luke (11:29–32), they will in fact be offered another sign—the death and resurrection of Jesus (the sign of Jonah); but to no avail.

d Other ancient authorities omit *Magadan* or *Magdala*   e Other ancient authorities read *the Herodians*

Jer 5:21
Mk 4:23
Ezek 12:2

Mk 6:41–44

Mk 8:6–9

Mk 7:18

you discuss the fact that you have no bread? Do you not yet perceive or understand? Are your hearts hardened? [18]Having eyes do you not see, and having ears do you not hear? And do you not remember? [19]When I broke the five loaves for the five thousand, how many baskets full of broken pieces did you take up?" They said to him, "Twelve." [20]"And the seven for the four thousand, how many baskets full of broken pieces did you take up?" And they said to him, "Seven." [21]And he said to them, "Do you not yet understand?"

Curing of a blind man at Bethsaida

Mk 6:56

Mk 7:32–33; 9:27
Jn 9:6

Mk 1:34; 5:43; 7:36

[22]And they came to Bethsaida. And some people brought to him a blind man, and begged him to touch him. [23]And he took the blind man by the hand, and led him out of the village; and when he had spit on his eyes and laid his hands upon him, he asked him, "Do you see anything?" [24]And he looked up and said, "I see men; but they look like trees, walking." [25]Then again he laid his hands upon his eyes; and he looked intently and was restored, and saw everything clearly. [26]And he sent him away to his home, saying, "Do not even enter the village."

Mt 16:13–20
Lk 9:18–21

Mk 6:14–15

Jn 6:67–69

Peter's profession of faith

[27]And Jesus went on with his disciples, to the villages of Caesarea Philippi; and on the way he asked his disciples, "Who do men say that I am?" [28]And they told him, "John the Baptist; and others say, Elijah; and others one of the prophets." [29]And he

auditis? Nec recordamini, [19]quando quinque panes fregi in quinque milia, quot cophinos fragmentorum plenos sustulistis?». Dicunt ei: «Duodecim». [20]«Quando illos septem in quattuor milia, quot sportas plenas fragmentorum tulistis?». Et dicunt ei: «Septem». [21]Et dicebat eis: «Nondum intellegitis?». [22]Et veniunt Bethsaida. Et adducunt ei caecum et rogant eum, ut illum tangat. [23]Et apprehendens manum caeci eduxit eum extra vicum et exspuens in oculos eius, impositis manibus ei, interrogabat eum: «Vides aliquid?». [24]Et aspiciens dicebat: «Video homines, quia velut arbores video ambulantes». [25]Deinde iterum imposuit manus super oculos eius; et coepit videre et restitutus est et videbat clare omnia. [26]Et misit illum in domum suam dicens: «Nec in vicum introieris». [27]Et egressus est Iesus et discipuli eius in castella Caesareae Philippi; et in via interrogabat discipulos suos dicens eis: «Quem me dicunt esse homines?». [28]Qui responderunt illi dicentes: «Ioannem Baptistam, alii Eliam, alii

8:22–26 As he did in the case of the deaf and speech-impaired man (see 7:31–37), Jesus here uses symbolic gestures to work a miracle. The cure of the blind man of Bethsaida marks, in the course of this Gospel, the climax of the messianic signs of Christ (cf. the note on 7:31–37); so it is fitting that it be followed by Peter's profession of faith (8:29). The fact that the cure takes effect gradually may symbolize the journey of faith made by Peter and the disciples, and indeed by everyone: by means of his signs, Jesus gradually cures our blindness until we "see everything clearly" (see v. 25) and are bold enough to confess him to be Christ, the Son of God and our Saviour: "Lord, give us light to see! We have more need of it than the blind man ... who wanted to see the light but could not. Now, Lord, people do not want to see: what an incurable evil! In this, Lord, you must show your power and your mercy" (St Teresa of Avila, *Exclamations*, 8).

8:27–30 St Mark here records one of the defining moments in the disciples' relationship with Jesus—the first acknowledgment by one of them that he is the Messiah. The dialogue shows how important Peter's reply is: the opinion of the crowd is that Jesus is the finest person a pious Jew could imagine—a prophet, perhaps even Elijah himself (cf. 9:11). But St Peter is not expressing a personal opinion; he is making a genuine profession of faith, the meaning of which is made explicit in Matthew 16:16–17. The firmness of Peter's faith and that of his successors helps to underpin the faith of believers: "Our faith, my beloved brothers, is the fruit of Peter's profession of faith. It was inspired in Peter's heart by the Father, overcomes all human doubt and is as firm as the rock that no violence can ever break. Peter professes his faith every day in the Church: 'You are the Christ, the Son of the living God'; every tongue that confesses faith in the Lord is following the example given

asked them, "But who do you say I am?" Peter answered him, "You are the Christ."
³⁰And he charged them to tell no one about him.

Mk 9:9

PART TWO

Jesus' ministry on the way to Jerusalem*

6. TEACHINGS ON THE CHRISTIAN LIFE*

Mt 16:21–28
Lk 9:22–27

Jesus foretells his passion and resurrection. Christian renunciation
³¹And he began to teach them that the Son of man must suffer many things, and be Mk 9:31; 10:32–34
rejected by the elders and the chief priests and the scribes, and be killed, and after
three days rise again. ³²And he said this plainly. And Peter took him, and began to

vero unum de prophetis». ²⁹Et ipse interrogabat eos: «Vos vero quem me dicitis esse?». Respondens Petrus ait ei: «Tu es Christus». ³⁰Et comminatus est eis, ne cui dicerent de illo. ³¹Et coepit docere illos: «Oportet Filium hominis multa pati et reprobari a senioribus et a summis sacerdotibus et scribis et occidi et post tres dies resurgere»; ³²et palam verbum loquebatur. Et apprehendens eum Petrus coepit increpare eum. ³³Qui conversus

in Peter's profession" (St Leo the Great, *Sermo 3 in ordinationi suae*).

Significantly, our Lord does not reject the title of "Christ" given him by Peter (v. 29), but he immediately replaces it with that of "Son of man" (8:31), thereby indicating that Peter's confession of faith is correct but incomplete. Jesus sees his mission as Messiah from the perspective of God, not from that of man: "We should bear in mind the fact that whereas the Lord refers to himself as the Son of man, Nathanael refers to him as the Son of God (Jn 1:49). [...] This distinction is part of the order of providence; it reflects the double nature of our Mediator, God and Lord: he is the Lord our God and a man. The Son of man gave strength to our human weakness; the Son of God gave the power of God to man. One name reflects his humility; the other, his majesty and power" (St Bede, *Homiliae*, 1, 17).

*8:31—10:52 After Peter's profession of faith, the focus of the Gospel changes. From now on, Jesus devotes more time to training his disciples, telling them directly that he must undergo his passion in order to enter into his glory (8:31—9:13). The three announcements of the passion (8:31; 9:31; 10:33–34) mark the time in this part of the Gospel. Mark's account here contains many teachings concerning the main virtues and

attributes that should characterize the lives of Jesus' disciples'—prayerfulness (9:14–29), humility (9:33–50), poverty (10:17–31), etc.

*8:31—9:50 The revelation of Jesus as the suffering Servant begins here. Christ accepted this way of the cross for himself (see 8:31), and it is the way that every Christian must follow (8:34). He prepares his disciples for this event by words and actions: the three disciples who will later witness his agony in the Garden of Olives (14:33) are now comforted with a vision of the glory that will later be his (9:2–13).

8:31—9:1 Jesus begins to teach his disciples about the true nature of his mission: salvation will come about through suffering and the cross, and therefore anyone who wants to follow him must be ready to renounce his own will and desires (8:34–38). The dialogue with Peter (8:31–33) provides an image of the paradox of Christianity: Peter finds it hard to see how Jesus' victory could possibly involve the cross. Jesus publicly rebukes him because this human way of looking at things is at odds with God's plan. We too need to be much less earth-bound in our thinking: "There is a kind of fear around, a fear of the Cross, of our Lord's Cross. What has happened is that people have begun to see as crosses

rebuke him. ³³But turning and seeing his disciples, he rebuked Peter, and said, "Get behind me, Satan! For you are not on the side of God, but of men."

Lk 14:27

³⁴And he called to him the multitude with his disciples, and said to them, "If any man would come after me, let him deny himself and take up his cross and follow

Mt 10:39
Jn 12:25

me. ³⁵For whoever would save his life will lose it: and whoever loses his life for my sake and the gospel's will save it. ³⁶For what does it profit a man to gain the whole

Mt 10:33

world and forfeit his life?* ³⁷For what can a man give in return for his life? ³⁸For whoever is ashamed of me and of my words in this adulterous and sinful generation, of him will the Son of man also be ashamed, when he comes in the glory of his Father with the holy angels."

Rom 1:4
Mk 14:62

9 ¹And he said to them, "Truly, I say to you, there are some standing here who will not taste death before they see the kingdom of God come with power."

Mt 17:1–13
Lk 9:28–36

The Transfiguration

²And after six days Jesus took with him Peter and James and John, and led them up a high mountain apart by themselves; and he was transfigured before them, ³and his

---

et videns discipulos suos comminatus est Petro et dicit: «Vade retro me, Satana, quoniam non sapis, quae Dei sunt, sed quae sunt hominum». ³⁴Et convocata turba cum discipulis suis, dixit eis: «Si quis vult post me sequi, deneget semetipsum et tollat crucem suam et sequatur me. ³⁵Qui enim voluerit animam suam salvam facere, perdet eam; qui autem perdiderit animam suam propter me et evangelium, salvam eam faciet. ³⁶Quid enim prodest homini, si lucretur mundum totum et detrimentum faciat animae suae? ³⁷Quid enim dabit homo commutationem pro anima sua? ³⁸Qui enim me confusus fuerit et mea verba in generatione ista adultera et peccatrice, et Filius hominis confundetur eum, cum venerit in gloria Patris sui cum angelis sanctis». [9] ¹Et dicebat illis: «Amen dico vobis: Sunt quidam de hic stantibus, qui non gustabunt mortem, donec videant regnum

---

all the unpleasant things that crop up in life, and they do not know how to take them as God's children should, with supernatural outlook. [...] In the Passion, the Cross ceased to be a symbol of punishment and became instead a sign of victory. It is the emblem of the Redeemer: *in quo est salus, vita et resurrectio nostra*: there lies our salvation, our life and our resurrection" (St Josemaría Escrivá, *The Way of the Cross*, 2, 5).

Jesus' words in 8:34–35 must have frightened his listeners, but they do convey the lengths one must go to follow him. A fleeting commitment, a burst of enthusiasm, is not enough; one needs to deny oneself, and take up one's own cross. This is because our Lord wants all of us to reach the beatitude of heaven. Our present life is transitory and of only relative value, and we need to see it in the light of eternal life if we are to reach heaven: "We should love the world, but we must love the Creator more than his creation. The world is beautiful, but the One who made the world is more beautiful. We must strive to ensure, beloved brothers, that love of the world does not weigh us down, that we do not fail to love the Creator more than his creation. God gave the whole world to us so that we would

love him with our whole heart and soul. [...] Just as we love more those who love us for who we are rather than what we have, so too God loves more those who value eternal life more than they love the things of this world" (St Caesarius of Arles, *Sermones*, 159, 5–6).

"Before they see the kingdom of God come with power" (9:1). This phrase sounds cryptic or vague, because it seems to refer to the end of time, the Parousia, when Jesus will come "in the glory of his Father with the holy angels" (8:38), "sitting at the right hand of Power" (14:62). However, Jesus is in fact referring to some of those present. We will better understand what he is saying if we remember that the Kingdom is like a seed which develops over time (4:30–32), and which will reach its full growth at the end of time when everything will be made manifest. Our Lord may be alluding to the wonderful spread of the Church during the apostles' lifetime. Or he may mean the glorious manifestation of the Lord at the end of time, a glimpse of which will be given at the Transfiguration.

9:2–13 Our Lord's transfiguration in the presence of his disciples (the three most beloved,

garments became glistening, intensely white, as no fuller on earth could bleach them. [4]And there appeared to them Elijah with Moses; and they were talking to Jesus. [5]And Peter said to Jesus, "Master,[f] it is well that we are here; let us make three booths, one for you and one for Moses and one for Elijah." [6]For he did not know what to say, for they were exceedingly afraid. [7]And a cloud overshadowed them, and a voice came out of the cloud, "This is my beloved Son;[g] listen to him." [8]And suddenly looking around they no longer saw any one with them but Jesus only.

[9]And as they were coming down the mountain, he charged them to tell no one what they had seen, until the Son of man should have risen from the dead. [10]So they kept the matter to themselves, questioning what the rising from the dead meant. [11]And they asked him, "Why do the scribes say that first Elijah must come?" [12]And he said to them, "Elijah does come first to restore all things; and how is it written of

Mk 14:40

Mk 1:11
2 Pet 1:17
Deut 18:15
Acts 3:22

Mk 8:30
Lk 17:15
Is 53:3

Mal 4:5

Dei venisse in virtute». [2]Et post dies sex assumit Iesus Petrum et Iacobum et Ioannem, et ducit illos in montem excelsum seorsum solos. Et transfiguratus est coram ipsis; [3]et vestimenta eius facta sunt splendentia, candida nimis, qualia fullo super terram non potest tam candida facere. [4]Et apparuit illis Elias cum Moyse, et erant loquentes cum Iesu. [5]Et respondens Petrus ait Iesu: «Rabbi, bonum est nos hic esse; et faciamus tria tabernacula: tibi unum et Moysi unum et Eliae unum». [6]Non enim sciebat quid responderet, erant enim exterriti. [7]Et facta est nubes obumbrans eos, et venit vox de nube: «Hic est Filius meus dilectus; audite illum». [8]Et statim circumspicientes neminem amplius viderunt nisi Iesum tantum secum. [9]Et descendentibus illis de monte, praecepit illis, ne cui, quae vidissent, narrarent, nisi cum Filius hominis a mortuis resurrexerit. [10]Et verbum continuerunt apud se, conquirentes quid esset illud: «a mortuis resurgere». [11]Et interrogabant eum dicentes: «Quid ergo dicunt scribae quia Eliam oportet venire primum?». [12]Qui ait illis: «Elias veniens primo, restituit omnia; et quomodo scriptum est super Filio hominis, ut multa patiatur et

who will later witness his agony: 14:33) is a counterpoint to his passion and an anticipation of its fruit—resurrection and glorification. Christians, too, need to learn to "consider that the sufferings of this present time are not worth comparing with the glory that is to be revealed to us" (Rom 8:18).

Mark shows in a number of ways the difficulty the disciples have in understanding what lies ahead for Christ (vv. 9–10). Similarly, in regard to Peter (who wants to attain heaven without undergoing the cross) he comments that "he did not know what to say" (v. 6): "Peter did not understand this when he wanted to remain with Christ on the mountain. It has been reserved for you, Peter, but for after death. For now, Jesus says: 'Go down to toil on earth, to serve on earth, to be scorned and crucified on earth.' Life goes down to be killed; Bread goes down to suffer hunger; the Way goes down to be exhausted on his journey; the Spring goes down to suffer thirst; and you refuse to suffer?" (St Augustine, *Sermones*, 78, 6; as quoted in *Catechism of the Catholic Church*, 556).

In the Transfiguration, the whole truth about Jesus is revealed. He is the Only Son of God, the "beloved Son", who, in order to save us, "emptied himself, taking the form of a servant" (Phil 2:7); he freely set aside divine glory and clothed

himself in vulnerable human flesh, becoming like us in all things except sin. The words that are spoken from the cloud are similar to those at the start of the first Song of the Servant of the Lord in the book of Isaiah (Is 42:1) and those spoken at Jesus' baptism (1:11; Mt 3:17; Lk 3:22); they show that Jesus is the Son of God who will fulfil the saving mission of the Servant of the Lord. The command "Listen to him" proclaims the authority of Jesus: his teachings and instructions have the authority of God himself: "This is my Son—not Moses or Elijah. Moses and Elijah were servants: this is my Son. This is my Son: that is, of one nature and substance with me, the Son who is with Me forever, who is all that I am. 'This is my beloved Son.' Moses and Elijah were beloved too, but he is the most beloved: 'listen to him'. Moses and Elijah foretold his coming, but you can listen to his words. They were servants as you are: he is the Lord. Moses and Elijah were servants who spoke of Christ. He is Christ the Lord: listen to him" (St Jerome, *Commentarium in Marcum*, 6).

As they make their way down from the mountain, there is a brief scene that is typical in this Gospel: the disciples do not understand what they have seen and heard. In this instance, they have seen Jesus in glory, but still they have questions. First they ask about the coming of Elijah

f Or *Rabbi*   g Or *my Son, my* (or the) *Beloved*

Mt 11:14

the Son of man, that he should suffer many things and be treated with contempt? [13]But I tell you that Elijah has come,* and they did to him whatever they pleased, as it is written of him."

Mt 17:14–20
Lk 9:37–43

Curing of an epileptic boy

[14]And when they came to the disciples, they saw a great crowd about them, and scribes arguing with them. [15]And immediately all the crowd, when they saw him, were greatly amazed, and ran up to him and greeted him. [16]And he asked them, "What are you discussing with them?" [17]And one of the crowd answered him, "Teacher, I brought my son to you, for he has a dumb spirit; [18]and wherever it seizes him, it dashes him down; and he foams and grinds his teeth and becomes rigid; and I asked your disciples to cast it out, and they were not able." [19]And he answered them, "O faithless generation, how long am I to be with you? How long am I to bear with you? Bring him to me." [20]And they brought the boy to him; and when the spirit saw him, immediately it convulsed the boy, and he fell on the ground and rolled about, foaming at the mouth. [21]And Jesus[h] asked his father, "How long has he had this?" And he said, "From childhood. [22]And it has often cast him into the fire and into the water, to destroy him; but if you can do anything, have pity on us and help

Deut 32:5–20
Num 14:26

contemnatur? [13]Sed dico vobis: Et Elias venit; et fecerunt illi, quaecumque volebant, sicut scriptum est de eo». [14]Et venientes ad discipulos viderunt turbam magnam circa eos et scribas conquirentes cum illis. [15]Et confestim omnis populus videns eum stupefactus est, et accurrentes salutabant eum. [16]Et interrogavit eos: «Quid inter vos conquiritis?». [17]Et respondit ei unus de turba: «Magister, attuli filium meum ad te habentem spiritum mutum; [18]et ubicumque eum apprehenderit, allidit eum, et spumat et stridet dentibus et arescit. Et dixi discipulis tuis, ut eicerent illum, et non potuerunt». [19]Qui respondens eis dicit: «O generatio incredula, quamdiu apud vos ero? Quamdiu vos patiar? Afferte illum ad me». [20]Et attulerunt illum ad eum. Et cum vidisset illum, spiritus statim conturbavit eum, et corruens in terram volutabatur spumans. [21]Et interrogavit patrem eius: «Quantum temporis est, ex quo hoc ei accidit?». At ille ait: «Ab infantia; [22]et frequenter eum etiam in ignem et in aquas misit, ut eum

(v. 11). Scribes and Pharisees interpreted the messianic prophecy of Malachi (Mal 3:1–2) to mean that Elijah would appear spectacularly in person, to be followed by a victorious Messiah who had not travelled along a path of pain or humiliation. Jesus tells them that Elijah has already come in the person of John the Baptist (cf. Mt 17:13) and that he has indeed prepared the ways of the Messiah, which are ways of trial and suffering (vv. 12–13). The other question remains unspoken: they dare not ask him what "rising from the dead" means (vv. 10). After Easter day they will see that the resurrection of Jesus means that he has entered into that glory of which they have already been given a preview.

9:14–29 With the miracle and the explanation that follows (vv. 28–29), Jesus shows us that prayer must be grounded on steadfast faith. In this conversation with the father of the epileptic boy we can see the method Jesus uses to lead the man to pray with confidence. To the man's imperfect faith (v. 22), our Lord replies with a lament (v. 23). But this lament is itself part of a dialogue; it is an invitation to the father of the boy to pray with true faith: "Without faith, prayer withers: who can ask for what he does not believe? Let us believe so that we can pray, and pray that the faith by which we pray may never wane. Faith is the food of prayer and, once it has been brought to life, prayer bears the fruit of firm faith" (St Augustine, *Sermones*, 115, 1).

Then (vv. 28–29), in a scene of a kind often found in St Mark, we find Jesus teaching his disciples in private. Jesus' reply (v. 29) also carries a message for the future: at present people are able to have direct recourse to him for remedies, but when he is no longer with them they will need to have recourse to prayer: "In teaching the apostles how to expel a spirit as evil as this he is teaching all of us how we should live, and telling us that prayer is the resource we should use to overcome even the severest temptations, whether they come from unclean spirits or from men" (St Bede, *In Marci Evangelium*, ad loc.).

h Greek *he*

us." [23]And Jesus said to him, "If you can! All things are possible to him who believes." [24]Immediately the father of the child cried out[i] and said, "I believe; help my unbelief!" [25]And when Jesus saw that a crowd came running together, he rebuked the unclean spirit, saying to it, "You dumb and deaf spirit, I command you, come out of him, and never enter him again." [26]And after crying out and convulsing him terribly, it came out, and the boy was like a corpse; so that most of them said, "He is dead." [27]But Jesus took him by the hand and lifted him up, and he arose. [28]And when he had entered the house, his disciples asked him privately, "Why could we not cast it out?" [29]And he said to them, "This kind cannot be driven out by anything but prayer and fasting."[j]

Lk 17:5

Mk 1:26

Mk 1:31; 5:41

Second announcement of the Passion

Mt 17:22–27
Lk 9:43–45

[30]They went on from there and passed through Galilee. And he would not have any one know it; [31]for he was teaching his disciples, saying to them, "The Son of man will be delivered into the hands of men, and they will kill him; and when he is killed, after three days he will rise." [32]But they did not understand the saying, and they were afraid to ask him.

Mk 8:31; 10:32–34

Service to others. On leading others astray

Mt 18:1–14
Lk 9:46–50;
17:1–2

[33]And they came to Capernaum; and when he was in the house he asked them, "What were you discussing on the way?" [34]But they were silent; for on the way they

perderet; sed si quid potes, adiuva nos, misertus nostri». [23]Iesus autem ait illi: «'Si potes!'. Omnia possibilia credenti». [24]Et continuo exclamans pater pueri aiebat: «Credo; adiuva incredulitatem meam». [25]Et cum videret Iesus concurrentem turbam, comminatus est spiritui immundo dicens illi: «Mute et surde spiritus, ego tibi praecipio: Exi ab eo et amplius ne introeas in eum». [26]Et clamans et multum discerpens eum exiit; et factus est sicut mortuus, ita ut multi dicerent: «Mortuus est!». [27]Iesus autem tenens manum eius elevavit illum, et surrexit. [28]Et cum introisset in domum, discipuli eius secreto interrogabant eum: «Quare nos non potuimus eicere eum?». [29]Et dixit illis: «Hoc genus in nullo potest exire nisi in oratione». [30]Et inde profecti peragrabant Galilaeam; nec volebat quemquam scire. [31]Docebat enim discipulos suos et dicebat illis: «Filius hominis traditur in manus hominum, et occident eum, et occisus post tres dies resurget». [32]At illi ignorabant verbum et timebant eum interrogare. [33]Et venerunt

9:30–32 From the time of Peter's confession of faith (8:29) until his arrival in Jerusalem (11:1), Jesus tries to escape from the crowds in order to train his disciples and instruct them about what will happen in the Holy City. The Gospel shows us the difficulty the disciples had in understanding what he told them (v. 32), a situation that will become very clear later, when, at the moment of truth, they leave him on his own (14:50, 66–71). The fact of the matter is that truths of this sort can only be understood with the help of grace: "What he told them was in accordance with what had been foretold by the prophets, about the death he would suffer in Jerusalem. [...] They also foretold why the unchanging Word of God willed to suffer the Passion: because it was the only way that mankind could be saved. These things were known only to him and to those to whom he chose to reveal them" (St Anastasius of Antioch, *Sermones*, 4, 1).

9:33–50 In this passage are reported a number of Jesus' teachings concerning the way the Church should function. In the first part (vv. 33–41) we read of two episodes in which Jesus deals with the kinds of attitudes Christians should have. The first starts from an argument that has gone on behind Jesus' back; he uses the occasion to instruct the disciples on how authority is to be exercised in the Church (vv. 33–35): those in charge must be not taskmasters but servants. He himself, who is the Head and the Lawgiver, came to serve, not to be served (10:45). If someone failed to cultivate that approach, he or she would be ill-equipped to exercise authority and, besides, would run the risk of acting out of ambition, pride and a desire to control others: "To be in charge of an apostolic undertaking demands readiness to suffer everything, from everybody, with infinite charity" (St Josemaría Escrivá, *The Way*, 951). Then, commenting on the man who cast out demons in the name of Jesus, our Lord

i Other ancient authorities add *with tears*   j Other ancient authorities omit *and fasting*

Mk 10:42–45
Lk 22:24
Mt 20:26

Mk 10:16

Mt 10:40
Jn 13:20

Num 11:27–28
Lk 9:49–50

1 Cor 12:3

Mt 12:30

Mt 10:42

Mt 18:6–9
Lk 17:1–2

Mt 5:30

Mt 5:29

Is 66:24

had discussed with one another who was the greatest. [35]And he sat down and called the twelve; and he said to them, "If any one would be first, he must be last of all and servant of all." [36]And he took a child, and put him in the midst of them; and taking him in his arms, he said to them, [37]"Whoever receives one such child in my name receives me; and whoever receives me, receives not me but him who sent me."

[38]John said to him, "Teacher, we saw a man casting out demons in your name,[k] and we forbade him, because he was not following us." [39]But Jesus said, "Do not forbid him; for no one who does a mighty work in my name will be able soon after to speak evil of me. [40]For he that is not against us is for us. [41]For truly, I say to you, whoever gives you a cup of water to drink because you bear the name of Christ, will by no means lose his reward.

[42]"Whoever causes one of these little ones who believe in me to sin,[l] it would be better for him if a great millstone were hung round his neck and he were thrown into the sea. [43]And if your hand causes you to sin,[l] cut it off; it is better for you to enter life maimed than with two hands to go to hell,[m] to the unquenchable fire.[n] [45]And if your foot causes you to sin,[l] cut it off; it is better for you to enter life lame than with two feet to be thrown into hell. [m, n] [47]And if your eye causes you to sin, [l]pluck it out; it is better for you to enter the kingdom of God with one eye than with two eyes to be thrown into hell,[m] [48]where their worm does not die, and the fire is not quenched.

Capharnaum. Qui cum domi esset, interrogabat eos: «Quid in via tractabatis?». [34]At illi tacebant. Siquidem inter se in via disputaverant, quis esset maior. [35]Et residens vocavit Duodecim et ait illis: «Si quis vult primus esse, erit omnium novissimus et omnium minister». [36]Et accipiens puerum, statuit eum in medio eorum; quem ut complexus esset, ait illis: [37]«Quisquis unum ex huiusmodi pueris receperit in nomine meo, me recipit; et, quicumque me susceperit, non me suscipit, sed eum qui me misit». [38]Dixit illi Ioannes: «Magister, vidimus quendam in nomine tuo eicientem daemonia, et prohibebamus eum, quia non sequebatur nos». [39]Iesus autem ait: «Nolite prohibere eum. Nemo est enim, qui faciat virtutem in nomine meo et possit cito male loqui de me; [40]qui enim non est adversum nos, pro nobis est. [41]Quisquis enim potum dederit vobis calicem aquae in nomine, quia Christi estis, amen dico vobis: Non perdet mercedem suam. [42]Et quisquis scandalizaverit unum ex his pusillis credentibus in me, bonum est ei magis, ut circumdetur mola asinaria collo eius, et in mare mittatur. [43]Et si scandalizaverit te manus tua, abscide illam: bonum est tibi debilem introire in vitam, quam duas manus habentem ire in gehennam, in ignem inexstinguibilem. [45]Et si pes tuus te scandalizat, amputa illum: bonum est tibi claudum introire in vitam, quam duos pedes habentem mitti in gehennam. [47]Et si oculus tuus scandalizat te, eice eum: bonum est tibi luscum introire in regnum Dei, quam duos oculos habentem mitti in gehennam, [48]ubi vermis eorum non moritur et ignis non exstinguitur; [49]omnis enim igne salietur. [50]Bonum est sal; quod si sal insulsum fuerit, in quo illud condietis? Habete in vobis sal et pacem habete inter vos».

tells his disciples that they need to be open-minded about the growth of the Kingdom of God (vv. 39–41) and he warns them (and us) against any tendency towards exclusivity.

Each episode is rounded off by a teaching given by Jesus on a number of occasions (cf. Mt 25:40, 45): Christians are to see Christ himself in the needy, in a child who cannot fend for himself (vv. 36–37) or in a disciple who has left everything behind in order to serve Christ (v. 41). What is important is not the amount one gives but the love that is behind the gift: "Do you see that glass of water or that piece of bread which a holy soul gives to a poor person for God's sake; it is a small matter, God knows, and in human judgment hardly worthy of consideration: God, notwithstanding, recompenses it, and forthwith gives for it some increase of charity" (St Francis de Sales, *Treatise on the Love of God*, 3, 2).

The following verses (vv. 42–50) have to do with the danger of causing scandal—by actions or attitudes that could lead others into sin (cf. the note on Mt 18:1–14). These exhortations show just how radical the Christian ethic can be, and they provide the foundation for moral teaching on the subject of "occasions of sin": we are under the same obligations to avoid proximate occasions of sin as we are to avoid sin itself. The eternal good of a person's soul is more valuable than any and every earthly good. Therefore, anything that might lead us to commit sin must be cut short and cast aside.

Some manuscripts add as two additional verses (44 and 46): "where their worm does not die, and the fire is not quenched". These words come from Isaiah 66:24, and do appear in all translations as v. 48.

k Other ancient authorities add *who does not follow us*   l Greek *stumble*   m Greek *Gehenna*   n Verses 44 and 46 (which are identical with verse 48) are omitted by the best ancient authorities

⁴⁹For every one will be salted with fire.º ⁵⁰Salt is good; but if the salt has lost its salt-
ness, how will you season it? Have salt in yourselves, and be at peace with one
another."

Lev 2:13
Mt 5:13
Lk 14:34
Col 4:6

7. HEADING FOR JUDEA AND JERUSALEM*

The indissolubility of marriage   Mt 19:1–12

10 ¹And he left there and went to the region of Judea and beyond the Jordan, and
crowds gathered to him again; and again, as his custom was, he taught them.
²And Pharisees came up and in order to test him asked, "Is it lawful for a man to
divorce his wife?" ³He answered them, "What did Moses command you?" ⁴They
said, "Moses allowed a man to write a certificate of divorce, and to put her away."

Deut 24:1
Mt 5:31–32

[10] ¹Et inde exsurgens venit in fines Iudaeae ultra Iordanem, et conveniunt iterum turbae ad eum, et, sicut consueverat, iterum docebat illos. ²Et
accedentes pharisaei interrogabant eum, si licet viro uxorem dimittere, tentantes eum. ³At ille respondens dixit eis: «Quid vobis praecepit
Moyses?». ⁴Qui dixerunt: «Moyses permisit *libellum repudii scribere et dimittere*». ⁵Iesus autem ait eis: «Ad duritiam cordis vestri scripsit vobis

*10:1–52 Jesus' journey towards Judea and
Jerusalem (10:1) sends the Gospel narrative in a
new direction. First comes an argument with
Pharisees (10:2–12), a foretaste of the open confrontation that will occur in the Holy City
(11:1 — 12:44). Jesus continues to tell his disciples about his future passion (10:32–45), but
most of this section deals with various aspects of
Christian life — marriage, commitment to Christ,
the call to poverty, etc.

10:1–12 This sort of scene occurs often in the
Gospel. The malice of some Pharisees sharply
contrasts with the simplicity of the crowd, who
listen attentively to Jesus' words. Jesus, well
aware of the duplicity of those who try to bait
him, asks them, "What did Moses command
you?" (v. 3). The Pharisees know that Moses
gave no command, and they reply that Moses
"allowed" the writing of a certificate of divorce
(v. 4). Having clarified this point, Jesus explains
that the real commandment is the one that God
made at the beginning of creation (Gen 2:24):
"The love of the spouses requires, of its very
nature, the unity and indissolubility of the
spouses' community of persons, which embraces
their entire life: 'so they are no longer two, but
one flesh' (Mt 19:6). They 'are called to grow
continually in their communion through day-to-
day fidelity to their marriage promise of total
mutual self-giving' (John Paul II, *Fam. cons.*,
19). This human communion is confirmed, puri-

fied, and completed by communion in Jesus
Christ, given through the sacrament of Matrimony. It is deepened by lives of the common
faith and by the Eucharist received together"
(*Catechism of the Catholic Church*, 1644).

Our Lord's words at the end of the passage
contain a clause (v. 12) which refers more to
Roman than Jewish law, given that the latter did
not envisage the possibility of a wife repudiating
her husband. The words seem to be an extension
of Jesus' teaching for the benefit of St Mark's
original readership. In any event, they tell us that
the presentation of Christ's teaching has to be
updated to take account of new circumstances
that may arise. Today, "To bear witness to the
inestimable value of the indissolubility and
fidelity of marriage is one of the most precious
and most urgent tasks of Christian couples in our
time. So […] I praise and encourage those
numerous couples who, though encountering no
small difficulty, preserve and develop the value
of indissolubility: thus, in a humble and courageous manner, they perform the role committed
to them of being in the world a 'sign' — a small
and precious sign, sometimes also subjected to
temptation, but always renewed — of the unfailing fidelity with which God and Jesus Christ
love each and every human being. But it is also
proper to recognize the value of the witness of
those spouses who, even when abandoned by
their partner, with the strength of faith and of
Christian hope have not entered a new union:

º Other ancient authorities add *and every sacrifice will be salted with salt*

5But Jesus said to them, "For your hardness of heart he wrote you this command-
Gen 1:27 ment. 6But from the beginning of creation, 'God made them male and female.' 7'For
Gen 2:24 this reason a man shall leave his father and mother and be joined to his wife,[p] 8and
the two shall become one.'[q] So they are no longer two but one.[q] 9What therefore God
has joined together, let not man put asunder."
Lk 16:18 10And in the house the disciples asked him again about this matter. 11And he said
to them, "Whoever divorces his wife and marries another, commits adultery against
her; 12and if she divorces her husband and marries another, she commits adultery."

Mt 19:13–15
Lk 18:15–17

Jesus and the children

13And they were bringing children to him, that he might touch them; and the disci-
Mt 18:3 ples rebuked them. 14But when Jesus saw it he was indignant, and said to them, "Let
the children come to me, do not hinder them; for to such belongs the kingdom of

praeceptum istud. 6Ab initio autem creaturae *masculum et feminam fecit eos*. 7*Propter hoc relinquet homo patrem suum et matrem et adhaerebit ad uxorem suam*, 8*et erunt duo in carne una*; itaque iam non sunt duo sed una caro. 9Quod ergo Deus coniunxit, homo non separet». 10Et domo iterum discipuli de hoc interrogabant eum. 11Et dicit illis: «Quicumque dimiserit uxorem suam et aliam duxerit, adulterium committit in eam; 12et si ipsa dimiserit virum suum et alii nupserit, moechatur». 13Et offerebant illi parvulos, ut tangeret illos; discipuli autem comminabantur eis. 14At

these spouses too give an authentic witness to fidelity, of which the world today has a great need" (John Paul II, *Familiaris consortio*, 20).

10:13–16 The Gospel helps us to see the features of Jesus as true Man—his look of indignation when he sees the hardness of people's hearts (3:5), his amazement when he finds his fellow countrymen in Nazareth so slow to believe (6:6), his exasperation when Pharisees show themselves to be duplicitous (see 8:12), his taking his disciples to task (v. 14) etc. In this vivid passage, Mark lets us see Jesus' attitude towards children; it is almost as if Mark cannot find words (see v. 16) to describe his affection for them.

This touching episode also carries a message: the Kingdom of heaven belongs to those who receive it like a child, that is, not as something they have merited but as a gift from their Father God. The life of spiritual childhood that some saints recommend stems from this attitude: "To be little you have to believe as children believe, to love as children love, to abandon yourself as children do … , to pray as children pray" (St Josemaría Escrivá, *Holy Rosary*, prologue).

10:17–31 There are three interlinked elements in this passage—the call that a rich young man rejects because he is attached to his wealth (vv. 17–22; cf. Mt 19:22); teachings about riches and the Kingdom (vv. 23–27); and the rewards promised to those who leave all things and follow Jesus (vv. 28–31).

Our Lord's meeting with this young man reminds us of the calling of the first disciples (1:16–20; 2:14). It begins differently but then proceeds in the same way—with Jesus' loving glance and then his direct command (v. 21). The evangelist manages to convey very vividly Jesus' regard for this upright young man (vv. 19–21), and the latter's sadness when he fails to respond generously to what God asks of him. The episode shows that knowledge and love of God are rooted in a response to our Lord's call. St Teresa uses this episode to explain how to become close to God: "If we turn our back on him and go away sorrowful like the young man in the Gospel whose face fell when he heard what had to be done in order to be good and inherit eternal life, what can His Majesty do? He rewards us for the love we have for him. This love, my daughters, is shown not in thoughts and words, but in deeds; not that he has need of our good works and deeds, but he wants us to be resolute" (*Interior Castle*, 3, 1, 7).

The behaviour of the rich young man gives Jesus an opportunity to comment on the use of material things (vv. 23–27). Attachment to them can be a kind of idolatry (see Mt 6:24 and Col 3:5) that prevents a person from entering the Kingdom of God (see Lk 6:20, 24). Our Lord uses here (v. 25) a metaphor, perhaps proverbial,

p Other ancient authorities omit *and be joined to his wife* q Greek *one flesh*

God. [15]Truly, I say to you, whoever does not receive the kingdom of God like a child shall not enter it." [16]And he took them in his arms and blessed them, laying his hands upon them.

Mk 9:36

The rich young man. Poverty and renunciation

Mt 19:16–30
Lk 18:18–30

[17]And as he was setting out on his journey, a man ran up and knelt before him, and asked him, "Good Teacher, what must I do to inherit eternal life?" [18]And Jesus said to him, "Why do you call me good? No one is good but God alone. [19]You know the commandments: 'Do not kill, Do not commit adultery, Do not steal, Do not bear false witness, Do not defraud, Honour your father and mother.'" [20]And he said to him, "Teacher, all these I have observed from my youth." [21]And Jesus looking upon him loved him, and said to him, "You lack one thing; go, sell what you have, and give to the poor, and you will have treasure in heaven; and come, follow me." [22]At that saying his countenance fell, and he went away sorrowful; for he had great possessions.

Ex 20:12–17
Deut 5:16–20; 24:14

[23]And Jesus looked around and said to his disciples, "How hard it will be for those who have riches to enter the kingdom of God!" [24]And the disciples were amazed at his words.* But Jesus said to them again, "Children, how hard it is for those who trust in riches[r] to enter the kingdom of God! [25]It is easier for a camel to go through the eye of a needle than for a rich man to enter the kingdom of God." [26]And they were exceedingly astonished, and said to him,[s] "Then who can be saved?" [27]Jesus

1 Tim 6:17

Gen 18:14

videns Iesus, indigne tulit et ait illis: «Sinite parvulos venire ad me. Ne prohibueritis eos; talium est enim regnum Dei. [15]Amen dico vobis: Quisquis non receperit regnum Dei velut parvulus, non intrabit in illud». [16]Et complexans eos benedicebat imponens manus super illos. [17]Et cum egrederetur in viam, accurrens quidam et, genu flexo ante eum, rogabat eum: «Magister bone, quid faciam ut vitam aeternam percipiam?». [18]Iesus autem dixit ei: «Quid me dicis bonum? Nemo bonus nisi unus Deus. [19]Praecepta nosti: ne occidas, ne adulteres, ne fureris, ne falsum testimonium dixeris, ne fraudem feceris, honora patrem tuum et matrem». [20]Ille autem dixit ei: «Magister, haec omnia conservavi a iuventute mea». [21]Iesus autem intuitus eum dilexit eum et dixit illi: «Unum tibi deest: vade, quaecumque habes, vende et da pauperibus et habebis thesaurum in caelo et veni, sequere me». [22]Qui contristatus in hoc verbo, abiit maerens: erat enim habens possessiones multas. [23]Et circumspiciens Iesus ait discipulis suis: «Quam difficile, qui pecunias habent, in regnum Dei introibunt». [24]Discipuli autem obstupescebant in verbis eius. At Iesus rursus respondens ait illis: «Filii, quam difficile est in regnum Dei introire. [25]Facilius est camelum per foramen acus transire quam divitem intrare in regnum Dei». [26]Qui magis admirabantur dicentes ad semetipsos: «Et quis potest salvus fieri?». [27]Intuens illos Iesus ait: «Apud homines impossibile est

which must have amused his listeners—a camel trying to manoeuvre himself through an impossibly narrow passage. Christian poverty, on the other hand, is something so precious that St Francis of Assisi used to say that Lady Poverty was the love of his life: "This is the virtue that allows the soul, still living in this world, to converse with the angels in heaven; it accompanied Christ on the cross, was buried with him in the tomb, rose with Christ, and with him ascended into heaven; souls in love with poverty receive, even in this life, the lightness to fly to heaven because it refines the powers of friendship, of humility and of love" (*Little Flowers*, 13).

In reply to Peter's question, Jesus speaks of the rewards that come from following him and the Gospel: in addition to gaining eternal life, a disciple of Jesus, because he is a son of God (and conscious that he is so) and a brother of his brethren, is given a hundred times what he gave.

Our Lord includes persecutions (v. 30) in that promise, but even these bring joy, when borne for Christ, as Peter and the apostles would discover (see Acts 5:40–41). But to go in the opposite direction, to close one's ears to the voice of God, is a recipe for sadness: "Ask yourself now (I too am examining my conscience) whether you are holding firmly and unshakable to your choice of Life? When you hear the most lovable voice of God urging you on to holiness, do you freely answer 'Yes'? Let us turn our gaze once more to Jesus, as he speaks to the people in the towns and countryside of Palestine. He doesn't want to force himself upon us. 'If you have a mind to be perfect …,' he says to the rich young man. The young man refused to take the hint, and the Gospel goes on to say: *abiit tristis*, he went away forlorn. [...] He lost his happiness because he refused to hand over his freedom to God" (St Josemaría Escrivá, *Friends of God*, 24).

r Other ancient authorities omit *for those who trust in riches*   s Other ancient authorities read *to one another*

looked at them and said, "With men it is impossible, but not with God; for all things are possible with God." [28]Peter began to say to him, "Lo, we have left everything and followed you." [29]Jesus said, "Truly, I say to you, there is no one who has left house or brothers or sisters or mother or father or children or lands, for my sake and for the gospel, [30]who will not receive a hundredfold now in this time, houses and brothers and sisters and mothers and children and lands, with persecutions, and in the age to come eternal life.* [31]But many that are first will be last, and the last first."

Mt 20:17–19
Lk 18:31:–34

Third announcement of the Passion

[32]And they were on the road, going up to Jerusalem, and Jesus was walking ahead of them; and they were amazed, and those who followed were afraid. And taking the

Mk 8:31; 9:31

twelve again, he began to tell them what was to happen to him, [33]saying, "Behold, we are going up to Jerusalem; and the Son of man will be delivered to the chief priests and the scribes, and they will condemn him to death, and deliver him to the Gentiles; [34]and they will mock him, and spit upon him, and scourge him, and kill him; and after three days he will rise."

Mt 20:20–28

The sons of Zebedee make a request

[35]And James and John, the sons of Zebedee, came forward to him, and said to him, "Teacher, we want you to do for us whatever we ask of you." [36]And he said to them,

sed non apud Deum: omnia enim possibilia sunt apud Deum». [28]Coepit Petrus ei dicere: «Ecce nos dimisimus omnia et secuti sumus te». [29]Ait Iesus: «Amen dico vobis: Nemo est, qui reliquerit domum aut fratres aut sorores aut matrem aut patrem aut filios aut agros propter me et propter evangelium, [30]qui non accipiat centies tantum nunc in tempore hoc, domos et fratres et sorores et matres et filios et agros cum persecutionibus, et in saeculo futuro vitam aeternam. [31]Multi autem erunt primi novissimi et novissimi primi». [32]Erant autem in via ascendentes in Hierosolymam, et praecedebat illos Iesus, et stupebant; illi autem sequentes timebant. Et assumens iterum Duodecim coepit illis dicere, quae essent ei eventura: [33]«Ecce ascendimus in Hierosolymam; et Filius hominis tradetur principibus sacerdotum et scribis, et damnabunt eum morte et tradent eum gentibus [34]et illudent ei et conspuent eum et flagellabunt eum et interficient eum, et post tres dies resurget». [35]Et accedunt ad eum Iacobus et Ioannes filii Zebedaei dicentes ei: «Magister, volumus, ut quodcumque petierimus a te, facias nobis». [36]At ille dixit eis: «Quid vultis, ut faciam vobis?».

10:32–45 As Jesus and his disciples make their way to Jerusalem, two related events occur. Jesus is committed to his plan to reach Jerusalem (v. 32); he knows what is going to happen there (vv. 33–34), that he is to redeem mankind through his passion and death (v. 45). The metaphors of the cup and the baptism (v. 38) convey how traumatic his passion will be (cf. 14:36; Rom 6:4–5). Jesus goes on to associate his followers with his own destiny: "The Lord's way of asking questions is a lure to his listeners, and an exhortation. He does not ask them: 'Are you prepared to suffer death?' or 'Are you prepared to spill your blood?' His question is: 'Are you able to drink the cup?', and to encourage them, he adds: 'the cup that I drink'. The thought that they are to drink the same cup as he will drink inspires a more generous response. He refers to his Passion as a 'baptism' to show that all his sufferings will be a purification on behalf of the whole world. They answer: 'We are able.' The zeal of his spirit provokes this response and though they do not realize what they are promising, they hope that by their answer their desire will be fulfilled" (St John Chrysostom, *In Matthaeum*, 65, 2).

At the end of the passage, our Lord tells us that, if he came to serve, then service should be a hallmark of those who follow after him (v. 43; cf. Jn 13:14–17). "The Church is not motivated by an earthly ambition but is interested in one thing only—to carry on the work of Christ under the guidance of the Holy Spirit, for he came into the world to bear witness to the truth, to save and not to judge, to serve and not to be served" (Vatican II, *Gaudium et spes*, 3).

Jesus' three announcements of his passion (8:31; 9:31, and 10:33–34) follow the same pattern: he tells his disciples what lies ahead; they object; and then he shows them that they are wrong. Similarly, we, like the disciples, need to continuously refine our understanding of Jesus.

"What do you want me to do for you?" [37]And they said to him, "Grant us to sit, one at your right hand and one at your left, in your glory." [38]But Jesus said to them, "You do not know what you are asking. Are you able to drink the cup that I drink, or to be baptized with the baptism with which I am baptized?" [39]And they said to him, "We are able." And Jesus said to them, "The cup that I drink you will drink; and with the baptism with which I am baptized, you will be baptized; [40]but to sit at my right hand or at my left is not mine to grant, but it is for those for whom it has been prepared." [41]And when the ten heard it, they began to be indignant at James and John. [42]And Jesus called them to him and said to them, "You know that those who are supposed to rule over the Gentiles lord it over them, and their great men exercise authority over them. [43]But it shall not be so among you; but whoever would be great among you must be your servant, [44]and whoever would be first among you must be slave of all. [45]For the Son of man also came not to be served but to serve, and to give his life as a ransom of many."

Lk 12:50
Rom 6:3

Acts 12:2
Rev 1:9

Lk 22:25–27

Mk 9:35

Bartimeus, the blind man of Jericho

Mt 20:29–34
Lk 18:35–43

[46]And they came to Jericho; and as he was leaving Jericho with his disciples and a great multitude, Bartimaeus, a blind beggar, the son of Timaeus, was sitting by the roadside. [47]And when he heard that it was Jesus of Nazareth, he began to cry out and

[37]Illi autem dixerunt ei: «Da nobis, ut unus ad dexteram tuam et alius ad sinistram sedeamus in gloria tua». [38]Iesus autem ait eis: «Nescitis quid petatis. Potestis bibere calicem, quem ego bibo, aut baptismum, quo ego baptizor, baptizari?». [39]At illi dixerunt ei: «Possumus». Iesus autem ait eis: «Calicem quidem, quem ego bibo, bibetis et baptismum, quo ego baptizor, baptizabimini; [40]sedere autem ad dexteram meam vel ad sinistram non est meum dare, sed quibus paratum est». [41]Et audientes decem coeperunt indignari de Iacobo et Ioanne. [42]Et vocans eos Iesus ait illis: «Scitis quia hi, qui videntur principari gentibus, dominantur eis, et principes eorum potestatem habent ipsorum. [43]Non ita est autem in vobis, sed quicumque voluerit fieri maior inter vos, erit vester minister; [44]et, quicumque voluerit in vobis primus esse, erit omnium servus; [45]nam et Filius hominis non venit, ut ministraretur ei, sed ut ministraret et daret animam suam redemptionem pro multis». [46]Et veniunt Iericho. Et proficiscente eo de Iericho et discipulis eius et plurima multitudine, filius Timaei Bartimaeus caecus sedebat iuxta viam mendicans. [47]Qui, cum audisset quia Iesus Nazarenus est, coepit clamare et dicere: «Fili David Iesu, miserere mei!». [48]Et comminabantur ei multi, ut taceret; at ille multo magis clam-

10:46–52 In his account of this miracle, Mark provides quite a lot of information about Bartimaeus himself (v. 46) and his attitude towards Jesus: this blind beggar is very determined and insistent (vv. 47–48); when he is called by Jesus, he forgets about his possessions (v. 50); and we can see his faith and simplicity in his conversation with Jesus (v. 51). Thanks to his faith, Bartimaeus' situation changes radically: previously he was blind and sitting by the roadside (v. 46); now that he can see, he follows Jesus on his way (v. 52).

Bartimaeus' journey of faith can be ours, too, if we act as he did. First, we need to pray like him, to cry out to Jesus, and our invocation can follow his example: Bartimaeus calls Jesus *rabbi*, "master", or *rabboni*, "my master" (v. 51); "Son of David", that is, Messiah King, merciful as God is merciful (v. 47); and, above all, "Jesus": "The one name that contains everything is the one that the Son of God received in his incarnation. [...] The name 'Jesus' contains all:

God and man and the whole economy of creation and salvation. To pray 'Jesus' is to invoke him and to call him within us" (*Catechism of the Catholic Church*, 2666).

But the faith of Bartimaeus goes beyond petition and entreaty: he takes action, throwing off his mantle and springing up to move close to Jesus (v. 50), and he follows him on his way to Jerusalem: "You have understood what our Lord was asking from you and you have decided to accompany him on his way. You are trying to walk in his footsteps, to clothe yourself in Christ's clothing, to be Christ himself: well, your faith, your faith in the light our Lord is giving you, must be both operative and full of sacrifice. Don't fool yourself. Don't think you are going to find new ways. The faith he demands of us is as I have said. We must keep in step with him, working generously and at the same time uprooting and getting rid of everything that gets in the way" (St Josemaría Escrivá, *Friends of God*, 198).

say, "Jesus, Son of David, have mercy on me!" [48]And many rebuked him, telling him to be silent; but he cried out all the more, "Son of David, have mercy on me!" [49]And Jesus stopped and said, "Call him." And they called the blind man, saying to him, "Take heart; rise, he is calling you." [50]And throwing off his mantle he sprang up and came to Jesus. [51]And Jesus said to him, "What do you want me to do for you?" And the blind man said to him, "Master,[t] let me receive my sight." [52]And Jesus said to him, "Go your way; your faith has made you well." And immediately he received his sight and followed him on the way.

Jn 20:16

PART THREE

Jesus' ministry in Jerusalem*

8. CLEANSING OF THE TEMPLE. CONTROVERSIES*

Mt 21:1–11
Lk 19:28–40
Jn 12:12–19

The Messiah enters the Holy City

Lk 23:53

11 [1]And when they drew near to Jerusalem, to Bethphage and Bethany, at the Mount of Olives, he sent two of his disciples, [2]and said to them, "Go into the

abat: «Fili David, miserere mei!». [49]Et stans Iesus dixit: «Vocate illum». Et vocant caecum dicentes ei: «Animaequior esto. Surge, vocat te». [50]Qui, proiecto vestimento suo, exsiliens venit ad Iesum. [51]Et respondens ei Iesus dixit: «Quid vis tibi faciam?». Caecus autem dixit ei: «Rabboni, ut videam». [52]Et Iesus ait illi: «Vade; fides tua te salvum fecit». Et confestim vidit et sequebatur eum in via. [11] [1]Et cum appropinquarent Hierosolymae, Bethphage et Bethaniae ad montem Olivarum, mittit duos ex discipulis suis [2]et ait illis: «Ite in castellum, quod est contra vos, et statim introe-

11:1—16:20 The final six chapters of Mark's Gospel cover the events in Jesus' life during his last days on earth. The structure of these chapters is that of Holy Week; and so we find the Church, in her liturgy, re-living these events in order, from Palm Sunday to the great day of the Resurrection: "Therefore Easter is not simply one feast among others, but the 'Feast of feasts,' the 'Solemnity of solemnities,' just as the Eucharist is the 'Sacrament of sacraments' (the Great Sacrament). St Athanasius calls Easter 'the Great Sunday' and the Eastern Churches call Holy Week 'the Great Week.' The mystery of the Resurrection, in which Christ crushed death, permeates with its powerful energy our old time, until all is subjected to him" (*Catechism of the Catholic Church*, 1169).

The importance of these events can be seen in the detailed information the Gospel provides on time and place. On the first day (11:1–19) Jesus enters Jerusalem in triumph and carries out the cleansing of the temple. The Pharisees' question about Jesus' authority to purify the temple (11:28) marks the start of a series of controver-

sies with leading priests, scribes, elders, Herodians and Sadducees (11:27—12:40); these controversies are interrupted by Jesus' Eschatological Discourse.

In addition to recounting the controversies, the Gospel three times (11:18; 12:12; 14:1–2) reports that the religious rulers were laying plans to arrest Jesus. An opportunity to do this arises when Judas volunteers to hand him over (14:10) and, from this point on, the Gospel records the suffering Jesus endured until his death. However, Jesus does not die because his enemies so decide; he dies because it is written that he should do so (14:21). Therefore, the last episode has to do not with Jesus' death but with his resurrection (see 14:28).

If the first part of the Gospel ended with Peter's confession of faith in which he proclaimed Jesus to be "the Christ" (8:29), this part reaches its climax with the centurion saying that Jesus is "the Son of God" (15:39). These two titles are the very ones that Mark uses to open his Gospel (see 1:1).

t Or *Rabbi*

village opposite you, and immediately as you enter it you will find a colt tied, on which no one has ever sat; untie it and bring it. ³If any one says to you, 'Why are you doing this?' say, 'The Lord has need of it and will send it back here immediately.'" ⁴And they went away, and found a colt tied at the door out in the open street; and they untied it. ⁵And those who stood there said to them, "What are you doing, untying the colt?" ⁶And they told them what Jesus had said; and they let them go. ⁷And they brought the colt to Jesus, and threw their garments on it; and he sat upon it. ⁸And many spread their garments on the road, and others spread leafy branches which they had cut from the fields. ⁹And those who went before and those who followed cried out, "Hosanna! Blessed is he who comes in the name of the Lord! ¹⁰Blessed is the kingdom of our father David that is coming! Hosanna in the highest!"

¹¹And he entered Jerusalem, and went into the temple; and when he had looked around at everything, as it was already late, he went out to Bethany with the twelve.

The barren fig tree. Expulsion of the money-changers
¹²On the following day, when they came from Bethany, he was hungry. ¹³And seeing in the distance a fig tree in leaf, he went to see if he could find anything on it. When

Mk 14:14

Ps 118:25–26

Lk 1:32
2 Sam 7:16

Mt 21:12–22
Lk 19:45–48
Jn 2:13–25

Lk 13:6–9

untes illud invenietis pullum ligatum, super quem nemo adhuc hominum sedit; solvite illum et adducite. ³Et si quis vobis dixerit: "Quid facitis hoc?", dicite: "Domino necessarius est, et continuo illum remittit iterum huc"». ⁴Et abeuntes invenerunt pullum ligatum ante ianuam foris in bivio et solvunt eum. ⁵Et quidam de illic stantibus dicebant illis: «Quid facitis solventes pullum?». ⁶Qui dixerunt eis, sicut dixerat Iesus; et dimiserunt eis. ⁷Et ducunt pullum ad Iesum et imponunt illi vestimenta sua; et sedit super eum. ⁸Et multi vestimenta sua straverunt in via, alii autem frondes, quas exciderant in agris. ⁹Et qui praeibant et qui sequebantur, clamabant: *«Hosanna! Benedictus, qui venit in nomine Domini! ¹⁰Benedictum, quod venit regnum patris nostri David! Hosanna in excelsis!»*. ¹¹Et introivit Hierosolymam in templum; et circumspectis omnibus, cum iam vespera esset hora, exivit in Bethaniam cum Duodecim. ¹²Et altera die cum exirent a Bethania, esuriit. ¹³Cumque vidisset a longe ficum habentem folia,

*11:1–12:44 This section begins with the account of Jesus' entry into Jerusalem and goes on to report the cleansing of the temple and arguments with the Jews. The first of these two chapters shows Jesus performing actions appropriate to the long-awaited Messiah. The parable of the wicked tenants (12:1) provides the key to the right interpretation of all the events that the evangelist tells us happened during this fateful week: Israel has rejected the gift of God and, therefore, God will create a new people through a new Covenant in his Son.

11:1–11 Jesus' entry into Jerusalem reveals him to be the promised Messiah (see Zech 9:9); and Jesus' gestures here help us to see his true grandeur. The crowds, like Bartimaeus earlier (10:47–48), see him as the Messiah descended from David, and Jesus amends this title (he will do so explicitly later: 12:35–37), by referring to himself as "the Lord" and showing that he does indeed have sovereign power over created things. However, his sovereignty is not imposed by force; it respects the freedom of human beings: "From the beginning of Christian history,

the assertion of Christ's lordship over the world and over history has implicitly recognized that man should not submit his personal freedom in an absolute manner to any earthly power, but only to God the Father and the Lord Jesus Christ" (*Catechism of the Catholic Church*, 450).

11:12–25 On the second day of the week Jesus performs further works that reveal his status as the Saviour Messiah: acting with apparent violence in the temple, he fulfils the prophecies that foretold the cleansing of the temple (Mal 3:1–5; Zech 14:21) in order to establish it as a place of prayer for all nations (Is 56:7).

This episode is framed by another, similar one—the cursing of the fig tree. By a symbolic action similar to some of those performed by prophets (see Jer 19:1–13; Ezek 4:1–3; 5:1–6), Jesus shows that Israel, like the fig tree, has failed to produce the fruit that God expected (cf. 12:1–12); he had come to his own people, to the Jews, eager to find fruit of holiness and good works, but all he found was external religion— no fruit, only leaves. Reference to the destruction of the temple (cf. 13:2) is thereby set within an

he came to it, he found nothing but leaves, for it was not the season for figs. [14]And he said to it, "May no one ever eat fruit from you again." And his disciples heard it.

[15]And they came to Jerusalem. And he entered the temple and began to drive out those who sold and those who bought in the temple, and he overturned the tables of the money-changers and the seats of those who sold pigeons; [16]and he would not allow any one to carry anything through the temple. [17]And he taught, and said to them, "Is it not written, 'My house shall be called a house of prayer for all the nations'? But you have made it a den of robbers." [18]And the chief priests and the scribes heard it and sought a way to destroy him; for they feared him, because all the multitude was astonished at his teaching. [19]And when evening came they[u] went out of the city.

[20]As they passed by in the morning, they saw the fig tree withered away to its roots. [21]And Peter remembered and said to him, "Master,[v] look! The fig tree which you cursed has withered." [22]And Jesus answered them, "Have faith in God. [23]Truly, I say to you, whoever says to this mountain, 'Be taken up and cast into the sea,' and does not doubt in his heart, but believes that what he says will come to pass, it will be done for him. [24]Therefore I tell you, whatever you ask in prayer, believe that you receive it, and you will. [25]And whenever you stand praying, forgive, if you have anything against any one; so that your Father also who is in heaven may forgive you your trespasses."[w]

Jesus' authority

[27]And they came again to Jerusalem. And as he was walking in the temple, the chief priests and the scribes and the elders came to him, [28]and they said to him, "By what

Margin references:
Is 56:7
Jer 7:11

Mk 11:14

Jn 14:1

Mt 17:20
Lk 17:6

Jn 14:13; 16:23
Mt 6:14–15

Mt 21:23–27
Lk 20:1–8

venit si quid forte inveniret in ea; et cum venisset ad eam, nihil invenit praeter folia: non enim erat tempus ficorum. [14]Et respondens dixit ei: «Iam non amplius in aeternum quisquam fructum ex te manducet». Et audiebant discipuli eius. [15]Et veniunt Hierosolymam. Et cum introisset in templum, coepit eicere vendentes et ementes in templo et mensas ñummulariorum et cathedras vendentium columbas evertit, [16]et non sinebat, ut quisquam vas transferret per templum. [17]Et docebat dicens eis: «Non scriptum est: *Domus mea domus orationis vocabitur omnibus gentibus*"? Vos autem fecistis eam *speluncam latronum*». [18]Quo audito, principes sacerdotum et scribae quaerebant quomodo eum perderent; timebant enim eum, quoniam universa turba admirabatur super doctrina eius. [19]Et cum vespera facta esset, egrediebantur de civitate. [20]Et cum mane transirent, viderunt ficum aridam factam a radicibus. [21]Et recordatus Petrus dicit ei: «Rabbi, ecce ficus, cui maledixisti, aruit». [22]Et respondens Iesus ait illis: «Habete fidem Dei! [23]Amen dico vobis: Quicumque dixerit huic monti: "Tollere et mittere in mare", et non haesitaverit in corde suo, sed crediderit quia, quod dixerit, fiat, fiet ei. [24]Propterea dico vobis: Omnia, quaecumque orantes petitis, credite quia iam accepistis, et erunt vobis. [25]Et cum statis in oratione, dimittite, si quid habetis adversus aliquem, ut et Pater vester, qui in caelis est, dimittat vobis peccata vestra». [27]Et veniunt rursus

episode about the need for purification. Engaging in external religious worship without having the right inner dispositions is something that everyone should avoid: "You also, if you do not wish to be condemned by Christ, [...] must be careful not to become a sterile tree, so that you can offer to Jesus, who made himself poor, the fruit of piety that he requires" (St Bede, *In Marci Evangelium*, ad loc.).

This episode, like so many others in Mark's Gospel, is brought to a close by Jesus with a message for his disciples—in this case, about the power of prayer (vv. 20–25). Charity (v. 25) is a prerequisite for prayer: when one approaches God in prayer, one must not harbour rancour or any other feeling that is unworthy of God. But if

a person approaches God with charity (Jesus teaches), he cannot but listen to prayer made in a spirit of faith: personal unworthiness or the fact that God is well aware of our needs is never a legitimate excuse for not turning to him: "O my God, can it be better to keep silent about my necessities, hoping that you will relieve them? No, indeed, for you, my Lord and my Joy, knowing how many they must be and how it will alleviate them if we speak to you of them, bid us pray to you and say that you will not fail to give" (St Teresa of Avila, *Exclamations*, 5). See the notes on Mt 6:1–18 and 7:1–12, and the RSV note **w**: this line may come from Mt 6:15.

11:27–33 Our Lord's third day in Jerusalem

u Other ancient authorities read *he*   v Or *Rabbi*   w Other ancient authorities add verse 26, *"But if you do not forgive, neither will your Father who is in heaven forgive your trespasses"*

authority are you doing these things, or who gave you this authority to do them?" [29]Jesus said to them, "I will ask you a question; answer me, and I will tell you by what authority I do these things. [30]Was the baptism of John from heaven or from men? Answer me." [31]And they argued with one another, "If we say, 'From heaven,' he will say, 'Why then did you not believe him?' [32]But shall we say, 'From men'?"—they were afraid of the people, for all held that John was a real prophet. [33]So they answered Jesus, "We do not know." And Jesus said to them, "Neither will I tell you by what authority I do these things."

Parable of the wicked tenants

Mt 21:33–46
Lk 20:9–19
Is 5:1–2
2 Chron 36:15ff

12 [1]And he began to speak to them in parables. "A man planted a vineyard, and set a hedge around it, and dug a pit for the wine press, and built a tower, and let it out to tenants, and went into another country. [2]When the time came, he sent a servant to the tenants, to get from them some of the fruit of the vineyard. [3]And they

Hierosolymam. Et cum ambularet in templo, accedunt ad eum summi sacerdotes et scribae et seniores [28]et dicebant illi: «In qua potestate haec facis? Vel quis tibi dedit hanc potestatem, ut ista facias?». [29]Iesus autem ait illis: «Interrogabo vos unum verbum, et respondete mihi, et dicam vobis, in qua potestate haec faciam: [30]Baptismum Ioannis de caelo erat an ex hominibus? Respondete mihi». [31]At illi cogitabant secum dicentes: «Si dixerimus: "De caelo", dicet: "Quare ergo non credidistis ei?"; [32]si autem dixerimus: "Ex hominibus?"». Timebant populum: omnes enim habebant Ioannem quia vere propheta esset. [33]Et respondentes dicunt Iesu: «Nescimus». Et Iesus ait illis: «Neque ego dico vobis in qua potestate haec faciam». [12] [1]Et coepit illis in parabolis loqui: «*Vineam pastinavit* homo *et circumdedit saepem et fodit lacum et aedificavit turrim* et locavit eam agricolis et peregre profectus est. [2]Et misit ad agricolas in tempore servum, ut ab agricolis acciperet de fructu vineae; [3]qui apprehensum eum

begins at this point. Much of Jesus' teaching in this passage occurs in the course of clashes with members of the Jewish establishment. It is likely that what most provoked these people was his cleansing of the temple (11:15–17). From then on, they try to find some way to destroy him (11:18). Now (v. 28) they ask him to explain his action, and later (14:58) they will distort its meaning to justify condemning him to death.

These people behave in a deceitful way: Jesus had already given them proof that he is the Messiah, and John the Baptist had also sworn testimony to him. Jesus is ready to engage in dialogue, but before replying to their question, he confronts them with the real question: Do they or do they not accept the ministry of John the Baptist as Precursor? For, if they accept John, they should also accept Jesus. But these people, the evangelist records, were not ready to acknowledge John, and their blindness led them to plan Jesus' death: "On the one hand, they were afraid of the people; on the other, of the truth. On the one hand, they were afraid; on the other, envious of him. One way or another, they were blind. Their blindness was caused by the fear in their hearts: they were afraid that if they said the baptism of John was from men, the people would stone them; and afraid that if they said it was

from heaven, Jesus would condemn them for their lack of faith" (St Augustine, *Sermones*, 308a, 7). This episode contains a lesson that is always valid: those who try to call God to account will never escape from their ignorance and confusion.

12:1–12 In this parable Jesus provides a summary of salvation history and of his own life and work. Using the allegory of the vineyard (cf. Is 5:1–7), he describes all the efforts made by God to encourage his Chosen People to yield fruit—and the reluctance of men (the rulers of Israel, especially) to do so. It seems clear from the tenor of the parable that the "beloved son" (v. 6) is Jesus himself (cf. 1:11; 9:7) and that the servants sent prior to the son are the prophets. The fact that the son was killed and thrown out of the vineyard (v. 8) is a prophetic announcement of the death of Jesus outside the walls of Jerusalem. However, by quoting words from Psalm 118, our Lord is saying that these actions of men are in keeping with God's plan, which is to found a new people on Christ, the new cornerstone: "The Lord God set the cornerstone not in one place, but throughout the world, to bear fruit in due season. The tower of God's chosen ones stands tall everywhere and is beautiful. The light of the

took him and beat him, and sent him away empty-handed. [4]Again he sent to them another servant, and they wounded him in the head, and treated him shamefully. [5]And he sent another, and him they killed; and so with many others, some they beat and some they killed. [6]He had still one other, a beloved son; finally he sent him to them, saying, 'They will respect my son.' [7]But those tenants said to one another, 'This is the heir; come, let us kill him, and the inheritance will be ours.' [8]And they took him and killed him, and cast him out of the vineyard. [9]What will the owner of the vineyard do? He will come and destroy the tenants, and give the vineyard to others. [10]Have you not read this scripture:

> 'The very stone which the builders rejected
> has become the head of the corner;
> [11]this was the Lord's doing,
> and it is marvellous in our eyes'?"

[12]And they tried to arrest him, but feared the multitude, for they perceived that he had told the parable against them; so they left him and went away.

Mk 1:11; 9:7

Gen 37:19–20

Heb 13:12

Ps 118:22–23

Paying tax to Caesar

Mt 22:15–22
Lk 20:20–26

Mk 3:6

[13]And they sent to him some of the Pharisees and some of the Herodians, to entrap him in his talk. [14]And they came and said to him, "Teacher, we know that you are true, and care for no man; for you do not regard the position of men, but truly teach the way of God. Is it lawful to pay taxes to Caesar, or not? [15]Should we pay them, or should we not?" But knowing their hypocrisy, he said to them, "Why put me to the test? Bring me a coin,[x] and let me look at it." [16]And they brought one. And he said to them, "Whose likeness and inscription is this?" They said to him, "Caesar's." [17]Jesus said to them, "Render to Caesar the things that are Caesar's, and to God the things that are God's." And they were amazed at him.

Rom 13:7

caeciderunt et dimiserunt vacuum. [4]Et iterum misit ad illos alium servum; et illum in capite vulneraverunt et contumeliis affecerunt. [5]Et alium misit, et illum occiderunt, et plures alios, quosdam caedentes, alios vero occidentes. [6]Adhuc unum habebat, filium dilectum. Misit illum ad eos novissimum dicens: "Reverebuntur filium meum". [7]Coloni autem illi dixerunt ad invicem: "Hic est heres. Venite, occidamus eum, et nostra erit hereditas". [8]Et apprehendentes eum occiderunt et eiecerunt extra vineam. [9]Quid ergo faciet dominus vineae? Veniet et perdet colonos et dabit vineam aliis. [10]Nec Scripturam hanc legistis: *"Lapidem quem reprobaverunt aedificantes, / hic factus est in caput anguli; / [11]a Domino factum est istud / et est mirabile in oculis nostris"*?». [12]Et quaerebant eum tenere et timuerunt turbam; cognoverunt enim quoniam ad eos parabolam hanc dixerit. Et relicto eo abierunt. [13]Et mittunt ad eum quosdam ex pharisaeis et herodianis, ut eum caperent in verbo. [14]Qui venientes dicunt ei: «Magister, scimus quia verax es et non curas quemquam, nec enim vides in faciem hominum, sed in veritate viam Dei doces. Licet dare tributum Caesari an non? Dabimus an non dabimus?». [15]Qui sciens versutiam eorum ait illis: «Quid me tentatis? Afferte mihi denarium, ut videam». [16]At illi attulerunt. Et ait illis: «Cuius est imago haec et inscriptio?». Illi autem dixerunt ei: «Caesaris». [17]Iesus autem dixit illis: «Quae sunt Caesaris, reddite Caesari et, quae sunt Dei, Deo». Et mirabantur super eo. [18]Et veniunt ad eum sadducaei, qui dicunt resurrectionem non esse, et interrogabant

Church shines out everywhere, and everywhere the winepress is at work, for people everywhere receive the Spirit" (St Irenaeus, *Adversus haereses*, 4, 36, 2).

12:13–17 In its simplicity, this episode shows the greatness of Jesus. Pharisees and Herodians, enemies though they are, join forces to try to entrap Jesus. Their manoeuvre is apparent even before they pose their trick question; their obsequious tone betrays their intent (v. 14). If the Jews are the People of God, whom they should serve, then to pay taxes to an oppressor could be

interpreted as a betrayal. But if Jesus were to answer that it is unlawful to pay the tax, then the Herodians could denounce him to the Roman authorities. Christ's answer leaves his questioners nonplussed (v. 17), and outlines the Christian attitude towards authorities and just laws (cf. Rom 13:1–7). "Therefore," St Justin comments, "to God alone do we pray; and you, princes and kings, we serve most readily as regards other things […] and we pray for you" (*Apologia*, 1, 17, 3). For more on this episode as a source of teaching about temporal authority and spiritual authority, see the note on Mt 22:15–22.

x Greek *a denarius*

The resurrection of the dead

Mt 22:23–33
Lk 20:27–40

[18]And Sadducees came to him, who say that there is no resurrection; and they asked him a question, saying, [19]"Teacher, Moses wrote for us that if a man's brother dies Deut 25:5–6
Gen 38:8 and leaves a wife, but leaves no child, the man[y] must take the wife, and raise up children for his brother. [20]There were seven brothers; the first took a wife, and when he died left no children; [21]and the second took her, and died, leaving no children; and the third likewise; [22]and the seven left no children. Last of all the woman also died. [23]In the resurrection whose wife will she be? For the seven had her as wife."

[24]Jesus said to them, "Is not this why you are wrong, that you know neither the scriptures nor the power of God? [25]For when they rise from the dead, they neither marry nor are given in marriage, but are like angels in heaven. [26]And as for the dead Ex 3:2, 6 being raised, have you not read in the book of Moses, in the passage about the bush, how God said to him, 'I am the God of Abraham, and the God of Isaac, and the God of Jacob'? [27]He is not God of the dead, but of the living; you are quite wrong." Rom 14:8

The greatest commandment of all

Mt 22:34–40
Lk 10:25–28

[28]And one of the scribes came up and heard them disputing with one another, and Lk 12:39 seeing that he answered them well, asked him, "Which commandment is the first of

eum dicentes: [19]«Magister, Moyses nobis scripsit, ut *si cuius frater mortuus fuerit* et reliquerit uxorem *et filium non reliquerit, accipiat frater eius uxorem et resuscitet semen fratri suo*. [20]Septem fratres erant: et primus accepit uxorem et moriens non reliquit semen; [21]et secundus accepit eam et mortuus est, non relicto semine; et tertius similiter; [22]et septem non reliquerunt semen. Novissima omnium defuncta est et mulier. [23]In resurrectione, cum resurrexerint, cuius de his erit uxor? Septem enim habuerunt eam uxorem». [24]Ait illis Iesus: «Non ideo erratis, quia non scitis Scripturas neque virtutem Dei? [25]Cum enim a mortuis resurrexerint, neque nubent neque nubentur, sed sunt sicut angeli in caelis. [26]De mortuis autem quod resurgant, non legistis in libro Moysis super rubum, quomodo dixerit illi Deus inquiens: *"Ego sum Deus Abraham et Deus Isaac et Deus*

12:18–27 It is now the turn of the Sadducees to try to ensnare Jesus. They devise a "case study" to try to make a nonsense of the doctrine of resurrection from the dead (cf. the notes on Mt 22:23–33 and Lk 20:27–40). Before dealing with the conundrum, Jesus shows where they have gone wrong: they have made the common human mistake of trying to reduce the greatness of God to the limitations of the human mind, even when God has already revealed the answer to their scholarly dilemma; moreover, they underestimate the power of God. Difficulties concerning the truths of faith can indeed arise (there is nothing surprising about that), for these truths are beyond human reason. But it makes no sense to try to find contradictions in the revealed word of God. Holy Scripture, and the things of God in general, should be approached with the humility that faith demands: "There is only one God, my brothers, and we can come to know him only through the Holy Scriptures. Therefore, we must strive to understand the things that we are told in the Scriptures and come to a deep understanding of what we are taught. We should come to know the Father as he desires to be

known, to glorify the Son as the Father wills that he be glorified, receive the Holy Spirit in the way the Father wills to send him to us. We should not act according to our own feelings or criteria, doing violence to the will of God, but in accordance with the ways that the Lord himself has laid down for us in the Holy Scriptures" (St Hippolytus, *Contra haeresim Noeti*, 9).

12:28–34 Over the course of these chapters, Mark has recorded traps set by the "chief priests and the scribes and the elders" (11:27), by "Pharisees and … Herodians" (12:13) and by "Sadducees" (12:18). The evangelist now notes that after Jesus' reply to the scribe, no one dared to ask him any more questions (v. 34). Even so, the well-intentioned question put by the scribe (v. 28) is quite different from the previous ones. Therefore, Jesus devotes time to instructing him, and the scribe is able to discern the profundity of Christ's reply. "The love of God is first in order of commandment, but the love of neighbour is first in order of action […]. Because you do not yet see God, by loving your neighbour you merit seeing Him; by loving your neighbour you

y Greek *his brother*

Deut 6:4–5

all?" [29]Jesus answered, "The first is, 'Hear, O Israel: The Lord our God, the Lord is one; [30]and you shall love the Lord your God with all your heart, and with all your

Lev 19:18
Jn 15:12

soul, and with all your mind, and with all your strength.' [31]The second is this, 'You shall love your neighbour as yourself.' There is no other commandment greater than

Deut 6:4; 4:35

these." [32]And the scribe said to him, "You are right, Teacher; you have truly said that

Josh 22:5
1 Sam 15:22

he is one, and there is no other than he; [33]and to love him with all the heart, and with all the understanding, and with all the strength, and to love one's neighbour as one-

Lk 12:40

self, is much more than all whole burnt offerings and sacrifices." [34]And when Jesus saw that he answered wisely, he said to him, "You are not far from the kingdom of God." And after that no one dared to ask him any question.

Mt 22:41–46
Lk 20:41–44

The divinity of the Messiah

Jn 7:42

[35]And as Jesus taught in the temple, he said, "How can the scribes say that the Christ is the son of David? [36]David himself, inspired by[z] the Holy Spirit, declared,

Ps 110:1

> 'The Lord said to my Lord,
> Sit at my right hand,
> till I put thy enemies under thy feet.'

Lk 19:48; 21:38

[37]David himself calls him Lord; so how is he his son?" And the great throng heard him gladly.

Mt 23:1–12
Lk 20:45–47

Jesus censures the scribes

[38]And in his teaching he said, "Beware of the scribes, who like to go about in long robes, and to have salutations in the market places [39]and the best seats in the syna-

---

Iacob"? [27]*Non est Deus mortuorum sed vivorum! Multum erratis*». [28]Et accessit unus de scribis, qui audierat illos conquirentes, videns quoniam bene illis responderit, interrogavit eum: «*Quod est primum omnium mandatum?*». [29]Iesus respondit: «*Primum est: "Audi, Israel: Dominus Deus noster Dominus unus est, [30]et diliges Dominum Deum tuum ex toto corde tuo et ex tota anima tua et ex tota mente tua et ex tota virtute tua"*. [31]*Secundum est illud: "Diliges proximum tuum tamquam teipsum"*. Maius horum aliud mandatum non est». [32]Et ait illi scriba: «Bene, Magister, in veritate dixisti: *"Unus est, et non est alius praeter eum,* [33]*et diligere eum ex toto corde et ex toto intellectu et ex tota fortitudine"* et: *"Diligere proximum tamquam seipsum"* maius est omnibus holocautomatibus et sacrificiis». [34]Et Iesus videns quod sapienter respondisset, dixit illi: «Non es longe a regno Dei». Et nemo iam audebat eum interrogare. [35]Et respondens Iesus dicebat docens in templo: «Quomodo dicunt scribae Christum filium esse David? [36]Ipse David dixit in Spiritu Sancto: *"Dixit Dominus Domino meo: Sede a dextris meis, / donec ponam inimicos tuos sub pedibus tuis"*. [37]Ipse David dicit eum Dominum, et unde est filius eius?». Et multa turba eum libenter audiebat. [38]Et dicebat in doctrina sua:

---

cleanse your eye for seeing God, as John clearly says: 'If you do not love your neighbour whom you see, how will you be able to love God whom you do not see?'" (St Augustine, *In Ioannis Evangelium*, 17, 8).

12:35–37 Over the course of the Gospel, our Lord has gradually revealed who he is, and people have begun to understand his revelation. St Peter acknowledged him as the Messiah (8:29). Bartimaeus, the blind man, gave him the title "Son of David" and sought his mercy (10:47–48), and the multitudes acclaimed him as the one sent by God (11:9). Here, in a veiled way, Jesus says that these titles are correct, but they are incomplete: he is the Messiah, the long-awaited Son of David, the one sent by God, but

he is this because, over and above all other things, he is the Son of God. That is the interpretation given by St Hilary of Poitiers when, commenting on the scribe's question, he says that he "was ignorant of the Law and did not know that Christ must be acknowledged as the Lord through the human nature with which he was born into this world. [...] He [Jesus] spoke in these terms so that the scribe who thought he was an ordinary man, born of Mary, of the line of David according to the flesh, would acknowledge him to be the Son of David according to the Spirit" (*De Trinitate*, 9, 26).

12:38–40 The other two Synoptic Gospels record a lengthy, severe criticism by Jesus of some scribes and Pharisees (see Mt 23:1–36; Lk

---

z Or *himself, in*

gogues and the places of honour at feasts, ⁴⁰who devour widows' houses and for a pretence make long prayers. They will receive the greater condemnation."

The widow's mite   Lk 21:1–4

⁴¹And he sat down opposite the treasury, and watched the multitude putting money into the treasury. Many rich people put in large sums. ⁴²And a poor widow came, and put in two copper coins, which make a penny. ⁴³And he called his disciples to him, and said to them, "Truly, I say to you, this poor widow has put in more than all those who are contributing to the treasury. ⁴⁴For they all contributed out of their abun-   2 Cor 8:12
dance; but she out of her poverty has put in everything she had, her whole living."

9. THE ESCHATOLOGICAL DISCOURSE*

Announcement of the destruction of the temple   Mt 24:1–2
                                                                                       Lk 21:5–6

13 ¹And as he came out of the temple, one of his disciples said to him, "Look, Teacher, what wonderful stones and what wonderful buildings!" ²And Jesus said to him, "Do you see these great buildings? There will not be left here one stone upon another, that will not be thrown down."

«Cavete a scribis, qui volunt in stolis ambulare et salutari in foro ³⁹et in primis cathedris sedere in synagogis et primos discubitus in cenis; ⁴⁰qui devorant domos viduarum et ostentant prolixas orationes. Hi accipient amplius iudicium». ⁴¹Et sedens contra gazophylacium aspiciebat quomodo turba iactaret aes in gazophylacium; et multi divites iactabant multa. ⁴²Et cum venisset una vidua pauper, misit duo minuta, quod est quadrans. ⁴³Et convocans discipulos suos ait illis: «Amen dico vobis: Vidua haec pauper plus omnibus misit, qui miserunt in gazophylacium: ⁴⁴omnes enim ex eo, quod abundabat illis, miserunt; haec vero de penuria sua omnia, quae habuit, misit, totum victum suum». [13] ¹Et cum egrederetur de templo, ait illi unus ex discipulis suis: «Magister, aspice quales lapides et quales structurae». ²Et Iesus ait illi: «Vides has magnas aedificationes?

11:37–54 and notes). St Mark records only the words in this passage, in which Jesus denounces any disordered desire for human honours: "We should notice that salutations in the marketplace are not forbidden, nor people taking the best seats if that befits their position; rather, the faithful are warned to avoid, as they would evil men, those who set too much store by such honours" (St Bede, *In Marci Evangelium*, ad loc.).

12:41–44 By contrast with the behaviour of scribes, that of the poor widow sets a good example. Jesus reproves the ostentation of scribes (12:38–40) and rich people (v. 41) but he praises the upright intention and generosity of this needy widow: "Didn't you see the light in Jesus' eyes as the poor widow left her little alms in the temple? Give him what you can: the merit is not in whether it is big or small, but in the intention with which you give it" (St Josemaría Escrivá, *The Way*, 829).

*13:1–37 The three Synoptic Gospels record this discourse of our Lord's (see Mt 24:1—25:46 and

Lk 21:5–36). It is often called the "Eschatological Discourse", or "Discourse on the Parousia", because it deals with events that will happen at the end of time. It is also called an "apocalyptic discourse", because of the language in which it is spoken and written (it is a revelation of hidden things, and therefore an apocalypse). This literary genre normally sounds a note of consolation, because it asserts the sovereignty of God over the world and expresses the certainty of ultimate victory for his children despite any difficulties they may meet. Still, the discourse is somewhat enigmatic—a fact that reinforces the central theme of what Jesus says: "Take heed! Watch!" (cf. 13:9, 23, 33, 35, 37).

13:1–2 The occasion when the speech was made provides some keys to its meaning. In Christ's time, the Jews (including the apostles) believed that a day of God's Judgment would come (Is 13:6, 9; Zeph 1:14–17) which would spell disaster for the impious but would be a day of triumph for the Chosen People. The imposing splendour of the temple was a symbol of this

The beginning of tribulation. Persecution on account of the Gospel

[3]And as he sat on the Mount of Olives opposite the temple, Peter and James and John and Andrew asked him privately, [4]"Tell us, when will this be, and what will be the sign when these are all to be accomplished?" [5]And Jesus began to say to them, "Take heed that no one leads you astray. [6]Many will come in my name, saying, 'I am he!' and they will lead many astray. [7]And when you hear of wars and rumours of wars, do not be alarmed; this must take place, but the end is not yet. [8]For nation will rise against nation, and kingdom against kingdom; there will be earthquakes in various places, there will be famines; this is but the beginning of the sufferings.

[9]"But take heed to yourselves; for they will deliver you up to councils, and you will be beaten in synagogues; and you will stand before governors and kings for my sake, to bear testimony before them. [10]And the gospel must first be preached to all nations.

Hic non relinquetur lapis super lapidem, qui non destruatur». [3]Et cum sederet in montem Olivarum contra templum, interrogabat eum separatim Petrus et Iacobus et Ioannes et Andreas: [4]«Dic nobis: Quando ista erunt, et quod signum erit, quando haec omnia incipient consummari?». [5]Iesus autem coepit dicere illis: «Videte, ne quis vos seducat. [6]Multi venient in nomine meo dicentes: "Ego sum", et multos seducent. [7]Cum audieritis autem bella et opiniones bellorum, ne timueritis; oportet fieri sed nondum finis. [8]Exsurget enim gens super gentem, et regnum super regnum, erunt terrae motus per loca, erunt fames; initium dolorum haec. [9]Videte autem vosmetipsos. Tradent vos conciliis et in synagogis vapulabitis et ante praesides et reges stabitis propter me in testimonium illis. [10]Et in omnes gentes primum oportet praedicari evangelium. [11]Et cum duxerint vos

glorious future. Our Lord corrects that interpretation: the temple will not survive; it will be destroyed by violence. But his disciples should learn to see that the destruction of the temple is itself a sign of the opposition they will encounter in their mission to spread the Gospel until the time when he, the Son of man, comes again in glory and power. So, two themes are interwoven throughout this discourse—the destruction of the temple, and the history of the Church.

13:3–13 At the start of the discourse, the disciples ask Jesus two questions: When will all this come about, and what signs will precede it? (v. 4). During the discourse he does not tell them the "when" they are preparing for, but he does tell them the "who": it will be he, the Son of man with glory and power, who will come to console his elect (vv. 24–27); and he gives them a motto to live by—watchfulness.

Jesus' first words have to do with "the beginning of the sufferings" (v. 8): the tribulation that will occur prior to the destruction of Jerusalem (vv. 6–8) is similar to what Christians will experience (vv. 9–13). In both instances, what he says is a call to serenity and hope (vv. 7, 11, 13).

Jesus warns them of the dangers that lie ahead (vv. 6–9, 12–13): when terrible things happen, his disciples must be alert to avoid succumbing to temptation and deception by false prophets; they will be persecuted and hated on account of his name; and they should bear witness to their faith. The experience of the early Church bore out the truth of what our Lord says here: merely to be a Christian meant that a person could be dragged before the courts. St Justin, in the second century, even said that "in our case you use the name alone as proof against us" (*Apologia*, 1, 4, 4). Over the course of history, countless Christians have experienced (and still do) the effect of overt or covert opposition to the Gospel in ways that affect their lives, good name and property. But all this is as nothing compared to the reward that those who persevere will receive (see Rom 8:18), as our Lord himself says in his call for perseverance (v. 13).

What Jesus says in this passage carries a message about providence: persecution and difficulties are an opportunity to bear witness to the Gospel (v. 9) and spread it to all nations (v. 10), because God will be with Christ's disciples, and the Spirit will tell them what they must say (vv. 11–12). That is the interpretation read in these words by Christian tradition: "[You, Lord, have enabled me to] constantly exalt and magnify your name in whatever place I have been, and not only in favourable circumstances, but also in pressing needs, so that whatever will have happened to me, either good or bad, I ought to undertake equally, and always to give thanks to God" (St Patrick, *Confessio*, 14).

11And when they bring you to trial and deliver you up, do not be anxious beforehand what you are to say; but say whatever is given you in that hour, for it is not you who speak, but the Holy Spirit. 12And brother will deliver up brother to death, and the father his child, and children will rise against parents and have them put to death; 13and you will be hated by all for my name's sake. But he who endures to the end will be saved.

Mic 7:6

Jn 15:21

The great tribulation

Mt 24:15–28
Lk 21:20–24

14"But when you see the desolating sacrilege set up where it ought not to be (let the reader understand), then let those who are in Judea flee to the mountains; 15let him who is on the housetop not go down, nor enter his house, to take anything away; 16and let him who is in the field not turn back to take his mantle. 17And alas for those who are with child and for those who give suck in those days! 18Pray that it may not happen in winter. 19For in those days there will be such tribulation as has not been from the beginning of the creation which God created until now, and never will be. 20And if the Lord had not shortened the days, no human being would be saved; but for the sake of the elect, whom he chose, he shortened the days. 21"And then if any one says to you, 'Look, here is the Christ!' or 'Look, there he is!' do not believe it. 22False Christs and false prophets will arise and show signs and wonders, to lead astray, if possible, the elect. 23But take heed; I have told you all things beforehand.

Dan 9:27;
11:31;12:11

Dan 12:1
Joel 2:2

Deut 13:1

The coming of the Son of man

Mt 24:29–31
Lk 21:25–28
Is 13:10
Is 34:4

24"But in those days, after that tribulation, the sun will be darkened, and the moon will not give its light, 25and the stars will be falling from heaven, and the powers in the

---

tradentes, nolite praecogitare quid loquamini, sed, quod datum vobis fuerit in illa hora, id loquimini: non enim estis vos loquentes sed Spiritus Sanctus. 12Et tradet frater fratrem in mortem, et pater filium; et consurgent filii in parentes et morte afficient eos; 13et eritis odio omnibus propter nomen meum. Qui autem sustinuerit in finem, hic salvus erit. 14Cum autem videritis *abominationem desolationis* stantem, ubi non debet, qui legit intellegat: tunc, qui in Iudaea sunt, fugiant in montes; 15qui autem super tectum, ne descendat nec introeat, ut tollat quid de domo sua; 16et, qui in agro erit, non revertatur retro tollere vestimentum suum. 17Vae autem praegnantibus et nutrientibus in illis diebus! 18Orate vero, ut hieme non fiat: 19erunt enim dies illi *tribulatio talis, qualis non fuit ab initio creaturae,* quam condidit Deus, *usque nunc,* neque fiet. 20Et nisi breviasset Dominus dies, non fuisset salva omnis caro. Sed propter electos, quos elegit, breviavit dies. 21Et tunc, si quis vobis dixerit: 'Ecce hic est Christus, ecce illic', ne credideritis. 22Exsurgent enim pseudochristi et pseudoprophetae et dabunt signa et portenta ad seducendos, si potest fieri, electos. 23Vos autem videte; praedixi vobis omnia. 24Sed in illis diebus post tribulationem illam *sol contenebrabitur, et luna non dabit splendorem suum,* 25et erunt stel-

---

13:14–23 In these verses, our Lord appears to regard the fall of Jerusalem as a metaphor for the end of the world. The "desolating sacrilege", literally "abomination of desolation" (v. 14), is a phrase taken from Daniel 9:27 meaning the profanation of the temple (1 Mac 1:54). Our Lord uses it to describe the terrible situation of the inhabitants of Jerusalem (vv. 14–20) when these days come: their plight will seem unbearable. He also speaks about the false messiahs and false prophets who will appear to work "signs and wonders" to deceive believers (vv. 21–22). This great "tribulation" (v. 19) is something that Christians should keep in mind when they feel they can endure no further trials. To cope with these difficulties, our Lord says, Christians must remember two things. First, he realizes that the dangers may well seem overwhelming, but God will not allow his chosen ones to be tempted beyond their endurance (v. 20). Also, they should remember that he has forewarned them: they must take heed and be watchful (v. 23). "The Word kept hidden from us the day and hour of the end of all things, and the day and hour of our own deaths. [...] Since we know neither the day nor the hour, we will walk onwards every day as we have been called, fixing our attention on what is truly important and ignoring whatever is of no real importance. If a man knew the day and hour of his death, he might waste all the time before it came. Since we know neither the day nor the hour, we must always be prepared" (St Athanasius, *Contra Arianos*, 3, 49).

13:24–27 After the age of the Church militant comes the time of the Son of man triumphant. The

Dan 7:13
Joel 2:10
Hag 2:6, 24
Zech 2:6
Deut 30:4
heavens will be shaken. ²⁶And then they will see the Son of man coming in clouds with great power and glory. ²⁷And then he will send out the angels, and gather his elect from the four winds, from the ends of the earth to the ends of heaven.

Mt 24:32–35
Lk 21:29–33
The end will surely come: the lesson of the fig tree
²⁸"From the fig tree learn its lesson: as soon as its branch becomes tender and puts forth its leaves, you know that summer is near. ²⁹So also, when you see these things taking place, you know that he is near, at the very gates. ³⁰Truly, I say to you, this

lae de caelo decidentes, et virtutes, quae sunt in caelis, movebuntur. ²⁶Et tunc videbunt *Filium hominis venientem in nubibus* cum virtute multa et gloria. ²⁷Et tunc mittet angelos et congregabit electos suos a quattuor ventis, a summo terrae usque ad summum caeli. ²⁸A ficu autem discite parabolam: cum iam ramus eius tener fuerit et germinaverit folia cognoscitis quia in proximo sit aestas. ²⁹Sic et vos, cum videritis haec fieri, scitote quod in proximo sit in ostiis. ³⁰Amen dico vobis: Non transiet generatio haec, donec omnia ista fiant. ³¹Caelum et terra transibunt, verba autem

world's fate will be sealed when Jesus comes in glory to judge the world and to save his elect (vv. 26–27). For Christians, sufferings are the path that leads to the second coming of the Son of man.

On two occasions, and in reference to two different events, our Lord spoke of his coming in glory as the Son of man. In the house of Caiaphas, he said to that high priest: "You will see the Son of man sitting at the right hand of Power, and coming with the clouds of heaven" (14:62); but here he speaks of an evidently more distant time when, at the end of the world, those who are still living "will see" the Son of man (v. 26). He appears to be referring to two different moments in time: in the house of Caiaphas he announces his glorious resurrection, which is a sign of his later advent in triumph. In both cases, the prophecy is reminiscent of that of the prophet Daniel about the glorious Son of man (Dan 7:1–28): kingdoms may arise that are opposed to the People of God, but in the end they will surrender to God and do him homage. The signs mentioned in the previous verses (vv. 24–25) also recall God's sentence against Babylon and Edom (Is 13:10; 34:4); God is determined to judge, reward and punish. St Augustine summed up the meaning of this passage when commenting on the return of the Son of man in majesty: "This passage can be read in two ways. The Son of Man may come to his Church in clouds, as he never ceases to come to the Church now, as it is written: 'And then they will see the Son of man coming in clouds'. He will come 'with great power and glory' because his divine power and majesty will be made more visible in his saints; he gives them strength to help them stand firm at

times of persecution. But it may mean that he will come in his Body, which sits at the right hand of the Father, the Body which suffered and died and rose" (*Epistolae*, 199, 11, 41).

13:28–37 The last verses of the discourse spell out what Christ's disciples' attitude should be: they must be vigilant, watchful (vv. 33, 35, 37). One thing is certain: the Lord will come. The two similes used here are very significant. The simile of the fig tree, the last tree to put forth leaves in spring, indicates that he may come later than some people expect, but come he will: it is as certain as the growth-cycle of the tree. Their hope should not waver.

The image of the householder (v. 34) indicates that it is unclear when exactly he will return: he could come at any time. His disciples must be faithful: "He wished to hide this from us so that we might remain on our guard and be aware that this might happen to us during our life. He said very clearly that he would come again, but without stating at what moment. Thus, through all generations and at all times his coming is ardently awaited" (St Ephrem, *Commentarii in Diatessaron*, 18, 15–17). In the Advent liturgy, the Church encourages us to keep our sense of watchfulness alive and vibrant.

"Of that day or that hour no one knows, not even the angels in heaven, nor the Son, but only the Father" (v. 32). Students of the Gospels have found it difficult to interpret this verse. It makes more sense in the context of Jesus' words in vv. 30–33. Apocalyptic texts typically give voice to new revelations about contemporary events and the future world or age (see v. 30). Speaking in

generation will not pass away before all these things take place. [31]Heaven and earth will pass away, but my words will not pass away.

The time of Christ's second coming

[32]"But of that day or that hour no one knows, not even the angels in heaven, nor the Son, but only the Father. [33]Take heed, watch and pray;[a] for you do not know when the time will come. [34]It is like a man going on a journey, when he leaves home and puts his servants in charge, each with his work, and commands the doorkeeper to be on the watch. [35]Watch therefore—for you do not know when the master of the house will come, in the evening, or at midnight, or at cockcrow, or in the morning—[36]lest he come suddenly and find you asleep. [37]And what I say to you I say to all: Watch."

Mt 24:36–44

Mt 25:13–15
Lk 19:12

Lk 12:38

10. PASSION, DEATH AND RESURRECTION OF JESUS*

Mt 26:3–5
Lk 22:1–2
Jn 1:45–57

The conspiracy against Jesus

14 [1]It was now two days before the Passover and the feast of Unleavened Bread. And the chief priests and the scribes were seeking how to arrest him by

mea non transibunt. [32]De die autem illo vel hora nemo scit, neque angeli in caelo neque Filius, nisi Pater. [33]Videte, vigilate; nescitis enim, quando tempus sit. [34]Sicut homo, qui peregre profectus reliquit domum suam et dedit servis suis potestatem, unicuique opus suum, ianitori quoque praecepit, ut vigilaret. [35]Vigilate ergo; nescitis enim quando dominus domus veniat, sero an media nocte an galli cantu an mane; [36]ne, cum venerit repente, inveniat vos dormientes. [37]Quod autem vobis dico, omnibus dico: Vigilate!». [14] [1]Erat autem Pascha et Azyma post biduum. Et quaere-

this context, Jesus is telling people not to pay heed to new revelations (v. 32): only his words have perennial value (v. 31), and those words can be expressed in one: "Watch" (v. 33). Read in this way, Jesus' words can be interpreted (as they are by some Fathers), not as meaning that Christ is ignorant as to when these things will take place, but simply as saying that it is not good for us to know the time (cf. the note on Mt 24:36–51); and they can also be interpreted as meaning that Jesus as man does not know the time of the final end: "When the disciples asked him about the day and hour of the end of all things, a natural question of the mortal body, he answered: not even the Son knows. As a man, not even he knew the day or the hour; and it is right and good that men should not know. But as the Word, as the One who is to come as Judge and Spouse, he knows the day and the hour. [...] As a man who hungered and felt thirst and suffered as all men do, he did not know; as God, the Word and Wisdom of the Father, there is nothing that he does not know" (St Athanasius, *Contra Arianos*, 3, 46).

*14:1—16:20 The last two chapters of St Mark are very tightly constructed. They show us the

roles played by the various actors in the drama of the passion—the Jewish authorities, determined to bring about Jesus' death, and the disciples, impotent witnesses who not only fail to see the significance of Christ's actions but abandon him at his time of greatest need. Throughout, the stateliness of Christ is plain to see: he knows what lies ahead, and he knows that it is all for the best. He takes the initiative at every juncture, voluntarily fulfilling Scripture (see 14:21, 27, 49) and letting the apostles know why these things are happening: he must die on the cross, but that death is only one stage on the road to his resurrection.

The saints frequently meditated on the story of the passion. To read these episodes is to live them and draw resolutions from them for our daily life: "May we imitate his Passion in our suffering, honour his blood with our blood, and climb up to his cross. If you are Simon of Cyrene, take up your cross and follow Christ. If you are crucified alongside him as a thief, put your trust in God as the good thief did. Christ was punished as an evildoer for you, on account of your sins, so that you would be made righteous. Worship the one who was crucified for you, and if you are

a Other ancient authorities omit *and pray*

stealth, and kill him; [2]for they said, "Not during the feast, lest there be a tumult of the people."

Mt 26:6–16
Lk 22:3–6
Jn 12:1–11

The anointing at Bethany and the treachery of Judas
[3]And while he was at Bethany in the house of Simon the leper, as he sat at table, a woman came with an alabaster jar of ointment of pure nard, very costly, and she broke the jar and poured it over his head. [4]But there were some who said to themselves indignantly, "Why was the ointment thus wasted? [5]For this ointment might have been sold for more than three hundred denarii,[b] and given to the poor." And they reproached her. [6]But Jesus said, "Let her alone; why do you trouble her? She

bant summi sacerdotes et scribae, quomodo eum dolo tenerent et occiderent; [2]dicebant enim: «Non in die festo, ne forte tumultus fieret populi». [3]Et cum esset Bethaniae in domo Simonis leprosi et recumberet, venit mulier habens alabastrum unguenti nardi puri pretiosi; fracto alabastro, effudit super caput eius. [4]Erant autem quidam indigne ferentes intra semetipsos: «Ut quid perditio ista unguenti facta est? [5]Poterat enim unguentum istud veniri plus quam trecentis denariis et dari pauperibus». Et fremebant in eam. [6]Iesus autem dixit: «Sinite eam; quid illi molesti estis?

crucified for your faults, turn your sin to good, winning salvation by your death. Enter into paradise with Jesus and see all the good things that you denied yourself. Meditate on the beauty of heaven, and see how the other thief, the blasphemer, is left outside for dead. If you are Joseph of Arimathea, claim the body of the Lord who was crucified and do penance for the sins of the whole world. If you are Nicodemus, who worshipped the Lord at night, come to bury him and anoint his body with oils and ointments. And if, at dawn, you are one of the two Marys, or Salome, or Joanna, try to be first to see the great stone rolled back, and you will see the angels too, and Jesus himself" (St Gregory Nazianzen, *In Sanctum Pascha*, 45, 23–24).

14:1–11 Almost from the beginning of the public ministry of Jesus, some scribes, chief priests and others sought "to destroy him" (3:6). Their determination increased in the days preceding the passion (11:18; 12:12). Now they try to arrest him "by stealth" (v. 1), and they find an ally in Judas, who has begun to look for an opportunity to betray Jesus (v. 11). We too should learn a lesson from this episode: "Today many people are horrified by Judas' crime—that he could be so cruel and so sacrilegious as to sell his Master and his God; and yet they fail to realize that when they for human reasons dismiss the rights of charity and truth, they are betraying God, who is charity and truth" (St Bede, *Homiliae*, 2, 43).

Between these two passages about betrayal comes the episode where Jesus is anointed by a woman in Bethany (vv. 3–9). The Gospel underlines two elements—the woman's generosity (v. 3) and the reactions of others. It was a custom at the time to honour distinguished guests by offering them perfumed water. This woman's refinement and generosity is interpreted by some as a waste of money (v. 4). Jesus himself gives the woman's gesture an interpretation that may be different from her own (v. 8). However, he says immediately that she has not made a mistake; the mistake lies with those who criticize her. In our relations with God, generosity is never out of place, whereas stinginess and calculation always are: "As he refuses to force our will, he takes what we give him but does not give himself wholly until he sees that we are giving ourselves wholly to him" (St Teresa of Avila, *Way of Perfection*, 48, 4).

"Wherever the Gospel is preached in the whole world, what she has done will be told in memory of her" (v. 9). The Gospel is the good news of all the wonderful things God has done through Jesus' words and works; and those wonderful things include the immortalizing of a little service done for Jesus: "Certainly we hear her story told in all the churches [...]. And yet hers was not an extraordinary deed, nor was she a distinguished person, nor was there a large audience, nor was the place one where she could easily be seen. She made no entrance onto a theatre stage to perform her service but did her good deed in a private house [...]. Nevertheless, today she is more illustrious than any king or queen; no passage of years has buried in oblivion this

b The denarius was a day's wage for a labourer

has done a beautiful thing to me. [7]For you always have the poor with you, and whenever you will, you can do good to them; but you will not always have me. [8]She has
done what she could; she has anointed my body beforehand for burying. [9]And truly,
I say to you, wherever the gospel is preached in the whole world, what she has done
will be told in memory of her."

[10]Then Judas Iscariot, who was one of the twelve, went to the chief priests in
order to betray him to them. [11]And when they heard it they were glad, and promised
to give him money. And he sought an opportunity to betray him."

Deut 15:11

Acts 3:6

Preparations for the Last Supper. Judas' treachery foretold

Mt 26:17–25
Lk 22:7–13
Jn 13:21–32

[12]And on the first day of Unleavened Bread, when they sacrificed the passover lamb,
his disciples said to him, "Where will you have us go and prepare for you to eat the
passover?" [13]And he sent two of his disciples, and said to them, "Go into the city,
and a man carrying a jar of water will meet you; follow him,* [14]and wherever he
enters, say to the householder, 'The Teacher says, Where is my guest room, where I
am to eat the passover with my disciples?' [15]And he will show you a large upper
room furnished and ready; there prepare for us." [16]And the disciples set out and went
to the city, and found it as he had told them; and they prepared the passover.

Mk 11:3

[17]And when it was evening he came with the twelve. [18]And as they were at table
eating, Jesus said, "Truly, I say to you, one of you will betray me, one who is eating
with me." [19]They began to be sorrowful, and to say to him one after another, "Is it
I?" [20]He said to them, "It is one of the twelve, one who is dipping bread in the same
dish with me. [21]For the Son of man goes as it is written of him, but woe to that man

Ps 41:9

Bonum opus operata est in me. [7]Semper enim pauperes habetis vobiscum et, cum volueritis, potestis illis bene facere; me autem non semper
habetis. [8]Quod habuit, operata est: praevenit ungere corpus meum in sepulturam. [9]Amen autem dico vobis: Ubicumque praedicatum fuerit evangelium in universo mundum, et, quod fecit haec, narrabitur in memoriam eius». [10]Et Iudas Iscarioth, unus de Duodecim, abiit ad summos sacerdotes, ut proderet eum illis. [11]Qui audientes gavisi sunt et promiserunt ei pecuniam se daturos. Et quaerebat quomodo illum opportune traderet.
[12]Et primo die Azymorum, quando Pascha immolabant, dicunt ei discipuli eius: «Quo vis eamus et paremus, ut manduces Pascha?». [13]Et mittit
duos ex discipulis suis et dicit eis: «Ite in civitatem, et occurret vobis homo lagoenam aquae baiulans; sequimini eum [14]et, quocumque introierit,
dicite domino domus: "Magister dicit: Ubi est refectio mea, ubi Pascha cum discipulis meis manducem?". [15]Et ipse vobis demonstrabit cenaculum grande stratum paratum; et illic parate nobis». [16]Et abierunt discipuli et venerunt in civitatem et invenerunt, sicut dixerat illis, et paraverunt
Pascha. [17]Et vespere facto venit cum Duodecim. [18]Et discumbentibus eis et manducantibus, ait Iesus: «Amen dico vobis: Unus ex vobis me tradet,
qui manducat mecum». [19]Coeperunt contristari et dicere ei singillatim: «Numquid ego?». [20]Qui ait illis: «Unus ex Duodecim, qui intingit mecum
in catino. [21]Nam Filius quidem hominis vadit, sicut scriptum est de eo. Vae autem homini illi, per quem Filius hominis traditur! Bonum est ei, si
non esset natus homo ille». [22]Et manducantibus illis, accepit panem et benedicens fregit et dedit eis et ait: «Sumite: hoc est corpus meum». [23]Et

service she performed" (St John Chrysostom,
Adversus Iudaeos, 5, 2).

14:12–21 Jesus' instructions for preparing for the
Passover (vv. 13–16) and, particularly, the
announcement of Judas' treachery as the fulfilment of a prophecy (vv. 18 and 21) show the
intersection of God's plans and the actions of
men. "Jesus' violent death was not the result of
chance in an unfortunate coincidence of circumstances, but is part of the mystery of God's plan,
as St Peter explains to the Jews of Jerusalem in
his first sermon on Pentecost: 'This Jesus [was]
delivered up according to the definite plan and
foreknowledge of God' (Acts 2:23). This biblical

language does not mean that those who handed
him over were merely passive players in a scenario written in advance by God" (*Catechism of
the Catholic Church*, 599). God's mysterious plan
does not do violence to that human freedom
which makes us responsible for our actions. "God
created all things and saw that they were good,
but whether people are good or bad depends on
the free decisions that each person makes. When
the Lord said, 'It would have been better for that
man if he had not been born' [Mk 14:21], he does
not lay a curse on what he himself created; he
curses the evil that has overcome the virtue of
free decision and the sins of the creature" (St John
Damascene, *De fide orthodoxa*, 4, 21).

by whom the Son of man is betrayed! It would have been better for that man if he
had not been born."

Mt 26:26–29
Lk 22:14–20
1 Cor 11:23–26
The institution of the Eucharist

²²And as they were eating, he took bread, and blessed, and broke it, and gave it to
them, and said, "Take; this is my body." ²³And he took a cup, and when he had given
Ex 24:8
Zech 9:11
thanks he gave it to them, and they all drank of it. ²⁴And he said to them, "This is my
blood of the^c covenant, which is poured out for many. ²⁵Truly, I say to you, I shall
not drink again of the fruit of the vine until that day when I drink it new in the kingdom of God."

Mt 26:30–35
Lk 22:31–34
Jn 13:36–38
The disciples will desert Jesus

Mt 26:30–35
Lk 22:39
Zech 13:7
²⁶And when they had sung a hymn, they went out to the Mount of Olives. ²⁷And
Jesus said to them, "You will all fall away; for it is written, 'I will strike the shep-

accepto calice, gratias agens dedit eis, et biberunt ex illo omnes. ²⁴Et ait illis: «Hic est sanguis meus novi testamenti, qui pro multis effunditur.
²⁵Amen dico vobis: Iam non bibam de genimine vitis usque in diem illum, cum illud bibam novum in regno Dei». ²⁶Et hymno dicto, exierunt in
montem Olivarum. ²⁷Et ait eis Iesus: «Omnes scandalizabimini, quia scriptum est: *"Percutiam pastorem, et dispergentur oves"*. ²⁸Sed posteaquam

14:22–25 St Mark's account of the institution of
the Eucharist is more matter-of-fact than those of
the other Synoptics (see Mt 26:26–29; Lk 22:14
–20 and notes). Still, in the light of Jesus' death
and resurrection, the sacrificial meaning of his
words and gestures must have been clear to the
apostles: "Christ's death is both the Paschal sacrifice that accomplishes the definitive redemption of men, through 'the Lamb of God, who
takes away the sin of the world' (Jn 1:29), and
the sacrifice of the New Covenant, which
restores man to communion with God by reconciling him to God through the 'blood of the
covenant, which was poured out for many for the
forgiveness of sins' (Mt 26:28)" (*Catechism of
the Catholic Church*, 613). This sacrifice is,
strictly speaking, the sacrifice of the cross, in
which Christ is at one and the same time Priest
and Victim. At the Last Supper, Jesus anticipates
that sacrifice in an unbloody manner, offering a
victim soon to be immolated; and in the Mass
the sacrifice is renewed, also in an unbloody
manner, with Christ offering himself as the
victim who has already been immolated on the
cross. The Council of Trent defined this truth as
follows: "If anyone says that in the Mass a true
and proper sacrifice is not offered to God, or that
the sacrifical offering consists merely in the fact
that Christ is given us to eat, let him be anathema" (*De SS. Missae sacrificio,* canon 1).

Our Lord's words here cannot rightly be
interpreted only in a symbolic or metaphorical
way; the Church has always read them as being
entirely realistic: "This is my body. That is to
say, what I am giving you now and what you are
taking is my body. For the bread is not only a
symbol of the body of Christ; it becomes his
very body, as the Lord has said: the bread which
I shall give for the life of the world is my flesh.
Therefore, the Lord conserves the appearances
of bread and wine but changes the bread and
wine into the reality of his flesh and his blood"
(Theophylact, *Enarratio in Evangelium Marci*,
ad loc.).

14:26–31 At the Passover meal Jews chant a collection of prayers known as the Hallel, which
includes Psalms 113–118; the last part of the
Hallel is sung at the end of the meal. After this
point, Jesus tells his disciples that they are going
to abandon him, but he comforts them with the
promise of his resurrection and a new beginning
in Galilee. The evangelist records the apostles'
protest (v. 31), particularly that of Peter (vv. 29
and 31). Over the course of his account, Mark
will note the fulfilment of this prophecy—the
apostles' flight (14:50), Peter's denial (14:66–72)
and the new calling and mission of the apostles
in Galilee (16:7).

Mark is the only evangelist to mention that

c Other ancient authorities insert *new*

herd, and the sheep will be scattered.' [28]But after I am raised up, I will go before you to Galilee." [29]Peter said to him, "Even though they all fall away, I will not." [30]And Jesus said to him, "Truly, I say to you, this very night, before the cock crows twice, you will deny me three times." [31]But he said vehemently, "If I must die with you, I will not deny you." And they all said the same.

Mk 16:7

Jn 13:36–38

Jesus' prayer and agony in the garden

[32]And they went to a place which was called Gethsemane; and he said to his disciples, "Sit here, while I pray." [33]And he took with him Peter and James and John, and began to be greatly distressed and troubled. [34]And he said to them, "My soul is very

Mt 26:36–46
Lk 22:39–46

Jn 18:1

Jn 12:27
Mk 5:37; 9:2

resurrexero, praecedam vos in Galilaeam». [29]Petrus autem ait ei: «Et si omnes scandalizati fuerint, sed non ego». [30]Et ait illi Iesus: «Amen dico tibi: Tu hodie, in nocte hac, priusquam bis gallus vocem dederit, ter me es negaturus». [31]At ille amplius loquebatur: «Et si oportuerit me commori tibi, non te negabo». Similiter autem et omnes dicebant. [32]Et veniunt in praedium, cui nomen Gethsemani, et ait discipulis suis: «Sedete hic, donec orem». [33]Et assumit Petrum et Iacobum et Ioannem secum et coepit pavere et taedere [34]et ait illis: «Tristis est anima mea usque ad mortem;

the cock crow in question was the second one, and that Peter had vehemently said he would not betray Jesus. This is a further sign that the Gospel according to Mark had a special connexion with Peter's preaching, and it is evidence of that apostle's humility: "Mark gives the most detailed account of Peter's weakness and terrible fear. Mark, who was a disciple of Peter's, learned all these details from Peter himself. We should marvel at the fact that he does not gloss over his master's weakness, but portrays it in a clearer light than any of the other evangelists" (St John Chrysostom, *In Matthaeum*, 85, 1).

14:32–42 In the solitude of the garden of Gethsemane Jesus' apprehension at what is about to happen becomes more acute. The evangelist tells us that Jesus "began to be greatly distressed and troubled" (v. 33), and that the three disciples could not stop themselves from falling asleep (vv. 37, 40–41). But Jesus steels his resolve and prays deeply. Mark records his filial appeal to God (v. 36): "Filial trust is tested—it proves itself—in tribulation. The principal difficulty concerns the prayer of petition, for oneself or for others in intercession" (*Catechism of the Catholic Church*, 2734). Jesus prays and asks his disciples to pray: prayer is indispensable for conquering temptation and staying faithful to God: "If our Lord had said only *watch*, we might expect that our own power would be sufficient, but when he adds *pray*, he shows that *if he keeps not* our souls in time of temptation, in vain shall they watch who keep them [cf. Ps 127:1]" (St

Francis de Sales, *Treatise on the Love of God*, 11, 1).

We, too, as the saints have done, can learn of Jesus' feelings by meditating on this text: "For a huge mass of troubles took possession of the tender and gentle body of our most holy Saviour. He knew that his ordeal was now imminent and just about to overtake him: the treacherous betrayer, the bitter enemies, binding ropes, false accusations, slanders, blows, thorns, nails, the cross, and horrible tortures stretched out over many hours. Over and above these, he was tormented by the thought of his disciples' terror, the loss of the Jews, even the destruction of the very man who so disloyally betrayed him, and finally the ineffable grief of his beloved Mother. The gathered storm of all these evils rushed into his most gentle heart and flooded it like the ocean sweeping through broken dikes" (St Thomas More, *The Sadness of Christ*, ad loc.).

However, it is not only Christ whom we should contemplate; we should look around us. Today, just as the apostles did then, we too can abandon Christ, to abuse by others: "See now, when Christ comes back to his apostles for the third time, there they are, buried in sleep, though he commanded them to bear up with him and to stay awake and pray because of the impending danger; but Judas the traitor at the same time was so wide awake and intent on betraying the Lord that the very idea of sleep never entered his mind. [...] For very many are sleepy and apathetic in sowing virtues among the people and maintaining the truth, while the enemies of

sorrowful, even to death; remain here, and watch."[d] [35]And going a little farther, he fell on the ground and prayed that, if it were possible, the hour might pass from him.

Gal 4:6

[36]And he said, "Abba, Father, all things are possible to thee; remove this cup from me; yet not what I will, but what thou wilt." [37]And he came and found them sleeping, and he said to Peter, "Simon, are you asleep? Could you not watch[d] one hour?

Rom 7:5

[38]Watch[d] and pray that you may not enter into temptation; the spirit indeed is willing, but the flesh is weak." [39]And again he went away and prayed, saying the same

Mk 9:6

words. [40]And again he came and found them sleeping, for their eyes were very heavy; and they did not know what to answer him. [41]And he came a third time, and said to them, "Are you still sleeping and taking your rest? It is enough; the hour has

Jn 14:31

come; the Son of man is betrayed into the hands of sinners. [42]Rise, let us be going; see, my betrayer is at hand."

Mt 26:47–56
Lk 22:47–53
Jn 18:1–12

Arrest of Jesus

[43]And immediately, while he was still speaking, Judas came, one of the twelve, and with him a crowd with swords and clubs, from the chief priests and the scribes and the elders. [44]Now the betrayer had given them a sign, saying, "The one I shall kiss is the man; seize him and lead him away safely." [45]And when he came, he went up to him at once, and said, "Master!"[e] And he kissed him. [46]And they laid hands on him and seized him. [47]But one of those who stood by drew his sword, and struck the slave of the high priest and cut off his ear. [48]And Jesus said to them, "Have you come out as against a robber, with swords and clubs to capture me? [49]Day after day I was with you in the temple teaching, and you did not seize me. But let the scrip-

Jn 16:32

tures be fulfilled." [50]And they all forsook him, and fled.

[51]And a young man followed him, with nothing but a linen cloth about his body; and they seized him, [52]but he left the linen cloth and ran away naked.*

---

sustinete hic et vigilate». [35]Et cum processisset paululum, procidebat super terram et orabat, ut, si fieri posset, transiret ab eo hora, [36]et dicebat: «Abba, Pater! Omnia tibi possibilia sunt. Transfer calicem hunc a me; sed non quod ego volo, sed quod tu». [37]Et venit et invenit eos dormientes et ait Petro: «Simon, dormis? Non potuisti una hora vigilare? [38]Vigilate et orate, ut non intretis in tentationem; spiritus quidem promptus, caro vero infirma». [39]Et iterum abiens oravit, eundem sermonem dicens. [40]Et veniens denuo invenit eos dormientes; erant enim oculi illorum ingravati, et ignorabant quid responderent ei. [41]Et venit tertio et ait illis: «Dormite iam et requiescite? Sufficit, venit hora: ecce traditur Filius hominis in manus peccatorum. [42]Surgite, eamus; ecce, qui me tradit, prope est». [43]Et confestim, adhuc eo loquente, venit Iudas unus ex Duodecim, et cum illo turba cum gladiis et lignis a summis sacerdotibus et scribis et senioribus. [44]Dederat autem traditor eius signum eis dicens: «Quemcumque osculatus fuero, ipse est; tenete eum et ducite caute». [45]Et cum venisset, statim accedens ad eum ait: «Rabbi», et osculatus est eum. [46]At illi manus iniecerunt in eum et tenuerunt eum. [47]Unus autem quidam de circumstantibus educens gladium percussit servum summi sacerdotis et amputavit illi auriculam. [48]Et respondens Iesus ait illis: «Tamquam ad latronem existis cum gladiis et lignis comprehendere me? [49]Cotidie eram apud vos in templo docens et non me tenuistis; sed adimpleantur Scripturae». [50]Et relinquentes eum omnes fugerunt. [51]Et adulescens quidam sequebatur eum amictus sindone super nudo, et tenent eum; [52]at ille, reiecta sindone, nudus profugit. [53]Et adduxerunt Iesum ad summum sacerdotem, et conveni-

---

Christ, in order to sow vices and uproot the faith [...], are wide awake" (ibid.).

14:43–52 This sober account of the arrest seems to indicate that Jesus expects it and offers no resistance. He sees beyond Judas' betrayal and the underhanded way he is arrested under cover of darkness; it is all a fulfilment of the Scriptures (cf. Is 52:13—53:12; Ps 41:9). St Mark is the only evangelist to mention the young man who runs away naked—something that many interpret as a discreet allusion to Mark himself. In any case, it

surely seems to be an instance of someone failing to follow Christ (as Peter, also, will be doing very soon). Christ's way, we need to remember, is the way that Christians must take: "Do not forget that being with Jesus means we shall most certainly come upon his Cross. When we abandon ourselves into God's hands, he frequently permits us to taste sorrow, loneliness, opposition, slander, defamation, ridicule, coming both from within and from outside. This is because he wants to mould us into his own image and likeness" (St Josemaría Escrivá, *Friends of God*, 301).

---

d Or *keep awake* e Or *Rabbi*

Jesus before the chief priests

Mt 26:57–68
Lk 22:66–71
Jn 18:13–24
Lk 22:54

⁵³And they led Jesus to the high priest; and all the chief priests and the elders and the scribes were assembled. ⁵⁴And Peter had followed him at a distance, right into the courtyard of the high priest; and he was sitting with the guards, and warming himself at the fire. ⁵⁵Now the chief priests and the whole council sought testimony against Jesus to put him to death, but they found none. ⁵⁶For many bore false witness against him, and their witness did not agree. ⁵⁷And some stood up and bore false witness against him saying, ⁵⁸"We heard him say, 'I will destroy this temple that is made with hands, and in three days I will build another, not made with hands.'" ⁵⁹Yet not even so did their testimony agree. ⁶⁰And the high priest stood up in the midst, and asked Jesus, "Have you no answer to make? What is it that these men testify against you?" ⁶¹But he was silent and made no answer. Again the high priest asked him, "Are you the Christ, the Son of the Blessed?" ⁶²And Jesus said, "I am;

Jn 2:19
Heb 9:11

Mk 15:5
Is 53:7
Dan 7:13
Ps 110:1

unt omnes summi sacerdotes et seniores et scribae. ⁵⁴Et Petrus a longe secutus est eum usque intro in atrium summi sacerdotis et sedebat cum ministris et calefaciebat se ad ignem. ⁵⁵Summi vero sacerdotes et omne concilium quaerebant adversus Iesum testimonium, ut eum morte afficerent, nec inveniebant. ⁵⁶Multi enim testimonium falsum dicebant adversus eum, et convenientia testimonia non erant. ⁵⁷Et quidam surgentes falsum testimonium ferebant adversus eum dicentes: ⁵⁸«Nos audivimus eum dicentem: "Ego dissolvam templum hoc manu factum et intra triduum aliud non manu factum aedificabo"». ⁵⁹Et ne ita quidem conveniens erat testimonium illorum. ⁶⁰Et exsurgens summus sacerdos in medium interrogavit Iesum dicens: «Non respondes quidquam ad ea, quae isti testantur adversum te?». ⁶¹Ille autem tacebat et nihil respondit. Rursum summus sacerdos interrogabat eum et dicit ei: «Tu es Christus filius Benedicti?». ⁶²Iesus autem dixit: «Ego sum, et *videbitis Filium hominis a dextris sedentem Virtutis et venientem cum nubibus caeli*». ⁶³Summus autem sacerdos scindens vestimenta sua ait: «Quid adhuc necessarii sunt nobis testes?»

14:53–72 This is a key episode in the second Gospel. The rulers of the people charge Jesus with having prophesied the destruction of the temple and its replacement with another (v. 58). Although the charge is baseless (see v. 57), their condemnation of Jesus to death will lead to the sacrifice of the cross and, therefore, true worship in a new temple: "Far from having been hostile to the Temple, where he gave the essential part of his teaching, Jesus was willing to pay the Temple-tax, associating with him Peter, whom he had just made the foundation of his future Church. He even identified himself with the Temple by presenting himself as God's definitive dwelling-place among men. Therefore his being put to bodily death presaged the destruction of the Temple, which would manifest the dawning of a new age in the history of salvation: 'The hour is coming when neither on this mountain nor in Jerusalem will you worship the Father' (Jn 4:21)" (*Catechism of the Catholic Church*, 586).

The episode reaches its climax in vv. 61–62. Jesus has made no reply to the absurd charges, but when the high priest asks him outright whether he is the Messiah, he openly confesses that he is—and, not only that, but the transcendent Messiah seen by Daniel (Dan 7:13–14). In fact, the words he uses to answer Caiaphas ("I

am") may have a deeper meaning, because "I am" is the translation of *Yhwh*, the proper name of God (see Ex 3:14).

The text then reports in detail the denials made by Peter (vv. 66–72). The tradition that sees the apostle's memory as the basis of Mark's Gospel is well supported by this passage. The opening verses (vv. 53–54) show us the two personalities—Jesus and Peter. Then the evangelist contrasts them: Jesus is being falsely accused, but he tells the truth and on that account he is condemned to death by the high priest and mocked by the servants (vv. 55–65); Peter, on the other hand, is taunted with being a follower of Jesus (which he is), but he denies the Master by telling lies and he escapes retribution (vv. 66–72). Clearly, Peter's greatness derives not from his bravery but from his contrition (v. 72; cf. Jn 21:15–19). "He wept bitter tears because he knew how to love, and the sweet caresses of love soon replaced the bitter pangs of sorrow" (St Augustine, *Sermones*, 295, 3). In describing his failings, St Mark reminds us that Peter the sinner was also the first to experience the saving grace of Jesus Christ. "God permitted the one he had chosen to lead the Church to be filled with fear at the words of a maid-servant and to deny Him. We know that this event forms part of provi-

and you will see the Son of man sitting at the right hand of Power, and coming with the clouds of heaven." [63] And the high priest tore his mantle, and said, "Why do we still need witnesses? [64] You have heard his blasphemy. What is your decision?" And they all condemned him as deserving death. [65] And some began to spit on him, and to cover his face, and to strike him, saying to him, "Prophesy!" And the guards received him with blows.

Jn 19:7

Mt 26:69–75
Lk 22:54–62
Jn 18:15–
18, 25–27

Peter's denial

Mt 2:23

[66] And as Peter was below in the courtyard, one of the maids of the high priest came; [67] and seeing Peter warming himself, she looked at him, and said, "You also were with the Nazarene, Jesus." [68] But he denied it, saying, "I neither know nor understand what you mean." And he went out into the gateway.[f] [69] And the maid saw him, and began again to say to the bystanders, "This man is one of them." [70] But again he denied it. And after a little while the bystanders said to Peter, "Certainly you are one of them; for you are a Galilean." [71] But he began to invoke a curse on himself and to swear, "I do not know this man of whom you speak." [72] And immediately the cock crowed a second time. And Peter remembered how Jesus had said to him, "Before the cock crows twice, you will deny me three times." And he broke down and wept.

Mk 14:30

Mt 27:11–26
Lk 23:1–25
Jn 18:28–19:16

Jesus before Pilate

Mt 27:1–2

15 [1] And as soon as it was morning the chief priests, with the elders and scribes, and the whole council held a consultation; and they bound Jesus and led him

[64] Audistis blasphemiam. Quid vobis videtur?». Qui omnes condemnaverunt eum esse reum mortis. [65] Et coeperunt quidam conspuere eum et velare faciem eius et colaphis eum caedere et dicere ei: «Prophetiza»; et ministri alapis eum caedebant. [66] Et cum esset Petrus in atrio deorsum, venit una ex ancillis summi sacerdotis [67] et, cum vidisset Petrum calefacientem se, aspiciens illum ait: «Et tu cum hoc Nazareno, Iesu, eras!». [68] At ille negavit dicens: «Neque scio neque novi quid tu dicas!». Et exiit foras ante atrium, et gallus cantavit. [69] Et ancilla, cum vidisset illum, rursus coepit dicere circumstantibus: «Hic ex illis est!». [70] At ille iterum negabat. Et post pusillum rursus, qui astabant, dicebant Petro: «Vere ex illis es, nam et Galilaeus es». [71] Ille autem coepit anathematizare et iurare: «Nescio hominem istum, quem dicitis!». [72] Et statim iterum gallus cantavit; et recordatus est Petrus verbi, sicut dixerat ei Iesus: «Priusquam gallus cantet bis, ter me negabis». Et coepit flere. [15] [1] Et confestim mane consilium facientes summi sacerdotes cum senioribus et scribis, id est universum concilium, vincientes Iesum duxerunt et tradiderunt Pilato. [2] Et interrogavit

dence: the pastor of the whole Church learns through his own weakness and failure how to feel pity and understanding for the sins of others. Thus, Peter first came to know himself as he was, so that afterwards he would know how to deal mercifully with the weakness and failings of others" (St Gregory the Great, *Homiliae in Evangelia*, 2, 21, 4).

15:1–15 The trial and death of Jesus must have been a shock for everyone—for the disciples, for the crowd, etc. How could this possibly have happened? St Mark gives a very matter-of-fact account of events, taking us through the roles played by the various participants: the Jewish authorities hand Jesus over (v. 1) out of envy (v. 10), wanting him executed even at the cost of having a murderer released (vv. 6–7); the crowd are simply a mouthpiece for groundless rage that

condemns a man to a violent death for no good reason (vv. 13–14); and then the indolent governor, Pilate, who has some regard for Jesus (v. 5) and seems to want to save him (v. 9), condemns him for the worst of reasons—to please the crowd (v. 15). When narrating these events and Jesus' attitude towards them, the evangelist identifies the real reason why things have gone this way: the death of Jesus is a consequence of man's sin, and Jesus accepts his death out of love for man, to atone for sin: "Jesus goes willingly to the Passion that had been foretold of him and which he himself had announced to his disciples. [...] He made no answer to the charges laid against him. Unlike on other occasions, when he escaped from the clutches of his enemies, although he could have gone into hiding, he did not. [...] He bore with patience the blows of the servants. He was beaten, spat upon, jeered at,

f Or *fore-court*. Other ancient authorities add *and the cock crowed*

away and delivered him to Pilate.* ²And Pilate asked him, "Are you the King of the Jews?" And he answered him, "You have said so." ³And the chief priests accused him of many things. ⁴And Pilate again asked him, "Have you no answer to make? See how many charges they bring against you." ⁵But Jesus made no further answer, so that Pilate wondered.

Mk 14:61
Is 53:7

⁶Now at the feast he used to release for them one prisoner whom they asked. ⁷And among the rebels in prison, who had committed murder in the insurrection, there was a man called Barabbas. ⁸And the crowd came up and began to ask Pilate to do as he was wont to do for them. ⁹And he answered them, "Do you want me to release for you the King of the Jews?" ¹⁰For he perceived that it was out of envy that the chief priests had delivered him up. ¹¹But the chief priests stirred up the crowd to have him release for them Barabbas instead. ¹²And Pilate again said to them, "Then what shall I do with the man whom you call the King of the Jews?" ¹³And they cried out again, "Crucify him." ¹⁴And Pilate said to them, "Why, what evil has he done?" But they shouted all the more, "Crucify him." ¹⁵So Pilate, wishing to satisfy the crowd, released for them Barabbas; and having scourged Jesus, he delivered him to be crucified.

Acts 3:13

The crowning with thorns

Mt 27:27–31
Jn 19:1–3

¹⁶And the soldiers led him away inside the palace (that is, the praetorium); and they called together the whole battalion. ¹⁷And they clothed him in a purple cloak, and

eum Pilatus: «Tu es rex Iudaeorum?». At ille respondens ait illi: «Tu dicis». ³Et accusabant eum summi sacerdotes in multis. ⁴Pilatus autem rursum interrogabat eum dicens: «Non respondes quidquam? Vide in quantis te accusant». ⁵Iesus autem amplius nihil respondit, ita ut miraretur Pilatus. ⁶Per diem autem festum dimittere solebat illis unum ex vinctis, quem peterent. ⁷Erat autem qui dicebatur Barabbas, vinctus cum seditiosis, qui in seditione fecerant homicidium. ⁸Et cum ascendisset turba, coepit rogare, sicut faciebat illis. ⁹Pilatus autem respondit eis et dixit: «Vultis dimittam vobis regem Iudaeorum?». ¹⁰Sciebat enim quod per invidiam tradidissent eum summi sacerdotes. ¹¹Pontifices autem concitaverunt turbam, ut magis Barabbam dimitteret eis. ¹²Pilatus autem iterum respondens aiebat illis: «Quid ergo vultis faciam regi Iudaeorum?». ¹³At illi iterum clamaverunt: «Crucifige eum!». ¹⁴Pilatus vero dicebat eis: «Quid enim mali fecit?». At illi magis clamaverunt: «Crucifige eum!». ¹⁵Pilatus autem, volens populo satisfacere, dimisit illis Barabbam et tradidit Iesum flagellis caesum, ut crucifigeretur. ¹⁶Milites autem duxerunt eum intro in atrium,

tortured, scourged and crucified. [...] By means of his suffering, he won salvation for us. All those who have fallen into the slavery of sin should suffer for the evil they have done; but he, free from all sin, who walked the path of righteousness to the end, suffered the torture of sinners and undid the ancient curse of evil on the cross" (Theodoret of Cyrrhus, *De incarnatione Domini*, 26).

Pilate "released for them Barabbas; and having scourged Jesus, he delivered him to be crucified" (v. 15): a very concise account of what occurred. In these words, with St Augustine, we can see the paradox involved in the condemnation of Christ: "The thief was set free; Christ was condemned to death. The criminal was pardoned; the one who pardons all those who confess their sins was condemned" (*In Ioannis Evangelium*, 31, 11). The Greek word translated here as "delivered" appears in all four Gospels

(cf. Mt 27:26; Lk 23:24–25; Jn 19:16); it appears (in one form or another) several times in St Mark (9:31; 10:33; 13:9), and is found throughout the New Testament and in later Christian teaching (cf. the note on 14:12–21). Though it seems that it is a man (Pilate) who delivers Jesus to death, in fact it is God who hands him over, for our salvation: "You loved us, Lord, and handed over your only, beloved Son for our salvation. He accepted and obeyed your will without complaint. Moreover, since he offered himself as the sacrifice, he went like an innocent lamb to the slaughter. Being God, he became man and submitted his will to you and was obedient unto you, God, his Father: he was 'obedient unto death, death on a cross'" (St John Damascene, *De fide orthodoxa*, 50).

15:16–20 After recounting how Jesus was rejected by Jews—by the chief priests (see

plaiting a crown of thorns they put it on him. [18]And they began to salute him, "Hail, King of the Jews!" [19]And they struck his head with a reed, and spat upon him, and they knelt down in homage to him. [20]And when they had mocked him, they stripped him of the purple cloak, and put his own clothes on him. And they led him out to crucify him.

Mt 27:32–56
Lk 23:26–49
Jn 19:17–30

The crucifixion and death of Jesus

[21]And they compelled a passer-by, Simon of Cyrene, who was coming in from the country, the father of Alexander and Rufus, to carry his cross. [22]And they brought

Ps 69:21

Ps 22:18

him to the place called Golgotha (which means the place of a skull). [23]And they offered him wine mingled with myrrh; but he did not take it. [24]And they crucified him, and divided his garments among them, casting lots for them, to decide what

quod est praetorium, et convocant totam cohortem. [17]Et induunt eum purpuram et imponunt ei plectentes spineam coronam, [18]et coeperunt salutare eum: «Ave, rex Iudaeorum!», [19]et percutiebant caput eius arundine et conspuebant eum et ponentes genua adorabant eum. [20]Et postquam illuserunt ei, exuerunt illum purpuram et induerunt eum vestimentis suis. Et educunt illum, ut crucifigerent eum. [21]Et angariant praetereuntem quempiam Simonem Cyrenaeum venientem de villa, patrem Alexandri et Rufi, ut tolleret crucem eius. [22]Et perducunt illum in Golgotha locum, quod est interpretatum Calvariae locus. [23]Et dabant ei myrrhatum vinum, ille autem non accepit. [24]Et crucifigunt eum et *dividunt vestimenta* eius, *mittentes*

14:64) and the crowd they incited (see 15:11–15)—the evangelist now describes how he was rejected by Gentile soldiers (cf. the note on Mt 27:27–31). Despite the sobriety of the narrative, the evangelist does register the mockery Jesus received in the high priest's palace (14:65), the scourging ordered by Pilate (15:15), and now the jeers of the soldiers, who render him mock homage. St Jerome comments that "the shame he endured has cleansed us of ours, the ropes which bound him have set us free, his crown of thorns has granted us the crown of the Kingdom, by his wounds we have been healed" (in *Catena aurea*, ad loc.).

The soldiers mock Jesus' kingship, yet without realizing it, they acknowledge him for what he is—a king. "When they dressed him in a purple robe to mock him, they acknowledged him for who he is: he is the King. And though they did so to mock him, they dressed him in the symbols of royalty. They crowned him with thorns, but still it was a crown; and he was crowned by soldiers, as a king is acclaimed by soldiers" (St Cyril of Jerusalem, *Homilia in paralyticum*, 12).

15:21–41 Crucifixion was a particularly painful form of punishment. Cicero calls it "the most cruel and terrible death" (*Pro Rabirio*, 5, 16). However, the evangelists refrain from that sort of comment: they are more interested in the fact of

the crucifixion and in its consequences for salvation. Mark's narrative specifies the various stages: at the third hour, that is, between nine o'clock and noon, Jesus was raised on the cross (v. 25); at the sixth hour, between noon and three, the whole land was covered in darkness (v. 33); and at the ninth hour, between three and six in the afternoon, Jesus died (v. 34). Mark also gives other pieces of information, such as the reference to the sons of Simon the Cyrene, whom the readers of the Gospel would have known (see Rom 16:3). However, the key to understanding the whole event is provided by our Lord on the cross when he says, "Elo-i, Elo-i, lama sabach-thani," the opening words of Psalm 22. That psalm is a very emotional prayer of a righteous man who undergoes persecution, but who will triumph in the end: through his sufferings the Lord will be praised in all the earth (Ps 22:29) and deliverance is assured to a people yet unborn (Ps 22:31). Among the offences suffered by the persecuted man of the psalm and by Jesus are: mockery by the people (Ps 22:7; v. 29), jeering because he calls on God (Ps 22:8; vv. 31–32, 36), and the dividing up of his garments (Ps 22:18; v. 24), etc. But Christ has triumphed. Mark sees proof of this in two events that occur after his death—the rending of the temple curtain (v. 38), which symbolizes the removal of barriers between the People of God and the Gentiles (cf. Ps 22:26); and a Gentile's

each should take. [25]And it was the third hour, when they crucified him. [26]And the inscription of the charge against him read, "The King of the Jews." [27]And with him they crucified two robbers, one on his right and one on his left.[g] [29]And those who passed by derided him, wagging their heads, and saying, "Aha! You who would destroy the temple and build it in three days, [30]save yourself, and come down from the cross!" [31]So also the chief priests mocked him to one another with the scribes, saying, "He saved others; he cannot save himself. [32]Let the Christ, the King of Israel, come down now from the cross, that we may see and believe." Those who were crucified with him also reviled him.

[33]And when the sixth hour had come, there was darkness over the whole land[h] until the ninth hour. [34]And at the ninth hour Jesus cried out with a loud voice, "Elo-i, Elo-i, lama sabach-thani?" which means, "My God, my God, why hast thou forsaken me?" [35]And some of the bystanders hearing it said, "Behold, he is calling Elijah." [36]And one ran and, filling a sponge full of vinegar, put it on a reed and gave it to him to drink, saying, "Wait, let us see whether Elijah will come to take him down." [37]And Jesus uttered a loud cry, and breathed his last. [38]And the curtain of the temple was torn in two, from top to bottom. [39]And when the centurion, who stood facing him, saw that he thus[i] breathed his last, he said, "Truly this man was the Son[x] of God!"

Margin references: Ps 22:7; 109:25 / Mk 14:58 / Ps 22:8 / Mt 16:1, 4 / Amos 8:9 / Ps 22:1 / Ps 69:21 / Mt 4:3

sortem super eis quis quid tolleret. [25]Erat autem hora tertia, et crucifixerunt eum. [26]Et erat titulus causae eius inscriptus: «Rex Iudaeorum». [27]Et cum eo crucifigunt duos latrones, unum a dextris et alium a sinistris eius. [29]Et praetereuntes blasphemabant eum *moventes capita* sua et dicentes: «Vah, qui destruit templum et in tribus diebus aedificat; [30]salvum fac temetipsum descendens de cruce!». [31]Similiter et summi sacerdotes ludentes ad alterutrum cum scribis dicebant: «Alios salvos fecit, seipsum non potest salvum facere. [32]Christus rex Israel descendat nunc de cruce, ut videamus et credamus». Etiam qui cum eo crucifixi erant, conviciabantur ei. [33]Et, facta hora sexta, tenebrae factae sunt per totam terram usque in horam nonam. [34]Et hora nona exclamavit Iesus voce magna: *«Heloi, Heloi, lema sabacthani?»*, quod est interpretatum: *«Deus meus, Deus meus, ut quid dereliquisti me?»*. [35]Et quidam de circumstantibus audientes dicebant: «Ecce Eliam vocat». [36]Currens autem unus et implens spongiam *aceto* circumponensque calamo *potum dabat* ei dicens: «Sinite, videamus, si veniat Elias ad deponendum eum». [37]Iesus autem, emissa voce magna, exspiravit. [38]Et velum templi scissum est in duo a sursum usque deorsum. [39]Videns autem centurio, qui ex adverso stabat, quia sic clamans exspirasset,

acknowledgment of Jesus' divinity (v. 39), which is a sign that all nations can now worship the Lord (cf. Ps 22:27–29). All this helps us understand the paradox that Jesus had tried to explain to his disciples: he is the Messiah and the Son of God (see 1:1), but his victory is closely linked to the cross. "O what marvellous power of the cross! What ineffable glory of the Passion! In them we can see the trial of the Lord, the judgment of the world, and the power of the Crucified Christ. [...] For your cross is the fountain of all blessings and the origin of all graces: in it believers find strength in their weakness, glory in shame, life in death itself" (St Leo the Great, *Sermo 8 de Passione Domini*, 7).

As he does at virtually every stage in the passion account, the evangelist contrasts the attitudes of the various people who encounter Jesus: passers-by insult him (v. 29), the chief priests and scribes mock him (v. 31), the two criminals on either side of him also revile him (v. 32), and even a gesture (perhaps a compassionate one) is

turned into a grotesque challenge (v. 36). Very different from all this is the centurion's tribute, when he acknowledges Jesus to be the Son of God (v. 39). But it is the women, above all, who deserve credit: earlier they had ministered to Christ (v. 41), and now, crushed and powerless, they witness the death of the One they love (v. 40). It is no surprise that Christian writers should focus on these women when they re-live this event. St Augustine, for example, clearly has them in mind when he says: "Look at the beauty of the one who loves you; meditate on the One who is equal to the Father and submits to the will of the Mother: the emperor of heaven who came to work as a servant here on earth, the creator of all things living as a creature among them. Look at how beautiful is that which the proud of heart mock as a delusion: in the light of your soul, contemplate the wounds of the one who was crucified, the blood he spilled as he died, the price of faith and the ransom of our redemption. Consider the value of all these things; weigh them on

g Other ancient authorities insert verse 28, *And the scripture was fulfilled which says, "He was reckoned with the transgressors"* h Or *earth* i Other ancient authorities insert *cried out and* x Or *a son*

Lk 8:2–3   **40**There were also women looking on from afar, among whom were Mary Magdalene, and Mary the mother of James the younger* and of Joses, and Salome,
41who, when he was in Galilee, followed him, and ministered to him; and also many
other women who came up with him to Jerusalem.

Mt 27:57–66
Lk 23:50–56
Jn 19:31–42

The burial of Jesus

42And when evening had come, since it was the day of Preparation, that is, the day
before the sabbath, **43**Joseph of Arimathea, a respected member of the council, who
was also himself looking for the kingdom of God, took courage and went to Pilate,

ait: «Vere homo hic Filius Dei erat». **40**Erant autem et mulieres de longe aspicientes, inter quas et Maria Magdalene et Maria Iacobi minoris et
Iosetis mater et Salome, **41**quae, cum esset in Galilaea, sequebantur eum et ministrabant ei, et aliae multae, quae simul cum eo ascenderant
Hierosolymam. **42**Et cum iam sero esset factum, quia erat Parasceve, quod est ante sabbatum, **43**venit Ioseph ab Arimathaea nobilis decurio, qui et
ipse erat exspectans regnum Dei, et audacter introivit ad Pilatum et petiit corpus Iesu. **44**Pilatus autem miratus est si iam obisset, et, accersito cen-

the scales of love, and give to him all the love
you have to give your loved ones" (*De sancta
virginitate*, 54–55, 55). See the RSV note **g**: cf.
Lk 22:37.

15:42–47 The Gospel underlines three things in
relation to Jesus' burial. Firstly, the attitude of
Joseph of Arimathea, a member of the Sanhedrin. The other Gospels tell us that he was
well-to-do (Mt 27:57), a disciple of our Lord,
though a hidden one (Jn 19:38), a good and
righteous man, who had taken no part in the
doings leading to the sentence passed on Jesus
(Lk 23:50–51). St Mark prefers to focus on his
boldness (v. 43) in approaching Pilate to ask for
our Lord's body. "Joseph of Arimathea and
Nicodemus visit Jesus secretly in ordinary times
and in the time of triumph. But they are courageous in the face of authority, declaring their
love for Christ *audacter* — 'boldly' — in the time
of cowardice. Learn" (St Josemaría Escrivá, *The
Way*, 841).

Secondly, the evangelist registers the fact that
Jesus truly died: Pilate himself had this confirmed (vv. 44–45). Rejecting any type of
Docetism (a heresy that denied that Christ was
truly man), the first Christians asserted that Jesus
truly died and that he truly rose from the dead:
"Close your ears to any words that do not come
from Christ Jesus, a descendent of the line of
David, the son of Mary, who was born, who ate
and drank as a man, who suffered under Pontius
Pilate, who was crucified and died in the presence of all the inhabitants of heaven and earth
and the abyss, and who was raised from the dead

by the power of the Father. God the Father will
also raise those who love Jesus Christ from the
dead, as he raised Jesus Christ himself, without
whom there is no true life" (St Ignatius of Antioch, *Ad Traianos*, 8–9).

Finally, the text mentions the tomb. Wealthy
Jews usually had graves on their property, excavated out of rock. A typical tomb had a small
vestibule in front of the tomb proper; the inner
vault had spaces inset in the walls and on these
the bodies of the dead were laid. In addition to
recording the refinement shown by Joseph (v.
46), the evangelist also mentions that the women
(v. 47) observed the whole procedure. This provides a link with the next episode and shows that
the person crucified and the person who rose
from the dead were one and the same: "The
Lord, being God, took on the nature of man. He
suffered because of what man suffered; he was
imprisoned instead of the one who was held captive; he was judged in the guilty man's stead; he
was laid in the tomb for the sake of the one who
was buried in the grave. And when he rose from
the dead, he cried out in a loud voice: 'Who
holds anything against me? Come close to me. I
am he who set free the one who was condemned.
I brought the dead to life. I raised the dead man
from his grave. Who will fight against me? I am
he — says Christ — who won victory over death,
who put the enemy in chains, who vanquished
hell, who bound the powers of evil, who raised
man up to the highest heavens. I am Christ.
Come, all of you who have fallen into evil ways,
and I will forgive you all your sins'" (Melito of
Sardes, *De Pascha*, 100–103).

and asked for the body of Jesus. [44]And Pilate wondered if he were already dead; and summoning the centurion, he asked him whether he was already dead.[j] [45]And when he learned from the centurion that he was dead, he granted the body to Joseph. [46]And he bought a linen shroud, and taking him down, wrapped him in the linen shroud, and laid him in a tomb which had been hewn out of the rock; and he rolled a stone against the door of the tomb. [47]Mary Magdalene and Mary the mother of Joses saw where he was laid.

The resurrection of Jesus. The empty tomb

Mt 28:1–10
Lk 24:1–12
Jn 20:1–10

16 [1]And when the sabbath was past, Mary Magdalene, and Mary the mother of James, and Salome, bought spices, so that they might go and anoint him.*

turione, interrogavit eum si iam mortuus esset, [45]et, cum cognovisset a centurione, donavit corpus Ioseph. [46]Is autem mercatus sindonem et deponens eum involvit sindone et posuit eum in monumento, quod erat excisum de petra, et advolvit lapidem ad ostium monumenti. [47]Maria autem Magdalene et Maria Iosetis aspiciebant, ubi positus esset. [16] [1]Et cum transisset sabbatum, Maria Magdalene et Maria Iacobi et Salome emerunt aromata, ut venientes ungerent eum. [2]Et valde mane, prima sabbatorum, veniunt ad monumentum, orto iam sole. [3]Et dicebant ad invicem: «Quis

16:1–8 From the very start of their preaching (cf. Acts 2:22–32; 3:13–15 and notes), the apostles made the point that "Christ died for our sins in accordance with the scriptures" (1 Cor 15:3). St Mark has shown that Christ truly died, and now he reports that he truly rose from the dead. "You seek Jesus of Nazareth, who was crucified. He has risen" (v. 6), the young man says. This is the same name that was written on the placard posted at the top of the cross, and now it is used to proclaim the glorious triumph of Jesus' resurrection. St Mark, by giving this information, leaves no room for doubt about the fact that the Crucified and the Risen are one and the same person.

The glorious resurrection of Jesus is the central mystery of our faith ("If Christ has not been raised, then our preaching is in vain and your faith is in vain": 1 Cor 15:14) and the foundation of our hope (see 1 Cor 15:20–22). The resurrection means that Jesus has triumphed over death, sin, pain and the power of the devil. True, as St Augustine says, "the Christian faith faces no greater opposition than in the question of the resurrection of the body" (*Enarrationes in Psalmos*, 88, 2, 5); however, that same faith confesses that "Christ is raised with his own body: 'See my hands and my feet, that it is I myself' (Lk 24:39); but he did not return to an earthly life. So, in him, 'all of them will rise again with their own bodies which they now bear,' but Christ 'will change our lowly body to be like his glorious body' (Phil 3:21), into a 'spiritual body' (Lateran

Council IV: DS 801; Phil 3:21; 1 Cor 15:44)" (*Catechism of the Catholic Church*, 999).

The announcement made by the young man at the tomb also contains instructions which sum up the life of the nascent Church: the disciples, and particularly Peter, are to be witnesses of the resurrection and all that it means. Their mission will start in Galilee. When Christ lived on earth, that region was a place where Jews and Gentiles lived together; now it becomes a symbol of the Church's mission to the world at large. And "the Church, spread throughout the whole world, carefully guards the faith and preaching it has received, as though living in one and the same house; and its faith is the same in every place, as if the Church had one soul and one heart, and whatever it preaches, teaches and transmits, it does so in unison, as if from one mouth" (St Irenaeus, *Adversus haereses*, 1, 10, 2).

From the earliest times of the Church, this first day after the sabbath was called "the Lord's day", because "after the sorrow of the sabbath, a joyful day breaks out, the day of greatest joy, lit up by the greatest light of all, for this day saw the triumph of the risen Christ" (St Jerome, *Commentarium in Marcum*, ad loc.). Therefore, "Christians saw the definitive time inaugurated by Christ as a new beginning, they made the first day after the Sabbath a festive day, for that was the day on which the Lord rose from the dead. The Paschal Mystery of Christ is the full revelation of the mystery of the world's origin, the climax of the history of salvation and the antici-

j Other ancient authorities read *whether he had been some time dead*

²And very early on the first day of the week they went to the tomb when the sun had risen. ³And they were saying to one another, "Who will roll away the stone for us from the door of the tomb?" ⁴And looking up, they saw that the stone was rolled back; for it was very large. ⁵And entering the tomb, they saw a young man on the

Mt 2:23

right side, dressed in a white robe; and they were amazed. ⁶And he said to them, "Do not be amazed; you seek Jesus of Nazareth, who was crucified. He has risen, he is

Mk 14:28

not here; see the place where they laid him. ⁷But go, tell his disciples and Peter that he is going before you to Galilee; there you will see him, as he told you." ⁸And they went out and fled from the tomb; for trembling and astonishment had come upon them; and they said nothing to any one, for they were afraid.

Jn 20:11-18

Jesus appears to Mary Magdalene
⁹Now when he rose early on the first day of the week, he appeared first to Mary

Lk 24:10-11

Magdalene, from whom he had cast out seven demons. ¹⁰She went and told those who had been with him, as they mourned and wept. ¹¹But when they heard that he was alive and had been seen by her, they would not believe it.

revolvet nobis lapidem ab ostio monumenti?». ⁴Et respicientes vident revolutum lapidem; erat quippe magnus valde. ⁵Et introeuntes in monumentum viderunt iuvenem sedentem in dextris, coopertum stola candida, et obstupuerunt. ⁶Qui dicit illis: «Nolite expavescere! Iesum quaeritis Nazarenum crucifixum. Surrexit, non est hic; ecce locus, ubi posuerunt eum. ⁷Sed ite, dicite discipulis eius et Petro: "Praecedit vos in Galilaeam. Ibi eum videbitis, sicut dixit vobis"». ⁸Et exeuntes fugerunt de monumento; invaserat enim eas tremor et pavor, et nemini quidquam dixerunt, timebant enim. ⁹Surgens autem mane, prima sabbati, apparuit primo Mariae Magdalenae, de qua eiecerat septem daemonia. ¹⁰Illa vadens nunti-

pation of the eschatological fulfilment of the world. What God accomplished in Creation and wrought for his People in the Exodus has found its fullest expression in Christ's Death and Resurrection" (John Paul II, *Dies Domini*, 18). Given that Sunday commemorates salvation, we can see why the Church says: "The duty to keep Sunday holy, especially by sharing in the Eucharist and by relaxing in a spirit of Christian joy and fraternity, is easily understood if we consider the many different aspects of this day" (ibid., 7).

16:9-20 The second Gospel ends with a very concise summary of the appearances of the risen Christ. The style of these verses is different from that of the rest of the Gospel, and they are not found in some of the manuscripts. But, be that as it may, whether Mark took this passage virtually unchanged from another document or whether it is a later addition, it is regarded as canonical and, therefore, inspired.

The passage does not disguise the initial incredulity of the apostles. The opening verses (vv. 9-13) report the appearances to Mary Magdalene and the disciples of Emmaus (cf. Lk 24:13-35), and in both instances the narrator notes that the

rest of the disciples did not believe (vv. 11, 13). At his appearance to the Eleven (vv. 14-18) Jesus summarizes the apostles' mission, which is now the mission of the Church—to preach salvation to the whole world, with Baptism the necessary gateway to that salvation. The Church's teaching is this: "Above all else, it must be firmly believed that 'the Church, a pilgrim now on earth, is necessary for salvation: the one Christ is the mediator and the way of salvation; he is present to us in his body which is the Church. He himself explicitly asserted the necessity of faith and baptism (cf. Mk 16:16; Jn 3:5), and thereby affirmed at the same time the necessity of the Church which men enter through baptism as through a door' (Vatican II, *Lumen gentium*, 14). This doctrine must not be set against the universal salvific will of God (cf. 1 Tim 2:4); 'it is necessary to keep these two truths together, namely, the real possibility of salvation in Christ for all mankind and the necessity of the Church for this salvation' (John Paul II, *Redemptoris missio*, 9). [...] The Church, guided by charity and respect for freedom, must be primarily committed to proclaiming to all people the truth definitively revealed by the Lord, and to announcing the necessity of conversion to Jesus Christ and of

Jesus appears to two disciples   Lk 24:13-35

[12]After this he appeared in another form to two of them, as they were walking into the country. [13]And they went back and told the rest, but they did not believe them.

Jesus appears to the Eleven. The apostles' mission   Mt 28:16-20
Lk 24:36-49
Jn 20:19-31

[14]Afterward he appeared to the eleven themselves as they sat at table; and he   1 Cor 15:5
upbraided them for their unbelief and hardness of heart, because they had not
believed those who saw him after he had risen. [15]And he said to them, "Go into all   Mk 13:10
the world and preach the gospel to the whole creation. [16]He who believes and is bap-   Acts 2:11; 10:46
tized will be saved; but he who does not believe will be condemned. [17]And these   Acts 2:4, 11; 10:46
signs will accompany those who believe: in my name they will cast out demons;
they will speak in new tongues; [18]they will pick up serpents, and if they drink any   Lk 10:19
Acts 28:3-6
deadly thing, it will not hurt them; they will lay their hands on the sick, and they will
recover."

The ascension of our Lord   Lk 24:50-53
Acts 1:6-11

[19]So then the Lord Jesus, after he had spoken to them, was taken up into heaven, and   Acts 2:33; 7:55
2 Kings 2:11
sat down at the right hand of God.

The apostles go forth and preach

[20]And they went forth and preached everywhere, while the Lord worked with them   Heb 2:4
and confirmed the message by the signs that attended it. Amen.k*

avit his, qui cum eo fuerant, lugentibus et flentibus; [11]et illi audientes quia viveret et visus esset ab ea, non crediderunt. [12]Post haec autem duobus ex eis ambulantibus ostensus est in alia effigie euntibus in villam; [13]et illi euntes nuntiaverunt ceteris, nec illis crediderunt. [14]Novissime recumbentibus illis Undecim apparuit, et exprobravit incredulitatem illorum et duritiam cordis, quia his, qui viderant eum resuscitatum, non crediderant. [15]Et dixit eis: «Euntes in mundum universum praedicate evangelium omni creaturae. [16]Qui crediderit et baptizatus fuerit, salvus erit; qui vero non crediderit, condemnabitur. [17]Signa autem eos, qui crediderint, haec sequentur: in nomine meo daemonia eicient, linguis loquentur novis, [18]serpentes tollent, et, si mortiferum quid biberint, non eos nocebit, super aegrotos manus imponent et bene habebunt». [19]Et Dominus quidem Iesus, postquam locutus est eis, assumptus est in caelum et sedit a dextris Dei. [20]Illi autem profecti praedicaverunt ubique, Domino cooperante et sermonem confirmante, sequentibus signis.

adherence to the Church through Baptism and the other sacraments, in order to participate fully in communion with God, the Father, Son and Holy Spirit. Thus, the certainty of the universal salvific will of God does not diminish, but rather increases the duty and urgency of the proclamation of salvation and of conversion to the Lord Jesus Christ" (Congregation for the Doctrine of the Faith, *Dominus Iesus*, 20 and 22).

Finally, the last two verses (vv. 19–20) tell us who Jesus is and what he does in this present age: he has been taken up and sits at the right hand of the Father, and he acts in his disciples, confirming the message they bear. The ascension of the Lord and his position at the right hand of

the Father form the sixth article of faith in the Apostles' Creed. Jesus Christ went up into heaven body and soul; in his human nature he has taken possession of heaven, and as man he holds the place of honour at God's side above all created things (see *Roman Catechism*, 1, 7, 2–3). With his "entry" into heaven, he attains a new mode of life in glory, a glory which we, too, in some way share (see Eph. 2:6). The *Catechism of the Catholic Church*, 666, sums up the salvific effect of the Ascension in these words: "Jesus Christ, the head of the Church, precedes us into the Father's glorious kingdom so that we, the members of his Body, may live in the hope of one day being with him for ever."

k Other ancient authorities omit verses 9–20. Some ancient authorities conclude Mark instead with the following: *But they reported briefly to Peter and those with him all that they had been told. And after this, Jesus himself sent out by means of them, from east to west, the sacred and imperishable proclamation of eternal salvation*

Jesus appears to two disciples.

After this he appeared in another form to two of them, as they were walking into the country. And they went back and told the rest, but they did not believe them.

Jesus appears to the Eleven. The apostolic commission.

Afterward he appeared to the eleven themselves, as they sat at table, and he upbraided them for their unbelief and hardness of heart, because they had not believed those who saw him after he had risen. And he said to them, "Go into all the world and preach the gospel to the whole creation. He who believes and is baptized will be saved; but he who does not believe will be condemned. And these signs will accompany those who believe: in my name they will cast out demons; they will speak in new tongues; they will pick up serpents, and if they drink any deadly thing, it will not hurt them; they will lay their hands on the sick, and they will recover."

The ascension of our Lord.

So then the Lord Jesus, after he had spoken to them, was taken up into heaven, and sat down at the right hand of God.

The apostles go forth and preach.

And they went forth and preached everywhere, while the Lord worked with them and confirmed the message by the signs that attended it. Amen.

THE GOSPEL ACCORDING TO

LUKE

Introduction

The Gospel of St Luke comes third in the list of New Testament books. In some Western codexes it follows Matthew and John because those two Gospels were written by apostles; but in most codexes the order is: Matthew, Mark, Luke and John. In the earliest period of the Church this was considered to be the order in which the books were written. Moreover, the fact that Luke comes after Mark makes sense because, if Mark records the preaching of Peter, Luke follows that of Paul. This reason for the ordering of the Gospels is mentioned very often in documents from the first four centuries. St Irenaeus, for example, writes: "Luke, the companion of Paul, wrote in a book the Gospel which he [Paul] preached."[1] The same comment is made in writings by Origen, Clement of Alexandria, Tertullian, Eusebius and St Jerome.

From the first centuries onwards, the Church has treasured the Gospel according to St Luke as a sacred book, using it in liturgical lectionaries and including it even in the earliest lists of canonical books, that is, texts which the Church holds to be inspired by God. As early as the fourth-century councils (Laodicea, Hippo, Carthage, Rome) it is stated time and again that the sacred books include the Gospels "according to Matthew, according to Mark, according to Luke, according to John".[2] The Councils of Florence and Trent repeat this statement of authority.

In the times of the Fathers we find homilies and commentaries on Luke in, for example, Origen, St Cyril of Alexandria, St John Chrysostom, St Ambrose and St Bede. There are more written commentaries on Luke than on Mark, but Luke is not commented on as frequently as Matthew.

1. STRUCTURE AND CONTENT

The book can be said to have three parts to it, each of more or less the same length; these deal with Jesus' ministry in Galilee, his ministry on the journey towards Jerusalem, and his ministry in Jerusalem. Before these come the prologue and the infancy narrative. Within this scheme of things, the most significant part of Luke's account is that dealing with the ministry on the way to Jerusalem: the other Synoptics give two or three chapters to this "journey", whereas it comprises ten in Luke. In these chapters Luke lays special emphasis on the fact that Jesus' call to salvation is addressed to all mankind.

INTRODUCTION (1:1—4:13). The book opens with a prologue (1:1–4) outlining the author's intention; the literary style of this passage is very elegant. This is followed by an account (1:5—2:52) of the births of John the Baptist and Jesus, and a couple of events in Jesus' childhood in which we are told who Jesus is—the promised Saviour, the Messiah, the Lord. Alongside Jesus we always find his Mother, who with her steadfast faith also played a role in God's plan of salvation. The introduction ends with an account of how Jesus prepared for his ministry; three themes dominate in this section—the role of John the Baptist, the temptation of Jesus, and Jesus' genealogy. In each of these we see the scope of the salvation brought about by Christ.

---

1 *Adversus haereses*, 3, 1, 1.   **2** See *EB* 12–22.

FIRST PART: JESUS' MINISTRY IN GALILEE (4:14—9:50). We learn about the early stages of Jesus' ministry, in Galilee. The opening scene has Jesus in the synagogue of Nazareth (4:16–30); we are given a summary of what his mission entails: the salvation promised by God comes about through the miracles worked by Jesus and the compassion he shows to all (4:38–41; 5:12–26; 7:1–23; 8:26–56; 9:11), through the forgiveness of sins (5:17–26; 7:36–50), etc. Jesus' ministry also involves preaching; this centres on the Sermon on the Plain (6:17–49) and the Kingdom parables (8:4–18). The evangelist likes to record the power and uniqueness of Jesus' words (4:31–37; 5:17–26; etc.), which have caused huge crowds to flock to his side (4:37, 40, 42; 5:1, 15, 19, 29; etc.). To help him carry out his plan of salvation, Jesus calls disciples (5:1–11, 27–28; 6:12–16), from among whom he chooses apostles. Jesus devotes special attention to the training of these apostles (8:10; 9:21; etc.); he gives them a vision of his glory (9:28–36), and sends them out to preach (9:1–6), as an anticipation of his later apostolic commission to go out into the whole world.

SECOND PART: JESUS' MINISTRY ON THE WAY TO JERUSALEM (9:51—19:27). Within the framework of the long journey to Jerusalem, Luke records many teachings of Jesus not found in the other Gospels—the parable of the good Samaritan (10:30–37), the parables of God's mercy (15:3–32), that of the Pharisee and the tax collector (18:9–14), etc. It is difficult to define any particular structure in this part of the Gospel, but its content has a certain coherence in that it deals with themes typical of the third Gospel—prayer, compassion, the universal scope of salvation, the joy of conversion, the value of poverty as distinct from riches, etc.

THIRD PART: MINISTRY IN JERUSALEM (19:28–24:53). Luke's account of this stage in Jesus' ministry is very similar to those found in the other Synoptics: he covers Christ's entry into Jerusalem and the cleansing of the temple (19:28–46), his controversies with Jewish authorities (20:1–47), and the Eschatological Discourse (21:5–36), and gives a long Last Supper and passion narrative (22:1–23; 56) and a Resurrection narrative (24:1–53). Luke foregrounds Jesus' sensitivity (19:41–44) and compassion (22:51; 23:28–29, 34, 43), his greatness of soul (22:21–30, 47–53; 23:26–49; etc.), and his constant recourse to prayer (22:32, 39–46; 23:34, 46). In all these respects, Jesus is presented as a model for Christians. The narrative ends with our Lord's instruction to his apostles to stay in Jerusalem until the Holy Spirit comes (24:48–49), and with Christ's ascension—events that overlap with the content of the opening pages of the Acts of the Apostles.

2. CONTEXT

The author

St Luke, a disciple and companion of St Paul, is the author of the third Gospel.[3] A statement to this effect is found in many writings by early ecclesiastical authors, along with further information about Luke: he was a physician, an Antiochene, an adept in the Greek language, who may well have written his Gospel in Achaia and Boeotia.[4]

---

3 The opening lines of the Muratorian Fragment repeat the ideas about the Gospel found in most early Christian writings: "The third book of the Gospel is that according to Luke. This Luke, a physician, after the ascension of Christ, was adopted by Paul [...]. He wrote down what he had heard, for he had not known the Lord in the flesh, and, having obtained such information as he could, he began his account with the birth of John" (*EB*, 1). **4** St Jerome writes: "Luke, a physician from Antioch, who was familiar with Greek as can be seen from his writings, a follower of the apostle Paul, and a companion on his journeys, wrote a

This information comes largely from comparing St Luke's two texts (his Gospel and the Acts of the Apostles) with other New Testament writings. For example, Acts contains a number of passages narrated in the first person plural (cf. Acts 16:10–17; 20:5–15; 21:1–18; 27:1—28:16), leading one to suppose that the narrator accompanied St Paul on his journeys. Of the companions that the Apostle of the Gentiles mentions in his letters, the Luke that Paul describes as "the beloved physician" and who is not a man "of the circumcision" but rather of Gentile background (see Col 4:10–14; 2 Tim 4:11; Philem 24) points to the author of the third Gospel. The Gospel itself shows that the author had medical knowledge and, whereas he is sometimes unsure of the geography and customs of Palestine, he is always conscious of the fact that salvation is open to all.

Both of Luke's books are addressed to "[most excellent] Theophilus" (Lk 1:3; Acts 1:1). This may be a general reference to all Christians, those "beloved by God", but the fact that in Luke 1:3 an adjective is attached to the name suggests that Theophilus was an actual person known to Luke. In any event, the book is clearly written for a Christian readership, because Luke says that he wrote it "that you may know the truth concerning the things of which you have been informed" (Lk 1:4). A reading of the book tells us nothing about Theophilus, other than what is evident—that he is a Christian of Gentile background, well-educated and open-minded. The author wants the reader to see the vitality and beauty of Christianity, and he does this by reporting the words and actions of Jesus, and, in the book of Acts, apostolic preaching in all its novelty and power.

Because we know so little about whom the book was written for, it is not easy to say where it was written. Three places have been suggested—Antioch in Syria, the region of Achaia and Boeotia (which included, for example, the flourishing church of Corinth), and Rome. Antioch is a possibility because Luke, especially in Acts, shows that he is very familiar with the way that the church in Antioch functioned, and with its strong evangelizing spirit. Rome is possible, because it is in that city that Acts comes to an end, and also because of the universal spirit of Luke's writings. The region of Achaia and Boeotia had similar features to Rome in that it was Gentile territory and the church there had a universal outlook; later tradition favours that region as the place of composition. A prologue to a copy of the Gospel dated to around the end of the second century says that "Luke was born in Antioch of Syria. He was a physician by profession, a disciple of the apostles, and, later, a companion of Paul, up to the time of the latter's martyrdom. He served the Lord with complete dedication. He did not marry or have children. He died at the age of eighty-four in Boeotia, full of the Holy Spirit."[5]

Some scholars look to the Acts of the Apostles to date the third Gospel. That second book by Luke ends with a description of St Paul's situation just before he is set free from his first imprisonment in Rome. Since Paul was released in the year 63, some think that the gospel account by Luke must have been written sometime in the period 67–80. The arguments for that latest year are mainly internal ones, based on the fact that Luke's work seems to have been written by someone who has witnessed the vitality and spread of the Gospel. If St Luke was a young man when he followed the first apostles, then by the year 80 he would have acquired the maturity needed to write a considered and well-balanced work such as the one under discussion.

Gospel" (*De vivis illustribus*, 1). And elsewhere he says: "Thirdly, Luke, a physician, a native of Antioch in Syria, a disciple of the apostle Paul, wrote the volume in Achaia and Boeotia; in this book, he covered, with a broader perspective, some things contained in other books and, as he admits in his prologue, he narrated things that he had heard about, not things that he had himself seen" (*Commentaria in Matthaeum*, prologue, 3–4). **5** *Prologi Monarchianorum*.

Literary and theological features

On reading this Gospel we quickly discover that its author is an educated man who appreciates elegance in style and possesses great refinement of soul. Very early on, St Jerome noted that Luke's knowledge and use of Greek is much more profound than that of the other evangelists.[6] He has a very extensive vocabulary, prefers compound verbs (which means his descriptions are more precise), avoids the use of jargon, and skims over details that might embarrass some readers and scenes that might appear too gruesome. However, when transcribing Jesus' words he often retains Semitic turns of phrase. This strange mixture of good Greek style combined with Semitic elements shows Luke's skill as a writer: he writes well and is scrupulously faithful to his sources.

This fidelity to sources is one of the many features that Luke's Gospel shares with all sound written history. Other such features can be found in the "prologue" to the Gospel. Here Luke follows the custom of Greek and Latin historians.[7] He uses the technical word "narrative" to show at the very start that he is writing as an historian. Features of this historical genre can be seen in his references to political history, and the other chronological information he gives, at the beginning of the Gospel (see 1:5; 2:1; 3:1–2, 23), and in the method he uses: he tells us that he aims to write an "orderly" account.

However, Luke is not writing history simply to satisfy his readers' curiosity: his aim is to teach the *history of salvation* from the moment when Christ became man to the spread of the Gospel among the Gentiles. He does this in his Gospel and the Acts of the Apostles, which effectively form two volumes of the same work. He reports "the things which have been accomplished among us", God's salvific action towards mankind, all of which is God's plan (see 1:1; 13:33; 17:25). Luke uses the verb "save" some twenty-five times in the Gospel and Acts, seeing the work of salvation not only in Christ's death and resurrection but also in everything that happens afterwards—Jesus' ascension into heaven and the spread of the Gospel. Viewing things from this perspective of salvation history, Luke uses the teaching handed down by eyewitnesses to produce his "orderly account" (1:3).

In the events reported in the two books, the evangelist discerns the fulfilment of Isaiah's prophecy: "It shall come to pass in the latter days that the mountain of the house of the Lord shall be established as the highest of the mountains, and shall be raised above the hills; and all the nations shall flow to it […]. For out of Zion shall go forth the law, and the word of the Lord from Jerusalem" (Is 2:2–3). This may explain the prominence given to *Jerusalem* in his account. Luke begins and ends his infancy narrative with two scenes in the temple of Jerusalem. In the temptations in the wilderness, he follows a different order from that found in Matthew's Gospel: the last temptation happens in Jerusalem (Lk 4:1–13; cf. Mt 4:1–11). From early on in his public life, Jesus is on a journey to Jerusalem (see Lk 9:51–53; 17:11; 19:28), where salvation history will reach its climax. St Luke mentions no appearances of the Risen Jesus in Galilee; instead, he focuses on his appearances in and near Jerusalem. And the Gospel ends with a scene set in the same place where it began, the temple in Jerusalem.[8]

Jerusalem is the place where salvation is consummated—not only because it is there that our Lord died, but also because his ascension took place there. St Luke writes two accounts of the

---

6 See *Epistolae*, 20, 4.   **7** See, for example, Flavius Josephus, *Contra Apion*. Scholars have noticed, too, that Luke usually follows the rules later laid down by Lucian of Samosata in his *Quomodo historia conscribenda sit*: good history writing should be orderly and chronological; it should not be just a list of facts. It should be selective; the historian should seek out good sources of information, avoid a panegyric tone and use sober language that is accessible to the reader.   **8** "And they worshipped him, and returned to Jerusalem with great joy, and were continually in the temple blessing God" (24:52–53).

ascension (cf. 24:51–53; Acts 1:6–11), providing important pieces of information: in the Gospel, Jesus takes leave of his disciples, for the ascension is the end of his life on earth. In Acts, the Ascension marks the Risen Lord's entry into heaven, from where he will send the Holy Spirit to give life to his Church.

The entire Gospel of St Luke takes its focus and tone from the account of the Ascension: that event is the last stage of Jesus' "journey".[9]

3. MESSAGE

In addition to these literary and theological aspects, the third Gospel has a great deal of doctrinal content. As is also true of the other Gospels, its main teaching is about Jesus Christ. It is significant that Luke depicts Jesus as Prophet, Saviour and Lord, but he also lays stress on other themes, such as, for example, the universal scope of salvation and such aspects of Christian life as the spirit of poverty, perseverance in prayer, compassion and joy. Finally, St Luke is the evangelist who most clearly presents the Blessed Virgin as a model of how to respond to God's gifts.

Jesus as Prophet, Saviour and Lord

Jesus is referred to as "prophet" in a number of places (see 7:16; 9:19; 13:33; 24:19). Because he is true God and true man, Jesus is the Prophet par excellence: like none other he can speak in God's name (see 4:18, 43). In the Old Testament, prophets were moved by the Spirit of God. St Luke underlines the deep, mysterious connexion between the *Holy Spirit* and the prophetic ministry of our Lord: for example, at Jesus' baptism, which marks the start of his public life, the Holy Spirit descends on him in visible form; later, the Spirit leads him into the wilderness (where he is tempted), into Galilee, etc. (see 3:22; 4:1, 14). Jesus applies to himself the role of prophet when in the synagogue of Nazareth he reads this passage from Isaiah: "The Spirit of the Lord is upon me, because he has anointed me to preach good news to the poor", and then he says, "Today this scripture has been fulfilled in your hearing" (see 4:16–30).

A message that runs right through Luke's Gospel is that Jesus is the *Saviour* of mankind. The infancy narrative makes it quite clear that the ancient promises of salvation made by God to the patriarchs and prophets of the Chosen People find fulfilment in Christ: the newborn Child is the Saviour come after centuries of waiting, as can be seen from the Benedictus, the Magnificat, the announcement to the shepherds and the canticle of Simeon. But salvation is made manifest, too, in the cures worked by Jesus and in his forgiveness of sins.[10]

Jesus is also the *Lord*. This was the title given God to avoid uttering his proper name (*Yhwh*). It was also used as a mark of respect when addressing people. St Luke uses this title much more

---

9 The Gospel contains passages that allude to the Ascension: at the Transfiguration (9:28–36) Jesus appears in glory. He talks with Moses and Elijah of his "departure" (his exodus), which will take place in Jerusalem; in 9:51 we learn that "when the days drew near for him to be received up, he set his face to go to Jerusalem"; and in 24:26 Jesus says that it was necessary that he should undergo his passion and thus "enter into his glory".   **10** A glance at Luke's terminology shows that the theme of *salvation* is central to his Gospel: the Blessed Virgin Mary rejoices in God her Saviour (1:47); at the Nativity, the angels announce that "to you is born this day in the city of David a Saviour, who is Christ the Lord" (2:11); God has "raised up a horn of salvation for us" (1:69), "that we should be saved from our enemies" (1:71); the Baptist is to proclaim this "to give knowledge of salvation to [God's] people", a salvation consisting in the forgiveness of sins (1:77); Simeon's eyes see salvation when he meets the Child Jesus (2:30); "all flesh shall see the salvation of God", as Isaiah prophesied (Is 40:5; Lk 3:6); and Jesus brings salvation to Zacchaeus (19:9). At other times, saving comes in the form of a cure —in the episodes of the woman with the haemorrhage (8:43–48), the blind man of Jericho (18:35–43), the raising of Jairus' daughter (8:50), etc. Salvation comes, too, for the sinful woman (7:50), the Samaritan cured of leprosy (17:19), etc.

than the other evangelists do—81 times in the Gospel, 107 in Acts. Jesus is the Lord in the most profound sense of the word from the time of his birth onwards, and he is revealed to be the Lord by his rising from the dead. Glory is his, as will become most evident when he returns at the end of time. He is also the Lord of history.

Salvation for all the world

Over the course of his two books, St Luke shows that the good things announced by the prophets find their fulfilment in Christ and in his Church in which he lives on, and that they are available not only to Jews but to all peoples. The universal reach of the salvation brought about by Jesus Christ is made plain in the Acts of the Apostles, but in many places in the Gospel we already find this idea being put forward. For example, Simeon in his canticle proclaims that he has seen the salvation that God has prepared "in the presence of all peoples" and that Jesus is "a light for revelation to the Gentiles" (2:29–32); St Luke also applies to the mission of John the Baptist the words of Isaiah 40:5 that read, "All flesh shall see the salvation of God" (3:6). In the synagogue of Nazareth, Jesus proclaims that non-Jews will hear the Gospel;[11] and later on he explains to his disciples that it was prophesied that he should suffer and then rise from the dead, and that repentance and forgiveness of sins would be preached to all nations (24:46–47). Many other things related to this theme could be mentioned, not least the way in which Jesus' dealings with Samaritans are reflected in the text.[12]

A call to Christian living

Luke shows us that, to Jesus, the proclamation of the Gospel means that the messianic age has come (4:16–21). If Christians are to imitate Christ, the Messiah, the first lesson to be learned is that of the cross. Christians should take up their cross *daily*, and they should practise the virtue of patience (see 9:23 and 21:19).

Similarly, the virtue of *poverty* must be practised if one is to respond to Christ's call and attain beatitude and eternal life. A person who follows Christ must be detached from *all things*. Riches end up having no value at all if they are treated as ends in themselves.[13] A standard of self-denial and renunciation is set by the first disciples, who, after the miraculous catch of fish in the lake of Gennesaret, "left everything and followed" the Master; similarly, the tax-collector Levi (Matthew), on hearing the Master's call, "left everything, and rose and followed him" (5:11, 28).

Finally other things on which the third Gospel lays special stress are the need for perseverance in prayer and for inner joy at all times. Here, too, Jesus' words and example set the tone for Christian living.

There are passages found only in Luke that mention Christ's own prayer, and Luke specifically mentions Christ praying at key points in his life—at his baptism; before choosing his apostles; at the Transfiguration; in Gethsemane; and on the cross.

The four Gospels, which record the proclamation of salvation and which are indeed "good news", are thus imbued with the *joy* of the redemption brought about by Christ. This note of joy

---

11 See Lk 4:24–27. There is a parallel between this passage and Acts 13:46–47, where the apostles, having been rejected by Jews, turn to Gentiles. **12** St Luke does not report the episode of the Canaanite woman (Mt 15:21–28; Mk 7:24–30), or the injunction about the Samaritans that is found in Matthew 10:5: "Go nowhere among the Gentiles, and enter no town of the Samaritans", which might imply that the disciples' mission was restricted to the land of the Jews. Jesus takes his disciples to task for calling for punishment to be visited on the Samaritans (9:55); he proposes the good Samaritan as a model of how to be a good neighbour (10:29–37); and of the ten lepers cured by Jesus, the one who comes back to thank him is a Samaritan (17:16). **13** See 4:18; 6:20; 7:22; 12:13–21; 16:9, 14–5, 19–31; 18:22.

is registered most noticeably in the Gospel of St Luke. For example, an angel tells Zechariah that he will have a son and that "many will *rejoice* at his birth"; in the annunciation to Mary, the archangel Gabriel begins with the Greek word *khaire*, which literally means "*rejoice*"; and the Master, after telling his disciples they will undergo persecution on account of their love for him, encourages them by saying, "*Rejoice* in that day and leap for *joy*." The birth of John the Baptist will bring Zechariah "*joy* and *gladness*"; the angel announces a great *joy* to the shepherds; in heaven there will be *joy* when a sinner repents; Elizabeth proclaims that her son leaped for *joy* in her womb; finally, after its account of the ascension of our Lord, the Gospel text ends with these words, "and they worshipped him, and returned to Jerusalem with *great joy*, and were continually in the temple blessing God".[14]

The Blessed Virgin Mary

The third Gospel (particularly in its first two chapters) depicts the Mother of Christ in a special light, gently revealing the greatness and beauty of her soul. (St Luke is said, too, to have painted a portrait of the Blessed Virgin.)[15] No one in the gospel story—except Jesus, of course—is described with such love and respect as Mary.

Nor has any other human being ever received such sublime and singular graces as she: she is "full of grace"; the Lord is with her; she has found favour with God; she conceived by the power of the Holy Spirit; she became the mother of Jesus and remained ever-virgin; intimately involved with the redemptive mystery of her Son, she will be blessed by all generations, for the Almighty has done great things for her.

Our Lady responded to these divine gifts in a most faithful and generous way: St Elizabeth exclaims that she is blessed because she has believed; Mary receives with humility the archangel's announcement that she is to become the Mother of God; in all simplicity she asks what she has to do to please God; she surrenders herself completely to God's plans; she shows appreciation of and gratitude for all that he has done for her; she faithfully observes God's laws and the pious customs of her people. She is distressed when the Child is lost and she makes tender complaint to him, but she meekly accepts what she does not yet understand. She has a contemplative sense of wonder towards divine mysteries, which she keeps in her heart and ponders over.

As Christian tradition has always taught, Mary is the Mother of God and Model of the Church. St Luke portrays her as someone who, on account of her faith and fidelity, epitomizes all the just people of the Old Testament who patiently awaited God's salvation, and as someone whose readiness to listen to the Word of God and put it into practice makes her a model for those of every generation who follow Christ (see 2:19, 51; 8:21; 11:28).

---

14 See 1:14, 28; 6:23; 15:7; 24:52. **15** In the sixth century Theodore the Reader says that there was in Jerusalem a portrait of Mary by St Luke. Reference is also made to Luke's painterly skills by Simeon Metaphrastus in the tenth century and by Nicephorus Calixtus in the fourteenth century.

Luke

Prologue

1 ¹Inasmuch as many have undertaken to compile a narrative of the things which have been accomplished among us, ²just as they were delivered to us by those who from the beginning were eyewitnesses and ministers of the word, ³it seemed good to me also, having followed all things closely[a] for some time past, to write an orderly account for you, most excellent Theophilus,* ⁴that you may know the truth concerning the things of which you have been informed.

Jn 15:27

Acts 1:1

1. THE INFANCY OF JOHN THE BAPTIST AND OF JESUS*

The birth of John the Baptist foretold

⁵*In the days of Herod, king of Judea, there was a priest named Zechariah,[b] of the division of Abijah; and he had a wife of the daughters of Aaron, and her name was

1 Chron 24:10

[1] ¹Quoniam quidem multi conati sunt ordinare narrationem, quae in nobis completae sunt, rerum, ²sicut tradiderunt nobis, qui ab initio ipsi viderunt et ministri fuerunt verbi, ³visum est et mihi, adsecuto a principio omnia, diligenter ex ordine tibi scribere, optime Theophile, ⁴ut cognoscas eorum verborum, de quibus eruditus es, firmitatem. ⁵Fuit in diebus Herodis regis Iudaeae sacerdos quidam nomine Zacharias de vice Abiae et uxor illi de filiabus Aaron, et nomen eius Elisabeth. ⁶Erant autem iusti ambo ante Deum, incedentes in omnibus mandatis et iustificationibus

1:1–4 In this prologue, which is brief and elegantly written, St Luke tells why he has written this book—to provide an orderly, documented account (v. 3) of the life of Christ, starting from the very beginning, and also to explain the salvific meaning of the things "which have been accomplished among us" (v. 1). It is, then, a history, but it also shows how events bear out promises made by God: "The Gospels do not claim to be a complete biography of Jesus in accordance with the canons of modern historical science. From them, nevertheless, the face of the Nazarene emerges with a solid historical foundation. The Evangelists took pains to represent him on the basis of trustworthy testimonies which they gathered (cf. Lk 1:3) and working with documents which were subjected to careful ecclesial scrutiny" (John Paul II, *Novo millennio ineunte*, 18).

*1:5—2:52 Luke and Matthew devote the first two chapters of their Gospels to episodes in the early life of our Lord. These opening chapters are usually referred to as the "infancy narrative".

From the very start one can see that Matthew and Luke relate different events (other than key events involving Jesus: see the note on Mt 1:1–2:23). Moreover, the two Gospels are quite different in tone—Matthew's with sudden shifts in time and place; Luke's, a combination of historical sobriety and evangelical joy.

Luke's infancy narrative comprises six episodes, structured in pairs, concerning the infancy of John the Baptist and that of Jesus—two annunciations (1:5–38), two births and circumcisions (1:39—2:21), and two scenes set in the temple (2:22–52). The accounts also include a number of canticles—the Magnificat (1:46–55), the Benedictus (1:68–79); the Gloria (2:14) and the Nunc dimittis (2:29–32)—all of which express joy at God's actions for the sake of man. The narratives, like the canticles, are replete with references to Old Testament passages—to show that the salvation promised by God has at last come to pass (see 1:1).

The central scene is the Annunciation to Mary and the Incarnation of the Word when Mary agrees to what God desires. These two dimensions—

a Or *accurately*   b Greek *Zacharias*

Ex 30:7

Elizabeth. ⁶And they were both righteous before God, walking in all the commandments and ordinances of the Lord blameless. ⁷But they had no child, because Elizabeth was barren, and both were advanced in years. ⁸Now while he was serving as priest before God when his division was on duty, ⁹according to the custom of the priesthood, it fell to him by lot to enter the temple of the Lord and burn incense. ¹⁰And the whole multitude of the people were praying outside at the hour of incense. ¹¹And there appeared to him an angel of the Lord standing on the right side of the altar of incense. ¹²And Zechariah was troubled when he saw him, and fear fell upon him. ¹³But the angel said to him, "Do not be afraid, Zechariah, for your prayer is heard, and your wife Elizabeth will bear you a son, and you shall call his name John.

Domini, irreprehensibiles. ⁷Et non erat illis filius eo quod esset Elisabeth sterilis, et ambo processissent in diebus suis. ⁸Factum est autem, cum sacerdotio fungeretur in ordine vicis suae ante Deum, ⁹secundum consuetudinem sacerdotii sorte exiit, ut incensum poneret ingressus in templum Domini; ¹⁰et omnis multitudo erat populi orans foris hora incensi. ¹¹Apparuit autem illi angelus Domini stans a dextris altaris incensi; ¹²et Zacharias turbatus est videns, et timor irruit super eum. ¹³Ait autem ad illum angelus: «Ne timeas, Zacharia, quoniam exaudita est deprecatio tua, et uxor

Christological and Mariological—are to be found in each episode. The Child born in Bethlehem is the promised Saviour (1:71, 77; 2:11, 30), the Messiah, the Lord (1:43; 76; 2:11, 26), and his mission is redemption (2:38). However, he will be a sign of contradiction, the cause of the ruin and rising of "many in Israel" (2:34), who can be saved only if they believe in him. Never far from Jesus is his Mother, and she for her part symbolizes that part of mankind that is faithful to God (1:46–56). Because she cooperates in God's plan of salvation (1:38) with a firm faith, God incorporates her not only into the Son's mission but also into the pain that that mission entails and which is part of God's plan (2:35): "enriched from the first instant of her conception with the splendour of an entirely unique holiness, [...] the virgin of Nazareth is hailed by the heralding angel, by divine command, as 'full of grace' (cf. Lk 1:28), and to the heavenly messenger she replies, 'Behold, the handmaid of the Lord, be it done unto me according to thy word' (Lk 1:38). Thus the daughter of Adam, Mary, consenting to the word of God, became the Mother of Jesus. Committing herself wholeheartedly to God's saving will and impeded by no sin, she devoted herself totally, as a handmaid of the Lord, to the person and work of her Son, under and with him, serving the mystery of Redemption, by the grace of Almighty God. Rightly, therefore, the Fathers see Mary not merely as passively engaged by God, but as freely cooperating in the work of man's salvation through faith and obedience" (Vatican II, *Lumen gentium*, 56).

1:5–25 As on other occasions (see 2:1ff; 3:1ff) Luke, being familiar with the way history should be written, begins his account by setting his story within a wider historical framework (v. 5). The event he goes on to describe will help the reader to date the Annunciation to the Blessed Virgin, which comes six months later (cf. 1:26).

The evangelist portrays Zechariah and his wife Elizabeth as exemplary devout Jews (v. 6). God intervenes dramatically in their lives, and this in turn will affect the lives of many other people (v. 14). Elizabeth, already an old woman, is going to have a child who will be named John (v. 13)—a name meaning "God is gracious"—and on him God will bestow exceptional holiness (v. 15) because he is to be the precursor of the long-awaited Messiah (v. 17) and will bring about the conversion of many in Israel (v. 16). Both the form of this scene (divine intervention, a state of confusion, an announcement, a difficulty, a sign) and its content seem to parallel and prepare for the Annunciation to Mary, which is the more important event. For example, Zechariah wanted to have an heir (v. 13) and could not; the Blessed Virgin, on the other hand, is not asking for a child (see 1:34), but God gives her one; both Zechariah and Mary are disconcerted by the angel's greeting (1:12, 29), but their attitudes are different: Zechariah fails to believe (v. 30) and he asks for a sign (v. 18), whereas Mary believes (1:38) and she is offered a sign she had not sought (1:36).

In the Gospel of St Luke, the story of Jesus begins in the temple of Jerusalem and ends there

¹⁴ And you will have joy and gladness,
   and many will rejoice at his birth;
¹⁵ for he will be great before the Lord,
   and he shall drink no wine nor strong drink,
   and he will be filled with the Holy Spirit,
   even from his mother's womb.
¹⁶ And he will turn many of the sons of Israel
   to the Lord their God,
¹⁷ and he will go before him in the spirit and power of Elijah,
   to turn the hearts of the fathers to the children,
   and the disobedient to the wisdom of the just,
   to make ready for the Lord a people prepared."

Num 6:3
Judg 13:4–5
1 Sam 1:11

Jer 1:5
Is 49:1, 5

Mt 17:11–13
Mal 3:1, 23–24;
4:5–6

¹⁸And Zechariah said to the angel, "How shall I know this? For I am an old man, and my wife is advanced in years." ¹⁹And the angel answered him, "I am Gabriel, who stand in the presence of God; and I was sent to speak to you, and to bring you this good news. ²⁰And behold, you will be silent and unable to speak until the day that these things come to pass, because you did not believe my words, which will be fulfilled in their time." ²¹And the people were waiting for Zechariah, and they wondered at his delay in the temple. ²²And when he came out, he could not speak to them, and they perceived that he had seen a vision in the temple; and he made signs to them and remained dumb. ²³And when his time of service was ended, he went to his home.

Gen 15:8

Dan 8:16; 9:21
Heb 1:14

²⁴After these days his wife Elizabeth conceived, and for five months she hid herself, saying, ²⁵"Thus the Lord has done to me in the days when he looked on me, to take away my reproach among men."

Gen 30:23

The annunciation and incarnation of the Son of God

Mt 1:18–25

²⁶In the sixth month the angel Gabriel was sent from God to a city of Galilee named Nazareth, ²⁷to a virgin betrothed to a man whose name was Joseph, of the house of

tua Elisabeth pariet tibi filium, et vocabis nomen eius Ioannem. ¹⁴Et erit gaudium tibi et exsultatio, et multi in nativitate eius gaudebunt: ¹⁵erit enim magnus coram Domino et vinum et siceram non bibet et Spiritu Sancto replebitur adhuc ex utero matris suae ¹⁶et multos filiorum Israel convertet ad Dominum Deum ipsorum. ¹⁷Et ipse praecedet ante illum in spiritu et virtute Eliae, *ut convertat corda patrum in filios* et incredibiles ad prudentiam iustorum, parare Domino plebem perfectam». ¹⁸Et dixit Zacharias ad angelum: «Unde hoc sciam? Ego enim sum senex et uxor mea processit in diebus suis». ¹⁹Et respondens angelus dixit ei: «Ego sum Gabriel, qui adsto ante Deum, et missus sum loqui ad te et haec tibi evangelizare. ²⁰Et ecce eris tacens et non poteris loqui usque in diem, quo haec fiant, pro eo quod non credidisti verbis meis, quae implebuntur in tempore suo». ²¹Et erat plebs exspectans Zachariam, et mirabantur quod tardaret ipse in templo. ²²Egressus autem non poterat loqui ad illos, et cognoverunt quod visionem vidisset in templo; et ipse erat innuens illis et permansit mutus. ²³Et factum est ut impleti sunt dies officii eius, abiit in domum suam. ²⁴Post hos autem dies concepit Elisabeth uxor eius et occultabat se mensibus quinque dicens: ²⁵«Sic mihi fecit Dominus in diebus, quibus respexit auferre opprobrium meum inter homines». ²⁶In mense autem sexto missus est angelus Gabriel a Deo in civitatem Galilaeae, cui nomen Nazareth, ²⁷ad virginem desponsatam viro, cui nomen erat Ioseph de domo David, et nomen virginis Maria. ²⁸Et ingressus ad eam dixit: «Ave, gratia plena,

(24:53). This helps to show the continuity between the salvation promised to Israel and that brought about by Jesus: "It is no accident that the angel makes his appearance in the temple, for this announces the imminent coming of the true Priest and prepares the heavenly sacrifice at which the angels will minister. Let it not be doubted, then, that the angels will be present when Christ is immolated" (St Ambrose, *Expositio Evangelii secundum Lucam*, ad loc.).

1:26–38 There are several significant dimensions to the mystery of the Incarnation. Mary is a virgin, yet she conceives a child; the Child, who is truly man because he is the son of Mary, is at the same time Son of God, in the fullest sense of that title. These truths are not spelt out "theologically", so to speak; they emerge from the story as it unfolds. The narrative, therefore, is very dense in meaning. Almost every word has special significance. The Fathers of the Church and

Zeph 3:14–15
Zech 2:14
Lk 1:14; 2:10

David; and the virgin's name was Mary. ²⁸And he came to her and said, "Hail, full of grace,ᵇ² the Lord is with you!"ᶜ ²⁹But she was greatly troubled at the saying, and considered in her mind what sort of greeting this might be. ³⁰And the angel said to

Is 7:14

her,* "Do not be afraid, Mary, for you have found favour with God. ³¹And behold you will conceive in your womb and bear a son, and you shall call his name Jesus.

Is 9:6
2 Sam 7:12–16

> ³² He will be great, and will be called the Son of the Most High;
>   and the Lord God will give to him the throne of his father David,

Mic 4:7
Dan 7:14

> ³³ and he will reign over the house of Jacob for ever;
>   and of his kingdom there will be no end."

Gen 1:2
Ex 40:34–36
Lk 1:18

³⁴And Mary said to the angel, "How can this be, since I have no husband?" ³⁵And the angel said to her,

Dominus tecum». ²⁹Ipsa autem turbata est in sermone eius et cogitabat qualis esset ista salutatio. ³⁰Et ait angelus ei: «Ne timeas, Maria; invenisti enim gratiam apud Deum. ³¹Et ecce concipies in utero et paries filium, et vocabis nomen eius Iesum. ³²Hic erit magnus et Filius Altissimi vocabitur, et dabit illi Dominus Deus sedem David patris eius, ³³et regnabit super domum Iacob in aeternum, et regni eius non erit finis». ³⁴Dixit autem Maria ad angelum: «Quomodo fiet istud, quoniam virum non cognosco?». ³⁵Et respondens angelus dixit ei: «Spiritus Sanctus superveniet

church tradition were quick to see this, and even today Christians relive this scene every time they say the Angelus.

The first aspect to focus on is the setting. The previous passage was set in the imposing temple of Jerusalem; this one takes place in Nazareth, a village in Galilee which is not mentioned even once in the Old Testament. Earlier, we met two upright people who wanted to have children but could not; and God came to their rescue (1:13); now we meet a virgin who has not prayed for a child—who, in fact, asks, How can this come about? (v. 34). Clearly, the angel's message refers to a unique action of the sovereign power of almighty God (see v. 35), one which recalls the act of creation (cf. Gen 1:2), when the Spirit moved over the face of the waters to create life, and also the time in the wilderness when God brought the people of Israel into being and made his presence known to them by means of a cloud that covered the ark of the Covenant (see Ex 40:34–38).

The picture of our Lady that emerges from this passage is very eloquent. To human eyes, Mary is "a virgin betrothed to a man whose name was Joseph, of the house of David" (v. 27); but God sees her as "full of grace" (v. 28), the most remarkable created being to have come into the world until this moment; and yet she regards herself as the "handmaid of the Lord" (v. 38). All this is possible because God "before all ages made choice of, and set in her proper place, a mother for his only-begotten Son from whom he,

after being made flesh, should be born in the blessed fullness of time: and he continued his persevering regard for her in preference to all other creatures, to such a degree that for her alone he had singular regard" (Pius IX, *Ineffabilis Deus*).

Amazed though we are that God should choose to make salvation dependent on our free response, we are not surprised that he should choose for this purpose a person as exceptional as Mary. When reflecting on this scene, we can readily make our own the prayer spoken by St Bernard: "You heard the annunciation, Blessed Virgin, that you would conceive and bear a son—not by knowing man, but by the power of the Holy Spirit. Look, the angel awaits your response. [...] We too, condemned to death by divine judgment, live in hope of hearing a word of mercy. The cost of our salvation is in your hands. If you say yes, we will be set free [...] because the consolation of the sorrowful, the liberation of slaves and prisoners, the redemption of all the children of Adam, your lineage, depends on your response. [...] Open your heart to faith, your mouth to consent, and your chaste body to the Creator" (*Laudes Mariae, Sermo*, 4, 8–9).

The passage also contains a revelation about Jesus. In his opening words (vv. 30–33), the angel states that the Child marks the fulfilment of God's promises. The phrases he uses are drawn from the Old Testament—"the throne of his father David" (v. 32; cf. Is 9:6), "he will

b2 Or *O favoured one*   c Other ancient authorities add *"Blessed are you among women!"*

"The Holy Spirit will come upon you,
and the power of the Most High will overshadow you;
therefore the child to be born[d] will be called holy,
the Son of God.
[36]And behold, your kinswoman Elizabeth in her old age has also conceived a son;
and this is the sixth month with her who was called barren. [37]For with God nothing
will be impossible." [38]And Mary said, "Behold, I am the handmaid of the Lord; let
it be to me according to your word." And the angel departed from her.

Gen 18:14
Jer 32:27
Job 42:2

The Visitation

[39]In those days Mary arose and went with haste into the hill country, to a city of
Judah, [40]and she entered the house of Zechariah and greeted Elizabeth. [41]And when
Elizabeth heard the greeting of Mary, the babe leaped in her womb; and Elizabeth

Lk 1:15

in te, et virtus Altissimi obumbrabit tibi: ideoque et quod nascetur sanctum, vocabitur Filius Dei. [36]Et ecce Elisabeth cognata tua et ipsa concepit filium in senecta sua, et hic mensis est sextus illi, quae vocatur sterilis, [37]*quia non erit impossibile apud Deum omne verbum»*. [38]Dixit autem Maria: «Ecce ancilla Domini; fiat mihi secundum verbum tuum». Et discessit ab illa angelus. [39]Exsurgens autem Maria in diebus illis abiit in montana cum festinatione in civitatem Iudae [40]et intravit in domum Zachariae et salutavit Elisabeth. [41]Et factum est ut audivit salutationem Mariae Elisabeth, exsultavit infans in utero eius, et repleta est Spiritu Sancto Elisabeth [42]et exclamavit voce magna et dixit: «Benedicta tu inter mulieres, et benedictus fructus ventris tui. [43]Et unde hoc mihi, ut veniat mater Domini mei ad me? [44]Ecce enim ut facta est vox salutationis tuae in auribus

reign over the house of Jacob" (v. 33; cf. Num 24:17), and "of his kingdom there will be no end" (v. 33; cf. 2 Sam 7:16; Dan 7:14; Mic 4:7). These formulae, steeped in Old Testament ideas and language, form part of God's promise to Israel-Jacob, which includes the oracles about a Messiah who will be a descendant of David and prophetic announcements about the Kingdom of God. For a person trained in the Israelite religion and piety, there can be no mistake about their meaning. Still, the description of the Child as "holy, the Son of God" (v. 35) goes beyond anything people could have imagined. The consequences of Mary's consent (v. 38) should be seen in the context of the whole history of mankind. "Hence not a few of the early Fathers gladly assert […] in their preaching: 'The knot of Eve's disobedience was untied by Mary's obedience: what the virgin Eve bound through her disbelief, Mary loosened by her faith.' Comparing Mary with Eve, they call her 'the Mother of the living,' and frequently claim: 'death through Eve, life through Mary'" (Vatican II, *Lumen gentium*, 56).

1:39–56 In this passage we see the greatness of Mary from other points of view. Elizabeth, filled with the Holy Spirit, proclaims Mary to be "the mother of my Lord" (v. 43). But Mary's being

"mother of God" is something which Mary, too, must accept on faith, and for her doing so Elizabeth praises her (v. 45). However, the Blessed Virgin's faith is not just a personal virtue of her own; it gives rise to the New Covenant: "Just as Abraham '*in hope believed against hope*, that he should become the father of many nations' (cf. Rom 4:18), so Mary, at the Annunciation, having professed her virginity ('How shall this be, since I have no husband?'), *believed* that through the power of the Most High, by the power of the Holy Spirit, she would become the Mother of God's Son in accordance with the angel's revelation" (John Paul II, *Redemptoris Mater*, 14).

The hill country of Judea was about 130 kilometres (80 miles) from Nazareth. According to a tradition that goes back to the fourth century, Zechariah's house was in what is now the village of Ain-Karim, about eight kilometres west of Jerusalem. There the infant John leaps in the womb of his mother. Theologians ancient and modern read this as a sign that the Baptist was sanctified in his mother's womb: "Reflect on how exact and perfect each word is: Elizabeth was the first to hear the voice, but John the first to experience grace; whereas the natural sound of words rang in his mother's ears, John rejoiced in the mystery of what they meant. Elizabeth felt Mary's presence at her side; John, the closeness

d Other ancient authorities add *of you*

Judg 5:24
Jud 13:23
was filled with the Holy Spirit [42]and she exclaimed with a loud cry, "Blessed are you among women, and blessed is the fruit of your womb! [43]And why is this granted me, that the mother of my Lord should come to me? [44]For behold, when the voice of Lk 11:28 your greeting came to my ears, the babe in my womb leaped for joy. [45]And blessed is she who believed that there would be[e] a fulfilment of what was spoken to her from the Lord."

The Magnificat

1 Sam 2: 1–10 [46]And Mary said,

"My soul magnifies the Lord,

Hab 3:18
Lk 1:38
1 Sam 1:11
Is 29:19; 61:10 [47] and my spirit rejoices in God my Saviour,

[48] for he has regarded the low estate of his handmaiden.

meis, exsultavit in gaudio infans in utero meo. [45]Et beata, quae credidit, quoniam perficientur ea, quae dicta sunt ei a Domino». [46]Et ait Maria: «Magnificat *anima mea Dominum*, / [47]et *exsultavit* spiritus meus *in Deo salvatore meo*, / [48]quia *respexit humilitatem ancillae* suae. / Ecce enim ex hoc beatam me dicent omnes generationes, / [49]quia fecit mihi magna, qui potens est, / et sanctum nomen eius, / [50]et misericordia eius in prog-

of the Lord. Elizabeth heard her cousin's greeting; John felt the presence of her Son. The two women spoke of grace, but their two sons experienced grace and communicated that gift to their mothers in such a way that, in a double miracle, both women began to prophesy, inspired by their sons" (St Ambrose, *Expositio Evangelii secundum Lucam*, ad loc.).

"Outstanding among the saints is Mary, Mother of the Lord and mirror of all holiness. In the Gospel of Luke we find her engaged in a service of charity to her cousin Elizabeth, with whom she remained for 'about three months' (1:56) so as to assist her in the final phase of her pregnancy. '*Magnificat anima mea Dominum*,' she says on the occasion of that visit, 'My soul magnifies the Lord' (Lk 1:46). In these words she expresses her whole programme of life: not setting herself at the centre, but leaving space for God, who is encountered both in prayer and in service of neighbour—only then does goodness enter the world. Mary's greatness consists in the fact that she wants to magnify God, not herself. She is lowly: her only desire is to be the handmaid of the Lord (cf. Lk 1:38, 48). She knows that she will only contribute to the salvation of the world if, rather than carrying out her own projects, she places herself completely at the disposal of God's initiatives. Mary is a woman of hope: only because she believes in God's promises and awaits the salvation of Israel, can the angel visit her and call her to the decisive service of these promises. Mary is a woman of faith:

'Blessed are you who believed', Elizabeth says to her (cf. Lk 1:45). The *Magnificat*—a portrait, so to speak, of her soul—is entirely woven from threads of Holy Scripture, threads drawn from the Word of God. Here we see how completely at home Mary is with the Word of God; with ease she moves in and out of it. She speaks and thinks with the Word of God; the Word of God becomes her word, and her word issues from the Word of God. Here we see how her thoughts are attuned to the thoughts of God, how her will is one with the will of God. Since Mary is completely imbued with the Word of God, she is able to become the Mother of the Word Incarnate. Finally, Mary is a woman who loves. How could it be otherwise? As a believer who in faith thinks with God's thoughts and wills with God's will, she cannot fail to be a woman who loves. We sense this in her quiet gestures, as recounted by the infancy narratives in the Gospel. We see it in the delicacy with which she recognizes the need of the spouses at Cana and makes it known to Jesus. We see it in the humility with which she recedes into the background during Jesus' public life, knowing that the Son must establish a new family and that the Mother's hour will come only with the Cross, which will be Jesus' true hour (cf. Jn 2:4; 13:1). When the disciples flee, Mary will remain beneath the Cross (cf. Jn 19:25–27); later, at the hour of Pentecost, it will be they who gather around her as they wait for the Holy Spirit (cf. Acts 1:14)" (Benedict XVI, *Deus caritas est*, 41).

e Or *believed, for there will be*

For behold, henceforth all generations will call me blessed;
⁴⁹ for he who is mighty has done great things for me,
and holy is his name.
⁵⁰ And his mercy is on those who fear him   Ps 103:13, 17
from generation to generation.
⁵¹ He has shown strength with his arm,   Ps 33:10; 89:10
he has scattered the proud in the imagination of their hearts,
⁵² he has put down the mighty from their thrones,   2 Sam 22:28
Ps 113:5–6; 147:6
and exalted those of low degree;   Job 12:19
⁵³ he has filled the hungry with good things,   Ps 107:9
and the rich he has sent empty away.
⁵⁴ He has helped his servant Israel,   Is 41:8
in remembrance of his mercy,   Ps 98:3
⁵⁵ as he spoke to our fathers,   Gen 17:7; 18:18;
22:15–18
to Abraham and to his posterity for ever."*   Mic 7:20
⁵⁶And Mary remained with her about three months, and returned to her home.   2 Sam 6:11

Birth and circumcision of John the Baptist

⁵⁷Now the time came for Elizabeth to be delivered, and she gave birth to a son.   Gen 25:24
⁵⁸And her neighbours and kinsfolk heard that the Lord had shown great mercy to her,   Lk 1:14
and they rejoiced with her. ⁵⁹And on the eighth day they came to circumcise the   Gen 17:12
child; and they would have named him Zechariah after his father, ⁶⁰but his mother   Lev 12:3
said, "Not so; he shall be called John." ⁶¹And they said to her, "None of your kin-   Lk 1:23
dred is called by this name." ⁶²And they made signs to his father, inquiring what he
would have him called. ⁶³And he asked for a writing tablet, and wrote, "His name is
John." And they all marvelled. ⁶⁴And immediately his mouth was opened and his   Lk 2:20
tongue loosed, and he spoke, blessing God. ⁶⁵And fear came on all their neighbours.

enies et progenies / timentibus eum. / ⁵¹Fecit potentiam in brachio suo, / dispersit superbos mente cordis sui; / ⁵²deposuit potentes de sede / et exaltavit humiles; / ⁵³esurientes implevit bonis / et divites dimisit inanes. / ⁵⁴Suscepit Israel puerum suum, / recordatus misericordiae, / ⁵⁵sicut locutus
est ad patres nostros, / Abraham et semini eius in saecula». ⁵⁶Mansit autem Maria cum illa quasi mensibus tribus et reversa est in domum suam.
⁵⁷Elisabeth autem impletum est tempus pariendi, et peperit filium. ⁵⁸Et audierunt vicini et cognati eius quia magnificavit Dominus misericordiam
suam cum illa, et congratulabantur ei. ⁵⁹Et factum est in die octavo venerunt circumcidere puerum et vocabant eum nomine patris eius Zachariam.
⁶⁰Et respondens mater eius dixit: «Nequaquam, sed vocabitur Ioannes». ⁶¹Et dixerunt ad illam: «Nemo est in cognatione tua, qui vocetur hoc
nomine». ⁶²Innuebant autem patri eius quem vellet vocari eum. ⁶³Et postulans pugillarem scripsit dicens: «Ioannes est nomen eius». Et mirati sunt
universi. ⁶⁴Apertum est autem ilico os eius et lingua eius, et loquebatur benedicens Deum. ⁶⁵Et factus est timor super omnes vicinos eorum, et

1:57–80 In two consecutive passages (1:57–80; 2:1–21), the Gospel recounts the births and circumcisions of John the Baptist and Jesus. There are interesting contrasts here: whereas John is born at home, surrounded by rejoicing and marvelling (vv. 58, 63–66), Jesus will be born away from home, with a manger for his crib, and only his parents and some shepherds to greet him (2:1–20).

In the case of John the Baptist, the focus is mainly on his circumcision, because that is when God's intervention is revealed. When Zechariah (v. 63) carries out the instruction given him by the angel (1:13), his speech returns: "With good

reason was his tongue loosed, because faith untied what had been tied by disbelief " (St Ambrose, *Expositio Evangelii secundum Lucam*, ad loc.).

God's part in these events causes the people to wonder what role he has planned for John. Zechariah, who already knows that his son is to be the precursor of God's Messiah (1:14–17), intones a canticle of praise (the Benedictus) in which he proclaims God's deliverance of Israel (vv. 68–75), which will culminate with the arrival of the Lord himself (vv. 76–79). These descriptions of God—Lord (v. 76) and Saviour (vv. 69, 71, 77)—are the same as those used to

And all these things were talked about through all the hill country of Judea; 66and all who heard them laid them up in their hearts, saying, "What then will this child be?" For the hand of the Lord was with him.

Canticle of Zechariah

67And his father Zechariah was filled with the Holy Spirit, and prophesied, saying,

Ps 41:13; 72:18;
106:48; 111:9

> 68 "Blessed be the Lord God of Israel,
>   for he has visited and redeemed his people,
> 69and has raised up a horn of salvation *for us
>   in the house of his servant David,

Lk 24:25, 44

> 70as he spoke by the mouth of his holy prophets from of old,

Ps 106:10

> 71that we should be saved from our enemies,
>   and from the hand of all who hate us;

Ps 105:8; 106:45
Gen 17:7

> 72to perform the mercy promised to our fathers,
>   and to remember his holy covenant,

Lev 26:42
Mic 5:20

> 73the oath which he swore to our father Abraham,

Mic 4:10

> 74to grant us that we, being delivered from the hand of our enemies,
>   might serve him without fear,
> 75in holiness and righteousness before him all the days of our life.

Ex 23:20
Mic 3:1
Is 40:3

> 76And you, child, will be called the prophet of the Most High;
>   for you will go before the Lord to prepare his ways,

Jer 31:34

> 77to give knowledge of salvation to his people
>   in the forgiveness of their sins,

Mic 3:1
Is 60:1–2

> 78through the tender mercy of our God,
>   when the day shall dawn upon[f] us from on high

Is 9:1; 42:7; 58:8
Ps 104:10

> 79to give light to those who sit in darkness and in the shadow of death,
>   to guide our feet into the way of peace."

80And the child grew and became strong in spirit, and he was in the wilderness till the day of his manifestation to Israel.

---

super omnia montana Iudaeae divulgabantur omnia verba haec. 66Et posuerunt omnes, qui audierant, in corde suo dicentes: «Quid putas puer iste erit?». Etenim manus Domini erat cum illo. 67Et Zacharias pater eius impletus est Spiritu Sancto et prophetavit dicens: 68«*Benedictus Dominus, Deus Israel,* / quia visitavit et fecit redemptionem plebi suae / 69et erexit cornu salutis nobis / in domo David pueri sui, / 70sicut locutus est per os sanctorum, / qui a saeculo sunt, prophetarum eius, / 71salutem ex inimicis nostris / et de manu omnium, qui oderunt nos; / 72ad faciendam misericordiam cum patribus nostris / et memorari testamenti sui sancti, / 73iusiurandum, quod iuravit ad Abraham patrem nostrum, / daturum se nobis, / 74ut sine timore, de manu inimicorum liberati, / serviamus illi / 75in sanctitate et iustitia coram ipso / omnibus diebus nostris. / 76Et tu, puer, propheta Altissimi vocaberis: / praeibis enim *ante faciem Domini parare vias eius,* / 77ad dandam scientiam salutis plebi eius / in remissionem peccatorum eorum, / 78per viscera misericordiae Dei nostri, / in quibus visitabit nos oriens ex alto, / 79*illuminare his, qui in tenebris et in umbra mortis sedent,* / ad dirigendos pedes nostros in viam pacis». 80Puer autem crescebat et confortabatur spiritu et erat in deserto usque in diem osten-

---

describe Jesus in the angel's announcement to the shepherds (2:11). This passage, then, speaks of John and of Jesus: "John's birth is the dividing line between the Old Testament and the New. [...] He personifies the Old and is the herald of the New. He was born of aged parents because he was to personify the Old Testament, and he was named a prophet in his mother's womb because he was to be the herald of the New. Before he was born, when the Virgin came, he leapt for joy in his mother's womb. That moment marked the start of his mission: he is the precursor, even before he himself can see or know his purpose. [...] He is born, and named, and his father's tongue is tied. [...] Zechariah's silence is an image of how the old prophecies were hidden, dark, closed before the preaching of Christ. Everything is made clear with the coming of the One of whom those prophecies speak" (St Augustine, *Sermones*, 293, 2–3).

---

f Or *whereby the dayspring will visit*. Other ancient authorities read *since the dayspring has visited*

The birth of Jesus

Mt 1:18–25

2 ¹In those days a decree went out from Caesar Augustus that all the world should be enrolled. ²This was the first enrolment, when Quirinius was governor of Syria. ³And all went to be enrolled, each to his own city. ⁴And Joseph also went up from Galilee, from the city of Nazareth, to Judea, to the city of David, which is called Bethlehem, because he was of the house and lineage of David, ⁵to be enrolled with Mary, his betrothed, who was with child. ⁶And while they were there, the time came for her to be delivered. ⁷And she gave birth to her first-born* son and wrapped him in swaddling cloths, and laid him in a manger, because there was no place for them in the inn.

Lk 1:27

sionis suae ad Israel. [2] ¹Factum est autem in diebus illis exiit edictum a Caesare Augusto, ut describeretur universus orbis. ²Haec descriptio prima facta est praeside Syriae Quirino. ³Et ibant omnes, ut profiterentur, singuli in suam civitatem. ⁴Ascendit autem et Ioseph a Galilaea de civitate Nazareth in Iudaeam in civitatem David, quae vocatur Bethlehem, eo quod esset de domo et familia David, ⁵ut profiteretur cum Maria desponsata sibi, uxore praegnante. ⁶Factum est autem cum essent ibi, impleti sunt dies, ut pareret, ⁷et peperit filium suum primogenitum; et pannis

2:1–7 The Gospel says very little about the birth of Jesus. However, it does indicate where it took place (Bethlehem), and the poverty and difficulties that marked it. This is an example of how God uses human events to put his plans into effect, and there is a message here for us to learn: "Is there any clearer way of declaring his mercy than by deigning to take on our miserable condition? Could there be anything more abounding in piety than that the Word of God should have made himself as one of such little worth as ourselves? Men ought to deduce from these facts what great concern God has for them; may they understand what God thinks and feels for them" (St Bernard, *In Epiphania Domini, Sermo*, 1, 2).

"A decree went out from Caesar" (v. 1). The only evidence from extrabiblical sources is of a general census in the time of Quirinius in AD 6, that is, some ten or twelve years after the birth of our Lord (see "The Dating of the Life of Our Lord Jesus Christ", pp. 34–35, above). But there may have been other general censuses and there certainly would have been local ones. Jesus' family may have gone to Bethlehem in connexion with one of these censuses, and perhaps the information available to Luke did not allow him to be more precise (see the note on Acts 5:34–42). In any case, the evangelist's intention here is quite clear: he wanted to pinpoint exactly when Jesus' birth took place, and, not having a general calendar of the type now available, he mentions Quirinius (v. 2), the governor of Syria, on which country Judea was politically dependent, and he

also mentions an edict of Caesar Augustus (v. 1), who reigned from 27 BC to AD 14. This reference also suggests a paradox: in his time Caesar presented himself as the saviour of mankind and, to perpetuate his memory, he supported the arts, to such a degree that his reign became known as the "century of Augustus". However, the true Saviour, as the angel will go on to say, is Jesus, and his birth will mark the start of a new age and a new dating system. Early Christian exegesis read this into that passage: "Being included in the census along with everybody else in the world, he could make them all holy [...]; he wrote their names in the book of the living: the names of those who believed in him were added to the census of the saints of God, to whom be glory and power for ever and ever" (Origen, *Homilia X in Lucam*, 6).

"She gave birth to her first-born son" (v. 7). The term "first-born", in biblical usage, does not necessarily imply subsequent births; it has to do with the child's dignity and rights (see Deut 21:17; 1 Kings 16:31; Heb 1:6 and 12:23). "Since the law of primogeniture applied also to a child who had no brothers or sisters, the term 'first-born' refers to the first child born of the mother's womb, not only to the first child in a family of children" (St Jerome, *Adversus Helvidium*, 9). The Church teaches as a truth of faith the perpetual virginity of Mary (see *Catechism of the Catholic Church*, 499); and some Fathers extended this teaching to include St Joseph: "You say that Mary was not ever-virgin, but I tell you that Joseph was also a virgin, through Mary,

The adoration of the shepherds

⁸And in that region there were shepherds out in the field, keeping watch over their flock by night. ⁹And an angel of the Lord appeared to them, and the glory of the Lord shone around them, and they were filled with fear. ¹⁰And the angel said to them, "Be not afraid; for behold, I bring you good news of a great joy which will come to all the people; ¹¹for to you is born this day in the city of David a Saviour, who is Christ the Lord. ¹²And this will be a sign for you: you will find a babe wrapped in swaddling cloths and lying in a manger." ¹³And suddenly there was with the angel a multitude of the heavenly host praising God and saying,

¹⁴"Glory to God in the highest,
and on earth peace among men with whom he is pleased!"^g

Jn 1:42

Ps 148:1
Lk 19:38
Is 57:19

eum involvit et reclinavit eum in praesepio, quia non erat eis locus in deversorio. ⁸Et pastores erant in regione eadem vigilantes et custodientes vigilias noctis supra gregem suum. ⁹Et angelus Domini stetit iuxta illos, et claritas Domini circumfulsit illos, et timuerunt timore magno. ¹⁰Et dixit illis angelus: «Nolite timere; ecce enim evangelizo vobis gaudium magnum, quod erit omni populo, ¹¹quia natus est vobis hodie Salvator, qui est Christus Dominus, in civitate David. ¹²Et hoc vobis signum: invenietis infantem pannis involutum et positum in praesepio». ¹³Et subito facta est cum angelo multitudo militiae caelestis laudantium Deum et dicentium: ¹⁴«Gloria in altissimis Deo, et super terram pax in hominibus bonae vol-

so that the virgin son was born of a virgin marriage. [...] If Joseph was more a protector than a spouse to Mary, it follows that the man deemed worthy to be the father of the Lord lived in perfect chastity with Mary" (St Jerome, *Adversus Helvidium*, 19). See the note on Mt 1:18–25.

"Because there was no place for them in the inn" (v. 7). By "inn" (*katalyma*) is probably meant the most spacious room in a house, which could be used as a reception room or a guestroom; the word occurs only twice more in the New Testament, where it refers to the room in which our Lord held the Last Supper (22:11; Mk 14:14). So, the evangelist may be saying that there was no suitable place in that room, and that the Holy Family wanted to preserve their privacy for the birth of Jesus. However, the poverty of the stable shows us "the grace of our Lord Jesus Christ, that though he was rich, yet for your sake he became poor, so that by his poverty you might become rich" (2 Cor 8:9). "Look at the poverty of the child wrapped in swaddling clothes and laid in a manger. What wonderful humility, what marvellous poverty! The King of angels, the Lord of heaven and earth, is laid in a manger. [...] Meditate on the humility, the sweet poverty, all the work and suffering that he endured to redeem the whole human race" (St Clare of Assisi, *Letter to Agnes of Prague*). This humility is not just an example for our benefit; it represents a gift from God, who lowers himself in order to be close to us. "God humbled himself to allow us to get near him, so that we could give

our love in exchange for his, so that our freedom might bow, not only at the sight of his power, but also before the wonder of his humility. The greatness of this Child who is God! His Father is the God who has made heaven and earth and there he is, in a manger, 'because there was no room at the inn' (Lk 2:7): there was nowhere else for the Lord of all creation" (St Josemaría Escrivá, *Christ Is Passing By*, 18).

2:8–20 The words of the angels to the shepherds reveal what Jesus' birth means. He is no ordinary child, but the Saviour, the Messiah, the Lord (v. 11). The divinity of the Child Jesus is not something obvious; that is why the angels make it known: "That which of itself is hidden needs to be manifested, but not that which is in itself is manifest. The flesh of him who was born was manifest, whereas his Godhead was hidden. And therefore it was fitting that this birth should be made known by angels, who are the ministers of God. This was why a certain *brightness* accompanied the angelic apparition, to indicate that He who was just born 'reflects the glory of God' (Heb 1:3)" (St Thomas Aquinas, *Summa theologiae*, 3, 36, 5 ad 1). The angels' words also proclaim that the coming of the Saviour into the world brings with it wonderful gifts—recognition of the glory of God, and peace for mankind (v. 14). Hence the deep significance of the adoration of the shepherds and the wise men (see Mt 2:11): the salvation brought by Christ is meant for people of every race and condition, and

g Other ancient authorities read *peace, good will among men*

¹⁵When the angels went away from them into heaven, the shepherds said to one another, "Let us go over to Bethlehem and see this thing that has happened, which the Lord has made known to us." ¹⁶And they went with haste, and found Mary and Joseph, and the babe lying in a manger. ¹⁷And when they saw it they made known the saying which had been told them concerning this child; ¹⁸and all who heard it wondered at what the shepherds told them. ¹⁹But Mary kept all these things, pondering them in her heart. ²⁰And the shepherds returned, glorifying and praising God for all they had heard and seen, as it had been told them.

Lk 2:51
Dan 7:28

The circumcision of Jesus

Mt 1:25

²¹And at the end of eight days, when he was circumcised, he was called Jesus, the name given by the angel before he was conceived in the womb.

Lk 59
Gen 17:12
Lev 12:3

The purification of Mary and the presentation of Jesus in the temple

²²And when the time came for their purification according to the law of Moses, they brought him up to Jerusalem to present him to the Lord ²³(as it is written in the law of the Lord, "Every male that opens the womb shall be called holy to the Lord") ²⁴and to offer a sacrifice according to what is said in the law of the Lord, "a pair of turtledoves, or two young pigeons."

Lev 12:2–8

Ex 13:2, 12

Lev 12:8

untatis». ¹⁵Et factum est ut discesserunt ab eis angeli in caelum, pastores loquebantur ad invicem: «Transeamus usque Bethlehem et videamus hoc verbum, quod factum est, quod Dominus ostendit nobis». ¹⁶Et venerunt festinantes et invenerunt Mariam et Ioseph et infantem positum in praesepio. ¹⁷Videntes autem notum fecerunt verbum, quod dictum erat illis de puero hoc. ¹⁸Et omnes, qui audierunt, mirati sunt de his, quae dicta erant a pastoribus ad ipsos. ¹⁹Maria autem conservabat omnia verba haec conferens in corde suo. ²⁰Et reversi sunt pastores glorificantes et laudantes Deum in omnibus, quae audierant et viderant, sicut dictum est ad illos. ²¹Et postquam consummati sunt dies octo, ut circumcideretur, vocatum est nomen eius Iesus, quod vocatum est ab angelo, priusquam in utero conciperetur. ²²Et postquam impleti sunt dies purgationis eorum secundum legem Moysis, tulerunt illum in Hierosolymam, ut sisterent Domino, ²³sicut scriptum est in lege Domini: «*Omne masculinum adaperiens vulvam*

therefore he chose to manifest himself to people from different nations and different backgrounds: "The shepherds were Israelites; the Magi, Gentiles. The first lived nearby; the latter, far away. Yet both came to the cornerstone, Christ" (St Augustine, *Sermones*, 202, 1).

The evangelist says that the shepherds went with haste (v. 16) to Bethlehem, and St Ambrose observes that "no one seeks Christ half-heartedly" (*Expositio Evangelii secundum Lucam,* ad loc.). Earlier, we are told that after the Annunciation, our Lady went with haste (1:39) to visit St Elizabeth. Souls who open their hearts to God experience great joy.

2:21 In the Old Testament, circumcision was the rite by which a boy or man became a member of the Chosen People: God commanded Abraham to institute circumcision as a sign of the covenant he had made with Abraham and his descendants (Gen 17:10–14). In addition to the actual circumcision, the rite involved blessings and the naming of the child. As on other occasions (see 2:22–24, 41),

Joseph and Mary fulfilled their obligations under the Law, like other Israelite families. This ceremony made Jesus a member of his people. At the council of Jerusalem, held around the year 49, the apostles declared that it was no longer necessary for this rite to be performed, since it had been replaced by Baptism, the sacrament that makes a person a member of the Church, the new People of God (see Acts 15:1–21 and *Catechism of the Catholic Church*, 527).

2:22–38 The Holy Family goes up to Jerusalem to fulfil two prescriptions of the Law of Moses— the purification of the mother (see Lev 12:1–8) and the redemption, or buying back, of the firstborn (see Ex 13:2, 12–13). This provides the occasion for Jesus to be manifested to Israel: "The presentation of Jesus in the temple shows him to be the firstborn Son who belongs to the Lord" (*Catechism of the Catholic Church*, 529). Simeon and Anna, both of them old people, stand for faithful Israel in their awaiting of the coming of their Saviour and Redeemer (vv. 25,

Simeon's prophecy

Is 40:1; 49:13
Gen 49:18 ·

²⁵Now there was a man in Jerusalem, whose name was Simeon, and this man was righteous and devout, looking for the consolation of Israel, and the Holy Spirit was upon him. ²⁶And it had been revealed to him by the Holy Spirit that he should not see death before he had seen the Lord's Christ. ²⁷And inspired by the Spirit[h] he came into the temple; and when the parents brought in the child Jesus, to do for him according to the custom of the law, ²⁸he took him up in his arms and blessed God and said,

²⁹"Lord, now lettest thou thy servant depart in peace,
according to thy word;

Is 40:5; 46:13
Is 52:10

³⁰for mine eyes have seen thy salvation
³¹which thou hast prepared in the presence of all peoples,

Is 42:6; 49:6
Acts 13:47

³²a light for revelation to the Gentiles,
and for glory to thy people Israel."

Is 8:14
Lk 20:17-18

³³And his father and his mother marvelled at what was said about him; ³⁴and Simeon blessed them and said to Mary his mother,

"Behold, this child is set for the fall* and rising of many in Israel,
and for a sign that is spoken against

Jn 19:25

³⁵(and a sword will pierce through your own soul also),
that thoughts out of many hearts may be revealed."

Anna the prophetess

³⁶And there was a prophetess Anna, the daughter of Phanuel, of the tribe of Asher; she was of a great age, having lived with her husband seven years from her virgin-

---

sanctum Domino vocabitur», ²⁴et ut darent hostiam secundum quod dictum est in lege Domini: *par turturum aut duos pullos columbarum*. ²⁵Et ecce homo erat in Ierusalem, cui nomen Simeon, et homo iste iustus et timoratus, exspectans consolationem Israel, et Spiritus Sanctus erat super eum, ²⁶et responsum acceperat ab Spiritu Sancto non visurum se mortem nisi prius videret Christum Domini. ²⁷Et venit in Spiritu in templum. Et cum inducerent puerum Iesum parentes eius, ut facerent secundum consuetudinem legis pro eo, ²⁸et ipse accepit eum in ulnas suas et benedixit Deum et dixit: ²⁹«Nunc dimittis servum tuum, Domine, / secundum verbum tuum in pace, / ³⁰quia viderunt oculi mei / salutare tuum, / ³¹quod parasti / ante faciem omnium populorum, / ³²lumen ad revelationem gentium / et gloriam plebis tuae Israel». ³³Et erat pater eius et mater mirantes super his, quae dicebantur de illo. ³⁴Et benedixit illis Simeon et dixit ad Mariam matrem eius: «Ecce positus est hic in ruinam et resurrectionem multorum in Israel et in signum, cui contradicetur ³⁵—et tuam ipsius animam pertransiet gladius— ut revelentur ex multis cordibus cogitationes». ³⁶Et erat Anna prophetissa, filia Phanuel, de tribu Aser. Haec processerat in diebus multis et vixerat cum viro annis septem a virginitate sua; ³⁷et

---

37) and who praise God for letting them see their hopes fulfilled (vv. 28–30, 38).

Among the Jews, first-born sons belonged to the Lord. Those not of the tribe of Levi had to be redeemed—in the temple, to show that they continued to be God's property (see the notes on Ex 13:1–2 and Num 3:11–13). This public redemption was usually carried out within one month of the child's birth. The redemption price was five silver shekels (see Num 18:16). A mother who had given birth to a male child was considered to be unclean for seven days and was obliged to go to the temple forty days after the birth, to undergo a purification rite and to make an offering—a lamb or, if she was poor, two turtledoves or two young pigeons (see Lev 12:1–8). The precept did not apply either to Jesus, the Son of God, or to the Virgin Mary, who had conceived

her Son without having intercourse and whose virginity was intact even after she had given birth. But this was a mystery of which no one outside the Holy Family was aware at the time. Joseph and Mary made the offering prescribed for the poor—not that laid down for the well-off, nor that applying to the truly needy: "Through this example, foolish child, won't you learn to fulfil the holy Law of God, regardless of any personal sacrifice? Purification! You and I certainly do need purification. Atonement and, more than atonement, Love. Love as a searing iron to cauterize our soul's uncleanness, and as a fire to kindle with divine flames the wretchedness of our hearts" (St Josemaría Escrivá, *Holy Rosary*, fourth joyful mystery).

Simeon is introduced as a man led by the Holy Spirit (vv. 25, 26, 27), and therefore what

h Or *in the Spirit*

ity, ³⁷and as a widow till she was eighty-four. She did not depart from the temple, worshipping with fasting and prayer night and day. ³⁸And coming up at that very hour she gave thanks to God, and spoke of him to all who were looking for the redemption of Jerusalem.

1 Tim 5:5
Jud 8:4–5

Is 52:9

The childhood of Jesus

³⁹And when they had performed everything according to the law of the Lord, they returned to Galilee, to their own city, Nazareth. ⁴⁰And the child grew and became strong, filled with wisdom; and the favour of God was upon him.

Mt 2:23

Lk 1:80; 2:52

haec vidua usque ad annos octoginta quattuor, quae non discedebat de templo, ieiuniis et obsecrationibus serviens nocte ac die. ³⁸Et haec ipsa hora superveniens confitebatur Deo et loquebatur de illo omnibus, qui exspectabant redemptionem Ierusalem. ³⁹Et ut perfecerunt omnia secundum legem Domini, reversi sunt in Galilaeam in civitatem suam Nazareth. ⁴⁰Puer autem crescebat et confortabatur plenus sapientia; et gratia Dei erat super illum. ⁴¹Et ibant parentes eius per omnes annos in Ierusalem in die festo Paschae. ⁴²Et cum factus esset annorum duodecim, ascendentibus

he has to say is particularly significant (vv. 29–32): he acknowledges Jesus as the expected Messiah, but also as "light" and "salvation" for all mankind. However, in the plan of God, Jesus will mean "the fall and rising of many in Israel", and his salvific mission will be a "sign" of contradiction. This marks the start of the sorrow and joy that together will punctuate the life of our Lord. Finally, "the sword of sorrow predicted for Mary announces Christ's perfect and unique oblation on the cross that will impart the salvation God had 'prepared in the presence of all peoples'" (*Catechism of the Catholic Church*, 529). The fact that Simeon says this to Mary shows us the fact that she shares in Christ's sacrifice: "Simeon's words seem like a second *Annunciation to Mary*, for they tell her of the actual historical situation in which the Son is to accomplish his mission, namely in misunderstanding and sorrow. While this announcement on the one hand confirms her faith in the accomplishment of the divine promises of salvation, on the other hand it also reveals to her that she will have to live her obedience of faith in suffering, at the side of the suffering Saviour, and that her motherhood will be mysterious and sorrowful" (John Paul II, *Redemptoris Mater*, 16). The Blessed Virgin and St Joseph marvelled (v. 33) when they learned of these new aspects of the mystery of their Son: he is to be not only the glory of his people, but the salvation of all mankind.

Anna's testimony (vv. 36–38) is very similar to Simeon's. Just as Simeon had been awaiting the consolation of Israel (v. 25), Anna had been looking to the redemption of Jerusalem (v. 38). This episode means that Christ's person and mission are already attested by three kinds of witnesses and in three different ways—first, by the angels who proclaim his coming; secondly, by the shepherds, after the angels appear to them; and thirdly by Simeon and Anna, moved by the Holy Spirit. Those who, like Simeon and Anna, persevere in their devotion and in the service of God become good messengers through whom the Holy Spirit can bring others to know Christ.

2:39–40 These two verses sum up Jesus' life in Nazareth. This town is not mentioned in the Old Testament, but archaeology has shown that it had been a place of settlement for over one thousand years prior to this time. It was no more than a cluster of poor dwellings, built into a hillside in Lower Galilee, home to a few Jewish families who subsisted by farming in one form or another; there would have been a craftsman, like Joseph, to supply for their various needs.

In Jesus' time there was a tradition (see Flavius Josephus, *Antiquitates iudaicae*, 2, 9, 6; 5, 4, 10; Philo, *De vita Moysis*, 5, 10, 4) that some personages, such as Moses and Samuel, showed amazing intelligence even as children. The evangelist here mentions Jesus' gifts, but he will immediately go on to show (see 2:49) that Jesus was much more remarkable than either Moses or Samuel. St Bede comments on this passage as follows: "Our Lord Jesus Christ as a child, that is, as one clothed in the fragility of human nature, had to grow and become stronger, but as the eternal Word of God he had no need to

The finding in the temple

Deut 16:16

⁴¹Now his parents went to Jerusalem every year at the feast of the Passover. ⁴²And when he was twelve years old, they went up according to custom; ⁴³and when the feast was ended, as they were returning, the boy Jesus stayed behind in Jerusalem. His parents did not know it, ⁴⁴but supposing him to be in the company they went a day's journey, and they sought him among their kinsfolk and acquaintances; ⁴⁵and when they did not find him, they returned to Jerusalem, seeking him. ⁴⁶After three days they found him in the temple, sitting among the teachers, listening to them and asking them questions; ⁴⁷and all who heard him were amazed at his understanding and his answers. ⁴⁸And when they saw him they were astonished; and his mother said to him, "Son, why have you treated us so? Behold, your father and I have been looking for you anxiously." ⁴⁹And he said to them, "How is it that you sought me? Did you not know that I must be in my Father's house?"* ⁵⁰And they did not understand the saying which he spoke to them.

Lk 4:22
Jn 7:15

Jn 2:16

illis secundum consuetudinem diei festi, ⁴³consummatisque diebus, cum redirent, remansit puer Iesus in Ierusalem, et non cognoverunt parentes eius. ⁴⁴Existimantes autem illum esse in comitatu, venerunt iter diei et requirebant eum inter cognatos et notos ⁴⁵et non invenientes regressi sunt in Ierusalem requirentes eum. ⁴⁶Et factum est post triduum invenerunt illum in templo sedentem in medio doctorum, audientem illos et interrogantem eos; ⁴⁷stupebant autem omnes, qui eum audiebant, super prudentia et responsis eius. ⁴⁸Et videntes eum admirati sunt, et dixit Mater eius ad illum: «Fili, quid fecisti nobis sic? Ecce pater tuus et ego dolentes quaerebamus te». ⁴⁹Et ait ad illos: «Quid est quod me quaerebatis? Nesciebatis quia in his, quae Patris mei sunt, oportet me esse?». ⁵⁰Et ipsi non intellexerunt verbum, quod locutus est ad illos. ⁵¹Et descendit cum eis et venit Nazareth et erat subditus illis. Et mater eius conservabat omnia verba in corde suo. ⁵²Et Iesus *proficiebat* sapientia et aetate *et gratia*

become stronger or to grow. Hence he is rightly described as full of wisdom and grace" (*In Lucae Evangelium*, ad loc.).

It is a feature of the infancy narrative that it contains almost nothing about things that Jesus did or said: we learn about who he is from the actions and words of other people in the accounts. The episode reported in this passage marks a change from this approach. At the Annunciation, the angel proclaimed Jesus to be the Son of God (1:35); the voice from heaven at Jesus' baptism will do the same (3:22); in between those two testimonies, Jesus himself refers to God as his Father (v. 49): "The finding of Jesus in the temple is the only event that breaks the silence of the Gospels about the hidden years of Jesus. Here Jesus lets us catch a glimpse of the mystery of his total consecration to a mission that flows from his divine sonship" (*Catechism of the Catholic Church*, 534).

The feast of the Unleavened Bread and the Passover, together, constituted one of the three feasts when the men of Israel were supposed to go on pilgrimage to the temple at Jerusalem (see Deut 16:16). Women and children were not obliged to fulfil this precept, but devout families normally brought even very young children with them. It is easy to see how Jesus could have

gone missing. At times like this, the population of Jerusalem was often three times its normal size. People used to travel in caravans, and in two groups, one made up of men, the other of women. Children could go with either group. When a stop was made on the journey, families would meet up again; maybe this was when Mary and Joseph realized that the Child had remained behind. The evangelist does not say much about this journey because what interests him is the dialogue between Jesus and his Mother. Jesus' parents find him "listening to [the teachers] and asking them questions" (v. 46), and all the people there are "amazed at his understanding" (v. 47). This prepares us for what follows: Jesus is not an ordinary child, or even a child who happens to be more clever than others: he is the Son of God. Jesus' reply to his Mother seems surprisingly remote, but to understand it one needs to remember that the Semitic mind relishes contrasts and antitheses. St Ambrose explains that Jesus "does not reproach them for having searched for their son; his words are intended to make them raise the eyes of their souls to see what is due to the One whose Eternal Son he is" (*Expositio Evangelii secundum Lucam*, ad loc.).

The hidden life of Jesus at Nazareth   Mt 2:23

⁵¹And he went down with them and came to Nazareth, and was obedient to them;   Lk 2:19
and his mother kept all these things in her heart.

⁵²And Jesus increased in wisdom and in stature,ⁱ and in favour with God and man.   Lk 1:80; 2:40
                                                                                          1 Sam 2:26

2. PRELUDE TO THE PUBLIC MINISTRY OF JESUS*

                                                                                          Mt 3:1–12
                                                                                          Mk 1:1–8
John the Baptist preaching in the wilderness   Jn 1:19–34

3 ¹In the fifteenth year of the reign of Tiberius Caesar, Pontius Pilate being governor of Judea, and Herod being tetrarch of Galilee, and his brother Philip tetrarch

apud Deum et homines. [3] ¹Anno autem quinto decimo imperii Tiberii Caesaris, procurante Pontio Pilato Iudaeam, tetrarcha autem Galilaeae
Herode, Philippo autem fratre eius tetrarcha Ituraeae et Trachonitidis regionis, et Lysania Abilinae tetrarcha, ²sub principe sacerdotum Anna et
Caipha, factum est verbum Dei super Ioannem Zachariae filium in deserto. ³Et venit in omnem regionem circa Iordanem praedicans baptismum

2:51–52 Luke ends his account of Jesus' childhood with a summary of the life led by Jesus and
Mary during those years—a few short phrases,
but they say a great deal; they are a refrain to the
infancy narrative (see 2:19, 39–40).

Jesus "was obedient to them". In the episode
just reported, Jesus was shown to be obedient to
the will of the Father (2:49); but, for Jesus, obedience to God includes obeying his parents:
"Christ, to whom the whole universe is subject,
was subject to his parents" (St Augustine, *Sermones*, 51, 19). By obeying his parents, Jesus
"increased in wisdom and stature" (v. 52).
Christ's entire life is a revelation of the Father;
these hidden years, too. "His hidden years are
not without significance, nor were they simply a
preparation for the years which were to come
after—those of his public life. [...] God wants
our Lord's whole life to be an example for Christians. [...] Our Lord wants many people to ratify
their vocation during years of quiet, unspectacu-
lar living" (St Josemaría Escrivá, *Christ Is Passing By*, 20).

We are told that Mary "kept all these things
in her heart" (v. 51). The term translated as
"things" could also mean "words". So, the evangelist is saying that not only was the word of the
Lord accomplished in Mary (1:38), she was
already practising something that Jesus identified
as basic to how his disciples should live: they
should listen to the word of God and live it out
(8:21; 11:28): "May all share in the soul of Mary,
to glorify the Lord, and in the spirit of Mary, to
rejoice in God. There is only one Mother of

Christ according to the flesh, but Christ is the
fruit of all mankind, for, as long as it is kept pure
and unstained by sin, every soul receives the
Word of God" (St Ambrose, *Expositio Evangelii
secundum Lucam*, ad loc.).

*3:1—4:13** St Luke outlines Jesus' preparation
for his public ministry by focusing on three
things—the figure of the Baptist (3:1–20), Jesus'
baptism (3:21–22) and the temptations in the
wilderness (4:1–13). To this he adds the genealogy (3:23–38). The third Gospel, typically, identifies the stages in the history of salvation and
where they occur; thus Luke mentions the
imprisonment of the Baptist earlier than the other
Synoptics do (3:19–20; cf. Mt 14:3–4; Mk 6:17–
18), because this helps to show that the time of
the Baptist comes before the public life of Jesus.
Similarly, he presents as the last temptation the
one in Jerusalem (4:9), because Jerusalem holds
a central position in his account: it was there that
the Lord was made manifest as a light for the
Gentiles (2:22–35); it will be from there that he
makes his "departure" (9:31); and it is there, too,
that he will charge his disciples with their mission to the whole world (24:47).

3:1–20 All four evangelists report John the Baptist's activity that preceded Christ's public life,
but Luke goes into the most detail, and his
account is the most carefully ordered: he
describes the general background (vv. 1–2),
John's mission (vv. 3–6), the content of his message (vv. 7–14), his connexion with the Messiah,

ⁱ Or *years*

Ezek 1:3
Jer 1:2
Hos 1:1
Lk 1:77 of the region of Ituraea and Trachonitis, and Lysanias tetrarch of Abilene, ²in the high-priesthood of Annas and Caiaphas,* the word of God came to John the son of Zechariah in the wilderness; ³and he went into all the region about the Jordan, preaching a baptism of repentance for the forgiveness of sins. ⁴As it is written in the book of the words of Isaiah the prophet,

Is 40:3–5
"The voice of one crying in the wilderness:
Prepare the way of the Lord,
make his paths straight.
⁵Every valley shall be filled,
and every mountain and hill shall be brought low,
and the crooked shall be made straight,
and the rough ways shall be made smooth;

Acts 28:28
⁶and all flesh shall see the salvation of God.'"

paenitentiae in remissionem peccatorum, ⁴sicut scriptum est in libro sermonum Isaiae prophetae: «Vox clamantis in deserto: / "Parate viam Domini, / rectas facite semitas eius. / ⁵Omnis vallis implebitur / et omnis mons et collis humiliabitur; / et erunt prava in directa, / et aspera in vias planas: / ⁶et videbit omnis caro salutare Dei"». ⁷Dicebat ergo ad turbas, quae exibant, ut baptizarentur ab ipso: «Genimina viperarum, quis osten-

who is now on his way (vv. 15–18), and finally his imprisonment (vv. 19–20).

Luke identifies precisely when and where John the Baptist began to preach (see vv. 1–2): The fifteenth year of the reign of Tiberius Caesar corresponds to AD 28/29 depending on which of two possible dating systems he might have used (see "The Dating of the Life of Our Lord Jesus Christ", pp. 35–36, above). Pontius Pilate was *praefectus* of Palestine (procurator, or governor, was the term used later) from about 26 to 36; his jurisdiction extended also to Samaria and Idumea. The Herod mentioned is Herod Antipas, who died in 39. Philip, a half-brother of Herod Antipas, was tetrarch of the region of Idumea and Trachonitis until the year 33 or 34; he is not the same man as Herod Philip, who was married to Herodias (mentioned in v. 19). The high priest was Caiaphas, who held the position from AD 18 to 36. Annas, his father-in-law, had been deposed by the Romans in the year 15 but was still very influential in Jewish political and religious life (see Jn 18:3; Acts 4:6). Many of the prophetical works of the Old Testament open with a reference to the historical background to the text, accompanied by the phrase "the word of God came to …" (v. 2); see Ezek 1:3; Hos 1:1; Mic 1:1; Zeph 1:1. The phrasing in 3:1–2 implies what Jesus will explicitly state later (16:16) — that John is the last of the prophets, and that through him God is giving the word (v. 2) for the last act in the history of salvation to begin.

The evangelist introduces the Baptist by quoting a passage from the book of Isaiah (vv. 4–6; Is 40:3–5) which tells the Jewish people that, after the Babylonian exile, a new exodus will take place, and that those who must make their way through the wilderness to the promised land will be led not by Moses but by God himself. The oracle of Isaiah quoted here appears in all four Gospels, but only St Luke includes the last verse: "and all flesh shall see the salvation of God". In this way, the universal scope of the Gospel is shown to be present even during the stage of the Precursor to the Messiah. Everyone, even tax collectors (vv. 12–13) and soldiers (v. 14), can attain salvation: "The Lord seeks to open up a path into the depth of your souls. […] The path that the word of God travels is the openness of the human heart. The human heart is deep and wide and open. […] Prepare the way for the Lord by upright conduct and make the path smooth with your good works so that the word of God can come straight to you" (Origen, *Commentarii in Ioannem*, 21, 5–7).

Because the arrival of the Lord is imminent, everyone should make ready, doing penance for their sins and mending their ways, to be able to receive the grace that the Messiah brings. Salvation does not depend on people's ancestry, or on whether or not they are descended from Abraham (v. 8): it is granted through repentance, which must find concrete expression in people's behaviour; what each person must do depends on his or her position (vv. 10–14).

[Mt 23:33]

[7]He said therefore to the multitudes that came out to be baptized by him, "You brood of vipers!* Who warned you to flee from the wrath to come? [8]Bear fruits that befit repentance, and do not begin to say to yourselves, 'We have Abraham as our father'; for I tell you, God is able from these stones to raise up children to Abraham. [9]Even now the axe is laid to the root of the trees; every tree therefore that does not bear good fruit is cut down and thrown into the fire."

[Acts 4:32, 35
Is 58:7
Ezek 18:7]

[10]And the multitudes asked him, "What then shall we do?" [11]And he answered them, "He who has two coats, let him share with him who has none; and he who has food, let him do likewise." [12]Tax collectors also came to be baptized, and said to him, "Teacher, what shall we do?" [13]And he said to them, "Collect no more than is appointed you." [14]Soldiers also asked him, "And we, what shall we do?" And he said to them, "Rob no one by violence or by false accusation, and be content with your wages."

[Jn 1:19–28
Acts 13:25]

[15]As the people were in expectation, and all men questioned in their hearts concerning John, whether perhaps he were the Christ, [16]John answered them all, "I baptize you with water; but he who is mightier than I is coming, the thong of whose sandal I am not worthy to untie; he will baptize you with the Holy Spirit and with fire. [17]His winnowing fork is in his hand, to clear his threshing floor, and to gather the wheat into his granary, but the chaff he will burn with unquenchable fire."

[18]So, with many other exhortations, he preached good news to the people.

dit vobis fugere a ventura ira? [8]Facite ergo fructus dignos paenitentiae et ne coeperitis dicere in vobis ipsis: "Patrem habemus Abraham"; dico enim vobis quia potest Deus de lapidibus istis suscitare Abrahae filios. [9]Iam enim et securis ad radicem arborum posita est; omnis ergo arbor non faciens fructum bonum exciditur et in ignem mittitur». [10]Et interrogabant eum turbae dicentes: «Quid ergo faciemus?». [11]Respondens autem dicebat illis: «Qui habet duas tunicas, det non habenti; et qui habet escas, similiter faciat». [12]Venerunt autem et publicani, ut baptizarentur, et dixerunt ad illum: «Magister, quid faciemus?». [13]At ille dixit ad eos: «Nihil amplius quam constitutum est vobis, faciatis». [14]Interrogabant autem eum et milites dicentes: «Quid faciemus et nos?». Et ait illis: «Neminem concutiatis, neque calumniam faciatis et contenti estote stipendiis vestris». [15]Existimante autem populo et cogitantibus omnibus in cordibus suis de Ioanne, ne forte ipse esset Christus, [16]respondit Ioannes dicens omnibus: «Ego quidem aqua baptizo vos. Venit autem fortior me, cuius non sum dignus solvere corrigiam calceamentorum eius; ipse vos baptizabit in Spiritu Sancto et igni, [17]cuius ventilabrum in manu eius ad purgandam aream suam et ad congregandum triticum in horreum suum, paleas autem comburet igni inexstinguibili». [18]Multa quidem et alia exhortans evangelizabat populum. [19]Herodes autem tetrarcha, cum corriperetur ab illo de

In v. 18 St Luke tells us that he has recorded only some of the exhortations with which the Baptist "preached good news to the people". Still, the summary he gives is very similar to that found in other documents of the time. Flavius Josephus records that John "was a good man who instructed the Jews in the practice of virtue, to be fair and just in their relationships with one another, to be pious before God, and to come to be baptized" (*Antiquitates iudaicae,*18, 5, 2).

The Baptist's message also makes reference to the Messiah (vv. 15–17). John tells people that he himself is not the Messiah, but that the latter will soon appear and will come with the power of a supreme judge, that is, wielding the authority of God himself, and that his status will be beyond all compare. "Learn directly from John a lesson of humility. People take him for the Messiah, and he tells them he is not; it does not occur to him to use another's mistake to his own advantage. [...]

He knows very well where their salvation lies; he knows that he is simply a lamp, and he wants to ensure that the wind of pride does not put it out" (St Augustine, *Sermones*, 293, 3).

Finally (vv. 19–20), the evangelist records the ultimate fate of John. The other Synoptic Gospels (see Mt 14:1–12; Mk 6:14–29) record how the Baptist criticized Herod for his adultery; St Luke also notes that John denounced "all the evil things" done by the tetrarch (v. 19). The arbitrariness of Herod's treatment of John can also be seen in Flavius Josephus' *Antiquitates iudaicae*, 18, 5, 2, where it is stated Herod was afraid that John the Baptist's authority "might lead his subjects to rebel against him and thought it better [...] to be rid of him; if he did not act against the Baptist, he might live to regret it when a revolution was begun. John was imprisoned in the stronghold at Makeronte because of Herod's suspicions." When Herod was defeated

Mt 14:3–4
Mk 6:17–29

John the Baptist imprisoned

[19]But Herod the tetrarch, who had been reproved by him for Herodias, his brother's wife, and for all the evil things that Herod had done, [20]added this to them all, that he shut up John in prison.

Mt 3:13–17
Mk 1:9–11

Ezek 1:1

Jn 1:32–34

Jesus is baptized

[21]Now when all the people were baptized, and when Jesus also had been baptized and was praying, the heaven was opened, [22]and the Holy Spirit descended upon him in bodily form, as a dove, and a voice came from heaven, "Thou art my beloved Son;[j] with thee I am well pleased."[k]

Mt 1:1–17

Lk 4:22

The ancestry of Jesus

[23]Jesus, when he began his ministry, was about thirty years of age, being the son (as was supposed) of Joseph,* the son of Heli, [24]the son of Matthat, the son of Levi, the

---

Herodiade uxore fratris sui et de omnibus malis, quae fecit Herodes, [20]adiecit et hoc supra omnia et inclusit Ioannem in carcere. [21]Factum est autem cum baptizaretur omnis populus et Iesu baptizato et orante, apertum est caelum, [22]et descendit Spiritus Sanctus corporali specie sicut columba super ipsum; et vox de caelo facta est: «Tu es Filius meus dilectus; in te complacui mihi». [23]Et ipse Iesus erat incipiens quasi annorum triginta, ut putabatur, filius Ioseph, qui fuit Heli, [24]qui fuit Matthat, qui fuit Levi, qui fuit Melchi, qui fuit Iannae, qui fuit Ioseph, [25]qui fuit Matthathiae,

---

later by his enemies, says Josephus, "many Jews saw his defeat as vengeance for the death of John the Baptist, as a punishment from God."

3:21–22 Jesus' baptism is covered by all three Synoptics. There are also references to it in the Gospel of St John (Jn 1:29–34) and in the Acts of the Apostles (Acts 1:5; 10:38). All these passages depict the baptism as marking the start of his ministry, or, more precisely, as being the immediate preparation for his public life. The baptism is highly significant: it means the manifestation (epiphany) of Jesus as the Messiah of Israel and the Son of God, and his acceptance of, and the first step taken in, his mission as "suffering Servant" (see the note on Mt 3:13–17). For mankind, Christ's baptism is also a sign of the world's reconciliation with God (see the note on Mk 1:9–11). This event, the adoration of the Magi (Mt 2:11) and the first miracle worked by our Lord (at the wedding at Cana: Jn 2:11) are the first three formal manifestations of the divinity of Christ; as such they are referred to in the liturgy of the solemnity of the Epiphany: "We venerate this holy day, lit up with three marvels: today, the star guides the Magi to the crib; today, the water is turned into wine at Cana; today, Christ was baptized by John in the Jordan in order to save us. Alleluia" (*Divine Office*, Magnificat antiphon, Second Vespers).

3:23–38 "Jesus was about thirty years of age" (v. 23). Apart from the fact that God planned that Jesus' ministry should start at this age, it is noteworthy too that the Jewish custom of the time was that no one should function as a teacher until he completed his thirtieth year. Jesus (like John the Baptist or, before him, Ezekiel: cf. Ezek 1:1 and note) may have explicitly observed this custom: "When he attained to the perfect age," St Thomas Aquinas comments, "when the time came for him to teach, to work miracles, and to draw men to himself, then was it fitting for his Godhead to be attested from on high by the Father's testimony, so that his teaching might become the more credible [...]: 'The Father himself who sent me has given testimony of me' [Jn 5:37]" (*Summa theologiae*, 3, 39, 8 ad 3).

The genealogies recorded by Luke and Matthew show similarities and differences. Some of the differences can be explained; we can only speculate about the reasons for others. Both genealogies have as one end point St Joseph, our Lord's immediate forebear, although both of them indicate, in different ways, that the Patriarch was not Jesus' father according to the flesh (v. 23; see Mt 1:16). Matthew's genealogy follows a descending order and begins with Abraham; Luke's is in ascending order and goes up to Adam. Neither genealogy lists all our Lord's ancestors, but this, too, is easy to explain:

---

j Or *my son* (or *the*) *Beloved*   k Other ancient authorities read *today I have begotten thee*

son of Melchi, the son of Jannai, the son of Joseph, [25]the son of Mattathias, the son of Amos, the son of Nahum, the son of Esli, the son of Naggai, [26]the son of Maath, the son of Mattathias, the son of Semein, the son of Josech, the son of Joda, [27]the son of Joanan, the son of Rhesa, the son of Zerubbabel, the son of Shealtiel,[l] the son of Neri, [28]the son of Melchi, the son of Addi, the son of Cosam, the son of Elmadam, the son of Er, [29]the son of Joshua, the son of Eliezer, the son of Jorim, the son of Matthat, the son of Levi, [30]the son of Simeon, the son of Judah, the son of Joseph, the son of Jonam, the son of Eliakim, [31]the son of Melea, the son of Menna, the son of Mattatha, the son of Nathan, the son of David, [32]the son of Jesse, the son of Obed, the son of Boaz, the son of Sala, the son of Nahshon, [33]the son of Amminadab, the son of Admin, the son of Arni, the son of Hezron, the son of Perez, the son of Judah, [34]the son of Jacob, the son of Isaac, the son of Abraham, the son of Terah, the son of Nahor, [35]the son of Serug, the son of Reu, the son of Peleg, the son of Eber, the son of Shelah, [36]the son of Cainan, the son of Arphaxad, the son of Shem, the son of Noah, the son of Lamech, [37]the son of Methuselah, the son of Enoch, the son of Jared, the son of Mahalaleel, the son of Cainan, [38]the son of Enos, the son of Seth, the son of Adam, the son of God.

1 Chron 3:4ff

1 Chron 2:1ff

1 Chron 1:24–27

1 Chron 1:1–4

Jesus fasts and is tempted in the wilderness

Mt 4:1–11
Mk 1:12–13

4 [1]And Jesus, full of the Holy Spirit, returned from the Jordan, and was led by the Spirit [2]for forty days in the wilderness, tempted by the devil. And he ate nothing

Lk 3:22

qui fuit Amos, qui fuit Nahum, qui fuit Esli, qui fuit Naggae, [26]qui fuit Maath, qui fuit Matthathiae, qui fuit Semei, qui fuit Iosech, qui fuit Ioda, [27]qui fuit Ioanna, qui fuit Resa, qui fuit Zorobabel, qui fuit Salathiel, qui fuit Neri, [28]qui fuit Melchi, qui fuit Addi, qui fuit Cosam, qui fuit Elmadam, qui fuit Her, [29]qui fuit Iesu, qui fuit Eliezer, qui fuit Iorim, qui fuit Matthat, qui fuit Levi, [30]qui fuit Simeon, qui fuit Iudae, qui fuit Ioseph, qui fuit Iona, qui fuit Eliachim, [31]qui fuit Melea, qui fuit Menna, qui fuit Matthatha, qui fuit Nathan, qui fuit David, [32]qui fuit Iesse, qui fuit Obed, qui fuit Booz, qui fuit Salmon, qui fuit Naasson, [33]qui fuit Aminadab, qui fuit Admin, qui fuit Arni, qui fuit Esrom, qui fuit Phares, qui fuit Iudae, [34]qui fuit Iacob, qui fuit Isaac, qui fuit Abrahae, qui fuit Thare, qui fuit Nachor, [35]qui fuit Seruch, qui fuit Ragau, qui fuit Phaleg, qui fuit Heber, qui fuit Sala, [36]qui fuit Cainan, qui fuit Arphaxad, qui fuit Sem, qui fuit Noe, qui fuit Lamech, [37]qui fuit Mathusala, qui fuit Henoch, qui fuit Iared, qui fuit Malaleel, qui fuit Cainan, [38]qui fuit Enos, qui fuit Seth, qui fuit Adam, qui fuit Dei. [4] [1]Iesus autem plenus Spiritu Sancto regressus est ab Iordane et agebatur in Spiritu in deserto [2]diebus quadraginta et tentabatur a Diabolo. Et nihil manducavit in diebus illis et, con-

genealogies in the Bible are not designed to simply list a person's forebears; their aim, rather, is to show his social and ethnic position and his belonging to a people (see the note on Mt 1:1–17). Matthew underlines the messianic character of our Lord (by running the genealogy from Abraham and through David); and Luke (by going back to Adam) highlights his priestly character and his mission as Saviour of all mankind. St Thomas, following St Augustine, has this to say: "Luke [...] sets forth Christ's genealogy not at the outset, but after Christ's baptism, and not in the descending but in the ascending order—as though giving prominence to the office of the Priest expiating our sins, to which the Baptist bore witness, saying, 'Behold him who takes away the sin of the world.' And in the ascending order, he passes Abraham and continues up to God, to whom we are reconciled

by cleansing and expiating" (*Summa theologiae*, 3, 31, 3 ad 3).

4:1–13 At the start of his mission as Saviour, our Lord fasts and is tempted by Satan (vv. 2–3; see the note on Mt 4:1–11). The three Synoptic Gospels say that this episode took place in the "wilderness" (v. 1). This word (see also 3:2) probably refers to the low valley on the banks of the Jordan, to the north of the Dead Sea. However, it also has a theological significance: it was in the wilderness that Moses and Israel succumbed to temptation; and it is in the wilderness that Jesus is tempted, but he is not defeated as others were: the devil wants to deflect Jesus from his mission, but Jesus defeats him. Since this Gospel in its genealogy of our Lord traces the line back to Adam, Christian Tradition has read this account as describing a victory of Jesus

l Greek *Salathiel*

in those days; and when they were ended, he was hungry. ³The devil said to him, "If you are the Son of God, command this stone to become bread." ⁴And Jesus answered him, "It is written, 'Man shall not live by bread alone.'" ⁵And the devil took him up, and showed him all the kingdoms of the world in a moment of time, ⁶and said to him, "To you I will give all this authority and their glory; for it has been delivered to me, and I give it to whom I will. ⁷If you, then, will worship me, it shall all be yours." ⁸And Jesus answered him, "It is written,

'You shall worship the Lord your God,
and him only shall you serve.'"

⁹And he took him to Jerusalem, and set him on the pinnacle of the temple, and said to him, "If you are the Son of God, throw yourself down from here; ¹⁰for it is written,

Deut 8:3

Jer 27:5

Deut 5:9; 6:13

Ps 91:11–12

summatis illis, esuriit. ³Dixit autem illi Diabolus: «Si Filius Dei es, dic lapidi huic, ut panis fiat». ⁴Et respondit ad illum Iesus: «Scriptum est: *"Non in pane solo vivet homo"*». ⁵Et sustulit illum et ostendit illi omnia regna orbis terrae in momento temporis; ⁶et ait ei Diabolus: «Tibi dabo potestatem hanc universam et gloriam illorum, quia mihi tradita est, et, cui volo, do illam: ⁷tu ergo, si adoraveris coram me, erit tua omnis». ⁸Et respondens Iesus dixit illi: «Scriptum est: *"Dominum Deum tuum adorabis et illi soli servies"*». ⁹Duxit autem illum in Ierusalem et statuit eum supra

as the antitype of Adam, thus inaugurating a renewed humanity: "As the first Adam was cast out of paradise and driven out into the wilderness, the second Adam came out of the wilderness and entered paradise. The damage is repaired by walking back over the same steps, and the divine order is restored by the return to origins" (St Ambrose, *Expositio Evangelii secundum Lucam*, ad loc.).

In the first temptation (v. 3), the devil puts Jesus' divine sonship to the test (God the Father had proclaimed it a short time earlier: cf. 3:22); in the second (vv. 5–7), he offers Jesus power over the world in exchange for worship of Satan; in the third (vv. 9–11), which takes place on the pinnacle of the temple, he suggests that Jesus escape death in a spectacular way because he is Son of God. Luke's account is very similar to Matthew's, but the temptations are given in a different order: the order of the second and third miracles is reversed. Given that the order in Matthew is the same as that of the temptations of Israel in the book of Exodus (see the note on Mt 4:1–11), and that, in St Luke's Gospel, Jerusalem, and particularly the temple, have a very high profile (they appear at the end of the infancy narrative, and at the end of the book itself), many scholars think that St Luke has changed the order here in order to give more prominence to the Holy City: Jerusalem is where our salvation will be accomplished, and it is also where Jesus conquers "every temptation" (v. 13). "As Ambrose says [...], Scripture would not

have said that 'all the temptation being ended, the devil departed from him', unless the matter of all sins were included in the three temptations already related. For the causes of temptation are the causes of desires—namely, 'lust of the flesh, desire for glory, eagerness for power'" (St Thomas Aquinas, *Summa theologiae*, 3, 41, 4 ad 4).

Jesus defeats the devil here, and the text says that Satan afterwards waits for an "opportune time" (v. 13). This must be a reference to Christ's passion and death; St Luke says that Satan "entered into Judas" (22:3) and precipitated the events of Holy Week (see the note on 22:1–6). But in the passion, too, Jesus will win victory through his filial acceptance of the Father's plans; he will deliver mankind from the one who wielded the power of death, that is, the devil (see Heb 2:14). Unlike Matthew and Mark, Luke does not mention that angels ministered to Christ after the temptations; but he will say later that an angel strengthened him during the agony in the garden of Gethsemane (22:43): "The Master wished to be tempted in every way as we are; he wished to suffer death as we suffer death; and he wished to rise from the dead so that we too may rise from the dead" (St Augustine, *Enarrationes in Psalmos*, 90, 2, 1).

This passage also shows us the methods to use to overcome temptation—prayer and fasting, not dialoguing with temptation, having words of God's Scripture on our lips, and putting our trust in the Lord.

'He will give his angels charge of you, to guard you,'

[11]and

'On their hands they will bear you up,
lest you strike your foot against a stone.'"

[12]And Jesus answered him, "It is said, 'You shall not tempt the Lord your God.'"
[13]And when the devil had ended every temptation, he departed from him until an opportune time.

Deut 6:16
Ex 17:1–17

Heb 4:15
Lk 22:3, 53
Jn 13:2, 27

PART ONE

Jesus' ministry in Galilee*

3. THE START OF JESUS' MINISTRY IN GALILEE*

[14]And Jesus returned in the power of the Spirit into Galilee, and a report concerning him went out through all the surrounding country. [15]And he taught in their synagogues, being glorified by all.

Mt 4:12–17
Lk 4:37; 5:15
Mk 1:14–15, 39

Lk 4:44

pinnam templi et dixit illi: «Si Filius Dei es, mitte te hinc deorsum. [10]Scriptum est enim: "*Angelis suis mandabit de te, / ut conservent te*" / [11]et: "*In manibus tollent te, / ne forte offendas ad lapidem pedem tuum*"». [12]Et respondens Iesus ait illi: «Dictum est: "*Non tentabis Dominum Deum tuum*"». [13]Et consummata omni tentatione, Diabolus recessit ab illo usque ad tempus. [14]Et regressus est Iesus in virtute Spiritus in Galilaeam. Et fama exiit per universam regionem de illo. [15]Et ipse docebat in synagogis eorum et magnificabatur ab omnibus. [16]Et venit Nazareth, ubi erat nutri-

*4:14—9:50 In this part of the Gospel, St Luke covers our Lord's early ministry in Galilee. In the synagogue of Nazareth, Jesus outlines what he will do (4:16–27). The "today" of salvation which he proclaims there will soon take the form of cures (see 4:38–41; 5:12–15; 7:1–23; 8:26–56), forgiveness of sins (see 5:17–26; 7:36–50), and acts of mercy and compassion (see 7:13; 9:11).

Jesus has been sent to preach good news (4:18). At the centre of his preaching we will find the Sermon on the Plain (6:17–49) and the Parables of the Kingdom (8:4–18). The evangelist likes to point out how effective and merciful Jesus' words are (see 4:31–37; 5:17–26), and how they attract huge crowds of people (see 4:37–40, 42; 5:1, 15, 19, 29).

To help him carry out his programme of salvation, Jesus chooses disciples (5:1–11, 27–28), some of whom he names as his apostles (6:12–16). He gives special training to these twelve (see 8:10; 9:21), manifests his glory to them (9:28–36) and sends them out to preach (9:1–5)—a commission which will later blossom

into the world-wide mission of the Church (see Acts 1:8).

Jesus' address in the synagogue also makes reference to this universal mission (4:25–27), which will be also seen in the episode of the centurion (7:1–10); but we will hear much more of it in the next part of the Gospel (9:51—19:27).

*4:14—6:11 The beginnings of Jesus' public ministry include his preaching in the synagogues of Galilee (4:14–15) and, later, of Judea (4:44). People are astonished by the authority with which Jesus speaks (4:32); and as a result more and more people hear of him (5:15). It comes as no surprise, then, that the Jewish authorities begin to argue with him (5:27—6:11).

4:14–15 Here Luke gives a brief summary of Jesus' activity prior to his proclamation in the synagogue of Nazareth. The central message here is not so much the preaching of the Kingdom of God (as in the other Synoptics) but the revelation of the Person of Jesus himself. In this very short summary, the Spirit is again men-

Mt 13:53–58
Mk 6:1–6

Preaching in Nazareth

Mt 11:5
Zeph 2:3
Is 58:6

[16]And he came to Nazareth, where he had been brought up; and he went to the synagogue, as his custom was, on the sabbath day.* And he stood up to read; [17]and there was given to him the book of the prophet Isaiah. He opened the book and found the place where it was written,

Is 61:1–12

[18] "The Spirit of the Lord is upon me,
because he has anointed me to preach good news to the poor.
He has sent me to proclaim release to the captives
and recovering of sight to the blind,
to set at liberty those who are oppressed,

Lev 25:10

[19] to proclaim the acceptable year of the Lord."

tus, et intravit secundum consuetudinem suam die sabbati in synagogam et surrexit legere. [17]Et traditus est illi liber prophetae Isaiae; et ut revolvit librum, invenit locum, ubi scriptum erat: [18]«Spiritus Domini super me; / propter quod unxit me / evangelizare pauperibus, / misit me praedicare captivis remissionem / et caecis visum, / dimittere confractos in remissione, / [19]praedicare annum Domini acceptum». [20]Et cum plicuisset librum,

tioned. The Holy Spirit, who intervened actively in the birth of Jesus and in the events of his infancy, is the One who directs his activity: after descending on him at his baptism (3:22), he leads him out into the wilderness (4:1) and empowers him for his mission in Galilee (v. 14), because "the humanity of Christ is one with his divinity, and he is moved by the power of God" (Nicholas of Lyra, *Postilla super Lucam*, 4).

4:16–30 This episode shows the procedure of synagogue ceremonies at the time. On the sabbath, the Jewish day for rest and prayer (see Ex 20:8–11), the people would gather to be instructed in Holy Scripture. At the beginning of this meeting they recited together the *Shema*, a summary of the Lord's precepts, and the "eighteen blessings". Then a passage was read from the book of the Law (the Pentateuch), and another from the Prophets. The leaders of the ceremony invited one of those present to address the gathering (see Acts 13:15). At times someone would volunteer to do so—as seems to have happened on this occasion. Jesus takes this opportunity to instruct the people (v. 16), and later on the apostles will do the same (see Acts 13:5, 15, 42–44; 14:1). The sabbath meeting concluded with a priestly blessing (see Num 6:22ff), recited by the leader or by a priest if one was present, and the people all answered "Amen".

Jesus reads the passage of Isaiah 61:1–2, where the prophet announces the coming of the Lord, who will free his people of their afflictions. So, the passage tells us about two things—

the salvation that God will bring about for his people, and the person chosen, anointed, by the Lord to effect it. Jesus tells them that these two elements of the divine plan have come to pass in him. For one thing, "by these actions and words Christ makes the Father present among men" (John Paul II, *Dives in misericordia*, 3). For another, by saying that the prophecy is now fulfilled in him (v. 21), Jesus implies that the message of salvation is in fact himself: "Since the 'Good News' is Christ, there is an identity between the message and the messenger, between saying, doing and being" (John Paul II, *Redemptoris missio*, 13).

"He has anointed me" (v. 18). "Christ was not anointed by men, nor was he anointed with oil or with any physical sign. The Father anointed him when he made him Saviour of the world, and he anointed him with the Holy Spirit" (St Cyril of Jerusalem, *Catecheses*, 21, 2).

"The acceptable year of the Lord" (v. 19). This is a reference to the jubilee year of the Jews, laid down by the Law (Lev 25:8ff) to happen every fifty years, to symbolize the age of redemption and deliverance that the Messiah would usher in. The age inaugurated by Christ, the time of the New Law, is "the age of grace", the time of mercy and redemption, which will be attained in their fullest form in eternal life. The Catholic Church also establishes Holy Years to announce and recall the redemption brought by Christ and its promised fullness in the afterlife.

The people of Nazareth are initially in awe of Jesus (v. 22), but soon they become filled with

²⁰And he closed the book, and gave it back to the attendant, and sat down; and the eyes of all in the synagogue were fixed on him. ²¹And he began to say to them, "Today this scripture has been fulfilled in your hearing." ²²And all spoke well of him, and wondered at the gracious words which proceeded out of his mouth; and they said, "Is not this Joseph's son?" ²³And he said to them, "Doubtless you will quote to me this proverb, 'Physician, heal yourself; what we have heard you did at Capernaum, do here also in your own country.'" ²⁴And he said, "Truly, I say to you, no prophet is acceptable in his own country. ²⁵But in truth, I tell you, there were many widows in Israel in the days of Elijah, when the heaven was shut up three years and six months, when there came a great famine over all the land; ²⁶and Elijah was sent to none of them but only to Zarephath, in the land of Sidon, to a woman who was a widow. ²⁷And there were many lepers in Israel in the time of the prophet Elisha; and none of them was cleansed, but only Naaman the Syrian." ²⁸When they heard this, all in the synagogue were filled with wrath. ²⁹And they rose up and put him out of the city, and led him to the brow of the hill on which their city was built, that they might throw him down headlong. ³⁰But passing through the midst of them he went away.

Jn 6:42

Mt 4:13

Jn 4:44

1 Kings 17:1; 18:1
Jas 5:17

1 Kings 17:9ff
2 Kings 5:9ff

In the synagogue in Capernaum

Mk 1:21–28

³¹And he went down to Capernaum, a city of Galilee. And he was teaching them on the sabbath; ³²and they were astonished at his teaching, for his word was with author-

Mt 7:28–29

reddidit ministro et sedit; et omnium in synagoga oculi erant intendentes in eum. ²¹Coepit autem dicere ad illos: «Hodie impleta est haec Scriptura in auribus vestris». ²²Et omnes testimonium illi dabant et mirabantur in verbis gratiae, quae procedebant de ore ipsius, et dicebant: «Nonne hic filius est Ioseph?». ²³Et ait illis: «Utique dicetis mihi hanc similitudinem: "Medice, cura teipsum; quanta audivimus facta in Capharnaum, fac et hic in patria tua"». ²⁴Ait autem: «Amen dico vobis: Nemo propheta acceptus est in patria sua. ²⁵In veritate autem dico vobis: Multae viduae erant in diebus Eliae in Israel, quando clausum est caelum annis tribus et mensibus sex, cum facta est fames magna in omni terra; ²⁶et ad nullam illarum missus est Elias nisi in Sarepta Sidoniae ad mulierem viduam. ²⁷Et multi leprosi erant in Israel sub Eliseo propheta; et nemo eorum mundatus est nisi Naaman Syrus». ²⁸Et repleti sunt omnes in synagoga ira haec audientes ²⁹et surrexerunt et eiecerunt illum extra civitatem et duxerunt illum usque ad supercilium montis, supra quem civitas illorum erat aedificata, ut praecipitarent eum. ³⁰Ipse autem transiens per medium illorum ibat. ³¹Et descendit in Capharnaum civitatem Galilaeae. Et docebat illos sabbatis, ³²et stupebant in doctrina eius, quia in potestate erat sermo ipsius.

anger over what he says (v. 28). In a sense this episode marks the fulfilment of Simeon's prophecy in the temple (2:34): Jesus is a cause of sorrow and joy. The unbelief of Jesus' fellow-townsmen made them want to challenge him to perform a miracle to back up his teaching. When Jesus did not oblige them, they may have decided that he was a false prophet, which would explain why they sought to be rid of him (v. 29; see Deut 13:1–5). The incident shows the narrow-mindedness that led them to fail to take our Lord's words for what they truly mean (v. 22). The episode shows us that to discover the truth about Jesus we need to be humble and unselfish.

4:31–37 Even early on in Jesus' ministry two things are evident to those who hear him: his words are backed up by works that reveal his authority (v. 32), and they actually have power to work wonders. These are the qualities that belong to the word of God in the Old Testament, for God confirms his words by actions (see Ex 19:3–6), and by means of his word he creates all things (Gen 1:3ff).

"The Holy One of God" (v. 34). The Holy One par excellence is the Anointed of God, the Messiah. By speaking as he does, the devil is telling the truth, but Jesus does not accept the testimony of this "father of lies" (see Jn 8:44). The devil sometimes utters true things in order to disguise error and to sow confusion. By telling the demon to be quiet, Jesus shows that we need to be prudent and not let ourselves be deceived by half-truths. "He commanded the demons to be silent [...] because he did not want the truth to be spoken from their unclean mouths, nor to allow them to insinuate the evil of their will into the hearts of men" (St Athanasius, *Epistula ad episcopos Aegypti et Libyae*, 3).

ity. ³³And in the synagogue there was a man who had the spirit of an unclean demon; and he cried out with a loud voice, ³⁴"Ah!^m What have you to do with us, Jesus of Nazareth? Have you come to destroy us? I know who you are, the Holy One of God." ³⁵But Jesus rebuked him, saying, "Be silent, and come out of him!" And when the demon had thrown him down in the midst, he came out of him, having done him no harm. ³⁶And they were all amazed and said to one another, "What is this word? For with authority and power he commands the unclean spirits, and they come out." ³⁷And reports of him went out into every place in the surrounding region.

Mt 8:29

Mt 8:14–15
Mk 1:29–31

Curing of Peter's mother-in-law

³⁸And he arose and left the synagogue, and entered Simon's house. Now Simon's mother-in-law was ill with a high fever, and they besought him for her. ³⁹And he stood over her and rebuked the fever, and it left her; and immediately she rose and served them.

Mt 8:16–17
Mk 1:32–34

Lk 13:13

Other cures

⁴⁰Now when the sun was setting, all those who had any that were sick with various diseases brought them to him; and he laid his hands on every one of them and healed them. ⁴¹And demons also came out of many, crying, "You are the Son of God!" But he rebuked them, and would not allow them to speak, because they knew that he was the Christ.

Mk 3:11–12

Mk 1:35–39

Lk 5:16

Jesus preaches in other cities in Judea

⁴²And when it was day he departed and went into a lonely place. And the people sought him and came to him, and would have kept him from leaving them; ⁴³but he

Lk 8:1

³³Et in synagoga erat homo habens spiritum daemonii immundi; et exclamavit voce magna: ³⁴«Sine; quid nobis et tibi, Iesu Nazarene? Venisti perdere nos? Scio te qui sis: Sanctus Dei». ³⁵Et increpavit illi Iesus dicens: «Obmutesce et exi ab illo!». Et cum proiecisset illum daemonium in medium, exiit ab illo nihilque illum nocuit. ³⁶Et factus est pavor in omnibus; et colloquebantur ad invicem dicentes: «Quod est hoc verbum, quia in potestate et virtute imperat immundis spiritibus, et exeunt?». ³⁷Et divulgabatur fama de illo in omnem locum regionis. ³⁸Surgens autem de synagoga introivit in domum Simonis. Socrus autem Simonis tenebatur magna febri; et rogaverunt illum pro ea. ³⁹Et stans super illam imperavit febri, et dimisit illam; et continuo surgens ministrabat illis. ⁴⁰Cum sol autem occidisset, omnes, qui habebant infirmos variis languoribus, ducebant illos ad eum; at ille singulis manus imponens curabat eos. ⁴¹Exibant autem daemonia a multis clamantia et dicentia: «Tu es Filius Dei». Et increpans

4:38–41 All three Synoptic Gospels report the cure of Peter's mother-in-law as one of a series of cures worked on the same day. Luke (alone) mentions people pleading for her (v. 38), so that we learn about both the effectiveness of prayer for others and the compassionate nature of our Lord: "When the sick asked our Lord to cure them, he immediately did so; he gives us to understand that he awaits the prayers of the faithful to heal the sufferings brought about by our sins" (St Jerome, in *Catena aurea*, ad loc.).

The evangelist notes that Jesus worked cures in a particular way: "he laid his hands on every one of them" (v. 40). This solicitude of Jesus for individuals carries a lesson for us. We should have concern for everyone and want them to know Christ: "No son or daughter of Holy

Church can lead a quiet life, without concern for the anonymous masses—a mob, a herd, a flock, as I once wrote. How many noble passions they have within their apparent listlessness! How much potential! We must serve all, laying our hands on each and every one, as Jesus did, *singulis manus imponens*, to bring them back to life, to enlighten their minds and strengthen their wills: so that they can become useful!" (St Josemaría Escrivá, *The Forge*, 901).

4:42–44 As in many other places in the Gospel (see 5:1, 15, 19, 29), the evangelist notes that people flocked in very large numbers to be with Jesus and to hear him. "Nobody can have all his desires satisfied in this life; no created thing can satisfy man's desire: God can satisfy in abun-

m Or *Let us alone*

said to them, "I must preach the good news of the kingdom of God to the other cities also; for I was sent for this purpose." ⁴⁴And he was preaching in the synagogues of Judea.ⁿ

The miraculous catch of fish and the calling of the first disciples

5 ¹While the people pressed upon him to hear the word of God, he was standing by the lake of Gennesaret. ²And he saw two boats by the lake; but the fishermen had gone out of them and were washing their nets. ³Getting into one of the boats, which was Simon's, he asked him to put out a little from the land. And he sat down and taught the people from the boat. ⁴And when he had ceased speaking, he said to Simon, "Put out into the deep and let down your nets for a catch." ⁵And Simon

non sinebat ea loqui, quia sciebant ipsum esse Christum. ⁴²Facta autem die, egressus ibat in desertum locum; et turbae requirebant eum et venerunt usque ad ipsum et detinebant illum, ne discederet ab eis. ⁴³Quibus ille ait: «Et aliis civitatibus oportet me evangelizare regnum Dei, quia ideo missus sum». ⁴⁴Et erat praedicans in synagogis Iudaeae. [5] ¹Factum est autem cum turba urgeret illum ut audiret verbum Dei, et ipse stabat secus stagnum Genesareth ²et vidit duas naves stantes secus stagnum; piscatores autem descenderant de illis et lavabant retia. ³Ascendens autem in unam navem, quae erat Simonis, rogavit eum a terra reducere pusillum; et sedens docebat de navicula turbas. ⁴Ut cessavit autem loqui, dixit ad Simonem: «Duc in altum et laxate retia vestra in capturam». ⁵Et respondens Simon dixit: «Praeceptor, per totam noctem laborantes nihil

dance, unto infinity" (St Thomas Aquinas, *Expositio in Credum*, 12, 1012).

5:1–11 St Luke records the calling of Peter and the other first apostles in a way that is slightly different from that of the other evangelists (see Mt 4:18–25; Mk 1:16–20; Jn 1:35–51). All the Gospels say that this took place early in Jesus' public life; and all the accounts record the authority with which Christ called them, and the immediacy of their response. However, Matthew, Mark and John, by this call as the first act of Jesus' ministry, seek to identify the disciples with their Master and his mission, whereas Luke's ordering of events places the calling of the twelve in the context of Jesus' ministry in Capernaum and his first dealings with the men that he would make his apostles.

From the narrative it is easy to see that Jesus has a special relationship with Peter: the whole conversation recorded here is between Jesus and Peter (see vv. 3, 4, 5, 8, 10). St Josemaría Escrivá makes a point based on this passage: "Before becoming apostles, we are fishermen. After becoming apostles, we are fishermen still. The same profession, before and after. What has changed? There is a change inside our soul, now that Christ has come aboard, as he went aboard Peter's boat. Its horizon has opened wider. It feels a greater ambition to serve and an irrepressible desire to tell all creation about the *magnalia Dei* (Acts 2:11), the marvellous doings of our Lord, if only

we let him work" (*Friends of God*, 264–265).

As events unfold, we learn something about the future mission of the Church: working on their own account, the disciples grow tired and see no results (v. 5), but when they begin to work in Christ's name and on his instructions, the fruit borne is vastly disproportionate to their efforts (vv. 6–10). "*Duc in altum!* These words ring out for us today, and they invite us to remember the past with gratitude, to live the present with enthusiasm and to look forward to the future with confidence: 'Jesus Christ is the same yesterday and today and for ever' (Heb 13:8)" (John Paul II, *Novo millennio ineunte*, 1). When Peter sees what the Lord has done, he is astonished (v. 9) and is acutely conscious of his personal unworthiness (v. 8). But like Zechariah (1:13), like the Blessed Virgin (1:30), like all those chosen by God for a mission, Peter is addressed by God with these encouraging words: "Do not be afraid" (v. 10). "If you feel for whatever reason that you cannot manage to go on, abandon yourself in God, telling him: Lord, I trust in you, I abandon myself in you, but do help me in my weakness! And filled with confidence, repeat: See, Jesus, what a filthy rag I am. My life seems to me so miserable. I am not worthy to be a son of yours. Tell him all this—and tell him so over and over again. It will not be long before you hear him say, *Ne timeas*—do not be afraid; and also: *Surge et ambula!*—Rise up and walk!" (St Josemaría Escrivá, *The Forge*, 287).

ⁿ Other ancient authorities read *Galilee*

answered, "Master, we toiled all night and took nothing! But at your word I will let down the nets." ⁶And when they had done this, they enclosed a great shoal of fish; and as their nets were breaking, ⁷they beckoned to their partners in the other boat to come and help them. And they came and filled both the boats, so that they began to sink. ⁸But when Simon Peter saw it, he fell down at Jesus' knees, saying, "Depart from me, for I am a sinful man, O Lord." ⁹For he was astonished, and all that were with him, at the catch of fish which they had taken; ¹⁰and so also were James and John, sons of Zebedee, who were partners with Simon. And Jesus said to Simon,

Mt 19:27
Lk 5:28; 14:33

"Do not be afraid; henceforth you will be catching men." ¹¹And when they had brought their boats to land, they left everything and followed him.

Mt 8:1–4
Mk 1:40–45

Curing of a leper

Lev 13:45–46

¹²While he was in one of the cities, there came a man full of leprosy; and when he saw Jesus, he fell on his face and besought him, "Lord, if you will, you can make me clean." ¹³And he stretched out his hand, and touched him, saying, "I will; be

Lev 13:49; 14:2–32

clean." And immediately the leprosy left him. ¹⁴And he charged him to tell no one; but "go and show yourself to the priest, and make an offering for your cleansing, as

Lk 4: 14, 37, 44

Moses commanded, for a proof to the people."° ¹⁵But so much the more the report went abroad concerning him; and great multitudes gathered to hear and to be healed

Mk 1:35

of their infirmities. ¹⁶But he withdrew to the wilderness and prayed.

Mt 9:1–8
Mk 2:1–12

Curing of a paralyzed man

¹⁷On one of those days, as he was teaching, there were Pharisees and teachers of the law sitting by, who had come from every village of Galilee and Judea and from

cepimus; in verbo autem tuo laxabo retia». ⁶Et cum hoc fecissent, concluserunt piscium multitudinem copiosam; rumpebantur autem retia eorum. ⁷Et annuerunt sociis, qui erant in alia navi, ut venirent et adiuvarent eos; et venerunt, et impleverunt ambas naviculas, ita ut mergerentur. ⁸Quod cum videret Simon Petrus, procidit ad genua Iesu dicens: «Exi a me, quia homo peccator sum, Domine». ⁹Stupor enim circumdederat eum et omnes, qui cum illo erant, in captura piscium, quos ceperant; ¹⁰similiter autem et Iacobum et Ioannem, filios Zebedaei, qui erant socii Simonis. Et ait ad Simonem Iesus: «Noli timere; ex hoc iam homines eris capiens». ¹¹Et subductis ad terram navibus, relictis omnibus, secuti sunt illum. ¹²Et factum est cum esset in una civitatum, et ecce vir plenus lepra; et videns Iesum et procidens in faciem rogavit eum dicens: «Domine, si vis, potes me mundare». ¹³Et extendens manum tetigit illum dicens: «Volo, mundare!»; et confestim lepra discessit ab illo. ¹⁴Et ipse praecepit illi, ut nemini diceret, sed: «Vade, ostende te sacerdoti et offer pro emundatione tua, sicut praecepit Moyses, in testimonium illis». ¹⁵Perambulabat autem magis sermo de illo, et conveniebant turbae multae, ut audirent et curarentur ab infirmitatibus suis; ¹⁶ipse autem secedebat in desertis et orabat. ¹⁷Et factum est in una dierum, et ipse erat docens, et erant pharisaei sedentes et legis doctores, qui venerant ex omni castello Galilaeae et Iudaeae et Ierusalem; et virtus Domini erat ei ad sanandum. ¹⁸Et ecce viri portantes in lecto hominem, qui erat paralyticus, et quaerebant eum inferre et

5:12–16 We can learn a lot about prayer by seeing the way various people in the Gospel approach Jesus: "Jesus hears the prayer of faith, expressed in words [...] or in silence [...]. Healing infirmities or forgiving sins, Jesus always responds to a prayer offered in faith: 'Your faith has made you well; go in peace'" (*Catechism of the Catholic Church*, 2616).

The Fathers saw a deeper significance in this cure. The man's disease made him very ugly, and people shunned him for fear of contagion. Sin has the same effects. We are all sinners and in need of forgiveness and the grace of God (see Rom 3:23–24). With humility and confidence, we will often borrow the leper's words and pray, "Lord, if you will, you can make me clean."

Here (v. 16) and elsewhere (cf. 6:12; 9:18; 11:1; 22:41), the Gospel shows us Jesus going off alone, to pray. We too need to set aside time for frequent, personal prayer in the midst of our daily activities.

5:17–26 The power of Jesus and his word (see the note on 4:31–37) is illustrated here by a miracle that demonstrates that his "authority on earth" (v. 24) derives from the Lord (v. 17). "According to Democritus, medicine cures the body's ailments. Wisdom frees the soul from the passions of the body. Our good Teacher, who is wisdom, the Logos of the Father, creator of man, cares for the whole creature: doctor to all mankind, he can cure men in soul and body. Our

° Greek *to them*

Jerusalem; and the power of the Lord was with him to heal.[p] [18]And behold, men were bringing on a bed a man who was paralyzed, and they sought to bring him in and lay him before Jesus;[q] [19]but finding no way to bring him in, because of the crowd, they went up on the roof and let him down with his bed through the tiles into the midst before Jesus. [20]And when he saw their faith he said, "Man, your sins are forgiven you." [21]And the scribes and the Pharisees began to question, saying, "Who is this that speaks blasphemies? Who can forgive sins but God only?" [22]When Jesus perceived their questionings, he answered them, "Why do you question in your hearts? [23]Which is easier, to say, 'Your sins are forgiven you,' or to say, 'Rise and walk'? [24]But that you may know that the Son of man has authority on earth to forgive sins"—he said to the man who was paralyzed—"I say to you, rise, take up your bed and go home." [25]And immediately he rose before them, and took up that on which he lay, and went home, glorifying God. [26]And amazement seized them all, and they glorified God and were filled with awe, saying, "We have seen strange things today."

Lk 7:49
Is 43:25; 55:7
Lk 6:8; 9:47

Jn 20:21–23

Jn 5:8

Lk 2:20

The calling of Matthew

Mt 9:9–13
Mk 2:13–17

[27]After this he went out, and saw a tax collector, named Levi, sitting at the tax office; and he said to him, "Follow me." [28]And he left everything, and rose and followed him.

Lk 5:11

ponere ante eum. [19]Et non invenientes qua parte illum inferrent prae turba, ascenderunt supra tectum et per tegulas summiserunt illum cum lectulo in medium ante Iesum. [20]Quorum fidem ut vidit, dixit: «Homo, remittuntur tibi peccata tua». [21]Et coeperunt cogitare scribae et pharisaei dicentes: «Quis est hic, qui loquitur blasphemias? Quis potest dimittere peccata nisi solus Deus?». [22]Ut cognovit autem Iesus cogitationes eorum, respondens dixit ad illos: «Quid cogitatis in cordibus vestris? [23]Quid est facilius, dicere: "Dimittuntur tibi peccata tua", an dicere: "Surge et ambula"? [24]Ut autem sciatis quia Filius hominis potestatem habet in terra dimittere peccata—ait paralytico—: Tibi dico: Surge, tolle lectulum tuum et vade in domum tuam». [25]Et confestim surgens coram illis tulit, in quo iacebat, et abiit in domum suam magnificans Deum. [26]Et stupor apprehendit omnes, et magnificabant Deum, et repleti sunt timore dicentes: «Vidimus mirabilia hodie». [27]Et post haec exiit et vidit publicanum

Saviour said to the man who was paralyzed, 'Rise, take up your bed and go home', and he was cured at once" (Clement of Alexandria, *Paedagogus*, 1, 6, 2).

The passage shows the active faith of the man's helpers, and of the man himself in allowing himself to be ferried around by them: "How great is the Lord who on account of the merits of some pardons others, and while praising the former absolves the latter! [...] Therefore, let you, who judge, learn to pardon; you, who are ill, learn to beg for forgiveness. And if the gravity of your sins causes you to doubt the possibility of being forgiven, have recourse to intercessors, have recourse to the Church, who will pray for you, and the Lord will grant you, out of love for her, what he might have refused you" (St Ambrose, *Expositio Evangelii secundum Lucam*, ad loc.).

5:27–32 In this episode we can see Jesus working in a way that continues in the Church. The call from Christ to follow him is not based

on a person's merits, and a person should respond gratefully to it (v. 29), generously and promptly (v. 28; cf. 5:11). "The Lord looked at him", says St Bede, "through the eyes of his love more than with the eyes of his body. Jesus looked at the publican and, because he loved him, he said: 'Follow me.' 'Follow me', which means: 'Be like me' [...]. 'And [he] rose and followed him.' We should not find it so strange that the tax-collector immediately forgot his concern for earthly things and left behind his goods and riches as soon as he heard the Lord's call and became a follower of one who had no possessions in this world. The Lord who called him to be his follower filled his mind with spiritual grace so that he would realize that the one who asked him to leave all worldly goods behind had the power to grant him a treasure in heaven that would never die" (*Homiliae*, 1, 22). St Luke's is the only Gospel that explicitly says that the meal with the tax-collector was a "great feast" put on by Levi at his house (v. 29) and that Jesus calls sinners "to repentance" (v. 32).

[p] Other ancient authorities read *was present to heal them*   [q] Greek *him*

Lk 7:36f; 14:1f; 15:1 ²⁹And Levi made him a great feast in his house; and there was a large company of tax collectors and others sitting at table^r with them. ³⁰And the Pharisees and their scribes murmured against his disciples, saying, "Why do you eat and drink with tax collectors and sinners?" ³¹And Jesus answered them, "Those who are well have no Lk 19:10 need of a physician, but those who are sick; ³²I have not come to call the righteous, but sinners to repentance."

Mt 9:14–17
Mk 2:18–22

A discussion on fasting

³³And they said to him, "The disciples of John fast often and offer prayers, and so Jn 3:29 do the disciples of the Pharisees, but yours eat and drink." ³⁴And Jesus said to them, Jn 16:20
Lk 17:22 "Can you make wedding guests fast while the bridegroom is with them? ³⁵The days will come, when the bridegroom is taken away from them, and then they will fast in those days." ³⁶He told them a parable also: "No one tears a piece from a new garment and puts it upon an old garment; if he does, he will tear the new, and the piece Job 32:19 from the new will not match the old. ³⁷And no one puts new wine into old wineskins; if he does, the new wine will burst the skins and it will be spilled, and the Sir 9:15 skins will be destroyed. ³⁸But new wine must be put into fresh wineskins. ³⁹And no one after drinking old wine desires new; for he says, 'The old is good.' "^s

---

nomine Levi sedentem ad teloneum et ait illi: «Sequere me». ²⁸Et relictis omnibus, surgens secutus est eum. ²⁹Et fecit ei convivium magnum Levi in domo sua; et erat turba multa publicanorum et aliorum, qui cum illis erant discumbentes. ³⁰Et murmurabant pharisaei et scribae eorum adversus discipulos eius dicentes: «Quare cum publicanis et peccatoribus manducatis et bibitis?». ³¹Et respondens Iesus dixit ad illos: «Non egent, qui sani sunt, medico, sed qui male habent. ³²Non veni vocare iustos sed peccatores in paenitentiam». ³³At illi dixerunt ad eum: «Discipuli Ioannis ieiunant frequenter et obsecrationes faciunt, similiter et pharisaeorum; tui autem edunt et bibunt». ³⁴Quibus Iesus ait: «Numquid potestis convivas nuptiarum, dum cum illis est sponsus, facere ieiunare? ³⁵Venient autem dies, et cum ablatus fuerit ab illis sponsus, tunc ieiunabunt in illis diebus». ³⁶Dicebat autem et similitudinem ad illos: «Nemo abscindit commissuram a vestimento novo et immittit in vestimentum vetus; alioquin et novum rumpet, et veteri non conveniet commissura a novo. ³⁷Et nemo mittit vinum novum in utres veteres; alioquin rumpet vinum novum utres, et ipsum effundetur, et utres peribunt; ³⁸sed vinum novum in utres novos mittendum est. ³⁹Et nemo bibens vetus vult novum; dicit enim: "Vetus melius est!"». [6] ¹Factum est autem in sabbato cum transiret per sata, et vellebant discipuli eius spicas et manducabant confricantes manibus.

The episode helps us to see Jesus' openness to all people, an openness which should characterize all apostolic work: "The conversion of one publican was a sign and example of repentance and forgiveness for many other publicans and sinners. It was a true and beautiful sign because Matthew, who was to become master and apostle to the gentiles, led many sinners onto the path of salvation through his first meeting with the Lord. From the first moment of his life of faith, Matthew began his ministry as teacher of the gospel which would reach its heights later when he had grown in virtue" (ibid.).

5:33–39 In the Old Testament certain days were laid down as days of fasting, the most prominent of which was the Day of Atonement, Yom Kippur (Num 29:7ff; cf. Acts 27:9). Moses and Elijah had fasted (Ex 34:28; 1 Kings 19:8), and our Lord himself fasted in the wilderness before starting his public ministry.

Jesus uses his response to the criticism from scribes and Pharisees to explain a little more about who he is and the claims of his teaching. His presence in the world causes a joy that reveals the relative importance of penitential practices like fasting (vv. 34–35). His teaching calls for new wineskins—deeper repentance, profound renewal (vv. 36–38)—and anyone who receives it with a sincere heart will see that it is like old wine (v. 39), that is, "better" wine, and will not want to go back to the sort of life he led before. Our Lord is not saying that fasting is outmoded (cf. v. 35); he gives it a deeper meaning: "The merit of our fasts consists not only in abstinence from food; there is no use in depriving the body of nourishment if the soul does not cut itself off from iniquity and if the tongue does not cease to speak evil" (St Leo the Great, *Sermo 4 in Quadragesima*, 2).

---

r Greek *reclining*   s Other ancient authorities read *better*

Mt 12:1–8
Mk 2:23–28

The law of the sabbath

6 [1]On a sabbath,[t] while he was going through the grainfields, his disciples plucked and ate some ears of grain, rubbing them in their hands. [2]But some of the Pharisees said, "Why are you doing what is not lawful to do on the sabbath?" [3]And Jesus answered, "Have you not read what David did when he was hungry, he and those who were with him: [4]how he entered the house of God, and took and ate the bread of the Presence, which it is not lawful for any but the priests to eat, and also gave it to those with him?" [5]And he said to them, "The Son of man is lord of the sabbath."

1 Sam 21:2–7

Lev 24:5–9

Curing of a man with a withered hand

[6]On another sabbath, when he entered the synagogue and taught, a man was there whose right hand was withered. [7]And the scribes and the Pharisees watched him, to see whether he would heal on the sabbath, so that they might find an accusation against him. [8]But he knew their thoughts, and he said to the man who had the withered hand, "Come and stand here." And he rose and stood there. [9]And Jesus said to them, "I ask you, is it lawful on the sabbath to do good or to do harm, to save life or to destroy it?" [10]And he looked around on them all, and said to him, "Stretch out your hand." And he did so, and his hand was restored. [11]But they were filled with fury and discussed with one another what they might do to Jesus.

Mt 12:9–14
Mk 3:1–6

Lk 13:10

Lk 11:54; 14:1

Lk 5:22; 9:47

Lk 11:53

4. JESUS' MIRACLES AND PREACHING IN GALILEE*

Mt 10:1–4
Mk 3:13–19

Jesus chooses twelve apostles

[12]In these days he went out into the hills to pray; and all night he continued in prayer to God. [13]And when it was day, he called his disciples, and chose from them twelve,

[2]Quidam autem pharisaeorum dixerunt: «Quid facitis, quod non licet in sabbatis?». [3]Et respondens Iesus ad eos dixit: «Nec hoc legistis, quod fecit David, cum esurisset ipse et qui cum eo erant? [4]Quomodo intravit in domum Dei et panes propositionis sumpsit et manducavit et dedit his, qui cum ipso erant, quos non licet manducare nisi tantum sacerdotibus?». [5]Et dicebat illis: «Dominus est sabbati Filius hominis». [6]Factum est autem in alio sabbato ut intraret in synagogam et doceret; et erat ibi homo, et manus eius dextra erat arida. [7]Observabant autem illum scribae et pharisaei si sabbato curaret, ut invenirent accusare illum. [8]Ipse vero sciebat cogitationes eorum et ait homini, qui habebat manum aridam: «Surge et sta in medium». Et surgens stetit. [9]Ait autem ad illos Iesus: «Interrogo vos si licet sabbato bene facere an male, animam salvam facere an perdere?». [10]Et circumspectis omnibus illis, dixit illi: «Extende manum tuam». Et fecit, et restituta est manus eius. [11]Ipsi autem repleti sunt insipientia et colloquebantur ad invicem quidnam facerent Iesu. [12]Factum est autem in illis diebus, exiit in montem orare et erat pernoctans in oratione

6:1–11 In these two controversies about the sabbath, Jesus manifests his divine power and authority and explains the right way to understand the sabbath rest (see the notes on Mt 12:1–8, 9–14; Mk 2:23–28; 3:1–6). But these scribes and Pharisees refuse to listen: "O Pharisee, you see him working wonders and healing the sick by using a higher power, yet out of envy you plot his death" (St Cyril of Alexandria, in *Catena aurea*, ad loc.). The episode helps us not to be so small-minded as to try to put in doubt the greatness of God: "The withered hand is cured, but the hardheartedness of the Jews is not softened because as they left the synagogue they discussed among themselves what was to be done with Jesus. Have you, too,

thought about what should be done with Jesus? Worship him as God, the miracle-worker; adore the Man who is greater than all men" (St Athanasius, *Homilia de semente*, 16).

*6:12–8:56 The establishment of the apostolic college marks the start of a new section of the Gospel in which Jesus carries out his mission with his apostles in Galilee. This phase consists in preaching—as can be seen mainly in the Sermon on the Plain (6:17–49) and in the parables (8:4–18)—and in the working of cures. The miracles reported here are virtually the same as those found in the other two Synoptics, but Luke is the only one to include the raising of the son of the widow of Nain, a miracle that Jesus performs out of

t Other ancient authorities read *On the second first sabbath* (on the second sabbath after the first)

Jn 1:42
Mt 16:18
Acts 1:13
whom he named apostles: ¹⁴Simon, whom he named Peter, and Andrew his brother, and James and John, and Philip and Bartholomew, ¹⁵and Matthew, and Thomas, and James the son of Alphaeus, and Simon who was called the Zealot, ¹⁶and Judas the son of James, and Judas Iscariot, who became a traitor.

Preaching on the plain

Mt 4:23–5:1
Mk 3:7–12
¹⁷And he came down with them and stood on a level place, with a great crowd of his disciples and a great multitude of people from all Judea and Jerusalem and the sea coast of Tyre and Sidon, who came to hear him and to be healed of their diseases; Lk 5:17; 8:46
Mk 5:30 ¹⁸and those who were troubled with unclean spirits were cured. ¹⁹And all the crowd sought to touch him, for power came forth from him and healed them all.

Dei. ¹³Et cum dies factus esset, vocavit discipulos suos et elegit Duodecim ex ipsis, quos et apostolos nominavit: ¹⁴Simonem, quem et cognominavit Petrum, et Andream fratrem eius et Iacobum et Ioannem et Philippum et Bartholomaeum ¹⁵et Matthaeum et Thomam et Iacobum Alphaei et Simonem, qui vocatur Zelotes, ¹⁶et Iudam Iacobi et Iudam Iscarioth, qui fuit proditor. ¹⁷Et descendens cum illis stetit in loco campestri, et turba multa discipulorum eius, et multitudo copiosa plebis ab omni Iudaea et Ierusalem et maritima Tyri et Sidonis, ¹⁸qui venerunt, ut audirent eum et sanarentur a languoribus suis; et qui vexabantur a spiritibus immundis, curabantur. ¹⁹Et omnis turba quaerebant eum tangere, quia virtus de illo

compassion (7:13)—which is in fact the virtue that defines the Sermon on the Plain (6:36).

6:12–16 Here again we see Jesus praying prior to an important event (v. 12), in this case his establishing of the group of twelve apostles. The selection of twelve men, to whom Jesus gives the special name of "apostles" (v. 13), along with other information found elsewhere (see the notes on Mt 10:1–4; Mk 3:13–19), points to the extension of Jesus' work through his Church. Jesus, sent by the Father, associates the apostles with his mission: "That divine mission, which was committed by Christ to the apostles, is destined to last until the end of the world (cf. Mt 28:20), since the Gospel, which they were charged to hand on, is, for the Church, the principle of all its life for all time. For that very reason the apostles were careful to appoint successors in this hierarchically constituted society" (Vatican II, *Lumen gentium*, 20).

In v. 13 a distinction is made between disciples in general and the apostles, the group of the Twelve. Jesus personally chooses these men by name, and "institutes" or "appoints" them. The four lists given for the Twelve in the New Testament are practically the same; the only significant difference between them is that St Luke calls one of the apostles "Judas the son of James" (v. 16; Acts 1:13) where Matthew and Mark (Mk 10:3; Mk 3:18) mention a "Thaddaeus"; he is the apostle that later hagiography calls "Judas Thaddaeus".

This virtual unanimity in the New Testament shows the importance the evangelists gave to providing a complete list of the Twelve, and the importance the Twelve will have when apostolic succession has to be decided.

6:17–19 These verses mark the start of a discourse which parallels the Sermon on the Mount in Matthew's Gospel (Mt 5:3–7:29), although this one is much shorter (30 verses rather than 107). Both evangelists record that there was a huge crowd of people present, though St Luke says the discourse took place on a plain, an area of level ground, after Jesus came down from the hills, whereas St Matthew sets it on a mountainside (v. 17; see Mt 5:1). Matthew may have wanted to associate it in people's minds with God's gift of the Law to his people on Mount Sinai (see Ex 19:1ff); St Luke, on the other hand, by recording that Jesus used to preach in open spaces which were easily accessible to the crowd, wants to show how available and open our Lord was to all people and how his message was directed to everyone.

Discrepancies between the Gospels (found here and elsewhere) do not limit their value as a true record; the Church teaches that these texts are a reliable chronicle of events, for the "sacred authors, in writing the four Gospels, selected certain of the many elements which had been handed on, either orally or already in written form, others they synthesized or explained with an eye to the situation of the churches, the while

The Beatitudes and the Woes   Mt 5: 1–12

²⁰And he lifted up his eyes on his disciples, and said:*   Jas 2:5

"Blessed are you poor, for yours is the kingdom of God.

²¹"Blessed are you that hunger now, for you shall be satisfied.   Rev 7:16–17
Ps 107:9; 126:5–6

"Blessed are you that weep now, for you shall laugh.   Is 61:3

²²"Blessed are you when men hate you, and when they exclude you and revile   Jn 15:19; 16:2
you, and cast out your name as evil, on account of the Son of man! ²³Rejoice in that
day, and leap for joy, for behold, your reward is great in heaven; for so their fathers
did to the prophets.

²⁴"But woe to you that are rich, for you have received your consolation.   Jas 5:1
Lk 16:25

²⁵"Woe to you that are full now, for you shall hunger.   Is 5:8
Is 5:22; 65:13

exibat et sanabat omnes. ²⁰Et ipse, elevatis oculis suis in discipulos suos, dicebat: «Beati pauperes, quia vestrum est regnum Dei. ²¹Beati, qui nunc esuritis, quia saturabimini. Beati, qui nunc fletis, quia ridebitis. ²²Beati eritis, cum vos oderint homines et cum separaverint vos et exprobraverint et eiecerint nomen vestrum tamquam malum propter Filium hominis. ²³Gaudete in illa die et exsultate, ecce enim merces vestra multa in caelo; secundum haec enim faciebant prophetis patres eorum. ²⁴Verumtamen vae vobis divitibus, quia habetis consolationem vestram! ²⁵Vae vobis, qui

sustaining the form of preaching, but always in such a fashion that they have told us the honest truth about Jesus" (Vatican II, *Dei Verbum*, 19). Comparing this passage of Luke to Matthew 5:3—7:29, we can deduce that the two Gospels draw on a common source (oral or, more likely, written) which recorded an important pro-gramme of teaching carried out by Jesus near the Sea of Galilee.

The Luke text could be said to have three parts—the Beatitudes and Woes (6:20–26), the teachings about love of enemies (6:27–38); and the teachings about sincerity of heart (6:39–49).

6:20–26 The eight (or nine) Beatitudes of the first Gospel (see Mt 5:3–12 and note) are summed up by Luke in four, to which are attached four antitheses or "Woes". But in both cases, "the beatitude we are promised confronts us with decisive moral choices. It invites us to purify our hearts of bad instincts and to seek the love of God above all else. It teaches us that true happiness is not found in riches or well-being, in human fame or power, or in any human achieve-ment—however beneficial it may be—such as science, technology, and art, or indeed in any creature, but in God alone, the source of every good and of all love" (*Catechism of the Catholic Church*, 1723).

In Matthew, the Beatitudes are couched in the third person plural, whereas in Luke they are phrased in the second person, as if they were being addressed directly to the people present. A disciple of Christ is blessed if he or she is truly "poor" (v. 20), or is "now" (v. 21) in a situation of need or persecution, because that very fact is a sign of blessing. People should not view their situations from a worldly perspective but from that of God. Therefore, these Beatitudes are not just about the *attitude* we should have towards material things and towards difficulties; they also imply the *behaviour* that should derive from the disciple's correct attitude: "The ordinary Chris-tian has to reconcile two aspects of his life that can at first sight seem contradictory. There is, on the one hand, *true poverty*, which is obvious and tangible and made up of definite things. This poverty should be an expression of faith in God and a sign that the heart is not satisfied with cre-ated things [...]. On the other hand, an ordinary Christian is and wants to be *one more among his fellow men*, sharing their way of life, their joys and happiness; working with them, loving the world and all the good things that exist in it; using all created things to solve the problems of human life and to establish a spiritual and mate-rial environment which will foster personal and social development" (St Josemaría Escrivá, *Con-versations*, 111).

For St Luke, the evangelist who in his Gospel most frequently uses the word "blessed" (*makarios*), the model of blessedness is the Virgin Mary (1:42, 45, 48; 11:27, 28), and she is also the mirror that a disciple of Christ should contemplate: "Blessed be the soul of the Virgin who, guided by the Spirit who dwelt within her,

"Woe to you that laugh now, for you shall mourn and weep.

Jas 4:4
Mic 2:11
[26]"Woe to you, when all men speak well of you, for so their fathers did to the false prophets.

Mt 5:38–48
Love of enemies
[27]"But I say to you that hear, Love your enemies, do good to those who hate you, [28]bless those who curse you, pray for those who abuse you. [29]To him who strikes you on the cheek, offer the other also; and from him who takes away your cloak do not withhold your coat as well. [30]Give to every one who begs from you; and of him who
Mt 7:12
Tob 4:15
takes away your goods do not ask them again. [31]And as you wish that men would do to you, do so to them.

Lk 14:12–14
[32]"If you love those who love you, what credit is that to you? For even sinners love those who love them. [33]And if you do good to those who do good to you, what

saturati estis nunc, quia esurietis! Vae vobis, qui ridetis nunc, quia lugebitis et flebitis! [26]Vae, cum bene vobis dixerint omnes homines! Secundum haec enim faciebant pseudoprophetis patres eorum. [27]Sed vobis dico, qui auditis: Diligite inimicos vestros, bene facite his, qui vos oderunt; [28]benedicite maledicentibus vobis, orate pro calumniantibus vos. [29]Ei qui te percutit in maxillam, praebe et alteram; et ab eo, qui aufert tibi vestimentum, etiam tunicam noli prohibere. [30]Omni petenti te tribue; et ab eo, qui aufert, quae tua sunt, ne repetas. [31]Et prout vultis, ut faciant vobis homines, facite illis similiter. [32]Et si diligitis eos, qui vos diligunt, quae vobis est gratia? Nam et peccatores diligentes se diligunt. [33]Et si bene

obeyed the commands of the Word of God at all times and in all things. She did not allow herself to be carried away by her own instincts or judgments; her outward actions always followed from the wisdom born of faith within her soul. Divine Wisdom, as he built the house of the Church in which he would live, used most Holy Mary as an example of observance of the law, purification of heart and mind, proper humility and spiritual sacrifice. Faithful soul, be like her. Look to the temple of your heart if you want to be spiritually pure and cleansed of all stain of sin" (St Lawrence Justinian, *Sermo 10 in festivitate Purificationis*).

Our Lord's words encapsulate a profound truth: Christians must follow Christ's way, a way that does not lead them through wealth and abundance, or worldly consolation and praise. The way that Christ took led him to condemnation (see 18:32–33; 22:63; 23:11, 36), and a Christian's way cannot be any different. St Peter reminds us of this: "Let none of you suffer as a murderer, or a thief, or a wrongdoer, or a mischief-maker; yet if one suffers as a Christian, let him not be ashamed, but under that name let him glorify God" (1 Pet 4:15–16). And the early Christians interpreted tribulation in the same way: "The only thing I think you need to ask for is fortitude, interior strength and outward determination, so that you may be wholly convinced of the words that you speak and be a Christian

not only in name and words, but also in deed. If I live a Christian life, I am worthy of the name 'Christian', and I will be truly faithful to Christ […]. When they are hated by the whole world, what Christians need is greatness of soul, not convincing words" (St Ignatius of Antioch, *Ad Romanos*, 5, 2).

6:27–38 These words, positioned immediately after the Beatitudes and Woes, could well be seen as the core of Jesus' teaching about the love and compassion that Christians should have towards others, and which they should demonstrate, especially through forgiveness. Throughout his earthly life, and particularly on the cross (see 23:34), Jesus sets an example for us: "In loving our enemies there shines forth in us some likeness to God our Father, who, by the death of his Son, ransomed from everlasting perdition and reconciled to himself the human race, which previously was most unfriendly and hostile to him" (*Roman Catechism*, 4, 14, 19).

In the opening verses (27–30), our Lord lists some trials and tribulations we might encounter and how we should respond to them. The Semitic style of teaching by way of drawing contrasts conveys very vividly this teaching, which is summed up in v. 31: "As you wish that men would do to you, do so to them."

Verses 32–34 prepare us for what Jesus will say is the real reason why we should act as he

credit is that to you? For even sinners do the same. ³⁴And if you lend to those from whom you hope to receive, what credit is that to you? Even sinners lend to sinners, to receive as much again. ³⁵But love your enemies, and do good, and lend, expecting nothing in return;ᵛ and your reward will be great, and you will be sons of the Most High; for he is kind to the ungrateful and the selfish. ³⁶Be merciful, even as your Father is merciful.

³⁷"Judge not, and you will not be judged; condemn not, and you will not be condemned; forgive, and you will be forgiven; ³⁸give, and it will be given to you; good measure, pressed down, shaken together, running over, will be put into your lap. For the measure you give will be the measure you get back."

Integrity

³⁹He also told them a parable: "Can a blind man lead a blind man? Will they not both fall into a pit? ⁴⁰A disciple is not above his teacher, but every one when he is fully taught will be like his teacher. ⁴¹Why do you see the speck that is in your brother's

Marginal references: Lev 25:35–36 · Mt 6:14 · Ex 34:6ff · Rom 14:10; Jas 2:13 · Mk 4:24 · Mt 7:1–5; 15–20; 24–27 · Mt 15:14; 23:16, 24 · Mt 10:24–25; Jn 13:16; 15:20

feceritis his, qui vobis bene faciunt, quae vobis est gratia? Siquidem et peccatores idem faciunt. ³⁴Et si mutuum dederitis his, a quibus speratis recipere, quae vobis gratia est? Nam et peccatores peccatoribus fenerantur, ut recipiant aequalia. ³⁵Verumtamen diligite inimicos vestros et bene facite et mutuum date nihil desperantes; et erit merces vestra multa, et eritis filii Altissimi, quia ipse benignus est super ingratos et malos. ³⁶Estote misericordes, sicut et Pater vester misericors est. ³⁷Et nolite iudicare et non iudicabimini; et nolite condemnare et non condemnabimini. Dimittite et dimittemini; ³⁸date, et dabitur vobis: mensuram bonam, confertam, coagitatam, supereffluentem dabunt in sinum vestrum; eadem quippe mensura, qua mensi fueritis, remetietur vobis». ³⁹Dixit autem illis et similitudinem: «Numquid potest caecus caecum ducere? Nonne ambo in foveam cadent? ⁴⁰Non est discipulus super magistrum; perfectus autem omnis erit sicut magister eius. ⁴¹Quid autem vides festucam in oculo fratris tui,

has described: it is the behaviour befitting a child of God (v. 35) who wants to imitate his or her merciful Father (v. 36). This verse ("Be merciful, even as your Father is merciful") parallels almost exactly what St Matthew records at the heart of the Sermon on the Mount: "You, therefore, must be perfect, as your heavenly Father is perfect" (Mt 5:48). Mercy is the way to a close union with God, and Jesus, the Son of God, is the incarnation of divine mercy: "Everyone wants to have mercy shown to them, but few show mercy to others. [...] How can you dare to ask for what you are not prepared to give? He who desires the mercy of heaven should show mercy here on earth. [...] There is earthly, human mercy and heavenly, divine mercy. What is human mercy? Human mercy is concern for the suffering of the poor. What is divine mercy? Divine mercy is forgiveness of sins. The human mercy we show during the pilgrimage of our life on earth will be repaid with divine mercy in our heavenly homeland. God suffers cold and hunger and thirst in the poor of this world, as he himself said: Whatever you do to the least of my people, you do to me. God, who gives all in heaven, wishes to receive from man in this world" (St Caesarius of Arles, *Sermones*, 25, 1).

By inviting us to be generous (vv. 37–38), Jesus underscores the idea of a reward in the next life, an idea already hinted at in v. 35: "The Lord adds one final, inescapable condition, which is at the same time both a commandment and a promise: that we ask pardon for our sins in the same measure as we pardon the sins of others against us. This condition makes it clear that our sins will not be forgiven if we do not forgive the offences others commit against us. For this reason, he says in another place: 'For the measure you give will be the measure you get back.' The servant in the gospel parable whose master waived his debt but who was not prepared to waive his fellow servant's debt was thrown into jail, because he would not forgive his fellow servant what he himself had been forgiven" (St Cyprian, *De Dominica oratione*, 23).

6:39–49 The discourse ends with some teachings that share a common theme: external expressions of piety or virtue have no value in themselves: what matters and gives meaning is one's inner disposition. Some comments that saints have made on this idea can help us put this teaching into practice.

At the start (vv. 39–42), emphasis is put on

v Other ancient authorities read *despairing of no man*

eye, but do not notice the log that is in your own eye? ⁴²Or how can you say to your brother, 'Brother, let me take out the speck that is in your eye,' when you yourself do not see the log that is in your own eye? You hypocrite, first take the log out of your own eye, and then you will see clearly to take out the speck that is in your brother's eye.

Jas 3:12
Mt 12:33—35

⁴³"For no good tree bears bad fruit, nor again does a bad tree bear good fruit; ⁴⁴for each tree is known by its own fruit. For figs are not gathered from thorns, nor are grapes picked from a bramble bush. ⁴⁵The good man out of the good treasure of his heart produces good, and the evil man out of his evil treasure produces evil; for out of the abundance of the heart his mouth speaks.

Mt 7:21

⁴⁶"Why do you call me 'Lord, Lord,' and not do what I tell you? ⁴⁷Every one who comes to me and hears my words and does them, I will show you what he is like: ⁴⁸he is like a man building a house, who dug deep, and laid the foundation upon rock; and when a flood arose, the stream broke against that house, and could not shake it, because it had been well built.ʷ ⁴⁹But he who hears and does not do them is like a man who built a house on the ground without a foundation; against which the stream broke, and immediately it fell, and the ruin of that house was great."

Mt 8:5—13
Jn 4:46—56

The centurion's faith

7 ¹After he had ended all his sayings in the hearing of the people he entered Capernaum. ²Now a centurion had a slave who was dearˣ to him, who was sick and at

trabem autem, quae in oculo tuo est, non consideras? ⁴²Quomodo potes dicere fratri tuo: "Frater, sine eiciam festucam, quae est in oculo tuo", ipse in oculo tuo trabem non videns? Hypocrita, eice primum trabem de oculo tuo et tunc perspicies, ut educas festucam, quae est in oculo fratris tui. ⁴³Non est enim arbor bona faciens fructum malum, neque iterum arbor mala faciens fructum bonum. ⁴⁴Unaquaeque enim arbor de fructu suo cognoscitur; neque enim de spinis colligunt ficus, neque de rubo vindemiant uvam. ⁴⁵Bonus homo de bono thesauro cordis profert bonum, et malus homo de malo profert malum: ex abundantia enim cordis os eius loquitur. ⁴⁶Quid autem vocatis me: "Domine, Domine", et non facitis, quae dico? ⁴⁷Omnis, qui venit ad me et audit sermones meos et facit eos, ostendam vobis cui similis sit: ⁴⁸similis est homini aedificanti domum, qui fodit in altum et posuit fundamentum supra petram; inundatione autem facta, illisum est flumen domui illi, et non potuit eam movere, bene enim aedificata erat. ⁴⁹Qui autem audivit et non fecit, similis est homini aedificanti domum suam supra terram sine fundamento, in quam illisus est fluvius, et continuo cecidit, et facta est ruina domus illius magna». [7] ¹Cum autem implesset omnia verba sua in aures plebis, intravit Capharnaum. ²Cen-

our need for purification if we are to see things clearly: "If you say to me 'Show me your God,' I would answer 'Show me the man that is within you' and I would show you my God. Show me that the eyes of your mind see and that the ears of your heart hear. [...] Those who are able to look at God can see him, because the eyes of their soul are open. Everyone has eyes, but the eyes of some are darkened and cannot see the light of the sun. The sun does not cease to shine because the blind cannot see it: the fault is in themselves and in their eyes. In the same way, the eyes of your soul are darkened by your sins and faults" (St Theophilus of Antioch, *Ad Autolycum*, 1, 2).

Jesus then goes on (vv. 43–45) to speak about purity of intention. Just as a tree's fruit tells us what kind of tree it is, a person's actions reveal the heart they stem from. The dispositions of our heart determine the true value of our actions (v. 45), for "what matters is not whether

or not we wear a religious habit; it is whether we try to practise the virtues and surrender our will to God and order our lives as His Majesty ordains, and not want to do our will but his" (St Teresa of Avila, *Interior Castle*, 3, 2, 6).

Finally, we are reminded that perseverance is built on good works (v. 47), and not just words or good intentions (v. 46): "Who can be a more faithful witness to the coming of Jesus Christ in the flesh than the one who keeps all the commandments of his gospel? The one who has heard the good news but does not put it into practice denies Christ; although he may testify to Christ by his words, he denies him by his deeds. [...] The true witness is the one who fulfils the commandments of our Lord Jesus in his deeds" (St Ambrose, *Expositio psalmi CXVIII*, 20, 48).

7:1–10 This account allows us to see some aspects of life in Capernaum: it was a commer-

w Other ancient authorities read *founded upon the rock*   x Or *valuable*

the point of death. ³When he heard of Jesus, he sent to him elders of the Jews, asking him to come and heal his slave. ⁴And when they came to Jesus, they besought him earnestly, saying, "He is worthy to have you do this for him, ⁵for he loves our nation, and he built us our synagogue." ⁶And Jesus went with them. When he was not far from the house, the centurion sent friends to him, saying to him, "Lord, do not trouble yourself, for I am not worthy to have you come under my roof; ⁷therefore I did not presume to come to you. But say the word, and let my servant be healed. ⁸For I am a man set under authority, with soldiers under me: and I say to one, 'Go,' and he goes; and to another, 'Come,' and he comes; and to my slave, 'Do this,' and he does it." ⁹When Jesus heard this he marvelled at him, and turned and said to the multitude that followed him, "I tell you, not even in Israel have I found such faith." ¹⁰And when those who had been sent returned to the house, they found the slave well.

The son of the widow of Nain restored to life

¹¹Soon afterwardʸ he went to a city called Nain, and his disciples and a great crowd went with him. ¹²As he drew near to the gate of the city, behold, a man who had died was being carried out, the only son of his mother, and she was a widow; and a large

1 Kings 17:10ff
Lk 9:38

turionis autem cuiusdam servus male habens erat moriturus, qui illi erat pretiosus. ³Et cum audisset de Iesu, misit ad eum seniores Iudaeorum, rogans eum, ut veniret et salvaret servum eius. ⁴At illi cum venissent ad Iesum, rogabant eum sollicite dicentes: «Dignus est, ut hoc illi praestes: ⁵diligit enim gentem nostram et synagogam ipse aedificavit nobis». ⁶Iesus autem ibat cum illis. At cum iam non longe esset a domo, misit centurio amicos dicens ei: «Domine, noli vexari; non enim dignus sum, ut sub tectum meum intres, ⁷propter quod et meipsum non sum dignum arbitratus, ut venirem ad te; sed dic verbo, et sanetur puer meus. ⁸Nam et ego homo sum sub potestate constitutus, habens sub me milites, et dico huic: "Vade", et vadit; et alii: "Veni", et venit; et servo meo: "Fac hoc", et facit». ⁹Quo audito, Iesus miratus est eum et conversus sequentibus se turbis dixit: «Dico vobis, nec in Israel tantam fidem inveni!». ¹⁰Et reversi, qui missi fuerant domum, invenerunt servum sanum. ¹¹Et factum est deinceps, ivit in civitatem, quae vocatur Naim, et ibant cum illo discipuli eius et turba copiosa. ¹²Cum autem appropinquaret portae civitatis, et ecce defunc-

cial city big enough to have a garrison commanded by a centurion, and it was a place where people of different backgrounds mixed easily (the centurion was not of the Jewish religion, but the Jewish leaders held him in high regard because he respected their people and had built them a synagogue: v. 5). Jesus, too, was respected by people of every rank—by the centurion (v. 3), some Jewish elders (vv. 4–5), a ruler of the synagogue (8:41), tax collectors (5:29), fishermen (5:2–3), etc. No one is foreign to Jesus, and his disciples, too, should put no limits on their apostolate: "The closer an apostle is to God, the more universal his desires. His heart expands and takes in everybody and everything in its longing to lay the universe at the feet of Jesus" (St Josemaría Escrivá, *The Way*, 764).

The passage is also a valuable lesson about the faith and humility needed to develop a relationship with Jesus. In the episode, we can see that even though the elders praise the centurion ("He is worthy to have you do this for him": v. 4), the man himself feels very unworthy (vv. 6–7). He has shown his faith by building a syna-

gogue (v. 5), and that faith becomes more evident still in what he says to Jesus and in Jesus' praise (vv. 6–9). The Church's liturgy gives us the centurion's beautiful prayer to recite, to prepare us to receive Holy Communion. "To know that he is unworthy to receive Jesus makes him worthy to receive him—if not in his body, then in his heart. He would not have been able to confess his unworthiness with true faith and humility if He, whom he was unworthy to receive, were not present in his heart. And he would not have rejoiced as greatly if the Lord had entered his house but not his body" (St Augustine, *Sermones*, 62, 1, 1).

7:11–17 The third Gospel often highlights God's compassion towards the needy and our duty to be merciful towards others (see 1:50, 54, 72, 78; 6:36; 10:33, 37; 15:20; etc.). Here, in a miracle that only St Luke reports, we can see Jesus' compassion towards those who are suffering; Christ is, in fact, "the definitive incarnation of mercy, its living sign" (John Paul II, *Dives in misericordia*, 8).

y Other ancient authorities read *Next day*

2 Kings 4:33–37
crowd from the city was with her. ¹³And when the Lord saw her, he had compassion on her and said to her, "Do not weep." ¹⁴And he came and touched the bier, and the Lk 9:42 bearers stood still. And he said, "Young man, I say to you, arise." ¹⁵And the dead Lk 1:68; 19:44 man sat up, and began to speak. And he gave him to his mother. ¹⁶Fear seized them all; and they glorified God, saying, "A great prophet has arisen among us!" and Lk 4:14 "God has visited his people!" ¹⁷And this report concerning him spread through the whole of Judea and all the surrounding country.

Mt 11:1–15   **Messengers from John the Baptist**
¹⁸The disciples of John told him of all these things. ¹⁹And John, calling to him two of his disciples, sent them to the Lord, saying, "Are you he who is to come, or shall we look for another?" ²⁰And when the men had come to him, they said, "John the Baptist has sent us to you, saying, 'Are you he who is to come, or shall we look for another?'" ²¹In that hour he cured many of diseases and plagues and evil spirits, and Is 26:19; 29:18; 33:5–6; 35:5; 61:1 on many that were blind he bestowed sight. ²²And he answered them, "Go and tell

tus efferebatur filius unicus matri suae, et haec vidua erat, et turba civitatis multa cum illa. ¹³Quam cum vidisset Dominus, misericordia motus super ea dixit illi: «Noli flere!». ¹⁴Et accessit et tetigit loculum; hi autem, qui portabant, steterunt. Et ait: «Adulescens, tibi dico: Surge!». ¹⁵Et resedit, qui erat mortuus, et coepit loqui; et dedit illum matri suae. ¹⁶Accepit autem omnes timor, et magnificabant Deum dicentes: «Propheta magnus surrexit in nobis» et: «Deus visitavit plebem suam». ¹⁷Et exiit hic sermo in universam Iudaeam de eo et omnem circa regionem. ¹⁸Et nuntiaverunt Ioanni discipuli eius de omnibus his. ¹⁹Et convocavit duos de discipulis suis Ioannes et misit ad Dominum dicens: «Tu es qui venturus es, an alium exspectamus?». ²⁰Cum autem venissent ad eum viri, dixerunt: «Ioannes Baptista misit nos ad te dicens: 'Tu es qui venturus es, an

It is interesting to see that the initiative here is taken by Jesus; no one makes any appeal to him (v. 12): "Jesus crosses paths again with a crowd of people. He could have passed by or waited until they called him. But he didn't. He took the initiative, because he was moved by a widow's sorrow. She had just lost all she had, her son. [...] Christ knows he is surrounded by a crowd which will be awed by the miracle and will tell the story all over the countryside. But he does not act artificially, merely to make an effect. Quite simply he is touched by that woman's suffering and cannot keep from consoling her. So he goes up to her and says, 'Do not weep.' It is like saying: 'I don't want to see you crying; I have come on earth to bring joy and peace.' And then comes the miracle, the sign of the power of Christ who is God. But first came his compassion, an evident sign of the tenderness of the heart of Christ the man" (St Josemaría Escrivá, *Christ Is Passing By*, 166).

Witnessing a miracle very similar to those worked by Elijah and Elisha (cf. 1 Kings 17:17–24; 2 Kings 4:18–37), the people take Jesus to be a great prophet (v. 16). The text immediately goes on to show what John the Baptist implied (cf. vv. 18–19), and Peter openly declares (see 9:20)—that Jesus is much more than a prophet;

he is the Messiah sent by God. The description of Jesus as a prophet is rounded off by something else the people say: "God has visited his people!" (v. 16). In the Old Testament (see Gen 21:1; 50:24; Ex 4:31; etc.), when such a phrase is used, it means an intervention by God in the history of his people. In the writings of St Luke (see 1:68, 78; Acts 15:14), it has the same meaning. It is remarkable that people should notice this saving intervention by God in miracles worked on behalf of a pagan man and a lowly woman, whereas Jerusalem failed to recognize the time of its visitation (19:44).

7:18–35 In his reply to John's disciples, Jesus shows that he is the promised Messiah, since he is performing the works that the Old Testament said would signal the messianic times (see the notes on Mt 11:1–15; Mk 7:31–37). He will go on to explain the special importance of John. John the Baptist is great on account of his exemplary life (vv. 24–25) and, especially, because he has the unique mission of being Christ's herald (vv. 26–27). However, John still belongs to the time of the promise (the Old Testament); the gift of the Kingdom that Jesus brings (that is, divine filiation) is a much greater gift than the one John received (vv. 28–29).

John what you have seen and heard: the blind receive their sight, the lame walk, lepers are cleansed, and the deaf hear, the dead are raised up, the poor have good news preached to them. ²³And blessed is he who takes no offence at me."

²⁴When the messengers of John had gone, he began to speak to the crowds concerning John: "What did you go out into the wilderness to behold? A reed shaken by the wind? ²⁵What then did you go out to see? A man clothed in soft raiment? Behold, those who are gorgeously apparelled and live in luxury are in kings' courts. ²⁶What then did you go out to see? A prophet? Yes, I tell you, and more than a prophet. ²⁷This is he of whom it is written,

> 'Behold, I send my messenger before thy face,
> who shall prepare thy way before thee.'

²⁸I tell you, among those born of women none is greater than John; yet he who is least in the kingdom of God is greater than he."* ²⁹(When they heard this all the people and the tax collectors justified God, having been baptized with the baptism of John; ³⁰but the Pharisees and the lawyers rejected the purpose of God for themselves, not having been baptized by him.)

Jesus reproaches his contemporaries

³¹"To what then shall I compare the men of this generation, and what are they like? ³²They are like children sitting in the market place and calling to one another,

> 'We piped to you, and you did not dance;
> we wailed, and you did not weep.'

³³For John the Baptist has come eating no bread and drinking no wine; and you say, 'He has a demon.' ³⁴The Son of man has come eating and drinking; and you say,

Margin references: Lk 1:76; Mal 3:1, Ex 23:20; Lk 1:15; Lk 3:7, 12, Mt 21:32; Acts 13:46; Mt 11:16–19; Lk 5:30; 15:1–2

alium exspectamus?'». ²¹In ipsa hora curavit multos a languoribus et plagis et spiritibus malis et caecis multis donavit visum. ²²Et respondens dixit illis: «Euntes nuntiate Ioanni, quae vidistis et audistis: *caeci vident*, claudi ambulant, leprosi mundantur et surdi audiunt, mortui resurgunt, *pauperes evangelizantur*; ²³et beatus est, quicumque non fuerit scandalizatus in me». ²⁴Et cum discessissent nuntii Ioannis, coepit dicere de Ioanne ad turbas: «Quid existis in desertum videre? Arundinem vento moveri? ²⁵Sed quid existis videre? Hominem mollibus vestimentis indutum? Ecce, qui in veste pretiosa sunt et deliciis, in domibus regum sunt. ²⁶Sed quid existis videre? Prophetam? Utique, dico vobis, et plus quam prophetam. ²⁷Hic est, de quo scriptum est: *"Ecce mitto angelum meum ante faciem tuam, / qui praeparabit viam tuam ante te"*. ²⁸Dico vobis: Maior inter natos mulierum Ioanne nemo est; qui autem minor est in regno Dei, maior est illo. ²⁹Et omnis populus audiens et publicani iustificaverunt Deum, baptizati baptismo Ioannis; ³⁰pharisaei autem et legis periti consilium Dei spreverunt in semetipsos, non baptizati ab eo. ³¹Cui ergo similes dicam homines generationis huius, et cui similes sunt? ³²Similes sunt pueris sedentibus in foro et loquentibus ad invicem, quod dicit: "Cantavimus vobis tibiis, et non saltastis; / lamentavimus, et non plorastis!". ³³Venit enim Ioannes Baptista neque manducans panem neque bibens vinum, et dicitis:

Finally, Jesus compares the response the Pharisees and lawyers gave to John's message with the response that his own message receives. The ordinary people and tax collectors listened to John (v. 29); but the Pharisees and lawyers refused to do so, and thereby rejected God's plan for them (v. 30). By what he says (vv. 31–35), Jesus clearly means that his own message of salvation will meet the same fate.

Given the intentions and styles of the four Gospels, the reader may find the Baptist's question (v. 19) disconcerting. A close reading of the texts, however, resolves any contradiction or lingering confusion: "It was not out of ignorance that John enquired about Christ's coming in the flesh, for he had already clearly professed his belief, saying, 'I have seen and have borne witness that this is the Son of God' (Jn 1:34). That is why he does not ask, 'Are you he who has come?' but rather, 'Are you he who is to come?' thus asking about the future, not about the past. Nor should we think that the Baptist did not know about Christ's future passion, for it was John who said, 'Behold the Lamb of God, who takes away the sins of the world' (Jn 1:29) [...]. It can also be replied [...], with St John Chrysostom, that John made this enquiry not from doubt or ignorance, but because he wished his disciples to be satisfied on this point by Christ. Therefore, Christ gave his reply to instruct these disciples, by pointing to the evidence of his miracles" (St Thomas Aquinas, *Summa theologiae*, 2–2, 2, 7 ad 2).

'Behold, a glutton and a drunkard, a friend of tax collectors and sinners!' [35]Yet wisdom is justified by all her children."

Forgiveness for a sinful woman

Lk 11:37

[36]One of the Pharisees asked him to eat with him, and he went into the Pharisee's house, and sat at table. [37]And behold, a woman of the city, who was a sinner, when she learned that he was sitting at table in the Pharisee's house, brought an alabaster

Mt 26:7–13
Mk 14:3–9
Jn 12:3–8

Jn 4:19

flask of ointment, [38]and standing behind him at his feet, weeping, she began to wet his feet with her tears; and wiped them with the hair of her head, and kissed his feet, and anointed them with the ointment. [39]Now when the Pharisee who had invited him saw it, he said to himself, "If this man were a prophet, he would have known who and what sort of woman this is who is touching him, for she is a sinner." [40]And Jesus answering said to him, "Simon, I have something to say to you." And he answered, "What is it, Teacher?" [41]"A certain creditor had two debtors; one owed five hundred denarii, and the other fifty. [42]When they could not pay, he forgave them both. Now which of them will love him more?" [43]Simon answered, "The one, I suppose, to whom he forgave more." And he said to him, "You have judged rightly." [44]Then turning toward the woman he said to Simon, "Do you see this woman? I entered your house, you gave me no water for my feet, but she has wet my feet with her

'Daemonium habet!'; [34]venit Filius hominis manducans et bibens, et dicitis: 'Ecce homo devorator et bibens vinum, amicus publicanorum et peccatorum!'. [35]Et iustificata est sapientia ab omnibus filiis suis». [36]Rogabat autem illum quidam de pharisaeis, ut manducaret cum illo; et ingressus domum pharisaei discubuit. [37]Et ecce mulier, quae erat in civitate peccatrix, ut cognovit quod accubuit in domo pharisaei, attulit alabastrum unguenti [38]et stans retro secus pedes eius flens lacrimis coepit rigare pedes eius et capillis capitis sui tergebat, et osculabatur pedes eius et unguento ungebat. [39]Videns autem pharisaeus, qui vocaverat eum, ait intra se dicens: «Hic si esset propheta sciret utique quae et qualis mulier, quae tangit eum, quia peccatrix est». [40]Et respondens Iesus dixit ad illum: «Simon, habeo tibi aliquid dicere». At ille ait: «Magister, dic». [41]«Duo debitores erant cuidam feneratori: unus debebat denarios quingentos, alius quinquaginta. [42]Non habentibus illis, unde redderent, donavit utrique. Quis ergo eorum plus diliget eum?». [43]Respondens Simon dixit: «Aestimo quia is, cui plus donavit». At ille dixit ei: «Recte iudicasti». [44]Et conversus ad mulierem, dixit Simoni: «Vides hanc mulierem? Intravi in domum tuam: aquam pedibus meis non dedisti; haec autem lacrimis rigavit pedes meos et capillis suis tersit. [45]Osculum mihi non dedisti; haec autem, ex quo intravi, non cessavit osculari pedes meos. [46]Oleo caput meum non unxisti;

7:36–50 This scene gives a very good idea of our Lord's teaching method, and it touches on a number of things—the divinity of Jesus, the connexion between forgiveness and love, the value of faith, how faith is and should be expressed, etc.

The account begins by introducing the main characters (Jesus, Simon, the woman) and the situation—a meal in Simon's house. The Pharisee may have invited Jesus in order to test him, but in any event he fails even to honour the demands of common courtesy (vv. 44–46). He has probably heard that since the raising of the son of the widow of Nain, the people have held Jesus to be a prophet (7:16). However, he himself appears to be convinced otherwise (v. 39). True, he does call Jesus "Teacher" (v. 40), but Jesus goes on to show him that he is something more, because he knows hidden things: he can read a person's thoughts, and he knows about the woman who brings the perfume. Since only God

can read hearts, the Pharisee should not be surprised (as others are: v. 49) that Jesus can forgive sins, a faculty reserved to God.

Jesus uses the motivation of the woman to explain the connexion between forgiveness and love. The last thing he says to Simon (v. 47) contains the key to the whole passage: love for God and forgiveness of sins are interconnected; forgiveness elicits love, and love wins forgiveness. The woman's behaviour sets a good example; Simon's does not; for if he failed to show love to Jesus (vv. 44–46), then he is far from obtaining forgiveness, and if he does not realize he needs forgiveness, he is far from having love.

At the end of the episode, just as he bestowed forgiveness on the paralyzed man in Capernaum (see 5:20–24), our Lord forgives the woman her sins. He addresses her, telling her that it is her faith that has saved her (v. 50). Faith is what saves, but love is what manifests faith: "It was not the ointment that the Lord loved", St

tears and wiped them with her hair. ⁴⁵You gave me no kiss, but from the time I came
in she has not ceased to kiss my feet. ⁴⁶You did not anoint my head with oil, but she
has anointed my feet with ointment. ⁴⁷Therefore I tell you, her sins, which are many,
are forgiven, for she loved much; but he who is forgiven little, loves little."* ⁴⁸And
he said to her, "Your sins are forgiven." ⁴⁹Then those who were at table with him
began to say among themselves, "Who is this, who even forgives sins?" ⁵⁰And he
said to the woman, "Your faith has saved you; go in peace."

Lk 5:20–21

Lk 8:48; 17:19;
18:42

The holy women

8 ¹Soon afterward he went on through cities and villages, preaching and bringing
the good news of the kingdom of God. And the twelve were with him, ²and also
some women who had been healed of evil spirits and infirmities: Mary, called Magdalene, from whom seven demons had gone out, ³and Joanna, the wife of Chuza,
Herod's steward, and Susanna, and many others, who provided for them[z] out of their
means.

Lk 4:43

Mt 27:55–56
Mk 15:40–41; 16:9
Lk 23:49

haec autem unguento unxit pedes meos. ⁴⁷Propter quod dico tibi: Remissa sunt peccata eius multa, quoniam dilexit multum; cui autem minus
dimittitur, minus diligit». ⁴⁸Dixit autem ad illam: «Remissa sunt peccata tua». ⁴⁹Et coeperunt, qui simul accumbebant, dicere intra se: «Quis est
hic, qui etiam peccata dimittit?». ⁵⁰Dixit autem ad mulierem: «Fides tua te salvam fecit; vade in pace!». [8] ¹Et factum est deinceps, et ipse iter
faciebat per civitatem et castellum praedicans et evangelizans regnum Dei, et Duodecim cum illo ²et mulieres aliquae, quae erant curatae ab spiritibus malignis et infirmitatibus, Maria, quae vocatur Magdalene, de qua daemonia septem exierant, ³et Ioanna uxor Chuza, procuratoris Herodis,
et Susanna et aliae multae, quae ministrabant eis de facultatibus suis. ⁴Cum autem turba plurima conveniret et de singulis civitatibus properarent

Ambrose comments, "but the affection; it was
the woman's faith that pleased him, her humility.
And you also, if you desire grace, increase your
love; pour over the body of Jesus Christ your
faith in the Resurrection, the perfume of the holy
Church and the ointment of charity towards
others" (St Ambrose, *Expositio Evangelii secundum Lucam*, ad loc.).

8:1–3 Our Lord receives devotion and assistance
from these women (cf. v. 3); they show appreciation for the goods and gifts they have received
(vv. 2–3), and they cooperate in the apostolic
task of preaching the Kingdom of God (v. 1).
Luke notes their attitude and gives the names of
three of the women—Mary Magdalene (who
will be the first witness to the Resurrection: Jn
20:11–18; Mk 16:9); Joanna, a person of high
social standing and also a witness to the Resurrection (24:10); and Susanna, about whom we
know nothing more than what is said here.

Not only in this passage but throughout the
Gospel, and in Acts, too, Luke reports the presence of women in the work of evangelization; he
does this more than any other evangelist. He
pays particular attention to the important role of
the Blessed Virgin (see the notes on 1:5—2:52),
and he also tells us about Martha and Mary

receiving Jesus into their home (10:38–42),
about the women who were greatly moved by
Christ's sufferings (23:27–31), about those who
were close to the Mother of our Lord and the
apostles (Acts 1:14), and about those, such as
Tabitha (Acts 9:36) and Lydia (Acts 16:15), who
ministered to their co-religionists, etc. In the
Church, man and woman have equal status, but
women have gifts and a dignity of their own that
should be reflected in their role in the Church:
"Unless one looks to the Mother of God, it is
impossible to understand the mystery of the
Church, her reality, her essential vitality. Indirectly we find here a reference to the biblical
exemplar of the 'woman' which is already
clearly outlined in the description of the 'beginning' (cf. Gen 3:15) and which proceeds from
creation, through sin to the Redemption. In this
way there is a confirmation of the profound
union between what is human and what constitutes the divine economy of salvation in human
history. The Bible convinces us of the fact that
one can have no adequate hermeneutic of man,
or of what is 'human', without appropriate reference to what is 'feminine'. There is an analogy
in God's salvific economy: if we wish to understand it fully in relation to the whole of human
history, we cannot omit, in the perspective of our

z Other ancient authorities read *him*

Mt 13:1–23
Mk 4:1–20

Hos 10:12

Jer 4:3ff

Deut 29:3

Parable of the sower. The meaning of parables

⁴And when a great crowd came together and people from town after town came to him, he said in a parable: ⁵"A sower went out to sow his seed; and as he sowed, some fell along the path, and was trodden under foot, and the birds of the air devoured it. ⁶And some fell on the rock; and as it grew up, it withered away, because it had no moisture. ⁷And some fell among thorns; and the thorns grew with it and choked it. ⁸And some fell into good soil and grew, and yielded a hundredfold." As he said this, he called out, "He who has ears to hear, let him hear."

ad eum, dixit per similitudinem: ⁵«Exiit, qui seminat, seminare semen suum. Et dum seminat ipse, aliud cecidit secus viam et conculcatum est, et volucres caeli comederunt illud. ⁶Et aliud cecidit super petram et natum aruit, quia non habebat umorem. ⁷Et aliud cecidit inter spinas, et simul exortae spinae suffocaverunt illud. ⁸Et aliud cecidit in terram bonam et ortum fecit fructum centuplum». Haec dicens clamabat: «Qui habet aures audiendi, audiat». ⁹Interrogabant autem eum discipuli eius quae esset haec parabola. ¹⁰Quibus ipse dixit: «Vobis datum est nosse mysteria regni

faith, the mystery of 'woman': virgin–mother–spouse" (John Paul II, *Mulieris dignitatem*, 22).

8:4–18 The Synoptic Gospels tell us a lot about Jesus' use of parables in his teaching (cf. the notes on Mt 13:1–52 and Mk 4:1–34). Luke reports the most—thirty-two in all, several of which do not appear in any other writings. However, in this Gospel the long discourse of parables about the Kingdom is not given the same importance as it has in the other Synoptics. The evangelist condenses the discourse to these few verses because he wants to show that Jesus used parables all the time (see 7:40–50; 10:30–37; 11:5–13; 12:16–21). Jesus normally uses parables to address the crowds; only six are addressed to his disciples. Moreover, the parables are not inscrutable or mysterious; they are a form of preaching that combines clear thinking with its application to the personal circumstances of the listeners.

The parable of the sower (vv. 4–15), as is the case in the other Gospels (see the note on Mt 13:1–23), speaks about the word and how it is received by people. However, Luke's version has distinctive features. In the first two Gospels (see Mt 13:21; Mk 4:17) what prevents the seed from growing is "tribulation or persecution" on account of the word; in St Luke the obstacle is "temptation" (v. 13). Similarly, the third Gospel stresses that there can be no fruit if a person lives a pleasure-focused life (v. 14); fruit comes when people are honest and determined (v. 15). So, this parable is a call to lead a sober life, with one's mind and heart on the Kingdom: "Let us root out the thorns because they strangle the word of God. As the rich know well, weeds and

thorns are useless here on earth, as well as in heaven. […] Harm to the soul springs from two sources: human worries and the desire for pleasure. Either, on its own, can shipwreck the soul; and shipwreck is certain if the soul yields to both. You should not be surprised that the Lord uses the image of thorns to describe worldly pleasures. If you do not see pleasures as thorns, it is because you are drunk on your own passions; the healthy and wise know that pleasures pierce much deeper than thorns" (St John Chrysostom, *In Matthaeum*, 44, 4).

Unlike those who choke the word with their worldly lifestyle, those who "hold it fast in an honest and good heart" (v. 15) produce fruit. The parable means that those who practise human virtues are able also to practise supernatural ones: "Human virtues acquired by education, by deliberate acts and by a perseverance ever-renewed in repeated efforts are purified and elevated by divine grace. With God's help, they forge character and give facility in the practice of the good. The virtuous man is happy to practise them" (*Catechism of the Catholic Church*, 1810).

The other parable (vv. 16–18) is scarcely more than a group of adages. This parable of the lamp should be read in connexion with 11:33–36: the light is Jesus' teaching taken to heart. And it is meant to be spread to others (v. 17): "We are children of God, bearers of the only flame that can light up the paths of the earth for souls, of the only brightness which can never be darkened, dimmed, or overshadowed. The Lord uses us as torches, to make that light shine out. Much depends on us; if we respond many people will remain in darkness no longer, but will walk

⁹And when his disciples asked him what this parable meant, ¹⁰he said, "To you it has been given to know the secrets of the kingdom of God; but for others they are in parables, so that seeing they may not see, and hearing they may not understand. ¹¹Now the parable is this: The seed is the word of God. ¹²The ones along the path are those who have heard; then the devil comes and takes away the word from their hearts, that they may not believe and be saved. ¹³And the ones on the rock are those who, when they hear the word, receive it with joy; but these have no root, they believe for a while and in time of temptation fall away. ¹⁴And as for what fell among the thorns, they are those who hear, but as they go on their way they are choked by the cares and riches and pleasures of life, and their fruit does not mature. ¹⁵And as for that in the good soil, they are those who, hearing the word, hold it fast in an honest and good heart, and bring forth fruit with patience.

Is 6:9–10

1 Pet 1:23

Lk 21:34

Jer 4:4

Parable of the lamp

¹⁶"No one after lighting a lamp covers it with a vessel, or puts it under a bed, but puts it on a stand, that those who enter may see the light. ¹⁷For nothing is hid that shall not be made manifest, nor anything secret that shall not be known and come to light. ¹⁸Take heed then how you hear; for to him who has will more be given, and from him who has not, even what he thinks that he has will be taken away."

Mk 4: 21–25
Lk 11:36
Mt 5:15

Lk 19:26
Mt 13:12; 25:29

Mt 12: 46–50
Mk 3:31–35
Lk 11:27–28

The true kinsmen of Jesus

¹⁹Then his mother and his brethren* came to him, but they could not reach him for the crowd. ²⁰And he was told, "Your mother and your brethren are standing outside, desiring to see you." ²¹But he said to them, "My mother and my brethren are those who hear the word of God and do it."

Mt 8: 23–27
Mk 4: 35–41

The calming of the storm

²²One day he got into a boat with his disciples and he said to them, "Let us go across to the other side of the lake." So they set out, ²³and as they sailed he fell asleep. And

Dei, ceteris autem in parabolis, ut *videntes non videant et audientes non intellegant*. ¹¹Est autem haec parabola: Semen est verbum Dei. ¹²Qui autem secus viam, sunt qui audiunt; deinde venit Diabolus et tollit verbum de corde eorum, ne credentes salvi fiant. ¹³Qui autem supra petram: qui cum audierint, cum gaudio suscipiunt verbum; et hi radices non habent, qui ad tempus credunt, et in tempore tentationis recedunt. ¹⁴Quod autem in spinis cecidit: hi sunt, qui audierunt et a sollicitudinibus et divitiis et voluptatibus vitae euntes suffocantur et non referunt fructum. ¹⁵Quod autem in bonam terram: hi sunt, qui in corde bono et optimo audientes verbum retinent et fructum afferunt in patientia. ¹⁶Nemo autem lucernam accendens operit eam vaso aut subtus lectum ponit, sed supra candelabrum ponit, ut intrantes videant lumen. ¹⁷Non enim est occultum, quod non manifestetur, nec absconditum, quod non cognoscatur et in palam veniat. ¹⁸Videte ergo quomodo auditis: qui enim habet, dabitur illi; et quicumque non habet, etiam quod putat se habere, auferetur ab illo». ¹⁹Venerunt autem ad illum mater et fratres eius, et non poterant adire ad eum prae turba. ²⁰Et nuntiatum est illi: «Mater tua et fratres tui stant foris volentes te videre». ²¹Qui respondens dixit ad eos: «Mater mea et fratres mei hi sunt,

instead along paths that lead to eternal life" (St Josemaría Escrivá, *The Forge*, 1).

8:19–21 This episode, set significantly just after the parable of the sower, serves to reveal the dignity of those who hear the word. If they hear it and keep it and bear fruit, they are disciples (8:15)—and now they are given a new title, that of brother and mother of Christ (v. 21). For Jesus and for the reader of the Gospel, there is clearly a reference here to Mary, who is a model disciple because she received the word and bore fruit in a pre-eminent way (see 1:38): "Mary is blessed

above all because she listened to the word of God and fulfilled it. She bore the body of Christ in her womb, but more importantly she tended the spirit of Christ in her soul. Christ is the truth, Christ has a body: Christ, the truth, was in Mary's heart; Christ made flesh, in her womb. What is in the heart is more important than what is borne in the womb" (St Augustine, *Sermones*, 25, 7).

For the meaning of the word "brethren", see the notes on Mt 12:46–50 and Mk 3:31–35.

8:22–25 This miracle makes manifest Jesus' power over the elements of nature, and the need

a storm of wind came down on the lake, and they were filling with water, and were in danger. [24]And they went and woke him, saying, "Master, Master, we are perishing!" And he awoke and rebuked the wind and the raging waves; and they ceased, and there was a calm. [25]He said to them, "Where is your faith?" And they were afraid, and they marvelled, saying to one another, "Who then is this, that he commands even wind and water, and they obey him?"

Lk 17:6

Mt 8: 28–34
Mk 5:1–20

The Gerasene demoniac

[26]Then they arrived at the country of the Gerasenes,[a] which is opposite Galilee. [27]And as he stepped out on land, there met him a man from the city who had demons; for a long time he had worn no clothes, and he lived not in a house but among the tombs. [28]When he saw Jesus, he cried out and fell down before him, and said with a loud voice, "What have you to do with me, Jesus, Son of the Most High God? I beseech you, do not torment me." [29]For he had commanded the unclean spirit to come out of the man. (For many a time it had seized him; he was kept under guard, and bound with chains and fetters, but he broke the bonds and was driven by the demon into the desert.) [30]Jesus then asked him, "What is your name?" And he said, "Legion"; for many demons had entered him. [31]And they begged him not to command them to depart into the abyss. [32]Now a large herd of swine was feeding there on the hillside; and they begged him to let them enter these. So he gave them leave. [33]Then the demons came out of the man and entered the swine, and the herd rushed down the steep bank into the lake and were drowned.

Lk 4:34

Rev 20:1–3

qui verbum Dei audiunt et faciunt». [22]Factum est autem in una dierum, et ipse ascendit in navem et discipuli eius, et ait ad illos: «Transfretemus trans stagnum». Et ascenderunt. [23]Navigantibus autem illis, obdormivit. Et descendit procella venti in stagnum, et complebantur et periclitabantur. [24]Accedentes autem suscitaverunt eum dicentes: «Praeceptor, praeceptor, perimus!». At ille surgens increpavit ventum et tempestatem aquae, et cessaverunt, et facta est tranquillitas. [25]Dixit autem illis: «Ubi est fides vestra?». Qui timentes mirati sunt dicentes ad invicem: «Quis putas hic est, quia et ventis imperat et aquae, et oboediunt ei?». [26]Enavigaverunt autem ad regionem Gergesenorum, quae est contra Galilaeam. [27]Et cum egressus esset ad terram, occurrit illi vir quidam de civitate, qui habebat daemonia et iam tempore multo vestimento non induebatur, neque in domo manebat sed in monumentis. [28]Is ut vidit Iesum, exclamans procidit ante illum et voce magna dixit: «Quid mihi et tibi est, Iesu, Fili Dei Altissimi? Obsecro te, ne me torqueas». [29]Praecipiebat enim spiritui immundo, ut exiret ab homine. Multis enim temporibus arripiebat illum, et vinciebatur catenis et compedibus custoditus; et ruptis vinculis, agebatur a daemonio in deserta. [30]Interrogavit autem illum Iesus dicens: «Quod tibi nomen est?». At ille dixit: «Legio», quia intraverunt daemonia multa in eum. [31]Et rogabant eum, ne imperaret illis, ut in abyssum irent. [32]Erat autem ibi grex porcorum multorum pascentium in monte; et rogaverunt eum, ut permitteret eis in illos ingredi. Et permisit illis. [33]Exierunt ergo daemonia ab homine et intraverunt in porcos, et impetu abiit grex per praeceps in stagnum et suffocatus est. [34]Quod ut viderunt factum, qui pasce-

for disciples to have faith (see the notes on Mt 8:23–27 and Mk 4:35–41). The scene has been interpreted as a paradigm of Jesus' presence and action in his Church (symbolized by the boat tossed by the waves) or in the individual soul. Sometimes we, too, feel that Jesus is asleep; but our persevering prayer "awakens" him, and he comes to our aid, and the waters are calm again: "Though the ship that sails across the ocean is threatened with a thousand dangers [...]—above all, the unruly passions—[...] there is no need to doubt or despair. When you are threatened by wild temptations, [...] use the human means you have at your disposal and [...] put your trust in God [...]: even at the height of the storm the sailor does not take his eye off the bright star that will guide the ship to port. In the same way, in

this life, we have to keep our eyes fixed on God, who alone can keep us safe from danger" (St Alphonsus Liguori, *Sermones*, 91).

8:26–39 This episode shows Jesus' authority over demons, and the universal scope of his mission (see the notes on Mt 8:28–34 and Mk 5:1–20): "The coming of God's kingdom means the defeat of Satan's [...]. Jesus' exorcisms free some individuals from the domination of demons. They anticipate Jesus' great victory over 'the ruler of this world'" (*Catechism of the Catholic Church*, 550). Jesus' victories over Satan, which began when he fasted and was tempted in the wilderness (4:1–13 and par.), reached their climax on the cross and will achieve their definitive goal at the end of time (see Rev 20:10).

a Other ancient authorities read *Gadarenes*, others *Gergesenes*

³⁴When the herdsmen saw what had happened, they fled, and told it in the city and in the country. ³⁵Then people went out to see what had happened, and they came to Jesus, and found the man from whom the demons had gone, sitting at the feet of Jesus, clothed and in his right mind; and they were afraid. ³⁶And those who had seen it told them how he who had been possessed with demons was healed. ³⁷Then all the people of the surrounding country of the Gerasenes^a asked him to depart from them; for they were seized with great fear; so he got into the boat and returned. ³⁸The man from whom the demons had gone begged that he might be with him; but he sent him away, saying, ³⁹"Return to your home, and declare how much God has done for you." And he went away, proclaiming throughout the whole city how much Jesus had done for him.*

Jairus' daughter is restored to life. Curing of the woman with a haemorrhage

Mt 9:18–26
Mk 5:21–43

⁴⁰Now when Jesus returned, the crowd welcomed him, for they were all waiting for him. ⁴¹And there came a man named Jairus, who was a ruler of the synagogue; and falling at Jesus' feet he besought him to come to his house, ⁴²for he had an only daughter, about twelve years of age, and she was dying.

As he went, the people pressed round him. ⁴³And a woman who had had a flow of blood for twelve years and had spent all her living upon physicians^b and could not be healed by any one, ⁴⁴came up behind him, and touched the fringe of his garment; and immediately her flow of blood ceased. ⁴⁵And Jesus said, "Who was it that

bant, fugerunt et nuntiaverunt in civitatem et in villas. ³⁵Exierunt autem videre, quod factum est, et venerunt ad Iesum, et invenerunt hominem sedentem, a quo daemonia exierant, vestitum ac sana mente ad pedes Iesu, et timuerunt. ³⁶Nuntiaverunt autem illis hi, qui viderant, quomodo sanus factus esset, qui a daemonio vexabatur. ³⁷Et rogaverunt illum omnis multitudo regionis Gergesenorum, ut discederet ab ipsis, quia timore magno tenebantur. Ipse autem ascendens navem reversus est. ³⁸Et rogabat illum vir, a quo daemonia exierant, ut cum eo esset. Dimisit autem eum dicens: ³⁹«Redi domum tuam et narra quanta tibi fecit Deus». Et abiit per universam civitatem praedicans quanta illi fecisset Iesus. ⁴⁰Cum autem rediret Iesus, excepit illum turba; erant enim omnes expectantes eum. ⁴¹Et ecce venit vir, cui nomen Iairus, et ipse princeps synagogae erat, et cecidit ad pedes Iesu rogans eum, ut intraret in domum eius, ⁴²quia filia unica erat illi fere annorum duodecim, et haec moriebatur. Et dum iret, a turbis comprimebatur. ⁴³Et mulier quaedam erat in fluxu sanguinis ab annis duodecim, quae in medicos erogaverat omnem substantiam suam, nec ab ullo potuit curari; ⁴⁴accessit retro et tetigit fimbriam vestimenti eius, et confestim stetit fluxus sanguinis eius. ⁴⁵Et ait Iesus: «Quis est qui me

8:40–56 This "miracle story within a miracle story", found in all the Synoptic Gospels, teaches us about the need for and value of faith in any approach to Jesus (see the notes on Mt 9:18–26 and Mk 5:21–43). But the evangelists like to stress that faith can be expressed in many different ways: "There are always sick people who, like Bartimaeus, pray with great faith and have no qualms about confessing their faith at the top of their voices. But notice how, among those whom Christ encounters, no two souls are alike. This woman, too, has great faith, but she does not cry aloud; she draws near to Jesus without anyone even noticing. For her it is enough just to touch his garment, because she is quite certain she will be cured" (St Josemaría Escrivá, *Friends of God*, 199).

This woman sets a good example of faith in Jesus: "Refined, religious, of deep faith, prudent in her humility (for there is humility and faith in

acknowledging one's infirmity and not despairing of a cure), this holy woman lightly touches the hem of the Lord's garment: she approaches him through faith and believes, devoutly and wisely, that she has been cured [...]. She touches Christ's garment with faith; she sees Christ with the eyes of faith. [...] If we wish to be healed, we too must touch the hem of Christ's garment with faith" (St Jerome, *Expositio in Lucam,* ad loc.). Jairus too sets a "good" example. But those people who "laugh at" Jesus (v. 53) are an example of lack of faith. When we don't have faith in the power of God, we become self-absorbed, consumed by our petty interests, inclined to judge everything through the prism of our limited minds. When that happens, it becomes difficult to see and understand the supernatural dimension. As St Paul puts it, in 1 Corinthians 2:14: "The unspiritual [or natural] man does not receive the gifts of the Spirit of God, for they are folly to him."

b Other ancient authorities omit *and had spent all her living upon physicians*

Lk 5:17; 6:19

touched me?" When all denied it, Peter[c] said, "Master, the multitudes surround you and press upon you!" ⁴⁶But Jesus said, "Some one touched me; for I perceive that power has gone forth from me." ⁴⁷And when the woman saw that she was not hidden, she came trembling, and falling down before him declared in the presence of all the people why she had touched him, and how she had been immediately

Lk 7:50

healed. ⁴⁸And he said to her, "Daughter, your faith has made you well; go in peace."

⁴⁹While he was still speaking, a man from the ruler's house came and said, "Your daughter is dead; do not trouble the Teacher any more." ⁵⁰But Jesus on hearing this answered him, "Do not fear; only believe, and she shall be well." ⁵¹And when he came to the house, he permitted no one to enter with him, except Peter and John and

Lk 7:13

James, and the father and mother of the child. ⁵²And all were weeping and bewail-

Lk 7:13

ing her; but he said, "Do not weep; for she is not dead but sleeping." ⁵³And they

Lk 7:14

laughed at him, knowing that she was dead. ⁵⁴But taking her by the hand he called,

Lk 7:13

saying, "Child, arise." ⁵⁵And her spirit returned, and she got up at once; and he

Lk 5:14
Mk 1:44; 7:36

directed that something should be given her to eat. ⁵⁶And her parents were amazed; but he charged them to tell no one what had happened.

5. JESUS TRAVELS WITH HIS APOSTLES*

Mt 10:5–15
Mk 6:6–13

The mission of the apostles

Lk 10:1

9 ¹And he called the twelve together and gave them power and authority over all demons and to cure diseases, ²and he sent them out to preach the kingdom of God and to heal. ³And he said to them, "Take nothing for your journey, no staff, nor

tetigit?». Negantibus autem omnibus, dixit Petrus: «Praeceptor, turbae te comprimunt et affligunt». ⁴⁶At dixit Iesus: «Tetigit me aliquis; nam et ego novi virtutem de me exisse». ⁴⁷Videns autem mulier quia non latuit, tremens venit et procidit ante eum et ob quam causam tetigerit eum indicavit coram omni populo et quemadmodum confestim sanata sit. ⁴⁸At ipse dixit illi: «Filia, fides tua te salvam fecit. Vade in pace». ⁴⁹Adhuc illo loquente, venit quidam e domo principis synagogae dicens: «Mortua est filia tua; noli amplius vexare magistrum». ⁵⁰Iesus autem, audito hoc verbo, respondit ei: «Noli timere; crede tantum, et salva erit». ⁵¹Et cum venisset domum, non permisit intrare secum quemquam nisi Petrum et Ioannem et Iacobum et patrem puellae et matrem. ⁵²Flebant autem omnes et plangebant illam. At ille dixit: «Nolite flere; non est enim mortua, sed dormit». ⁵³Et deridebant eum scientes quia mortua esset. ⁵⁴Ipse autem tenens manum eius clamavit dicens: «Puella, surge!». ⁵⁵Et reversus est spiritus eius, et surrexit continuo; et iussit illi dari manducare. ⁵⁶Et stupuerunt parentes eius, quibus praecepit, ne alicui dicerent, quod factum erat.   [9] ¹Convocatis autem Duodecim, dedit illis virtutem et potestatem super omnia daemonia et ut languores curarent, ²et misit illos praedicare regnum Dei

*9:1–50 The sending-out of the apostles marks the start of a new section, in which Jesus' ministry in Galilee draws to a close. These fifty verses contain important episodes such as the apostolic mission, the miracle of the loaves, Peter's confession of faith, and the Transfiguration. The passage reflects primarily upon Jesus' relationship with the apostles. The central scene is Peter's profession of faith (9:18–21). Up to this point, the apostles have only accompanied our Lord and assisted him in ways and cooperated in his mission; but from then onwards Jesus engages in preparing them to understand the greater meaning of the events that will take place in Jerusalem, and in showing them the sort of life expected of a disciple of Christ. It is no accident that our Lord's teaching comes to us

through the apostles: "The whole Church is apostolic, in that she remains, through the successors of St Peter and the other apostles, in communion of faith and life with her origin: and in that she is 'sent out' into the whole world. All members of the Church share in this mission, though in various ways" (*Catechism of the Catholic Church*, 863).

9:1–6 The apostles cooperate in Christ's mission and extend it. Luke has described the power and authority with which Jesus proclaimed the Gospel and cured the sick; now the same power (v. 1) and the same mission (v. 2) are conferred by Christ on the Twelve. They engaged in that mission and passed it on to the Church: "During his life on this earth, Jesus Christ our Lord

c Other ancient authorities add *and those who were with him*

bag, nor bread, nor money; and do not have two tunics. [4]And whatever house you enter, stay there, and from there depart. [5]And wherever they do not receive you, when you leave that town shake off the dust from your feet as a testimony against them." [6]And they departed and went through the villages, preaching the gospel and healing everywhere.

Lk 10:5–7
Acts 9:43; 16:15
Lk 10:11
Acts 13:51

Herod's opinion about Jesus

Mt 14:1–2
Mk 6:14–16

[7]Now Herod the tetrarch heard of all that was done, and he was perplexed, because it was said by some that John had been raised from the dead, [8]by some that Elijah had appeared, and by others that one of the old prophets had risen. [9]Herod said, "John I beheaded; but who is this about whom I hear such things?" And he sought to see him.

Deut 18:15, 18
Mal 3:23
Lk 9:19

Return of the apostles. First miracle of the loaves and fish

Mt 14:13–21
Mk 6:30–44
Jn 6:1–15

[10]On their return the apostles told him what they had done. And he took them and withdrew apart to a city called Bethsaida. [11]When the crowds learned it, they followed him; and he welcomed them and spoke to them of the kingdom of God, and

et sanare infirmos; [3]et ait ad illos: «Nihil tuleritis in via, neque virgam neque peram neque panem neque pecuniam, neque duas tunicas habeatis. [4]Et in quamcumque domum intraveritis, ibi manete et inde exite. [5]Et quicumque non receperint vos, exeuntes de civitate illa pulverem pedum vestrorum excutite in testimonium supra illos». [6]Egressi autem circumibant per castella evangelizantes et curantes ubique. [7]Audivit autem Herodes tetrarcha omnia, quae fiebant, et haesitabat, eo quod diceretur a quibusdam: «Ioannes surrexit a mortuis»; [8]a quibusdam vero: «Elias apparuit»; ab aliis autem: «Propheta unus de antiquis surrexit». [9]Et ait Herodes: «Ioannem ego decollavi; quis autem est iste, de quo audio ego talia?». Et quaerebat videre eum. [10]Et reversi apostoli narraverunt illi, quaecumque fecerunt. Et assumptis illis, secessit seorsum ad civitatem, quae vocatur Bethsaida. [11]Quod cum cognovissent turbae, secutae sunt illum. Et excepit illos et loquebatur illis de regno Dei, et eos, qui cura indigebant, san-

revealed who he really is, who he has always been, the saving plan of the Father that he was to fulfil in the world, and how men ought to respond to God's providence. He sometimes taught in public and sometimes in private, with his disciples, especially the twelve that he had chosen to be closest to him and whom he would send out as teachers to all nations. [...] The apostles [...] bore witness to their faith in Jesus Christ first in Judea, and established churches there; then they went out into the whole world to preach the same teaching and the same faith. They founded churches everywhere they went, and the faith and doctrine of the first churches were the seed and shoots of faith and doctrine in the later ones. Insofar as they grew out of the first apostolic churches, those later churches, too, are apostolic. All things are defined by their origins. Therefore, all churches form part of the one Church established by the apostles and from which all others come" (Tertullian, *De praescriptione haereticorum*, 20–21).

9:7–9 Jesus' doings provoke the key question: "Who is he?" The Gospel points out that the people were unsure as to the answer (vv. 7–8; cf. 9:18–19), and that Herod was perplexed (v. 7); but it records that Peter acknowledged our Lord as the Messiah (9:20). We can see that Herod's interest stemmed from mere curiosity (v. 9; cf. 23:8), whereas Peter made a genuine act of faith that involved his personal commitment: "The crowds are able to sense a definitely exceptional religious dimension to this rabbi who speaks in such a spellbinding way, but they are not able to put him above those men of God who had distinguished the history of Israel. Jesus is really far different! It is precisely this further step of awareness, concerning as it does the deeper level of his being, which he expects from those who are close to him [...]. Only the faith proclaimed by Peter, and with him by the Church in every age, truly goes to the heart, and touches the depth of the mystery" (John Paul II, *Novo millennio ineunte*, 19).

9:10–17 The salvific actions of Christ are symbolized very clearly in this miracle which leads to Peter's confession of faith (9:18–21). Prior to the miracle, we see (in v. 11) Jesus engaged in actions typical of his messianic

cured those who had need of healing. [12]Now the day began to wear away; and the twelve came and said to him, "Send the crowd away, to go into the villages and country round about, to lodge and get provisions; for we are here in a lonely place."

2 Kings 4:43

[13]But he said to them, "You give them something to eat." They said, "We have no more than five loaves and two fish—unless we are to go and buy food for all these people." [14]For there were about five thousand men. And he said to his disciples, "Make them sit down in companies, about fifty each." [15]And they did so, and made

Mt 26:26

them all sit down. [16]And taking the five loaves and the two fish he looked up to heaven, and blessed and broke them, and gave them to the disciples to set before the

Ps 78:29

crowd. [17]And all ate and were satisfied. And they took up what was left over, twelve baskets of broken pieces.

Mt 16:13-20
Mk 8:27-30

Peter's profession of faith

[18]Now it happened that as he was praying alone the disciples were with him; and he

Lk 9:7-8

asked them, "Who do the people say that I am?" [19]And they answered, "John the Baptist; but others say, Elijah; and others, that one of the old prophets has risen."

Jn 6:68-69

[20]And he said to them, "But who do you say that I am?" And Peter answered, "The Christ of God."

abat. [12]Dies autem coeperat declinare; et accedentes Duodecim dixerunt illi: «Dimitte turbam, ut euntes in castella villasque, quae circa sunt, divertant et inveniant escas, quia hic in loco deserto sumus». [13]Ait autem ad illos: «Vos date illis manducare». At illi dixerunt: «Non sunt nobis plus quam quinque panes et duo pisces, nisi forte nos eamus et emamus in omnem hanc turbam escas». [14]Erant enim fere viri quinque milia. Ait autem ad discipulos suos: «Facite illos discumbere per convivia ad quinquagenos». [15]Et ita fecerunt et discumbere fecerunt omnes. [16]Acceptis autem quinque panibus et duobus piscibus, respexit in caelum et benedixit illis et fregit et dabat discipulis suis, ut ponerent ante turbam. [17]Et manducaverunt et saturati sunt omnes; et sublatum est, quod superfuit illis, fragmentorum cophini duodecim. [18]Et factum est cum solus esset orans, erant cum illo discipuli, et interrogavit illos dicens: «Quem me dicunt esse turbae?». [19]At illi responderunt et dixerunt: «Ioannem Baptistam, alii autem

mission (and he has just charged his disciples to engage in the same: 9:2, 6)—proclaiming the Gospel and curing the sick: cf. 4:18). The miracle of the loaves introduces a new note—the superabundance of gifts that is a sign and proof of the messianic age (cf. Is 25:6). This provision of the people with food in a "lonely place" (v. 12) recalls the episodes during the Exodus when God provided his people with food and water (cf. Ex 16:1ff), and it prefigures the Eucharist, the nourishment that Christians enjoy as they make their way towards God: "Communion with the Body and Blood of Christ increases the communicant's union with the Lord, forgives his venial sins, and preserves him from grave sins. Since receiving this sacrament strengthens the bonds of charity between the communicant and Christ, it also reinforces the unity of the Church as the Mystical Body of Christ" (*Catechism of the Catholic Church*, 1416).

9:18-21 The first three Gospels report Peter's confession of faith. Luke's account is the shortest (cf. the notes on Mt 16:13-20; Mk 8:27-30);

and, whereas the other two Gospels say that it happened at Caesarea Philippi, Luke makes no reference to place. However, he does mention that Jesus was praying (v. 18). Jesus seems always to have prayed at key moments in his ministry (cf. 3:21; 6:12; 9:28; etc.).

In one way or another, each Gospel shows Peter to have been the leading apostle. Here (unlike Mt 16:17-19) there is no mention of Peter's primacy; but in his account of the Last Supper (cf. 22:31-34 and note) Luke does bear witness to Peter's special role in the apostolic college: "Peter was chosen to be the leader of the universal mission of the Church, to be first among the apostles and the Fathers of the Church. Although there are many priests and pastors in the Church, all are under Peter's authority and are ruled above all by the authority of Christ. Divine goodness has given an extraordinary share in God's power to this one man, and all the power that other church leaders may possess is granted to them through the power of Peter" (St Leo the Great, *Sermo 4 in anniversario ordinationis suae*, 2).

First announcement of the Passion

²¹But he charged and commanded them to tell this to no one, ²²saying, "The Son of man must suffer many things, and be rejected by the elders and chief priests and scribes, and be killed, and on the third day be raised."

The need for self-denial

²³And he said to all, "If any man would come after me, let him deny himself and take up his cross daily and follow me. ²⁴For whoever would save his life will lose it;

and whoever loses his life for my sake, he will save it. ²⁵For what does it profit a man if he gains the whole world and loses or forfeits himself? ²⁶For whoever is

ashamed of me and of my words, of him will the Son of man be ashamed when he comes in his glory and the glory of the Father and of the holy angels. ²⁷But I tell you truly, there are some standing here who will not taste death before they see the kingdom of God."

The Transfiguration

²⁸Now about eight days after these sayings he took with him Peter and John and James, and went up on the mountain to pray. ²⁹And as he was praying, the appearance of his countenance was altered, and his raiment became dazzling white. ³⁰And behold,

Eliam, alii vero: Propheta unus de prioribus surrexit». ²⁰Dixit autem illis: «Vos autem quem me esse dicitis?». Respondens Petrus dixit: «Christum Dei». ²¹At ille increpans illos praecepit, ne cui dicerent hoc, ²²dicens: «Oportet Filium hominis multa pati et reprobari a senioribus et principibus sacerdotum et scribis et occidi et tertia die resurgere». ²³Dicebat autem ad omnes: «Si quis vult post me venire, abneget semetipsum et tollat crucem suam cotidie et sequatur me. ²⁴Qui enim voluerit animam suam salvam facere, perdet illam; qui autem perdiderit animam suam propter me, hic salvam faciet illam. ²⁵Quid enim proficit homo, si lucretur universum mundum, se autem ipsum perdat vel detrimentum sui faciat? ²⁶Nam qui me erubuerit et meos sermones, hunc Filius hominis erubescet, cum venerit in gloria sua et Patris et sanctorum angelorum. ²⁷Dico autem vobis vere: Sunt aliqui hic stantes, qui non gustabunt mortem, donec videant regnum Dei». ²⁸Factum est autem post haec verba fere dies octo, et assumpsit Petrum et Ioannem et Iacobum et ascendit in montem, ut oraret. ²⁹Et facta est, dum oraret, species vultus eius altera, et vestitus eius

9:22–27 St Luke makes no mention of Jesus' taking Peter to task (cf. Mt 16:21–28; Mk 8:31–9:1) when he reacted negatively to the announcement of the passion. Jesus is the Christ and, as the Transfiguration will show, he will ultimately be glorified. But his path runs via the cross. Therefore, anyone who wants to follow him must take the same road. The passion, the cross, is the defining episode in Christ's life, and therefore it is the first step in the Christian life: "There is no doubt about it: a person who loves pleasure, who seeks comfort, who flies from anything that might spell suffering, who is overanxious, who complains, who blames and who becomes impatient at the least little thing which does not go his way—a person like that is a Christian only in name; he is only a dishonour to his religion, for Jesus Christ has said so: Anyone who wishes to come after me, let him deny himself and take up his cross every day of his life, and follow me" (St John Vianney, *Ash Wednesday Sermon on Penance*).

Significantly, our Lord specifies that a Chris-

tian should take up his cross "daily" (v. 23), because salvation comes at a precise time, "today", "immediately" (4:21; 5:25; 19:9, 42), and therefore any moment may be the key time of salvation: "You ask me, 'Why that wooden cross?' And I quote from a letter: 'As I raise my eyes from the microscope, my sight comes to rest on the cross—black and empty. That cross without a corpus is a symbol; it has a meaning others won't see. And I, tired out and on the point of abandoning my work, once again bring my eyes close to the lens and continue. For that lonely cross is calling for a pair of shoulders to bear it'" (St Josemaría Escrivá, *The Way*, 277).

9:28–36 The Transfiguration is one of the few episodes in the Gospel that is explicitly connected in time with another: it happened "about eight days after" (v. 28; "six days after", according to Mt 17:1 and Mk 9:2) Peter's confession of faith. There is also a thematic link between the two episodes: what "he was to accomplish at Jerusalem" (v. 31) was the route Jesus had to

Lk 24:27
two men talked with him, Moses and Elijah, [31]who appeared in glory and spoke of his departure, which he was to accomplish at Jerusalem. [32]Now Peter and those who were with him were heavy with sleep but kept awake, and they saw his glory and the two Lev 23:42
Zech 14:16–19 men who stood with him. [33]And as the men were parting from him, Peter said to Jesus, "Master, it is well that we are here; let us make three booths, one for you and one for Moses and one for Elijah"—not knowing what he said. [34]As he said this, a cloud came Lk 3:22
2 Pet 1:15–18
Ps 2:7
Is 42:1 and overshadowed them; and they were afraid as they entered the cloud. [35]And a voice came out of the cloud, saying, "This is my Son, my Chosen;[d] listen to him!" [36]And when the voice had spoken, Jesus was found alone. And they kept silence and told no one in those days anything of what they had seen.

Mt 17:14–20
Mk 9:14–29 ### Curing of an epileptic boy

[37]On the next day, when they had come down from the mountain, a great crowd met Lk 7:12 him. [38]And behold, a man from the crowd cried, "Teacher, I beg you to look upon my son, for he is my only child; [39]and behold, a spirit seizes him and he suddenly

albus refulgens. [30]Et ecce duo viri loquebantur cum illo, et erant Moyses et Elias, [31]qui visi in gloria dicebant exodum eius, quem completurus erat in Ierusalem. [32]Petrus vero et qui cum illo gravati erant somno; et evigilantes viderunt gloriam eius et duos viros, qui stabant cum illo. [33]Et factum est cum discederent ab illo, ait Petrus ad Iesum: «Praeceptor, bonum est nos hic esse; et faciamus tria tabernacula: unum tibi et unum Moysi et unum Eliae», nesciens quid diceret. [34]Haec autem illo loquente, facta est nubes et obumbravit eos; et timuerunt intrantibus illis in nubem. [35]Et vox facta est de nube dicens: «Hic est Filius meus electus; ipsum audite». [36]Et dum fieret vox, inventus est Iesus solus. Et ipsi tacuerunt et nemini dixerunt in illis diebus quidquam ex his, quae viderant. [37]Factum est autem in sequenti die, descendentibus illis de monte, occurrit illi turba multa. [38]Et ecce vir de turba exclamavit dicens: «Magister, obsecro te, respice in filium meum, quia unicus est mihi; [39]et ecce spiritus apprehen-

take to reach "glory" (v. 32); the cross foretold a little earlier (9:22–23) is not the final outcome; it is simply a stage on the way to glory: "For a moment Jesus discloses his divine glory, confirming Peter's confession. He also reveals that he will have to go by the way of the cross at Jerusalem in order to 'enter into his glory'. Moses and Elijah had seen God's glory on the Mountain; the Law and the Prophets had announced the Messiah's sufferings. Christ's Passion is the will of the Father: the Son acts as God's servant. The cloud indicates the presence of the Holy Spirit. 'The whole Trinity appeared: the Father in the voice; the Son in the man; the Spirit in the shining cloud' (St Thomas Aquinas, *Summa Theologiae*, 3, 45, 4 ad 2)" (*Catechism of the Catholic Church*, 555).

In his transfiguration, Jesus strengthens his disciples' faith by giving them an insight into the glory that his human nature will possess after the Resurrection. It is no accident that the three disciples who witness the Transfiguration (v. 28) are those who are closest to him during his agony in Gethsemane (see Mt 26:37; Mk 14:33). Their hope is strengthened by this vision: "For a person to go straight along the road, he must have some knowledge of the end [...]. This is particularly

necessary if the road is hard and rough, the going heavy, and the end delightful" (St Thomas Aquinas, *Summa theologiae*, 3, 45, 1).

9:37–43 In the context of this cure of the epileptic boy the other evangelists give Jesus' teaching about the value of faith (see Mt 17:14–20 and note) and prayer (see Mk 9:14–29 and note). Luke, for his part, shows us the father's concern for his only child (v. 38) and Jesus' compassion in giving the boy back to his father (v. 42). In these respects, the miracle is reminiscent of the raising of the son of the widow of Nain, an only son (7:12) returned to his mother (7:15). The reaction of those present is also similar. If the crowds earlier glorified God for having "visited his people" (7:16), now they are "astonished at the majesty of God" (v. 43; cf. 4:32; 8:26; 11:14). Jesus does not work miracles to enhance his own reputation, but rather to make manifest the nature of God: "In Christ and through Christ, God also becomes especially visible in His mercy [...]. Not only does he speak of it and explain it by the use of comparisons and parables, but above all he himself makes it incarnate and personifies it. He himself, in a certain sense, is mercy" (John Paul II, *Dives in misericordia*, 2).

d Other ancient authorities read *my Beloved*

cries out; it convulses him till he foams, and shatters him, and will hardly leave him. ⁴⁰And I begged your disciples to cast it out, but they could not." ⁴¹Jesus answered, "O faithless and perverse generation, how long am I to be with you and bear with you? Bring your son here." ⁴²While he was coming, the demon tore him and convulsed him. But Jesus rebuked the unclean spirit, and healed the boy, and gave him back to his father. ⁴³And all were astonished at the majesty of God.

Deut 32:5

Second announcement of the Passion

But while they were all marvelling at everything he did, he said to his disciples, ⁴⁴"Let these words sink into your ears; for the Son of man is to be delivered into the hands of men." ⁴⁵But they did not understand this saying, and it was concealed from them, that they should not perceive it; and they were afraid to ask him about this saying.

Mt 17:22–27
Mk 9:30–32
Lk 9:22; 24:26

Lk 18:34

Humility and tolerance

⁴⁶And an argument arose among them as to which of them was the greatest. ⁴⁷But when Jesus perceived the thought of their hearts, he took a child and put him by his side, ⁴⁸and said to them, "Whoever receives this child in my name receives me, and whoever receives me receives him who sent me; for he who is least among you all is the one who is great."

Mt 18:1–14
Mk 9:33–50

Lk 9:48

Mt 10:40
Lk 22:26
Jn 13:20

dit illum, et subito clamat et dissipat eum cum spuma et vix discedit ab eo dilanians eum; ⁴⁰et rogavi discipulos tuos, ut eicerent illum, et non potuerunt». ⁴¹Respondens autem Iesus dixit: «O generatio infidelis et perversa, usquequo ero apud vos et patiar vos? Adduc huc filium tuum». ⁴²Et cum accederet, elisit illum daemonium et dissipavit. Et increpavit Iesus spiritum immundum et sanavit puerum et reddidit illum patri eius. ⁴³Stupebant autem omnes in magnitudine Dei. Omnibusque mirantibus in omnibus, quae faciebat, dixit ad discipulos suos: ⁴⁴«Ponite vos in auribus vestris sermones istos: Filius enim hominis futurum est ut tradatur in manus hominum». ⁴⁵At illi ignorabant verbum istud, et erat velatum ante eos, ut non sentirent illud, et timebant interrogare eum de hoc verbo. ⁴⁶Intravit autem cogitatio in eos, quis eorum maior esset. ⁴⁷At Iesus sciens cogitationem cordis illorum, apprehendens puerum statuit eum secus se ⁴⁸et ait illis: «Quicumque susceperit puerum istum in nomine meo, me

9:43–45 Once again, this time after the vision of his glory, Jesus speaks of his forthcoming passion and death; but his disciples miss his meaning: "No one should be scandalized to see how imperfect the apostles were. The mystery of the cross lay in the future, and the grace of the Holy Spirit had not yet been given to them" (St John Chrysostom, *In Matthaeum*, 65, 2). Also, unlike the other announcements, this one contains mention only of Christ's humiliation, not his glorification—of his betrayal into the hands of men, but not the victory of his resurrection. It is a further reminder that love for the cross is a sign of a person's identification with Jesus: "Suffer death on the cross with him, and like him, crucify your nature through a life of mortification and self-denial. Give yourself up to the terrible suffering of the cross which leads to the death that God ordains and allows. The more closely you take part in and endure this crucifixion the closer you will be to the One who was crucified, and the more you will partake of the divine life" (St Teresa Benedicta

of the Cross, *The Science of the Cross*, 53).

9:46–50 In contrast to the suffering that Jesus sees awaiting him (9:44), this episode exposes the flawed outlook of the apostles. Jesus counterpoints the ambition of these all-too-typical adults with the simplicity of a child (vv. 46–48). His teaching about humility and the simplicity was not lost on the early Christians: "You will be simple of heart and rich in spirit [...]. You will not praise yourself, but be humble in everything. You will not seek [your own] glory. You will not harbour evil intentions against your neighbour, nor fill your soul with recklessness" (*Epistula Barnabae*, 19, 2–3).

Later, our Lord corrects the intolerant, exclusivist attitude of the apostles, by inviting them to find room for all people in their hearts: "Rejoice when you see others working in good apostolic activities. And ask God to grant them abundant grace and correspondence to that grace. Then, you, on your way. Convince yourself that it's the only way for you" (St Josemaría Escrivá, *The Way*, 965).

Lk 11:23
Phil 1:18
⁴⁹John answered, "Master, we saw a man casting out demons in your name, and we forbade him, because he does not follow with us." ⁵⁰But Jesus said to him, "Do not forbid him; for he that is not against you is for you."

PART TWO

Jesus' ministry on the way to Jerusalem*

6. THE JOURNEY BEGINS*

Samaritans refuse to receive Jesus

Jn 4:4, 9
⁵¹When the days drew near for him to be received up, he set his face to go to Jerusalem.* ⁵²And he sent messengers ahead of him, who went and entered a village of the Samaritans, to make ready for him; ⁵³but the people would not receive him,
Mt 19:1
Mk 10:1, 39
1 Kings 1:10, 17
because his face was set toward Jerusalem.* ⁵⁴And when his disciples James and John saw it, they said, "Lord, do you want us to bid fire come down from heaven and consume them?"ᵉ ⁵⁵But he turned and rebuked them.ᶠ ⁵⁶And they went on to another village.

recipit; et, quicumque me receperit, recipit eum, qui me misit; nam qui minor est inter omnes vos, hic maior est». ⁴⁹Respondens autem Ioannes dixit: «Praeceptor, vidimus quendam in nomine tuo eicientem daemonia, et prohibuimus eum, quia non sequitur nobiscum». ⁵⁰Et ait ad illum Iesus: «Nolite prohibere; qui enim non est adversus vos, pro vobis est». ⁵¹Factum est autem dum complerentur dies assumptionis eius, et ipse faciem suam firmavit, ut iret Ierusalem, ⁵²et misit nuntios ante conspectum suum. Et euntes intraverunt in castellum Samaritanorum, ut pararent illi. ⁵³Et non receperunt eum, quia facies eius erat euntis Ierusalem. ⁵⁴Cum vidissent autem discipuli Iacobus et Ioannes dixerunt: «Domine, vis dicamus, ut *ignis descendat de caelo et consumat* illos?». ⁵⁵Et conversus increpavit illos. ⁵⁶Et ierunt in aliud castellum. ⁵⁷Et euntibus illis in via, dixit quidam

*9:51—19:27 All three Synoptic Gospels contain extensive accounts of Jesus' journey from Galilee to Jerusalem. But, at almost ten full chapters, Luke's account is much longer than the others, and comprises many of our Lord's teachings that are not recorded in the other Gospels— the parables of the good Samaritan (10:23–37), of mercy (15:30–32), of the Pharisee and the tax collector (18:10–14), and the conversion of Zacchaeus (19:1–10).

By giving so extended an account of Jesus' journey to Jerusalem, Luke makes clear the importance of the Holy City in the history of salvation. The Lord's public ministry begins in Galilee (4:14—9:50); Jesus travels through Samaria on his way to Jerusalem (9:51—19:27); and our salvation is won in the Holy City (19:28—24:53). The Acts of the Apostles plots a reverse trajectory: the Church takes root in Jerusalem (Acts 1:1—7:60) and spreads through Samaria (Acts 8:1–25) to the ends of the earth (Acts 8:26—28:31).

*9:51—10:24 Events during Jesus' journey to Jerusalem recall similar occurrences during his ministry in Galilee. The Samaritans' rejection of the Lord (9:53) parallels the response he received in Nazareth (4:28–30); the sending-out of seventy-two disciples (10:1–12; 17–20) mirrors the mission of the Twelve (9:1–6, 10); and finally, Jesus' reproaches of the unbelieving cities (10:13–15) echo his reproach to the "men of this generation" for their lack of faith (7:31–35).

9:51–56 By making his way purposefully towards Jerusalem, to the cross, Jesus is voluntarily advancing his Father's plan (cf. 9:31) that he should suffer and die before rising in glory and ascending into heaven. "The days […] for him to be received up", literally "the days of his assumption" (v. 51), are when he will leave this world and ascend into heaven. The evangelist describes Jesus' journey to Jerusalem as an ascent to a point where salvation will be effected, but it

e Other ancient authorities read *as Elijah did*   f Other ancient authorities add *and he said, "You do not know what manner of spirit you are of; for the Son of man came not to destroy men's lives but to save them"*

Requirements for following Jesus

Mt 8:18–22

⁵⁷As they were going along the road, a man said to him, "I will follow you wherever you go." ⁵⁸And Jesus said to him, "Foxes have holes, and birds of the air have nests; but the Son of man has nowhere to lay his head." ⁵⁹To another he said, "Follow me."

Lk 14:26, 33

But he said, "Lord, let me first go and bury my father." ⁶⁰But he said to him, "Leave the dead to bury their own dead; but as for you, go and proclaim the kingdom of God." ⁶¹Another said, "I will follow you, Lord; but let me first say farewell to those

1 Kings 19:19–21

at my home." ⁶²Jesus said to him, "No one who puts his hand to the plough and looks back is fit for the kingdom of God."

The mission of the seventy disciples

10 ¹After this the Lord appointed seventyᵍ others, and sent them on ahead of him, two by two, into every town and place where he himself was about to

Mt 10:7–16
Mk 6:8–11
Ex 24:1
Lk 9:1–2

ad illum: «Sequar te, quocumque ieris». ⁵⁸Et ait illi Iesus: «Vulpes foveas habent et volucres caeli nidos, Filius autem hominis non habet, ubi caput reclinet». ⁵⁹Ait autem ad alterum: «Sequere me». Ille autem dixit: «Domine, permitte mihi primum ire et sepelire patrem meum». ⁶⁰Dixitque ei Iesus: «Sine, ut mortui sepeliant mortuos suos; tu autem vade, annuntia regnum Dei». ⁶¹Et ait alter: «Sequar te, Domine, sed primum permitte mihi renuntiare his, qui domi sunt». ⁶²Ait ad illum Iesus: «Nemo mittens manum suam in aratrum et aspiciens retro, aptus est regno Dei».   [10] ¹Post haec autem designavit Dominus alios septuaginta duos et misit illos binos ante faciem suam in omnem civitatem et locum, quo erat ipse

is a journey that necessarily entails the cross. Hence the double meaning that "cross" has in Christian language: "The cross is also the glory and exaltation of Christ. It is the overflowing cup of which the psalm speaks, and the crown of all the suffering that Christ endured for us. [...] Christ himself tells us that the cross is his glory [...]; he tells us that the cross is his exaltation: 'And when I am lifted up above the earth, I will draw all things to myself'. The cross is the glory and exaltation of Christ" (St Andrew of Crete, *Sermo 10 in Exaltatione Sanctae Cruce*).

"But the people would not receive him" (v. 53). The hostility between Samaritans and Jews stemmed from the time when Jews intermarried with Gentile settlers introduced into Samaria by the Assyrians around the eighth century BC (see 2 Kings 17:24–41). Friction increased when Jews returned from exile in Babylon and rebuilt Jerusalem (see Neh 13:4–31). For these and other reasons, the Samaritans did not recognize the temple of Jerusalem as the only place where ritual sacrifices could properly be offered, so they built their own temple on Mount Gerizim (see Jn 4:20). Jesus reproves his disciples' desire for revenge (vv. 54–56) because it is out of keeping with his mission as Messiah; he has come to save people, not destroy them. This helps them to see that zeal for the things of God should never be bitter or violent: "The Lord does everything in an admirable way [...]. He acts in this

way to teach us that perfect virtue retains no desire for vengeance, and that where there is true charity there is no room for anger—in other words, that weakness should not be treated with harshness but should be helped" (St Ambrose, *Expositio Evangelii secundum Lucam*, ad loc.).

See the RSV note **f** about an addition to v. 55 found in some Greek manuscripts (and followed by the Vulgate).

9:57–62 As happened at the start of his ministry (see 5:1–11), now too we find people who feel called to follow Jesus. Peter and the other apostles "left everything and followed him" (see 5:11, 28); but these other people still have attachments to their old life and their attitude is quite different from that of Jesus, whom the Gospel has shown to be resolutely committed to his journey to Jerusalem (see 9:51). To follow Jesus requires a radical decision and commitment: "Sometimes [the will] seems to be fixed on serving Christ, but at the same time seeks the applause and approval of men [...]. It struggles to win future goods but without leaving behind those of the present life. A will like this will never enable us to achieve genuine holiness" (John Cassian, *Collationes*, 4, 12).

10:1–12 Jesus now sends out another seventy (or, according to some manuscripts, seventy-two) disciples to "every town and place" on his

g Other ancient authorities read *seventy-two*

Mt 9:37–38
Jn 4:35, 38

Lk 22:35

1 Tim 5:18

1 Cor 10:27

Acts 13:51; 18:6

come. ²And he said to them, "The harvest is plentiful, but the labourers are few; pray therefore the Lord of the harvest to send out labourers into his harvest. ³Go your way; behold, I send you out as lambs in the midst of wolves. ⁴Carry no purse, no bag, no sandals; and salute no one on the road. ⁵Whatever house you enter, first say, 'Peace be to this house!' ⁶And if a son of peace is there, your peace shall rest upon him; but if not, it shall return to you. ⁷And remain in the same house, eating and drinking what they provide, for the labourer deserves his wages; do not go from house to house. ⁸Whenever you enter a town and they receive you, eat what is set before you; ⁹heal the sick in it and say to them, 'The kingdom of God has come near to you.' ¹⁰But whenever you enter a town and they do not receive you, go into its streets and say, ¹¹'Even the dust of your town that clings to our feet, we wipe off against you; nevertheless know this, that the kingdom of God has come near.' ¹²I tell you, it shall be more tolerable on that day for Sodom than for that town.

Mt 11:20–24

Jon 3:6

Jesus reproaches cities for their unbelief

¹³"Woe to you, Chorazin! woe to you, Bethsaida! for if the mighty works done in you had been done in Tyre and Sidon, they would have repented long ago, sitting in

---

venturus. ²Et dicebat illis: «Messis quidem multa, operarii autem pauci; rogate ergo Dominum messis, ut mittat operarios in messem suam. ³Ite; ecce ego mitto vos sicut agnos inter lupos. ⁴Nolite portare sacculum, neque peram neque calceamenta, et neminem per viam salutaveritis. ⁵In quamcumque domum intraveritis, primum dicite: "Pax huic domui". ⁶Et si ibi fuerit filius pacis, requiescet super illam pax vestra; sin autem ad vos revertetur. ⁷In eadem autem domo manete edentes et bibentes, quae apud illos sunt: dignus enim est operarius mercede sua. Nolite transire de domo in domum. ⁸Et in quamcumque civitatem intraveritis, et susceperint vos, manducate, quae apponuntur vobis, ⁹et curate infirmos, qui in illa sunt, et dicite illis: "Appropinquavit in vos regnum Dei". ¹⁰In quamcumque civitatem intraveritis, et non receperint vos, exeuntes in plateas eius dicite: ¹¹"Etiam pulverem, qui adhaesit nobis ad pedes de civitate vestra, extergimus in vos; tamen hoc scitote quia appropinquavit regnum Dei". ¹²Dico vobis quia Sodomis in die illa remissius erit quam illi civitati. ¹³Vae tibi, Chorazin! Vae tibi, Bethsaida! Quia si in Tyro et Sidone factae

---

itinerary (v. 1), charged with a mission similar to the one he earlier gave the Twelve (see 9:1–5). The number seventy-two may be an allusion to the descendants of Noah (see Gen 10:1ff) who were founders of nations prior to the scattering of Babel (see Gen 10:32—11:9). In any case, the mission appears to show the universal thrust of Christ's mission. Jesus' instructions, moreover, have a ring of urgency to them. Universality and zeal will always be part of the Church's missionary activity: "Today, all Christians, the particular [local] Churches and the universal Church, are called to have the same courage that missionaries of the past, and the same readiness to listen to the voice of the inspired Spirit" (John Paul II, *Redemptoris missio*, 30).

Those who followed Jesus and received a call from him (see Lk 9:57–62) made up a large number of disciples. Of these, we know the names of few, but among them must have been some who were with him right from the time of his baptism by John until his ascension; for example, the Joseph known as Barsabbas, and Matthias (see Acts 1:23), and Cleophas and his

companion, to whom the Risen Christ appeared on the way to Emmaus (see 24:13–35). From among these many disciples, our Lord chooses out about seventy, and he requires of them (as he did of the apostles) total detachment and abandonment to divine providence (v. 4). "Such should be the confidence the preacher places in God that even if he is not provided with the necessities of life, he is convinced that they will come his way. This will ensure that worry about providing temporal things for himself does not distract him from providing others with eternal things" (St Gregory the Great, *Homiliae in Evangelia*, 17).

10:13–16 As examples of places where the disciples may not receive a good welcome, Jesus mentions two fishing villages, Chorazin and Bethsaida (v. 16; cf. 10:10–12). These were Jewish towns that had witnessed the things God had done through Jesus, yet failed to mend their ways. The comparison with the pagan towns of Tyre and Sidon shows how blameworthy the Jewish towns were, because "every one to whom

sackcloth and ashes. [14]But it shall be more tolerable in the judgment for Tyre and
Sidon than for you. [15]And you, Capernaum, will you be exalted to heaven? You shall
be brought down to Hades.

Is 14:13–15

[16]"He who hears you hears me, and he who rejects you rejects me, and he who
rejects me rejects him who sent me."

Mt 10:40
Jn 5:23; 15:23

The seventy return from their mission

[17]The seventy[g] returned with joy, saying, "Lord, even the demons are subject to us
in your name!" [18]And he said to them, "I saw Satan fall like lightning from heaven.*
[19]Behold, I have given you authority to tread upon serpents and scorpions, and over
all the power of the enemy; and nothing shall hurt you. [20]Nevertheless do not rejoice
in this, that the spirits are subject to you; but rejoice that your names are written in
heaven."

Jn 12:31

Rev 12:8–9
Mk 16:18
Ps 91:13

Ex 32:32
Rev 10:15
Mt 7:22

Jesus gives thanks

Mt 11:25–30

[21]In that same hour he rejoiced in the Holy Spirit and said, "I thank thee, Father,
Lord of heaven and earth, that thou hast hidden these things from the wise and
understanding and revealed them to babes; yea, Father, for such was thy gracious
will.[h] [22]All things have been delivered to me by my Father; and no one knows who

Jn 17:25

---

fuissent virtutes, quae in vobis factae sunt, olim in cilicio et cinere sedentes paeniterent. [14]Verumtamen Tyro et Sidoni remissius erit in iudicio
quam vobis. [15]Et tu, Capharnaum, numquid *usque in caelum exaltaberis? Usque ad infernum demergeris!* [16]Qui vos audit, me audit; et qui vos
spernit, me spernit; qui autem me spernit, spernit eum, qui me misit». [17]Reversi sunt autem septuaginta duo cum gaudio dicentes: «Domine, etiam
daemonia subiciuntur nobis in nomine tuo!». [18]Et ait illis: «Videbam Satanam sicut fulgur de caelo cadentem. [19]Ecce dedi vobis potestatem cal-
candi supra serpentes et scorpiones et supra omnem virtutem inimici; et nihil vobis nocebit. [20]Verumtamen in hoc nolite gaudere quia spiritus
vobis subiciuntur; gaudete autem quod nomina vestra scripta sunt in caelis». [21]In ipsa hora exsultavit Spiritu Sancto et dixit: «Confiteor tibi, Pater,
Domine caeli et terrae, quod abscondisti haec a sapientibus et prudentibus et revelasti ea parvulis; etiam, Pater, quia sic placuit ante te. [22]Omnia

---

much is given, of him will much be required"
(12:48). The actions and words of the disciples
are, like those of Jesus (v. 16), a call from God to
repentance (v. 13), which must come from the
heart: "Interior repentance is a radical reorienta-
tion of our whole life, a return, a conversion to
God with all our heart, an end of sin, a turning
away from evil, with repugnance toward the evil
actions we have committed. At the same time it
entails the desire and resolution to change one's
life, with hope in God's mercy and trust in the
help of his grace. This conversion of heart is
accompanied by a salutary pain and sadness
which the Fathers called *animi cruciatus* (affliction of spirit) and *compunctio cordis* (repentance
of heart)" (*Catechism of the Catholic Church*,
1431).

10:17–20 The disciples rejoice at having played
a part in Christ's mission and at having seen its
power (v. 17). However, our Lord asks them to
look deeper: the fact that God has chosen them is
what calls for real celebration: "Don't doubt it:

your vocation is the greatest grace our Lord
could have given you. Thank him for it" (St
Josemaría Escrivá, *The Way*, 913).

10:21–24 This passage, found also in Matthew
(see Mt 11:25–27 and note), is often called
Jesus' "hymn of joy". It marks one of the few
times when we find him expressing his joy, in
this case on seeing that humble people understand him and accept the word of God (v. 21):
"Children do not worry about the wealth of their
parents. However, the parents, if they hold the
throne or have great riches, do not hesitate to satisfy all their little ones' desires [...]. Neither
riches nor glory (not even the glory of heaven)
fills the heart of a small child [...]. What he
demands is love [...]. He can do but one thing,
Jesus — love you!" (St Thérèse of Lisieux, *Autobiographical Writings*, 9).

Here Jesus openly declares who he is: he is
the one who knows God the Father and who
reveals him; he is at the same time both revealer
and revelation. In Jesus, God makes himself

---

h Or *so it was well-pleasing before thee*

the Son is except the Father, or who the Father is except the Son and any one to whom the Son chooses to reveal him."

Mt 13:16–17

1 Pet 1:10

23Then turning to the disciples he said privately, "Blessed are the eyes which see what you see! 24For I tell you that many prophets and kings desired to see what you see, and did not see it, and to hear what you hear, and did not hear it."

7. FURTHER PREACHING*

Mt 22:34–40
Mk 12:28–34

Lk 18:18–20
Mt 19:17
Mk 10:17

Deut 6:5
Lev 19:18

Parable of the good Samaritan

25And behold, a lawyer stood up to put him to the test, saying, "Teacher, what shall I do to inherit eternal life?" 26He said to him, "What is written in the law? How do you read?" 27And he answered, "You shall love the Lord your God with all your heart, and with all your soul, and with all your strength, and with all your mind: and your neighbour as yourself." 28And he said to him, "You have answered right; do this, and you will live."

29But he, desiring to justify himself, said to Jesus, "And who is my neighbour?" 30Jesus replied, "A man was going down from Jerusalem to Jericho, and he fell among robbers, who stripped him and beat him, and departed, leaving him half dead. 31Now by chance a priest was going down that road; and when he saw him he passed by on the other side. 32So likewise a Levite, when he came to the place and saw him, passed by on the other side. 33But a Samaritan, as he journeyed, came to where he

mihi tradita sunt a Patre meo; et nemo scit qui sit Filius nisi Pater, et qui sit Pater nisi Filius et cui voluerit Filius revelare». 23Et conversus ad discipulos seorsum dixit: «Beati oculi, qui vident, quae videtis. 24Dico enim vobis: Multi prophetae et reges voluerunt videre, quae vos videtis, et non viderunt, et audire, quae auditis, et non audierunt». 25Et ecce quidam legis peritus surrexit tentans illum dicens: «Magister, quid faciendo vitam aeternam possidebo?». 26At ille dixit ad eum: «In Lege quid scriptum est? Quomodo legis?». 27Ille autem respondens dixit: «*Diliges Dominum Deum tuum ex toto corde tuo et ex tota anima tua et ex omnibus viribus tuis* et ex omni mente tua et *proximum tuum sicut teipsum*». 28Dixitque illi: «Recte respondisti; hoc fac et vives». 29Ille autem, volens iustificare seipsum, dixit ad Iesum: «Et quis est meus proximus?». 30Suscipiens autem Iesus dixit: «Homo quidam descendebat ab Ierusalem in Iericho et incidit in latrones, qui etiam despoliaverunt eum et, plagis impositis, abierunt, semivivo relicto. 31Accidit autem, ut sacerdos quidam descenderet eadem via et, viso illo, praeterivit; 32similiter et Levita, cum esset secus locum et videret eum, pertransiit. 33Samaritanus autem quidam iter faciens, venit secus eum et videns eum misericordia motus est, 34et

accessible to man: "What idea of God could man have made but an idol after his own heart? God was beyond reach and comprehension, invisible and superior to all human thought. But now he has willed to be seen and understood, to make himself known to human understanding. How? By lying in a manger, by preaching on a mountainside, by spending the whole night in prayer; by hanging on the cross in the agony of death, and freed from death, overcoming the power of death, rising from the dead on the third day, showing the apostles the marks of the nails as a sign of his victory, and finally, ascending to the heights of heaven before their very eyes. Is any part of his life unworthy of profound and pious meditation? When I contemplate these events, my mind is on God, and through them, my thoughts can reach God" (St Bernard, *Sermo in Nativitate B. Virginis Mariae*).

*10:25—11:54 This section consists of a series of passages in which the event described is the pretext for a report of the teachings of our Lord—on compassion, prayer, etc.

10:25–37 Jesus praises the summary of the Law given by the scribe (this summary is an amalgam of Deuteronomy 6:5 and Leviticus 19:18). But by telling the parable of the good Samaritan, Christ extends horizons that had been narrowed by legalistic attitudes and interpretations. "The concept of 'neighbour' [prior to this] was understood as referring essentially to one's countrymen and to foreigners who had settled in the land of Israel; in other words, to the closely-knit community of a single country or people. This limit is now abolished. Anyone who needs me, and whom I can help, is my neighbour. The concept of 'neighbour' is now universalized, yet it

was; and when he saw him, he had compassion, ³⁴and went to him and bound up his wounds, pouring on oil and wine; then he set him on his own beast and brought him to an inn, and took care of him. ³⁵And the next day he took out two denarii[i] and gave them to the inn-keeper, saying, 'Take care of him; and whatever more you spend, I will repay you when I come back.' ³⁶Which of these three, do you think, proved neighbour to the man who fell among the robbers?" ³⁷He said, "The one who showed mercy on him." And Jesus said to him, "Go and do likewise."

Is 1:6

Martha and Mary welcome our Lord

³⁸Now as they went on their way, he entered a village; and a woman named Martha received him into her house. ³⁹And she had a sister called Mary, who sat at the

Jn 11:1; 12:2-3

appropians alligavit vulnera eius infundens oleum et vinum; et imponens illum in iumentum suum duxit in stabulum et curam eius egit. ³⁵Et altera die protulit duos denarios et dedit stabulario et ait: "Curam illius habe, et, quodcumque supererogaveris, ego, cum rediero, reddam tibi". ³⁶Quis horum trium videtur tibi proximus fuisse illi, qui incidit in latrones?». ³⁷At ille dixit: «Qui fecit misericordiam in illum». Et ait illi Iesus: «Vade et tu fac similiter». ³⁸Cum autem irent, ipse intravit in quoddam castellum, et mulier quaedam Martha nomine excepit illum. ³⁹Et huic erat soror nomine Maria, quae etiam sedens secus pedes Domini audiebat verbum illius. ⁴⁰Martha autem satagebat circa frequens ministerium; quae stetit

remains concrete. Despite being extended to all mankind, it is not reduced to a generic, abstract and undemanding expression of love, but calls for my own practical commitment here and now" (Benedict XVI, *Deus caritas est*, 15).

By mentioning the priest and the Levite (vv. 31–32), our Lord may have sought to define the limits of legal prescriptions. The victim may well have appeared to have been dead (see v. 30); and according to the Mosaic Law (cf. Lev 21:1–4, 10–11; Num 19:11–22), a person who touched a dead body became unclean. Through this parable Jesus shows (and the scribe sees this, too) that adherence to legal precepts should never prevent one from showing compassion.

The reader can also see that Jesus is the incarnation of divine mercy and acts in the same merciful way as his Father (cf. 15:1–32 and notes). Therefore, it is not surprising that from very early on this parable was interpreted as an allegory. St Augustine (who comments on it in a number of places), followed by other Fathers, sees the good Samaritan as standing for our Lord, and the man fallen among robbers as Adam, the origin and symbol of fallen mankind: "Our God wanted to be our neighbour, and Jesus Christ our Lord presented the good Samaritan as a symbol of himself: he came to the aid of a man struck down by thieves at the side of the road and left only half alive" (*De doctrina christiana*, 1, 33). Moreover, the man left on the roadside is healed of his wounds in the Church: "My soul,

where are you, where are you laid while you are cured of your wounds and pains by the one who has made reparation for your sins? You are in the same inn to which the good Samaritan brought the man that he had found lying at the side of the road, beaten by a band of thieves and left only half alive" (idem, *De Trinitate*, 15, 27, 50).

10:38–42 St John's Gospel, too, tells us about this family (Lazarus, Martha and Mary) to whom Jesus was a close friend. Jesus' words to Martha are not really a reproach; they are warm praise for Mary's interest in hearing our Lord speak. "The former busied herself, the latter got nourished; the former had many things to attend to, the latter concentrated on one. Both occupations were good" (St Augustine, *Sermones*, 103, 3).

Martha is sometimes seen as a symbol of the active life, and Mary as a symbol of the contemplative life. There are different vocations within the Church, but action and contemplation are to be found in every Christian life. All baptized people are called to have an integrated life in which a personal relationship with God merges harmoniously with their responsibilities. As St Josemaría Escrivá put it, "In this life, the contemplation of supernatural reality, the action of grace in our souls, our love for our neighbour as a result of our love for God—all these are already a foretaste of heaven, a beginning that is destined to grow from day to day. We Christians cannot resign ourselves to leading a double

i The denarius was a day's wage for a labourer

Lord's feet and listened to his teaching. [40]But Martha was distracted with much serving; and she went to him and said, "Lord, do you not care that my sister has left me to serve alone? Tell her then to help me." [41]But the Lord answered her, "Martha, Martha, you are anxious and troubled about many things; [42]one thing is needful.[j] Mary has chosen the good portion, which shall not be taken away from her."

Mt 6:33

The Our Father

Mt 6:9–13
Lk 5:33; 6:12; 9:29

11 [1]He was praying in a certain place, and when he ceased, one of his disciples said to him, "Lord, teach us to pray, as John taught his disciples." [2]And he said to them, "When you pray, say:

et ait: «Domine, non est tibi curae quod soror mea reliquit me solam ministrare? Dic ergo illi, ut me adiuvet». [41]Et respondens dixit illi Dominus: «Martha, Martha, sollicita es et turbaris erga plurima, [42]porro unum est necessarium; Maria enim optimam partem elegit, quae non auferetur ab ea». [11] [1]Et factum est cum esset in loco quodam orans, ut cessavit, dixit unus ex discipulis eius ad eum: «Domine, doce nos orare, sicut et Ioannes docuit discipulos suos». [2]Et ait illis: «Cum oratis, dicite: Pater, sanctificetur nomen tuum, / adveniat regnum tuum; / [3]panem nostrum cotidianum da nobis cotidie, / [4]et dimitte nobis peccata nostra, / siquidem et ipsi dimittimus omni debenti nobis, / et ne nos inducas in tenta-

life—our life must be a strong and simple unity into which all our actions converge. Christ awaits us. […] Let us be contemplative souls, carrying on an unceasing dialogue with our Lord at all hours—from the first thought of the day to the last, turning our heart constantly toward our Lord Jesus Christ, going to him through our Mother, Holy Mary, and through him to the Father and the Holy Spirit" (*Christ Is Passing By*, 126). And elsewhere he says: "You must understand now, more clearly, that God is calling you to serve him *in and from* the ordinary, material and secular activities of human life. […] Understand this well: there is something holy, something divine, hidden in the most ordinary situations, and it is up to each one of you to discover it" (*Conversations*, 114).

11:1–4 The Our Father is also to be found in St Matthew's Gospel, where it is found in the Sermon on the Mount (see the note on Mt 6:1–18). Here it comes as a reply by Jesus to a request from his disciples, who are impressed by the way their Teacher prays (v. 1); this helps us see the close connexion between the prayer of Jesus, the Son of God, and that of Christians: "The prayer that comes to us from Jesus is truly unique: it is 'of the Lord'. On the one hand, in the words of this prayer the only Son gives us the words the Father gave him: he is the master of our prayer. On the other, as Word incarnate, he knows in his human heart the needs of his human brothers and sisters and reveals them to

us: he is the model of our prayer" (*Catechism of the Catholic Church*, 2765).

It is very consoling to be able to call God "Father". If Jesus, the Son of God, teaches us to invoke God as Father, it is because we truly are and should feel ourselves to be his children: "I am that daughter, the child who receives the concerned love of a Father who sent the Word not to save the righteous, but to save sinners. He wants me to love him because he has forgiven me— and not just part, or most: he has forgiven me everything. He did not expect me to love him as much as Mary Magdalene did, but he wants me to know how much he loves me, with a providential love, so that now I love him madly …!" (St Thérèse of Lisieux, *Autobiographical Writings*, 4, 39).

The text of the Our Father is shorter here than in St Matthew, but it contains the same invocations and petitions: "If you study all the prayers in Holy Scripture, you will find nothing that is not contained in the Lord's Prayer. In your prayer, you can put the petitions it contains into different words, but you should not change the petitions themselves to ask for different things. […] This prayer is, to my mind, an explanation of what prayer should be, what should be asked for in prayer. This is not my teaching; it is what we have all been taught by the one who deigned to be our Master" (St Augustine, *Ad Probam*, 12–13).

One of the things we ask for in the Our Father (cf. the note on Mt 6:1–18) is our daily

j Other ancient authorities read *few things are meaningful, or only one*

"Father, hallowed be thy name. Thy kingdom come. ³Give us each day our daily bread;ᵏ ⁴and forgive us our sins, for we ourselves forgive every one who is indebted to us; and lead us not into temptation."

Effective prayer

Mt 7:7–11
Lk 18:1–5

⁵And he said to them, "Which of you who has a friend will go to him at midnight and say to him, 'Friend, lend me three loaves; ⁶for a friend of mine has arrived on a journey, and I have nothing to set before him'; ⁷and he will answer from within, 'Do not bother me; the door is now shut, and my children are with me in bed; I cannot get up and give you anything'? ⁸I tell you, though he will not get up and give him anything because he is his friend, yet because of his importunity he will rise and give him whatever he needs. ⁹And I tell you, Ask, and it will be given you; seek, and you will find; knock, and it will be opened to you. ¹⁰For every one who asks receives, and he who seeks finds, and to him who knocks it will be opened. ¹¹What father among you,

Jn 14:13–14

tionem». ⁵Et ait ad illos: «Quis vestrum habebit amicum et ibit ad illum media nocte et dicet illi: "Amice, commoda mihi tres panes, ⁶quoniam amicus meus venit de via ad me, et non habeo, quod ponam ante illum"; ⁷et ille de intus respondens dicat: "Noli mihi molestus esse; iam ostium clausum est, et pueri mei mecum sunt in cubili; non possum surgere et dare tibi". ⁸Dico vobis: Et si non dabit illi surgens, eo quod amicus eius sit, propter improbitatem tamen eius surget et dabit illi, quotquot habet necessarios. ⁹Et ego vobis dico: Petite, et dabitur vobis; quaerite, et invenietis; pulsate, et aperietur vobis. ¹⁰Omnis enim qui petit, accipit; et, qui quaerit, invenit; et pulsanti aperietur. ¹¹Quem autem ex vobis patrem filius

bread (v. 3). We petition God for the food we need every day—not for plenty, nor for bare subsistence (cf. Prov 30:8). The Fathers of the Church interpreted this "bread" as meaning not only ordinary food but also the Eucharist, which our soul needs for survival. The Church offers us this food every day in the Mass, and we will learn its nourishing value if we receive it daily: "If the bread we ask God for is 'our daily bread', why do you only go to receive it once a year? Receive daily what enriches every day, and live your daily life in such a way as to be worthy to receive it" (St Ambrose, *De Sacramentis*, 5, 4).

We also ask for strength to deal with temptation (v. 4). But "we do not ask to be freed from temptation, for temptation marks the life of man on earth (cf. Job 7:1). [...] What we ask for here is that with the help of God we will not give in to temptation, nor yield to temptation out of discouragement. The grace of God is never slow to come to our aid, which should be a comfort and support to us when we feel our own lack of strength" (*Roman Catechism*, 4, 15, 14).

11:5–13 After the Our Father come teachings about prayer of petition, which begin with a brief but very vivid vignette (vv. 5–8). Archaeological investigation has discovered that some dwellings in Nazareth in the time of Jesus consisted simply of a space hollowed out of the hillside with a

building projecting out just a few metres. Little shelves were made in the rock for storage. The man who requests the three loaves makes a nuisance of himself, because to reach the bread the owner will have to wake his whole house (v. 7). Jesus concludes the illustration with a word about the effectiveness of prayer (vv. 9–10). The truth of what he says has been discovered by the Church time and time again: "Once, when I was pestering the Lord a lot with my petitions, [...] I was afraid that he could not hear my prayers because of my many sins. Then, as he has at other times, he appeared to me, and began to show me the wound in his left hand, [...] and told me that one who has suffered in that way for me would grant me greater things than I could ask him for. He promised me that he would not deny me a single thing because he knew that I prayed for things for the greater glory of God" (St Teresa of Avila, *Life*, 39, 1).

The vignette and image of the father (vv. 11–13) guarantees to all Christians the greatest gift of all, the Holy Spirit: "Through communion with him, the Holy Spirit makes us spiritual, he returns us to Paradise, brings us to the Kingdom of heaven and into adoption as sons, he gives us the confidence to call God Father and to participate in the grace of Christ, to be called a child of light and to partake in eternal glory" (St Basil, *De Spiritu Sancto*, 15, 36).

k Or *our bread for the morrow*

Jn 14:13–16

if his son asks for¹ a fish, will instead of a fish give him a serpent; ¹²or if he asks for an egg, will give him a scorpion? ¹³If you then, who are evil, know how to give good gifts to your children, how much more will the heavenly Father give the Holy Spirit to those who ask him!"

Mt 12:22–37, 43–45
Mk 3:22–27
Mt 9:32–34

The Kingdom of God and the kingdom of Satan

Mt 16:1
Mk 8:11

¹⁴Now he was casting out a demon that was dumb; when the demon had gone out, the dumb man spoke, and the people marvelled. ¹⁵But some of them said, "He casts out demons by Beelzebul, the prince of demons"; ¹⁶while others, to test him, sought from him a sign from heaven. ¹⁷But he, knowing their thoughts, said to them, "Every kingdom divided against itself is laid waste, and house falls upon house. ¹⁸And if Satan also is divided against himself, how will his kingdom stand? For you say that I cast out demons by Beelzebul. ¹⁹And if I cast out demons by Beelzebul, by whom do your sons cast them out? Therefore they shall be your judges. ²⁰But if it is by the finger of God that I cast out demons, then the kingdom of God has come upon you. ²¹When a strong man, fully armed, guards his own palace, his goods are in peace; ²²but when one stronger than he assails him and overcomes him, he takes away his armour in which he trusted, and divides his spoil. ²³He who is not with me is against me, and he who does not gather with me scatters.

Lk 17:21

Col 2:15
Is 49:24ff
Jn 12:31; 16:33
Lk 9:50

Jn 5:14

²⁴"When the unclean spirit has gone out of a man, he passes through waterless places seeking rest; and finding none he says, 'I will return to my house from which I came.' ²⁵And when he comes he finds it swept and put in order. ²⁶Then he goes and brings seven other spirits more evil than himself, and they enter and dwell there; and the last state of that man becomes worse than the first."

petierit piscem, numquid pro pisce serpentem dabit illi? ¹²Aut si petierit ovum, numquid porriget illi scorpionem? ¹³Si ergo vos, cum sitis mali, nostis dona bona dare filiis vestris, quanto magis Pater de caelo dabit Spiritum Sanctum petentibus se». ¹⁴Et erat eiciens daemonium, et illud erat mutum; et factum est cum daemonium exisset, locutus est mutus. Et admiratae sunt turbae; ¹⁵quidam autem ex eis dixerunt: «In Beelzebul principe daemoniorum eicit daemonia». ¹⁶Et alii tentantes signum de caelo quaerebant ab eo. ¹⁷Ipse autem sciens cogitationes eorum dixit eis: «Omne regnum in seipsum divisum desolatur, et domus supra domum cadit. ¹⁸Si autem et Satanas in seipsum divisus est, quomodo stabit regnum ipsius? Quia dicitis in Beelzebul eicere me daemonia. ¹⁹Si autem ego in Beelzebul eicio daemonia, filii vestri in quo eiciunt? Ideo ipsi iudices vestri erunt. ²⁰Porro si in digito Dei eicio daemonia, profecto pervenit in vos regnum Dei. ²¹Cum fortis armatus custodit atrium suum, in pace sunt ea, quae possidet; ²²si autem fortior illo superveniens vicerit eum, universa arma eius auferet, in quibus confidebat, et spolia eius distribuet. ²³Qui non est mecum, adversum me est; et, qui non colligit mecum, dispergit. ²⁴Cum immundus spiritus exierit de homine, perambulat per loca inaquosa quaerens requiem et non inveniens dicit: 'Revertar in domum meam unde exivi'. ²⁵Et cum venerit, invenit scopis mundatam et exornatam. ²⁶Et

11:14–26 Jesus' critics now approach him making a grave charge—that the devil is acting through him. Jesus refutes this, and at the same time gives them a serious warning (cf. the notes on Mt 12:22–37 and Mk 3:22–30). He makes a comparison (vv. 24–26) to show them the danger they are in: thanks to God's action among them they have seen people freed from the devil, but their obstinate attitude towards Christ gives the evil one new scope to do his worst. Elsewhere in the New Testament (see Heb 6:4–6; 2 Pet 2:20–22) sacred writers express their worry that Christians might find themselves in a similar situation.

In its understandably polemical tone (vv. 15–16), the passage spells out some blunt truths. The

strong man well-armed (v. 21) is the devil, who has enslaved mankind; but Jesus, who is stronger than he, has come and defeated him, and he has been cast out of his former domain. However, even though the devil has been overcome by Christ, it falls to us to make room in our lives for the Kingdom of Christ: "The devil lived in all of us, beloved brothers and sisters, before we were baptised; at our baptism, we were made into temples of the Holy Spirit. [...] And since Christ at his coming cast the devil out of our hearts to make his temple and dwelling-place there, we should do everything in our power, with the help of his grace, to ensure that Christ is not dishonoured by our sins" (St Caesarius of Arles, *Sermones*, 229, 1–3).

¹ Other ancient authorities insert *bread, will give him a stone; or if he asks for*

Responding to the word of God
Lk 8:19–21

[27]As he said this, a woman in the crowd raised her voice and said to him, "Blessed is the womb that bore you, and the breasts that you sucked!" [28]But he said, "Blessed rather are those who hear the word of God and keep it!"

Lk 2:19, 51

The sign of Jonah
Mt 12:38–42

[29]When the crowds were increasing, he began to say, "This generation is an evil generation; it seeks a sign, but no sign shall be given to it except the sign of Jonah. [30]For as Jonah became a sign to the men of Nineveh, so will the Son of man be to this generation. [31]The queen of the South will arise at the judgment with the men of this generation and condemn them; for she came from the ends of the earth to hear the wisdom of Solomon, and behold, something greater than Solomon is here. [32]The men of Nineveh will arise at the judgment with this generation and condemn it; for they repented at the preaching of Jonah, and behold, something greater than Jonah is here.

1 Cor 1:22

Mk 8:11–12
Jon 3:1f

1 Kings 10:1ff

Jon 3:5

The lamp of the body, the light of the soul
Mt 5:15;
6:22–23

[33]"No one after lighting a lamp puts it in a cellar or under a bushel, but on a stand, that those who enter may see the light. [34]Your eye is the lamp of your body; when

Lk 8:16
Mk 4:21

tunc vadit et assumit septem alios spiritus nequiores se, et ingressi habitant ibi; et sunt novissima hominis illius peiora prioribus». [27]Factum est autem cum haec diceret, extollens vocem quaedam mulier de turba dixit illi: «Beatus venter, qui te portavit, et ubera, quae suxisti!». [28]At ille dixit: «Quinimmo beati, qui audiunt verbum Dei et custodiunt!». [29]Turbis autem concurrentibus, coepit dicere: «Generatio haec generatio nequam est; signum quaerit, et signum non dabitur illi nisi signum Ionae. [30]Nam sicut Ionas fuit signum Ninevitis, ita erit et Filius hominis generationi isti. [31]Regina austri surget in iudicio cum viris generationis huius et condemnabit illos, quia venit a finibus terrae audire sapientiam Salomonis, et ecce plus Salomone hic. [32]Viri Ninevitae surgent in iudicio cum generatione hac et condemnabunt illam, quia paenitentiam egerunt ad praedicationem Ionae, et ecce plus Iona hic. [33]Nemo lucernam accendit et in abscondito ponit, neque sub modio, sed supra candelabrum, ut, qui ingrediuntur,

11:27–28 The Tradition of the Church has always read these words as great praise for the Blessed Virgin, for "in the course of her Son's preaching she [Mary] received the words whereby, in extolling a kingdom beyond the concerns and ties of flesh and blood, he declared blessed those who heard and kept the word of God (cf. Mk 3:35; Lk 11:27–28) as she was faithfully doing (cf. Lk 2:19, 51)" (Vatican II, *Lumen gentium*, 58). Mary believed the word of God (1:38), and now Jesus pays "a compliment to his Mother on her *fiat*, her 'be it done' (Lk 1:38). She lived it sincerely, unstintingly, fulfilling its every consequence, but never amid fanfare, rather in the hidden and silent sacrifice of each day" (St Josemaría Escrivá, *Christ Is Passing By*, 172). "Throughout her life and until her last ordeal, when Jesus her son died on the cross, Mary's faith never wavered. She never ceased to believe in the fulfilment of God's word. And so the Church venerates in Mary the purest realization of faith" (*Catechism of the Catholic Church*, 149).

11:29–32 What Jesus says here is a reply to the provocation just reported by St Luke (11:16). The signs that Jesus works, and his wisdom, are clear to those who wish to see. The Ninevites did penance because they acknowledged the prophet Jonah and accepted his message. Jesus is greater than Jonah. And he is also greater than Solomon, the man that Israel held to be the epitome of wisdom. The "queen of the South", the queen of Sheba, visited Solomon (see 1 Kings 10:1–13) and marvelled at the wisdom God had given him. The Ninevites and the pagan queen will confront Jews who do not repent or seek the truth. Christ's life and preaching are a call to conversion, but some of those who hear his preaching are reluctant to take it to heart and therefore fail to understand it. See the note on Mt 12:38–45.

11:33–36 A person who has good eyesight sees things clearly; similarly, those who are morally upright and pure of heart are able to see God at work in the world. Christ makes an appeal here;

your eye is sound, your whole body is full of light; but when it is not sound, your body is full of darkness. [35]Therefore be careful lest the light in you be darkness. [36]If then your whole body is full of light, having no part dark, it will be wholly bright, as when a lamp with its rays gives you light."

Mt 23:1–36   **Jesus reproaches scribes and Pharisees**
Lk 7:36; 14:1   [37]While he was speaking, a Pharisee asked him to dine with him; so he went in and
Mt 15:2   sat at table. [38]The Pharisee was astonished to see that he did not first wash before
Mk 7:2, 5   dinner. [39]And the Lord said to him, "Now you Pharisees cleanse the outside of the cup and of the dish, but inside you are full of extortion and wickedness. [40]You fools!

lumen videant. [34]Lucerna corporis est oculus tuus. Si oculus tuus fuerit simplex, totum corpus tuum lucidum erit; si autem nequam fuerit, etiam corpus tuum tenebrosum erit. [35]Vide ergo, ne lumen, quod in te est, tenebrae sint. [36]Si ergo corpus tuum totum lucidum fuerit, non habens aliquam partem tenebrarum, erit lucidum totum, sicut quando lucerna in fulgore suo illuminat te». [37]Et cum loqueretur, rogavit illum quidam pharisaeus, ut pranderet apud se; et ingressus recubuit. [38]Pharisaeus autem videns miratus est quod non baptizatus esset ante prandium. [39]Et ait Dominus ad illum: «Nunc vos pharisaei, quod de foris est calicis et catini, mundatis, quod autem intus est vestrum, plenum est rapina et iniquitate. [40]Stulti! Nonne, qui fecit, quod de foris est, etiam id, quod de intus est, fecit? [41]Verumtamen, quae insunt, date eleemosynam, et ecce omnia munda sunt

if people repent, they will be able to discern the truth: "Clear sight is the mother of all virtue, and everyone should have this discernment in order to give spiritual guidance to others or to bring order to one's own life. Human judgment is true and just when it is in line with God's will; and human intentions are good when they are trained wholly on God. If our sight is clear, our life and each one of our actions will shine; and our sight is clear when we see clearly what must be done and, acting on our good intention, do what must be done without duplicity. No error can come from good judgment, nor can good intentions lead us to lie. The definition of discernment is the combination of good intention with true judgment. All our actions should be guided by the light of clear discernment, bearing in mind always that we work in God's presence and for his glory" (Baldwin of Canterbury, *Tractatus*, 6).

11:37–54 In this passage (few in the Gospel contain stronger language) Jesus determinedly unmasks the vice that was largely responsible for the Judaic establishment's rejection of his teaching—hypocrisy cloaked in legalism. There are those who, in the guise of doing good, keep to the mere letter of the Law and fail to keep its spirit; they close themselves off from the love of God and neighbour; and, though apparently very upright, they turn others away from fervent pursuit of God because they make religion distasteful and burdensome. Jesus identifies three results of their false approach: it can cause others to

transgress laws without realizing they are doing so (v. 44); it can even lead to the death of the righteous (vv. 48–51); and it can make it impossible for people to attain salvation (v. 52).

The passage begins with a Pharisee inviting Jesus to dine with him. The attitude of this Pharisee, who is surprised to "see" (v. 38) that Jesus does not wash his hands, illustrates what our Lord has said a few minutes earlier: "when your eye is sound, your whole body is full of light; but when it is not sound, your body is full of darkness" (11:34). The Pharisee is focused on external things, and Jesus wants him to look deeper than that: this is the thrust of the comparisons our Lord goes on to draw (vv. 39–44). According to the Law of Moses, Jews were supposed to tithe their harvests (cf. Lev 27:30–33; Deut 14:22ff) to pay for the upkeep of temple worship; insignificant products were not subject to this law, but the Pharisees, who were excessively precise in everything, insisted that they too should be tithed. Our Lord does not condemn them for this (v. 42), but he does say that justice and love of God should take precedence: "He told them that they were only concerned with external things, that they did not value what is within man's heart, for they failed to see that more important than the cleansing of the body is the cleansing of the soul" (Hegemonius, *Acta disputationis Archelai episcopi Mesopotamiae et Manetis haeresiarchae*, 21). The Law also stipulated that anyone who touched a grave would remain

Did not he who made the outside make the inside also? ⁴¹But give for alms those things which are within; and behold, everything is clean for you.

Lk 12:33

⁴²"But woe to you Pharisees! for you tithe mint and rue and every herb, and neglect justice and the love of God; these you ought to have done, without neglecting the others. ⁴³Woe to you Pharisees! for you love the best seat in the synagogues and salutations in the market places. ⁴⁴Woe to you! for you are like graves which are not seen, and men walk over them without knowing it."

Lk 20:46
Mk 12:38–39

⁴⁵One of the lawyers answered him, "Teacher, in saying this you reproach us also." ⁴⁶And he said, "Woe to you lawyers also! for you load men with burdens hard to bear, and you yourselves do not touch the burdens with one of your fingers. ⁴⁷Woe to you! for you build the tombs of the prophets whom your fathers killed. ⁴⁸So you are witnesses and consent to the deed of your fathers; for they killed them, and you build their tombs. ⁴⁹Therefore also the Wisdom of God said, 'I will send them prophets and apostles, some of whom they will kill and persecute,' ⁵⁰that the blood of all the prophets, shed from the foundation of the world, may be required of this generation, ⁵¹from the blood of Abel to the blood of Zechariah, who perished between the altar and the sanctuary. Yes, I tell you, it shall be required of this generation. ⁵²Woe to you lawyers! for you have taken away the key of knowledge; you did not enter yourselves, and you hindered those who were entering."

Gen 4:8
2 Chron 24:20–21

⁵³As he went away from there, the scribes and the Pharisees began to press him hard, and to provoke him to speak of many things, ⁵⁴lying in wait for him, to catch at something he might say.

Lk 20:20

vobis. ⁴²Sed vae vobis pharisaeis, quia decimatis mentam et rutam et omne holus et praeteritis iudicium et caritatem Dei! Haec autem oportuit facere et illa non omittere. ⁴³Vae vobis pharisaeis, quia diligitis primam cathedram in synagogis et salutationes in foro! ⁴⁴Vae vobis, quia estis ut monumenta, quae non parent, et homines ambulantes supra nesciunt!». ⁴⁵Respondens autem quidam ex legis peritis ait illi: «Magister, haec dicens etiam nobis contumeliam facis». ⁴⁶At ille ait: «Et vobis legis peritis: Vae, quia oneratis homines oneribus, quae portari non possunt, et ipsi uno digito vestro non tangitis sarcinas! ⁴⁷Vae vobis, quia aedificatis monumenta prophetarum, patres autem vestri occiderunt illos! ⁴⁸Profecto testificamini et consentitis operibus patrum vestrorum, quoniam ipsi quidem eos occiderunt, vos autem aedificatis. ⁴⁹Propterea et sapientia Dei dixit: Mittam ad illos prophetas et apostolos, et ex illis occident et persequentur, ⁵⁰ut requiratur sanguis omnium prophetarum, qui effusus est a constitutione mundi, a generatione ista, ⁵¹a sanguine Abel usque ad sanguinem Zachariae, qui periit inter altare et aedem. Ita dico vobis: Requiretur ab hac generatione. ⁵²Vae vobis legis peritis, quia tulistis clavem scientiae! Ipsi non introistis et eos, qui introibant, prohibuistis». ⁵³Cum autem inde exisset, coeperunt scribae et pharisaei graviter insistere et eum allicere in sermone de multis ⁵⁴insidiantes ei, ut caperent aliquid ex ore eius.

unclean for seven days (Num 19:16). Therefore, graves had to be marked lest, with the passage of time, people should inadvertently step on them. The Pharisees have no light with which to show people the way (cf. 11:33), and they can cause the faithful to wander astray (v. 44).

Next (in vv. 46–52), Jesus replies to a remark made by a lawyer. Lawyers, doctors of the Law (usually called scribes), were people who were reasonably well versed in the Law and its interpretation. Both the Pharisees and Sadducees had their scribes. The criticism made here by our Lord is shorter than that recorded by St Matthew (see Mt 23:1–36 and note), but it is equally severe. Using language reminiscent of the prophets, Jesus reminds them of all the blood spilt from the time of Abel, at the start of the Bible (see Gen 4:8), to that of Zechariah, the

prophet whose martyrdom is recounted in the last of the sacred books in the Hebrew Bible (2 Chron 24:20–22). By doing so, he announces his own fate, as readers can already sense in the attitude of the scribes and Pharisees (see vv. 53–54); but readers also realize at the same time that it is Jesus' attitude they must imitate: "Do not trouble yourself with worries about who is with you and who against you, but strive to ensure that God is with you and in everything you do. If your conscience is clear, God will protect you; no harm can come to one under God's protection. If you know how to suffer in silence, be sure that God will come to your aid. He knows the time and way to set you free from suffering. Offer yourself wholly to him. God helps and saves all those who suffer" (Thomas à Kempis, *De imitatione Christi*, 2, 2).

8. ANNOUNCEMENT OF THE END*

Mt 10:16–42   **Various teachings**
Mk 8:15

12 ¹In the meantime, when so many thousands of the multitude had gathered together that they trod upon one another, he began to say to his disciples first,

Lk 8:17   "Beware of the leaven of the Pharisees, which is hypocrisy. ²Nothing is covered up that will not be revealed, or hidden that will not be known. ³Whatever you have said in the dark shall be heard in the light, and what you have whispered in private rooms shall be proclaimed upon the housetops.

⁴"I tell you, my friends, do not fear those who kill the body, and after that have no more that they can do. ⁵But I will warn you whom to fear: fear him who, after he has killed, has power to cast into hell;ᵐ yes, I tell you, fear him! ⁶Are not five sparrows sold

Lk 21:18
Acts 27:34   for two pennies? And not one of them is forgotten before God. ⁷Why, even the hairs of your head are all numbered. Fear not; you are of more value than many sparrows.

Mk 8:38   ⁸"And I tell you, every one who acknowledges me before men, the Son of man
Lk 9:26   also will acknowledge before the angels of God; ⁹but he who denies me before men

[12] ¹Interea multis circumstantibus, ita ut se invicem conculcarent, coepit dicere ad discipulos suos primum: «Attendite a fermento pharisaeorum, quod est hypocrisis. ²Nihil autem opertum est, quod non reveletur, neque absconditum, quod non sciatur. ³Quoniam, quae in tenebris dixistis, in lumine audientur, et quod in aurem locuti estis in cubiculis, praedicabitur in tectis. ⁴Dico autem vobis amicis meis: Ne terreamini ab his, qui occidunt corpus, et post haec non habent amplius, quod faciant. ⁵Ostendam autem vobis quem timeatis: Timete eum, qui postquam occiderit, habet potestatem mittere in gehennam. Ita dico vobis: Hunc timete. ⁶Nonne quinque passeres veneunt dipundio? Et unus ex illis non est in oblivione coram Deo. ⁷Sed et capilli capitis vestri omnes numerati sunt. Nolite timere; multis passeribus pluris estis. ⁸Dico autem vobis: Omnis,

*12:1—14:35 This new section, like the previous one, largely comprises some teachings of Jesus. However, the main theme is the coming of the End. Christ's words are an invitation to be vigilant and to look to the Kingdom of the future (12:1—13:9; 13:22–30; 14:15–24). Other themes characteristic of St Luke appear here, too—true poverty, humility, etc.

12:1–12 Chapter 12 consists almost entirely of instructions given by Jesus to his disciples. Many of them are also to be found in the Mission Discourse in the first Gospel (Mt 10:5–42). The text makes it clear that these instructions are specifically addressed to Christ's disciples, even though St Luke notes that "many thousands of the multitude" were present (v. 1). Everything Jesus says here is addressed to all Christians.

The teaching begins with some forthright statements. The previous episode ended with Jesus' enemies deciding to press him, provoke him and try to catch him out (see 11:53–54). Christ now warns his disciples that they will experience similar persecution: they too will face the hypocrisy of the Pharisees (v. 1); and just as his adversaries went so far as to attribute his own works to Beelzebul (11:15), the same accusation

will be made against his disciples. They will be accused, not only in synagogues (or religious tribunals of some sort), but by authorities in general (v. 11). But Jesus asks them to be steadfast and to bear witness to him fearlessly (vv. 4, 8), because God in his providence will take care of them (vv. 6–7) and will endow them with the wisdom of the Spirit (v. 12). From the times of early Christians (like St Ignatius and St Polycarp) down to our own days, these teachings are echoed in the words of many martyrs. In a letter from Margaret Roper, St Thomas More's daughter, to Alice Alington, Margaret reports him as saying: "And finally, Marget, this wot I well, that without my fault he will not let me be lost. I shall therefore with good hope commit myself wholly to him. [...] But in good faith, Meg, I trust that his tender pity shall keep my poor soul safe and make me commend his mercy. And therefore mine own good daughter, never trouble thy mind for any thing that ever shall happen me in this world. Nothing can come but that that God will. And I make me very sure that what so ever that be, seme it never so bad in sight, it shall in dede be the best" (Letter 206, in *The Correspondence of Sir Thomas More*, ed. Rogers (Princeton, 1947), p. 1434.

ᵐ Greek Gehenna

will be denied before the angels of God. [10]And every one who speaks a word against the Son of man will be forgiven; but he who blasphemes against the Holy Spirit will not be forgiven. [11]And when they bring you before the synagogues and the rulers and the authorities, do not be anxious how or what you are to answer or what you are to say; [12]for the Holy Spirit will teach you in that very hour what you ought to say."

Mt 12:32
Mk 3:28–29

Lk 21:12–15
Mk 13:11

Parable of the rich fool

[13]One of the multitude said to him, "Teacher, bid my brother divide the inheritance with me." [14]But he said to him, "Man, who made me a judge or divider over you?" [15]And he said to them, "Take heed, and beware of all covetousness; for a man's life does not consist in the abundance of his possessions." [16]And he told them a parable, saying, "The land of a rich man brought forth plentifully; [17]and he thought to himself, 'What shall I do, for I have nowhere to store my crops?' [18]And he said, 'I will do this: I will pull down my barns, and build larger ones; and there I will store all my grain and my goods. [19]And I will say to my soul, Soul, you have ample goods laid up for many years; take your ease, eat, drink, be merry.' [20]But God said to him, 'Fool! This night your soul is required of you; and the things you have prepared, whose will they be?' [21]So is he who lays up treasure for himself, and is not rich toward God."

1 Tim 6:9–10

Jas 4:13–15
Prov 27:1
Sir 11:19
Eccles 2:17–23

Trust in God's fatherly providence

Mt 6:19–34

[22]And he said to his disciples, "Therefore I tell you, do not be anxious about your life, what you shall eat, nor about your body, what you shall put on. [23]For life is

quicumque confessus fuerit in me coram hominibus, et Filius hominis confitebitur in illo coram angelis Dei; [9]qui autem negaverit me coram hominibus, denegabitur coram angelis Dei. [10]Et omnis, qui dicet verbum in Filium hominis, remittetur illi; ei autem qui in Spiritum Sanctum blasphemaverit, non remittetur. [11]Cum autem inducent vos in synagogas et ad magistratus et potestates, nolite solliciti esse qualiter aut quid respondeatis aut quid dicatis: [12]Spiritus enim Sanctus docebit vos in ipsa hora, quae oporteat dicere». [13]Ait autem quidam ei de turba: «Magister, dic fratri meo, ut dividat mecum hereditatem». [14]At ille dixit ei: «Homo, quis me constituit iudicem aut divisorem super vos?». [15]Dixitque ad illos: «Videte et cavete ab omni avaritia, quia si cui res abundant, vita eius non est ex his, quae possidet». [16]Dixit autem similitudinem ad illos dicens: «Hominis cuiusdam divitis uberes fructus ager attulit. [17]Et cogitabat intra se dicens: "Quid faciam, quod non habeo, quo congregem fructus meos?". [18]Et dixit: "Hoc faciam: destruam horrea mea et maiora aedificabo, et illuc congregabo omne triticum et bona mea, [19]et dicam animae meae: Anima, habes multa bona posita in annos plurimos; requiesce, comede, bibe, epulare". [20]Dixit autem illi Deus: "Stulte! Hac nocte animam tuam repetunt a te; quae autem parasti, cuius erunt?". [21]Sic est qui sibi thesaurizat et non fit in Deum dives». [22]Dixitque ad discipulos suos: «Ideo

12:13–21 The doctrinal context here is the same as that of the previous discourse—valuing earthly things in the light of heaven. Here Jesus shows how dangerous it is to put one's faith in riches: "Increased possession is not the ultimate goal of nations nor of individuals. All growth is ambivalent. It is essential if man is to develop as a man, but in a way it imprisons man if he considers it the supreme good, and it restricts his vision" (Paul VI, *Populorum progressio*, 19).

The parable that our Lord uses to communicate this teaching is very interesting. At first sight, we might assume that this rich man was acting prudently: if one has a good harvest, one should store it and not let it go to waste. Jesus says we need to look far beyond practical needs and values. This life, lived for its own sake, does not amount to much; the riches we should seek are spiritual ones (v. 21). So, it enriches our life to be always conscious of death: "A person who lives as if he were to die every day—given that our life is uncertain by definition—will not sin, for good fear extinguishes most of the disorder of our appetites; whereas he who thinks he has a long life ahead of him will easily let himself be dominated by pleasures" (St Athanasius, *Vita Antonii*).

12:22–34 This passage contains further teaching about riches and the use of temporal things. The key to it lies in the last verse. Each of us has something of value—and wherever we put it, that is where we are putting our heart. The rich fool set his heart on himself (12:20–21), and Jesus invites us to be "rich toward God" (12:21), laying up our treasure in heaven (v. 33): "We

Ps 147:9

more than food, and the body more than clothing. ²⁴Consider the ravens: they neither sow nor reap, they have neither storehouse nor barn, and yet God feeds them. Of how much more value are you than the birds! ²⁵And which of you by being anxious can add a cubit to his span of life?^{n} ²⁶If then you are not able to do as small a thing as that, why are you anxious about the rest? ²⁷Consider the lilies, how they grow; they neither toil nor spin;^{o} yet I tell you, even Solomon in all his glory was not arrayed like one of these. ²⁸But if God so clothes the grass which is alive in the field today and tomorrow is thrown into the oven, how much more will he clothe you, O men of little faith! ²⁹And do not seek what you are to eat and what you are to drink, nor be of anxious mind. ³⁰For all the nations of the world seek these things; and your Father knows that you need them. ³¹Instead, seek his^{p} kingdom, and these things shall be yours as well.

Is 41:14

Lk 18:22
Tob 4:8–10

³²"Fear not, little flock, for it is your Father's good pleasure to give you the kingdom. ³³Sell your possessions, and give alms; provide yourselves with purses that do not grow old, with a treasure in the heavens that does not fail, where no thief approaches and no moth destroys. ³⁴For where your treasure is, there will your heart be also.

Mt 24:45–51

The need for vigilance; the parable of the steward

Mt 25:1–13

1 Pet 1:13

³⁵"Let your loins be girded and your lamps burning, ³⁶and be like men who are waiting for their master to come home from the marriage feast, so that they may open to

---

dico vobis: nolite solliciti esse animae quid manducetis, neque corpori quid vestiamini. ²³Anima enim plus est quam esca, et corpus quam vestimentum. ²⁴Considerate corvos quia non seminant neque metunt, quibus non est cellarium neque horreum, et Deus pascit illos; quanto magis vos pluris estis volucribus. ²⁵Quis autem vestrum cogitando potest adicere ad aetatem suam cubitum? ²⁶Si ergo neque, quod minimum est, potestis, quid de ceteris solliciti estis? ²⁷Considerate lilia quomodo crescunt: non laborant, neque nent; dico autem vobis: Nec Salomon in omni gloria sua vestiebatur sicut unum ex istis. ²⁸Si autem fenum, quod hodie in agro est et cras in clibanum mittitur, Deus sic vestit, quanto magis vos, pusillae fidei. ²⁹Et vos nolite quaerere quid manducetis aut quid bibatis, et nolite solliciti esse. ³⁰Haec enim omnia gentes mundi quaerunt; Pater autem vester scit quoniam his indigetis. ³¹Verumtamen quaerite regnum eius; et haec adicientur vobis. ³²Noli timere, pusillus grex, quia complacuit Patri vestro dare vobis regnum. ³³Vendite, quae possidetis, et date eleemosynam. Facite vobis sacculos, qui non veterescunt, thesaurum non deficientem in caelis, quo fur non appropiat, neque tinea corrumpit; ³⁴ubi enim thesaurus vester est, ibi et cor vestrum erit. ³⁵Sint lumbi vestri praecincti et lucernae ardentes, ³⁶et vos similes hominibus exspectantibus dominum suum, quando revertatur a nuptiis, ut, cum venerit et pulsaverit, con-

---

must strive to bear the fruit of true repentance. Let us love our neighbour as ourselves, be humble, show charity and give alms to those in need: these deeds cleanse the soul of sin. Man must leave everything behind when he leaves this world; but the Lord will repay his charity and almsgiving with a great reward" (St Francis of Assisi, *Letter to All the Faithful*).

This radical choice of the Kingdom of God over and above material things, good health etc. (vv. 22–30), is part and parcel of the universal call to holiness: "All the faithful are invited and obliged to holiness and the perfection of their own state of life. Accordingly let all of them see that they direct their affections rightly, lest they be hindered in their pursuit of perfect love by the use of worldly things and by an adherence to riches which is contrary to the spirit of evangelical poverty" (Vatican II, *Lumen gentium*, 42).

12:35–48 In Christ's preaching (cf. Mt 24:42; 25:13; Mk 13:5) and that of his apostles, calls to vigilance frequently occur—because the enemy is always trying to trap us (see 1 Pet 5:8) and, besides, because a person in love never sleeps (see Song 5:2). This watchfulness is to be seen in one's spirit of prayer (see 21:36; 1 Pet 4:7) and one's firmness of faith (see 1 Cor 16:13).

In his appeal for vigilance here, Jesus uses two metaphors—being dressed for the occasion, and having one's lamp always lit (v. 35). The Jews tucked their flowing garments inside a belt when they had to do certain kinds of work or go on a journey, etc., so having one's "loins girded" means showing that one is on the alert and prepared (cf. Jer 1:17; Eph 6:14; 1 Pet 1:13). Similarly, a lamp is kept burning if one is on guard duty or waiting for someone to arrive. Our Lord then goes on to describe how we should be on

---

n Or *to his stature*   o Other ancient authorities read *Consider the lilies; they neither spin nor weave*   p Other ancient authorities read *God's*

him at once when he comes and knocks. [37]Blessed are those servants whom the master finds awake when he comes; truly, I say to you, he will gird himself and have them sit at table, and he will come and serve them. [38]If he comes in the second watch, or in the third, and finds them so, blessed are those servants! [39]But know this, that if the householder had known at what hour the thief was coming, he would have been awake and[q] would not have left his house to be broken into. [40]You also must be ready; for the Son of man is coming at an hour you do not expect."

[41]Peter said, "Lord, are you telling this parable for us or for all?" [42]And the Lord said, "Who then is the faithful and wise steward, whom his master will set over his household, to give them their portion of food at the proper time? [43]Blessed is that servant whom his master when he comes will find so doing. [44]Truly I tell you, he will set him over all his possessions. [45]But if that servant says to himself, 'My master is delayed in coming,' and begins to beat the menservants and the maidservants, and to eat and drink and get drunk, [46]the master of that servant will come on a day when he does not expect him and at an hour he does not know, and will punish[r] him, and put him with the unfaithful. [47]And that servant who knew his master's will, but did not make ready or act according to his will, shall receive a severe beating. [48]But he who did not know, and did what deserved a beating, shall receive a light beating. Every one to whom much is given, of him will much be required; and of him to whom men commit much they will demand the more.

Margin references: Lk 22:27; Jn 13:4ff; Mk 13:35; 1 Thess 5:2; 1 Pet 4:10; Jas 4:17

festim aperiant ei. [37]Beati servi illi, quos cum venerit dominus invenerit vigilantes. Amen dico vobis, quod praecinget se et faciet illos discumbere, et transiens ministrabit illis. [38]Et si venerit in secunda vigilia et si in tertia vigilia venerit et ita invenerit, beati sunt illi. [39]Hoc autem scitote quia, si sciret pater familias qua hora fur veniret, non sineret perfodi domum suam. [40]Et vos estote parati, quia, qua hora non putatis, Filius hominis venit». [41]Ait autem Petrus: «Domine, ad nos dicis hanc parabolam an et ad omnes?». [42]Et dixit Dominus: «Quis putas est fidelis dispensator et prudens, quem constituet dominus super familiam suam, ut det illis in tempore tritici mensuram? [43]Beatus ille servus, quem cum venerit dominus eius invenerit ita facientem. [44]Vere dico vobis: Supra omnia, quae possidet, constituet illum. [45]Quod si dixerit servus ille in corde suo: "Moram facit dominus meus venire", et coeperit percutere pueros et ancillas et edere et bibere et inebriari, [46]veniet dominus servi illius in die, qua non sperat, et hora, qua nescit, et dividet eum partemque eius cum infidelibus ponet. [47]Ille autem servus, qui cognovit voluntatem domini sui et non praeparavit vel non fecit secundum voluntatem eius, vapulabit multis; [48]qui autem non cognovit et fecit digna plagis, vapulabit paucis. Omni autem, cui multum datum est, multum quaeretur ab eo, et cui commendaverunt multum, plus petent ab eo. [49]Ignem veni mittere in terram et quid

the lookout, certain that he is on his way—like a servant waiting for his master, or a householder protecting himself against a thief: servant and householder both know that the other will come and that their future depends on what will happen when he arrives. Verse 37 seems shocking in the context of life in Jesus' time: it is difficult to believe that a master would prepare a meal for his servants simply because they had waited up to greet him. But that is what the Lord does for his faithful servants: he girds himself and renders them service (see Jn 13:1–20).

In reply to St Peter (v. 41), Jesus touches on the responsibility of those who hold official positions (vv. 42–48a) and on responsibility in general (v. 48b). He explains that faithful souls (vv. 43–44) will be judged differently from the calculating (vv. 46–46), and the lazy and noncompliant (v. 47) differently from the ignorant (v.

48). "The classes and duties of life are many, but holiness is one—that sanctity which is cultivated by all who are moved by the Spirit of God, and who obey the voice of the Father and worship God the Father in spirit and in truth. These people follow the poor Christ, the humble and cross-bearing Christ, in order to be worthy of being sharers in His glory. Every person must walk unhesitatingly according to his own personal gifts and duties in the path of living faith, which arouses hope and works through charity. In the first place, the shepherds of Christ's flock must holily and eagerly, humbly and courageously carry out their ministry, in imitation of the eternal high Priest, the Shepherd and Guardian of our souls. They ought to fulfil this duty in such a way that it will be the principal means also of their own sanctification" (Vatican II, *Lumen gentium*, 41).

q Other ancient authorities omit *would have been awake and*   r Or *cut him to pieces*

<table>
<tr><td>Mt 10:34–36
Mk 10:38</td><td>

Jesus brings division, not peace

⁴⁹"I came to cast fire upon the earth; and would that it were already kindled! ⁵⁰I have a baptism to be baptized with; and how I am constrained until it is accomplished! ⁵¹Do you think that I have come to give peace on earth? No, I tell you, but rather division; ⁵²for henceforth in one house there will be five divided, three against two and two against three; ⁵³they will be divided, father against son and son against father, mother against daughter and daughter against her mother, mother-in-law against daughter-in-law and daughter-in-law against her mother-in-law."
</td></tr>
</table>

Mic 7:6

Mt 5:25–26;
16:2–3

The signs of the times

⁵⁴He also said to the multitudes, "When you see a cloud rising in the west, you say at once, 'A shower is coming'; and so it happens. ⁵⁵And when you see the south wind blowing, you say, 'There will be scorching heat'; and it happens. ⁵⁶You hypocrites! You know how to interpret the appearance of earth and sky; but why do you not know how to interpret the present time?

⁵⁷"And why do you not judge for yourselves what is right? ⁵⁸As you go with your accuser before the magistrate, make an effort to settle with him on the way, lest he drag you to the judge, and the judge hand you over to the officer, and the officer put you in prison. ⁵⁹I tell you, you will never get out till you have paid the very last copper."

volo? Si iam accensus esset! ⁵⁰Baptisma autem habeo baptizari et quomodo coartor, usque dum perficiatur! ⁵¹Putatis quia pacem veni dare in terram? Non, dico vobis, sed separationem. ⁵²Erunt enim ex hoc quinque in domo una divisi: tres in duo et duo in tres; ⁵³dividentur pater in filium et *filius in patrem*, mater in filiam et *filia in matrem*, socrus in nurum suam et *nurus in socrum*». ⁵⁴Dicebat autem et ad turbas: «Cum videritis nubem orientem ab occasu, statim dicitis: "Nimbus venit", et ita fit; ⁵⁵et cum austrum flantem, dicitis: "Aestus erit", et fit. ⁵⁶Hypocritae, faciem terrae et caeli nostis probare, hoc autem tempus quomodo nescitis probare? ⁵⁷Quid autem et a vobis ipsis non iudicatis, quod iustum est? ⁵⁸Cum autem vadis cum adversario tuo ad principem, in via da operam liberari ab illo, ne forte trahat te apud iudicem, et iudex tradat te exactori, et exac-

12:49–53 There is nothing dull about God's ardent love for us. By speaking of fire and baptism (see the note on Mt 10:16–42), Jesus reveals his vibrant and abounding desire to give his life on our behalf. Christians should follow his example: "O Jesus, strengthen our souls, open out the way for us, and, above all, intoxicate us with your Love. Make us into blazing fires to enkindle the earth with the heavenly fire you brought us" (St Josemaría Escrivá, *The Forge*, 31). However, Jesus knows that he is bound to be "sign of contradiction" (cf. 2:34–35), and that his disciples too will provoke responses of both joy and opposition.

12:54–59 In the complaint he makes here, Jesus plays on two meanings of the word "time"—the one having connexions with the weather, and the other having to do with stages in salvation history. People seemed to be using two kinds of reasoning: they apply logic to understand earthly things, but no logic at all in their judgments of him. The signs he has given them (miracles, his life and his teaching) should be enough to con-

vince them that he is the Messiah. However, they have failed to understand the signs and they have misunderstood him. It was not only many of Jesus' contemporaries who behaved like this. It happens today as well, when people ignore God's signs or his voice when he speaks to their conscience: "Those who wilfully try to drive God from their heart and to avoid all questions about religion, not following the biddings of their conscience, are not free from blame" (Vatican II, *Gaudium et spes*, 19).

In vv. 58–59, using the parallel of the accuser and the judge, Jesus tells "the multitudes" that they still have time to correct their line of conduct—not much time, because they are on their way to the judgment seat, but enough time to avoid being condemned: "Strive to partake in the first resurrection now if you wish to escape the eternal punishment of the second death. Those who leave evil behind and embrace good through fear of God pass from death to life in this world, and their humble nature will later be made glorious" (St Fulgentius of Ruspe, *De remissione peccatorum*, 12, 4).

The need for repentance

13 ¹There were some present at that very time who told him of the Galileans whose blood Pilate had mingled with their sacrifices. ²And he answered them, "Do you think that these Galileans were worse sinners than all the other Galileans, because they suffered thus? ³I tell you, No; but unless you repent you will all likewise perish. ⁴Or those eighteen upon whom the tower in Siloam fell and killed them, do you think that they were worse offenders than all the others who dwelt in Jerusalem? ⁵I tell you, No; but unless you repent you will all likewise perish."

Jn 9:2

Parable of the barren fig tree

⁶And he told this parable: "A man had a fig tree planted in his vineyard; and he came seeking fruit on it and found none. ⁷And he said to the vinedresser, 'Lo, these three years I have come seeking fruit on this fig tree, and I find none. Cut it down; why should it use up the ground?' ⁸And he answered him, 'Let it alone, sir, this year also, till I dig about it and put on manure. ⁹And if it bears fruit next year, well and good; but if not, you can cut it down.'"

Lk 3:9
Mt 21:19
Mk 11:13

tor mittat te in carcerem. ⁵⁹Dico tibi: Non exies inde, donec etiam novissimum minutum reddas». [13] ¹Aderant autem quidam ipso in tempore nuntiantes illi de Galilaeis, quorum sanguinem Pilatus miscuit cum sacrificiis eorum. ²Et respondens dixit illis: «Putatis quod hi Galilaei prae omnibus Galilaeis peccatores fuerunt, quia talia passi sunt? ³Non, dico vobis, sed nisi paenitentiam egeritis, omnes similiter peribitis. ⁴Vel illi decem et octo, supra quos cecidit turris in Siloam et occidit eos, putatis quia et ipsi debitores fuerunt praeter omnes homines habitantes in Ierusalem? ⁵Non, dico vobis, sed si non paenitentiam egeritis, omnes similiter peribitis». ⁶Dicebat autem hanc similitudinem: «Arborem fici habebat quidam plantatam in vinea sua et venit quaerens fructum in illa et non invenit. ⁷Dixit autem ad cultorem vineae: "Ecce anni tres sunt, ex quo venio quaerens fructum in ficulnea hac, et non invenio. Succide ergo illam. Ut quid etiam terram evacuat?". ⁸At ille respondens dicit illi: "Domine, dimitte illam et hoc anno, usque dum fodiam circa illam et mittam stercora, ⁹et siquidem fecerit fructum in futurum; sin autem succides eam"». ¹⁰Erat autem docens in una synagogarum sabbatis. ¹¹Et ecce mulier, quae habebat spiritum infirmitatis annis decem et octo, et erat incli-

13:1–5 Here Jesus is drawing on current events in his teaching. He explains that, contrary to the general opinion, the causes of two recent tragic events (vv. 1, 4) should not be attributed to the people who died in them. These events, in their way, were a call to repentance. Every event carries a message from God, and therefore can help us turn back to God: "Going over all the stages of history again, we will see that in each era the Lord has given a chance to repent to anyone who wanted to convert to him" (St Clement of Rome, *Ad Corinthios*, 7, 5).

13:6–9 The parable of the barren fig tree is a gloss on the last verse of the previous passage (13:5), on the need to repent in order to avoid eternal death. In the other two Synoptics (see Mt 21:18–22; Mk 11:12–25) the barren fig tree symbolizes the temple, which appeared to be functioning properly but was in fact ineffective. In some Old Testament passages (e.g. Jer 8:13; Joel 1:12), the fig tree symbolizes Israel, the People of God, when it fails to produce the fruit

it should. The vineyard (v. 6) is also an image often used to symbolize Israel (see Is 3:14; 5:7; Jer 12:10). In the background to this parable, we recognize Jesus as the vinedresser (v. 7) through whom God gives his people a last chance. For the people who heard this parable, and for ourselves, there is a revelation and a warning here: God does not desire the death of the sinner; he wants him to repent and live (see Ezek 33:11) and he does not wish that "any should perish, but that all should reach repentance" (2 Pet 3:9); but he does require us to produce good works as evidence of our conversion: "Man's greatness is the measure of God's likeness that he reflects. If a man lives out the virtues planted like seeds in his soul, he will be like God. In the commandments, God teaches us that we are to offer him the fruit of the virtues that he planted in our souls when he created us. [...] Our love of God makes his likeness shine out through us. [...] But true love is more than good words: true love is good works" (St Columbanus, *Instructiones*, 11, 1–2).

Jesus cures a woman on the sabbath

^{Lk 6:6–11; 14:1–6} ¹⁰Now he was teaching in one of the synagogues on the sabbath. ¹¹And there was a woman who had had a spirit of infirmity for eighteen years; she was bent over and could not fully straighten herself. ¹²And when Jesus saw her, he called her and said to her, "Woman, you are freed from your infirmity." ¹³And he laid his hands upon her, and immediately she was made straight, and she praised God. ¹⁴But the ruler of the synagogue, indignant because Jesus had healed on the sabbath, said to the people, "There are six days on which work ought to be done; come on those days and be healed, and not on the sabbath day." ¹⁵Then the Lord answered him, "You hypocrites! Does not each of you on the sabbath untie his ox or his ass from the manger, and lead it away to water it? ¹⁶And ought not this woman, a daughter of Abraham whom Satan bound for eighteen years, be loosed from this bond on the sabbath day?" ¹⁷As he said this, all his adversaries were put to shame; and all the people rejoiced at all the glorious things that were done by him.

^{Ex 20:9}
^{Deut 5:13}

^{Lk 14:5}
^{Mt 12:11}

^{Lk 19:9}

^{Mt 13:31–35}
^{Mk 4:30–32} ### Parables of the mustard seed and of the leaven

¹⁸He said therefore, "What is the kingdom of God like? And to what shall I compare it? ¹⁹It is like a grain of mustard seed which a man took and sowed in his garden; and it grew and became a tree, and the birds of the air made nests in its branches."

^{Ezek 17:23; 31:6} ²⁰And again he said, "To what shall I compare the kingdom of God? ²¹It is like leaven which a woman took and hid in three measures of meal, till it was all leavened."

---

nata nec omnino poterat sursum respicere. ¹²Quam cum vidisset Iesus vocavit et ait illi: «Mulier, dimissa es ab infirmitate tua», ¹³et imposuit illi manus; et confestim erecta est et glorificabat Deum. ¹⁴Respondens autem archisynagogus, indignans quia sabbato curasset Iesus, dicebat turbae: «Sex dies sunt, in quibus oportet operari; in his ergo venite et curamini et non in die sabbati». ¹⁵Respondit autem ad illum Dominus et dixit: «Hypocritae, unusquisque vestrum sabbato non solvit bovem suum aut asinum a praesepio et ducit adaquare? ¹⁶Hanc autem filiam Abrahae, quam alligavit Satanas ecce decem et octo annis, non oportuit solvi a vinculo isto die sabbati?». ¹⁷Et cum haec diceret, erubescebant omnes adversarii eius, et omnis populus gaudebat in universis, quae gloriose fiebant ab eo. ¹⁸Dicebat ergo: «Cui simile est regnum Dei, et cui simile existimabo illud? ¹⁹Simile est grano sinapis, quod acceptum homo misit in hortum suum, et crevit et factum est in arborem, et volucres caeli requieverunt in ramis eius». ²⁰Et iterum dixit: «Cui simile aestimabo regnum Dei? ²¹Simile est fermento, quod acceptum mulier abscondit in farinae sata tria, donec fermentaretur totum». ²²Et ibat per civitates et castella docens et iter faciens in Hierosolymam. ²³Ait autem illi quidam: «Domine, pauci sunt, qui sal-

---

13:10–17 Elsewhere in the Gospels (see 6:6–11; 14:1–6; Jn 5:2–18, 9:1–16) we find episodes similar to this one. By performing this cure on a sabbath, Jesus shows his divine magnanimity and exposes the narrow-mindedness of his critics. This account adds a new perspective: God blessed the sabbath (Ex 20:11) and gave it to man as a day of rest (Ex 23:12); therefore it is a day for praise of God and a day of joy. That is why it made sense to cure the woman on the sabbath (v. 16). The fact that the people rejoice over the cure (v. 17) attests to how right Jesus was to work it.

13:18–21 These two parables teach us not to measure the power of the Kingdom by our own limited criteria: the Kingdom is like a little seed, but it has an amazing power to grow (vv.

18–19): Our Lord "with the parable of the mustard seed encourages them to have faith and shows them that the Gospel preaching will spread in spite of everything. The Lord's disciples were the weakest of men, but nevertheless, because of the great power that was in them, the Gospel has been spread to every part of the world" (St John Chrysostom, *In Matthaeum*, 46). Leaven is even more effective: the three measures are about 40 kilos (88 pounds), and the amount of bread that can be made is out of all proportion to the weight of leaven. The Kingdom has the power to transform anything it touches. The early Christians could see this for themselves; as Tertullian boasted, in the second century AD: "We are but of yesterday and yet we are everywhere" (*Apologeticum*, 37).

The narrow gate

Mt 7:13–14, 21–23
Lk 9:51

²²He went on his way through towns and villages, teaching, and journeying toward Jerusalem. ²³And some one said to him, "Lord, will those who are saved be few?" And he said to them, ²⁴"Strive to enter by the narrow door; for many, I tell you, will seek to enter and will not be able. ²⁵When once the householder has risen up and shut the door, you will begin to stand outside and to knock at the door, saying, 'Lord, open to us.' He will answer you, 'I do not know where you come from.' ²⁶Then you will begin to say, 'We ate and drank in your presence, and you taught in our streets.' ²⁷But he will say, 'I tell you, I do not know where you come from; depart from me, all you workers of iniquity!' ²⁸There you will weep and gnash your teeth, when you see Abraham and Isaac and Jacob and all the prophets in the kingdom of God and you yourselves thrust out. ²⁹And men will come from east and west, and from north and south, and sit at table in the kingdom of God. ³⁰And behold, some are last who will be first, and some are first who will be last."

Mt 25:11–12

Mt 8:11–12

Is 49:12
Ps 107:3
Mt 19:30; 20:16
Mk 10:31

Jesus' reply to Herod

³¹At that very hour some Pharisees came, and said to him, "Get away from here, for Herod wants to kill you." ³²And he said to them, "Go and tell that fox, 'Behold, I cast out demons and perform cures today and tomorrow, and the third day I finish

vantur?». Ipse autem dixit ad illos: ²⁴«Contendite intrare per angustam portam, quia multi, dico vobis, quaerent intrare et non poterunt. ²⁵Cum autem surrexerit pater familias et clauserit ostium, et incipietis foris stare et pulsare ostium dicentes: "Domine, aperi nobis"; et respondens dicet vobis: "Nescio vos unde sitis". ²⁶Tunc incipietis dicere: "Manducavimus coram te et bibimus, et in plateis nostris docuisti"; ²⁷et dicet loquens vobis: "Nescio vos unde sitis; discedite a me, omnes operarii iniquitatis". ²⁸Ibi erit fletus et stridor dentium, cum videritis Abraham et Isaac et Iacob et omnes prophetas in regno Dei, vos autem expelli foras. ²⁹Et venient ab oriente et occidente et aquilone et austro et accumbent in regno Dei. ³⁰Et ecce sunt novissimi, qui erunt primi, et sunt primi, qui erunt novissimi». ³¹In ipsa hora accesserunt quidam pharisaeorum dicentes illi:

13:22–30 In reply to a question, Jesus here expounds teaching about salvation. Salvation does not depend on race (v. 26: "We ate and drank in your presence": Jews would not eat with Gentiles); it is available to those who struggle to obtain it (v. 27), eschewing sin. "[God] desires all men to be saved" (1 Tim 2:4), but for this to happen, Christians need to "use the strength dealt out to them by Christ's gift, so that, following in his footsteps and conformed to his image, doing the will of God in everything, they may wholeheartedly devote themselves to the glory of God and to the service of their neighbour" (Vatican II, *Lumen gentium*, 40). This is what the "narrow door" means; this passage puts us on our guard against the danger of having a false sense of security. To belong to the people of God, or to have known Christ and heard him teach, is no guarantee of the reward of heaven. God will judge us on what we actually do—on our response to grace.

On a number of occasions Jesus describes eternal life as a banquet (v. 29; cf. 12:35–40; 14:15–24; Mt 8:11) to which all are invited:

"Those who, through no fault of their own, do not know the Gospel of Christ or his Church, but who nevertheless seek God with a sincere heart and, moved by grace, try in their actions to do his will as they know it through the dictates of their conscience: those too may achieve eternal salvation. Nor shall divine providence deny the assistance necessary for salvation to those who, without any fault of theirs, have not yet arrived at an explicit knowledge of God, and who, not without grace, strive to lead a good life" (ibid., 16).

13:31–35 This passage is a record of two episodes. The first (vv. 31–33) seems to have occurred in the Perea region, which came within the jurisdiction of Herod Antipas (cf. 3:1); it was relatively close to Jerusalem. The second (vv. 34–35) seems to have occurred even closer to Jerusalem. The whole passage reveals a great deal about how Jesus saw his life. "Jesus freely accepted his Passion and death: 'No one takes [my life] from me, but I lay it down of my own accord' (Jn 10:18). Hence the sovereign freedom of God's Son as he went out to his death" (*Cate-*

my course. ³³Nevertheless I must go on my way today and tomorrow and the day following; for it cannot be that a prophet should perish away from Jerusalem.'

Mt 23:37–39v
Lk 19:41–44

Jer 12:7; 22:5

Ps 69:25; 117:26

Jerusalem admonished

³⁴"O Jerusalem, Jerusalem, killing the prophets and stoning those who are sent to you! How often would I have gathered your children together as a hen gathers her brood under her wings, and you would not! ³⁵Behold, your house is forsaken. And I tell you, you will not see me until you say, 'Blessed is he who comes in the name of the Lord.'"

Jesus cures a dropsical man on the sabbath

Lk 6:6–11; 13:10–17
Lk 7:36

Mk 3:4

Mt 12:11

14 ¹One sabbath when he went to dine at the house of a ruler who belonged to the Pharisees, they were watching him. ²And behold, there was a man before him who had dropsy. ³And Jesus spoke to the lawyers and Pharisees, saying, "Is it lawful to heal on the sabbath, or not?" ⁴But they were silent. Then he took him and healed him, and let him go. ⁵And he said to them, "Which of you, having an ass^s or an ox that has fallen into a well, will not immediately pull him out on a sabbath day?" ⁶And they could not reply to this.

«Exi et vade hinc, quia Herodes vult te occidere». ³²Et ait illis: «Ite, dicite vulpi illi: "Ecce eicio daemonia et sanitates perficio hodie et cras et tertia consummor. ³³Verumtamen oportet me hodie et cras et sequenti ambulare, quia non capit prophetam perire extra Ierusalem". ³⁴Ierusalem, Ierusalem, quae occidis prophetas et lapidas eos, qui missi sunt ad te, quotiens volui congregare filios tuos, quemadmodum avis nidum suum sub pinnis, et noluistis. ³⁵Ecce *relinquitur vobis domus vestra*. Dico autem vobis: Non videbitis me, donec veniat cum dicetis: "*Benedictus, qui venit in nomine Domini*"». [14] ¹Et factum est, cum intraret in domum cuiusdam principis pharisaeorum sabbato manducare panem, et ipsi observabant eum. ²Et ecce homo quidam hydropicus erat ante illum. ³Et respondens Iesus dixit ad legis peritos et pharisaeos dicens: «Licet sabbato curare an non?». ⁴At illi tacuerunt. Ipse vero apprehensum sanavit eum ac dimisit. ⁵Et ad illos dixit: «Cuius vestrum filius aut bos in puteum cadet, et non continuo extrahet illum die sabbati?». ⁶Et non poterant ad haec respondere illi. ⁷Dicebat autem ad invitatos parabolam, intendens quomodo

chism of the Catholic Church*, 609). Jesus is aware, moreover, that the failure of his mission to the Jews is only a temporary one, for the time will come when they will acknowledge him as the Messiah (v. 35).

The warning given by the Pharisees (v. 31) allows us to see (as happens elsewhere: see 7:36; 11:37) that Jesus had a lot of contact with them, and that even though he criticized their behaviour, he did so only to expose their faults so that they could correct them.

In vv. 34–35, Jesus lets us see how profoundly saddened he is by Jerusalem's resistance to the love of God—a love of which there was much evidence. By using the simile of the hen and her chicks, he shows that his actions are those of God (cf. Mt 23:37–39 and note). St Augustine explores the meaning of this touching simile, saying: "You see, brethren, how a hen becomes weak with her chickens. No other bird, when it is a mother, shows its maternity so clearly. [...] But the hen is so enfeebled over her brood that even if the chickens are not following her, even if you do not see the young ones, you

still know her at once to be a mother. With her wings drooping, her feathers ruffled, her note hoarse, in all her limbs she becomes so sunken and abject that, as I have said, even though you cannot see her young, you can see she is a mother. That is the way Jesus feels" (*In Ioannis Evangelium*, 15, 7).

14:1–6 This account suggests that the scenario was carefully planned: the Pharisees invite Jesus to dinner, bring in a man suffering from dropsy, and wait to see what happens. In Jesus' time it was commonly thought that this particular disease (also called edema, it involved the retention of a lot of liquid, usually in the stomach or lungs area) was contracted due to some sin, and therefore (among other reasons) could not lawfully be cured on a sabbath. Our Lord's line of argument also shows how he conceived his mission towards men: just as someone would not fail to rescue *his* child or *his* ox on a sabbath, Jesus cures this man because he sees each of us as precious to him, and all our needs as being his own.

Our Lord's attitude stands in sharp contrast

s Other ancient authorities read *a son*

A lesson about humility

7Now he told a parable to those who were invited, when he marked how they chose
the places of honour, saying to them, 8"When you are invited by any one to a marriage feast, do not sit down in a place of honour, lest a more eminent man than you
be invited by him; 9and he who invited you both will come and say to you, 'Give
place to this man,' and then you will begin with shame to take the lowest place.
10But when you are invited, go and sit in the lowest place, so that when your host
comes he may say to you, 'Friend, go up higher'; then you will be honoured in the
presence of all who sit at table with you. 11For every one who exalts himself will be
humbled, and he who humbles himself will be exalted."

Mt 23:6
Prov 25:6f
Lk 18:14
Mt 23:12

The right attitude to the poor

12He said also to the man who had invited him, "When you give a dinner or a banquet, do not invite your friends or your brothers or your kinsmen or rich neighbours,
lest they also invite you in return, and you be repaid. 13But when you give a feast,
invite the poor, the maimed, the lame, the blind, 14and you will be blessed, because
they cannot repay you. You will be repaid at the resurrection of the just."

Deut 14:29

primos accubitus eligerent, dicens ad illos: 8«Cum invitatus fueris ab aliquo ad nuptias, non discumbas in primo loco, ne forte honoratior te sit
invitatus ab eo, 9et veniens is, qui te et illum vocavit, dicat tibi: "Da huic locum"; et tunc incipias cum rubore novissimum locum tenere. 10Sed
cum vocatus fueris, vade, recumbe in novissimo loco, ut, cum venerit qui te invitavit, dicat tibi: "Amice, ascende superius"; tunc erit tibi gloria
coram omnibus simul discumbentibus. 11Quia omnis, qui se exaltat, humiliabitur; et, qui se humiliat, exaltabitur». 12Dicebat autem et ei, qui se
invitaverat: «Cum facis prandium aut cenam, noli vocare amicos tuos neque fratres tuos neque cognatos neque vicinos divites, ne forte et ipsi te
reinvitent et fiat tibi retributio. 13Sed cum facis convivium, voca pauperes, debiles, claudos, caecos; 14et beatus eris, quia non habent retribuere

to the fundamentalism of these men. Fundamentalism, fanaticism, is always wrong. It often
blinds people, causing them to reject (as in this
case) elementary principles of charity and justice
and even to deny basic human concern. We
should never be fanatical about anything—no
matter how sacred it is. Hence the Second Vatican Council's teaching that "no one is to be
forced to act in a manner contrary to his own
beliefs, whether privately or publicly, whether
alone or in association with others, within due
limits. The Council further declares that the right
to religious freedom has its foundation in the
very dignity of the human person as this dignity
is known through the revealed word of God and
by reason itself" (*Dignitatis humanae*, 2).

14:7–11 Jesus avails himself of this dinner party
to speak on a number of subjects, including
humility. "I was wondering once why our Lord
so dearly loved this virtue of humility; and all of
a sudden—without, I believe, my having previously thought of it—the following reason came
into my mind: that it is because God is Sovereign Truth and to be humble is to walk in truth,
for it is absolutely true to say that we have no

good thing in ourselves, but only misery and
nothingness; and anyone who fails to understand
this is walking in falsehood. He who best understands it is most pleasing to Sovereign Truth
because he is walking in truth. May it please
God, sisters, to grant us grace never to fail to
have this knowledge of ourselves. Amen" (St
Teresa of Avila, *Interior Castle*, 6, 10, 8).

14:12–14 Here again Jesus uses the simile of a
banquet to develop his teaching. He speaks not
about the guest but about the host, and shows
that humility must be complemented by charity.
When exercising generosity, we must avoid any
trace of vainglory or seeking of human reward;
our primary focus should be on God (cf. 12:22–
34 and note), from whom we have received
everything: "Who has given you rain and land,
food and home, art and law and society, a pleasant life, the friends and family with whom you
are bound by the bonds of true kinship? [...] Was
it not God, who now asks you to be kind and
generous in and above all the things he has given
you? After all we have received from him, and
hope to receive from him, we should be ashamed
of ourselves if we fail to repay him with our

Mt 22:1–14   Parable of the invited guests

[15]When one of those who sat at table with him heard this, he said to him, "Blessed is he who shall eat bread in the kingdom of God!" [16]But he said to him, "A man once gave a great banquet, and invited many; [17]and at the time for the banquet he sent his servant to say to those who had been invited, 'Come; for all is now ready.' [18]But they all alike began to make excuses. The first said to him, 'I have bought a field, and I must go out and see it; I pray you, have me excused.' [19]And another said, 'I have bought five yoke of oxen, and I go to examine them; I pray you, have me excused.' [20]And another said, 'I have married a wife, and therefore I cannot come.' [21]So the servant came and reported this to his master. Then the householder in anger said to his servant, 'Go out quickly to the streets and lanes of the city, and bring in the poor and maimed and blind and lame.' [22]And the servant said, 'Sir, what you commanded has been done, and still there is room.' [23]And the master said to the servant, 'Go out to the highways and hedges, and compel people to come in, that my house may be filled. [24]For I tell you, none of these men who were invited shall taste my banquet.'"

tibi. Retribuetur enim tibi in resurrectione iustorum». [15]Haec cum audisset quidam de simul discumbentibus, dixit illi: «Beatus, qui manducabit panem in regno Dei». [16]At ipse dixit ei: «Homo quidam fecit cenam magnam et vocavit multos"; [17]et misit servum suum hora cenae dicere invitatis: "Venite, quia iam paratum est". [18]Et coeperunt simul omnes excusare. Primus dixit ei: "Villam emi et necesse habeo exire et videre illam; rogo te, habe me excusatum". [19]Et alter dixit: "Iuga boum emi quinque et eo probare illa; rogo te, habe me excusatum". [20]Et alius dixit: "Uxorem duxi et ideo non possum venire". [21]Et reversus servus nuntiavit haec domino suo. Tunc iratus pater familias dixit servo suo: "Exi cito in plateas et vicos civitatis et pauperes ac debiles et caecos et claudos introduc huc". [22]Et ait servus: "Domine, factum est ut imperasti, et adhuc locus est". [23]Et ait dominus servo: "Exi in vias et saepes, et compelle intrare, ut impleatur domus mea. [24]Dico autem vobis quod nemo virorum illorum, qui

kindness and generosity. If our God and Lord has deigned to call himself our Father, how can we refuse our brothers anything? My brothers and friends, we cannot allow ourselves to use badly what has been given to us as a gift from God" (St Gregory the Great, *De pauperum amore*, 23–24).

14:15–24 The banquet simile now takes on a new meaning; for Jesus uses it to describe the Kingdom of God. In this parable we see the Church taking shape in response to a universal call to holiness. God chose Israel to mediate salvation (cf. Is 45:20–25), but when everything was ready (v. 17) and he sent his Son, the majority of those he called first (the ostensibly great and good of Israel) rejected him. Therefore God will now found his Church, to be made up of the poor and despised of Israel (v. 21) and the pagans (v. 23).

This parable contains many useful ideas about apostolate and the mission of Christians. God's call often entails a sacrifice of personal interests, and there will be some who fail to grasp the greatness of God's gift (vv. 16–20), but even so the Lord's servants should keep looking for new guests because there is still room at the banquet (vv. 21–22). The Gospel contains a phrase that might seem contrary to its spirit: "Compel people to come in" (v. 23). It is, obviously, not a matter of coercing anyone's freedom but of helping people to make the right decision, to shrug off any sort of human respect, to avoid occasions of sin, to do what they can to discover the truth: "In the parable of the wedding feast, when the master of the house finds out that some guests have declined his invitation with poor excuses, he tells his servant, 'Go out into the highways and hedgerows and compel—*compelle intrare*—people to come in'. Surely this is coercion, an act of violence against the legitimate freedom of each individual conscience? If we meditate on the Gospel and reflect on the teachings of Jesus, we will not mistake these commands for coercion. [...] His *compelle intrare* implies no violence, either physical or moral. Rather, it reflects the power of attraction of Christian example, which shows in its way of acting the power of God: 'See how the Father attracts. He delights in teaching, and not in imposing necessity on men. That is how he attracts men towards himself' (St Augustine, *In Ioannis Evangelium tractatus*, 26, 7)" (St Josemaría Escrivá, *Friends of God*, 37). We can and

Conditions for following Jesus

Mt 10:37–38; 5:13
Lk 18:29–30

²⁵Now great multitudes accompanied him; and he turned and said to them, ²⁶"If any one comes to me and does not hate his own father and mother and wife and children and brothers and sisters, yes, and even his own life, he cannot be my disciple.* ²⁷Whoever does not bear his own cross and come after me, cannot be my disciple. ²⁸For which of you, desiring to build a tower, does not first sit down and count the cost, whether he has enough to complete it? ²⁹Otherwise, when he has laid a foundation, and is not able to finish, all who see it begin to mock him, ³⁰saying, 'This man began to build, and was not able to finish.' ³¹Or what king, going to encounter another king in war, will not sit down first and take counsel whether he is able with ten thousand to meet him who comes against him with twenty thousand? ³²And if not, while the other is yet a great way off, he sends an embassy and asks terms of peace. ³³So therefore, whoever of you does not renounce all that he has cannot be my disciple.

Lk 9:23
Mt 10:38
Mk 8:34

vocati sunt, gustabit cenam meam"». ²⁵Ibant autem turbae multae cum eo, et conversus dixit ad illos: ²⁶«Si quis venit ad me et non odit patrem suum et matrem et uxorem et filios et fratres et sorores, adhuc et animam suam, non potest esse meus discipulus. ²⁷Et, qui non baiulat crucem suam et venit post me, non potest esse meus discipulus. ²⁸Quis enim ex vobis volens turrem aedificare, non prius sedens computat sumptus, si habet ad perficiendum? ²⁹Ne, posteaquam posuerit fundamentum et non potuerit perficere, omnes, qui vident, incipiant illudere ei ³⁰dicentes: "Hic homo coepit aedificare et non potuit consummare". ³¹Aut quis rex, iturus committere bellum adversus alium regem, non sedens prius cogitat si possit cum decem milibus occurrere ei, qui cum viginti milibus venit ad se? ³²Alioquin, adhuc illo longe agente, legationem mittens rogat ea, quae pacis sunt. ³³Sic ergo omnis ex vobis, qui non renuntiat omnibus, quae possidet, non potest meus esse discipulus. ³⁴Bonum est sal; si autem sal

should "compel people to come in" through prayer, sacrifice, the example of a good Christian life, and friendship.

14:25–35 The evangelist now presents Jesus in a different context. Jesus is attracting huge crowds (v. 25)—and telling them that to truly follow him it is not enough to find his teaching attractive. "The doctrine that the Son of God came to teach was contempt for all things in order to receive as a reward the Spirit of God in himself. For, as long as the soul does not reject all things, it has no capacity to receive the Spirit of God in pure transformation" (St John of the Cross, *Ascent of Mount Carmel*, 1, 5, 2). What our Lord says in v. 26 may seem harsh; but we need to read this verse in the overall context of the demands he makes and the biblical language he is using. In many passages of the Old Testament, "loving" this person or thing and "hating" another means simply that the one is better than, or preferred to, the other: the difference between them marks a choice. For example, in Genesis 29:30 we read that Jacob "loved Rachel more than Leah", but literally what is said is "he loved Rachel and hated Leah"; in Malachi 1:2–3 (and Romans 9:13), we read "I have loved Jacob but I have hated Esau": what these statements mean is that

Rachel was the one chosen by Jacob, and Jacob was the object of God's election. Therefore, Jesus' words here should be read as meaning that one must put Christ first and commit oneself decisively to him: being a disciple of Christ means taking God's side and not compromising in any way. That is how the passage has been read in the Tradition of the Church: "We should have charity towards all—towards relatives and towards strangers—but without separating ourselves from the love of God out of love for them" (St Gregory the Great, *Homiliae in Evangelia*, 37, 3). The Second Vatican Council makes a similar point when it teaches that Christians strive "to please God rather than men, always ready to abandon everything for Christ" (*Apostolicam actuositatem*, 4).

The two later comparisons, about the man who begins to build and the king who embarks on a campaign (vv. 28–32), set out what is involved in giving up everything to follow Jesus, as Jesus explains in v. 33. Unless our commitment finds expression in everyday action, we won't be able to finish what we started or keep earthly things at bay; people will jeer at us (v. 30) or we will simply be defeated: "If you cannot set aside all the things of this life, at the very least own and use them in a way that does

Mk 9:50 ³⁴"Salt is good; but if salt has lost its taste, how shall its saltness be restored? ³⁵It is fit neither for the land nor for the dunghill; men throw it away. He who has ears to hear, let him hear."

9. PARABLES OF GOD'S MERCY*

Mt 18:12–14
Lk 5:30; 7:34; 19:7 **The lost sheep**

15 ¹Now the tax collectors and sinners were all drawing near to hear him. ²And the Pharisees and the scribes murmured, saying, "This man receives sinners and eats with them."

quoque evanuerit, in quo condietur? ³⁵Neque in terram neque in sterquilinium utile est, sed foras proiciunt illud. Qui habet aures audiendi, audiat».
[15] ¹Erant autem appropinquantes ei omnes publicani et peccatores, ut audirent illum. ²Et murmurabant pharisaei et scribae dicentes: «Hic peccatores recipit et manducat cum illis». ³Et ait ad illos parabolam istam dicens: ⁴«Quis ex vobis homo, qui habet centum oves, et si perdiderit unam

not bind you wholly to this world. You should be the owner of worldly things, not possessed by them [...]. Worldly goods are for our use; the things of heaven are the objects of our true desires [...]. Let us make use, then, of earthly things, while desiring all the time to take possession of the heavenly" (St Gregory the Great, *Homiliae in Evangelia*, 2, 36, 11).

The final verses of the passage presuppose what Jesus has said about his disciples being the light and the salt of the world (Mt 5:13–16). If they lose their identity, their lives will prove useless: "You need interior life and doctrinal formation. Be demanding on yourself! As a Christian man or woman, you have to be the salt of the earth and the light of the world, for you are obliged to give good example with holy shamelessness. The charity of Christ should compel you. Feeling and knowing yourself to be another Christ from the moment you told him that you would follow him, you must not separate yourself from your equals—your relatives, friends, and colleagues—any more than you would separate salt from the food it is seasoning. Your interior life and your formation must include the piety and the principles a child of God must have in order to give flavour to everything by his active presence there. Ask the Lord that you may always be that good seasoning in the lives of others" (St Josemaría Escrivá, *The Forge*, 450).

*15:1–32 All Jesus' actions and words reveal God's love and compassion for us. However, "the Gospel writer who particularly treats of these themes in Christ's teaching is Luke, whose Gospel has earned the title of 'the Gospel of mercy'" (John Paul II, *Dives in misericordia*, 3). In this chapter, St Luke records three parables in which Jesus graphically describes the infinite, pastoral mercy of God, the care he takes of each of us, and his joy when a sinner repents. Meditation on this passage will help us to be optimistic and confident: "What joy to remember that our Lord is just; that he makes allowances for all our shortcomings, and knows full well how weak we are. What have I to fear, then? Surely the God of infinite justice who pardons the prodigal son with such mercy will be just with me 'who am always with Him'" (St Thérèse of Lisieux, *Autobiographical Writings*, 8).

15:1–10 Jesus uses the criticism made by Pharisees and scribes to show that God desires to save each and every person. Clearly, the climax of God's initiative in this regard begins with the incarnation of God the Son. Therefore, Christian Tradition, drawing also on other Gospel passages, sees Christ in this depiction of the shepherd: "He put the sheep on his shoulders because, on taking on human nature, he burdened himself with our sins" (St Gregory the Great, *Homiliae in Evangelia*, 2, 14, 3).

The passage starts by giving us the background to these teachings—the accusation that Jesus receives sinners and eats with them. It is the very same criticism as will be made by the elder son against the father in the parable of the prodigal son: he has welcomed home the son

Ezek 34:11–16

³So he told them this parable: ⁴"What man of you, having a hundred sheep, if he has lost one of them, does not leave the ninety-nine in the wilderness, and go after the one which is lost, until he finds it? ⁵And when he has found it, he lays it on his shoulders, rejoicing. ⁶And when he comes home, he calls together his friends and his neighbours, saying to them, 'Rejoice with me, for I have found my sheep which was lost.' ⁷Just so, I tell you, there will be more joy in heaven over one sinner who repents than over ninety-nine righteous persons who need no repentance.

The lost coin

⁸"Or what woman, having ten silver coins,ᵗ if she loses one coin, does not light a lamp and sweep the house and seek diligently until she finds it? ⁹And when she has found it, she calls together her friends and neighbours, saying, 'Rejoice with me, for I have found the coin which I had lost.' ¹⁰Just so, I tell you, there is joy before the angels of God over one sinner who repents."

The prodigal son

¹¹And he said, "There was a man who had two sons; ¹²and the younger of them said to his father, 'Father, give me the share of property that falls to me.' And he divided

ex illis, nonne dimittit nonaginta novem in deserto et vadit ad illam, quae perierat, donec inveniat illam? ⁵Et cum invenerit eam, imponit in umeros suos gaudens ⁶et veniens domum convocat amicos et vicinos dicens illis: "Congratulamini mihi, quia inveni ovem meam, quae perierat". ⁷Dico vobis: Ita gaudium erit in caelo super uno peccatore paenitentiam agente quam super nonaginta novem iustis, qui non indigent paenitentia. ⁸Aut quae mulier habens drachmas decem, si perdiderit drachmam unam, nonne accendit lucernam et everrit domum et quaerit diligenter, donec inveniat? ⁹Et cum invenerit, convocat amicas et vicinas dicens: "Congratulamini mihi, quia inveni drachmam, quam perdideram». ¹⁰Ita dico vobis: Gaudium fit coram angelis Dei super uno peccatore paenitentiam agente». ¹¹Ait autem: «Homo quidam habebat duos filios. ¹²Et dixit adulescentior ex illis patri: "Pater, da mihi portionem substantiae, quae me contingit". Et divisit illis substantiam. ¹³Et non post multos dies, congregatis

who has committed every possible sin, and has organized a feast to celebrate his return. The parable serves to explain why Jesus acts as he does; and it also warns us that anyone who judges another will be judged, in turn, on the same basis and in the same way.

The parables of the lost sheep and the lost coin (vv. 3–10) are structured in a similar way to each other—first the parable; then a comment by the protagonist (vv. 6, 9), in which he or she rejoices over finding what was lost; then Jesus says that there will be the same joy in heaven when a sinner repents (vv. 7, 10). The listener can see that God's actions towards us are like those of the shepherd and the woman. In the face of our weakness, God does not stand idly by: he goes out in search of what is lost and makes every effort to find it (vv. 4, 8). But, above all, he rejoices—as he does when we seek him: "Love, if it is pure, has another power: we forget our own happiness and are wholly concerned with the happiness of the one we love. Although the tasks we face may seem great and burdensome, if we carry them out for the love of God they

will be sweet and light" (St Teresa of Avila, *Book of Foundations*, 5, 7).

15:11–32 This is one of Jesus' most beautiful parables. God's immense love and infinite compassion, described in the previous parables, are further revealed in this vivid portrayal of the Father's love (vv. 20–24, 31–32).

The phenomenon of conversion looms large in the parable: "The process of conversion and repentance was described by Jesus in the parable of the prodigal son, the centre of which is the merciful father: the fascination of illusory freedom, the abandonment of the father's house; the extreme misery in which the son finds himself after squandering his fortune; his deep humiliation at finding himself obliged to feed swine, and still worse, at wanting to feed on the husks the pigs ate; his reflection on all he has lost; his repentance and decision to declare himself guilty before his father; the journey back; the father's generous welcome; the father's joy—all these are characteristic of the process of conversion. The beautiful robe, the ring, and the festive ban-

t The drachma, rendered here by *silver coin*, was about a day's wage for a labourer

Prov 29:3

his living between them. ¹³Not many days later, the younger son gathered all he had and took his journey into a far country, and there he squandered his property in loose living. ¹⁴And when he had spent everything, a great famine arose in that country, and he began to be in want. ¹⁵So he went and joined himself to one of the citizens of that country, who sent him into his fields to feed swine. ¹⁶And he would gladly have fed on^u the pods that the swine ate; and no one gave him anything. ¹⁷But when he came to himself he said, 'How many of my father's hired servants have bread enough and to spare, but I perish here with hunger! ¹⁸I will arise and go to my father, and I will say to him, "Father, I have sinned against heaven and before you; ¹⁹I am no longer worthy to be called your son; treat me as one of your hired servants.' " ²⁰And he arose and came to his father. But while he was yet at a distance, his father saw him and had compassion, and ran and embraced him and kissed him. ²¹And the son said to him, 'Father, I have sinned against heaven and before you; I am no longer worthy to be called your son.'^v ²²But the father said to his servants, 'Bring quickly the best robe, and put it on him; and put a ring on his hand, and shoes on his feet; ²³and bring

Jer 3:12–13
Is 55:7

Jer 31:20

omnibus, adulescentior filius peregre profectus est in regionem longinquam et ibi dissipavit substantiam suam vivendo luxuriose. ¹⁴Et postquam omnia consummasset, facta est fames valida in regione illa, et ipse coepit egere. ¹⁵Et abiit et adhaesit uni civium regionis illius, et misit illum in villam suam, ut pasceret porcos; ¹⁶et cupiebat saturari de siliquis, quas porci manducabant, et nemo illi dabat. ¹⁷In se autem reversus dixit: "Quanti mercennarii patris mei abundant panibus, ego autem hic fame pereo. ¹⁸Surgam et ibo ad patrem meum et dicam illi: Pater, peccavi in caelum et coram te ¹⁹et iam non sum dignus vocari filius tuus; fac me sicut unum de mercennariis tuis". ²⁰Et surgens venit ad patrem suum. Cum autem adhuc longe esset, vidit illum pater ipsius et misericordia motus est et accurrens cecidit supra collum eius et osculatus est illum. ²¹Dixitque ei filius: "Pater, peccavi in caelum et coram te; iam non sum dignus vocari filius tuus". ²²Dixit autem pater ad servos suos: "Cito proferte stolam primam et induite illum et date anulum in manum eius et calceamenta in pedes ²³et adducite vitulum saginatum, occidite et manducemus et epule-

quet are symbols of that new life—pure, worthy and joyful—of anyone who returns to God and to the bosom of his family, which is the Church. Only the heart of Christ who knows the depths of his Father's love could reveal to us the abyss of his mercy in so simple and beautiful a way" (*Catechism of the Catholic Church*, 1439).

The parable, at once simple and profound, is narrated from three perspectives—that of the younger son, that of the father, and that of the older son. The young man's story is a classic account of a sinner's career: he cuts himself off from his home, goes away to a distant country where he cannot practise his religion or be helped by or help his family, and ends up living with swine, etc. (vv. 13–15). "That son [...] in a certain sense is the man of every period, beginning with the one who was the first to lose the inheritance of grace and original justice. [...] The parable indirectly touches upon every breach of the covenant of love, every loss of grace, every sin" (John Paul II, *Dives in misericordia*, 5). But eventually a moment comes when he decides to turn back. This decision has many elements to it: the son realizes that not only has he offended his father, he has also

offended God (v. 18); and he is acutely conscious of the gravity of his sin: "At the centre of the prodigal son's consciousness, the sense of lost dignity is emerging, the sense of that dignity that springs from the relationship of the son with the father. And it is with this decision that he sets out" (ibid.; see vv. 19–20).

The focus then moves on to the father. He acts in a surprising way, just as God does towards us. Human fathers also forgive, but this one, in addition to forgiving, calls for the best robe, a ring, shoes and the killing of the fatted calf: "The father of the prodigal son *is faithful to his fatherhood, faithful to the love* that he had always lavished on his son. This fidelity is expressed in the parable not only by his immediate readiness to welcome him home when he returns after having squandered his inheritance; it is expressed even more fully by that joy, that merrymaking for the squanderer after his return" (ibid., 6).

The parable then turns to its third character— the older son, who feels offended by what his father has done. In the historical context of Jesus' public ministry, the older son epitomizes the attitude of those Jews who thought them-

u Other ancient authorities read *filled his belly with*   v Other ancient authorities add *treat me as one of your hired servants*

the fatted calf and kill it, and let us eat and make merry; ^{24}for this my son was dead, and is alive again; he was lost, and is found.' And they began to make merry.

Eph 2:1–5

^{25}"Now his elder son was in the field; and as he came and drew near to the house, he heard music and dancing. ^{26}And he called one of the servants and asked what this meant. ^{27}And he said to him, 'Your brother has come, and your father has killed the fatted calf, because he has received him safe and sound.' ^{28}But he was angry and refused to go in. His father came out and entreated him, ^{29}but he answered his father, 'Lo, these many years I have served you, and I never disobeyed your command; yet you never gave me a kid, that I might make merry with my friends. ^{30}But when this son of yours came, who has devoured your living with harlots, you killed for him the fatted calf!' ^{31}And he said to him, 'Son, you are always with me, and all that is mine is yours. ^{32}It was fitting to make merry and be glad, for this your brother was dead, and is alive; he was lost, and is found.'"

10. VARIOUS TEACHINGS*

The unjust steward

16 ^{1}He also said to the disciples, "There was a rich man who had a steward, and charges were brought to him that this man was wasting his goods. ^{2}And he

mur, ^{24}quia hic filius meus mortuus erat et revixit, perierat et inventus est". Et coeperunt epulari. ^{25}Erat autem filius eius senior in agro et, cum veniret et appropinquaret domui, audivit symphoniam et choros, ^{26}et vocavit unum de servis et interrogavit quae haec essent. ^{27}Isque dixit illi: "Frater tuus venit, et occidit pater tuus vitulum saginatum, quia salvum illum recepit". ^{28}Indignatus est autem et nolebat introire. Pater ergo illius egressus coepit rogare illum. ^{29}At ille respondens dixit patri suo: "Ecce tot annis servio tibi et numquam mandatum tuum praeterii, et numquam dedisti mihi haedum, ut cum amicis meis epularer, ^{30}sed postquam filius tuus hic, qui devoravit substantiam tuam cum meretricibus, venit, occidisti illi vitulum saginatum". ^{31}At ipse dixit illi: "Fili, tu semper mecum es, et omnia mea tua sunt; ^{32}epulari autem et gaudere oportebat, quia frater tuus hic mortuus erat et revixit, perierat et inventus est"». [16] ^{1}Dicebat autem et ad discipulos: «Homo quidam erat dives, qui habebat vilicum, et hic diffamatus est apud illum quasi dissipasset bona ipsius. ^{2}Et vocavit illum et ait illi: "Quid hoc audio de te? Redde rationem vilicationis tuae;

selves "righteous" (18:9) and felt that God owed them a reward; they felt offended that Jesus should be so compassionate towards sinners. "Man—every human being—is also this elder brother. Selfishness makes him jealous, hardens his heart, blinds him and shuts him off from other people and from God. The loving kindness and mercy of the father irritate and enrage him; for him the happiness of the brother who has been found again has a bitter taste. From this point of view he too needs to be converted in order to be reconciled" (John Paul II, *Reconciliatio et paenitentia*, 6).

*16:1—19:27 This section contains a broad range of teachings, as the second part of this Gospel does. It begins with further parables (16:1–31), but on the theme of riches and the dangers they often provoke. Later (18:18–30), Jesus will return to this theme in connexion with the failure of the rich young man to answer Jesus' call, and in the more positive episode con-

cerning the conversion of Zacchaeus (19:1–10). Other parables (18:1–14) about prayer and humility are complemented by Jesus' preaching in the middle of the section (17:1–10). At the end of the section the theme of the End is dealt with in both our Lord's discourse (17:20–37) and the parable of the pounds (19:11–27).

The section comes to a climax with the third announcement of the Passion (18:31–34) and the messianic confession of the blind man at Jericho (18:38); these prepare us for the events that take place in Jerusalem.

16:1–15 The parable of the unjust steward may disconcert us a little if we forget that parables are simply devices to convey teachings. Our Lord takes it as understood that the steward has acted unethically, but he uses the steward's behaviour to show his disciples that they must be astute and clever (v. 8) if they are to spread the Kingdom of God: "What zeal people put into their earthly affairs: dreaming of honours, striving for riches,

called him and said to him, 'What is this that I hear about you? Turn in the account of your stewardship, for you can no longer be steward.' ³And the steward said to himself, 'What shall I do, since my master is taking the stewardship away from me? I am not strong enough to dig, and I am ashamed to beg. ⁴I have decided what to do, so that people may receive me into their houses when I am put out of the steward-ship.' ⁵So, summoning his master's debtors one by one, he said to the first, 'How much do you owe my master?' ⁶He said, 'A hundred measures of oil.' And he said to him, 'Take your bill, and sit down quickly and write fifty.' ⁷Then he said to another, 'And how much do you owe?' He said, 'A hundred measures of wheat.' He said to him, 'Take your bill, and write eighty.' ⁸The master commended the dishon-est steward for his prudence; for the sons of this world[w] are wiser in their own gen-eration than the sons of light.* ⁹And I tell you, make friends for yourselves by means of unrighteous mammon, so that when it fails they may receive you into the eternal habitations.

¹⁰"He who is faithful in a very little is faithful also in much; and he who is dis-honest in a very little is dishonest also in much. ¹¹If then you have not been faithful in the unrighteous mammon, who will entrust to you the true riches? ¹²And if you have not been faithful in that which is another's, who will give you that which is your own? ¹³No servant can serve two masters; for either he will hate the one and love the other, or he will be devoted to the one and despise the other. You cannot serve God and mammon."

¹⁴The Pharisees, who were lovers of money, heard all this, and they scoffed at him. ¹⁵But he said to them, "You are those who justify yourselves before men, but God knows your hearts; for what is exalted among men is an abomination in the sight of God.

Lk 12:21, 33
Mt 6:20

Lk 19:17

Mt 6:24

Mt 23:14

Mt 6:1
Mt 23:28

iam enim non poteris vilicare". ³Ait autem vilicus intra se: "Quid faciam, quia dominus meus aufert a me vilicationem? Fodere non valeo, men-dicare erubesco. ⁴Scio quid faciam, ut, cum amotus fuero a vilicatione, recipiant me in domos suas". ⁵Convocatis itaque singulis debitoribus domini sui, dicebat primo: "Quantum debes domino meo?". ⁶At ille dixit: "Centum cados olei". Dixitque illi: "Accipe cautionem tuam et sede cito, scribe quinquaginta". ⁷Deinde alii dixit: "Tu vero quantum debes?". Qui ait: "Centum coros tritici". Ait illi: "Accipe litteras tuas et scribe octoginta". ⁸Et laudavit dominus vilicum iniquitatis, quia prudenter fecisset, quia filii huius saeculi prudentiores filiis lucis in generatione sua sunt. ⁹Et ego vobis dico: Facite vobis amicos de mammona iniquitatis, ut, cum defecerit, recipiant vos in aeterna tabernacula. ¹⁰Qui fidelis est in minimo, et in maiori fidelis est; et qui in modico iniquus est, et in maiori iniquus est. ¹¹Si ergo in iniquo mammona fideles non fuistis, quod verum est, quis credet vobis? ¹²Et si in alieno fideles non fuistis, quod vestrum est, quis dabit vobis? ¹³Nemo servus potest duobus dominis servire: aut enim unum odiet et alterum diliget, aut uni adhaerebit et alterum contemnet. Non potestis Deo servire et mammonae». ¹⁴Audiebant autem omnia haec phar-isaei, qui erant avari, et deridebant illum. ¹⁵Et ait illis: «Vos estis qui iustificatis vos coram hominibus; Deus autem novit corda vestra, quia, quod hominibus altum est, abominatio est ante Deum. ¹⁶Lex et Prophetae usque ad Ioannem; ex tunc regnum Dei evangelizatur, et omnis in illud vim

bent on sensuality! Men and women, rich and poor, old and middle-aged and young and even children: all of them alike. When you and I put the same zeal into the affairs of our souls, we will have a living and working faith. And there will be no obstacle that we cannot overcome in our apost-olic works" (St Josemaría Escrivá, *The Way*, 317).

After the parable, the Gospel records some sayings of Jesus (vv. 9–15), prefaced by the forceful expression "And I tell you" (v. 9). There are a number of ideas here, but they all serve to make the same point—that at all times, in little things and big things, in wealth or poverty, our focus should be on God. Maybe the core idea

comes in v. 13, where attachment to riches is presented as a kind of idolatry: "All bow down before wealth. Wealth is that to which the multitude of men pay an instinctive homage. They measure happiness by wealth; and by wealth they measure respectability. ... It is a homage resulting from a profound faith. ... Wealth is one idol of the day and notoriety is a second. ... Notoriety, or the making of a noise in the world—it may be called 'newspaper fame'—has come to be considered a great good in itself, and a ground of veneration" (John Henry Newman, as quoted in *Catechism of the Catholic Church*, 1723).

w Greek *age*

The law and the Gospel

Mt 5:17, 32;
11:12–13; 19:9
Mk 10:11

¹⁶"The law and the prophets were until John; since then the good news of the kingdom of God is preached, and every one enters it violently. ¹⁷But it is easier for
heaven and earth to pass away, than for one dot of the law to become void.

Mt 5:18

¹⁸"Every one who divorces his wife and marries another commits adultery, and
he who marries a woman divorced from her husband commits adultery.

Lazarus and the rich man

¹⁹"There was a rich man, who was clothed in purple and fine linen and who feasted
sumptuously every day. ²⁰And at his gate lay a poor man named Lazarus, full of
sores, ²¹who desired to be fed with what fell from the rich man's table; moreover the

facit. ¹⁷Facilius est autem caelum et terram praeterire, quam de Lege unum apicem cadere. ¹⁸Omnis, qui dimittit uxorem suam et ducit alteram,
moechatur; et qui dimissam a viro ducit, moechatur. ¹⁹Homo quidam erat dives et induebatur purpura et bysso et epulabatur cotidie splendide.
²⁰Quidam autem pauper nomine Lazarus iacebat ad ianuam eius ulceribus plenus ²¹et cupiens saturari de his, quae cadebant de mensa divitis; sed

16:16–18 Here the evangelist records sayings of
Jesus on disparate themes, but the background is
clearly salvation history (see v. 16). Jesus has
come not to abolish the Law (v. 17), but to bring
it to perfection: his teaching on marriage (v. 18)
is an instance of his doing this.

Verse 16 deals with a theme that recurs often
in the work of St Luke: God has a plan; he
chooses when and where things happen, as a
prelude to the salvation made available to all
mankind in Jesus: "The economy of the Old
Testament, in fact, was essentially ordered to
preparing and proclaiming the coming of Christ,
the Redeemer of the universe, and of his
Messianic Kingdom. The books of the Old
Covenant are thus a permanent witness to a
careful divine pedagogy. In Christ this pedagogy
achieves its purpose: Jesus does not in fact
merely speak 'in the name of God' like the
Prophets, but he is God himself speaking in his
Eternal Word made flesh. [...] Jesus Christ is
the new beginning of everything. In him all
things come into their own; they are taken up
and given back to the Creator from whom they
first came. Christ is thus the fulfilment of the
yearning of all the world's religions and, as
such, he is their sole and definitive completion.
Just as God in Christ speaks to humanity of
himself, so in Christ all humanity and the whole
of creation speaks of itself to God—indeed, it
gives itself to God. Everything thus returns to its
origin. Jesus Christ is the recapitulation of
everything (cf. Eph 1:10) and at the same time
the fulfilment of all things in God: a fulfilment

which is the glory of God" (John Paul II, *Tertio
millennio adveniente*, 6–7).

16:19–31 The parable of Lazarus and the rich
man negates two erroneous ideas—the idea that
the soul does not survive after death (and therefore there is no such thing as judgment or retribution in an afterlife), and the idea that material
prosperity is a reward for moral probity and,
conversely, that misfortune in this world is a
punishment for sin.

The parable illustrates teaching recorded in
16:1–15. It does not explicitly say that the rich
man did anything evil; but all we know is that he
lived a life of luxury (v. 19); and that this
lifestyle has prevented his seeing Lazarus as a
neighbour, and caused him to be deaf to the
voice of God even when it speaks very clearly to
him (vv. 29, 31): "Wishing to come down to
topics that are practical and of some urgency, the
Council lays stress on respect for the human
person: everyone should look upon his neighbour (without any exception) as another self,
bearing in mind above all his life and the means
necessary for living it in a dignified way lest he
follow the example of the rich man who ignored
Lazarus, the poor man" (Vatican II, *Gaudium et
spes*, 27).

Christian doctrine, drawing on sacred texts,
says that "Abraham's bosom" (v. 22) means the
state in which holy souls found themselves prior
to Christ's resurrection. There, feeling no pain,
and confident that they would in due course be
redeemed, they were at peace; and Christ set

dogs came and licked his sores. [22]The poor man died and was carried by the angels to Abraham's bosom. The rich man also died and was buried; [23]and in Hades, being in torment, he lifted up his eyes, and saw Abraham far off and Lazarus in his bosom. [24]And he called out, 'Father Abraham, have mercy upon me, and send Lazarus to dip the end of his finger in water and cool my tongue; for I am in anguish in this flame.' [25]But Abraham said, 'Son, remember that you in your lifetime received your good things, and Lazarus in like manner evil things, but now he is comforted here, and you are in anguish. [26]And besides all this, between us and you a great chasm has been fixed, in order that those who would pass from here to you may not be able, and none may cross from there to us.' [27]And he said, 'Then I beg you, father, to send him to my father's house, [28]for I have five brothers, so that he may warn them, lest they also come into this place of torment.' [29]But Abraham said, 'They have Moses and the prophets; let them hear them.' [30]And he said, 'No, father Abraham; but if some one goes to them from the dead, they will repent.' [31]He said to him, 'If they do not hear Moses and the prophets, neither will they be convinced if some one should rise from the dead'.''

Lk 6:24

2 Tim 3:16

Jn 5:46; 11:45–53

Mt 18:6–7
Mk 9:42

On leading others astray

17 [1]And he said to his disciples, "Temptations to sin[x] are sure to come; but woe to him by whom they come! [2]It would be better for him if a millstone were

et canes veniebant et lingebant ulcera eius. [22]Factum est autem ut moreretur pauper et portaretur ab angelis in sinum Abrahae; mortuus est autem et dives et sepultus est. [23]Et in inferno elevans oculos suos cum esset in tormentis, videbat Abraham a longe et Lazarum in sinu eius. [24]Et ipse cla-mans dixit: "Pater Abraham, miserere mei et mitte Lazarum, ut intingat extremum digiti sui in aquam, ut refrigeret linguam meam, quia crucior in hac flamma". [25]At dixit Abraham: "Fili, recordare quia recepisti bona tua in vita tua, et Lazarus similiter mala; nunc autem hic consolatur, tu vero cruciaris. [26]Et in his omnibus inter nos et vos chaos magnum firmatum est, ut hi, qui volunt hinc transire ad vos, non possint, neque inde ad nos transmeare". [27]Et ait: "Rogo ergo te, Pater, ut mittas eum in domum patris mei [28] —habeo enim quinque fratres— ut testetur illis, ne et ipsi veniant in locum hunc tormentorum". [29]Ait autem Abraham: "Habent Moysen et Prophetas; audiant illos". [30]At ille dixit: "Non, pater Abraham, sed si quis ex mortuis ierit ad eos, paenitentiam agent". [31]Ait autem illi: "Si Moysen et Prophetas non audiunt, neque si quis ex mortuis resur-rexerit, credent"». [17] [1]Et ad discipulos suos ait: «Impossibile est ut non veniant scandala; vae autem illi, per quem veniunt! [2]Utilius est illi si

them free when he descended into the under-world and rose from the dead (see *Roman Cathechism*, 1, 6, 3; *Catechism of the Catholic Church*, 633). The rich man, when he died, went not to Abraham's bosom but to "Hades", hell (v. 23). His conversation with Abraham is a device used by our Lord to engrave his teaching on the minds of his listeners (in fact, there is no room in hell for feelings of compassion): "When Abra-ham said to the rich man 'between us and you a great chasm has been fixed', he showed that after death and resurrection there will be no scope for any kind of penance. The impious will not repent and enter the Kingdom, nor will the just sin and go down into hell. This is the unbridgable abyss" (Aphraates, *Demonstra-tiones*, 20, 12).

17:1–10 This passage contains teachings addressed to disciples (v. 1) and apostles (v. 5) all on the same basic theme—the conduct

expected of people (especially those who hold office) in the future Church.

Our Lord's graphic teaching on the sin of scandal (vv. 1–2) makes it clear that this sin is very serious indeed. Hence the need for great prudence: "Not only should we strive to live a good life, my brothers, but the goodness of our life should also be seen by others. We should be concerned not only with having a clean con-science, but also […] with ensuring that our weaker brothers are not given even the slightest cause for scandal. If we have been given fresh grass to eat and clear water to drink, let us make sure that the weaker sheep do not feed on tram-pled grass and drink muddied water" (St Augus-tine, *Sermones*, 47, 12–14).

In vv. 3–4 our Lord calls for generosity in forgiving offences. His teaching implies two things—firstly, that every sin, within the Church, should be condemned; and secondly, that repen-tance merits forgiveness. Grudges should never

x Greek *stumbling blocks*

hung round his neck and he were cast into the sea, than that he should cause one of these little ones to sin.[y]

Forgiving offences

Mt 18:15–17, 21–22

[3]Take heed to yourselves; if your brother sins, rebuke him, and if he repents, forgive him; [4]and if he sins against you seven times in the day, and turns to you seven times, and says, 'I repent,' you must forgive him."

The power of faith

Mt 21:21
Mk 11:22–24
Mk 9:24
Mt 17:20

[5]The apostles said to the Lord, "Increase our faith!" [6]And the Lord said, "If you had faith as a grain of mustard seed, you could say to this sycamine tree, 'Be rooted up, and be planted in the sea,' and it would obey you.

Humble service

[7]"Will any one of you, who has a servant ploughing or keeping sheep, say to him when he has come in from the field, 'Come at once and sit down at table'? [8]Will he not rather say to him, 'Prepare supper for me, and gird yourself and serve me, till I eat and drink; and afterward you shall eat and drink'? [9]Does he thank the servant because he did what was commanded? [10]So you also, when you have done all that is commanded you, say, 'We are unworthy servants; we have only done what was our duty.'"

Cure of ten lepers

[11]On the way to Jerusalem he was passing along between Samaria and Galilee. [12]And as he entered a village, he was met by ten lepers, who stood at a distance [13]and lifted

Lev 13:45ff

lapis molaris imponatur circa collum eius et proiciatur in mare, quam ut scandalizet unum de pusillis istis. [3]Attendite vobis! Si peccaverit frater tuus, increpa illum, et si paenitentiam egerit, dimitte illi; [4]et si septies in die peccaverit in te et septies conversus fuerit ad te dicens: "Paenitet me", dimittes illi». [5]Et dixerunt apostoli Domino: «Adauge nobis fidem!». [6]Dixit autem Dominus: «Si haberetis fidem sicut granum sinapis, diceretis huic arbori moro: "Eradicare et transplantare in mare", et oboediret vobis. [7]Quis autem vestrum habens servum arantem aut pascentem, qui regresso de agro dicet illi: "Statim transi, recumbe", [8]et non dicet ei: "Para, quod cenem, et praecinge te et ministra mihi, donec manducem et bibam, et post haec tu manducabis et bibes"? [9]Numquid gratiam habet servo illi, quia fecit, quae praecepta sunt? [10]Sic et vos, cum feceritis omnia, quae praecepta sunt vobis, dicite: "Servi inutiles sumus; quod debuimus facere, fecimus"». [11]Et factum est dum iret in Ierusalem, et ipse transi-

be harboured, for "God does not reject and repudiate as man often does by constantly recalling the offences committed against him, hardening his heart and stoking the fire of anger in his soul" (St John Chrysostom, *De proditione Iudae*, 2).

The apostles realize that this teaching is very demanding, so Christ adds that nothing is impossible if one has faith in God (vv. 5–6). Finally, he stresses that there is no room for feelings of self-importance (vv. 7–10). Clearly he is not recommending or praising the landowner's behaviour. But he is saying that the virtue shown in keeping God's commandments will win us the admiration of others and bring us inner consolation, and that when that happens, we should not think we are special but should instead remind ourselves

that we are only doing what God requires: "Do not boast unworthily of the fact that you are a son of God: remember the power of grace, and your own poor nature. Do not glory in your service to the Lord: it is no more than your duty. The sun shines, and the moon, and the angels do their duty. [...] We should not praise ourselves, nor tempt God's judgment [...]. God's judgment will come in his good time" (St Ambrose, *Expositio Evangelii secundum Lucam*, ad loc.).

17:11–19 According to the Law of Moses (see Lev 13:45–46), to avoid contagion, people suffering from leprosy were to live away from settlements and let others know that they had the disease; that is why the ten lepers keep their distance from Jesus and shout out their appeal to

y Greek *stumble*

Lk 5:14
Mk 1:44

up their voices and said, "Jesus, Master, have mercy on us." [14]When he saw them he said to them, "Go and show yourselves to the priests." And as they went they were cleansed. [15]Then one of them, when he saw that he was healed, turned back, prais-

Lk 10:33

ing God with a loud voice; [16]and he fell on his face at Jesus' feet, giving him thanks. Now he was a Samaritan. [17]Then said Jesus, "Were not ten cleansed? Where are the nine? [18]Was no one found to return and give praise to God except this foreigner?"

Lk 7:50; 8:48

[19]And he said to him, "Rise and go your way; your faith has made you well."

The coming of the Kingdom of God

[20]Being asked by the Pharisees when the kingdom of God was coming, he answered

Mt 24:23, 26ff

them, "The kingdom of God is not coming with signs to be observed;* [21]nor will

bat per mediam Samariam et Galilaeam. [12]Et cum ingrederetur quoddam castellum, occurrerunt ei decem viri leprosi, qui steterunt a longe, [13]et levaverunt vocem dicentes: «Iesu praeceptor, miserere nostri!». [14]Quos ut vidit, dixit: «Ite, ostendite vos sacerdotibus». Et factum est dum irent, mundati sunt. [15]Unus autem ex illis, ut vidit quia sanatus est, regressus est cum magna voce magnificans Deum [16]et cecidit in faciem ante pedes eius gratias agens ei; et hic erat Samaritanus. [17]Respondens autem Iesus dixit: «Nonne decem mundati sunt? Et novem ubi sunt? [18]Non sunt inventi qui redirent, ut darent gloriam Deo, nisi hic alienigena?». [19]Et ait illi: «Surge, vade; fides tua te salvum fecit». [20]Interrogatus autem a pharisaeis: «Quando venit regnum Dei?», respondit eis et dixit: «Non venit regnum Dei cum observatione, [21]neque dicent: "Ecce hic" aut: "Illic"; ecce enim

him (vv. 12–13). The location of this episode explains how a Samaritan came to be in a group with Jews. There was hostility between these peoples (see Jn 4:9), but the disease they shared led them to overlook the antagonism between the two peoples.

These men put their faith in Jesus' instruction to show themselves to the priests (v. 14), but only one of them comes back to thank him—a Samaritan. He, as Jesus put it, "gave thanks to God" (v. 18), with the result that, of the ten who were cured, only one, through faith, was made well, that is, saved, as the Latin makes clear ("fides tua te salvum fecit": v. 19). The scene bears out what Jesus, in the synagogue of Nazareth, had said would happen (see 4:27). It is also an invitation to us to show gratitude to God: "What better prayer can we think in our mind, or utter with our tongue, or express with our pen than 'Thanks be to God'? Nothing can be said more briefly than this, or heard more joyfully, or used more faithfully" (St Augustine, *Epistolae*, 41, 1).

17:20–37 Jesus' dialogue with the Pharisees (vv. 20–21) and the things he says later to his disciples (vv. 22–37) reveal much about the coming of the Kingdom of God. In both situations, he says that it won't happen in such a way that people will be able to say, "Look, here it is!" (vv. 21, 23).

The Pharisees were expecting God to estab-

lish his Kingdom in a spectacular way, but Jesus tells them that it has already arrived. The Greek words translated as "the kingdom of God is in the midst of you" (v. 21) could also be translated as "[…] is within you" or "[…] among you". The Fathers of the Church and other commentators translate it and interpret it in both senses. If it is translated as "the kingdom of God is among you", it refers to Jesus and his activity; that is how St Ephrem explains: "in saying this ['the kingdom of God is in the midst of you'], he was speaking of himself, for he was in our midst when he spoke" (*Commentarii in Diatessaron*, 18). However, it is more common to find a spiritual interpretation being offered, such as this one: "When our outward senses are stilled and we rejoice in the presence of God within us and retire from the noise and troubles of this world, then we see the Kingdom of God within us, for as Jesus said, the Kingdom of God is within us" (St John Damascene, *Homilia in Transfigurationem Domini*, 9). Souls who are close to God have passed on their own experience of this: "The Doctor of doctors teaches us without the sound of words. I have never heard him speak, and yet I know he is within my soul. Every moment he is guiding and inspiring me, and, just at the moment I need them, 'lights' till then unseen are granted me. Most often it is not at prayer that they come but while I go about my daily duties" (St Thérèse of Lisieux, *Story of a Soul*, 8).

they say, 'Lo, here it is!' or 'There!' for behold, the kingdom of God is in the midst of you."[z]

The day of Christ's coming

Mt 24:36–41

[22]And he said to the disciples, "The days are coming when you will desire to see one of the days of the Son of man, and you will not see it. [23]And they will say to you, 'Lo, there!' or 'Lo, here!' Do not go, do not follow them. [24]For as the lightning flashes and lights up the sky from one side to the other, so will the Son of man be in his day.[a] [25]But first he must suffer many things and be rejected by this generation. [26]As it was in the days of Noah, so will it be in the days of the Son of man. [27]They ate, they drank, they married, they were given in marriage, until the day when Noah entered the ark, and the flood came and destroyed them all. [28]Likewise as it was in the days of Lot—they ate, they drank, they bought, they sold, they planted, they built, [29]but on the day when Lot went out from Sodom fire and brimstone rained from heaven and destroyed them all— [30]so will it be on the day when the Son of man is revealed. [31]On that day, let him who is on the housetop, with his goods in the house, not come down to take them away; and likewise let him who is in the field not turn back. [32]Remember Lot's wife. [33]Whoever seeks to gain his life will lose it, but whoever loses his life will preserve it. [34]I tell you, in that night there will be two men in one bed; one will be taken and the other left. [35]There will be two women grinding together; one will be taken and the other left."[b] [37]And they said to him, "Where, Lord?" He said to them, "Where the body is, there the eagles[c] will be gathered together."

Lk 21:8
Mk 13:21
Mt 24:27

Lk 9:22

Gen 7:7–23

Gen 18:20
Gen 19:1–29

Mt 24:17–18
Lk 21:21
Mk 13:15ff

Lk 9:24
Gen 19:26
Lk 9:24
Mt 10:39

Job 39:30

regnum Dei intra vos est». [22]Et ait ad discipulos: «Venient dies, quando desideretis videre unum diem Filii hominis et non videbitis. [23]Et dicent vobis: "Ecce hic", "Ecce illic"; nolite ire neque sectemini. [24]Nam sicut fulgur coruscans de sub caelo in ea, quae sub caelo sunt, fulget, ita erit Filius hominis in die sua. [25]Primum autem oportet illum multa pati et reprobari a generatione hac. [26]Et sicut factum est in diebus Noe, ita erit et in diebus Filii hominis: [27]edebant, bibebant, uxores ducebant, dabantur ad nuptias, usque in diem, qua intravit Noe in arcam, et venit diluvium et perdidit omnes. [28]Similiter sicut factum est in diebus Lot: edebant, bibebant, emebant, vendebant, plantabant, aedificabant; [29]qua die autem exiit Lot a Sodomis, pluit ignem et sulphur de caelo et omnes perdidit. [30]Secundum haec erit, qua die Filius hominis revelabitur. [31]In illa die, qui fuerit in tecto et vasa eius in domo, ne descendat tollere illa, et qui in agro, similiter non redeat retro. [32]Memores estote uxoris Lot. [33]Quicumque quaesierit animam suam salvam facere, perdet illam; et, quicumque perdiderit illam, vivificabit eam. [34]Dico vobis: Illa nocte erunt duo in lecto uno: unus assumetur, et alter relinquetur; [35]duae erunt molentes in unum: una assumetur, et altera relinquetur». [37]Respondentes dicunt illi: «Ubi,

Jesus' words to his disciples (vv. 22–35) are on a different line. He is not speaking now about the Kingdom being present, but about the end of the world. As he explained in many parables, the Kingdom is meant to grow: "First announced to the children of Israel, this messianic kingdom is intended to accept men of all nations" (*Catechism of the Catholic Church*, 543). At an exact time in the future, the End will come. But that will not be soon; first, Jesus must be rejected by "his generation" (v. 25). Because of this, Jesus' disciples need to be on guard—in order not to be led astray by false signs (v. 23), and also because if we become impatient for the Master's coming and grow forgetful of what lies ahead, we may begin to take things easy (vv. 26–33). Jesus will come as the glorified Son of man, suddenly, unexpectedly: hence the need to

live our lives as if the Lord could call us to account at any time.

"Where, Lord?" (v. 37). After asking about the "when" of his coming, his disciples now ask Jesus about the "where" of its taking place. His reply sounds proverbial; it is somewhat enigmatic, as if he does not want to give a clear answer. However, the image he uses (the speed with which a bird of prey descends on its quarry) shows that it will happen very suddenly. This is a further warning about the need to live every moment as if it were our last, as if it were the defining moment of our life: "A true Christian is always ready to appear before God. Because, if he is fighting to live as a man of Christ, he is ready at every moment to fulfil his duty" (St Josemaría Escrivá, *Furrow*, 875).

See the RSV note **b** and Mt 24:40.

[z] Or *within you* [a] Other ancient authorities omit *in his day* [b] Other ancient authorities add v. 36 *"two men will be in the field; one will be taken and the other left"* [c] Or *vultures*

Persevering prayer. Parable of the unjust judge

Rom 12:12
Col 4:2
1 Thess 5:17

18 ¹And he told them a parable, to the effect that they ought always to pray and not lose heart. ²He said, "In a certain city there was a judge who neither feared God nor regarded man; ³and there was a widow in that city who kept coming to him and saying, 'Vindicate me against my adversary.' ⁴For a while he refused; but Lk 11:7–8 afterward he said to himself, 'Though I neither fear God nor regard man, ⁵yet because this widow bothers me, I will vindicate her, or she will wear me out by her continual coming.'" ⁶And the Lord said, "Hear what the unrighteous judge says. ⁷And will not God vindicate his elect, who cry to him day and night? Will he delay long over them? ⁸I tell you, he will vindicate them speedily. Nevertheless, when the Son of man comes, will he find faith on earth?"

Parable of the Pharisee and the tax collector

⁹He also told this parable to some who trusted in themselves that they were righteous and despised others: ¹⁰"Two men went up into the temple to pray, one a Pharisee and

Domine?». Qui dixit eis: «Ubicumque fuerit corpus, illuc congregabuntur et aquilae».   [18] ¹Dicebat autem parabolam ad illos quoniam oportet semper orare et non deficere, ²dicens: «Iudex quidam erat in quadam civitate, qui Deum non timebat et hominem non reverebatur. ³Vidua autem erat in civitate illa et veniebat ad eum dicens: "Vindica me de adversario meo". ⁴Et nolebat per multum tempus; post haec autem dixit intra se: "Etsi Deum non timeo nec hominem revereor, ⁵tamen quia molesta est mihi haec vidua, vindicabo illam, ne in novissimo veniens suggillet me"». ⁶Ait autem Dominus: «Audite quid iudex iniquitatis dicit; ⁷Deus autem non faciet vindictam electorum suorum clamantium ad se die ac nocte, et patientiam habebit in illis? ⁸Dico vobis: Cito faciet vindictam illorum. Verumtamen Filius hominis veniens, putas, inveniet fidem in terra?». ⁹Dixit

18:1–8 The parable of the unjust judge is a very eloquent lesson about the effectiveness of perseverance in prayer. Verse 1 has been a touchstone of Christian catechesis on prayer: "We were not commanded to work and stand watch and fast constantly: we were commanded to pray without ceasing" (Evagrius, *Capita practica ad Anatolium*, 49). To do this one needs to overcome laziness and raise one's eyes to God at every turn: "A man can pray devoutly whether he is standing in the public square or during a quiet walk; seated at his study desk or while he works at other tasks, he can raise his heart and soul to God" (St John Chrysostom, *De Anna*, 4, 5). We will succeed in this only if we pray and live a consistently Christian life: "He prays without ceasing who prays with good works and works with a prayerful spirit. Only thus can we pray without ceasing as we have been commanded" (Origen, *De oratione*, 12). See *Catechism of the Catholic Church*, 2742–2745.

At the end of the passage, our Lord links the effectiveness of prayer to faith (v. 8): prayer nourishes faith, but faith, in turn, grows when it is enlivened by prayer: "You grew in the face of difficulties in the apostolate when you prayed: 'Lord, you are the same as ever. Give me the faith of those men who knew how to correspond

to your grace, who worked great miracles, real marvels, in your Name ...' And you finished off: 'I know that you will do it: but I also know that you want to be asked. You want to be sought out. You want us to knock hard at the door of your Heart.' At the end you renewed your resolve to persevere in humble and trusting prayer" (St Josemaría Escrivá, *The Forge*, 653).

18:9–14 Besides constancy, prayer requires humility. That is the message of the parable of the Pharisee and the tax collector: "When we pray, do we speak from the height of our pride and will, or 'out of the depths' (Ps 130:1) of a humble and contrite heart? He who humbles himself will be exalted; *humility* is the foundation of prayer. Only when we humbly acknowledge that 'we do not know how to pray as we ought' (Rom 8:26), are we ready to receive freely the gift of prayer. 'Man is a beggar before God' (St Augustine, *Sermo*, 56, 6, 9)" (*Catechism of the Catholic Church*, 2559).

The parable shows us contrasting types of prayer. The Pharisee is very self-satisfied: he prays standing up (v. 11), boasts to God about all the good he does, considers himself to be without sin, and therefore, feels no need to repent. He performs all his religious duties, going beyond

the other a tax collector. [11]The Pharisee stood and prayed thus with himself, 'God, I thank thee that I am not like other men, extortioners, unjust, adulterers, or even like this tax collector. [12]I fast twice a week, I give tithes of all that I get.' [13]But the tax collector, standing far off, would not even lift up his eyes to heaven, but beat his breast, saying, 'God, be merciful to me a sinner!' [14]I tell you, this man went down to his house justified rather than the other; for every one who exalts himself will be humbled, but he who humbles himself will be exalted."

Is 58:2–3
Lk 16:15

Mt 23:23
Ps 51:1

Lk 14:11
Mt 23:12

Jesus blesses the children

[15]Now they were bringing even infants to him that he might touch them; and when the disciples saw it, they rebuked them. [16]But Jesus called them to him, saying, "Let the children come to me, and do not hinder them; for to such belongs the kingdom of God. [17]Truly, I say to you, whoever does not receive the kingdom of God like a child shall not enter it."

Mt 19:13–15
Mk 10:13–16

Lk 9:47ff

Mt 18:3

The rich young man. Christian poverty and renunciation

[18]And a ruler asked him, "Good Teacher, what shall I do to inherit eternal life?" [19]And Jesus said to him, "Why do you call me good? No one is good but God alone. [20]You know the commandments: 'Do not commit adultery, Do not kill, Do not steal,

Mt 19:16–30
Mk 10:17–31

Lk 10:25–28

Ex 20:12–16
Deut 5:16–20

autem et ad quosdam, qui in se confidebant tamquam iusti et aspernabantur ceteros, parabolam istam: [10]«Duo homines ascenderunt in templum, ut orarent: unus pharisaeus et alter publicanus. [11]Pharisaeus stans haec apud se orabat: "Deus, gratias ago tibi quia non sum sicut ceteri hominum, raptores, iniusti, adulteri, velut etiam hic publicanus; [12]ieiuno bis in sabbato, decimas do omnium, quae possideo". [13]Et publicanus a longe stans nolebat nec oculos ad caelum levare, sed percutiebat pectus suum dicens: "Deus, propitius esto mihi peccatori". [14]Dico vobis: Descendit hic iustificatus in domum suam ab illo. Quia omnis, qui se exaltat, humiliabitur; et, qui se humiliat, exaltabitur». [15]Afferebant autem ad illum et infantes, ut eos tangeret; quod cum viderent, discipuli increpabant illos. [16]Iesus autem convocans illos dixit: «Sinite pueros venire ad me et nolite eos vetare; talium est enim regnum Dei. [17]Amen dico vobis: Quicumque non acceperit regnum Dei sicut puer, non intrabit in illud». [18]Et interrogavit eum quidam princeps dicens: «Magister bone, quid faciens vitam aeternam possidebo?». [19]Dixit autem ei Iesus: «Quid me dicis bonum? Nemo bonus nisi solus Deus. [20]Mandata nosti: *non moechaberis, non occides, non furtum facies, non falsum testimonium dices, honora patrem tuum et*

what is laid down (v. 12), fasting twice a week, whereas rabbis said once was enough, and paying tithes on everything, not just items that the Law said should be tithed. His words are not true prayer because they are not addressed to God: he prays "with himself" and despises others (v. 11). The tax collector is the exact opposite. He recognizes his unworthiness and is sincerely sorry for his sins; he puts all his trust in divine mercy (v. 13). His prayer is genuine and he has all the right dispositions for approaching God. And he, this tax collector, goes home justified (v. 14): "[It is not without reason that some have said that prayer justifies;] for repentant prayer or supplicant repentance, raising up the soul to God and re-uniting it to his goodness, without doubt obtains pardon in virtue of the holy love which gives it this sacred movement" (St Francis de Sales, *Treatise on the Love of God*, 2, 20).

18:15–17 This episode shows us two things—

Jesus' regard for children (v. 16), and our need to be like children if we are to enter the Kingdom of heaven (v. 17): "Why, then, does he say that children are fit for the Kingdom of heaven? Perhaps because usually they are without malice, nor are they deceptive, nor do they dare to avenge themselves; they have no experience of lust, do not covet riches and are not ambitious. But the virtue of all this does not lie in ignorance of evil, but in its rejection; it does not consist in not being able to sin but rather in not consenting to sin. Therefore, the Lord is not referring to childhood as such, but to the innocence which children have in their simplicity" (St Ambrose, *Expositio Evangelii secundum Lucam*, ad loc.).

18:18–30 All the Synoptic Gospels report the episode of this rich young ruler, and the words of Peter and Jesus that follow it. Luke's account is the most sober of the three, but it spells out the key aspects of Christ's teaching, the essence of which is expressed in Jesus' final words to Peter:

Do not bear false witness, Honour your father and mother.'" [21]And he said, "All these I have observed from my youth." [22]And when Jesus heard it, he said to him, "One thing you still lack. Sell all that you have and distribute to the poor, and you will have treasure in heaven; and come, follow me." [23]But when he heard this he became sad, for he was very rich. [24]Jesus looking at him said, "How hard it is for those who have riches to enter the kingdom of God! [25]For it is easier for a camel to go through the eye of a needle than for a rich man to enter the kingdom of God." [26]Those who heard it said, "Then who can be saved?" [27]But he said, "What is impossible with men is possible with God." [28]And Peter said, "Lo, we have left our homes and followed you." [29]And he said to them, "Truly, I say to you, there is no man who has left house or wife or brothers or parents or children, for the sake of the kingdom of God, [30]who will not receive manifold more in this time, and in the age to come eternal life."

Mt 6:20
Lk 12:33

matrem». [21]Qui ait: «Haec omnia custodivi a iuventute». [22]Quo audito Iesus ait ei: «Adhuc unum tibi deest: omnia, quaecumque habes, vende et da pauperibus et habebis thesaurum in caelo et veni, sequere me». [23]His ille auditis, contristatus est, quia dives erat valde. [24]Videns autem illum Iesus tristem factum dixit: «Quam difficile, qui pecunias habent, in regnum Dei intrant. [25]Facilius est enim camelum per foramen acus transire, quam divitem intrare in regnum Dei». [26]Et dixerunt, qui audiebant: «Et quis potest salvus fieri?». [27]Ait autem illis: «Quae impossibilia sunt apud homines, possibilia sunt apud Deum». [28]Ait autem Petrus: «Ecce nos dimisimus nostra et secuti sumus te». [29]Qui dixit eis: «Amen dico vobis: Nemo est, qui reliquit domum aut uxorem aut fratres aut parentes aut filios propter regnum Dei, [30]et non recipiat multo plura in hoc tempore et in

a person who leaves everything for the sake of the Kingdom of God will receive much more than he has denied himself. Thus, "Jesus' call to the rich young man to follow him, in the obedience of a disciple and in the observance of the Commandments, is joined to the call to poverty and chastity" (*Catechism of the Catholic Church*, 2053).

The episode begins with the question put by the rich young man, the same question as was put on another occasion by a lawyer (see 10:25): What must I do to be saved? The difference in Jesus' replies shows his teaching method: the demands he makes vary depending on the person's capacity to understand and respond. In the case of the lawyer, Jesus reminded him about practising the commandments of love of God and neighbour; in the case of this man, Jesus confronts him with further challenges. Jesus first reiterates here the commandments in the second table of the Law, but he prefaces them with a warning: "No one is good but God alone" (v. 19). Jesus declines to be called "good", possibly because he does not want a quality pertaining to God to be reduced to the level of a formula of courtesy: "Before answering the question, Jesus wishes the young man to have a clear idea of why he asked his question. The 'Good Teacher' points out to him—and to all of us—that the answer to the question, 'What good must I do to have eternal life?' can only be found by turning one's

mind and heart to the 'One' who is good: 'No one is good but God alone' (Mk 10:18; cf. Lk 18:19). *Only God can answer the question about what is good, because he is the Good itself*" (John Paul II, *Veritatis splendor*, 9). In this way, our Lord prepares the young man for the challenge he gives in v. 22: "Since God is good, and more good still to those who are faithful to him, let us cling to him with our whole heart and soul, with all the determination of which we are capable. [...] No one is good but God alone: everything that is good is divine, and everything divine is good" (St Ambrose, *De fuga mundi*, 6, 36).

Jesus responds to the uneasiness felt by Peter and the other disciples (vv. 26–30) with words of reassurance for all those who, after they have given everything to the Lord, feel a sense of regret at one moment or another. The promise Jesus makes far exceeds anything the world can give. Those who follow him generously will obtain, while on earth, a joy and a peace that far exceed mere human joys and consolations, for they are an anticipation of eternal bliss: "Try to find on earth anyone who repays so generously!" (St Josemaría Escrivá, *The Way*, 670). However, we need to take care, because, as St Teresa of Avila used to say, "Sometimes it seems as if we are giving God everything when all we have really given him is the interest or the fruit, and we keep the principal or root for ourselves" (*Life*, 11, 2).

Third announcement of the Passion
Mt 20:17-19
Mk 10:32-34
Lk 9:22, 44, 51

³¹And taking the twelve, he said to them, "Behold, we are going up to Jerusalem, and everything that is written of the Son of man by the prophets will be accomplished. ³²For he will be delivered to the Gentiles, and will be mocked and shamefully treated and spit upon; ³³they will scourge him and kill him, and on the third day he will rise." ³⁴But they understood none of these things; this saying was hid from them, and they did not grasp what was said.

Lk 9:45

Curing of the blind man of Jericho
Mt 20:29-34
Mk 10:46-52

³⁵As he drew near to Jericho, a blind man was sitting by the roadside begging; ³⁶and hearing a multitude going by, he inquired what this meant. ³⁷They told him, "Jesus of Nazareth is passing by." ³⁸And he cried, "Jesus, Son of David, have mercy on me!" ³⁹And those who were in front rebuked him, telling him to be silent; but he cried out all the more, "Son of David, have mercy on me!" ⁴⁰And Jesus stopped, and commanded him to be brought to him; and when he came near, he asked him, ⁴¹"What do you want me to do for you?" He said, "Lord, let me receive my sight."

saeculo venturo vitam aeternam». ³¹Assumpsit autem Duodecim et ait illis: «Ecce ascendimus Ierusalem, et consummabuntur omnia, quae scripta sunt per Prophetas de Filio hominis: ³²tradetur enim gentibus et illudetur et contumeliis afficietur et conspuetur, ³³et, postquam flagellaverint, occident eum, et die tertia resurget». ³⁴Et ipsi nihil horum intellexerunt; et erat verbum istud absconditum ab eis, et non intellegebant, quae dicebantur. ³⁵Factum est autem cum appropinquaret Iericho, caecus quidam sedebat secus viam mendicans. ³⁶Et cum audiret turbam praetereuntem, interrogabat quid hoc esset. ³⁷Dixerunt autem ei: «Iesus Nazarenus transit». ³⁸Et clamavit dicens: «Iesu, fili David, miserere mei!». ³⁹Et qui praeibant, increpabant eum, ut taceret; ipse vero multo magis clamabat: «Fili David, miserere mei!». ⁴⁰Stans autem Iesus iussit illum adduci ad se. Et cum appropinquasset, interrogavit illum: ⁴¹«Quid tibi vis faciam?». At ille dixit: «Domine, ut videam». ⁴²Et Iesus dixit illi: «Respice! Fides

18:31-34 This is Jesus' third announcement of his passion; it appears in all the Synoptics. Luke records the largest number of intimations of the passion and resurrection (see 12:50; 13:32; 17:25), as well as the difficulty the disciples had in understanding what Jesus meant (v. 34). That difficulty is not surprising. Really, suffering only makes sense when seen in the light of Christ's death and resurrection, for "by suffering for us [Christ] not only gave us an example so that we might follow in his footsteps, but he also opened up a way. If we follow this path, life and death become holy and acquire a new meaning" (Vatican II, *Gaudium et spes*, 22). See also the note on 2 Thess 1:3-4.

18:35-43 This passage reads almost as though the information came from the blind man himself. He hears the crowd and asks what is happening (v. 36). When he learns that Jesus is passing by, he prays with all his might (vv. 38-39): "The thing I fear is that Jesus should pass by and not return" (St Augustine, *Sermones*, 88, 13). When the other people tell him to keep quiet, he cries out even louder (v. 39). He replies in all simplicity to Jesus' question (v. 41). His

faith earns his cure, which causes all the people to praise God (v. 43). The man paid no heed to what people might have thought of him—and he was cured: "When a Christian begins to live a good life and to do good works without regard to the judgments of this world, he may suffer the criticism and scorn of half-hearted Christians; but if he perseveres, he will win them over by his perseverance, and those who once scorned and rebuked him will come to greatly esteem him" (St Augustine, *Sermones*, 88, 18).

"Lord, let me receive my sight" (v. 41). We would do well to make our own this simple appeal in moments of doubt, when we cannot understand why God lets certain things happen; when we find it difficult to have faith; when our self-denial seems to serve no purpose. It is a good prayer for use by non-believers, that is, those who are seeking God in all sincerity: "Place yourself before the Lord each day and tell him slowly and in all earnestness, like the man in the Gospel who was in such great need, *Domine, ut videam!*—Lord, that I may see; that I may see what you expect from me, and struggle to be faithful to you" (St Josemaría Escrivá, *The Forge*, 318).

Lk 8:48

⁴²And Jesus said to him, "Receive your sight; your faith has made you well." ⁴³And immediately he received his sight and followed him, glorifying God; and all the people, when they saw it, gave praise to God.

The conversion of Zacchaeus

19 ¹He entered Jericho and was passing through. ²And there was a man named Zacchaeus; he was a chief tax collector, and rich. ³And he sought to see who Jesus was, but could not, on account of the crowd, because he was small of stature. ⁴So he ran on ahead and climbed up into a sycamore tree to see him, for he was to pass that way. ⁵And when Jesus came to the place, he looked up and said to him, "Zacchaeus, make haste and come down; for I must stay at your house today." ⁶So he

Lk 5:30; 15:2

Ex 21:37
Lk 12:33
2 Sam 12:6

made haste and came down, and received him joyfully. ⁷And when they saw it they all murmured, "He has gone in to be the guest of a man who is a sinner." ⁸And Zacchaeus stood and said to the Lord, "Behold, Lord, the half of my goods I give to the poor; and if I have defrauded any one of anything, I restore it fourfold." ⁹And Jesus said to

Ezek 34:16
Lk 13:6
1 Tim 1:15

him, "Today salvation has come to this house, since he also is a son of Abraham. ¹⁰For the Son of man came to seek and to save the lost."

tua te salvum fecit». ⁴³Et confestim vidit et sequebatur illum magnificans Deum. Et omnis plebs, ut vidit, dedit laudem Deo.   [19] ¹Et ingressus perambulabat Iericho. ²Et ecce vir nomine Zacchaeus, et hic erat princeps publicanorum et ipse dives. ³Et quaerebat videre Iesum quis esset, et non poterat prae turba, quia statura pusillus erat. ⁴Et praecurrens ascendit in arborem sycomorum, ut videret illum, quia inde erat transiturus. ⁵Et cum venisset ad locum, suspiciens Iesus dixit ad eum: «Zacchaee, festinans descende, nam hodie in domo tua oportet me manere». ⁶Et festinans descendit et excepit illum gaudens. ⁷Et cum viderent, omnes murmurabant dicentes: «Ad hominem peccatorem divertit!». ⁸Stans autem Zacchaeus dixit ad Dominum: «Ecce dimidium bonorum meorum, Domine, do pauperibus, et, si quid aliquem defraudavi, reddo quadruplum». ⁹Ait autem Iesus ad eum: «Hodie salus domui huic facta est, eo quod et ipse filius sit Abrahae; ¹⁰venit enim Filius hominis quaerere et salvum facere, quod perierat». ¹¹Haec autem illis audientibus, adiciens dixit parabolam, eo quod esset prope Ierusalem, et illi existimarent quod confestim regnum Dei manifestaretur. ¹²Dixit ergo: «Homo quidam nobilis abiit in regionem longinquam accipere sibi regnum et reverti. ¹³Vocatis autem decem

19:1–10 In several of his parables (cf. 15:1–32) Jesus vividly described the mercy shown by God when a sinner repents. The story of Zacchaeus is a case in point. This man is a son of Abraham (v. 9) who has not been living according to the demands of the Covenant (cf. vv. 2, 7). But Jesus has come to save everyone, even those who have strayed (cf. 15:1–7 and Ezek 34:16: "I will seek the lost, and I will bring back the strayed, and I will bind up the crippled, and I will strengthen the weak ..."). And so, in response to Zacchaeus' curiosity, Jesus calls him by his name and welcomes him (v. 5). That meeting with Christ results in joy (v. 6) and salvation (vv. 9–10).

Many lessons flow from this episode. Firstly, that our Lord looks for us, no matter what situation we find or place ourselves in. Zacchaeus was a tax collector working for the Roman authorities; because of this, and because these collectors abused their position, they were despised by the people. "[Our Lord] chooses a chief tax collector: who can despair when such a man obtains grace?" (St Ambrose, *Expositio*

Evangelii secundum Lucam, ad loc.).

We can learn, too, from Zacchaeus' attitude. From the way he behaves, the reader can sense that it was on account of something more than curiosity that he "ran on ahead" and climbed into a sycamore tree (v. 4). Perhaps that was why Jesus called out to him. Our search for God should be like that of Zacchaeus: we should not care what people may think. "Convince yourself that there is no such thing as ridicule for whoever is doing what is best" (St Josemaría Escrivá, *The Way*, 392).

Finally, there is the way Zacchaeus responds to grace. By resolving to restore fourfold anything he has wrongly appropriated, he fulfils the Law of Moses (see Ex 21:37); and, in addition, he gives away half his property: "Let the rich learn", St Ambrose comments, "that evil does not consist in having wealth, but in not putting it to good use; for just as riches are an obstacle to evil people, they are also a means of virtue for good people" (*Expositio Evangelium secundum Lucam*, ad loc.).

Parable of the pounds

Mt 25:14–30

[11]As they heard these things, he proceeded to tell a parable, because he was near to Jerusalem, and because they supposed that the kingdom of God was to appear immediately. [12]He said therefore, "A nobleman went into a far country to receive kingly power[d] and then return. [13]Calling ten of his servants, he gave them ten pounds,[e] and said to them, 'Trade with these till I come.' [14]But his citizens hated him and sent an embassy after him, saying, 'We do not want this man to reign over us.' [15]When he returned, having received the kingly power,[d] he commanded these servants, to whom he had given the money, to be called to him, that he might know what they had gained by trading. [16]The first came before him, saying, 'Lord, your pound has made ten pounds more.' [17]And he said to him, 'Well done, good servant! Because you have been faithful in a very little, you shall have authority over ten cities.' [18]And the second came, saying, 'Lord, your pound has made five pounds.' [19]And he said to him, 'And you are to be over five cities.' [20]Then another came, saying, 'Lord, here is your pound, which I kept laid away in a napkin; [21]for I was afraid of you, because you are a severe man; you take up what you did not lay down, and reap what you did not sow.' [22]He said to him, 'I will condemn you out of your own mouth, you wicked servant! You knew that I was a severe man, taking up what I did not lay down and reaping what I did not sow? [23]Why then did you not put my money into the bank, and at my coming I should have collected it with interest?' [24]And he said to those who stood by, 'Take the pound from him, and give it to him who has the ten pounds.' [25](And they said to him, 'Lord, he has ten pounds!') [26]'I tell you, that to every one who has will more be given; but from him who has not,

Acts 1:6

Ps 2:2f

Lk 16:10

Lk 8:18
Mt 13:12
Mk 4:25

servis suis, dedit illis decem minas, et ait ad illos: "Negotiamini, dum venio". [14]Cives autem eius oderant illum et miserunt legationem post illum dicentes: "Nolumus hunc regnare super nos!". [15]Et factum est ut rediret, accepto regno, et iussit ad se vocari servos illos, quibus dedit pecuniam, ut sciret quantum negotiati essent. [16]Venit autem primus dicens: "Domine, mina tua decem minas acquisivit". [17]Et ait illi: "Euge, bone serve; quia in modico fidelis fuisti, esto potestatem habens supra decem civitates". [18]Et alter venit dicens: "Mina tua, domine, fecit quinque minas". [19]Et huic ait: "Et tu esto supra quinque civitates". [20]Et alter venit dicens: "Domine, ecce mina tua, quam habui repositam in sudario; [21]timui enim te, quia homo austerus es: tollis, quod non posuisti, et metis, quod non seminasti". [22]Dicit ei: "De ore tuo te iudico, serve nequam! Sciebas quod ego austerus homo sum, tollens quod non posui et metens quod non seminavi? [23]Et quare non dedisti pecuniam meam ad mensam? Et ego veniens cum usuris utique exegissem illud". [24]Et adstantibus dixit: "Auferte ab illo minam et date illi, qui decem minas habet". [25]Et dixerunt ei: "Domine, habet decem minas!". [26]Dico vobis: "Omni habenti dabitur; ab eo autem, qui non habet, et, quod habet, auferetur". [27]Verumtamen inimicos meos

19:11–27 The parable of the pounds would have reminded Jesus' audience of recent events. Flavius Josephus records that after the death of Herod (around the year 4 or 3 BC), Herod's son Archelaus went to Rome to have his royal title confirmed. However, some leading Jews, who considered him a ruthless man, travelled after him to petition Caesar not to grant him the title. In Archelaus' absence, some of his aides administered his property (see *Antiquitates iudaicae*, 17, 299–314; *De bello iudaico*, 2:1–19). The "mina" (v. 13), here translated as "pound", was not a coin but a measure of value worth 570 grammes (20 ounces) of silver, the equivalent of 100 drachmas.

The parable is similar to the parable of the talents, narrated, by St Matthew, but each account has its unique features (see Mt 25:14–30 and note). Jesus tells this parable to correct the idea people had of a Messiah who would immediately set up in glory and power the Kingdom of God (see v. 11). He tells them that he will come as King and Judge; his disciples should pay no heed to the enemies of the Kingdom (v. 14) but, rather, concentrate on developing the inheritance they have received. If we appreciate the treasures God has given us (life, the gift of faith, grace), we will strive to make them bear fruit—by performing our duties, by working hard and doing apostolate. "Don't let your life be barren. Be useful. Make yourself felt. Shine forth with the torch of your faith and your love. With your apostolic life, wipe out the trail of filth and slime left by the corrupt sowers of hatred. And set aflame all the ways of the earth with the fire of Christ that you bear in your heart" (St Josemaría Escrivá, *The Way*, 1).

d Greek *a kingdom* e The mina, rendered here by *pound*, was about three months' wages for a labourer

Ps 2:9 even what he has will be taken away. ²⁷But as for these enemies of mine, who did not want me to reign over them, bring them here and slay them before me.'"

PART THREE

The Jerusalem ministry*

11. CLEANSING OF THE TEMPLE. CONTROVERSIES*

Mt 21:1–11
Mk 11:1–11
Jn 12:12–19

The Messiah enters the Holy City

²⁸And when he had said this, he went on ahead, going up to Jerusalem. ²⁹When he drew near to Bethphage and Bethany, at the mount that is called Olivet, he sent two of the disciples, ³⁰saying, "Go into the village opposite, where on entering you will find a colt tied, on which no one has ever yet sat; untie it and bring it here. ³¹If any one asks you, 'Why are you untying it?' you shall say this, 'The Lord has need of

illos, qui noluerunt me regnare super se, adducite huc et interficite ante me!». ²⁸Et his dictis, praecedebat ascendens Hierosolymam. ²⁹Et factum est cum appropinquasset ad Bethfage et Bethaniam, ad montem, qui vocatur Oliveti, misit duos discipulos ³⁰dicens: «Ite in castellum, quod contra est, in quod introeuntes invenietis pullum asinae alligatum, cui nemo umquam hominum sedit; solvite illum et adducite. ³¹Et si quis vos interrogaverit: "Quare solvitis?", sic dicetis: "Dominus eum necessarium habet"». ³²Abierunt autem, qui missi erant, et invenerunt, sicut dixit illis. ³³Sol-

*19:28—24:53 Luke's account of Jesus' last week in Jerusalem deals with the following events—his entry into the Holy City and the cleansing of the temple (19:28–48), controversies with Jewish authorities (20:1–44), the eschatological discourse (21:5–36), and a lengthy narrative of the passion (22:1—23:56) and the resurrection (24:1–53). Throughout his account, Luke highlights Jesus' feelings of compassion (19:41–44) and mercy (22:51; 23:34, 43), his greatness of soul (22:21–30, 47–53; 23:26–49) and his constant recourse to prayer (22:32, 39–46; 23:34, 46). Jesus is presented as the model that Christians should imitate.

This third part of the Gospel ends with our Lord commanding his apostles to stay in Jerusalem until the coming of the Holy Spirit, and with an account of the Ascension (24:49–53)—the same events as are covered in the opening chapters of the Acts of the Apostles (Acts 1:4–11), the volume in which Luke describes the public manifestation of the Church and its spread across the empire.

*19:28—21:38 The cleansing of the temple and the controversies with the Jewish authorities in

the days prior to our Lord's passion are covered by the three Synoptics in much the same way. Luke expressly notes the authorities' desire to do away with Jesus (19:47–48; 20:19, 20, 26). These events fulfil the prophecy that Jesus would be the cornerstone (20:17–18) established "for the fall and rising of many in Israel, and for a sign that is spoken against" (2:34). Luke's account of the Eschatological Discourse is shorter than those given in the other Synoptics, because much of what their discourses contain has been reported previously by Luke in his account of Jesus' journey to Jerusalem.

19:28–40 Jerusalem, the goal of the long journey, will be where the redemptive sacrifice of the cross takes place. Jesus' triumphal entry into the Holy City manifests him to be the Messiah. By riding on an ass, he fulfils another prophetic oracle: "Rejoice greatly, O daughter of Zion! Shout aloud, O daughter of Jerusalem! Lo, your king comes to you; triumphant and victorious is he, humble and riding on an ass, on a colt the foal of an ass" (Zech 9:9). The disciples' acclamation (v. 38) is their acknowledgment of him as King and Messiah, for they honour him with

it.'" ³²So those who were sent went away and found it as he had told them. ³³And as they were untying the colt, its owners said to them, "Why are you untying the colt?" ³⁴And they said, "The Lord has need of it." ³⁵And they brought it to Jesus, and throwing their garments on the colt they set Jesus upon it. ³⁶And as he rode along, they spread their garments on the road. ³⁷As he was now drawing near, at the descent of the Mount of Olives, the whole multitude of the disciples began to rejoice and praise God with a loud voice for all the mighty works that they had seen, ³⁸saying, *Ps 118:26* "Blessed is the King who comes in the name of the Lord! Peace in heaven and glory in the highest!" ³⁹And some of the Pharisees in the multitude said to him, "Teacher, rebuke your disciples." ⁴⁰He answered, "I tell you, if these were silent, the very *Hab 2:11* stones would cry out."

Jesus weeps over Jerusalem

⁴¹And when he drew near and saw the city he wept over it, ⁴²saying, "Would that *Lk 13:34–35* *Mt 23:37, 39* even today you knew the things that make for peace! But now they are hid from your eyes. ⁴³For the days shall come upon you, when your enemies will cast up a *Lk 21:20–24;* *23:28–31* bank about you and surround you, and hem you in on every side, ⁴⁴and dash you to *Lk 21:6*

ventibus autem illis pullum, dixerunt domini eius ad illos: «Quid solvitis pullum?». ³⁴At illi dixerunt: «Dominus eum necessarium habet». ³⁵Et duxerunt illum ad Iesum; et iactantes vestimenta sua supra pullum imposuerunt Iesum. ³⁶Eunte autem illo, substernebant vestimenta sua in via. ³⁷Et cum appropinquaret iam ad descensum montis Oliveti, coeperunt omnis multitudo discipulorum gaudentes laudare Deum voce magna super omnibus, quas viderant, virtutibus ³⁸dicentes: «*Benedictus, qui venit rex in nomine Domini!* / Pax in caelo et gloria in excelsis!». ³⁹Et quidam pharisaeorum de turbis dixerunt ad illum: «Magister, increpa discipulos tuos!». ⁴⁰Et respondens dixit: «Dico vobis: Si hi tacuerint, lapides clamabunt!». ⁴¹Et ut appropinquavit, videns civitatem flevit super illam ⁴²dicens: «Si cognovisses et tu in hac die, quae ad pacem tibi! Nunc autem abscondita sunt ab oculis tuis. ⁴³Quia venient dies in te, et circumdabunt te inimici tui vallo et obsidebunt te et coangustabunt te undique ⁴⁴et ad terram prosternent te et filios tuos, qui in te sunt, et non relinquent in te lapidem super lapidem, eo quod non cognoveris tempus visitationis tuae». ⁴⁵Et ingres-

words from a messianic coronation psalm (cf. Ps 118:26: "Blessed be he who enters in the name of the Lord!") and receive him as Saviour (cf. 2:11–14). Maybe because they are afraid of possible civil unrest, the Pharisees reproach Jesus for his behaviour, but he replies to them with a proverb, meaning by it that his being the Messiah is so self-evident that, if people refused to admit it, nature itself would burst into praise (v. 40). "Let us go out to meet Christ. He is making his way back from Bethany and, according to his will, making haste towards his most holy Passion, to open the mystery of salvation to all mankind. [...] Let us make haste as he makes haste towards his Passion, and go out to meet him as those who went out to meet him did. Not to lay olive branches or garments or palm branches on the path beneath his feet, but to prostrate ourselves before him, with the greatest humility of which we are capable, and the best intentions, to welcome the Word as he comes, and thus encounter God whom we can never fully embrace on our own. [...] The palm branches will be our praise for the final victory

of the cross. We will acclaim his coming not with olive branches, but with our generosity and love for one another. We will cover the ground he walks on not with garments, but with our heart's desires, so that by walking on us he may come within us and join us to himself as he joins himself to us" (St Andrew of Crete, *Sermo 9 de Dominica in Palmis*).

19:41–44 When the procession reaches a place that looks out on a good view of the city, the disciples' joy is disturbed by Jesus' unexpected weeping. His lament (Luke is the only evangelist to record it) expresses his heartfelt desire, and is, at the same time, a last appeal to Jerusalem. Zechariah, the father of John the Baptist, was able to see in the events surrounding his son's birth the "visit" of God and his Messiah to his people (see 1:68, 78); but Jerusalem, which has witnessed so many signs worked by Jesus, has failed to acknowledge him for what he is (vv. 42, 44). The eventual destruction of the temple and the Holy City by the armies of the Roman general Titus in the

the ground, you and your children within you, and they will not leave one stone upon another in you; because you did not know the time of your visitation."*

Mt 21:12–17
Mk 11:15–19
Jn 2:13–25

Jesus in the temple

Mt 21:12–16
Is 56:7
Jer 7:11

⁴⁵And he entered the temple and began to drive out those who sold, ⁴⁶saying to them, "It is written, 'My house shall be a house of prayer'; but you have made it a den of robbers."

Lk 20:19; 22:53
Jn 18:20

⁴⁷And he was teaching daily in the temple. The chief priests and the scribes and the principal men of the people sought to destroy him; ⁴⁸but they did not find anything they could do, for all the people hung upon his words.

Mt 21:23–27
Mk 11:27–33

Jesus' authority

20 ¹One day, as he was teaching the people in the temple and preaching the gospel, the chief priests and the scribes with the elders came up ²and said to him, "Tell us by what authority you do these things, or who it is that gave you this authority." ³He answered them, "I also will ask you a question; now tell me, ⁴Was the baptism of John from heaven or from men?" ⁵And they discussed it with one another, saying, "If we say, 'From heaven,' he will say, 'Why did you not believe him?' ⁶But if we say, 'From men,' all the people will stone us; for they are convinced that John was a prophet." ⁷So they answered that they did not know whence it was. ⁸And Jesus said to them, "Neither will I tell you by what authority I do these things."

sus in templum, coepit eicere vendentes ⁴⁶dicens illis: «Scriptum est: "*Et erit domus mea domus orationis*". Vos autem fecistis illam *speluncam latronum*». ⁴⁷Et erat docens cotidie in templo. Principes autem sacerdotum et scribae et principes plebis quaerebant illum perdere ⁴⁸et non inveniebant quid facerent; omnis enim populus suspensus erat audiens illum.   [20] ¹Et factum est in una dierum, docente illo populum in templo et evangelizante, supervenerunt principes sacerdotum et scribae cum senioribus ²et aiunt dicentes ad illum: «Dic nobis: In qua potestate haec facis aut quis est qui dedit tibi hanc potestatem?». ³Respondens autem dixit ad illos: «Interrogabo vos et ego verbum; et dicite mihi: ⁴Baptismum Ioannis de caelo erat an ex hominibus?». ⁵At illi cogitabant inter se dicentes: «Si dixerimus: "De caelo", dicet: "Quare non credidistis illi?"; ⁶si autem dixerimus: "Ex hominibus", plebs universa lapidabit nos; certi sunt enim Ioannem prophetam esse». ⁷Et responderunt se nescire unde esset. ⁸Et Iesus ait illis: «Neque ego dico vobis in qua potestate haec facio». ⁹Coepit autem dicere ad plebem parabolam hanc: «Homo *plantavit vineam* et

year 70, prophesied here by our Lord (vv. 43–44), is a sign that the Old Covenant has ceased to operate and is being replaced by the New Covenant that will be sealed on Calvary. We, too, are each of us visited by Jesus; he comes as our Saviour and teaches us through the Church's preaching; he grants us forgiveness and grace through the sacraments. If we are faithful and attentive to his word, we can ensure that our Lord has not come in vain. St Ambrose is addressing virgins when he makes the following point, but it applies to everyone: "Look after the house, clean the most secluded rooms; when the house is perfectly clean, the spiritual house founded on the cornerstone, the spiritual priesthood will be built and the Holy Spirit come to live there. Those who seek Christ in this way, who pray to Christ in this way, will find that he is always close, and will often come to stay in their home" (*De virginitate*, 13, 78).

19:45–48 What Jesus foretold now reaches fulfilment: he cleanses the temple, and the rulers of the people begin to plan his death. Apart from its prophetic meaning (cf. the notes on Mt 21:12–17 and Mk 11:12–25), Jesus' cleansing of the temple is a reminder of the respect due to the House of the Lord. Christian temples that house the Blessed Eucharist are worthy of even greater reverence.

20:1–8 This exchange takes the form of a theological dispute in which our Lord has the last word. It should come as no surprise that he refused to answer these elders. "Jesus has no time for calculations, for astuteness, for the cruelty of cold hearts, for attractive but empty beauty. What he likes is the cheerfulness of a young heart, a simple step, a natural voice, clean eyes, attention to his affectionate word of advice" (St Josemaría Escrivá, *Christ Is Passing By*, 181).

Parable of the wicked tenants

Mt 21:33–46
Mk 12:1–12
Is 5:1
2 Chron 36:15–17

⁹And he began to tell the people this parable: "A man planted a vineyard, and let it out to tenants, and went into another country for a long while. ¹⁰When the time came, he sent a servant to the tenants, that they should give him some of the fruit of the vineyard; but the tenants beat him, and sent him away empty-handed. ¹¹And he sent another servant; him also they beat and treated shamefully, and sent him away empty-handed. ¹²And he sent yet a third; this one they wounded and cast out. ¹³Then the owner of the vineyard said, 'What shall I do? I will send my beloved son; it may be they will respect him.' ¹⁴But when the tenants saw him, they said to themselves, 'This is the heir; let us kill him, that the inheritance may be ours.' ¹⁵And they cast him out of the vineyard and killed him. What then will the owner of the vineyard do to them? ¹⁶He will come and destroy those tenants, and give the vineyard to others." When they heard this, they said, "God forbid!" ¹⁷But he looked at them and said, "What then is this that is written:

Ps 118:22

'The very stone which the builders rejected
has become the head of the corner'?

¹⁸Every one who falls on that stone will be broken to pieces; but when it falls on any one it will crush him."

Is 8:14
Dan 2:34–44

¹⁹The scribes and chief priests tried to lay hands on him at that very hour, but they feared the people; for they perceived that he had told this parable against them.

Lk 19:47–48

Tribute to Caesar

Mt 22:15–22
Mk 12:13–17
Lk 11:54

²⁰So they watched him, and sent spies, who pretended to be sincere, that they might take hold of what he said, so as to deliver him up to the authority and jurisdiction of

locavit eam colonis et ipse peregre fuit multis temporibus. ¹⁰Et in tempore misit ad cultores servum, ut de fructu vineae darent illi; cultores autem caesum dimiserunt eum inanem. ¹¹Et addidit alterum servum mittere; illi autem hunc quoque caedentes et afficientes contumelia dimiserunt inanem. ¹²Et addidit tertium mittere; qui et illum vulnerantes eiecerunt. ¹³Dixit autem dominus vineae: "Quid faciam? Mittam filium meum dilectum; forsitan hunc verebuntur". ¹⁴Quem cum vidissent coloni, cogitaverunt inter se dicentes: "Hic est heres. Occidamus illum, ut nostra fiat hereditas". ¹⁵Et eiectum illum extra vineam occiderunt. Quid ergo faciet illis dominus vineae? ¹⁶Veniet et perdet colonos istos et dabit vineam aliis». Quo audito, dixerunt: «Absit!». ¹⁷Ille autem aspiciens eos ait: «Quid est ergo hoc, quod scriptum est: / "Lapidem, quem reprobaverunt aedificantes, / hic factus est in caput anguli"? ¹⁸Omnis, qui ceciderit supra illum lapidem, conquassabitur; supra quem autem ceciderit, comminuet illum». ¹⁹Et quaerebant scribae et principes sacerdotum mittere in illum manus in illa hora et timuerunt populum; cognoverunt enim quod ad ipsos dixerit similitudinem istam. ²⁰Et observantes miserunt insidiatores, qui se iustos simularent, ut caperent eum in sermone, et sic traderent illum

20:9–19 Given the immediate context in which it was told, the parable of the wicked tenants must have had an unnerving effect (cf. the notes on Mt 21:28–46 and Mk 12:1–12). Jesus clearly identifies himself as the beloved son (v. 13; cf. 3:22) who is cast out of the vineyard (v. 15), Jerusalem, to be put to death. And Jesus is also the cornerstone of the new house of God (v. 17; cf. Ps 118:22), the stone seen by the prophet Daniel (Dan 2:34–35) which, becoming detached from the mountain "by no human hand", crushes human empires (v. 18). We see here the fulfilment of Simeon's prophecy (see 2:34): those who reject him meet their downfall.

20:20–26 For a third time, St Luke records the machinations of the Jewish authorities to do away with Jesus (v. 20; see 6:7; 14:1), though the flattery with which these men preface their questions shows that their astuteness to be increasingly insidious (vv. 21–22). A refusal to pay tribute to Rome would have allowed them to report Jesus to the Roman authorities as a rebel (see v. 20). But the Teacher sees through their questions and asks them to hand him a coin, a denarius. An image of the head of Caesar is stampled on it, along with the words "Tiberius Caesar, son of divine Augustus", and Jesus uses this design to confound his adversaries: payment of tax (and his questioners themselves paid it) does not mean acknowledging Caesar to be God. Jesus is the Messiah, but he rejects political messianism; he has no intention of sitting in political judgment on the authority of Rome, for the

the governor. [21]They asked him, "Teacher, we know that you speak and teach rightly, and show no partiality, but truly teach the way of God. [22]Is it lawful for us to give tribute to Caesar, or not?" [23]But he perceived their craftiness, and said to them, [24]"Show me a coin.[f] Whose likeness and inscription has it?" They said, "Caesar's."

Rom 13:7

[25]He said to them, "Then render to Caesar the things that are Caesar's, and to God the things that are God's." [26]And they were not able in the presence of the people to catch him by what he said; but marvelling at his answer they were silent.

Mt 22:23–33
Mk 12:18–27

The resurrection of the dead

Mt 22:23–33, 46

Gen 38:8
Deut 25:5–6

[27]There came to him some Sadducees, those who say that there is no resurrection, [28]and they asked him a question, saying, "Teacher, Moses wrote for us that if a man's brother dies, having a wife but no children, the man[g] must take the wife and raise up children for his brother. [29]Now there were seven brothers; the first took a wife, and died without children; [30]and the second [31]and the third took her, and likewise all seven left no children and died. [32]Afterward the woman also died. [33]In the resurrection, therefore, whose wife will the woman be? For the seven had her as wife."

[34]And Jesus said to them, "The sons of this age marry and are given in marriage;

Phil 3:11

1 Jn 3:1–2

[35]but those who are accounted worthy to attain to that age and to the resurrection from the dead neither marry nor are given in marriage, [36]for they cannot die any more, because they are equal to angels and are sons of God, being sons of the res-

principatui et potestati praesidis. [21]Et interrogaverunt illum dicentes: «Magister, scimus quia recte dicis et doces et non accipis personam, sed in veritate viam Dei doces. [22]Licet nobis dare tributum Caesari an non?». [23]Considerans autem dolum illorum dixit ad eos: [24]«Ostendite mihi denarium. Cuius habet imaginem et inscriptionem?». [25]At illi dixerunt: «Caesaris». Et ait illis: «Reddite ergo, quae Caesaris sunt, Caesari et, quae Dei sunt, Deo». [26]Et non potuerunt verbum eius reprehendere coram plebe et mirati in responso eius tacuerunt. [27]Accesserunt autem quidam sadducaeorum, qui negant esse resurrectionem, et interrogaverunt eum [28]dicentes: «Magister, Moyses scripsit nobis, si frater alicuius mortuus fuerit habens uxorem et hic sine filiis fuerit, ut accipiat eam frater eius uxorem et suscitet semen fratri suo. [29]Septem ergo fratres erant: et primus accepit uxorem et mortuus est sine filiis; [30]et sequens [31]et tertius accepit illam, similiter autem et septem non reliquerunt filios et mortui sunt. [32]Novissima mortua est et mulier. [33]Mulier ergo in resurrectione cuius eorum erit uxor? Siquidem septem habuerunt eam uxorem». [34]Et ait illis Iesus: «Filii saeculi huius nubunt et traduntur ad nuptias; [35]illi autem, qui digni habentur saeculo illo et resurrectione ex mortuis, neque nubunt, neque ducunt uxores. [36]Neque enim ultra mori possunt: aequales enim angelis sunt et filii sunt Dei, cum sint filii resurrectionis. [37]Quia vero resurgant mortui et

Kingdom of God that he preaches and practises is of a different sort entirely. What he says here does spell out how a Christian should act in society: "As we have been instructed by him [Jesus], we before all others try everywhere to pay your appointed officials the ordinary and special taxes" (St Justin, *Apologia*, 1, 17, 1). The Church avails herself of these texts to spell out the way church/state relations should operate: "The political community and the Church are autonomous and independent of each other in their own fields. Nevertheless, both are devoted to the personal vocation of man, though under different titles. This service will redound the more effectively to the welfare of all insofar as both institutions practise better cooperation according to the local and prevailing situation" (Vatican II, *Gaudium et spes*, 76).

20:27–40 The Sadducees were very literal in

their interpretation of what "Moses wrote for us" and did not believe in the resurrection of the body, whereas the Pharisees (see Acts 23:8) did accept that doctrine as found in some texts of Scripture (especially Dan 12:2–3) and in oral tradition. In reply to the sly question put to him here, Jesus touches on some aspects of the general resurrection (cf. the note on Mt 22:23–33): in the afterlife there will be no need for marriage, for after the resurrection there will be a new kind of life which is not the result of intercourse between man and woman; it comes directly from God himself (v. 38). "For man, this consummation will be the final realization of the unity of the human race, which God willed from creation [...]. The beatific vision, in which God opens himself in an inexhaustible way to the elect, will be the ever-flowing well-spring of happiness, peace, and mutual communion" (*Catechism of the Catholic Church*, 1045).

f Greek *denarius* g Greek *his brother*

urrection. ³⁷But that the dead are raised, even Moses showed, in the passage about
the bush, where he calls the Lord the God of Abraham and the God of Isaac and the
God of Jacob.* ³⁸Now he is not God of the dead, but of the living; for all live to
him." ³⁹And some of the scribes answered, "Teacher, you have spoken well." ⁴⁰For
they no longer dared to ask him any question.

Ex 3:6

Rom 14:8
Mk 12:34

The divinity of the Messiah
⁴¹But he said to them, "How can they say that the Christ is David's son? ⁴²For David
himself says in the Book of Psalms,
    'The Lord said to my Lord,
      Sit at my right hand,
      ⁴³till I make thy enemies a stool for thy feet.'
⁴⁴David thus calls him Lord; so how is he his son?"

Mt 22:41–46
Mk 12:35–37
Jn 7:42

Ps 110:1

Jesus condemns the scribes
⁴⁵And in the hearing of all the people he said to his disciples, ⁴⁶"Beware of the
scribes, who like to go about in long robes, and love salutations in the market places
and the best seats in the synagogues and the places of honour at feasts, ⁴⁷who devour
widow's houses and for a pretence make long prayers. They will receive the greater
condemnation."

Mt 23:1–36
Mk 12:38–40
Lk 11:43; 14:7

Lk 18:9–12

The widow's mite
21 ¹He looked up and saw the rich putting their gifts into the treasury; ²and he
saw a poor widow put in two copper coins. ³And he said, "Truly I tell you,
this poor widow has put in more than all of them; ⁴for they all contributed out of
their abundance, but she out of her poverty put in all the living that she had."

Mk 12:41–44

2 Cor 8:12
Lk 12:15

Moyses ostendit secus rubum, sicut dicit: "*Dominum Deum Abraham et Deum Isaac et Deum Iacob*". ³⁸Deus autem non est mortuorum sed vivorum:
omnes enim vivunt ei». ³⁹Respondentes autem quidam scribarum dixerunt: «Magister, bene dixisti». ⁴⁰Et amplius non audebant eum quidquam interrogare. ⁴¹Dixit autem ad illos: «Quomodo dicunt Christum filium David esse? ⁴²Ipse enim David dicit in libro Psalmorum: "*Dixit Dominus Domino meo:
Sede a dextris meis,/ ⁴³donec ponam inimicos tuos scabellum pedum tuorum*". ⁴⁴David ergo Dominum illum vocat; et quomodo filius eius est?». ⁴⁵Audi-
ente autem omni populo, dixit discipulis suis: ⁴⁶«Attendite a scribis, qui volunt ambulare in stolis et amant salutationes in foro et primas cathedras in synagogis et primos discubitus in conviviis, ⁴⁷qui devorant domos viduarum et simulant longam orationem. Hi accipient damnationem maiorem». [21]
¹Respiciens autem vidit eos, qui mittebant munera sua in gazophylacium, divites. ²Vidit autem quandam viduam pauperculam mittentem illuc minuta

20:41–44 "Lord" ("Kyrios") was the word in
common use among Greek-speaking Jews to
refer to God. In this passage (cf. the notes on Mt
22:41–46 and Mk 12:35–37), "Jesus ascribes this
title to himself in a veiled way when he disputes
with the Pharisees about the meaning of Psalm
110 [...]. Throughout his public life, he demon-
strated his divine sovereignty by works of power
over nature, illnesses, demons, death and sin."
(*Catechism of the Catholic Church*, 447).

20:45–47 What Jesus says here amplifies what
he said on another occasion (see 11:43). According to Jewish traditions of the time, later
recorded in the Talmud, the best seats in the synagogue were reserved for doctors of the Law,
and the places of honour at meals were for elders

or people of eminence. Our Lord is not taking
issue with this; he is saying that people who
desire only to be prominent (v. 46) are headed
for a fall (v. 47). There is a lesson here for everyone: "Let us flee from vanity, and hate all the
sins found on the wrong path; do not set yourself
apart or withdraw into yourself, as though you
had already been justified" (*Epistula Barnabae*,
4, 10–11).

21:1–4 Jesus draws attention to this poor
widow's good deed (vv. 1–2)—which is in sharp
contrast to the way scribes devoured the property
of widows (20:47). His comments (vv. 3–4)
show that she has set an example that all should
follow in their behaviour towards God: "The
Lord does not look at the amount offered but at

12. THE ESCHATOLOGICAL DISCOURSE*

Mt 24:1–2
Mk 13:1–2
Announcement of the destruction of the temple

Lk 19:44
⁵And as some spoke of the temple, how it was adorned with noble stones and offerings, he said, ⁶"As for these things which you see, the days will come when there shall not be left here one stone upon another that will not be thrown down."

Mt 24:3–14
Mk 13:3–13
The beginning of tribulation. Persecution on account of the Gospel

⁷And they asked him, "Teacher, when will this be, and what will be the sign when this is about to take place?" ⁸And he said, "Take heed that you are not led astray;

duo ³et dixit: «Vere dico vobis: Vidua haec pauper plus quam omnes misit. ⁴Nam omnes hi ex abundantia sua miserunt in munera; haec autem ex inopia sua omnem victum suum, quem habebat, misit». ⁵Et quibusdam dicentibus de templo quod lapidibus bonis et donis ornatum esset dixit: ⁶«Haec, quae videtis, venient dies in quibus non relinquetur lapis super lapidem, qui non destruatur». ⁷Interrogaverunt autem illum dicentes: «Praeceptor, quando ergo haec erunt, et quod signum, cum fieri incipient?». ⁸Qui dixit: «Videte, ne seducamini. Multi enim venient in nomine meo dicentes: "Ego

the affection with which it is offered. It is not a question of giving a little of what you have, but, like the widow, of giving everything you have" (St John Chrysostom, *In Hebraeos*, 1, 4).

*21:5–36 The three Synoptic Gospels (cf. Mt 24:1–51; Mk 13:1–37, and notes) record this discourse of Jesus outside the temple, in which he speaks about the destruction of Jerusalem and the end of time. Three themes are interwoven in the discourse—the destruction of Jerusalem (which took place some forty years later); the signs that will presage the end of the world; and the second coming of Christ, in glory and majesty. Our Lord's words here are in the style and language of the genre of apocalyptic writing (cf. the "Introduction" to the book of Revelation, below)—an imagistic style and a symbolic language that are not always easy to interpret.

21:5–6 This discourse is sparked off by the disciples' amazement at the magnificence of the temple "adorned with noble stones and offerings" (v. 5). In the year 20 BC Herod the Great had set about rebuilding and extending the temple, which dated from the years after the exile in Babylon (sixth century BC). The work was completed in AD 64; that is, just a few years before the Romans razed it to the ground. The process of rebuilding must have been quite far advanced when this episode occurred. Every Jew of the time must have been proud of the temple's sheer scale, its harmonious ornamentation, and the richness of the materials used (see Flavius

Josephus, *De bello iudaica*, 184–237; *Antiquitates iudaicae*, 15, 11). The disciples, too, were in awe of the temple; and Jesus' prediction must have truly surprised them.

21:7–19 The disciples' question (v. 7) leads Jesus to announce the destruction of the temple. That event will be preceded by the appearance of false messiahs (v. 8), wars and revolutions (v. 9). These things should not alarm them: they should "take heed" not to be led astray (v. 8), "not be terrified" (v. 9). Jesus also says that they are not signs that the world is coming to an end (v. 9). First, the "times of the Gentiles" must come (21:24).

He goes on (vv. 10–19) to predict further disasters (vv. 10–11), and the trials his disciples must undergo to spread the Kingdom of God—persecution, misunderstanding, hatred etc. (vv. 12, 16, 17). However, a positive message runs through what our Lord is saying. Firstly, he promises them help from God (vv. 14–15): divine providence takes account of all these difficulties, severe though they may be. They occur because God permits them, being able to use them to advantage. Persecution will give the disciples an opportunity to bear witness to him. In the famous wording of early Christian apologetics: "Sanguis martyrum semen Christianorum", "The blood of martyrs is the seed of new Christians" (Tertullian, *Apologeticum*, 50, 13).

Our Lord also promises them special help: he will give them his wisdom to defend themselves, and even apparent disaster will be a foretaste of glory. They will prove victorious if they are

for many will come in my name, saying, 'I am he!' and, 'The time is at hand!' Do not go after them. [9]And when you hear of wars and tumults, do not be terrified; for this must first take place, but the end will not be at once."

[10]Then he said to them, "Nation will rise against nation, and kingdom against kingdom; [11]there will be great earthquakes, and in various places famines and pestilences; and there will be terrors and great signs from heaven. [12]But before all this they will lay their hands on you and persecute you, delivering you up to the synagogues and prisons, and you will be brought before kings and governors for my name's sake. [13]This will be a time for you to bear testimony. [14]Settle it therefore in your minds, not to meditate beforehand how to answer; [15]for I will give you a mouth and wisdom, which none of your adversaries will be able to withstand or contradict. [16]You will be delivered up even by parents and brothers and kinsmen and friends, and some of you they will put to death; [17]you will be hated by all for my name's sake. [18]But not a hair of your head will perish. [19]By your endurance you will gain your lives.

Dan 2:28

Is 19:2
2 Chron 15:6
Lk 12:11
Mt 10:17–22
Jn 15:20; 16:1–2

Lk 12:11–12
Acts 6:10

Mt 10:21–22

Lk 12:7
Mt 10:30
Heb 10:36, 39

The great tribulation in Jerusalem

Mt 24:15–28
Mk 13:14–23

[20]"But when you see Jerusalem surrounded by armies, then know that its desolation has come near. [21]Then let those who are in Judea flee to the mountains, and let those who are inside the city depart, and let not those who are out in the coun-

sum" et: "Tempus appropinquavit". Nolite ergo ire post illos. [9]Cum autem audieritis proelia et seditiones, nolite terreri; oportet enim primum haec fieri, sed non statim finis». [10]Tunc dicebat illis: «Surget gens contra gentem et regnum adversus regnum; [11]et terrae motus magni et per loca fames et pestilentiae erunt, terroresque et de caelo signa magna erunt. [12]Sed ante haec omnia inicient vobis manus suas et persequentur tradentes in synagogas et custodias, et trahemini ad reges et praesides propter nomen meum; [13]continget autem vobis in testimonium. [14]Ponite ergo in cordibus vestris non praemeditari quemadmodum respondeatis; [15]ego enim dabo vobis os et sapientiam, cui non poterunt resistere vel contradicere omnes adversarii vestri. [16]Trademini autem et a parentibus et fratribus et cognatis et amicis, et morte afficient ex vobis, [17]et eritis odio omnibus propter nomen meum. [18]Et capillus de capite vestro non peribit. [19]In patientia vestra possidebitis animas vestras. [20]Cum autem videritis circumdari ab exercitu Ierusalem, tunc scitote quia appropinquavit desolatio eius. [21]Tunc, qui in Iudaea sunt, fugiant in montes; et, qui in medio eius, discedant;

steadfast and patient (vv. 18–19). Patience is an integral part of fortitude: "Virtue is needed if reason is not to be overcome by sadness, so that reason does not succumb to sorrow. This virtue is patience, which, as St Augustine says, 'allows us to withstand sufferings without loss of heart— that is, without sinking into sorrow; may we respond to trials with patience, for through impatience we fail to appreciate the good things that lead to greater things'" (St Thomas Aquinas, *Summa theologiae*, 2–2, 136, 1). So, as Jesus says here (v. 19), endurance (patience) will save us, because "it is through patience that man remains the master of his own soul, in so far as he is able to root out the worry and alarm caused by the contradictions that would deprive his soul of peace" (ibid., 2–2, 136, 2 ad 2).

21:20–24 The discourse continues to foreshadow the destruction of Jerusalem, with signs which are also signs of the end of the world. The focus

is especially on the fall of the city after it is besieged by armies (v. 20). Years later, when Christians saw the armies circling the city, they remembered our Lord's words and fled to Transjordan (see Eusebius of Caesarea, *Historia ecclesiastica*, 3, 5). Christian Tradition, drawing on the Scriptures, sees Jerusalem as a symbol of the Church (cf. Rev 21:2). Therefore, the trials undergone by the Holy City can be read as a figure of the pilgrim Church: "She herself takes her place among the creatures which groan and travail yet and await the revelation of the children of God" (Vatican II, *Lumen gentium*, 48). Verse 24 can also be read in this sense: Israel's captivity, that is, its disappearance as a nation, is a sign that "the times of the Gentiles" have come, that is, the epoch during which the Gentiles, who do not belong to the people of Israel, will come to belong to the new People of God, the Church; at the end of time the Jews will be converted (see Rom 11:25–32).

Deut 32:35
Hos 9:7

1 Thess 2:16

Deut 28:64
Dan 9:26; 12:7, 11

try enter it; ²²for these are days of vengeance, to fulfil all that is written. ²³Alas for those who are with child and for those who give suck in those days! For great distress shall be upon the earth and wrath upon this people; ²⁴they will fall by the edge of the sword, and be led captive among all nations; and Jerusalem will be trodden down by the Gentiles, until the times of the Gentiles* are fulfilled.

Mt 24:29–31
Mk 13:24–27

Ps 65:6
Is 34:4

Dan 7:13
Hag 2:6, 21

The coming of the Son of man
²⁵"And there will be signs in sun and moon and stars, and upon the earth distress of nations in perplexity at the roaring of the sea and the waves, ²⁶men fainting with fear and foreboding of what is coming on the world; for the powers of the heavens will be shaken. ²⁷And then they will see the Son of man coming in a cloud with power and great glory. ²⁸Now when these things begin to take place, look up and raise your heads, because your redemption is drawing near."

Mt 24:32–35
Mk 13:28–31

The end will surely come—the lesson of the fig tree
²⁹And he told them a parable: "Look at the fig tree, and all the trees; ³⁰as soon as they come out in leaf, you see for yourselves and know that the summer is already near. ³¹So also, when you see these things taking place, you know that the kingdom

---

et, qui in regionibus, non intrent in eam. ²²Quia dies ultionis hi sunt, ut impleantur omnia, quae scripta sunt. ²³Vae autem praegnantibus et nutrientibus in illis diebus! Erit enim pressura magna super terram et ira populo huic, ²⁴et cadent in ore gladii et captivi ducentur in omnes gentes, et Ierusalem calcabitur a gentibus, donec impleantur tempora nationum. ²⁵Et erunt signa in sole et luna et stellis, et super terram pressura gentium prae confusione sonitus maris et fluctuum, ²⁶arescentibus hominibus prae timore et exspectatione eorum, quae supervenient orbi, nam *virtutes caelorum* movebuntur. ²⁷Et tunc videbunt *Filium hominis venientem in nube* cum potestate et gloria magna. ²⁸His autem fieri incipientibus, respicite et levate capita vestra, quoniam appropinquat redemptio vestra». ²⁹Et dixit illis similitudinem: «Videte ficulneam et omnes arbores: ³⁰cum iam germinaverint, videntes vosmetipsi scitis quia iam prope est aestas. ³¹Ita et vos, cum videritis haec fieri, scitote quoniam prope est regnum

---

21:25–28 The misfortunes that befall Jerusalem are signs of what will happen before the Son of man comes: all creation (heavens, earth, sea) will be affected by the distress of nations (v. 25), their fear and foreboding. Christians, however, won't feel this distress; they will hold their heads high (v. 28), because Christ's victory (v. 27) is their victory, too. They will see how well-founded their hope was when they bore trials patiently (21:10–19): "My brothers, we must be patient and persevere, so that having been given hope of truth and freedom, we may embrace truth and freedom themselves. [...] Let no one abandon good works through impatience or, overcome by temptation, renounce the good life halfway along the path; he would lose the fruit of what he had done because he did not finish what he had begun" (St Cyprian, *De bono patientiae*, 13 and 15).

21:29–36 As is also the case in the other Synoptics (see the notes on Mt 24:32–41; Mk 13:28–37), the final part of the discourse is concerned with the second coming of Christ. Drawing a

comparison with the fig tree and other trees (vv. 29–33), our Lord assures his listeners that all that he has said will come to pass. Some readers may find v. 32 puzzling. "This generation", in apocalyptic language, can mean the entire period, from now until the moment when the Lord comes again and makes all things new. Also, read in context, "this generation" refers to what Jesus has just been talking about (v. 31), that is, the signs that will precede the fall of Jerusalem (21:7). But the events having to do with the End (of which the destruction of the city is a foretaste and a symbol) will happen without any warning (v. 35). The fact that Jerusalem did fall should serve as a warning to be alert, for the "Son of man" could come at any time; hence the final exhortation, to "watch at all times": if we pray (v. 36) and live a temperate life (v. 34) we will be ready for Jesus when he comes (see 21:28): "Let us be temperate in order to dedicate our soul to prayer, persevere in fasting and make our prayers to God who sees all things. [...] Let us cling tightly to our hope and to Jesus Christ, the pledge of our salvation. [...] Let us imitate his

of God is near. ³²Truly, I say to you, this generation will not pass away till all has taken place. ³³Heaven and earth will pass away, but my words will not pass away.

Lk 9:27

Lk 16:17

The need for vigilance

³⁴"But take heed to yourselves lest your hearts be weighed down with dissipation and drunkenness and cares of this life, and that day come upon you suddenly like a snare; ³⁵for it will come upon all who dwell upon the face of the whole earth. ³⁶But watch at all times, praying that you may have strength to escape all these things that will take place, and to stand before the Son of man."

Lk 17:27
Mt 24:49
Is 5:11–13

Is 24:17
Eccles 9:1
1 Thess 5:3

Eph 6:18

Jesus teaches in the temple

³⁷And every day he was teaching in the temple, but at night he went out and lodged on the mount called Olivet. ³⁸And early in the morning all the people came to him in the temple to hear him.

Lk 19:47
Jn 8:1f; 18:12

Mk 11:11, 19

13. THE PASSION, DEATH AND RESURRECTION OF JESUS*

Judas' treachery

22 ¹Now the feast of Unleavened Bread drew near, which is called the Passover. ²And the chief priests and the scribes were seeking how to put him to death; for they feared the people.

Mt 26:3–5, 14–16
Mk 14:1–2, 10–11

Jn 11:47–53
Lk 20:9

Dei. ³²Amen dico vobis: Non praeteribit generatio haec, donec omnia fiant. ³³Caelum et terra transibunt, verba autem mea non transibunt. ³⁴Attendite autem vobis, ne forte graventur corda vestra in crapula et ebrietate et curis huius vitae, et superveniat in vos repentina dies illa; ³⁵tamquam laqueus enim superveniet in omnes, qui sedent super faciem omnis terrae. ³⁶Vigilate itaque omni tempore orantes, ut possitis fugere ista omnia, quae futura sunt, et stare ante Filium hominis». ³⁷Erat autem diebus docens in templo, noctibus vero exiens morabatur in monte, qui vocatur Oliveti. ³⁸Et omnis populus manicabat ad eum in templo audire eum. [22] ¹Appropinquabat autem dies festus Azymorum, qui dicitur Pascha. ²Et quaerebant principes sacerdotum et scribae quomodo eum interficerent; timebant vero plebem. ³Intravit autem Satanas in Iudam, qui cog-

patience and, if we must suffer for his name, give him glory, for that is the example he gave us, that is what we believe" (St Polycarp, *Ad Philippenses*, 7–8).

21:37–38 The other two Synoptics suggest that Jesus spent these days in Bethany (see Mt 21:17; 26:6; Mk 11:11; 14:3). Mount Olivet (v. 37) lay between Jerusalem and Bethany. A little further on, in connexion with the agony in the garden, St Luke tells us that Jesus used to go there often. He probably went there to pray. Verse 37 may be another example of the importance that Jesus gave to daily prayer: "Each day try to find a few minutes of that blessed solitude you need so much to keep your interior life going" (St Josemaría Escrivá, *The Way*, 304).

*22:1—24:53 In all the Gospels, the account of the passion, death and resurrection of Jesus is presented in vivid and dramatic terms. In his nar-

rative of the passion, St Luke highlights Jesus' compassion; even in the midst of suffering, our Lord shows concern for those he meets: he cures the servant wounded by the sword (22:51), consoles some women (23:28ff), and promises Paradise to the good thief (23:43). After the Resurrection, it is the third Gospel (as compared with the other Synoptics) that has most to say about Jesus' appearances in Jerusalem. This is the city where the passion and death of Christ took place, and it is from here that salvation will spread throughout the world. Therefore, Jerusalem is not only where the drama of Jesus was played out but, more importantly, the place where our salvation was achieved.

Christians have always nurtured their repentance by meditating on these chapters: "What I call meditation is when we allow our mind to reason in this way: we begin by thinking of God's mercy in giving us his only Son, and go on to consider all the mysteries of his glorious

Jn 13:2, 27
Acts 5:3

³Then Satan entered into Judas called Iscariot, who was of the number of the twelve; ⁴he went away and conferred with the chief priests and captains how he might betray him to them. ⁵And they were glad, and engaged to give him money. ⁶So he agreed and sought an opportunity to betray him to them in the absence of the multitude.

Mt 26:17–19
Mk 14:12–16

Preparations for the Last Supper

Mk 14:12–17
Ex 12:18–20

⁷Then came the day of Unleavened Bread, on which the passover lamb had to be sacrificed. ⁸So Jesus[h] sent Peter and John, saying, "Go and prepare the passover for us, that we may eat it." ⁹They said to him, "Where will you have us prepare it?" ¹⁰He said to them, "Behold, when you have entered the city, a man carrying a jar of water

nominabatur Iscarioth, unum de Duodecim; ⁴et abiit et locutus est cum principibus sacerdotum et magistratibus quemadmodum illum traderet eis. ⁵Et gavisi sunt et pacti sunt pecuniam illi dare. ⁶Et spopondit et quaerebat opportunitatem, ut eis traderet illum sine turba. ⁷Venit autem dies Azymorum, in qua necesse erat occidi Pascha. ⁸Et misit Petrum et Ioannem dicens: «Euntes parate nobis Pascha, ut manducemus». ⁹At illi dixerunt ei: «Ubi vis paremus?». ¹⁰Et dixit ad eos: «Ecce introeuntibus vobis in civitatem occurret vobis homo amphoram aquae portans; sequimini eum

life. Or we begin with his prayer in the garden of Gethsemane and follow him from there to the cross. Or we join him at one moment in his Passion—when he is arrested, for example—and go deep into this mystery, reflecting in detail on what he must have thought and felt at Judas' betrayal, the flight of the apostles and all the rest: this is good and valuable prayer. [...] The soul can understand these mysteries in a very deep way; and when they have been meditated on, they are absorbed into our memory in such a way that the simple thought of our Lord stretched out on the ground in the garden will be food for our prayer not only for an hour, but for days; we will see him as he is and realize how indifferent and ungrateful we have been for so much suffering. Then from our will springs the desire to respond to such great mercy, to suffer for the one who suffered so much; and many other thoughts and desires will spring from our memory and understanding" (St Teresa of Avila, *Interior Castle*, 6, 4, 10–11).

22:1–6 After the third temptation in the wilderness, the devil went away "until an opportune time" (4:13). Now, availing himself of Judas (v. 3), he makes another appearance. It is his hour, the hour of "the power of darkness" (22:53). But this apparent success of Satan proves his undoing, because Christ, through his death, destroys the one who had the power of death, that is, the devil, and sets free those who "through fear of death were subject to lifelong bondage" (Heb

2:15). "The tree of man's defeat became his tree of victory; where life was lost, there life has been restored" (*Roman Missal*, Preface of the feast of the Triumph of the Cross).

22:7–20 In Jesus' time, the area inside the walls of Jerusalem was only 1,500 by 800 metres (*c*.300 acres). Tradition places the Cenacle, the supper room, in the southwest corner of the city, very near the house of the high priest and Herod's palace. There is a street of steps (part of which survives) that leads to the Kidron brook and the Mount of Olives. Presumably Jesus went down along this street on the night of Thursday, and was brought back up along it to the high priest's house. It may be that Jesus gave these cryptic instructions to Peter and John in order to avoid the Sanhedrin's knowing where he was going to have the Passover supper.

Preparations for the Passover (v. 7) involved a series of time-consuming operations—sacrificing the lamb in the temple in the early evening; burning anything in the house that had been leavened, and assembling the side dishes for the supper—five types of bitter herbs, parsley, wine, oil, unleavened bread, honey, figs and almonds. At the meal, four goblets of wine mixed with water were drunk; Luke mentions two of them, the second being the cup of the Consecration.

In one way or another, all the Gospels report the essential aspects of what Jesus does during this Supper: it anticipates the sacrifice on the cross, which is offered for the forgiveness of sins,

h Greek *he*

will meet you; follow him into the house which he enters, [11]and tell the householder,
'The Teacher says to you, Where is the guest room, where I am to eat the passover
with my disciples?' [12]And he will show you a large upper room furnished; there
make ready." [13]And they went, and found it as he had told them; and they prepared
the passover.

Lk 19:32

Mt 26:26–29
Mk 14:22–25
1 Cor 11:23–26

The institution of the Eucharist

[14]And when the hour came, he sat at table, and the apostles with him. [15]And he said
to them, "I have earnestly desired to eat this passover with you before I suffer; [16]for
I tell you I shall not eat it[i] until it is fulfilled in the kingdom of God." [17]And he took
a cup, and when he had given thanks he said, "Take this, and divide it among yourselves; [18]for I tell you that from now on I shall not drink of the fruit of the vine until
the kingdom of God comes." [19]And he took bread, and when he had given thanks he
broke it and gave it to them, saying, "This is my body which is given for you. Do
this in remembrance of me." [20]And likewise the cup after supper, saying, "This cup
which is poured out for you is the new covenant in my blood.[j]

Ex 12:14

Jer 31:31
Ex 24:8

in domum, in quam intrat. [11]Et dicetis patri familias domus: "Dicit tibi Magister: Ubi est deversorium ubi Pascha cum discipulis meis manducem?". [12]Ipse vobis ostendet cenaculum magnum stratum; ibi parate». [13]Euntes autem invenerunt, sicut dixit illis, et paraverunt Pascha. [14]Et
cum facta esset hora, discubuit, et apostoli cum eo. [15]Et ait illis: «Desiderio desideravi hoc Pascha manducare vobiscum, antequam patiar. [16]Dico
enim vobis: Non manducabo illud, donec impleatur in regno Dei». [17]Et accepto calice, gratias egit et dixit: «Accipite hoc et dividite inter vos.
[18]Dico enim vobis: Non bibam amodo de generatione vitis, donec regnum Dei veniat». [19]Et accepto pane, gratias egit et fregit et dedit eis dicens:
«Hoc est corpus meum, quod pro vobis datur. Hoc facite in meam commemorationem». [20]Similiter et calicem, postquam cenavit, dicens: «Hic
calix novum testamentum est in sanguine meo, qui pro vobis funditur. [21]Verumtamen ecce manus tradentis me mecum est in mensa; [22]et quidem

and which implies a New Covenant between God
and mankind. At this meal our Lord institutes the
sacrament of the Eucharist, which is "thanksgiving and praise to the *Father*; the sacrificial
memorial of *Christ* and his Body; the presence of
Christ by the power of his word and of his *Spirit*"
(*Catechism of the Catholic Church*, 1358). See
also the note on Mt 26:26–29.

Of all the evangelists, Luke is the one who
most clearly records that Jesus established this
rite as a memorial of his Passover, to be celebrated and renewed in his Church. In fact, the
Passover meal was itself a "memorial", that is, it
put before people's minds God's deliverance of
each member of his people (the recitation of
prayers from Deuteronomy 26:5–10 served this
purpose). Jesus' opening words (vv. 15–18)
show that the old rite has ceased to apply, and
the words he says over the bread and wine (vv.
19–20) institute something new: his body given,
his blood poured out "for you", bring into being
the New Covenant between God and mankind,
for the sake of man's salvation. Jesus established
this rite as a memorial ("Do this in remembrance
of me": v. 19) which takes place in the Church
every time the sacrifice of the altar is renewed in

an unbloody manner: "When the Church celebrates the Eucharist, she commemorates Christ's
Passover, and it is made present: the sacrifice
Christ offered once for all on the cross remains
ever present: 'As often as the sacrifice of the
Cross by which "Christ our Pasch has been sacrificed" is celebrated on the altar, the work of our
redemption is carried out' (*Lumen gentium*, 3)"
(ibid., 1364).

From this need to perpetuate the sacrifice of
the cross we can deduce that by what he says
here Jesus "made his apostles priests" and
"decreed that they and other priests should offer
his body and blood" (Council of Trent, *De SS.
Missae sacrificio*, can. 2). The Church reminds
priests that "they exercise their sacred function
especially in the eucharistic worship or the celebration of the Mass by which, acting in the
person of Christ and proclaiming his Mystery,
they unite the prayers of the faithful with the sacrifice of their Head and renew and apply in the
sacrifice of the Mass until the coming of the
Lord the only sacrifice of the New Testament,
namely that of Christ offering himself once for
all a spotless Victim to the Father" (Vatican II,
Lumen gentium, 28).

i Other ancient authorities read *never eat it again*   j Some ancient authorities omit *which is given for you. Do this in remembrance of me.*" [20]*And likewise the cup after
supper, saying, "This cup which is poured out for you is the new covenant in my blood*

Mt 26:20–25
Mk 14:17–21
Jn 13:21–32
The treachery of Judas foretold

²¹"But behold the hand of him who betrays me is with me on the table. ²²For the Son of man goes as it has been determined; but woe to that man by whom he is betrayed!" ²³And they began to question one another, which of them it was that would do this.

A dispute among the apostles

Lk 9:46ff
²⁴A dispute also arose among them, which of them was to be regarded as the great-
Mt 20:25–27
Mk 10:42–45
est. ²⁵And he said to them. "The kings of the Gentiles exercise lordship over them; and those in authority over them are called benefactors. ²⁶But not so with you; rather let the greatest among you become as the youngest, and the leader as one who
Jn 13:4–14
serves. ²⁷For which is the greater, one who sits at table, or one who serves? Is it not the one who sits at table? But I am among you as one who serves.

Jn 6:67
Jn 15:27
Lk 12:32
²⁸"You are those who have continued with me in my trials; ²⁹as my Father appointed a kingdom for me, so do I appoint for you ³⁰that you may eat and drink at my table in my kingdom, and sit on thrones judging the twelve tribes of Israel.

Mt 26:30–35
Mk 14:26–31
Jn 13:36–38
Peter's denial foretold

Amos 9:9–35
³¹"Simon, Simon, behold, Satan demanded to have you,[k] that he might sift you[k] like
Mt 16:19
Jn 21:15–17
wheat, ³²but I have prayed for you that your faith may not fail; and when you have turned again, strengthen your brethren." ³³And he said to him, "Lord, I am ready to go with you to prison and to death." ³⁴He said, "I tell you, Peter, the cock will not crow this day, until you three times deny that you know me."

Filius hominis, secundum quod definitum est, vadit; verumtamen vae illi homini, per quem traditur!». ²³Et ipsi coeperunt quaerere inter se quis esset ex eis, qui hoc facturus esset. ²⁴Facta est autem et contentio inter eos, quis eorum videretur esse maior. ²⁵Dixit autem eis: «Reges gentium dominantur eorum et, qui potestatem habent super eos, benefici vocantur. ²⁶Vos autem non sic, sed qui maior est in vobis, fiat sicut iunior; et, qui praecessor est, sicut ministrator. ²⁷Nam quis maior est: qui recumbit, an qui ministrat? Nonne qui recumbit? Ego autem in medio vestrum sum sicut qui ministrat. ²⁸Vos autem estis qui permansistis mecum in tentationibus meis; ²⁹et ego dispono vobis, sicut disposuit mihi Pater meus regnum, ³⁰ut edatis et bibatis super mensam meam in regno meo, et sedeatis super thronos iudicantes duodecim tribus Israel. ³¹Simon, Simon, ecce Satanas expetivit vos, ut cribraret sicut triticum; ³²ego autem rogavi pro te, ut non deficiat fides tua. Et tu, aliquando conversus, confirma fratres tuos». ³³Qui dixit ei: «Domine, tecum paratus sum et in carcerem et in mortem ire». ³⁴Et ille dixit: «Dico tibi, Petre, non cantabit hodie gallus

22:21–30 Throughout his Gospel (and especially in his account of the passion), Luke likes to note that the way Jesus deals with difficulties sets an example for us to follow. These two episodes contrast with the previous one, in that they give us a glimpse into our Lord's loneliness and his deepest feelings (so different from those of his disciples). Even so, our Lord's words bolster their hope. Although they are still blinded by their worldly outlook (v. 24; cf. Mt 20:20–28; Mk 10:35–45; and notes), because they share in Jesus' trials and humiliation (v. 28) they will also share in his triumph (vv. 29–30).

"Sit on thrones judging the twelve tribes of Israel" (v. 30). The throne is a symbol of royal power, and the twelve tribes of Israel symbolize the universal nature of the authority that Jesus confers on the apostles. The tradition of the Church is that this apostolic authority continues

to exist in bishops: "The bishops, as vicars and legates of Christ, govern the particular Churches assigned to them by their counsels, exhortations and example, but over and above that also by the authority and sacred power which indeed they exercise exclusively for the spiritual development of their flock in truth and holiness, keeping in mind that he who is greater should become as the lesser, and he who is the leader as the servant" (Vatican II, *Lumen gentium*, 27).

22:31–34 After the Supper, and before his arrest in Gethsemane, Jesus warns his disciples (Peter, in particular) about the test that their faith will face (vv. 31–32) because of their failing to grasp the redemptive nature of his mission and death (22:37–38). Luke gives more information about this episode than the other Synoptics, and he records Jesus' prayer for Peter. The passion is

k The Greek word for *you* here is plural; in verse 32 it is singular

Appeal to the apostles

³⁵And he said to them, "When I sent you out with no purse or bag or sandals, did you lack anything?" They said, "Nothing." ³⁶He said to them, "But now, let him who has a purse take it, and likewise a bag. And let him who has no sword sell his mantle and buy one. ³⁷For I tell you that this scripture must be fulfilled in me, 'And he was reckoned with transgressors'; for what is written about me has its fulfilment." ³⁸And they said, "Look, Lord, here are two swords." And he said to them, "It is enough."

Lk 9:3; 10:4

Lk 12:51
Mt 10:34

Is 53:12
Lk 23:32

Jesus' prayer and agony in the garden

³⁹And he came out, and went, as was his custom, to the Mount of Olives; and the disciples followed him. ⁴⁰And when he came to the place he said to them, "Pray that

Mt 26:36–46
Mk 14:32–42

Lk 21:37
Jn 18:38

donec ter abneges nosse me». ³⁵Et dixit eis: «Quando misi vos sine sacculo et pera et calceamentis, numquid aliquid defuit vobis?». At illi dixerunt: «Nihil». ³⁶Dixit ergo eis: «Sed nunc, qui habet sacculum, tollat, similiter et peram; et, qui non habet, vendat tunicam suam et emat gladium. ³⁷Dico enim vobis: Hoc, quod scriptum est, oportet impleri in me, illud: "Cum iniustis deputatus est". Etenim ea, quae sunt de me, adimpletionem habent». ³⁸At illi dixerunt: «Domine, ecce gladii duo hic». At ille dixit eis: «Satis est». ³⁹Et egressus ibat secundum consuetudinem in montem Olivarum; secuti sunt autem illum et discipuli. ⁴⁰Et cum pervenisset ad locum, dixit illis: «Orate, ne intretis in tentationem». ⁴¹Et ipse

presented as a battle between Satan and Jesus. Satan is successful with Judas (22:3) and with the Jewish authorities whose "hour" coincides with that of "the power of darkness" (22:53). Here the battleground extends to Peter and the other apostles (v. 31). Although the weakness of Peter is plain to see, he will not fall away, because his faith is supported by Jesus' prayer for him. The Church teaches that, thanks to Jesus' special help to Peter for his mission, "because of the faith he confessed, Peter will remain the unshakeable rock of the Church. His mission will be to keep this faith from every lapse and to strengthen his brothers in it" (*Catechism of the Catholic Church*, 552). This applies also to the Pope, in his capacity as Peter's successor: "The See of Peter always remained unstained by all error, according to the divine promise that our Saviour made to the chief of his disciples [...]. Therefore this charism of truth and unfailing faith was divinely given to Peter and his successors in this chair so that they might fulfil their high office for the salvation of all" (Vatican I, *Pastor aeternus*, 3). See the notes on Mt 16:13–20 and John 21:15–23.

22:35–38 Here Jesus announces his passion by applying to himself Isaiah's prophecy about the suffering Servant (Is 53:12) and by pointing out that the other prophecies about the Redeemer's sufferings also find fulfilment in him. As in all the rest of these episodes, there is a sharp difference

between Jesus' view of events and that of the disciples. Jesus knows what is going to happen, and therefore he prepares the Passover with the benefit of prophetic insight (22:7–13): he knows that Judas will betray him (22:21), that Peter will deny him (22:34), and that the moment of truth has arrived (22:53). But he refuses to allow weapons to be used to defend him (22:51), and he does not reply to jeers and insults (22:63–65) or attempt to defend himself before the Sanhedrin (22:66–71) or before Pilate (23:3). He is blameless, as Pilate (23:4, 14, 22) and the centurion (23:47) assert. Rejected, and unjustly condemned, he offers forgiveness to his executioners (23:34). Clearly, the way he behaves sets the standard for all those who suffer without just cause. But he is not sacrificing himself in the service of some abstract ideal: he does this to fulfil his Father's will: "He submitted himself wholly to the will of the Father; and the Father's will was that his holy and glorious Son, whom he gave to us and who was born for us, should offer himself as victim and sacrifice on the cross, shedding his blood, not for himself, through whom all things were made, but for our sins. He is the example that we must follow. May we all be saved through him, and receive him with a pure heart and a chaste body" (St Francis of Assisi, *Letter to All the Faithful*, 2, 10–15).

22:39–46 In the garden, Jesus expresses his readiness to accept an appalling death to fulfil

you may not enter into temptation." [41]And he withdrew from them about a stone's throw, and knelt down and prayed, [42]"Father, if thou art willing, remove this cup from me; nevertheless not my will, but thine, be done." [43]And there appeared to him an angel from heaven, strengthening him. [44]And being in an agony he prayed more earnestly; and his sweat became like great drops of blood falling down upon the ground.[l] [45]And when he rose from prayer, he came to the disciples and found them sleeping for sorrow, [46]and he said to them, "Why do you sleep? Rise and pray that you may not enter into temptation."

Mt 6:10
1 Kings 19:5–7

Mt 26:47–56
Mk 14:43–52
Jn 18:1–12

Arrest of Jesus

[47]While he was still speaking, there came a crowd, and the man called Judas, one of the twelve, was leading them. He drew near to Jesus to kiss him; [48]but Jesus said to him, "Judas, would you betray the Son of man with a kiss?" [49]And when those who were about him saw what would follow, they said, "Lord, shall we strike with the sword?" [50]And one of them struck the slave of the high priest and cut off his right

avulsus est ab eis, quantum iactus est lapidis, et, positis genibus, orabat [42]dicens: «Pater, si vis, transfer calicem istum a me; verumtamen non mea voluntas sed tua fiat». [43]Apparuit autem illi angelus de caelo confortans eum. Et factus in agonia prolixius orabat. [44]Et factus est sudor eius sicut guttae sanguinis decurrentis in terram. [45]Et cum surrexisset ab oratione et venisset ad discipulos, invenit eos dormientes prae tristitia [46]et ait illis: «Quid dormitis? Surgite; orate, ne intretis in tentationem». [47]Adhuc eo loquente, ecce turba, et qui vocabatur Iudas, unus de Duodecim, antecedebat eos, et appropinquavit Iesu, ut oscularetur eum. [48]Iesus autem dixit ei: «Iuda, osculo Filium hominis tradis?». [49]Videntes autem hi, qui circa ipsum erant, quod futurum erat, dixerunt: «Domine, si percutimus in gladio?». [50]Et percussit unus ex illis servum principis sacerdotum et amputavit auriculam eius dextram. [51]Respondens autem Iesus ait: «Sinite usque huc!». Et cum tetigisset auriculam eius, sanavit eum. [52]Dixit autem

his Father's will. His prayer must have lasted for a long time, but St Luke only describes a few key moments. Almost every verse here mentions prayer: the passage begins and ends with Jesus asking the disciples to pray in order not to fall into temptation; and Jesus sets an example in that "being in an agony he prayed more earnestly" (v. 44). Our Lord's prayer is a perfect example of abandonment into and union with the will of God: "Are things going against you? Are you going through a rough time? Say very slowly, as if relishing it, this powerful and manly prayer: 'May the most just and most lovable will of God be done, be fulfilled, be praised and eternally exalted above all things. Amen, Amen.' I assure you that you will find peace" (St Josemaría Escrivá, *The Way*, 691).

Jesus' prayer is intense, but his distress is no less so: in fact, so deep is his sorrow that an angel comes to strengthen him, and he sweats blood (vv. 43–44). This is the greatest evidence yet of our Lord's truly human capacity to feel pain: "The fear of death and torments carries no stigma of guilt but rather is an affliction of the sort Christ came to suffer, not to escape. We should not immediately consider it cowardice for someone to feel fear and horror at the thought of

torments" (St Thomas More, *The Sadness of Christ*). Here, as always, our Lord's actions and words are a model for us: "It is right and good that, out of pity for the weakest, the Master, our true Saviour, show in his own person that the martyrs should never lose hope if, because of the frailty of human nature, they were to feel sorrow in their hearts during their time of suffering. They have already overcome sorrow and despair by putting the will of God before their own, and God knows what is best for those who turn to him" (St Augustine, *De consensus Evangelistarum*, 3, 4).

22:47–53 When narrating this episode, all four evangelists manage to convey the majesty of Jesus and the significance of what is happening—the crush of the crowd (see Mt 26:47), Judas' treachery, the wounding of the high priest's servant, etc. Luke also notes the compassion shown by our Lord when he cures the wounded servant (v. 51), and the apparent victory of the devil (v. 53). In reading this passage, one cannot but think about Judas: "Since God showed his great mercy in so many ways even toward Judas, an apostle turned traitor, since he

l Other ancient authorities omit verses 43 and 44

ear. ⁵¹But Jesus said, "No more of this!" And he touched his ear and healed him.
⁵²Then Jesus said to the chief priests and captains of the temple and elders, who had
come out against him,* "Have you come out as against a robber, with swords and
clubs? ⁵³When I was with you day after day in the temple, you did not lay hands on
me. But this is your hour, and the power of darkness."

Lk 19:47
Jn 7:30; 18:20

Peter's denials

Mt 26:69–75
Mk 14:66–72
Jn 18:13–18, 25–27

⁵⁴Then they seized him and led him away, bringing him into the high priest's house.
Peter followed at a distance; ⁵⁵and when they had kindled a fire in the middle of the
courtyard and sat down together, Peter sat among them. ⁵⁶Then a maid, seeing him
as he sat in the light and gazing at him, said, "This man also was with him." ⁵⁷But
he denied it, saying, "Woman, I do not know him." ⁵⁸And a little later some one else
saw him and said, "You also are one of them." But Peter said, "Man, I am not."
⁵⁹And after an interval of about an hour still another insisted, saying, "Certainly this
man also was with him; for he is a Galilean." ⁶⁰But Peter said, "Man, I do not know
what you are saying." And immediately, while he was still speaking, the cock
crowed. ⁶¹And the Lord turned and looked at Peter. And Peter remembered the word
of the Lord, how he had said to him, "Before the cock crows today, you will deny
me three times." ⁶²And he went out and wept bitterly.

Mt 26:57–58
Mk 14:53–54

Lk 22:34

Iesus ad eos, qui venerant ad se principes sacerdotum et magistratus templi et seniores: «Quasi ad latronem existis cum gladiis et fustibus? ⁵³Cum
cotidie vobiscum fuerim in templo, non extendistis manus in me; sed haec est hora vestra et potestas tenebrarum». ⁵⁴Comprehendentes autem
eum, duxerunt et introduxerunt in domum principis sacerdotum. Petrus vero sequebatur a longe. ⁵⁵Accenso autem igni in medio atrio et cir-
cumsedentibus illis, sedebat Petrus in medio eorum. ⁵⁶Quem cum vidisset ancilla quaedam sedentem ad lumen et eum fuisset intuita, dixit: ⁵⁷«Et
hic cum illo erat!». At ille negavit eum dicens: ⁵⁸«Mulier, non novi illum!». Et post pusillum alius videns eum dixit: «Et tu de illis es!». Petrus
vero ait: «O homo, non sum!». ⁵⁹Et intervallo facto quasi horae unius, alius quidam affirmabat dicens: «Vere et hic cum illo erat, nam et Galilaeus

invited him to forgiveness so often and did not
allow him to perish except through despair
alone, certainly there is no reason why, in this
life, anyone should despair of any imitator of
Judas" (St Thomas More, *The Sadness of Christ*,
p. 50).

22:54–71 The first two evangelists (see Mt
26:57–75; Mk 14:53–72; and notes) show in
contrast the different ways in which Jesus and
Peter are questioned and respond. Luke's
account keeps closer to the chronology of
events: at night Jesus is brought to the house of
Caiaphas, where Peter denies him and the servants revile him; in the morning (v. 66) the Sanhedrin meets and condemns him to death. Of the
events that occur at night, only Luke records the
incident of Jesus' looking at Peter (22:61) that
leads the latter to repent. The saints frequently
pause to reflect on Christ's glance (so often mentioned in this Gospel: see 5:20, 27; 6:10, 20): "I
often think, my Christ, how delectable and
happy your eyes seem to those who love you,
when you, my God, are pleased to look on them

with love. I think that even one such gentle
glance bestowed on souls whom you count as
your own is sufficient reward for many years of
service" (St Teresa of Avila, *Exclamations*, 14).
Peter's tears are the true reaction of a noble heart
when it is moved by the grace of God; they are a
sign of true contrition, which involves "a sorrow
of mind, and detestation for sin committed, with
the purpose of not sinning for the future" (Council of Trent, *De Paenitentia*, 4).

The coldness of those who have no faith (vv.
66–71) is in sharp contrast to the tears shed by
Peter. The charges brought by the Sanhedrin are
so contradictory that they cannot provide
grounds for condemning Jesus. But they elicit
from him a statement that does compromise him
(he is of course aware of this): he asserts formally that he is not only the Christ (cf. Dan
7:13–14) but also the Son of God. The members
of the Sanhedrin know exactly what Jesus
means; and they call for his death, claiming that
he has blasphemed and so must die. They do not
have the faith necessary to acknowledge Jesus as
Messiah (vv. 67–68).

Mt 26:67–68
Mk 14:65

Jesus abused by the guards

⁶³Now the men who were holding Jesus mocked him and beat him; ⁶⁴they also blind-folded him and asked him, "Prophesy! Who is it that struck you?" ⁶⁵And they spoke many other words against him, reviling him.

Mt 26:57–68
Mk 14:53–65
Jn 18:13–24

Jesus before the chief priests

Jn 8:45; 10:24

⁶⁶When day came, the assembly of the elders of the people gathered together, both chief priests and scribes; and they led him away to their council, and they said, ⁶⁷"If you are the Christ, tell us." But he said to them, "If I tell you, you will not believe;

Dan 7:13
Ps 110:1

⁶⁸and if I ask you, you will not answer. ⁶⁹But from now on the Son of man shall be seated at the right hand of the power of God." ⁷⁰And they all said, "Are you the Son of God, then?" And he said to them, "You say that I am." ⁷¹And they said, "What further testimony do we need? We have heard it ourselves from his own lips."

Mt 27:11–14
Mk 15:1–5
Jn 18:28–40

Mt 27:2

Lk 20:25

Jesus before Pilate

23 ¹Then the whole company of them arose, and brought him before Pilate. ²And they began to accuse him, saying, "We found this man perverting our nation, and forbidding us to give tribute to Caesar, and saying that he himself is

est!». ⁶⁰Et ait Petrus: «Homo, nescio quid dicis!». Et continuo adhuc illo loquente cantavit gallus. ⁶¹Et conversus Dominus respexit Petrum; et recordatus est Petrus verbi Domini, sicut dixit ei: «Priusquam gallus cantet hodie, ter me negabis». ⁶²Et egressus foras flevit amare. ⁶³Et viri, qui tenebant illum, illudebant ei caedentes, ⁶⁴et velaverunt eum et interrogabant eum dicentes: «Prophetiza: Quis est, qui te percussit?». ⁶⁵Et alia multa blasphemantes dicebant in eum. ⁶⁶Et ut factus est dies, convenerunt seniores plebis et principes sacerdotum et scribae et duxerunt illum in con-cilium suum ⁶⁷dicentes: «Si tu es Christus, dic nobis». Et ait illis: «Si vobis dixero, non credetis; ⁶⁸si autem interrogavero, non respondebitis mihi. ⁶⁹Ex hoc autem erit *Filius hominis sedens a dextris virtutis Dei*». ⁷⁰Dixerunt autem omnes: «Tu ergo es Filius Dei?». Qui ait ad illos: «Vos dicitis quia ego sum». ⁷¹At illi dixerunt: «Quid adhuc desideramus testimonium? Ipsi enim audivimus de ore eius!». [23] ¹Et surgens omnis multitudo eorum, duxerunt illum ad Pilatum. ²Coeperunt autem accusare illum dicentes: «Hunc invenimus subvertentem gentem nostram et prohibentem tributa dare Caesari et dicentem se Christum regem esse». ³Pilatus autem interrogavit eum dicens: «Tu es rex Iudaeorum?». At ille respondens

23:1–25 Luke's account of the condemnation of Jesus parallels the later prayer of Christians in Jerusalem recorded in Acts 4:27–28: "Truly in this city there were gathered together against thy holy servant Jesus, whom thou didst anoint, both Herod and Pontius Pilate, with the Gentiles and the peoples of Israel, to do whatever thy hand and thy plan had predestined to take place." In line with that description, St Luke shows us three scenes in sequence—Jesus before Pilate, before Herod, and before Pilate again. Presented with the evidence, readers may have their own view as to how the blame should be apportioned, but, along with the evangelist, they realize that God's plans are being implemented, independ-ently of what anyone decides about that.

In the first scene (vv. 1–5) we see the cun-ning of Jesus' accusers: they deftly change the charge. The Sanhedrin condemned Jesus for call-ing himself the Christ (Messiah) and Son of God (22:66–71) but now he is being charged with calling himself "Christ a king" and stirring up the people (v. 2). Pilate immediately sees that

there are no grounds for the charges (v. 4), but he tries to buy time and uses the first opportunity that presents itself (vv. 6–7) to avoid making any decision. Commentators are quick to notice the composed and dignified stance of Jesus in this scene: "This wonderful passage fills the hearts of men with patience so that they may face trials with an untroubled spirit. The Lord is accused, and he remains silent; and because he is in no need of defence, he is right to remain silent: the struggle to defend is for those who fear they may be overcome. The Lord does not accept the accu-sation by his silence; rather, he undoes it by his refusal to respond. [...] He wanted to show his royal status, rather than proclaim it in words, so that they would have no grounds to condemn him with a false accusation" (St Ambrose, *Expo-sitio Evangelii secundum Lucam*, ad loc.).

The following scene (vv. 6–12) reveals the various protagonists for what they are—Herod, a frivolous, almost grotesque man; the chief priests and rulers, bent on Jesus' execution (v. 10); our Lord, a majestic figure standing apart

Christ a king."* ³And Pilate asked him, "Are you the King of the Jews?" And he
answered him, "You have said so." ⁴And Pilate said to the chief priests and the multitudes, "I find no crime in this man." ⁵But they were urgent, saying, "He stirs up the
people, teaching throughout all Judea, from Galilee even to this place."

1 Tim 6:13

Jesus before Herod

⁶When Pilate heard this, he asked whether the man was a Galilean. ⁷And when he
learned that he belonged to Herod's jurisdiction, he sent him over to Herod, who was
himself in Jerusalem at that time. ⁸When Herod saw Jesus, he was very glad, for he
had long desired to see him, because he had heard about him, and he was hoping to
see some sign done by him. ⁹So he questioned him at some length; but he made no
answer. ¹⁰The chief priests and the scribes stood by, vehemently accusing him. ¹¹And
Herod with his soldiers treated him with contempt and mocked him; then, arraying
him in gorgeous apparel, he sent him back to Pilate. ¹²And Herod and Pilate became
friends with each other that very day, for before this they had been at enmity with
each other.

Lk 3:1

Lk 9:9

Acts 4:27

Jesus is condemned to death

¹³Pilate then called together the chief priests and the rulers and the people, ¹⁴and said
to them, "You brought me this man as one who was perverting the people; and after
examining him before you, behold, I did not find this man guilty of any of your
charges against him;* ¹⁵neither did Herod, for he sent him back to us. Behold, nothing deserving death has been done by him; ¹⁶I will therefore chastise him and release
him."ᵐ

Mt 27:15–26
Mk 15:6–15
Jn 19:4–16

Acts 28:18–19
Jn 18:38

ait: «Tu dicis». ⁴Ait autem Pilatus ad principes sacerdotum et turbas: «Nihil invenio causae in hoc homine». ⁵At illi invalescebant dicentes: «Com-
movet populum docens per universam Iudaeam et incipiens a Galilaea usque huc!». ⁶Pilatus autem audiens interrogavit si homo Galilaeus esset
⁷et ut cognovit quod de Herodis potestate esset, remisit eum ad Herodem, qui et ipse Hierosolymis erat illis diebus. ⁸Herodes autem, viso Iesu,
gavisus est valde: erat enim cupiens ex multo tempore videre eum, eo quod audiret de illo et sperabat signum aliquod videre ab eo fieri. ⁹Interro-
gabat autem illum multis sermonibus; at ipse nihil illi respondebat. ¹⁰Stabant etiam principes sacerdotum et scribae constanter accusantes eum.
¹¹Sprevit autem illum Herodes cum exercitu suo et illusit indutum veste alba et remisit ad Pilatum. ¹²Facti sunt autem amici inter se Herodes et
Pilatus in ipsa die, nam antea inimici erant ad invicem. ¹³Pilatus autem, convocatis principibus sacerdotum et magistratibus et plebe, ¹⁴dixit ad
illos: «Obtulistis mihi hunc hominem quasi avertentem populum, et ecce ego coram vobis interrogans nullam causam inveni in homine isto ex
his, in quibus eum accusatis, ¹⁵sed neque Herodes: remisit enim illum ad nos. Et ecce nihil dignum morte actum est ei. ¹⁶Emendatum ergo illum

from their attitudes and actions, saying nothing.
Here is St Ambrose's comment on the scene:
"When Herod wanted him to perform miracles,
he remained silent and did nothing because the
cruel king did not deserve to see the workings of
divine power, nor did Jesus ever boast of his
Lordship and power. Herod may be regarded as
an example of all wicked men: if they do not
believe in the Law and the Prophets, they will
not be able to see Christ's miracles in the
Gospel" (ibid., ad loc.).

When Jesus is brought back to Pilate, the
governor three times declares Jesus to be innocent (vv. 14, 20, 22). But the crowd, each time,
clamours for his death (vv. 18, 21, 23). Paradoxically, Barabbas is released from prison (v. 25) in
spite of having being guilty of sedition and

murder (v. 19). The whole scene is proof of the
sad effects of indolence: neither Herod nor Pilate
has found him guilty, though each has taken
advantage of the cruel intentions of the other.
Pilate washes his hands, but he cannot wipe
away his actions; given his position as a judge,
he should not have yielded to hatred and fear, to
the extent of spilling innocent blood. His wife
warned him, grace having enlightened her during
the night; the Godhead influenced her; but even
so Pilate went on and handed down a sacrilegious sentence. I see in him an early reflection of
all those who will in future times condemn those
whom they know to be innocent" (ibid., ad loc.).
"A man, a 'gentleman', ready to compromise
would condemn Jesus to death again" (St Josemaría Escrivá, *The Way*, 393).

ᵐ Here, or after verse 19, other ancient authorities add verse 17, *Now he was obliged to release one man to them at the festival*

¹⁸But they all cried out together, "Away with this man, and release to us Barabbas" — ¹⁹a man who had been thrown into prison for an insurrection started in the city, and for murder. ²⁰Pilate addressed them once more, desiring to release Jesus; ²¹but they shouted out, "Crucify, crucify him!" ²²A third time he said to them, "Why, what evil has he done? I have found in him no crime deserving death; I will therefore chastise him and release him." ²³But they were urgent, demanding with loud cries that he should be crucified. And their voices prevailed. ²⁴So Pilate gave sentence that their demand should be granted. ²⁵He released the man who had been thrown into prison for insurrection and murder, whom they asked for; but Jesus he delivered up to their will.

Mt 27:32–56
Mk 15:21–41
Jn 19:17–30

The crucifixion and death of Jesus

²⁶And as they led him away, they seized one Simon of Cyrene, who was coming in from the country, and laid on him the cross, to carry it behind Jesus. ²⁷And there followed him a great multitude of the people, and of women who bewailed and lamented him. ²⁸But Jesus turning to them said, "Daughters of Jerusalem, do not weep for me, but weep for yourselves and for your children. ²⁹For behold, the days are coming when they will say, 'Blessed are the barren, and the wombs that never bore, and the breasts that never gave suck!' ³⁰Then they will begin to say to the mountains, 'Fall on us'; and to the hills, 'Cover us.' ³¹For if they do this when the wood is green, what will

Hos 10:8
Rev 6:16; 9:6

Ezek 21:38

dimittam». ¹⁸Exclamavit autem universa turba dicens: «Tolle hunc et dimitte nobis Barabbam!», ¹⁹qui erat propter seditionem quandam factam in civitate et homicidium missus in carcerem. ²⁰Iterum autem Pilatus locutus est ad illos volens dimittere Iesum, ²¹at illi succlamabant dicentes: «Crucifige, crucifige illum!». ²²Ille autem tertio dixit ad illos: «Quid enim mali fecit iste? Nullam causam mortis invenio in eo; corripiam ergo illum et dimittam». ²³At illi instabant vocibus magnis postulantes, ut crucifigeretur, et invalescebant voces eorum. ²⁴Et Pilatus adiudicavit fieri petitionem eorum: ²⁵dimisit autem eum, qui propter seditionem et homicidium missus fuerat in carcerem, quem petebant, Iesum vero tradidit voluntati eorum. ²⁶Et cum abducerent eum, apprehenderunt Simonem quendam Cyrenensem venientem de villa et imposuerunt illi crucem portare post Iesum. ²⁷Sequebatur autem illum multa turba populi et mulierum, quae plangebant et lamentabant eum. ²⁸Conversus autem ad illas Iesus dixit: «Filiae Ierusalem, nolite flere super me, sed super vos ipsas flete et super filios vestros, ²⁹quoniam ecce venient dies, in quibus dicent: "Beatae steriles et ventres, qui non genuerunt, et ubera, quae non lactaverunt!". ³⁰Tunc incipient *dicere montibus: "Cadite super nos!"*, *et collibus: "Operite*

23:26–49 Like the other evangelists, St Luke describes the crucifixion and death of Jesus as the fulfilment of God's plans; Jesus becomes the suffering Servant of Yahweh (cf. the notes on Mt 27:32–56; Mk 15:21–41).

Jesus' behaviour is depicted as an example for all Christians: it provokes the admiration of the centurion and the repentance of the crowd (vv. 47–48). Jesus is a model of compassion and forgiveness: he consoles some women (vv. 28–29), pardons his executioners (v. 34) and opens the gates of Paradise to the good thief (v. 43). In his other book, St Luke shows us the first martyr, St Stephen, imitating Christ in this respect (see Acts 7:60): "Forgiveness demonstrates the presence in the world of *the love which is more powerful than sin*. Forgiveness is also the fundamental condition for reconciliation, not only in the relationship of God with man, but also in relationships between people" (John Paul II, *Dives in misericordia*, 14).

Jesus draws his strength from prayer. He twice addresses his Father (vv. 34, 46); in fact, his very last words are spoken to him: "Father, into thy hands I commit my spirit!" (v. 46). "All the troubles, for all time, of humanity enslaved by sin and death, all the petitions and intercessions of salvation history are summed up in this cry of the incarnate Word. Here the Father accepts them and, beyond all hope, answers them by raising his Son. Thus is fulfilled and brought to completion the drama of prayer in the economy of creation and salvation" (*Catechism of the Catholic Church*, 2606).

As elsewhere in the Gospel, people are seen in their true light in the way they relate to Jesus. The kindness of those women (vv. 27–29) shows that, though Jesus has enemies, there are also those who love him. "Among the people watching our Lord as he passes by are a number of women who are unable to restrain their compassion and break into tears [...]. But our Lord

happen when it is dry?"* [32]Two others also, who were criminals, were led away to be put to death with him. [33]And when they came to the place which is called The Skull, there they crucified him, and the criminals, one on the right and one on the left. [34]And Jesus said, "Father, forgive them; for they know not what they do."[n] And they cast lots to divide his garments. [35]And the people stood by, watching; but the rulers scoffed at him, saying, "He saved others; let him save himself, if he is the Christ of God, his Chosen One!" [36]The soldiers also mocked him, coming up and offering him vinegar, [37]and saying, "If you are the King of the Jews, save yourself!" [38]There was also an inscription over him,[o] "This is the King of the Jews."

[39]One of the criminals who were hanged railed at him, saying, "Are you not the Christ? Save yourself and us!" [40]But the other rebuked him, saying, "Do you not fear God, since you are under the same sentence of condemnation? [41]And we indeed justly; for we are receiving the due reward of our deeds; but this man has done nothing wrong." [42]And he said, "Jesus, remember me when you come in your kingly power."[p] [43]And he said to him, "Truly, I say to you, today you will be with me in Paradise."

Lk 22:37
Is 53:12

Mt 5:44
Ps 22:18
Acts 7: 60

Ps 22:7

Ps 69:21

---

nos!", [31]quia si in viridi ligno haec faciunt, in arido quid fiet?». [32]Ducebantur autem et alii duo nequam cum eo, ut interficerentur. [33]Et postquam venerunt in locum, qui vocatur Calvariae, ibi crucifixerunt eum et latrones, unum a dextris et alterum a sinistris. [34]Iesus autem dicebat: «Pater, dimitte illis, non enim sciunt quid faciunt». *Dividentes* vero *vestimenta eius miserunt sortes.* [35]Et stabat populus *exspectans.* Et *deridebant* illum et principes dicentes: «Alios salvos fecit; se salvum faciat, si hic est Christus Dei electus!». [36]Illudebant autem ei et milites accedentes, *acetum* offerentes illi [37]et dicentes: «Si tu es rex Iudaeorum, salvum te fac!». [38]Erat autem et superscriptio super illum: «Hic est rex Iudaeorum». [39]Unus autem de his, qui pendebant, latronibus blasphemabat eum dicens: «Nonne tu es Christus? Salvum fac temetipsum et nos!». [40]Respondens autem alter increpabat illum dicens: «Neque tu times Deum, quod in eadem damnatione es? [41]Et nos quidem iuste, nam digna factis recipimus! Hic vero nihil mali gessit». [42]Et dicebat: «Iesu, memento mei cum veneris in regnum tuum». [43]Et dixit illi: «Amen dico tibi: Hodie mecum eris in paradiso».

---

wishes to channel their weeping towards a more supernatural motive, and he invites them to weep for sins, which are the cause of the Passion [...]. Your sins, my sins, the sins of all men, rise up. All the evil we have done and the good that we have neglected to do. The desolate panorama of the countless crimes and iniquities which we would have committed, if he, Jesus, had not strengthened us with the light of his most loving glance. How little a life is for making atonement!" (St Josemaría Escrivá, *The Way of the Cross*, 8).

The episode of the "good thief" (vv. 39–43) appears only in Luke's Gospel. This man shows signs of repentance, recognizes Jesus' innocence, and makes an act of faith in him. Jesus, for his part, promises him Paradise. "The Lord," St Ambrose comments, "always grants more than one asks: the thief only asked him to remember him, but the Lord says to him, 'Truly, I say to you, today you will be with me in Paradise.' Life consists in dwelling with Jesus Christ, and where Jesus Christ is there is his Kingdom" (*Expositio Evangelii secundum Lucam*, ad loc.). This episode also invites us to admire the designs of divine providence, how grace and human free-

dom relate to one another. These two criminals have found themselves in the same position. One of them despairs and goes on blaspheming, but the other repents, makes a prayerful appeal to Christ, and wins the promise of immediate salvation. "Among men, confession is followed by punishment; whereas confession to God is followed by salvation" (St John Chrysostom, *De Cruce et latrone*).

The word "Paradise" (v. 45), Persian in origin, occurs (in the sense used here) in a few places in the Old Testament (Song 4:13; Neh 2:8; Eccles 2:5) and in two others in the New (2 Cor 12:4; Rev 2:7); here Jesus is telling the good thief that happiness awaits him soon, at Jesus' side: "We believe in eternal life. We believe that the souls of all those who die in the grace of Christ—whether they must still make expiation in the fire of purgatory, or whether from the moment they leave their bodies they are received by Jesus into Paradise like the good thief—go to form that People of God which succeeds death, death which will be totally destroyed on the day of the resurrection when these souls are reunited with their bodies" (Paul VI, *Creed of the People of God*).

---

n Other ancient authorities omit the sentence *And Jesus ... what they do*   o Other ancient authorities add *in letters of Greek and Latin and Hebrew*   p Greek *kingdom*

Amos 8:9

⁴⁴It was now about the sixth hour, and there was darkness over the whole land�q until the ninth hour, ⁴⁵while the sun's light failed;ʳ and the curtain of the temple was torn in two. ⁴⁶Then Jesus, crying with a loud voice, said, "Father, into thy hands I commit my spirit!" And having said this he breathed his last. ⁴⁷Now when the centurion saw what had taken place, he praised God, and said, "Certainly this man was innocent!" ⁴⁸And all the multitudes who assembled to see the sight, when they saw what had taken place, returned home beating their breasts. ⁴⁹And all his acquaintances and the women who had followed him from Galilee stood at a distance and saw these things.

Acts 7:59
Ps 31:5
Lk 7:16

Zech 12:10

Ps 88:8
Lk 8:2–3

Mt 27:57–61
Mk 15:42–47
Jn 19:31–42

The burial

⁵⁰Now there was a man named Joseph from the Jewish town of Arimathea. He was a member of the council, a good and righteous man, ⁵¹who had not consented to their purpose and deed, and he was looking for the kingdom of God. ⁵²This man went to Pilate and asked for the body of Jesus. ⁵³Then he took it down and wrapped it in a linen shroud, and laid him in a rock-hewn tomb, where no one had ever yet been laid. ⁵⁴It was the day of Preparation, and the sabbath was beginning.ˢ ⁵⁵The women who had come with him from Galilee followed, and saw the tomb, and how his body was laid; ⁵⁶then they returned, and prepared spices and ointments.

Lk 8:2–3

Ex 12:16; 20:10
Lev 23:8

On the sabbath they rested according to the commandment.

Mt 28:1–10
Mk 16:1–8
Jn 20:1–10

The resurrection of Jesus. The empty tomb

24 ¹But on the first day of the week, at early dawn, they went to the tomb, taking the spices which they had prepared. ²And they found the stone rolled

---

⁴⁴Et erat iam fere hora sexta, et tenebrae factae sunt in universa terra usque in horam nonam, ⁴⁵et obscuratus est sol, et velum templi scissum est medium. ⁴⁶Et clamans voce magna Iesus ait: «Pater, *in manus tuas commendo spiritum meum*»; et haec dicens exspiravit. ⁴⁷Videns autem centurio, quod factum fuerat, glorificavit Deum dicens: «Vere hic homo iustus erat!». ⁴⁸Et omnis turba eorum, qui simul aderant ad spectaculum istud, et videbant, quae fiebant, percutientes pectora sua revertebantur. ⁴⁹Stabant autem omnes noti eius a longe, et mulieres, quae secutae erant eum a Galilaea, haec videntes. ⁵⁰Et ecce vir nomine Ioseph, qui erat decurio, vir bonus et iustus ⁵¹— hic non consenserat consilio et actibus eorum— ab Arimathaea civitate Iudaeorum, qui exspectabat regnum Dei, ⁵²hic accessit ad Pilatum et petiit corpus Iesu, ⁵³et depositum involvit sindone et posuit eum in monumento exciso, in quo nondum quisquam positus fuerat. ⁵⁴Et dies erat Parasceves, et sabbatum illucescebat. ⁵⁵Subsecutae autem mulieres, quae cum ipso venerant de Galilaea, viderunt monumentum et quemadmodum positum erat corpus eius, ⁵⁶et revertentes paraverunt aromata et unguenta et sabbato quidem siluerunt secundum mandatum. [24] ¹Prima autem sabbatorum, valde diluculo venerunt ad monumentum portantes, quae paraverant, aromata. ²Et invenerunt lapidem revolutum a monumento ³et ingressae non invenerunt corpus Domini Iesu. ⁴Et factum est, dum mente haesitarent de

---

23:50–56 This passage provides pieces of information that prove that the one who is buried is the one who is raised. Jesus' body was placed in a tomb "where no one had ever yet been laid" (v. 53), and the women were witnesses to "how his body was laid" (v. 55): "God did not prevent death from separating [Christ's] soul from the body in accordance with the necessary order of nature, but he reunited them once again, one to the other, by means of the Resurrection so that he himself might become the point of contact between life and death, ending in himself the decomposition of the nature which produces death and inaugurating in himself the principle of reunion of the two separated parts" (St Gregory of Nyssa, *Oratio catechetica*, 16).

It is all over. Joseph of Arimathea, a man of considerable standing, shows great refinement in doing all that was required to give Jesus' body pious burial. His action sets an example for all of Christ's disciples: love for their Lord should lead them to risk honour, position and money. It is time to reflect on the work of Jesus, who "as an innocent lamb [...] merited for us life by the free shedding of His own blood. In Him God reconciled us to Himself and among ourselves [...]. He blazed a trail, and if we follow it, life and death are made holy and take on a new meaning" (Vatican II, *Gaudium et spes*, 22).

24:1–12 St Luke is the Synoptic author who goes into the most detail about the announce-

---

q Or *earth*   r Or *the sun was eclipsed*. Other ancient authorities read the *sun was darkened*   s Greek *was dawning*

away from the tomb, [3]but when they went in they did not find the body.[t] [4]While they were perplexed about this, behold, two men stood by them in dazzling apparel; [5]and as they were frightened and bowed their faces to the ground, the men said to them, "Why do you seek the living among the dead? He is not here, but has risen.[u] [6]Remember how he told you, while he was still in Galilee, [7]that the Son of man must be delivered into the hands of sinful men, and be crucified, and on the third day rise." [8]And they remembered his words, [9]and returning from the tomb they told all this to the eleven and to all the rest. [10]Now it was Mary Magdalene and Joanna and Mary the mother of James and the other women with them who told this to the apostles; [11]but these words seemed to them an idle tale, and they did not believe them. [12]But Peter rose and ran to the tomb; stooping and looking in, he saw the linen cloths by themselves; and he went home wondering at what had happened.[v]

Rom 1:4
Acts 1:10
Rev 1:18

Mt 17:22
Lk 9:22

Mk 16:10–14
Jn 20:18

Lk 8:2–3

Lk 24:24

The road to Emmaus

Mk 16:12–13

[13]That very day two of them were going to a village named Emmaus, about seven miles[w] from Jerusalem, [14]and talking with each other about all these things that had happened. [15]While they were talking and discussing together, Jesus himself drew

isto, ecce duo viri steterunt secus illas in veste fulgenti. [5]Cum timerent autem et declinarent vultum in terram, dixerunt ad illas: «Quid quaeritis viventem cum mortuis? [6]Non est hic, sed surrexit. Recordamini qualiter locutus est vobis, cum adhuc in Galilaea esset, [7]dicens: "Oportet Filium hominis tradi in manus hominum peccatorum et crucifigi et die tertia resurgere"». [8]Et recordatae sunt verborum eius [9]et regressae a monumento nuntiaverunt haec omnia illis Undecim et ceteris omnibus. [10]Erat autem Maria Magdalene et Ioanna et Maria Iacobi; et ceterae cum eis dicebant ad apostolos haec. [11]Et visa sunt ante illos sicut deliramentum verba ista, et non credebant illis. [12]Petrus autem surgens cucurrit ad monumentum et procumbens videt linteamina sola; et rediit ad sua mirans, quod factum fuerat. [13]Et ecce duo ex illis ibant ipsa die in castellum, quod erat in spatio stadiorum sexaginta ab Ierusalem nomine Emmaus, [14]et ipsi loquebantur ad invicem de his omnibus, quae acciderant. [15]Et factum est, dum fabularentur et secum quaer-

ment of the Resurrection and the appearances of Jesus. And what comes across very clearly is the difficulty the disciples had in accepting the Resurrection. However, as the "two men" remind the women (v. 7), Jesus' death was oriented to his Resurrection. The Resurrection completes the work of our redemption: "For just as by dying he endured all evil to deliver us from evil, so was he glorified in rising again to advance us towards good things, according to Romans 4:25 which says that 'he was put to death for our trespasses and raised for our justification'" (St Thomas Aquinas, *Summa theologiae*, 3, 53, 1c).

The opening verses of this passage describe the women's reaction. They are disconcerted by the empty tomb and the presence of the "two men" (v. 4) and are "frightened" (v. 5). They believe in the Resurrection only when reminded that it had all been foretold by Jesus (vv. 7–8). The Gospels are unanimous in recording that the women were the first witnesses to the Resurrection. St Bede (making no reference to the tradition that the risen Jesus appeared first to his Mother) sees in this fact a providential act of God, in that if a woman, Eve, was the first to

yield to temptation, a woman was the first to announce the news of the Resurrection: "As woman was the first to taste death, so woman was the first to witness the Resurrection [...] and as original sin first came to man through woman, so too grace came to man through woman" (*In Marci Evangelium*, 4, 16, 9–10).

The narrative then goes on to describe the attitude of the apostles (vv. 11–12). They do not believe what the women tell them. The women's account sows doubts in Peter's mind, and presumably in the minds of the others, too (24:24; cf. Jn 20:3–8), but this does not lead to an act of faith on their part; it simply causes them to wonder (v. 12). Their reactions show how difficult it was for the apostles to believe in the Resurrection.

24:13–35 The Emmaus episode forms a bridge between the announcement of the Resurrection and Jesus' appearances to the Eleven. It complements the previous episode because, when these two disciples arrive back in Jerusalem, the Eleven, thanks to Peter's testimony (vv. 33–34), already believe in the Resurrection. And like the

t Other ancient authorities add *of the Lord Jesus*   u Other ancient authorities omit *He is not here, but has risen*   v Other ancient authorities omit verse 12   w Greek *sixty stadia*; other ancient authorities read *a hundred and sixty stadia*

Lk 24:31 near and went with them. ¹⁶But their eyes were kept from recognizing him. ¹⁷And he said to them, "What is this conversation which you are holding with each other as you walk?" And they stood still, looking sad. ¹⁸Then one of them, named Cleopas, Mt 21:11
Acts 2:22 answered him, "Are you the only visitor to Jerusalem who does not know the things that have happened there in these days?" ¹⁹And he said to them, "What things?" And they said to him, "Concerning Jesus of Nazareth, who was a prophet mighty in deed and word before God and all the people, ²⁰and how our chief priests and rulers deliv- Lk 1:68; 2:38; 19:11
Acts 1:6 ered him up to be condemned to death, and crucified him. ²¹But we had hoped that he was the one to redeem Israel. Yes, and besides all this, it is now the third day Lk 24:1–11
Jn 20:2 since this happened. ²²Moreover, some women of our company amazed us. They were at the tomb early in the morning ²³and did not find his body; and they came back saying that they had even seen a vision of angels, who said that he was alive. Jn 20:3–10
Lk 24:12 ²⁴Some of those who were with us went to the tomb, and found it just as the women had said; but him they did not see." ²⁵And he said to them, "O foolish men, and slow

erent, et ipse Iesus appropinquans ibat cum illis; ¹⁶oculi autem illorum tenebantur, ne eum agnoscerent. ¹⁷Et ait ad illos: «Qui sunt hi sermones, quos confertis ad invicem ambulantes?». Et steterunt tristes. ¹⁸Et respondens unus, cui nomen Cleopas, dixit ei: «Tu solus peregrinus es in Ierusalem et non cognovisti, quae facta sunt in illa his diebus?». ¹⁹Quibus ille dixit: «Quae?». Et illi dixerunt ei: «De Iesu Nazareno, qui fuit vir propheta, potens in opere et sermone coram Deo et omni populo, ²⁰et quomodo eum tradiderunt summi sacerdotes et principes nostri in damnationem mortis, et cru- cifixerunt eum. ²¹Nos autem sperabamus quia ipse esset redempturus Israel; at nunc super haec omnia tertia dies hodie quod haec facta sunt. ²²Sed et mulieres quaedam ex nostris terruerunt nos, quae ante lucem fuerunt ad monumentum ²³et, non invento corpore eius, venerunt dicentes se etiam visionem angelorum vidisse, qui dicunt eum vivere. ²⁴Et abierunt quidam ex nostris ad monumentum et ita invenerunt, sicut mulieres dixerunt, ipsum

episode that follows (24:36–49), in which the physical reality of Christ's true body is made clear, the Emmaus episode serves to show that those who love Jesus will always come to recog- nize him (cf. Jn 20:11–17).

The scene is very easy to visualize. These two disciples are downhearted (v. 17) and with- out hope (v. 21), because they had been expect- ing a dramatic victory (vv. 19–21). They are well-intentioned, but too human in their think- ing. Meanwhile, Jesus joins them and they listen to what he has to say: "As he is walking along, Christ meets two men who have nearly lost all hope. They are beginning to feel that life has no meaning for them. Christ understands their sorrow; he sees into their heart and communi- cates to them some of the life he carries within himself" (St Josemaría Escrivá, *Christ Is Pass- ing By*, 105).

Jesus responds to the earthbound thinking of the disciples by giving them divine wisdom: he explains recent events as a fulfilment of the Scriptures, and this sets their hearts aflame (cf. v. 32), so they want him to stay with them and not continue on his journey alone (vv. 28–29). Jesus acts in the same way towards us: "This Lord of ours never forces himself on us. He wants us to turn to him freely, when we begin to grasp the purity of his Love which he has placed in our souls. [...] Deep down what we are really think- ing is: 'Stay with us, because our souls are shrouded in darkness and You alone are the light. You alone can satisfy this longing that consumes us'" (St Josemaría Escrivá, *Friends of God*, 314).

Eventually, they recognize Jesus in the break- ing of the bread (v. 31). He has opened their minds and hearts: "Illumined by his grace, they heard the call of faith; and as he interpreted the Scriptures to them, their cold, sad hearts began to burn within them. Their eyes were opened at the breaking of the bread when they sat with Him, and they were able to see and contemplate Christ's glorified nature" (St Leo the Great, *Sermo I de ascensione Domini*, 3). This account also illustrates the importance that Holy Scrip- ture and the Eucharist have in the Church, for the nourishment of people's faith. As a medieval writer on Christian living put it, "The holy books are a consolation and a mirror to my life, and your holy Body my refuge and my strength. [...] Without these, I could not live a good life, for the word of God is the light of my soul, and the Sacrament is the bread that gives life forever" (Thomas à Kempis, *De imitatione Christi*, 4, 11, 3–4).

of heart to believe all that the prophets have spoken! [26]Was it not necessary that the
Christ should suffer these things and enter into his glory?" [27]And beginning with
Moses and all the prophets, he interpreted to them in all the scriptures the things
concerning himself.

Lk 9:22; 17:25

[28]So they drew near to the village to which they were going. He appeared to be
going further, [29]but they constrained him, saying, "Stay with us, for it is toward
evening and the day is now far spent." So he went in to stay with them. [30]When he
was at table with them, he took the bread and blessed, and broke it, and gave it to
them. [31]And their eyes were opened and they recognized him; and he vanished out
of their sight. [32]They said to each other, "Did not our hearts burn within us while he
talked to us on the road, while he opened to us the scriptures?" [33]And they rose that
same hour and returned to Jerusalem; and they found the eleven gathered together
and those who were with them, [34]who said, "The Lord has risen indeed, and has
appeared to Simon!" [35]Then they told what had happened on the road, and how he
was known to them in the breaking of the bread.

Lk 22:19

1 Cor 15:4–5

Jesus appears to the disciples in the upper room

Mt 28:16–20
Mk 16:14–18
Jn 20:19–31

[36]As they were saying this, Jesus himself stood among them, and said to them,
"Peace to you!"[x] [37]But they were startled and frightened, and supposed that they saw
a spirit. [38]And he said to them, "Why are you troubled, and why do questionings rise
in your hearts?* [39]See my hands and my feet, that it is I myself; handle me, and see;
for a spirit has not flesh and bones as you see that I have." [40]And when he had said
this, he showed them his hands and his feet.[y] [41]And while they still disbelieved for

1 Cor 15:5
Mt 14:26

1 Jn 1:1

vero non viderunt». [25]Et ipse dixit ad eos: «O stulti et tardi corde ad credendum in omnibus, quae locuti sunt Prophetae! [26]Nonne haec oportuit pati
Christum et intrare in gloriam suam?». [27]Et incipiens a Moyse et omnibus Prophetis interpretabatur illis in omnibus Scripturis, quae de ipso erant.
[28]Et appropinquaverunt castello, quo ibant, et ipse se finxit longius ire. [29]Et coegerunt illum dicentes: «Mane nobiscum, quoniam advesperascit et
inclinata est iam dies». Et intravit, ut maneret cum illis. [30]Et factum est, dum recumberet cum illis, accepit panem et benedixit ac fregit et porrigebat
illis. [31]Et aperti sunt oculi eorum et cognoverunt eum; et ipse evanuit ab eis. [32]Et dixerunt ad invicem: «Nonne cor nostrum ardens erat in nobis, dum
loqueretur nobis in via et aperiret nobis Scripturas?». [33]Et surgentes eadem hora regressi sunt in Ierusalem et invenerunt congregatos Undecim et eos,
qui cum ipsis erant, [34]dicentes: «Surrexit Dominus vere et apparuit Simoni». [35]Et ipsi narrabant, quae gesta erant in via, et quomodo cognoverunt eum
in fractione panis. [36]Dum haec autem loquuntur, ipse stetit in medio eorum et dicit eis: «Pax vobis!». [37]Conturbati vero et conterriti existimabant se
spiritum videre. [38]Et dixit eis: «Quid turbati estis, et quare cogitationes ascendunt in corda vestra? [39]Videte manus meas et pedes meos, quia ipse ego
sum! Palpate me et videte, quia spiritus carnem et ossa non habet, sicut me videtis habere». [40]Et cum hoc dixisset, ostendit eis manus et pedes. [41]Adhuc
autem illis non credentibus prae gaudio et mirantibus, dixit eis: «Habetis hic aliquid, quod manducetur?». [42]At illi obtulerunt ei partem piscis assi.

24:36–49 From the narrative of the apparitions
we can see how Jesus went about explaining the
Resurrection to his disciples. Once they are convinced that he has indeed risen (24:34), he shows
them that he is not a spirit or a ghost (see v. 37):
he has flesh and bones (vv. 39, 41–43) and is the
same person as died on the cross (vv. 39–40):
"For myself, I know and believe that our Lord
was in the flesh even after the Resurrection. And
when he came to Peter and his companions, he
said to them: 'Here, feel me and see that I am not
a bodiless ghost.' They touched him and
believed, and were convinced that he was flesh
and spirit [...]. Moreover, after the Resurrection,
he ate and drank with them like a man of flesh
and blood, though spiritually one with the

Father" (St Ignatius of Antioch, *Ad Smyrnaeos*,
3, 1–3).

After proving who he is and before he returns
to his Father's side, Jesus entrusts his disciples
with their mission. These final words of our Lord
sum up everything that St Luke will go on to
recount in the book of the Acts of the Apostles: it
is God's plan that the mysteries to which they
are witnesses (v. 48) should be preached (vv. 46–
47) to bring salvation to all nations (v. 47). This
apostolic mission will begin in Jerusalem (v. 47)
because it is from there that Jesus will make his
"departure" (see 9:31) and there, too, that the
mission of the Holy Spirit will begin (v. 49). If
Galilee is the land of the promises (24:6),
Jerusalem will be where they find fulfilment.

x Other ancient authorities omit *and said to them, "Peace to you!"*   y Other ancient authorities omit verse 40

Jn 21:5–10, 13

Acts 10:41

Lk 18:31–33
Jn 5:46

Lk 24:25–27
1 Tim 3:16
Lk 9:22

Acts 1:4, 8; 3:15;
5:32

Jn 15:26

joy, and wondered, he said to them, "Have you anything here to eat?" [42]They gave him a piece of broiled fish, [43]and he took it and ate before them.

[44]Then he said to them, "These are my words which I spoke to you, while I was still with you, that everything written about me in the law of Moses and the prophets and the psalms must be fulfilled." [45]Then he opened their minds to understand the scriptures, [46]and said to them, "Thus it is written, that the Christ should suffer and on the third day rise from the dead, [47]and that repentance and forgiveness of sins should be preached in his name to all nations,[z] beginning from Jerusalem. [48]You are witnesses of these things. [49]And behold, I send the promise of my Father upon you; but stay in the city, until you are clothed with power from on high."

Mk 16:19
Acts 1:6–11

The ascension of our Lord

[50]Then he led them out as far as Bethany, and lifting up his hands he blessed them. [51]While he blessed them, he parted from them, and was carried up into heaven.[a] [52]And they worshipped him, and[b] returned to Jerusalem with great joy, [53]and were continually in the temple blessing God.

[43]Et sumens coram eis manducavit. [44]Et dixit ad eos: «Haec sunt verba, quae locutus sum ad vos, cum adhuc essem vobiscum, quoniam necesse est impleri omnia, quae scripta sunt in Lege Moysis et Prophetis et Psalmis de me». [45]Tunc aperuit illis sensum, ut intellegerent Scripturas. [46]Et dixit eis: «Sic scriptum est, Christum pati et resurgere a mortuis die tertia, [47]et praedicari in nomine eius paenitentiam in remissionem peccatorum in omnes gentes, incipientibus ab Ierusalem. [48]Vos estis testes horum. [49]Et ecce ego mitto promissum Patris mei in vos; vos autem sedete in civitate, quoadusque induamini virtutem ex alto». [50]Eduxit autem eos foras usque in Bethaniam et, elevatis manibus suis, benedixit eis. [51]Et factum est dum benediceret illis, recessit ab eis et ferebatur in caelum. [52]Et ipsi adoraverunt eum et regressi sunt in Ierusalem cum gaudio magno [53]et erant semper in templo benedicentes Deum.

24:50–53 The Ascension marks the culmination of salvation. Jesus, as High Priest, blesses his faithful. His entry into heaven means not only that his human nature now receives the glory it deserves; it also signals the fact that our human nature already shares the glory of the Godhead in him: "The apostles and the other disciples, who had been so troubled by his death on the cross and had doubted the truth of his resurrection, were not filled with sorrow at his ascension into heaven; rather, they were filled with a great joy. Truly it was an occasion of great, indescribable joy, when human nature ascended into heaven and was raised above all the heavenly beings, [...] higher than the archangels, raised and exalted to a height that no human measure can comprehend, until He was received by the Father, led to the throne and given the glory of the One whose divine nature he shares in the person of the Son" (St Leo the Great, *Sermo I de ascensione Domini*, 4).

z Or *nations. Beginning from Jerusalem you are witnesses*   a Other ancient authorities omit *and was carried up into heaven*   b Other ancient authorities omit *worshipped him, and*

THE GOSPEL ACCORDING TO

JOHN

Introduction

This book completes the canon of Gospels defined as sacred by the Church. Like the Synoptics it is a "Gospel", a proclamation of the Good News, but it provides a deeper understanding than they do of the life and teaching of our Lord. This is why it is positioned after them, although in some early Western codexes it is placed second, not fourth.

Evidence from the early second century shows this Gospel to have enjoyed great prestige, for even then we find it quoted verbatim and references being made to the meanings of some of the expressions it contains. For example, St Ignatius of Antioch (*c*.110) speaks of the Spirit that knows "whence it comes or whither it goes",[1] and says that the Word, the Son of God, pleases in every respect him who sent him (cf. Jn 1:14; 7:28; 8:29). St Polycarp, in his *Letter to the Philippians* (*c*.110), also echoes phrases from the Gospel of John, as does St Justin (*c*.150) when he says that it is necessary to be born again in order to enter the Kingdom of heaven.[2] Moreover, a fragment of the fourth Gospel is conserved in a papyrus, P[52], in the John Rylands Library, Manchester, which was discovered in El Faiyûm, Egypt, and which has been dated to the first half of the second century; this indicates that the fourth Gospel was widely known by that early date; the papyrus is the earliest text we have of any Gospel.

A reference to the fourth Gospel, with attribution of it to St John, is found in the work of St Irenaeus, bishop of Lyons, who was born around the year 130 in Smyrna (Asia Minor), where he knew St Polycarp. His testimony is particularly valuable because, as we know from Tertullian, Polycarp had been appointed bishop of Smyrna by St John himself.[3] What Irenaeus actually says is: "John, the Lord's disciple, the very one who leant on his breast, published the Gospel during his stay at Ephesus."[4] Another important testimony is that of Papias, whom, through Eusebius of Caesarea, we know to have been a disciple of St John. Although in a passage quoted by Eusebius,[5] Papias speaks of a "John the apostle", and of a "John the presbyter", both St Irenaeus and Eusebius understand him to mean that it was the apostle who wrote the Gospel. From the fourth century onwards, widespread and consistent tradition attributes the fourth Gospel to the apostle St John, and that tradition is upheld by the Magisterium of the Church.[6]

1. STRUCTURE AND CONTENT

St John and the Synoptics follow the general scheme used by the apostles in their oral preaching (cf. Acts 10:38–41): Jesus begins his public ministry after his baptism in the Jordan by John the Baptist; he preaches and works miracles in Galilee and Jerusalem; and his life on earth ends with his passion and glorious resurrection. Within this general framework St John follows a plan of his own, structured around various Jewish feasts and showing how Jesus gradually revealed himself to be the Messiah and the Son of God. The structure of the fourth Gospel is more or less the following:

---

1 St Ignatius of Antioch, *Ad Philadelphos*, 7, 1, referring to John 3:8. **2** See St Polycarp, *Ad Philippenses*, 7, 1, 2; St Justin, *Apologia*, 1:61; see Jn 3:5. **3** Tertullian, *De praescriptionibus adversus haereticos*, 32. **4** St Irenaeus, *Adversus haereses*, 3, 1, 1. **5** *Historia ecclesiastica*, 3, 39, 1. **6** See DS, 180–182, 200–202 and 475.

PROLOGUE (1:1–18). Here Jesus is praised as the eternal Word of God, who with the Father created the world; he enlightens all mankind, having been made man in order to make known to the world the truth about God and to enable those who believe in him to become children of God.

PART ONE: JESUS IS REVEALED AS THE MESSIAH BY HIS SIGNS AND WORDS (1:19—12:50). This part runs from the Baptist's testimony regarding Jesus to the Passover during which he dies. After an introduction that includes the Baptist's first testimony (1:19–34) and the calling of the first disciples (1:35–51), we read of the first manifestation of Jesus as the bearer of salvation, and expressions of faith in him (2:1—4:54). This manifestation of Jesus comes in the account of his ministry in Galilee, a first journey to Jerusalem for the Passover, and his return to Galilee by way of Samaria. Jesus then goes on to reveal his divinity (5:1–47) during another visit to Jerusalem for another feast. After this we find him in Galilee again when he portrays himself as the Bread of Life (6:1–71), and in Jerusalem, during the feast of Tabernacles, he reveals himself as the one sent by the Father, and as the Light of the world and the Good Shepherd (7:1—10:21). In a further confrontation with Jews in Jerusalem during the feast of the Dedication, Jesus says that he is one with the Father (10:22–42), and in Bethany, near Jerusalem, where Jesus raises Lazarus to life, he shows himself to be the one who grants man resurrection and eternal life (11:1–57). Finally, after Mary anoints Jesus at Bethany, he is acclaimed in Jerusalem as the Messiah King (12:1–50).

PART TWO: JESUS IS REVEALED AS THE MESSIAH, THE SON OF GOD, IN HIS PASSION, DEATH AND RESURRECTION (13:1—21:25). This part begins with the Last Supper, in the course of which Jesus makes known his inner thoughts and feelings (13:1—17:26); the account of his passion and death follows (18:1–19:42); and then the risen Jesus appears to his disciples on a number of occasions (20:1—21:25). The empty tomb and Jesus' appearances prove that the Resurrection has truly taken place. The risen Jesus breathes the Holy Spirit into the apostles, empowering them to forgive sins, and charges Peter to lead his Church.

2. CONTEXT

The author and the circumstances in which the book was written
When one is reading the fourth Gospel, certain transitions that disrupt the flow of the narrative become evident, which might lead one to suspect that the book was composed in stages. The most significant examples of this are as follows: chapter 5's description of Jesus' activity in Jerusalem on the occasion of a Jewish festival (unspecified) does not fit well between chapters 4 and 6, which place Jesus in Galilee; at the Last Supper, Jesus says at the end of chapter 14, "Rise, let us go hence", whereas his discourse continues in chapter 15; the account of the appearance of Jesus in chapter 21 has an ending similar to that of chapter 20, so that chapter 21 appears to be a later addition. These and other literary features suggest that the present form of the Gospel is the work of a later editor who has reconstructed material already written and given it the shape it now has. That last editor, when ending the book, speaks in the first person plural ("we know that his testimony is true"), as if he were echoing the view of the community, while, at the same time, he identifies "the disciple whom Jesus loved" as the one "who is bearing witness to these things, and who has written these things" (21:20, 24).

The "disciple whom Jesus loved" and, therefore, the true author of this Gospel is the apostle St John, a fact which is corroborated by a comparing of information in the Gospel itself with that provided by the Synoptics. Besides, many literary features of the fourth Gospel confirm that the author is a Jew, who was very familiar with the geography of Palestine and with Jewish customs and feasts (see 3:23; 4:5–6; 7:2; 10:22; 11:18). The language and grammatical constructions used in the Gospel are markedly Semitic. The Tradition of the Fathers of the Church and ecclesiastical writers from the second century onwards confirms that St John was the author, and gives Ephesus as the place where it was written—the city to which John had moved to preach the Gospel.

Implicit in the Gospel itself is the supposition that it was written in a context where Christians no longer had any involvement with Judaism. For example, it speaks of "the Jews", and not just the Jewish authorities, as being a body opposed to Jesus (see Jn 1:19; 2:18; 5:10) and it speaks, too, of Christians being expelled from the synagogues (see Jn 9:22; 16:2). Reference to the Jewish feasts as the context in which Jesus established a new economy of salvation indicates that the community for which this Gospel was written is regarded as the true, new Israel, distinct and separate from the old Jewish institutions; the new religion is seen as taking the place of Judaism. This confrontation with Judaism and the expulsion of Christians from the synagogue would have happened around the end of the first century, so that Tradition would appear to be correct in saying that the Gospel was written in the decade of the 90s.

The author's purpose in writing; comparison with the Synoptic Gospels

As the author himself explains, his intention in writing is "that you may believe that Jesus is the Christ, the Son of God, and that believing you may have life in his name" (20:31). That is to say, he seeks to form and strengthen his readers' faith. To achieve the purpose outlined at the end of the book, the author follows a plan different from that of the Synoptics. He focuses mainly on Jesus' activity in Judea, and especially in the temple of Jerusalem, to which our Lord goes up at least three times in connexion with feasts (see 2:13; 7:10; 12:12), and makes little comment on Jesus' activity in Galilee. He does mention that Jesus passed through Samaria (see 4:1–42). In contrast, the first three Gospels mention only one visit by Jesus to Jerusalem in the course of his public ministry—the one during which he meets his death, at the Passover feast.

Of the twenty-nine miracles recorded by the Synoptics, St John includes only two (see 6:11, 19), and he reports five additional ones (see 2:1–11; 4:46–54; 5:1–9; 9:1–41; 11:33–44). But what comes across very clearly is that he wants to present the miracles as "signs", for he makes use of them to expound meanings that are not immediately apparent. For example, the changing of water into wine (the first of the signs) displays Jesus' glory, reveals the start of the messianic age, and allows us to glimpse the role of his Blessed Mother in the Redemption (Jn 2:1–11); the miracle of the loaves and fish, reported also in the Synoptics, supports what Christ says when he portrays himself as the Bread of Life (Jn 6); the curing of the man blind from birth together with Jesus' reiterated claim to be the Light of the world (Jn 9); and the raising of Lazarus teaches that only Jesus is the Resurrection and the Life (Jn 11).

The fourth Gospel's account of the passion, death and resurrection of our Lord is similar to those found in the Synoptics, but, again, John has his own distinctive perspective: he looks at these events in the light of Christ's glorification. This is when Jesus' "hour" comes, when the Father glorifies the Son, who, through his death, defeats the devil, sin and death, and is exalted above all things (12:32–33). Thus, whereas the announcements Jesus makes about his passion in the Synoptics focus on the appropriateness of the Son of Man *suffering* (see Mt 16:21 and par.),

St John stresses that it is fitting and right that the Son of Man should be *lifted up* (see 3:14–15; 8:28; 12:32–33).

The fourth Gospel also gives nuances to Jesus' teaching that are not discernible in the Synoptics. For example, only twice do we find the simple expression "kingdom of God", whereas in the Synoptics (especially Matthew) it appears often (see, e.g., Mt 3:2; 4:23; 5:3; 11:12; 13:24). Many themes that recur often in the Synoptics are not dealt with by St John, such as the question of the sabbath, the legalism of the Pharisees, etc.; instead, he centres his account on life, truth, light, glory—ideas that are very rarely found in the earlier Gospels.

As we are told at the end of the book, the aim of the author is to bear witness to things that he has seen (19:35; 21:24). Evidence of this intention appears throughout the text, and the author favours the use of "to bear witness" and "to teach", rather than "to evangelize" or "to preach". His narrative focus is always on Jesus Christ. For example, he presents the Baptist's preaching as an historical event that bears witness to Christ (1:7, 19–34; 3:26; 5:33). But, above all, he records the testimony given by the Father to the one he has sent (5:36–37), and Jesus bears witness himself: he says that he knows where he has come from and where he is going (8:14), and that he is testifying to what he has seen (3:11). The Scriptures, too, bear witness to him (5:39), as the Holy Spirit will when he is sent (15:26). Finally, our Lord tells the apostles: "You also are witnesses, because you have been with me from the beginning" (15:27). The written Gospel is itself "witness" borne to and accepted by the Church (21:24).

3. MESSAGE

The revelation of God

The most important religious/doctrinal message of the fourth Gospel is its depiction of the invisible God who makes himself known through Jesus Christ: "No one has ever seen God; the only Son, who is in the bosom of the Father, he has made him known" (1:18). Only Jesus could reveal the inner life of God, for he is the Logos or Word of God, the eternal Son, who truly knows the Father, and his revelation is possible because, thanks to his intercession and in his name, God has sent his Holy Spirit to make all truth known. In the Prologue we are told that "in the beginning" the Word was God; by saying that the Word was with God, the text implicitly asserts that the Word is consubstantial with the Father.

The Word is the only-begotten Son of the Father (1:14). Throughout the Gospel, Jesus speaks about his Father, and on the three occasions when he prays out loud, he begins by invoking the Father (11:41; 12:28; 17:1). Besides making this distinction between himself and the Father, Jesus expressly says that the Father and the Son share the same nature: "I and the Father are one" (10:30).

Jesus also speaks of the Spirit as being a Person. At the Last Supper, and after the Resurrection, he speaks to his followers about the Spirit and his role as Revealer. He tells them that he himself will ask the Father to give them another "Counsellor", the Spirit of truth (14:16–17; 15:26; 16:13), and that the Father will hear his prayer and will send this Counsellor (14:26), who is also sent by the Son (16:7), and receives from him the message he is to proclaim (16:13–15).

The action of the Spirit accompanies the work of Christ. In the account of the baptism of Jesus, the sign that reveals him to be the Son of God is the descent upon him of the Spirit in the form of a dove (1:32); the Baptist himself preaches that, in contrast to the way he baptizes, Jesus baptizes with the Holy Spirit (1:32–34). It is the Spirit, along with water, that gives man a new form of being, a form of rebirth: "unless one is born again of water and the Spirit, he cannot enter the kingdom of God" (3:5). This connexion between water and the Spirit appears again in 7:37–39, where our Lord says that rivers of living water will flow from his heart, and the evangelist adds the explanation: "Now this he said about the Spirit, which those who believed in him were to receive, for as yet the Spirit had not been given, because Jesus was not yet glorified" (7:39). It is the Spirit who will remind the disciples about, and enable them to know, the works and words of Jesus, the revealer of the Father (cf. 14:26), guiding them to full truth and leading them to glorify Jesus (cf. 16:13). The Spirit, too, will be the one who brings about man's deliverance through the ministry of the apostles: "Receive the Holy Spirit. If you forgive the sins of any, they are forgiven; if you retain the sins of any, they are retained" (20:22–23).

Knowledge of God: faith and love

According to the fourth Gospel, belief involves knowing the truth about Christ. The verbs "believe" and "know" are often used together in the same phrase; in fact, on occasion seem to be interchangeable (see, e.g., 6:69; 17:8). "Knowing" is not something purely intellectual, a mere grasping the truth. In line with the Old Testament meaning of the word, it signifies full commitment to the Word; and the Word is Jesus Christ. Therefore, faith includes both the act of trusting self-surrender and that of knowing. This knowledge results from the testimony of the author of the Gospel and the action of the Spirit of truth. Thus, faith is, at the same time, both a free gift from God and a free act on the part of man. And so we find Jesus constantly exhorting people to believe in him, that is, to desire to believe in him, and not to deliberately close themselves to the truth (see, e.g., 3:36; 5:24; 8:24).

A person who believes in Jesus Christ comes to have eternal life, that is, to share in the very life of God which is given him or her through union with Jesus, in the same way that the branches form part of the vine (15:1–8). The aim of divine revelation is to pass this life on to the human person: "God so loved the world that he gave his only Son, that whoever believes in him should not perish but have eternal life" (3:16). The new life granted to a person who believes in Jesus Christ ("He who believes in the Son has eternal life": 3:36; cf. 3:18; 5:24) is also a guarantee of resurrection at the end of time: "This is the will of my Father, that every one who sees the Son and believes in him should have eternal life; and I will raise him up at the last day" (6:40).

Eternal life consists in knowing the Father and the Son, through faith: "This is eternal life, that they know thee the only true God, and Jesus Christ whom thou hast sent" (17:3). At the same time, this knowledge means sharing in the love that obtains between the Father and the Son: "I made known to them thy name, and I will make it known, that the love with which thou hast loved me may be in them, and I in them" (17:26).

The faith that gives man eternal life is therefore completely bound up with love, for it consists precisely in entering into the relationship of love between the Father and the Son: "As the Father has loved me, so have I loved you; abide in my love" (15:9). Therefore it should be made manifest, too, in fraternal love (the commandment of fraternal love is the only one laid down by Jesus in this Gospel); Jesus says that he is the model for this love.[7]

---

7 See Jn 15:9–17. In 1 John 3:23 Jesus' commandment appears in a different form, but it is essentially the same as the one in the Gospel: "This is his commandment, that we should believe in the name of his Son Jesus Christ and love one another, just as he has commanded us."

The Church and the sacraments

Although the word "church" does not appear in the fourth Gospel, each of the authors implies that he sees himself as a member of the group made up of Jesus' disciples. This happens, for example, when the writer uses the first person plural both to bear witness to Christ ("we have seen his glory": 1:14) and when the secondary author does so to underwrite the truth of what is being passed on by the apostle ("we know that his testimony is true": 21:24). The Gospel reports Christ's words describing those who believe in him as a sheepfold whose gate is Christ himself (10:1–6), and statements of his later in which, referring to Old Testament prophecies about the renewal of the people of Israel (see Ezek 34), Jesus portrays himself as the Good Shepherd who creates a single flock that will comprise all mankind (10:11–18). This sheepfold and this flock stand for the Church. And the Church is also symbolized in the vine to which the branches stay joined (15:1–8). These and later images show that it is Jesus who rules and gives life to his Church; and he himself asks the Father to give his disciples the same unity as he has with the Father (17:20–23).

The later community of those who believe in Jesus—that is, the on-going Church—is in continuity with the group of disciples who knew him and bore witness to him. Among these, the "disciple whom Jesus loved" has a special place, and it is through his testimony that the reader of the Gospel comes to know Christ (20:31; 21:24). However, the disciple who is first among the apostles is Peter, as can be seen from the fact that he is the first to enter the empty tomb (20:3–8), and it is to him that the risen Christ gives charge of the whole flock of believers (21:15–19).

It could be said that in the fourth Gospel the actions performed by Jesus have a sacramental character, for in them, through outward signs, divine gifts are communicated. Jesus promises his disciples that they too will perform works like his (14:12); and, after he has risen, he gives the apostles the Holy Spirit to enable them to forgive sins, that is, to give people salvation (20:22–23). The Gospel effectively tells us that the gifts of salvation reach believers through actions performed by disciples of Christ, that is, through sacramental actions. A person, then, enters the Church, Christ's flock, by adhering to Christ through faith and through rebirth by "water and the Spirit" (cf. 3:5), an expression that refers to the rite of Christian Baptism, which is also symbolized in the account of the curing of the man blind from birth (9:1–41). Christ's flock also receives the nourishment of the Bread of life, the body and blood of Christ, who offers himself in the Eucharist to believers in the Eucharist (cf. 6:48–59).

The Blessed Virgin Mary

One particularly noteworthy feature of the fourth Gospel is the prominent treatment of women— Martha and Mary, Mary Magdalene, and, particularly, the Lord's Mother, the Virgin Mary. Although the Blessed Virgin appears only twice, these appearances come, significantly, at the start and at the close of the revelation of Jesus as Messiah and Son of God—in 2:1–11, in the account of the wedding at Cana, the scene of "the first of his signs"; and in 19:25–27, when he is dying on the cross. These passages are written to be read in parallel: in both, the Blessed Virgin is referred to not by name, but simply as Jesus' mother, and in both our Lord calls her "Woman". At both Cana and Calvary Jesus' "hour" is referred to, the hour which encompasses his whole life (cf. 7:30; 8:20; 12:23, 27; 13:1; 17:1); in the first case, it is a reference to a future time; in the second, to a present reality.

About Jesus' calling Mary "Woman": because there is something formal and emphatic about the use of the word in this context, most commentators are inclined to read it as an allusion to

Genesis 3:15, which speaks of the "woman" and "her seed" who will triumph over the "serpent", the symbol of the devil. Many Fathers of the Church speak of a parallel between Eve and Mary, similar to that between Adam and Christ (cf. Rom 5:12–14). Victory over the devil is won by Christ's death because, by dying, Christ redeems us from slavery to the devil. "Mors per Evam, vita per Mariam" ("Death through Eve, life through Mary").[8] "The first Eve", St Irenaeus teaches, "disobeyed God; but the second obeyed him; thus the Virgin Mary became the advocate of the virgin Eve."[9] And Origen comments: "We dare to say that the Gospels are the flower of the Scriptures, and the flower of the Gospels is that of St John. But no one can penetrate its meaning who has not rested on Jesus' breast and taken Mary as his Mother. To be like John one must be, as he was, pointed out by Jesus as another Jesus. And so, if Mary had no other children but Jesus, and Jesus says to his Mother, 'Behold, your Son', and not 'Behold another son', then it is as if he were saying, 'Behold, Jesus, to whom you have given life.' And so it is: anyone who has identified himself with Christ, no longer lives for himself, but Christ lives in him (cf. Gal 2:20), and since Christ lives in him, Jesus says of him to Mary, 'Behold, your son—Christ'."[10]

8 St Jerome, *Epistola ad Eustochium*, 22, 21.   **9** *Adversus haereses*, 5, 19, 1.   **10** *In Ioannem commentarium*, on Jn 19:26–27.

John

PROLOGUE

1 ¹In the beginning was the Word, and the Word was with God, and the Word was God.* ²He was in the beginning with God; ³all things were made through him, and without him was not anything made that was made. ⁴In him was life,ᵃ and the life was the light of men. ⁵The light shines in the darkness,* and the darkness has not overcome it.

1 Jn 1:1–4
Rev 19:13; Gen 1:1–5
Prov 8:22–27

Sir 24

Ps 33; Sir 43:28
Col 1:15–20
1 Cor 8:6; Heb 1:1–3
Jn 5:26; 8:12; 12:46;
1 Jn 5:11

Jn 3:19; 12:35–36

[1] ¹In principio erat Verbum, et Verbum erat apud Deum, et Deus erat Verbum. ²Hoc erat in principio apud Deum. ³Omnia per ipsum facta sunt, et sine ipso factum est nihil, quod factum est; ⁴in ipso vita erat, et vita erat lux hominum, ⁵et lux in tenebris lucet, et tenebrae eam non comprehenderunt. ⁶Fuit homo missus a Deo, cui nomen erat Ioannes; ⁷hic venit in testimonium, ut testimonium perhiberet de lumine, ut omnes creder-

1:1–18 These verses act as a prologue to the whole Gospel, and are a hymn in praise of Jesus Christ.

As a prologue, they mention the key themes that will be developed over the course of the narrative: Jesus is the Logos, the eternal Word of God (as the Word, he expresses God's Thought), who, on being sent into the world, communicates, through his words and works, the truth about God and about himself (see 8:31; 10:29; 14:6–13), and gives mankind divine life, eternal life (see 3:16; 5:26; 6:35; 11:25; 15:5). Prior to his coming, man was able to see God only indirectly: he could know God only through things and events, through reflections of his greatness. But now that the fullness of time has come, God is revealed through the human nature of Jesus Christ, who is the visible image of the invisible God (cf. Col 1:15); there can be no greater revelation of God to the world. In fact, Jesus himself assures us: "He who has seen me has seen the Father" (14:9). "The most intimate truth which this revelation gives us about God and the salvation of man shines forth in Christ, who is himself both the mediator and the sum total of Revelation" (Vatican II, *Dei Verbum*, 2). The prologue also mentions those who have been witnesses to Jesus' life on earth—John the Baptist (vv. 6–8, 15) and many others, disciples who believed in Jesus (v. 16), and those people who rejected him (v. 11). St Augustine comments: "But it may be that the dull hearts of some cannot yet receive this light. Their sins weigh them down, and they cannot discern it. Let them not think, however, that, because they cannot discern it, therefore it is not present with them. For they themselves, because of their sins, are darkness. Just as if you place a blind person in the sunshine, although the sun is present to him, yet he is absent from the sun" (*In Ioannis Evangelium*, 1, 19).

As a hymn to Jesus Christ, these verses proclaim the divinity and eternity of the Word (v. 1), his role in creation (v. 3), the fact that he enlightens the soul of man (vv. 4–5), his coming into the world and being rejected by it (vv. 9–11), the gifts he brings to those who believe in him (vv. 12–13). Even though he shared our human condition, his divine glory shone out (v. 14); and he (as only he could) has made known to us the saving mercy of God (vv. 16–18). To summarize: the Gospel proclaims (as St Paul does elsewhere: see Col 1:15–20; Phil 2:5–11) who Jesus Christ really is, where he comes from, how he came into the world and what he has done for mankind. To this end it portrays Jesus in a way similar to that in which Wisdom is personified in the Old Testament—as eternal, and active in creation and in the instruction of man (see Prov 8:22–31; Sir 24:1–22; Wis 7:22). It also tells us something about the role of the Word of God in the creation of the world (cf. Gen 1:1).

Verse 14, in a very condensed way, introduces the mystery of the Incarnation. The Greek verb used by St John and translated in the RSV as "dwelt" etymologically means "pitched his tent", that is, settled down to stay in a particular

ᵃ Or *was not anything made. That which has been made was life in him*

Lk 1:3–17, 57–60
Mt 3:1; Mk 1:4
Jn 3:28
Is 6:8; Jer 25:4
Jn 1:19–34; Lk 3:3
Jn 5:35
Jn 3:19; 8:12; 12:46
Jn 1:3; 14:17
Mt 21:38–43
Jn 4:44; 16:32
Gal 3:26
Jn 10:35; 20:31
1 Jn 3:2; 5:13
Jn 3:3–6; 1 Jn 5:1
Ex 25:8; Sir 24:8
Jn 7:3; Is 60:1
1 Jn 4:2
2 Pet 1:16–17
Rev 21:3; Lk 9:28–35
Jn 1:30
Col 1:19; 2:9–10
Ex 34:6
Rom 3:24; 6:14; 10:4
Ps 24:10; 40:10; 85:10
Ex 33:20, 23
Jn 6:46; 14:9
Mt 11:27; Lk 10:22
1 Tim 6:16

[6]There was a man sent from God, whose name was John. [7]He came for testimony, to bear witness to the light, that all might believe through him. [8]He was not the light, but came to bear witness to the light.

[9]The true light that enlightens every man was coming into the world. [10]He was in the world, and the world was made through him, yet the world knew him not. [11]He came to his own home, and his own people received him not. [12]But to all who received him, who believed in his name, he gave power to become children of God; [13]who were born, not of blood nor of the will of the flesh nor of the will of man, but of God.

[14]And the Word became flesh and dwelt among us, full of grace and truth; we have beheld his glory, glory as of the only Son from the Father. [15](John bore witness to him, and cried, "This was he of whom I said, 'He who comes after me ranks before me, for he was before me.'") [16]And from his fullness have we all received, grace upon grace. [17]For the law was given through Moses; grace and truth came through Jesus Christ. [18]No one has ever seen God; the only Son,[b] who is in the bosom of the Father, he has made him known.

ent per illum. [8]Non erat ille lux, sed ut testimonium perhiberet de lumine. [9]Erat lux vera, quae illuminat omnem hominem, veniens in mundum. [10]In mundo erat, et mundus per ipsum factus est, et mundus eum non cognovit. [11]In propria venit, et sui eum non receperunt. [12]Quotquot autem acceperunt eum, dedit eis potestatem filios Dei fieri, his, qui credunt in nomine eius, [13]qui non ex sanguinibus neque ex voluntate carnis neque ex voluntate viri, sed ex Deo nati sunt. [14]Et Verbum caro factum est et habitavit in nobis; et vidimus gloriam eius, gloriam quasi Unigeniti a Patre, plenum gratiae et veritatis. [15]Ioannes testimonium perhibet de ipso, et clamat dicens: «Hic erat, quem dixi: Qui post me venturus est, ante me factus est, quia prior me erat». [16]Et de plenitudine eius nos omnes accepimus, et gratiam pro gratia; [17]quia lex per Moysen data est, gratia et veritas per Iesum Christum facta est. [18]Deum nemo vidit umquam; Unigenitus Deus, qui est in sinum Patris, ipse enarravit. [19]Et hoc est testimonium

place. It calls to mind the tabernacle or tent from the time of the Exodus, where God manifested his presence in the midst of the people of Israel by means of signs of his glory such as the cloud that settled over the tent (see e.g. Ex 25:8; 40:34–35). The Old Testament also proclaims that God, and particularly his Wisdom, chose a place to dwell among the people (cf. e.g. Sir 24:8; Jer 7:3; Ezek 43:9). The Son of God's coming to live among men also fulfils the promise in Isaiah of the Immanuel or "God with us" (Is 7:14; cf. Mt 1:23). So, reading these verses of the Gospel or saying the Angelus is a valuable opportunity to make a deep act of faith and thanksgiving, and to adore the Holy Human Nature of our Lord, who, by becoming man, gives us the possibility of becoming children of God: "The Son of God became man", St Athanasius explains, "in order that the sons of men, the sons of Adam, might become sons of God. [...] He is the Son of God by nature; we, by grace" (*De Incarnatione contra Apollinarium*, 8). And John Paul II teaches: "Christ's union with man is power and the source of power, as St John stated

so incisively in the prologue of his Gospel: '[The Word] gave power to become children of God.' Man is transformed inwardly by this power as the source of a new life that does not disappear and pass away but lasts to eternal life (cf. Jn 4:14)" (*Redemptor hominis*, 18). The divine filiation that we acquire by union with Christ through Baptism enables us to share God's own life in a real, supernatural way (cf. 2 Pet 1:4); it draws us into the inner life of the Blessed Trinity.

The words "grace" and "truth" are, in this context, synonymous with "steadfast love and faithfulness", two attributes that the Old Testament constantly applies to God (see e.g. Ex 34:6; Ps 117 and 136; Hos 2:16–22). "Grace upon grace" or "grace for grace" (v. 16) means the replacement of the salvific economy of the Old Testament by the new economy of grace brought by Christ. It may also refer to the superabundance of gifts given by Jesus—grace piled on grace, all of it flowing from Christ, who has fullness of grace and therefore is an inexhaustible source of it.

b Other ancient authorities read *God*

PART ONE

Jesus is manifested as the Messiah by his signs and words*

1. INTRODUCTION*

The witness of John the Baptist

¹⁹And this is the testimony of John, when the Jews sent priests and Levites from Jerusalem to ask him, "Who are you?" ²⁰He confessed, he did not deny, but confessed, "I am not the Christ." ²¹And they asked him, "What then? Are you Elijah?" He said, "I am not." "Are you the prophet?" And he answered, "No." ²²They said to him then, "Who are you? Let us have an answer for those who sent us. What do you say about yourself?" ²³He said, "I am the voice of one crying in the wilderness, 'Make straight the way of the Lord,' as the prophet Isaiah said."

Mt 3:1–12
Mk 1:1–8
Lk 3:1–18

Jn 1:6; 5:33

Acts 13:25

Jn 6:14; 7:40
Mt 17:10
Deut 18:15

Is 40:3
Mt 3:3

Ioannis, quando miserunt ad eum Iudaei ab Hierosolymis sacerdotes et Levitas, ut interrogarent eum: «Tu quis es?». ²⁰Et confessus est et non negavit; et confessus est: «Non sum ego Christus». ²¹Et interrogaverunt eum: «Quid ergo? Elias es tu?». Et dicit: «Non sum». «Propheta es tu?». Et respondit: «Non». ²²Dixerunt ergo ei: «Quis es? Ut responsum demus his, qui miserunt nos. Quid dicis de teipso?». ²³Ait: «*Ego vox clamantis in deserto: / "Dirigite viam Domini"*», sicut dixit Isaias propheta». ²⁴Et qui missi fuerant, erant ex pharisaeis; ²⁵et interrogaverunt eum et dixerunt

*1:19—12:50 Jesus gradually reveals who he is by working miracles (signs of his divinity) and by preaching in which he declares himself to be the Messiah, and the Son of God, equal to the Father. This builds to a dramatic crescendo that culminates in Jesus' "hour", that is, his death and resurrection, which are recounted in the second part of the Gospel. Because of its content, this first part of the Gospel of John is called by many scholars the "book of signs".

*1:19–51 These verses are an introduction to the first part of the Gospel; they cover the testimony borne by the Baptist (1:19–36; cf. 3:22–36) and the calling of the first disciples (1:35–51).

1:19–34 John bears witness not only that Jesus is the Messiah but that he will redeem the world from sin by his violent death. The Baptist's testimony is portrayed as a model of the witness that Christians should bear to what they have seen and experienced through their belief in Jesus Christ: "All Christians by the example of their lives and the witness of the word, wherever they live, have an obligation to manifest the new man which they put on in Baptism, and to reveal the power of the Holy Spirit by whom they were strengthened at Confirmation, so that others, seeing their good works, might glorify the Father

and more perfectly perceive the true meaning of human life and the universal solidarity of mankind" (Vatican II, *Ad gentes*, 11).

In calling Jesus the "Lamb of God" (v. 29), John alludes to Christ's redemptive sacrifice. Isaiah compared the sufferings of the Servant, the Messiah, with the offering of a lamb (see Is 53:7). Moreover, at the time of the Exodus the blood of the Passover lamb, smeared on the doorposts of houses, kept the first-born of Israel safe from death (see Ex 12:6–7). After Jesus' death and resurrection, his disciples recognize him to be the true Passover Lamb: before receiving Christ in Holy Communion, that is, when about to share in the "marriage supper of the Lamb", they make this act of faith.

When John the Baptist says that Jesus "was before me" (v. 30) he acknowledges Jesus' divinity. As St Gregory puts it, it is as if he were saying: "Although I was born before him, he is not limited by the ties of his birth; for although he is born of his mother in time, he was generated by his Father outside of time" (*Homiliae in Evangelia*, 7). The witness borne by John at Jesus' baptism also reveals the mystery of the Blessed Trinity (see vv. 32–34). The dove is the symbol of the Holy Spirit, who hovered over the face of the waters at the dawn of creation (see Gen 1:2).

Mt 16:14; 21:25

Mt 3:11
Mk 1:7ff

Jn 3:26; 7:27–39
Acts 3:25
Jn 3:23, 26; 10:40
Mt 3:6–13
Jn 1:36
Hos 4:16
1 Jn 3:5
Is 53:7, 12
Ex 12:1–14
Rev 5:6
Jn 1:15, 17
Mt 3:16
Mk 1:10
Lk 3:22
Mt 3:17
Jn 1:18; 20:31

Mt 4:18–25
Mk 1:16–20
Lk 5:1–11
Jn 1:29
Is 53:7

Prov 8:17

²⁴Now they had been sent from the Pharisees. ²⁵They asked him, "Then why are you baptizing, if you are neither the Christ, nor Elijah, nor the prophet?" ²⁶John answered them, "I baptize with water; but among you stands one whom you do not know, ²⁷even he who comes after me, the thong of whose sandal I am not worthy to untie." ²⁸This took place in Bethany beyond the Jordan, where John was baptizing.

²⁹The next day he saw Jesus coming toward him, and said, "Behold, the Lamb of God, who takes away the sin of the world!* ³⁰This is he of whom I said, 'After me comes a man who ranks before me, for he was before me.' ³¹I myself did not know him; but for this I came baptizing with water, that he might be revealed to Israel." ³²And John bore witness, "I saw the Spirit descend as a dove from heaven, and it remained on him. ³³I myself did not know him; but he who sent me to baptize with water said to me, 'He on whom you see the Spirit descend and remain, this is he who baptizes with the Holy Spirit.' ³⁴And I have seen and borne witness that this is the Son of God."

The calling of the first disciples

³⁵The next day again John was standing with two of his disciples; ³⁶and he looked at Jesus as he walked, and said, "Behold, the Lamb of God!" ³⁷The two disciples heard him say this, and they followed Jesus. ³⁸Jesus turned, and saw them following, and

---

ei: «Quid ergo baptizas, si tu non es Christus neque Elias neque propheta?». ²⁶Respondit eis Ioannes dicens: «Ego baptizo in aqua; medius vestrum stat, quem vos non scitis, ²⁷qui post me venturus est, cuius ego non sum dignus, ut solvam eius corrigiam calceamenti». ²⁸Haec in Bethania facta sunt trans Iordanem, ubi erat Ioannes baptizans. ²⁹Altera die videt Iesum venientem ad se et ait: «Ecce agnus Dei, qui tollit peccatum mundi. ³⁰Hic est, de quo dixi: Post me venit vir, qui ante me factus est, quia prior me erat. ³¹Et ego nesciebam eum, sed ut manifestetur Israel, propterea veni ego in aqua baptizans». ³²Et testimonium perhibuit Ioannes dicens: «Vidi Spiritum descendentem quasi columbam de caelo, et mansit super eum; ³³et ego nesciebam eum, sed, qui misit me baptizare in aqua, ille mihi dixit: 'Super quem videris Spiritum descendentem et manentem super eum, hic est qui baptizat in Spiritu Sancto'. ³⁴Et ego vidi et testimonium perhibui quia hic est Filius Dei». ³⁵Altera die iterum stabat Ioannes et ex discipulis eius duo, ³⁶et respiciens Iesum ambulantem dicit: «Ecce agnus Dei». ³⁷Et audierunt eum duo discipuli loquentem et secuti sunt Iesum. ³⁸Conversus autem Iesus et videns eos sequentes se dicit eis: «Quid quaeritis?». Qui dixerunt ei: «Rabbi —quod dicitur interpretatum Magister—

1:35–51 This account of the calling of the first disciples contains mention of a number of Jesus' titles—Rabbi (Teacher), Messiah (Christ), Son of God, King of Israel, Son of man. Together they reveal Jesus to be the Messiah promised in the Old Testament and acknowledged by the Church: "St John the Apostle, who pours into his narrative so much that is first-hand, tells of his first unforgettable conversation with Christ. '"Master, where are you staying?" He said to them, "Come and see." They went and saw where he was staying; and they stayed with him that day, for it was about the tenth hour' (Jn 1:38–39). This divine and human dialogue completely changed the life of John and Andrew, and Peter and James and so many others. It prepared their hearts to listen to the authoritative teaching which Jesus gave them beside the Sea of Galilee" (St Josemaría Escrivá, *Christ Is Passing By*, 108).

The evangelist shows us that some of these early disciples came to know Jesus through introductions from people who were already among his followers. This is an instance of Christian apostolate. Commenting on v. 41, St John Chrysostom says: "This response is the expression of a soul who greatly desired the coming of the Messiah; filled with joy when he saw that his hope had been realized, he ran to tell his brothers the good news" (*In Ioannem*, 19, 1).

"You shall be called Cephas" (v. 42). The act of naming is equivalent to taking possession of the thing or person named (cf. Gen 17:5; 32:29). "Cephas" is a re-transliteration, from Greek, of an Aramaic word which means stone or rock, and, from this moment on, "Peter". That is why the evangelist (who is writing in Greek) explains the meaning of the word used by Jesus. "Cephas" was not a proper name, but our Lord gives it to Simon to indicate the role he will have as Christ's vicar (as will be revealed later: see Mt 16:16–18).

"Follow me" (v. 43) is what Jesus usually says when he calls disciples (see e.g. Mt 4:19; 8:22;

said to them, "What do you seek?" And they said to him, "Rabbi" (which means Teacher), "where are you staying?" [39]He said to them, "Come and see." They came and saw where he was staying; and they stayed with him that day, for it was about the tenth hour. [40]One of the two who heard John speak, and followed him, was Andrew, Simon Peter's brother. [41]He first found his brother Simon, and said to him, "We have found the Messiah" (which means Christ). [42]He brought him to Jesus. Jesus looked at him, and said, "So you are Simon the son of John? You shall be called Cephas" (which means Peter[c]).

[43]The next day Jesus decided to go to Galilee. And he found Philip and said to him, "Follow me." [44]Now Philip was from Bethsaida, the city of Andrew and Peter. [45]Philip found Nathanael, and said to him, "We have found him of whom Moses in the law and also the prophets wrote, Jesus of Nazareth, the son of Joseph." [46]Nathanael said to him, "Can anything good come out of Nazareth?" Philip said to him, "Come and see." [47]Jesus saw Nathanael coming to him, and said to him, "Behold, an Israelite indeed, in whom is no guile!" [48]Nathanael said to him, "How do you know me?" Jesus answered him, "Before Philip called you, when you were under the fig tree, I saw you." [49]Nathanael answered him, "Rabbi, you are the Son of God! You are the King of Israel!" [50]Jesus answered him, "Because I said to you, I saw you under the fig tree, do you believe? You shall see greater things than these." [51]And he said to him, "Truly, truly, I say to you, you will see heaven opened, and the angels of God ascending and descending upon the Son of man."

Mt 4:18

Mt 16:18
Mk 3:16
Lk 6:14

Mt 8:22; 9:9
Lk 9:59

Deut 18:18

Jn 7:41, 52
Mt 13:54ff

Is 11:2
Jn 2:24–24; 14:17–19

1 Kings 5:5
Jn 6:61, 64, 69
2 Sam 7:14
Mic 4:4
Ps 2:7
Mt 14:33; 16:16

Gen 28:12
Rev 19:11

2. JESUS, THE AUTHOR OF THE NEW ECONOMY OF SALVATION. FIRST SIGNS OF FAITH*

The wedding at Cana—the first sign worked by Jesus

2 [1]On the third day there was a marriage at Cana in Galilee, and the mother of Jesus was there; [2]Jesus also was invited to the marriage, with his disciples. [3]When

Hos 2:16–25
Is 25:6; 54:4–5
Ezek 16:8, 60
Mt 22:1–10
Rev 19:7–9

ubi manes?». [39]Dicit eis: «Venite et videbitis». Venerunt ergo et viderunt, ubi maneret, et apud eum manserunt die illo; hora erat quasi decima. [40]Erat Andreas, frater Simonis Petri, unus ex duobus, qui audierant ab Ioanne et secuti fuerant eum. [41]Invenit hic primum fratrem suum Simonem et dicit ei: «Invenimus Messiam» —quod est interpretatum Christus—; [42]adduxit eum ad Iesum. Intuitus eum Iesus dixit: «Tu es Simon filius Ioannis; tu vocaberis Cephas» —quod interpretatur Petrus—. [43]In crastinum voluit exire in Galilaeam et invenit Philippum. Et dicit ei Iesus: «Sequere me». [44]Erat autem Philippus a Bethsaida, civitate Andreae et Petri. [45]Invenit Philippus Nathanael et dicit ei: «Quem scripsit Moyses in Lege et Prophetae invenimus, Iesum filium Ioseph a Nazareth». [46]Et dixit ei Nathanael: «A Nazareth potest aliquid boni esse?». Dicit ei Philippus: «Veni et vide». [47]Vidit Iesus Nathanael venientem ad se et dicit de eo: «Ecce vere Israelita, in quo dolus non est». [48]Dicit ei Nathanael: «Unde me nosti?». Respondit Iesus et dixit ei: «Priusquam te Philippus vocaret, cum esses sub ficu, vidi te». [49]Respondit ei Nathanael: «Rabbi, tu es Filius Dei, tu rex es Israel!». [50]Respondit Iesus et dixit ei: «Quia dixi tibi: Vidi te sub ficu, credis? Maiora his videbis». [51]Et dicit ei: «Amen, amen

9:9). During Jesus' lifetime, this invitation meant accompanying him in his public ministry, listening to his teaching, and imitating his lifestyle. When our Lord ascended into heaven, to "follow him" meant to live Christ's life, to make his sentiments one's own: "It is no longer I who live, but Christ who lives in me" (Gal 2:20).

Verses 50–51, about those "greater things than these", seem to refer to Jesus' glorification. Jesus' words are reminiscent of the dream that Jacob had, in which he saw a ladder linking heaven and earth, and angels ascending and

descending (Gen 28:12), and they also recall to mind the figure of the "son of man" in the book of Daniel (Dan 7:13). There is already a reference here to the glorification of Christ that will come about through his death on the cross (see 12:23; 13:31): on dying, Jesus becomes the one who will judge mankind (the Son of man) and the way to salvation—the ladder whereby we are enabled to reach heaven.

*2:1—4:54 This section deals with Jesus' ministry in Galilee, Jerusalem and Samaria.

c From the word for *rock* in Aramaic and Greek respectively

Jn 19:26
Sir 31:27–28
Judg 11:12
Mt 12:48; Mk 1:24
Gen 41:55; Ex 19:8
Ps 26:6; Mk 7:2–4
the wine failed, the mother of Jesus said to him, "They have no wine." [4]And Jesus said to her, "O woman, what have you to do with me?* My hour has not yet come." [5]His mother said to the servants, "Do whatever he tells you." [6]Now six stone jars were standing there, for the Jewish rites of purification, each holding twenty or thirty gallons. [7]Jesus said to them, "Fill the jars with water." And they filled them up to the brim. [8]He said to them, "Now draw some out, and take it to the steward of the feast."

dico vobis: Videbitis *caelum* apertum et *angelos Dei ascendentes et descendentes* supra Filium hominis». [2] [1]Et die tertio nuptiae factae sunt in Cana Galilaeae, et erat mater Iesu ibi; [2]vocatus est autem et Iesus et discipuli eius ad nuptias. [3]Et deficiente vino, dicit mater Iesu ad eum: «Vinum non habent». [4]Et dicit ei Iesus: «Quid mihi et tibi, mulier? Nondum venit hora mea». [5]Dicit mater eius ministris: «Quodcumque dixerit vobis, facite». [6]Erant autem ibi lapideae hydriae sex positae secundum purificationem Iudaeorum, capientes singulae metretas binas vel ternas.

What gives the section unity is Jesus' revelation of himself as the Messiah who proclaims and implements God's new plans of salvation, which replace the temple and the Law of Moses. This can be seen in his turning of water into wine at Cana of Galilee (2:9), in the evangelist's comment on the episode of the cleansing of the temple ("he spoke of the temple of his body": 2:21), in the revelation to Nicodemus about rebirth through Baptism (3:5), and in Jesus' conversation with the Samaritan woman, when he says that true worship of God must be "in spirit and truth" (4:23–24). No one can be indifferent to these revelations of Jesus, and St John reports the first stirrings of faith in the disciples and in others, and the first sign of rejection by some Jews.

2:1–12 Cana in Galilee may be what is now Kefr Kenna, which is about seven kilometres (four miles) northeast of Nazareth. The first guest to be mentioned is Mary. St Joseph is not mentioned—which cannot be attributed to forgetfulness on John's part; his silence about him here and at other significant moments in the Gospel implies that Joseph was no longer alive.

The miracle at the wedding feast of Cana marks the start of the messianic times and of the gradual manifestation of Jesus' eternal glory. The miracle—or, as the text puts it literally, "the sign"—of the water being turned into wine anticipates the "hour" of Jesus' glorification (v. 4). Jesus sometimes used the term "hour" to refer to his second coming in glory (see 5:28), but usually it meant the time of his passion, death and resurrection (cf. 7:30; 12:23; 13:1; 17:1). John notes the generosity of the gift provided by our Lord: it was at least 480 litres of wine, or 120

gallons. This largesse is a sign that the messianic times have come; and the wine itself is a symbol of the supernatural gifts that Christ offers us.

In the fourth Gospel, the "mother of Jesus" (John's only way of referring to our Lady) appears only twice—once here (v. 1), and again at Calvary (19:25). Her appearances indicate Mary's role in the Redemption; they occur at the start and the close of our Lord's public life, as if to suggest that Mary played a part in all that Jesus did, acting as a true mother and being especially solicitous about people's needs. At Cana, she appeals for the newly-weds when her Son's "hour" has not yet come; on Calvary, when the hour has come, she offers the redemptive death of her Son to the Father and accepts the mission that Jesus confers on her to be the Mother of all believers, as represented by the beloved disciple.

The episode of Cana reveals a new dimension of Mary's motherhood: "The description of the Cana event outlines what is actually manifested as a new kind of motherhood according to the spirit and not just according to the flesh, that is to say *Mary's solicitude for human beings*, her coming to them in the wide variety of their wants and needs. At Cana in Galilee there is shown only one concrete aspect of human need, apparently a small one of little importance ('They have no wine'). But it has a symbolic value: this coming to the aid of human needs means, at the same time, bringing those needs within the radius of Christ's messianic mission and salvific power. Thus there is a mediation: Mary places herself between her Son and mankind in the reality of their wants, needs and sufferings. *She puts herself 'in the middle,'* that is to say *she acts as a mediatrix not as an out-*

So they took it. [9]When the steward of the feast tasted the water now become wine, and did not know where it came from (though the servants who had drawn the water knew), the steward of the feast called the bridegroom [10]and said to him, "Every man serves the good wine first; and when men have drunk freely, then the poor wine; but you have kept the good wine till now." [11]This, the first of his signs, Jesus did at Cana in Galilee, and manifested his glory; and his disciples believed in him.

[12]After this he went down to Capernaum, with his mother and his brethren* and his disciples; and there they stayed for a few days.

Jn 4:11; 8:14
Gen 24:20

Mk 2:22
Lk 5:39

Jn 4:54; 11:40

Mt 4:13

Cleansing of the temple—Christ, God's new temple

Mt 21:12–17
Mk 11:15–19
Lk 19:45–48

[13]The Passover of the Jews was at hand, and Jesus went up to Jerusalem. [14]In the temple he found those who were selling oxen and sheep and pigeons, and the

Jn 2:23; 6:4; 11:55; 12:1
Ex 12:11, 48
Deut 16:1

[7]Dicit eis Iesus: «Implete hydrias aqua». Et impleverunt eas usque ad summum. [8]Et dicit eis: «Haurite nunc et ferte architriclino». Illi autem tulerunt. [9]Ut autem gustavit architriclinus aquam vinum factam et non sciebat unde esset, ministri autem sciebant, qui haurierant aquam, vocat sponsum architriclinus [10]et dicit ei: «Omnis homo primum bonum vinum ponit et, cum inebriati fuerint, id quod deterius est; tu servasti bonum vinum usque adhuc». [11]Hoc fecit initium signorum Iesus in Cana Galilaeae et manifestavit gloriam suam, et crediderunt in eum discipuli eius. [12]Post hoc descendit Capharnaum ipse et mater eius et fratres eius et discipuli eius, et ibi manserunt non multis diebus. [13]Et prope erat Pascha

sider, but in her position as mother. She knows that as such she can point out to her Son the needs of mankind, and in fact, she 'has the right' to do so. Her mediation is thus in the nature of intercession: Mary 'intercedes' for mankind. And that is not all. As a mother she also wishes the messianic power of her Son to be manifested, that salvific power of his which is meant to help man in his misfortunes, to free him from the evil which in various forms and degrees weighs heavily upon his life" (John Paul II, Redemptoris Mater, 21).

The sentence rendered "What have you to do with me?" is the subject of an RSVCE note: see the end matter of this volume. It can also be translated as "What does this have to do with you and me?" The sentence is an Eastern idiom which can be used to express various shades of meaning. Jesus' reply seems to indicate that although in principle it was not part of God's plan for him to use his power to solve the crisis at the wedding feast, our Lady's request moves him to act. Christian piety has referred to our Lady's "supplicant omnipotence". "Mary's heart cannot but take pity on the unfortunate couple [...]; it stirs her to act as intercessor and ask her Son for the miracle, even though no one asks her to. [...] If our Lady acted like this without being asked, what would she not have done if they actually asked her to intervene?" (St Alphonsus Liguori, Short Sermons, 48, 2, 1).

The Church regards our Lord's presence at

this wedding as highly significant, reading it as confirmation of the goodness of marriage and as an announcement that henceforth marriage will be an effective sign of the presence of Christ (see Catechism of the Catholic Church, 1613). "At the beginning of his mission, we find Jesus at Cana in Galilee, taking part in a wedding banquet, together with Mary and with the first disciples (cf. Jn 2:1–11). He thus wishes to make clear to what extent the truth about the family is part of God's revelation and the history of salvation" (John Paul II, Letter to Families, 18).

In connexion with the addition of "mysteries of light" to the Rosary, John Paul II comments: "The revelation made directly by the Father at the Baptism in the Jordan and echoed by John the Baptist is placed upon Mary's lips at Cana, and it becomes the great maternal counsel which Mary addresses to the Church of every age: 'Do whatever he tells you' (Jn 2:5). This counsel is a fitting introduction to the words and signs of Christ's public ministry and it forms the Marian foundation of all the 'mysteries of light'" (Rosarium Virginis Mariae, 21).

On the "brethren" of Jesus (v. 12), see the note on Mt 12:46:50.

2:13–25 St John links Jesus' ministry to the celebration of Jewish feasts. The events reported here are set in the context of a Passover—which gives the "cleansing of the temple" greater significance than it has in the other Gospels: Jesus

money-changers at their business. [15]And making a whip of cords, he drove them all, with the sheep and oxen, out of the temple; and he poured out the coins of the money-changers and overturned their tables. [16]And he told those who sold the pigeons, "Take these things away; you shall not make my Father's house a house of trade." [17]His disciples remembered that it was written, "Zeal for thy house will consume me." [18]The Jews then said to him, "What sign have you to show us for doing this?" [19]Jesus answered them, "Destroy this temple, and in three days I will raise it up." [20]The Jews then said, "It has taken forty-six years to build this temple, and will you raise it up in three days?" [21]But he spoke of the temple of his body. [22]When therefore he was raised from the dead, his disciples remembered that he had said this; and they believed the scripture and the word which Jesus had spoken.

[23]Now when he was in Jerusalem at the Passover feast, many believed in his name when they saw the signs which he did; [24]but Jesus did not trust himself to them, [25]because he knew all men and needed no one to bear witness of man; for he himself knew what was in man.

Nicodemus visits Jesus

3 [1]Now there was a man of the Pharisees, named Nicodemus, a ruler of the Jews. [2]This man came to Jesus[d] by night and said to him, "Rabbi, we know that you are a teacher come from God; for no one can do these signs that you do, unless God is

Margin references:
Lev 1:1–17; 5:7
Zech 14:21
Lk 2:49

Hos 5:6–7
Ps 69:9

Mt 21:23

Mt 26:61; 27:40
Hos 6:2

1 Cor 3:17; 6:19

Jn 2:18; 6:26

1 Kings 8:39
Lk 16:15

Jn 7:48, 50; 12:42;
19:39

Mt 22:16

Iudaeorum, et ascendit Hierosolymam Iesus. [14]Et invenit in templo vendentes boves et oves et columbas, et nummularios sedentes; [15]et, cum fecisset flagellum de funiculis, omnes eiecit de templo, oves quoque et boves, et nummulariorum effudit aes et mensas subvertit; [16]et his, qui columbas vendebant, dixit: «Auferte ista hinc! Nolite facere domum Patris mei domum negotiationis». [17]Recordati sunt discipuli eius quia scriptum est: «*Zelus domus tuae comedit me*». [18]Responderunt ergo Iudaei et dixerunt ei: «Quod signum ostendis nobis, quia haec facis?». [19]Respondit Iesus et dixit eis: «Solvite templum hoc et in tribus diebus excitabo illud». [20]Dixerunt ergo Iudaei: «Quadraginta et sex annis aedificatum est templum hoc, et tu tribus diebus excitabis illud?». [21]Ille autem dicebat de templo corporis sui. [22]Cum ergo resurrexisset a mortuis, recordati sunt discipuli eius quia hoc dicebat, et crediderunt Scripturae et sermoni, quem dixit Iesus. [23]Cum autem esset Hierosolymis in Pascha, in die festo, multi crediderunt in nomine eius, videntes signa eius, quae faciebat. [24]Ipse autem Iesus non credebat semetipsum eis, eo quod ipse nosset omnes, [25]et quia opus ei non erat, ut quis testimonium perhiberet de homine: ipse enim sciebat quid esset in homine. [3] [1]Erat autem homo ex pharisaeis, Nicodemus nomine, princeps Iudaeorum; [2]hic venit ad eum nocte et dixit ei: «Rabbi, scimus quia a Deo venisti magister: nemo enim potest haec signa facere,

---

not only reveals himself as the Messiah (cf. Mt 21:12–13); he explains that he is the new, definitive Temple of God among men.

When Jesus compares the temple of Jerusalem to his own body, he reveals the most profound truth about himself—the Incarnation, that is, the fact that he is the Word of God who has come to dwell among us (cf. 1:14). The evangelist notes, however, that the full meaning of what Jesus said could not be grasped until the events of his last Passover had taken place (v. 22).

In what Jesus says about the temple in v. 19 there is nothing derogatory, contrary to what will later be claimed by false witnesses (Mt 26:61; Mk 14:58) and by those who jeer at him when he is dying on the cross (Mt 27:40; Mk 15:29; cf. Acts 6:14). The sign he refers to is his own resurrection on the third day (cf. Mt 16:4: "the sign of Jonah"). To express how great the miracle of his resurrection will be, Jesus uses metaphorical

language. He is in effect saying: "Do you see this temple? Well, imagine if it were destroyed. Would it not be a great miracle if it were rebuilt in three days? That is the sign that I will work. For you will destroy my body, which is the temple par excellence, and I will raise it up again on the third day." None of his listeners understand Jesus' description of himself as the temple of God. His disciples, as well as others, think that he is speaking about rebuilding the temple whose construction was begun by Herod the Great around 19–20 BC. Only later will the disciples understand the true meaning of what Jesus says (v. 22).

3:1–21 Nicodemus was probably a member of the Jerusalem Sanhedrin, or supreme council (cf. 7:50). He must also have been an educated man, possibly a scribe or teacher of the Law: Jesus addresses him as a "teacher of Israel" (v. 10). He

d Greek *him*

with him." ³Jesus answered him, "Truly, truly, I say to you, unless one is born anew,ᵉ he cannot see the kingdom of God." ⁴Nicodemus said to him, "How can a man be born when he is old? Can he enter a second time into his mother's womb and be born?" ⁵Jesus answered, "Truly, truly, I say to you, unless one is born of water and the Spirit, he cannot enter the kingdom of God. ⁶That which is born of the flesh is flesh, and that which is born of the Spirit is spirit.ᶠ ⁷Do not marvel that I said to you, 'You must be born anew.'ᵉ ⁸The windᶠ blows where it wills, and you hear the sound of it, but you do not know whence it comes or whither it goes; so it is with every one who is born of the Spirit." ⁹Nicodemus said to him, "How can this be?" ¹⁰Jesus answered him, "Are you a teacher of Israel, and yet you do not understand this?

Mt 18:3
1 Pet 1:23

Is 44:3
Ezek 36:25–27
Eph 5:26; Tit 3:5
Jn 18:36
1 Jn 3:9; 5:1

Jn 1:13; Gen 6:3

Eccles 11:5

Lk 1:34

quae tu facis, nisi fuerit Deus cum eo». ³Respondit Iesus et dixit ei: «Amen, amen dico tibi: Nisi quis natus fuerit desuper, non potest videre regnum Dei». ⁴Dicit ad eum Nicodemus: «Quomodo potest homo nasci, cum senex sit? Numquid potest in ventrem matris suae iterato introire et nasci?». ⁵Respondit Iesus: «Amen, amen dico tibi: Nisi quis natus fuerit ex aqua et Spiritu, non potest introire in regnum Dei. ⁶Quod natum est ex carne, caro est; et, quod natum est ex Spiritu, spiritus est. ⁷Non mireris quia dixi tibi: Oportet vos nasci denuo. ⁸Spiritus, ubi vult, spirat, et vocem eius audis, sed non scis unde veniat et quo vadat; sic est omnis, qui natus est ex Spiritu». ⁹Respondit Nicodemus et dixit ei: «Quomodo possunt haec fieri?». ¹⁰Respondit Iesus et dixit ei: «Tu es magister Israel et haec ignoras? ¹¹Amen, amen dico tibi: Quod scimus, loquimur et, quod

would have been what we would call an intellectual—a person who reasons things out; someone with an inquiring mind, for whom the search for truth is a basic part of life. He would, naturally, have been much influenced by the Jewish intellectual climate of his time. However, if divine things are to be understood, reason is not enough: a person also needs grace and humility. Nicodemus needs to realize that, despite all his studies, he is still ignorant of the things of God.

In the course of this conversation between Jesus and Nicodemus, the clear teaching emerges about who Jesus is, what salvation means, and what one must do to attain it: one must have the faith that comes through Baptism from the Holy Spirit. (The Greek word *anothen*, which can be translated as "from above" [see RSV note **e**] can also mean "anew", which is how Nicodemus understands it: cf. v. 4.) The image of a new birth illustrates how a person is transformed by Baptism. He or she enjoys a new form of being, born of the Spirit of God; by Baptism one becomes a child of God endowed with the freedom proper to a child of God: "All those who believed in Christ were given the grace to become children of God—that is, children of the Holy Spirit—so that they might partake of God's own nature; and to show that He is the One who gives life to the children of God, the Spirit says in the words of Christ: 'unless one is born of water and the Spirit, he cannot enter the kingdom of God'" (Didymus of Alexandria, *De Trinitate*,

2, 12). "Whereas there are two births, he [Nicodemus] knew only of one. One is of earth, the other of heaven; one of the flesh, the other of the Spirit; one of mortality, the other of eternity; one of male and female, the other of God and the Church. But the two are each unique; neither one nor the other can be repeated" (St Augustine, *In Ioannis Evangelium*, 11, 6).

Jesus explains to Nicodemus that he needs faith if he is to understand what he is being told (vv. 9–15). He compares his future crucified self to the bronze serpent that, on God's instructions, Moses raised on a pole during the Exodus to cure the people who had been bitten by snakes (Num 21:8–9). In the same way, Jesus, when he is raised on the cross, is salvation for all who look at him with faith—and he is condemnation for those who do not believe. "The words of Christ are at once words of judgment and grace, of life and death. For it is only by putting to death that which is old that we can come to newness of life. [...] No one is freed from sin by himself or by his own efforts, no one is raised above himself or completely delivered from his own weakness, solitude or slavery; all have need of Christ, who is the model, master, liberator, saviour, and giver of life" (Vatican II, *Ad gentes*, 8).

The last words in the passage (vv. 16–21) are a summary showing that Jesus' death is the greatest expression of God's love for mankind. Both for the original hearers of the Gospel and for all who read it, these words are a challenge to

e Or *from above* f The same Greek word means both *wind* and spirit

Jn 7:16; 8:26ff; 12:49
Lk 22:67
Wis 9:16-17

Prov 30:4
Eph 4:9

Jn 8:28; 12:32-54;
18:32
Num 21:8-9
Is 52:13

Rom 5:8; 8:32
Gal 1:4; 1 Jn 4:9
Jn 5:22; 12:47
Lk 19:10; Acts 17:31
Jn 3:36; 5:24

Jn 1:5, 9-11; 12:48
Rom 13:12
Eph 5:8-12

Jn 7:7; 13:27, 30
Eph 5:13
Gen 1:3-5
Jn 5:29; 7:26

[11]Truly, truly, I say to you, we speak of what we know, and bear witness to what we have seen; but you do not receive our testimony. [12]If I have told you earthly things and you do not believe, how can you believe if I tell you heavenly things? [13]No one has ascended into heaven but he who descended from heaven, the Son of man.[g] [14]And as Moses lifted up the serpent in the wilderness, so must the Son of man be lifted up, [15]that whoever believes in him may have eternal life."[h]

[16]For God so loved the world that he gave his only Son, that whoever believes in him should not perish but have eternal life. [17]For God sent the Son into the world, not to condemn the world, but that the world might be saved through him. [18]He who believes in him is not condemned; he who does not believe is condemned already, because he has not believed in the name of the only Son of God. [19]And this is the judgment, that the light has come into the world, and men loved darkness rather than light, because their deeds were evil. [20]For every one who does evil hates the light, and does not come to the light, lest his deeds should be exposed. [21]But he who does what is true comes to the light, that it may be clearly seen that his deeds have been wrought in God.

The Baptist again bears witness

Jn 1:19-34; 2:12;
4:2; 5:1; 6:1; 7:1

Mt 4:12

Lk 3:20

[22]After this Jesus and his disciples went into the land of Judea; there he remained with them and baptized.* [23]John also was baptizing at Aenon near Salim, because there was much water there; and people came and were baptized. [24]For John had not yet been put in prison.*

vidimus, testamur, et testimonium nostrum non accipitis. [12]Si terrena dixi vobis, et non creditis, quomodo, si dixero vobis caelestia, credetis? [13]Et nemo ascendit in caelum, nisi qui descendit de caelo, Filius hominis. [14]Et sicut Moyses exaltavit serpentem in deserto, ita exaltari oportet Filium hominis, [15]ut omnis, qui credit, in ipso habeat vitam aeternam». [16]Sic enim dilexit Deus mundum, ut Filium suum unigenitum daret, ut omnis, qui credit in eum, non pereat, sed habeat vitam aeternam. [17]Non enim misit Deus Filium in mundum, ut iudicet mundum, sed ut salvetur mundus per ipsum. [18]Qui credit in eum, non iudicatur; qui autem non credit, iam iudicatus est, quia non credidit in nomen Unigeniti Filii Dei. [19]Hoc est autem iudicium: Lux venit in mundum, et dilexerunt homines magis tenebras quam lucem; erant enim eorum mala opera. [20]Omnis enim, qui mala agit, odit lucem et non venit ad lucem, ut non arguantur opera eius; [21]qui autem facit veritatem, venit ad lucem, ut manifestentur eius opera, quia in Deo sunt facta. [22]Post haec venit Iesus et discipuli eius in Iudaeam terram, et illic demorabatur cum eis et baptizabat. [23]Erat autem et Ioannes bap-

respond to the love that God has shown us: "Let us remember with what love [the Lord] has shown us mercy and the greatness of God [...]: love draws forth love. [...] Let us strive to keep sight of this always, and awaken ourselves to love" (St Teresa of Avila, *Life*, 22, 14).

John Paul II made this comment on the words of v. 16: "they also express the very essence of Christian soteriology, that is, the theology of salvation. Salvation means liberation from evil, and for this reason it is closely bound up with the problem of suffering. According to the words spoken to Nicodemus, God gives his son to 'the world' to free man from evil, which bears within itself the definitive and absolute perspective on suffering. At the same time, the very word *'gives'* ('gave') indicates that this liberation must be achieved by the only-begotten Son through his own suffering. And in this, love is manifested, the infinite love both of that only-begotten Son and of the Father who for this

reason 'gives' his Son. This is love for man, love for the 'world': it is salvific love" (*Salvifici doloris*, 14).

Jesus' self-surrender is a pressing call to respond to his great love for us: "If it is true that God has created us, that he has redeemed us, that he loves us so much that he has given up his only-begotten Son for us (cf. Jn 3:16), that he waits for us—every day!—as eagerly as the father of the prodigal son did (cf. Lk 15:11-32), how can we doubt that he wants us to respond to him with all our love? The strange thing would be not to talk to God, to draw away and forget him, and busy ourselves in activities which are closed to the constant promptings of his grace" (St Josemaría Escrivá, *Friends of God*, 251).

3:22-36 A little further on (4:2), the evangelist makes it clear that it was not Jesus himself who baptized, but his disciples. The rite referred to here was not yet Christian Baptism, because

g Other ancient authorities add *who is in heaven*   h Some interpreters hold that the quotation continues through verse 21

²⁵Now a discussion arose between John's disciples and a Jew over purifying. ²⁶And they came to John, and said to him, "Rabbi, he who was with you beyond the Jordan, to whom you bore witness, here he is, baptizing, and all are going to him." ²⁷John answered, "No one can receive anything except what is given him from heaven. ²⁸You yourselves bear me witness, that I said, I am not the Christ, but I have been sent before him. ²⁹He who has the bride is the bridegroom; the friend of the bridegroom, who stands and hears him, rejoices greatly at the bridegroom's voice; therefore this joy of mine is now full. ³⁰He must increase, but I must decrease."ⁱ

³¹He who comes from above is above all; he who is of the earth belongs to the earth, and of the earth he speaks; he who comes from heaven is above all. ³²He bears witness to what he has seen and heard, yet no one receives his testimony; ³³he who receives his testimony sets his seal to this, that God is true. ³⁴For he whom God has

(marginal references) Jn 19:11; Heb 5:4 / 1 Cor 4:7 / Jn 1:20, 23, 27 / Mt 11:10; Mk 1:2 / Mt 9:15; 22:2 / 2 Sam 3:1 / Jn 8:23 / Jn 3:11 / Jn 1:33–34

tizans in Enon iuxta Salim, quia aquae multae erant illic, et adveniebant et baptizabantur; ²⁴nondum enim missus fuerat in carcerem Ioannes. ²⁵Facta est ergo quaestio ex discipulis Ioannis cum Iudaeo de purificatione. ²⁶Et venerunt ad Ioannem et dixerunt ei: «Rabbi, qui erat tecum trans Iordanem, cui tu testimonium perhibuisti, ecce hic baptizat et omnes veniunt ad eum!». ²⁷Respondit Ioannes et dixit: «Non sum ego Christus, sed: Missus sum ante illum. ²⁹Qui habet sponsam, sponsus est; amicus autem sponsi, qui stat et audit eum, gaudio gaudet propter vocem sponsi. Hoc ergo gaudium meum impletum est. ³⁰Illum oportet crescere, me autem minui». ³¹Qui de sursum venit, supra omnes est; qui est de terra, de terra est et de terra loquitur. Qui de caelo venit, supra omnes est; ³²et quod vidit et audivit, hoc testatur, et testimonium eius nemo accipit. ³³Qui accipit eius testimonium, signavit quia Deus verax est. ³⁴Quem enim misit Deus, verba Dei loquitur, non enim ad mensuram dat Spiritum. ³⁵Pater diligit Filium et omnia dedit

that sacrament received its full effectiveness only after the resurrection of Christ (cf. 7:39; 16:7; Mt 28:19). "Aenon" (v. 23) derives from an Aramaic word that means "wells". Salim was situated to the northeast of Samaria, south of the town of Scythopolis or Bethshan, near the west bank of the Jordan, about 20 kilometres (13 miles) to the south of the lake of Gennesaret.

In this new testimony, the Baptist once again asserts that Jesus is greater than he. The "friend of the bridegroom" (v. 29), by Jewish custom, was the man who stood next to the groom at the very start of the wedding, and he had a special role in the wedding festivities. Obviously, as the Baptist says, there is a great difference between the best man and the bridegroom, who is the most important man at the wedding.

With its symbolism of a wedding, in which Jesus is the Bridegroom (cf. Mk 2:19) and the Church the Bride (cf. Eph 5:24–32; Rev 19:7–9), this passage is evocative of the union by which Christ incorporates the Church into himself. The Baptist's joy is caused by the fact that the Messiah has already begun to act; his joy is full (v. 29) because he witnesses Jesus calling people to follow him, and many people responding. His joy is an earnest of the Church's joy when new members join the Body of Christ.

The Baptist sees his mission as that of a Precursor, who must disappear from the scene once the Messiah arrives (v. 30); it is a mission that he performs faithfully and humbly. Similarly, Christians should avoid any desire to stand out and be noticed in the apostolate: it is really Christ's apostolate; Christians need to empty themselves of self, so that Christ can fill their lives: "It is necessary for Christ to grow in you, for you to progress in your knowledge and love of him: for, the more you know him and love him, the more he grows in you" (St Thomas Aquinas, *Super Evangelium Ioannis*, ad loc.).

The words at the end of the chapter (vv. 31–36) reveal the divinity of Christ and show the Messiah he is. Only he can reveal God the Father to mankind, and he can do this because he is the Son of God. "Christ, the Son of God made man, is the Father's one, perfect, and unsurpassable Word. In him he has said everything; there will be no other word than this one" (*Catechism of the Catholic Church*, 65; see also the notes on Mt 17:1–13 and Heb 1:1–4). The works and words of Jesus, human as they truly are, are at the same time works and words of God in human history, because the Incarnate Word is one with the Father and the Holy Spirit. In Jesus Christ, there is only one Person—that of the Word—and all his actions flow from who he is.

i Some interpreters hold that the quotation continues through verse 36

Jn 5:20; 17:2
Mt 11:27
Jn 1:18; 20:31
1 Jn 5:12
sent utters the words of God, for it is not by measure that he gives the Spirit; ³⁵the Father loves the Son, and has given all things into his hand. ³⁶He who believes in the Son has eternal life; he who does not obey the Son shall not see life, but the wrath of God rests upon him.

Jesus and the Samaritan woman

Jn 3:22, 26
1 Cor 1:17

Josh 24:32
4 ¹Now when the Lord knew that the Pharisees had heard that Jesus was making and baptizing more disciples than John ²(although Jesus himself did not baptize, but only his disciples), ³he left Judea and departed again to Galilee. ⁴He had to pass through Samaria. ⁵So he came to a city of Samaria, called Sychar, near the field that

in manu eius. ³⁶Qui credit in Filium, habet vitam aeternam; qui autem incredulus est Filio, non videbit vitam, sed ira Dei manet super eum.   [4] ¹Ut ergo cognovit Iesus quia audierunt pharisaei quia Iesus plures discipulos facit et baptizat quam Ioannes, ²—quamquam Iesus ipse non baptizaret sed discipuli eius— ³reliquit Iudaeam et abiit iterum in Galilaeam. ⁴Oportebat autem eum transire per Samariam. ⁵Venit ergo in civitatem Samariae, quae dicitur Sichar, iuxta praedium, quod dedit Iacob Ioseph filio suo; ⁶erat autem ibi fons Iacob. Iesus ergo fatigatus ex itinere sede-

4:1–45 Jerusalem is where hostility to Jesus on the part of the Pharisees first raises its head (vv. 1–2). Our Lord then withdraws to the north, to Galilee (v. 3), where the Pharisees wield less influence. This prevents them from destroying him prior to the time appointed by God the Father. This action of Jesus shows us that divine providence is no reason for a believer not to use his intelligence and will-power (as Jesus did) to prudently discover what God wants of him.

There were two main routes from Judea to Galilee. The shorter one went through the city of Samaria; the other followed the course of the Jordan. Jesus takes the Samaria route (v. 4). In his approach to that city, near Sychar (present-day Askar), at the foot of Mount Ebal, he meets the Samaritan woman. The political and religious tensions between the Jews and the Samaritans should be borne in mind in the reading of this passage (see vv. 9, 27). The latter were descendants of Jews who had stayed in the north after the destruction of the capital of the Northern kingdom, Samaria, in the year 722 BC, and who had intermarried with colonists settled there by the Assyrians. The Samaritans always claimed to be true heirs of patriarchal and Mosaic tradition, but as far back as the seventh century BC other Jews regarded them as heterodox in their religion and practices (see 2 Kings 17:24–40). Schism in the proper sense of the word took place in the fifth century BC, and it was exacerbated when the Samaritans built a temple on Mount Gerizim in honour of the Lord, the God of Israel. During the period of Syrian influence

(second century BC), according to Flavius Josephus (*Antiquitates iudaicae*, 12, 5, 5), the Samaritans asked Antiochus to dedicate their temple to the Greek god Zeus. The Jewish king John Hyrcanus I destroyed that temple, and from then onwards enmity prevailed between Jews and Samaritans. The latter still saw themselves as true upholders of the Hebrew religion, and they observed many of the ancient traditions. They revered the Pentateuch as the only sacred book (see also the note on Lk 9:51–56).

The Gospels (particularly St John's) often mention details which seem unimportant, but they always have some significance. Jesus, like us, really does get tired (v. 6); he needs rest to recover his energy; he experiences hunger and thirst; however, even when he is exhausted he does not miss an opportunity to do good for souls. "Recollect yourselves and go over the scene again slowly in your minds. Jesus Christ, *perfectus Deus, perfectus homo*, is tired out from his travels and his apostolic work. Perhaps there have been times when the same thing has happened to you and you have ended up worn out, because you have reached the limit of your resources. It is a touching sight to see our Master so exhausted. He is hungry too—his disciples have gone to a neighbouring village to look for food. And he is thirsty. But tired though his body is, his thirst for souls is even greater. So, when the Samaritan woman, the sinner, arrives, Christ with his priestly heart turns eagerly to save the lost sheep, and he forgets his tiredness, his hunger and his thirst. [...] Whenever we get tired—in our work,

Jacob gave to his son Joseph. ⁶Jacob's well was there, and so Jesus, wearied as he Gen 29:2–10
Num 21:16–18 was with his journey, sat down beside the well. It was about the sixth hour.

⁷There came a woman of Samaria to draw water. Jesus said to her, "Give me a drink." ⁸For his disciples had gone away into the city to buy food. ⁹The Samaritan Lk 9:53 woman said to him, "How is it that you, a Jew, ask a drink of me, a woman of Samaria?" For Jews have no dealings with Samaritans. ¹⁰Jesus answered her, "If you Jn 7:38–39
Zech 14:8 knew the gift of God, and who it is that is saying to you, 'Give me a drink,' you would have asked him, and he would have given you living water." ¹¹The woman said to him, "Sir, you have nothing to draw with, and the well is deep; where do you get that living water? ¹²Are you greater than our father Jacob, who gave us the well, Gen 28:10
Jn 8:53 and drank from it himself, and his sons, and his cattle?" ¹³Jesus said to her, "Every Jn 6:58

bat sic super fontem; hora erat quasi sexta. ⁷Venit mulier de Samaria haurire aquam. Dicit ei Iesus: «Da mihi bibere»; ⁸discipuli enim eius abierant in civitatem, ut cibos emerent. ⁹Dicit ergo ei mulier illa Samaritana: «Quomodo tu Iudaeus cum sis, bibere a me poscis, quae sum mulier Samaritana?». Non enim coutuntur Iudaei Samaritanis. ¹⁰Respondit Iesus et dixit ei: «Si scires donum Dei et quis est, qui dicit tibi: "Da mihi bibere", tu forsitan petisses ab eo et dedisset tibi aquam vivam». ¹¹Dicit ei mulier: «Domine, neque in quo haurias habes, et puteus altus est; unde ergo habes aquam vivam? ¹²Numquid tu maior es patre nostro Iacob, qui dedit nobis puteum, et ipse ex eo bibit et filii eius et pecora eius?».

in our studies, in our apostolic endeavours—when our horizon is darkened by lowering clouds, then let us turn our eyes to Jesus, to Jesus who is so good, and who also gets tired; to Jesus who is hungry and suffers thirst. Lord, how well you make yourself understood! How lovable you are! You show us that you are just like us, in everything but sin, so that we can feel utterly sure that, together with you, we can conquer all our evil inclinations, all our faults. For neither weariness nor hunger matters, nor thirst, nor tears … since Christ also grew weary, knew hunger, was thirsty, and wept. What is important is that we struggle to fulfil the will of our heavenly Father (cf. Jn 4:34), battling away good-heartedly, for our Lord is always at our side" (St Josemaría Escrivá, *Friends of God*, 176 and 201).

In this moving dialogue between Jesus and the Samaritan woman (vv. 7–26), St John once again outlines the doctrine of grace, God's gift to man through the Holy Spirit after the incarnation of his Son. As he has done in his conversation with Nicodemus (3:1–21), Jesus uses observations on ordinary, concrete needs to explain supernatural things. What is written here is the seed of the Church's later teaching about the sacraments. Just as water is necessary for human life, the water that can truly quench man's spiritual thirst is the grace of Christ: "According to the Gospel of John, the Holy Spirit is given to us with the new life, as Jesus foretells and promises on the great day of the Feast of Tabernacles: 'If

any one thirst, let him come to me and drink. He who believes in me as the scripture has said, "Out of his heart shall flow rivers of living water"' (Jn 7:37–38). And the Evangelist explains: '*This he said about the Spirit*, which those who believed in him were to receive' (7:39). It is the same simile of water which Jesus uses in his conversation with the Samaritan woman, when he speaks of 'a spring of water welling up to eternal life' (Jn 4:14), and in his conversation with Nicodemus when he speaks of the need for a new *birth* 'of water and the Spirit' in order to 'enter the kingdom of God' (cf. Jn 3:5)" (John Paul II, *Dominum et Vivificantem*, 1).

This episode also shows that the salvation brought by Christ is available to everyone. His love extends to all souls (vv. 9, 31–42). Jesus asks for a drink not only because he is thirsty but also to show that he thirsts for people to discover the love of God: "He was thirsty … But when he said 'Give me a drink', what the Creator of the universe meant was that he was thirsty for the love of his poor creature. He thirsted for love … and, now more than ever, I realise that Jesus is thirsty. Among his disciples in this world—his own disciples!—he sees only ungrateful and indifferent souls. How few pledge their hearts wholly to him; how few truly understand the tenderness of his infinite love!" (St Thérèse of Lisieux, *Story of a Soul*, 9).

The episode at the well of Sychar helps us see that prayer is an encounter with Christ: "The

Jn 6:27, 35; 7:37–39
Sir 24:20–22
Is 58:11
one who drinks of this water will thirst again, ¹⁴but whoever drinks of the water that I shall give him will never thirst; the water that I shall give him will become in him a spring of water welling up to eternal life." ¹⁵The woman said to him, "Sir, give me this water, that I may not thirst, nor come here to draw."

¹⁶Jesus said to her, "Go, call your husband, and come here." ¹⁷The woman answered him, "I have no husband." Jesus said to her, "You are right in saying, 'I have no husband'; 1 Cor 14:24–25 ¹⁸for you have had five husbands, and he whom you now have is not your husband; this you said truly." ¹⁹The woman said to him, "Sir, I perceive that Deut 12:5 you are a prophet. ²⁰Our fathers worshipped on this mountain;* and you say that in Jerusalem is the place where men ought to worship." ²¹Jesus said to her, "Woman, believe me, the hour is coming when neither on this mountain nor in Jerusalem will 2 Kings 17:29–41
Is 2:3
Deut 13:3, 7, 14 you worship the Father. ²²You worship what you do not know; we worship what we know, for salvation is from the Jews. ²³But the hour is coming, and now is, when the 1 Kings 12:25, 33
Ezra 4:1–3
Jn 1:14 true worshippers will worship the Father in spirit and truth, for such the Father seeks Rom 12:1
2 Cor 3:17 to worship him. ²⁴God is spirit, and those who worship him must worship in spirit and truth." ²⁵The woman said to him, "I know that Messiah is coming (he who is Jn 1:41 called Christ); when he comes, he will show us all things." ²⁶Jesus said to her, "I Jn 9:37; 10:25 who speak to you am he."

²⁷Just then the disciples came. They marvelled that he was talking with a woman, but none said, "What do you wish?" or, "Why are you talking with her?" ²⁸So the woman left her water jar, and went away into the city, and said to the people,

¹³Respondit Iesus et dixit ei: «Omnis, qui bibit ex aqua hac, sitiet iterum; ¹⁴qui autem biberit ex aqua, quam ego dabo ei, non sitiet in aeternum, sed aqua, quam dabo ei, fiet in eo fons aquae salientis in vitam aeternam». ¹⁵Dicit ad eum mulier: «Domine, da mihi hanc aquam, ut non sitiam, neque veniam huc haurire». ¹⁶Dicit ei: «Vade, voca virum tuum et veni huc». ¹⁷Respondit mulier et dixit ei: «Non habeo virum». Dicit ei Iesus: «Bene dixisti: "Non habeo virum"; ¹⁸quinque enim viros habuisti, et nunc, quem habes, non est tuus vir. Hoc vere dixisti». ¹⁹Dicit ei mulier: «Domine, video quia propheta es tu. ²⁰Patres nostri in monte hoc adoraverunt, et vos dicitis quia in Hierosolymis est locus, ubi adorare oportet». ²¹Dicit ei Iesus: «Crede mihi, mulier, quia venit hora quando neque in monte hoc neque in Hierosolymis adorabitis Patrem. ²²Vos adoratis, quod nescitis; nos adoramus, quod scimus, quia salus ex Iudaeis est. ²³Sed venit hora et nunc est, quando veri adoratores adorabunt Patrem in Spiritu et veritate; nam et Pater tales quaerit, qui adorent eum. ²⁴Spiritus est Deus, et eos, qui adorant eum, in Spiritu et veritate oportet adorare». ²⁵Dicit ei mulier: «Scio quia Messias venit —qui dicitur Christus—; cum venerit ille, nobis annuntiabit omnia». ²⁶Dicit ei Iesus: «Ego sum, qui loquor tecum». ²⁷Et continuo venerunt discipuli eius et mirabantur quia cum muliere loquebatur; nemo tamen dixit: «Quid quaeris aut quid loqueris cum

wonder of prayer is revealed beside the well where we come seeking water: there, Christ comes to meet every human being. It is he who first seeks us and asks us for a drink. Jesus thirsts; his asking arises from the depths of God's desire for us. Whether we realize it or not, prayer is the encounter of God's thirst with ours. God thirsts that we may thirst for him" (*Catechism of the Catholic Church*, 2560).

Reference is made to God's designs (vv. 20–26). The Samaritans were unaware of much of God's plan because they ignored any revelation not found in the Law of Moses; the Jews were closer to the truth about the Messiah because they read and believed the Prophets and the Psalms. But both Samaritans and Jews needed to open themselves to the new Revelation of Jesus Christ. The arrival of the Messiah (whom both peoples believed would come) marks the start of

a new, definitive Covenant in which neither Gerizim (the mountain where the Samaritans worshipped) nor the temple of Jerusalem would have a role: what pleases the Father is that everyone should acknowledge the Messiah, his Son, as the new Temple of God (see 2:21) and should offer God worship that wells up within the heart (see 2 Tim 2:22), fanned by the Spirit himself (see Rom 8:14–16).

The effect of grace on this woman is remarkable (vv. 28–29). All her thoughts now centre on Jesus, and, forgetting what brought her to the well, she leaves the water jar there and goes off to tell the people what she has discovered. "The apostles, when they were called, left their nets; this woman leaves her water jar and proclaims the Gospel, calling not just one person but influencing the whole city" (St John Chrysostom, *In Ioannem*, 33).

²⁹"Come, see a man who told me all that I ever did. Can this be the Christ?" ³⁰They went out of the city and were coming to him.

³¹Meanwhile the disciples besought him, saying, "Rabbi, eat." ³²But he said to them, "I have food to eat of which you do not know." ³³So the disciples said to one another, "Has any one brought him food?" ³⁴Jesus said to them, "My food is to do the will of him who sent me, and to accomplish his work. ³⁵Do you not say, 'There are yet four months, then comes the harvest'? I tell you, lift up your eyes, and see how the fields are already white for harvest. ³⁶He who reaps receives wages, and gathers fruit for eternal life, so that sower and reaper may rejoice together. ³⁷For here the saying holds true, 'One sows and another reaps.' ³⁸I sent you to reap that for which you did not labour; others have laboured, and you have entered into their labour."

³⁹Many Samaritans from that city believed in him because of the woman's testimony, "He told me all that I ever did." ⁴⁰So when the Samaritans came to him, they asked him to stay with them; and he stayed there two days. ⁴¹And many more believed because of his word. ⁴²They said to the woman, "It is no longer because of your words that we believe, for we have heard for ourselves, and we know that this is indeed the Saviour of the world."

⁴³After the two days he departed to Galilee. ⁴⁴For Jesus himself testified that a prophet has no honour in his own country. ⁴⁵So when he came to Galilee, the Galileans welcomed him, having seen all that he had done in Jerusalem at the feast, for they too had gone to the feast.

Curing of a royal official's son — the second sign worked by Jesus

⁴⁶So he came again to Cana in Galilee, where he had made the water wine. And at Capernaum there was an official whose son was ill. ⁴⁷When he heard that Jesus had

Marginal references: Prov 9:5; Ps 119:103; Sir 24:20-22; Jn 5:36; 17:4; Is 17:5; Mt 9:37; Lk 10:2; Jn 3:29; 15:11; Josh 24:13; Deut 6:10-12; Mic 6:15; 1 Jn 4:14; 1 Tim 4:10; Mt 4:12; Mt 13:57; Mk 6:4; Lk 4:24; Jn 2:23; Mt 8:5-13; Lk 7:1-10; Jn 2:1-12

ea?». ²⁸Reliquit ergo hydriam suam mulier et abiit in civitatem et dicit illis hominibus: ²⁹«Venite, videte hominem, qui dixit mihi omnia, quaecumque feci; numquid ipse est Christus?». ³⁰Exierunt de civitate et veniebant ad eum. ³¹Interea rogabant eum discipuli dicentes: «Rabbi, manduca». ³²Ille autem dixit eis: «Ego cibum habeo manducare, quem vos nescitis». ³³Dicebant ergo discipuli ad invicem: «Numquid aliquis attulit ei manducare?». ³⁴Dicit eis Iesus: «Meus cibus est, ut faciam voluntatem eius, qui misit me, et ut perficiam opus eius. ³⁵Nonne vos dicitis: "Adhuc quattuor menses sunt, et messis venit"? Ecce dico vobis: Levate oculos vestros et videte regiones quia albae sunt ad messem! Iam ³⁶qui metit, mercedem accipit et congregat fructum in vitam aeternam, ut et qui seminat, simul gaudeat et qui metit. ³⁷In hoc enim est verbum verum: Alius est qui seminat, et alius est qui metit. ³⁸Ego misi vos metere, quod vos non laborastis; alii laboraverunt, et vos in laborem eorum introistis». ³⁹Ex civitate autem illa multi crediderunt in eum Samaritanorum propter verbum mulieris testimonium perhibentis: «Dixit mihi omnia, quaecumque feci!». ⁴⁰Cum venissent ergo ad illum Samaritani, rogaverunt eum, ut apud ipsos maneret; et mansit ibi duos dies. ⁴¹Et multo plures crediderunt propter sermonem eius; ⁴²et mulieri dicebant: «Iam non propter tuam loquelam credimus; ipsi enim audivimus et scimus quia hic est vere Salvator mundi!». ⁴³Post duos autem dies exiit inde in Galilaeam; ⁴⁴ipse enim Iesus testimonium perhibuit quia propheta in sua patria honorem non habet. ⁴⁵Cum ergo venisset in Galilaeam, exceperunt eum Galilaei, cum omnia vidissent, quae fecerat Hierosolymis in die festo; et ipsi enim venerant in diem festum. ⁴⁶Venit ergo iterum in Cana Galilaeae, ubi fecit aquam vinum. Et erat quidam regius, cuius filius infirmabatur Capharnaum;

The episode shows a whole process of evangelization at work, beginning with the Samaritan woman's enthusiasm (vv. 39-42). "The same thing happens today with those who are outside, who are not Christians: they receive tidings of Christ through Christian friends; like that woman, they learn of Christ through the Church; then they come to Christ, that is, they believe in Christ through this report, and then Jesus stays two days among them and many more believe, and believe more firmly, that he indeed is the Saviour of the world" (St Augustine, *In Ioannis Evangelium*, 15, 33).

The woman's conversion and the return of the disciples lead on to another of this Gospel's recurring themes—the fact that Jesus has come to do the Father's will (v. 34). It is the Father's desire that all who see the Son and believe in him should have eternal life and be raised up at the last day (see 6:39-40).

4:46-54 In the first part of his Gospel, John reports miracles worked by Jesus in Cana of Galilee. The first one led some people to believe in him (see 2:1-11); in this second miracle, the official (possibly a pagan at the court of Herod

Jn 2:18
1 Cor 1:22

come from Judea to Galilee, he went and begged him to come down and heal his son, for he was at the point of death. [48]Jesus therefore said to him, "Unless you see signs and wonders you will not believe." [49]The official said to him, "Sir, come down before my child dies." [50]Jesus said to him, "Go, your son will live." The man believed the word that Jesus spoke to him and went his way. [51]As he was going down, his servants met him and told him that his son was living. [52]So he asked them the hour when he began to mend, and they said to him, "Yesterday at the seventh hour the fever left him." [53]The father knew that was the hour when Jesus had said to

Jn 2:11–23

him, "Your son will live"; and he himself believed, and all his household. [54]This was now the second sign that Jesus did when he had come from Judea to Galilee.

3. JESUS REVEALS HIS DIVINITY*

Curing of a paralyzed man

Jn 2:13

5 [1]After this there was a feast of the Jews, and Jesus went up to Jerusalem. [2]Now there is in Jerusalem by the Sheep Gate a pool, in Hebrew called Bethzatha,[j] which has five porticoes. [3]In these lay a multitude of invalids, blind, lame, para-

[47]hic cum audisset quia Iesus advenerit a Iudaea in Galilaeam, abiit ad eum et rogabat ut descenderet et sanaret filium eius; incipiebat enim mori. [48]Dixit ergo Iesus ad eum: «Nisi signa et prodigia videritis, non credetis». [49]Dicit ad eum regius: «Domine, descende priusquam moriatur puer meus». [50]Dicit ei Iesus: «Vade. Filius tuus vivit». Credidit homo sermoni, quem dixit ei Iesus, et ibat. [51]Iam autem eo descendente, servi eius occurrerunt ei dicentes quia puer eius vivit. [52]Interrogabat ergo horam ab eis, in qua melius habuerit. Dixerunt ergo ei: «Heri hora septima reliquit eum febris». [53]Cognovit ergo pater quia illa hora erat, in qua dixit ei Iesus: «Filius tuus vivit», et credidit ipse et domus eius tota. [54]Hoc iterum secundum signum fecit Iesus, cum venisset a Iudaea in Galilaeam. [5] [1]Post haec erat dies festus Iudaeorum, et ascendit Iesus Hierosolymam. [2]Est autem Hierosolymis, super Probatica, piscina, quae cognominatur Hebraice Bethsatha, quinque porticus habens. [3]In his iacebat multitudo languen-

Antipas) puts faith in Jesus even before he sees the miracle. He in fact already had a faith that, though imperfect, was enough to bring him the 33 kilometres (20 miles) from Capernaum to Cana, and he came to ask Jesus' help even though he was a man of high rank. Jesus is pleased to see his perseverance and humility.

The Fathers of the Church compare this miracle with the cure of the centurion's servant (Mt 8:5–13; Lk 7:1–10), and note how different that Roman officer's remarkable faith is from the initially imperfect faith of this royal official. St John Chrysostom comments: "Here was a robust faith [in the case of this official]; therefore, Jesus made him the promise, so that we might learn from this man's devotion; his faith was as yet imperfect, and he did not clearly realize that Jesus could effect the cure at a distance; thus, the Lord, by not agreeing to go down to the man's house, wished us to learn the need to have faith" (*In Ioannem*, 35).

Our Lord wants faith in him to be acceptance of his words rather than desire for miracles. Miracles are a call to faith and provide reasons for

believing. In our own time, miracles also happen; they are a sign of God's mercy and a call to trust in his power.

*5:1–47 In this section John reports the cure of a paralyzed man at the pool of Bethzatha and a discourse in which Jesus reveals that he is the Son of God, and that, as such, he always acts in union with the Father. These events took place on "a feast of the Jews" (v. 1), possibly the Passover, or perhaps, Pentecost, which comes fifty days after the Passover. John makes it quite clear here that Jesus is divine; it can be seen both from the miracle and from the discourse. He also notes the open hostility shown by some Jews, who want to kill Jesus because of his claims to be the Son of God (v. 18).

5:1–18 The pool of Bethzatha (v. 2), situated on the outskirts of Jerusalem, was near the Sheep Gate, which was in the northeastern section of the city wall (cf. Neh 3:1–33; 12:39). The livestock for temple sacrifices were driven through the Sheep Gate. Around the end of the nineteenth

j Other ancient authorities read *Bethesda*, others *Bethsaida*

lyzed.[k] [5]One man was there, who had been ill for thirty-eight years. [6]When Jesus saw him and knew that he had been lying there a long time, he said to him, "Do you want to be healed?" [7]The sick man answered him, "Sir, I have no man to put me into the pool when the water is troubled, and while I am going another steps down before me." [8]Jesus said to him, "Rise, take up your pallet, and walk." [9]And at once the man was healed, and he took up his pallet and walked.

Lk 5:24

Jn 9:14

Now that day was the sabbath. [10]So the Jews said to the man who was cured, "It is the sabbath, it is not lawful for you to carry your pallet." [11]But he answered them, "The man who healed me said to me, 'Take up your pallet, and walk.'" [12]They asked him, "Who is the man who said to you, 'Take up your pallet, and walk'?" [13]Now the man who had been healed did not know who it was, for Jesus had withdrawn, as there was a crowd in the place. [14]Afterward, Jesus found him in the temple, and said to him, "See, you are well! Sin no more, that nothing worse befall you." [15]The man

Ex 16:23
Lev 23:24, 39
Jer 17:21
Lk 6:2

Jn 8:11

tium, caecorum, claudorum, aridorum. [5]Erat autem quidam homo ibi triginta et octo annos habens in infirmitate sua. [6]Hunc cum vidisset Iesus iacentem, et cognovisset quia multum iam tempus habet, dicit ei: «Vis sanus fieri?». [7]Respondit ei languidus: «Domine, hominem non habeo, ut, cum turbata fuerit aqua, mittat me in piscinam; dum autem venio ego, alius ante me descendit». [8]Dicit ei Iesus: «Surge, tolle grabatum tuum et ambula». [9]Et statim sanus factus est homo, et sustulit grabatum suum et ambulabat. Erat autem sabbatum in illo die. [10]Dicebant ergo Iudaei illi, qui sanatus fuerat: «Sabbatum est, et non licet tibi tollere grabatum tuum». [11]Ille autem respondit eis: «Qui me fecit sanum, ille mihi dixit: "Tolle grabatum tuum et ambula"». [12]Interrogaverunt eum: «Quis est ille homo, qui dixit tibi: "Tolle et ambula"?». [13]Is autem, qui sanus fuerat effectus, nesciebat quis esset; Iesus enim declinavit a turba constituta in loco. [14]Postea invenit eum Iesus in templo, et dixit illi: «Ecce sanus factus es; iam noli peccare, ne deterius tibi aliquid contingat». [15]Abiit ille homo et nuntiavit Iudaeis quia Iesus esset, qui fecit eum sanum. [16]Et propterea perse-

century, the remains of a pool were discovered: excavated out of rock, it was trapezoidal in shape and surrounded by four galleries or porches; a fifth porch divided the pool in two.

[The Sixto-Clementine edition of the Vulgate includes here as a second part of v. 3 and all v. 4 the words given in RSV note **k**. The New Vulgate relegates these words to a footnote; they are absent from many important codexes and Greek papyri, nor are they to be found in many early translations.]

In the cure of the paralyzed man, Jesus shows that he acts with the power of God, and that because he has that power he is above the law of the sabbath and able to forgive people's sins. Jesus' subsequent meeting with the man (v. 14) shows that the man's physical cure was a sign that his sins had been forgiven. What Jesus says here should be read in the context of an idea prevalent among Jews at the time: that there is always a direct cause-and-effect relation between sin and sickness. Jesus does not concur with this idea (cf. 9:3). But the paralyzed man may well have thought that his condition was due to sin; and Jesus tells him that sin, not sickness, is the true evil, and, once a person has received God's forgiveness, he or she should strive not to sin again.

The Law of Moses established the sabbath as a day of rest (see Ex 20:8–11). By keeping the sabbath, Jews felt they were imitating God, who rested from the work of creation on the seventh day. St Thomas Aquinas explains why Jesus rejects this strict interpretation that "the Jews" gave to the sabbath law: "[Those Jews], in their desire to imitate God, did nothing on the sabbath, as if God on that day had ceased absolutely to act. It is true that he rested on the sabbath from his work of creating new creatures, but he is always continually at work, maintaining them in existence. [...] God is the cause of all things in the sense that he also maintains them in existence; for if for one moment he were to stop exercising his power, at that very moment everything that nature contains would cease to exist" (*Super Evangelium Ioannis*, ad loc.). That is what Jesus means when he says, "My Father is working still, and I am working" (v. 17). God does not cease to be active after creating the world. Because the Son acts along with the Father (and they with the Holy Spirit are the one God), our Lord, the Son of God, is able to say that he never stops working. These words spoken by Jesus imply his own divine nature—and that was what the Jews understood them to mean. They considered him to be blaspheming, which

k Other ancient authorities insert, wholly or in part, *waiting for the moving of the water;* [4] *for an angel of the Lord went down at certain seasons into the pool, and troubled the water: whoever stepped in first after the troubling of the water was healed of whatever disease he had*

Mt 12:14

Jn 9:4

Jn 7:1, 19, 30;
10:33, 36

went away and told the Jews that it was Jesus who had healed him. [16]And this was why the Jews persecuted Jesus, because he did this on the sabbath. [17]But Jesus answered them, "My Father is working still, and I am working." [18]This was why the Jews sought all the more to kill him, because he not only broke the sabbath* but also called God his Father, making himself equal with God.

The authority of the Son of God

Jn 3:11, 32; 5:30

Jn 3:35

Deut 32:39
1 Sam 2:6
2 Kings 5:7

Dan 7:10, 13, 14
Acts 10:42

Lk 10:16
Phil 2:10, 11
1 Jn 2:23

[19]Jesus said to them, "Truly, truly, I say to you, the Son can do nothing of his own accord, but only what he sees the Father doing; for whatever he does, that the Son does likewise. [20]For the Father loves the Son, and shows him all that he himself is doing; and greater works than these will he show him, that you may marvel. [21]For as the Father raises the dead and gives them life, so also the Son gives life to whom he will. [22]The Father judges no one, but has given all judgment to the Son, [23]that all may honour the Son, even as they honour the Father. He who does not honour the

quebantur Iudaei Iesum, quia haec faciebat in sabbato. [17]Iesus autem respondit eis: «Pater meus usque modo operatur, et ego operor». [18]Propterea ergo magis quaerebant eum Iudaei interficere, quia non solum solvebat sabbatum, sed et Patrem suum dicebat Deum, aequalem se faciens Deo. [19]Respondit itaque Iesus et dixit eis: «Amen, amen dico vobis: Non potest Filius a se facere quidquam, nisi quod viderit Patrem facientem; quaecumque enim ille faciat, haec et Filius similiter facit. [20]Pater enim diligit Filium et omnia demonstrat ei, quae ipse facit, et maiora his demonstrabit ei opera, ut vos miremini. [21]Sicut enim Pater suscitat mortuos et vivificat, sic et Filius, quos vult, vivificat. [22]Neque enim Pater iudicat quemquam, sed iudicium omne dedit Filio, [23]ut omnes honorificent Filium, sicut honorificant Patrem. Qui non honorificat Filium, non honorificat Patrem, qui misit illum. [24]Amen, amen dico vobis: Qui verbum meum audit et credit ei, qui misit me, habet vitam aeternam et in iudicium non

was why they sought to do away with him (v. 18).

5:19–47 This long discourse in which Jesus explains who he is and what his mission is deals with the defining themes of St John's Gospel—that Christ reveals the Father, and that he has received from him the power to give people true life.

In the opening verses Jesus speaks of the equality and also the distinction between the Father and the Son. They are equal to one another: all the Son's power is the Father's; all the things the Son does are done by the Father. But they are also distinct from one another: it is the Father who sends the Son. When Jesus performs actions that are proper to God, he is showing his own divine status (cf. v. 36).

The "greater works" (v. 20; cf. 1:50; 14:12) will begin with Christ's resurrection, the cause and pledge of our own (cf. 1 Cor 15:20 ff), and the Son has received from the Father the authority to judge mankind: "Christ is Lord of eternal life. Full right to pass definitive judgment on the works and hearts of men belongs to him as redeemer of the world. He 'acquired' this right by his cross. The Father has given 'all judgment to the Son' (Jn 5:22). Yet the Son did not come to

judge, but to save and to give the life he has in himself. By rejecting grace in this life, one already judges oneself, receives according to one's works, and can even condemn oneself for all eternity by rejecting the Spirit of love" (*Catechism of the Catholic Church*, 679). The words of v. 22 are very consoling: "We have, I admit, a rigorous account to give of our sins; but who will be our judge? The Father [...] has given all judgment to the Son. Let us be comforted: the eternal Father has placed our cause in the hands of our Redeemer himself. St Paul encourages us, saying, Who is [the judge] who is to condemn us? It is Jesus Christ, who died, [...] who indeed intercedes for us (Rom 8:34). It is the Saviour himself, who, in order that he should not condemn us to eternal death, has condemned himself to death for our sake, and who, not content with this, still continues to intercede for us in heaven with God his Father" (St Alphonsus Liguori, *Practice of the Love of Jesus Christ*, 3).

Verses 24–30 close the first part of this discourse. They connect the new life that Christ has already conferred on those who believe in him (vv. 24–27) with life after death (vv. 28–29). In both situations what we receive is a share in God's own life; in fact, even now, in this world, man enjoys "eternal life" (v. 24). "Christ, 'the

Son does not honour the Father who sent him. ²⁴Truly, truly, I say to you, he who hears my word and believes him who sent me, has eternal life; he does not come into judgment, but has passed from death to life.

²⁵"Truly, truly, I say to you, the hour is coming, and now is, when the dead will hear the voice of the Son of God, and those who hear will live. ²⁶For as the Father has life in himself, so he has granted the Son also to have life in himself, ²⁷and has given him authority to execute judgment, because he is the Son of man. ²⁸Do not marvel at this; for the hour is coming when all who are in the tombs will hear his voice ²⁹and come forth, those who have done good, to the resurrection of life, and those who have done evil, to the resurrection of judgment.

³⁰"I can do nothing on my own authority; as I hear, I judge; and my judgment is just, because I seek not my own will but the will of him who sent me. ³¹If I bear witness to myself, my testimony is not true; ³²there is another who bears witness to me, and I know that the testimony which he bears to me is true. ³³You sent to John, and he has borne witness to the truth. ³⁴Not that the testimony which I receive is from

Jn 3:16, 18; 8:51
1 Jn 3:14

Mt 8:22
Eph 2:5, 6; 5:14
Jn 1:1–4; 6:53, 57

Mk 8:38
Dan 7:9–10, 13, 14, 22

Jn 6:40
Dan 12:2
Acts 24:15
Mt 16:27

Jn 5:19; 6:38

Deut 17:6; 19:15
Jn 8:14

Jn 5:36, 37
1 Jn 5:9

Jn 1:6–9, 19–34

venit, sed transiit a morte in vitam. ²⁵Amen, amen dico vobis: Venit hora, et nunc est, quando mortui audient vocem Filii Dei et, qui audierint, vivent. ²⁶Sicut enim Pater habet vitam in semetipso, sic dedit et Filio vitam habere in semetipso; ²⁷et potestatem dedit ei iudicium facere, quia Filius hominis est. ²⁸Nolite mirari hoc, quia venit hora, in qua omnes, qui in monumentis sunt, audient vocem eius ²⁹et procedent, qui bona fecerunt, in resurrectionem vitae, qui vero mala egerunt, in resurrectionem iudicii. ³⁰Non possum ego a meipso facere quidquam; sicut audio, iudico, et iudicium meum iustum est, quia non quaero voluntatem meam, sed voluntatem eius, qui misit me. ³¹Si ego testimonium perhibeo de meipso, testimonium meum non est verum; ³²alius est, qui testimonium perhibet de me, et scio quia verum est testimonium, quod perhibet de me. ³³Vos misistis ad Ioannem, et testimonium perhibuit veritati; ³⁴ego autem non ab homine testimonium accipio, sed haec dico, ut vos salvi sitis.

first-born from the dead' (Col 1:18), is the principle of our own resurrection, even now by the justification of our souls, and one day by the new life he will impart to our bodies" (*Catechism of the Catholic Church*, 658).

To understand what Jesus says in vv. 25–30, we must remember that he—who is a single (divine) Person, one subject of operations, one I—is expressing in human words not only his feelings as a man but also the deepest dimension of his being: he is the Son of God, eternally begotten by the Father and begotten also in time through his human nature.

In the second part of the discourse (vv. 31–40), in anticipation of possible objections that it is not enough for a person to testify in his own cause (cf. Deut 19:15), Jesus explains that what he says is vouched for by four witnesses—John the Baptist (vv. 32–36; cf. 1:34), the kind of works he himself does (v. 36; cf. 2:1–11; 4:46–54; 5:1–18), the Father (vv. 37–38; cf. 1:31–34; 12:28–30), and the Scriptures (v. 39). Jesus invites his hearers to examine the Scriptures, the Word of God, because they will find there the explanation for what is happening (for what he says and does), provided they are not blinded by prejudice. "The economy of the Old Testament was deliberately so orientated that it should prepare for and declare in prophecy the coming of Christ, redeemer of all men, and of the messianic kingdom (cf. Lk 24:44; Jn 5:39; 1 Pet 1:10), and should indicate it by means of different types (cf. 1 Cor 10:11). [...] Christians should accept with veneration these writings which give expression to a lively sense of God, which are a storehouse of sublime teaching on God and of sound wisdom on human life, as well as a wonderful treasury of prayers; in them, too, the mystery of our salvation is present in a hidden way" (Vatican II, *Dei Verbum*, 15).

Finally (vv. 41–47), Jesus spells out three things that prevent his hearers from acknowledging him to be the Messiah and the Son of God— their lack of love for God, their desire for human glory, and their prejudiced reading of Scripture. Better dispositions are needed if one is to discover who Christ really is: "That Christ you see is not Jesus. At best it is only the pitiful image that your blurred eyes are able to form ... Purify yourself. Make your sight sharper with humility and penance. Then the pure light of love will not fail you. And you will have perfect vision. The image you see will really be his: Jesus himself" (St Josemaría Escrivá, *The Way*, 212).

Jn 1:8
Lk 1:17

Jn 1:33; 3:2
1 Jn 5:9

Ex 19:5; 24:17
Deut 4:12
Mt 3:17

Lk 24:27, 44
2 Tim 3:15–17
1 Pet 1:11

Deut 18:15, 18

Jn 7:18; 12:43
Mt 23:5–7
Rom 2:29

Deut 31:26

Jn 7:19
Deut 18:15
Lk 16:31

man; but I say this that you may be saved. [35]He was a burning and shining lamp, and you were willing to rejoice for a while in his light. [36]But the testimony which I have is greater than that of John; for the works which the Father has granted me to accomplish, these very works which I am doing, bear me witness that the Father has sent me. [37]And the Father who sent me has himself borne witness to me. His voice you have never heard, his form you have never seen; [38]and you do not have his word abiding in you, for you do not believe him whom he has sent. [39]You search the scriptures, because you think that in them you have eternal life; and it is they that bear witness to me; [40]yet you refuse to come to me that you may have life. [41]I do not receive glory from men. [42]But I know that you have not the love of God within you. [43]I have come in my Father's name, and you do not receive me; if another comes in his own name, him you will receive. [44]How can you believe, who receive glory from one another and do not seek the glory that comes from the only God? [45]Do not think that I shall accuse you to the Father; it is Moses who accuses you, on whom you set your hope. [46]If you believed Moses, you would believe me, for he wrote of me. [47]But if you do not believe his writings, how will you believe my words?"

4. JESUS IS THE BREAD OF LIFE*

Mt 14:13–21
Mk 6:30–44
Lk 9:10–17

Miracle of the loaves and fish

6 [1]After this Jesus went to the other side of the Sea of Galilee, which is the Sea of Tiberias. [2]And a multitude followed him, because they saw the signs which he

[35]Ille erat lucerna ardens et lucens, vos autem voluistis exsultare ad horam in luce eius. [36]Ego autem habeo testimonium maius Ioanne; opera enim, quae dedit mihi Pater, ut perficiam ea, ipsa opera, quae ego facio, testimonium perhibent de me quia Pater me misit; [37]et, qui misit me, Pater, ipse testimonium perhibuit de me. Neque vocem eius umquam audistis, neque speciem eius vidistis, [38]et verbum eius non habetis in vobis manens, quia, quem misit ille, huic vos non creditis. [39]Scrutamini Scripturas, quia vos putatis in ipsis vitam aeternam habere; et illae sunt, quae testimonium perhibent de me. [40]Et non vultis venire ad me, ut vitam habeatis. [41]Gloriam ab hominibus non accipio, [42]sed cognovi vos, quia dilectionem Dei non habetis in vobis. [43]Ego veni in nomine Patris mei, et non accipitis me; si alius venerit in nomine suo, illum accipietis. [44]Quomodo potestis vos credere, qui gloriam ab invicem accipitis, et gloriam, quae a solo est Deo, non quaeritis? [45]Nolite putare quia ego accusaturus sim vos apud Patrem; est qui accuset vos: Moyses, in quo vos speratis. [46]Si enim crederetis Moysi, crederetis forsitan et mihi; de me enim ille scripsit. [47]Si autem illius litteris non creditis, quomodo meis verbis credetis?». [6] [1]Post haec abiit Iesus trans mare Galilaeae, quod est Tiberiadis. [2]Et sequebatur

*6:1–71 This chapter (the fourth section of the Gospel) is structured in a similar way to the previous one. It opens with two signs or miracles—that of the loaves and fish, and that of Jesus walking on the water; this is followed by the discourse in the synagogue of Capernaum in which he manifests himself as the Bread of Life. St John notes that this took place when "the Passover, the feast of the Jews, was at hand" (v. 4); he seems to imply that the Eucharistic banquet will, in due course, be the New Passover. Many of Jesus' followers are shocked by what he says; in general, those who do not believe go away (v. 66), and those who do are drawn more closely to him (v. 69).

6:1–15 St John's Gospel reports only seven of Jesus' miracles, selecting those which best illustrate aspects of the mystery of Christ. The miracle of the loaves and fish, performed some days before the Passover, prefigures the Christian Easter and the mystery of the Eucharist, and is positioned as a lead-up to the discourse on the Bread of Life (6:26–58), in which Jesus promises himself as nourishment for the soul. The connexion between miracle and discourse is strengthened by what is said in v. 11, which reads like the accounts of the institution of the Eucharist in the Synoptics and St Paul (see Mt 26:26; Mk 14:22; Lk 22:17; and 1 Cor 11:23–24).

Jesus is sensitive to people's needs, both material and spiritual (v. 5). Here he takes the initiative to relieve the hunger of the thousands of people who have been following him. In his conversations with the disciples and in the miracle that follows, he tells them that they must

did on those who were diseased. ³Jesus went up into the hills, and there sat down with his disciples. ⁴Now the Passover, the feast of the Jews, was at hand. ⁵Lifting up his eyes, then, and seeing that a multitude was coming to him, Jesus said to Philip, "How are we to buy bread, so that these people may eat?" ⁶This he said to test them, for he himself knew what he would do. ⁷Philip answered him, "Two hundred denarii¹ would not buy enough bread for each of them to get a little." ⁸One of his disciples, Andrew, Simon Peter's brother, said to him, ⁹"There is a lad here who has five barley loaves and two fish; but what are they among so many?" ¹⁰Jesus said, "Make the people sit down." Now there was much grass in the place; so the men sat down, in number about five thousand. ¹¹Jesus then took the loaves, and when he had given thanks, he distributed them to those who were seated; so also the fish, as much as they wanted. ¹²And when they had eaten their fill, he told his disciples, "Gather up the fragments left over, that nothing may be lost." ¹³So they gathered them up and filled twelve baskets with fragments from the five barley loaves, left by those who had eaten. ¹⁴When the people saw the sign which he had done, they said, "This is indeed the prophet who is to come into the world!"

¹⁵Perceiving then that they were about to come and take him by force to make him king, Jesus withdrew again to the hills by himself.

Mt 5:1

Jn 2:13; 11:55
Lk 22:1
Jn 1:44
Mk 8:1–10

Jn 1:40

2 Kings 4:42–44

Jn 10:9
Acts 4:4

Deut 18:15

Ex 32:30; 34:3
Jn 12:13; 18:36

eum multitudo magna, quia videbant signa, quae faciebat super his, qui infirmabantur. ³Subiit autem in montem Iesus et ibi sedebat cum discipulis suis. ⁴Erat autem proximum Pascha, dies festus Iudaeorum. ⁵Cum sublevasset ergo oculos Iesus et vidisset quia multitudo magna venit ad eum, dicit ad Philippum: «Unde ememus panes, ut manducent hi?». ⁶Hoc autem dicebat tentans eum; ipse enim sciebat quid esset facturus. ⁷Respondit ei Philippus: «Ducentorum denariorum panes non sufficiunt eis, ut unusquisque modicum quid accipiat!». ⁸Dicit ei unus ex discipulis eius, Andreas frater Simonis Petri: ⁹«Est puer hic, qui habet quinque panes hordeaceos et duos pisces; sed haec quid sunt propter tantos?». ¹⁰Dixit Iesus: «Facite homines discumbere». Erat autem fenum multum in loco. Discubuerunt ergo viri numero quasi quinque milia. ¹¹Accepit ergo panes Iesus et, cum gratias egisset, distribuit discumbentibus, similiter et ex piscibus, quantum volebant. ¹²Ut autem impleti sunt, dicit discipulis suis: «Colligite, quae superaverunt, fragmenta, ne quid pereat». ¹³Collegerunt ergo et impleverunt duodecim cophinos fragmentorum ex quinque panibus hordeaceis, quae superfuerunt his, qui manducaverunt. ¹⁴Illi ergo homines, cum vidissent quod fecerat signum, dicebant: «Hic est vere propheta, qui venit in mundum!». ¹⁵Iesus ergo, cum cognovisset quia venturi essent, ut raperent eum et facerent eum regem, secessit iterum in

trust in him when difficulties arise in their future apostolate; they must embark on that apostolate as best they can, even if they lack sufficient resources, as is the case at present (v. 9). He will provide what they need. As Christians, we have to put everything at God's disposal, even if it does not seem to amount to much. Our Lord will put it to good use: "Jesus relied not on a sufficient supply of material goods but on the boy's generosity in offering the little he had. [...] What human reason could not dare to hope came true in Jesus through the generous heart of a young boy" (John Paul II, *Message*, 8 September 1997).

The reaction to the miracle (v. 14) shows that the beneficiaries acknowledge Jesus as the Prophet, the Messiah promised in the Old Testament (see Deut 18:15), but they have too earthly, too rationalistic, an idea of the Messiah's role: they want Jesus to be a king who will provide them with earthly things in abundance and set them free from the Romans.

Later (see 6:26–27) Jesus will explain the true meaning of the miracle of the loaves; but for the moment he simply withdraws from that place, to avoid popular acclaim that has nothing to do with his true mission. In his conversation with Pilate (see 18:36) he will explain that his kingdom is "not of this world". "The Gospels clearly show that for Jesus anything that would alter his mission as the Servant of Yahweh was a temptation (cf. Mt 4:8; Lk 4:5). He does not accept the position of those who mixed the things of God with merely political attitudes (cf. Mt 22:21; Mk 12:17; Jn 18:36). [...] The perspective of his mission is much deeper. It consists in complete salvation through transforming, peacemaking, pardoning, and reconciling love. There is no doubt, moreover, that all this makes many demands on the Christian who wishes truly to serve his least brethren, the poor, the needy, the outcast; in a word, all those who in their lives reflect the sorrowing face of the Lord (cf. *Lumen gentium*, 8)" (John Paul II, *Address to Latin-American Bishops*, 28 January 1979).

1 The denarius was a day's wage for a labourer

Jesus walks on water

Mt 14:22–33
Mk 6:45–52

[16]When evening came, his disciples went down to the sea, [17]got into a boat, and started across the sea to Capernaum. It was now dark, and Jesus had not yet come to

Mt 8:24
Ps 77:19

them. [18]The sea rose because a strong wind was blowing. [19]When they had rowed about three or four miles,[m] they saw Jesus walking on the sea and drawing near to

Ex 3:14
Jn 4:26

the boat. They were frightened, [20]but he said to them, "It is I; do not be afraid." [21]Then they were glad to take him into the boat, and immediately the boat was at the land to which they were going.

The people look for Jesus*

Jn 6:17

[22]On the next day the people who remained on the other side of the sea saw that there had been only one boat there, and that Jesus had not entered the boat with his disciples, but that his disciples had gone away alone. [23]However, boats from Tiberias came near the place where they ate the bread after the Lord had given thanks. [24]So when the people saw that Jesus was not there, nor his disciples, they themselves got into the boats and went to Capernaum, seeking Jesus. [25]When they found him on the other side of the sea, they said to him, "Rabbi, when did you come here?"

The discourse on the Bread of Life

[26]Jesus answered them, "Truly, truly, I say to you, you seek me, not because you saw

Dan 7:14
Jn 3:33; 4:14; 5:36

signs, but because you ate your fill of the loaves. [27]Do not labour for the food which

montem ipse solus. [16]Ut autem sero factum est, descenderunt discipuli eius ad mare [17]et, cum ascendissent navem, veniebant trans mare in Capharnaum. Et tenebrae iam factae erant, et nondum venerat ad eos Iesus. [18]Mare autem, vento magno flante, exsurgebat. [19]Cum remigassent ergo quasi stadia viginti quinque aut triginta, vident Iesum ambulantem super mare et proximum navi fieri, et timuerunt. [20]Ille autem dicit eis: «Ego sum, nolite timere!». [21]Volebant ergo accipere eum in navem, et statim fuit navis ad terram, in quam ibant. [22]Altera die turba, quae stabat trans mare, vidit quia navicula alia non erat ibi nisi una et quia non introisset cum discipulis suis Iesus in navem, sed soli discipuli eius abiissent; [23]aliae supervenerunt naves a Tiberiade iuxta locum, ubi manducaverant panem, gratias agente Domino. [24]Cum ergo vidisset turba quia Iesus non esset ibi neque discipuli eius, ascenderunt ipsi naviculas et venerunt Capharnaum quaerentes Iesum. [25]Et cum invenissent eum trans mare, dixerunt ei:

6:16–21 This miracle, which is also reported by Matthew and Mark, is beyond the comprehension of the disciples, their faith being still weak. In this miracle Jesus shows that his power exceeds that of Moses; to allow him and the Israelites to cross the sea, God just had Moses divide the waters (see Ex 14:15–31). The words "It is I" (v. 20) are reminiscent of what God said when he revealed his name to Moses (cf. 8:28; Ex 3:14). This miracle and the discourse on the Bread of Life strengthen the disciples' faith.

Christian tradition has seen the boat of this episode as a symbol of the Church, which will have to cope with many difficulties and which our Lord has promised to aid at all times (cf. Mt 28:20); his help will ensure that the Church remains firm in the faith. St Thomas Aquinas comments: "The wind symbolizes the temptations and persecution the Church will suffer due to lack of love. For, as St Augustine says, when love grows cold, the sea becomes rougher and

the boat begins to founder. Yet the wind, the storm, the waves and the darkness will fail to put it off course and wreck it" (*Super Evangelium Ioannis*, ad loc.).

*6:22–59 Capernaum was Jesus' base for his ministry in Galilee (cf. the note on Lk 7:1–10). Its synagogue (v. 59) is the scene of the discourse on the Bread of Life (vv. 26–58), in which Jesus reveals who he is, where he comes from, and the great gifts he will grant us—faith, the Eucharist, eternal life.

6:26–34 The discourse begins with a conversation between Jesus and the Jews in which he speaks about the messianic gifts he brings. These people thought that the manna (the food the Israelites received every day during their journey through the wilderness: see Ex 16:13–36) was a symbol of the gifts the Messiah would provide; that is why they ask Jesus to work a similar, dra-

m Greek *twenty-five or thirty stadia*

perishes, but for the food which endures to eternal life, which the Son of man will give to you; for on him has God the Father set his seal." ²⁸Then they said to him, "What must we do, to be doing the works of God?" ²⁹Jesus answered them, "This is the work of God, that you believe in him whom he has sent." ³⁰So they said to him, "Then what sign do you do, that we may see, and believe you? What work do you perform? ³¹Our fathers ate the manna in the wilderness; as it is written, 'He gave them bread from heaven to eat.'" ³²Jesus then said to them, "Truly, truly, I say to you, it was not Moses who gave you the bread from heaven; my Father gives you the true bread from heaven. ³³For the bread of God is that which comes down from heaven, and gives life to the world." ³⁴They said to him, "Lord, give us this bread always."

1 Jn 3:23
Jn 2:18–12
Mk 8:11
Lk 11:29–30
Wis 16:20
Ps 78:24
Ex 16:15
Wis 16:20
Jn 6:49
Jn 6:51
Jn 4:15

Jesus is the one who reveals the Father

³⁵Jesus said to them, "I am the bread of life; he who comes to me shall not hunger, and he who believes in me shall never thirst. ³⁶But I said to you that you have seen me and

Jn 4:14; 6:48; 7:37
Sir 24:20
Jn 6:26, 29

«Rabbi, quando huc venisti?». ²⁶Respondit eis Iesus et dixit: «Amen, amen dico vobis: Quaeritis me non quia vidistis signa, sed quia manducastis ex panibus et saturati estis. ²⁷Operamini non cibum, qui perit, sed cibum, qui permanet in vitam aeternam, quem Filius hominis vobis dabit; hunc enim Pater signavit Deus!». ²⁸Dixerunt ergo ad eum: «Quid faciemus, ut operemur opera Dei?». ²⁹Respondit Iesus et dixit eis: «Hoc est opus Dei, ut credatis in eum, quem misit ille». ³⁰Dixerunt ergo ei: «Quod ergo tu facis signum, ut videamus et credamus tibi? Quid operaris? ³¹Patres nostri manna manducaverunt in deserto, sicut scriptum est: *"Panem de caelo dedit eis manducare"*». ³²Dixit ergo eis Iesus: «Amen, amen dico vobis: Non Moyses dedit vobis panem de caelo, sed Pater meus dat vobis panem de caelo verum: ³³panis enim Dei est, qui descendit de caelo et dat vitam mundo». ³⁴Dixerunt ergo ad eum: «Domine, semper da nobis panem hunc».³⁵Dixit eis Iesus: «Ego sum panis vitae. Qui venit ad me, non esuriet; et, qui credit in me, non sitiet umquam. ³⁶Sed dixi vobis quia et vidistis me, et non creditis. ³⁷Omne, quod dat mihi Pater, ad me veniet, et eum,

matic miracle. But they could never have imagined that the manna prefigured a truly wonderful messianic gift from God to men—his own Son present in the mystery of the Holy Eucharist. In this conversation, Jesus tries to lead them to make an act of faith in him as a preparation for his revelation about the Eucharist.

"On him has God the Father set his seal" (v. 27): this phrase expresses why it is that only he, the Son of man, can provide the heavenly gifts he has referred to: he is God and man, and his human nature is the instrument through which the Second Person of the Blessed Trinity acts. St Thomas Aquinas comments on these words as follows: "What the Son of man will give he possesses through his superiority over all other men in his singular and outstanding fullness of grace [...]. When a seal is impressed on wax, the wax receives the complete form of the seal. So it is that the Son received the entire form of the Father. This occurred in two ways; eternally (eternal generation), which is not referred to here because the seal and the sealed are different in nature from one another; what is referred to here is the other manner, that is, the mystery of the Incarnation, whereby God the Father impressed

on human nature the Word, who is the reflection and the very stamp of God's nature, as Hebrews [1:3] says" (*Super Evangelium Ioannis*, ad loc.).

6:35–47 In this first main part of the discourse, Jesus portrays himself as the Bread of Life. He speaks about (1) faith in himself; faith involves "coming to him" (see vv. 35, 37, 44, 45), accepting his signs (miracles) and his teaching; (2) the resurrection of believers (vv. 39, 40, 44, 47), which begins in this life, through faith, and will come about definitively at the end of time; (3) predestination—the plan of our Father in heaven that all should be saved (vv. 39, 40).

"They shall all be taught by God" (v. 45) is evocative of Isaiah 54:13 and Jeremiah 31:31–34, where those prophets speak of the future covenant that God will establish with his people when the Messiah comes; that covenant will be sealed with the blood of the Messiah forever, and God will write it on men's hearts. "Coming to Jesus", going to him (v. 35), means believing in him, because we approach him through faith. Using the images of food and drink, Jesus is saying that he will satisfy all man's noble aspirations: "How beautiful is our Catholic faith! It

Jn 17:6–8
Mt 8:12

Jn 4:34; 5:30

Jn 10:28, 29; 17:12

Jn 5:29; 11:42

Ex 16:7; 17:3
Num 11:1
Ps 106:25
Jn 6:61
Lk 4:22
Mk 6:1–6
Jer 31:3
Hos 2:16; 11:4
Jn 6:65
Is 54:13
Jer 31:33, 34
Jn 1:18
Jn 3:16

yet do not believe. ³⁷All that the Father gives me will come to me; and him who comes to me I will not cast out. ³⁸For I have come down from heaven, not to do my own will, but the will of him who sent me; ³⁹and this is the will of him who sent me, that I should lose nothing of all that he has given me, but raise it up on the last day. ⁴⁰For this is the will of my Father, that every one who sees the Son and believes in him should have eternal life; and I will raise him up at the last day."

⁴¹The Jews then murmured at him, because he said, "I am the bread which came down from heaven." ⁴²They said, "Is not this Jesus, the son of Joseph, whose father and mother we know? How does he now say, 'I have come down from heaven'?" ⁴³Jesus answered them, "Do not murmur among yourselves. ⁴⁴No one can come to me unless the Father who sent me draws him; and I will raise him up on the last day. ⁴⁵It is written in the prophets, 'And they shall all be taught by God.' Every one who has heard and learned from the Father comes to me. ⁴⁶Not that any one has seen the Father except him who is from God; he has seen the Father. ⁴⁷Truly, truly, I say to you, he who believes has eternal life.

Jesus is the Bread of Life in the Eucharist

Num 14:35
Josh 5:6
Ps 95:7–11
Jn 6:31–35
1 Cor 10:3–5

⁴⁸I am the bread of life. ⁴⁹Your fathers ate the manna in the wilderness, and they died. ⁵⁰This is the bread which comes down from heaven, that a man may eat of it and not

qui venit ad me, non eiciam foras, ³⁸quia descendi de caelo, non ut faciam voluntatem meam sed voluntatem eius, qui misit me. ³⁹Haec est autem voluntas eius, qui misit me, ut omne, quod dedit mihi, non perdam ex eo, sed resuscitem illud in novissimo die. ⁴⁰Haec est enim voluntas Patris mei, ut omnis, qui videt Filium et credit in eum, habeat vitam aeternam; et resuscitabo ego eum in novissimo die». ⁴¹Murmurabant ergo Iudaei de illo quia dixisset: «Ego sum panis, qui de caelo descendi», ⁴²et dicebant: «Nonne hic est Iesus filius Ioseph, cuius nos novimus patrem et matrem? Quomodo dicit nunc: "De caelo descendi"?». ⁴³Respondit Iesus et dixit eis: «Nolite murmurare in invicem. ⁴⁴Nemo potest venire ad me, nisi Pater, qui misit me, traxerit eum; et ego resuscitabo eum in novissimo die. ⁴⁵Est scriptum in Prophetis: "Et erunt omnes docibiles Dei". Omnis, qui audivit a Patre et didicit, venit ad me. ⁴⁶Non quia Patrem vidit quisquam, nisi is qui est a Deo, hic vidit Patrem. ⁴⁷Amen, amen dico vobis: Qui credit, habet vitam aeternam. ⁴⁸Ego sum panis vitae. ⁴⁹Patres vestri manducaverunt in deserto manna et mortui sunt. ⁵⁰Hic est panis de caelo descendens, ut, si quis ex ipso manducaverit, non moriatur. ⁵¹Ego sum panis vivus, qui de caelo descendi. Si quis manducaverit ex hoc pane, vivet in aeter-

provides a solution for all our anxieties, calms our minds and fills our hearts with hope" (St Josemaría Escrivá, *The Way*, 582).

Verse 42 mentions St Joseph for the second and last time in this Gospel, and registers the generally held, but mistaken, opinion of those who knew Jesus and thought him to be the son of Joseph the carpenter (cf. 1:45; Mt 13:55; Lk 3:23; 4:22). Conceived in the virginal womb of Mary through the action of the Holy Spirit, Jesus had only one Father—God himself (cf. 5:18). However, St Joseph acted as his father on earth, as God had planned (cf. the notes on Mt 1:1–25): "Not only does Joseph deserve the name of father: he deserves it more than anyone else. In what way was he a father? As profoundly as his fatherhood was chaste. Some people thought that he was the father of our Lord Jesus Christ in the same way as others are fathers, begetting according to the flesh and not receiving their children as fruit of their spiritual affection. That is why St Luke says that they supposed he was the father

of Jesus. Why does he say that they only supposed it? Because human thoughts and judgments are based on what normally happens. And our Lord was not born of the seed of Joseph. However, to the piety and charity of Joseph a son was born to him of the Virgin Mary, who was the Son of God" (St Augustine, *Sermones*, 51, 20).

6:48–59 In this second main part of the discourse, Christ reveals the mystery of the Eucharist. His words have such a declarative realism that they cannot be interpreted in a figurative way. His hearers knew exactly what he meant (see v. 52), and they could not accept it. If they had taken Jesus' language as figurative or symbolic, it would not have shocked them as it did, and no argument would have ensued. What Jesus says here is the root of the Church's belief that, by the transformation of bread and wine into his Body and Blood, Christ becomes present in the Eucharist: "The Council of Trent summarizes the Catholic faith by declaring: 'Because

die. ⁵¹I am the living bread* which came down from heaven; if any one eats of this

Prov 9:5
Heb 10:5–10

bread, he will live for ever; and the bread which I shall give for the life of the world is my flesh."

⁵²The Jews then disputed among themselves, saying, "How can this man give us

Jn 6:60

his flesh to eat?"* ⁵³So Jesus said to them, "Truly, truly, I say to you, unless you eat

Jn 5:26

the flesh of the Son of man and drink his blood, you have no life in you; ⁵⁴he who eats

Gen 9:4
Lev 17:10–16

my flesh and drinks my blood has eternal life, and I will raise him up on the last day. ⁵⁵For my flesh is food indeed, and my blood is drink indeed. ⁵⁶He who eats my flesh

Ezek 36:28
Jn 15:4; 17:21, 26
1 Jn 2:24; 3:24

and drinks my blood abides in me, and I in him. ⁵⁷As the living Father sent me, and I live because of the Father, so he who eats me will live because of me. ⁵⁸This is the bread which came from heaven, not such as the fathers ate and died; he who eats this bread will live for ever." ⁵⁹This he said in the synagogue, as he taught in Capernaum.

Jn 6:24

The disciples' reaction

⁶⁰Many of his disciples, when they heard of it, said, "This is a hard saying; who can

Jn 6:41

listen to it?" ⁶¹But Jesus, knowing in himself that his disciples murmured at it, said

Jn 6:41

num; panis autem, quem ego dabo, caro mea est pro mundi vita». ⁵²Litigabant ergo Iudaei ad invicem dicentes: «Quomodo potest hic nobis carnem suam dare ad manducandum?». ⁵³Dixit ergo eis Iesus: «Amen, amen dico vobis: Nisi manducaveritis carnem Filii hominis et biberitis eius sanguinem, non habetis vitam in vobismetipsis. ⁵⁴Qui manducat meam carnem et bibit meum sanguinem, habet vitam aeternam; et ego resuscitabo eum in novissimo die. ⁵⁵Caro enim mea verus est cibus, et sanguis meus verus est potus. ⁵⁶Qui manducat meam carnem et bibit meum sanguinem, in me manet, et ego in illo. ⁵⁷Sicut misit me vivens Pater, et ego vivo propter Patrem; et, qui manducat me, et ipse vivet propter me. ⁵⁸Hic est panis, qui de caelo descendit, non sicut manducaverunt patres et mortui sunt; qui manducat hunc panem, vivet in aeternum». ⁵⁹Haec dixit in synagoga docens in Capharnaum. ⁶⁰Multi ergo audientes ex discipulis eius dixerunt: «Durus est hic sermo! Quis potest eum audire?». ⁶¹Sciens autem Iesus

Christ our Redeemer said that it was truly his body that he was offering under the species of bread, it has always been the conviction of the Church of God, and this holy Council now declares again, that by the consecration of the bread and wine there takes place a change of the whole substance of the bread into the substance of the body of Christ our Lord and of the whole substance of the wine into the substance of his blood. This change the holy Catholic Church has fittingly and properly called transubstantiation'" (*Catechism of the Catholic Church*, 1376).

Three times (see vv. 31–32, 49, 58) Jesus compares the true Bread of Life, his own Body, to the manna God provided as daily food during the Isrealites' forty years in the desert. He is inviting us to partake often of his Body, as nourishment for our souls: "From this comparison of the Food of angels with bread and with manna, it was easily to be understood by his disciples that, as the body is daily nourished with bread, and as the Hebrews were daily fed with manna in the desert, so the Christian soul might daily partake of this heavenly bread and be refreshed thereby. Moreover, we are bidden in the Lord's Prayer to ask for 'our daily bread', by which words, the holy Fathers of the

Church all but unanimously teach, must be understood not so much that material bread which is the support of the body as the Eucharistic bread which ought to be our daily food" (St Pius X, *Sacra Tridentina Synodus*, 20 December 1905).

6:60–71 These verses tell how Jesus' disciples reacted to his discourse. Even when revealing the Eucharistic mystery, this most outlandish-sounding thing, he expects them to believe in his words. What he is revealing is not to be understood according to the flesh, that is, in terms perceptible to the senses, or from an earth-bound point of view: it needs to be accepted as revelation from God, who is "spirit and life". As on other occasions (see 1:51; 5:20), Jesus' reference to future events (in this case, his glorious ascension) helps to strengthen his disciples' faith and that of all believers when they see his words fulfilled (v. 62): "I have told you before it takes place, so that when it does take place, you may believe" (14:29).

The promise of the Eucharist causes these people in Capernaum to dispute among themselves (6:52) and scandalizes (v. 61) and alienates many of Jesus' followers (v. 66). He has

Jn 3:13

to them, "Do you take offence at this? [62]Then what if you were to see the Son of

Dan 7:13–14
2 Cor 3:6

man ascending where he was before?* [63]It is the spirit that gives life, the flesh is of

Jn 1:47–48; 2:24–25;
13:11

no avail; the words that I have spoken to you are spirit and life. [64]But there are some of you that do not believe." For Jesus knew from the first who those were that did

Jn 6:44

not believe, and who it was that should betray him. [65]And he said, "This is why I told you that no one can come to me unless it is granted him by the Father."

[66]After this many of his disciples drew back and no longer went with him. [67]Jesus

Mk 8:27–30

said to the twelve, "Will you also go away?" [68]Simon Peter answered him, "Lord, to

Lev 21:6–7
Jn 1:49; 11:27
Mt 14:33; 16:16

whom shall we go? You have the words of eternal life; [69]and we have believed, and have come to know, that you are the Holy One of God." [70]Jesus answered them,

Jn 6:64

"Did I not choose you, the twelve, and one of you is a devil?" [71]He spoke of Judas the son of Simon Iscariot, for he, one of the twelve, was to betray him.

5. JESUS, SENT BY THE FATHER, IS THE LIGHT OF THE WORLD AND THE GOOD SHEPHERD*

Jesus goes up to Jerusalem during the feast of Tabernacles*

Jn 4:44–45; 5:16–18
Mk 9:30

Ex 23:14
Lev 23:34
Zech 14:16–19

7 [1]After this Jesus went about in Galilee; he would not go about in Judea, because the Jews[n] sought to kill him. [2]Now the Jews' feast of Tabernacles was at hand.

apud semetipsum quia murmurarent de hoc discipuli eius, dixit eis: «Hoc vos scandalizat? [62]Si ergo videritis Filium hominis ascendentem, ubi erat prius? [63]Spiritus est, qui vivificat, caro non prodest quidquam; verba, quae ego locutus sum vobis, Spiritus sunt et vita sunt. [64]Sed sunt quidam ex vobis, qui non credunt». Sciebat enim ab initio Iesus, qui essent non credentes, et quis traditurus esset eum. [65]Et dicebat: «Propterea dixi vobis: Nemo potest venire ad me, nisi fuerit ei datum a Patre». [66]Ex hoc multi discipulorum eius abierunt retro et iam non cum illo ambulabant. [67]Dixit ergo Iesus ad Duodecim: «Numquid et vos vultis abire?». [68]Respondit ei Simon Petrus: «Domine, ad quem ibimus? Verba vitae aeternae habes; [69]et nos credidimus et cognovimus quia tu es Sanctus Dei». [70]Respondit eis Iesus: «Nonne ego vos Duodecim elegi? Et ex vobis unus Diabolus est?». [71]Dicebat autem Iudam Simonis Iscariotis: hic enim erat traditurus eum, cum esset unus ex Duodecim.   [7] [1]Et post haec ambulabat Iesus

revealed to them a wonderful, salvific truth, but those disciples reject divine grace, because they are not prepared to accept something that goes far beyond their limited horizons. The mystery of the Eucharist calls for a special act of faith. St John Chrysostom therefore advised Christians: "Let us in everything believe God, and gainsay him in nothing, though what is said be contrary to our thoughts and senses. [...] Let us act likewise in respect to the [Eucharistic] mysteries, not looking at the things set before us, but keeping in mind his words. For his word cannot deceive" (*In Matthaeum*, 82).

Speaking for the Twelve, Peter expresses faith in Jesus' words because he knows them to come from God—in the same kind of way as he acknowledged at Caesarea Philippi (see Mt 16:13–20; Mk 8:27–30) that Jesus was the Messiah. Peter's confession of faith, and that of his successors, stands for the communion of faith of believers in Christ, which enables them to discern that what they believe is true.

*7:1—10:21 The fifth section of the Gospel comprises almost four chapters, in which John recounts Jesus' activity in Jerusalem at the festival of Tabernacles—the occasion of another visit by our Lord to the Holy City. A new meaning is added to those that this feast traditionally had: Jesus is portrayed as the Messiah who inaugurates a new order of salvation centred on grace, an order higher than that previously enjoyed by God's people, which was centred on the Law (see 1:17). Once again we are told that Jesus has been sent by the Father, and that the Holy Spirit is to come (chap. 7). Jesus is the Judge who pardons the adulterous woman (chap. 8), and the Light of the world who restores sight to the man blind from birth; but he denounces those who refuse to see (chap. 9). He is the Door through which people enter eternal life, and the Good Shepherd who gives his life for mankind (10:1–21).

*7:1–30 The name of this feast recalls the time when the Israelites were in the wilderness, living

n Or *Judeans*

³So his brethren* said to him, "Leave here and go to Judea, that your disciples may see the works you are doing. ⁴For no man works in secret if he seeks to be known openly. If you do these things, show yourself to the world." ⁵For even his brethren did not believe in him. ⁶Jesus said to them, "My time has not yet come, but your time is always here. ⁷The world cannot hate you, but it hates me because I testify of it that its works are evil. ⁸Go to the feast yourselves; I am not° going up to this feast, for my time has not fully come." ⁹So saying, he remained in Galilee.

Jn 2:11–12
Mt 12:46

Mk 1:15

Jn 3:19; 15:18

¹⁰But after his brethren had gone up to the feast, then he also went up, not publicly but in private. ¹¹The Jews were looking for him at the feast, and saying, "Where is he?" ¹²And there was much muttering about him among the people. While some said, "He is a good man," others said, "No, he is leading the people astray." ¹³Yet for fear of the Jews no one spoke openly of him.

Mt 27:63

Mt 27:63
Deut 13:6; 18:22
Jn 9:22; 12:42

Jesus' teaching comes from God

¹⁴About the middle of the feast Jesus went up into the temple and taught. ¹⁵The Jews marvelled at it, saying, "How is it that this man has learning,ᵖ when he has never

Mt 13:54–57
Lk 2:47

Mk 6:2

in Galilaeam; non enim volebat in Iudaeam ambulare, quia quaerebant eum Iudaei interficere. ²Erat autem in proximo dies festus Iudaeorum, Scenopegia. ³Dixerunt ergo ad eum fratres eius: «Transi hinc et vade in Iudaeam, ut et discipuli tui videant opera tua, quae facis. ⁴Nemo quippe in occulto quid facit et quaerit ipse in palam esse. Si haec facis, manifesta teipsum mundo». ⁵Neque enim fratres eius credebant in eum. ⁶Dicit ergo eis Iesus: «Tempus meum nondum adest, tempus autem vestrum semper est paratum. ⁷Non potest mundus odisse vos, me autem odit, quia ego testimonium perhibeo de illo quia opera eius mala sunt. ⁸Vos ascendite ad diem festum, ego non ascendo ad diem festum istum, quia meum tempus nondum impletum est». ⁹Haec autem cum dixisset, ipse mansit in Galilaea. ¹⁰Ut autem ascenderunt fratres eius ad diem festum, tunc et ipse ascendit, non manifeste sed quasi in occulto. ¹¹Iudaei ergo quaerebant eum in die festo et dicebant: «Ubi est ille?». ¹²Et murmur multus de eo erat in turba. Alii quidem dicebant: «Bonus est!»; alii autem dicebant: «Non, sed seducit turbam!». ¹³Nemo tamen palam loquebatur de illo

in tents (cf. Lev 23:33–43). The feast, held at the beginning of autumn, lasted eight days (see Neh 8:13–18) and commemorated the protection God had given the Israelites during those forty years of pilgrimage. Because it coincided with the end of the harvest, it was also called the feast of Ingathering. It was one of the three annual feasts when every male Israelite had to present himself before the Lord (see Ex 23:14–17; Deut 16:16).

7:1–13 John records the refusal of the relatives of Jesus to believe in him, and also our Lord's refusal to seek human, earthly glory. These relatives know that he has the power to work great miracles; yet they do not believe in him. They do not understand the true meaning of the signs Jesus works. Miracles, on their own, cannot produce faith.

On the "brethren" of Jesus, see the note on Mt 12:46–50; on the meaning of the word "world", see 17:1–26.

7:14–24 Jesus has the authority and status of the Revealer of the Father. Some Jews, having never seen Jesus attend any of the schools run by teachers of the Law, are amazed by his teaching,

and they ask a question laced with a certain malice: "How is it that this man has learning, when he has never studied?" (v. 15). They are accusing him of being a false prophet. Jesus uses the occasion to state clearly that his teaching comes from God; but he also points out that a person must be sincere to be able to discern the truth (v. 24). And he gives them a way to tell that his work as a teacher is valid: his teaching comes not from himself but from God; this can be seen from the fact that he seeks not personal fame but the glory of God.

Following the example of Christ, the Church in her apostolate seeks not earthly acclaim but the good of souls and the glory of God: "Only God is fully glorified, when men fully and consciously accept the work of salvation which he accomplished in Christ. By means of it God's plan is realized, a plan to which Christ lovingly and obediently submitted for the glory of the Father who sent him in order that the whole human race might become one People of God, form one body of Christ, and be built up into one temple of the Holy Spirit" (Vatican II, *Ad gentes*, 7).

o Other ancient authorities add *yet* p Or *this man knows his letters*

Jn 3:11; 12:49

studied?" ¹⁶So Jesus answered them, "My teaching is not mine, but his who sent me;
¹⁷if any man's will is to do his will, he shall know whether the teaching is from God

Deut 18:18, 22
Jn 5:41–44; 8:50
Rom 2:17–23

or whether I am speaking on my own authority. ¹⁸He who speaks on his own authority seeks his own glory; but he who seeks the glory of him who sent him is true, and

Acts 7:53
Mt 23:23

in him there is no falsehood. ¹⁹Did not Moses give you the law? Yet none of you

Jn 10:20
Mk 3:22–27

keeps the law. Why do you seek to kill me?" ²⁰The people answered, "You have a
demon! Who is seeking to kill you?" ²¹Jesus answered them, "I did one deed, and

Gen 17:10–12
Lev 12:3

you all marvel at it. ²²Moses gave you circumcision (not that it is from Moses, but

Jn 5:16
Mk 3:4
Mt 12:1–5

from the fathers), and you circumcise a man upon the sabbath. ²³If on the sabbath a
man receives circumcision, so that the law of Moses may not be broken, are you

Jn 8:15
Is 11:3
Zech 7:9

angry with me because on the sabbath I made a man's whole body well? ²⁴Do not
judge by appearances, but judge with right judgment."

Jesus comes from God

Jn 5:18

²⁵Some of the people of Jerusalem therefore said, "Is not this the man whom they
seek to kill? ²⁶And here he is, speaking openly, and they say nothing to him! Can it

Jn 1:26

be that the authorities really know that this is the Christ? ²⁷Yet we know where this
man comes from; and when the Christ appears, no one will know where he comes

Jn 8:19

from." ²⁸So Jesus proclaimed, as he taught in the temple, "You know me, and you
know where I come from? But I have not come of my own accord; he who sent me

propter metum Iudaeorum. ¹⁴Iam autem die festo mediante, ascendit Iesus in templum et docebat. ¹⁵Mirabantur ergo Iudaei dicentes: «Quomodo hic litteras scit, cum non didicerit?». ¹⁶Respondit ergo eis Iesus et dixit: «Mea doctrina non est mea sed eius, qui misit me. ¹⁷Si quis voluerit voluntatem eius facere, cognoscet de doctrina utrum ex Deo sit, an ego a meipso loquar. ¹⁸Qui a semetipso loquitur, gloriam propriam quaerit; qui autem quaerit gloriam eius, qui misit illum, hic verax est, et iniustitia in illo non est. ¹⁹Nonne Moyses dedit vobis legem? Et nemo ex vobis facit legem. Quid me quaeritis interficere?». ²⁰Respondit turba: «Daemonium habes! Quis te quaerit interficere?». ²¹Respondit Iesus et dixit eis: «Unum opus feci, et omnes miramini. ²²Propterea Moyses dedit vobis circumcisionem —non quia ex Moyse est sed ex patribus— et in sabbato circumciditis hominem. ²³Si circumcisionem accipit homo in sabbato, ut non solvatur lex Moysis, mihi indignamini quia totum hominem sanum feci in sabbato? ²⁴Nolite iudicare secundum faciem, sed iustum iudicium iudicate». ²⁵Dicebant ergo quidam ex Hierosolymitis: «Nonne hic est, quem quaerunt interficere? ²⁶Et ecce palam loquitur, et nihil ei dicunt. Numquid vere cognoverunt principes quia hic est Christus? ²⁷Sed hunc scimus unde sit, Christus autem cum venerit, nemo scit unde sit». ²⁸Clamavit ergo docens in templo Iesus et dicens: «Et me scitis et unde sim scitis. Et a meipso non veni, sed est verus, qui misit me, quem vos non scitis. ²⁹Ego scio eum, quia ab ipso sum, et ipse me misit». ³⁰Quaerebant ergo eum apprehendere, et nemo misit in illum manus, quia nondum venerat hora eius. ³¹De turba autem multi crediderunt in eum et dicebant: «Christus

7:25–30 St John shows that some people in
Jerusalem could not recognize who Jesus was
(vv. 25–27). Although it was known that the
Messiah would be born in Bethlehem and of the
line of David (7:42), during Jesus' time some
people thought that the Messiah would remain
absent from public life until the day came for
him to manifest himself (see 1:33; 14:22).

Jesus asks them to be honest and accept that
he has power to bring salvation; his words
should make this obvious. As a result, they plot
his arrest, because he makes himself out to be
God's equal, which they consider blasphemy—
an offence which, according to the Law (see Lev
24:16, 23), carries the mandatory penalty of
stoning. This is not the first time that St John
mentions hostility shown by Jews (see 5:18),
nor will it be the last (see 8:59; 10:31–33). He
records this hostility because it is a historical

fact, and also, perhaps, to show that Jesus was a
free agent: he would give himself up to his
enemies (in accordance with the Father's will)
when and only when his "hour" came (cf. 18:4–
8). "He did not therefore mean an hour when he
would be forced to die, but one when he would
allow himself to be put to death. For he was
waiting for the time in which he should die,
even as he waited for the time in which he
should be born" (St Augustine, *In Ioannis
Evangelium*, 31, 5).

The first step towards belief that Jesus is
divine is to acknowledge sincerely the things that
he does. Acknowledging Jesus requires a conversion of heart and mind: "He who desires,
therefore, to fully understand and appreciate the
words of Christ must strive to conform his entire
life to him" (Thomas à Kempis, *De imitatione
Christi*, 1, 1, 2).

is true, and him you do not know. ²⁹I know him, for I come from him, and he sent   Jn 1:1; 8:55
Mt 11:27
me." ³⁰So they sought to arrest him; but no one laid hands on him, because his hour   Jn 7:6, 44; 8:20
Lk 4:29; 22:53
had not yet come.

Jesus must return to the Father

³¹Yet many of the people believed in him; they said, "When the Christ appears, will
he do more signs than this man has done?" ³²The Pharisees heard the crowd thus
muttering about him, and the chief priests and Pharisees sent officers to arrest him.
³³Jesus then said, "I shall be with you a little longer, and then I go to him who sent
me; ³⁴you will seek me and you will not find me; where I am you cannot come."   Amos 8:11–12
³⁵The Jews said to one another, "Where does this man intend to go that we shall not   Jn 8:21; 13:33; 17:24
find him? Does he intend to go to the Dispersion among the Greeks and teach the   Jn 12:20–22
Is 55:6

cum venerit, numquid plura signa faciet quam quae hic fecit?». ³²Audierunt pharisaei turbam murmurantem de illo haec et miserunt pontifices et
pharisaei ministros, ut apprehenderent eum. ³³Dixit ergo Iesus: «Adhuc modicum tempus vobiscum sum et vado ad eum, qui misit me. ³⁴Quaeretis
me et non invenietis; et ubi sum ego, vos non potestis venire». ³⁵Dixerunt ergo Iudaei ad seipsos: «Quo hic iturus est, quia nos non inveniemus
eum? Numquid in dispersionem Graecorum iturus est et docturus Graecos? ³⁶Quis est hic sermo, quem dixit: "Quaeretis me et non invenietis" et:

7:31–39 Jesus speaks here of his being glorified
at his Father's side and of the sending of the
Holy Spirit. The feast of Tabernacles was a
festival of joy and thanksgiving. On the last of
the eight days of the feast, the high priest went
to the pool of Siloam (cf. the note on 9:1–23)
and, using a golden cup, took water from it
which he then sprinkled on the altar of the
temple, in remembrance of the water that sprang
up miraculously in the desert (cf. Ex 17:1–7),
and asked God to send rain in plenty. While he
did this, a passage from the prophet Isaiah was
chanted (Is 12:3) which told of the coming of
the Saviour and of the outpouring of heavenly
gifts that would accompany him. Ezekiel
47:1–12 was also read, a passage that speaks of
the torrents of water that will one day stream out
of the temple. Jesus now proclaims that that
happy time has come: "If any one thirst, let him
come to me and drink ..." (v. 37). This
invitation is reminiscent of one made by divine
Wisdom in the Old Testament: "Come to me,
you who desire me, and eat your fill of my
produce" (Sir 24:19; cf. Prov 9:4–5)—which
suggests that Jesus is the Wisdom of God
incarnate. Only he can quench our thirst:
"'Thirst' is the desire for something we greatly
need, without which we would die. Water,
which would kill us if we did not have it, can
also kill us if we have too much: so many
people drown. Lord, drown us in a flood of
living water!" (St Teresa, *Way of Perfection*, 19).

On the words of Jesus in v. 37 St Alphonsus
Liguori makes a very moving commentary, full
of love for our Saviour: "In Jesus Christ we have
three fountains of grace. The first is the fountain
of mercy, where we can be purified of all the
stains of our sins. [...] The second is that of love:
no one who meditates on the suffering and
shame that Jesus Christ undergoes out of love for
us, from his birth to his death, can fail to be kindled by that happy fire which comes down on
earth to set on fire the hearts of all men. [...] The
third is the fountain of peace: let him who seeks
peace of heart come to me, who is the God of
peace" (*Meditations for Advent*, 1, 8).

The expression "rivers of living water" (v.
38) probably refers to the prophecy in Ezekiel
36:25ff, which announces that in the messianic
times the people will be cleansed by pure water,
will receive a new spirit, and will be given hearts
of flesh to replace their hearts of stone.

Once Jesus is exalted as befits his position as
Son of God, he will send the Holy Spirit, at Pentecost, to change the hearts of those who believe
in him: "Just as clear, transparent things in nature
reflect the bright light of the sun, souls filled
with the Holy Spirit shine the light of grace on
others. The Holy Spirit grants the soul knowledge of future events and of hidden truths,
understanding of mysteries, a plethora of gifts,
citizenship of heaven, speech in the tongues of
angels. From him comes never-ending joy, perseverance, and likeness to God, the greatest gift

Deut 4:29
Prov 1:28
Hos 5:6–7

Jn 4:10–14
Is 55:1, 3
Is 12:3
Ezek 47:1–12
Ps 78:15–16
Zech 13:1
Joel 3:1, 23
Jn 16:7; 19:34
Acts 2:1–13

Deut 18:15

Jn 1:46
2 Sam 7:12
Ps 89:3–4
Mic 5:1–2
Mt 2:6; 22:42
Lk 2:4–11

Jn 9:16

Jn 7:30

Greeks? [36]What does he mean by saying, 'You will seek me and you will not find me,' and, 'Where I am you cannot come'?"

[37]On the last day of the feast, the great day, Jesus stood up and proclaimed, "If any one thirst, let him come to me and drink. [38]He who believes in me, as[q] the scripture has said, 'Out of his heart shall flow rivers of living water.'" [39]Now this he said about the Spirit, which those who believed in him were to receive; for as yet the Spirit had not been given, because Jesus was not yet glorified.

Different opinions about Jesus

[40]When they heard these words, some of the people said, "This is really the prophet." [41]Others said, "This is the Christ." But some said, "Is the Christ to come from Galilee? [42]Has not the scripture said that the Christ is descended from David, and comes from Bethlehem, the village where David was?" [43]So there was a division among the people over him. [44]Some of them wanted to arrest him, but no one laid hands on him.

"Ubi sum ego, vos non potestis venire"?». [37]In novissimo autem die magno festivitatis stabat Iesus et clamavit dicens: «Si quis sitit, veniat ad me et bibat, [38]qui credit in me. Sicut dixit Scriptura, flumina de ventre eius fluent aquae vivae». [39]Hoc autem dixit de Spiritu, quem accepturi erant qui crediderant in eum. Nondum enim erat Spiritus, quia Iesus nondum fuerat glorificatus. [40]Ex illa ergo turba, cum audissent hos sermones, dicebant: «Hic est vere propheta!»; [41]alii dicebant: «Hic est Christus!»; quidam autem dicebant: «Numquid a Galilaea Christus venit? [42]Nonne Scriptura dixit: "Ex semine David, et de Bethlehem castello, ubi erat David, venit Christus"?». [43]Dissensio itaque facta est in turba propter eum. [44]Quidam autem ex ipsis volebant apprehendere eum, sed nemo misit super illum manus. [45]Venerunt ergo ministri ad pontifices et pharisaeos, et

imaginable: the soul is made like God" (St Basil, *De Spiritu Sancto*, 9, 23).

"How", St Augustine asks, "are the words of the Evangelist to be understood: 'The Spirit had not yet been given, since Jesus was not yet glorified', if not in the sense that, after the glorification of Christ, there would certainly be a giving or sending of the Holy Spirit of such a kind as there had never been before?" (*De Trinitate*, 4, 20): clearly, our Lord was referring, to the coming of the Holy Spirit after his ascension (v. 39), an outpouring of grace that St John sees symbolized in advance when Christ's side is pierced by a lance and blood and water flow out (19:34). The Fathers of the Church saw in this the birth of the Church and the sanctifying power of the sacraments, especially those of Baptism and the Eucharist.

7:40–53 "The prophet" (v. 40) is a reference to Deuteronomy 18:14–18, which predicts the coming of a last prophet or second Moses, one to whom all must listen (cf. 1:21; 6:14). "The Christ" ("the Messiah") was the title most used in Judaism to designate that future saviour whom God would send.

Verses 40–44 show the range of people's views about Jesus. Many Jews—not having

made the effort to establish the truth—did not know that he had been born in Bethlehem, the city of David, where the prophet Micah said the Messiah would be born. This ignorance on their part was their excuse for not accepting Jesus as the Christ. The evangelist, writing for Christians who were well aware of the true origin of Jesus Christ, the Son of God, born in Bethlehem, suggests a certain irony when he implies those people's ignorance of this might in itself be a proof that Jesus was the Messiah they were expecting (see 7:27).

Others, however, realized from his miracles that he must be the Messiah (see 7:31); and there were those, including even some officers of the authorities, who could not gainsay the fact that Jesus spoke in a most powerful way (vv. 45–46): "Notice that the Pharisees and scribes derive no benefit either from witnessing miracles or reading the Scriptures; whereas their servants, without these helps, were captivated by a single discourse [...]. Not only is their prudence admirable, for they did not need signs; it is also impressive that they were won over by his teaching on its own; they did not say, in effect, 'No man has ever worked such miracles,' but 'No man ever spoke like this man.' Their conviction also is worthy of admiration: they go to the Pharisees, who were

q Or *let him come to me, and let him who believes in me drink. As*

⁴⁵The officers then went back to the chief priests and Pharisees, who said to them, "Why did you not bring him?" ⁴⁶The officers answered, "No man ever spoke like this man!" ⁴⁷The Pharisees answered them, "Are you led astray, you also? ⁴⁸Have any of the authorities or of the Pharisees believed in him? ⁴⁹But this crowd, who do not know the law, are accursed." ⁵⁰Nicodemus, who had gone to him before, and who was one of them, said to them, ⁵¹"Does our law judge a man without first giving him a hearing and learning what he does?" ⁵²They replied, "Are you from Galilee too? Search and you will see that no prophet is to rise from Galilee." ⁵³They went each to his own house, ¹but Jesus went to the Mount of Olives.

Mt 7:28; 13:54–56

Jn 12:42

Deut 27:26; 28:15
Ps 119:21

Jn 3:1–2

Deut 1:16–17; 14:4
Jn 1:46; 7:41

Mk 11:1
Lk 21:37–38
Mk 14:49

The adulterous woman—Jesus as judge

8 ²Early in the morning he came again to the temple; all the people came to him, and he sat down and taught them. ³The scribes and the Pharisees brought a woman who had been caught in adultery, and placing her in the midst ⁴they said to him, "Teacher, this woman has been caught in the act of adultery. ⁵Now in the law Moses commanded us to stone such. What do you say about her?" ⁶This they said to test him, that they might have some charge to bring against him. Jesus bent down and wrote with his finger on the ground. ⁷And as they continued to ask him, he stood up and said to them, "Let him who is without sin among you be the first to throw a

Lev 20:10
Deut 22:22–24

Mt 22:15
Lk 20:20

Deut 17:7
Dan 13:52–62
Rom 2:1, 22

dixerunt eis illi: «Quare non adduxistis eum?». ⁴⁶Responderunt ministri: «Numquam sic locutus est homo». ⁴⁷Responderunt ergo eis pharisaei: «Numquid et vos seducti estis? ⁴⁸Numquid aliquis ex principibus credidit in eum aut ex pharisaeis? ⁴⁹Sed turba haec, quae non novit legem, maledicti sunt!». ⁵⁰Dicit Nicodemus ad eos, ille qui venit ad eum antea, qui unus erat ex ipsis: ⁵¹«Numquid lex nostra iudicat hominem, nisi audierit ab ipso prius et cognoverit quid faciat?». ⁵²Responderunt et dixerunt ei: «Numquid et tu ex Galilaea es? Scrutare et vide quia propheta a Galilaea non surgit!». ⁵³Et reversi sunt unusquisque in domum suam. [8] ¹Iesus autem perrexit in montem Oliveti. ²Diluculo autem iterum venit in templum, et omnis populus veniebat ad eum, et sedens docebat eos. ³Adducunt autem scribae et pharisaei mulierem in adulterio deprehensam et statuerunt eam in medio ⁴et dicunt ei: «Magister, haec mulier manifesto deprehensa est in adulterio. ⁵In lege autem Moyses mandavit nobis huiusmodi lapidare; tu ergo quid dicis?». ⁶Hoc autem dicebant tentantes eum, ut possent accusare eum. Iesus autem inclinans se deorsum digito scribebat in terra. ⁷Cum autem perseverarent interrogantes eum, erexit se et dixit eis: «Qui sine peccato est vestrum, primus in illam lapidem mittat»; ⁸et iterum

opposed to Christ, and address them in the way they do" (St John Chrysostom, *In Ioannem*, 9).

8:1–11 This passage is absent from many ancient codexes (see RSV note **r**) but the Church holds it to be inspired and canonical. It may be that some people of a very strict frame of mind thought that because it showed Jesus to be so merciful, it might lead to a relaxation of moral standards. In any event, the episode demonstrates how Jesus sees his role as Judge (see 8:15): he is the Just One, but he does not condemn; whereas these critics, even though they are sinners, want to apply the death penalty. "But it should also be pointed out that we should never act in such a way in view of God's mercy, that we forget about his justice; nor should we attend to his justice forgetting about his mercy; for hope should have in it an element of fear, and fear an element of hope" (Fray Luis de Granada, *Life of Jesus*, 13).

Jesus' reply (v. 7) refers to the way stoning

was carried out: those who witnessed the crime cast the first stones, and then others joined in, combining forces to blot out the slur on the people that the sin implied (cf. Deut 17:7). The question put to Jesus is couched in legal terms; he raises it to the moral sphere (the basis and justification of all laws), appealing to the consciences of those present. He does not violate the Law, St Augustine notes, nor at the same time does he want to lose sight of the true object that he has in mind—for he has come to save that which was lost: "His answer is so full of justice, gentleness and truth. [...] O true answer of Wisdom. You have heard: Keep the Law, let the woman be stoned. But how can sinners keep the Law and punish this woman? Let each of them look inside himself and enter the tribunal of his heart and conscience; there he will discover that he is a sinner. Let this woman be punished, but not by sinners; let the Law be applied, but not by its transgressors" (St Augustine, *In Ioannis Evangelium*, 33, 5).

stone at her." [8]And once more he bent down and wrote with his finger on the ground. [9]But when they heard it, they went away, one by one, beginning with the eldest, and Jesus was left alone with the woman standing before him. [10]Jesus looked up and said to her, "Woman, where are they? Has no one condemned you?" [11]She said, "No one, Lord." And Jesus said, "Neither do I condemn you; go, and do not sin again."[r]*

Jn 5:14
Ezek 33:11

Jesus, the light of the world

Jn 1:5–9; 12:46
Ps 27:1
Is 42:6–7; 49:6
Mt 5:14
Lk 2:32
Jn 5:31

[12]Again Jesus spoke to them, saying, "I am the light of the world; he who follows me will not walk in darkness, but will have the light of life." [13]The Pharisees then said to him, "You are bearing witness to yourself; your testimony is not true." [14]Jesus answered, "Even if I do bear witness to myself, my testimony is true, for I know whence I have come and whither I am going, but you do not know whence I have come or whither I am going. [15]You judge according to the flesh, I judge no one. [16]Yet even if I do judge, my judgment is true, for it is not I alone that judge, but I and he[s] who sent me. [17]In your law it is written that the testimony of two men is true; [18]I bear

Jn 7:24; 12:47
Jn 5:30; 8:29
Num 35:30
Deut 17:6; 19:15

se inclinans scribebat in terra. [9]Audientes autem unus post unum exibant, incipientes a senioribus, et remansit solus, et mulier in medio stans. [10]Erigens autem se Iesus dixit ei: «Mulier, ubi sunt? Nemo te condemnavit?». [11]Quae dixit: «Nemo, Domine». Dixit autem Iesus: «Nec ego te condemno; vade et amplius iam noli peccare». [12]Iterum ergo locutus est eis Iesus dicens: «Ego sum lux mundi; qui sequitur me, non ambulabit in tenebris, sed habebit lucem vitae». [13]Dixerunt ergo ei pharisaei: «Tu de teipso testimonium perhibes; testimonium tuum non est verum». [14]Respondit Iesus et dixit eis: «Et si ego testimonium perhibeo de meipso, verum est testimonium meum, quia scio unde veni et quo vado; vos autem nescitis unde venio aut quo vado. [15]Vos secundum carnem iudicatis, ego non iudico quemquam. [16]Et si iudico ego, iudicium meum verum est, quia solus non sum, sed ego et, qui me misit, Pater. [17]Sed et in lege vestra scriptum est quia duorum hominum testimonium verum est. [18]Ego sum, qui

8:12–20 Jesus now reveals himself as the Light of the world. On the first night of the feast of Tabernacles it was the custom to fill the "court of the women" in the temple with the light of four huge lamps, a light so bright that it lit up the sky over the city. This brought to mind the bright cloud of God's presence that guided the Israelites through the wilderness during the Exodus (see Ex 13:21–22; 16:10). This context may explain why Jesus portrays himself as "the Light", an image used elsewhere too (see Mt 4:16) to describe the Messiah (see also Lk 1:78; 2:30–32).

Jesus is the Light in two senses: he is the light that enlightens our minds, for he is the fullness of divine Revelation, and he is also the light that shines in our hearts to enable us to accept that Revelation and to live by it. "In Christ and through Christ God has revealed himself fully to mankind and has definitively drawn close to it; at the same time, in Christ and through Christ man has acquired full awareness of his dignity, of the heights to which he is raised, of the surpassing worth of his own humanity, and of the meaning of his existence" (John Paul II, *Redemptoris hominis*, 11).

To the Pharisees' implied objection that he is a man (v. 13), Jesus replies by asserting his union with the Father; as St Bede says, "he wanted to make the Father known. The Son gives glory to the Father. He glorifies the One who sent him" (*In Ioannis Evangelium expositio*, ad loc.).

The question put to Jesus in v. 19 is intended to entrap him; the Pharisees think that he cannot show them the Father. But to know Jesus and accept the mystery of his divinity means that one also knows the Father. This same message will be expressed again, in different words (see 12:44–45). And our Lord will say the same thing to Philip in a tone of reproach: "Have I been with you so long, and yet you do not know me, Philip? He who has seen me has seen the Father" (14:9). Jesus is the visible manifestation of the invisible God, the fullest and the definitive revelation of God to man (see Heb 1:1–3). Jesus Christ "completed and perfected Revelation [...]. He did this by the total fact of his presence and self-manifestation—by words and works, signs and miracles, but above all by his death and glorious resurrection from the dead, and finally by sending the Spirit of truth. He revealed that God was with us, to deliver us from the darkness of sin and death, and to raise us up to eternal life" (Vatican II, *Dei Verbum*, 4).

r Some ancient authorities insert 7:53–8:11 either at the end of this gospel or after Lk 21:38, with variations of the text. Others omit it altogether   s Other ancient authorities read *the Father*

witness to myself, and the Father who sent me bears witness to me." [19]They said to him therefore, "Where is your Father?" Jesus answered, "You know neither me nor my Father; if you knew me, you would know my Father also." [20]These words he spoke in the treasury, as he taught in the temple; but no one arrested him, because his hour had not yet come.

1 Jn 5:9
Jn 12:45; 14:7

Jn 6:59; 13:1
Lk 21:1

Jesus says he has been sent by the Father

[21]Again he said to them, "I go away, and you will seek me and die in your sin;* where I am going, you cannot come." [22]Then said the Jews, "Will he kill himself, since he says, 'Where I am going, you cannot come'?" [23]He said to them, "You are from below, I am from above; you are of this world, I am not of this world. [24]I told you that you would die in your sins, for you will die in your sins unless you believe that I am he." [25]They said to him, "Who are you?" Jesus said to them, "Even what I have told you from the beginning.[t] [26]I have much to say about you and much to judge; but he who sent me is true, and I declare to the world what I have heard from

Jn 7:32-36; 13:33, 36
Prov 1:28

Jn 7:35

Jn 3:31

Ex 3:14
Is 43:10

Jn 5:36; 7:28; 8:18;
12:48-50

testimonium perhibeo de meipso, et testimonium perhibet de me, qui misit me, Pater». [19]Dicebant ergo ei: «Ubi est Pater tuus?». Respondit Iesus: «Neque me scitis neque Patrem meum; si me sciretis, forsitan et Patrem meum sciretis». [20]Haec verba locutus est in gazophylacio docens in templo; et nemo apprehendit eum, quia necdum venerat hora eius. [21]Dixit ergo iterum eis: «Ego vado, et quaeretis me et in peccato vestro moriemini! Quo ego vado, vos non potestis venire». [22]Dicebant ergo Iudaei: «Numquid interficiet semetipsum, quia dicit: "Quo ego vado, vos non potestis venire"?». [23]Et dicebat eis: «Vos de deorsum estis, ego de supernis sum; vos de mundo hoc estis, ego non sum de hoc mundo. [24]Dixi ergo vobis quia moriemini in peccatis vestris; si enim non credideritis quia ego sum, moriemini in peccatis vestris». [25]Dicebant ergo ei: «Tu quis es?». Dixit eis Iesus: «In principio: id quod et loquor vobis! [26]Multa habeo de vobis loqui et iudicare; sed, qui misit me, verax est, et ego, quae audivi ab eo,

8:21-30 In response to the authorities' rejection of him, Jesus warns them that he will leave and go to heaven, from where he came, and that they will live on in hope of a Messiah to come, but will never find him because they look for him in the wrong place (*he* is the Messiah); nor can they follow him now, for they don't believe in him. The categorical expression "I am", found (in the Greek) also in several other places in the Gospel (vv. 24, 28; 4:26; 8:58; 13:19; 18:5, 8), points to the divine nature of Jesus. This was the name of God revealed to Moses: "I am who I am" or "I am he who is" (Ex 3:14). "The divine name, 'I Am' or 'He Is', expresses God's faithfulness: despite the faithlessness of men's sin and the punishment it deserves, he keeps 'steadfast love for thousands' (Ex 34:7). By going so far as to give up his own Son for us, God reveals that he is 'rich in mercy' (Eph 2:4). By giving his life to free us from sin, Jesus reveals that he himself bears the divine name: 'When you have lifted up the Son of man, then you will realize that 'I Am' (Jn 8:28 [Gk.])'" (*Catechism of the Catholic Church*, 211).

The question asked by the Pharisees in v. 25 is one that is asked by many people in our own time when the Church proclaims Christ. A little further on, Jesus provides the key to the right

answer—a sincere search for truth (see 8:32).

Jesus' reply (v. 25) has several possible interpretations. It can be understood to mean that Jesus confirms what he has just been saying, or to mean, "Why, in the first place, am I speaking to you?" or "Why should I speak to you at all?" But it could also mean "The Beginning, just as I have been telling you" (in which case it is an assertion of his divine origin); see Rev 1:8 and 3:14.

In vv. 28-29 Jesus refers to his passion and death (cf. 12:32-33). Complementing, as it does, the Synoptic Gospels and the letters of St Paul, the fourth Gospel portrays the cross as, above all, a royal throne, where Christ, "lifted up", offers mankind the fruits of salvation (cf. 3:14-15; Num 21:8-9; Wis 16:5-6). Jesus is saying that when that time comes, the Jews will know who he is, and know his close union with the Father, because many of them will discover, through the grace of his death and resurrection, that he is the Messiah. Even a non-Jew will realize that he is the Son of God (see Mk 15:39). Those "many" who believed in him in Jerusalem (v. 30) are a foreshadowing of the thousands who will believe in him when the Holy Spirit comes (see Acts 2:41; 4:4).

t Or *Why do I talk to you at all?*

Num 16:28
Jn 3:14; 5:30; 6:38;
12:32

Jn 4:34; 16:32

him." [27]They did not understand that he spoke to them of the Father. [28]So Jesus said, "When you have lifted up the Son of man, then you will know that I am he, and that I do nothing on my own authority but speak thus as the Father taught me. [29]And he who sent me is with me; he has not left me alone, for I always do what is pleasing to him." [30]As he spoke thus, many believed in him.

"The truth will set you free"

Jn 15:14

Gen 12:–4; 22:1–19
Mt 3:9

Rom 6:17–20

Gen 21:1–21
Ex 21:2
Gal 4:30

Gal 5:1
Jn 5:38

[31]Jesus then said to the Jews who had believed in him, "If you continue in my word, you are truly my disciples, [32]and you will know the truth, and the truth will make you free." [33]They answered him, "We are descendants of Abraham, and have never been in bondage to any one. How is it that you say, 'You will be made free'?" [34]Jesus answered them, "Truly, truly, I say to you, every one who commits sin is a slave of sin. [35]The slave does not continue in the house for ever; the son continues for ever. [36]So if the Son makes you free, you will be free indeed. [37]I know that you are descendants of Abraham; yet you seek to kill me, because my word finds no

haec loquor ad mundum». [27]Non cognoverunt quia Patrem eis dicebat. [28]Dixit ergo eis Iesus: «Cum exaltaveritis Filium hominis, tunc cognoscetis quia ego sum, et a meipso facio nihil, sed, sicut docuit me Pater, haec loquor. [29]Et qui me misit, mecum est; non reliquit me solum, quia ego, quae placita sunt ei, facio semper». [30]Haec illo loquente, multi crediderunt in eum. [31]Dicebat ergo Iesus ad eos, qui crediderunt ei, Iudaeos: «Si vos manseritis in sermone meo, vere discipuli mei estis [32]et cognoscetis veritatem, et veritas liberabit vos». [33]Responderunt ei: «Semen Abrahae sumus et nemine servivimus umquam? Quomodo tu dicis: "Liberi fietis"?». [34]Respondit eis Iesus: «Amen, amen dico vobis: Omnis, qui facit peccatum, servus est. [35]Servus autem non manet in domo in aeternum; filius manet in aeternum. [36]Si ergo Filius vos liberaverit, vere liberi eritis. [37]Scio quia semen Abrahae estis; sed quaeritis me interficere, quia sermo meus non capit in vobis. [38]Ego, quae vidi apud Patrem, loquor; et vos ergo, quae audivistis a patre, facitis». [39]Responderunt et dixerunt ei: «Pater noster Abraham est». Dicit eis Iesus: «Si filii Abrahae essetis, opera Abrahae fac-

8:31–38 Faith in Jesus must be more than superficial enthusiasm: it entails true discipleship; Jesus' words should affect a person's whole life. To have a deep faith in Jesus is to know the truth and become a truly free person. According to Christian faith and the Church's teaching, "only the freedom which submits to the truth leads the human person to his true good. The good of the person is to be in the truth and to *do* the Truth" (John Paul II, *Veritatis splendor*, 84).

"The truth will set you free" (v. 32). "These words contain both a fundamental requirement and a warning: the requirement of an honest relationship with regard to truth as a condition for authentic freedom, and the warning to avoid every kind of illusory freedom, every superficial unilateral freedom, every freedom that fails to enter into the whole truth about man and the world. Today also, even after two thousand years, we see Christ as the one who brings man freedom based on truth, frees man from what curtails, diminishes and as it were breaks off this freedom at its root, in man's soul, his heart and his conscience" (John Paul II, *Redemptor hominis*, 12).

Reminding those hostile Jews about the two sons of Abraham (see Gen 21:1–21)—Ishmael,

the son of the slave woman (Hagar), and Isaac, born of the free woman (Sarah) and who alone will be the heir of God's promises—Jesus tells them that possessing freedom is not a matter of being descended from Abraham but of knowing the truth, which in the last analysis means knowing Christ himself. This is the only kind of knowledge that sets us free, for it liberates us from our slavery to sin, which is the real cause of every kind of human slavery. "Freedom finds its true meaning when it is put to the service of the truth which redeems, when it is spent in seeking God's infinite Love which liberates us from all forms of slavery. Each passing day increases my yearning to proclaim to the four winds this inexhaustible treasure that belongs to Christianity: 'the glorious freedom of the children of God!' (Rom 8:21). [...] Where does our freedom come from? It comes from Christ our Lord. This is the freedom with which he has ransomed us (cf. Gal 4:31). That is why he teaches, 'If the Son makes you free, you will be free indeed' (Jn 8:36). We Christians do not have to ask anyone to tell us the true meaning of this gift, because the only freedom that can save man is Christian freedom" (St Josemaría Escrivá, *Friends of God*, 27 and 35).

place in you. [38]I speak of what I have seen with my Father, and you do what you
have heard from your father."

Jn 3:11

The true children of Abraham

[39]They answered him, "Abraham is our father." Jesus said to them, "If you were
Abraham's children, you would do what Abraham did, [40]but now you seek to kill
me, a man who has told you the truth which I heard from God; this is not what
Abraham did. [41]You do what your father did." They said to him, "We were not born
of fornication; we have one Father, even God."* [42]Jesus said of them, "If God were
your Father, you would love me, for I proceeded and came forth from God; I came
not of my own account, but he sent me. [43]Why do you not understand what I say? It
is because you cannot bear to hear my word. [44]You are of your father the devil, and
your will is to do your father's desires. He was a murderer from the beginning, and
has nothing to do with the truth, because there is no truth in him. When he lies, he
speaks according to his own nature, for he is a liar and the father of lies.
[45]But, because I tell the truth, you do not believe me. [46]Which of you convicts me of
sin? If I tell the truth, why do you not believe me? [47]He who is of God hears the
words of God; the reason why you do not hear them is that you are not of God."

[48]The Jews answered him, "Are we not right in saying that you are a Samaritan
and have a demon?" [49]Jesus answered, "I have not a demon; but I honour my Father,
and you dishonour me. [50]Yet I do not seek my own glory; there is One who seeks it
and he will be the judge. [51]Truly, truly, I say to you, if any one keeps my word, he
will never see death."

Hos 11:1
Is 62:16
Mal 2:10
1 Jn 5:1

Jn 6:70; 13:2, 27
1 Jn 3:8–15
Gen 3:1–4
Wis 2:24
Rom 5:19
2 Pet 2:4
Rev 12:9

2 Cor 5:21
1 Pet 2:22

Jn 8:41; 18:37
Deut 4:10, 13
1 Jn 4:6

Jn 7:20
Mk 3:21ff

Jn 5:41; 7:18

Jn 5:24–28; 6:40, 47;
11:25

eretis. [40]Nunc autem quaeritis me interficere, hominem, qui veritatem vobis locutus sum, quam audivi a Deo; hoc Abraham non fecit. [41]Vos facitis opera patris vestri». Dixerunt itaque ei: «Nos ex fornicatione non sumus nati; unum patrem habemus Deum!». [42]Dixit eis Iesus: «Si Deus pater
vester esset, diligeretis me; ego enim ex Deo processi et veni, neque enim a meipso veni, sed ille me misit. [43]Quare loquelam meam non cognoscitis? Quia non potestis audire sermonem meum. [44]Vos ex patre Diabolo estis et desideria patris vestri vultis facere. Ille homicida erat ab initio et
in veritate non stabat, quia non est veritas in eo. Cum loquitur mendacium, ex propriis loquitur, quia mendax est et pater eius. [45]Ego autem quia
veritatem dico non creditis mihi. [46]Quis ex vobis arguit me de peccato? Si veritatem dico, quare vos non creditis mihi? [47]Qui est ex Deo, verba
Dei audit; propterea vos non auditis, quia ex Deo non estis». [48]Responderunt Iudaei et dixerunt ei: «Nonne bene dicimus nos quia Samaritanus es
tu et daemonium habes?». [49]Respondit Iesus: «Ego daemonium non habeo, sed honorifico Patrem meum, et vos inhonoratis me. [50]Ego autem non
quaero gloriam meam; est qui quaerit et iudicat. [51]Amen, amen dico vobis: Si quis sermonem meum servaverit, mortem non videbit in aeternum».

8:39–51 These Jews claim to be children of
Abraham, but they are really his descendants
only "according to the flesh, for they squandered
their spiritual inheritance when they failed to live
by the faith of their great ancestor" (St
Augustine, *In Ioannis Evangelium*, 42, 1). Those
who live by faith (St Paul says) are the true
children of Abraham, and they, like Abraham,
will be blessed by God (see Gal 3:7–9). The
Jews also claim to be the children of God (v. 41)
on the basis of some phrases found in the Old
Testament (see Ex 4:22; Deut 32:6; Is 63:16; Jer
3:4; 31:9; Mal 1:6). However, the attitude they
adopt towards Jesus contradicts this: if they were
children of God, they would accept Jesus,
because, as he tells them, he is the one sent by
the Father.

Those who deliberately oppose the truth as
revealed in Jesus' actions and words act as parti-
sans or children of God's enemy, the devil. The
devil is the father of lies: by lying he seduced
our first parents, and now he deceives those who
listen to him and remain in a state of sin. "The
reason the Son of God appeared was to destroy
the works of the devil" (1 Jn 3:8). The father of
lies promised Adam and Eve immortality; Jesus
truthfully promises eternal life to those who
accept his teachings and live by them (v. 51).

Wild accusations are made against Jesus—
that he is possessed by the devil (cf. Mt 12:24
and Mk 3:21–22), and that he is a Samaritan (v.
48): in other words, he is a heretic and violator
of the Law (see the note on 4:1–45). Jesus' reply
is mild: he leaves judgment to God the Father (v.
50). However, he tells them again that he is the
Saviour (v. 51).

"Before Abraham was, I am"

Jn 7:20
[52]The Jews said to him, "Now we know that you have a demon. Abraham died, as did the prophets; and you say, 'If any one keeps my word, he will never taste death.'
Zech 1:5
Jn 4:12
[53]Are you greater than our father Abraham, who died? And the prophets died! Who do you claim to be?" [54]Jesus answered, "If I glorify myself, my glory is nothing; it
Jn 5:32; 7:28–29;
8:41
is my Father who glorifies me, of whom you say that he is your God. [55]But you have not known him; I know him. If I said, I do not know him, I should be a liar like you;
Gen 17:17; 18:1
Mt 13:17–18
but I do know him and I keep his word. [56]Your father Abraham rejoiced that he was to see my day; he saw it* and was glad." [57]The Jews then said to him, "You are not
Jn 8:24
yet fifty years old, and have you seen Abraham?"u [58]Jesus said to them, "Truly, truly,
Jn 10:31
Lk 4:29ff
I say to you, before Abraham was, I am."* [59]So they took up stones to throw at him; but Jesus hid himself, and went out of the temple.

Curing of the man born blind

Ex 20:5; 34:7
Deut 5:9
Num 14:18
Tob 3:3; Lk 13:2
Jn 11:4
9 [1]As he passed by, he saw a man blind from his birth. [2]And his disciples asked him, "Rabbi, who sinned, this man or his parents, that he was born blind?" [3]Jesus answered, "It was not that this man sinned, or his parents, but that the works of God

[52]Dixerunt ergo ei Iudaei: «Nunc cognovimus quia daemonium habes. Abraham mortuus est et prophetae, et tu dicis: "Si quis sermonem meum servaverit, non gustabit mortem in aeternum". [53]Numquid tu maior es patre nostro Abraham, qui mortuus est? Et prophetae mortui sunt! Quem teipsum facis?». [54]Respondit Iesus: «Si ego glorifico meipsum, gloria mea nihil est; est Pater meus, qui glorificat me, quem vos dicitis: "Deus noster est!", [55]et non cognovistis eum. Ego autem novi eum. Et si dixero: Non scio eum, ero similis vobis, mendax; sed scio eum et sermonem eius servo. [56]Abraham pater vester exsultavit, ut videret diem meum, et vidit et gavisus est». [57]Dixerunt ergo Iudaei ad eum: «Quinquaginta annos nondum habes et Abraham vidisti?». [58]Dixit eis Iesus: «Amen, amen dico vobis: Antequam Abraham fieret, ego sum». [59]Tulerunt ergo lapides, ut iacerent in eum; Iesus autem abscondit se et exivit de templo.   [9] [1]Et praeteriens vidit hominem caecum a nativitate. [2]Et interrogaverunt eum discipuli sui dicentes: «Rabbi, quis peccavit, hic aut parentes eius, ut caecus nasceretur?». [3]Respondit Iesus: «Neque hic peccavit neque parentes

8:52–59 Misinterpreting Jesus' words, thinking that he is referring to physical death, the Jews continue to accuse him of telling lies and of claiming (falsely) to be greater than the patriarchs and prophets. He points again to the works that he does, which are signs of God's power ("it is my Father who glorifies me": v. 54) and again claims to be the Messiah, the Saviour promised by God to the patriarchs (v. 56). Abraham was given a foretaste of messianic joy in the form of a prophecy about the birth of his son Isaac, and again when Isaac was restored to him alive after God tested Abraham by asking him to sacrifice his son (Gen 22:1–18). That latter event prefigured the resurrection that Christ would have after performing the sacrifice that would bring about Redemption.

Jesus' reply to the skeptical remarks of these Jews contains a revelation of his divinity. When he says, "Before Abraham was, I am" (v. 58), he is claiming to be eternal; and only God is eternal.

9:1–23 The cure of the man blind from birth shows that Jesus is indeed the Light of the world (see 8:12) and bears out what is stated in the pro-

logue to the Gospel: "The true light that enlightens every man was coming into the world" (1:9). Jesus not only gives light to the eyes of the blind man; he also enlightens his mind, enabling him to make an act of faith in his divinity (9:38). This episode also shows the struggle within those who refuse to do anything about their blindness. Jesus proclaims himself to be the Light of the world, because his life among men has enabled us to see the true meaning of the world and of the life of each and every person. Without Jesus, all creation is in darkness; it cannot work out the meaning of life or know where it is headed. "Only in the mystery of the Incarnate Word does the mystery of man take on light. [...] Through Christ and in Christ, the riddles of sorrow and death grow meaningful; apart from his Gospel they overwhelm us" (Vatican II, *Gaudium et spes*, 22). Jesus warns us, as he will do more clearly in 12:35–36, of the need to be guided by the Light, which is himself (cf. 1:9–13).

In his conversation with the disciples (vv. 1–5), Jesus corrects the widely-held view that sickness and all other kinds of misfortune are attributable to personal sins of one's own or to

u Other ancient authorities read *has Abraham seen you?*

might be made manifest in him. ⁴We must work the works of him who sent me, while it is day; night comes, when no one can work.* ⁵As long as I am in the world, I am the light of the world." ⁶As he said this, he spat on the ground and made clay of the spittle and anointed the man's eyes with the clay, ⁷saying to him, "Go, wash in the pool of Siloam" (which means Sent). So he went and washed and came back seeing. ⁸The neighbours and those who had seen him before as a beggar, said, "Is not this the man who used to sit and beg?" ⁹Some said, "It is he"; others said, "No, but he is like him." He said, "I am the man." ¹⁰They said to him, "Then how were your eyes opened?" ¹¹He answered, "The man called Jesus made clay and anointed my eyes and said to me, 'Go to Siloam and wash'; so I went and washed and received my sight." ¹²They said to him, "Where is he?" He said, "I do not know."

¹³They brought to the Pharisees the man who had formerly been blind. ¹⁴Now it was a sabbath day when Jesus made the clay and opened his eyes. ¹⁵The Pharisees again asked him how he had received his sight. And he said to them, "He put clay

Jn 3:21; 5:17, 20; 11:9–10
Is 42:6
Jn 8:12; 12:35
Is 8:6
Jn 5:9
Mt 12:10–11
Lk 13:10ff

eius, sed ut manifestentur opera Dei in illo. ⁴Nos oportet operari opera eius, qui misit me, donec dies est; venit nox, quando nemo potest operari. ⁵Quamdiu in mundo sum, lux sum mundi». ⁶Haec cum dixisset, exspuit in terram et fecit lutum ex sputo et linivit lutum super oculos eius ⁷et dixit ei: «Vade, lava in natatoria Siloae!»—quod interpretatur Missus—. Abiit ergo et lavit et venit videns. ⁸Itaque vicini et, qui videbant eum prius quia mendicus erat, dicebant: «Nonne hic est, qui sedebat et mendicabat?»; ⁹alii dicebant: «Hic est!»; alii dicebant: «Nequaquam, sed similis est eius!». Ille dicebat: «Ego sum!». ¹⁰Dicebant ergo ei: «Quomodo igitur aperti sunt oculi tibi?». ¹¹Respondit ille: «Homo, qui dicitur Iesus, lutum fecit et unxit oculos meos et dixit mihi: 'Vade ad Siloam et lava!'. Abii ergo et lavi et vidi». ¹²Et dixerunt ei: «Ubi est ille?». Ait: «Nescio». ¹³Adducunt eum ad pharisaeos, qui caecus fuerat. ¹⁴Erat autem sabbatum, in qua die lutum fecit Iesus et aperuit oculos eius. ¹⁵Iterum ergo interrogabant

those of one's forebears. At the same time, by curing the blind man, he shows that he has come to take away the sin of the world, which in the last analysis is the cause of all mankind's misfortunes.

"Siloam" (v. 7). The pool of Siloam was a reservoir built inside the walls of Jerusalem (to the south) to store the water that came from a natural spring. A channel built by King Hezekiah in the eighth century BC (see 2 Kings 20:20; 2 Chron 32:30) fed this water to the city; the prophets saw these waters as a sign of divine favour (see Is 8:6; 22:11). John may be using the broader sense of the etymology of the word "Siloam" (the Hebrew word is the participial adjective "sent" in its masculine form, and refers here perhaps to the water, "water" being masculine in Hebrew), to show that Jesus is the One sent by the Father. With words and gestures reminiscent of the miracle worked for Naaman, the Syrian general who was cured of leprosy by the prophet Elisha (see 2 Kings 5:1ff), Jesus requires that the man believe in him. "What an example of firm faith the blind man gives us! [...] What power could the water possibly contain that when the blind man's eyes were moistened with it they were cured? Surely some mysterious eye salve, or a precious medicine made up in the laboratory of some wise alchemist, would have

done better? But the man believed; he acted upon the command of God, and he returned with eyes full of light" (St Josemaría Escrivá, *Friends of God*, 193).

The episode shows us the different ways in which people reacted to Jesus and his miracles. Sincere and honest people, like the blind man, believe in Jesus as one sent by God, as a prophet (v. 17; cf. 9:33) and as the Son of God (9:35–38; see RSV note v). Those who are self-centred and claim to have no need of salvation, such as the Pharisees mentioned here, stubbornly refuse to see or believe, despite the evidence before their eyes. The Pharisees, to avoid having to acknowledge Jesus' divinity, reject the only possible explanation for the miracle; whereas the blind man (like any other open-minded souls who accept the truth) finds in the miracle proof that Jesus acts with divine power (9:33): "He supported and confirmed his preaching by miracles to arouse the faith of his hearers and give them assurance, but not to coerce them" (Vatican II, *Dignitatis humanae*, 11).

Church tradition has seen this miracle as a symbol of the sacrament of Baptism, in which water is used to cleanse the soul and give it the light of faith. "This blind man represents the human race [...]. If the blindness represents lack

Jn 3:2; 7:43; 9:31, 33 on my eyes, and I washed, and I see." [16]Some of the Pharisees said, "This man is not from God, for he does not keep the sabbath." But others said, "How can a man who Jn 4:19
Mt 16:14 is a sinner do such signs?" There was a division among them. [17]So they again said to the blind man, "What do you say about him, since he has opened your eyes?" He said, "He is a prophet."

[18]The Jews did not believe that he had been blind and had received his sight, until they called the parents of the man who had received his sight, [19]and asked them, "Is this your son, who you say was born blind? How then does he now see?" [20]His parents answered, "We know that this is our son, and that he was born blind; [21]but how he now sees we do not know, nor do we know who opened his eyes. Ask him; he is Jn 7:13; 12:42
16:2 of age, he will speak for himself." [22]His parents said this because they feared the Jews, for the Jews had already agreed that if any one should confess him to be Christ, he was to be put out of the synagogue. [23]Therefore his parents said, "He is of age, ask him."

The blindness of the Jews
Josh 7:19
Rev 11:13 [24]So for the second time they called the man who had been blind, and said to him, "Give God the praise; we know that this man is a sinner." [25]He answered, "Whether he is a sinner, I do not know; one thing I know, that though I was blind, now I see."

et eum pharisaei quomodo vidisset. Ille autem dixit eis: «Lutum posuit super oculos meos, et lavi et video». [16]Dicebant ergo ex pharisaeis quidam: «Non est hic homo a Deo, quia sabbatum non custodit!»; alii autem dicebant: «Quomodo potest homo peccator haec signa facere?». Et schisma erat in eis. [17]Dicunt ergo caeco iterum: «Tu quid dicis de eo quia aperuit oculos tuos?». Ille autem dixit: «Propheta est!». [18]Non crediderunt ergo Iudaei de illo quia caecus fuisset et vidisset, donec vocaverunt parentes eius, qui viderat. [19]Et interrogaverunt eos dicentes: «Hic est filius vester, quem vos dicitis quia caecus natus est? Quomodo ergo nunc videt?». [20]Responderunt ergo parentes eius et dixerunt: «Scimus quia hic est filius noster et quia caecus natus est. [21]Quomodo autem nunc videat nescimus, aut quis eius aperuit oculos nos nescimus; ipsum interrogate. Aetatem habet; ipse de se loquetur!». [22]Haec dixerunt parentes eius, quia timebant Iudaeos; iam enim conspiraverant Iudaei, ut, si quis eum confiteretur Christum, extra synagogam fieret. [23]Propterea parentes eius dixerunt: «Aetatem habet; ipsum interrogate!». [24]Vocaverunt ergo rursum hominem,

of faith, enlightenment represents faith. [...]. He washed his eyes in the pool whose name means 'Who has been sent': he was baptized in Christ" (St Augustine, *In Ioannis Evangelium*, 44, 1–2).

9:24–41 The conversation between the man and the Jewish authorities shows that a person who acknowledges Christ is (at least in that respect) doing the will of God. The expression "Give God the praise" (v. 24) was a solemn call upon a person to admit the truth.

The man's being expelled for believing in Christ (v. 34) serves as a reminder to Christians that they should hold fast to their beliefs even if it means that people shun them. Everyone can see that a miracle has taken place, but these Pharisees are so hard-hearted that they will not accept the evidence—not even after they have spoken both with the man himself and with his parents (9:13–23). "The sin of the Pharisees did not consist in not seeing God in Christ, but in voluntarily shutting themselves up within themselves, in not letting Jesus, who is the light, open

their eyes" (St Josemaría Escrivá, *Christ Is Passing By*, 71).

The man who has been cured professes his belief in the divinity of Jesus (v. 38). His subsequent meeting with Jesus does not seem accidental. The Pharisees threw the man out of the synagogue; our Lord not only welcomes him but helps him make an act of faith in his divinity. "Now with the face of his heart washed and with his conscience cleansed, he acknowledges him to be not only Son of man but Son of God" (St Augustine, *In Ioannis Evangelium*, 44, 15). Jesus' dialogue with the man at this point is reminiscent of his conversation with the woman at the well of Sychar (cf. 4:26).

The contrast between the man's faith and the Pharisees' obstinacy leads our Lord to say what he does in v. 39. He has come not to condemn the world but to save it (cf. 3:17); but his presence among us already involves a judgment, for each of us has to decide on whether to accept Jesus or to reject him. Christ's coming implies the fall of some and the salvation of others (cf. Lk 2:34).

²⁶They said to him, "What did he do to you? How did he open your eyes?" ²⁷He answered them, "I have told you already, and you would not listen. Why do you want to hear it again? Do you too want to become his disciples?" ²⁸And they reviled him, saying, "You are his disciple, but we are disciples of Moses. ²⁹We know that God has spoken to Moses, but as for this man, we do not know where he comes from." ³⁰The man answered, "Why, this is a marvel! You do not know where he comes from, and yet he opened my eyes. ³¹We know that God does not listen to sinners, but if any one is a worshipper of God and does his will, God listens to him. ³²Never since the world began has it been heard that any one opened the eyes of a man born blind. ³³If this man were not from God, he could do nothing." ³⁴They answered him, "You were born in utter sin, and would you teach us?" And they cast him out.

³⁵Jesus heard that they had cast him out and having found him he said, "Do you believe in the Son of man?"ᵛ ³⁶He answered, "And who is he, sir, that I may believe in him?" ³⁷Jesus said to him, "You have seen him, and it is he who speaks to you." ³⁸He said, "Lord, I believe"; and he worshipped him. ³⁹Jesus said, "For judgment I came into this world, that those who do not see may see, and that those who see may become blind." ⁴⁰Some of the Pharisees near him heard this, and they said to him, "Are we also blind?" ⁴¹Jesus said to them, "If you were blind, you would have no guilt; but now that you say, 'We see,' your guilt remains."

Cross-references: Ex 33:9–11; Num 12:8; Deut 34:10; Is 1:15; Prov 15:29; Ps 34:15; Acts 10:35; Jn 9:16; Jn 9:2; Jn 1:51; 8:28; Jn 4:26; Jn 8:12; Mt 13:13; Mt 15:14; Is 6:10; Ezek 12:2; Jer 5:21; Mk 3:29; Jn 3:36; Prov 26:12

The Good Shepherd

10 ¹"Truly, truly, I say to you, he who does not enter the sheepfold by the door but climbs in by another way, that man is a thief and a robber; ²but he who

Cross-references: Zech 11:4–17; Ezek 34:1–31; Jer 23:1–3; Mt 10:6; Mk 6:34

qui fuerat caecus, et dixerunt ei: «Da gloriam Deo! Nos scimus quia hic homo peccator est». ²⁵Respondit ergo ille: «Si peccator est nescio; unum scio quia caecus cum essem, modo video». ²⁶Dixerunt ergo illi: «Quid fecit tibi? Quomodo aperuit oculos tuos?». ²⁷Respondit eis: «Dixi vobis iam, et non audistis; quid iterum vultis audire? Numquid et vos vultis discipuli eius fieri?». ²⁸Et maledixerunt ei et dixerunt: «Tu discipulus illius es, nos autem Moysis discipuli sumus. ²⁹Nos scimus quia Moysi locutus est Deus, hunc autem nescimus unde sit». ³⁰Respondit homo et dixit eis: «In hoc enim mirabile est quia vos nescitis unde sit, et aperuit meos oculos! ³¹Scimus quia peccatores Deus non audit, sed si quis Dei cultor est et voluntatem eius facit, hunc exaudit. ³²A saeculo non est auditum quia aperuit quis oculos caeci nati; ³³nisi esset hic a Deo, non poterat facere quidquam». ³⁴Responderunt et dixerunt ei: «In peccatis tu natus es totus et tu doces nos?». Et eiecerunt eum foras. ³⁵Audivit Iesus quia eiecerunt eum foras et, cum invenisset eum, dixit ei: «Tu credis in Filium hominis?». ³⁶Respondit ille et dixit: «Et quis est, Domine, ut credam in eum?». ³⁷Dixit ei Iesus: «Et vidisti eum et, qui loquitur tecum, ipse est». ³⁸At ille ait: «Credo, Domine!»; et adoravit eum. ³⁹Et dixit Iesus: «In iudicium ego in hunc mundum veni, ut, qui non vident, videant, et, qui vident, caeci fiant». ⁴⁰Audierunt haec ex pharisaeis, qui cum ipso erant, et dixerunt ei: «Numquid et nos caeci sumus?». ⁴¹Dixit eis Iesus: «Si caeci essetis, non haberetis peccatum. Nunc vero dicitis: "Videmus!"; peccatum vestrum manet». [10] ¹«Amen, amen dico vobis: Qui non intrat per ostium in ovile ovium, sed ascendit aliunde, ille fur est et latro; ²qui autem intrat per

Jesus' words sting the Pharisees, who are always trying to catch him out in what he says. They realize that he is referring to them, and they ask him, "Are we also blind?" Our Lord's reply is unambiguous: they are able to see, but they do not want to see—hence their guilt. "What terrible blindness in the eyes of your soul! Such bright light, and yet so blind! Such loud voices, and yet so deaf! Can you not see that the more you seek greatness and glory, the smaller and more miserable you become? Despite all the great gifts you have been given, you remain unaware of the truth and unworthy!" (St John of the Cross, *Spiritual Canticle*, 39, 7).

10:1–21 Here we see how to attain salvation

through faith in Christ and by means of his grace. Jesus is the gateway to eternal life, the Good Shepherd who guides us and who has given his life for us. The imagery of the shepherd, the sheep and the sheepfold echoes a favourite theme of the Old Testament prophets: the Chosen People is the flock, and the Lord is its shepherd (see Ps 23). The prophets, particularly Jeremiah and Ezekiel (Jer 23:1–4; Ezek 34:1–31), in view of the infidelity of kings and priests, to whom the title of "shepherd" was also applied, promise a change of shepherds. In fact, Ezekiel says that God will raise up one Shepherd, a man like David, who will pasture his sheep and keep them safe (Ezek 34:23–31). Jesus presents himself as that Good Shepherd

ᵛ Other ancient authorities read *the Son of God*

enters by the door is the shepherd of the sheep. ³To him the gatekeeper opens; the sheep hear his voice, and he calls his own sheep by name and leads them out. ⁴When he has brought out all his own, he goes before them, and the sheep follow him, for they know his voice. ⁵A stranger they will not follow, but they will flee from him, for they do not know the voice of strangers." ⁶This figure Jesus used with them, but they did not understand what he was saying to them.

⁷So Jesus again said to them, "Truly, truly, I say to you, I am the door of the sheep. ⁸All who came before me are thieves and robbers; but the sheep did not heed them. ⁹I am the door; if any one enters by me, he will be saved, and will go in and out and find pasture. ¹⁰The thief comes only to steal and kill and destroy; I came that they may have life, and have it abundantly. ¹¹I am the good shepherd. The good shepherd lays down his life for the sheep. ¹²He who is a hireling and not a shepherd, whose own the sheep are not, sees the wolf coming and leaves the sheep and flees; and the wolf snatches them and scatters them. ¹³He flees because he is a hireling and cares nothing for the sheep. ¹⁴I am the good shepherd;* I know my own and my own know me, ¹⁵as the Father knows me and I know the Father; and I lay down my life for the sheep.

Margin references:
Jn 10:27
Mt 13:10–17
Ps 118:20
Ob 5
Bar 6:57
Jn 3:17
Is 49:9–10
Ezek 34:23–24
Ezek 34:23–24
Ps 23:1ff
Lk 15:4–7
Zech 11:17
Acts 20:29
1 Pet 2:25; 5:2–3
2 Tim 2:19
Mt 11:25–27

ostium, pastor est ovium. ³Huic ostiarius aperit, et oves vocem eius audiunt, et proprias oves vocat nominatim et educit eas. ⁴Cum proprias omnes emiserit, ante eas vadit, et oves illum sequuntur, quia sciunt vocem eius; ⁵alienum autem non sequentur, sed fugient ab eo, quia non noverunt vocem alienorum». ⁶Hoc proverbium dixit eis Iesus; illi autem non cognoverunt quid esset, quod loquebatur eis. ⁷Dixit ergo iterum Iesus: «Amen, amen dico vobis: Ego sum ostium ovium. ⁸Omnes, quotquot venerunt ante me, fures sunt et latrones, sed non audierunt eos oves. ⁹Ego sum ostium: per me si quis introierit, salvabitur et ingredietur et egredietur et pascua inveniet. ¹⁰Fur non venit, nisi ut furetur et mactet et perdat; ego veni, ut vitam habeant et abundantius habeant. ¹¹Ego sum pastor bonus: bonus pastor animam suam ponit pro ovibus; ¹²mercennarius et, qui non est pastor, cuius non sunt oves propriae, videt lupum venientem et dimittit oves et fugit —et lupus rapit eas et dispergit— ¹³quia mercennarius est, et non pertinet ad eum de ovibus. ¹⁴Ego sum pastor bonus: et cognosco meas, et cognoscunt me meae, ¹⁵sicut cognoscit me Pater, et ego cognosco Patrem; et animam meam pono pro ovibus. ¹⁶Et alias oves habeo, quae non sunt ex hoc ovili, et illas oportet me adducere, et vocem meam audi-

who looks after his sheep. In him, therefore, the ancient prophecies find fulfilment. From very early on, Christian artists have drawn inspiration from this touching image of the Good Shepherd and used it to illustrate Christ's love for all mankind.

To understand better what Jesus says in vv. 3–5, it is helpful to remember that in those times it was the practice to bring a number of flocks to the same sheepfold, where they would be guarded for the night by a lookout. Then at dawn, each shepherd would come back, the lookout would open the gate, and the shepherd would call his sheep, which would come out of the pen and follow him; he would keep letting them hear his voice, to prevent any sheep from straying, and he would walk ahead of them, to bring them out to pasture. Our Lord uses this image (one very familiar to his listeners) to make an important point: since there are alien voices in the air, we need to be able to recognize the voice of Christ (which speaks continually through the Church's magisterium) and follow him, if we are to get the nourishment our soul requires. Jesus' words have special relevance for those who hold

the office of pastors in the Church: "*I am the Good Shepherd*. These words are intended as a spark and fire to your love, for no one can be a good shepherd if he is not made one with Christ, the Good Shepherd, through love" (St Thomas Aquinas, *Super Evangelium Ioannis*, ad loc.).

Christ applies the image of the door (v. 7) to himself; through that door people enter the Church, his sheepfold. The sheepfold houses both shepherds and sheep: both must enter by the door, which is Christ. "I, seeking to enter in among you, that is, into your heart, preach Christ: if I were to preach other than that, I should be trying to enter by some other way. Through Christ I enter in, not to your houses but to your hearts. Through him I enter and you have willingly heard me speak of him. Why? Because you are Christ's sheep and you have been purchased with Christ's blood" (St Augustine, *In Ioannis Evangelium*, 47, 2, 3). "The Church is," Vatican II teaches, "a sheepfold, the sole and necessary gateway to which is Christ (see Jn 10:1–10). It is also a flock, of which God foretold that he himself would be the shepherd (cf. Is 40:11; Ezek 34:11f), and whose sheep, although

¹⁶And I have other sheep, that are not of this fold; I must bring them also, and they will heed my voice. So there shall be one flock, one shepherd. ¹⁷For this reason the Father loves me, because I lay down my life, that I may take it again. ¹⁸No one takes it from me, but I lay it down of my own accord. I have power to lay it down, and I have power to take it again; this charge I have received from my Father."*

Is 11:10
Mt 8:11
Jn 3:16; 4:42; 7:35;
11:52
Ezek 37:24
Jn 5:26

¹⁹There was again a division among the Jews because of these words. ²⁰Many of them said, "He has a demon, and he is mad; why listen to him?" ²¹Others said, "These are not the sayings of one who has a demon. Can a demon open the eyes of the blind?"

Jn 7:43; 9:16
Jn 7:20; 8:48
Mk 3:21
Jn 9:17
Is 42:6–7
Lk 4:18

6. JESUS AND THE FATHER*

Jesus and the Father are one

²²It was the feast of the Dedication at Jerusalem; ²³it was winter, and Jesus was walking in the temple, in the portico of Solomon. ²⁴So the Jews gathered round him and said

1 Mac 4:36, 59
Jn 7:26; 8:20–59;
10:39
Acts 3:11

ent et fient unus grex, unus pastor. ¹⁷Propterea me Pater diligit, quia ego pono animam meam, ut iterum sumam eam. ¹⁸Nemo tollit eam a me, sed ego pono eam a meipso. Potestatem habeo ponendi eam et potestatem habeo iterum sumendi eam. Hoc mandatum accepi a Patre meo». ¹⁹Dissensio iterum facta est inter Iudaeos propter sermones hos. ²⁰Dicebant autem multi ex ipsis: «Daemonium habet et insanit! Quid eum auditis?». ²¹Alii dicebant: «Haec verba non sunt daemonium habentis! Numquid daemonium potest caecorum oculos aperire?». ²²Facta sunt tunc Encaenia

watched over by human shepherds, are nevertheless at all times led and brought to pasture by Christ himself, the Good Shepherd and prince of shepherds (cf. Jn 10:11; 1 Pet 5:4), who gave his life for his sheep (cf. Jn 10:11–15)" (*Lumen gentium*, 6).

The Good Shepherd knows each of his sheep; he calls each by its name (v. 14, cf. v. 3). There is a message here for future pastors of the Church, as St Peter will later explain: "Tend the flock of God that is your charge, not by constraint but willingly, not for shameful gain but eagerly, not as domineering over those in your charge but being examples to the flock" (1 Pet 5:2). "Let them remember that their priestly ministry ... is—in a special way —'ordered' to the great solicitude of the Good Shepherd, solicitude for the salvation of every human being. And this we must all remember: that it is not lawful for any one of us to deserve the name of 'hireling', that is to say, the name of one 'to whom the sheep do not belong', one who, 'since he is not the shepherd and the sheep do not belong to him, abandons the sheep and runs away as soon as he sees the wolf coming, and then the wolf attacks and scatters the sheep; this is because he is only a hired man and has no concern for the sheep.' The solicitude of every good shepherd is that all people 'may have life and have it to the full', so

that none of them may be lost, but should have eternal life. Let us endeavour to make this solicitude penetrate deeply into our souls; let us strive to live it. May it characterize our personality, and be at the foundation of our priestly identity" (John Paul II, *Letter to All Priests*, 7).

As often happens in the course of the Gospel, an explicit reference is made here to the redemptive effect of Christ's sacrifice (cf. vv. 15–17). Jesus gives his life even for those sheep that do not belong to the flock of Israel. His mission is to the whole world, for he calls all the children of God to gather together in his Church (v. 16).

At the end of the passage (vv. 19–21), the evangelist reports the different reactions to what Jesus has been saying (cf. 6:52; 7:12, 25–27, 31, 40, 43). The same range of responses persists through the ages. "Jesus: wherever you have passed no heart remains indifferent. You are either loved or hated" (St Josemaría Escrivá, *The Way*, 687).

*10:22–42 The events in this section occur during Hanukkah, the feast of the Dedication of the Temple, which commemorates the time when Judas Maccabeus cleansed the temple after it had been profaned by Antiochus IV Epiphanes (see 1 Mac 1:54; 4:36–59; 2 Mac 1:1—2:18). Jesus reveals himself as the Son of God, equal to the

Lk 22:67

Jn 5:24, 36; 6:38;
7:16; 8:16

Jn 10:3–4, 14
Prov 28:5
1 Cor 2:14

Jn 6:39; 10:10;
17:12
Rom 8:33–39

Deut 32:39
1 Jn 4:4

Jn 1:1; 14:10–11

to him, "How long will you keep us in suspense? If you are the Christ, tell us plainly." ²⁵Jesus answered them, "I told you, and you do not believe. The works that I do in my Father's name, they bear witness to me; ²⁶but you do not believe, because you do not belong to my sheep. ²⁷My sheep hear my voice, and I know them, and they follow me; ²⁸and I give them eternal life, and they shall never perish, and no one shall snatch them out of my hand. ²⁹My Father, who has given them to me,ʷ is greater than all, and no one is able to snatch them out of the Father's hand. ³⁰I and the Father are one."

An attempt to stone Jesus

Jn 8:59

Lev 24:16
Mk 14:60–64

³¹The Jews took up stones again to stone him. ³²Jesus answered them, "I have shown you many good works from the Father; for which of these do you stone me?" ³³The

in Hierosolymis. Hiems erat; ²³et ambulabat Iesus in templo in porticu Salomonis. ²⁴Circumdederunt ergo eum Iudaei et dicebant ei: «Quousque animam nostram tollis? Si tu es Christus, dic nobis palam!». ²⁵Respondit eis Iesus: «Dixi vobis, et non creditis; opera, quae ego facio in nomine Patris mei, haec testimonium perhibent de me. ²⁶Sed vos non creditis, quia non estis ex ovibus meis. ²⁷Oves meae vocem meam audiunt, et ego cognosco eas, et sequuntur me, ²⁸et ego vitam aeternam do eis, et non peribunt in aeternum, et non rapiet eas quisquam de manu mea. ²⁹Pater meus quod dedit mihi, maius omnibus est, et nemo potest rapere de manu Patris. ³⁰Ego et Pater unum sumus». ³¹Sustulerunt iterum lapides Iudaei, ut lapidarent eum. ³²Respondit eis Iesus: «Multa opera bona ostendi vobis ex Patre; propter quod eorum opus me lapidatis?». ³³Responderunt ei

Father, and this provokes reactions in those present: some of them believe him, but others (particularly the Jewish authorities) reject what he says and are so hostile to him that they attempt his arrest (v. 39). However, it will happen only when the Lord permits it.

10:22–30 Given people's doubts about whether Jesus is the Messiah, St John once more emphasizes the fact that Jesus himself says that he and the Father are one. Jesus again uses the image of the shepherd. As St Gregory the Great comments, it is as if he were saying: "the proof that I know the Father, and that the Father knows me, is the love with which I lay down my life for my sheep" (*Homiliae in Evangelia*, 14, 3). People who will not accept that Jesus is acting on behalf of the Father will not be able to believe in him. Jesus gives his grace to all; but some put obstacles in its path and do not want to believe: "I can see, thanks to the light of the sun; but if I close my eyes, I cannot see: this is no fault of the sun, it is my own fault, because by closing my eyes, I prevent the sunlight from reaching me" (St Thomas Aquinas, *Super Evangelium Ioannis*, ad loc.).

In v. 30 Jesus reveals that he and the Father are one in being. Earlier he has proclaimed that God is his Father, thereby "making himself equal with God"—which is why the authorities have often thought of doing away with him (cf. 5:18; 8:59). Now he speaks about the mystery of God, which is something we can know only with the

help of Revelation. Later on, at the Last Supper, he will reveal more about this mystery (14:10; 17:21–22). It is a truth that the evangelist reflects on at the very beginning of his Gospel, in the prologue (see 1:1 and note). "Listen to the Son himself," St Augustine invites us. "'I and the Father are one.' He did not say, 'I am the Father' or 'I and the Father are one [Person].' But when he says 'I and the Father are one,' notice the two words '[we are]' and 'one' [...]. For if they are one, then they are not diverse; if '[we] are', then there is both a Father and a Son" (*In Ioannis Evangelium*, 36, 9). Jesus reveals that he is one in substance with the Father as far as the divine essence or nature is concerned, but he also reveals that the Father and the Son are distinct Persons: "We believe then in the Father who eternally begets the Son; in the Son, the Word of God, who is eternally begotten; in the Holy Spirit, the uncreated Person who proceeds from the Father and the Son as their eternal Love. Thus in the three divine Persons, *coaeternae sibi et coaequales*, the life and beatitude of God perfectly One superabound and are consummated in the supreme excellence and glory proper to uncreated Being, and always 'there should be venerated Unity in the Trinity and Trinity in the Unity'" (Paul VI, *Creed of the People of God*, 10).

10:31–42 We can only become aware of the substantial unity between Jesus and the Father by means of divine revelation. These people under-

---

ʷ Other ancient authorities read *What my Father has given to me*

Jews answered him, "We stone you for no good work but for blasphemy; because you, being a man, make yourself God." ³⁴Jesus answered them, "Is it not written in your law, 'I said, you are gods'? ³⁵If he called them gods to whom the word of God came (and scripture cannot be broken), ³⁶do you say of him whom the Father consecrated and sent into the world, 'You are blaspheming,' because I said, 'I am the Son of God'? ³⁷If I am not doing the works of my Father, then do not believe me; ³⁸but if I do them, even though you do not believe me, believe the works, that you may know and understand that the Father is in me and I am in the Father." ³⁹Again they tried to arrest him, but he escaped from their hands.

⁴⁰He went away again across the Jordan to the place where John at first baptized, and there he remained. ⁴¹And many came to him; and they said, "John did no sign, but everything that John said about this man was true." ⁴²And many believed in him there.

Jn 5:18
Mt 26:65–66

Ps 82:6

Mt 5:17

Sir 45:4; 49:7
Jer 1:5

Jn 2:11; 5:17–22

Jn 7:30; 8:20, 59
Lk 4:30

Jn 1:28–38
Mt 19:1

Jn 2:23; 8:30

7. JESUS IS THE RESURRECTION AND THE LIFE*

Jesus' reaction to the death of Lazarus

11 ¹Now a certain man was ill, Lazarus of Bethany, the village of Mary and her sister Martha. ²It was Mary who anointed the Lord with ointment and wiped

Mk 14:3

Jn 12:3
Lk 7:37

Iudaei: «De bono opere non lapidamus te sed de blasphemia, et quia tu, homo cum sis, facis teipsum Deum». ³⁴Respondit eis Iesus: «Nonne scriptum est in lege vestra: *"Ego dixi: Dii estis?"* ³⁵Si illos dixit deos ad quos sermo Dei factus est, et non potest solvi Scriptura, ³⁶quem Pater sanctificavit et misit in mundum, vos dicitis: "Blasphemas!", quia dixi: Filius Dei sum? ³⁷Si non facio opera Patris mei, nolite credere mihi; ³⁸si autem facio, et si mihi non vultis credere, operibus credite, ut cognoscatis et sciatis quia in me est Pater, et ego in Patre». ³⁹Quaerebant ergo iterum eum prehendere; et exivit de manibus eorum. ⁴⁰Et abiit iterum trans Iordanem, in eum locum, ubi erat Ioannes baptizans primum, et mansit illic. ⁴¹Et multi venerunt ad eum et dicebant: «Ioannes quidem signum fecit nullum; omnia autem, quaecumque dixit Ioannes de hoc, vera erant». ⁴²Et multi crediderunt in eum illic. [11] ¹Erat autem quidam languens Lazarus a Bethania, de castello Mariae et Marthae sororis eius. ²Maria autem erat,

stand that Jesus is saying he is God, but they wrongly interpret his words as blasphemy, and they accuse him of claiming to be God when what he is is a mere man (v. 33). Jesus replies with a dual defence—the witness of Scripture (prophecies), and that of his own actions (miracles).

He cites Psalm 82, in which God reproaches some judges for acting unjustly and says to them in warning: "You are gods, sons of the Most High, all of you" (Ps 82:6); nevertheless, you shall die like men and fall like any prince. If, according to that psalm, the children of Israel are gods and children of God, with how much more reason should he be called God who has been sent by God the Father and proved by him to be sanctified. Christ's human nature, having been assumed by the Word, is sanctified completely and comes to the world to sanctify man. Jesus' works prove as much: "The Fathers of the Church constantly proclaim that what was not assumed by Christ was not healed. Now Christ took a complete human nature just as it is found

in us poor unfortunates, but one that was without sin, [for] Christ said of himself [that he was the one 'whom the Father consecrated and sent into the world']" (Vatican II, *Ad gentes*, 3).

Although some people oppose Christ (see 10:20, 31, 39), others do believe in him and seek him out when he withdraws to beyond the Jordan (v. 41). The preparatory work done by John the Baptist continues to bear fruit: people who followed John's teaching now draw near to Christ and believe in him; John had announced that Jesus is the Messiah, the Son of God, and Jesus' own words and works bear that out. Work sincerely done in the name of the Lord is never useless or fruitless. Similarly, the apostolic example given by true Christians is never fruitless, even if results are not immediately evident.

*11:1–57 In this chapter Jesus is revealed as "the resurrection and the life" (v. 25) for those who believe in him. Martha's faith in him comes across strongly, as does the Jewish authorities' hatred of him, which leads them to plot his

his feet with her hair, whose brother Lazarus was ill. ³So the sisters sent to him,
saying, "Lord, he whom you love is ill." ⁴But when Jesus heard it he said, "This illness is not unto death; it is for the glory of God, so that the Son of God may be glorified by means of it."

⁵Now Jesus loved Martha and her sister and Lazarus. ⁶So when he heard that he
was ill, he stayed two days longer* in the place where he was. ⁷Then after this he
said to the disciples, "Let us go into Judea again." ⁸The disciples said to him,
"Rabbi, the Jews were but now seeking to stone you, and are you going there
again?" ⁹Jesus answered, "Are there not twelve hours in the day? If any one walks
in the day, he does not stumble, because he sees the light of this world. ¹⁰But if any
one walks in the night, he stumbles, because the light is not in him." ¹¹Thus he
spoke, and then he said to them, "Our friend Lazarus has fallen asleep, but I go to
awake him out of sleep." ¹²The disciples said to him, "Lord, if he has fallen asleep,
he will recover." ¹³Now Jesus had spoken of his death, but they thought that he
meant taking rest in sleep. ¹⁴Then Jesus told them plainly, "Lazarus is dead; ¹⁵and for
your sake I am glad that I was not there, so that you may believe. But let us go to
him." ¹⁶Thomas, called the Twin, said to his fellow disciples, "Let us also go, that
we may die with him."

Marginal references:
Jn 9:3; 12:23
Jn 10:40
Jn 8:59; 10:31, 39
Jn 9:4
1 Jn 2:10–11
Jn 12:35
Mt 9:24
1 Thess 4:13
Jn 14:5; 20:24–29
Mk 10:32

quae unxit Dominum unguento et extersit pedes eius capillis suis, cuius frater Lazarus infirmabatur. ³Miserunt ergo sorores ad eum dicentes: «Domine, ecce, quem amas, infirmatur».⁴Audiens autem Iesus dixit: «Infirmitas haec non est ad mortem sed pro gloria Dei, ut glorificetur Filius Dei per eam».⁵Diligebat autem Iesus Martham et sororem eius et Lazarum. ⁶Ut ergo audivit quia infirmabatur, tunc quidem mansit in loco, in quo erat, duobus diebus; ⁷deinde post hoc dicit discipulis: «Eamus in Iudaeam iterum». ⁸Dicunt ei discipuli: «Rabbi, nunc quaerebant te Iudaei lapidare, et iterum vadis illuc?».⁹Respondit Iesus: «Nonne duodecim horae sunt diei? Si quis ambulaverit in die, non offendit, quia lux non est in eo». ¹¹Haec ait et post hoc dicit eis: «Lazarus amicus noster dormit, sed vado, ut a somno exsuscitem eum». ¹²Dixerunt ergo ei discipuli: «Domine, si dormit, salvus erit». ¹³Dixerat autem Iesus de morte eius, illi autem putaverunt quia de dormitione somni diceret. ¹⁴Tunc ergo dixit eis Iesus manifeste: «Lazarus mortuus est, ¹⁵et gaudeo propter vos, ut credatis, quoniam non eram ibi; sed eamus ad eum». ¹⁶Dixit ergo Thomas, qui dicitur Didymus, ad condiscipulos: «Eamus et nos, ut moriamur cum eo!». ¹⁷Venit itaque Iesus et invenit eum quattuor dies iam in monumento habentem. ¹⁸Erat autem Bethania iuxta Hierosolymam quasi stadiis quindecim.

death. The evangelist's observation that "the Passover of the Jews was at hand" (v. 55) implies that these events herald the redemptive death of Christ and his glorious resurrection, that is, the Christian Passover, or Easter.

11:1–44 The miracle of the raising of Lazarus, a sign of our own future resurrection, shows Jesus' power over death. The evangelist begins his account by describing the initial situation; this is followed by Jesus' conversation with Lazarus' sisters and then the miracle that takes place four days after the death of Lazarus.

Bethany was about three kilometres (two miles) from Jerusalem (v. 18). In the days before his passion, Jesus will often visit this family, to whom he is very close. St John notes the great affection Jesus has for them (vv. 3, 5, 36), and the fact that he knows in advance what is going to happen (vv. 11, 14).

From his initial conversation with Martha (vv. 20–27), one of the clearest revelations about

Jesus emerges: he is the Resurrection and the Life. He is the Resurrection because his victory over death is the cause of the resurrection of all men. He is the Life because he gives us a share in the life of God which will reach its climax in eternal life. That is why the Christian can say, "Lord, for your faithful people life is changed, not ended. When the body of our earthly dwelling lies in death we gain an everlasting dwelling place in heaven" (*Roman Missal*, Preface of Christian Death I). Martha's faith sets an example for us: we must believe in Jesus if we are to be raised from the dead and live in him (vv. 25–27).

The depth of Jesus' feeling can be seen from the tears he sheds for Lazarus (v. 35). This is the shortest verse in the Bible (two words in English, three in Greek and Latin). It seems as if, when the text was being divided up into verses (in the twelfth century), the editor(s) intended to give special emphasis to Jesus' tears: this is an indication that he truly was human, and a testi-

¹⁷Now when Jesus came, he found that Lazarus^x had already been in the tomb four days. ¹⁸Bethany was near Jerusalem, about two miles^y off, ¹⁹and many of the Jews had come to Martha and Mary to console them concerning their brother. ²⁰When Martha heard that Jesus was coming, she went to meet him, while Mary sat in the house. ²¹Martha said to Jesus, "Lord, if you had been here, my brother would not have died. ²²And even now I know that whatever you ask from God, God will give you." ²³Jesus said to her, "Your brother will rise again." ²⁴Martha said to him, "I know that he will rise again in the resurrection at the last day." ²⁵Jesus said to her, "I am the resurrection and the life,^z he who believes in me, though he die, yet shall he live, ²⁶and whoever lives and believes in me shall never die. Do you believe this?" ²⁷She said to him, "Yes, Lord; I believe that you are the Christ, the son of God, he who is coming into the world."

²⁸When she had said this, she went and called her sister Mary, saying quietly, "The Teacher is here and is calling for you." ²⁹And when she heard it, she rose quickly and went to him. ³⁰Now Jesus had not yet come to the village, but was still in the place where Martha had met him. ³¹When the Jews who were with her in the house, consoling her, saw Mary rise quickly and go out, they followed her, supposing that she was going to the tomb to weep there. ³²Then Mary, when she came to where Jesus was and saw him, fell at his feet, saying to him, "Lord, if you had been here, my brother would not have died." ³³When Jesus saw her weeping, and the Jews who came with her also weeping, he was deeply moved in spirit and troubled; ³⁴and

Lk 10:38ff

Mt 11:43
Mk 11:24
Dan 12:2
2 Mac 7:9, 23
Jn 5:25; 6:40
Acts 24:15
Jn 3:3–7; 5:24; 8:51

Mk 1:1
Jn 6:69; 20:31
Mt 16:16

Jn 11:21

Jn 11:38; 13:21

¹⁹Multi autem ex Iudaeis venerant ad Martham et Mariam, ut consolarentur eas de fratre. ²⁰Martha ergo ut audivit quia Iesus venit, occurrit illi; Maria autem domi sedebat. ²¹Dixit ergo Martha ad Iesum: «Domine, si fuisses hic, frater meus non esset mortuus! ²²Sed et nunc scio quia, quaecumque poposceris a Deo, dabit tibi Deus». ²³Dicit illi Iesus: «Resurget frater tuus». ²⁴Dicit ei Martha: «Scio quia resurget in resurrectione in novissimo die». ²⁵Dixit ei Iesus: «Ego sum resurrectio et vita. Qui credit in me, et si mortuus fuerit, vivet; ²⁶et omnis, qui vivit et credit in me, non morietur in aeternum. Credis hoc?». ²⁷Ait illi: «Utique, Domine; ego credidi quia tu es Christus Filius Dei, qui in mundum venisti». ²⁸Et cum haec dixisset, abiit et vocavit Mariam sororem suam silentio dicens: «Magister adest et vocat te». ²⁹Illa autem ut audivit, surrexit cito et venit ad eum; ³⁰nondum enim venerat Iesus in castellum, sed erat adhuc in illo loco, ubi occurrerat ei Martha. ³¹Iudaei igitur, qui erant cum ea in domo et consolabantur eam, cum vidissent Mariam quia cito surrexit et exiit, secuti sunt eam putantes: «Vadit ad monumentum, ut ploret ibi». ³²Maria ergo, cum venisset, ubi erat Iesus, videns eum cecidit ad pedes eius dicens ei: «Domine, si fuisses hic, non esset mortuus frater meus!». ³³Iesus ergo, ut

mony to God's love for us: "Jesus is your friend. The Friend. With a human heart, like yours. With loving eyes that wept for Lazarus. And he loves you as much as he loved Lazarus" (St Josemaría Escrivá, *The Way*, 422).

Before working the miracle, Jesus prays and gives thanks (vv. 41–42). His gratitude to his Father for always hearing him "implies that Jesus, on his part, *constantly made such petitions*. Jesus' prayer, characterized by thanksgiving, reveals to us how to ask: *before* the gift is given, Jesus commits himself to the One who in giving gives himself. The Giver is more precious than the gift; he is the 'treasure'; in him abides his Son's heart; the gift is given 'as well' (cf. Mt 6:21, 33)" (*Catechism of the Catholic Church*, 2604).

St Augustine sees in the raising of Lazarus a symbol of the sacrament of Penance: in the same way as Lazarus comes out of the tomb, he says, "when you confess, you come forth. For what

does 'come forth' mean if not emerging from what is hidden, to be made manifest. But for you to confess is God's doing; he calls you with an urgent voice, by an extraordinary grace. And just as the dead man came out still bound, so you go to confession still guilty. In order that his sins be loosed, the Lord said this to his ministers: 'Unbind him and let him go'—which means: 'What you will loose on earth will be loosed also in heaven' (Mt 18:18)" (St Augustine, *In Ioannis Evangelium*, 49, 24).

"Bound with bandages" (v. 44). The Jews prepared the body for burial by washing it and anointing it with aromatic ointments to delay decomposition and counteract offensive odours; they then wrapped the body in linen cloths and bandages, covering the mouth with a napkin—a method very like the Egyptians', but not extending to full embalming, which involved removal of some internal organs.

x Greek *he* y Greek *fifteen stadia* z Other ancient authorities omit *and the life*

Lk 19:41

he said, "Where have you laid him?" They said to him, "Lord, come and see." ³⁵Jesus wept. ³⁶So the Jews said, "See how he loved him!" ³⁷But some of them said, "Could not he who opened the eyes of a blind man have kept this man from dying?"

The raising of Lazarus

³⁸Then Jesus, deeply moved again, came to the tomb; it was a cave, and a stone lay upon it. ³⁹Jesus said, "Take away the stone." Martha, the sister of the dead man, said to him, "Lord, by this time there will be an odour, for he has been dead four days." ⁴⁰Jesus said to her, "Did I not tell you that if you would believe you would see the glory of God?" ⁴¹So they took away the stone. And Jesus lifted his eyes and said,

Jn 12:30

"Father, I thank thee that thou hast heard me. ⁴²I knew that thou hearest me always, but I have said this on account of the people standing by, that they may believe that

Jn 5:27–29

thou didst send me." ⁴³When he had said this, he cried with a loud voice, "Lazarus, come out." ⁴⁴The dead man came out, his hands and feet bound with bandages, and his face wrapped with a cloth. Jesus said to them, "Unbind him, and let him go."

Mt 26:3–5
Mk 14:1–2

The Sanhedrin decides on the death of Jesus

⁴⁵Many of the Jews therefore, who had come with Mary and had seen what he did,

Lk 16:31

believed in him; ⁴⁶but some of them went to the Pharisees and told them what Jesus

vidit eam plorantem et Iudaeos, qui venerant cum ea, plorantes, fremuit spiritu et turbavit seipsum ³⁴et dixit: «Ubi posuistis eum?». Dicunt ei: «Domine, veni et vide». ³⁵Lacrimatus est Iesus. ³⁶Dicebant ergo Iudaei: «Ecce quomodo amabat eum!». ³⁷Quidam autem dixerunt ex ipsis: «Non poterat hic, qui aperuit oculos caeci, facere, ut et hic non moreretur?». ³⁸Iesus ergo rursum fremens in semetipso, venit ad monumentum; erat autem spelunca, et lapis superpositus erat ei. ³⁹Ait Iesus: «Tollite lapidem!». Dicit ei Martha, soror eius, qui mortuus fuerat: «Domine, iam foetet; quatriduanus enim est!». ⁴⁰Dicit ei Iesus: «Nonne dixi tibi quoniam si credideris, videbis gloriam Dei?». ⁴¹Tulerunt ergo lapidem. Iesus autem, elevatis sursum oculis, dixit: «Pater, gratias ago tibi quoniam audisti me. ⁴²Ego autem sciebam quia semper me audis, sed propter populum, qui circumstat dixi, ut credant quia tu me misisti». ⁴³Et haec cum dixisset, voce magna clamavit: «Lazare, veni foras!». ⁴⁴Prodiit, qui fuerat mortuus, ligatus pedes et manus institis; et facies illius sudario erat ligata. Dicit Iesus eis: «Solvite eum et sinite eum abire». ⁴⁵Multi ergo ex Iudaeis, qui venerant ad Mariam et viderant, quae fecit, crediderunt in eum; ⁴⁶quidam autem ex ipsis abierunt ad pharisaeos et dixerunt eis, quae fecit Iesus. ⁴⁷Collegerunt ergo pontifices et pharisaei concilium et dicebant: «Quid facimus, quia hic homo multa signa facit? ⁴⁸Si dimittimus eum sic, omnes

11:45–57 Once again, Jesus proves to be a sign of contradiction. Some believe in him, others denounce him. Caiaphas' words in vv. 49–50 (which have a dual meaning, as John notes) point to the foundation of the new Israel, the Church, which will come about through the death of Christ on the cross. And so it happens that one of the last high priests of the Old Covenant prophesies the investiture of the High Priest of the New Covenant, the covenant sealed by his own blood.

When St John says that Christ was going to die "to gather into one the children of God who are scattered abroad" (v. 52), he is referring to what our Lord had said regarding the salvific effects of his death (see 10:15–16). The prophets had already announced the future assembly of faithful Israelites to form the new people of Israel (cf. Is 43:5; Jer 23:3–5; Ezek 34:23; 37:21–24). These prophecies are fulfilled in the death of Christ, who, raised on the cross, draws and gathers together the true People of God, made up of all

believers, Israelite and Gentile (cf. 12:32). "All men are called to belong to the new People of God. This people therefore, whilst remaining one and only one, is to be spread throughout the whole world and to all ages in order that the design of God's will may be fulfilled: he made human nature one in the beginning and has decreed that all his children who were scattered should be finally gathered together as one (cf. Jn 11:52). It was for this purpose that God sent his Son; whom he appointed heir of all things (cf. Heb 1:2), that he might be teacher, king and priest of all, the head of the new and universal People of God's sons" (Vatican II, *Lumen gentium*, 13).

In the fourth century, St John Chrysostom explained the universality, the catholicity, of the Church in these words: "What is the meaning of 'to gather into one those who are scattered abroad'? He made them one body. He who dwells in Rome knows that the Christians of India are his members" (*In Ioannem*, 651).

had done. [47]So the chief priests and the Pharisees gathered the council, and said, Jn 7:32, 45
"What are we to do? For this man performs many signs. [48]If we let him go on thus,
every one will believe in him, and the Romans will come and destroy our holy place[a]
and our nation." [49]But one of them, Caiaphas, who was high priest that year, said to Jn 18:31
Lk 3:2
them, "You know nothing at all; [50]you do not understand that it is expedient for you
that one man should die for the people, and that the whole nation should not
perish."* [51]He did not say this of his own accord, but being high priest that year he
prophesied that Jesus should die for the nation, [52]and not for the nation only, but to Is 56:1–8
Jer 31:8, 11
Ezek 11:17
Jn 10:16
1 Jn 2:2
Mt 12:14
gather into one the children of God who are scattered abroad. [53]So from that day on
they took counsel how to put him to death.

[54]Jesus therefore no longer went about openly among the Jews, but went from
there to the country near the wilderness, to a town called Ephraim; and there he
stayed with the disciples.

[55]Now the Passover of the Jews was at hand, and many went up from the coun- Jn 2:13; 6:4
Num 9:6–13
try to Jerusalem before the Passover, to purify themselves. [56]They were looking for 2 Chron 30:15–20
Jn 7:11
Jesus and saying to one another as they stood in the temple, "What do you think?
That he will not come to the feast?" [57]Now the chief priests and the Pharisees had
given orders that if any one knew where he was, he should let them know, so that
they might arrest him.

8. JESUS IS ACCLAIMED AS THE MESSIANIC KING*

Mary anoints our Lord at Bethany Mt 26:6–16
Mk 14:3–11

12 *[1]Six days before the Passover, Jesus came to Bethany, where Lazarus was, Jn 11:1ff
whom Jesus had raised from the dead. [2]There they made him a supper; Lk 10:40

credent in eum, et venient Romani et tollent nostrum et locum et gentem!». [49]Unus autem ex ipsis, Caiaphas, cum esset pontifex anni illius, dixit
eis: «Vos nescitis quidquam, [50]nec cogitatis quia expedit vobis, ut unus moriatur homo pro populo, et non tota gens pereat!». [51]Hoc autem a
semetipso non dixit, sed cum esset pontifex anni illius, prophetavit quia Iesus moriturus erat pro gente [52]et non tantum pro gente sed et ut filios
Dei, qui erant dispersi, congregaret in unum. [53]Ab illo ergo die cogitaverunt, ut interficerent eum. [54]Iesus ergo iam non in palam ambulabat apud
Iudaeos, sed abiit inde in regionem iuxta desertum, in civitatem, quae dicitur Ephraim, et ibi morabatur cum discipulis. [55]Proximum autem erat
Pascha Iudaeorum, et ascenderunt multi Hierosolymam de regione ante Pascha, ut sanctificarent seipsos. [56]Quaerebant ergo Iesum et colloquebantur ad invicem in templo stantes: «Quid videtur vobis? Numquid veniet ad diem festum?». [57]Dederant autem pontifices et pharisaei mandatum, ut si quis cognoverit, ubi sit, indicet, ut apprehendant eum. [12] [1]Iesus ergo ante sex dies Paschae venit Bethaniam, ubi erat Lazarus, quem
suscitavit a mortuis Iesus. [2]Fecerunt ergo ei cenam ibi, et Martha ministrabat, Lazarus vero unus erat ex discumbentibus cum eo. [3]Maria ergo

"Ephraim" (v. 54). We cannot be sure where
this town was. Some scholars think that it was
what is now et-Taiyibeh, which is about 20 kilometres (12 miles) northwest of Jerusalem.

The reference to the Passover (vv. 55–57)
sets the scene for the events that follow, and
underlines the fact that Christ is the true, definitive Passover (cf. 1 Cor 5:7).

*12:1–50 This section brings to an end the first
main part of the Gospel, which focuses on Jesus'
revelation of himself through his preaching and
miracles (signs). The anointing at Bethany and
the triumphal entry into Jerusalem herald the
redemptive death of Jesus and his glorification
after rising from the dead. Our Lord himself

announces that the hour has come for his death
on the cross and his resurrection (vv. 23–33).
After his last invitation to people to believe in
him, many do turn to him, but others prefer the
praise of men more than that of God (vv. 42–43).

12:1–11 Jesus pays another visit to his friends in
Bethany (cf. 11:5). It is touching to see that Jesus
has this friendship, so divine and so human,
expressed in frequent visits and meetings. Jesus
appears to have been anointed on two different
occasions, and for different reasons—firstly at
the start of his public ministry (see Lk 7:36–50)
and secondly at the end of his life, at Bethany.
The second occasion is narrated here by St John;
the same episode is reported by Matthew (26:6–

a Greek *our place*

Song 1:12
Lk 7:38

Martha served, and Lazarus was one of those at table with him. ³Mary took a pound of costly ointment of pure nard and anointed the feet of Jesus and wiped his feet with her hair; and the house was filled with the fragrance of the ointment. ⁴But Judas

Jn 6:70–71

Iscariot, one of his disciples (he who was to betray him), said, ⁵"Why was this oint-

Jn 13:29

ment not sold for three hundred denarii[b] and given to the poor?" ⁶This he said, not that he cared for the poor, but because he was a thief, and as he had the money box he used to take what was put into it. ⁷Jesus said, "Let her alone, let her keep it for

Deut 15:11

the day of my burial. ⁸The poor you always have with you, but you do not always have me."

Jn 11:56ff

⁹When the great crowd of the Jews learned that he was there, they came, not only on account of Jesus but also to see Lazarus, whom he had raised from the dead. ¹⁰So

Jn 11:45

the chief priests planned to put Lazarus also to death, ¹¹because on account of him many of the Jews were going away and believing in Jesus.

Mt 21:1–11
Mk 11:1–11
Lk 19:28–40

The Messiah's entry into Jerusalem

¹²The next day a great crowd who had come to the feast heard that Jesus was coming

Lev 23:40
Neh 8:15
1 Mac 13:51

to Jerusalem. ¹³So they took branches of palm trees and went out to meet him,

accepit libram unguenti nardi puri, pretiosi et unxit pedes Iesu et extersit capillis suis pedes eius; domus autem impleta est ex odore unguenti. ⁴Dicit autem Iudas Iscariotes, unus ex discipulis eius, qui erat eum traditurus: ⁵«Quare hoc unguentum non veniit trecentis denariis et datum est egenis?». ⁶Dixit autem hoc, non quia de egenis pertinebat ad eum, sed quia fur erat et, loculos habens, ea, quae mittebantur, portabat. ⁷Dixit ergo Iesus: «Sine illam, ut in diem sepulturae meae servet illud. ⁸Pauperes enim semper habetis vobiscum, me autem non semper habetis». ⁹Cognovit ergo turba multa ex Iudaeis quia illic est, et venerunt non propter Iesum tantum, sed ut et Lazarum viderent, quem suscitavit a mortuis. ¹⁰Cogitaverunt autem principes sacerdotum, ut et Lazarum interficerent, ¹¹quia multi propter illum abibant ex Iudaeis et credebant in Iesum. ¹²In crastinum turba multa, quae venerat ad diem festum, cum audissent quia venit Iesus Hierosolymam, ¹³acceperunt ramos palmarum et processerunt

13) and Mark (14:3–9), but in St John the account is more personal. We are told the names of the person who anoints Jesus (Mary: v. 3) and of the one who criticizes her action (Judas: v. 4). The presence of Lazarus (recently raised from the dead) and the reference to the burial of Jesus (v. 7) suggest that Jesus will die for our sake. Mary of Bethany and Mary Magdalene have sometimes been confused because of a mistaken identification of this anointing with that reported by St Luke (Lk 7:36), performed by a sinful woman in Galilee also in the context of a meal. That sinful woman is often said to be Mary Magdalene, the woman out of whom Jesus had cast seven demons (see cf. Lk 8:2). However, there are no good grounds for making these identifications; the texts, in fact, seem to indicate that the episodes involved three different women.

The pound (v. 3) was a measure of weight equivalent to 300 grammes (10.5 ounces); a denarius (v. 5), as indicated elsewhere, was a day's wage for a farmhand (see Mt 20:2–13); therefore the cost of the flask of perfume would have amounted to almost a year's wages. Church Tradition has seen in this gesture of Mary's a

measure of the generosity with which we should respond to Christ's love: "What a shining proof of magnanimity is this 'extravagance' on Mary's part! [...] Don't be mean and grudging with people who, without counting the cost, have given of their all, everything they have, for your sake" (St Josemaría Escrivá, *Friends of God*, 126).

As well as praising Mary's generosity, our Lord indirectly announces the imminence of his death (v. 7), implying that it will happen so precipitously that there will hardly be time to prepare his body for burial in the normal way (cf. 19:39–40; Lk 23:56). Jesus does not mean that almsgiving is without virtue (he often praised it: see Lk 11:41; 12:33); nor that people should have no concern for the poor (cf. Lk 14:12–14); rather, he seeks to expose the hypocrisy of people like Judas who deceitfully profess noble motives in order to avoid giving God the honour he is due (see also the notes on Mt 26:6–16 and Mk 14:1–11).

12:12–19 Jesus' triumphal entry into Jerusalem anticipates the glorification he will receive in his

b The denarius was a day's wage for a labourer

crying, "Hosanna! Blessed is he who comes in the name of the Lord, even the King of Israel! [14]And Jesus found a young ass and sat upon it; as it is written,

Rev 7:9
Ps 118:25–26
Jn 1:49; 6:15

[15]"Fear not, daughter of Zion;
    behold, your king is coming,
    sitting on an ass's colt!"

Zech 9:9
Zeph 3:16
Is 40:9

[16]His disciples did not understand this at first; but when Jesus was glorified, then they remembered that this had been written of him and had been done to him. [17]The crowd that had been with him when he called Lazarus out of the tomb and raised him from the dead bore witness. [18]The reason why the crowd went to meet him was that they heard he had done this sign. [19]The Pharisees then said to one another, "You see that you can do nothing; look, the world has gone after him."

Jn 2:22; 7:39

Jn 11:47–48

Jesus announces his glorification

[20]Now among those who went up to worship at the feast were some Greeks. [21]So these came to Philip, who was from Bethsaida in Galilee, and said to him, "Sir, we wish to see Jesus." [23]Philip went and told Andrew; Andrew went with Philip and they told Jesus. [23]And Jesus answered them, "The hour has come for the Son of man

Acts 8:26
Jn 1:44; 7:34–35;
11:55

Jn 2:4; 7:30

obviam ei et clamabant: «*Hosanna! / Benedictus, qui venit in nomine Domini, / et rex Israel!*». [14]Invenit autem Iesus asellum et sedit super eum, sicut scriptum est: [15]«*Noli timere, filia Sion. / Ecce rex tuus venit / sedens super pullum asinae*». [16]Haec non cognoverunt discipuli eius primum, sed quando glorificatus est Iesus, tunc recordati sunt quia haec erant scripta de eo, et haec fecerunt ei. [17]Testimonium ergo perhibebat turba, quae erat cum eo, quando Lazarum vocavit de monumento et suscitavit eum a mortuis. [18]Propterea et obviam venit ei turba, quia audierunt eum fecisse hoc signum. [19]Pharisaei ergo dixerunt ad semetipsos: «Videtis quia nihil proficitis? Ecce mundus post eum abiit!». [20]Erant autem Graeci quidam ex his, qui ascenderant, ut adorarent in die festo; [21]hi ergo accesserunt ad Philippum, qui erat a Bethsaida Galilaeae, et rogabant eum dicentes: «Domine, volumus Iesum videre». [22]Venit Philippus et dicit Andreae; venit Andreas et Philippus et dicunt Iesu. [23]Iesus autem respondet eis dicens:

resurrection. When the crowd use the words "Blessed is he who comes in the name of the Lord" (Ps 118:26), they acclaim Jesus as the Messiah. The phrase "the King of Israel" (not all of which is included in the Synoptic accounts) underlines an aspect that St John likes to stress—Christ's royalty; the Messiah is the King of Israel in an absolute sense; but his Kingdom is not of this world (cf. 18:36). "Christ", St Augustine teaches, "was not king of Israel for exacting tribute, or arming a host with the sword; but king of Israel to rule souls, to counsel them for eternal life, to bring to the Kingdom of heaven those that believe, hope and love" (*In Ioannis Evangelium*, 51, 4).

Jesus' entry into the Holy City riding on an ass makes a very precise point: he is the king of peace announced by the prophets (see Zech 9:9). Only after his death will his disciples see the true significance of this sign—as the evangelist himself notes (v. 16). Christ acquires his kingdom through humility and by means of the cross. "Christ should reign first and foremost in our soul. But how would we reply if he asked us: 'How do you go about letting me reign in you?'

I would reply that I need lots of his grace. Only that way can my every heartbeat and breath, my least intense look, my most ordinary word, my most basic feeling be transformed into a hosanna to Christ my king" (St Josemaría Escrivá, *Christ Is Passing By*, 181).

12:20–36 The "Greeks" (v. 20) who wish to see Jesus are probably converts to Judaism, and they stand for the Gentile world (cf. 7:35). On hearing about them, Jesus again mentions his imminent glorification and makes reference to the universal nature of his mission: he is, as it were, a seed that perishes and thereby produces abundant fruit (v. 24). He draws everyone to himself (v. 32).

There is an apparent paradox in vv. 24–25 between Christ's humiliation and his glorification. However, "it was appropriate that the loftiness of his glorification should be preceded by the lowliness of his passion" (St Augustine, *In Ioannis Evangelium*, 51, 8). This is the same idea we find in St Paul, when he says that Christ "humbled himself and became obedient unto death, even death on a cross," and that therefore God the Father "highly exalted him" to far above

Is 53:10–12
Jn 10:11; 1 Cor 15:36
to be glorified. ²⁴Truly, truly, I say to you, unless a grain of wheat falls into the earth
Mt 16:25
Mk 8:35; Lk 9:24
and dies, it remains alone; but if it dies, it bears much fruit. ²⁵He who loves his life
Mk 10:45; Jn 14:3
loses it, and he who hates his life in this world will keep it for eternal life. ²⁶If any
one serves me, he must follow me; and where I am, there shall my servant be also;
if any one serves me, the Father will honour him.

Mk 14:34–36
Jn 11:33; Ps 6:2
Mt 26:38; Heb 5:7–8
²⁷"Now is my soul troubled. And what shall I say? 'Father, save me from this
hour'? No, for this purpose I have come to this hour. ²⁸Father, glorify thy name."
Mt 6:9; 17:5; Jn 5:37
Then a voice came from heaven, "I have glorified it, and I will glorify it again."
Ex 19:19
Job 37:5; Lk 22:43
²⁹The crowd standing by heard it and said that it had thundered. Others said, "An
angel has spoken to him." ³⁰Jesus answered, "This voice has come for your sake, not
1 Cor 15:25–26
Jn 3:18, 19; 14:30;
16:11
for mine. ³¹Now is the judgment of this world, now shall the ruler of this world be
Lk 10:18; Rev 12:9
cast out; ³²and I, when I am lifted up* from the earth, will draw all men to myself."
Jn 6:44; 8:28
³³He said this to show by what death he was to die. ³⁴The crowd answered him, "We
Dan 7:14; Jn 1:51
have heard from the law that the Christ remains for ever. How can you say that the

«Venit hora, ut glorificetur Filius hominis. ²⁴Amen, amen dico vobis: Nisi granum frumenti cadens in terram mortuum fuerit, ipsum solum manet; si autem mortuum fuerit, multum fructum affert. ²⁵Qui amat animam suam, perdit eam; et, qui odit animam suam in hoc mundo, in vitam aeternam custodiet eam. ²⁶Si quis mihi ministrat, me sequatur, et ubi sum ego, illic et minister meus erit; si quis mihi ministraverit, honorificabit eum Pater. ²⁷Nunc anima mea turbata est. Et quid dicam? Pater, salvifica me ex hora hac? Sed propterea veni in horam hanc. ²⁸Pater, glorifica tuum nomen!». Venit ergo vox de caelo: «Et glorificavi et iterum glorificabo». ²⁹Turba ergo, quae stabat et audierat, dicebat tonitruum factum esse; alii dicebant: «Angelus ei locutus est». ³⁰Respondit Iesus et dixit: «Non propter me vox haec facta est sed propter vos. ³¹Nunc iudicium est huius mundi, nunc princeps huius mundi eicietur foras; ³²et ego, si exaltatus fuero a terra, omnes traham ad meipsum». ³³Hoc autem dicebat significans,

all created beings (Phil 2:8–9). This is a lesson and an encouragement to Christians, who should see every type of suffering and contradiction as a sharing in Christ's cross, which redeems us and exalts us. To be supernaturally effective, a person needs to die to himself, without a thought to his own comfort or personal desires and plans.

Now, when Jesus' "hour" is imminent, St John records a prayer of our Lord's (vv. 27–28) that has the same tone as the Gethsemane prayer reported by the other evangelists (see Mk 14:34–36 and par.). Jesus feels very ill at ease and he turns to his Father for support, for help to carry out his mission, whereby God will manifest his glory (to "glorify" means to demonstrate the presence of the holiness and power of God in that person). The voice of the Father is a solemn attesting of the fact that the fullness of the Godhead dwells in Jesus Christ (cf. Col 2:9). The episode evokes other occasions when the Father testifies to the divinity of Jesus—at his baptism (see Mt 3:13–17 and par.) and at his transfiguration (Mt 17:1–13 and par.). When Christ is raised on the cross, the world and the ruler of the world (Satan) will be judged (vv. 31–33). Jesus, nailed to the cross, is the supreme sign of contradiction for all mankind: those who acknowledge him as the Son of God will be saved; those who reject

him will be condemned (see 3:18). Christ crucified is the greatest expression of the Father's love for us; the clearest proof of the malice of sin that its remedy should have cost so high a price (see Rom 8:32); the sign raised on high that was prefigured in the bronze serpent raised up by Moses in the wilderness (3:14–15). The Israelites who spoke and complained against God during the exodus from Egypt and were bitten by poisonous snakes could be cured by looking at that serpent (see Num 21:9); so, too, faith in Jesus Christ raised on the cross brings salvation to us who are wounded by sin.

Christians must show others the saving power of the cross. "The Cross must also be inserted in the very heart of the world. Jesus wants to be raised on high, there: in the noise of the factories and workshops, in the silence of libraries, in the loud clamour of the streets, in the stillness of the fields, in the intimacy of the family, in crowded gatherings, in stadiums ... Wherever there is a Christian striving to lead an honourable life, he should, with his love, set up the Cross of Christ, who attracts all things to himself" (St Josemaría Escrivá, *The Way of the Cross*, 11, 3). "Christ our Lord was crucified; from the height of the cross he redeemed the world, thereby restoring peace between God and

Son of man must be lifted up? Who is this Son of man?" [35]Jesus said to them, "The Jn 7:33; 8:12; 9:5;
11:10
light is with you for a little longer. Walk while you have the light, lest the darkness
overtake you; he who walks in the darkness does not know where he goes. [36]While Jer 13:16
Lk 16:8
you have the light, believe in the light, that you may become sons of light." Rom 13:12
1 Thess 5:5

When Jesus had said this, he departed and hid himself from them. Eph 5:8

Jesus appeals for faith in himself

[37]Though he had done so many signs before them, yet they did not believe in him;
[38]it was that the word spoken by the prophet Isaiah might be fulfilled:

"Lord, who has believed our report, *Is 53:1*
and to whom has the arm of the Lord been revealed?" Rom 10:16

[39]Therefore they could not believe. For Isaiah again said,

[40] "He has blinded their eyes and hardened their heart, *Is 6:9–10*
lest they should see with their eyes and perceive with their heart, Jer 5:20–23
Ezek 12:2
and turn for me to heal them." Mt 13:14ff
Acts 28:26–27
Rom 11:8

qua morte esset moriturus. [34]Respondit ergo ei turba: «Nos audivimus ex lege quia Christus manet in aeternum; et quomodo tu dicis: "Oportet
exaltari Filium hominis"? Quis est iste Filius hominis?». [35]Dixit ergo eis Iesus: «Adhuc modicum tempus lumen in vobis est. Ambulate, dum
lucem habetis, ut non tenebrae vos comprehendant; et qui ambulat in tenebris, nescit quo vadat. [36]Dum lucem habetis, credite in lucem, ut filii
lucis fiatis». Haec locutus est Iesus et abiit et abscondit se ab eis. [37]Cum autem tanta signa fecisset coram eis, non credebant in eum, [38]ut sermo
Isaiae prophetae impleretur, quem dixit: «*Domine, quis credidit auditui nostro, / et brachium Domini cui revelatum est?*». [39]Propterea non poterant credere, quia iterum dixit Isaias: [40]«*Excaecavit oculos eorum / et induravit eorum cor, / ut non videant oculis / et intellegant corde et conver-*

men. Jesus reminds all of us: *Et ego, si exaltatus fuero a terra, omnia traham ad meipsum*— 'and I, when I am lifted up from the earth, will draw all things to myself' (Jn 12:32). If you put me at the centre of all earthly activities, he is saying, by fulfilling the duty of each moment, in what appears important and what appears unimportant, I will draw everything to myself. My kingdom among you will be a reality!" (idem, *Christ Is Passing By*, 183).

The revelation made by Jesus here leads some of his listeners to ask questions about the Messiah (v. 34). Jesus does not give any direct answer, but he implies that his presence among them is light enough by which to glimpse the mystery and believe in him, before it is too late.

On the "Son of man" (cf. 1:51; 3:13–14; 5:27), see the note on Mt 8:18–28.

12:37–50 St John explains here why many Jews did not believe in Jesus despite having seen his miracles and heard his teaching. He quotes two prophecies from the book of Isaiah. From the first (Is 53:1), we can see that faith is a gift from God, an act whereby "man yields voluntary obedience to God himself by assenting to and cooperating with his grace, which he is able to resist" (Vatican I, *Dei Filius*, chap. 3). The second

prophecy (Is 6:10, which is also quoted in other books of the New Testament: Mt 13:14–15 and par.; Acts 28:26–27; Rom 11:7–8) shows that the unbelief of the Jews, a possible source of scandal to early Christians, was in fact foreseen and predicted (cf. the note on Mk 4:1–20). "Some, then, mutter in themselves and, when they can, now and then cry out, saying, What did the Jews do or what was their faith, for it to be necessary for the words of the prophet Isaiah to be fulfilled? To this we answer that the Lord, who knows the future, predicted by the prophet the unbelief of the Jews; he predicted it, but he was not its cause. Just as God compels no one to sin, though he knows already man's future sins. [...] Consequently, what the Jews did was sin; but they were not compelled to do so by him who hates sin; and it was only predicted that they would sin, by him from whom nothing is hidden. If they had wished to do not evil but good, they would not have been hindered; but then God would have foreseen this, for he knows what each man will do, and what he will render him according to his works" (St Augustine, *In Ioannis Evangelium*, 53, 4).

We saw earlier how, when he was cured, the man born blind refused to retract his belief in Jesus despite the attitude of the Jewish authori-

Is 6:1
Jn 7:26, 48; 9:22

⁴¹Isaiah said this because he saw his glory and spoke of him. ⁴²Nevertheless many even of the authorities believed in him, but for fear of the Pharisees they did not con-

Mt 10:32–33
Jn 5:44

fess it, lest they should be put out of the synagogue: ⁴³for they loved the praise of men more than the praise of God.

Mt 10:40
Jn 3:16–18
Jn 14:7–9
Jn 8:12; 9:5; 12:53
Lk 8:21
Jn 3:16–18
Heb 4:12
Deut 18:18–19
Jn 8:26–28

⁴⁴And Jesus cried out and said, "He who believes in me, believes not in me, but in him who sent me. ⁴⁵And he who sees me sees him who sent me. ⁴⁶I have come as light into the world, that whoever believes in me may not remain in darkness. ⁴⁷If any one hears my sayings and does not keep them, I do not judge him; for I did not come to judge the world but to save the world. ⁴⁸He who rejects me and does not receive my sayings has a judge; the word that I have spoken will be his judge on the last day. ⁴⁹For I have not spoken on my own authority; the Father who sent me has himself given me commandment what to say and what to speak. ⁵⁰And I know that his commandment is eternal life. What I say, therefore, I say as the Father has bidden me."

PART TWO

Jesus is manifested as the Messiah Son of God in his passion, death and resurrection*

9. THE LAST SUPPER*

Jesus washes his disciples' feet

Jn 2:4; 5:24; 7:30;
8:20; 15:13; 19:30
1 Jn 3:16

13 *¹Now before the feast of the Passover, when Jesus knew that his hour had come to depart out of this world to the Father, having loved his own who

tantur, / et sanem eos». ⁴¹Haec dixit Isaias, quia vidit gloriam eius et locutus est de eo. ⁴²Verumtamen et ex principibus multi crediderunt in eum, sed propter pharisaeos non confitebantur, ut de synagoga non eicerentur; ⁴³dilexerunt enim gloriam hominum magis quam gloriam Dei. ⁴⁴Iesus autem clamavit et dixit: «Qui credit in me, non credit in me sed in eum, qui misit me; ⁴⁵et, qui videt me, videt eum, qui misit me. ⁴⁶Ego lux in mundum veni, ut omnis, qui credit in me, in tenebris non maneat. ⁴⁷Et si quis audierit verba mea et non custodierit, ego non iudico eum; non enim veni, ut iudicem mundum, sed ut salvificem mundum. ⁴⁸Qui spernit me et non accipit verba mea, habet, qui iudicet eum: sermo, quem locutus sum, ille iudicabit eum in novissimo die, ⁴⁹quia ego ex meipso non sum locutus, sed, qui misit me, Pater, ipse mihi mandatum dedit quid dicam et quid loquar. ⁵⁰Et scio quia mandatum eius vita aeterna est. Quae ergo ego loquor, sicut dixit mihi Pater, sic loquor». [13] ¹Ante diem autem

ties (9:30–41); now, in this very tense situation, the Jewish authorities mentioned here back away from a public acknowledgment of Jesus (v. 42). When Christians experience opposition, they should remember that the glory of God takes priority over praise from men (cf. 1 Pet 5:9).

The evangelist ends his account of Jesus' preaching with a summary of the main themes developed in the previous chapters—faith in Christ as the One sent by the Father (v. 44; cf. 3:16, 36; 5:24); the Father and the Son are one but distinct (v. 45; cf. 5:19–30); Jesus is the Light and Life of the world (vv. 46, 50; cf. 8:12; 11:25); people will be judged in accordance with whether they accept or reject what Jesus has

revealed about God (vv. 47–50; cf. 5:22–29; 7:14–24). Christ has come to save the world, offering himself up as a sacrifice for our sins and bringing us eternal life (cf. 3:17). He has been made Judge of the living and the dead (cf. 5:27; Acts 10:42; 17:31).

*13:1—21:25 In this second part of the Gospel we can distinguish three sections based on their subject-matter—the Last Supper and farewell discourse; Christ's passion and death; and the Resurrection. In each section we see again the revelation of Christ and the different ways in which people react to him. This part of the Gospel is sometimes called the "book of glory",

were in the world, he loved them to the end. [2]And during supper, when the devil had Lk 22:3
already put it into the heart of Judas Iscariot, Simon's son, to betray him, [3]Jesus, Jn 1:1; 3:35; 16:28; 17:2
knowing that the Father had given all things into his hands, and that he had come
from God and was going to God, [4]rose from supper, laid aside his garments, and Mt 11:29; 20:28 Lk 7:44; 12:37
girded himself with a towel. [5]Then he poured water into a basin, and began to wash
the disciples' feet, and to wipe them with the towel with which he was girded. [6]He
came to Simon Peter, and Peter said to him, "Lord, do you wash my feet?" [7]Jesus Jn 13:12ff; 14:26
answered him, "What I am doing you do not know now, but afterward you will

festum Paschae, sciens Iesus quia venit eius hora, ut transeat ex hoc mundo ad Patrem, cum dilexisset suos, qui erant in mundo, in finem dilexit eos. [2]Et in cena, cum Diabolus iam misisset in corde, ut traderet eum Iudas Simonis Iscariotis, [3]sciens quia omnia dedit ei Pater in manus et quia a Deo exivit et ad Deum vadit, [4]surgit a cena et ponit vestimenta sua et, cum accepisset linteum, praecinxit se. [5]Deinde mittit aquam in pelvem et coepit lavare pedes discipulorum et extergere linteo, quo erat praecinctus. [6]Venit ergo ad Simonem Petrum. Dicit ei: «Domine, tu mihi lavas pedes?». [7]Respondit Iesus et dixit ei: «Quod ego facio, tu nescis modo, scies autem postea». [8]Dicit ei Petrus: «Non lavabis mihi pedes in aeternum!». Respondit Iesus ei: «Si non lavero te, non habes partem mecum». [9]Dicit ei Simon Petrus: «Domine, non tantum pedes meos, sed et manus

because Jesus' "hour" has come, that is, the hour of his passion, death and resurrection, which John presents as the time of the glorification and exaltation of Jesus Christ.

*13:1—17:26 These chapters comprise the revelation made by Jesus to his disciples during the private gathering for the Last Supper. John relates to us some things which are not recounted in the other Gospels (the washing of the feet, for example), and he omits the institution of the Eucharist—an event already covered by the Synoptics and by St Paul, and one whose meaning has already been discussed at length in this Gospel in chapter 6. Up to this point "life" and "light" were the defining terms and images; now the key word is "love".

In 13:33—17:26 John gives an account of the Supper or "farewell" discourse: 13:33–38 and chapter 14 are about Jesus' departure and return; chapters 15 and 16 are about Christ and his Church; and chapter 17 is taken up with the priestly prayer of Jesus. The main themes are: (a) love, which derives from Christ's own love and becomes the "Lord's commandment"; (b) the consolation that Jesus gives his disciples when he is about to leave them, and his promise to return and send the Holy Spirit; (c) Christ's unity with his followers (the image of the vine and branches), which is based on love and on their keeping of his commandments.

13:1–20 The chapter begins with a signalling of the meaning of the occasion. The Passover, the commemoration of the liberation of the Israelites

from their slavery under Pharaoh, was a prefigurement of what Jesus Christ had come to do—redeem mankind from slavery to sin through his sacrifice on the cross. As St Bede explains, "The mystical meaning of the Passover is that the Lord must pass over from this world to the Father; his disciples, freed from all worldly desires and slavery to sin through the ceaseless practice of virtue, are to follow him into the promised homeland of heaven" (*In Ioannis Evangelium expositio*, ad loc.). Jesus knows that his death and resurrection are imminent (cf. 18:4); so his words acquire a special tone of intimacy and love for those whom he will leave behind in the world: "He himself wished to give that encounter such a fullness of meaning, such a richness of memories, such a moving image of words and thoughts, such a newness of acts and precepts, that we can never exhaust our reflection and exploration of it. It was a testamentary supper, infinitely affectionate and immensely sad, and at the same time a mysterious revelation of divine promises, of supreme visions. Death was imminent, with silent omens of betrayal, of abandonment, of immolation; the conversation dies down but Jesus continues to speak in words that are new and beautifully reflective, in almost supreme intimacy, almost hovering between life and death" (Paul VI, *Homily on Holy Thursday*, 27 March 1975).

What Christ did for his own can be summed up in the words "he loved them to the end" (v. 1): his love is so great that he gives up his life for their sake; but his love does not end with his death, for Christ lives on and continues to love us

understand." [8]Peter said to him, "You shall never wash my feet." Jesus answered him, "If I do not wash you, you have no part in me." [9]Simon Peter said to him, "Lord, not my feet only but also my hands and my head!" [10]Jesus said to him, "He who has bathed does not need to wash, except for his feet,[c] but he is clean all over; and you are clean, but not all of you." [11]For he knew who was to betray him; that was why he said, "You are not all clean."

Jn 6:64, 70–71

[12]When he had washed their feet, and taken his garments, and resumed his place, he said to them, "Do you know what I have done to you? [13]You call me Teacher and Lord; and you are right, for so I am. [14]If I then, your Lord and Teacher, have washed your feet, you also ought to wash one another's feet. [15]For I have given you an example, that you also should do as I have done to you. [16]Truly, truly, I say to you, a servant[d] is not greater than his master; nor is he who is sent greater than he who sent him. [17]If you know these things, blessed are you if you do them. [18]I am not speaking of you all; I know whom I have chosen; it is that the scripture may be fulfilled, 'He who ate my bread has lifted his heel against me.' [19]I tell you this now,

Mt 23:8, 10
Lk 22:27
1 Tim 5:10
Jn 13:35; 15:12
Phil 2:5; Col 3:13
1 Pet 2:21; 5:3
Mt 10:24
Lk 6:40; Jn 15:20
Jas 1:25
Jn 6:70
Mk 14:18
Ps 41:9
Ex 3:14

et caput!». [10]Dicit ei Iesus: «Qui lotus est non indiget nisi ut pedes lavet, sed est mundus totus; et vos mundi estis, sed non omnes». [11]Sciebat enim quisnam esset, qui traderet eum; propterea dixit: «Non estis mundi omnes». [12]Postquam ergo lavit pedes eorum et accepit vestimenta sua, cum recubuisset iterum, dixit eis: «Scitis quid fecerim vobis? [13]Vos vocatis me: "Magister" et: "Domine", et bene dicitis; sum etenim. [14]Si ergo ego lavi vestros pedes, Dominus et Magister, et vos debetis alter alterius lavare pedes. [15]Exemplum enim dedi vobis, ut, quemadmodum ego feci vobis, et vos faciatis. [16]Amen, amen dico vobis: Non est servus maior domino suo, neque apostolus maior eo, qui misit illum. [17]Si haec scitis, beati estis, si facitis ea. [18]Non de omnibus vobis dico, ego scio, quos elegerim, sed ut impleatur Scriptura: *"Qui manducat meum panem, levavit contra me*

infinitely. "It is love 'to the end' (Jn 13:1) that confers on Christ's sacrifice its value as redemption and reparation, as atonement and satisfaction. He knew and loved us all when he offered his life [...]. No man, not even the holiest, was ever able to take on himself the sins of all men and offer himself as a sacrifice for all. The existence in Christ of the divine person of the Son, who at once surpasses and embraces all human persons and constitutes himself as the Head of all mankind, makes possible his redemptive sacrifice *for all*" (*Catechism of the Catholic Church*, 616).

In washing the disciples' feet, Jesus performs a service normally done by household slaves. The passage is reminiscent of the hymn in the Letter to the Philippians: "Jesus, [...] though he was in the form of God, did not count equality with God a thing to be grasped, but emptied himself, taking the form of a servant" (Phil 2:6–7). St Peter, at the time, could not understand why Jesus would want to humble himself in such a way. Jesus' gesture is a simple and symbolic one which shows that he "came not to be served but to serve", and that his service consisted in "[giving] his life as a ransom for many" (Mk 10:45). It makes clear to the apostles, and, through them, to all who would enter the

Church, that humble service of others likens the disciple to the Master. "If, in the light of this attitude of Christ's, 'being a king' is truly possible only by 'being a servant', then 'being a servant' also demands so much spiritual maturity that it must really be described as 'being a king'" (John Paul II, *Redemptor hominis*, 21).

Jesus' entire life was an example of service to others, doing the Father's will, to the point of dying on a cross. In v. 17 our Lord promises that if we imitate him in disinterested service, which always involves sacrifice, we will find true happiness that no one can take away (cf. 16:22; 17:13). "'I have given you an example' (Jn 13:15), he tells his disciples after washing their feet, on the night of the Last Supper. Let us reject from our hearts any pride, any ambition, any desire to dominate; and peace and joy will reign around us and within us, as a consequence of our personal sacrifice" (St Josemaría Escrivá, *Christ Is Passing By*, 94).

Our Lord tells the apostles in advance about Judas' treachery (vv. 18–19). When they see Jesus' predictions come true, they realize that he had divine foreknowledge and that, in him, the Old Testament scriptures found fulfilment (cf. 2:22). On the words "I am he" (v. 19) see the note on 8:21–30.

c Other ancient authorities omit *except for his feet* d Or *slave*

before it takes place, that when it does take place you may believe that I am he. Jn 8:24, 28; 14:29; 16:4
Mt 10:40
Mk 9:37
Lk 9:48
²⁰Truly, truly, I say to you, he who receives any one whom I send receives me; and
he who receives me receives him who sent me."

Mt 26:20–25
Mk 14:17–21
Lk 22:21–23

The treachery of Judas foretold

Jn 12:27

²¹When Jesus had thus spoken, he was troubled in spirit, and testified, "Truly, truly,
I say to you, one of you will betray me." ²²The disciples looked at one another,
uncertain of whom he spoke. ²³One of his disciples, whom Jesus loved, was lying Jn 19:26; 20:2; 21:7, 20
close to the breast of Jesus; ²⁴so Simon Peter beckoned to him and said, "Tell us who
it is of whom he speaks." ²⁵So lying thus, close to the breast of Jesus, he said to him,
"Lord, who is it?" ²⁶Jesus answered, "It is he whom I shall give this morsel when I
have dipped it." So when he had dipped the morsel, he gave it to Judas, the son of
Simon Iscariot. ²⁷Then after the morsel, Satan entered into him. Jesus said to him, Jn 13:2
Lk 22:3
"What you are going to do, do quickly," ²⁸Now no one at the table knew why he said
this to him. ²⁹Some thought that, because Judas had the money box, Jesus was telling Jn 12:6
him, "Buy what you need for the feast"; or, that he should give something to the
poor. ³⁰So, after receiving the morsel, he immediately went out; and it was night. Jn 8:12
Lk 22:53
1 Cor 11:23

calcaneum suum". ¹⁹Amodo dico vobis priusquam fiat, ut credatis cum factum fuerit, quia ego sum. ²⁰Amen, amen dico vobis: Qui accipit, si quem misero, me accipit; qui autem me accipit, accipit eum, qui me misit». ²¹Cum haec dixisset Iesus, turbatus est spiritu et protestatus est et dixit: «Amen, amen dico vobis: Unus ex vobis tradet me». ²²Aspiciebant ad invicem discipuli, haesitantes de quo diceret. ²³Erat recumbens unus ex discipulis eius in sinu Iesu, quem diligebat Iesus. ²⁴Innuit ergo huic Simon Petrus, ut interrogaret: «Quis est, de quo dicit?». ²⁵Cum ergo recumberet ille ita supra pectus Iesu, dicit ei: «Domine, quis est?». ²⁶Respondet Iesus: «Ille est, cui ego intinctam buccellam porrexero». Cum ergo intinxisset buccellam dat Iudae Simonis Iscariotis. ²⁷Et post buccellam tunc introivit in illum Satanas. Dicit ergo ei Iesus: «Quod facis, fac citius». ²⁸Hoc autem nemo scivit discumbentium ad quid dixerit ei; ²⁹quidam enim putabant quia loculos habebat Iudas, quia dicit ei Iesus: «Eme ea, quae opus

13:21–30 In the context of the announcement of Judas' betrayal, Jesus' special love for one of his true disciples is put on record. It is a model of his love for all his true disciples, and of their love for him. When reading this passage, it is useful to remember the customary layout of the furniture. The diners usually reclined on divans; each would support himself on an elbow, and three or more people would share a single divan. The divans were ranged round a low table. The intimacy of the meal and this moment is made obvious.

The morsel that Jesus offers Judas (v. 26) is a sign of friendship, and therefore an invitation to him to renounce his evil plot. But Judas rejects the chance he is offered. "What he received is good", St Augustine comments, "but he received it to his own perdition, because he, being evil, received in an evil manner what is good" (*In Ioannis Evangelium*, 61, 6). "Satan entered him" (v. 27)—at this point, Judas yields to temptation; there will be no going back. "These details have been recorded that we may not bear ill will against those who wrong us, but may reproach them and weep over them. Indeed, not those who are wronged, but those who do wrong deserve

our tears. For the covetous man and the slanderer, and the man guilty of any other wrongdoing injure themselves most of all. [...] Christ repaid the man who was going to betray him with just the opposite. For example, he washed his feet, reproved him without bitterness, censured him in private, ministered to him, allowed him to share in his table and his kiss. Yet, though Judas did not become better because of these things, Jesus himself persevered in his course of action" (St John Chrysostom, *In Ioannem*, 71, 4).

The mention that "it was night" (v. 30) is a reference to darkness as a symbol of sin; at this point, the power of darkness seems to take over (cf. Lk 22:53), and is pitched against the true Light, Christ, whom the darkness does not overcome (1:5). The point when he is to be "glorified" has come (vv. 31–32); this refers above all to the glory that Christ will receive once he is raised on the cross. The evangelist underlines that Christ's death both is the beginning of his triumph and also gives glory to the Father. A disciple of Christ will also find his greatest joy in identifying himself with his Master's obedience; as St Paul puts it, "Far be it

Mt 26:30–35
Mk 14:26–31
Lk 22:31–34

Jn 12:32–34; Phil 2:9
Deut 7:13–14

Jn 7:33, 34; 8:21

Mk 12:28–31
Jn 15:12, 13, 17
1 Jn 2:8

Lev 19:18
Jn 17:23

Acts 4:32

Jn 21:18, 19

The new commandment. The disciples' desertion foretold

[31]When he had gone out, Jesus said, "Now is the Son of man glorified, and in him God is glorified; [32]if God is glorified in him, God will also glorify him in himself, and glorify him at once. [33]Little children, yet a little while I am with you. You will seek me; and as I said to the Jews so now I say to you, 'Where I am going you cannot come.' [34]A new commandment* I give to you, that you love one another; even as I have loved you, that you also love one another. [35]By this all men will know that you are my disciples, if you have love for one another."

[36]Simon Peter said to him, "Lord, where are you going?" Jesus answered, "Where I am going you cannot follow me now; but you shall follow afterward." [37]Peter said to him, "Lord, why cannot I follow you now? I will lay down my life for you." [38]Jesus answered, "Will you lay down your life for me? Truly, truly, I say to you, the cock will not crow, till you have denied me three times.

Jesus reveals the Father

Jn 14:27

14 [1]"Let not your hearts be troubled; believe[e] in God, believe also in me. [2]In my Father's house are many rooms; if it were not so, would I have told you that I

sunt nobis ad diem festum», aut egenis ut aliquid daret. [30]Cum ergo accepisset ille buccellam, exivit continuo; erat autem nox. [31]Cum ergo exisset, dicit Iesus: «Nunc clarificatus est Filius hominis, et Deus clarificatus est in eo; [32]si Deus clarificatus est in eo, et Deus clarificabit eum in semetipso, et continuo clarificabit eum. [33]Filioli, adhuc modicum vobiscum sum; quaeretis me, et sicut dixi Iudaeis: Quo ego vado, vos non potestis venire, et vobis dico modo. [34]Mandatum novum do vobis, ut diligatis invicem; sicut dilexi vos, ut et vos diligatis invicem. [35]In hoc cognoscent omnes quia mei discipuli estis: si dilectionem habueritis ad invicem». [36]Dicit ei Simon Petrus: «Domine, quo vadis?». Respondit Iesus: «Quo vado, non potes me modo sequi, sequeris autem postea». [37]Dicit ei Petrus: «Domine, quare non possum te sequi modo? Animam meam pro te ponam». [38]Respondet Iesus: «Animam tuam pro me pones? Amen, amen dico tibi: Non cantabit gallus, donec me ter neges. [14] [1]Non turbe-

from me to glory except in the cross of our Lord Jesus Christ" (Gal 6:14).

13:31–38 Our Lord's precepts can be summed up in one—the New Commandment of love (v. 34). It contains all the law of the Church and is the distinguishing characteristic of Christians: "Anyone can bless himself with the sign of the cross of Christ: anyone can answer 'Amen'; anyone can sing Alleluia; anyone can be baptized, enter churches, build the walls of basilicas. But the only thing that distinguishes the children of God is charity. Those who practise charity are born of God; those who do not practise it are not born of God. It is indeed an important sign, an essential difference. No matter what you have, if you do not have this one thing, everything else is of no avail; and if you lack everything, and have nothing else but charity, then you have kept the law" (St Augustine, *In Epistolam Ioannis ad Parthos*, 5, 7). The words "even as I have loved you" give the precept a new content and a new meaning: Christian love is measured by no one's heart but Christ's (cf. Mt 5:43–48).

Christ's prediction about Peter's denials pre-

pares the ground for the last dialogue in the Gospel, where Jesus asks Peter if he loves him (21:15–19). Straightforward and sincere as usual, Peter tells the Master that he is prepared to follow him to the end, even to death (vv. 36–38). But Peter is not yet ready to do as he says he will. He speaks from the heart, he is enthusiastic, but he is weak. Later on he will acquire strength based on humility; and at the end of his life, considering himself unworthy to die like his Master, he will be crucified upside-down. The solid Petrine rock endures in those who succeed him and forms the foundation on which the Church is built and made perfect. Peter's denials, a sign of his weakness, were more than compensated for by his repentance. "Let everyone draw from this example of contrition, and if he has fallen let him not despair, but always remember that he can become worthy of forgiveness" (St Bede, *In Ioannis Evangelium expositio*, ad loc.). Even so, faithfulness to Christ depends on love: "And what is the secret of perseverance? Love. Fall in Love, and you will not leave him" (St Josemaría Escrivá, *The Way*, 999).

14:1–14 The prediction of Peter's denial seems

e Or *you believe*

go to prepare a place for you? [3]And when I go and prepare a place for you, I will come again and will take you to myself, that where I am you may be also. [4]And you know the way where I am going."[f] [5]Thomas said to him, "Lord, we do not know where you are going; how can we know the way?" [6]Jesus said to him, "I am the way, and the truth, and the life; no one comes to the Father, but by me. [7]If you had known me, you would have known my Father also; henceforth you know him and have seen him."

[8]Philip said to him, "Lord, show us the Father, and we shall be satisfied." [9]Jesus said to him, "Have I been with you so long, and yet you do not know me, Philip? He who has seen me has seen the Father; how can you say, 'Show us the Father'? [10]Do you not believe that I am in the Father and the Father in me? The words that I say to

Heb 6:19–20

Is 40:3
Ps 119
Jn 11:25
Mt 11:27
Rom 5:1ff
Heb 10:20

Jn 12:44–46
Heb 1:3

Jn 12:49

tur cor vestrum. Creditis in Deum et in me credite. [2]In domo Patris mei mansiones multae sunt; si quo minus, dixissem vobis quia vado parare vobis locum? [3]Et si abiero et praeparavero vobis locum, iterum venio et accipiam vos ad meipsum, ut, ubi sum ego, et vos sitis. [4]Et quo ego vado, scitis viam». [5]Dicit ei Thomas: «Domine, nescimus quo vadis; quomodo possumus viam scire?». [6]Dicit ei Iesus: «Ego sum via et veritas et vita; nemo venit ad Patrem nisi per me. [7]Si cognovistis me, et Patrem meum utique cognoscetis; et amodo cognoscitis eum et vidistis eum». [8]Dicit ei Philippus: «Domine, ostende nobis Patrem, et sufficit nobis». [9]Dicit ei Iesus: «Tanto tempore vobiscum sum, et non cognovisti me, Philippe? Qui vidit me, vidit Patrem. Quomodo tu dicis: "Ostende nobis Patrem"? [10]Non credis quia ego in Patre, et Pater in me est? Verba, quae ego loquor

to have depressed the disciples. Jesus cheers them up by telling them that he is going away to prepare a place for them in heaven, for they will eventually attain heaven, despite their shortcomings and failures and setbacks.

Inspired by the words of v. 2, St Teresa wrote her famous work *Interior Castle*, in which she says this: "Just as there are many rooms in the Father's house, the soul is like a crystal or diamond castle with many rooms. If we think about it deeply, sisters, is not the soul of the just man or woman and the paradise filled with His delights one and the same? The castle where the most powerful, wise, pure King, filled with everything that is good, takes his ease and his delight is your soul!" (*Interior Castle*, 1, 1); and later she adds: "The gateway to this castle is prayer" (ibid., 2, 11).

Jesus' death means that he takes leave of the apostles to be with the Father, with whom he is one because he is God (see v. 10). The apostles don't really understand what he is telling them here; hence Thomas' question (v. 5). Our Lord explains that he is the way to the Father: "It was necessary for him to say 'I am the Way' to show them that they really knew what they thought they were ignorant of, because they knew him" (St Augustine, *In Ioannis Evangelium*, 66, 2).

What Jesus says in v. 6, about being the Way, the Truth and the Life, goes beyond the question asked him by Thomas. The Word-made-flesh is by his nature Truth and Life: as St John says in the prologue, he is "full of grace and truth"

(1:14). He is Truth because his coming into the world proves that God is true to his promises, and because he teaches the truth about God and tells us that true worship must be "in spirit and truth" (4:23). He is Life because from all eternity he shares in divine life with the Father (cf. 1:4), and because he allows us, through grace, to partake of that divine life. That is why he now says: "This is eternal life, that they know thee, the only true God, and Jesus Christ whom thou hast sent" (17:3). In his reply to Thomas, Jesus is, as St Augustine points out, saying in effect, "Where do you want to go? I am the Way. Where do you want to reach? I am the Truth. Where do you hope to stay? I am the Life. [...] Every man is capable of understanding the Truth and the Life but not all find the Way. The wise men of the world understand God as eternal life and as a truth which is knowable; [...] however, the word of God, which is Truth and Life in the presence of the Father, has become the Way on assuming a human nature. Look at his humility and you will attain God" (*Sermones*, 142, and 141, 1, 4). And St Thomas tells us, "If you are looking for where you must go, stay close to Christ within you for he is the way [...]. It is better to limp along the right road than to run down the wrong path. Although his progress is slow, the one who limps along the right road is always drawing nearer to his goal; whereas the one who runs faster and faster down the wrong path is always moving further and further from where he wants to go" (*Super Evangelium Ioannis*, ad loc.).

f Other ancient authorities read *where I am going you know, and the way you know*

you I do not speak on my own authority; but the Father who dwells in me does his
Jn 10:25, 38; 14:20 works. ¹¹Believe me that I am in the Father and the Father in me; or else believe me
for the sake of the works themselves.

Mk 16:19, 20 ¹²Truly, truly, I say to you, he who believes in me will also do the works that I do;
Jn 14:24, 26; 15:7, 16
Mk 11:24
1 Jn 5:14 and greater works than these will he do; because I go to the Father. ¹³Whatever you
ask in my name, I will do it, that the Father may be glorified in the Son; ¹⁴if you ask^g
Jn 16:23, 24 anything in my name, I will do it.

1 Jn 5:3 **Promise of the Holy Spirit**

Mk 13:11
Jn 14:26; 15:26; 16:7
1 Jn 2:1 ¹⁵"If you love me, you will keep my commandments. ¹⁶And I will pray the Father,
and he will give you another Counsellor, to be with you for ever, ¹⁷even the Spirit of
Jn 7:35, 39; 16:13
Mt 10:20
Rom 8:26
1 Jn 5:6 truth, whom the world cannot receive, because it neither sees him nor knows him;
you know him, for he dwells with you, and will be in you.

Jn 6:57; 16:16 ¹⁸"I will not leave you desolate; I will come to you. ¹⁹Yet a little while, and the
world will see me no more, but you will see me; because I live, you will live also.

vobis, a meipso non loquor; Pater autem in me manens facit opera sua. ¹¹Credite mihi quia ego in Patre, et Pater in me est; alioquin propter opera
ipsa credite. ¹²Amen, amen dico vobis: Qui credit in me, opera, quae ego facio, et ipse faciet et maiora horum faciet, quia ego ad Patrem vado.
¹³Et quodcumque petieritis in nomine meo, hoc faciam, ut glorificetur Pater in Filio; ¹⁴si quid petieritis me in nomine meo, ego faciam. ¹⁵Si diligitis me, mandata mea servabitis; ¹⁶et ego rogabo Patrem, et alium Paraclitum dabit vobis, ut maneat vobiscum in aeternum, ¹⁷Spiritum veritatis,
quem mundus non potest accipere, quia non videt eum nec cognoscit. Vos cognoscitis eum, quia apud vos manet; et in vobis erit. ¹⁸Non relinquam
vos orphanos, venio ad vos. ¹⁹Adhuc modicum, et mundus me iam non videt; vos autem videtis me, quia ego vivo et vos vivetis. ²⁰In illo die vos

Verse 9 expresses a dazzling truth: to know
Christ is to know God; Jesus is the face of God:
"Christ's whole earthly life—his words and
deeds, his silences and sufferings, indeed his
manner of being and speaking—is *Revelation* of
the Father. Jesus can say: 'Whoever has seen me
has seen the Father' (Jn 14:9), and the Father can
say: 'This is my Son, my Chosen; listen to him!'
(Lk 9:35). Because our Lord became man in
order to do his Father's will, even the least characteristics of his mysteries manifest 'God's love
… among us' (1 Jn 4:9)" (*Catechism of the
Catholic Church*, 516).

Before leaving this world, our Lord promises
the apostles a share in his power so that God's
salvation can be made known through them. The
"works" that Jesus refers to (see vv. 11–12) are
miracles worked in the name of Jesus (cf. Acts
3:1–10; 5:15–16) and, above all, conversions to
the Christian faith, and the sanctification of men
through preaching and the sacraments. Works of
the Church might be said to be "greater" than
Jesus' own in the sense that the apostles will
preach the Gospel not only in Palestine but to the
ends of the earth.

Jesus will be constantly interceding in
heaven; hence his promise that everything we
ask for in his name will be done (v. 13). To ask

in his name (cf. 15:7, 16; 16:23–24) means to
appeal to the power of the risen Christ, believing
him to be almighty and merciful because he is
true God; and it also means to ask for whatever
is conducive to our salvation, for Jesus Christ is
the Saviour. So, "whatever you ask" means
whatever is good for the person in question.
When our Lord does not give us what we ask for,
it is because it is not part of his plan for our salvation; so, he shows himself to be our Saviour
both when he gives us what we ask for and when
he denies our petition.

14:15–31 Jesus announces here that, after his
resurrection, he will send the Holy Spirit to the
apostles, to guide them and recall to their minds
and explain the things that Jesus said. The Holy
Spirit is revealed in this way as another divine
Person together with the Father and the Son.
This constitutes an announcement of the mystery
of the Blessed Trinity, which will be definitively
revealed when the Holy Spirit comes.

Genuine love must express itself in deeds (v.
15). "This indeed is love, obeying and believing
in the loved one" (St John Chrysostom, *In Ioannem*, 74). Therefore, Jesus wants us to see that, if
we truly love God, that love must be reflected in
a life of generous and faithful self-giving, obedi-

g Other ancient authotities add *me*

²⁰In that day you will know that I am in my Father, and you in me, and I in you. ²¹He who has my commandments and keeps them, he it is who loves me; and he who loves me will be loved by my Father, and I will love him and manifest myself to him. ²²Judas (not Iscariot) said to him, "Lord, how is it that you will manifest yourself to us, and not to the world?" ²³Jesus answered him, "If a man loves me, he will keep my word, and my Father will love him, and we will come to him and make our home with him. ²⁴He who does not love me does not keep my words; and the word which you hear is not mine but the Father's who sent me.

²⁵"These things I have spoken to you, while I am still with you. ²⁶But the Counsellor, the Holy Spirit, whom the Father will send in my name, he will teach you all things,* and bring to your remembrance all that I have said to you. ²⁷Peace I leave with you; my peace I give to you; not as the world gives do I give to you. Let not your hearts be troubled, neither let them be afraid. ²⁸You heard me say to you, 'I go away, and I will come to you.' If you loved me, you would have rejoiced, because I

Jn 17:21–23
1 Jn 5:3

Prov 8:17
Eph 3:17
2 Cor 6:16

Ex 25:8
Zech 2:14

Jn 7:16
1 Jn 2:5

Jn 14:16
Mt 10:19ff
1 Jn 2:27

Is 9:5–6
Zech 9:10
Jn 14:1; 16:33
Acts 10:36
Eph 2:14, 18

Jn 14:3, 6, 18
Lk 24:52

cognoscetis quia ego sum in Patre meo, et vos in me et ego in vobis. ²¹Qui habet mandata mea et servat ea, ille est qui diligit me; qui autem diligit me, diligetur a Patre meo, et ego diligam eum et manifestabo ei meipsum». ²²Dicit ei Iudas, non ille Iscariotes: «Domine, et quid factum est, quia nobis manifestaturus es teipsum et non mundo?». ²³Respondit Iesus et dixit ei: «Si quis diligit me, sermonem meum servabit, et Pater meus diliget eum, et ad eum veniemus et mansionem apud eum faciemus; ²⁴qui non diligit me, sermones meos non servat. Et sermo quem auditis, non est meus, sed eius qui misit me, Patris. ²⁵Haec locutus sum vobis apud vos manens. ²⁶Paraclitus autem, Spiritus Sanctus, quem mittet Pater in nomine meo, ille vos docebit omnia et suggeret vobis omnia, quae dixi vobis. ²⁷Pacem relinquo vobis, pacem meam do vobis; non quomodo mundus dat, ego do vobis. Non turbetur cor vestrum neque formidet. ²⁸Audistis quia ego dixi vobis: Vado et venio ad vos. Si diligeretis me, gauderetis quia vado

ent to the will of God: the person who accepts God's commandments and obeys them is the one who loves him (see v. 21).

"Counsellor" (v. 15): the Greek word sometimes anglicized as "paraclete" means someone "called to the side" of someone else, to accompany, console, protect, defend that other person. Hence the word is translated as "counsellor", "advocate" etc. Jesus speaks of the Holy Spirit as being "another Counsellor" because Jesus himself is our Advocate and Mediator in heaven beside the Father (see 1 Jn 2:1), and the Holy Spirit will be given to the disciples in his place when he ascends into heaven, as an Advocate or Protector who will aid them on earth.

As we make our way in this world, the Holy Spirit is our Counsellor, amid difficulties and against the temptation to feel disheartened. "In spite of our great limitations, we can look up to heaven with confidence and joy: God loves us and frees us from our sins. The presence and the action of the Holy Spirit in the Church are a foretaste of eternal happiness, of the joy and peace for which we are destined by God" (St Josemaría Escrivá, *Christ Is Passing By*, 128).

The apostles are surprised (v. 22) because they interpret Jesus' words as meant for them alone, whereas the commonly held opinion among Jews was that when the Messiah came he would be revealed to the whole world as a king and saviour. Jesus' reply (v. 23) may seem evasive but, in fact, in telling them how the Messiah will manifest himself, he is explaining why his glory is not manifest to the world at large: he makes himself known to those who love him and keep his commandments. God revealed himself repeatedly in the Old Testament, and promised that he would stay in the midst of his people (see Ex 29:45; Ezek 37:26–27) but here Jesus speaks of a presence in each person. St Paul refers to the same truth when he says that each of us is a temple of the Holy Spirit (see 1 Cor 6:19; 2 Cor 6:16).

The saints have drawn much consolation from the realization that the Trinity dwells in the soul of each person. "It was a sweet dream that shed light throughout my life, converting it into a heaven on earth" (Bl. Elizabeth of the Trinity, *Epistula*, 1906). And St Josemaría Escrivá, meditating on the indwelling of the Trinity in the soul, writes: "Our heart now needs to distinguish and adore each one of the divine Persons. The soul is, as it were, making a discovery in the supernatural life, like a little child opening his eyes to the world about him. The soul spends time lovingly with the Father and the Son and

go to the Father; for the Father is greater than I. [29]And now I have told you before it

Mk 14:36, 41–42
Jn 12:31
Eph 2:2

Mt 26:46
Mk 14:42

takes place, so that when it does take place, you may believe. [30]I will no longer talk much with you, for the ruler of this world is coming. He has no power over me; [31]but I do as the Father has commanded me, so that the world may know that I love the Father. Rise, let us go hence.

The vine and the branches

Hos 10:1
Is 5:1–7
Ezek 15:1–8
Jer 2:21
Ps 80:8–15, 18
Mt 15:13; 21:33
Jn 13:10

15 [1]"I am the true vine, and my Father is the vinedresser. [2]Every branch of mine that bears no fruit, he takes away, and every branch that does bear fruit he prunes that it may bear more fruit. [3]You are already made clean by the word which I have spoken to you. [4]Abide in me, and I in you. As the branch cannot bear fruit by

ad Patrem, quia Pater maior me est. [29]Et nunc dixi vobis, priusquam fiat, ut, cum factum fuerit, credatis. [30]Iam non multa loquar vobiscum, venit enim princeps mundi et in me non habet quidquam, [31]sed, ut cognoscat mundus quia diligo Patrem, et sicut mandatum dedit mihi Pater, sic facio. Surgite, eamus hinc.   [15] [1]Ego sum vitis vera, et Pater meus agricola est. [2]Omnem palmitem in me non ferentem fructum, tollit eum; et omnem, qui fert fructum, purgat eum, ut fructum plus afferat. [3]Iam vos mundi estis propter sermonem, quem locutus sum vobis. [4]Manete in me, et ego in vobis. Sicut palmes non potest ferre fructum a semetipso, nisi manserit in vite, sic nec vos, nisi in me manseritis. [5]Ego sum vitis, vos palmites.

the Holy Spirit, and readily submits to the work of the life-giving Paraclete, who gives himself to us with no merit on our part, bestowing his gifts and the supernatural virtues!" (*Friends of God*, 306).

The word translated here as "bring to [...] your remembrance" also includes the idea of suggestion: the Holy Spirit will remind the apostles' of what they have already heard Jesus say, and he will give them light to enable them to discover the depth and richness of it all. Thus, "the apostles handed on to their hearers what he had said and done, but with that fuller understanding which they, instructed by the glorious events of Christ and enlightened by the Spirit of truth, now enjoyed" (Vatican II, *Dei Verbum*, 18). "And so the Holy Spirit did teach them and remind them: he taught them what Christ had not said because they could not have taken it in, and he reminded them of what the Lord had taught and which, either because of the obscurity of the things or because of the dullness of their minds, they had not been able to retain" (Theophylact, *Enarratio in Evangelium Ioannis*, ad loc.).

Along with the gift of the Holy Spirit, the Christian also receives peace (v. 27), that is, reconciliation with God and with others (cf. Gal 5:22–23). The peace that Jesus sends transcends that of this world, which can be superficial and sometimes co-exist with great injustice.

When Jesus says that the Father is greater than he (v. 28), he is thinking of his human nature. As

man, Jesus will be glorified; he will *ascend* to the right hand of the Father. Jesus Christ "is equal to the Father in his divinity, less than the Father in his humanity" (Athanasian Creed).

The "world" (v. 30), as in many other passages, refers to all those who reject Christ; thus, the devil is the prince of that world (cf. 1:10; 7:7; 15:18–19; 16:8–11; 17:16). The devil has been opposing the work of Jesus from the start of his public life when he tempted him in the wilderness (see Mt 4:1–11 and par.). Now is the hour of the power of darkness (see Lk 22:53), when the devil, using Jesus' betrayer (see 13:27; Lk 22:1–6), succeeds in having our Lord arrested and crucified.

15:1–8 The image of the vine is used in the Old Testament to symbolize the people of Israel (Ps 80:8ff; Is 5:1–7; cf. Mt 21:33–43). Now, speaking of the branches, Jesus uses this image to describe how he and those united to him form the new Israel of God, the Church, whose head is Christ. To bear fruit, people must be joined to the true, new Vine, Christ. It is not a matter of simply belonging to a community but of living the life of Christ, the life of grace, which is the sap that gives life to believers and enables them to bear fruit of eternal life. "Through Christ and in him, we have been reborn in the Spirit to bear the fruit of life—not the old, spent life, but the new life rooted in love. This life is ours as long as we are united to him, as if grafted onto him. If

itself, unless it abides in the vine, neither can you, unless you abide in me. ⁵I am the ^{1 Cor 12:12, 27}
vine, you are the branches. He who abides in me, and I in him, he it is that bears ^{2 Cor 3:5}
much fruit, for apart from me you can do nothing. ⁶If a man does not abide in me, ^{Mt 3:10; 13:6, 40, 43}
he is cast forth as a branch and withers; and the branches are gathered, thrown into
the fire and burned. ⁷If you abide in me, and my words abide in you, ask whatever ^{Mk 11:24}
you will, and it shall be done for you. ⁸By this my Father is glorified, that you bear ^{Mt 5:16
Rom 7:4}
much fruit, and so prove to be my disciples.

The law of love

⁹As the Father has loved me, so have I loved you; abide in my love. ¹⁰If you keep ^{Jn 14:15; 8:29
1 Jn 2:4, 8}
my commandments, you will abide in my love, just as I have kept my Father's
commandments and abide in his love. ¹¹These things I have spoken to you, that my ^{Jn 16:24; 17:13
1 Jn 1:4}
joy may be in you, and that your joy may be full.
   ¹²"This is my commandment, that you love one another as I have loved you. ^{Jn 13:34–35
1 Jn 3:11
Mk 12:31}
¹³Greater love has no man than this, that a man lay down his life for his friends. ^{Jn 10:11
1 Jn 3:16}

Qui manet in me, et ego in eo, hic fert fructum multum, quia sine me nihil potestis facere. ⁶Si quis in me non manserit, missus est foras sicut palmes et aruit, et colligunt eos et in ignem mittunt, et ardent. ⁷Si manseritis in me, et verba mea in vobis manserint, quodcumque volueritis, petite, et fiet vobis. ⁸In hoc clarificatus est Pater meus, ut fructum multum afferatis et efficiamini mei discipuli. ⁹Sicut dilexit me Pater, et ego dilexi vos; manete in dilectione mea. ¹⁰Si praecepta mea servaveritis, manebitis in dilectione mea, sicut ego Patris mei praecepta servavi et maneo in eius dilectione. ¹¹Haec locutus sum vobis, ut gaudium meum in vobis sit, et gaudium vestrum impleatur. ¹²Hoc est praeceptum meum, ut diligatis invicem, sicut dilexi vos; ¹³maiorem hac dilectionem nemo habet, ut animam suam quis ponat pro amicis suis. ¹⁴Vos amici mei estis, si feceritis,

we faithfully carry out the commandments he gave us and carefully guard his great gifts, and strive with all our might never to sadden the Spirit that lives in our hearts in even the slightest way, then through him God will dwell in our souls" (St Cyril of Alexandria, *Commentarium in Ioannem*, 10, 2).

   The Second Vatican Council, quoting this passage from St John, has this to say about the apostolate that Christians should carry out: "Christ, sent by the Father, is the source of the Church's whole apostolate. Clearly then, the fruitfulness of the apostolate of lay people depends on their living union with Christ; as the Lord said himself: 'He who abides in me, and I in him, he it is that bears much fruit, for apart from me you can do nothing.' This life of intimate union with Christ in the Church is maintained by the spiritual helps common to all the faithful, chiefly by active participation in the liturgy. Laymen should make such a use of these helps that, while meeting their human obligations in the ordinary conditions of life, they do not separate their union with Christ from their ordinary life; but through the very performance of their tasks, which are God's will for them, actually promote the growth of their union with him" (*Apostolicam actuositatem*, 4).

   The image of the vine also helps us see what the unity of the Church, Christ's Mystical Body, entails; all its members are intimately united to the Head and thereby to one another (see 1 Cor 12:12–27; Rom 12:4–5; Eph 4:15–16). A person not united to Christ through grace will end up like a dead branch on the fire (v. 6). There is a clear parallel between this image and others used by our Lord in his preaching about hell—those of the sound tree versus the bad tree (Mt 7:16–20), of the net (Mt 13:47–50), of the guest without the wedding garment (Mt 22:11–14), etc.

15:9–17 Having a genuine love for Jesus involves making an effort to keep God's commandments, particularly the commandment of brotherly love, his keeping of which led Christ to the cross. Love, not fear, is what should inspire us to keep the commandments: it is a matter of responding to the One who first loved us and who proved his love for us on the cross. The friendship between Christ and every Christian, which our Lord expresses so clearly in this passage, led St John of the Cross to write: "Call him Beloved to spur him to answer your prayers, for when God is loved he is not slow to respond to the petitions of the one who loves him. [...] The

Jn 8:31
Mt 12:50; 28:10
Jn 12:26
Jn 13:18
Rom 6:20–23

[14]You are my friends if you do what I command you. [15]No longer do I call you servants,[h] for the servant[i] does not know what his master is doing; but I have called you friends, for all that I have heard from my Father I have made known to you. [16]You did not choose me, but I chose you and appointed you that you should go and bear fruit and that your fruit should abide; so that whatever you ask the Father in my name, he may give it to you. [17]This I command you, to love one another.

A hostile world

Jn 7:7
1 Jn 3:13
Jn 17:14–16
1 Jn 4:5
Jn 13:16
Mt 10:24

[18]"If the world hates you, know that it has hated me before it hated you.* [19]If you were of the world, the world would love its own; but because you are not of the world, but I chose you out of the world, therefore the world hates you. [20]Remember the word that I said to you, 'A servant[i] is not greater than his master.' If they persecuted me, they will persecute you; if they kept my word, they will keep yours also.

Mt 5:11; 10:23
Mk 13:13
Lk 6:22
Acts 5:41
1 Pet 4:14
Jn 5:23
1 Jn 2:23
Jn 9:41; 14:11
Ps 35:19; 109:3
Lk 24:49
Jn 14:16–17, 26
Lk 1:2
Acts 1:8; 5:32

[21]But all this they will do to you on my account, because they do not know him who sent me. [22]If I had not come and spoken to them, they would not have sin; but now they have no excuse for their sin. [23]He who hates me hates my Father also. [24]If I had not done among them the works which no one else did, they would not have sin; but now they have seen and hated both me and my Father. [25]It is to fulfil the word that is written in their law, 'They hated me without a cause.' [26]But when the Counsellor comes, whom I shall send to you from the Father, even the Spirit of truth, who proceeds from the Father, he will bear witness to me; [27]and you also are witnesses, because you have been with me from the beginning.

quae ego praecipio vobis. [15]Iam non dico vos servos, quia servus nescit quid facit dominus eius; vos autem dixi amicos, quia omnia, quae audivi a Patre meo, nota feci vobis. [16]Non vos me elegistis, sed ego elegi vos et posui vos, ut vos eatis et fructum afferatis, et fructus vester maneat, ut quodcumque petieritis Patrem in nomine meo, det vobis. [17]Haec mando vobis, ut diligatis invicem. [18]Si mundus vos odit, scitote quia me priorem vobis odio habuit. [19]Si de mundo essetis, mundus, quod suum est, diligeret; quia vero de mundo non estis, sed ego elegi vos de mundo, propterea odit vos mundus. [20]Mementote sermonis, quem ego dixi vobis: Non est servus maior domino suo. Si me persecuti sunt, et vos persequentur; si sermonem meum servaverunt, et vestrum servabunt. [21]Sed haec omnia facient vobis propter nomen meum, quia nesciunt eum, qui misit me. [22]Si non venissem et locutus fuissem eis, peccatum non haberent; nunc autem excusationem non habent de peccato suo. [23]Qui me odit, et Patrem meum odit. [24]Si opera non fecissem in eis, quae nemo alius fecit, peccatum non haberent; nunc autem et viderunt et oderunt et me et Patrem meum. [25]Sed ut impleatur sermo, qui in lege eorum scriptus est: *"Odio me habuerunt gratis"*. [26]Cum autem venerit Paraclitus, quem ego mittam vobis a Patre, Spiritum veritatis, qui a Patre procedit, ille testimonium perhibebit de me; [27]sed et vos testimonium perhibetis, quia ab initio mecum estis.

Christian soul can truly call him Beloved when his mind and heart are set on him alone" (*Spiritual Canticle*, 1, 13).

15:18–27 Sin appears to triumph in the world, but Jesus makes it clear that there can be no compromise between him and the world: everyone who does evil hates the light (see 3:19–20). That is the root cause of people's persecution of Christ, and the reason why they will persecute the apostles: "The hostility of the perverse sounds like praise for our life," St Gregory the Great says, "because it shows that we have at least some rectitude if we are an annoyance to those who do not love God; no one can be pleasing to God and to God's enemies at the same time. He who seeks to please those who oppose God is no friend of God; and he who submits

himself to the truth will fight against those who strive against the truth" (*Homiliae in Ezechielem*, 1, 9, 14).

Those who deny Christ would not be guilty of sin for that, had he not revealed himself by his works. It would be different if the Light had not shone in the darkness; but as it is, they have no excuse: by rejecting Christ, they reject God's truth (cf. Ps 35:19): "This is the sin," St Augustine comments, "that they did not believe in what Christ said and did. We are not to suppose that they had no sin before he spoke to them and worked miracles among them; but this sin, their not believing in him, is mentioned in this way, because in this sin of unbelief are all other sins rooted. For if they had believed in him, the rest would be forgiven" (*In Ioannis Evangelium*, 91, 1).

h Or *slaves* i Or *slave*

The action of the Holy Spirit

16 ¹"I have said all this to you to keep you from falling away. ²They will put you out of the synagogues; indeed, the hour is coming when whoever kills you will think he is offering service to God. ³And they will do this because they have not known the Father, nor me. ⁴But I have said these things to you, that when their hour comes you may remember that I told you of them.

"I did not say these things to you from the beginning, because I was with you. ⁵But now I am going to him who sent me; yet none of you asks me, 'Where are you going?' ⁶But because I have said these things to you, sorrow has filled your hearts. ⁷Nevertheless I tell you the truth: it is to your advantage that I go away, for if I do not go away, the Counsellor will not come to you; but if I go, I will send him to you. ⁸And when he comes, he will convince the world of sin and of righteousness and of judgment: ⁹of sin, because they do not believe in me; ¹⁰of righteousness, because I

Jn 9:22; 12:42
1 Thess 2:14
Mt 5:11; 24:9
Lk 6:22
Jn 15:21
Jn 17:12

Jn 7:33; 13:36; 14:5

Jn 14:15–16, 26; 26:28

1 Cor 14:24

Jn 8:24; 15:22
Rom 1:18

[16] ¹Haec locutus sum vobis, ut non scandalizemini. ²Absque synagogis facient vos; sed venit hora, ut omnis, qui interficit vos, arbitretur obsequium se praestare Deo. ³Et haec facient, quia non noverunt Patrem neque me. ⁴Sed haec locutus sum vobis, ut, cum venerit hora eorum, reminiscamini eorum, quia ego dixi vobis. Haec autem vobis ab initio non dixi, quia vobiscum eram. ⁵At nunc vado ad eum, qui me misit, et nemo ex vobis interrogat me: "Quo vadis?". ⁶Sed quia haec locutus sum vobis, tristitia implevit cor vestrum. ⁷Sed ego veritatem dico vobis: Expedit vobis, ut ego vadam. Si enim non abiero, Paraclitus non veniet ad vos; si autem abiero, mittam eum ad vos. ⁸Et cum venerit ille, arguet mundum de peccato et de iustitia et de iudicio: ⁹de peccato quidem, quia non credunt in me; ¹⁰de iustitia vero, quia ad Patrem vado, et iam non videtis me; ¹¹de iudicio autem, quia princeps mundi huius iudicatus est. ¹²Adhuc multa habeo vobis dicere, sed non potestis portare modo. ¹³Cum autem venerit

16:1–15 Jesus predicts that those who do not know the Father or his Christ will persecute Jesus' disciples just as they persecuted him and put him to death (cf. 15:18–20). And they will believe that they are serving God by doing so (v. 2). Fanaticism can lead people to think it is lawful to commit crimes in the service of religion (cf. the note on Lk 14:1–6).

The persecutions and trials that Christ's followers will inevitably experience should not scandalize or dishearten them. On the contrary, being, as they are, consoled and comforted by the Holy Spirit, Christians should turn difficulties to good purpose and let their faith be seen. St Bede points out that our Lord comes to their aid "so that their souls, which have not yet been fully formed, will not be troubled by a sudden, unexpected time of trial, even if that time lasts only for a short while; rather, by knowing of it in advance, and through patient acceptance of its coming, the time of trouble will lead them to eternal life" (*In Ioannis Evangelium expositio*, ad loc.).

Jesus mentions the Paraclete three times in the Supper Sermon. On the first occasion (14:15ff), he says another Consoler will be sent by the Father to stay with them for ever; on the second (14:26), he says that the Father will send the Holy Spirit in his name to teach them all things; and in this third passage (vv. 1–15) he

announces that his ascension will lead to the sending of the Holy Spirit and the work of the Spirit, which the world and Jesus' disciples will see for themselves. The Holy Spirit will lead the disciples to a full understanding of the truth revealed by Christ. (Cf. the note on 14:15–31.)

In vv. 8–11, the word "world" means those who do not believe in Christ and have rejected him (cf. 14:30). These the Spirit will convince "of sin and of righteousness and of judgment" (v. 8) — "of sin", on account of their unbelief; "of righteousness", because Jesus was the Just One who never committed sin (cf. 8:46; Heb 4:15) and therefore sits in glory at the Father's side; and "of judgment", by making it clear that the devil, the prince of this world, has been vanquished by Christ's death which has redeemed man from the power of the Evil One and enabled him, through grace, to escape the devil's snares. "Men believe in Christ so that they will not stand accused of the sin of infidelity, and thus be stripped of all God's great gifts. They count themselves among the faithful so that they will not be condemned by the just lives of those who have been justified in Christ. They hope to be spared future condemnation so that they will not be judged with the prince of this world, who has been judged and condemned" (St Bede, *In Ioannis Evangelium expositio*, ad loc.).

Jn 12:31; 14:30 go to the Father, and you will see me no more;* [11]of judgment, because the ruler of this world is judged.

Jn 14:26
Is 42:9
Dan 2:20–22
Jn 17:10;12:26
1 Jn 2:27

[12]"I have yet many things to say to you, but you cannot bear them now. [13]When the Spirit of truth comes, he will guide you into all the truth; for he will not speak of his own authority, but whatever he hears he will speak, and he will declare to you the things that are to come. [14]He will glorify me, for he will take what is mine and declare it to you. [15]All that the Father has is mine; therefore I said that he will take what is mine and declare it to you.

Fullness of joy

Jn 7:33; 12:35;
13:33; 14:19

[16]"A little while, and you will see me no more; again a little while, and you will see me." [17]Some of his disciples said to one another, "What is this that he says to us, 'A little while, and you will not see me, and again a little while, and you will see me'; and, 'because I go to the Father'?" [18]They said, "What does he mean by 'a little

Lk 9:45 while'? We do not know what he means." [19]Jesus knew that they wanted to ask him; so he said to them, "Is this what you are asking yourselves, what I meant by saying, 'A little while, and you will not see me, and again a little while, and you will see

Jn 11:31, 33; 20:11,
13, 15
Rev 11:10 me'? [20]Truly, truly, I say to you, you will weep and lament, but the world will rejoice; you will be sorrowful, but your sorrow will turn into joy. [21]When a woman

Is 26:17–18; 66:14
Mic 4:9–10 is in travail she has sorrow, because her hour has come; but when she is delivered of

---

ille, Spiritus veritatis, deducet vos in omnem veritatem; non enim loquetur a semetipso, sed quaecumque audiet, loquetur et, quae ventura sunt, annuntiabit vobis. [14]Ille me clarificabit, quia de meo accipiet et annuntiabit vobis. [15]Omnia, quaecumque habet Pater, mea sunt; propterea dixi quia de meo accipit et annuntiabit vobis. [16]Modicum, et iam non videtis me, et iterum modicum, et videbitis me». [17]Dixerunt ergo ex discipulis eius ad invicem: «Quid est hoc, quod dicit nobis: "Modicum, et non videtis me, et iterum modicum et videbitis me" et: "Vado ad Patrem"?». [18]Dicebant ergo: «Quid est hoc, quod dicit: "Modicum"? Nescimus quid loquitur». [19]Cognovit Iesus quia volebant eum interrogare et dixit eis: «De hoc quaeritis inter vos quia dixi: "Modicum, et non videtis me, et iterum modicum, et videbitis me"? [20]Amen, amen dico vobis quia plorabitis et flebitis vos, mundus autem gaudebit; vos contristabimini, sed tristitia vestra vertetur in gaudium. [21]Mulier, cum parit, tristitiam habet, quia venit hora eius; cum autem pepererit puerum, iam non meminit pressurae propter gaudium quia natus est homo in mundum. [22]Et vos igitur nunc quidem tris-

---

Verses 14 and 15 reveal special aspects of the mystery of the Trinity. They show the equality of the three divine Persons: everything that the Father has is the Son's, and everything that the Son has is the Father's, and the Holy Spirit also has what is common to the Father and the Son, that is, the divine essence.

16:16–33 The apostles fail to grasp what Jesus says about his death and resurrection (vv. 16–18). When he tells them that after suffering tribulation they will be filled with a joy that they will never lose (v. 22; 17:13), he is referring primarily to the joy of the Resurrection (cf. Lk 24:41), as well as to that of their definitive encounter with Christ in heaven (cf. 17:24).

The image of the woman giving birth (v. 21), often used in the Old Testament to describe intense pain, is also used by the prophets with reference to the birth of the new messianic people (see Is 26:17; Jer 30:6; Hos 13:13; Mic

4:9–10). The birth of the new People of God (Christ's Church) will involve intense pain, not only for Christ but also, to some degree, for the apostles. But this pain, like the pain of labour, will be made up for by the joy that the Kingdom has come at last (cf. Rom 8:18).

After his resurrection Jesus will speak plainly to his apostles, and they will begin to understand the mystery of his passion and the greatness of God's love that led him to send his Son into the world. In the meantime, the disciples' faith is firmly based on the conviction that the Lord reads all hearts and knows all things (v. 30; cf. 2:25). His prediction that they will leave him on his own (v. 32) will be a consolation to them when they remember it after his resurrection, when they gather round him again. When they undergo trials and suffer at the hands of those who reject Christ, Jesus' words will resound in their ears: "Be of good cheer, I have overcome the world" (v. 33).

the child, she no longer remembers the anguish, for joy that a child[j] is born into the world. [22]So you have sorrow now, but I will see you again and your hearts will rejoice, and no one will take your joy from you. [23]In that day you will ask nothing of me. Truly, truly, I say to you, if you ask anything of the Father, he will give it to you in my name. [24]Hitherto you have asked nothing in my name; ask, and you will receive, that your joy may be full.

[25]"I have said this to you in figures; the hour is coming when I shall no longer speak to you in figures but tell you plainly of the Father. [26]In that day you will ask in my name; and I do not say to you that I shall pray the Father for you; [27]for the Father himself loves you, because you have loved me and have believed that I came from the Father. [28]I came from the Father and have come into the world; again, I am leaving the world and going to the Father."

[29]His disciples said, "Ah, now you are speaking plainly, not in any figure! [30]Now we know that you know all things, and need none to question you; by this we believe that you came from God." [31]Jesus answered them, "Do you now believe? [32]The hour is coming, indeed it has come, when you will be scattered, every man to his home, and will leave me alone; yet I am not alone, for the Father is with me. [33]I have said this to you, that in me you may have peace. In the world you have tribulation; but be of good cheer, I have overcome the world."

The priestly prayer of Jesus

17 [1]When Jesus had spoken these words, he lifted his eyes to heaven and said,* "Father, the hour has come, glorify thy Son that the Son may glorify thee,

Margin references:
Jn 20:20
Jn 14:13, 20; 16:15
1 Jn 5:14
Mt 7:7
Jn 15:11
1 Jn 1:4
Jn 10:6; 14:6
Mt 13:34–35
Jn 14:21, 23
Jn 16:25
Jn 2:25
Mt 26:31, 45, 56
Mk 14:27, 50
Jn 8:29; 18:10–27
Jn 8:16, 29; 14:27
Rom 5:1
1 Cor 15:54–58
1 Jn 5:4
Mt 11:25–27
Mk 14:36
Jn 11:41; 13:31

titiam habetis; iterum autem videbo vos, et gaudebit cor vestrum, et gaudium vestrum nemo tollit a vobis. [23]Et in illo die me non rogabitis quidquam. Amen, amen dico vobis: Si quid petieritis Patrem in nomine meo, dabit vobis. [24]Usque modo non petistis quidquam in nomine meo. Petite et accipietis, ut gaudium vestrum sit plenum. [25]Haec in proverbiis locutus sum vobis; venit hora, cum iam non in proverbiis loquar vobis, sed palam de Patre annuntiabo vobis. [26]Illo die in nomine meo petetis, et non dico vobis quia ego rogabo Patrem de vobis; [27]ipse enim Pater amat vos, quia vos me amastis et credidistis quia ego a Deo exivi. [28]Exivi a Patre et veni in mundum; iterum relinquo mundum et vado ad Patrem». [29]Dicunt discipuli eius: «Ecce nunc palam loqueris, et proverbium nullum dicis. [30]Nunc scimus quia scis omnia et non opus est tibi, ut quis te interroget; in hoc credimus quia a Deo existi». [31]Respondit eis Iesus: «Modo creditis? [32]Ecce venit hora et iam venit, ut dispergamini unusquisque in propria et me solum relinquatis; et non sum solus, quia Pater mecum est. [33]Haec locutus sum vobis, ut in me pacem habeatis; in mundo pressuram habetis, sed confidite, ego vici mundum». [17] [1]Haec locutus est Iesus; et sublevatis oculis suis in caelum dixit: «Pater, venit hora: clarifica Filium tuum, ut Filius clarificet te, [2]sicut dedisti ei potestatem omnis carnis, ut omne, quod dedisti ei, det eis vitam aeternam. [3]Haec est autem vita

17:1–26 At the end of the discourse, Jesus addresses his Father in a very moving dialogue in which, as Priest, he offers up to him the imminent sacrifice of his passion and death. This section is known as the "Priestly Prayer of Jesus".

In the first part of this prayer (vv. 1–5), Jesus asks for the glorification of his holy human nature and for the acceptance by the Father of his sacrifice on the cross. The word "glory" here refers to the splendour, power and honour that belong to God. The glorification of Jesus has three aspects to it. (1) It reveals the glory of the Father, because Christ, in obedience to God's redemptive decree, makes the Father known (v. 4). (2) Christ's divinity is manifested through his human nature (vv. 2 and 5). (3) Christ, through his glorification, makes it possible for man to

attain eternal life, and this in turn redounds to the glorification of the Father and of Jesus (vv. 2–3). "The Son glorifies you, making you known to all those you have given him. Furthermore, if the knowledge of God is life eternal, we the more tend to life, the more we advance in this knowledge. [...] There shall the praise of God be without end, where there shall be full knowledge of God; and because in heaven this knowledge shall be full, there shall glorifying be of the highest" (St Augustine, *In Ioannis Evangelium*, 105, 3).

In the second part of the prayer (vv. 6–19) Jesus prays for his disciples, whom he sends into the world to spread the good news of redemption. He asks for them to be given perseverance, joy and holiness. By asking the Father to keep them in his name (v. 11), he is asking for their

j Greek *a human being*

Is 40:5

Wis 15:3
Jer 31:31–34
Jn 3:15, 16
1 Jn 5:20

Jn 4:34

Jn 17:24; 1:1
Phil 2:6–11

Jn 12:45; 14:9; 17:9
Mt 6:9

Jn 14:21, 24; 16:30

Jn 6:37, 44, 65

Jn 16:15
Lk 15:31

Jn 6:44; 10:30
Mt 6:13

Jn 6:39

2 Thess 2:3
Jn 13:18; 15:11
Acts 1:16, 20
1 Jn 1:4

Jn 15:19

²since thou hast given him power over all flesh, to give eternal life to all whom thou hast given him. ³And this is eternal life, that they know thee the only true God, and Jesus Christ whom thou hast sent. ⁴I glorified thee on earth, having accomplished the work which thou gavest me to do; ⁵and now, Father, glorify thou me in thy own presence with the glory which I had with thee before the world was made.*

⁶"I have manifested thy name to the men whom thou gavest me out of the world; thine they were, and thou gavest them to me, and they have kept thy word. ⁷Now they know that everything that thou hast given me is from thee; ⁸for I have given them the words which thou gavest me, and they have received them and know in truth that I came from thee; and they have believed that thou didst send me. ⁹I am praying for them; I am not praying for the world but for those whom thou hast given me, for they are thine; ¹⁰all mine are thine, and thine are mine, and I am glorified in them. ¹¹And now I am no more in the world, but they are in the world, and I am coming to thee. Holy Father, keep them in thy name, which thou hast given me, that they may be one, even as we are one. ¹²While I was with them, I kept them in my name, which thou hast given me; I have guarded them, and none of them is lost but the son of perdition, that the scripture might be fulfilled. ¹³But now I am coming to thee; and these things I speak in the world, that they may have my joy fulfilled in themselves. ¹⁴I have given them thy word; and the world has hated them because

aeterna, ut cognoscant te solum verum Deum et, quem misisti, Iesum Christum. ⁴Ego te clarificavi super terram: opus consummavi, quod dedisti mihi, ut faciam; ⁵et nunc clarifica me tu, Pater, apud temetipsum claritate, quam habebam, priusquam mundus esset, apud te. ⁶Manifestavi nomen tuum hominibus, quos dedisti mihi de mundo. Tui erant, et mihi eos dedisti, et sermonem tuum servaverunt. ⁷Nunc cognoverunt quia omnia, quae dedisti mihi, abs te sunt, ⁸quia verba, quae dedisti mihi, dedi eis, et ipsi acceperunt et cognoverunt vere quia a te exivi, et crediderunt quia tu me misisti. ⁹Ego pro eis rogo; non pro mundo rogo, sed pro his, quos dedisti mihi, quia tui sunt, ¹⁰et mea omnia tua sunt et tua mea; et clarificatus sum in eis. ¹¹Et iam non sum in mundo, et hi in mundo sunt, et ego ad te venio. Pater sancte, serva eos in nomine tuo, quod dedisti mihi, ut sint unum sicut nos. ¹²Cum essem cum eis, ego servabam eos in nomine tuo, quod dedisti mihi et custodivi, et nemo ex his periit nisi filius perditio-

fidelity to his teaching (cf. v. 6) and for their communion with him. One result of this communion is unity among themselves, which is a reflection of the unity of the three divine Persons, among whom mutual love and self-giving reign. "The Lord Jesus, when praying to the Father 'that they may all be one … even as we are one' (Jn 17:21–22), has opened up new horizons closed to human reason by implying that there is a certain parallel between the union existing among the divine persons and the union of the sons of God in truth and love. It follows, then, that if man is the only creature on earth that God has wanted for its own sake, man can fully discover his true self only in a sincere giving of himself" (Vatican II, *Gaudium et spes*, 24).

Our Lord also prays for those who, though living in the world, are not of the world—that they may be sanctified in the truth of God's word (v. 17) and carry out the mission he entrusts to them, just as he will have carried out the work his Father gave him to do (v. 18). The term "world" has a number of meanings in the Gospel

of St John (cf. the note on 14:15–31). Firstly, it means the whole of creation, including the human race, of which God loves each member most tenderly for who he or she is (see 1:10; 3:16; 13:1); but "world" also refers to the things of this world, which do not last, and to the people who live solely for them and have no interest in the things of the spirit (see 7:7; 8:23). So, Jesus' prayer to the Father (v. 15) implies an invitation to his disciples to respond to God's love: "Be men and women of the world, but don't be worldly men and women" (St Josemaría Escrivá, *The Way*, 939).

By his death on the cross, Jesus consecrates himself to God in order to sanctify us (vv. 17–19): "When he says *sanctifico* [v. 19: 'I consecrate myself'] we should read 'I dedicate myself to God' or 'I offer myself as the sweet, immaculate host'. According to the Law, what was offered on the altar in the temple was sanctified or consecrated to God. Christ offered his body for our sake, and true life was granted to us" (St Cyril of Alexandria, *Commentarium in Ioannem*, 4, 2).

they are not of the world, even as I am not of the world. [15]I do not pray that thou shouldst take them out of the world, but that thou shouldst keep them from the evil one.[k] [16]They are not of the world, even as I am not of the world. [17]Sanctify them in the truth; thy word is truth. [18]As thou didst send me into the world, so I have sent them into the world. [19]And for their sake I consecrate myself, that they also may be consecrated in truth.

[20]"I do not pray for these only, but also for those who believe in me through their word, [21]that they may all be one; even as thou, Father, art in me, and I in thee, that they also may be in us, so that the world may believe that thou hast sent me. [22]The glory which thou hast given me I have given to them, that they may be one even as we are one, [23]I in them and thou in me, that they may become perfectly one, so that the world may know that thou hast sent me and hast loved them even as thou has loved me. [24]Father, I desire that they also, whom thou hast given me, may be with me where I am, to behold my glory which thou has given me in thy love for me before the foundation of the world. [25]O righteous Father, the world has not known thee, but I have known thee; and these know that thou hast sent me. [26]I made known to them thy name, and I will make it known, that the love with which thou has loved me may be in them, and I in them."

2 Thess 3:3
1 Jn 5:18
Mt 6:13

Jn 16:13
Jn 20:21

Heb 2:11; 9:13–14
Jn 17:9

Gal 3:28

Acts 4:32

1 Cor 6:17
Gal 2:20

Jn 10:29; 12:26, 32;
14:3
Eph 1:4

Ps 116:5
Rom 3:26

Ex 3:13
Lev 26:11–12
Jer 31:31
Ezek 36:28; 37:27
Jn 17:6

nis, ut Scriptura impleatur. [13]Nunc autem ad te venio et haec loquor in mundo, ut habeant gaudium meum impletum in semetipsis. [14]Ego dedi eis sermonem tuum, et mundus odio eos habuit, quia non sunt de mundo, sicut ego non sum de mundo. [15]Non rogo, ut tollas eos de mundo, sed ut serves eos ex Malo. [16]De mundo non sunt, sicut ego non sum de mundo. [17]Sanctifica eos in veritate; sermo tuus veritas est. [18]Sicut me misisti in mundum, et ego misi eos in mundum; [19]et pro eis ego sanctifico meipsum, ut sint et ipsi sanctificati in veritate. [20]Non pro his autem rogo tantum, sed et pro eis, qui credituri sunt per verbum eorum in me, [21]ut omnes unum sint, sicut tu, Pater, in me et ego in te, ut et ipsi in nobis unum sint: ut mundus credat quia tu me misisti. [22]Et ego claritatem, quam dedisti mihi, dedi illis, ut sint unum, sicut nos unum sumus; [23]ego in eis, et tu in me, ut sint consummati in unum: ut cognoscat mundus quia tu me misisti et dilexisti eos, sicut me dilexisti. [24]Pater, quod dedisti mihi, volo, ut ubi ego sum, et illi sint mecum, ut videant claritatem meam, quam dedisti mihi, quia dilexisti me ante constitutionem mundi. [25]Pater iuste, et mundus te non cognovit; ego autem te cognovi et hi cognoverunt quia tu me misisti, [26]et notum feci eis nomen tuum et notum faciam, ut dilectio, qua dilex-

In the third part of his priestly prayer (vv. 20–26), Jesus again asks that all who believe in him should remain united throughout history: this is his prayer for the Church, which should be one just as the Father and the Son are one: "When we have received one and the same Spirit, the Holy Spirit, we are made one with one another and with God. Although we are many, and Christ brings the Spirit of the Father to live in each one of us, this one, indivisible Spirit makes of many, one — different as we are, unique, the Spirit makes us one" (ibid., 11, 11).

The main fruit of the unity of the Church will be belief in Christ and in his divine mission (vv. 21, 23). "Jesus Christ wishes his people to increase [...] and he perfects its fellowship in unity: in the confession of one faith, in the common celebration of divine worship, and in the fraternal harmony of the family of God. [...] The highest exemplar and source of this mystery is the unity, in the Trinity of Persons, of one God, the Father and the Son in the Holy Spirit" (Vatican II, *Unitatis redintegratio*, 2). Following Christ's example, the same Council repeatedly calls for prayer for the unity of Christians, defining that unity as "the soul of the ecumenical movement" (ibid., 8).

Jesus concludes his prayer by expressing his desire that all Christians attain the blessedness of heaven (vv. 24–26). The words he uses ("I desire", not "I pray") indicate that he is asking for the most important thing of all; and it is what the Father desires — that all may be saved and come to a knowledge of the truth (cf. 1 Tim 2:4).

God's revelation of himself through Christ begins our participation in the divine life, and this will reach its climax in heaven: "God alone can give us the right and full knowledge of this reality by revealing himself as Father, Son and Holy Spirit, in whose eternal life we are by grace called to share, here below in the obscurity of faith and after death in eternal light" (Paul VI, *Creed of the People of God*).

k Or *from evil*

10. THE PASSION AND DEATH OF JESUS*

Arrest of Jesus

18 ¹When Jesus had spoken these words, he went forth with his disciples across the Kidron valley, where there was a garden, which he and his disciples

entered. ²Now Judas, who betrayed him, also knew the place; for Jesus often met there with his disciples. ³So Judas, procuring a band of soldiers and some officers from the chief priests and the Pharisees, went there with lanterns and torches and

weapons. ⁴Then Jesus, knowing all that was to befall him, came forward and said to them, "Whom do you seek?" ⁵They answered him, "Jesus of Nazareth." Jesus said

to them, "I am he." Judas, who betrayed him, was standing with them. ⁶When he said to them, "I am he," they drew back and fell to the ground. ⁷Again he asked

isti me, in ipsis sit, et ego in ipsis». [18] ¹Haec cum dixisset Iesus, egressus est cum discipulis suis trans torrentem Cedron, ubi erat hortus, in quem introivit ipse et discipuli eius. ²Sciebat autem et Iudas, qui tradebat eum, locum, quia frequenter Iesus convenerat illuc cum discipulis suis. ³Iudas ergo, cum accepisset cohortem et a pontificibus et pharisaeis ministros, venit illuc cum lanternis et facibus et armis. ⁴Iesus itaque, sciens omnia, quae ventura erant super eum, processit et dicit eis: «Quem quaeritis?». ⁵Responderunt ei: «Iesum Nazarenum». Dicit eis: «Ego sum!». Stabat autem et Iudas, qui tradebat eum, cum ipsis. ⁶Ut ergo dixit eis: «Ego sum!», abierunt retrorsum et ceciderunt in terram. ⁷Iterum ergo eos interrogavit: «Quem quaeritis?». Illi autem dixerunt: «Iesum Nazarenum». ⁸Respondit Iesus: «Dixi vobis: Ego sum! Si ergo me quaeritis, sinite

*18:1—19:42 The Gospel of St John portrays the passion and death of Christ as his glorification. It goes into great detail in order to demonstrate that these events constitute the supreme manifestation of Jesus as the Messiah King. For example, when he replies, "I am he", those who have come to arrest him draw back and fall to the ground (18:5–8); when he is before Pilate, he declares himself to be a king (18:33–37; cf. 19:2–3, 19–22); and, throughout, his dignified serenity shows his complete understanding and control of events (18:4; 19:28), all of which are in keeping with the Father's will (18:11; 19:30).

The passion is also the point when Jesus' enemies and the world vent their hatred most savagely: it is the hour of a darkness that engulfs even his disciples, for they run away and deny they know him (18:25–27). But at the foot of the cross we witness the supreme act of faith: it is made by Mary, his Mother, whom he makes a Mother to all mankind in the person of the beloved disciple (19:25–27). Christ is the new Passover Lamb, by whose redemptive death the sin of the world is washed away (19:31–42; 1:29, 36). And there flows from our Lord's side, along with blood, water that symbolizes Baptism and the Holy Spirit that Jesus has promised (see 7:37–39), that is to say, the sacramental life of the Church.

18:1–12 On the other side of the Kidron valley

(v. 1) is situated what the Synoptics call Gethsemane. It is the first of five settings where the sufferings of Christ take place. St John does not record Jesus' agony in the Garden of Olives, but he is the only one to report that the people who come to arrest Jesus draw back and fall to the ground when Jesus identifies himself (vv. 4–6). This passage is reminiscent of Psalm 56:9, the first part of which reads, "Then my enemies will be turned back in the day when I call." Our Lord's majesty is clear to see: he surrenders himself of his own free will. "Had he not allowed himself to be taken by them, they would have been unable to effect their plan, but neither would he have done what he came to do. They in their rage sought him to put him to death; but he also sought us by dying for us" (St Augustine, *In Ioannis Evangelium*, 112, 3).

It is moving to see how Jesus is concerned about the fate of his disciples when it is himself who is in danger (v. 8). He promised that none of his own would perish, except Judas Iscariot (see 6:39; 17:12); although that promise was a promise to protect them from eternal punishment, our Lord is also concerned about their immediate safety, for they are not yet ready to face martyrdom.

Once again we can see Peter's impetuous nature and his loyalty: he comes to Jesus' defence, risking his own life (v. 10). However, Peter still does not understand God's plan of sal-

them, "Whom do you seek?" And they said, "Jesus of Nazareth," [8]Jesus answered, "I told you that I am he; so, if you seek me, let these men go." [9]This was to fulfil the word which he had spoken, "Of those whom you gavest me I lost not one." [10]Then Simon Peter, having a sword, drew it and struck the high priest's slave and cut off his right ear. The slave's name was Malchus. [11]Jesus said to Peter, "Put your sword into its sheath; shall I not drink the cup which the Father has given me?"

[12]So the band of soldiers and their captain and the officers of the Jews seized Jesus and bound him.

Jesus before the chief priests. Peter's denials

[13]First they led him to Annas; for he was the father-in-law of Caiaphas, who was high priest that year.* [14]It was Caiaphas who had given counsel to the Jews that it was expedient that one man should die for the people.

[15]Simon Peter followed Jesus, and so did another disciple. As this disciple was known to the high priest, he entered the court of the high priest along with Jesus, [16]while Peter stood outside at the door. So the other disciple, who was known to the high priest, went out and spoke to the maid who kept the door, and brought Peter in. [17]The maid who kept the door said to Peter, "Are not you also one of this man's dis-

Margin references:
Jn 6:39; 17:12

Mt 26:39
Mk 10:38
Jn 10:17–18

Mt 26:57–75
Mk 14:53–72
Lk 22:54–71

Lk 3:2
Acts 4:6
Jn 11:49, 50

Jn 20:2–4
Acts 3:1

hos abire», [9]ut impleretur sermo quem dixit: «Quos dedisti mihi, non perdidi ex ipsis quemquam». [10]Simon ergo Petrus, habens gladium, eduxit eum et percussit pontificis servum et abscidit eius auriculam dextram. Erat autem nomen servo Malchus. [11]Dixit ergo Iesus Petro: «Mitte gladium in vaginam; calicem, quem dedit mihi Pater, non bibam illum?». [12]Cohors ergo et tribunus et ministri Iudaeorum comprehenderunt Iesum et ligaverunt eum [13]et adduxerunt ad Annam primum; erat enim socer Caiphae, qui erat pontifex anni illius. [14]Erat autem Caiphas, qui consilium dederat Iudaeis: «Expedit unum hominem mori pro populo». [15]Sequebatur autem Iesum Simon Petrus et alius discipulus. Discipulus autem ille erat notus pontifici et introivit cum Iesu in atrium pontificis; [16]Petrus autem stabat ad ostium foris. Exivit ergo discipulus alius, qui erat notus pontifici,

vation: he cannot come to terms with the idea of Christ's self-sacrifice, any more than he could when Jesus first announced his passion (see Mt 16:21–22). Our Lord does not tolerate Peter's turning to violence on his behalf; he refers back to what he said in his prayer in the Garden of Olives (see Mt 26:39), during which he freely accepted his Father's will in order to carry out the Redemption; then he gives himself up to his captors without a show of resistance. This passage tells us that we should seek to do God's will as readily and as obediently as Christ accepted his passion.

18:13–27 The second scene of the passion takes place in the house of Annas. Jesus, who had unbound Lazarus (11:44), is led here bound. Isaac, too, was bound in preparation for being offered in sacrifice (see Gen 22:9), and he put up no resistance, thereby prefiguring Jesus' voluntary self-offering. During the interrogation (vv. 19–24), Jesus lays stress on the fact that he has acted openly: everyone has had an opportunity to listen to him and to witness his miracles—which is why people have acclaimed him as the Mes-

siah. The chief priests themselves have seen him in the temple and in the synagogues, but, not wishing to believe, they allege that he has a hidden, sinister agenda.

Peter's denials are treated in less detail here than in the Synoptics. Peter's repentance is not mentioned, but it is implied by the reference to cock crowing (v. 27): the very brevity of John's account points to the fact that that episode was well known to the first Christians. After the Resurrection, the full scope of Jesus' forgiveness will be evident when he confirms Peter in his role as guide of the Church (cf. 21:15–17). There is a lesson to be learned here: "In this adventure of love we should not be depressed by our falls, not even by serious falls, if we go to God in the sacrament of Penance contrite and resolved to improve. A Christian is not a neurotic collector of good behaviour reports. Jesus Christ our Lord was moved as much by Peter's repentance after his fall as by John's innocence and faithfulness. Jesus understands our weakness and draws us to himself on an inclined plane. He wants us to make an effort to climb a little each day" (St Josemaría Escrivá, *Christ Is Passing By*, 75).

ciples?" He said, "I am not." [18]Now the servants[1] and officers had made a charcoal fire, because it was cold, and they were standing and warming themselves; Peter also was with them, standing and warming himself.

[19]The high priest then questioned Jesus about his disciples and his teaching. [20]Jesus answered him, "I have spoken openly to the world; I have always taught in synagogues and in the temple, where all Jews come together; I have said nothing secretly. [21]Why do you ask me? Ask those who have heard me, what I said to them; they know what I said." [22]When he had said this, one of the officers standing by struck Jesus with his hand, saying, "Is that how you answer the high priest?" [23]Jesus answered him, "If I have spoken wrongly, bear witness to the wrong; but if I have spoken rightly, why do you strike me?" [24]Annas then sent him bound to Caiaphas the high priest.

[25]Now Simon Peter was standing and warming himself. They said to him, "Are not you also one of his disciples?" He denied it and said, "I am not." [26]One of the servants[1] of the high priest, a kinsman of the man whose ear Peter had cut off, asked, "Did I not see you in the garden with him?" [27]Peter again denied it; and at once the cock crowed.

The trial before Pilate: Jesus is King*

[28]Then they led Jesus from the house of Caiaphas to the praetorium. It was early. They themselves did not enter the praetorium, so that they might not be defiled, but

Marginal references:
Jn 7:14, 28; 8:20
Mt 10:27
Is 45:19

Ex 22:27
Jn 19:3
Acts 23:2

Jn 8:46; 15:25

Jn 11:47–53

Jn 18:18

Jn 13:38

Mt 27:11–14
Mk 15:1–15
Lk 23:1–5
Jn 20:1
Acts 10:28

et dixit ostiariae et introduxit Petrum. [17]Dicit ergo Petro ancilla ostiaria: «Numquid et tu ex discipulis es hominis istius?». Dicit ille: «Non sum!». [18]Stabant autem servi et ministri, qui prunas fecerant, quia frigus erat, et calefaciebant se; erat autem cum eis et Petrus stans et calefaciens se. [19]Pontifex ergo interrogavit Iesum de discipulis suis et de doctrina eius. [20]Respondit ei Iesus: «Ego palam locutus sum mundo; ego semper docui in synagoga et in templo, quo omnes Iudaei conveniunt, et in occulto locutus sum nihil. [21]Quid me interrogas? Interroga eos, qui audierunt quid locutus sum ipsis; ecce hi sciunt, quae dixerim ego». [22]Haec autem cum dixisset, unus assistens ministrorum dedit alapam Iesu dicens: «Sic respondes pontifici?». [23]Respondit ei Iesus: «Si male locutus sum, testimonium perhibe de malo; si autem bene, quid me caedis?». [24]Misit ergo eum Annas ligatum ad Caipham pontificem. [25]Erat autem Simon Petrus stans et calefaciens se. Dixerunt ergo ei: «Numquid et tu ex discipulis eius es?». Negavit ille et dixit: «Non sum!». [26]Dicit unus ex servis pontificis, cognatus eius, cuius abscidit Petrus auriculam: «Nonne ego te vidi in horto cum illo?». [27]Iterum ergo negavit Petrus; et statim gallus cantavit. [28]Adducunt ergo Iesum a Caipha in praetorium. Erat autem mane. Et ipsi non introierunt in praetorium, ut non contaminarentur, sed manducarent Pascha. [29]Exivit ergo Pilatus ad eos foras et dicit: «Quam accusationem

*18:28–19:16 St John gives a longer and more detailed account of the trial before Pilate than those found in the Synoptics. This trial is the third of the five scenes in John's passion account. What comes across very clearly here is the majesty of Jesus the Messiah King, and his rejection by the Jews.

There are seven stages in the trial, marked by Pilate's entrances and exits. First (18:29–32), the Jews indict Jesus in a general way as an "evil-doer". Then follows the dialogue between Pilate and Jesus (18:33–38), culminating in Jesus' statement: "You say that I am a king" (or "You have said it: I am a king"). In the third stage Pilate tries to save our Lord (18:38–40) by asking the people if they want him to release "the King of the Jews". The central scene, the fourth stage, is the crowning with thorns, when the soldiers mockingly make obeisance to Christ

as "King of the Jews" (19:1–3). Then comes the point when our Lord is introduced by the words "Ecce homo", crowned with thorns, a purple cloak draped around him; and the Jewish authorities change their accusation and charge Jesus with having made himself the Son of God (19:4–7).

In the sixth stage, Pilate has a further conversation with Jesus in the praetorium (19:8–11) and tries to discover who exactly he is: this is the point when the crowd concentrate their hatred in an explicitly political indictment: "every one who makes himself a king sets himself against Caesar" (19:12). Eventually Pilate shows them Jesus and says, "Here is your King!" (19:14). The solemnity of this moment is signalled by the fact that we are told the precise place—the Pavement (Greek, lithostrotos), the day (the day of Preparation for the Passover, the Parasceve) and

[1] Or slaves

might eat the passover.* ²⁹So Pilate went out to them and said, "What accusation do you bring against this man?"* ³⁰They answered him, "If this man were not an evildoer, we would not have handed him over." ³¹Pilate said to them, "Take him yourselves and judge him by your own law." The Jews said to him, "It is not lawful for us to put any man to death."* ³²This was to fulfil the word which Jesus had spoken to show by what death he was to die.

³³Pilate entered the praetorium again and called Jesus, and said to him, "Are you the King of the Jews?" ³⁴Jesus answered, "Do you say this of your own accord, or did others say it to you about me?" ³⁵Pilate answered, "Am I a Jew? Your own nation and the chief priests have handed you over to me; what have you done?" ³⁶Jesus answered, "My kingship is not of this world; if my kingship were of this world, my servants would fight, that I might not be handed over to the Jews; but my kingship is not from the world." ³⁷Pilate said to him, "So you are a king?" Jesus answered, "You say that I am a king. For this I was born, and for this I have come into the world, to bear witness to the truth. Every one who is of the truth hears my voice." ³⁸Pilate said to him, "What is truth?"

After he had said this, he went out to the Jews again, and told them, "I find no crime in him. ³⁹But you have a custom that I should release one man for you at the Passover; will you have me release for you the King of the Jews?" ⁴⁰They cried out again, "Not this man, but Barabbas!" Now Barabbas was a robber.

Marginal references:
Jn 10:33; 11:47; 19:42
Jn 19:6, 7 Acts 18:15
Jn 3:14; 8:28; 12:32, 33
Mk 15:26 Jn 19:14, 19
Mt 20:19 Mk 10:33 Lk 18:32
Jn 8:23 1 Tim 6:13
Jn 3:16, 32; 14:6
Mt 27:15–23 Mk 15:6–14 Lk 23:17–23

affertis adversus hominem hunc?». ³⁰Responderunt et dixerunt ei: «Si non esset hic malefactor, non tibi tradidissemus eum». ³¹Dixit ergo eis Pilatus: «Accipite eum vos et secundum legem vestram iudicate eum!». Dixerunt ei Iudaei: «Nobis non licet interficere quemquam», ³²ut sermo Iesu impleretur, quem dixit, significans qua esset morte moriturus. ³³Introivit ergo iterum in praetorium Pilatus et vocavit Iesum et dixit ei: «Tu es rex Iudaeorum?». ³⁴Respondit Iesus: «A temetipso tu hoc dicis, an alii tibi dixerunt de me?». ³⁵Respondit Pilatus: «Numquid ego Iudaeus sum? Gens tua et pontifices tradiderunt te mihi; quid fecisti?». ³⁶Respondit Iesus: «Regnum meum non est de mundo hoc; si ex hoc mundo esset regnum meum, ministri mei decertarent, ut non traderer Iudaeis; nunc autem meum regnum non est hinc». ³⁷Dixit itaque ei Pilatus: «Ergo rex es tu?». Respondit Iesus: «Tu dicis quia rex sum. Ego in hoc natus sum et ad hoc veni in mundum, ut testimonium perhibeam veritati; omnis, qui est ex veritate, audit meam vocem». ³⁸Dicit ei Pilatus: «Quid est veritas?». Et cum hoc dixisset, iterum exivit ad Iudaeos et dicit eis: «Ego nullam invenio in eo causam. ³⁹Est autem consuetudo vobis, ut unum dimittam vobis in Pascha; vultis ergo dimittam vobis regem Iudaeorum?». ⁴⁰Clamaverunt

the time (around midday). The chief priests openly reject the One who is the true King spoken of by the prophets.

"Praetorium" (18:28, 33; 19:9): the official Jerusalem residence of the procurator or prefect. Pilate's main residence was on the coast, at Maritime Caesarea, but he usually moved to Jerusalem for the major festival periods, bringing additional troops to be called upon in the event of civil disorder. In Jerusalem, at this time and later, the procurator resided in Herod's palace (in the western part of the city). However, it is not known for certain whether the praetorium mentioned by St John was that palace or some other building in the city.

18:28–40 When Jesus appeared before the high priest, the charge laid against him was a religious one (that he claimed to be the Son of God; cf. Mt 26:57–68). Now, before Pilate, the charge against him is political. Jesus' accusers seek to involve the authority of the Roman empire in the affair: they make out that, by declaring himself to be the Messiah and the King of the Jews, Jesus is a revolutionary who conspired against Caesar. It is not part of Pilate's brief to interfere in religious matters, but because the charge now laid against Jesus has to do with public and political order, his interrogation begins with a question that goes to the central issue: "Are you the King of the Jews?" (v. 33).

In replying with another question, Jesus is not refusing to answer, but he wants to make quite clear, as he has always done, that his mission is a spiritual one. And really Pilate's was not an easy question to answer, because, to a Gentile, a king of the Jews meant simply a subverter of the empire; and to a Jewish nationalist, the Messiah King was a politico-religious liberator who would obtain independence from Rome. The true character of Jesus' role as Messiah transcends both these approaches—and that is the

Mt 27:27–31
Mk 15:16–20

Is 50:6
Jn 18:22

Jn 1:29, 36

Lev 24:16
Deut 13:1–11
Jn 5:18; 10:33

The scourging at the pillar and the crowning with thorns

19 ¹Then Pilate took Jesus and scourged him. ²And the soldiers plaited a crown of thorns, and put it on his head, and arrayed him in a purple robe; ³they came up to him, saying, "Hail, King of the Jews!" and struck him with their hands. ⁴Pilate went out again, and said to them, "Behold, I am bringing him out to you, that you may know that I find no crime in him." ⁵So Jesus came out, wearing the crown of thorns and the purple robe. Pilate said to them, "Here is the man!" ⁶When the chief priests and the officers saw him, they cried out, "Crucify him, crucify him!" Pilate said to them, "Take him yourselves and crucify him, for I find no crime in him." ⁷The Jews answered him, "We have a law, and by that law he ought to die, because he has made

ergo rursum dicentes: «Non hunc, sed Barabbam!». Erat autem Barabbas latro.   [19] ¹Tunc ergo apprehendit Pilatus Iesum et flagellavit. ²Et milites, plectentes coronam de spinis, imposuerunt capiti eius et veste purpurea circumdederunt eum; ³et veniebant ad eum et dicebant: «Ave, rex Iudaeorum!», et dabant ei alapas. ⁴Et exiit iterum Pilatus foras et dicit eis: «Ecce adduco vobis eum foras, ut cognoscatis quia in eo invenio causam nullam». ⁵Exiit ergo Iesus foras, portans spineam coronam et purpureum vestimentum. Et dicit eis: «Ecce homo!». ⁶Cum ergo vidissent eum pontifices et ministri, clamaverunt dicentes: «Crucifige, crucifige!». Dicit eis Pilatus: «Accipite eum vos et crucifigite; ego enim non invenio in eo causam». ⁷Responderunt ei Iudaei: «Nos legem habemus, et secundum legem debet mori, quia Filium Dei se fecit». ⁸Cum ergo audisset Pilatus

point Jesus is making to the procurator (v. 36), although he knows how very difficult it is for Pilate to grasp what this different kingship really involves. "Truth and justice, peace and joy in the Holy Spirit. That is the kingdom of Christ: the divine activity which saves men and which will reach its culmination when history ends and the Lord comes from the heights of paradise finally to judge men" (St Josemaría Escrivá, *Christ Is Passing By*, 180). This is what Jesus' kingship really is: his kingdom is "a kingdom of truth and life, a kingdom of holiness and grace, a kingdom of justice, love, and peace" (*Roman Missal*, Preface of the Mass of Christ the King). Christ reigns over those who accept and practise this truth revealed by him—the fact that his Father loves the world (3:16; 1 Jn 4:9–11).

19:1–3 The crowning with thorns, which occurs in the centre of the narrative, serves to underline Christ's kingship (about which Pilate has been cross-examining him), even though the soldiers are only mocking him when they proclaim him as King of the Jews. With Christ wearing the insignia of royalty, albeit in a parody, his majesty as King of Kings is projected in some way, and one is able to see that his kingdom is different from the sort of kingdom people tend to envisage (18:36).

Spiritual writers have been very moved by the sight of Jesus being ill-treated in this way: "Imagine that divine face: swollen by blows, covered in spittle, torn by thorns, furrowed with blood, here fresh blood, there ugly dried blood.

And, since the sacred Lamb had his hands tied, he could not use them to wipe away the blood running into his eyes, and so those two luminaries of heaven were eclipsed and almost blinded and made mere pieces of flesh. Finally, so disfigured was he that one could not make out who he was; he scarcely seemed human; he had become an altarpiece depicting suffering, painted by those cruel artists and their evil president, producing this pitiful figure to plead his case before his enemies" (Fray Luis de Granada, *Life of Jesus Christ*, 24). Christ is undergoing all this suffering in order to atone for our sins: "Therefore, sins—yours and mine, like everyone else's—were the executioners who bound him and lashed him and crowned him with thorns and put him on the cross. So you can see how right it is for you to feel the enormity and malice of your sins, for it was these which really caused so much suffering" (ibid., 15).

19:4–16 Pilate finds that Jesus is not guilty of any crime. It is clear to him that this man is not the revolutionary his accusers allege him to be. And so, because the procurator does not wish to judge a religious question (vv. 6–7; 18:31), the Jewish authorities now shift their charge to the political arena, even though that involves violating their consciences by proclaiming Caesar to be their true king (v. 15). When Pilate hears them accuse Jesus of proclaiming himself the Son of God, he becomes even more alarmed (v. 8). Pilate's question, "Where are you from?" (v. 9),

himself the Son of God."* [8]When Pilate heard these words, he was the more afraid; [9]he entered the praetorium again and said to Jesus, "Where are you from?"* But Jesus gave no answer. [10]Pilate therefore said to him, "You will not speak to me? Do you not know that I have the power to release you, and the power to crucify you?" [11]Jesus answered him, "You would have no power over me unless it had been given you from above; therefore he who delivered me to you has the greater sin."

Jn 7:27–29; 9:29

Jn 10:18; 18:37
Acts 2:23

Mt 27:15–26
Mk 15:6–15
Lk 23:13–25

Pilate hands Jesus over

[12]Upon this Pilate sought to release him, but the Jews cried out, "If you release this man, you are not Caesar's friend; every one who makes himself a king sets himself against Caesar." [13]When Pilate heard these words, he brought Jesus out and sat down on the judgment seat at a place called The Pavement, and in Hebrew, Gabbatha. [14]Now it was the day of Preparation for the Passover; it was about the sixth hour. He said to the Jews, "Here is your King!" [15]They cried out, "Away with him, away with him, crucify him!" Pilate said to them, "Shall I crucify your King?" The chief priests answered, "We have no king but Caesar." [16]Then he handed him over to them to be crucified.

Jn 18:33
Acts 17:7

Jn 18:33–37

Jn 19:6

hunc sermonem, magis timuit [9]et ingressus est praetorium iterum et dicit ad Iesum: «Unde es tu?». Iesus autem responsum non dedit ei. [10]Dicit ergo ei Pilatus: «Mihi non loqueris? Nescis quia potestatem habeo dimittere te et potestatem habeo crucifigere te?». [11]Respondit Iesus: «Non haberes potestatem adversum me ullam, nisi tibi esset datum desuper; propterea qui tradidit me tibi, maius peccatum habet». [12]Exinde quaerebat Pilatus dimittere eum; Iudaei autem clamabant dicentes: «Si hunc dimittis, non es amicus Caesaris! Omnis, qui se regem facit, contradicit Caesari». [13]Pilatus ergo, cum audisset hos sermones, adduxit foras Iesum et sedit pro tribunali in locum, qui dicitur Lithostrotos, Hebraice autem Gabbatha. [14]Erat autem Parasceve Paschae, hora erat quasi sexta. Et dicit Iudaeis: «Ecce rex vester!». [15]Clamaverunt ergo illi: «Tolle, tolle, crucifige eum!». Dicit eis Pilatus: «Regem vestrum crucifigam?». Responderunt pontifices: «Non habemus regem nisi Caesarem». [16]Tunc ergo tradidit eis illum, ut crucifigeretur. Susceperunt ergo Iesum. [17]Et baiulans sibi crucem exivit in eum, qui dicitur Calvariae locum, quod Hebraice dicitur Gol-

really means, "Who are you?"; that is to say, he is asking him about the mystery of his Person. But Jesus makes no reply: "Although Jesus often responded to those who questioned him, the occasions, like this one, when he chose not to respond remind us of his likeness to the lamb: 'Like the lamb before the shearers ... he opened not his mouth' (Is 53:7)—his silence is not the silence of the guilty, but of the innocent" (St Bede, *In Ioannis Evangelium expositio*, ad loc.).

Christ's majesty is further underlined by what he says about God's being as the source of Pilate's authority (vv. 8–11). In the last analysis, though people speak of the sovereignty of the king or of the people, civil authority is never absolute; it is subject to the absolute sovereignty of God; and, therefore, a human law not in accord with divine law cannot be just or, as a consequence, binding in conscience.

Even though Pilate wants to set Jesus free (v. 12), the uproar provoked by the Jewish authorities overwhelms him; he gives in to pressure and allows Jesus to be crucified.

"The Pavement" (v. 13): the Greek word *lithostrotos* means a flagstone pavement. The

Hebrew word *gabbatha*, on the other hand, probably means an elevated place. Both words refer to the same place; however, its precise location is uncertain, as is also that of the praetorium (cf. the note on 18:28—19:26).

The "day of Preparation for the Passover" (v. 14). The Hebrew word *Parasceve* denoted to the day prior to the sabbath and the day of Preparation for the Passover (see Mk 15:42). The sixth hour (v. 14) began at midday. Around that time all leavened bread was removed from houses and replaced by the unleavened bread to be eaten at the Passover meal (see Ex 12:15ff) and the lamb was officially sacrificed in the temple. St John notes that this was the time at which Jesus was condemned, thereby underlining the fact that the death sentence was handed down at the same time as the Passover lamb was sacrificed (cf. 1:29). The fact that Jesus was sentenced on the Preparation day suggests that in holding the Last Supper the previous evening, Jesus and his disciples may have been using a calendar, adhered to by some Jews, which put the Passover day one day earlier than the day specified by the claendar in general use.

Mt 27:32–56
Mk 15:21–41
Lk 23:26–49

Gen 22:6
Is 53:12

Jn 4:42; 18:5
Heb 13:12

Ps 22:18

The crucifixion and death of Jesus

[17]So they took Jesus, and he went out, bearing his own cross, to the place called the place of a skull, which is called in Hebrew Golgotha. [18]There they crucified him, and with him two others, one on either side, and Jesus between them. [19]Pilate also wrote a title and put it on the cross; it read, "Jesus of Nazareth, the King of the Jews." [20]Many of the Jews read this title, for the place where Jesus was crucified was near the city; and it was written in Hebrew, in Latin, and in Greek. [21]The chief priests of the Jews then said to Pilate, "Do not write, 'The King of the Jews,' but 'This man said, I am King of the Jews.'" [22]Pilate answered, "What I have written I have written."

[23]When the soldiers had crucified Jesus they took his garments and made four parts, one for each soldier; also his tunic. But the tunic was without seam, woven from top to bottom; [24]so they said to one another, "Let us not tear it, but cast lots for it to see whose it shall be." This was to fulfil the scripture,

"They parted my garments among them,
and for my clothing they cast lots."

gotha, [18]ubi eum crucifixerunt et cum eo alios duos hinc et hinc, medium autem Iesum. [19]Scripsit autem et titulum Pilatus et posuit super crucem; erat autem scriptum: «Iesus Nazarenus Rex Iudaeorum». [20]Hunc ergo titulum multi legerunt Iudaeorum, quia prope civitatem erat locus, ubi crucifixus est Iesus; et erat scriptum Hebraice, Latine, Graece. [21]Dicebant ergo Pilato pontifices Iudaeorum: «Noli scribere: Rex Iudaeorum, sed: Ipse dixit: 'Rex sum Iudaeorum'». [22]Respondit Pilatus: «Quod scripsi, scripsi!». [23]Milites ergo cum crucifixissent Iesum, acceperunt vestimenta eius et fecerunt quattuor partes, unicuique militi partem, et tunicam. Erat autem tunica inconsutilis, desuper contexta per totum. [24]Dixerunt ergo ad invicem: «Non scindamus eam, sed sortiamur de illa, cuius sit», ut Scriptura impleatur dicens: *«Partiti sunt vestimenta mea sibi / et in vestem*

19:17–30 "The place of a skull" or Calvary (from the Aramaic name Golgotha, which means "skull") seems to have got its name from the fact that it was shaped like a skull; it was a disused quarry on the outskirts of Jerusalem. And it is the fourth scene of the passion. St John is the only evangelist who clearly states that Jesus carried his own cross; the other three mention only the help given him by Simon of Cyrene (Mt 27:32; Mk 15:21; Lk 23:26). Jesus carrying his cross to Calvary is something to which no one can be indifferent; it calls for a decision—to be for or against him: "He was going therefore to the place where he was to be crucified, bearing his own Cross. An extraordinary spectacle: to impiety, something to jeer at; to piety, a great mystery. [...] Impiety looks on and laughs at a king bearing, instead of a sceptre, the wood of his punishment; piety looks on and sees the King bearing that cross for himself to be fixed on, a cross which would thereafter shine on the brows of kings; an object of contempt in the eyes of the impious, but something in which hereafter the hearts of the saints should glorify" (St Augustine, *In Ioannis Evangelium*, 117, 3).

The crucifixion scene summarizes the life and teaching of Jesus. The seamless tunic which the soldiers do not tear (v. 24) symbolizes the unity of the Church, the unity for which Jesus asked the Father during his priestly prayer (see 17:20–26). The presence of the Blessed Virgin and the beloved disciple (vv. 25–27), and the outflow of blood and water from Christ's side (v. 34), recall the wedding at Cana (2:1–11) and symbolize the Church and believers who become members of it through Baptism and the Eucharist. Jesus' thirst (v. 28) brings to mind the episode of his meeting with the Samaritan woman (see 4:7) and the things he said during the feast of Tabernacles (see 7:37), and it shows his deep desire to save all souls. The words he says just before giving up his spirit (v. 30) make it clear that he is truly dying, and they also indicate that he is about to send into the world the Holy Spirit so often promised during his public life (see 14:26; 15:26; 16:7–15). And he also gives his Mother to the disciples (represented by the beloved disciple) to be their Mother (vv. 25–27).

The "title" (v. 19) was the technical term used at the time in Roman law to indicate the crime for which the person had been executed. Usually written on a board prominently displayed, it summarized the official document which was being forwarded to the legal archives in Rome. This explains why, when the chief priests ask Pilate to change the wording of the inscription (v.

²⁵So the soldiers did this. But standing by the cross of Jesus were his mother, and his mother's sister, Mary the wife of Clopas, and Mary Magdalene. ²⁶When Jesus saw his mother, and the disciple whom he loved standing near, he said to his mother, "Woman, behold, your son!" ²⁷Then he said to the disciple, "Behold, your mother!" And from that hour the disciple took her to his own home.*

²⁸After this Jesus, knowing that all was now finished, said (to fulfil the scripture), "I thirst." ²⁹A bowl full of vinegar stood there; so they put a sponge full of vinegar on hyssop and held it to his mouth. ³⁰When Jesus had received the vinegar, he said, "It is finished"; and he bowed his head and gave up his spirit.

Jn 2:4; 13:23

Jn 2:4

Jn 13:1

Ps 22:15; 69:21
Jn 4:7

Jesus' side is pierced. The burial

Mt 27:57–66
Mk 15:42–47
Lk 23:50–56
Deut 21:22–23

³¹Since it was the day of Preparation, in order to prevent the bodies from remaining on the cross on the sabbath (for that sabbath was a high day), the Jews asked Pilate

---

meam miserunt sortem». Et milites quidem haec fecerunt. ²⁵Stabant autem iuxta crucem Iesu mater eius et soror matris eius, Maria Cleopae, et Maria Magdalene. ²⁶Cum vidisset ergo Iesus matrem et discipulum stantem, quem diligebat, dicit matri: «Mulier, ecce filius tuus». ²⁷Deinde dicit discipulo: «Ecce mater tua». Et ex illa hora accepit eam discipulus in sua. ²⁸Post hoc sciens Iesus quia iam omnia consummata sunt, ut consummaretur Scriptura, dicit: «Sitio». ²⁹Vas positum erat aceto plenum; spongiam ergo plenam aceto hyssopo circumponentes, obtulerunt ori eius. ³⁰Cum ergo accepisset acetum, Iesus dixit: «Consummatum est!». Et inclinato capite tradidit spiritum. ³¹Iudaei ergo, quoniam Parasceve erat, ut

---

21), the procurator is adamant in his refusal to do so: the sentence, once handed down, was irrevocable; that is what he means when he says, "What I have written I have written" (v. 22). All the evangelists bear witness to this title, though only St John mentions that it was written in a number of languages. It thus proclaims the universal Kingship of Christ, for it could be read by people from all over the world who had come to celebrate the Passover—and confirms our Lord's words: "You say that I am a king. For this I was born, and for this I have come into the world, to bear witness to the truth" (18:37).

Jesus' words to Mary and the beloved disciple (vv. 25–27) show Jesus' filial love for his Mother. By declaring her to be the Mother of the beloved disciple, he gives her a new role in his work of salvation, at the moment when it reaches its climax. He thereby establishes Mary's spiritual motherhood: "The Blessed Virgin advanced in her pilgrimage of faith, and faithfully persevered in her union with her Son unto the cross, where she stood, in keeping with the divine plan, enduring with her only begotten Son the intensity of his suffering, associating herself with his sacrifice in her mother's heart, and lovingly consenting to the immolation of this victim who was born of her. Finally, she was given by the same Christ Jesus dying on the cross as a mother to his disciple" (Vatican II, *Lumen gentium*, 58).

All Christians, who are represented in the person of John, are children of Mary. "Entrusting himself to Mary in a filial manner, the Christian, like the Apostle John, 'welcomes' the Mother of Christ 'into his own home' and brings her into everything that makes up his inner life, that is to say, into his human and Christian 'I'" (John Paul II, *Redemptoris Mater*, 45). "John, the disciple whom Jesus loved, brought Mary into his home, into his life. Spiritual writers have seen these words of the Gospel as an invitation to all Christians to bring Mary into their lives. Mary certainly wants us to invoke her, to approach her confidently, to appeal to her as our mother, asking her to 'show that you are our mother' (hymn *Ave Maris Stella*)" (St Josemaría Escrivá, *Christ Is Passing By*, 140).

The detail of Jesus' drinking vinegar (vv. 28–30) was also predicted in the Old Testament: "For my thirst they gave me vinegar to drink" (Ps 69:21). This does not mean that the vinegar was given to increase Jesus' suffering: it was customary to offer crucifixion victims water mixed with vinegar to relieve their thirst. In addition to the natural dehydration caused by crucifixion, we see in Jesus' thirst an expression of his burning desire to do his Father's will and to save all souls.

19:31–37 On the eve of the Passover the paschal

that their legs might be broken, and that they might be taken away. ³²So the soldiers came and broke the legs of the first, and of the other who had been crucified with him; ³³but when they came to Jesus and saw that he was already dead, they did not break his legs. ³⁴But one of the soldiers pierced his side with a spear, and at once there came out blood and water. ³⁵He who saw it has borne witness—his testimony is true, and he knows that he tells the truth—that you also may believe. ³⁶For these things took place that the scripture might be fulfilled, "Not a bone of him shall be broken." ³⁷And again another scripture says, "They shall look on him whom they have pierced."

³⁸After this Joseph of Arimathea, who was a disciple of Jesus, but secretly, for fear of the Jews, asked Pilate that he might take away the body of Jesus, and Pilate gave him leave. So he came and took away his body. ³⁹Nicodemus also, who had at first come to him by night, came bringing a mixture of myrrh and aloes, about a hundred pounds' weight. ⁴⁰They took the body of Jesus, and bound it in linen cloths with the spices, as is the burial custom of the Jews. ⁴¹Now in the place where he was

Margin references:
1 Jn 5:6–8
Jn 7:37–39; 10:11
Ex 12:46
Num 9:12
Ps 34:20
Zech 12:10
Rev 1:7
Prov 7:17
Song 3:6
Ps 45:8; Mt 2:11
Jn 3:1–2; 7:50–51; 11:53
Jn 11:44

non remanerent in cruce corpora sabbato, erat enim magnus dies illius sabbati, rogaverunt Pilatum, ut frangerentur eorum crura, et tollerentur. ³²Venerunt ergo milites et primi quidem fregerunt crura et alterius, qui crucifixus est cum eo; ³³ad Iesum autem cum venissent, ut viderunt eum iam mortuum, non fregerunt eius crura, ³⁴sed unus militum lancea latus eius aperuit, et continuo exivit sanguis et aqua. ³⁵Et qui vidit, testimonium perhibuit, et verum est eius testimonium, et ille scit quia vera dicit, ut et vos credatis. ³⁶Facta sunt enim haec, ut Scriptura impleatur: «Os non comminuetur eius», ³⁷et iterum alia Scriptura dicit: «Videbunt in quem transfixerunt». ³⁸Post haec autem rogavit Pilatum Ioseph ab Arimathaea, qui erat discipulus Iesu, occultus autem propter metum Iudaeorum, ut tolleret corpus Iesu; et permisit Pilatus. Venit ergo et tulit corpus eius. ³⁹Venit autem et Nicodemus, qui venerat ad eum nocte primum, ferens mixturam myrrhae et aloes quasi libras centum. ⁴⁰Acceperunt ergo corpus Iesu et

lambs were officially sacrificed in the temple. The Law laid down that not a bone of the lamb should be broken (cf. Ex 12:46). The combined mention of the facts that it was to the Preparation day and that the soldiers did not break Jesus' legs (vv. 31–33) points to his being the true Paschal Lamb who takes away the sin of the world.

The blood and water that flow from Jesus' pierced side are figures of Baptism and the Eucharist, of all the sacraments, and of the Church itself. "Here was opened wide the door of life, from which the sacraments of the Church have flowed out, without which there is no entering in unto life which is true life. [...] Here the second Adam with bowed head slept upon the cross, that thence a wife might be formed of him, flowing from his side while he slept. O death, by which the dead come back to life! Is there anything purer than this blood, any wound more healing?" (St Augustine, *In Ioannis Evangelium*, 120, 2). The Second Vatican Council, for its part, teaches: "The origin and growth of the Church are symbolized by the blood and water which flowed from the open side of the crucified Jesus" (*Lumen gentium*, 3).

The account of the crucifixion and death of Jesus ends (v. 37) with the quotation from Zechariah 12:10. By citing this text, the evangelist is saying that the salvation won by Christ on the cross is the fulfilment of God's promise of redemption.

19:38–42 The fifth and final scene of the passion account is the new, unused tomb. Our Lord's sacrifice begins to bear its first fruit: people who up to this have been afraid now boldly confess themselves disciples of Christ and attend to his burial with exquisite refinement and generosity. Many of the Fathers go into the mystical meaning of the garden that housed the tomb—usually to point out that Christ, who was arrested in a garden (the Garden of Olives) and buried in a garden (the one that the tomb was in), has redeemed us superabundantly from the first sin, which was also committed in a garden, the garden of Eden. They also note that, because no one else had been buried in this tomb, there could be no doubt that it was Jesus and not someone else who rose from the dead. St Augustine observes that "just as in the womb of the Virgin Mary none was conceived before him, none after him, so in this tomb none before him, none was buried after him" (*In Ioannis Evangelium*, 120, 5).

crucified there was a garden, and in the garden a new tomb where no one had ever been laid. ⁴²So because of the Jewish day of Preparation, as the tomb was close at hand, they laid Jesus there.

Gen 2:8
Song 4:12, 15–16

11. APPEARANCES OF THE RISEN CHRIST*

Mt 28:1–10
Mk 16:1–8
Lk 24:1–12

The empty tomb

20 ¹Now on the first day of the week Mary Magdalene came to the tomb early, while it was still dark, and saw that the stone had been taken away from the tomb. ²So she ran, and went to Simon Peter and the other disciple, the one whom Jesus loved, and said to them, "They have taken the Lord out of the tomb, and we do not know where they have laid him." ³Peter then came out with the other disciple, and they went toward the tomb. ⁴They both ran, but the other disciple outran Peter and reached the tomb first; ⁵and stooping to look in, he saw the linen cloths lying there, but he did not go in. ⁶Then Simon Peter came, following him, and went into the tomb; he saw the linen cloths lying, ⁷and the napkin, which had been on his

Song 3:1

Jn 13:23

Deut 17:6; 19:15
Jn 8:17

Jn 19:40

ligaverunt illud linteis cum aromatibus, sicut mos Iudaeis est sepelire. ⁴¹Erat autem in loco, ubi crucifixus est, hortus, et in horto monumentum novum, in quo nondum quisquam positus erat. ⁴²Ibi ergo propter Parascevem Iudaeorum, quia iuxta erat monumentum, posuerunt Iesum.   [20] ¹Prima autem sabbatorum Maria Magdalene venit mane, cum adhuc tenebrae essent, ad monumentum, et videt lapidem sublatum a monumento. ²Currit ergo et venit ad Simonem Petrum et ad alium discipulum, quem amabat Iesus, et dicit eis: «Tulerunt Dominum de monumento, et nescimus, ubi posuerunt eum!». ³Exiit ergo Petrus et ille alius discipulus, et veniebant ad monumentum. ⁴Currebant autem duo simul, et ille alius discipulus praecucurrit citius Petro et venit primus ad monumentum; ⁵et cum se inclinasset, videt posita linteamina, non tamen introivit. ⁶Venit

*20:1—21:25 This last section of the Gospel completes the glorious revelation of Jesus as Messiah and Son of God, whose story John has recounted to bolster the faith of believers. It includes the appearances of the risen Lord to the apostles; Jesus helps them to understand the meaning of the Scriptures in the light of his teaching and miracles (see 20:8–9), and gives them the Holy Spirit and the power to forgive sins (20:22–23). The miraculous catch of fish in the Sea of Tiberias (21:1–14) prefigures the host of peoples that the apostolate of the Church will win for Christ. The next part of chapter 21 is also devoted to the Church; it recounts the commission given to St Peter to be her leader (21:15–19). The Gospel ends with a vouching for the truthfulness of the witness borne by the evangelist, who has seen and heard all the things he has reported (21:24–25).

20:1–10 All four Gospels report the testimony of the holy women and the apostles regarding Christ's glorious resurrection—first the empty tomb and then the appearances of the risen Jesus. St John makes it clear that although Mary Magdalene was the first to go to the tomb, it was the two apostles who were the first to go inside and to see the evidence that Christ had risen (the empty tomb, the linen cloths and the napkin in a place by itself ...). The beloved disciple verifies that Jesus' body is missing; and the state of the tomb, especially the linen cloths "laying there" (flattened, "deflated", fallen), shows that no human hand could have been responsible for what has happened, and that Jesus has not come back to life in the way that Lazarus did. That is why John notes that he "saw" and "believed" (v. 8).

The empty tomb and the other evidence that Peter and John saw were perceptible to the senses: but the Resurrection, even though it had effects that could be proven by experience, requires faith if it is to be truly accepted. As St Thomas Aquinas says, "the individual arguments taken alone are not sufficient proof of Christ's resurrection, but taken together, in a cumulative way, they manifest it perfectly. Particularly important in this regard are the scriptural proofs [cf. especially Lk 24:25–27], the angelic testimony [cf. Lk 24:4–7] and Christ's own post-resurrection word confirmed by miracles" (*Summa theologiae*, 3, 55, 6 ad 1).

Jn 2:22

Ps 16:9
1 Cor 15:4
Acts 2:24–32

head, not lying with the linen cloths but rolled up in a place by itself. ⁸Then the other disciple, who reached the tomb first, also went in, and he saw and believed; ⁹for as yet they did not know the scripture, that he must rise from the dead. ¹⁰Then the disciples went back to their homes.

Mt 28:1–10
Mk 16:9–11

Jn 1:51;11:33

2 Mac 3:26
Heb 1:14

The appearance to Mary Magdalene

¹¹But Mary stood weeping outside the tomb, and as she wept she stooped to look into the tomb; ¹²and she saw two angels in white, sitting where the body of Jesus had lain, one at the head and one at the feet. ¹³They said to her, "Woman, why are you weeping?" She said to them, "Because they have taken away my Lord, and I do not know where they have laid him." ¹⁴Saying this, she turned round and saw Jesus standing, but she did not know that it was Jesus. ¹⁵Jesus said to her, "Woman, why are you weeping? Whom do you seek?" Supposing him to be the gardener, she said to him, "Sir, if you have carried him away, tell me where you have laid him, and I will take him away." ¹⁶Jesus said to her, "Mary." She turned and said to him in Hebrew, "Rabboni!" (which means Teacher). ¹⁷Jesus said to her, "Do not hold me, for I have not yet ascended to the Father; but go to my brethren and say to them, I am ascending to my Father and your Father, to my God and your God."* ¹⁸Mary Magdalene went and said to the disciples, "I have seen the Lord"; and she told them that he had said these things to her.

Jn 21:4
Acts 7:55
Rev 5:6

Song 3:2, 3
Wis 6:12
Lk 24:16
Jn 16:16–33

Jer 33:11
Mk 10:51

Heb 2:11
Rom 8:29
Ps 22:22

1 Cor 9:1

ergo et Simon Petrus sequens eum et introivit in monumentum; et videt linteamina posita ⁷et sudarium, quod fuerat super caput eius, non cum linteaminibus positum, sed separatim involutum in unum locum. ⁸Tunc ergo introivit et alter discipulus, qui venerat primus ad monumentum, et vidit et credidit. ⁹Nondum enim sciebant Scripturam quia oportet eum a mortuis resurgere. ¹⁰Abierunt ergo iterum ad semetipsos discipuli. ¹¹Maria autem stabat ad monumentum foris plorans. Dum ergo fleret, inclinavit se in monumentum ¹²et videt duos angelos in albis sedentes, unum ad caput et unum ad pedes, ubi positum fuerat corpus Iesu. ¹³Et dicunt ei illi: «Mulier, quid ploras?». Dicit eis: «Tulerunt Dominum meum, et nescio, ubi posuerunt eum». ¹⁴Haec cum dixisset, conversa est retrorsum et videt Iesum stantem et non sciebat quia Iesus est. ¹⁵Dicit ei Iesus: «Mulier, quid ploras? Quem quaeris?». Illa, existimans quia hortulanus esset, dicit ei: «Domine, si tu sustulisti eum, dicito mihi, ubi posuisti eum, et ego eum tollam». ¹⁶Dicit ei Iesus: «Maria!». Conversa illa dicit ei Hebraice: «Rabbuni!»—quod dicitur Magister—. ¹⁷Dicit ei Iesus: «Iam noli me tenere, nondum enim ascendi ad Patrem; vade autem ad fratres meos et dic eis: Ascendo ad Patrem meum et Patrem vestrum, et Deum meum et Deum vestrum». ¹⁸Venit Maria Magdalene annuntians discipulis: «Vidi Dominum!», et quia haec dixit ei. ¹⁹Cum esset ergo sero die illa prima

20:11–18 The Gospel shows us that Jesus manifests himself to those who seek him in all sincerity. Mary Magdalene is the model for those who seek Jesus. "What we must try to understand in this episode is the depth of love that burns in the woman's heart, the way she stays close to the tomb even when all the disciples have gone away. In tears, she sought the one who could not be found, and aflame with love, she burned with a pure desire for the one she thought had been taken away forever. She alone saw him then because she had stayed close by to look for him. Perseverance gives good works their power" (St Gregory the Great, *Homiliae in Evangelia*, 25, 1–2 and 4–5). Here we see Jesus as the Good Shepherd who "calls his own sheep by name" (10:3)—"Mary"—and she does "know his voice" (10:4); she cries, "Rabboni!" Mary, in turn, bears witness to the Resurrection and tells the others that she has seen the Lord. That is why

in the Eastern tradition, Mary has been called "isapóstolos", that is, equal to the apostles, and in the Western tradition "apostola apostolorum", apostle of apostles. Jesus, whose glorified human body transcends this material world, must return to the Father. Significantly, the apostles are no longer "servants" or even "friends" (15:15) but "brethren" (v. 17)—an indication that after the death and glorious resurrection of Jesus, those who believe in him receive the gift of divine filiation (cf. 1:12), which makes them sons of God and brothers of Christ.

"Do not hold me" (v. 17). In the original, the verb is in the present imperative, implying that Mary was clinging to our Lord. The negative instruction (reflected in the Latin, "Noli me tangere") means that our Lord is telling Mary to release her hold on him, to let him go, for she will have another chance to see him before his ascension into heaven.

Jesus' first appearance to the disciples

Mt 28:16–20
Mk 16:14–18
Lk 24:36–49

[19]On the evening of that day, the first day of the week, the doors being shut where the disciples were, for fear of the Jews, Jesus came and stood among them and said to them, "Peace be with you." [20]When he had said this, he showed them his hands and his side. Then the disciples were glad when they saw the Lord. [21]Jesus said to them again, "Peace be with you. As the Father has sent me, even so I send you." [22]And when he had said this, he breathed on them, and said to them, "Receive the Holy Spirit. [23]If you forgive the sins of any, they are forgiven; if you retain the sins of any, they are retained."

Is 26:20–21
Jn 7:13; 14:27; 19:38

Ex 12:12–23
1 Jn 1:1

Jn 15:16; 17:18
Mt 28:18ff

Jn 7:39
Gen 2:7
1 Cor 15:45

Mt 16:19; 18:18
Jn 1:29, 33; 3:18;
14:25–26

A second appearance with Thomas present

[24]Now Thomas, one of the twelve, called the Twin, was not with them when Jesus came. [25]So the other disciples told him, "We have seen the Lord." But he said to them, "Unless I see in his hand the print of the nails, and place my finger in the mark of the nails, and place my hand in his side, I will not believe."

[26]Eight days later, his disciples were again in the house, and Thomas was with them. The doors were shut, but Jesus came and stood among them, and said, "Peace

Jn 11:16; 14:5

Jn 19:34
1 Jn 1:1

Jn 20:19

sabbatorum, et fores essent clausae, ubi erant discipuli propter metum Iudaeorum, venit Iesus et stetit in medio et dicit eis: «Pax vobis!». [20]Et hoc cum dixisset, ostendit eis manus et latus. Gavisi sunt ergo discipuli, viso Domino. [21]Dixit ergo eis iterum: «Pax vobis! Sicut misit me Pater, et ego mitto vos». [22]Et cum hoc dixisset, insufflavit et dicit eis: «Accipite Spiritum Sanctum. [23]Quorum remiseritis peccata, remissa sunt eis; quorum retinueritis, retenta sunt». [24]Thomas autem, unus ex Duodecim, qui dicitur Didymus, non erat cum eis, quando venit Iesus. [25]Dicebant ergo ei alii discipuli: «Vidimus Dominum!». Ille autem dixit eis: «Nisi videro in manibus eius signum clavorum et mittam digitum meum in signum clavorum et mittam manum meam in latus eius, non credam». [26]Et post dies octo iterum erant discipuli eius intus, et Thomas cum eis. Venit Iesus ianuis

20:19–23 In the Gospel of St John, the point when the glorified Jesus appears to the disciples and breathes the Holy Spirit onto them is equivalent to Pentecost in St Luke's second book, the Acts of the Apostles. "God's plan of salvation for the world had been fulfilled, but it was God's will that we should participate in the divine nature of the Word, leaving our old way of life behind to enter into a new and holy life. This transformation could be brought about only through the gift of the Holy Spirit" (St Cyril of Alexandria, *Commentarium in Ioannem*, 10).

The commission that our Lord gives the apostles (vv. 22–23) can be seen as a parallel to that recorded at the end of St Matthew's Gospel (Mt 28:18ff), since it shows the divine origin of the Church's mission and her authority to forgive sins. "The Lord then especially instituted the sacrament of Penance when, after being risen from the dead, he breathed upon his disciples and said: 'Receive the Holy Spirit ...'. The consensus of all the Fathers has always acknowledged that by this action so sublime and words so clear the power of forgiving and retaining sins was given to the Apostles and their lawful successors for reconciling the faithful who have

fallen after Baptism" (Council of Trent, *De Paenitentia*, chap. 1).

20:24–31 In this new appearance, eight days later, St Thomas plays a key role; and, just as Mary Magdalene became a model for those who seek Jesus (20:1–11), Thomas exemplifies those who at first doubt both his divinity and his humanity but are later completely converted. The Risen One is the very same person as the Crucified One. Our Lord once again makes it clear that the testimony of those who saw him after the Resurrection is a ground of faith for believers who do not have that personal experience. "Surely you do not think", St Gregory the Great comments, "that it was a pure accident that that chosen disciple was missing; who on his return was told about the appearance and on hearing about it doubted; doubting, so that he might touch and believe by touching? It was not an accident; God arranged that it should happen. His clemency acted in this wonderful way so that through the doubting disciple touching the wounds in his Master's body, our own wounds of incredulity might be healed. [...] And so the disciple, doubting and touching, was changed

Lk 24:25

be with you." ²⁷Then he said to Thomas, "Put your finger here, and see my hands; and put out your hand, and place it in my side; do not be faithless, but believing."

Ps 35:23
Jn 1:1, 18; 13
Jn 1:50
1 Pet 1:8

²⁸Thomas answered him, "My Lord and my God!" ²⁹Jesus said to him, "Have you believed because you have seen me? Blessed are those who have not seen and yet believe."

Jn 2:11; 21:25

³⁰Now Jesus did many other signs in the presence of the disciples, which are not written in this book; ³¹but these are written that you may believe that Jesus is the Christ, the Son of God, and that believing you may have life in his name.

Jn 1:12
1 Jn 5:13
Rom 1:17
Acts 3:16

The miraculous catch of fish*

Mt 26:32; 28:7

Jn 1:45–49; 11:16;
20:26–29

21 *¹After this Jesus revealed himself again to the disciples by the Sea of Tiberias; and he revealed himself in this way. ²Simon Peter, Thomas called the Twin, Nathanael of Cana in Galilee, the sons of Zebedee, and two others of his disciples were together. ³Simon Peter said to them, "I am going fishing." They said to him, "We will go with you." They went out and got into the boat; but that night they caught nothing.

Lk 5:5

Jn 20:14
Lk 24:16

Lk 24:41

⁴Just as day was breaking, Jesus stood on the beach; yet the disciples did not know that it was Jesus. ⁵Jesus said to them, "Children, have you any fish?" They

clausis et stetit in medio et dixit: «Pax vobis!». ²⁷Deinde dicit Thomae: «Infer digitum tuum huc et vide manus meas et affer manum tuam et mitte in latus meum, et noli fieri incredulus sed fidelis!». ²⁸Respondit Thomas et dixit ei: «Dominus meus et Deus meus!». ²⁹Dicit ei Iesus: «Quia vidisti me, credidisti. Beati, qui non viderunt et crediderunt!». ³⁰Multa quidem et alia signa fecit Iesus in conspectu discipulorum suorum, quae non sunt scripta in libro hoc; ³¹haec autem scripta sunt, ut credatis quia Iesus est Christus Filius Dei, et ut credentes vitam habeatis in nomine eius.   [21] ¹Postea manifestavit se iterum Iesus discipulis ad mare Tiberiadis; manifestavit autem sic. ²Erant simul Simon Petrus et Thomas, qui dicitur Didymus, et Nathanael, qui erat a Cana Galilaeae, et filii Zebedaei et alii ex discipulis eius duo. ³Dicit eis Simon Petrus: «Vado piscari». Dicunt ei: «Venimus et nos tecum». Exierunt et ascenderunt in navem; et illa nocte nihil prendiderunt. ⁴Mane autem iam facto, stetit Iesus in litore; non

into a witness of the truth and of the Resurrection" (*Homiliae in Evangelia*, 26, 7).

Verses 30–31 are the first epilogue or conclusion to the Gospel. They sum up the inspired writer's whole purpose in writing his Gospel — to have people believe that Jesus is the Christ, the Messiah announced by the Old Testament prophets, and the Son of God; this belief enables us to share in eternal life even now.

*21:1–25 This chapter is an addition to the Gospel, written either by the evangelist himself or by one of his disciples (see v. 24). The main theme is the Church; and the communion that exists between the beloved disciple and Peter is plain to see. By recounting the commission given by Jesus to Peter to lead his Church (vv. 15–17), the beloved disciple acknowledges Peter's authority, and implicitly submits his entire testimony, written and oral, to his judgment.

21:1–14 This passage about the miraculous catch of fish is reminiscent of that earlier one after which our Lord promised Peter that he would

make him a fisher of men (see Lk 5:1–11). The account underlines the beloved disciple's love, which enables him to recognize Jesus (v. 7). "God allows himself to be seen and recognized by those who are pure of heart" (St Gregory of Nyssa, *De beatitudinibus*, 6). It also shows us Peter's faith (witness the fact that he reaches Jesus before the other disciples do) and how the Risen Jesus repeatedly proves that he is not a ghost: he ate with them before, and now he eats with them again (vv. 10–14). "He passes by, close to his Apostles, close to those souls who have given themselves to him and they don't realize he is there. How often Christ is not only near us, but in us; yet we still live in such a human way! [...] 'Whereupon the disciple whom Jesus loved said to Peter, "It is the Lord!"' Love, love is farsighted. Love is the first to appreciate kindness. The adolescent apostle, who felt a deep and firm affection for Jesus, because he loved Christ with all the purity and tenderness of a heart that had never been corrupted, exclaimed: 'It is the Lord!' 'When Simon Peter heard that it was the Lord, he put on his clothes

answered him, "No." [6]He said to them, "Cast the net on the right side of the boat, _{Lk 5:4–7 Jn 15:5} and you will find some." So they cast it and now they were not able to haul it in, for the quantity of fish. [7]That disciple whom Jesus loved* said to Peter, "It is the Lord!" When Simon Peter heard that it was the Lord, he put on his clothes, for he was stripped for work, and sprang into the sea. [8]But the other disciples came in the boat, dragging the net full of fish, for they were not far from the land, but about a hundred yards[m] off.

[9]When they got out on land, they saw a charcoal fire there, with fish lying on it, and bread. [10]Jesus said to them, "Bring some of the fish that you have just caught." [11]So Simon Peter went aboard and hauled the net ashore, full of large fish, a hundred and fifty-three of them; and although there were so many, the net was not torn. [12]Jesus said to them, "Come and have breakfast." Now none of the disciples dared ask him, "Who are you?" They knew it was the Lord. [13]Jesus came and took the bread and gave it to them, and so with the fish. [14]This was now the third time that Jesus was revealed to the disciples after he was raised from the dead.

Reference notes in margin:
- Lk 5:4–7
- Jn 15:5
- Jn 13:23
- Ezek 47:8–10
- Jn 6:11
- Jn 20:19, 26
- Rom 4:25

Peter's primacy

[15]When they had finished breakfast, Jesus said to Simon Peter, "Simon, son of John, _{Jn 1:42 Mt 16:17} do you love me more than these?" He said to him, "Yes, Lord; you know that I love

tamen sciebant discipuli quia Iesus est. [5]Dicit ergo eis Iesus: «Pueri, numquid pulmentarium habetis?». Responderunt ei: «Non». [6]Ille autem dixit eis: «Mittite in dexteram navigii rete et invenietis». Miserunt ergo et iam non valebant illud trahere a multitudine piscium. [7]Dicit ergo discipulus ille, quem diligebat Iesus, Petro: «Dominus est!». Simon ergo Petrus, cum audisset quia Dominus est, tunicam succinxit se, erat enim nudus, et misit se in mare; [8]alii autem discipuli navigio venerunt, non enim longe erant a terra, sed quasi cubitis ducentis, trahentes rete piscium. [9]Ut ergo descenderunt in terram, vident prunas positas et piscem superpositum et panem. [10]Dicit eis Iesus: «Afferte de piscibus, quos prendidistis nunc». [11]Ascendit ergo Simon Petrus et traxit rete in terram, plenum magnis piscibus centum quinquaginta tribus; et cum tanti essent, non est scissum rete. [12]Dicit eis Iesus: «Venite, prandete». Nemo autem audebat discipulorum interrogare eum: «Tu quis es?», scientes quia Dominus est. [13]Venit Iesus et accipit panem et dat eis et piscem similiter. [14]Hoc iam tertio manifestatus est Iesus discipulis, cum resurrexisset a mortuis. [15]Cum ergo prandissent, dicit Simoni Petro Iesus: «Simon Ioannis, diligis me plus his?». Dicit ei: «Etiam, Domine, tu scis quia amo te». Dicit ei: «Pasce agnos

and sprang into the sea.' Peter personifies faith. Full of marvellous daring, he leaps into the sea. With a love like John's and a faith like Peter's, what is there that can stop us?" (St Josemaría Escrivá, *Friends of God*, 265–266).

The Fathers and Doctors of the Church have often commented on the mystical meaning of this episode: the boat is the Church, whose unity is symbolized by the net that does not tear; the sea is the world; Peter in the boat stands for supreme authority in the Church; the number of fish signifies the number of the elect.

21:15–23 Despite Peter's denials of him during the passion, Jesus, as the Good Shepherd who takes the best possible care of his sheep (10:11; cf. Ezek 34:16; Lk 15:4–7), now confers on him the primacy he earlier promised. "Jesus entrusted a specific authority to Peter: 'I will give you the keys of the kingdom of heaven, and whatever you bind on earth shall be bound in heaven, and whatever you loose on earth shall be loosed in

heaven' (Mt 16:19). The 'power of the keys' designates authority to govern the house of God, which is the Church. Jesus, the Good Shepherd, confirmed this mandate after his Resurrection: 'Feed my sheep' (Jn 21:15–17). The power to 'bind and loose' connotes the authority to absolve sins, to pronounce doctrinal judgments, and to make disciplinary decisions in the Church. Jesus entrusted this authority to the Church through the ministry of the apostles and in particular through the ministry of Peter, the only one to whom he specifically entrusted the keys of the kingdom" (*Catechism of the Catholic Church*, 553).

Alongside the authority of Peter, the role of St John is also recognized; it is alluded to especially in v. 23, which disabuses people of the idea that the beloved disciple would never die. According to St Irenaeus (see *Adversus haereses*, 2, 22, 5; 3, 3, 4), St John lived much longer than the other apostles, into the reign of Trajan (AD 98–117).

m Greek *two hundred cubits*

1 Pet 5:2, 4
you." He said to him, "Feed my lambs." [16]A second time he said to him, "Simon, son of John, do you love me?" He said to him, "Yes, Lord; you know I love you." He
Jn 13:38; 18:17, 25, 27
said to him, "Tend my sheep." [17]He said to him the third time, "Simon, son of John, do you love me?" Peter was grieved because he said to him the third time, "Do you love me?" And he said to him, "Lord, you know everything; you know that I love
Mt 16:22
Lk 22:31–32
you." Jesus said to him, "Feed my sheep.* [18]Truly, truly, I say to you, when you were young, you girded yourself and walked where you would; but when you are old, you will stretch out your hands, and another will gird you and carry you where
Jn 13:36
you do not wish to go." [19](This he said to show by what death he was to glorify God.) And after this he said to him, "Follow me."

Jn 13:23
[20]Peter turned and saw following them the disciple whom Jesus loved, who had lain close to his breast at the supper and had said, "Lord, who is it that is going to betray you?" [21]When Peter saw him, he said to Jesus, "Lord, what about this man?" [22]Jesus said to him, "If it is my will that he remain until I come, what is that to you? Follow me!" [23]The saying spread abroad among the brethren that this disciple was not to die; yet Jesus did not say to him that he was not to die, but, "If it is my will that he remain until I come, what is that to you?"

Conclusion
Jn 19:35
3 Jn 12
[24]This is the disciple who is bearing witness to these things, and who has written these things; and we know that his testimony is true.

Jn 20:30
[25]But there are also many other things which Jesus did; were every one of them to be written, I suppose that the world itself could not contain the books that would be written.

meos». [16]Dicit ei iterum secundo: «Simon Ioannis, diligis me?». Ait illi: «Etiam, Domine, tu scis quia amo te». Dicit ei: «Pasce oves meas». [17]Dicit ei tertio: «Simon Ioannis, amas me?». Contristatus est Petrus quia dixit ei tertio: «Amas me?», et dicit ei: «Domine, tu omnia scis, tu cognoscis quia amo te». Dicit ei: «Pasce oves meas. [18]Amen, amen dico tibi: Cum esses iunior, cingebas teipsum et ambulabas, ubi volebas; cum autem senueris, extendes manus tuas, et alius te cinget et ducet, quo non vis». [19]Hoc autem dixit significans qua morte clarificaturus esset Deum. Et hoc cum dixisset, dicit ei: «Sequere me». [20]Conversus Petrus videt illum discipulum, quem diligebat Iesus, sequentem, qui et recubuit in cena super pectus eius et dixit: «Domine, quis est qui tradit te?». [21]Hunc ergo cum vidisset Petrus, dicit Iesu: «Domine, hic autem quid?». [22]Dicit ei Iesus: «Si eum volo manere donec veniam, quid ad te? Tu me sequere». [23]Exivit ergo sermo iste in fratres quia discipulus ille non moritur. Non autem dixit ei Iesus: «Non moritur», sed: «Si eum volo manere donec veniam, quid ad te?». [24]Hic est discipulus, qui testimonium perhibet de his et scripsit haec, et scimus quia verum est testimonium eius. [25]Sunt autem et alia multa, quae fecit Iesus, quae si scribantur per singula, nec ipsum arbitror mundum capere eos, qui scribendi sunt, libros.

21:24–25 The witness borne by the disciple "whom Jesus loved" (21:20) is offered as a guarantee that all the things he has been reporting throughout the book are worthy of belief. John's narrative, written under the inspiration of the Holy Spirit, has as its aim to strengthen the faith of believers by reflecting on what Jesus did and taught. We will never be able to capture the full richness and depth of our Lord's personality—nor does the fourth Gospel manage to do so. "Once we begin to be interested in Christ, one's interest can never cease. There is always something more to be known, to be said—infinitely more. St John the Evangelist ends his Gospel making this very point (Jn 21:25). Everything to do with Christ is so rich, there are such depths for us to explore; such light, strength, joy, desire have their source in him. [...] His coming to the world, his presence in history and culture and [...] his vital relationship with our conscience: everything suggests that it is unseemly, unscientific and irreverent ever to think that we need not and cannot advance further in contemplation of Jesus Christ" (Paul VI, General Audience, 20 February 1974).

THE
ACTS OF THE APOSTLES

Introduction

The English title of this work—"Acts of the Apostles"—corresponds to the Latin "Actus Apostolorum" and the Greek "Praxeis Apostolon". From the middle of the second century on, this title is found in the Greek manuscripts, in early translations, and in references to the book in the works of the Fathers of the Church and other ecclesiastical writers. However, the title seems not to have come from the author but to have been given to the text somewhat later. It is not so much an account of the apostles' activity as a history of the early stages of Christianity linked to the missionary work of the two most prominent apostles, Peter and Paul.

In the early collections of New Testament books, Acts is sometimes found alongside the letters of St Paul; and sometimes it comes just before or after the Catholic Letters. So, it acts as a kind of bridge between the Gospels and the apostles' letters, showing how the early disciples imitated their Master and what their oral preaching was prior to its being written down; it helps the reader see where and when almost all the authors of the rest of the New Testament were working.

The opening lines of the Gospel of St Luke and those of Acts clearly show that these two books had the same author and were part of the same project. Nowadays, commentators tend to agree that these two books of St Luke form a single unit, but in ancient times they are almost always found separately, and Christian writers comment on them separately. In the early Church, Acts clearly had great authority, for we find it quoted in the main patristic writings of the early centuries.[1] Perhaps the most important testimony is that of St Irenaeus, who uses it to defend the apostolic status of St Paul against the Ebionites, and to combat Marcion, who accepted only the Gospel of Luke and the letters of Paul as inspired writings.[2]

As regards the actual content of Acts, it has come down to us via two traditions—the Eastern, or Alexandrian, text found in most codexes, and the Western text, found in an occasional codex (the Beza codex, for example), in some papyri and in Latin and Syriac translations. The Western tradition of the text is about one-tenth longer than the Eastern, the additions being explanations and small paraphrases provided for clarity's sake. Some scholars have suggested that Luke himself may have written this longer text in Rome, to clarify certain things for readers. But the most likely explanation for the existence of the longer text is that, whereas the Church recognized the Gospel of Luke as canonical and inspired from the very beginning, Acts, although it had authority from the start, took some time to be acknowledged as canonical—and therefore some copyists would have felt freer to add in brief notes and clarifications.

A small number of commentaries from the early centuries are extant—a series of homilies by St John Chrysostom and some glosses on the texts of Acts, the best known being that of St Ephrem. St Bede's commentary, which dates from a later period, mostly draws on ideas in earlier ones.

---

1 St Justin (*Apologia*, 39, 49; 50, 12) appears to quote the book. It is expressly mentioned in the Muratorian Canon (end of second century) and in the *Antimarcionite Prologues*. From the third century onwards, references to the book occur repeatedly in the writings of Clement of Alexandria, Origen, Tertullian, Cyril of Jerusalem, and other Fathers. **2** See St Irenaeus, *Adversus haereses*, 3, 14–15.

1. STRUCTURE AND CONTENT

The Acts of the Apostles gives an account of how the Church was originally established and of the spread of the Gospel in the years after the ascension of our Lord. One could describe it as a history book, an account of the early history of Christianity. However, it is not a simple chronicle of events. The author has succeeded in combining history and theology remarkably well. In relating the early history of the Church, his primary aim is to strengthen the faith of Christians, to show that their beliefs are solidly grounded. Secondarily, the book anticipates the kind of writing typical of the apologists of the second and third centuries, by arguing that Christ's disciples should be extended the same freedom and the same respect that the empire gave to what were called "lawful" religions, which included Judaism. Christianity is presented as a deep-rooted faith, trusting in God and confident, one that has no time for obscurantism or the kind of secrecy typical of sects and one that is not afraid to debate its principles and convictions with all comers. The whole narrative is imbued with an extraordinary spiritual joy—a joy that comes from the Holy Spirit, from certainty about the supernatural origin of the Church, from contemplation of the marvels that God works in support of the preachers of his Gospel, and from the protection he gives his disciples despite the persecution they experience.

Commentators have suggested a number of ways to divide the book into parts, to help readers understand it better. From the point of view of God's plan of salvation, which the book reflects, the twenty-eight chapters divide into two main sections—before and after the "council" of Jerusalem, which is recounted at the start of chapter 15. The gathering at Jerusalem is certainly the theological centre of the book, because of the unique role it played in explaining, as God wished it to do, the catholic nature of the Church and the primacy of grace over the Mosaic Law, and because of the impetus its decision gave to the spread of the Gospel throughout the world.

From another point of view, the book is a detailed description of how Jesus' words to the disciples just before his ascension were borne out: "You shall be my witnesses in Jerusalem and in all Judea and Samaria and to the end of the earth" (1:8). From this perspective, Acts describes the first, tentative steps of the church of Jerusalem, its spread to the neighbouring regions of Judea and Samaria, and its further development in the regions around the Mediterranean and then on into Rome, the capital of the empire. At every moment, the Holy Spirit is present, guiding the actions of the disciples.

However, within this general plan, it becomes clear to the reader that the first twelve chapters (except for the account of Paul's conversion) hinge largely on the person of Peter; whereas from chapter 13 onwards (except for the account of the council of Jerusalem, where Peter is the protagonist), the narrative follows in the footsteps of Paul. This dual narrative focus extends to the account of the geographical growth of the Church: the early chapters report the mission of evangelization from Jerusalem (led by Peter); thereafter the apostolic outreach of the church of Antioch (led by Paul) receives most attention.

If one looks at the book in terms of the episodes it contains—stages, as it were, in the history of the preaching of the Gospel—Acts can be divided into four parts, which are prefaced by a short introduction.

INTRODUCTION (1:1–11). This links up with the Gospel of St Luke. The prologue (1:1–5) harks back to the opening words of the Gospel (Lk 1:1–4), and the account of the Ascension (1:6–11) echoes the Gospel's closing verses (Lk 24:50–53).

FIRST PART: THE CHURCH IN JERUSALEM (1:12—7:60). These chapters tell of the life of the early Christian community in Jerusalem. Once Matthias is elected to fill the vacancy in the Twelve (1:15–26), we are told about the coming of the Holy Spirit at Pentecost (2:1–13) and about early apostolic preaching concerning Jesus. The narrative goes on to cover the growth of the community around Peter and the other apostles (2:14–17). Miracles and other extraordinary events (3:1–10; 5:1–16) accompany the preaching of the Twelve. Brief summaries seeded in the text (1:14; 2:42–47; 4:32–37; 5:12–16) show the spiritual vitality of the early Church. The increase in the number of believers (2:41, 47; 4:4, 5:14; 6:1) leads to the election of deacons (6:1–5). The persecution unleashed against "Hellenist" Christians in Jerusalem (that is, people from the Jewish diaspora) and the martyrdom of Stephen (6:8—7:60), bring this section to a close, and the scene changes to regions bordering on Judea.

SECOND PART: THE SPREAD OF THE CHURCH BEYOND JERUSALEM (8:1—12:25). We are now told about how the Hellenist Christians, driven out of Jerusalem by persecution, start preaching the Gospel in Judea, Samaria and Syria. The persecution has been providential; it leads to the Church opening her doors to the Gentiles. We learn of the conversion of the Ethiopian courtier (8:26–39), as well as that of many Samaritans (8:14–17). The text goes into considerable detail about the calling of Paul to be the Apostle of the Gentiles (9:1–19) and about the conversion of the centurion Cornelius (10:1—11:18), a key event in overcoming ethnic barriers to the spread of the Gospel. This part ends with the death of James, the brother of John, and the arrest and miraculous release of St Peter (12:1–19).

THIRD PART: THE SPREAD OF THE CHURCH AMONG THE GENTILES, AND THE MISSIONARY JOURNEYS OF ST PAUL (13:1—20:38). Paul was the main person chosen by God to open the doors of salvation to the pagan world. This third part of Acts recounts his journeys to spread the Gospel, and the establishment of new communities of Christians. From the very start, the missionary work of the church of Antioch is very significant; still, the book does show that in every new thrust to spread the Gospel, Jerusalem is involved (see 9:26; 15:2; 20:16; 21:15).

FOURTH PART: ST PAUL, IN PRISON, BEARS WITNESS TO THE GOSPEL (21:1—28:31). St Paul's arrival in Jerusalem marks the start of the last part of the book, which deals with the Apostle's imprisonment. As the Lord himself tells him (23:11), he will become his witness in Rome. St Luke narrates Paul's journey as a prisoner, up to the point when Paul reaches Rome. The paths of the Gospel will now open up from Rome across the world.

2. CONTEXT

The author, and place and date of composition
Since this book and the third Gospel form part of the same project, its authorship and the various circumstances of its composition have been dealt with in the "Introduction to the Gospel of St Luke", above. In fact, as was pointed out there, theories about the author, and about the place and date of composition, are based more on Acts than on the third Gospel: Acts tells us more about the general plan and purpose that the author had before he began to write.

Literary and theological features

The Acts of the Apostles is a history book; but the author is not only writing history: he is teaching as well. Rationalist criticism in centuries past argued that the narratives in these books were the product of the imagination of a later, anonymous author with a particular agenda—to project his own image of Paul and the Church. These critics did not accept that Acts was genuine history; in their view, it was a propaganda piece designed to gloss over tensions between churches of Jewish background and those made up of Gentile converts: in this sense the book marked the start of Catholicism, for its author tried to project an idea of communion and a hierarchy onto the Church which (these authors claimed) never truly existed in it. For other commentators, the book marked the start of the sort of Christianity that has predominated from the second century onwards. According to these, Jesus Christ centred his preaching on the idea that the end of the world was nigh; St Paul followed suit; but St Luke, when he realized that the second coming of Christ was not imminent, drew the conclusion that there were stages in salvation history: the stage in which we live is the last stage, and what we must do is imitate Jesus Christ and await his second coming.

However, contemporary scholars find these interpretations somewhat arbitrary and superficial. It is true that the book seeks to contribute to the spread of the Gospel, but even though that is Luke's purpose, he assembled, checked and evaluated his sources very well: there is every reason to read him as a good historian.

With regard to St Paul, the events narrated in Acts, when checked against the Apostle's letters, can be seen to be historically accurate. It is true that Luke portrays Paul as a fully mature Christian personality from the day of his conversion forward; but this understandable simplification does not prevent us from recognizing the Paul of Acts and the Paul of the Letters as being the same person. The Paul of Acts is the real Paul, seen retrospectively by a disciple who is also a friend.[3]

Luke's historical accuracy is also borne out by Flavius Josephus' *Antiquitates iudaicae*, written some twenty years after Acts, and by later archaeological discoveries. Josephus enables us to establish the chronology of the reign of Herod Agrippa I (the date he gives for the king's sudden death is the same as that given by Luke).[4] Josephus also helps us to understand Luke's references to two Jewish rebels, Judas of Galilee and Theudas.[5] Luke's profiles of the two governors Felix and Festus and of Herod Agrippa II are also confirmed and developed by Josephus. Another instance of corroboration is that Acts 18:12 describes Gallio as being proconsul of Achaia and this has been borne out by an inscription found at Delphi, near Corinth. Moreover, especially as regards judicial procedures and titles and names of Roman officials, Acts has been shown to be a useful source of information about the customs and institutions of the period.

The *speeches* that the book contains[6] have been the subject of many detailed studies. The actual address in each instance would have been longer than the version given in the book, and

---

3 The connexions between Acts and the Letters point to one and the same Paul. His activity as persecutor of the Church is recorded in the same sort of language in Acts (8:3; 9:1) as it is in Galatians 1:13 and 1 Corinthians 15:9. Galatians 1:17 confirms what Acts says (9:3) about his conversion taking place in Damascus. In Acts 9:23–27 and Galatians 1:18 we are told that after his conversion Paul's first journey was to Jerusalem. In Acts 9:30 and Galatians 1:21 we are told that Paul was sent to Tarsus after his stay in Jerusalem (Tarsus was the capital of Cilicia). His missionary companions after the split with Barnabas —namely, Silas and Timothy (cf. Acts 15:22, 40; 16:1)—figure in the letters written during this period; the itinerary in Acts 16–19 (Philippi—Thessalonica—Athens—Corinth—Ephesus—Macedonia—Achaia) is confirmed in the letters (see 1 Thess 2:2; 3:1; 1 Cor 2:1; 16:5–9; 2 Cor 12:14ff; Rom 15:26). **4** See Acts 12:20–23 and *Antiquitates iudaicae*, 19, 274–363. **5** See Acts 5:36–37 and *Antiquitates iudaicae*, 20, 169–172. Here there are discrepancies between the information given in Luke and Josephus; however, scholars find more contradictions in Josephus' two works (the *Antiquitates* and *De bello iudaico*) than they do in Acts. **6**. In particular, the important speeches by Peter (see 2:14ff; 3:12ff; 10:34ff; 11:5ff), Stephen (see 7:1ff) and Paul (see 13:16ff; 17:22ff; 20:18ff; 22:1ff; 24:10ff; 26:2ff).

Luke would have had more to draw on for some than for others. Still, the texts reflect traditional Jewish styles of quotation and interpretation of Holy Scripture. Although the speeches are similar in structure to each other, they remain quite diverse. They reflect in obvious ways the differences of speaker, location and audience in each case, and they give a good idea of the Church's earliest form of preaching.

In line with the usual style of Jewish and Hellenist writers, Luke made use of sources when writing. He was not an eyewitness to everything he reported, and he would not have settled for simple rumour or verbal reports: he would have used documents of various kinds, such as short narrative accounts, summaries of speeches, notes, travel diaries, etc. Very probably, for the earlier part of the book he used material collected from the various churches or from the main people involved. Some scholars think that he used (a) an Antiochene source containing information about Stephen, Philip, Barnabas and Paul; (b) a collection of accounts concerning St Peter; and, of course, the author's own notes, expressed in the first person plural. But this is only a theory.

Nor is it possible to say whether Luke included all the material available to him or instead selected and edited his material. He clearly seems to have used his own judgment as to which items to incorporate into his narrative and which to omit. One indication of this is that whereas the first three years of the Church take up the first nine chapters, the rest of the book (nineteen chapters) cover over twenty-five years. Luke probably omitted any material that he did not think necessary for his purpose, and he must sometimes have decided to shorten, repeat, amalgamate or separate pieces of data that had come his way, according to their significance. Whatever the method, he gave a remarkable unity to his work, every page of which provides evidence of the Holy Spirit actively guiding the Church.

3. MESSAGE

Acts is a compendium of the Christian faith in action. St Luke's purposes, which are to inform and to instruct, lead him to cover all the principal truths of the Christian religion and to show the main outlines of the liturgical and sacramental life of the infant Church. His book also gives valuable insights into the way the Church was structured and managed, and into the attitudes of Christians towards political and social questions of their time.

Its teachings on Christ, the Holy Spirit and the Church merit special attention.

Jesus Christ

The teaching in Acts about Christ is based on his life on earth and on his glorification, which are the core of the Gospel message. All aspects of the paschal mystery—the passion, death, resurrection and ascension of our Lord—are given prominence. The apostles are "witnesses" to these events, which are shown to have fulfilled the plans of God announced long before in the Old Testament prophecies. Various Christological titles are applied to Jesus which show his divinity and his redemptive mission—titles such as Lord, Saviour, Servant of the Lord, the Righteous One, the Holy One, and especially Christ (Messiah), which becomes his proper name.

The Holy Spirit

St Luke stresses the key role of the Holy Spirit in all aspects of the life of the Church. He is mentioned by name fifty-seven times in the book. The Holy Spirit, who is at one and the same time the Spirit of God the Father and the Spirit of Jesus Christ, comes down on the disciples at Pentecost to make the Church manifest and enable it to begin its saving work; he is also sent to the centurion Cornelius in what has been called the "Pentecost of the Gentiles". The Spirit is the personal possession and the common inheritance of Christians, and the source of their joy and spiritual vitality. It is the Spirit who guides and supports in a special way those Christians who are ordained to carry out the various sacred ministries; and it is he who guides the Church in its choice of rulers and missionaries, and impels and protects it in its work of evangelization. With very good reason, this second book by St Luke has been called "the Gospel of the Holy Spirit".

The Church
Acts is an indispensable source of information about the life of the Church during its first three decades. In it we see the Church as the instrument God uses to implement the Old Testament promises. The Church is, then, the true Israel, a new people, a worldwide community joined by spiritual links, a body that is essentially missionary.

The Church enjoys the invisible but real presence of its risen Lord, who is the centre of Christian worship and the only Name by which one can be saved. Jesus' presence is real and substantial, brought about in the "breaking of the bread", that is, in the Eucharistic sacrifice, which his disciples already celebrate on Sunday, the first day of the week.

Acts describes the way of life of the early Christians in a direct and moving way. Their life centres on prayer, the Eucharist and the apostles' teaching, and it expresses itself in attitudes and actions of detachment, concord and love. St Luke offers this lifestyle as a model and patrimony for future generations of disciples.

Two aspects of Christianity are deliberately drawn together in the pages of this book—expectation of the Lord's second coming (which expectation runs right through the New Testament) and the need to commit oneself, through prayer, work and cheerful sacrifice, to the building up of the Kingdom of God on earth.

Acts also tells us a great deal about the structure of the Church in its earliest years, and provides us with a very valuable account of the first council of the Church.

The Acts of the Apostles

Prologue

1 ¹In the first book,* O Theophilus, I have dealt with all that Jesus began to do and teach, ²until the day when he was taken up, after he had given commandment through the Holy Spirit to the apostles whom he had chosen. ³To them he presented himself alive after his passion by many proofs, appearing to them during forty days, and speaking of the kingdom of God. ⁴And while staying^a with them he charged them not to depart from Jerusalem, but to wait for the promise of the Father, which, he said, "you heard from me, ⁵for John baptized with water, but before many days you shall be baptized with the Holy Spirit."

Lk 1:4
Mt 28:20
Lk 6:13; 24:49–51
Jn 20:22
1 Tim 3:16
Acts 10:40–41; 13:31
Lk 24:49
Mt 3:11
Lk 3:16
Acts 11:16

The Ascension

Mk 16:19
Lk 24:50–53

⁶So when they had come together, they asked him, "Lord, will you at this time restore the kingdom of Israel?" ⁷He said to them, "It is not for you to know times or

Lk 19:11; Dan 2:21
Mt 24:36; Mk 13:52
1 Thess 5:1–2
Mt 28:19

[1] ¹Primum quidem sermonem feci de omnibus, o Theophile, quae coepit Iesus facere et docere, ²usque in diem, qua, cum praecepisset apostolis per Spiritum Sanctum, quos elegit, assumptus est; ³quibus et praebuit seipsum vivum post passionem suam in multis argumentis, per dies quadraginta apparens eis et loquens ea, quae sunt de regno Dei. ⁴Et convescens praecepit eis ab Hierosolymis ne discederent, sed exspectarent promissionem Patris: «Quam audistis a me, ⁵quia Ioannes quidem baptizavit aqua, vos autem baptizabimini in Spiritu Sancto non post multos hos dies». ⁶Igitur qui convenerant, interrogabant eum dicentes: «Domine, si in tempore hoc restitues regnum Israeli?». ⁷Dixit autem eis: «Non est

1:1–5 As he has done in his Gospel (see Lk 1:1–4), St Luke begins his narrative with a prologue similar to those found in secular history books. He makes mention of events covered at the end of the first volume of his work, and then he will move on to describe the origins and early spread of Christianity, which are achieved through the power of the Holy Spirit, the main protagonist of his whole account. The spiritual dimension of this book, which is one of a piece with the third Gospel, nourished the souls of the first generations of Christians by providing them with a chronicle of God's faithful and loving support for the new Israel, the Church. So, although Luke's narrative style is akin to that of historians generally, this is a history book with a difference: "The Acts of the Apostles seems to be a straightforward historical account of the early years of the nascent Church. But if we bear in mind it is written by Luke the physician, who is praised in the Gospel [see 2 Cor 8:18], we will realize that everything he says is medicine for the ailing soul" (St Jerome, *Epistulae*, 53, 9).

"Theophilus" (v. 1), to whom the book is dedicated, may have been an educated Christian in comfortable circumstances; but this reference to a person may simply be a literary device, for the name means "beloved of God".

The third Gospel relates appearances of the risen Jesus to the disciples of Emmaus and to the apostles, indicating that they happened on the same day (see Lk 24:13–26). Here St Luke says that he appeared to them "during forty days" (v. 3). The figure of forty may be symbolic as well as literal. In Holy Scripture, periods of forty days and of forty years have a clearly salvific meaning: they are periods during which God prepares or effects important elements of his plans. The great flood lasted forty days (Gen 7:17); the Israelites journeyed forty years in the wilderness on their way to the promised land (Ps 95:10); Moses spent forty days on Mount Sinai, to receive God's revelation of the Covenant (Ex 24:18); Elijah walked forty days and forty nights on the strength of a loaf of bread sent him by God (1 Kings 19:8); and our Lord fasted in the wilderness for forty days in preparation for his public life (Mt 4:2).

1:6–11 The apostles' question (v. 6) shows that they are still thinking in terms of the restoration

a Or *eating*

Lk 24:47–48
Acts 10:39
Mk 16:15

Jn 6:62
Eph 4:8–10
1 Pet 3:22

Lk 24:4

Mt 24:30; 25:31;
26:64
Rev 1:7

seasons which the Father has fixed by his own authority. [8]But you shall receive power when the Holy Spirit has come upon you; and you shall be my witnesses in Jerusalem and in all Judea and Samaria and to the end of the earth." [9]And when he had said this, as they were looking on, he was lifted up, and a cloud took him out of their sight. [10]And while they were gazing into heaven as he went, behold, two men stood by them in white robes, [11]and said, "Men of Galilee, why do you stand looking into heaven? This Jesus, who was taken up from you into heaven, will come in the same way as you saw him go into heaven."

PART ONE

The Church in Jerusalem*

1. THE DISCIPLES IN JERUSALEM*

The apostolic college

Lk 24:50
Mt 10:2–4
Lk 6:14–16

[12]Then they returned to Jerusalem from the mount called Olivet, which is near Jerusalem, a sabbath day's journey away; [13]and when they had entered, they went up

vestrum nosse tempora vel momenta, quae Pater posuit in sua potestate, [8]sed accipietis virtutem superveniente Sancto Spiritu in vos et eritis mihi testes et in Ierusalem et in omni Iudaea et Samaria et usque ad ultimum terrae». [9]Et cum haec dixisset, videntibus illis, elevatus est, et nubes suscepit eum ab oculis eorum. [10]Cumque intuerentur in caelum eunte illo, ecce duo viri astiterunt iuxta illos in vestibus albis, [11]qui et dixerunt: «Viri Galilaei, quid statis aspicientes in caelum? Hic Iesus, qui assumptus est a vobis in caelum, sic veniet quemadmodum vidistis eum euntem in caelum». [12]Tunc reversi sunt in Ierusalem a monte, qui vocatur Oliveti, qui est iuxta Ierusalem sabbati habens iter. [13]Et cum introissent, in cenaculum ascenderunt, ubi manebant et Petrus et Ioannes et Iacobus et Andreas, Philippus et Thomas, Bartholomaeus et Matthaeus, Iacobus Alphaei et Simon Zelotes et Iudas Iacobi. [14]Hi omnes erant perseverantes unanimiter in oratione cum mulieribus et Maria matre Iesu et fratribus eius. [15]Et

of an earthly Davidic kingdom. It would seem that for them (as for many other Jews of their time) hope in the Kingdom went no further than expectation of a world-wide Jewish hegemony to be established with God's help. Our Lord's reply shows them that that hope is a false illusion: God's plans operate on a much higher plane; they have nothing to do with political objectives, but seek to transform people through the action of the Holy Spirit: "It seems to me that they had not any clear notion of the nature of the Kingdom, for the Spirit had not yet instructed them" (St John Chrysostom, *In Acta Apostolorum*, 2).

In correcting his disciples' ideas, our Lord tells them very clearly what their mission is—to be his witnesses to the ends of the earth (v. 8): "Concern for souls is a response to a command of love given us by our Lord. As he goes up to heaven, Jesus sends us out as his witnesses throughout the whole world. Our responsibility is great, because to be Christ's witness implies

first of all that we should try to behave according to his doctrine, that we should struggle to make our actions remind others of Jesus and his most lovable personality" (St Josemaría Escrivá, *Christ Is Passing By*, 122).

After this, our Lord ascends into heaven. As regards the present state of the risen body of Jesus, "Christ's Ascension into heaven signifies his participation, in his humanity, in God's power and authority. Jesus Christ is Lord: he possesses all power in heaven and on earth. [...] As Lord, Christ is also head of the Church, which is his Body. Taken up to heaven and glorified after he had thus fully accomplished his mission, Christ dwells on earth in his Church" (*Catechism of the Catholic Church*, 668–669).

*1:12—7:60 The first seven chapters of Acts describe the life of the nascent Church in Jerusalem. After Matthias is elected to fill the ranks of the Twelve (1:15–26), the Holy Spirit

to the upper room, where they were staying, Peter and John and James and Andrew, Philip and Thomas, Bartholomew and Matthew, James the son of Alphaeus and Simon the Zealot and Judas the son of James. [14]All these with one accord devoted themselves to prayer, together with the women and Mary the mother of Jesus, and with his brethren.*

Mt 13:55
Lk 8:2–3; 24:10
Acts 12:12

in diebus illis exsurgens Petrus in medio fratrum dixit—erat autem turba hominum simul fere centum viginti—: [16]«Viri fratres, oportebat impleri Scripturam, quam praedixit Spiritus Sanctus per os David de Iuda, qui fuit dux eorum, qui comprehenderunt Iesum, [17]quia connumeratus erat in nobis et sortitus est sortem ministerii huius. [18]Hic quidem possedit agrum de mercede iniquitatis et pronus factus crepuit medius, et diffusa sunt

comes at Pentecost (2:1–13) and the apostles begin to preach Jesus Christ (2:14–42).

We learn about the growth of the community around Peter and the other apostles. Miracles and prodigies (3:1–10; 5:1–16) accompany the preaching of the Twelve. In occasional summaries in the text (1:14; 2:42–47; 4:32–37; 5:12–16) Luke gives us an idea of the spiritual vitality of the early Church. The steady growth in numbers (2:41, 47; 4:4; 5:14; 6:1) makes the election of the Seven necessary (6:1–6). This part of the book ends with an account of the persecution unleashed against the Church, the martyrdom of Stephen (6:8–7:60); and the narrative focus then changes to the regions bordering on Judea (8:1ff).

*1:12–26 St Luke introduces us to the small group of disciples, the nucleus of the nascent Church, prior to the coming of the Holy Spirit. He names the members of the apostolic college (1:13)—which will be completed by the election of Matthias (1:26)—and he mentions Mary the Mother of Jesus (1:14).

In a way similar to how the Holy Spirit descended on Mary "full of grace" (Lk 1:28), he will now descend on this group gathered together in prayer (1:14, 24).

1:12–14 There are a number of interesting aspects to this short description of the group of disciples gathered prior to the coming of the Holy Spirit. Firstly, the author mentions the Eleven, who were witnesses to Jesus' public life and to his resurrection; "the women", who witnessed his death, burial and resurrection; Mary, the Lord's Mother, the privileged witness of his infancy and hidden life; and other relatives of his. This first community is well-placed and well-qualified to bear witness to Christ with authority.

The text also tells us about a highly significant feature of the early times of the Church: "We are told this time and again in the passage narrating the lives of the first followers of Christ. 'All these with one accord devoted themselves to prayer' (Acts 1:14). [...] Prayer was then, as it is today, the only weapon, the most powerful means, for winning the battles of our interior struggle" (St Josemaría Escrivá, *Friends of God*, 242).

The sacred writer makes a point of noting Mary's presence alongside the apostles. By meditating on this vignette, Tradition has concluded that it provides evidence of Mary's role as Mother of the whole Church, from its inception and forever thereafter. "In the redemptive economy of grace, brought about through the action of the Holy Spirit, there is a unique correspondence between the moment of the Incarnation of the Word and the moment of the birth of the Church. The person who links these two moments is Mary: *Mary at Nazareth* and *Mary in the Upper Room at Jerusalem*. In both cases her discreet yet essential presence indicates the path of 'birth from the Holy Spirit.' Thus she who is present in the mystery of Christ as Mother becomes—by the will of the Son and the power of the Holy Spirit—present in the mystery of the Church. In the Church too she continues to be *a maternal presence*" (John Paul II, *Redemptoris Mater*, 24).

The passage refers to the "brethren" of Jesus (v. 14), a term that is found also in the Gospels and which has the broad meaning of "relatives", without specifying the precise degree of kinship. The Church, guided by the Holy Spirit, has always held that the Blessed Virgin had no children other than Jesus: see the notes on Mt 1:18–25; 12:46–50; Mk 3:31–35; Lk 8:19–21.

The election of Matthias

Ps 41:9
Lk 22:47
Jn 13:18

[15]In those days Peter stood up among the brethren (the company of persons was in all about a hundred and twenty), and said, [16]"Brethren, the scripture had to be fulfilled, which the Holy Spirit spoke beforehand by the mouth of David, concerning Judas who was guide to those who arrested Jesus. [17]For he was numbered among us,

Mt 27:3–10

and was allotted his share in this ministry. [18](Now this man bought a field with the reward of his wickedness; and falling headlong[b] he burst open in the middle and all his bowels gushed out. [19]And it became known to all the inhabitants of Jerusalem, so that the field was called in their language Akeldama, that is, Field of Blood.) [20]For it is written in the Book of Psalms,

Ps 69:25; 109:8

'Let his habitation become desolate,
and let there be no one to live in it';

and

'His office let another take.'

Jn 15:27

[21]So one of the men who have accompanied us during all the time that the Lord

Lk 1:2
Acts 4:20

Jesus went in and out among us, [22]beginning from the baptism of John until the day when he was taken up from us—one of these men must become with us a witness to

omnia viscera eius. [19]Et notum factum est omnibus habitantibus Ierusalem, ita ut appellaretur ager ille lingua eorum Aceldamach, hoc est ager Sanguinis. [20]Scriptum est enim in libro Psalmorum: *"Fiat commoratio eius deserta, / et non sit qui inhabitet in ea"* / et: *"Episcopatum eius accipiat alius"*. [21]Oportet ergo ex his viris, qui nobiscum congregati erant in omni tempore, quo intravit et exivit inter nos Dominus Iesus, [22]incipiens a baptismate Ioannis usque in diem, qua assumptus est a nobis, testem resurrectionis eius nobiscum fieri unum ex istis». [23]Et statuerunt duos,

---

1:15–26 The episode of Matthias' election has important things to say about the constitution of the Church, such as the number of the Twelve and the place Peter holds in the community.

The initiative for the election comes from Peter, whom Jesus has commissioned to confirm the faith of his brethren (Lk 22:32). Peter first calls to mind the violent death of Judas (vv. 18–19; cf. Mt 27:3–10) and proposes that someone be elected as an apostle in Judas' place. Later on, when James the Greater dies (12:2), no mention is made of this sort of procedure; so Peter's action seems to indicate that the group of the Twelve was needed to be in position before the Holy Spirit came and the Church became publicly made known.

The Christian community uses the method of casting lots (used in the Old Testament: see e.g. 1 Sam 14:41) because, as they see it, God has already made his choice and he will reveal it when the lots are cast: "They all pray together, saying: 'Lord, who knowest the hearts of all men, show [us]'. They rightly asked Him to open their hearts, for it was He alone who could make the choice. In their need for the election of a new apostle, their prayer is trusting and confident. They do not tell God to choose, but to 'show

which one of these two thou hast chosen', because they know that God has foreseen all things. 'And they cast lots' because they did not consider themselves worthy to make the choice alone and chose instead to rely on a sign from God" (St John Chrysostom, *In Acta Apostolorum*, 3, 3).

Luke usually reserves the term "apostles" for the Twelve (see e.g. 6:6), or the Eleven plus Peter, who is presented as the head of the apostolic college (see 2:14). Throughout Acts, the apostles have as their main functions: to be witnesses to the resurrection of Jesus (1:21–22) and to express this testimony through the ministry of the Word (6:4), accompanied by signs and wonders that illustrate the salvation they proclaim (see 2:14–21, 43; 3:1—11:16). The Twelve are also responsible for the management of the Church—collecting resources for needy brethren (4:35), electing people to church office (6:2–3), intervening to ensure unity among the faithful (11:1–18; 15:2), etc.

Luke focuses a lot of attention on Peter, mentioning him by name 56 times in his book. Peter is always the central focus of attention in scenes and episodes where he appears with other apostles or disciples. In events having to do with the

b Or *swelling up*

his resurrection."* ²³And they put forward two, Joseph called Barsabbas, who was Jer 11:20
Lk 16:15
Acts 15:8
surnamed Justus, and Matthias. ²⁴And they prayed and said, "Lord, who knowest the Rev 2:23
hearts of all men, show which one of these two thou hast chosen ²⁵to take the place
in this ministry and apostleship from which Judas turned aside, to go to his own
place." ²⁶And they cast lots for them, and the lot fell on Matthias; and he was 1 Sam 14:41
Prov 16:33
enrolled with the eleven apostles.

2. PENTECOST*

The coming of the Holy Spirit

2 ¹When the day of Pentecost had come, they were all together in one place. ²And Lev 23:15–21
Deut 16:9–11
suddenly a sound came from heaven like the rush of a mighty wind, and it filled Jn 3:8
Acts 4:31
all the house where they were sitting. ³And there appeared to them tongues as of fire,
distributed and resting on each one of them. ⁴And they were all filled with the Holy Ps 104:30
Mt 3:11
Spirit and began to speak in other tongues, as the Spirit gave them utterance. Acts 10:44–46; 19:6

Ioseph, qui vocabatur Barsabbas, qui cognominatus est Iustus, et Matthiam. ²⁴Et orantes dixerunt: «Tu, Domine, qui corda nosti omnium, ostende quem elegeris ex his duobus unum ²⁵accipere locum ministerii huius et apostolatus, de quo praevaricatus est Iudas, ut abiret in locum suum». ²⁶Et dederunt sortes eis, et cecidit sors super Matthiam, et annumeratus est cum undecim apostolis. [2] ¹Et cum compleretur dies Pentecostes, erant omnes pariter in eodem loco. ²Et factus est repente de caelo sonus tamquam advenientis spiritus vehementis et replevit totam domum, ubi erant sedentes. ³Et apparuerunt illis dispertitae linguae tamquam ignis, seditque supra singulos eorum; ⁴et repleti sunt omnes Spiritu Sancto et coeperunt loqui aliis linguis, prout Spiritus dabat eloqui illis. ⁵Erant autem in Ierusalem habitantes Iudaei, viri religiosi ex omni natione, quae sub caelo

Jerusalem community, Peter acts as the spokesman of the Twelve (2:14, 37–38; 5:29); and he plays a key role in the opening up of the Gospel to pagans.

The college of the twelve apostles, with Peter at its head, subsists in the episcopacy of the Church, whose head is the bishop of Rome, Peter's successor and the vicar of Christ: "Just as, in accordance with the Lord's decree, St Peter and the rest of the apostles constitute a unique apostolic college, so in like fashion the Roman pontiff, Peter's successor, and the bishops, the successors of the apostles, are related with and united to one another" (Vatican II, *Lumen gentium*, 22).

*2:1–47 In Acts, Pentecost marks the point at which the Church takes its first steps, animated by the Holy Spirit; it is the new People of God, commissioned to proclaim the Gospel to all nations and to console all those whom God has called. The outpouring of the Holy Spirit is seen by the apostles as a form of revelation; later on, St Peter will see the descent of the Spirit on Cornelius and his family and friends (10:24, 44–48; 11:15–17) as a clear sign that Gentiles, too, are called by God, without the biblical condition of circumcision being required.

2:1–13 This account of the coming of the Holy Spirit is full of symbolism. Pentecost was one of the three great Jewish feasts; it was held on the fiftieth day after the Passover, and many Israelites went on pilgrimage to Jerusalem for that day. The feast originated as a thanksgiving for the grain harvest, and involved an offering of the first fruits. Later it was given the added dimension of commemorating the promulgation of the Law given by God to Moses on Sinai. The noise, like that of a strong wind, and the fire (vv. 2–3) are powerfully evocative of the way God manifested himself on Mount Sinai (see Ex 19:16, 18; Ps 29), when, on giving them the Law, God established Israel as his own people. Now, with the same signs, he reveals himself to his new people, the Church; the wind signals that he is about to act in a completely new way in the history of man (cf. *Catechism of the Catholic Church*, 691); and "fire symbolizes the transforming energy of the Holy Spirit's actions" (ibid., 696).

The listing of the countries where these people came from (vv. 5, 9–11), juxtaposed with the fact that they can all understand what the apostles are saying (vv. 4, 6, 8, 11), is reminiscent, by way of contrast, of the confusion

Mk 16:17

Gen 11:1–9
Col 1:23

⁵Now there were dwelling in Jerusalem Jews, devout men from every nation under heaven. ⁶And at this sound the multitude came together, and they were bewildered, because each one heard them speaking in his own language. ⁷And they were amazed and wondered, saying, "Are not all these who are speaking Galileans? ⁸And how is it that we hear, each of us in his own native language? ⁹Parthians and Medes and Elamites and residents of Mesopotamia, Judea and Cappadocia, Pontus and Asia, ¹⁰Phrygia and Pamphylia, Egypt and the parts of Libya belonging to Cyrene, and visitors from Rome, both Jews and proselytes, ¹¹Cretans and Arabians, we hear

1 Cor 14:22–25

them telling in our own tongues the mighty works of God." ¹²And all were amazed and perplexed, saying to one another, "What does this mean?" ¹³But others mocking said, "They are filled with new wine."

Peter's address

Acts 15:7

¹⁴But Peter,* standing with the eleven, lifted up his voice and addressed them, "Men of Judea and all who dwell in Jerusalem, let this be known to you, and give ear to my words. ¹⁵For these men are not drunk, as you suppose, since it is only the third hour of the day; ¹⁶but this is what was spoken by the prophet Joel:

Joel 3:1–5

> ¹⁷'And in the last days it shall be, God declares,
> that I will pour out my Spirit upon all flesh,
> and your sons and your daughters shall prophesy,
> and your young men shall see visions,
> and your old men shall dream dreams;

Rom 5:5

> ¹⁸yea, and on my menservants and my maidservants in those days
> I will pour out my Spirit; and they shall prophesy.

est; ⁶facta autem hac voce, convenit multitudo et confusa est, quoniam audiebat unusquisque lingua sua illos loquentes. ⁷Stupebant autem et mirabantur dicentes: «Nonne ecce omnes isti, qui loquuntur, Galilaei sunt? ⁸Et quomodo nos audimus unusquisque propria lingua nostra, in qua nati sumus? ⁹Parthi et Medi et Elamitae, et qui habitant Mesopotamiam, Iudaeam quoque et Cappadociam, Pontum et Asiam, ¹⁰Phrygiam quoque et Pamphyliam, Aegyptum et partes Libyae, quae est circa Cyrenem, et advenae Romani, ¹¹Iudaei quoque et proselyti, Cretes et Arabes, audimus loquentes eos nostris linguis magnalia Dei». ¹²Stupebant autem omnes et haesitabant ad invicem dicentes: «Quidnam hoc vult esse?»; ¹³alii autem irridentes dicebant: «Musto pleni sunt isti». ¹⁴Stans autem Petrus cum Undecim levavit vocem suam et locutus est eis: «Viri Iudaei et, qui habitatis Ierusalem universi, hoc vobis notum sit, et auribus percipite verba mea. ¹⁵Non enim, sicut vos aestimatis, hi ebrii sunt, est enim hora diei tertia, ¹⁶sed hoc est, quod dictum est per prophetam Ioel: ¹⁷"*Et erit*: in novissimis diebus, dicit Deus, / *effundam de Spiritu meo super omnem carnem, / et prophetabunt filii vestri et filiae vestrae, / et iuvenes vestri visiones videbunt, / et seniores vestri somnia somniabunt*; / ¹⁸*et quidem*

of language that took place at Babel (see Gen 11:1–9). "Without doubt, the Holy Spirit was at work in the world before Christ was glorified. On the day of Pentecost, however, he came down on the disciples that he might remain with them forever (cf. Jn 14:16); on that day the Church was openly displayed to the crowds and the spread of the Gospel among the nations, through preaching, was begun. Finally, on that day was foreshadowed the union of all peoples in the catholicity of the faith by means of the Church of the New Alliance, a Church which speaks every language, understands and embraces all tongues in charity, and thus overcomes the dispersion of Babel" (Vatican II, *Ad gentes*, 4). The gift of the Spirit is ongoing; we, too, need it, for at all times and places we should bear witness to Christ:

"Every generation of Christians [...] must understand and share the desires of other men—their equals—in order to make known to them, with a 'gift of tongues', how they are to respond to the action of the Holy Spirit, to that permanent outflow of rich treasures that comes from our Lord's heart. We Christians are called upon to announce, in our own time, to this world to which we belong and in which we live, the message—old and at the same time new—of the Gospel" (St Josemaría Escrivá, *Christ Is Passing By*, 132).

2:14–36 Peter now speaks in the name of the Twelve, as he will do on many other occasions. His speech is full of quotations from the Old Testament which he uses to explain the meaning of what has just happened: "The prophetic texts

¹⁹ And I will show wonders in the heaven above
    and signs on the earth beneath,
    blood, and fire, and vapour of smoke;
²⁰ the sun shall be turned into darkness
    and the moon into blood,
    before the day of the Lord comes,
    the great and manifest day.
²¹ And it shall be that whoever calls on the name of the Lord shall be saved.'

²²"Men of Israel, hear these words: Jesus of Nazareth a man attested to you by God with mighty works and wonders and signs which God did through him in your midst, as you yourselves know—²³this Jesus, delivered up according to the definite plan and foreknowledge of God, you crucified and killed by the hands of lawless men. ²⁴But God raised him up, having loosed the pangs of death, because it was not possible for him to be held by it. ²⁵For David says concerning him,

    'I saw the Lord always before me,
    for he is at my right hand that I may not be shaken;
²⁶ therefore my heart was glad, and my tongue rejoiced;
    moreover my flesh will dwell in hope.
²⁷ For thou wilt not abandon my soul to Hades,
    nor let thy Holy One see corruption.
²⁸ Thou hast made known to me the ways of life;
    thou wilt make me full of gladness with thy presence.'

²⁹"Brethren, I may say to you confidently of the patriarch David that he both died and was buried, and his tomb is with us to this day. ³⁰Being therefore a prophet, and

Marginal references:
Acts 5:12
Rev 6:12
Mt 24:29

Rom 10:9–13

Jn 3:2; 5:36

Lk 23:33, 46
Jn 19:6, 11
Acts 3:15

2 Sam 22:6
Ps 18:5
Acts 13:34–37

Ps 16:8–11

1 Kings 2:10

2 Sam 7:12–13
Ps 132:11

super servos meos et super ancillas meas / in diebus illis effundam de Spiritu meo,/ et prophetabunt. / ¹⁹Et dabo prodigia in caelo sursum et signa in terra deorsum,/ sanguinem et ignem et vaporem fumi;/ ²⁰sol convertetur in tenebras / et luna in sanguinem,/ antequam veniat dies Domini / magnus et manifestus. / ²¹Et erit: / omnis quicumque invocaverit nomen Domini, salvus erit". ²²Viri Israelitae, audite verba haec: Iesum Nazarenum, virum approbatum a Deo apud vos virtutibus et prodigiis et signis, quae fecit per illum Deus in medio vestri, sicut ipsi scitis, ²³hunc definito consilio et praescientia Dei traditum per manum iniquorum affigentes interemistis, ²⁴quem Deus suscitavit solutis doloribus mortis, iuxta quod impossibile erat teneri illum ab ea. ²⁵David enim dicit circa eum: "Providebam Dominum coram me semper, / quoniam a dextris meis est, ne commovear. / ²⁶Propter hoc laetatum est cor meum, / et exsultavit lingua mea; / insuper et caro mea requiescet in spe. / ²⁷Quoniam non dere- linques animam meam in inferno / neque dabis Sanctum tuum videre corruptionem. / ²⁸Notas fecisti mihi vias vitae, / replebis me iucunditate cum facie tua". ²⁹Viri fratres, liceat audenter dicere ad vos de patriarcha David quoniam et defunctus est et sepultus est et sepulcrum eius est apud nos usque in hodiernum diem; ³⁰propheta igitur cum esset et sciret quia iure iurando iurasset illi Deus de fructu lumbi eius sedere super sedem eius,

that directly concern the sending of the Holy Spirit are oracles by which God speaks to the heart of his people in the language of the prom-ise, with the accents of 'love and fidelity' […]. According to these promises, at the 'end time' the Lord's Spirit will renew the hearts of men, engraving a new law in them. He will gather and reconcile the scattered and divided peoples; he will transform the first creation, and God will dwell there with men in peace" (*Catechism of the Catholic Church*, 715).

In his address Peter outlines the content of the apostolic proclamation (the *kérygma*), the content of preaching and belief. This proclama-tion bears witness to the death and resurrection of Jesus and his subsequent glorification; it recalls the main aspects of Christ's mission, announced by John the Baptist, confirmed by miracles and concluding with the appearances of the risen Lord and the outpouring of the Holy Spirit; Peter tells people that the messianic time foretold by the prophets has come to pass, and he calls on everyone to repent, in order to prepare for the Parousia—the second coming of Christ, in glory. These central ideas are essentially the same as those passed on to us in the written Gospels, particularly the Synoptics.

Commenting on this passage, St John Chrysostom draws attention to the change worked in Peter by the Holy Spirit, and to the apostle's daring: "Listen to him preach and argue so boldly, who shortly before had trembled at the

knowing that God had sworn with an oath to him that he would set one of his

Ps 16:10
Lk 24:48
Acts, 5:31;7:55–56
Rom 8:34
Phil 2:9

Ps 110:1
Mt 22:44

Acts 5:30–31

descendants upon his throne, ³¹he foresaw and spoke of the resurrection of the Christ, that he was not abandoned to Hades, nor did his flesh see corruption. ³²This Jesus God raised up, and of that we all are witnesses. ³³Being therefore exalted at the right hand of God, and having received from the Father the promise of the Holy Spirit, he has poured out this which you see and hear. ³⁴For David did not ascend into the heavens; but he himself says,

'The Lord said to my Lord, Sit at my right hand,
    ³⁵till I make thy enemies a stool for thy feet.'

³⁶Let all the house of Israel therefore know assuredly that God has made him both Lord and Christ, this Jesus whom you crucified."

Many baptisms

Lk 3:10, 12, 14

Mt 3:2
Lk 13:3
Acts 3:19; 8:16

Is 57:19
Joel 3:5
Acts 3:26; 13:46
Eph 2:13–17

Deut 32:5
Ps 78:8
Mt 17:17

Acts 5:14; 6:7

³⁷Now when they heard this they were cut to the heart, and said to Peter and the rest of the apostles, "Brethren, what shall we do?" ³⁸And Peter said to them, "Repent, and be baptized every one of you in the name of Jesus Christ for the forgiveness of your sins; and you shall receive the gift of the Holy Spirit. ³⁹For the promise is to you and to your children and to all that are far off, every one whom the Lord our God calls to him." ⁴⁰And he testified with many other words and exhorted them, saying, "Save yourselves from this crooked generation." ⁴¹So those who received his word were baptized, and there were added that day about three thousand souls.

³¹providens locutus est de resurrectione Christi quia *neque derelictus est in inferno, neque* caro eius *vidit corruptionem*. ³²Hunc Iesum resuscitavit Deus, cuius omnes nos testes sumus. ³³Dextera igitur Dei exaltatus et, promissione Spiritus Sancti accepta a Patre, effudit hunc, quem vos videtis et auditis. ³⁴Non enim David ascendit in caelos; dicit autem ipse: "*Dixit Dominus Domino meo: Sede a dextris meis, / ³⁵donec ponam inimicos tuos scabellum pedum tuorum*". ³⁶Certissime ergo sciat omnis domus Israel quia et Dominum eum et Christum Deus fecit, hunc Iesum, quem vos crucifixistis». ³⁷His auditis, compuncti sunt corde et dixerunt ad Petrum et reliquos apostolos: «Quid faciemus, viri fratres?». ³⁸Petrus vero ad illos: «Paenitentiam, inquit, agite, et baptizetur unusquisque vestrum in nomine Iesu Christi in remissionem peccatorum vestrorum, et accipietis donum Sancti Spiritus; ³⁹vobis enim est repromissio et filiis vestris et omnibus, qui longe sunt, quoscumque advocaverit Dominus Deus noster». ⁴⁰Aliis etiam verbis pluribus testificatus est et exhortabatur eos dicens: «Salvamini a generatione ista prava». ⁴¹Qui ergo, recepto sermone eius, baptizati sunt; et appositae sunt in illa die animae circiter tria milia. ⁴²Erant autem perseverantes in doctrina apostolorum et communicatione, in fractione

word of a servant girl! This boldness is a significant proof of the resurrection of his Master: Peter preaches to men who mock and laugh at his enthusiasm. [...] Calumny ('they are filled with new wine') does not deter the apostles; sarcasm does not undermine their courage, for the coming of the Holy Spirit has made new men of them, men who can put up with every kind of human test. When the Holy Spirit enters into hearts he does so to elevate their affections and to change earthly souls, souls of clay, into chosen souls, people of real courage [...]. Look at the harmony that exists among the apostles. See how they allow Peter to speak on behalf of them all. Peter raises his voice and speaks to the people with full assurance. That is the kind of courage a man has when he is the instrument of the Holy Spirit. [...] Just as a burning coal does not lose its heat when it falls on a haystack but

instead is enabled to release its heat, so Peter, now that he is in contact with the life-giving Spirit, spreads his inner fire to those around him" (*In Acta Apostolorum*, 4).

2:37–41 The Baptism that Peter prescribes is not that of John the Baptist, for it includes the gift of the Holy Spirit (v. 38; cf. 1:5; Lk 3:3, 16). "Be baptized [...] in the name of Jesus Christ": this is not a liturgical form of words used by the apostles, substituting for the Trinitarian formula found in Matthew 28:19. In the *Didache* or *Teaching of the Twelve Apostles* (written around the year 100) it is stated that Baptism should be given in the name of the Father and of the Son and of the Holy Spirit; but Christians are also often referred to here and in other places as "those baptized in the name of the Lord" (see *Didache*, 7, 1; 9, 5). "Baptized in the name of

The early Christians

⁴²And they devoted themselves to the apostles' teaching and fellowship, to the breaking of bread and the prayers.

⁴³And fear came upon every soul; and many wonders and signs were done through the apostles. ⁴⁴And all who believed were together and had all things in common; ⁴⁵and they sold their possessions and goods and distributed them to all, as any had need. ⁴⁶And day by day, attending the temple together and breaking bread in their homes, they partook of food with glad and generous hearts, ⁴⁷praising God and having favour with all the people. And the Lord added to their number day by day those who were being saved.

Acts 5:11–12

Acts 4:32, 34–35

Lk 24:53
Acts 16:34

Acts 13:48

panis et orationibus. ⁴³Fiebat autem omni animae timor; multa quoque prodigia et signa per apostolos fiebant. ⁴⁴Omnes autem, qui crediderant erant pariter et habebant omnia communia ⁴⁵et possessiones et substantias vendebant et dividebant illas omnibus, prout cuique opus erat; ⁴⁶cotidie quoque perdurantes unanimiter in templo et frangentes circa domos panem, sumebant cibum cum exsultatione et simplicitate cordis, ⁴⁷collaudantes Deum et habentes gratiam ad omnem plebem. Dominus autem augebat, qui salvi fierent cotidie in idipsum.   [3] ¹Petrus autem et

Christ", therefore, refers to the sacrament instituted by Jesus Christ, the sacrament through which a person becomes a Christian.

2:42–47 This is the second of the four summaries found early on in Acts (cf. 1:14; 4:32–37; 5:12–16). It begins (v. 42) by describing in simple terms the key elements of the ascetical and sacramental life of the first Christians. "This sequence is characteristic of the Church's prayer: founded on the apostolic faith; authenticated by charity; nourished in the Eucharist" (*Catechism of the Catholic Church*, 2624).

The "apostles' teaching" means the instruction normally given to new converts. Distinct from the proclamation of the Gospel to non-Christians, it is a type of *catechesis* (which, with time, became more structured and systematic) designed to explain to disciples the basic truths of the Faith (these explanations soon gave rise to the Church's creeds and statements of belief) which they needed to hold to and to practise in order to attain salvation. Catechesis, ongoing preaching and explanation of the Gospel within the bosom of the Church, has been there from its very beginning. "An evangelizer, the Church begins by evangelizing itself. A community of believers, a community of hope practised and transmitted, a community of fraternal love, it has a need to listen unceasingly to what it must believe, to the reasons for its hope, to the new commandment of love" (Paul VI, *Evangelii nuntiandi*, 15).

"Fellowship" (v. 42) is the union of hearts which is brought about by the Holy Spirit. This profound solidarity among the disciples came from their practice of the faith and their appreciation of it as a shared treasure, a gift to them from God through Jesus Christ (cf. Gal 2:9). This mutual affection enabled them to be detached from material things and to generously support those in need (vv. 45–46): "This voluntary poverty and detachment strike at the selfish root of many evils, and the new disciples showed that they had understood the Gospel teaching" (Chrysostom, *In Acta Apostolorum*, 7).

"The breaking of bread" (v. 42) is one of the names given to the Blessed Eucharist. It is called this "because Jesus used this rite, part of a Jewish meal, when as master of the table he blessed and distributed the bread, above all at the Last Supper. It is by this action that his disciples will recognize him after his Resurrection, and it is this expression that the first Christians will use to designate their Eucharistic assemblies; by doing so they signified that all who eat the one broken bread, Christ, enter into communion with him and form but one body in him" (*Catechism of the Catholic Church*, 1329). Other names were also used, such as "Eucharist", which puts the stress on the idea of thanksgiving (see *Didache*, 9, 1). From Pentecost onwards, the Mass and Holy Communion form the core of Christian worship.

"The prayers" (v. 42) probably means the psalms and hymns that were part of the celebra-

3. THE APOSTLES' WORK IN JERUSALEM*

Curing of a man lame from birth

Acts 14:8–10

3 ¹Now Peter and John were going up to the temple at the hour of prayer, the ninth hour.* ²And a man lame from birth was being carried, whom they laid daily at the gate of the temple which is called Beautiful to ask alms of those who entered the temple. ³Seeing Peter and John about to go into the temple, he asked for alms. ⁴And Peter directed his gaze at him, with John, and said, "Look at us." ⁵And he fixed his attention upon them, expecting to receive something from them. ⁶But Peter said, "I have no silver and gold, but I give you what I have; in the name of Jesus Christ of

Is 35:6
Lk 7:22

Nazareth, walk." ⁷And he took him by the right hand and raised him up; and imme-

Jn 5:14

diately his feet and ankles were made strong. ⁸And leaping up he stood and walked and entered the temple with them, walking and leaping and praising God. ⁹And all the people saw him walking and praising God, ¹⁰and recognized him as the one who sat for alms at the Beautiful Gate of the temple; and they were filled with wonder and amazement at what had happened to him.

Ioannes ascendebant in templum ad horam orationis nonam. ²Et quidam vir, qui erat claudus ex utero matris suae, baiulabatur, quem ponebant cotidie ad portam templi, quae dicitur Speciosa, ut peteret eleemosynam ab introeuntibus in templum; ³is cum vidisset Petrum et Ioannem incipientes introire in templum, rogabat, ut eleemosynam acciperet. ⁴Intuens autem in eum Petrus cum Ioanne dixit: «Respice in nos». ⁵At ille intendebat in eos, sperans se aliquid accepturum ab eis. ⁶Petrus autem dixit: «Argentum et aurum non est mihi; quod autem habeo, hoc tibi do: In nomine Iesu Christi Nazareni surge et ambula!». ⁷Et apprehensa ei manu dextera, allevavit eum; et protinus consolidatae sunt bases eius et tali, ⁸et exsiliens stetit et ambulabat et intravit cum illis in templum, ambulans et exsiliens et laudans Deum. ⁹Et vidit omnis populus eum ambulantem et laudantem Deum; ¹⁰cognoscebant autem illum quoniam ipse erat, qui ad eleemosynam sedebat ad Speciosam portam templi, et impleti sunt stupore et exstasi in eo, quod contigerat illi. ¹¹Cum teneret autem Petrum et Ioannem, concurrit omnis populus ad eos ad porticum, qui appellatur

tion of the Eucharist. The fact that the text says "the" prayers, and "prayers" rather than "prayer", indicates that specific prayers were involved. These early Jerusalem Christians did go to the temple because, initially, it was one of the centres of their liturgical and prayer life (v. 46). The temple was for them the house of God. However, it was not the only place where they met for prayer and worship. When the text speaks of their "breaking bread in their homes", it is probably referring to the breaking of the bread mentioned earlier (v. 42): the Christian community of Jerusalem (like the communities later founded by St Paul) did not have buildings set apart for liturgical assemblies; the liturgy took place in private houses, in dignified settings. It was not until the third century that buildings designed solely for liturgical use were built.

*3:1—5:42 Strengthened by the Holy Spirit whom they received at Pentecost, the apostles press on with their proclamation of the Gospel, the truth of which is borne out by their works. They soon meet with opposition from the Jewish authorities (4:1–3; 5:17–18), and the faults and failings of some church members are not slow to

appear (5:1–11), but the text does show the radical optimism of those guided by the Spirit: they were held in high regard by the people (5:15–16); prominent just men such as Gamaliel treated them with respect (5:34–39); the Spirit gave them courage (4:31); and the Lord consoled them by increasing the number of the faithful and helping the early community to grow in virtue (4:4, 32–37), for "the sight of events like this can indeed cause conviction and faith in those who love the truth, who are not swayed by opinions and who do not let their evil passions gain the upper hand" (St Justin, *Apologia*, 1, 53).

3:1–10 This episode bears out what Luke has said in summary form in 2:42–47: it shows the apostles to be men of prayer and workers of miracles who are praised by the people. Peter and John go to the temple at the time of the evening sacrifice, which began around three and lasted until sunset. Many pious Jews usually attended it. (In the morning there was another, similar sacrifice, beginning at dawn and lasting until the third hour, that is, around nine in the morning.) The cure of the lame man is the first miracle worked by the apostles, who must have sensed

Peter's address in the temple

[11]While he clung to Peter and John, all the people ran together to them in the portico called Solomon's, astounded. [12]And when Peter saw it he addressed the people, "Men of Israel, why do you wonder at this, or why do you stare at us, as though by our own power or piety we had made him walk? [13]The God of Abraham and of Isaac and of Jacob, the God of our fathers, glorified his servant[c] Jesus, whom you delivered up and denied in the presence of Pilate, when he had decided to release him. [14]But you denied the Holy and Righteous One, and asked for a murderer to be granted to you, [15]and killed the Author of life, whom God raised from the dead. To this we are witnesses. [16]And his name, by faith in his name, has made this man strong whom you see and know; and the faith which is through Jesus[d] has given the man this perfect health in the presence of you all.

[17]"And now, brethren, I know that you acted in ignorance, as did also your rulers. [18]But what God foretold by the mouth of all the prophets, that his Christ should suffer, he thus fulfilled. [19]Repent therefore, and turn again, that your sins may be blotted out, that times of refreshing may come from the presence of the Lord, [20]and that he may send the Christ appointed for you, Jesus, [21]whom heaven must receive until the time for establishing all that God spoke by the mouth of his holy prophets from of old. [22]Moses said, 'The Lord God will raise up for you a prophet from your brethren as he raised me up. You shall listen to him in whatever he tells you. [23]And it shall be that every soul that does not listen to that prophet shall be destroyed from

Jn 10:23
Acts 5:12

Ex 3:6, 15
Is 52:13
Lk 1:35; 23:22
Jn 18:38; 19:4
Lk 1:35; 23:25
Jn 6:69:18:40
Acts 7:52

Mt 27:20, 21
Acts 1:8; 13:31

Acts 4:10

Acts 13:27

1 Cor 2:8

1 Tim 1:13
Lk 18:31; 24:27

Acts 2:38
Rev 10:7

Acts 1:11
Rev 10:7

Deut 18:15, 19
Acts 7:37

Salomonis, stupentes. [12]Videns autem Petrus respondit ad populum: «Viri Israelitae, quid miramini in hoc aut nos quid intuemini, quasi nostra virtute aut pietate fecerimus hunc ambulare? [13]*Deus Abraham et Deus Isaac et Deus Iacob, Deus patrum nostrorum* glorificavit puerum suum Iesum, quem vos quidem tradidistis et negastis ante faciem Pilati, iudicante illo dimitti; [14]vos autem Sanctum et Iustum negastis et petistis virum homicidam donari vobis, [15]ducem vero vitae interfecistis, quem Deus suscitavit a mortuis, cuius nos testes sumus. [16]Et in fide nominis eius hunc, quem videtis et nostis, confirmavit nomen eius, et fides, quae per eum est, dedit huic integritatem istam in conspectu omnium vestrum. [17]Et nunc, fratres, scio quia per ignorantiam fecistis, sicut et principes vestri; [18]Deus autem, quae praenuntiavit per os omnium prophetarum pati Christum suum, implevit sic. [19]Paenitemini igitur et convertimini, ut deleantur vestra peccata, [20]ut veniant tempora refrigerii a conspectu Domini, et mittat eum, qui praedestinatus est vobis Christus, Iesum, [21]quem oportet caelum quidem suscipere usque in tempora restitutionis omnium, quae locutus est Deus per os sanctorum a saeculo suorum prophetarum. [22]Moyses quidem dixit: *"Prophetam vobis suscitabit Dominus Deus vester de fratribus vestris tamquam me; ipsum audietis iuxta omnia, quaecumque locutus fuerit* vobis. [23]*Erit autem: omnis anima, quae non audierit prophetam illum,*

that the time had come for the power of God to manifest itself through them in this way. Jesus had promised that they would indeed work miracles, visible signs showing the Kingdom of God had come (cf. Mt 16:17-20). Now they perform in the Lord's name the same sort of wonders as Jesus did: "The word of Peter cures the man born with a deformity: he who could not give the likeness of Caesar stamped on a coin to that man seeking alms, gave him instead the likeness of Christ by restoring him to health. This treasure enriched not only the man who regained the ability to walk; it also benefited those five thousand men who, on witnessing that miraculous cure, believed in Peter's preaching" (St Leo the Great, *Sermones*, 95, 3).

The miracles in the New Testament occur in situations where divine grace is especially abundant. However, they are not confined to a

particular time in the Christian economy of salvation. They happen in a variety of circumstances, for God's power is drawn down by people's good dispositions and trusting faith: "The same is true of us. If we struggle daily to become saints, each of us in his own situation in the world and through his own job or profession, in our ordinary lives, then I assure you that God will make us into instruments that can work miracles and, if necessary, miracles of the most extraordinary kind" (St Josemaría Escrivá, *Friends of God*, 262).

3:11-26 After the curing of the lame man comes this second address by St Peter. There are two parts to it: in the first (vv. 12-16), the apostle explains that the miracle has been worked in the name of Jesus and through faith in his name; in the second (vv. 17-26), he stresses that the Old

c Or *child* d Greek *him*

Acts 10:43

Gen 12:3; 22:18;
26:18
Acts 13:32–34;
26:6–8
Gal 3:8

the people.' ²⁴And all the prophets who have spoken, from Samuel and those who came afterwards, also proclaimed these days. ²⁵You are the sons of the prophets and of the covenant which God gave to your fathers, saying to Abraham, 'And in your posterity shall all the families of the earth be blessed.' ²⁶God having raised up his servant,ᶜ sent him to you first, to bless you in turning every one of you from your wickedness."

Peter and John are arrested

Lk 22:4, 52
Acts 5:24

Mt 22:23
Acts 23:6–8
1 Cor 15:20–23

Acts 5:18

Acts 2:47

4 ¹And as they were speaking to the people, the priests and the captain of the temple and the Sadducees came upon them, ²annoyed because they were teaching the people and proclaiming in Jesus the resurrection from the dead.* ³And they arrested them and put them in custody until the morrow, for it was already evening. ⁴But many of those who heard the word believed; and the number of the men came to about five thousand.

Address to the Sanhedrin

Acts 5:21

Lk 3:2

Mt 21:23
Lk 20:2

Mt 10:19–20
Lk 12:11–12

⁵On the morrow their rulers and elders and scribes were gathered together in Jerusalem, ⁶with Annas the high priest and Caiaphas and John and Alexander, and all who were of the high-priestly family. ⁷And when they had set them in the midst, they inquired, "By what power or by what name did you do this?" ⁸Then Peter, filled with the Holy Spirit, said to them, "Rulers of the people and elders, ⁹if we are being

---

exterminabitur de plebe". ²⁴Et omnes prophetae a Samuel et deinceps quotquot locuti sunt, etiam annuntiaverunt dies istos. ²⁵Vos estis filii prophetarum et testamenti, quod disposuit Deus ad patres vestros dicens ad Abraham: "*Et in semine tuo benedicentur omnes familiae terrae*". ²⁶Vobis primum Deus suscitans Puerum suum, misit eum benedicentem vobis in avertendo unumquemque a nequitiis vestris». [4] ¹Loquentibus autem illis ad populum, supervenerunt eis sacerdotes et magistratus templi et sadducaei, ²dolentes quod docerent populum et annuntiarent in Iesu resurrectionem ex mortuis, ³et iniecerunt in eos manus et posuerunt in custodiam in crastinum; erat enim iam vespera. ⁴Multi autem eorum, qui audierant verbum, crediderunt; et factus est numerus virorum quinque milia. ⁵Factum est autem in crastinum, ut congregarentur principes eorum et seniores et scribae in Ierusalem, ⁶et Annas princeps sacerdotum et Caiphas et Ioannes et Alexander et quotquot erant de genere sacerdotali, ⁷et statuentes eos in medio interrogabant: «In qua virtute aut in quo nomine fecistis hoc vos?». ⁸Tunc Petrus repletus Spiritu Sancto dixit ad eos:

Testament prophecies were fulfilled in Jesus, and he calls to repentance this crowd of people who were responsible to some degree for Jesus' death. At the end of the speech (vv. 25–26) he makes a point that often recurs in apostolic preaching (cf. 2:39): salvation is offered in the first instance to the Chosen People, but it is intended for all nations. When referring to Jesus, Peter uses terms that Jews readily associated with the Messiah. He calls him Christ (vv. 18, 20) and also "prophet" (v. 22), and even the Author of life (v. 15). The expressions "the Holy One" and "the Righteous One" mean the same thing, as do the words "holiness" and "righteousness".

As St Paul will later (13:27), St Peter in v. 17 does point out that the people and their rulers were acting in ignorance when they condemned our Lord; this is an echo of what Jesus said on the cross (Lk 23:34). Similarly, the public conversion of thousands of people in Peter's audi-

ence (4:4) is reminiscent of the point when the crowd beat their breasts after the death of our Lord (Lk 23:48). It is clear, as the apostle says at the end of his speech (vv. 25–26), that there is no break but, rather, a continuity between Israel and the Church (cf. the note on Rom 11:1–12). Jesus Christ is of the Jewish people, as is his Mother, the Blessed Virgin, and as are the apostles—the foundation and pillars of the Church—and the other first disciples who proclaim the Gospel of Christ to the world. For this reason, the Church in her charity prays to God for the Jewish people: "Christ, God and man, who is the Lord of David and his children, we beseech you that in keeping with the prophecies and promises, Israel recognize you as Messiah" (*Divine Office*, Morning Prayer, 31 December).

4:1–22 This passage deals with the first clash between the apostles and the Jerusalem authori-

ᶜ Or *child*

examined today concerning a good deed done to a cripple, by what means this man has been healed, ¹⁰be it known to you all, and to all the people of Israel, that by the name of Jesus Christ of Nazareth, whom you crucified, whom God raised from the dead, by him this man is standing before you well. ¹¹This is the stone which was rejected by you builders, but which has become the head of the corner. ¹²And there is salvation in no one else, for there is no other name under heaven given among men by which we must be saved."

¹³Now when they saw the boldness of Peter and John, and perceived that they were uneducated, common men, they wondered; and they recognized that they had been with Jesus. ¹⁴But seeing the man that had been healed standing beside them, they had nothing to say in opposition. ¹⁵But when they had commanded them to go aside out of the council, they conferred with one another, ¹⁶saying, "What shall we do with these men? For that a notable sign has been performed through them is manifest to all the inhabitants of Jerusalem, and we cannot deny it. ¹⁷But in order that it may spread no further among the people, let us warn them to speak no more to any one in this name." ¹⁸So they called them and charged them not to speak or teach at all in the name of Jesus. ¹⁹But Peter and John answered them, "Whether it is right in the sight of God to listen to you rather than to God, you must judge; ²⁰for we cannot

Margin references: Acts 3:16 · Ps 118:22; Mt 21:42; Lk 20:17; 1 Pet 2:4–7 · Joel 3:5; Mt 1:21; Jn 1:12; Acts 2:21 · Lk 21:12–15; Jn 7:15 · Jn 11:47 · Acts 5:28 · Acts 5:29 · 1 Cor 9:16; 2 Tim 1:7–8

«Principes populi et seniores, ⁹si nos hodie diiudicamur in benefacto hominis infirmi, in quo iste salvus factus est, ¹⁰notum sit omnibus vobis et omni plebi Israel quia in nomine Iesu Christi Nazareni, quem vos crucifixistis, quem Deus suscitavit a mortuis, in hoc iste astat coram vobis sanus. ¹¹Hic est *lapis, qui reprobatus est a vobis aedificatoribus, / qui factus est in caput anguli.* ¹²Et non est in alio aliquo salus, nec enim nomen aliud est sub caelo datum in hominibus, in quo oportet nos salvos fieri». ¹³Videntes autem Petri fiduciam et Ioannis, et comperto quod homines essent sine litteris et idiotae, admirabantur et cognoscebant eos quoniam cum Iesu fuerant; ¹⁴hominem quoque videntes stantem cum eis, qui curatus fuerat, nihil poterant contradicere. ¹⁵Iubentes autem eos foras extra concilium secedere, conferebant ad invicem ¹⁶dicentes: «Quid faciemus hominibus istis? Quoniam quidem notum signum factum est per eos omnibus habitantibus in Ierusalem manifestum, et non possumus negare; ¹⁷sed ne amplius divulgetur in populum, comminemur eis, ne ultra loquantur in nomine hoc ulli hominum». ¹⁸Et vocantes eos denuntiaverunt, ne omnino loquerentur neque docerent in nomine Iesu. ¹⁹Petrus vero et Ioannes respondentes dixerunt ad eos: «Si iustum est in conspectu Dei vos potius audire quam Deum, iudicate; ²⁰non enim possumus nos, quae vidimus et audivimus, non loqui». ²¹At illi ultra comminantes dimiserunt eos,

ties. The episode is a paradigmatic example of the reactions to deeds of God that were evident in the earliest times of the Church. The spiritual leaders had closed their hearts and minds to the miracles that Jesus worked in his time—and now the apostles encounter the same calculated ignorance. Despite the abrupt ending of Peter's speech, caused by the Jewish authorities' intrusion and Peter's subsequent arrest, his words prove to be a channel of grace that causes faith to well up in the hearts of many of his listeners.

Even in the very early days of Christianity, Jesus' prediction to his disciples (cf. Lk 21:12–15) is borne out: when persecution arises, he gives them a wisdom that overwhelms the mighty of this world. The key to the whole passage must surely be what the apostles say at the end (vv. 19–20). This sort of boldness is expected not just of leaders, but of all of us: "Christians should approach those who are outside wisely, 'in the Holy Spirit, genuine love, truthful speech' (2 Cor 6:6–7), and should strive,

even to the shedding of their blood, to spread the light of life with all confidence and apostolic courage. The disciple has a grave obligation to Christ, his Master, to grow daily in his knowledge of the truth he has received from him, to be faithful in announcing it and vigorous in defending it" (Vatican II, *Dignitatis humanae*, 14).

The words of v. 12 are striking: God has given mankind no saviour other than Jesus of Nazareth. The message is very succinct and clear. God saves us in his Son, Jesus Christ, in line with the mysterious plan which took shape over centuries and was implemented in the "fullness of time" (see Eph 1:7–10): "The Redeemer of man, Jesus Christ, is the centre of the universe and of history. [...] God entered the history of humanity and, as a man, became an actor in that history, one of the thousands of millions of human beings but at the same time Unique. Through the Incarnation God gave human life the dimension that he intended man to have from his first beginning; he has granted that dimension

but speak of what we have seen and heard." [21]And when they had further threatened them, they let them go, finding no way to punish them, because of the people; for all men praised God for what had happened. [22]For the man on whom this sign of healing was performed was more than forty years old.

The Church's thanksgiving prayer

[23]When they were released they went to their friends and reported what the chief priests and the elders had said to them. [24]And when they heard it, they lifted their voices together to God and said, "Sovereign Lord, who didst make the heaven and the earth and the sea and everything in them, [25]who by the mouth of our father David, thy servant,[c] didst say by the Holy Spirit,

> 'Why did the Gentiles rage,
> and the peoples imagine vain things?
> [26]The kings of the earth set themselves in array,
> and the rulers were gathered together,
> against the Lord and against his Anointed' —[e]

[27]for truly in this city there were gathered together against thy holy servant[c] Jesus, whom thou didst anoint, both Herod and Pontius Pilate, with the Gentiles, and the peoples of Israel, [28]to do whatever thy hand and thy plan had predestined to take place. [29]And now, Lord, look upon their threats, and grant to thy servants[f] to speak thy word with all boldness, [30]while thou stretchest out thy hand to heal, and signs and

Marginal references:
Ps 146:6
Is 37:16
Jer 32:17

Rev 10:6
Ps 2:1–2

Lk 23:12

Acts 2:23

Eph 6:19

---

nequaquam invenientes, quomodo punirent eos, propter populum, quia omnes glorificabant Deum in eo, quod acciderat; [22]annorum enim erat amplius quadraginta homo, in quo factum erat signum istud sanitatis. [23]Dimissi autem venerunt ad suos et annuntiaverunt quanta ad eos principes sacerdotum et seniores dixissent. [24]Qui cum audissent unanimiter levaverunt vocem ad Deum et dixerunt: «Domine, tu, qui *fecisti caelum et terram et mare et omnia, quae in eis sunt,* [25]qui Spiritu Sancto per os patris nostri David pueri tui dixisti: "*Quare fremuerunt gentes, / et populi meditati sunt inania? / [26]Astiterunt reges terrae, / et principes convenerunt in unum / adversus Dominum et adversus Christum eius*". [27]Convenerunt enim vere in civitate ista adversus sanctum puerum tuum Iesum, quem unxisti, Herodes et Pontius Pilatus cum gentibus et populis Israel [28]facere, quaecumque manus tua et consilium praedestinavit fieri. [29]Et nunc, Domine, respice in minas eorum et da servis tuis cum omni fiducia loqui verbum tuum, [30]in eo quod manum tuam extendas ad sanitatem et signa et prodigia facienda per nomen sancti pueri tui Iesu». [31]Et cum orassent, motus est locus, in quo erant congregati, et repleti sunt omnes Sancto Spiritu et loquebantur verbum Dei cum fiducia. [32]Multitudinis

---

definitively—in the way that is peculiar to him alone, in keeping with his eternal love and mercy, with the full freedom of God—and he has granted it also with the bounty that enables us, in considering the original sin and the whole history of the sins of humanity, and in considering the errors of the human intellect, will and heart, to repeat with amazement the words of the Sacred Liturgy: 'O happy fault ... which gained us so great a Redeemer!'" (John Paul II, *Redemptor hominis*, 1).

4:23–31 The release of the apostles is followed not by a celebration but by prayer. This particular prayer is a model for Christians in their own prayer and reliance on God's help. The Christians ask God for the strength to proclaim the Word boldly, and not to be deflected by persecution; they also ask that the truth of their preaching be attested to by signs and wonders.

The events of Jesus' life and of the times after it mark the fulfilment of Psalm 2, which is quoted in part in this passage (vv. 25–26). The sacred writer twice mentions the Holy Spirit (vv. 25, 31), for "the Spirit who teaches the Church and recalls for her everything that Jesus said was also to form her in the life of prayer" (*Catechism of the Catholic Church*, 2623). In their prayer, the first Christians have recourse to Holy Scripture: "Like the inspired writers of the New Testament, the first Christian communities read the Book of Psalms in a new way, singing in it the mystery of Christ. In the newness of the Spirit, they also composed hymns and canticles in the light of the unheard-of event that God accomplished in his Son: his Incarnation, his death which conquered death, his Resurrection, and Ascension to the right hand of the Father. Doxology, the praise of God, arises from this 'marvellous work' of the whole economy of salvation" (ibid., 2641).

c Or *child* e Or *Christ* f Or *slaves*

wonders are performed through the name of thy holy servant^c Jesus." ³¹And when
they had prayed, the place in which they were gathered together was shaken; and
they were all filled with the Holy Spirit and spoke the word of God with boldness.

Acts 2:1–4

The way of life of the early Christians

³²Now the company of those who believed were of one heart and soul, and no one
said that any of the things which he possessed was his own, but they had everything
in common.* ³³And with great power the apostles gave their testimony to the resurrection of the Lord Jesus, and great grace was upon them all. ³⁴There was not a
needy person among them, for as many as were possessors of lands or houses sold
them, and brought the proceeds of what was sold ³⁵and laid it at the apostles' feet;
and distribution was made to each as any had need. ³⁶Thus Joseph who was surnamed by the apostles Barnabas (which means, Son of encouragement), a Levite, a
native of Cyprus, ³⁷sold a field which belonged to him, and brought the money and
laid it at the apostles' feet.

Jn 17:11, 21
Phil 1:27; 2:5
Acts 2:44

Acts 1:8, 22

Deut 15:7–8
Lk 12:33

Acts 11:22, 30;
12:25; 13:1–15
1 Cor 9:6
Gal 2:1–13
Col 4:10

Deception by Ananias and Sapphira

5 ¹But a man named Ananias with his wife Sapphira sold a piece of property, ²and
with his wife's knowledge he kept back some of the proceeds, and brought only
a part and laid it at the apostles' feet. ³But Peter said, "Ananias, why has Satan filled

Acts 4:35, 37

---

autem credentium erat cor et anima una, nec quisquam eorum, quae possidebant, aliquid suum esse dicebat, sed erant illis omnia communia. ³³Et
virtute magna reddebant apostoli testimonium resurrectionis Domini Iesu, et gratia magna erat super omnibus illis. ³⁴Neque enim quisquam egens
erat inter illos; quotquot enim possessores agrorum aut domorum erant, vendentes afferebant pretia eorum, quae vendebant, ³⁵et ponebant ante
pedes apostolorum; dividebatur autem singulis, prout cuique opus erat. ³⁶Ioseph autem, qui cognominatus est Barnabas ab apostolis—quod est
interpretatum filius Consolationis—Levites, Cyprius genere, ³⁷cum haberet agrum, vendidit et attulit pecuniam et posuit ante pedes apostolorum.
[5] ¹Vir autem quidam nomine Ananias cum Sapphira uxore sua vendidit agrum ²et subtraxit de pretio, conscia quoque uxore, et afferens partem

---

4:32–37 In his second summary (see 2:42–47
and note), as well as in his first (1:14), Luke
reported mainly on the prayer life of the first
church; now, in another summary, he emphasizes
the fact that they "had everything in common";
later on (see 5:12–16), he will focus on the wondrous works of the apostles. He is conscious of
the importance of true detachment from material
things and so he mentions a notable example, the
case of Barnabas (vv. 36–37), which will be followed by a counter-example, that of Ananias and
Sapphira (5:1–11): "Without doubt, it is easier
for a poor man to grow in humility than for a
rich man, for the life of the poor man leads him
to be meek, whereas the life of the rich man
leads him to be proud. Nevertheless, there are
many rich men who are humble, who do not take
pride in the riches they possess, but use them
instead in charitable work. [...] The gift of
poverty is given to men from all walks of life, no
matter what the circumstances of their lives. [...]
After our Lord, the Apostles were the first to
give us good example of wholehearted poverty.

[...] When they had been converted to the faith,
many of the first Christians set aside all their
goods and possessions and embraced poverty
with their heart and soul; they rejoiced in following the teaching of the Apostles, having nothing in this world and possessing all things in
Christ" (St Leo the Great, *Sermones*, 95, 2).

The generosity of Barnabas can be seen in
many other places (mostly in Acts) from the
prominent role he plays in the spread of the
Gospel. It will be he who introduces the new
convert Saul to the apostles (9:27). Later, the
apostles will send him to Antioch when the
Gospel is first preached to the Gentiles (11:22).
He will be Paul's companion on his first journey
(13:2–3) and he will go up to Jerusalem with
him in connexion with the controversy about the
circumcision of Gentile converts (15:1–2). St
Paul praises Barnabas' zeal and selflessness in
the cause of the Gospel (cf. 1 Cor 9:6).

5:1–11 Acts mentions different ways in which
the virtues of poverty and charity towards others

c Or *child*

your heart to lie to the Holy Spirit and to keep back part of the proceeds of the land? [4]While it remained unsold, did it not remain your own? And after it was sold, was it not at your disposal? How is it that you have contrived this deed in your heart? You have not lied to men but to God." [5]When Ananias heard these words, he fell down and died. And great fear came upon all who heard of it. [6]The young men rose and wrapped him up and carried him out and buried him.

[7]After an interval of about three hours his wife came in, not knowing what had happened. [8]And Peter said to her, "Tell me whether you sold the land for so much." And she said, "Yes, for so much." [9]But Peter said to her, "How is it that you have agreed together to tempt the Spirit of the Lord? Hark, the feet of those that have buried your husband are at the door, and they will carry you out." [10]Immediately she fell down at his feet and died. When the young men came in they found her dead, and they carried her out and buried her beside her husband. [11]And great fear came upon the whole church,* and upon all who heard of these things.

Growth of the Church

[12]Now many signs and wonders were done among the people by the hands of the apostles. And they were all together in Solomon's Portico. [13]None of the rest dared

Margin references:
Acts 5:10–11
1 Cor 10:9
Jn 10:23
Acts 2:19, 46; 3:11

---

quandam ad pedes apostolorum posuit. [3]Dixit autem Petrus: «Anania, cur implevit Satanas cor tuum mentiri te Spiritui Sancto et subtrahere de pretio agri? [4]Nonne manens tibi manebat et venumdatum in tua erat potestate? Quare posuisti in corde tuo hanc rem? Non es mentitus hominibus sed Deo!». [5]Audiens autem Ananias haec verba cecidit et exspiravit; et factus est timor magnus in omnes audientes. [6]Surgentes autem iuvenes involverunt eum et efferentes sepelierunt. [7]Factum est autem quasi horarum trium spatium, et uxor ipsius nesciens, quod factum fuerat, introivit. [8]Respondit autem ei Petrus: «Dic mihi si tanti agrum vendidistis?». At illa dixit: «Etiam, tanti». [9]Petrus autem ad eam: «Quid est quod convenit vobis tentare Spiritum Domini? Ecce pedes eorum, qui sepelierunt virum tuum, ad ostium et efferent te». [10]Confestim cecidit ante pedes eius et exspiravit; intrantes autem iuvenes invenerunt illam mortuam et efferentes sepelierunt ad virum suum. [11]Et factus est timor magnus super universam ecclesiam et in omnes, qui audierunt haec. [12]Per manus autem apostolorum fiebant signa et prodigia multa in plebe; et erant unanimiter omnes in porticu Salomonis. [13]Ceterorum autem nemo audebat coniungere se illis, sed magnificabat eos populus; [14]magis autem addebantur cre-

---

were practised in the early Church. In the previous episode, we learned that property was in some way held in common in the Jerusalem church (4:32); we saw the concern the Church had for those in need (4:34–35), and Barnabas' generosity (4:36–37). Later, Luke will report the efforts Christians made to look after widows (6:1–6); he will sing the praises of people who gave alms, such as Tabitha (9:36) and Cornelius (10:2); and he will tell of the collection made by Antiochene Christians to bring relief to their brethren in Judea (11:29). There was a rich culture of generosity. But from this passage we can see that Christians were free to donate their property or not (v. 4). The fault exposed here is not only one of greed; in fact, the main sin is that Ananias and his wife seek to deceive the Church and therefore God (vv. 3, 9). God punished this couple, St Ephrem says, "not only because they stole something and concealed it, but because they were quite brazen and sought to deceive those in whom dwelt the Holy Spirit who knows everything" (*Commentarii in Acta*, ad loc.). The

punishment they receive befits the circumstances: the Church was in a foundation period, when people had a special responsibility to be faithful and when God's help was manifestly effective and abundant.

The episode shows in a vivid way how much God detests hypocrisy, and from it we can deduce the value of the virtue of truthfulness. Veracity inclines people to bring what they say and what they do into line with their convictions, and to be people of their word. It is closely connected to the virtue of fidelity/loyalty, which helps one to stay true to promises made (see St Thomas Aquinas, *Summa theologiae*, 2–2, 80, 1). Only someone who is truthful and loyal can keep the Lord's commandment, "Let what you say be simply 'Yes' or 'No'" (Mt 5:37).

5:12–16 In this fourth summary (cf. 1:14; 2:42–47; 4:32–37), Luke concentrates on the apostles' power to work miracles. Like those worked directly by Christ (see 2:22; Mk 6:56; Lk 7:18–23), these miracles confirm to people that the

join them, but the people held them in high honour. ¹⁴And more than ever believers were added to the Lord, multitudes both of men and women, ¹⁵so that they even carried out the sick into the streets, and laid them on beds and pallets, that as Peter came by at least his shadow might fall on some of them. ¹⁶The people also gathered from the towns around Jerusalem, bringing the sick and those afflicted with unclean spirits, and they were all healed.

Mk 6:56
Acts 19:11–12

Acts 8:6–7

The apostles are arrested and miraculously freed

¹⁷But the high priest rose up and all who were with him, that is, the party of the Sadducees, and filled with jealousy ¹⁸they arrested the apostles and put them in the common prison. ¹⁹But at night an angel of the Lord opened the prison doors and brought them out and said, ²⁰"Go and stand in the temple and speak to the people all the words of this Life."* ²¹And when they heard this, they entered the temple at daybreak and taught.

Acts 4:1, 6; 13:45

Acts 12:7–10

Acts 7:38; 13:26
Phil 2:16
1 Jn 1:1
Acts 4:5

Now the high priest came and those who were with him and called together the council and all the senate of Israel, and sent to the prison to have them brought. ²²But when the officers came, they did not find them in the prison, and they returned and reported, ²³"We found the prison securely locked and the sentries standing at the

---

dentes Domino, multitudines virorum ac mulierum, ¹⁵ita ut et in plateas efferrent infirmos et ponerent in lectulis et grabatis, ut, veniente Petro, saltem umbra illius obumbraret quemquam eorum. ¹⁶Concurrebat autem et multitudo vicinarum civitatum Ierusalem, afferentes aegros et vexatos ab spiritibus immundis, qui curabantur omnes. ¹⁷Exsurgens autem princeps sacerdotum et omnes, qui cum illo erant, quae est haeresis sadducaeorum, repleti sunt zelo ¹⁸et ieiecerunt manus in apostolos et posuerunt illos in custodia publica. ¹⁹Angelus autem Domini per noctem aperuit ianuas carceris et educens eos dixit: ²⁰«Ite et stantes loquimini in templo plebi omnia verba vitae huius». ²¹Qui cum audissent, intraverunt diluculo in templum et docebant. Adveniens autem princeps sacerdotum et, qui cum eo erant, convocaverunt concilium et omnes seniores filiorum Israel et miserunt in carcerem, ut adducerentur illi. ²²Cum venissent autem ministri, non invenerunt illos in carcere; reversi autem nuntiaverunt ²³dicentes: «Carcerem invenimus clausum cum omni diligentia et custodes stantes ad ianuas, aperientes autem intus neminem invenimus!». ²⁴Ut audierunt

---

Kingdom of God has indeed come among them: "If they had not worked miracles and wonders, Jesus' disciples could not have moved their hearers to give up their traditional religion for new teachings and truths, and to embrace, at the risk of their lives, the teachings which were being proclaimed to them" (Origen, *Contra Celsum*, 1, 46).

Miracles accompany God's revelation to men, and are part of it. They are signs and consequences of grace: "Grace is first and foremost the gift of the Spirit who justifies and sanctifies us. But grace also includes the gifts that the Spirit grants us to associate us with his work, to enable us to collaborate in the salvation of others and in the growth of the Body of Christ, the Church. There are *sacramental graces*, gifts proper to the different sacraments. There are furthermore *special graces*, also called *charisms* after the Greek term used by St Paul and meaning 'favour', 'gratuitous gift', 'benefit'. Whatever their character—sometimes it is extraordinary, such as the gift of miracles or of tongues—

charisms are oriented toward sanctifying grace and are intended for the common good of the Church. They are at the service of charity which builds up the Church" (*Catechism of the Catholic Church*, 2003).

5:17–33 This episode contains mention of two orders given to the apostles—one from the angel (v. 20) and the other from the Sanhedrin (v. 28). The apostles' response to the implied reiteration of the latter is very significant: God must be obeyed before men (v. 29).

The early verses (vv. 17–25) deal with the apostles' imprisonment and their release thanks to the help of an angel. In Holy Scripture we read of angels serving as messengers of God and also as mediators, guardians and ministers of divine justice. Abraham sent his most trusted servant on a mission to his kindred and told him, "[God] will send his angel with you and prosper your way" (Gen 24:40; see also Gen 24: 2, 7). Tobit, Lot and his family, Daniel and his companions, Judith, etc. also experienced the help of

doors, but when we opened it we found no one inside." ²⁴Now when the captain of the temple and the chief priests heard these words, they were much perplexed about them, wondering what this would come to. ²⁵And some one came and told them, "The men whom you put in prison are standing in the temple and teaching the people."

The apostles before the Sanhedrin

Lk 20:19; 22:2

²⁶Then the captain with the officers went and brought them, but without violence, for they were afraid of being stoned by the people.

²⁷And when they had brought them, they set them before the council. And the

Mt 27:25
Acts 4:18

high priest questioned them, ²⁸saying, "We strictly charged you not to teach in this name, yet here you have filled Jerusalem with your teaching and you intend to bring

Acts 4:19

this man's blood upon us." ²⁹But Peter and the apostles answered, "We must obey

Gal 3:13

God rather than men. ³⁰The God of our fathers raised Jesus whom you killed by

Acts 2:33; 10:43;
13:38
Heb 2:10
Lk 24:48
Jn 7:39; 15:26–27

hanging him on a tree. ³¹God exalted him at his right hand as Leader and Saviour, to give repentance to Israel and forgiveness of sins. ³²And we are witnesses to these things, and so is the Holy Spirit whom God has given to those who obey him."

³³When they heard this they were enraged and wanted to kill them.

Gamaliel's intervention

Acts 22:3

³⁴But a Pharisee in the council named Gamaliel,* a teacher of the law, held in honour by all the people, stood up and ordered the men to be put outside for a while.

autem hos sermones, magistratus templi et principes sacerdotum ambigebant de illis quidnam fieret illud. ²⁵Adveniens autem quidam nuntiavit eis: «Ecce viri, quos posuistis in carcere, sunt in templo stantes et docentes populum». ²⁶Tunc abiens magistratus cum ministris adducebat illos, non per vim, timebant enim populum, ne lapidarentur. ²⁷Et cum adduxissent illos, statuerunt in concilio. Et interrogavit eos princeps sacerdotum ²⁸dicens: «Nonne praecipiendo praecepimus vobis, ne doceretis in nomine isto? Et ecce replevistis Ierusalem doctrina vestra et vultis inducere super nos sanguinem hominis istius». ²⁹Respondens autem Petrus et apostoli dixerunt: «Oboedire oportet Deo magis quam hominibus. ³⁰Deus patrum nostrorum suscitavit Iesum, quem vos interemistis suspendentes in ligno; ³¹hunc Deus Ducem et Salvatorem exaltavit dextera sua ad dandam paenitentiam Israel et remissionem peccatorum. ³²Et nos sumus testes horum verborum, et Spiritus Sanctus, quem dedit Deus oboedientibus sibi». ³³Haec cum audissent, dissecabantur et volebant interficere illos. ³⁴Surgens autem quidam in concilio pharisaeus nomine Gamaliel,

angels. The psalms speak of trust in the angels and the continuous help they render people in their obedience to God's commands (see Ps 34:7; 91:11–14). This means that the angels should always have a place in a Christian's piety. "I ask our Lord that, during our stay on this earth of ours, we may never be parted from our divine travelling companion. To ensure this, let us also become firmer friends of the Holy Guardian Angels. We all need a lot of company, company from heaven and company on earth. Have great devotion to the Holy Angels!" (St Josemaría Escrivá, *Friends of God*, 315).

The passage goes on to show (vv. 26–33) how the apostles proclaim the key elements of Christian teaching even to members of the Sanhedrin (see vv. 30–32). They are more concerned about the spiritual welfare of their judges than they are about their own safety. St

John Chrysostom comments: "God allowed the apostles to be brought to trial so that their adversaries might be instructed, if they so desired. [...] The apostles are not irritated by the judges; they plead with them compassionately, with tears in their eyes, and their only aim is to free them from error and from divine wrath" (*In Acta Apostolorum*, 13). Gamaliel's intervention a little later on (5:34–39) shows that their approach and attitude bear fruit.

5:34–42 Gamaliel's is the first in a series of testimonies in Acts which show that, even in the eyes of non-believers, Christianity was a religion that had good grounds for claiming credibility (cf. 10:1ff; 13:7; 18:12; 22:25ff; 24:1ff). Gamaliel was St Paul's teacher (see 22:3), and he belonged to a moderate grouping among the Pharisees. He was a prudent man, impartial, with

³⁵And he said to them, "Men of Israel, take care what you do with these men. ³⁶For before these days Theudas arose, giving himself out to be somebody, and a number of men, about four hundred, joined him; but he was slain and all who followed him were dispersed and came to nothing. ³⁷After him Judas the Galilean arose in the days of the census and drew away some of the people after him; he also perished, and all who followed him were scattered. ³⁸So in the present case I tell you, keep away from these men and let them alone; for if this plan or this undertaking is of men, it will fail; ³⁹but if it is of God, you will not be able to overthrow them. You might even be found opposing God!"

Jn 7:50–51

Lk 2:2; 13:2–3

*2 Mac 7:19
Wis 12:13–14
Mt 15:13*

The apostles are flogged

⁴⁰So they took his advice, and when they had called in the apostles, they beat them and charged them not to speak in the name of Jesus, and let them go. ⁴¹Then they left the presence of the council, rejoicing that they were counted worthy to suffer dishonour for the name. ⁴²And every day in the temple and at home they did not cease teaching and preaching Jesus as the Christ.

*Mt 10:17
Acts 22:19*

*Mt 5:10–12
1 Pet 4:13–14*

Acts 18:5

---

legis doctor honorabilis universae plebi, iussit foras ad breve homines fieri ³⁵dixitque ad illos: «Viri Israelitae, attendite vobis super hominibus istis quid acturi sitis. ³⁶Ante hos enim dies exstitit Theudas dicens esse se aliquem, cui consensit virorum numerus circiter quadringentorum; qui occisus est, et omnes, quicumque credebant ei, dissipati sunt et redacti sunt ad nihilum. ³⁷Post hunc exstitit Iudas Galilaeus in diebus census et avertit populum post se; et ipse periit, et omnes, quotquot consentiebant ei, dispersi sunt. ³⁸Et nunc dico vobis: Discedite ab hominibus istis et sinite illos. Quoniam si est ex hominibus consilium hoc aut opus hoc, dissolvetur; ³⁹si vero ex Deo est, non poteritis dissolvere eos, ne forte et adversus Deum pugnantes inveniamini!». Consenserunt autem illi ⁴⁰et convocantes apostolos, caesis denuntiaverunt, ne loquerentur in nomine Iesu, et dimiserunt eos. ⁴¹Et illi quidem ibant gaudentes a conspectu concilii quoniam digni habiti sunt pro nomine contumeliam pati; ⁴²et omni

---

a profoundly religious sensibility. The Fathers of the Church often propose him as an example of an upright man awaiting the Kingdom of God, and they praise him for daring to defend the apostles. The revolts of Theudas and Judas, mentioned in this passage, are referred to by Flavius Josephus (in *Antiquitates iudaicae*, 18, 4–10; 20, 169–172); but they appear to have occurred around the time of Jesus' birth. Both Theudas and Judas attracted considerable support; as they saw it, the Jewish people, God's chosen people, should not be subject to the power of foreigners, such as Herod or the Roman empire, or have to pay tax to such overlords.

Gamaliel's argument impresses the Sanhedrin to some extent. They do let the apostles go—but only after beating them and giving them a warning. However, in punishing them they only bring to fulfilment something our Lord had foretold to his disciples: their suffering for him is a reason for their rejoicing (see Mt 5:11–12; Mk 10:30; Lk 6:22–23). At the end of the passage Luke shows that the apostles' faith and resolve has not been weakened in the least: "In this case the apostles, as they did earlier by their

miracles, showed forth the power of God. He does not say that they did not suffer, but that they rejoiced over having to suffer" (St John Chrysostom, *In Acta Apostolorum*, 14).

In a Jewish context, a scourging or flogging (v. 40) was much less cruel than the similar Roman punishment. The scourge was not fitted with bits of iron or bone, and the maximum number of lashes was thirty-nine, to ensure that the limit of forty laid down in Deuteronomy 25:3 was not exceeded. St Paul was flogged on five occasions on the orders of Jewish authorities (see 2 Cor 11:24).

We cannot but notice the contrast between the Peter who denied Jesus (Lk 22:54–62) and this Peter who is sifted like wheat (see Lk 22:31) and does not yield, thanks to Jesus' prayer (see Lk 22:32): "It is not difficult to see how the Spirit transforms the souls of those in whom he lives: from love of earthly things, the Spirit leads us to hope in the things of heaven; and where once we were cowardly and full of fright, He makes us spiritually brave and dauntless" (St Cyril of Alexandria, *Commentarium in Ioannem*, 10).

4. THE "DEACONS". ST STEPHEN*

Appointment of the seven deacons

6 [1]Now in these days when the disciples were increasing in number, the
Hellenists* murmured against the Hebrews because their widows were neglected in the daily distribution. [2]And the twelve summoned the body of the disciples
and said, "It is not right that we should give up preaching the word of God to serve
tables. [3]Therefore, brethren, pick out from among you seven men of good repute,
full of the Spirit and of wisdom, whom we may appoint to this duty. [4]But we will
devote ourselves to prayer and to the ministry of the word." [5]And what they said
pleased the whole multitude, and they chose Stephen, a man full of faith and of the

Ex 18:17–23

1 Tim 3:8–10

Acts 8:5; 21:8

die in templo et circa domos non cessabant docentes et evangelizantes Christum, Iesum. [6] [1]In diebus autem illis, crescente numero discipulorum, factus est murmur Graecorum adversus Hebraeos, eo quod neglegerentur in ministerio cotidiano viduae eorum. [2]Convocantes autem
Duodecim multitudinem discipulorum, dixerunt: «Non est aequum nos derelinquentes verbum Dei ministrare mensis; [3]considerate vero, fratres,
viros ex vobis boni testimonii septem plenos Spiritu et sapientia, quos constituemus super hoc opus; [4]nos vero orationi et ministerio verbi instantes
erimus». [5]Et placuit sermo coram omni multitudine, et elegerunt Stephanum, virum plenum fide et Spiritu Sancto, et Philippum et Prochorum et
Nicanorem et Timonem et Parmenam et Nicolaum proselytum Antiochenum, [6]quos statuerunt ante conspectum apostolorum, et orantes impo-

*6:1–7:60 Here St Luke deals with themes sim-
ilar to those in the previous section (cf. the note
on 3:1–5:42), but this time the focus is on the
Hellenists. Hellenist Christians experienced difficulties, both within the Church, because
widows in their ranks were not fairly treated
(6:1), and from outside the Church, in that they
suffered harassment at the hands of some Jews
(6:9). Luke likes to show that divine providence
lies behind such events. The problem of the
widows is solved by the appointment of seven
table-servers, and this contributes to an increase
in the number of the faithful, including the conversions even of many priests (6:7). Persecution
from some Hellenist Jews leads to the martyrdom of Stephen, which is the seed of the conversion of Saul: "If Stephen had not prayed to God,
the Church would not have had Paul" (St
Augustine, *Sermones*, 315, 7).

6:1–7 At the start of this section we are introduced to two groups of disciples, identified by
their background prior to conversion—the
"Hellenists" and the "Hebrews". The
"Hellenists" were Jews who had been born and
who had lived for a time outside Palestine. They
spoke Greek and had synagogues of their own in
which Greek translations of Scripture were used.
They belonged to a Greek culture, to some
degree, as the "Hebrews" also did, though to a
lesser degree. The "Hebrews" were Jews born in
Palestine: they spoke Aramaic and used the

Hebrew Bible in their synagogues. Naturally,
this difference of backgrounds carried over into
the Christian community in its early years, but it
would be wrong to think that there were two
opposed groups in early Christianity.

This chapter deals with the apostles' establishment of "the Seven": this is the second identifiable group of disciples (the first being "the
Twelve") to be given a ministry in the Church.
Luke uses the term *diakonía* (help, service, ministry; vv. 1, 4), and the verbal form *diakonein* (to
serve; v. 2), though he does not call "deacons"
the seven men picked "to serve tables" (v. 2). We
do not know for certain whether the diaconate as
we know it derives directly from the Seven.
Christian documents from the early centuries
mention many deacons who were martyrs of the
Lord, who had a role in the liturgy and who provided assistance to the poor and needy, and who
helped in various ways to foment unity in the
Church: "I urge you to strive to do all things in
the peace of God, under the authority of the
bishop, who is God's representative on earth,
and of the priests, who represent the Apostles.
The deacons, whom I dearly love, should carry
out the mission entrusted to them by Jesus
Christ, who is one with the Father from before
all times and who was revealed to the world in
these latter days. In accordance with God's
plans, we should love and respect one another.
Your respect for your brothers should not be a
merely human respect: you should love one

Holy Spirit, and Philip, and Prochorus, and Nicanor, and Timon, and Parmenas, and
Nicolaus, a proselyte of Antioch. [6]These they set before the apostles, and they
prayed and laid their hands upon them.

[7]And the word of God increased; and the number of the disciples multiplied
greatly in Jerusalem, and a great many of the priests were obedient to the faith.

2 Tim 1:6

Acts 12:24; 19:20

Stephen's arrest

[8]And Stephen, full of grace and power, did great wonders and signs among the
people. [9]Then some of those who belonged to the synagogue of the Freedmen (as it
was called), and of the Cyrenians, and of the Alexandrians, and of those from Cilicia
and Asia, arose and disputed with Stephen. [10]But they could not withstand the
wisdom and the Spirit with which he spoke. [11]Then they secretly instigated men,
who said, "We have heard him speak blasphemous words against Moses and God."
[12]And they stirred up the people and the elders and the scribes, and they came upon

Lk 21:15

Acts 1:8
Mt 26:59–66

Mt 10:17

suerunt eis manus. [7]Et verbum Dei crescebat, et multiplicabatur numerus discipulorum in Ierusalem valde; multa etiam turba sacerdotum
oboediebat fidei. [8]Stephanus autem plenus gratia et virtute faciebat prodigia et signa magna in populo. [9]Surrexerunt autem quidam de synagoga,
quae appellatur Libertinorum et Cyrenensium et Alexandrinorum et eorum, qui erant a Cilicia et Asia, disputantes cum Stephano, [10]et non poterant resistere sapientiae et Spiritui, quo loquebatur. [11]Tunc submiserunt viros, qui dicerent: «Audivimus eum dicentem verba blasphema in Moysen
et Deum»; [12]et commoverunt plebem et seniores et scribas, et concurrentes rapuerunt eum et adduxerunt in concilium [13]et statuerunt testes falsos
dicentes: «Homo iste non cessat loqui verba adversus locum sanctum et legem; [14]audivimus enim eum dicentem quoniam Iesus Nazarenus hic

another in Jesus Christ at all times. Let nothing
separate you from one another: you have been
made one body with the bishop and the elders of
the assembly as a model and example of immortality" (St Ignatius of Antioch, *Ad Magnesios*, 6).

In another brief summary (v. 7), St Luke
points to the growth of the Church, this time
mentioning the conversions of many priests.
Some scholars think that these men were of the
lower rank of the priesthood (as was Zechariah:
see Lk 1:5), rather than of the great priestly families, which belonged to the Sadducee party, an
uncompromising opponent of the early Church
(see 4:1; 5:17).

6:8–15 St Stephen was the first Christian martyr,
which is why Luke devotes so much attention to
his death; in his account, he focuses especially on
the way Stephen followed the Master in words
and deeds. Stephen has the unassailable wisdom
that Jesus promised his disciples (see Lk 21:15).
Like Jesus (see Mt 26:57–68 and par.) he is
accused of blasphemy (the gravest charge that
could be laid against a Jew). Later, just before he
dies, Stephen has a vision of the Son of man in
glory (7:55–56), a scene which Jesus had
prophesied (see Mt 26:64 and par.). Finally, as
Christ did (see Lk 23:34), Stephen forgives those
who put him to death and accepts God's

providence (7:59–60): "How fitting it was for him
to be Christ's first martyr, so that by being,
through his glorious death, the model of all the
martyrs that would come after him, he should not
only be a preacher of the Lord's Passion, but
should also imitate it in his meekness and
immense patience" (St Cyprian, *De bono
patientiae*, 16). But imitation of Christ and
bearing witness to him can take many forms:
"The holy martyrs imitated him by the spilling of
their blood, and their deaths were like his Passion;
but the martyrs are not alone in imitating him.
The bridge did not collapse after they crossed it,
nor did the spring dry up after they drank from it.
In the Lord's garden, as well as the roses of the
martyrs, are the lilies of the virgins, the ivy of
married couples, the violets of widows. No man,
no matter what the circumstances of his life,
should despair of his calling: Christ suffered and
died for all" (St Augustine, *Sermones*, 304, 2–3).

The synagogue "of the Freedmen" (v. 9)
seems to be Luke's way of describing Jews coming from Hellenist areas of the "diaspora". These
"freedmen" are probably those Hellenists who
later fall into dispute with St Paul and seek his
death (9:29). Just as in this instance they are
overwhelmed by Stephen's wisdom (v. 10), they
will not be able to withstand for long the force of
the new faith.

Jer 26:11
Acts 21:28

him and seized him, and brought him before the council, ¹³and set up false witnesses who said, "This man never ceases to speak words against this holy place and the

Mk 14:58

law; ¹⁴for we have heard him say that this Jesus of Nazareth will destroy this place, and will change the customs which Moses delivered to us." ¹⁵And gazing at him, all who sat in the council saw that his face was like the face of an angel.

Stephen's address to the Sanhedrin

Acts 24:9

7 ¹And the high priest said, "Is this so?" ²And Stephen said: "Brethren and fathers, hear me. The God of glory appeared to our father Abraham, when he was in

Gen 12:1, 5; 15:7
Gen 11:32; 12:5

Mesopotamia, before he lived in Haran, ³and said to him, 'Depart from your land and from your kindred and go into the land which I will show you.' ⁴Then he departed from the land of the Chaldeans, and lived in Haran. And after his father

Gen 12:7; 13:15; 17:8
Gal 3:16

died, God removed him from there into this land in which you are now living; ⁵yet he gave him no inheritance in it, not even a foot's length, but promised to give it to

Deut 2:5
Gen 15:13
Ex 12:40
Gen 15:14

him in possession and to his posterity after him, though he had no child. ⁶And God spoke to this effect, that his posterity would be aliens in a land belonging to others, who would enslave them and ill-treat them four hundred years. ⁷'But I will judge the

Ex 3:12

nation which they serve,' said God, 'and after that they shall come out and worship

Gen 17:10–14; 21:4

me in this place.' ⁸And he gave him the covenant of circumcision. And so Abraham became the father of Isaac, and circumcised him on the eighth day; and Isaac became the father of Jacob, and Jacob of the twelve patriarchs.

Gen 37:11, 28; 45:5
Wis 10:13
Gen 39:21;
41:40–41

⁹"And the patriarchs, jealous of Joseph, sold him into Egypt; but God was with him, ¹⁰and rescued him out of all his afflictions, and gave him favour and wisdom before Pharaoh, king of Egypt, who made him governor over Egypt and over all his

Gen 41:54

household. ¹¹Now there came a famine throughout all Egypt and Canaan, and great

Gen 42:1–2

affliction, and our fathers could find no food. ¹²But when Jacob heard that there was

Gen 45:17–18

grain in Egypt, he sent forth our fathers the first time. ¹³And at the second visit Joseph made himself known to his brothers, and Joseph's family became known to

Gen 46:27
Ex 1:5

Pharaoh. ¹⁴And Joseph sent and called to him Jacob his father and all his kindred,

Gen 46:6; 49:33

seventy-five souls; ¹⁵and Jacob went down into Egypt. And he died, himself and our

Gen 23:2–20; 33:19;
49:29–30; 50:7–13

fathers, ¹⁶and they were carried back to Shechem and laid in the tomb that Abraham had bought for a sum of silver from the sons of Hamor in Shechem.

destruet locum istum et mutabit consuetudines, quas tradidit nobis Moyses». ¹⁵Et intuentes eum omnes, qui sedebant in concilio, viderunt faciem eius tamquam faciem angeli.   [7] ¹Dixit autem princeps sacerdotum: «Si haec ita se habent?». ²Qui ait: «Viri fratres et patres, audite. Deus gloriae apparuit patri nostro Abraham, cum esset in Mesopotamia, priusquam moraretur in Charran, ³*et dixit ad illum: "Exi de terra tua et de cognatione tua, et veni in terram, quam tibi monstravero"*. ⁴Tunc egressus de terra Chaldaeorum habitavit in Charran. Et inde postquam mortuus est pater eius, transtulit illum in terram istam, in qua nunc vos habitatis, ⁵et non dedit illi hereditatem in ea nec passum pedis et repromisit *dare illi eam in possessionem et semini eius post ipsum,* cum non haberet filium. ⁶Locutus est autem sic Deus: *"Erit semen eius accola in terra aliena, et servituti eos subicient et male tractabunt annis quadringentis;* ⁷*et gentem, cui servierint, iudicabo ego,* dixit Deus, *et post haec exibunt et deservient mihi in* loco *isto"*. ⁸Et dedit illi testamentum circumcisionis; et sic genuit Isaac et circumcidit eum die octava, et Isaac Iacob, et Iacob duodecim patriarchas. ⁹Et patriarchae aemulantes Ioseph vendiderunt in Aegyptum; et erat Deus cum eo, ¹⁰et eripuit eum ex omnibus tribulationibus eius, et *dedit ei gratiam* et sapientiam *in conspectu pharaonis regis Aegypti, et constituit eum praepositum super Aegyptum et super omnem domum suam.* ¹¹*Venit autem fames in universam Aegyptum et Chanaan* et tribulatio magna, et non inveniebant cibos patres nostri. ¹²Cum audisset autem Iacob esse frumentum in Aegypto, misit patres nostros primum; ¹³et in secundo cognitus est Ioseph a fratribus suis, et manifestatum est pharaoni genus Ioseph. ¹⁴Mittens autem Ioseph accersivit Iacob patrem suum et omnem cognationem in animabus septuaginta quinque,

7:1–53. The discourse delivered by Stephen is the longest one in Acts. He gives a panoramic overview of Israel's history, covering its three main stages—that of the patriarchs (vv. 2–16); that of Moses (vv. 17–43); and that of the building of the temple (vv. 44–50). The passage ends with verses that draw the elements of his argument together (vv. 51–53).

Stephen does not defend himself by answering the specific charges made against him. Instead, he answers his accusers by surveying the history of salvation to show that

Ex 1:8

¹⁷"But as the time of the promise drew near, which God had granted to Abraham, the people grew and multiplied in Egypt ¹⁸till there arose over Egypt another king who had not known Joseph. ¹⁹He dealt craftily with our race and forced our fathers to expose their infants, that they might not be kept alive. ²⁰At this time Moses was born, and was beautiful before God. And he was brought up for three months in his father's house; ²¹and when he was exposed, Pharaoh's daughter adopted him and brought him up as her own son. ²²And Moses was instructed in all the wisdom of the Egyptians, and he was mighty in his words and deeds.

Ex 1:10, 22

Ex 2:2–15
Heb 11:23

²³"When he was forty years old, it came into his heart to visit his brethren, the sons of Israel. ²⁴And seeing one of them being wronged, he defended the oppressed man and avenged him by striking the Egyptian. ²⁵He supposed that his brethren understood that God was giving them deliverance by his hand, but they did not understand. ²⁶And on the following day he appeared to them as they were quarrelling and would have reconciled them, saying, 'Men, you are brethren, why do you wrong each other?' ²⁷But the man who was wronging his neighbour thrust him aside, saying, 'Who made you a ruler and a judge over us? ²⁸Do you want to kill me as you killed the Egyptian yesterday?' ²⁹At this retort Moses fled, and became an exile in the land of Midian, where he became the father of two sons.

Ex 2:14
Lk 12:14

Ex 2:15–22; 18:3

³⁰"Now when forty years had passed, an angel appeared to him in the wilderness of Mount Sinai, in a flame of fire in a bush. ³¹When Moses saw it he wondered at the sight; and as he drew near to look, the voice of the Lord came, ³²'I am the God of your fathers, the God of Abraham and of Isaac and of Jacob.' And Moses trembled and did not dare to look. ³³And the Lord said to him, 'Take off the shoes from your feet, for the place where you are standing is holy ground. ³⁴I have surely seen the ill-treatment of my people that are in Egypt and heard their groaning, and I have come down to deliver them. And now come, I will send you to Egypt.'

Ex 3:1–2
Deut 33:16

Ex 3:6
Mt 22:32

Ex 3:7–10

³⁵"This Moses whom they refused, saying, 'Who made you a ruler and a judge?' God sent as both ruler and deliverer by the hand of the angel that appeared to him in the bush. ³⁶He led them out, having performed wonders and signs in Egypt and at the Red Sea, and in the wilderness for forty years. ³⁷This is the Moses who said to the

Ex 2:14

Ex 7:3; 14:21
Num 14:33

Deut 18:15
Acts 3:22

¹⁵et descendit Iacob in Aegyptum. Et defunctus est ipse et patres nostri, ¹⁶et translati sunt in Sichem et positi sunt in sepulcro, quod emit Abraham pretio argenti a filiis Hemmor in Sichem. ¹⁷Cum appropinquaret autem tempus repromissionis, quam confessus erat Deus Abrahae, crevit populus et multiplicatus est in Aegypto, ¹⁸quoadusque *surrexit rex alius super Aegypto, qui non sciebat Ioseph*. ¹⁹Hic circumveniens genus nostrum, afflixit patres, ut exponerent infantes suos, ne vivi servarentur. ²⁰Eodem tempore natus est Moyses et erat formosus coram Deo; qui nutritus est tribus mensibus in domo patris. ²¹Exposito autem illo, sustulit eum filia pharaonis et enutrivit eum sibi in filium; ²²et eruditus est Moyses in omni sapientia Aegyptiorum et erat potens in verbis et in operibus suis. ²³Cum autem impleretur ei quadraginta annorum tempus, ascendit in cor eius, ut visitaret fratres suos filios Israel. ²⁴Et cum vidisset quendam iniuriam patientem, vindicavit et fecit ultionem ei, qui opprimebatur, percusso Aegyptio. ²⁵Existimabat autem intellegere fratres quoniam Deus per manum ipsius daret salutem illis, at illi non intellexerunt. ²⁶Atque sequenti die apparuit illis litigantibus et reconciliabat eos in pacem dicens: "Viri, fratres estis; ut quid nocetis alterutrum?". ²⁷Qui autem iniuriam faciebat proximo, reppulit eum dicens: *"Quis te constituit principem et iudicem super nos? ²⁸Numquid interficere me tu vis, quemadmodum interfecisti heri Aegyptium?"*. ²⁹Fugit autem Moyses propter verbum istud et factus est advena in terra Madian, ubi generavit filios duos. ³⁰Et expletis annis quadraginta, *apparuit illi in deserto montis* Sinai *angelus in ignis flamma rubi*. ³¹Moyses autem videns admirabatur visum; accedente autem illo, ut consideraret, facta est vox Domini: ³²*Ego Deus patrum tuorum, Deus Abraham et Isaac et Iacob*". Tremefactus autem Moyses non audebat considerare. ³³Dixit autem illi Dominus: *"Solve calceamentum pedum tuorum; locus enim, in quo stas, terra sancta est. ³⁴Videns vidi afflictionem populi mei, qui est in Aegypto, et gemitum eorum audivi et descendi liberare eos; et nunc veni, mittam te in Aegyptum"*. ³⁵Hunc Moysen, quem negaverunt dicentes: *"Quis te constituit principem et iudicem?"*, hunc Deus et principem et redemptorem misit cum manu angeli, qui apparuit illi

the temple and the Law have already fulfilled their purposes. He tells them that he continues to respect the Mosaic Law and the temple, but that, he now being a Christian, his idea of God's law is more universal and more profound, his concept of the temple more spiritual, for God can be worshipped anywhere in the world. This approach, which respects and perfects the religious values of Judaism (because it reveals their true meaning and brings them to fulfilment), is reinforced by the way the figure of Moses is presented. Stephen shows Moses as

Israelites, 'God will raise up for you a prophet from your brethren as he raised me up.' ³⁸This is he who was in the congregation in the wilderness with the angel who spoke to him at Mount Sinai, and with our fathers; and he received living oracles to give to us. ³⁹Our fathers refused to obey him, but thrust him aside, and in their hearts they turned to Egypt, ⁴⁰saying to Aaron, 'Make for us gods to go before us; as for this Moses who led us out from the land of Egypt, we do not know what has become of him.' ⁴¹And they made a calf in those days, and offered a sacrifice to the idol and rejoiced in the works of their hands. ⁴²But God turned and gave them over to worship the host of heaven, as it is written in the book of the prophets:

'Did you offer to me slain beasts and sacrifices,
        forty years in the wilderness, O house of Israel?
    ⁴³ And you took up the tent of Moloch,
        and the star of the god Rephan,
        the figures which you made to worship;
        and I will remove you beyond Babylon.'

⁴⁴"Our fathers had the tent of witness in the wilderness, even as he who spoke to Moses directed him to make it, according to the pattern that he had seen. ⁴⁵Our fathers in turn brought it in with Joshua when they dispossessed the nations which God thrust out before our fathers. So it was until the days of David, ⁴⁶who found favour in the sight of God and asked leave to find a habitation for the God of Jacob. ⁴⁷But it was Solomon who built a house for him. ⁴⁸Yet the Most High does not dwell in houses made with hands; as the prophet says,

    ⁴⁹ 'Heaven is my throne,
        and earth my footstool.
        What house will you build for me, says the Lord,
        or what is the place of my rest?
    ⁵⁰ Did not my hand make all these things?'

⁵¹"You stiff-necked people, uncircumcised in heart and ears, you always resist the Holy Spirit. As your fathers did, so do you. ⁵²Which of the prophets did not your fathers persecute? And they killed those who announced beforehand the coming of

Marginal references (left column):

Ex 19:3
Deut 4:10; 5:4–22; 9:10
Gal 3:19
Heb 2:2
Num 14:3
Ex 32:1, 23

Ex 32:4, 6

Jer 7:18; 19:13
Amos 5:25–27

Ex 25:40; 27:21
Heb 8:5
Josh 3:14; 18:1

2 Sam 7:2–16
Ps 132:5

1 Kings 6:1, 14; 8:19–20
Is 66:1
Acts 17:24
Heb 9:11, 24

Ex 32:9; 33:3
Lev 26:41
Is 63:10
Jer 4:4; 6:10; 9:25
Mt 23:31
Acts 3:14
2 Chron 36:16

---

in rubo. ³⁶Hic eduxit illos faciens prodigia et signa in terra Aegypti et in Rubro mari et in deserto annis quadraginta. ³⁷Hic est Moyses, qui dixit filiis Israel: "*Prophetam vobis suscitabit Deus de fratribus vestris tamquam me*". ³⁸Hic est qui fuit in ecclesia in solitudine cum angelo, qui loquebatur ei in monte Sinai et cum patribus nostris, qui accepit verba viva dare nobis, ³⁹cui noluerunt oboedire patres nostri, sed reppulerunt et aversi sunt in cordibus suis in Aegyptum ⁴⁰dicentes ad Aaron: "*Fac nobis deos, qui praecedant nos; Moyses enim hic, qui eduxit nos de terra Aegypti, nescimus quid factum sit ei*". ⁴¹Et vitulum fecerunt in illis diebus et obtulerunt hostiam simulacro et laetabantur in operibus manuum suarum. ⁴²Convertit autem Deus et tradidit eos servire militiae caeli, sicut scriptum est in libro Prophetarum: "*Numquid victimas et hostias obtulistis mihi / annis quadraginta in deserto, domus Israel? / ⁴³Et suscepistis tabernaculum Moloch / et sidus dei vestri Rhaephan, / figuras, quas fecistis* ad adorandum eas. / *Et transferam vos trans Babylonem*". ⁴⁴Tabernaculum testimonii erat patribus nostris in deserto, sicut disposuit, qui loquebatur ad Moysen, ut faceret illud secundum formam, quam viderat; ⁴⁵quod et induxerunt suscipientes patres nostri cum Iesu in possessionem gentium, quas expulit Deus a facie patrum nostrorum usque in diebus David, ⁴⁶qui invenit gratiam ante Deum et petiit, ut inveniret tabernaculum domui Iacob. ⁴⁷Salomon autem aedificavit illi domum. ⁴⁸Sed non Altissimus in manufactis habitat, sicut propheta dicit: ⁴⁹"*Caelum mihi thronus est, / terra autem scabellum pedum meorum. / Quam domum aedificabitis mihi, dicit Dominus, / aut quis locus requietionis meae? / ⁵⁰Nonne manus mea fecit haec omnia?*". ⁵¹Duri cervice et incircumcisi cordibus et auribus, vos semper Spiritui Sancto resistitis, sicut patres vestri et vos. ⁵²Quem prophetarum non sunt persecuti patres vestri? Et occiderunt eos, qui praenuntiabant de adventu Iusti, cuius vos nunc proditores et homicidae fuistis, ⁵³qui accepistis legem in dispositionibus angelorum et non custodistis». ⁵⁴Audientes autem haec, dissecabantur cordibus suis et stridebant den-

---

a "type" or figure of Christ: Christ therefore is the new Moses. Small elucidations of the Greek text of the Old Testament help to get these ideas across. In the books of the Old Testament, expressions like "whom they refused" and "deliverer" (v. 35) were not applied to Moses; but in the Judaism of Stephen's time they were, and they are used in this speech to point to Jesus Christ: Moses had a mission from God, but he met with hostility and rebellion from the Israelites; now they oppose Jesus, too—a much more serious fault.

the Righteous One, whom you have now betrayed and murdered, ⁵³you who received the law as delivered by angels and did not keep it."

Acts 7:38

Martyrdom of St Stephen

⁵⁴Now when they heard these things they were enraged, and they ground their teeth against him. ⁵⁵But he, full of the Holy Spirit, gazed into heaven and saw the glory of God, and Jesus standing at the right hand of God; ⁵⁶and he said, "Behold, I see the heavens opened, and the Son of man standing at the right hand of God." ⁵⁷But they cried out with a loud voice and stopped their ears and rushed together upon him. ⁵⁸Then they cast him out of the city and stoned him; and the witnesses laid down their garments at the feet of a young man named Saul. ⁵⁹And as they were stoning Stephen, he prayed, "Lord Jesus, receive my spirit." ⁶⁰And he knelt down and cried with a loud voice, "Lord, do not hold this sin against them." And when he had said this, he fell asleep. ¹ᵃAnd Saul was consenting to his death.

Ps 35:16; 37:12; 112:10
Dan 7:13
Mt 26:64
Lk 3:21; 20:42; 22:69
Acts 22:20
Ps 31:5
Lk 23:46
Lk 23:34

tibus in eum. ⁵⁵Cum autem esset plenus Spiritu Sancto, intendens in caelum vidit gloriam Dei et Iesum stantem a dextris Dei ⁵⁶et ait: «Ecce video caelos apertos et Filium hominis a dextris stantem Dei». ⁵⁷Exclamantes autem voce magna continuerunt aures suas et impetum fecerunt unanimiter in eum ⁵⁸et eicientes extra civitatem lapidabant. Et testes deposuerunt vestimenta sua secus pedes adulescentis, qui vocabatur Saulus. ⁵⁹Et lapidabant Stephanum invocantem et dicentem: «Domine Iesu, suscipe spiritum meum». ⁶⁰Positis autem genibus clamavit voce magna: «Domine, ne statuas illis hoc peccatum»; et cum hoc dixisset, obdormivit. [8] ¹Saulus autem erat consentiens neci eius. Facta est autem in illa die persecutio

7:54–60 Luke's account, with its parallels between Jesus' death and Stephen's (cf. the note on 6:8–15), marks a new moment in salvation history: whereas Jesus addresses God the Father (Lk 23:46), Stephen addresses his similar prayer to the Lord Jesus (v. 59), thereby confessing what he has just seen in his vision (vv. 55–56)—the divinity of Christ. "It is clear", St Ephrem comments, "that those who suffer for Christ enjoy the glory of the whole Trinity. Stephen saw the Father and Jesus at his side, because Jesus appears only to his own, as was the case with the apostles after the Resurrection. While the champion of the faith stood there helpless in the midst of those who had killed the Lord, just at the point when the first martyr was to be crowned, he saw the Lord, holding a crown in his right hand, as if to encourage him to conquer death and to show that he inwardly helps those who are about to die on his account. He therefore reveals what he sees, that is, the heavens opened, which were closed to Adam and only opened to Christ at the Jordan, but open now after the cross to all those who share Christ's sufferings, and in the first instance open to this man. See how Stephen reveals why his face was lit up: it was because he was on the point of contemplating this wondrous mission. That is why he took on the appearance of an angel—so that his testi-

mony might be more reliable" (*Catena armenia super Acta*, ad loc.).

Towards the end of the passage (v. 58), St Luke introduces Saul, to imply perhaps that Stephen's charity, seen in his forgiving his persecutors, will soon bear fruit. Many Christian preachers have made this point: "To win the crown that is his, Stephen wielded love as his weapon, and through love he triumphed over all things. Through love of God, he did not yield to the attacks of his persecutors; through love of neighbour, he prayed for those who stoned him. Through love, he argued with those who were in error so that they might see and correct their mistakes, and he prayed for those who stoned him so that they might not suffer punishment. The power of his love overcame Saul's cruelty, and his persecutor in this world became his companion in heaven. Stephen's holy and unquenchable love conquered with prayer those who could not be won over with words. Now Paul rejoices with Stephen, rejoices with Stephen in the love of Christ, and triumphs with him and reigns with him. The path laid out by Stephen when he was martyred by Saul's stones has been followed by Paul with the help of Stephen's prayers. [...] Love is the source and origin of all good things, sure protection and the path to heaven" (St Fulgentius of Ruspe, *Sermones*, 3, 5–6).

PART TWO

The Church spreads beyond Jerusalem*

5. THE CHURCH IN SAMARIA*

Persecution of the Church

Jn 16:2
Acts 11:19; 26:10

8 ¹ᵇAnd on that day a great persecution arose against the church in Jerusalem; and they were all scattered throughout the region of Judea and Samaria, except the

Acts 9:1; 22:4
Gal 1:13
1 Cor 15:9
1 Tim 1:13

apostles. ²Devout men buried Stephen, and made great lamentation over him. ³But Saul laid waste the church, and entering house after house, he dragged off men and women and committed them to prison.

Acts 11:19

⁴Now those who were scattered went about preaching the word.

Philip's preaching in Samaria

Acts 6:5

⁵Philip went down to a city of Samaria, and proclaimed to them the Christ. ⁶And the multitudes with one accord gave heed to what was said by Philip, when they heard

magna in ecclesiam, quae erat Hierosolymis; et omnes dispersi sunt per regiones Iudaeae et Samariae praeter apostolos. ²Sepelierunt autem Stephanum viri timorati et fecerunt planctum magnum super illum. ³Saulus vero devastabat ecclesiam per domos intrans et trahens viros ac mulieres tradebat in custodiam. ⁴Igitur qui dispersi erant, pertransierunt evangelizantes verbum. ⁵Philippus autem descendens in civitatem

*8:1—12:25 This part of the book relates how Christians come to be scattered due to persecution, so that the Gospel now reaches Judea, Samaria and Syria. Jerusalem has begun to stifle the spread of the Gospel (in both geographical and religious terms), and the Church starts to open its gates to Gentiles: we hear about the conversion of many of them, including an Ethiopian (8:26–39) and many Samaritans (8:14–17).

Luke deals in some detail with the calling of Paul, the Apostle of the Gentiles (9:1–30), and the conversion of the centurion Cornelius and his family (10:1–11:18), a highly significant development, for it shows the Gospel to transcend ethnic barriers. This part of the book ends with the death of James the brother of John, and the arrest and miraculous release of Peter.

*8:1–40 The spread of the Church across Samaria is the first step towards the fulfilment of our Lord's words at the Ascension (1:8). Philip, one of the Seven (6:5), plays a large part in this spreading of the faith (8:4–8), but in Acts full reception of the Holy Spirit is always linked to the apostles and to the union of all Christians with the mother church in Jerusalem (8:14–17).

8:1–4 Stephen's death marks the start of a violent persecution in Jerusalem. Given that the apostles and a considerable number of the other believers stayed on in the Holy City, many scholars think that the persecution was aimed primarily against Hellenist Christians (see 6:1–7 and note). St Luke does not actually say this; aware of the role that Paul will play in the early Church, he prefers to point out, twice (vv. 1, 3), his involvement in the persecution: "Christianity has been too often in what seemed deadly peril that we should fear for it any new trial now. So far is certain; on the other hand, what is uncertain […] is the particular mode by which, in the event, Providence rescues and saves His elect inheritance. Sometimes our enemy is turned into a friend; sometimes he is despoiled of that special virulence of evil which was so threatening; sometimes he falls to pieces himself; sometimes he does just so much as is beneficial, and then is removed. Commonly the Church has nothing more to do than to go on in her own proper duties, in confidence and peace; to stand still and to see the salvation of God" (Cardinal John Henry Newman, *Biglietto Speech*).

8:5–8 The Philip mentioned here is not the apostle Philip (1:13) but one of the Seven chosen to

him and saw the signs which he did. [7]For unclean spirits came out of many who Mt 8:29; 10:1
Mk 16:17
were possessed, crying with a loud voice; and many who were paralyzed or lame
were healed. [8]So there was much joy in that city. Jn 4:38–41

Simon the magician

[9]But there was a man named Simon who had previously practised magic in the city
and amazed the nation of Samaria, saying that he himself was somebody great.
[10]They all gave heed to him, from the least to the greatest, saying, "This man is that
power of God which is called Great." [11]And they gave heed to him, because for a
long time he had amazed them with his magic. [12]But when they believed Philip as
he preached good news about the kingdom of God and the name of Jesus Christ,

Samariae praedicabat illis Christum. [6]Intendebant autem turbae his, quae a Philippo dicebantur, unanimiter, audientes et videntes signa, quae
faciebat; [7]ex multis enim eorum, qui habebant spiritus immundos clamantes voce magna exibant; multi autem paralytici et claudi curati sunt.
[8]Factum est autem magnum gaudium in illa civitate. [9]Vir autem quidem nomine Simon iampridem erat in civitate magias faciens et dementans
gentem Samariae, dicens esse se aliquem magnum, [10]cui attendebant omnes a minimo usque ad maximum dicentes: «Hic est virtus Dei, quae
vocatur Magna». [11]Attendebant autem eum propter quod multo tempore magiis dementasset eos. [12]Cum vero credidissent Philippo evangelizanti

minister to the needy (6:5). The Gospel now reaches beyond the borders of Judea: "See how, in the middle of misfortune, the Christians keep up their preaching instead of neglecting it" (St John Chrysostom, *In Acta Apostolorum*, 18). Apostolic fruitfulness in Samaria is the first consequence of the persecution: "The religion founded by the mystery of the cross of Christ cannot be destroyed by any form of cruelty. The Church is not diminished by persecutions; on the contrary, they make for its increase. The field of the Lord is clothed in a richer harvest. When the grain which falls dies, it is reborn and multiplied" (St Leo the Great, *In natali Apostolorum Petri et Pauli*, 6).

8:9–13 St Luke makes use of the episode of Simon the magician to show the difference between the genuine miracles worked by the apostles in the name of Jesus and with his authority, and the real or apparent wonders worked by a charlatan: "As in the time of Moses, so now the distinction is made between different kinds of prodigies. Magic was practised, but it was easy to see the difference between it and genuine miracles. [...] Unclean spirits, in great numbers, went out of possessed people, protesting as they went. This showed that they were being expelled. Those who practised magic did just the opposite: they reinforced the bonds that bound the possessed" (St John Chrysostom, *In Acta Apostolorum*, 18, 3).

Magic (an attempt to control occult forces) and superstition (trying to obtain supernatural effects by methods that cannot produce them) are symptoms of debased or corrupt religion. Natural religion per se is a legitimate and necessary search for God in a desire to worship him. It is cleansed and perfected by supernatural revelation, whereby God seeks man out, to assuage his inner restlessness and raise him up and steer him in the right direction. Without such supernatural intervention, natural religion can easily lose its original impulse and become useless or even harmful. Simon's behaviour seems indicative of this breakdown: he believes, is baptized and follows Philip (v. 13) but he does not understand how true religion works (8:18–19). Still, he has a certain piety; he does ask the apostles to pray to the Lord for him (8:24). But without the help of revelation, man at best can only stumble blindly after God (see 17:27). The difficulty pagans had in arriving at the whole truth (in religion or philosophy) was something that the first Christian apologists noted: "Our teaching surpasses all human teaching because the fullness of the Word has been given to us in Christ, who was revealed body, soul and word. All the just and noble principles defined by philosophers and lawmakers are the traces of the Word that they have been able to discern; and it is because they do not know the Word, who is Christ, that they so often contradict one another" (St Justin, *Apologia*, 2, 7, 3).

they were baptized, both men and women. [13]Even Simon himself believed, and after being baptized he continued with Philip. And seeing signs and great miracles performed, he was amazed.

Peter and John in Samaria

Acts 11:1, 22

Acts 2:38

Acts 19:2–6
1 Tim 4:14

[14]Now when the apostles at Jerusalem heard that Samaria had received the word of God, they sent to them Peter and John, [15]who came down and prayed for them that they might receive the Holy Spirit; [16]for it had not yet fallen on any of them, but they had only been baptized in the name of the Lord Jesus. [17]Then they laid their hands on them and they received the Holy Spirit.

The sin of simony

Mt 10:8
Acts 2:38; 10:45–48;
11:15–17

Ps 78:37
Lk 11:13

Heb 12:15

[18]Now when Simon saw that the Spirit was given through the laying on of the apostles' hands, he offered them money, [19]saying, "Give me also this power, that any one on whom I lay my hands may receive the Holy Spirit." [20]But Peter said to him, "Your silver perish with you, because you thought you could obtain the gift of God with money!* [21]You have neither part nor lot in this matter, for your heart is not right before God. [22]Repent therefore of this wickedness of yours, and pray to the Lord

de regno Dei et nomine Iesu Christi, baptizabantur viri ac mulieres. [13]Tunc Simon et ipse credidit et, cum baptizatus esset, adhaerebat Philippo; videns etiam signa et virtutes magnas fieri stupens admirabatur. [14]Cum autem audissent apostoli, qui erant Hierosolymis, quia recepit Samaria verbum Dei, miserunt ad illos Petrum et Ioannem, [15]qui cum descendissent, oraverunt pro ipsis, ut acciperent Spiritum Sanctum; [16]nondum enim super quemquam illorum venerat, sed baptizati tantum erant in nomine Domini Iesu. [17]Tunc imposuerunt manus super illos, et accipiebant Spiritum Sanctum. [18]Cum vidisset autem Simon quia per impositionem manuum apostolorum daretur Spiritus, obtulit eis pecuniam [19]dicens: «Date et mihi hanc potestatem, ut cuicumque imposuero manus, accipiat Spiritum Sanctum». [20]Petrus autem dixit ad eum: «Argentum tuum tecum sit in perditionem, quoniam donum Dei existimasti pecunia possideri! [21]Non est tibi pars neque sors in verbo isto, cor enim tuum non est rectum coram Deo. [22]Paenitentiam itaque age ab hac nequitia tua et roga Dominum, si forte remittatur tibi haec cogitatio cordis tui; [23]in felle enim amar-

"That power of God which is called Great" (v. 10): it is not very clear where this expression comes from. The naïveté and credulity of those Samaritans seems to have led them to believe that the gods themselves were implicated in some way in any magic trick performed by a human being. In any event, they attributed some sort of divine power to Simon.

8:14–25 The apostles oversaw the first spread of the Church outside Jerusalem (v. 14). Tradition has seen in vv. 15–17 a first manifestation of the sacrament of Confirmation: "The apostles, in fulfilment of the will of Christ, communicate the gift of the Holy Spirit to the neophytes by the laying on of hands, and so bring the grace of Baptism to completion in them (cf. Acts 8:15–17; 19:5–6). This explains why the doctrine of Baptism and the laying on of hands is recalled as one of the fundamental elements of Christian formation in the Letter to the Hebrews (cf. Heb 6:2). Catholic tradition has justifiably taken the act of the laying on of hands as the primitive

origin of the sacrament of Confirmation, which, in a certain way, preserves the grace of Pentecost in the Church" (Paul VI, *Divinae consortium naturae*).

Peter and John do not act here on the strength of an independent power that they have or control: rather, divine power acts through them (vv. 15, 17). Christians work miracles through prayer, never by resorting to magical actions or words. St Luke will again point out the difference between Christian miracles and magic when he deals with the episodes of Elymas the magician (13:6ff), the girl with a spirit of divination (16:16ff), and the sons of Sceva the priest (19:13ff).

Simon's proposal—he offers the apostles money in exchange for the power to call down the Holy Spirit (vv. 18–19)—gave rise to the term "simony". "Simony is defined as the buying or selling of spiritual things. To Simon the magician, who wanted to buy the spiritual power he saw at work in the apostles, St Peter responded: 'Your silver perish with you, because

that, if possible, the intent of your heart may be forgiven you. [23]For I see that you are in the gall of bitterness and in the bond of iniquity." [24]And Simon answered, "Pray for me to the Lord, that nothing of what you have said may come upon me."

[25]Now when they had testified and spoken the word of the Lord, they returned to Jerusalem, preaching the gospel to many villages of the Samaritans.

Deut 29:17

Ex 8:4

Jn 4:35

Philip baptizes an Ethiopian official

[26]But an angel of the Lord said to Philip, "Rise and go toward the south[g] to the road that goes down from Jerusalem to Gaza." This is a desert road. [27]And he rose and went. And behold, an Ethiopian, a eunuch, a minister of Candace the queen of the Ethiopians, in charge of all her treasure, had come to Jerusalem to worship [28]and was returning; seated in his chariot, he was reading the prophet Isaiah. [29]And the Spirit said to Philip, "Go up and join this chariot." [30]So Philip ran to him, and heard him reading Isaiah the prophet, and asked, "Do you understand what you are reading?" [31]And he said, "How can I, unless some one guides me?" And he invited Philip to come up and sit with him. [32]Now the passage of the scripture which he was reading was this:

Acts 1:8
Ps 68:31
Is 56:3–7

Jn 16:13
Rom 10:14
Is 53:7–8
Lk 18:31

> "As a sheep led to the slaughter
> or a lamb before its shearer is dumb,

itudinis et obligatione iniquitatis video te esse». [24]Respondens autem Simon dixit: «Precamini vos pro me ad Dominum, ut nihil veniat super me horum, quae dixistis». [25]Et illi quidem testificati et locuti verbum Domini, redibant Hierosolymam, et multis vicis Samaritanorum evangelizabant. [26]Angelus autem Domini locutus est ad Philippum dicens: «Surge et vade contra meridianum ad viam, quae descendit ab Ierusalem in Gazam; haec est deserta». [27]Et surgens abiit; et ecce vir Aethiops eunuchus potens Candacis reginae Aethiopum, qui erat super omnem gazam eius, qui venerat adorare in Ierusalem [28]et revertebatur sedens super currum suum et legebat prophetam Isaiam. [29]Dixit autem Spiritus Philippo: «Accede et adiunge te ad currum istum». [30]Accurrens autem Philippus audivit illum legentem Isaiam prophetam et dixit: «Putasne intellegis, quae legis?». [31]Qui ait: «Et quomodo possum, si non aliquis ostenderit mihi?». Rogavitque Philippum, ut ascenderet et sederet secum. [32]Locus autem Scripturae,

you thought you could obtain God's gift with money!' (Acts 8:20) Peter thus held to the words of Jesus: 'You received without pay, give without pay' (Mt 10:8; cf. Is 55:1). It is impossible to appropriate to oneself spiritual goods and behave toward them as their owner or master, for they have their source in God. One can receive them only from him, without payment" (*Catechism of the Catholic Church*, 2121). However, sacred ministers do not commit simony when they accept reasonable alms, in cash or in kind, for their own maintenance or for expenses incurred in the liturgy; in such things there is no question of paying for a spiritual benefit. Jesus taught that the apostle needs an appropriate wage (see Lk 10:7), and St Paul wrote to the same effect (see 1 Cor 9:14). See *Catechism of the Catholic Church*, 2122.

8:26–40 The baptizing of the Ethiopian official marks an important step in the spread of Christianity. This episode encapsulates the various

stages in apostolate: Christ's disciple, moved by the Spirit (vv. 29, 39), readily obeys his command; he bases his teaching on Holy Scripture (as Jesus did with the disciples in Emmaus: Lk 24:27); and thus brings the person to receive Baptism.

After relating the angel's command to Philip, St Luke introduces the official. The Ethiopia referred to was the kingdom of Nubia, to the south of Egypt, above Aswan, the first waterfall on the Nile; it is part of present-day Sudan. Candace is not a proper name but the dynastic title of the queens of that country, which at that time was ruled by women (see Eusebius, *Historia ecclesiastica*, 2, 1, 13). The term "eunuch", like its equivalent in Hebrew, was often used even if the person was not physically a eunuch; court officials in general were often termed eunuchs (see e.g. Gen 39:1; 2 Kings 25:19). The man in this episode held a high office, equivalent to the post of minister of finance. We do not know if he was a member of the Jewish race, a proselyte (a Jew not by race

g Or *at noon*

so he opens not his mouth.
³³ In his humiliation justice was denied him.
Who can describe his generation?
For his life is taken up from the earth."

³⁴And the eunuch said to Philip, "About whom, pray, does the prophet say this, about himself or about some one else?" ³⁵Then Philip opened his mouth, and beginning with this scripture he told him the good news of Jesus. ³⁶And as they went along the road they came to some water, and the eunuch said, "See, here is water! What is to prevent my being baptized?"^h ³⁸And he commanded the chariot to stop, and they both went down into the water, Philip and the eunuch, and he baptized him. ³⁹And when they came up out of the water, the Spirit of the Lord caught up Philip; and the eunuch saw him no more, and went on his way rejoicing. ⁴⁰But Philip was found at Azotus, and passing on he preached the gospel to all the towns till he came to Caesarea.

Lk 24:27

Acts 10:47; 11:17

1 Kings 18:12
Lk 24:31–32

Acts 21:8

---

quem legebat, erat hic: «*Tamquam ovis ad occisionem ductus est / et sicut agnus coram tondente se sine voce, / sic non aperit os suum. / *³³*In humilitate eius iudicium eius sublatum est. / Generationem illius quis enarrabit? / Quoniam tollitur de terra vita eius*». ³⁴Respondens autem eunuchus Philippo dixit: «Obsecro te, de quo propheta dicit hoc? De se an de alio aliquo?». ³⁵Aperiens autem Philippus os suum et incipiens a Scriptura ista, evangelizavit illi Iesum. ³⁶Et dum irent per viam, venerunt ad quandam aquam, et ait eunuchus: «Ecce aqua; quid prohibet me baptizari?». ³⁸Et iussit stare currum, et descenderunt uterque in aquam Philippus et eunuchus, et baptizavit eum. ³⁹Cum autem ascendissent de aqua, Spiritus Domini rapuit Philippum, et amplius non vidit eum eunuchus; ibat autem per viam suam gaudens. ⁴⁰Philippus autem inventus est in Azoto et pertransiens evangelizabat civitatibus cunctis, donec veniret Caesaream. [9] ¹Saulus autem, adhuc spirans minarum et caedis in discipulos Domini, accessit ad principem sacerdotum ²et petiit ab eo epistulas in Damascum ad synagogas, ut si quos invenisset huius viae, viros ac mulieres,

---

but by religion) or a "God-fearer", a pagan who was well disposed towards the Jewish religion. The book of Deuteronomy (see Deut 23:2) prescribed that no eunuch could belong to the people of Israel; but Isaiah 56:8 stated that, when salvation eventually came, God would also call "the outcasts of Israel" to form his assembly. This may be what the passage is about: it shows that salvation is being extended to the ends of the earth (see 1:8), even to those who were previously excluded from the Lord's assembly.

The conversation between Philip and the Ethiopian (vv. 30–35) shows the importance that Holy Scripture has in evangelization. And it also shows that we need people to help us interpret Scripture: "I am not (to speak in passing of myself) more learned or more holy than that eunuch who travelled to the temple from Ethiopia, that is, from the end of the earth: he left the royal palace and such was his desire for divine knowledge that he was even reading the sacred words in his chariot. And yet ... he did not realize whom he was venerating in that book. Philip comes along, he reveals to him Jesus

hidden and as it were imprisoned in the text [...], and in that very moment he believes, is baptized, is faithful and holy. [...] I tell you this to show you that, unless you have a guide who goes ahead of you to show you the way, you cannot enter the holy Scriptures" (St Jerome, *Epistulae*, 53, 5–6). That guide is the sure interpretation provided by the Church, to whom God has entrusted the inspired books. Hence Vatican II's teaching: "If we are to derive their true meaning from the sacred texts," we must devote attention not only to their content but to the "unity of the whole of Scripture, taking account of the Tradition of the entire Church and the analogy of faith. [...] Everything to do with the interpretation of Scripture is ultimately subject to the judgment of the Church, which exercises the divinely conferred commission and ministry of watching over and interpreting the Word of God" (*Dei Verbum*, 12).

Verse 37 (see RSV note **h**), present in the Latin Vulgate, is not to be found in some Greek codexes or in the more authoritative translations. It may be a very ancient gloss, inspired by baptismal liturgy.

---

h Other ancient authorities add all or most of verse 37, *And Philip said, "If you believe with all your heart, you may." And he replied, "I believe that Jesus Christ is the Son of God."*

6. THE CONVERSION OF ST PAUL*

Saul on his way to Damascus

9 ¹But Saul, still breathing threats and murder against the disciples of the Lord, went to the high priest ²and asked him for letters to the synagogues at Damascus, so that if he found any belonging to the Way, men or women, he might bring them bound to Jerusalem. ³Now as he journeyed he approached Damascus, and suddenly a light from heaven flashed about him. ⁴And he fell to the ground and heard a voice saying to him, "Saul, Saul, why do you persecute me?" ⁵And he said, "Who are you, Lord?" And he said, "I am Jesus, whom you are persecuting;* ⁶but rise and enter the city, and you will be told what you are to do." ⁷The men who were travelling with him stood speechless, hearing the voice but seeing no one. ⁸Saul arose from the ground; and when his eyes were opened, he could see nothing; so they led him by the hand and brought him into Damascus. ⁹And for three days he was without sight, and neither ate nor drank.

(margin) Acts 22:5–16; 26:10–18 Gal 1:12–17 Acts 8:3

(margin) 1 Cor 15:8

(margin) Dan 10:7

vinctos perduceret in Ierusalem. ³Et cum iter faceret, contigit ut appropinquaret Damasco, et subito circumfulsit eum lux de caelo, ⁴et cadens in terram audivit vocem dicentem sibi: «Saul, Saul, quid me persequeris?». ⁵Qui dixit: «Quis es, Domine?». Et ille: «Ego sum Iesus, quem tu persequeris! ⁶Sed surge et ingredere civitatem, et dicetur tibi quid te oporteat facere». ⁷Viri autem illi, qui comitabantur cum eo, stabant stupefacti, audientes quidem vocem, neminem autem videntes. ⁸Surrexit autem Saulus de terra apertisque oculis nihil videbat; ad manus autem illum trahentes introduxerunt Damascum. ⁹Et erat tribus diebus non videns et non manducavit, neque bibit. ¹⁰Erat autem quidam discipulus Damasci nomine

*9:1–31 This is the first of three accounts in Acts about the calling of Saul (see 22:5–16; 26:9–20), which probably occurred between the years 34 and 36; where important events are concerned, Luke sees the importance of repetition as a form of teaching. In this first account, the events are described from two different viewpoints—that of Paul (vv. 1–9) and that of Ananias (vv. 10–19). In vv. 19–30 we see how quickly the Apostle commits himself to the ministry of preaching.

9:1–19 The Roman authorities recognized the moral authority of the Sanhedrin and even allowed it to exercise a certain jurisdiction over members of Jewish communities outside Palestine—as was the case with Damascus, a city about 250 kilometres (155 miles) from Jerusalem. The Sanhedrin even had the right to extradite Jews (cf. 1 Mac 15:21). This explains Saul's assignment (vv. 1–3).

On his way to Damascus, Saul had this vision, which marked the beginning of his vocation. From the very beginning, Jesus made Saul see that there is an identity between Christ and Christians: Christ *is* his Church. This truth was etched on the Apostle's soul, and it led him, much later, to speak in his letters about the Mystical Body of Christ (see Col 1:18; Eph

1:22f). Some of the Fathers spell this idea out in their commentaries: "Jesus does not say, 'Why do you persecute my members?', but, 'Why do you persecute me?', because he himself still suffers affronts in his body, which is the Church" (St Bede, *Expositio Actuum Apostolorum*, ad loc.).

However, our Lord does not tell Saul what his mission will be. His calling to be the Apostle of the Gentiles is revealed by Jesus to Ananias (v. 15), and Ananias tells Saul (see 22:12–15). Despite the dramatic start to Saul's vocation, God chose to train him and make his will known to him through other members of the Christian community. That may be why ascetical traditions, dating back to the early centuries of the Church, use this passage to show how useful spiritual guidance is, for there is this principle in the governance of men: "no one can be a good judge on his own cause, because everyone judges according to his own inclinations" (John Cassian, *Collationes*, 16, 11). "Our Lord Jesus Christ, without whom we can do nothing, will not give his grace to him who, though he has access to an expert guide, rejects this precious means of sanctification, thinking that he can look after on his own everything that touches on his salvation. He who has a director, whom he

Ananias baptizes Saul

1 Sam 3:4

10Now there was a disciple at Damascus called Ananias. The Lord said to him in a vision, "Ananias." And he said, "Here I am, Lord." **11**And the Lord said to him, "Rise and go to the street called Straight, and inquire in the house of Judas for a man

Mk 8:23–25

of Tarsus named Saul; for behold, he is praying, **12**and he has seen a man named Ananias come in and lay his hands on him so that he might regain his sight." **13**But Ananias answered, "Lord, I have heard from many about this man, how much evil he has done to thy saints* at Jerusalem; **14**and here he has authority from the chief

1 Cor 4:9–13

priests to bind all who call upon thy name." **15**But the Lord said to him, "Go, for he is a chosen instrument of mine to carry my name before the Gentiles and kings and

Rom 1:5
2 Cor 11:23–28
2 Tim 3:11–12

the sons of Israel; **16**for I will show him how much he must suffer for the sake of my name." **17**So Ananias departed and entered the house. And laying his hands on him

Acts 15:8; 22:14–16

he said, "Brother Saul, the Lord Jesus who appeared to you on the road by which you came, has sent me that you may regain your sight and be filled with the Holy

Tob 11:10–15

Spirit." **18**And immediately something like scales fell from his eyes and he regained his sight. Then he rose and was baptized, **19**and took food and was strengthened.

Paul begins his apostolate

Gal 1:16

For several days he was with the disciples at Damascus. **20**And in the synagogues immediately he proclaimed Jesus, saying, "He is the Son of God." **21**And all who heard him were amazed, and said, "Is not this the man who made havoc in

Ananias, et dixit ad illum in visu Dominus: «Anania». At ille ait: «Ecce ego, Domine». **11**Et Dominus ad illum: «Surgens vade in vicum, qui vocatur Rectus, et quaere in domo Iudae Saulum nomine Tarsensem; ecce enim orat **12**et vidit virum Ananiam nomine introeuntem et imponentem sibi manus, ut visum recipiat». **13**Respondit autem Ananias: «Domine, audivi a multis de viro hoc, quanta mala sanctis tuis fecerit in Ierusalem; **14**et hic habet potestatem a principibus sacerdotum alligandi omnes, qui invocant nomen tuum». **15**Dixit autem ad eum Dominus: «Vade, quoniam vas electionis est mihi iste, ut portet nomen meum coram gentibus et regibus et filiis Israel; **16**ego enim ostendam illi quanta oporteat eum pro nomine meo pati». **17**Et abiit Ananias et introivit in domum et imponens ei manus dixit: «Saul frater, Dominus misit me, Iesus qui apparuit tibi in via, qua veniebas, ut videas et implearis Spiritu Sancto». **18**Et confestim ceciderunt ab oculis eius tamquam squamae, et visum recepit. Et surgens baptizatus est **19**et, cum accepisset cibum, confortatus est. Fuit autem cum discipulis, qui erant Damasci, per dies aliquot **20**et continuo in synagogis praedicabat Iesum, quoniam hic est Filius Dei. **21**Stupebant autem omnes, qui audiebant et dicebant: «Nonne hic est, qui expugnabat in Ierusalem eos, qui invocabant nomen istud, et huc ad hoc venerat, ut vinctos illos duceret ad principes sacerdotum?». **22**Saulus autem magis con-

obeys in everything, will reach his goal more easily and more quickly than if he acted as his own guide, even if he be very intelligent and have the very best of spiritual books" (St Vincent Ferrer, *Treatise on the Spiritual Life*, 2, 1).

Ananias refers to the first followers of Christ as "saints" (v. 13). This name was in common use among the first Christians (see 9:32, 41; Rom 8:27; 1 Cor 1:2). God is *the* "Holy One" (see Is 6:3), and those who approach God and keep his commandments share in this holiness: "The Lord said to Moses, 'Say to all the congregation of the people of Israel, You shall be holy; for I the Lord your God am holy'" (Lev 19:1–2). "What a moving name—saints!—the early Christians used to address each other! ... Learn to be a brother to your brothers" (St Josemaría Escrivá, *The Way*, 469).

9:19–30 Luke shows us the energy that Saul put into his preaching: the same fervour that Saul brought to his persecution of Christians (9:1–2) he now invests in his controversies with Jews, whether they be of Palestinian (v. 22) or Greek (v. 29) origin. But at the same time the power of God is clear to see: the persecutor (v. 21) feared by all (v. 26) has been converted by God to the gospel of Christ.

In Galatians 1:15–17, St Paul tells how, after his conversion, he withdrew to Arabia and then later returned to Damascus. Almost three years elapsed between these two visits to Damascus, and it may have been during this second period in the city that Paul preached there the divinity of Jesus, with all his learning and ardour now placed at the service of Christ (vv. 20–22). This amazed and confounded the Jews, leading them to plot his death. The flight reported in vv. 23–26

Jerusalem of those who called on this name? And he has come here for this purpose, to bring them bound before the chief priests." ²²But Saul increased all the more in strength, and confounded the Jews who lived in Damascus by proving that Jesus was the Christ.

Acts 18:5, 28

Paul flees from Damascus

²³When many days had passed, the Jews plotted to kill him, ²⁴but their plot became known to Saul. They were watching the gates day and night, to kill him; ²⁵but his disciples took him by night and let him down over the wall, lowering him in a basket.

2 Cor 11:32–33

Barnabas and Paul in Jerusalem

²⁶And when he had come to Jerusalem he attempted to join the disciples; and they were all afraid of him, for they did not believe that he was a disciple. ²⁷But Barnabas took him, and brought him to the apostles, and declared to them how on the road he had seen the Lord, who spoke to him, and how at Damascus he had preached boldly in the name of Jesus. ²⁸So he went in and out among them at Jerusalem, ²⁹preaching boldly in the name of the Lord. And he spoke and disputed against the Hellenists; but they were seeking to kill him. ³⁰And when the brethren knew it, they brought him down to Caesarea, and sent him off to Tarsus.

Gal 1:18f

Acts 11:25
Gal 1:21

Growth of the Church

³¹So the church throughout all Judea and Galilee and Samaria had peace and was built up; and walking in the fear of the Lord and in the comfort of the Holy Spirit it was multiplied.

Acts 2:46

valescebat et confundebat Iudaeos, qui habitabant Damasci, affirmans quoniam hic est Christus. ²³Cum implerentur autem dies multi, consilium fecerunt Iudaei, ut eum interficerent; ²⁴notae autem factae sunt Saulo insidiae eorum. Custodiebant autem et portas die ac nocte, ut eum interficerent; ²⁵accipientes autem discipuli eius nocte per murum dimiserunt eum submittentes in sporta. ²⁶Cum autem venisset in Ierusalem, tentabat iungere se discipulis; et omnes timebant eum, non credentes quia esset discipulus. ²⁷Barnabas autem apprehensum illum duxit ad apostolos, et narravit illis quomodo in via vidisset Dominum et quia locutus est ei, et quomodo in Damasco fiducialiter egerit in nomine Iesu. ²⁸Et erat cum illis intrans et exiens in Ierusalem, fiducialiter agens in nomine Domini. ²⁹Loquebatur quoque et disputabat cum Graecis; illi autem quaerebant occidere eum. ³⁰Quod cum cognovissent, fratres deduxerunt eum Caesaream et dimiserunt Tarsum. ³¹Ecclesia quidem per totam Iudaeam et

is also recounted by St Paul himself in 2 Corinthians 11:32–33. The person who tried to arrest him at the instigation of the Damascus Jews was the governor of the Nabataean king Aretas IV.

The passage goes on (vv. 26–28) to give a short account of Paul's first visit to Jerusalem after his conversion. He spent a fortnight with Peter (see Gal 1:18) to confirm that his preaching was in line with that of the apostles. Barnabas (cf. the note on 4:32–37) dispelled the initial (and understandable) reservations that the early community had about their former persecutor.

For a second time Paul has to flee for his life (vv. 29–30). Commenting on this episode, St John Chrysostom explains that, in addition to grace, human resourcefulness has a significant part to play in apostolic activity: "The disciples

were afraid that the Jews would cause Saul's martyrdom as they did Stephen's. [...] They sent him to preach the Gospel in his native city, where the risk would be less. From this action of the apostles you can see that God does not do everything directly by his grace and that he often permits his disciples to apply the rule of prudence" (*In Acta Apostolorum*, 21).

9:31 After describing Paul's early activity, Luke interrupts his narrative to give an overview of the steady progress of the Church as a whole and of the various communities that have grown up as a result of the Christians' flight from Jerusalem (see also 2:41, 47; 4:4, 5:14; 6:1, 7; 11:21, 24; 16:5). Although he mentions the expansion of the Church through Galilee and Judea, he has not yet given any details about

7. ST PETER'S ACTIVITY*

Curing of a paralyzed man at Lydda

Acts 8:4

³²Now as Peter went here and there among them all, he came down also to the saints that lived at Lydda. ³³There he found a man named Aeneas, who had been bedridden

Acts 3:7

for eight years and was paralyzed. ³⁴And Peter said to him, "Aeneas, Jesus Christ heals you; rise and make your bed." And immediately he rose. ³⁵And all the residents of Lydda and Sharon saw him, and they turned to the Lord.

Peter raises Tabitha to life

Lk 12:33

³⁶Now there was at Joppa a disciple named Tabitha, which means Dorcas or Gazelle. She was full of good works and acts of charity. ³⁷In those days she fell sick and died; and when they had washed her, they laid her in an upper room. ³⁸Since Lydda was near Joppa, the disciples, hearing that Peter was there, sent two men to him entreating him, "Please come to us without delay." ³⁹So Peter rose and went with them. And when he had come, they took him to the upper room. All the widows stood beside

Galilaeam et Samariam habebat pacem, aedificabatur et ambulabat in timore Domini et consolatione Sancti Spiritus crescebat. ³²Factum est autem Petrum, dum pertransiret universos, devenire et ad sanctos, qui habitabant Lyddae. ³³Invenit autem ibi hominem quendam nomine Aeneam ab annis octo iacentem in grabato, qui erat paralyticus. ³⁴Et ait illi Petrus: «Aenea, sanat te Iesus Christus; surge et sterne tibi». Et continuo surrexit. ³⁵Et viderunt illum omnes, qui inhabitabant Lyddam et Saron, qui conversi sunt ad Dominum. ³⁶In Ioppe autem erat quaedam discipula nomine Tabitha, quae interpretata dicitur Dorcas; haec erat plena operibus bonis et eleemosynis, quas faciebat. ³⁷Factum est autem in diebus illis ut infirmata moreretur; quam cum lavissent posuerunt in cenaculo. ³⁸Cum autem prope esset Lydda ab Ioppe, discipuli audientes quia Petrus esset in ea, miserunt duos viros ad eum rogantes: «Ne pigriteris venire usque ad nos!». ³⁹Exsurgens autem Petrus venit cum illis; et cum advenisset, duxerunt illum in cenaculum et circumsteterunt illum omnes viduae flentes et ostendentes tunicas et vestes, quas faciebat Dorcas, cum esset cum illis.

events in Galilee; and now is the point when he begins to cover the expansion of the Church in Judea. In summary, he underlines the peace and consolation brought by the Holy Spirit. This is a note of justified optimism and of trust in God's help and comfort.

*9:32–12:25 Luke continues his narrative with an account of St Peter's activity outside Jerusalem. Apparently there were a considerable number of Christians in Lydda (9:32) and Joppa (9:36–38). But the main event of Peter's journey is the conversion of the centurion Cornelius in Maritime Caesarea (10:1–11:18), because it demonstrates the fact that the Church can admit converts who have not undergone circumcision. Throughout his account, Luke (as does Peter himself in his address in Jerusalem: 11:4–17) stresses that the evangelical initiative always comes from the Holy Spirit. The significance of the event will be seen at other important moments in the life of the early Church (see 15:3–11).

9:32–35 Jesus cured a paralyzed man (Mt 9:1–8 and par.) by telling him to take up his bed and

walk. He did this in his own name and at the same time he forgave sins, being God. But St Peter cures Aeneas in the name of Jesus: "This name must be preached so that it shines out and is not hidden. But it should not be preached from an impure heart or by a tainted tongue: the name must be guarded and spoken from a worthy vessel" (St Bernardine of Siena, *Sermones*, 49, 2).

9:36–43 Joppa (present-day Jaffa) was a seaside town with a small harbour; today it is part of Tel-Aviv. Maritime Caesarea (as distinct from Caesarea Philippi: see Mt 16:13 and par.) was on the Mediterranean coast, north of Joppa, and was the city where the Roman prefect of Palestine was based. Observant Jews considered the trade of tanning (v. 43) to be unclean because it involved contact with dead animals (see Lev 11:39).

The miracle (vv. 36–41) is performed to awaken faith in those well-disposed people who witness it or hear of it, provided they have good dispositions and desire to believe (v. 42), but, in this case, it is also a kindness that God shows Tabitha to reward her for her good works: "In

him weeping, and showing coats and garments which Dorcas made while she was
with them. ⁴⁰But Peter put them all outside and knelt down and prayed; then turning
to the body he said, "Tabitha, rise." And she opened her eyes, and when she saw
Peter she sat up. ⁴¹And he gave her his hand and lifted her up. Then calling the saints
and widows he presented her alive. ⁴²And it became known throughout all Joppa,
and many believed in the Lord. ⁴³And he stayed in Joppa for many days with one
Simon, a tanner.

Mk 5:40–41

Lk 7:15
Acts 3:7

Acts 10:6

The vision of the centurion Cornelius

10 ¹At Caesarea there was a man named Cornelius, a centurion of what was
known as the Italian Cohort, ²a devout man who feared God with all his
household, gave alms liberally to the people, and prayed constantly to God. ³About
the ninth hour of the day he saw clearly in a vision an angel of God coming in and
saying to him, "Cornelius." ⁴And he stared at him in terror, and said, "What is it,
Lord?" And he said to him, "Your prayers and your alms have ascended as a memorial before God. ⁵And now send men to Joppa, and bring one Simon who is called
Peter; ⁶he is lodging with Simon, a tanner, whose house is by the seaside." ⁷When
the angel who spoke to him had departed, he called two of his servants and a devout
soldier from among those that waited on him, ⁸and having related everything to
them, he sent them to Joppa.

Lk 7:2, 5

Tob 12:12
Lk 1:12

Lk 6:14

⁴⁰Eiectis autem omnibus foras Petrus, et ponens genua oravit et conversus ad corpus dixit: «Tabitha, surge!». At illa aperuit oculos suos et, viso
Petro, resedit. ⁴¹Dans autem illi manum erexit eam et, cum vocasset sanctos et viduas, exhibuit eam vivam. ⁴²Notum autem factum est per universam Ioppen, et crediderunt multi in Domino. ⁴³Factum est autem ut dies multos moraretur in Ioppe apud quendam Simonem coriarium.   [10]
¹Vir autem quidam in Caesarea nomine Cornelius, centurio cohortis, quae dicitur Italica, ²religiosus et timens Deum cum omni domo sua, faciens
eleemosynas multas plebi et deprecans Deum semper, ³vidit in visu manifeste quasi hora nona diei angelum Dei introeuntem ad se et dicentem
sibi: «Corneli». ⁴At ille intuens eum et timore correptus dixit: «Quid est, domine?». Dixit autem illi: «Orationes tuae et eleemosynae tuae ascenderunt in memoriam in conspectu Dei. ⁵Et nunc mitte viros in Ioppen et accersi Simonem quendam, qui cognominatur Petrus; ⁶hic hospitatur apud
Simonem quendam coriarium, cui est domus iuxta mare». ⁷Ut autem discessit angelus, qui loquebatur illi, cum vocasset duos domesticos suos et
militem religiosum ex his, qui illi parebant, ⁸et narrasset illis omnia, misit illos in Ioppen. ⁹Postera autem die iter illis facientibus et appropin-
quantibus civitati, ascendit Petrus super tectum, ut oraret circa horam sextam. ¹⁰Et cum esuriret, voluit gustare; parantibus autem eis, cecidit super

the Acts of the Apostles," St Cyprian writes, "it
is clear that alms not only free us from spiritual
death, but also from temporal death. Tabitha, a
woman who did many 'good works and acts of
charity,' had taken ill and died: and Peter was
sent for. No sooner had he arrived, with all the
diligence of his apostolic charity, than he was
surrounded by widows in tears […], praying for
the dead woman more by gestures than by
words. Peter believed that he could obtain what
they were asking for so insistently and that
Christ's help would be available in answer to the
prayers of the poor in whose persons he himself
had been clothed. […] And so it was: he did
come to Peter's aid, to whom he had said in the
Gospel that he would grant everything asked for
in his name. For this reason he stops the course
of death and the woman returns to life, and to the
amazement of all she revives, restoring her risen
body to the light of day. Such was the power of

works of mercy, of good deeds" (*De opere et
eleemosynis*, 6).

10:1–48 The conversion of the centurion
Cornelius is one of the high points in the book of
Acts, for it demonstrates that the Gospel is
addressed to all mankind, and shows that the
power of the Holy Spirit knows no limits and
transcends all boundaries and differences. That is
why Luke recounts the episode twice in this
chapter, following the order of events and sup-
plying details that underline and illustrate the
main moments and events, and yet again in the
next chapter (11:1–18), when Peter justifies his
action to the brethren in Jerusalem.

At the start of the account Cornelius is introduced as a pious and God-fearing man (vv. 2, 4).
People were described as "fearing God" if they
worshipped the God of the Bible, attended services in the synagogue (cf. 13–16) and obeyed the

Peter's vision

⁹The next day, as they were on their journey and coming near the city, Peter went up on the housetop to pray, about the sixth hour. ¹⁰And he became hungry and desired something to eat; but while they were preparing it, he fell into a trance ¹¹and saw the heaven opened, and something descending, like a great sheet, let down by four corners upon the earth. ¹²In it were all kinds of animals and reptiles and birds of the air. ¹³And there came a voice to him, "Rise, Peter; kill and eat." ¹⁴But Peter said, "No, Lord; for I have never eaten anything that is common or unclean." ¹⁵And the voice came to him again a second time, "What God has cleansed, you must not call common." ¹⁶This happened three times, and the thing was taken up at once to heaven.*

¹⁷Now while Peter was inwardly perplexed as to what the vision which he had seen might mean, behold, the men that were sent by Cornelius, having made inquiry for Simon's house, stood before the gate ¹⁸and called out to ask whether Simon who was called Peter was lodging there. ¹⁹And while Peter was pondering the vision, the Spirit said to him, "Behold, three men are looking for you. ²⁰Rise and go down, and accompany them without hesitation; for I have sent them." ²¹And Peter went down to the men and said, "I am the one you are looking for; what is the reason for your coming?" ²²And they said, "Cornelius, a centurion, an upright and God-fearing man, who is well spoken of by the whole Jewish nation, was directed by a holy angel to send for you to come to his house, and to hear what you have to say." ²³So he called them in to be his guests.

Marginal references:
Lev 11:1–47
Ezek 4:14
Mt 15:11
Mk 7:19
Rom 14:14
1 Tim 4:4

Acts 13:2

Lk 7:5

Peter in the house of Cornelius

The next day he rose and went off with them, and some of the brethren from Joppa accompanied him. ²⁴And on the following day they entered Caesarea. Cornelius was

eum mentis excessus, ¹¹et videt caelum apertum et descendens vas quoddam velut linteum magnum quattuor initiis submitti in terram, ¹²in quo erant omnia quadrupedia et serpentia terrae et volatilia caeli. ¹³Et facta est vox ad eum: «Surge, Petre, occide et manduca!». ¹⁴Ait autem Petrus: «Nequaquam, Domine, quia numquam manducavi omne commune et immundum». ¹⁵Et vox iterum secundo ad eum: «Quae Deus purificavit, ne tu commune dixeris». ¹⁶Hoc autem factum est per ter, et statim receptum est vas in caelum. ¹⁷Et dum intra se haesitaret Petrus quidnam esset visio, quam vidisset, ecce viri, qui missi erant a Cornelio, inquirentes domum Simonis astiterunt ad ianuam ¹⁸et, cum vocassent, interrogabant si Simon, qui cognominatur Petrus, illic haberet hospitium. ¹⁹Petro autem cogitante de visione, dixit Spiritus ei: «Ecce viri tres quaerunt te; ²⁰surge itaque et descende et vade cum eis nihil dubitans, quia ego misi illos». ²¹Descendens autem Petrus ad viros dixit: «Ecce ego sum, quem quaeritis; quae causa est, propter quam venistis?». ²²Qui dixerunt: «Cornelius centurio, vir iustus et timens Deum et testimonium habens ab universa gente Iudaeorum, responsum accepit ab angelo sancto accersire te in domum suam et audire verba abs te». ²³Invitans igitur eos recepit hospitio. Sequenti autem die surgens profectus est cum eis, et quidam ex fratribus ab Ioppe comitati sunt eum. ²⁴Altera autem die introivit Caesaream; Cornelius

main commandments of the Jewish Law, without formally becoming Jews by undergoing circumcision. Although God's gifts are unmerited, the angel tells the centurion that his good works have won him God's favour (see v. 4): "Do you see how the work of the Gospel begins among the Gentiles? Through a devout man, whose deeds have made him worthy of this favour" (St John Chrysostom, *In Acta Apostolorum*, 22, 2).

The focus then switches to Peter, who receives two instructions from the Holy Spirit — to eat meat of the kinds of animals he is shown in the vision (cf. vv. 10–15) and to accompany Cornelius' messengers (cf. v. 20). Of the two

instructions (both of which ran counter to Peter's normal Jewish observance), Peter resisted only the first. His reaction to the Lord's order (v. 14) is that of a good Jew who has loved and observed the divine Law in which he was raised and educated. He has always adhered to the regulations concerning food, and respected the Mosaic distinction between clean and unclean food (see Lev 11:1ff). However, Peter is docile to the Spirit's instructions; although the vision perplexes him, he does not resist the order to accompany the messengers: "Christian tradition has summarized the attitude we should adopt toward the Holy Spirit in just one idea: docility.

expecting them and had called together his kinsmen and close friends. [25]When Peter entered, Cornelius met him and fell down at his feet and worshipped him. [26]But Peter lifted him up, saying, "Stand up; I too am a man." [27]And as he talked with him, he went in and found many persons gathered; [28]and he said to them, "You yourselves know how unlawful it is for a Jew to associate with or to visit any one of another nation; but God has shown me that I should not call any man common or unclean. [29]So when I was sent for, I came without objection. I ask then why you sent for me."

[30]And Cornelius said, "Four days ago, about this hour, I was keeping the ninth hour of prayer in my house; and behold, a man stood before me in bright apparel, [31]saying, 'Cornelius, your prayer has been heard and your alms have been remembered before God. [32]Send therefore to Joppa and ask for Simon who is called Peter; he is lodging in the house of Simon, a tanner, by the seaside.' [33]So I sent for you at once, and you have been kind enough to come. Now therefore we are all here present in the sight of God, to hear all that you have been commanded by the Lord."

Peter preaches to Cornelius

[34]And Peter opened his mouth and said: "Truly I perceive that God shows no partiality, [35]but in every nation any one who fears him and does what is right is acceptable to him. [36]You know the word which he sent to Israel, preaching good news of peace by Jesus Christ (he is Lord of all), [37]the word which was proclaimed throughout all Judea, beginning from Galilee after the baptism which John preached: [38]how God anointed Jesus of Nazareth with the Holy Spirit and with power; how he went about doing good and healing all that were oppressed by the devil, for God was with him. [39]And we are witnesses to all that he did both in the country of the Jews and in

Margin references: Mt 8:8; Acts 14:15; Rev 19:10; Wis 7:1; Gal 2:12; Lk 24:4; Deut 10:17; 2 Chron 19:7; Rom 2:11; Gal 2:6; 1 Pet 1:17; Is 56:7; Ps 107:20; Rom 15:16; Is 52:7; Nahum 2:1; Is 61:1; Lk 4:18; Mt 3:16; Acts 1:8

vero exspectabat illos, convocatis cognatis suis et necessariis amicis. [25]Et factum est cum introisset Petrus, obvius ei Cornelius procidens ad pedes adoravit. [26]Petrus vero levavit eum dicens: «Surge, et ego ipse homo sum». [27]Et loquens cum illo intravit et invenit multos, qui convenerant, [28]dixitque ad illos: «Vos scitis quomodo illicitum sit viro Iudaeo coniungi aut accedere ad alienigenam. Et mihi ostendit Deus neminem communem aut immundum dicere hominem; [29]propter quod sine dubitatione veni accersitus. Interrogo ergo quam ob causam accersistis me». [30]Et Cornelius ait: «A nudius quarta die usque in hanc horam orans eram hora nona in domo mea, et ecce vir stetit ante me in veste candida [31]et ait: "Corneli, exaudita est oratio tua, et eleemosynae tuae commemoratae sunt in conspectu Dei. [32]Mitte ergo in Ioppen et accersi Simonem, qui cognominatur Petrus; hic hospitatur in domo Simonis coriarii iuxta mare". [33]Confestim igitur misi ad te, et tu bene fecisti veniendo. Nunc ergo omnes nos in conspectu Dei adsumus audire omnia, quaecumque tibi praecepta sunt a Domino». [34]Aperiens autem Petrus os dixit: «In veritate comperio quoniam non est personarum acceptor Deus, [35]sed in omni gente, qui timet eum et operatur iustitiam, acceptus est illi. [36]Verbum misit filiis Israel evangelizans pacem per Iesum Christum; hic est omnium Dominus. [37]Vos scitis quod factum est verbum per universam Iudaeam incipiens a Galilaea post baptismum, quod praedicavit Ioannes: [38]Iesum a Nazareth, quomodo unxit eum Deus Spiritu Sancto et virtute, qui pertransivit benefaciendo et sanando omnes oppressos a Diabolo, quoniam Deus erat cum illo. [39]Et nos testes sumus omnium, quae fecit in regione Iudaeorum et Ierusalem; quem et occiderunt suspendentes in ligno. [40]Hunc Deus suscitavit tertia die et dedit eum manifestum fieri [41]non omni populo, sed testibus prae-

That means we should be aware of the work of the Holy Spirit all around us, and in our own selves we should recognize the gifts he distributes, the movements and institutions he inspires, the affections and decisions he provokes in our hearts. The Holy Spirit carries out in the world the works of God. He is, as we read in a liturgical hymn, the giver of grace, the light of our hearts, the soul's guest, our rest in work, our consolation in sorrow. Without his help there is nothing innocent or valuable in man, since he is the one who cleanses the soiled, heals what is sick, sets on fire what is cold, straightens what is bent and guides men toward the safe harbour of

salvation and eternal joy" (St Josemaría Escrivá, *Christ Is Passing By*, 130).

When he reaches Cornelius' house, Peter discovers that God has been guiding his every step (vv. 24, 27); and when he hears Cornelius' explanation (vv. 30–33), he realizes the full meaning of what he heard Jesus say, and sees that, in the saving plans of God, Jews and Gentiles are equal. A direct divine intervention was required to allow him to make this simple and vital discovery.

However, the action of the Holy Spirit goes much further than that of men. The angel had simply told Cornelius to send for Peter and hear

1 Cor 15:4

Lk 24:30–43
Jn 14:22

Acts 17:31
2 Tim 4:1
Is 33:24; 53:5–6
Jer 31:34

Jerusalem. They put him to death by hanging him on a tree; ⁴⁰but God raised him on the third day and made him manifest; ⁴¹not to all the people but to us who were chosen by God as witnesses, who ate and drank with him after he rose from the dead. ⁴²And he commanded us to preach to the people, and to testify that he is the one ordained by God to be judge of the living and the dead. ⁴³To him all the prophets bear witness that every one who believes in him receives forgiveness of sins through his name."

The baptism of Cornelius and his household

Acts 11:15; 15:8

Acts 2:4, 11; 19:6

Acts 8:36; 11:17

⁴⁴While Peter was still saying this, the Holy Spirit fell on all who heard the word. ⁴⁵And the believers from among the circumcised who came with Peter were amazed, because the gift of the Holy Spirit had been poured out even on the Gentiles. ⁴⁶For they heard them speaking in tongues and extolling God. Then Peter declared, ⁴⁷"Can any one forbid water for baptizing these people who have received the Holy Spirit just as we have?" ⁴⁸And he commanded them to be baptized in the name of Jesus Christ. Then they asked him to remain for some days.

In Jerusalem Peter justifies his conduct

Acts 10:28, 48
Gal 2:12

Eph 2:11

Acts 10:9–48

11 ¹Now the apostles and the brethren who were in Judea heard that the Gentiles also had received the word of God. ²So when Peter went up to Jerusalem, the circumcision party criticized him, ³saying, "Why did you go to uncircumcised men and eat with them?" ⁴But Peter began and explained to them in order: ⁵"I was in the

ordinatis a Deo, nobis, qui manducavimus et bibimus cum illo postquam resurrexit a mortuis; ⁴²et praecepit nobis praedicare populo et testificari quia ipse est, qui constitutus est a Deo iudex vivorum et mortuorum. ⁴³Huic omnes Prophetae testimonium perhibent remissionem peccatorum accipere per nomen eius omnes, qui credunt in eum». ⁴⁴Adhuc loquente Petro verba haec, cecidit Spiritus Sanctus super omnes, qui audiebant verbum. ⁴⁵Et obstupuerunt, qui ex circumcisione fideles, qui venerant cum Petro, quia et in nationes gratia Spiritus Sancti effusa est; ⁴⁶audiebant enim illos loquentes linguis et magnificantes Deum. Tunc respondit Petrus: ⁴⁷«Numquid aquam quis prohibere potest, ut non baptizentur hi, qui Spiritum Sanctum acceperunt sicut et nos?». ⁴⁸Et iussit eos in nomine Iesu Christi baptizari. Tunc rogaverunt eum, ut maneret aliquot diebus. [11] ¹Audierunt autem apostoli et fratres, qui erant in Iudaea, quoniam et gentes receperunt verbum Dei. ²Cum ascendisset autem Petrus in Ierusalem, disceptabant adversus illum, qui erant ex circumcisione, ³dicentes: «Introisti ad viros praeputium habentes et manducasti cum illis!». ⁴Incipiens autem Petrus exponebat illis ex ordine dicens: ⁵«Ego eram in civitate Ioppe orans et vidi in excessu mentis visionem, descendens vas

what he had to say (vv. 5, 22, 33), and therefore Peter, in a compact speech, which constitutes a summary of the entire Gospel (vv. 36–43; cf. the note on Mk 1:14 — 8:30), preaches the truth about Christ Jesus. In his speech at Pentecost, Peter presented Jesus to a Jewish audience as "Lord and Christ" (2:36); now he portrays him as "judge of the living and the dead" (v. 42), something that according to the Old Testament only God is or could be. Cornelius and the other people in his house, some of them probably also officials of the Roman empire, were well aware that in the human sphere supreme judicial power was vested in Caesar. The apostles teach that no human authority can have the last word about the justice of men's actions.

After Peter preaches, the initiative is again taken by the Holy Spirit, who manifests himself in ways similar to those seen and heard at Pentecost (v. 46), and provokes the action of the apostle (vv. 47–48). Peter instructs that Baptism be administered to these Gentiles, without requiring them to be circumcised. This is the first time this happens, and it happens because of the action of the Holy Spirit, sent by Christ "to defend and sanctify the Church, as a guide to souls, the ship's captain in times of storm, a light to those in darkness, one who watches over the struggles and crowns the victorious" (St Cyril of Jerusalem, *Catecheses*, 17, 3).

11:1–18 The community of the circumcised, alarmed to hear what has happened, reproach Peter for eating with uncircumcised people and preaching the word of God to them (vv. 1–3). To understand the attitude of the Jerusalem Christians, who were of course brought up in a strict Jewish tradition, we need to bear in mind

city of Joppa praying; and in a trance I saw a vision, something descending, like a great sheet, let down from heaven by four corners; and it came down to me. [6]Looking at it closely I observed animals and beasts of prey and reptiles and birds of the air. [7]And I heard a voice saying to me, 'Rise, Peter; kill and eat.' [8]But I said, 'No, Lord; for nothing common or unclean has ever entered my mouth.' [9]But the voice answered a second time from heaven, 'What God has cleansed you must not call common.' [10]This happened three times, and all was drawn up again into heaven. [11]And that very moment three men arrived at the house in which we were, sent to me from Caesarea. [12]And the Spirit told me to go with them, making no distinction. These six brethren also accompanied me, and we entered the man's house. [13]And he told us how he had seen the angel standing in this house and saying, 'Send to Joppa and bring Simon called Peter; [14]he will declare to you a message by which you will be saved, you and all your household.' [15]As I began to speak, the Holy Spirit fell on them just as on us at the beginning. [16]And I remembered the word of the Lord, how he said, 'John baptized with water, but you shall be baptized with the Holy Spirit.' [17]If then God gave the same gift to them as he gave to us when we believed in the Lord Jesus Christ, who was I that I could withstand God?" [18]When they heard this they were silenced. And they glorified God, saying, "Then to the Gentiles also God has granted repentance unto life."

Acts 1:8

Acts 2:1–4

Acts 1:5

Acts 15:8–9; 10:47

Acts 14:27

quoddam velut linteum magnum quattuor initiis submitti de caelo, et venit usque ad me; [6]in quod intuens considerabam et vidi quadrupedia terrae et bestias et reptilia et volatilia caeli. [7]Audivi autem et vocem dicentem mihi: "Surgens, Petre, occide et manduca!". [8]Dixi autem: Nequaquam, Domine, quia commune aut immundum numquam introivit in os meum. [9]Respondit autem vox secundo de caelo: "Quae Deus mundavit, tu ne commune dixeris". [10]Hoc autem factum est per ter, et retracta sunt rursum omnia in caelum. [11]Et ecce confestim tres viri astiterunt in domo, in qua eramus, missi a Caesarea ad me. [12]Dixit autem Spiritus mihi, ut irem cum illis nihil haesitans. Venerunt autem mecum et sex fratres isti, et ingressi sumus in domum viri. [13]Narravit autem nobis quomodo vidisset angelum ad domum suam stantem et dicentem: "Mitte in Ioppen et accersi Simonem, qui cognominatur Petrus, [14]qui loquetur tibi verba, in quibus salvus eris tu et universa domus tua". [15]Cum autem coepissem loqui, decidit Spiritus Sanctus super eos sicut et super nos in initio. [16]Recordatus sum autem verbi Domini sicut dicebat: "Ioannes quidem baptizavit aqua, vos autem baptizabimini in Spiritu Sancto". [17]Si ergo aequale donum dedit illis Deus sicut et nobis, qui credidimus in Dominum Iesum Christum, ego quis eram qui possem prohibere Deum?». [18]His autem auditis acquieverunt et glorificaverunt Deum dicentes: «Ergo et gentibus

that Christianity was born within Judaism and portrayed itself not as a new religion but as the fulfilment of the Old Testament promises and prophecies. Ever since the return from exile in Babylon, the Israelites had interpreted salvation as a matter of keeping scrupulously to the Mosaic Law in its every detail. As a result, by the time Christ came, legal casuistry had led to such an accumulation of rules that observance of the Law had become very difficult indeed, and people were so stifled by regulations that they lost sight of the essential purpose of the Law — love of God and neighbour. Still, this "circumcision party" found it difficult to see how there could be preached the New Law without the preservation of the Old Law in every detail.

In a long address, St Peter explains that he did not act on his own initiative: at every stage he obeyed the Holy Spirit. The new departure marked in this address, as compared with the account in chapter 10, comes in verses 15–17, in

which Peter establishes a connexion between what happened when the Holy Spirit came at Pentecost (2:1ff) and the fact that he descended on the Gentile converts (10:44–46) in Caesarea. This makes it clear to everyone (see v. 18) that to enter the Church a man does not need to first become part of the Jewish people through the rite of circumcision: "Men, women and children, of all different races, nations, languages, social classes and cultures [...] form the Church by the power of the Spirit. The Spirit sets the same divine seal on each of them; and each is given a new, unbreakable nature. [...] Therefore, we are all united in a truly catholic way. No one stands outside the community of the Church, for we are all united by the unbreakable bonds of faith. Christ is all in all things: by his power, he draws all to himself and gives his goodness to all. [...] The creatures of the one God are no longer strangers or enemies to one another" (St Maximus the Confessor, *Mistagogia*, 1).

Beginning of the Church in Antioch

Acts 8:1, 4

[19]Now those who were scattered because of the persecution that arose over Stephen travelled as far as Phoenicia and Cyprus and Antioch, speaking the word to none except Jews. [20]But there were some of them, men of Cyprus and Cyrene, who on

Acts 2:47

coming to Antioch spoke to the Greeks[i] also, preaching the Lord Jesus. [21]And the hand of the Lord was with them, and a great number that believed turned to the

Acts 4:36; 8:14

Lord. [22]News of this came to the ears of the church in Jerusalem, and they sent Barnabas to Antioch. [23]When he came and saw the grace of God, he was glad; and he exhorted them all to remain faithful to the Lord with steadfast purpose; [24]for he was a good man, full of the Holy Spirit and of faith. And a large company was added

Acts 9:30
1 Pet 4:16

to the Lord. [25]So Barnabas went to Tarsus to look for Saul; [26]and when he had found him, he brought him to Antioch. For a whole year they met with[j] the church, and taught a large company of people; and in Antioch the disciples were for the first time called Christians.

Antioch helps the Church in Judea

Acts 21:10

[27]Now in these days prophets came down from Jerusalem to Antioch. [28]And one of them named Agabus stood up and foretold by the Spirit that there would be a great

---

Deus paenitentiam ad vitam dedit». [19]Et illi quidem, qui dispersi fuerant a tribulatione, quae facta fuerat sub Stephano, perambulaverunt usque Phoenicen et Cyprum et Antiochiam, nemini loquentes verbum nisi solis Iudaeis. [20]Erant autem quidam ex eis viri Cyprii et Cyrenaei, qui cum introissent Antiochiam, loquebantur et ad Graecos evangelizantes Dominum Iesum. [21]Et erat manus Domini cum eis; multusque numerus credentium conversus est ad Dominum. [22]Auditus est autem sermo in auribus ecclesiae, quae erat in Ierusalem, super istis, et miserunt Barnabam usque Antiochiam; [23]qui cum pervenisset et vidisset gratiam Dei, gavisus est et hortabatur omnes proposito cordis permanere in Domino, [24]quia erat vir bonus et plenus Spiritu Sancto et fide. Et apposita est turba multa Domino. [25]Profectus est autem Tarsum, ut quaereret Saulum; [26]quem cum invenisset, perduxit Antiochiam. Factum est autem eis ut annum totum conversarentur in ecclesia et docerent turbam multam, et cognominarentur primum Antiochiae discipuli Christiani. [27]In his autem diebus supervenerunt ab Hierosolymis prophetae Antiochiam; [28]et surgens unus ex eis nomine Agabus, significavit per Spiritum famem magnam futuram in universo orbe terrarum; quae facta est sub Claudio. [29]Discipuli autem,

---

11:19–26 This account is tied in with that of the "dispersion" of Christians which occurred after the martyrdom of Stephen (see 8:1–4). We are told about the spread of the Gospel to Antioch, the capital of the Roman province of Syria. Antioch was the first major city in the ancient world where Jesus Christ was preached. After Rome and Alexandria, it and Ephesus were the most important cities in the empire. Antioch had a population of around 150,000, including a sizeable Jewish colony. It was a significant cultural, commercial and religious centre. And the proclamation of the Gospel in Antioch was not confined to Jews and Jewish proselytes; it was directed to everyone and was part of the normal, spontaneous everyday activity of Hellenist Jews who had settled in the city after the martyrdom of Stephen. The Christian mission at Antioch was hugely important in the spread of Christianity; the centre of gravity of the Christian Church began to shift from Jerusalem to this city, which would later be the springboard for the evangelization of the pagan world. That is why

St Luke stresses the communion between the two churches: the church of Jerusalem (see v. 22) feels responsible and solicitous for the entire Christian mission; thus, Barnabas, a man in whom the apostles placed full trust, is sent to Antioch. When he sees the immense panorama opening up for the Gospel, Barnabas goes to Tarsus in search of Paul, to involve him in this apostolate. For its part, the church of Antioch is the first to take action to relieve the needs of the mother church in Jerusalem (see 11:27–30).

Luke also records (v. 26) the origin of the name "Christians", a happy development that identifies the faithful of Christ: "Although the holy apostles were our teachers and have given us the Gospel of the Saviour, it is not from them that we have taken our name: we are *Christians* through Christ and it is for him that we are called in this way" (St Athanasius, *Contra Arianos*, 1, 2).

11:27–30 Acts mentions prophets a number of times. In addition to Agabus (vv. 27–28), Judas and Silas (15:32), the daughters of Philip the

---

i Other ancient authorities read *Hellenists* j Or *were guests of*

famine over all the world; and this took place in the days of Claudius. ²⁹And the disciples determined, every one according to his ability, to send relief to the brethren who lived in Judea; ³⁰and they did so, sending it to the elders by the hand of Barnabas and Saul.

Gal 2:10

Acts 12:25

Persecution by Herod. Peter's arrest and miraculous deliverance

12 ¹About that time Herod the king laid violent hands upon some who belonged to the church.* ²He killed James the brother of John with the sword; ³and when he saw that it pleased the Jews, he proceeded to arrest Peter also. This was during the days of Unleavened Bread. ⁴And when he had seized him, he put him in prison, and delivered him to four squads of soldiers to guard him, intending after the Passover to bring him out to the people. ⁵So Peter was kept in prison; but earnest prayer for him was made to God by the church.

Mt 20:22–23

Jas 5:16

prout quis habebat, proposuerunt singuli eorum in ministerium mittere habitantibus in Iudaea fratribus; ³⁰quod et fecerunt, mittentes ad presbyteros per manum Barnabae et Sauli. [12] ¹Illo autem tempore misit Herodes rex manus, ut affligeret quosdam de ecclesia. ²Occidit autem Iacobum fratrem Ioannis gladio. ³Videns autem quia placeret Iudaeis, apposuit apprehendere et Petrum—erant autem dies Azymorum—⁴quem cum apprehendisset, misit in carcerem tradens quattuor quaternionibus militum custodire eum, volens post Pascha producere eum populo. ⁵Et Petrus quidem servabatur in carcere; oratio autem fiebat sine intermissione ab ecclesia ad Deum pro eo. ⁶Cum autem producturus eum esset Herodes, in ipsa

deacon (21:9), and some other people (13:1) are described as prophets. In the early Church the prophetic office was subordinate to the apostolic ministry, and was exercised under the aegis of the apostles in the service of the growing Christian community (see 1 Cor 12:10–11, 28–29; 13:2; 14:1–3, 29–40).

The charism of prophecy as found in the early years of the Church is not apparent in later times. But the gifts of the Holy Spirit are still to be found in all the members of Christ's Mystical Body, in accordance with the ecclesial role that each person has: "Whether extraordinary or simple and humble, charisms are graces of the Holy Spirit which directly or indirectly benefit the Church, ordered as they are to her building up, to the good of men, and to the needs of the world" (*Catechism of the Catholic Church*, 799).

During the reign of Claudius (AD 41–54), the empire suffered a severe food crisis (sometime within the years 47–49) which affected, among other places, Rome, Greece, Syria and Palestine; this famine is probably the one that Agabus predicted (v. 28). The imminent shortage prompts the Antioch community to send relief to the Christians of the mother church in Jerusalem. Like the Christians in the very first days of the Church (cf. 4:34), the Antiochene disciples show their charity in a practical way to their brethren in need; it proves that they truly are Christians. Their example has helped to shape church teach-

ing: "The stronger and richer nations must have a sense of moral *responsibility* for the other nations, so that a *real international system* may be established which will rest on the foundation of the *equality* of all peoples and on the necessary respect for their legitimate differences. The economically weaker countries, or those still at subsistence level, must be enabled, with the assistance of other peoples and of the international community, to make a contribution of their own to the common good with their treasures of *humanity* and *culture*, which otherwise would be lost forever" (John Paul II, *Sollicitudo rei socialis*, 39).

12:1–19 This Herod (v. 1) is the third prince of that name to appear in the New Testament. He was grandson to Herod the Great, who built the new temple of Jerusalem and was responsible for the massacre of the Holy Innocents (cf. Mt 2:16), and a nephew of Herod Antipas, the tetrarch of Galilee at the time of our Lord's death. Known as Herod Agrippa I, he enjoyed the favour of the emperor Caligula, who gradually gave him more territory and allowed him to use the title of king. A sophisticated person, a diplomat, Herod Agrippa I consolidated his power by being a master of intrigue and a shrewd opportunist. The martyrdom of James the Greater (v. 2) must have taken place around the year 42 or 43. He was the first of the twelve apostles to be martyred, and

⁶The very night when Herod was about to bring him out, Peter was sleeping between two soldiers, bound with two chains, and sentries before the door were guarding the prison; ⁷and behold, an angel of the Lord appeared, and a light shone in the cell; and he struck Peter on the side and woke him, saying, "Get up quickly." And the chains fell off his hands. ⁸And the angel said to him, "Dress yourself and put on your sandals." And he did so. And he said to him, "Wrap your mantle around you and follow me." ⁹And he went out and followed him; he did not know that what was done by the angel was real, but thought he was seeing a vision. ¹⁰When they had passed the first and the second guard, they came to the iron gate leading into the city. It opened to them of its own accord, and they went out and passed on through one street; and immediately the angel left him. ¹¹And Peter came to himself, and said, "Now I am sure that the Lord has sent his angel and rescued me from the hand of Herod and from all that the Jewish people were expecting."

¹²When he realized this, he went to the house of Mary, the mother of John whose other name was Mark, where many were gathered together and were praying. ¹³And when he knocked at the door of the gateway, a maid named Rhoda came to answer. ¹⁴Recognizing Peter's voice, in her joy she did not open the gate but ran in and told that Peter was standing at the gate. ¹⁵They said to her, "You are mad." But she insisted that it was so. They said, "It is his angel!" ¹⁶But Peter continued knocking;

and when they opened, they saw him and were amazed. ¹⁷But motioning to them with his hand to be silent, he described to them how the Lord had brought him out of the prison. And he said, "Tell this to James and to the brethren." Then he departed and went to another place.

nocte erat Petrus dormiens inter duos milites vinctus catenis duabus, et custodes ante ostium custodiebant carcerem. ⁷Et ecce angelus Domini astitit, et lumen refulsit in habitaculo; percusso autem latere Petri, suscitavit eum dicens: «Surge velociter!». Et ceciderunt catenae de manibus eius. ⁸Dixit autem angelus ad eum: «Praecingere et calcea te sandalia tua!». Et fecit sic. Et dicit illi: «Circumda tibi vestimentum tuum et sequere me!». ⁹Et exiens sequebatur et nesciebat quia verum est, quod fiebat per angelum; aestimabat autem se visum videre. ¹⁰Transeuntes autem primam custodiam et secundam venerunt ad portam ferream, quae ducit ad civitatem, quae ultro aperta est eis, et exeuntes processerunt vicum unum, et continuo discessit angelus ab eo. ¹¹Et Petrus ad se reversus dixit: «Nunc scio vere quia misit Dominus angelum suum et eripuit me de manu Herodis et de omni exspectatione plebis Iudaeorum». ¹²Consideransque venit ad domum Mariae matris Ioannis, qui cognominatur Marcus, ubi erant multi congregati et orantes. ¹³Pulsante autem eo ostium ianuae, processit puella ad audiendum, nomine Rhode; ¹⁴et ut cognovit vocem Petri prae gaudio non aperuit ianuam, sed intro currens nuntiavit stare Petrum ante ianuam. ¹⁵At illi dixerunt ad eam: «Insanis!». Illa autem affirmabat sic se habere. Illi autem dicebant: «Angelus eius est». ¹⁶Petrus autem perseverabat pulsans; cum autem aperuissent, viderunt eum et obstupuerunt. ¹⁷Annuens

the only one whose death is mentioned in the New Testament.

Luke's descriptions of the Church's attitude towards the persecution and towards the imprisonment of St Peter (v. 5) are as precise as his report on Herod (vv. 1–4): "Notice the feelings of the faithful towards their pastors. They do not riot or rebel; they have recourse to prayer, which can solve all problems. They do not say to themselves: 'We do not count, there is no point in our praying for him.' Their love led them to pray and they did not think along those lines. Have you noticed what these persecutors did without intending to? They made [their victims] more determined to stand the test, and [the faithful] more zealous and loving" (St John Chrysostom, *In Acta Apostolorum*, 26, 2).

The account of the miraculous release of Peter through the help of an angel shows God's providence at work (v. 11). An angel also came to Peter's rescue during a previous imprisonment (5:19ff). This protection illustrates the role God entrusts to angels: "From its beginning until death, human life is surrounded by their watchful care and intercession. 'Beside each believer stands an angel as protector and shepherd leading him to life' (St Basil, *Adv. Eunomium*, 3, 1)" (*Catechism of the Catholic Church*, 336). But the account also shows the early Christians' conviction about the power and work of angels (see v. 15): "Drink at the clear fountain of the Acts of the Apostles. In the twelfth chapter, Peter, freed from prison by the ministry of angels, comes to the house of the mother of Mark. Those inside

[18]Now when day came, there was no small stir among the soldiers over what had become of Peter. [19]And when Herod had sought for him and could not find him, he examined the sentries and ordered that they should be put to death. Then he went down from Judea to Caesarea, and remained there.

Death of Herod

[20]Now Herod was angry with the people of Tyre and Sidon; and they came to him in a body, and having persuaded Blastus, the king's chamberlain, they asked for peace, because their country depended on the king's country for food. [21]On an appointed day Herod put on his royal robes, took his seat upon the throne, and made an oration to them. [22]And the people shouted, "The voice of a god, and not of man!" [23]Immediately an angel of the Lord smote him, because he did not give God the glory; and he was eaten by worms and died.

Ezek 28:2

Dan 5:20
2 Mac 9:5, 28

Barnabas and Paul return

[24]But the word of God grew and multiplied. [25]And Barnabas and Saul returned from[k] Jerusalem when they had fulfilled their mission, bringing with them John whose other name was Mark.

Acts 6:7

Acts 11:29; 12:12

autem eis manu, ut tacerent, enarravit quomodo Dominus eduxisset eum de carcere dixitque: «Nuntiate Iacobo et fratribus haec». Et egressus abiit in alium locum. [18]Facta autem die erat non parva turbatio inter milites, quidnam de Petro factum esset. [19]Herodes autem cum requisisset eum et non invenisset, interrogatis custodibus iussit eos abduci; descendensque a Iudaea in Caesaream ibi commorabatur. [20]Erat autem iratus Tyriis et Sidoniis; at illi unanimes venerunt ad eum et persuaso Blasto, qui erat super cubiculum regis, postulabant pacem, eo quod aleretur regio eorum ab annona regis. [21]Statuto autem die, Herodes, vestitus veste regia, sedens pro tribunali, contionabatur ad eos; [22]populus autem acclamabat: «Dei vox et non hominis!». [23]Confestim autem percussit eum angelus Domini, eo quod non dedisset gloriam Deo, et consumptus a vermibus exspiravit. [24]Verbum autem Dei crescebat et multiplicabatur. [25]Barnabas autem et Saulus reversi sunt in Ierusalem expleto ministerio, assumpto Ioanne,

will not believe the servant girl, who says that Peter is at the door. '*Angelus eius est!* It must be his angel!' they said. See on what intimate terms the early Christians were with their guardian angels. And what about you?" (St Josemaría Escrivá, *The Way*, 570).

12:20–23 Herod Agrippa I died in Caesarea in the year 44, during the games in honour of Claudius. St Luke's brief account is corroborated by that of Flavius Josephus: "On the morning of the second day, as the king made his way towards the theatre, sunlight flashed brightly on his silver clothes and a crowd of his followers praised him loudly. They called him a god and said: 'Be gracious to us. Until now, we have thought of you as a man; from now on, we will honour you as more than mortal man.' The king listened to their blasphemy in silence, but at once his body was wracked by terrible pains and within five days he was dead" (*Antiquitates iudaicae*, 19, 344–345). The painful and unex-

pected death of this king who persecuted the Church is reminiscent of the death of Antiochus IV Epiphanes, another declared enemy of God's elect and of the divine Law: "The all-seeing Lord, the God of Israel, struck him an incurable and unseen blow" (2 Mac 9:5).

12:24–25 John Mark (v. 25) was a cousin of Barnabas (Col 4:10). A little earlier we were told that the church used to meet for prayer in the house of his mother (12:12). A number of ecclesiastical traditions say that his was the house of the Cenacle, where the Last Supper was held. Mark will accompany Barnabas and Paul on their first apostolic journey (13:2–5) but only for a short time (see 13:13). Paul decided against taking him with him on the second apostolic journey (15:37–39), but later he is again counted among the Apostle's co-workers (see Col 4:10; 2 Tim 4:11); and we find him as a disciple and aide to St Peter (1 Pet 5:13). Church Tradition attributes to him the writing of the second Gospel.

k Other ancient authorities read *to*

PART THREE

The spread of the Church among the Gentiles.
Missionary journeys of St Paul*

8. ST PAUL'S FIRST APOSTOLIC JOURNEY*

Paul and Barnabas are sent on a mission

Acts 4:36; 11:20, 27   **13** ¹Now in the church at Antioch there were prophets and teachers, Barnabas, Symeon who was called Niger, Lucius of Cyrene, Manaen a member of the court of Herod the tetrarch, and Saul. ²While they were worshipping the Lord and fasting, the Holy Spirit said, "Set apart for me Barnabas and Saul for the work to which I have called them." ³Then after fasting and praying they laid their hands on them and sent them off.

Gal 1:15

Acts 6:6

qui cognominatus est Marcus.   [13] ¹Erant autem in ecclesia, quae erat Antiochiae, prophetae et doctores: Barnabas et Simeon, qui vocabatur Niger, et Lucius Cyrenensis, et Manaen, qui erat Herodis tetrarchae collactaneus, et Saulus. ²Ministrantibus autem illis Domino et ieiunantibus, dixit Spiritus Sanctus: «Separate mihi Barnabam et Saulum in opus, ad quod vocavi eos». ³Tunc ieiunantes et orantes imponentesque eis manus

*13:1—20:38 The narrative in Acts describes how salvation spread from Jerusalem to the limits of the known world. Paul is the principal instrument used by God to carry out this endeavour (9:15). This third part of the book covers his apostolic journeys to preach the Gospel and establish new communities. It is worth noting that, from this point onwards, the church of Antioch's missionary work is given great prominence (see 13:1; 14:26; 15:35; 18:22). However, St Luke never fails to point out that at every new stage Jerusalem is also involved (9:26; 12:25; 15:2; 19:21; 20:16; 21:15; 25:1).

*13:1–14:28 Following a short description of the community of Antioch (13:1), Luke focuses his attention on the first apostolic journey by St Paul and St Barnabas through the countries of Asia Minor. They probably left Antioch in the spring of the year 45, returning four years later. Their ministry took them to Cyprus and much of Cilicia, Pamphylia, Lycaonia and Pisidia (all what is now southern Turkey); they preached to Jews and Gentiles and founded communities in the areas through which they travelled. Later, they will go back to these places to confirm Christians in the faith.

13:1–3 The narrative now focuses on the church of Antioch and the spread of Christianity in the

pagan world. The Antiochene church was a flourishing community, with an organizational structure similar to that of the church of Jerusalem, with some notable differences. It had ordained some ministers who were responsible for its government and who preached and administered the sacraments (see v. 2). Alongside these are "prophets" and "teachers"—specially trained members of the community (v. 1; see also Cor 12:28). In the early churches, "teachers" were disciples who were well-versed in Holy Scripture and who were in charge of catechesis. A second-century document continues this first-person description of the Christian teacher: "I do not speak of passing things nor do I go in search of new things, but, like the disciple of the apostles that I am, I become a teacher of peoples. I do nothing but hand on what was given me by those who made themselves worthy disciples of the truth" (*Epistula ad Diognetum*, 11, 1). On prophets, see the note on 11:27–30.

The sending out on mission of Paul and Barnabas (vv. 2–3) is the work of the Holy Spirit and, at the same time, of the Church: the Church gives specific shape to God's plans and to the vocation of its two emissaries. Fasting and prayer prepare Paul and Barnabas for the spiritual enterprise they are to undertake: "First, prayer; then, atonement; in the third place, very

Paul and Barnabas in Cyprus

⁴So, being sent out by the Holy Spirit, they went down to Seleucia; and from there they sailed to Cyprus. ⁵When they arrived at Salamis, they proclaimed the word of God in the synagogues of the Jews. And they had John to assist them. ⁶When they had gone through the whole island as far as Paphos, they came upon a certain magician, a Jewish false prophet, named Bar-Jesus. ⁷He was with the proconsul, Sergius Paulus, a man of intelligence, who summoned Barnabas and Saul and sought to hear the word of God. ⁸But Elymas the magician (for that is the meaning of his name) withstood them, seeking to turn away the proconsul from the faith. ⁹But Saul, who is also called Paul, filled with the Holy Spirit, looked intently at him ¹⁰and said, "You son of the devil, you enemy of all righteousness, full of all deceit and villainy, will you not stop making crooked the straight paths of the Lord? ¹¹And now, behold, the hand of the Lord is upon you, and you shall be blind and unable to see the sun

Acts 12:12

2 Tim 3:8

Prov 10:9
Hos 14:10
Jn 8:44

Jn 9:39

dimiserunt illos. ⁴Et ipsi quidem missi ab Spiritu Sancto devenerunt Seleuciam et inde navigaverunt Cyprum ⁵et, cum venissent Salamina, praedicabant verbum Dei in synagogis Iudaeorum; habebant autem et Ioannem ministrum. ⁶Et cum perambulassent universam insulam usque Paphum, invenerunt quendam virum magum pseudoprophetam Iudaeum, cui nomen Bariesu, ⁷qui erat cum proconsule Sergio Paulo, viro prudente. Hic accitis Barnaba et Saulo, quaesivit audire verbum Dei; ⁸resistebat autem illis Elymas, magus, sic enim interpretatur nomen eius, quaerens avertere proconsulem a fide. ⁹Saulus autem, qui et Paulus, repletus Spiritu Sancto, intuens in eum ¹⁰dixit: «O plene omni dolo et omni fallacia, fili Diaboli, inimice omnis iustitiae, non desines subvertere vias Domini rectas? ¹¹Et nunc ecce manus Domini super te: et eris caecus, non videns

much 'in the third place', action" (St Josemaría Escrivá, *The Way*, 82). The apostles are well aware that their mission is not a human, earthly one, and that it will produce results only with God's help. The prayer and penance that accompany apostolate are not just aimed at obtaining grace from God for others: they are designed to purify hearts and lips, so that the Lord will be at their side to ensure that none of their words "fall to the ground" (see 1 Sam 3:19).

13:4–12 We are told in passing that Saul is now known as "Paul" (v. 9). This is the name used hereafter in the New Testament. The previous episode twice (13:1, 2) mentions "Saul" in the last place. From now on, when a number of missionaries are named, Paul will usually be mentioned first. This signals the important role he has in the apostolic mission of the Church: "Not only should we reflect upon the Apostle's great virtues, the strength of his soul and his willingness to serve, which led him to be counted among the great apostles, we should also remember that his nature was human nature, exactly like ours. Thus, the things we find more difficult to do will appear lighter to carry and easier to carry out; if we struggle during the brief span of our life in this world, we will win the immortal and incorruptible crown of victory through the grace and mercy of our Lord Jesus Christ" (St John Chrysostom, *De*

laudibus sancti Pauli apostoli, 2).

In each city he visits, Paul's usual practice is to begin his preaching in the synagogue, if there is one (see v. 5 and 17:1–2). This is not simply a clever, human tactic; it is in line with what Paul knows to be God's plan of salvation. Like Jesus, he feels obliged to proclaim the Kingdom first to the Jews, because "to them belong the sonship, the glory, the covenants, the giving of the law, the worship, and the promises; to them belong the patriarchs, and of their race, according to the flesh, is the Christ" (Rom 9:4–5). The Jews have a right to be the first to whom the Gospel is preached, for they were the first to receive the promises (see 13:46).

Paul's punishment of Bar-Jesus (who is also called Elymas) is one of the few punitive miracles in the New Testament; commentators note that the punishment is medicinal and temporary (see v. 11). "Paul chooses to convert him by means of a miracle similar to that by which he himself was converted. 'For a time' is not the wording of one who punishes but of one who converts" (St John Chrysostom, *In Acta Apostolorum*, 28, 1). The punishment of Elymas helps bring Sergius Paulus' conversion, but it is not crucial to it. The text makes it clear (see v. 12) that the proconsul was already attracted to the faith by the coherence and sublimity of the Christian message.

Lk 4:32

for a time." Immediately mist and darkness fell upon him and he went about seeking people to lead him by the hand. [12]Then the proconsul believed, when he saw what had occurred, for he was astonished at the teaching of the Lord.

Paul and Barnabas cross into Asia Minor

Acts 15:38

[13]Now Paul and his company set sail from Paphos, and came to Perga in Pamphylia. And John left them and returned to Jerusalem; [14]but they passed on from Perga and came to Antioch of Pisidia.

Preaching in the synagogue of Antioch of Pisidia

Acts 15:21

And on the sabbath day they went into the synagogue and sat down. [15]After the reading of the law and the prophets, the rulers of the synagogue sent to them, saying, "Brethren, if you have any word of exhortation for the people, say it." [16]So Paul stood up, and motioning with his hand said:*

Ex 3:15; 6:1, 6;
12:51

"Men of Israel, and you that fear God, listen. [17]The God of this people Israel chose our fathers and made the people great during their stay in the land of Egypt,

Ex 16:35
Num 14:34
Deut 1:31

and with uplifted arm he led them out of it. [18]And for about forty years he bore with[m]

Deut 7:1
Josh 14:2

them in the wilderness. [19]And when he had destroyed seven nations in the land of Canaan, he gave them their land as an inheritance, for about four hundred and fifty

Gen 15:13

years. [20]And after that he gave them judges until Samuel the prophet. [21]Then they

Judg 2:16
1 Sam 3:20
1 Sam 10:20–21

asked for a king; and God gave them Saul the son of Kish, a man of the tribe of Benjamin, for forty years. [22]And when he had removed him, he raised up David to

*1 Sam 13:14;
16:12–13
Ps 89:20*

be their king; of whom he testified and said, 'I have found in David the son of Jesse

solem usque ad tempus». Et confestim cecidit in eum caligo et tenebrae, et circumiens quaerebat, qui eum manum darent. [12]Tunc proconsul, cum vidisset factum, credidit admirans super doctrinam Domini. [13]Et cum a Papho navigassent, qui erant cum Paulo, venerunt Pergen Pamphyliae; Ioannes autem discedens ab eis reversus est Hierosolymam. [14]Illi vero pertranseuntes, a Perge venerunt Antiochiam Pisidiae, et ingressi synagogam die sabbatorum sederunt. [15]Post lectionem autem Legis et Prophetarum, miserunt principes synagogae ad eos dicentes: «Viri fratres, si quis est in vobis sermo exhortationis ad plebem, dicite!». [16]Surgens autem Paulus et manu silentium indicens ait: «Viri Israelitae et qui timetis Deum, audite. [17]Deus plebis huius Israel elegit patres nostros et plebem exaltavit, cum essent incolae in terra Aegypti, et in brachio excelso eduxit eos ex ea [18]et per quadraginta fere annorum tempus mores eorum sustinuit in deserto [19]et destruens gentes septem in terra Chanaan sorte distribuit terram eorum, [20]quasi quadringentos et quinquaginta annos. Et post haec dedit iudices usque ad Samuel prophetam. [21]Et exinde postulaverunt regem, et dedit illis Deus Saul filium Cis, virum de tribu Beniamin, annis quadraginta. [22]Et amoto illo, suscitavit illis David in regem, cui et testimonium perhibens dixit: "*Inveni David* filium Iesse, *virum secundum cor meum*, qui faciet omnes voluntates meas". [23]Huius Deus ex semine secundum

13:13–43 By the first century AD, sabbath services in the synagogue (see vv. 14–15) were a well-established custom. They consisted of readings from Holy Scripture, preaching and public prayer. No one was specifically appointed to preside over these services; the president or ruler of the synagogue could ask any member of the community to do the readings etc.; he supervised the preparations and made sure the service was carried out properly.

Paul's address in the synagogue of the other Antioch (in Pisidia) is an excellent illustration of the method he used to present the Gospel to a mixed congregation of Jews and proselytes. He gives a general outline of salvation history and then shows Jesus to be the long-awaited Messiah in whom all the lines of salvation history and all

God's promises converge. The various moments in history that have led up to Jesus Christ, including the life and work of John the Baptist, are staging posts on the path. Provisional earlier elements must be set aside to accommodate the new, definitive situation: "Christ is the end of the Law. He led us out of the slavery of the Law into the freedom of the Spirit. The Law was directed towards him as its fulfilment; and he, the supreme Lawgiver, fulfilled it by transforming the letter of the Law into pure spirit. [...] As light grows, shadows fade: grace replaces the letter of the Law with the freedom of the Spirit" (St Andrew of Crete, *Sermones*, 1).

Paul's address contains all the main themes of apostolic preaching—God's taking the initiative to save Israel, over the centuries (vv. 17–22); the

m Other ancient authorities read *cared for* (Deut 1:31)

a man after my heart, who will do all my will.' ²³Of this man's posterity God has
brought to Israel a Saviour, Jesus, as he promised. ²⁴Before his coming John had
preached a baptism of repentance to all the people of Israel. ²⁵And as John was fin-
ishing his course, he said, 'What do you suppose that I am? I am not he. No, but
after me one is coming, the sandals of whose feet I am not worthy to untie.'

²⁶"Brethren, sons of the family of Abraham, and those among you that fear God,
to us has been sent the message of this salvation. ²⁷For those who live in Jerusalem
and their rulers, because they did not recognize him nor understand the utterances
of the prophets which are read every sabbath, fulfilled these by condemning him.
²⁸Though they could charge him with nothing deserving death, yet they asked Pilate
to have him killed. ²⁹And when they had fulfilled all that was written of him, they
took him down from the tree, and laid him in a tomb. ³⁰But God raised him from the
dead; ³¹and for many days he appeared to those who came up with him from Galilee
to Jerusalem, who are now his witnesses to the people. ³²And we bring you the good
news that what God promised to the fathers, ³³this he has fulfilled to us their children by raising Jesus; as also it is written in the second psalm,

> 'Thou art my Son,
> today I have begotten thee.'

³⁴And as for the fact that he raised him from the dead, no more to return to corrup-
tion, he spoke in this way,

> 'I will give you the holy and sure blessings of David.'

³⁵Therefore he says also in another psalm,

> 'Thou wilt not let thy Holy One see corruption.'

Margin references:
2 Sam 7:12
Lk 3:3, 16
Mt 3:11
Jn 1:20, 27
Lk 23:21–23
Acts 3:17
Mt 27:22–23
Mt 27:59–60
Lk 23:53; Acts 5:30
Acts 1:3; 3:15; 10:40
Lk 24:48
Acts 13:23
Ps 2:7
Is 55:3
Ps 16:10

promissionem eduxit Israel salvatorem Iesum, ²⁴praedicante Ioanne ante adventum eius baptismum paenitentiae omni populo Israel. ²⁵Cum
impleret autem Ioannes cursum suum, dicebat: "Quid me arbitramini esse? Non sum ego; sed ecce venit post me, cuius non sum dignus calceamenta pedum solvere". ²⁶Viri fratres, filii generis Abraham et qui in vobis timent Deum, nobis verbum salutis huius missum est. ²⁷Qui enim habitabant Ierusalem et principes eorum, hunc ignorantes et voces Prophetarum, quae per omne sabbatum leguntur, iudicantes impleverunt, ²⁸et nullam
causam mortis invenientes petierunt a Pilato, ut interficeretur; ²⁹cumque consummassent omnia, quae de eo scripta erant, deponentes eum de ligno
posuerunt in monumento. ³⁰Deus vero suscitavit eum a mortuis; ³¹qui visus est per dies multos his, qui simul ascenderant cum eo de Galilaea in
Ierusalem, qui nunc sunt testes eius ad plebem. ³²Et nos vobis evangelizamus eam, quae ad patres promissio facta est, ³³quoniam hanc Deus adim-
plevit filiis eorum, nobis resuscitans Iesum, sicut et in Psalmo secundo scriptum est: *"Filius meus es tu; ego hodie genui te"*. ³⁴Quod autem suscitaverit eum a mortuis, amplius iam non reversurum in corruptionem, ita dixit: *"Dabo vobis sancta David fidelia"*. ³⁵Ideoque et in alio dicit: *"Non
dabis Sanctum tuum videre corruptionem"*. ³⁶David enim sua generatione cum administrasset voluntati Dei, dormivit et appositus est ad patres

coming of the Precursor (vv. 24–25); the
proclamation of the Gospel, or *kérygma* (vv. 26b–
31a); the reference to Jerusalem (v. 31b); proofs
from Scripture (vv. 33–37), completed by doctrine
and apostolic tradition (vv. 38–39); and a final
exhortation, eschatological in style, a warning
about the future (vv. 40–41). Paul's address has
many similarities to St Peter's discourses (see
2:14ff; 3:12ff; 4:8ff; 10:34ff), especially in the
proclamation of Jesus as Messiah and citing the
the many quotations from Holy Scripture cited to
show that the momentous event of Jesus'
resurrection is confirmation that he is divine.

Two different styles are discernible in the
address: the first part (vv. 16–31) is more or less a
narrative, a history of salvation which culminates
in Jesus; the second part (vv. 32–41), on the other
hand, deals with our Lord's resurrection, and Paul
replaces straight narrative with argument. He
portrays the Resurrection as marking the
fulfilment by God of the promises found in the
sacred texts (Ps 2:7; Is 55:3; Ps 16:10). This
argument leads to the conclusion drawn in vv. 38–
39: we are not justified by the Law of Moses but
by faith in the risen Christ. Christian doctrine tells
us that justification "is the *most excellent work of
God's love* made manifest in Christ Jesus and
granted by the Holy Spirit. It is the opinion of St
Augustine that 'the justification of the wicked is a
greater work than the creation of heaven and
earth,' because 'heaven and earth will pass away
but the salvation and justification of the elect ...
will not pass away' (*In Ioannis Evangelium*, 72,
3)" (*Catechism of the Catholic Church*, 1994).

1 Kings 2:10
Acts 2:29

Rom 3:20

Acts 15:11

Hab 1:5
Rom 10:4
Heb 10:1–4

Acts 11:23

Mt 10:6
Lk 7:30

Is 49:6

Rom 8:28–30

³⁶For David, after he had served the counsel of God in his own generation, fell asleep, and was laid with his fathers, and saw corruption; ³⁷but he whom God raised up saw no corruption. ³⁸Let it be known to you therefore, brethren, that through this man forgiveness of sins is proclaimed to you, ³⁹and by him every one that believes is freed from everything from which you could not be freed by the law of Moses. ⁴⁰Beware, therefore, lest there come upon you what is said in the prophets:

⁴¹'Behold, you scoffers, and wonder, and perish;
for I do a deed in your days,
a deed you will never believe, if one declares it to you.'"

⁴²As they went out, the people begged that these things might be told them the next sabbath. ⁴³And when the meeting of the synagogue broke up, many Jews and devout converts to Judaism followed Paul and Barnabas, who spoke to them and urged them to continue in the grace of God.

Paul and Barnabas preach to the pagans

⁴⁴The next sabbath almost the whole city gathered together to hear the word of God. ⁴⁵But when the Jews saw the multitudes, they were filled with jealousy, and contradicted what was spoken by Paul, and reviled him. ⁴⁶And Paul and Barnabas spoke out boldly, saying, "It was necessary that the word of God should be spoken first to you. Since you thrust it from you, and judge yourselves unworthy of eternal life, behold, we turn to the Gentiles. ⁴⁷For so the Lord has commanded us, saying,

'I have set you to be a light for the Gentiles,
that you may bring salvation to the uttermost parts of the earth.'"

⁴⁸And when the Gentiles heard this, they were glad and glorified the word of God; and as many as were ordained to eternal life believed. ⁴⁹And the word of the

suos et vidit corruptionem; ³⁷quem vero Deus suscitavit, non vidit corruptionem. ³⁸Notum igitur sit vobis, viri fratres, quia per hunc vobis remissio peccatorum annuntiatur; ab omnibus, quibus non potuistis in lege Moysi iustificari, ³⁹in hoc omnis, qui credit, iustificatur. ⁴⁰Videte ergo, ne superveniat, quod dictum est in Prophetis: ⁴¹"*Videte, contemptores, / et admiramini et disperdimini, / quia opus operor ego in diebus vestris, / opus, quod non credetis, si quis enarraverit vobis!*"». ⁴²Exeuntibus autem illis, rogabant, ut sequenti sabbato loquerentur sibi verba haec. ⁴³Cumque dimissa esset synagoga, secuti sunt multi Iudaeorum et colentium proselytorum Paulum et Barnabam, qui loquebantur eis, ut permanerent in gratia Dei. ⁴⁴Sequenti vero sabbato paene universa civitas convenit audire verbum Domini. ⁴⁵Videntes autem turbas Iudaei repleti sunt zelo et contradicebant his, quae a Paulo dicebantur, blasphemantes. ⁴⁶Tunc audenter Paulus et Barnabas dixerunt: «Vobis oportebat primum loqui verbum Dei; sed quoniam repellitis illud et indignos vos iudicatis aeternae vitae, ecce convertimur ad gentes. ⁴⁷Sic enim praecepit nobis Dominus: "*Posui te in lumen gentium, / ut sis in salutem usque ad extremum terrae*"». ⁴⁸Audientes autem gentes gaudebant et glorificabant verbum Domini, et crediderunt, quotquot erant praeordinati ad vitam aeternam; ⁴⁹ferebatur autem verbum Domini per universam regionem. ⁵⁰Iudaei autem conci-

13:44–52 Paul may have hoped that Christianity would take root among the Jews in such a way that they would peacefully and religiously accept the Gospel as the logical fulfilment of God's plans. His experience proved otherwise: he encountered the terrible mystery of the infidelity of the greater part of the Chosen People, his own people (see Rom 9:1 — 11:36). However, the evangelization of the pagan world did not happen because of the Jews' lack of response to the Gospel message: it had to happen, because the Christian message is universal; it offers to everyone the only grace that brings salvation, a grace perfecting the Law of Moses and reaching out beyond the ethnic and geographical boundaries of Judaism.

Paul and Barnabas quote Isaiah 49:6 in support of their decision to preach to the Gentiles (vv. 46–47; see also 18:6; 28:28). However, Acts shows that they continued to address Jews first. In this, they were following Christ's example: "Paul spoke the truth when he said that Christ dedicated his public ministry to the Jewish people so that the promises made to their forefathers might be fulfilled, and so that the pagan peoples might receive God's mercy and give glory to Him as the creator and maker, saviour and redeemer of all. In this way, divine mercy was opened to all, including the pagans, and the plan of God's wisdom in Christ was fulfilled: the world was saved through the mercy of God"

Lord spread throughout all the region. ⁵⁰But the Jews incited the devout women of high standing and the leading men of the city, and stirred up persecution against Paul and Barnabas, and drove them out of their district. ⁵¹But they shook off the dust from their feet against them, and went to Iconium. ⁵²And the disciples were filled with joy and with the Holy Spirit.

Mt 10:14
Lk 9:5; 10:11
Acts 18:6

Iconium evangelized. Persecution

14 ¹Now at Iconium they entered together into the Jewish synagogue, and so spoke that a great company believed, both of Jews and of Greeks. ²But the unbelieving Jews stirred up the Gentiles and poisoned their minds against the brethren. ³So they remained for a long time, speaking boldly for the Lord, who bore witness to the word of his grace, granting signs and wonders to be done by their hands. ⁴But the people of the city were divided; some sided with the Jews, and some with the apostles. ⁵When an attempt was made by both Gentiles and Jews, with their rulers, to molest them and to stone them, ⁶they learned of it and fled to Lystra and Derbe, cities of Lycaonia, and to the surrounding country; ⁷and there they preached the gospel.

Acts 13:14, 44
1 Thess 2:14

Mk 16:17–20
Heb 2:4

2 Tim 3:11
Mt 10:23
Acts 11:19–20

Curing of a cripple at Lystra

⁸Now at Lystra there was a man sitting, who could not use his feet; he was a cripple from birth, who had never walked. ⁹He listened to Paul speaking; and Paul, looking

Jn 9:1
Acts 3:2; 9:33

taverunt honestas inter colentes mulieres et primos civitatis et excitaverunt persecutionem in Paulum et Barnabam et eiecerunt eos de finibus suis. ⁵¹At illi, excusso pulvere pedum in eos, venerunt Iconium; ⁵²discipuli quoque replebantur gaudio et Spiritu Sancto. [14] ¹Factum est autem Iconii, ut eodem modo introirent synagogam Iudaeorum et ita loquerentur, ut crederet Iudaeorum et Graecorum copiosa multitudo. ²Qui vero increduli fuerunt Iudaei, suscitaverunt et exacerbaverunt animas gentium adversus fratres. ³Multo igitur tempore demorati sunt, fiducialiter agentes in Domino, testimonium perhibente verbo gratiae suae, dante signa et prodigia fieri per manus eorum. ⁴Divisa est autem multitudo civitatis: et quidam quidem erant cum Iudaeis, quidam vero cum apostolis. ⁵Cum autem factus esset impetus gentilium et Iudaeorum cum principibus suis, ut contumeliis afficerent et lapidarent eos, ⁶intellegentes confugerunt ad civitates Lycaoniae, Lystram et Derben et ad regionem in circuitu, ⁷et ibi evangelizantes erant. ⁸Et quidam vir in Lystris infirmus pedibus sedebat, claudus ex utero matris suae, qui numquam ambulaverat. ⁹Hic audivit Paulum loquentem; qui intuitus eum et videns quia haberet fidem, ut salvus fieret, ¹⁰dixit magna voce: «Surge super pedes tuos rectus!». Et

(St Cyril of Alexandria, *Commentarium in Romanos*, 15, 7).

14:1–7 Luke here describes Paul and Barnabas as "apostles" (v. 4). Even though neither of them belongs to the group of the Twelve (for whom Luke usually reserves the name of "apostles"), Paul is seen, by himself and others, as an "apostle" by virtue of his unique vocation (see 1 Cor 15:9; 2 Cor 11:5) and his tireless preaching to the Gentiles. When the Fathers of the Church mention in their writings "the apostle", without being any more specific than that, they mean St Paul, because he is the apostle most quoted and commented on, due to the numerous letters written by him that belong to the canon of Scripture.

This brief overview of the apostles' activity in Iconium shows that their efforts bear out what the Gospel predicted would happen—signs and wonders give authority to their preaching (v. 3;

see Mk 16:15–18); Jesus is a sign of contradiction (v. 4; see Lk 2:34; etc.).

14:8–18 This account of Paul's activity in Lystra has parallels with Peter's ministry. Peter, too, cured a lame man (3:1–10), and Peter (as Paul does now: v. 15) had to explain to people that he was like any other man (see 10:26). The Fathers pointed out the significance of these parallels: "Just as the lame man whom Peter and John cured at the gate of the temple prefigured the salvation of the Jews, so too this cripple represents the Gentile peoples distanced from the religion of the Law and the temple, but now brought in through the preaching of the apostle Paul" (St Bede, *Expositio Actuum Apostolorum*, ad loc.).

This account also shows that natural religion can help to prepare people to accept supernatural revelation: "Throughout history even to the present day, there is found among different peoples a

intently at him and seeing that he had faith to be made well, [10]said in a loud voice,

Mt 9:6–7

"Stand upright on your feet." And he sprang up and walked. [11]And when the crowds saw what Paul had done, they lifted up their voices, saying in Lycaonian, "The gods have come down to us in the likeness of men!" [12]Barnabas they called Zeus, and Paul, because he was the chief speaker, they called Hermes. [13]And the priest of Zeus, whose temple was in front of the city, brought oxen and garlands to the gates and wanted to offer sacrifice with the people. [14]But when the apostles Barnabas and Paul heard of it, they tore their garments and rushed out among the multitude, crying,

Ps 146:6
Acts 10:26;
17:22–30

[15]"Men, why are you doing this? We also are men, of like nature with you, and bring you good news, that you should turn from these vain things to a living God who made the heaven and the earth and the sea and all that is in them. [16]In past genera-

Jer 5:24
Ps 147:8

tions he allowed all the nations to walk in their own ways; [17]yet he did not leave himself without witness, for he did good and gave you from heaven rains and fruitful seasons, satisfying your hearts with food and gladness." [18]With these words they scarcely restrained the people from offering sacrifice to them.

Paul is stoned

2 Cor 11:25
2 Tim 3:11
2 Thess 2:14–16

[19]But Jews came there from Antioch and Iconium; and having persuaded the people, they stoned Paul and dragged him out of the city, supposing that he was dead. [20]But

exsilivit et ambulabat. [11]Turbae autem cum vidissent, quod fecerat Paulus, levaverunt vocem suam Lycaonice dicentes: «Dii similes facti hominibus descenderunt ad nos!»; [12]et vocabant Barnabam Iovem, Paulum vero Mercurium, quoniam ipse erat dux verbi. [13]Sacerdos quoque templi Iovis, quod erat ante civitatem, tauros et coronas ad ianuas afferens cum populis, volebat sacrificare. [14]Quod ubi audierunt apostoli Barnabas et Paulus, conscissis tunicis suis, exsilierunt in turbam clamantes [15]et dicentes: «Viri, quid haec facitis? Et nos mortales sumus similes vobis homines, evangelizantes vobis ab his vanis converti ad Deum vivum, *qui fecit caelum et terram et mare et omnia, quae in eis sunt*. [16]Qui in praeteritis generationibus permisit omnes gentes ambulare in viis suis; [17]et quidem non sine testimonio semetipsum reliquit benefaciens, de caelo dans vobis pluvias et tempora fructifera, implens cibo et laetitia corda vestra». [18]Et haec dicentes vix sedaverunt turbas, ne sibi immolarent. [19]Supervenerunt autem ab Antiochia et Iconio Iudaei et persuasis turbis lapidantesque Paulum trahebant extra civitatem aestimantes eum mortuum esse. [20]Circumdantibus autem eum discipulis, surgens intravit civitatem. Et postera die profectus est cum Barnaba in Derben. [21]Cumque

certain awareness of a hidden power, which lies behind the course of nature and the events of human life. At times there is present even a recognition of a supreme being, or still more of a Father. This awareness and recognition results in a way of life that is imbued with a deep religious sense" (Vatican II, *Nostra aetate*, 2). This passage also shows the difficulty the apostles had (see v. 18) ensuring that new converts did not allow their faith to be contaminated by idolatry: "The saints and holy men refused to accept the honours and tributes due only to God. Paul and Barnabas made their refusal clear when the people of Lycaonia tried to offer sacrifices to them, as to gods, for the miracles they had performed among them: they tore their garments and cried out loudly to convince the people that they were not gods, and so prevented the offering of false sacrifices. But what we teach is one thing, and what we see and hear around us another; what we say ought to be done and what,

on the other hand, we must correct; while we search for the best way to correct old ways, we will have to withstand many errors" (St Augustine, *Contra Faustinum*, 20, 21).

14:19–28 Staying with his account of Paul's preaching (see v. 22), Luke points out in these verses the fruitful progress made by the Word of God, without hiding the fact that its preachers encountered the cross: "Cross, toil, anguish: such will be your lot as long as you live. That was the way Christ went, and the disciple is not above his Master" (St Josemaría Escrivá, *The Way*, 699). In 2 Corinthians 11:25, St Paul refers to this stoning at Lystra. The text says that Paul and Barnabas did "appoint" (the Greek verb literally means "to extend one's hands in order to charge someone with an assignment") "elders [...] in every church" (v. 23). These elders are given priestly ordination, although they are not called "priests" because that term, in the early days of the growth

when the disciples gathered about him, he rose up and entered the city; and on the next day he went on with Barnabas to Derbe.

Return journey to Antioch

²¹When they had preached the gospel to that city and had made many disciples, they returned to Lystra and to Iconium and to Antioch, ²²strengthening the souls of the disciples, exhorting them to continue in the faith, and saying that through many tribulations we must enter the kingdom of God. ²³And when they had appointed elders for them in every church, with prayer and fasting, they committed them to the Lord in whom they believed.

²⁴Then they passed through Pisidia, and came to Pamphylia. ²⁵And when they had spoken the word in Perga, they went down to Attalia; ²⁶and from there they sailed to Antioch, where they had been commended to the grace of God for the work which they had fulfilled. ²⁷And when they arrived, they gathered the church together and declared all that God had done with them, and how he had opened a door of faith to the Gentiles. ²⁸And they remained no little time with the disciples.

Mt 28:19

Mt 10:22
Acts 11:23
1 Thess 3:3
Heb 10:36
Acts 13:3

Acts 13:1

Acts 15:4

9. THE COUNCIL OF JERUSALEM*

Dissension at Antioch; Judaizers

15 ¹But some men came down from Judea and were teaching the brethren, "Unless you are circumcised according to the custom of Moses, you cannot

Gen 17:10
Gal 5:2

evangelizassent civitati illi et docuissent multos, reversi sunt Lystram et Iconium et Antiochiam ²²confirmantes animas discipulorum, exhortantes, ut permanerent in fide, et quoniam per multas tribulationes oportet nos intrare in regnum Dei. ²³Et cum ordinassent illis per singulas ecclesias presbyteros et orassent cum ieiunationibus, commendaverunt eos Domino, in quem crediderant. ²⁴Transeuntesque Pisidiam venerunt Pamphyliam, ²⁵et loquentes in Perge verbum descenderunt in Attaliam. ²⁶Et inde navigaverunt Antiochiam, unde erant traditi gratiae Dei in opus, quod compleverunt. ²⁷Cum autem venissent et congregassent ecclesiam, rettulerunt quanta fecisset Deus cum illis et quia aperuisset gentibus ostium fidei.

and development of Christianity, connoted the idea of a minister (*hieréus*) in pagan religions in the Greek world or a Levitical priest (*kôhen*) in the Jewish world. Among the Jews, "elders" (*presbýteroi*, in Greek) were those who presided over the community. By the using of this name to describe church ministers, a possible confusion was avoided; in Greek, the word "presbyter" could be used of a minister without any particular religion being implied. Eventually Paul and Barnabas return to Syrian Antioch, travelling back through the cities they have already visited (vv. 24–26). At the port of Attalia they board ship for Syria, and they arrive at Antioch soon afterwards. The missionary journey has taken around four years. Despite the hostility and persecution experienced previously, the two missionaries are not afraid to return to the cities they have visited earlier. They want to complete arrangements for the government of the new churches and to consolidate the disciples' faith.

*15:1–35 Chapter 15 could be said to be the centre of the book of Acts, not only because it is positioned in the middle of the text, but also because it covers the key event connected with the universality of the Gospel and resulting in its unrestricted spread among the Gentiles. It is directly linked to the conversion of the pagan Cornelius, all the consequences of which will now be drawn out: the baptizing of Cornelius was not a one-time exception to the rule; it signalled what God wants to happen as a matter of course. In his usual orderly way, Luke tells us how the controversy arose (vv. 1–5), what happened at the meeting in Jerusalem (vv. 6–29), and the outcome of the meeting for the Church (vv. 30–35).

15:1–5 Some Christians with a Pharisee background ("certain men [coming] from James": Gal 2:12), come to Antioch and insist that salvation is impossible unless a person is circumcised and lives according to the Law of Moses. They

Gal 2:1–2 be saved." ²And when Paul and Barnabas had no small dissension and debate with them, Paul and Barnabas and some of the others were appointed to go up to Jerusalem to the apostles and the elders about this question.

Paul and Barnabas go to Jerusalem
³So, being sent on their way by the church, they passed through both Phoenicia and Samaria, reporting the conversion of the Gentiles, and they gave great joy to all the Acts 14:27; 21:17 brethren. ⁴When they came to Jerusalem, they were welcomed by the church and the Gal 2:4–9 apostles and the elders, and they declared all that God had done with them. ⁵But some believers who belonged to the party of the Pharisees rose up, and said, "It is necessary to circumcise them, and to charge them to keep the law of Moses."

Peter's address to the council
⁶The apostles and the elders were gathered together to consider this matter. ⁷And after there had been much debate, Peter rose and said to them, "Brethren, you know that in the early days God made choice among you, that by my mouth the Gentiles

²⁸Morati sunt autem tempus non modicum cum discipulis. [15] ¹Et quidam descendentes de Iudaea docebant fratres: «Nisi circumcidamini secundum morem Moysis, non potestis salvi fieri». ²Facta autem seditione et conquisitione non minima Paulo et Barnabae adversum illos, statuerunt, ut ascenderent Paulus et Barnabas et quidam alii ex illis ad apostolos et presbyteros in Ierusalem super hac quaestione. ³Illi igitur deducti ab ecclesia pertransiebant Phoenicen et Samariam narrantes conversionem gentium et faciebant gaudium magnum omnibus fratribus. ⁴Cum autem venissent Hierosolymam, suscepti sunt ab ecclesia et apostolis et presbyteris et annuntiaverunt quanta Deus fecisset cum illis. ⁵Surrexerunt autem quidam de haeresi pharisaeorum, qui crediderant, dicentes: «Oportet circumcidere eos, praecipere quoque servare legem Moysis!». ⁶Conveneruntque apostoli et presbyteri videre de verbo hoc. ⁷Cum autem magna conquisitio fieret, surgens Petrus dixit ad eos: «Viri fratres, vos

accept (see 11:18) that Gentile converts can be baptized and be full members of the Church, but they do not properly understand the new economy of the Gospel; they think that converts must first embrace Judaism and abide by all the Mosaic precepts and rites. Their assertions greatly trouble the disciples at Antioch, and put the Church's whole programme of evangelization at risk. So, a decision is taken to appeal to the apostles and elders in Jerusalem who form the government of the Church.

"Party" (v. 5): the Greek and the New Vulgate both literally say "heresy". However, in this context the word doesn't have a pejorative meaning. It is a correct use of language in view of the religious exclusivity and strict separation practised by the Pharisees. It is also used where St Paul mentions that he belonged to "the strictest party of our religion" (26:5), and where he speaks of "the party of the Sadducees" (5:17). Jews referred to Christianity as a "sect" or party (24:5, 14: 28:22).

15:6–11 St Luke records three important events touching on this issue—Peter's address (vv. 7–11), that of James (15:13–21), and the text of the

decree sent to the churches (15:23–29). Peter's short speech proves decisive. Referring back to what God gave him to understand in connexion with the baptism of Cornelius (see 10:1ff), Peter sums up the long debate (v. 7) and proposes a line of thought which corresponds to that of Paul and Barnabas: it is grace, not the Law, that saves, and therefore circumcision and the Law itself have been superseded by faith in Jesus (v. 11): "No one can be sanctified after sin," St Thomas Aquinas says, "unless it be through Christ. [...] Just as the ancient fathers were saved by faith in the Christ who was to come, so we are saved by faith in the Christ who was born and suffered" (*Summa theologiae*, 3, 61, 3 and 4).

Once again, Peter plays a decisive role in maintaining the Church's unity. Not only does he draw together the various legitimate views of those trying to arrive at the truth: he points out where the truth is to be found. This meeting (probably held in the year 49 or 50) was the first general council of the Church, and a prototype of all later ecumenical councils: "Who can doubt that the keys to the kingdom of heaven were given to Peter? The whole church is built on the faith and teaching of Peter until we are made the

should hear the word of the gospel and believe.[8]And God who knows the heart bore witness to them, giving them the Holy Spirit just as he did to us; [9]and he made no distinction between us and them, but cleansed their hearts by faith. [10]Now therefore why do you make trial of God by putting a yoke upon the neck of the disciples which neither our fathers nor we have been able to bear? [11]But we believe that we shall be saved through the grace of the Lord Jesus, just as they will."

Acts 10:44; 11:15

Mt 11:30; 23:4
Gal 5:1

Gal 2:15–21;
3:22–26
Eph 2:1–10

James' speech

[12]And all the assembly kept silence; and they listened to Barnabas and Paul as they related what signs and wonders God had done through them among the Gentiles. [13]After they finished speaking, James replied, "Brethren, listen to me. [14]Symeon has related how God first visited the Gentiles, to take out of them a people for his name. [15]And with this the words of the prophets agree, as it is written,

Acts 14: 3–27

Gal 2:9
Acts 2:17
Lk 1:68

Jer 12, 15
Amos 9:11–12

> [16]'After this I will return,
> And I will rebuild the dwelling of David, which has fallen;
> I will rebuild its ruins,
> and I will set it up,
> [17] that the rest of men may seek the Lord,
> and all the Gentiles who are called by my name,

scitis quoniam ab antiquis diebus in vobis elegit Deus per os meum audire gentes verbum evangelii et credere; [8]et qui novit corda, Deus testimonium perhibuit illis dans Spiritum Sanctum sicut et nobis [9]et nihil discrevit inter nos et illos fide purificans corda eorum. [10]Nunc ergo quid tentatis Deum imponere iugum super cervicem discipulorum, quod neque patres nostri neque nos portare potuimus? [11]Sed per gratiam Domini Iesu credimus salvari quemadmodum et illi». [12]Tacuit autem omnis multitudo, et audiebant Barnabam et Paulum narrantes quanta fecisset Deus signa et prodigia in gentibus per eos. [13]Et postquam tacuerunt, respondit Iacobus dicens: «Viri fratres, audite me. [14]Simeon narravit quemadmodum primum Deus visitavit sumere ex gentibus populum nomini suo, [15]et huic concordant verba Prophetarum, sicut scriptum est: [16]"*Post haec revertar* / *et reaedificabo tabernaculum David, quod decidit,* / *et diruta eius reaedificabo et erigam illud,* / [17]*ut requirant reliqui hominum Dominum* / *et omnes*

perfect man in the unity of the faith and knowledge of the Son of God. Many must sow and many water if the preaching is to spread and the churches grow. [...] God will not grant growth to anyone who sows or waters unless he sows and waters the soil of Peter's faith and teaching" (St Thomas à Becket, *Epistulae*, 74).

15:12–21 Using proofs from Scripture, James backs up what Peter has said: God desires that his new people be drawn from every nation. The three prohibitions he recommends all come from Leviticus: (1) the eating of meat from animals used in sacrifices to idols, because the eating of that meat would involve Jews in some way in idolatry (Lev 17:7–9); (2) irregular sexual unions (see Lev 18:6ff), and other sins against sexual morality (some of these norms would later be included in the matrimonial law of the Church); (3) the eating of meat that had blood in it (the meat from strangled animals always contains blood), or of food that had blood as an ingredient (see Lev 17:10ff): this last prohibition was

rooted in the belief that blood was the vessel of life and as such belonged to God alone; a Jew would find it virtually impossible to overcome his religious and cultural revulsion at the thought of anyone's consuming blood. The Law laid down (see Lev 17:8, 10, 13, 15) that not only Israelites but also foreigners living in Israel had to adhere to these rules; they were what were called the "commandments of Noah", that is, commandments given by God to Noah and his sons (see Gen 9:4–5) and were thought to be the Law as applied to Gentiles. However, James also makes it clear that this decision is a prudential one which is temporary and changeable, one designed to avoid giving scandal to those who still kept the Law of Moses throughout the diaspora (v. 21). St Paul will adopt the same position with regard to meat from animals sacrificed to idols (1 Cor 8:1–13), and in the case of the Corinthian "living with his father's wife" (1 Cor 5:1), who had probably infringed one of the rules to do with the "unchastity" referred to here (v. 20; see Lev 18:6ff).

Is 45:21

Gen 9:4
Lev 3:17; 17:11–14
1 Cor 8:10

[18] says the Lord, who has made these things known from of old.'

[19] Therefore my judgment is that we should not trouble those of the Gentiles who turn to God, [20] but should write to them to abstain from the pollutions of idols and from unchastity and from what is strangled[n] and from blood. [21] For from early generations Moses has had in every city those who preach him, for he is read every sabbath in the synagogues."

The council's decision

[22] Then it seemed good to the apostles and the elders, with the whole church, to choose men from among them and send them to Antioch with Paul and Barnabas. They sent Judas called Barsabbas, and Silas, leading men among the brethren, [23] with the following letter: "The brethren, both the apostles and the elders, to the brethren

Acts 15:1
Gal 2:12

who are of the Gentiles in Antioch and Syria and Cilicia, greeting. [24] Since we have heard that some persons from us have troubled you with words, unsettling your minds, although we gave them no instructions, [25] it has seemed good to us in assem-

Acts 21:13

bly to choose men and send them to you with our beloved Barnabas and Paul, [26] men who have risked their lives for the sake of our Lord Jesus Christ. [27] We have therefore sent Judas and Silas, who themselves will tell you the same things by word of

Acts 5:32; 1:8

mouth. [28] For it has seemed good to the Holy Spirit and to us to lay upon you no greater burden than these necessary things: [29] that you abstain from what has been sacrificed to idols and from blood and from what is strangled[n] and from unchastity. If you keep yourselves from these, you will do well. Farewell."

---

gentes, super quas invocatum est nomen meum, / dicit Dominus faciens haec [18] nota a saeculo". [19] Propter quod ego iudico non inquietari eos, qui ex gentibus convertuntur ad Deum, [20] sed scribere ad eos, ut abstineant se a contaminationibus simulacrorum et fornicatione et suffocato et sanguine. [21] Moyses enim a generationibus antiquis habet in singulis civitatibus, qui eum praedicent in synagogis, ubi per omne sabbatum legitur». [22] Tunc placuit apostolis et presbyteris cum omni ecclesia electos viros ex eis mittere Antiochiam cum Paulo et Barnaba: Iudam, qui cognominatur Barsabbas, et Silam, viros primos in fratribus, [23] scribentes per manum eorum: «Apostoli et presbyteri fratres his, qui sunt Antiochiae et Syriae et Ciliciae fratribus ex gentibus, salutem! [24] Quoniam audivimus quia quidam ex nobis quibus non mandavimus, exeuntes turbaverunt vos verbis evertentes animas vestras, [25] placuit nobis collectis in unum eligere viros et mittere ad vos cum carissimis nobis Barnaba et Paulo, [26] hominibus, qui tradiderunt animas suas pro nomine Domini nostri Iesu Christi. [27] Misimus ergo Iudam et Silam, qui et ipsi verbis referent eadem. [28] Visum est enim Spiritui Sancto et nobis nihil ultra imponere vobis oneris quam haec necessario: [29] abstinere ab idolothytis et sanguine et suffocatis et fornicatione; a quibus custodientes vos bene agetis. Valete». [30] Illi igitur dimissi descenderunt Antiochiam et, congregata multitudine, tradiderunt epistulam; [31] quam cum legissent, gavisi sunt super consolatione. [32] Iudas quoque et Silas, cum et ipsi essent prophetae, verbo plurimo consolati sunt

---

15:22–29 The apostolic decree sums up the deliberations of the council—how the controversy has arisen, what it has consisted of, and what the solution is to be. Significantly, the apostles describe their decision as being that of the Holy Spirit (v. 28): "As I see it, the richness of these great events cannot be explained unless it be with help from the same Holy Spirit who was their author" (Origen, *Homiliae in Exodum*, 4, 5). Here is what a Spanish theologian of the sixteenth century has to say about the matter: "We should take the same road that the apostle Paul considered to be the one best suited to solving all matters to do with the doctrine of the faith. [...] The Gentiles could have sought satisfaction from the Council because it seemed to take from the

freedom granted them by Jesus Christ, and because it imposed on the disciples certain rites as necessary, when in fact they were not, since faith is the key to salvation. Nor did the Jews object by invoking Sacred Scripture against the Council's decision on the grounds that Scripture seems to support their view that circumcision is necessary for salvation. So, by respecting the Council they gave us all the criteria which should be observed in all later times, that is, to place full faith in the authority of synods confirmed by Peter and his legitimate successors. They say, 'It has seemed good to the Holy Spirit and to us'; thus, the Council's decision is the decision of the Holy Spirit himself " (Melchor Cano, *De loci theologicis*, 5, 4).

---

n Other early authorities omit *and from what is strangled*

Reception of the council's decree

[30] So when they were sent off, they went down to Antioch; and having gathered the congregation together, they delivered the letter. [31] And when they read it, they rejoiced at the exhortation. [32] And Judas and Silas, who were themselves prophets, exhorted the brethren with many words and strengthened them. [33] And after they had spent some time, they were sent off in peace by the brethren to those who had sent them.° [35] But Paul and Barnabas remained in Antioch, teaching and preaching the word of the Lord, with many others also.

Acts 11:27

Acts 14:28

10. ST PAUL'S SECOND APOSTOLIC JOURNEY*

Silas, Paul's new companion

[36] And after some days Paul said to Barnabas, "Come, let us return and visit the brethren in every city where we proclaimed the word of the Lord, and see how they are." [37] And Barnabas wanted to take with them John called Mark. [38] But Paul thought

Acts 12:12

Acts 13:13

fratres et confirmaverunt. ³³Facto autem tempore, dimissi sunt cum pace a fratribus ad eos, qui miserant illos. ³⁵Paulus autem et Barnabas demorabantur Antiochiae docentes et evangelizantes cum aliis pluribus verbum Domini. ³⁶Post aliquot autem dies dixit ad Barnabam Paulus: «Revertentes visitemus fratres per universas civitates, in quibus praedicavimus verbum Domini, quomodo se habeant». ³⁷Barnabas autem volebat secum assumere et Ioannem, qui cognominatur Marcus; ³⁸Paulus autem iudicabat eum, qui discessisset ab eis a Pamphylia et non isset cum

15:30–35 Paul and Barnabas, accompanied by Judas and Silas (see 15:22, 27, 32) return to Antioch (the one in Syria) to reassure the community and bring them the apostles' decree. Silas is a Christian from Jerusalem and a Roman citizen who, like Paul, has two names, Silas and Silvanus (see 2 Cor 1:19; 1 Thess 1:1; 2 Thess 1:1; 1 Pet 5:12). Paul and Silas then set off to visit the places evangelized in Paul's first missionary journey (see 15:39–41), to tell the brethren there about the decisions made in Jerusalem (see 16:4).

Some manuscripts add (as v. 34): "But it seemed good to Silas to remain there, so that only Judas returned to Jerusalem".

*15:36—18:22 This section covers St Paul's second journey. As before, he sets out from Antioch and returns a few years later; this time perhaps around the spring of the year 53. The initial plan was to visit the brethren in the cities previously evangelized, and to confirm them in the faith. The journey comprises almost three full chapters, and the third apostolic journey begins immediately after it (18:23).

Paul and Silas pass through Syria and Cilicia (Paul's native region) and travel on to Derbe and then to Lystra (16:1), where Timothy joins them. They make their way across most of Asia Minor

(see 16:6) and reach Troas (16:8), where they board a ship bound for Macedonia (16:10–12). The sea journey from Troas to Neapolis is about 230 kilometres (143 miles); from Neapolis they press on to Philippi, a Roman colony, where the rest of the events described in chapter 16 take place. From there they go to Thessalonica (17:1), the seat of government of the Roman province of Macedonia. Due to the violent opposition they encounter there, they have to leave and go to Beroea (17:10); and then Jewish hostility again forces Paul to leave suddenly. He then sails to Athens (17:14), where he makes his famous speech in the Areopagus. Without tarrying in Athens, he goes to Corinth (18:1), where he will spend a considerable amount of time (perhaps a year and a half) because he finds the Corinthians very responsive to the Lord's call. After this long stay (see 18:18) he travels by sea to Antioch, with brief stops at Ephesus (18:19) and Caesarea (18:22).

15:36–41 The journey begins here, but this time Paul and Barnabas go in different directions due to a disagreement over Mark. However, it is all part of God's plan and everything works out well in the end: "The gifts of the two men differ, and clearly this difference is itself a gift. [...]

o Other ancient authorities insert verse 34, *But it seemed good to Silas to remain there*

Col 4:10
2 Tim 4:11

best not to take with them one who had withdrawn from them in Pamphylia, and had not gone with them to the work. [39]And there arose a sharp contention, so that they separated from each other; Barnabas took Mark with him and sailed away to Cyprus, [40]but Paul chose Silas and departed, being commended by the brethren to the grace of the Lord. [41]And he went through Syria and Cilicia, strengthening the churches.

Timothy joins Paul

Phil 2:19–22
2 Tim 1:5

Gal 2:3–5

16 [1]And he came also to Derbe and to Lystra. A disciple was there, named Timothy, the son of a Jewish woman who was a believer; but his father was a Greek. [2]He was well spoken of by the brethren at Lystra and Iconium. [3]Paul wanted Timothy to accompany him; and he took him and circumcised him because of the Jews that were in those places, for they all knew that his father was a Greek.

Tour of the churches of Asia Minor

Acts 15:23–29

Acts 2:41

[4]As they went on their way through the cities, they delivered to them for observance the decisions which had been reached by the apostles and elders who were at Jerusalem. [5]So the churches were strengthened in the faith, and they increased in numbers daily.

Acts 18:23
Gal 4:13–15

[6]And they went through the region of Phrygia and Galatia, having been forbidden by the Holy Spirit to speak the word in Asia. [7]And when they had come oppo-

---

eis in opus, non debere recipi eum. [39]Facta est autem exacerbatio, ita ut discederent ab invicem, et Barnabas assumpto Marco navigaret Cyprum. [40]Paulus vero, electo Sila, profectus est traditus gratiae Domini a fratribus; [41]perambulabat autem Syriam et Ciliciam confirmans ecclesias. [16] [1]Pervenit autem in Derben et Lystram. Et ecce discipulus quidam erat ibi nomine Timotheus, filius mulieris Iudaeae fidelis, patre autem Graeco; [2]huic testimonium reddebant, qui in Lystris erant et Iconii fratres. [3]Hunc voluit Paulus secum proficisci et assumens circumcidit eum propter Iudaeos, qui erant in illis locis; sciebant enim omnes quod pater eius Graecus esset. [4]Cum autem pertransirent civitates, tradebant eis custodire dogmata, quae erant decreta ab apostolis et presbyteris, qui essent Hierosolymis. [5]Ecclesiae quidem confirmabantur fide et abundabant numero cotidie. [6]Transierunt autem Phrygiam et Galatiae regionem, vetati a Sancto Spiritu loqui verbum in Asia; [7]cum venissent autem circa Mysiam,

---

Observe that there is nothing wrong in their separating if this means that they can evangelize all the Gentiles. If they go different ways, in order to teach and convert people, there is nothing wrong about that. What should be emphasized is not their difficulties but what unites them. [...] If only all our divisions were motivated by zeal for preaching!" (St John Chrysostom, *In Acta Apostolorum*, 34, 1–2). This disagreement does not mean that the two apostles were estranged. Paul always praised Barnabas for his zeal (see 1 Cor 9:6; Gal 2:9), and later he is quite happy to have Mark work with him as a co-missionary (see Col 4:10).

16:1–3 At this point Paul is joined for the first time by Timothy, a man who will later be a real help to him in his apostolate (cf. 17:14–15f; 18:5; 19:22; 20:4) and to whom he will write two letters that are incorporated into the canon of the New Testament. Timothy's mother, Eunice, and his grandmother Lois were Christians (cf. 2 Tim 1:5),

and they had passed the faith on to him. As St Luke explains (v. 3), Paul has Timothy circumcised for reasons of pastoral prudence: "He took Timothy and circumcised him. Paul did not do this without deliberation: he always acted prudently; but given that Timothy was being trained to preach the Gospel to Jews everywhere, and to avoid their not giving him a good hearing because he was not circumcised, he decided to circumcise him. In doing this he was not aiming to show that circumcision was necessary—he had been the one most instrumental in eliminating it—but to avoid putting the Gospel at risk" (St Ephrem, *Commentarii in Acta*, ad loc.).

16:4–10 The brief summary contained in vv. 4–5 makes it understood that the decrees of the assembly at Jerusalem were received by Christians in a spirit of obedience and joy; they saw them as coming from the mother church, from the apostles, and as providing a satisfactory solution to a delicate problem.

site Mysia, they attempted to go into Bithynia, but the Spirit of Jesus did not allow
them; [8]so, passing by Mysia, they went down to Troas. [9]And a vision appeared to
Paul in the night: a man of Macedonia was standing beseeching him and saying,
"Come over to Macedonia and help us." [10]And when he had seen the vision, immediately we sought to go on into Macedonia, concluding that God had called us to
preach the gospel to them.*

Rom 8:9

Macedonia

[11]Setting sail therefore from Troas we made a direct voyage to Samothrace, and the
following day to Neapolis, [12]and from there to Philippi, which is the leading city of
the district[x] of Macedonia, and a Roman colony.

tentabant ire Bithyniam, et non permisit eos Spiritus Iesu; [8]cum autem praeterissent Mysiam, descenderunt Troadem. [9]Et visio per noctem Paulo
ostensa est: vir Macedo quidam erat stans et deprecans eum et dicens: «Transiens in Macedoniam, adiuva nos!». [10]Ut autem visum vidit, statim
quaesivimus proficisci in Macedoniam, certi facti quia vocasset nos Deus evangelizare eis. [11]Navigantes autem a Troade recto cursu venimus
Samothraciam et sequenti die Neapolim [12]et inde Philippos, quae est prima partis Macedoniae civitas, colonia. Eramus autem in hac urbe diebus
aliquot commorantes. [13]Die autem sabbatorum egressi sumus foras portam iuxta flumen, ubi putabamus orationem esse, et sedentes loquebamur

As soon as Paul and his companions set out
on this work of evangelization, the Holy Spirit
(here called the "Spirit of Jesus": v. 7) is once
again, as always, their guide: "There is hardly a
page in the Acts of the Apostles where we fail to
read about the Spirit and the action by which he
guides, directs and enlivens the life and work of
the early Christian community. It is he who
inspires the preaching of St Peter (cf. Acts 4:8),
who strengthens the faith of the disciples (cf.
Acts 4:31), who confirms with his presence the
calling of the Gentiles (cf. Acts 10:44–47), who
sends Saul and Barnabas to the distant lands
where they will open new paths for the teaching
of Jesus (cf. Acts 13:2–4). In a word, his presence and doctrine are everywhere" (St Josemaría
Escrivá, *Christ Is Passing By*, 127).

"Asia" (v. 6): the name of the Roman
province that had Ephesus as its capital.
"Macedonia" (vv. 9–10; see the note on 15:36—
18:22) was regarded as the gateway to Europe,
so the events recounted here show God working
in a special way to see that the Gospel will
spread in that continent: "There can be no doubt
that, in Europe's complex history, Christianity
has been a central and defining element [...].
The Christian faith has shaped the culture of the
Continent and is inextricably bound up with its
history [...]. The path to the future cannot overlook this fact, and Christians are called to renew
their awareness of it, in order to demonstrate
faith's perennial potential. In the building up of

Europe, Christians have a duty to make a specific contribution, one which will be all the more
valid and effective to the extent that they themselves are renewed in the light of the Gospel. In
this way they will carry forward that long history
of holiness which has traversed the various
regions of Europe in the course of these two mil-
lennia" (John Paul II, Letter proclaiming St
Bridget of Sweden, St Catherine of Siena and St
Teresa Benedicta of the Cross Co-patronesses of
Europe).

In verse 10 the narrative shifts into the first
person plural, giving us to understand that Luke
accompanied Paul on this journey (see 16:10–17;
20:5–15; 21:1–18; 27:1—28:16). Luke must
have joined the missionaries at Troas and then
stayed on later at Philippi.

16:11–15 Philippi was a prosperous city founded
by the father of Alexander the Great (in the
fourth century BC). Augustus raised it to the
status of a *colonia* and endowed it with many
privileges. Very few Jews lived in the city, as can
be seen from the fact that it had no synagogue
(for there to be a synagogue there had to be at
least ten Jewish men in a town or neighbourhood). The text mentions only a group of women
who meet for prayer by the river—a location
probably chosen to allow for purification rites.

This brief and beautiful episode shows a
drama of the divine gift of vocation and a grateful human response. It is God who opens this

x The Greek text is uncertain

The conversion of Lydia

Acts 13:5, 14

We remained in this city some days; [13]and on the sabbath day we went outside the gate to the riverside, where we supposed there was a place of prayer;* and we sat down and spoke to the women who had come together. [14]One who heard us was a woman named Lydia, from the city of Thyatira, a seller of purple goods, who was a worshipper of God. The Lord opened her heart to give heed to what was said by

Acts 10:44, 48

Paul. [15]And when she was baptized, with her household, she besought us, saying, "If you have judged me to be faithful to the Lord, come to my house and stay." And she prevailed upon us.

Curing of a possessed girl. Imprisonment of Paul

Acts 19:15, 24

Mt 8:29

Mk 16:17

[16]As we were going to the place of prayer, we were met by a slave girl who had a spirit of divination and brought her owners much gain by soothsaying. [17]She followed Paul and us, crying, "These men are servants of the Most High God, who proclaim to you the way of salvation." [18]And this she did for many days. But Paul was annoyed, and turned and said to the spirit, "I charge you in the name of Jesus Christ to come out of her." And it came out that very hour.

mulieribus, quae convenerant. [14]Et quaedam mulier nomine Lydia, purpuraria civitatis Thyatirenorum colens Deum, audiebat, cuius Dominus aperuit cor intendere his, quae dicebantur a Paulo. [15]Cum autem baptizata esset et domus eius, deprecata est dicens: «Si iudicastis me fidelem Domino esse, introite in domum meam et manete»; et coegit nos. [16]Factum est autem euntibus nobis ad orationem, puellam quandam habentem spiritum pythonem obviare nobis, quae quaestum magnum praestabat dominis suis divinando. [17]Haec subsecuta Paulum et nos clamabat dicens: «Isti homines servi Dei Altissimi sunt, qui annuntiant vobis viam salutis». [18]Hoc autem faciebat multis diebus. Dolens autem Paulus et conversus spiritui dixit: «Praecipio tibi in nomine Iesu Christi exire ab ea»; et exiit eadem hora. [19]Videntes autem domini eius quia exivit spes quaestus eorum,

woman's heart (v. 14), for "no one can give his assent to the Gospel message in a truly salvific way except it be by the light and inspiration of the Holy Spirit: he it is who gives to all the power necessary for affirming and believing the truth" (Vatican I, *Dei Filius*, chap. 3). But then (v. 15) Lydia shows her appreciation in a practical way: "Look at her wisdom, how full of humility her words are: 'If you have judged me to be faithful to the Lord.' [...] See how she straightaway bears fruit and accounts her calling a great gain" (St John Chrysostom, *In Acta Apostolorum*, 35, 1). The first fruit of Christianity in Europe is the response of this woman to her calling: "These women, and others afterwards, *played an active and important role in the life of the early Church*, in building up from its foundations the first Christian community—and subsequent communities—*through their own charisms and their varied service*. The apostolic writings note their names [...]. The same thing is repeated down the centuries, from one generation to the next, as the *history of the Church* demonstrates. By defending the dignity of women and their vocation, the Church has shown honour and gratitude for those women

who —faithful to the Gospel—have shared in every age in the apostolic mission of the whole People of God. They are the holy martyrs, virgins, and mothers of families, who bravely bore witness to their faith and passed on the Church's faith and tradition by bringing up their children in the spirit of the Gospel. [...] In our own days too the Church is constantly enriched by the witness of the many women who fulfil their vocation to holiness. Holy women are an incarnation of the feminine ideal; they are also a model for all Christians, a model of the *'sequela Christi'*, an example of how the Bride must respond with love to the love of the Bridegroom" (John Paul II, *Mulieris dignitatem*, 27).

16:16–24 In Greek mythology Python was a serpent which uttered the Delphic oracles; hence *spiritus pythonis*, the "spirit of divination" (v. 16) attributed to this slave girl. St Paul decides that it is the devil who is at work in her, and he decides to cast him out: "The apostles were displeased to be honoured and praised by the evil spirit, just as our Lord rejected the devil who proclaimed him to the Jews" (St Ephrem, *Commentarii in Acta*, ad loc.).

¹⁹But when her owners saw that their hope of gain was gone, they seized Paul and Silas and dragged them into the market place before the rulers; ²⁰and when they had brought them to the magistrates they said, "These men are Jews and they are disturbing our city. ²¹They advocate customs which it is not lawful for us Romans to accept or practise." ²²The crowd joined in attacking them; and the magistrates tore the garments off them and gave orders to beat them with rods. ²³And when they had inflicted many blows upon them, they threw them into prison, charging the jailer to keep them safely. ²⁴Having received this charge, he put them into the inner prison and fastened their feet in the stocks.

1 Kings 18:17

2 Cor 11:25
Phil 1:30
1 Thess 2:2
2 Cor 11:25

Baptism of the jailer

²⁵But about midnight Paul and Silas were praying and singing hymns to God, and the prisoners were listening to them, ²⁶and suddenly there was a great earthquake, so that the foundations of the prison were shaken; and immediately all the doors were opened and every one's fetters were unfastened. ²⁷When the jailer woke and saw that the prison doors were open, he drew his sword and was about to kill himself, supposing that the prisoners had escaped. ²⁸But Paul cried with a loud voice, "Do not harm yourself, for we are all here." ²⁹And he called for lights and rushed in, and

Col 3:16

Acts 12:6-11

Acts 12:18-19

apprehendentes Paulum et Silam traxerunt in forum ad principes ²⁰et producentes eos magistratibus dixerunt: «Hi homines conturbant civitatem nostram, cum sint Iudaei, ²¹et annuntiant mores, quos non licet nobis suscipere neque facere cum simus Romani». ²²Et concurrit plebs adversus eos, et magistratus scissis tunicis eorum iusserunt virgis caedi ²³et, cum multas plagas eis imposuissent, miserunt eos in carcerem, praecipientes custodi, ut caute custodiret eos; ²⁴qui cum tale praeceptum accepisset, misit eos in interiorem carcerem et pedes eorum strinxit in ligno. ²⁵Media autem nocte Paulus et Silas orantes laudabant Deum, et audiebant eos, qui in custodia erant; ²⁶subito vero terraemotus factus est magnus, ita ut moverentur fundamenta carceris, et aperta sunt statim ostia omnia, et universorum vincula soluta sunt. ²⁷Expergefactus autem custos carceris et videns apertas ianuas carceris, evaginato gladio volebat se interficere, aestimans fugisse vinctos. ²⁸Clamavit autem Paulus magna voce dicens: «Nihil feceris tibi mali; universi enim hic sumus». ²⁹Petitoque lumine intro cucurrit et tremefactus procidit Paulo et Silae ³⁰et producens eos foras

By casting out this spirit, for the first time Paul comes into conflict with non-Jews. The opposition does not take the form of a riot, as it did in cities of Asia Minor (13:50; 14:5, 19), but of a civil suit before local magistrates. Their ruling seems disproportionate to the circumstances, and quite unjustified. That may be why Paul later demands a form of reparation (see 16:35-40).

16:25-34 Paul and Silas spend the night in prayer (v. 25). St John Chrysostom uses this passage to encourage people to sanctify night-time rest: "Show by your example that the night-time is not just for recovering the strength of your body: it is also a help in sanctifying your soul. [...] You do not have to say long prayers; one prayer, said well, is enough. [...] Offer God this sacrifice of a moment of prayer and he will reward you" (*In Acta Apostolorum*, 36). St Bede focuses on the example that Paul and Silas give to Christians who are going through a time of trial: "The piety and energy which fires the heart

of the apostles expresses itself in prayer and brings them to sing hymns even in prison. Their praise causes the earth to move, the foundations to quake, the doors to open and even their fetters to break. Similarly, that Christian who rejoices when he is happy, let him rejoice also in his weakness, when he is tempted, so that Christ's strength comes to his aid. And then let him praise the Lord with hymns, as Paul and Silas did in the darkness of their prison, and sing with the psalmist, 'Thou dost encompass me with deliverance' (Ps 32:7)" (*Expositio Actuum Apostolorum*, ad loc.).

Here, as also happens in other places in the New Testament (see 16:15; 18:8; 1 Cor 1:16), reference is made to the baptism of a whole household (v. 33). When the Church recommends that children be baptized, she notes that this practice goes back to the apostles: "The practice of infant Baptism is an immemorial tradition of the Church. There is explicit testimony to this practice from the second century on, and it is quite possible that, from the beginning of the

trembling with fear he fell down before Paul and Silas, ³⁰and brought them out and said, "Men, what must I do to be saved?" ³¹And they said, "Believe in the Lord Jesus, and you will be saved, you and your household." ³²And they spoke the word of the Lord to him and to all that were in his house. ³³And he took them the same hour of the night, and washed their wounds, and he was baptized at once with all his family. ³⁴Then he brought them up into his house, and set food before them; and he rejoiced with all his household that he had believed in God.

Acts 8:38–39

Release from jail and departure from Philippi

³⁵But when it was day, the magistrates sent the police, saying, "Let those men go." ³⁶And the jailer reported the words to Paul, saying, "The magistrates have sent to let you go; now therefore come out and go in peace." ³⁷But Paul said to them, "They have beaten us publicly, uncondemned, men who are Roman citizens, and have thrown us into prison; and do they now cast us out secretly? No! let them come themselves and take us out." ³⁸The police reported these words to the magistrates, and they were afraid when they heard that they were Roman citizens; ³⁹so they came and apologized to them. And they took them out and asked them to leave the city. ⁴⁰So they went out of the prison, and visited Lydia; and when they had seen the brethren, they exhorted them and departed.

Acts 22:25

Acts 22:29

Difficulties with Jews in Thessalonica

1 Thess 2:2

Lk 4:16

17 ¹Now when they had passed through Amphipolis and Apollonia, they came to Thessalonica, where there was a synagogue of the Jews. ²And Paul went in, as was his custom, and for three weeksᵖ he argued with them from the scriptures,

ait: «Domini, quid me oportet facere, ut salvus fiam?». ³¹At illi dixerunt: «Crede in Domino Iesu et salvus eris tu et domus tua». ³²Et locuti sunt ei verbum Domini cum omnibus, qui erant in domo eius. ³³Et tollens eos in illa hora noctis lavit eos a plagis, et baptizatus est ipse et omnes eius continuo; ³⁴cumque perduxisset eos in domum, apposuit mensam et laetatus est cum omni domo sua credens Deo. ³⁵Et cum dies factus esset, miserunt magistratus lictores dicentes: «Dimitte homines illos!». ³⁶Nuntiavit autem custos carceris verba haec Paulo: «Miserunt magistratus, ut dimittamini; nunc igitur exeuntes ite in pace». ³⁷Paulus autem dixit eis: «Caesos nos publice indemnatos, cum homines Romani essemus, miserunt in carcerem; et nunc occulte nos eiciunt? Non ita, sed veniant et ipsi nos educant». ³⁸Nuntiaverunt autem magistratibus lictores verba haec. Timueruntque audito quod Romani essent, ³⁹et venientes deprecati sunt eos et educentes rogabant, ut egrederentur urbem. ⁴⁰Exeuntes autem de carcere introierunt ad Lydiam et, visis fratribus, consolati sunt eos et profecti sunt. [17] ¹Cum autem perambulassent Amphipolim et Apolloniam, venerunt Thessalonicam, ubi erat synagoga Iudaeorum. ²Secundum consuetudinem autem suam Paulus introivit ad eos et per sabbata tria dis-

apostolic preaching, when whole 'households' received baptism, infants may also have been baptized" (*Catechism of the Catholic Church*, 1252). This practice is not simply a tradition; it has a sound doctrinal basis: "The sheer gratuitousness of the grace of salvation is particularly manifest in infant Baptism. The Church and the parents would deny a child the priceless grace of becoming a child of God were they not to confer Baptism shortly after birth" (ibid., 1250).

16:35–40 The fact that St Paul claims his rights under the law as a Roman citizen is a reminder that Christians do not cease to be citizens just because they are Christians. Although ancient Roman law forbade the flogging of Roman citizens, from the start of the empire it became per-

missible—though, of course, the person had first to be found guilty.

"Magistrates" (v. 36): in the Roman empire a *praetor* was a magistrate exercising jurisdiction in Rome or in the provinces. The "police" (*lictores*: v. 35) were officials who walked in front of higher magistrates bearing the insignia of Roman justice. The magistrates' fear is very understandable given the context of the time: only very few people had the privilege of Roman citizenship, and the provincial authorities ensured that Romans were always treated properly.

17:1–9 Thessalonica was the seat of the Roman governor of the province of Macedonia; it was about 150 kilometres (93 miles) from Philippi.

p Or *sabbaths*

³explaining and proving that it was necessary for the Christ to suffer and to rise from the dead, and saying, "This Jesus, whom I proclaim to you, is the Christ." ⁴And some of them were persuaded, and joined Paul and Silas; as did a great many of the devout Greeks and not a few of the leading women. ⁵But the Jews were jealous, and taking some wicked fellows of the rabble, they gathered a crowd, set the city in an uproar, and attacked the house of Jason, seeking to bring them out to the people. ⁶And when they could not find them, they dragged Jason and some of the brethren before the city authorities, crying, "These men who have turned the world upside down have come here also, ⁷and Jason has received them; and they are all acting against the decrees of Caesar, saying that there is another king, Jesus." ⁸And the people and the city authorities were disturbed when they heard this. ⁹And when they had taken security from Jason and the rest, they let them go.

Lk 24:25–27, 46–47
Acts 18:5
Acts 17:12

1 Thess 2:14

Acts 24:5

Lk 23:2
Jn 19:12–15

Reception in Beroea

¹⁰The brethren immediately sent Paul and Silas away by night to Beroea; and when they arrived they went into the Jewish synagogue. ¹¹Now these Jews were more noble than those in Thessalonica, for they received the word with all eagerness, examining the scriptures daily to see if these things were so. ¹²Many of them there-

serebat eis de Scripturis ³adaperiens et comprobans quia Christum oportebat pati et resurgere a mortuis, et: «Hic est Christus, Iesus, quem ego annuntio vobis». ⁴Et quidam ex eis crediderunt et adiuncti sunt Paulo et Silae et de colentibus Graecis multitudo magna et mulieres nobiles non paucae. ⁵Zelantes autem Iudaei assumentesque de foro viros quosdam malos et turba facta concitaverunt civitatem, et assistentes domui Iasonis quaerebant eos producere in populum. ⁶Et cum non invenissent eos, trahebant Iasonem et quosdam fratres ad politarchas clamantes: «Qui orbem concitaverunt, isti et huc venerunt, ⁷quos suscepit Iason; et hi omnes contra decreta Caesaris faciunt, regem alium dicentes esse, Iesum». ⁸Concitaverunt autem plebem et politarchas audientes haec; ⁹et accepto satis ab Iasone et a ceteris, dimiserunt eos. ¹⁰Fratres vero confestim per noctem dimiserunt Paulum et Silam in Beroeam; qui cum advenissent, in synagogam Iudaeorum introierunt. ¹¹Hi autem erant nobiliores eorum, qui sunt Thessalonicae, qui susceperunt verbum cum omni aviditate, cotidie scrutantes Scripturas si haec ita se haberent. ¹²Et multi quidem cre-

Founded in the fourth century BC and declared a "free city" by Augustus in 42 BC, it contained a Jewish colony, as can be seen from the fact that there was a synagogue. Paul must have stayed in Thessalonica for a number of weeks, during which time he received donations from the Christians at Philippi (see Phil 4:16) but had to work "night and day" to earn his keep (cf. 1 Thess 2:9). It was a time of difficulties (cf. vv. 5–8) and consolations (cf. v. 4), as he would recall later in his letters to the Thessalonians (see 1 Thess 1:6–7; 2 Thess 3:7–8).

St Luke refers to the magistrates of Thessalonica as "politarchs" (v. 6). Recently discovered inscriptions confirm that this term was then in use. Thessalonica, as a "free city", had a popular assembly empowered to investigate the charges brought against people. The Jews accuse Paul of two crimes—causing civil unrest, and putting forward "another king"; in other words, high treason. These are exactly the same crimes as were levelled against our Lord (see Lk 23:2; Jn 19:12). His accusers have clearly distorted

Paul's teaching (he would certainly have spoken of Christ as the Lord); he preached about the messianic Kingdom, but they alleged that he had claimed an earthly king was about to arrive and usurp the existing powers: "God opens the lips of those who utter divine words", Origen writes, "but I fear that it is the devil who opens other people's mouths" (*Homiliae in Exodum*, 3, 2). The magistrates listen to the charges, but they accept Jason's security and the charges are dropped.

17:10–15 The Jews of Beroea have more open hearts and minds, which facilitates their belief in the Lord. Luke explicitly mentions their nobility, interest and diligence (see v. 11): "It is a fact that the teaching of the truth is differently received depending on the listeners' dispositions. The Word shows everyone what is good and what is bad; if a person is predisposed to do what is proclaimed to him, his soul is in the light; if he is not and he has not decided to fix his soul's gaze on the light of truth, then he will remain in the

fore believed, with not a few Greek women of high standing as well as men. [13]But when the Jews of Thessalonica learned that the word of God was proclaimed by Paul at Beroea also, they came there too, stirring up and inciting the crowds. [14]Then the brethren immediately sent Paul off on his way to the sea, but Silas and Timothy remained there. [15]Those who conducted Paul brought him as far as Athens; and receiving a command for Silas and Timothy to come to him as soon as possible, they departed.

Acts 14:2

Paul in Athens

[16]Now while Paul was waiting for them at Athens, his spirit was provoked within him as he saw that the city was full of idols. [17]So he argued in the synagogue with the Jews and the devout persons, and in the market place every day with those who chanced to be there. [18]Some also of the Epicurean and Stoic philosophers met him. And some said, "What would this babbler say?" Others said, "He seems to be a preacher of foreign divinities"—because he preached Jesus and the resurrection. [19]And they took hold of him and brought him to the Areopagus, saying, "May we know what this new teaching is which you present? [20]For you bring some strange things to our ears; we wish to know therefore what these things mean." [21]Now all the Athenians and the foreigners who lived there spent their time in nothing except telling or hearing something new.

Acts 14:7–17

diderunt ex eis et Graecarum mulierum honestarum et virorum non pauci. [13]Cum autem cognovissent in Thessalonica Iudaei quia et Beroeae annuntiatum est a Paulo verbum Dei, venerunt et illuc commoventes et turbantes multitudinem. [14]Statimque tunc Paulum dimiserunt fratres, ut iret usque ad mare; Silas autem et Timotheus remanserunt ibi. [15]Qui autem deducebant Paulum, perduxerunt usque Athenas, et accepto mandato ad Silam et Timotheum, ut quam celerrime venirent ad illum, profecti sunt. [16]Paulus autem cum Athenis eos exspectaret, irritabatur spiritus eius in ipso videns idololatriae deditam civitatem. [17]Disputabat igitur in synagoga cum Iudaeis et colentibus et in foro per omnes dies ad eos, qui aderant. [18]Quidam autem ex Epicureis et Stoicis philosophi disserebant cum eo. Et quidam dicebant: «Quid vult seminiverbius hic dicere?»; alii vero: «Novorum daemoniorum videtur annuntiator esse», quia Iesum et resurrectionem evangelizabat. [19]Et apprehensum eum ad Areopagum duxerunt dicentes: «Possumus scire quae est haec nova, quae a te dicitur doctrina? [20]Mira enim quaedam infers auribus nostris; volumus ergo scire quidnam velint haec esse». [21]Athenienses autem omnes et advenae hospites ad nihil aliud vacabant nisi aut dicere aut audire aliquid novi. [22]Stans autem Paulus in medio Areopagi ait: «Viri Athenienses, per omnia quasi superstitiosiores vos video; [23]praeteriens enim et videns simulacra vestra inveni

darkness of ignorance" (St Gregory of Nyssa, *De vita Moysis*, 2, 65).

17:16–21 The account of Paul's stay in Athens is detailed and nuanced. It depicts the first hearing of the Gospel by pagans in Greece. The audience included both ordinary people and intellectuals. This is an important episode in the transmission of the Christian message, for we see the capacity of Gospel preaching to adapt itself to people of different outlooks and levels of culture, while remaining completely true to itself. In the Tradition of the Church, particularly in the early times, preachers were well aware that pagan peoples, too, had a certain understanding of the Truth that prepared them to accept Christ, who *is* Truth: "I declare that I prayed and strove with all my might to be known as a Christian, not because the teachings of Plato are completely different from those of Christ, but because they are not in

all respects the same; neither are those of other writers, Stoics, the poets and the historians. For each discoursed rightly, seeing through his participation in the seminal divine Word what related to it. But they that have uttered contrary opinions clearly do not have sound knowledge and irrefutable wisdom. Whatever has been uttered aright by any man in any place belongs to Christians; for, next to God, we worship and love the Word which is from the unbegotten and ineffable God. [...] The profane authors could only dimly perceive the truth, and that only through the seed of reason [*logos*, word] implanted in them" (St Justin, *Apologia*, 2, 13, 2–5).

At the start of his account, Luke notes the Apostle's zeal (v. 16) and shows how it expresses itself in the way he evangelizes Jews and pagans. Following his normal practice, Paul preaches in the synagogue, but he also speaks in the "market place" (v. 17), the *ágora*, the city's

Paul's speech in the Areopagus

²²So Paul, standing in the middle of the Areopagus, said: "Men of Athens, I perceive that in every way you are very religious. ²³For as I passed along, and observed the objects of your worship, I found also an altar with this inscription, 'To an unknown god.' What therefore you worship as unknown, this I proclaim to you. ²⁴The God who made the world and everything in it, being Lord of heaven and earth, does not live in shrines made by man, ²⁵nor is he served by human hands, as though he needed anything, since he himself gives to all men life and breath and everything. ²⁶And he made from one every nation of men to live on all the face of the earth, having determined allotted periods and the boundaries of their habitation, ²⁷that they should seek God, in the hope that they might feel after him and find him. Yet he is not far from each one of us, ²⁸for

'In him we live and move and have our being';
as even some of your poets have said,
'For we are indeed his offspring.'

Is 42:5
Acts 14:15
Ps 50:10–12
1 Kings 8:27

Deut 32:8
2 Mac 7:23
Deut 4:29
Is 55:6
Ps 145:18
Jer 23:23
Rom 1:19

et aram in qua scriptum erat: "Ignoto deo". Quod ergo ignorantes colitis, hoc ego annuntio vobis. ²⁴Deus, qui fecit mundum et omnia, quae in eo sunt, hic, caeli et terrae cum sit Dominus, non in manufactis templis inhabitat, ²⁵nec manibus humanis colitur indigens aliquo, cum ipse det omnibus vitam et inspirationem et omnia; ²⁶fecitque ex uno omne genus hominum inhabitare super universam faciem terrae, definiens statuta tempora et terminos habitationis eorum, ²⁷quaerere Deum si forte attrectent eum et inveniant, quamvis non longe sit ab unoquoque nostrum. ²⁸In ipso enim vivimus et movemur et sumus, sicut et quidam vestrum poetarum dixerunt: "Ipsius enim et genus sumus". ²⁹Genus ergo cum simus Dei, non

main square where people gathered to debate the political questions of the day, though it was also used for informal, everyday social and commercial exchanges, being also a marketplace. The "Areopagus" (v. 19) was originally the name of a hill to the northwest of the acropolis of Athens; later it became the name of the tribunal where legal cases were heard. In Paul's time, the name applied both to the hill and to the tribunal, which, for some time past, had been transferred to the Royal Gate in the *ágora*.

Luke shows us Paul in conversation with Epicureans and Stoics (v. 18). The Epicureans, disciples of Epicurus (341–270 BC) tended to be rather materialistic; they argued that there were no gods, or that, if there were any, they took no interest in the doings of mortals; Epicurean ethics stressed the importance of pleasure and a life of ease. The Stoics, who followed Zeno of Citium (340–265 BC) saw the *logos* as the cause that shapes and directs the entire universe and the lives of those who inhabit it; the cause which is the Reason for everything that exists; the ultimate principle, immanent in matter. This is a pantheistic notion of the world. Stoic ethics stresses individual responsibility and self-sufficiency, but although this philosophy speaks a great deal about freedom, it sees Fate as playing a determining role in people's lives.

17:22–34 This is not Paul's first address to pagans that is reported in Acts (see 14:8–18), but it is the longest, and it is probably the first model we have of the Christian apologetical method. Paul seeks to show the reasonableness of Christianity and the fact that this religion can hold its own with the best of human thought. The speaker is clearly the same person who wrote the first three chapters of the Letter to the Romans— someone who has had a great deal of experience in preaching the Gospel to pagans, who uses a method that consists in speaking first about the one, true, living God and then proclaiming Jesus Christ, the divine Saviour of all mankind (cf. 2 Tim 1:9–10).

The central point of the address is that human beings have been created by God and, therefore, retain a "nostalgia" for God that impels them to seek him. The Fathers of the Church like to expand on this idea: "If a man raises his eyes above the immediate, physical horizons of this world and, freed from the slavery of his wild passions, examines his soul sincerely and honestly, he will discover in his own nature God's love for us and the Creator's plan for the world. He will see that man's desire for the good and the beautiful is natural and intrinsic to him, and that his unwavering and joyous love for the blessed Image of which he himself is a copy is a

Acts 19:26
Rom 1:22–23

Rom 3:25–26

Lk 24:47
Ps 9:7; 96:13; 98:9
Acts 10:42
1 Pet 4:5

²⁹Being then God's offspring, we ought not to think that the Deity is like gold, or silver, or stone, a representation by the art and imagination of man. ³⁰The times of ignorance God overlooked, but now he commands all men everywhere to repent, ³¹because he has fixed a day on which he will judge the world in righteousness by a man whom he has appointed, and of this he has given asssurance to all men by raising him from the dead."

³²Now when they heard of the resurrection of the dead, some mocked; but others said, "We will hear you again about this." ³³So Paul went out from among them. ³⁴But some men joined him and believed, among them Dionysius the Areopagite and a woman named Damaris and others with them.

Paul in Corinth, with Aquila and Priscilla

Rom 16:3
1 Cor 16:19
2 Tim 4:19

18 ¹After this he left Athens and went to Corinth. ²And he found a Jew named Aquila, a native of Pontus, lately come from Italy with his wife Priscilla,

debemus aestimare auro aut argento aut lapidi, sculpturae artis et cogitationis hominis, divinum esse simile. ³⁰Et tempora quidem ignorantiae despiciens Deus, nunc annuntiat hominibus, ut omnes ubique paenitentiam agant, ³¹eo quod statuit diem, in qua iudicaturus est orbem in iustitia in viro, quem constituit, fidem praebens omnibus suscitans eum a mortuis». ³²Cum audissent autem resurrectionem mortuorum, quidam quidem irridebant, quidam vero dixerunt: «Audiemus te de hoc iterum». ³³Sic Paulus exivit de medio eorum. ³⁴Quidam vero viri adhaerentes ei crediderunt, in quibus et Dionysius Areopagita et mulier nomine Damaris et alii cum eis. [18] ¹Post haec discedens ab Athenis venit Corinthum. ²Et inveniens quendam Iudaeum nomine Aquilam, Ponticum genere, qui nuper venerat ab Italia, et Priscillam uxorem eius, eo quod praecepisset

seed within his soul" (St Gregory of Nyssa, *De instituto christiano*).

After an introduction designed to catch listeners' attention and register the main theme (vv. 22–23), the speech appears to be structured in three parts, communicating these truths: (1) God is the Lord of the world and does not need to live in temples built by human hands (vv. 24–25a); (2) man has been created by God and is dependent on him for everything (vv. 25b–27a); (3) there is a special relationship between God and man, such that idolatry is a serious error (vv. 27a–29). Then, in his conclusion, Paul exhorts his listeners to shed their mistaken notions about God and repent their sins, being ever-mindful of the fact that there will be a Last Judgment conducted by the risen Jesus (vv. 30–31).

The quotation cited by St Paul in v. 28 is taken from the Stoic poet Aratus (third century BC), where it is spoken in the first person. The plural form used by the Apostle seems to come from a nearly identical line in a hymn to Zeus written by Cleanthes (also third century BC). Paul is trying to win over his listeners, to encourage them to be well-disposed to what he has to say; moreover, these invocations of pagan writers show the respect that Paul and Christians in general have for every manifestation of truth to be found in human culture: "There are aspects of profane culture

which should not be rejected when the time comes to grow in virtue. Natural moral philosophy can, in fact, be the companion of one who wants to lead a higher life [...], provided that its fruit does not carry any alien contamination" (St Gregory of Nyssa, *De vita Moysis*, 2, 37).

But Paul's address provokes different responses at different moments. As soon as he speaks about the resurrection of the dead, there is loud controversy: "It is very commonly accepted that the life of the human person continues in a spiritual fashion after death. But how can we believe that this body, so clearly mortal, could rise to everlasting life?" (*Catechism of the Catholic Church*, 996). For this, faith is required, and God gives faith and understanding to those who seek him with a sincere heart (see v. 34): "We firmly believe that human nature cannot look for God or see him clearly if it does not receive help from the one for whom it seeks. He is seen by those who have done all they can in their search for him and have discovered that they need him" (Origen, *Contra Celsum*, 7, 42).

18:1–11 Paul must have arrived in Corinth somewhat dejected by his reception in Athens, and very short of money. Some time later he would write: "And I was with you in weakness and in much fear and trembling; and my speech

because Claudius had commanded all the Jews to leave Rome. And he went to see
them; 3and because he was of the same trade he stayed with them, and they worked, 1 Cor 4:12
for by trade they were tentmakers. 4And he argued in the synagogue every sabbath,
and persuaded Jews and Greeks.

Preaching to Jews and Gentiles

5When Silas and Timothy arrived from Macedonia, Paul was occupied with preach- Acts 17:14–15
ing, testifying to the Jews that the Christ was Jesus. 6And when they opposed and Lk 9:5; 10:11 Acts 13:46, 51; 20:26; 28:28
reviled him, he shook out his garments and said to them, "Your blood be upon your
heads! I am innocent. From now on I will go to the Gentiles." 7And he left there and
went to the house of a man named Titius[q] Justus, a worshipper of God; his house
was next door to the synagogue. 8Crispus, the ruler of the synagogue, believed in the 1 Cor 1:14
Lord, together with all his household; and many of the Corinthians hearing Paul
believed and were baptized. 9And the Lord said to Paul one night in a vision, "Do 1 Cor 2:3

Claudius discedere omnes Iudaeos a Roma, accessit ad eos 3et, quia eiusdem erat artis, manebat apud eos et operabatur; erant autem scenofactoriae artis. 4Disputabat autem in synagoga per omne sabbatum suadebatque Iudaeis et Graecis. 5Cum venissent autem de Macedonia Silas et Timotheus, instabat verbo Paulus testificans Iudaeis esse Christum Iesum. 6Contradicentibus autem eis et blasphemantibus, excutiens vestimenta dixit ad eos: «Sanguis vester super caput vestrum! Mundus ego. Ex hoc nunc ad gentes vadam». 7Et migrans inde intravit in domum cuiusdam nomine Titi Iusti, colentis Deum, cuius domus erat coniuncta synagogae. 8Crispus autem archisynagogus credidit Domino cum omni domo sua, et multi Corinthiorum audientes credebant et baptizabantur. 9Dixit autem Dominus nocte per visionem Paulo: «Noli timere, sed loquere et ne

and my message were not in plausible words of wisdom, but in demonstration of the Spirit and power" (1 Cor 2:3–4). Corinth was a very cosmopolitan city and an important centre of trade. It stood on an isthmus between two gulfs (today linked by a canal). Ships came into Corinth from all over the world. Low moral standards, an obsession with money-making, and the vulgar cult of Aphrodite made Corinth appear not to be the best ground in which to sow the word of God (see Paul's description of the pagan world in Romans 1:18–32, which he in fact wrote in Corinth). However, God's Word is more powerful than human beings; and his message of salvation can change hearts.

In his work at Corinth, Paul receives a great deal of help from Aquila and Priscilla (vv. 2–4), a married couple who later travel with him to Ephesus (see 18:18) and later still will return to Rome (see Rom 16:3). The contribution made by this Christian husband and wife in the early years of the spread of the Gospel stands as an example of what the Church expects of her faithful: "The Christian family's faith and evangelizing mission also possesses this catholic missionary inspiration. The sacrament of marriage takes up and reproposes the task of defending and spreading the faith, a task that has its roots in Baptism and Confirmation, and makes Christian married couples and parents witnesses of Christ 'to the end of the earth' (Acts 1:8) [...] Just as at the dawn of Christianity Aquila and Priscilla were presented as a missionary couple (cf. Acts 18; Rom 16:3f), so today the Church shows forth her perennial newness and fruitfulness by the presence of Christian couples who [...] work in missionary territories, proclaiming the Gospel and doing service to their fellow man in the love of Jesus Christ" (John Paul II, *Familiaris consortio*, 54).

Claudius was emperor of Rome in the years 41–54. His edict expelling the Jews from the city (v. 2), mentioned also by the Roman historian Seutonius, was issued before the year 50. St Paul earns his own living while at Corinth, but he continues to preach the Gospel (vv. 3–4). "This teaching of Christ on work, based on the example of his life during his years in Nazareth, finds a particularly lively echo *in the teaching of the Apostle Paul*. Paul boasts of working at his trade (he was probably a tentmaker: cf. Acts 18:3), and thanks to that work he was able even as an Apostle to earn his own bread" (John Paul II, *Laborem exercens*, 26). During his year and a half at Corinth, Paul writes letters to the Thessalonians urging them not to neglect their everyday work and responsibilities (see 2 Thess 3:10–12). St John Chrysostom, commenting on

q Other early authorities read *Titus*

Is 41:10; 43:5
Jer 1:8
Jn 10:16

not be afraid, but speak and do not be silent; [10]for I am with you, and no man shall attack you to harm you; for I have many people in this city." [11]And he stayed a year and six months, teaching the word of God among them.

Paul before Gallio

1 Thess 2:14

Acts 25:18–19

Jn 18:31
Acts 23:29

[12]But when Gallio was proconsul of Achaia, the Jews made a united attack upon Paul and brought him before the tribunal, [13]saying, "This man is persuading men to worship God contrary to the law." [14]But when Paul was about to open his mouth, Gallio said to the Jews, "If it were a matter of wrongdoing or vicious crime, I should have reason to bear with you, O Jews; [15]but since it is a matter of questions about words and names and your own law, see to it yourselves; I refuse to be a judge of these things." [16]And he drove them from the tribunal. [17]And they all seized Sosthenes, the ruler of the synagogue, and beat him in front of the tribunal. But Gallio paid no attention to this.

taceas, [10]quia ego sum tecum, et nemo apponetur tibi, ut noceat te, quoniam populus est mihi multus in hac civitate». [11]Sedit autem annum et sex menses docens apud eos verbum Dei. [12]Gallione autem proconsule Achaiae, insurrexerunt uno animo Iudaei in Paulum et adduxerunt eum ad tribunal [13]dicentes: «Contra legem hic persuadet hominibus colere Deum». [14]Incipiente autem Paulo aperire os, dixit Gallio ad Iudaeos: «Si quidem esset iniquum aliquid aut facinus pessimum, o Iudaei, merito vos sustinerem; [15]si vero quaestiones sunt de verbo et nominibus et lege vestra, vos

this passage in Acts, says, "Work is man's natural state. Idleness is against his nature. God has placed man in this world to work, and the natural thing for the soul is to be active and not passive" (*In Acta Apostolorum*, 35).

The blindness of the Jews in Corinth (vv. 5–6) once again causes Paul profound sorrow: here is further evidence of the mysterious resistance shown the faith by many of the Chosen People. As he did in Pisidian Antioch (see 13:14, 51), the Apostle shakes the dust of the town from his clothes. The words "From now on I will go to the Gentiles" (v. 6) refer to his preaching in Corinth, for he will continue to evangelize Jews as well as Gentiles wherever his work takes him (see 18:19; 28:17). "The Jews, in truth, who had the prophecies and always looked for the coming of Christ, not only did not recognize him, but, far beyond that, even mistreated him. But the Gentiles, who had never even heard anything of Christ until his apostles went from Jerusalem and preached about him and gave them the prophecies, were filled with joy and faith, and turned away from their idols, and dedicated themselves to the Unbegotten God through Christ" (St Justin, *Apologia*, 1, 49, 5).

However, Paul's preaching in Corinth does begin to bear fruit (see vv. 7–8) among some Jews, such as Crispus and his family, as well as among many Gentiles. The extraordinary gifts that Paul receives, such as the vision in which our Lord speaks to him (vv. 9–10), reflect the degree of heroism and commitment that God has asked of him. When people receive consolation in prayer, this is not designed to lessen the effort involved in their following Christ; rather, it means the person should make even greater efforts and accept even greater responsibility with the help of our Lord: "I am well aware that the trials given by God to contemplatives are intolerable; and they are of such a kind that, were he not to feed them with consolations, they could not be borne. It is clear that [...] the more he loves them, the greater will be their trials" (St Teresa of Avila, *Way of Perfection*, 18, 1).

18:12–17 The proconsul Gallio was a brother of the Stoic philosopher Seneca. From an inscription found at Delphi *c*.1900, we learn that Gallio began his proconsulship of Achaia (of which Corinth was the capital), in July 51. Paul must have appeared before Gallio around the end of that year. This is one of the most exact established dates in the life of the Apostle.

Sosthenes (v. 17), who must have been sympathetic to the Christian message, suffered as a result of this persecution. Some scholars have speculated that this is the same person who later appears as either the co-author or the amanuensis of 1 Corinthians (see 1 Cor 1:1).

Return to Antioch via Ephesus

[18]After this Paul stayed many days longer and then took leave of the brethren and sailed for Syria, and with him Priscilla and Aquila. At Cenchreae he cut his hair, for he had a vow. [19]And they came to Ephesus, and he left them there; but he himself went into the synagogue and argued with the Jews. [20]When they asked him to stay for a longer period, he declined; [21]but on taking leave of them he said, "I will return to you if God wills," and he set sail from Ephesus.

[22]When he had landed at Caesarea, he went up and greeted the church, and then went down to Antioch.

Rom 16:3–4
Acts 21:24
Num 6:18

Acts 19:8

1 Cor 4:19

Acts 21:15

11. ST PAUL'S THIRD APOSTOLIC JOURNEY*

Galatia and Phrygia

[23]After spending some time there he departed and went from place to place through the region of Galatia and Phrygia, strengthening all the disciples.

ipsi videritis; iudex ego horum nolo esse». [16]Et minavit eos a tribunali. [17]Apprehendentes autem omnes Sosthenen, principem synagogae, percutiebant ante tribunal; et nihil horum Gallioni curae erat. [18]Paulus vero, cum adhuc sustinuisset dies multos, fratribus valefaciens navigabat Syriam, et cum eo Priscilla et Aquila, qui sibi totonderat in Cenchreis caput; habebat enim votum. [19]Deveneruntque Ephesum, et illos ibi reliquit, ipse vero ingressus synagogam disputabat cum Iudaeis. [20]Rogantibus autem eis, ut ampliore tempore maneret, non consensit, [21]sed valefaciens et dicens: «Iterum revertar ad vos Deo volente», navigavit ab Epheso; [22]et descendens Caesaream ascendit et salutavit ecclesiam et descendit Antiochiam. [23]Et facto ibi aliquanto tempore, profectus est perambulans ex ordine Galaticam regionem et Phrygiam, confirmans omnes discipu-

18:18–22 The Apostle now, for the first time, visits Ephesus, the capital of proconsular Asia; it had a population of around 200,000 and was one of the richest cities of the empire. Its most famous building, the Artemision, or temple of Artemis (Diana), was one of the seven wonders of the ancient world. The city's huge amphitheatre could accommodate 23,000 spectators. On this visit, Paul does not stay long, but on his next journey to the region the city will be the centre of his missionary work.

The vow mentioned in v. 18 may have been the vow taken by a Nazirite, a person "consecrated" to God. The Nazirite vow described in Numbers involved (among other things) letting one's hair grow uncut (to symbolize that one was allowing God to take over) and abstaining from all fermented beverages (to show one's resolve to practise self-denial). In the Greek text it is not clear whether it was Paul or Aquila who took the vow, but most commentators are inclined to think it was Paul.

*18:23—20:38 Like the earlier missions, Paul's third apostolic journey starts at Antioch. This one will end in Miletus, with the Apostle leaving for Jerusalem. It is a long journey, but Luke focuses mainly on events in Ephesus.

To begin with, Paul revisits the cities already evangelized in Galatia and Phrygia; this phase may have lasted from the last months of 53 into early 54. He then goes to Ephesus, where he stays almost three years and encounters all kinds of obstacles and difficulties (see 2 Cor 1:8), as he describes in a letter he sends to the Corinthians from there: "To the present hour we hunger and thirst, we are ill-clad and buffeted and homeless [...]. We have become, and are now, as the refuse of the world, the offscouring of all things" (1 Cor 4:11, 13). Despite this suffering, or perhaps because of it, his apostolate is very fruitful and the Christian message spreads across all proconsular Asia (present-day western Turkey), to important cities such as Colossae, Laodicea and Hierapolis; as he writes in 1 Corinthians 16:9, "a wide door for effective work has opened to me".

Leaving Ephesus on account of the revolt of the silversmiths, the Apostle travels to Macedonia and Achaia to visit the churches founded on his second journey—those at Philippi, Thessalonica and Corinth. He stays in that area for three months, during the winter of

Apollos in Ephesus and Corinth

1 Cor 3:6
Tit 3:13

2 Cor 3:1
Acts 19:1

Acts 9:22

Jn 7:39
Acts 8:15–17

Mt 3:6, 11
Acts 13:24

24Now a Jew named Apollos, a native of Alexandria, came to Ephesus. He was an eloquent man, well versed in the scriptures. **25**He had been instructed in the way of the Lord; and being fervent in spirit, he spoke and taught accurately the things concerning Jesus, though he knew only the baptism of John. **26**He began to speak boldly in the synagogue; but when Priscilla and Aquila heard him, they took him and expounded to him the way of God more accurately. **27**And when he wished to cross to Achaia, the brethren encouraged him, and wrote to the disciples to receive him. When he arrived, he greatly helped those who through grace had believed, **28**for he powerfully confuted the Jews in public, showing by the scriptures that the Christ was Jesus.

Disciples of John the Baptist at Ephesus

19 **1**While Apollos was at Corinth, Paul passed through the upper country and came to Ephesus. There he found some disciples. **2**And he said to them, "Did you receive the Holy Spirit when you believed?" And they said, "No, we have never even heard that there is a Holy Spirit." **3**And he said, "Into what then were you baptized?" They said, "Into John's baptism." **4**And Paul said, "John baptized with the bap-

los. **24**Iudaeus autem quidam Apollo nomine, Alexandrinus natione, vir eloquens, devenit Ephesum, potens in Scripturis. **25**Hic erat catechizatus viam Domini et fervens spiritu loquebatur et docebat diligenter ea, quae sunt de Iesu, sciens tantum baptisma Ioannis. **26**Hic ergo coepit fiducialiter agere in synagoga; quem cum audissent Priscilla et Aquila, assumpserunt eum et diligentius exposuerunt ei viam Dei. **27**Cum autem vellet transire in Achaiam, exhortati fratres scripserunt discipulis, ut susciperent eum; qui cum venisset, contulit multum his, qui crediderant per gratiam; **28**vehementer enim Iudaeos revincebat publice ostendens per Scripturas esse Christum Iesum. [**19**] **1**Factum est autem cum Apollo esset Corinthi, ut Paulus, peragratis superioribus partibus, veniret Ephesum et inveniret quosdam discipulos, **2**dixitque ad eos: «Si Spiritum Sanctum accepistis credentes?». At illi ad eum: «Sed neque si Spiritus Sanctus est audivimus». **3**Ille vero ait: «In quo ergo baptizati estis?». Qui dixerunt: «In Ioannis

57/58. On his return journey (to Jerusalem, to bring the money that has been collected), he goes through Macedonia to circumvent a plot against him. He boards ship at Neapolis, the port near Philippi, and stops off at Miletus. There he meets the elders of Ephesus by arrangement. From Miletus he sails to Caesarea and succeeds in reaching Jerusalem in time for Pentecost.

18:24–28 This episode shows just how dedicated Aquila and Priscilla were. Evidence of the same sort of zeal is reflected often in early Christian writings: "We do our very best to warn them [Jews and heretics], as we do you, not to be deluded, for we know full well that whoever can speak out the truth and fails to do so shall be condemned by God" (St Justin, *Dialogus cum Tryphone*, 82, 3).

The apostolic zeal of this married couple proves very effective: they befriend Apollos, a man who becomes a disciple and a powerful preacher (vv. 27–28): "A glimmer of Christ's light had already filtered into the mind of this man. He had heard about our Lord and he passed the news

on to others. But he still had some way to go. He needed to know more if he was to acquire the fullness of the faith and so come to love our Lord truly. A Christian couple, Aquila and Priscilla, hear him speaking; they are not inactive or indifferent. They do not think: 'This man already knows enough; it's not our business to teach him.' They were souls who were really eager to do apostolate and so they approach Apollos" (St Josemaría Escrivá, *Friends of God*, 269).

19:1–7 The presence in Ephesus of a group of disciples who had received only the baptism of John is open to various interpretations. Since they were aware of the Baptist's teachings (they had received his baptism), Paul might have considered them to be already Christian. However, in the New Testament to be a Christian always requires being baptized with the Baptism of Jesus and receiving the Holy Spirit (see 11:16; Jn 3:5; Rom 8:9; 1 Cor 12:3; Gal 3:2), and this is what now happens in the case of these disciples. "The baptism of John did not confer grace, but only prepared the way for grace; and this in three

tism of repentance, telling the people to believe in the one who was to come after him, that is, Jesus." ⁵On hearing this, they were baptized in the name of the Lord Jesus. ⁶And when Paul had laid his hands upon them, the Holy Spirit came on them; and they spoke with tongues and prophesied. ⁷There were about twelve of them in all.

Acts 11:15–16

Paul's preaching and miracles at Ephesus

⁸And he entered the synagogue and for three months spoke boldly, arguing and pleading about the kingdom of God; ⁹but when some were stubborn and disbelieved, speaking evil of the Way before the congregation, he withdrew from them, taking the disciples with him, and argued daily in the hall of Tyrannus.ʳ ¹⁰This continued for two years, so that all the residents of Asia heard the word of the Lord, both Jews and Greeks.

Acts 13:5, 45–47; 14:3

¹¹And God did extraordinary miracles by the hands of Paul, ¹²so that handkerchiefs or aprons were carried away from his body to the sick, and diseases left them and the evil spirits came out of them. ¹³Then some of the itinerant Jewish exorcists undertook to pronounce the name of the Lord Jesus over those who had evil spirits, saying, "I adjure you by the Jesus whom Paul preaches." ¹⁴Seven sons of a Jewish

Mk 6:56
Lk 8:44–47
Acts 5:15
Mk 9:38
Lk 9:49

baptismate». ⁴Dixit autem Paulus: «Ioannes baptizavit baptisma paenitentiae, populo dicens in eum, qui venturus esset post ipsum ut crederent, hoc est in Iesum». ⁵His auditis, baptizati sunt in nomine Domini Iesu; ⁶et cum imposuisset illis manus Paulus, venit Spiritus Sanctus super eos, et loquebantur linguis et prophetabant. ⁷Erant autem omnes viri fere duodecim. ⁸Introgressus autem synagogam cum fiducia loquebatur per tres menses disputans et suadens de regno Dei. ⁹Cum autem quidam indurarentur et non crederent maledicentes viam coram multitudine, discedens ab eis segregavit discipulos, cotidie disputans in schola Tyranni. ¹⁰Hoc autem factum est per biennium, ita ut omnes, qui habitabant in Asia, audirent verbum Domini, Iudaei atque Graeci. ¹¹Virtutesque non quaslibet Deus faciebat per manus Pauli, ¹²ita ut etiam super languidos deferrentur a corpore eius sudaria vel semicinctia, et recederent ab eis languores, et spiritus nequam egrederentur. ¹³Tentaverunt autem quidam et de circumeuntibus Iudaeis exorcistis invocare super eos, qui habebant spiritus malos, nomen Domini Iesu dicentes: «Adiuro vos per Iesum, quem

ways: first by John's teaching, which led people to faith in Christ; second, by accustoming people to the rite of Christ's Baptism; and third, through penance, preparing them to receive the effect of Christ's Baptism" (St Thomas Aquinas, *Summa theologiae*, 3, 38, 3).

In this scene, we can see (in v. 6), as elsewhere in Acts (see 3:1–10 and 14:8–18; 12:1–12 and 16:25–34) many parallels between Paul's ministry and Peter's (see 8:14–17). The unity of spirit and practice in these two apostles in the mission of the Church continued to express itself in many ways: "We celebrate the martyrdom of these two Apostles on the same day. Though they were martyred on different days, their martyrdom was one: first Peter, then Paul. Today's feast is made holy by the blood of the Apostles. We must strive to imitate their faith, their lives, their good works, their suffering and witness and teaching" (St Augustine, *Sermones*, 295, 8).

19:8–20 During the time of the early Church there were many magicians, fortune-tellers and exorcists who were ready to invoke any and

every god they knew of in the Hellenic world. We know, for example, of a papyrus containing a wording similar to the one used by the exorcists who appear in this passage (v. 13); it reads: "I adjure you by Jesus, the God of the Hebrews." But the power of Christian witness cannot be contained in a formula of words: "For the preacher's instruction to exercise its full force," writes St John of the Cross, "there must be two kinds of preparation — that of the preacher and that of the hearer; for, as a rule, the benefit derived from instruction depends on the preparation of the teacher. For this reason it is said, Like master, like pupil. For, when in the Acts of the Apostles those seven sons of that chief priest of the Jews used to cast out devils in the same way as St Paul did, the devil rose up against them [...] and then, attacking them, stripped and wounded them. This was only because they had not the proper preparation" (*Ascent of Mount Carmel*, 3, 45).

The cures worked by Paul are reminiscent of those worked by Peter: just as the people brought their sick so that Peter's shadow would cure

r Other ancient authorities add *from the fifth hour to the tenth*

Lk 4:41
Acts 16:17
high priest named Sceva were doing this. [15]But the evil spirit answered them, "Jesus I know, and Paul I know; but who are you?" [16]And the man in whom the evil spirit was leaped on them, mastered all of them, and overpowered them, so that they fled out of that house naked and wounded.

Books of magic burned

Lk 5:26
Acts 3:10
[17]And this became known to all residents of Ephesus, both Jews and Greeks; and fear fell upon them all; and the name of the Lord Jesus was extolled. [18]Many also of those who were now believers came, confessing and divulging their practices. [19]And a number of those who practised magic arts brought their books together and burned them in the sight of all; and they counted the value of them and found it came to fifty Acts 6:7 thousand pieces of silver. [20]So the word of the Lord grew and prevailed mightily.

Paul's plans for further journeys

Acts 23:11
Rom 15:22–23

Rom 1:13
[21]Now after these events Paul resolved in the Spirit to pass through Macedonia and Achaia and go to Jerusalem, saying, "After I have been there, I must also see Rome." [22]And having sent into Macedonia two of his helpers, Timothy and Erastus, he himself stayed in Asia for a while.

Paulus praedicat». [14]Erant autem cuiusdam Scevae Iudaei principis sacerdotum septem filii, qui hoc faciebant. [15]Respondens autem spiritus nequam dixit eis: «Iesum novi et Paulum scio, vos autem qui estis?». [16]Et insiliens homo in eos, in quo erat spiritus malus, dominatus amborum invaluit contra eos, ita ut nudi et vulnerati effugerent de domo illa. [17]Hoc autem notum factum est omnibus Iudaeis atque Graecis, qui habitabant Ephesi, et cecidit timor super omnes illos, et magnificabatur nomen Domini Iesu. [18]Multique credentium veniebant confitentes et annuntiantes actus suos. [19]Multi autem ex his, qui fuerant curiosa sectati, conferentes libros combusserunt coram omnibus; et computaverunt pretia illorum et invenerunt argenti quinquaginta milia. [20]Ita fortiter verbum Domini crescebat et convalescebat. [21]His autem expletis, proposuit Paulus in Spiritu, transita Macedonia et Achaia, ire Hierosolymam, dicens: «Postquam fuero ibi, oportet me et Romam videre». [22]Mittens autem in Macedoniam

them (5:15), now they flock to Paul seeking cures (vv. 11–12). But what Paul's activity in Ephesus brings most to mind is that of Jesus in Galilee when the crowds jostled around him, trying to touch his garments and be cured (see Mk 6:56). Jesus' way, working miracles that confirmed the truth of his message, is also reflected in Paul's life: "Did the disciples of Jesus learn to do miracles and thereby convince their hearers, or did they not do any? It is quite absurd to say that they did not do any miracles of any kind, and that, in blind faith, [...] they went off everywhere to propagate a new teaching; for what would have kept their spirits up when they had to teach something which was so completely new? But if they did also work miracles, how on earth could these magicians have faced so many dangers to spread a teaching which explicitly forbade the use of magic?" (Origen, *Contra Celsum*, 1, 38).

A holy fear of offending God led the Christians of Ephesus to shun anything that might separate them from him, beginning with the magic arts and the books on those topics.

19:21–41 Artemis was the Greek name of the goddess the Romans called Diana, but through syncretism she was also identified with an oriental goddess of fertility; a statue of Diana was worshipped in the Artemision. Her festivals were celebrated with orgies and attracted large crowds from neighbouring regions. Demetrius and his fellow craftsmen did a brisk trade selling statuettes of Diana to many visitors as souvenirs.

The success of Paul's apostolate at Ephesus can be seen not only in the fact that the silversmiths became alarmed, fearful that their sales would decline, but also in the fact that Paul was on good terms with some of the leaders, the Asiarchs (see v. 31). The text shows that whereas all that concerned the silversmiths was their profits, the town clerk was much more circumspect and measured in his attitude (vv. 35–40). The words of a Christian writer suggest that the Christian message can make a good impression on anyone who examines it calmly and closely. Christians, he says, "obey all the laws laid down, but go beyond the law in their lives. They love all men, and are persecuted by all. They are dis-

The silversmiths' riot in Ephesus

²³About that time there arose no little stir concerning the Way. ²⁴For a man named Demetrius, a silversmith, who made silver shrines of Artemis, brought no little business to the craftsmen. ²⁵These he gathered together, with the workmen of like occupation, and said, "Men, you know that from this business we have our wealth. ²⁶And you see and hear that not only at Ephesus but almost throughout all Asia this Paul has persuaded and turned away a considerable company of people, saying that gods made with hands are not gods. ²⁷And there is danger not only that this trade of ours may come into disrepute but also that the temple of the great goddess Artemis may count for nothing, and that she may even be deposed from her magnificence, she whom all Asia and the world worship."

²⁸When they heard this they were enraged, and cried out, "Great is Artemis of the Ephesians!" ²⁹So the city was filled with the confusion; and they rushed together into the theatre, dragging with them Gaius and Aristarchus, Macedonians who were Paul's companions in travel. ³⁰Paul wished to go in among the crowd, but the disciples would not let him; ³¹some of the Asiarchs also, who were friends of his, sent to him and begged him not to venture into the theatre. ³²Now some cried one thing, some another; for the assembly was in confusion, and most of them did not know why they had come together. ³³Some of the crowd prompted Alexander, whom the Jews had put forward. And Alexander motioned with his hand, wishing to make a defence to the people. ³⁴But when they recognized that he was a Jew, for about two hours they all with one voice cried out, "Great is Artemis of the Ephesians!" ³⁵And when the town clerk had quieted the crowd, he said, "Men of Ephesus, what man is there who does not know that the city of the Ephesians is temple keeper of the great Artemis, and of the sacred stone* that fell from the sky?ˢ ³⁶Seeing then that these things cannot be contradicted, you ought to be quiet and do nothing rash. ³⁷For you have brought these men here who are neither sacrilegious nor blasphemers of our

1 Cor 1:8

Acts 20:4; 27:2

Acts 16:20

duos ex ministrantibus sibi, Timotheum et Erastum, ipse remansit ad tempus in Asia. ²³Facta est autem in illo tempore turbatio non minima de via. ²⁴Demetrius enim quidam nomine, argentarius, faciens aedes argenteas Dianae praestabat artificibus non modicum quaestum; ²⁵quos congregans et eos, qui eiusmodi erant opifices, dixit: «Viri, scitis quia de hoc artificio acquisitio est nobis ²⁶et videtis et auditis quia non solum Ephesi, sed paene totius Asiae Paulus hic suadens avertit multam turbam dicens quoniam non sunt dii, qui manibus fiunt. ²⁷Non solum autem haec periclitatur nobis pars in redargutionem venire, sed et magnae deae Dianae templum in nihilum reputari, et destrui incipiet maiestas eius, quam tota Asia et orbis colit». ²⁸His auditis, repleti sunt ira et clamabant dicentes: «Magna Diana Ephesiorum!», ²⁹et impleta est civitas confusione, et impetum fecerunt uno animo in theatrum, rapto Gaio et Aristarcho Macedonibus, comitibus Pauli. ³⁰Paulo autem volente intrare in populum, non permiserunt discipuli; ³¹quidam autem de Asiarchis, qui erant amici eius, miserunt ad eum rogantes, ne se daret in theatrum. ³²Alii autem aliud clamabant; erat enim ecclesia confusa, et plures nesciebant qua ex causa convenissent. ³³De turba autem instruxerunt Alexandrum, propellentibus eum Iudaeis; Alexander ergo, manu silentio postulato, volebat rationem reddere populo. ³⁴Quem ut cognoverunt Iudaeum esse, vox facta est una omnium quasi per horas duas clamantium: «Magna Diana Ephesiorum!». ³⁵Et cum sedasset scriba turbam dixit: «Viri Ephesii, quis enim est hominum, qui nesciat Ephesiorum civitatem cultricem esse magnae Dianae et simulacri a Iove delapsi? ³⁶Cum ergo his contradici non possit, oportet vos sedatos esse et nihil temere agere. ³⁷Adduxistis enim homines istos neque sacrilegos neque blasphemantes deam nostram. ³⁸Quod si Demetrius et, qui cum eo sunt, artifices habent adversus aliquem causam, conventus forenses aguntur, et proconsules sunt: accusent invicem. ³⁹Si

owned and condemned. They are condemned to death, and thus are born to new life. They are poor, and enrich many by their poverty; they lack all, and possess all. They are dishonoured, and by dishonour they are glorified; they are maligned, and that is proof of their righteousness. They are cursed, and they bless; they are humiliated, and they honour others. They do what is good, and are punished as evildoers; when they are condemned to death, they respond

as though they had been granted new life. The Jews persecute them as strangers, as do the gentiles, though neither can explain the reasons for their hatred. To put it in a few, short words: Christians are in the world as the soul in the body" (*Epistula ad Diognetum*, 5).

Luke refers to Christianity and the Church as "the Way" (v. 23; see 9:2; 19:9; 22:4; 24:14, 22). The term was probably quite commonly used with this meaning by Christians at the time. It

ˢ The meaning of the Greek is uncertain

Acts 18:12

goddess. [38]If therefore Demetrius and the craftsmen with him have a complaint against any one, the courts are open, and there are proconsuls; let them bring charges against one another. [39]But if you seek anything further,[t] it shall be settled in the regular assembly. [40]For we are in danger of being charged with rioting today, there being no cause that we can give to justify this commotion." [41]And when he had said this, he dismissed the assembly.

Paul goes into Macedonia and begins his return journey

20 [1]After the uproar ceased, Paul sent for the disciples and having exhorted them took leave of them and departed for Macedonia. [2]When he had gone through these parts and had given them much encouragement, he came to Greece.

1 Cor 16:5–6

[3]There he spent three months, and when a plot was made against him by the Jews as he was about to set sail for Syria, he determined to return through Macedonia. [4]Sopater of Beroea, the son of Pyrrhus, accompanied him; and of the Thessalonians, Aristarchus and Secundus; and Gaius of Derbe, and Timothy; and the Asians, Tychicus and Trophimus. [5]These went on and were waiting for us at Troas, [6]but we sailed away from Philippi after the days of Unleavened Bread, and in five days we came to them at Troas, where we stayed for seven days.

Celebration of the Eucharist. Eutychus' fall and recovery

Acts 2:42

[7]On the first day of the week, when we were gathered together to break bread,* Paul talked with them, intending to depart on the morrow; and he prolonged his speech until midnight. [8]There were many lights in the upper chamber where we were gathered. [9]And a young man named Eutychus was sitting in the window. He sank into a

---

quid autem ulterius quaeritis, in legitima ecclesia poterit absolvi. [40]Nam et periclitamur argui seditionis hodiernae, cum nullus obnoxius sit, de quo non possimus reddere rationem concursus istius». Et cum haec dixisset, dimisit ecclesiam. [20] [1]Postquam autem cessavit tumultus, accersitis Paulus discipulis et exhortatus eos, valedixit et profectus est, ut iret in Macedoniam. [2]Cum autem perambulasset partes illas et exhortatus eos fuisset multo sermone, venit ad Graeciam; [3]cumque fecisset menses tres, factae sunt illi insidiae a Iudaeis navigaturo in Syriam, habuitque consilium, ut reverteretur per Macedoniam. [4]Comitabatur autem eum Sopater Pyrrhi Beroeensis, Thessalonicensium vero Aristarchus et Secundus et Gaius Derbeus et Timotheus, Asiani vero Tychicus et Trophimus. [5]Hi cum praecessissent, sustinebant nos Troade; [6]nos vero navigavimus post dies Azymorum a Philippis, et venimus ad eos Troadem in diebus quinque, ubi demorati sumus diebus septem. [7]In una autem sabbatorum cum convenissemus ad frangendum panem, Paulus disputabat eis, profecturus in crastinum, protraxitque sermonem usque in mediam noctem. [8]Erant

---

has biblical roots: see Deuteronomy 11:26–33 and 30:15–20, where it means moral and religious lifestyle, and even a rule of conduct: "The preaching of the Gospel is rightly called 'a way', for it is the path that truly leads to the Kingdom of heaven" (St John Chrysostom, *In Acta Apostolorum*, 41, 1).

20:1–6 The sacred writer now picks up the thread of his account of the third journey of St Paul, from which he veered in 19:23. In v. 5 Luke again shifts into first person plural: he may have joined Paul at Philippi, and now be accompanying him. This journey to Macedonia is probably the one mentioned in 2 Corinthians 2:12–13: "When I came to Troas to preach the gospel of Christ, a door was opened for me in the Lord; but my mind could not rest because I

did not find my brother Titus there. So I took leave of them and went on to Macedonia."

20:7–12 In v. 7 we find the first explicit mention in scripture of the Christian custom of meeting on the first day of the week to celebrate the Eucharist (cf. 2:42; 1 Cor 10:16). This custom will be referred to in many later Christian documents: "On the day named after the sun, all the people gather in one place, those who live in the city and those who live in the countryside, and they read the gospels of the apostles and the writings of the prophets, as time allows. Then, when the reading is finished, the one who presides over the gathering preaches, addressing words of exhortation to his listeners, to encourage them to imitate the wonderful deeds they have read about. Then we stand and pray together; and when the

---

t Other ancient authorities read *about their own matters*

deep sleep as Paul talked still longer; and being overcome by sleep, he fell down from the third storey and was taken up dead. [10]But Paul went down and bent over him, and embracing him said, "Do not be alarmed, for his life is in him." [11]And when Paul had gone up and had broken bread and eaten, he conversed with them a long time, until daybreak, and so departed. [12]And they took the lad away alive, and were not a little comforted.

1 Kings 17:17–24

From Troas to Miletus

[13]But going ahead to the ship, we set sail for Assos, intending to take Paul aboard there; for so he had arranged, intending himself to go by land. [14]And when he met us at Assos, we took him on board and came to Mitylene. [15]And sailing from there we came the following day opposite Chios; the next day we touched at Samos; and[u] the day after that we came to Miletus. [16]For Paul had decided to sail past Ephesus, so that he might not have to spend time in Asia; for he was hastening to be at Jerusalem, if possible, on the day of Pentecost.

Acts 18:21

Farewell address to the elders of Ephesus

[17]And from Miletus he sent to Ephesus and called to him the elders of the church. [18]And when they came to him he said to them:

1 Thess 1:5

"You yourselves know how I lived among you all the time from the first day that I set foot in Asia, [19]serving the Lord with all humility and with tears and with trials which befell me through the plots of the Jews; [20]how I did not shrink from declaring to you anything that was profitable, and teaching you in public and from house to

2 Cor 11:23–31
Phil 2:3
2 Tim 4:2

autem lampades copiosae in cenaculo, ubi eramus congregati; [9]sedens autem quidam adulescens nomine Eutychus super fenestram, cum mergeretur somno gravi disputante diutius Paulo, eductus somno cecidit de tertio cenaculo deorsum et sublatus est mortuus. [10]Cum descendisset autem Paulus incubuit super eum et complexus dixit: «Nolite turbari, anima enim ipsius in eo est!». [11]Ascendens autem frangensque panem et gustans satisque allocutus usque in lucem, sic profectus est. [12]Adduxerunt autem puerum viventem et consolati sunt non minime. [13]Nos autem praecedentes navi enavigavimus in Asson, inde suscepturi Paulum, sic enim disposuerat volens ipse per terram iter facere. [14]Cum autem convenisset nos in Asson, assumpto eo, venimus Mitylenen [15]et inde navigantes sequenti die pervenimus contra Chium et alia applicuimus Samum et sequenti venimus Miletum. [16]Proposuerat enim Paulus transnavigare Ephesum, ne qua mora illi fieret in Asia; festinabat enim, si possibile sibi esset, ut diem Pentecosten faceret Hierosolymis. [17]A Mileto autem mittens Ephesum convocavit presbyteros ecclesiae. [18]Qui cum venissent ad eum, dixit eis: «Vos scitis a prima die, qua ingressus sum in Asiam, qualiter vobiscum per omne tempus fuerim, [19]serviens Domino cum omni humilitate et

prayers are ended, the bread, wine and water are brought to the one who presides over the gathering, who offers fervent prayers and gives thanks to God for them. The people answer 'Amen' to his prayers, and then the offerings for which God has been thanked are distributed amongst them all; they receive the communion, and the deacons are charged with bringing communion to all the faithful who are not present at the gathering. [...] We gather together on Sundays because this day was the first of creation, when God began his work on darkness and matter, and also because it is the day of Jesus Christ, our Saviour, who was raised from the dead" (St Justin, *Apologia*, 1, 67).

As St Peter did earlier (see 9:36–41), Paul raises someone from the dead. St Bede sees in this event a certain spiritual symbolism: "The restoring of this young man to life is brought about in the course of preaching. Thereby Paul's preaching is confirmed by the kindness of the miracle and the teaching; the effort involved in the long vigil is repaid with interest; and all those present are reminded vividly of their departed Master" (*Expositio Actuum Apostolorum*, ad loc.).

20:13–38 Paul's address to the elders of Ephesus is his third long speech recorded in Acts, the previous two being his addresses to Jews at Pisidian Antioch (13:16ff) and to pagans at Athens (17:22ff). This speech is, really, a heartfelt farewell to the churches he founded. It is reminiscent of our Lord's discourse at the Last Supper (see Lk 22:21–38), and contains similar warnings about the future of the Church, the role of ministers and the duties of pastors. The main

u Other ancient authorities add *after remaining at Trogyllium*

house, ²¹testifying both to Jews and to Greeks of repentance to God and of faith in our Lord Jesus Christ. ²²And now, behold, I am going to Jerusalem, bound in the Spirit, not knowing what shall befall me there; ²³except that the Holy Spirit testifies to me in every city that imprisonment and inflictions await me. ²⁴But I do not account my life of any value nor as precious to myself, if only I may accomplish my course and the ministry which I received from the Lord Jesus, to testify to the gospel of the grace of God. ²⁵And now, behold, I know that all you among whom I have gone about preaching the kingdom will see my face no more. ²⁶Therefore I testify to you this day that I am innocent of the blood of all of you, ²⁷for I did not shrink from declaring to you the whole counsel of God. ²⁸Take heed to yourselves and to all the flock, in which the Holy Spirit has made you guardians, to feed the church of the Lord^v which he obtained with his own blood.^w ²⁹I know that after my departure fierce wolves will come in among you, not sparing the flock; ³⁰and from among your own selves will arise men speaking perverse things, to draw away the disciples after them. ³¹Therefore be alert, remembering that for three years I did not cease night or day to admonish every one with tears. ³²And now I commend you to God and to the word of his grace, which is able to build you up and to give you the inheritance among all those who are sanctified. ³³I coveted no one's silver or gold or apparel.

Acts 21:4, 11

Acts 26:16–18
2 Tim 4:7

Acts 18:6

1 Tim 4:16
1 Pet 2:9; 5:2
Ps 74:2

Mt 7:15
Jn 10:12
2 Pet 2:1–2
1 Jn 2:19

i Thess 2:11
1 Pet 5:8–9
Deut 33:3
Wis 5:5
Eph 2:20–22

lacrimis et tentationibus, quae mihi acciderunt in insidiis Iudaeorum; ²⁰quomodo nihil subtraxerim utilium, quominus annuntiarem vobis et docerem vos publice et per domos, ²¹testificans Iudaeis atque Graecis in Deum paenitentiam et fidem in Dominum nostrum Iesum. ²²Et nunc ecce alligatus ego Spiritu vado in Ierusalem, quae in ea eventura sint mihi ignorans, ²³nisi quod Spiritus Sanctus per omnes civitates protestatur mihi dicens quoniam vincula et tribulationes me manent. ²⁴Sed nihili facio animam meam pretiosam mihi, dummodo consummem cursum meum et ministerium, quod accepi a Domino Iesu, testificari evangelium gratiae Dei. ²⁵Et nunc ecce ego scio quia amplius non videbitis faciem meam vos omnes, per quos transivi praedicans regnum; ²⁶quapropter contestor vos hodierna die quia mundus sum a sanguine omnium, ²⁷non enim subterfugi, quominus annuntiarem omne consilium Dei vobis. ²⁸Attendite vobis et universo gregi, in quo vos Spiritus Sanctus posuit episcopos, pascere ecclesiam Dei, quam acquisivit sanguine suo. ²⁹Ego scio quoniam intrabunt post discessionem meam lupi graves in vos non parcentes gregi, ³⁰et ex vobis ipsis exsurgent viri loquentes perversa, ut abstrahant discipulos post se. ³¹Propter quod vigilate memoria retinentes quoniam per triennium nocte et die non cessavi cum lacrimis monens unumquemque vestrum. ³²Et nunc commendo vos Deo et verbo gratiae ipsius, qui potens est aed-

thing that comes across is the Apostle's humility, which must have impressed these elders, teaching them something about how they should choose to live their own lives. That is the first lesson to be learned from the address—the example that it sets: "Those who rule the community must perform worthily the tasks of government. [...] There is a danger that some who concern themselves with others and guide them towards eternal life may ruin themselves without realizing it. Those who are in charge must work harder than others, must be humbler than those under them, must in their own lives give an example of service, and must regard their subjects as a deposit which God has given them in trust" (St Gregory of Nyssa, *De instituto christiano*).

The address can be divided into two parts. The first (vv. 18–27) is a brief summary of Paul's life of dedication to the church he established at Ephesus, with some indications of the difficulties he expects to meet within the immediate future. Two parallel sections (vv. 18–21

and 26–27) frame the central passage in this part (vv. 22–25). Clearly Paul is convinced that God guides his steps and watches over him; but naturally (he is only human), a question-mark hangs over his future: "Grace does not work on its own. It respects men in the actions they take, it influences them, it awakens and does not entirely dispel their restlessness" (St John Chrysostom, *In Acta Apostolorum*, 37). Paul has managed to love Jesus Christ to the point that he gives himself no importance; for him, the only thing that matters is trying to complete the task God has entrusted to him (see 2 Cor 4:7; Phil 1:19–26; Col 1:24). The Apostle sees holiness as a constant, uninterrupted striving, full of love and good works, towards his encounter with the Lord (v. 24), and the Fathers of the Church teach that this indeed is the ideal of Christian perfection: "On the subject of virtue," writes St Gregory of Nyssa, for example, "we have learned from the apostle himself that the only limit to perfection of virtue is that there is no limit. This fine, noble

v Other ancient authorities read *of God*   w Or *with the blood of his Own*

³⁴You yourselves know that these hands ministered to my necessities, and to those who were with me.* ³⁵In all things I have shown you that by so toiling one must help the weak, remembering the words of the Lord Jesus, how he said, 'It is more blessed to give than to receive.'"

³⁶And when he had spoken thus, he knelt down and prayed with them all. ³⁷And they all wept and embraced Paul and kissed him, ³⁸sorrowing most of all because of the word he had spoken, that they should see his face no more. And they brought him to the ship.

Acts 18:3
1 Cor 4:12
1 Thess 2:9
Mt 10:8

Acts 21:5
1 Pet 5:14
Acts 20:25

PART FOUR

St Paul, in imprisonment, bears witness to Christ*

12. ST PAUL IN JERUSALEM*

From Miletus to Caesarea

21 ¹And when we had parted from them and set sail, we came by a straight course to Cos, and the next day to Rhodes, and from there to Patara.ˣ ²And having found a ship crossing to Phoenicia, we went aboard, and set sail. ³When we had come in sight of Cyprus, leaving it on the left we sailed to Syria, and landed at

ificare et dare hereditatem in sanctificatis omnibus. ³³Argentum aut aurum aut vestem nullius concupivi; ³⁴ipsi scitis quoniam ad ea, quae mihi opus erant et his, qui mecum sunt, ministraverunt manus istae. ³⁵Omnia ostendi vobis quoniam sic laborantes oportet suscipere infirmos, ac meminisse verborum Domini Iesu, quoniam ipse dixit: "Beatius est magis dare quam accipere!"». ³⁶Et cum haec dixisset, positis genibus suis, cum omnibus illis oravit. ³⁷Magnus autem fletus factus est omnium, et procumbentes super collum Pauli osculabantur eum ³⁸dolentes maxime in verbo, quod dixerat, quoniam amplius faciem eius non essent visuri. Et deducebant eum ad navem. [21] ¹Cum autem factum esset ut navigaremus abstracti ab eis, recto cursu venimus Cho et sequenti die Rhodum et inde Patara; ²et cum invenissemus navem transfretantem in Phoenicen, ascen-

man, this divine apostle, never ceases, when running on the course of virtue, to 'strain forward to what lies ahead' (Phil 3:13). He realizes it is dangerous to stop. Why? Because all good, by its very nature, is unlimited: its only limit is where it meets its opposite: thus, the limit of life is death, of light darkness, and in general of every good its opposite. Just as the end of life is the beginning of death, so too if one ceases to follow the path of virtue one is beginning to follow the path of vice" (*De vita Moysis*, 1, 5).

In the second part of the address, the Apostle speaks movingly about the duties of elders. Here again, two series of counsels (vv. 28–31 and 33–35) hinge on a central verse (v. 32): "Christians should not believe that the winning of the crown depends wholly on their human strength and efforts in the struggle for victory; their hope to win the great reward must come from their trust in the will of God" (St Gregory of Nyssa, *De instituto christiano*).

*21:1—28:31 Paul's arrival in Jerusalem marks the start of the last part of the book, which describes the Apostle's imprisonment. As our Lord foretells (see 23:11), Paul will, from now on, bear witness to Christ and the Gospel as a prisoner. His journey to Rome as a prisoner is described in detail. Once he is in Rome, the way is open for the Gospel to extend across the world.

*21:1—23:21 During his last stay in Jerusalem, the Apostle is warmly received by the Christians (21:17) but bitterly persecuted by some Jews (21:27–32). Adverse circumstances provide Paul with an opportunity to make an apologia for his actions and thus also for the Gospel (22:1–21). His enemies seem to be on the point of taking his life, but God's providence is at work all the time and ensures that Paul will bring the Gospel to Gentiles and to Rome itself (22:21; 23:11).

21:1–14 Just like Jesus in his time, Paul travels

x Other ancient authorities add *and Myra*

Acts 20–23

Acts 20:36

Tyre; for there the ship was to unload its cargo. ⁴And having sought out the disciples, we stayed there for seven days. Through the Spirit they told Paul not to go* on to Jerusalem. ⁵And when our days there were ended, we departed and went on our journey; and they all, with wives and children, brought us on our way till we were outside the city; and kneeling down on the beach we prayed and bade one another farewell. ⁶Then we went on board the ship, and they returned home.

Acts 6:5; 8:40

Acts 2:17

⁷When we had finished the voyage from Tyre, we arrived at Ptolemais; and we greeted the brethren and stayed with them for one day. ⁸On the morrow we departed and came to Caesarea; and we entered the house of Philip the evangelist, who was one of the seven, and stayed with him. ⁹And he had four unmarried daughters, who prophesied.

The prophet Agabus

Acts 11:27–28

Acts 21:31–33

Mt 16:22

Mt 26:42
Lk 22:42

¹⁰While we were staying for some days, a prophet named Agabus came down from Judea. ¹¹And coming to us he took Paul's girdle and bound his own feet and hands, and said, "Thus says the Holy Spirit, 'So shall the Jews at Jerusalem bind the man who owns this girdle and deliver him into the hands of the Gentiles.'" ¹²When we heard this, we and the people there begged him not to go up to Jerusalem. ¹³Then Paul answered, "What are you doing, weeping and breaking my heart? For I am ready not only to be imprisoned but even to die at Jerusalem for the name of the Lord Jesus." ¹⁴And when he would not be persuaded, we ceased and said, "The will of the Lord be done."

Paul arrives in Jerusalem and meets the Christians

¹⁵After these days we made ready and went up to Jerusalem. ¹⁶And some of the disciples from Caesarea went with us, bringing us to the house of Mnason of Cyprus, an early disciple, with whom we should lodge.

dentes navigavimus. ³Cum paruissemus autem Cypro, et relinquentes eam ad sinistram navigabamus in Syriam et venimus Tyrum, ibi enim navis erat exposita onus. ⁴Inventis autem discipulis, mansimus ibi diebus septem; qui Paulo dicebant per Spiritum, ne iret Hierosolymam. ⁵Et explicitis diebus, profecti ibamus, deducentibus nos omnibus cum uxoribus et filiis usque foras civitatem; et positis genibus in litore orantes, ⁶valefecimus invicem et ascendimus in navem, illi autem redierunt in sua. ⁷Nos vero navigatione explicita, a Tyro devenimus Ptolemaida et salutatis fratribus mansimus die una apud illos. ⁸Alia autem die profecti venimus Caesaream et intrantes in domum Philippi evangelistae, qui erat de septem, mansimus apud eum. ⁹Huic autem erant filiae quattuor virgines prophetantes. ¹⁰Et cum moraremur plures dies, supervenit quidam a Iudaea propheta nomine Agabus; ¹¹is cum venisset ad nos et tulisset zonam Pauli, alligans sibi pedes et manus dixit: «Haec dicit Spiritus Sanctus: Virum, cuius est zona haec, sic alligabunt in Ierusalem Iudaei et tradent in manus gentium». ¹²Quod cum audissemus, rogabamus nos et, qui loci illius erant, ne ipse ascenderet Ierusalem. ¹³Tunc respondit Paulus: «Quid facitis flentes et affligentes cor meum? Ego enim non solum alligari sed et mori in Ierusalem paratus sum propter nomen Domini Iesu». ¹⁴Et cum ei suadere non possemus, quievimus dicentes: «Domini voluntas fiat!».

to Jerusalem fully aware of what awaits him. The Holy Spirit's instructions and warnings (vv. 4, 11; cf. 20:23) strengthen his resolve to accept God's will and endure all the difficulties he has been told to expect (v. 13; cf. 20:23–24). His serenity contrasts with the concern felt by those around him, which stems from their affection for him. His long years of dedication and self-forgetfulness explain why he can face trial so calmly: "Accepting the will of God wholeheartedly is a sure way of finding joy and peace: happiness in the cross. Then we realize that Christ's yoke is sweet and that his burden is not heavy" (St Josemaría Escrivá, *The Way*, 758).

Paul's example impresses the disciples and helps them to accept what God has ordained. "Let God's will be done," they say, echoing Jesus' words in Gethsemane (v. 14; see Lk 22:42). "This consists mainly or entirely in our ceasing to care about ourselves and our own pleasures, for the least that anyone who is beginning to serve the Lord can truly offer Him is his life. Once he has surrendered his will to Him, what has he to fear?" (St Teresa of Avila, *Way of Perfection*, 12, 1).

21:15–26 Paul and his companions are welcomed by James (probably the relative of our

¹⁷When we had come to Jerusalem, the brethren received us gladly. ¹⁸On the following day Paul went in with us to James; and all the elders were present. ¹⁹After
greeting them, he related one by one the things that God had done among the
Gentiles through his ministry. ²⁰And when they heard it, they glorified God. And
they said to him, "You see, brother, how many thousands there are among the Jews
of those who have believed; they are all zealous for the law, ²¹and they have been
told about you that you teach all the Jews who are among the Gentiles to forsake
Moses, telling them not to circumcise their children or observe the customs. ²²What
then is to be done? They will certainly hear that you have come. ²³Do therefore what
we tell you. We have four men who are under a vow; ²⁴take these men and purify
yourself along with them and pay their expenses, so that they may shave their heads.
Thus all will know that there is nothing in what they have been told about you but
that you yourself live in observance of the law. ²⁵But as for the Gentiles who have
believed, we have sent a letter with our judgment that they should abstain from what
has been sacrificed to idols and from blood and from what is strangled[y] and from
unchastity." ²⁶Then Paul took the men, and the next day he purified himself with
them and went into the temple, to give notice when the days of purification would
be fulfilled and the offering presented for every one of them.

Marginal references:
Acts 12:17
Gal 1:19
Acts 15:4

Rom 2:25–29
Gal 2:3
1 Cor 7:17–20

Num 6:5, 13ff

Acts 15:28–29

1 Cor 9:20, 29

¹⁵Post dies autem istos praeparati ascendebamus Hierosolymam; ¹⁶venerunt autem et ex discipulis a Caesarea nobiscum adducentes apud quem hos-
pitaremur, Mnasonem quendam Cyprium, antiquum discipulum. ¹⁷Et cum venissemus Hierosolymam, libenter exceperunt nos fratres. ¹⁸Sequenti
autem die introibat Paulus nobiscum ad Iacobum, omnesque collecti sunt presbyteri. ¹⁹Quos cum salutasset, narrabat per singula, quae fecisset
Deus in gentibus per ministerium ipsius. ²⁰At illi cum audissent, glorificabant Deum dixeruntque ei: «Vides, frater, quot milia sint in Iudaeis, qui
crediderunt, et omnes aemulatores sunt legis; ²¹audierunt autem de te quia discessionem doceas a Moyse omnes, qui per gentes sunt, Iudaeos,
dicens non debere circumcidere eos filios suos, neque secundum consuetudines ambulare. ²²Quid ergo est? Utique audient te supervenisse. ²³Hoc
ergo fac, quod tibi dicimus. Sunt nobis viri quattuor votum habentes super se; ²⁴his assumptis, sanctifica te cum illis et impende pro illis, ut radant
capita, et scient omnes quia, quae de te audierunt, nihil sunt, sed ambulas et ipse custodiens legem. ²⁵De his autem, qui crediderunt, gentibus nos

Lord), the head of the church of Jerusalem in
those years (cf. 12:17; 15:13; 1 Cor 15:7; Gal
1:19), and by the elders who were his aides in
the government and spiritual care of the community. Since Luke usually distinguishes between
elders and apostles, the other apostles, including
Peter, may well have left the Holy City by this
time. Those in charge of the church in Jerusalem
are delighted to hear about the abundant fruit of
Paul's apostolate (v. 20), but they are also aware
of rumours circulating about him (v. 21). These
rumours are well-founded, because Paul saw the
Mosaic Law as secondary to the conditions for
salvation laid down by Jesus, and did not consider circumcision necessary for Christians (see
Rom 2:25–29; Gal 4:9; 5:11). However, the
actual charge made against him is groundless.
Paul never exhorted Christians of Jewish background not to circumcise their sons, and he himself took care to see that Timothy was
circumcised (see 16:3). In Corinth, he supported
the idea that women should follow the Jewish
custom of wearing a veil at liturgical ceremonies

(see 1 Cor 11:2–16); etc. "Paul was calumniated
by those who did not understand the Spirit with
which these customs should be kept by Jewish
Christians, that is, in a spirit of homage to the
divine authority and prophetic holiness of these
signs — and not in order to attain salvation, which
had been revealed with Christ and applied
through the sacrament of Baptism. Those who
calumniated him were people who wanted to
observe these customs as if believers in the
Gospel could not attain salvation without them"
(St Bede, *Expositio Actuum Apostolorum*, ad
loc.).

Even so, the Christians of Jerusalem, for reasons of prudence (vv. 23–24), advise Paul to
publicly show his respect for the Law by joining
with some men who have taken a vow and by
going so far as to pay their expenses. The text
does not say what kind of vow this was; it may
have been a Nazirite vow (see 18:18; Num 6:1–
21). Verse 25 is somewhat surprising, because
earlier we learned that this letter to the churches
was in fact delivered by Paul and Barnabas (cf.

y Other early authorities omit *and from what is strangled*

Paul is arrested in the temple

Ezek 44:9
Acts 6:13

²⁷When the seven days were almost completed, the Jews from Asia, who had seen him in the temple, stirred up all the crowd, and laid hands on him, ²⁸crying out, "Men of Israel, help! This is the man who is teaching men everywhere against the people and the law and this place; moreover he also brought Greeks into the temple,

Acts 20:4

and he has defiled this holy place." ²⁹For they had previously seen Trophimus the Ephesian with him in the city, and they supposed that Paul had brought him into the temple. ³⁰Then all the city was aroused, and the people ran together; they seized Paul and dragged him out of the temple, and at once the gates were shut. ³¹And as they were trying to kill him, word came to the tribune of the cohort that all Jerusalem was in confusion. ³²He at once took soldiers and centurions, and ran down to them; and

Acts 21:11

when they saw the tribune and the soldiers, they stopped beating Paul. ³³Then the tribune came up and arrested him, and ordered him to be bound with two chains. He inquired who he was and what he had done. ³⁴Some in the crowd shouted one thing, some another; and as he could not learn the facts because of the uproar, he ordered him to be brought into the barracks. ³⁵And when he came to the steps, he was actu-

scripsimus iudicantes, ut abstineant ab idolothyto et sanguine et suffocato et fornicatione». ²⁶Tunc Paulus, assumptis viris, postera die purificatus cum illis intravit in templum annuntians expletionem dierum purificationis, donec offerretur pro unoquoque eorum oblatio. ²⁷Dum autem septem dies consummarentur, hi, qui de Asia erant, Iudaei cum vidissent eum in templo, concitaverunt omnem turbam et iniecerunt ei manus ²⁸clamantes: «Viri Israelitae, adiuvate! Hic est homo, qui adversus populum et legem et locum hunc omnes ubique docens, insuper et Graecos induxit in templum et polluit sanctum locum istum». ²⁹Viderant enim Trophimum Ephesium in civitate cum ipso, quem aestimabant quoniam in templum induxisset Paulus. ³⁰Commotaque est civitas tota, et facta est concursio populi, et apprehendentes Paulum trahebant eum extra templum, et statim clausae sunt ianuae. ³¹Quaerentibus autem eum occidere, nuntiatum est tribuno cohortis quia tota confunditur Ierusalem, ³²qui statim, assumptis militibus et centurionibus, decucurrit ad illos; qui cum vidissent tribunum et milites, cessaverunt percutere Paulum. ³³Tunc accedens tribunus apprehendit eum et iussit alligari catenis duabus et interrogabat quis esset et quid fecisset. ³⁴Alii autem aliud clamabant in turba; et cum non posset certum cognoscere prae tumultu, iussit duci eum in castra. ³⁵Et cum venisset ad gradus, contigit ut portaretur a militibus propter vim turbae;

16:4); it may be that James and the elders mention these decisions of the council of Jerusalem for the benefit of Gentiles not evangelized by Paul.

After v. 18 the use of the first person plural is discontinued, and it is not taken up again until Luke begins his account of the journey to Rome (27:1).

21:27–40 Some Jews arriving from the Roman province of Asia (v. 27), probably having come from Ephesus (see v. 29) for the feast of Pentecost (see 20:16), stir up the crowd against Paul. They accuse him, falsely, of profaning the temple by bringing pagans into it. Under Jewish law it was a crime punishable by death for a Gentile to cross the balustrade that separated the Court of the Gentiles from the inner courtyards, but, as the text indicates (v. 29), Paul had not brought Trophimus into the temple. The general tenor of the accusations made against Paul (v. 28) is very like that of those laid against Jesus in his time (see Mt 26:61; 27:40) and against Stephen (see 6:11–14).

The intervention of some Roman soldiers rescues Paul from certain death (vv. 31–36). The Egyptian rebel (v. 38) is also mentioned by Flavius Josephus (*De bello iudaico*, 2, 261–263). The "Assassins" (Latin: *Sicarii*) referred to here were so named because they always carried a dagger (*sica*); together with the Zealots, they would be noted for the violent part they played in the war against Rome some years later.

In the speech that the Apostle is given permission to make, he once again trusts to God to put the right words on his lips, and does not content himself with simply reproaching these people for their behaviour, for he knows that "truth is not preached with swords and lances or with the aid of soldiers, but rather by means of persuasion and counsel" (St Athanasius, *Historia Arianorum*, 33).

Luke goes into some detail about what happens to Paul after his arrest—his imprisonment (21:33—22:30), his appearances in court at Jerusalem and Caesarea (chaps. 23–26), and his going to Rome (27:1—28:16) to appear before the imperial tribunal. From this point onwards, Paul

ally carried by the soldiers because of the violence of the crowd; [36]for the mob of the Lk 23:18
Acts 22:22
people followed, crying, "Away with him!"

[37]As Paul was about to be brought into the barracks, he said to the tribune, "May I say something to you?" And he said, "Do you know Greek? [38]Are you not the Egyptian, then, who recently stirred up a revolt and led the four thousand men of the Assassins out into the wilderness?" [39]Paul replied, "I am a Jew, from Tarsus in Cilicia, a citizen of no mean city; I beg you, let me speak to the people." [40]And when he had given him leave, Paul, standing on the steps, motioned with his hand to the people; and when there was a great hush, he spoke to them in the Hebrew language, saying:

Paul defends himself before the crowd

22 [1]"Brethren and fathers, hear the defence which I now make before you." Acts 7:2
[2]And when they heard that he addressed them in the Hebrew language, they were the more quiet. And he said:

[3]"I am a Jew, born at Tarsus in Cilicia, but brought up in this city at the feet of Acts 26:4–5
Rom 10:2
2 Cor 11:22
Gal 1:14
Phil 3:5–6
Gamaliel, educated according to the strict manner of the law of our fathers, being zealous for God as you all are this day. [4]I persecuted this Way to the death, binding Acts 8:3
and delivering to prison both men and women, [5]as the high priest and the whole Acts 9:1–18; 26:9–18
council of elders bear me witness. From them I received letters to the brethren, and I journeyed to Damascus to take those also who were there and bring them in bonds to Jerusalem to be punished.

[6]"As I made my journey and drew near to Damascus, about noon a great light from heaven suddenly shone about me. [7]And I fell to the ground and heard a voice

---

[36]sequebatur enim multitudo populi clamantes: «Tolle eum!». [37]Et cum coepisset induci in castra, Paulus dicit tribuno: «Si licet mihi loqui aliquid ad te?». Qui dixit: «Graece nosti? [38]Nonne tu es Aegyptius, qui ante hos dies tumultum concitasti et eduxisti in desertum quattuor milia virorum sicariorum?». [39]Et dixit Paulus: «Ego homo sum quidem Iudaeus a Tarso Ciliciae, non ignotae civitatis municeps; rogo autem te, permitte mihi loqui ad populum». [40]Et cum ille permisisset, Paulus stans in gradibus annuit manu ad plebem et, magno silentio facto, allocutus est Hebraea lingua dicens: [22] [1]«Viri fratres et patres, audite a me, quam ad vos nunc reddo, rationem». [2]Cum audissent autem quia Hebraea lingua loquebatur ad illos, magis praestiterunt silentium. Et dixit: [3]«Ego sum vir Iudaeus, natus Tarso Ciliciae, enutritus autem in ista civitate, secus pedes Gamaliel eruditus iuxta veritatem paternae legis, aemulator Dei sicut et vos omnes estis hodie. [4]Qui hanc viam persecutus sum usque ad mortem, alligans et tradens in custodias viros ac mulieres, [5]sicut et princeps sacerdotum testimonium mihi reddit et omne concilium; a quibus et epistulas accipiens ad fratres, Damascum pergebam, ut adducerem et eos, qui ibi essent, vinctos in Ierusalem, uti punirentur. [6]Factum est autem eunte me

---

will not be so much the tireless missionary and founder of churches as a Gospel witness in chains.

22:1–21 This address to the Jews of Jerusalem is the first of three personal defences (cf. 24:10–21; 26:1–23) in which the Apostle tries to show that Christianity deserves neither the hostility shown by Jews nor the suspicion shown by Romans. He presents himself as a pious Jew full of respect for his people and their sacred traditions. He earnestly desires his brethren to see that there are compelling reasons for his commitment to Jesus: "Many have come to Christianity", Origen says, "as if against their will, for a certain spirit, appearing to them, in sleep or when they are awake, suddenly silences their mind, and they change from hating the Word to dying for him" (*Contra Celsum*, 1, 46).

The address, however, is not an apologia in the strict sense. Paul's primary aim is not to answer the charge of sacrilege laid against him, but to use the occasion to bear witness to Jesus Christ, whose commandments justify the way he has acted. Paul's words are really a call to his hearers to listen to the voice of the Lord and to obey it.

The account that Paul gives here of his call on the road to Damascus contains details not found in the other two accounts (9:3–19; 26:9–18)—for example, that Jesus identified himself as "Jesus of Nazareth" and that Paul asked him what he should do. He then mentions his return to Jerusalem (which happened three years after his conversion: see Gal 1:18), and makes a point of mentioning his custom of praying in the temple. He also tells of a spiritual ecstasy he

Mt 2:23

Wis 18:1

Acts 3:13–14

1 Jn 1:1–3

Acts 9:26
Gal 1:18

Acts 13:46–48; 18:6;
28:25–28

Acts 7:58; 8:1

Acts 9:15
Gal 2:7–9

Acts 25:24

saying to me, 'Saul, Saul, why do you persecute me?' [8]And I answered, 'Who are you, Lord?' And he said to me, 'I am Jesus of Nazareth whom you are persecuting.' [9]Now those who were with me saw the light but did not hear the voice of the one who was speaking to me. [10]And I said, 'What shall I do, Lord?' And the Lord said to me, 'Rise, and go into Damascus, and there you will be told all that is appointed for you to do.' [11]And when I could not see because of the brightness of that light, I was led by the hand by those who were with me, and came into Damascus.

[12]"And one Ananias, a devout man according to the law, well spoken of by all the Jews who lived there, [13]came to me, and standing by me said to me, 'Brother Saul, receive your sight.' And in that very hour I received my sight and saw him. [14]And he said, 'The God of our fathers appointed you to know his will, to see the Just One and to hear a voice from his mouth; [15]for you will be a witness for him to all men of what you have seen and heard.[16]And now why do you wait? Rise and be baptized, and wash away your sins, calling on his name.'

[17]"When I had returned to Jerusalem and was praying in the temple, I fell into a trance [18]and saw him saying to me, 'Make haste and get quickly out of Jerusalem, because they will not accept your testimony about me.' [19]And I said, 'Lord, they themselves know that in every synagogue I imprisoned and beat those who believed in thee. [20]And when the blood of Stephen thy witness* was shed, I also was standing by and approving, and keeping the garments of those who killed him.' [21]And he said to me, 'Depart; for I will send you far away to the Gentiles.'"

Paul, the Roman citizen

[22]Up to this word they listened to him; then they lifted up their voices and said, "Away with such a fellow from the earth! For he ought not to live." [23]And as they

et appropinquante Damasco, circa mediam diem subito de caelo circumfulsit me lux copiosa, [7]et decidi in terram et audivi vocem dicentem mihi: "Saul, Saul, quid me persequeris?". [8]Ego autem respondi: "Quis es, Domine?". Dixitque ad me: "Ego sum Iesus Nazarenus, quem tu persequeris". [9]Et qui mecum erant, lumen quidem viderunt, vocem autem non audierunt eius, qui loquebatur mecum. [10]Et dixi: "Quid faciam, Domine?". Dominus autem dixit ad me: "Surgens vade Damascum, et ibi tibi dicetur de omnibus, quae statutum est tibi, ut faceres". [11]Et cum non viderem prae claritate luminis illius, ad manum deductus a comitibus veni Damascum. [12]Ananias autem quidam vir religiosus secundum legem testimonium habens ab omnibus habitantibus Iudaeis, [13]veniens ad me et astans dixit mihi: "Saul frater, respice!". Et ego eadem hora respexi in eum. [14]At ille dixit: "Deus patrum nostrorum praeordinavit te, ut cognosceres voluntatem eius et videres Iustum et audires vocem ex ore eius, [15]quia eris testis illi ad omnes homines eorum, quae vidisti et audisti. [16]Et nunc quid moraris? Exsurgens baptizare et ablue peccata tua, invocato nomine ipsius". [17]Factum est autem revertenti mihi in Ierusalem et oranti in templo fieri me in stupore mentis [18]et videre illum dicentem mihi: "Festina et exi velociter ex Ierusalem, quoniam non recipient testimonium tuum de me". [19]Et ego dixi: "Domine, ipsi sciunt quia ego eram concludens in carcerem et caedens per synagogas eos, qui credebant in te; [20]et cum funderetur sanguis Stephani testis tui, et ipse astabam et consentiebam et custodiebam vestimenta interficientium illum". [21]Et dixit ad me: "Vade, quoniam ego in nationes longe mittam te"». [22]Audiebant autem eum usque

experienced, a vision of Jesus (vv. 17–21) in which he was commanded to preach to the Gentiles. Interestingly, this vision was not intended to comfort Paul, but to give him a mission: "Those who walked most closely at Christ's side were entrusted with the greatest tasks: see the lives of his glorious Mother and his glorious apostles. How did Paul withstand all the suffering he had to endure? In Paul we see the real effects of true visions and contemplation of our Lord, not the deceptions of our own imagination or of the devil. Did Paul try to hide away in them, to rejoice in God's gift and to avoid their message to him? No: from what we read of

his life, he never had a day's rest, nor a night's, for he worked at night to earn his living" (St Teresa of Avila, *Interior Castle*, 7, 4, 5).

22:22–29 Roman legal practice allowed for the flogging of suspects and slaves in order to extract confessions. When Paul tells the authorities that he is a Roman citizen—as he did in Philippi (see 16:37), though here he anticipates what the authorities might do and avoids being flogged—the reason why the tribune convokes the Sanhedrin (22:30) may simply be to apprise himself of the grounds for the charges (now that "evidence" cannot be extracted from Paul by torture).

cried out and waved their garments and threw dust into the air, ²⁴the tribune commanded him to be brought into the barracks, and ordered him to be examined by
scourging, to find out why they shouted thus against him. ²⁵But when they had tied
him up with the thongs, Paul said to the centurion who was standing by, "Is it lawful
for you to scourge a man who is a Roman citizen, and uncondemned?" ²⁶When the
centurion heard that, he went to the tribune and said to him, "What are you about to
do? For this man is a Roman citizen." ²⁷So the tribune came and said to him, "Tell
me, are you a Roman citizen?" And he said, "Yes." ²⁸The tribune answered, "I bought
this citizenship for a large sum." Paul said, "But I was born a citizen." ²⁹So those who
were about to examine him withdrew from him instantly; and the tribune also was
afraid, for he realized that Paul was a Roman citizen and that he had bound him.

Acts 16:22, 37

Acts 16:38–39

Speech before the Sanhedrin

³⁰But on the morrow, desiring to know the real reason why the Jews accused him, he
unbound him, and commanded the chief priests and all the council to meet, and he
brought Paul down and set him before them.

23 ¹And Paul, looking intently at the council, said, "Brethren, I have lived
before God in all good conscience up to this day." ²And the high priest
Ananias commanded those who stood by him to strike him on the mouth. ³Then Paul
said to him, "God shall strike you, you whitewashed wall! Are you sitting to judge
me according to the law, and yet contrary to the law you order me to be struck?"
⁴Those who stood by said, "Would you revile God's high priest?" ⁵And Paul said, "I
did not know, brethren, that he was the high priest; for it is written, 'You shall not
speak evil of a ruler of your people.'"
    ⁶But when Paul perceived that one part were Sadducees and the other Pharisees,
he cried out in the council, "Brethren, I am a Pharisee, a son of Pharisees; with

Acts 24:16
Heb 13:18
Jn 18:22–23

Ezek 13:10–15
Lev 19:15
Mt 23:27

Ex 22:27

Acts 26:5
Phil 3:5

ad hoc verbum et levaverunt vocem suam dicentes: «Tolle de terra eiusmodi, non enim fas est eum vivere!». ²³Vociferantibus autem eis et proici-
entibus vestimenta sua et pulverem iactantibus in aerem, ²⁴iussit tribunus induci eum in castra dicens flagellis eum interrogari, ut sciret propter
quam causam sic acclamarent ei. ²⁵Et cum astrinxissent eum loris, dixit astanti centurioni Paulus: «Si hominem Romanum et indemnatum licet
vobis flagellare?». ²⁶Quo audito, centurio accedens ad tribunum nuntiavit dicens: «Quid acturus es? Hic enim homo Romanus est». ²⁷Accedens
autem tribunus dixit illi: «Dic mihi, tu Romanus es?». At ille dixit: «Etiam». ²⁸Et respondit tribunus: «Ego multa summa civitatem hanc consecutus sum». Et Paulus ait: «Ego autem et natus sum». ²⁹Protinus ergo discesserunt ab illo, qui eum interrogaturi erant; tribunus quoque timuit,
postquam rescivit quia Romanus esset et quia alligasset eum. ³⁰Postera autem die volens scire diligenter qua ex causa accusaretur a Iudaeis, solvit
eum et iussit principes sacerdotum convenire et omne concilium et producens Paulum statuit coram illis. [23] ¹Intendens autem concilium Paulus
ait: «Viri fratres, ego omni conscientia bona conversatus sum ante Deum usque in hodiernum diem». ²Princeps autem sacerdotum Ananias praecepit astantibus sibi percutere os eius. ³Tunc Paulus ad eum dixit: «Percutiet te Deus, paries dealbate! Et tu sedes iudicans me secundum legem
et contra legem iubes me percuti?». ⁴Et qui astabant, dixerunt: «Summum sacerdotem Dei maledicis?». ⁵Dixit autem Paulus: «Nesciebam, fratres,
quia princeps est sacerdotum; scriptum est enim: "*Principem populi tui non maledices*"». ⁶Sciens autem Paulus quia una pars esset sadducaeo-

22:30—23:11 On a number of occasions in
Acts, St Luke makes a point of showing that
Paul's behaviour and what follows it parallel in
some ways what happened with Jesus. In
connexion with the charges brought before the
Sanhedrin, he lets us know that Paul, like Jesus
(see Jn 18:22) was struck on the order of the
high priest in an effort to force him to tell the
truth (23:1–2). This high priest, Ananias, should
not be confused with Annas (see 4:6). Ananias
was appointed high priest in the year 47; he was
deposed around the year 59, and was

assassinated in 66 by Jews opposed to Rome.
Flavius Josephus says that he was an arrogant
and hot-tempered man (*Antiquitates iudaicae*,
20, 199).
    However, the hearing takes a different direc-
tion at this point. Jesus did not answer the
charges brought against him, whereas Paul introduces a subject (in 23:1) that sets his judges in
dispute with one another; this allows him to
emerge unscathed. God has another mission in
mind for him—to bear witness to the Gospel in
Rome (see 23:11).

respect to the hope and the resurrection of the dead I am on trial." [7]And when he had said this, a dissension arose between the Pharisees and the Sadducees; and the assembly was divided. [8]For the Sadducees say that there is no resurrection, nor angel, nor spirit; but the Pharisees acknowledge them all. [9]Then a great clamour arose; and some of the scribes of the Pharisees' party stood up and contended, "We find nothing wrong in this man. What if a spirit or an angel spoke to him?" [10]And when the dissension became violent, the tribune, afraid that Paul would be torn in pieces by them, commanded the soldiers to go down and take him by force from among them and bring him into the barracks.

[11]The following night the Lord stood by him and said, "Take courage, for as you have testified about me at Jerusalem, so you must bear witness also at Rome."

Mt 22:23

Lk 23:4, 14, 22
Jn 18:38

Acts 18:9–10; 27:24

Acts 9:23; 20:3

A Jewish plot against Paul

[12]When it was day, the Jews made a plot and bound themselves by an oath neither to eat nor drink till they had killed Paul. [13]There were more than forty who made this conspiracy. [14]And they went to the chief priests and elders, and said, "We have strictly bound ourselves by an oath to taste no food till we have killed Paul. [15]You therefore, along with the council, give notice now to the tribune to bring him down to you, as though you were going to determine his case more exactly. And we are ready to kill him before he comes near."

[16]Now the son of Paul's sister heard of their ambush; so he went and entered the barracks and told Paul. [17]And Paul called one of the centurions and said, "Bring this young man to the tribune; for he has something to tell him." [18]So he took him and brought him to the tribune and said, "Paul the prisoner called me and asked me to bring this young man to you, as he has something to say to you." [19]The tribune took him by the hand, and going aside asked him privately, "What is it that you have to tell me?" [20]And he said, "The Jews have agreed to ask you to bring Paul down to the council tomorrow, as though they were going to inquire somewhat more closely

rum et altera pharisaeorum, exclamabat in concilio: «Viri fratres, ego pharisaeus sum, filius pharisaeorum; de spe et resurrectione mortuorum ego iudicor». [7]Et cum haec diceret, facta est dissensio inter pharisaeos et sadducaeos, et divisa est multitudo. [8]Sadducaei enim dicunt non esse resurrectionem neque angelum neque spiritum; pharisaei autem utrumque confitentur. [9]Factus est autem clamor magnus, et surgentes scribae quidam partis pharisaeorum pugnabant dicentes: «Nihil mali invenimus in homine isto: quod si spiritus locutus est ei aut angelus»; [10]et cum magna dissensio facta esset, timens tribunus ne discerperetur Paulus ab ipsis, iussit milites descendere, ut raperent eum de medio eorum ac deducerent in castra. [11]Sequenti autem nocte assistens ei Dominus ait: «Constans esto! Sicut enim testificatus es, quae sunt de me in Ierusalem, sic te oportet et Romae testificari». [12]Facta autem die, faciebant concursum Iudaei et devoverunt se dicentes neque manducaturos neque bibituros, donec occiderent Paulum. [13]Erant autem plus quam quadraginta, qui hanc coniurationem fecerant; [14]qui accedentes ad principes sacerdotum et seniores dixerunt: «Devotione devovimus nos nihil gustaturos, donec occidamus Paulum. [15]Nunc ergo vos notum facite tribuno cum concilio, ut producat illum ad vos, tamquam aliquid certius cognituri de eo; nos vero priusquam appropiet, parati sumus interficere illum». [16]Quod cum audisset filius sororis Pauli insidias, venit et intravit in castra nuntiavitque Paulo. [17]Vocans autem Paulus ad se unum ex centurionibus ait: Adulescentem hunc perduc ad tribunum, habet enim aliquid indicare illi». [18]Et ille quidem assumens eum duxit ad tribunum et ait: «Vinctus Paulus vocans rogavit me hunc adulescentem perducere ad te habentem aliquid loqui tibi». [19]Apprehendens autem tribunus manum illius, secessit cum eo seorsum et interrogabat: «Quid est quod habes indicare mihi?». [20]Ille autem dixit: «Iudaei constituerunt rogare te, ut crastina die Paulum producas in concilium, quasi

23:12–21 Blinded by fanaticism, a small group of Jews take an oath to do away with Paul. "But there can be no wisdom nor prudence nor plots against God [...]. So although they swear oaths and plot and scheme against Paul, he will be spared so that he may bear witness to Christ in Rome as he had said he would" (St Bede, *Expositio Actuum Apostolorum*, ad loc.). On other occasions, apostles were miraculously released from prison. Now God uses ordinary means (family connexions) to ensure that Paul stays in confinement, so that he can live long enough to carry out God's plan for him. With or without miracles, divine providence is at work.

This is the only information we have about Paul's sister and nephew, although in his Letter to the Romans (16:7, 11) he does mention other relatives.

about him. [21]But do not yield to them; for more than forty of their men lie in ambush for him, having bound themselves by an oath neither to eat nor drink till they have killed him; and now they are ready, waiting for the promise from you."

13. FROM JERUSALEM TO ROME*

Paul is moved to Caesarea

[22]So the tribune dismissed the young man, charging him, "Tell no one that you have informed me of this."

[23]Then he called two of the centurions and said, "At the third hour of the night get ready two hundred soldiers with seventy horsemen and two hundred spearmen to go as far as Caesarea. [24]Also provide mounts for Paul to ride, and bring him safely to Felix the governor." [25]And he wrote a letter to this effect:

[26]"Claudius Lysias to his Excellency the governor Felix, greeting. [27]This man was seized by the Jews, and was about to be killed by them, when I came upon them with the soldiers and rescued him, having learned that he was a Roman citizen. [28]And desiring to know the charge on which they accused him, I brought him down to their council. [29]I found that he was accused about questions of their law, but charged with nothing deserving death or imprisonment. [30]And when it was disclosed to me that there would be a plot against the man, I sent him to you at once, ordering his accusers also to state before you what they have against him."

Acts 21:31–33; 22:25–29

Acts 25:18–19; 26:31

aliquid certius inquisiturum sit de illo. [21]Tu ergo ne credideris illis; insidiantur enim ei ex eis viri amplius quadraginta, qui se devoverunt non manducare neque bibere, donec interficiant eum, et nunc parati sunt exspectantes promissum tuum». [22]Tribunus igitur dimisit adulescentem praecipiens, ne cui eloqueretur quoniam «haec nota mihi fecisti». [23]Et vocatis duobus centurionibus, dixit: «Parate milites ducentos, ut eant usque Caesaream, et equites septuaginta et lancearios ducentos, a tertia hora noctis, [24]et iumenta praeparate», ut imponentes Paulum salvum perducerent ad Felicem praesidem, [25]scribens epistulam habentem formam hanc: [26]«Claudius Lysias optimo praesidi Felici salutem. [27]Virum hunc comprehensum a Iudaeis et incipientem interfici ab eis, superveniens cum exercitu eripui, cognito quia Romanus est. [28]Volensque scire causam, propter quam accusabant illum, deduxi in concilium eorum; [29]quem inveni accusari de quaestionibus legis ipsorum, nihil vero dignum morte aut vinculis habentem crimen. [30]Et cum mihi perlatum esset de insidiis, quae in virum pararentur, confestim misi ad te denuntians et accusatoribus, ut dicant adversum eum apud te». [31]Milites ergo, secundum praeceptum sibi assumentes Paulum, duxerunt per noctem in Antipatridem; [32]et postera die

*23:22—28:31 In the last section of his book, Luke describes in great detail both Paul's trial and his journey to Rome. Over the course of these pages, we will see that all the various authorities who heard Paul speak or sat in judgement over him asserted his innocence of the charges laid against him: Christianity is a religion that does not run counter to the constitutional principles of the Roman empire.

23:22–35 Luke outlines, here and in the next three chapters, how Paul came to be tried under Roman law. The information he gives about both the legal process and the figures who took part in it (Felix, Festus etc.) fits in with information available to us from secular sources.

Felix had been governor or procurator of Judea since the year 52. He was a freedman who had risen remarkably high, but, according to Tacitus, the Roman historian, he "exerted royal power with the mind of a slave" (*Historiae*, 5, 9). He put down a number of revolts, but his excessive severity led to his being recalled in about the year 60 (see 24:27). The letter to him from the tribune Claudius Lysias (vv. 25–30) is the only secular letter transcribed in the New Testament. Antipatris was halfway between Jerusalem and Caesarea. Felix acts here in accordance with Roman law. He could have referred the case to the legate of the province of Syria, which at this time included Cilicia (Paul came from there), but he prefers to hear the case himself.

"Herod's praetorium" (v. 35) was a palace built by Herod the Great in Caesarea; it later became a residence of the Roman governor in Judea.

³¹So the soldiers, according to their instructions, took Paul and brought him by night to Antipatris. ³²And on the morrow they returned to the barracks, leaving the horsemen to go on with him. ³³When they came to Caesarea and delivered the letter to the governor, they presented Paul also before him. ³⁴On reading the letter, he asked to what province he belonged. When he learned that he was from Cilicia ³⁵he said, "I will hear you when your accusers arrive." And he commanded him to be guarded in Herod's praetorium.

The trial before Felix

Lk 23:2
Acts 16:20

24 ¹And after five days the high priest Ananias came down with some elders and a spokesman, one Tertullus. They laid before the governor their case against Paul; ²and when he was called, Tertullus began to accuse him, saying:

"Since through you we enjoy much peace, and since by your provision, most excellent Felix, reforms are introduced on behalf of this nation, ³in every way and everywhere we accept this with all gratitude. ⁴But, to detain you no further, I beg you in your kindness to hear us briefly. ⁵For we have found this man a pestilent fellow, an agitator among all the Jews throughout the world, and a ringleader of the sect of the Nazarenes. ⁶He even tried to profane the temple, but we seized him.ᶻ ⁸By examining him yourself you will be able to learn from him about everything of which we accuse him."

⁹The Jews also joined in the charge, affirming that all this was so.

¹⁰And when the governor had motioned to him to speak, Paul replied:

Acts 20:16

"Realizing that for many years you have been judge over this nation, I cheerfully make my defence. ¹¹As you may ascertain, it is not more than twelve days since I went up to worship at Jerusalem; ¹²and they did not find me disputing with any one or stirring up a crowd, either in the temple or in the synagogues, or in the city.

Acts 17:6
Mt 2:23

Acts 21:28

dimissis equitibus, ut abirent cum eo, reversi sunt ad castra. ³³Qui cum venissent Caesaream et tradidissent epistulam praesidi, statuerunt ante illum et Paulum. ³⁴Cum legisset autem et interrogasset de qua provincia esset et cognoscens quia de Cilicia: ³⁵«Audiam te, inquit, cum et accusatores tui venerint»; iussitque in praetorio Herodis custodiri eum. [24] ¹Post quinque autem dies descendit princeps sacerdotum Ananias cum senioribus quibusdam et Tertullo quodam oratore, qui adierunt praesidem adversus Paulum. ²Et citato eo coepit accusare Tertullus dicens: «Cum in multa pace agamus per te, et multa corrigantur genti huic per tuam providentiam, ³semper et ubique suscipimus, optime Felix, cum omni gratiarum actione. ⁴Ne diutius autem te protraham, oro breviter audias nos pro tua clementia. ⁵Invenimus enim hunc hominem pestiferum et concitantem seditiones omnibus Iudaeis, qui sunt in universo orbe, et auctorem seditionis sectae Nazarenorum, ⁶qui etiam templum violare conatus est, quem et apprehendimus, ⁸a quo poteris ipse diiudicans de omnibus istis cognoscere, de quibus nos accusamus eum». ⁹Adiecerunt autem et Iudaei dicentes haec ita se habere. ¹⁰Respondit autem Paulus, annuente sibi praeside dicere: «Ex multis annis esse te iudicem genti huic sciens bono animo de causa mea rationem reddam, ¹¹cum possis cognoscere quia non plus sunt dies mihi quam duodecim, ex quo ascendi adorare in Ierusalem, ¹²et neque in templo invenerunt me cum aliquo disputantem aut concursum facientem turbae neque in synagogis neque in civitate, ¹³neque pro-

24:1–27 Sent to Caesarea by the tribune Lysias, Paul now enters Roman jurisdiction. The Jews will not succeed in their attempt to have him judged by the Sanhedrin. The Apostle's case is now handled in the Roman judicial process known as *cognitio extra ordinem*, which was also used in criminal law cases and which would eventually (in the second century) replace trials held before "permanent tribunals" (*quaestiones perpetuae*). The main feature that distinguished *cognitio extra ordinem* from the previous system of trials before a permanent tribunal was that the case was heard by the emperor or, in his name, by a magistrate or an imperial official aided by an advisory council. Another difference was that the newer type of legal process, the one applied in Paul's case, was based on an inquisitorial rather than an accusatory model of justice. This allowed the judge greater scope for gathering evidence and for judging the case; and he had the power to vary the penalty according to the seriousness of the offence.

Chapters 24 and 25 of Acts are in fact an important source of information about the functioning of *cognitio extra ordinem* in criminal cases; they accurately report various elements in

z Other ancient authorities add *and we would have judged him according to our law.* ⁷*But the chief captain Lysias came and with great violence took him out of our hands,* ⁸*commanding his accusers to come before you*

[13]Neither can they prove to you what they now bring up against me. [14]But this I admit to you, that according to the Way, which they call a sect, I worship the God of our fathers, believing everything laid down by the law or written in the prophets, [15]having a hope in God which these themselves accept, that there will be a resurrection of both the just and the unjust. [16]So I always take pains to have a clear conscience toward God and toward men. [17]Now after some years I came to bring to my nation alms and offerings. [18]As I was doing this, they found me purified in the temple, without any crowd or tumult. But some Jews from Asia—[19]they ought to be here before you and to make an accusation, if they have anything against me. [20]Or else let these men themselves say what wrongdoing they found when I stood before the council, [21]except this one thing which I cried out while standing among them, 'With respect to the resurrection of the dead I am on trial before you this day.'"

[22]But Felix, having a rather accurate knowledge of the Way, put them off, saying, "When Lysias the tribune comes down, I will decide your case." [23]Then he gave orders to the centurion that he should be kept in custody but should have some liberty, and that none of his friends should be prevented from attending to his needs.

Mt 5:17
Rom 16:26

Dan 12:2
Jn 5:28–29; 15:29
Acts 23:1
Rom 15:25
Gal 2:10
Acts 21:27

A further appearance before Felix

[24]After some days Felix came with his wife Drusilla, who was a Jewess; and he sent for Paul and heard him speak upon faith in Christ Jesus. [25]And as he argued about justice and self-control and future judgment, Felix was alarmed and said, "Go away for the present; when I have an opportunity I will summon you." [26]At the same time he hoped that money would be given him by Paul. So he sent for him often and conversed with him. [27]But when two years had elapsed, Felix was succeeded by Porcius Festus; and desiring to do the Jews a favour, Felix left Paul in prison.

Mk 6:17–20
Jn 16:8

Acts 25:9

bare possunt tibi, de quibus nunc accusant me. [14]Confiteor autem hoc tibi quod secundum viam, quam dicunt haeresim, sic deservio patrio Deo credens omnibus, quae secundum Legem sunt et in Prophetis scripta, [15]spem habens in Deum, quam et hi ipsi exspectant, resurrectionem futuram iustorum et iniquorum. [16]In hoc et ipse studeo sine offendiculo conscientiam habere ad Deum et ad homines semper. [17]Post annos autem plures eleemosynas facturus in gentem meam veni et oblationes, [18]in quibus invenerunt me purificatum in templo, non cum turba neque cum tumultu; [19]quidam autem ex Asia Iudaei, quos oportebat apud te praesto esse et accusare si quid haberent adversum me [20]aut hi ipsi dicant quid invenerint iniquitatis, cum starem in concilio, [21]nisi de una hac voce, qua clamavi inter eos stans: De resurrectione mortuorum ego iudicor hodie apud vos!». [22]Distulit autem illos Felix certissime sciens ea, quae de hac via sunt, dicens: «Cum tribunus Lysias descenderit, cognoscam causam vestram», [23]iubens centurioni custodiri eum et habere mitigationem, nec quemquam prohibere de suis ministrare ei. [24]Post aliquot autem dies adveniens Felix cum Drusilla uxore sua, quae erat Iudaea, vocavit Paulum et audivit ab eo de fide, quae est in Christum Iesum. [25]Disputante autem illo de iustitia et continentia et de iudicio futuro, timefactus Felix respondit: «Quod nunc attinet, vade; tempore autem opportuno accersiam te», [26]simul et sper-

the trial process. In the narrative we are told about the charges laid by the Jews against Paul (see 23:35; 24:1); the correct legal terminology is used with reference to hearings by the judge (see 25:6, 17); mention is made of the council that assists the magistrate (see 25:12); the charges are described in some detail and we see the kind of discretion that the magistrates (Felix and Festus) had in the way they heard the case and weighed the evidence.

In the speech he makes in his own defence (vv. 10–21), St Paul argues (vv. 14–16) that Christianity cannot be defined as a sect of Judaism. He also asserts that he has always acted within the law and has never done anything that was at odds with the civil authority's jurisdiction over its citizens. "A Christian", Tertullian will write, "is an enemy of no one, least of all the emperor. Since he knows him to be appointed by his own God, he must love, reverence, honour, and wish him well, together with the whole Roman empire, as long as the world shall last" (*Liber ad Scapulum*, 2).

Later (vv. 24–27), we hear about Paul's encounter with Felix and his wife, Drusilla. Drusilla, a daughter of Herod Agrippa I (cf. 12:1f), had left her lawful husband to marry the Roman governor. It is very daring of Paul to speak about justice, self-control and future judgment (v. 25) to a couple who were effectively

Festus resumes the trial. Paul appeals to Caesar

25 ¹Now when Festus had come into his province, after three days he went up to Jerusalem from Caesarea. ²And the chief priests and the principal men of the Jews informed him against Paul; and they urged him, ³asking as a favour to have the man sent to Jerusalem, planning an ambush to kill him on the way. ⁴Festus replied that Paul was being kept at Caesarea, and that he himself intended to go there shortly. ⁵"So," said he, "let the men of authority among you go down with me, and if there is anything wrong about the man, let them accuse him."

⁶When he had stayed among them not more than eight or ten days, he went down to Caesarea; and the next day he took his seat on the tribunal and ordered Paul to be brought. ⁷And when he had come, the Jews who had gone down from Jerusalem stood about him, bringing against him many serious charges which they could not prove. ⁸Paul said in his defence, "Neither against the law of the Jews, nor against the temple, nor against Caesar have I offended at all." ⁹But Festus, wishing to do the Jews a favour, said to Paul, "Do you wish to go up to Jerusalem, and there be tried on these charges before me?" ¹⁰But Paul said, "I am standing before Caesar's tribunal, where I ought to be tried; to the Jews I have done no wrong, as you know very well. ¹¹If then I am a wrongdoer, and have committed anything for which I deserve to die, I do not seek to escape death; but if there is nothing in their charges against

living in concubinage: "Observe that, when he has the opportunity to converse with the governor, Paul does not say anything which might influence his decision or flatter him: he says things which shock him and disturb his conscience" (St John Chrysostom, *In Acta Apostolorum*, 51). Felix (see v. 26) may well have hoped he could get some of the money Paul had collected and brought to Jerusalem: Paul had mentioned it during his defence speech (v. 17).

See the RSV note **z** (p. 538 above).

25:1–12 Felix's venality can be seen from what Luke reports in 24:26–27. His successor now takes over the case. Porcius Festus, we learn from secular sources, governed Judea well during the two or three years he spent in the position (he died in 61 or 62). The text seems to confirm that Festus was a fair-minded man. He has no intention of handing the case over to the

Jewish authorities; but his political prudence leads him to accede partly to the requests of Paul's accusers: he allows the Sanhedrin a voice in the proceedings. He had a right to make the Sanhedrin a *consilium*, to hear its advice; that is the import of his offer to Paul to hear the charges in Jerusalem (v. 9).

In point of fact, the governor's offer to Paul is a rhetorical one: it is notification of a decision he has already made. Paul realizes what Festus intends to do, so he appeals to Caesar in order to avoid being tried in a hostile venue, Jerusalem. Accused citizens had the right to appeal (*provocare*) to the throne when they felt that a magistrate had misused his authority. This right lay at the heart of the Roman way of thinking; it was a legal protection of a citizen's political freedom.

Provocatio, by the way, should not be confused with *apellatio*, an appeal against a sen-

Acts 23:15

Mt 26:59–60
Lk 23:14–15

Acts 24:14–15

Acts 24:27

me, no one can give me up to them. I appeal to Caesar." [12]Then Festus, when he had conferred with his council, answered, "You have appealed to Caesar; to Caesar you shall go."

Festus briefs Agrippa

[13]Now when some days had passed, Agrippa the king and Bernice arrived at Caesarea to welcome Festus. [14]And as they stayed there many days, Festus laid Paul's case before the king, saying, "There is a man left prisoner by Felix; [15]and when I was at Jerusalem, the chief priests and the elders of the Jews gave information about him, asking for sentence against him. [16]I answered them that it was not the custom of the Romans to give up any one before the accused met the accusers face to face, and had opportunity to make his defence concerning the charge laid against him. [17]When therefore they came together here, I made no delay, but on the next day took my seat on the tribunal and ordered the man to be brought in. [18]When the accusers stood up, they brought no charge in his case of such evils as I supposed; [19]but they had certain points of dispute with him about their own superstition and about one Jesus, who was dead, but whom Paul asserted to be alive. [20]Being at a loss how to investigate these questions, I asked whether he wished to go to Jerusalem and be tried there regarding them. [21]But when Paul had appealed to be kept in custody for the decision of the emperor, I commanded him to be held until I send him to Caesar." [22]And Agrippa said to Festus, "I should like to hear the man myself." "Tomorrow," said he, "you shall hear him."

Acts 24:1; 25:2

Acts 18:5; 23:29
1 Cor 15:14

Lk 23:8

consilio locutus respondit: «Caesarem appellasti; ad Caesarem ibis». [13]Et cum dies aliquot transacti essent, Agrippa rex et Berenice descenderunt Caesaream et salutaverunt Festum. [14]Et cum dies plures ibi demorarentur, Festus regi indicavit de Paulo dicens: «Vir quidam est derelictus a Felice vinctus, [15]de quo cum essem Hierosolymis, adierunt me principes sacerdotum et seniores Iudaeorum postulantes adversus illum damnationem; [16]ad quos respondi quia non est consuetudo Romanis donare aliquem hominem, priusquam is, qui accusatur, praesentes habeat accusatores locumque defendendi se ab accusatione accipiat. [17]Cum ergo huc convenissent, sine ulla dilatione sequenti die sedens pro tribunali iussi adduci virum; [18]de quo cum stetissent accusatores, nullam causam deferebant, de quibus ego suspicabar malis, [19]quaestiones vero quasdam de sua superstitione habebant adversus eum et de quodam Iesu defuncto, quem affirmabat Paulus vivere. [20]Haesitans autem ego de huiusmodi quaestione, dicebam si vellet ire Hierosolymam et ibi iudicari de istis. [21]Paulo autem appellante, ut servaretur ad Augusti cognitionem, iussi servari eum, donec mittam eum ad Caesarem». [22]Agrippa autem ad Festum: «Volebam et ipse hominem audire!». «Cras, inquit, audies eum». [23]Altera autem die, cum venisset Agrippa et Berenice cum multa ambitione, et introissent in auditorium cum tribunis et viris principalibus civitatis, et iubente Festo, adductus est Paulus. [24]Et dicit Festus: «Agrippa rex et omnes, qui simul adestis nobiscum viri, videtis hunc, de quo omnis multitudo Iudaeorum inter-

tence (none had so far been passed against Paul).

These various legal proceedings, foreseen by Providence, ensure that Paul can fulfil the task that God has marked out for him and foretold (see 23:11) "He appeals to Caesar and hastens to Rome to persist still longer in preaching, and thereby go to Christ crowned with the many who thereby will come to believe, as well as those who already believe [through him]" (St Bede, *Expositio Actuum Apostolorum*, ad loc.).

25:13–27 Herod Agrippa II was a son of Herod Agrippa I (cf. the note on 12:1–19), and therefore a great-grandson of Herod the Great. He was born in the year 27. Like his father, he had won favour with Rome and had been granted various territories in northern Palestine, which he was allowed to rule with the title of king. Bernice was his sister.

Festus' words, on the two occasions that he addresses the king (vv. 14–21; 24–27) show that none of the charges brought against Paul has any basis. Agrippa's reply in v. 22 is somewhat reminiscent of the desire expressed by his great-uncle, Herod Antipas, to see Jesus (see Lk 9:9; 23:8). Commentators have not been slow to see the hand of God in this process: "His conversation with the governor awakens in Agrippa a strong desire to hear Paul. Festus meets his wish [...]. This is the outcome of the machinations against him: without them no judge would have deigned to listen to such things, nor would anyone have heard them with such rapt attention" (St John Chrysostom, *In Acta Apostolorum*, 51, 4).

Paul before Agrippa

23So on the morrow Agrippa and Bernice came with great pomp, and they entered the audience hall with the military tribunes and the prominent men of the city. Then by command of Festus Paul was brought in. 24And Festus said, "King Agrippa and all who are present with us, you see this man about whom the whole Jewish people petitioned me, both at Jerusalem and here, shouting that he ought not to live any longer. 25But I found that he had done nothing deserving death; and as he himself appealed to the emperor, I decided to send him. 26But I have nothing definite to write to my lord about him. Therefore I have brought him before you, and, especially before you, King Agrippa, that, after we have examined him, I may have something to write. 27For it seems to me unreasonable, in sending a prisoner, not to indicate the charges against him."

Paul's speech in the presence of Agrippa

26 1Agrippa said to Paul, "You have permission to speak for yourself." Then Paul stretched out his hand and made his defence:

2"I think myself fortunate that it is before you, King Agrippa, I am to make my defence today against all the accusations of the Jews, 3because you are especially familiar with all customs and controversies of the Jews; therefore I beg you to listen to me patiently.

4"My manner of life from my youth, spent from the beginning among my own nation and at Jerusalem, is known by all the Jews. 5They have known for a long time, if they are willing to testify, that according to the strictest party of our religion I have lived as a Pharisee. 6And now I stand here on trial for hope in the promise made by God to our fathers, 7to which our twelve tribes hope to attain, as they earnestly worship night and day. And for this hope I am accused by Jews, O king! 8Why is it thought incredible by any of you that God raises the dead?

9"I myself was convinced that I ought to do many things in opposing the name of Jesus of Nazareth. 10And I did so in Jerusalem; I not only shut up many of the

Acts 22:3
Gal 1:14
Phil 3:5–6
Acts 23:6

Dan 12:1–3
2 Mac 7

Jn 16:2
Acts 9:13; 22:20

pellavit me Hierosolymis et hic, clamantes non oportere eum vivere amplius. 25Ego vero comperi nihil dignum eum morte fecisse, ipso autem hoc appellante Augustum, iudicavi mittere. 26De quo quid certum scribam domino, non habeo; propter quod produxi eum ad vos et maxime ad te, rex Agrippa, ut, interrogatione facta, habeam quid scribam: 27sine ratione enim mihi videtur mittere vinctum et causas eius non significare». [26] 1Agrippa vero ad Paulum ait: «Permittitur tibi loqui pro temetipso». Tunc Paulus, extenta manu, coepit rationem reddere: 2«De omnibus, quibus accusor a Iudaeis, rex Agrippa, aestimo me beatum, apud te cum sim defensurus me hodie, 3maxime te sciente omnia, quae apud Iudaeos sunt consuetudines et quaestiones; propter quod obsecro patienter me audias. 4Et quidem vitam meam a iuventute, quae ab initio fuit in gente mea et in Hierosolymis, noverunt omnes Iudaei, 5praescientes me ab initio, si velint testimonium perhibere, quoniam secundum diligentissimam sectam nostrae religionis vixi pharisaeus. 6Et nunc propter spem eius, quae ad patres nostros repromissionis facta est a Deo, sto iudicio subiectus, 7in quam duodecim tribus nostrae cum perseverantia nocte ac die deservientes sperant devenire; de qua spe accusor a Iudaeis, rex! 8Quid incredibile iudicatur apud vos, si Deus mortuos suscitat? 9Et ego quidem existimaveram me adversus nomen Iesu Nazareni debere multa contraria agere; 10quod et feci Hierosolymis, et multos sanctorum ego in carceribus inclusi, a principibus sacerdotum potestate accepta, et cum occiderentur, detuli

26:1–23 In his speech given before Agrippa, Paul once again describes how he came to receive his call from God—which was rather in the way that the prophets of old were called (cf. Ezek 1:28—2:2; Is 42:6ff). God makes known his intentions, calling his chosen one to a radical change of life. But there is a special nuance to this description: his vocation made Paul a witness (see v. 16), just like the original apostles (see 1:8, 22; 3:15).

In the second part of his speech (vv. 19–23), Paul explains why he has acted as he has. He makes it clear that he embraced Christianity not blindly, but with a profound and reasonable conviction. He explains his change of heart in terms of docility and obedience to the vision he received (v. 19). Paul's experience is repeated in different ways (usually in less dramatic and intense terms) in the life of every man and woman. God calls us and invites us to a new

saints in prison, by authority from the chief priests, but when they were put to death I cast my vote against them. [11]And I punished them often in all the synagogues and tried to make them blaspheme; and in raging fury against them, I persecuted them even to foreign cities.

[12]"Thus I journeyed to Damascus with the authority and commission of the chief priests. [13]At midday, O king, I saw on the way a light from heaven, brighter than the sun, shining round me and those who journeyed with me. [14]And when we had all fallen to the ground, I heard a voice saying to me in the Hebrew language, 'Saul, Saul, why do you persecute me? It hurts you to kick against the goads.' [15]And I said, 'Who are you, Lord?' And the Lord said, 'I am Jesus whom you are persecuting. [16]But rise and stand upon your feet; for I have appeared to you for this purpose, to appoint you to serve and bear witness to the things in which you have seen me and to those in which I will appear to you, [17]delivering you from the people and from the Gentiles — to whom I send you [18]to open their eyes, that they may turn from darkness to light and from the power of Satan to God, that they may receive forgiveness of sins and a place among those who are sanctified by faith in me.'

[19]"Wherefore, O King Agrippa, I was not disobedient to the heavenly vision, [20]but declared first to those at Damascus, then at Jerusalem and throughout all the country of Judea, and also to the Gentiles, that they should repent and turn to God and perform deeds worthy of their repentance. [21]For this reason the Jews seized me in the temple and tried to kill me. [22]To this day I have had the help that comes from God, and so I stand here testifying both to small and great, saying nothing but what the prophets and Moses said would come to pass: [23]that the Christ must suffer, and that, by being the first to rise from the dead, he would proclaim light both to the people and to the Gentiles."

Ezek 2:1

1 Chron 16:15
Jer 1:7
Is 35:5; 42:7, 16;
61:1
Jn 8:12
Acts 9:17–18
Deut 33:3–4
Wis 5:5
Col 1:12–14
Gal 1:16

Acts 21:30–31

Lk 24:44
Acts 13:47; 17:3

Is 42:6; 49:6
1 Cor 15:20–23
Col 1:18

sententiam, [11]et per omnes synagogas frequenter puniens eos compellebam blasphemare, et abundantius insaniens in eos persequebar usque in exteras civitates. [12]In quibus dum irem Damascum cum potestate et permissu principum sacerdotum, [13]die media in via vidi, rex, de caelo supra splendorem solis circumfulgens me lumen et eos, qui mecum simul ibant; [14]omnesque nos cum decidissemus in terram, audivi vocem loquentem mihi Hebraica lingua: "Saul, Saul, quid me persequeris? Durum est tibi contra stimulum calcitrare". [15]Ego autem dixi: "Quis es, Domine?". Dominus autem dixit: "Ego sum Iesus, quem tu persequeris. [16]Sed exsurge et sta super pedes tuos; ad hoc enim apparui tibi, ut constituam te ministrum et testem eorum, quae vidisti, et eorum, quibus apparebo tibi, [17]eripiens te de populo et de gentibus, in quas ego mitto te [18]aperire oculos eorum, ut convertantur a tenebris ad lucem et de potestate Satanae ad Deum, ut accipiant remissionem peccatorum et sortem inter sanctificatos per fidem, quae est in me". [19]Unde, rex Agrippa, non fui incredulus caelestis visionis, [20]sed his, qui sunt Damasci primum et Hierosolymis, et in omnem regionem Iudaeae et gentibus annuntiabam, ut paenitentiam agerent et converterentur ad Deum digna paenitentiae opera facientes. [21]Hac ex causa me Iudaei, cum essem in templo comprehensum, tentabant interficere. [22]Auxilium igitur assecutus a Deo usque in hodiernum diem sto testificans minori atque maiori, nihil extra dicens quam ea, quae prophetae sunt locuti futura esse et Moyses, [23]si passibilis Christus, si primus ex

conversion that draws us out of sin or lukewarmness. What we must do is listen carefully to that calling and obey it. "We should let our Lord get involved in our lives, admitting him trustingly, removing from his way any obstacles or excuses. We tend to be on the defensive, to be attached to our selfishness. We always want to be in charge, even if it's only to be in charge of our wretchedness. That is why we must go to Jesus, so to have him make us truly free. Only then will we be able to serve God and all men" (St Josemaría Escrivá, *Christ Is Passing By*, 17).

The speech also shows how diligently Paul strove to respond to the grace he received (see v.

22). In this regard, too, he sets an example for all Christians: "The grace of the Holy Spirit is given to each person in the hope that each will multiply and increase what he receives" (St Gregory of Nyssa, *De instituto christiano*). The same idea is expressed by St Teresa when she says that "we must seek new strength with which to serve Him, and endeavour not to be ungrateful, for that is the condition on which the Lord bestows His jewels. Unless we make good use of His treasures, and of the high estate to which He brings us, He will take these treasures back from us, and we shall be poorer than before, and His Majesty will give the jewels to some other

Reactions to Paul's speech

Jn 10:20
Jn 18:37

[24]And as he thus made his defence, Festus said with a loud voice, "Paul, you are mad; your great learning is turning you mad." [25]But Paul said, "I am not mad, most excellent Festus, but I am speaking the sober truth. [26]For the king knows about these things, and to him I speak freely; for I am persuaded that none of these things has escaped his notice, for this was not done in a corner. [27]King Agrippa, do you believe

Acts 11:26
1 Pet 4:16

the prophets? I know that you believe." [28]And Agrippa said to Paul, "In a short time you think to make me a Christian!" [29]And Paul said, "Whether short or long, I would to God that not only you but also all who hear me this day might become such as I am—except for these chains."

Acts 28:20

[30]Then the king rose, and the governor and Bernice and those who were sitting with them; [31]and when they had withdrawn, they said to one another, "This man is

Acts 23:29

doing nothing to deserve death or imprisonment." [32]And Agrippa said to Festus, "This man could have been set free if he had not appealed to Caesar."

Departure for Rome. Voyage to Crete

27 [1]And when it was decided that we should sail for Italy, they delivered Paul and some other prisoners to a centurion of the Augustan Cohort, named

Acts 19:29

Julius. [2]And embarking in a ship of Adramyttium, which was about to sail to the ports along the coast of Asia, we put to sea, accompanied by Aristarchus, a

Acts 24:23; 28:16

Macedonian from Thessalonica. [3]The next day we put in at Sidon; and Julius treated Paul kindly, and gave him leave to go to his friends and be cared for. [4]And putting

---

resurrectione mortuorum lumen annuntiaturus est populo et gentibus». [24]Sic autem eo rationem reddente, Festus magna voce dixit: «Insanis, Paule; multae te litterae ad insaniam convertunt!». [25]At Paulus: «Non insanio, inquit, optime Feste, sed veritatis et sobrietatis verba eloquor. [26]Scit enim de his rex, ad quem et audenter loquor; latere enim eum nihil horum arbitror, neque enim in angulo hoc gestum est. [27]Credis, rex Agrippa, prophetis? Scio quia credis». [28]Agrippa autem ad Paulum: «In modico suades me Christianum fieri!». [29]Et Paulus: «Optarem apud Deum et in modico et in magno non tantum te sed et omnes hos, qui audiunt me hodie, fieri tales, qualis et ego sum, exceptis vinculis his!». [30]Et exsurrexit rex et praeses et Berenice et, qui assidebant eis, [31]et cum secessissent, loquebantur ad invicem dicentes: «Nihil morte aut vinculis dignum quid facit homo iste». [32]Agrippa autem Festo dixit: «Dimitti poterat homo hic, si non appellasset Caesarem». [27] [1]Ut autem iudicatum est navigare nos in Italiam, tradiderunt et Paulum et quosdam alios vinctos centurioni nomine Iulio, cohortis Augustae. [2]Ascendentes autem navem Hadramyttenam, incipientem navigare circa Asiae loca, sustulimus, perseverante nobiscum Aristarcho Macedone Thessalonicensi; [3]sequenti autem

---

person who can display them to advantage and to his own profit and that of others" (*Life*, 10, 6).

26:24–32 Festus cannot make sense of what Paul is saying; he lacks any understanding or belief, even though he does seem to harbour a certain sympathy for the Apostle. The fact is that divine wisdom sometimes does not make sense to someone who sees things only in pragmatic terms. "He regarded it as madness for a man in chains not to deal with the calumnies that threatened him but, instead, to be speaking about the convictions which enlightened him from within" (St Bede, *Expositio Actuum Apostolorum*, ad loc.).

Paul's apostolic zeal, so evident in this episode, still has the power to inspire those who read it: "How admirably he behaves! Imprisoned for spreading the teachings of Christ, he misses

no opportunity to preach the Gospel. [...] The apostle does not silence or hide his faith, or his apostolic preaching that had brought down on him the hatred of his persecutors. He continues preaching salvation to everyone he meets. [...]. Where did St Paul get all his strength from? *Omnia possum in eo qui me confortat!* (Phil 4:13). I can do all things in him who strengthens me. I can do all things, because God alone gives me this faith, this hope, this charity" (St Josemaría Escrivá, *Friends of God*, 270–271).

At the end of this scene (vv. 30–32), impartial judges again declare Paul innocent. However, to set him free now, after he has appealed to Caesar, would cause offence both to the emperor and to the Jewish authorities.

27:1–44 The account of St Paul's sea journey (27:1–28:16) is so exact in its terminology that it

to sea from there we sailed under the lee of Cyprus, because the winds were against us. [5]And when we had sailed across the sea which is off Cilicia and Pamphylia, we came to Myra in Lycia. [6]There the centurion found a ship of Alexandria sailing for Italy, and put us on board. [7]We sailed slowly for a number of days, and arrived with difficulty off Cnidus, and as the wind did not allow us to go on, we sailed under the lee of Crete off Salmone. [8]Coasting along it with difficulty, we came to a place called Fair Havens, near which was the city of Lasaea.

The voyage is resumed against Paul's advice

[9]As much time had been lost, and the voyage was already dangerous because the fast had already gone by, Paul advised them, [10]saying, "Sirs, I perceive that the voyage will be with injury and much loss, not only of the cargo and the ship, but also of our lives." [11]But the centurion paid more attention to the captain and to the owner of the ship than to what Paul said. [12]And because the harbour was not suitable to winter in, the majority advised to put to sea from there, on the chance that somehow they could reach Phoenix, a harbour of Crete, looking northeast and southeast,[a] and winter there.

A storm

[13]And when the south wind blew gently, supposing that they had obtained their purpose, they weighed anchor and sailed along Crete, close inshore. [14]But soon a tempestuous wind, called the northeaster, struck down from the land; [15]and when the ship was caught and could not face the wind, we gave way to it and were driven. [16]And running under the lee of a small island called Cauda,[b] we managed with difficulty to secure the boat; [17]after hoisting it up, they took measures[c] to undergird the

die devenimus Sidonem, et humane tractans Iulius Paulum permisit ad amicos ire et curam sui agere. [4]Et inde cum sustulissemus, subnavigavimus Cypro, propterea quod essent venti contrarii, [5]et pelagus Ciliciae et Pamphyliae navigantes venimus Myram, quae est Lyciae. [6]Et ibi inveniens centurio navem Alexandrinam navigantem in Italiam transposuit nos in eam. [7]Et cum multis diebus tarde navigaremus et vix devenissemus contra Cnidum, prohibente nos vento, subnavigavimus Cretae secundum Salmonem, [8]et vix iuxta eam navigantes venimus in locum quendam, qui vocatur Boni Portus, cui iuxta erat civitas Lasaea. [9]Multo autem tempore peracto, et cum iam non esset tuta navigatio, eo quod et ieiunium iam praeterisset, monebat Paulus [10]dicens eis: «Viri, video quoniam cum iniuria et multo damno non solum oneris et navis sed etiam animarum nostrarum incipit esse navigatio». [11]Centurio autem gubernatori et nauclero magis credebat quam his, quae a Paulo dicebantur. [12]Et cum aptus portus non esset ad hiemandum, plurimi statuerunt consilium enavigare inde, si quo modo possent devenientes Phoenicen hiemare, portum Cretae respicientem ad africum et ad caurum. [13]Aspirante autem austro, aestimantes propositum se tenere, cum sustulissent, propius legebant Cretam. [14]Non post multum autem misit se contra ipsam ventus typhonicus, qui vocatur euroaquilo; [15]cumque arrepta esset navis et non posset conari in ventum, data nave flatibus, ferebamur. [16]Insulam autem quandam decurrentes, quae vocatur Cauda, potuimus vix obtinere scapham, [17]qua sublata,

has been read as an important source of information on seafaring in ancient times. It is full of detail, all of it accurate. Events and situations are so vividly drawn that the narrative must be based on the memories, and maybe the notes, of an eyewitness, someone who accompanied the Apostle on the journey. (And, in fact, they are written in the first person plural from this point on until the end of the book.) The ship from Alexandria on which they embarked (v. 6) must have been one of the cargo boats that brought grain from Egypt to Rome. These wide, heavy boats had one mast amidship and another further forward, towards the prow; the hull was covered by a deck that had openings or moveable timbers allowing access to the hold, where the cargo was stored and where passengers could take shelter in bad weather. At that time travel on the high seas was considered unsafe as of the middle of September, and entirely out of the question from November to March. The "fast" (v. 9) was that prescribed for all Jews on the Day of Atonement (see Lev 16:29–31); in the year 60 it fell at the end of October. Prior to this, Paul had suffered shipwreck three times (see 2 Cor 11:25), and he knew how risky the voyage would be, but most of those on board were in favour of making for some more suitable port to winter in.

The account notes God's special providence towards Paul (vv. 24, 44), and the active interest

a Or *southwest and northwest*   b Other ancient authorities read *Clauda*   c Greek *helps*

ship; then, fearing that they should run on the Syrtis, they lowered the gear, and so were driven. [18]As we were violently storm-tossed, they began next day to throw the cargo overboard; [19]and the third day they cast out with their own hands the tackle of the ship. [20]And when neither sun nor stars appeared for many a day, and no small tempest lay on us, all hope of our being saved was at last abandoned.

Paul's vision. He rallies his companions

[21]As they had been long without food, Paul then came forward among them and said, "Men, you should have listened to me, and should not have set sail from Crete and incurred this injury and loss. [22]I now bid you to take heart; for there will be no loss of life among you, but only of the ship. [23]For this very night there stood by me an angel of the God to whom I belong and whom I worship, [24]and he said, 'Do not be afraid, Paul; you must stand before Caesar; and lo, God has granted you all those who sail with you.' [25]So take heart, men, for I have faith in God that it will be exactly as I have been told. [26]But we shall have to run on some island."

[27]When the fourteenth night had come, as we were drifting across the sea of Adria, about midnight the sailors suspected that they were nearing land. [28]So they sounded and found twenty fathoms; a little farther on they sounded again and found fifteen fathoms. [29]And fearing that we might run on the rocks, they let out four anchors from the stern, and prayed for day to come. [30]And as the sailors were seeking to escape from the ship, and had lowered the boat into the sea, under pretence of laying out anchors from the bow, [31]Paul said to the centurion and the soldiers, "Unless these men stay in the ship, you cannot be saved." [32]Then the soldiers cut away the ropes of the boat, and let it go.

[33]As day was about to dawn, Paul urged them all to take some food, saying, "Today is the fourteenth day that you have continued in suspense and without food, having taken nothing. [34]Therefore I urge you to take some food; it will give you strength, since not a hair is to perish from the head of any of you." [35]And when he

Jn 1:5

Acts 27:33

Acts 23:11

1 Sam 14:45
2 Sam 14:11
Mt 10:30
Lk 12:7
Lk 22:19
1 Tim 4:4

adiutoriis utebantur accingentes navem; et timentes, ne in Syrtim inciderent, submisso vase, sic ferebantur. [18]Valide autem nobis tempestate iactatis, sequenti die iactum fecerunt [19]et tertia die suis manibus armamenta navis proiecerunt. [20]Neque sole autem neque sideribus apparentibus per plures dies, et tempestate non exigua imminente, iam auferebatur spes omnis salutis nostrae. [21]Et cum multa ieiunatio fuisset, tunc stans Paulus in medio eorum dixit: «Oportebat quidem, o viri, audito me, non tollere a Creta lucrique facere iniuriam hanc et iacturam. [22]Et nunc suadeo vobis bono animo esse, nulla enim amissio animae erit ex vobis praeterquam navis; [23]astitit enim mihi hac nocte angelus Dei, cuius sum ego, cui et deservio, [24]dicens: "Ne timeas, Paule; Caesari te oportet assistere, et ecce donavit tibi Deus omnes, qui navigant tecum". [25]Propter quod bono animo estote, viri; credo enim Deo quia sic erit, quemadmodum dictum est mihi. [26]In insulam autem quandam oportet nos incidere». [27]Sed posteaquam quarta decima nox supervenit, cum ferremur in Hadria, circa mediam noctem suspicabantur nautae apparere sibi aliquam regionem. [28]Qui submittentes bolidem invenerunt passus viginti et pusillum inde separati et rursum submittentes invenerunt passus quindecim; [29]timentes autem, ne in aspera loca incideremus, de puppi mittentes ancoras quattuor optabant diem fieri. [30]Nautis vero quaerentibus fugere de navi, cum demisissent scapham in mare sub obtentu, quasi a prora inciperent ancoras extendere, [31]dixit Paulus centurioni et militibus: «Nisi hi in navi manserint, vos salvi fieri non potestis». [32]Tunc absciderunt milites funes scaphae et passi sunt eam excidere. [33]Donec autem lux inciperet fieri, rogabat Paulus omnes sumere cibum dicens: «Quarta decima hodie die exspectantes ieiuni permanetis nihil accipientes; [34]propter quod rogo vos accipere cibum, hoc enim pro salute vestra est, quia nullius vestrum capillus de capite peribit». [35]Et cum haec dixisset et sumpsisset panem, gratias egit Deo in conspectu omnium et, cum fregisset, coepit manducare. [36]Animaequiores autem facti omnes et ipsi assumpserunt cibum. [37]Eramus vero universae animae in navi ducentae septuaginta sex. [38]Et satiati cibo alleviabant navem iactantes triticum in mare. [39]Cum autem dies factus

the Apostle takes in his fellow passengers' welfare (vv. 33–36), though they don't always reciprocate his good will (v. 42). The Tradition of the Church draws lessons from this episode for the faithful in general: "Why did God not save the boat from shipwreck? So that the travellers would realize the scale of the danger and that they were saved from it not by any human help but by God, who saved their lives after the boat broke up. In like manner the just are well off even in storms and tempests, on the high seas or in a rough bay, because they are protected from everything and even come to the rescue of others. Aboard a ship in danger of being engulfed by the waves, the enchained prisoners and the whole crew owe their safety to the pres-

had said this, he took bread, and giving thanks to God in the presence of all he broke it and began to eat. ³⁶Then they all were encouraged and ate some food themselves. ³⁷(We were in all two hundred and seventy-six[d] persons in the ship.) ³⁸And when they had eaten enough, they lightened the ship, throwing out the wheat into the sea.

Shipwreck and rescue

³⁹Now when it was day, they did not recognize the land, but they noticed a bay with a beach, on which they planned if possible to bring the ship ashore. ⁴⁰So they cast off the anchors and left them in the sea, at the same time loosening the ropes that tied the rudders; then hoisting the foresail to the wind they made for the beach. ⁴¹But striking a shoal[e] they ran the vessel aground; the bow struck and remained immovable, and the stern was broken up by the surf. ⁴²The soldiers' plan was to kill the prisoners, lest any should swim away and escape; ⁴³but the centurion, wishing to save Paul, kept them from carrying out their purpose. He ordered those who could swim to throw themselves overboard first and make for the land, ⁴⁴and the rest on planks or on pieces of the ship. And so it was that all escaped to land.

Acts 12:18–19

Waiting in Malta

28 ¹After we had escaped, we then learned that the island was called Malta. ²And the natives showed us unusual kindness, for they kindled a fire and welcomed us all, because it had begun to rain and was cold. ³Paul had gathered a bundle of sticks and put them on the fire, when a viper came out because of the heat and fastened on his hand. ⁴When the natives saw the creature hanging from his hand, they said to one another, "No doubt this man is a murderer. Though he has escaped from the sea, justice has not allowed him to live." ⁵He, however, shook off the creature into the fire and suffered no harm. ⁶They waited, expecting him to swell up or suddenly fall down dead; but when they had waited a long time and saw no misfortune come to him, they changed their minds and said that he was a god.

2 Cor 11:27

Mk 16:18
Lk 10:19
Acts 14:11

esset, terram non agnoscebant, sinum vero quendam considerabant habentem litus, in quem cogitabant si possent eicere navem. ⁴⁰Et cum ancoras abstulissent, committebant mari simul laxantes iuncturas gubernaculorum et, levato artemone, secundum flatum aurae tendebant ad litus. ⁴¹Et cum incidissent in locum dithalassum, impegerunt navem; et prora quidem fixa manebat immobilis, puppis vero solvebatur a vi fluctuum. ⁴²Militum autem consilium fuit, ut custodias occiderent, ne quis, cum enatasset, effugeret; ⁴³centurio autem volens servare Paulum prohibuit eos a consilio, iussitque eos, qui possent natare, mittere se primos et ad terram exire ⁴⁴et ceteros, quosdam in tabulis, quosdam vero super ea, quae de navi essent; et sic factum est ut omnes evaderent ad terram.   [28] ¹Et cum evasissemus, tunc cognovimus quia Melita insula vocatur. ²Barbari vero praestabant non modicam humanitatem nobis; accensa enim pyra suscipiebant nos omnes propter imbrem, qui imminebat et frigus. ³Cum congregasset autem Paulus sarmentorum aliquantam multitudinem et imposuisset super ignem, vipera, a calore cum processisset, invasit manum eius. ⁴Ut vero viderunt barbari pendentem bestiam de manu eius, ad invicem dicebant: «Utique homicida est homo hic, qui cum evaserit de mari, Ultio non permisit vivere». ⁵Et ille quidem excutiens bestiam in ignem, nihil mali passus est; ⁶at illi exspectabant eum in tumorem convertendum

ence of Paul. See how useful it is to live in the company of a devout and saintly person. Frequent and terrible storms buffet our souls. God can free us from them if we are as sensible as those sailors and pay attention to the saints' advice. […] Not only were they saved from shipwreck but they embraced the faith. Let us believe St Paul. Even if we be in the midst of storms we shall be set free from dangers; even if we be fasting for forty days, we shall stay alive; even if we fall into darkness and obscurity, if we believe in him we shall be freed" (St John

Chrysostom, *In Acta Apostolorum*, 53, 4–5).

28:1–10 The local people (natives, literally "barbarians": v. 2) show kindness to the travellers, but they are very superstitious (vv. 4, 6). St Paul's actions here bear out promises of Jesus: "And these signs will accompany those who believe: in my name they will cast out demons; they will speak in new tongues; they will pick up serpents, and if they drink any deadly thing, it will not hurt them; they will lay their hands on the sick, and they will recover" (Mk 16:17–18).

d Other ancient authorities read *seventy-six* or *about seventy-six* e Greek *place of two seas*

⁷Now in the neighbourhood of that place were lands belonging to the chief man of the island, named Publius, who received us and entertained us hospitably for three days. ⁸It happened that the father of Publius lay sick with fever and dysentery; and Paul visited him and prayed, and putting his hands on him healed him. ⁹And when this had taken place, the rest of the people on the island who had diseases also came and were cured. ¹⁰They presented many gifts to us;ᶠ and when we sailed, they put on board whatever we needed.

Lk 4:38–40; 10:9
Acts 5:15–16

Arrival in Rome

¹¹After three months we set sail in a ship which had wintered in the island, a ship of Alexandria, with the Twin Brothers as figureheads. ¹²Putting in at Syracuse, we stayed there for three days. ¹³And from there we made a circuit and arrived at Rhegium; and after one day a south wind sprang up, and on the second day we came to Puteoli. ¹⁴There we found brethren, and were invited to stay with them for seven days. And so we came to Rome. ¹⁵And the brethren there, when they heard of us, came as far as the Forum of Appius and Three Taverns to meet us. On seeing them Paul thanked God and took courage. ¹⁶And when we came into Rome, Paul was allowed to stay by himself, with the soldier that guarded him.

Paul and the Roman Jews

¹⁷After three days he called together the local leaders of the Jews; and when they had gathered, he said to them, "Brethren, though I had done nothing against the people

aut subito casurum et mori. Diu autem illis exspectantibus et videntibus nihil mali in eo fieri, convertentes se dicebant eum esse deum. ⁷In locis autem illis erant praedia principis insulae nomine Publii, qui nos suscipiens triduo benigne hospitio recepit. ⁸Contigit autem patrem Publii febribus et dysenteria vexatum iacere, ad quem Paulus intravit et, cum orasset et imposuisset ei manus, sanavit eum. ⁹Quo facto et ceteri, qui in insula habebant infirmitates, accedebant et curabantur; ¹⁰qui etiam multis honoribus nos honoraverunt et navigantibus imposuerunt, quae necessaria erant. ¹¹Post menses autem tres navigavimus in navi Alexandrina, quae in insula hiemaverat, cui erat insigne Castorum. ¹²Et cum venissemus Syracusam, mansimus ibi triduo; ¹³inde solventes devenimus Rhegium. Et post unum diem, superveniente austro, secunda die venimus Puteolos, ¹⁴ubi inventis fratribus rogati sumus manere apud eos dies septem; et sic venimus Romam. ¹⁵Et inde cum audissent de nobis fratres, occurrerunt nobis usque ad Appii Forum et Tres Tabernas; quos cum vidisset Paulus, gratias agens Deo, accepit fiduciam. ¹⁶Cum introissemus autem Romam, permissum

28:11–16 Syracuse (v. 12) was at that time the main city in Sicily. From Syracuse the boat went along the east coast and crossed the straits of Messina to reach Rhegium, where it lay at anchor for a day. Eventually, the passengers and crew disembarked at Puteoli (present-day Pozzuoli), the principal port on the Gulf of Naples (v. 13). The Forum of Appius and Three Taverns were 69 kilometres (43 miles) and 51 kilometres (32 miles), respectively, from Rome. They were located on the Appian Way, the main road linking Rome and the south. We do not know much about the Christian community in Rome at this time or how it came to be established. There is a tradition that it was founded by St Peter, which does not necessarily mean that no other Christians had travelled there before him (see 18:2). Its original members could perhaps have been some of the "visitors from Rome" (2:10) who were in Jerusalem on the day

of Pentecost, when the Holy Spirit first descended on the apostolic community.

The text (cf. vv. 14–16) shows us the friendliness and supernatural outlook of these Roman Christians. The sincere affection they showed Paul must have warmed his heart and helped him recover his strength after the tiring months of travel. "The principal apostolate we Christians must carry out in the world, and the best witness we can give of our faith, is to help bring about a climate of genuine charity within the Church. For who indeed could feel attracted to the Gospel if those who say they preach the Good News do not really love one another, but spend their time attacking one another, spreading slander and rancour" (St Josemaría Escrivá, *Friends of God*, 226).

28:17–28 Paul must have arrived in Rome around the year 61. He was allowed to stay in a

f Or *honoured us with many honours*

or the customs of our fathers, yet I was delivered prisoner from Jerusalem into the hands of the Romans. [18]When they had examined me, they wished to set me at lib- Acts 21:30–38; 23:29 erty, because there was no reason for the death penalty in my case. [19]But when the Acts 25:11; 26:32 Jews objected, I was compelled to appeal to Caesar—though I had no charge to bring against my nation. [20]For this reason therefore I have asked to see you and speak with you, since it is because of the hope of Israel that I am bound with this chain." [21]And they said to him, "We have received no letters from Judea about you, and none of the brethren coming here has reported or spoken any evil about you. [22]But we desire to hear from you what your views are; for with regard to this sect we Lk 2:34 know that everywhere it is spoken against." Acts 17:19; 24:14–16

Acts 13:15–41

[23]When they had appointed a day for him, they came to him at his lodging in great numbers. And he expounded the matter to them from morning till evening, testifying to the kingdom of God and trying to convince them about Jesus both from the law of Moses and from the prophets. [24]And some were convinced by what he Acts 13:46–47 said, while others disbelieved. [25]So, as they disagreed among themselves, they departed, after Paul had made one statement: "The Holy Spirit was right in saying to your fathers through Isaiah the prophet:

[26] 'Go to this people, and say, Is 6:9–10
Mt 13:14
   You shall indeed hear but never understand,
   and you shall indeed see but never perceive.
[27] For this people's heart has grown dull, Jn 12:39
2 Cor 3:14
   and their ears are heavy of hearing,
   and their eyes they have closed;
   lest they should perceive with their eyes,
   and hear with their ears,
   and understand with their heart,
   and turn for me to heal them.'

est Paulo manere sibimet cum custodiente se milite. [17]Factum est autem ut post tertium diem convocaret primos Iudaeorum; cumque convenissent dicebat eis: «Ego, viri fratres, nihil adversus plebem faciens aut mores paternos, vinctus ab Hierosolymis traditus sum in manus Romanorum, [18]qui cum interrogationem de me habuissent, volebant dimittere eo quod nulla causa esset mortis in me; [19]contradicentibus autem Iudaeis, coactus sum appellare Caesarem, non quasi gentem meam habens aliquid accusare. [20]Propter hanc igitur causam rogavi vos videre et alloqui; propter spem enim Israel catena hac circumdatus sum». [21]At illi dixerunt ad eum: «Nos neque litteras accepimus de te a Iudaea, neque adveniens aliquis fratrum nuntiavit aut locutus est quid de te malum. [22]Rogamus autem a te audire quae sentis, nam de secta hac notum est nobis quia ubique ei contradicitur». [23]Cum constituissent autem illi diem, venerunt ad eum in hospitium plures, quibus exponebat testificans regnum Dei, suadensque eos de Iesu ex Lege Moysis et Prophetis a mane usque ad vesperam. [24]Et quidam credebant his quae dicebantur, quidam vero non credebant; [25]cumque invicem non essent consentientes, discedebant, dicente Paulo unum verbum: «Bene Spiritus Sanctus locutus est per Isaiam prophetam ad patres vestros [26]dicens: *"Vade ad populum istum et dic: / Auditu audietis et non intellegetis, / et videntes videbitis et non perspicietis. / [27]Incrassatum est enim cor populi huius, / et auribus graviter audierunt, / et oculos suos compresserunt, / ne forte videant oculis / et auribus audiant / et corde*

private house; he was under *custodia militaris*, pending his trial, the only restriction being that he was guarded by a soldier at all times. In keeping with his normal missionary practice, he first seeks out the local Jews. His preaching has the same sort of results as before (v. 24; cf. 13:44–47; 18:6), and because many Jews reject his message, he proclaims himself to have fulfilled his self-imposed duty to announce the Gospel to Jews before he can begin to preach to Gentiles (v. 28). What he says in vv. 25–28 suggests that it is the Christians who have understood the meaning of the promises made by God to the Chosen People, and that they are the true Israel. "We are the true, spiritual people of Israel," St Justin writes, "the race of Judah, and of Jacob, and of Isaac and of Abraham, he who was testified to by God even while he was still uncircumcised, he who was blessed and named the father of many nations" (*Dialogus cum Tryphone*, 11, 5).

See the RSV note **g**.

Ps 67:1; 98:3
Is 40:5
Lk 3:6

28Let it be known to you then that this salvation of God has been sent to the Gentiles; they will listen."g

Paul's ministry in Rome

Phil 1:14
2 Tim 2:9

30And he lived there two whole years at his own expense,h and welcomed all who came to him, **31**preaching the kingdom of God and teaching about the Lord Jesus Christ quite openly and unhindered.

intellegant et convertantur, / et sanabo illos". 28Notum ergo sit vobis quoniam gentibus missum est hoc salutare Dei; ipsi et audient!».(29) 30Mansit autem biennio toto in suo conducto; et suscipiebat omnes qui ingrediebantur ad eum, 31praedicans regnum Dei et docens quae sunt de Domino Iesu Christo cum omni fiducia sine prohibitione.

28:30–31 The apparently abrupt ending of the book shows in fact that our Lord's promise to his apostles has been fulfilled: they are indeed his witnesses to the ends of the earth (1:8). To describe St Paul's approach to the work of evangelization, St Luke uses in v. 31 the word *parrhesia*, "the beautiful, characteristically Christian expression [connoting] straightforward simplicity, filial trust, joyous assurance, humble boldness, the certainty of being loved" (*Catechism of the Catholic Church*, 2778).

"He lived there two whole years" (v. 30), literally "a full biennium". It is not clear whether this refers (as it does in 24:27) to the maximum period a person could be confined under Roman law while awaiting trial. We do not know exactly what happened at the end of the two years. Paul was set free. Nevertheless, the task that God gave Luke when he inspired him to write this book has been accomplished. "If you ask me", St John Chrysostom observes, "why St Luke, who stayed with the Apostle up to his martyrdom, did not bring his narrative up to that point, I will reply that the Book of the Acts, in the form that has come down to us, perfectly fulfils its author's purpose. For the evangelists' only aim was to write down the most essential things" (St John Chrysostom, *In Acta Apostolorum*, 1).

g Other ancient authorities add verse 29, *And when he had said these words, the Jews departed, holding much dispute among themselves* h Or *in his own hired dwelling*

Introduction to the Writings of St Paul

After the historical or narrative books (the Gospels and the Acts of the Apostles), the New Testament brings us sacred writings that develop in theological terms the original core of apostolic preaching, expound the saving power of Christ's divine work, and apply his teaching to the everyday situations in which Christians live.[1] Foremost among these are fourteen letters in which St Paul is named as the writer or which, as in the case of the Letter to the Hebrews, show strong evidence of the Apostle's influence and authority.

In the classical world, correspondence took two forms—*letters* about family, business or other such matters, and *epistles*, which were small treatises or essays on a theme, dedicated to an important personage or to a friend or relative. St Paul's writings are both epistle and letter: they are letters because they have a family tone, with personal greetings, recommendations of people, and lines of farewell; and they are epistles in that they contain teaching concerning doctrine or moral matters.

The order in which St Paul's letters come in most ancient codexes and printed editions of the Bible is conventional rather than chronological; the earlier ones are those addressed to communities, followed by those written to individuals; within this structure, the longer letters and those more important to the life of the Church come first, the exception being the Letter to the Hebrews, which usually comes at the end.

1. ST PAUL

St Paul was a man commissioned by God to play a key role in the evangelization of the Gentiles. This plan to extend salvation across the world was part of our Lord's own mission, but the personality and work of St Paul played a decisive part in spreading the Good News of the Gospel throughout the known world.

The proclamation of the Gospel to the Gentiles was not an idea original to Paul himself; it was part and parcel of the essence of the Gospel message. What St Paul did was to respond to this call to proclaim the good news that he heard in the Gospel. Thus, he speaks of a "mystery" that had lain hidden in God for centuries and was now revealed, and of which he was conscious of being a minister—the salvation of Jews and Gentiles, and their forming one Body, which is the Church. Paul showed his awareness of this one Body—for example, in the fact that he always tried to act in line with the apostolic college, consulting the apostles and elders of Jerusalem about his evangelizing methods. They ratified his mission to preach to the Gentiles, whereas St Peter was to minister more to Jews. However, Paul was not alone in this huge task, for the Twelve travelled to proclaim the Gospel to other nations and other countries that had no connexion with Judaism; that is evident from the ancient traditions about their lives, from information provided by the first Christian writers, and from the letters of the New Testament itself (the so-called "catholic letters") that are also addressed to Christians of Gentile background.

St Paul's early life: a Jew of the diaspora

St Paul received a formation during his youth that would serve him very well in the mission God had in store for him. He was certainly a Jew, but he was a Jew born and reared in the diaspora, in

---

1 Cf. Vatican II, *Dei Verbum*, 20.

a Greek environment. He himself speaks with pride of his Jewishness: he was of the tribe of Benjamin (hence his name, Saul); his family were observant Jews; he was a Pharisee in his interpretation of the Law, and zealously kept to the traditions he received from his forebears (see Gal 1:14; 2 Cor 11:22; Rom 11:1; Phil 3:5–6). His thinking was imbued with Holy Scripture, which he often explicitly quotes and comments on; he was firmly focused on the salvation promised to Israel; and his theological outlook was permeated with a sense of history and Jewish tradition.

This Jewish man received an excellent rabbinical training at the feet of Gamaliel (cf. Acts 22:3), and, prior to that, a good grounding in Hellenistic culture in Tarsus, his native city. We do not know what course of study he took, but, given the way he wrote and many other features of his thinking, he must have been well trained in rhetoric, and he seems to have had a considerable understanding of Stoic thought. We do know that Tarsus was a place of residence of important Stoic thinkers,[2] and that it had a renowned school of oratory.[3]

In addition to his Jewish background and Hellenistic education, a third factor to bear in mind is that St Paul was a Roman citizen by birth and proud of his status as such (see Acts 22:25–28; 16:37). This suggests that his father had managed to acquire Roman citizenship and the right to pass it on—which would lead one to think that Paul's family, good Jews though they were, did not belong to any of the more closed Jewish groups such as the Zealots. This openness of mind, combined with deep religious convictions, explains many of the encouraging things we find in Paul's words to Gentiles, such as this example from the Letter to the Philippians: "Finally, brethren, whatever is true, whatever is honourable, whatever is just, whatever is pure, whatever is lovely, whatever is gracious, if there is any excellence, if there is anything worthy of praise, think about these things. What you have learned and received and heard and seen in me, do; and the God of peace will be with you" (Phil 4:8–9).

St Paul's calling and mission

The Acts of the Apostles gives us three accounts of how Paul was called by God on the road to Damascus (9:1–19; 22:5–16; 26:10–18). In the first account, God himself reveals to Ananias what Paul's mission is to be: "The Lord said to him, 'Go, for he is a chosen instrument of mine to carry my name before the Gentiles and kings and the sons of Israel; for I will show him how much he must suffer for the sake of my name'" (Acts 9:15–16). The second account tells how Ananias revealed to Saul his mission: "The God of our fathers appointed you to know his will, to see the Just One and to hear a voice from his mouth; for you will be a witness for him to all men of what you have seen and heard" (Acts 22:14–15). In the third account, Paul describes how he became aware of this divine mission: "And the Lord said, 'I am Jesus whom you are persecuting. But rise and stand upon your feet, for I have appeared to you for this purpose, to appoint you to serve and bear witness to the things in which you have seen me and to those in which I will appear to you, delivering you from the people and from the Gentiles—to whom I send you to open their eyes, that they may turn from darkness to light and from the power of Satan to God, that they may receive forgiveness of sins and a place among those who are sanctified by faith in me'" (Acts 26:15–18). The small differences in detail in the three passages are not surprising, and cause no great difficulty. These accounts derived from different contexts and came down to Luke through different traditions: the first probably came from the Jerusalem church; and the other two came from Paul's preaching to Jews and Gentiles, respectively. Still, they all have one element in common, which is worth noting: God assigned to St Paul the specific mission of proclaiming the Gospel to all mankind, first to Jews and then to Gentiles.

---

2 Chrysippus, the second founder of the Stoa, came from Soli, in Cilicia; and Posidonius, one of the leaders of the middle Stoa, came from Apamea, in Syria. **3** One of the graduates of this school was Athenodorus the Bald, who became a tutor to Octavius. **4** *Historia Ecclesiastica*, 2, 25, 4–8.

On receiving this revelation and understanding that Jesus was the glorified Messiah, Paul had to radically change his whole outlook, which was that of a fervent Pharisee. Previously, as he saw it, the road to God was the Law; now he has become convinced that the Law on its own is inadequate, because Jesus, the Messiah and Son of God, was condemned according to the Law, became accursed of the Law (see Gal 3:13). Previously, he thought that the true Israel was still the one descended from Abraham according to the flesh, and so he observed the Law; but now he sees that the true Israel is the followers of Jesus, with whom Jesus identifies himself (see Acts 9:5): in meeting Christ on the road to Damascus, St Paul sees God's plans in a wholly new way, and that insight will be the basis of his thinking and theology from then on.

Immediately after his encounter with Jesus, St Paul addressed the Jews of Damascus (see Acts 9:20), and when he went to Jerusalem he preached to the Hellenists, that is, Jews who were not of Palestinian origin (see Acts 9:28–29). His first apostolic contact with Gentiles did not take place until much later, when he went to Antioch, to help Barnabas in his work of evangelization (see Acts 11:25). Later, when the Holy Spirit chose Barnabas and Paul for a special mission (see Acts 13:2), he went to Cyprus and began to preach in the synagogues of Salamis (see Acts 13:5). He did the same, along with Barnabas, in Antioch of Pisidia (see Acts 13:14), as he would in Iconium (see Acts 14:1), Philippi (see Acts 16:12), Thessalonica (see Acts 17:1), Beroea (see Acts 17:10), Corinth (see Acts 18:4), Ephesus (see Acts 19:8) and Rome (see Acts 28:17–28). In Pisidian Antioch, Corinth and Ephesus he met persistent opposition from Jews, and declared that he was going to devote his attention to the Gentiles, as he in fact went on to do, but even so he always kept in close contact with members of his people, and always spoke well of them (cf. 1 Cor 9:20–23; Rom 9:1–5).

The introduction of Christianity to a Hellenist culture

St Paul chose to write his letters to Christian communities in Greek. That is not surprising, given that it was the everyday language of those Christians; but it meant, very importantly, that the message of the faith was being expressed in new ways. The earliest New Testament letter is, possibly, a letter of St Paul's, the First Letter to the Thessalonians, written around AD 51–52, and originally in Greek.

It is worth remembering that most of the Old Testament, where earlier divine Revelation is found, was written in Hebrew, with some passages in Aramaic, and it was not until times quite close to the Christian era that some books were written in Greek. The great task of making biblical revelation accessible to people of Greek culture began with the translation into Greek of the Old Testament (the Septuagint version), and would be continued and completed in the New Testament, whose books were written in that language. The Apostle's decision to write in Greek was the first step in creating a Christian culture in the Greek language; this trend, which would continue for centuries, marked a development in Christian thought (it was not until the end of the second century AD that Christian writers in Latin first appeared).

Before St Paul's time, various attempts were made by Jews to integrate Jewish thought and Greek culture. One of the leading figures in this project was Philo of Alexandria, who lived about fifty years before the Apostle. However, St Paul managed to assimilate ideas from a range of cultures and to express them in Christian language and ideas: for example, he adopted from Greek culture such notions as "conscience" (*synéidesis*), "knowledge" (*gnosis*), "glorious manifestation" (*epipháneia*), "love of mankind" (*philantrópia*), and "regeneration" (*palingennesia*).

Establishing dates for St Paul's life

It is not possible to establish an exact chronology of the Saint's life, because the main sources for our knowledge of Paul (his letters and the Acts of the Apostles) do not give importance to dates or times. Nevertheless, the most significant moments in the Apostle's life can be dated with a relatively high degree of accuracy.

Scholars are inclined to think that Paul was born in Tarsus of Cilicia (see Acts 9:11; 21:39; 22:3) between the years AD 5 and 10, given that Luke describes Saul as *neanías*, "young", in his account of the martyrdom of St Stephen (see Acts 7:58), which occurred not long after our Lord's death in the year 30.

As regards the date of *Christ's appearance to Paul near Damascus*, the main references occur in the Letter to the Galatians, where Paul says that three years after that event he went up to Jerusalem (see Gal 1:18) and that he went there again fourteen years later (see Gal 2:1). However, it is not possible to work out whether those fourteen years between the Damascus vision and Paul's second visit to Jerusalem, accompanied by Barnabas and Titus (when the meeting with James, Peter and John took place: see Gal 2:1–10; Acts 15:1–41), include the three years mentioned in Galatians 1:18, or whether they should be added on, making a total of seventeen years.

In any case, taking into account that the assembly at Jerusalem took place in the year 48 or 49, the vision on the road to Damascus is likely to have occurred in the year 32 or 35.

The most definite piece of information that can help us establish dates for the Apostle's work as a missionary comes from an inscription found in Delphi (published in 1905) in which there is a reference to Junius Gallio as proconsul of Achaia. Gallio held this office between the years 51 and 52. According to the account in Acts, when Paul was in Corinth during his second missionary journey angry Jews brought him before Gallio's judgment seat (but, when he heard that the problem at issue involved matters to do with the Jewish Law, the proconsul refused to intervene): cf. Acts 18:12–17. Paul must have appeared before Gallio towards the end of the year 51 or a little later.

St Paul's *captivity in maritime Caesarea* can also be dated fairly exactly. According to Acts, Paul was taken from Jerusalem to Caesarea on the orders of the tribune Claudius Lysias, to appear before the prefect Antonius Felix (see Acts 23:24—24:27). During Paul's imprisonment in Caesarea, Antonius Felix was replaced by Porcius Festus. A few days after Festus' arrival, Paul appealed his case to Caesar (see Acts 25:11). When did all these events take place? The historians Tacitus and Flavius Josephus, who also mention Festus' replacement of Felix, do not give exact dates, but most modern scholars argue it was in the year 60.

The Acts of the Apostles does not mention the *death of Paul*. An ancient tradition, recorded in the fourth century by Eusebius,[4] says that he was beheaded in Rome[5] during Nero's persecution (in which Peter, too, died a martyr's death, by crucifixion); that persecution happened in the years 64–67. St Clement of Rome (around the year 95) refers to Paul "journeying to the farthest limits of the West"[6] before bearing witness to Christ by his death. Is St Clement here referring to a historical fact or is he assuming that Paul made this journey because of what is implied in Romans 15:24, 28? The other ancient documents that refer to a possible journey to Spain date from much later,[7] and are historically less reliable (the Acts of the Apostles and the Letters say nothing that conflicts with those ancient traditions). St Paul is considered to have been between 55 and 60 years old at the time of his martyrdom.

2. THE PAULINE COMMUNITIES AND LETTERS

St Paul's letters, written to particular Christian communities, deal with specific needs, but they have perennial value because they also contain a rich source of doctrine and theology. Moreover,

---

5 This event is commemorated by the Roman basilica of St Paul Without the Walls.   **6** St Clement of Rome, *Letter to the Corinthians*, 5, 7.   **7** Muratorian Fragment, *c.* AD 180.

they tell us a lot about the Apostle's activity and the environment in which he carried out his work. The information to be gleaned from the letters, together with that given in Acts, allows us to trace, at least in broad outline, the impact he made during the early days of Christianity.

The Pauline communities

In the first instance, the Gospel spread around the rim of the Mediterranean among the Jewish communities of the diaspora. Wherever Jews lived, some Christians were soon to be found. The finest cities were those whose importance stemmed from the fact that they were at major cross-roads and were centres of trade or the capitals of regions or provinces of the empire. Before AD 50, Christians were already to be found in Rome, Alexandria, Antioch, Caesarea and Damascus.

In his evangelizing work, St Paul focused particularly on centres of population where roads and sea-routes met and where there was a good deal of trade and cultural interchange. Thessalonica is a case in point: it was a port 150 kilometres (95 miles) west of Philippi on the Via Egnatia, a route that linked the Adriatic Sea with the plains of Asia Minor. The same could be said of Corinth and Ephesus, where the Apostle stayed for a number of years and which were strategically placed in the sense that they were good bases for missionary work in the surrounding areas. For example, Ephesus, the capital of the Roman province of "Asia", was the base for the spread of the Gospel throughout the valley of a river on whose banks stood Hierapolis, Laodicea and Colossae.

After Jerusalem, the next Christian community in order of importance was that of Antioch, the ancient capital of the Seleucid kingdom. As far as we can make out from the Acts of the Apostles, the community at Antioch was made up mainly of people of pagan background. It was at Antioch that believers in Christ first came to be called "Christians" (Acts 11:26). This community had a lively missionary spirit and a refined sense of brotherhood and solidarity with the community in Jerusalem (see Acts 11:27–30). The Christians of Antioch seem to have included some who were quite wealthy—which would explain how they managed to raise a considerable sum of money to relieve their brethren in Jerusalem. The book of Acts implies that the community was guided by a group of "prophets and teachers", who made up a sort of presbyterate (see Acts 13:1). This leads to the conclusion that church organization developed in parallel with that of civil society, which had a people's assembly (*boulé*) and a council of elders (*gerousía*). It is likely that one of the members of the presbyterate acted as head of the community, as Barnabas did when the community was first founded.

Antioch was the base for Paul's apostolic journeys, which are described in great detail in Acts.[8] These journeys took him, first, across Asia Minor (Galatia, Pamphilia, Lycaonia) and then to the continent of Europe (Thessalonica, Philippi, Athens, Corinth); in the course of his journeys, Paul not only converted and baptized but also established structured communities with people assigned to giving instruction in the faith, administering the sacraments and preaching the Gospel.

These early Christian communities could be ethnically quite different and located quite far from each other, but they had features in common: firstly, they included Gentiles ("Greeks") and Jews, without discrimination of any kind (see Gal 3:28; 1 Cor 12:13; Col 3:11); there was equality, too, between free men and slaves, and between men and women. All had been redeemed by Christ and had been given the status of children of God. The various other features of Christian life rested on these bases of equality.

The Pauline letters

St Paul's letters have to do with specific needs of the communities he founded, preparations for journeys he plans to make, the personal circumstances of the addressees, etc. Therefore, we do

---

8 For where Paul went and what he did, see Acts 13:1—28:31. The maps on pages 11–13 give an overview of his journeys.

not find in them a system of ideas or a structured theology; he writes out of his experience of the mystery of Christ, which he wants to spread to everyone, both to communities and individuals. To this end, he avails himself of all kinds of literary and oratorical resources and devices.

From the historical point of view, there is enough evidence for us to be confident that the first of Paul's letters conserved in the Bible is that written to the Thessalonians during his second missionary journey (1 Thessalonians), and, after it, written during his third journey, the Letter to the Galatians, 1 and 2 Corinthians, and the Letter to the Romans. As far as the other letters are concerned, there is no consensus among scholars as to when exactly the Apostle wrote them.[9]

Studies of the letters attributed to the Apostle undertaken by historians and literary experts show that some of them have distinctive features that remove any substantive doubt about their authorship. These letters are: Romans, 1 and 2 Corinthians, Galatians, Philippians, 1 Thessalonians and Philemon; neither in ancient times nor in our own day has Pauline authorship been seriously questioned. However, recent times have seen differences of opinion as to the authorship of 2 Thessalonians, Ephesians, Colossians, 1 and 2 Timothy, and the Letter to Titus. The debate centres on whether these letters can be said to have been written by Paul personally or whether, although they contain Pauline teaching, the final composition of the letters in question should be attributed instead to one or more of his disciples.[10] The authorship of the Letter to the Hebrews is the most contested instance, not least because Paul's name does not appear at the heading of the letter (as it does in the case of the others). In any event, the Church has accepted all these letters as divinely inspired, as a source of Christian Revelation of enduring value and as precious testimonies to the life and thought of the Apostle, of his co-workers and of the first Christian communities.

3. THE MAIN DOCTRINAL THEMES OF ST PAUL'S LETTERS

The letters of St Paul contain a great wealth of doctrine. The main features of each letter are discussed in the various Introductions. However, because certain themes recur frequently (sometimes expressed in different words, sometimes complementing things said in other letters), it is useful to be conscious of them from the beginning in order to appreciate the Apostle's thinking.

The resurrection of Christ

The appearance of the risen Christ to Paul on the road to Damascus is the key to the Apostle's faith and teaching. In every other respect, Paul echoes the apostolic *kérygma*, which held the glorious resurrection of Jesus to be the foremost proof of the truth of what he said and did, of the mystery of who he is. Paul explicitly says that Christ's resurrection is also proof that we too will rise again. The rite of immersion in the water of Baptism signifies and brings about our death in Christ to sin, and emerging from the water signals the birth of a new creature to a life of grace and to hope in a future, glorious resurrection (cf. Rom 6:5–11).

Jesus Christ, the only Saviour

Prior to his conversion, Paul was faithful to the fundamental tenets of Judaism: God had chosen Israel as his people, who had been entrusted with the promises which he made to the patriarchs and which found expression in the Covenant and the Law of Moses, and who were convinced that salvation lay in observance of the Law. Nothing is said in the Letters or in the Acts that reflects

9 As regards the circumstances in which each was written, see the Introductions to the various letters in this volume. **10** In the Introduction to each letter, we examine the matter in a little more detail to see whether the letter may have had a somewhat more complex history of authorship.

how the young Paul might have envisioned the Messiah announced by the prophets, or what sort of divine deliverance he would bring. Prior to his experience on the road to Damascus, Paul certainly shared the view of many of his co-religionists that Jesus of Nazareth was not the Messiah; as he saw it, the few dissident Jews who held that view were a menace that needed to be dealt with severely in order to safeguard the Jewish religion (see Gal 1:13–14; Acts 22:3–5). But when the risen Jesus revealed himself, Paul immediately saw the truth: Jesus Christ is alive! He is the Messiah! And the graces that Paul subsequently received deepened his understanding of the faith: Jesus is the Son of God, and Paul must proclaim him to the world (see Gal 1:15–16).

What he later preached and wrote about stemmed from his own, living experience of the mystery of Christ. His divine calling was to proclaim the "Good News", the Gospel of Jesus Christ, which is "the power of God for salvation to every one who has faith" (Rom 1:16). This is the core message that he will expound in his letters from a variety of different perspectives. This basic message is always the same: Jesus Christ is the only Saviour, the redeemer of Jews and Gentiles alike (cf. Rom 3:22–23).

The salvific mystery

"The Gospel of Paul" is the proclamation of God's plan for the salvation of all mankind. This plan was foretold by the prophets in the Old Testament, but it was only through Christ that it came to be revealed to the apostles. Paul describes the saving plan of God in Christ using expressions like "the mystery of Christ", "of the Gospel", "of God", "of faith", etc., or simply "the mystery", to show that it was a truth that lay hidden until it was revealed in Christ. What was revealed to Paul was simply this: *the mystery has been fulfilled in Christ*. The Damascus vision and the graces Paul subsequently received did not mean that now there was a "new religion": rather, Paul now had a deeper understanding of *one* revelation, which had started with the patriarchs and reached its fullness in Jesus Christ. The "light" he received on the road to Damascus was not strictly speaking a "conversion" to God, but an illumination showing him that the "mystery" had been fulfilled in Christ.

The divinity of Jesus Christ

The letters make it very clear that Jesus is the Son of God. Paul uses a number of titles for Christ, already found in apostolic preaching—"the Lord", "the Son of God", "the Saviour". In Romans 9:5 and Titus 2:13 he calls Jesus "God", "God over all, blessed for ever" and "our great God"; and in Colossians 1:15–17 he speaks of Christ's having existed eternally, prior to being sent into the world, prior even to the creation of the world. Jesus Christ is co-eternal with the Father, and has been sent by the Father out of love for mankind.

The Incarnation of the Son of God

The Son of God took on human form; "born of woman, born under the law" (Gal 4:4), he "emptied himself" (Phil 2:7), and "in [his own] flesh he condemned sin" (see Rom 8:3; Col 1:22). In this way, all the elements of life that had enslaved human beings (sin, flesh, death, Law) were overcome by Christ. His death is the supreme proof of God's love for man (see Rom 5:8). By making the human condition his own, Christ becomes the representative and "head" of mankind, as the "new Adam" (see 1 Cor 15:20–22; 2 Cor 5:14; Rom 5:14; Col 1:18). Christ's death has won for us forgiveness of sins and has brought us into a new way of being (see Rom 4:25).

"Justice" and "justification"

Paul refers often to the "justice" (or righteousness) of God, by which he means the saving power of God that expresses itself in Christ's work of redemption; by believing in Jesus, a person gains access to this redemption. "Justification" is the word used to describe the new relationship that a human being has with God, through the workings of divine grace. From the time of the Lutheran reformation onwards, the whole question of "justice/justification" has become a key theme in Pauline scholarship; some writers see it as the cornerstone of his theology. But "justice/justification" is the consequence of the salvific mystery of the "event" of Christ himself. The core of Paul's teaching, as we have said, stems from his living experience of Jesus Christ as the only Saviour; salvation reaches man through faith. Every other idea and teaching flows from this belief.

As St Paul sees it, the process of justification involves three stages. First, the initiative comes from God; a person does not obtain justification thanks to previous actions on his or her part (see Rom 8:29–30). Second, God wants everyone to be saved (cf. 1 Tim 2:3–4). Third, although it is God who takes the initiative, and his action is the decisive force in justification, every human being must respond personally to God's grace.

Christian life in Christ

Through joining ourselves to Christ by means of faith, we become children of God: "Because you are sons, God has sent the Spirit of his Son into our hearts, crying, 'Abba! Father!' So through God you are no longer a slave but a son, and if a son then an heir" (Gal 4:6–7; cf. Rom 8:14–17). Life in Christ, or Christ's life in each Christian (Gal 2:19–20), means having divine sonship/filiation and the gift of the Holy Spirit whereby God's love is poured into our hearts (cf. Rom 5:5).

Being a Christian involves obedience to serious ethical imperatives. In the first century AD, Greco-Roman society was so morally decadent that Christian converts had to shed many of their old ideas about morality and many habits of behaviour that were often sinful. For this to happen, God's grace was needed as well as the individual's cooperation (see 1 Cor 6:9–11). Paul identifies the source of a Christian's dignity when he says, "your body is a temple of the Holy Spirit" (1 Cor 6:19).

The Church

Of all the inspired writers of the New Testament, St Paul is the one who speaks most often about the Church, and the one who delves deepest into its mystery. His insight into this mystery begins at the very moment of his conversion, when he hears Jesus identify himself with Christians: "Saul, Saul, why do you persecute me?" (Acts 9:4). After this initial, direct revelation, Paul will receive other revelations and have other experiences which further develop his understanding of the Church.

Although in his letters Paul sometimes describes as "churches" the Christian communities in the various places or regions (see 1 Thess 1:1; 1 Cor 1:2; 2 Cor 1:1), he was, from the beginning, clearly aware that the Church was one, single entity: there is only one Church. The Church is one, and Christians are one with Christ and with each other; alongside this belief we find, deeply rooted in Paul's thinking, the idea that the Church is the Body of Christ and the People of God;[11] this fact underlines the profound and mysterious relationship that exists between Christ and the Church, enabling her to be the instrument of the world's salvation (see Eph 3:9–11).

---

11 See, e.g., Rom 12:5; 1 Cor 10:16, 12:13; Col 1:18, 24; 2:19; 3:15; Eph 1:10.

THE LETTER OF PAUL TO THE

ROMANS

Introduction

The Letter to the Romans, the longest of Paul's letters in the New Testament, is also generally regarded as the most important. In it the Apostle deals with key points of doctrine about Christ's work of redemption and the Christian life. The letter expands on and delves deeper into themes found in the Letter to the Galatians, and outlines in a more structured way how Jesus Christ the Saviour acts in the believer and what consequences flow from that action. The manuscripts of Paul's letters place this one first; this order is retained from the earliest extant papyrus (second century) to the codexes of the late Middle Ages (14th–15th century). If the letters were arranged chronologically, Romans would not come first, so the fact that it is placed first shows that from ancient times it was judged to be the Apostle's masterpiece. It is a letter or epistle in the form of a treatise focusing on the salvation brought by Christ, a salvation that is an unmerited gift from God and one attained through faith, not by observance of the precepts of the Mosaic Law.

In the Latin Vulgate edition, and in the New Vulgate, too, the letter comes immediately after the Acts of the Apostles (the last of the historical books), as the first in a series of books in epistle form. An outstanding expression of divine revelation comes down to us through the Apostle. The letters that follow Romans in the New Testament provide us with further insights into aspects of the teaching found in Romans.

1. STRUCTURE AND CONTENT

Although the letter deals with a single theme, it can be divided into four parts: an introduction (1:1–17); a discourse on doctrine (1:18—11:36); a section dealing with Christian morality (12:1—15:13); and an unusually extensive expression of farewell (15:14—16:27).

In his greeting (1:1–17) St Paul portrays himself as a servant of Jesus Christ. In the doctrinal part (1:18—11:36), we are first given an overview of unredeemed mankind, estranged from and hostile to God from the fall of Adam onwards (1:18—3:31). The moral degeneracy of the Gentiles (1:18–32) and the sins of the Jews (2:1–29) show that mankind is in absolute need of the Redemption worked by Christ; otherwise there can be no forgiveness of sin, no grace of God (3:1–31). This first doctrinal passage ends by recalling Abraham, a man justified by faith before the Law's existence (4:1–25). St Paul then goes on to deal with things that run counter to justification (5:1—7:25). He discusses four ideas here: sin and death (5:12–21), the flesh and the Law (7:1–25) are impediments on the path to justification. Mankind in its fallen state is at the mercy of these forces, and the only way it can be free of them is through the Redemption brought by Christ Jesus. God gives man salvation only through Jesus Christ our Lord, and man must cleave to it through faith, which is an unmerited gift from God and not a reward for good works. But once Christians have attained faith (through Baptism, which draws a person into Christ: 6:1–23), they can and should do good, with the help of the grace of the Holy Spirit who dwells in them and completes the work of justification done by Christ, so that they become saints and adoptive children of the Father (8:1–39). Through Baptism a person is moved from a situation of estrangement from God to one of friendship with him; from a state of unredemption to the state of grace; the old condemnation no longer stands; he or she has become a new creation, open to the hope of the glory of the children of God. A new section (9:1 — 11:36) then looks at the unfaithfulness of the people of Israel (9:1 — 10:21), God's election of a new people, and the eventual conversion of a remnant of Israel (11:1–32). The doctrinal part of the letter ends with a hymn to the Wisdom of God and a doxology (11:33–36).

In the second part of the letter (12:1 — 15:13), Paul applies what he has been saying to the daily life of Christians; and, in conclusion, he spells out the moral demands entailed by faith, that is, by "life in the Spirit" (12:1 — 13:14), providing practical advice about how Christians should lead their lives in a world that is as yet unredeemed but which they should lead to salvation (14:1 — 15:13).

The epilogue (15:14 — 16:24) has two sections: in the first, Paul outlines journeys he plans to make (15:15–33); in the second, he sends affectionate good wishes to many Christians, both men and women, living in Rome (16:1–23). The letter ends with an elaborate doxology (16:25–27).

2. CONTEXT

The Letter to the Romans is one of the group of letters that everyone agrees was written by St Paul. It is one of what are known as his "great letters" (Galatians, 1 and 2 Corinthians, and Romans) that comprise the substance of the Apostle's theology.

During his third missionary journey (in the years AD 53–58), St Paul wrote from Ephesus to the Galatians and began a correspondence with the community of Corinth. The two letters to the Corinthians, written when times were difficult for Paul, bore good fruit, and that community enjoyed spiritual health and fervour. Reports about the other churches founded by the Apostle indicated that things were going well, thanks to the grace of the Spirit. Paul's work in the eastern regions of the empire had created stable, healthy churches. The Gospel of Christ had been preached all the way from Jerusalem to the regions of Illyria, that is, the eastern coast of the Adriatic (cf. Rom 15:19), and because of this Paul plans to extend his apostolate to Spain (Rom 15:28), spending a considerable time in Rome on the way there (there was already a sizeable Christian community in the capital city).

In order to prepare the ground for his planned visit, Paul writes his Letter to the Romans from Corinth, in the winter-spring of 57–58. That is the date that most scholars of recent decades assign to the letter, although a minority argue for an earlier date (the year 52). Corinth is thought to be the place of writing because of the reference to "Phoebe, a deaconess of the church at Cenchreae", the port of Corinth on the Aegean Sea (Rom 16:1). If Phoebe was about to embark for Rome, it is reasonable to suppose that this was at the end of the winter or in early spring of Paul's last stay in Corinth.

We do not know when the first Christian community in Rome came into being, but it must have been there for quite some time, since Paul says, "I have longed for many years to come to you" (15:23) and "your faith is proclaimed in all the world" (1:8). We know from contemporary sources that there was a substantial flow of traffic by land and sea between Palestine and Rome during this period, and the city had a number of synagogues. So it is reasonable to suppose that some Christians from Judea and the surrounding regions had gone to Rome for a variety of reasons, including trade. It is possible, then, that the Christian community of Rome, made up of people of both Jewish and Gentile background, was more inclined to adhere to Jewish traditions than were those founded by Paul in the East. That might explain why Paul is more cautious in the

Letter to the Romans than he is in Galatians when he discusses the value of the Law and other Jewish traditions (compare, for example, Romans 3:1–2 with Galatians 5:2). Another thing to bear in mind in this connexion is the fact that, of the letters whose Pauline authorship is not contested, Romans is the one that contains most words and expressions drawn from the liturgy of sacrifice: in it Christ is described as an expiatory sacrifice (see 3:25); the faithful are exhorted to offer their bodies "as a living sacrifice" (12:1); etc. References like these would seem to make more sense if the letter was addressed to people who were familiar with the liturgy of the temple in Jerusalem.

In any event, the Apostle thought it important to explain the effects of Christ's salvation to these Christians of different backgrounds, to show them that they were all now made one and the same by faith. Also, given that Paul had completed his work in the countries of the Eastern Mediterranean, he hoped to begin to work in the West, specifically in Spain, the *fines terrae* (end of the world), and Rome would be the best base for this new spread of the Gospel.

3. MESSAGE

St Paul wrote two letters about the salvation that God gratuitously grants through Jesus Christ to those who believe in him. The first, the Letter to the Galatians, was written at the height of his debate with Judaizers. The second is Romans, but, although the same polemic is still present in the background, in this letter Paul goes deeper into the subject and works on a wider canvas, writing very calmly and organizing his arguments well. In Romans he devotes more of his attention to showing that Jesus Christ delivered us from the Law, from the religious regimentation of the Law, and he explains the profound newness of the Gospel and how the grace of God transforms believers, so that they become children of God in Christ through his Spirit. He speaks about the privileges that are Israel's (its calling, God's promises, the Law, the prophets), all of which spell hope for the ultimate salvation of the Chosen People and provide the theological basis for man's vocation and predestination. He also outlines how the moral and spiritual life of Christians must be in line with the new dignity conferred on them thanks to the salvific work of Jesus Christ. Twenty years of experience in the field of apostolate (and, moreover, the divine revelations he has received) allow Paul to make these very deep religious and theological reflections.

The Letter to the Romans is not a complete exposition of the Apostle's teaching. The pre-eminent importance given it in Luther's exegesis and the controversy that followed is detrimental if, as a result, the range of teaching found in the other Pauline letters is limited to the outlines of teaching found in the Letter to the Romans. However, Romans does convey the basic message of Paul's "Gospel", and it is the best synthesis. Some passages of Galatians find their best exegesis in the parallel passages of Romans, and Romans also helps to unlock the meaning of many passages in other letters.

Because the letter is quite long, it is not easy to say that it has one main doctrinal point, or focuses on one key idea in its discussion on morals. Many scholars argue that the main "thesis" of the letter is summarized in 1:16–17—salvation through the righteousness of God which is revealed to us through faith. As in the Letter to the Galatians, but without the same, rather polemical tone, the Apostle, by God's inspiration, wants to make it clear that the "righteousness of God", or justification (the action whereby God makes a human being righteous), is a divine grace, the first grace on the road to salvation; that is, it is a gift from God, and does not reach a person because he or she has fulfilled all the works prescribed by the Law of Moses; in fact, it is not possible to keep that Law unless grace comes to our aid. In other words, God reveals through St Paul that the beginning of justification and salvation is faith, which God himself gives a person irrespective of his or her merits. This central assertion, together with Paul's remonstration that all men are sinners, comprises the first four chapters of the letter, before he goes on to deal with other matters, as corollaries, so to speak—original sin, and Christ's being the new head of mankind, who redeems us from it (chap. 5); the need for Baptism and what Baptism is (chap. 6); man's struggle against concupiscence (chap. 7); life in the Holy Spirit (chap. 8). He rounds off his argument by reflecting on salvation history and on the future of the people of Israel (chaps. 9–11), and by giving an outline of Christian life, concentrating on charity and self-surrender in God (chaps. 12–14).

The Letter to the Romans has always been read as a key text in St Paul's thinking, and as a key source of Revelation. That explains why it is used so much in the liturgy. It contains some very poetic passages, such as the end of chapter 8 (8:28–39), certain verses about the Holy Spirit (8:14–17), and its two main doxologies—11:33–36 (the hymn to Wisdom) and 16:25–27. The letter seems to draw to a close in 15:33, with the usual words of farewell: this would explain why a very ancient papyrus puts the doxology of 16:25–27 there; some other manuscripts have it at the end of chapter 14, and most of them repeat it at the very end of the epistle. It is not difficult to offer an explanation for this. The liturgical reading of Romans usually omitted chapters 15 and 16 because they contained mainly personal information and "news items"; however, not wanting to lose the beautiful doxology at the very end, the liturgy brought it forward, and appended it to the text proper, so to speak. Liturgical reading influenced the copying of the manuscripts and thereby gave rise to the variations referred to.

Commentaries on Romans by Origen (conserved in a Latin translation by Rufinus) and by St John Chrysostom opened the way for extensive patristic exegesis. The main Eastern commentaries include those by St Ephrem, Theodore of Mopsuestia and Theodoret of Cyrrhus; in the West, commentaries were written by, among others, Marius Victorinus, Ambrosiaster (an unknown author whose commentary was attributed to St Ambrose), Pelagius and St Augustine. Because of these commentaries the main ideas in the letter proved influential in medieval scholarship theology.

During the Protestant Reformation, Luther, Calvin and Melanchthon based their ideas on justification and salvation, predestination and free will on a very lopsided view of Romans. Theological experts at the Council of Trent (1545–1563) studied the letter in depth, in the context of Christian discourse as a whole, making use of works by Fathers of the Church, and the main result of their work was the decree *De iustificatione*, a very unambiguous and insightful work. In the twentieth century, Karl Barth's commentary on Romans was very influential in a theological movement against the Liberal Protestantism of the nineteenth century. The past century has also seen many Catholic studies of Romans and an increased awareness of its importance. It is true to say that Romans has played an important role in European Christian thinking—even to the extent of splitting Western Christendom down the middle (this phenomenon was neither inevitable nor even reasonable, but it is certainly lamentable). Many of the interpretations given the text have been bound up with confessional interests that have nothing whatever to do with the Apostle's own thinking, and are equally out of touch with the lives of Christians today. At the present time it is common knowledge that theologians and exegetes are converging on a shared interpretation of the text, and this cannot but facilitate ecumenical dialogue and understanding.

Romans

1. INTRODUCTION*

Greeting

1 ¹Paul, a servant[a] of Jesus Christ, called to be an apostle, set apart for the gospel of God ²which he promised beforehand through his prophets in the holy scriptures, ³the gospel concerning his Son, who was descended from David according to the flesh ⁴and designated[a²] Son of God in power according to the Spirit of holiness by his resurrection from the dead, Jesus Christ our Lord, ⁵through whom we have received grace and apostleship to bring about the obedience of faith for the sake of his name among all the nations, ⁶including yourselves who are called to belong to Jesus Christ;

⁷To all God's beloved in Rome, who are called to be saints:

Grace to you and peace from God our Father and the Lord Jesus Christ.*

Gal 1:10, 15
Phil 1:1
Acts 26:16-18

2 Sam 7
Mt 9:27
2 Tim 2:8
Rev 22:16

Acts 9:15

Acts 9:13
1 Cor 8:6

[1] ¹Paulus servus Christi Iesu, vocatus apostolus, segregatus in evangelium Dei, ²quod ante promiserat per prophetas suos in Scripturis sanctis ³de Filio suo, qui factus est ex semine David secundum carnem, ⁴qui constitutus est Filius Dei in virtute secundum Spiritum sanctificationis ex resurrectione mortuorum, Iesu Christo Domino nostro, ⁵per quem accepimus gratiam et apostolatum ad oboeditionem fidei in omnibus gentibus pro nomine eius, ⁶in quibus estis et vos vocati Iesu Christi, ⁷omnibus, qui sunt Romae dilectis Dei, vocatis sanctis: gratia vobis et pax a Deo Patre nostro et Domino Iesu Christo. ⁸Primum quidem gratias ago Deo meo per Iesum Christum pro omnibus vobis, quia fides vestra annuntiatur in

*1:1–17 The letter begins with an elaborate greeting (vv. 1–7), an act of thanksgiving that is also an exhortation (vv. 8–15) and a preview of the letter's theme (vv. 16–17).

1:1–7 When introducing himself (v. 1), the Apostle shows that he sees himself as (a) "a servant of Jesus Christ", just as Moses and the ancient prophets saw themselves as servants of God; (b) "called to be an apostle", which puts him in the same company as the Twelve; and (c) "set apart for the gospel of God". In this way, he justifies his writing to the faithful in Rome even though he has never been there. In this opening passage he also reminds them about God the Father's plan of redemption, put into effect by Christ, through the Holy Spirit, here called "the Spirit of holiness" (v. 4), an expression not used elsewhere in the New Testament; and he calls his addressees "God's beloved" and "saints" (v. 7). This is not just a way of speaking; it expresses something quite profound—the fact that Christians are chosen by God and "called", just as the Israelites were so often called through Moses (see Num 10:1–4). Christians are called to form

the new People of God, whose distinguishing mark is holiness (cf. the notes on 15:22–33; Acts 9:1–19; and 1 Cor 6:1–11).

The word "gospel", frequently used by St Paul, means the good news about the salvation effected by Christ. The apostles were charged by Jesus with spreading the Gospel to all creation (Mk 16:15; Mt 28:19). Paul has been chosen just as they were, with a special commission to proclaim the Gospel to the Gentiles (v. 5), who include the Romans. For him, the Gospel necessarily includes believing that Jesus Christ is the Son of God, as his resurrection from the dead (v. 4) goes to prove. So, the Gospel is at one and the same time the saving power of the grace obtained by Jesus Christ, the truths revealed by him, and the efforts of the Church to spread divine salvation to all mankind. In Paul's writings, the expressions "the gospel of God" and "the gospel of Christ" mean the same thing (cf. the note on Mk 1:1–13).

The "obedience of faith" (v. 5) means acceptance of the Gospel, an act involving the human mind and will but one which only comes to fruition when done with faith.

a Or *slave*   a² Or *constituted*

Act of thanksgiving

Rom 16:19
1 Thess 2:5,10

[8]First, I thank my God through Jesus Christ for all of you, because your faith is proclaimed in all the world. [9]For God is my witness, whom I serve with my spirit in the gospel of his Son, that without ceasing I mention you always in my prayers, [10]asking that somehow by God's will I may now at last succeed in coming to you.* [11]For I long to see you, that I may impart to you some spiritual gift to strengthen you, [12]that is, that we may be mutually encouraged by each other's faith, both yours and mine. [13]I want you to know, brethren, that I have often intended to come to you (but thus

Rom 15:23
Acts 19:21

far have been prevented), in order that I may reap some harvest* among you as well as among the rest of the Gentiles. [14]I am under obligation both to Greeks and to barbarians, both to the wise and to the foolish:[15]so I am eager to preach the gospel to you also who are in Rome.

Theme of the letter

1 Cor 1:18–25; 2:1–5
2 Cor 12:9f
1 Thess 2:13

Gal 3:11
Heb 10:38
Hab 2:4

[16]For I am not ashamed of the gospel: it is the power of God for salvation to every one who has faith, to the Jew first and also to the Greek. [17]For in it the righteousness of God is revealed through faith for faith; as it is written, "He who through faith is righteous shall live."[b]

---

universo mundo; [9]testis enim mihi est Deus, cui servio in spiritu meo in evangelio Filii eius, quomodo sine intermissione memoriam vestri faciam [10]semper in orationibus meis obsecrans si quo modo tandem aliquando prosperum iter habeam in voluntate Dei veniendi ad vos. [11]Desidero enim videre vos, ut aliquid impertiar gratiae vobis spiritalis ad confirmandos vos, [12]id est una vobiscum consolari per eam, quae invicem est, fidem vestram atque meam. [13]Nolo autem vos ignorare, fratres, quia saepe proposui venire ad vos et prohibitus sum usque adhuc, ut aliquem fructum habeam et in vobis, sicut et in ceteris gentibus. [14]Graecis ac barbaris, sapientibus et insipientibus debitor sum. [15]Itaque, quod in me est, promptus sum et vobis, qui Romae estis, evangelizare. [16]Non enim erubesco evangelium: virtus enim Dei est in salutem omni credenti, Iudaeo primum et Graeco. [17]Iustitia enim Dei in eo revelatur ex fide in fidem, sicut scriptum est: *«Iustus autem ex fide vivet»*. [18]Revelatur enim ira Dei de caelo super

---

1:8–15 In this passage, as well as giving thanks to God, Paul mentions his plan to visit the faithful in Rome in order to preach the Gospel to them (v. 15), and so that they and he should be consoled and strengthened in the faith they share. Paul feels an obligation to make this journey (v. 14), because "Greeks" and "barbarians", that is, all Gentiles, including those in Rome, have a right to hear his preaching; it is his God-given mission (cf. 15:15–19; Gal 2:7; Acts 9:15).

1:16–17 Here the Apostle spells out the theme of the letter—righteousness (justification) that comes through faith. The expression "righteousness of God" is one of the most important used by St Paul, and it is rich in meaning. It means (a) the divine attribute whereby God is always just

in his treatment of others; (b) God's faithfulness to his promises; and (c) the mercy he shows sinful man by forgiving him and making him righteous. St Paul is using the last meaning here (see the note on 3:21–31). "Through faith for faith" shows that divine righteousness in man begins with faith and is perfected by faith.

The words "He who through faith is righteous shall live" or "The righteous man shall live by [or through] faith" are a quotation from Habakkuk 2:4. The prophet was referring to an historical situation involving an invasion: those who trust in God's promises will not perish. The Apostle applies this passage to Christians to stress that faith is the beginning of salvation, since it is through faith that man becomes justified in God's sight. He will elaborate on aspects of this theme over the course of the letter.

b Or *The righteous shall live by faith*

PART ONE

Justification through Jesus Christ*

2. JUSTIFICATION BY FAITH*

The fault of the Gentiles, and their punishment

[18]For the wrath of God is revealed from heaven against all ungodliness and wickedness of men who by their wickedness suppress the truth. [19]For what can be known about God is plain to them, because God has shown it to them. [20]Ever since the creation of the world his invisible nature, namely, his eternal power and deity, has been clearly perceived in the things that have been made. So they are without excuse; [21]for although they knew God they did not honour him as God or give thanks to him, but they became futile in their thinking and their senseless minds were darkened. [22]Claiming to be wise, they became fools, [23]and exchanged the glory of the immortal God for images resembling mortal man or birds or animals or reptiles.

[24]Therefore God gave them up in the lusts of their hearts to impurity, to the dishonouring of their bodies among themselves, [25]because they exchanged the truth about God for a lie and worshipped and served the creature rather than the Creator, who is blessed for ever! Amen.

Ps 85: 3–5; 69:24
Mic 7:9
Zeph 1:15

Wis 13:1–9
Acts 17:24–29
Sir 17:8

Is 40:26–28
Eph 4:17–18

1 Cor 1:19–20
Gen 1:26–27
Ps 106:20; Ex 32
Jer 2:5, 11
Deut 4:16–18
Wis 11:15; 12:24;
13:10f

Eph 4:19

Rom 16:27

omnem impietatem et iniustitiam hominum, qui veritatem in iniustitia detinent, [19]quia, quod noscibile est Dei, manifestum est in illis; Deus enim illis manifestavit. [20]Invisibilia enim ipsius a creatura mundi per ea, quae facta sunt, intellecta conspiciuntur, sempiterna eius et virtus et divinitas, ut sint inexcusabiles; [21]quia, cum cognovissent Deum, non sicut Deum glorificaverunt aut gratias egerunt, sed evanuerunt in cogitationibus suis, et obscuratum est insipiens cor eorum. [22]Dicentes se esse sapientes, stulti facti sunt, [23]et mutaverunt gloriam incorruptibilis Dei in similitudinem imaginis corruptibilis hominis et volucrum et quadrupedum et serpentium. [24]Propter quod tradidit illos Deus in concupiscentiis cordis eorum in immunditiam, ut ignominia afficiant corpora sua in semetipsis, [25]qui commutaverunt veritatem Dei in mendacio et coluerunt et servierunt creaturae potius quam Creatori, qui est benedictus in saecula. Amen. [26]Propterea tradidit illos Deus in passiones ignominiae. Nam et feminae eorum

*1:18—11:36 These chapters, which make up the "doctrinal" part of the letter, deal with the nature and effects of the justification won for us by Christ. After asserting that only through Christ and through faith in him can man become righteous or just in God's eyes (1:18—4:25), St Paul explains how, through Baptism, we are enabled to partake of the reconciliation with God that Christ's sacrifice brought about; he also shows what consequences flow from that—freedom, life in the Spirit, divine filiation (5:1—8:39). Finally, he describes the role Israel will have in the definitive manifestation of the justifying action of God (9:1—11:36).

*1:18—4:25 The underlying thesis of this section is that justification through faith is the only route to salvation; all are sinners—pagans on account of their idolatry and immorality (1:18–32), Jews because of their sins and infringement of the Law (2:17–24). Everyone—Jews (despite

circumcision and the promises made to Israel: 2:1–16, 2:25–3:8) and Gentiles—are sinners in God's sight (3:9–20), and therefore all need to be justified by the grace which he bestows on those who believe in Christ (3:21–31). This can be seen in Scripture: God blessed Abraham with the promises, not because of Abraham's works but because of his faith (4:1–25).

1:18–32 Taking his cue perhaps from Wisdom 13:1–9 and his perception of how things stand in the cities of the Hellenic world (not least Corinth, where he is writing from), Paul outlines the situation of the Gentiles—one of idolatry through their own fault (vv. 18–23)—and then spells out what this situation leads to (vv. 24–32).

He tells the Romans that God can be known through the greatness and beauty of the physical universe, but, by falling into idolatry, men have lost their senses (v. 22) and have rejected God. They have earned the "wrath of God" (v. 18),

²⁶For this reason God gave them up to dishonourable passions. Their women exchanged natural relations for unnatural, ²⁷and the men likewise gave up natural relations with women and were consumed with passion for one another, men committing shameless acts with men and receiving in their own persons the due penalty for their error.

²⁸And since they did not see fit to acknowledge God, God gave them up to a base mind and to improper conduct. ²⁹They were filled with all manner of wickedness, evil, covetousness, malice. Full of envy, murder, strife, deceit, malignity, they are gossips, ³⁰slanderers, haters of God, insolent, haughty, boastful, inventors of evil, disobedient to parents, ³¹foolish, faithless, heartless, ruthless. ³²Though they know God's decree that those who do such things deserve to die, they not only do them but approve those who practise them.

immutaverunt naturalem usum in eum, qui est contra naturam; ²⁷similiter et masculi, relicto naturali usu feminae, exarserunt in desideriis suis in invicem, masculi in masculos turpitudinem operantes et mercedem, quam oportuit, erroris sui in semetipsis recipientes. ²⁸Et sicut non probaverunt Deum habere in notitia, tradidit eos Deus in reprobum sensum, ut faciant, quae non conveniunt, ²⁹repletos omni iniquitate, malitia, avaritia, nequitia, plenos invidia, homicidio, contentione, dolo, malignitate, susurrones, ³⁰detractores, Deo odibiles, contumeliosos, superbos, elatos, inventores malorum, parentibus non oboedientes, ³¹insipientes, incompositos, sine affectione, sine misericordia. ³²Qui cum iudicium Dei cognovissent, quoniam qui talia agunt, digni sunt morte, non solum ea faciunt, sed et consentiunt facientibus. [2] ¹Propter quod inexcusabilis es, o homo omnis,

which is a way of saying that those who cut themselves off from God are punished by him: St Thomas Aquinas says that "anger and other passions are ascribed to God by an analogy drawn from their effects. Because it is characteristic of an angry person to punish (the guilty party), divine retribution is metaphorically termed 'anger'", that is, wrath (*Summa theologiae*, 1, 3, 2 ad 2). In any case, we should remember that when God is said to punish someone, we need to interpret that as meaning that he acts in the same way as a father does when he corrects his children. So, just as the "righteousness of God" means the action whereby he saves sinful man by pouring grace into his soul, so too God's "wrath" expresses in some way his fatherly attitude towards those who persist in sin. The "wickedness" (v. 18), injustice/ unrighteousness, refers to rejection of the truth about God (for human beings are capable of knowing the existence of God on a natural level). How God's plan to save sinners ("righteousness", in the sense of a desire to save) can be comparable with punishing sins (the "wrath of God") is a mystery of God's perfect justice, his even greater mercy, and man's personal freedom.

This passage does not mean that all Gentiles are base. Paul is making a general judgment on the basis of his own experience, Old Testament

wisdom insights and, above all, what Jesus has revealed.

On the basis of vv. 19–20 and other biblical passages (see Wis 13:1–9; Acts 14:15–17; 17:24–29), the Church teaches that a person can acquire a natural knowledge of God through observation of the physical universe: "God, the origin and end of all things, can be known with certainty by the natural light of human reason from the things he created" (Vatican I, *Dei Filius*, chap. 2). "The world and man attest that they contain within themselves neither their first principle nor their final end, but rather that they participate in Being itself, which alone is without origin or end. Thus, in different ways, man can come to know that there exists a reality which is the first cause and final end of all things, a reality 'that everyone calls "God"' (St Thomas Aquinas, *S. Th.*, 1, 2, 3)" (*Catechism of the Catholic Church*, 34). See the note on Wis 13:1–9.

Verses 24–27 show the connexion between rejection of God and sexual immorality, especially homosexual behaviour. "This judgment of Scripture does not of course permit us to conclude that all those who suffer from this anomaly are personally responsible for it, but it does attest to the fact that homosexual acts are intrinsically disordered and can in no case be approved of" (Congregation for the Doctrine of the Faith, *Persona humana*, 8). Cf. Jude 7.

The Jews are guilty, too

2 ¹Therefore you have no excuse, O man, whoever you are, when you judge another; for in passing judgment upon him you condemn yourself, because you, the judge, are doing the very same things. ²We know that the judgment of God rightly falls upon those who do such things. ³Do you suppose, O man, that when you judge those who do such things and yet do them yourself, you will escape the judgment of God? ⁴Or do you presume upon the riches of his kindness and forbearance and patience? Do you not know that God's kindness is meant to lead you to repentance? ⁵But by your hard and impenitent heart you are storing up wrath for yourself on the day of wrath when God's righteous judgment will be revealed. ⁶For he will render to every man according to his works: ⁷to those who by patience in well-doing seek for glory and honour and immortality, he will give eternal life; ⁸but for those who are factious and do not obey the truth, but obey wickedness, there will be wrath and fury. ⁹There will be tribulation and distress for every human being who does evil, the Jew first and also the Greek, ¹⁰but glory and honour and peace for every one who does good, the Jew first and also the Greek. ¹¹For God shows no partiality.

¹²All who have sinned without the law will also perish without the law, and all who have sinned under the law will be judged by the law. ¹³For it is not the hearers

Jn 8:7
Jas 4:1
Mt 7:2

Eph 2:3

Wis 11.23
Sir 5:4
2 Pet 3:15

Rom 1:18; Rev 6:17
Zeph 1:14–18
Acts 7:51

Ps 62:12
2 Thess 1:5–10
2 Cor 5:10
Heb 11:16

Mt 16:27; Jn 5:29
Ezek 18:21–22
2 Thess 1:8

Rom 1:16; 3:9
2 Cor 5:10

Wis 6:7–8
Deut 10:17
Acts 10:34

Rom 3:19
Jas 2:12; 1 Jn 3, 7

qui iudicas. In quo enim iudicas alterum, teipsum condemnas; eadem enim agis, qui iudicas. ²Scimus enim quoniam iudicium Dei est secundum veritatem in eos, qui talia agunt. ³Existimas autem hoc, o homo, qui iudicas eos, qui talia agunt, et facis ea, quia tu effugies iudicium Dei? ⁴An divitias benignitatis eius et patientiae et longanimitatis contemnis, ignorans quoniam benignitas Dei ad paenitentiam te adducit? ⁵Secundum duritiam autem tuam et impaenitens cor thesaurizas tibi iram in die irae et revelationis iusti iudicii Dei, ⁶qui reddet unicuique secundum opera eius: ⁷his quidem, qui secundum patientiam boni operis gloriam et honorem et incorruptionem quaerunt, vitam aeternam; ⁸his autem, qui ex contentione et non oboediunt veritati, oboediunt autem iniquitati, ira et indignatio. ⁹Tribulatio et angustia in omnem animam hominis operantis malum, Iudaei primum et Graeci; ¹⁰gloria autem et honor et pax omni operanti bonum, Iudaeo primum et Graeco. ¹¹Non est enim personarum acceptio apud

2:1–24 In the style of a "diatribe" (a form of dispute in Stoic philosophy), St Paul sets up a conversation with an imaginary person who represents the Jewish people (see v. 17), to make the point that no one can consider himself to be righteous/just: all men, Gentiles and Jews, are sinners in God's sight. Paul argues that it is not enough to have the Law in order to be saved. God is always impartial; he judges every human being according to how he or she has kept his law. First he will judge the Jews, according to the Law of Moses; and then the Gentiles, according to the natural law written on their hearts. By acting in accordance with nature they would be adhering to the same moral precepts that God made explicit in the Ten Commandments (v. 14).

These verses show that God is fair in his rewards and punishments, bestowing eternal life or retribution, depending on whether a person has kept the Law; he is an impartial Judge who makes no distinction between Jew and Gentile: all he takes into consideration is the good a person has done; a time will come when the Lord will deliver judgment. The Church uses this

passage and other texts from Scripture to teach that there are two points when a person must appear before the Lord. The first is on leaving this life, the so-called "particular judgment", and the other "occurs when on the same day and in the same place all men shall stand together before the tribunal of their judge, that in the presence and hearing of all human beings of all times each may know his final doom and sentence" (*Roman Catechism*, 18, 3).

The teaching expressed in vv. 14–15 is very important. It states that there is a law "written and engraved on the mind of every man, and this is nothing but our reason, commanding us to do right and forbidding sin" (Leo XIII, *Libertas praestantissimum*, 8), and that conscience and law complement one another: conscience applies the law to particular situations. That is why conscience has been called "the voice of God" that "ever calling him to love and to do what is good and to avoid evil, tells him inwardly at the right moment: do this, shun that. [...] Conscience is the most secret core and sanctuary of a man. There he is alone with God, whose voice echoes in his

Mt 7:21, 26
Jas 1:22, 25
Lk 8:21

Jer 31:33
2 Tim 2:8
Rom 2:6–8
1 Cor 4:5

Jas 2:19
Phil 3:4–6
Mt 3:7–9
Jn 8:33–40
Is 48:1–4

Phil 1:10
Amos 5:21
Mt 15:14
Lk 6:39
Jn 9:40–41

Ps 50:16–21

Jas 2:7
2 Pet 2:2
Is 52:5 (LXX)
Ezek 36:20

1 Cor 7:19
Gal 5:3, 6
Jer 4:4; 9:24–25

Mt 12:41f

of the law who are righteous before God, but the doers of the law who will be justified. [14]When Gentiles who have not the law do by nature what the law requires, they are a law to themselves, even though they do not have the law. [15]They show that what the law requires is written on their hearts, while their conscience also bears witness and their conflicting thoughts accuse or perhaps excuse them [16]on that day when, according to my gospel, God judges the secrets of men by Christ Jesus.

[17]But if you call yourself a Jew and rely upon the law and boast of your relation to God [18]and know his will and approve what is excellent, because you are instructed in the law, [19]and if you are sure that you are a guide to the blind, a light to those who are in darkness, [20]a corrector of the foolish, a teacher of children, having in the law the embodiment of knowledge and truth—[21]you then who teach others, will you not teach yourself? While you preach against stealing, do you steal? [22]You who say that one must not commit adultery, do you commit adultery? You who abhor idols, do you rob temples? [23]You who boast in the law, do you dishonour God by breaking the law? [24]For, as it is written, "The name of God is blasphemed among the Gentiles because of you."

Real circumcision, a matter of the heart

[25]Circumcision indeed is of value if you obey the law; but if you break the law, your circumcision becomes uncircumcision. [26]So, if a man who is uncircumcised keeps the precepts of the law, will not his uncircumcision be regarded as circumcision? [27]Then those who are physically uncircumcised but keep the law will condemn you

Deum! [12]Quicumque enim sine lege peccaverunt, sine lege et peribunt; et quicumque in lege peccaverunt, per legem iudicabuntur. [13]Non enim auditores legis iusti sunt apud Deum, sed factores legis iustificabuntur. [14]Cum enim gentes, quae legem non habent, naturaliter, quae legis sunt, faciunt, eiusmodi legem non habentes ipsi sibi sunt lex; [15]qui ostendunt opus legis scriptum in cordibus suis, testimonium simul reddente illis conscientia ipsorum, et inter se invicem cogitationibus accusantibus aut etiam defendentibus, [16]in die cum iudicabit Deus occulta hominum secundum evangelium meum per Christum Iesum. [17]Si autem tu Iudaeus cognominaris et requiescis in lege et gloriaris in Deo, [18]et nosti Voluntatem et discernis potiora instructus per legem, [19]et confidis teipsum ducem esse caecorum, lumen eorum, qui in tenebris sunt, [20]eruditorem insipientium, magistrum infantium, habentem formam scientiae et veritatis in lege. [21]Qui ergo alium doces, teipsum non doces? Qui praedicas non furandum, furaris? [22]Qui dicis non moechandum, moecharis? Qui abominaris idola, templa spolias? [23]Qui in lege gloriaris, per praevaricationem legis Deum inhonoras? [24]«Nomen enim *Dei propter vos blasphematur inter gentes*», sicut scriptum est. [25]Circumcisio quidem prodest, si legem observes; si autem praevaricator legis sis, circumcisio tua praeputium facta est. [26]Si igitur praeputium iustitias legis custodiat, nonne praeputium illius in circumcisionem reputabitur? [27]Et iudicabit, quod ex natura est praeputium legem consummans, te, qui per litteram et circumcisionem praevaricator

depths" (Vatican II, *Gaudium et spes*, 16). Even so, conscience encounters real difficulties in its attempt to discover all the implications of the law; fuzzy thinking, weakness of the will, disordered senses, imagination, passions—all play their part; the net result is that people can easily convince themselves that something they don't want to believe is true is in fact untrue or at least doubtful. To help man deal with these difficulties, God chose to reveal the *natural* law in a *supernatural* way and to give his Church authority to spell out the implications of the natural law.

In vv. 17–24 of this imaginary dispute, Paul shows the inconsistency of those who have clear criteria of truth in the Law but fail to apply them, and what bad example they give to the Gentiles. Here Paul is talking about Jews, but what he says is also a call to Christians to live in accordance

with their beliefs: "Good example does not only have outward effects, it also acts deep within the other to produce the most precious and powerful good: identity with his own Christian vocation" (John Paul II, *Address*, 20 February 1980).

2:25 – 3:8 The argument about how Jews need to be justified by grace now focuses on circumcision (2:25–29) and the promises made by God to Israel (3:1–8).

Circumcision was the rite whereby a person came to share in the covenant God made with Abraham (Gen 17:10–11) and became an heir to the promises. By virtue of that Covenant, a circumcised Hebrew was obliged to keep the entire Law of Moses—but that was beyond man's natural powers. On the other hand, the Gentiles, though they were not circumcised, were able to

who have the written code and circumcision but break the law. ²⁸For he is not a real Jew who is one outwardly, nor is true circumcision something external and physical. ²⁹He is a Jew who is one inwardly, and real circumcision is a matter of the heart, spiritual and not literal. His praise is not from men but from God.

Jn 7:24

Col 2:11
2 Cor 10:18
Jer 4:4
Rom 7:6; 8:2–4
2 Cor 3:6
Phil 3:2–3
Eph 2:11

3 ¹Then what advantage has the Jew? Or what is the value of circumcision? ²Much in every way. To begin with, the Jews are entrusted with the oracles of God. ³What if some were unfaithful? Does their faithlessness nullify the faithfulness of God? ⁴By no means! Let God be true though every man be false, as it is written,

Ps 147:19–20
Rom 9:4–7
Deut 4:7–8

Ps 89:30–37
2 Tim 2:13

Ps 116:11

"That thou mayest be justified in thy words,
and prevail when thou art judged."

Ps 51:4 (LXX)

⁵But if our wickedness serves to show the justice of God, what shall we say? That God is unjust to inflict wrath on us? (I speak in a human way.) ⁶By no means! For then how could God judge the world? ⁷But if through my falsehood God's truthfulness abounds to his glory, why am I still being condemned as a sinner? ⁸And why not do evil that good may come?—as some people slanderously charge us with saying. Their condemnation is just.

Job 34:12, 17
Rom 1:18

Rom 9:19

Rom 6:1–15

All are sinners—Jews and Gentiles alike

⁹What then? Are we Jews any better off?^c No, not at all; for I^d have already charged that all men, both Jews and Greeks, are under the power of sin, ¹⁰as it is written:

Rom 2:9ff; 11:32

legis es. ²⁸Non enim, qui manifesto Iudaeus est, neque quae manifesto in carne circumcisio, ²⁹sed qui in abscondito Iudaeus est, et circumcisio cordis in spiritu non littera, cuius laus non ex hominibus sed ex Deo est.   [3] ¹Quid ergo amplius est Iudaeo, aut quae utilitas circumcisionis? ²Multum per omnem modum. Primum quidem, quia credita sunt illis eloquia Dei. ³Quid enim, si quidam non crediderunt? Numquid incredulitas illorum fidem Dei evacuabit? ⁴Absit! Exstet autem Deus verax, omnis autem homo mendax, sicut scriptum est: *«Ut iustificeris in sermonibus tuis et vincas cum iudicaris»*. ⁵Si autem iniustitia nostra iustitiam Dei commendat, quid dicemus? Numquid iniustus Deus, qui infert iram? Secundum hominem dico. ⁶Absit! Alioquin quomodo iudicabit Deus mundum? ⁷Si enim veritas Dei in meo mendacio abundavit in gloriam ipsius, quid adhuc

keep some commandments of the Law, and at times even better than the Jews were. From this it follows that what carries weight with God is not physical circumcision but man's readiness to do what God commands. Real circumcision, Paul argues, is not physical circumcision but circumcision of the heart (2:29), that is, obedient observance of the law of God. God, who can read all hearts, does not judge people on the basis of external appearances.

On hearing this argument, an imaginary Jewish questioner might ask, "If that is the case, what advantages do Jews have, what point is there in circumcision?" (see 3:1). Paul's reply is that God gave the Jews his "oracles", that is, the promises and the Law; in spite of that, some Jews rejected Christ and crucified him. However, that in turn led to the promises of salvation being fulfilled: their unbelief did not prevent God's plans being carried out (3:3).

Still replying to objections from an imaginary questioner, Paul responds to another question: If

the sin of those Jews did not lessen God's faithfulness but actually redounded to his glory (see 3:7), is God not unjust when he rejects Jews who do not believe in Christ (3:5, 7)? Paul replies in 3:6 with a question that shows that the idea is absurd: If God is unjust, how then can he judge the world? This argument carries a lot of weight for a Jew, because, being familiar with the Old Testament, he knows that God will indeed judge all men (see Joel 3:12). Finally, Paul says that if his questioner's false reasoning were pushed to its logical conclusion, one could legitimately do evil in order to achieve good. So he concludes that those who argue along these lines are rightly condemned (3:8b). Paul's message is clear: God is faithful, and our own infidelity makes God's plans of salvation all the more evident.

3:9–20 In an exposition woven with quotations from the Old Testament after the style of the rabbis, Paul returns to the subject of guilt: all are sinners, Jews included. After an introduction (v.

c Or *at any disadvantage*   d Greek *we*

Ps 14:1–3; 55:1–3

"None is righteous, no, not one;

Eccles 7:20

[11] no one understands, no one seeks for God.

[12] All have turned aside, together they have gone wrong;
no one does good, not even one."

Ps 5:9; 140:3

[13] "Their throat is an open grave,
they use their tongues to deceive."
"The venom of asps is under their lips."

Ps 10:7

[14] "Their mouth is full of curses and bitterness."

Is 59:7–8
Prov 1:16

[15] "Their feet are swift to shed blood,
[16] in their paths are ruin and misery,
[17] and the way of peace they do not know."

Ps 36:1

[18] "There is no fear of God before their eyes."

Rom 2:12
Jn 10:34

[19] Now we know that whatever the law says it speaks to those who are under the law, so that every mouth may be stopped, and the whole world may be held account-

Ps 143:2
Gal 2:16; 3:22
Rom 7:7

able to God. [20] For no human being will be justified in his sight by works of the law, since through the law comes knowledge of sin.

Righteousness, a free gift through faith in Christ*

1 Kings 8:46
Acts 10:43
Rom 1:16
Gal 2:16

[21] But now the righteousness of God has been manifested apart from law, although the law and the prophets bear witness to it, [22] the righteousness of God through faith

et ego tamquam peccator iudicor? [8] Et non sicut blasphemamur et sicut aiunt quidam nos dicere: «Faciamus mala, ut veniant bona?». Quorum damnatio iusta est. [9] Quid igitur? Praecellimus eos? Nequaquam! Antea enim causati sumus Iudaeos et Graecos omnes sub peccato esse, [10] sicut scriptum est: «Non est iustus quisquam, / [11] non est intellegens, non est requirens Deum. / [12] Omnes declinaverunt, simul inutiles facti sunt; / non est qui faciat bonum, non est usque ad unum. / [13] Sepulcrum patens est guttur eorum, / linguis suis dolose agebant, / venenum aspidum sub labiis eorum, / [14] quorum os maledictione et amaritudine plenum est; / [15] veloces pedes eorum ad effundendum sanguinem, / [16] contritio et infelicitas in viis eorum, / [17] et viam pacis non cognoverunt. / [18] Non est timor Dei ante oculos eorum». [19] Scimus autem quoniam, quaecumque lex loquitur, his,

9), he describes the universal apostasy that the psalmist had already spoken of (vv. 10–12); he then lists the sins, by word (vv. 13–14) and by action (v. 15), that the prophets denounced (see Is 5:8–25; 59:2–8; Jer 8:8; Amos 5:11; Mal 2:8). Those who are guilty of such sins will come to a sorry end; they will have no peace, and no fear of God (vv. 17–18); moreover, the Law is not strong enough on its own to make man righteous (vv. 19–20). The implication is that if, as Scripture says, all have sinned, then all need the righteousness that comes from God (justification); no one is justified by works of the Law. This teaching to the effect that all men sin implies, in turn, that redemption extends to all (cf. 3:21–31): "What divine revelation makes known to us agrees with experience. Examining his heart, man finds that he has inclinations toward evil too, and is engulfed by manifold ills which cannot come from his good Creator. Often refusing to acknowledge God as his beginning, man has disrupted also his proper relationship to his own ultimate goal as well as his whole relation-

ship toward himself and others and all created things" (Vatican II, *Gaudium et spes*, 13). Of course, the depressing panorama painted by Paul does not mean that there were no just and devout people (in Israel or elsewhere) who received divine grace and performed good works by virtue of the future merits of Christ.

*3:21—4:25 In 1:18—3:20, the Apostle argued that Jews and Gentiles are in a similar situation with regard to sin and reward or punishment. Now he goes on to show that they are all equally in need of the justification made possible by the redemption worked by Christ. All need to join themselves to Christ through faith. The form of argument is similar to that used in the previous section—first the teaching is put forward (3:21–22a); then it is developed in detail (3:22b–26) and explained by questions and answers (3:27–31); and there is a lengthy conclusion which draws on evidence from Scripture (4:1–25).

3:21–31 These verses contain key aspects of the

in Jesus Christ for all who believe. For there is no distinction; [23]since all have sinned and fall short of the glory of God, [24]they are justified by his grace as a gift, through the redemption which is in Christ Jesus, [25]whom God put forward as an expiation by his blood, to be received by faith. This was to show God's righteousness, because in his divine forbearance he had passed over former sins; [26]it was to prove at the present time that he himself is righteous and that he justifies him who has faith in Jesus.

Rom 3:9; 5:1
Dan 9:24
Eph 2:8
Tit 3:7
Heb 9:5–15
1 Jn 2:2; 4:10
2 Cor 5:19
Lev 16
Acts 17:30
Is 53:11

[27]Then what becomes of our boasting? It is excluded. On what principle? On the principle of works? No, but on the principle of faith.* [28]For we hold that a man is justified by faith apart from works of law. [29]Or is God the God of Jews only? Is he not the God of Gentiles also? Yes, of Gentiles also, [30]since God is one; and he will justify the circumcised on the ground of their faith and the uncircumcised through their faith. [31]Do we then overthrow the law by this faith? By no means! On the contrary, we uphold the law.

Rom 2:17; 4:2–3;
5:2, 8; 11:18
Gal 6:13–14
Eph 2:9
Rom 9:24
Gal 3:6
Rom 6:15
Mt 5:17

qui in lege sunt, loquitur, ut omne os obstruatur, et obnoxius fiat omnis mundus Deo; [20]quia ex operibus legis *non iustificabitur omnis caro coram illo*, per legem enim cognitio peccati. [21]Nunc autem sine lege iustitia Dei manifestata est, testificata a Lege et Prophetis, [22]iustitia autem Dei per fidem Iesu Christi, in omnes qui credunt. Non enim est distinctio: [23]omnes enim peccaverunt et egent gloria Dei, [24]iustificati gratis per gratiam ipsius per redemptionem, quae est in Christo Iesu; [25]quem proposuit Deus propitiatorium per fidem in sanguine ipsius ad ostensionem iustitiae suae, cum praetermisisset praecedentia delicta [26]in sustentatione Dei, ad ostensionem iustitiae eius in hoc tempore, ut sit ipse iustus et iustificans eum, qui ex fide est Iesu. [27]Ubi est ergo gloriatio? Exclusa est. Per quam legem? Operum? Non, sed per legem fidei. [28]Arbitramur enim iustificari hominem per fidem sine operibus legis. [29]An Iudaeorum Deus tantum? Nonne et gentium? Immo et gentium, [30]quoniam quidem unus Deus, qui

teaching in this letter. First (vv. 21–26) the Apostle explains how man is justified by God: the righteousness of God which makes men righteous and which was announced in the books of the Old Testament (see Ps 103:6; Is 46:13; Jer 9:24) has been definitively revealed in Christ and in the Gospel. God the Father, the source of all goodness, has given us his Son to redeem us; in Jesus Christ, who shed his blood on the cross, we are justified; faith is the divine gift whereby God enables man to accept the gift of his redemption in Christ.

St Paul teaches that God's righteousness is bound up with his mercy: all men are justified by a *gratuitous* action on God's part (v. 24). The assertion that grace is a gift that God bestows without our meriting it in any way is so important that the Council of Trent, when citing this passage from St Paul, decided to define exactly what it meant: nothing that precedes and disposes man for justification—whether it be faith or works—*merits* the grace whereby man is justified (*De iustificatione*, chap. 8).

The Apostle adds that justification by grace is attained "through the redemption which is in Christ Jesus" (v. 24). That is to say, when a sinner is justified, there is a "passing from the state in which man is born a son of the first Adam, to the state of grace and adoption as sons of God through the second Adam, Jesus Christ, our Saviour" (Council of Trent, *De iustificatione*, chap. 4). This has been made possible because our Lord saved us by handing himself over as our ransom. The Greek word translated as "redemption" refers to the ransom money paid to free a person from slavery. Christ has delivered us from the slavery of sin by paying, so to speak, the price of our freedom (see 6:23), though that price is not so much his suffering in itself as the love for the Father with which it was endured. St Paul asserts that God has made Jesus the true "expiation" (propitiation, mercy seat). The "mercy seat" was the cover on top of the ark of the Covenant on which were set two figures of cherubim. The mercy seat was considered to be God's throne on earth (see Ps 80:1; 99:1), from which he spoke to Moses (see Ex 37:6), and the place where the people asked God for forgiveness of sins during the expiation offering on the Day of Expiation, Yom Kippur (see Lev 16:1–34); on that day, the high priest sprinkled the mercy seat with the blood of animals offered as victims to atone for the sins of the priest and the people. By saying that Jesus is an "expiation", Paul teaches that he is the only one who can obtain remission of sins by his blood.

The *Catechism of the Catholic Church*, in summing up this teaching, says: "Justification is

Abraham's exemplary faith

Gal 3:6–9
Jas 2:20–24
Gen 12:12

Jas 3:6
Gen 15:6
Gal 3:6

Ps 32:1–2

Gal 3:6
Jas 2:23
Gen 15:6

Jas 2:23
Gen 17:10–11
Gal 3:7

4 ¹What then shall we say about[e] Abraham, our forefather according to the flesh? ²For if Abraham was justified by works, he has something to boast about, but not before God. ³For what does the scripture say? "Abraham believed God, and it was reckoned to him as righteousness." ⁴Now to one who works, his wages are not reckoned as a gift but as his due. ⁵And to one who does not work but trusts him who justifies the ungodly, his faith is reckoned as righteousness. ⁶So also David pronounces a blessing upon the man to whom God reckons righteousness apart from works:

⁷"Blessed are those whose iniquities are forgiven, and whose sins are covered;
⁸ blessed is the man against whom the Lord will not reckon his sin."

⁹Is this blessing pronounced only upon the circumcised, or also upon the uncircumcised? We say that faith was reckoned to Abraham as righteousness. ¹⁰How then was it reckoned to him? Was it before or after he had been circumcised? It was not after, but before he was circumcised. ¹¹He received circumcision as a sign or seal of the righteousness which he had by faith while he was still uncircumcised. The purpose was to make him the father of all who believe without being circumcised and

iustificabit circumcisionem ex fide et praeputium per fidem. ³¹Legem ergo destruimus per fidem? Absit, sed legem statuimus. [4] ¹Quid ergo dicemus invenisse Abraham progenitorem nostrum secundum carnem? ²Si enim Abraham ex operibus iustificatus est, habet gloriam, sed non apud Deum. ³Quid enim Scriptura dicit? *«Credidit autem Abraham Deo, et reputatum est illi ad iustitiam»*. ⁴Ei autem, qui operatur, merces non reputatur secundum gratiam sed secundum debitum; ⁵ei vero, qui non operatur, sed credit in eum, qui iustificat impium, reputatur fides eius ad iustitiam, ⁶sicut et David dicit beatitudinem hominis, cui Deus reputat iustitiam sine operibus: ⁷*«Beati, quorum remissae sunt iniquitates / et quorum tecta sunt peccata. / ⁸Beatus vir, cui non imputabit Dominus peccatum»*. ⁹Beatitudo ergo haec in circumcisione an etiam in praeputio? Dicimus enim: *«Reputata est Abrahae fides ad iustitiam»*. ¹⁰Quomodo ergo reputata est? In circumcisione an in praeputio? Non in circumcisione sed in

at the same time *the acceptance of God's righteousness* through faith in Jesus Christ. Righteousness (or 'justice') here means the rectitude of divine love. With justification, faith, hope, and charity are poured into our hearts, and obedience to the divine will is granted us. Justification has been *merited for us by the Passion of Christ* who offered himself on the cross as a living victim, holy and pleasing to God, and whose blood has become the instrument of atonement for the sins of all men. Justification is conferred in Baptism, the sacrament of faith. It conforms us to the righteousness of God, who makes us inwardly just by the power of his mercy. Its purpose is the glory of God and of Christ, and the gift of eternal life" (*Catechism of the Catholic Church*, 1991 and 1992).

Verses 27–31 show that there is no reason, then, why anyone should think himself better than others: not even Jews should think like that, although God has shown them special favour. St Paul solemnly declares: no one should boast before God, as if he were just or holy, on the grounds that he has kept the Law (vv. 27–28); if a man is just, it is because God has made him just, by sheer grace, and man becomes just/right-

eous, that is, he is justified, when he accepts, through faith, the grace God offers him through Jesus Christ. The Apostle puts such stress on the point that man is justified by faith, and not by works of the Law, that it becomes a kind of refrain that is repeated throughout the letter (see vv. 22, 26, 28, 30; 4:5; 11:6; and see also Gal 2:16; 3:11).

Nowadays, Christian exegetes, Catholic and non-Catholic alike, are agreed on this basic teaching of St Paul's: salvation is offered to man in Jesus Christ, and God justifies man through faith in Christ. It is therefore faith that justifies. Not faith "alone", however (which is a misinterpretation that might be made on the basis of Luther's translation of the text), but faith that works through love (see Gal 5:6). It will be, therefore, by virtue of faith, not circumcision, that the Jews will be justified, and "by means of faith" that the uncircumcised, too, will be saved. Faith has not annulled the law, but confirms it, giving it its true meaning and bringing it to perfection.

4:1–25 This passage rounds out the idea that Paul briefly referred to in 1:16–17, that the right-

e Other ancient authorities read *was gained by*

who thus have righteousness reckoned to them, ¹²and likewise the father of the cir- 1 Pet 2:21
cumcised who are not merely circumcised but also follow the example of the faith
which our father Abraham had before he was circumcised.

¹³The promise to Abraham and his descendants, that they should inherit the world, Gal 3:16–18, 29
did not come through the law but through the righteousness of faith. ¹⁴If it is the Gen 12:3, 7; 18:18; 22:15–18
adherents of the law who are to be the heirs, faith is null and the promise is void. Gal 3:10, 19–22
¹⁵For the law brings wrath, but where there is no law there is no transgression. Rom 3:20; 5:13, 20; 7:7–11

¹⁶That is why it depends on faith, in order that the promise may rest on grace and
be guaranteed to all his descendants—not only to the adherents of the law but also
to those who share the faith of Abraham, for he is the father of us all, ¹⁷as it is writ- 2 Cor 1:9
ten, "I have made you the father of many nations"—in the presence of the God in Gen 17:5
whom he believed, who gives life to the dead and calls into existence the things that Is 48:13 Heb 11:17–19
do not exist. ¹⁸In hope he believed against hope, that he should become the father of Deut 32:39
many nations; as he had been told, "So shall your descendants be." ¹⁹He did not Gen 15:5
weaken in faith when he considered his own body, which was as good as dead Gen 17:1, 17

praeputio: ¹¹et signum accepit circumcisionis, signaculum iustitiae fidei, quae fuit in praeputio, ut esset pater omnium credentium per praeputium, ut reputetur illis iustitia, ¹²et pater circumcisionis his non tantum, qui ex circumcisione sunt, sed et qui sectantur vestigia eius, quae fuit in praeputio, fidei patris nostri Abrahae. ¹³Non enim per legem promissio Abrahae aut semini eius, ut heres esset mundi, sed per iustitiam fidei; ¹⁴si enim qui ex lege heredes sunt, exinanita est fides, et abolita est promissio. ¹⁵Lex enim iram operatur; ubi autem non est lex, nec praevaricatio. ¹⁶Ideo ex fide, ut secundum gratiam, ut firma sit promissio omni semini, non ei, qui ex lege est solum sed et ei, qui ex fide est Abrahae—qui est pater omnium nostrum, ¹⁷sicut scriptum est: «*Patrem multarum gentium posui te*»—, ante Deum, cui credidit, qui vivificat mortuos et vocat ea, quae non sunt, quasi sint; ¹⁸qui contra spem in spe credidit, ut fieret *pater multarum gentium*, secundum quod dictum est: «*Sic erit semen tuum*». ¹⁹Et non infirmatus fide consideravit corpus suum iam emortuum, cum fere centum annorum esset, et emortuam vulvam Sarae; ²⁰in repromissione

eousness of God makes man righteous through faith, not through nature or through the Law.

Paul begins by citing Scripture to back up his teaching on justification: Abraham was not justified by works of the Law but by faith (vv. 1–8), as Genesis 15:6 says and as David confirms in the psalms (vv. 6–8). When he says "it was reckoned to him [by God]" (v. 3), God is being compared to a master who keeps accounts of his servants' debts and credits. In the case of Abraham, God noted in the credit column not his works but his faith, and that is why his faith was reckoned to him as righteousness (holiness, justice), as wages due to him. The gratuitous character of justification is being emphasized here. The first step towards justification is the act of faith. It is not, therefore, good works that produce justification: it is justification that makes works good and deserving of eternal life: "The source of justification is faith in God, who justifies. This faith, when it is justified, is like a root on which rain falls in the soil of the soul. When the root begins to grow in accordance with the law, it sends out branches which bear the fruit of good works. The root of justice is not good works; rather, good works spring from the root

of justice" (Origen, *Commentarii in Romanos*, 4, 1).

The Apostle stresses (vv. 9–12) that Abraham's righteousness was not a consequence of circumcision, for he received that righteousness (see Gen 15:6) prior to being circumcised (Gen 17:1–24). He also points out that what Abraham believed in was God's promise to him that he would be the father of many nations and that all the nations of the earth would be blessed in his offspring (see Gen 12:1–3; 15:5–6). Thus, the promise made to Abraham was not linked to the Law, because it was made before the Law was given to Moses, and because it was addressed to all Abraham's descendants, not only to the Jews.

Paul also points out that Abraham's faith in a promise that seemed impossible in human terms sets an example for Christian faith (vv. 18–25; cf. *Catechism of the Catholic Church*, 144). The promise made to him is fulfilled in us when we believe in Christ who died and rose again for all men (vv. 23–25); in this belief our faith and that of the patriarch are made one.

Verse 25, about the significance of Jesus' death and resurrection, is very apposite; it shows us that faith in Christ is fully sufficient for attain-

Heb 11:8–12
Lk 1:37
Mk 9:23

Jer 32:17

Rom 4:3
Gen 15:6

1 Cor 10:6

Rom 1–4

Is 53:4–6
1 Cor 15:17
1 Pet 1:21

because he was about a hundred years old, or when he considered the barrenness of Sarah's womb. ²⁰No distrust made him waver concerning the promise of God, but he grew strong in his faith as he gave glory to God, ²¹fully convinced that God was able to do what he had promised. ²²That is why his faith was "reckoned to him as righteousness." ²³But the words, "it was reckoned to him," were written not for his sake alone, ²⁴but for ours also. It will be reckoned to us who believe in him that raised from the dead Jesus our Lord, ²⁵who was put to death for our trespasses and raised for our justification.

3. SALVATION AND THE CHRISTIAN LIFE*

Reconciliation through Christ's sacrifice, the basis of our hope

Is 53:5; 6:12
Jn 14:27
Rom 3:22–24, 28
Eph 2:18; 3:12

2 Cor 12:9–10
Jas 1:2–4
1 Cor 13:13
1 Pet 1:5–7;
4:13–14
Rev 1:9
Rom 8:4–16
Gal 4:4–6

5 ¹Therefore, since we are justified by faith, weᶠ have peace with God through our Lord Jesus Christ. ²Through him we have obtained accessᵍ to this grace in which we stand, and weʰ rejoice in our hope of sharing the glory of God. ³More than that, weʰ rejoice in our sufferings, knowing that suffering produces endurance, ⁴and endurance produces character, and character produces hope, ⁵and hope does not disappoint us, because God's love has been poured into our hearts through the Holy Spirit who has been given to us.

autem Dei non haesitavit diffidentia, sed confortatus est fide, dans gloriam Deo, ²¹et plenissime sciens quia, quod promisit, potens est et facere. ²²Ideo et *reputatum est illi ad iustitiam*. ²³Non est autem scriptum tantum propter ipsum: *reputatum est illi*, ²⁴sed et propter nos, quibus reputabitur, credentibus in eum, qui suscitavit Iesum Dominum nostrum a mortuis, ²⁵qui traditus est propter delicta nostra et suscitatus est propter iustificationem nostram. [5] ¹Iustificati igitur ex fide, pacem habemus ad Deum per Dominum nostrum Iesum Christum, ²per quem et accessum habemus fide in gratiam istam, in qua stamus et gloriamur in spe gloriae Dei. ³Non solum autem, sed et gloriamur in tribulationibus, scientes quod tribulatio patientiam operatur, ⁴patientia autem probationem, probatio vero spem; ⁵spes autem non confundit, quia caritas Dei diffusa est in

ing justification. Jesus Christ has won everything for us through his death and resurrection; by his death he atoned for our sins; and his resurrection proves that God accepted that atonement and put everything to rights, that is, he has restored the order destroyed by sin.

*5:1—8:39 The line of argument in chapters 1–4 stressed that faith is the route by which one attains justification. Now Paul describes the effects of justification. He outlines what the basis of believers' hope is, and what hope entails. By his blood-sacrifice Christ reconciles us with the Father, and his resurrection is the ground of our hope (5:1–11); he delivers us from sin and death, giving us back the eternal life and the life of grace which the first man's sin stole from us (5:12–21); this life is restored to us through Baptism (6:1–11). Christ also makes it possible for us to be freed from our personal sins (6:12–23) and from the slavery of the Law, by giving us a new kind of freedom, a freedom of spirit, not a freedom bound to the letter of the Law (7:1–6)

or conditioned by our own tendency to sin. Nevertheless, there may remain in the hearts of those who have embraced faith some trace of nervousness about the future. Because of this, a Christian needs to be constant and valiant in the struggle against temptation (7:14–25). Still, the most important aspect of justification is the new life that the Spirit bestows (8:1–13). Through the action of the Spirit, Christians have become children of God (8:14–30) and filled with confidence and hope, even in the midst of contradictions (8:31–39).

5:1–11. The new life that justification brings works through faith and hope (vv. 1–2) which are supported by the love of God (v. 5). Faith, hope and charity—"the divine interlacing of the three theological virtues which form the backing upon which the true life of every Christian man or woman has to be woven" (St Josemaría Escrivá, *Friends of God*, 205), continue to act on us, and allow our life of grace to grow. The fruit of this growth is a peace (v. 1) which is a kind of

f Other ancient authorities read *let us*   g Other ancient authorities add *by faith*   h Or *let us*

⁶While we were still weak, at the right time Christ died for the ungodly. ⁷Why, one will hardly die for a righteous man—though perhaps for a good man one will dare even to die. ⁸But God shows his love for us in that while we were yet sinners Christ died for us. ⁹Since, therefore, we are now justified by his blood, much more shall we be saved by him from the wrath of God. ¹⁰For if while we were enemies we were reconciled to God by the death of his Son, much more, now that we are reconciled, shall we be saved by his life. ¹¹Not only so, but we also rejoice in God through our Lord Jesus Christ, through whom we have now received our reconciliation.

Rom 3:26
1 Pet 3:18

Rom 8:32
Jn 3:16
1 Jn 4:9–10, 19
1 Thess 1:10

Col 1:21–22
Jn 15:13

2 Cor 5:18

Adam's original sin

¹²Therefore as sin came into the world through one man and death through sin, and so death spread to all men because all men sinned—*¹³sin indeed was in the world before the law was given, but sin is not counted where there is no law. ¹⁴Yet death reigned from Adam to Moses, even over those whose sins were not like the transgression of Adam, who was a type of the one who was to come.

¹⁵But the free gift is not like the trespass. For if many died through one man's trespass, much more have the grace of God and the free gift in the grace of that one

Wis 2:24
1 Cor 15:21–22, 45
Rom 3:23; 6:23
Gen 3:17–19

Rom 3:23;
4:15; 7:7–10

1 Tim 2:5

cordibus nostris per Spiritum Sanctum, qui datus est nobis. ⁶Adhuc enim Christus, cum adhuc infirmi essemus, secundum tempus pro impiis mortuus est. ⁷Vix enim pro iusto quis moritur; nam pro bono forsitan quis et audeat mori. ⁸Commendat autem suam caritatem Deus in nos, quoniam, cum adhuc peccatores essemus, Christus pro nobis mortuus est. ⁹Multo igitur magis iustificati nunc in sanguine ipsius, salvi erimus ab ira per ipsum! ¹⁰Si enim cum inimici essemus reconciliati sumus Deo per mortem Filii eius, multo magis reconciliati salvi erimus in vita ipsius; ¹¹non solum autem, sed et gloriamur in Deo per Dominum nostrum Iesum Christum, per quem nunc reconciliationem accepimus. ¹²Propterea, sicut per unum hominem peccatum in hunc mundum intravit et per peccatum mors, et ita in omnes homines mors pertransiit, eo quod omnes peccaverunt. ¹³Usque ad legem enim peccatum erat in mundo; peccatum autem non imputatur, cum lex non est, ¹⁴sed regnavit mors ab Adam usque ad Moysen etiam in eos, qui non peccaverunt in similitudine praevaricationis Adae, qui est figura futuri. ¹⁵Sed non sicut delictum, ita et donum; si enim unius

anticipation (in some way unalterable, but still imperfect) of eternal life. This peace is not the apathy of someone who wants to have no problems; it is a resoluteness, full of hope, that produces the "character" (v. 4) that enables a person to rise above suffering and be faithful and loyal. "A person who hopes for something and strives eagerly to attain it is ready to endure all kinds of difficulty and distress. Thus, for example, a sick person, if he is eager to be healthy, is happy to take the bitter medicine which will cure him" (St Thomas Aquinas, *Super Romanos*, ad loc.).

The love spoken of in v. 5 is, at one and the same time, God's love for us (manifested by his sending the Holy Spirit) and the love that God places in our souls to enable us to love him. The Second Council of Orange, quoting St Augustine, explains this as follows: "To love God is entirely a gift of God. He, without being loved, loves us and enabled us to love him. We were loved when we were still displeasing to him, so that we might be given something whereby we might please him. So it is that the Spirit of the Father and the Son, whom we love with the

Father and the Son, pours charity into our hearts" (*De gratia*, can. 25; cf. St Augustine, *In Ioannis Evangelium*, 102, 5).

Verses 6–11 tell us that the scale of God's love for us can be seen in the "reconciliation" that came about through Christ's sacrifice on the cross, when he put to death in himself the old enmity that existed, and re-established peace (cf. Eph 2:15–16). If, when we were still sinners, God manifested this love, then how much more, now that we are reconciled, should we not be confident that God will save us? This reconciliation in Christ is spelt out quite clearly: it is not that God was hostile towards mankind; rather, we showed hostility towards God by our sins; it was not God who needed a change of heart, but man; however, God has taken the initiative in Christ's death, so that man can return to God's friendship.

5:12–21 The Apostle explains what has been accomplished by Christ for Adam's descendants. He contrasts grace and life with sin and death. Whereas Adam's transgression caused all to be

man Jesus Christ abounded for many.* [16]And the free gift is not like the effect of that one man's sin. For the judgment following one trespass brought condemnation, but the free gift following many trespasses brings justification. [17]If, because of one man's trespass, death reigned through that one man, much more will those who receive the abundance of grace and the free gift of righteousness reign in life through the one man Jesus Christ.

1 Cor 15:22

Is 53:11

Rom 3:23; 4:15;
5:13; 7:7–10
Gal 3:19
Rom 11:32

[18]Then as one man's trespass led to condemnation for all men, so one man's act of righteousness leads to acquittal and life for all men. [19]For as by one man's disobedience many were made sinners, so by one man's obedience many will be made righteous. [20]Law came in, to increase the trespass; but where sin increased, grace abounded all the more, [21]so that, as sin reigned in death, grace also might reign through righteousness to eternal life through Jesus Christ our Lord.

Baptism

Rom 3:5–8
Col 2:12–13
Tit 3:5–7
1 Pet 4:1-2

1 Pet 3:21–22

6 [1]What shall we say then? Are we to continue in sin that grace may abound? [2]By no means! How can we who died to sin still live in it? [3]Do you not know that all

delicto multi mortui sunt, multo magis gratia Dei et donum in gratia unius hominis Iesu Christi in multos abundavit. [16]Et non sicut per unum, qui peccavit, ita et donum; nam iudicium ex uno in condemnationem, gratia autem ex multis delictis in iustificationem. [17]Si enim unius delicto mors regnavit per unum, multo magis, qui abundantiam gratiae et donationis iustitiae accipiunt, in vita regnabunt per unum Iesum Christum. [18]Igitur sicut per unius delictum in omnes homines in condemnationem, sic et per unius iustitiam in omnes homines in iustificationem vitae; [19]sicut enim per inoboedientiam unius hominis peccatores constituti sunt multi, ita et per unius oboeditionem iusti constituentur multi. [20]Lex autem subintravit, ut abundaret delictum; ubi autem abundavit peccatum, superabundavit gratia, [21]ut sicut regnavit peccatum in morte, ita et gratia regnet per iustitiam in vitam aeternam per Iesum Christum Dominum nostrum.   [6] [1]Quid ergo dicemus? Permanebimus in peccato, ut gratia abundet? [2]Absit! Qui enim mortui sumus peccato, quomodo adhuc vivemus in illo? [3]An ignoratis quia, quicumque baptizati sumus in Christum Iesum, in mortem

condemned, Christ's obedience and righteousness leads everyone to justification and eternal life.

Four important points emerge from this passage: (1) Adam's sin and its consequences, which include death, are things that affect all mankind (vv. 12–14); (2) the contrast between the effects of original sin and those of the Redemption brought about by Christ (vv. 15–19); (3) the role of the Mosaic Law in relation to sin (vv. 13, 20), which anticipates a theme that will be explored further in chapter 7; (4) the final victory of the Kingdom of grace (vv. 20–21); grace, personified as sin was, is a divine power that leads men to salvation.

This passage is fundamental to the Christian theology of original sin. St Paul shows us that the light of the death and resurrection of Christ enables us to see that we are all implicated in Adam's sin. "We […] hold, with the Council of Trent, that original sin is transmitted with human nature, 'by propagation, not by imitation' and that it is … 'proper to each'" (Paul VI, *Creed of the People of God*, quoted in *Catechism of the Catholic Church*, 419). Just as sin entered the world through the action of a person represent-

ing all mankind, so too righteousness reaches us all through one man, the "new Adam", Jesus Christ, "the first-born of all creation" and "the head of the body, the church" (Col 1:15, 18). By his obedience to the Father's will, Christ countered the disobedience of Adam, restoring to us the happiness and eternal life we lost—and even more than that: for "where sin increased, grace abounded all the more" (v. 20).

Original sin is not a theory; it is a truth of faith. In his *Creed of the People of God*, Paul VI stated: "We believe that in Adam all have sinned. From this it follows that, on account of the original offence, human nature, which is common to all men, is reduced to that condition in which it must suffer the consequences of that fall […]. Consequently, fallen human nature is deprived of the economy of grace which it formerly enjoyed. It is wounded in its natural powers and subjected to the dominion of death which is transmitted to all men. It is in this sense that every man is born in sin."

6:1–11 The grace of Christ comes to us through Baptism and frees us from the slavery of sin. The sacrament reproduces in us not only the passion,

of us who have been baptized into Christ Jesus were baptized into his death? ⁴We were buried* therefore with him by baptism into death, so that as Christ was raised from the dead by the glory of the Father, we too might walk in newness of life.

⁵For if we have been united with him in a death like his, we shall certainly be united with him in a resurrection like his. ⁶We know that our old self was crucified with him so that the sinful body might be destroyed, and we might no longer be enslaved to sin. ⁷For he who has died is freed from sin. ⁸But if we have died with Christ, we believe that we shall also live with him. ⁹For we know that Christ being raised from the dead will never die again; death no longer has dominion over him. ¹⁰The death he died he died to sin, once for all, but the life he lives he lives to God. ¹¹So you also must consider yourselves dead to sin and alive to God in Christ Jesus.

Ex 24:6–8
Gal 3:27

2 Tim 2:11
Eph 2;4–7
Col 2:12
1 Pet 4:1
Rom 8:11
Phil 3:10–11

Gal 5:24
Col 3:3–4, 9–10
Rom 6:14
1 Pet 4:1
Acts 13:34
2 Tim 1:10
1 Cor 15:26
Heb 2:14
Rev 1:18

Gal 2:19
Heb 7:27; 9:28
1 Pet 2:24; 3:18
2 Cor 5:15

Liberation from sin

¹²Let not sin therefore reign in your mortal bodies, to make you obey their passions. ¹³Do not yield your members to sin as instruments of wickedness, but yield your-

1 Cor 6:15
Sir 18:30

Rom 7:14–24; 12:1
Gen 4:7
Eph 2:5; 5:14

ipsius baptizati sumus? ⁴Consepulti ergo sumus cum illo per baptismum in mortem, ut quemadmodum suscitatus est Christus a mortuis per gloriam Patris, ita et nos in novitate vitae ambulemus. ⁵Si enim complantati facti sumus similitudini mortis eius, sed et resurrectionis erimus; ⁶hoc scientes quia vetus homo noster simul crucifixus est, ut destruatur corpus peccati, ut ultra non serviamus peccato. ⁷Qui enim mortuus est, iustificatus est a peccato. ⁸Si autem mortui sumus cum Christo, credimus quia simul etiam vivemus cum eo; ⁹scientes quod Christus suscitatus ex mortuis iam non moritur, mors illi ultra non dominatur. ¹⁰Quod enim mortuus est, peccato mortuus est semel; quod autem vivit, vivit Deo. ¹¹Ita et vos existimate vos mortuos quidem esse peccato, viventes autem Deo in Christo Iesu. ¹²Non ergo regnet peccatum in vestro mortali corpore, ut oboe-

death and burial of Christ, symbolized by immersion in water (vv. 3–4, 6), but also gives us a new life, the life of grace, which is poured into the soul and allows us to share in the resurrection of Christ (vv. 4–5).

The Fathers of the Church used this Pauline teaching to develop their own thinking on the meaning of Christian Baptism and its spiritual effects. "The Lord," St Ambrose tells the newly baptized, "who wanted his benefactions to endure, the serpent's plans to be turned to naught, and the harm done to be put right, delivered a sentence on mankind: 'You are dust, and to dust you shall return' (Gen 3:19), and made man subject to death […]. The remedy was given him: man would die and rise again […]. You ask me how? […] Pay attention. So that in this world too the devil's snare would be broken, a rite was instituted whereby man would die, being alive, and rise again, being alive" (*De Sacramentis*, 2, 6). And St John Chrysostom explains: "Baptism is for us what the Cross and burial were for Christ; but with this difference: the Saviour died physically, he was physically buried, whereas we ought to die spiritually. That is why the Apostle does not say we are 'united with him in his death', but 'in a death *like his*'" (*In Romanos*, 10). Moreover, just as a grafted branch and its host plant share the

same life, when Christians are inserted into Christ, becoming members of him through Baptism, they truly share his divine life.

In its teaching on Baptism, the *Catechism of the Catholic Church*, 1214, says this: "This sacrament is called *Baptism*, after the central rite by which it is carried out: to baptize (Greek *baptizein*) means to 'plunge' or 'immerse'; the 'plunge' into the water symbolizes the catechumen's burial into Christ's death, from which he rises up by resurrection with him, as 'a new creature' (2 Cor 5:17; Gal 6:15)".

The ordinary form of Baptism nowadays (pouring water over the head), as distinct from Baptism by immersion, was already used in apostolic times and became the norm for obvious practical reasons.

In vv. 9–11, St Paul spells out his teaching further: with the death of Christ on the cross and with his resurrection, the bonds of death were broken, both for Christ and for all his followers. He has won the victory, winning a new life for his human nature and for Christians. These events in Christ's life are reproduced anew when a person is baptized.

6:12–23 Sin retains its power even after Christ has won grace for us. Therefore, using the

selves to God as men who have been brought from death to life, and your members to God as instruments of righteousness. [14]For sin will have no dominion over you, since you are not under law but under grace.

[15]What then? Are we to sin because we are not under law but under grace? By no means!* [16]Do you not know that if you yield yourselves to any one as obedient slaves, you are slaves of the one whom you obey, either of sin, which leads to death, or of obedience, which leads to righteousness? [17]But thanks be to God, that you who were once slaves of sin have become obedient from the heart to the standard of teaching to which you were committed, [18]and, having been set free from sin, have become slaves of righteousness. [19]I am speaking in human terms, because of your natural limitations. For just as you once yielded your members to impurity and to greater and greater iniquity, so now yield your members to righteousness for sanctification.

[20]When you were slaves of sin, you were free in regard to righteousness. [21]But then what return did you get from the things of which you are now ashamed? The end of those things is death. [22]But now that you have been set free from sin and have become slaves of God, the return you get is sanctification and its end, eternal life. [23]For the wages of sin is death, but the free gift of God is eternal life in Christ Jesus our Lord.

The Christian is not bound by the Law

7 [1]Do you not know, brethren—for I am speaking to those who know the law—that the law is binding on a person only during his life? [2]Thus a married woman is bound by law to her husband as long as he lives; but if her husband dies she is dis-

Margin references:
1 Jn 3:6
Rom 3:8; 6:1
Rom 1:5
Jn 8:34
2 Pet 2:19
Rom 16:17
Jn 8:34–36
Gal 5:13
1 Pet 1:14–16
Rom 7:5; 8:6, 13
Deut 30:15–20
1 Pet 1:9
Jn 15:8, 16
Rom 5:12, 21
Gal 6:7–9
Jas 1:15
Acts 15:10–11
Gal 2:19
1 Cor 7:39

diatis concupiscentiis eius, ¹³neque exhibeatis membra vestra arma iniustitiae peccato, sed exhibete vos Deo tamquam ex mortuis viventes et membra vestra arma iustitiae Deo. ¹⁴Peccatum enim vobis non dominabitur; non enim sub lege estis sed sub gratia. ¹⁵Quid ergo? Peccabimus, quoniam non sumus sub lege sed sub gratia? Absit! ¹⁶Nescitis quoniam, cui exhibetis vos servos ad oboedientiam, servi estis eius, cui oboeditis, sive peccati ad mortem, sive oboeditionis ad iustitiam? ¹⁷Gratias autem Deo quod fuistis servi peccati, oboedistis autem ex corde in eam formam doctrinae, in quam traditi estis, ¹⁸liberati autem a peccato servi facti estis iustitiae. ¹⁹Humanum dico propter infirmitatem carnis vestrae. Sicut enim exhibuistis membra vestra servientia immunditiae et iniquitati ad iniquitatem, ita nunc exhibete membra vestra servientia iustitiae ad sanctificationem. ²⁰Cum enim servi essetis peccati, liberi eratis iustitiae. ²¹Quem ergo fructum habebatis tunc, in quibus nunc erubescitis? Nam finis illorum mors! ²²Nunc vero liberati a peccato, servi autem facti Deo, habetis fructum vestrum in sanctificationem, finem vero vitam aeternam! ²³Stipendia enim peccati mors, donum autem Dei vita aeterna in Christo Iesu Domino nostro.   [7] ¹An ignoras, fratres—scientibus enim legem loquor—, quia lex in homine dominatur, quanto tempore vivit? ²Nam quae sub viro est mulier, viventi viro alligata est lege; si autem mortuus

imagery of slavery and freedom, Paul exhorts Christians to live as befits baptized people and not to let sin reassert itself. It could be that some feared that, by neglecting to preach the need to conform to the Mosaic Law, Paul might lead people to ignore the restraints of morality. It may be that the Apostle adds these warnings about the snares of passion in order to prevent people from misinterpreting his teaching in that way. Christians must live in a way that is consistent with their justification (v. 22). "Our past sins have been wiped out by the action of grace. Now, so as to stay dead to sin after Baptism, personal effort is called for, even though the grace of God continues to help us mightily" (St John Chrysostom, *In Romanos*, 11, 1).

The dialectical line of argument in vv. 15–23 (slaves of sin / set free from sin / slaves of right-

eousness) has a pedagogical ring to it: if once we bore with being slaves of sin unto death, then surely we should be ready now to be slaves of righteousness unto eternal life. "We were all slaves to sin, but when we heard the good news and decided to heed it, not only in word, but completely, wholeheartedly, we were freed from slavery to sin, and became servants of justice" (Origen, *Commentarii in Romanos*, 6, 3).

7:1–6 Here St Paul returns to the theme of the Mosaic Law. Although that Law cannot in any way be equated with sin, it might nevertheless "awaken" our sinful passions (cf. the note on 7:7–13). The Apostle teaches that because a Christian, through Baptism, shares in Christ's death, he or she is "dead" to the Law (depicted in vv. 2–3 as a husband), that is, is free from the

charged from the law concerning the husband. ³Accordingly, she will be called an adulteress if she lives with another man while her husband is alive. But if her husband dies she is free from that law, and if she marries another man she is not an adulteress.

⁴Likewise, my brethren, you have died to the law through the body of Christ, so that you may belong to another, to him who has been raised from the dead in order that we may bear fruit for God. ⁵While we were living in the flesh, our sinful passions, aroused by the law, were at work in our members to bear fruit for death. ⁶But now we are discharged from the law, dead to that which held us captive, so that we serve not under the old written code but in the new life of the Spirit.

Rom 6:5–7; 8:11
Col 2:13–14
Gal 2:19
Jn 15:8

Rom 6:22; 7:7, 10;
8:6, 13
Rom 6:4
2 Cor 3:6
Mt 9:16–17
Gal 2:19

The Law and concupiscence

⁷What then shall we say? That the law is sin? By no means! Yet, if it had not been for the law, I should not have known sin. I should not have known what it is to covet if the law had not said, "You shall not covet." ⁸But sin, finding opportunity in the commandment, wrought in me all kinds of covetousness. Apart from the law sin lies dead. ⁹I was once alive apart from the law, but when the commandment came, sin revived and I died; ¹⁰the very commandment which promised life proved to be death to me. ¹¹For sin, finding opportunity in the commandment, deceived me and by it killed me. ¹²So the law is holy, and the commandment is holy and just and good.

¹³Did that which is good, then, bring death to me?* By no means! It was sin, working death in me through what is good, in order that sin might be shown to be sin, and through the commandment might become sinful beyond measure.

Rom 3:20; 4:15;
5:13, 20

Ex 20:17
Deut 5:21
Jas 1:14–15
1 Cor 15:56

Gen 2:17; 3:19, 22

Gal 3:12
Lev 18:5
Heb 3:13–19

2 Cor 11:3
Gen 3:13
Deut 4:8
1 Tim 1:8

Rom 5:20

fuerit vir, soluta est a lege viri. ³Igitur vivente viro vocabitur adultera, si fuerit alterius viri; si autem mortuus fuerit vir, libera est a lege, ut non sit adultera, si fuerit alterius viri. ⁴Itaque, fratres mei, et vos mortificati estis legi per corpus Christi, ut sitis alterius, eius qui ex mortuis suscitatus est, ut fructificaremus Deo. ⁵Cum enim essemus in carne, passiones peccatorum, quae per legem sunt, operabantur in membris nostris, ut fructificarent morti; ⁶nunc autem soluti sumus a lege, mortui ei, in qua detinebamur, ita ut serviamus in novitate Spiritus et non in vetustate litterae. ⁷Quid ergo dicemus? Lex peccatum est? Absit! Sed peccatum non cognovi nisi per legem, nam concupiscentiam nescirem nisi lex diceret: «Non concupisces». ⁸Occasione autem accepta, peccatum per mandatum operatum est in me omnem concupiscentiam; sine lege enim peccatum mortuum erat. ⁹Ego autem vivebam sine lege aliquando; sed, cum venisset mandatum, peccatum revixit, ¹⁰ego autem mortuus sum, et inventum est mihi mandatum, quod erat ad vitam, hoc esse ad mortem; ¹¹nam peccatum, occasione accepta, per mandatum seduxit me et per illud occidit. ¹²Itaque lex quidem sancta, et mandatum sanctum et iustum et bonum. ¹³Quod ergo bonum est, mihi factum est mors? Absit! Sed peccatum, ut

Law—free, however, to be good, to "bear fruit for God", the fruit of a good life, because he or she is one with Christ (v. 4).

The grace of the cross frees us from the tyranny of sin, enabling us to serve God of our own free will, not out of fear of punishment but out of filial love. That is the freedom of spirit that Christians should practise—doing what God wants, because it is what we ourselves want to do. "Just think: the Almighty, who through his providence rules the whole universe, does not want the forced service of slaves; he prefers to have children who are free. Although we are born *proni ad peccatum*, inclined to sin, due to the fall of our first parents, he has placed in the soul of each and every one of us a spark of his infinite intelligence, an attraction towards the good, a yearning for everlasting peace. And he

brings us to understand that we will attain truth, happiness and freedom if we strive to nurture within us the seed of eternal life" (St Josemaría Escrivá, *Friends of God*, 33).

The term "flesh" (v. 5) means both human weakness, and thus the source of concupiscence which moves a person to commit sin, and the human condition after original sin.

7:7–13 Here the Apostle sets out the connexions between "the law", sin and man himself, the nature of each of which he goes on to describes: "the law" is specifically the Law of Moses, but it also encompasses the precepts of the natural law. Legal rules make man aware of what sin is, of what is sinful; and sin (depicted here as a power, a person) makes use of these precepts to provoke temptation.

Interior struggle

Job 14:4
Ps 51:5
Jn 3:6
Rom 7:5

Phil 2:13
Gen 6:5; 8:21
Rom 3:10–18; 7:5
Gal 2:20

Eph 3:16

Gal 5:17

[14]We know that the law is spiritual; but I am carnal, sold under sin. [15]I do not understand my own actions. For I do not do what I want, but I do the very thing I hate. [16]Now if I do what I do not want, I agree that the law is good. [17]So then it is no longer I that do it, but sin which dwells within me. [18]For I know that nothing good dwells within me, that is, in my flesh. I can will what is right, but I cannot do it. [19]For I do not do the good I want, but the evil I do not want is what I do. [20]Now if I do what I do not want, it is no longer I that do it, but sin which dwells within me.

[21]So I find it to be a law that when I want to do right, evil lies close at hand. [22]For I delight in the law of God, in my inmost self, [23]but I see in my members another law

appareat peccatum, per bonum mihi operatum est mortem; ut fiat supra modum peccans peccatum per mandatum. [14]Scimus enim quod lex spiritalis est; ego autem carnalis sum, venumdatus sub peccato. [15]Quod enim operor, non intellego; non enim, quod volo, hoc ago, sed quod odi, illud facio. [16]Si autem, quod nolo, illud facio, consentio legi quoniam bona. [17]Nunc autem iam non ego operor illud, sed, quod habitat in me, peccatum. [18]Scio enim quia non habitat in me, hoc est in carne mea, bonum; nam velle adiacet mihi, operari autem bonum, non! [19]Non enim, quod volo bonum, facio, sed, quod nolo malum, hoc ago. [20]Si autem, quod nolo, illud facio, iam non ego operor illud, sed, quod habitat in me, peccatum. [21]Invenio igitur hanc legem volenti mihi facere bonum, quoniam mihi malum adiacet. [22]Condelector enim legi Dei secundum interiorem hominem;

At the same time, St Paul makes it clear that, although sin can draw on the Law to tempt man, the Law is not in itself bad; on the contrary, it is holy, just and good: "The Law is a pedagogy and a prophecy of things to come" (St Irenaeus, *Adversus haereses*, 4, 15, 1; as quoted in *Catechism of the Catholic Church*, 1964). The Law is good because it is a gift from God, it reveals the right order established by divine Wisdom, it prohibits evil of any kind, it helps man to see where his duty lies, and it has prepared the way for the coming of the Redeemer (see 3:19–20; 5:20; Gal 3:19, 24). However, the Law is insufficient, because it does not empower a person to defeat sin. The "I" that appears a number of times in 7:7–25 can be read as meaning Paul himself (before his conversion?), or Jews subject to the Law or, more likely, mankind in general. Certainly, the personalization of the situation makes this one of the most dramatic passages in the letter.

7:14–25 St Paul appeals to everyone's experience of another "law" distinct from the law of God, an inclination that runs counter to the law of the Spirit, the good that God causes us to desire with the help of his grace.

The phrase "the law of sin which dwells in my members" (v. 23) emphasizes how strongly our evil desires oppose "the law of the mind". The "law of sin" disorients our faculties and, although it is not itself sinful, it does incline us to commit sin: "The new life received in Chris-

tian initiation has not abolished the frailty and weakness of human nature, nor the inclination to sin that tradition calls *concupiscence*, which remains in the baptized such that with the help of the grace of Christ they may prove themselves in the struggle of Christian life. This is the struggle of *conversion* directed toward holiness and eternal life to which the Lord never ceases to call us" (*Catechism of the Catholic Church*, 1426).

Some commentators interpreted these verses as a description of Paul's inner struggle to observe the Mosaic Law prior to his conversion. Martin Luther adopted this interpretation. As he saw it, original sin totally corrupted human nature with the result that man lost his freedom and was powerless to perform morally good acts. According to Luther, man is always a sinner; sin continues to live in him; but thanks to justification, his sins are no longer imputed to him (although they are never erased), and he is considered to be just not on account of his own actions but through the grace of Jesus Christ. That is what he means by his famous assertion: "At once just and a sinner", which he bases on 7:15–20. The Church's teaching on this point is given in the Council of Trent's *Decree on Justification* (see also *Catechism of the Catholic Church*, 1987–1992). According to that decree, the sanctifying grace given by the sacraments makes us intrinsically just and pleasing to God, because it has wiped out sin and made us children of God. Grace renews man's being. It is true that because of our wounded nature we still

at war with the law of my mind and making me captive to the law of sin which
dwells in my members. ²⁴Wretched man that I am! Who will deliver me from this
body of death? ²⁵Thanks be to God through Jesus Christ our Lord! So then, I of
myself serve the law of God with my mind, but with my flesh I serve the law of sin.

Jas 1:14
1 Pet 2:11
Wis 1:4

1 Cor 15:57
Rom 5:21; 6:23

Life in the Spirit

8 ¹There is therefore now no condemnation for those who are in Christ Jesus. ²For
the law of the Spirit of life in Christ Jesus has set me free from the law of sin and
death. ³For God has done what the law, weakened by the flesh, could not do: sending his own Son in the likeness of sinful flesh and for sin,ⁱ he condemned sin in the
flesh, ⁴in order that the just requirement of the law might be fulfilled in us, who walk

Ezek 36:27
Wis 1:4
Rom 7:7; 3:27

Acts 13:38–39;
15:10–11
2 Cor 5:21
Jn 1:14
Phil 2:7
Rom 6:10
Gal 3:13
Mt 5:17

²³video autem aliam legem in membris meis repugnantem legi mentis meae et captivantem me in lege peccati, quae est in membris meis. ²⁴Infe-
lix ego homo! Quis me liberabit de corpore mortis huius? ²⁵Gratias autem Deo per Iesum Christum Dominum nostrum! Igitur ego ipse mente
servio legi Dei, carne autem legi peccati.   [8] ¹Nihil ergo nunc damnationis est his, qui sunt in Christo Iesu; ²lex enim Spiritus vitae in Christo
Iesu liberavit te a lege peccati et mortis. ³Nam, quod impossibile erat legi, in quo infirmabatur per carnem, Deus Filium suum mittens in similitudine carnis peccati et pro peccato, damnavit peccatum in carne, ⁴ut iustitia legis impleretur in nobis, qui non secundum carnem ambulamus, sed
secundum Spiritum. ⁵Qui enim secundum carnem sunt, quae carnis sunt, sapiunt; qui vero secundum Spiritum, quae sunt Spiritus. ⁶Nam sapien-

have an inclination to sin, but our freedom has
not been destroyed and it is left to our freedom
to choose to respond to grace.

8:1–13 St Paul has stated that Jesus Christ has
freed us from death and sin and given us new
life; but, how can any Christian lead that life if
he is still a man of flesh and the flesh is not subject to the law of God? The Apostle's response is
that we should not live according to the flesh
but, rather, according to the Spirit of God who
raised Jesus from the dead.

First, he points out that no one can free himself from sin—not even with the help of the Old
Law (vv. 1–4). However, what is impossible for
human beings is not impossible for God; in fact,
God did free us from sin by sending his own Son
to conquer sin by his death. Through the merits
of Christ and through sharing in his resurrection,
we too can conquer sin.

By assuming human nature, Jesus Christ
chose to take on the likeness of sinful flesh (but
not sin itself), becoming subject to the trials of
this life. These deficiencies (hunger, fatigue, suffering and, above all, death) are the "likeness of
sinful flesh" (v. 3); by taking them to himself,
Christ redeemed them and turned them into a
path to holiness so that through them we are
enabled to become identified with him.

St Paul specifies two ways in which someone
can live in this world (vv. 5–8). One way is
"according to the Spirit"—seeking God above all

things and, with his grace, striving against the
inclinations of concupiscence. The other is life
"according to the flesh"—letting one's passions
have free rein. Life according to the Spirit has its
source in grace, and cannot be reduced to mere
passivity and the routine performance of some
regular practices. It means living in accordance
with God's will, so that a person's thoughts,
yearnings, desires and actions are in line with
what God demands of him; in everything Christians do, they should try to follow the inspirations of the Holy Spirit. "We need to submit to
the Spirit, to wholeheartedly commit ourselves
and strive to keep the flesh in its place. By so
doing, our flesh will become spiritual again. Otherwise, if we give in to the easy life, this will
lower our soul to the level of the flesh and make
it carnal again […]. Through the Spirit, the soul
belongs to Christ, possesses him […]. The flesh
is crucified in the Spirit, and the soul tastes eternal life" (St John Chrysostom, *In Romanos*, 13).

Christ himself lives in those who live
according to the Spirit (v. 10; cf. Gal 2:20; 1 Cor
15:20–23), and therefore they can be confident of
their future resurrection (vv. 9–13). Hence
Origen's comment: "Everyone should look within
himself to see if he has the Spirit of Christ […].
He who has [wisdom, justice, peace, love,
holiness] can be sure that he possesses the Spirit
of Christ, and can live in hope that his mortal
body will be brought to life by the Spirit of Christ
within him" (*Commentarii in Romanos*, 6, 13).

i Or *and as a sin offering*

Heb 2:14–18; 4:15
Rom 3:31; 9:30–31;
10:4
Gal 5:16–23
Rom 6:21
Gal 6:8

Jn 3:8; Jas 4:4
1 Jn 2:15–16
Rom 7:5–6

Jn 3:5–6
1 Cor 3:16; 12:3

1 Cor 3:23
Gal 2:20
Phil 1:21
Rom 5:12
1 Cor 6:14
Ezek 37:10
1 Pet 4:6
Rom 1:4; 6:4, 8–11

Rom 6:6, 18

Gal 6:8
Gen 6:3
Eph 4:22–24

Gal 4:4–7; 5:18

Jn 1:12; 15:15
1 Jn 3:1; 4:18
Rom 5:5

not according to the flesh but according to the Spirit. [5]For those who live according to the flesh set their minds on the things of the flesh, but those who live according to the Spirit set their minds on the things of the Spirit. [6]To set the mind on the flesh is death, but to set the mind on the Spirit is life and peace. [7]For the mind that is set on the flesh is hostile to God; it does not submit to God's law, indeed it cannot; [8]and those who are in the flesh cannot please God.

[9]But you are not in the flesh, you are in the Spirit, if in fact the Spirit of God dwells in you. Any one who does not have the Spirit of Christ does not belong to him. [10]But if Christ is in you, although your bodies are dead because of sin, your spirits are alive because of righteousness. [11]If the Spirit of him who raised Jesus from the dead dwells in you, he who raised Christ Jesus from the dead will give life to your mortal bodies also through his Spirit who dwells in you.

[12]So then, brethren, we are debtors, not to the flesh, to live according to the flesh—[13]for if you live according to the flesh you will die, but if by the Spirit you put to death the deeds of the body you will live.

Christians are children of God

[14]For all who are led by the Spirit of God are sons of God. [15]For you did not receive the spirit of slavery to fall back into fear, but you have received the spirit of sonship. When we cry, "Abba! Father!" [16]it is the Spirit himself bearing witness with our

tia carnis mors, sapientia autem Spiritus vita et pax; [7]quoniam sapientia carnis inimicitia est in Deum, legi enim Dei non subicitur, nec enim potest. [8]Qui autem in carne sunt, Deo placere non possunt. [9]Vos autem in carne non estis, sed in Spiritu, si tamen Spiritus Dei habitat in vobis. Si quis autem Spiritum Christi non habet, hic non est eius. [10]Si autem Christus in vobis est, corpus quidem mortuum est propter peccatum, spiritus vero vita propter iustitiam. [11]Quod si Spiritus eius, qui suscitavit Iesum a mortuis, habitat in vobis, qui suscitavit Christum a mortuis, vivificabit et mortalia corpora vestra per inhabitantem Spiritum suum in vobis. [12]Ergo, fratres, debitores sumus, non carni, ut secundum carnem vivamus. [13]Si enim secundum carnem vixeritis, moriemini; si autem Spiritu opera corporis mortificatis, vivetis. [14]Quicumque enim Spiritu Dei aguntur, hi filii Dei sunt. [15]Non enim accepistis spiritum servitutis iterum in timorem, sed accepistis Spiritum adoptionis filiorum, in quo clamamus: «Abba, Pater!».

"Your bodies are dead because of sin" (v. 10) means that, because of sin, the human body is destined to die; it is as though it were already dead.

8:14–30 The people of Israel knew that they were God's first-born, and his children insofar as they were members of his people (cf. Ex 4:22–23; Is 1:2); however, St Paul now explains that man's relationship with God has been re-established in a new and unimaginable way, through the spirit of Jesus Christ, the only and true Son of God. By the power of the Holy Spirit, Christians are able to share in the life of Christ, who is God's Son by nature. This sharing is "[adoptive] sonship" (v. 15), enabling each to cry out to God, "Abba! Father!", just as Jesus did. Becoming, by adoption, true children of God, Christians have a right (so to speak) to share also in Christ's inheritance—eternal life in the glory of heaven (vv. 14–18).

In line with the teaching of the prophets,

who announced "new heavens and a new earth" (see Is 65:17; 66:22), Paul extends to the material cosmos the deliverance brought about by Christ (vv. 19–22). The cosmos was "subjected to futility" (v. 20); that is, vitiated by the sin of Adam (see Gen 3:17–19; 5:29). Now, developing the contrast he drew between Christ and Adam (see 5:12–21), Paul concludes that the liberation of the cosmos follows from the liberation of man. Although we cannot yet see evidence of this, we expect that it will happen, through the work of the Spirit who helps us in our weakness (vv. 23–27). Until it does happen, there is a tension between what we already have and are, and what we yearn to be. But we know that in no sense does God leave the future to chance (vv. 28–30). Election, predestination, vocation, justification and resurrection form part of his plan of salvation: "in everything God works for good with those who love him" (v. 28). Awareness of our divine filiation shows us that all the events of our life are guided by the

spirit that we are children of God, [17]and if children, then heirs, heirs of God and fellow heirs with Christ, provided we suffer with him in order that we may also be glorified with him.

[18]I consider that the sufferings of this present time are not worth comparing with the glory that is to be revealed to us. [19]For the creation waits with eager longing for the revealing of the sons of God;* [20]for the creation was subjected to futility, not of its own will but by the will of him who subjected it in hope; [21]because the creation itself will be set free from its bondage to decay and obtain the glorious liberty of the children of God. [22]We know that the whole creation has been groaning in travail together until now; [23]and not only the creation, but we ourselves, who have the first fruits of the Spirit, groan inwardly as we wait for adoption as sons, the redemption of our bodies. [24]For in this hope we were saved. Now hope that is seen is not hope. For who hopes for what he sees? [25]But if we hope for what we do not see, we wait for it with patience.

[26]Likewise the Spirit helps us in our weakness; for we do not know how to pray as we ought, but the Spirit himself intercedes for us with sighs too deep for words. [27]And he who searches the hearts of men knows what is the mind of the Spirit, because[j] the Spirit intercedes for the saints according to the will of God.

[28]We know that in everything God works for good[k] with those who love him,[l] who are called according to his purpose. [29]For those whom he foreknew he also predestined to be conformed to the image of his Son, in order that he might be the first-born

Margin references:
Gal 3:26–29, 16
Lk 22:28–30; 24:26
Phil 3:10–11
Rev 21:7
1 Pet 4:13
Rom 5:2–5
2 Cor 4:17;
Col 3:3–4;
1 Jn 3:2
Wis 3:5
Rom 6:20
Gen 3:17–19
Hos 4:3
2 Pet 3:12–13
Rev 21:1

2 Cor 5:2–7
Gal 5:5
Phil 3:20–21
Rom 3:24; 7:24

Heb 11:1
2 Cor 5:7

Rom 5:5; 8:15
1 Cor 2:10–13
Jn 3:8
Gal 4:6
Ps 139:1
Jer 11:20
Jas 4:3, 5

Eph 1:4–14
Gen 50:20
Jas 1:12

Acts 13:48
1 Cor 15:49
Phil 3:21
Col 1:18

---

[16]Ipse Spiritus testimonium reddit una cum spiritu nostro quod sumus filii Dei. [17]Si autem filii, et heredes: heredes quidem Dei, coheredes autem Christi, si tamen compatimur, ut et conglorificemur. [18]Existimo enim quod non sunt condignae passiones huius temporis ad futuram gloriam, quae revelanda est in nobis. [19]Nam exspectatio creaturae revelationem filiorum Dei exspectat; [20]vanitati enim creatura subiecta est, non volens sed propter eum, qui subiecit, in spem, [21]quia et ipsa creatura liberabitur a servitute corruptionis in libertatem gloriae filiorum Dei. [22]Scimus enim quod omnis creatura congemiscit et comparturit usque adhuc; [23]non solum autem, sed et nos ipsi primitias Spiritus habentes, et ipsi intra nos gemimus adoptionem filiorum exspectantes, redemptionem corporis nostri. [24]Spe enim salvi facti sumus; spes autem, quae videtur, non est spes; nam, quod videt, quis sperat? [25]Si autem, quod non videmus, speramus, per patientiam exspectamus. [26]Similiter autem et Spiritus adiuvat infirmitatem nostram; nam quid oremus, sicut oportet, nescimus, sed ipse Spiritus interpellat gemitibus inenarrabilibus; [27]qui autem scrutatur corda, scit quid desideret Spiritus, quia secundum Deum postulat pro sanctis. [28]Scimus autem quoniam diligentibus Deum omnia cooperantur in bonum, his, qui secundum propositum vocati sunt. [29]Nam, quos praescivit, et praedestinavit conformes fieri imaginis Filii eius, ut sit ipse primogenitus in multis fratribus; [30]quos autem praedestinavit, hos et vocavit; et quos vocavit, hos et iustificavit; quos autem iustificavit, illos et glorificavit. [31]Quid

---

loving Will of God, and that conviction fills us with hope and peace.

The inspired words of the Apostle helped St Josemaría Escrivá have a sense of divine filiation in his life and catechesis: "We've got to be convinced that God is always near us. We live as though he were far away, in the heavens high above, and we forget that he is also continually by our side. He is there like a loving Father. He loves each of us more than all the mothers in the world can love their children—helping us, inspiring us, blessing ... and forgiving. [...] We've got to be filled, to be imbued with the idea that our Father, and very much our Father, is God who is both near us and in heaven" (*The Way*, 267). "Divine filiation [...] fills all our spiritual life, it shows us how to speak to God, to know and love our Father in heaven. And it

makes our interior struggle overflow with hope, and gives us the trusting simplicity of little children. More than that: precisely because we are children of God, we can contemplate in love and wonder everything as coming from the hands of our Father, God the Creator. And so we become contemplatives in the middle of the world, loving the world" (idem, *Christ Is Passing By*, 65). "The whole world seems to be coming down on top of you. Whichever way you turn you find no way out. This time, it is impossible to overcome the difficulties. But, have you again forgotten that God is your Father?—all-powerful, infinitely wise, full of mercy. [...] That thing that is worrying you is good for you, even though those earthbound eyes of yours may not be able to see it now. *Omnia in bonum!*" (idem, *The Way of the Cross*, 9, 4).

j Or *that*   k Other ancient authorities read *in everything he works for good, or everything works for good*   l Greek *God*

among many brethren. [30]And those whom he predestined he also called; and those whom he called he also justified; and those whom he justified he also glorified.

Trust in God

Ps 118:6
1 Cor 13:1
Jn 3:16
Gen 22:16
Is 50:7-9
Rom 5:6-11
2 Cor 5:14-21
1 Jn 4:9-10
Zech 3:1f
Ps 109:1
Acts 2:23
Heb 1:3; 7:25; 12:2
1 Jn 2:1

2 Cor 4:11
2 Tim 3:12

Ps 44:22
1 Thess 3:4

Jn 16:33
Col 2:15
1 Pet 3:22
Eph 1:21

[31]What then shall we say to this? If God is for us, who is against us? [32]He who did not spare his own Son but gave him up for us all, will he not also give us all things with him? [33]Who shall bring any charge against God's elect? It is God who justifies; [34]who is to condemn? Is it Christ Jesus, who died, yes, who was raised from the dead, who is at the right hand of God, who indeed intercedes for us?[m] [35]Who shall separate us from the love of Christ? Shall tribulation, or distress, or persecution, or famine, or nakedness, or peril, or sword? [36]As it is written,

> "For thy sake we are being killed all the day long;
> we are regarded as sheep to be slaughtered."

[37]No, in all these things we are more than conquerors through him who loved us. [38]For I am sure that neither death, nor life, nor angels, nor principalities, nor things present, nor things to come, nor powers, [39]nor height, nor depth, nor anything else in all creation, will be able to separate us from the love of God in Christ Jesus our Lord.

4. GOD'S PLAN FOR THE CHOSEN PEOPLE*

The privileges of Israel and God's fidelity

2 Cor 11:29
2 Cor 12:7

9 [1]I am speaking the truth in Christ, I am not lying; my conscience bears me witness in the Holy Spirit, [2]that I have great sorrow and unceasing anguish in my heart.

ergo dicemus ad haec? Si Deus pro nobis, quis contra nos? [32]Qui Filio suo non pepercit, sed pro nobis omnibus tradidit illum, quomodo non etiam cum illo omnia nobis donabit? [33]Quis accusabit adversus electos Dei? Deus, qui iustificat? [34]Quis est qui condemnet? Christus Iesus, qui mortuus est, immo qui suscitatus est, qui et est ad dexteram Dei, qui etiam interpellat pro nobis? [35]Quis nos separabit a caritate Christi? Tribulatio an angustia an persecutio an fames an nuditas an periculum an gladius? [36]Sicut scriptum est: *«Propter te mortificamur tota die, / aestimati sumus ut oves occisionis».* [37]Sed in his omnibus supervincimus per eum, qui dilexit nos. [38]Certus sum enim quia neque mors neque vita neque angeli neque principatus neque instantia neque futura neque virtutes [39]neque altitudo neque profundum neque alia quaelibet creatura poterit nos separare a caritate Dei, quae est in Christo Iesu Domino nostro. [9] [1]Veritatem dico in Christo, non mentior, testimonium mihi perhibente conscientia mea in Spir-

8:31–39 These verses, a sort of summary of what the Apostle has been saying, show him at his most eloquent: the almighty power of God, who loves mankind to the point of handing over his Only-begotten Son to be put to death, will ensure that we emerge victorious from any kind of threat or suffering. Provided they are determined to accept all God's help, Christians can be confident of attaining salvation, for God will never withhold from them the graces they need. "It is not science that redeems man: man is redeemed by love. This applies even in terms of this present world. When someone has the experience of a great love in his life, this is a moment of 'redemption' which gives a new meaning to his life. But soon he will also realise that the love bestowed upon him cannot by itself resolve the question of his life. It is a love that remains fragile. It can be destroyed by death.

The human being needs unconditional love. He needs the certainty which makes him say [what St Paul says in Romans 8:38–39]. If this absolute love exists, with its absolute certainty, then—only then—is man 'redeemed', whatever should happen to him in his particular circumstances. This is what it means to say: Jesus Christ has 'redeemed' us. Through him we have become certain of God, a God who is not a remote 'first cause' of the world, because his only-begotten Son has become man and of him everyone can say: 'I live by faith in the Son of God, who loved me and gave himself for me' (Gal 2:20)" (Benedict XVI, *Spe salvi*, 26).

*9:1—11:36 These three chapters are the last section in the doctrinal part of the letter. Here St Paul responds to a question in the light of what

m Or *It is Christ Jesus . . . for us*

³For I could wish that I myself were accursed and cut off from Christ for the sake of my
brethren, my kinsmen by race. ⁴They are Israelites, and to them belong the sonship, the
glory, the covenants, the giving of the law, the worship, and the promises; ⁵to them
belong the patriarchs, and of their race, according to the flesh, is the Christ, who is God
over all, blessed for ever.ⁿ Amen.

    ⁶But it is not as though the word of God had failed. For not all who are descended
from Israel belong to Israel, ⁷and not all are children of Abraham because they are his
descendants; but "Through Isaac shall your descendants be named." ⁸This means that
it is not the children of the flesh who are the children of God, but the children of the
promise are reckoned as descendants. ⁹For this is what the promise said, "About this
time I will return and Sarah shall have a son." ¹⁰And not only so, but also when Rebecca

Ex 32:32
Gal 1:9

Ex 4:22
Deut 7:6; 14:1–2
Rom 1:3
Mt 1
1 Cor 3:23-24
Lk 3:23–34

Num 23:19
Is 55:10–11
Rom 2:28–29

Eph 2:12
Gen 21:12
Mt 3:9

Jn 8:31–44

Gen 18:10

itu Sancto, ²quoniam tristitia est mihi magna et continuus dolor cordi meo. ³Optarem enim ipse ego anathema esse a Christo pro fratribus meis,
cognatis meis secundum carnem, ⁴qui sunt Israelitae, quorum adoptio est filiorum et gloria et testamenta et legislatio et cultus et promissiones,
⁵quorum sunt patres, et ex quibus Christus secundum carnem: qui est super omnia Deus benedictus in saecula. Amen. ⁶Non autem quod exciderit
verbum Dei. Non enim omnes, qui ex Israel, hi sunt Israel; ⁷neque quia semen sunt Abrahae, omnes filii, sed: *«In Isaac vocabitur tibi semen»*. ⁸Id
est, non qui filii carnis, hi filii Dei, sed qui filii sunt promissionis, aestimantur semen; ⁹promissionis enim verbum hoc est: *«Secundum hoc tempus
veniam, et erit Sarae filius»*. ¹⁰Non solum autem, sed et Rebecca ex uno concubitum habens, Isaac patre nostro; ¹¹cum enim nondum nati fuissent

he has been saying: How can justification
through faith in Christ be compatible with the
promises God made to Israel? If, from the start,
God had a plan that culminated in the coming of
the Messiah, how is it that the Jews—the recipients of the promises made to the patriarchs, and
of the Law and of the works of the Prophets—
have rejected Christ?

    Returning to what he has already said in 3:1–
2, the Apostle discusses the Hebrew people's
great privilege of being the first to receive divine
revelation (9:1–5). The Gentiles have heard
God's call, but, he says, even though his Jewish
brethren have rejected Christ, God's promises to
Israel still apply. The Old Testament makes clear
that God chooses whomever he so wishes (9:6–
13); that is the mystery of divine predestination
(9:14–33). Moreover, although the first chosen
people were unfaithful to their calling, even their
infidelity produced good results, for it led to the
extension of divine mercy to the Gentiles (10:1–
21). Israel has not been rejected by God, because
a remnant have listened to the Gospel (11:1–12).
The Gentiles should be very conscious of the gift
they have received (11:13–24), and they should
also know that divine Wisdom has disposed that
eventually Israel will be converted and all
believers will be as one (11:25–36).

9:1–13 Descent from Jacob (Israel) was the basis
of the divine privileges given to Israel over the
centuries. However, St Paul (demonstrating here

his great love for those of his own race) says that
the singular honour bestowed on the Chosen
People is to be seen most clearly in the fact that
God himself chose to assume a human nature
that had all the features of the Israelite race (vv.
1–5). Jesus is descended from Israelites "according to the flesh", and he is also true God because
he is "God over all, blessed for ever" (v. 5). This
statement appears here as a sort of doxology or
praise of God, one of the most solemn ways of
extolling God in the Old Testament (see Ps
41:13; 72:18–19; 106:48; Neh 9:5; Dan 2:20).

    Isaac was chosen to be the heir of the prom-
ise made to Abraham, and after him Jacob (not
Esau, his first-born); Paul uses this fact to
explain that no one should be surprised to see
Gentiles being called to the faith, for God
chooses in accordance with his promise and not
according to the flesh (vv. 6–13). The true Israel,
then, is not that descended from Abraham
"according to the flesh", but that established by
bonds of the Spirit.

    Exploring this idea, St Thomas Aquinas
points out the difference between the way we
love and the way God loves: "Man's will is
moved to love by the attraction of the good he
finds in the thing loved; that is why he chooses it
in preference to something else […]. God's will,
on the other hand, is the cause of every good to
be found in a created thing […]. Hence God
does not love a person because he finds in him
something which leads him to choose that

n Or *Christ. God who is over all be blessed for ever*

Rom 11:5–6
Gen 25:21–23 had conceived children by one man, our forefather Isaac, [11]though they were not yet born and had done nothing either good or bad, in order that God's purpose of election might continue, not because of works but because of his call, [12]she was told, "The elder Mal 1:2–3
Gen 25:23 will serve the younger." [13]As it is written, "Jacob I loved, but Esau I hated."

Israel's vocation

Deut 32:4
Rom 3:5 [14]What shall we say then? Is there injustice on God's part? By no means! [15]For he Ex 33:19 says to Moses, "I will have mercy on whom I have mercy, and I will have compassion Ps 147:10–11
1 Cor 3:7
Eph 2:8 on whom I have compassion." [16]So it depends not upon man's will or exertion, but upon God's mercy. [17]For the scripture says to Pharaoh, "I have raised you up for the Ex 9:16 very purpose of showing my power in you, so that my name may be proclaimed in Ex 4:21; 9:12; 14:4;
17 all the earth." [18]So then he has mercy upon whomever he wills, and he hardens the heart of whomever he wills.

aut aliquid egissent bonum aut malum, ut secundum electionem propositum Dei maneret, [12]non ex operibus sed ex vocante dictum est ei: «*Maior serviet minori*»; [13]sicut scriptum est: «*Iacob dilexi, Esau autem odio habui*». [14]Quid ergo dicemus? Numquid iniustitia apud Deum? Absit! [15]Moysi enim dicit: «*Miserebor, cuius misereor, et misericordiam praestabo, cui misericordiam praesto*». [16]Igitur non volentis neque currentis, sed miserentis Dei. [17]Dicit enim Scriptura pharaoni: «*In hoc ipsum excitavi te, ut ostendam in te virtutem meam, et ut annuntietur nomen meum in universa terra*». [18]Ergo, cuius vult, miseretur et, quem vult, indurat. [19]Dices itaque mihi: «Quid ergo adhuc queritur? Voluntati enim eius quis

person: he chooses him rather than others because he loves him" (*Super Romanos*, ad loc.). The story of Jacob, the calling of the apostles, the election of Paul himself and of so many other people over the course of history show that God is pleased to pick precisely those who seem quite unsuitable in the eyes of men. "You realize you are weak. And so indeed you are. In spite of that—rather, just because of that—God has chosen you. He always uses inadequate instruments, so that the 'work' will be seen to be his. Of you, he only asks docility" (St Josemaría Escrivá, *The Way*, 475).

"Esau I hated" (v. 13): this is a Semitic way of speaking, of a sort often found in Scripture. God loves Esau, too, but compared with his preferential love for Jacob, his love for Esau looks like "hate". Exaggeration is being used to make a point. Our Lord sometimes uses similar language in the Gospel—for example, when he compares the love he is owed with the love a person owes his parents (see Mt 10:37 and the note on Lk 14:25–35). God loves everything and everyone he has made (see Wis 11:24).

9:14–33 St Paul now backs up what he has been saying with quotations from Scripture. Israel's calling leads him to speak about the profound mystery of predestination, giving as examples: the choosing of the people of Israel in preference

to all other nations (v. 15); the hardening of Pharaoh's heart (vv. 16–18); individual salvation or rejection, illustrated by the simile of the vessel of clay (vv. 20–26). God, who is almighty and all-knowing, not only knows all future events but arranges them so as to accomplish his designs: divine Wisdom, Scripture tells us, "reaches mightily from one end of the earth to the other, and she orders all things well" (Wis 8:1). Our limited minds cannot grasp how the infallibility of God's plans can be compatible with human freedom. That in fact is the *mystery* of predestination. It involves three things: (a) the absolute freedom of God and his generosity in granting us his grace; (b) God's desire that all men be saved by the death of Christ on the cross; and (c) the fact that in the work of salvation God counts on our free cooperation and inspires us, through his grace, to respond. "To God, all moments of time are present in their immediacy. When therefore he establishes his eternal plan of 'predestination', he includes in it each person's free response to his grace" (*Catechism of the Catholic Church*, 600). St Augustine says that when men freely follow the will of God, even when they do what they do voluntarily, their will is nevertheless the will of God, for God orders all things and ordains what men desire (cf. *In Ioannis Evangelium*, 19, 19).

God is not unjust, Paul says, when he distrib-

[19]You will say to me then, "Why does he still find fault? For who can resist his will?"* [20]But who are you, a man, to answer back to God? Will what is moulded say to its moulder, "Why have you made me thus?" [21]Has the potter no right over the clay, to make out of the same lump one vessel for beauty and another for menial use? [22]What if God, desiring to show his wrath and to make known his power, has endured with much patience the vessels of wrath made for destruction, [23]in order to make known the riches of his glory for the vessels of mercy, which he has prepared beforehand for glory, [24]even us whom he has called, not from the Jews only but also from the Gentiles? [25]As indeed he says in Hosea,

> "Those who were not my people
> I will call 'my people,'
> and her who was not beloved
> I will call 'my beloved.'"

Is 29:16; 45:9; 64–7
Jer 18:1–6
Wis 12:12; 15:7
Sir 33:12–13

Is 13:5
Rom 2:4; 3:25–26
Prov 16:4
Eph 1:3–12; 2:1–7
Rom 8:29
Wis 12:20–21

1 Pet 2:10

Hos 2:23

restitit?». [20]O homo, sed tu quis es, qui respondeas Deo? *Numquid dicet figmentum ei, qui se finxit:* «Quid me fecisti sic?». [21]An non habet potestatem *figulus luti* ex eadem massa facere aliud quidem vas in honorem, aliud vero in ignominiam? [22]Quod si volens Deus ostendere iram et notam facere potentiam suam sustinuit in multa patientia vasa irae aptata in interitum [23]et ut ostenderet divitias gloriae suae in vasa misericordiae, quae praeparavit in gloriam, [24]quos et vocavit nos non solum ex Iudaeis sed etiam ex gentibus? [25]Sicut et in Osee dicit: «*Vocabo Non plebem meam Plebem meam / et Non dilectam Dilectam.* [26]*Et erit: in loco, ubi dictum est eis: / "Non plebs mea vos", / ibi vocabuntur Filii Dei vivi*». [27]Isaias

utes his grace unequally among men (vv. 14–18). He has mercy on whomever he chooses without that meaning he is unfair. However, if a person in the exercise of his freedom rejects God's gifts, God respects that decision. Therefore, when Paul says that God "hardens the heart of whomever he wills" (v. 18), this should be read as a typically biblical way of speaking—attributing to God's action things that he merely permits. A sinner is always responsible for his own hardness of heart. St Thomas Aquinas explains this by using a simile: "Although the sun, for its part, enlightens all bodies, if it encounters an obstacle in a body it leaves the body in darkness, as happens to a house whose window shutters are closed. Clearly, the sun is not the cause of the house being darkened, since it does not act of its own accord in failing to light up the interior of the house; the cause of the darkness is the person who closed the shutters. So God chooses not to give [the light of] grace to those who put an obstacle in its way" (*Summa theologiae*, 1–2, 79, 3). All we need to remember, then, is that God always offers man the opportunity to change and repent. Hence the psalmist's call not to close our heart to God's invitations: "O that today you would hearken to his voice! Harden not your hearts" (Ps 95:7–8).

The image of the potter making vessels for different uses (vv. 20–23) appears in Scripture a number of times, with different symbolic meanings. In the words of the prophets, it refers to God's power over human events: the potter is God, and the vessel the Chosen People (cf. Is 29:16; 45:9; Jer 18:1ff). In the wisdom books the idea is applied to the individual believer, who is subject to God, like clay in the hands of the potter, for God made all human beings from the dust of the earth (cf. Sir 33:10–13; Wis 15:7). Paul uses the metaphor to make the point that we should not try to call God to account for his actions (vv. 19–26); his will far exceeds man's capacity to understand it; however, we can be sure that God always seeks our good; and our personal freedom and responsibility are never lessened by his concern.

Finally, the Apostle shows that the true Israel is not in fact those descended from Abraham "according to the flesh" (see 9:7), who seek to justify themselves by works rather than by faith; the true Israel is the "remnant" of which the prophets spoke (vv. 27–28; cf. 11:4): following Abraham's example, the remnant live by faith, as do the Gentiles who have accepted the Gospel. So, the Church, made up of one portion of Israel and another of Gentiles, is the true Israel, which is established on the cornerstone foretold in Scripture (v. 33), Christ, and which is bound together not by the bonds of human descent but by the bonds of the Spirit (vv. 30–33).

Hos 1:10
²⁶"And in the very place where it was said to them,
'You are not my people,'
they will be called 'sons of the living God.'"

Is 10:22–23
Rom 11:5
²⁷And Isaiah cries out concerning Israel: "Though the number of the sons of Israel be as the sand of the sea, only a remnant of them will be saved; ²⁸for the Lord will execute his sentence upon the earth with rigour and dispatch." ²⁹And as Isaiah predicted,

Is 1:9
"If the Lord of hosts had not left us children,
we would have fared like Sodom and been made like Gomorrah."

Rom 10:20–21; 11:7
Wis 2:11
³⁰What shall we say, then? That Gentiles who did not pursue righteousness have attained it, that is, righteousness through faith; ³¹but that Israel who pursued the righteousness which is based on law did not succeed in fulfilling that law. ³²Why? Because they did not pursue it through faith, but as if it were based on works. They

Rom 10:11
Ps 118:22–23
Is 8:14; 28: 16–17
Mt 21:42–44
Eph 2:20
1 Pet 2:6–8
have stumbled over the stumbling stone, ³³as it is written,

"Behold, I am laying in Zion a stone that will make men stumble,
a rock that will make them fall;
and he who believes in him will not be put to shame."

Israel's infidelity

10 ¹Brethren, my heart's desire and prayer to God for them is that they may be saved.* ²I bear them witness that they have a zeal for God, but it is not enlight-

Acts 22:3
Prov 19:2
ened. ³For, being ignorant of the righteousness that comes from God, and seeking to

Rom 9:31–32
Phil 3:9
establish their own, they did not submit to God's righteousness. ⁴For Christ is the end

Heb 8:13
Mt 5:17
Jn 1:17–18
Gal 3:24
of the law, that every one who has faith may be justified.

Lev 18:5
Gal 3:12
Rom 3:21
⁵Moses writes that the man who practises the righteousness which is based on the law shall live by it. ⁶But the righteousness based on faith says, Do not say in your

autem clamat pro Israel: «Si fuerit numerus filiorum Israel tamquam arena maris, reliquiae salvae fient. ²⁸Verbum enim consummans et brevians faciet Dominus super terram». ²⁹Et sicut praedixit Isaias: «Nisi Dominus Sabaoth reliquisset nobis semen, / sicut Sodoma facti essemus / et sicut Gomorra similes fuissemus». ³⁰Quid ergo dicemus? Quod gentes, quae non sectabantur iustitiam, apprehenderunt iustitiam, iustitiam autem, quae ex fide est; ³¹Israel vero sectans legem iustitiae in legem non pervenit. ³²Quare? Quia non ex fide sed quasi ex operibus; offenderunt in lapidem offensionis, ³³sicut scriptum est: «Ecce pono in Sion lapidem offensionis et petram scandali; / et, qui credit in eo, non confundetur». [10] ¹Fratres, voluntas quidem cordis mei et obsecratio ad Deum pro illis in salutem. ²Testimonium enim perhibeo illis quod aemulationem Dei habent, sed non secundum scientiam; ³ignorantes enim Dei iustitiam et suam iustitiam quaerentes statuere, iustitiae Dei non sunt subiecti; ⁴finis enim legis

10:1–21 Paul's aim here seems to be to show that almighty God is able to draw from a grave evil (the infidelity of Israel) a greater good (the call of the Gentiles). He points out that, by hoping to find justification in observance of the Law, Jews have failed to see that God justifies those who believe in Christ—and yet the Law was given to Israel with a view to Christ ("Christ is the end of the Law": v. 4). He also says that there is no excuse for Jews not accepting Christ as Lord: they cannot say they have not heard the Gospel preached; the problem is their failure to accept it and to respond to God's call. He backs this up with quotations from Scripture in the style of rabbis of his time.

In vv. 5–8, the Apostle teaches that, if the

Law given to Moses made God's will manifest and therefore easier to comply with, faith in Christ has opened up a much easier path to God. Jesus Christ, by coming down from heaven in the Incarnation and by rising from the dead and ascending into heaven, has fulfilled the prophecy of Moses about the nearness of the word of God (see Deut 30:11–14); through his work of redemption, Christ has drawn very close to those who believe in him.

Verses 9–10 show the need to acknowledge the divinity of Christ internally and to profess that faith externally also. Hence the importance of the confession or "profession" of faith, a practice in the Church from earliest times. The title of "Lord" (v. 9; Hebrew, *Adonai*), from the third century BC

heart, "Who will ascend into heaven?" (that is, to bring Christ down) [7]or "Who will descend into the abyss?" (that is, to bring Christ up from the dead). [8]But what does it say? The word is near you, on your lips and in your heart (that is, the word of faith which we preach); [9]because, if you confess with your lips that Jesus is Lord and believe in your heart that God raised him from the dead, you will be saved. [10]For man believes with his heart and so is justified, and he confesses with his lips and so is saved. [11]The scripture says, "No one who believes in him will be put to shame." [12]For there is no distinction between Jew and Greek; the same Lord is Lord of all and bestows his riches upon all who call upon him. [13]For, "every one who calls upon the name of the Lord will be saved."

[14]But how are men to call upon him in whom they have not believed? And how are they to believe in him of whom they have never heard? And how are they to hear without a preacher? [15]And how can men preach unless they are sent? As it is written, "How beautiful are the feet of those who preach good news!" [16]But they have not all obeyed the gospel; for Isaiah says, "Lord, who has believed what he has heard from us?" [17]So faith comes from what is heard, and what is heard comes by the preaching of Christ.

[18]But I ask, have they not heard? Indeed they have; for

Deut 9:4;30:12–14
Eph 4:7–10
1 Pet 3:19
Ps 107:26

Sir 21:26

Phil 2:11
Mk 9:38–40
2 Cor 4:5
Acts 2:36–39
1 Cor 12:3
Rom 1:4
Is 28:16

Rom 1:16
Col 3:11
Gal 3:26–28, 32–33
Acts 10:34–36; 15:7–9
Joel 3:5
Acts 2:14–21
Act 8:31

Is 52:7
Eph 6:15
Rom 1:5
Is 53:1
Jn 12:37–40

Christus ad iustitiam omni credenti. [5]Moyses enim scribit de iustitia, quae ex lege est: «*Qui fecerit homo, vivet in eis*». [6]Quae autem ex fide est iustitia, sic dicit: «*Ne dixeris* in corde tuo: *Quis ascendet in caelum?*», id est Christum deducere; [7]aut: «*Quis descendet in abyssum?*», hoc est Christum ex mortuis revocare. [8]Sed quid dicit? «*Prope te est verbum, in ore tuo et in corde tuo*»; hoc est verbum fidei, quod praedicamus. [9]Quia si confitearis in ore tuo: «*Dominum Iesum!*», et in corde tuo credideris quod Deus illum excitavit ex mortuis, salvus eris. [10]Corde enim creditur ad iustitiam, ore autem confessio fit in salutem. [11]Dicit enim Scriptura: «Omnis, *qui credit in illo, non confundetur*». [12]Non enim est distinctio Iudaei et Graeci, nam idem Dominus omnium, dives in omnes, qui invocant illum: [13]*Omnis* enim, *quicumque invocaverit nomen Domini, salvus erit*. [14]Quomodo ergo invocabunt, in quem non crediderunt? Aut quomodo credent ei, quem non audierunt? Quomodo autem audient sine praedicante? [15]Quomodo vero praedicabunt nisi mittantur? Sicut scriptum est: «*Quam speciosi pedes evangelizantium bona*». [16]Sed non omnes oboedierunt evangelio; Isaias enim dicit: «*Domine, quis credidit auditui nostro?*». [17]Ergo fides ex auditu, auditus autem per verbum Christi. [18]Sed dico: Numquid non audierunt? Quin immo, *in omnem terram exiit sonus eorum, / et in fines orbis terrae verba eorum*. [19]Sed dico: Numquid Israel

onwards, was used by Jews in preference to *Yhwh* (which was not uttered, out of respect for the name of God): here it is applied to Jesus Christ—an acknowledgment of his divinity. The subject of the verb "to confess" in v. 9 ("you") makes no distinction between Jew and Gentile (cf. v. 12). The prophecy of Joel (v. 13) has been fulfilled.

Staying with the same point (in vv. 14–21) St Paul argues that the Jews have very little excuse for failing to acknowledge Christ: the Gospel (the "good news") was proclaimed of old by the prophets (v. 15; cf. Is 52:7) and has been spread far and wide (v. 18; see Ps 19:4), but many of the Jews have not believed it (vv. 16, 21; cf. Is 53:1; 65:2). They did not listen to Moses, either (v. 19; cf. Deut 32:21). Instead, God has been found by people who did not seek him (v. 20; cf. Is 65:1–2).

The words of vv. 14–15 are a stirring call to spread the word of God in line with the charge that our Lord gave the apostles (cf. Mk 16:15–16). "The 'feet' the text refers to is the coming of the apostles, who travel throughout the whole

world to preach the coming of the Kingdom of God. Their coming is a light for all mankind, which illuminates the path of peace to God" (Ambrosiaster, *Ad Romanos*, ad loc.). Like the Apostles, Christ's disciples should spread the Gospel by word and example. Commenting on v. 14, Paul VI said: "This law once laid down by the Apostle Paul maintains its full force today. Preaching, the verbal proclamation of a message, is indeed always indispensable" (*Evangelii nuntiandi*, 42). But proclaiming the Gospel is not enough: "For the Church, the first means of evangelization is the witness of an authentically Christian life, given over to God in a communion that nothing should destroy and at the same time given to one's neighbour with limitless zeal. As we said recently to a group of lay people, 'Modern man listens more willingly to witnesses than to teachers, and if he does listen to teachers, it is because they are witnesses.' [...] It is therefore primarily by her conduct and by her life that the Church will evangelize the

Ps 19:3–4
Mt 24:14

"Their voice has gone out to all the earth,
and their words to the ends of the world."

¹⁹Again I ask, did Israel not understand? First Moses says,

Deut 32:21
Rom 11:11

"I will make you jealous of those who are not a nation;
with a foolish nation I will make you angry."

²⁰Then Isaiah is so bold as to say,

Is 65:1
Rom 9:30

"I have been found by those who did not seek me;
I have shown myself to those who did not ask for me."

Is 65:2

²¹But of Israel he says, "All day long I have held out my hands to a disobedient and contrary people."

Part of Israel will be saved

Ps 94:14; 44:9
1 Sam 12:22
2 Cor 11:22
Phil 3:4–5

1 Kings 19:10, 14

11 ¹I ask, then, has God rejected his people? By no means! I myself am an Israelite, a descendant of Abraham, a member of the tribe of Benjamin. ²God has not rejected his people whom he foreknew. Do you not know what the scripture says of Elijah, how he pleads with God against Israel? ³"Lord, they have killed thy prophets, they have demolished thy altars, and I alone am left, and they seek my

non cognovit? Primus Moyses dicit: «*Ego ad aemulationem vos adducam per Non gentem: / per gentem insipientem ad iram vos provocabo*». ²⁰Isaias autem audet et dicit: «*Inventus sum in non quaerentibus me; palam apparui his, qui me non interrogabant*». ²¹Ad Israel autem dicit: «*Tota die expandi manus meas ad populum non credentem et contradicentem*». [11] ¹Dico ergo: Numquid reppulit Deus populum suum? Absit! Nam et ego Israelita sum, ex semine Abraham, tribu Beniamin. ²*Non reppulit Deus plebem suam*, quam praescivit. An nescitis in Elia quid dicit Scriptura? Quemadmodum interpellat Deum adversus Israel: ³«Domine, *prophetas tuos occiderunt, altaria tua suffoderunt, et ego relictus sum solus, et quaerunt animam meam*». ⁴Sed quid dicit illi responsum divinum? «*Reliqui* mihi *septem milia virorum, qui non curvaverunt genu Baal*». ⁵Sic

world, in other words, by her living witness of fidelity to the Lord Jesus—the witness of poverty and detachment, of freedom in the face of the powers of this world, in short, the witness of sanctity" (ibid., 41).

11:1–12 Feeling himself to be a true Israelite, one who is a descendant of Abraham, of the tribe of Benjamin, the Apostle emphatically asserts that, despite all that he has said, God has not rejected Israel (v. 1). Citing the prophet Elijah's complaints to God about the infidelity of most of the people (v. 3) and God's reply (v. 4), Paul returns again to the biblical theme of the "remnant of Israel" (see 9:27–28). That phrase, often found (with variations in wording) in the prophets (see Is 4:2–3; Jer 3:14; Ezek 9:8; Amos 3:12; Mic 4:7; Zeph 2:7, 9), was used to designate those Israelites who stayed true to God at times of widespread infidelity. Paul uses it to explain why only a small number of Jews have believed in the Gospel message: they are the "remnant" chosen by God so that the promises might be fulfilled in them; Paul himself is one of that remnant and a sign that Israel will return to its God.

On reading these verses, Christians can see that, just like what happened in Israel, many people, in our own time, and in earlier times, have fallen away from the faith. During times of crisis, we should trust in God's promises and remember that the Lord wants to use a remnant of the people and their holy lives in order to redeem the whole. "I'll tell you a secret, an open secret: these world crises are crises of saints. God wants a handful of men 'of his own' in every human activity. Then ... '*pax Christi in regno Christi*' — 'the peace of Christ in the kingdom of Christ'" (St Josemaría Escrivá, *The Way*, 301).

The words of v. 1 should also encourage Christians to love the Jewish people. The Second Vatican Council teaches: "The Church of Christ acknowledges that, according to God's saving design, the beginnings of her faith and her election are found already among the Patriarchs, Moses and the prophets. She professes that all who believe in Christ—Abraham's sons according to faith (cf. Gal 3:7)—are included in the same Patriarch's call, and likewise that the salvation of the Church is mysteriously foreshadowed by the Chosen People's exodus from the land of bondage.

life." [4]But what is God's reply to him? "I have kept for myself seven thousand men who have not bowed the knee to Baal." [5]So too at the present time there is a remnant, chosen by grace. [6]But if it is by grace, it is no longer on the basis of works; otherwise grace would no longer be grace.

1 Kings 19:18

Rom 4:4; 12:17

[7]What then? Israel failed to obtain what it sought. The elect obtained it, but the rest were hardened, [8]as it is written,

Gal 2:16; 3:18
Eph 2:8

> "God gave them a spirit of stupor,
> eyes that should not see and ears that should not hear,
> down to this very day."

Deut 29:3
Is 6:9; 29:10
Mt 13:13–15
Jn 12:40
Acts 28:26

[9]And David says,

> "Let their table become a snare and a trap,
> a pitfall and a retribution for them;
> [10] let their eyes be darkened so that they cannot see,
> and bend their backs for ever."

Ps 69:22–23; 35:8

Rom 10:19
Mt 8:11–12;
21:43–46
Acts 13:46–48
Deut 32:21
Acts 13:5

[11]So I ask, have they stumbled so as to fall? By no means! But through their trespass salvation has come to the Gentiles, so as to make Israel jealous. [12]Now if their trespass means riches for the world, and if their failure means riches for the Gentiles, how much more will their full inclusion mean!

Acts 9:15

ergo et in hoc tempore reliquiae secundum electionem gratiae factae sunt. [6]Si autem gratia, iam non ex operibus, alioquin gratia iam non est gratia. [7]Quid ergo? Quod quaerit Israel, hoc non est consecutus, electio autem consecuta est; ceteri vero excaecati sunt, [8]sicut scriptum est: *«Dedit illis Deus spiritum soporis, / oculos, ut non videant, / et aures, ut non audiant, / usque in hodiernum diem»*. [9]Et David dicit: *«Fiat mensa eorum in laqueum* et in captionem, / *et in scandalum et in retributionem illis*. / [10]*Obscurentur oculi eorum, ne videant, / et dorsum illorum semper incurva!»*. [11]Dico ergo: Numquid sic offenderunt, ut caderent? Absit! Sed illorum casu salus gentibus, ut illi ad aemulationem adducantur. [12]Quod si casus illorum divitiae sunt mundi et deminutio eorum divitiae gentium, quanto magis plenitudo eorum! [13]Vobis autem dico gentibus: Quantum quidem

The Church, therefore, cannot forget that she received the revelation of the Old Testament through the people with whom God in his inexpressible mercy concluded the Ancient Covenant. Nor can she forget that she draws sustenance from the root of that well-cultivated olive tree onto which have been grafted the wild shoots, the Gentiles (cf. Rom 11:17–24). Indeed, the Church believes that by his cross Christ, Our Peace, reconciled Jews and Gentiles, making both one in himself (cf. Eph 2:14–16). The Church keeps ever in mind the words of the Apostle about his kinsmen: 'theirs is the sonship and the glory and the covenants and the law and the worship and the promises; theirs are the fathers and from them is the Christ according to the flesh' (Rom 9:4–5), the Son of the Virgin Mary. She also recalls that the Apostles, the Church's main-stay and pillars, as well as most of the early disciples who proclaimed Christ's Gospel to the world, sprang from the Jewish people" (*Nostra aetate*, 4). John Paul II speaks in the same vein; referring to the existence of the people of Israel, he points out "this people was gathered together and led by God, the Creator of heaven and earth. Thus its existence is not a mere fact of nature or culture, in the sense that through culture man displays the resources of his own nature. It is a supernatural fact. This people perseveres in spite of everything because they are the people of the Covenant, and despite human infidelities, the Lord is faithful to his Covenant. To ignore this primary fact is to embark on the way of a Marcionism against which the Church immediately and vigorously reacted, in the awareness of her vital link with the Old Testament, without which the New Testament itself would be emptied of its meaning. The Scriptures cannot be separated from the people and its history, which leads to Christ, the promised and awaited Messiah, the Son of God made man. […] That is why those who regard the fact that Jesus was a Jew and that his milieu was the Jewish world as mere cultural accidents […] not only ignore the meaning of salvation history, but more radically challenge the very truth of the Incarnation" (Address to the symposium on "The Roots of Anti-Semitism in Christian Cultures", 31 October 1997).

The new Chosen People

1 Cor 9:19–23

[13]Now I am speaking to you Gentiles. Inasmuch then as I am an apostle to the Gentiles, I magnify my ministry [14]in order to make my fellow Jews jealous, and thus save some of them. [15]For if their rejection means the reconciliation of the world,

Ezek 44:30
Num 15:17–21

what will their acceptance mean but life from the dead? [16]If the dough offered as first fruits is holy, so is the whole lump; and if the root is holy, so are the branches.

Eph 2:11–18

[17]But if some of the branches were broken off, and you, a wild olive shoot, were

Rom 3:27–28;
14:1–5
1 Cor 1:31; 10:12

grafted in their place to share the richness[o] of the olive tree, [18]do not boast over the branches. If you do boast, remember it is not you that support the root, but the root that supports you. [19]You will say, "Branches were broken off so that I might be grafted in." [20]That is true. They were broken off because of their unbelief, but you stand

Lk 23:31
Jer 49:12

fast only through faith. So do not become proud, but stand in awe. [21]For if God did not

Jn 15:2
Heb 3:14–15

spare the natural branches, neither will he spare you. [22]Note then the kindness and the severity of God: severity toward those who have fallen, but God's kindness to you, provided you continue in his kindness; otherwise you too will be cut off. [23]And even the others, if they do not persist in their unbelief, will be grafted in, for God has the power to graft them in again. [24]For if you have been cut from what is by nature a wild olive tree, and grafted, contrary to nature, into a cultivated olive tree, how much more will these natural branches be grafted back into their own olive tree.

The conversion of the Jews

Prov 3:7
Rom 12:16;
16:25–27

[25]Lest you be wise in your own conceits, I want you to understand this mystery, brethren: a hardening has come upon part of Israel, until the full number of the Gentiles

Rom 11:11

come in, [26]and so all Israel will be saved; as it is written,

ego sum gentium apostolus, ministerium meum honorifico, [14]si quo modo ad aemulandum provocem carnem meam et salvos faciam aliquos ex illis. [15]Si enim amissio eorum reconciliatio est mundi, quae assumptio nisi vita ex mortuis? [16]Quod si primitiae sanctae sunt, et massa; et si radix sancta, et rami. [17]Quod si aliqui ex ramis fracti sunt, tu autem, cum oleaster esses, insertus es in illis et consocius radicis pinguedinis olivae factus es, [18]noli gloriari adversus ramos; quod si gloriaris, non tu radicem portas, sed radix te. [19]Dices ergo: «Fracti sunt rami, ut ego inserar». [20]Bene; incredulitate fracti sunt, tu autem fide stas. Noli altum sapere, sed time: [21]si enim Deus naturalibus ramis non pepercit, ne forte nec tibi parcat. [22]Vide ergo bonitatem et severitatem Dei: in eos quidem, qui ceciderunt, severitatem; in te autem bonitatem Dei, si permanseris in bonitate, alioquin et tu excideris. [23]Sed et illi, si non permanserint in incredulitate, inserentur; potens est enim Deus iterum inserere illos! [24]Nam si tu ex naturali excisus es oleastro et contra naturam insertus es in bonam olivam, quanto magis hi, qui secundum naturam sunt, inserentur suae olivae. [25]Nolo enim vos ignorare, fratres, mysterium hoc, ut non sitis vobis ipsis sapientes, quia caecitas ex parte contigit in Israel, donec plenitudo gentium

11:13–24 The conversion of the Gentiles should make the Jews envious and lead them, too, to conversion. The cultivated olive tree stands for the faithful of the Old Testament and, at the same time, the new Israel of God—that is, the Church. The natural branches that remain on the olive tree are those Jews who have embraced the Christian faith; the broken-off branches are the unbelieving Jews; the branches of the wild olive, now grafted onto the original tree, are the Gentiles who have taken the place of the unbelieving Jews and now profess the same faith as the patriarchs and prophets, and have a share in the blessings God has promised.

The Apostle is trying to do two things here: on the one hand, he wants to check any boasting by Christians of Gentile background, for, if the natural branches have been broken off, this can much more easily happen to branches that are mere grafts; on the other hand, he wants to raise the hopes of Christians of Jewish background: wild branches (the Gentiles) have been grafted onto the olive tree, so it will be much easier for natural branches to be reunited to the stem from which they have become detached.

11:25–36 St Paul announces that, in keeping with God's plans, all nations will eventually be converted. "Together with the prophets and the Apostle himself, the Church awaits the day, known to God alone, when all peoples will call on God with one voice and 'serve him with one accord' (Zeph 3:9)" (Vatican II, *Nostra aetate*, 4). However, he is not any more specific than

o Other ancient authorities read *rich root*

"The Deliverer will come from Zion,
   he will banish ungodliness from Jacob";
  [27]"and this will be my covenant with them
    when I take away their sins."

       Is 59:20–21
       Ps 14:7

       Is 27:9
       Jer 31:31–33

[28]As regards the gospel they are enemies of God, for your sake; but as regards election they are beloved for the sake of their forefathers. [29]For the gifts and the call of God are irrevocable. [30]Just as you were once disobedient to God but now have received mercy because of their disobedience, [31]so they have now been disobedient in order that by the mercy shown to you they also may[p] receive mercy. [32]For God has consigned all men to disobedience, that he may have mercy upon all.

       Heb 6:17–18
       Rom 9:6
       Num 23:19
       1 Sam 15:29
       Rom 3:26
       Rom 11:11
       Gal 3:22
       Ezek 18:23–32

    [33]O the depth of the riches and wisdom and knowledge of God! How unsearchable are his judgments and how inscrutable his ways!

       Ps 139:6, 17–18
       Job 11:6–8
       Sir 1:1–3
       Is 55:8–9

     [34]"For who has known the mind of the Lord,
       or who has been his counsellor?"

       Is 40:13
       Job 15:8; 41:3
       Jer 23:18

     [35]"Or who has given a gift to him
       that he might be repaid?"

       1 Cor 2:11, 16
       Wis 9:13

[36]For from him and through him and to him are all things. To him be glory for ever. Amen.

       1 Cor 8:6
       Col 1:16
       Heb 2:10

---

intraret, ²⁶et sic omnis Israel salvus fiet, sicut scriptum est: «*Veniet ex Sion, qui eripiat,* / *avertet impietates ab Iacob*; / ²⁷*et hoc illis a me testamentum,* / *cum abstulero peccata eorum*». ²⁸Secundum evangelium quidem inimici propter vos, secundum electionem autem carissimi propter patres; ²⁹sine paenitentia enim sunt dona et vocatio Dei! ³⁰Sicut enim aliquando vos non credidistis Deo, nunc autem misericordiam consecuti estis propter illorum incredulitatem, ³¹ita et isti nunc non crediderunt propter vestram misericordiam, ut et ipsi nunc misericordiam consequantur. ³²Conclusit enim Deus omnes in incredulitatem, ut omnium misereatur! ³³O altitudo divitiarum et sapientiae et scientiae Dei! Quam incomprehensibilia sunt iudicia eius et investigabiles viae eius! ³⁴*Quis* enim *cognovit sensum Domini?* / *Aut quis consiliarius eius fuit?* / ³⁵*Aut quis prior*

---

this about its happening. Acceptance of the Messiah by the Jews is a "mystery" (v. 25); it will happen when God so ordains. Certainly, God keeps his promises; he never breaks them. Therefore, the calling of the Jewish people to be the Chosen People is irreversible (v. 29). Despite their disobedience, God loves them with an everlasting love, as he promised the patriarchs he would and in line with the merits that have accrued to them because of their fidelity (cf. 9:4–5). It is the unchanging nature of God's love that makes it possible for "all Israel" (v. 26) to be saved. St Paul, then, sees the conversion of the Gentiles as a stage in the mission of the people of Israel, for Scripture says that God's promise to Abraham holds good forever: "I will bless those who bless you, and him who curses you I will curse; and by you all the families of the earth shall bless themselves" (Gen 12:3).

    It does not necessarily follow from the words quoted in vv. 26–27 that the conversion of the Jewish people presages the end of the world. In any event, they mean that the history of the Jewish people has a special place in salvation history and that redemption extends to all mankind, both Jews and Gentiles (provided that individuals are open to its power). Hence the Church's appeal to God to listen to her prayers "that the people you first made your own may arrive at the fullness of redemption" (*Roman Missal*, Liturgy of Good Friday, Bidding Prayer).

    God's admirable kindness in letting Jews and Gentiles disobey him and then taking pity on their wretchedness (v. 32) causes the Apostle to pour out his heart in praise of God's mysterious design (vv. 33–35); his praise ends with a doxology: "To him be glory for ever. Amen" (v. 36). And Origen comments: "The 'Amen' is added at the end to remind us that this happiness is ours through Him, of whom is written in Revelations, 'the words of the Amen' (Rev 3:14)" (*Commentarii in Romanos*, 8, 13).

---

p Other ancient authorities add *now*

PART TWO

Living in charity*

5. CHRISTIAN BEHAVIOUR*

Solidarity in the mystical body of Christ

Rom 1:9; 6:12–13
1 Pet 2:5
Jn 4:23–24
Acts 10:35

Rom 2:18; 8:5, 14,
20
Eph 4:23; 5:10–17
Phil 1:10
Heb 5:14

Eph 4:7
Rom 3:24–26
1 Cor 12:9–11
Phil 2:3

1 Cor 12:12–14,
28–30

Eph 4:7–11, 25
1 Pet 4:10–11

12 ¹I appeal to you therefore, brethren, by the mercies of God, to present your bodies as a living sacrifice, holy and acceptable to God, which is your spiritual worship. ²Do not be conformed to this world^q but be transformed by the renewal of your mind, that you may prove what is the will of God, what is good and acceptable and perfect.^r

³For by the grace given to me I bid every one among you not to think of himself more highly than he ought to think, but to think with sober judgment, each according to the measure of faith which God has assigned him. ⁴For as in one body we have many members, and all the members do not have the same function, ⁵so we, though many, are one body in Christ, and individually members one of another.

dedit illi, / et retribuetur ei? ³⁶Quoniam ex ipso et per ipsum et in ipsum omnia. Ipsi gloria in saecula. Amen.   [12] ¹Obsecro itaque vos, fratres, per misericordiam Dei, ut exhibeatis corpora vestra hostiam viventem, sanctam, Deo placentem, rationabile obsequium vestrum; ²et nolite conformari huic saeculo, sed transformamini renovatione mentis, ut probetis quid sit voluntas Dei, quid bonum et bene placens et perfectum. ³Dico enim per gratiam, quae data est mihi, omnibus, qui sunt inter vos, non altius sapere quam oportet sapere, sed sapere ad sobrietatem, unicuique

*12:1—16:27 A revelation of how all are united in Christ opens the part of the letter that deals with morality, the central theme of which is the importance of living in accordance with charity (12:1—13:14). This entails certain demands, as Christ's example illustrates (14:1—15:13). The Apostle's own life accords with this spirit (15:14—16:27).

*12:1—13:14 Addressing the Christians of Rome, but conveying a message meant for all, St Paul spells out the general principle that should govern Christians' lives: charity, love, is what binds people together as members of Christ's Body, the Church. We all form one body in Christ, and are members of one another (12:1–8); that is why we must practise brotherly love (12:9–21). Within this context, obedience to authority, which comes from God and is oriented to the service of God (13:1–7), must also be imbued with love of God. For all these reasons, love is the fullness of the Law (13:8–14).

12:1–8 In the light of the grace given him (v. 3), Paul now outlines how to live in accordance with God's will and one's Christian dignity. The idea

he wants to get across is summarized in v. 2: "Do not be conformed to this world".

First, he lays the groundwork for his exhortation. Those who have been justified in Christ should offer themselves unreservedly to God, as a kind of act of worship (vv. 1–2). "It is by the apostolic preaching of the Gospel that the People of God is called together and gathered so that all who belong to this people, sanctified as they are by the Holy Spirit, may offer themselves 'a living sacrifice, holy and acceptable to God' (Rom 12:1)" (Vatican II, *Presbyterorum ordinis*, 2). It is then a matter (as Jesus told the Samaritan woman) of rendering God worship that is not purely material, external and formal, but interior and spiritual (see Jn 4:23–24). This means that a Christian's whole life must have a priestly character: "If I renounce everything I possess, if I carry the cross and follow Christ, I have offered a holocaust on the altar of God. [...] If I mortify my body and abstain from all concupiscence, if the world is crucified unto me and not me unto the world, then I have offered a holocaust on the altar of God and I am become a priest of my own sacrifice" (Origen, *In Leviticum homilia*, 9, 9). Or, as St Josemaría Escrivá put it: "Through

q Greek *age*   r Or *what is the good and acceptable and perfect will of God*

⁶Having gifts that differ according to the grace given to us, let us use them: if
prophecy, in proportion to our faith; ⁷if service, in our serving; he who teaches, in
his teaching; ⁸he who exhorts, in his exhortation; he who contributes, in liberality;
he who gives aid, with zeal; he who does acts of mercy, with cheerfulness.

Charity towards all

⁹Let love be genuine; hate what is evil, hold fast to what is good; ¹⁰love one another
with brotherly affection; outdo one another in showing honour. ¹¹Never flag in zeal,
be aglow with the Spirit, serve the Lord. ¹²Rejoice in your hope, be patient in tribulation, be constant in prayer. ¹³Contribute to the needs of the saints, practise hospitality.

¹⁴Bless those who persecute you; bless and do not curse them. ¹⁵Rejoice with those
who rejoice, weep with those who weep. ¹⁶Live in harmony with one another; do not be
haughty, but associate with the lowly;ˢ never be conceited. ¹⁷Repay no one evil for evil,
but take thought for what is noble in the sight of all. ¹⁸If possible, so far as it depends
upon you, live peaceably with all. ¹⁹Beloved, never avenge yourselves, but leave itᵗ to the
wrath of God; for it is written, "Vengeance is mine, I will repay, says the Lord." ²⁰No, "if
your enemy is hungry, feed him; if he is thirsty, give him drink; for by so doing you will
heap burning coals upon his head." ²¹Do not be overcome by evil, but overcome evil
with good.

1 Cor 12:8–10, 28–30
Acts 11:27
Mt 6:2–4
2 Cor 9:7
Tit 1:5–9
2 Cor 6:6
Is 1:17; Phil 1:22
1 Pet 1:22
Jn 13:12–17
1 Cor 13:13
Col 4:2
2 Pet 1:7
Acts 1:14; 6:4; 9:13
1 Thess 5:17
Heb 13:2
1 Pet 4:9
Mt 5:38–48
1 Cor 4:12
Acts 7:59–60
1 Cor 12:26
Sir 7:34
Prov 3:7
Is 5:21
2 Cor 8:21
Prov 3:4 (LXX)
1 Thess 5:15
1 Pet 3:9
Mk 9:50
Heb 12:14
1 Cor 6:6–7
Deut 32:35
Lev 19:17–18
Prov 20:22
Gen 50:19
Mt 5:38–42
Prov 25:21–22
Mt 5:44
Jas 5:4

sicut Deus divisit mensuram fidei. ⁴Sicut enim in uno corpore multa membra habemus, omnia autem membra non eundem actum habent, ⁵ita multi
unum corpus sumus in Christo, singuli autem alter alterius membra. ⁶Habentes autem donationes secundum gratiam, quae data est nobis, differ-
entes: sive prophetiam, secundum rationem fidei; ⁷sive ministerium, in ministrando; sive qui docet, in doctrina; ⁸sive qui exhortatur, in exhor-
tando; qui tribuit, in simplicitate; qui praeest, in sollicitudine; qui miseretur, in hilaritate. ⁹Dilectio sine simulatione. Odientes malum, adhaerentes
bono; ¹⁰caritate fraternitatis invicem diligentes, honore invicem praevenientes, ¹¹sollicitudine non pigri, spiritu ferventes, Domino servientes, ¹²spe
gaudentes, in tribulatione patientes, orationi instantes, ¹³necessitatibus sanctorum communicantes, hospitalitatem sectantes. ¹⁴Benedicite persequentibus; benedicite et nolite maledicere! ¹⁵Gaudere cum gaudentibus, flere cum flentibus. ¹⁶Idipsum invicem sentientes, non alta sapientes, sed
humilibus consentientes. Nolite esse prudentes apud vosmetipsos. ¹⁷Nulli malum pro malo reddentes; *providentes bona coram* omnibus *hominibus*;
¹⁸si fieri potest, quod ex vobis est, cum omnibus hominibus pacem habentes; ¹⁹non vosmetipsos vindicantes, carissimi, sed date locum irae, scriptum est enim: «*Mihi vindicta, ego retribuam*», dicit Dominus. ²⁰Sed *si esurierit inimicus tuus, ciba illum; si sitit, potum da illi. Hoc enim faciens,*

Baptism all of us have been made priests of our
lives, 'to offer spiritual sacrifices acceptable to
God through Jesus Christ' (1 Pet 2:5). Everything we do can be an expression of our obedience to God's will and so perpetuate the mission
of the God-man" (*Christ Is Passing By*, 96). See
also the note on 1 Pet 2:4–10.

In vv. 3–8, Paul echoes ideas found in 1
Corinthians (see 1 Cor 12:8–10, 28). Once again
he describes the range of gifts or charisms to be
found in the Church, using the metaphor of the
body to illustrate how unity and diversity combine: each person has a defined role and should
work for the benefit of all, seeking his or her
own spiritual betterment while so doing (cf. 1
Cor 12:12–31). Gifts, or charisms, are special,
transitory, divine graces, granted not so much for
the personal benefit of the recipient as for the
general good of the Church. The term "charism"
[rendered as "gift" in the RSV] was brought into
the Church by St Paul.

12:9–21 Having discussed those gifts entrusted
only to some, the Apostle now teaches that charity is common to all (cf. St Thomas Aquinas,
Super Romanos, ad loc.). Love, charity,
expresses itself in a number of ways, depending
on the needs and capacity of each person; it
always necessarily involves seeking good and
avoiding evil (vv. 9, 15–16), and it is to be practised towards both Christians (vv. 10–13) and
those who are not yet Christians (vv. 14, 17–21);
in fact, charity shown to the latter will help to
draw them closer to the faith. "We have to
understand everyone; we must live peaceably
with everyone; we must forgive everyone. We
shall not call injustice justice; we shall not say
that an offence against God is not an offence
against God, or that evil is good. When con-
fronted by evil we shall not reply with another
evil, but rather with sound doctrine and good
actions—drowning evil in an abundance of good
(cf. Rom 12:21). That is how Christ will reign in

s Or *give yourselves to humble tasks*   t Greek *give place*

Submission to authority

Mt 22:16–21
Jn 19:11
Tit 3:1
1 Pet 2:13–15
1 Tim 2:1–2
Wis 6:3
Prov 8:15–16

13 ¹Let every person be subject to the governing authorities. For there is no authority except from God, and those that exist have been instituted by God. ²Therefore he who resists the authorities resists what God has appointed, and those who resist will incur judgment. ³For rulers are not a terror to good conduct, but to bad. Would you have no fear of him who is in authority? Then do what is good, and you will receive his approval, ⁴for he is God's servant for your good. But if you do wrong, be afraid, for he does not bear the sword in vain; he is the servant of God to execute his wrath on the wrongdoer. ⁵Therefore one must be subject, not only to avoid God's wrath but also for the sake of conscience. ⁶For the same reason you also pay taxes, for the authorities are ministers of God, attending to this very thing. ⁷Pay all of them their dues, taxes to whom taxes are due, revenue to whom revenue is due, respect to whom respect is due, honour to whom honour is due.

Mt 22:21
Mk 12:17
Lk 20:25

Love, the fullness of the Law

Gal 5:14
Col 3:14
1 Tim 1:5
Mt 22:34–40
Jn 13:34–35
Ex 20:13–17
Deut 5:17–21
Jas 2:8

⁸Owe no one anything, except to love one another; for he who loves his neighbour has fulfilled the law. ⁹The commandments, "You shall not commit adultery, You

carbones ignis congeres super caput eius. ²¹Noli vinci a malo, sed vince in bono malum.   [13] ¹Omnis anima potestatibus sublimioribus subdita sit. Non est enim potestas nisi a Deo; quae autem sunt, a Deo ordinatae sunt. ²Itaque, qui resistit potestati, Dei ordinationi resistit; qui autem resistunt ipsi, sibi damnationem acquirent. ³Nam principes non sunt timori bono operi sed malo. Vis autem non timere potestatem? Bonum fac, et habebis laudem ex illa; ⁴Dei enim ministra est tibi in bonum. Si autem malum feceris, time; non enim sine causa gladium portat; Dei enim ministra est, vindex in iram ei, qui malum agit. ⁵Ideo necesse est subditos esse, non solum propter iram sed et propter conscientiam. ⁶Ideo enim et tributa praestatis; ministri enim Dei sunt in hoc ipsum instantes. ⁷Reddite omnibus debita: cui tributum tributum, cui vectigal vectigal, cui timorem timorem, cui honorem honorem. ⁸Nemini quidquam debeatis, nisi ut invicem diligatis: qui enim diligit proximum, legem implevit. ⁹Nam:

our souls and in the souls of the people around us" (St Josemaría Escrivá, *Christ Is Passing By*, 182).

13:1–7 Here St Paul shows the impact of charity on a Christian's civic duties. God created man with a need to live and develop within a community, and thereby attain his last end. Civil authority (provided it is lawful, of course, and respects the dignity of the human person) is part of the divine scheme of things (see Prov 8:15–16; Wis 6:3). From the very beginning, Christians have sought to fulfil their civic obligations even if they are victims of persecution. "Christians live in their own countries, but are seen as outsiders; they play their part as citizens and endure all things [...]. They obey all the laws laid down, but go beyond the law in their lives. They love all men, and are persecuted by all. They are disowned and condemned [...]. They are dishonoured, and by dishonour they are glorified" (*Epistula ad Diognetum*, 5, 5–14). "It is clear", Vatican II says, "that the political community and public authority are based on human nature, and therefore that they belong to an order estab-

lished by God; nevertheless, the choice of the political regime and the appointment of rulers are left to the free decisions of the citizens" (*Gaudium et spes*, 74). Because of its divine origin, civil authority should be obeyed provided it is exercised within the limits of the moral order and promotes the common good. If, however, a civil authority abuses its power and imposes laws that are unjust and that are damaging to human dignity and freedom (see Rev 13:1–10), people have a duty in conscience to defend human rights by political argument and legal means. Therefore, the Apostle's counsels about Christians having to be exemplary citizens are not absolute.

In line with this teaching, the Church also teaches that "submission to authority and co-responsibility for the common good make it morally obligatory to pay taxes, to exercise the right to vote, and to defend one's country" (*Catechism of the Catholic Church*, 2240).

13:8–14 Verses 8–10 bring us back to our Lord's teaching (cf. Mt 22:36–40): love is the fullness of the Law. This does not mean that

shall not kill, You shall not steal, You shall not covet," and any other commandment, are summed up in this sentence, "You shall love your neighbour as yourself." [10]Love does no wrong to a neighbour; therefore love is the fulfilling of the law.

Lev 18:19
1 Cor 13:4–7

[11]Besides this you know what hour it is, how it is full time now for you to wake from sleep. For salvation is nearer to us now than when we first believed; [12]the night is far gone, the day is at hand. Let us then cast off the works of darkness and put on the armour of light; [13]let us conduct ourselves becomingly as in the day, not in revelling and drunkenness, not in debauchery and licentiousness, not in quarrelling and jealousy. [14]But put on the Lord Jesus Christ, and make no provision for the flesh, to gratify its desires.

1 Cor 7:26, 29–31
Eph 5:14–16
Col 4:5
1 Thess 5:4–8
1 Jn 2:8
Eph 5:11–14
2 Tim 1:10
Jn 8:12
Lk 21:34
Eph 5:18; 6:1

Gal 3:27
Eph 4:24
Rom 1:29

6. SENSITIVITY TOWARDS OTHERS*

Seeing things from the other person's point of view

14 [1]As for the man who is weak in faith, welcome him, but not for disputes over opinions.* [2]One believes he may eat anything, while the weak man eats only vegetables. [3]Let not him who eats despise him who abstains, and let not him who

1 Cor 8:7–13;
10:14–33

Gen 1:29; 9:3

1 Cor 10:14–33
Col 2:16–17

Non adulterabis, Non occides, Non furaberis, Non concupisces, et si quod est aliud mandatum, in hoc verbo recapitulatur: *Diliges proximum tuum tamquam teipsum*. [10]Dilectio proximo malum non operatur; plenitudo ergo legis est dilectio. [11]Et hoc scientes tempus quia hora est iam vos de somno surgere, nunc enim propior est nobis salus quam cum credidimus. [12]Nox processit, dies autem appropiavit. Abiciamus ergo opera tenebrarum et induamur arma lucis. [13]Sicut in die honeste ambulemus: non in comissationibus et ebrietatibus, non in cubilibus et impudicitiis, non in contentione et aemulatione; [14]sed induite Dominum Iesum Christum et carnis curam ne feceritis in concupiscentiis. [14] [1]Infirmum autem in fide assumite, non in disceptationibus cogitationum. [2]Alius enim credit manducare omnia; qui autem infirmus est, holus manducat. [3]Is qui manducat,

other moral rules cease to apply. "The faithful are obliged to acknowledge and respect the specific moral precepts declared and taught by the Church in the name of God, the Creator and Lord. When the Apostle Paul sums up the fulfilment of the law in the precept of love of neighbour as oneself (cf. Rom 13: 8-10), he is not weakening the commandments but reinforcing them, since he is revealing their requirements and their gravity. *Love of God* and of one's neighbour can not be separated from the observance of the commandments of the covenant renewed in the blood of Jesus Christ and in the gift of the Spirit" (John Paul II, *Veritatis splendor*, 76).

In his exhortation in vv. 11–14, Paul invites his readers to be vigilant, to "know what hour it is" (v. 11), that is, to remember that Christ has already obtained salvation for us, and that he will come again at the end of time. Jesus came into the world by his Incarnation; he enters to souls through grace; and he will come at the end of time as Judge. Rising like the sun, he dispelled the darkness when he came into the world, and he continues to dispel whatever darkness

remains in souls as his influence on the hearts of men increases. Theodoret of Cyrrhus comments, "Thus, the age of ignorance is referred to as 'night' and 'day' dawns with the coming of our Lord" (*Interpretatio in Romanos*, ad loc.). The Church uses this Pauline text in the liturgy for Advent, the time preceding the annual celebration of Christ's birth, to help us prepare for the definitive coming of the Lord.

14:1–15:13 The early Christian communities frequently met for fraternal meals linked to the celebration of the Eucharist (cf. 1 Cor 11:17–22 and note); so the question of lawful and unlawful types of food was of practical relevance. It is likely that the first evangelizers in Rome included people who had come from Jerusalem and still held to Mosaic prescriptions and Jewish traditions (concerning food and how it was to be prepared, and observance of the Jewish calendar, with its sabbaths and various feastdays), and they may have influenced other Jewish converts. However, other Christians, of pagan background, did not consider themselves bound by these rules, for they knew that Jesus Christ had freed

Mt 7:1
Jas 4:11–12
Rom 6:15

Gal 4:10

1 Cor 10:30
1 Tim 4:4
Col 2:16

Rom 6:10–11

2 Cor 5:15
1 Thess 5:10
Lk 20:38
Gal 2:19
Acts 10:42

Mt 25:31
Acts 17:31
2 Cor 5:10
Rom 2:6–8

Is 45:23; 49:18
Phil 2:10–11

Gal 6:5

abstains pass judgment on him who eats; for God has welcomed him. [4]Who are you to pass judgment on the servant of another? It is before his own master that he stands or falls. And he will be upheld, for the Master is able to make him stand.

[5]One man esteems one day as better than another, while another man esteems all days alike. Let every one be fully convinced in his own mind. [6]He who observes the day, observes it in honour of the Lord. He also who eats, eats in honour of the Lord, since he gives thanks to God; while he who abstains, abstains in honour of the Lord and gives thanks to God. [7]None of us lives to himself, and none of us dies to himself. [8]If we live, we live to the Lord, and if we die, we die to the Lord; so then, whether we live or whether we die, we are the Lord's. [9]For to this end Christ died and lived again, that he might be Lord both of the dead and of the living.

[10]Why do you pass judgment on your brother? Or you, why do you despise your brother? For we shall all stand before the judgment seat of God; [11]for it is written,

"As I live, says the Lord, every knee shall bow to me,
and every tongue shall give praise[u] to God."

[12]So each of us shall give account of himself to God.

non manducantem non spernat; et qui non manducat, manducantem non iudicet, Deus enim illum assumpsit. [4]Tu quis es, qui iudices alienum servum? Suo domino stat aut cadit; stabit autem, potens est enim Dominus statuere illum. [5]Nam alius iudicat inter diem et diem, alius iudicat omnem diem; unusquisque in suo sensu abundet. [6]Qui sapit diem, Domino sapit; et qui manducat, Domino manducat, gratias enim agit Deo; et qui non manducat, Domino non manducat et gratias agit Deo. [7]Nemo enim nostrum sibi vivit et nemo sibi moritur; [8]sive enim vivimus, Domino vivimus, sive morimur, Domino morimur. Sive ergo vivimus, sive morimur, Domini sumus. [9]In hoc enim Christus et mortuus est et vixit, ut et mortuorum et vivorum dominetur. [10]Tu autem quid iudicas fratrem tuum? Aut tu quare spernis fratrem tuum? Omnes enim stabimus ante tribunal Dei; [11]scriptum est enim: «Vivo ego, dicit Dominus, / mihi flectetur omne genu, / et omnis lingua confitebitur Deo». [12]Itaque unusquisque nostrum pro se rationem reddet Deo. [13]Non ergo amplius invicem iudicemus, sed hoc iudicate magis, ne ponatis offendiculum fratri vel scandalum.

them from observance of the Law. The "strong" (15:1) seems to mean Christians who were confident about eating any kind of food; the "weak" were those who (whether of Jewish or Gentile background) had qualms about eating food declared in the Old Testament to be unclean. However, it was not a matter of there being groups or factions within the Roman community, as was the case in Corinth at that time (cf. 1 Cor 1:10–17).

Paul tells the Romans that the criteria they should apply are love and mutual respect: they should put themselves in the shoes of their neighbour (14:1–12), always avoid injuring others (14:13–23), and in all things follow the example set by Christ (15:1–13), being understanding and accommodating (see 15:7). It is a catechesis that "also teaches us to deal with cases of conscience in the light of our relationship to Christ and to the Church" (*Catechism of the Catholic Church*, 1971).

14:1–12 It appears that the "strong" looked down on the "weak", who in turn were shocked by the freedom of spirit of the former and

harshly criticized them. The Apostle addresses them all in a fatherly way, exhorting the weak not to rashly judge the strong, and appealing to the strong to show their respect for the weak. Charity is a necessary virtue, as is respect for the freedom of others.

The Apostle gives theological reasons for the practice of fraternal charity and freedom (vv. 7–9): no Christian lives or dies to himself alone; every Christian must also live and die "to the Lord", to whom, eventually, an account must be given. In this connexion, St John Chrysostom comments: "Our God wants us to live, and not to die; and he wills these more than we do ourselves" (*In Romanos*, 25, 3). And St Gregory the Great says: "The saints, therefore, do not live and do not die for themselves. They do not live for themselves, because in all that they do they strive for spiritual gain: by praying, preaching and persevering in good works, they seek the increase of the citizens of the heavenly fatherland. Nor do they die for themselves because men see them glorifying God by their death, hastening to reach him through death" (*Homiliae in Ezechielem*, 2, 9, 16).

u Or *confess*

Not leading others astray

[13]Then let us no more pass judgment on one another, but rather decide never to put a stumbling block or hindrance in the way of a brother. [14]I know and am persuaded in the Lord Jesus that nothing is unclean in itself; but it is unclean for any one who thinks it unclean.* [15]If your brother is being injured by what you eat, you are no longer walking in love. Do not let what you eat cause the ruin of one for whom Christ died. [16]So do not let your good be spoken of as evil. [17]For the kingdom of God is not food and drink but righteousness and peace and joy in the Holy Spirit; [18]he who thus serves Christ is acceptable to God and approved by men. [19]Let us then pursue what makes for peace and for mutual upbuilding. [20]Do not, for the sake of food, destroy the work of God. Everything is indeed clean, but it is wrong for any one to make others fall by what he eats; [21]it is right not to eat meat or drink wine or do anything that makes your brother stumble.[v] [22]The faith that you have, keep between yourself and God; happy is he who has no reason to judge himself for what he approves. [23]But he who has doubts is condemned, if he eats, because he does not act from faith; for whatever does not proceed from faith is sin.[w]

Mt 15:10–20
Acts 10:15
1 Cor 8:9–10

1 Cor 10:25
1 Tim 4:3–4
Tit 1:15

1 Cor 8:10–13

Gal 5:22
1 Cor 8:8

Rom 12:17–18
1 Thess 1:6
Tit 1:15

1 Cor 8:13

Jas 4:17–44
1 Cor 8:7

The example of Christ

15 [1]We who are strong ought to bear with the failings of the weak, and not to please ourselves; [2]let each of us please his neighbour for his good, to edify him. [3]For Christ did not please himself; but, as it is written, "The reproaches of those who reproached thee fell on me." [4]For whatever was written in former days was writ-

1 Cor 9:19, 22;
10:24, 33
Gal 6:2
Rom 14:19
1 Cor 8:1
2 Cor 13:5
Ps 69:9
1 Cor 6:6, 11
2 Tim 3:16

[14]Scio et certus sum in Domino Iesu quia nihil commune per seipsum, nisi ei, qui existimat quid commune esse, illi commune est. [15]Si enim propter cibum frater tuus contristatur, iam non secundum caritatem ambulas. Noli cibo tuo illum perdere, pro quo Christus mortuus est! [16]Non ergo blasphemetur bonum vestrum! [17]Non est enim regnum Dei esca et potus, sed iustitia et pax et gaudium in Spiritu Sancto; [18]qui enim in hoc servit Christo, placet Deo et probatus est hominibus. [19]Itaque, quae pacis sunt, sectemur et quae aedificationis sunt in invicem. [20]Noli propter escam destruere opus Dei! Omnia quidem munda sunt, sed malum est homini, qui per offendiculum manducat. [21]Bonum est non manducare carnem et non bibere vinum neque id, in quo frater tuus offendit. [22]Tu, quam fidem habes, penes temetipsum habe coram Deo. Beatus, qui non iudicat semetipsum in eo quod probat. [23]Qui autem discernit si manducaverit, damnatus est, quia non ex fide; omne autem, quod non ex fide, peccatum est. [15][1]Debemus autem nos firmiores imbecillitates infirmorum sustinere, et non nobis placere. [2]Unusquisque nostrum proximo placeat in bonum ad aedificationem; [3]etenim Christus non sibi placuit, sed sicut scriptum est: «Improperia improperantium tibi ceciderunt super me».

14:13–23 These verses are a call to Christians to help one another for the sake of "mutual upbuilding" and peace (v. 19) and to avoid giving scandal, not only by sin but by doing anything which in itself is morally neutral but which could scandalize others. However, in trying to avoid any forms of behaviour that might shock others, we should not act against our conscience. Jesus himself experienced the offence taken by Pharisees (see Mt 15:14): theirs was a false scandal, for they were only seeking excuses to avoid accepting the truth.

When he declared that all food was clean, Jesus pointed out that "the things which come out of a man are what defile him" (Mk 7:15; cf. Mt 15:16–20). The Apostle applies this teaching here (vv. 22–23) and says that "nothing is unclean in itself" (vv. 14; cf. v. 20). Therefore, there is nothing wrong in the behaviour of the "strong", but there would be if it caused their

brethren to stumble (cf. vv. 20–21; 1 Cor 8:9–13). And he adds: "whatever does not proceed from faith is sin" (v. 23). "Faith" here means the certain conviction of the judgment of conscience which dictates that something is to be done or avoided; but the authority of conscience is not absolute: a person may do something wrong and yet think it good—in which case his conscience is "certain" but not "right". Therefore, we should try to develop a right conscience in order to seek and follow God's will as found in his revelation; and if we find we are in error, we should take corrective measures immediately.

15:1–13 The reason why the strong should help the weak and not simply please themselves (v. 1) comes from Christ's example: he "did not please himself" (v. 3) but bore our sins in his body and healed us by his wounds (see 1 Pet 2:24; Is 53:5–6). Jesus died so that we should all "with one voice" (v.

v Other ancient authorities add *or be upset or be weakened*   w Other authorities, some ancient, insert here Ch 16:25–27

1 Mac 12:9
2 Mac 15:9
ten for our instruction, that by steadfastness and by the encouragement of the scriptures we might have hope. [5]May the God of steadfastness and encouragement grant you

Phil 2:1–4
to live in such harmony with one another, in accord with Christ Jesus, [6]that together you may with one voice glorify the God and Father of our Lord Jesus Christ.

Mt 15:24
Acts 3:25–26
[7]Welcome one another, therefore, as Christ has welcomed you, for the glory of God. [8]For I tell you that Christ became a servant to the circumcised to show God's

Ex 34:6
truthfulness, in order to confirm the promises given to the patriarchs, [9]and in order that the Gentiles might glorify God for his mercy. As it is written,

Ps 18:49
> "Therefore I will praise thee among the Gentiles,
>   and sing to thy name";

[10]and again it is said,

Deut 32:43 (LXX)
> "Rejoice, O Gentiles, with his people";

[11]and again,

Ps 117:1
> "Praise the Lord, all Gentiles,
>   and let all the peoples praise him";

[12]and further Isaiah says,

Is 11:10
Rev 5:5
Gen 49:10
> "The root of Jesse shall come,
>   he who rises to rule the Gentiles;
> in him shall the Gentiles hope."

[13]May the God of hope fill you with all joy and peace in believing, so that by the power of the Holy Spirit you may abound in hope.

7. CONCLUSION AND FAREWELL*

Paul's ministry

Phil 1:9–10
[14]I myself am satisfied about you, my brethren, that you yourselves are full of goodness, filled with all knowledge, and able to instruct one another. [15]But on some

[4]Quaecumque enim antea scripta sunt, ad nostram doctrinam scripta sunt, ut per patientiam et consolationem Scripturarum spem habeamus. [5]Deus autem patientiae et solacii det vobis idipsum sapere in alterutrum secundum Christum Iesum, [6]ut unanimes uno ore glorificetis Deum et Patrem Domini nostri Iesu Christi. [7]Propter quod suscipite invicem, sicut et Christus suscepit vos, in gloriam Dei. [8]Dico enim Christum ministrum fuisse circumcisionis propter veritatem Dei ad confirmandas promissiones patrum, [9]gentes autem propter misericordiam glorificare Deum, sicut scriptum est: «Propter hoc confitebor tibi in gentibus, / et nomini tuo cantabo». [10]Et iterum dicit: «Laetamini, gentes, cum plebe eius». [11]Et iterum: «Laudate, omnes gentes, Dominum, / et magnificent eum omnes populi». [12]Et rursus Isaias ait: «Erit radix Iesse, / et qui exsurget regere gentes: in

6) glorify God. And, although Christ addressed the Jews in the first instance, he also offered his welcome to Gentiles. By his life he brought to fulfilment the promises made to the Israelites that the Gentiles too would glorify God. This shows that God is faithful to his promises (v. 8) and his mercy extends to all: his blessings extend also to those who do not belong to Israel according to the flesh. In support of what he says, Paul cites the Prophets, the Law and the Writings, the three Jewish divisions of Holy Scripture (vv. 9–12).

The teaching is very clear: we need to practise charity by having the same mind as Christ had (cf. Phil 2:5–8), to the point of loving others as he loves them (cf. Jn 13:34–35; 15:12–13; 1 Jn 3:16; 4:11; Eph 5:1–2), excluding no one:

"Turn your gaze constantly to Jesus who, without ceasing to be God, humbled himself and took the nature of a slave (cf. Phil 2:6–7), in order to serve us. Only by following in his direction will we find ideals that are worthwhile. Love seeks union, identification with the beloved. United to Christ, we shall be drawn to imitate his life of dedication, his unlimited love and his sacrifice unto death. Christ brings us face to face with the ultimate choice: either we spend our life in selfish isolation, or we devote ourselves and all our energies to the service of others" (St Josemaría Escrivá, *Friends of God*, 236).

*15:14—16:27 In the form of an epilogue, St Paul explains why he has written to the faithful in

points I have written to you very boldly by way of reminder, because of the grace Rom 1:5-6,13
given me by God ¹⁶to be a minister of Christ Jesus to the Gentiles in the priestly Rom 1:9; 11:13; 12:1
Phil 2:17
service of the gospel of God, so that the offering of the Gentiles may be acceptable, 2 Cor 3:5–6
sanctified by the Holy Spirit.* ¹⁷In Christ Jesus, then, I have reason to be proud of Heb 5:1
Gal 2:7
my work for God. ¹⁸For I will not venture to speak of anything except what Christ Rom 3:27
has wrought through me to win obedience from the Gentiles, by word and deed, ¹⁹by Mk 16:17
2 Cor 12:12
the power of signs and wonders, by the power of the Holy Spirit, so that from Acts 1:8
Col 1:25
Jerusalem and as far round as Illyricum I have fully preached the gospel of Christ, 2 Cor 10:15–16;
12:12
²⁰thus making it my ambition to preach the gospel, not where Christ has already 1 Cor 3:10–12
been named, lest I build on another man's foundation, ²¹but as it is written,

> "They shall see who have never been told of him, Is 52:15
> and they shall understand who have never heard of him."

Journeys planned Rom 1:10–15
1 Thess 2:18

²²This is the reason why I have so often been hindered from coming to you. ²³But
now, since I no longer have any room for work in these regions, and since I have 1 Cor 16:6
longed for many years to come to you, ²⁴I hope to see you in passing as I go to Acts 11:29–30;19:21

eo gentes sperabunt». ¹³Deus autem spei repleat vos omni gaudio et pace in credendo, ut abundetis in spe in virtute Spiritus Sancti. ¹⁴Certus sum autem, fratres mei, et ego ipse de vobis, quoniam et ipsi pleni estis bonitate, repleti omni scientia, ita ut possitis et alterutrum monere. ¹⁵Audacius autem scripsi vobis ex parte, tamquam in memoriam vos reducens propter gratiam, quae data est mihi a Deo, ¹⁶ut sim minister Christi Iesu ad gentes, consecrans evangelium Dei, ut fiat oblatio gentium accepta, sanctificata in Spiritu Sancto. ¹⁷Habeo igitur gloriationem in Christo Iesu ad Deum; ¹⁸non enim audebo aliquid loqui eorum, quae per me non effecit Christus in oboedientiam gentium, verbo et factis, ¹⁹in virtute signorum et prodigiorum, in virtute Spiritus, ita ut ab Ierusalem et per circuitum usque in Illyricum repleverim evangelium Christi, ²⁰sic autem contendens praedicare evangelium, non ubi nominatus est Christus, ne super alienum fundamentum aedificarem, ²¹sed sicut scriptum est: «*Quibus non est annuntiatum de eo, videbunt; / et, qui non audierunt, intellegent*». ²²Propter quod et impediebar plurimum venire ad vos; ²³nunc vero ulterius locum non habens in his regionibus, cupiditatem autem habens veniendi ad vos ex multis iam annis, ²⁴cum in Hispaniam proficisci coepero, spero enim quod praeteriens videam vos et a vobis deducar illuc, si vobis primum ex parte fruitus fuero. ²⁵Nunc autem proficiscor in Ierusalem minis-

Rome (15:14–21), outlines his future plans (15:22–33), and ends his letter with a long and warm series of greetings and introductions (16:1–24). The final verses are in praise of God through Jesus Christ (16:25–27), so the letter ends as it began, in the name of God and of Jesus Christ.

15:14–21 The part of the letter dealing with morality began by exhorting readers to offer themselves as a sacrifice pleasing to God (12:1). Now Paul ends by explaining that the reason he was inspired to write the letter has to do with the ministry Christ entrusted to him—to preach the Gospel to the Gentiles (cf. 1:5) so as to make them an offering acceptable to God. Previously, only the Jewish people could be considered a priestly people (see Ex 19:5–6), but with the coming of Christ, the Gentiles too are an offering "acceptable, sanctified by the Holy Spirit" (v. 16). This mission to the Gentiles has brought Paul across the empire from Jerusalem as far as Illyricum, that is, the eastern Adriatic (v. 19); it is why he is writing to the Romans (vv. 14–17)

and why he plans to journey to Spain (15:24, 28–29).

15:22–33 Paul sees his work in the East as having achieved a certain stability; now he prepares to journey west, to Spain, to regions where the Gospel has not yet been proclaimed (see 15:20). For this he counts on help from the faithful in Rome (v. 24), which he plans to visit after bringing the collections taken up in Macedonia and Achaia to Jerusalem (vv. 25–27; cf. 2 Cor 8:1—9:15). He appeals to the Romans for prayers for the success of his trip (vv. 30–33), "because when many humble souls gather together in prayer, they form a great multitude, and their prayers cannot go unheard" (Ambrosiaster, *Ad Romanos*, ad loc.).

The first Christians saw themselves as being bound together by charity and by their shared vocation to holiness, so they had no reservations about referring to each other as "saints" (v. 25; see also 1:7; Acts 9:13; 1 Cor 1:2; Heb 3:1; 13:24; Jude 3).

Spain, and to be sped on my journey there by you, once I have enjoyed your company for a little. ²⁵At present, however, I am going to Jerusalem with aid for the saints. ²⁶For Macedonia and Achaia have been pleased to make some contribution for the poor among the saints at Jerusalem; ²⁷they were pleased to do it, and indeed they are in debt to them, for if the Gentiles have come to share in their spiritual blessings, they ought also to be of service to them in material blessings. ²⁸When therefore I have completed this, and have delivered to them what has been raised,ˣ I shall go on by way of you to Spain; ²⁹and I know that when I come to you I shall come in the fullness of the blessingʸ of Christ.

³⁰I appeal to you, brethren, by our Lord Jesus Christ and by the love of the Spirit, to strive together with me in your prayers to God on my behalf, ³¹that I may be delivered from the unbelievers in Judea, and that my service for Jerusalem may be acceptable to the saints, ³²so that by God's will I may come to you with joy and be refreshed in your company. ³³The God of peace be with you all. Amen.

Greetings and recommendations

16 ¹I commend to you our sister Phoebe, a deaconess of the church at Cenchreae, ²that you may receive her in the Lord as befits the saints, and help her in whatever she may require from you, for she has been a helper of many and of myself as well.

³Greet Prisca and Aquila, my fellow workers in Christ Jesus, ⁴who risked their necks for my life, to whom not only I but also all the churches of the Gentiles give thanks; ⁵greet also the church in their house. Greet my beloved Epaenetus, who was the first convert in Asia for Christ. ⁶Greet Mary, who has worked hard among you. ⁷Greet Andronicus and Junias, my kinsmen and my fellow prisoners; they are men of note among the apostles, and they were in Christ before me. ⁸Greet Ampliatus, my beloved in the Lord. ⁹Greet Urbanus, our fellow worker in Christ, and my beloved Stachys. ¹⁰Greet Apelles, who is approved in Christ. Greet those who belong

Marginal references:
Acts 20:22–23
1 Cor 16:1
2 Cor 8:1–6; 9: 1-2
Rom 12:13
1 Cor 9:11
Gal 6:6
Rom 11:17
2 Cor 1:11
Phil 1:27
Col 4:2–3
2 Thess 3:1
Acts 20:3, 23; 21:10, 17, 27
Phil 4:9
1 Cor 14:33
2 Cor 13:11
1 Thess 5:23
2 Thess 3:16
Acts 18:18
Acts 18:2–3, 26
1 Cor 16:19
2 Tim 4:19
Col 4:15
Philem 2
1 Cor 16:15, 19

trare sanctis; ²⁶probaverunt enim Macedonia et Achaia communicationem aliquam facere in pauperes sanctorum, qui sunt in Ierusalem. ²⁷Placuit enim eis, et debitores sunt eorum; nam si spiritalibus eorum communicaverunt gentes, debent et in carnalibus ministrare eis. ²⁸Hoc igitur cum consummavero et assignavero eis fructum hunc, proficiscar per vos in Hispaniam; ²⁹scio autem quoniam veniens ad vos, in abundantia benedictionis Christi veniam. ³⁰Obsecro autem vos, fratres, per Dominum nostrum Iesum Christum et per caritatem Spiritus, ut concertemini mecum in orationibus pro me ad Deum, ³¹ut liberer ab infidelibus, qui sunt in Iudaea, et ministerium meum pro Ierusalem acceptum sit sanctis, ³²ut veniens ad vos in gaudio per voluntatem Dei refrigerer vobiscum. ³³Deus autem pacis sit cum omnibus vobis. Amen. [16] ¹Commendo autem vobis Phoebem sororem nostram, quae est ministra ecclesiae, quae est Cenchreis, ²ut eam suscipiatis in Domino digne sanctis et assistatis ei in quocumque negotio vestri indiguerit, etenim ipsa astitit multis et mihi ipsi. ³Salutate Priscam et Aquilam adiutores meos in Christo Iesu, ⁴qui pro anima mea suas cervices supposuerunt, quibus non solus ego gratias ago, sed et cunctae ecclesiae gentium, ⁵et domesticam eorum ecclesiam. Salutate Epaenetum dilectum mihi, primitias Asiae in Christo. ⁶Salutate Mariam, quae multum laboravit in vobis. ⁷Salutate Andronicum et Iuniam cognatos meos et concaptivos meos, qui sunt nobiles in apostolis, qui et ante me fuerunt in Christo. ⁸Salutate Ampliatum dilectissimum mihi in Domino. ⁹Salutate Urbanum adiutorem nostrum in Christo et Stachyn dilectum meum. ¹⁰Salutate Apellem probatum in Christo. Salutate eos, qui sunt ex Aristobuli.

16:1–23 This long sequence of affectionate greetings shows that the early Christians formed one family, in which each saw the others as brothers and sisters. They included people of every walk of life, all united by the same faith and the bond of charity: "[They were] families who lived in union with Christ and who made him known to others. Small Christian communities which were centres for the spreading of the Gospel and its message. Families no different from other families of those times, but living with a new spirit, which spread to all those who were in contact with them. This is what the first Christians were, and this is what we have to be—sowers of peace and joy, the peace and joy that Jesus has brought to us" (St Josemaría Escrivá, *Christ Is Passing By*, 30).

As we can see from the names mentioned here, the Romans included people from many parts of the empire, from different cultures and social classes. Some have Greek names, some Latin or Jewish. As many as twenty-seven people

x Greek *sealed to them this fruit*   y Other ancient authorities insert *of the gospel*

to the family of Aristobulus. ¹¹Greet my kinsman Herodion. Greet those in the Lord who belong to the family of Narcissus. ¹²Greet those workers in the Lord, Tryphaena and Tryphosa. Greet the beloved Persis, who has worked hard in the Lord. ¹³Greet Rufus, eminent in the Lord, also his mother and mine. ¹⁴Greet Asyncritus, Phlegon, Hermes, Patrobas, Hermas, and the brethren who are with them. ¹⁵Greet Philologus, Julia, Nereus and his sister, and Olympas, and all the saints who are with them. ¹⁶Greet one another with a holy kiss. All the churches of Christ greet you.*

Mk 15:21

¹⁷I appeal to you, brethren, to take note of those who create dissensions and difficulties, in opposition to the doctrine which you have been taught; avoid them. ¹⁸For such persons do not serve our Lord Christ, but their own appetites,ᶻ and by fair and flattering words they deceive the hearts of the simple-minded. ¹⁹For while your obedience is known to all, so that I rejoice over you, I would have you wise as to what is good and guileless as to what is evil; ²⁰then the God of peace will soon crush Satan under your feet. The grace of our Lord Jesus Christ be with you.ᵃ

Acts 20:37
1 Thess 5: 26
1 Cor 16:20
2 Cor 13:12
1 Pet 5:14
Mt 7:15
Gal 6:11
1 Tim 1:3
2 Jn 10
Rom 6:17
2 Pet 2:3
Phil 3:19
Col 2:4
Tit 1:10
Phil 3:19
Rom 1:5, 8
Mt 10:16
1 Cor 14:20
Gen 3:15

²¹Timothy, my fellow worker, greets you; so do Lucius and Jason and Sosipater, my kinsmen.

²²I Tertius, the writer of this letter, greet you in the Lord.

²³Gaius, who is host to me and to the whole church, greets you. Erastus, the city treasurer, and our brother Quartus, greet you.ᵇ

Acts 16:1; 13:1;
17:5; 19:22; 20:4
Phil 2:19
1 Cor 1:14

Doxology

²⁵Now to him who is able to strengthen you according to my gospel and the preaching of Jesus Christ, according to the revelation of the mystery which was kept secret for long ages ²⁶but is now disclosed and through the prophetic writings is made known to all nations, according to the command of the eternal God, to bring about the obedience of faith—²⁷to the only wise God be glory for evermore through Jesus Christ! Amen.

Eph 1:9; 3:5, 9
Col 1:26

Acts 15:14
1 Pet 1:20
Eph 3:4
Rom 1:5
2 Tim 1:10
1 Tim 1:17
Jude 25
Rom 1:25

¹¹Salutate Herodionem cognatum meum. Salutate eos, qui sunt ex Narcissi, qui sunt in Domino. ¹²Salutate Tryphaenam et Tryphosam, quae laborant in Domino. Salutate Persidam carissimam, quae multum laboravit in Domino. ¹³Salutate Rufum electum in Domino et matrem eius et meam. ¹⁴Salutate Asyncritum, Phlegonta, Hermen, Patroban, Hermam et, qui cum eis sunt, fratres. ¹⁵Salutate Philologum et Iuliam, Nereum et sororem eius et Olympam et omnes, qui cum eis sunt, sanctos. ¹⁶Salutate invicem in osculo sancto. Salutant vos omnes ecclesiae Christi. ¹⁷Rogo autem vos, fratres, ut observetis eos, qui dissensiones et offendicula praeter doctrinam, quam vos didicistis, faciunt, et declinate ab illis; ¹⁸huiusmodi enim Domino nostro Christo non serviunt sed suo ventri, et per dulces sermones et benedictiones seducunt corda innocentium. ¹⁹Vestra enim oboedientia ad omnes pervenit; gaudeo igitur in vobis, sed volo vos sapientes esse in bono et simplices in malo. ²⁰Deus autem pacis conteret Satanam sub pedibus vestris velociter. Gratia Domini nostri Iesu vobiscum. ²¹Salutat vos Timotheus adiutor meus et Lucius et Iason et Sosipater cognati mei. ²²Saluto vos ego Tertius, qui scripsi epistulam in Domino. ²³Salutat vos Gaius hospes meus et universae ecclesiae. Salutat vos Erastus arcarius civitatis et Quartus frater.⁽²⁴⁾ ²⁵Ei autem, qui potens est vos confirmare iuxta evangelium meum et praedicationem Iesu Christi secundum revelationem mysterii temporibus aeternis taciti, ²⁶manifestati autem nunc, et per scripturas Prophetarum secundum praeceptum aeterni Dei ad oboeditionem fidei in cunctis gentibus patefacti, ²⁷soli sapienti Deo per Iesum Christum, cui gloria in saecula. Amen.

were mentioned by name; some appear elsewhere in the New Testament; most do not. Paul introduces Phoebe at some length (vv. 1–2); a deaconess with the church at Cenchreae (Corinth's port on the Aegean), she seems to have been the bearer of the letter; this suggests that Paul was in Corinth when he wrote the letter.

The warning in vv. 17–18 probably refers to Judaizers who were making a parade of their religiosity and preaching a way of life they claimed to be more perfect than that of others.

16:25–27 St Paul finishes this letter, unusually, with a doxology—to "the only wise God", through Jesus Christ. A very ancient papyrus places this verse in 15:33; other manuscripts put it at the end of chapter 14 and then repeat it at the end of the letter. These variations derive from the liturgical use of the letter: chapters 15 and 16 were sometimes not read out because of their more personal nature.

z Greek *their own belly* (Phil 3:19) a Other ancient authorities omit this sentence b Other ancient authorities insert verse 24, *The grace of our Lord Jesus Christ be with you all. Amen*

THE FIRST LETTER OF PAUL TO THE

CORINTHIANS

Introduction

In the New Testament's collection of St Paul's letters, the two letters to the Corinthians come immediately after that to the Romans—a sign of the importance given them from the very beginning, on account of their length, the range of themes they cover and the way these themes are explored. From very early on Christians held these letters in high regard: they had been written by Paul, to a community founded by himself in an important city of the empire. A city that enjoyed great fame during the Greek period, Corinth was re-founded by Julius Caesar in 44 BC and soon became very influential. Set on the isthmus of the same name, with two ports, one on the Aegean Sea and one on the Adriatic, it was the capital of the Roman province of Achaia and a key Mediterranean centre of commerce. It was also one of the largest cities of its kind, with a population of around 100,000, and it was notorious for its decadent moral climate.

1. STRUCTURE AND CONTENT

The many problems encountered in the church of Corinth (and dealt with in the letter) and the markedly pastoral nature of the text make it difficult to divide into sections. Still, we can see that it has an introduction, and an epilogue, with the body of the letter falling into three parts.

The introduction (1:1–9) contains the usual words of greeting (vv. 1–3) and a thanksgiving hymn (vv. 4–9). The first of the three parts (1:10—4:21) deals with divisions among the faithful and contains forthright criticism of factions and rival groups. The second part (5:1—11:34) consists of the Apostle's reply to major problems brought to his attention by third parties or by the Corinthians themselves—a painful case of incest (5:1–13), appeals made to pagan courts to solve internal church problems (6:1–11), and prevalent sins against chastity (6:12–20). Among the matters raised by the Corinthians themselves, Paul deals at length with marriage and celibacy (7:1–40), the question of eating food that has been sacrificed to idols (8:1–10:33), and how the faithful should comport themselves at liturgical assemblies (11:1–34). The third part (12:1—15:58) covers two very theological subjects—the diverse gifts and their relationship to charity, on the one hand; and, on the other, the resurrection of Christ, and of all the dead. The epilogue (16:1–24) deals with the collection to be made to relieve the Christians in Jerusalem and outlines the next journeys planned by the Apostle.

2. CONTEXT

The church of Corinth was founded by St Paul with the help of Silas and Timothy in the year 50–51, during his second missionary journey (which took place in 50 to 53; see Acts 18:1–18). St Paul had arrived in the city "in much fear and trembling" (1 Cor 2:3); he had just been in Athens where, despite his brilliant discourse in the Areopagus, he failed to make many converts (see Acts 17:16–34). Initially he stayed and worked in the home of Aquila and Priscilla, a Christian couple who had been expelled from Rome because of Claudius' recent edict against Jews (see Acts 18:2). In line with his custom, he preached in the synagogue to begin with—to Jews and to Greeks who believed in the God of Israel. Later, because of the opposition he encountered from Jews, he decided to focus on preaching to Gentiles (see Acts 18:5–6).

Paul made many converts in Corinth—Crispus, the ruler of the synagogue, being particularly prominent—but he experienced his share of setbacks, too, during the year and a half that he spent in the city. In fact, on one occasion our Lord appeared to him in a vision, at night, to raise his spirits (cf. Acts 18:7–10). Increasing opposition from Jews ultimately led to charges being brought against Paul to Gallio, the Roman proconsul (see Acts 18:12–17). Paul appeared before Gallio around the end of 51 or the start of 52. He left Corinth shortly after that, boarding a ship bound for Syria with Aquila and Priscilla (see Acts 18:18).

The Apostle made a number of subsequent visits to the city. During his third missionary journey, at the time when he was founding the church in Ephesus (see Acts 19:1–41), he probably paid a visit to Corinth, in the year 57 (cf. the note on 2 Cor 1:15—2:4); on that occasion, he, or one of his co-workers, was the subject of an especially serious insult (cf. the note on 2 Cor 2:5–11). Later, after writing the Second Letter to the Corinthians from Macedonia, he spent the winter of 57–58 in the city (see Acts 20:1–3).

All the indications are that he wrote this first letter at the end of his stay in Ephesus, probably in the spring of 57, around Passover time (see 1 Cor 16:8), given that he mentions the feast of Unleavened Bread (see 1 Cor 5:7–8) and compares the self-denial that Christians practise to the athletic training of runners in the stadium (see 1 Cor 9:24–27), an allusion to the Isthmus Games held in springtime every second year.[1]

Given the close and frequent commercial ties between Corinth and Ephesus, it is not surprising that St Paul (living in Ephesus at the time) was well aware of the situation in the church of Corinth. In the letter, he mentions that he has been told "by Chloe's people" (1 Cor 1:11) about certain abuses that had found their way into that community: there were various parties in dispute (see 1 Cor 1:11ff); great laxity applied in the area of chastity (see 1 Cor 6:12ff): there was even a case of incest (see 1 Cor 5:1ff); Christians had brought cases before pagan courts (see 1 Cor 6:1ff); some women behaved without due decorum at liturgical assemblies (see 1 Cor 11:2ff; 14:34ff); and there were irregularities in the celebration of the Eucharist (see 1 Cor 11:17ff). Moreover, the community itself had sent a delegation to Paul, composed of Stephanas, Fortunatus and Achaicus (see 1 Cor 16:17), bearing a letter seeking the Apostle's advice on a number of matters[2]—marriage and virginity (see 1 Cor 7:1ff), the lawfulness of eating food offered to idols (see 1 Cor 8:1ff), charisms and their proper use (see 1 Cor 12:1ff), and the resurrection of the dead (see 1 Cor 15:1ff).

3. MESSAGE

The First Letter to the Corinthians is particularly important for its doctrinal content. Its themes include divine wisdom and human wisdom, criteria that should govern Christian conduct, various aspects of morality, and the life to come. The Apostle's rich personality is portrayed very clearly, and he managed to combine theological depth and pastoral generosity of spirit. All the themes of the letter deserve commentary; this is provided in the notes, but there are three themes that deserve special attention—the Church, the Eucharist and the resurrection of the dead.

---

1 See Xenophon, *Hellenica*, 4, 5, 1.   **2** Cf. 1 Cor 7:1; similar points are raised in 7:25; 8:1; 12:1.

The Church

The letter's basic premise is that the Church is a supernatural reality: it has been founded by Christ, Christ is its head, and it is Christ who governs it, through his ministers. Christ is the basis of the life of the Church and of its unity and, therefore, Christians belong to Christ and no one else (cf. 1 Cor 3:23; and also 2 Cor 10:7). There is no room for factions or rival groups (cf. 1 Cor 1:10–11); people do not belong to the party of Paul or Apollos or Cephas; these messengers are not the source of Christian life.

The mystery of the Church and its fundamental unity are made very clear in the metaphors Paul uses in the letter: the Church is a field planted by God (see 1 Cor 3:6–9), a building he has erected (see 1 Cor 3:9, 11, 16). It is true that none of these metaphors can wholly explain the Church, but they do make it plain that the source of unity is God, who gives life to each of the plants in the field,[3] and who causes all the parts to form one building.[4] "We are the house of God [...]. The first stirrings of faith in our soul are like the cutting of wood in the forest or the quarrying of stone in the mountains. The catechumens are instructed, baptised and formed as wood and stone are carved and planed in the hands of craftsmen and carpenters. But they only form the house of God when they are held together by Love."[5]

Of key importance to a good understanding of the Church is its description as the Body of Christ. Paul's notion of the Church as a body goes beyond that of a social corporation, for between Christ and the Church, between Christ and Christians, a unity exists that is not just an agreement on goals, or a coming together for meetings; it is a living unity: Christ is the life of the Church and of Christians; Christ and the Church are inseparable. St Augustine writes: "Let us rejoice and give thanks to God, for not only have we become Christians, we have been made into Christ. Do you understand, brothers? Are you aware of the grace of God that is within us? Rejoice and be glad: we have been made into Christ. If he is the Head and we are his members, then the whole man is him and ourselves in him. The apostle Paul says so: the fullness of Christ is the Head and its members. What does 'the Head and its members' mean? Christ and the Church."[6]

The union between Christ and the Church does not prevent a person from being himself or herself. A Christian's personality does not disappear when he or she becomes a member of Christ, nor does the Church lose her identity on being configured to Christ. By differentiating Christ too much from the Church, one runs the risk of a kind of Nestorianism (which held that there were two distinct persons in Christ, one divine, one human); but if one conceived the unity of Christ and the Church in a way that denied each its own distinct personality, one would be making the same sort of mistake as the Monophysites, who refused to accept that Christ has two natures, one divine and one human.

The unity that exists among the members of the Mystical Body is not only an interior, spiritual unity; it also has a visible, structural dimension; this means that the variety of offices and ministries in the Church in no way detracts from a unity that is both spiritual and hierarchical: "As all the members of the human body, though they are many, form one body, so also are the faithful in Christ (cf. 1 Cor 12:12). Also, in the building up of Christ's Body various members and functions have their part to play. There is only one Spirit who, according to his own richness and the needs of the ministries, gives his different gifts for the welfare of the Church (cf. 1 Cor 12:1–11). What has a special place among these gifts is the grace of the apostles to whose author-

---

3 Cf. the allegory of the vine in Jn 15:1–8; and that of the olive tree in Rom 11:17–24. **4** This metaphor occurs in many New Testament passages; see, e.g., Mt 16:18; 1 Tim 3:15; Heb 3:1–6. **5** St Augustine, *Sermo*, 136, 1. **6** St Augustine, *In Ioannis Evangelium*, 21, 8.

ity the Spirit himself subjected even those who were endowed with charisms (cf. 1 Cor 14). Giving the body unity through himself and through his power and inner joining of the members, this same Spirit produces and urges love among the believers. From all this it follows that if one member endures anything, all the members co-endure it, and if one member is honoured, all the members together rejoice (cf. 1 Cor 12:26)."[7]

The Eucharist

At two points in the letter the Apostle mentions the Eucharist—first as an aside, when he is explaining why Christians may not attend banquets at pagan shrines (cf. 1 Cor 10:14–22); and later, in the course of correcting abuses that have arisen during the Eucharistic celebrations in Corinth (cf. 1 Cor 11:17–34). These two passages comprise the basic truths about the Eucharist— its institution by Christ himself; the fact that it is a sacrifice; the real presence of Christ under the appearances of bread and wine; and the connexions between our Lord's sacramental Body and his mystical Body, the Church.

St Paul narrates the institution of the Eucharist (see 1 Cor 11:23–25) in much the same way as St Luke. He also teaches that the Eucharist is *the* sacrifice, far beyond and incompatible with pagan sacrifices, and that the victim in the Eucharist was prefigured in the victims in Old Testament oblations (see 1 Cor 10:14–22).

Furthermore, Paul asserts the real presence of Christ in the Eucharist under the sacramental species of bread and wine: "Whoever eats, therefore, the bread or drinks the cup of the Lord in an unworthy manner will be guilty of profaning the body and blood of the Lord" (1 Cor 11:27). And he clearly establishes the connexions between the Eucharist (the sacramental Body of Christ) and the Church (his mystical Body): "Really partaking of the body of the Lord in the breaking of the Eucharistic bread, we are taken up into communion with Him and with one another. 'Because the bread is one, we, though many, are one body, all of us who partake of the one bread' (1 Cor 10:17). In this way all of us are made members of his body (cf. 1 Cor 12:27), 'but severally members one of another' (Rom 12:5)."[8]

The resurrection of the dead

The Christians of Corinth did not find it easy to accept the resurrection of the dead (see 1 Cor 15:12), for this truth of faith was very much at odds with Greek thought of the time. According to the Acts of the Apostles, Paul found this out for himself when he spoke in the Areopagus of Athens: "When they heard of the resurrection of the dead, some mocked; but others said, 'We will hear you again about this'" (Acts 17:32).

Here, as an introduction to this difficult truth, Paul deals first with the resurrection of Christ. The passage, written less than thirty years after the event, is very important as an argument for the historicity of the Resurrection, particularly because Christ's resurrection is presented as a truth deriving from apostolic Tradition: "I delivered to you as of first importance what I also received" (1 Cor 15:3). "The mystery of Christ's resurrection is a real event, with manifestations that were historically verified, as the New Testament bears witness."[9] The Apostle presents a long list of witnesses to the risen Christ—Peter, James the Less, all the apostles and five hundred brethren, most of whom were still alive and could testify to what they had seen (see 1 Cor 15:5–7). At the end, he adds his own testimony (see 1 Cor 15:8).

---

7 Vatican II, *Lumen gentium*, 7.   **8** Ibid.   **9** *Catechism of the Catholic Church*, 639.

However, the resurrection of Christ is not only an historical fact; it is also a mystery. The mystery centres on the glorified condition of the risen Christ. Thus, St Paul repeats several times the fact that Christ "appeared" (literally, "was seen", cf. 1 Cor 15:5, 6, 7, 8), giving us to understand that he showed himself only to those he chose to see him. "Christ's Resurrection was not a return to earthly life, as was the case with the raisings from the dead that he had performed before Easter: Jairus' daughter, the young man of Naim, Lazarus. [...] Christ's Resurrection is essentially different. In his risen body he passes from the state of death to another life beyond time and space. At Jesus' Resurrection his body is filled with the power of the Holy Spirit: he shares the divine life in his glorious state, so that St Paul can say that Christ is 'the man of heaven' (cf. 1 Cor 15:35–50)."[10]

Christ's resurrection is the sure ground on which our faith is based: "'If Christ has not been raised, then our preaching is in vain and your faith is in vain'" (1 Cor 15:14). The Resurrection above all constitutes the confirmation of all Christ's works and teachings. All truths, even those most inaccessible to human reason, find their justification if Christ by his Resurrection has given the definitive proof of his divine authority, which he had promised."[11]

Our faith makes sense only if Christ is alive. Specifically, our incorporation into Christ through Baptism, by which we share in his death and resurrection, has value only if Christ has risen; if he did not rise, then we are still lost to sin (see 1 Cor 15:17): "It is no great thing to believe that Christ has died, for the Jews and pagans and wicked men believe as much: they all believe that he has died. The faith of Christians is the Resurrection of Christ. This is our great belief: that he is risen."[12]

Christ's resurrection is also the basis for our hope in our own resurrection: "Since Christ has risen from the dead, we have the firm hope that we too shall rise from the dead, for the members of the body follow its head."[13] The resurrection of Christ is, above all, the "efficient cause" of our own. St Paul explains this by his metaphor of the "first fruits" (see 1 Cor 15:20, 23) and by his counterposing of Christ and Adam: just as death came through a man, so will resurrection from the dead come through a man; "for, as in Adam all die, so also in Christ shall all be made alive" (1 Cor 15:22).

Finally, the Apostle explains at length our form of existence after rising from the dead (see 1 Cor 15:35–53). Glorious resurrection, which will happen on the last day, at the second coming of Christ (see 1 Cor 15:23), will involve a total transformation of our bodies (see 1 Cor 15:51); they will cease to have a natural mode of existence, and will be raised to a spiritual mode (see 1 Cor 15:44–46). By this, St Paul does not mean that the risen body is not material (that would be a contradiction in terms); what he means is that the spirit will have complete control over the body. As a consequence of this control, the body will be incorruptible (see 1 Cor 15:42), glorious (see 1 Cor 15:43), strong (see 1 Cor 15:44) and immortal (see 1 Cor 15:53–54). "Then, with death overcome, the sons of God will be raised up in Christ, and what was sown in weakness and corruption will be invested with incorruptibility (cf. 1 Cor 15:42, 53). Enduring with charity and its fruits (cf. 1 Cor 13:8), all that creation (cf. Rom 8:19–21) which God made on man's account will be unchained from the bondage of vanity."[14]

10 Ibid., 646. **11** Ibid., 651. **12** St Augustine, *Enarrationes in Psalmos*, 120. **13** *Roman Catechism*, 1, 6, 12. **14** Vatican II, *Gaudium et spes*, 39.

1 Corinthians

1. INTRODUCTION*

Greeting

1 ¹Paul, called by the will of God to be an apostle of Christ Jesus, and our brother Sosthenes,

²To the church of God which is at Corinth, to those sanctified in Christ Jesus, called to be saints* together with all those who in every place call on the name of our Lord Jesus Christ, both their Lord and ours:

³Grace to you and peace from God our Father and the Lord Jesus Christ.

Rom 1:1

1 Cor 6:11
Rom 1:7

Phil 1:2
Col 1:2

[1] ¹Paulus, vocatus apostolus Christi Iesu per voluntatem Dei, et Sosthenes frater, ²ecclesiae Dei, quae est Corinthi, sanctificatis in Christo Iesu, vocatis sanctis cum omnibus, qui invocant nomen Domini nostri Iesu Christi in omni loco ipsorum et nostro: ³gratia vobis et pax a Deo Patre nostro et Domino Iesu Christo. ⁴Gratias ago Deo meo semper pro vobis in gratia Dei, quae data est vobis in Christo Iesu, ⁵quia in omnibus divites

*1:1–9 St Paul begins the letter with the usual opening greeting (vv. 1–3) and an act of thanksgiving that mentions the main gifts and virtues of the Christians to whom he is writing (vv. 4–9).

1:1–3 The Apostle introduces himself (vv. 1–2) by giving his name and mentioning three things that identify him and his role in the Church—his divine calling, his office as an apostle of Jesus Christ, and the will of God, the source of his mission. Paul is "called"; he is very conscious of the fact that Christ changed the whole direction of his life when he appeared to him on the road to Damascus (see Acts 9:1–9; Rom 1:1). The title "apostle of Christ Jesus" shows what his mission is and the source of his authority to praise, teach, admonish and correct by preaching and in writing. Christ Jesus is named nine times in the first nine verses, leaving it in no doubt that he is central to Christian life. "By the will of God" identifies the ultimate authority for Paul's ministry.

"Sosthenes": given the way his name is mentioned in the letter, Sosthenes must have been someone well known to the Corinthians, perhaps because he often accompanied St Paul. He may have been the person who actually wrote down the letter (see 16:21). There are not sufficient grounds for identifying him with the ruler of the synagogue in Corinth (see Acts 18:17).

"The church of God which is at Corinth" (v. 2) is the immediate recipient of the letter. Even the grammar of the phrase emphasizes the fact that the Church is not the sum total of the various local communities; rather, each community (here the Christians of Corinth) represents the whole Church, which is one and indivisible: "The Apostle calls it [the community] 'the Church of God' in order to show that unity is one of its essential and necessary characteristics. The Church of God is one in its members and forms nothing but a single Church with all the communities spread throughout the world, for the word 'church' does not mean schism: it means unity, harmony, concord" (St John Chrysostom, *In 1 Corinthios*, 1, ad loc.).

"Those sanctified in Christ Jesus" (v. 2). The formula "in Christ Jesus" is used up to 65 times in the Pauline letters; here it indicates that Baptism grafts people onto Christ so that they become like branches on a vine (see Jn 15:1ff). This link with Christ makes them saints, that is, people who share in God's own holiness and are called to live perfect lives: "The faithful, although offending in many things and violating the commitments to which they had pledged themselves, are still called holy, because they have been made the People of God and have consecrated themselves to Christ by faith and Baptism. Hence, St Paul calls the Corinthians sanctified and holy, although it is certain that among them there were some whom he severely rebuked as carnal, and charged with grosser crimes" (*Roman Catechism*, 1, 10, 15).

615

Thanksgiving

Phil 1:3

2 Cor 7:9

Tit 2:13

Phil 1:10
1 Thess 3:13
Jude 24
2 Cor 1:18

[4]I give thanks to God[a] always for you because of the grace of God which was given you in Christ Jesus, [5]that in every way you were enriched in him with all speech and all knowledge—[6]even as the testimony to Christ was confirmed among you—[7]so that you are not lacking in any spiritual gift, as you wait for the revealing of our Lord Jesus Christ; [8]who will sustain you to the end, guiltless in the day of our Lord Jesus Christ. [9]God is faithful, by whom you were called into the fellowship of his Son, Jesus Christ our Lord.

PART ONE

Correction of abuses*

2. DIVISIONS AMONG THE CORINTHIANS*

An appeal for unity

Rom 15:5

[10]I appeal to you, brethren, by the name of our Lord Jesus Christ, that all of you agree and that there be no dissensions among you, but that you be united in the same

facti estis in illo, in omni verbo et in omni scientia, [6]sicut testimonium Christi confirmatum est in vobis, [7]ita ut nihil vobis desit in ulla donatione, exspectantibus revelationem Domini nostri Iesu Christi; [8]qui et confirmabit vos usque ad finem sine crimine in die Domini nostri Iesu Christi. [9]Fidelis Deus, per quem vocati estis in communionem Filii eius Iesu Christi Domini nostri. [10]Obsecro autem vos, fratres, per nomen Domini nostri

In the Greco-Roman world, letters usually began with the word "*chairein*", greetings; but Paul uses a more personal, more explicitly Christian, salutation: "Grace [...] and peace" (see v. 3). "There is no true peace, just as there is no true grace, other than the grace and peace which come from God," St John Chrysostom teaches. "Possess this divine peace and you will have nothing to fear, even if you be threatened by the direst danger, whether from men or even from the demons themselves; whereas see how everything is a cause of fear for the man who is at war with God through sin" (*In 1 Corinthios*, 1, ad loc.).

1:4–9 Acts of thanksgiving are often to be found in Paul's letters, but this one is particularly rich in doctrine: Paul reminds the Corinthians that they owe their privileged position to God (v. 4); he has enriched them "with all speech and all knowledge" (v. 5), and they live in hope of the glorious second coming of Christ (vv. 7–9).

Elsewhere in the letter (12:1ff), Paul will discuss spiritual gifts and charisms in detail. Here he stresses that the Corinthians are rich in "speech" and "knowledge" (v. 5), that is, they are familiar

with Christian teaching and are able to express it clearly: "There are those who have the gift of knowledge but not that of speech; and there are others who have the gift of speech but not knowledge. The faithful in general, who are uneducated, know these truths, but they cannot clearly explain what they have in their soul. You, on the other hand, St Paul says, are different; you know these truths and you can speak about them; you are rich in the gift of speech and in that of knowledge" (St John Chrysostom, *1 Corinthios*, 2, ad loc.).

"Who will sustain you to the end" (v. 8). It is important for people to focus on their own personal end and on the end of the world. There were some who thought they had already reached the height of perfection; Paul tells them that Christian life requires a struggle until the "day of our Lord" comes (v. 8), that is, the day of judgment, the day when Jesus Christ, as Judge, will come in glory (see 2 Cor 1:14; 1 Thess 5:2). Hope in the Day of the Lord will be discussed later (see 15:50–58).

*1:10—6:20 The first part of the letter directly confronts some abuses that have arisen in the

a Other ancient authorities read *my God*

mind and the same judgment. [11]For it has been reported to me by Chloe's people that there is quarrelling among you, my brethren. [12]What I mean is that each one of you says, "I belong to Paul," or "I belong to Apollos," or "I belong to Cephas,"* or "I belong to Christ." [13]Is Christ divided? Was Paul crucified for you? Or were you baptized in the name of Paul? [14]I am thankful[b] that I baptized none of you except Crispus and Gaius; [15] lest any one should say that you were baptized in my name. [16](I did baptize also the household of Stephanas. Beyond that, I do not know whether I baptized any one else.) [17]For Christ did not send me to baptize but to preach the gospel, and not with eloquent wisdom, lest the cross of Christ be emptied of its power.

1 Cor 3:4

Eph 4:5

Acts 18:8

Acts 16:15

Mt 28:19

Iesu Christi, ut idipsum dicatis omnes, et non sint in vobis schismata, sitis autem perfecti in eodem sensu et in eadem sententia. [11]Significatum est enim mihi de vobis, fratres mei, ab his, qui sunt Chloes, quia contentiones inter vos sunt. [12]Hoc autem dico, quod unusquisque vestrum dicit: «Ego quidem sum Pauli», «Ego autem Apollo», «Ego vero Cephae», «Ego autem Christi». [13]Divisus est Christus? Numquid Paulus crucifixus est pro vobis, aut in nomine Pauli baptizati estis? [14]Gratias ago Deo quod neminem vestrum baptizavi nisi Crispum et Gaium, [15]ne quis dicat quod in nomine meo baptizati sitis. [16]Baptizavi autem et Stephanae domum; ceterum nescio si quem alium baptizaverim. [17]Non enim misit me Christus

Christian community at Corinth. Firstly, Paul talks about divisions among Christians—clear evidence that they have forgotten the Gospel of the cross that he preached to them (1:10—4:21). Then, in the light of the Gospel, he judges three specific cases, having to do with incest (5:1–13), legal disputes among Christians (6:1–11), and questions of sexual morality (6:12–20).

*1:10—4:21 The first problem St Paul deals with is the strife in their community. After denouncing these divisions (1:10–17), he goes on to show that the Corinthians have not discovered true wisdom (1:18—3:3) or what apostolic ministry is about (3:4—4:13). He ends with words of admonishment (4:14–21).

1:10–17 St Paul takes the Corinthians to task for the divisions in their ranks—not, it seems, quarrels over matters of doctrine, but disagreements due to preferences for certain teachers. His warning is "by the name of our Lord Jesus Christ" (v. 10) and his appeal perfectly clear—"that all of you agree [...], that you be united in the same mind and the same judgment". Basic to church unity is unity of faith, as handed down by Tradition: "Any meaning of the sacred dogmas that has once been declared by holy Mother Church must always be retained; and there must never be any deviation from that meaning on the specious grounds of a more profound understanding. 'Therefore, let there be growth [...] and all possible progress in understanding, knowledge, and wisdom whether in single individuals or in the

whole body, in each man as well as in the entire Church, according to the stage of their development but only within proper limits, that is, in the same doctrine, in the same meaning, and in the same purport [eodem sensu eademque sententia]' (St Vincent of Lerins, Commonitorium, 28)" (Vatican I, Dei Filius, chap. 4).

St Paul refers to the "dissensions" he has learned about through "Chloe's people". Presumably, Chloe was a woman well known in the church at Corinth; her "people" could mean members of her family or of her domestic church who visited the Apostle in Ephesus.

From what Paul says, parties of followers had gathered around important people in the church at Corinth. "Apollos" (v. 12) was a Jewish convert from Alexandria (Egypt), a renowned speaker and a man very learned in the Scriptures, who preached in Corinth (cf. Acts 18:24—19:1). The people who claimed to belong "to Cephas" may have met Peter when he passed through Corinth (though there is no evidence he was ever in the city) or they could have been disciples of Peter or of people whom he had brought to the faith and who had later moved to Corinth. It is not easy to define the group who claimed to "belong to Christ": they may have been people who had gravitated towards Judaizing preachers who had come from Jerusalem, or Christians who were disgusted at the petty squabbling of the other groups and who had decided (with good reason) to make the point that they acknowledged only one leader, Christ; but it could be (if the passage is given

b. Other ancient authorities read *I thank God*

The wisdom of the cross and the wisdom of the world

2 Cor 4:3
Rom 1:16

¹⁸For the word of the cross is folly to those who are perishing, but to us who are being saved it is the power of God. ¹⁹For it is written,

Is 29:14
Ps 33:10

"I will destroy the wisdom of the wise,
and the cleverness of the clever I will thwart."

baptizare sed evangelizare, non in sapientia verbi, ut non evacuetur crux Christi. ¹⁸Verbum enim crucis pereuntibus quidem stultitia est, his autem, qui salvi fiunt, id est nobis, virtus Dei est. ¹⁹Scriptum est enim: «*Perdam sapientiam sapientium / et prudentiam prudentium reprobabo*». ²⁰Ubi sapiens? Ubi scriba? Ubi conquisitor huius saeculi? Nonne stultam fecit Deus sapientiam huius mundi? ²¹Nam quia in Dei sapientia non cognovit mundus per sapientiam Deum, placuit Deo per stultitiam praedicationis salvos facere credentes. ²²Quoniam et Iudaei signa petunt, et Graeci sapi-

different punctuation) that Paul is speaking ironically, to show how nonsensical the divisions at Corinth are—as if to say: "You say that you belong to Paul, to Apollos, to Peter ... well, then I belong to Christ."

Of the people baptized by Paul (vv. 13–16) we know a little more: Crispus was, or had been, the ruler of the Corinth synagogue, and had been converted by Paul's preaching (see Acts 18:8). Gaius, another convert of Paul's, had given Paul lodging during his stay in Corinth (see Rom 16:23). The household of Stephanas was the first family to be converted in the province of Achaia (see 16:15–17).

"Christ did not send me to baptize but to preach the gospel" (v. 17). The Apostle says this to show the Corinthians that he has no favourites, and to show that no one can claim him to be the leader of their party. He is certainly not counterposing preaching the Gospel and administering sacraments. Paul VI had occasion to criticize that line of thinking: "In a certain sense it is a mistake to make a contrast between evangelization and sacramentalization, as is sometimes done. It is indeed true that a certain way of administering the Sacraments, without the solid support of catechesis regarding these same Sacraments and a global catechesis, could end up by depriving them of their effectiveness to a great extent. The role of evangelization is precisely to educate people in the faith so as to lead each individual Christian to live the Sacraments as true Sacraments of faith" (*Evangelii nuntiandi*, 47).

1:18–19 The Corinthians have failed to discover where true wisdom lies—in the cross. The cross of Christ is a seal of wisdom and judgment, a touchstone. There are those who think that the message of the cross ("the word of the cross") is foolishness: these people are "perishing" (literally, are "heading towards perdition"). However, others, those who are on the road to salvation, can see that the cross is "the power of God", because through it the devil and sin have been defeated. Hence the Church's anthem: "This is the wood of the cross, on which hung the Saviour of the world" (*Roman Missal*, Good Friday liturgy); hence, too, the saints' promises: "O most precious gift of the Cross! How splendid it looks! [...] It is a tree which begets life, without causing death; which sheds light, without casting shadows; which leads to Paradise and does not expel anyone therefrom; it is the wood which Christ ascended, as a king mounting his chariot, to defeat the devil who had usurped the power of death, and to set mankind free from the thrall in which the devil held it. This wood, on which the Lord, valiant fighter in the combat, was wounded in his divine hands and feet and side, healed the effects of sins and the wounds which the pernicious dragon had inflicted on our nature [...]. That supreme wisdom, which, so to speak, burgeoned on the cross, exposed the boasts and the foolish arrogance of the wisdom of the world" (St Theodore the Studite, *Oratio in adorationem crucis*).

The words of Isaiah (Is 29:14) quoted by St Paul in v. 19 were fulfilled in the cross. "The message of Christ's cross", St Thomas Aquinas says, "contains something which to human wisdom seems impossible—that God should die, or that the Almighty should give himself up into the power of violent men. It also contains things which seem to be contrary to worldly prudence—for instance, someone who is free to flee from contradictions and yet does not do so" (*Super 1 Corinthios*, ad loc.).

²⁰Where is the wise man? Where is the scribe? Where is the debater of this age? Has not God made foolish the wisdom of the world? ²¹For since, in the wisdom of God, the world did not know God through wisdom, it pleased God through the folly of what we preach to save those who believe. ²²For Jews demand signs and Greeks seek wisdom, ²³but we preach Christ crucified, a stumbling block to Jews and folly to Gentiles, ²⁴but to those who are called, both Jews and Greeks, Christ the power of God and the wisdom of God. ²⁵For the foolishness of God is wiser than men, and the weakness of God is stronger than men.

²⁶For consider your call, brethren; not many of you were wise according to worldly standards, not many were powerful, not many were of noble birth; ²⁷but God chose what is foolish in the world to shame the wise, God chose what is weak in the

Is 19:12; 33:18

Rom 1:20

Mt 12:38
Rom 9:32
1 Cor 2:14
Gal 5:11

Col 2:3
2 Cor 13:4

Jn 7:48

2 Cor 4:7

entiam quaerunt, ²³nos autem praedicamus Christum crucifixum, Iudaeis quidem scandalum, gentibus autem stultitiam; ²⁴ipsis autem vocatis, Iudaeis atque Graecis, Christum Dei virtutem et Dei sapientiam, ²⁵quia quod stultum est Dei, sapientius est hominibus, et quod infirmum est Dei, fortius est hominibus. ²⁶Videte enim vocationem vestram, fratres, quia non multi sapientes secundum carnem, non multi potentes, non multi nobiles; ²⁷sed, quae stulta sunt mundi elegit Deus, ut confundat sapientes, et infirma mundi elegit Deus, ut confundat fortia, ²⁸et ignobilia mundi et contemptibilia elegit Deus, quae non sunt, ut ea, quae sunt, destrueret, ²⁹ut non glorietur omnis caro in conspectu Dei. ³⁰Ex ipso autem vos estis

1:20–25 The "wisdom of the world" is human thinking that has gone awry and therefore cannot come to know God (see Rom 1:19–25), because it accepts only physical evidence or only rational arguments.

For many Jews, only signs will do; they want to base their faith on things the senses can perceive. For people with that attitude, Christ's cross is a stumbling block, an obstacle that prevents their gaining access to divine things. Greeks (here Paul means the rationalists of his time) tend to think that they are the arbiters of truth and that anything that cannot be irrefutably proved in rational terms is a nonsense: "For the world, that is, for the prudent of the world, their wisdom turned into blindness; it could not lead them to see God [...]. Therefore, since the world had become puffed up by the vanity of its dogmas, the Lord set in place the faith whereby believers would be saved by what seemed unworthy and foolish, so that, all human conjecture being of no avail, only the grace of God might reveal what the human mind cannot take in" (St Leo the Great, *Sermo 5 de Nativitate*).

1:26–31 As in the case of the apostles ("You did not choose me, but I chose you": Jn 15:16), it is the Lord who chooses, who gives each Christian his vocation (vv. 26–29). It was God who chose these Corinthians to be Christians, and he did not base his choice on human criteria—intelligence, influence, family descent: "God is no respecter of

persons (cf. 2 Chron 19:7; Rom 2:1; Eph 6:9; Col 3:25; etc.). When he invites a soul to live a life fully in accordance with the faith, he does not set store by merits of fortune, nobility, blood or learning. God's call precedes all merits [...]. Vocation comes first. God loves us before we even know how to go toward him, and he places in us the love with which we can respond to his call" (St Josemaría Escrivá, *Christ Is Passing By*, 33).

However, vv. 27–28 should not lead us to think that the early Christians did not include people who were educated, learned, influential, or otherwise important from a human point of view. The Acts of the Apostles mentions converts such as a minister at the Ethiopian court, the centurion Cornelius, Apollos, Dionysius the Areopagite, etc. "It would appear that worldly excellence is not godly unless God uses it for his honour. And therefore, although at the beginning they were indeed few, later God chose many humanly outstanding people for the ministry of preaching. Hence the gloss which says, 'If the fisherman had not faithfully led the way, the orator would not have humbly followed.' That He led the great of this world to Himself through the work of the humble is part of God's glory" (St Thomas Aquinas, *Super 1 Corinthios*, ad loc.).

Christ is our "wisdom" from God (v. 30), and to know him is true wisdom, the most important wisdom of all. He is our "righteousness", because the merits accruing from his incarnation, death and resurrection have made us truly right-

Jas 2:5
1 Sam 16:7
Col 2:3

Jer 9:22f
2 Cor 10:17

2 Cor 11:6
Gal 6:14
2 Cor 7:15; 10:10
1 Cor 4:20
Eph 1:17, 19
Acts 1:8

Mt 13:35
Eph 3:10
1 Pet 1:12
Is 19:11, 13
Bar 3:14
Ps 19:4

world to shame the strong, [28]God chose what is low and despised in the world, even things that are not, to bring to nothing things that are, [29]so that no human being might boast in the presence of God. [30]He is the source of your life in Christ Jesus, whom God made our wisdom, our righteousness and sanctification and redemption; [31]therefore, as it is written, "Let him who boasts, boast of the Lord."

Paul's preaching in Corinth

2 [1]When I came to you, brethren, I did not come proclaiming to you the testimony[c] of God in lofty words or wisdom. [2]For I decided to know nothing among you except Jesus Christ and him crucified.* [3]And I was with you in weakness and in much fear and trembling; [4]and my speech and my message were not in plausible words of wisdom, but in demonstration of the Spirit and of power, [5]that your faith might not rest in the wisdom of men but in the power of God.

Divine wisdom

[6]Yet among the mature we do impart wisdom, although it is not a wisdom of this age or of the rulers of this age, who are doomed to pass away. [7]But we impart a secret and hidden wisdom of God, which God decreed before the ages for our glorification. [8]None of the rulers of this age understood this; for if they had, they would not have crucified the Lord of glory. [9]But, as it is written,

in Christo Iesu, qui factus est sapientia nobis a Deo et iustitia et sanctificatio et redemptio, [31]ut quemadmodum scriptum est: *«Qui gloriatur in Domino glorietur».* [2] [1]Et ego, cum venissem ad vos, fratres, veni non per sublimitatem sermonis aut sapientiae annuntians vobis mysterium Dei. [2]Non enim iudicavi scire me aliquid inter vos nisi Iesum Christum et hunc crucifixum. [3]Et ego in infirmitate et timore et tremore multo fui apud vos, [4]et sermo meus et praedicatio mea non in persuasibilibus sapientiae verbis, sed in ostensione Spiritus et virtutis, [5]ut fides vestra non sit in sapientia hominum sed in virtute Dei. [6]Sapientiam autem loquimur inter perfectos, sapientiam vero non huius saeculi neque principum huius saeculi, qui destruuntur, [7]sed loquimur Dei sapientiam in mysterio, quae abscondita est, quam praedestinavit Deus ante saecula in gloriam nos-

eous (just) in God's sight. He is also our "sanctification", the source of all holiness; holiness in fact consists in identification with him. Through Christ, who became our ransom, our "redemption", we have been rescued from the slavery of sin. "How well the Apostle orders his ideas: God has made us wise by rescuing us from error; and then he has made us just and holy by giving us his spirit" (St John Chrysostom, *In 1 Corinthios,* 5, ad loc.).

Christians, for their part, should try to see to it that those around them "desire to know Jesus Christ and him crucified and that they be firmly convinced and with the most heartfelt piety and devotion believe that no other name under heaven has been given to men by which we may be saved (cf. Acts 4:12), since he is the expiation for our sins (cf. 1 Jn 2:2)" (*Roman Catechism,* Introduction, 10).

2:1–5. The centre of Paul's message is Christ, Christ crucified, for, instead of being based on human wisdom, faith is grounded on the cross

and on the power of God; this is what gives it its enduring solidity. The Christian message "is unique. It cannot be replaced. It does not permit indifference, syncretism or accommodation. It is a question of people's salvation. It is the beauty of the Revelation that it represents. It brings with it a wisdom that is not of this world. It is able to stir up by itself faith—faith that rests on the power of God (cf. 1 Cor 2:5). It is truth. It merits having the apostle consecrate to it all his time and all his energies, and to sacrifice for it, if necessary, his own life" (Paul VI, *Evangelii nuntiandi,* 5).

2:6–16 Divine wisdom, in which human beings are called to share, is the divine plan of salvation revealed by the Father through the Holy Spirit. The wisdom that Paul proclaims here does not contradict human wisdom, but it does go far beyond it: it is "secret and hidden" (v. 7) and therefore man cannot take it all in, just as he can never totally understand who God is; however, he can acquire knowledge of God through reve-

c Other ancient authorities read *mystery* (or *secret*)

"What no eye has seen, nor ear heard,

nor the heart of man conceived,

what God has prepared for those who love him,"

Is 64:3
Jer 3:16

[10]God has revealed to us through the Spirit. For the Spirit searches everything, even the depths of God. [11]For what person knows a man's thoughts except the spirit of the man which is in him? So also no one comprehends the thoughts of God except the Spirit of God. [12]Now we have received not the spirit of the world, but the Spirit which is from God, that we might understand the gifts bestowed on us by God. [13]And we impart this in words not taught by human wisdom but taught by the Spirit, interpreting spiritual truths to those who possess the Spirit.[d]

2 Cor 13:13

Prov 20:27
Rom 11:34

Jn 14:26

tram, [8]quam nemo principum huius saeculi cognovit; si enim cognovissent, numquam Dominum gloriae crucifixissent. [9]Sed sicut scriptum est: «*Quod oculus non vidit, nec auris audivit*, nec in cor hominis ascendit, quae praeparavit Deus his, qui diligunt illum». [10]Nobis autem revelavit Deus per Spiritum; Spiritus enim omnia scrutatur, etiam profunda Dei. [11]Quis enim scit hominum, quae sint hominis, nisi spiritus hominis, qui in ipso est? Ita et, quae Dei sunt, nemo cognovit nisi Spiritus Dei. [12]Nos autem non spiritum mundi accepimus, sed Spiritum, qui ex Deo est, ut sciamus, quae a Deo donata sunt nobis; [13]quae et loquimur non in doctis humanae sapientiae, sed in doctis Spiritus verbis, spiritalibus spiritalia comparantes. [14]Animalis autem homo non percipit, quae sunt Spiritus Dei, stultitia enim sunt illi, et non potest intellegere, quia spiritaliter examinantur;

lation (see Lk 8:10; Col 1:26), a knowledge that will reach its fullness in heaven. There are, then, three ways of looking at this wisdom-mystery-salvation: it is part of God's plan from all eternity; it is made manifest in revelation and especially in Jesus Christ, who died and then rose; it is attained partially in this life and fully in heaven: "How blessed, how marvellous, are the gifts of God. Some of them, indeed, already lie within our comprehension—the life that knows no death, the shining splendour of righteousness, truth in freedom, trusting faith, the holiness of chastity. But what of the things that God has prepared for those who hope in him? Only the Creator and Father of eternity knows them. Let us strive earnestly to be counted among those who wait patiently in order to earn a share in his promised gifts" (St Clement of Rome, *Ad Corinthios*, 30). The words of Isaiah 64:4 in v. 9 sum up what God's wisdom involves—all those gifts that man's mind cannot grasp (see Eph 3:19) and which God has prepared from all eternity for those who love him. Because these gifts are only fully attained in the next life, Christian tradition sees in these words a description of heaven.

"The spirit of the world" (v. 12) means all the most negative aspects of human society, which inevitably impact to some degree on Christians. The "spirit of the man" (v. 11) means the innermost being of a person, his or her whole person. The "Spirit of God", which should be taken as meaning God's innermost self and God himself,

is the Holy Spirit: "One cannot believe in Jesus Christ without sharing in his Spirit. It is the Holy Spirit who reveals to men who Jesus is. [...] Only God knows God completely: we believe in the Holy Spirit because he is God" (*Catechism of the Catholic Church*, 152).

"The unspiritual man" (v. 14). The original text says "*psychikos*", the "physical man", as distinct from the "spiritual man"; some translations say "natural man"; others say "animal man", which is what the Vulgate (followed by the New Vulgate) does—meaning someone who uses only his human faculties (intelligence and will) and cannot see beyond the things of the earth. The spiritual man, on the other hand, is the Christian reborn through God's grace; grace raises his faculties to enable him to do actions that have a supernatural value—acts of faith, hope and charity: "We have no alternative. There are only two possible ways of living on this earth: either we live a supernatural life, or we live an animal life. And you and I can only live the life of God, a supernatural life" (St Josemaría Escrivá, *Friends of God*, 200). People who live the life of the Spirit are able to perceive what is good for souls and what is harmful: "A person who is awake rightly perceives both that he is awake and that the other person is asleep; but the person who is asleep cannot form a correct judgment concerning either himself or someone who is awake. [...] And so the Apostle says that 'the spiritual man judges all things': for a person whose understanding is enlightened and whose

d Or *interpreting spiritual truths in spiritual language*; or *comparing spiritual things with spiritual*

Jn 10:26
Mt 16:23

1 Jn 2:20
1 Cor 15:49
Is 40:13
1 Cor 7:40
Wis 9:13

1 Thess 2:7

Heb 5:12
1 Pet 2:2

1 Cor 1:10; 11:18

¹⁴The unspiritual^e man does not receive the gifts of the Spirit of God, for they are folly to him, and he is not able to understand them because they are spiritually discerned. ¹⁵The spiritual man judges all things, but is himself to be judged by no one. ¹⁶"For who has known the mind of the Lord so as to instruct him?" But we have the mind of Christ.

The Corinthians are still unspiritual

3 ¹But I, brethren, could not address you as spiritual men, but as men of the flesh, as babes in Christ. ²I fed you with milk, not solid food; for you were not ready for it; and even yet you are not ready, ³for you are still of the flesh. For while there is jealousy and strife among you, are you not of the flesh, and behaving like ordinary men?

¹⁵*spiritalis autem iudicat omnia, et ipse a nemine iudicatur.* ¹⁶*Quis enim cognovit sensum Domini, / qui instruat eum?* Nos autem sensum Christi habemus. [3] ¹*Et ego, fratres, non potui vobis loqui quasi spiritalibus, sed quasi carnalibus, tamquam parvulis in Christo.* ²*Lac vobis potum dedi, non escam, nondum enim poteratis. Sed ne nunc quidem potestis,* ³*adhuc enim estis carnales. Cum enim sit inter vos zelus et contentio, nonne carnales estis et secundum hominem ambulatis?* ⁴*Cum enim quis dicit: «Ego quidem sum Pauli», alius autem: «Ego Apollo», nonne homines estis?*

affections are ordered by the Holy Spirit forms correct judgments on particular matters having to do with salvation. He who is unspiritual has a darkened understanding and disordered affection as far as spiritual things are concerned, and therefore the spiritual man cannot be judged by the unspiritual man, just as the sleeping person cannot judge the one who is awake" (St Thomas Aquinas, *Super 1 Corinthios*, ad loc.).

3:1–3 The Corinthians have not yet attained true wisdom; they are still "of the flesh" (v. 3). They are responsible for the divisions that have arisen among them, for they have confused the Gospel with the personal wisdom and talents of its preachers. When Paul draws the contrast between "spiritual men" and "men of the flesh", he obviously does not mean that there are two kinds of people in the Church; rather, he is reproaching them in a fatherly way: by Baptism they are called to become fully mature and have a deep understanding of spiritual things; but because they let human criteria rule their actions, they are still at a very early stage of development. The reason for this, St John Chrysostom comments, is that "unclean living makes it difficult for a person to know the truth. Just as a man who is blinded by error cannot for long keep to the right road, so too is it very difficult for someone who is leading a bad life to accept the demands our sublime mysteries make on us. To embrace truth one needs to be detached from all

one's passions […]. This freedom of soul must be total, if one is to attain truth" (*In 1 Corinthios*, 8, ad loc.).

"As babes in Christ" (v. 1). Here (and elsewhere) the Apostle uses the images of child and adult to urge people to be strong in the faith (see 13:11; Gal 4:1–3; Eph 4:14). He is not referring to the spiritual childhood taught by Jesus (see Mt 18:1–6; cf. 1 Pet 2:2). He makes the comparison to show that Christians need to make progress in the spiritual life by developing the infused virtues they received at Baptism. To be more specific, the Apostle mentions "jealousy and strife" (v. 3) as two serious sins that are draining the Corinthians of spiritual vitality. They leave Christians in a lamentable, unspiritual state and prevent authentic spiritual development.

3:4–23 One sign of the Corinthians' too-human vision of things (v. 4) is their failure to see that ministers are not trying to win a following of their own: they want to build up the Church; every individual and the entire Church belong only to God and to Christ. All apostolic work derives from God: it is he "who gives the growth" (v. 7). God works through people; these are "servants" (v. 5), "God's fellow workers" (v. 9), and the foundation they build on is Christ (v. 11). Paul expands on this idea, using images taken from farming (vv. 6–9) and building (vv. 10–17).

e Or *natural*

Apostolic ministry

[4]For when one says, "I belong to Paul," and another, "I belong to Apollos," are you not merely men?

1 Cor 1:12

[5]What then is Apollos? What is Paul? Servants through whom you believed, as the Lord assigned to each. [6]I planted, Apollos watered, but God gave the growth. [7]So neither he who plants nor he who waters is anything, but only God who gives the growth. [8]He who plants and he who waters are equal, and each shall receive his wages according to his labour. [9]For we are God's fellow workers;[f] you are God's field, God's building.

Acts 18:24, 27

Eph 2:20

[10]According to the grace of God given to me, like a skilled master builder I laid a foundation, and another man is building upon it. Let each man take care how he builds upon it. [11]For no other foundation can any one lay than that which is laid, which is Jesus Christ. [12]Now if any one builds on the foundation with gold, silver,

1 Cor 15:10
2 Pet 3:15

1 Pet 2:4
Acts 4:12

[5]Quid igitur est Apollo? Quid vero Paulus? Ministri, per quos credidistis, et unicuique sicut Dominus dedit. [6]Ego plantavi, Apollo rigavit, sed Deus incrementum dedit; [7]itaque neque qui plantat, est aliquid, neque qui rigat, sed qui incrementum dat, Deus. [8]Qui plantat autem et qui rigat unum sunt; unusquisque autem propriam mercedem accipiet secundum suum laborem. [9]Dei enim sumus adiutores: Dei agricultura estis, Dei aedificatio estis. [10]Secundum gratiam Dei, quae data est mihi, ut sapiens architectus fundamentum posui; alius autem superaedificat. Unusquisque autem videat quomodo superaedificet; [11]fundamentum enim aliud nemo potest ponere praeter id, quod positum est, qui est Iesus Christus. [12]Si quis autem superaedificat supra fundamentum aurum, argentum, lapides pretiosos, ligna, fenum, stipulam, [13]uniuscuiusque opus manifestum erit; dies

3:6–9 The comparison of apostolate with farming shows that God wants to use people to produce supernatural results that are totally disproportionate to their abilities: "We must remember that we are only instruments," St Josemaría Escrivá points out. "[Text of 1 Cor 3:4–6]. The teaching, the message which we have to communicate, has in its own right an infinite effectiveness which comes not from us, but from Christ. It is God himself who is bent on bringing about salvation, on redeeming the world" (*Christ Is Passing By*, 159).

"God's field, God's building" (v. 9). The Second Vatican Council uses these images to describe how the Church functions: "Often, too, the Church is called the building of God (1 Cor 3:9). The Lord compared himself to the stone which the builders rejected, but which was made into the cornerstone (Mt 21:42; cf. Acts 4:11; 1 Pet 2:7; Ps 117:22). On this foundation the Church is built by the Apostles (cf. 1 Cor 3:11) and from it the Church receives solidity and unity. This edifice has many names to describe it—the house of God in which his family dwells; the household of God in the Spirit (Eph 2:19:22); the dwelling-place of God among men (Rev 21:3); and, especially, the holy temple. This temple, symbolized in places of worship built out of stone, is praised by the Fathers and, not without reason, is compared in the liturgy to the

Holy City, the New Jerusalem. As living stones we here on earth are built into it (1 Pet 2:5). It is this holy city that is seen by John as it comes down out of heaven from God when the world is made anew, prepared like a bride adorned for her husband (Rev 21:1f)" (*Lumen gentium*, 6).

3:10–17 Christ is the only foundation (v. 11), and therefore a Christian "needs not only to be linked to Jesus Christ, but to adhere to him, to be firmly attached to him. [...] He is the foundation, we the building; he is the vine, we the branches; he the spouse, we the bride; he is the shepherd, we the flock" (St John Chrysostom, *In 1 Corinthios*, 8, 4). Developing the building metaphor, St Paul appeals to church ministers to act responsibly, reminding them that a "Day" of judgment will come (vv. 10–17).

The image of God's temple (vv. 16–17), often used by St Paul (see 6:19–20; 2 Cor 6:16), helps explain how the Holy Trinity dwells in the soul in grace; "by means of grace, God dwells in the just soul as in a temple, in a special and intimate manner" (Leo XIII, *Divinum illud munus*, 10). It is consoling and helpful to know that "the divine persons are said to indwell inasmuch as they are present to intellectual creatures in a way that transcends human comprehension, and are known and loved (cf. *Summa theologiae*, 1, 43, 3) by them, yet in a way that is unique, purely

[f] Or *fellow workers for God*

precious stones, wood, hay, straw—[13]each man's work will become manifest; for the Day* will disclose it, because it will be revealed with fire, and the fire will test what sort of work each one has done. [14]If the work which any man has built on the foundation survives, he will receive a reward. [15]If any man's work is burned up, he will suffer loss, though he himself will be saved, but only as through fire.

1 Cor 6:19
2 Cor 6:16
Rom 8:9

[16]Do you not know that you are God's temple* and that God's Spirit dwells in you? [17]If any one destroys God's temple, God will destroy him. For God's temple is holy, and that temple you are.

Rev 3:17
1 Cor 1:17–25; 4:10

[18]Let no one deceive himself. If any one among you thinks that he is wise in this age, let him become a fool that he may become wise. [19]For the wisdom of this world is folly with God. For it is written, "He catches the wise in their craftiness," [20]and again, "The Lord knows that the thoughts of the wise are futile." [21]So let no one boast of men. For all things are yours, [22]whether Paul or Apollos or Cephas or the world or life or death or the present or the future, all are yours; [23]and you are Christ's; and Christ is God's.

Job 5:12f

Ps 94:11

2 Cor 10:7

Servants of Christ

Tit 1:7
Col 1:25
1 Pet 4:10
Lk 12:42

4 [1]This is how one should regard us, as servants of Christ and stewards of the mysteries of God. [2]Moreover it is required of stewards that they be found trustworthy. [3]But with me it is a very small thing that I should be judged by you or by any human court. I do not even judge myself. [4]I am not aware of anything against

Ps 143:2
2 Cor 5:10

enim declarabit: quia in igne revelatur, et uniuscuiusque opus quale sit ignis probabit. [14]Si cuius opus manserit, quod superaedificavit, mercedem accipiet; [15]si cuius opus arserit, detrimentum patietur, ipse autem salvus erit, sic tamen quasi per ignem. [16]Nescitis quia templum Dei estis et Spiritus Dei habitat in vobis? [17]Si quis autem templum Dei everterit, evertet illum Deus; templum enim Dei sanctum est, quod estis vos. [18]Nemo se seducat; si quis videtur sapiens esse inter vos in hoc saeculo, stultus fiat, ut sit sapiens. [19]Sapientia enim huius mundi stultitia est apud Deum. Scriptum est enim: «Qui apprehendit sapientes in astutia eorum»; [20]et iterum: «Dominus novit cogitationes sapientium / quoniam vanae sunt». [21]Itaque nemo glorietur in hominibus. Omnia enim vestra sunt, [22]sive Paulus sive Apollo sive Cephas sive mundus sive vita sive mors sive praesentia sive futura, omnia enim vestra sunt, [23]vos autem Christi, Christus autem Dei.　　[4] [1]Sic nos existimet homo ut ministros Christi et dispensatores mysteriorum Dei. [2]Hic iam quaeritur inter dispensatores, ut fidelis quis inveniatur. [3]Mihi autem pro minimo est, ut a vobis iudicer aut ab humano die. Sed neque meipsum iudico; [4]nihil enim mihi conscius sum, sed non in hoc iustificatus sum. Qui autem iudicat me, Dominus est!

supernatural, and in the deepest sanctuary of the soul" (Pius XII, *Mystici Corporis*).

The presence of the Blessed Trinity in the soul in grace invites Christians to try to have a personal and direct relationship with God, whom we can at all times seek in the intimacy of our soul: "Get to know the Holy Spirit, the Great Stranger, on whom depends your sanctification. Don't forget that you are God's temple. The Advocate is in the centre of your soul: listen to him and be docile to his inspirations" (St Josemaría Escrivá, *The Way*, 57).

3:18–23 Paul uses two biblical quotations (Job 5:13; Ps 94:11) to show that an exclusively human approach is always doomed to failure. But Christians, who belong only to Christ (v. 23), are lords of all they survey: "Mine are the heavens and mine is the earth", St John of the Cross explains; "mine are the people, the right-

eous are mine, and the Mother of God, and all things are mine; and God himself is mine and for me, for Christ is mine and all for me. What, then, do you ask for and seek, my soul? All this is yours, and it is all for you. Do not despise yourself, do not despise the crumbs that fall from your Father's table" (*Prayer of the Soul Aflame with Love*).

4:1–7 The features of apostles ("servants of Christ", "stewards of the mysteries of God": v. 1) entail that they put their ministry beyond grudges and petty squabbling.

The Church has often applied the words of v. 1 to the Christian priesthood: "The priest is the minister of Christ, an instrument, that is to say, in the hands of the divine Redeemer. He continues the work of the redemption in all its universality and divine efficacy, that work that wrought so marvellous a transformation in the world. Thus

myself, but I am not thereby acquitted. It is the Lord who judges me. [5]Therefore do
not pronounce judgment before the time, before the Lord comes, who will bring to
light the things now hidden in darkness and will disclose the purposes of the heart.
Then every man will receive his commendation from God.

Rom 2:16

[6]I have applied all this to myself and Apollos for your benefit, brethren, that you
may learn by us not to go beyond what is written, that none of you may be puffed up
in favour of one against another. [7]For who sees anything different in you? What have
you that you did not receive? If then you received it, why do you boast as if it were
not a gift?

Jn 3:27
Rom 12:3

Trials experienced by apostles

[8]Already you are filled! Already you have become rich! Without us you have
become kings! And would that you did reign, so that we might share the rule with
you! [9]For I think that God has exhibited us apostles as last of all, like men sentenced
to death; because we have become a spectacle to the world, to angels and to men.
[10]We are fools for Christ's sake, but you are wise in Christ. We are weak, but you are
strong. You are held in honour, but we in disrepute. [11]To the present hour we hunger

Rev 3:17

Rom 8:26

1 Cor 3:18
2 Cor 11:23–27

[5]Itaque nolite ante tempus quidquam iudicare, quoadusque veniat Dominus, qui et illuminabit abscondita tenebrarum et manifestabit consilia
cordium; et tunc laus erit unicuique a Deo. [6]Haec autem, fratres, transfiguravi in me et Apollo propter vos, ut in nobis discatis illud: «Ne supra
quae scripta sunt», ne unus pro alio inflemini adversus alterum. [7]Quis enim te discernit? Quid autem habes, quod non accepisti? Si autem accepisti,
quid gloriaris, quasi non acceperis? [8]Iam saturati estis, iam divites facti estis. Sine nobis regnastis; et utinam regnaretis, ut et nos vobiscum reg-
naremus. [9]Puto enim, Deus nos apostolos novissimos ostendit tamquam morti destinatos, quia spectaculum facti sumus mundo et angelis et
hominibus. [10]Nos stulti propter Christum, vos autem prudentes in Christo; nos infirmi, vos autem fortes; vos gloriosi, nos autem ignobiles. [11]Usque
in hanc horam et esurimus et sitimus et nudi sumus et colaphis caedimur et instabiles sumus [12]et laboramus operantes manibus nostris; maledicti

the priest, as is said with good reason, is indeed
'another Christ', for, in some way, he is himself
a continuation of Christ […]. A priest is
appointed 'steward of the mysteries of God' (cf.
1 Cor 4:1) for the benefit of the members of the
mystical body of Christ, since he is the ordinary
minister of nearly all the sacraments—those
channels through which the grace of the Saviour
flows for the good of humanity" (Pius XI, *Ad
catholici sacerdotii*, 17).

"Not to go beyond what is written" (v. 6).
This phrase is open to various interpretations. It
may be a proverb familiar to the Corinthians,
meaning that one should keep to safe ground (in
this case, the Apostle's guidelines). "What is
written" could also mean all Holy Scripture, or
the quotations Paul has been taking from it (see
1:19, 31; 3:19). In any event, he does make the
point to the Corinthians that it is their own
immaturity and pride that have caused the dissension in their community through the exalting
of one preacher at the expense of others. Paul
and Apollos have behaved quite properly and
cannot be held responsible for the divisions that
have arisen.

4:8–13 The Apostle uses irony to expose the
Corinthians' conceit, and then he spells out the
kinds of suffering that followers of Christ are
happy to endure: like people sentenced to death
in the arena, they are a spectacle for everyone to
watch; like people cast out of Greek cities, they
have become "the refuse of the world, the offs-
couring of all things" (v. 13). These remarks may
refer to an appalling custom that existed in some
Greek cities: in the face of some public calamity,
a citizen, in exchange for being treated as royalty
for a period of time, agreed to be sacrificed to
the gods; on the day of his sacrifice, the people
had the right to heap every kind of insult and
filth upon him: he was "the offscouring" of
everyone. This sacrifice was supposed to free the
city from the effects of magic spells. If the words
in the letter do refer to this custom, they have a
deeper meaning, too: the apostle must put up
with abuse out of love for Christ and his fellow
men: "I will tell you which are man's treasures
on earth," St Josemaría Escrivá writes, "so that
you won't let them go to waste: hunger, thirst,
heat, cold, pain, dishonour, poverty, loneliness,
betrayal, slander, prison …" (*The Way*, 194).

2 Thess 2:9
Rom 12:14
and thirst, we are ill-clad and buffeted and homeless, [12]and we labour, working with our own hands. When reviled, we bless; when persecuted, we endure; [13]when slandered, we
Lam 3:45
try to conciliate; we have become, and are now, as the refuse of the world, the offs-couring of all things.

Admonishment

1 Thess 2:11
Gal 4:19
[14]I do not write this to make you ashamed, but to admonish you as my beloved children. [15]For though you have countless guides in Christ, you do not have many fathers. For I became your father in Christ Jesus through the gospel. [16]I urge you,
2 Thess 3:7
Acts 19:22
Phil 2:19
then, be imitators of me. [17]Therefore I sent[g] to you Timothy, my beloved and faithful child in the Lord, to remind you of my ways in Christ, as I teach them everywhere in every church. [18]Some are arrogant, as though I were not coming to you.
Jas 4:16
Acts 18:21
[19]But I will come to you soon, if the Lord wills, and I will find out not the talk of these arrogant people but their power. [20]For the kingdom of God does not consist in
2 Cor 10:2; 13:1–10
talk but in power. [21]What do you wish? Shall I come to you with a rod, or with love in a spirit of gentleness?

3. A CASE OF INCEST*

Punishment of the sinner

Lev 18:8
Deut 27:20
5 [1]It is actually reported that there is immorality among you, and of a kind that is not found even among pagans; for a man is living with his father's wife.* [2]And

benedicimus, persecutionem passi sustinemus, [13]blasphemati obsecramus; tamquam purgamenta mundi facti sumus, omnium peripsema, usque adhuc. [14]Non ut confundam vos, haec scribo, sed ut quasi filios meos carissimos moneam; [15]nam si decem milia paedagogorum habeatis in Christo, sed non multos patres, nam in Christo Iesu per evangelium ego vos genui. [16]Rogo ergo vos: imitatores mei estote! [17]Ideo misi ad vos Timotheum, qui est filius meus carissimus et fidelis in Domino, quae vos commonefaciat vias meas, quae sunt in Christo, sicut ubique in omni ecclesia doceo. [18]Tamquam non venturus sim ad vos, sic inflati sunt quidam; [19]veniam autem cito ad vos, si Dominus voluerit, et cognoscam non sermonem eorum, qui inflati sunt, sed virtutem; [20]non enim in sermone est regnum Dei sed in virtute. [21]Quid vultis? In virga veniam ad vos an in caritate et spiritu mansuetudinis?   [5] [1]Omnino auditur inter vos fornicatio et talis fornicatio, qualis nec inter gentes, ita ut uxorem patris aliquis habeat. [2]Et vos inflati estis et non magis luctum habuistis, ut tollatur de medio vestrum, qui hoc opus fecit? [3]Ego quidem absens corpore, praesens autem spir-

4:14–21 St Paul introduces the subject of the spiritual paternity of the Corinthians because it was he who begot them in the faith. Given that fact, his reproaches carry special weight, and gentleness, too: it is not his aim to make these Christians feel ashamed, but to encourage them to grow in virtue, and to help build up the Church. The Saints have always seen authority in these terms: "We ought to regard those under our authority as our children. We place ourselves at their service as Jesus did" (St John Bosco, *Letter,* in the *Divine Office,* office of readings, 31 January).

The Apostle is very conscious of being the pastor of this Christian community. He desires always to act "in a spirit of gentleness" (v. 21), not locking horns with anyone or causing distress. However, he is ready to go against his inclinations and brandish the "rod", that is, to

speak out boldly, if the good of the faithful requires it—energetically admonishing people, or even excommunicating them, cutting them off from ecclesial communion, if they become a danger to the faith of Christians.

*5:1–13 The second serious matter facing the community was the case of a Christian and his mother-in-law who were living as man and wife. After dealing with the particular case (vv. 1–8), the Apostle has something to say about people who refuse to mend their sinful ways (vv. 9–13).

5:1–8 Incest, which "corrupts family relationships and marks a regression toward animality" (*Catechism of the Catholic Church,* 2388), was, even in that culture, seen as reprehensible. The

g Or *am sending*

you are arrogant! Ought you not rather to mourn? Let him who has done this be removed from among you.

Deut 13:16

³For though absent in body I am present in spirit, and as if present, I have already pronounced judgment ⁴in the name of the Lord Jesus on the man who has done such a thing. When you are assembled, and my spirit is present, with the power of our Lord Jesus, ⁵you are to deliver this man to Satan* for the destruction of the flesh, that his spirit may be saved in the day of the Lord Jesus.ʰ

Col 2:5

Mt 16:19

1 Tim 1:20
1 Pet 4:6

⁶Your boasting is not good. Do you not know that a little leaven leavens the whole lump? ⁷Cleanse out the old leaven that you may be a new lump, as you really are unleavened. For Christ, our paschal lamb, has been sacrificed. ⁸Let us, therefore, celebrate the festival, not with the old leaven, the leaven of malice and evil, but with the unleavened bread of sincerity and truth.

Gal 5:9
Ex 12:21
Jn 1:29
1 Pet 1:19
Ex 12:3–20

Obstinate sinners are to be shunned

⁹I wrote to you in my letter not to associate with immoral men;* ¹⁰not at all meaning the immoral* of this world, or the greedy and robbers, or idolaters, since then you would need to go out of the world. ¹¹But rather I wroteⁱ to you not to associate with any one who bears the name of brother if he is guilty of immorality* or greed, or is an idolater, reviler, drunkard, or robber—not even to eat with such a one. ¹²For what have I to do with judging outsiders? Is it not those inside the church whom you are to judge? ¹³God judges those outside. "Drive out the wicked person from among you."

1 Jn 5:19
Eph 5:3
Tit 3:10
1 Tim 6:3

Rom 1:29
Col 4:5

Mt 4:11

Deut 13:6

itu, iam iudicavi ut praesens eum, qui sic operatus est, ⁴in nomine Domini nostri Iesu, congregatis vobis et meo spiritu cum virtute Domini nostri Iesu, ⁵tradere huiusmodi Satanae in interitum carnis, ut spiritus salvus sit in die Domini. ⁶Non bona gloriatio vestra. Nescitis quia modicum fermentum totam massam corrumpit? ⁷Expurgate vetus fermentum, ut sitis nova consparsio, sicut estis azymi. Etenim Pascha nostrum immolatus est Christus! ⁸Itaque festa celebremus, non in fermento veteri neque in fermento malitiae et nequitiae, sed in azymis sinceritatis et veritatis. ⁹Scripsi vobis in epistula: Ne commisceamini fornicariis. ¹⁰Non utique fornicariis huius mundi aut avaris aut rapacibus aut idolis servientibus, alioquin debueratis de hoc mundo exisse! ¹¹Nunc autem scripsi vobis non commisceri, si is qui frater nominatur, est fornicator aut avarus aut idolis serviens aut maledicus aut ebriosus aut rapax; cum eiusmodi nec cibum sumere. ¹²Quid enim mihi de his, qui foris sunt, iudicare? Nonne de his, qui intus

Corinthians have taken no action about this case; not so St Paul, who formally decrees the man's excommunication (vv. 4–5), to prevent any further harm being done to the community. With the image of the unleavened dough used to make the bread for the Azymes (the days before Passover), Paul explains that Christians, likewise, should shed any gravely sinful habit: "Therefore, when in our own life or in that of others we notice something that isn't going well, something that requires the spiritual and human help which, as children of God, we can and ought to provide, the prudent thing to do is to apply the appropriate remedy by going to the root of the trouble, resolutely, lovingly and sincerely. There is no room here for inhibitions, for it is a great mistake to think that problems can be solved by omissions or procrastination" (St Josemaría Escrivá, *Friends of God*, 157).

5:9–13 Here Paul warns the Corinthians not to associate with people, nominally Christians, who persist in committing sins of the types he lists. Christians should do whatever they can to save others; only when someone constitutes a danger to one's own soul, should that person be shunned.

This passage twice mentions a letter (vv. 9, 11) that has not come down to us; scholars often refer to it as the "precanonical" letter to the Corinthians.

The list of sins in v. 11 is very similar to that given in the next chapter (see 6:9–10), and follows much in line with the other lists (up to thirteen) of grave sins found in the Pauline letters. In devout, educated circles at that time, it was quite common for lists of sins to circulate (Jewish lists differing from Greek ones). St Paul is not providing an exhaustive list here; rather, he is warning his addressees about the sins they are most in danger of committing.

h Other ancient authorities omit *Jesus* i Or *now I write*

4. RECOURSE TO PAGAN COURTS*

Dan 7:22–26
Wis 3:8
Rev 3:21; 20:4
Mt 19:28
Acts 9:13
Gal 5:6
Jude 5–6
2 Pet 2:4
1 Cor 15:34

6 ¹When one of you has a grievance against a brother, does he dare go to law before the unrighteous* instead of the saints? ²Do you not know that the saints will judge the world? And if the world is to be judged by you, are you incompetent to try trivial cases? ³Do you not know that we are to judge angels? How much more, matters pertaining to this life! ⁴If then you have such cases, why do you lay them before those who are least esteemed by the church? ⁵I say this to your shame. Can it be that there is no man among you wise enough to decide between members of the brotherhood, ⁶but brother goes to law against brother, and that before unbelievers?

Mt 5:39
Lk 6:26
1 Thess 5:15
1 Pet 3:9
Rom 12:17–21

⁷To have lawsuits at all with one another is defeat for you. Why not rather suffer wrong? Why not rather be defrauded? ⁸But you yourselves wrong and defraud, and that even your own brethren.

Gal 5:19–21
Eph 5:5
Rom 1:29-31
Rev 21:8; 22:15
1 Cor 15:50

⁹Do you not know that the unrighteous will not inherit the kingdom of God? Do not be deceived; neither the immoral,* nor idolaters, nor adulterers, nor homosexuals,ʲ* ¹⁰nor thieves, nor the greedy, nor drunkards, nor revilers, nor robbers will inherit the kingdom of God. ¹¹And such were some of you. But you were washed,

Tit 3:3–7
Gal 5:21
Eph 2:1–7
Jn 3:5
1 Jn 2:12
1 Pet 3:21

you were sanctified, you were justified in the name of the Lord Jesus Christ and in the Spirit of our God.

5. FORNICATION, A GRAVE SIN*

1 Cor 10:23
Rom 6:15
Gen 4:7
1 Thess 4:3–8
Mt 15:17
Col 2:22

Respect for the body

¹²"All things are lawful for me," but not all things are helpful. "All things are lawful for me," *but I will not be enslaved by anything. ¹³"Food is meant for the stomach and

sunt, vos iudicatis? ¹³Nam eos, qui foris sunt, Deus iudicabit. *Auferte malum ex vobis ipsis!* [6] ¹Audet aliquis vestrum habens negotium adversus alterum iudicari apud iniquos et non apud sanctos? ²An nescitis quoniam sancti de mundo iudicabunt? Et si in vobis iudicabitur mundus, indigni estis minimis iudiciis? ³Nescitis quoniam angelos iudicabimus, quanto magis saecularia? ⁴Saecularia igitur iudicia si habueritis, contemptibiles, qui sunt in ecclesia, illos constituite ad iudicandum? ⁵Ad verecundiam vestram dico! Sic non est inter vos sapiens quisquam, qui possit iudicare inter fratrem suum? ⁶Sed frater cum fratre iudicio contendit, et hoc apud infideles? ⁷Iam quidem omnino defectio est vobis, quod iudicia habetis inter vosmetipsos! Quare non magis iniuriam accipitis, quare non magis fraudem patimini? ⁸Sed vos iniuriam facitis et fraudatis, et hoc fratribus! ⁹An nescitis quia iniqui regnum Dei non possidebunt? Nolite errare: neque fornicarii neque idolis servientes neque adulteri neque molles neque masculorum concubitores ¹⁰neque fures neque avari, non ebriosi, non maledici, non rapaces regnum Dei possidebunt. ¹¹Et haec quidam fuistis. Sed abluti estis, sed sanctificati estis, sed iustificati estis in nomine Domini Iesu Christi et in Spiritu Dei nostri ! ¹²«Omnia mihi licent!».

*6:1–11 The third matter the Apostle deplores is the fact that Christians are taking suits against one another in pagan courts, instead of trying to resolve matters within their own community.

The advice he gives here is in line with the Jewish practice of using special Jewish courts. He wants Christians to practise fraternity and resolve their differences among themselves. Going before pagan courts could hinder the spread of the Gospel: what attraction could a community hold if it was divided within itself and as litigious as any other? St John Chrysostom lists the Corinthians' faults as follows: "For one thing, not bearing injuries patiently; for another, offending others; then looking for arbitrators to decide on the matter; finally, making

use of these means in a dispute with a Christian, a brother in the faith" (*In 1 Corinthios*, ad loc.).

The Apostle rounds off his admonitions by reminding the Corinthians of the dignity conferred on them by Baptism. "The followers of Christ, called by God not in virtue of their works but by his design and grace, and justified in the Lord Jesus, have been made sons of God in baptism, the sacrament of faith, and partakers of the divine nature, and so are truly sanctified. They must therefore hold on to and perfect in their lives that sanctification which they have received from God" (Vatican II, *Lumen gentium*, 40).

*6:12–20 The Apostle now deals with the gravity of sins against chastity, showing that they

ʲ Two Greek words are rendered by this expression

the stomach for food"—and God will destroy both one and the other. The body is not
meant for immorality,* but for the Lord, and the Lord for the body. ¹⁴And God raised   ^{1 Cor 8:11; 15:15–20}
                                                                                          ^{2 Cor 4:14}
the Lord and will also raise us up by his power.   ^{Rom 1:4; 8:11}

Offence to Christ and the Holy Spirit

¹⁵Do you not know that your bodies are members of Christ? Shall I therefore take   1 Cor 12:12, 27
the members of Christ and make them members of a prostitute? Never! ¹⁶Do you not   Rom 6:12–13; 12:5
                                                                                        Gen 2:24
know that he who joins himself to a prostitute becomes one body with her? For, as
it is written, "The two shall become one flesh."ᵏ ¹⁷But he who is united to the Lord   Jn 17:21ff
                                                                                         Rom 8:9–10
becomes one spirit with him. ¹⁸Shun immorality.* Every other sin which a man com-   2 Cor 3:17
mits is outside the body; but the immoral man sins against his own body. ¹⁹Do you   1 Cor 3:16f, 23
                                                                                         Rom 5:5
not know that your body is a temple of the Holy Spirit within you, which you have   1 Thess 4:4–8
from God? You are not your own; ²⁰you were bought with a price. So glorify God in   1 Cor 6:15; 7:23
                                                                                         Phil 1:20
your body.   1 Pet 1:18

Sed non omnia expediunt. «Omnia mihi licent!». Sed ego sub nullius redigar potestate. ¹³«Esca ventri et venter escis!». Deus autem et hunc et has
destruet. Corpus autem non fornicationi sed Domino, et Dominus corpori; ¹⁴Deus vero et Dominum suscitavit et nos suscitabit per virtutem suam.
¹⁵Nescitis quoniam corpora vestra membra Christi sunt? Tollens ergo membra Christi faciam membra meretricis? Absit! ¹⁶An nescitis quoniam,
qui adhaeret meretrici, unum corpus est? «Erunt enim, inquit, duo in carne una». ¹⁷Qui autem adhaeret Domino, unus Spiritus est. ¹⁸Fugite fornicationem! Omne peccatum, quodcumque fecerit homo, extra corpus est; qui autem fornicatur, in corpus suum peccat. ¹⁹An nescitis quoniam
corpus vestrum templum est Spiritus Sancti, qui in vobis est, quem habetis a Deo, et non estis vestri? ²⁰Empti enim estis pretio! Glorificate ergo

profoundly harm the person and are incompatible with a Christian's calling.

6:12–14 Apparently, a false idea of freedom was
widespread among the Corinthians—the idea
that Christians, because they owed no obedience
to the Law, could operate without reference to
God's commandments: "All things are lawful for
me" (v. 12). The Apostle points out that there are
actions and attitudes (having to do with chastity,
for example) that are bad for people because
they turn them into slaves.

Another serious mistake they were making
was to present the sexual appetite as being
equivalent to the need for food. On this point the
Apostle's teaching leaves no room for doubt:
things involving food have no relevance after
death, whereas the body, being an integral part of
the person, shares in union with Christ, will in
due course experience resurrection, and therefore
has a dignity which must be respected.

6:15–20 The Christian, body and soul, is a
member of Christ (v. 15). This striking assertion
is very central to Paul's teaching and to Christian
doctrine in general: Christians become part of
Christ's body through Baptism, and from then on
they are meant to be closely united to him, to live
his life (see Gal 2:20), to be "one spirit with him"

(v. 17). They are, that is to say, *members* of his
Body (see 12:27; Rom 12:5). A person who sins
against chastity is profaning his own body, for it
is a temple of the Holy Spirit. Paul's advice is
clear: flee from sexual immorality (v. 18). "One
does not win by putting up resistance, because the
more one thinks about the thing, the more
influenced one becomes; one wins by fleeing—
that is, by avoiding unclean thoughts completely
and by avoiding all occasions of sin" (St Thomas
Aquinas, *Super 1 Corinthios*, ad loc.). A Christian
has all kinds of resources for being chaste: "The
first is to be very vigilant about what we look at,
and what we think and say and do; second, to
have recourse to prayer; third, to frequent the
sacraments worthily; fourth, to fly from anything
which might tempt us to sin; fifth, to have great
devotion to the Blessed Virgin. If we do all that,
then, no matter what our enemies do, no matter
how frail this virtue be, we can be quite sure of
holding on to it" (St John Vianney, *Sermon on the
Seventeenth Sunday after Pentecost*).

St Paul concludes this passage (v. 20) by
stressing the wonderful condition in which the
baptized find themselves: "Christian, remember
who you are; you have been given a share in
God's very nature; do not, therefore, even think
of reverting by unworthy conduct to your earlier
evil ways" (St Leo the Great, *Sermo 1 de Nativ-*

k Greek *one flesh*

PART TWO

Answers to various questions*

6. MARRIAGE AND VIRGINITY*

Relations between husband and wife

Mt 19:10
1 Tim 4:3
1 Thess 4:3

Eph 5:21–29

7 ¹Now concerning the matters about which you wrote. It is well for a man not to touch a woman. ²But because of the temptation to immorality, each man should have his own wife and each woman her own husband.* ³The husband should give to his wife her conjugal rights, and likewise the wife to her husband. ⁴For the wife does not rule over her own body, but the husband does; likewise the husband does not rule over his own body, but the wife does. ⁵Do not refuse one another except perhaps by agreement for a season, that you may devote yourselves to prayer; but then come together again, lest Satan tempt you through lack of self-control. ⁶I say this by way of concession, not of command. ⁷I wish that all were as I myself am. But each has his own special gift from God, one of one kind and one of another.

2 Cor 8:8

Mt 19:12

Deum in corpore vestro. [7] ¹De quibus autem scripsistis, bonum est homini mulierem non tangere; ²propter fornicationes autem unusquisque suam uxorem habeat, et unaquaeque suum virum habeat. ³Uxori vir debitum reddat; similiter autem et uxor viro. ⁴Mulier sui corporis potestatem non habet sed vir; similiter autem et vir sui corporis potestatem non habet sed mulier. ⁵Nolite fraudare invicem, nisi forte ex consensu ad tempus,

itate). On this dignity deriving from Baptism the Apostle grounds chastity in its highest forms.

*7:1–15:58 In the second part of the letter, the Apostle replies to matters raised by the faithful of Corinth, matters to do with everyday life: relations between husband and wife, and whether or not to marry at all (7:1–40); purchasing food in the public market that comes from animals used in pagan sacrifices (8:1—10:33); the celebration of the Eucharist (11:1–34); gifts and charisms (12:1—14:40); and, finally, hope in the resurrection of the dead (15:1–58). Throughout, the main principle that should apply is mutual love, charity (13:1–13), and therefore people should avoid actions or attitudes that could cause scandal or imply disrespect for others. Questions raised by some people on the subject of resurrection of the dead lead St Paul to remind his readers that the resurrection of Jesus is a truth of the Gospel as preached from the very beginning, and it is a basic tenet of Christian faith (15:1–4).

*7:1–40 The first matter (v. 1) raised with Paul on the subject of marriage and celibacy seems to have come from some people who considered marital relations to be evil and therefore thought

that celibacy/virginity was the only valid state in life for Christians. Paul will deal with these questions here, and will also comment on the situation of widows.

7:1–9 The Apostle briefly states that marriage is something quite lawful. Absolutely speaking, virginity is on a higher plane than marriage (see 7:25–35), but marriage is something good and holy for those who are called to it: "Whoever condemns marriage also deprives virginity of its glory; whereas whoever praises it makes virginity more attractive and luminous. Something which seems good only when compared with something bad, is not very valuable; but when it is greater than things which everyone gives great value to, then indeed it is good to a superlative degree" (St John Chrysostom, *De virginitate*, 10).

To practise virginity and celibacy, special grace from God is needed. If people do not receive that gift, it is better for them to be married; marriage, like virginity, is a gift from God (v. 7). "Marriage is a divine path on earth. [...] Those who are called to the married state will, with the grace of God, find within their state everything they need to be holy, to identify

1 Tim 5:14
1 Cor 11:14

[8]To the unmarried and the widows I say that it is well for them to remain single as I do. [9]But if they cannot exercise self-control, they should marry. For it is better to marry than to be aflame with passion.

Indissolubility of marriage

Mt 5:32
Mk 10:11f
Lk 16:18
Mt 19:3–9

[10]To the married I give charge, not I but the Lord, that the wife should not separate from her husband [11](but if she does, let her remain single or else be reconciled to her husband)—and that the husband should not divorce his wife.

The Pauline privilege

[12]To the rest I say, not the Lord, that if any brother has a wife who is an unbeliever, and she consents to live with him, he should not divorce her. [13]If any woman has a husband who is an unbeliever, and he consents to live with her, she should not divorce him. [14]For

Rom 11:16

the unbelieving husband is consecrated through his wife, and the unbelieving wife is consecrated through her husband. Otherwise, your children would be unclean, but as it is they are holy. [15]But if the unbelieving partner desires to separate, let it be so; in such a

Rom 14:19
1 Cor 14:33

case the brother or sister is not bound. For God has called us[l] to peace. [16]Wife, how do

1 Pet 3:1–2

you know whether you will save your husband? Husband, how do you know whether you will save your wife?

ut vacetis orationi et iterum sitis in idipsum, ne tentet vos Satanas propter incontinentiam vestram. [6]Hoc autem dico secundum indulgentiam, non secundum imperium. [7]Volo autem omnes homines esse sicut meipsum; sed unusquisque proprium habet donum ex Deo: alius quidem sic, alius vero sic. [8]Dico autem innuptis et viduis: Bonum est illis si sic maneant sicut et ego; [9]quod si non se continent, nubant. Melius est enim nubere quam uri. [10]His autem, qui matrimonio iuncti sunt, praecipio, non ego sed Dominus, uxorem a viro non discedere [11]—quod si discesserit, maneat innupta aut viro suo reconcilietur—et virum uxorem non dimittere. [12]Ceteris autem ego dico, non Dominus: Si quis frater uxorem habet infidelem, et haec consentit habitare cum illo, non dimittat illam; [13]et si qua mulier habet virum infidelem, et hic consentit habitare cum illa, non dimittat virum. [14]Sanctificatus est enim vir infidelis in muliere, et sanctificata est mulier infidelis in fratre. Alioquin filii vestri immundi essent; nunc autem sancti sunt. [15]Quod si infidelis discedit, discedat. Non est enim servituti subiectus frater aut soror in eiusmodi; in pace autem vocavit nos Deus. [16]Quid enim scis, mulier, si virum salvum facies? Aut quid scis, vir, si mulierem salvam facies? [17]Nisi unicuique, sicut divisit Dominus,

themselves each day more with Jesus Christ, and to lead those with whom they live to God" (St Josemaría Escrivá, *Conversations*, 91).

The Apostle has inspiring things to say about the duties of husband and wife towards each other (vv. 2–5); there must be complete reciprocity, he says (three times); this is quite different from Greek and Jewish practice at the time, with all rights pertaining to the husband. Husband and wife no longer have exclusive ownership of their own bodies; they belong to each other, owing themselves to each other in strict justice.

"Remain single as I do" (v. 8); literally, "remain as I am". From these words, all we can deduce is that St Paul lived as a celibate; we do not know whether at any stage he was married; he may have been a widower; but v. 7 supports the commonly held view that he never married.

7:10–11 Referring to the indissolubility of marriage, Paul makes it quite clear that it is a commandment of God, not a teaching of his own

design:: "It is a fundamental duty of the Church to reaffirm strongly […] the doctrine of the indissolubility of marriage. […] He [God] wills and he communicates the indissolubility of marriage as a fruit, a sign and a requirement of the absolutely faithful love that God has for man and that the Lord Jesus has for the Church. […] To bear witness to the inestimable value of the indissolubility and fidelity of marriage is one of the most precious and most urgent tasks of Christian couples in our time" (John Paul II, *Familiaris consortio*, 20).

7:12–16 Church discipline follows the solution outlined by St Paul: when a husband or wife becomes a Christian, the marriage bond remains in place; but if the pagan spouse makes married life impossible or does not allow the Christian spouse to live in accordance with his or her faith, then the Christian spouse is free to leave him or her and to marry again (cf. *Code of Canon Law*, canons 1143–1147).

l Other ancient authorities read *you*

Leading the life God has assigned

Rom 12:3
1 Cor 7:20-24
1 Mac 1:15
Gal 5:1

[17]Only, let every one lead the life which the Lord has assigned to him, and in which God has called him. This is my rule in all the churches. [18]Was any one at the time of his call already circumcised? Let him not seek to remove the marks of circumcision. Was any one at the time of his call uncircumcised? Let him not seek circumcision.

Rom 2:25–29
Gal 5:6; 6:15

[19]For neither circumcision counts for anything nor uncircumcision, but keeping the commandments of God.

1 Cor 7:17–24
Col 3:22; 4:1
Eph 6:5–9
Rom 3:24

[20]Every one should remain in the state in which he was called. [21]Were you a slave when called? Never mind. But if you can gain your freedom, avail yourself of the opportunity.[x] [22]For he who was called in the Lord as a slave is a freedman of the

Rom 6:19

Lord. Likewise he who was free when called is a slave of Christ. [23]You were bought with a price; do not become slaves of men. [24]So, brethren, in whatever state each was called, there let him remain with God.

Excellence of virginity

Mt 19:12
1 Cor 7:10, 40
1 Tim 1:12–14
2 Cor 8:10
1 Cor 10:11

[25]Now concerning the unmarried,[x2] I have no command of the Lord, but I give my opinion as one who by the Lord's mercy is trustworthy. [26]I think that in view of the present[m] distress it is well for a person to remain as he is. [27]Are you bound to a wife? Do not seek to be free. Are you free from a wife? Do not seek marriage. [28]But if you

unumquemque, sicut vocavit Deus, ita ambulet; et sic in omnibus ecclesiis doceo. [18]Circumcisus aliquis vocatus est? Non adducat praeputium! In praeputio aliquis vocatus est? Non circumcidatur! [19]Circumcisio nihil est, et praeputium nihil est, sed observatio mandatorum Dei. [20]Unusquisque, in qua vocatione vocatus est, in ea permaneat. [21]Servus vocatus es? Non sit tibi curae; sed et si potes liber fieri, magis utere! [22]Qui enim in Domino vocatus est servus, libertus est Domini; similiter, qui liber vocatus est, servus est Christi! [23]Pretio empti estis! Nolite fieri servi hominum. [24]Unusquisque, in quo vocatus est, fratres, in hoc maneat apud Deum. [25]De virginibus autem praeceptum Domini non habeo, consilium autem do, tamquam misericordiam consecutus a Domino ut sim fidelis. [26]Existimo ergo hoc bonum esse propter instantem necessitatem, quo-

7:17–24 Some Corinthians may have been misapplying the consequences of being "reborn" through Baptism, making out that it brought about a total change in a person's life, not only internally but externally as well. The Apostle explains (by giving two examples—circumcision and slavery) that external circumstances do not determine or inhibit a person's Christian life; in fact, God designs these circumstances as a positive help for Christian living. The Christian calling does not take anyone out of his or her place, nor is there any reason why it should entail changing one's circumstances. "Our calling discloses to us the meaning of our existence. It means being convinced, through faith, of the reason for our life on earth. Our life, present, past and future, acquires a new dimension, a depth we did not perceive before. All happenings and events now fall into proper perspective: we understand where God is leading us" (St Josemaría Escrivá, *Christ Is Passing By*, 45).

7:25–38 The excellence of virginity, whether of men or women, derives from the love of God, to which a celibate person can devote himself or herself exclusively in a way that a married person cannot. "The response to the divine call is an answer of love to the love which Christ has shown us so sublimely (Jn 15:13; 3:16) [...]. Grace with a divine force increases the longings of love. And love, when it is genuine, is total, exclusive, stable and lasting, an irresistible spur to all forms of heroism. And so, the free choice of sacred celibacy has always been considered by the Church 'as something that signifies and stimulates charity' (*Lumen gentium*, 42). It signifies a love without reservations, it stimulates to a charity which is open to all" (Paul VI, *Sacerdotalis caelibatus*, 24).

Verses 36–38 are difficult to interpret. They may refer to a social context where parents decided on the marriage of their children; in which case the word "betrothed" (v. 36) should be read as "daughter". Another interpretation is that "betrothed" means what it normally does: in such a case, a man who decided to remain celibate would have to consider his choice in light of the burden it might pose for his betrothed. While

x. Or *make use of your present condition instead*   x2 Greek *virgins*   m Or *present*

marry, you do not sin, and if a girl[m2] marries she does not sin. Yet those who marry will have worldly troubles, and I would spare you that. [29]I mean, brethren, the appointed time has grown very short; from now on, let those who have wives live as though they had none, [30]and those who mourn as though they were not mourning, and those who rejoice as though they were not rejoicing, and those who buy as though they had no goods, [31]and those who deal with the world as though they had no dealings with it. For the form of this world is passing away.

[32]I want you to be free from anxieties. The unmarried man is anxious about the affairs of the Lord, how to please the Lord; [33]but the married man is anxious about worldly affairs, how to please his wife, [34]and his interests are divided. And the unmarried woman or girl[m2] is anxious about the affairs of the Lord, how to be holy in body and spirit; but the married woman is anxious about worldly affairs, how to please her husband. [35]I say this for your own benefit, not to lay any restraint upon you, but to promote good order and to secure your undivided devotion to the Lord.

[36]If any one thinks that he is not behaving properly toward his betrothed,[m2] if his passions are strong, and it has to be, let him do as he wishes: let them marry—it is no sin. [37]But whoever is firmly established in his heart, being under no necessity but having his desire under control, and has determined this in his heart, to keep her as his betrothed,[m2] he will do well. [38]So that he who marries his betrothed[m2] does well; and he who refrains from marriage will do better.

Advice to widows

[39]A wife is bound to her husband as long as he lives. If the husband dies, she is free to be married to whom she wishes, only in the Lord. [40]But in my judgment she is happier if she remains as she is. And I think that I have the Spirit of God.

Lk 14:26
1 Pet 4:7
2 Cor 6:2
Rom 13:11
2 Cor 6:8–10

1 Jn 2:15ff

Lk 14:20
Eph 5:29

Lk 10:39, 42

Rom 7:2

niam bonum est homini sic esse. [27]Alligatus es uxori? Noli quaerere solutionem. Solutus es ab uxore? Noli quaerere uxorem. [28]Si autem acceperis uxorem, non peccasti; et si nupserit virgo, non peccavit. Tribulationem tamen carnis habebunt huiusmodi, ego autem vobis parco. [29]Hoc itaque dico, fratres, tempus breviatum est; reliquum est, ut et qui habent uxores, tamquam non habentes sint, [30]et qui flent, tamquam non flentes, et qui gaudent, tamquam non gaudentes, et qui emunt, tamquam non possidentes, [31]et qui utuntur hoc mundo, tamquam non abutentes; praeterit enim figura huius mundi. [32]Volo autem vos sine sollicitudine esse. Qui sine uxore est, sollicitus est, quae Domini sunt, quomodo placeat Domino; [33]qui autem cum uxore est, sollicitus est, quae sunt mundi, quomodo placeat uxori, [34]et divisus est. Et mulier innupta et virgo cogitat, quae Domini sunt, ut sit sancta et corpore et spiritu; quae autem nupta est, cogitat, quae sunt mundi, quomodo placeat viro. [35]Porro hoc ad utilitatem vestram dico, non ut laqueum vobis iniciam, sed ad id quod honestum est et ut assidue cum Domino sitis sine distractione. [36]Si quis autem turpem se videri existimat super virgine sua quod sit superadulta, et ita oportet fieri, quod vult, faciat; non peccat: nubant. [37]Qui autem statuit in corde suo firmus, non habens necessitatem, potestatem autem habet suae voluntatis, et hoc iudicavit in corde suo servare virginem suam, bene faciet; [38]igitur et, qui matrimonio iungit virginem suam, bene facit; et, qui non iungit, melius faciet. [39]Mulier alligata est, quanto tempore vir eius vivit; quod si dormierit vir eius, libera est, cui vult nubere, tantum in Domino. [40]Beatior autem erit, si sic permanserit secundum meum consilium; puto autem quod et

Paul always defends the excellence of virginity, he also encourages men and women to make their decisions of their own free will.

7:39–40 Following what St Paul says here, the Church has always taught that the marriage bond is broken by the death of one of the spouses, and the other then becomes free to marry again. It is not very clear what is meant by "only in the Lord" (v. 39). The most likely meaning is that the Apostle is recommending that a widow marry a Christian, to avoid the danger of apos-

tasy that a mixed marriage might involve. In any event, as in the case of unmarried persons, he recommends, as the more perfect route to take, staying unmarried, consecrated to the service of God.

In his first Letter to Timothy, the Apostle gives more explicit directions about the life of widows; some should be supported by their families; some should remarry: some should dedicate themselves to the service of the Church in a permanent way; and all should behave with the decorum proper to their state (see 1 Tim 5:9–16).

m2 Greek *virgin*

7. FOOD OFFERED TO IDOLS*

Idols have no real existence

Acts 15:29

Rom 15:1–2

Gal 4:9
Deut 6:4
1 Cor 10:19; 13:12

Ps 82:6
Jn 10:34

Ex 20:3
Jn 1:3
1 Tim 2:5
Mal 2:10
Rom 11:36
Eph 4:5–6
Col 1:16–17

8 ¹Now concerning food offered to idols:* we know that "all of us possess knowledge." "Knowledge" puffs up, but love builds up. ²If any one imagines that he knows something, he does not yet know as he ought to know. ³But if one loves God, one is known by him.

⁴Hence, as to the eating of food offered to idols, we know that "an idol has no real existence," and that "there is no God but one." ⁵For although there may be so-called gods in heaven or on earth—as indeed there are many "gods" and many "lords"—⁶yet for us there is one God, the Father, from whom are all things and for whom we exist, and one Lord, Jesus Christ, through whom are all things and through whom we exist.

Not scandalizing the weak

Heb 1:2
1 Cor 10:27; 15:1–2, 7
1 Thess 5:14

Rom 14:17
Col 2:21–23
Heb 13:9

⁷However, not all possess this knowledge. But some, through being hitherto accustomed to idols, eat food as really offered to an idol; and their conscience, being weak, is defiled. ⁸Food will not commend us to God. We are no worse off if we do

ego Spiritum Dei habeo. [8] ¹De idolothytis autem, scimus quia omnes scientiam habemus. Scientia inflat, caritas vero aedificat. ²Si quis se existimat scire aliquid, nondum cognovit, quemadmodum oporteat eum scire; ³si quis autem diligit Deum, hic cognitus est ab eo. ⁴De esu igitur idolothytorum, scimus quia nullum idolum est in mundo et quod nullus deus nisi Unus. ⁵Nam et si sunt, qui dicantur dii sive in caelo sive in terra, siquidem sunt dii multi et domini multi, ⁶nobis tamen unus Deus Pater, ex quo omnia et nos in illum, et unus Dominus Iesus Christus, per quem omnia et nos per ipsum. ⁷Sed non in omnibus est scientia; quidam autem consuetudine usque nunc idoli quasi idolothytum manducant, et conscientia ipsorum, cum sit infirma, polluitur. ⁸Esca autem nos non commendat Deo; neque si non manducaverimus, deficiemus, neque si mandu-

---

*8:1—10:33 In pagan rites, some of the meat of animals sacrificed to the gods could be sold in the market and eaten in private houses. Some Christians—afraid that by eating this meat they were in some way taking part in idolatrous worship (see Acts 15:23–29)—had posed a number of practical questions in this regard. The Apostle first outlines the general principles that apply: meat of this kind may be eaten, since idols have no real existence (8:1–6), but charity can sometimes dictate that people do abstain from it (8:7–13). He illustrates what he says by mentioning what he himself does (9:1–27) and by drawing lessons from the history of Israel (10:1–13). Finally, he deals with particular cases involving meat from pagan sacrifices (10:14–33).

8:1–6 Some Corinthians boasted to others that they knew that the pagan gods were mere figments of imagination and therefore meat from pagan sacrifices could be eaten without any qualms (see 10:25–27). St Paul tells them they must not rely on this "knowledge"; they have to take account of charity, too: "'Knowledge' puffs up, but love builds up" (v. 1). "The source of all

the Corinthians' problems", St John Chrysostom comments, "was not their lack of knowledge but their lack of charity and lack of concern for their neighbour. This was the cause of the divisions in that church, the cause of the vanity which blinded them and of all the disorder for which the Apostle has censured them and will censure them. [...] Have love: that way your knowledge will not lead you astray. I should like your knowledge to outstrip that of your brethren. If you love them, far from being aloof and looking down on them, you will strive to have them share your insights" (*In 1 Corinthios*, 20, ad loc.).

8:7–13 Charity requires that one abstain from food sacrificed to idols, if eating it might prove to be a "stumbling block" to the weak. In this area, charity should prevail over freedom, because scandal could harm a weak person, and Christ died for all, including the weak. "Scandal takes on a particular gravity by reason of the authority of those who cause it or the weakness of those who are scandalized" (*Catechism of the Catholic Church*, 2285).

not eat, and no better off if we do. [9]Only take care lest this liberty of yours somehow become a stumbling block to the weak. [10]For if any one sees you, a man of knowledge, at table in an idol's temple, might he not be encouraged, if his conscience is weak, to eat food offered to idols? [11]And so by your knowledge this weak man is destroyed, the brother for whom Christ died. [12]Thus, sinning against your brethren and wounding their conscience when it is weak, you sin against Christ. [13]Therefore, if food is a cause of my brother's falling, I will never eat meat, lest I cause my brother to fall.

Gal 5:13
Rom 6:15

Rom 14:15
Mt 10:40
Acts 9:5
Rom 14:13, 20–21

The right of apostles to receive maintenance from the faithful

9 [1]Am I not free? Am I not an apostle? Have I not seen Jesus our Lord? Are not you my workmanship in the Lord? [2]If to others I am not an apostle, at least I am to you; for you are the seal of my apostleship in the Lord.

Acts 9:17; 22:17;
26:16
Gal 5:1, 13
Rom 1:1; 6:15
1 Cor 4:15; 15:8
2 Cor 3:2

[3]This is my defence to those who would examine me.* [4]Do we not have the right to our food and drink? [5]Do we not have the right to be accompanied by a wife,[n]* as the other apostles and the brethren of the Lord and Cephas? [6]Or is it only Barnabas and I who have no right to refrain from working for a living? [7]Who serves as a soldier at his own expense? Who plants a vineyard without eating any of its fruit? Who tends a flock without getting some of the milk?

Lk 10:8
1 Cor 4:3
Lk 8:2–3
Mt 8:14; 12:43
Jn 1:42
Acts 4:36; 11:22ff;
18:3
2 Thess 3:9
2 Tim 2:6

[8]Do I say this on human authority? Does not the law say the same? [9]For it is written in the law of Moses, "You shall not muzzle an ox when it is treading out the grain." Is it for oxen that God is concerned? [10]Does he not speak entirely for our sake? It was written for our sake, because the ploughman should plough in hope and the thresher thresh in hope of a share in the crop. [11]If we have sown spiritual good among you, is it too much if we reap your material benefits? [12]If others share this rightful claim upon you, do not we still more?

Deut 25:4
Lk 12:6, 24
1 Tim 5:18
1 Cor 10:11

Rom 15:27
Philem 19
2 Cor 11:9
1 Cor 4:12
Rev 20:23

caverimus, abundabimus. [9]Videte autem, ne forte haec licentia vestra offendiculum fiat infirmis. [10]Si enim quis viderit eum, qui habet scientiam, in idolio recumbentem, nonne conscientia eius, cum sit infirma, aedificabitur ad manducandum idolothyta? [11]Peribit enim infirmus in tua scientia, frater, propter quem Christus mortuus est! [12]Sic autem peccantes in fratres et percutientes conscientiam eorum infirmam, in Christum peccatis. [13]Quapropter si esca scandalizat fratrem meum, non manducabo carnem in aeternum, ne fratrem meum scandalizem.   [9] [1]Non sum liber? Non sum apostolus? Nonne Iesum Dominum nostrum vidi? Non opus meum vos estis in Domino? [2]Si aliis non sum apostolus, sed tamen vobis sum; nam signaculum apostolatus mei vos estis in Domino. [3]Mea defensio apud eos, qui me interrogant, haec est. [4]Numquid non habemus potestatem manducandi et bibendi? [5]Numquid non habemus potestatem sororem mulierem circumducendi sicut et ceteri apostoli et fratres Domini et Cephas? [6]Aut solus ego et Barnabas non habemus potestatem non operandi? [7]Quis militat suis stipendiis umquam? Quis plantat vineam et fructum eius non edit? Aut quis pascit gregem et de lacte gregis non manducat? [8]Numquid secundum hominem haec dico? An et lex haec non dicit? [9]Scriptum est enim in Lege Moysis: «Non alligabis os bovi trituranti». Numquid de bobus cura est Deo? [10]An propter nos utique dicit? Nam propter nos scripta sunt, quoniam debet in spe, qui arat, arare et, qui triturat, in spe fructus percipiendi. [11]Si nos vobis spiritalia seminavimus, magnum est, si nos carnalia vestra metamus? [12]Si alii potestatis vestrae participes sunt, non potius nos? Sed non usi sumus hac potestate, sed omnia sustinemus, ne quod offendiculum demus evangelio Christi. [13]Nescitis quoniam, qui sacra operantur, quae de sacrario sunt edunt; qui altari

9:1–14 St Paul gives an example from his own life to show that charity should take precedence over personal rights. First, he has rights as an apostle— witness the fact that he has seen Jesus Christ (v. 1; cf. Acts 9:1–19; 1 Cor 15:8) and founded the church at Corinth (cf. Acts 18:1–18). He then mentions rights he has not exercised—to be accompanied by a wife or a female helper (vv. 5–6), and to be supported by the faithful (vv. 7–14); he uses the examples of a soldier, a farmer, a shepherd, to show he has the right to be given his upkeep: "Completely devoted as they are to the service of God in the fulfilment of the office entrusted to them, priests are entitled to receive a just remuneration. For 'the labourer deserves his wages' (Lk 10:7), and 'the Lord commanded that they who proclaim the Gospel should get their living by the Gospel' (1 Cor 9:14). For this reason, insofar as provision is not made from some other source for the just remuneration of priests, the faithful are bound by a real obligation to see to it that the necessary provision for a decent and fitting livelihood for the priests is available" (Vatican II, *Presbyterorum ordinis*, 20).

n Greek *a woman, a sister*

Nevertheless, we have not made use of this right, but we endure anything rather

Num 18:8, 31
Deut 18:1–8

than put an obstacle in the way of the gospel of Christ. [13]Do you not know that those

who are employed in the temple service get their food from the temple, and those who

Mt 10:10
Lk 10:7
Gal 6:6

serve at the altar share in the sacrificial offerings? [14]In the same way, the Lord commanded that those who proclaim the gospel should get their living by the gospel.

St Paul does not exercise that right

Acts 18:3

[15]But I have made no use of any of these rights, nor am I writing this to secure any

such provision. For I would rather die than have any one deprive me of my ground

Jer 20:9

for boasting. [16]For if I preach the gospel, that gives me no ground for boasting. For

Acts 4:20; 9:15–16;
22:14–15; 26:16–18
2 Cor 11:7

necessity is laid upon me. Woe to me if I do not preach the gospel! [17]For if I do this

of my own will, I have a reward; but if not of my own will, I am entrusted with a

commission. [18]What then is my reward? Just this: that in my preaching I may make

the gospel free of charge, not making full use of my right in the gospel.

Mt 20:26ff
Rom 6:15
Gal 4:4–5
1 Cor 10:33
Rev 16:3; 21:20
Gal 4:12

[19]For though I am free from all men, I have made myself a slave to all, that I might

win the more. [20]To the Jews I became as a Jew, in order to win Jews; to those under the

law I became as one under the law—though not being myself under the law—that I

might win those under the law. [21]To those outside the law I became as one outside the

law—not being without law toward God but under the law of Christ—that I might win

2 Cor 11:29
Rom 15:1

those outside the law. [22]To the weak I became weak, that I might win the weak. I have

become all things to all men, that I might by all means save some. [23]I do it all for the

sake of the gospel, that I may share in its blessings.

The need for asceticism

Gal 5:7
Wis 4:2; 5:16
Phil 3:14

[24]Do you not know that in a race all the runners compete, but only one receives the

prize? So run that you may obtain it. [25]Every athlete exercises self-control in all

deserviunt, cum altari participantur? [14]Ita et Dominus ordinavit his, qui evangelium annuntiant, de evangelio vivere. [15]Ego autem nullo horum usus sum. Non scripsi autem haec, ut ita fiant in me; bonum est enim mihi magis mori quam ut gloriam meam quis evacuet. [16]Nam si evangelizavero, non est mihi gloria; necessitas enim mihi incumbit. Vae enim mihi est, si non evangelizavero! [17]Si enim volens hoc ago, mercedem habeo; si autem invitus, dispensatio mihi credita est. [18]Quae est ergo merces mea? Ut evangelium praedicans sine sumptu ponam evangelium, ut non abutar potestate mea in evangelio. [19]Nam cum liber essem ex omnibus, omnium me servum feci, ut plures lucri facerem. [20]Et factus sum Iudaeis tamquam Iudaeus, ut Iudaeos lucrarer; his, qui sub lege sunt, quasi sub lege essem, cum ipse non essem sub lege, ut eos, qui sub lege erant, lucri facerem; [21]his, qui sine lege erant, tamquam sine lege essem, cum sine lege Dei non essem, sed in lege essem Christi, ut lucri facerem eos, qui sine lege erant; [22]factus sum infirmis infirmus, ut infirmos lucri facerem; omnibus omnia factus sum, ut aliquos utique facerem salvos. [23]Omnia autem facio propter evangelium, ut compar ticeps eius efficiar. [24]Nescitis quod hi, qui in stadio currunt, omnes quidem currunt, sed unus

9:15–23 Every Christian has a duty to proclaim Jesus Christ (v. 18): "The true apostle is on the lookout for occasions of announcing Christ by word, either to unbelievers to draw them towards the faith, or to the faithful to instruct them, strengthen them, incite them to a more fervent life; 'for Christ's love urges us on' (2 Cor 5:14), and in the hearts of all should the Apostle's words find echo: 'Woe to me if I do not preach the Gospel' (1 Cor 9:16)" (Vatican II, *Apostolicam actuositatem*, 6). "I have become all things to all men" (v. 22). St Paul excludes no one from the scope of his apostolate. "A Christian has to be ready to share his life with everyone at all times, giving to everyone

the chance to come nearer to Christ Jesus. He has to sacrifice his own desires willingly for the sake of others, without separating people into watertight compartments, without pigeonholing them or putting tags on them as though they were merchandise or insect specimens. A Christian cannot afford to separate himself from others, because, if he did that, his life would be miserably selfish. He must become 'all things to all men, in order to save all men' (1 Cor 9:22)" (St Josemaría Escrivá, *Christ Is Passing By*, 124).

9:24–27 The Isthmus Games were held in Corinth every second year. That may explain

things. They do it to receive a perishable wreath, but we an imperishable. ²⁶Well, I do not run aimlessly, I do not box as one beating the air; ²⁷but I pommel my body and subdue it, lest after preaching to others I myself should be disqualified.

2 Tim 4:7f
1 Pet 5:4
Jas 1:12
2 Tim 2:4–6; 4:7–8;
Rev 2:10; 3:11
Rom 8:13; 13:14

The lesson of Israel's history

10 ¹I want you to know, brethren, that our fathers were all under the cloud, and all passed through the sea, and all were baptized into Moses in the cloud and in the sea, ²and all ate the same supernatural° food ³and all drank the same supernatural° drink. ⁴For they drank from the supernatural° Rock which followed them, and the Rock was Christ. ⁵Nevertheless with most of them God was not pleased; for they were overthrown in the wilderness.

Ex 13:21; 14:22
Ps 78:13

Ps 78:29
Ex 16:4–35
Deut 8:3
Ex 17:5-6
Num 20:7-11
Wis 78:15
Num 14:16, 23, 30

⁶Now these things are warnings for us, not to desire evil as they did. ⁷Do not be idolaters as some of them were; as it is written, "The people sat down to eat and drink and rose up to dance." ⁸We must not indulge in immorality as some of them did, and twenty-three thousand fell in a single day. ⁹We must not put the Lord^p to the test, as some of them did and were destroyed by serpents; ¹⁰nor grumble, as some of them did and were destroyed by the Destroyer. ¹¹Now these things happened to them as a warning, but they were written down for our instruction, upon whom the end of the ages has come. ¹²Therefore let any one who thinks that he stands take heed lest he fall. ¹³No temptation has overtaken you that is not common to man. God is faithful, and he will not let you be tempted beyond your strength, but with the temptation will also provide the way of escape, that you may be able to endure it.

Num 11:4, 34

Ex 32:6

Num 25:1–9

Num 21:5f

Num 14:2–36; 17:6–
15
Ex 16:2

Ex 12:23
Rom 15:4
2 Tim 3:16

Gal 6:1
1 Pet 4:7
Sir 15:11–20
Mt 6:13; 26:41
Jas 1:13–15
1 Cor 1:9

---

accipit bravium? Sic currite, ut comprehendatis. ²⁵Omnis autem, qui in agone contendit, ab omnibus se abstinet, et illi quidem, ut corruptibilem coronam accipiant, nos autem incorruptam. ²⁶Ego igitur sic curro non quasi in incertum, sic pugno non quasi aerem verberans; ²⁷sed castigo corpus meum et in servitutem redigo, ne forte, cum aliis praedicaverim, ipse reprobus efficiar. [10] ¹Nolo enim vos ignorare, fratres, quoniam patres nostri omnes sub nube fuerunt et omnes mare transierunt ²et omnes in Moyse baptizati sunt in nube et in mari ³et omnes eandem escam spiritalem manducaverunt ⁴et omnes eundem potum spiritalem biberunt; bibebant autem de spiritali, consequente eos petra: petra autem erat Christus ⁵ Sed non in pluribus eorum complacuit sibi Deus, nam prostrati sunt in deserto. ⁶Haec autem figurae fuerunt nostrae, ut non simus concupiscentes malorum, sicut et illi concupierunt. ⁷Neque idolorum cultores efficiamini, sicut quidam ex ipsis; quemadmodum scriptum est: «Sedit populus manducare et bibere, et surrexerunt ludere». ⁸Neque fornicemur, sicut quidam ex ipsis fornicati sunt, et ceciderunt una die viginti tria milia. ⁹Neque tentemus Christum, sicut quidam eorum tentaverunt, et a serpentibus perierunt. ¹⁰Neque murmuraveritis, sicut quidam eorum murmuraverunt et perierunt ab exterminatore. ¹¹Haec autem in figura contingebant illis; scripta sunt autem ad correptionem nostram, in quos fines saeculorum devenerunt. ¹²Itaque, qui se existimat stare, videat, ne cadat. ¹³Tentatio vos non apprehendit nisi humana; fidelis autem Deus, qui non patietur vos tentari super id quod potestis, sed faciet cum tentatione etiam proventum, ut possitis sustinere. ¹⁴Propter quod, carissimi mihi, fugite ab idolorum

---

why Paul uses metaphors taken from athletics to illustrate what Christian asceticism involves. In Christian life, as in sport, personal limitations and temptations of different kinds are always a stimulus to press on: "During our pilgrimage through this world, our life cannot be free from temptation, for it is precisely through temptation that we make our way forward; no one can truly know himself if he is not tempted, nor be crowned if he has not been victorious, nor be victorious if he has not fought, nor fight if he has no enemies and temptations" (St Augustine, *Enarrationes in Psalmos*, 60, 3).

10:1–13 The exodus of the Israelites from Egypt to the promised land marked a key stage in

salvation history and illustrated God's special love for his people. In spite of all the wonders he worked on their behalf during that period, most of the Israelites died before the journey was over as a consequence of their many infidelities. St Paul points out that there is a lesson here: if we rely too much on ourselves, we run the risk of being unfaithful to God and being rejected by him: "God's gifts to the Hebrews were figures of the gifts of Baptism and the Eucharist which we were to be given; and the punishments meted out to them are figures of the punishment which our ingratitude will deserve; hence his reminder to be watchful" (St John Chrysostom, *In 1 Corinthios*, 23, ad loc.).

o Greek *spiritual*   p Other ancient authorities read *Christ*

Idolatry and the Eucharist, incompatible

1 Jn 5:21
Mt 26:27
Acts 2:42
1 Cor 11:23ff
1 Cor 12:12, 27
Rom 12:4–5
Lev 3:1–17; 7:11–37
Deut 18:1–4
1 Cor 8:4
Ps 106:37
2 Cor 6:15f
Rev 9:20
Mal 1:7, 12
2 Cor 6:14–16
Deut 4:24; 32:21

14Therefore, my beloved, shun the worship of idols. 15I speak as to sensible men;
judge for yourselves what I say. 16The cup of blessing which we bless, is it not a participation[q] in the blood of Christ? The bread which we break, is it not a participation
in the body of Christ? 17Because there is one bread, we who are many are one body,
for we all partake of the one bread. 18Consider the people of Israel; are not those who
eat the sacrifices partners in the altar? 19What do I imply then? That food offered to
idols is anything, or that an idol is anything? 20No, I imply that what pagans sacrifice they offer to demons and not to God. I do not want you to be partners with
demons.* 21You cannot drink the cup of the Lord and the cup of demons. You cannot
partake of the table of the Lord and the table of demons. 22Shall we provoke the
Lord to jealousy? Are we stronger than he?

Practical solutions to certain questions

1 Cor 6:12
Rom 14:19; 15:2
1 Cor 10:33
Phil 12:4
Rom 14:2–10

23"All things are lawful," but not all things are helpful. "All things are lawful," but not
all things build up. 24Let no one seek his own good, but the good of his neighbour. 25Eat
whatever is sold in the meat market without raising any question on the ground of con-

cultura. 15Ut prudentibus loquor; vos iudicate, quod dico: 16Calix benedictionis, cui benedicimus, nonne communicatio sanguinis Christi est? Et panis, quem frangimus, nonne communicatio corporis Christi est? 17Quoniam unus panis, unum corpus multi sumus, omnes enim de uno pane participamur. 18Videte Israel secundum carnem: nonne, qui edunt hostias, communicantes sunt altari? 19Quid ergo dico? Quod idolothytum sit aliquid? Aut quod idolum sit aliquid? 20Sed, quae immolant, daemoniis immolant et non Deo; nolo autem vos communicantes fieri daemoniis. 21Non potestis calicem Domini bibere et calicem daemoniorum; non potestis mensae Domini participes esse et mensae daemoniorum. 22An aemulamur Dominum? Numquid fortiores illo sumus? 23«Omnia licent!» Sed non omnia expediunt. «Omnia licent!». Sed non omnia aedificant. 24Nemo, quod suum est, quaerat, sed quod alterius. 25Omnes, quod in macello venit, manducate, nihil interrogantes propter conscientiam; 26*Domini enim est terra et plenitudo eius*. 27Si quis vocat vos infidelium, et vultis ire, omne, quod vobis apponitur, manducate, nihil interrogantes propter

10:14–22 St Paul returns here to the subject of food offered to idols (see 8:1–6). Although an idol is nothing, Christians should never have anything to do with pagan sacrifices (v. 20). He backs this up by comparing pagan sacrificial banquets with the Eucharistic sacrifice. The key word here is "participation" (v. 16), or "communion", signifying intimacy, a becoming one with. The main effect of the Eucharist is intimate union with Christ. The Fathers of the Church have always emphasized this: "What in fact is the bread? The body of Christ. What do they become who receive Communion? The body of Christ" (St John Chrysostom, *In 1 Corinthios*, 24, ad loc.). Therefore, participation in idolatrous banquets is incompatible with Eucharistic communion, because it violates the Christian's union with Christ and with other Christians. What St Paul says here contains two basic truths about the Eucharist—that it is a sacrifice (a truth adverted to here by the parallel drawn between it and pagan sacrifices: v. 21), and that it is the real presence of Christ (he says that the Eucharist is communion with the Body and Blood of Christ: v. 16): "In the divine sacrifice that is offered in the Mass, the same Christ who offered himself once in a bloody manner on the altar of the cross is present and is offered in an unbloody manner (cf. Heb 9:27). [...] For it is one and the same victim—he who now makes the offering through the ministry of priests and he who then offered himself on the cross; the only difference is in the manner of the offering" (Council of Trent, *De SS. Missae sacrificio*, chap. 2).

10:23–33 St Paul deals with some specific scenarios here and reaffirms the guidelines he has already recommended—avoid giving scandal, and do everything for the glory of God (v. 31): "When you sit down to eat," St Basil says, commenting on this verse, "pray. When you eat bread, do so thanking him for being so generous to you. Similarly, when the sun goes down and when it rises, when you are asleep and awake, give thanks to God, who created and arranged all things for your benefit, to have you know, love and praise their Creator" (*Homilia in martyrem Julittam*).

q Or *communion*

science. ²⁶For "the earth is the Lord's, and everything in it." ²⁷If one of the unbelievers invites you to dinner and you are disposed to go, eat whatever is set before you without raising any question on the ground of conscience. ²⁸(But if some one says to you, "This has been offered in sacrifice," then out of consideration for the man who informed you, and for conscience' sake—²⁹I mean his conscience, not yours—do not eat it.) For why should my liberty be determined by another man's scruples? ³⁰If I partake with thankfulness, why am I denounced because of that for which I give thanks?

³¹So, whether you eat or drink, or whatever you do, do all to the glory of God. ³²Give no offence to Jews or to Greeks or to the church of God, ³³just as I try to please all men in everything I do, not seeking my own advantage, but that of many, that they may be saved.

Ps 24:1
Lk 10:8

1 Cor 8:7

Rom 14:6
1 Tim 4:3–5

Col 3:17
1 Pet 4:11
1 Cor 9:19ff
Rom 15:1–2
1 Cor 10:24

8. THE CELEBRATION OF THE EUCHARIST*

Women in church

11 ¹Be imitators of me, as I am of Christ. ²I commend you because you remember me in everything and maintain the traditions even as I have delivered them to you. ³But I want you to understand that the head of every man is Christ, the head of a woman is her husband, and the head of Christ is God. ⁴Any man who prays or prophesies with his head covered dishonours his head, ⁵but any woman who prays or prophesies with her head unveiled dishonours her head—it is the same as if her head were shaven. ⁶For if a woman will not veil herself, then she should cut off her hair; but if it is disgraceful for a woman to be shorn or shaven, let her wear a veil. ⁷For a man ought not to cover his head, since he is the image and glory of God; but woman is the glory of man. ⁸(For man was not made from woman, but woman from man. ⁹Neither was man created for woman, but woman for man.) ¹⁰That is why a woman ought to have a veil^r on her head, because of the angels. ¹¹(Nevertheless, in the Lord woman is not independent of man nor man of woman; ¹²for as woman was made from man, so man is now born of

1 Cor 4:16
Phil 3:17; 4:9
2 Thess 3:7

1 Thess 2:13; 4-2
2 Thess 2:15
1 Cor 15:1–3
Gen 3:16
Eph 4:15; 5:23
1 Cor 3:23; 12:10;
14:1
Acts 11:27
2 Cor 3:18
1 Cor 11:15

Gen 1:26

Gen 2:18–23
1 Tim 2:13

Gen 3:16; 6:2
1 Cor 14:34

conscientiam. ²⁸Si quis autem vobis dixerit: «Hoc immolaticium est idolis», nolite manducare, propter illum, qui indicavit, et propter conscientiam; ²⁹conscientiam autem dico non tuam ipsius, sed alterius. Ut quid enim libertas mea iudicatur ab alia conscientia? ³⁰Si ego cum gratia participo, quid blasphemor pro eo, quod gratias ago? ³¹Sive ergo manducatis sive bibitis sive aliud quid facitis, omnia in gloriam Dei facite. ³²Sine offensione estote Iudaeis et Graecis et ecclesiae Dei, ³³sicut et ego per omnia omnibus placeo, non quaerens, quod mihi utile est, sed quod multis, ut salvi fiant.   [11] ¹Imitatores mei estote sicut et ego Christi. ²Laudo autem vos quod omnia mei memores estis et, sicut tradidi vobis, traditiones meas tenetis. ³Volo autem vos scire quod omnis viri caput Christus est, caput autem mulieris vir, caput vero Christi Deus. ⁴Omnis vir orans aut prophetans velato capite, deturpat caput suum; ⁵omnis autem mulier orans aut prophetans non velato capite, deturpat caput suum: unum est enim atque si decalvetur. ⁶Nam si non velatur mulier, et tondeatur! Si vero turpe est mulieri tonderi aut decalvari, veletur. ⁷Vir quidem non debet velare caput, quoniam imago et gloria est Dei; mulier autem gloria viri est. ⁸Non enim vir ex muliere est, sed mulier ex viro; ⁹etenim non est creatus vir propter mulierem, sed mulier propter virum. ¹⁰Ideo debet mulier potestatem habere supra caput propter angelos. ¹¹Verumtamen neque mulier sine viro, neque vir sine muliere in Domino; ¹²nam sicut mulier de viro, ita et vir per mulierem, omnia autem ex Deo. ¹³In vobis ipsi iudicate: Decet

*11:1–34 In this section St Paul deals with matters having to do with public worship—the place and behaviour of women during liturgical assemblies (vv. 1–16), and the respect and decorum that should mark the celebration of the Eucharist (vv. 17–34).

11:1–16 The use of the veil by women during liturgical assemblies was not a matter of great importance, but it caused some concern among a

number of the Corinthians (v. 16). The Apostle's reply is in line with Jewish customs of his time, the "traditions" (v. 2) he has handed down. It may well be that the veil question was a touchstone for a deeper issue—hence Paul's insistence that, while man and woman have equal status (v. 11; cf. Gal 3:28), their roles and responsibilities differ. One thing at least can be clearly deduced from what he says here: external behaviour at public worship is important because it reflects inner dispositions.

r Greek *authority* (the veil being a symbol of this)

woman. And all things are from God.) [13]Judge for yourselves; is it proper for a woman to pray to God with her head uncovered? [14]Does not nature itself teach you that for a man to wear long hair is degrading to him, [15]but if a woman has long hair, it is her pride? For her hair is given to her for a covering. [16]If any one is disposed to be contentious, we recognize no other practise, nor do the churches of God.

1 Cor 1:2; 4:17; 7:17; 14:33

Abuses in the celebration of the Eucharist

1 Cor 1:10; 11:22

1 Cor 1:10; 3:3

[17]But in the following instructions I do not commend you, because when you come together it is not for the better but for the worse. [18]For, in the first place, when you assemble as a church, I hear that there are divisions among you; and I partly believe it, [19]for there must be factions among you in order that those who are genuine among you may be recognized. [20]When you meet together, it is not the Lord's supper that you eat.* [21]For in eating, each one goes ahead with his own meal, and one is hungry and another is drunk. [22]What! Do you not have houses to eat and drink in? Or do you despise the church of God and humiliate those who have nothing? What shall I say to you? Shall I commend you in this? No, I will not.

1 Cor 1:2
Jas 2:5

Mt 26:26–29
Mk 14:22–25
Lk 22:14-20

The institution of the Eucharist and its worthy reception

1 Cor 15:3

Ex 12:14
Deut 16:3

Ex 24:8
Jer 31:31
Lk 22:20
Heb 8:6–13

Mt 26:29
Mk 14:25
Lk 22:16–18
1 Cor 16:22

[23]For I received from the Lord what I also delivered to you, that the Lord Jesus on the night when he was betrayed took bread, [24]and when he had given thanks, he broke it, and said, "This is my body which is for[s] you. Do this in remembrance of me." [25]In the same way also the cup, after supper, saying, "This cup is the new covenant in my blood. Do this, as often as you drink it, in remembrance of me." [26]For as often as you eat this bread and drink the cup, you proclaim the Lord's death until he comes.

mulierem non velatam orare Deum? [14]Nec ipsa natura docet vos quod vir quidem, si comam nutriat, ignominia est illi, [15]mulier vero, si comam nutriat, gloria est illi? Quoniam coma pro velamine ei data est. [16]Si quis autem videtur contentiosus esse, nos talem consuetudinem non habemus, neque ecclesiae Dei. [17]Hoc autem praecipio non laudans quod non in melius sed in deterius convenitis. [18]Primum quidem convenientibus vobis in ecclesia, audio scissuras inter vos esse et ex parte credo. [19]Nam oportet et haereses inter vos esse, ut et, qui probati sunt, manifesti fiant in vobis. [20]Convenientibus ergo vobis in unum, non est dominicam cenam manducare; [21]unusquisque enim suam cenam praesumit in manducando, et alius quidem esurit, alius autem ebrius est. [22]Numquid domos non habetis ad manducandum et bibendum? Aut ecclesiam Dei contemnitis et confunditis eos, qui non habent? Quid dicam vobis? Laudabo vos? In hoc non laudo? [23]Ego enim accepi a Domino, quod et tradidi vobis, quoniam Domi-

11:17–22 St Paul addresses a serious abuse here. In the early days of the Church Christians used to combine the celebration of the Eucharist with a meal in common. This meal was intended to be a sign of charity and solidarity (which was why it was called an *ágape* or fraternal meal) and it provided an opportunity to help those most in need. However, certain abuses had arisen, and these meals were in sharp contrast with the Eucharist, the source of charity and unity. Very early on in the Church, the Eucharist was set apart from these meals, when they became simple fraternal meals with no liturgical significance.

11:23–34 The teaching about the Eucharist passed on here by St Paul shows the importance of apostolic Tradition (v. 23). Together with the

passages in Matthew, Mark and Luke, verses 23–25 are one of the four New Testament accounts of the institution of the Eucharist. The passage contains the basic elements of Christian belief in the mystery of the Eucharist—the institution of this sacrament by Jesus Christ, the fact that his presence in the Eucharist is real, the institution of the Christian priesthood, and the fact that the Eucharist is a sacrifice: "Do this in remembrance of me." This instruction means the Eucharist is a commemoration, renewal and representation of the paschal sacrifice of Calvary. The Church reads these words as implying the institution of Christian priesthood: The Council of Trent teaches that Jesus Christ our Lord, at the Last Supper, "offered his body and blood under the species of bread and wine to God the Father and

s Other ancient authorities read *broken for*

²⁷Whoever, therefore, eats the bread or drinks the cup of the Lord in an unworthy
manner will be guilty of profaning the body and blood of the Lord. ²⁸Let a man
examine himself, and so eat of the bread and drink of the cup. ²⁹For any one who
eats and drinks without discerning the body eats and drinks judgment upon himself.
³⁰That is why many of you are weak and ill, and some have died.^t ³¹But if we judged
ourselves truly, we should not be judged. ³²But when we are judged by the Lord, we
are chastened^u so that we may not be condemned along with the world.

³³So then, my brethren, when you come together to eat, wait for one another—³⁴if
any one is hungry, let him eat at home—lest you come together to be condemned.
About the other things I will give directions when I come.

Rev 22:17−20
Heb 10:29
2 Cor 13:5

1 Thess 5:6−7

Deut 8:5
Heb 12:5
Prov 3:11−12
Wis 11:9−10

9. GIFTS AND GRACES*

Kinds of spiritual gifts

12 ¹Now concerning spiritual gifts, brethren, I do not want you to be unin-
formed.* ²You know that when you were heathen, you were led astray to

1 Cor 14:1
Gal 4:8

nus Iesus, in qua nocte tradebatur, accepit panem ²⁴et gratias agens fregit et dixit: «*Hoc est corpus meum, quod pro vobis est; hoc facite in meam
commemorationem*»; ²⁵similiter et calicem, postquam cenatum est, dicens: «*Hic calix novum testamentum est in meo sanguine; hoc facite, quoti-
escumque bibetis, in meam commemorationem*». ²⁶Quotiescumque enim manducabitis panem hunc et calicem bibetis, mortem Domini annunti-
atis, donec veniat. ²⁷Itaque, quicumque manducaverit panem vel biberit calicem Domini indigne, reus erit corporis et sanguinis Domini. ²⁸Probet
autem seipsum homo, et sic de pane illo edat et de calice bibat; ²⁹qui enim manducat et bibit, iudicium sibi manducat et bibit non diiudicans
corpus. ³⁰Ideo inter vos multi infirmi et imbecilles et dormiunt multi. ³¹Quod si nosmetipsos diiudicaremus, non utique iudicaremur; ³²dum iudica-
mur autem, a Domino corripimur, ut non cum hoc mundo damnemur. ³³Itaque, fratres mei, cum convenitis ad manducandum, invicem exspectate.
³⁴Si quis esurit, domi manducet, ut non in iudicium conveniatis. Cetera autem, cum venero, disponam. [12] ¹De spiritalibus autem, fratres, nolo

he gave his body and blood under the same
species to the apostles to receive, making them
priests of the New Testament at that time. [...] He
ordered the apostles and their successors in the
priesthood to offer this sacrament when he said,
'Do this in remembrance of me', as the Catholic
Church has always understood and taught" (*De
SS. Missae sacrificio*, chap. 1; cf. can. 2).

The application of this teaching to what is
happening in Corinth (vv. 27–32) gives rise to an
unambiguous statement of the real presence of
Jesus Christ under the appearance of the bread
and wine. That explains why a person needs to
be properly prepared, body and soul, to receive
the Eucharist, and why receiving it unworthily
has such grave consequences (vv. 27–29). Divisions and quarrels can have no place in the
reception of the Body of Christ, and that condition holds good for any kind of grave sin:
"Anyone conscious of a grave sin must receive
the sacrament of Reconciliation before coming
to communion" (*Catechism of the Catholic
Church*, 1385; cf. *Code of Canon Law*, can. 919,
1). Apropos of what St Paul says in v. 28, John
Paul II has written: "This call by the Apostle

indicates at least indirectly the close link
between the Eucharist and Penance. Indeed, if
the first word of Christ's teaching, the first
phrase of the Gospel Good News, was 'Repent,
and believe in the gospel' (*metanoeite*: Mk 1:15),
the Sacrament of the Passion, Cross and Resurrection seems to strengthen and consolidate in an
altogether special way this call in our souls. The
Eucharist and Penance thus become in a sense
two closely connected dimensions of authentic
life in accordance with the spirit of the Gospel,
of truly Christian life. The Christ who calls to the
Eucharistic banquet is always the same Christ
who exhorts us to penance and repeats his
'Repent'" (*Redemptor hominis*, 20).

*12:1−14:40 St Paul here takes up a new
theme, that of spiritual gifts or charisms, which
were being used in a disordered and disruptive
way even during liturgical assemblies. This gives
him the opportunity to stress that the greatest gift
is love, charity (13:1–13).

12:1−11 Apparently, in pagan circles in Corinth
there were some instances of religious exaltation,

t Greek *have fallen asleep* (as in 15:6, 20) u Or *when we are judged we are being chastened by the Lord*

Jn 14:26
1 Jn 4:1–3
Acts 2:21, 26
Rom 10:9
Phil 2:11

dumb idols, however you may have been moved. ³Therefore I want you to understand that no one speaking by the Spirit of God ever says "Jesus be cursed!" and no one can say "Jesus is Lord" except by the Holy Spirit.

Rom 12:6
Eph 4:4–6

⁴Now there are varieties of gifts, but the same Spirit; ⁵and there are varieties of service, but the same Lord; ⁶and there are varieties of working, but it is the same

1 Cor 8:6

God who inspires them all in every one. ⁷To each is given the manifestation of the

1 Cor 12:28–30
Eph 4:7
Rom 12:6–8
Eph 4:11
Acts 11:27
Acts 2:4
1 Jn 4:1–3

Spirit for the common good. ⁸To one is given through the Spirit the utterance of wisdom, and to another the utterance of knowledge according to the same Spirit, ⁹to another faith by the same Spirit, to another gifts of healing by the one Spirit, ¹⁰to another the working of miracles, to another prophecy, to another the ability to distinguish between spirits, to another various kinds of tongues, to another the inter-

Rom 12:3
Eph 4:7
1 Pet 4:10

pretation of tongues. ¹¹All these are inspired by one and the same Spirit, who apportions to each one individually as he wills.

Unity and variety in the mystical body of Christ

Rom 12:4–5
1 Cor 10:17; 12:27

Gal 3:28
Eph 4:4–6
Col 3:11
Philem 16

¹²For just as the body is one and has many members, and all the members of the body, though many, are one body, so it is with Christ. ¹³For by one Spirit we were all baptized into one body—Jews or Greeks, slaves or free—and all were made to drink of one Spirit.

vos ignorare. ²Scitis quoniam, cum gentes essetis, ad simulacra muta, prout ducebamini, euntes. ³Ideo notum vobis facio quod nemo in Spiritu Dei loquens dicit: «Anathema Iesus!», et nemo potest dicere: «Dominus Iesus», nisi in Spiritu Sancto. ⁴Divisiones vero gratiarum sunt, idem autem Spiritus; ⁵et divisiones ministrationum sunt, idem autem Dominus; ⁶et divisiones operationum sunt, idem vero Deus, qui operatur omnia in omnibus. ⁷Unicuique autem datur manifestatio Spiritus ad utilitatem. ⁸Alii quidem per Spiritum datur sermo sapientiae, alii autem sermo scientiae secundum eundem Spiritum, ⁹alteri fides in eodem Spiritu, alii donationes sanitatum in uno Spiritu, ¹⁰alii operationes virtutum, alii prophetatio, alii discretio spirituum, alii genera linguarum, alii interpretatio linguarum; ¹¹haec autem omnia operatur unus et idem Spiritus, dividens singulis, prout vult. ¹²Sicut enim corpus unum est et membra habet multa, omnia autem membra corporis, cum sint multa, unum corpus sunt, ita

such as people going into trances and sometimes speaking in foreign tongues: such things featured at services at the shrine of the Delphic Oracle, near Corinth. St Paul provides a general principle for distinguishing pagan phenomena of this kind from genuine gifts of the Holy Spirit, which always acknowledge and praise Jesus (v. 3).

He lists and evaluates those charisms and ministries which, through the action of the Holy Spirit, help to build up the Church (vv. 7–10). "It is not only through the sacraments and the ministrations of the Church that the Holy Spirit makes holy the people, leads them and enriches them with his virtues. Allotting his gifts according as he wills (cf. Cor 12:11), he also distributes special graces among the faithful of every rank. By these gifts he makes them fit and ready to undertake various tasks and offices for the renewal and building up of the Church, as it is written, 'To each is given the manifestation of the Spirit for the common good' (1 Cor 12:7). Whether these charisms be very remarkable or more simple and widely diffused, they are to be

received with thanksgiving and consolation since they are fitting and useful for the needs of the Church. Extraordinary gifts are not to be rashly desired, nor is it from them that the fruits of apostolic labours are to be presumptuously expected" (Vatican II, *Lumen gentium*, 12).

12:12–31 St Paul uses the comparison of the Church with a body to point out two important facts—the identification of the Church with Christ (v. 12) and the fact that the Holy Spirit is the life-principle of the Church. The identification of the Church with Christ is not a metaphor: "The complete Christ is made up of the head and the body, as I am sure you know well. The head is our Saviour himself, who suffered under Pontius Pilate and now, after rising from the dead, is seated at the right hand of the Father. And his body is the Church. Not this or that church, but the Church which is to be found all over the world. Nor is it only that which exists among us today, for also belonging to it are those who lived before us and those who will live in the future,

¹⁴For the body does not consist of one member but of many. ¹⁵If the foot should
say, "Because I am not a hand, I do not belong to the body," that would not make it
any less a part of the body. ¹⁶And if the ear should say, "Because I am not an eye, I
do not belong to the body," that would not make it any less a part of the body. ¹⁷If
the whole body were an eye, where would be the hearing? If the whole body were
an ear, where would be the sense of smell? ¹⁸But as it is, God arranged the organs in
the body, each one of them, as he chose. ¹⁹If all were a single organ, where would
the body be? ²⁰As it is, there are many parts, yet one body. ²¹The eye cannot say to
the hand, "I have no need of you," nor again the head to the feet, "I have no need of
you." ²²On the contrary, the parts of the body which seem to be weaker are indispensable, ²³and those parts of the body which we think less honourable we invest
with the greater honour, and our unpresentable parts are treated with greater modesty, ²⁴which our more presentable parts do not require. But God has so composed
the body, giving the greater honour to the inferior part, ²⁵that there may be no discord in the body, but that the members may have the same care for one another. ²⁶If
one member suffers, all suffer together; if one member is honoured, all rejoice
together.

[1 Cor 12:20]

[1 Cor 12:14]

[Rom 12:15]

et Christus; ¹³etenim in uno Spiritu omnes nos in unum corpus baptizati sumus, sive Iudaei sive Graeci sive servi sive liberi, et omnes unum Spiritum potati sumus. ¹⁴Nam et corpus non est unum membrum sed multa. ¹⁵Si dixerit pes: «Non sum manus, non sum de corpore», non ideo non est
de corpore; ¹⁶et si dixerit auris: «Non sum oculus, non sum de corpore», non ideo non est de corpore. ¹⁷Si totum corpus oculus est, ubi auditus?
Si totum auditus, ubi odoratus? ¹⁸Nunc autem posuit Deus membra, unumquodque eorum in corpore, sicut voluit. ¹⁹Quod si essent omnia unum
membrum, ubi corpus? ²⁰Nunc autem multa quidem membra, unum autem corpus. ²¹Non potest dicere oculus manui: «Non es mihi necessaria!»,
aut iterum caput pedibus: «Non estis mihi necessarii!». ²²Sed multo magis, quae videntur membra corporis infirmiora esse, necessaria sunt; ²³et,
quae putamus ignobiliora membra esse corporis, his honorem abundantiorem circumdamus; et, quae inhonesta sunt nostra, abundantiorem hon-
estatem habent, ²⁴honesta autem nostra nullius egent. Sed Deus temperavit corpus, ei, cui deerat, abundantiorem tribuendo honorem, ²⁵ut non sit
schisma in corpore, sed idipsum pro invicem sollicita sint membra. ²⁶Et sive patitur unum membrum, compatiuntur omnia membra; sive glorifi-
catur unum membrum, congaudent omnia membra. ²⁷Vos autem estis corpus Christi et membra ex parte. ²⁸Et quosdam quidem posuit Deus in

right up to the end of the world. All this Church,
made up of the assembly of the faithful—for all
the faithful are members of Christ—has Christ as
its head, governing his body from heaven. And
although this head is located out of sight of the
body, he is, however, joined to it by love" (St
Augustine, *Enarrationes in Psalmos*, 56, 1).

The source of the organic unity of the Church
is the Holy Spirit, who not only assembles the
faithful into a society but also imbues and vivi-
fies its members, in the same way as the soul
gives life to the physical body: "In order that we
might be unceasingly renewed in him (cf. Eph
4:23), he has shared with us his Spirit who,
being one and the same in head and members,
gives life to, unifies and moves the whole body.
Consequently, his work could be compared by
the Fathers to the function that the principle of
life, the soul, fulfils in the human body" (Vatican
II, *Lumen gentium*, 7).

The fact that Christians are in living union
with one another and influence one another by
their lives (v. 26) is something that the Church

has always taught: it is found in the profession of
faith, the Creed, where it is called the "communion of saints": "this expression refers first to the
'holy things' (*sancta*), above all the Eucharist, by
which 'the unity of believers, who form one
body in Christ, is both represented and brought
about' (*Lumen gentium*, 3). The term 'communion of saints' refers also to the communion of
'holy persons' (*sancti*) in Christ who 'died for
all,' so that what each one does or suffers in and
for Christ bears fruit for all" (*Catechism of the
Catholic Church*, 960 and 961).

"Earnestly desire the higher gifts" (v. 31).
What some Greek manuscripts have here can be
translated as "earnestly seek the greater gifts". St
Paul is encouraging his Christians to put greater
value on those gifts of the Spirit that contribute
most to the good of the Church. "The first and
most necessary gift is charity, by which we love
God above all things and our neighbour because
of him. [...] [L]ove, as the bond of perfection
and fullness of the law (cf. Col 3:14, Rom.
13:10), governs, gives meaning to, and perfects

Rom 12:7–11
Eph 5:30

Rom 1:1
Eph 4:11
Acts 11:27

Eph 5:30
Rom 12:5

1 Cor 14:1

²⁷Now you are the body of Christ and individually members of it. ²⁸And God has appointed in the church first apostles, second prophets, third teachers, then workers of miracles, then healers, helpers, administrators, speakers in various kinds of tongues. ²⁹Are all apostles? Are all prophets? Are all teachers? Do all work miracles? ³⁰Do all possess gifts of healing? Do all speak with tongues? Do all interpret? ³¹But earnestly desire the higher gifts.

And I will show you a still more excellent way.*

Hymn to charity

Mt 7:22

Mt 17:20; 21:22
Mk 11:23
1 Cor 14:3, 5
Jas 2:14–17

Dan 3:28
Mt 6:22; 9:21

Rom 13:9–10
1 Thess 5:14f
1 Pet 4:8

13 ¹If I speak in the tongues of men and of angels, but have not love, I am a noisy gong or a clanging cymbal. ²And if I have prophetic powers, and understand all mysteries and all knowledge, and if I have all faith, so as to remove mountains, but have not love, I am nothing. ³If I give away all I have, and if I deliver my body to be burned,ᵛ but have not love, I gain nothing.

⁴Love is patient and kind; love is not jealous or boastful; ⁵it is not arrogant or rude. Love does not insist on its own way; it is not irritable or resentful; ⁶it does not

ecclesia primum apostolos, secundo prophetas, tertio doctores, deinde virtutes, exinde donationes curationum, opitulationes, gubernationes, genera linguarum. ²⁹Numquid omnes apostoli? Numquid omnes prophetae? Numquid omnes doctores? Numquid omnes virtutes? ³⁰Numquid omnes donationes habent curationum? Numquid omnes linguis loquuntur? Numquid omnes interpretantur? ³¹Aemulamini autem charismata maiora. Et adhuc excellentiorem viam vobis demonstro.   [13] ¹Si linguis hominum loquar et angelorum, caritatem autem non habeam, factus sum velut aes sonans aut cymbalum tinniens. ²Et si habuero prophetiam et noverim mysteria omnia et omnem scientiam, et si habuero omnem fidem, ita ut montes transferam, caritatem autem non habuero, nihil sum. ³Et si distribuero in cibos omnes facultates meas et si tradidero corpus meum, ut glo-

all the means of sanctification. Hence the true disciple of Christ is marked by love both of God and of his neighbour" (Vatican II, *Lumen gentium*, 42).

13:1–13 This hymn to charity is one of the most beautiful passages in Pauline writing. The Apostle sings the praises of love from three points of view—the superiority of, and absolute need for, this gift (vv. 1–3); its features and practical expression (vv. 4–7); and the fact that charity endures forever (vv. 8–13).

Charity is so excellent a gift that without it all other gifts can have neither meaning nor value (vv. 1–3). To make this point clear, St Paul mentions those gifts that seem to be most exceptional—the gift of tongues, knowledge, and heroic actions; charity is more useful and valuable than any of those gifts: "Our love is not to be confused with sentimentality or mere good fellowship, nor with that somewhat questionable zeal to help others in order to convince ourselves of our superiority. Rather, it means living in peace with our neighbour, venerating the image of God that is found in each and every person and doing all we can to get them in their turn to contemplate that image and learn to turn to

Christ" (St Josemaría Escrivá, *Friends of God*, 230).

In the list of the virtues of charity (vv. 4–7), the most important are patience and kindness, two qualities that the Bible attributes to God (see Ps 145:8): "Love is patient," St Gregory the Great comments, "because it bears serenely the injury it suffers. It is kind, because it repays evil with good. It is not jealous, because it covets nothing in this world: it does not know what it is to envy worldly prosperity. It is not boastful, because it yearns only for spiritual reward, and it is not carried away by external things. It is not arrogant, because it thrives only on the love of God and neighbour and avoids whatever would take it from the path of righteousness. It is not covetous, because although it ardently pursues its own spiritual goals, it does not desire the goods of others. It does not insist on its own way, because it scorns as alien those things it temporarily possesses here below: it seeks to hold on only to what is enduring. It is not irritable, and even though injuries seek to provoke it, it does not let itself have any desire for vengeance, for no matter how difficult a time it may have in this life, it hopes for greater rewards in the next. It is not resentful, because it has

v Other ancient authorities read *body that I may glory*

rejoice at wrong, but rejoices in the right. ⁷Love bears all things, believes all things, hopes all things, endures all things.

Rom 12:9
Prov 10:12

⁸Love never ends; as for prophecies, they will pass away; as for tongues, they will cease; as for knowledge, it will pass away. ⁹For our knowledge is imperfect and our prophecy is imperfect; ¹⁰but when the perfect comes, the imperfect will pass away. ¹¹When I was a child, I spoke like a child, I thought like a child, I reasoned like a child; when I became a man, I gave up childish ways. ¹²For now we see in a mirror dimly, but then face to face. Now I know in part; then I shall understand fully, even as I have been fully understood. ¹³So faith, hope, love abide, these three; but the greatest of these is love.

1 Cor 13:13
Acts 2:4; 11:27
1 Pet 4:8

Num 12:8
2 Cor 5:7
Jas 1:23
1 Jn 3:2
Gal 4:9

1 Thess 1:3
1 Jn 4:16
Heb 10:22–24
Col 3:14

Prophecy, the gift of tongues, and interpretation of tongues

14 ¹Make love your aim, and earnestly desire the spiritual gifts, especially that you may prophesy. ²For one who speaks in a tongue speaks not to men but to God; for no one understands him, but he utters mysteries in the Spirit. ³On the other hand, he who prophesies speaks to men for their upbuilding and encouragement and consolation. ⁴He who speaks in a tongue edifies himself, but he who prophesies edifies the church. ⁵Now I want you all to speak in tongues, but even more to prophesy. He who prophesies is greater than he who speaks in tongues, unless some one interprets, so that the church may be edified.

1 Cor 12:10, 31
Acts 11:27; 2:4
Rom 1:9
1 Thess 5:20

Num 11:29

⁶Now, brethren, if I come to you speaking in tongues, how shall I benefit you unless I bring you some revelation or knowledge or prophecy or teaching? ⁷If even

1 Cor 12:8

---

rier, caritatem autem non habuero, nihil mihi prodest. ⁴Caritas patiens est, benigna est caritas, non aemulatur, non agit superbe, non inflatur, ⁵non est ambitiosa, non quaerit, quae sua sunt, non irritatur, non cogitat malum, ⁶non gaudet super iniquitatem, congaudet autem veritati; ⁷omnia suffert, omnia credit, omnia sperat, omnia sustinet. ⁸Caritas numquam excidit. Sive prophetiae, evacuabuntur; sive linguae, cessabunt; sive scientia, destruetur. ⁹Ex parte enim cognoscimus et ex parte prophetamus; ¹⁰cum autem venerit, quod perfectum est, evacuabitur, quod ex parte est. ¹¹Cum essem parvulus, loquebar ut parvulus, sapiebam ut parvulus, cogitabam ut parvulus; quando factus sum vir, evacuavi, quae erant parvuli. ¹²Videmus enim nunc per speculum in aenigmate, tunc autem facie ad faciem; nunc cognosco ex parte, tunc autem cognoscam, sicut et cognitus sum. ¹³Nunc autem manet fides, spes, caritas, tria haec; maior autem ex his est caritas. [14] ¹Sectamini caritatem, aemulamini spiritalia, magis autem, ut prophetetis. ²Qui enim loquitur lingua, non hominibus loquitur, sed Deo; nemo enim audit, spiritu autem loquitur mysteria. ³Qui autem prophetat, hominibus loquitur aedificationem et exhortationem et consolationes. ⁴Qui loquitur lingua, semetipsum aedificat; qui autem prophetat, ecclesiam aedificat. ⁵Volo autem omnes vos loqui linguis, magis autem prophetare; maior autem est qui prophetat quam qui loquitur linguis, nisi

---

invested its thought in the love of purity, and having rooted out all hatred it is incapable of harbouring in its heart any type of aversion. It does not rejoice at wrong, because it feels affection for others and does not rejoice at seeing the ruin of its enemies. It rejoices in the right, because by loving others as it loves itself, it is as pleased to see goodness in them as if it were indeed something to its own personal advantage" (*Moralia*, 10, 7–8, 10).

Charity is the greatest of God's gifts (v. 13). Other gifts are given to help us achieve perfection and lasting happiness; but charity is beatitude itself.

14:1–25 In these verses, St Paul continues his teaching on charity, and stresses the importance of prophecy. Here the gift of prophecy means the

faculty of speaking on impulse in the name of God to console and edify hearers; it does not necessarily include the ability to foretell the future or reveal hidden things. The gift of tongues was seen as a supernatural faculty to pray or sing the praises of God with great enthusiasm, using strange words that often required the help of an interpreter to be understood. This gift often impressed people, non-believers included (v. 22), but it did little to instruct; whereas prophecy does help to communicate the truth (v. 24).

"So that the church may be edified" (v. 5). According to this criterion for discerning gifts, the gift of prophecy deserves pride of place: "This is the rule", St John Chrysostom comments, "constantly followed by St Paul—to give preference to the gifts that make for the edifying

lifeless instruments, such as the flute or the harp, do not give distinct notes, how will any one know what is played? [8]And if the bugle gives an indistinct sound, who will get ready for battle? [9]So with yourselves; if you in a tongue utter speech that is not intelligible, how will any one know what is said? For you will be speaking into the air. [10]There are doubtless many different languages in the world, and none is without meaning; [11]but if I do not know the meaning of the language, I shall be a foreigner to the speaker and the speaker a foreigner to me. [12]So with yourselves; since you are eager for manifestations of the Spirit, strive to excel in building up the church.

1 Cor 14:1–4

[13]Therefore, he who speaks in a tongue should pray for the power to interpret. [14]For if I pray in a tongue, my spirit prays but my mind is unfruitful. [15]What am I to do? I will pray with the spirit and I will pray with the mind also; I will sing with the spirit and I will sing with the mind. [16]Otherwise, if you bless[w] with the spirit, how can any one in the position of an outsider[x] say the "Amen" to your thanksgiving when he does not know what you are saying? [17]For you may give thanks well enough, but the other man is not edified. [18]I thank God that I speak in tongues more than you all; [19]nevertheless, in church I would rather speak five words with my mind, in order to instruct others, than ten thousand words in a tongue.

1 Cor 12:10

Eph 5:19

1 Chron 16:36
Neh 8:6
2 Cor 1:20

[20]Brethren, do not be children in your thinking; be babes in evil, but in thinking be mature. [21]In the law it is written, "By men of strange tongues and by the lips of foreigners will I speak to this people, and even then they will not listen to me, says the Lord." [22]Thus, tongues are a sign not for believers but for unbelievers, while prophecy is not for unbelievers but for believers. [23]If, therefore, the whole church assembles and all speak in tongues, and outsiders or unbelievers enter, will they not say that you are mad? [24]But if all prophesy, and an unbeliever or outsider enters, he is convicted by all, he is called to account by all, [25]the secrets of his heart are disclosed; and so, falling on his face, he will worship God and declare that God is really among you.

Rom 16:19
Eph 4:14
Phil 3:12, 15

Is 28:11f

Is 45:14
Zech 8:23

forte interpretetur, ut ecclesia aedificationem accipiat. [6]Nunc autem, fratres, si venero ad vos linguis loquens, quid vobis prodero, nisi vobis loquar aut in revelatione aut in scientia aut in prophetia aut in doctrina? [7]Tamen, quae sine anima sunt vocem dantia, sive tibia sive cithara, nisi distinctionem sonituum dederint, quomodo scietur quod tibia canitur aut quod citharizatur? [8]Etenim si incertam vocem det tuba, quis parabit se ad bellum? [9]Ita et vos per linguam nisi manifestum sermonem dederitis, quomodo scietur id, quod dicitur? Eritis enim in aera loquentes. [10]Tam multa, ut puta, genera linguarum sunt in mundo, et nihil sine voce est. [11]Si ergo nesciero virtutem vocis, ero ei, qui loquitur, barbarus; et, qui loquitur, mihi, barbarus. [12]Sic et vos, quoniam aemulatores estis spirituum, ad aedificationem ecclesiae quaerite, ut abundetis. [13]Et ideo, qui loquitur lingua, oret, ut interpretetur. [14]Nam si orem lingua, spiritus meus orat, mens autem mea sine fructu est. [15]Quid ergo est? Orabo spiritu, orabo et mente; psallam spiritu, psallam et mente. [16]Ceterum si benedixeris in spiritu, qui supplet locum idiotae, quomodo dicet «Amen!» super tuam benedictionem, quoniam quid dicas nescit? [17]Nam tu quidem bene gratias agis, sed alter non aedificatur. [18]Gratias ago Deo quod omnium vestrum magis linguis loquor; [19]sed in ecclesia volo quinque verba sensu meo loqui, ut et alios instruam, quam decem milia verborum in lingua. [20]Fratres, nolite pueri effici sensibus, sed malitia parvuli estote, sensibus autem perfecti estote. [21]In lege scriptum est: «*In aliis linguis et in labiis aliorum / loquar populo huic, / et nec sic exaudient me*», dicit Dominus. [22]Itaque linguae in signum sunt non fidelibus sed infidelibus, prophetia autem non infidelibus sed fidelibus. [23]Si ergo conveniat universa ecclesia in unum, et omnes linguis loquantur, intrent autem idiotae aut infideles, nonne dicent quod insanitis? [24]Si autem omnes prophetent, intret autem quis infidelis vel idiota, convincitur ab omnibus, diiudicatur ab omnibus, [25]occulta cordis eius manifesta fiunt, et ita cadens in faciem adorabit Deum pronuntians: «Vere Deus in vobis est!». [26]Quid ergo est, fratres? Cum convenitis, unusquisque psalmum habet, doctrinam habet, apocalypsim habet, linguam habet, interpretationem habet: omnia ad aedificationem fiant. [27]Sive

of the Church. Someone will ask, 'Is it possible for someone to speak in tongues without speaking to the benefit of his brethren?' Listen: those Christians do speak [in tongues], but what they say is less helpful to the edification, exhortation and consolation of souls than the gift of prophecy. Both [prophets and those who speak in tongues] are acting as the voice of the Holy Spirit who moves and inspires them; but what the prophet says is useful to those faithful who hear him, whereas the gift of tongues does not lead to understanding unless the hearers themselves have received the same supernatural gift" (*In 1 Corinthios*, 35, ad loc.).

w That is, *give thanks to God*   x Or *him that is without gifts*

Regulation of liturgical assemblies

²⁶What then, brethren? When you come together, each one has a hymn, a lesson, a revelation, a tongue, or an interpretation. Let all things be done for edification. ²⁷If any speak in a tongue, let there be only two or at most three, and each in turn; and let one interpret. ²⁸But if there is no one to interpret, let each of them keep silence in church and speak to himself and to God. ²⁹Let two or three prophets speak, and let the others weigh what is said. ³⁰If a revelation is made to another sitting by, let the first be silent. ³¹For you can all prophesy one by one, so that all may learn and all be encouraged; ³²and the spirits of prophets are subject to prophets. ³³For God is not a God of confusion but of peace.

As in all the churches of the saints, ³⁴the women should keep silence in the churches. For they are not permitted to speak, but should be subordinate, as even the law says. ³⁵If there is anything they desire to know, let them ask their husbands at home. For it is shameful for a woman to speak in church. ³⁶What! Did the word of God originate with you, or are you the only ones it has reached?

³⁷If any one thinks that he is a prophet, or spiritual, he should acknowledge that what I am writing to you is a command of the Lord. ³⁸If any one does not recognize this, he is not recognized. ³⁹So, my brethren, earnestly desire to prophesy, and do not forbid speaking in tongues; ⁴⁰but all things should be done decently and in order.

Margin references:
Eph 4:12
1 Cor 11:18, 20

Acts 17:11
1 Thess 5:21

Acts 9:13
Gen 3:16
1 Cor 11:16
Eph 5:22
1 Thess 2:12
Tit 2:5
1 Tim 2:11-14

1 Jn 4:6
1 Cor 2:16; 7:40;
15:34

1 Cor 14:1, 5

Col 2:5

---

lingua quis loquitur, secundum duos aut ut multum tres, et per partes, et unus interpretetur; ²⁸si autem non fuerit interpres, taceat in ecclesia, sibi autem loquatur et Deo. ²⁹Prophetae duo aut tres dicant, et ceteri diiudicent; ³⁰quod si alii revelatum fuerit sedenti, prior taceat. ³¹Potestis enim omnes per singulos prophetare, ut omnes discant et omnes exhortentur, ³²et spiritus prophetarum prophetis subiecti sunt; ³³non enim est dissensionis Deus sed pacis. Sicut in omnibus ecclesiis sanctorum, ³⁴mulieres in ecclesiis taceant, non enim permittitur eis loqui; sed subditae sint, sicut et lex dicit. ³⁵Si quid autem volunt discere, domi viros suos interrogent; turpe est enim mulieri loqui in ecclesia. ³⁶An a vobis verbum Dei processit aut in vos solos pervenit? ³⁷Si quis videtur propheta esse aut spiritalis, cognoscat, quae scribo vobis, quia Domini est mandatum. ³⁸Si quis autem ignorat, ignorabitur. ³⁹Itaque, fratres mei, aemulamini prophetare et loqui linguis nolite prohibere; ⁴⁰omnia autem honeste et secundum

---

14:26–40 In their assemblies, the Corinthians could become so fired up with enthusiasm (possibly taking a cue from what happened at pagan religious rites) that there was a danger of the celebration slipping out of control. Therefore, the Apostle gives some guidelines on how the faithful should conduct themselves at liturgical assemblies. He addresses those who speak in tongues (vv. 27–28), those who prophesy (vv. 29–33), and women (vv. 34–35). Then he summarizes everything he has been saying (vv. 36–40).

As regards women (v. 34), St Paul is not opposed to their prophesying (cf. 11:5; what he says has to be read in the context of the circumstances that had arisen in assemblies at Corinth. "The prohibition solely concerns the official function of teaching in the Christian assembly. [...] Nor should it be forgotten that we owe to St Paul one of the most vigorous texts in the New Testament on the fundamental equality of men and women, as children of God in Christ (cf. Gal 3:28)" (Congregation for the Doctrine of the Faith, *Inter insigniores*, 4, 20). Men and women are fundamentally equal, but that does not mean there is not a variety of roles in the Church, which allows for the condition that ministerial priesthood is restricted to men. But we need to remember that "the greatest in the Kingdom of heaven are not the ministers but the saints" (ibid., 6, 39). In this connexion, John Paul II has taught this: "Both in her earliest days and in her successive development, the Church, albeit in different ways and with diverse emphases, has always known women who have exercised an oftentimes decisive role in the Church herself and accomplished tasks of considerable value on her behalf. History is marked by grand works, quite often lowly and hidden, but not for this reason any less decisive to the growth and the holiness of the Church. It is necessary that this history continue" (*Christifideles laici*, 49).

10. THE RESURRECTION OF THE DEAD*

Christ's resurrection and his appearances

1 Thess 2:13
Gal 1:11
1 Cor 15:14
Is 53:8ff
Lk 1:2
1 Cor 11:2, 23
Acts 2:23
Rom 2:24
1 Pet 2:24

Lk 24:34–43
Acts 2:20–32

Hos 6:2

1 Tim 1:15–16
Gal 1:13–14
Acts 8:3; 9:1–2
Eph 3:8

1 Tim 1:14
2 Cor 11:5, 23
1 Cor 3:10

Acts 2:22–24
2 Tim 2:18

Mt 22:23

15 ¹Now I would remind you, brethren, in what terms I preached to you the gospel, which you received, in which you stand, ²by which you are saved, if you hold it fast—unless you believed in vain.

³For I delivered to you as of first importance what I also received, that Christ died for our sins in accordance with the scriptures, ⁴that he was buried, that he was raised on the third day in accordance with the scriptures, ⁵and that he appeared to Cephas, then to the twelve. ⁶Then he appeared to more than five hundred brethren at one time, most of whom are still alive, though some have fallen asleep. ⁷Then he appeared to James, then to all the apostles. ⁸Last of all, as to one untimely born, he appeared also to me. ⁹For I am the least of the apostles, unfit to be called an apostle, because I persecuted the church of God. ¹⁰But by the grace of God I am what I am, and his grace toward me was not in vain. On the contrary, I worked harder than any of them, though it was not I, but the grace of God which is with me. ¹¹Whether then it was I or they, so we preach and so you believed.

The basis of our faith

¹²Now if Christ is preached as raised from the dead, how can some of you say that there is no resurrection of the dead? ¹³But if there is no resurrection of the dead, then

ordinem fiant. [15] ¹Notum autem vobis facio, fratres, evangelium, quod evangelizavi vobis, quod et accepistis, in quo et statis, ²per quod et salvamini, qua ratione evangelizaverim vobis, si tenetis, nisi si frustra credidistis! ³Tradidi enim vobis in primis, quod et accepi, quoniam Christus mortuus est pro peccatis nostris secundum Scripturas ⁴et quia sepultus est et quia suscitatus est tertia die secundum Scripturas ⁵et quia visus est Cephae et post haec Duodecim; ⁶deinde visus est plus quam quingentis fratribus simul, ex quibus plures manent usque adhuc, quidam autem dormierunt; ⁷deinde visus est Iacobo, deinde apostolis omnibus; ⁸novissime autem omnium, tamquam abortivo, visus est et mihi. ⁹Ego enim sum minimus apostolorum, qui non sum dignus vocari apostolus, quoniam persecutus sum ecclesiam Dei; ¹⁰gratia autem Dei sum id, quod sum, et gratia eius in me vacua non fuit, sed abundantius illis omnibus laboravi, non ego autem, sed gratia Dei mecum. ¹¹Igitur sive ego sive illi, sic praedicamus, et sic credidistis. ¹²Si autem Christus praedicatur quod suscitatus est a mortuis, quomodo quidam dicunt in vobis quoniam resurrectio mortuorum non est? ¹³Si autem resurrectio mortuorum non est, neque Christus suscitatus est! ¹⁴Si autem Christus non suscitatus est, inanis

*15:1–58 Some of the Christians at Corinth objected to the doctrine of the resurrection of the dead, because this was a belief with which the Greeks were unfamiliar, even those who held the soul to be immortal. Given the importance of the subject, St Paul replies at length, pointing first to the historical fact of Christ's resurrection (vv. 1–11) and its connexion with the resurrection of the dead in general (vv. 12–34). He then goes on to discuss what form this resurrection will take (vv. 35–58).

15:1–11 Paul reminds the people of the Gospel as preached from the very beginning by the apostles—that Jesus died, was buried and rose on the third day (vv. 1–4). The appearances of the risen Christ are a convincing proof that he did indeed rise from the dead; they are also the credentials of the authority of the apostles, Paul included, for they are all "witnesses of the Risen One" (see *Catechism of the Catholic Church*, 642). This passage is particularly significant in that it is the earliest New Testament account (earlier than that of any of the Gospels) of our Lord's resurrection; it was written not thirty years after the event: "The Apostle speaks here of the living tradition of the Resurrection which he had learned after his conversion at the gates of Damascus" (ibid., 639). The testimony of the Scriptures and of the apostles to whom Jesus appeared in his risen, glorious body is the guarantee for Christians of the historical fact of the Resurrection.

15:12–19 By rising from the dead, Christ completed his work of Redemption. If by dying on the cross he overcame sin, it was necessary that he should also rise, thereby overcoming death, the consequence of sin (see Rom 5:12). "The Resurrection above all constitutes the confirma-

Christ has not been raised;* [14]if Christ has not been raised, then our preaching is in vain and your faith is in vain. [15]We are even found to be misrepresenting God, because we testified of God that he raised Christ, whom he did not raise if it is true that the dead are not raised. [16]For if the dead are not raised, then Christ has not been raised. [17]If Christ has not been raised, your faith is futile and you are still in your sins. [18]Then those also who have fallen asleep in Christ have perished. [19]If for this life only we have hoped in Christ, we are of all men most to be pitied.

Acts 2:22

Acts 1:8; 5:32;
20:16, 24

Rom 4:24–25; 10:9
1 Cor 6:14
1 Thess 4:14

The cause of our resurrection

[20]But in fact Christ has been raised from the dead, the first fruits of those who have fallen asleep. [21]For as by a man came death, by a man has come also the resurrection of the dead. [22]For as in Adam all die, so also in Christ shall all be made alive. [23]But each in his own order: Christ the first fruits, then at his coming those who belong to Christ. [24]Then comes the end, when he delivers the kingdom to God the Father after destroying every rule and every authority and power. [25]For he must reign until he has put all his enemies under his feet. [26]The last enemy to be destroyed is death. [27]"For God[z] has put all things in subjection under his feet." But when it says, "All things are

Acts 26:23
Rom 8:11
Col 1:18
1 Thess 4:14
Gen 3:17–19
Rom 5:12, 18, 21
1 Cor 15:45–49
1 Thess 4:16
Rev 20:5
Dan 12:2

Ps 110:1
Mt 22:44

Ps 8:2, 6
Eph 1:22
Heb 2:6–8
Col 3:11

est ergo praedicatio nostra, inanis est et fides vestra, [15]invenimur autem et falsi testes Dei, quoniam testimonium diximus adversus Deum quod suscitaverit Christum, quem non suscitavit, si revera mortui non resurgunt. [16]Nam si mortui non resurgunt, neque Christus resurrexit; [17]quod si Christus non resurrexit, stulta est fides vestra, adhuc estis in peccatis vestris [18]Ergo et, qui dormierunt in Christo, perierunt. [19]Si in hac vita tantum in Christo sperantes sumus, miserabiliores sumus omnibus hominibus. [20]Nunc autem Christus resurrexit a mortuis, primitiae dormientium. [21]Quoniam enim per hominem mors, et per hominem resurrectio mortuorum: [22]sicut enim in Adam omnes moriuntur, ita et in Christo omnes vivificabuntur. [23]Unusquisque autem in suo ordine: primitiae Christus; deinde hi, qui sunt Christi, in adventu eius; [24]deinde finis, cum tradiderit regnum Deo et Patri, cum evacuaverit omnem principatum et omnem potestatem et virtutem. [25]Oportet autem illum regnare, *donec ponat* omnes *inimicos sub pedibus* eius. [26]Novissima autem inimica destruetur mors; [27]*omnia* enim *subiecit sub pedibus eius*. Cum autem dicat: «Omnia subiecta sunt»,

tion of all Christ's works and teachings. All truths, even those most inaccessible to human reason, find their justification if Christ by his Resurrection has given the definitive proof of his divine authority, which he had promised" (*Catechism of the Catholic Church*, 651).

These verses contain indirect arguments for the truth of our Lord's resurrection, for they show what an absurd situation Christians would be in if Jesus had not risen: their faith would be in vain (vv. 14, 17, 18), as would their hope (v. 19); the apostles would be false witnesses and their preaching valueless (vv. 14–15); and sinners would remain unredeemed (v. 17). Christians, in other words, would be "of all men most to be pitied" (v. 19).

15:20–34 The union of Christians with Christ goes so deep that Christ's resurrection is the principle and cause of their own. Just as Adam's disobedience brought death for all, so Jesus Christ, the new Adam, has merited that all should rise from the dead (vv. 21–23). Christian salvation reaches its culmination with the resurrection of

the body at the end of time (vv. 24–25). "Belief in the resurrection of the dead has been an essential element of the Christian faith from its beginnings. 'The confidence of Christians is the resurrection of the dead; believing this we live' (Tertullian, *De resurrectione mortuorum*, 1, 1)" (*Catechism of the Catholic Church*, 991).

St Paul outlines very succinctly the entire messianic and redemptive work of Christ (vv. 25–28): by the Father's decree, Christ has been made Lord of the universe, in fulfilment of the Scriptures (Ps 110:1 and 8:6). Christ's sovereignty over all creation (v. 28) has come about in history, but it will achieve its final, complete, form at the end of time when God will be everything to everyone. Each year, on the last Sunday in Ordinary Time, the Church celebrates the feast of Christ, Universal King, as a reminder of his absolute dominion over all things.

The meaning of v. 29 is unclear; it may refer to a (short-lived) practice of associating with one's own Baptism loved ones who had already died. If that was the case, it would only have had value and meaning as a prayer for the dead.

z Greek *he*

Phil 3:21
Rom 9:5
Eph 4:6
1 Cor 8:6
Rom 11:36

2 Mac 12:44

2 Cor 4:10f

Is 22:13
Wis 2:6

Acts 26:8
Rom 13:11
Eph 5:14
1 Cor 14:38
1 Thess 5:6–8

Jn 12:24

Gen 1:11
1 Cor 12:18

put in subjection under him," it is plain that he is excepted who put all things under him. ²⁸When all things are subjected to him, then the Son himself will also be subjected to him who put all things under him, that God may be everything to every one.

²⁹Otherwise, what do people mean by being baptized on behalf of the dead? If the dead are not raised at all, why are people baptized on their behalf? * ³⁰Why am I in peril every hour? ³¹I protest, brethren, by my pride in you which I have in Christ Jesus our Lord, I die every day! ³²What do I gain if, humanly speaking, I fought with beasts at Ephesus? If the dead are not raised, "Let us eat and drink, for tomorrow we die." ³³Do not be deceived: "Bad company ruins good morals." ³⁴Come to your right mind, and sin no more. For some have no knowledge of God. I say this to your shame.

The manner of the resurrection of the dead

³⁵But some one will ask, "How are the dead raised? With what kind of body do they come?" ³⁶You foolish man! What you sow does not come to life unless it dies. ³⁷And what you sow is not the body which is to be, but a bare kernel, perhaps of wheat or of some other grain. ³⁸But God gives it a body as he has chosen, and to each kind of seed its own body. ³⁹For not all flesh is alike, but there is one kind for men, another for animals, another for birds, and another for fish. ⁴⁰There are celestial bodies and there are terrestrial bodies; but the glory of the celestial is one, and the glory of the

sine dubio praeter eum, qui subiecit ei omnia. ²⁸Cum autem subiecta fuerint illi omnia, tunc ipse Filius subiectus erit illi, qui sibi subiecit omnia, ut sit Deus omnia in omnibus. ²⁹Alioquin quid facient, qui baptizantur pro mortuis? Si omnino mortui non resurgunt, ut quid et baptizantur pro illis? ³⁰Ut quid et nos periclitamur omni hora? ³¹Cotidie morior, utique per vestram gloriationem, fratres, quam habeo in Christo Iesu Domino nostro! ³²Si secundum hominem ad bestias pugnavi Ephesi, quid mihi prodest? Si mortui non resurgunt, *manducemus et bibamus, cras enim moriemur*. ³³Nolite seduci: «Corrumpunt mores bonos colloquia mala». ³⁴Evigilate iuste et nolite peccare! Ignorantiam enim Dei quidam habent; ad reverentiam vobis loquor. ³⁵Sed dicet aliquis: «Quomodo resurgunt mortui? Quali autem corpore veniunt?». ³⁶Insipiens! Tu, quod seminas, non

15:35–56 To help explain what the resurrection of the dead involves, the Apostle uses comparisons taken from the vegetable, animal and mineral worlds (vv. 36–41). "This 'how' [how the dead are raised] exceeds our imagination and understanding; it is accessible only to faith. Yet our participation in the Eucharist already gives us a foretaste of Christ's transfiguration of our bodies: 'Just as bread that comes from the earth, after God's blessing has been invoked upon it, is no longer ordinary bread, but Eucharist, formed of two things, the one earthly and the other heavenly: so too our bodies, which partake of the Eucharist, are no longer corruptible, but possess the hope of resurrection'" (*Catechism of the Catholic Church*, 1000).

The Apostle uses vivid images to describe the qualities of the resurrected body; these help to convey a sense of the splendour of the "glorious body" (see Phil 3:21). "The bodies of the dead will be raised, as Christ rose from the dead; but the risen will have no bodily needs, just as Christ, when he rose from the dead, ate only because he wanted to, not because he needed to.

There will be no hunger […], nor will men pray for rain so the wheat for bread will grow, nor lament when there is drought. There will be no fear, no tiredness, no pain, no blight, no scarcity, no weakness, no laziness. None of these things will exist, but the body will" (St Augustine, *Sermones*, 242a, 3). St Paul calls it a "spiritual body" (v. 44). "It is called a spiritual body," St Augustine says, "not because it has become a spirit but because it is in such a way subject to the spirit, to fit it for its heavenly abode, that every kind of earthly weakness and imperfection is changed into heavenly permanence" (idem, *De fide et symbolo*, 6).

"We shall not all sleep, but we shall all be changed" (v. 51). In apocalyptic language (the trumpet sound, use of the first person plural), the Apostle shares a "mystery" which at first glance may seem difficult to reconcile with the fact that death will affect everyone because it is a consequence of original sin. But he is not teaching here about death or the actual moment of the Second Coming: he is talking about resurrection, and means that everyone (living and dead, he says,

terrestrial is another. [41]There is one glory of the sun, and another glory of the moon, and another glory of the stars; for star differs from star in glory.

[42]So is it with the resurrection of the dead. What is sown is perishable, what is raised is imperishable. [43]It is sown in dishonour, it is raised in glory. It is sown in weakness, it is raised in power. [44]It is sown a physical body, it is raised a spiritual body. If there is a physical body, there is also a spiritual body. [45]Thus it is written, "The first man Adam became a living being"; the last Adam became a life-giving spirit. [46]But it is not the spiritual which is first but the physical, and then the spiritual. [47]The first man was from the earth, a man of dust; the second man is from heaven. [48]As was the man of dust, so are those who are of the dust; and as is the man of heaven, so are those who are of heaven. [49]Just as we have borne the image of the man of dust, we shall[a] also bear the image of the man of heaven. [50]I tell you this, brethren: flesh and blood cannot inherit the kingdom of God, nor does the perishable inherit the imperishable.

[51]Lo! I tell you a mystery. We shall not all sleep, but we shall all be changed, [52]in a moment, in the twinkling of an eye, at the last trumpet. For the trumpet will sound, and the dead will be raised imperishable, and we shall be changed. [53]For this perishable nature must put on the imperishable, and this mortal nature must put on immortality. [54]When the perishable puts on the imperishable, and the mortal puts on immortality, then shall come to pass the saying that is written:

"Death is swallowed up in victory."

[55] "O death, where is thy victory?

O death, where is thy sting?"

[56]The sting of death is sin, and the power of sin is the law. [57]But thanks be to God, who gives us the victory through our Lord Jesus Christ.

[58]Therefore, my beloved brethren, be steadfast, immovable, always abounding in the work of the Lord, knowing that in the Lord your labour is not in vain.

Margin references:

Phil 3:20f
Col 3:4

Gen 2:7
Jn 6:63
1 Cor 15:20–28
2 Cor 3:6, 17

Gen 2:7
Dan 7:13
Jn 3:13

Gen 5:3
Rom 8:29
Phil 3:21

Jn 3:5
1 Cor 6:9–10

1 Thess 4:5–17
Num 10:3
Joel 2:1
Mt 24:31
2 Cor 5:4

2 Cor 5:1-5

Is 25:8

Hos 13:14
Rev 20:14; 15:56

1 Cor 16-13
Rom 5:12; 7:7, 13
Heb 6:1
2 Chron 15:7
1 Chron 16:13
Rev 14:13

---

vivificatur, nisi prius moriatur; [37]et quod seminas, non corpus, quod futurum est, seminas, sed nudum granum, ut puta tritici aut alicuius ceterorum. [38]Deus autem dat illi corpus sicut voluit, et unicuique seminum proprium corpus. [39]Non omnis caro eadem caro, sed alia hominum, alia caro pecorum, alia caro volucrum, alia autem piscium. [40]Et corpora caelestia et corpora terrestria, sed alia quidem caelestium gloria, alia autem terrestrium. [41]Alia claritas solis, alia claritas lunae et alia claritas stellarum; stella enim a stella differt in claritate. [42]Sic et resurrectio mortuorum: seminatur in corruptione, resurgit in incorruptione; [43]seminatur in ignobilitate, resurgit in gloria; seminatur in infirmitate, resurgit in virtute; [44] seminatur corpus animale, resurgit corpus spiritale. Si est corpus animale, est et spiritale. [45]Sic et scriptum est: «*Factus est primus homo* Adam *in animam viventem*»; novissimus Adam in Spiritum vivificantem. [46]Sed non prius, quod spiritale est, sed quod animale est; deinde quod spiritale. [47]Primus homo de terra terrenus, secundus homo de caelo. [48]Qualis terrenus, tales et terreni, et qualis caelestis, tales et caelestes; [49]et sicut portavimus imaginem terreni, portabimus et imaginem caelestis. [50]Hoc autem dico, fratres, quoniam caro et sanguis regnum Dei possidere non possunt, neque corruptio incorruptelam possidebit. [51]Ecce mysterium vobis dico: Non omnes quidem dormiemus, sed omnes immutabimur, [52]in momento, in ictu oculi, in novissima tuba; canet enim, et mortui suscitabuntur incorrupti, et nos immutabimur. [53]Oportet enim corruptibile hoc induere incorruptelam, et mortale induere immortalitatem. [54]Cum autem corruptibile hoc induerit incorruptelam, et mortale hoc induerit immortalitatem, tunc fiet sermo, qui scriptus est: «*Absorpta est mors in victoria. / [55]Ubi est, mors, victoria tua? / Ubi est, mors, stimulus tuus?*» [56]Stimulus autem mortis peccatum est, virtus vero peccati lex. [57]Deo autem gratias, qui dedit nobis victoriam per Dominum nostrum Iesum Christum. [58]Itaque, fratres mei dilecti, stabiles estote, immobiles, abundantes in opere Domini semper, scientes quod labor vester non est inanis in Domino.

---

thus underscoring the importance of his point) will find their mortal body transformed into a glorious body (cf. 1 Thess 4:13–18). The image of "putting on" new garb is a graphic way of showing that life will definitely vanquish death.

15:57–58 Thanksgiving to God is based on the

hope that everything good we have enjoyed on earth we will again find in greater abundance in heaven: "Do not ever forget that after death, you will be welcomed by Love itself. And in that love of God you will find as well all the noble loves which you had on earth" (St Josemaría Escrivá, *Friends of God*, 221).

a Other ancient authorities read *let us*

11. MESSAGES AND WORDS OF FAREWELL*

Collection for the church of Jerusalem

Gen 2:10
2 Cor 8:9
Acts 9:13
Gal 2:10
Rom 15:26

Mt 28:1
Acts 20:7

Rev 1:10
2 Cor 8:20f

16 ¹Now concerning the contribution for the saints:* as I directed the churches of Galatia, so you also are to do. ²On the first day of every week, each of you is to put something aside and store it up, as he may prosper, so that contributions need not be made when I come. ³And when I arrive, I will send those whom you accredit by letter to carry your gift to Jerusalem. ⁴If it seems advisable that I should go also, they will accompany me.

Plans for the months ahead

Acts 19:21; 20:21ff
2 Cor 1:16
Rom 15:24
Tit 3:12

Acts 18:21; 20:2

Acts 19:1-10

Acts 14:27
2 Cor 2:12

⁵I will visit you after passing through Macedonia, for I intend to pass through Macedonia, ⁶and perhaps I will stay with you or even spend the winter, so that you may speed me on my journey, wherever I go. ⁷For I do not want to see you now just in passing; I hope to spend some time with you, if the Lord permits. ⁸But I will stay in Ephesus until Pentecost, ⁹for a wide door for effective work has opened to me, and there are many adversaries.

[16]¹De collectis autem, quae fiunt in sanctos, sicut ordinavi ecclesiis Galatiae, ita et vos facite. ²Per primam sabbati unusquisque vestrum apud se ponat recondens, quod ei beneplacuerit, ut non, cum venero, tunc collectae fiant. ³Cum autem praesens fuero, quos probaveritis, per epistulas hos mittam perferre gratiam vestram in Ierusalem; ⁴quod si dignum fuerit, ut et ego eam, mecum ibunt. ⁵Veniam autem ad vos, cum Macedoniam pertransiero, nam Macedoniam pertransibo; ⁶apud vos autem forsitan manebo vel etiam hiemabo, ut vos me deducatis, quocumque iero. ⁷Nolo enim vos modo in transitu videre; spero enim me aliquantum temporis manere apud vos, si Dominus permiserit. ⁸Permanebo autem Ephesi usque

---

*16:1–24 The last chapter is an epilogue comprised of messages and greetings. Paul gives instructions for the collection to relieve the Christians in Jerusalem (vv. 1–4), outlines where he plans to visit next (vv. 5–12) and adds some warm recommendations and good wishes (vv. 13–20).

16:1–4 In line with an appeal to him by the apostles to "remember the poor" (see Gal 2:10), Paul gives advice about how to collect money for the church of Jerusalem. Helping those in need is one of the messages at the heart of the Gospel: "Wherever people are to be found who are in want of food and drink, of clothing, housing, medicine, work, education, the means necessary for leading a truly human life, wherever there are people racked by misfortune or illness, people suffering exile or imprisonment, Christian charity should go in search of them and find them out, comfort them with devoted care and give them the help that will relieve their needs. This obligation binds first and foremost the more affluent individuals and nations" (Vatican II, *Apostolicam actuositatem*, 8). We should be more than willing to perform this duty to help

others, for "our Lord, who loves the poor, loves those who love the poor. [...] Therefore, we who have sought to love the poor hope that we will be beloved of God" (St Vincent de Paul, *Letter*, in the *Divine Office*, office of readings, 27 September). "The first day of every week" (v. 2), that is Sunday: "Ever since Apostolic times, the Sunday gathering has in fact been for Christians a moment of fraternal sharing with the very poor. 'On the first day of every week...' (1 Cor 16:2), says Saint Paul, referring to the collection organized for the poor Churches of Judea. In the Sunday Eucharist, the believing heart opens wide to embrace all aspects of the Church. But the full range of the apostolic summons needs to be accepted: far from trying to create a narrow 'gift' mentality, Paul calls rather for a demanding *culture of sharing*, to be lived not only among the members of the community itself but also in society as a whole" (John Paul II, *Dies Domini*, 70).

16:5–12 St Paul mentions the journeys he is planning and his intention to stay a long time in Corinth; he clearly has great affection for this community that he himself founded.

¹⁰When Timothy comes, see that you put him at ease among you, for he is doing the work of the Lord, as I am. ¹¹So let no one despise him. Speed him on his way in peace, that he may return to me; for I am expecting him with the brethren.

Col 4:3
Rev 3:8
1 Cor 4:17
Phil 2:20

¹²As for our brother Apollos, I strongly urged him to visit you with the other brethren, but it was not at all his will[b] to come now. He will come when he has opportunity.

1 Tim 4:12
Acts 18:24
1 Cor 3:5

Exhortations and greetings

¹³Be watchful, stand firm in your faith, be courageous, be strong. ¹⁴Let all that you do be done in love.

Josh 1:7
Ps 31:25
1 Cor 15:58
1 Pet 5:8–9
Rom 16:5
1 Cor 1:16

¹⁵Now, brethren, you know that the household of Stephanas were the first converts in Achaia, and they have devoted themselves to the service of the saints; ¹⁶I urge you to be subject to such men and to every fellow worker and labourer. ¹⁷I rejoice at the coming of Stephanas and Fortunatus and Achaicus, because they have made up for your absence; ¹⁸for they refreshed my spirit as well as yours. Give recognition to such men.

Phil 3:17
1 Thess 5:12

¹⁹The churches of Asia send greetings. Aquila and Prisca, together with the church in their house, send you hearty greetings in the Lord. ²⁰All the brethren send greetings. Greet one another with a holy kiss.

Acts 18:2, 18, 26
Rev 1:4–11
Rom 16:3–5, 16
2 Cor 13:12

²¹I, Paul, write this greeting with my own hand. ²²If any one has no love for the Lord, let him be accursed. Our Lord, come![c] ²³The grace of the Lord Jesus be with you. ²⁴My love be with you all in Christ Jesus. Amen.

1 Thess 3:17
Col 4:18
Gal 1:8
Rom 16:24
Rev 22:20

ad Pentecosten; ⁹ostium enim mihi apertum est magnum et efficax, et adversarii multi. ¹⁰Si autem venerit Timotheus, videte, ut sine timore sit apud vos, opus enim Domini operatur sicut et ego; ¹¹ne quis ergo illum spernat. Deducite autem illum in pace, ut veniat ad me; expecto enim illum cum fratribus. ¹²De Apollo autem fratre, multum rogavi eum, ut veniret ad vos cum fratribus, et utique non fuit voluntas, ut nunc veniret; veniet autem, cum ei opportunum fuerit. ¹³Vigilate, state in fide, viriliter agite, confortamini; ¹⁴omnia vestra in caritate fiant. ¹⁵Obsecro autem vos, fratres: nostis domum Stephanae, quoniam sunt primitiae Achaiae et in ministerium sanctorum ordinaverunt seipsos; ¹⁶ut et vos subditi sitis eiusmodi et omni cooperanti et laboranti. ¹⁷Gaudeo autem in praesentia Stephanae et Fortunati et Achaici, quoniam id, quod vobis deerat, ipsi suppleverunt, ¹⁸refecerunt enim et meum spiritum et vestrum. Cognoscite ergo, qui eiusmodi sunt. ¹⁹Salutant vos ecclesiae Asiae. Salutant vos in Domino multum Aquila et Prisca cum domestica sua ecclesia. ²⁰Salutant vos fratres omnes. Salutate invicem in osculo sancto. ²¹Salutatio mea manu Pauli. ²²Si quis non amat Dominum, sit anathema. Marana tha! ²³Gratia Domini Iesu vobiscum. ²⁴Caritas mea cum omnibus vobis in Christo Iesu.

Timothy was still a young man (see 1 Tim 4:12; 5:1; 2 Tim 1:6–8), and Apollos was well known to the Christians of Corinth, having lived with them for quite long periods of time (cf. Acts 19:1; 1 Cor 1:11–12).

16:13–24 St Paul summarizes here the main points he has made in the letter—that the Christian life is a struggle against one's passions and against temptations from the devil, and that everything a Christian does should be inspired by charity.

"Let him be accursed", *Anathema sit* (v. 22): this is a standard formula of words used to curse or punish someone (see 12:3; Gal 1:8); apparently, a person shunned in this way was excluded from church meetings.

"Our Lord, come!" is a translation of an Aramaic prayer. According to the *Didache*, 10, 6, this invocation was used in early Christian times after the Eucharistic Prayer. It also appears in Revelation 22:20, translated into Greek; see RSV note **c**.

St Paul's final greeting, which the Liturgy uses in the introductory rite of the Mass, is a form of blessing that comprises a confession of faith in our Lord's presence among Christians and a prayer that it be fruitful. Commenting on these words, St John Chrysostom says: "Every good shepherd and every teacher has the duty to help his brethren with advice but, above all, with prayers and entreaty" (*In 1 Corinthios*, 44, ad loc.).

b Or *God's will for him*   c Greek *Maranatha*

THE SECOND LETTER OF PAUL TO THE

CORINTHIANS

Introduction

The Second Letter to the Corinthians, written towards the end of autumn in the year 57, some months after the First Letter, tells us a lot about St Paul's ministry and the richness of his personality; clearly he was a man passionately in love with Jesus Christ and zealous for the welfare of his faithful. Except in the cases of a few specific passages (see 6:14–7:2) the Pauline authorship of this letter has not been called into question, even though the earliest documents to mention the letter (the canon drawn up by Marcion and the Muratorian Fragment) date to as late as the middle of the second century.

1. STRUCTURE AND CONTENT

The letter divides naturally into three parts. The first (chaps. 1–7) is largely about the character and attributes of the Christian evangelizer. Paul's apologia for himself and his ministry delineates the role of apostles, the pillars of the Church. The second part concerns the collection being made for the Jerusalem Christians (chaps. 8–9); as he did in 1 Corinthians, St Paul encourages these wealthier Christians to help their brethren in Jerusalem who are experiencing severe hardship because of persecution and penury. In the third part, the Apostle defends himself against his detractors (chaps. 10–13), answering, one by one, the lies that have been told about him, and giving the faithful ample arguments to set the record straight. At the end of the letter, he gives some instructions having to do with his next visit to Corinth (his third visit, which took place at the beginning of the year 58).

2. CONTEXT

The main question that arises in the case of this letter concerns its composition and whether it was originally a single letter. Since the late eighteenth century, scholars have been coming round to the view that the text is an amalgam of material from a number of letters written by the Apostle to the Christians of Corinth (it is very likely that he engaged in extensive correspondence with them). This idea is put forward to explain why the letter touches on such a broad range of themes and why the tone varies often throughout. The current consensus is that two letters have been combined to make this one—the letter written "with many tears" (chaps. 10–13; see 2:4) in which the Apostle, with pain and with determination, takes issue with the agitators who were trying to undermine the community he had built up at such personal cost; and the "letter of reconciliation" which accounts for most of the first seven chapters; the letter of reconciliation would have been written after the letter of tears, when the community's enemies no longer held great sway. The section of the letter that deals with the collection for Jerusalem is also judged to be made up of two elements—chapter 8, the conclusion of the "letter of reconciliation", and chapter 9 (which does not refer back to what had been already written in the previous chapter) which appears to derive from a letter that has disappeared.

In recent years, given that it seems impossible to work out exactly how the text acquired its present form, scholars prefer to take the letter at face value, convinced that, despite the likelihood that it contains fragments from other letters, the whole is the work of the same writer, the Apostle.

Likewise, scholars have been unable to work out the exact nature of the conflict that forms the background to the letter. It seems likely that, on the occasion of a brief visit to Corinth, the Apostle or one of his co-workers was treated very badly by some particular person, who went as far as to ridicule Paul and his work: "They say, 'His letters are weighty and strong, but his bodily presence is weak, and his speech of no account'" (10:10). The people who really caused Paul grief were the "false teachers", without doubt a group of Judaizing Christians come from outside with teachings in conflict with the true Gospel. Maybe both things happened at the same time—insults made by some particular individual, and arrogance shown by "superlative apostles"; both factors caused the Apostle a great deal of pain and provoked the apologia contained in the letter.

3. MESSAGE

The central theme of the letter is the apostolic ministry, dealt with in a positive way in the first part, and in the third with arguments (occasionally ironic in tone) designed to refute lies being spread about the Apostle. The middle part of the letter, dealing with the collection for Christians in Jerusalem, stresses the religious and social value of coming to the aid of those most in need.

The apostolic ministry

Even in his opening greetings, St Paul expresses his profound conviction of being "an apostle of Christ Jesus by the will of God" (1:1), and he will later claim that it was by the mercy of God that he was entrusted this ministry (cf. 4:1). God, who called him despite his shortcomings, also equips him to carry out this task (see 3:5–6).

Christian apostolate is portrayed as a participation in the redemptive work of Christ: the apostle is God's co-worker (see 6:1), Christ's ambassador (cf. 5:20), and a minister of the reconciliation that God brought about through Christ (see 5:18–19). For these reasons, an apostle's mission is to preach Christ faithfully—Christ in whom God's promises find fulfilment (see 1:18–20)—and to spread the sweet fragrance of Christ's goodness everywhere (see 2:14).

Christ's work of redemption reached its climax in his passion and death; the Christian apostle, too, encounters suffering (cf. 1:5). St Paul was profoundly convinced that redemption came about through suffering; this conviction became the driving force of his life and of his preaching. This explains why a number of times in the letter he speaks about his own experience of suffering. To begin with, he deals with the subject in general terms (see 2 Cor 4:7–12), pointing out that God allows his apostle to suffer "to show that the transcendent power belongs to God and not to us" (4:7). Later on, speaking in more concrete terms, he lists a series of tribulations he has suffered, to show that "as servants of God we commend ourselves in every way" (6:4). Then, near the end of the letter, he gives a long, detailed list (though, no doubt, not an exhaustive one) of what he has done and suffered for Christ (cf. 11:23–33). All of this can be summed up in a single sentence: "the love of Christ controls us …", "caritas Christi urget nos" (5:14f).

To these trials he adds his disinterested preaching of the Gospel (cf. 11:7ff): he never seeks his own advantage; all that interests him is the glory of God and the salvation of the souls entrusted to him (cf. 12:13ff). A love similar to that between parents and their children links him to the faithful (see 6:11–13; 12:14). They are his letters of recommendation, his credentials (see 3:2–3), and one day they will be his boast before the Lord (cf. 1:14). That is why he is so jealous for them on God's behalf and will not allow anyone to lead them astray (see 11:2ff).

In the course of defending his apostolic work against the false teachers who have wormed their way into the ranks of the Corinthians, St Paul demonstrates the superiority of the New Covenant (of which he is a minister) over the Old. He does this by drawing a series of vivid contrasts: the Old is given in a written code that "kills", the New is given in the Spirit who gives life; the former led to death and condemnation, the latter brings life and justification; the Old was a temporary phenomenon, the New lasts forever (see 3:6–11).

Sharing worldly goods

The collection for the faithful of Jerusalem was designed to relieve an urgent need, and St Paul instructs that it be taken up in Corinth, just as he arranged to have done in the other churches he founded (see Rom 15:26; 1 Cor 16:1). He asked Titus to organize the collection, and he encourages all to make generous donations and to do so without delay.

As well as meeting immediate needs, collections of this sort have deep religious significance. Firstly, they are a concrete expression of Christian solidarity. By relieving their brethren in this way, Christians put their resources to good use and learn to give of themselves. Here we find that the generosity of Christians in Macedonia is used to encourage the Corinthians to imitate their good example.

By contributing to relieve the needs of others, the faithful imitate Jesus, for, "though he was rich, yet for your sake he became poor, so that by his poverty you might become rich" (8:9). In his hymn in the Letter to the Philippians (Phil 2:5–11), the Apostle shows us that Christ's self-giving is made evident in a tangible (physical) way in the Incarnation. This bold Christological argument raises the human value of solidarity to the status of a supernatural virtue which identifies the Christian with Jesus Christ.

Finally, generosity in almsgiving strengthens the Christian's relationship with God, who "loves a cheerful giver" (9:7). God, who enriches the generous giver, will "increase the harvest of your righteousness" (9:10), that is, of a Christian's holiness.

2 Corinthians

1. INTRODUCTION*

Greeting

1 ¹Paul, an apostle of Christ Jesus by the will of God, and Timothy our brother. To the church of God which is at Corinth, with all the saints who are in the whole of Achaia:

²Grace to you and peace from God our Father and the Lord Jesus Christ.

Acts 9:13; 16:1
1 Cor 1:1
Rom 1:1

Rom 1:7
Phil 1:2
1 Cor 1:3

Thanksgiving

³Blessed be the God and Father of our Lord Jesus Christ, the Father of mercies and God of all comfort, ⁴who comforts us in all our affliction, so that we may be able to comfort those who are in any affliction, with the comfort with which we ourselves are comforted by God. ⁵For as we share abundantly in Christ's sufferings, so through Christ we share abundantly in comfort too.ᵃ ⁶If we are afflicted, it is for your com-

Eph 1:3
1 Pet 1:3

Col 1:24
Phil 1:20

[1] ¹Paulus apostolus Christi Iesu per voluntatem Dei, et Timotheus frater, ecclesiae Dei, quae est Corinthi, cum sanctis omnibus, qui sunt in universa Achaia: ²gratia vobis et pax a Deo Patre nostro et Domino Iesu Christo. ³Benedictus Deus et Pater Domini nostri Iesu Christi, Pater misericordiarum et Deus totius consolationis, ⁴qui consolatur nos in omni tribulatione nostra, ut possimus et ipsi consolari eos, qui in omni pressura sunt, per exhortationem, qua exhortamur et ipsi a Deo; ⁵quoniam, sicut abundant passiones Christi in nobis, ita per Christum abundat et consolatio nostra. ⁶Sive autem tribulamur, pro vestra exhortatione et salute; sive exhortamur, pro vestra exhortatione, quae operatur in tolerantia earun-

*1:1–11 The letter begins in St Paul's customary way—with a greeting in which the Apostle introduces himself (vv. 1–2), and an ardent act of thanksgiving to God (vv. 3–11).

1:1–2 St Paul's way of introducing himself—as "an apostle of Christ Jesus by the will of God"—takes on special significance in this letter, much of which is a defence of his calling as apostle against people who, seemingly, have claimed that he has no right to the title (see chaps. 10–13).

"Grace [...] and peace" (v. 2). This pious greeting has been incorporated into Eucharistic liturgy: "Grace is the first good, because it is the source of all good things [...]. The last of all good things is peace, because it is the general goal of the mind. For, whichever way this word 'peace' is used, it is in the sense of a goal or end; in eternal glory, in government and in one's manner of living, peace has the sense of 'end'" (St Thomas Aquinas, *Super 2 Corinthios*, ad loc.).

1:3–11 The act of thanksgiving here is rather different from those in other letters, where Paul thanks God for the favours enjoyed by the Christians to whom he is writing, in order to make them more appreciative of their calling. Here he thanks God for the consolation he himself is receiving in the midst of his trials, though he is not forgetful of the many benefits his addressees enjoy. The way he expresses his gratitude shows the profound union that exists among members of Christ's mystical body and between them and Christ, its head. This very close communion and intercommunication allows the Apostle to say that his sufferings are "Christ's sufferings" (v. 5), and to speak about the close connexion between his own afflictions and consolations and those of the faithful in Corinth.

"The Father of mercies" (v. 3). This is a Hebraic way of saying that God is merciful. Thanks to God's mercy, the Apostle is consoled in his sufferings, and therefore is able to offer consolation to others. The God of mercies has been revealed to us by Jesus Christ: "The truth, revealed in Christ, about God the 'Father of mercies' (2 Cor 1:3), enables us to 'see' him as particularly close to man especially when man is suffering, when he is under threat at the very

a Or *For as the suffering of Christ abound for us, so also our comfort abounds through Christ*

fort and salvation; and if we are comforted, it is for your comfort, which you experience when you patiently endure the same sufferings that we suffer. [7]Our hope for you is unshaken; for we know that as you share in our sufferings, you will also share in our comfort.

Acts 19:23
1 Cor 15:32

[8]For we do not want you to be ignorant, brethren, of the affliction* we experienced in Asia; for we were so utterly, unbearably crushed that we despaired of life itself.

Rom 4:17

[9]Why, we felt that we had received the sentence of death; but that was to make us rely

Rom 8:28
2 Tim 4:18

not on ourselves but on God who raises the dead; [10]he delivered us from so deadly a peril, and he will deliver us; on him we have set our hope that he will deliver us again.

Rom 15:30
2 Cor 4:15; 9:12

[11]You also must help us by prayer, so that many will give thanks on our behalf for the blessing granted us in answer to many prayers.

PART ONE

St Paul's defence against his enemies*

2. HIS SIMPLICITY AND SINCERITY*

The evidence of his actions and his letters

2 Cor 2:17
1 Cor 1:17

[12]For our boast is this, the testimony of our conscience that we have behaved in the world, and still more toward you, with holiness and godly sincerity, not by earthly

2 Cor 5:12

wisdom but by the grace of God. [13]For we write you nothing but what you can read

dem passionum, quas et nos patimur. [7]Et spes nostra firma pro vobis, scientes quoniam, sicut socii passionum estis, sic eritis et consolationis. [8]Non enim volumus ignorare vos, fratres, de tribulatione nostra, quae facta est in Asia, quoniam supra modum gravati sumus supra virtutem, ita ut taedaret nos etiam vivere; [9]sed ipsi in nobis ipsis responsum mortis habuimus, ut non simus fidentes in nobis, sed in Deo, qui suscitat mortuos: [10]qui de tanta morte eripuit nos et eruet, in quem speramus, et adhuc eripiet, [11]adiuvantibus et vobis in oratione pro nobis, ut propter eam, quae ex multis personis in nos est, donationem per multos gratiae agantur pro nobis. [12]Nam gloria nostra haec est, testimonium conscientiae nostrae, quod in simplicitate et sinceritate Dei et non in sapientia carnali sed in gratia Dei conversati sumus in mundo, abundantius autem ad vos. [13]Non enim alia scribimus vobis quam quae legitis aut etiam cognoscitis; spero autem quod usque in finem cognoscetis, [14]sicut et cognovistis nos ex parte, quia

heart of his existence and dignity" (John Paul II, *Dives in misericordia*, 2).

"We despaired of life itself" (v. 8). We do not know exactly what kind of affliction St Paul is referring to. He may mean the riot caused by Demetrius the silversmith in Ephesus, which forced the Apostle to leave the city (see Acts 19:23–41). Whatever the precise cause, St Paul uses the occasion to stress that we need to put our trust in God, for only he can deliver us from all danger.

*1:12—7:16 In this first part of the letter, St Paul explains how he has acted out of concern for them, and takes issue with the criticisms that some have levelled against him: the reason why he has delayed his visit to Corinth and altered his plans stems from his total commitment to his ministry (1:12—2:17); he makes a passionate defence of

his apostleship (3:1—6:10); and he declares that what will most please him is to win back the trust and affection of the Corinthians (6:11—7:16).

*1:12–2:17 The first criticism that Paul deals with is that he is weak and timid. His failure to visit Corinth despite his having said he would has been interpreted by some as a sign of weakness; Paul justifies his behaviour vehemently, in arguments that also contain a wealth of teaching.

1:12–14 The Apostle is very eager to regain the Corinthians' affection and trust which are in danger of eroding due to the constant carping of his detractors. He replies to their accusations by appealing to his own conscience, which assures him he has always acted rightly.

"That you can be proud of us" (v. 14). The Apostle is confident of the Corinthians' respect

and understand; I hope you will understand fully, [14]as you have understood in part, that you can be proud of us as we can be of you, on the day of the Lord Jesus.

Phil 2:16; 4:1
1 Thess 2:19–20
1 Cor 1:8

Why he has not visited Corinth

[15]Because I was sure of this, I wanted to come to you first, so that you might have a double pleasure;[b] [16]I wanted to visit you on my way to Macedonia, and to come back to you from Macedonia and have you send me on my way to Judea. [17]Was I vacillating when I wanted to do this? Do I make my plans like a worldly man, ready to say Yes and No at once? [18]As surely as God is faithful, our word to you has not been Yes and No. [19]For the Son of God, Jesus Christ, whom we preached among you, Silvanus and Timothy and I, was not Yes and No; but in him it is always Yes. [20]For all the promises of God find their Yes in him. That is why we utter the Amen through him, to the glory of God. [21]But it is God who establishes us with you in Christ, and has commissioned us; [22]he has put his seal upon us and given us his Spirit in our hearts as a guarantee.

1 Cor 16:5–9
Acts 19:21
Rom 7:5
2 Cor 1:12; 5:16
1 Cor 1:9
Mt 5:37
Acts 16:1; 18:5
Rom 16:27
Rev 3:14
1 Cor 1:6
1 Jn 2:20, 27
Rom 5:5; 6:4; 8:16
Eph 1:13f

[23]But I call God to witness against me—it was to spare you that I refrained from coming to Corinth. [24]Not that we lord it over your faith; we work with you for your joy, for you stand firm in your faith. [1]I made up my mind not to make you another 2 painful visit. [2]For if I cause you pain, who is there to make me glad but the one whom I have pained? [3]And I wrote as I did, so that when I came I might not suffer pain from those who should have made me rejoice, for I felt sure of all of you, that my joy would be the joy of you all. [4]For I wrote you out of much affliction and anguish of

2 Cor 11:31
Rom 1:9
1 Pet 5:3
2 Cor 12, 21
2 Cor 7:8

gloria vestra sumus sicut et vos nostra in die Domini nostri Iesu. [15]Et hac confidentia volui prius venire ad vos, ut secundam gratiam haberetis, [16]et per vos transire in Macedoniam, et iterum a Macedonia venire ad vos et a vobis deduci in Iudaeam. [17]Cum hoc ergo voluissem, numquid levitate usus sum? Aut, quae cogito, secundum carnem cogito, ut sit apud me «Est, est» et «Non, non»? [18]Fidelis autem Deus, quia sermo noster, qui fit apud vos, non est «Est» et «Non»! [19]Dei enim Filius Iesus Christus, qui in vobis per nos praedicatus est, per me et Silvanum et Timotheum, non fuit «Est» et «Non», sed «Est» in illo fuit. [20]Quotquot enim promissiones Dei sunt, in illo «Est»; ideo et per ipsum «Amen» Deo ad gloriam per nos. [21]Qui autem confirmat nos vobiscum in Christum et qui unxit nos Deus, [22]et qui signavit nos et dedit arrabonem Spiritus in cordibus nostris. [23]Ego autem testem Deum invoco in animam meam quod parcens vobis non veni ultra Corinthum. [24]Non quia dominamur fidei vestrae, sed adiutores sumus gaudii vestri, nam fide stetistis. [2] [1]Statui autem hoc ipse apud me, ne iterum in tristitia venirem ad vos; [2]si enim ego contristo vos, et quis est qui me laetificet, nisi qui contristatur ex me? [3]Et hoc ipsum scripsi, ut non, cum venero, tristitiam habeam de quibus oportebat me gaudere, confidens in omnibus vobis, quia meum gaudium omnium vestrum est. [4]Nam ex multa tribulatione et angustia cordis scripsi vobis per

and love in spite of the lies and insults spread by his enemies. After all, he founded the church at Corinth and has nurtured it.

1:15—2:4 Paul had planned a journey with this route: Corinth–Macedonia–Corinth–Judea. However, the visit to Corinth was postponed for some reason unknown to us—perhaps on account of an unpleasant incident that may have occurred on a previous visit (cf. 2:5–11). St Paul gives three reasons for his change of plan—faithfulness to God and to Christ who is the "Yes" of the Father (1:19); obedience to God, shown when we say "the Amen" (1:20); and a desire not to upset the Corinthians (1:23).

"He has put his seal on us" (1:22). This seal, similar to anointing, signifies one of the main effects of the Holy Spirit: "Because this seal indicates the indelible effect of the anointing with the Holy Spirit in the sacraments of Baptism, Confirmation and Holy Orders, the image of the seal (*sphragis*) has been used in some theological traditions to express the indelible 'character' imprinted by these three unrepeatable sacraments" (*Catechism of the Catholic Church*, 698). As elsewhere in the letter (see 3:3; 13:14), the three Persons of the Holy Trinity are mentioned here—God (the Father), who has "commissioned us" (1:21), the Son, Christ, who sustains us, and the Holy Spirit, who is given us as an earnest or pledge.

"I wrote you … with many tears" (2:4). This letter (see the Introduction) was occasioned by Paul's sadness (caused, no doubt by the way he was treated on his earlier visit), but both it and his emotion stemmed, above all, from his warm affection for the people in Corinth.

b Other ancient authorities read *favour*

heart and with many tears, not to cause you pain but to let you know the abundant love that I have for you.

Forgiveness for those who offend us

⁵But if any one has caused pain, he has caused it not to me, but in some measure —not to put it too severely—to you all. ⁶For such a one this punishment by the majority is enough; ⁷so you should rather turn to forgive and comfort him, or he may be overwhelmed by excessive sorrow. ⁸So I beg you to reaffirm your love for him. ⁹For this is why I wrote, that I might test you and know whether you are obedient in everything. ¹⁰Any one whom you forgive, I also forgive. What I have forgiven, if I have forgiven anything, has been for your sake in the presence of Christ, ¹¹to keep Satan from gaining the advantage over us; for we are not ignorant of his designs.

Col 3:13

2 Cor 7:15

Lk 22:31
Eph 4:27

Paul's eagerness for news

¹²When I came to Troas to preach the gospel of Christ, a door was opened for me in the Lord; ¹³but my mind could not rest because I did not find my brother Titus there. So I took leave of them and went on to Macedonia.

¹⁴But thanks be to God, who in Christ always leads us in triumph, and through us spreads the fragrance of the knowledge of him everywhere. ¹⁵For we are the aroma of Christ to God among those who are being saved and among those who are perishing, ¹⁶to one a fragrance from death to death, to the other a fragrance from life to life. Who

1 Cor 16:9

2 Cor 7:6

Col 2:15

1 Cor 1:18
Lk 2:34

multas lacrimas, non ut contristemini, sed ut sciatis quam caritatem habeo abundantius in vos. ⁵Si quis autem contristavit, non me contristavit, sed ex parte, ut non onerem, omnes vos. ⁶Sufficit illi, qui eiusmodi est, obiurgatio haec, quae fit a pluribus, ⁷ita ut e contra magis donetis et consolemini, ne forte abundantiore tristitia absorbeatur, qui eiusmodi est. ⁸Propter quod obsecro vos, ut confirmetis in illum caritatem; ⁹ideo enim et scripsi, ut cognoscam probationem vestram, an in omnibus oboedientes sitis. ¹⁰Cui autem aliquid donatis, et ego; nam et ego, quod donavi, si quid donavi, propter vos in persona Christi, ¹¹ut non circumveniamur a Satana, non enim ignoramus cogitationes eius. ¹²Cum venissem autem Troadem ob evangelium Christi, et ostium mihi apertum esset in Domino, ¹³non habui requiem spiritui meo, eo quod non invenerim Titum fratrem meum, sed valefaciens eis profectus sum in Macedoniam. ¹⁴Deo autem gratias, qui semper triumphat nos in Christo et odorem notitiae suae manifestat per nos in omni loco. ¹⁵Quia Christi bonus odor sumus Deo in his, qui salvi fiunt, et in his, qui pereunt: ¹⁶aliis quidem odor ex morte in

2:5–11 What the Apostle says here has often been taken to refer to the case of the man guilty of incest (the one whom Paul took to task in 1 Corinthians 5:1–5). However, he may in fact be referring to someone who gravely insulted Paul (or one of Paul's co-workers) during a previous visit to Corinth. The offender may have been a Judaizer who had the support of a minority of the faithful. The person in question seems to have repented after being reprimanded and punished by the community, and St Paul now asks them to show clemency. Forgiveness, the central theme of this section, is clear proof that justice is at work, and justice leads to the peace which every community needs.

2:12–17 St Paul feels concern for his flock, and his fellow workers are never far from his thoughts: he is saddened by the way Titus was treated (Titus was his envoy to Corinth), and he

rejoices when he meets him again in Macedonia.

"The aroma of Christ" (v. 15). "The Gospel continues to spread everywhere a sweet and precious savour, even though some are lost who do not believe it: it is not the Gospel but their own perverseness that brings about their perdition" (St John Chrysostom, *In 2 Corinthios*, 5). It follows that all Christians should seek to mirror Christ in their behaviour: "Every Christian should make Christ present among men. He ought to act in such a way that those who know him sense 'the aroma of Christ' (2 Cor 2:15). People should be able to recognize the Master in his disciples" (St Josemaría Escrivá, *Christ Is Passing By*, 105).

Verse 17 and the second part of v. 16 serve as an introduction to the Apostle's defence of his ministry in the chapters that follow (3:16—6:10). Here he contrasts the sincerity of his preaching with the way the false disciples (who are

is sufficient for these things? [17]For we are not, like so many, pedlars of God's word; but as men of sincerity, as commissioned by God, in the sight of God we speak in Christ.

1 Pet 4:11
2 Cor 1:12; 12:19

3. THE IMPORTANCE OF APOSTOLIC OFFICE*

Paul's letter of recommendation

3 [1]Are we beginning to commend ourselves again? Or do we need, as some do, letters of recommendation to you, or from you? [2]You yourselves are our letter of recommendation, written on your[c] hearts, to be known and read by all men; [3]and you show that you are a letter from Christ delivered by us, written not with ink but with the Spirit of the living God, not on tablets of stone but on tablets of human hearts.

2 Cor 15:12;
10:12; 11:8
Acts 18:27
1 Cor 9:2

Ex 24:12
Jer 31:33
Ezek 11:19; 36:26

Christian ministry is greater than that of the Old Covenant

[4]Such is the confidence that we have through Christ toward God. [5]Not that we are competent of ourselves to claim anything as coming from us; our competence is from God, [6]who has made us competent to be ministers of a new covenant, not in a

Jn 3:27

Jer 31:31
Rom 2:29; 7:6
1 Cor 11:25
Col 1:23, 25
Eph 3:7

mortem, aliis autem odor ex vita in vitam. Et ad haec quis idoneus? [17]Non enim sumus sicut plurimi adulterantes verbum Dei, sed sicut ex sinceritate, sed sicut ex Deo coram Deo in Christo loquimur. [3][1]Incipimus iterum nosmetipsos commendare? Aut numquid egemus sicut quidam commendaticiis epistulis ad vos aut ex vobis? [2]Epistula nostra vos estis, scripta in cordibus nostris, quae scitur et legitur ab omnibus hominibus; [3]manifestati quoniam epistula estis Christi ministrata a nobis, scripta non atramento sed Spiritu Dei vivi, non in tabulis lapideis sed in tabulis cordis carnalibus. [4]Fiduciam autem talem habemus per Christum ad Deum. [5]Non quod sufficientes simus cogitare aliquid a nobis quasi ex nobis, sed sufficientia nostra ex Deo est, [6]qui et idoneos nos fecit ministros Novi Testamenti, non litterae sed Spiritus: littera enim occidit, Spiritus autem

trying to undermine his authority) adulterate the word of God; they are more interested in personal prestige and success than in Christ's cause. "Adulterating the word of God", St Gregory the Great explains, "is either seeing in it something which is not really there, or seeking from it not spiritual fruit but the adulterous offspring of human praise. Sincere preaching [of the word of God] means seeking the glory of its author and creator" (*Moralia*, 22, 12).

*3:1—6:10 Another criticism put out by Paul's opponents was that he was arrogant and proud in the performance of his office (see 10:12–18). He here appeals to God, and he puts forward important reasons in support of the dignity of his apostolic ministry: that office has to do with the New Covenant, which is greater than the Old Covenant (3:4–18); he performs it conscientiously (4:1–6); he patiently bears the trials that it involves (4:7—5:10); and he portrays it as a ministry of reconciliation (5:11—6:10).

3:1–3 Evidence from contemporary documents shows that letters of recommendation were commonly used in St Paul's time (cf. e.g. Acts 9:2;

15:22–30). Apparently Paul's enemies had arrived in Corinth with a letter of this sort. The Apostle, whose credentials come from the Lord (see 10:18), is further vouched for by the Corinthians themselves, whom he has brought to the faith: "They [the people of Corinth] were an adequate letter to explain who St Paul was and how beneficial his presence had been. And he says that this letter is one which all can know and read, because anyone, no matter how uncultured he may be, even if he does not understand the language of words, can understand the language of good example and virtue, whose results he can see, and so can come to esteem greatly one who has such fine disciples" (St John of Avila, *Audi, filia*, 34).

3:4–18 Apparently, there were some in Corinth who, influenced by the Judaizers, considered Paul's teaching to be his own invention and to be a fruit of his arrogance (see v. 5). Paul replies to this charge by appealing to God as his witness, and he makes three significant points in support of his ministry as an apostle: it belongs to the New Covenant, which is superior to the Old (vv. 4–6); more "splendour" attaches to it than to

c Other ancient authorities read *our*

Ex 32:15; 34:30

written code but in the Spirit; for the written code kills, but the Spirit gives life.
[7]Now if the dispensation of death, carved in letters on stone, came with such splendour that the Israelites could not look at Moses' face because of its brightness, fading as this was, [8]will not the dispensation of the Spirit be attended with greater splendour? [9]For if there was splendour in the dispensation of condemnation, the dispensation of righteousness must far exceed it in splendour. [10]Indeed, in this case, what once had splendour has come to have no splendour at all, because of the splendour that surpasses it. [11]For if what faded away came with splendour, what is permanent must have much more splendour.

Gal 3:8; 3:21

Ex 34:33

[12]Since we have such a hope, we are very bold, [13]not like Moses, who put a veil over his face so that the Israelites might not see the end of the fading splendour. [14]But their minds were hardened; for to this day, when they read the old covenant, that same veil remains unlifted, because only through Christ is it taken away. [15]Yes, to this day whenever Moses is read a veil lies over their minds; [16]but when a man turns to the Lord the veil is removed. [17]Now the Lord is the Spirit, and where the

Rom 10:4

Rom 11: 7–10

Ex 34:34
Rom 11:7–27

Rom 8:2

vivificat. [7]Quod si ministratio mortis litteris deformata in lapidibus fuit in gloria, ita ut non possent intendere filii Israel in faciem Moysis propter gloriam vultus eius, quae evacuatur, [8]quomodo non magis ministratio Spiritus erit in gloria? [9]Nam si ministerium damnationis gloria est, multo magis abundat ministerium iustitiae in gloria. [10]Nam nec glorificatum est, quod claruit in hac parte, propter excellentem gloriam; [11]si enim, quod evacuatur, per gloriam est, multo magis, quod manet, in gloria est. [12]Habentes igitur talem spem multa fiducia utimur, [13]et non sicut Moyses: ponebat velamen super faciem suam, ut non intenderent filii Israel in finem illus, quod evacuatur. [14]Sed obtusi sunt sensus eorum. Usque in hodiernum enim diem idipsum velamen in lectione Veteris Testamenti manet non revelatum, quoniam in Christo evacuatur; [15]sed usque in hodiernum diem, cum legitur Moyses, velamen est positum super cor eorum. [16]*Quando autem conversus fuerit ad Dominum, aufertur velamen.* [17]Dominus

Moses' ministry (vv. 7–11); and it is founded on the Spirit of truth and freedom, not on a written text obscured by a veil (vv. 12–18).

"The written code kills, but the Spirit gives life" (v. 6; cf. Rom 2:29; 7:6). The prophets announced that there would be a New Covenant, its novelty lying in the fact that God would write it on people's hearts, and He would give them a new spirit (cf. Jer 31:31). The New Law is "Spirit", because it is the Holy Spirit himself who through grace imbues the hearts of the faithful with charity, and charity is the fullness of the Law: "What is predominant in the law of the New Testament, and whereon all its efficacy is based, is the grace of the Holy Spirit, which is given through faith in Christ" (St Thomas Aquinas, *Summa theologiae*, 1–2, 106, 1).

In a typically rabbinical exegesis, Paul invokes the image of the veil with which Moses covered his face after his meetings with God (vv. 13–18; cf. Ex 34:29–35). The splendour of the Lord that shone out from Moses was so bright that the Israelites could not look at him directly. The Apostle says that this veil served not only to hide the radiance of Moses' face but also to hide the fact that the radiance was temporary; Paul uses the veil as a symbol of the provisional

nature of the Old Testament, a sign that it was impossible to communicate directly with God through Moses and the Law. Christ, he says, causes the veil to fall away; only by means of the light brought by Christ, the fullness of revelation, can one understand the true meaning of the sacred books. "God, the inspirer and author of the books of both Testaments, in his wisdom has so brought it about that the New should be hidden in the Old and that the Old should be made manifest in the New. [...] The books of the Old Covenant, all of them caught up into the Gospel message, attain and show forth their full meaning in the New Testament (cf. Mt 5:17; Lk 24:27; Rom 16:25–26; 2 Cor 3:14–16) and, in their turn, shed light on it and explain it" (Vatican II, *Dei Verbum*, 16). The final message is clear: in Christ, through the Holy Spirit, we are able to share in the life of God. Just as Moses reflected in his face the splendour of God after being with him on Sinai, Christians reflect in their lives the splendour of Christ, whom they contemplate through faith: "The Christian who has been cleansed by the Holy Spirit in the sacrament of regeneration", St John Chrysostom comments, "is changed, as the Apostle puts it, into the likeness of Jesus Christ himself. Not

Spirit of the Lord is, there is freedom. ¹⁸And we all, with unveiled face, beholding^d the glory of the Lord, are being changed into his likeness from one degree of glory to another; for this comes from the Lord who is the Spirit.*

Rom 8:29
1 Jn 3:2
2 Cor 4:6

Paul's sincere conduct

4 ¹Therefore, having this ministry by the mercy of God,^e we do not lose heart. ²We have renounced disgraceful, underhanded ways; we refuse to practise cunning or to tamper with God's word, but by the open statement of the truth we would commend ourselves to every man's conscience in the sight of God. ³And even if our gospel is veiled, it is veiled only to those who are perishing. ⁴In their case the god of this world has blinded the minds of the unbelievers, to keep them from seeing the light of the gospel of the glory of Christ, who is the likeness of God. ⁵For what we preach is not ourselves, but Jesus Christ as Lord, with ourselves as your servants^f for Jesus' sake. ⁶For it is the God who said, "Let light shine out of darkness," who has shone in our hearts to give the light of the knowledge of the glory of God in the face of Christ.

Rom 1:16
1 Cor 7:25
1 Thess 2:3–5
2 Cor 2:17
Heb 1:3
2 Thess 2:10–12
Rom 8:29
Col 1:15
Heb 1:3
2 Cor 1:24
Gen 1:3
Job 37:15
Jn 8:12
Eph 1:18
Heb 1:3
Rom 3:23

Trials that Paul has experienced

⁷But we have this treasure* in earthen vessels, to show that the transcendent power belongs to God and not to us. ⁸We are afflicted in every way, but not crushed; per-

Acts 9:15
2 Cor 12:9
1 Cor 4:9–13
2 Cor 6:4–10

autem Spiritus est; ubi autem Spiritus Domini, ibi libertas. ¹⁸Nos vero omnes revelata facie gloriam Domini speculantes, in eandem imaginem transformamur a claritate in claritatem tamquam a Domini Spiritu. [4] ¹Ideo habentes hanc ministrationem, iuxta quod misericordiam consecuti sumus, non deficimus, ²sed abdicavimus occulta dedecoris non ambulantes in astutia, neque adulterantes verbum Dei, sed in manifestatione veritatis commendantes nosmetipsos ad omnem conscientiam hominum coram Deo. ³Quod si etiam velatum est evangelium nostrum, in his, qui pereunt, est velatum, ⁴in quibus deus huius saeculi excaecavit mentes infidelium, ut non fulgeat illuminatio evangelii gloriae Christi, qui est imago Dei. ⁵Non enim nosmetipsos praedicamus sed Iesum Christum Dominum; nos autem servos vestros per Iesum. ⁶Quoniam Deus qui dixit: «De tenebris lux splendescat», ipse illuxit in cordibus nostris ad illuminationem scientiae claritatis Dei in facie Iesu Christi. ⁷Habemus autem thesaurum istum in vasis fictilibus, ut sublimitas sit virtutis Dei, et non ex nobis. ⁸In omnibus tribulationem patimur, sed non angustiamur; aporiamur, sed non destituimur; ⁹persecutionem patimur, sed non derelinquimur; deicimur, sed non perimus; ¹⁰semper mortificationem Iesu in corpore

only does he behold the glory of the Lord but he takes on some of the features of God's glory [...]. The soul who is regenerated by the Holy Spirit receives and radiates the splendour of the heavenly glory that has been given him" (*In 2 Corinthios*, 7).

4:1–6 A theme running through this first part of the letter is the sincere and genuine character of Paul's ministry. Unlike the false apostles, he preaches the truth about Jesus Christ without deviation or compromise. If, in spite of that, there are still some who cannot see the truth of the Gospel, the reason lies in their own bad dispositions and attitudes, which give entry to the devil, "the god of this world" (v. 4).

"Jesus Christ as Lord" (v. 5). This is a veiled assertion of the divinity of Jesus Christ: *Kyrios* (Lord) is the way the Greek version of the Old Testament translates the proper name of God, *Yhwh*.

4:7–12 The sufferings of the Apostle mirror those of Christ in his passion and death, and reflect, too, the life of the risen Christ. Pain and difficulties of one kind or another are never absent from the life of Christ's disciples: "If it is your ambition to win the esteem of men, if you desire to be well-regarded and seek only a life of ease, you have gone astray [...]. In the city of the saints, entrance is given, and rest and eternal rule with the King, only to those who have made their way along the rough, narrow path of trial and tribulation" (Pseudo-Macarius, *Homiliae*, 12, 5).

Christ's minister is weak, but he manages to stay the course of his ministry. The image of the earthenware vessel (v. 7; cf. Jer 18:6) serves to show the fragility of the apostle, but he bears a message that is a treasure: "God has entrusted his gifts to the weakness and fragility of human freedom. We can be certain of the help of God's power, but our lust, our love of comfort and our

d Or *reflecting* e Greek *as we have received mercy* f Or *slaves*

Col 1:24

1 Cor 15:31

plexed, but not driven to despair; ⁹persecuted, but not forsaken; struck down, but not destroyed; ¹⁰always carrying in the body the death of Jesus, so that the life of Jesus may also be manifested in our bodies. ¹¹For while we live we are always being given up to death for Jesus' sake, so that the life of Jesus may be manifested in our mortal flesh. ¹²So death is at work in us, but life in you.*

Paul is sustained by hope of heaven

Ps 116:10

Rom 1:4; 8:11
1 Cor 6:14
1 Thess 4:14

2 Cor 1:11
Rom 3:24

Eph 3:16
Rom 7:22

Rom 8:17-18
Mt 5:11-12

Heb 11:1–3
Rom 8:24–25
Col 1:16

¹³Since we have the same spirit of faith as he had who wrote, "I believed, and so I spoke," we too believe, and so we speak, ¹⁴knowing that he who raised the Lord Jesus will raise us also with Jesus and bring us with you into his presence. ¹⁵For it is all for your sake, so that as grace extends to more and more people it may increase thanksgiving, to the glory of God.

¹⁶So we do not lose heart. Though our outer nature is wasting away, our inner nature is being renewed every day. ¹⁷For this slight momentary affliction is preparing for us an eternal weight of glory beyond all comparison, ¹⁸because we look not to the things that are seen but to the things that are unseen; for the things that are seen are transient, but the things that are unseen are eternal.

circumferentes, ut et vita Iesu in corpore nostro manifestetur. ¹¹Semper enim nos, qui vivimus, in mortem tradimur propter Iesum, ut et vita Iesu manifestetur in carne nostra mortali. ¹²Ergo mors in nobis operatur, vita autem in vobis. ¹³Habentes autem eundem spiritum fidei, sicut scriptum est: «Credidi, propter quod locutus sum», et nos credimus, propter quod et loquimur, ¹⁴scientes quoniam, qui suscitavit Dominum Iesum, et nos cum Iesu suscitabit et constituet vobiscum. ¹⁵Omnia enim propter vos, ut gratia abundans per multos gratiarum actionem abundare faciat in gloriam Dei. ¹⁶Propter quod non deficimus, sed licet is, qui foris est, noster homo corrumpitur, tamen is, qui intus est, noster renovatur de die in diem. ¹⁷Id enim, quod in praesenti est, leve tribulationis nostrae supra modum in sublimitatem aeternum gloriae pondus operatur nobis, ¹⁸non contemplantibus nobis, quae videntur, sed quae non videntur; quae enim videntur, temporalia sunt, quae autem non videntur, aeterna sunt.

pride sometimes cause us to reject his grace and to fall into sin. [...] What is most important in the Church is not how we humans react but how God acts. This is what the Church is: Christ present in our midst" (St Josemaría Escrivá, *Christ Is Passing By*, 131).

4:13—5:10 The Apostle is strengthened by his hope in the resurrection and of attaining heaven (4:14). Our outer nature (our corruptible nature) is eroded by all kinds of afflictions and suffering, but our inner nature (the life of the soul) develops and is renewed day after day until it attains its full growth in heaven. This comes across clearly in the lives of the saints; though life takes its toll on them, their souls are constantly being rejuvenated, their joy ever on the increase. "[Yet 'our inner nature is being renewed every day.'] How? By faith, by hope and by charity. Therefore, we must brave these dangers which threaten us. In proportion as our body suffers our soul must grow in hope and become brighter, as gold becomes brighter the stronger the heat in which it is refined" (St John Chrysostom, *In 2 Corinthios*, 9).

The reference to the tent (5:1) emphasizes the impermanence of life, but we have the Spirit (5:5) as a guarantee that another life awaits us, like that of the risen Christ: "This earth is not our homeland; we are passing through it, as pilgrims. [...] Our homeland is heaven, which we merit by the grace of God and our own good works" (St Alphonsus Mary de Liguori, *Short Sermons*, 16, 1, 2).

St Paul yearns to be in heaven with Christ (5:8), but he is very conscious that he must strive in this present life to please God (5:9–10). This passage confirms there is a judgment that takes place immediately after death: "Each man receives his eternal retribution in his immortal soul at the very moment of his death, in a particular judgment that refers his life to Christ" (*Catechism of the Catholic Church*, 1022). Whether a person is rewarded or punished depends on the merits of his life: no more merit can be earned after death. St Paul's words exhort us to strive to please our Lord throughout our lives: "Does your soul not burn with the desire to make your Father-God happy when he has to judge you?" (St Josemaría Escrivá, *The Way*, 746).

5 [1]For we know that if the earthly tent we live in is destroyed, we have a building from God, a house not made with hands, eternal in the heavens. [2]Here indeed we groan, and long to put on our heavenly dwelling, [3]so that by putting it on we may not be found naked. [4]For while we are still in this tent, we sigh with anxiety; not that we would be unclothed, but that we would be further clothed, so that what is mortal may be swallowed up by life. [5]He who has prepared us for this very thing is God, who has given us the Spirit as a guarantee.

[6]So we are always of good courage; we know that while we are at home in the body we are away from the Lord, [7]for we walk by faith, not by sight. [8]We are of good courage, and we would rather be away from the body and at home with the Lord. [9]So whether we are at home or away, we make it our aim to please him. [10]For we must all appear before the judgment seat of Christ, so that each one may receive good or evil, according to what he has done in the body.

The ministry of reconciliation

[11]Therefore, knowing the fear of the Lord, we persuade men; but what we are is known to God, and I hope it is known also to your conscience. [12]We are not com-

Marginal references:
Wis 9:15
Is 38:12
1 Cor 15:44–49
2 Pet 1:13–14
Rom 8:23
Phil 3:20
Col 3:4
1 Cor 15:51-58
1 Thess 4:15
Rom 8:22–23
1 Cor 1:22
Ps 39:12
1 Pet 1:1
1 Cor 13:12
Phil 1:21–23
1 Cor 12, 12
Rom 8:24
Mt 25:31–44
Jn 5:27
Rom 2:6–11, 16;
14:10
Heb 11:6
2 Cor 4:2

---

[5] [1]Scimus enim quoniam si terrestris domus nostra huius tabernaculi dissolvatur, aedificationem ex Deo habemus domum non manufactam, aeternam in caelis. [2]Nam et in hoc ingemiscimus habitationem nostram, quae de caelo est, superindui cupientes, [3]si tamen et exspoliati, non nudi inveniamur. [4]Nam et, qui sumus in tabernaculo, ingemiscimus gravati, eo quod nolumus exspoliari sed supervestiri, ut absorbeatur, quod mortale est, a vita. [5]Qui autem effecit nos in hoc ipsum, Deus, qui dedit nobis arrabonem Spiritus. [6]Audentes igitur semper et scientes quoniam, dum praesentes sumus in corpore, peregrinamur a Domino; [7]per fidem enim ambulamus et non per speciem. [8]Audemus autem et bonam voluntatem habemus magis peregrinari a corpore et praesentes esse ad Dominum. [9]Et ideo contendimus sive praesentes sive absentes placere illi. [10]Omnes enim nos manifestari oportet ante tribunal Christi, ut referat unusquisque pro eis, quae per corpus gessit, sive bonum sive malum. [11]Scientes ergo tim-

---

5:11–21 The Apostle returns to the justification of his ministry. He has always been honest, he says (vv. 11–13), "the love of Christ" (v. 14) urging him on (here this phrase can be taken to mean both Christ's love for us and our love for Christ). In speaking of this love, the Apostle sums up the meaning of the Redemption (vv. 15–17): God has reconciled mankind to himself through Jesus Christ, who took our sins upon himself and died for all: "We know all that the Son of God did and taught for the reconciliation of the world not only through history and the accounts of his life, but because we can feel the power of the work he continues to do in the present time" (St Leo the Great, *Tractatus*, 63; cf. *De passione Domini*, 12, 6). Moreover, God has made the apostles his ambassadors, who bring his message of reconciliation (v. 19) to all mankind: "This pastoral activity would be lacking an essential aspect of its being and failing in an indispensable function if the 'message of reconciliation' (cf. 2 Cor 5:20) were not proclaimed with clarity and tenacity, in season and out of season, and if the gift of reconciliation were not offered to the world. But it is worth repeating that the importance of this ecclesial service of reconciliation extends beyond the confines of the Church to the whole world" (John Paul II, *Reconciliatio et paenitentia*, 23).

Prior to his conversion, Paul only saw Christ from a human point of view, but now he has an altogether different knowledge of him (see v. 16).

"The love of Christ controls us", urges us (v. 14). The love of Christ should inspire all Christians to try to bring the salvation won by Christ to all souls. "We are urged on by the charity of Christ (cf. 2 Cor 5:14) to take upon our shoulders a part of this task of saving souls. [...] As a result, we will foster in ourselves a vehement desire to live as co-redeemers with Christ, to save all souls with him" (St Josemaría Escrivá, *Christ Is Passing By*, 120–121).

"He made him to be sin" (v. 21). In the context of the ritual sacrifices of the Old Testament, the word "sin" refers less to the sinful act as such than to the act of offering a sacrifice and to what is offered in sacrifice (the "victim"). Therefore, these words in v. 21 mean that God "made him a victim for sin" or "a sacrifice (offering) for sin",

2 Cor 3:1
mending ourselves to you again but giving you cause to be proud of us, so that you may be able to answer those who pride themselves on a man's position and not on his heart. [13]For if we are beside ourselves, it is for God; if we are in our right mind, it is

Gal 2:20
Rom 6:4–11
1 Tim 2:6
Rom 7:1; 14:7–8
Rom 9:5; 7:5; 1:3
for you. [14]For the love of Christ controls us, because we are convinced that one has died for all; therefore all have died. [15]And he died for all, that those who live might live no longer for themselves but for him who for their sake died and was raised.

[16]From now on, therefore, we regard no one from a human point of view; even

Is 43:18
Rom 8:1–10
Gal 6:15

Rom 5:10
Eph 2:10, 15
Col 1:19-20

1 Cor 1:24
though we once regarded Christ from a human point of view, we regard him thus no longer. [17]Therefore, if any one is in Christ, he is a new creation;[g] the old has passed away, behold, the new has come. [18]All this is from God, who through Christ reconciled us to himself and gave us the ministry of reconciliation; [19]that is, in Christ God was reconciling[h] the world to himself,* not counting their trespasses against them, and entrusting to us the message of reconciliation. [20]So we are ambassadors for Christ, God making his appeal through us. We beseech you on behalf of Christ, be

Is 53:5-17
Gal 3:13
1 Pet 2:24
1 Jn 3:5
Rom 8:3
reconciled to God. [21]For our sake he made him to be sin* who knew no sin, so that in him we might become the righteousness of God.

Paul, a true servant of Christ

1 Cor 3:9
6 [1]Working together with him, then, we entreat you not to accept the grace of God in vain. [2]For he says,

Is 49:8
"At the acceptable time I have listened to you,
   and helped you on the day of salvation."

orem Domini hominibus suademus, Deo autem manifesti sumus; spero autem et in conscientiis vestris manifestos nos esse. [12]Non iterum nos commendamus vobis, sed occasionem damus vobis gloriandi pro nobis, ut habeatis ad eos, qui in facie gloriantur et non in corde. [13]Sive enim mente excedimus, Deo; sive sobrii sumus, vobis. [14]Caritas enim Christi urget nos, aestimantes hoc quoniam, si unus pro omnibus mortuus est, ergo omnes mortui sunt; [15]et pro omnibus mortuus est, ut et, qui vivunt, iam non sibi vivant, sed ei, qui pro ipsis mortuus est et resurrexit. [16]Itaque nos ex hoc neminem novimus secundum carnem; et si cognovimus secundum carnem Christum, sed nunc iam non novimus. [17]Si quis ergo in Christo, nova creatura; vetera transierunt, ecce, facta sunt nova. [18]Omnia autem ex Deo, qui reconciliavit nos sibi per Christum et dedit nobis ministerium reconciliationis, [19]quoniam quidem Deus erat in Christo mundum reconcilians sibi, non reputans illis delicta ipsorum, et posuit in nobis verbum reconciliationis. [20]Pro Christo ergo legatione fungimur tamquam Deo exhortante per nos: obsecramus pro Christo, reconciliamini Deo. [21]Eum, qui non noverat peccatum, pro nobis peccatum fecit, ut nos efficeremur iustitia Dei in ipso. [6] [1]Adiuvantes autem et exhortamur, ne in vacuum gra-

for Christ could never be guilty of any sin. "Christ had no sin; he bore sins, but he did not commit them" (St Augustine, *Enarrationes in Psalmos*, 68, 1, 10). Burdened with our sins, and offering himself on the cross as a victim for them, Jesus brought about the Redemption: "In the Passion and death of Christ—in the fact that the Father did not spare his own Son, but 'for our sake made him sin' (2 Cor 5:21)—absolute justice is expressed, for Christ undergoes the Passion and Cross because of the sins of humanity. [...] The *divine dimension of redemption* is put into effect not only by bringing justice to bear upon sin, but also by restoring to love that creative power in man thanks to which he once more has access to the fullness of life and holiness that come from God. In this way, redemption involves the revelation of mercy in its fullness" (John Paul II, *Dives in misericordia*, 7).

6:1–10 Paul concludes his long defence of his apostolic ministry by appealing, as God's minister, to the Corinthians to have a sense of responsibility; he quotes Isaiah 49:8 to show they should not vacillate. He then goes on to summarize the trials and sufferings he has encountered in his ministry.

The "acceptable time" (v. 2) extends to when Christ returns in glory at the end of time—and, in the case of each individual, until the moment of death. Until that day and hour comes, every day is the day of salvation: "*Ecce nunc dies salutis*, the day of salvation is here before us. The call of the good shepherd has reached us: '*ego vocavi te nomine tuo*, I have called you by name' (Is 43:1). Since love repays love, we must reply: '*ecce ego quia vocasti me*, Here I am, for you called me' (1 Sam 3:5) [...]. I will be converted, I will turn again to the Lord and love him

g Or *creature*   h Or *in Christ God was reconcilling*

Behold, now is the acceptable time; behold, now is the day of salvation. ³We put no
obstacle in any one's way, so that no fault may be found with our ministry, ⁴but as
servants of God we commend ourselves in every way: through great endurance, in
afflictions, hardships, calamities, ⁵beatings, imprisonments, tumults, labours, watching, hunger; ⁶by purity, knowledge, forbearance, kindness, the Holy Spirit, genuine
love, ⁷truthful speech, and the power of God; with the weapons of righteousness for
the right hand and for the left; ⁸in honour and dishonour, in ill repute and good
repute. We are treated as impostors, and yet are true; ⁹as unknown, and yet well
known; as dying, and behold we live; as punished, and yet not killed; ¹⁰as sorrowful, yet always rejoicing; as poor, yet making many rich; as having nothing, and yet
possessing everything.

(margin references) 2 Cor 8:21 · 1 Cor 4:9–13 · 2 Cor 4:8–10; 11:23–27 · Eph 6:11 · 2 Cor 10:4 · 2 Cor 4:11 · Rom 8:32 · 1 Cor 1:7

4. ST PAUL OPENS HIS HEART*

His love for the Corinthians

¹¹Our mouth is open to you, Corinthians; our heart is wide. ¹²You are not restricted by
us, but you are restricted in your own affections. ¹³In return—I speak as to children—
widen your hearts also.

(margin reference) 1 Cor 4:14

Contact with unbelievers

¹⁴Do not be mismated with unbelievers. For what partnership have righteousness and
iniquity? Or what fellowship has light with darkness? ¹⁵What accord has Christ with
Belial?ⁱ Or what has a believer in common with an unbeliever? ¹⁶What agreement

(margin references) Deut 22:10 · Jn 8:12 · Deut 13:14

tiam. Dei recipiatis ²—ait enim: «*Tempore accepto exaudivi te / et in die salutis adiuvi te*»; ecce nunc tempus acceptabile, ecce nunc dies salutis—
, ³nemini dantes ullam offensionem, ut non vituperetur ministerium, ⁴sed in omnibus exhibentes nosmetipsos sicut Dei ministros in multa patientia, in tribulationibus, in necessitatibus, in angustiis, ⁵in plagis, in carceribus, in seditionibus, in laboribus, in vigiliis, in ieiuniis, ⁶in castitate,
in scientia, in longanimitate, in suavitate, in Spiritu Sancto, in caritate non ficta, ⁷in verbo veritatis, in virtute Dei; per arma iustitiae a dextris et
sinistris, ⁸per gloriam et ignobilitatem, per infamiam et bonam famam; ut seductores et veraces, ⁹sicut qui ignoti et cogniti, quasi morientes, et
ecce vivimus, ut castigati et non mortificati, ¹⁰quasi tristes, semper autem gaudentes, sicut egentes, multos autem locupletantes, tamquam nihil
habentes et omnia possidentes. ¹¹Os nostrum patet ad vos, o Corinthii, cor nostrum dilatatum est. ¹²Non angustiamini in nobis, sed angustiamini
in visceribus vestris; ¹³eandem autem habentes remunerationem, tamquam filiis dico, dilatamini et vos. ¹⁴Nolite iugum ducere cum infidelibus!

as he wants to be loved" (St Josemaría Escrivá,
Christ Is Passing By, 59).

The list of tribulations (v. 5) is a reminder to
us to be resolute and resilient in the face of the
contradictions that inevitably arise: "Let nothing
trouble you, / Let nothing frighten you, / Everything passes, / God never changes, / Patience /
Obtains all; / He who has God / Wants for nothing: / God alone is enough" (St Teresa of Avila,
Poems, 30).

*6:11—7:16 This section, which concludes the
first part of the letter (cf. the note on 1:12–7:16),
is a vibrant appeal by Paul to the Corinthians in
an attempt to win back their trust and affection.
The personality of the Apostle comes across very
clearly here, and his warmheartedness and concern for his flock. He implores them most ten-

derly to respond to his ceaseless zeal for them
(6:11–13), gives them guidelines concerning
their relationships with people who do not
belong to the Church (6:14—7:1), and ends by
registering his joy when he is reassured as to the
Corinthians' fidelity.

6:11–13 Paul makes a direct appeal to the
Corinthians to reciprocate his affection: "For
nothing is bigger than Paul's heart which loved
all the faithful with more ardour than even the
most passionate of hearts; his love was not
divided and therefore weakened: it abided in him
and communicated itself to all equally" (St John
Chrysostom, *In 2 Corinthios*, 13, 1).

6:14—7:1 Paul does not mean that Christians
should avoid all contact with unbelievers; if they

i Greek *Beliar*

has the temple of God with idols? For we are the temple of the living God; as God said,

Lev 26:12
Ezek 37:27
1 Cor 3:16
> "I will live in them and move among them,
>> "and I will be their God,
>> "and they shall be my people.

Is 52:11
Jer 51:45
> [17] Therefore come out from them,
>> and be separate from them, says the Lord,
>> and touch nothing unclean;
>> then I will welcome you,
> [18] and I will be a father to you,

2 Sam 7, 14
Is 43:6
Jer 31:9
>> and you shall be my sons and daughters,
>> says the Lord Almighty."

Heb 10:22
2 Cor 1:9
Rom 1:9; 7:5
7 [1] Since we have these promises, beloved, let us cleanse ourselves from every defilement of body and spirit, and make holiness perfect in the fear of God.

Paul's joy at the news brought by Titus

2 Cor 6:11–13
Col 1:24
[2] Open your hearts to us; we have wronged no one, we have corrupted no one, we have taken advantage of no one. [3] I do not say this to condemn you, for I said before

---

Quae enim participatio iustitiae cum iniquitate? Aut quae societas luci ad tenebras? [15] Quae autem conventio Christi cum Beliar, aut quae pars fideli cum infideli? [16] Qui autem consensus templo Dei cum idolis? Vos enim estis templum Dei vivi; sicut dicit Deus: «*Inhabitabo in illis et inambulabo / et ero illorum Deus, et ipsi erunt mihi populus.* / [17] *Propter quod exite de medio eorum / et separamini, dicit Dominus, / et immundum ne tetigeritis; / et ego recipiam vos / [18] et ero vobis in Patrem, / et vos eritis mihi in fi lios et filias, / dicit Dominus omnipotens».*   [7] [1] Has igitur habentes promissiones, carissimi, mundemus nos ab omni inquinamento carnis et spiritus, perficientes sanctificationem in timore Dei. [2] Capite nos! Neminem laesimus, neminem corrupimus, neminem circumvenimus. [3] Non ad condemnationem dico; praedixi enim quod in cordibus nos-

---

did that, they would deprive them of the chance of conversion; but they should certainly avoid any contact that puts their own faith at risk. In v. 14, the original text uses a verbal construction that means "not yoking two different sorts of animals together"—the metaphor being designed to show that a believer is of a different "species" from an unbeliever and cannot live just like an unbeliever. "Belial" (v. 15): the etymology of this word is uncertain; it may mean "useless", "perverse" or "without-law" (see Deut 13:13)— hence its frequent application to the devil.

"We are the temple of the living God" (v. 16). This image, also found elsewhere (cf. 1 Cor 3:16–17; 6:19–20.), shows that the Blessed Trinity dwells in the soul in grace: "What more do you desire, O soul," St John of the Cross asks, quoting this verse, "and what more do you seek outside yourself, for within yourself you have your riches, your delights, your satisfaction, your fullness and your kingdom, which is your Beloved, whom your soul desires and seeks? Rejoice and be glad in your inner recollection with him; for you have him so near. There desire him, there adore him, and do not go to seek him outside yourself, for that will only make you weary and distracted, and you will not find him, or enjoy him more surely or more quickly or more intimately than within yourself" (*Spiritual Canticle*, 1, 8).

7:2–16 Paul wants to regain the full confidence and affection of the Corinthians. What he says here refers back to what he had begun to tell them in chapter 2 and then interrupted to make his long apologia. He explains why he wrote his letter—to move them to repentance; God will have proof of their change of heart, when they show Paul their affection. We can see here that when Paul converts someone, he always seeks the good of that person: "We should correct out of love, not out of a desire to hurt others, but with the affectionate intention of helping them to change. If we correct others in that way we fulfil the precept very well, 'If your brother sins against you, go and tell him his fault, between you and him alone' (Mt 18:15)" (St Augustine, *Sermones*, 82, 4).

that you are in our hearts, to die together and to live together. ⁴I have great confi- 2 Cor 12:10
dence in you; I have great pride in you; I am filled with comfort. With all our affliction, I am overjoyed.

⁵For even when we came into Macedonia, our bodies had no rest but we were Acts 20:1–2
afflicted at every turn — fighting without and fear within. ⁶But God, who comforts 2 Cor 2:13
the downcast, comforted us by the coming of Titus, ⁷and not only by his coming
but also by the comfort with which he was comforted in you, as he told us of your
longing, your mourning, your zeal for me, so that I rejoiced still more. ⁸For even 2 Cor 2:4
if I made you sorry with my letter, I do not regret it (though I did regret it), for I
see that that letter grieved you, though only for a while. ⁹As it is, I rejoice, not
because you were grieved, but because you were grieved into repenting; for you
felt a godly grief, so that you suffered no loss through us. ¹⁰For godly grief produces a repentance that leads to salvation and brings no regret, but worldly grief
produces death. ¹¹For see what earnestness this godly grief has produced in you,
what eagerness to clear yourselves, what indignation, what alarm, what longing,
what zeal, what punishment! At every point you have proved yourselves guiltless
in the matter. ¹²So although I wrote to you, it was not on account of the one who
did the wrong, nor on account of the one who suffered the wrong, but in order that
your zeal for us might be revealed to you in the sight of God. ¹³Therefore we are
comforted.

And besides our own comfort we rejoiced still more at the joy of Titus, because
his mind has been set at rest by you all. ¹⁴For if I have expressed to him some pride 2 Cor 8:23
in you, I was not put to shame; but just as everything we said to you was true, so our
boasting before Titus has proved true. ¹⁵And his heart goes out all the more to you, 1 Cor 2:3
as he remembers the obedience of you all, and the fear and trembling with which
you received him. ¹⁶I rejoice, because I have perfect confidence in you.

tris estis ad commoriendum et ad convivendum. ⁴Multa mihi fiducia est apud vos, multa mihi gloriatio pro vobis; repletus sum consolatione, super-
abundo gaudio in omni tribulatione nostra. ⁵Nam et cum venissemus Macedoniam, nullam requiem habuit caro nostra, sed omnem tribulationem
passi: foris pugnae, intus timores. ⁶Sed qui consolatur humiles, consolatus est nos Deus in adventu Titi; ⁷non solum autem in adventu eius sed
etiam in solacio, quo consolatus est in vobis, referens nobis vestrum desiderium, vestrum fletum, vestram aemulationem pro me, ita ut magis gaud-
erem. ⁸Quoniam etsi contristavi vos in epistula, non me paenitet; etsi paeniteret — video quod epistula illa, etsi ad horam, vos contristavit — ⁹nunc
gaudeo, non quia contristati estis, sed quia contristati estis ad paenitentiam; contristati enim estis secundum Deum, ut in nullo detrimentum patiamini ex nobis. ¹⁰Quae enim secundum Deum tristitia, paenitentiam in salutem stabilem operatur; saeculi autem tristitia mortem operatur. ¹¹Ecce
enim hoc ipsum secundum Deum contristari: quantam in vobis operatum est sollicitudinem, sed defensionem, sed indignationem, sed timorem,
sed desiderium, sed aemulationem, sed vindictam! In omnibus exhibuistis vos incontaminatos esse negotio. ¹²Igitur etsi scripsi vobis, non propter
eum, qui fecit iniuriam, nec propter eum, qui passus est, sed ad manifestandam sollicitudinem vestram, quam pro nobis habetis, ad vos coram
Deo. ¹³Ideo consolati sumus. In consolatione autem nostra abundantius magis gavisi sumus super gaudium Titi, quia refectus est spiritus eius ab
omnibus vobis; ¹⁴et si quid apud illum de vobis gloriatus sum, non sum confusus, sed sicut omnia vobis in veritate locuti sumus, ita et gloriatio
nostra, quae fuit ad Titum, veritas facta est. ¹⁵Et viscera eius abundantius in vos sunt, reminiscentis omnium vestrum oboedientiam, quomodo cum
timore et tremore excepistis eum. ¹⁶Gaudeo quod in omnibus confido in vobis.   [8] ¹Notam autem facimus vobis, fratres, gratiam Dei, quae data

Paul eagerly confides in the Corinthians his
delight at the good news brought by Titus (v. 6;
cf. the note on 2 Cor 2:12–17): the faithful at
Corinth have shown their respect and appreciation for this co-worker of Paul's (v. 15) and have
responded very well (vv. 7, 9, 11) to the letter
"written in tears" (see 2:3–4).

"Godly grief" (v. 10) is the sorrow of a soul
that grieves for having sinned and hopes to

receive forgiveness: "The sadness which healthy
repentance produces is proper to the obedient,
affable, humble, sweet, gentle and patient man,
because it comes from the love of God. [...]
Diabolical sadness is the very opposite. It
is rough, impatient, full of bitterness and
disgust, and it also involves a kind of painful
despair" (John Cassian, *De institutis coenob-
iorum*, 9, 11).

PART TWO

The collection for the church of Jerusalem*

The Macedonians' good example

Rom 3:26–28
1 Cor 16:5

8 ¹We want you to know, brethren, about the grace of God which has been shown in the churches of Macedonia, ²for in a severe test of affliction, their abundance of joy and their extreme poverty have overflowed in a wealth of liberality on their part. ³For they gave according to their means, as I can testify, and beyond their means, of their own free will, ⁴begging us earnestly for the favour of taking part in the relief of the saints—⁵and this, not as we expected, but first they gave themselves to the Lord and to us by the will of God. ⁶Accordingly we have urged Titus that as he had already made a beginning, he should also complete among you this gracious work.

Acts 11:29
2 Cor 9:1
1 Cor 16:1–2

Appeal for generosity

1 Cor 1:5

⁷Now as you excel in everything—in faith, in utterance, in knowledge, in all earnestness, and in your love for us—see that you excel in this gracious work also.

1 Cor 7:6
2 Cor 9:7
Phil 8:14

⁸I say this not as a command, but to prove by the earnestness of others that your love also is genuine. ⁹For you know the grace of our Lord Jesus Christ, that though he

est in ecclesiis Macedoniae, ²quod in multo experimento tribulationis abundantia gaudii ipsorum et altissima paupertas eorum abundavit in divitias simplicitatis eorum; ³quia secundum virtutem, testimonium reddo, et supra virtutem voluntarii fuerunt ⁴cum multa exhortatione obsecrantes nos gratiam et communicationem ministerii, quod fit in sanctos. ⁵Et non sicut speravimus, sed semetipsos dederunt primum Domino, deinde nobis per voluntatem Dei, ⁶ita ut rogaremus Titum, ut, quemadmodum coepit, ita et perficiat in vos etiam gratiam istam. ⁷Sed sicut in omnibus abundatis, fide et sermone et scientia et omni sollicitudine et caritate ex nobis in vobis, ut et in hac gratia abundetis. ⁸Non quasi imperans dico, sed per aliorum sollicitudinem etiam vestrae caritatis ingenitum bonum comprobans; ⁹scitis enim gratiam Domini nostri Iesu Christi, quoniam propter

*8:1—9:15 These chapters form the second part of the letter, in which the Apostle deals with the collection for the faithful in Jerusalem (other churches founded by Paul are involved in this collection: cf. Rom 15:26; 1 Cor 16:1). He explains with some enthusiasm the theological reasons why Christians should share their resources with one another. He praises what the Macedonians have done in this regard: it sets an example for the Corinthians (8:1–15); then he gives Titus and others some practical suggestions about the collection (8:16–9:5), and finishes by describing the fruits borne by effects of generous almsgiving (9:6–15).

8:1–6 The Macedonians have been remarkably generous: they could easily have felt excused from coming to the aid of their brothers, in view of their own poverty; instead, they were more than generous in their response. In this passage it is interesting to note how delicately the Apostle broaches the subject: he does not talk about

"money", "alms", "collection", but instead uses more spiritual vocabulary—such expressions as "favour", "gracious work", "love" (vv. 4, 6; 8:7) or "relief of the saints" (v. 4).

8:7–15 Jesus is the supreme example of detachment and generosity (v. 9). "If you do not believe that poverty is enriching, think of our Lord and you will doubt me no longer. For had he not become poor, you could not have become rich. By a miracle which men cannot understand, poverty has produced these riches—the knowledge of God and godliness, liberation from sin, justification, sanctification, the countless good things which he has bestowed on us and will bestow on us in the future. All those things have accrued to us through his poverty—through his taking our flesh and becoming man and suffering what he suffered. And yet, unlike us, he did not deserve punishment and suffering" (St John Chrysostom, *In 2 Corinthios*, 17). Jesus' self-giving is the point of reference for the donations

was rich, yet for your sake he became poor, so that by his poverty you might become rich. ¹⁰And in this matter I give my advice: it is best for you now to complete what a year ago you began not only to do but to desire, ¹¹so that your readiness in desiring it may be matched by your completing it out of what you have. ¹²For if the readiness is there, it is acceptable according to what a man has, not according to what he has not. ¹³I do not mean that others should be eased and you burdened, ¹⁴but that as a matter of equality your abundance at the present time should supply their want, so that their abundance may supply your want, that there may be equality. ¹⁵As it is written, "He who gathered much had nothing over, and he who gathered little had no lack."

Mt 5:3
Phil 2:6–7

Prov 3:27–28

Rom 15:26–27

Ex 16:18

Paul praises Titus and Timothy

¹⁶But thanks be to God who puts the same earnest care for you into the heart of Titus. ¹⁷For he not only accepted our appeal, but being himself very earnest he is going to you of his own accord. ¹⁸With him we are sending the brother who is famous among all the churches for his preaching of the gospel; ¹⁹and not only that, but he has been appointed by the churches to travel with us in this gracious work which we are carrying on, for the glory of the Lord and to show our good will. ²⁰We intend that no one should blame us about this liberal gift which we are administering, ²¹for we aim at what is honourable not only in the Lord's sight but also in the sight of men. ²²And with them we are sending our brother whom we have often tested and found earnest in many matters, but who is now more earnest than ever because of his great confidence in you. ²³As for Titus, he is my partner and fellow

1 Cor 16:3

Prov 3:4
Rom 12:17

2 Cor 7:13; 12:18

vos egenus factus est, cum esset dives, ut illius inopia vos divites essetis. ¹⁰Et consilium in hoc do. Hoc enim vobis utile est, qui non solum facere sed et velle coepistis ab anno priore; ¹¹nunc vero et facto perficite, ut, quemadmodum promptus est animus velle, ita sit et perficere ex eo, quod habetis. ¹²Si enim voluntas prompta est, secundum id quod habet, accepta est, non secundum quod non habet. ¹³Non enim, ut aliis sit remissio, vobis autem tribulatio; sed ex aequalitate ¹⁴in praesenti tempore vestra abundantia illorum inopiam suppleat, ut et illorum abundantia vestram inopiam suppleat, ut fiat aequalitas, sicut scriptum est: ¹⁵«*Qui multum, non abundavit; et, qui modicum, non minoravit*». ¹⁶Gratias autem Deo, qui dedit eandem sollicitudinem pro vobis in corde Titi, ¹⁷quoniam exhortationem quidem suscepit, sed, cum sollicitior esset, sua voluntate profectus est ad vos. ¹⁸Misimus etiam cum illo fratrem, cuius laus est in evangelio per omnes ecclesias ¹⁹—non solum autem sed et ordinatus ab ecclesiis comes noster cum hac gratia, quae ministratur a nobis ad Domini gloriam et destinatam voluntatem nostram—²⁰devitantes hoc, ne quis nos vituperet in hac plenitudine, quae ministratur a nobis; ²¹*providemus* enim *bona* non solum *coram Domino* sed *etiam* coram *hominibus*. ²²Misimus autem cum illis et fratrem nostrum, quem probavimus in multis saepe sollicitum esse, nunc autem multo sollicitiorem, confidentia multa in vos.

made by the faithful: "From the very beginning Christians have brought, along with the bread and wine for the Eucharist, gifts to share with those in need. This custom of the *collection*, ever appropriate, is inspired by the example of Christ, who became poor to make us rich" (*Catechism of the Catholic Church*, 1351).

In almsgiving a person's dispositions are more important than the amount of his gift (v. 12). "If you put out your hand to give [something], but you do not have pity in your heart, your gesture is useless; whereas, if you have pity in your heart, even if you have nothing to give with your hand, God accepts your alms" (St Augustine, *Enarrationes in Psalmos*, 125, 5*)*.

8:16–24 As well as Titus, who in all probability was the bearer of this letter, two other brethren are

mentioned, but no names are given. It has been suggested that the first (see vv. 18–19) was St Luke, who may have been with St Paul at the time and who afterwards travelled with him to Jerusalem (cf. Acts 20:5ff). On the basis of 1 Corinthians 16:12, some think that the other envoy (see v. 22) could have been Apollos, who was well known to the Corinthians (see 1 Cor 1:12).

"The glory of Christ" (v. 23): praise indeed for Titus and the Apostle's other aides. Paul VI applies the description to priests: "In this way, in our world, which needs God's glory (cf. Rom 3:23), priests, ever more perfectly conformed to the one and supreme Priest, will be a real glory to Christ (2 Cor 8:23), and, through them, the glory of the grace of God will be magnified in the world of today (cf. Eph 1:6)" (*Sacerdotalis caelibatus*, 45).

worker in your service; and as for our brethren, they are messengers[j] of the churches, the glory of Christ. [24]So give proof, before the churches, of your love and of our boasting about you to these men.

Appeal for speediness

2 Cor 8:4

[9] [1]Now it is superfluous* for me to write to you about the offering for the saints, [2]for I know your readiness, of which I boast about you to the people of Macedonia, saying that Achaia has been ready since last year; and your zeal has stirred up most of them. [3]But I am sending the brethren so that our boasting about you may not prove vain in this case, so that you may be ready, as I said you would be; [4]lest if some Macedonians come with me and find that you are not ready, we be humiliated—to say nothing of you—for being so confident. [5]So I thought it necessary to urge the brethren to go on to you before me, and arrange in advance for this gift you have promised, so that it may be ready not as an exaction but as a willing gift.

Blessings to be expected

Prov 11:24–25

Sir 35:8
Rom 12:8
2 Cor 8:8
Prov 22:8
Rom 3:24

[6]The point is this: he who sows sparingly will also reap sparingly, and he who sows bountifully will also reap bountifully. [7]Each one must do as he has made up his mind, not reluctantly or under compulsion, for God loves a cheerful giver. [8]And God is able to provide you with every blessing in abundance, so that you may always have enough of everything and may provide in abundance for every good work. [9]As it is written,

Ps 112:9

> "He scatters abroad, he gives to the poor;
> his righteousness[k] endures for ever."

[23]Sive pro Tito, est socius meus et in vos adiutor; sive fratres nostri, apostoli ecclesiarum, gloria Christi. [24]Ostensionem ergo, quae est caritatis vestrae et nostrae gloriationis pro vobis, in illos ostendite in faciem ecclesiarum. [9] [1]Nam de ministerio, quod fit in sanctos, superfluum est mihi scribere vobis; [2]scio enim promptum animum vestrum, pro quo de vobis glorior apud Macedonas, quoniam Achaia parata est ab anno praeterito, et vestra aemulatio provocavit plurimos. [3]Misi autem fratres, ut ne, quod gloriamur de vobis, evacuetur in hac parte, ut, quemadmodum dixi, parati sitis, [4]ne, cum venerint mecum Macedones et invenerint vos imparatos, erubescamus nos, ut non dicam vos, in hac substantia. [5]Necessarium ergo existimavi rogare fratres, ut praeveniant ad vos et praeparent repromissam benedictionem vestram, ut haec sit parata sic quasi benedictionem, non quasi avaritiam. [6]Hoc autem: qui parce seminat, parce et metet; et, qui seminat in benedictionibus, in benedictionibus et metet. [7]Unusquisque prout destinavit corde suo, non ex tristitia aut ex necessitate, *hilarem* enim *datorem* diligit *Deus*. [8]Potens est autem Deus omnem gratiam abundare facere in vobis, ut, in omnibus semper omnem sufficientiam habentes, abundetis in omne opus bonum, [9]sicut scriptum est: *«Dispersit, dedit pauperibus; / iustitia eius manet in aeternum»*. [10]Qui autem administrat semen seminanti, et panem ad manducandum praestabit et multiplicabit semen vestrum

9:1–5 By praising the Macedonians (see also 8:1–5), Paul uses the friendly rivalry between the two Christian communities to stir the Corinthians to generosity. He has already boasted to the Macedonians (see v. 2) of the zeal and readiness of those in Corinth, who were the first to set about making the collection. Now he asks the Corinthians not to let him down; it would embarrass him if they did not live up to his boasts.

9:6–15 Another reason why the Apostle encourages them to be generous is the reward they will receive from God. The harvest they reap from sowing is proof of how generous God is: "For if even to those who sow the earth and to those who are concerned about the needs of the body,

God gives in great abundance, much more will he give to those who till the soil of heaven and apply themselves to the salvation of their souls [...]. Therefore he asks that we should not simply give alms, but give alms generously. That is why he calls alms 'seed'. Just as corn sown in the ground produces a crop, so generous alms produce righteousness in an abundant harvest" (St John Chrysostom, *In 2 Corinthios*, 20).

"God loves a cheerful giver" (v. 7). This is a loose translation of the Septuagint version of Proverbs 22:8, which puts the emphasis on the joy that almsgiving brings: "If you give bread and it makes you sad to do so," St Augustine comments, "you lose both the bread and the reward" (*Enarrationes in Psalmos*, 42, 8).

j Greek *apostles* k Or *benevolence*

[10]He who supplies seed to the sower and bread for food will supply and multiply your resources[l] and increase the harvest of your righteousness.[k] [11]You will be enriched in every way for great generosity, which through us will produce thanksgiving to God; [12]for the rendering of this service not only supplies the wants of the saints but also overflows in many thanksgivings to God. [13]Under the test of this service, you[m] will glorify God by your obedience in acknowledging the gospel of Christ, and by the generosity of your contribution for them and for all others; [14]while they long for you and pray for you, because of the surpassing grace of God in you. [15]Thanks be to God for his inexpressible gift!

Is 55:10
Hos 10:12
2 Cor 1:11

2 Cor 8:14

Acts 2:42

2 Cor 8:9

PART THREE

Paul justifies his conduct*

5. A REPLY TO ACCUSATIONS*

Paul's readiness to use his apostolic authority

10 [1]I, Paul, myself entreat you, by the meekness and gentleness of Christ—I who am humble when face to face with you, but bold to you when I am away!*— [2]I beg of you that when I am present I may not have to show boldness with such

Mt 11:29
Phil 2:1
1 Cor 2:3

1 Cor 4:21

et augebit incrementa frugum iustitiae vestrae. [11]In omnibus locupletati in omnem simplicitatem, quae operatur per nos gratiarum actionem Deo [12]—quoniam ministerium huius officii non solum supplet ea, quae desunt sanctis, sed etiam abundat per multas gratiarum actiones Deo—[13]per probationem ministerii huius glorificantes Deum in oboedientia confessionis vestrae in evangelium Christi et simplicitate communionis in illos et in omnes, [14]et ipsorum obsecratione pro vobis, desiderantium vos propter eminentem gratiam Dei in vobis. [15]Gratias Deo super inenarrabili dono eius. [10] [1]Ipse autem ego Paulus obsecro vos per mansuetudinem et modestiam Christi, qui in facie quidem humilis inter vos, absens autem confido in vobis; [2]rogo autem, ne praesens audeam per eam confidentiam, quae existimo audere in quosdam, qui arbitrantur nos tamquam

*10:1—13:10 In these chapters St Paul justifies himself to his opponents in Corinth. The tone of the preceding chapters was one of affection, but now the Apostle is outspoken and fiery in his words, because he realizes the harm that would befall this fledgling community if they broke with their founder and apostle. He begins by defending himself against the charge of being weak and vainglorious (10:11–18). Then he compares his entitlement to boast with that of his adversaries (11:1—12:18). And finally he explains that his apologia is designed to encourage the Corinthians to repent of their behaviour prior to his next visit (12:19—13:10).

*10:1—18 The Apostle tackles head-on the charges levelled by those trying to discredit him. It seems that they were Judaizers, and claimed to have a knowledge of God superior to Paul's.

10:1–11 In this passage Paul defends his apostolic authority against people who misread his meekness and gentleness for faintheartedness. Paul was fully aware of the apostolic authority given him by Christ, but, if at all possible, he preferred to use it only to build up people's faith, and to edify them by his own example, not to criticize.

"We live in the world", "in the flesh" (v. 3): this has a positive meaning, referring to the life we have when we are here on earth. But "acting in worldly fashion" (v. 2) is the same thing as acting from purely human motives: "Acting in a worldly fashion applies to people who make worldly things their goal and therefore design their actions so as to obtain worldly things. Since these things can be taken away from them by men, those who have a tendency to be drawn towards worldly things behave in a deferential and mild way towards others" (St Thomas Aquinas, *Super 2 Corinthios*, ad loc.).

k Or *benevolence* l Greek *sowing* m Or *they*

confidence as I count on showing against some who suspect us of acting in worldly

Rom 7:5

fashion. [3]For though we live in the world we are not carrying on a worldly war, [4]for

Eph 6:11–17
2 Cor 6:7

the weapons of our warfare are not worldly but have divine power to destroy strong-

Is 2:11–18
1 Cor 1:25

holds. [5]We destroy arguments and every proud obstacle to the knowledge of God,

Rom 1:5

and take every thought captive to obey Christ, [6]being ready to punish every disobedience, when your obedience is complete.

1 Cor 1:12
2 Cor 11:23

[7]Look at what is before your eyes. If any one is confident that he is Christ's, let

Jer 1:10
2 Cor 13:10

him remind himself that as he is Christ's, so are we. [8]For even if I boast a little too
much of our authority, which the Lord gave for building you up and not for destroying you, I shall not be put to shame. [9]I would not seem to be frightening you with letters. [10]For they say, "His letters are weighty and strong, but his bodily presence is

2 Cor 13, 10

weak, and his speech of no account." [11]Let such people understand that what we say
by letter when absent, we do when present.

Paul's province includes Corinth

2 Cor 3:1; 5:12
Gal 6:4

[12]Not that we venture to class or compare ourselves with some of those who commend themselves. But when they measure themselves by one another, and compare
themselves with one another, they are without understanding.

Rom 15:17–20

[13]But we will not boast beyond limit, but will keep to the limits God has appor-

Col 1:25

tioned us, to reach even to you. [14]For we are not overextending ourselves, as though
we did not reach you; we were the first to come all the way to you with the gospel of
Christ. [15]We do not boast beyond limit, in other men's labours; but our hope is that as

Acts 19:21

your faith increases, our field among you may be greatly enlarged, [16]so that we may
preach the gospel in lands beyond you, without boasting of work already done in

Jer 9:22–23
1 Cor 1:31

another's field. [17]"Let him who boasts, boast of the Lord." [18]For it is not the man who
commends himself that is accepted, but the man whom the Lord commends.

secundum carnem ambulemus. [3]In carne enim ambulantes, non secundum carnem militamus [4]—nam arma militiae nostrae non carnalia sed potentia Deo ad destructionem munitionum—consilia destruentes [5]et omnem altitudinem extollentem se adversus scientiam Dei, et in captivitatem redi-
gentes omnem intellectum in obsequium Christi, [6]et in promptu habentes ulcisci omnem inoboedientiam, cum impleta fuerit vestra oboedientia.
[7]Quae secundum faciem sunt, videte. Si quis confidit sibi Christi se esse, hoc cogitet iterum apud se, quia sicut ipse Christi est, ita et nos. [8]Nam
et si amplius aliquid gloriatus fuero de potestate nostra, quam dedit Dominus in aedificationem et non in destructionem vestram, non erubescam,
[9]ut non existimer tamquam terrere vos per epistulas; [10]quoniam quidem «Epistulae—inquiunt—graves sunt et fortes, praesentia autem corporis
infirma et sermo contemptibilis». [11]Hoc cogitet, qui eiusmodi est, quia quales sumus verbo per epistulas absentes, tales et praesentes in facto.
[12]Non enim audemus inserere aut comparare nos quibusdam, qui seipsos commendant; sed ipsi se in semetipsis metientes, et comparantes semetipsos sibi, non intellegunt. [13]Nos autem non ultra mensuram gloriabimur, sed secundum mensuram regulae, quam impertitus est nobis Deus, mensuram pertingendi usque ad vos. [14]Non enim quasi non pertingentes ad vos superextendimus nosmetipsos, usque ad vos enim pervenimus in
evangelio Christi; [15]non ultra mensuram gloriantes in alienis laboribus, spem autem habentes, crescente fide vestra, in vobis magnificari secundum regulam nostram in abundantiam, [16]ad evangelizandum in iis, quae ultra vos sunt, et non in aliena regula gloriari in his, quae praeparata sunt.
[17]Qui autem *gloriatur, in Domino glorietur*; [18]non enim qui seipsum commendat, ille probatus est, sed quem Dominus commendat.   [11] [1]Utinam

10:12–18 Here Paul answers the accusation that
he prides himself on his ministry in Corinth.
True, he is pleased with the results, but he has
never claimed for himself the achievements of
others. He relies solely on God, in line with the
words of Jeremiah 9:23 (v. 17). The opinions of
men matter very little. "My brothers, if I had to
present myself before your tribunal, rightly
would I be happy to receive your praise. And if I
had to be judged by my own conscience and
make do with my own opinion of myself, I
would be glad of my self-esteem. But since I
have to appear, not before your judgment or my
own, but before the judgment of God, how foolish, how deluded I would be to take refuge in
your testimony or in my own, especially since
God is such that everything is bare and open to
his gaze, and he has no need of anyone's testimony about man" (St Bernard, *Sermones de
diversis*, 7, 2).

6. THE APOSTLE'S GROUNDS FOR BOASTING*

His zeal

11 ¹I wish you would bear with me in a little foolishness. Do bear with me! ²I feel a divine jealousy for you, for I betrothed you to Christ to present you as a pure bride to her one husband. ³But I am afraid that as the serpent deceived Eve by his cunning, your thoughts will be led astray from a sincere and pure devotion to Christ. ⁴For if some one comes and preaches another Jesus than the one we preached, or if you receive a different spirit from the one you received, or if you accept a different gospel from the one you accepted, you submit to it readily enough. ⁵I think that I am not in the least inferior to these superlative apostles. ⁶Even if I am unskilled in speaking, I am not in knowledge; in every way we have made this plain to you in all things.

Deut 4:24
Eph 5:25–27
Hos 1:2
Rev 21:2,9
Gen 3:1–6, 13
Gen 3:1–6, 9
Eph 5:27
Rev 21:2, 9
Gal 1:6–9

2 Cor 12:11

1 Cor 2:1–5

Paul accepted no material support in payment for preaching

⁷Did I commit a sin in abasing myself so that you might be exalted, because I preached God's gospel without cost to you? ⁸I robbed other churches by accepting support from them in order to serve you. ⁹And when I was with you and was in want, I did not burden any one, for my needs were supplied by the brethren who

1 Cor 9:18
Acts 18:3
Phil 4:10, 15
2 Cor 8:1–4
1 Cor 9:15

sustineretis modicum quid insipientiae meae; sed et supportate me! ²Aemulor enim vos Dei aemulatione; despondi enim vos uni viro virginem castam exhibere Christo. ³Timeo autem, ne, sicut serpens Evam seduxit astutia sua, ita corrumpantur sensus vestri a simplicitate et castitate, quae est in Christum. ⁴Nam si is qui venit, alium Christum praedicat, quem non praedicavimus, aut alium Spiritum accipitis, quem non accepistis, aut aliud evangelium, quod non recepistis, recte pateremini. ⁵Existimo enim nihil me minus fecisse magnis apostolis; ⁶nam etsi imperitus sermone, sed non scientia, in omni autem manifestantes in omnibus ad vos. ⁷Aut numquid peccatum feci meipsum humilians, ut vos exaltemini, quoniam gratis evangelium Dei evangelizavi vobis? ⁸Alias ecclesias exspoliavi accipiens stipendium ad ministerium vestrum ⁹et, cum essem apud vos et

*11:1 — 12:18 To counter the criticism spread by his adversaries, Paul feels he must justify himself; he speaks about his constant sincerity (11:7–15), the sufferings he has experienced in the course of preaching the Gospel (11:21–33), and the visions he has received (12:1–10). He apologizes to his readers for having to "boast" in this way (see 11:1–6, 16–21; 12:11–13).

11:1–6 The apologies in v. 1 (repeated as many as seven times: cf. 11:1, 16, 18, 21, 23; 12:1, 6, 11) refer to the rather brazen tone of this passage— sometimes called by scholars "the fool's speech", because the Apostle depicts himself as acting like a fool. He uses this literary device to make a series of bold statements, filled with zeal for souls. He assumes the role of the "friend of the bridegroom" (see Jn 3:29), whose responsibility is to protect the bride's virginity (see v. 2), and he is very conscious of the harm his enemies could do (see v. 3). "The Apostle", St Thomas Aquinas comments, "is saying that the Church is like Eve; the devil sometimes attacks her openly by the actions of tyrants and powers, in which case he is

'like a roaring lion [who] prowls around seeking someone to devour' (1 Pet 5:8). At other times he molests her in a hidden way through heresies which promise the truth and pretend to be sound—in which case he is like the serpent who seduces in an astute way, promising things he cannot give" (*Super 2 Corinthios*, ad loc.).

Paul sarcastically describes the false teachers as "superlative apostles" (v. 5; cf. 11:13), perhaps because they claim to have apostolic authority.

11:7–15 St Paul appeals to his detachment (see 1 Cor 9:4–15) as proof that his ministry is genuine. There will be those who interpret this disinterest in money as dishonest façade, but Paul's conduct is motivated by love (v. 11): "What did the holy apostles teach us? What do they teach us?", St Bernard asks himself. "Not the skill of the fisherman, not how to make tents, nor any of those things […]. They taught us how to live […]. The upright life I judge to consist in suffering evils, doing good and persevering faithfully until death" (*In festo SS. Petri et Pauli*, 3).

came from Macedonia. So I refrained and will refrain from burdening you in any way. [10]As the truth of Christ is in me, this boast of mine shall not be silenced in the regions of Achaia. [11]And why? Because I do not love you? God knows I do!

[12]And what I do I will continue to do, in order to undermine the claim of those who would like to claim that in their boasted mission they work on the same terms as we do. [13]For such men are false apostles, deceitful workmen, disguising themselves as apostles of Christ. [14]And no wonder, for even Satan disguises himself as an angel of light. [15]So it is not strange if his servants also disguise themselves as servants of righteousness. Their end will correspond to their deeds.

Paul apologizes for boasting

[16]I repeat, let no one think me foolish; but even if you do, accept me as a fool, so that I too may boast a little. [17](What I am saying I say not with the Lord's authority but as a fool, in this boastful confidence; [18]since many boast of worldly things, I too will boast.) [19]For you gladly bear with fools, being wise yourselves! [20]For you bear it if a man makes slaves of you, or preys upon you, or takes advantage of you, or puts on airs, or strikes you in the face. [21]To my shame, I must say, we were too weak for that!

What Paul has suffered for Christ

But whatever any one dares to boast of—I am speaking as a fool—I also dare to boast of that. [22]Are they Hebrews? So am I. Are they Israelites? So am I. Are they descendants of Abraham? So am I. [23]Are they servants of Christ? I am a better one— I am talking like a madman—with far greater labours, far more imprisonments, with countless beatings, and often near death. [24]Five times I have received at the hands of the Jews the forty lashes less one. [25]Three times I have been beaten with rods; once

Phil 3:2

Eph 6:8

2 Cor 3:1
Rom 7:5

Phil 3:4–6

Phil 3:4–6
Acts 22:3
Rom 11:1
Gal 1:13–14
1 Cor 15:10
2 Cor 10:7
Deut 25:3
Acts 14:19; 16:22

egerem, nulli onerosus fui; nam, quod mihi deerat, suppleverunt fratres, qui venerunt a Macedonia; et in omnibus sine onere me vobis servavi et servabo. [10]Est veritas Christi in me, quoniam haec gloria non infringetur in me in regionibus Achaiae. [11]Quare? Quia non diligo vos? Deus scit! [12]Quod autem facio et faciam, ut amputem occasionem eorum, qui volunt occasionem, ut in quo gloriantur, inveniantur sicut et nos. [13]Nam eiusmodi pseudoapostoli, operarii subdoli, transfigurantes se in apostolos Christi. [14]Et non mirum, ipse enim Satanas transfigurat se in angelum lucis; [15]non est ergo magnum, si et ministri eius transfigurentur velut ministri iustitiae, quorum finis erit secundum opera ipsorum. [16]Iterum dico, ne quis me putet insipientem esse; alioquin velut insipientem accipite me, ut et ego modicum quid glorier. [17]Quod loquor, non loquor secundum Dominum, sed quasi in insipientia in hac substantia gloriationis. [18]Quoniam multi gloriantur secundum carnem, et ego gloriabor. [19]Libenter enim suffertis insipientes, cum sitis ipsi sapientes; [20]sustinetis enim, si quis vos in servitutem redigit, si quis devorat, si quis accipit, si quis extollitur, si quis in faciem vos caedit. [21]Secundum ignobilitatem dico, quasi nos infirmi fuerimus; in quo quis audet, in insipientia dico, audeo et ego. [22]Hebraei sunt? Et ego. Israelitae sunt? Et ego. Semen Abrahae sunt? Et ego. [23]Ministri Christi sunt? Minus sapiens dico, plus ego: in laboribus plurimis, in carceribus abundantius, in plagis supra modum, in mortibus frequenter; [24]a Iudaeis quinquies quadragenas una minus accepi, [25]ter virgis caesus

11:16–21 Paul's words in vv. 19–20 are heavily ironic, to caricature the foolishness of the Corinthians, who consider themselves to be sensible and prudent (cf. 1 Cor 1:18–20) and yet have allowed themselves to be taken advantage of (even materially) by intruders and false teachers.

11:21–33 St Paul begins his apologia proper by referring to his background and merits, as against those of his adversaries. As a Jew he is their equal (v. 22), and as a minister of Christ he has clearly done much more than they. Pain and the cross are always present in a Christian's life:

"When we set out seriously along the 'royal highway', that of following Christ and behaving as children of God, we soon realize what awaits us—the Holy Cross. We must see it as the central point upon which to rest our hope of being united with our Lord. Let me warn you that the programme ahead is not an easy one. It takes an effort to lead the kind of life our Lord wants. Listen to the account St Paul gives of the incidents and sufferings he encountered in carrying out the will of Jesus: 'Five times I have received at the hands of the Jews the forty lashes less one' (2 Cor 11:24–28)" (St Josemaría Escrivá, *Friends of God*, 212).

I was stoned. Three times I have been shipwrecked; a night and a day I have been adrift at sea; ²⁶on frequent journeys, in danger from rivers, danger from robbers, danger from my own people, danger from Gentiles, danger in the city, danger in the wilderness, danger at sea, danger from false brethren; ²⁷in toil and hardship, through many a sleepless night, in hunger and thirst, often without food, in cold and exposure. ²⁸And, apart from other things, there is the daily pressure upon me of my anxiety for all the churches. ²⁹Who is weak, and I am not weak? Who is made to fall, and I am not indignant?

³⁰If I must boast, I will boast of the things that show my weakness. ³¹The God and Father of the Lord Jesus, he who is blessed for ever, knows that I do not lie. ³²At Damascus, the governor under King Aretas guarded the city of Damascus in order to seize me, ³³but I was let down in a basket through a window in the wall, and escaped his hands.

1 Cor 4:11
2 Thess 3:8

Rom 9:2
1 Cor 9:22

2 Cor 12:5
2 Cor 1:23
Acts 9:23–25

Visions and revelations

12 ¹I must boast; there is nothing to be gained by it, but I will go on to visions and revelations of the Lord. ²I know a man in Christ who fourteen years ago was caught up to the third heaven—whether in the body or out of the body I do not know, God knows. ³And I know that this man was caught up into Paradise—whether in the body or out of the body I do not know, God knows—⁴and he heard things that cannot be told, which man may not utter. ⁵On behalf of this man I will boast, but on my own behalf I will not boast, except of my weaknesses. ⁶Though if I wish to boast, I shall not be a fool, for I shall be speaking the truth. But I refrain from it, so that no one may think more of me than he sees in me or hears from me. ⁷And to keep me from being too elated by the abundance of revelations, a thorn* was given me in the flesh, a messenger of Satan, to harass me, to keep me from being too elated. ⁸Three times I besought

Ex 33:20

Lk 23:43
Rev 2:7
2 Cor 11:30

2 Cor 10:8; 11:6

Job 2:6–7
Rom 9:2

Mt 26:39, 42–44

sum, semel lapidatus sum, ter naufragium feci, nocte et die in profundo maris fui; ²⁶in itineribus saepe, periculis fluminum, periculis latronum, periculis ex genere, periculis ex gentibus, periculis in civitate, periculis in solitudine, periculis in mari, periculis in falsis fratribus, ²⁷in labore et aerumna, in vigiliis saepe, in fame et siti, in ieiuniis frequenter, in frigore et nuditate; ²⁸praeter illa, quae extrinsecus sunt, instantia mea cotidiana, sollicitudo omnium ecclesiarum. ²⁹Quis infirmatur, et non infirmor? Quis scandalizatur, et ego non uror? ³⁰Si gloriari oportet, quae infirmitatis meae sunt, gloriabor. ³¹Deus, et Pater Domini Iesu scit, qui est benedictus in saecula, quod non mentior. ³²Damasci praepositus gentis Aretae regis custodiebat civitatem Damascenorum, ut me comprehenderet, ³³et per fenestram in sporta dimissus sum per murum et effugi manus eius. [12] ¹Gloriari oportet; non expedit quidem, veniam autem ad visiones et revelationes Domini. ²Scio hominem in Christo ante annos quattuordecim—sive in corpore nescio, sive extra corpus nescio, Deus scit—raptum eiusmodi usque ad tertium caelum. ³Et scio huiusmodi hominem—sive in corpore sive extra corpus nescio, Deus scit—⁴quoniam raptus est in paradisum et audivit arcana verba, quae non licet homini loqui. ⁵Pro eiusmodi gloriabor, pro me autem nihil gloriabor nisi in infirmitatibus meis. ⁶Nam et si voluero gloriari, non ero insipiens, veritatem enim dicam; parco autem, ne quis in me existimet supra id, quod videt me aut audit ex me, ⁷et ex magnitudine revelationum. Propter quod, ne extollar, datus est mihi stimulus carni, angelus Satanae, ut me colaphizet, ne extollar. ⁸Propter quod ter Dominum rogavi, ut discederet a me; ⁹et dixit mihi: «Sufficit tibi gratia mea, nam virtus in infirmitate perficitur». Libentissime igitur potius gloriabor in infirmitatibus meis, ut inhabitet

12:1–10 Paul seems to have had many visions and revelations in the course of his life (see Acts 9:1–8; 16:9–10; 22:17–21; Gal 2:1–2). Now he says that he was even taken up into the third heaven, that is, to where God himself dwells (v. 2). In this way, too, he stands above his adversaries (who are, it appears, in thrall to the extraordinary and the miraculous).

"A thorn was given me in the flesh" (v. 7). St John Chrysostom reads this as meaning the trials and constant persecution previously mentioned. St Augustine thinks that it means some chronic

and debilitating physical illness. Not until St Gregory the Great do commentators interpret it as meaning temptations of concupiscence. In any event, the Apostle's candour and the reply from God, "My grace is sufficient for you" (v. 9), carry many lessons about the ascetical struggle, the first of which is to trust in God when we become all too conscious of our own weakness. "God frees us from strife not by making our troubles disappear, [...] but by helping us not to be overcome by suffering" (Origen, *De oratione*, 30, 1).

the Lord about this, that it should leave me; [9]but he said to me, "My grace is sufficient for you, for my power is made perfect in weakness." I will all the more gladly boast of my weaknesses, that the power of Christ may rest upon me. [10]For the sake of Christ, then, I am content with weaknesses, insults, hardships, persecutions, and calamities; for when I am weak, then I am strong.

Paul again apologizes for boasting

[11]I have been a fool! You forced me to it, for I ought to have been commended by you. For I was not at all inferior to these superlative apostles, even though I am nothing. [12]The signs of a true apostle were performed among you in all patience, with signs and wonders and mighty works. [13]For in what were you less favoured than the rest of the churches, except that I myself did not burden you? Forgive me this wrong!*

[14]Here for the third time I am ready to come to you. And I will not be a burden, for I seek not what is yours but you; for children ought not to lay up for their parents, but parents for their children. [15]I will most gladly spend and be spent for your souls. If I love you the more, am I to be loved the less? [16]But granting that I myself did not burden you, I was crafty, you say, and got the better of you by guile. [17]Did I take advantage of you through any of those whom I sent to you? [18]I urged Titus to go, and sent the brother with him. Did Titus take advantage of you? Did we not act in the same spirit? Did we not take the same steps?

7. THE APOSTLE'S NEXT VISIT*

The reason for his apologia

[19]Have you been thinking all along that we have been defending ourselves before you? It is in the sight of God that we have been speaking in Christ, and all for your upbuild-

Margin references:
Is 40:29
2 Cor 4:7
Rom 3:4

Col 1:24, 29
2 Cor 7:4
Phil 4:13

1 Cor 15:10
2 Cor 11:5

Rom 15:19
1 Cor 2:4
1 Thess 2:4
Acts 1:8; 18:3
2 Cor 11:9

2 Cor 13:1

Phil 2:17

2 Cor 8:6, 16–22

2 Cor 2:17

---

in me virtus Christi. [10]Propter quod placeo mihi in infirmitatibus, in contumeliis, in necessitatibus, in persecutionibus et in angustiis, pro Christo: cum enim infirmor, tunc potens sum. [11]Factus sum insipiens. Vos me coegistis; ego enim debui a vobis commendari. Nihil enim minus fui ab his, qui sunt supra modum apostoli, tametsi nihil sum; [12]signa tamen apostoli facta sunt super vos in omni patientia, signis quoque et prodigiis et virtutibus. [13]Quid est enim quod minus habuistis prae ceteris ecclesiis, nisi quod ego ipse non gravavi vos? Donate mihi hanc iniuriam. [14]Ecce tertio hoc paratus sum venire ad vos et non ero gravis vobis; non enim quaero, quae vestra sunt, sed vos, nec enim debent filii parentibus thesaurizare, sed parentes filiis. [15]Ego autem libentissime impendam et superimpendar ipse pro animabus vestris. Si plus vos diligo, minus diligar? [16]Esto quidem, ego vos non gravavi; sed cum essem astutus, dolo vos cepi. [17]Numquid per aliquem eorum, quos misi ad vos, circumveni vos? [18]Rogavi Titum et misi cum illo fratrem; numquid Titus vos circumvenit? Nonne eodem spiritu ambulavimus? Nonne iisdem vestigiis? [19]Olim putatis quod excusemus nos apud vos? Coram Deo in Christo loquimur; omnia autem, carissimi, propter vestram aedificationem. [20]Timeo enim, ne forte, cum

---

12:11–18 In this epilogue to "the fool's speech", Paul again mentions the most obvious proof of his apostolic credentials—the fact that he has no interest in money: he has always sought the good of the Corinthians, never their money (v. 14). Nor have his co-workers lived at the expense of the faithful. Ministers of the Church should never put their personal gain or advantage before the welfare of the faithful: "Enlighten men's minds with divine truth; guide their consciences in the way of uprightness; strengthen and refresh the souls that are tossed by doubt or tortured with suffering. These are the chief activities of your apostolate. Whatever other activities our times demand, these

too you must engage in. But let it be clear that, in all that he does, the priest aims only at the good of souls and that he looks only to Christ, to whom he must dedicate not only his energy but also himself" (Pius XII, *Menti nostrae*).

*__12:19—13:10__ The Apostle ends the letter by explaining that he has made this personal apologia for the benefit of the Corinthians (12:19–21); then he makes a number of suggestions about preparations for his next visit to Corinth (13:1–10).

12:19–21 Paul's apologia was not intended simply to prove his apostolic credentials to the

ing, beloved. [20]For I fear that perhaps I may come and find you not what I wish, and that you may find me not what you wish; that perhaps there may be quarrelling, jealousy, anger, selfishness, slander, gossip, conceit, and disorder. [21]I fear that when I come again my God may humble me before you, and I may have to mourn over many of those who sinned before and have not repented of the impurity, immorality, and licentiousness which they have practised.

Rom 1:29ff
1 Cor 3:1
Gal 5:20

1 Cor 5:1
2 Cor 2:1; 13:2

Preparation for his next visit

13 [1]This is the third time I am coming to you. Any charge must be sustained by the evidence of two or three witnesses. [2]I warned those who sinned before and all the others, and I warn them now while absent, as I did when present on my second visit, that if I come again I will not spare them—[3]since you desire proof that Christ is speaking in me. He is not weak in dealing with you, but is powerful in you. [4]For he was crucified in weakness, but lives by the power of God. For we are weak in him, but in dealing with you we shall live with him by the power of God.

Deut 19:15
Mt 18:16
1 Tim 5:19
2 Cor 12:14

Rom 1:4; 8:11
Phil 2:7–11

[5]Examine yourselves, to see whether you are holding to your faith. Test yourselves. Do you not realize that Jesus Christ is in you?—unless indeed you fail to meet the test! [6]I hope you will find out that we have not failed. [7]But we pray God that you may not do wrong—not that we may appear to have met the test, but that you may do what is right, though we may seem to have failed. [8]For we cannot do anything against the truth, but only for the truth. [9]For we are glad when we are weak and you are strong. What we pray for is your improvement. [10]I write this while I am

1 Cor 11:28

Acts 4:20

Jer 1:10
2 Cor 2:3; 10:4–8, 11

venero, non quales volo, inveniam vos, et ego inveniar a vobis, qualem non vultis, ne forte contentiones, aemulationes, animositates, dissensiones, detractiones, susurrationes, inflationes, seditiones sint; [21]ne iterum, cum venero, humiliet me Deus meus apud vos, et lugeam multos ex his, qui ante peccaverunt et non egerunt paenitentiam super immunditia et fornicatione et impudicitia, quam gesserunt. [13] [1]Ecce tertio hoc venio ad vos: *in ore duorum vel trium testium stabit omne verbum.* [2]Praedixi et praedico, ut praesens bis et nunc absens his, qui ante peccaverunt, et ceteris omnibus, quoniam si venero iterum, non parcam, [3]quoniam experimentum quaeritis eius, qui in me loquitur, Christi, qui in vos non infirmatur, sed potens est in vobis. [4]Nam etsi crucifixus est in infirmitate, sed vivit ex virtute Dei. Nam et nos infirmi sumus in illo, sed vivemus cum eo ex virtute Dei in vos. [5]Vosmetipsos tentate, si estis in fide; ipsi vos probate. An non cognoscitis vos ipsos quia Iesus Christus in vobis est? Nisi forte reprobi estis. [6]Spero autem quod cognoscetis quia nos non sumus reprobi. [7]Oramus autem Deum, ut nihil mali faciatis, non ut nos probati pareamus, sed ut vos, quod bonum est, faciatis, nos autem ut reprobi simus. [8]Non enim possumus aliquid adversus veritatem, sed pro veritate. [9]Gaudemus enim, quando nos infirmi sumus, vos autem potentes estis; hoc et oramus, vestram consummationem. [10]Ideo haec absens scribo, ut non

Corinthians, as if he were someone on trial. He has been speaking in the presence of God (who is the only Judge), and he asserts that his only aim at all times has been the good of souls, their "upbuilding" (v. 19). At the end of the letter we get a glimpse of the sorts of difficulties and misunderstanding Paul has encountered. He senses that some people may not understand him correctly, and he fears that he may still find his beloved faithful mired in the sins he warned them against in his earlier letter—pride, which causes disunity and discord (cf. 1 Cor 1:18—4:21), and impurity, which prevents a person from advancing towards God (cf. 1 Cor 6:12ff).

13:1–10 The Apostle offers the Corinthians three words of advice here—to misinterpret his attitude not as weakness, but rather as meek, Christ-

like conduct (vv. 1–4); to examine their hearts to ensure that their faith is intact (v. 5); and to be alive to doing what is right (vv. 6–10). A combination of gentleness and firmness in the exercise of authority shows that a person is making prudent decisions, in line with the counsel in Deuteronomy 19:15 (v.1) and in imitation, too, of Christ, who in his earthly life chose to be weak but by rising from the dead has manifested his power.

"We pray God that you may not do wrong" (v. 7): St Thomas Aquinas reminds us that "in order to avoid sin two things are necessary—free choice and the grace of God. [...] Therefore, showing that both things are necessary, the Apostle asks God to provide grace, and admonishes them to exercise their free choice to avoid evil and do good" (*Super 2 Corinthios*, ad loc.).

away from you, in order that when I come I may not have to be severe in my use of the authority which the Lord has given me for building up and not for tearing down.

8. WORDS OF FAREWELL

Rom 15:33
Phil 3:1; 4:4
1 Cor 16:20

[11]Finally, brethren, farewell. Mend your ways, heed my appeal, agree with one another, live in peace, and the God of love and peace will be with you. [12]Greet one another with a holy kiss. [13]All the saints greet you.

[14]The grace of the Lord Jesus Christ and the love of God and the fellowship of[n] the Holy Spirit be with you all.

praesens durius agam secundum potestatem, quam Dominus dedit mihi in aedificationem et non in destructionem. [11]De cetero, fratres, gaudete, perfecti estote, exhortamini invicem, idem sapite, pacem habete, et Deus dilectionis et pacis erit vobiscum. [12]Salutate invicem in osculo sancto. Salutant vos sancti omnes. [13]Gratia Domini Iesu Christi et caritas Dei et communicatio Sancti Spiritus cum omnibus vobis.

13:11–13 In his words of farewell, the Apostle again shows his great affection and pastoral concern for the faithful at Corinth: "Live in peace, and the God of love and peace will be with you, for God is a God of love and a God of peace, and in these he takes his delight. Love will give you peace and remove every evil from your church" (St John Chrysostom, *In 2 Corinthios*, 30).

Verse 14, used in the liturgy as one of the opening salutations at Mass, expresses belief in the Blessed Trinity, and prays for the granting of all kinds of supernatural gifts: "The grace of Christ, by which we are justified and saved; the love of God the Father, by which we are united to him; and the fellowship of the Holy Spirit, who distributes the divine gifts to us" (St Thomas Aquinas, *Super 2 Corinthios*, ad loc.).

n Or *and participation in*

THE LETTER OF PAUL TO THE

GALATIANS

Introduction

The Letter to the Galatians is chronologically the first of St Paul's "great" letters (Romans, 1 and 2 Corinthians, Galatians), but in manuscripts and printed editions of the New Testament it is usually placed fourth (after Romans and 1 and 2 Corinthians), simply because it is by far the shortest of them.

In terms of content, it obviously has a close connexion with the Letter to the Romans, which was written a short time afterwards. Galatians introduces the basic theme (justification by faith in Christ, not by works of the Mosaic Law) which Romans will develop at greater length, and in greater depth. (Romans also covers some other themes not dealt with in Galatians.) There are also certain similarities between Galatians and one part of 2 Corinthians—the rather polemical line of argument against Judaizers.

1. STRUCTURE AND CONTENT

Because the literary structure of the letter is not at all clear, almost every commentator divides it into parts differently. This is quite understandable, given the nature of the text—a "family" letter dictated to a secretary. One possible way of dividing the letter up is as follows:

First comes an INTRODUCTION with greetings and some outspoken words of warning (1:1–10). This is followed by two parts:

1. THE GOSPEL PREACHED BY PAUL (1:11—4:31). This part, dealing with subjects which today are classed under the heading of dogmatic theology, carries the core message of the letter. It includes an apologia for St Paul's apostolate, rich in autobiographical detail (1:11—2:21), and a doctrinal exposition (3:1—4:31) containing most of the theological and scriptural arguments that form part of the Apostle's teaching, that is, the "Gospel" he preaches (justification by faith; the Law and the Promise; divine filiation).

2. CHRISTIAN FREEDOM AND CHARITY (5:1—6:18). In this part of the letter, where the tone is one of exhortation, the Apostle applies doctrine to everyday Christian life. First come exhortations about Christian freedom, the fruits of the Spirit and the works of the flesh, and fraternal charity (5:1—6:10). Then, to conclude, he exposes the selfish agenda of those who have tried to unsettle the faith of the Galatians, and reasserts that he has been sincere and correct in his own proclamation of the Gospel (6:11–18).

This outline of the letter shows that it encompasses quite a mixture of styles and themes, but one central theme does stand out—namely, that Christ alone has power to justify and save; therefore anyone who preaches a gospel that distorts the Gospel of Christ commits a grave error (see 1:4—5:8); so, Christians are under no obligation to adhere to the prescriptions of the Mosaic Law and the complicated apparatus that has accrued to it in the tradition of the scribes (*Halajôt*). The

Judaizers argued that to belong to the true Israel, a person had to be circumcised; the Apostle takes issue with this idea; he will not accept it as a valid teaching: only faith in Jesus Christ can make a man righteous in God's eyes.

2. CONTEXT

Galatia was an inland region of Asia Minor occupying the central plains of present-day Turkey. In St Paul's time, the Roman province of Galatia also included the territory of Lycaonia, in which were located four cities referred to often in Acts of the Apostles—Derbe, Lystra, Iconium and Pisidian Antioch. The common view among historians is that the Galatians were of Celtic stock (the *keltoi* or *galatai* of the Greeks, and the *galli* of the Romans); like the Celts of the West, they had originated in Asia and probably reached central Asia Minor (Turkey) not long before the arrival of Alexander the Great (356–323 BC); in due course they became Hellenized.

During his first apostolic journey (in the years 45–49) Paul came into contact with Galatians when he was evangelizing the southern part of the province. But it must have been during his second journey (in 50–52) that his more systematic ministry took place, possibly because illness forced him to stay there for a period (Gal 4:13; Acts 16:1–8). The Galatians welcomed him with open arms (Gal 4:14). The Apostle paid a further visit there in the year 53 or 54 (Acts 18:23).

In the meantime, some Jewish Christians had moved into Galatia. They were strongly attached to their religious traditions, to the point that they believed it was necessary to conform to the prescriptions of the Law of Moses, particularly circumcision (see Gal 5:2), in order to be saved. Some of these "false brethren" (Gal 2:4) probably intended to correct the message that Paul had been preaching during his second missionary journey (Acts 16:6), as they had already sought to do at the council of Jerusalem. We do not know exactly who these people were. But they certainly constituted a threat to the integrity of the faith, and they had put pressure on the apostles themselves, and were responsible for some compromises, or the appearance of compromise, on St Peter's part (Gal 2:11–14).

On becoming aware of the danger from Judaizers, Paul writes this letter to the Galatians, a letter full of anguish and love. Probably written in Ephesus in the year 54/55, it is in fact the best commentary there is on the decisions of the council of Jerusalem (cf. Acts 15:23–29) to the effect that Christians of Gentile background were under no obligation to keep to Jewish rules and regulations. The differences between Paul and the troublemakers in Galatia ran deep. The point at issue, he knew, was a crucial one: it involved the role of Christ in salvation history, the very nature of Christianity, the connexion between the Gospel and the Mosaic Law. Reading between the lines, it seems that the Judaizers had run a campaign to discredit Paul on the grounds that he was not one of the Twelve and because he preached that Gentiles who became Christians did not need to observe the prescriptions of the Law.

3. MESSAGE

The "Galatian crisis" leads Paul to tease out the practical implications of belief in Christ. The letter shows that the Apostle is worried by the news that has reached him. In interpreting the letter, the reader should bear in mind the dispute with the Judaizers.

As the Christian faith began to be preached in non-Jewish areas, and more and more pagans were converted, differences between Christians of Jewish and Gentile background became more evident—particularly on subjects to do with what food could be eaten, the celebration of the breaking of the bread (the Eucharist), that is, the context of the meal which preceded or followed that rite, and the status of sacramental rites such as Baptism. This set of problems was addressed at the council of Jerusalem which was held around the year 49, and the decision handed down was that Christians of Gentile background need not conform to the prescriptions of the Jewish Law. In other words, salvation and justification by God do not depend on the performance of works of the Law but on belief in Jesus Christ as the only Saviour and the Son of God. In Abraham, who acted by faith, long before the Law was established, all the nations of the earth were blessed: that promise, made to the Patriarch, was fulfilled in Jesus Christ. Salvation is not obtained through fulfilment of the Law of Moses and the prescriptions pertaining to it; it is offered to all mankind in Jesus Christ. "For as many of you as were baptized into Christ have put on Christ. There is neither Jew nor Greek, there is neither slave nor free, there is neither male nor female; for you are all one in Christ Jesus. And if you are Christ's, then you are Abraham's offspring, heirs according to promise" (3:27–29).

This is the "gospel" that Paul proclaims, and it accords with that preached by Peter, James, John and the other apostles of Jerusalem (2:6–10). When Paul speaks of "my gospel" (see Rom 2:16; 16:25) or "the gospel which was preached by me" (1:11), he means what he has preached to the Gentiles. There is only one Gospel. There are different ways of presenting it—one type of evangelization for the circumcised, another for the uncircumcised (just as later on it will be presented in different ways to other nations and cultures); but the Gospel's content, its message, its ethical principles, never vary.

Christians' identity derives from the fact that they are sons and daughters of God through faith in Christ Jesus (3:26–29). What matters to Paul is to ensure that the gospel message remains unvarying and clear: the salvation won by Christ is available to all who accept the faith. Salvation came about when "God sent forth his Son, born of woman, born under the law, to redeem those who were under the law, so that we might receive adoption as sons. And because you are sons, God has sent the Spirit of his Son into our hearts, crying, 'Abba! Father!'" (4:4–6). That is the source of Christian freedom, the freedom of the children of God: "For freedom Christ has set us free" (5:1). The Christian life is lived in a sphere of freedom, on the basis of divine filiation and belief in Jesus Christ who has died and risen (see 5:24). Christians receive their life from the Spirit, and they should "also walk by the Spirit" (5:25), who will produce in them his fruits (cf. 5:22–23).

St Paul's single-mindedness, especially evident in this letter and in his ministry at Antioch and Corinth, was very important to the early Church. If he had failed to take a stand against the imposition of circumcision and other prescriptions of the Mosaic Law, it would have been difficult for Christianity to be anything other than a sect of Judaism that believed in Jesus as the Messiah; the efficacy and truth of Jesus' saving action for all mankind would have been compromised.

Galatians

1. INTRODUCTION*

Greeting

1 ¹Paul an apostle—not from men nor through man, but through Jesus Christ and God the Father, who raised him from the dead—²and all the brethren who are with me,

To the churches of Galatia:

³Grace to you and peace from God the Father and our Lord Jesus Christ, ⁴who gave himself for our sins to deliver us from the present evil age, according to the will of our God and Father; ⁵to whom be the glory for ever and ever. Amen.

A warning

⁶I am astonished that you are so quickly deserting him who called you in the grace of Christ and turning to a different gospel—*⁷not that there is another gospel, but there are some who trouble you and want to pervert the gospel of Christ. ⁸But even if we, or an angel from heaven, should preach to you a gospel contrary to that which we preached to you, let him be accursed. ⁹As we have said before, so now I say again, If any one is preaching to you a gospel contrary to that which you received, let him be accursed.

Rom 1:1
Gal 1:11

1 Cor 1:2; 16:9
2 Cor 1:11
Rom 1:7

1 Cor 1:3
Phil 1:2

1 Tim 2:6
Tit 2:14
1 Jn 5:19

Phil 1:11
Rom 16:27
2 Tim 4:18

2 Thess 2:2
2 Cor 11:4

2 Cor 11:4
Acts 15:1–24
Gal 5:10; 6:12

1 Cor 16:22
Rom 9:3

1 Cor 11:2; 12:3

[1] ¹Paulus apostolus, non ab hominibus neque per hominem, sed per Iesum Christum et Deum Patrem, qui suscitavit eum a mortuis, ²et, qui mecum sunt, omnes fratres, ecclesiis Galatiae: ³gratia vobis et pax a Deo Patre nostro et Domino Iesu Christo, ⁴qui dedit semetipsum pro peccatis nostris, ut eriperet nos de praesenti saeculo nequam secundum voluntatem Dei et Patris nostri, ⁵cui gloria in saecula saeculorum. Amen. ⁶Miror quod tam cito transferimini ab eo, qui vos vocavit in gratia Christi, in aliud evangelium; ⁷quod non est aliud, nisi sunt aliqui, qui vos conturbant et volunt convertere evangelium Christi. ⁸Sed licet nos aut angelus de caelo evangelizet vobis praeterquam quod evangelizavimus vobis, anath-

*1:1–10 This short introduction includes the greeting (vv. 1–5) and explains the reason for the letter—to warn the addressees against distortions of the Gospel (vv. 6–10).

1:1–5 Paul loses no time in reminding the Galatians that his authority, like that of the other apostles, comes from Jesus Christ himself (v. 1), and he encapsulates the theological message of the letter in a single phrase: by giving himself up for us, Christ has made our redemption possible (v. 4). Chapters 1 and 2 comprise Paul's proof that his authority comes from God; and the rest of the letter concerns the nature of the redemption brought about by Christ. Beginning the letter as he does, Paul takes issue immediately with the misconceptions being spread by some Christians of Jewish background who claimed that he had no proper authority and that all Christians were bound by observance of the Mosaic Law, circumcision.

1:6–10 "The gospel of Christ" (v. 7), which Paul had preached to the Galatians, as can be deduced from this and other passages in his letters, marks the fulfilment of the promise proclaimed by the Old Testament prophets. It is the good news that "when the time had fully come, God sent forth his Son, born of woman" (4:4), Jesus Christ, the only Saviour of mankind. This is the core of the Gospel, and it must never be altered or distorted. Although the Apostle does not yet explain how exactly some people had tried to distort the Gospel, he twice launches an anathema against them ("anathema sit!": vv. 8–9), for daring to be so bold; this shows that something very serious is happening, and it serves as a reminder that there is no "new Christianity" waiting to be discovered; Christ is the pinnacle and fullness of Revelation: "The Christian economy, therefore, since it is the new and definitive covenant, will never pass away; and no new public revelation is to be expected before the glorious manifest-

1 Thess 2:4
2 Cor 5:11

^{10}Am I now seeking the favour of men, or of God? Or am I trying to please men? If I were still pleasing men, I should not be a servant^a of Christ.*

PART ONE

The Gospel preached by St Paul*

2. ST PAUL ARGUES IN HIS OWN DEFENCE*

Paul's vocation

Mt 16:17
Eph 3:3

Acts 8:1-3; 9:1
Phil 3:4–6
1 Cor 15:9

Acts 26:4–5
Phil 3:5

Acts 9:3–19
Jer 1:5
Is 49:1
1 Cor 15:8–10
Acts 9:3–5; 26:16

^{11}For I would have you know, brethren, that the gospel which was preached by me is not man's^b gospel. ^{12}For I did not receive it from man, nor was I taught it, but it came through a revelation of Jesus Christ. ^{13}For you have heard of my former life in Judaism, how I persecuted the church of God violently and tried to destroy it; ^{14}and I advanced in Judaism beyond many of my own age among my people, so extremely zealous was I for the traditions of my fathers. ^{15}But when he who had set me apart before I was born, and had called me through his grace, ^{16}was pleased to reveal his

ema sit! ^{9}Sicut praediximus, et nunc iterum dico: Si quis vobis evangelizaverit praeter id, quod accepistis, anathema sit! ^{10}Modo enim hominibus suadeo aut Deo? Aut quaero hominibus placere? Si adhuc hominibus placerem, Christi servus non essem! ^{11}Notum enim vobis facio, fratres, evangelium, quod evangelizatum est a me, quia non est secundum hominem; ^{12}neque enim ego ab homine accepi illud neque didici, sed per revelationem Iesu Christi. ^{13}Audistis enim conversationem meam aliquando in Iudaismo quoniam supra modum persequebar ecclesiam Dei et expugnabam illam ^{14}et proficiebam in Iudaismo supra multos coaetaneos in genere meo, abundantius aemulator existens paternarum mearum traditionum. ^{15}Cum autem placuit Deo, qui me segregavit de utero matris meae et vocavit per gratiam suam, ^{16}ut revelaret Filium suum in me, ut

ation of our Lord Jesus Christ" (Vatican II, *Dei Verbum*, 4).

In v. 10 Paul is presumably replying to a charge made against him to the effect that, to make conversion easier for people, he was not requiring them to be circumcised and thus was "seeking the favour of men". The Apostle's spirited defence of his position reminds us that we should not be cowed by people's possible reaction to the truth: "The preacher of the Gospel will therefore be a person who even at the price of personal renunciation and suffering always seeks the truth that he must transmit to others. He never betrays or hides truth out of a desire to please men, in order to astonish or to shock, nor for the sake of originality or a desire to make an impression. He does not refuse truth" (Paul VI, *Evangelii nuntiandi*, 78).

*1:11–4:31 The Gospel that Paul preached did not require Gentiles to first become Jews (by circumcision and submission to the prescriptions of the Law) in order to accept the call to Christian-

ity. This policy met with opposition from people whose way of thinking prevented them from seeing the newness of Christian salvation. Paul answers them by appealing to the fact that he is an apostle and is in communion with the other apostles (1:11–2:21), and then by using Scripture to show that only Christ, and not the Law of Moses, can make a person just in the eyes of God (3:1–4:31).

*1:11–2:21 To prove that his mission is God-given and his Gospel true, the Apostle outlines key stages in his life—his call from God (1:11–24), his journey to Jerusalem with Barnabas and Titus, probably in connexion with the special meeting of the apostles (2:1–10), and the episode in Antioch when he took St Peter to task for behaving in a manner open to misinterpretation (2:11–21).

1:11–24 The way that Paul received his vocation shows the validity of his teaching. His Gospel (which differs in no respect from that proclaimed

a Or *slave*   b Greek *according to man*

Son to^c me, in order that I might preach him among the Gentiles, I did not confer with flesh and blood, ¹⁷nor did I go up to Jerusalem to those who were apostles before me, but I went away into Arabia; and again I returned to Damascus.

¹⁸Then after three years I went up to Jerusalem to visit Cephas, and remained with him fifteen days. ¹⁹But I saw none of the other apostles except James the Lord's brother. ²⁰(In what I am writing to you, before God, I do not lie!) ²¹Then I went into the regions of Syria and Cilicia. ²²And I was still not known by sight to the churches of Christ in Judea; ²³they only heard it said, "He who once persecuted us is now preaching the faith he once tried to destroy." ²⁴And they glorified God because of me.

Rom 1:5
Acts 9:22-25
2 Cor 11:32

Visit to Jerusalem

2 ¹Then after fourteen years I went up again to Jerusalem with Barnabas, taking Titus along with me. ²I went up by revelation; and I laid before them (but privately before those who were of repute) the gospel which I preach among the Gentiles, lest somehow I should be running or had run in vain. ³But even Titus, who was with me, was not compelled to be circumcised, though he was a Greek. ⁴But because of false brethren secretly brought in, who slipped in to spy out our freedom which we have in Christ Jesus, that they might bring us into bondage—⁵to them we did not

Acts 11:30; 15:2
1 Cor 9:6; 24–27
Phil 2:16
Gal 5:7
Acts 16:3
Acts 15:1, 24–29
Rom 6:15, 18–22
Gal 5:1

evangelizarem illum in gentibus, continuo non contuli cum carne et sanguine ¹⁷neque ascendi Hierosolymam ad antecessores meos apostolos, sed abii in Arabiam et iterum reversus sum Damascum. ¹⁸Deinde post annos tres ascendi Hierosolymam videre Cepham et mansi apud eum diebus quindecim; ¹⁹alium autem apostolorum non vidi nisi Iacobum fratrem Domini. ²⁰Quae autem scribo vobis, ecce coram Deo quia non mentior. ²¹Deinde veni in partes Syriae et Ciliciae. ²²Eram autem ignotus facie ecclesiis Iudaeae, quae sunt in Christo; ²³tantum autem auditum habebant: «Qui persequebatur nos aliquando, nunc evangelizat fidem, quam aliquando expugnabat», ²⁴et in me glorificabant Deum. [2] ¹Deinde post annos quattuordecim iterum ascendi Hierosolymam cum Barnaba, assumpto et Tito; ²ascendi autem secundum revelationem; et contuli cum illis evangelium, quod praedico in gentibus, seorsum autem his, qui observabantur, ne forte in vacuum currerem aut cucurrissem. ³Sed neque Titus, qui mecum erat, cum esset Graecus, compulsus est circumcidi. ⁴Sed propter subintroductos falsos fratres, qui subintroierunt explorare libertatem nostram, quam habemus in Christo Iesu, ut nos in servitutem redigerent; ⁵quibus neque ad horam cessimus subicientes nos, ut veritas evangelii permaneat apud vos. ⁶Ab his autem, qui videbantur esse aliquid—quales aliquando fuerint, nihil mea interest; Deus personam hominis non

by the other apostles: 2:2; 1 Cor 15:3) comes not from any mere man but from the revelation of Jesus Christ (v. 12). His calling, like that of other messengers from God (see Jer 1:5; Is 49:1–5; Lk 1:14), had nothing to do with his personal merits; it came from God. When God made his will known to Paul on the road to Damascus (see Acts 9:3–6), his life changed radically (vv. 13–17): without that change, which gave the Christian communities in Judea great joy (vv. 22–24) and which the Galatians had seen for themselves, his claims about his calling and mission would have been empty words.

Paul tells us that after withdrawing into Arabia for a while (probably to the kingdom of the Nabateans, to the south of Damascus), he returned to the capital of Syria (v. 17) and later went to Jerusalem (vv. 18–20; cf. Acts 9:26–30; 22:18) to see Cephas. The fact that he met and stayed with Peter shows that Paul recognized the pre-eminence of Simon Peter's authority: "He refers to him as a renowned and important

person; he did not say, 'Look to Peter', but 'Visit Peter', like those who speak of great and marvellous cities" (St John Chrysostom, *In Galatas*, 1, 1, 18). In the same spirit, over the centuries, Christians have shown their love for Peter and his successors by going on pilgrimage to Rome "to visit Cephas", "*videre Cepham*" (v. 18).

After his short stay in Jerusalem, Paul spent time in Syria and Cilicia (v. 21), but he does not say how long he stayed in each place.

"James the Lord's brother" (v. 19) is probably the man who was head of the Christian community at Jerusalem for some time and to whom the Letter of James is attributed (see Jas 1:1). On the expression "the Lord's brother", see the note on Mt 12:46–50.

2:1–10 Some Christians who had converted from Judaism thought that Gentile converts should conform to the prescriptions of the Mosaic Law and undergo circumcision. These views gave rise to considerable controversy in

c Greek *in*

Deut 10:17
Gal 2:14
Acts 10:34
Rom 2:11
1 Pet 1:17
Col 1:5

Acts 15:3f, 12;
22:21
Rom 1:5; 15:16–18

Gal 1:19
Acts 12:17

Acts 11:29
1 Cor 16:1
Rom 15:26
2 Cor 8:9, 14

yield submission even for a moment, that the truth of the gospel might be preserved for you. [6]And from those who were reputed to be something (what they were makes no difference to me; God shows no partiality)—those, I say, who were of repute added nothing to me; [7]but on the contrary, when they saw that I had been entrusted with the gospel to the uncircumcised, just as Peter had been entrusted with the gospel to the circumcised [8](for he who worked through Peter for the mission to the circumcised worked through me also for the Gentiles), [9]and when they perceived the grace that was given to me, James and Cephas and John, who were reputed to be pillars, gave to me and Barnabas the right hand of fellowship, that we should go to the Gentiles and they to the circumcised; [10]only they would have us remember the poor, which very thing I was eager to do.

The incident at Antioch

Jn 1:42
Acts 15

Acts 10:13–17, 28

[11]But when Cephas came to Antioch I opposed him to his face, because he stood condemned. [12]For before certain men came from James, he ate with the Gentiles; but when they came he drew back and separated himself, fearing the circumcision party. [13]And with him the rest of the Jews acted insincerely, so that even Barnabas was car-

accipit—mihi enim, qui observabantur, nihil contulerunt, [7]sed e contra, cum vidissent quod creditum est mihi evangelium praeputii, sicut Petro circumcisionis[8]—qui enim operatus est Petro in apostolatum circumcisionis operatus est et mihi inter gentes—[9]et cum cognovissent gratiam, quae data est mihi, Iacobus et Cephas et Ioannes, qui videbantur columnae esse, dexteras dederunt mihi et Barnabae communionis, ut nos in gentes, ipsi autem in circumcisionem; [10]tantum ut pauperum memores essemus, quod etiam sollicitus fui hoc ipsum facere. [11]Cum autem venisset Cephas Antiochiam, in faciem ei restiti, quia reprehensibilis erat. [12]Prius enim quam venirent quidam ab Iacobo, cum gentibus comedebat; cum autem venissent, subtrahebat et segregabat se, timens eos, qui ex circumcisione erant. [13]Et simulationi eius consenserunt ceteri Iudaei, ita ut et Barnabas

Jerusalem. This passage in Galatians shows that Paul, on receiving a revelation from God, travelled to Jerusalem, from Antioch, with Barnabas and Titus, to raise this issue and to have it clarified that Christ's redemption (and it alone) brings salvation: to accept the stand taken by Judaizers would have emptied Christ's life, death and resurrection of redemptive value. Those in authority at Jerusalem, the "pillars" of the Church (see v. 9), acknowledged that Paul's teaching was correct and that his mission to preach the Gospel to Gentiles was further evidence of God's mercy.

Just as Peter had been chosen to preach mainly to the Jews, so Paul had been designated to evangelize Gentiles. This distinction does not mean that Peter and Paul were limited as to whom they could preach to—Peter only to the Jews, Paul only to the Gentiles (vv. 7–9).

The decision handed down at Jerusalem refers to the primary mission of each at the time. Paul was faithful to the charge to be attentive to the needs of the poor. His collections for the poor in Jerusalem evidence his communion with the first Christian church (see v. 10; 1 Cor 16:1–3; 2 Cor 8:1–15; 9:11–15).

2:11–21 When necessary, the Apostle did yield somewhat in secondary matters (see Acts 16:3; 21:22–26; Rom 14:1–12; 1 Cor 10:23–30), but he always stood firm about the freedom of Christians in regard to observation of the Mosaic Law. The church at Antioch was made up of both Jewish and Gentile converts, for example. By ceasing to attend meals held by Christians of Gentile background (Jews were forbidden to do so), St Peter gave the impression that he felt obliged to keep the Mosaic Law. Paul could not let the situation continue without comment or correction, because Peter's behaviour, that of the visible head of the Church, could have serious consequences for all the faithful. We should bear in mind that the meals referred to may have been closely connected to the Eucharist (see 1 Cor 11:17–34), so there was a danger of a serious rift in the community.

"Certain men came from James" (v. 12): this refers to Jewish Christians who had come from Jerusalem, where James assumed leadership of the church after Peter was forced to flee (see Acts 12:17). The faithful of Jerusalem, having been brought up in the Jewish religion, are still following Jewish customs (that is understand-

Gal 2:5

ried away by their insincerity. ¹⁴But when I saw that they were not straightforward about the truth of the gospel, I said to Cephas before them all, "If you, though a Jew, live like a Gentile and not like a Jew, how can you compel the Gentiles to live like Jews?" ¹⁵We ourselves, who are Jews by birth and not Gentile sinners, ¹⁶yet who know that a man is not justified[d] by works of the law but through faith in Jesus Christ, even we have believed in Christ Jesus, in order to be justified by faith in Christ, and not by works of the law,* because by works of the law shall no one be justified. ¹⁷But if, in our endeavour to be justified in Christ, we ourselves were found to be sinners, is Christ then an agent of sin? Certainly not! ¹⁸But if I build up again those things which I tore down, then I prove myself a transgressor. ¹⁹For I through the law died to the law, that I might live to God. ²⁰I have been crucified with Christ; it is no longer I who live, but Christ who lives in me; and the life I now live in the flesh I live by faith in the Son of God, who loved me and gave himself for me. ²¹I do not nullify the grace of God; for if justification[e] were through the law, then Christ died to no purpose.

Gal 3:11, 26; 4:5
Phil 3:9
Acts 15:7–11
Rom 3:20–28
Eph 2:8

Ps 143:2

Rom 15:20–21
1 Cor 3:10
Rom 6:10–11
Gal 6:14
Rom 8:9–11
Col 3:3–4
Gal 6:14
1 Jn 3:16, 24
2 Cor 5:14

Rom 3:24
Jn 15:13
Eph 5:2
Gal 5:4, 11

simul abduceretur illorum simulatione. ¹⁴Sed cum vidissem quod non recte ambularent ad veritatem evangelii, dixi Cephae coram omnibus: «Si tu, cum Iudaeus sis, gentiliter et non Iudaice vivis, quomodo gentes cogis iudaizare?». ¹⁵Nos natura Iudaei et non ex gentibus peccatores, ¹⁶scientes autem quod non iustificatur homo ex operibus legis nisi per fidem Iesu Christi, et nos in Christum Iesum credidimus, ut iustificemur ex fide Christi et non ex operibus legis, quoniam ex operibus legis *non iustificabitur omnis* caro. ¹⁷Quodsi quaerentes iustificari in Christo, inventi sumus et ipsi peccatores, numquid Christus peccati minister est? Absit! ¹⁸Si enim, quae destruxi, haec iterum aedifico, praevaricatorem me constituo. ¹⁹Ego enim per legem legi mortuus sum, ut Deo vivam. Christo confixus sum cruci: ²⁰vivo autem iam non ego, vivit vero in me Christus; quod autem nunc vivo in carne, in fide vivo Filii Dei, qui dilexit me et tradidit seipsum pro me. ²¹Non irritam facio gratiam Dei; si enim per legem iusti-

able); but St Paul is aware of the dangers that underlie this attachment, and therefore he asserts the newness of the Christian faith: only by joining ourselves wholly to Christ can we be justified in God's sight. To argue that Christians must adhere to the rituals and other disciplinary aspects of the Jewish Law would imply that these external actions have salvific value; and, consequently, that those who gave up such practices in order to follow Christ would commit sin by doing so (v. 18), and Christ would be the minister or agent of that sin (v. 17)—an absurd line of logic and belief. To expose this erroneous line of thought, the Apostle highlights the consequences of justification: by joining ourselves to Christ through faith, he lives in us, and thus, with him and like him, we live to God (vv. 19–20). As St Augustine comments: "In the believer Christ is formed gradually by faith in the depth of his heart. The believer is called to freedom under grace, to be gentle and humble of heart, not boasting about the merits of his deeds, because in themselves they don't have any value. [...] Christ is formed in him who assimilates the form of Christ, and he assimilates the form of Christ who unites himself to him in spiritual

love" (*Expositio in Galatas*, 38). Therefore, a Christian "should live as Christ lived, making the affections of Christ his own, so that he can exclaim with St Paul: 'It is now no longer I who live, but Christ lives in me'. [...] We have to join him through faith, letting his life show forth in ours to such an extent that each Christian is not simply *alter Christus*: another Christ, but *ipse Christus*: Christ himself!" (St Josemaría Escrivá, *Christ Is Passing By*, 103 and 104).

All this is a consequence of Christ's love: he freely gave himself up to death out of love for each of us (v. 20). If we reflect on that truth, we will receive a great deal of consolation and encouragement: "Only of Him can we truthfully say in St Paul's words: '[He] loved me and gave himself for me' (Gal 2:20). This is the root of your deepest joy, your mainstay, the source of all your strength. If you taste bitterness in this life, suffer trials, meet with misunderstanding, or fall into sin, turn to the One who loves you always, with the infinite love of God, who will help you to overcome all obstacles, fill your emptiness, forgive your sins, and encourage you to return to the path of truth with a new confidence and joy" (John Paul II, *Address*, 1 March 1980).

d Or *reckoned righteous*; and so elsewhere   e Or *righteousness*

3. DOCTRINAL MATTERS*

Justification by faith

Lk 24:25
1 Cor 1, 2:2
Gal 5:7
Rom 2:15; 5:5
Gal 2:16; 4:6

Acts 1:8
1 Thess 4:8

Gen 15:6
Jn 8:39
Rom 1:16; 4:3
Acts 3:25

Gen 12:3

Rom 4:16; 7:7–8
Gal 5:3; Jas 2:10
Deut 27:26
Rom 1:17; 3:19–20
Heb 10:38
Hab 2:4

Lev 18:5
Rom 10:5

Acts 5:30
Phil 2, 8
Rom 4:13; 5:5
Deut 21:23

Joel 3:1
Is 44:3
Eph 1:3
Rom 4:13; 5:5

3 ¹O foolish Galatians! Who has bewitched you, before whose eyes Jesus Christ was publicly portrayed as crucified? ²Let me ask you only this: Did you receive the Spirit* by works of the law, or by hearing with faith? ³Are you so foolish? Having begun with the Spirit, are you now ending with the flesh? ⁴Did you experience so many things in vain?—if it really is in vain. ⁵Does he who supplies the Spirit to you and works miracles among you do so by works of the law, or by hearing with faith?

⁶Thus Abraham "believed God, and it was reckoned to him as righteousness." ⁷So you see that it is men of faith who are the sons of Abraham. ⁸And the scripture, foreseeing that God would justify the Gentiles by faith, preached the gospel beforehand to Abraham, saying, "In you shall all the nations be blessed." ⁹So then, those who are men of faith are blessed with Abraham who had faith.

¹⁰For all who rely on works of the law are under a curse; for it is written, "Cursed be every one who does not abide by all things written in the book of the law, and do them." ¹¹Now it is evident that no man is justified before God by the law; for "He who through faith is righteous shall live";ᶠ ¹²but the law does not rest on faith, for "He who does them shall live by them." ¹³Christ redeemed us from the curse of the law, having become a curse for us—for it is written, "Cursed be every one who hangs on a tree"— ¹⁴that in Christ Jesus the blessing of Abraham might come upon the Gentiles, that we might receive the promise of the Spirit through faith.

tia, ergo Christus gratis mortuus est.   [3] ¹O insensati Galatae, quis vos fascinavit, ante quorum oculos Iesus Christus descriptus est crucifixus? ²Hoc solum volo a vobis discere: Ex operibus legis Spiritum accepistis an ex auditu fidei? ³Sic stulti estis? Cum Spiritu coeperitis, nunc carne consummamini? ⁴Tanta passi estis sine causa? Si tamen et sine causa! ⁵Qui ergo tribuit vobis Spiritum et operatur virtutes in vobis, ex operibus legis an ex auditu fidei? ⁶Sicut Abraham *credidit Deo, et reputatum est ei ad iustitiam.* ⁷Cognoscitis ergo quia qui ex fide sunt, hi sunt filii Abrahae. ⁸Providens autem Scriptura quia ex fide iustificat gentes Deus, praenuntiavit Abrahae: *«Benedicentur in te omnes gentes».* ⁹Igitur, qui ex fide sunt, benedicuntur cum fideli Abraham. ¹⁰Quicumque enim ex operibus legis sunt, sub maledicto sunt; scriptum est enim: *«Maledictus omnis, qui non permanserit in omnibus, quae scripta sunt in libro legis, ut faciat ea».* ¹¹Quoniam autem in lege nemo iustificatur apud Deum manifestum

*3:1—4:31 The doctrinal part of the letter deals with the subject of justification through faith in Jesus Christ, not through works of the Mosaic Law, which was designed to prepare the way for the law of Christ. This is the very essence of the redemptive work of Christ (3:1–14). In him God's promises to Abraham have found fulfilment (3:15–29). Christians, who are children of God, free men and not slaves, are heirs of God their Father (4:1–31).

3:1–14 Paul's love for the Galatians causes him suffering, for they have forgotten that only Jesus, and not the Law, brings salvation. They should know very well that they received justification without even having heard of the Law, for the Holy Spirit came down upon them prior to the arrival of the Judaizers. All they need do is remember the charisms they received through their faith in Christ (vv. 1–5). Besides, Holy Scripture shows that justification is attained through faith: witness the case of Abraham (vv. 6–9). God promised Abraham that his offspring would be blessed; he made a covenant with him and justified him, not because he performed works of the Law (the Law was not established until later), but on account of his faith (cf. Rom 4:1ff). Similarly, all those who believe in God, like Abraham, are his true descendants and will receive God's blessing. But there is another fact to be considered. Far from bringing salvation, the Law is in some way the cause of spiritual death (a "curse"), insofar as every precept carries a penalty in the case of transgression (vv. 10–14; cf. Rom 7:7–12). Christ redeemed us from this curse of the Law by freely taking upon himself the punishment that our sins deserved (v. 13; cf. Is 53:4; Mt 8:17; Rom 3:21–26; 5:6–10). To sum up, to submit to the Law again would mean that our Redeemer's sacrifice had served no purpose.

f Or *the righteous shall live by faith*

The Law and the promise

[15]To give a human example, brethren: no one annuls even a man's will,[g] or adds to it, once it has been ratified. [16]Now the promises were made to Abraham and to his offspring. It does not say, "And to offsprings," referring to many; but, referring to one, "And to your offspring," which is Christ. [17]This is what I mean: the law, which came four hundred and thirty years afterward, does not annul a covenant previously ratified by God, so as to make the promise void. [18]For if the inheritance is by the law, it is no longer by promise; but God gave it to Abraham by a promise.

[19]Why then the law? It was added because of transgressions, till the offspring should come to whom the promise had been made; and it was ordained by angels through an intermediary. [20]Now an intermediary implies more than one; but God is one.

[21]Is the law then against the promises of God? Certainly not; for if a law had been given which could make alive, then righteousness would indeed be by the law. [22]But the scripture consigned all things to sin, that what was promised to faith in Jesus Christ might be given to those who believe.

[23]Now before faith came, we were confined under the law, kept under restraint until faith should be revealed. [24]So that the law was our custodian until Christ came, that we might be justified by faith. [25]But now that faith has come, we are no longer under a custodian; [26]for in Christ Jesus you are all sons of God, through faith. [27]For

Margin references: Heb 9:16; Gal 4:1; Jn 8:56; Gen 12:7; 22:17; Ex 12:40; Rom 4:13; 11:6; Acts 7:38; Heb 2:2; Rom 5, 20; 7:7; Gal 4:3; Col 2:15; Rom 3:31; 7:10; 8:2–4; Ps 14:1–3; Rom 3:9–20, 23; 11:32; Gal 4:3; 1 Cor 4:15; Rom 10:4; Rom 6:14; Jn 1:12; Gal 4:5–7; Rom 8:14f, 29

est, quia *iustus ex fide vivet*; [12]lex autem non est ex fide, sed *qui fecerit ea, vivet in illis.* [13]Christus nos redemit de maledicto legis factus pro nobis maledictum, quia scriptum est: «*Maledictus omnis, qui pendet in ligno*», [14]ut in gentes benedictio Abrahae fieret in Christo Iesu, ut promissionem Spiritus accipiamus per fidem. [15]Fratres, secundum hominem dico, tamen hominis confirmatum testamentum nemo irritum facit aut superordinat. [16]Abrahae autem dictae sunt promissiones *et semini eius.* Non dicit: «*Et seminibus*» quasi in multis, sed quasi in uno: «*Et semini tuo*», qui est Christus. [17]Hoc autem dico: Testamentum confirmatum a Deo, quae post quadringentos et triginta annos facta est lex, non irritum facit, ad evacuandam promissionem. [18]Nam si ex lege hereditas, iam non ex promissione; Abrahae autem per promissionem donavit Deus. [19]Quid igitur lex? Propter transgressiones apposita est, donec veniret semen, cui promissum est, ordinata per angelos in manu mediatoris. [20]Mediator autem unius non est, Deus autem unus est. [21]Lex ergo adversus promissa Dei? Absit. Si enim data esset lex, quae posset vivificare, vere ex lege esset iustitia. [22]Sed conclusit Scriptura omnia sub peccato, ut promissio ex fide Iesu Christi daretur credentibus. [23]Prius autem quam veniret fides, sub lege custodiebamur conclusi in eam fidem, quae revelanda erat. [24]Itaque lex paedagogus noster fuit in Christum, ut ex fide iustificemur; [25]at ubi venit fides,

3:15–29 Here Paul returns to the subject of God's promise to Abraham and his descendants as an argument in favour of justification by faith: the promise referred to Christ (vv. 15–16), and it is like a last will or testament: it cannot be changed (vv. 17–18). Since God always keeps his promises (cf. Ex 34:6) and does what he says he will do, what God promised Abraham cannot be rendered void by the Law of Moses, which was promulgated a long time afterwards (cf. Rom 4:13–17).

The Law was established to identify and punish transgressions prior to the coming of Christ (vv. 19–22), but it did not undo the promise made to Abraham; on the contrary, the Law identified what was sinful, and how that sin would have to be paid for. So, the Law was designed by God to be a tutor or pedagogue (a "custodian"—the sort of servant who, in St Paul's time, had charge of the children and

brought them to school) to show men the way to Christ (vv. 23–25). Now that Christ has brought redemption (v. 26), man comes of age and is in no need of this tutor. Through faith in Christ and by means of Baptism, he becomes a son of God (v. 27), "[and the clothing we are given] is not just something beautiful and costly: it is Jesus Christ himself, who is the sum total of all beauty, all value, all richness" (St John of Avila, *Lecciones sobre Galatas*, ad loc.). From that point onwards, all differences among believers disappear (v. 28); all become descendants of Abraham and sharers in the divine promises (v. 29): "So there is only one race, the race of the children of God. There is only one colour, the colour of the children of God. And there is only one language, the language which speaks to the heart and to the mind, without the noise of words, making us know God and love one another" (St Josemaría Escrivá, *Christ Is Passing By*, 106).

g Or *covenant* (as in verse 17)

Rom 6:4; 13:14
1 Cor 12:13
Rom 10:12
Col 3:11

Jn 17:21f
Rom 9:7-13
Gal 3:7, 14–18
as many of you as were baptized into Christ have put on Christ. ²⁸There is neither Jew nor Greek, there is neither slave nor free, there is neither male nor female; for you are all one in Christ Jesus. ²⁹And if you are Christ's, then you are Abraham's offspring, heirs according to promise.

Divine sonship

Gal 3:15

Gal 3:23; 5:1
Col 2:8, 20

Mk 1:15

Gal 3:13
Rom 3:24; 8:15–17
4 ¹I mean that the heir, as long as he is a child, is no better than a slave, though he is the owner of all the estate; ²but he is under guardians and trustees until the date set by the father. ³So with us; when we were children, we were slaves to the elemental spirits of the universe. ⁴But when the time had fully come, God sent forth his Son, born of woman, born under the law, ⁵to redeem those who were under the law,

iam non sumus sub paedagogo. ²⁶Omnes enim filii Dei estis per fidem in Christo Iesu. ²⁷Quicumque enim in Christum baptizati estis, Christum induistis: ²⁸non est Iudaeus neque Graecus, non est servus neque liber, non est masculus et femina; omnes enim vos unus estis in Christo Iesu. ²⁹Si autem vos Christi, ergo Abrahae semen estis, secundum promissionem heredes.   [4] ¹Dico autem: Quanto tempore heres parvulus est, nihil differt a servo, cum sit dominus omnium, ²sed sub tutoribus est et actoribus usque ad praefinitum tempus a patre. ³Ita et nos, cum essemus parvuli, sub elementis mundi eramus servientes; ⁴at ubi venit plenitudo temporis, misit Deus Filium suum, factum ex muliere, factum sub lege, ⁵ut eos,

4:1–11 In line with the idea of the Law as a tutor and the image of those under the Law as children or minors (see 3:24–25), St Paul goes on to explain that with the coming of Christ we have now reached maturity. In Christ, God offers to all men and women the opportunity to become his sons and daughters, and he sends us the Spirit of his Son: "Every man who believes […] no longer belongs to the ancestry of his father in the flesh, but to the seed of the Saviour, who made himself the Son of man so that we might become sons of God" (St Leo the Great, *Sermo 6 in Nativitate*, 2).

In the fullness of time (see v. 4), with the Incarnation history reaches its defining moment; when it becomes definitively oriented towards God: "Speaking of the birth of the Son of God, Saint Paul places this event in the 'fullness of time' (cf. Gal 4:4). *Time is indeed fulfilled by the very fact that God, in the Incarnation, came down into human history.* Eternity entered into time: what 'fulfilment' could be greater than this? What other 'fulfilment' would be possible?" (John Paul II, *Tertio millennio adveniente*, 9).

The words "born of woman" (see v. 4) underline the fact that Jesus is truly man, and they point to the role of the Blessed Virgin, the New Eve, in the work of salvation: "'God sent forth his Son' (Gal 4:4), but to prepare a body for him, he wanted the free co-operation of a creature. For this, from all eternity God chose for the mother of his Son a daughter of Israel, a young

Jewish woman of Nazareth in Galilee, 'a virgin betrothed to a man whose name was Joseph, of the house of David; and the virgin's name was Mary' (Lk 1:26–27)" (*Catechism of the Catholic Church*, 488).

Probably out of respect for God's majesty, the Jews did not use the word "Abba" (v. 6)—the name that small children called their father—when addressing God. Jesus does not hesitate to use it to address God the Father, thereby showing his special relationship to him as Son, his trust in him and his submission to his will (see Mk 14:36). St Paul echoes that tradition and teaches that it is the Spirit of Jesus, the Holy Spirit, who enables us to see that we are children of God (see Rom 8:16–17): the Christian is a son in the Son through the Holy Spirit: "If we have a constant relationship with the Holy Spirit, we shall become spiritual ourselves, we shall realize that we are Christ's brothers and children of God, and we shall not hesitate to call upon our Father" (St Josemaría Escrivá, *Christ Is Passing By*, 136).

It is not clear what is meant by "the elemental spirits of the universe" (v. 3). St Paul may be referring pejoratively to practices of the Jewish Law (see vv. 9–10). In any event, he is trying to show the Galatians how sad it would be if, having converted to the faith, they were now to submit themselves to observances that had been superseded by the coming of Christ. In effect, they would revert to their former Gentile state.

so that we might receive adoption as sons. ⁶And because you are sons, God has sent the Spirit of his Son into our hearts, crying, "Abba! Father!" ⁷So through God you are no longer a slave but a son, and if a son then an heir.

Jn 15:15
Mk 14:36
Rom 8:15–17
Gal 3:26

⁸Formerly, when you did not know God, you were in bondage to beings that by nature are no gods; ⁹but now that you have come to know God, or rather to be known by God, how can you turn back again to the weak and beggarly elemental spirits, whose slaves you want to be once more? ¹⁰You observe days, and months, and seasons, and years! ¹¹I am afraid I have laboured over you in vain.

1 Cor 8:4; 12:2
1 Thess 1:9–10; 4:5
Col 2:20
Rom 8: 28–30
1 Cor 13:12
Rom 14:5
Col 2:16-20
Phil 2:16
1 Thess 3:5

A fatherly appeal by Paul

¹²Brethren, I beseech you, become as I am, for I also have become as you are. You did me no wrong; ¹³you know it was because of a bodily ailment that I preached the gospel to you at first; ¹⁴and though my condition was a trial to you, you did not scorn or despise me, but received me as an angel of God, as Christ Jesus. ¹⁵What has become of the satisfaction you felt? For I bear you witness that, if possible, you would have plucked out your eyes and given them to me. ¹⁶Have I then become your enemy by telling you the truth?ʰ ¹⁷They make much of you, but for no good purpose; they want to shut you out, that you may make much of them. ¹⁸For a good purpose it is always good to be made much of, and not only when I am present with you. ¹⁹My little children, with whom I am again in travail until Christ be formed in you! ²⁰I could wish to be present with you now and to change my tone, for I am perplexed about you.

1 Cor 9:19–23
2 Thess 3:7–10
Acts 16:6
1 Cor 2:3–5
Mt 10:40–42
Gal 5:7
2 Cor 12:15ff
Gal 1:7; 6:12
2 Cor 12:15
Philem 10
Rom 15:14–33
1 Cor 4:14–15
2 Cor 6:13
1 Thess 2:7
1 Jn 2:1, 12
1 Cor 4:14–21
Phil 2:19–24

The two covenants—Hagar and Sarah

²¹Tell me, you who desire to be under law, do you not hear the law? ²²For it is written that Abraham had two sons, one by a slave and one by a free woman. ²³But the

Gen 16:15; 21:2

qui sub lege erant, redimeret, ut adoptionem filiorum reciperemus. ⁶Quoniam autem estis filii, misit Deus Spiritum Filii sui in corda nostra clamantem: «Abba, Pater!». ⁷Itaque iam non es servus sed filius; quod si filius, et heres per Deum. ⁸uidem ignorantes Deum, his, qui natura non sunt dii, servistis; ⁹nunc autem, cum cognoveritis Deum, immo cogniti sitis a Deo, quomodo convertimini iterum ad infirma et egena elementa, quibus rursus ut antea servire vultis? ¹⁰Dies observatis et menses et tempora et annos! ¹¹Timeo vos, ne forte sine causa laboraverim in vobis. ¹²Estote sicut ego, quia et ego sicut vos, fratres, obsecro vos. Nihil me laesistis; ¹³scitis autem quia per infirmitatem carnis pridem vobis evangelizavi, ¹⁴et tentationem vestram in carne mea non sprevistis neque respuistis, sed sicut angelum Dei excepistis me, sicut Christum Iesum. ¹⁵beatitudo vestra? Testimonium enim perhibeo vobis, quia, si fieri posset, oculos vestros eruissetis et dedissetis mihi. ¹⁶Ergo inimicus vobis factus sum verum dicens vobis? ¹⁷Aemulantur vos non bene, sed excludere vos volunt, ut illos aemulemini. ¹⁸Bonum est autem aemulari in bono semper, et non tantum cum praesens sum apud vos, ¹⁹filioli mei, quos iterum parturio, donec formetur Christus in vobis! ²⁰Vellem autem esse apud vos modo et mutare vocem meam, quoniam incertus sum in vobis. ²¹Dicite mihi, qui sub lege vultis esse: Legem non auditis? ²²Scriptum est enim quoniam Abraham duos filios habuit, unum de ancilla et unum de libera. ²³Sed qui de ancilla, secundum carnem natus est, qui autem de libera, per promissionem.

4:12–20 The Apostle changes his tone at this point. He tenderly recalls the time when the Galatians were converted to Christ, and the sincere joy with which they received him when he first visited them (probably during the journey narrated in Acts 16:6). Although he was ill at the time (we do not know what Paul suffered from), they received him "as an angel of God, as Christ Jesus" himself (v. 14). His only desire is to draw them back to the Gospel and to Christ. "Having spoken to them in another passage as a father speaks (cf. 1 Cor 4:18) [...], he no longer speaks to them as a father, but as their mother in Christ so that they will see the love of a mother and the

tenderness of a father in his concern for them" (St Jerome, *Commentarii in Galatas*, 2, 4, 19). And St John Chrysostom comments: "He is like a mother who worries about her children, *until Christ be formed in you!* See his fatherly tenderness. Mark the sorrow of the good Apostle. See how his cry bursts forth, louder than a mother in her labour pains" (*In Galatas*, 4, 3, 4).

4:21–31 The example of Abraham is again used to explain the freedom that Christ won for us. Sarah, Abraham's wife, was barren; thus, the patriarch, in line with the customs of his time, had a child by her slave, Hagar—Ishmael (cf. Gen 16:1–4,

h Or *by dealing truly with you*

Gen 17:16
Rom 4:19; 9:7–9

son of the slave was born according to the flesh, the son of the free woman through

Ex 19:20
Jn 8:32–33
Heb 12:18–24
Gen 16:1

promise. ²⁴Now this is an allegory: these women are two covenants. One is from Mount Sinai, bearing children for slavery; she is Hagar. ²⁵Now Hagar is Mount Sinai in Arabia;ⁱ she corresponds to the present Jerusalem, for she is in slavery with her

Rev 21:2
Phil 3:20
1 Sam 2:5
Is 54:1
Ps 86:5; 113:9

children. ²⁶But the Jerusalem above is free, and she is our mother. ²⁷For it is written,

> "Rejoice, O barren one that dost not bear;
> break forth and shout, thou who art not in travail;
> for the desolate hath more children
> than she who hath a husband."

Gen 21:9
1 Thess 2:14–15

²⁸Now we,ʲ brethren, like Isaac, are children of promise. ²⁹But as at that time he who was born according to the flesh persecuted him who was born according to the Spirit,

Gen 21:10

so it is now. ³⁰But what does the scripture say? "Cast out the slave and her son; for the son of the slave shall not inherit with the son of the free woman." ³¹So, brethren, we are not children of the slave but of the free woman.

PART TWO

Christian freedom and charity*

4. EXHORTATIONS*

Christian freedom

Gal 2:4; 4:5, 9
Mt 11:29–30
Rom 6:17–22

5 ¹For freedom Christ has set us free; stand fast therefore, and do not submit again to a yoke of slavery.

²⁴Quae sunt per allegoriam dicta; ipsae enim sunt duo Testamenta, unum quidem a monte Sinai, in servitutem generans, quod est Agar. ²⁵Illud vero Agar mons est Sinai in Arabia, respondet autem Ierusalem, quae nunc est; servit enim cum filiis suis. ²⁶Illa autem, quae sursum est Ierusalem, libera est, quae est mater nostra; ²⁷scriptum est enim: «*Laetare, sterilis, quae non paris, / erumpe et exclama, quae non parturis, / quia multi filii desertae / magis quam eius, quae habet virum*». ²⁸Vos autem, fratres, secundum Isaac promissionis filii estis. ²⁹Sed quomodo tunc, qui secundum carnem natus fuerat, persequebatur eum, qui secundum spiritum, ita et nunc. ³⁰Sed quid dicit Scriptura? «*Eice ancillam et filium eius; non enim heres erit filius ancillae cum filio* liberae». ³¹Itaque, fratres, non sumus ancillae filii sed liberae. [5] ¹Hac libertate nos Christus liberavit; state igitur et nolite iterum iugo servitutis detineri. ²Ecce ego Paulus dico vobis quoniam, si circumcidamini, Christus vobis nihil proderit. ³Testificor

15–16). However, God had promised Abraham that he would have a son by Sarah, and this came about. Although Abraham and Sarah were both in their old age, Sarah gave birth to Isaac (Gen 17:19; 21:1–7). St Paul sees an allegory here: the slave woman represents the Jewish people, who are subject to the Law; the free wife prefigures the Church (cf. Rev 21:2, 10), the fruit of the divine promise. Christians resemble Isaac because they exist by virtue of the promise, not of the Law.

Since Jerusalem (v. 25) is located on a hill (Mount Zion), Paul sees a symbolic parallel between this hill and Mount Sinai, where the Old Covenant was ratified (vv. 24–25), because Sinai is situated in Arabia, whose inhabitants are the descendants of Ishmael, the son of Abraham and Hagar.

Verse 29 glosses the scene in Genesis 21:9, following a rabbinical tradition (cf. *Talmud*, Sotah Treatise, 6, 6) according to which Ishmael ill-treated Isaac during a game. Similarly, Paul says, those born according to the flesh (Jews) are persecuting those born according to the Spirit (Christians). In this persecution Paul sees another indication that the ancient promises are being fulfilled.

*5:1—6:18 In this part of the letter St Paul shows what the salvation worked by Christ implies for everyday Christian living. Only if we are free in the Spirit can we practise charity, and charity, in turn, guides our freedom and ensures that it develops properly (5:1—6:10). Paul ends the letter by showing how he himself practises that freedom (6:11–18).

i Other ancient authorities read *For Sinai is a mountain in Arabia*   j Other ancient authorities read *you*

²Now I, Paul, say to you that if you receive circumcision, Christ will be of no advantage to you. ³I testify again to every man who receives circumcision that he is bound to keep the whole law. ⁴You are severed from Christ, you who would be justified by the law; you have fallen away from grace. ⁵For through the Spirit, by faith, we wait for the hope of righteousness. ⁶For in Christ Jesus neither circumcision nor uncircumcision is of any avail, but faith working through love. ⁷You were running well; who hindered you from obeying the truth? ⁸This persuasion is not from him who called you. ⁹A little leaven leavens the whole lump. ¹⁰I have confidence in the Lord that you will take no other view than mine; and he who is troubling you will bear his judgment, whoever he is. ¹¹But if I, brethren, still preach circumcision, why am I still persecuted? In that case the stumbling block of the cross* has been removed. ¹²I wish those who unsettle you would mutilate themselves!

Rom 2:25
Jas 2:10
Gal 2:21; 3:10; 6:13
Rom 3:24–26
Rom 8:23, 25
Phil 3:20
1 Cor 7:19
Gal 3:28; 6:15;
13:13ff
Jas 2:14
Phil 3:12
Gal 1:6
Mk 8:15
Mt 13:33
1 Cor 5:6
Gal 1:7
1 Cor 1:23; 3:17
2 Cor 11:23–29
Gal 6:12, 24
Phil 3:2

autem rursum omni homini circumcidenti se quoniam debitor est universae legis faciendae. ⁴Evacuati estis a Christo, qui in lege iustificamini, a gratia excidistis. ⁵Nos enim Spiritu ex fide spem iustitiae exspectamus. ⁶Nam in Christo Iesu neque circumcisio aliquid valet neque praeputium, sed fides, quae per caritatem operatur. ⁷Currebatis bene; quis vos impedivit veritati non oboedire? ⁸Haec persuasio non est ex eo, qui vocat vos. ⁹Modicum fermentum totam massam corrumpit. ¹⁰Ego confido in vobis in Domino quod nihil aliud sapietis; qui autem conturbat vos, portabit iudicium, quicumque est ille. ¹¹Ego autem, fratres, si circumcisionem adhuc praedico, quid adhuc persecutionem patior? Ergo evacuatum est scandalum crucis. ¹²Utinam et abscidantur, qui vos conturbant! ¹³Vos enim in libertatem vocati estis, fratres; tantum ne libertatem in occasionem detis

*5:1—6:10 The law of Christ, unlike the law of the circumcised, is a law of freedom (5:1–12). The works of the New Law, works of the Spirit, stand in opposition to the works of the flesh and sin (5:13–26). Charity is the precept that underpins the law of Christ (6:1–10).

5:1–12 Christians owe their freedom to the redemptive work of Christ. By the grace of redemption, believers desire righteousness/justice (holiness), their souls being moved by the Holy Spirit. Their background no longer matters—whether they be Jew or Gentile, circumcised or uncircumcised. The important thing is faith working through love (v. 6), a faith that stirs them to love Christ and, with that same love, to love all others.

The faith that St Paul is speaking about here is the supernatural virtue of faith—what is called "living faith", that is, faith that translates into a deep conviction which moves a person to love. In Christian tradition, faith that does not lead to action is called "dead faith", which is a caricature of faith, for "faith, unless it be joined to hope and charity, neither makes us one with Christ nor loving members of his body. That is why it is rightly said that 'faith by itself, if it has no works, is dead' (Jas 2:17), and that 'in Christ Jesus neither circumcision nor uncircumcision is of any avail, but faith working through love' (Gal 5:6; 6:15)" (Council of Trent, *De iustificatione*, chap. 7).

Love, in turn, is a reflection of faith (see Jn 13:35). "When one asks if someone is good," St Augustine says, "one does not check to see what he believes or what he hopes for, but what it is he loves. For someone who loves rightly certainly also believes and hopes rightly; but he who does not love believes in vain, even if what he believes in is true [...]. Therefore, this is the faith in Christ which the Apostle extols—'faith which works through love'" (*Enchiridion*, 117).

In vv. 7–12 Paul refers again to the time when the Galatians were first converted, and he warns them to be on their guard against the false preachers who would lead them astray. He still has every hope that they will return to the true faith he preached to them (v. 10). Verse 11 seems to indicate that some opponents of Paul have been criticizing him for continuing to preach circumcision. Their grounds for saying he is doing this may have been the fact that he had Timothy circumcised (see Acts 16:1–3). But this he did simply for reasons of prudence; he denies that he ever preached the *need* for circumcision: if he had done so, they would not persist in attacking him, and the cross would no longer be a scandal, a stumbling-block. Verse 12 may be written in irony: if his critics are so convinced of the need for circumcision, then let them not only circumcise themselves but (as St Thomas Aquinas interprets the passage) actually castrate themselves (see *Super Galatas*, ad loc.), a reference perhaps

The fruits of the Spirit and the works of the flesh

1 Pet 2:16
1 Cor 8:9
Rom 6:19

Mt 5:43; 22:39
Lev 19:18
Mk 12:31
Rom 13:8–10
Lk 10:27

Rom 7:14, 23;
8:1–5, 14
1 Pet 2:11

Rom 6:14; 8: 1-2, 14
Rom 1:29–31
1 Cor 6:9

Eph 5:3–4
2 Cor 6, 9
Col 3:5, 8
Rev 22:15

1 Cor 6:10

1 Cor 13:4–7
2 Cor 6:6–10
Rom 12:9-12
1 Tim 1:9

¹³For you were called to freedom, brethren; only do not use your freedom as an opportunity for the flesh, but through love be servants of one another. ¹⁴For the whole law is fulfilled in one word, "You shall love your neighbour as yourself." ¹⁵But if you bite and devour one another take heed that you are not consumed by one another.

¹⁶But I say, walk by the Spirit, and do not gratify the desires of the flesh. ¹⁷For the desires of the flesh are against the Spirit, and the desires of the Spirit are against the flesh; for these are opposed to each other, to prevent you from doing what you would. ¹⁸But if you are led by the Spirit you are not under the law. ¹⁹Now the works of the flesh are plain: immorality, impurity, licentiousness, ²⁰idolatry, sorcery, enmity, strife, jealousy, anger, selfishness, dissension, party spirit, ²¹envy,ᵏ drunkenness, carousing, and the like. I warn you, as I warned you before, that those who do such things shall not inherit the kingdom of God. ²²But the fruit of the Spirit is love, joy, peace, patience, kindness, goodness, faithfulness, ²³gentleness, self-control; against

carni, sed per caritatem servite invicem. ¹⁴Omnis enim lex in uno sermone impletur, in hoc: *Diliges proximum tuum sicut teipsum*. ¹⁵Quod si invicem mordetis et devoratis, videte, ne ab invicem consumamini! ¹⁶Dico autem: Spiritu ambulate et concupiscentiam carnis ne perfeceritis. ¹⁷Caro enim concupiscit adversus Spiritum, Spiritus autem adversus carnem; haec enim invicem adversantur, ut non, quaecumque vultis, illa faciatis. ¹⁸Quod si Spiritu ducimini, non estis sub lege. ¹⁹Manifesta autem sunt opera carnis, quae sunt fornicatio, immunditia, luxuria, ²⁰idolorum servitus, veneficia, inimicitiae, contentiones, aemulationes, irae, rixae, dissensiones, sectae, ²¹invidiae, ebrietates, comissationes et his similia, quae praedico vobis, sicut praedixi, quoniam, qui talia agunt, regnum Dei non consequentur. ²²Fructus autem Spiritus est caritas, gaudium, pax,

to ritual castration in the cult of Artemis, a goddess very popular in Asia Minor at that time (see Acts 19:23–38). (A person who was castrated was excluded from the community of Israel by that fact: see Deut 23:2.)

5:13–26 For Paul, freedom does not mean license: the law of Christ confirms the Decalogue and gives it greater depth (vv. 13–15). Christ gave the Ten Commandments new life and showed that the key to and essence of the commandments is Love—love of God, which necessarily brings with it love of one's neighbour. "It might also be asked", St Augustine comments, "why the Apostle here speaks only of love of neighbour, saying that this way the whole Law is fulfilled [...], when in fact charity is perfect only if one practises the two precepts of love of God and love of neighbour [...]. But who can love his neighbour, that is, all men, as himself, if he does not love God, since it is only by God's precept and gift that one can love one's neighbour? So, since neither precept can be kept unless the other be kept, it is enough to mention one of them" (*Expositio in Galatas*, 45). See also the note on Rom 13:8–10.

Freedom means that man is able to make his way to God, his true and ultimate end (vv. 16–

26). A person is free when he is led by the Spirit of God, who enables him to overcome the inclinations of the flesh, which the Law denounces (vv. 19–21), and to produce fruit which is on a plane above the Law (vv. 22–23). It follows that when someone does not live according to the Spirit, he is allowing his sensual appetites free rein. "It is said that someone lives according to the flesh when he lives for himself. Therefore, in this case, by 'flesh' is meant the whole person. For everything which stems from a disordered love of oneself is called work of the flesh" (St Augustine, *De civitate Dei*, 14, 2). That is why we find included in the "works of the flesh" not only sins of impurity (v. 19) and intemperance (v. 21) but also sins against the virtue of religion and fraternal charity (v. 20). On the other hand, when someone allows the Spirit to move him, his life is transformed into a life "by the Spirit" (v. 25), a life that is no longer merely human but also divine. The soul then becomes a good tree known by its fruit. In Christian tradition, these actions that reveal the presence of the Paraclete and give a person spiritual delight, a foretaste of eternal life, are called fruits of the Holy Spirit (see *Summa theologiae*, 1–2, 70, 1). "Those blessed fruits enumerated by the Apostle (Gal 5:22) the Spirit produces and shows forth in the

ᵏ Other ancient authorities add *murder*

such there is no law. ²⁴And those who belong to Christ Jesus have crucified the flesh with its passions and desires.

2 Pet 1:5–7

²⁵If we live by the Spirit, let us also walk by the Spirit. ²⁶Let us have no self-conceit, no provoking of one another, no envy of one another.

Rom 6:6; 8:9
Col 3:5
Gal 5:16
Rom 8:4,14
Phil 2:3

Fraternal charity

6 ¹Brethren, if a man is overtaken in any trespass, you who are spiritual should restore him in a spirit of gentleness. Look to yourself, lest you too be tempted. ²Bear one another's burdens, and so fulfil the law of Christ. ³For if any one thinks he is something, when he is nothing, he deceives himself. ⁴But let each one test his own work, and then his reason to boast will be in himself alone and not in his neighbour. ⁵For each man will have to bear his own load.

Mt 18:15
1 Cor 10:12
2 Thess 3:15
2 Tim 2:25
Jas 5:19
Jn 13, 34
Col 3:13
Rom 15:1
1 Cor 4:7; 8:2, 9
2 Cor 12:11; 13:5
Rom 14:12
1 Cor 3:8

⁶Let him who is taught the word share all good things with him who teaches.

Lk 10:7
Rom 15:27

⁷Do not be deceived; God is not mocked, for whatever a man sows, that he will also reap. ⁸For he who sows to his own flesh will from the flesh reap corruption; but

Job 4:8; 13:9
2 Cor 9:6
Jn 3:6; 6:63
Rom 6:21–22; 8:12–13

longanimitas, benignitas, bonitas, fides, ²³mansuetudo, continentia; adversus huiusmodi non est lex. ²⁴Qui autem sunt Christi Iesu, carnem crucifixerunt cum vitiis et concupiscentiis. ²⁵Si vivimus Spiritu, Spiritu et ambulemus. ²⁶Non efficiamur inanis gloriae cupidi, invicem provocantes, invicem invidentes. [6] ¹Fratres, et si praeoccupatus fuerit homo in aliquo delicto, vos, qui spiritales estis, huiusmodi instruite in spiritu lenitatis, considerans teipsum, ne et tu tenteris. ²Alter alterius onera portate et sic adimplebitis legem Christi. ³Nam si quis existimat se aliquid esse, cum sit nihil, ipse se seducit; ⁴opus autem suum probet unusquisque et sic in semetipso tantum gloriationem habebit et non in altero. ⁵Unusquisque enim onus suum portabit. ⁶Communicet autem is, qui catechizatur verbum, ei qui se catechizat, in omnibus bonis. ⁷Nolite errare: Deus non irride-

just, even in this mortal life—fruits replete with all sweetness and joy. Such must, indeed, be from the Spirit 'who in the Trinity is the love of the Father and the Son, filling all creatures with immeasurable sweetness' (St Augustine, *De Trinitate*, 5, 9)" (Leo XIII, *Divinum illud munus*). Drawing on vv. 22 and 23, and using the Vulgate (which also mentions generosity, chastity, patience, faith—or fidelity—and modesty), Christian catechesis speaks of there being twelve such fruits.

6:1–10 In line with what was said in 5:14, the Apostle again says that the law of Christ is love. That is what Jesus himself teaches. "Jesus makes charity the *new commandment* (cf. Jn 13:34). By loving his own 'to the end' (Jn 13:1), he makes manifest the Father's love which he receives. By loving one another, the disciples imitate the love of Jesus which they themselves receive" (*Catechism of the Catholic Church*, 1823).

One of the signs of mutual love is fraternal correction (v. 1), which one should practise in a spirit of meekness and humility, seeking only the other person's good and with a clear awareness of one's own shortcomings. "We should never take issue with another's sin," St Augustine comments, "without first examining our own con-

science by inner questioning and by then replying, before God, without ambiguity, that we are acting out of love" (*Expositio in Galatas*, 57). Paul also exhorts his readers, as an expression of charity, to bear the burdens of others as well as their own: "Charity, which is like a generous overflowing of justice, demands first of all the fulfilment of one's duty. The way to start is to be just; the next step is to do what is most equitable…; but in order to love, great refinement is required, and much thoughtfulness, and respect, and kindliness in rich measure. In other words, it involves following the Apostle's advice: 'carry one another's burdens, and thus you will fulfil the law of Christ' (Gal 6:2). Then indeed we shall be living charity fully and carrying out the commandment of Jesus" (St Josemaría Escrivá, *Friends of God*, 173).

Some Jews thought that, on account of their observing the prescriptions of the Law, they were superior to others (vv. 3–5; cf. Lk 18:9–14). That pride stemmed from lack of self-knowledge. Hence the Apostle's exhortation to all to examine themselves sincerely, in the sight of God, who sees everything.

Verses 7–10 imply that the time for gaining merit ends with death. That is why the Apostle stresses the need to strive to live an honest life,

1 Cor 15:35–49
1 Thess 5:15
2 Thess 3:13
Rom 2:10
2 Pet 1:5–7

he who sows to the Spirit will from the Spirit reap eternal life. ⁹And let us not grow weary in well-doing, for in due season we shall reap, if we do not lose heart. ¹⁰So then, as we have opportunity, let us do good to all men, and especially to those who are of the household of faith.

5. CONCLUSION*

1 Cor 16:21
2 Thess 3:17

Col 2:18
Gal 5:2, 11
Phil 3:18

Rom 3:27

Gal 3:1; 5:24
1 Cor 1:18, 31; 2:2

¹¹See with what large letters I am writing to you with my own hand. ¹²It is those who want to make a good showing in the flesh that would compel you to be circumcised, and only in order that they may not be persecuted for the cross of Christ. ¹³For even those who receive circumcision do not themselves keep the law, but they desire to have you circumcised that they may glory in your flesh. ¹⁴But far be it from me to glory except in the cross of our Lord Jesus Christ, by which[l] the world has been cru-

tur. Quae enim seminaverit homo, haec et metet; ⁸quoniam, qui seminat in carne sua, de carne metet corruptionem, qui autem seminat in Spiritu, de Spiritu metet vitam aeternam. ⁹Bonum autem facientes infatigabiles, tempore enim suo metemus non deficientes. ¹⁰Ergo dum tempus habemus, operemur bonum ad omnes, maxime autem ad domesticos fidei. ¹¹Videte qualibus litteris scripsi vobis mea manu. ¹²Quicumque volunt placere in carne, hi cogunt vos circumcidi, tantum ut crucis Christi persecutionem non patiantur; ¹³neque enim, qui circumciduntur, legem custodiunt, sed volunt vos circumcidi, ut in carne vestra glorientur. ¹⁴Mihi autem absit gloriari nisi in cruce Domini nostri Iesu Christi, per quem mihi

"for whatever a man sows, that he will also reap" (v. 7). The metaphor of sowing, often found in the Bible, is rich in content (see Ps 107:37; Prov 6:19; Mt 13:4ff; Jn 4:37; 1 Cor 9:11). St John of Avila makes the following comment on these verses: "He had said that to do good was to sow; and when one sows, at first there is nothing but loss: the sower divests himself of what he has for the sake of what he hopes to gain. He is referring to the same metaphor, and says that we should not grow weary, we should not give up doing good, we should put our hope in God" (*Lecciones sobre Galatas*, loc. cit.).

*6:11–18 Paul ends the letter with words written in his own hand and added to the manuscript written by the scribe to whom he has been dictating (cf. 1 Cor 16:21; Col 4:18; 2 Thess 3:17). Before signing off, Paul provides a brief summary of the teaching contained in the letter, exposing the agenda of those who have been leading the Galatians astray.

St Paul was well aware that preaching Christ crucified was a stumbling block to Jews and folly to Gentiles (see 1 Cor 1:23). Nevertheless, the mystery of the cross was the very essence of apostolic preaching (see Acts 2:22–24; 3:13–15), for it opens the only possible way to eternal life and salvation. The Judaizers boasted of bearing

in their bodies the sign of the Old Covenant, circumcision; but Paul shows that there is only one sign, only one ground for boasting—the cross of our Lord Jesus Christ, by which he sealed the New Covenant and brought about the Redemption. The cross is the sign that identifies the Christian. Far from being folly, it is the strength and the wisdom of God.

In line with what St Paul says here, Christian tradition has produced writings of extraordinary piety. The anonymous author of a second-century homily has this to say, for example: "When I am overtaken by fear of God, the cross is my protection; when I stumble, it is my help and my support; when I engage in combat, my prize; when I conquer, my crown. The cross is for me a narrow path, a narrow way—Jacob's ladder, which angels ascend and descend, at the top of which the Lord is to be found." St Anselm, for his part, comments: "O Cross, chosen and designed to do such ineffable good: you are praised and exalted not so much by the minds and tongues of men, or even angels, as by the works that have been done thanks to you. O Cross, in whom and by whom salvation and life have come to me, in whom and by whom all good things come to me: God would not have me glory unless it be in you (cf. Gal 6:14)" (*Meditationes et orationes*, 4). And St Teresa Benedicta (Stein) writes: "The soul

l Or *through whom*

cified to me, and I to the world. ¹⁵For neither circumcision counts for anything, nor uncircumcision, but a new creation. ¹⁶Peace and mercy be upon all who walk by this rule, upon the Israel of God.

Gal 5:6
1 Cor 7:19

Ps 125:4
Phil 3:3, 15

¹⁷Henceforth let no man trouble me; for I bear on my body the marks of Jesus.

2 Cor 4:10; 12:7

¹⁸The grace of our Lord Jesus Christ be with your spirit, brethren. Amen.

Phil 4:23
2 Tim 4:22
Philem 25

mundus crucifixus est, et ego mundo. ¹⁵Neque enim circumcisio aliquid est neque praeputium, sed nova creatura. ¹⁶Et quicumque hanc regulam secuti fuerint, pax super illos et misericordia et super Israel Dei. ¹⁷De cetero nemo mihi molestus sit; ego enim stigmata Iesu in super corpore meo porto. ¹⁸Gratia Domini nostri Iesu Christi cum spiritu vestro, fratres. Amen.

was created for union with God through the cross, redeemed by the cross, consumed and sanctified by the cross, so that it would be marked with the sign of the cross for all eternity" (*The Science of the Cross*, 337).

The expression "new creation" (v. 15) indicates the fact that divine grace transcends every human action; things exist because they have been created, but man lives in a supernatural order of being because he has been "re-created". "We have been created," St Thomas comments, "and we have received our natural being through Adam; but that creature grew old, and died, and therefore the Lord, by constituting us in the state of grace, worked a kind of new creation [...]. Thus, by means of the new creation, that is, through faith in Christ and through the love of God, which has been poured into our hearts, we are renewed and we are united to Christ" (*Super Galatas,* ad loc.).

The "marks" mentioned in v. 17 are reminiscent of the way slaves used to be branded to show which family they belonged to. St Paul may be referring to that custom: he declares himself to be a slave of the Lord, marked by the scars and sufferings caused by his proclamation of the Gospel—marks more glorious than those made by circumcision.

THE LETTER OF PAUL TO THE

EPHESIANS

Introduction

In the canon of the New Testament, the great Pauline letters (Romans, Galatians, and 1 and 2 Corinthians) are followed by what are usually called the "Captivity Letters" because they contain references that imply they were written from prison. The Letter to the Ephesians is placed first among these because it is the longest and the most significant from a doctrinal point of view. It contains a refined synthesis of the thinking that runs through all Paul's letters.

It is possible that this was a circular letter for all the churches of Phrygia, a region that included not only Ephesus, but other cities such as Colossae and Laodicea: some of the oldest and most important manuscripts do not mention Ephesus in 1:1 [see RSV note **a**]; moreover, no specific individuals are mentioned, and there are none of the usual messages and greetings at the end.

1. STRUCTURE AND CONTENT

Like all of St Paul's other letters, Ephesians opens with a greeting and blessing in which the writer and the addressees, the Ephesians, are mentioned.

The letter can be divided into six sections. The introductory section, which is formal in tone, focuses on the main theme—the salvific mystery of God brought into being in the Church, whose Head is Christ (1:3–23). The other five sections are a series of concentric circles which centre on the mission of St Paul, which is to preach God's plan to bring all mankind together as a single people (fourth section).

Within this understanding of the letter as a whole, the second section (2:1–10) is about the Gentiles becoming part of the Church; God, who is rich in mercy, has called them to a new life. In the third section (2:11–22) we are told that Christ has brought Gentiles and Jews together to form one people; those who were Gentiles have become fellow citizens with the saints and members of God's household.

Having dealt with these themes, the letter reaches its defining point in the fourth section (3:1–21), which deals with the Apostle's mission—to proclaim to the Gentiles that they too are called to be members of Christ's body; here Paul beseeches God to strengthen his readers, so that Christ may dwell in their hearts.

In the fifth section (4:1–16), which links up with the third, the Apostle returns to the theme of the unity of the Church and the duty incumbent on all Christians to protect it. The sixth and final section (4:17—6:20) is about the new life in Christ and in the Church: all should strive to practise those virtues that create harmony and make it a delight for all to be members of Christ's Body. Christian holiness also affects family life: Paul devotes quite an extensive section of the letter to showing the implications of Christian teaching for husband and wife, parents and children, and masters and servants.

The letter ends with references to the bearer, and a blessing (6:21–24).

2. CONTEXT

As already mentioned, this may well have been a circular letter to the churches of the Phrygian region. The words "at Ephesus" (see 1:1; and RSV note **a**) do not appear in the oldest and most important Greek manuscripts; papyrus 46 does not contain them; nor did they appear, it seems, in the manuscripts available to Tertullian and Origen. The letter contains no reference to Paul's having preached in the city, a reference which would have helped to date when, more or less, the letter was written in relation to other episodes in Paul's life. It does mention that Paul is a prisoner at the time of writing (cf. 3:1 and 4:1), but this is not a very useful detail because, according to the Acts of the Apostles, St Paul was imprisoned for long periods and in a number of places—and he served more sentences in prison than are mentioned in that book.

This means that we need to look at the literary style and the content of the text to see where the Letter to the Ephesians fits into the Pauline corpus. As regards the language of the letter, the Greek original contains many very long sentences, far more relatively speaking than are to be found in the "great" letters (Romans, Galatians, 1 and 2 Corinthians) or in the First Letter to the Thessalonians, which were the first letters written with the Apostle's authority. The Greek text of Ephesians contains many words and turns of phrase that are not found in those letters but which often appear in later Christian writings. This evidence suggests that this text was written sometime after the first Pauline letters.

Even though there are these differences between Ephesians and the "great" letters, the letter is (in both form and content) quite similar to the Letter to the Colossians, and, therefore, scholars have concluded that Ephesians and Colossians were written in similar circumstances. It is quite likely that Colossians was written first, and then, using some of the ideas in Colossians but omitting any specific reference to that Christian community, the Letter to the Ephesians was written.

The letter is addressed to Christians of Gentile background (see 2:11), to whom the Gospel has already been preached (see 4:20–21), to help them come to a deeper understanding of God's plan of salvation effected in Christ and the Church, and not to yield to the temptation to repudiate all things Jewish, for Christ "has made us both [Jews and Gentiles] one, and has broken down the dividing wall of hostility" (2:14).

Study of the literary features of the letter does not enable us to say with certainty whether it was written by St Paul himself or (and this is what many scholars nowadays think more likely) by a successor of his who holds in high regard the "holy apostles and prophets" (see 3:5) and who, inspired by the Holy Spirit, wrote the letter in order to shed further light on the faith held by people who owed their conversion to apostolic preaching. Certainly, Tradition has always regarded the letter as having been written by St Paul himself. The Church has taken it to be a book of sacred writing and has, from the start, included it in the canon of Holy Scripture.

3. MESSAGE

The information available to us from both biblical and extrabiblical sources indicates that the Christian communities founded by St Paul had to defend themselves against ideas that were widespread in their cultures and which some Christians would later try to formulate as aspects of Christian belief. These ideas may be traceable to a sense of *angst* or an existential crisis prevalent at the time in the Hellenistic world in Asia and Egypt, of which there is abundant evidence in writings from the first and second centuries. There was a perception that mankind was at the mercy of forces it could not control, and that man was in some way a stranger to, or not at home in, the world. According to this way of thinking, the cosmos had been invaded by dark powers of evil, and only those who had been initiated into knowledge (*gnosis*) of the divine mysteries could survive against that evil: this *gnosis* enabled them to exist in their true fatherland, the world of "divine plenitude" (*pléroma*). The world existed in the abyss between darkness and light. Later on, in the second century, all these ideas were developed even further, giving rise to what is called "Gnosticism".

In opposition to these Hellenistic-Gnostic notions, Paul's letters argue, in various ways and different passages, that Christ is superior to all powers, be they earthly or celestial: he is Lord of all, and he is the only Saviour; nothing lies outside the lordship of Jesus Christ, whose Body is the Church.

This conviction leads to a profound doctrinal reflection on the nature of the Church and on how mankind will find its unity within it. Both these themes are approached from the perspective of belief in Christ and all that it entails and implies: he, who has universal lordship, is the one who brings redeemed mankind together in a harmonious unity, and he is the Head of the Church, which is his Body.

The theological response to the problem of the human condition found in the Letter to the Ephesians is detailed and coherent, and invites us to consider key aspects of the Christian life— acceptance of the Word of God (cf. Eph 1:13) and Baptism (cf. 4:5).

Jesus Christ is Lord of all

Harmony among mankind, and even within the entire cosmos, derives primarily from the dominion that Jesus Christ has and exercises over all creation. There can be no question of a conflict between two equally powerful entities, a power of good and a power of evil, for Christ is Lord of all things. In him is fulfilled what the psalmist said—that God has placed all things under his feet (see Ps 8:6). God's power was displayed in its fullness when he raised Christ from the dead and exalted him in glory, placing him at his right hand in heaven. That is why he is "far above all rule and authority and power and dominion, and above every name that is named, not only in this age but also in that which is to come" (1:21).

In Christ its Head, the entire universe finds cohesion (see 1:10), and it is he, too, who gives peace and unity to the new people, making it one body with himself, which he nourishes with all the graces it needs for its "upbuilding in love" (see 4:16). This leads St Paul to comment further on Christ as the Head and "Saviour" of the body (5:23). The emphasis with which Jesus Christ is called "Saviour" marks his role with respect to the Church. He is its head not only in the sense of being the primary and most perfect member of the Church: the Church's life of grace flows from Christ (the Head) to his body (the Church). The Second Vatican Council recalls this teaching when it says that "by the greatness of his power he [Christ] rules heaven and earth, and with his all-surpassing perfection and activity he fills the whole body with the riches of his glory."[1]

The Church

That Christ is Lord of all things can be appreciated in its fullness by the fact that he is the Head of the Church, which he establishes, gives life to and loves. Jesus Christ "assembles" not only the

---

1 Vatican II, *Lumen gentium*, 7.

"scattered people of Israel" but also those who do not belong to Israel, the Gentiles. These two peoples, Jews and Gentiles, are destined by God's will to form a single people, the People of God, an image which is deeply rooted in the Bible and which Vatican II's Dogmatic Constitution *Lumen gentium* takes up and develops in its second chapter.[2]

The idea of the Church as the Body of Christ is found in other Pauline letters,[3] but it is given special emphasis in this letter. Here, most of all, the focus is on the Church universal. In the earlier Pauline letters the word *ekklesía* is normally used to designate a particular community, but now the Church is depicted as something "catholic", universal, not just local.

The entire Letter to the Ephesians is a call for unity with the one Lord, Christ. There are no divisions that separate members of Christ's body from one another. The fact that he is the Head means that the Church, which encompasses all Christians, forms one body with Christ (see 4:4). Christ the Head distributes his gifts and charisms to the faithful: "His gifts were that some should be apostles, some prophets, some evangelists, some pastors and teachers, for the equipment of the saints, for the work of ministry, for building up the body of Christ" (4:11–12). Paul later underlines this teaching when he says that Christ loves the Church as something that belongs to him, which he cherishes (see 5:29) and nourishes with an abundance of grace.

The Church is also depicted in this letter as the temple of God, a dwelling place of God built on the foundation of the apostles and prophets, with Christ himself as the cornerstone, "in whom the whole structure is joined together and grows into a holy temple in the Lord" (2:21). Christians are depicted as living stones, harmoniously "built into it for a dwelling place of God in the Spirit" (2:22). Those who form part of this building are no longer strangers to one another but "fellow citizens with the saints and members of the household of God" (2:19).

Enlightened by the Holy Spirit, St Paul delves further into the mystery of the Church, showing it to be a supernatural institution with features that make it different from any merely human institution, for the Church is Christ's Spouse (see 5:21–23). The image of the spouse, often used in the Old Testament, is used also in the New, to describe God's relationship with his people; of course, the prophets and sacred writers also employed many other similes to describe God's great love for and mercy towards mankind.[4]

By the highlighting of Christ's role as Saviour of mankind, the salvific role of the Church also becomes evident. For it is through the Church that people come to know the mystery of Redemption that God had kept hidden from all eternity (see 1:9). This Redemption which is brought about and revealed in Christ (see 3:3, 9) reaches mankind through the Church. "Since the Church, in Christ, is in the nature of a sacrament—a sign and instrument, that is, of communion with God and of unity among men—she [...] proposes, for the benefit of the faithful and of the whole world, to set forth as clearly as possible [...] her own nature and universal mission."[5]

---

2 See Vatican II, *Lumen gentium*, 9–17. 3 See Rom 12:5; 1 Cor 10:16; 12:13, 27; Col 1:18, 24; 2:19; 3:15. 4 See, e.g., Is 1:21; 49:18; Jer 2:2; Ezek 16; Hos 2:16–18; Mk 2:19; Jn 3:29; Rev 19:7–9. 5 See Vatican II, *Lumen gentium*, 1.

Ephesians

1. INTRODUCTION*

Greeting

1 [1]Paul, an apostle of Christ Jesus by the will of God,
To the saints who are* also faithful[a] in Christ Jesus:
[2]Grace to you and peace from God our Father and the Lord Jesus Christ.

1 Cor 1:1–17
Rom 1:7
1 Cor 1:1

1 Cor 1:2

Christ, head of the Church and source of unity

[3]Blessed be the God and Father of our Lord Jesus Christ, who has blessed us in Christ with every spiritual blessing in the heavenly places, [4]even as he chose us in him before

Tob 13:1
Acts 2:33
1 Pet 1:3
2 Cor 1:3
Jn 17:24
Eph 5:27
Col 1:12–22; 3:14
Phil 2:15
1 Cor 1:8–9

[1][1]Paulus apostolus Christi Iesu per voluntatem Dei sanctis, qui sunt Ephesi, et fidelibusin Christo Iesu: [2]gratia vobis et pax a Deo Patre nostro et Domino Iesu Christo. [3]Benedictus Deus et Pater Domini nostri Iesu Christi, / qui benedixit nos in omni benedictione spiritali in caelestibus in Christo, / [4]sicut elegit nos in ipso ante mundi constitutionem, / ut essemus sancti et immaculati in conspectu eius in caritate, / [5]qui praedestinavit

*1:1–23 The central theme of the letter is the Church, whose Head is Christ. This section outlines the divine plan of salvation, presenting it as part of the mystery of God's eternity, revealed in time and history through Christ and the Church.

1:1–2 The letter opens in much the same way as the previous ones did—a greeting, followed by a thanksgiving hymn (1:3–14; cf. Rom 1:1ff; 1 Cor 1:1ff). Given that the words "in Ephesus" are absent from many manuscripts, it may be that this was a circular letter to the churches in the general Ephesus area. It contains no references to the circumstances of any particular Christian community.

1:3–14 Paul begins with a hymn of praise (vv. 3–10), listing the benefits or blessings that are part of God's plan of salvation; in this and other Pauline letters this is called the "mystery" of his will (v. 9). It ranges from God's eternal plan for the salvation of all human beings, through the redemption brought about by Christ, to the point when all things in heaven and earth are united ("recapitulated") in Christ. He then goes on to explain that that divine plan of salvation encompasses both Jews (vv. 11–12) and Gentiles (vv. 13–14).

1:4 "He chose us". The word translated here as "chose" is the same one as is used in the Greek translation of the Old Testament with reference to God's election of Israel. "In him", in Christ, the invitation to form part of the People of God is extended to everyone: we are all called to holiness (cf. the notes on Mt 5:17–48 and Lk 12:22–34). In the same way as in the Old Testament a victim offered to God had to be perfect, unblemished (see Ex 12:5; Lev 9:3), the holiness to which God has destined us admits of no imperfection. St Jerome, distinguishing between the "holy" and the "blameless" comments: "'Holy' does not always mean 'immaculate'. Children, for example, are immaculate, for they have not committed any sin with any part of their bodies; yet they are not holy, for holiness is won by good, firm will and long struggle. 'Immaculate' is the one who has not sinned; 'holy' is the one who is full of virtue" (*Commentarii in Ephesios, 1, 1, 4*).

"In love" (v. 5) refers to God's love for us, but also our love for him: he is the ultimate reason for the effort we make to live a blameless life, for "virtue will save no one, unless there be love" (St John Chrysostom, *In Ephesios*, 1, 1, 5, 14).

The holiness to which we are called becomes attainable through Christ (see 1:5): "Think about what the Holy Spirit says, and let yourself be filled with awe and gratitude: *Elegit nos ante mundi constitutionem*—he chose us before the foundation of the world, *ut essemus sancti in conspectu eius!*—that we might be holy in his

a Other ancient authorities read *who are at Ephesus and faithful*

Jn 1:12
Rom 18:14–17, 20
Gal 4:5–7
1 Jn 3:1
Mt 3:17; 17:5
Lk 1:28
2 Cor 1:14
Phil 1:11
Rom 3:24-25
Eph 2:7
Col 1:13–14
Eph 1:18; 3:17–19
1 Cor 1:5, 30; 2:12
Col 1:9
Rom 3:25; 16:25
1 Cor 2:1, 7; 4:1
Mk 1:15
1 Cor 15:25–27
Gal 4:4ff
Col 1:16, 20
Phil 2:10–11
Deut 7:6
Dan 4:32
Rom 8:17, 28, 30
Gal 3:29
Rom 10:9, 14–17
2 Cor 1:21–22
Gal 2:5; 3:12, 14
Col 1:5
1 Thess 1:6; 2:3
Eph 4:30

the foundation of the world, that we should be holy and blameless before him. [5]He destined us in love[b] to be his sons through Jesus Christ, according to the purpose of his will, [6]to the praise of his glorious grace which he freely bestowed on us in the Beloved. [7]In him we have redemption through his blood, the forgiveness of our trespasses, according to the riches of his grace [8]which he lavished upon us. [9]For he has made known to us in all wisdom and insight the mystery of his will, according to his purpose which he set forth in Christ [10]as a plan for the fullness of time, to unite* all things in him, things in heaven and things on earth.

[11]In him, according to the purpose of him who accomplishes all things according to the counsel of his will, [12]we who first hoped in Christ have been destined and appointed to live for the praise of his glory. [13]In him you also, who have heard the word of truth, the gospel of your salvation, and have believed in him, were sealed with the promised Holy Spirit, [14]who is the guarantee of our inheritance until we acquire possession of it, to the praise of his glory.

nos in adoptionem filiorum / per Iesum Christum in ipsum, / secundum beneplacitum voluntatis suae, / [6]in laudem gloriae gratiae suae, / in qua gratificavit nos in Dilecto, / [7]in quo habemus redemptionem per sanguinem eius, / remissionem peccatorum, / secundum divitias gratiae eius, / [8]quam superabundare fecit in nobis / in omni sapientia et prudentia / [9]notum faciens nobis mysterium voluntatis suae, / secundum beneplacitum eius, quod proposuit in eo, / [10]in dispensationem plenitudinis temporum: / recapitulare omnia in Christo, / quae in caelis et quae in terra, in ipso; [11]in quo etiam sorte vocati sumus, praedestinati secundum propositum eius, qui omnia operatur secundum consilium voluntatis suae, [12]ut simus in laudem gloriae eius, qui ante speravimus in Christo; [13]in quo et vos cum audissetis verbum veritatis, evangelium salutis vestrae, in quo et cre-

presence. To be holy isn't easy, but it isn't difficult either. To be holy is to be a good Christian, to resemble Christ. The more closely a person resembles Christ, the more Christian he is, the more he belongs to Christ, the holier he is" (St Josemaría Escrivá, *The Forge*, 10).

1:5–6 God treats the people of Israel with a father's affection, as his child: "When Israel was a child, I loved him, and out of Egypt I called my son" (Hos 11:1). In Jesus Christ all mankind is destined to become part of the People of God and to be his sons and daughters ("*in adoptionem filiorum*"), no longer in a merely metaphorical sense, but in fact: God's only Son, one in substance with the Father, took on human nature in order to make us sons and daughters of God by adoption (cf. Rom 8:15, 29; 9:4; Gal 4:5). God's glory has been made manifest through his merciful love, which has led him to make us his children in accordance with the eternal purpose of his will. This eternal design "flows from 'fountain-like love', the love of God the Father [...]. God in his great and merciful kindness freely creates us and, moreover, graciously calls us to share in his life and glory. He generously pours out, and never ceases to pour out, his divine goodness, so that he who is Creator of all things might at last become

'everything to everyone' (1 Cor 15:28), thus simultaneously assuring his own glory and our happiness" (Vatican II, *Ad gentes*, 2).

Jesus Christ, the "Beloved" of the Father (1:6), brought about our redemption. To "redeem" means to "set free". God redeemed the people of Israel from slavery in Egypt. By smearing the lintels of their doors with the blood of the lamb, the Israelites were enabled to protect their first-born sons from death (see Ex 12:21–28). However, that redemption from slavery in Egypt was only a foreshadowing of the Redemption that Christ would bring about: "Christ our Lord achieved this task [of redeeming mankind and giving perfect glory to God] principally by the paschal mystery of his blessed passion, resurrection from the dead, and glorious ascension" (Vatican II, *Sacrosanctum Concilium*, 5). By shedding his blood on the cross, Jesus has redeemed us from the slavery of sin: "When we reflect that we have been ransomed 'not with perishable things such as silver or gold but with the precious blood of Christ, like that of a lamb without blemish or spot' (1 Pet 1:18f), we are naturally led to conclude that we could have received no gift more salutary than this power [given to the Church] of forgiving sins, which proclaims the ineffable providence of God and

b Or *before him in love, having destined us*

Thanksgiving and prayer

Is 43:21(LXX)
Rom 3:24; 8:23
2 Cor 1:22; 5:5
1 Pet 2:9
Rom 1:8
Col 1:3, 9
1 Cor 1:4
Col 1:3
Rom 1:9
Phil 1:9
Col 1:9
Eph 3:16
Jn 5:20
Rom 5:4–5; 8:24–25
Col 1:5
2 Cor 4:36
Acts 9:13
1 Cor 1:18
2 Cor 13:4
Acts 2:24–33
Rom 1:4; 4:24
Col 2:12
Dan 7:14
Phil 2:9
Col 2:10, 15
1 Pet 3:22
Ps 8:6
Mt 28:18
1 Cor 1:25–27
Col 1:18–19
Eph 4:12
Col 1:18; 3:11
Rom 12:5

¹⁵For this reason, because I have heard of your faith in the Lord Jesus and your love^c toward all the saints, ¹⁶I do not cease to give thanks for you, remembering you in my prayers, ¹⁷that the God of our Lord Jesus Christ, the Father of glory, may give you a spirit of wisdom and of revelation in the knowledge of him, ¹⁸having the eyes of your hearts enlightened, that you may know what is the hope to which he has called you, what are the riches of his glorious inheritance in the saints, ¹⁹and what is the immeasurable greatness of his power in us who believe, according to the working of his great might ²⁰which he accomplished in Christ when he raised him from the dead and made him sit at his right hand in the heavenly places, ²¹far above all rule and authority and power and dominion, and above every name that is named, not only in this age but also in that which is to come; ²²and he has put all things under his feet and has made him the head over all things for the church, ²³which is his body, the fullness of him who fills all in all.

dentes signati estis Spiritu promissionis Sancto, ¹⁴qui est arrabon hereditatis nostrae in redemptionem acquisitionis, in laudem gloriae ipsius. ¹⁵Propterea et ego audiens fidem vestram, quae est in Domino Iesu, et dilectionem in omnes sanctos, ¹⁶non cesso gratias agens pro vobis memoriam faciens in orationibus meis, ¹⁷ut Deus Domini nostri Iesu Christi, Pater gloriae, det vobis Spiritum sapientiae et revelationis in agnitione eius, ¹⁸illuminatos oculos cordis vestri, ut sciatis quae sit spes vocationis eius, quae divitiae gloriae hereditatis eius in sanctis ¹⁹et quae sit supereminens magnitudo virtutis eius in nos, qui credimus, secundum operationem potentiae virtutis eius, ²⁰quam operatus est in Christo, suscitans illum a mortuis et constituens ad dexteram suam in caelestibus ²¹supra omnem principatum et potestatem et virtutem et dominationem et omne nomen, quod nominatur non solum in hoc saeculo sed et in futuro; ²²et *omnia subiecit sub pedibus eius*, et ipsum dedit caput supra omnia ecclesiae, ²³quae est corpus ipsius, plenitudo eius, qui omnia in omnibus adimpletur.   [2] ¹Et vos, cum essetis mortui delictis et peccatis vestris, ²in quibus ali-

the excess of his love towards us" (*Roman Catechism*, 1, 11, 10).

1:9–14 The "mystery" (v. 9) is God's design to save mankind in Christ. To begin with, this plan was known to God alone; then it began to take effect and to be revealed in a harmonious way, in different stages or at different times (*kairoí*) over the course of history. It began with the "choice" (see 1:4) made by God; this was followed by the call to mankind to be "adoptive sons" (see 1:5–6), which led to "redemption" (1:7–8), and it will reach its fullness when all things are united ("recapitulated") in Christ (v. 10), who draws to himself a people that includes, along with Israel (vv. 11–12), men and women of every race and nation who have believed in the Gospel and have been sealed with the Holy Spirit to receive the inheritance of God's children (vv. 13–14).

"What does 'recapitulate' [v. 10: 'to unite'] mean?", St John Chrysostom asks himself. "To 'recapitulate'," he comments, "is to unite one thing with another. But we want to come closer to the truth. According to convention and common use, to recapitulate is to express a long discourse in more concise terms. The same

meaning applies here, too: all of history is recapitulated, is united in Christ [...]. Something else is revealed here also, which is that there is one Head for all creation, for angels as well as men" (*In Ephesios*, 1, 1, 10, 19).

1:15–23 The faithful to whom St Paul is writing, most of them Gentile in background, were very eager to "know" the divine mysteries (cf. the Introduction to this letter, above). This desire may have been influenced by doctrinal and cultural trends of the time; but it was, in general, a well-intentioned curiosity. And so we find Paul asking God for a spirit of wisdom and revelation, so that they are enabled to know what is truly important, Jesus Christ in whom all fullness dwells. Knowledge of the mystery of Christ provides a solid ground for love (v. 18): "The Apostle speaks of the future as though it had already been fulfilled, which is true to the power of God, for everything that must come about in the fullness of time is already present in Christ, who is all fullness. All that has yet to happen is not and will not be new, but the fulfilment of the plan of salvation" (St Hilary of Poitiers, *De Trinitate*, 11, 31).

c Other ancient authorities omit *your love*

2. SALVATION IN CHRIST*

Rom 5:12–14;
7:11, 13; 8:10
Col 1:21; 2:13
Jn 12:31
Acts 26:18
Gal 5:17
Col 3:7
Ex 34:6
Rom 5:8; 8:39
1 Pet 1:3
Rom 5:8; 6:4
Col 2:12–13; 3:1–4
Eph 1:20
Phil 3:20
Ps 22:30–31
Eph 1:7; 3:10
Rom 1:16; 3:24; 5:1;
9:23; 3:27
Gal 2:16, 21
Rom 3:27
1 Cor 1:29, 31
Gal 1:4; 5:16
Col 1:10

2 ¹And you he made alive, when you were dead through the trespasses and sins ²in which you once walked, following the course of this world, following the prince of the power of the air, the spirit that is now at work in the sons of disobedience. ³Among these we all once lived in the passions of our flesh, following the desires of body and mind, and so we were by nature children of wrath, like the rest of mankind. ⁴But God, who is rich in mercy, out of the great love with which he loved us, ⁵even when we were dead through our trespasses, made us alive together with Christ (by grace you have been saved), ⁶and raised us up with him, and made us sit with him in the heavenly places in Christ Jesus, ⁷that in the coming ages he might show the immeasurable riches of his grace in kindness toward us in Christ Jesus. ⁸For by grace you have been saved through faith; and this is not your own doing, it is the gift of God—⁹not because of works, lest any man should boast. ¹⁰For we are his workmanship, created in Christ Jesus for good works, which God prepared beforehand, that we should walk in them.

quando ambulastis secundum saeculum mundi huius, secundum principem potestatis aeris, spiritus, qui nunc operatur in filios diffidentiae; ³in quibus et nos omnes aliquando conversati sumus in concupiscentiis carnis nostrae, facientes voluntates carnis et cogitationum, et eramus natura filii irae sicut et ceteri. ⁴Deus autem, qui dives est in misericordia, propter nimiam caritatem suam, qua dilexit nos, ⁵et cum essemus mortui peccatis, convivificavit nos Christo—gratia estis salvati—⁶et conresuscitavit et consedere fecit in caelestibus in Christo Iesu, ⁷ut ostenderet in saeculis supervenientibus abundantes divitias gratiae suae in bonitate super nos in Christo Iesu. ⁸Gratia enim estis salvati per fidem; et hoc non ex vobis, Dei donum est: ⁹non ex operibus, ut ne quis glorietur. ¹⁰Ipsius enim sumus factura, creati in Christo Iesu in opera bona, quae praeparavit

*2:1–10 The main body of the letter is made up of five sections, all of which centre on a single, key theme—St Paul's mission as an apostle of Christ. The Apostle has been called to preach God's saving mystery, his plan to draw together all mankind to form one, Jew and Gentile alike. This people is a Body whose Head is Christ. The central section (3:1–21) deals with this theme; in the preceding and subsequent sections, Paul deals with various aspects of the unity of the Church (2:11–22 and 4:1–16). At the beginning and the end of the letter, he focuses on those Gentiles who have become members of Christ, to help them appreciate their undeserved gift (vv. 1–10) and to draw practical consequences for their new lives as members of Christ and the Church (4:17—6:20).

2:1–7 Some of the faithful to whom the letter was written came to believe that (the much sought-after) "knowledge" of the divine mysteries was all that a person needed in order to be saved. St Paul now explains that Christian initiation, and the new lifestyle it entails, is not something purely human, that is, it is not about attaining salvation through one's own efforts: it

is a response to God's love; he of his own initiative has given us grace, without our meriting it. Even though both Gentiles and Jews were in a state of sin (vv. 1–3), almighty God in his mercy has given them all life in Christ (vv. 4–7). The initiative comes from God, who is "rich in mercy" (v. 4): "The richness of mercy consists in giving to those who have not asked for anything. Such is God's love for us that, having made us, He does not want us to grow lazy; therefore, you should love his work" (Ambrosiaster, *Ad Ephesios*, ad loc.).

The "prince of the power of the air" (v. 2; cf. 6:12) is one of the beings generically referred to elsewhere in New Testament writings as "principalities and powers" (see 3:10; Col 1:16; 2:15; 1 Pet 3:22). These were superhuman entities which, according to thinking prevalent at the time, inhabited regions located between heaven and earth and which exercised a baneful influence on the world. Christ has defeated them and, by his death on the cross, ensured that they have no power over us (see Col 1:20; 2:14–15).

2:8–10 In his Letter to the Romans, St Paul taught that, contrary to what Jews believed, sal-

3. MEMBERSHIP OF THE CHURCH*

[11]Therefore remember that at one time you Gentiles in the flesh, called the uncircumcision by what is called the circumcision, which is made in the flesh by
hands—[12]remember that you were at that time separated from Christ, alienated
from the commonwealth of Israel, and strangers to the covenants of promise,
having no hope and without God in the world. [13]But now in Christ Jesus you who
once were far off have been brought near in the blood of Christ.[14]For he is our
peace, who has made us both one, and has broken down the dividing wall* of hostility, [15]by abolishing in his flesh the law of commandments and ordinances, that
he might create in himself one new man in place of the two, so making peace,
[16]and might reconcile us both to God in one body through the cross, thereby bringing the hostility to an end. [17]And he came and preached peace to you who were far
off and peace to those who were near; [18]for through him we both have access in
one Spirit to the Father. [19]So then you are no longer strangers and sojourners, but
you are fellow citizens with the saints and members of the household of God,

Rom 2:25–29
Col 2:11, 13

Rom 9:4
Gal 4:8–9
Col 1:21–27

Is 57:19
Acts 2:39
Col 1:20
Eph 2:17

Jn 14:27
Gal 3:28
Jn 14:27
Rom 5:1
Col 1:20, 22; 2:14
Eph 4:24
Col 2:14
2 Cor 5:17
Rom 5:9–11
2 Cor 5:18–21
Col 1:20, 22
Is 57:19
Eph 3:12; 4:4
Ex 12:48ff
Heb 12:22

Deus, ut in illis ambulemus. [11]Propter quod memores estote quod aliquando vos gentes in carne, qui dicimini praeputium ab ea, quae dicitur circumcisio in carne manufacta, [12]quia eratis illo in tempore sine Christo, alienati a conversatione Israel et extranei testamentorum promissionis,
spem non habentes et sine Deo in mundo. [13]Nunc autem in Christo Iesu vos, qui aliquando eratis longe, facti estis prope in sanguine Christi. [14]Ipse
est enim pax nostra, qui fecit utraque unum et medium parietem maceriae solvit, inimicitiam, in carne sua, [15]legem mandatorum in decretis evac-
uans, ut duos condat in semetipso in unum novum hominem, faciens pacem, [16]et reconciliet ambos in uno corpore Deo per crucem interficiens
inimicitiam in semetipso. [17]Et veniens *evangelizavit pacem* vobis, *qui longe fuistis, et pacem his, qui prope*; [18]quoniam per ipsum habemus accessum ambo in uno Spiritu ad Patrem. [19]Ergo iam non estis extranei et advenae, sed estis concives sanctorum et domestici Dei, [20]superaedificati

vation is not to be found in observance of the
prescriptions of the Law of Moses; it is a gratuitous gift from God (see the notes on Romans
from Rom 2:18 to Rom 4:2, especially Rom
3:21–31). Now, in a different context, writing to
Christians from the Greek world, where there
were many different groups hoping to find salvation through initiation into powerful mysteries, Paul once more proclaims that salvation does
not come from man but is an unmerited gift that
God grants through faith in Jesus Christ. He is
emphatic about the gratuitous nature of salvation
because he wants to "ensure that no one may
begin to think, even privately, that 'we save ourselves by our good works; or, if not by our good
works, by our faith; one way or another, we save
ourselves.' Thus, the Apostle went on to explain
that faith is not a fruit of our own will but a gift
of God. This does not mean that man is not free,
but that man's free will itself comes from God.
We do all things by the grace of God, and it is
through him that we can love what is good" (St
Jerome; *Commentarii in Ephesios*, 1, 2, 8–9).

*2:11–22 Still addressing Christians of Gentile
background, the Apostle stresses that, when con-

sidering the mystery of Christ, they must not
boast of self-reliance. The redemption won by
Christ on the cross has brought Jews and Gentiles together in peace (vv. 13–15) and reconciled
them both to God (vv. 16–18). They need to
remember that, through Christ, they and the Jews
have been made into one people and therefore,
as Gentiles, they have been given a share in the
heritage that God promised Israel. They have
been called, along with the Jews, to be members
of God's household, the Church, which is built
on the apostles and prophets, and bound together
by and in Christ (vv. 19–22). "With our eyes
fixed on the mystery of Golgotha we should be
reminded always of that *'vertical' dimension* of
division and reconciliation concerning the relationship between man and God, a dimension
which in the eyes of faith always prevails over
the *'horizontal' dimension*, that is to say, over the
reality of division between people and the need
for reconciliation between them. For we know
that reconciliation between people is and can
only be the fruit of the redemptive act of Christ,
who died and rose again to conquer the kingdom
of sin, to re-establish the covenant with God and
thus break down the dividing wall which sin had

Is 28:16
Rev 21:14
Rom 15:20
1 Cor 3:9–11
1 Pet 2:4–5
²⁰built upon the foundation of the apostles and prophets, Christ Jesus himself being the cornerstone, ²¹in whom the whole structure is joined together and grows into a holy temple in the Lord; ²²in whom you also are built into it for a dwelling place of God in the Spirit.

1 Cor 3:16–17; 6:19
2 Cor 6:16
1 Pet 2:5
Rev 21:3

4. PAUL'S MISSION*

Revelation of the mystery of Christ

Eph 4:1
Phil 1:7, 13, 17
Col 1:24–29
2 Tim 2:9
1 Cor 4:2; 9:17
Rom 16:25
Gal 1:1, 11f, 15f
Eph 1:9
Col 1:26
2 Cor 11:5–6
Col 1:26
1 Pet 1:10–12
3 ¹For this reason I, Paul, a prisoner for Christ Jesus on behalf of you Gentiles — ²assuming that you have heard of the stewardship of God's grace that was given to me for you, ³how the mystery* was made known to me by revelation, as I have written briefly. ⁴When you read this you can perceive my insight into the mystery of Christ, ⁵which was not made known to the sons of men in other generations as it has now been revealed to his holy apostles and prophets by the Spirit; ⁶that is, how the Gentiles are fellow heirs, members of the same body, and partakers of the promise in Christ Jesus through the gospel.

Eph 2:12–19
Col 1:27; 3:10–11

Rom 15:15ff
2 Cor 3:6
Col 1:23, 25, 29
⁷Of this gospel I was made a minister according to the gift of God's grace which was given me by the working of his power. ⁸To me, though I am the very least of all the saints, this grace was given, to preach to the Gentiles the unsearchable riches

Rom 1:5
Gal 1:16; 2:8

super fundamentum apostolorum et prophetarum, ipso summo angulari lapide Christo Iesu, ²¹in quo omnis aedificatio compacta crescit in templum sanctum in Domino, ²²in quo et vos coaedificamini in habitaculum Dei in Spiritu.   [3] ¹Huius rei gratia ego Paulus vinctus Christi Iesu pro vobis gentibus—²si tamen audistis dispensationem gratiae Dei, quae data est mihi pro vobis, ³quoniam secundum revelationem notum mihi factum est mysterium, sicut supra scripsi in brevi, ⁴prout potestis legentes intellegere prudentiam meam in mysterio Christi, ⁵quod aliis generationibus non innotuit filiis hominum, sicuti nunc revelatum est sanctis apostolis eius et prophetis in Spiritu, ⁶esse gentes coheredes et comparticipes promissionis in Christo Iesu per evangelium, ⁷cuius factus sum minister secundum donum gratiae Dei, quae data est mihi secundum operationem virtutis eius. ⁸Mihi omnium sanctorum minimo data est gratia haec: gentibus evangelizare investigabiles divitias Christi ⁹et illuminare

raised up between people" (John Paul II, *Reconciliatio et paenitentia*, 7).

The Redemption has brought something new into being—the Church, which is portrayed as a holy temple, built on the foundation of the apostles and prophets with Christ as its cornerstone (vv. 19–22). "The Church will shake if its foundation shakes, but can Christ shake? As long as Christ does not shake, so shall the Church never weaken until the end of time" (St Augustine, *Enarrationes in Psalmos*, 103).

*3:1–21 The mystery of Christ, the Head of the Church, is not just one more element in Paul's message; it is the essence of the message he has been sent to proclaim (vv. 1–13); hence his fervent prayer that the faithful come to understand his role and his teaching well (vv. 14–21).

3:1–13 St Paul has been sent to reveal the "mystery" to the Gentiles (v. 3). When he preaches, he is acting as a "minister" (v. 7) of the Gospel of

Jesus Christ. As St Thomas Aquinas comments: "I am not carrying out this task as if it were an initiative of my own; I am performing it as a service, a task which comes from God" (*Super Ephesios*, ad loc.).

3:14–21 St Paul conveys the immensity of the mystery of Christ by using a graphic image—a cross, whose extremities extend in every direction, encompassing the entire universe. "Everything comes under the influence of the work of redemption through the Word of God; the Son of God was crucified for all [mankind], and has drawn the sign of the cross on all things" (St Irenaeus, *Demonstratio praedicationis apostolicae*, 34). Knowledge of salvation history and of the "mystery" of Christ allows us to realize the scale of God's love for us; Christian life is based on this understanding: "O Jesus, most meek, the greatest joy of our heart, our endless good, your love embraces us" (*Divine Office*, Solemnity of the Sacred Heart of Jesus, Lauds hymn).

of Christ, [9]and to make all men see what is the plan of the mystery hidden for ages in[d] God who created all things; [10]that through the church the manifold wisdom of God might now be made known to the principalities and powers in the heavenly places. [11]This was according to the eternal purpose which he has realized in Christ Jesus our Lord, [12]in whom we have boldness and confidence of access through our faith in him. [13]So I ask you not to[e] lose heart over what I am suffering for you, which is your glory.

Rom 16:25
Col 1:26

Eph 2:7
1 Pet 1:12
1 Cor 1:21; 2:7–9

Rom 8:34
Eph 1:4

Jn 14:6
2 Cor 1:6–7
Eph 1:4
Eph 2:18
Rom 5:1
Phil 2:17–18
Col 1:24

Prayer for the faithful

[14]For this reason I bow my knees before the Father, [15]from whom every family in heaven and on earth is named, [16]that according to the riches of his glory he may grant you to be strengthened with might through his Spirit in the inner man, [17]and that Christ may dwell in your hearts through faith; that you, being rooted and grounded in love, [18]may have power to comprehend with all the saints what is the breadth and length and height and depth, [19]and to know the love of Christ which surpasses knowledge, that you may be filled with all the fullness of God.

Col 1:9
1 Thess 3:10
1 Cor 8:6
Acts 1:8
Rom 5:5; 8:26
2 Cor 4:16
Col 1:11

Rom 8:10
Gal 2:20
Col 1:23; 2:7
Job 11:7–9
Col 2:2
Eph 1:23
Jn 1:16
2 Cor 5:14–16
Phil 3:8–11
Col 2:2–39

Doxology

[20]Now to him who by the power at work within us is able to do far more abundantly than all that we ask or think, [21]to him be glory in the church and in Christ Jesus to all generations, for ever and ever. Amen.

Eph 1:19
Rom 11:33;
16:25–27
Col 1:29
Rom 15:5–6
2 Cor 1:20

---

omnes, quae sit dispensatio mysterii absconditi a saeculis in Deo, qui omnia creavit, [10]ut innotescat nunc principatibus et potestatibus in caelestibus per ecclesiam multiformis sapientia Dei [11]secundum propositum saeculorum, quod fecit in Christo Iesu Domino nostro, [12]in quo habemus fiduciam et accessum in confidentia per fidem eius. [13]Propter quod peto, ne deficiatis in tribulationibus meis pro vobis, quae est gloria vestra. [14]Huius rei gratia flecto genua mea ad Patrem, [15]ex quo omnis paternitas in caelis et in terra nominatur, [16]ut det vobis secundum divitias gloriae suae virtute corroborari per Spiritum eius in interiorem hominem, [17]habitare Christum per fidem in cordibus vestris, in caritate radicati et fundati, [18]ut valeatis comprehendere cum omnibus sanctis quae sit latitudo et longitudo et sublimitas et profundum, [19]scire etiam supereminentem scientiae caritatem Christi, ut impleamini in omnem plenitudinem Dei. [20]Ei autem, qui potens est supra omnia facere superabundanter quam petimus aut intellegimus, secundum virtutem, quae operatur in nobis, [21]ipsi gloria in ecclesia et in Christo Iesu in omnes generationes saeculi saeculorum. Amen. [4] [1]Obsecro itaque vos ego vinctus in Domino, ut digne ambuletis vocatione, qua vocati estis, [2]cum omni humilitate et mansuetudine,

---

3:14 "I bow my knees". The Jews generally prayed standing up. Only at moments of special solemnity did they kneel or prostrate themselves as a sign of adoration. By introducing this almost liturgical gesture, the Apostle is expressing the intensity of his prayer, and the humility that inspires it. The passage also makes the point that the bodily gestures (genuflection, bowing one's head, beating one's breast, etc.) that accompany prayer should be sincere expressions of devotion. They allow the whole person, body and soul, to show by words and gestures his or her filial love for God.

3:15 To be named "from" something means to come from, to originate from it, and the word translated here as "family" (*patría* in Greek) means a group of individuals who are descended from the same father; it could also be translated as "paternity", as it is in the New Vulgate. The Apostle means that every grouping that can be considered a family, whether on earth (like the Church, the family, etc.) or in heaven (like the Church in triumph), takes its name and origin from God, the only father in the full meaning of the word. So, the word "Father" can be correctly used to designate not only physical but also spiritual fatherhood. The parenthood of married people, in turn, is an outstanding reflection of the love of God, the Creator of all things. Hence, "when they become parents, spouses receive from God the gift of a new responsibility. Their parental love is called to become for the children the visible sign of the very love of God, 'from whom every family in heaven and on earth is named'" (John Paul II, *Familiaris consortio*, 14).

d Or *by*   e Or *I ask that I may not*

5. UNITY IN THE CHURCH*

Bases of unity

Rom 6:4
Phil 1:27
Col 1:10; 2:6
Rom 12:9–16
Phil 2:1–4
Col 3:12–15
Phil 4:7
Rom 5:5; 12:5
Col 3:14
1 Cor 10:17; 12:12
Jn 10:16
1 Cor 8:6; 12:4–6
Rom 12:3, 6
1 Cor 12:7, 11
Col 2:15

Ps 68:18

Jn 1:14; 3:13
Rom 10:6–7
Lk 24:51
Jn 1:16
Acts 1:1–10

4 ¹I therefore, a prisoner for the Lord, beg you to lead a life worthy of the calling to which you have been called, ²with all lowliness and meekness, with patience, forbearing one another in love, ³eager to maintain the unity of the Spirit in the bond of peace. ⁴There is one body and one Spirit, just as you were called to the one hope that belongs to your call, ⁵one Lord, one faith, one baptism, ⁶one God and Father of us all, who is above all and through all and in all. ⁷But grace was given to each of us according to the measure of Christ's gift. ⁸Therefore it is said,

> "When he ascended on high he led a host of captives,
>   and he gave gifts to men."

⁹(In saying, "He ascended," what does it mean but that he had also descended into the lower parts of the earth? ¹⁰He who descended is he who also ascended far above all the heavens, that he might fill all things.)

Building up Christ's body

Rom 12:3, 6
1 Cor 12:28
Eph 2:21; 4:16
Col 2:19
1 Pet 2:5

¹¹And his gifts were that some should be apostles, some prophets, some evangelists, some pastors and teachers, ¹²to equip the saints for the work of ministry, for build-

cum longanimitate, supportantes invicem in caritate, ³solliciti servare unitatem spiritus in vinculo pacis; ⁴unum corpus et unus Spiritus, sicut et vocati estis in una spe vocationis vestrae; ⁵unus Dominus, una fides, unum baptisma; ⁶unus Deus et Pater omnium, qui super omnes et per omnia et in omnibus. ⁷Unicuique autem nostrum data est gratia secundum mensuram donationis Christi. ⁸Propter quod dicit: «*Ascendens in altum captivam duxit captivitatem, / dedit dona hominibus*». ⁹Illud autem «ascendit» quid est, nisi quia et descendit in inferiores partes terrae? ¹⁰Qui descendit, ipse est et qui ascendit super omnes caelos, ut impleret omnia. ¹¹Et ipse dedit quosdam quidem apostolos, quosdam autem prophetas, alios vero evangelistas, alios autem pastores et doctores ¹²ad instructionem sanctorum in opus ministerii, in aedificationem corporis Christi, ¹³donec occurramus omnes in unitatem fidei et agnitionis Filii Dei, in virum perfectum, in mensuram aetatis plenitudinis Christi, ¹⁴ut iam non simus parvuli

*4:1–16 Christ has drawn together all men and women, Jew and Gentile alike, to form a single family in Him. Christians must strive to safeguard the unity of the Body of Christ (vv. 1–10). The unity of the Church is perfectly compatible with the variety of gifts and tasks that Christ has entrusted to his members, who serve the Body from their respective places and roles in the Church and in the world (vv. 11–16).

4:1–10 The unity of the Body of Christ, as described here, is clearly the touchstone of what Paul said in the first part of the letter. It requires humility and persistence on the part of Christians. Church unity (one body, one spirit: v. 4) derives from the fact that there is only one God, one Lord, one faith, one Baptism (vv. 5–6). "It is the Holy Spirit, dwelling in believers and pervading and ruling over the entire Church, who brings about that wonderful communion of the faithful and joins them together so intimately in Christ, for he [the Spirit] is the principle of the Church's unity" (Vatican II, *Unitatis redintegratio*, 2).

The quotation in v. 8 comes from Psalm 68:18, where God enters Zion in triumph, and his people receive him, pay him homage, and offer him gifts. Jewish tradition applied these words of the psalm to Moses, introducing a slight change to the meaning: Moses ascended on high, that is, climbed Mount Sinai, and brought down gifts for men, that is, the Law of God. St Paul is saying that this psalm finds its fulfilment in Jesus Christ, for it is through him that God's gifts reach us. He sees Jesus from the glory of heaven, where he now is, distributing to mankind the gifts he gained by his Redemption.

4:11–16 The unity of the Church is sustained by Christ, its Head, who inspires the ministries that arise within it. When members fulfil their given roles, and perform the tasks that have been assigned to them, the body steadily develops. "In the organism of a living body no member plays a purely passive part; sharing in the life of the body it shares at the same time in its activity. The same is true for the mystical Body of Christ, the Church:

ing up the body of Christ, [13]until we all attain to the unity of the faith and of the Eph 1:23; 3, 11–19
Phil 3:8

knowledge of the Son of God, to mature manhood, to the measure of the stature of the Col 1:19, 23, 28
1 Cor 14:20

fullness of Christ; [14]so that we may no longer be children, tossed to and fro and car- Eph 5:6
Jas 1:6

ried about with every wind of doctrine, by the cunning of men, by their craftiness in

deceitful wiles. [15]Rather, speaking the truth in love, we are to grow up in every way Eph 1:22; 5:23
1 Cor 11:3

into him who is the head, into Christ, [16]from whom the whole body, joined and knit Gal 5:13
Rom 12:5; 15:2

together by every joint with which it is supplied, when each part is working prop- Col 2:19

erly, makes bodily growth and upbuilds itself in love.

6. NEW LIFE IN CHRIST AND IN THE CHURCH*

Corruption, a thing of the past

[17]Now this I affirm and testify in the Lord, that you must no longer live as the Gentiles Rom 1:18, 21
1 Cor 3:20

do, in the futility of their minds; [18]they are darkened in their understanding, alienated 1 Pet 1:18; 4:3

from the life of God because of the ignorance that is in them, due to their hardness of Col 1:21
Eph 2:12

heart; [19]they have become callous and have given themselves up to licentiousness, 2 Cor 3:14

greedy to practise every kind of uncleanness. [20]You did not so learn Christ!—[21]assum- Rom 1:26, 28
1 Thess 4:4–5
2 Pet 2:20

ing that you have heard about him and were taught in him, as the truth is in Jesus. [22]Put Mt 23:10

Rom 6:17
1 Cor 15:11

fluctuantes et circumacti omni vento doctrinae in fallacia hominum, in astutia ad circumventionem erroris; [15]veritatem autem facientes in caritate crescamus in illum per omnia, qui est caput Christus, [16]ex quo totum corpus compactum et conexum per omnem iuncturam subministrationis secundum operationem in mensura uniuscuiusque partis augmentum corporis facit in aedificationem sui in caritate. [17]Hoc igitur dico et testificor in Domino, ut iam non ambuletis, sicut et gentes ambulant in vanitate sensus sui [18]tenebris obscuratum habentes intellectum, alienati a vita Dei propter ignorantiam, quae est in illis propter caecitatem cordis ipsorum; [19]qui indolentes semetipsos tradiderunt impudicitiae in operationem immunditiae omnis in avaritia. [20]Vos autem non ita didicistis Christum, [21]si tamen illum audistis et in ipso edocti estis, sicut est veritas in Iesu:

'the whole body achieves full growth in depend-ence on the full functioning of each part' (Eph 4:16)" (Vatican II, *Apostolicam actuositatem*, 2).

*4:17–6:24 In this last (and longest) section of the letter, St Paul outlines the moral implications of being a member of the Church. To understand the argument here it is helpful to bear in mind that in that culture people who desired to have "knowledge" of divine mysteries saw the world as being divided into two elements—one of darkness, which had invaded the world and which controlled it; the other of "initiates" who rejected that world because they saw themselves as part of the divine *pléroma*. That kind of out-look would later be taken up and developed by Gnosticism; St Paul makes use of it in a way in the morality section of this letter, correcting it, of course, in the light of Christian faith.

He explains, therefore, that the Christian no longer has the "old nature"; he is no longer the "old" person who lived in the darkness of evil (see 4:17–32), but rather a "new" one, who should reflect God in his behaviour (see 5:1–7):

he lives in the light of the Lord, as a wise man, full of the Spirit, in the midst of the world (5:8–20). His family and social life, too, should reflect the fact that he is a new person (5:21—6:9). In order not to succumb to the power of evil that is present in the world, he must always be vigilant, to keep up the fight, using the weapons of the Spirit (6:10–20).

4:17–32 A Christian's new life in Christ requires him to help build up the Body of Christ (see 4:12, 16). He must shed the vanity and sin that marked him before his conversion (vv. 17–19) and put on Christ instead, being faithful to him at all times (vv. 20–24). "A person is renewed, made new by God, when he puts on Christ. It is clear, then, that he who has put on Christ is become a new man, and this new man has been created by God" (St Gregory of Nyssa, *Contra Eunomium*, 3, 1, 52).

The first consequence of the new life is the practice of virtues which make it possible for Christians to live in harmony as members of one body of Christ (vv. 25–32).

Rom 6:6; 8:13
Col 3:5, 8-9
Rom 12:2
2 Cor 4:16; 5:16–17
Gen 1:26
Rom 13:14
Gal 3:27
Eph 2:15
Col 3:10
Zech 8:16
Col 3:9
Jas 3:14
Ps 4:4
Mt 5:22
2 Cor 2:11
Acts 18:3; 20:34–35
1 Thess 4:11
2 Thess 3:12
Mt 15:11
Jas 3:1–12
Col 4:6
Is 63:10
2 Cor 1:21–22
Eph 1:13
Rev 7:2
Col 3:8
Rom 1:29
Lk 6:27–38
Mt 6:12, 14–15
Rom 13:8–10
2 Cor 5:19–21
Col 2:13; 3:13
Jas 2:13

Mt 5:48

Rom 3:25; 5:6, 9
1 Cor 5:7
Gal 2:20

off your old nature which belongs to your former manner of life and is corrupt through deceitful lusts, ²³and be renewed in the spirit of your minds, ²⁴and put on the new nature, created after the likeness of God in true righteousness and holiness.

²⁵Therefore, putting away falsehood, let every one speak the truth with his neighbour, for we are members one of another. ²⁶Be angry but do not sin; do not let the sun go down on your anger, ²⁷and give no opportunity to the devil. ²⁸Let the thief no longer steal, but rather let him labour, doing honest work with his hands, so that he may be able to give to those in need. ²⁹Let no evil talk come out of your mouths, but only such as is good for edifying, as fits the occasion, that it may impart grace to those who hear. ³⁰And do not grieve the Holy Spirit of God, in whom you were sealed for the day of redemption. ³¹Let all bitterness and wrath and anger and clamour and slander be put away from you, with all malice, ³²and be kind to one another, tenderhearted, forgiving one another, as God in Christ forgave you.

The purity of life of God's children

5 ¹Therefore be imitators of God, as beloved children. ²And walk in love, as Christ loved us and gave himself up for us, a fragrant offering and sacrifice to God.

²²deponere vos secundum pristinam conversationem veterem hominem, qui corrumpitur secundum desideria erroris, ²³renovari autem spiritu mentis vestrae ²⁴et induere novum hominem, qui secundum Deum creatus est in iustitia et sanctitate veritatis. ²⁵Propter quod deponentes mendacium *loquimini veritatem unusquisque cum proximo suo*, quoniam sumus invicem membra. ²⁶*Irascimini et nolite peccare*; sol non occidat super iracundiam vestram, ²⁷et nolite locum dare Diabolo. ²⁸Qui furabatur, iam non furetur, magis autem laboret operando manibus bonum, ut habeat unde tribuat necessitatem patienti. ²⁹Omnis sermo malus ex ore vestro non procedat, sed si quis bonus ad aedificationem opportunitatis, ut det gratiam audientibus. ³⁰Et nolite contristare Spiritum Sanctum Dei, in quo signati estis in diem redemptionis. ³¹Omnis amaritudo et ira et indignatio et clamor et blasphemia tollatur a vobis cum omni malitia. ³²Estote autem invicem benigni, misericordes, donantes invicem, sicut et Deus in Christo donavit vobis. [5] ¹Estote ergo imitatores Dei sicut filii carissimi ²et ambulate in dilectione, sicut et Christus dilexit nos et tradidit seipsum pro nobis oblationem et hostiam Deo in odorem suavitatis. ³Fornicatio autem et omnis immunditia aut avaritia nec nominetur in vobis, sicut

To put the Gospel into practice, Christians do not need to flee the world. They should try to find God in the every day circumstances of ordinary life, where they carry out their work (v. 28), and to change the world by practising the Christian virtues, following the example of Christ, not least by forgiving one another.

4:30 When the time came for Israel's redemption from slavery in Egypt, the blood of the Passover lamb, which had been smeared on the doors of the Israelites' houses, acted as the mark that identified those to be saved. In an analogous way, the seal of the Holy Spirit which is given in Baptism is the permanent sign engraved on the souls of those who are called to salvation by virtue of the Redemption achieved by Christ. The three sacraments of Baptism, Confirmation and Holy Orders confer, in addition to grace, "a sacramental *character* or 'seal' by which the Christian shares in Christ's priesthood and is made a member of the Church according to different states and functions. This configuration to Christ and to the Church, brought about by the Spirit, is indelible. It remains for ever in the Christian as a positive disposition for grace, a promise and guarantee of divine protection, and as a vocation to divine worship and to the service of the Church. Therefore these sacraments can never be repeated" (*Catechism of the Catholic Church*, 1121). See also the note on 2 Cor 1:15—2:4.

5:1–7 To be sanctified means to enter the sphere of God, who is the Only Holy One. The path to holiness is the imitation of Christ's love and self-surrender (vv. 1–2). Here, and elsewhere (see Rom 1:18–32; Gal 5:19–21; 1 Cor 6:9–10), Paul warns that those who lead immoral lives will find no place in the Kingdom of God.

Christ gave himself up to death of his own free will, out of love for man. The words "a fragrant offering and sacrifice" (v. 2) call to mind the sacrifices of the Old Law; they underline the sacrificial nature of Christ's death and show that his obedience was pleasing to God the Father. Christians are called to imitate that self-giving:

³But fornication and all impurity or covetousness must not even be named among you, as is fitting among saints. ⁴Let there be no filthiness, nor silly talk, nor levity, which are not fitting; but instead let there be thanksgiving. ⁵Be sure of this, that no fornicator or impure man, or one who is covetous (that is, an idolater), has any inheritance in the kingdom of Christ and of God. ⁶Let no one deceive you with empty words, for it is because of these things that the wrath of God comes upon the sons of disobedience. ⁷Therefore do not associate with them,

1 Cor 10:8
Gal 5:19
1 Thess 4:3–8
Col 3:5
Col 3:8
1 Cor 6:9–10
Col 3:5
Heb 13:4–5
Rev 21:8; 22:15
Col 2:4–8; 3:6
1 Thess 4:6
1 Cor 5:9

Walking in the light

⁸for once you were darkness, but now you are light in the Lord; walk as children of light ⁹(for the fruit of light is found in all that is good and right and true), ¹⁰and try to learn what is pleasing to the Lord. ¹¹Take no part in the unfruitful works of darkness, but instead expose them. ¹²For it is a shame even to speak of the things that they do in secret; ¹³but when anything is exposed by the light it becomes visible, for anything that becomes visible is light. ¹⁴Therefore it is said,

Mt 5:14
Jn 3:19–24; 8:12;
12:36
Rom 13:12
1 Pet 2:9
Gal 5:22
1 Thess 5:4–8
Rom 2:2; 13:12
2 Pet 2:17
Rom 1:24
Jn 3:20–21; 8:12

"Awake, O sleeper, and arise from the dead,
    and Christ shall give you light."*

¹⁵Look carefully then how you walk, not as unwise men but as wise, ¹⁶making the most of the time, because the days are evil. ¹⁷Therefore do not be foolish, but under-

Is 26:19; 60:1
Rom 13:11–12
1 Jn 1:5–7
1 Cor 3:18
Rom 13:11
Col 1:9

decet sanctos, ⁴et turpitudo et stultiloquium aut scurrilitas, quae non decent, sed magis gratiarum actio. ⁵Hoc enim scitote intellegentes quod omnis fornicator aut immundus aut avarus, id est idolorum cultor, non habet hereditatem in regno Christi et Dei. ⁶Nemo vos decipiat inanibus verbis; propter haec enim venit ira Dei in filios diffidentiae. ⁷Nolite ergo effici comparticipes eorum; ⁸eratis enim aliquando tenebrae, nunc autem lux in Domino. Ut filii lucis ambulate ⁹— fructus enim lucis est in omni bonitate et iustitia et veritate— ¹⁰probantes quid sit beneplacitum Domino; ¹¹et nolite communicare operibus infructuosis tenebrarum, magis autem et redarguite; ¹²quae enim in occulto fiunt ab ipsis, turpe est et dicere; ¹³omnia autem, quae arguuntur, a lumine manifestantur, ¹⁴omne enim, quod manifestatur, lumen est. Propter quod dicit: «Surge, qui dormis, et exsurge a mortuis, et illuminabit te Christus». ¹⁵Videte itaque caute quomodo ambuletis, non quasi insipientes sed ut sapientes, ¹⁶redimentes tempus, quo-

"Anyone who struggles against sin to the point of shedding his blood or giving his life for the salvation of others walks the path of Love and follows in the footsteps of Christ, who loved us so much that he bore the Cross for our sake" (St Jerome, *Commentarii in Ephesios*, 3, 5, 2).

5:3–5 No matter how corrupt public morality may be, Christians should strive to counter it with all their strength, especially by giving an example of upright living that befits people who aspire to holiness because they are temples of the Holy Spirit (see 1 Cor 6:19) and members of Christ (see 1 Cor 6:15).

The warning given in v. 3 could also be translated as " … should not be mentioned in connexion with you"; that is, Christians should be so refined in the practice of chastity and its attendant virtues that non-Christians have no grounds whatever for accusing them of impurity.

Christians should also strive to avoid greed, a vice that makes a person a slave to power and money, each of which can become a kind of idol

(see Mt 6:24); they should avoid being bound in any way to the things of this world: "The Lord does not command us to demolish our house and have no dealings with money. What he does desire is that we remove from our soul the priority given to possessions, uncontrolled greed and desire for riches, the cares, the thorns of this life, which smother the seed of the true life" (Clement of Alexandria, *Quis dives salvetur*, 11).

5:8–20 Another practical consequence is the leading of clean lives that produce the "fruit of light" proper to those who have received the light of Christ in Baptism and have been filled with the Holy Spirit. The sacrament of Baptism is also called "enlightenment", because it enlightens the minds of those who have heard apostolic preaching (see St Justin, *Apologia*, 1, 61, 12). The quotation in v. 14 probably comes from a baptismal liturgy.

The new life people receive in Baptism is characterized by a wisdom that contrasts with the foolishness of those who try to ignore God

Prov 23:29f
1 Pet 4:3f
Lk 21:34
Ps 33:2
Col 3:17f
1 Thess 5:18
stand what the will of the Lord is. [18]And do not get drunk with wine, for that is debauchery; but be filled with the Spirit, [19]addressing one another in psalms and hymns and spiritual songs, singing and making melody to the Lord with all your heart, [20]always and for everything giving thanks in the name of our Lord Jesus Christ to God the Father.

Gal 5:13
Eph 1:22–23; 4:15
1 Pet 5:5
Col 3:18
1 Cor 11:3
1 Pet 3:1–6
1 Cor 15:25

Col 3:19
1 Pet 3:7
Eph 5:2
1 Cor 6:11
Tit 2:14; 3:5–7
Eph 1:4
Col 1:22
2 Cor 11:2
Rev 21:2, 10;
19:7–8

Marriage compared to Christ's union with the Church

[21]Be subject to one another out of reverence for Christ. [22]Wives, be subject to your husbands, as to the Lord. [23]For the husband is the head of the wife as Christ is the head of the church, his body, and is himself its Saviour. [24]As the church is subject to Christ, so let wives also be subject in everything to their husbands. [25]Husbands, love your wives, as Christ loved the church and gave himself up for her, [26]that he might sanctify her, having cleansed her by the washing of water with the word, [27]that he might present the church to himself in splendour, without spot or wrinkle or any such thing, that

niam dies mali sunt. [17]Propterea nolite fieri imprudentes, sed intellegite, quae sit voluntas Domini. [18]Et nolite inebriari vino, in quo est luxuria, sed implemini Spiritu [19]loquentes vobismetipsis in psalmis et hymnis et canticis spiritalibus, cantantes et psallentes in cordibus vestris Domino. [20]Gratias agentes semper pro omnibus in nomine Domini nostri Iesu Christi, Deo et Patri, [21]subiecti invicem in timore Christi. [22]Mulieres viris suis sicut Domino, [23]quoniam vir caput est mulieris, sicut et Christus caput est ecclesiae, ipse salvator corporis. [24]Sed ut ecclesia subiecta est Christo, ita et mulieres viris in omnibus. [25]Viri, diligite uxores, sicut et Christus dilexit ecclesiam et seipsum tradidit pro ea, [26]ut illam sanctificaret mundans lavacro aquae in verbo, [27]ut exhiberet ipse sibi gloriosam ecclesiam non habentem maculam aut rugam aut aliquid eiusmodi, sed ut sit sancta et immaculata. [28]Ita et viri debent diligere uxores suas ut corpora sua. Qui suam uxorem diligit, seipsum diligit; [29]nemo enim umquam

(see 1 Cor 1:18). This wisdom leads people to "make the most of the time" God gives them for their sanctification (v. 16), to be temperate (v. 18) and to praise God (v. 19). "What a wonderful thing it is to imitate on earth the choir of the angels", St Basil explains, "preparing oneself for prayer at the first hour of the day and glorifying the Creator with hymns and praise. And later, when the sun is at its height, full of splendour and light, doing one's work to the accompaniment of prayer on all sides, seasoning one's actions, so to speak, with the salt of ejaculatory prayers" (*Epistula*, 2, 3).

Verse 20 implies the truth stated in Romans 8:28. St Jerome comments on it as follows: "*Always and for everything giving thanks*: we should reflect on the Apostle's words in two ways. We should give thanks to God at all times and for all things, for what we consider to be good; but we should also cry out in grateful praise to God for those things that cause us suffering or seem to go against us and our will" (*Commentarii in Ephesios*, 3, 5, 20).

5:21–33 The supernatural grandeur and dignity of Christian marriage is based on the fact that it reflects the union between Christ and his Church. In exhorting married couples to live as befits their

membership of the Church, the Apostle establishes an analogy in which the husband stands for Christ and the wife for the Church. "Christ our Lord has abundantly blessed this love, which is rich in its various features, coming as it does from the spring of divine love and modelled on Christ's own union with the Church. Just as of old God encountered his people with a covenant of love and fidelity, so our Saviour, the spouse of the Church, now encounters Christian spouses through the sacrament of marriage. He abides with them in order that by their mutual self-giving spouses will love each other with enduring fidelity, as he loved the Church and delivered himself for it. Authentic married love is caught up into divine love and is directed and enriched by the redemptive power of Christ and the salvific action of the Church, with the result that the spouses are effectively led to God and are helped and strengthened in their lofty role as fathers and mothers" (Vatican II, *Gaudium et spes*, 48). Marriage, therefore, is a way of holiness: "For a Christian, marriage is not just a social institution, much less a mere remedy for human weakness. It is a real supernatural calling. A great sacrament, in Christ and in the Church, says St Paul. [...] It is a sacred sign that sanctifies, an action of Jesus; he fills the souls of husband and wife and invites

she might be holy and without blemish. [28]Even so husbands should love their wives as their own bodies. He who loves his wife loves himself. [29]For no man ever hates his own flesh, but nourishes and cherishes it, as Christ does the church, [30]because we are members of his body. [31]"For this reason a man shall leave his father and mother and be joined to his wife, and the two shall become one flesh." [32]This mystery is a profound one, and I mean in reference to Christ and the church; [33]however, let each one of you love his wife as himself, and let the wife see that she respects her husband.

1 Pet 3:7

Mk 10:8
1 Thess 2:7

Rom 12:5; 15:5
1 Cor 12:12
Gen 2:24
Mk 10:7
Rev 19:7; 22:17
1 Cor 6:16
Mt 19:5f

Col 3:19

Advice to children and parents

6 [1]Children, obey your parents in the Lord, for this is right. [2]"Honour your father and mother" (this is the first commandment with a promise), [3]"that it may be well with you and that you may live long on the earth." [4]Fathers, do not provoke your children to anger, but bring them up in the discipline and instruction of the Lord.

Prov 6:20
Col 3:20
Ex 20:12
Mt 10:37
Deut 5:16

Prov 13:24ff
Col 3:21
Heb 12:9–12

Advice to servants and masters

[5]Slaves, be obedient to those who are your earthly masters, with fear and trembling, in singleness of heart, as to Christ; [6]not in the way of eye-service, as men-pleasers,

Col 3:22; 4:1
1 Pet 2:18
1 Tim 6:1ff
Tit 2:4
Gal 1:10
1 Thess 2:4
Tit 2:9–10

carnem suam odio habuit, sed nutrit et fovet eam sicut et Christus ecclesiam, [30]quia membra sumus corporis eius. [31]*Propter hoc relinquet homo patrem et matrem et adhaerebit uxori suae, et erunt duo in carne una.* [32]Mysterium hoc magnum est; ego autem dico de Christo et ecclesia! [33]Verumtamen et vos singuli unusquisque suam uxorem sicut seipsum diligat; uxor autem timeat virum.   [6] [1]Filii, oboedite parentibus vestris in Domino, hoc enim est iustum. [2]*Honora patrem tuum et matrem,* quod est mandatum primum cum promissione, [3]*ut bene sit tibi et sis longaevus*

them to follow him; he transforms their whole married life into an occasion for God's presence on earth" (St Josemaría Escrivá, *Christ Is Passing By*, 23).

When, in line with the customs of the time, St Paul exhorts wives to be subject to their husbands (v. 22), he is inviting every wife, in the way she relates to her husband, to reflect the Church herself, who always is submissive to Christ. The husband, for his part, is asked to be submissive to his wife, for he is a reflection of Jesus Christ, who offered himself up, even to death, out of love for the Church. "By virtue of the sacramentality of their marriage, spouses are bound to one another in the most profoundly indissoluble manner. Their belonging to each other is the real representation, by means of the sacramental sign, of the very relationship of Christ with the Church. Spouses are therefore the permanent reminder to the Church of what happened on the Cross; they are for one another and for the children witnesses to the salvation in which the sacrament makes them sharers" (John Paul II, *Familiaris consortio*, 13).

Those who keep this commandment receive spiritual rewards, but also temporal rewards of peace and prosperity (see *Catechism of the Catholic Church*, 2200). He goes on to speak about the duties of parents. "Parents must regard their children as *children of God* and respect them as *human persons*. Showing themselves obedient to the will of the Father in heaven, they educate their children to fulfil God's law" (ibid., 2222). "It is therefore the duty of parents to create a family atmosphere inspired by love and devotion to God and their fellow-men which will promote an integrated, personal and social education of their children [...]. It is therefore above all in the Christian family, enriched by the grace and the responsibility of the sacrament of matrimony, that children should be taught to know and worship God and to love their neighbour, in accordance with the faith which they have received in earliest infancy in the sacrament of Baptism [...]. Finally, it is through the family that they are gradually initiated into association with their fellow-men in civil life and as members of the People of God" (Vatican II, *Gravissimum educationis*, 3).

6:1–4 The Apostle reminds his readers about the fourth commandment (see Ex 20:12; Deut 5:16).

6:5–9 In St Paul's time labour relations were largely based on a system of slavery. The Apos-

Col 3:23–24
Job 31:13–15
Rom 2:6
2 Cor 5:10
Col 3:25
Deut 10:17
Acts 10:34
Col 4:1
Rom 2:11
Jas 5:1ff
but as servants[f] of Christ, doing the will of God from the heart, [7]rendering service with a good will as to the Lord and not to men, [8]knowing that whatever good any one does, he will receive the same again from the Lord, whether he is a slave or free. [9]Masters, do the same to them, and forbear threatening, knowing that he who is both their Master and yours is in heaven, and that there is no partiality with him.

Weapons for spiritual combat

1 Pet 5:8–9

2 Cor 2:11
Jas 4:7
Eph 1:21; 2:2
1 Pet 5:8

Lk 22:36
Rom 13:12

Is 11:5; 59:17
Lk 12:35
Is 52:7; 40:3–9
Eph 2:17
Acts 10:36
Is 52:7; 40:3–9
Wis 5:19
1 Jn 5:4

Is 49:2
1 Thess 5:8
Heb 4:12
Lk 18:1; 21:36
Col 4:2
1 Thess 5:17
[10]Finally, be strong in the Lord and in the strength of his might. [11]Put on the whole armour of God, that you may be able to stand against the wiles of the devil. [12]For we are not contending against flesh and blood, but against the principalities, against the powers, against the world rulers of this present darkness, against the spiritual hosts of wickedness in the heavenly places. [13]Therefore take the whole armour of God, that you may be able to withstand in the evil day, and having done all, to stand. [14]Stand therefore, having girded your loins with truth, and having put on the breastplate of righteousness, [15]and having shod your feet with the equipment of the gospel of peace; [16]besides all these, taking the shield of faith, with which you can quench all the flaming darts of the evil one. [17]And take the helmet of salvation, and the sword of the Spirit, which is the word of God. [18]Pray at all times in the Spirit, with all prayer and supplication. To that end keep alert with all perseverance, making supplication for all the saints, [19]and also for me, that utterance may be given me in

super terram. [4]Et, patres, nolite ad iracundiam provocare filios vestros, sed educate illos in disciplina et correptione Domini. [5]Servi, oboedite dominis carnalibus cum timore et tremore, in simplicitate cordis vestri sicut Christo [6]non ad oculum servientes quasi hominibus placentes, sed ut servi Christi facientes voluntatem Dei ex animo, [7]cum bona voluntate servientes, sicut Domino et non hominibus, [8]scientes quoniam unusquisque, si quid fecerit bonum, hoc percipiet a Domino, sive servus sive liber. [9]Et, domini, eadem facite illis, remittentes minas, scientes quia et illorum et vester Dominus est in caelis, et personarum acceptio non est apud eum. [10]De cetero confortamini in Domino et in potentia virtutis eius. [11]Induite armaturam Dei, ut possitis stare adversus insidias Diaboli. [12]Quia non est nobis colluctatio adversus sanguinem et carnem sed adversus principatus, adversus potestates, adversus mundi rectores tenebrarum harum, adversus spiritalia nequitiae in caelestibus. [13]Propterea accipite armaturam Dei, ut possitis resistere in die malo et, omnibus perfectis, stare. [14]State ergo *succincti lumbos* vestros *in veritate* et *induti loricam iustitiae* [15]et calceati *pedes in praeparatione evangelii pacis,* [16]in omnibus sumentes scutum fidei, in quo possitis omnia tela Maligni ignea exstinguere; [17]et *galeam salutis* assumite *et gladium Spiritus,* quod est *verbum Dei,* [18]per omnem orationem et obsecrationem orantes omni tempore in Spiritu, et in ipso vigilantes in omni instantia et obsecratione pro omnibus sanctis [19]et pro me, ut detur mihi sermo in aperitione oris mei cum fiducia notum

tle sets out how relations between masters and servants should operate. By emphasizing the dignity of the human person, he is clearly teaching that human relationships should be raised to a supernatural level, that is, should be seen and lived in the light of Christ. Centuries later the values he identifies would be invoked in the struggle to abolish slavery.

6:10–20 The letter ends by rallying Christians to wage war on evil, fully aware of the weapons that will bring them victory. Using armour and weapons as a metaphor, the Apostle invites all to put on godly armour and fight the good fight; and he exhorts his readers to persevere in prayer, and to include him in their prayers. It is a call to draw their strength from God: "To be strong in the Lord is to be strong in word, in wisdom, in contem-

plation of the truth and all the teachings of Christ" (Origen, *Fragmenta in Ephesios*, 32). Among the spiritual resources to be used to avoid the snares of the devil, prayer merits special mention (v. 18): "For 'we have not been commanded to work, to keep watch and to fast constantly, but it has been laid down that we are to pray without ceasing' (Evagrius Ponticus, *Pract.* 49). This tireless fervour can come only from love. Against our dullness and laziness, the battle of prayer is that of humble, trusting, and persevering *love*" (*Catechism of the Catholic Church*, 2742).

Verse 12 speaks about "principalities", "powers", "world rulers"—all terms borrowed from Jewish literature of the time; here they refer to dark forces that strive to keep men and women separate from Christ and never cease to lay traps for all mankind (see 1 Pet 5:8).

f Or *slaves*

opening my mouth boldly to proclaim the mystery of the gospel, [20]for which I am an ambassador in chains; that I may declare it boldly, as I ought to speak.

Rom 15:30; 16:35
2 Thess 3:1

Conclusion and blessing

[21]Now that you also may know how I am and what I am doing, Tychicus the beloved brother and faithful minister in the Lord will tell you everything. [22]I have sent him to you for this very purpose, that you may know how we are, and that he may encourage your hearts.

1 Thess 5:25
Col 4:4, 10, 18
Acts 20:4
Col 4:7
2 Tim 4:12
Tit 3:12
Col 4:8

 [23]Peace be to the brethren, and love with faith, from God the Father and the Lord Jesus Christ. [24]Grace be with all who love our Lord Jesus Christ with love undying.

Gal 5:6
Phil 4:7–9
1 Cor 15:42

facere mysterium evangelii, [20]pro quo legatione fungor in catena, ut in ipso audeam, prout oportet me loqui. [21]Ut autem et vos sciatis, quae circa me sunt, quid agam, omnia nota vobis faciet Tychicus, carissimus frater et fidelis minister in Domino, [22]quem misi ad vos in hoc ipsum, ut cognoscatis, quae circa nos sunt, et consoletur corda vestra. [23]Pax fratribus et caritas cum fide a Deo Patre et Domino Iesu Christo. [24]Gratia cum omnibus, qui diligunt Dominum nostrum Iesum Christum in incorruptione.

6:21–24 Tychicus' mission is almost exactly the same as the one he is given in Colossians 4:7–8. He accompanied St Paul on his third journey to Jerusalem and would later be entrusted with tasks in Crete and Ephesus (see Acts 20:4; 2 Tim 4:12; Tit 3:12).

THE LETTER OF PAUL TO THE

PHILIPPIANS

Introduction

In the New Testament canon, the Letter to the Philippians comes immediately after that to the Ephesians; like it, it is described as a "Captivity Letter" because it is clear from certain statements in it that the Apostle was in prison when he wrote it. It is addressed to a Christian community very close to Paul's heart: "I hold you in my heart" (1:7), "my brethren, whom I love and long for, my joy and crown" (4:1).

Its content and familiar and affectionate tone make it one of the easiest of Paul's letters to read.

1. STRUCTURE AND CONTENT

Philippians is a letter from a friend, written in a personal, intimate style. This explains why it does not have a well-defined structure and why it is not possible to divide it, as other letters have been, into doctrinal and moral sections.

It begins with a greeting, very simple in style, followed by an act of thanksgiving. St Paul then mentions his being in prison, and how this situation has helped the spread of the Gospel (1:1–26).

He then exhorts his readers to behave as befits children of God, portraying our Lord Jesus Christ as the model we should imitate in all things (he does this especially in a hymn extolling the humiliation and later exaltation of Christ: 2:5–11).

The letter then changes direction to deal with items of news, etc.; the Apostle tells his readers that he is going to send Timothy to them, and that he himself plans to visit soon but, for the moment, he will send in his stead Epaphroditus, whom they will be happy to find recovered from his illness (2:19–30).

Before the letter ends, there is a warning about the harm that can be done by Judaizers who have found their way to Philippi, and an exhortation to persevere and be joyful, following the example set by the Apostle himself (3:1–4:9).

The letter ends with words of thanks and further greetings.

2. CONTEXT

There were close bonds between the Apostle and the church of Philippi. The letter itself, as it has come down to us, contains personal reminiscences, news about St Paul's imprisonment, and references to the contact he has maintained with the faithful at Philippi through Timothy and Epaphroditus. Moreover, there are indications that this was not the only letter Paul sent to the Philippians (see 3:1).

As early as the first third of the second century, St Polycarp, in a letter of his own to this church, refers to letters sent by Paul: "He [Paul], when living among you, clearly and steadfastly taught the word of truth to the people of his time. And when he was absent he wrote you letters;

by reading these attentively you will be able to strengthen yourselves in the faith that has been given to you."[1]

Internal analysis of the letter shows that its structure is not as well-defined as that of other letters by the Apostle. This has led scholars to speculate that it is an amalgam of a number of letters that Paul sent this community. It is noticeable, for example, that after his announcing his plans and giving news (see 2:19–29)—usually a sign that the letter is coming to an end—we get a further section, more polemical in tone than the earlier part of the letter, about preachers of a Judaizing tendency, whose influence is beginning to be felt in Philippi. Also, the section in which St Paul thanks the Philippians for help received (see 4:10–20) stands almost as a unit on its own, as if it had originally been a separate, short personal letter.

Evidence of this sort has led some to the conclusion that the text that has come down to us may be a combination of two or three letters sent to the Philippians at different times from different places. The first of these could be Philippians 4:10–20; another, Philippians 1:1—3:1, with some verses from chapter 4; and a possible third, the criticism of Judaizers in Philippians 3:2—4:1, along with some verses from the last chapter.

The first (4:10–20) would be a short personal letter written in St Paul's own hand (like the Letter to Philemon), thanking the Philippians for coming to his aid.

The second (1:1—3:1), sent from prison, gives news of his situation and of how he still succeeds in preaching the Gospel; it also exhorts readers to be humble and to stay united. Apparently, the Philippians, always ready to help the Apostle when necessary and when they could, decided to send Epaphroditus to him, to assist him during his imprisonment (see 2:25). But Epaphroditus took ill and was even in danger of death. Once he recovers, St Paul decides that he should return home, to be a consolation to the Philippians (see 2:26–30).

The third (3:2—4:1) would have been written to confirm them in the faith taught to them by Paul, in case they were tempted by the Judaizers in their midst to wander astray from the true faith.

In any event, the language and literary style of these three parts (whether they were three separate letters later collated into one, or are three parts of a single letter) show no substantial variations from the ways St Paul expresses himself in other letters, such as those to the Corinthians, the Romans, the Galatians and the Thessalonians; there is no good reason for thinking that they may have been written by someone other than Paul himself.

As regards the date of composition, the most likely time-frame seems to be during Paul's first imprisonment in Rome (in the years 61–62), if one takes Paul's reference to his being confined in the praetorium (see 1:13), and the greetings he sends on behalf of "those of Caesar's household" (4:22) in the most obvious, literal sense. However, it is possible (this is a widely held view nowadays) that the letter was written in Ephesus, at a time when the Apostle was imprisoned in that city, during what is called his "third journey", before he moved on again to Macedonia (between the years 54 and 57).[2] The basis for this theory is the impression given in the letter that the Apostle and the Philippians are in fairly regular contact with one another—which would not be easy to explain if the Apostle was in a city as far away from Philippi as Rome.[3] Moreover, if the letter was in fact written from Rome, it is strange that he should speak about the Philippians not having had an opportunity to show him their affection since the time they came to his aid in

---

1 St Polycarp, *Ad Philippenses*, 3. **2** This may be the imprisonment implied in 2 Corinthians 1:8. **3** See 2:19–24: this passage gives the impression that St Paul is writing from somewhere relatively near Philippi, possibly Ephesus.

Thessalonica (see 4:10, 16), given that prior to his imprisonment he had twice visited Philippi, in the course of his third apostolic journey (see Acts 16:12; 20:1–3, 6). Also, the reference to imprisonment in the "praetorium" does not necessarily imply that he was in Rome at the time of writing, for "praetorium" could also mean the palace of the governor of a province. "Those of Caesar's household" may be a reference to imperial officials, who were to be found in every province (and Ephesus had a particularly strong Roman presence). If the letter was in fact written from Ephesus, it should be dated to the period AD 54–57.

3. MESSAGE

The primary purpose of the letter seems to be to give encouragement, rather than to teach. In affectionate and informal language, St Paul gives his readers news about the spread of the Gospel. From prison, he encourages them to put his teachings into practice and to grow in Christian virtues. Nevertheless, despite its brevity, the letter does deal with important points of doctrine.

What the Christian calling entails

Even in this life Christians can be called "saints" (1:1) because of sanctifying grace; but this does not mean that they can be said to have reached definitive holiness, to a state of being "already perfect" (3:12). St Paul points out the way that leads to holiness—sharing in Christ's suffering, and becoming like him in his death (see 3:10–11). To be a Christian, therefore, means to become identified with Christ, by trying to have "this mind among yourselves, which was in Christ Jesus" (2:5), and following the example he set; he is our true model, a perfect model, having been "obedient unto death, even death on a cross" (2:8).

Christians who strive to be one with Christ will, like him, be exalted (see 2:9) in the glory of heaven. Whatever sufferings they experience in this life, even of shedding their blood, if it comes to that, are a cause of joy for them (see 2:17); for they know that one's life on earth, and the death of one's body, make for the glory of God as long as one is one with Christ (cf. 1:20).

Christians in the world

For the most part, Christians live ordinary lives in the world, shoulder to shoulder with all kinds of people; many non-Christian men and women act honourably and are motivated by high ideals, but some allow ambition and greed to take hold of them (see 2:15). There is always a risk that a Christian might give in to the temptations present in the environment.

Therefore, no matter where they happen to be, Christians should remember that they are citizens of heaven (see 3:20) and should always act in a manner worthy of the Gospel (see 1:27); that is, they should be humble, motivated not by self-interest but by the good of others (see 2:3–4). They should always be joyful (see 4:4), blameless and innocent (see 2:15), and observably considerate of others (see 4:5). In this way, the good lives of the children of God will shine out as "lights in the world" (2:15), showing everyone the way to God by the light of Christ.

The mystery of Jesus Christ the Redeemer

The Apostle sets before us as our model the life of Christ. In the hymn that forms part of Philippians (2:5–11), he provides a wonderful summary of the life and redemptive work of Christ; there he praises the glorification of Christ's human nature, a glory given it after his life on earth, inspired as it was in all things by a freely accepted obedience, whereby he humbled himself even unto death on a cross. The hymn, which is very profound, proclaims the divine nature of Christ that pre-existed before the Incarnation, and thus his oneness in substance with God the Father. Without ceasing to be God, he lowered himself by taking on a human nature. The hymn extols Christ's death and his glorious resurrection (cf. 2:9–11). Christ raised on high is the Man-God who was born, and who died on a cross for our sake.

The language and content of this hymn make it clear that the Revelation made by God in the Old Testament reaches its fulfilment in Jesus Christ. By his redeeming death, Jesus atones for the disorder caused by Adam, the first man. In Christ, the new Adam (see Rom 5:14), the salvation promised in the proto-Gospel comes about (see Gen 3:15). Jesus takes the form of a servant by freely following the way of obedience. As was foretold of the Servant of the Lord in the book of Isaiah, his humiliation and death are the cause of salvation for all (see Is 53:2–11). In Christ, in fact, all the prophecies find fulfilment. What St Paul says in 2:9–11 allows us to see that Jesus Christ is also the One who is to come on the clouds of heaven, "like a son of man" (see Dan 7:13–14; Is 45:23). By using an image taken from the book of Daniel, the letter unequivocally proclaims the lordship of Christ.

St Paul centres his attention on the Son of God made man—on his life on earth, as well as his glorification in heaven. Jesus Christ is portrayed as being truly man (see 2:7–8); but his divine personality is shrouded in mystery. We see him as a man, but his origin and status belong to an infinitely higher plane. It is precisely because he is both God and man that his life on earth, summarized so beautifully in this text, is of such singular importance and culminates with his exaltation in glory.

Philippians

1. INTRODUCTION*

Greeting

1 ¹Paul and Timothy, servantsª of Christ Jesus,
To all the saints in Christ Jesus who are at Philippi, with the bishopsᵇ and deacon:
²Grace to you and peace from God our Father and the Lord Jesus Christ.

Acts 9:13; 16:1
Rom 1:1
1 Cor 1:2
2 Cor 1:1
Rom 1:7–8
Gal 1:3
1 Cor 1:4

Thanksgiving. Paul's affection and love

³I thank my God in all my remembrance of you, ⁴always in every prayer of mine for you all making my prayer with joy, ⁵thankful for your partnership in the gospel from the first day until now. ⁶And I am sure that he who began a good work in you will

1 Thess 1:2
Rom 1:9
Amos 5:20
1 Cor 1:6–8
Phil 1:10; 2:16

[1] ¹Paulus et Timotheus servi Christi Iesu omnibus sanctis in Christo Iesu, qui sunt Philippis, cum episcopis et diaconis: ²gratia vobis et pax a Deo Patre nostro et Domino Iesu Christo. ³Gratias ago Deo meo in omni memoria vestri ⁴semper in omni oratione mea pro omnibus vobis cum gaudio deprecationem faciens ⁵ super communione vestra in evangelio a prima die usque nunc, ⁶confidens hoc ipsum, quia, qui coepit in vobis

*1:1–26 In this letter St Paul opens his heart to the faithful at Philippi. He begins by telling them how happy he feels, despite his imprisonment (1:1–26), when he thinks of them and of the Gospel. He asks that they, despite his absence, complete his joy by being united to one another in humility. Christ's own self-abasement is an example for them (1:27—2:18). Paul makes up for his absence from Philippi by sending some brethren to be with the people there (2:19–30) and by writing this letter in which, to strengthen their Christian life, he warns them against certain false teachers, enlivens their hope in heaven, and thanks them for the help they have given him (3:1—4:23).

One feature of this letter is that it shows, more vividly than any other, St Paul's appreciation of and affection for the Christians of the communities he founded. In addition to the opening greeting (vv. 1–2) and the act of thanksgiving for the fidelity of those he is addressing (vv. 3–11)—features always found in his letters—the Apostle also offers some reflections on his own personal circumstances (vv. 12–26).

1:1–2 The Greek word *epískopos* means "watchman", "guardian", "overseer", and *diákonos*, "servant", "keeper". In the early times of the Church, the words "bishop" and "deacon" did not have the precise meanings they have now; but their use here does show that, even at this early stage, local churches had some form of hierarchical structure.

1:3–11 A sense of joy is one of the most obvious features of the letter (see 3:1; 4:4); it derives especially from the good spirit and upright living of the Philippians. Joy, as Paul tells us in Galatians 5:22, is one of the fruits of the Holy Spirit. It comes from union with God and recognition of his loving providence towards all creation, and particularly towards his children. Joy gives Christians peace, serenity and clarity of purpose in all their doings. St Paul is so identified with Christ that he is able to say that he has the same feelings of affection for all these people as the Lord has for them (v. 8).

On the basis of v. 6, the Magisterium of the Church, in response to the Pelagian heresy, has taught that the beginnings of faith, as also increase of faith and the act of faith whereby we believe, are the result of grace and of our free response to that gift (see Second Council of Orange, can. 5). Centuries later, the Council of Trent repeated this teaching: just as God has begun the good work, so will he bring it to completion, if we for our part cooperate with the grace that is given us (see *De iustificatione*, chap.

a Or *slaves* b Or *overseers*

Acts 25:16
2 Tim 4:16

Rom 1:9
2 Cor 1:23
Col 1:9-10

Rom 12:ff
Heb 5:14

Jn 15:8
Gal 5:22
Eph 5:9
Phil 3:9
Heb 12:11
Jas 3:18

2 Tim 2:9

Mt 27:27
Jn 18:28

Eph 3:1

Job 13:16
1 Thess 5:25
2 Cor 1:11

1 Cor 6:20
Rom 8:19

bring it to completion at the day of Jesus Christ. [7]It is right for me to feel thus about you all, because I hold you in my heart, for you are all partakers with me of grace, both in my imprisonment and in the defence and confirmation of the gospel. [8]For God is my witness, how I yearn for you all with the affection of Christ Jesus. [9]And it is my prayer that your love may abound more and more, with knowledge and all discernment, [10]so that you may approve what is excellent, and may be pure and blameless for the day of Christ, [11]filled with the fruits of righteousness which come through Jesus Christ, to the glory and praise of God.

Paul's own circumstances

[12]I want you to know, brethren, that what has happened to me has really served to advance the gospel, [13]so that it has become known throughout the whole praetorian guard[c] and to all the rest that my imprisonment is for Christ; [14]and most of the brethren have been made confident in the Lord because of my imprisonment,* and are much more bold to speak the word of God without fear.

[15]Some indeed preach Christ from envy and rivalry, but others from good will. [16]The latter do it out of love, knowing that I am put here for the defence of the gospel; [17]the former proclaim Christ out of partisanship, not sincerely but thinking to afflict me in my imprisonment. [18]What then? Only that in every way, whether in pretence or in truth, Christ is proclaimed; and in that I rejoice.

[19]Yes, and I shall rejoice. For I know that through your prayers and the help of the Spirit of Jesus Christ this will turn out for my deliverance, [20]as it is my eager expec-

opus bonum, perficiet usque in diem Christi Iesu; [7]sicut est mihi iustum hoc sentire pro omnibus vobis, eo quod habeam in corde vos et in vinculis meis et in defensione et confirmatione evangelii socios gratiae meae omnes vos esse. [8]Testis enim mihi Deus, quomodo cupiam omnes vos in visceribus Christi Iesu. [9]Et hoc oro, ut caritas vestra magis ac magis abundet in scientia et omni sensu, [10]ut probetis potiora, ut sitis sinceri et sine offensa in diem Christi, [11]repleti fructu iustitiae, qui est per Iesum Christum, in gloriam et laudem Dei. [12]Scire autem vos volo, fratres, quia, quae circa me sunt, magis ad profectum venerunt evangelii, [13]ita ut vincula mea manifesta fierent in Christo in omni praetorio et in ceteris omnibus, [14]et plures e fratribus in Domino confidentes vinculis meis abundantius audere sine timore verbum loqui. [15]Quidam quidem et propter invidiam et contentionem, quidam autem et propter bonam voluntatem Christum praedicant; [16]hi quidem ex caritate scientes quoniam in defensionem evangelii positus sum, [17]illi autem ex contentione Christum annuntiant, non sincere, existimantes pressuram se suscitare vinculis meis. [18]Quid enim? Dum omni modo, sive sub obtentu sive in veritate, Christus annuntietur, et in hoc gaudeo; sed et gaudebo, [19]scio enim quia hoc mihi

13). As well as trust in divine help, we must make a personal effort to respond to grace, for, in the words of St Augustine, "God who created you without your cooperation will not save you without your cooperation" (*Sermones*, 169, 13).

1:9 Growth in charity helps a person to have greater "knowledge" of God. "The lover", St Thomas Aquinas says, "is not satisfied with superficial knowledge of the beloved, but strives to gain an intimate knowledge of everything pertaining to him, so as to penetrate his very soul" (*Summa theologiae*, 1–2, 28, 2c).

1:12–20 Paul sees an advantage to his being in prison: it gives him an opportunity to bear witness to and spread the Gospel in special ways. Like Paul, Christians nowadays "stir up irresistible questions in the hearts of those who see

how they live: Why are they like this? Why do they live in this way? What or who is it that inspires them? Why are they in our midst? Such a witness is already a silent proclamation of the Good News and a very powerful and effective one [...]. Nevertheless, this always remains insufficient, because even the finest witness will prove ineffective in the long run if it is not [...] made explicit by a clear and unequivocal proclamation of the Lord Jesus" (Paul VI, *Evangelii nuntiandi*, 21–22).

We do not know who or exactly what Paul is speaking of when he says there are some who "preach Christ from envy and rivalry" (v. 15); still, whatever their motives may be, he rejoices that the Gospel is being preached (cf. Mt 9:38–40).

1:21–26 The Greek word translated as "depart" in v. 23 is normally used to connote casting off

c Greek *in the whole praetorium*

tation and hope that I shall not be at all ashamed, but that with full courage now as
always Christ will be honoured in my body,* whether by life or by death. [21]For to
me to live is Christ, and to die is gain. [22]If it is to be life in the flesh, that means fruitful labour for me. Yet which I shall choose I cannot tell. [23]I am hard pressed between
the two. My desire is to depart and be with Christ, for that is far better. [24]But
to remain in the flesh is more necessary on your account. [25]Convinced of this, I
know that I shall remain and continue with you all, for your progress and joy in the
faith, [26]so that in me you may have ample cause to glory in Christ Jesus, because of
my coming to you again.

Col 1:24

Phil 3:8
Gal 2:20
Col 3:3

2 Cor 5:6–9

1 Cor 4:21
2 Cor 1:14; 5:12
Phil 1:4; 2:16
1 Thess 2:19

2. TEACHINGS*

Appeal for steadfastness

[27]Only let your manner of life be worthy of the gospel of Christ, so that whether I
come and see you or am absent, I may hear of you that you stand firm in one spirit,
with one mind striving side by side for the faith of the gospel, [28]and not frightened
in anything by your opponents. This is a clear omen to them of their destruction, but
of your salvation, and that from God. [29]For it has been granted to you that for the
sake of Christ you should not only believe in him but also suffer for his sake, [30]engaged in the same conflict which you saw and now hear to be mine.

Phil 3:20
Eph 2:19; 4:1
Col 1:10; 2:5
1 Thess 2:12

1 Cor 1:18

2 Thess 1:4–7

Acts 16:19–22; 20:22
Phil 11:7
Col 1:24
1 Thess 2:2

proveniet in salutem per vestram orationem et subministrationem Spiritus Iesu Christi, [20]secundum exspectationem et spem meam quia in nullo
confundar, sed in omni fiducia sicut semper et nunc magnificabitur Christus in corpore meo, sive per vitam sive per mortem. [21]Mihi enim vivere
Christus est et mori lucrum. [22]Quod si vivere in carne, hic mihi fructus operis est, et quid eligam ignoro. [23]Coartor autem ex his duobus: desiderium
habens dissolvi et cum Christo esse, multo magis melius; [24]permanere autem in carne magis necessarium est propter vos. [25]Et hoc confidens scio
quia manebo et permanebo omnibus vobis ad profectum vestrum et gaudium fidei, [26]ut gloriatio vestra abundet in Christo Iesu in me per meum
adventum iterum ad vos. [27]Tantum digne evangelio Christi conversamini, ut sive cum venero et videro vos, sive absens audiam de vobis quia statis
in uno Spiritu unanimes concertantes fide evangelii [28]et in nullo perterriti ab adversariis, quod est illis indicium perditionis, vobis autem salutis,

(as sailors do, when they leave harbour) or
pulling up stakes (as when an army decamps).
Paul sees death as a liberation from earthly ties,
a liberation which will allow him to go away and
"be with Christ". Because of Christ, death now
makes sense: it is "gain" (v. 21), because it
allows a person to see God forever, face to face
(cf. 1 Cor 13:12), and to "be with Christ" forever
in heaven (see Jn 14:3; Phil 1:23; 1 Thess 4:17).
Upon dying, the elect live "in Christ" even more;
or, better, they find their true identity, receive a
new name, in him: "To live in heaven is 'to be
with Christ'. The elect live 'in Christ', but they
retain, or rather find, their true identity, their own
name (cf. Rev 2:17). 'For life is to be with
Christ; where Christ is, there is life, there is the
kingdom' (St Ambrose, *In Luc.* 10, 121)" (*Catechism of the Catholic Church*, 1025) .

This desire to rejoice in the presence of God
in heaven caused St Teresa of Avila to say: "I am
living and yet I am not really living, for I place

my hopes on such a higher life that I am dying
because I do not die" (*Poems*, 2). However, Paul
is eager to live on in this world for now, for there
is much work still to be done (vv. 25–26). "The
Apostle's great love for the faithful is shown by
the fact that he did not say or do only the things
that it pleased him to say or do; rather, he wanted
as many people as possible to profit by his
words, for the salvation of many is pleasing to
God" (Ambrosiaster, *Ad Philippenses*).

*1:27—2:18 Not everything was going well for
the Philippians: there may have been a degree of
persecution, and rivalries had developed, provoked, it seems, by some preachers. St Paul
exhorts the Philippians to be steadfast (1:27–30)
and to have a unity based on Christ-like humility
(2:1–18).

1:27–30 The Greek expression translated here as
"let your manner of life be" (v. 27) has also a

Unity and humility

2 Cor 13:13

Phil 1:4
1 Cor 1:10f
Rom 12:10
Gal 5:26

1 Cor 10:24, 33

2 ¹So if there is any encouragement in Christ, any incentive of love, any participation in the Spirit, any affection and sympathy, ²complete my joy by being of the same mind, having the same love, being in full accord and of one mind. ³Do nothing from selfishness or conceit, but in humility count others better than yourselves. ⁴Let each of you look not only to his own interests, but also to the interests of others.

Hymn in praise of Christ's self-emptying

Heb 1:3
Col 1:15–30
Rom 1:2–4

Is 53:3, 12
Mt 20:28
Gal 4:4

⁵Have this mind among yourselves, which was in Christ Jesus, ⁶who, though he was in the form of God,* did not count equality with God a thing to be grasped, ⁷but emptied himself,* taking the form of a servant,ᵈ being born in the likeness of men.

et hoc a Deo; ²⁹quia vobis hoc donatum est pro Christo, non solum ut in eum credatis, sed ut etiam pro illo patiamini ³⁰idem certamen habentes, quale vidistis in me et nunc auditis in me. [2] ¹Si qua ergo consolatio in Christo, si quod solacium caritatis, si qua communio spiritus, si quae viscera et miserationes, ²implete gaudium meum, ut idem sapiatis, eandem caritatem habentes, unanimes, id ipsum sapientes, ³nihil per contentionem neque per inanem gloriam, sed in humilitate superiores sibi invicem arbitrantes, ⁴non, quae sua sunt, singuli considerantes, sed et ea, quae aliorum. ⁵Hoc sentite in vobis, quod et in Christo Iesu: / ⁶qui cum in forma Dei esset, / non rapinam arbitratus est esse se aequalem Deo, / ⁷sed semetipsum exinanivit formam servi accipiens, / in similitudinem hominum factus; / et habitu inventus ut homo, / ⁸humiliavit semetipsum

more specific meaning: "live as good citizens". St Paul may be referring to the Philippians' right to Roman citizenship, a right they were very proud of. He is pointing out here that, as well as having a position in society, Christians are citizens of heaven (see 3:20). They should live their lives on earth as good citizens of the Kingdom of God, realizing that "hope in a life to come does not take away from the importance of the duties of this life on earth, but rather adds to it by giving new motives for fulfilling these duties" (Vatican II, *Gaudium et spes*, 21).

Sufferings and difficulties are opportunities that God offers us to help us identify more closely with Christ by fearlessly embracing his cross (v. 29). "What does suffering matter if we accept it to console, to please God our Lord, with a spirit of reparation, united with him on his cross—in a word, if we suffer for Love?" (St Josemaría Escrivá, *The Way*, 182).

2:1–4 What makes the Apostle particularly happy is when Christians are at one with each other, in a union based on love and on the example set by Christ—the greatest example of humility, as is reflected in the verses that follow.

2:5–11 This is one of the earliest New Testament texts about the divinity of Jesus Christ. It is possible that Paul is transcribing an early liturgical hymn, adding some details or emphases of his own. The hymn extols the humiliation and exal-

tation of Christ. Conscious throughout of Christ's divinity, the Apostle focuses on his death on the cross, the supreme example of humility and obedience: "What is more humble", St Gregory of Nyssa asks, "than the King of all creation entering into communion with our poor nature? The King of kings and Lord of lords clothes himself with the form of our enslavement; the Judge of the universe comes to pay tribute to the princes of this world; the Lord of creation is born in a cave; he who encompasses the world cannot find room in the inn [...]; the pure and incorrupt one puts on the filthiness of our nature and experiences all our needs, experiences even death itself" (*De beatitudinibus*, 1).

2:6–8 These verses bring to mind the contrast between Jesus and Adam: Adam, a mere man, wanted to be like God (see Gen 3:5); Jesus, although he was God, "emptied himself" (v. 7). "When the text says that he 'emptied himself', it means that he took the form of a servant, not that he ceased to be God. His divine nature, the same as that of God the Father, was unchanged; but he took on our changing human nature when he was conceived in the Virgin's womb" (St Augustine, *Contra Faustum*, 3, 6).

Christ's obedience, even to death on a cross (v. 8), makes up for the disobedience of the first man. "The Only-begotten Son of God, the Word and Wisdom of the Father, who co-existed with God in glory before the creation of the world,

d Or *slave*

⁸And being found in human form he humbled himself and became obedient unto death, even death on a cross. ⁹Therefore God has highly exalted him and bestowed on him the name which is above every name, ¹⁰that at the name of Jesus every knee should bow, in heaven and on earth and under the earth, ¹¹and every tongue confess that Jesus Christ is Lord, to the glory of God the Father.

1 Cor 1:23; 2:2
Gal 3:13
Rom 5:19
Heb 12:2
Is 52:13
Rom 14:9
Acts 2:33
Is 45:23
Rev 5:3
Rom 1:4; 10:9
1 Cor 12:3
Acts 12:11

The children of God, the light of the world

¹²Therefore, my beloved, as you have always obeyed, so now, not only as in my presence but much more in my absence, work out your own salvation with fear and trembling; ¹³for God is at work in you, both to will and to work for his good pleasure.

¹⁴Do all things without grumbling or questioning, ¹⁵that you may be blameless and innocent, children of God without blemish in the midst of a crooked and per-

1 Cor 2:3
2 Cor 7:15
Eph 2:10
Eph 3:20
Heb 13:21
1 Pet 4:9
Deut 32:5
Mt 5:14–16; 12:39;
17:17
Eph 5:8

factus oboediens usque ad mortem, / mortem autem crucis. / ⁹Propter quod et Deus illum exaltavit / et donavit illi nomen, / quod est super omne nomen, / ¹⁰ut in nomine Iesu *omne genu flectatur* / caelestium et terrestrium et infernorum, / ¹¹*et omnis lingua confiteatur*: / «Dominus Iesus Christus!», / in gloriam Dei Patris. ¹²Itaque, carissimi mei, sicut semper oboedistis, non ut in praesentia mei tantum sed multo magis nunc in absentia mea, cum metu et tremore vestram salutem operamini; ¹³Deus est enim, qui operatur in vobis et velle et perficere pro suo beneplacito. ¹⁴Omnia

emptied himself, took the form of a servant and was obedient unto death in order to teach obedience to those who can be saved only if they learn to obey" (Origen, *De principiis*, 3, 5, 6).

2:9–11 On raising Jesus from the dead and setting him at his right hand, God the Father enabled the human nature of Jesus to manifest the glory of the divinity that is his. (The "name which is above every name" means the name of God.) St Athanasius points out that "this expression, 'he exalted him', does not mean that the nature of the Word was raised up [...]. Terms such as 'humbled' and 'exalted' refer only to the sphere of humanity, since only what is human can be exalted" (*Contra Arianos*, 1, 41).

All created beings are subject to Christ's authority, so mankind should acknowledge the fundamental truth of Christian belief that "Jesus Christ is Lord". The Greek word used here by St Paul—*Kyrios*—is the word used in the Septuagint, the early Greek version of the Old Testament, to translate the Hebrew name of God. Therefore, this sentence means, "Jesus Christ is God".

2:12–18 Reflection on the example set by Christ should help his disciple to persevere generously in his service. The upright, honest and generous lives of Christians should be a beacon to all those who meet them. Verse 13 shows that in all this we can count on the help of God's grace. "The more we will what is good, the more does

God strengthen our good will" (St John Chrysostom, *In Philippenses*, 8, 2, 12–13). "The truth that God is at work in all the actions of his creatures is inseparable from faith in God the Creator. God is the first cause who operates in and through secondary causes [...]. Far from diminishing the creature's dignity, this truth enhances it. Drawn from nothingness by God's power, wisdom and goodness, it can do nothing if it is cut off from its origin, for 'without a Creator the creature vanishes' (*Gaudium et spes*, 36, 3). Still less can a creature attain its ultimate end without the help of God's grace" (*Catechism of the Catholic Church*, 308). We can do nothing that leads to eternal life unless we are moved by God. However, grace does not overpower our freedom, because it is *we* who will and *we* who act. Our inability to perform meritorious actions on our own should not demoralize us. On the contrary, it is an additional reason why we should be grateful to God, for he is always ready to give us the help of his grace; grace enables us to do good works which in turn enable us to merit heaven. St Francis de Sales gives this example to show the wonderful way God works: "When an affectionate mother is teaching her little child to walk, she helps him and holds him if necessary, directing him to safer places and more level ground, holding him by the hand and keeping him there, or lifting him up in her arms. Our Lord similarly watches over the steps his children take" (*Treatise on the Love of God*, 3, 4).

Is 49:4
Gal 2:2; 4:11; 5:7
1 Thess 1:6–8
Is 65:23
2 Tim 4:6
Rom 1:9

Phil 1:4; 3:1; 4:4
verse generation, among whom you shine as lights in the world, ¹⁶holding fast the word of life, so that in the day of Christ I may be proud that I did not run in vain or labour in vain. ¹⁷Even if I am to be poured as a libation upon the sacrificial offering of your faith, I am glad and rejoice with you all. ¹⁸Likewise you also should be glad and rejoice with me.

3. PLANS AND NEWS*

Timothy's mission

1 Cor 4:17; 16:10
Acts 16:1

1 Cor 16:10

Phil 1:15–27
Gal 1:7

Phil 1:25
¹⁹I hope in the Lord Jesus to send Timothy to you soon, so that I may be cheered by news of you. ²⁰I have no one like him, who will be genuinely anxious for your welfare. ²¹They all look after their own interests, not those of Jesus Christ. ²²But Timothy's worth you know, how as a son with a father he has served with me in the gospel. ²³I hope therefore to send him just as soon as I see how it will go with me; ²⁴and I trust in the Lord that shortly I myself shall come also.

Epaphroditus' mission

Phil 4:18
²⁵I have thought it necessary to send to you Epaphroditus my brother and fellow worker and fellow soldier, and your messenger and minister to my need, ²⁶for he has been longing for you all, and has been distressed because you heard that he was ill. ²⁷Indeed he was ill, near to death. But God had mercy on him, and not only on him but on me also, lest I should have sorrow upon sorrow. ²⁸I am the more eager to send him, therefore, that you may rejoice at seeing him again, and that I may be less anxious.
1 Cor 16:18

Acts 20:24
1 Cor 16:17
²⁹So receive him in the Lord with all joy; and honour such men, ³⁰for he nearly died for the work of Christ, risking his life to complete your service to me.

facite sine murmurationibus et haesitationibus, ¹⁵ut efficiamini sine querela et simplices, filii Dei sine reprehensione in medio generationis pravae et perversae, inter quos lucetis sicut luminaria in mundo, ¹⁶verbum vitae firmiter tenentes ad gloriam meam in die Christi, quia non in vacuum cucurri, neque in vacuum laboravi. ¹⁷Sed et si delibor supra sacrificium et obsequium fidei vestrae, gaudeo et congaudeo omnibus vobis; ¹⁸idipsum autem et vos gaudete et congaudete mihi. ¹⁹Spero autem in Domino Iesu Timotheum cito me mittere ad vos, ut et ego bono animo sim, cognitis, quae circa vos sunt. ²⁰Neminem enim habeo tam unanimem, qui sincere pro vobis sollicitus sit; ²¹omnes enim sua quaerunt, non quae sunt Iesu Christi. ²²Probationem autem eius cognoscitis, quoniam sicut patri filius mecum servivit in evangelium. ²³Hunc igitur spero me mittere, mox ut videro, quae circa me sunt; ²⁴confido autem in Domino, quoniam et ipse cito veniam. ²⁵Necessarium autem existimavi Epaphroditum fratrem et cooperatorem et commilitonem meum, vestrum autem apostolum et ministrum necessitatis meae, mittere ad vos, ²⁶quoniam omnes vos desiderabat et maestus erat, propterea quod audieratis illum infirmatum. ²⁷Nam et infirmatus est usque ad mortem, sed Deus misertus est eius; non solum autem eius, verum et mei, ne tristitiam super tristitiam haberem. ²⁸Festinantius ergo misi illum, ut, viso eo, iterum gaudeatis, et ego sine tristitia sim. ²⁹Excipite itaque illum in Domino cum omni gaudio et eiusmodi cum honore habetote, ³⁰quoniam propter opus Christi usque ad mortem

*2:19–30 There is a rather abrupt change of subject at this point, where the Apostle passes on some news to the Philippians.

2:19–24 Timothy has been the Apostle's coworker in the evangelization of the Philippians, his companion on apostolic journeys (see Acts 16:1, 3, 10ff; 20:4) and his special envoy (see Acts 19:22). Paul praises Timothy for a number of qualities, particularly the way he identifies with and supports the Apostle; he is a good example of the sort of communion Christians should have with legitimate pastors of the Church.

2:25–30 Paul's imprisonment was part of God's plan. It stirred the love and generosity of the Philippians to send Epaphroditus to minister to his needs. "Suffering is present in the world in order to release love, to give birth to works of love towards neighbour, to transform the whole of human civilization into a 'civilization of love'" (John Paul II, *Salvifici doloris*, 30). It is very touching to see the sensitive way the first Christians practised fraternity with one another, and the respect and affection they had for their pastors.

4. THE CHRISTIAN LIFE*

A warning about Judaizers

3 ¹Finally, my brethren, rejoice in the Lord. To write the same things to you is not irksome to me, and is safe for you.

Philem 21
2 Cor 13:11
Phil 2:18; 4:4

²Look out for the dogs, look out for the evil-workers, look out for those who mutilate the flesh. ³For we are the true circumcision, who worship God in spirit,ᵉ and glory in Christ Jesus, and put no confidence in the flesh. ⁴Though I myself have reason for confidence in the flesh also. If any other man thinks he has reason for confidence in the flesh, I have more: ⁵circumcised on the eighth day, of the people of Israel, of the tribe of Benjamin, a Hebrew born of Hebrews; as to the law a Pharisee, ⁶as to zeal a persecutor of the church, as to righteousness under the law blameless.

Jer 4:4
Rom 2:25–29
Col 2:11

2 Cor 11:18, 21
Rom 7:5
Gen 17:10
Lev 12:3
2 Cor 11:22
Rom 11:1
Acts 22:3; 26:4

Acts 8:1, 3; 24:4
1 Cor 15:9
Gal 1:13–14

The righteousness of God exceeds that of the Law

⁷But whatever gain I had, I counted as loss for the sake of Christ. ⁸Indeed I count everything as loss because of the surpassing worth of knowing Christ Jesus my Lord. For his sake I have suffered the loss of all things, and count them as refuse, in

Mt 13:44–46
Mk 4:17–22
Lk 14:33
Phil 1:21

---

accessit in interitum tradens animam suam, ut suppleret id, quod vobis deerat ministerii erga me. [3] ¹De cetero, fratres mei, gaudete in Domino. Eadem vobis scribere mihi quidem non pigrum, vobis autem securum. ²Videte canes, videte malos operarios, videte concisionem! ³Nos enim sumus circumcisio, qui Spiritu Dei servimus et gloriamur in Christo Iesu et non in carne fiduciam habentes, ⁴quamquam ego habeam confidentiam et in carne. Si quis alius videtur confidere in carne, ego magis: ⁵circumcisus octava die, ex genere Israel, de tribu Beniamin, Hebraeus ex Hebraeis, secundum legem pharisaeus, ⁶secundum aemulationem persequens ecclesiam, secundum iustitiam, quae in lege est, conversatus sine querela. ⁷Sed, quae mihi erant lucra, haec arbitratus sum propter Christum detrimentum. ⁸Verumtamen existimo omnia detrimentum esse propter

---

*3:1—4:23 After giving news about himself and his co-workers, St Paul encourages the Philippians to be faithful and to continue to grow in the Christian life. He offers himself as an example: first, to answer the Judaizers, he describes the change he experienced when he became a Christian (3:1–16); then he speaks about the goal they must strive to reach, that of heaven (3:17–21); finally, he tells them how happy and grateful he feels when he thinks of them (4:1–20).

3:1–6 It was common for Roman houses to have a notice at the entrance that read, "*Cave canem*", Beware of the dog. St Paul uses these words as a colourful way to tell the Philippians to be on their guard against those "evil-workers" who, instead of helping to construct Christ's building, are doing damage to it. In the Old Testament, circumcision showed that a man belonged to the people of Israel; it guaranteed the promises of salvation made by God on Sinai. But some Christian preachers of a Judaizing tendency were arguing that circumcision was also a prerequisite for converting from paganism to Christianity. The Apostle calls them "those who mutilate the flesh", because they were promoting something

purely external, circumcision of the flesh, whereas what Christians should glory in is the fact that they have been remade in the image of Christ, through Baptism. The Apostle boasts of the fact that he is a Jew, in order to show the Philippians that he has moral authority to argue on this matter against these Judaizers.

3:7–11 Everything in which he gloried prior to his conversion Paul now regards as worthless when compared with the grace of knowing Christ. Christ makes a person righteous, not the Law of Moses (see Rom 3:21). Therefore, one needs to leave everything else behind for Christ's sake, and to strive to be like Christ until one eventually attains the glory of resurrection. St Teresa of Avila explains just how we should strive: "It is important—all-important, indeed—that they [those who want to take the high road to heaven] should begin well by making an earnest and most determined resolve not to halt until they reach their goal, whatever may come, whatever may happen to them, however hard they may have to labour, whoever may complain of them, whether they reach their goal or die on the road or have no heart to confront the trials

---

e Other ancient authorities read *worship by the Spirit of God*

Gal 2:16; 6:17
Rom 3:21–22; 10:3

Gal 6:17
Rom 6:1:4; 6:4;
8:11, 17
1 Pet 4:13

order that I may gain Christ ⁹and be found in him, not having a righteousness of my own, based on law, but that which is through faith in Christ, the righteousness from God that depends on faith; ¹⁰that I may know him and the power of his resurrection, and may share his sufferings, becoming like him in his death, ¹¹that if possible I may attain the resurrection from the dead.

The spiritual athlete

Phil 2:16
Gal 5:7
Rev 20:4ff

Lk 9:62

1 Cor 9:24ff

1 Cor 2:6

Gal 6:16

¹²Not that I have already obtained this or am already perfect; but I press on to make it my own, because Christ Jesus has made me his own.* ¹³Brethren, I do not consider that I have made it my own; but one thing I do, forgetting what lies behind and straining forward to what lies ahead, ¹⁴I press on toward the goal for the prize of the upward call of God in Christ Jesus. ¹⁵Let those of us who are mature be thus minded; and if in anything you are otherwise minded, God will reveal that also to you. ¹⁶Only let us hold true to what we have attained.

Citizens of heaven

Phil 4:9
1 Cor 4:16; 11:1
Gal 4:12
2 Thess 3:7
Rom 16:18
Gal 6:12
Col 3:2

¹⁷Brethren, join in imitating me, and mark those who so live as you have an example in us. ¹⁸For many, of whom I have often told you and now tell you even with tears, live as enemies of the cross of Christ. ¹⁹Their end is destruction, their god is

eminentiam scientiae Christi Iesu Domini mei, propter quem omnia detrimentum feci et arbitror ut stercora, ut Christum lucri faciam ⁹et inveniar in illo non habens meam iustitiam, quae ex lege est, sed illam, quae per fidem est Christi, quae ex Deo est iustitia in fide, ¹⁰ad cognoscendum illum et virtutem resurrectionis eius et communionem passionum illius, conformans me morti eius, ¹¹si quo modo occurram ad resurrectionem, quae est ex mortuis. ¹²Non quod iam acceperim aut iam perfectus sim, persequor autem si umquam comprehendam, sicut et comprehensus sum a Christo Iesu. ¹³Fratres, ego me non arbitror comprehendisse; unum autem: quae quidem retro sunt, obliviscens, ad ea vero, quae ante sunt, extendens me ¹⁴ad destinatum persequor, ad bravium supernae vocationis Dei in Christo Iesu. ¹⁵Quicumque ergo perfecti, hoc sentiamus; et si quid aliter sapitis, et hoc vobis Deus revelabit; ¹⁶verumtamen, ad quod pervenimus, in eodem ambulemus. ¹⁷Coimitatores mei estote, fratres, et observate eos, qui ita ambulant, sicut habetis formam nos. ¹⁸Multi enim ambulant, quos saepe dicebam vobis, nunc autem et flens dico, inimicos crucis Christi, ¹⁹quorum finis interitus, quorum deus venter et gloria in confusione ipsorum, qui terrena sapiunt. ²⁰Noster enim municipatus in caelis est, unde

which they meet, whether the whole world dissolves before them" (*Way of Perfection*, 21).

3:12–16 Growth in holiness always entails an effort. To make this point, St Paul uses a vivid comparison—the races in the stadium. He depicts asceticism as a kind of supernatural athletics, where one's goal is to progress in the interior life. "You should always be unhappy with what you are, if you want to attain what you are not yet. For when you were content with yourself, you stayed where you were, because if you say 'Enough', you are finished that very minute. Always grow, always walk on, always advance; do not stop on the way, do not turn back, do not go off course. One who does not advance is standing still; one who returns to the things he already abandoned is going backwards; one who goes off course commits apostasy. It is better to hobble along the road than run on any other route" (St Augustine, *Sermones*, 169, 18).

3:17–21 Imitation of the saints (and not of those opposed to Christ's cross) is a sure way to serve God and others. As fellow citizens of heaven, Christians should always be joyful and confident; as children of God, their lives should be based on hope in the Lord's coming and their own future resurrection.

St Paul's pastoral spirit is worth noting. He practises what he preaches: "There is no better teaching than the teacher's own example," St John Chrysostom exclaims, commenting on this passage; "by taking this course the teacher is sure of getting his disciple to follow him. Speak wisely, instruct as eloquently as you can […], but your example will make a greater impression and be more decisive […]. When your actions are in line with your words, nobody will be able to find fault with you" (St John Chrysostom, *In Philippenses*, ad loc.). Paul's exhortation in v. 17 should not be taken as meaning that he was lacking in humility. This is not the only letter in

the belly, and they glory in their shame, with minds set on earthly things.* ²⁰But our commonwealth is in heaven, and from it we await a Saviour, the Lord Jesus Christ, ²¹who will change our lowly body to be like his glorious body, by the power which enables him even to subject all things to himself.

Col 3:1-4
Acts 3:20–21
Gal 4:26
Heb 11:13–16; 12:22
1 Cor 15:47–49
Rom 8:23, 29
Col 3:4

Exhortation to perseverance and joy

4 ¹Therefore, my brethren, whom I love and long for, my joy and crown, stand firm thus in the Lord, my beloved.

1 Thess 2:19–20
Phil 1:4
1 Cor 9:25
2 Cor 1:14

²I entreat Euodia and I entreat Syntyche to agree in the Lord. ³And I ask you also, true yokefellow, help these women, for they have laboured side by side with me in the gospel together with Clement and the rest of my fellow workers, whose names are in the book of life.

Dan 12:1
Lk 10:20
Rev 20:12

⁴Rejoice in the Lord always; again I will say, Rejoice. ⁵Let all men know your forbearance. The Lord is at hand. ⁶Have no anxiety about anything, but in everything by prayer and supplication with thanksgiving let your requests be made known to God. ⁷And the peace of God, which passes all understanding, will keep your hearts and your minds in Christ Jesus.

2 Cor 13:11
Heb 10:37
Rom 13:11
Jas 5:8–9
Mt 6:25–34
Eph 5:19–20
Jn 14:27
Col 3:15
Eph 5:20

etiam salvatorem exspectamus Dominum Iesum Christum, ²¹qui transfigurabit corpus humilitatis nostrae, ut illud conforme faciat corpori gloriae suae secundum operationem, qua possit etiam subicere sibi omnia.   [4] ¹Itaque, fratres mei carissimi et desideratissimi, gaudium et corona mea, sic state in Domino, carissimi! ²Evodiam rogo et Syntychen deprecor idipsum sapere in Domino. ³Etiam rogo et te, germane compar, adiuva illas, quae mecum concertaverunt in evangelio cum Clemente et ceteris adiutoribus meis, quorum nomina sunt in libro vitae. ⁴Gaudete in Domino semper. Iterum dico: Gaudete! ⁵Modestia vestra nota sit omnibus hominibus. Dominus prope. ⁶Nihil solliciti sitis, sed in omnibus oratione et obse-

which he encourages Christians to imitate him. But in 1 Corinthians 11:1 he specifies that they should imitate him only insofar as he imitates Christ. True humility is not at odds with recognizing one's own virtues, provided one remembers that everything good in us comes from God.

4:1–3 St Paul speaks very tenderly here (v. 1) and makes a plea to two Christian women to bury their differences (v. 2). There is no room for rancour in a fervent Christian community. "Yokefellow" (v. 3): the same word in Greek seems to have been used as a proper name— Syzygus; St Paul may be addressing a third person, a co-worker named Syzygus (we know nothing else about him), calling on him to help these two women; he puns on the meaning of his name to remind him affectionately to live up to it—to be a yokefellow and bear a burden for the sake of the Gospel.

4:4 What St Paul says here is particularly striking if one bears in mind that he is writing from prison. True joy cannot be marred or strained by difficulties or problems. "This is the difference between us and those who do not know God," St Cyprian says: "they complain in

adversity; but difficulties do not draw us away from virtue or from the true faith. On the contrary, our virtue and faith are reinforced in affliction" (*De mortalitate*, 13).

4:5–7 "The Lord is at hand" (v. 5): the Apostle reminds the faithful of the nearness of our Lord; he wants to encourage them to bring joy to others and to always show understanding. These words must surely have brought to people's minds the exclamation *Marana tha* (Come, Lord), which was often on their lips at liturgical celebrations (see 1 Cor 16:21–24). In the sort of hostile environment that many of them lived in, the early Christians put their hope in their Saviour, Jesus Christ. Like them, we should be convinced that, while we await his coming in glory, the Lord is also with us, caring for us in his providence. There is no reason, then, for us to feel ill at ease or worried. All we need do is speak to him, trustingly, in prayer, with the simplicity of children. Constant prayer helps us to be serene, for, as St Bernard teaches, prayer "regulates our affections, directs our actions, corrects our faults, guides our conduct, beautifies and orders our life; it brings with it, too, knowledge of things divine and things human. It determines

Rom 12:17

⁸Finally, brethren, whatever is true, whatever is honourable, whatever is just, whatever is pure, whatever is lovely, whatever is gracious, if there is any excellence,

Rom 15:33; 16:20
Phil 3:17
1 Cor 14:33
1 Thess 5:23
2 Thess 3:7, 16

if there is anything worthy of praise, think about these things. ⁹What you have learned and received and heard and seen in me, do; and the God of peace will be with you.

Thanks for help received

Phil 1:4

¹⁰I rejoice in the Lord greatly that now at length you have revived your concern for me; you were indeed concerned for me, but you had no opportunity. ¹¹Not that I complain of want; for I have learned, in whatever state I am, to be content. ¹²I know how to be abased, and I know how to abound; in any and all circumstances I have learned the secret of facing plenty and hunger, abundance and want. ¹³I can do all things in him who strengthens me.

Heb 13:5
1 Tim 6:6
1 Cor 4:11–13
2 Cor 6:3–10
2 Cor 12:10
Col 1:29
1 Thess 2:3–9
Acts 16:12f

¹⁴Yet it was kind of you to share my trouble. ¹⁵And you Philippians yourselves know that in the beginning of the gospel, when I left Macedonia, no church entered into partnership with me in giving and receiving except you only; ¹⁶for even in Thessalonica you sent me help[f] once and again. ¹⁷Not that I seek the gift; but I seek the fruit which increases to your credit. ¹⁸I have received full payment, and more; I am filled, having received from Epaphroditus the gifts you sent, a fragrant offering, a sacrifice acceptable and pleasing to God. ¹⁹And my God will supply every need of yours according to his riches in glory in Christ Jesus. ²⁰To our God and Father be glory for ever and ever. Amen.

2 Cor 11:9
1 Cor 9:11
Gen 8:21
Ex 29:18
Phil 2:15
Eph 5:2
2 Cor 2:15
Rom 16:27

cratione cum gratiarum actione petitiones vestrae innotescant apud Deum. ⁷Et pax Dei, quae exsuperat omnem sensum, custodiet corda vestra et intellegentias vestras in Christo Iesu. ⁸De cetero, fratres, quaecumque sunt vera, quaecumque pudica, quaecumque iusta, quaecumque casta, quaecumque amabilia, quaecumque bonae famae, si qua virtus et si qua laus, haec cogitate; ⁹quae et didicistis et accepistis et audistis et vidistis in me, haec agite; et Deus pacis erit vobiscum. ¹⁰Gavisus sum autem in Domino vehementer quoniam tandem aliquando refloruistis pro me sentire, sicut et sentiebatis, opportunitate autem carebatis. ¹¹Non quasi propter penuriam dico, ego enim didici, in quibus sum, sufficiens esse. ¹²Scio et humiliari, scio et abundare; ubique et in omnibus institutus sum et satiari et esurire et abundare et penuriam pati. ¹³Omnia possum in eo, qui me confortat. ¹⁴Verumtamen bene fecistis communicantes tribulationi meae. ¹⁵Scitis autem et vos, Philippenses, quod in principio evangelii, quando profectus sum a Macedonia, nulla mihi ecclesia communicavit in ratione dati et accepti nisi vos soli; ¹⁶quia et Thessalonicam et semel et bis in usum mihi misistis. ¹⁷Non quia quaero datum, sed requiro fructum, qui abundet in rationem vestram. ¹⁸Accepi autem omnia et abundo; repletus sum acceptis ab Epaphrodito, quae misistis odorem suavitatis, hostiam acceptam, placentem Deo. ¹⁹Deus autem meus implebit omne desiderium

what we ought to do and reflects on what we have done, in such a way that our heart never becomes wanton or in need of discipline" (*De consideratione*, 1, 7).

4:8–9 All earthly things, everything noble in this world, have a divine value; they are good, and they help to lead a Christian to God (v. 8). "Your daily encounter with Christ takes place where your fellow men, your yearnings, your work and your affections are" (St Josemaría Escrivá, *Conversations*, 113).

4:10–20 The difficulties that may arise in a person's life never form an insuperable obstacle and should never take away one's peace. Christians can always count on God's support.

St Paul is touched by the Philippians' generosity (vv. 14–20). He is not asking them for donations: what interests him is the good that will come to them as a reward for their almsgiving: "He does not want for anything, he says, nor does he ask for anything he needs. We should rely only on good will and charity, so that we may reap the rewards of good will and charity" (Marius Victorinus, *In epistolam Pauli ad Philippenses*, 4, 17).

Since God rewards men for their actions, a person who gives alms gains more than he who receives them. "Whoever gives alms should do so with detachment and joy, for the less he keeps back for himself, the greater will be his reward" (St Leo the Great, *Sermo 10 de Quadragesima*, 5).

f Other ancient authorities read *money for my needs*

Words of farewell

[21]Greet every saint in Christ Jesus. The brethren who are with me greet you. [22]All the saints greet you, especially those of Caesar's household.

[23]The grace of the Lord Jesus Christ be with your spirit.

2 Cor 13:12
Phil 1:13

Gal 6:18

vestrum secundum divitias suas in gloria in Christo Iesu. [20]Deo autem et Patri nostro gloria in saecula saeculorum. Amen. [21] Salutate omnem sanctum in Christo Iesu. Salutant vos, qui mecum sunt, fratres. [22]Salutant vos omnes sancti, maxime autem, qui de Caesaris domo sunt. [23]Gratia Domini Iesu Christi cum spiritu vestro. Amen.

4:21–23 "Those of Caesar's household": these are civil servants, employees of the imperial government, who have become Christians. The expression applies equally to people based in Rome or to those based in any important city of the empire.

THE LETTER OF PAUL TO THE

COLOSSIANS

Introduction

The Letters to the Ephesians and the Philippians are followed by another (Colossians) which also contains references to the Apostle's being in prison, and on this account it is included among the so-called Captivity Letters.

Colossians has many features in common with Ephesians where content and literary style are concerned. For this reason, when studying either letter, it is useful to note what is said in the other. Colossians assumes that its addressees are aware of the letter to Philemon; in fact, almost all the personal reference in Colossians are also found to be in the short letter written by St Paul to Philemon, one of the Christians at Colossae.

1. STRUCTURE AND CONTENT

The Letter to the Colossians begins with a short greeting followed by a hymn to Christ and an act of thanksgiving to God (1:3–23). The most significant passage in this section is the in praise of Christ's lordship over all creation.

St Paul then goes on to register that his authority is at the service of the Gospel (1:24—2:5). The possibility of having to undergo suffering in order to carry out his God-given mission does not alarm him; he does what he must.

Later, he encourages those who have accepted Christ, and who have been raised up with him in Baptism, to be steadfast in the faith they have received, and not to allow themselves to be led astray by false beliefs (2:6–23).

The moral conduct of Christians should be grounded on their union with Christ, which begins at Baptism (a true spiritual resurrection) and is perfected by the other sacraments and a life of prayer. Christians' new life in Christ should be reflected in their family life and the way they conduct themselves in society (3:1—4:18).

2. CONTEXT

There is no evidence that St Paul actually preached the Gospel in Colossae during any of his apostolic journeys; but his co-worker Epaphras (see Col 1:7; 4:12) was apparently sent to preach there and in the neighbouring cities of Hierapolis and Laodicea (see 4:12–13). Colossians 2:1 indicates that the Apostle was not personally familiar with the church in Colossae. Therefore, any attempt to reconstruct the background to the letter must be based on the few references contained in it to particular people and events.

The letter addresses the unease and unrest caused in the communities of the Phrygian region by the teachings of preachers who had come from outside.

Syncretic beliefs and practices were beginning to spread; these were a mixture of the Christian Gospel, Jewish apocalyptic thinking and Hellenistic "mystery" religions—early forms of Gnosticism. Gnostics claimed that theirs was a higher form of wisdom; all other religions (including Judaism) were viewed by them as inadequate explanations of reality, suitable only for the general mass of uneducated and unenlightened people. Gnostics saw the world and human history as subject to manipulation by superhuman powers that were on a level lower than the true God but that were, nevertheless, in control of everything. Only those aware of these powers could win their favour or escape their influence. Therefore, knowledge (*gnosis*) of this suprahuman world was the path to salvation. The Gnostic sects that are known about (through later references to them by St Justin, St Irenaeus etc.) believed that initiates (and they alone) could attain salvation through "knowledge" of the divine mysteries; this knowledge gave them access to their true goal and proper home, the world of "divine fullness" (*pléroma*). People who wanted to be initiates had to undergo rigorous ascetical training.

The early Gnostics seem to have tried to merge their own ideas with Christianity. They regarded Christ as one of the divine beings that made up the *pléroma*. Their cosmos was a divided one: there was the sphere of the true God, who was unknown to man; and the sphere of the lower god, the Demiurge, and his subordinates, who controlled the world. These beliefs led them to the practice of a rigorous asceticism which required outright rejection of the created world in which ordinary human life is lived.

St Paul wrote this letter to combat these esoteric ideas; and so, although it follows the general lines of Pauline letters, its thrust is markedly polemical. However, it is also very profound in theological terms, because it explores key aspects of the mystery of Christ's being (Christology) and his infinite superiority and his lordship over all things (see 1:15–20). St Paul also makes some powerful statements, such as when he says that in Christ "the whole fulness [*pléroma*] of deity dwells bodily" (2:9).

This letter has certain features not found elsewhere in Paul's writings. There are new words or terms which seem to have come from the doctrines he is arguing against, but here they are charged with special shades of meaning. As regards the literary style, the original Greek of this letter (like that of the letter to the Ephesians) contains much longer sentences than are found in the Greek original of the "great" letters (Romans, Galatians, 1 and 2 Corinthians) and the First Letter to the Thessalonians, which were Paul's earliest letters.

There are new subjects and themes in this letter, too, mainly concerning the subject of Christ's lordship over all creation. In other letters St Paul expounds at length about God's plan for salvation of *man*, but here he teaches that *all* created things share in the fruits of Redemption.[1]

We have no information as to precisely when the Christian communities in Phrygia experienced the upheaval reflected in the letter, but it must have been at some point early in the second half of the first century. We cannot say exactly when the letter was written. However, Colossae was destroyed by an earthquake in the year 60 or 61, so the letter must have been written before then.[2]

Irrespective of what actually provoked the letter, or when it was written, it is traditionally attributed to St Paul and it tells us a great deal about Christian belief in the early Church. The later Church always regarded this letter to have been inspired by the Holy Spirit, which is why it is included in the canon of Holy Scripture.

---

1 This was a theme previously treated at some length only in Romans 8:19–22.   **2** However, it is not entirely impossible that these new philosophical-religious ideas began to spread in Phrygia after the disastrous earthquake, when the city of Laodicea was being rebuilt, and that this letter is addressed mainly to Christians of that city (the letter contains kind words for the community at Laodicea, and an explicit request that they read it: see 2:1–2; 4:15–16); in the letter the Apostle emphasizes the authority he has, to ensure that people are not led astray by these new ideas.

3. MESSAGE

The dangerous doctrinal confusion that was beginning to spread to Christian communities of Phrygia moved St Paul to reflect, from the perspective of the Gospel, on the theme of the creation and governance of the universe, and on God's plan of salvation for mankind, which also encompasses all earthly realities.

Christ is Lord of all creation

Taking issue with the bizarre ideas being spread in that region, St Paul asserts categorically that the Lord Jesus reigns supreme over all created beings, in heaven and on earth; his dominion is absolute, and he is infinitely beyond any created entity (see 1:15–20). This is the case because "in him [Christ] all the fulness [*pléroma*] of God was pleased to dwell, and through him to reconcile to himself all things" (1:19–20). The sphere of Christ's influence is not limited in any way; he fills all things, for "in him the whole fulness of deity dwells bodily" (2:9). Christ is not one of many suprahuman entities that populate the cosmos; he is the head, the one through whom salvation is made available to us.

Our Lord is head of the cosmos not only because of what he is on the level of being (God and Man) but also because he is the Saviour. Salvation has been brought about definitively by Christ, but its effect is an ongoing reality, because its benefits have to reach every single human being; it will eventually reach its culmination when the "recapitulation" of all things in Christ is made complete.

Christ is the head of the Church

Since the time of St Thomas Aquinas it has been customary to identify three elements in the fact that Christ is the head of the Church—his pre-eminence, his perfection and his life-giving power.[3] Colossians contains two key passages about Christ as head of the Church (1:18 and 2:19). The first defines headship in terms of pre-eminence, while the second speaks more clearly of Christ as the life-force of the Church; both these aspects are, however, intimately linked in the two passages. Colossians 1:15–20 is a hymn extolling Christ as absolutely supreme over all creation and over each of the grades of life and existence within it. In the course of the hymn it is stated that "he is [also] the head of the body, the church" (1:18). The subject of this sentence ("he") is the indivisible Christ, the God-Man. This verse adds to the proclamation of Christ's supremacy over creation the notion of his being the head of the Church.

The description of the Church as Christ's body is wonderfully expressive of how the mystery of salvation works. It explains the supernatural life and growth of each and every member of the entire Christian community. Because of the organic unity the Church has as the body of Christ, her members are enabled to grow in charity, each supporting the others while performing his or her own special function as a living member of the organism. Salvation thus works its way organically and systematically to encompass all members of the Church.

Indeed, through the intimate union between body and head, the body extends the action of the head: without the body's cooperation, the head would in some way be incomplete insofar as its life-giving action is concerned. Therefore, in a certain sense, the Christian can "complete" the redemptive passion of Christ himself: "Now I rejoice in my sufferings for your sake, and in my

---

3 See St Thomas Aquinas, *Summa theologiae*, 3, 8, 1c.

flesh I complete what is lacking in Christ's afflictions for the sake of his body, that is, the church" (1:24).

Christ is Lord of all temporal realities

The fact that Christ is lord of the cosmos is closely linked with his headship of the Church. Since the members of the Church are involved in temporal realities, "profane" affairs, the Letter to the Colossians takes account not only of Christ's lordship in heaven and in the human soul, but also of his supremacy over earthly affairs, all human interests and activities. Temporal realities are, in themselves, capable of being "Christianized"; in fact, they *should* be Christianized, sanctified.

It is not simply a matter of invoking the name of Jesus as one goes about one's business; it is a matter of directing everything one does towards Christ, for he "is before all things, and in him all things hold together" (1:17). In this sense, Christ should be placed at the summit of all these realities, as their head, their source of salvation and the point at which they converge, for he is the ultimate goal towards which everything that man does should be directed.

Colossians

1. INTRODUCTION*

Greeting

1 ¹Paul, an apostle of Christ Jesus by the will of God, and Timothy our brother, ²To the saints and faithful brethren in Christ at Colossae: Grace to you and peace from God our Father.

Acts 9:13
Eph 1:1
Rom 1:1, 7

Thanksgiving for the Colossians' response to the Gospel

³We always thank God, the Father of our Lord Jesus Christ, when we pray for you, ⁴because we have heard of your faith in Christ Jesus and of the love which you have for all the saints, ⁵because of the hope laid up for you in heaven. Of this you have heard before in the word of the truth, the gospel ⁶which has come to you, as indeed in the whole world it is bearing fruit and growing—so among yourselves, from the day you heard and understood the grace of God in truth, ⁷as you learned it from Epaphras our beloved fellow servant. He is a faithful minister of Christ on our[a] behalf ⁸and has made known to us your love in the Spirit.

Eph 1:15–16
Philem 4–5
Eph 1:13
1 Pet 1:4

2 Cor 6:1
Eph 1:13
Acts 14:3; 20:24, 32

1 Thess 2:13
1 Tim 3:16

1 Cor 13:1

[1] ¹Paulus apostolus Christi Iesu per voluntatem Dei et Timotheus frater ²his, qui sunt Colossis, sanctis et fidelibus fratribus in Christo: gratia vobis et pax a Deo Patre nostro. ³Gratias agimus Deo Patri Domini nostri Iesu Christi semper pro vobis orantes, ⁴audientes fidem vestram in Christo Iesu et dilectionem, quam habetis in sanctos omnes, ⁵propter spem, quae reposita est vobis in caelis, quam ante audistis in verbo veritatis evangelii, ⁶quod pervenit ad vos, sicut et in universo mundo est fructificans et crescens sicut et in vobis ex ea die, qua audistis et cognovistis gratiam Dei in veritate; ⁷sicut didicistis ab Epaphra carissimo conservo nostro, qui est fidelis pro nobis minister Christi, ⁸qui etiam manifestavit nobis

*1:1–23 After the usual words of greeting (vv. 1–2), St Paul begins the letter by thanking God for the way in which the Colossians have responded to the gifts that God has given them (vv. 3–8). There follows a heartfelt prayer for their growth in holiness (vv. 9–10), and an exhortation to be grateful for the wonderful things God has done in them (vv. 9–14). These introductory words lead Paul to proclaim a beautiful hymn in praise of Christ as head of all creation and of the Church: there is nothing that does not receive the redemptive benefit of the blood Christ shed on the cross (vv. 15–20).

1:3–14 Colossae had not been evangelized by St Paul, but by Epaphras. Paul confirms Epaphras' preaching and ministry and rejoices at the Colossians' faith.

Syncretic teachings being spread among the churches of Phrygia were beginning to make people there very interested in "knowledge" (*gnosis*) of divine mysteries. Paul's earnest prayer tells them that they need to discern what

true knowledge of God involves (v. 9); it comes from the Gospel, not from erroneous teachings that promise salvation to those initiated into the *gnosis* (see the Introduction to this letter). The Gnostics conceived the cosmos as divided in two parts—a realm of darkness, and the divine *pléroma* (fullness) where initiates who shunned this world would enjoy salvation. Alluding to this sort of language, but changing its meaning somewhat, the Apostle speaks now about "the dominion of darkness" (v. 13), to describe the condition of enslavement in which sinful people find themselves, and about the "light" (v. 12), the clarity that surrounds those who lead lives worthy of God.

The Apostle prays unceasingly that the Colossians may grow in true knowledge of God (vv. 9–10), and he exhorts them to express, by way of good works, their appreciation to God, for all the divine gifts they have received through Christ. "The Apostle speaks here, as he does in many other places, of faith and good works, for faith and the good life must always be

a Other ancient authorities read *your*

753

Eph 1:16
Col 3:10
Phil 1:9

Rom 12:2
Eph 2:10; 4:1

Rom 15:5
1 Cor 1:5
Eph 3:16

Acts 26:18
1 Pet 2:9
Eph 1:11–13, 18
Lk 22:53
Jn 8:12
Acts 26:18
1 Pet 2:9
Eph 1:6–7
Rom 3:24

⁹And so, from the day we heard of it, we have not ceased to pray for you, asking that you may be filled with the knowledge of his will in all spiritual wisdom and understanding, ¹⁰to lead a life worthy of the Lord, fully pleasing to him, bearing fruit in every good work and increasing in the knowledge of God. ¹¹May you be strengthened with all power, according to his glorious might, for all endurance and patience with joy, ¹²giving thanks to the Father, who has qualified us[b] to share in the inheritance of the saints in light. ¹³He has delivered us from the dominion of darkness and transferred us to the kingdom of his beloved Son, ¹⁴in whom we have redemption, the forgiveness of sins.

Hymn in praise of Christ, the head of all creation

Wis 7:26
Col 1:18
Rom 8:29
2 Cor 4:4
Jn 1:3
Heb 1:2f
Eph 1:10, 21
1 Cor 8:6
Heb 1:2f
Prov 8:2
Eph 1:22–23; 5:23f
Rom 8:29

¹⁵He is the image of the invisible God, the first-born* of all creation; ¹⁶for in him all things were created, in heaven and on earth, visible and invisible, whether thrones or dominions or principalities or authorities—all things were created through him and for him. ¹⁷He is before all things, and in him all things hold together. ¹⁸He is the head of the body, the church; he is the beginning, the first-born from the dead, that

dilectionem vestram in Spiritu. ⁹Ideo et nos, ex qua die audivimus, non cessamus pro vobis orantes et postulantes, ut impleamini agnitione voluntatis eius in omni sapientia et intellectu spiritali, ¹⁰ut ambuletis digne Domino per omnia placentes, in omni opere bono fructificantes et crescentes in scientia Dei, ¹¹in omni virtute confortati secundum potentiam claritatis eius in omnem patientiam et longanimitatem, cum gaudio ¹²gratias agentes Patri, / qui idoneos vos fecit in partem sortis sanctorum in lumine; / ¹³qui eripuit nos de potestate tenebrarum / et transtulit in regnum Filii dilectionis suae, / ¹⁴in quo habemus redemptionem, / remissionem peccatorum; / ¹⁵qui est imago Dei invisibilis, / primogenitus omnis creaturae, / ¹⁶quia in ipso condita sunt universa in caelis et in terra, / visibilia et invisibilia, / sive throni sive dominationes / sive principatus sive potestates. / Omnia per ipsum et in ipsum creata sunt, / ¹⁷et ipse est ante omnia, / et omnia in ipso constant. / ¹⁸Et ipse est caput corporis ecclesiae; / qui est

considered together [...]. How great must be the virtue of one who knows God and is deemed worthy to be His servant, or even his son!" (St John Chrysostom, *In Colossenses*, 2).

1:15–20 St Paul counters the erroneous ideas by extolling the mystery of Christ and his mission as Redeemer. These verses are a beautiful hymn in praise of Christ's lordship over all creation. The first stanza (vv. 15–17) asserts that Christ's dominion encompasses the entire cosmos and stems from the fact that he is its Creator. This passage is reminiscent of the prologue to St John's Gospel and of the early verses of Genesis. The second stanza (vv. 18–20) describes the new creation that has come about through the grace won by Christ in his death on the cross. He is the Mediator, and the head of the Church. He has re-established peace and has reconciled all things to God.

When St Paul describes the Son as "the image of the invisible God" (v. 15), he anticipates the later Christian teaching that the Father and the Son have the same nature, and he points out that the Son proceeds from the Father. Only the second Person of the Blessed Trinity, the Son, is the perfect image of the Father. "He is

called 'the image of God' because he is consubstantial with the Father. He proceeds from the Father; the Father does not proceed from him" (St Gregory Nazianzen, *De theologia*, 30, 20). And St Thomas explains: "The image [likeness] of a thing may be found in something in two ways; in one way it is found in something of the same specific nature—as the image of the king is found in his son. In another way it is found in something of a different nature, as the king's image on the coin. In the first sense the Son is the Image of the Father; in the second sense man is called the image of God; and therefore in order to express the imperfect character of the divine image in man, man is not simply called the image but is referred to as being *the image*, whereby is expressed a certain movement or tendency to perfection. But it cannot be said that the Son of God is according *to the image*, because He is the perfect Image of the Father" (*Summa theologiae*, 1, 35, 2, ad 3).

When the Apostle calls Christ "the first-born of all creation" (v. 15), the description means that Christ has pre-eminence and headship over all created things. "He is called 'the first-born' not because he is begotten of the Father but because in

b Other ancient authorities read *you*

in everything he* might be pre-eminent. ¹⁹For in him all the fullness of God was
pleased to dwell, ²⁰and through him to reconcile to himself all things, whether on
earth or in heaven, making peace by the blood of his cross.

Col 1:15, 24
1 Cor 15:20
Rev 1:5

The effect of Christ's saving action

²¹And you, who once were estranged and hostile in mind, doing evil deeds, ²²he has
now reconciled in his body of flesh by his death, in order to present you holy and
blameless and irreproachable before him, ²³provided that you continue in the faith,
stable and steadfast, not shifting from the hope of the gospel which you heard, which
has been preached to every creature under heaven, and of which I, Paul, became a
minister.

Eph 4:18–19
Eph 2:14–16

Mk 16:15
1 Tim 3:16
Eph 3:17

principium, primogenitus ex mortuis, / ut sit in omnibus ipse primatum tenens, / ¹⁹quia in ipso complacuit omnem plenitudinem habitare / ²⁰et per
eum reconciliare omnia in ipsum, / pacificans per sanguinem crucis eius, sive quae in terris sive quae in caelis sunt. ²¹Et vos, cum essetis aliquando
alienati et inimici sensu in operibus malis, ²²nunc autem reconciliavit in corpore carnis eius per mortem exhibere vos sanctos et immaculatos et
irreprehensibiles coram ipso, ²³si tamen permanetis in fide fundati et stabiles et immobiles a spe evangelii, quod audistis, quod praedicatum est
in universa creatura, quae sub caelo est, cuius factus sum ego Paulus minister. ²⁴Nunc gaudeo in passionibus pro vobis et adimpleo ea quae desunt
passionum Christi in carne mea pro corpore eius, quod est ecclesia, ²⁵cuius factus sum ego minister secundum dispensationem Dei, quae data est

Him all things were made […]. If the Word were a
creature, Scripture would say that he was 'the
first-born of all creatures'. When the holy writers
say that he is 'the first-born of all creation', they
show that the Son of God is not a creature and that
he stands above all creation" (St Athanasius,
Contra Arianos, 2, 63). He is the first-born not
only because he existed before all created things
but also because they were all created "in him"
and "through him" and "for him"; *in* Christ: he is
their source, their centre and their model or
exemplary cause; *through* him, because God the
Father, through God the Son, creates all things;
and *for* him, because Christ is the last end, the
goal or purpose of all creation (see Eph 1:10).
And, Paul adds, "in him all things hold together",
that is to say, Christ maintains everything in being.

In v. 18 Paul uses the image of a body and its
head to describe the Church and Christ (cf. 2:19
and Eph 1:23 and 4:15). "We Christians know
that the resurrection has come about in the Head
and that it will be brought about in the members
of the body. The head of the Church is Christ,
and the members of his body, the Church. What
comes to pass in the head will later be fulfilled in
the body. This is our hope" (St Augustine, *Enarrationes in Psalmos*, 65, 1).

Since Christ is above all created things, the
Father chose to reconcile all things to himself
through him (v. 20). Sin had cut man off from
God, rupturing the perfect order that had once
reigned in the created world. By shedding his

blood on the cross, Christ obtained peace for us;
nothing in the universe falls outside the scope of
the power of his peace: "The history of salvation—the salvation of the whole of humanity as
well as of every human being of whatever
period—is the wonderful history of a reconciliation: the reconciliation whereby God, as Father,
in the Blood and the Cross of his Son made man,
reconciles the world to himself and thus brings
into being a new family of those who have been
reconciled. Reconciliation becomes necessary
because there has been the break of sin from
which derive all the other forms of break within
man and about him. Reconciliation therefore, in
order to be complete, necessarily requires liberation from sin, which is to be rejected in its
deepest roots. Thus a close internal link unites
conversion and *reconciliation*. It is impossible to
split these two realities or to speak of one and
say nothing of the other" (John Paul II, *Reconciliatio et paenitentia*, 4).

1:21–23 In the light of Christ's saving action, St
Paul now introduces three themes which he will
discuss (in reverse order) in the remaining sections
of the letter—the duty of Christians to live
irreproachable lives, now that they have become
members of Christ (vv. 21–22); their need to be
steadfast in the faith and true to the Gospel given
them (v. 23); and the Apostle's own authority to
speak as he does: he is a servant of the Gospel (v.
23).

2. PAUL'S MISSION*

Proclamation of the Mystery

Eph 3:1, 13
2 Cor 1:5

Eph 3:2, 7
2 Cor 3:6

Rom 16:25

Eph 3:9
Phil 4:13

Eph 4:13

[24]Now I rejoice in my sufferings for your sake, and in my flesh I complete what is lacking* in Christ's afflictions for the sake of his body, that is, the church, [25]of which I became a minister according to the divine office which was given to me for you, to make the word of God fully known, [26]the mystery hidden for ages and generations[c] but now made manifest to his saints. [27]To them God chose to make known how great among the Gentiles are the riches of the glory of this mystery, which is Christ in you, the hope of glory. [28]Him we proclaim, warning every man and teaching every man in all wisdom, that we may present every man mature in Christ. [29]For this I toil, striving with all the energy which he mightily inspires within me.

Paul's concern for the faithful

Col 1:24

2 Cor 1:4
Col 1:9

2 [1]For I want you to know how greatly I strive for you, and for those at Laodicea, and for all who have not seen my face, [2]that their hearts may be encouraged as

mihi in vos, ut impleam verbum Dei, [26]mysterium, quod absconditum fuit a saeculis et generationibus, nunc autem manifestatum est sanctis eius, [27]quibus voluit Deus notas facere divitias gloriae mysterii huius in gentibus, quod est Christus in vobis, spes gloriae; [28]quem nos annuntiamus, commonentes omnem hominem et docentes omnem hominem in omni sapientia, ut exhibeamus omnem hominem perfectum in Christo; [29]ad quod et laboro certando secundum operationem eius, quae operatur in me in virtute.   [2] [1]Volo enim vos scire qualem sollicitudinem habeam pro vobis et pro his, qui sunt Laodiciae, et quicumque non viderunt faciem meam in carne, [2]ut consolentur corda ipsorum instructi in caritate et in omnes

Christ's holy human nature is an instrument of salvation: through his passion and death "in his body of flesh" (v. 22) our Lord overpowered sin and obtained the grace necessary to cleanse man of his faults and make him presentable to God. The incarnation of the Word means that the Christian faith is opposed to the kind of dualism that was being disseminated at the time, which depicted spirit and matter as being at war with one another. The human body and purely material things are not an obstacle to sanctification. "There is only one life, made of flesh and spirit. And it is that life which has to become, in both body and soul, holy and filled with God: we discover the invisible God in the most visible and material things" (St Josemaría Escrivá, *Conversations*, 114).

*1:24—2:5 In this section St Paul declares that his life has been devoted to his God-given mission to reveal the divine mystery to the Gentiles, no matter what suffering that might entail for him (1:24–29). The Apostle was always very concerned to ensure that the faithful kept to the faith they received; he did not want them to be led astray by unorthodox ideas (2:1–5).

1:24–29 What does St Paul mean when he talks about "what is lacking in Christ's afflictions" (v.

24)? The most common explanation of this statement is summarized by St Alphonsus as follows: "Can it be that Christ's passion alone was insufficient to save us? It left nothing more to be done, it was entirely sufficient to save all men. However, for the merits of the Passion to be applied to us, according to St Thomas [*Summa theologiae*, 3, 49, 3], we need to cooperate [subjective redemption] by patiently bearing the trials God sends us, so as to become like our head, Christ" (*Reflections on the Passion*, 10). That is to say, we can cooperate with God's plans through our prayers and actions, and even our sufferings, which give us a share in the sufferings of Christ. When a person suffers "in the spiritual dimension of the work of Redemption *he is serving*, like Christ, *the salvation of his brothers and sisters*" (John Paul II, *Salvifici doloris*, 27).

"The proclamation of the economy of Redemption is called a 'mystery' [v. 26] because no one knew of it in ancient times but God alone" (Theodoret of Cyrrhus, *Interpretatio in Colossenses*, ad loc.). On the "mystery", see also the note on Eph 1:3–14.

2:1–5 Christ is the fullest manifestation of the "mystery" or divine plan for man's salvation. To

c Or *from angels and men*

they are knit together in love, to have all the riches of assured understanding and the   Eph 3:18–19
Rom 16:25
knowledge of God's mystery, of Christ, ³in whom are hid all the treasures of wisdom   Is 45:3
Prov 2:4–5
and knowledge. ⁴I say this in order that no one may delude you with beguiling   Eph 5:6
speech. ⁵For though I am absent in body, yet I am with you in spirit, rejoicing to see   Rom 16:18
1 Thess 2:17
your good order and the firmness of your faith in Christ.   1 Cor 5:3–4

3. FIRMNESS IN THE FAITH*

A warning about heresy

⁶As therefore you received Christ Jesus the Lord, so live in him, ⁷rooted and built up in   Acts 2:22
him and established in the faith, just as you were taught, abounding in thanksgiving.   Eph 2:20; 3:17; 4:21
2 Thess 2:1

⁸See to it that no one makes a prey of you by philosophy and empty deceit,   Gal 4:3
Eph 5:6
according to human tradition, according to the elemental spirits of the universe, and   Col 2:16
not according to Christ. ⁹For in him the whole fullness of deity dwells bodily, ¹⁰and   Jn 1:14
Col 1:16–19; 2:15
you have come to fullness of life in him, who is the head of all rule and authority.   Eph 1:21f; 3:19

divitias plenitudinis intellectus, in agnitionem mysterii Dei, Christi, ³in quo sunt omnes thesauri sapientiae et scientiae absconditi. ⁴Hoc dico, ut nemo vos decipiat in subtilitate sermonum. ⁵Nam etsi corpore absens sum, sed spiritu vobiscum sum, gaudens et videns ordinem vestrum et firmamentum eius, quae in Christum est, fidei vestrae. ⁶Sicut ergo accepistis Christum Iesum Dominum, in ipso ambulate, ⁷radicati et superaedificati in ipso et confirmati fide, sicut didicistis, abundantes in gratiarum actione. ⁸Videte, ne quis vos depraedetur per philosophiam et inanem fallaciam secundum traditionem hominum, secundum elementa mundi et non secundum Christum; ⁹quia in ipso inhabitat omnis plenitudo divinitatis corporaliter, ¹⁰et estis in illo repleti, qui est caput omnis principatus et potestatis, ¹¹in quo et circumcisi estis circumcisione non manufacta in

counter the "beguiling speech" of false teachers (v. 4), St Paul exhorts the faithful to strive for a deeper understanding of the Gospel they have received. An infinite treasure of wisdom and knowledge lies hidden in Christ (v. 3); this means that reflection on his life and teachings is an inexhaustible source of nourishment for the soul. "There are great depths to be fathomed in Christ. For he is like an abandoned mine with many recesses containing treasures, of which, for all that men try to fathom them, the end and bottom is never reached; rather in each recess men continue to find new veins of new riches on all sides" (St John of the Cross, *Spiritual Canticle*, 37, 3).

*2:6–23 Those who have accepted Christ and been raised with him through Baptism should persevere in the faith they have received, and not allow themselves to be deflected by vain beliefs (vv. 6–15), or adopt religious practices which bring them no benefit or are so rigorous that they undermine genuine Christian piety (vv. 16–23).

2:6–15 St Paul draws attention to the implications of Christians' faith in the Incarnation, the mystery from which Christ's headship over the cosmos derives. Speaking against those who

sought to enter the sphere of divine fullness (*pléroma*) by means of *gnosis* (and all sorts of complicated initiation rites), St Paul asserts that in Christ "the whole fulness [*pléroma*] of deity dwells bodily" (v. 9). Paul is not simply developing his argument here; what he says also has profound theological content: St John of Avila explains: "It does not dwell in him merely by grace—as in the case of the saints (men and angels both), but in another way of greater substance and value, that is, by way of personal union" (St John of Avila, *Audi filia*, 84). Christian teaching will later spell out that there are two natures in Christ, divine and human, joined in one Person, who is divine. This "hypostatic union" does not prevent each nature from having all its own proper features, for, as St Leo the Great defined, "the Word has not changed into flesh, nor has flesh changed into Word; but each remains, in a unity" (*Licet per nostros*, 2).

Just as an Israelite becomes part of the People of God through circumcision, a Christian becomes part of the Church through Baptism (vv. 11–12). Using imagery similar to that found in Romans 6:4, and referring to the rite of Baptism by immersion, St Paul speaks of the sacrament as a kind of burial (a sure sign that

Jer 4:4
Phil 3:3
Rom 2:25–29
Rom 1:4; 6:4; 8:11

Eph 2:1, 5, 6

Eph 2:15
1 Pet 2:24
Lk 11:22
Eph 1:21
2 Cor 2:14
Col 1:16; 2:10
1 Pet 3:22

[11]In him also you were circumcised with a circumcision made without hands, by putting off the body of flesh in the circumcision of Christ; [12]and you were buried with him in baptism, in which you were also raised with him through faith in the working of God, who raised him from the dead. [13]And you, who were dead in trespasses and the uncircumcision of your flesh, God made alive together with him, having forgiven us all our trespasses, [14]having cancelled the bond which stood against us with its legal demands; this he set aside, nailing it to the cross. [15]He disarmed the principalities and powers and made a public example of them, triumphing over them in him.[d]

Rejection of false asceticism

Rom 14:1, 5–6
Gal 4:3
Heb 8:5; 10:1

Gal 6:12

[16]Therefore let no one pass judgment on you in questions of food and drink or with regard to a festival or a new moon or a sabbath. [17]These are only a shadow of what is to come; but the substance belongs to Christ. [18]Let no one disqualify you, insisting on self-abasement and worship of angels, taking his stand on visions, puffed up without reason by his sensuous mind, [19]and not holding fast to the Head, from whom

exspoliatione corporis carnis, in circumcisione Christi, [12]consepulti ei in baptismo, in quo et conresuscitati estis per fidem operationis Dei, qui suscitavit illum a mortuis; [13]et vos, cum mortui essetis in delictis et praeputio carnis vestrae, convivificavit cum illo, donans nobis omnia delicta, [14]delens, quod adversum nos erat, chirographum decretis, quod erat contrarium nobis, et ipsum tulit de medio affigens illud cruci; [15]exspolians principatus et potestates traduxit confidenter, triumphans illos in semetipso. [16]Nemo ergo vos iudicet in cibo aut in potu aut ex parte diei festi aut neomeniae aut sabbatorum, [17]quae sunt umbra futurorum, corpus autem Christi. [18]Nemo vos bravio defraudet complacens sibi in humilitate et religione angelorum propter ea, quae vidit, ingrediens, frustra inflatus sensu carnis suae [19]et non tenens caput, ex quo totum corpus per nexus et coni-

someone has died to sin), and a resurrection to a new life, the life of grace. By this sacrament we are drawn into Christ's death and burial so as to be able to rise with him. "Christ by his resurrection came to signify our new life, reborn out of the old death which submerged us in sin. This is what is brought about in us by the great sacrament of Baptism: all those who receive this grace die to sin [...] and are reborn to the new life" (St Augustine, *Enchiridion*, 41–42).

Christ is the only mediator because he is both God and Man. The basic purpose of his mediation is to reconcile men to God by forgiveness of sin and the gift of the life of grace, which is a sharing in God's own life. Verse 14 states how Christ accomplished this purpose—by dying on the cross. All who were under the yoke of sin and the Law have been set free through his death. The Mosaic Law, to which scribes and Pharisees added so many precepts as to make it unbearable had become (to use Paul's comparison) like a charge sheet against man, because it imposed heavy burdens but did not provide the grace needed to bear them. The Apostle says very graphically that this charge sheet or "bond which stood against us" (v. 14) was taken out of the reckoning and nailed to the cross. "The King

came to cancel our debts, and signed His name on another bill to make Himself our debtor" (St Ephrem, *Hymnus de Nativitate*, 4, 12).

On the "principalities and powers" (v. 15), see the note on Eph 6:10–20.

2:16–23 The days of the "new moon" (see Lev 23:24) were Jewish festivals that had been celebrated for centuries. The sabbath, the weekly Jewish holy day, was the day reserved to the Lord, for he himself marked it out as holy, and to be dedicated to rest (see Ex 20:8–11). Abstinence from certain types of food and drink was specified in detail in the Old Testament (see Lev 10:9; 11:1–47; Num 6:3), as were the festivals celebrated in the Lord's honour (see Num 28:1–26). These precepts were useful in that they brought people into the world of things divine, but now that the fullness of Revelation has come with Jesus Christ they no longer apply (preachers who came from outside may have been telling the Colossians otherwise). When a person is baptized, he or she dies with Christ to the "spirits of the universe" (v. 20) and is freed from slavery to the Law and to sin, to be born into a new kind of life—a teaching which will be the subject of the chapters that follow.

d Or *in it* (that is, the cross)

the whole body, nourished and knit together through its joints and ligaments, grows with a growth that is from God.

Eph 2:21, 22; 4:15–16

²⁰If with Christ you died to the elemental spirits of the universe, why do you live as if you still belonged to the world? Why do you submit to regulations, ²¹"Do not handle, Do not taste, Do not touch" ²²(referring to things which all perish as they are used), according to human precepts and doctrines? ²³These have indeed an appearance of wisdom in promoting rigor of devotion and self-abasement and severity to the body, but they are of no value in checking the indulgence of the flesh.ᵉ

Gal 4:3–9

Is 29:13
Mt 15:9
1 Cor 6:13; 8:8
Rom 13:14
1 Tim 4:3

4. NEW LIFE IN CHRIST*

Seeking the things that are above

3 ¹If then you have been raised with Christ, seek the things that are above, where Christ is, seated at the right hand of God. ²Set your minds on things that are above, not on things that are on earth. ³For you have died, and your life is hid with Christ in God. ⁴When Christ who is our life appears, then you also will appear with him in glory.

Eph 2:6
Phil 3:20

Ps 110:1
Mt 6:33

Col 2:12

1 Jn 3:2
Rom 8:19
Col 1:27; 2:12
1 Cor 15:43

Avoiding sin

⁵Put to death therefore what is earthly in you: fornication, impurity, passion, evil desire, and covetousness, which is idolatry. ⁶On account of these the wrath of God

Mt 15:9
Rom 1:29; 6:12; 8:13
Eph 4:19; 5:3–5
Eph 5:6

unctiones subministratum et compaginatum crescit in augmentum Dei. ²⁰Si mortui estis cum Christo ab elementis mundi, quid tamquam viventes in mundo decretis subicimini: ²¹«Ne tetigeris neque gustaveris neque contrectaveris», ²²quae sunt omnia in corruptionem ipso usu secundum praecepta et doctrinas hominum? ²³Quae sunt rationem quidem habentia sapientiae in superstitione et humilitate, et non parcendo corpori, non in honore aliquo ad saturitatem carnis.   [3] ¹Igitur si conresurrexistis Christo, quae sursum sunt quaerite, ubi Christus est in dextera Dei sedens; ²quae sursum sunt sapite, non quae supra terram. ³Mortui enim estis, et vita vestra abscondita est cum Christo in Deo! ⁴Cum Christus apparuerit, vita vestra, tunc et vos apparebitis cum ipso in gloria. ⁵Mortificate ergo membra, quae sunt super terram: fornicationem, immunditiam, libidinem, concupiscentiam malam et avaritiam, quae est simulacrorum servitus, ⁶propter quae venit ira Dei super filios incredulitatis; ⁷in quibus et vos ambulastis ali-

*3:1—4:18 Christian ethics are based on the fact that the person is linked to Christ; this link is formed by Baptism, which is a spiritual resurrection, and perfected by the other sacraments and by prayer. Christians need, therefore, to always seek the "things that are above", where Christ dwells (3:1–4). The Christian path begins with a clear rejection of the vices of the "old nature"; one must instead put on the "new nature" (3:5–11), and then grow in virtue (3:12–17). All this should show itself in family life (3:18—4:1) and public life. Paul invites Christians to draw their strength from prayer; their upright lifestyle will help bring others closer to the faith (4:2–6).

3:1–4 Through Baptism Christians share in the glorious life of the risen Jesus, so Christ should be present in everything they do. "My love is crucified […]. Neither the food that decays nor the pleasures of this world satisfy me. What I want is the bread of God, which is the flesh of Christ, born of the descendants of David, and I desire no other drink but his blood, which is the charity that is never corrupted" (St Ignatius of Antioch, *Ad Romanos*, 6, 1—9, 3). Eagerness to live in Christ's presence gives people a different perspective on life and the world around them: "In their pilgrimage to the heavenly city Christians are to seek and relish the things that are above (cf. Col 3:1–2): this involves not a lesser, but a greater commitment to working with all men to build a world that is more human" (Vatican II, *Gaudium et spes*, 57).

3:5–11 The "old man" (v. 9) is a person who allows himself to be dominated by the disorders in his nature. The disciple of Christ, who has been renewed by the Lord and lives for him, has a new and more perfect understanding of God and of the world; he sees things from a higher

e Or *are of no value, serving only to indulge the flesh*

Eph 2:2–3
Tit 3:3
Eph 4:25–31; 5:4
Eph 4:22, 25

Gen 1:26f
Col 1:9
Rom 12:2

Eph 2:15
Gal 3:27–28
1 Cor 2:13; 15:28

is coming.[f] [7]In these you once walked, when you lived in them. [8]But now put them all away: anger, wrath, malice, slander, and foul talk from your mouth. [9]Do not lie to one another, seeing that you have put off the old nature with its practices [10]and have put on the new nature, which is being renewed in knowledge after the image of its creator. [11]Here there cannot be Greek and Jew, circumcised and uncircumcised, barbarian, Scythian, slave, free man, but Christ is all, and in all.

Progress in the spiritual life

Eph 4:2, 32
1 Pet 2:9

[12]Put on then, as God's chosen ones, holy and beloved, compassion, kindness, lowliness, meekness, and patience, [13]forbearing one another and, if one has a complaint against another, forgiving each other; as the Lord has forgiven you, so you also must forgive. [14]And above all these put on love, which binds everything together in perfect harmony. [15]And let the peace of Christ rule in your hearts, to which indeed you were called in the one body. And be thankful. [16]Let the word of Christ dwell in you richly, teach and admonish one another in all wisdom, and sing psalms and hymns and spiritual songs with thankfulness in your hearts to God. [17]And whatever you do, in word or deed, do everything in the name of the Lord Jesus, giving thanks to God the Father through him.

1 Cor 10:31
Eph 5:20

Morals in family life

Eph 5:22; 6:9
1 Pet 2:13, 18; 3:1–7
Tit 2:10

[18]Wives, be subject to your husbands, as is fitting in the Lord.* [19]Husbands, love your wives, and do not be harsh with them. [20]Children, obey your parents in every-

quando, cum viveretis in illis. [8]Nunc autem deponite et vos omnia: iram, indignationem, malitiam, blasphemiam, turpem sermonem de ore vestro; [9]nolite mentiri invicem, qui exuistis vos veterem hominem cum actibus eius [10]et induistis novum, eum, qui renovatur in agnitionem secundum imaginem eius, qui creavit eum, [11]ubi non est Graecus et Iudaeus, circumcisio et praeputium, barbarus, Scytha, servus, liber, sed omnia et in omnibus Christus. [12]Induite vos ergo sicut electi Dei, sancti et dilecti, viscera misericordiae, benignitatem, humilitatem, mansuetudinem, longanimitatem, [13]supportantes invicem et donantes vobis ipsis, si quis adversus aliquem habet querelam; sicut et Dominus donavit vobis, ita et vos; [14]super omnia autem haec: caritatem, quod est vinculum perfectionis. [15]Et pax Christi dominetur in cordibus vestris, ad quam et vocati estis in uno corpore. Et grati estote. [16]Verbum Christi habitet in vobis abundanter, in omni sapientia docentes et commonentes vosmetipsos psalmis, hymnis, canticis spiritalibus, in gratia cantantes in cordibus vestris Deo; [17]et omne, quodcumque facitis in verbo aut in opere, omnia in nomine Domini Iesu gratias agentes Deo Patri per ipsum. [18]Mulieres, subditae estote viris, sicut oportet in Domino. [19]Viri, diligite uxores et nolite amari esse ad

perspective, with supernatural vision: "he allows himself to be moved and directed by the hand of the maker of all good things" (St Ignatius of Loyola, *Letters*, 4, 561–562).

3:12–17 The virtues that the Apostle lists as features of a person who lives by a "new nature" are all expressions of the love that is the "bond of perfection" (cf. v. 14), "None of the commandments are fulfilled where there is no love, for we turn away from sin and set our minds on doing good only when we love one another" (St Severinus of Gabala, *Fragmenta in Colossenses*). All genuinely human things can and should be sanctified; they are made holy when they are done well and done out of love (v. 17). "I assure you […] that when a Christian carries out with love the most insignificant everyday action, that action overflows with the transcendence of God.

That is why I have told you repeatedly, and hammered away once and again on the idea, that the Christian vocation consists in making heroic verse out of the prose of each day. Heaven and earth seem to merge […] on the horizon. But where they really meet is in your hearts, when you sanctify your everyday lives" (St Josemaría Escrivá, *Conversations*, 116).

3:18–21 This application to family life of the doctrine in the previous passage is based on charity and on the duty to live in the presence of God. The roles of father, mother, children take on a new meaning. In every family there should be an "educational exchange between parents and children (cf. Eph 6:1–4; Col 3:20–21) in which each gives and receives. By means of love, respect and obedience towards their parents, children offer their specific and irreplace-

f Other ancient authorities add *upon the sons of disobedience*

thing, for this pleases the Lord. [21]Fathers, do not provoke your children, lest they become discouraged. [22]Slaves, obey in everything those who are your earthly masters, not with eyeservice, as men-pleasers, but in singleness of heart, fearing the Lord. [23]Whatever your task, work heartily, as serving the Lord and not men, [24]knowing that from the Lord you will receive the inheritance as your reward; you are serving the Lord Christ. [25]For the wrongdoer will be paid back for the wrong he has done, and there is no partiality.

1 Tim 2:9–15

1 Cor 7:21:23
Philem 16
1 Pet 2:18
1 Tim 6:1
Tit 2:9

Rom 12:11

Lev 25:43, 53
Rom 2:11

4 [1]Masters, treat your slaves justly and fairly, knowing that you also have a Master in heaven.

1 Pet 2:18

Prayer and upright conduct

[2]Continue steadfastly in prayer, being watchful in it with thanksgiving; [3]and pray for us also, that God may open to us a door for the word, to declare the mystery of Christ, on account of which I am in prison, [4]that I may make it clear, as I ought to speak.

Rom 12:12
Eph 6:18–20
1 Thess 5:17
Rom 15:30
1 Cor 16:9
2 Thess 3:1
Eph 6:20
1 Thess 4:12
Eph 5:15

illas. [20]Filii, oboedite parentibus per omnia, hoc enim placitum est in Domino. [21]Patres, nolite ad indignationem provocare filios vestros, ut non pusillo animo fiant. [22]Servi, oboedite per omnia dominis carnalibus, non ad oculum servientes, quasi hominibus placentes, sed in simplicitate cordis, timentes Dominum. [23]Quodcumque facitis, ex animo operamini sicut Domino et non hominibus, [24]scientes quod a Domino accipietis retributionem hereditatis. Domino Christo servite; [25]qui enim iniuriam facit, recipiet id quod inique gessit, et non est personarum acceptio. [4] [1]Domini, quod iustum est et aequum, servis praestate, scientes quoniam et vos Dominum habetis in caelo. [2]Orationi instate, vigilantes in ea in gratiarum actione, [3]orantes simul et pro nobis, ut Deus aperiat nobis ostium sermonis ad loquendum mysterium Christi, propter quod etiam vinc-

able contribution to the construction of an authentically human and Christian family (cf. *Gaudium et spes*, 48). They will be aided in this if parents exercise their unrenounceable authority as a true and proper 'ministry', that is, as a service to the human and Christian well-being of their children, and in particular as a service aimed at helping them acquire a truly responsible freedom" (John Paul II, *Familiaris consortio*, 21).

3:22—4:1 God makes no distinction between slave and free man (see 3:11); he shows "no partiality" (3:25). Christians should keep this radical equality in mind in the context of the workplace and labour relations, for example, for "there is no doubt that human work has an ethical value of its own, which clearly and directly remains linked to the fact that the one who carries it out is a person, a conscious and free subject, that is to say, a subject that decides about himself […]. Such a concept practically does away with the very basis of the ancient differentiation of people into classes according to the kind of work done" (John Paul II, *Laborem exercens*, 6). Over the centuries, improvements have at times been made in the world of work,

but much remains to be done: "An inner effort on the part of the human spirit, guided by faith, hope and charity, is needed in order that through these points the *work* of the individual human being may *be given the meaning which it has in the eyes of God* and by means of which work enters into the salvation process on a par with the other ordinary yet particularly important components of its texture" (ibid., 24).

4:2–6 Perseverance in prayer is something often emphasized in the New Testament as a necessary feature of the lives of Christians (see Lk 18:1; Rom 12:12; 1 Thess 5:17). Prayer gave the early Christians the strength to spread the message of Christ far and wide, by their word and example. The daily effort it takes to orient one's ordinary activities towards God is a powerful reason for personal prayer. "How many occasions present themselves in the course of the day for a soul desirous of its own sanctification and the salvation of others, to raise itself to God—secret anguish, powerful and obstinate temptations, countless offences and omissions, and, lastly, fear of divine judgment" (St Pius X, *Haerent animo*, 10). All these things stimulate us to persevere in humble, trusting prayer, which wins us

Wis 8:9
Mk 9:50
Eph 5:16
2 Cor 6:2
1 Pet 3:15

⁵Conduct yourselves wisely toward outsiders, making the most of the time. ⁶Let your speech always be gracious, seasoned with salt, so that you may know how you ought to answer every one.

Conclusion

Acts 20:4
Eph 6:21–22

Philem 10

⁷Tychicus will tell you all about my affairs; he is a beloved brother and faithful minister and fellow servant in the Lord. ⁸I have sent him to you for this very purpose, that you may know how we are and that he may encourage your hearts, ⁹and with him Onesimus, the faithful and beloved brother, who is one of yourselves. They will tell you of everything that has taken place here.

Acts 12:12; 15:26f,
37, 39; 19:29; 20:4;
27:2

Philem 24

Col 1:7
Rom 15:30

2 Tim 4:9f
Philem 24

1 Thess 5:27
1 Tim 4:13

Philem 2

¹⁰Aristarchus my fellow prisoner greets you, and Mark the cousin of Barnabas* (concerning whom you have received instructions—if he comes to you, receive him), ¹¹and Jesus who is called Justus. These are the only men of the circumcision among my fellow workers for the kingdom of God, and they have been a comfort to me. ¹²Epaphras, who is one of yourselves, a servant^g of Christ Jesus, greets you, always remembering you earnestly in his prayers, that you may stand mature and fully assured in all the will of God. ¹³For I bear him witness that he has worked hard for you and for those in Laodicea and in Hierapolis. ¹⁴Luke the beloved physician* and Demas greet you. ¹⁵Give my greetings to the brethren at Laodicea, and to Nympha and the church in her house. ¹⁶And when this letter has been read among you, have it read also in the church of the Laodiceans; and see that you read also the letter from Laodicea. ¹⁷And say to Archippus, "See that you fulfil the ministry which you have received in the Lord."

2 Thess 3:17
Gal 6:11
Eph 3:1, 2; 6:20
1 Cor 16:21

¹⁸I, Paul, write this greeting with my own hand. Remember my fetters. Grace be with you.

tus sum, ⁴ut manifestem illud, ita ut oportet me loqui. ⁵In sapientia ambulate ad eos, qui foris sunt, tempus redimentes. ⁶Sermo vester semper sit in gratia, sale conditus, ut sciatis quomodo oporteat vos unicuique respondere. ⁷Quae circa me sunt, omnia vobis nota faciet Tychicus, carissimus frater et fidelis minister et conservus in Domino, ⁸quem misi ad vos ad hoc ipsum, ut cognoscatis, quae circa nos sunt, et consoletur corda vestra, ⁹cum Onesimo fideli et carissimo fratre, qui est ex vobis; omnia, quae hic aguntur, nota facient vobis. ¹⁰Salutat vos Aristarchus concaptivus meus et Marcus, consobrinus Barnabae, de quo accepistis mandata—si venerit ad vos, excipite illum—¹¹et Iesus, qui dicitur Iustus, qui sunt ex circumcisione, hi soli adiutores in regno Dei, qui mihi fuerunt solacio. ¹²Salutat vos Epaphras, qui ex vobis est, servus Christi Iesu, semper certans pro vobis in orationibus, ut stetis perfecti et impleti in omni voluntate Dei. ¹³Testimonium enim illi perhibeo quod habet multum laborem pro vobis et pro his, qui sunt Laodiciae et qui Hierapoli. ¹⁴Salutat vos Lucas, medicus carissimus, et Demas. ¹⁵Salutate fratres, qui sunt Laodiciae, et Nympham et, quae in domo eius est, ecclesiam. ¹⁶Et cum lecta fuerit apud vos epistula, facite ut et in Laodicensium ecclesia legatur, et eam, quae ex Laodicia est, vos quoque legatis. ¹⁷Et dicite Archippo: «Vide ministerium, quod accepisti in Domino, ut illud impleas». ¹⁸Salutatio mea manu Pauli. Memores estote vinculorum meorum. Gratia vobiscum.

God's favour and makes us rely more on his grace. "This is your duty: to give thanks to God in your prayers, both for the benefits you are conscious of having received and for those which God has given you without your realizing it. Thank him both for the favours you have sought from him and for those which he has done you despite yourselves. Thank him both for the heaven where he promises you happiness and for the hell from which he sets you free. In a word, thank him for everything—afflictions and joys, disasters and happiness" (St John Chrysostom, *In Colossenses*, ad loc.).

4:7–18 This letter (like that written to the Ephesians) is being delivered by Tychicus. With him goes Onesimus, a runaway slave (see Philem 8–10).

Of the people mentioned here, some are well known to us—for example, Mark, Barnabas and Luke. Demas will later desert Paul because he is "in love with this present world" (2 Tim 4:10). Archippus could be a son of Philemon (cf. Philem 2).

On the greeting written "with my own hand" (v. 18), see the note on 2 Thess 3:16–18.

g Or *slave*

THE FIRST LETTER OF PAUL TO THE

THESSALONIANS

Introduction

In the canon of Scripture, the Letters to the Thessalonians come after the "great" Pauline letters (Romans, Galatians, 1 and 2 Corinthians) and after the Captivity Letters (Ephesians, Philippians and Colossians).

The First Letter to the Thessalonians is the earliest book in the New Testament. Unlike the letters to the Romans and the Galatians, which expound doctrine at some length, this is a much shorter text, full of personal memories recalled in the light of faith and love. The style is simple and direct, but the content is still rich in doctrine.

1. STRUCTURE AND CONTENT

In addition to the opening words of greeting, there are two main sections in the letter.

In the first the Apostle looks back and recalls the early days of evangelization in Thessalonica (1:2–3:11). Paul remembers how he preached to the Thessalonians, and how they responded to him and to his teachings. In the course of doing so, he explains why he is writing this letter: he had to leave the city in haste, and he is anxious to return (he is sure God will allow him to do so); his return will be of great benefit to the Thessalonians' faith.

The second section is an exhortation to live in accordance with the Gospel preached to them and accepted by them (4:1—5:24). The Apostle devotes a good deal of attention in the letter to what he considers the faithful stand most in need of—steadfast hope that the difficulties they are experiencing will turn into joy when the Lord comes again; as they wait for that day, they should be both patient and active; not knowing when that time will come, they should always be ready to receive the Lord.

The letter ends with a few words of farewell (5:25–28).

2. CONTEXT

Paul's visit to Thessalonica with Silas and Timothy led to many conversions, and established in the first stage of his second apostolic journey a Christian community that gave him a holy sense of pride. However, only a few months after his arrival there, he unexpectedly had to leave the city due to opposition from some quarters; this meant that the instruction of the recent converts was cut short (see Acts 17:1–10). As soon as it was possible to do so, he sent Timothy from Athens (see 1 Thess 3:1–2) to see how they had responded to the difficulties that had arisen and to confirm them in faith, hope and charity.

In the meantime, Paul went to Corinth, where he met Timothy on his return from Thessalonica (see Acts 18:5; Thessalonica was in Macedonia). Timothy reported that the Thessalonians were persevering in faith and charity, despite persecution (see 3:6). On hearing this, the Apostle saw that the Gospel had taken root among them; they were keeping the faith.

Nevertheless, Paul remains worried by the fact that the Thessalonians needed reassurance about the fate of those who would die prior to the Lord's second coming. Because he had to leave the city so suddenly, Paul was unable to complete their instruction in Jesus' teachings; this meant that they did not have enough resources of doctrine to bolster their hope.

This is the context in which, in the winter of 50–51, the Apostle writes them this first letter. He recalls with joy and gratefulness to God the work done so far and their response to the Gospel, and he rounds off his earlier preaching by giving them a firm ground for hope, a strong basis for the faith and charity that is already theirs.

3. MESSAGE

Bearing in mind the background to the letter, and the tone in which the Apostle writes—he confides in them affectionately and recalls with joy the apostolate he did in Thessalonica—we can learn a lot from this letter about what that evangelization involved—about how Paul preached and what he preached. This letter (which, as was noted above, is probably the earliest New Testament book) deals in one way or another with the main aspects of the Christian faith.

The preaching of the Gospel

The first three chapters bear witness to Paul's great work of evangelization in Thessalonica—a work which is a model of how the Gospel should be proclaimed.

The inspiration to evangelize comes from God; and it is he who causes Gospel preaching to bear fruit. The election of the Christian is God's doing, and it stems from his love (1:4); his Son, Jesus, "who delivers us from the wrath to come" (1:10), sustains our hope (1:3); the action of the Holy Spirit renders the preacher's word persuasive and fills with joy those who listen to it, no matter what they may suffer in this life (1:5–6).

The core of preaching is the "Gospel", that is, the Good News of salvation foretold by the prophets and brought to fulfilment by our Lord Jesus Christ. This proclamation tells those who hear and are attentive to it that they are "beloved by God", and have been specially chosen by him (1:4–5). They are called to turn to God (1:9), who will grant the three theological virtues (faith, hope and charity) to those who accept the Christian message. The good example of those who respond faithfully and promptly to the word of God reinforces the effectiveness of preaching (1:3–9).

The attitude of the evangelizer plays a key role. St Paul exhorts others by his own example; he has no wish to shine himself. He contributes his voice and example, but it is the Holy Spirit who moves the hearts of his listeners (see 1:5). A person who is called to be a minister of the Gospel must always act with upright intention (God "tests our hearts"), so the Word of God must be preached simply and faithfully (2:1–12). A teacher of Christian doctrine does not act for earthly reward; what motivates him is love of God and love of others (see 2:6–9). The Apostle relies on prayer to make his work fruitful (see 3:10) and as far as possible tries to encourage and instruct people individually, showing them what they must do to live in accordance with their Christian calling (see 2:7–9).

The foundations of faith, morality and prayer

This letter touches on the main truths of faith as well as the foundations of Christian morality and the inspiration and motivations for Christian prayer. The main articles of faith, which Christian

Tradition will later formulate in the Apostles' Creed, are to be found here—in a letter which was written only nineteen years after Christ's death. St Paul teaches that God is our Father (cf. 1:3) and Jesus his Son (see 1:10). Salvation comes "through our Lord Jesus Christ, who died for us" and "rose again" (5:9–10; 4:14; see also 1:10). He will come again in power and majesty to judge the living and the dead (see 1:10; 2:19; 3:13; 4:16–17). God the Father sends the Holy Spirit (see 4:8), who moves us to accept with joy the preaching of the word of God (see 1:6).

The moral teaching contained in the letter derives from the fact that all Christians are called to holiness: "For this is the will of God, your sanctification" (4:3; cf. 4:7–8; 5:9). To attain this goal, we need to share in Christ's own life (see 5:10) and rely on the strength of the theological virtues: we must "put on the breastplate of faith and love, and for a helmet the hope of salvation" (5:8). Our relationships with others should be based on brotherly love: therefore, all Christians should give good example, convert those who act waywardly, help the weak, support the sick and be patient with all (see 4:9; 5:11, 14). We must be watchful, exercise self-control and sobriety (cf. 5:16–18), and work conscientiously (cf. 4:11–12).

As well as setting out the truths of faith and moral guidelines, Christian instruction has always laid stress on prayer, so this is another theme of the letter. People are advised to "pray constantly" (5:17) and are given direction on the content of prayer.

The letter contains, in one way or another, the basic elements of the Lord's Prayer in the form in which it is most commonly used in Christian Tradition, that is, the version found in St Matthew's Gospel (Mt 6:9–13). God is our Father (cf. 1:3; 3:11, 13), who with his Son is in heaven (see 1:10; 4:16). Christians should strive to do his will, which means sanctification (see 4:3), while doing their work and waiting for his Kingdom to come (see 2:12). The exhortation not to repay evil with evil (see 5:15) is reminiscent of the Prayer's petition, "Forgive us our trespasses, as we forgive those who trespass against us". Also, just as we pray for all in the Church, "And lead us not into temptation", we can see that the Apostle was concerned that possibly "somehow the tempter had tempted you" (3:5). And when, in addition to the evil influence of the tempter on others, we have to contend with assaults from him on our own selves ("I, Paul, again and again [wanted to come to you], but Satan hindered us": 2:18), we can readily understand why our Lord should teach us to pray, "Deliver us from evil."

Eschatology

Christian teaching on the end of the world and the last things is given special attention in this letter. St Paul wants to bolster the hope of recent converts who experience trials and suffering.

Man's life does not end with death. Believers therefore should not be saddened by the deaths of others or by the prospect of their own dying, for if Christ has risen, we too will rise with him (see 4:13–14).

We hope in the resurrection of our bodies (at the end of time, when our Lord Jesus Christ returns in glory). The Apostle describes the Second Coming in solemn words: "For the Lord himself will descend from heaven with a cry of command, with the archangel's call, and with the sound of the trumpet of God" (4:16). The apocalyptic language used here highlights the mystery and power of God. After the Parousia, or Second Coming, the resurrection of the dead will take place. Bodies will come back to life, and those who are still alive on that day, together with their brethren who have died, will go to meet the Lord (4:16–17). Those who died before the Parousia will not receive different treatment compared with those still alive at the time.

St Paul is not specific about the timing of the Parousia, for "as to the times and the seasons, brethren, you have no need to have anything written to you" (5:1). He simply exhorts the Thessalonians to be always on the watch, for "the day of the Lord will come like a thief in the night" (5:2), when it is least expected.

1 Thessalonians

Greeting*

1 ¹Paul, Silvanus, and Timothy,* To the church of the Thessalonians in God the Father and the Lord Jesus Christ:
Grace to you and peace.

2 Thess 1:1–2
Acts 15:22; 16:1

1. THE APOSTLE REJOICES OVER THE CHURCH OF THESSALONICA*

The evangelizing of Thessalonica

²We give thanks to God always for you all, constantly mentioning you in our prayers, ³remembering before our God and Father your work of faith and labour of love and steadfastness of hope in our Lord Jesus Christ. ⁴For we know, brethren beloved by God, that he has chosen you; ⁵for our gospel came to you not only in word, but also in power and in the Holy Spirit and with full conviction. You know what kind of men we proved to be among you for your sake. ⁶And you became imitators of us and of the Lord, for you received the word in much affliction, with joy inspired by the Holy Spirit; ⁷so that you became an example to all the believers in Macedonia and in Achaia. ⁸For not only has the word of the Lord sounded forth from you in Macedonia and Achaia, but your faith in God has gone forth everywhere, so

2 Thess 1:3
1 Thess 2:13
1 Cor 13:13
1 Thess 5:8
Col 1:4–5
2 Thess 2:13
Acts 1:8
1 Thess 2:13
1 Cor 2:4

Mt 13:20–21
1 Cor 4:16; 11:1
2 Thess 3:7

2 Cor 8:2
Phil 3:17
1 Thess 4:10

Rom 1:8; 16:19
2 Cor 9:2

[1] ¹Paulus et Silvanus et Timotheus ecclesiae Thessalonicensium in Deo Patre et Domino Iesu Christo: gratia vobis et pax. ²Gratias agimus Deo semper pro omnibus vobis, memoriam facientes in orationibus nostris, sine intermissione ³memores operis fidei vestrae et laboris caritatis et sustinentiae spei Domini nostri Iesu Christi ante Deum et Patrem nostrum, ⁴scientes, fratres, dilecti a Deo, electionem vestram, ⁵quia evangelium nostrum non fuit ad vos in sermone tantum, sed et in virtute et in Spiritu Sancto et in plenitudine multa, sicut scitis quales fuerimus vobis propter vos. ⁶Et vos imitatores nostri facti estis et Domini, excipientes verbum in tribulatione multa cum gaudio Spiritus Sancti, ⁷ita ut facti sitis forma omnibus credentibus in Macedonia et in Achaia. ⁸A vobis enim diffamatus est sermo Domini non solum in Macedonia et in Achaia, sed in omni loco fides

*1:1 This is the earliest letter of St Paul that has come down to us (it dates from the year 51–52). After greeting the community which he himself founded, he thanks God for the abundant fruit of his evangelization and for the faithfulness of these Christians (1:2—3:13). Later, moved by the Thessalonians' sorrow over the deaths of their loved ones, he exhorts them to live holy lives in the hope of the second coming of Christ (4:1—5:24).

The letter opens in the way letters usually did at the time—with the names of the sender and addressees, and some words of greeting. The tone is affectionate, but it is not an ordinary family letter; it is an official text and names two witnesses who vouch for its content. The Greek work *ekklesía* (translated as "church") means "assembly, gathering of the people", and was

used from the apostolic age onwards to describe the new People of God. St Thomas uses this verse to define the Church as "the assembly of the faithful brought together in God the Father and in the Lord Jesus Christ, through faith in the Trinity and in the divinity and humanity of Christ" (*Super 1 Thessalonicenses*, ad loc.).

*1:2—3:13 The Apostle's thanksgiving encompasses both the spread of the Gospel in Thessalonica (1:2—2:16) and the reports that have reached him about how these Christians are persevering in the faith (2:17—3:10). The section ends with a prayer for them (3:11–13).

1:2–10 It makes St Paul very happy to see how effective the action of divine grace has been among the Thessalonians. The theological

Jer 10:10
1 Cor 12:2
Jn 17:3
Acts 3:19; 14:15–17
1 Cor 12:2
Mt 3:7
Acts 17:31
Tit 2:13
Eph 2:3
1 Thess 4:16–17
Rom 1:18; 2:5ff; 3:5; 5:9

1 Thess 1:9

Acts 13:46;
16:19–40; 17:1–5
Phil 1:30
2 Cor 3:12
2 Cor 2:17

Jer 11:20
Gal 1:10
1 Tim 1:11
2 Cor 5:9

Acts 20:19

that we need not say anything. ⁹For they themselves report concerning us what a welcome we had among you, and how you turned to God from idols, to serve a living and true God, ¹⁰and to wait for his Son from heaven, whom he raised from the dead, Jesus who delivers us from the wrath to come.

Gospel preaching in Thessalonica—the early days recalled

2 ¹For you yourselves know, brethren, that our visit to you was not in vain; ²but though we had already suffered and been shamefully treated at Philippi, as you know, we had courage in our God to declare to you the gospel of God in the face of great opposition. ³For our appeal does not spring from error or uncleanness, nor is it made with guile; ⁴but just as we have been approved by God to be entrusted with the gospel, so we speak, not to please men, but to please God who tests our hearts. ⁵For we never used either words of flattery, as you know, or a cloak for greed, as God is witness;

vestra, quae est ad Deum, profecta est, ita ut non sit nobis necesse quidquam loqui; ⁹ipsi enim de nobis annuntiant qualem introitum habuerimus ad vos, et quomodo conversi estis ad Deum a simulacris, servire Deo vivo et vero ¹⁰et exspectare Filium eius de caelis, quem suscitavit ex mortuis, Iesum, qui eripit nos ab ira ventura. [2] ¹Nam ipsi scitis, fratres, introitum nostrum ad vos quia non inanis fuit, ²sed ante passi et contumeliis affecti, sicut scitis, in Philippis, fiduciam habuimus in Deo nostro loqui ad vos evangelium Dei in multa sollicitudine. ³Exhortatio enim nostra non ex errore neque ex immunditia neque in dolo, ⁴sed sicut probati sumus a Deo, ut crederetur nobis evangelium, ita loquimur non quasi

virtues have taken root in them, not due to their own personal merits but because they have been loved and chosen by God (see v. 4). The Holy Spirit is the main agent of evangelization (v. 5), working in the souls of those who accept the word of God in all simplicity: "The power of the Spirit purifies those who are united to the Spirit by a pure heart, a full faith, and a clear conscience" (St Gregory of Nyssa, *De instituto christiano*).

The Apostle's work of evangelization is a model of how the Christian message should be proclaimed. Just as the Apostle imitated Christ (cf. 1 Cor 11:1) and led others to the faith (v. 6), Christians should act in such a way that others see Christ in them "as in a mirror. If the mirror is as it ought to be, it will capture our Saviour's most lovable face without distorting it or making a caricature of it; and then other people will have an opportunity of admiring him and following him" (St Josemaría Escrivá, *Friends of God*, 299).

2:1–12 St Paul and his companions arrived at Thessalonica from Philippi, where a persecution had occurred. But in Thessalonica, too, uproar broke out, instigated by Jews, and Paul and Silas were forced to leave that city (see Acts 16:19–17:10). The Apostle recalls these difficulties, and he makes the point that he always acted in an upright way (with this last argument, he may be responding to criticism or allegations made by Jews or pagans in Thessalonica).

St Paul describes as "uncleanness" (v. 3) any attempt to change Christ's teaching. When he says that his preaching does not spring from uncleanness, he means that he does not do violence to or alter the Christian message; his one desire has always been to know and teach the truth: "The preacher of the Gospel will be a person who even at the price of personal renunciation and suffering always seeks the truth that he must transmit to others. He never betrays or hides truth out of a desire to please men, in order to astonish or to shock, nor for the sake of originality or a desire to make an impression. He does not refuse truth. He does not obscure revealed truth by being too idle to search for it, or for the sake of his own comfort, or out of fear. He does not neglect to study it. He serves it generously, without making it serve him" (Paul VI, *Evangelii nuntiandi*, 78).

The work of evangelization requires that the preacher love all those he teaches. His love should be more than the love of teacher; it should be the love of a father, or greater still, the love of a mother (vv. 7–12) who is attentive to all her child's immediate needs, and, at the same time, constantly looks beyond the present moment. The Apostle looks after fledgling Chris-

[6]nor did we seek glory from men, whether from you or from others, though we might have made demands as apostles of Christ. [7]But we were gentle[a] among you, like a nurse taking care of her children. [8]So, being affectionately desirous of you, we were ready to share with you not only the gospel of God but also our own selves, because you had become very dear to us.

[9]For you remember our labour and toil, brethren; we worked night and day, that we might not burden any of you, while we preached to you the gospel of God. [10]You are witnesses, and God also, how holy and righteous and blameless was our behaviour to you believers; [11]for you know how, like a father with his children, we exhorted each one of you and encouraged you and charged you [12]to lead a life worthy of God, who calls you into his own kingdom and glory.

Jn 5:41–44
1 Cor 3:2
Rom 9:3
2 Cor 12:15
Gal 2:10; 4:19

Acts 18:3; 20:34
1 Cor 4:12; 9:12–18
2 Thess 3:8
1 Thess 4:11
Rom 1:9

1 Cor 4:15ff

Mt 4:17
Eph 4:1; 5:1–2
2 Tim 2:24–25
1 Thess 5:24
Eph 4:1; 5:1–2
2 Thess 1:5
Phil 1:27

The Thessalonians' patience

[13]And we also thank God constantly for this, that when you received the word of God which you heard from us, you accepted it not as the word of men but as what it

1 Thess 1:2–10
Heb 4:2
2 Thess 2:13
1 Cor 11:2
Gal 1:11

hominibus placentes, sed Deo, qui probat corda nostra. [5]Neque enim aliquando fuimus in sermone adulationis, sicut scitis, neque sub praetextu avaritiae, Deus testis, [6]nec quaerentes ab hominibus gloriam, neque a vobis neque ab aliis, [7]cum possemus oneri esse ut Christi apostoli, sed facti sumus parvuli in medio vestrum, tamquam si nutrix foveat filios suos, [8]ita desiderantes vos, cupide volebamus tradere vobis non solum evangelium Dei, sed etiam animas nostras, quoniam carissimi nobis facti estis. [9]Memores enim estis, fratres, laboris nostri et fatigationis; nocte et die operantes, ne quem vestrum gravaremus, praedicavimus in vobis evangelium Dei. [10]Vos testes estis et Deus, quam sancte et iuste et sine querela vobis, qui credidistis, fuimus; [11]sicut scitis qualiter unumquemque vestrum, tamquam pater filios suos, [12]deprecantes vos et consolantes testificati sumus, ut ambularetis digne Deo, qui vocat vos in suum regnum et gloriam. [13]Ideo et nos gratias agimus Deo sine intermissione, quoniam cum

tians "as a mother feeds her child and wants him to grow strong. She carries him in her arms, comforts him with her touch, gives him her milk to drink. She does all these things for him because she wants him to grow strong: she wants her child to grow strong so that he will not always have to be cared for in this way" (St Augustine, *Sermones*, 23, 3). Similarly, a preacher should be as attentive and concerned as a mother; but he must also offer people the firm ground of the truth based on the word of God, which will allow their faith to take root and develop.

St Paul did not confine his preaching to synagogues or other public places, or to liturgical assemblies of Christians. He took an interest in people as individuals (v. 11), giving advice and consolation in a friendly way, and teaching them how to live their lives in accordance with the faith. The Second Vatican Council pointed out that one form of personal apostolate very suited to our times is "the witness of a whole lay life issuing from faith, hope and charity [...]. Then, by the apostolate of the word, which in certain circumstances is absolutely necessary, the laity proclaim Christ, explain and spread his teachings, each one according to his conditions and

competence, and profess those teachings with fidelity" (*Apostolicam actuositatem*, 16). In the last analysis it is a matter of helping those around us to find God. "When you come across something useful, you try to bring other people to it," St Gregory comments. "So, you should want other people to join you on the way of the Lord. If you are going to the forum or the baths and you meet someone who has nothing to do, you invite him to go along with you. Apply this earthly custom to the spiritual sphere and, as you make your way to God, do not go alone" (St Gregory the Great, *Homiliae in Evangelia*, 6, 6).

2:13–16 Preaching is truly "the word of God" (v. 13), not only inasmuch as it faithfully passes on divine revelation, but also in that God himself speaks through those who proclaim the Gospel (see 2 Cor 5:20). "The Word of God is living and active" (Heb 4:12). "By the saving Word of God faith is aroused in the hearts of unbelievers and is nourished in the hearts of believers. By this faith, then, the community of believers begins and develops" (Vatican II, *Presbyterorum ordinis*, 4).

Those who embrace the faith will suffer on that account (v. 14). However, opposition should

a Other ancient authorities read *babes*

Acts 2:23; 4:12; 17:5
2 Thess 3:17
Gal 1:22

Mt 5:11–12
Acts 2:23; 7:52
1 Cor 2:8
Rom 11:28

Gen 15:16
2 Mac 6:14
Dan 8:23
Mt 23:13, 32
Rom 1:18

really is, the word of God, which is at work in you believers. ¹⁴For you, brethren, became imitators of the churches of God in Christ Jesus which are in Judea; for you suffered the same things from your own countrymen as they did from the Jews, ¹⁵who killed both the Lord Jesus and the prophets, and drove us out, and displease God and oppose all men ¹⁶by hindering us from speaking to the Gentiles that they may be saved—so as always to fill up the measure of their sins. But God's wrath has come upon them at last!ᵇ

Paul's solicitude

Col 2:5
1 Thess 3:10

Rom 1:10–11

Prov 16:31
Ezek 6:12; 23:42
Phil 2:16; 4:1
2 Cor 8:24; 10:17
2 Cor 1:14

¹⁷But since we were bereft of you, brethren, for a short time, in person not in heart, we endeavored the more eagerly and with great desire to see you face to face; ¹⁸because we wanted to come to you—I, Paul,* again and again—but Satan hindered us. ¹⁹For what is our hope or joy or crown of boasting before our Lord Jesus at his coming? Is it not you? ²⁰For you are our glory and joy.

accepissetis a nobis verbum auditus Dei, accepistis non ut verbum hominum sed, sicut est vere, verbum Dei, quod et operatur in vobis, qui creditis. ¹⁴Vos enim imitatores facti estis, fratres, ecclesiarum Dei, quae sunt in Iudaea in Christo Iesu, quia eadem passi estis et vos a contribulibus vestris, sicut et ipsi a Iudaeis, ¹⁵qui et Dominum occiderunt Iesum et prophetas et nos persecuti sunt et Deo non placent et omnibus hominibus adversantur, ¹⁶prohibentes nos gentibus loqui, ut salvae fiant, ut impleant peccata sua semper. Pervenit autem ira Dei super illos usque in finem. ¹⁷Nos autem, fratres, desolati a vobis ad tempus horae, facie non corde, abundantius festinavimus faciem vestram videre cum multo desiderio. ¹⁸Propter quod voluimus venire ad vos, ego quidem Paulus et semel et iterum, et impedivit nos Satanas. ¹⁹Quae est enim nostra spes aut gaudium aut corona gloriae —nonne et vos— ante Dominum nostrum Iesum in adventu eius? ²⁰Vos enim estis gloria nostra et gaudium.   [3] ¹Propter quod

not be seen as an obstacle but rather as a stimulus to spread the Gospel: "Therefore, count yourselves blessed. Consider that you have performed a mighty deed, if one of you suffers for God" (*Shepherd of Hermas*, 9, 28, 6).

In vv. 14–16 we can see how energetically St Paul reacts to the opposition that here comes from some Jews when he preaches to Gentiles; but in no way do these verses imply condemnation of the Jewish people; Paul himself was a Jew. His harsh words apply only to those who made it difficult for him to preach the Gospel to all who wanted to hear it. But he leaves a door of hope open even for those people. The last words of v. 16 are reminiscent of 2 Chronicles 36:16: "They kept mocking the messengers of God, and scoffing at his prophets, till the wrath of God rose against his people, till there was no remedy." That passage foretold the siege and fall of Jerusalem, the burning of the temple and the deportation to Babylon that occurred in the year 587 BC. It is almost as if St Paul foresees here a similar catastrophe (which in fact happened in the year AD 70 with the destruction of Jerusalem by the Romans). However, the Apostle was well aware that the events of 587 BC did not mark a definitive end-point, for the Lord went on to show his people mercy. So what St Paul says

here does not rule out a later reconciliation with those who oppose the preaching of the Gospel (see Rom 11:25–36). On the wrath of God (v. 16), see also Rom 1:18.

2:17—3:10 Paul delights in the Thessalonians' fidelity. "Thanks to the work of the master, the disciple is obedient, in such a way that his good behaviour brings about improvement in the master; the fruit reveals the master's work. Moreover, the effort of the disciple to do good crowns the master in the judgment of Christ" (St Thomas Aquinas, *Super 1 Thessalonicenses*, ad loc.).

Paul gives us here the first mention in the New Testament of the "coming" of Christ, using the Greek word *parousía* (2:19). In secular language at the time, *parousía* was the formal entry into a city of a ruler accompanied by all his entourage. In the New Testament, the word refers to the coming of Christ in glory, with all his power and majesty, to judge mankind; and in this letter it refers to that definitive and solemn coming at the end of time.

A disciple is no greater than his master (see Mt 10:24). St Luke reports that from the time of his first missionary journeys St Paul told the disciples that "through many tribulations we must

b Or *completely*, or *for ever*

3 ¹Therefore when we could bear it no longer, we were willing to be left behind at Athens alone, ²and we sent Timothy, our brother and God's servant in the gospel of Christ, to establish you in your faith and to exhort you, ³that no one be moved by these afflictions. You yourselves know that this is to be our lot. ⁴For when we were with you, we told you beforehand that we were to suffer affliction; just as it has come to pass, and as you know. ⁵For this reason, when I could bear it no longer, I sent that I might know your faith, for fear that somehow the tempter had tempted you and that our labour would be in vain. ⁶But now that Timothy has come to us from you, and has brought us the good news of your faith and love and reported that you always remember us kindly and long to see us, as we long to see you—⁷for this reason, brethren, in all our distress and affliction we have been comforted about you through your faith; ⁸for now we live, if you stand fast in the Lord. ⁹For what thanksgiving can we render to God for you, for all the joy which we feel for your sake before our God, ¹⁰praying earnestly night and day that we may see you face to face and supply what is lacking in your faith?

Acts 17:14

Acts 16:1–3;
17:14–16
1 Cor 3:9
2 Cor 6:1

1 Thess 1:6
Mt 16:24
Tim 3:2
Heb 10:32

Mt 4:9
Gal 4:11
1 Pet 5:9
Phil 2:16

Acts 18:5
2 Thess 1:3
2 Cor 7:7

2 Thess 1:4

1 Cor 16:13
Phil 1:3
2 Thess 1:3

1 Thess 2:17; 4:1–12;
5:1–11

Paul's prayer for the Thessalonians

¹¹Now may our God and Father himself, and our Lord Jesus, direct our way to you; ¹²and may the Lord make you increase and abound in love to one another and to all

Mt 5:43–44
Gal 6:10
Rom 12:17–18
Col 3:14
Tit 3:2

non sustinentes amplius, placuit nobis, ut relinqueremur Athenis soli, ²et misimus Timotheum, fratrem nostrum et cooperatorem Dei in evangelio Christi, ad confirmandos vos et exhortandos pro fide vestra, ³ut nemo turbetur in tribulationibus istis. Ipsi enim scitis quod in hoc positi sumus; ⁴nam et cum apud vos essemus, praedicebamus vobis passuros nos tribulationes, sicut et factum est et scitis. ⁵Propterea et ego amplius non sustinens, misi ad cognoscendam fidem vestram, ne forte tentaverit vos is qui tentat, et inanis fiat labor noster. ⁶Nunc autem veniente Timotheo ad nos a vobis et annuntiante nobis fidem et caritatem vestram et quia memoriam nostri habetis bonam semper, desiderantes nos videre, sicut nos quoque vos, ⁷ideo consolati sumus, fratres, propter vos in omni necessitate et tribulatione nostra per vestram fidem, ⁸quoniam nunc vivimus, si vos statis in Domino. ⁹Quam enim gratiarum actionem possumus Deo retribuere pro vobis in omni gaudio, quo gaudemus propter vos ante Deum nostrum, ¹⁰nocte et die abundantius orantes ut videamus faciem vestram et compleamus ea, quae desunt fidei vestrae? ¹¹Ipse autem Deus et Pater noster et

enter the kingdom of God" (Acts 14:22), and the same idea appears in Paul's last letter: "All who desire to live a godly life in Christ Jesus will be persecuted" (2 Tim 3:12). "Therefore, you should not be troubled, says Paul, for what is happening is neither strange nor unexpected; and these words were enough to give them new heart. Christ spoke to his disciples in the same way and for the same reason, so that they would understand: 'And now I have told you before it takes place, so that when it does take place, you may believe' (Jn 14:29)" (St John Chrysostom, *In 1 Thessalonicenses*, ad loc.).

The "tempter" (3:5) is Satan (see Mt 4:3), who tempts men, not to test their virtue and find them faithful, but to lead them astray and cause them to abandon the path of faith. "When tempting us", St Thomas Aquinas explains, "he acts very cunningly. Like a skilful general laying siege to a fortress, the demon looks for the weak points of the person he wants to overcome, and goes for his weakest flank. He tempts man to

those sins to which (after subduing the flesh) he is most inclined: for example, anger, pride and the other spiritual sins" (*On the Lord's Prayer*). A Christian therefore needs to be vigilant ("Watch and pray that you may not enter into temptation": Mt 26:41) and to humbly ask God for help: "And lead us not into temptation, but deliver us from evil" (Mt 6:13).

3:6–10 The fact that the Thessalonians are steadfast in the faith despite persecution is not a result of their own efforts alone; their faithfulness rests on the grace of God.

3:11–13 Since we do not know when the second coming of the Lord will take place (cf. 5:2), we should concentrate at all times on leading lives worthy of Christ, lives in which love reigns supreme. Supernatural love, or charity, extends to everyone, without exception: "Loving one person and showing indifference to others is characteristic of purely human affection; but St

Zech 14:5
1 Thess 2:19, 5, 23
2 Thess 1:7–10
1 Cor 1:8; 15:23
men, as we do to you, ¹³so that he may establish your hearts unblamable in holiness before our God and Father, at the coming of our Lord Jesus with all his saints.

2. ADVANCEMENT IN THE CHRISTIAN LIFE*

Holiness and purity

1 Cor 11:1–2
Rom 12:1–2
2 Thess 3:6
1 Thess 4:13

1 Pet 1:16

Acts 15:20
1 Cor 6:13–15

Eph 4:19

4 ¹Finally, brethren, we beseech and exhort you in the Lord Jesus, that as you learned from us how you ought to live and to please God, just as you are doing, you do so more and more. ²For you know what instructions we gave you through the Lord Jesus. ³For this is the will of God, your sanctification:* that you abstain from unchastity;* ⁴that each one of you know how to control his own body in holiness and honour, ⁵not in the passion of lust like heathen who do not know God; ⁶that no man

Dominus noster Iesus dirigat viam nostram ad vos; ¹²vos autem Dominus abundare et superabundare faciat caritate in invicem et in omnes, quemadmodum et nos in vos, ¹³ad confirmanda corda vestra sine querela in sanctitate ante Deum et Patrem nostrum, in adventu Domini nostri Iesu cum omnibus sanctis eius. Amen. [4] ¹De cetero ergo, fratres, rogamus vos et obsecramus in Domino Iesu, ut æquemadmodum accepistis a nobis quomodo vos oporteat ambulare et placere Deo, sicut et ambulatis — ut abundetis magis. ²Scitis enim, quae praecepta dederimus vobis per Dominum Iesum. ³Haec est enim voluntas Dei, sanctificatio vestra, ⁴ut abstineatis a fornicatione, ut sciat unusquisque vestrum suum vas possidere in sanctificatione et honore, ⁵non in passione desiderii, sicut et gentes, quae ignorant Deum, ⁶ut ne quis supergrediatur neque circumveniat in nego-

Paul tells us that our love should not be restricted in any way" (St John Chrysostom, *In 1 Thessalonicenses*, ad loc.). When we unreservedly practise this virtue, we grow in holiness: we become "unblamable […] before our God and Father" (v. 13).

*4:1—5:28 The thought of the second coming of the Lord leads the Apostle to make the exhortations that form the second section of the letter. They are all designed to encourage the Thessalonians to progress steadily in holiness (4:1–8) and in love (4:9–12), and to enliven their hope in future resurrection (4:13—5:11). The section concludes with encouragement to live in peace and joy and to pray at all times (5:12–22).

4:1–8 The exhortations the Apostle now begins to make are based on God's call to holiness, a call addressed not to a select few but to all mankind: "All in the Church, whether they belong to the hierarchy or are cared for by it, are called to holiness" (Vatican II, *Lumen gentium*, 39). This calling derives from the fact that we are, each of us, the object of God's special choice: "Let us not forget, then, that we are in our Master's sheepfold in order to achieve that goal. […] What does matter is that we engrave, that we burn upon our souls the conviction that Christ's invitation to holiness, which he

addresses to all men without exception, puts each one of us under an obligation to cultivate our interior life and to struggle daily to practise the Christian virtues; and not just in any way whatsoever, nor in a way which is above average or even excellent. No; we must strive to the point of heroism, in the strictest and most exacting sense of the word" (St Josemaría Escrivá, *Friends of God*, 2 and 3).

Holiness requires that Christians practise the virtue of chastity. Christian chastity is not only a virtue vital to the dignity of the human person, who is created in the likeness of God; it is also a requirement of the new dignity that a person acquires through Baptism, which makes his or her body a temple of the Holy Spirit (cf. 1 Cor 6:19–20).

The word translated as "body" in v. 4 means, literally, "vessel", and in Jewish texts of the time it was used to refer both to a person's body and to someone's wife. If it means "wife" here, the passage can be interpreted as an exhortation to fidelity in marriage and to virtuous living between husband and wife. St Augustine gives it this interpretation: "Not only should the Christian husband not use another's 'vessel', which is the case of those who covet their neighbour's wife; he should also recognize that his own wife is not for his use, as the object only of his carnal desire. But the apostle's injunction should not be

transgress, and wrong his brother in this matter,ᶜ because the Lord is an avenger in all these things, as we solemnly forewarned you. ⁷For God has not called us for uncleanness, but in holiness. ⁸Therefore whoever disregards this, disregards not man but God, who gives his Holy Spirit to you.

Jer 10:25
Ps 79:6; 94:4–6
Deut 32:35
Rom 1 :24-28
2 Thess 2:13
Lk 10:16
Ezek 37:14
2 Cor 1:22; 5:5

Charity and good use of time

⁹But concerning love of the brethren you have no need to have any one write to you, for you yourselves have been taught by God to love one another; ¹⁰and indeed you do love all the brethren throughout Macedonia. But we exhort you, brethren, to do so more and more, ¹¹to aspire to live quietly, to mind your own affairs, and to work with your hands, as we charged you;* ¹²so that you may command the respect of outsiders, and be dependent on nobody.

Jer 31:31–34
Is 54:13
Jn 6:45; 13:34
1 Thess 1:7–8

Acts 18:3
Eph 4:28
2 Thess 3:6–12
Col 4:5
1 Cor 5:12

Hope

¹³But we would not have you ignorant, brethren, concerning those who are asleep, that you may not grieve as others do who have no hope.* ¹⁴For since we believe that Jesus died and rose again, even so, through Jesus, God will bring with him those

Eph 2:12
2 Thess 2:1–12
1 Cor 15:20
Rom 1:4; 8:11; 10:9;
14:9
1 Cor 6:14; 15:3, 20
Jn 11:11

tio fratrem suum, quoniam vindex est Dominus de his omnibus, sicut et praediximus vobis et testificati sumus. ⁷Non enim vocavit nos Deus in immunditiam sed in sanctificationem. ⁸Itaque, qui spernit, non hominem spernit sed Deum, qui etiam dat Spiritum suum Sanctum in vos. ⁹De caritate autem fraternitatis non necesse habetis, ut vobis scribam; ipsi enim vos a Deo edocti estis, ut diligatis invicem; ¹⁰etenim facitis illud in omnes fratres in universa Macedonia. Rogamus autem vos, fratres, ut abundetis magis ¹¹et operam detis, ut quieti sitis et ut vestrum negotium agatis et operemini manibus vestris, sicut praecipimus vobis, ¹²ut honeste ambuletis ad eos, qui foris sunt, et nullius aliquid desideretis. ¹³Nolumus autem vos ignorare, fratres, de dormientibus, ut non contristemini sicut et ceteri, qui spem non habent. ¹⁴Si enim credimus quod Iesus mortuus est et resurrexit, ita et Deus eos, qui dormierunt, per Iesum adducet cum eo. ¹⁵Hoc enim vobis dicimus in verbo Domini, quia nos, qui vivimus, qui relin-

read as a condemnation of all conjugal relationships; that is, any union between a man and a woman which is licit and good" (*De nuptiis et concupiscentia*, 1, 8, 9).

In any event, the sacred text tells us that God calls us to exercise self-control in holiness and honour (cf. v. 4); the body and its various capacities should be used in the ways God means them to be used. The Lord of life has entrusted to men and women the mission of conserving life and transmitting it in a manner that befits human dignity: "Man's sexuality and the faculty of reproduction wondrously surpass the endowments of lower forms of life; therefore the acts proper to married life are to be ordered according to authentic human dignity and must be honoured with the greatest reverence" (Vatican II, *Gaudium et spes*, 51).

4:9–12 Alongside love, as a key aspect of Christian living, St Paul mentions the need to do one's work well (it follows on from love, in fact). Similar advice is often to be found in early Christian writings: "If somebody wishes to settle among you, let him find a job and work and so feed himself. If he has no job, provide for him as your own prudent judgement allows, so that there may be no idle Christian among you" (*Didache*, 12, 3–5). Love of God gives work a greater meaning: "An inner effort on the part of the human spirit, guided by faith, hope and charity, is needed in order that through these points the *work* of the individual human being may *be given the meaning which it has in the eyes of God*" (John Paul II, *Laborem exercens*, 24).

4:13—5–11 The fact that the Apostle was forced to leave Thessalonica meant that the people's instruction in the faith was not complete. "Would those who had already died be at a disadvantage, compared with those who were still alive, when the day of judgment came?" was a doubt in their minds. Paul's response to them consists of two teachings: all will be judged equally, whether they are alive or dead when the day comes (4:15–18); and we do not know when Christ will come again in glory (5:1–2).

4:13–14 "Those who are asleep" (v. 13). This expression, already to be found in some pagan

ᶜ Or *defraud his brother in business*

Sir 48:11
1 Cor 15:51

Mk 24:30–31
1 Cor 15:23
2 Thess 1:7

Dan 7:13
Jn 12:26; 14:2–3;
17:24
1 Thess 5:10
1 Thess 5:11

Mt 24:36
Acts 1:7
Lk 12:39
Rev 3:3; 16:15

Jer 4:31; 6:15
Lk 21:34:35
Mt 24:8, 38
Is 13:8
Hos 13:13
Eph 5:8
Jn 8:12
Eph 5:8
Rom 13:12–13
Mt 24:42
1 Pet 4:7; 5:8

who have fallen asleep. [15]For this we declare to you by the word of the Lord, that we who are alive, who are left until the coming of the Lord, shall not precede those who have fallen asleep. [16]For the Lord himself will descend from heaven with a cry of command, with the archangel's call, and with the sound of the trumpet of God. And the dead in Christ will rise first; [17]then we who are alive, who are left, shall be caught up together with them in the clouds to meet the Lord in the air; and so we shall always be with the Lord.* [18]Therefore comfort one another with these words.

5 [1]But as to the times and the seasons, brethren, you have no need to have anything written to you. [2]For you yourselves know well that the day of the Lord will come like a thief in the night. [3]When people say, "There is peace and security," then sudden destruction will come upon them as travail comes upon a woman with child, and there will be no escape. [4]But you are not in darkness, brethren, for that day to surprise you like a thief. [5]For you are all sons of light and sons of the day; we are not of the night or of darkness. [6]So then let us not sleep, as others do, but let us keep awake and be sober. [7]For those who sleep sleep at night, and those who get drunk

quimur in adventum Domini, non praeveniemus eos, qui dormierunt; [16]quoniam ipse Dominus in iussu, in voce archangeli et in tuba Dei descendet de caelo, et mortui, qui in Christo sunt, resurgent primi; [17]deinde nos, qui vivimus, qui relinquimur, simul rapiemur cum illis in nubibus obviam Domino in aera, et sic semper cum Domino erimus. [18]Itaque consolamini invicem in verbis istis.   [5] [1]De temporibus autem et momentis, fratres, non indigetis, ut scribatur vobis; [2]ipsi enim diligenter scitis quia dies Domini sicut fur in nocte ita veniet. [3]Cum enim dixerint: «Pax et securitas», tunc repentinus eis superveniet interitus, sicut dolor in utero habenti, et non effugient. [4]Vos autem, fratres, non estis in tenebris, ut vos dies ille tamquam fur comprehendat; [5]omnes enim vos filii lucis estis et filii diei. Non sumus noctis neque tenebrarum; [6]igitur non dormiamus sicut ceteri,

writings, was often used by the early Christians to refer to those who had died in the faith of Christ.

In Christian writings this expression makes much more sense, given Christian belief in the resurrection of Jesus and the conviction that all will eventually rise from the dead. It is no mere euphemism: it underlines the fact that death is not a definitive ending. "Why does it say that they are asleep", St Augustine asks, "if not because they will be raised when their day comes?" (*Sermones*, 93, 6). The resurrection of the dead is one of the basic truths of our faith, found in both the Apostles' Creed and the Nicene Creed (see also the notes on 1 Cor 15).

4:15–18 St Paul gives reasons for our hope in the resurrection of the dead. He speaks of meeting our Lord when he comes again; but he gives no indication here as to when it will happen. A little later on, he will add that the only thing we do know is that it will come about unexpectedly (cf. 5:1–3). In any case, the question of timing is irrelevant, for what really matters is to be with Christ forever. At the Parousia, those still alive will have no advantage over those have already reached the end of their earthly life "in Christ" (v. 16).

St Ambrose explains this passage by linking it to comments that the Apostle makes elsewhere: "All will be raised from the dead; but no one should lose heart or feel sorry for himself at this thought, nor expect some special reward for his own virtue. All are raised from the dead, as the Apostle says, but 'each in his own order' (1 Cor 15:23). The gift of divine mercy is open to all, but it is not the same as the order of merit. The day will dawn for all, and the sun shine on all, and the rain fall to water the ground for all. We are all born, and we are all raised, but the gifts of life and resurrection are different, each in its own order. We are urged to live as Paul lives, so that we too can say: *we who are alive ... shall not precede those who have fallen asleep* (cf. 1 Thess 4:15). His words refer not to ordinary life, but to the gift of resurrection" (*De excessu fratris sui Satyri*, 2, 92–93).

5:2 "The day of the Lord" is an expression used a number of times in Holy Scripture to refer to the point in time when God will intervene decisively and irreversibly in human history. In St Paul's letters, as in other New Testament writings, it is the day of the general judgment, when Christ will appear in the fullness of glory to judge mankind (see 1 Cor 1:8; 2 Cor 1:14). But

are drunk at night. [8]But, since we belong to the day, let us be sober, and put on the breastplate of faith and love, and for a helmet the hope of salvation. [9]For God has not destined us for wrath, but to obtain salvation through our Lord Jesus Christ, [10]who died for us so that whether we wake or sleep we might live with him. [11]Therefore encourage one another and build one another up, just as you are doing.

Rom 13:12–13
Eph 6:11, 14–17
Is 59:17
1 Cor 13:13
1 Thess 1:3, 10
2 Thess 2:14, 17
1 Thess 4:14
Rom 14:8
Rom 14:19
1 Thess 4:18
Eph 2:20
Jude 20

Various counsels

[12]But we beseech you, brethren, to respect those who labour among you and are over you in the Lord and admonish you, [13]and to esteem them very highly in love because of their work. Be at peace among yourselves.^{c2} [14]And we exhort you, brethren, admonish the idlers, encourage the fainthearted, help the weak, be patient with them all. [15]See that none of you repays evil for evil, but always seek to do good to one another and to all. [16]Rejoice always, [17]pray constantly, [18]give thanks in all circumstances; for this is the will of God in Christ Jesus for you. [19]Do not quench the Spirit, [20]do not despise prophesying, [21]but test everything; hold fast what is good, [22]abstain from every form of evil.

1 Cor 16:16, 18
1 Tim 5:17
Heb 13:17
1 Gal 6:6

2 Thess 3:6–15
Rom 14:1

Prov 20:22
Mt 5:43–48
Rom 12:17
1 Pet 3:9
Phil 3:1; 4:4–6
Lk 18:1
Rom 12:12
Eph 5:20; 6:18
Col 4:2
1 Cor 12:10; 14:1
Job 1:1, 8; 2:3
1 Jn 4:1

sed vigilemus et sobrii simus. [7]Qui enim dormiunt, nocte dormiunt; et, qui ebrii sunt, nocte inebriantur. [8]Nos autem, qui diei sumus, sobrii simus, induti loricam fidei et caritatis et *galeam* spem *salutis*; [9]quoniam non posuit nos Deus in iram sed in acquisitionem salutis per Dominum nostrum Iesum Christum, [10]qui mortuus est pro nobis, ut sive vigilemus sive dormiamus, simul cum illo vivamus. [11]Propter quod consolamini invicem et aedificate alterutrum, sicut et facitis. [12]Rogamus autem vos, fratres, ut noveritis eos, qui laborant inter vos et praesunt vobis in Domino et monent vos, [13]ut habeatis illos superabundanter in caritate propter opus illorum. Pacem habete inter vos. [14]Hortamur autem vos, fratres: corripite inquietos, consolamini pusillanimes, suscipite infirmos, longanimes estote ad omnes. [15]Videte, ne quis malum pro malo alicui reddat, sed semper, quod bonum est, sectamini et in invicem et in omnes. [16]Semper gaudete, [17]sine intermissione orate, [18]in omnibus gratias agite; haec enim voluntas Dei est in Christo Iesu erga vos. [19]Spiritum nolite exstinguere, [20]prophetias nolite spernere; [21]omnia autem probate, quod bonum est tenete, [22]ab omni specie mala abstinete vos. [23]Ipse autem Deus pacis sanctificet vos per omnia, et integer spiritus vester et anima et corpus sine querela in adventu

death is a moment when we meet the Lord face to face (see 2 Cor 5:6; Phil 1:23). A Christian, therefore, should always be vigilant, for he can never know which day will be his last.

5:12–22 These counsels include one to respect and venerate those who form the hierarchy of the Church: "Those who rule serve those whom they seem to rule. The reason for this is that they do not command out of a desire to be in authority, but because their ministry is to look after others; it is love, not pride, which leads them to look after others" (St Augustine, *De civitate Dei*, 19, 14).

St Paul goes on to urge Christians to practise brotherly love (vv. 14–15): "The Apostle's words are addressed not only to priests and ministers, but to all laymen and women as well: *admonish the idlers, encourage the fainthearted, help the weak*. No matter what the sin, if you correct one another with love, the enemy will never be able to ambush you; and if the enemy does attack you, the damage that he tries to inflict on you will be easily repaired or undone; what is written will be fulfilled in you: 'A brother is a better

defence than a strong city' (Prov 18:19); and 'whoever brings back a sinner from the error of his way will save his soul from death and will cover a multitude of sins' (Jas 5:20)" (St Caesarius of Arles, *Sermones*, 74, 4).

Being at peace with God and with others fills a person with joy and serenity (v. 16). Even pains and sorrows, if borne with faith, cannot undermine our joy: "If we feel we are beloved sons of our Heavenly Father, as indeed we are, how can we fail to be happy all the time? Think about it" (St Josemaría Escrivá, *The Forge*, 266).

Constant prayer (v. 17) will help a person to take Paul's advice to heart "The Apostle commands us to pray at all times. For the saints, sleep itself is prayer. Nevertheless, we should set out particular times of prayer so that if we become absorbed in our work the timetable [of our day] will remind us to fulfil our duty" (St Jerome, *Epistulae*, 22, 37).

This intention and struggle requires the effective power and grace of the Holy Spirit (vv. 19–21): "Because he did not want the grace of the Spirit to die down in us, the holy Apostle Paul wrote: 'Do not quench the Spirit.' If we are faith-

^{c2} Or *with them*

Closing prayer and farewell

Is 11:6
2 Thess 3:16
1 Thess 3:13
2 Thess 3:3
1 Cor 1:9
²³May the God of peace himself sanctify you wholly; and may your spirit and soul and body be kept sound and blameless at the coming of our Lord Jesus Christ. ²⁴He who calls you is faithful, and he will do it.

2 Thess 3:1
Rom 16:16
2 Cor 13:12
1 Cor 16:20
²⁵Brethren, pray for us.

²⁶Greet all the brethren with a holy kiss.

Col 4:16

2 Thess 3:18

Rom 16:20
²⁷I adjure you by the Lord that this letter be read to all the brethren.

²⁸The grace of our Lord Jesus Christ be with you.

Domini nostri Iesu Christi servetur. ²⁴Fidelis est, qui vocat vos, qui etiam faciet. ²⁵Fratres, orate etiam pro nobis. ²⁶Salutate fratres omnes in osculo sancto. ²⁷Adiuro vos per Dominum, ut legatur epistula omnibus fratribus. ²⁸Gratia Domini nostri Iesu Christi vobiscum.

ful to the end to the Spirit that he gave us in the beginning, we will belong to Christ forever. He said 'Do not quench the Spirit' not because man has the power to put out the Spirit, but because sinful and ungrateful men show the desire to put Him out, and by their sinful behaviour they lead the Spirit to flee" (St Athanasius, *Epistulae festales*, 3, 4).

5:23–28 The sanctification that God works in man affects his entire being. In the last analysis, Christian holiness is the fullness of the order established by God at the creation and restored after man's fall from grace. Therefore, the Apostle invokes God as "the God of peace" (v. 23), that is, of "tranquillity in order", which is a theological definition of peace. Holiness gives all man's faculties, physical as well as spiritual, their perfection and wholeness, and thus completes and perfects the natural order without changing it.

"He who calls you" (v. 24). The Greek text conveys the idea of continuous action—"he who is calling you". The calling that God addresses to a person is not an isolated event, occurring at a single moment in his or her life; it is a permanent attitude of God: he is always calling believers to be holy. Faithfulness is a "property" of God: he

always keeps his promises and he never goes back on his desire to save man: "He who began a good work in you will bring it to completion" (Phil 1:6). So, holiness depends on divine grace, which is always available, and on man's response to it. Final perseverance is a grace, but it will not be denied to anyone who strives to act in an upright way. "Buoyed up by this hope, let us bind our souls to him who is true to his word and righteous in his judgments. He who has forbidden us to use any deception can much less be a deceiver himself" (St Clement of Rome, *Ad Corinthios*, 1, 27).

Kissing (see v. 26) is mentioned on three other occasions in St Paul's letters (Rom 16:16; 1 Cor 16:20; 2 Cor 13:12), always with the adjective "holy" (v. 26). The kiss was normally used in Eastern cultures as a form of greeting and farewell (cf. Ex 4:27; 1 Sam 20:41; 2 Sam 19:39; Lk 7:45), but St Paul gives it a religious significance; it is now a sign of supernatural charity (cf. 1 Pet 5:14) and of shared faith. It had this meaning even in early Eucharistic liturgy: "The kiss of peace", Tertullian says, "is the seal of prayer" (*De oratione*, 14). The Roman Missal notes that, when pastoral considerations make this advisable, so advise, a kiss or another sign of peace may be offered just before Holy Communion.

THE SECOND LETTER OF PAUL TO THE

THESSALONIANS

Introduction

The fact that, in the Greek codexes, the Second Letter to the Thessalonians follows the First is because the content is somewhat similar in places and, of course, because it is written to the same community. It does not necessarily mean that it was the next letter written by Paul after 1 Thessalonians.

1. STRUCTURE AND CONTENT

The letter opens in a very similar way to the First Letter. The rest of the letter can be divided into three sections; the main content being found in the middle part.

The first part (as in the First Letter) begins with an act of thanksgiving to God for the exemplary way the Thessalonians are growing in virtue, and then focuses in on the subject of divine retribution—when, at the coming of the Lord Jesus, God in his justice will reward those who work for his Kingdom and will punish those who oppose him (1:3–12).

Paul goes on to spell out the main theme of the letter: the day of the Lord is not imminent, as the Thessalonians have been told since they were first instructed in the faith (2:1–17). Some people have been misled by Satan and have turned away from the tradition they received, putting their faith not in truth but in lies; all those who persist in doing this will be condemned. Paul exhorts the faithful to remain steadfast in the truth and to live in accordance with the traditions they were taught.

Following on from what he has said, and convinced that God is always faithful, Paul has every hope that the word of God will continue to bear fruit among the Thessalonians and spread to others throughout the world. They must also remember what the Apostle has told them about the need to work hard in their ordinary occupations and to show a fraternal concern for others (3:1–15). These exhortations end with a prayer to the Lord to give them peace at all times. The letter ends with a few words of farewell (3:16–18).

2. CONTEXT

The First Letter to the Thessalonians contains many references to the evangelization carried out by Paul, Silas and Timothy in Thessalonica—some so precise that we know that Paul's work in that city must have been carried out during the course of his second apostolic journey. However, the references in the Second Letter are so general and say so little about time and dates that it is not possible to establish when exactly it was written.

On the one hand, the wording at the start of the letter, the way the writer structures his ideas, and some specific references are similar in style to those in the First Letter. However, there are differences in nuance: in the Second Letter there is a much greater emphasis on the fact that the Lord's coming is not imminent (see 2 Thess 2:1–2 as compared with 1 Thess 4:15–17); and the need to hold onto the traditions received from Paul is also stressed several times (cf. 2 Thess 2:15 and 3:6)—a concern that is not expressed in the First Letter. For this reason, many scholars nowadays think that the Second Letter is by a disciple of St Paul writing in his name to reassure the Thessalonians, encouraging them to work patiently and always be prepared for the Second

Coming. Be that as it may, the Church has always accepted the letter as part of the canon because the churches of East and West were never in any doubt about its status as an inspired text.

Accepting as a given the fact that it is not possible (or indeed necessary) to say when exactly the letter was written, and therefore what the exact circumstances were at the time, we can see from the text itself that it is written to a Christian community in which the idea that the second coming of Jesus Christ is imminent has become widespread and prominent—to the point that some people have stopped doing their customary work and are wandering from place to place. The letter calls on the Thessalonians to remain calm, and urges each of them to stick to their appointed task and role in life.

3. MESSAGE

There are two main themes in the letter. The first, more doctrinal, subject is that of the need to stay true to the tradition that has been handed down. The second, which has more to do with contemporary issues, is that of when the Parousia will take place. An examination of the structure of the argument reveals that the writer's main aim is to convince readers that the day of the Lord is not imminent, and to have them see that they must live in accordance with Paul's teaching.

The Second Coming

On the subject of the "when" of the Parousia, the author, using apocalyptic language, offers arguments showing that it is not imminent (see 2:3–10). The expressions used—"rebellion (i.e., apostasy), "the man of lawlessness", "the son of perdition", "what is restraining him now", "the lawless one", "the mystery of lawlessness"—have given rise to a wide variety of interpretations (as is typical of apocalyptic language). However, to grasp what the letter is saying, there is no need to delve into the meanings of these expressions in any great detail. The main point is made very clear: no one should become agitated or alarmed, as if "the day of the Lord has come" (2:2).

When the Lord does come in all his power and glory, he will deliver "the righteous judgment of God" (1:5), when those who "do not know God" and "do not obey the gospel of our Lord Jesus" shall "suffer the punishment of eternal destruction and exclusion from the presence of the Lord and from the glory of his might" (1:8–9), whereas those who have suffered for the Kingdom of God will be found worthy of it (see 1:5).

Tradition and Christian life

One of the main points being made in the letter is the need to remember what was taught from the beginning and to hold on to apostolic tradition.

It explicitly warns against subscribing to new teachings which claim to be authoritative, whether they come in the form of new revelations, general rumours, or even letters allegedly written by Paul (see 2:2), if it is the case that those teachings are at odds with what the Apostle taught when he himself evangelized that community, that is, "when I was still with you" (2:5). Hence the admonition to keep to the traditions taught by him (see 2:15). This applies not only to points of doctrine, but also to the way Christians live their lives: "You yourselves know how you ought to imitate us" (3:7). They should avoid those who do not live "in accord with the tradition that you received from us" (3:6).

The Pauline tradition is, then, a rule of faith and a set of criteria for action. Hence the prayer that God, who loves and consoles his chosen ones, will help them to persevere along the right path: "May [he …] comfort your hearts and establish them in every good work and word" (2:17).

2 Thessalonians

Greeting*

1 ¹Paul, Silvanus, and Timothy,
To the church of the Thessalonians in God our Father and the Lord Jesus Christ: ²Grace to you and peace from God the Father and the Lord Jesus Christ.

Acts 15:22; 16:1
1 Thess 1:1

Rom 1:7

1. HOPE IN A DIVINE REWARD*

Thanksgiving

³We are bound to give thanks to God always for you, brethren, as is fitting, because your faith is growing abundantly, and the love of every one of you for one another is increasing. ⁴Therefore we ourselves boast of you in the churches of God for your steadfastness and faith in all your persecutions and in the afflictions which you are enduring.

1 Thess 1:2; 3:6–12;
4:9–10
2 Thess 2:13
1 Cor 1:4

1 Thess 2:19–20
Mk 4:17
2 Cor 8:2, 23–24

Divine retribution

⁵This is evidence of the righteous judgment of God, that you may be made worthy of the kingdom of God, for which you are suffering—⁶since indeed God deems it just

Mt 4:17
1 Thess 2:12, 14;3:4
Acts 14:22
Rom 12:19
Rev 18:6

[1] ¹Paulus et Silvanus et Timotheus ecclesiae Thessalonicensium in Deo Patre nostro et Domino Iesu Christo: ²gratia vobis et pax a Deo Patre nostro et Domino Iesu Christo. ³Gratias agere debemus Deo semper pro vobis, fratres, sicut dignum est, quoniam supercrescit fides vestra, et abundat caritas uniuscuiusque omnium vestrum in invicem, ⁴ita ut et nos ipsi in vobis gloriemur in ecclesiis Dei pro patientia vestra et fide in omnibus persecutionibus vestris et tribulationibus, quas sustinetis, ⁵indicium iusti iudicii Dei, ut digni habeamini regno Dei, pro quo et patimini, ⁶siquidem

*1:1–2 This second letter to the faithful at Thessalonica is in many respects similar to the first one. Apparently, some Christians there did not properly understand parts of the Apostle's teaching, and their faith was weakening in the face of persecution. St Paul gives them instruction about the justice and retribution God will deal out to each and all eventually (1:3–12), and about the timing of the Lord's second coming (2:1–17); then he exhorts them to pray and work (3:1–16).

*1:3–12 After greeting the community, he encourages them by comparing the demands of their faith and the great reward they will earn for their faithfulness (1:5, 7, 10), and contrasting it with the punishment their persecutors will receive in due course (1:6, 9).

1:3–4 The Apostle gives thanks for the Thessalonians' steadfastness and patience in the face of difficulties. John Paul II, commenting on this passage, wrote: "Thus to share in the sufferings of Christ is, at the same time, to suffer for the Kingdom of God. [...] Christ has led us

into this Kingdom through his suffering. And also through suffering those surrounded by the mystery of Christ's Redemption become mature enough to enter this Kingdom" (*Salvifici doloris*, 21).

"Your faith is growing" (v. 3). Faith needs to grow, it needs to be alive; and it grows when it is joined to love. The Apostle is delighted to see that the Thessalonians are active in their practice of faith and love; it explains why the level of morale among them is so good despite persecutions and afflictions: "Observe how the love and mutual solidarity of the believers is a great help in resisting evils and bearing affliction," St John Chrysostom says. "That deep fraternity was a great source of consolation. It is only a weak faith and an imperfect charity that afflictions cause to waver; but a solid, robust faith is in fact strengthened by affliction. A weak, languid soul derives no benefit from suffering, whereas a generous soul finds in suffering a source of new energy" (*In 2 Thessalonicenses*, ad loc.).

1:5–10 The Lord is just, and will give to each his just reward. The threat of punishment should not

Mt 25:31
Rev 18:6; 14:13
Ex 3:2
1 Thess 3:13; 4:16

Is 66:4, 15
Jer 10:25

Is 2:10, 19, 21
Ps 79:6

1 Thess 3:13
Ps 89:7
Is 2:11–17; 49:3; 66:3 to repay with affliction those who afflict you, [7]and to grant rest with us to you who are afflicted, when the Lord Jesus is revealed from heaven with his mighty angels in flaming fire, [8]inflicting vengeance upon those who do not know God and upon those who do not obey the gospel of our Lord Jesus. [9]They shall suffer the punishment of eternal destruction and exclusion from the presence of the Lord and from the glory of his might, [10]when he comes on that day to be glorified in his saints, and to be marvelled at in all who have believed, because our testimony to you was believed.

Prayer for perseverance

Jn 17:10
2 Thess 1:3
Phil 2:13; 4:13
Eph 4:1
Is 24:15; 66:5
Mal 1:11
2 Thess 2:14 [11]To this end we always pray for you, that our God may make you worthy of his call, and may fulfil every good resolve and work of faith by his power, [12]so that the name of our Lord Jesus may be glorified in you, and you in him, according to the grace of our God and the Lord Jesus Christ.

2. THE COMING OF THE LORD*

The day of the Lord is not imminent

Mt 24:31
1 Thess 4:13–17
Mt 24:6
Mk 13:7

1 Cor 1:8

1 Tim 4:1
1 Jn 2:18; 4:3 2 [1]Now concerning the coming of our Lord Jesus Christ and our assembling to meet him, we beg you, brethren, [2]not to be quickly shaken in mind or excited, either by spirit or by word, or by letter purporting to be from us, to the effect that the day of the Lord has come.* [3]Let no one deceive you in any way; for that day will not

iustum est apud Deum retribuere tribulationem his, qui vos tribulant, [7]et vobis, qui tribulamini, requiem nobiscum in revelatione Domini Iesu de caelo cum angelis virtutis eius, [8]*in igne flammae, dantis vindictam his, qui non noverunt Deum* et qui non oboediunt evangelio Domini nostri Iesu, [9]qui poenas dabunt interitu aeterno *a facie Domini et a gloria virtutis eius*, [10]cum venerit glorificari in sanctis suis et admirabilis fieri in omnibus, qui crediderunt, quia creditum est testimonium nostrum super vos in die illo. [11]Ad quod etiam oramus semper pro vobis, ut dignetur vos vocatione sua Deus noster et impleat omnem voluntatem bonitatis et opus fidei in virtute, [12]ut glorificetur nomen Domini nostri Iesu Christi in vobis, et vos in illo, secundum gratiam Dei nostri et Domini Iesu Christi. [2] [1]Rogamus autem vos, fratres, circa adventum Domini nostri Iesu Christi et nostram congregationem in ipsum, [2]ut non cito moveamini a sensu neque terreamini, neque per spiritum neque per verbum neque per epistu-

be the main reason for loyalty to God (one's primary motivation should be love); however, it should always be remembered that there is a risk that one could be cut off from God permanently. That is what happens to anyone who freely separates himself from God through sin and maintains that distance to the end of his life. Hence, the Church's prayer at Mass, just before the Consecration: "Father, accept this offering from your whole family. Grant us your peace in this life, save us from final damnation, and count us among those you have chosen" (*Roman Missal*, Eucharistic Prayer I).

1:11–12 The Greek phrase translated as "according to the grace of our God and of the Lord Jesus Christ" (v. 12) could also be given as "according to the grace of our God and Lord Jesus Christ"— which is a profession of faith in Christ as God and Lord. This phrase, which came to be used

very widely in later times, is of great value and significance on account of its antiquity.

*2:1–17 Here we reach the main theme of the letter—the time of our Lord's second coming or Parousia, which some people thought was imminent. This passage has bested interpreters; it is very difficult to discern its exact meaning and all kinds of explanations have been offered, both nowadays and in earlier times. The general meaning is clear: it is an exhortation to the Thessalonians to remain calm and to continue with the ordinary business of their lives, for the events that will signal the Second Coming have not yet occurred.

2:1–12 Against those who misled the Thessalonians by telling them that the Second Coming was imminent, St Paul uses Old Testament images and symbols to assert that two things

come, unless the rebellion comes first, and the man of lawlessness[a]* is revealed, the son of perdition, [4]who opposes and exalts himself against every so-called god or object of worship, so that he takes his seat in the temple of God, proclaiming himself to be God. [5]Do you not remember that when I was still with you I told you this? [6]And you know what is restraining him now so that he may be revealed in his time. [7]For the mystery of lawlessness is already at work; only he who now restrains it will do so until he is out of the way.* [8]And then the lawless one will be revealed, and the Lord Jesus will slay him with the breath of his mouth and destroy him by his appearing and his coming. [9]The coming of the lawless one by the activity of Satan will be with all power and with pretended signs and wonders, [10]and with all wicked deception for those who are to perish, because they refused to love the truth and so be saved. [11]Therefore God sends upon them a strong delusion, to make them believe what is false, [12]so that all may be condemned who did not believe the truth but had pleasure in unrighteousness.

Rev 13:1–8

Dan 11:36
Ezek 28:2
Is 14:13
1 Jn 2:18

Is 11:4
Job 4:9
Rev 19:11–21
Rev 13:13–17
Jn 8:44
Mt 24:24
Mt 24:12
Is 6:10
Rom 1:28
1 Kings 22:22
2 Tim 4:4
Jn 3:19; 3:39
Rom 1:32

Iam tamquam per nos, quasi instet dies Domini. [3]Ne quis vos seducat ullo modo; quoniam nisi venerit discessio primum, et revelatus fuerit homo iniquitatis, filius perditionis, [4]qui adversatur et extollitur supra omne, quod dicitur Deus aut quod colitur, ita ut in templo Dei sedeat, ostendens se quia sit Deus. [5]Non retinetis quod, cum adhuc essem apud vos, haec dicebam vobis? [6]Et nunc quid detineat scitis, ut ipse reveletur in suo tempore. [7]Nam mysterium iam operatur iniquitatis; tantum qui tenet nunc, donec de medio fiat. [8]Et tunc revelabitur ille *iniquus*, quem Dominus Iesus *interficiet spiritu oris sui* et destruet illustratione adventus sui, [9]eum, cuius est adventus secundum operationem Satanae in omni virtute et signis et prodigiis mendacibus [10]et in omni seductione iniquitatis his, qui pereunt, eo quod caritatem veritatis non receperunt, ut salvi fierent. [11]Et ideo mittit illis Deus operationem erroris, ut credant mendacio, [12]ut iudicentur omnes, qui non crediderunt veritati, sed consenserunt iniquitati. [13]Nos

must happen first—"rebellion" and the appearance of the "man of lawlessness" (v. 3). Our Lord himself predicted this rebellion (see Mark 13:22); he said that when it had run its course, the End would come, and the Last Judgment. We do not know what the Apostle means by "the man of lawlessness"; it may be all the forces of evil brought together as a tool in Satan's hands, although the description of this adversary of God is very like that of the "antichrist" given by St John (see 1 Jn 2:18–22). Verse 2 talks about "spirit"; this could be a reference to people who claimed to have a charismatic gift of prophecy (supposedly from the Holy Spirit), and who were spreading their own ideas as if they came from God. Others preferred to present what they had to say as though it came from St Paul (orally or in writing).

It is difficult to say what "the mystery of lawlessness" means or who or what is restraining it (v. 6). Some think that this mystery is the activity of the "man of lawlessness" (vv. 3–4). As regards the obstacle that restrains it, some scholars suggest that this refers to the laws of the Roman empire, an instrument manipulated by God. Others think that it refers to the proclamation of the Gospel and the active presence of Christians in the world, who through word and

example bring Christ's teaching and grace to many. If Christians let their zeal grow cold (these people say), then the curb on evil will cease to apply and apostasy will ensue. Others link the mystery to God, who, according to Jewish thinking, would keep evil angels enchained until the day of Judgment. Many other interpretations have been proposed, but none is wholly reliable. The *Catechism of the Catholic Church* teaches: "Before Christ's second coming the Church must pass through a final trial that will shake the faith of many believers. The persecution that accompanies her pilgrimage on earth will unveil the 'mystery of iniquity' in the form of a religious deception offering men an apparent solution to their problems at the price of apostasy from the truth. The supreme religious deception is that of the Antichrist, a pseudo-messianism by which man glorifies himself in place of God and of his Messiah come in the flesh. The Antichrist's deception already begins to take shape in the world every time the claim is made to realize within history that messianic hope which can only be realized beyond history through the eschatological judgment. The Church has rejected even modified forms of this falsification of the kingdom to come under the name of millenarianism, especially the 'intrinsically per-

a Other ancient authorities read *sin*

Belief in the truth

Deut 33:12
Eph 1:4
Rom 8:29f
1 Thess 1:2, 4; 2:13;
4:3–8
1 Thess 4:7; 5:9
Col 2:6
1 Thess 3:8
1 Cor 11:2

[13]But we are bound to give thanks to God always for you, brethren beloved by the Lord, because God chose you from the beginning[b] to be saved, through sanctification by the Spirit[c] and belief in the truth. [14]To this he called you through our gospel, so that you may obtain the glory of our Lord Jesus Christ. [15]So then, brethren, stand firm and hold to the traditions which you were taught by us, either by word of mouth or by letter.

Prayer for encouragement

2 Cor 1:4

Rom 5:2
1 Thess 3:11–13

[16]Now may our Lord Jesus Christ himself, and God our Father, who loved us and gave us eternal comfort and good hope through grace, [17]comfort your hearts and establish them in every good work and word.

autem debemus gratias agere Deo semper pro vobis, fratres, dilecti a Domino, quod elegerit vos Deus primitias in salutem, in sanctificatione Spiritus et fide veritatis: [14]ad quod et vocavit vos per evangelium nostrum in acquisitionem gloriae Domini nostri Iesu Christi. [15]Itaque, fratres, state et tenete traditiones, quas didicistis sive per sermonem sive per epistulam nostram. [16]Ipse autem Dominus noster Iesus Christus et Deus Pater noster, qui dilexit nos et dedit consolationem aeternam et spem bonam in gratia, [17]consoletur corda vestra et confirmet in omni opere et sermone bono. [3] [1]De cetero, fratres, orate pro nobis, ut sermo Domini currat et glorificetur sicut et apud vos, [2]et ut liberemur ab importunis et malis

verse' political form of a secular messianism" (nos. 675–676). See also the notes on 1 Jn 2:18–29 and Rev 20:1–6.

"God sends upon them a strong delusion" (v. 11). This type of expression appears quite often in the Bible—attributing to the action of God things that he simply *permits*. God wants everyone to be saved and never encourages anyone to do evil; however, out of respect for man's freedom, he allows people who persist in wrongdoing to damn themselves.

Uncertainty as to when the Parousia will happen is no obstacle to leading a genuine Christian life, nor should it make people uneasy; in fact, as St Athanasius points out, it has certain advantages: "Not to know the day of the Second Coming or the day of his own death is good for man. For if he did know, he would not value the time in between; he would think only of the last days before his death and the end of all things. For this reason, the day and hour of death is kept secret, so that man will not grow proud and live most of his life unthinkingly. (The end of all things contains the death of each man; and the death of each man foreshadows the end of all things.) The Word has kept the hour of the Second Coming and of his death hidden from man so that his life will be a time of uncertainty and hope: each day he will respond and grow as he has been called to do, 'forgetting what lies behind, and straining

forward to what lies ahead' (Phil 3:13)" (*Contra Arianos*, 3, 49).

In any event, and given that this is a difficult passage to understand, an individual must choose either to "love the truth" (see v. 10), the truth offered by Christ, or to follow the signs and arguments put forward by the Evil One. "All men are bound to seek the truth, especially in what concerns God and his Church, and to embrace it. And hold on to it as they come to know it" (Vatican II, *Dignitatis humanae*, 1).

2:13–17 Even though there are some who do not accept the truth, the Apostle feels moved to thank God for the good results his grace has worked in the Thessalonians. The mention of the three divine Persons reminds us that salvation is the joint work of the Blessed Trinity: "God", the Father, calls people so that they may attain the glory of "our Lord Jesus Christ" through the action of "the Spirit" (vv. 13–14).

To avoid being led astray by unsound teaching, people need to hold fast to the faith they received and to apostolic traditions. The term "traditions" in v. 15 seems to refer primarily to the Christian teaching that St Paul himself received and preached; but it is also equivalent to the "deposit" of faith: "The Church, in her doctrine, life and worship, perpetuates and transmits to every generation all that she herself is, all that she believes" (Vatican II, *Dei Verbum*, 8).

b Other ancient authorities read *as the first converts*   c Or *of spirit*

3. STEADFASTNESS*

May the word of the Lord speed on

3 [1]Finally, brethren, pray for us, that the word of the Lord may speed on and triumph, as it did among you, [2]and that we may be delivered from wicked and evil men; for not all have faith. [3]But the Lord is faithful; he will strengthen you and guard you from evil.[d] [4]And we have confidence in the Lord about you, that you are doing and will do the things which we command. [5]May the Lord direct your hearts to the love of God and to the steadfastness of Christ.

1 Thess 5:25
Col 4:3
Eph 6:19f
Rom 10:16; 15:21
Mt 6:13
1 Cor 10:13
1 Jn 2:14
2 Cor 7:16
1 Thess 4:2, 10
1 Cor 13:13

Avoiding idleness. Earning one's living

[6]Now we command you, brethren, in the name of our Lord Jesus Christ, that you keep away from any brother who is living in idleness and not in accord with the tradition that you received from us. [7]For you yourselves know how you ought to imitate us; we were not idle when we were with you, [8]we did not eat any one's bread without paying, but with toil and labour we worked night and day, that we might not burden any of you. [9]It was not because we have not that right, but to give you in our conduct an example to imitate. [10]For even when we were with you, we gave you this command: If any one will not work, let him not eat. [11]For we hear that some of you

1 Thess 4:1, 11–12;
5:14
2 Thess 2:15
Rom 16:17
1 Thess 2:9
1 Cor 11:1
Acts 18:3
1 Cor 4:11–12;
9:1–129
Mt 10:10
Phil 3:17
1 Cor 4:16; 11:1;
9:6, 14

hominibus; non enim omnium est fides. [3]Fidelis autem Dominus est, qui confirmabit vos et custodiet a Malo. [4]Confidimus autem de vobis in Domino, quoniam, quae praecipimus, et facitis et facietis. [5]Dominus autem dirigat corda vestra in caritatem Dei et patientiam Christi. [6]Praecipimus autem vobis, fratres, in nomine Domini nostri Iesu Christi, ut subtrahatis vos ab omni fratre ambulante inordinate et non secundum traditionem, quam acceperunt a nobis. [7]Ipsi enim scitis quemadmodum oporteat imitari nos, quoniam non inordinati fuimus inter vos [8]neque gratis panem manducavimus ab aliquo sed in labore et fatigatione, nocte et die operantes, ne quem vestrum gravaremus; [9]non quasi non habuerimus potestatem, sed ut nosmetipsos formam daremus vobis ad imitandum nos. [10]Nam et cum essemus apud vos, hoc praecipiebamus vobis: Si quis non vult operari, nec manducet. [11]Audimus enim inter vos quosdam ambulare inordinate, nihil operantes sed curiose agentes; [12]his autem, qui eius-

*3:1–18 From this point onwards, the letter focuses on matters concerning Christian conduct, particularly the attitude the Thessalonians should have towards work.

3:1–5 St John Chrysostom comments on St Paul's approach: "The Apostle [...] now encourages them to offer prayers to God for him, but he does not ask them to pray God to free him from dangers he ought to face up to (for they are an unavoidable consequence of his ministry); rather, he asks them to pray 'that the word of the Lord may speed on and triumph'" (*In 2 Thessalonicenses*, ad loc.).

The phrase "speed and triumph" (v. 1) is evocative of the Games which were a great Greek institution: the winner of a race was given a victory wreath. The triumph, the prize, of the word of the Lord is that it be proclaimed to and accepted by all.

In contrast to the unfaithfulness of some Christians, the Apostle calls for trust in God (v. 3), who is always faithful. We must respond to

grace: God created us without our cooperation, but he has willed to save us only with our cooperation (see St Augustine, *Sermones*, 169, 13).

3:6–15 Some Thessalonians, wrongly thinking that the Parousia was about to happen, had given up working. So the Apostle reminds them that when he was among them he worked hard to keep himself and was a burden to no one. Christians should, "as citizens of both cities, perform their duties faithfully in the spirit of the Gospel. [... By their faith they] are bound all the more to fulfil these responsibilities according to the vocation of each one (cf. 2 Thess 3:6–13; Eph 4:28)" (Vatican II, *Gaudium et spes*, 43). This is the way that every responsible Christian should act—working hard to give glory to God, to look after the needs of one's family, and to serve the whole community. "Everyone, in his job, in whatever place he has in society, must feel obliged to make his work God's work, sowing everywhere the peace and joy of the Lord" (St Josemaría Escrivá, *Friends of God*, 70).

d Or *the evil one*

Gen 3:19
1 Thess 4:11

Gal 6:9

1 Cor 5:5, 9–13
2 Thess 3:6
Mt 18:15–18
2 Cor 2:7
Gal 6:1
1 Thess 5:14

Jn 14:27
1 Thess 5:23
Rom 15:33

Gal 6:11
1 Cor 16:21

1 Thess 5:28
Rom 16:20–24

are living in idleness, mere busybodies, not doing any work. [12]Now such persons we command and exhort in the Lord Jesus Christ to do their work in quietness and to earn their own living. [13]Brethren, do not be weary in well-doing.

[14]If any one refuses to obey what we say in this letter, note that man, and have nothing to do with him, that he may be ashamed. [15]Do not look on him as an enemy, but warn him as a brother.

Words of farewell

[16]Now may the Lord of peace himself give you peace at all times in all ways. The Lord be with you all.

[17]I, Paul, write this greeting with my own hand. This is the mark in every letter of mine; it is the way I write. [18]The grace of our Lord Jesus Christ be with you all.

modi sunt, praecipimus et obsecramus in Domino Iesu Christo, ut cum quiete operantes suum panem manducent. [13]Vos autem, fratres, nolite deficere benefacientes. [14]Quod si quis non oboedit verbo nostro per epistulam, hunc notate, non commisceamini cum illo, ut confundatur; [15]et nolite quasi inimicum existimare, sed corripite ut fratrem. [16]Ipse autem Dominus pacis det vobis pacem sempiternam in omni modo. Dominus cum omnibus vobis. [17]Salutatio mea manu Pauli, quod est signum in omni epistula, ita scribo. [18]Gratia Domini nostri Iesu Christi cum omnibus vobis.

3:13 In the Gospels we are told that "he who endures to the end will be saved" (Mt 10:22), and also that "no one who puts his hand to the plough and looks back is fit for the kingdom of God" (Lk 9:62). These are teachings which, given man's natural inconsistency and changeability, encourage us to make a real effort to do things well and never take things easy, because only those who are faithful unto death will receive the crown of life (see Rev 2:10).

3:16–18 In ancient times, letters were usually dictated to an amanuensis or secretary; St Paul followed that custom (see Rom 16:22). Often the person dictating the letter would add a few words at the end in his own handwriting, out of courtesy and to vouch for the document's authority; this happens in the case of some of Paul's letters (cf. 1 Cor 16:21; Gal 6:11; Col 4:18). The words of farewell in this letter have become a liturgical greeting in the Church.

THE FIRST LETTER OF PAUL TO

TIMOTHY

Introduction

In printed editions of the New Testament, the letters of St Paul to Christian communities are followed by those written to particular people. In this group, too, they are arranged in order of length. First come the two letters to Timothy, then the letter to Titus, and finally the short letter to Philemon.

The first three of these (1 and 2 Timothy, and Titus) are given the collective title of "Pastoral Letters", a name which was coined early in the eighteenth century and which derives from the letters' original addressees and content. Timothy and Titus were co-workers of the Apostle who were in charge of the local communities of Ephesus and Crete, respectively. The letters are about pastoral matters; in them St Paul gives rulings and advice about the governance of those communities, which were under threat at the time from false teachers. Guidelines about church organization and about the roles of ministers are also given. All three letters are written in a simple, friendly style, which reflects the writer's desire to train those men to be good shepherds of their flocks. However, each letter has distinctive features of its own which are worth pointing out.

1. STRUCTURE AND CONTENT

The First Letter to Timothy is written to defend "sound doctrine" (1:10)—that is, teaching which truly leads to salvation and which comes from the Apostle's own preaching—to counter heterodox ideas and to reaffirm that the Church should be organized in line with the teaching of the Gospel.

After a short greeting (1:1–2), Paul in the first section of the letter urges Timothy to defend sound doctrine against the ideas being spread by false teachers (1:3–20). Then, having laid down the firm ground of the doctrine of the faith, he deals with some aspects of its practice. Given that the most important element of faith is how one relates to God, in the second section the Apostle instructs his disciple about matters having to do with divine worship, particularly prayer and attendance at liturgical assemblies (2:1–15). The instructions in the third section of the letter concern the qualifications necessary for those who hold a ministry in a Christian community: the persons involved must live lives that edify all the faithful—and also present an accurate and attractive image of the Church to outsiders (3:1–16). Finally, in an even more informal and friendly tone than before (such that it is not easy to identify any particular order to the themes touched on), the Apostle exhorts and advises Timothy about his attitude and behaviour towards others—older people, younger people, widows, elders, slaves, well-to-do people, false teachers; he has pastoral duties towards them all (4:11—6:19). The letter ends with a few words of farewell in which Paul returns to the main point of the letter—the need for Timothy to guard the faith entrusted to him (6:20–21).

2. CONTEXT

At the time of the writing of this letter, Timothy is the head of the Christian community established at Ephesus, one that is experiencing the typical growing pains of a young church. The pagan environment, doctrines of false teachers, and the lax moral behaviour of some Christians are matters of concern to the Apostle. Timothy is charged with holding fast to the teaching handed down, and with helping the people entrusted to him to lead Christian lives.

Elsewhere in the New Testament we meet Timothy as a co-worker of St Paul. In Philippians 2:22, Paul says that "as a son with a father he has served with me in the gospel". The Acts of the Apostles tells us that Timothy was the son of a Gentile father and a Jewish mother who had become a devout Christian, and that during his second missionary journey, when passing through Lystra, Paul received excellent reports about this Christian youth (Acts 16:1–3). Having had him circumcised, he took him along as a helper in the foundation of the churches of Philippi and Thessalonica (Acts 16:12). We know that he was with Paul in Beroea (Acts 17:14), and that the Apostle sent him from Athens to Thessalonica (1 Thess 3:2). He appears alongside Paul again in Corinth (Acts 18:5), and he accompanies him to Ephesus (Acts 19:22), Macedonia (1 Cor 4:17; 16:10; 2 Cor 1:1) and Asia Minor (Acts 20:4), during his third apostolic journey. In the Captivity Letters we are told that he was with Paul when the Apostle was in prison (Col 1:1; Phil 1:1; 2:19). The Letter to the Hebrews speaks of Timothy's having been "released", though nothing is said about why or where he was imprisoned (Heb 13:23).

Timothy comes across as a very loyal follower of St Paul. He must have been still very young when the Apostle called on the Christians at Corinth to treat him with respect (see 1 Cor 16:11), and he could not have been much older when he was given charge of the church at Ephesus (see 1 Tim 4:12; 2 Tim 2:22).

This letter provides us with information about St Paul's activity that is not mentioned elsewhere in the New Testament. We are told, for example, that the Apostle leaves Timothy in Ephesus when he went to Macedonia (1 Tim 1:3), and that he planned to meet with him there later (1 Tim 3:14; 4:13). It is not easy to match these movements with any of the Apostle's journeys mentioned in Acts, for when Paul leaves Ephesus for Macedonia on his third journey no reference is made to Timothy's having stayed on in that city; on the contrary, as has already been noted, we are told that he travelled with the Apostle. Also, the account in Acts about the emotional leave-taking at Ephesus (implying that the elders would never see Paul again: Acts 20:25, 38), suggests that the Apostle never returned to that city. Yet, what is said in this letter leads one to think that the Apostle did return after his imprisonment in Rome and that that visit accords with references in this letter and in the Letter to Titus.

Aside from this new information, the letter tells us about the situation in a Christian community founded by Paul that has seen the arrival of preachers peddling ideas at odds with the "deposit" of faith passed on by the Apostle; hence the urgent need to distinguish sound teaching from the ideas being put out by false teachers

Both of the letters to Timothy and the one sent to Titus are somewhat different from the other Pauline letters: the vocabulary and the style are different; the content has to do with moral and practical matters—as compared with the more theological concerns of other letters; the hierarchical organization of the Church and the kinds of errors referred to seem to belong to a period after Paul's lifetime; it is, in the end, not easy to say when the letters might have been written. This has led some scholars to query whether they were in fact written by St Paul. However, regardless of whether they were written by a secretary or by some more or less close disciple of St Paul, or by St Paul himself, the letters do reflect the mind and authority of the Apostle.

3. MESSAGE

The central theme of the First Letter to Timothy is the salvation dispensed by the Church, which makes present and extends the saving work of Christ. This theme is developed from a number of different but complementary points of view—first from a theological perspective, in terms of the Christ-event, which is the core and basis of the Christian life; but then from a more practical angle, in terms of church administration (Timothy's own calling and that of others entrusted with church ministries of different kinds).

Jesus Christ and salvation

The basic idea in the Pastoral Letters (and therefore one that often recurs) is that of salvation: God is described as being our "Saviour" (cf. 1:1; 2:3; 4:10), who, in his infinite love, "desires all men to be saved and to come to the knowledge of the truth" (2:4).

This design of God's has been revealed and accomplished by Jesus Christ, the "one mediator" (2:5), who "came into the world to save sinners" (1:15). Faith in these truths leads to salvation; they constitute the "sound doctrine" (1:10) of the Gospel preached by St Paul (see 1:11, 15–16).

This faith is put at risk by false teaching that leads Christians away from the truth (see 1:3, 6; 4:1–2; 6:3–5). In fact, one of the main problems confronting the early generations of Christians, in Ephesus and elsewhere, was that of distinguishing sound teaching from teaching contaminated by ideas peculiar to Jewish tradition or to Greek religions, none of which had any place in the Christian message.

The Church

The cordial and at the same time demanding tone of the letter shows how the Church is a family, "the household of God" (3:15), in which all not only share the same beliefs but also practise them. The Church is "the pillar and bulwark of the truth" (3:15); Timothy is enjoined to conserve and pass on intact the deposit of faith —"what has been entrusted" to him (6:20). All who, like Timothy, have received the grace of ministry by the laying-on of hands (cf. 4:14) have the duty to teach others how to keep the faith (see 1:18–19) and ensure that erroneous teaching is kept at bay (see 1:3).

At the time when this letter was written, the terminology of church offices was still fluid, and the roles of the different ministries were not as clearly defined as they would be by the time of St Irenaeus, in the early second century. The letter refers to someone being a "bishop", *epískopos* (3:2), meaning that the person headed up a particular community; it also speaks of "deacons" (*diákonoi*), "elders" or "presbyters" (*presbýteroi*), and even of there being a special group of "widows" (see 5:9). In line with the ministry a person received, the role of each was to preside, assist, or instruct—and a high standard of Christian living was expected of all ministers.

1 Timothy

1 Tim 2:3; 4:10
Tit 1:3; 3:4
Col 1:27

2 Tim 1:2
Tit 1:4
Acts 16:1
2 Jn 1:3
Rom 1:7
1 Cor 1:3

Greeting*

1 ¹Paul, an apostle of Christ Jesus by command of God our Saviour and of Christ Jesus our hope,
²To Timothy, my true child in the faith:*
Grace, mercy, and peace from God the Father and Christ Jesus our Lord.

1. SOUND DOCTRINE*

False teachers to be admonished

Acts 20:1

2 Tim 2:14, 16, 23;
4:4
Tit 3:9
1 Tim 4:7; 6:4, 20

Gal 5:14
Rom 13:10

³As I urged you when I was going to Macedonia, remain at Ephesus that you may charge certain persons not to teach any different doctrine, ⁴nor to occupy themselves with myths and endless genealogies* which promote speculations rather than the divine training[a] that is in faith; ⁵whereas the aim of our charge is love that issues from a pure heart and a good conscience and sincere faith. ⁶Certain persons by

[1] ¹ Paulus apostolus Christi Iesu secundum praeceptum Dei salvatoris nostri et Christi Iesu spei nostrae, ²Timotheo germano filio in fide: gratia, misericordia, pax a Deo Patre et Christo Iesu Domino nostro. ³Sicut rogavi te, ut remaneres Ephesi, cum irem in Macedoniam, ut praeciperes quibusdam, ne aliter docerent ⁴neque intenderent fabulis et genealogiis interminatis, quae quaestiones praestant magis quam dispensationem Dei, quae est in fide; ⁵finis autem praecepti est caritas de corde puro et conscientia bona et fide non ficta, ⁶a quibus quidam aberrantes conversi sunt in vaniloquium, ⁷volentes esse legis doctores, non intelligentes neque quae loquuntur neque de quibus affirmant. ⁸Scimus autem quia bona est lex,

*1:1–2 This letter instructs Timothy, a disciple of St Paul, about his duties as the minister in charge of the church at Ephesus. It urges him to defend sound doctrine (1:3–20) and gives him guidelines about community prayer (2:1–15), qualifications for church ministers (3:1–16) and the way in which ministers (and certain other groups of people—such as widows and slaves) should conduct themselves (4:1—6:19).

"God our Saviour" (v. 1). In the Greco-Roman world the title of "saviour" was applied to emperors and gods. In the Pastoral Letters, in line with Old Testament usage, it is applied to God (2:3; 4:10; Tit 1:3; 2:10; 3:4), who effects his plan of salvation through Jesus Christ. St John Chrysostom comments: "We suffer many evils, but we harbour great hopes; we are exposed to dangers and snares, but we have a Saviour, who is not just man, but God. Strength will never fail our Saviour, for he is God; no matter how great the dangers, we will overcome them" (*In 1 Timotheum*, ad loc.).

"Grace, mercy and peace" (v. 2). A wish for mercy is added here to the now customary wish for "grace and peace" (see Rom 1:7; 1 Cor 1:3; 2

Cor 1:2) perhaps to underline the salvation accomplished by Christ, for in the language of the Bible petitioning for mercy means the same as asking for salvation.

*1:3–20 The exhortation to Timothy focuses on his duty to ensure that believers receive sound teaching (vv. 3–7) and are not exposed to mistaken interpretations (vv. 8–11). Paul's message is not a plan of his own devising; it is the "glorious gospel" (v. 11) of God.

1:3–7 One of the main challenges facing the Christian communities, including that at Ephesus, during the early stages of their development was that of distinguishing sound teaching from false, for there were those who never managed to move away from their very fixed Jewish outlook—and others who tried to import Greek, pagan, ideas into the Christian message. The first duty, then, of someone in charge of a Christian community is to ensure sound teaching; he should not impose personal ideas of his own, but should inculcate the growth and practice of charity. "Faith teaches the truth, and a pure faith

a Or *stewardship*, or *order*

swerving from these have wandered away into vain discussion, [7]desiring to be teachers of the law, without understanding either what they are saying or the things about which they make assertions.

The purpose of the Law

[8]Now we know that the law is good, if any one uses it lawfully, [9]understanding this, that the law is not laid down for the just but for the lawless and disobedient, for the ungodly and sinners, for the unholy and profane, for murderers of fathers and murderers of mothers, for manslayers, [10]immoral persons, sodomites, kidnappers, liars, perjurers, and whatever else is contrary to sound doctrine, [11]in accordance with the glorious gospel of the blessed God with which I have been entrusted.

2 Tim 2:16
Tit 1:10

Rom 7:7, 12, 16
Rom 1:29; 7:7–12
Gal 5:18, 23

1 Tim 6:3

Jn 1:14
2 Cor 4:4
1 Thess 2:4
Tit 1:3

si quis ea legitime utatur, [9]sciens hoc quia iusto lex non est posita, sed iniustis et non subiectis, impiis et peccatoribus, sceleratis et contaminatis, patricidis et matricidis, homicidis, [10]fornicariis, masculorum concubitoribus, plagiariis, mendacibus, periuris, et si quid aliud sanae doctrinae adversatur, [11]secundum evangelium gloriae beati Dei, quod creditum est mihi. [12]Gratiam habeo ei, qui me confortavit, Christo Iesu Domino nostro,

gives rise to charity" (St John Chrysostom, *In 1 Timotheum*, 2, 1). St Thomas Aquinas explains that this is the case because "those who do not hold the true faith cannot love God, for a person who believes things about God that are untrue no longer loves God" (*Super 1 Timotheum*, ad loc.); at best, such a person could love the caricature of God that he believes in.

In line with this apostolic teaching, the Church tries to ensure that religious instruction covers the basics of the faith, which we are to be taught simply and clearly; this saves time and avoids the confusion that can result from people being exposed to unreliable speculation, or to theories marginal to the faith. John Paul II refers to this passage from St Paul when he says that catechists "must refuse to trouble the minds of children and young people, at this stage of their catechesis, with outlandish theories, useless questions and unproductive discussions, things that St Paul often condemned in his pastoral letters" (*Catechesi tradendae*, 61).

1:8–11 The previous exhortation to promote sound teaching does not imply rejecting that contained in the Law of Moses: that law is still valid for Christians, but they have to see it in a new light. St Paul taught that Christians do not come under the rule of the Law; they must live by faith in Christ (Gal 3:24–26; 4:3–7); they come under the rule of grace (Rom 6:14–15). Believers avoid everything that the Law forbids, and they do all that it commands—and more besides. The Law of Moses is good, but it is

inadequate: it tells us what is sinful but it does not provide the means to conquer sin; whereas "the law of the Spirit of life in Christ Jesus" (Rom 8:2) enables us to attain what the Law on its own cannot grant us—salvation (cf. Rom 8:1–4). That is why it says here that "the law is not laid down for the just" (v. 9), that is, for the person justified by Christ; for the just or righteous man acts not at the diktat of the prescriptions of the Mosaic Law, which do not apply to him; rather, what motivates him is faith in God and love of God. False teachers do not seem to realize what the justification worked by Christ achieves, because they continue to argue over interpretations of the Old Testament, as if salvation depended on its observance.

"Sound doctrine" or some equivalent expression appears often in the Pastoral Letters. In Greek literature of the time, "sound" means more or less the same as "reasonable", so the idea is that faith and morals are not at odds with sound human reasoning; rather, they help to guide reason and raise it beyond what it can attain on its own: "Man is able to recognize good and evil thanks to that discernment of good from evil which he himself carries out by his *reason, in particular by his reason enlightened by divine revelation and by faith,* through the law which God gave to the Chosen People, beginning with the commandments on Sinai. Israel was called to accept and to live out *God's law as a particular gift and sign of its election and of the divine Covenant,* and also as a pledge of God's blessing" (John Paul II, *Veritatis splendor*, 44).

Paul recalls his own conversion

[12]I thank him who has given me strength for this, Christ Jesus our Lord, because he judged me faithful by appointing me to his service, [13]though I formerly blasphemed and persecuted and insulted him; but I received mercy because I had acted ignorantly in unbelief, [14]and the grace of our Lord overflowed for me with the faith and love that are in Christ Jesus. [15]The saying is sure and worthy of full acceptance, that Christ Jesus came into the world to save sinners. And I am the foremost of sinners; [16]but I received mercy for this reason, that in me, as the foremost, Jesus Christ might display his perfect patience for an example to those who were to believe in him for eternal life. [17]To the King of ages, immortal, invisible, the only God, be honour and glory for ever and ever.[b] Amen.

Acts 9:15
Gal 1:15–16
1 Cor 15:9–10
Acts 9:12
Phil 4:13
Gal 1:13–16
Phil 3:6
1 Cor 15:9
2 Pet 3:15

Lk 15:2; 19:10
Mt 9:13
1 Tim 3:1; 4:9

2 Thess 3:7
1 Cor 15:9–10
Eph 3:1, 7–9
Col 1:24

1 Tim 2:5; 6:16
Rom 16:27
Col 1:15
Rev 4:11; 7:12

Timothy's responsibilities

[18]This charge I commit to you, Timothy, my son, in accordance with the prophetic utterances which pointed to you, that inspired by them you may wage the good warfare, [19]holding faith and a good conscience. By rejecting conscience, certain persons

1 Tim 4:14; 6:12
2 Tim 4:7

1 Tim 3:9

quia fidelem me existimavit ponens in ministerio, [13]qui prius fui blasphemus et persecutor et contumeliosus; sed misericordiam consecutus sum, quia ignorans feci in incredulitate, [14]superabundavit autem gratia Domini nostri cum fide et dilectione, quae sunt in Christo Iesu. [15]Fidelis sermo et omni acceptione dignus: Christus Iesus venit in mundum peccatores salvos facere; quorum primus ego sum, [16]sed ideo misericordiam consecutus sum, ut in me primo ostenderet Christus Iesus omnem longanimitatem, ad informationem eorum, qui credituri sunt illi in vitam aeternam. [17]Regi autem saeculorum, incorruptibili, invisibili, soli Deo honor et gloria in saecula saeculorum. Amen. [18]Hoc praeceptum commendo tibi, fili Timothee, secundum praecedentes super te prophetias, ut milites in illis bonam militiam [19]habens fidem et bonam conscientiam, quam quidam

1:12–17 Awareness of one's own limitations or unworthiness is not a valid reason for not accepting a position of responsibility that involves the preaching and defence of sound teaching in the Church. The example a minister sets should help dispel any feelings of mistrust or doubt that people might harbour. Paul is very conscious that it was not merit on his part that earned him his calling to be a minister of faith and love.

Verse 15 sums up very succinctly the redemptive work of Christ. It opens with a form of words signalling that an important statement is about to be made. "The salvation of sinners was the only reason for the Lord's coming. If all wounds and illnesses are cured, there is no need for medicine. The great doctor came down from heaven to cure the terrible illness that was everywhere in the world; the one who suffered this illness was all mankind" (St Augustine, *Sermones*, 175, 1). This is in fact one of the basic truths of the Christian faith, and it is clearly affirmed in the Creed: "For us men and for our salvation he came down from heaven".

The passage ends with a solemn doxology (v. 17), a formal statement in praise of God. In contrast to the energetic attempts by civil authorities of the time to foster emperor-worship, Christians proclaim that God is Lord of the universe and the King who will reign forever.

1:18–20 Just as St Paul himself never failed to protect sound teaching, that safeguarding is also Timothy's duty. In the New Testament "prophetic utterances" (v. 18) do not normally have to do with predicting future events. Here such utterances seems to be a reference to the mission given to Timothy when hands were laid upon him (see 4:14; 2 Tim 1:6) and to the words of exhortation addressed to him by St Paul when he first instructed him in the faith.

Faith is an unmerited gift that God gives a person; and it can be lost. One must strive to protect it, and this means having a "good", rightly formed, conscience (v. 19), for a corrupt conscience tries to justify actions that are at odds with the faith. St John Chrysostom warns of this: "He who says goodbye to right Christian living devises for himself a faith that suits his moral behaviour" (*In 1 Timotheum*, ad loc.).

Delivering someone over to Satan (v. 20) means excommunicating them from the Church—a pastoral, therapeutic recourse designed to protect the flock and to reform those who have strayed from the faith. We do not

b Greek *to the ages of ages*

2 Tim 2:17
1 Cor 5:5

have made shipwreck of their faith, [20]among them Hymenaeus and Alexander, whom I have delivered to Satan* that they may learn not to blaspheme.

2. REGULATIONS ABOUT PRAYER*

God desires the salvation of all

Eph 6:18
Phil 4:6
Rom 13:1–7
Tit 3:1

1 Tim 1:1
Ezek 18:23
Jn 8:32
2 Pet 3:9;
Tit 3:4

2 [1]First of all, then, I urge that supplications, prayers, intercessions, and thanksgivings be made for all men, [2]for kings and all who are in high positions, that we may lead a quiet and peaceable life, godly and respectful in every way. [3]This is good, and it is acceptable in the sight of God our Saviour, [4]who desires all men to be saved

repellentes circa fidem naufragaverunt; [20]ex quibus est Hymenaeus et Alexander, quos tradidi Satanae, ut discant non blasphemare.　[2] [1]Obsecro igitur primo omnium fieri obsecrationes, orationes, postulationes, gratiarum actiones pro omnibus hominibus, [2]pro regibus et omnibus, qui in sublimitate sunt, ut quietam et tranquillam vitam agamus in omni pietate et castitate. [3]Hoc bonum est et acceptum coram salvatore nostro Deo, [4]qui omnes homines vult salvos fieri et ad agnitionem veritatis venire. [5]Unus enim Deus, unus et mediator Dei et hominum, homo Christus Iesus,

know much about the two people St Paul mentions in v. 20. Hymenaeus could be the same heretic that Paul warns Timothy about in his second letter—the one who believed that the resurrection of the dead had already taken place (2 Tim 2:17). Alexander was a much more common name—which makes this man more difficult to identify. He may be the coppersmith whom Paul warns Timothy about in 2 Timothy 4:14–15; in Acts there is also a reference to an Alexander at Ephesus (see Acts 19:33–34).

*2:1–15 Having dealt with the key matter of safeguarding sound teaching (1:3–20), the Apostle now gives his disciple some guidelines about the regulation of worship—particularly public prayer and how people should conduct themselves at liturgical assemblies.

2:1–7 Paul stipulates that prayers should be said for all, not just for friends and benefactors, and not just for Christians. The Church helps people to do as Paul suggests by means of the Bidding Prayers (General Intercessions) at Mass, where the people, exercising their priestly function, intercede for all mankind (*Roman Missal*, General Introduction, 45).

God's desire that all should be saved is a subject that is closely linked to the fact that Christ our Saviour is the only mediator between God and us. St Augustine asserts that "without Christ, the way to salvation for all, who has never once failed man, no one has been set free,

no one is set free, no one will be set free" (*De civitate Dei*, 10, 32, 2). And the Second Vatican Council repeats this perennial Christian belief: "The Church firmly believes that Christ, who died and was raised up for all, can through His Spirit offer man the light and the strength to measure up to his supreme destiny. Nor has any other name under heaven been given to man by which he can be saved" (*Gaudium et spes*, 10). However, the saving work of Jesus Christ, with and through his Spirit, extends beyond the visible confines of the Church; it extends to all mankind. We find Vatican II also stating that "the unique mediation of the Redeemer does not exclude but rather gives rise to a manifold cooperation which is but a sharing in this one source" (*Lumen gentium*, 62). John Paul II invited us to reflect on how that cooperation in mediation works: it is based on the uniqueness of the mediation exercised by Christ: "Although participated forms of mediation of different kinds and degrees are not excluded, they acquire meaning and value only from Christ's own mediation, and they cannot be understood as parallel or complementary to his" (*Redemptoris missio*, 5). Hence the reminder from the Congregation for the Doctrine of the Faith that "it must therefore be firmly believed as a truth of Catholic faith that the universal salvific will of the One and Triune God is offered and accomplished once for all in the mystery of the incarnation, death, and resurrection of the Son of God" (*Dominus Iesus*, 14).

and to come to the knowledge of the truth. [5]For there is one God, and there is one mediator between God and men, the man Christ Jesus, [6]who gave himself as a ransom for all,* the testimony to which was borne at the proper time. [7]For this I was appointed a preacher and apostle (I am telling the truth, I am not lying), a teacher of the Gentiles in faith and truth.

1 Cor 13:13
Heb 8:6; 9:15
1 Cor 8:6
Mk 10:45
Gal 1:4
2 Cor 5:15
Eph 5:2
Tit 2:14
Col 1:25-29

Men at prayer, women at prayer

[8]I desire then that in every place the men should pray, lifting holy hands without anger or quarrelling; [9]also that women should adorn themselves modestly and sensibly in seemly apparel, not with braided hair or gold or pearls or costly attire [10]but by good deeds, as befits women who profess religion. [11]Let a woman learn in silence

Acts 9:15
1 Pet 3:3–5
Is 3:16–23
1 Pet 3:1–5
1 Tim 5:10
Is 3:16-23
Gen 3:16

[6]qui dedit redemptionem semetipsum pro omnibus, testimonium temporibus suis; [7]in quod positus sum ego praedicator et apostolus —veritatem dico, non mentior— doctor gentium in fide et veritate. [8]Volo ergo viros orare in omni loco levantes puras manus sine ira et disceptatione; [9]similiter et mulieres in habitu ornato cum verecundia et sobrietate ornantes se, non in tortis crinibus et auro aut margaritis vel veste pretiosa, [10]sed, quod decet mulieres, profitentes pietatem per opera bona. [11]Mulier in tranquillitate discat cum omni subiectione; [12]docere autem mulieri non permitto neque dominari in virum, sed esse in tranquillitate. [13]Adam enim primus formatus est, deinde Eva; [14]et Adam non est seductus, mulier autem

2:8–15 Having just asked that prayers be offered for everyone (including Gentiles) because God desires all to be saved, Paul now adds that prayer should be done in a discreet, decorous way, humbly and modestly, with no extravagant gestures. Men should pray with hands upraised (a gesture used in the Hellenic world for appeals to the deity); and women, when they pray, should be soberly dressed and discreet in their speech and responses, as was likewise the custom. The most important thing for men to determine is that their conscience is clear when they pray, "without anger or quarrelling" (v. 8); and women should prove their piety by good deeds (cf. v. 10). Abuses should be corrected. Men should not try to flaunt their power or social importance, nor should women distract people by the way they dress or by speaking at inappropriate times or in inappropriate ways. The substance of these guidelines is valid for all cultures. "Humility in prayer is pleasing to God and wins us His favour [...]. The one who is humble, who does not claim his rights, nor appeals for what he believes is his due, nor stakes his claim on his own reputation, is rich before God, before Whom no one is rich. Humility makes man rich because it is a gift from God. Paul also says that prayer should be modest and dignified. He wants us to see that humility comes before and illuminates the path of prayer that we should follow" (St Ambrose, *De mysteriis*, 1, 18, 70).

This passage of the letter giving guidelines about prayer should not be taken as establishing permanent rules about the roles of men and women in the liturgy. Paul is speaking here against the background of how things were done at the time, and he is using the sort of rationale that would have been considered appropriate at the time. When he says that no woman should teach (v. 12), this cannot be taken as an absolute ban; it should be interpreted in the light of how public worship was conducted at the time. Some commentators think that what is said here is directed at well-to-do women who had come under the influence of false teachers and were being used by these teachers as mouthpieces. The false doctrines being spread seem to have included the notion that marriage was sinful (see 4:3); hence the rather strange remark about "bearing children" (v. 15). In any event, the teaching given here continues to be valid (particularly in contexts where the importance of the role of woman as mother is undervalued). And so we find John Paul II, for example, teaching that "the true advancement of women requires that clear recognition be given to the value of their maternal and family role, by comparison with all other public roles and all other professions [...]. While it must be recognized that women have the same right as men to perform various public functions, society must be structured in such a way that wives and mothers are *not in practice compelled* to work outside the home, and that their families can live and pros-

1 Cor 14:34–35
Eph 5:22

Gen 2:7, 18, 21–22
1 Cor 11:3, 8–12
Gen 3:6, 12–13
2 Cor 11:3

1 Tim 5:14
1 Cor 13:13
with all submissiveness. [12]I permit no woman to teach or to have authority over men; she is to keep silent. [13]For Adam was formed first, then Eve; [14]and Adam was not deceived, but the woman was deceived and became a transgressor. [15]Yet woman will be saved through bearing children,[c] if she continues[d] in faith and love and holiness, with modesty.

3. CHURCH OFFICE*

Qualifications for bishops

Tit 1:6–9

Mk 10:1–11
2 Tim 2:24
1 Pet 5:3
1 Tim 3:12
Tit 2:6

1 Tim 3:12

1 Cor 1:2
3 [1]The saying is sure: If any one aspires to the office of bishop,* he desires a noble task. [2]Now a bishop must be above reproach, the husband of one wife, temperate, sensible, dignified, hospitable, an apt teacher, [3]no drunkard, not violent but gentle, not quarrelsome, and no lover of money. [4]He must manage his own household well, keeping his children submissive and respectful in every way; [5]for if a man does not know how to manage his own household, how can he care for God's church? [6]He must not be a recent convert, or he may be puffed up with conceit and fall into the condemnation of the devil;[f] [7]moreover he must be well thought of by outsiders, or he may fall into reproach and the snare of the devil.[f]

Mk 4:1
1 Tim 5:10
2 Cor 8:21
1 Cor 5:12

Qualifications for deacons

Acts 6:1–3

2 Tim 1:3
Rom 16:25
1 Tim 5:22
Tit 2:3–5
[8]Deacons likewise must be serious, not double-tongued, not addicted to much wine, not greedy for gain; [9]they must hold the mystery of the faith with a clear conscience.

seducta in praevaricatione fuit. [15]Salvabitur autem per filiorum generationem, si permanserint in fide et dilectione et sanctificatione cum sobrietate. [3] [1]Fidelis sermo: si quis episcopatum appetit, bonum opus desiderat. [2]Oportet ergo episcopum irreprehensibilem esse, unius uxoris virum, sobrium, prudentem, ornatum, hospitalem, doctorem, [3]non vinolentum, non percussorem, sed modestum, non litigiosum, non cupidum, [4]suae domui bene praepositum, filios habentem in subiectione cum omni castitate [5] — si quis autem domui suae praeesse nescit, quomodo ecclesiae Dei curam habebit?—, [6]non neophytum, ne in superbia elatus in iudicium incidat Diaboli. [7]Oportet autem illum et testimonium habere bonum

per in a dignified way even when they themselves devote their full time to their own family" (*Familiaris consortio*, 23).

*3:1–16 These instructions focus on the guidelines that a church minister should go by. The welfare of the faithful is at stake here, and the image that the Church projects to outsiders.

3:1–7 When the Pastoral Letters were being written, the titles and responsibilities attaching to the various church offices in the hierarchy had not yet become fixed; from the writings of St Ignatius of Antioch (early second century) we can see that "bishops" (*epískopoi*) were those who headed up a particular community. Their mission as ministers of the Church involved teaching, presiding and giving good example of Christian living.

"The husband of one wife" (v. 2): this condition, which also applies to "deacons" (3:12), clearly is not a forbidding of polygamy

(polygamy is forbidden to everyone, not just sacred ministers); it means that no one who has been married more than once can be a minister. In the apostolic age, celibacy was not a requirement for someone who presided over a Christian community (not least because many people became Christians when they were adults and already married). However, it very soon became customary to require that sacred ministers be celibate. "In Christian antiquity the Fathers and ecclesiastical writers testify to the spread through the East and the West of the voluntary practice of celibacy by sacred ministers because of its profound suitability for their total dedication to the service of Christ and his Church. The Church of the West, from the beginning of the fourth century, strengthened, spread, and approved this practice by means of various provincial councils and through the Supreme Pontiffs" (Paul VI, *Sacerdotalis caelibatus*, 35–36).

3:8–13 "Deacons" were ministers who per-

c Or *by the birth of the child*   d Greek *they continue*   f Or *slanderer*

¹⁰And let them also be tested first; then if they prove themselves blameless let them serve as deacons. ¹¹The women* likewise must be serious, no slanderers, but temperate, faithful in all things. ¹²Let deacons be the husband of one wife, and let them manage their children and their households well; ¹³for those who serve well as deacons gain a good standing for themselves and also great confidence in the faith which is in Christ Jesus.

1 Tim 3:2, 4
1 Tim 3:1

The Church is God's household

¹⁴I hope to come to you soon, but I am writing these instructions to you so that, ¹⁵if I am delayed, you may know how one ought to behave in the household of God, which is the church of the living God, the pillar and bulwark of the truth.

1 Tim 4:13
1 Cor 1:2
Eph 2:20
Tit 1:7

The mystery of our religion

¹⁶Great indeed, we confess, is the mystery of our religion:

Heʰ was manifested in the flesh,

Jn 1:14
Rom 1:3; 16:25
Mk 16:19
1 Pet 1:12
Acts 1:2, 11
Phil 2:9–11

ab his, qui foris sunt, ut non in opprobrium incidat et laqueum Diaboli. ⁸Diaconos similiter pudicos, non bilingues, non multo vino deditos, non turpe lucrum sectantes, ⁹habentes mysterium fidei in conscientia pura. ¹⁰Et hi autem probentur primum, deinde ministrent nullum crimen habentes. ¹¹Mulieres similiter pudicas, non detrahentes, sobrias, fideles in omnibus. ¹²Diaconi sint unius uxoris viri, qui filiis suis bene praesint et suis domibus; ¹³qui enim bene ministraverint, gradum sibi bonum acquirent et multam fiduciam in fide, quae est in Christo Iesu. ¹⁴Haec tibi scribo sperans venire ad te cito; ¹⁵si autem tardavero, ut scias quomodo oporteat in domo Dei conversari, quae est ecclesia Dei vivi, columna et firmamentum veritatis. ¹⁶Et omnium confessione magnum est pietatis mysterium: Qui manifestatus est in carne, / iustificatus est in Spiritu, / apparuit

formed their functions under the authority of presiding elders. The origins of the diaconate probably go back to the "seven men of good repute" elected to help the apostles (see Acts 6:1–6). The term *diákonos* ordinarily meant a helper, or servant; in the Christian context it referred to the office of helping bishops and priests—until it eventually acquired the specific meaning it has nowadays.

Very little information is available to us as to the actual status of the women being referred to here (v. 11); they must have been assigned some role of service in the early community. In Romans 16:1, Phoebe is described as a "deaconess"—but the word does not refer there to a sacred ministry. We do know from a fourth-century document that some women helped in the instruction of catechumens prior to baptism, looked after the sick and performed other types of service (cf. *Constitutiones apostolicae*, 2, 26; 3, 15).

3:14–15 God acts in and through the Church the way a good father does within the family. The Church is not a purely human society where ministers can exercise their roles as they think fit, for she depends on God and must do his bidding.

The expression "household of God", or "house of God" (*domus Domini*), conveys the idea of a family and also the idea that Christians should have cohesion, should "cohere" in the way that elements combine to form a building, a spiritual building in this case: the children of God, assembled together by the will of God, make up the Church, a house and a temple in which God dwells in a fuller way than he did in the ancient temple of Jerusalem (see 1 Kings 8:12–64). "Pillar and bulwark of the truth": these features, extending the building metaphor, graphically convey the idea of the Church's stability and permanence as the guardian and teacher of the truth, "the deposit of revelation [...] which must be religiously guarded and courageously expounded" (Vatican II, *Lumen gentium*, 25).

3:16 "The mystery of our religion" is spelt out in the form of a hymn, a canticle in honour of Christ; it is the opposite of the "mystery of lawlessness" (2 Thess 2:7). The text may even have been a sort of response to idolatrous chants such as that one heard in pagan Ephesus: "Great is Artemis of the Ephesians!" (Acts 19:28). The "mystery of our religion" is the bringing about of the reconciliation and union of mankind with

h Greek *Who*; other ancient authorities read *God*; others, *Which*

2 Tim 1:10
Tit 2:11; 3:4–5
1 Cor 6:11

vindicated[i] in the Spirit,
seen by angels,
preached among the nations,
believed on in the world,
taken up in glory.

4. PASTORAL DIRECTIVES*

Mt 24:23–24
Acts 20:29, 30
2 Tim 3:1
2 Pet 2:1; 3:3
1 Jn 2:18; 4:1
2 Thess 2:3
Jude 18

Gen 9:3
Rom 9:3
1 Cor 10:30–31
Col 2:16–23

Gen 1:31
Mt 15:11
Acts 10:15
Rom 14:14, 20
1 Cor 10:25, 30
1 Tim 6:3; 1:10
2 Tim 4:3
1 Tim 1:4; 6:20
Tit 1:14

What to do about false teachers

4 ¹Now the Spirit expressly says that in later times some will depart from the faith by giving heed to deceitful spirits and doctrines of demons, ²through the pretensions of liars whose consciences are seared, ³who forbid marriage* and enjoin abstinence from foods* which God created to be received with thanksgiving by those who believe and know the truth. ⁴For everything created by God is good, and nothing is to be rejected if it is received with thanksgiving; ⁵for then it is consecrated by the word of God and prayer.

⁶If you put these instructions before the brethren, you will be a good minister of Christ Jesus, nourished on the words of the faith and of the good doctrine which you have followed. ⁷Have nothing to do with godless and silly myths. Train yourself in

angelis, / praedicatus est in gentibus, / creditus est in mundo, / assumptus est in gloria. [4] ¹Spiritus autem manifeste dicit quia in novissimis temporibus discedent quidam a fide, attendentes spiritibus seductoribus et doctrinis daemoniorum, ²in hypocrisi loquentium mendacium et cauteriatam habentium suam conscientiam, ³prohibentium nubere, abstinere a cibis, quos Deus creavit ad percipiendum cum gratiarum actione fidelibus et his, qui cognoverunt veritatem. ⁴Quia omnis creatura Dei bona, et nihil reiciendum, quod cum gratiarum actione percipitur, ⁵sanctificatur enim per verbum Dei et orationem. ⁶Haec proponens fratribus bonus eris minister Christi Iesu, enutritus verbis fidei et bonae doctrinae, quam assecutus es; ⁷profanas autem et aniles fabulas devita. Exerce teipsum ad pietatem; ⁸nam corporalis exercitatio ad modicum utilis est, pietas autem

God, in Christ: he took our flesh without ceasing to be God; the nations of the earth will acknowledge him just as the angels do; he dwells in the hearts of men through faith, but his abode is in heaven, at the Father's side.

*4:1—6:21 The letter has an even more familial and affectionate tone in these last chapters, which are rather unstructured, dealing as they do with particular groups of people—false teachers, older men, widows, elders, slaves, the well-to-do, and others. However, the exhortations and counsels do hinge on certain themes—in chapter 4, on Timothy himself and the example he should give; in chapter 5 on how he should relate to the faithful; in chapter 6 on policy in regard to false teachers. The general message is that a pastor cannot afford to overlook anything that happens in the community.

4:1–11 In chapter 1 Timothy was exhorted to fulfil his duty to see to it that sound doctrine was being taught. This passage deals with errors in

the area of morality that derived from the false teaching to which this community had been exposed—prohibition of marriage and a ban on foods considered to be unclean (whereas our Lord in his teaching, and apostles in theirs, defended marriage as good, and said that every sort of food may be eaten).

Paul's advice to Timothy is that practising godliness is the way to ensure one's faith is not contaminated. St Augustine, commenting on v. 8, says: "Piety, true service of the True God, is valuable in all things. It undoes or softens the sufferings of this life, and leads to that state of life or health in which we suffer no evil and are filled with joy and goodness forever. I urge you, as I urge myself, to struggle to be pious always, to persevere to the end in piety" (*Epistulae*, 155, 4, 17). To this end, we need to use the resources available to us: "Interior life is strengthened by a daily struggle in your practices of piety, which you should fulfil—or rather which you should *live*—lovingly, for the path we travel as children of God is a path of Love" (St Josemaría Escrivá, *The Forge*, 83).

i Or *justified*

godliness; [8]for while bodily training is of some value, godliness is of value in every way, as it holds promise for the present life and also for the life to come. [9]The saying is sure and worthy of full acceptance. [10]For to this end we toil and strive,[j] because we have our hope set on the living God, who is the Saviour of all men, especially of those who believe.

[11]Command and teach these things.

2 Pet 1:3, 6–7
Col 2:23
2 Tim 2:11
1 Tim 1:1; 2:3–4
Jude 25
Tit 1:3; 2:10; 3:4
Tit 2:7-8
1 Tim 2:7-8

Pastoral advice to Timothy

[12]Let no one despise your youth, but set the believers an example in speech and conduct, in love, in faith, in purity. [13]Till I come, attend to the public reading of scripture, to preaching, to teaching. [14]Do not neglect the gift you have, which was given you by prophetic utterance when the council of elders laid their hands upon you. [15]Practise these duties, devote yourself to them, so that all may see your progress. [16]Take heed to yourself and to your teaching; hold to that, for by so doing you will save both yourself and your hearers.

Tit 2:15; 2:7–8
1 Tim 6:11
2 Thess 3:7
Lk 4:16–21
Acts 6:6
1 Tim 5:22
Acts 20:28
2 Tim 3:14

The pastor and the faithful in general

5 [1]Do not rebuke an older man but exhort him as you would a father; treat younger men like brothers, [2]older women like mothers, younger women like sisters, in all purity.

Lev 19:32
Tit 2:2ff

Widows, their role and lifestyle

[3]Honour widows who are real widows.* [4]If a widow has children or grandchildren, let them first learn their religious duty to their own family and make some return to

1 Tim 5:5, 16

ad omnia utilis est promissionem habens vitae, quae nunc est, et futurae. [9]Fidelis sermo et omni acceptione dignus: [10]in hoc enim laboramus et certamus, quia sperantes sumus in Deum vivum, qui est salvator omnium hominum, maxime fidelium. [11]Praecipe haec et doce. [12]Nemo adulescentiam tuam contemnat, sed exemplum esto fidelium in verbo, in conversatione, in caritate, in fide, in castitate. [13]Dum venio, attende lectioni, exhortationi, doctrinae. [14]Noli neglegere donationem, quae in te est, quae data est tibi per prophetiam cum impositione manuum presbyterii. [15]Haec meditare, in his esto, ut profectus tuus manifestus sit omnibus. [16]Attende tibi et doctrinae; insta in illis; hoc enim faciens et teipsum salvum facies et eos, qui te audiunt. [5] [1]Seniorem ne increpaveris, sed obsecra ut patrem, iuvenes ut fratres, [2]anus ut matres, iuvenculas ut sorores in omni castitate. [3]Viduas honora, quae vere viduae sunt. [4]Si qua autem vidua filios aut nepotes habet, discant primum domum suam pie regere et mutuam vicem reddere parentibus, hoc enim acceptum est coram Deo. [5]Quae autem vere vidua est et desolata, sperat in Deum et instat obsecrationibus et

4:12–16 "Reading", "preaching" and "teaching" (v. 13)—all these were features of the liturgical assembly in early Christian times. Priestly ordination was conferred by liturgical prayer ("prophetic utterance") and the laying-on of hands (see v. 14). The Apostle's pastoral advice also stresses the importance of preaching by good example: "We speak through them [our good works] when we show them to others in our life. Our deeds speak: they are living words" (St Anthony of Padua, *Sermon*, in the *Divine Office*, 13 June).

5:1–2 The Apostle now begins to give Timothy a series of practical rules for the governance of the Christian community. He first states a general principle that a pastor should operate by towards

everyone: he should treat them like members of his own family, even when he has to correct or rebuke them for some reason. "There are also men, our brothers, who have fallen into sin or fallen away altogether; they should be corrected and exhorted with the proper authority for the sake of love" (St Leo the Great, *Epistulae*, 14, 1).

5:3–16 This passage contains rules for widows. In the early Christian communities, widows formed a group or "institution" to some degree; they did charitable work and looked after the needy (see Acts 9:36–39). These widows seem to have been women without personal resources (see vv. 5 and 16), for whose upkeep the Church took responsibility (see Acts 6:1). These were

j Other ancient authorities read *suffer reproach*

Jud 8:4–5
Jer 49:11
Lk 2:37; 18

Rev 3:1

Lk 7:44
Jn 13:14
1 Tim 2:10; 3:7
Heb 13:2
Rom 12:13

Rev 2:4
2 Thess 3:11
Tit 1:11

1 Cor 7:9
1 Tim 2:15
Tit 2:15

Phil 2:29
1 Pet 5:1–5
1 Thess 5:12
Deut 25:4

their parents; for this is acceptable in the sight of God. [5]She who is a real widow, and is left all alone, has set her hope on God and continues in supplications and prayers night and day; [6]whereas she who is self-indulgent is dead even while she lives. [7]Command this, so that they may be without reproach. [8]If any one does not provide for his relatives, and especially for his own family, he has disowned the faith and is worse than an unbeliever.

[9]Let a widow be enrolled if she is not less than sixty years of age, having been the wife of one husband; [10]and she must be well attested for her good deeds, as one who has brought up children, shown hospitality, washed the feet of the saints, relieved the afflicted, and devoted herself to doing good in every way. [11]But refuse to enrol younger widows; for when they grow wanton against Christ they desire to marry, [12]and so they incur condemnation for having violated their first pledge.* [13]Besides that, they learn to be idlers, gadding about from house to house, and not only idlers but gossips and busybodies, saying what they should not. [14]So I would have younger widows marry, bear children, rule their households, and give the enemy no occasion to revile us. [15]For some have already strayed after Satan. [16]If any believing woman[1] has relatives who are widows, let her assist them; let the church not be burdened, so that it may assist those who are real widows.

Criteria for choosing elders

[17]Let the elders who rule well be considered worthy of double honour, especially those who labour in preaching and teaching; [18]for the scripture says, "You shall not

orationibus nocte ac die; [6]nam quae in deliciis est vivens, mortua est. [7]Et haec praecipe, ut irreprehensibiles sint. [8]Si quis autem suorum et maxime domesticorum curam non habet, fidem negavit et est infideli deterior. [9]Vidua adscribatur non minus sexaginta annorum, quae fuerit unius viri uxor, [10]in operibus bonis testimonium habens: si filios educavit, si hospitio recepit, si sanctorum pedes lavit, si tribulationem patientibus subministravit, si omne opus bonum subsecuta est. [11]Adulescentiores autem viduas devita; cum enim luxuriatae fuerint adversus Christum, nubere volunt, [12]habentes damnationem, quia primam fidem irritam fecerunt; [13]simul autem et otiosae discunt circumire domos, non solum otiosae sed et verbosae et curiosae, loquentes quae non oportet. [14]Volo ergo iuniores nubere, filios procreare, dominas domus esse, nullam occasionem dare adversario maledicti gratia; [15]iam enim quaedam conversae sunt retro Satanam. [16]Si qua fidelis habet viduas, subministret illis, et non gravetur ecclesia, ut his, quae vere viduae sunt, sufficiat. [17]Qui bene praesunt presbyteri, duplici honore digni habeantur, maxime qui laborant in verbo et doctrina; [18]dicit enim Scriptura: «Non infrenabis os bovi trituranti» et: «Dignus operarius mercede sua». [19]Adversus presbyterum accusationem noli

"real widows" (see v. 5)—as distinct from younger widows who might easily be somewhat frivolous. The "wantonness" mentioned in v. 11 may refer to passions of the flesh, or it could mean simply the passing enthusiasm of young people. Maybe Paul wants to avoid the risk that young widows, having committed themselves fully to the service of the Church, might break that commitment by marrying again. However, it is also possible that unhappy experience (see v. 15) leads Paul to favour the idea that young widows without domestic responsibilities should marry again (and thus free themselves from many of the temptations to waywardness).

5:17–25 These words show that it would be a serious thing to do laying on of hands on someone without proper screening of candidates. The Church tries to ensure that only worthy and

properly trained ones receive ordination; candidates for the priesthood need to be personally committed to what they are called to do—"labour in word and doctrine (cf. 1 Tim 5:17), believing what they have read and meditated upon in the law of God, teaching what they have believed, and putting in practice in their own lives what they have taught" (Vatican II, *Lumen gentium*, 28). The requirement that candidates commit themselves to lead holy lives can never leave the Church unprovided with priestly vocations, for our faith assures us that "God never abandons his Church, leaving the faithful without a sufficient number of suitable ministers to meet their needs, if worthy [candidates] are encouraged and the unworthy rejected" (St Thomas Aquinas, *Summa theologiae*, *supp.*, 36, 4, 1).

Verse 18 quotes from Deuteronomy 25:4 and then repeats words of our Lord found in Luke

1 Other ancient authorities read *man or woman*; others, simply *man*

muzzle an ox when it is treading out the grain," and, "The labourer deserves his wages." ¹⁹Never admit any charge against an elder except on the evidence of two or three witnesses. ²⁰As for those who persist in sin, rebuke them in the presence of all, so that the rest may stand in fear. ²¹In the presence of God and of Christ Jesus and of the elect angels I charge you to keep these rules without favour, doing nothing from partiality. ²²Do not be hasty in the laying on of hands, nor participate in another man's sins; keep yourself pure.

²³No longer drink only water, but use a little wine for the sake of your stomach and your frequent ailments.

²⁴The sins of some men are conspicuous, pointing to judgment, but the sins of others appear later. ²⁵So also good deeds are conspicuous; and even when they are not, they cannot remain hidden.

Slaves and their moral obligations

6 ¹Let all who are under the yoke of slavery regard their masters as worthy of all honour, so that the name of God and the teaching may not be defamed. ²Those who have believing masters must not be disrespectful on the ground that they are brethren; rather they must serve all the better since those who benefit by their service are believers and beloved.

Teach and urge these duties.

False teachers described

³If any one teaches otherwise and does not agree with the sound words of our Lord Jesus Christ and the teaching which accords with godliness, ⁴he is puffed up with

Margin references:
Lk 10:7
Mt 18:16; 2 Cor 13:1; Heb 10:28; *Deut 19:15*
Acts 6:6; Mk 5:32; 2 Jn 11; Rev 18:4
Mt 5:16; 10:26; 1 Tim 5:10
1 Pet 2:18; Eph 6:5; Col 3:22–25; Tit 2:9f; 1 Cor 7:21–22
Rom 2:24; 6:15; Philem 16
1 Tim 1:10; 4:6; 2 Tim 1:13; 4:3; Gal 1:6–9; 2 Tim 2:14, 23; *Tit 1:9*

---

recipere, nisi *sub duobus vel tribus testibus*. ²⁰Peccantes coram omnibus argue, ut ceteri timorem habeant. ²¹Testificor coram Deo et Christo Iesu et electis angelis, ut haec custodias sine praeiudicio nihil faciens in aliquam partem declinando. ²²Manus cito nemini imposueris neque communicaveris peccatis alienis; teipsum castum custodi. ²³Noli adhuc aquam bibere, sed vino modico utere propter stomachum et frequentes tuas infirmitates. ²⁴Quorundam hominum peccata manifesta sunt praecedentia ad iudicium, quosdam autem et subsequuntur; ²⁵similiter et facta bona manifesta sunt, et, quae aliter se habent, abscondi non possunt. [6] ¹Quicumque sunt sub iugo, servi dominos suos omni honore dignos arbitrentur, ne nomen Dei et doctrina blasphemetur. ²Qui autem fideles habent dominos, non contemnant, quia fratres sunt, sed magis serviant, quia fideles sunt et dilecti, qui beneficii participes sunt. Haec doce et exhortare. ³Si quis aliter docet et non accedit sanis sermonibus Domini nostri Iesu

---

10:7. This may indicate that Paul acknowledges the Gospel of St Luke to be "scripture", although this second quotation could of course come from some other written source predating Luke's Gospel.

6:1–2 The Apostle does not deal with the question of slavery in a direct way (cf. Col 3:22—4:1), but that does not mean he approves of slavery (see the notes on Philem 21 and Eph 6:5–9). It is estimated that about half the population of Ephesus at that time were slaves, so quite a number of the Christians at Ephesus would have been members of that class. In fact, for many pagans the example set by their slaves was how they came to know Christianity: that is one reason it was vital that slaves' conduct reflect their faith (v. 1). If the masters, too, were Chris-

tians, then slaves had an additional, fraternal, reason for trying to do their work well (v. 2). Over the course of history Christian belief has contributed to the cause of abolishing every kind of slavery, for "the ferment of the Gospel has aroused and continues to arouse in the hearts of men an unquenchable thirst for human dignity" (Vatican II, *Gaudium et spes*, 26).

6:3–10 What the Apostle has to say about unmasking false teachers shows that he is pained by the harm they are doing. They seek personal advantage (v. 10), whereas good teachers are content with basic provisions and shelter. Detachment has always been a prerequisite for apostolic success: it sets a person free: "Only he who lives for Christ is truly free. He is beyond the reach of evil, and if he does not will harm to

Rom 1:29
1 Tim 1:4

2 Tim 3:8; 4:4
Tit 1:14

Phil 4:11

Job 1:21

Mt 6:11
Prov 30:8
Prov 23:4; 28:22
Lk 12:15
Mt 6:24

conceit, he knows nothing; he has a morbid craving for controversy and for disputes about words, which produce envy, dissension, slander, base suspicions, ⁵and wrangling among men who are depraved in mind and bereft of the truth, imagining that godliness is a means of gain. ⁶There is great gain in godliness with contentment; ⁷for we brought nothing into the world, andᵐ we cannot take anything out of the world; ⁸but if we have food and clothing, with these we shall be content. ⁹But those who desire to be rich fall into temptation, into a snare, into many senseless and hurtful desires that plunge men into ruin and destruction. ¹⁰For the love of money is the root of all evils; it is through this craving that some have wandered away from the faith and pierced their hearts with many pangs.

An appeal to defend the faith

2 Tim 2:22
1 Cor 13:13
Gal 5:22
2 Tim 4:7
1 Cor 9:25–26
1 Tim 1:18; 2:6
Jude 3

Jn 18:36–37
2 Tim 4:1
Mt 27:11

2 Tim 4:18

Deut 10:17
2 Mac 13:4
Ps 136:3
Rev 17:14
Ps 104 :2
Ex 23:20; 33:20
1 Tim 1:17

¹¹But as for you, man of God, shun all this; aim at righteousness, godliness, faith, love, steadfastness, gentleness. ¹²Fight the good fight of the faith; take hold of the eternal life to which you were called when you made the good confession in the presence of many witnesses. ¹³In the presence of God who gives life to all things, and of Christ Jesus who in his testimony before Pontius Pilate made the good confession, ¹⁴I charge you to keep the commandment unstained and free from reproach until the appearing of our Lord Jesus Christ; ¹⁵and this will be made manifest at the proper time by the blessed and only Sovereign, the King of kings and Lord of lords, ¹⁶who alone has immortality and dwells in unapproachable light, whom no man has ever seen or can see. To him be honour and eternal dominion. Amen.

Christi et ei, quae secundum pietatem est, doctrinae, ⁴superbus est, nihil sciens, sed languens circa quaestiones et pugnas verborum, ex quibus oriuntur invidiae, contentiones, blasphemiae, suspiciones malae, ⁵conflictationes hominum mente corruptorum et qui veritate privati sunt, existimantium quaestum esse pietatem. ⁶Est autem quaestus magnus pietas cum sufficientia. ⁷Nihil enim intulimus in mundum, quia nec auferre quid possumus; ⁸habentes autem alimenta et quibus tegamur, his contenti erimus. ⁹Nam qui volunt divites fieri, incidunt in tentationem et laqueum et desideria multa stulta et nociva, quae mergunt homines in interitum et perditionem; ¹⁰radix enim omnium malorum est cupiditas, quam quidam appetentes erraverunt a fide et inseruerunt se doloribus multis. ¹¹Tu autem, o homo Dei, haec fuge; sectare vero iustitiam, pietatem, fidem, caritatem, patientiam, mansuetudinem. ¹²Certa bonum certamen fidei, apprehende vitam aeternam, ad quam vocatus es, et confessus es bonam confessionem coram multis testibus. ¹³Praecipio tibi coram Deo, qui vivificat omnia, et Christo Iesu, qui testimonium reddidit sub Pontio Pilato bonam confessionem, ¹⁴ut serves mandatum sine macula irreprehensibile usque in adventum Domini nostri Iesu Christi, ¹⁵quem suis temporibus ostendet beatus et solus potens, Rex regnantium et Dominus dominantium, ¹⁶qui solus habet immortalitatem, lucem habitans inaccessibilem, quem vidit nullus hominum nec videre potest; cui honor et imperium sempiternum. Amen. ¹⁷Divitibus huius saeculi praecipe non superbe sapere neque sper-

himself, nothing shall ever harm him. The servant of Christ cannot be attacked or defeated. Loss of money does not affect him, for *we brought nothing into the world, and we cannot take anything out of the world*. He is not ruled by ambition, he is not vainglorious, because he knows that man's true home is in heaven. He does not feel pain when he suffers wounds or blows. For the Christian, there is only one real disgrace: an offence against God. Compared to this, he does not consider anything—loss of property or of his home, threats to his life—to be truly evil. Death, our leaving this world, which makes all men tremble, is more beautiful to him than life itself" (St John Chrysostom, *Ad Theodorum lapsum*, 2, 5).

6:11–16 Paul stresses the need to be loyal and to do one's duty as laid down in the teaching of the faith; he calls God the Father and Jesus as witnesses—Jesus, who himself bore witness to his kingship before Pontius Pilate.

This beautiful hymn to Christ's kingship (vv. 15–16) may have been taken from the liturgy. Like the other hymns found in this letter (1:17 and 3:16), it shows how aware the early Christians were that man's true purpose in life is to give glory to God: "We do not live for the world, or for our own honour, but for the honour of God, for the glory of God, for the service of God. That is what should motivate us!" (St Josemaría Escrivá, *The Forge*, 851).

m Other ancient authorities insert *it is certain that*

The right way to use wealth

[17]As for the rich in this world, charge them not to be haughty, nor to set their hopes on uncertain riches but on God who richly furnishes us with everything to enjoy. [18]They are to do good, to be rich in good deeds, liberal and generous, [19]thus laying up for themselves a good foundation for the future, so that they may take hold of the life which is life indeed.

Rom 12:16
Jas 1:10
Ps 62:10
Lk 12:20
1 Tim 5:10
Mt 6:20; 19:21
Lk 12:33
Phil 4:17
2 Cor 9:8

Words of farewell

[20]O Timothy, guard what has been entrusted to you. Avoid the godless chatter and contradictions of what is falsely called knowledge, [21]for by professing it some have missed the mark as regards the faith.
    Grace be with you.

Tit 2:1
2 Tim 1:12, 14; 2:2;
3:14; 4:7
1 Tim 1:4, 6
2 Tim 2:18
Tit 3:15

are in incerto divitiarum, sed in Deo, qui praestat nobis omnia abunde ad fruendum, [18]bene agere, divites fieri in operibus bonis, facile tribuere, communicare, [19]thesaurizare sibi fundamentum bonum in futurum, ut apprehendant veram vitam. [20]O Timothee, depositum custodi, devitans profanas vocum novitates et oppositiones falsi nominis scientiae, [21]quam quidam profitentes circa fidem aberraverunt. Gratia vobiscum.

6:17–19 Material things are meant to be used with a sense of social responsibility, and with detachment, because true wealth is that which never perishes (see Lk 12:33). "It is necessary to state once more the characteristic principle of Christian social doctrine: the goods of this world are *originally meant for all*. The right to private property is *valid and necessary*, but it does not nullify the value of this principle" (John Paul II, *Sollicitudo rei socialis*, 42).

6:20–21 These verses summarize the letter's teaching. "What has been entrusted" is sometimes translated as "deposit" ("*depositum*" in Latin). A *depositum* was something (usually a sum of money) entrusted to someone for them to keep and protect until the depositor claimed it back. St Paul applies the idea to Revelation and the faith, and it has found its way into theological tradition. "What is this 'deposit'? It is something entrusted to you, not something you have discovered [...]. It is what you must believe, not what you invented; what you received, not what you thought up yourself; it is the outcome of teaching, not the result of ingenuity; what comes from public tradition, not from private plundering. It is something which has come down to you, but which you have not produced; something of which you are not the author but the guardian; not the leader but the one led. [...] Keep inviolate and spotless the talent of the catholic faith. What you have believed hold fast to, and pass it on to another" (St Vincent Lerins, *Commonitorium*, 22, 4).

THE SECOND LETTER OF PAUL TO

TIMOTHY

Introduction

The Second Letter to Timothy, shorter than the first, comes immediately after it in the canon. It is one of the three "Pastoral Letters", but it has features that differentiate it from the First Letter to Timothy and the Letter to Titus. The tone is very informal and affectionate, and it contains many personal references. Paul senses that his death is near, so the letter takes the form of a kind of "last will and testament".

1. STRUCTURE AND CONTENT

The first thing the reader notices here is the urgent call that the Apostle makes to Timothy to stay true to the teaching he has received and to his calling as a pastor: he must surmount any obstacles he meets, no matter how daunting—even if death threatens. The teaching entrusted by God to St Paul, the deposit of faith, has been passed on in turn to Timothy, without any additions or subtractions. Now it is up to Timothy to conserve it and to teach it to others in all its purity. Paul also instructs Timothy in the responsibilities of a pastor and specifically the protection of the faith from ideas being spread by false teachers. These two great themes—the deposit of faith, and pastoral teaching—form the thread that runs throughout the letter.

After the usual greeting, which in this instance reveals the fond affection that Paul has for his disciple (1:1–5), comes the first section of the letter, about the care Timothy must take of the truth entrusted to him; included, too, are some anecdotes and advice about how to preach the Gospel message (1:6—2:13), and a call to keep before his mind Jesus Christ, risen from the dead, who has overcome death and who is ever faithful (2:8–13).

The second section focuses more on pastoral teaching, especially the defence of sound doctrine (2:14—4:8). Paul advises Timothy on how to steer clear of error, be patient with those who go astray, and shelter them from harmful influences; the best recourse for this is to keep firmly to the teaching handed down, and to draw strength from Holy Scripture. This section ends with a solemn charge to persevere in sound teaching (4:1–8).

The letter ends with various personal messages, a few pieces of news, and words of farewell (4:9–22).

2. CONTEXT

The Second Letter to Timothy has no particular connexion with the first. It contains no reference to there having been an earlier letter from St Paul to his disciple, so the fact that it is called "second" does not necessarily mean it was written after the "first"; it is simply placed after it in the canon of the Bible.

In this letter the Apostle mentions that he is a prisoner in Rome (1:16–17; 2:9) and that he thinks his death is near (4:6–7). If one goes along with the theory that Paul was set free after the Roman imprisonment that marks the end of the Acts of the Apostles, and that he subsequently made other journeys, including one to Ephesus, where he left Timothy and set out for Macedonia (this being the context of the First Letter to Timothy), then the Second Letter could have been written during a second imprisonment in Rome (the first suggestion that there was such an imprisonment comes as late as the fourth century).[1]

Literary analysis shows that the vocabularies used in 1 and 2 Timothy is very similar, and the picture each paints of a Christian community and its circumstances suggests that they both refer to the same community. For this reason (as is also the case with the First Letter), some scholars question whether this is truly a letter written by St Paul—arguing instead that its author was a disciple who was more or less close to the Apostle and who wrote on his authority. However, the very personal tone of this letter—one written very much from the heart—makes it likely that this letter was written by St Paul himself, more likely even than that he wrote 1 Timothy.

The letter does have features that fit the "genre" of a farewell address. It is presented as a spiritual testament in which St Paul, seeing that his life is nearing its end (cf. 4:6–8), reflects on his (and Timothy's) solicitude for the churches he has founded, and sends Timothy words of encouragement and some last pieces of advice.

3. MESSAGE

The tone of the Second Letter to Timothy is even warmer and more personal than that of the first. Paul repeatedly exhorts Timothy to persevere in his preaching and other pastoral duties, and not to let himself be deflected by either external opposition or inner fatigue. He also charges him to reinforce the way the local church is organized. The themes in the letter are very much the same as those in the other Pastoral Letters. Special mention is made here of the contribution Holy Scripture can make in preaching and in the Christian life.

The deposit of faith

From the very start of the letter we see how concerned Paul is to defend the Gospel from false teachers who are causing confusion. These people seem to have been Christians who did not have a clear knowledge of what Christianity was; they may have been Jews of the diaspora who had a poor understanding of Greek religions and cultural ideas to begin with, and who did not know where Christianity and philosophy met (or did not meet). The writer refers to "stupid, senseless controversies" that "breed quarrels" (2:23); these can only lead to rejection of the "sound teaching" (4:3) given them by the Apostle.

Given this doctrinal confusion, a good pastor should never be remiss in preaching the Gospel, for people need "knowledge of the truth" (3:7; cf. 2:25), obtained by repentance and conversion, if they are to lead Christian lives (see 2:25).

Central to the teaching contained in this letter is "the appearing [manifestation] of our Saviour Christ Jesus, who abolished death and brought life and immortality to light through the gospel" (1:10). Christians must never lose sight of Jesus Christ, and must cling fast to the faith they have received (see 2:8–13). Preachers must teach the gospel truth in its fullness, and not deviate from it as false teachers have been doing (see 2:14–18). It is essential that ministers preach the word of God; Timothy must give pride of place to this work of spreading the Gospel—convincing, rebuking and exhorting people at every opportunity (see 4:2, 5).

1 Eusebius of Caesarea, *Historia ecclesiastica*, 2, 22, 2.

The "sacred writings"

An outstanding feature of the Second Letter to Timothy is the passage that deals with Holy Scripture and the part it plays in building up the Church: "As for you, continue in what you have learned and have firmly believed, knowing from whom you learned it and how from childhood you have been acquainted with the sacred writings which are able to instruct you for salvation through faith in Christ Jesus. All scripture is inspired by God and profitable for teaching, for reproof, for correction, and for training in righteousness, that the man of God may be complete, equipped for every good work" (3:14–17).

This exhortation comes in the context of Timothy's ministry. The Apostle is warning him against false teachers, who delude themselves and others (cf. 3:13); he encourages Timothy to stay true to what he has been taught from childhood onwards by his mother and his grandmother and by Paul himself. The phrase translated here as "sacred writings" (3:15) is often used in Jewish writings of the Greek diaspora, but this is the only place where it occurs in the Bible. The description of these writings as "sacred", or "holy", distinguishes them from profane or secular writings and implies a recognition of their canonical authority.

In line with the tradition of the people of Israel, Paul says that Scripture can "instruct you", but this instruction or wisdom, which in the wisdom tradition of the Old Testament is linked to the Torah, now derives from and is directed to "salvation through faith in Christ Jesus". This is an instance of Christian apologetics making the point that the Old Testament prophecies refer to Christ.

The expression "all scripture" (v. 16) may refer to the entire canonical Bible as a unit in the sense of its being "inspired by God", but in this context it could mean each and every passage of the Bible. Both interpretations are possible. However, the question does arise as to whether this expression encompasses the New Testament texts known to the author of the letter. He is referring directly and expressly to the Old Testament, for he speaks of "sacred writings" that Timothy knew through his mother (see 3:15), "a Jewish woman who was a believer" (Acts 16:1). Indirectly and by extension, the phrase "all scripture" in 2 Timothy 3:16 could also include those writings which at the time the letter was written were held to be "inspired" and therefore part of "scripture"—texts that form part of the New Testament as we know it. This is not pure speculation, for there is another passage in Paul's writings that can be read in the same way—1 Timothy 5:17–18, which quotes *as scripture*, along with a passage from Deuteronomy, a saying of Jesus that is found in the Gospel of St Luke. This passage reads: "Let the elders who rule well be considered worthy of double honour, especially those who labour in preaching and teaching; for the scripture says, 'You shall not muzzle an ox when it is treading out the grain [Deut 25:4]' and "the labourer deserves his wages.'"

2 Timothy

Greeting*

1 ¹Paul, an apostle of Christ Jesus by the will of God according to the promise of the life which is in Christ Jesus,

²To Timothy, my beloved child:

Grace, mercy, and peace from God the Father and Christ Jesus our Lord.

³I thank God whom I serve with a clear conscience, as did my fathers, when I remember you constantly in my prayers. ⁴As I remember your tears, I long night and day to see you, that I may be filled with joy. ⁵I am reminded of your sincere faith, a faith that dwelt first in your grandmother Lois and your mother Eunice and now, I am sure, dwells in you.

Rom 1:1
1 Cor 1:1

Acts 16:1
1 Cor 4:17
1 Tim 1:2
2 Jn 3

Rom 1:9
Phil 3:5
1 Tim 3:9

2 Tim 4:9, 21
2 Tim 3:14–15
Acts 16:1

1. PREACHING THE GOSPEL MESSAGE*

Response to grace

⁶Hence I remind you to rekindle the gift of God that is within you through the laying on of my hands; ⁷for God did not give us a spirit of timidity but a spirit of power and love and self-control.

Mt 9:18
Acts 6:6; 14:23
1 Tim 4:14

Rom 8:15
1 Jn 4:18
1 Tim 4:14

[1] ¹Paulus apostolus Christi Iesu per voluntatem Dei secundum promissionem vitae, quae est in Christo Iesu, ²Timotheo carissimo filio: gratia, misericordia, pax a Deo Patre et Christo Iesu Domino nostro. ³Gratias ago Deo, cui servio a progenitoribus in conscientia pura, quod sine intermissione habeo tui memoriam in orationibus meis nocte ac die ⁴desiderans te videre, memor lacrimarum tuarum, ut gaudio implear, ⁵recordationem accipiens eius fidei, quae est in te non ficta, quae et habitavit primum in avia tua Loide et matre tua Eunice, certus sum autem quod et in te. ⁶Propter quam causam admoneo te, ut resuscites donationem Dei, quae est in te per impositionem manuum mearum; ⁷non enim dedit nobis

*1:1–5 In this letter Paul focuses on the Gospel; it can make all kinds of tribulation worthwhile (1:6–2:13), and it is a salutary teaching that must be conserved, defended and spread (2:14—4:17). Over the course of the letter, the Apostle gives pieces of news about himself, ending with some messages for Timothy (4:9–22).

The opening lines (vv. 1–5) show the Apostle's deep affection for his disciple. They are somewhat reminiscent of the elders' farewell to Paul at Miletus (see Acts 20:37). The reference to Timothy's mother and grandmother (typical of the intimate tone of the letter) is a reminder of how grateful we should be to those who have passed the faith on to us. "For Christians a special gratitude is due to those from whom they have received the gift of faith, the grace of Baptism, and life in the Church. These may include parents, grandparents, other members of the family, pastors, catechists, and other teachers or friends" (*Catechism of the Catholic Church*, 2220).

*1:6—2:13 The first section of the letter concerns the hardship experienced by Paul on account of the Gospel; hardship is part of the Christian calling, and Timothy should take it in his stride.

1:6–7 The rite of laying on of hands, also mentioned in 1 Timothy 4:14, passed on the gift of apostolic ministry. The Church has preserved intact these essential elements of the sacrament of Holy Orders—the imposition of hands and the bishop's words of consecration (see Paul VI, *Pontificalis Romani recognitio*). The "gift of God" (v. 6) refers to the indelible "character" or mark impressed on the soul at ordination. The gifts which God confers on the priest "are not transitory or temporary in him, but stable and permanent, attached as they are to an indelible character, impressed on his soul, by which he is made a priest forever (cf. Ps 109:4), in the likeness of Him in whose priesthood he has been

St Paul, herald of the Gospel

Lk 9:26
Rom 1:16; 5:3
Eph 3:13
⁸Do not be ashamed then of testifying to our Lord, nor of me his prisoner, but share in suffering for the gospel in the power of God, ⁹who saved us and called us with a holy calling, not in virtue of our works but in virtue of his own purpose and the
Rom 8:28; 16:25f
Tit 3:5
Eph 1:4, 11
Tit 3:5
Eph 1:4, 11
Heb 2:14–15
Tit 1:4; 2:11, 13;
3:4, 6
1 Tim 2:7
1 Col 1:8
2 Tim 2:7
1 Tim 1:10; 4:6; 6:3
Tit 1:9; 2:1
2 Tim 4:3
Rom 5:5
1 Tim 6:20
grace which he gave us in Christ Jesus ages ago, ¹⁰and now has manifested through the appearing of our Saviour Christ Jesus, who abolished death and brought life and immortality to light through the gospel. ¹¹For this gospel I was appointed a preacher and apostle and teacher, ¹²and therefore I suffer as I do. But I am not ashamed, for I know whom I have believed, and I am sure that he is able to guard until that Day what has been entrusted to me.ᵃ ¹³Follow the pattern of the sound words which you have heard from me, in the faith and love which are in Christ Jesus; ¹⁴guard the truth that has been entrusted to you by the Holy Spirit who dwells within us.

Attitudes towards certain disciples

2 Tim 4:16
¹⁵You are aware that all who are in Asia* turned away from me, and among them
2 Tim 4:19
Phygelus and Hermogenes. ¹⁶May the Lord grant mercy to the household of One-

Deus Spiritum timoris sed virtutis et dilectionis et sobrietatis. ⁸Noli itaque erubescere testimonium Domini nostri neque me vinctum eius, sed collabora evangelio secundum virtutem Dei, ⁹qui nos salvos fecit et vocavit vocatione sancta, non secundum opera nostra sed secundum propositum suum et gratiam, quae data est nobis in Christo Iesu ante tempora saecularia, ¹⁰manifestata autem nunc per illustrationem salvatoris nostri Iesu Christi, qui destruxit quidem mortem, illuminavit autem vitam et incorruptionem per evangelium, ¹¹in quo positus sum ego praedicator et apostolus et doctor. ¹²Ob quam causam etiam haec patior, sed non confundor; scio enim, cui credidi, et certus sum quia potens est depositum meum servare in illum diem. ¹³Formam habe sanorum verborum, quae a me audisti, in fide et dilectione, quae sunt in Christo Iesu; ¹⁴bonum depositum custodi per Spiritum Sanctum, qui habitat in nobis. ¹⁵Scis hoc quod aversi sunt a me omnes, qui in Asia sunt, ex quibus est Phygelus et Hermo-

made to share" (Pius XI, *Ad catholici sacerdotii*, 22). The language St Paul uses here is quite graphic: through the sacrament of Orders a person receives a divine gift that stays with him forever as a kind of ember which must be fanned from time to time to make it glow and give forth its warmth. St Thomas Aquinas comments that "the grace of God is like a fire, which does not glow when it is covered by ashes; the same thing happens when grace is covered over by sluggishness or natural fear" (*Super 2 Timotheum*, ad loc.). The Council of Trent uses these two verses in its solemn definition of Holy Orders as a sacrament instituted by Christ (see *De sacramento Ordinis*, chap. 7).

1:8–14 The Holy Spirit manifested himself and poured himself out on the Church on the day of Pentecost, and he continues to act in her to sanctify the faithful and to ensure that pastors (especially the successors of Peter) "will guard in a holy way the revelation, that is, the deposit of the faith, given them by the apostles, and pass it on faithfully to others" (Vatican I, *Pastor Aeternus*, 4).

"I know whom I have believed" (v. 12). "By faith man freely commits his entire life to God,

making 'the full submission of his intellect and will to God who reveals' (Vatican I, Dogm. Const. *De Fide*, c. 3), and willingly assenting to the Revelation given by him. Before this faith can be exercised, man must have the grace of God to move and assist him; he must have the interior helps of the Holy Spirit, who moves the heart and converts it to God, who opens the eyes of the mind and 'makes it easy for all to accept and believe the truth' (Second Council of Orange, can. 7)" (Vatican II, *Dei Verbum*, 5).

"What has been entrusted to me" (v. 12). See the note on 1 Tim 6:20–21. St John Chrysostom interprets it in this way: "What does he mean when he speaks of 'what has been entrusted to me'? He means the faith and the duty to preach. The one who entrusted these things to me is able to guard them safely. I am prepared to suffer all things in order to safeguard this treasure from theft or destruction. I will not shy away from any suffering that may befall me; the only reward that I seek is that what has been entrusted to me be kept whole and safe" (*In 2 Timotheum*, ad loc.).

1:15–18 We do not know anything about these disciples who deserted St Paul, but they were

a Or *what I have entrusted to him*

siphorus, for he often refreshed me; he was not ashamed of my chains, ¹⁷but when he arrived in Rome he searched for me eagerly and found me—¹⁸may the Lord grant him to find mercy from the Lord on that Day—and you well know all the service he rendered at Ephesus.

2 Tim 1:8

Jude 21

Bearing one's share of suffering

2 ¹You then, my son, be strong in the grace that is in Christ Jesus, ²and what you have heard from me before many witnesses entrust to faithful men who will be able to teach others also. ³Share in suffering as a good soldier of Christ Jesus. ⁴No soldier on service gets entangled in civilian pursuits, since his aim is to satisfy the one who enlisted him. ⁵An athlete is not crowned unless he competes according to the rules. ⁶It is the hard-working farmer who ought to have the first share of the crops. ⁷Think over what I say, for the Lord will grant you understanding in everything.

Eph 6:10
2 Tim 3:14
1 Tim 4:14; 6:12

2 Tim 1:8

1 Cor 9:24, 25
2 Tim 4:8

1 Cor 9:3:6–9; 7:10

Phil 3:15
Prov 2:6

genes. ¹⁶Det misericordiam Dominus Onesiphori domui, quia saepe me refrigeravit et catenam meam non erubuit, ¹⁷sed cum Romam venisset, sollicite me quaesivit et invenit ¹⁸ —det illi Dominus invenire misericordiam a Domino in illa die— et quanta Ephesi ministravit, melius tu nosti. [2] ¹Tu ergo, fili mi, confortare in gratia, quae est in Christo Iesu; ²et quae audisti a me per multos testes, haec commenda fidelibus hominibus, qui idonei erunt et alios docere. ³Collabora sicut bonus miles Christi Iesu. ⁴Nemo militans implicat se saeculi negotiis, ut ei placeat, qui eum elegit; ⁵si autem certat quis agone, non coronatur nisi legitime certaverit. ⁶Laborantem agricolam oportet primum de fructibus accipere. ⁷Intellege, quae dico; dabit enim tibi Dominus in omnibus intellectum. ⁸Memor esto Iesum Christum resuscitatum esse a mortuis, ex semine David, secundum

probably well known at Ephesus. Onesiphorus' faithfulness, on the other hand, must have inspired Christians to help one another: "What good would it do the bishop to be faithful", St John Chrysostom asks himself, "if he were unable to pass the faith on to others, or if, settling for not betraying the faith, he was unable to awake it in other believers? So, both conditions are necessary in the training of teachers—to be faithful and to have a capacity to teach" (*In 2 Timotheum*, ad loc.). The Apostle prays for Onesiphorus and his household; there is a play on words in vv. 17–18: just as Onesiphorus "searched" eagerly for Paul, God in his kindness will have him "find" mercy on the day of Judgment, as a reward for his good actions.

2:1–7 Faithfulness has always been seen as a virtue essential for those in positions of responsibility; hence its significance for bishops (the Greek word *epíscopos* means "watchman"). The "faithful men" given this office must be "able to teach others also" (v. 2): "What good would it do the bishop to be faithful", St John Chrysostom asks himself, "if he were unable to pass the faith on to others, or if, settling for not betraying the faith, he was unable to awake it in other believers? So, both conditions are necessary in the training of teachers—to be faithful and to have a capacity to teach" (*In 2 Timotheum*, ad loc.). The

Second Vatican Council recalls this teaching when it says: "The Shepherd and Bishop of our souls so constituted his Church that the people whom he chose and acquired by his blood would have its priests to the end of time, and that Christians would never be like sheep without a shepherd. Recognizing Christ's desire, and at the inspiration of the Holy Spirit, the apostles considered it their duty to select men 'who will be capable of teaching others' (2 Tim 2:2). This duty, then, is a part of the priestly mission by which every priest becomes a sharer in the care of the whole Church, lest ministers be ever lacking for the People of God on earth. Since, however, there is common cause between the captain of a ship and the sailors, let all Christian people be taught that it is their duty to cooperate in one way or another, by constant prayer and other means at their disposal, that the Church will always have a sufficient number of priests to carry out her divine mission" (*Presbyterorum ordinis*, 11).

The soldier, the athlete and the farmer are three examples of people whose jobs involve discipline, dedication and effort—qualities also requisite for all those engaged in apostolic undertakings in communion with the pastors of the Church. "Listen to the bishop through whom God reveals himself to you. I would give my life for those who listen to and obey the bishop, the

Jesus, the Apostle's model

⁸Remember Jesus Christ, risen from the dead, descended from David, as preached in my gospel, ⁹the gospel for which I am suffering and wearing fetters like a criminal. But the word of God is not fettered. ¹⁰Therefore I endure everything for the sake of the elect, that they also may obtain the salvation which in Christ Jesus goes with eternal glory. ¹¹The saying is sure:

If we have died with him, we shall also live with him;
¹²if we endure, we shall also reign with him;
if we deny him, he also will deny us;
¹³if we are faithless, he remains faithful—
for he cannot deny himself.

2. DEFENDING THE GOSPEL*

Avoiding useless arguments

¹⁴Remind them of this, and charge them before the Lord[b] to avoid disputing about words, which does no good, but only ruins the hearers. ¹⁵Do your best to present yourself to God as one approved, a workman who has no need to be ashamed, rightly handling the word of truth. ¹⁶Avoid such godless chatter, for it will lead

priests and deacons. May you, like them, have new life in God! United to them and to one another, may you work, struggle, walk, suffer, sleep and wake as servants of God. Please him for whom you work, and who will give you your just reward. May you never harbour a deserter in your ranks. Let your baptism be your seal; faith, your helmet; your love, a lance; your patience, a suit of armour" (St Ignatius of Antioch, *Ad Polycarpum*, 6, 1–2).

2:8–13 The trials that Paul experienced—imprisoned as he was for preaching the Gospel—are a gift of entitlement to heaven, for martyrdom makes the disciple like his Master. Salvation is attained through the merits of Christ. Moreover, no external difficulty is an insurmountable obstacle to the spread of the Gospel: "The word of God is not fettered" (v. 9). "Just as a ray of sunlight cannot be trapped or locked indoors, the preaching of the word of God cannot be tied down. Moreover, even when the teacher is bound in chains, the words of the Gospel remain free; when the preacher was in prison, his teaching

flew throughout the whole world as though it had wings" (St John Chrysostom, *Ad populum Antiochenum*, 16, 12).

The hymn in vv. 11–13 is a call to be faithful in hostile circumstances, even to the point of martyrdom. It shows the closeness of the baptized person to Christ who died and rose from the dead; it sings the praises of Christian perseverance grounded on the eternal fidelity of the Lord, who "cannot deny himself" (v. 13). St Augustine explains that this "cannot" does not mean that God's omnipotence is somehow restricted: "The only thing the Almighty cannot do is what he does not will be done. (...) Justice cannot do what is unjust, nor wisdom what is foolish, nor the truth what is false" (*Sermones*, 214, 4).

***2:14—4:8** Pointless argument and disorderly conduct undermine sound teaching. The second section of the letter warns of these dangers.

2:14–21 Given that errors and misconceptions were prevalent, the emphasis here is on the solid-

people into more and more ungodliness, [17]and their talk will eat its way like gangrene. Among them are Hymenaeus and Philetus, [18]who have swerved from the truth by holding that the resurrection is past already.* They are upsetting the faith of some. [19]But God's firm foundation stands, bearing this seal: "The Lord knows those who are his," and, "Let every one who names the name of the Lord depart from iniquity."

[20]In a great house there are not only vessels of gold and silver but also of wood and earthenware, and some for noble use, some for ignoble. [21]If any one purifies himself from what is ignoble, then he will be a vessel for noble use, consecrated and useful to the master of the house, ready for any good work.

1 Cor 15:12, 19, 22

Sir 7:2
Lev 24:16
Num 16:5, 26
Is 26:13
Jn 10:14
Eph 2:10
1 Cor 8:3
Rev 21:27
Is 26:13; 29:16
Wis 15:7
1 Cor 3:12
Rom 9:21

Patience towards those in error

[22]So shun youthful passions and aim at righteousness, faith, love, and peace, along with those who call upon the Lord from a pure heart. [23]Have nothing to do with stupid, senseless controversies; you know that they breed quarrels. [24]And the Lord's servant must not be quarrelsome but kindly to every one, an apt teacher, forbearing, [25]correcting his opponents with gentleness. God may perhaps grant that they will

1 Tim 6:11
Gal 5:22
Tit 1:14; 3:9
1 Tim 1:4; 6:4
Is 42:3
Mt 12:19
1 Tim 3:2
Tit 1:7; 3:2
1 Tim 2:4

exhibere Deo, operarium inconfusibilem, recte tractantem verbum veritatis. [16]Profana autem inaniloquia devita, magis enim proficient ad impietatem, [17]et sermo eorum ut cancer serpit; ex quibus est Hymenaeus et Philetus, [18]qui circa veritatem aberraverunt dicentes resurrectionem iam factam, et subvertunt quorundam fidem. [19]Sed firmum fundamentum Dei stat habens signaculum hoc: *Cognovit Dominus, qui sunt eius, et: Discedat ab iniquitate omnis, qui nominat nomen Domini.* [20]In magna autem domo non solum sunt vasa aurea et argentea sed et lignea et fictilia, et quaedam quidem in honorem, quaedam autem in ignominiam; [21]si quis ergo emundaverit se ab istis, erit vas in honorem, sanctificatum, utile Domino, ad omne opus bonum paratum. [22]Iuvenilia autem desideria fuge, sectare vero iustitiam, fidem, caritatem, pacem cum his, qui invocant Dominum de corde puro. [23]Stultas autem et sine disciplina quaestiones devita, sciens quia generant lites; [24]servum autem Domini non oportet litigare, sed mansuetum esse ad omnes, aptum ad docendum, patientem, [25]cum mansuetudine corripientem eos, qui resistunt, si quando det illis Deus

ity of the Church; the metaphor used is taken from building (v. 19). It was customary to attach a "foundation document" (a "seal") to the first stone of a building; in the case of a temple or other religious building, that document indicated the intention of the builders. St Paul develops this metaphor by envisaging two inscriptions on the seal: the first, from Numbers 16:5, reminds Timothy that God does the choosing and that he takes care of those he chooses; the second, from Isaiah 26:13, affirms the need for holiness: "You are holy, O Church, my Mother, because the Son of God, who is holy, founded you. You are holy because the Father, source of all holiness, so ordained it. You are holy, because the Holy Spirit, who dwells in the souls of the faithful, assists you" (St Josemaría Escrivá, *In Love with the Church*, 8).

On the other hand, just as different kinds of containers and instruments can be found in a house (vv. 20–21), we should not be scandalized to find that there are sinners in the Church, or people whose behaviour leaves a lot to be desired; rather we should pray for their conver-

sion, for everyone is called to be holy and each should be ready to fulfil the function assigned to him or her: "Each one of us, who has been instructed in the Word, is a servant of all the things we have been taught in the Gospel. In this great house which is the Church, not only are there all kinds of vessels—of gold and silver, of wood and earth—there are also all kinds of work. There are hunters, travellers, architects, builders, farmers, shepherds, athletes and soldiers in the house of God, the Church of the living God" (St Basil, *Homilia in illud: Attende tibi ipsi*, 4).

2:22–26 This is an appeal for patience and serenity; when faced with error, we should try to bring the other person round to the truth, to help him mend his ways. "The superior should only reprove those who have fallen or failed when he is calm. If he were to speak in anger or indignation, he would not free the other from his sin, but only add new sin to old. It is for this reason that Scripture says: *correcting his opponents with gentleness*. He should not become angry even if

1 Jn 2:14
1 Cor 5:5
Gal 6:1
repent and come to know the truth, ²⁶and they may escape from the snare of the
devil, after being captured by him to do his will.^c

Preventing error from doing harm

1 Tim 4:1
2 Pet 3:3
Rom 1:29–32
1 Tim 1:10
3 ¹But understand this, that in the last days there will come times of stress. ²For
men will be lovers of self, lovers of money, proud, arrogant, abusive, disobedi-
ent to their parents, ungrateful, unholy, ³inhuman, implacable, slanderers, profligates,
fierce, haters of good, ⁴treacherous, reckless, swollen with conceit, lovers of pleas-

Mt 7:15–21;
24:4–24
Tit 1:16
Col 2:23
Rom 2:19–20
ure rather than lovers of God, ⁵holding the form of religion but denying the power
of it. Avoid such people. ⁶For among them are those who make their way into households and capture weak women, burdened with sins and swayed by various

1 Tim 2:4
Jn 8:32
Acts 12:21
Ex 7:11
Jn 8:32
Acts 13:8
1 Tim 3:13
2 Tim 3:13
1 Cor 13:13
impulses, ⁷who will listen to anybody and can never arrive at a knowledge of the
truth. ⁸As Jannes and Jambres opposed Moses, so these men also oppose the truth,
men of corrupt mind and counterfeit faith; ⁹but they will not get very far, for their
folly will be plain to all, as was that of those two men.

Ps 34:17, 19
Acts 13:50;
14:2, 5, 19, 22
2 Cor 1:10
¹⁰Now you have observed my teaching, my conduct, my aim in life, my faith, my
patience, my love, my steadfastness, ¹¹my persecutions, my sufferings, what befell
me at Antioch, at Iconium, and at Lystra, what persecutions I endured; yet from

Col 1:24
Phil 3:10
1 Thess 3:4–5
Eph 3:1
Mk 10:30
them all the Lord rescued me. ¹²Indeed all who desire to live a godly life in Christ
Jesus will be persecuted, ¹³while evil men and impostors will go on from bad to
worse, deceivers and deceived.

---

paenitentiam ad cognoscendam veritatem, ²⁶et resipiscant a Diaboli laqueo, a quo capti tenentur ad ipsius voluntatem.   [3] ¹Hoc autem scito,
quod in novissimis diebus instabunt tempora periculosa. ²Erunt enim homines seipsos amantes, cupidi, elati, superbi, blasphemi, parentibus
inoboedientes, ingrati, scelesti, ³sine affectione, sine foedere, criminatores, incontinentes, immites, sine benignitate, ⁴proditores, protervi, tumidi,
voluptatum amatores magis quam Dei, ⁵habentes speciem quidem pietatis, virtutem autem eius abnegantes; et hos devita. ⁶Ex his enim sunt, qui
penetrant domos et captivas ducunt mulierculas oneratas peccatis, quae ducuntur variis concupiscentiis, ⁷semper discentes et numquam ad scientiam veritatis pervenire valentes. ⁸Quemadmodum autem Iannes et Iambres restiterunt Moysi, ita et hi resistunt veritati, homines corrupti mente,
reprobi circa fidem; ⁹sed ultra non proficient, insipientia enim eorum manifesta erit omnibus, sicut et illorum fuit. ¹⁰Tu autem assecutus es meam
doctrinam, institutionem, propositum, fidem, longanimitatem, dilectionem, patientiam, ¹¹persecutiones, passiones, qualia mihi facta sunt Antiochiae, Iconii, Lystris, quales persecutiones sustinui; et ex omnibus me eripuit Dominus. ¹²Et omnes, qui volunt pie vivere in Christo Iesu, persecutionem patientur; ¹³mali autem homines et seductores proficient in peius, in errorem mittentes et errantes. ¹⁴Tu vero permane in his, quae

---

someone rejects his correction; he should always
be gentle with the sinner, and become angry only
at the sin that has been committed" (St Basil,
Regulae morales, 50).

We should do everything we can to prevent a
breach of faith and the consequent danger that
people might be lost to the Church. "The pastor
of souls needs great patience and diligence and
perseverance to look after one who has wandered off the path of true faith. The sinner cannot
be obliged to repent through force or fear; rather,
he must be led back gently to the truth from
which he has fallen away. The pastor must be a
very generous soul if he is not to despair or grow
discouraged in his efforts to save the one who
has wandered away from the truth; he should
remind himself of what the Apostle wrote: 'God
may perhaps grant that they will repent and
come to know the truth, and they may escape

from the snares of the devil'" (St John Chrysostom, *De sacerdotio*, 2, 4).

3:1–13 The "last days" (v. 1) means the period
between the Incarnation of Christ and his second
coming in glory. Among the men burdened with
sin (vv. 2–5), those do most harm who spread
ideas that go against the faith and good morality.
Jannes and Jambres (v. 8) were, according to
Jewish tradition, the names of the Egyptian
magicians summoned by Pharaoh to perform
miracles in reply to the prodigies worked by
Moses and Aaron in his presence (cf. Ex 7:11).
In literature they epitomized evil men.

Paul's brief references to his own experiences (vv. 10–13), with which Timothy would
have been familiar (since he came from Lystra),
are designed to be an encouragement to Timothy: "A true athlete wins despite the blows he

---

c Or *by him, to do his* (that is, God's) *will*

Staying true to Holy Scripture

¹⁴But as for you, continue in what you have learned and have firmly believed, knowing from whom you learned it ¹⁵and how from childhood you have been acquainted with the sacred writings which are able to instruct you for salvation through faith in Christ Jesus. ¹⁶All scripture is inspired by God and^d profitable for teaching, for reproof, for correction, and for training in righteousness,* ¹⁷that the man of God may be complete, equipped for every good work.

2 Tim 1:5
2 Pet 1:20

Jn 5:39
Jude 3
Jn 5:39
2 Cor 3:14-18
2 Pet 1:21
Rom 15:4
1 Cor 10:6

Dedication to preaching

4 ¹I charge you in the presence of God and of Christ Jesus who is to judge the living and the dead, and by his appearing and his kingdom: ²preach the word, be urgent in season and out of season, convince, rebuke, and exhort, be unfailing in patience and in teaching. ³For the time is coming when people will not endure sound teaching, but having itching ears they will accumulate for themselves teachers to suit their own likings, ⁴and will turn away from listening to the truth and wander into myths. ⁵As for you, always be steady, endure suffering, do the work of an evangelist, fulfil your ministry.

Rom 14:9
Acts 10:42
1 Tim 5:21; 6:11, 14
1 Pet 4:5
2 Pet 1:12
Jude 17
Tit 1:13
2 Pet 3:3
Tit 1:9; 2:1-10
Jude 18
1 Tim 1:10; 4:1, 6;
6:3
1 Tim 1:4; 4:7
Tit 1:14
2 Thess 2:11
2 Tim 2:3

didicisti et credita sunt tibi, sciens a quibus didiceris, ¹⁵et quia ab infantia Sacras Litteras nosti, quae te possunt instruere ad salutem per fidem, quae est in Christo Iesu. ¹⁶Omnis Scriptura divinitus inspirata est et utilis ad docendum, ad arguendum, ad corrigendum, ad erudiendum in iustitia, ¹⁷ut perfectus sit homo Dei, ad omne opus bonum instructus.   [4] ¹Testificor coram Deo et Christo Iesu, qui iudicaturus est vivos ac mortuos, per adventum ipsius et regnum eius: ²praedica verbum, insta opportune, importune, argue, increpa, obsecra in omni longanimitate et doctrina. ³Erit enim tempus, cum sanam doctrinam non sustinebunt, sed ad sua desideria coacervabunt sibi magistros prurientes auribus, ⁴et a veritate quidem auditum avertent, ad fabulas autem convertentur. ⁵Tu vero vigila in omnibus, labora, opus fac evangelistae, ministerium tuum imple. ⁶Ego

suffers. Bear all things [adversity] for God, so that he, too, will bear us up" (St Ignatius of Antioch, *Ad Polycarpum*, 3, 1).

3:14-17 Paul exhorts Timothy to read Holy Scripture (the Old Testament), which his mother and grandmother taught him to revere ever since he was a child, for the books of the Bible are inspired by God. That is why they enjoy special authority in the Church: "the divinely revealed realities, which are contained and presented in the Holy Scriptures, have been written down under the inspiration of the Holy Spirit [...]. All that the inspired authors, or sacred writers, affirm should be regarded as affirmed by the Holy Spirit; we must acknowledge that the books of Scripture, firmly, faithfully and without error, teach that truth which God, for the sake of our salvation, wished to see confided to the Holy Scriptures" (Vatican II, *Dei Verbum*, 11). "Read the divine Scriptures very often, or, to say it better, never let the holy Scriptures fall from your hands" (St Jerome, *Epistulae*, 52, 7).

"Man of God" (v. 17). The Old Testament describes in this way people who carried out some special God-given mission—for example,

Moses (Deut 33:1; Josh 14:6), Samuel (1 Sam 9:6-7), Elijah and Elisha (1 Kings 17:18; 2 Kings 4:7, 27, 42). The description is applied to Timothy here because, through ordination, God has given him a ministry in the Church. By ordination "the priest is a consecrated man, a *man of God* (1 Tim 6:11). [...] The ministerial priesthood in the People of God is more than a public office and a sacred ministry: above all, it is the mysterious and sacramental transformation of the priest into Christ himself, the only mediator between God and man (cf. 1 Tim 2:5)" (Alvaro del Portillo, *On Priesthood*).

4:1-5 The solemnity of this exhortation is signalled by a form of words at the beginning similar to that found in Greco-Roman wills, which laid on the heirs an obligation to carry out the testator's wishes: "I charge you most solemnly" or "I adjure you". It is clear that the preaching of the Gospel is a serious duty incumbent on a person who has charge of a Christian community. The Second Vatican Council has this to say: "Among the principal duties of bishops the preaching of the Gospel occupies an eminent place. For bishops are

d Or *Every scripture inspired by God is also*

The crown of righteousness

⁶For I am already on the point of being sacrificed;* the time of my departure has come. ⁷I have fought the good fight, I have finished the race, I have kept the faith. ⁸Henceforth there is laid up for me the crown of righteousness, which the Lord, the righteous judge, will award to me on that Day, and not only to me but also to all who have loved his appearing.

3. FINAL ADVICE*

News and messages

⁹Do your best to come to me soon. ¹⁰For Demas, in love with this present world, has deserted me and gone to Thessalonica; Crescens has gone to Galatia,ᵉ Titus to Dalmatia. ¹¹Luke alone is with me. Get Mark and bring him with you; for he is very useful in serving me. ¹²Tychicus I have sent to Ephesus. ¹³When you come, bring the cloak that I left with Carpus at Troas, also the books, and above all the parchments. ¹⁴Alexander the coppersmith did me great harm; the Lord will requite him for his deeds. ¹⁵Beware of him yourself, for he strongly opposed our message. ¹⁶At my first defence no one took my part; all deserted me. May it not be charged against them!

enim iam delibor, et tempus meae resolutionis instat. ⁷Bonum certamen certavi, cursum consummavi, fidem servavi; ⁸in reliquo reposita est mihi iustitiae corona, quam reddet mihi Dominus in illa die, iustus iudex, non solum autem mihi sed et omnibus, qui diligunt adventum eius. ⁹Festina venire ad me cito. ¹⁰Demas enim me dereliquit diligens hoc saeculum et abiit Thessalonicam, Crescens in Galatiam, Titus in Dalmatiam; ¹¹Lucas est mecum solus. Marcum assumens adduc tecum, est enim mihi utilis in ministerium. ¹²Tychicum autem misi Ephesum. ¹³Paenulam, quam reliqui Troade apud Carpum, veniens affer, et libros, maxime autem membranas. ¹⁴Alexander aerarius multa mala mihi ostendit. Reddet ei Dominus secundum opera eius; ¹⁵quem et tu devita, valde enim restitit verbis nostris. ¹⁶In prima mea defensione nemo mihi affuit, sed omnes me dereli-

preachers of the faith, who lead new disciples to Christ, and they are authentic teachers, that is, teachers endowed with the authority of Christ, who preach to the people committed to them the faith they must believe and put into practice, and by the light of the Holy Spirit illustrate that faith. They bring forth from the treasury of Revelation new things and old (cf. Mt 13:52), making it bear fruit and vigilantly warding off any errors that threaten their flock (cf. 2 Tim 4:1–4)" (*Lumen gentium*, 25).

The words of the Apostle, so full of prudence and wisdom, have often been cited in Christian tradition in connexion with this subject. St Benedict, for example, writes: "As he governs, the abbot should always obey the law laid down by the Apostle: convince, rebuke, and exhort; that is, he should bear in mind the time and circumstances, combine severity and gentleness, and act with both the strictness of a teacher and the tenderness of a father" (*Regula*, 2, 23–25).

4:6–8 Conscious that his life is coming to an

end, Paul portrays death as an offering to God, like the libations poured out on an altar of sacrifice. He depicts the Christian life as a spiritual sport, a competition that is watched and judged by God himself. Hope of attaining eternal life is a virtue that all Christians should have: "We who know about the eternal joys of the heavenly fatherland should hasten to reach it" (St Gregory the Great, *Homiliae in Evangelia*, 1, 3).

*4:9–22 The last section of the letter is very moving. It consists largely of news items and messages. We see here St Paul's state of mind as he stands on the brink of martyrdom. The fact that he mentions so many disciples by name shows the Apostle's generosity of spirit: he tried his best with everyone; some failed to persevere, but most did stay loyal. Other letters and the Acts of the Apostles tell us a little more about some of these people; as for the rest, this reference in 2 Timothy is all we know about them. Certainly, they must all have been very much in the heart of St Paul, who made himself "all

ᵉ Other ancient authorities read *Gaul*

[17]But the Lord stood by me and gave me strength to proclaim the message fully, that all the Gentiles might hear it. So I was rescued from the lion's mouth. [18]The Lord will rescue me from every evil and save me for his heavenly kingdom. To him be the glory for ever and ever. Amen.

Ps 22:21
Mt 10:19
Acts 23:11; 27:33
Ps 22:21
Phil 1:19
Col 4:3
Rom 15:9
2 Cor 1:10
2 Pet 2:9

Greetings and final good wishes

[19]Greet Prisca and Aquila, and the household of Onesiphorus. [20]Erastus remained at Corinth; Trophimus I left ill at Miletus. [21]Do your best to come before winter. Eubulus sends greetings to you, as do Pudens and Linus* and Claudia and all the brethren.
[22]The Lord be with your spirit. Grace be with you.

Acts 18:2
1 Cor 16:19
2 Tim 1:16
Rom 16:23
Acts 19:22; 21:29
2 Tim 4:9

1 Tim 6:21
Tit 3:15
Gal 6:18
Col 4:18

querunt. Non illis reputetur; [17]Dominus autem mihi astitit et confortavit me, ut per me praedicatio impleatur, et audiant omnes gentes, et liberatus sum de ore leonis. [18]Liberabit me Dominus ab omni opere malo et salvum faciet in regnum suum caeleste; cui gloria in saecula saeculorum. Amen. [19]Saluta Priscam et Aquilam et Onesiphori domum. [20]Erastus remansit Corinthi, Trophimum autem reliqui infirmum Mileti. [21]Festina ante hiemem venire. Salutat te Eubulus et Pudens et Linus et Claudia et fratres omnes. [22]Dominus cum spiritu tuo. Gratia vobiscum.

things to all men, that I might by all means save some" (1 Cor 9:22).

"The Lord be with your spirit" (v. 22): an early Christian greeting invoking God's help, protection and blessing. Although it may be a Semitic turn of phrase meaning "The Lord be with you", some Fathers interpreted it, in this context, as alluding to the grace conferred on Timothy by the sacrament of Orders—in which case the Apostle is calling on God to help Timothy in his work as a minister of the Church.

THE LETTER OF PAUL TO

TITUS

Introduction

The Letter to Titus is the shortest of the three Pastoral Letters. In printed editions of the New Testament it comes after the two letters to Timothy, and directly before the very short Letter to Philemon, the last of the letters addressed to individuals and the last of the letters, written, either directly or indirectly, by St Paul. In style and content it is very similar to the First Letter to Timothy.

1. STRUCTURE AND CONTENT

The Letter to Titus invites the reader to focus his attention on Jesus, our Saviour, and on the change in lifestyle and attitudes that Christian initiation implies. The pastoral work entrusted to Titus and to church ministers in general is at the service of these beliefs and demands.

Typical of a letter of St Paul, it begins with an elaborate greeting (1:1–4), which in this case refers both to "God" and to "Christ Jesus" as "our Saviour" and allows us to see the Apostle's affectionate regard for this disciple.

At the start of the first section of the letter, Paul sends Titus instructions on the way in which the Christian communities in Crete should be organized: each of them is to be led by a minister with the necessary moral qualities; and the responsibilities of the minister include correcting those who stray and striving to prevent the spread of ideas and theories harmful to the faith (1:5–16).

The second section (2:1—3:11), somewhat longer than the first, is arranged in a series of concentric circles that centre on the idea that God's saving grace has been made manifest to all in Jesus Christ, and Christians should therefore turn their backs on sin and live godly lives (2:11–15). Paul spells out the duties of Christians depending on their age and circumstances (2:1–10), and then duties common to all; all this is set against the background of respect for lawful authority and the need to avoid doctrinal quarrels, because they are a waste of time (3:1–11).

The letter ends with some personal messages and words of farewell (3:12–15).

2. CONTEXT

As has already been mentioned, the Letter to Titus has features very similar to those of the First Letter to Timothy. It could be that these two letters, sent to the ministers in charge of the Pauline communities in Crete and Ephesus, and written against similar backgrounds, date from around the same time.

Titus, the son of pagan parents (see Gal 2:3), must have been converted by St Paul, given the special affection the Apostle has for him (see 1:4). Along with Barnabas he accompanied Paul on his visit to Jerusalem to confirm with church leaders that the message being preached to the Gentiles was authoritative (see Gal 2:1–5). Titus is not named in the Acts of the Apostles, but there are references in Pauline letters to his being sent to Corinth on two delicate missions—the first, to deliver a letter that has not come down to us (see 2 Cor 7:14); and later, to organize a collection and deliver the Second Letter to the Corinthians (see 2 Cor 8:6, 16–23; 12:18).

The Letter to Titus shows that St Paul had left this disciple behind on the island of Crete to continue the missionary work that they had jointly started there (see 1:5). This same source tells us that Titus stayed on in Crete until he was relieved by Artemas or Tychicus (cf. 3:12).

The background discernible in the letter is very similar to that in the First Letter to Timothy—a Christian community founded by St Paul which needs to have suitable ministers, capable of preaching the "sound doctrine" given them by the Apostle (see 1:9; 2:1), and thereby countering the work of false teachers.

As has already been noted, the language and literary style of the Pastoral letters are somewhat different from what is found in the other Pauline writings. Because of this, some scholars query whether they were in fact written by Paul, although it seems fairly clear that they were written in line with the teaching and on the authority of the Apostle, and were received as apostolic writings in the communities associated with Timothy and Titus.

3. MESSAGE

The main themes of this letter are the same as those mentioned in connexion with the First Letter to Timothy—the organization of the Church, defence of sound teaching, and faith in Jesus Christ our Saviour as the basis of Christian life.

Jesus Christ our Saviour

As often happens in the Pastoral Letters, Christ is called Saviour here (1:4; 2:13; 3:6). The emphasis is on his human nature, in which his divinity is made manifest (2:11; 3:4): he is "our great God and Saviour Jesus Christ" (2:13).

Like 1 Timothy, the letter denounces deviations from the "sure word" preached by St Paul, to which Titus must closely adhere in his preaching (1:9).

The Church

The letter does not give a formal exposition of the nature of the Church, but it does describe important features of the Church and its organization. In connexion with the central idea (salvation for all mankind won by Jesus Christ), the letter teaches that the Church is the vessel of God's plan of salvation. Jesus Christ establishes the New Covenant in his blood, making "a people of his own" (2:14), that is, the Church, which makes present and extends to everyone the saving actions of Christ; the Church is the people redeemed from all iniquity and purified by means of Christ's sacrifice (2:14).

Church ministers have the essential role of preaching the word of God. In sharp contrast to false teachers who distort the truth, they must make sure they "give instruction in sound doctrine" (1:9); they should foster "sound speech" (2:8) and try to ensure that people are "sound in the faith" (1:13; cf. 2:2).

The structure of the Church, as evidenced in this letter and in 1 and 2 Timothy, is that of the stage when "apostolic succession" begins. Initially there is the authority of the Apostle, whether he be present or absent. Then the Apostle delegates his authority to his representative. Titus had previously been given specific and local assignments, but here he has broader responsibilities—teaching, preaching and governance of the community (2:1–10). And, because the mission entrusted to him must be given continuity, he must appoint others who in their turn will guide the community—*presbýteroi* and *epískopoi*.[1] Although there was as yet no clear distinction between the episcopacy and the presbyterate (such as is found in the writings of St Ignatius of Antioch early in the second century),[2] it is already possible to discern the origins of the various levels of ministry in the church hierarchy.

The Christian life

Christians are called to lead upright lives because Christ "gave himself for us to redeem us from all iniquity" (2:14). Through Baptism and new life in the Holy Spirit we are justified and become "heirs in hope of eternal life" (3:7). The source of Christian life is the salvation achieved for us by Christ; all moral rules are based on it. The grace of God guides us "to renounce irreligion and worldly passions, and to live sober, upright, and godly lives in this world" (2:12). Christians should apply themselves to good deeds because they believe in God (3:8), because they know that they have been redeemed by Christ from all iniquity (2:14) and because grace gives them the strength to do so.

---

1 The meanings of these terms had not yet been fixed; sometimes both terms are applied to the same person (see 1:5 and 1:7).
2 See *Ad Magnesios*, 6, 1; *Ad Trallianos*, 7, 2; *Ad Philadelphos*, 7, 1.

Titus

Greeting*

1 [1]Paul, a servant[a] of God and an apostle of Jesus Christ, to further the faith of God's elect and their knowledge of the truth which accords with godliness, [2]in hope of eternal life which God, who never lies, promised ages ago [3]and at the proper time manifested in his word through the preaching with which I have been entrusted by command of God our Saviour;

[4]To Titus, my true child in a common faith:

Grace and peace from God the Father and Christ Jesus our Saviour.

1 Tim 2:4
2 Tim 2:25; 3:7
Rom 1:1

Num 23:19
2 Tim 2:13
Eph 1:9
Acts 1:7
Eph 1:9
1 Tim 1:1, 11; 2:6;
6:15
Rom 3:6; 16:25–26
Tit 2:10; 3:4
1 Tim 1:2, 11; 2:3;
4:10
2 Cor 2:13
2 Tim 1:10
2 Pet 1:1, 11; 3:18

1. TITUS' MISSION IN CRETE*

Qualifications for elders

[5]This is why I left you in Crete, that you might amend what was defective, and appoint elders* in every town as I directed you, [6]if any man is blameless, the husband of one wife, and his children are believers and not open to the charge of being profligate or insubordinate. [7]For a bishop, as God's steward, must be blameless; he must not be arrogant or quick-tempered or a drunkard or violent or greedy for gain,

Acts 14:23; 20:17,
28; 27:8
1 Tim 3:2–4
Prov 28:7
2 Tim 2:24–26
1 Pet 5:2
1 Cor 4:1
1 Tim 1:10; 3:6–7;
6:3-4
Tit 2:1–10
2 Tim 1:13; 2:24; 4:3

[1] [1]Paulus servus Dei, apostolus autem Iesu Christi secundum fidem electorum Dei et agnitionem veritatis, quae secundum pietatem est [2]in spem vitae aeternae, quam promisit, qui non mentitur, Deus ante tempora saecularia, [3]manifestavit autem temporibus suis verbum suum in praedicatione, quae credita est mihi secundum praeceptum salvatoris nostri Dei, [4]Tito germano filio secundum communem fidem: gratia et pax a Deo Patre et Christo Iesu salvatore nostro. [5]Huius rei gratia reliqui te Cretae, ut ea, quae desunt, corrigas et constituas per civitates presbyteros, sicut ego tibi disposui, [6]si quis sine crimine est, unius uxoris vir, filios habens fideles, non in accusatione luxuriae aut non subiectos. [7]Oportet enim episcopum sine crimine esse sicut Dei dispensatorem, non superbum, non iracundum, non vinolentum, non percussorem, non turpis lucri cupidum,

*1:1–4 In content and purpose this letter is very similar to the two letters to Timothy. The Apostle seeks to support and encourage his co-workers in their government of the churches. The letter also contains instructions about how the community should be organized and governed (1:5–16) and about what is expected of Christians depending on their circumstances (2:1—3:11).

The initial greeting is longer and more formal than those found in the other Pastoral Letters. It emphasizes the fact that Paul is an apostle and the importance of the message he preaches.

*1:5–16 Paul reminds Titus that he has been charged to organize the Christian community in Crete and its hierarchy, and to defend the faithful from the false teachings that some were beginning to spread.

1:5–9 As he does in 1 Timothy (3:2–7), Paul declares that a minister should be a model of holiness for his flock. At the time when the Pastoral Letters were written, the names and responsibilities of the various sacred orders in the church hierarchy had not yet become fixed (cf. the note on 1 Tim 3:1–7). Here the words used for "elders", priests (*presbýteroi*: v. 5) and bishops (*epískopoi*: v. 7) seem to refer to the same people. In the first case the emphasis is more on the maturity and experience expected of "elders" (*presbýteros* means "elder"), and in the other the stress is on the function of overseeing (*epískopos* means "watchman"): they have to "watch out for", look after, the faithful. But in both cases the terms refer to those who preside over each Christian community.

This passage is not meant to spell out all the values needed of the clergy. Still, it does seem to stress four aspects of good character—irre-

a Or *slave*

Rom 12:13

1 Pet 5:2
1 Tim 1:10–11; 4:3
2 Tim 1:13
1 Tim 1:10

[8]but hospitable, a lover of goodness, master of himself, upright, holy, and self-controlled; [9]he must hold firm to the sure word as taught, so that he may be able to give instruction in sound doctrine and also to confute those who contradict it.

Attitudes towards false teachers

1 Tim 1:6; 4:1
2 Tim 3:13
Acts 15:1
2 Tim 3:6
1 Tim 3:6; 6:10
2 Tim 4:2
1 Tim 1:10
1 Tim 5:20
1 Tim 1:4, 10; 4:7
2 Tim 2:16
Mt 15:11
Mk 7:15
Rom 14:14–20
1 Tim 4:4
1 Jn 1:6; 2:4
2 Tim 3:5

[10]For there are many insubordinate men, empty talkers and deceivers, especially the circumcision party; [11]they must be silenced, since they are upsetting whole families by teaching for base gain what they have no right to teach. [12]One of themselves, a prophet of their own, said, "Cretans are always liars, evil beasts, lazy gluttons." [13]This testimony is true. Therefore rebuke them sharply, that they may be sound in the faith, [14]instead of giving heed to Jewish myths or to commands of men who reject the truth. [15]To the pure all things are pure, but to the corrupt and unbelieving nothing is pure; their very minds and consciences are corrupted. [16]They profess to know God, but they deny him by their deeds; they are detestable, disobedient, unfit for any good deed.

2. MORAL DEMANDS OF THE CHRISTIAN FAITH*

Duties of Christians in different situations

1 Tim 1:10; 4:6; 6:3
2 Tim 1:13
1 Tim 5:1–2; 6:11
1 Cor 13:13
1 Tim 3:11
1 Pet 3:1–5
1 Tim 5:14

2 [1]But as for you, teach what befits sound doctrine. [2]Bid the older men be temperate, serious, sensible, sound in faith, in love, and in steadfastness. [3]Bid the older women likewise to be reverent in behaviour, not to be slanderers or slaves to drink; they are to teach what is good, [4]and so train the young women to love their husbands

[8]sed hospitalem, benignum, sobrium, iustum, sanctum, continentem, [9]amplectentem eum, qui secundum doctrinam est, fidelem sermonem, ut potens sit et exhortari in doctrina sana et eos, qui contradicunt, arguere. [10]Sunt enim multi et non subiecti vaniloqui et seductores, maxime qui de circumcisione sunt, [11]quibus oportet silentium imponere, quia universas domos subvertunt docentes, quae non oportet, turpis lucri gratia. [12]Dixit quidam ex illis, proprius ipsorum propheta: «Cretenses semper mendaces, malae bestiae, ventres pigri». [13]Testimonium hoc verum est. Quam ob causam increpa illos dure, ut sani sint in fide, [14]non intendentes Iudaicis fabulis et mandatis hominum aversantium veritatem. [15]Omnia munda mundis; coinquinatis autem et infidelibus nihil mundum, sed inquinatae sunt eorum et mens et conscientia. [16]Confitentur se nosse Deum, factis autem negant, cum sunt abominati et inoboedientes et ad omne opus bonum reprobi. [2] [1]Tu autem loquere, quae decent sanam doctrinam. [2]Senes, ut sobrii sint, pudici, prudentes, sani fide, dilectione, patientia. [3]Anus similiter in habitu sanctae, non criminatrices, non vino multo deditae, bene docentes, [4]ut prudentiam doceant adulescentulas, ut viros suos ament, filios diligant, [5]prudentes sint, castae, domus curam habentes,

proachable behaviour (vv. 6–7), being an exemplary family man (v. 6), having an upright character and being a welcoming person (vv. 7–8), and having a good understanding of the Gospel (v. 9). These are qualities the Church expects to find in its ministers; they "should abound in every spiritual good and bear a living witness of God to all" (Vatican II, *Lumen gentium*, 41).

1:10–16 In Crete, as in Ephesus (see 1 Tim 1:6), some philosophers (a number of them of Jewish background) had met with some success by their use of sophistry and fallacious arguments. Here the Apostle resorts to irony, quoting a verse from "a prophet of their own" (possibly the poet Epimenides, sixth century BC) about the Cretans' reputation for telling lies.

"To the pure all things are pure" (v. 15). "God made all things pure and clean. If there are things which are unclean, their impurity is a quality that has been produced in them by others" (Severinus of Gabala, *Fragmenta in Titum*). Interior purity (see Mt 23:25–26) is the source of Christian freedom; it makes no sense for people to claim to have Christian beliefs and yet live corrupt lives.

*2:1–3:11 Here Paul spells out the duties of Christians that vary according to their age and circumstances; but all are called to be devout and to play their part in society.

2:1–10 The counsels given here are similar to those found in other Pauline passages (cf. Eph

and children, [5]to be sensible, chaste, domestic, kind, and submissive to their husbands, that the word of God may not be discredited. [6]Likewise urge the younger men to control themselves. [7]Show yourself in all respects a model of good deeds, and in your teaching show integrity, gravity, [8]and sound speech that cannot be censured, so that an opponent may be put to shame, having nothing evil to say of us. [9]Bid slaves to be submissive to their masters and to give satisfaction in every respect; they are not to be refractory, [10]nor to pilfer, but to show entire and true fidelity, so that in everything they may adorn the doctrine of God our Saviour.

Eph 5:22
Col 3:18
1 Cor 14:34
1 Tim 2:12
1 Tim 6:1
1 Jn 2:14
1 Tim 4:12; 5:10
1 Pet 3:15; 5:3
1 Pet 1:15; 3:16
1 Tim 1:10; 5:14
Eph 6:5
Col 3:22
1 Pet 2:18
1 Tim 6:1
Tit 1:3; 3:4
1 Tim 1:1; 2:3; 4:10;
6:1–2

The Incarnation, the basis of Christian ethics and piety

[11]For the grace of God has appeared for the salvation of all men, [12]training us to renounce irreligion and worldly passions, and to live sober, upright, and godly lives in this world, [13]awaiting our blessed hope, the appearing of the glory of our great God and Saviour[c] *Jesus Christ, [14]who gave himself for us to redeem us from all iniquity and to purify for himself a people of his own who are zealous for good deeds.

[15]Declare these things; exhort and reprove with all authority. Let no one disregard you.

Tit 3:4
2 Tim 1:10
1 Jn 2:16
Eph 1:4
1 Cor 1:7
Rom 5:2
Phil 3:20
2 Tim 4:18
1 Tim 6:14
Eph 2:10
Ps 130:8
Ex 19:5
Deut 4:20; 7:6; 14:2
1 Tim 1:1; 2:6; 4:1
Eph 2:10; 5:25

benignae, subditae suis viris, ut non blasphemetur verbum Dei. [6]Iuvenes similiter hortare, ut sobrii sint. [7]In omnibus teipsum praebens exemplum bonorum operum, in doctrina integritatem, gravitatem, [8]in verbo sano irreprehensibilem, ut is, qui ex adverso est, vereatur, nihil habens malum dicere de nobis. [9]Servos dominis suis subditos esse in omnibus, placentes esse, non contradicentes, [10]non fraudantes, sed omnem fidem bonam ostendentes, ut doctrinam salutaris nostri Dei ornent in omnibus. [11]Apparuit enim gratia Dei salutaris omnibus hominibus [12]erudiens nos, ut abnegantes impietatem et saecularia desideria sobrie et iuste et pie vivamus in hoc saeculo, [13]exspectantes beatam spem et adventum gloriae magni Dei et salvatoris nostri Iesu Christi, [14]qui dedit semetipsum pro nobis, ut nos redimeret ab omni iniquitate et mundaret sibi populum peculiarem,

5:21–6:9; Col 3:18—4:6) where there is an underlying notion of the Church as God's family, made up of different kinds of members. As against the falseness of people whose sinful behaviour is at odds with what they claim to believe in, Paul urges Titus to teach people to live in line with their faith. Clearly, an important feature of Christian morality is that Christians should not reduce it to an abstract ethical code with no theological content; rather, it should flow from "sound doctrine" (v. 1), that is, from the true faith that they profess. "There is a connection between purity of heart, of body and of faith: the faithful must believe the articles of the Creed 'so that by believing they may obey God, by obeying they may live well, by living well may purify their hearts, and with pure hearts may understand what they believe' (St Augustine, *De fide et symbolo* 10, 25)" (*Catechism of the Catholic Church*, 2518).

Christian faith entails that a person should strive not only to be very upright, to live in a way consistent with one's beliefs, but also to offer others the attractive and credible witness of a clean life. "And so, living among our equals in a Christian way, we will be Christ present among

men. And we will do this in a natural way, consistent with our faith" (St Josemaría Escrivá, *Christ Is Passing By*, 112).

2:11–15 The duties just outlined all point to a Christian way of life (v. 12) based on hope (v. 13). By his work of redemption Christ has enabled us to live and hope in this way. We receive this grace from the Eucharist, which we celebrate "'awaiting the blessed hope and the coming of our Saviour, Jesus Christ,' asking 'to share in your glory when every tear will be wiped away. On that day we shall see you, our God, as you are. We shall become like you and praise you for ever through Christ our Lord'" (*Catechism of the Catholic Church*, 1404).

Verse 14 is an elegant summary of what the Redemption is; it identifies four elements in our salvation—Christ's self-giving; redemption from all iniquity; purification; and Christ's establishment of "a people of his own who are zealous for good deeds". The reference to Christ's self-giving obviously means his voluntary sacrifice on the cross (see Gal 1:4; 2:20; Eph 5:2; 1 Tim 2:6), whereby we are set free from the slavery of sin. Christ's sacrifice is the cause of the freedom

c Or *of the great God and our Saviour*

Respect for lawful authority

1 Tim 2:2
Rom 13:1–7
1 Pet 2:13–14, 17
Phil 4:5
2 Tim 2:24

3 ¹Remind them to be submissive to rulers and authorities, to be obedient, to be ready for any honest work, ²to speak evil of no one, to avoid quarrelling, to be gentle, and to show perfect courtesy toward all men.

Renewal of the Christian life in the Holy Spirit

Rom 1:29; 3:21–26
1 Pet 4:3
1 Thess 3:12
Col 3:5–7
Phil 4:5
Eph 2:3–10; 5:8

Rom 3:21–26
1 Cor 6:11
Tit 1:13; 2:11

Eph 2:4, 8; 5:26
Rom 5:5; 6:4; 7:6
Gal 2:16
2 Tim 1:9

Eph 2:8; 4:23; 5:26
Acts 2:17
Rom 8:17, 24
1 Tim 1:15; 5:10
Tit 3:14

³For we ourselves were once foolish, disobedient, led astray, slaves to various passions and pleasures, passing our days in malice and envy, hated by men and hating one another; ⁴but when the goodness and loving kindness of God our Saviour appeared, ⁵he saved us, not because of deeds done by us in righteousness, but in virtue of his own mercy, by the washing of regeneration and renewal in the Holy Spirit, ⁶which he poured out upon us richly through Jesus Christ our Saviour, ⁷so that we might be justified by his grace and become heirs in hope of eternal life.* ⁸The saying is sure.

I desire you to insist on these things, so that those who have believed in God may be careful to apply themselves to good deeds;ᵈ these are excellent and profitable to men.

sectatorem bonorum operum. ¹⁵Haec loquere et exhortare et argue cum omni imperio. Nemo te contemnat! [3] ¹Admone illos principibus, potestatibus subditos esse, dicto oboedire, ad omne opus bonum paratos esse, ²neminem blasphemare, non litigiosos esse, modestos, omnem ostendentes mansuetudinem ad omnes homines. ³Eramus enim et nos aliquando insipientes, inoboedientes, errantes, servientes concupiscentiis et voluptatibus variis, in malitia et invidia agentes, odibiles, odientes invicem. ⁴Cum autem benignitas et humanitas apparuit salvatoris nostri Dei, ⁵non ex operibus iustitiae, quae fecimus nos, sed secundum suam misericordiam salvos nos fecit per lavacrum regenerationis et renovationis Spiritus Sancti, ⁶quem effudit super nos abunde per Iesum Christum salvatorem nostrum, ⁷ut iustificati gratia ipsius heredes simus secundum spem vitae aeternae. ⁸Fidelis sermo, et volo te de his confirmare, ut curent bonis operibus praeesse, qui crediderunt Deo. Haec sunt bona et utilia

of the children of God (analogously, God's action during the Exodus liberated the people of Israel and made them a people of his own [cf. Ex 19:4–6]). Through the New Covenant of his blood, Jesus brings into being the Church, his chosen people, which is open to all mankind: "As Israel according to the flesh which wandered in the desert was already called the Church of God, so, too, the new Israel, which advances in this present era in search of a future and permanent city, is called also the Church of Christ. It is Christ indeed who has purchased it with his own blood; he has filled it with his Spirit; he has provided means adapted to its visible and social union" (Vatican II, *Lumen gentium*, 9).

3:1–2 The freedom of the children of God which Christ has won for us does not give us any right to oppose lawful civil authority, nor does it imply that Christians are opposed in principle to existing social structures; rather, it means that we desire to improve the world around us by becoming better people ourselves: "Therefore it is only by making an appeal to the 'moral poten-

tial' of the person and to the constant need for interior conversion, that social change will be brought about which will be truly in the service of man" (Congregation for the Doctrine of the Faith, *Libertatis nuntius*, 9, 8). Christians should obey lawful authority (see Rom 13:1–7; 1 Tim 2:2; 1 Pet 2:13–14).

3:3–8 The theological basis of the social obligations that must be met is the main theme of this chapter. It is summed up in a beautiful hymn in praise of Jesus Christ (vv. 4–7), about the Incarnation, the Redemption and the application of salvation to the individual person. Every baptized person is a witness to salvation history, to the transition from sin to grace, from the era of slavery and blindness to that of freedom and rebirth inaugurated by Christ. Experience of forgiveness fills a person with joy and moves him or her to give thanks. "If there were no forgiveness of sins in the Church, there could be no hope of freedom and eternal life. We give thanks to God for this great gift to His Church" (St Augustine, *Sermones*, 213, 9).

d Or *enter honourable occupations*

Further advice

⁹But avoid stupid controversies, genealogies, dissensions, and quarrels over the law, for they are unprofitable and futile. ¹⁰As for a man who is factious, after admonishing him once or twice, have nothing more to do with him, ¹¹knowing that such a person is perverted and sinful; he is self-condemned.

2 Tim 2:14; 16:23
1 Tim 1:4; 4:7
Mt 18:15–17
Rom 16:17

3. CONCLUSION*

Final messages

¹²When I send Artemas or Tychicus to you, do your best to come to me at Nicopolis, for I have decided to spend the winter there. ¹³Do your best to speed Zenas the lawyer and Apollos on their way; see that they lack nothing. ¹⁴And let our people learn to apply themselves to good deeds,ᵈ so as to help cases of urgent need, and not to be unfruitful.

Acts 20:4
2 Tim 4:12
Acts 18:24
3 Jn 6
Tit 2:14
1 Tim 5:10
Eph 4:28

Words of farewell

¹⁵All who are with me send greetings to you. Greet those who love us in the faith.
   Grace be with you all.

1 Tim 6:21
2 Tim 4:22

hominibus; ⁹stultas autem quaestiones et genealogias et contentiones et pugnas circa legem devita, sunt enim inutiles et vanae. ¹⁰Haereticum hominem post unam et secundam correptionem devita, ¹¹sciens quia subversus est, qui eiusmodi est, et delinquit, proprio iudicio condemnatus. ¹²Cum misero ad te Artemam aut Tychicum, festina ad me venire Nicopolim; ibi enim statui hiemare. ¹³Zenam legis peritum et Apollo sollicite instrue, ut nihil illis desit. ¹⁴Discant autem et nostri bonis operibus praeesse ad usus necessarios, ut non sint infructuosi. ¹⁵Salutant te, qui mecum sunt, omnes. Saluta, qui nos amant in fide. Gratia cum omnibus vobis.

3:9–11 The Church is not a place for strife. "Factious" (v. 10) refers here to those false teachers who reject sound doctrine and create divisions. In due course, the meaning of such terms as "heresy" and "schism" became more precise: "Heresy is the obstinate denial or doubt, after Baptism, of a truth which must be believed by divine and Catholic faith. Apostasy is the total repudiation of the Christian faith. Schism is the withdrawal of submission to the [Pope] or from communion with the members of the Church subject to him" (*Code of Canon Law*, 751).

*3:12–15 The messages at the end of the letter show the importance that the early Christians gave to hospitality.

Tychicus accompanied St Paul on his third missionary journey (see Acts 20:4) and delivered Paul's letters to the Ephesians and the Colossians. Apollos, too, is mentioned in Acts and is described as an educated and eloquent man (Acts 18:24–26); in addition to his evangelizing work in Ephesus, he also contributed to the development of the church at Corinth (see 1 Cor 1:12; 3:4–6, 22; 16:12).

"Those who love us in the faith" (v. 15), or, less literally, "our friends in the faith", means Christians; this love for one another has a supernatural origin. St Jerome comments: "If everyone who loves loved in the faith, St Paul would not have added faith to love; mothers love their children and are ready to give their lives for them, but that kind of love is not necessarily love in the faith; and wives love their husbands and often even die for them, yet that is not love in the faith. Only saints love in the faith, for their love embraces also unbelievers; indeed, they love even their enemies; that is love in the faith, for it is a love based on Him who has promised the reward to those who keep the *new commandment*" (*Commentarii in Titum*, ad loc.).

d Or *enter honourable occupations*

THE LETTER OF PAUL TO

PHILEMON

Introduction

The Letter to Philemon, the shortest of the Pauline letters, is placed at the end of the series of letters by Paul and before the Letter to the Hebrews which, though it is "Pauline", has features that put it in a category of its own.

Philemon, apparently, was a well-to-do Colossian (see Col 4:8–9) whom St Paul had converted to the Christian faith (cf. Philem 19), probably during his three-year stay in Ephesus, when people from throughout the region heard St Paul preach. Paul calls him his "fellow worker" (v. 1) and treats him with great affection and trust (see Philem 8, 17, 19, 21).

1. STRUCTURE AND CONTENT

This is a letter written from one friend to another; brief and straightforward though it is, it follows the typical pattern of a Pauline letter.

It begins, as usual, with a few words of greeting, containing the names of the sender and of the addressees (vv. 1–3).

The body of the letter begins with words expressing gratitude to God for Philemon's charity and faith, and a desire that his faith be truly active and vibrant (vv. 4–7). Then comes the main part of the letter, which is a plea (based on their mutual friendship and their faith in Jesus Christ) on behalf of Onesimus, a fugitive slave who is returning to Colossae to work for Philemon (vv. 8–21). The letter ends with the usual personal messages and greetings (vv. 22–25).

2. CONTEXT

Onesimus, a slave belonging to Philemon, had fled his house, possibly after stealing some money or other valuables (see v. 18); fearing punishment, Onesimus is reluctant to return to his master. In the course of his absence from Philemon, Onesimus met up with Paul, who was in prison at the time. Paul's friendliness and zeal soon drew Onesimus to the Gospel, and he was converted to the Christian faith.

Initially Paul may have thought of keeping Onesimus with him, to be a help to him (see vv. 13–14), but he soon changed his mind and decided to send him back to Philemon.

Because the literary style and language and line of argument of this letter are typically Pauline, few scholars question its authenticity. However, because the only concrete piece of information here about the time-frame is the fact that the writer (Paul) is in prison, it is not possible to be sure when exactly it was written, given that the Apostle was imprisoned a number of times. The most likely place and time of composition is Ephesus, at some point during the years 54–57.[1] Of all the places where Paul was imprisoned, Ephesus is the nearest to Colossae, and the place to which a slave from Colossae would have been most likely to flee. However, it is also possible

---

1 This may be the imprisonment implied in 2 Corinthians 1:8 and 11:23.

that the letter was written from Rome, during the Apostle's first imprisonment there—in which case the letter should be dated to between AD 61 and 63.

3. MESSAGE

This very short letter is a masterpiece of its type; it exudes sensitivity and refined charity. The Apostle does not write as a superior laying down what must be done (though he had the authority to do so); instead, he makes a humble appeal, on the strength of his being an "old man" and a "prisoner" for Christ (see v. 9 and RSV note **a**).

Although the letter is largely a private one, it does contain some doctrine—and important doctrine, despite the brevity of the treatment. In fact, the letter has been called the "magna carta" of Christian freedom. St Paul does not directly ask Philemon to liberate Onesimus, but he does ask him to receive him as "a beloved brother" (v. 16), as if he were Paul himself in person (cf. v. 17). The Apostle expects that Philemon, by acting in this way, will do "even more than I say" (v. 21). What might "more" mean? The question being left in the air, so to speak, the thrust of the letter is clear. The Apostle does not deal with the question of slavery directly, but he does provide the Christian principles which in due course will lead to abolition of slavery. These principles are grounded on the freedom that Christ has won for us on the cross, which makes us truly sons and daughters of God and brothers and sisters who share the same faith. The Letter to Philemon shows that "the new freedom procured by the grace of Christ should necessarily have effects on the social level".[2] That is the meaning of the "more" that St Paul expects of Philemon—that he should treat Onesimus as a true brother in the faith, as his equal, for there is no justification for discriminating against anyone on the basis of class or social standing.

2 Congregation for the Doctrine of the Faith, *Libertatis nuntius*, 4, 13.

Philemon

Greeting*

1 ¹Paul, a prisoner for Christ Jesus, and Timothy our brother,

To Philemon our beloved fellow worker ²and Apphia our sister and Archippus our fellow soldier, and the church in your house:

³Grace to you and peace from God our Father and the Lord Jesus Christ.

A plea on behalf of Onesimus

2 Cor 8:8; 9:7

[8]Accordingly, though I am bold enough in Christ to command you to do what is required, [9]yet for love's sake I prefer to appeal to you—I, Paul, an ambassador[a] and now a prisoner also for Christ Jesus—[10]I appeal to you for my child, Onesimus, whose father I have become in my imprisonment. [11](Formerly he was useless to you, but now he is indeed useful[b] to you and to me.) [12]I am sending him back to you, sending my very heart. [13]I would have been glad to keep him with me, in order that he might serve me on your behalf during my imprisonment for the gospel; [14]but I preferred to do nothing without your consent in order that your goodness might not be by compulsion but of your own free will.

1 Cor 4:15
Col 4:9
Gal 4:19

Phil 2:30

2 Cor 9:7
1 Pet 5:2

1 Tim 6:2

Col 3:22—4:1

[15]Perhaps this is why he was parted from you for a while, that you might have him back for ever, [16]no longer as a slave but more than a slave, as a beloved brother, especially to me but how much more to you, both in the flesh and in the Lord. [17]So if you consider me your partner, receive him as you would receive me. [18]If he has wronged you at all, or owes you anything, charge that to my account. [19]I, Paul, write this with my own hand, I will repay it—to say nothing of your owing me even your own self. [20]Yes, brother, I want some benefit from you in the Lord. Refresh my heart in Christ.

Gal 6:11
2 Thess 3:17
Col 4:18
1 Cor 9:11

cro, cum sim talis ut Paulus senex, nunc autem et vinctus Christi Iesu; [10]obsecro te de meo filio, quem genui in vinculis, Onesimo, [11]qui tibi aliquando inutilis fuit, nunc autem et tibi et mihi utilis, [12]quem remisi tibi: eum, hoc est viscera mea; [13]quem ego volueram mecum detinere, ut pro te mihi ministraret in vinculis evangelii. [14]Sine consilio autem tuo nihil volui facere, uti ne velut ex necessitate bonum tuum esset sed voluntarium. [15]Forsitan enim ideo discessit ad horam, ut aeternum illum reciperes, [16]iam non ut servum sed plus servo, carissimum fratrem, maxime mihi, quanto autem magis tibi et in carne et in Domino. [17]Si ergo habes me socium, suscipe illum sicut me. [18]Si autem aliquid nocuit tibi aut debet, hoc mihi imputa. [19]Ego Paulus scripsi mea manu, ego reddam; ut non dicam tibi quod et teipsum mihi debes. [20]Ita, frater! Ego te fruar in Domino;

8–21 St Paul begot Onesimus, this fugitive slave of Philemon's, in the faith. The Apostle plays on the meaning of the word "*onesimus*" (useful) in order to intercede on the man's behalf with his old master and to have Philemon take him back again.

We should remember that the Apostle brought the Gospel message to all sorts of people, making no distinction on grounds of class or social status; in fact, he had special regard for people who were disadvantaged; in contrast to views held by so many, in his day and ours, he did not see them as inferior in any way; for him they were dearly beloved brothers and sisters in the faith. "Look at Paul writing on behalf of Onesimus, a runaway slave; he is not ashamed to call him his child, his very heart, his brother" (St John Chrysostom, *In Philemonem ad loc.*).

The truth of the matter is that Christians are called to regard everyone as their brothers and sisters; they have the dignity of human persons and the rights that follow from that status. No Christian has a right to adopt any other attitude; if he or she did harbour prejudices of that sort, it would amount to committing a sin against God and against human society. Pope John Paul II made this point very clearly: "The term *social* applies to every sin against justice in interpersonal relationships, committed either by the individual against the community or by the community against the individual. Also *social* is every sin against the rights of the human person, beginning with the right to life and including the life of the unborn, or against a person's physical integrity. Likewise *social* is every sin against others' freedom, especially against the supreme freedom to believe in God and adore him; *social* is every sin against the dignity and honour of one's neighbour. Also *social* is every sin against the common good and its exigencies in relation to the whole broad spectrum of the rights and duties of citizens. The term *social* can be applied to sins of commission or omission—on the part of political, economic or trade union leaders, who though in a position to do so do not work diligently and wisely for the improvement and transformation of society according to the requirements and potential of the given historic moment; as also on the part of workers who

a Or *an old man*   b The name Onesimus meant *useful* or (compare verse 20) *beneficial*

²¹Confident of your obedience, I write to you, knowing that you will do even more than I say.

Words of farewell

²²At the same time, prepare a guest room for me, for I am hoping through your prayers to be granted to you.

Phil 2:24

²³Epaphras, my fellow prisoner in Christ Jesus, sends greetings to you, ²⁴and so do Mark, Aristarchus, Demas, and Luke, my fellow workers.

Col 1:7
Col 4:10, 14

²⁵The grace of the Lord Jesus Christ be with your spirit.

Gal 6:18
2 Tim 4:22

refice viscera mea in Christo! ²¹Confidens oboedientia tua scripsi tibi, sciens quoniam et super id, quod dico, facies. ²²Simul autem et para mihi hospitium, nam spero per orationes vestras donari me vobis. ²³Salutat te Epaphras, concaptivus meus in Christo Iesu, ²⁴Marcus, Aristarchus, Demas, Lucas, adiutores mei. ²⁵Gratia Domini Iesu Christi cum spiritu vestro.

through absenteeism or non-cooperation fail to ensure that their industries can continue to advance the well-being of the workers themselves, of their families, and of the whole of society" (*Reconciliatio et paenitentia*, 16).

21 The Apostle appeals, politely, for behaviour in keeping with the Gospel message. This is the "more" he asks of Philemon: he should treat Onesimus as a true brother in the faith, on an equal level, not discriminating against him. "Be convinced that justice alone is never enough to solve the great problems of mankind. When justice alone is done, don't be surprised if people are hurt. The dignity of man, who is a son of God, requires much more. Charity must penetrate and accompany justice because it sweetens and deifies everything: 'God is love' (1 Jn 4:16). Our motive in everything we do should be the Love of God, which makes it easier for us to love our neighbour and which purifies all earthly love and raises it on to a higher level" (St Josemaría Escrivá, *Friends of God*, 172).

22–25 These are the words of farewell, together with greetings from people who happen to be with Paul at the time of writing (they are mentioned also in Colossians 4:10–14). Obviously Philemon and his family were important members of the infant church at Colossae. The whole letter is a reminder of the significant role played by Christian families in the spread of the Gospel (cf. the note on Rom 16:1–23).

THE LETTER TO THE

HEBREWS

Introduction

The Letter to the Hebrews is one of the most important and sophisticated texts in the New Testament. It appears at the end of the Pauline letters, linking them with the Catholic Letters. Historically and doctrinally it has connexions with the letters of St Paul, being a faithful echo of his preaching. However, the elegance and technical perfection with which it is written, in polished, educated Greek, contrasts sharply with Paul's spontaneous, vigorous Greek and style. Moreover, the way in which this letter approaches its themes and, in particular, its treatment of the Old Testament are not the same as those found in writings by the Apostle. For these reasons doubts had already arisen in the first century of the Church with regard to the Pauline authorship of the letter, and on that account it was not easily accepted as Holy Writ by all the churches.

In the East it was widely accepted as Pauline from early on. St Polycarp was acquainted with it (though he does not name its author), and, according to Eusebius, Clement of Alexandria says that it was written by St Paul but translated from Hebrew by Luke.[1] Origen, in the second century, speculated that the letter was written by an editor using ideas provided by the true author, Paul. "The ideas of the epistle", the Alexandrian exegete writes, "certainly belong to the Apostle; however, the language and composition seem to belong to someone else, someone who wished to record Paul's thinking, as one writing down the words of the Master."[2] However, he acknowledges that "only God knows" who the actual writer was.[3] St John Chrysostom, who was a great admirer of the writings of the Teacher of the Gentiles, and who was very familiar with them, held that Paul was the author. Eusebius, having investigated church tradition on the matter, included the book in his list of canonical writings.[4]

In the West, on the other hand, the tradition was less unanimous. St Clement of Rome did make use of the letter, but without explicitly quoting from it. The author of the first Latin-language commentary on all the letters of St Paul, the anonymous writer known as "Ambrosiaster", does not comment on Hebrews. St Jerome himself touches on the question and expresses some doubts as to whether it can be directly attributed to St Paul—as does St Augustine. However, both Augustine and Jerome, with the passing of time and the increasing weight of tradition, came to accept not only that it is an inspired letter but also that it is Pauline.[5] Around the end of the fourth century Hebrews appears in the lists produced by African councils, and from the sixth to the sixteenth century the letter was unanimously regarded as Pauline. The Council of Trent solemnly pronounced it to be canonical and inspired.[6]

Some Renaissance scholars, among them Erasmus and Cardinal Cajetan, reopened the question of Pauline authorship. From that time onwards, most exegetes have been of the view that, at least in the Greek form that has come down to us, the letter was not written by St Paul. However, we should point out that this does not affect the letter's canonicity. The Letter to the Hebrews is an inspired, canonical book, one that is linked in many ways to Paul's teaching; we simply cannot say for certain who the author was.

---

1 Eusebius of Caesarea, *Historia ecclesiastica*, 6, 14, 2. **2** Ibid., 6, 25, 14. **3** Ibid. **4** Ibid., 3, 25, 2–3. **5** St Jerome, *Commentarium in Matthaeum*, 4, 26. **6** Session IV, 1546. See Dz-Sch, 2176.

1. STRUCTURE AND CONTENT

The literary structure of Hebrews has been the subject of much detailed study, but it has proven very difficult to define. Over the course of the letter, doctrinal, explanatory, parts alternate with passages of exhortation. The exhortatory parts, those about morals, are intentionally interwoven with the dogmatic material, truths of faith being presented as grounds for the lines of conduct the author proposes as being incumbent on Christians. From this point of view, the letter is a good illustration of the coherence that should exist between doctrine and life (so appropriate to the New Testament); it is a model of Christian religious writing.

The five doctrinal sections in the letter are readily identifiable:

1. Christ's pre-existence, his divinity and his activity as creator (1:1–4);
2. Christ's superiority over the angels (1:5—2:18);
3. Christ's superiority over Moses (3:1—4:13);
4. Christ's priesthood is on a higher level than the Levitical priesthood (4:14—7:28);
5. Christ's sacrifice is worth more than all the sacrifices of the Old Law (8:1—10:18).

The letter's ascetic, exhortatory and moral content, which is interlaced with the doctrinal parts, deals with the following themes:

1. To attain salvation, a person must follow Jesus (2:1–4).
2. We need to imitate those faithful souls who accepted Revelation, if we are to enter God's "rest" (3:7—4:13).
3. Joyful hope and rules for Christian living (5:11—6:20).
4. Reasons why a believer should persevere in the faith despite difficulties (10:19—12:29); and the good example set by people who have gone before.
5. A final appeal (13:1–19).

Verses 7–17 of chapter 13, which seem to sum up the main points of the letter, contain a final exhortation to the upright conduct and faithful witness that define the Christian life.

2. CONTEXT

The letter was written by an educated Christian of Jewish background, a person very familiar with the Scriptures and with the theological issues being debated at the time; he must also have been someone very close to St Paul in thinking and in the kind of apostolic work he engaged in. The content of the letter shows its author to have been a man of Hellenistic culture and great pastoral zeal, and someone steeped in the religious life of the Jewish people and the rites of the temple of Jerusalem. In writing, he seems to have deliberately effaced his own character and life in order not to detract attention from the sublimity and importance of his theme. Many attempts have been made to identify the author-editor; among the names put forward are Barnabas, Luke,

Clement of Rome, Philip, Silvanus, and the disciple Apollos (mentioned in Acts 18:24f). However, none of these hypotheses is entirely convincing.

The letter belongs to a mixed genre that combines the style of an ordinary letter with that of a written discourse or sermon (see 13:22, where the author speaks of his "word of exhortation"). Its structure and method of presentation is rather like those of a theological essay. Its majestic flow and the sublimity of its subject-matter explain why the Church makes such extensive use of it in her liturgy. It is written in very correct and elegant Greek; a rich vocabulary is used, and the author supports his argument with lots of stylistic devices, quotations and examples drawn from Holy Scripture. From a literary point of view this is the most accomplished piece of writing in the New Testament after the works of St Luke.

The title was probably not added until the second century, but it is very appropriate, given the nature and theme of the letter. It is very likely that the "Hebrews", the supposed addressees of the letter, were Christians of Jewish background who were familiar with both the Greek language and Jewish culture, particularly the rites of the temple at Jerusalem. The primary purpose of the letter is to show that Christianity is superior to the Old Law; however, neither the style nor the intention of the author is polemical.

The letter shows the New Law to be the perfection and fulfilment of the Old Law, which it also supersedes. The author focuses mainly on Christ's priesthood and sacrifice, to show that these are on a plane higher than that of Levitical priesthood and sacrifices; and this point provides the doctrinal basis for the writer's exhortations to his readers to persevere in the faith (the other main purpose of the letter).

As regards when the letter was written, the range AD 60 to 69 has been suggested, that is to say, prior to the destruction of Jerusalem by the Roman armies of Vespasian and Titus in the year 70, for no mention is made of the city's fall, and many passages in the letter imply that the temple and Mosaic worship continued unhindered and unchanged.[7] A substantial number of scholars opt for the year 67 as the date of composition. However, a later date in the first century cannot be ruled out—but no later than the decade of 90–100, when St Clement of Rome's first letter to the Corinthians was written (because that letter quotes from Hebrews).

Because of the message in 13:24 ("Those who come from Italy send you greetings"), Rome has been suggested as the place of composition. However, this remark could also be interpreted as a greeting from a group of Italian Christians who had moved from somewhere to live in a different city or place, one unknown to us, from which the letter is being sent. Palestine and Alexandria have also been proposed as possible points of origin for the letter.

3. MESSAGE

The teaching contained in the letter is centred on Christ. Jesus Christ, God and man and the High Priest of the New Law, is the focus of the letter, linking all its sections and giving a remarkable unity to the entire text.

Christology
The sacred writer's main theme is the redemption of mankind brought about by Jesus Christ the Mediator, through his sacrifice on the cross and the shedding of his blood. Christ is at one and the

---

7 See Heb 8:4; 9:7, 13, 25; 10:1–2; 13:11.

same time the perfect Victim who atones for all the sins of mankind and the true High Priest who offers to God the Father worship that is acceptable and everlasting. This theme is central to Pauline theology. However, in the opening verses, before entering into the subjects of redemption and priesthood, the author of the letter makes a brief but solemn proclamation of the eternal pre-existence of the Word, his role as creator, and his equality with the Father (see 1:1–3); these verses are reminiscent of what the prologue to St John's Gospel reveals about the Word.

In line with the general theme of the letter, that is, the salvation brought about by Jesus Christ, true God and true Man, the sacred writer concentrates on our Lord's priesthood, which not only places our Lord far beyond the angels, superior to the legislator of the Old Law, and higher, too, than the Levitical priesthood, but also reveals him to be superabundantly fitted to redeem mankind. The Redemption wrought by Christ is a universal remedy for a universal need.

Christ's sacrifice, unlike the Old Testament sacrifices, does not involve the ritual shedding of the blood of animals; it cannot be repeated; its saving effects have been produced once and for all. Christ's intercession on our behalf is infinite in its effectiveness. What each of the redeemed must do is apply to himself or herself, through faith, the effects of Christ's sacrifice, and grow in the charity that brings salvation.

Jesus Christ manifests who he is and his priestly role both in his self-abasement and in his glorification. Both are necessary to the performance of his role as priest and redeemer. His self-abasement and humiliation show us his utter obedience to the will of the Father; they also show the weight of temptation that pressed down on his human nature, and the extraordinary sufferings he experienced in the mortal flesh he chose to assume (cf. 5:7).

The sacred writer's reflections, full of emotion and pathos, reach a climax in the assertion that forms the core of the letter: "We have such a high priest, one who is seated at the right hand of the throne of the Majesty in heaven" (8:1). This central truth of Christian dogma is also, as the letter makes clear, a great encouragement to hope. In addition to showing Jesus and his work in terms of his eternal Priesthood and explaining the implications of his role as Priest and Redeemer, the writer applies to Christ four important titles—Son, Messiah, Jesus and Lord—each of which reveals different aspects of our Saviour. He is also given the titles of Sanctified, Heir, Mediator and Apostle (this in fact is the only place in the New Testament where the word "apostle" is used with reference to him). Thus, the sacred writer underlines the enduring importance of Christ as Priest and definitive Mediator for each and every Christian: "Jesus Christ is the same yesterday and today and forever" (13:8).

Judaism and Christianity

Without engaging in polemic, the sacred writer shows that the objective superiority of Christianity is the cornerstone of salvation history. The letter's line of argument is not designed to undermine or discredit the Jewish religion but rather to assign it its proper place as a preparatory stage in God's plan of salvation. The central idea of the letter is that the Mosaic Law was incapable of saving a mankind sunk in a fallen state because of Adam's sin. In line with this, it proclaims the temporary, transitional nature of the Old Law; Christ has abolished it and replaced it with the Law of the Gospel. This is another key idea in Pauline thought.

The superiority of the New Testament over the Old does not, however, affect the unity there is between them: they form a continuum. The letter reflects this unity mainly by its use of Old Testament figures or "types". All the Old Testament figures look to Christ and hope in him. Moses and Melchizedek are, respectively, "types" of the Messiah and Priest of the New Law.

Christianity is, then, the culmination of Judaism, so much so in fact that the Mosaic religion cannot be properly understood without reference to the Gospel.

Faith and Revelation

The Letter to the Hebrews is a "word of exhortation" (13:22) to persevere in the faith. There are many references to this theme in the letter, but Hebrews 11:1 offers an especially rich and concise definition of faith, one which has become classical in the commentaries of the Fathers and Doctors of the Church. Faith, as seen in the letter, is a habit or a disposition which moves a person to adhere firmly to what God has revealed and promised. But the content of these promises was Jesus Christ himself and the benefits he would obtain for mankind through his redemptive sacrifice. Faith, in fact, is anchored in Jesus, "the pioneer and perfecter of our faith" (12:2): he is the cause of our faith, and it is in him that we believe in the first instance. We start out from faith in Jesus, and we shall eventually see him face to face in heaven—hence faith's close connexion with hope. Faith in Christ is the foundation of Christian hope. Christ has entered heaven, thereby opening the way for all mankind to do so. That is why suffering makes sense; that is why it is worthwhile to endure affliction (cf. 10:19ff).

But faith in Christ is faith in Revelation; Christ is the fullest revelation of the Father. God has made himself manifest to us in his own Son, the perfect Word spoken by the Father to mankind.[8] Faith in Christ requires, therefore, that we not only believe in him, in his person, but also believe in his precepts and teachings. Hence the letter's numerous exhortations to Christian living which are closely interwoven with its dogmatic teaching; these exhortations derive naturally from belief in the Son of God and in what he has revealed to us.

Eschatology

The entire letter is imbued with a spirit of eschatology. It provides the key to interpreting the connexion between the provisional covenant of Judaism and the definitive covenant of Christianity. Judaism was a preparation for Christianity, and Christianity perfects and completes Mosaic religion. Christianity, for its part, has two dimensions: it begins here on earth but will find its true fulfilment only in heaven. It is true that the land promised to Abraham was Palestine, but the promise meant much more than that: it meant the grace of Christ, which is our pledge of heaven. The Promised Land, which we are all called to enter, is heaven. The exodus in which Moses led the people to take possession of the Promised Land was a foreshadowing of the journey of Christian life: Jesus, the new Moses, will lead his people into their definitive Homeland. Hence the letter's repeated exhortation to the followers of Moses: "Today, when you hear his voice, do not harden your hearts" (3:7; 4:7). This means a number of things: it is an invitation to make an act of faith, similar to Abraham's, that is, to enjoy, through faith, the peace, the rest, that grace provides; but it is also an invitation to stay faithful right to the end of our lives, and so enter the eternal rest of heaven. This focus on the other life beyond the grave runs right through the epistle. It contributes to a portrayal of the Christian life as a journey from salvation which is already brought about and which has yet to take its final form, towards the Kingdom of the future city, whose builder is God (see 11:10) and which is ruled over by Christ.

The sacred writer also speaks frequently of the second coming of Christ, the Parousia, when he will judge the living and the dead (see 10:25), and it announces the Judgment to come (see 10:27) and refers to the final re-creation of the world (see 12:26–28).

---

8 See Heb 1:1–2; Vatican II, *Dei Verbum*, 4.

The Christian's present life

The letter depicts Christians' life on earth as a pilgrimage towards their heavenly home, where they will "rest" in God. In keeping with this perspective, it frequently emphasizes faith and hope, virtues necessary to man while he is still a pilgrim. As we make our way towards heaven on this pilgrim journey, we will meet with obstacles and difficulties, but Christ will be our guide along the way. There is, we could say, an "exodus" theology here, seen from a Christian or New Testament perspective. Christians are engaged in a new exodus, in which they leave both Judaism and sin behind, and they have the conviction that they will indeed reach the true Promised Land (see 4:11; 9:11; 11:8–10; 13:14).

Hebrews

The greatness of the incarnate Son of God

1 ¹In many and various ways God spoke of old to our fathers by the prophets; ²but in these last days he has spoken to us by a Son, whom he appointed the heir of all things, through whom also he created the world. ³He reflects the glory of God and bears the very stamp of his nature, upholding the universe by his word of power. When he had made purification for sins, he sat down at the right hand of the Majesty on high, ⁴having become as much superior to angels as the name he has obtained is more excellent than theirs.*

Lk 1:55

Gal 4:4
Jn 1:3, 18; 10:34
Col 1:16
Wis 7:22–26
2 Cor 4:4
Col 1:17
Heb 8:1; 10:12
Ps 110:1
Mk 14:62
Phil 2:9
Eph 1:20f
1 Pet 3:22
Ps 113:5
Col 1:15
Mk 16:19

PART ONE

Excellence of the religion revealed by Christ*

1. CHRIST IS GREATER THAN THE ANGELS*

Proof from Holy Scripture

⁵ For to what angel did God ever say,

"Thou art my Son,

today I have begotten thee"?

Heb 5:5
Ps 2:7
2 Sam 7:14
1 Chron 17:13

[1]¹ Multifariam et multis modis olim Deus locutus patribus in prophetis, ²in novissimis his diebus locutus est nobis in Filio, quem constituit heredem universorum, per quem fecit et saecula; ³qui, cum sit splendor gloriae et figura substantiae eius et portet omnia verbo virtutis suae, purgatione peccatorum facta, consedit ad dexteram maiestatis in excelsis, ⁴tanto melior angelis effectus, quanto differentius prae illis nomen hereditavit.⁵Cui enim dixit aliquando angelorum: «*Filius meus es tu; / ego hodie genui te*» et rursum: «*Ego ero illi in patrem, et ipse erit mihi in filium*»?

1:1–4 Like the opening of St John's Gospel, the first four verses of this letter are a prologue identifying the theme that its author will go on to develop from different perspectives—the exalted status of Christ, God's own eternal Son, the universal Mediator, eternal Priest; after his sacrifice he was glorified and sat down at the right hand of the Father, receiving "the name which is above every name" (Phil 2:6–11; cf. Jn 1:3, 14). The "name he has obtained" (v. 4) is, then, that of "Son", which means that he is higher than the angels. The epistle is an exhortation to Christians to ground their entire lives on belief in Christ, the Son of God.

God has made himself known to mankind not just through prophets, as in times past, but through his Son (v. 2). Christ is spoken of here in language reminiscent of Old Testament passages about divine Wisdom (v. 3; cf. Wis 7:25–27). What in the Old Testament is presented as an attribute of God is now revealed as a divine

Person, the Word Incarnate. Jesus Christ is portrayed as the fullness of salvific revelation. Because he is the only, perfect and unsurpassable Word of the Father, there is no room or need for further revelation (cf. *Catechism of the Catholic Church*, 65). St John of the Cross comments on this passage in a very beautiful way: "The Apostle gives us to understand that God has rendered himself dumb because he has nothing left to say: what he said before in part, through the prophets, he has now said completely through him [Christ]" (*Ascent of Mount Carmel*, 2, 22, 4).

The liturgy of the Church uses this passage in the third Mass of Christmas Day, along with Isaiah 52:7–10 (the messenger's announcement of peace) and the prologue of the fourth Gospel (Jn 1:1–18).

***1:5—10:18** Although doctrinal and moral teachings are interwoven throughout the letter,

Or again,

"I will be to him a father,

and he shall be to me a son"?

Deut 32:43
Ps 97:7
1 Chron 17:13
Rom 8:29
Col 1:15–18
[6]And again, when he brings the first-born into the world, he says,

"Let all God's angels worship him."

Ps 104:4
[7]Of the angels he says,

"Who makes his angels winds,

and his servants flames of fire."

[8]But of the Son he says,

"Thy throne, O God,[a] is for ever and ever,

Ps 45:6–7
the righteous sceptre is the sceptre of thy[b] kingdom.

[9] Thou hast loved righteousness and hated lawlessness;

therefore God, thy God, has anointed thee

with the oil of gladness beyond thy comrades."

[10]And,

Ps 102:25–27
"Thou, Lord, didst found the earth in the beginning,

and the heavens are the work of thy hands;

Mt 24:35
[11]they will perish, but thou remainest;

Rev 6:14
[12]they will all grow old like a garment,

[6]Cum autem iterum introducit primogenitum in orbem terrae, dicit: «*Et adorent eum omnes angeli Dei*». [7]Et ad angelos quidem dicit: «*Qui facit angelos suos spiritus / et ministros suos flammam ignis*»; [8]ad Filium autem: «*Thronus tuus, Deus, in saeculum saeculi, / et virga aequitatis virga regni tui.* / [9]*Dilexisti iustitiam et odisti iniquitatem, / propterea unxit te Deus, Deus tuus, / oleo exsultationis prae participibus tuis*» [10]et: «*Tu in principio, Domine, terram fundasti; / et opera manuum tuarum sunt caeli.* / [11]*Ipsi peribunt, tu autem permanes; / et omnes ut vestimentum veterascent,* / [12]*et velut amictum involves eos,* / sicut vestimentum *et mutabuntur.* / *Tu autem idem es, et anni tui non deficient*». [13]Ad quem autem

the first ten chapters are mainly doctrinal in character: the sacred writer deals with Christ's superiority (as Son of God) over the main figures of the Old Testament—angels (1:5—2:18) and Moses (3:1—4:13)—and the superiority of his priesthood over that of the Old Law, both from the viewpoint of priesthood itself (4:14—7:28) and from that of sacrifice (8:1—10:18).

*1:5–2:18 The exposition begins by proving that Christ is greater than the angels (1:5–14). Because veneration of angels was widespread in the Jewish world (angels were seen as "sons of God" and mediators of the Law) there was a danger that because Christ had a human nature he would be seen as inferior to angels. Christ, being the Son of God (1:2, 5, 8) has a greater right to be obeyed than angels have (2:1–4). And because the Son is man, he is our brother and can mediate on our behalf (2:5–18).

1:5–14 These verses are very rich in Christological terms. The sacred writer links a series of quotations from the Old Testament to show that Jesus is the Messiah King and that he is the Son

of God, by nature as distinct from adoption (v. 5); the angels owe him worship because their nature is lower than his (vv. 6–7): he has the prerogatives of the Messiah King, the Anointed One (vv. 8–9), and it was through him that the world came into being (vv. 10–12). The role of the angels, on the other hand, is to serve God, in worship of him (vv. 7–8, 14). That is why St Thomas says, commenting on v. 7: "As ministers they are flames of fire, for of all the elements fire is the most active and most powerful" (*Super Hebraeos*, ad loc.). And Origen says: "We say that they [the angels] rise up to bring the prayers of men to the purest places of the world, the heavens. [...] And from there they descend, carrying the benefits that God has given them for each man as he deserves. [...] And so we call them angels or messengers because of their role" (*Contra Celsum*, 5, 4).

Verses 8–12 constitute one of the most important New Testament passages about the divinity of Jesus Christ (see also Jn 1:1; 20:28; Rom 9:5; Tit 2:13; 2 Pet 1:1). The words of Psalm 45:6–7 are interpreted as words of God the Father addressed to the Son; here Jesus

a Or *God is thy throne* b Other ancient authorities read *his*

like a mantle thou wilt roll them up,
and they will be changed.^c
But thou art the same,
and thy years will never end."

¹³ But to what angel has he ever said,
"Sit at my right hand,
till I make thy enemies
a stool for thy feet"?

Ps 110:1
Mt 22:44
Acts 2:33–35

¹⁴Are they not all ministering spirits sent forth to serve, for the sake of those who are to obtain salvation?

Ps 91:11
Mt 4:11; 18:10;
26–53
Dan 7:10
Tob 5:11
Lk 1:26

An appeal for faith

2 ¹Therefore we must pay the closer attention to what we have heard, lest we drift away from it. ²For if the message declared by angels* was valid and every transgression or disobedience received a just retribution, ³how shall we escape if we neglect such a great salvation? It was declared at first by the Lord, and it was attested to us by those who heard him, ⁴while God also bore witness by signs and wonders and various miracles and by gifts of the Holy Spirit distributed according to his own will.

Acts 8:6
2 Pet 3:17

Acts 7:53
Gal 3:19

Heb 12:25
Lk 1:2
1 Cor 1:6
Acts 10:37

Mk 16:20
Acts 1:8; 8:13
Rom 15:19
1 Cor 12:11
2 Cor 12:12

Jesus, man's brother, was crowned with glory and honour above the angels

⁵For it was not to angels that God subjected the world to come, of which we are speaking. ⁶It has been testified somewhere,

---

angelorum dixit aliquando: «*Sede a dextris meis, / donec ponam inimicos tuos scabellum pedum tuorum*»? ¹⁴Nonne omnes sunt administratorii spiritus, qui in ministerium mittuntur propter eos, qui hereditatem capient salutis?   [2] ¹Propterea abundantius oportet observare nos ea, quae audivimus, ne forte praeterfluamus. ²Si enim, qui per angelos dictus est, sermo factus est firmus, et omnis praevaricatio et inoboedientia accepit iustam mercedis retributionem, ³quomodo nos effugiemus si tantam neglexerimus salutem? Quae, cum initium accepisset enarrari per Dominum,

---

Christ is explicitly called "God", the name that in the New Testament is usually reserved for the Person of the Father. Similarly, in vv. 10–12 the words of Psalm 102:25–27, which originally were addressed to God the Creator, are applied to Christ. Something similar happens in v. 6 in connexion with the Greek translation of Deuteronomy 32:43. Christ's infinite superiority over the angels derives from the mystery of his being not only a man but God. Angels are created spiritual beings with a subordinate role in the plan of salvation. "Christ is the centre of the angelic world. [...] They belong to him because they were created *through* and *for* him [...]. They belong to him still more because he has made them messengers of his saving plan" (*Catechism of the Catholic Church*, 331; cf. the notes on Mk 1:1–13 and Acts 5:17–33).

2:1–4 Here the writer inserts an appeal based on the teaching he has just outlined. If Jesus is above the angels, more obedience is due to his teaching and Law than to "the message declared by angels" (v. 2), that is, the Law given to Moses

on Sinai, which, according to a Jewish tradition, was communicated through angels (cf. Gal 3:19). Hence the exhortation to be on guard against possible infidelity to the New Covenant established in Jesus Christ; for the divine word of salvation promulgated by him is infinitely precious. It is the greatest gift a human being can receive, because it equips one to know and praise God and at the same time attain one's own temporal and eternal happiness.

"It was attested to us by those who heard him" (v. 3): this is an explicit reference to the preaching of the apostles, which is what confirms and transmits the proclamation of salvation instituted by Christ's own preaching (cf. 1 Cor 11:23; 15:3).

On the spiritual, created nature of angels and on their subordinate mission in the plan of salvation, see the notes on Genesis 18:1–15 and 32:2–3.

2:5–18 Having spoken about the glory and divinity of Jesus Christ, the sacred writer now goes on to speak of his human nature and his self-emptying.

---

c Other ancient authorities add *like a garment*

Ps 8:4–6 (LXX)

"What is man that thou art mindful of him,
or the son of man, that thou carest for him?
[7]Thou didst make him for a little while lower than the angels,
thou hast crowned him with glory and honour,[d]

1 Cor 15:25–27
Eph 1:20–23
Phil 3:21
Phil 2:8–9

[8]putting everything in subjection under his feet."
Now in putting everything in subjection to him, he left nothing outside his control.
As it is, we do not yet see everything in subjection to him. [9]But we see Jesus, who
for a little while was made lower than the angels, crowned with glory and honour
because of the suffering of death, so that by the grace of God he might taste death
for every one.

Rom 11:36
1 Cor 8:6
Heb 5:9; 12:2
Acts 3:15

Heb 10:10; 13:12

Jn 17:6

[10]For it was fitting that he, for whom and by whom all things exist, in bringing
many sons to glory, should make the pioneer of their salvation perfect through suffering.* [11]For he who sanctifies and those who are sanctified have all one origin.
That is why he is not ashamed to call them brethren, [12]saying,

Is 8:17-18 (LXX)

"I will proclaim thy name to my brethren,
in the midst of the congregation I will praise thee."
[13]And again,
"I will put my trust in him."

ab eis, qui audierunt, in nos confirmata est, [4]contestante Deo signis et portentis et variis virtutibus et Spiritus Sancti distributionibus secundum
suam voluntatem. [5]Non enim angelis subiecit orbem terrae futurum, de quo loquimur. [6]Testatus est autem in quodam loco quis dicens: *«Quid est
homo, quod memor es eius, / aut filius hominis, quoniam visitas eum? / [7]Minuisti eum paulo minus ab angelis, / gloria et honore coronasti eum,
/ [8]omnia subiecisti sub pedibus eius»*. In eo enim quod ei omnia subiecit, nihil dimisit non subiectibile ei. Nunc autem necdum videmus omnia
subiecta ei; [9]eum autem, qui *paulo minus ab angelis minoratus est*, videmus Iesum propter passionem mortis *gloria et honore coronatum*, ut gratia
Dei pro omnibus gustaverit mortem. [10]Decebat enim eum, propter quem omnia et per quem omnia, qui multos filios in gloriam adduxit, ducem
salutis eorum per passiones consummare. [11]Qui enim sanctificat et qui sanctificantur, ex uno omnes; propter quam causam non erubescit fratres
eos vocare [12]dicens: *«Nuntiabo nomen tuum fratribus meis, / in medio ecclesiae laudabo te»*; [13]et iterum: *«Ego ero fidens in eum»*; et iterum: *«Ecce*

Christians ought to be faithful to Christ,
because, as well as being the cause and beginning of salvation, he has been made Lord of the
universe. To him, as man, all things have been
made subject, as has "the world to come" (v.
5)—an expression often used by Jews to refer to
the period immediately after the coming of the
Messiah. That world has begun with the resurrection and glorification of Jesus, but it will not
reach its fullness until his second coming (v. 8).

The words of Psalm 8 are applied to Christ
(words praising the greatness of God and the
dignity of man), because Christ is the perfection
of mankind; he is the perfect man, who in his
obedience and humility, his passion and death,
was made lower than the angels, but who
thereby merited to be crowned with glory and
honour (cf. Phil 2:6–11; 1 Pet 2:21–25). Thus, on
account of his sufferings (v. 9), Christ is the
Lord, and everything, even death itself (cf. 1 Cor
15:22–28), has been subjected to him.

The passage is one of the most beautiful texts
concerning the Incarnation. In order to bring
about the salvation of mankind, Jesus Christ had
to have, like them, a human nature. God the
Father made his Son "perfect through suffering"
(v. 10) in the sense that, by his becoming man,
and therefore able to suffer and die, he is entirely
equipped to be the representative of his
"brethren", all the members of the human race
(vv. 11–15). "He partook of the same food as we
do," writes Theodoret of Cyrrhus, "and he
worked; he experienced sadness in his soul and
shed tears; he suffered death" (*Interpretatio ad
Hebraeos*, ad loc.).

Being God and man, Jesus Christ is the only
mediator between God and mankind; he exercises this mediation as High Priest (v. 17), and,
through his love, bridges the abyss separating the
sinful stock of Adam from God. Christ's priesthood consists in making atonement by a sacrifice
of expiation and a peace-offering for the sins of
mankind; he takes our place and atones on our
behalf. His suffering strengthens us and sets us
an example as to how to deal with pain and difficulty (v. 18): "By taking our weaknesses upon

d Other ancient authorities insert *and didst set him over the works of thy hands*

And again,

"Here am I, and the children God has given me."

2 Sam 22:3

[14]Since therefore the children share in flesh and blood, he himself likewise partook of the same nature, that through death he might destroy him who has the power of death, that is, the devil, [15]and deliver all those who through fear of death were subject to lifelong bondage. [16]For surely it is not with angels that he is concerned but with the descendants of Abraham. [17]Therefore he had to be made like his brethren in every respect, so that he might become a merciful and faithful high priest in the service of God, to make expiation for the sins of the people. [18]For because he himself has suffered and been tempted, he is able to help those who are tempted.

Rom 8:3
1 Cor 15:54–56
1 Jn 3:8

Jn 3:8
Jn 12:31
Rom 5:12f
Rev 12:10
Is 41:8–10

Heb 5:1
Rom 3:25; 8:3, 29
1 Sam 2:35
Ex 4:16
1 Jn 2:2

1 Cor 10:13
Job 1:12–15
Mt 4:1–11
Lk 4:1–3
1 Jn 2:2; 4:10

2. CHRIST IS GREATER THAN MOSES*

Moses' ministry and that of Christ compared

3 [1]Therefore, holy brethren, who share in a heavenly call, consider Jesus, the apostle and high priest of our confession. [2]He was faithful to him who appointed him, just as Moses also was faithful in[e] God's house. [3]Yet Jesus has been counted worthy of as much more glory than Moses as the builder of a house has more honour than the house. [4](For every house is built by some one, but the builder of all things is God.) [5]Now Moses was faithful in all God's house as a servant, to testify to the

Eph 1:18; 4:1
Heb 11:16; 12:22
Phil 3:14
Heb 4:14; 10:23
Num 12:7
Heb 8:6
2 Cor 3:7–11
Acts 7:20–44

Ps 127:1
Num 12:7
Deut 34:10–12

ego et pueri, quos mihi dedit Deus». [14]Quia ergo pueri communicaverunt sanguini et carni, et ipse similiter participavit iisdem, ut per mortem destrueret eum, qui habebat mortis imperium, id est Diabolum, [15]et liberaret eos, qui timore mortis per totam vitam obnoxii erant servituti. [16]Nusquam enim angelos apprehendit, sed semen Abrahae apprehendit. [17]Unde debuit per omnia fratribus similari, ut misericors fieret et fidelis pontifex in iis, quae sunt ad Deum, ut repropitiaret delicta populi; [18]in quo enim passus est ipse tentatus, potens est eis, qui tentantur, auxiliari. [3] [1]Unde, fratres sancti, vocationis caelestis participes, considerate apostolum et pontificem confessionis nostrae Iesum, [2]qui fidelis est ei, qui fecit illum, sicut et Moyses in tota domo illius. [3]Amplioris enim gloriae iste prae Moyse dignus est habitus, quanto ampliorem honorem habet quam domus, qui fabricavit illam. [4]Omnis namque domus fabricatur ab aliquo; qui autem omnia fabricavit, Deus est. [5]Et Moyses quidem fidelis

himself Christ has obtained for us the strength to overcome our natural infirmity. On the night before his passion, by choosing to suffer fear, anguish and sorrow in the garden of Gethsemane he won for us strength to resist harassment by those who seek our downfall; he obtained for us strength to overcome the fatigue we experience in prayer, in mortification and in other acts of devotion, and, finally, the fortitude to bear adversity with peace and joy" (St Alphonsus Liguori, *Reflections on the Passion*, 9, 1).

*3:1—4:13 The Jews regarded Moses as the true founder, liberator and lawgiver of the Chosen People. These two chapters teach that Jesus Christ, the "new Moses", is greater than Moses (cf. the notes on Mt 2:13–18; 4:1–11; 5:17–48), because Christ is the Son and Moses the servant.

3:1–6 Starting out from the faithfulness of

Moses and, pre-eminently, that of Jesus, the sacred writer shows the superiority of the latter by using the metaphor of a house—sometimes in the sense of a building and on other occasions as an image of a family: the architect is greater than the house he builds, and the son of the house has more status than a servant on its staff. Our hope is grounded on Christ (v. 6).

The titles of "apostle" and "high priest" (v. 1) delineate the Son's mission in the world. Jesus is God's messenger or envoy to mankind, and he is man's representative before God (cf. Mal 2:7). St Justin says that "Christ is called messenger and apostle because he proclaims what must be made known and is sent to reveal what the Father has to tell us. The Lord himself gave us to understand this when he said, 'he who hears me, hears him who sent me'" (*Apologia*, 1, 63, 5). The Christian call is a "heavenly call" (v. 1); it comes from heaven and draws us to heaven; it is a personal call to follow Jesus in the Church.

e Other ancient authorities insert *all*

Josh 1:1–2
Jn 8:35
1 Cor 3:9
Eph 2:19
1 Pet 2:4–5
1 Tim 3:15
Heb 1:2; 3:14; 4:16;
10:23

Ps 95:8–11

Ex 17:7
Num 20:2–5

Num 14:21–23

Jer 16:10–13;
18:11–12
2 Thess 2:3

Heb 10:25
1 Thess 5:11
2 Thess 2:10

things that were to be spoken later, [6]but Christ was faithful over God's[f] house as a son. And we are his house if we hold fast our confidence and pride in our hope.[g]

The need for faith. The bad example given by the Chosen People

[7]Therefore, as the Holy Spirit says,

"Today, when you hear his voice,
    [8]do not harden your hearts as in the rebellion,
    on the day of testing in the wilderness,
    [9]where your fathers put me to the test
and saw my works for forty years.
    [10]Therefore I was provoked with that generation,
    and said, 'They always go astray in their hearts;
    they have not known my ways.'
    [11]As I swore in my wrath,
    'They shall never enter my rest.'"*

[12]Take care, brethren, lest there be in any of you an evil, unbelieving heart, leading you to fall away from the living God. [13]But exhort one another every day, as long as it is called "today," that none of you may be hardened by the deceitfulness of sin.

erat in tota domo eius tamquam *famulus* in testimonium eorum, quae dicenda erant, [6]Christus vero tamquam Filius super domum illius; cuius domus sumus nos, si fiduciam et gloriationem spei retineamus. [7]Quapropter, sicut dicit Spiritus Sanctus: «*Hodie, si vocem eius audieritis, / *[8]*nolite obdurare corda vestra sicut in exacerbatione, / secundum diem tentationis in deserto, /* [9]*ubi tentaverunt me patres vestri in probatione / et viderunt opera mea* [10]*quadraginta annos. / Propter quod infensus fui generationi huic / et dixi: Semper errant corde. / Ipsi autem non cognoverunt vias meas; /* [11]*sicut iuravi in ira mea: / Non introibunt in requiem meam*». [12]Videte, fratres, ne forte sit in aliquo vestrum cor malum incredulitatis discedendi a Deo vivo, [13]sed adhortamini vosmetipsos per singulos dies, donec illud «*hodie*» vocatur, ut non obduretur quis ex vobis fallacia peccati; [14]participes enim Christi effecti sumus, si tamen initium substantiae usque ad finem firmum retineamus, [15]dum dicitur: «*Hodie, si vocem eius*

3:7–19 Because of the discouragement that threatens his readers, the writer exhorts them to stay true to Christ. And, since his readers come from a Jewish background, he uses arguments from Scripture that draw on the life of Moses. Rest was prescribed in the Old Testament as an imitation of what God did when he finished his work of creation (see Gen 2:2; Ex 20:10–11). Similarly, the Exodus was seen as a kind of new creation, and it too was followed by a type of rest, that is, the attainment of the promised land. The author of the letter gives the Exodus a Christian interpretation: it was a foreshadowing of the redemption whereby Christ, like a new Moses, leads us to eternal rest. Hence the need to remain faithful. The writer quotes from Psalm 95, which contains a reference to a rebellion by the Israelites that took place in the wilderness when a shortage of water gave rise to complaints against God (see Ex 17:1–7), and he exhorts his readers to imitate those who stayed faithful at that time and put their faith in the promise that they would enter God's "rest". He makes the point that the word of the Holy Spirit is enduring;

it continues to apply "today" (v. 13). God punished the Israelites for not having faith in him and in Moses, and for all their complaints and disobedience; this fact should induce Christians of every era to be steadfast; for a Christian could, through infidelity, fail to attain eternal life. If people persist in not listening to God's calls, their resistance to grace can eventually lead to loss of faith. Unbelief is not normally something that happens all of a sudden; it is usually the outcome of a process of interior disobedience. Hence the need to continually respond to grace. The early Christians set a standard in this regard, preferring to die rather than "fall away from the living God" (v. 12). In the following words from St Justin we can see the holy pride he took in the lives and deaths of the early martyrs: "They cut our heads off, they nail us to crosses, they throw us to wild beasts, imprison us and burn us, and we submit to every kind of torture; yet everyone knows that we do not betray our faith. Rather, the worse our sufferings, the more there are who embrace faith and devotion in the name of Jesus" (*Dialogus cum Tryphone*, 110, 4).

f Greek *his* g Other ancient authorities insert *firm to the end*

¹⁴For we share in Christ, if only we hold our first confidence firm to the end, ¹⁵while it is said,

> "Today, when you hear his voice,
> do not harden your hearts as in the rebellion."

¹⁶Who were they that heard and yet were rebellious? Was it not all those who left Egypt under the leadership of Moses? ¹⁷And with whom was he provoked forty years? Was it not with those who sinned, whose bodies fell in the wilderness? ¹⁸And to whom did he swear that they should never enter his rest, but to those who were disobedient? ¹⁹So we see that they were unable to enter because of unbelief.

Heb 6:11; 11:1
Rom 7:11
Mk 4:19

Ps 95:8

Num 14:1–35
1 Cor 10:5–10
Ex 17:1ff
Num 14:29

Num 14:22

Heb 4:6

Through faith we can attain God's "rest"

4 ¹Therefore, while the promise of entering his rest remains, let us fear lest any of you be judged to have failed to reach it. ²For good news came to us just as to them; but the message which they heard did not benefit them, because it did not meet with faith in the hearers.ʰ ³For we who have believed enter that rest, as he has said,

Ps 95:11
1 Thess 2:13
Judg 1:21–25
1 Cor 10:1–13

> "As I swore in my wrath,
> 'They shall never enter my rest,'"

Heb 3:11; 12:15

Ps 95:11

although his works were finished from the foundation of the world. ⁴For he has somewhere spoken of the seventh day in this way, "And God rested on the seventh day from all his works." ⁵And again in this place he said,

Gen 2:1–3

> "They shall never enter my rest."

Ps 95:11

⁶Since therefore it remains for some to enter it, and those who formerly received the good news failed to enter because of disobedience, ⁷again he sets a certain day, "Today," saying through David so long afterward, in the words already quoted,

Heb 3:9

---

audieritis, / nolite obdurare corda vestra quemadmodum in illa exacerbatione». ¹⁶Qui sunt enim qui audientes exacerbaverunt? Nonne universi, qui profecti sunt ab Aegypto per Moysen? ¹⁷Quibus autem *infensus fuit quadraginta annos?* Nonne illis, qui peccaverunt, quorum *membra ceciderunt in deserto?* ¹⁸Quibus autem *iuravit non introire in requiem ipsius,* nisi illis, qui increduli fuerunt? ¹⁹Et videmus quia non potuerunt introire propter incredulitatem. [4] ¹Timeamus ergo, ne forte, relicta pollicitatione introeundi in requiem eius, existimetur aliquis ex vobis deesse; ²etenim et nobis evangelizatum est quemadmodum et illis, sed non profuit illis sermo auditus, non commixtis fide cum iis, qui audierant. ³Ingredimur enim in requiem, qui credidimus, quemadmodum dixit: *«Sicut iuravi in ira mea: / Non introibunt in requiem meam»,* et quidem operibus ab institutione mundi factis. ⁴Dixit enim quodam loco de die septima sic: *«Et requievit Deus die septima ab omnibus operibus suis»;* ⁵et in isto rursum: *«Non introibunt in requiem meam».* ⁶Quoniam ergo superest quosdam introire in illam, et hi, quibus prioribus evangelizatum est, non introierunt propter inoboedientiam, ⁷iterum terminat diem quendam, «Hodie», in David dicendo post tantum temporis, sicut supra dictum est:

4:1–11 Developing what he has just said in 3:18–19, the writer repeats his call to faithfulness, and extends the comparison of Christ and Moses to Israelites and Christians. Moses had tried to get the people of Israel to stay true to God and thereby enter their place of rest (see Deut 12:9–10). He laid down the precept of sabbath rest (see Deut 5:12–15; Ex 20:8–11; 35:1–3; Num 15:32–36) as a memorial of God's day of rest after the work of creation, as a sign of the Covenant and as a symbol of eternal rest (v. 4). However, the people failed to obtain that rest, and did not even manage to do so when they eventually entered the promised land under the leadership of Joshua (v. 8). They were found lacking in faith (v. 2) and obedience (v. 6). The promise sung in Psalm 95 (written

after the people had reached the promised land) remains open, even "today" (see vv. 1 and 7). And, since Christ promised a new, definitive rest—life in his Father's house (cf. Jn 14:1–3)—Christians have been given a further invitation by God to enter divine rest (vv. 2–3). Another "today" begins, another point when we can attain the true Promised Land, as a reward for our fidelity: "This, indeed, will be that ultimate sabbath that has no evening and which the Lord foreshadowed in the account of his creation [...]. Only when we are remade by God and perfected by a greater grace shall we have the eternal stillness of that rest in which we shall see that he is God. Then only shall we be filled with him when he will be all in all" (St Augustine, *De civitate Dei*, 22, 30). Loss of this promised

---

ʰ Other manuscripts read *they were not united in faith with the hearers*

Ps 95:8

"Today, when you hear his voice,
do not harden your hearts."

Deut 31:7
Josh 22:4
⁸For if Joshua had given them rest, God[i] would not speak later of another day. ⁹So
Gen 2:2
Rev 14:13
Ps 95:11
then, there remains a sabbath rest for the people of God; ¹⁰for whoever enters God's
rest also ceases from his labours as God did from his.

¹¹Let us therefore strive to enter that rest, that no one fall by the same sort of disobedience.

The power of God's word

1 Pet 1:23
Rev 1:16
Is 49:2
Wis 7:22–30
Jn 12:48
1 Pet 1:23
Rev 1:16
¹²For the word of God is living and active, sharper than any two-edged sword, piercing
to the division of soul and spirit, of joints and marrow, and discerning the thoughts and
intentions of the heart. ¹³And before him no creature is hidden, but all are open and laid
bare to the eyes of him with whom we have to do.

Job 34:21–22
Wis 1:6–11
Ps 33:13–15

3. CHRIST, OUR HIGH PRIEST, IS GREATER THAN THE PRIESTS OF THE MOSAIC LAW*

Our confidence is based on Christ's priesthood

Heb 3:1; 6:20; 7:26;
8:1; 9:11, 24; 5:5, 10
¹⁴Since then we have a great high priest who has passed through the heavens, Jesus,
Mt 4:1–11
Rom 8:1–4
the Son of God, let us hold fast our confession. ¹⁵For we have not a high priest who

«Hodie, si vocem eius audieritis, / nolite obdurare corda vestra». ⁸Nam si eis Iesus requiem praestitisset, non de alio loqueretur posthac die.
⁹Itaque relinquitur sabbatismus populo Dei; ¹⁰qui enim ingressus est in requiem eius, etiam ipse requievit ab operibus suis, sicut a suis Deus. ¹¹Fes-
tinemus ergo ingredi in illam requiem, ut ne in idipsum quis incidat inoboedientiae exemplum. ¹²Vivus est enim Dei sermo et efficax et penetra-
bilior omni gladio ancipiti et pertingens usque ad divisionem animae ac spiritus, compagum quoque et medullarum, et discretor cogitationum et
intentionum cordis; ¹³et non est creatura invisibilis in conspectu eius, omnia autem nuda et aperta sunt oculis eius, ad quem nobis sermo.
¹⁴Habentes ergo pontificem magnum, qui penetravit caelos, Iesum Filium Dei, teneamus confessionem. ¹⁵Non enim habemus pontificem, qui non
possit compati infirmitatibus nostris, tentatum autem per omnia secundum similitudinem absque peccato; ¹⁶adeamus ergo cum fiducia ad thronum

"rest" is the only thing a person should truly
fear.

4:12–13 To enter this rest, one needs to accept
the Word of God. In these verses, the "word"
may mean Revelation as a whole, which finds its
fullest and most perfect form in Jesus Christ, on
whom the life of the Church is grounded: "Such
is the force and power of the Word of God that it
can serve the Church as her support and vigour,
and the children of the Church as strength for
their faith, food for the soul, and a pure and lasting fount of spiritual life" (Vatican II, *Dei
Verbum*, 21).

The Word is said to be living and active; but
there is also something in it that inspires fear and
reverence; it is not to be taken lightly. The depths
of a person's heart, his deepest thoughts, attitudes and intentions, lie open to God's all-seeing
eye. Commenting on this passage, Baldwin of
Canterbury observes: "[The word of God is]

sharper than any two-edged sword for anyone
who believes in it and loves it. Nothing is impossible for the one who believes, nor difficult for
the one who loves. When the word of God rings
out, it pierces the heart of the believer like an
arrow and penetrates to depths of the soul. The
word of God is sharper than any two-edged
sword; it cuts deeper than any other power or
force; it is more subtle than any human strata-
gem, more penetrating than all the wisdom and
wise words of the learned" (*Tractatus*, 6).

*4:14—7:28 The main theme of the epistle—the
priesthood of Christ—is dealt with in this section; his priesthood is greater than that of priests
of the Mosaic Law.

4:14–16 A Christian should put all his trust in the
new high priest, Christ, who has entered heaven,
and in his mercy, for he sympathizes with our
weakness: "The believers were at that time in a

i Greek *he*

is unable to sympathize with our weaknesses, but one who in every respect has been _{2 Cor 5:21} _{Jn 8:46}
tempted as we are, yet without sin. ¹⁶Let us then with confidence draw near to the _{Heb 10:19–23, 25f} _{Rom 3:25}
throne of grace, that we may receive mercy and find grace to help in time of need. _{2 Cor 5:21} _{1 Jn 3:21}

Christ has been made high priest by God the Father

5 ¹For every high priest chosen from among men is appointed to act on behalf of _{Heb 2:17; 7:28; 8:3–4}
men in relation to God, to offer gifts and sacrifices for sins. ²He can deal gently _{Heb 4:15}
with the ignorant and wayward, since he himself is beset with weakness. ³Because of _{Lev 9:7–24; 16:6, 15} _{Ex 28:1–5}
this he is bound to offer sacrifice for his own sins as well as for those of the people. _{Jn 3:27}
⁴And one does not take the honour upon himself, but he is called by God, just as Aaron
was. ⁵So also Christ did not exalt himself to be made a high priest, but was appointed _{Ps 2:7} _{Heb 1:5; 4:14}
by him who said to him,

gratiae, ut misericordiam consequamur et gratiam inveniamus in auxilium opportunum. [5] ¹Omnis namque pontifex ex hominibus assumptus pro hominibus constituitur in his, quae sunt ad Deum, ut offerat dona et sacrificia pro peccatis, ²qui aeque condolere possit his, qui ignorant et errant, quoniam et ipse circumdatus est infirmitate ³et propter eam debet, quemadmodum et pro populo, ita etiam pro semetipso offerre pro peccatis. ⁴Nec quisquam sumit sibi illum honorem, sed qui vocatur a Deo tamquam et Aaron. ⁵Sic et Christus non semetipsum glorificavit, ut pon-

storm of temptation; that is why the Apostle is consoling them, saying that our high priest not only knows, as God, the weakness of our nature: as man, he has also experienced the sufferings that affect us, although he was free from sin. Since he knows our weakness so well, he can give us the help we need, and when he comes to judge us, he will take that weakness into account in his sentence" (Theodoret of Cyrrhus, *Interpretatio ad Hebraeos*, ad loc.). We should respond to the Lord's goodness by staying true to our profession of faith.

The fact that Christ could not commit sin, to which Holy Scripture attests (cf. Jn 8:46; Rom 8:2; 2 Cor 5:21; 1 Pet 1:19; 2:21–24), is a logical consequence of his divinity and of his integrity and human holiness. The weakness of Christ, "who in every respect has been tempted as we are" (v. 15), a condition that he chose to experience on account of his love for us, is the reason why we can be confident that he will give us the strength to resist sin. "What security should be ours in considering the mercy of the Lord! 'He has but to cry for redress, and I, the ever merciful, will listen to him' (Ex 22:27). It is an invitation, a promise that he will not fail to fulfill. 'Let us then with confidence draw near to the throne of grace, that we may receive mercy and find grace to help in time of need' (Heb 4:16). The enemies of our sanctification will be rendered powerless if the mercy of God goes before us. And if through our own fault and human weak-

ness we should fall, the Lord comes to our aid and raises us up" (St Josemaría Escrivá, *Christ Is Passing By*, 7).

5:1–10 Christ is the high priest, a high priest who is truly able to free us from sin. In fact, he is the only perfect Priest: other priests (in natural religions as well as in the Jewish religion) are only prefigurements of Christ. Jesus Christ is the true priest, for he was chosen by God (vv. 5–6; cf. Ex 28:1–5), just as Aaron was, but not according to the "order" of the Levitical priesthood, to which Aaron belonged (see Ex 4:14; Num 3:1–10); Christ belongs to a higher order, the order of Melchizedek (see 5:11–14; 7:1–28). The term "order" is used here in the sense it had for the Romans, meaning a specific rank in the army or in a civil institution. The word was used mainly in respect of the ranks charged with duties of governance. This meaning of the term found its way into the Church in the expression "the sacrament of Orders". The words of v. 1 are a precise and succinct definition of what a priest is. "The proper office of the priest is to be a mediator between God and man, in so far as, on the one hand, he gives the divine things to the people, from which the name 'sacerdos' [priest] comes, 'he who gives the sacred things …', and, on the other, he offers to God the prayers of the people, and makes reparation for the sins of the people against God" (St Thomas Aquinas, *Summa theologiae*, 3, 22, 1).

Heb 7:1–28

Ps 110:4

Mt 26:36–46
Mk 14:32–42
Lk 22:39–46

Phil 110:4

Heb 9:12

Ps 110:4

> "Thou art my Son,
>   today I have begotten thee";*
> ⁶as he says also in another place,
> "Thou art a priest for ever,
>   after the order of Melchizedek."

⁷In the days of his flesh, Jesus[j] offered up prayers and supplications, with loud cries and tears, to him who was able to save him from death, and he was heard for his godly fear. ⁸Although he was a Son, he learned obedience through what he suffered; ⁹and being made perfect he became the source of eternal salvation to all who obey him, ¹⁰being designated by God a high priest after the order of Melchizedek.

The need for religious instruction

Heb 6:1
1 Cor 3:1–3

1 Pet 2:2

¹¹About this we have much to say which is hard to explain, since you have become dull of hearing. ¹²For though by this time you ought to be teachers, you need some

tifex fieret, sed qui locutus est ad eum: *«Filius meus es tu; / ego hodie genui te»*; ⁶quemadmodum et in alio dicit: *«Tu es sacerdos in aeternum secundum ordinem Melchisedech»*. ⁷Qui in diebus carnis suae, preces supplicationesque ad eum, qui possit salvum illum a morte facere, cum clamore valido et lacrimis offerens et exauditus pro sua reverentia, ⁸et quidem cum esset Filius, didicit ex his, quae passus est, oboedientiam; ⁹et, consummatus, factus est omnibus oboedientibus sibi auctor salutis aeternae, ¹⁰appellatus a Deo pontifex *iuxta ordinem Melchisedech*. ¹¹De quo grandis nobis sermo et ininterpretabilis ad dicendum, quoniam segnes facti estis ad audiendum. ¹²Etenim cum deberetis magistri esse propter tempus, rursum indigetis, ut vos doceat aliquis elementa exordii sermonum Dei, et facti estis, quibus lacte opus sit, non solido cibo. ¹³Omnis enim,

The letter says that Christ exercised his priesthood especially in his passion (vv. 7–10). As high priest, he interceded for mankind by his prayer: the sacred writer uses expressions that are reminiscent of Christ's agony in Gethsemane (see Mt 26:39 and par.); and he offered himself in a redemptive sacrifice by dying on the cross in perfect obedience to his Father's will. Therefore there is no contradiction between the fact that he was heard by the Father (v. 7) and the fact that he suffered (v. 8), for Jesus did not ask God the Father to save him from death; he prayed that his Father's will be done (see Mk 14:36). His obedience was so pleasing to the Father that Jesus, by dying, caused death's defeat; he was "made perfect [and] he became the source of eternal salvation" (v. 9). The *Catechism of the Catholic Church*, 2825, quotes v. 8 and adds: "How much more reason have we sinful creatures to learn obedience—we who in him have become children of adoption. We ask our Father to unite our will to his Son's, in order to fulfill his will, his plan of salvation for the life of the world. We are radically incapable of this, but united with Jesus and with the power of his Holy Spirit, we can surrender our will to him and decide to choose what his Son has always chosen: to do what is pleasing to the Father (cf. Jn 8:29)".

The Church uses vv. 5 and 7–9 (along with

4:15–16) in the Good Friday liturgy prior to the reading of the Passion.

5:11—6:3 Before developing further the teaching he has given in 5:1–10, the writer interrupts the thread of his discourse to make another short exhortation. He sees himself as the teacher and spiritual father of his readers. Like little children, they need to deepen their knowledge of the first principles of the faith, because they are as yet unprepared to grasp the "word of righteousness", that is, the mystery of justification (see Rom 6:16; 9:30). He invites his readers to become spiritually adult, for a Christian needs to attain the wisdom and maturity of the perfect human being, to the measure of the stature and fullness of Christ (see Eph 4:13; 1 Cor 14:20; Col 1:28).

In 6:1–3 we find a summary of the teachings that should be explained (and which need to be accepted) before a person is baptized; these are basic truths, from which one can proceed to grow in knowledge of Jesus Christ. "The laying on of hands" refers to the outpouring of the Holy Spirit, which comes about in a special way through the sacraments (see Acts 8:17; 19:6; 1 Tim 4:14; 5:22; 2 Tim 1:6; Jas 5:14). This passage is a constant encouragement to Christians to study the teaching given by the Church in her catechesis.

j Greek *he*

one to teach you again the first principles of God's word. You need milk, not solid food; ¹³for every one who lives on milk is unskilled in the word of righteousness, for he is a child. ¹⁴But solid food is for the mature, for those who have their faculties trained by practise to distinguish good from evil.

6 ¹Therefore let us leave the elementary doctrine of Christ and go on to maturity, not laying again a foundation of repentance from dead works and of faith toward God, ²with instruction^k about ablutions, the laying on of hands, the resurrection of the dead, and eternal judgment. ³And this we will do if God permits.^l

The danger of apostasy and the need for perseverance

⁴For it is impossible* to restore again to repentance those who have once been enlightened, who have tasted the heavenly gift, and have become partakers of the Holy Spirit, ⁵and have tasted the goodness of the word of God and the powers of the age to come, ⁶if they then commit apostasy, since they crucify the Son of God on their own account and hold him up to contempt. ⁷For land which has drunk the rain that often falls upon it, and brings forth vegetation useful to those for whose sake it is cultivated, receives a blessing from God. ⁸But if it bears thorns and thistles, it is worthless and near to being cursed; its end is to be burned.

Marginal references:
1 Cor 3:1–3; 13:9–12
Eph 4:13f
Gen 2:17
Rom 16:19
Phil 1:10
1 Cor 2:14–16
Heb 9:14
Mt 3:2
Acts 20:21
Acts 6:6
1 Tim 4:14
2 Tim 1:6
Heb 10:32
1 Pet 2:3
Rom 5:5
Mt 12:31–32
2 Pet 2:20–22
1 Jn 5:16–17
Gen 1:11f
Mk 4:20
2 Tim 2:6
Heb 10:26–31; 12:17
Gen 1:11–12
Gen 3:17f
Mt 7:16

qui lactis est particeps, expers est sermonis iustitiae, parvulus enim est; ¹⁴perfectorum autem est solidus cibus, eorum, qui pro consuetudine exercitatos habent sensus ad discretionem boni ac mali. [6] ¹Quapropter praetermittentes inchoationis Christi sermonem ad perfectionem feramur, non rursum iacientes fundamentum paenitentiae ab operibus mortuis et fidei ad Deum, ²baptismatum doctrinae, impositionis quoque manuum, ac resurrectionis mortuorum et iudicii aeterni. ³Et hoc faciemus siquidem permiserit Deus. ⁴Impossibile est enim eos, qui semel sunt illuminati, gustaverunt etiam donum caeleste et participes sunt facti Spiritus Sancti ⁵et bonum gustaverunt Dei verbum virtutesque saeculi venturi ⁶et prolapsi sunt, rursus renovari ad paenitentiam rursum crucifigentes sibimetipsis Filium Dei et ostentui habentes. ⁷Terra enim saepe venientem super se bibens imbrem et generans herbam opportunam illis propter quos et colitur, accipit benedictionem a Deo; ⁸*proferens* autem *spinas ac tribulos*

6:4–12 Christian maturity (see 6:1) implies a responsibility. Christians have been "enlightened", that is, they have received Baptism, "which is the principle of spiritual rebirth whereby the mind is enlightened by faith" (St Thomas Aquinas, *Super Hebraeos*, ad loc.). Christians have been filled with the "heavenly gift", that is, the Holy Spirit himself, who fills the soul with sweetness (see 1 Pet 2:3), and they have tasted the goodness of the Gospel and that power of the Kingdom of God which will reach its climax with the second coming of Christ. Therefore, if they were to intentionally and persistently reject the Son of God, it would not be possible for them to be converted again (vv. 4–6). This is not to say that no forgiveness is available to those who commit apostasy; the problem lies in the fact that the sin itself is a rejection of God's mercy. This teaching is reminiscent of what our Lord said about sins against the Holy Spirit (see the note on Mt 12:22–37), and what the Second Letter of Peter has to say about apostasy (see 2 Pet 2:20–22). The parable of the good

soil and the barren soil reinforces this exhortation (vv. 7–8). Even so, in the midst of this dramatic warning comes a very positive invitation to trust in God (vv. 9–12). God is not unjust, he does not forget his own, and, if they are steadfast, he will reward them: "Eternal life should be set before those who persevere in good works 'to the end' (cf. Mt 10:22) and who hope in God; it should be set before them as being the grace that God, through Jesus Christ, has mercifully promised his sons and 'as the reward' which, according to God's personal undertaking, most assuredly will be given them for their good works and merits (cf. St Augustine, *De natura et gratia*, 8, 20)" (Council of Trent, *De iustificatione*, chap. 16).

6:6 These words are a striking reminder for us that not only apostates, but all sinners, are the cause of Christ's passion and death; as long as we remain turned away from him, we crucify Christ again and insult him because we show contempt for the fruit of our Lord's passion. "In

k Other ancient manuscripts read *of instruction*   l Other ancient manuscripts read *let us do this if God permits*

Col 1:3–4
1 Thess 1:3
Eph 1:15
Heb 3:14
2 Cor 8:4
Rom 12:11–12
1 Cor 11:1
Eph 1:11–13
Gal 3:14, 29
1 Cor 11:1
Phil 3:17; 4:9

⁹Though we speak thus, yet in your case, beloved, we feel sure of better things that belong to salvation. ¹⁰For God is not so unjust as to overlook your work and the love which you showed for his sake in serving the saints, as you still do. ¹¹And we desire each one of you to show the same earnestness in realizing the full assurance of hope until the end, ¹²so that you may not be sluggish, but imitators of those who through faith and patience inherit the promises.

The promises made to Abraham were confirmed by oath and cannot be broken

Rom 4:20
Gen 22:16

Gen 22:17
Sir 44:21
Rom 4:19–21

¹³For when God made a promise to Abraham, since he had no one greater by whom to swear, he swore by himself, ¹⁴saying, "Surely I will bless you and multiply you." ¹⁵And thus Abraham,ᵐ having patiently endured, obtained the promise. ¹⁶Men indeed swear by a greater than themselves, and in all their disputes an oath is final for confirmation.

Num 23:19
1 Sam 15:29
Col 1:5
Tit 1:2
2 Tim 2:13
Lev 16:2, 12, 15
Heb 9:3; 10:20
Mt 27:51
Heb 1:2; 5:10

¹⁷So when God desired to show more convincingly to the heirs of the promise the unchangeable character of his purpose, he interposed with an oath, ¹⁸so that through two unchangeable things, in which it is impossible that God should prove false, we who have fled for refuge might have strong encouragement to seize the hope set before us. ¹⁹We have this as a sure and steadfast anchor of the soul, a hope that enters into the

reproba est et *maledicto* proxima, cuius finis in combustionem. ⁹Confidimus autem de vobis, dilectissimi, meliora et viciniora saluti, tametsi ita loquimur; ¹⁰non enim iniustus Deus, ut obliviscatur operis vestri et dilectionis, quam ostendistis nomini ipsius, qui ministrastis sanctis et ministratis. ¹¹Cupimus autem unumquemque vestrum eandem ostentare sollicitudinem ad expletionem spei usque in finem, ¹² ut non segnes efficiamini, verum imitatores eorum, qui fide et patientia hereditant promissiones. ¹³Abrahae namque promittens Deus, quoniam neminem habuit, per quem iuraret maiorem, *iuravit per semetipsum* ¹⁴dicens: «*Utique benedicens benedicam te et multiplicans multiplicabo te*»; ¹⁵et sic longanimiter ferens adeptus est repromissionem. ¹⁶Homines enim per maiorem sui iurant, et omnis controversiae eorum finis ad confirmationem est iuramentum; ¹⁷in quo abundantius volens Deus ostendere pollicitationis heredibus immobilitatem consilii sui, se interposuit iure iurando, ¹⁸ut per duas res immo-

her Magisterial teaching of the faith and in the witness of her saints, the Church has never forgotten that 'sinners were the authors and the ministers of all the sufferings that the divine Redeemer endured' (*Roman Catechism* I, 5, 11). […] 'Nor did demons crucify him; it is you who have crucified him and crucify him still, when you delight in your vices and sins' (St Francis of Assisi, *Admonitio* 5, 3)" (*Catechism of the Catholic Church*, 598).

6:13–20 God is worthy of our trust (see 6:9–12), because he is faithful to his promises. We can see this from the life of Abraham, to whom God bound himself by oath. That promise, which is evidence of his unswerving intention, was the basis of the Israelites' hope (vv. 13–18). "Through two unchangeable things" (v. 18)—that is, the oath and the promise, God being the swearer and the guarantor. Therefore, the promise and God's oath are an anchor (v. 19) of faith, a source of reassurance at all times. Christians, who are Abraham's true descendants through faith (see Rom 4:12) and the recipients of his promise (see Gal 3:14, 16, 29), can be confident,

therefore, that God will stay true to his promise. Their hope should not waver, because it is based on the enduring nature of Christ's sacrifice and priesthood. In the Old Covenant, the high priest went behind the curtain of the temple on one day a year—the Day of Atonement—and entered the Holy of Holies, the inner shrine (see v. 19); but Christ, by his sacrifice on the cross, entered the true Shrine of heaven and made it possible for all to follow him. The passage says that the Christians should "seize the hope set before us" (v. 18). Hope, in some way, puts one in possession of what has been promised: it is "a sure and steadfast anchor" (v. 19), "for just as the anchor thrown overboard prevents the ship from moving, and keeps it in one place even if it is being battered by countless winds, hope has the same effect" (St John Chrysostom, *In Hebraeos* 11).

From the early centuries onwards, the anchor has been used in Christian art as a symbol, not just of safety at a human level, but as an expression of faith in the resurrection of our Lord and of personal resurrection born of close union with Christ.

m Greek *he*

inner shrine behind the curtain, [20]where Jesus has gone as a forerunner on our behalf, having become a high priest for ever after the order of Melchizedek.

Ps 110:4

Jesus Christ is a priest after the order of Melchizedek

7 [1]For this Melchizedek, king of Salem, priest of the Most High God, met Abraham returning from the slaughter of the kings and blessed him; [2]and to him Abraham apportioned a tenth part of everything. He is first, by translation of his name, king of righteousness, and then he is also king of Salem, that is, king of peace. [3]He is without father or mother or genealogy, and has neither beginning of days nor end of life,* but resembling the Son of God he continues a priest for ever.

Gen 14:17−20

*Mt 3:31−35
Jn 1:1−2; 7:27−28;
8:19
Ps 110:4*

Melchizedek's priesthood is greater than that of Abraham's line

[4]See how great he is! Abraham the patriarch gave him a tithe of the spoils. [5]And those descendants of Levi who receive the priestly office have a commandment in the law to take tithes from the people, that is, from their brethren, though these also are descended from Abraham. [6]But this man who has not their genealogy received

*Gen 14:20
Num 18:21−32
Deut 14:22−29
Gen 14:20*

biles, in quibus impossibile est mentiri Deum, fortissimum solacium habeamus, qui confugimus ad tenendam propositam spem, [19]quam sicut ancoram habemus animae, tutam ac firmam et incedentem usque in interiora velaminis, [20]ubi praecursor pro nobis introivit Iesus, *secundum ordinem Melchisedech* pontifex factus *in aeternum.* [7] [1]Hic enim *Melchisedech, rex Salem, sacerdos Dei summi,* qui *obviavit Abrahae regresso a caede regum et benedixit ei,* [2]cui et *decimam omnium* divisit *Abraham,* primum quidem, qui interpretatur rex iustitiae, deinde autem et *rex Salem,* quod est rex Pacis, [3]sine patre, sine matre, sine genealogia, neque initium dierum neque finem vitae habens, assimilatus autem Filio Dei, manet sacerdos in perpetuum. [4]Intuemini autem quantus sit hic, cui et decimam dedit de praecipuis Abraham patriarcha. [5]Et illi quidem, qui de filiis Levi sac-

7:1−3 After the exhortation, and linking with 6:20, where Melchizedek is mentioned, the writer returns to his main theme (see 5:1−10)— the superiority of Christ's priesthood over that of the Old Law. Now he argues his point on the basis of the higher status of Melchizedek's priesthood. He refers to two passages from the Old Testament (Gen 14:17−20 and Ps 110), both of which speak of a mysterious king without father or mother or genealogy. Psalm 110:4 says that David belongs to an eternal priesthood. It is an eternal priesthood in the sense that God, who is faithful to his promises, promised David an enduring throne (see 2 Sam 7:16), that of Jerusalem. This throne had priestly dignity and status, but the dignity it had was one in accord with the status (the "order") of Melchizedek, who had blessed the faith of the people, in Abraham (Gen 14:17−20). David's priesthood does not come via family descent (as was the case with the Levitical priesthood), but derives directly from God. Thus, Melchizedek can be seen as a figure or type of Christ, as Messiah King and Son of God, clothed in a priesthood higher than the Levitical priesthood.

7:4−19 The tithes and blessing show that

Melchizedek is greater than Abraham. Melchizedek, who is not of the line of Abraham (see v. 6), received tithes from the latter (v. 9), and Abraham was blessed by him, which shows that Melchizedek was superior to him (v. 7). The conclusion is clear: since Melchizedek was greater than Abraham (and, therefore, than the Levites, Abraham's descendants) and Christ's priesthood belongs to the order of Melchizedek (see 5:10), Christ's priesthood is superior to that of the Levites.

The author then emphasizes another aspect of his teaching (vv. 11−19): the superiority of Christ's priesthood can be seen in its "perfection", that is, in its effectiveness. The priesthood of the order of Levi did serve God and man in accord with the Mosaic Law, but it could not open the way to God for men; therefore, a new priesthood was needed—not according to the order of Aaron, or by "bodily descent" (linked to the tribe of Levi: vv. 12−16), but to the order established "by the power of an indestructible life" (v. 16), that is, through the grace of resurrection. The Law was designed, so to speak, to announce a future, better, law (that of Christ), one full of hope, which opens the gates of eternal life (v. 19).

tithes from Abraham and blessed him who had the promises. ⁷It is beyond dispute that the inferior is blessed by the superior. ⁸Here tithes are received by mortal men; there, by one of whom it is testified that he lives. ⁹One might even say that Levi himself, who receives tithes, paid tithes through Abraham, ¹⁰for he was still in the loins of his ancestor when Melchizedek met him.

Gen 14:17

¹¹Now if perfection had been attainable through the Levitical priesthood (for under it the people received the law), what further need would there have been for another priest to arise after the order of Melchizedek, rather than one named after the order of Aaron? ¹²For when there is a change in the priesthood, there is necessarily a change in the law as well. ¹³For the one of whom these things are spoken belonged to another tribe, from which no one has ever served at the altar. ¹⁴For it is evident that our Lord was descended from Judah, and in connection with that tribe Moses said nothing about priests.

Ps 110:4

Heb 8:6

Is 11:1, 10
Mic 5:1–3
Lk 1:78
Rom 1:3
Rev 5:5

¹⁵This becomes even more evident when another priest arises in the likeness of Melchizedek, ¹⁶who has become a priest, not according to a legal requirement concerning bodily descent but by the power of an indestructible life. ¹⁷For it is witnessed of him,

Heb 5:6; 6:20
Rom 1:4

Ps 110:4

> "Thou art a priest for ever,
> after the order of Melchizedek."

¹⁸On the one hand, a former commandment is set aside because of its weakness and uselessness ¹⁹(for the law made nothing perfect); on the other hand, a better hope is introduced, through which we draw near to God.

Rom 7:7

Heb 9:9; 11:40
Rom 8:3

erdotium accipiunt, mandatum habent decimas sumere a populo secundum legem, id est a fratribus suis, quamquam et ipsi exierunt de lumbis Abrahae; ⁶hic autem, cuius generatio non annumeratur in eis, decimam sumpsit ab Abraham, et eum, qui habebat repromissiones, benedixit. ⁷Sine ulla autem contradictione, quod minus est, a meliore benedicitur. ⁸Et hic quidem decimas morientes homines sumunt, ibi autem testimonium accipiens, quia vivit. ⁹Et ut ita dictum sit, per Abraham et Levi, qui decimas accipit, decimatus est, ¹⁰adhuc enim in lumbis patris erat, quando *obviavit ei Melchisedech*. ¹¹Si ergo consummatio per sacerdotium leviticum erat, populus enim sub ipso legem accepit, quid adhuc necessarium *secundum ordinem Melchisedech* alium surgere *sacerdotem* et non *secundum ordinem* Aaron dici? ¹²Translato enim sacerdotio, necesse est, ut et legis translatio fiat. ¹³De quo enim haec dicuntur, ex alia tribu est, ex qua nullus altari praesto fuit; ¹⁴manifestum enim quod ex Iuda ortus sit Dominus noster, in quam tribum nihil de sacerdotibus Moyses locutus est. ¹⁵Et amplius adhuc manifestum est, si *secundum* similitudinem *Melchisedech* exsurgit alius *sacerdos*, ¹⁶qui non secundum legem mandati carnalis factus est sed secundum virtutem vitae insolubilis, ¹⁷testimonium enim accipit: «*Tu es sacerdos in aeternum secundum ordinem Melchisedech*». ¹⁸Reprobatio quidem fit praecedentis mandati propter infirmitatem eius et inutilitatem, ¹⁹nihil enim ad perfectum adduxit lex, introductio vero melioris spei, per quam proximamus ad Deum. ²⁰Et quantum non est sine iure iurando, illi quidem sine iure iurando sacerdotes facti sunt, ²¹hic autem cum iure iurando per eum, qui dicit ad illum: «*Iuravit Dominus et non paenitebit eum:*

7:20–28 The superiority of Christ's priesthood is further proven by the fact that it endures forever and there is no other. Since Christ has the priesthood of Melchizedek in the way that corresponds to God's oath in Psalm 110:4, his priesthood is everlasting and unique. Christ is the only true high priest: whereas previously there were many Levitical high priests because "they were prevented by death from continuing in office" (v. 23), Jesus always lives to intercede for us (v. 25).

The end of the passage sums up and rounds off the point. Christ's holiness and self-offering made his sacrifice effective once and for all (vv. 26–27). The oath—the new and definitive word of God which replaces the Old Law—has made the Son a high priest who "has been made perfect for ever" (v. 28). Christ, so to speak, is forever offering to the Father the sacrifice of his patience and humility, his obedience and his love. That is why it is possible for us to approach him at any time to find salvation: "Through Christ and in the Holy Spirit, a Christian has access to the intimacy of God the Father, and he spends his life looking for the Kingdom which is not of this world, but which is initiated and prepared in this world" (St Josemaría Escrivá, *Christ Is Passing By*, 116). Christ's priesthood is the ground and source of all ministerial priesthood in the Church. "The redemptive sacrifice of Christ is unique, accomplished once for all; yet it is made present in the Eucharistic sacrifice of the Church. The same

Christ is perfect high priest and his priesthood endures forever

²⁰And it was not without an oath. ²¹Those who formerly became priests took their office without an oath, but this one was addressed with an oath,

> "The Lord has sworn
>
> and will not change his mind,
>
> 'Thou art a priest for ever.'"

²²This makes Jesus the surety of a better covenant.

²³The former priests were many in number, because they were prevented by death from continuing in office; ²⁴but he holds his priesthood permanently, because he continues for ever. ²⁵Consequently he is able for all time to save those who draw near to God through him, since he always lives to make intercession for them.

²⁶For it was fitting that we should have such a high priest, holy, blameless, unstained, separated from sinners, exalted above the heavens. ²⁷He has no need, like those high priests, to offer sacrifices daily, first for his own sins and then for those of the people; he did this once for all when he offered up himself. ²⁸Indeed, the law appoints men in their weakness as high priests, but the word of the oath, which came later than the law, appoints a Son who has been made perfect for ever.

Ps 110:4

Heb 8:6–9:15; 12:24

Ps 110:4

Rom 8:34
1 Jn 2:1
Rev 1:18
Heb 9:24; 10:19

Heb 3:1

Heb 9:25–26;
10:11–14
Ex 29:38–42
Lev 9:7; 16:6, 11, 15
Num 28:3–8

Heb 5:1–29

4. CHRIST'S SACRIFICE IS MORE EXCELLENT THAN ALL THE SACRIFICES OF THE OLD LAW

Christ is high priest of a New Covenant, which replaces the Old

8 ¹Now the point in what we are saying is this: we have such a high priest, one who is seated at the right hand of the throne of the Majesty in heaven, ²a minister in the sanctuary and the true tentⁿ which is set up not by man but by the Lord. ³For every high priest is appointed to offer gifts and sacrifices; hence it is necessary for

Ps 2:7; 110:4
Heb 4:14; 6:20; 10:12

Mt 22:44
Mk 16:19
Acts 2:33
Eph 1:20
Ps 110:1

Heb 5:1

/ *Tu es sacerdos in aeternum*», ²²in tantum et melioris testamenti sponsor factus est Iesus. ²³Et illi quidem plures facti sunt sacerdotes, idcirco quod morte prohibebantur permanere; ²⁴hic autem eo quod manet in aeternum, intransgressibile habet sacerdotium, ²⁵unde et salvare in perpetuum potest accedentes per semetipsum ad Deum, semper vivens ad interpellandum pro eis. ²⁶Talis enim et decebat, ut nobis esset pontifex, sanctus, innocens, impollutus, segregatus a peccatoribus et excelsior caelis factus, ²⁷qui non habet necessitatem cotidie, quemadmodum pontifices, prius pro suis delictis hostias offerre, deinde pro populi; hoc enim fecit semel semetipsum offerendo. ²⁸Lex enim homines constituit pontifices infirmitatem habentes, sermo autem iuris iurandi, quod post legem est, Filium in aeternum consummatum. [8] ¹Caput autem super ea, quae dicuntur: talem habemus pontificem, qui consedit in dextera throni Maiestatis in caelis, ²sanctorum minister et tabernaculi veri, quod fixit Dominus, non homo. ³Omnis enim pontifex ad offerenda munera et hostias constituitur; unde necesse erat et hunc habere aliquid, quod offerret. ⁴Si ergo esset super

is true of the one priesthood of Christ; it is made present through the ministerial priesthood without diminishing the uniqueness of Christ's priesthood" (*Catechism of the Catholic Church*, 1545).

*8:1–10:18 The text now demonstrates the superiority of Christ's priesthood from the point of view of sacrifice, which is the essential and specific function of a priest. The Old Covenant finds its perfection and fulfilment in Christ: in the Old Covenant God was worshipped by means of sacrifices and offerings; now that Christ has come, the New Covenant begins, with a new sacrifice and a new temple.

8:1–13 The fact that Jesus is a high priest (v. 1; cf. 7:1–28) leads the writer to formally proclaim the key "argument" or teaching of the epistle — the superiority of Christ's priesthood. Christ exercises his ministry in heaven, at the right hand of the Majesty on high (v. 1; cf. 1:3), in a new sanctuary and a new tabernacle or tent, the "true" one (v. 2), unlike the sanctuary and tent of Moses (cf. Ex 25:40), which were only a foreshadowing of the truth. For this reason, too, the Levitical priests who served in the "shadow" sanctuary (v. 5) have a lesser ministry than Christ's; whereas the high priest (who is not explicitly named until 9:11), performs a more

n Or *tabernacle*

Heb 7:13

Heb 9:23; 10:1
Acts 7:44
Rev 11:19

Ex 25:40

Heb 7:22; 9:15;
12:24
1 Tim 2:5

1 Cor 11:25
Mt 26:28

Jer 31:31–34

Ex 19:5f

Heb 10:16
Ex 6:4–8
2 Cor 3:2; 6:16–18

Hos 6:6

this priest also to have something to offer. [4]Now if he were on earth, he would not be a priest at all, since there are priests who offer gifts according to the law. [5]They serve a copy and shadow of the heavenly sanctuary; for when Moses was about to erect the tent,[n] he was instructed by God, saying, "See that you make everything according to the pattern which was shown you on the mountain." [6]But as it is, Christ[o] has obtained a ministry which is as much more excellent than the old as the covenant he mediates is better, since it is enacted on better promises. [7]For if that first covenant had been faultless, there would have been no occasion for a second.

[8]For he finds fault with them when he says:

"The days will come, says the Lord,
when I will establish a new covenant with the house of Israel
and with the house of Judah;
[9]not like the covenant that I made with their fathers
on the day when I took them by the hand
to lead them out of the land of Egypt;
for they did not continue in my covenant,
and so I paid no heed to them, says the Lord.
[10]This is the covenant that I will make with the house of Israel
after those days, says the Lord:
I will put my laws into their minds,
and write them on their hearts,
and I will be their God,
and they shall be my people.
[11]And they shall not teach every one his fellow
or every one his brother, saying, 'Know the Lord,'
for all shall know me,
from the least of them to the greatest.*

terram, nec esset sacerdos, cum sint qui offerant secundum legem munera; [5]qui figurae et umbrae deserviunt caelestium, sicut responsum est Moysi, cum consummaturus esset tabernaculum: «*Vide* enim, inquit, *omnia facies secundum exemplar, quod tibi ostensum est in monte*». [6]Nunc autem differentius sortitus est ministerium, quanto et melioris testamenti mediator est, quod in melioribus repromissionibus sancitum est. [7]Nam si illud prius culpa vacasset, non secundi locus inquireretur; [8]vituperans enim eos dicit: «*Ecce dies veniunt, dicit Dominus, et consummabo super domum Israel et super domum Iudae testamentum novum;* [9]*non secundum testamentum, quod feci patribus eorum, in die, qua apprehendi manum illorum, ut educerem illos de terra Aegypti; quoniam ipsi non permanserunt in testamento meo, et ego neglexi eos, dicit Dominus.* [10]*Quia hoc est testamentum, quod testabor domui Israel post dies illos, dicit Dominus, dando leges meas in mentem eorum, et in corde eorum superscribam eas; et ero eis in Deum, et ipsi erunt mihi in populum.* [11]*Et non docebit unusquisque civem suum, et unusquisque fratrem suum dicens: "Cognosce Dominum"; quoniam omnes scient me, a minore usque ad maiorem eorum,* [12]*quia propitius ero iniquitatibus eorum et peccatorum illorum iam*

excellent mediation (v. 6), because he offered on the cross a sacrifice that sealed a New Covenant. Christ, in heaven, continually offers to the Father the fruit of his sacrifice on the cross. That heavenly liturgy is also made present in earthly liturgy, especially in the Sacrifice of the Mass. In it, Jesus Christ, the only Priest of the New Law, offers through priests, his ministers, the same victim—his own self, which was immolated in a bloody manner, once and for all, on the cross. "In the earthly liturgy we take part in a foretaste of that heavenly liturgy which is celebrated in the Holy City of Jerusalem toward which we journey as pilgrims, where Christ is sitting at the

right hand of God, Minister of the holies and of the true tabernacle" (Vatican II, *Sacrosanctum Concilium*, 8).

The words of Jeremiah 31:31–34, which prophesy God's making a New Covenant between himself and his people on account of their persistent infringement of the Covenant of Sinai, have been borne out by the Covenant established by Jesus: this is that New Covenant in which God truly forgives men's sins and remembers them no more. The Old Covenant was not "faultless", that is to say, it was imperfect (v. 7); it could not put people on truly intimate terms with God (v. 10).

n Or *tabernacle* o Greek *he*

¹²For I will be merciful toward their iniquities,
        and I will remember their sins no more."

Heb 10:17

¹³In speaking of a new covenant he treats the first as obsolete. And what is becoming obsolete and growing old is ready to vanish away.

2 Cor 5:17
Rev 21:4f

The rites of the Old Covenant prefigure those of the New

9 ¹Now even the first covenant had regulations for worship and an earthly sanctuary. ²For a tent[p] was prepared, the outer one, in which were the lampstand and the table and the bread of the Presence;[q] it is called the Holy Place. ³Behind the second curtain stood a tent[p] called the Holy of Holies, ⁴having the golden altar of incense and the ark of the covenant covered on all sides with gold, which contained a golden urn holding the manna, and Aaron's rod that budded, and the tables of the covenant; ⁵above it were the cherubim of glory overshadowing the mercy seat. Of these things we cannot now speak in detail.

Ex 25:22, 30, 40
2 Chron 13:11
Mk 2:25–26
Ex 26:31–33

Ex 16:32–34;
25:10–22; 10:22
Deut 9:9; 10: 3–5

Ex 25:18, 22

⁶These preparations having thus been made, the priests go continually into the outer tent,[p] performing their ritual duties; ⁷but into the second only the high priest goes, and he but once a year, and not without taking blood which he offers for himself and for the errors of the people. ⁸By this the Holy Spirit indicates that the way into the sanctuary is not yet opened as long as the outer tent is still standing ⁹(which is symbolic for the present age). According to this arrangement, gifts and sacrifices are offered which cannot perfect the conscience of the worshipper, ¹⁰but deal only

Num 18:3–7

Ex 30:10
Lev 16:2, 11f
Heb 7:27

Heb 10:20

Heb 10:1–2; 11:40
1 Cor 10:6

Lev 11:2; 15:18
Num 19:11–22
Col 2:16f

non memorabor». ¹³Dicendo «*novum*» veteravit prius; quod autem antiquatur et senescit, prope interitum est.   [9] ¹Habuit ergo et prius praecepta cultus et Sanctum huius saeculi. ²Tabernaculum enim praeparatum est primum, in quo inerat candelabrum et mensa et propositio panum, quod dicitur Sancta; ³post secundum autem velamentum, tabernaculum, quod dicitur Sancta Sanctorum, ⁴aureum habens turibulum et arcam testamenti circumtectam ex omni parte auro, in qua urna aurea habens manna et virga Aaron, quae fronduerat, et tabulae testamenti, ⁵superque eam cherubim gloriae obumbrantia propitiatorium; de quibus non est modo dicendum per singula. ⁶His vero ita praeparatis, in prius quidem tabernaculum semper intrant sacerdotes sacrorum officia consummantes, ⁷in secundum autem semel in anno solus pontifex, non sine sanguine, quem offert pro suis et populi ignorantiis, ⁸hoc significante Spiritu Sancto, nondum propalatam esse sanctorum viam, adhuc priore tabernaculo habente statum; ⁹quae parabola est temporis instantis, iuxta quam munera et hostiae offeruntur, quae non possunt iuxta conscientiam perfectum facere servientem, ¹⁰solummodo in cibis et in potibus et variis baptismis, quae sunt praecepta carnis usque ad tempus correctionis imposita. ¹¹Christus autem cum

9:1–10 To show the excellence of the sacrifice of the New Covenant, to which the text has just referred (see 8:13), the author now describes the sanctuary of the Old Law—the tabernacle or tent in which the Lord dwelt when the people of Israel were making their way through the wilderness after their escape from Egypt and during their early years in the promised land (see Ex 25:1—26:36). He also refers (v. 7) to the liturgy that took place in it for the expiation of sins—the sacrifice on the Day of Atonement or Yom Kippur (see Lev 16:1–34; 23:26–32; Num 29:7–11). Along with the Passover, Pentecost, Tabernacles and the festival of the New Year, Yom Kippur, which was celebrated on 10/11 Tishri (September–October), was one of the great Jewish festivals; on it all Israel was reconciled to God by means of purification and the forgiveness of sins committed during the previous year which had not yet been atoned for.

The author shows that Old Testament worship was ineffective; it was only a prefigurement of a new form of worship, at the centre of which stands the atoning sacrifice offered by Christ, the only sacrifice that can sanctify man (open the way into the sanctuary, that is, the way to God), the only sacrifice that can "perfect the conscience of the worshipper" (v. 9). Symbolic of the inability of the old form of worship to bring about man's justification was the fact that there was another tent that prevented access to the inner tent. Now that the curtain or veil blocking man's way has ceased to exist, he is in a position to attain union with God, holiness, which is symbolized by entry into the "Holy of Holies". By his death, Christ tore the curtain (cf. Mt 27:51). He is the Way (see Jn 14:6), the Gate (see Jn 10:7), by which we can enter the heavenly sanctuary.

p Or *tabernacle*   q Greek *the presentation of the loaves*

with food and drink and various ablutions, regulations for the body imposed until the time of reformation.

Christ sealed the New Covenant with his blood once and for all

Heb 8:2; 9:24
2 Cor 5:1

[11]But when Christ appeared as a high priest of the good things that have come,[r] then through the greater and more perfect tent[p] (not made with hands, that is, not of this

Heb 7:27; 9:19; 10:4;
13:12
Rom 3:24
Mt 20:28
Lk 24:21

creation) [12]he[s] entered once for all into the Holy Place, taking not the blood of goats and calves but his own blood, thus securing an eternal redemption. [13]For if the sprin-

Dan 9:24
Lev 16:3, 14f
Num 19:1–10, 17–22

kling of defiled persons with the blood of goats and bulls and with the ashes of a heifer sanctifies for the purification of the flesh, [14]how much more shall the blood of

Heb 6:1
1 Pet 1:18f
1 Jn 1:7

Christ, who through the eternal Spirit offered himself without blemish to God, purify your[t] conscience from dead works to serve the living God.

Heb 7:22; 8:6; 12:24
1 Tim 2:5
Gal 3:19; 4:1–7

[15]Therefore he is the mediator of a new covenant, so that those who are called may receive the promised eternal inheritance, since a death has occurred which redeems

Gal 3:15-18

them from the transgressions under the first covenant.[u] [16]For where a will is involved, the death of the one who made it must be established. [17]For a will[u] takes effect only at

Ex 24:3–8
Lev 14:4
Num 19:6

death, since it is not in force as long as the one who made it is alive. [18]Hence even the first covenant was not ratified without blood. [19]For when every commandment of the

advenit pontifex futurorum bonorum, per amplius et perfectius tabernaculum, non manufactum, id est non huius creationis, [12]neque per sanguinem hircorum et vitulorum sed per proprium sanguinem introivit semel in Sancta, aeterna redemptione inventa. [13]Si enim sanguis hircorum et tauro-rum et cinis vitulae aspersus inquinatos sanctificat ad emundationem carnis, [14]quanto magis sanguis Christi, qui per Spiritum aeternum semetip-sum obtulit immaculatum Deo, emundabit conscientiam nostram ab operibus mortuis ad serviendum Deo viventi. [15]Et ideo novi testamenti mediator est, ut, morte intercedente, in redemptionem earum praevaricationum, quae erant sub priore testamento, repromissionem accipiant, qui vocati sunt aeternae hereditatis. [16]Ubi enim testamentum, mors necesse est afferatur testatoris; [17]testamentum autem in mortuis est confirmatum, nondum enim valet, dum vivit, qui testatus est. [18]Unde ne prius quidem sine sanguine dedicatum est; [19]enuntiato enim omni mandato secundum

9:11–28 In the Old Law, the shedding of blood was required in sacrifices of reconciliation or purification and as part of a pact or covenant. The sacred writer shows that Christ's priestly mediation is the only one that can win forgive-ness for mankind and give people access to God, because he shed his own blood to ratify the New Covenant (vv. 11–14), and by his risen body (the "tent": v. 11; cf. Jn 2:19–22) opened for us the gates of heaven. "The eternal Spirit" (v. 14) may refer to the Godhead present in Christ or to the Holy Spirit, who "acted in a special way in this absolute self-giving of the Son of Man, in order to transform this suffering into redemptive love" (John Paul II, *Dominum et Vivificantem*, 40). Christians can also make their lives a sacrifice to God, by uniting themselves to Christ's sacrifice: "Through Him, who was so great as to sacrifice Himself for us, our sacrifice is made pleasing in the eyes of God" (St Fulgentius of Ruspe, *Epis-tulae*, 14, 36).

As the RSV note points out, the Greek word (*diatheke*) in vv. 15–17 can be translated as either "covenant" or "will". This word, which lit-

erally means a "disposition", was the word used in Greek translations of the Old Testament for the covenant made on Sinai. The author of Hebrews uses both these meanings—pact and last will (disposition, testament)—to explain that Christ's death on the cross was a true covenant sacrifice, like that made on Sinai (vv. 18–22; cf. Ex 24:3–8). He also teaches that Christ's death is God's last disposition: he has willed man heaven as his inheritance (vv. 15 and 28).

The entire passage reveals the redemptive power of Christ's blood; this is something that should move our hearts, as it has moved the hearts of saints: "We should focus our minds and hearts on the blood of Christ and on how pre-cious it is to his Father because, since it has been shed for our sake, it has won the grace of repen-tance for the whole world" (St Clement of Rome, *Ad Corinthios*, 7, 4). "Do you want to discover by yet another means the power of this blood [of Christ]? Notice where it flows from, and what its source is. It began to flow from the cross itself, and its source was the Lord's side. [...] The soldier pierced his side, the wall of the

p Or *tabernacle*   r Other manuscripts read *good things to come*   s Greek *through*   t Other manuscripts read *our*   u The Greek word here used means both *covenant* and *will*

law had been declared by Moses to all the people, he took the blood of calves and goats, with water and scarlet wool and hyssop, and sprinkled both the book itself and all the people, ²⁰saying, "This is the blood of the covenant which God commanded you." ²¹And in the same way he sprinkled with the blood both the tentᵖ and all the vessels used in worship. ²²Indeed, under the law almost everything is purified with blood, and without the shedding of blood there is no forgiveness of sins.

²³Thus it was necessary for the copies of the heavenly things to be purified with these rites, but the heavenly things themselves with better sacrifices than these. ²⁴For Christ has entered, not into a sanctuary made with hands, a copy of the true one, but into heaven itself, now to appear in the presence of God on our behalf. ²⁵Nor was it to offer himself repeatedly, as the high priest enters the Holy Place yearly with blood not his own; ²⁶for then he would have had to suffer repeatedly since the foundation of the world. But as it is, he has appeared once for all at the end of the age to put away sin by the sacrifice of himself. ²⁷And just as it is appointed for men to die once, and after that comes judgment, ²⁸so Christ, having been offered once to bear the sins of many, will appear a second time, not to deal with sin but to save those who are eagerly waiting for him.

The sacrifices of the Old Covenant could not take away sins

10 ¹For since the law has but a shadow of the good things to come instead of the true form of these realities, it can never, by the same sacrifices which are continually offered year after year, make perfect those who draw near.* ²Otherwise,

Marginal refs: Mt 26:28; Ex 24:8; Lev 8:15, 19; Ex 40:9; Lev 17:11; Eph 1:7; Heb 8:5; 9:11; Heb 7:25; Heb 7:27; Gal 4:4; 1 Tim 3:16; 1 Pet 1:20; 3:18; Jn 1:29; Heb 7:19; 8:5; Col 2:17

legem a Moyse universo populo, accipiens sanguinem vitulorum et hircorum cum aqua et lana coccinea et hyssopo, ipsum librum et omnem populum aspersit ²⁰dicens: «Hic sanguis testamenti, quod mandavit ad vos Deus»; ²¹etiam tabernaculum et omnia vasa ministerii sanguine similiter aspersit. ²²Et omnia paene in sanguine mundantur secundum legem, et sine sanguinis effusione non fit remissio. ²³Necesse erat ergo figuras quidem caelestium his mundari, ipsa autem caelestia melioribus hostiis quam istis. ²⁴Non enim in manufacta Sancta Christus introivit, quae sunt similitudo verorum, sed in ipsum caelum, ut appareat nunc vultui Dei pro nobis; ²⁵neque ut saepe offerat semetipsum, quemadmodum pontifex intrat in Sancta per singulos annos in sanguine alieno. ²⁶Alioquin oportebat eum frequenter pati ab origine mundi; nunc autem semel in consummatione saeculorum ad destitutionem peccati per sacrificium sui manifestatus est. ²⁷Et quemadmodum statutum est hominibus semel mori, post hoc autem iudicium, ²⁸sic et Christus, se mel oblatus ad multorum auferenda peccata, secundo sine peccato apparebit exspectantibus se in salutem. [10] ¹Umbram enim habens lex bonorum futurorum, non ipsam imaginem rerum, per singulos annos iisdem ipsis hostiis, quas offerunt indesinen-

holy temple was breached, and I find the hidden treasure and rejoice over the richness I have found" (St John Chrysostom, *Catecheses ad illuminandos*, 3, 16). And St Catherine of Siena writes: "Be washed in the blood of the crucified Christ; wash yourself in his blood; drink your fill of his blood; be drunk on his blood; clothe yourself in his blood; suffer your weakness in his blood; rejoice in his blood; grow strong in his blood; shed your weakness and blindness through the blood of the immaculate Lamb; and, in his blood, fight like a noble soldier for the honour of God, for the good of his holy Church and of all souls" (*Letters*, 333).

In verse 24, the writer again makes the point (cf. 7:25) that Christ exercises his priesthood from heaven on our behalf: "Jesus Christ, having entered the sanctuary of heaven once and for all, intercedes constantly for us as the mediator who assures

us of the permanent outpouring of the Holy Spirit" (*Catechism of the Catholic Church*, 667).

Verses 27 and 28 deal with three basic Christian truths about the last things: (1) death is a one-time event (there is no reincarnation); (2) there is a judgment immediately after death; and (3) Christ will come again: "Death is the end of man's earthly pilgrimage, of the time of grace and mercy which God offers him so as to work out his earthly life in keeping with the divine plan, and to decide his ultimate destiny" (*Catechism of the Catholic Church*, 1013).

The expression "not to deal with sin" (v. 28) means that at his second coming Christ will not have to make expiation for sin or be offered as a victim for sin.

10:1–18 The writer concludes his comparison of Old Testament sacrifices and the sacrifice of

u The Greek word here used means both *covenant* and *will*   p Or *tabernacle*

Heb 10:19; 11:40

Num 5:15

Heb 7:18–19;
9:12–13
Is 1:11
would they not have ceased to be offered? If the worshippers had once been cleansed, they would no longer have any consciousness of sin. ³But in these sacrifices there is a reminder of sin year after year. ⁴For it is impossible that the blood of bulls and goats should take away sins.

Christ's offering of himself has infinite value

Heb 9:13

Ps 40:5–8
⁵Consequently, when Christ^v came into the world, he said,

"Sacrifices and offerings thou hast not desired,
but a body hast thou prepared for me;

Hos 6:6
Mt 9:13
⁶in burnt offerings and sin offerings thou hast taken no pleasure.
⁷Then I said, 'Lo, I have come to do thy will, O God,'
as it is written of me in the roll of the book."

1 Sam 15:22
Ps 40:6
⁸When he said above, "Thou hast neither desired nor taken pleasure in sacrifices and offerings and burnt offerings and sin offerings" (these are offered according to the

Ps 40:7a–8a
Jn 6:38

Heb 9:14, 28; 2:11;
7:27; 10:12, 14
Eph 5:2
law), ⁹then he added, "Lo, I have come to do thy will." He abolishes the first in order to establish the second. ¹⁰And by that will we have been sanctified through the offering of the body of Jesus Christ once for all.

Deut 10:8
Ex 29:38–39
Heb 10:1–4

Heb 7:27; 9:28; 10:10
¹¹And every priest stands daily at his service, offering repeatedly the same sacrifices, which can never take away sins. ¹²But when Christ^w had offered for all time a

ter, numquam potest accedentes perfectos facere. ²Alioquin nonne cessassent offerri, ideo quod nullam haberent ultra conscientiam peccatorum cultores semel mundati? ³Sed in ipsis commemoratio peccatorum per singulos annos fit. ⁴Impossibile enim est sanguinem taurorum et hircorum auferre peccata. ⁵Ideo ingrediens mundum dicit: «Hostiam et oblationem noluisti, / corpus autem aptasti mihi; / ⁶holocautomata et sacrificia pro peccato / non tibi placuerunt. / ⁷Tunc dixi: Ecce venio, / in capitulo libri scriptum est de me, / ut faciam, Deus, voluntatem tuam». ⁸Superius dicens: «Hostias et oblationes et holocautomata et sacrificia pro peccato noluisti, nec placuerunt tibi», quae secundum legem offeruntur, ⁹tunc dixit: «Ecce venio, ut faciam voluntatem tuam». Aufert primum, ut secundum statuat; ¹⁰in qua voluntate sanctificati sumus per oblationem corporis Christi Iesu in semel. ¹¹Et omnis quidem sacerdos stat cotidie ministrans et easdem saepe offerens hostias, quae numquam possunt auferre peccata. ¹²Hic autem, una pro peccatis oblata hostia, in sempiternum consedit in dextera Dei, ¹³de cetero exspectans, donec ponantur inimici eius

Christ, from the point of view of efficacy (see 7:27; 9:9–14). He uses Old Testament passages to show that Christ's sacrifice is superior to those of the Old Law. The latter had to be offered repeatedly (see vv. 1–3) and they could not take away sin (v. 11), whereas Christ's sacrifice on the cross is a "single" and perfect one "offered for all time" (vv. 12–14). Those who share in this sacrifice are made perfect, that is, they attain forgiveness of sins, purity of conscience and access to and union with God. In other words, the sacrifice of Calvary is the source of man's holiness.

The efficacy of Christ's sacrifice stems from his perfect obedience to the will of his Father (see 5:9). This obedience is the reason for the Incarnation, which is referred to in vv. 5–7 in a quotation from the Greek version of Psalm 40. That is why this passage (vv. 4–10) appears a number of times in the liturgy of the Church, notably that for the solemnity of the Annunciation of the Lord. The words of this psalm "allow us as it were to sound the unfathomable depths

of this self-abasement of the Word, his humiliation of himself for love of men even to death on the cross [...]. Why this obedience, this self-abasement, this suffering? The Creed gives us the answer: 'for us men and for our salvation' Jesus came down from heaven so as to give man full entitlement to ascend [to heaven] and by becoming a son in the Son to regain the dignity [man] lost through sin [...]. Let us welcome him. Let us say to him, 'Here I am; I have come to do your will'" (John Paul II, General Audience, 25 March 1981).

It is important to remember that the Mass is the renewal of Christ's unique sacrifice and that it is not a repetition of it in the way that the old sacrifices were repeated: "The sacrifice of Christ and the sacrifice of the Eucharist are *one single sacrifice*: 'The victim is one and the same: the same now offers through the ministry of priests, who then offered himself on the cross; only the manner of offering is different' (Council of Trent: DS 1743)" (*Catechism of the Catholic Church*, 1367).

v Greek *he*   w Greek *this one*

single sacrifice for sins, he sat down at the right hand of God, [13]then to wait until his enemies should be made a stool for his feet. [14]For by a single offering he has perfected for all time those who are sanctified. [15]And the Holy Spirit also bears witness to us; for after saying,

Ps 110:1
Acts 2:33
Mt 22:44

Jn 17:19

> [16]"This is the covenant that I will make with them
> after those days, says the Lord:
> I will put my laws on their hearts,
> and write them on their minds,"

Jer 31:33–34

[17]then he adds,

Heb 8:12

> "I will remember their sins and their misdeeds no more."

Jer 31:34

[18]Where there is forgiveness of these, there is no longer any offering for sin.

PART TWO

Faith and perseverance in faith*

5. A CALL FOR LOYALTY*

Motives for staying loyal to Christ

[19]Therefore, brethren, since we have confidence to enter the sanctuary by the blood of Jesus, [20]by the new and living way which he opened for us through the curtain, that is, through his flesh, [21]and since we have a great priest over the house of God,

Heb 9:8, 11
Eph 3:12
Jn 14:6

Heb 3:6; 4:14

---

scabellum pedum eius; [14]una enim oblatione consummavit in sempiternum eos, qui sanctificantur. [15]Testificatur autem nobis et Spiritus Sanctus; postquam enim dixit: [16]*«Hoc est testamentum, quod testabor ad illos post dies illos, dicit Dominus, dando leges meas in cordibus eorum et in mente eorum superscribam eas;* [17]*et peccatorum eorum et iniquitatum eorum iam non recordabor amplius».* [18]Ubi autem horum remissio, iam non oblatio pro peccato. [19]Habentes itaque, fratres, fiduciam in introitum Sanctorum in sanguine Iesu, [20]quam initiavit nobis viam novam et viventem per velamen, id est carnem suam, [21]et sacerdotem magnum super domum Dei, [22]accedamus cum vero corde in plenitudine fidei, aspersi corda a conscientia mala et abluti corpus aqua munda; [23]teneamus spei confessionem indeclinabilem, fidelis enim est, qui repromisit; [24]et consideremus

---

*10:19—13:25 From here until the end of the letter the writer's emphasis is on moral matters; the keynote is an exhortation to an active, steadfast faith (10:19—11:40), which helps a person draw closer to Christ, both in the midst of trials and sufferings and in behaviour that is always guided by charity (12:1—13:19). These chapters are a call to respond, to let one's soul be influenced by the redemption brought about by Christ on the cross, which has been the subject of the earlier chapters.

*10:19—11:40 First comes an exhortation to reap the reward of Christ's sacrifice, and the writer then offers a series of considerations and outstanding examples which are designed to encourage the believer to persevere in faith despite difficulties.

10:19–39 Christians should put their trust in the efficacy of Christ's sacrifice (vv. 19–21). When the text says that Christ's flesh is a "curtain" (v. 20), it not only calls to mind the veil of the temple separating the "Holy of Holies" from the rest of the sanctuary, but also implies that Christ's human nature is at the same time a "way" because it reveals his divinity, and a "curtain", because it screens it. Christians' union with the priesthood of Christ comes about through faith, hope and charity (vv. 19–24), which are manifested externally in the forms of good example and public worship (v. 25). Therefore, we need to hold fast to the faith we have received and professed in Baptism and to the purity that we have been given through the sacrament (vv. 26–31). The writer warns against the risk of the sin of apostasy and about its grav-

[22]let us draw near with a true heart in full assurance of faith, with our hearts sprinkled clean from an evil conscience and our bodies washed with pure water. [23]Let us hold fast the confession of our hope without wavering, for he who promised is faithful; [24]and let us consider how to stir up one another to love and good works, [25]not neglecting to meet together, as is the habit of some, but encouraging one another, and all the more as you see the Day drawing near.

[26]For if we sin deliberately after receiving the knowledge of the truth, there no longer remains a sacrifice for sins, [27]but a fearful prospect of judgment, and a fury of fire which will consume the adversaries. [28]A man who has violated the law of Moses dies without mercy at the testimony of two or three witnesses. [29]How much worse punishment do you think will be deserved by the man who has spurned the Son of God, and profaned the blood of the covenant by which he was sanctified, and outraged the Spirit of grace? [30]For we know him who said, "Vengeance is mine, I will repay." And again, "The Lord will judge his people." [31]It is a fearful thing to fall into the hands of the living God.

[32]But recall the former days when, after you were enlightened, you endured a hard struggle with sufferings, [33]sometimes being publicly exposed to abuse and affliction, and sometimes being partners with those so treated. [34]For you had compassion on the prisoners, and you joyfully accepted the plundering of your property, since you knew that you yourselves had a better possession and an abiding one. [35]Therefore do not throw away your confidence, which has a great reward. [36]For you have need of endurance, so that you may do the will of God and receive what is promised.

[37]"For yet a little while,
          and the coming one shall come and shall not tarry;

invicem in provocationem caritatis et bonorum operum, [25]non deserentes congregationem nostram, sicut est consuetudinis quibusdam, sed exhortantes, et tanto magis quanto videtis appropinquantem diem. [26]Voluntarie enim peccantibus nobis, post acceptam notitiam veritatis, iam non relinquitur pro peccatis hostia, [27]terribilis autem quaedam exspectatio iudicii et ignis aemulatio, quae consumptura est adversarios. [28]Irritam quis faciens legem Moysis sine ulla miseratione *duobus vel tribus testibus moritur;* [29]quanto deteriora putatis merebitur supplicia, qui Filium Dei conculcaverit et sanguinem testamenti communem duxerit, in quo sanctificatus est, et Spiritui gratiae contumeliam fecerit? [30]Scimus enim eum, qui dixit: «*Mihi vindicta, ego retribuam*» et iterum: «*Iudicabit Dominus populum suum*». [31]Horrendum est incidere in manus Dei viventis. [32]Rememoramini autem pristinos dies, in quibus illuminati magnum certamen sustinuistis passionum; [33]in altero quidem opprobriis et tribulationibus spectaculum facti, in altero autem socii taliter conversantium effecti; [34]nam et vinctis compassi estis et rapinam bonorum vestrorum cum gaudio suscepistis, cognoscentes vos habere meliorem substantiam et manentem. [35]Nolite itaque abicere confidentiam vestram, quae magnam habet remunerationem; [36]patientia enim vobis necessaria est, ut voluntatem Dei facientes reportetis promissionem. [37]Adhuc enim *modicum quantulum,* / qui *venturus est,*

ity; it is, he says, an outrage against the Holy Spirit (cf. the notes on 6:4–12 and Mt 12:22–37). In v. 31, we come to the end of a passage that is aimed at inspiring horror of deliberate grave sin and at instilling a holy fear of God: "'*Timor Domini sanctus*. The fear of God is holy.' Fear which is the veneration of a son for his Father; never a servile fear, for your Father-God is not a tyrant" (St Josemaría Escrivá, *The Way*, 435).

To help people endure persecution (vv. 32–34), the sacred writer urges perseverance (vv. 35–39). He asks his readers to think back on the early days of their Christian vocation, when they were "enlightened" (v. 32), that is, when they received Baptism. They should act like people who compete and strive in the public eye without fear of being a spectacle to others (cf. 1 Cor 4:9), without losing

"confidence" (v. 35; cf. 3:6; 4:16; 10:19). The Greek word he uses here (*parrhesía*) suggests the sense of freedom and assurance with which a person speaks to a good friend and to God. This exhortation to perseverance is backed up by two quotations from Scripture. The first (v. 37a), in line with the Greek translation of Isaiah 26:20, reminds readers of the letter that God will not be slow to judge the sinful. The second (vv. 37b–38), from Habakkuk 2.4 (a passage quoted also in Romans 1:17; Galatians 3:11), foretells the future liberation of the people of Israel. The ancient prophecies have found fulfilment in Christ, "the coming one" (v. 37), that is, the one who will come a second time. The Christian, then, should face and endure persecution loyally and with "endurance" (v. 36; cf. 12:1–13) and "faith" (v. 39; cf. 11:1–40).

³⁸ but my righteous one shall live by faith,

and if he shrinks back,

my soul has no pleasure in him."

³⁹ But we are not of those who shrink back and are destroyed, but of those who have faith and keep their souls.

Rom 1:17
Gal 3:11

1 Thess 5:9
1 Pet 1:9
1 Tim 6:9

The good example of the patriarchs

11 ¹Now faith is the assurance of things hoped for, the conviction of things not seen. ²For by it the men of old received divine approval. ³By faith we understand that the world was created by the word of God, so that what is seen was made out of things which do not appear.

⁴By faith Abel offered to God a more acceptable sacrifice than Cain, through which he received approval as righteous, God bearing witness by accepting his gifts; he died, but through his faith he is still speaking. ⁵By faith Enoch was taken up so that he should not see death; and he was not found, because God had taken him. Now before he was taken he was attested as having pleased God. ⁶And without faith it is impossible to please him. For whoever would draw near to God must believe that he exists and that he rewards those who seek him.* ⁷By faith Noah, being warned by God concerning events as yet unseen, took heed and constructed an ark for the saving of his household; by this he condemned the world and became an heir of the righteousness which comes by faith.

Heb 3:14
Rom 8:24–25
2 Cor 4:18–19
Gen 1:1–2, 4
Ps 33:6–9
Rom 1:20
2 Pet 3:5

Heb 12:24
Gen 3–10
Mt 23:35
1 Jn 3:12
Job 16:18
Sir 44:16
Wis 4:10
Gen 5:22–24
Is 55:6
Jer 29:12–14
Amos 5:4, 14
Mk 1:35–37
Heb 7:25; 10:35
Gen 6:8; 7:1
Sir 44:17–18
Mt 24:34–39
2 Pet 2:5
1 Pet 3:20
Rom 1:16; 3:22

veniet et non tardabit. / ³⁸*Iustus autem meus ex fide vivet*; / quod *si subtraxerit se*, / *non sibi complacet in eo anima mea.* ³⁹Nos autem non sumus subtractionis in perditionem, sed fidei in acquisitionem animae. [11] ¹Est autem fides sperandorum substantia, rerum argumentum non apparentium. ²In hac enim testimonium consecuti sunt seniores. ³Fide intellegimus aptata esse saecula verbo Dei, ut ex invisibilibus visibilia facta sint. ⁴Fide ampliorem hostiam Abel quam Cain obtulit Deo, per quam testimonium consecutus est esse iustus, testimonium perhibente muneribus eius Deo, et per illam defunctus adhuc loquitur. ⁵Fide Henoch translatus est ne videret mortem, et *non inveniebatur, quia transtulit illum Deus*; ante translationem enim testimonium accepit *placuisse Deo.* ⁶Sine fide autem impossibile placere; credere enim oportet accedentem ad Deum quia est

11:1–22 In these verses that last exhortation to faith (10:39) inspires heartfelt praise of our forefathers in the faith; their faith won "approval" (v. 2), that is, God acknowledged it. To start with (v. 1), the writer defines the essence of faith—that it gives the believer firm reliance on God's promises and a hold on the really good things, those of heaven. Faith, which is necessary for salvation, includes in the first place acknowledging the existence of God and the creation of all things out of nothing (v. 3).

"He died, but through his faith he is still speaking" (v. 4): this is reminiscent of the passage in Genesis where God tells Cain that "the voice of your brother's blood is crying to me from the ground" (Gen 4:10). Abel continues to have relevance because he confesses God's greatness by his faith, his sacrifice and his generosity.

Based on a reading of Genesis 5:21–24, one Jewish tradition held that Enoch (v. 5) did not die, but that, like Elijah, he was simply taken up into the presence of God and was preparing the way for the Messiah's coming. Enoch's example leads the sacred writer to assert that faith is absolutely necessary for salvation (v. 6). Faith is the "beginning of man's salvation" (St Fulgentius of Ruspe, *De fide ad Petrum*, 1). "Believing in Jesus Christ and in the One who sent him for our salvation is necessary for obtaining that salvation. Since 'without faith it is impossible to please [God]' (Heb 11:6) and to attain to the fellowship of his sons, therefore without faith no one has ever attained justification, nor will anyone obtain eternal life 'but he who endures to the end' (Mt 10:22; 24:13)" (*Catechism of the Catholic Church*, 161). So, "although in ways known to himself God can lead those who, through no fault of their own, are ignorant of the Gospel to that faith without which it is impossible to please him (Heb 11:6), the Church, nevertheless, still has the obligation [cf. 1 Cor 9:16] and also the sacred right to evangelize" (Vatican II, *Ad gentes*, 7).

Gen 12:1–5
Acts 7:2–4
Rom 1:5

Gen 23:5; 26:3;
35:12, 27

Heb 12:22
Rev 21:10–23

Gen 17:19;
18:10–15; 21:1–2
Rom 4:19–21
Heb 10:23

Is 51:2
Gen 15:7; 22:17;
32:13
Dan 3:36 (LXX)
Ex 32:13

Jn 8:56
1 Chron 29:15
Ps 39:12
1 Pet 1:1; 2:11
Eph 2:19–20
Phil 3:20

Ex 3:6, 14–15
Jn 14:2–3
Mt 22:32
Heb 13:14

Gen 22
Jas 2:21
1 Mac 2:52

Gen 21:12
Rom 9:7–8
Rom 4:17–21

Gen 27:1–40
Gen 47:31; 48:8–20

Gen 50:24–25

⁸By faith Abraham obeyed when he was called to go out to a place which he was to receive as an inheritance; and he went out, not knowing where he was to go. ⁹By faith he sojourned in the land of promise, as in a foreign land, living in tents with Isaac and Jacob, heirs with him of the same promise. ¹⁰For he looked forward to the city which has foundations, whose builder and maker is God. ¹¹By faith Sarah herself received power to conceive, even when she was past the age, since she considered him faithful who had promised. ¹²Therefore from one man, and him as good as dead, were born descendants as many as the stars of heaven and as the innumerable grains of sand by the seashore.

¹³These all died in faith, not having received what was promised, but having seen it and greeted it from afar, and having acknowledged that they were strangers and exiles on the earth. ¹⁴For people who speak thus make it clear that they are seeking a homeland. ¹⁵If they had been thinking of that land from which they had gone out, they would have had opportunity to return. ¹⁶But as it is, they desire a better country, that is, a heavenly one. Therefore God is not ashamed to be called their God, for he has prepared for them a city.

¹⁷By faith Abraham, when he was tested, offered up Isaac, and he who had received the promises was ready to offer up his only son, ¹⁸of whom it was said, "Through Isaac shall your descendants be named." ¹⁹He considered that God was able to raise men even from the dead; hence, he did receive him back, and this was a symbol. ²⁰By faith Isaac invoked future blessings on Jacob and Esau. ²¹By faith Jacob, when dying, blessed each of the sons of Joseph, bowing in worship over the head of his staff. ²²By faith Joseph, at the end of his life, made mention of the exodus of the Israelites and gave directions concerning his burial.ˣ

The faith of Moses, the judges and the prophets

Ex 2:2f
Acts 7:20

²³By faith Moses, when he was born, was hid for three months by his parents, because they saw that the child was beautiful; and they were not afraid of the king's edict. ²⁴By

---

et inquirentibus se remunerator fit. ⁷Fide Noe responso accepto de his, quae adhuc non videbantur, reveritus aptavit arcam in salutem domus suae; per quam damnavit mundum, et iustitiae, quae secundum fidem est, heres est institutus. ⁸Fide vocatus Abraham oboedivit in locum exire, quem accepturus erat in hereditatem, et exivit nesciens quo iret. ⁹Fide peregrinatus est in terra promissionis tamquam in aliena in casulis habitando cum Isaac et Iacob, coheredibus promissionis eiusdem; ¹⁰exspectabat enim fundamenta habentem civitatem, cuius artifex et conditor Deus. ¹¹Fide — et ipsa Sara sterilis — virtutem in conceptionem seminis accepit etiam praeter tempus aetatis, quoniam fidelem credidit esse, qui promiserat; ¹²propter quod et ab uno orti sunt, et hoc emortuo, *tamquam sidera caeli* in multitudine *et sicut arena, quae est ad oram maris innumerabilis*. ¹³Iuxta fidem defuncti sunt omnes isti, non acceptis promissionibus, sed a longe eas aspicientes et salutantes, et confitentes quia peregrini et hospites sunt supra terram; ¹⁴qui enim haec dicunt, significant se patriam inquirere. ¹⁵Et si quidem illius meminissent, de qua exierant, habebant utique tempus revertendi; ¹⁶nunc autem meliorem appetunt, id est caelestem. Ideo non confunditur Deus vocari Deus eorum, paravit enim illis civitatem. ¹⁷Fide obtulit Abraham Isaac, cum tentaretur, et unigenitum offerebat ille, qui susceperat promissiones, ¹⁸ad quem dictum erat: «*In Isaac vocabitur tibi semen*», ¹⁹arbitratus quia et a mortuis suscitare potens est Deus; unde eum et in parabola reportavit. ²⁰Fide et de futuris benedixit Isaac Iacob et Esau. ²¹Fide Iacob moriens singulis filiorum Ioseph benedixit et *adoravit super fastigium virgae suae*. ²²Fide Ioseph moriens de profectione filiorum Israel memoratus est et de ossibus suis mandavit. ²³Fide Moyses natus occultatus est mensibus tribus a parentibus suis, eo quod vidissent

---

Noah "condemned the world" (v. 7), in the sense that his upright conduct exposed the unbelief of his contemporaries: "He showed up the world as deserving of punishment, because even though they saw him building [the ark] they did not mend their ways or repent" (St John Chrysostom, *In Hebraeos*, 23, 1).

The most outstanding example of faith to be found in the Old Testament is Abraham (vv. 8–19; cf. 6:13ff; Gen 12:1–4; Rom 4:1ff; Gal 3:6–9). "To

obey (from the Latin *ob-audire*, to 'hear or listen to') in faith is to submit freely to the word that has been heard, because its truth is guaranteed by God, who is Truth itself. Abraham is the model of such obedience offered us by Sacred Scripture. The Virgin Mary is its most perfect embodiment" (*Catechism of the Catholic Church*, 144).

11:23–40 After the patriarchs, Moses was the figure most venerated among the Jewish people;

---

x Greek *bones*

faith Moses, when he was grown up, refused to be called the son of Pharaoh's daughter, [25]choosing rather to share ill-treatment with the people of God than to enjoy the fleeting pleasures of sin. [26]He considered abuse suffered for the Christ greater wealth than the treasures of Egypt, for he looked to the reward. [27]By faith he left Egypt, not being afraid of the anger of the king; for he endured as seeing him who is invisible. [28]By faith he kept the Passover and sprinkled the blood, so that the Destroyer of the first-born might not touch them.

[29]By faith the people crossed the Red Sea as if on dry land; but the Egyptians, when they attempted to do the same, were drowned. [30]By faith the walls of Jericho fell down after they had been encircled for seven days. [31]By faith Rahab the harlot did not perish with those who were disobedient, because she had given friendly welcome to the spies.

[32]And what more shall I say? For time would fail me to tell of Gideon, Barak, Samson, Jephthah, of David and Samuel and the prophets—[33]who through faith conquered kingdoms, enforced justice, received promises, stopped the mouths of lions, [34]quenched raging fire, escaped the edge of the sword, won strength out of weakness, became mighty in war, put foreign armies to flight. [35]Women received their dead by resurrection. Some were tortured, refusing to accept release, that they might rise

Ex 2:10-12
Acts 7:23

Ps 69:9; 89:50
Heb 10:35; 12:2;
13:13
Phil 3:7–8

Ex 2:15

Ex 12:11–30

Ex 14:21–31
1 Cor 10:10
Wis 18:25

Josh 6:12–21

Josh 2:8–14;
6:17, 22–25
Jas 2:25

Judg 6:11; 4:6; 13:24

2 Sam 8:1–15
Dan 6:1–28
Judg 4:15

1 Kings 19:10
Dan 3:22–24
Ps 46:6 (LXX)

1 Kings 17:17–24
2 Kings 4:25–36

formosum infantem et non timuerunt regis edictum. [24]Fide Moyses grandis factus negavit se dici filium filiae pharaonis, [25]magis eligens affligi cum populo Dei quam temporalem peccati habere iucunditatem, [26]maiores divitias aestimans thesauris Aegypti improperium Christi; aspiciebat enim in remunerationem. [27]Fide reliquit Aegyptum non veritus animositatem regis, invisibilem enim tamquam videns sustinuit. [28]Fide celebravit Pascha et sanguinis effusionem, ne, qui vastabat primogenita, tangeret ea. [29]Fide transierunt mare Rubrum tamquam per aridam terram, quod experti Aegyptii devorati sunt. [30]Fide muri Iericho ruerunt circuiti diebus septem. [31]Fide Rahab meretrix non periit cum incredulis, quia exceperat exploratores cum pace. [32]Et quid adhuc dicam? Deficiet enim me tempus enarrantem de Gedeon, Barac, Samson, Iephte, David et Samuel atque prophetis, [33]qui per fidem devicerunt regna, operati sunt iustitiam, adepti sunt repromissiones, obturaverunt ora leonum, [34]exstinxerunt impetum ignis, effugerunt aciem gladii, convaluerunt de infirmitate, fortes facti sunt in bello, castra verterunt exterorum; [35]acceperunt mulieres de resurrectione mortuos suos; alii autem distenti sunt, non suscipientes redemptionem, ut meliorem invenirent resurrectionem; [36]alii vero ludibria et ver-

he was for them the lawgiver and ultimate human authority (see 3:1–5). The central part of this passage is the twofold choice that faith requires us to make—on the one hand, to give up sinful pleasures and embrace the suffering of the People of God (vv. 24–25) and, on the other, have no use for "the treasures of Egypt" and opt instead for "abuse suffered for the Christ" (v. 26). The latter expression suggests that the sufferings endured by the Israelites in Egypt prefigured the sufferings of the Messiah. In the light of this idea, Christians should see that no human advantage can compare to union with the Lord by means of grace. No suffering is too much, provided one can follow the Master and become like unto him.

Then (vv. 30–40), recalling the exploits and sufferings of those who won victory through their faith, the writer mentions the testimony of faith given by heroes, judges, prophets and martyrs from the years when the Israelites first gained possession of the promised land up until the time of the Maccabees (the marginal notes refer the reader to the relevant biblical passages). Not following any strict chronological order, he cites some of the more prominent judges (Gideon, Barak, Samson and Jephthah), the greatest of the kings (David), the most famous early prophet (Samuel) and even a woman whose life was not in every way beyond reproach (Rahab). Finally, he refers to other exploits and deeds inspired by faith and fidelity, without mentioning anyone by name.

The passage ends with the assertion that the righteous of the Old Testament "did not receive what was promised, since God had foreseen something better" (vv. 39–40). They had to await the grace that would flow from Christ's sacrifice. God is like a good father, St John Chrysostom comments, who tells his beloved children, after they have come to the end of their work, that he will not give them their food until they are joined by their brethren. "For if we are all the one body, this body will the more rejoice if all are crowned at the same time and not one by one" (*In Hebraeos*, 28).

2 Mac 6:18; 7:42
1 Kings 22:26–27
Jer 20:2–18; 37:15
2 Chron 24:21
Mt 23:30–36
Acts 7:59
1 Cor 4:10–13
1 Sam 13:6
again to a better life. ³⁶Others suffered mocking and scourging, and even chains and imprisonment. ³⁷They were stoned, they were sawn in two,ʸ they were killed with the sword; they went about in skins of sheep and goats, destitute, afflicted, ill-treated—³⁸of whom the world was not worthy—wandering over deserts and mountains, and in dens and caves of the earth.

1 Pet 1:10–12
³⁹And all these, though well attested by their faith, did not receive what was Heb 12:23 promised, ⁴⁰since God had foreseen something better for us, that apart from us they should not be made perfect.

6. THE EXAMPLE OF CHRIST AND THE DUTIES OF CHRISTIANS*

The example of Christ

1 Tim 6:12
1 Cor 9:24–27
Phil 3:14
2 Tim 4:7
Gen 4:7
Gal 5:7
12 ¹Therefore, since we are surrounded by so great a cloud of witnesses, let us also lay aside every weight, and sin which clings so closely, and let us run with perseverance the race that is set before us,* ²looking to Jesus the pioneer and Lk 2:34; 21:28
Jn 12:32; 19:37
Heb 2:10
Acts 2:33
Phil 2:6–8 perfecter of our faith, who for the joy that was set before him endured the cross, despising the shame, and is seated at the right hand of the throne of God.

Mt 11:28–30
Gal 5:1; 6:9
Lk 2:34
³Consider him who endured from sinners such hostility against himself, so that you may not grow weary or fainthearted.

Perseverance in the midst of trials

Heb 10:32–39
⁴In your struggle against sin you have not yet resisted to the point of shedding your blood. ⁵And have you forgotten the exhortation which addresses you as sons?—

bera experti sunt, insuper et vincula et carcerem; ³⁷lapidati sunt, secti sunt, in occisione gladii mortui sunt, circumierunt in melotis, in pellibus caprinis, egentes, angustiati, afflicti, ³⁸quibus dignus non erat mundus, in solitudinibus errantes et montibus et speluncis et in cavernis terrae. ³⁹Et hi omnes testimonium per fidem consecuti non reportaverunt promissionem, ⁴⁰Deo pro nobis melius aliquid providente, ut ne sine nobis consummarentur. [12] ¹Ideoque et nos tantam habentes circumpositam nobis nubem testium, deponentes omne pondus et circumstans nos peccatum, per patientiam curramus propositum nobis certamen, ²aspicientes in ducem fidei et consummatorem Iesum, qui pro gaudio sibi proposito sustinuit crucem, confusione contempta, atque in dextera throni Dei sedet. ³Recogitate enim eum, qui talem sustinuit a peccatoribus adversum

*12:1—13:25 Now that the reader has been reminded of the standards of faith and fidelity set by the righteous of the Old Testament, the writer of the letter outlines the moral lesson to be learned and practised: Christians must be no less faithful.

12:1–3 The "cloud of witnesses" (v. 1) and the reference to Jesus as the "pioneer and perfecter of our faith" link up with the foregoing passage (see 11:4–38, 40). Christ is a perfect example of the endurance mentioned in 10:36, and he is its cornerstone. None was more obedient, none closer to the Father; none bore suffering as patiently as he did. Christ is portrayed as a strong, unselfish athlete who runs a good race (cf. 1 Cor 9:24; Phil 2:16; 1 Tim 6:12; 2 Tim 2:5); he starts and finishes at the right time; his

commitment does not flag, and he attains victory. Christians should try to live as he did. This passage is reminiscent of Philippians 2:5–9: "Have this mind among yourselves, which was in Christ Jesus ...". His example helps us to put up with criticism from others, and reminds us that we should not be surprised if, instead of success and joy, we encounter humiliation and hostility (cf. Mt 10:24–25; Jn 15:20). "What does Christ teach you from the height of the cross, from which he chose not to come down, but that you should arm yourself with valour against those who revile you, and be strong with the strength of God?" (St Augustine, *Enarrationes in Psalmos*, 70, 1).

12:4–13 Following the example of Jesus, who gave his life "to redeem us from all iniquity" (Tit

y Other manuscripts add *they were tempted*

"My son, do not regard lightly the discipline of the Lord,

   nor lose courage when you are punished by him.

   ⁶For the Lord disciplines him whom he loves,

   and chastises every son whom he receives."

⁷It is for discipline that you have to endure. God is treating you as sons; for what son is there whom his father does not discipline? ⁸If you are left without discipline, in which all have participated, then you are illegitimate children and not sons. ⁹Besides this, we have had earthly fathers to discipline us and we respected them. Shall we not much more be subject to the Father of spirits and live? ¹⁰For they disciplined us for a short time at their pleasure, but he disciplines us for our good, that we may share his holiness. ¹¹For the moment all discipline seems painful rather than pleasant; later it yields the peaceful fruit of righteousness to those who have been trained by it.

¹²Therefore lift your drooping hands and strengthen your weak knees, ¹³and make straight paths for your feet, so that what is lame may not be put out of joint but rather be healed.

Prov 3:1–12

Rev 3:19

Deut 8:5
2 Sam 7:14–15
Sir 30:1–2
Ps 73:14
Num 16:22; 27:16
2 Mac 3:24

2 Pet 1:4

Jn 16:20
Gal 5:22
Jas 1:2–4; 3:18
1 Pet 1:6–7
2 Cor 4:17; 7:8–11

Job 4:3-4
Is 35:3; 40:29–31
Prov 4:26
Lk 1:79; 3:4–6

Striving for peace. Purity. Reverent worship

¹⁴Strive for peace with all men, and for the holiness without which no one will see the Lord. ¹⁵See to it that no one fail to obtain the grace of God; that no "root of bitterness" spring up and cause trouble, and by it the many become defiled; ¹⁶that no one be immoral or irreligious like Esau, who sold his birthright for a single meal.

Mt 5:9

Acts 8:23

Gen 25:31–34

semetipsum contradictionem, ut ne fatigemini animis vestris deficientes. ⁴Nondum usque ad sanguinem restitistis adversus peccatum repugnantes ⁵et obliti estis exhortationis, quae vobis tamquam filiis loquitur: «*Fili mi, noli neglegere disciplinam Domini, / neque deficias, dum ab eo argueris: / ⁶quem enim diligit, Dominus castigat, / flagellat autem omnem filium, quem recipit*». ⁷Ad disciplinam suffertis; tamquam filios vos tractat Deus. Quis enim filius, quem non corripit pater? ⁸Quod si extra disciplinam estis, cuius participes facti sunt omnes, ergo adulterini et non filii estis! ⁹Deinde patres quidem carnis nostrae habebamus eruditores et reverebamur; non multo magis obtemperabimus Patri spirituum et vivemus? ¹⁰Et illi quidem ad tempus paucorum dierum, secundum quod videbatur illis, castigabant, hic autem ad id, quod utile est ad participandam sanctitatem eius. ¹¹Omnis autem disciplina in praesenti quidem videtur non esse gaudii sed maeroris, postea autem fructum pacificum exercitatis per eam reddit iustitiae. ¹²Propter quod *remissas manus et soluta genua erigite* ¹³*et gressus rectos facite pedibus* vestris, ut, quod claudum est, non extorqueatur, magis autem sanetur. ¹⁴Pacem sectamini cum omnibus et sanctificationem, sine qua nemo videbit Dominum, ¹⁵providentes, ne quis desit gratiae Dei, ne qua radix amaritudinis sursum germinans perturbet et per illam inquinentur multi, ¹⁶ne quis fornicator aut profanus ut Esau,

2:14), Christians should strive to avoid sin and persevere in times of tribulation and persecution, because, if such adversity arises, it means that the Lord permits it for our good. God is a good Father, who brings up his children tenderly but firmly. He disciplines us, by means of setbacks, in order to make us saints (see v. 10). So, an illness, or anything else that people might naturally see as negative or difficult, can be the means God plans to help us atone for sins and become more like Christ. Sufferings are a sign of God's paternal love and at the same time a proof that we are truly his children. It is to our advantage to accept them calmly, because they are for our own good. "God is my Father, even though he may send me suffering. He loves me tenderly, even while wounding me. [...] And I, who also wish to fulfil the most holy Will of God, follow-

ing in the footsteps of the Master, can I complain if I too meet suffering as my travelling companion? It will be a sure sign of my sonship, because God is treating me as he treated his own divine Son" (St Josemaría Escrivá, *The Way of the Cross*, 1, 1).

12:14–29 The writer exhorts Christians to lead exemplary lives and thereby render worship to God (see v. 28). By way of contrast, he mentions Esau (vv. 16–17), and compares two scenes (vv. 18–24)—the awesome events that marked the establishment of the Covenant on Sinai (cf. Ex 19:12–16; 20:18), and the wonderful vision of the heavenly city on Mount Zion, the abode of the angels and the blessed.

The crux of his argument is the key moment when the New Covenant is made (v. 24)—the

Gen 27:30–40
Heb 6:4–6

Deut 4:11–12
Ex 19:16, 19;
20:19

Ex 19:12-13

Deut 9:19

Gal 4:26
Rev 5:11; 14:1;
21:10
Lk 10:20
Ps 50:6
2 Tim 4:8
Rom 2:6

Heb 7:22; 8:6; 9:15;
11:4

Jn 4:10
Heb 2:1–3

Ex 19:19
Judg 5:4–5
Hag 2:6, 21
Mt 24:29

2 Pet 3:10–33
Rev 21:1
Mt 24:35

Dan 7:14, 18
Heb 9:14; 13:21

Is 33:1
Deut 4:24

Jn 13:34
1 Pet 4:9
Gen 18:2; 19:1
Tob 5:4

¹⁷For you know that afterward, when he desired to inherit the blessing, he was rejected, for he found no chance to repent, though he sought it with tears.

¹⁸For you have not come to what may be touched, a blazing fire, and darkness, and gloom, and a tempest, ¹⁹and the sound of a trumpet, and a voice whose words made the hearers entreat that no further messages be spoken to them. ²⁰For they could not endure the order that was given, "If even a beast touches the mountain, it shall be stoned." ²¹Indeed, so terrifying was the sight that Moses said, "I tremble with fear." ²²But you have come to Mount Zion and to the city of the living God, the heavenly Jerusalem, and to innumerable angels in festal gathering, ²³and to the assembly[z] of the first-born who are enrolled in heaven, and to a judge who is God of all, and to the spirits of just men made perfect, ²⁴and to Jesus, the mediator of a new covenant, and to the sprinkled blood that speaks more graciously than the blood of Abel.

²⁵See that you do not refuse him who is speaking. For if they did not escape when they refused him who warned them on earth, much less shall we escape if we reject him who warns from heaven. ²⁶His voice then shook the earth; but now he has promised, "Yet once more I will shake not only the earth but also the heaven." ²⁷This phrase, "Yet once more," indicates the removal of what is shaken, as of what has been made, in order that what cannot be shaken may remain. ²⁸Therefore let us be grateful for receiving a kingdom that cannot be shaken, and thus let us offer to God acceptable worship, with reverence and awe; ²⁹for our God is a consuming fire.

Duties towards others—charity, hospitality, fidelity in marriage

13 ¹*Let brotherly love continue. ²Do not neglect to show hospitality to strangers, for thereby some have entertained angels unawares. ³Remember those who are

qui propter unam escam vendidit primogenita sua. ¹⁷Scitis enim quoniam et postea cupiens hereditare benedictionem reprobatus est, non enim invenit paenitentiae locum, quamquam cum lacrimis inquisisset eam. ¹⁸Non enim accessistis ad tractabilem et ardentem ignem et turbinem et caliginem et procellam ¹⁹et tubae sonum et vocem verborum, quam qui audierunt, recusaverunt, ne ultra eis fieret verbum; ²⁰non enim portabant mandatum: «Et si bestia tetigerit montem, lapidabitur»; ²¹et ita terribile erat, quod videbatur, Moyses dixit: «Exterritus sum et tremebundus». ²²Sed accessistis ad Sion montem et civitatem Dei viventis, Ierusalem caelestem, et multa milia angelorum, frequentiam ²³et ecclesiam primogenitorum, qui conscripti sunt in caelis, et iudicem Deum omnium et spiritus iustorum, qui consummati sunt, ²⁴et testamenti novi mediatorem Iesum et sanguinem aspersionis, melius loquentem quam Abel. ²⁵Videte, ne recusetis loquentem; si enim illi non effugerunt recusantes eum, qui super terram loquebatur, multo magis nos, qui de caelis loquentem avertimus; ²⁶cuius vox movit terram tunc, modo autem pronuntiavit dicens: «Adhuc semel ego movebo» non solum terram sed et caelum». ²⁷Hoc autem «adhuc semel» declarat mobilium translationem tamquam factorum, ut maneant ea, quae sunt immobilia. ²⁸Itaque, regnum immobile suscipientes, habeamus gratiam, per quam serviamus placentes Deo cum reverentia et metu; ²⁹etenim Deus noster ignis consumens est.   [13] ¹Caritas fraternitatis maneat. ²Hospitalitatem nolite oblivisci, per hanc enim quidam nescientes hospitio receperunt angelos. ³Mementote vinctorum tamquam simul vincti, laborantium tamquam et ipsi in corpore morantes. ⁴Hon-

shedding of our Lord's blood that seals it and purifies the sins of mankind (cf. Ex 24:8; Heb 9:12–14, 20; 1 Pet 1:2). That blood "speaks more graciously than the blood of Abel" (v. 24; cf. 11:4), because "the shedding of Abel's blood called for vengeance, whereas the blood of Christ claims forgiveness" (St Thomas Aquinas, *Super Hebraeos*, ad loc.). "Sinners, says the Letter, you are fortunate indeed, for after you sin you have recourse to the crucified Jesus, who shed all his blood so that he might stand as mediator to make peace between God and sinners, and win you forgiveness from him. If your evildoing shouts against you, the Redeemer's blood cries out in your favour, and divine justice cannot but listen to

what this blood says" (St Alphonsus Liguori, *The Love of Our Lord Jesus Christ*, 3).

Christians have a heavy responsibility. Quoting the prophet Haggai (v. 26), the writer points out that just as the earth shook at Sinai when God sealed the Covenant with Moses, so too earth, and heaven, have trembled with the making of the New Covenant (cf. Mt 27:51–52). If the Old Covenant called for obedience and fear (vv. 20–21), the New one requires greater acceptance of God (v. 25) and lives led in grace that are true worship worthy of God (v. 28).

13:1–6 This passage contains moral lessons drawn from what has just been said (see 12:28).

z Or angels, and to the festal gathering and assembly

in prison, as though in prison with them; and those who are ill-treated, since you also
are in the body. [4]Let marriage be held in honour among all, and let the marriage bed be
undefiled; for God will judge the immoral and adulterous. [5]Keep your life free from
love of money, and be content with what you have; for he has said, "I will never fail
you nor forsake you." [6]Hence we can confidently say,

> "The Lord is my helper,
> I will not be afraid;
> what can man do to me?"

Religious duties—obeying lawful pastors; religious worship

[7]Remember your leaders, those who spoke to you the word of God; consider the outcome of their life, and imitate their faith. [8]Jesus Christ is the same yesterday and
today and for ever. [9]Do not be led away by diverse and strange teachings; for it is
well that the heart be strengthened by grace, not by foods, which have not benefited
their adherents.* [10]We have an altar from which those who serve the tent[a] have no
right to eat. [11]For the bodies of those animals whose blood is brought into the sanctuary by the high priest as a sacrifice for sin are burned outside the camp. [12]So Jesus
also suffered outside the gate in order to sanctify the people through his own blood.
[13]Therefore let us go forth to him outside the camp and bear the abuse he endured.*

Margin references:
Heb 10:34; 11:36
Mt 25:36
Mt 19:9
Gal 5:19, 21
1 Cor 5:11; 7:2–4
Eph 5:5
Wis 3:13
Phil 4:11–12
Deut 31:6, 8
Gen 28:15
Josh 1:5
Ps 118:6; 27:1–3
Rom 8:31–39
Heb 13:17, 24
Lk 22:26
1 Tim 5:17
Rev 1:8, 17–18
Eph 4:14
2 Pet 1:16
Col 2:78, 21
1 Tim 1:6; 4:3
1 Cor 8:8
Heb 8:4–5
Lev 16:27
Mt 21:39
Jn 19:17–20
Lev 24:14
Num 15:35–36

orabile conubium in omnibus et torus immaculatus, fornicatores enim et adulteros iudicabit Deus. [5]Sint mores sine avaritia; contenti praesentibus.
Ipse enim dixit: «*Non te deseram, neque derelinquam*», [6]ita ut confidenter dicamus: «*Dominus mihi adiutor est, non timebo; / quid faciet mihi
homo?*». [7]Mementote praepositorum vestrorum, qui vobis locuti sunt verbum Dei, quorum intuentes exitum conversationis imitamini fidem. [8]Iesus
Christus heri et hodie idem, et in saecula! [9]Doctrinis variis et peregrinis nolite abduci; optimum enim est gratia stabiliri cor, non escis, quae non
profuerunt ambulantibus in eis. [10]Habemus altare, de quo edere non habent potestatem, qui tabernaculo deserviunt. [11]Quorum enim animalium
infertur sanguis pro peccato in Sancta per pontificem, horum corpora cremantur extra castra. [12]Propter quod et Iesus, ut sanctificaret per suum sanguinem populum, extra portam passus est. [13]Exeamus igitur ad eum extra castra, improperium eius portantes; [14]non enim habemus hic manentem

True worship cannot be separated from good
moral conduct (cf. 13:15–16). Being faithful to
Christ means being true to him, and to his teaching in our lives.

Verse 2 alludes to episodes in the lives of
Abraham and Sarah (see Gen 18:1–16), Lot (see
Gen 19), Manoah (see Judg 13:2–22) and Tobit
(see Tob 12:1–22), all of whom gave hospitality
to wayfarers who turned out to be angels.

Verses 3–4 are a call to practise charity and
chastity. The writer is categorical in his praise of
marriage. "When there is chastity in the love of
married persons, their marital life is authentic;
husband and wife are true to themselves, they
understand each other and develop the union
between them. When the divine gift of sex is
perverted, their intimacy is destroyed, and they
can no longer look openly at one another" (St
Josemaría Escrivá, *Christ Is Passing By*, 25).

In verses 5–6 the writer exhorts Christians
not to set their heart on riches or become
attached to material things. He quotes some
words spoken by Moses (see Deut 31:6), and

adds to them Psalm 118:6, to make it clear that it
is God himself who has told man he will never
abandon him. "If Christ is yours, then wealth is
yours; he satisfies all your wants. He will look
after you, manage all your affairs for you most
dutifully; you will need no human support to rely
on [...]. Put all your trust in God; centre in him
all your fear and all your love; he will make himself responsible for you, and all will go well as
he sees best" (Thomas à Kempis, *The Imitation
of Christ*, 2, 1, 2–3).

13:7–19 These verses are an appeal to readers to
persevere in the faith they have received (vv. 7–
9, 17). The value of their lives derives from the
"altar" of the cross, that is, from the sacrifice of
Christ that is renewed in the Eucharist (v. 10).
Verses 11–13 should be read against the background of the Old Testament rites for the Day of
Atonement (cf. 9:1–10 and note). Jesus Christ,
crucified outside the walls of Jerusalem, has fulfilled what was prefigured by the sacrificed victims that were burned outside the encampment

a Or *tabernacle*

1 Cor 7:29–31
Phil 3:20

2 Chron 29:31
Ps 50:14, 23
Rom 10:9
Mal 1:11

Heb 13:21
2 Cor 8:4

Is 62:6
1 Pet 5:2–5
Acts 20:28–31
1 Thess 5:12
Eph 6:18–19
Rom 15:30
Col 4:3
2 Thess 3:1
Philem 22
Acts 12:5

¹⁴For here we have no lasting city, but we seek the city which is to come. ¹⁵Through him then let us continually offer up a sacrifice of praise to God, that is, the fruit of lips that acknowledge his name. ¹⁶Do not neglect to do good and to share what you have, for such sacrifices are pleasing to God.

¹⁷Obey your leaders and submit to them; for they are keeping watch over your souls, as men who will have to give account. Let them do this joyfully, and not sadly, for that would be of no advantage to you.

¹⁸Pray for us, for we are sure that we have a clear conscience, desiring to act honourably in all things. ¹⁹I urge you the more earnestly to do this in order that I may be restored to you the sooner.

Words of farewell

Jn 10:11
Is 55:3; 63:11
1 Pet 2:25; 5:4
Jer 32:40
2 Cor 5:9
Rom 16:27

²⁰Now may the God of peace who brought again from the dead our Lord Jesus, the great shepherd of the sheep, by the blood of the eternal covenant, ²¹equip you with

civitatem, sed futuram inquirimus. ¹⁵Per ipsum ergo offeramus hostiam laudis semper Deo, id est fructum labiorum confitentium nomini eius. ¹⁶Beneficientiae autem et communionis nolite oblivisci, talibus enim hostiis oblectatur Deus. ¹⁷Oboedite praepositis vestris et subiacete eis, ipsi enim pervigilant pro animabus vestris quasi rationem reddituri, ut cum gaudio hoc faciant et non gementes, hoc enim non expedit vobis. ¹⁸Orate pro nobis; confidimus enim quia bonam conscientiam habemus, in omnibus bene volentes conversari. ¹⁹Amplius autem deprecor vos hoc facere, ut quo celerius restituar vobis. ²⁰Deus autem pacis, qui eduxit de mortuis pastorem magnum ovium in sanguine testamenti aeterni, Dominum nos-

on that day. Because he was the one to sacrifice the heifer and the male goat to atone for the sins of the people, the high priest was permitted to enter the sanctuary; so too the shedding of Christ's blood has opened the way to the sanctuary of heaven. By their taking part in that sacrifice, it becomes possible for Christians to give their lives a supernatural meaning (v. 14), by exercising a spiritual priesthood through a sacrifice of prayer and good works (vv. 15–16). Finally, the writer asks for obedience to pastors and for prayers for himself (vv. 17–19).

If, as some think, this letter was originally addressed to the church in Rome, v. 7 may be a reference to Peter and Paul.

Verse 8 is a profound confession of faith that sums up the basis for all Christian practice. Christ's teaching is as unchangeable as he himself is, and it will eventually transform the world. All human things—work, family life, social life, affections, setbacks—acquire a new, definitive meaning in Christ. "The Church believes that Christ, who died and was raised for the sake of all, can show man the way and strengthen him through the Spirit in order to be worthy of his destiny: nor is there any other name under heaven given among men by which they can be saved. The Church likewise believes that the key, the centre and the purpose of the

whole of man's history is to be found in its Lord and Master. She also maintains that beneath all that changes there is much that is unchanging, much that has its ultimate foundation in Christ, who is the same yesterday, and today, and forever" (Vatican II, *Gaudium et spes*, 10). This is the source of the Christian's confidence. "Jesus is the way. Behind him on this earth of ours he has left the clear outlines of his footprints. They are indelible signs which neither the erosion of time nor the treachery of the evil one have been able to erase. *Iesus Christus heri, et hodie; ipse et in saecula*. How I love to recall these words! Jesus Christ, the very Jesus who was alive yesterday for his Apostles and the people who sought him out—this same Jesus lives today for us, and will live forever" (St Josemaría Escrivá, *Friends of God*, 127).

13:20–25 The ending of the letter is similar to the endings of the Pauline letters—a doxology, followed by some words of farewell. The body of the letter is referred to as a "word of exhortation", which conveys the idea of a discourse or treatise designed to provide consolation and encouragement. The phrase could even be an allusion to the types of addresses given in synagogues (see Acts 13:15).

Jesus Christ is called the "great shepherd of

everything good that you may do his will, working in you[b] that which is pleasing in his sight, through Jesus Christ; to whom be glory for ever and ever. Amen.

[22]I appeal to you, brethren, bear with my word of exhortation, for I have written to you briefly. [23]You should understand that our brother Timothy has been released, with whom I shall see you if he comes soon. [24]Greet all your leaders and all the saints. Those who come from Italy send you greetings. [25]Grace be with all of you. Amen.

2 Tim 4:3
1 Pet 5:12

Acts 16:1

Heb 13:7–17
Tit 3:15
2 Cor 1:1

trum Iesum, [21]aptet vos in omni bono, ut faciatis voluntatem eius, faciens in nobis, quod placeat coram se per Iesum Christum, cui gloria in saecula saeculorum. Amen. [22]Rogo autem vos, fratres, sufferte sermonem exhortationis, etenim perpaucis scripsi vobis. [23]Cognoscite fratrem nostrum Timotheum dimissum esse, cum quo si celerius venerit, videbo vos. [24]Salutate omnes praepositos vestros et omnes sanctos. Salutant vos, qui de Italia sunt. [25]Gratia cum omnibus vobis.

the sheep" (v. 20; cf. 1 Pet 2:25), greater even than Moses, who was also thought of as the shepherd of a flock (see Is 63:11). Once again a parallel is implied between the Exodus (and the Old Covenant) and entry into heaven.

Verse 21 is a reference to Christian teaching about the need for and the efficacy of grace, and about the need to respond to that grace.

"Those who come from Italy" (v. 24). Many Fathers of the Church and early commentators on the text take this as an indication that the letter was written in Rome, but the phrase could also refer to a group of Christians who originally came from Italy but who now lived elsewhere.

On the "saints" (cf. 3:1), see the note on Rom 15:22–33.

b Other ancient authorities read *us*

Introduction to the Catholic Letters

After the writings traditionally attributed to St Paul, the New Testament has a group of seven letters usually described as the "Catholic Letters"—one written by St James, two by St Peter, three by St John and one by St Jude. They belong to the same literary genre as the writings of St Paul: they are letters intended to instruct people about Jesus and his work of redemption. All the letters are quite short, and were written for the whole Church, in the sense that they are not addressed to particular communities or (except for 3 John) particular individuals—hence the collective title "catholic". These texts have not always been placed where they are now in the New Testament canon, or in the same sequence: in the great early codexes (except for the Sinaitic) they appear after the Acts of the Apostles, and that is where they are still found in the canon of the Eastern Church. Their present position serves to show that St Paul's teaching is rounded off and borne out by that of the other apostles. The letter of St Jude, which comments on some aspects of Jewish apocalyptic writing, acts as a natural introduction to the Revelation to St John (or, Apocalypse) which follows it.

As early as the end of the fourth century, these seven letters that do not form part of the Pauline corpus were grouped together under the general title of "catholic" letters.[1] It is not clear how they got this name. Clement of Alexandria (2nd–3rd century) gave the title of "catholic" epistle to the letter sent out by the council of Jerusalem (Acts 15:23–29) because it was written by all the apostles.[2] Origen described the First Letter of St Peter as "catholic".[3] Denys of Alexandria (d. 264) gave the same title to 1 John to distinguish it from 2 and 3 John, on the grounds that it mentions no particular addressee but is, rather, addressed to all and is therefore "universal" or "catholic".[4] The title of "catholic" appears to mean, at different times, "addressed to all the churches" and "accepted by all the churches", that is, canonical. It may be that originally they were called "catholic" because they were to be sent from church to church as "encyclical" letters and that, later on, the description was applied also to the letters addressed to individuals (3 John, for example),[5] as a confirmation of their authority.

Five of these letters (James, 2 Peter, 2 and 3 John, and Jude) were not immediately or unanimously accepted as canonical; therefore, they are sometimes called "deuterocanonical". Eusebius, in his famous canon, put these five among the debated letters (*antilegómena*), acknowledging at the same time that most people regarded them as inspired books.[6] From the fourth century on, the Western Church has held unanimously that the letters are authoritative and canonical, as the teachings of the Council of Hippo (AD 393) and the third and fourth Councils of Carthage (397 and 419) attest. From that time on, in the Eastern Church, doubts about their canonicity also dissipated; from the seventh century on, the entire Church has accepted them as being inspired. In the sixteenth century, when Protestants began to resurrect early doubts about the canonicity of some of the Catholic Letters, the Council of Trent solemnly defined what Tradition taught—that all of these letters are to be received "as sacred and canonical in their entirety, with all their parts, according to the text usually read in the Catholic Church".[7]

---

1 Cf. St Jerome, *De viris illustribus*, 2, 4. 2 Clement of Alexandria, *Stromata*, 4, 15. 3 See Eusebius, *Historia ecclesiastica*, 6, 25, 8. 4 See ibid., 7, 25, 7. 5 See St Isidore of Seville, *Etymologiae*, 6, 24. 6 See Eusebius, *Historia ecclesiastica*, 3, 25, 3. 7 Council of Trent, *De libris sacris*.

Each letter has a specific purpose and content of its own, and they have very few features in common. St Augustine says that all were written to refute errors that had begun to appear.[8] Certainly, all of them are examples of the teaching and catechesis given to the early Christian communities. For the most part, the tone of each is pastoral and the letters contain religious instruction and moral teaching which encourage people to lead deeply Christian lives.

---

8 Cf. *De fide et operibus*, 14, 21.

THE LETTER OF

JAMES

Introduction

The Letter of James comes first among the "catholic" letters, and the position it now occupies in the canon (just after the Pauline letters) is an apt one, since it deals with the theme of consistency between faith and behaviour, and the need for works always to accompany faith (see 2:14–26)— ideas very much in line with St Paul's teaching. Also, St James' connexion with Jerusalem and the Christian communities of Palestine recalls the theme of the Letter to the Hebrews, the text that comes directly before James. Over a span of many centuries this letter received little commentary, probably because it did not easily come to be accepted universally as canonical and because it deals more with moral than doctrinal matters.

The first extant acknowledgment of the letter comes from Origen (c.185–255), although it is possible that it was also known to St Clement of Rome, Clement of Alexandria, and the author of the *Shepherd of Hermas*. By the end of the fourth century it is already accepted by almost all the churches and appears in all the lists of inspired books. Martin Luther described it as a "letter of straw", as compared with the genuine gold of the Gospel, for (as he saw it) it appears to be at odds with St Paul's teaching on the subject of justification by faith. Even so, Protestant tradition still retained the letter as part of the Bible. The Council of Trent confirmed it to be canonical and inspired.

The dearth of early commentary, and the complexity of the letter's language (a very educated Greek with a clearly Semitic background), explain why scholars nowadays continue to query its authorship, date of composition, etc. In recent decades it has attracted considerable attention on account of the fact that it faithfully reflects the spontaneity and vitality with which the Christian message was transmitted in the early communities, and because it clearly shows the continuity between the Old and the New Testaments.

1. STRUCTURE AND CONTENT

Given its nature and content, the letter is not structured as a systematic thesis. Like Jewish wisdom writings, its structure is pedagogical and psychological. One word leads to another, one idea introduces another, different, one; the same idea is often repeated a number of times; the writer's thought moves in a series of concentric circles, as it were, and he uses language that has the rhythm of recitation and often takes the form of brief maxims, etc. While the letter does not have a clearly defined structure, it can usefully be divided into four sections:

1. The first section (1:1—2:13) consists of a series of interlinked assertions about the value of suffering, the need to put teaching into practice, and the need to be determined not to be inhibited by what people might think.

2. The second section (2:14–26) focuses on the central idea that a faith that does not translate into good works is a dead faith. This point is made a number of times, citing the examples of well-known figures from the Bible.

3. In the third section (3:1–5:6), practical applications of this teaching come one after another, woven together. Christians are exhorted to take care in what they say, to seek true wisdom, to avoid discord, and to be on their guard against pride and a desire for wealth. The section ends with some severe words of warning to the well-to-do.

4. The fourth section (5:7–20) contains a call to stay faithful until the Lord comes, and various instructions about Christian living: Christians should draw their strength from prayer, and take an active role in the salvation of others.

2. CONTEXT

The opening greeting—"James, a servant of God and of the Lord Jesus Christ, To the twelve tribes in the Dispersion" (1:1)—along with other details in the body of the letter, suggests that James was someone who enjoyed considerable authority as a pastor and a teacher among some Christians living outside Palestine. Tradition identifies him as the James who was the Lord's "brother" and "bishop" of Jerusalem, the one whom we know to have been a relative of Jesus. This man was a son of Cleophas and Mary (one of the women who was with the Blessed Virgin at the foot of the cross); he was the brother of Joseph and Joses (see Mk 15:40; Mt 27:56; Jn 19:25) and Jude (see Jude 1). Along with St Peter he received St Paul when he visited Jerusalem after his conversion (see Gal 1:19), and after Peter left the city he stayed on as head of the Jerusalem community (see Acts 12:17; 15:13; 21:18–19; 1 Cor 15:7). He was martyred around the year 62 at the instigation of the high priest Annas II.[1] Some Fathers of the Church identify him as James the son of Alphaeus, one of the twelve apostles.

As regards what led him to write the letter, we know little more than the text itself tells us. Apparently, the Christian communities to which it was addressed (which were probably made up of Christians of Jewish background) had begun to show signs of defects that threatened their spiritual progress. Almost all the failings denounced in the letter concern people's treatment of one another—grumbling, envy, jealousy, backbiting, etc. (5:9; 3:14–16; 4:1–3, 11), and especially tension between the poor and the well-to-do: the writer addresses some very blunt words to the wealthy (see 2:1–13; 5:1–6), making it very clear that people must not selfishly turn their backs on the disadvantaged.

There is some disagreement among scholars as to the time and place of composition. Many think that the letter was written during the period AD 60–70 and that the author may have been a disciple writing after James' death and passing on some of his teachings. Others think it was written earlier, and some scholars, noting that the letter was not easily accepted as canonical, and drawing attention to certain internal features in the text, are of the view that it was written towards the end of the first century. Jerusalem is regarded as the most likely place of composition.

3. MESSAGE

What gives the letter unity is its teaching on the need for consistency between a believer's faith and life: a Christian's behaviour should always reflect the faith that he or she professes. Doctri-

---

1 See Flavius Josephus, *Antiquitates iudaicae*, 20, 9, 1; Eusebius of Caesarea, *Historia ecclesiastica*, 2, 23, 19–23.

nal themes, even though for the most part they are not dealt with directly, underlie the whole letter. Attributes and actions of God are frequently mentioned: he is Creator, Father, Redeemer and Judge, Merciful Saviour (1:17, 27; 2:13; 4:12; 5:4; 3:9).

Except in 1:1 and 2:1, Jesus Christ is not mentioned by name, but throughout the letter he is spoken of as the Lord and Saviour; there is mention of the Lord's second coming and of the fact that he is our Judge (5:8–9); and his teachings are echoed throughout. The letter speaks of the Church as a community of believers (2:2), in which teachers and elders (3:1; 5:14) have specific offices in government and in the administration of the sacraments (1:18; 5:14).

The letter contains many exhortations and warnings concerning setbacks and temptations; on controlling one's tongue and not complaining; about detachment from riches, care for the poor and needy, the practice of prayer, and bringing back those who go astray. Many of these exhortations are reminiscent of things that Jesus says in the Gospels, particularly in his Sermon on the Mount.[2] Among the themes that merit special attention are faith in relation to works, and the sacrament of the Anointing of the Sick.

Faith and works

In a very direct and vivid way, the sacred writer expounds teaching about faith and works, particularly in 2:14–26, a passage whose tone is reminiscent of the wisdom books of the Old Testament. He teaches that "faith by itself, if it has no works, is dead" (2:17). Until the sixteenth century, this teaching presented no difficulty for believers. However, Luther saw it as an obstacle to his theory of justification by faith alone, a theory based on his interpretation of St Paul. From that point onwards, some have sought to find an opposition between St James and the Pauline texts, specifically Galatians 2:16 ("a man is not justified by works of the law but through faith in Jesus Christ"; see also 3:2, 5, 11) and Romans 3:28 ("a man is justified by faith apart from works of the law").

Any opposition, however, is unreal. It is true that the terms being used are identical, but the perspective in each case is different. When St James speaks about "works" he means the moral behaviour of someone who already believes in Jesus, a behaviour that should be in line with the faith he or she has accepted; for St Paul, in his controversy with Judaizers, "works" means the legal rites of the Old Law, which could not lead to justification, since Jesus had promulgated the New Law. For both sacred authors, a person needs to live in union with God, to have a faith that expresses itself in a Christian life that accords with that faith. This coherence between faith and works that is called for by St James is also required by St Paul when he says that only "faith working through love" is of any avail (Gal 5:6), and when he says in connexion with the just judgment of God that "he will render to every man according to his works" (Rom 2:6). In fact, far from being a contradiction or correction of St Paul's teaching, the Letter of St James may even be taking issue with a misinterpretation of Paul's teaching, arguing that faith should be reflected in a person's behaviour.

The Anointing of the Sick

Apart from the allusion to anointing with oil[3] in Mark 6:13 ("and [the disciples] cast out many demons and anointed with oil many that were sick and healed them"), this letter is the only place

---

2 See, e.g., Jas 1:12 and Mt 5:11–12; Jas 2:5 and Mt 5:3; Jas 2:13 and Mt 5:7; and Jas 5:12 and Mt 5:37. **3** Oil was used in ancient times for medical purposes and also in exorcisms: Leviticus 14:10–32 mentions anointing with oil to confirm that a leper has been cured; Isaiah 1:6 refers to wounds being dressed with oil; Jeremiah 8:22 implies that oil of balsam was believed to have curative power.

in the New Testament where there is an explicit account of the Anointing of the Sick: "Is any among you sick? Let him call for the elders of the church, and let them pray over him, anointing him with oil in the name of the Lord; and the prayer of faith will save the sick man, and the Lord will raise him up; and if he has committed sins, he will be forgiven" (5:14–15). The passage shows that prayer over a sick person and anointment by recognized ministers ("elders") to bring about his cure constituted a sacred action that is in line with what Jesus did.[4] This congruence with his actions may also be what is meant by "in the name of the Lord", where "Lord" probably refers to Jesus rather than God the Father.[5]

In the controversies that arose during the Reformation as regards the number of sacraments, the Church used this passage to prove that the Anointing of the Sick is one of the seven sacraments instituted by Christ, and that it was promulgated by St James. Trent also teaches that the "elders" in this passage should be read as meaning not people older in age or leaders of the people, but, rather, ordained ministers (bishops or priests), and that one of the effects of this sacrament is the forgiveness of sins.[6]

---

4 Mark 6:13 and Matthew 10:1 include anointing and curing among the tasks assigned to the Twelve. **5** There are many passages having to do with casting out devils and curing in the name of Jesus; see, e.g., Mt 7:22; Lk 10:17; Mk 16:17; Acts 3:6; 4:30; 16:18. **6** Council of Trent (DS 1695); cf. *Catechism of the Catholic Church*, 1499–1532.

James

Greeting*

1 ¹James, a servant of God and of the Lord Jesus Christ,
To the twelve tribes* in the Dispersion:
Greeting.

1 Pet 1:1
Acts 26:7
Jn 7:35

1. OPENING INSTRUCTIONS*

The value of suffering

²Count it all joy, my brethren, when you meet various trials, ³for you know that the testing of your faith produces steadfastness. ⁴And let steadfastness have its full effect, that you may be perfect and complete, lacking in nothing.

⁵If any of you lacks wisdom, let him ask God, who gives to all men generously and without reproaching, and it will be given him. ⁶But let him ask in faith, with no doubt-

Heb 12:11
1 Pet 1:6–7; 4:13–14
Mt 5:11
Rom 5:3
Mt 5:48
Jas 1:25

1 Kings 3:7ff
Prov 2:6
Wis 8:21ff
Mt 7:7; 21:21
Is 57:20

[1] ¹Iacobus, Dei et Domini Iesu Christi servus, duodecim tribubus, quae sunt in dispersione, salutem. ²Omne gaudium existimate, fratres mei, cum in tentationibus variis incideritis, ³scientes quod probatio fidei vestrae patientiam operatur; ⁴patientia autem opus perfectum habeat, ut sitis perfecti et integri, in nullo deficientes. ⁵Si quis autem vestrum indiget sapientia, postulet a Deo, qui dat omnibus affluenter et non improperat, et dabitur ei. ⁶Postulet autem in fide nihil haesitans; qui enim haesitat, similis est fluctui maris, qui a vento movetur et circumfertur. ⁷Non ergo aes-

*1:1 This sacred text reads not so much as a letter addressed to people known to the writer but as a homily or short treatise, in the style of wisdom writing. The counsels it gives come in no particular order. First there are injunctions to be patient in the midst of trials and to treat the poor with respect (1:2—2:13). The author shows that faith must be accompanied by good works (2:14–26), and then come more specific pieces of advice (3:1—5:20)—notably warnings addressed to the well-to-do (5:1–6) and comments on the value of prayer and the anointing of the sick.

In the Old Testament the title of "servant of God" was given to people outstanding for their fidelity to the Lord, such as Moses, David and the prophets. In the New it is applied to all Christians, but especially the apostles (see Acts 4:29; 16:17; Rev 1:1), to make the point that they were humble bearers of a divine message.

"In the Dispersion": this description originally applied to Jews who lived outside Palestine. In the New Testament it often refers to Christians who saw themselves as the new Israel. Here, it very likely means Jews who had been converted to Christianity.

*1:2–2:13 This passage contains a number of interconnected instructions that exhort readers to be steadfast in order to ensure that there is no contradiction between their beliefs and their everyday conduct: the author stresses that their suffering of various trials is good for them (1:2–12); from God only good can come (1:13–18); to accept what comes from God, one needs to put into practice the word one has heard (1:19–27) and not discriminate among people in any way (2:1–13).

1:2–12 St James points out how Christians should act in the face of trials and sufferings: they should be received joyfully (vv. 2–4) and, when we find it difficult to make sense of them, we should ask God to give us the necessary wisdom (vv. 5–8). Both poverty and wealth are kinds of tests (vv. 9–11; cf. 5:1–6; Lk 6:20, 24). Finally, he reminds readers that the reward promised by God to those who endure trials is blessedness (v. 12). The whole passage is imbued with the teaching of the Sermon on the Mount (see Mt 5:1—7:27).

The problem of suffering experienced by the righteous and (by contrast) the prosperity

ing, for he who doubts is like a wave of the sea that is driven and tossed by the wind.
Jas 4:8   [7,8]For that person must not suppose that a double-minded man, unstable in all his ways, will receive anything from the Lord.

Jer 9:22–23   [9]Let the lowly brother boast in his exaltation, [10]and the rich in his humiliation,
1 Pet 1:24
Is 40:6–7   because like the flower of the grass he will pass away. [11]For the sun rises with its scorching heat and withers the grass; its flower falls, and its beauty perishes. So will the rich man fade away in the midst of his pursuits.

Wis 5:16   [12]Blessed is the man who endures trial, for when he has stood the test he will
1 Cor 9:25
Rev 2:10   receive the crown of life which God has promised to those who love him.
Mt 5:3
Dan 12:12

The source of temptation

Sir 15:11–20   [13]Let no one say when he is tempted, "I am tempted by God"; for God cannot be
Mt 6:13
Rom 7:7–8   tempted with evil and he himself tempts no one; [14]but each person is tempted when he
Rom 5:12, 20; 6:23
Heb 6:1   is lured and enticed by his own desire. [15]Then desire when it has conceived gives
Gen 1:14–18   birth to sin; and sin when it is full-grown brings forth death.
Mt 7:11
Jn 3:3, 27; 8:12   [16]Do not be deceived, my beloved brethren. [17]Every good endowment and every per-
1 Jn 1:5
1 Pet 1:23   fect gift is from above, coming down from the Father of lights with whom there is no
Rev 14:4

timet homo ille quod accipiat aliquid a Domino, [8]vir duplex animo, inconstans in omnibus viis suis. [9]Glorietur autem frater humilis in exaltatione sua, [10]dives autem in humilitate sua, quoniam sicut flos feni transibit. [11]Exortus est enim sol cum ardore et arefecit fenum, et flos eius decidit, et decor vultus eius deperiit; ita et dives in itineribus suis marcescet. [12]Beatus vir, qui suffert tentationem, quia, cum probatus fuerit, accipiet coronam vitae, quam repromisit Deus diligentibus se. [13]Nemo, cum tentatur, dicat: «A Deo tentor»; Deus enim non tentatur malis, ipse autem neminem tentat. [14]Unusquisque vero tentatur a concupiscentia sua abstractus et illectus; [15]dein concupiscentia, cum conceperit, parit peccatum, peccatum vero, cum consummatum fuerit, generat mortem. [16]Nolite errare, fratres mei dilectissimi. [17]Omne datum optimum et omne donum per-

enjoyed by the ungodly in this life is often dealt with in the Old Testament, notably in the Psalms and the book of Job. But it was not fully and finally solved until the coming of Christ. The "wisdom" that James speaks of (v. 5) is, then, the wisdom of the cross (cf. 1 Cor 1:18ff).

We need to pray with faith (v. 6): "If a man has faith, let him ask; and if he does not have faith, let him not ask; for if he does not have faith, he will not receive what he asks for" (Ecumenius, *Commentarium in Iacobum*, ad loc.). The "double-minded man" (v. 8) is someone who cannot make up his mind whether to trust God or not. St Bede comments: "A double-minded person is one who kneels down to ask God for things and beseeches him to grant them, and yet feels so accused by his conscience that he distrusts his ability to pray. A double-minded person is also one who, when he does good deeds, looks for external approval rather than interior reward. [...] He wants to rejoice in the life of this world, and reign in the other world with God" (*In Epistolam Iacobi*, ad loc.). And St Josemaría Escrivá makes a similar point: "It's wrong to have two candles lighted—one to St Michael and another to the devil. We must snuff

out the devil's candle: we must spend our life completely in the service of the Lord" (*Christ Is Passing By*, 59).

1:13–18 As regards the sorts of difficulties his readers were experiencing, St James leaves no room for doubt: from God only good can come. We are never justified in attributing to God our tendency towards sin (cf. Sir 15:11–13). Nor is it right to say that since God has given us freedom, he is the cause of the sins we commit. Sin is committed when we give in to the pull of our passions. We are responsible for our actions, even if we are tempted to act wrongly. And so, when we pray in the Our Father, "Lead us not into temptation", we are asking God not to "allow us to take the way that leads to sin" (*Catechism of the Catholic Church*, 2846).

"The Father of lights" (v. 17): this is a reference to God as the Creator of the heavenly bodies (cf. Gen 1:14ff; Ps 136:7–9) and, given the symbolism of light, as the source of all good things. Christians, having been brought forth by God through the Gospels, "the word of truth" (v. 18), belong to God as his "first fruits" (v. 18; cf. Deut 26:1–11).

variation or shadow due to change.[a] [18]Of his own will he brought us forth by the word of truth that we should be a kind of first fruits of his creatures.

Prov 10:19
Sir 5:11

Doers of the word, not hearers only

[19]Know this, my beloved brethren. Let every man be quick to hear, slow to speak, slow to anger, [20]for the anger of man does not work the righteousness of God. [21]Therefore put away all filthiness and rank growth of wickedness and receive with meekness the implanted word, which is able to save your souls.

Prov 14:7
Mt 5:22
Jn 3:11
Col 3:8
1 Pet 2:1–2
Gal 5:19

[22]But be doers of the word, and not hearers only, deceiving yourselves.* [23]For if any one is a hearer of the word and not a doer, he is like a man who observes his natural face in a mirror; [24]for he observes himself and goes away and at once forgets what he was like. [25]But he who looks into the perfect law, the law of liberty, and perseveres, being no hearer that forgets but a doer that acts, he shall be blessed in his doing.

Mt 7:24–27
Lk 8:21
Rom 8:2
1 Jn 3:17

Ps 19:7
Mt 5:17
Jn 13:17
Rom 7:12; 8:2

[26]If any one thinks he is religious, and does not bridle his tongue but deceives his heart, this man's religion is vain. [27]Religion that is pure and undefiled before God and the Father is this: to visit orphans and widows in their affliction, and to keep oneself unstained from the world.

Jas 3:2

Ps 68:5
Ex 22:21
Is 1:10–20

Impartiality

2 [1]My brethren, show no partiality as you hold the faith of our Lord Jesus Christ, the Lord of glory. [2]For if a man with gold rings and in fine clothing comes into your assembly, and a poor man in shabby clothing also comes in, [3]and you pay atten-

Deut 1:17
Jas 2:9
Rom 2:11

fectum de sursum est, descendens a Patre luminum, apud quem non est transmutatio nec vicissitudinis obumbratio. [18]Voluntarie genuit nos verbo veritatis, ut simus primitiae quaedam creaturae eius. [19]Scitis, fratres mei dilecti. Sit autem omnis homo velox ad audiendum, tardus autem ad loquendum et tardus ad iram; [20]ira enim viri iustitiam Dei non operatur. [21]Propter quod abicientes omnem immunditiam et abundantiam malitiae in mansuetudine suscipite insitum verbum, quod potest salvare animas vestras. [22]Estote autem factores verbi et non auditores tantum fallentes vosmetipsos. [23]Quia si quis auditor est verbi et non factor, hic comparabitur viro consideranti vultum nativitatis suae in speculo; [24]consideravit enim se et abiit, et statim oblitus est qualis fuerit. [25]Qui autem perspexerit in lege perfecta libertatis et permanserit, non auditor obliviosus factus sed factor operis, hic beatus in facto suo erit. [26]Si quis putat se religiosum esse non freno circumducens linguam suam sed seducens cor suum, huius vana est religio. [27]Religio munda et immaculata apud Deum et Patrem haec est: visitare pupillos et viduas in tribulatione eorum, immaculatum se custodire ab hoc saeculo.   [2] [1]Fratres mei, nolite in personarum acceptione habere fidem Domini nostri Iesu Christi gloriae. [2]Etenim si introierit

1:19–27 In v. 18 the sacred writer spoke of the "word of truth" and its supernatural effectiveness. Here, he uses vivid imagery to make the point that, while it has that power, it is not enough just to hear the word: one needs to be attentive and docile and to take the word to heart (vv. 19–21): "He who speaks often lives to regret his words; he who holds his peace, never does" (Ecumenius, *Commentarium in Iacobum*, ad loc.); and one must let it influence one's way of acting (see vv. 22–27; cf. Mt 7:24; Lk 11:28). St James will insist on this point again later (cf. 2:14–26).

"The perfect law, the law of liberty" (v. 25): this is the good news brought by Christ, whose life and teaching have made us children of God and who has set us free from the slavery of the Old Law and the slavery of the devil and sin and death.

2:1–13 Apparently some of those to whom this letter was addressed were guilty of discriminating against people on the basis of social standing (vv. 1–4)—a clear instance of inconsistency between faith and actions. The Law of Moses condemned discrimination and partiality (see Deut 1:17; Lev 19:15; Is 5:23). Such behaviour also goes against the Gospel (vv. 5–7), for Jesus took issue with narrow-minded interpretations of the Law (vv. 8–11). St James makes it plain that this type of behaviour will be severely punished by God when the day of judgment comes (vv. 12–13).

The letter reminds us of the Church's special regard for the poor (v. 5; cf. Mt 5:3; Lk 6:20) and invites us to make a real effort to practise justice: "The evil inequities and oppression of every kind which afflict millions of men and women today openly contradict Christ's Gospel and

a Other ancient authorities read *variation due to a shadow of turning*

Jas 4:11–12

Mt 5:3
1 Cor 1:26–29
Rev 2:9
Gal 3:29

Jas 1:12

Is 52:5
Rom 2:24

Lev 19:18
Mt 22:39
Rom 13:8–10
Prov 24:33

Mt 5:19
Gal 3:10
Deut 27:26

Ex 20:13–14
Deut 5:17–18

Rom 2:12

Mt 6:14–15; 18:35
Lk 6:36–37

tion to the one who wears the fine clothing and say, "Have a seat here, please," while you say to the poor man, "Stand there," or, "Sit at my feet," [4]have you not made distinctions among yourselves, and become judges with evil thoughts? [5]Listen, my beloved brethren. Has not God chosen those who are poor in the world to be rich in faith and heirs of the kingdom which he has promised to those who love him? [6]But you have dishonoured the poor man. Is it not the rich who oppress you, is it not they who drag you into court? [7]Is it not they who blaspheme that honourable name which was invoked over you?*

[8]If you really fulfil the royal law, according to the scripture, "You shall love your neighbour as yourself," you do well. [9]But if you show partiality, you commit sin, and are convicted by the law as transgressors. [10]For whoever keeps the whole law but fails in one point has become guilty of all of it.* [11]For he who said, "Do not commit adultery," said also, "Do not kill." If you do not commit adultery but do kill, you have become a transgressor of the law. [12]So speak and so act as those who are to be judged under the law of liberty. [13]For judgment is without mercy to one who has shown no mercy; yet mercy triumphs over judgment.

2. FAITH AND GOOD WORKS*

Faith without good works is dead

Gal 5:6
1 Cor 13:3
Mt 7:21; 25:41–45

[14]What does it profit, my brethren, if a man says he has faith but has not works? Can his faith save him?* [15]If a brother or sister is ill-clad and in lack of daily food, [16]and

in synagogam vestram vir aureum anulum habens in veste candida, introierit autem et pauper in sordido habitu, [3]et intendatis in eum, qui indutus est veste praeclara, et dixeritis: «Tu sede hic bene», pauperi autem dicatis: «Tu sta illic aut sede sub scabello meo», [4]nonne iudicatis apud vosmetipsos et facti estis iudices cogitationum iniquarum? [5]Audite, fratres mei dilectissimi. Nonne Deus elegit, qui pauperes sunt mundo, divites in fide et heredes regni, quod repromisit diligentibus se? [6]Vos autem exhonorastis pauperem. Nonne divites opprimunt vos et ipsi trahunt vos ad iudicia? [7]Nonne ipsi blasphemant bonum nomen, quod invocatum est super vos? [8]Si tamen legem perficitis regalem secundum Scripturam: «*Diliges proximum tuum sicut teipsum*», bene facitis; [9]si autem personas accipitis, peccatum operamini, redarguti a lege quasi transgressores. [10]Quicumque autem totam legem servaverit, offendat autem in uno, factus est omnium reus. [11]Qui enim dixit: «*Non moechaberis*», dixit et: «*Non occides*»; quod si non moecharis, occidis autem, factus es transgressor legis. [12]Sic loquimini et sic facite sicut per legem libertatis iudicandi. [13]Iudicium enim sine misericordia illi, qui non fecit misericordiam; superexsultat misericordia iudicio. [14]Quid proderit, fratres mei, si fidem quis dicat se habere, opera autem non habeat? Numquid poterit fides salvare eum? [15]Si frater aut soror nudi sunt et indigent victu cotidiano, [16]dicat autem aliquis de vobis

cannot leave the conscience of any Christian indifferent" (Congregation for the Doctrine of the Faith, *Libertatis conscientia*, 57). The basis for this teaching is to be found in Holy Scripture: love for one's neighbour sums up the Law and the commandments. Jesus drew out the full implications of this precept (see Mt 22:34–40) and formulated the "new commandment" (cf. Jn 13:34). Moreover, in the Old Law (vv. 10–11), as in the New, "to transgress one commandment is to infringe all the others. One cannot honour another person without blessing God his Creator. One cannot adore God without loving all men, his creatures" (*Catechism of the Catholic Church*, 2069). And, as St Augustine comments, "that is why whoever would keep the whole law but sins against one commandment has become

guilty of all, for he has acted against charity, on which the whole law depends. One becomes guilty by all the commandments when one sins against that (virtue) from which they all derive" (*Epistolae*, 167, 5, 16).

2:7 The "honourable name" can mean both "Jesus", called down on them at Baptism, and "Christians", a name already being given to those first followers of the Master (see Acts 11:26).

*2:14–26 This passage summarizes the central theme of the letter: faith that produces no works is a dead faith (vv. 14–19)—and this is shown with the help of examples taken from the Bible (vv. 20–26). When St James speaks of "works",

one of you says to them, "Go in peace, be warmed and filled," without giving them the things needed for the body, what does it profit? [17]So faith by itself, if it has no works, is dead.

[18]But some one will say, "You have faith and I have works." Show me your faith apart from your works, and I by my works will show you my faith. [19]You believe that God is one; you do well. Even the demons believe — and shudder.

Deut 6:4
Mk 1:24; 5:7
Mt 8:29

Examples from the Bible

[20]Do you want to be shown, you shallow man, that faith apart from works is barren? [21]Was not Abraham our father justified by works, when he offered his son Isaac upon the altar? [22]You see that faith was active along with his works, and faith was completed by works, [23]and the scripture was fulfilled which says, "Abraham believed God, and it was reckoned to him as righteousness"; and he was called the friend of

Gen 2:16
Heb 11:17
Rom 4:1–25
Gal 2:16

Gen 15:6
Is 41:8
Rom 4:3
Gal 3:6

illis: «Ite in pace, calefacimini et saturamini», non dederitis autem eis, quae necessaria sunt corporis, quid proderit? [17]Sic et fides, si non habeat opera, mortua est in semetipsa. [18]Sed dicet quis: «Tu fidem habes, et ego opera habeo». Ostende mihi fidem tuam sine operibus, et ego tibi ostendam ex operibus meis fidem. [19]Tu credis quoniam unus est Deus? Bene facis; et daemones credunt et contremiscunt! [20]Vis autem scire, o homo inanis, quoniam fides sine operibus otiosa est? [21]Abraham pater noster nonne ex operibus iustificatus est offerens Isaac filium suum super altare? [22]Vides quoniam fides cooperabatur operibus illius, et ex operibus fides consummata est, [23]et suppleta est Scriptura dicens: «Credidit Abraham Deo, et reputatum est illi ad iustitiam», et amicus Dei appellatus est. [24]Videtis quoniam ex operibus iustificatur homo et non ex fide tantum.

he obviously does not mean the works of the Law of Moses (cf. the Introduction, above).

St James returns repeatedly throughout the passage to this key idea: that a faith that has no works cannot save a person (vv. 14, 17, 18, 20, 26). This teaching is perfectly in line with that of the Master: "Not everyone who says to me, 'Lord, Lord', shall enter the kingdom of heaven, but he who does the will of my Father who is in heaven" (Mt 7:21). The rhetorical question at the start (v. 14) and the simple, vivid example given in vv. 15–16 catch readers' attention and predispose them to accept the core message (v. 17). The text retains the conversational tone typical of a Greco-Roman debate, as the author offers three instances of faith as examples. First he gives a negative example — the faith of demons, which produces no good fruit at all (vv. 18–19); this he contrasts with the faith of Abraham, who is a model for believers, and is their father (vv. 20–23); and finally he mentions the faith of a sinful woman (Rahab the prostitute) whose works brought her salvation (vv. 24–25). The closing sentence repeats the essential idea of the passage (v. 26).

*2:14–19 The brief example given in vv. 15–16 is similar to that in 1 John: "If anyone has the world's goods and sees his brother in need, yet closes his heart to him, how does God's love abide in him?" (1 Jn 3:17). The conclusion drawn by John is similar too: "Little children, let us not love in word and speech but in deed and in truth" (1 Jn 3:18). St Paul for his part says: "The kingdom of God does not consist in talk but in power", that is, in action (1 Cor 4:20). Works are the standard by which the authenticity of Christian life and belief will be judged: "Just as we know the life of the body through its movements, we come to see the life of faith through good works. The body is given life by the soul through which it moves and feels; likewise, charity is the life-force of faith [...]. Just as the body dies when the soul leaves it, faith dies when the ardour of charity is cooled" (St Bernard, *In Octava Paschae, Sermo*, 2, 1).

Christian teaching also describes as "dead" faith (see v. 17) the faith of a person in mortal sin. "The gift of faith remains in one who has not sinned against it. But [...] when it is deprived of hope and love, faith does not fully unite the believer to Christ and does not make him a living member of his Body" (*Catechism of the Catholic Church*, 1815).

2:20–26 St James supports his arguments by referring to Genesis 15:6 (a passage also used by St Paul to show Abraham's faith) and the episode of Rahab (see Josh 2:1–21; 6:17–25). The justification spoken of here is the moral perfection that presupposes faith and which is attained, with

God. ²⁴You see that a man is justified by works and not by faith alone. ²⁵And in the same way was not also Rahab the harlot justified by works when she received the messengers and sent them out another way? ²⁶For as the body apart from the spirit is dead, so faith apart from works is dead.

3. PRACTICAL APPLICATIONS*

Controlling one's tongue

3 ¹Let not many of you become teachers, my brethren, for you know that we who teach shall be judged with greater strictness. ²For we all make many mistakes, and if any one makes no mistakes in what he says he is a perfect man, able to bridle the whole body also. ³If we put bits into the mouths of horses that they may obey us, we guide their whole bodies. ⁴Look at the ships also; though they are so great and are driven by strong winds, they are guided by a very small rudder wherever the will

²⁵Similiter autem et Rahab meretrix nonne ex operibus iustificata est suscipiens nuntios et alia via eiciens? ²⁶Sicut enim corpus sine spiritu emortuum est, ita et fides sine operibus mortua est.   [3] ¹Nolite plures magistri fieri, fratres mei, scientes quoniam maius iudicium accipiemus. ²In multis enim offendimus omnes. Si quis in verbo non offendit, hic perfectus est vir, potens etiam freno circumducere totum corpus. ³Si autem equorum frenos in ora mittimus ad oboediendum nobis, et omne corpus illorum circumferimus. ⁴Ecce et naves, cum tam magnae sint et a ventis validis

the help of grace, by the practice of virtue. In Paul (Rom 4:1–25; Gal 3:6–9), justification means union with God through grace, but also the practice of charity (cf. Gal 5:6).

The biblical examples cited show clearly that God calls everyone to believe, and that all can and should manifest their faith by exemplary living.

The Magisterium of the Church quotes vv. 22–24 when it teaches that justification, righteousness, received as a free gift in the sacrament of Baptism, grows stronger as the Christian responds to grace by keeping the commandments of God and of the Church. The righteous "increase in the very justice which they have received through the grace of Christ, 'faith active with works' (cf. Jas 2:22), and are justified the more, as it is written 'Let the righteous still do right' (Rev 22:11)" (Council of Trent, *De iustificatione*, chap. 10).

*3:1—5:6 The principle that our behaviour should be consistent with our faith is exemplified in several ways in this passage—to take care in what we say (3:12); to tell the difference between true and false wisdom (3:13–3:18); to identify the sources of discord (4:1–12); to put our trust fully in divine providence and not be taken up entirely by our own affairs (4:13–17) or by the pursuit of wealth, for that pursuit gives rise to flagrant injustice (5:1–6).

3:1–12 Sins of the tongue are easy to commit, but they can do a great deal of harm (vv. 3–12). St James provides examples, in the style of the Old Testament wisdom books (see Prov 10:11–21; Sir 5:9–15; 28:13–26), to show how, particularly in the case of those in positions of authority (vv. 1–2), a tiny cause can have disproportionately large consequences (vv. 3–12). The thread of the passage covers three points. Summing up in a positive way everything that follows, he says: "If anyone makes no mistakes in what he says he is a perfect man" (v. 2). He goes on to show the harm that speech can do, providing three graphic examples, typical of the style of the letter (vv. 3–6); finally, he counsels control of one's speech, to avoid doing irreparable damage (vv. 7–12). His teaching is clear: one should always speak aware of the presence of God and seeking the good of one's neighbour: "Every good Christian must act more promptly to save the position of his neighbour, and not condemn it; if he cannot save it, he should enquire how his neighbour understands it, and if he misunderstands his position he should be corrected through love; if that is not enough, all the appropriate means should be put into action to ensure that his neighbour, through a perfect understanding of his situation, is saved" (St Ignatius of Loyola, *Spiritual Exercises*, 22).

of the pilot directs. [5]So the tongue is a little member and boasts of great things. How great a forest is set ablaze by a small fire!

[6]And the tongue is a fire. The tongue is an unrighteous world among our members, staining the whole body, setting on fire the cycle of nature,[b] and set on fire by hell.[c] [7]For every kind of beast and bird, of reptile and sea creature, can be tamed and has been tamed by humankind, [8]but no human being can tame the tongue—a restless evil, full of deadly poison. [9]With it we bless the Lord and Father, and with it we curse men, who are made in the likeness of God. [10]From the same mouth come blessing and cursing. My brethren, this ought not to be so. [11]Does a spring pour forth from the same opening fresh water and brackish? [12]Can a fig tree, my brethren, yield olives, or a grapevine figs? No more can salt water yield fresh.

Prov 16:27; 26:18–21
Mt 5:22; 15:18

Gen 1:26; 9:2

Ps 140:3

Gen 1:27

Eph 4:29

Mt 7:16

True and false wisdom

[13]Who is wise and understanding among you? By his good life let him show his works in the meekness of wisdom. [14]But if you have bitter jealousy and selfish ambition in your hearts, do not boast and be false to the truth. [15]This wisdom is not such as comes down from above, but is earthly, unspiritual, devilish. [16]For where jealousy and selfish ambition exist, there will be disorder and every vile practise. [17]But the wisdom from above is first pure, then peaceable, gentle, open to reason, full of mercy and good fruits, without uncertainty or insincerity. [18]And the harvest of righteousness is sown in peace by those who make peace.

Sir 19:18–27
Eph 4:1–2

1 Cor 2:14; 3:3
2 Cor 1:12
Jas 1:5, 17

Is 32:17
Mt 5:9

The source of discord

4 [1]What causes wars, and what causes fightings among you? Is it not your passions that are at war in your members? [2]You desire and do not have; so you kill. And

Rom 7:23
1 Pet 2:11
Gal 5:17

minentur, circumferuntur a minimo gubernaculo, ubi impetus dirigentis voluerit; [5]ita et lingua modicum quidem membrum est et magna exsultat. Ecce quantus ignis quam magnam silvam incendit! [6]Et lingua ignis est, universitas iniquitatis; lingua constituitur in membris nostris, quae maculat totum corpus et inflammat rotam nativitatis et inflammatur a gehenna. [7]Omnis enim natura et bestiarum et volucrum et serpentium et etiam cetorum domatur et domita est a natura humana; [8]linguam autem nullus hominum domare potest, inquietum malum, plena veneno mortifero. [9]In ipsa benedicimus Dominum et Patrem et in ipsa maledicimus homines, qui ad similitudinem Dei facti sunt; [10]ex ipso ore procedit benedictio et maledictio. Non oportet, fratres mei, haec ita fieri. [11]Numquid fons de eodem foramine emanat dulcem et amaram aquam? [12]Numquid potest, fratres mei, ficus olivas facere aut vitis ficus? Neque salsa dulcem facere potest aquam. [13]Quis sapiens et disciplinatus inter vos? Ostendat ex bona conversatione operationem suam in mansuetudine sapientiae. [14]Quod si zelum amarum habetis et contentiones in cordibus vestris, nolite gloriari et mendaces esse adversus veritatem. [15]Non est ista sapientia desursum descendens, sed terrena, animalis, diabolica; [16]ubi enim zelus et contentio, ibi inconstantia et omne opus pravum. [17]Quae autem desursum est sapientia primum quidem pudica est, deinde pacifica, modesta, suadibilis, plena misericordia et fructibus bonis, non iudicans, sine simulatione; [18]fructus autem iustitiae in pace seminatur facientibus pacem. [4] [1]Unde bella et unde lites in vobis? Nonne hinc, ex concupiscentiis vestris, quae militant in membris vestris? [2]Concupiscitis et non habetis; occiditis et zelatis et non potestis adipisci; litigatis et belligeratis. Non habetis, propter quod non postulatis; [3]petitis et non accipitis, eo quod male petitis, ut in concu-

"A perfect man" (v. 2). This does not mean that a person will not commit other sins; but it does mean that by controlling one's tongue one can gain self-control, and that will help a person resist other temptations. Using this verse, the Church teaches that man cannot get through life without committing venial sins, "except by a special privilege granted by God, as the Church teaches happened in the case of the Blessed Virgin" (Council of Trent, *De iustificatione*, chap. 23; cf. chap. 16).

3:13–18 These verses point out the qualities of

Christian wisdom (cf. 1:5). Unlike the false wisdom of the world, true wisdom (cf. 1 Cor 1:18—3:3) produces meekness, mercy and peace (cf. Mt 5:4, 7, 9; Gal 5:22).

4:1–12 In contrast to what he has just been saying (see 3:17–18), St James mentions the discord and disagreement that can undermine harmonious relations with others. He lists the main causes of disunity—greed and envy (vv 1–3), disordered love for things of this world, and pride (vv. 4–10), and, stemming from there, grumbling and defamation (vv. 11–12).

b Or *wheel of birth* c Greek *Gehenna*

you covet[d] and cannot obtain; so you fight and wage war. You do not have, because
you do not ask. [3]You ask and do not receive, because you ask wrongly, to spend it on
your passions. [4]Unfaithful creatures! Do you not know that friendship with the world
is enmity with God? Therefore whoever wishes to be a friend of the world makes
himself an enemy of God. [5]Or do you suppose it is in vain that the scripture says,
"He yearns jealously over the spirit which he has made to dwell in us"? [6]But he
gives more grace; therefore it says, "God opposes the proud, but gives grace to the
humble." [7]Submit yourselves therefore to God. Resist the devil and he will flee from
you. [8]Draw near to God and he will draw near to you. Cleanse your hands, you sinners, and purify your hearts, you men of double mind. [9]Be wretched and mourn and
weep. Let your laughter be turned to mourning and your joy to dejection. [10]Humble
yourselves before the Lord and he will exalt you.

[11]Do not speak evil against one another, brethren. He that speaks evil against a
brother or judges his brother, speaks evil against the law and judges the law. But if
you judge the law, you are not a doer of the law but a judge. [12]There is one lawgiver
and judge, he who is able to save and to destroy. But who are you that you judge
your neighbour?

Trust in divine providence

[13]Come now, you who say, "Today or tomorrow we will go into such and such a
town and spend a year there and trade and get gain"; [14]whereas you do not know
about tomorrow. What is your life? For you are a mist that appears for a little time

Marginal references:
Ps 66:18
Rom 8:7
Mt 6:5–13, 24
Mt 6:24
1 Jn 2:15–17
Gen 2:7
1 Pet 5:5–9
Prov 3:34 (LXX)
Eph 6:11
Mic 3:7
Zech 1:3
Jas 1:8
Mt 23:12
Lev 19:16
Mt 7:1–5
Mt 10:28
Rom 14:4
Deut 32:39
1 Sam 2:6
Prov 27:1
Lk 12:19f
Job 7:7–9; 14:2
Ps 39:5–6

piscentiis vestris insumatis. ⁴Adulteri, nescitis quia amicitia huius mundi inimica est Dei? Quicumque ergo voluerit amicus esse saeculi huius,
inimicus Dei constituitur. ⁵Aut putatis quia inaniter Scriptura dicat: «Ad invidiam concupiscit Spiritus, qui inhabitat in nobis?». ⁶Maiorem autem
dat gratiam; propter quod dicit: *«Deus superbis resistit, / humilibus autem dat gratiam»*. ⁷Subicimini igitur Deo; resistite autem Diabolo, et fugiet
a vobis. ⁸Appropiate Deo, et appropinquabit vobis. Emundate manus, peccatores, et purificate corda, duplices animo. ⁹Miseri estote et lugete et
plorate; risus vester in luctum convertatur et gaudium in maerorem. ¹⁰Humiliamini in conspectu Domini, et exaltabit vos. ¹¹Nolite detrahere
alterutrum, fratres; qui detrahit fratri aut qui iudicat fratrem suum, detrahit legi et iudicat legem; si autem iudicas legem, non es factor legis sed
iudex. ¹²Unus est legislator et iudex, qui potest salvare et perdere; tu autem quis es, qui iudicas proximum? ¹³Age nunc, qui dicitis: «Hodie aut
crastino ibimus in illam civitatem et faciemus quidem ibi annum et mercabimur et lucrum faciemus», ¹⁴qui ignoratis, quae erit in crastinum vita
vestra! Vapor enim estis ad modicum parens, deinceps exterminatur; ¹⁵pro eo ut dicatis: «Si Dominus voluerit, et vivemus et faciemus hoc aut

The quotation in v. 5 does not seem to come
directly from the Bible. St James may be referring
not so much to a specific passage as to an image
often found in the Bible when God is depicted as
a jealous lover (see Ex 20:5; 34:14; Zech 1:14;
8:2). The quotation in v. 6 comes from the Greek
translation of Proverbs 3:34 (it is also cited in 1
Pet 5:5), and it acts as a sort of summary for the
whole passage. St Augustine comments that
"there is hardly a single page in the whole of
Holy Scripture where it is not written that *God
resists the proud and gives his grace to the
humble*" (*De doctrina christiana*, 3, 23, 33). The
basic idea of the passage is that if one is to return
to God one needs to acknowledge one's sin and
one's sinfulness (see also the note on Rev 2:1–7).

4:4 "Unfaithful creatures!" The Greek says,
simply, "Adulterers!", in the feminine, and the
New Vulgate renders it in the masculine. St James
does not seem to be referring to the sin of adultery; rather he is berating those whose excessive
love for the things of this world makes them
unfaithful to God (in line with the biblical tradition
of the spousal relationship between God and his
people: see Hos 1:2ff: Jer 3:6–10). Some interpret
the expression to mean "adulterous souls".

4:13–17 Overweening self-importance is a type
of pride because it means one is forgetful of
God, who, in his providence, rules over the lives
of men (cf. Prov 27:1). The phrase in v. 15 ("if
the Lord wills"), used also by St Paul (see 1 Cor
4:19), has found its way into popular Christian
speech. It shows a readiness to leave one's future
in God's hands, trusting in divine providence. As
elsewhere in the letter (see 1:12; 2:13, 3:18), the
passage ends with a general maxim (v. 17)—

d Or *you kill and you covet*

and then vanishes. [15]Instead you ought to say, "If the Lord wills, we shall live and
we shall do this or that." [16]As it is, you boast in your arrogance. All such boasting is
evil. [17]Whoever knows what is right to do and fails to do it, for him it is sin.

Acts 18:21
Rom 1:10
1 Cor 4:19
Jas 1:22–25

A warning to the rich

5 [1]Come now, you rich, weep and howl for the miseries that are coming upon you.
[2]Your riches have rotted and your garments are moth-eaten. [3]Your gold and silver
have rusted, and their rust will be evidence against you and will eat your flesh like
fire. You have laid up treasure[e]* for the last days. [4]Behold, the wages of the labourers who mowed your fields, which you kept back by fraud, cry out; and the cries of
the harvesters have reached the ears of the Lord of hosts. [5]You have lived on the
earth in luxury and in pleasure; you have fattened your hearts in a day of slaughter.
[6]You have condemned, you have killed the righteous man; he does not resist you.

Amos 8:4–8
Prov 11:4, 28
Lk 6:24
Sir 29:10–12
Mt 6:19–21
Lev 19:23
Deut 24:14–15
Jer 22:13
Sir 34:21–22
Ex 22:22
Wis 2:10–20

4. FINAL COUNSELS*

A call for constancy

[7]Be patient, therefore, brethren, until the coming of the Lord. Behold, the farmer waits
for the precious fruit of the earth, being patient over it until it receives the early and

Mk 4:26–29

illud». [16]Nunc autem gloriamini in superbiis vestris; omnis gloriatio talis maligna est. [17]Scienti igitur bonum facere et non facienti, peccatum est
illi! [5] [1]Age nunc, divites, plorate ululantes in miseriis, quae advenient vobis. [2]Divitiae vestrae putrefactae sunt, et vestimenta vestra a tineis
comesta sunt, [3]aurum et argentum vestrum aeruginavit, et aerugo eorum in testimonium vobis erit et manducabit carnes vestras sicut ignis: the-
saurizastis in novissimis diebus. [4]Ecce merces operariorum, qui messuerunt regiones vestras, quae fraudata est a vobis, clamat, et clamores eorum,
qui messuerunt, in aures Domini Sabaoth introierunt. [5]Epulati estis super terram et in luxuriis fuistis, enutristis corda vestra in die occisionis.
[6]Addixistis, occidistis iustum. Non resistit vobis. [7]Patientes igitur estote, fratres, usque ad adventum Domini. Ecce agricola exspectat pretiosum

here, a warning about sins of omission (cf. Lk
12:47).

5:1–6 In tones reminiscent of the prophets, St
James reproves the well-to-do for their pride,
greed and pleasure-seeking, warning them that
the judgment of God is near at hand. His
description of the lifestyle of those wealthy
people brings to mind the parable of Lazarus
and the rich man (see Lk 16:19ff). The Church
has constantly reminded people of the need to
get rid of unjust inequalities (so often
denounced in Scripture). Those who have plenty
should use their wealth to benefit others. The
Church teaches that "men [...] are morally
obliged not to keep capital in reserve and
unproductive. Looking at it another way, they
must have regard for the common good before
all other things [...]. The right to private
property must not be conceived of without
reference to the common good. It is subordinate
to the universal end of all material goods"
(Congregation for the Doctrine of the Faith,
Libertatis conscientiae, 87).

"You have laid up treasure for the last days"
(v. 3). This refers to the Day of Judgment, as
does the "day of slaughter" in v. 5 (cf. Is 34:6;
Jer 12:3; 25:34).

Cheating workers of their earnings (v. 4) was
condemned in the Old Testament (see, for example, Lev 19:13; Deut 24:14–15; Mal 3:5). It is
one of the sins that "cries out to heaven" for
immediate and exemplary punishment; the same
applies to murder (see Gen 4:10), sodomy (see
Gen 18:20–21) and the oppression of widows
and orphans (see Ex 22:21–23).

St Bede (see *In Epistolam Iacobi*, ad loc.)
reads "the righteous man" (v. 6) as a reference to
Jesus, the just man par excellence (see, for
example, Acts 3:14; 7:52). James may mean,
therefore, that we should see Jesus Christ himself in the needy (cf. Mt 25:31–45).

*5:7–20 This section contains concluding words
of advice about patience and steadfastness (5:7–
11), the value of prayer (5:13–18), and finally
the care that Christians should take of one
another (5:19–20).

e Or *will eat your flesh, since you have stored up fire*

Deut 11:14
Jer 5:24
Mt 24:33
Rev 1:3
Mk 13:29

Jas 1:2–3
Heb 11:36–38

Job 42:10–17
Ps 103:8
the late rain. ⁸You also be patient. Establish your hearts, for the coming of the Lord is at hand. ⁹Do not grumble, brethren, against one another, that you may not be judged; behold, the Judge is standing at the doors. ¹⁰As an example of suffering and patience, brethren, take the prophets who spoke in the name of the Lord. ¹¹Behold, we call those happy who were steadfast. You have heard of the steadfastness of Job, and you have seen the purpose of the Lord, how the Lord is compassionate and merciful.

On oath-taking

Mt 5:34–37
¹²But above all, my brethren, do not swear, either by heaven or by earth or with any other oath, but let your yes be yes and your no be no, that you may not fall under condemnation.

The value of prayer. The sacrament of the Anointing of the Sick

Mk 6:13
Acts 3:16; 28:8
¹³Is any one among you suffering? Let him pray. Is any cheerful? Let him sing praise. ¹⁴Is any among you sick? Let him call for the elders of the church, and let them pray over him, anointing him with oil in the name of the Lord; ¹⁵and the prayer of faith will save the sick man, and the Lord will raise him up; and if he has com-

---

fructum terrae, patienter ferens, donec accipiat *imbrem temporaneum et serotinum*. ⁸Patientes estote et vos, confirmate corda vestra, quoniam adventus Domini appropinquavit. ⁹Nolite ingemiscere, fratres, in alterutrum, ut non iudicemini; ecce iudex ante ianuam assistit. ¹⁰Exemplum accipite, fratres, laboris et patientiae prophetas, qui locuti sunt in nomine Domini. ¹¹Ecce beatificamus eos, qui sustinuerunt; sufferentiam Iob audistis et finem Domini vidistis, quoniam *misericors est Dominus et miserator*. ¹²Ante omnia autem, fratres mei, nolite iurare, neque per caelum neque per terram, neque aliud quodcumque iuramentum; sit autem vestrum «Est» est, et «Non» non, uti non sub iudicio decidatis. ¹³Tristatur aliquis vestrum? Oret. Aequo animo est? Psallat. ¹⁴Infirmatur quis in vobis? Advocet presbyteros ecclesiae, et orent super eum, unguentes eum oleo in nomine Domini. ¹⁵Et oratio fidei salvabit infirmum, et allevabit eum Dominus; et si peccata operatus fuerit, dimittentur ei. ¹⁶Confitemini

---

5:7–11 Here St James renews his appeal for patience, found at the start of the letter (see 1:2–4, 12). He calls for serenity, based on hope in the Lord's coming: "It may be said that it is through patience that man possesses his soul (cf. Lk 21:29), because patience destroys at the root all the tribulations that deprive the soul of peace" (St Thomas Aquinas, *Summa theologiae*, 2–2, 136, 2 ad 2).

"You have seen the purpose of the Lord" (v. 11). Another possible translation is "You have seen the outcome the Lord gave him", a reference to Job, who, having patiently borne the trials that the Lord permitted to happen, was rewarded with the double of everything he had lost (see Job 42:10ff). The RSV's wording (probably less correct, but still valid) refers to the example of patience set by Jesus in his passion and death on the cross; that is the way St Bede and St Augustine interpret the text.

5:12 This exhortation, made at a time when people tended to make oaths all too readily, is almost an exact echo of our Lord's words, "Let what you say be simply 'Yes' or 'No'; anything more than this comes from evil" (Mt 5:37). "Dis-

cretion in calling upon God is allied with a respectful awareness of his presence, which all our assertions either witness to or mock" (*Catechism of the Catholic Church*, 2153).

5:13–18 Prayer is a necessary and effective counter to sadness ("suffering": v. 13); the elders' prayer, along with anointing with oil, cures sin and illness (vv. 14–15); prayer for one another helps us to admit ("confess") and obtain forgiveness of sins (v. 16). This is confirmed by the effectiveness of Elijah's prayer (vv. 17–18).

The Greek phrase usually translated as "Is any among you sad?" (v. 13) includes the idea of suffering under some evil; this is why spiritual tradition has seen sadness as a sort of sickness of the soul. "Being children of God, how can we be sad? Sadness is the end product of selfishness. If we truly want to live for God, we will never lack cheerfulness, even when we discover our errors and wretchedness. Cheerfulness finds its way into our life of prayer, so much so that we cannot help singing for joy. For we are in love, and singing is a thing that lovers do" (St Josemaría Escrivá, *Friends of God*, 92).

mitted sins, he will be forgiven.* [16]Therefore confess your sins to one another, and pray for one another, that you may be healed. The prayer of a righteous man has great power in its effects. [17]Elijah was a man of like nature with ourselves and he prayed fervently that it might not rain, and for three years and six months it did not rain on the earth. [18]Then he prayed again and the heaven gave rain, and the earth brought forth its fruit.

Prov 28:13
Lev 5:5
Sir 4:26

1 Kings 17:1;
18:1, 45
Sir 48:2
Lk 4:25
Rev 11:6

Concern for one another

[19]My brethren, if any one among you wanders from the truth and some one brings him back, [20]let him know that whoever brings back a sinner from the error of his way will save his soul from death and will cover a multitude of sins.

Mt 18:12–13, 15
Gal 6:1

1 Jn 5:16
Prov 10:12
1 Pet 4:8

ergo alterutrum peccata et orate pro invicem, ut sanemini. Multum enim valet deprecatio iusti operans. [17]Elias homo erat similis nobis passibilis et oratione oravit, ut non plueret, et non pluit super terram annos tres et menses sex; [18]et rursum oravit, et caelum dedit pluviam, et terra germinavit fructum suum. [19]Fratres mei, si quis ex vobis erraverit a veritate et converterit quis eum, [20]scire debet quoniam, qui converti fecerit peccatorem ab errore viae eius, salvabit animam suam a morte et operiet multitudinem peccatorum.

The Magisterium of the Church teaches that this text (vv. 14–15) promulgates the sacrament of the Anointing of the Sick (see the note on Mk 6:6–13). "The sacrament of Anointing of the Sick has as its purpose the conferral of a special grace on the Christian experiencing the difficulties inherent in the condition of grave illness or old age" (*Catechism of the Catholic Church*, 1527). Vatican II observes, "By the sacred anointing of the sick and the prayer of her priests the whole Church commends the sick to the suffering and glorified Lord, asking that He may lighten their suffering and save them; she exhorts them, moreover, to contribute to the welfare of the whole People of God by associating themselves freely with the passion and death of Christ" (*Lumen gentium*, 11). The special grace of this sacrament includes these effects: "the uniting of the sick person to the passion of Christ, for his own good and that of the whole Church; the strengthening, peace, and courage to endure in a Christian manner the sufferings of illness or old age; the forgiveness of sins, if the sick person was not able to obtain it through the sacrament of Penance; the restoration of health, if it is conducive to the salvation of his soul; the preparation for passing over to eternal life" (*Catechism of the Catholic Church*, 1532).

The prophet Elijah's prayer of intercession (vv. 17–18; cf. 1 Kings 17—18; Sir 48:3) shows the tremendous power of prayer, and its effectiveness to obtain God's help even in regard to material needs.

5:19–20 The letter ends with an encouraging call to apostolic zeal, which is an expression of true charity (cf. 1 Pet 4:8). "He (God) prizes the soul which by his mercy, and through our diligence and prayer, we may have gained for him, more than all the other services we can render him" (St Teresa of Avila, *Book of Foundations*, 1, 7).

THE FIRST LETTER OF

PETER

Introduction

After the Letter of St James, written for people familiar with Jewish traditions, comes the First Letter of St Peter, a document addressed to Christians who were, for the most part, of Gentile background.[1] The letter is a sign and an example of the close ties between Jerusalem (James), Asia Minor (Paul) and Rome (Peter),[2] and the early Church's unity in its evangelization of a world estranged from God. It reflects the form that Christian presence in the world should take, and the practical consequences of Baptism for Christians who live in a hostile environment. Baptism and the cross are two points of reference that recur in the letter.

From very early on, this letter was unanimously recognized as canonical. We find echoes of it in the *Fourth Letter of Clement* (AD 97), in Polycarp's *Letter to the Philippians*, and in the writings of St Justin Martyr. The first reference to its existence comes from Papias of Hierapolis.[3] St Irenaeus of Lyons (around the end of the second century) quotes the letter a number of times, and attributes it explicitly to St Peter.[4] Clement of Alexandria (d. 214) appears to have been the first to write a commentary on 1 Peter, but that has not come down to us.[5] Eusebius (d. 339 or 340) sums up Christian tradition to date when he says that the letter belongs to the category of New Testament texts that all without exception acknowledge as canonical.[6]

1. STRUCTURE AND CONTENT

It is not easy to discern a clear structure in the letter. Doctrinal themes are often raised and discussed in the context of exhortations. Nevertheless, the letter can be said to have this basic structure:

1. The customary greeting (1:1–2) and an introductory hymn of thanksgiving (1:3–12), which speaks of the dignity of the Christian person, which is the general theme of the letter.

2. The body of the letter (1:13—5:11), which, without following any strict order, can be said to contain three sections and to conclude with some final exhortations (5:12–14).

The first of the three sections (1:13—2:10) contains features of a baptismal catechesis. It is an enthusiastic invitation to seek holiness, a consequence of the vocation a person receives in Baptism, the sacrament that makes him or her a member of a priestly people, the Church.

The second section (2:11—3:12) focuses on the duties incumbent on Christians living in a hostile environment: they should lead exemplary lives in public and in private, whether in the presence of strangers or of other Christians.

The third (3:13—4:19) examines further the stance that Christians should take towards persecution and setbacks; all form part of the redemptive mystery of Christ.

---

1 Both letters are, however, addressed to Christians in the 'Dispersion' or diaspora (see 1 Pet 1:1 and Jas 1:1). **2** The mentions of Silvanus (Silas) and Mark (see 1 Pet 5:12–13) also suggest this link, given that both men had been in Jerusalem, and that they eventually were to be found with Peter in Rome. Both were also well known among Christians as co-workers of Paul (see Acts 15:36–41). **3** See Eusebius, *Historia ecclesiastica*, 3, 39, 17. **4** See *Adversus haereses*, 4, 9, 2; 16, 5; 5, 7, 2. **5** See *Stromata*, 4, 7, 47; *Hypothyposeis*. **6** See *Historia ecclesiastica*, 3, 3, 1; 3, 25, 2.

At the end of the letter (5:1–14), St Peter addresses some exhortations to priests and to the faithful in general, encouraging them to trust in the Lord.

2. CONTEXT

In the opening words of greeting, the author identifies himself as "Peter, an apostle of Jesus Christ", who, as we later learn, is also a witness to the sufferings of Christ (see 1:1; 5:1). From very early times, Tradition attributed the letter to the apostle St Peter. We know little about Peter in the period after he left Jerusalem, in the first years of the Church. There are some indications that he spent time in Antioch, and he was in Jerusalem again at the assembly of apostles (see Gal 2:11–14; Acts 15:7–11); and, according to a reliable tradition, he was at the head of the church of Rome when he was put to death under Nero. However, it is not known when he arrived in Rome or how long he stayed there—or in what year he was martyred (it was between 64 and 67). The letter itself can be dated to between 57/58 (the year St Paul wrote his Letter to the Romans, which makes no reference to Peter—a fact that suggests that Peter was not in Rome at the time) and the year of his martyrdom. However, a later date is not impossible, if the letter was put together by Silvanus,[7] Paul's associate in the evangelization of Asia Minor (also known as Silas),[8] for example, or by some other disciple, collecting St Peter's teaching. Both of these theories would help to explain the points of contact between this letter and the Pauline letters.

The First Letter of Peter is addressed to Christian communities in various regions in Asia Minor. These Christians lived in an environment hostile to the faith, which meant that their perseverance was at risk. Many of them were recent converts from paganism[9]—hence the constant reminders in the letter about their Baptism (1:3, 23; 2:2; 3:21).

The letter is written in refined Greek, almost as educated as that in the Letter of James, with a rich vocabulary and a simple but studied style. As the words of farewell indicate, the letter was written in "Babylon", that is, Rome, the capital of the empire, which was often given that symbolic title.[10]

3. MESSAGE

The main purpose of the letter appears to be to console Christians and to exhort them to stand firm in the midst of difficulties and persecution, conscious of the implications of the vocation they received at Baptism.

Persecutions
The persecutions mentioned above may well have been the reason why the letter was written. They took various forms—calumny, insults etc. (see 1:6–7; 2:12–15; 3:9–17; 4:4); St Peter goes so far as to speak of a "fiery ordeal" (cf. 4:12–16) that could cause them to waver in their faith. It is unlikely that this means official persecution: the persecution instigated by Nero did not

---

7 "By Silvanus, a faithful brother as I regard him, I have written briefly to you" (1 Pet 5:12). **8** See Acts 15:22—18:5; 2 Cor 1:19; 1 Thess 1:1; 2 Thess 1:1. **9** See 1 Pet 1:14, 18; 2:9–10, 25; 4:2–4. **10** See 1 Pet 5:13; Rev 14:8; 16:19; 17:5; 18:2, 10, 21.

extend to the provinces of Asia Minor; and it was not until much later that empire-wide persecutions were unleashed—under Domitian (d. 96) and Trajan (d. 117). Moreover, those persecutions were so severe that if the letter had been written then, the language would surely have been much more dramatic. The letter must be referring, rather, to opposition of different kinds from the pagan world in which these people lived, a world that felt affronted by their upright lifestyle and that therefore discriminated against them in various ways (cf. 4:4). Christians must have felt alienated by their fellow citizens at a community level (cf. 2:11–12), but the clash of lifestyles must have occurred also within the family circle, where slaves had to endure injustice from their masters (cf. 2:18–25) and wives intolerance from their husbands (cf. 3:1–3). The letter is clearly written in a tone of consolation and exhortation. It makes the point that trials have a positive dimension; Christians should see them as a means of purification, remembering that what matters is God's judgment, not that of others (see 4:19). They should realize that their imitation of Christ, their sufferings, will bear good fruit and might even attract their persecutors to the faith (see 2:12). The sacred writer does not confine himself to giving occasional advice on humility (see 5:5–7) but tells them, in line with our Lord's teaching (see Mt 5:10–12), that they are blessed, and encourages them to bear their trials joyfully (see 4:13). He develops one particularly profound and consoling idea: Christians are members of Christ and share in his paschal mystery; just as Jesus, in order to redeem man, underwent his passion and death and afterwards was raised to everlasting life, so too Christians will attain their salvation, and that of many others, by bearing trials well. Jesus is their model, and it is also he who gives full meaning to the sufferings that they endure (see 4:12–19).

Baptism

Although he explicitly mentions Baptism only once, St Peter frequently alludes to this sacrament which makes us members of Jesus Christ and which marks the start of a new life. By God's "great mercy we have been born anew to a living hope" (1:3). Forms of words like this one help us to identify elements of baptismal liturgy and pre-baptismal catechetical instruction in the letter. We can draw three ideas from the letter's teachings: (1) Baptism brings about a rebirth: Christians are "born anew" of imperishable seed (cf. 1:23; 1:3), and Peter encourages them, as "newborn babes" (2:2), to live in goodness and simplicity, hungry for the spiritual nourishment available in the Word of God and in the sacraments. (2) Baptism is a liberation from sin. Christians have broken with sin (see 4:1–6), and have passed from slavery to the freedom of the children of God, because they have been ransomed "with the precious blood of Christ, like that of a lamb without blemish or spot".[11] Without explicitly quoting from the Old Testament, the sacred writer often alludes to the Exodus of the Israelites from Egypt, the ancient deliverance worked by God that prefigures what happens in Baptism.[12] (3) Baptism brings about salvation, prefigured in Noah; it is in this context that the only explicit reference to Baptism is made (see 3:21). St Peter does not draw an exact parallel between Noah's salvation and Baptism; rather, he points clearly to the effectiveness of the sacrament of Baptism. Water on its own serves to remove only dirt (see 3:21), but Baptism cleanses the soul of original sin and any other sin, purifying the heart of every stain, when the body of the person is bathed in pure water (see Heb 10:22).

---

11 1 Pet 1:19. See the note on 1:1–2. **12** See, e.g., 1 Pet 1:19 and Ex 12:5; 1 Pet 1:18 and Ex 12:11; and 1 Pet 2:9 and Ex 19:5–6.

Other doctrinal aspects

On the basis of this baptismal catechesis the letter presents other doctrinal teaching important for helping Christians to stay true to their faith (see 5:9). For example, it points to the action of the three divine Persons (see 1:2–12; 4:14), the divinity of Jesus Christ with the title of *Kyrios*–Lord (see 1:3; 2:3; 3:15), and his work of redemption: by his passion, death and resurrection he has obtained salvation for all mankind (see 1:18–21; 3:18–22). Moreover, although the Church is not named as such, its reality is reflected throughout the letter: Christians, who are brothers and sisters to one another, are living stones in the spiritual building which has Christ as its cornerstone (see 2:4–10); they are the new priestly people established by God (see 2:9); Christ is their Shepherd (see 2:25) and in his name pastors must tend the flock lovingly and without partiality (see 5:1–4).

Hope of eternal life should encourage Christians on their earthly pilgrimage (see 1:1, 17; 2:11); they have been reborn so as to obtain an imperishable inheritance (see 1:4); the difficulties and trials they experience will not last for long, for the hour is coming when the faithful will receive their definitive, glorious reward, and when the guilty will be punished (see 4:17–19). This hope is a distinctive mark of believers, and they should always be ready to demonstrate it by giving witness of their faith to other people through their exemplary lives (see 3:15).

Finally, the reference to Jesus preaching to "the spirits in prison" (3:18–22) is a very important passage for the doctrine of Christ's descent into hell, showing that the Redemption has a universal scope.

1 Peter

Greeting*

1 ¹Peter, an apostle of Jesus Christ, To the exiles of the Dispersion in Pontus, Galatia, Cappadocia, Asia, and Bithynia,* ²chosen and destined by God the Father and sanctified by the Spirit for obedience to Jesus Christ and for sprinkling with his blood:

May grace and peace be multiplied to you.

Jas 1:1
Jn 7:35

Rom 8:29
Heb 12:24
2 Thess 2:13
Eph 1:4
Ex 24:68

Praise and thanksgiving to God

³Blessed be the God and Father of our Lord Jesus Christ! By his great mercy we have been born anew to a living hope through the resurrection of Jesus Christ from the dead, ⁴and to an inheritance which is imperishable, undefiled, and unfading, kept in heaven for you, ⁵who by God's power are guarded through faith for a salvation

Eph 2:4; 1:3
2 Cor 1:3
1 Pet 1:23
Jn 3:5

Col 1:5, 12; 3:3–4
1 Jn 2:29; 3:9

Heb 12:11
Jn 16:20

[1] ¹Petrus apostolus Iesu Christi electis advenis dispersionis Ponti, Galatiae, Cappadociae, Asiae et Bithyniae, ²secundum praescientiam Dei Patris, in sanctificatione Spiritus, in oboedientiam et aspersionem sanguinis Iesu Christi: gratia vobis et pax multiplicetur. ³Benedictus Deus et Pater Domini nostri Iesu Christi, qui secundum magnam misericordiam suam regeneravit nos in spem vivam per resurrectionem Iesu Christi ex mortuis, ⁴in hereditatem incorruptibilem et incontaminatam et immarcescibilem, conservatam in caelis propter vos, ⁵qui in virtute Dei custodimini per fidem in salutem paratam revelari in tempore novissimo. ⁶In quo exsultatis, modicum nunc si oportet contristati in variis tentationibus,

*1:1–2 The author addresses this letter mainly to Christians of Gentile background. In it, after thanking God for having saved us through Jesus Christ (1:3–12), he looks at some aspects of Christian life that follow on from Baptism—the call to holiness (1:13—2:10), the exemplary way Christians should act in everyday life (2:11—3:12), patience in the midst of trials, big or small (3:13—4:19), and, finally, the way priests should behave towards their flocks and vice versa (5:1–11). The author ends by giving some information about the circumstances in which the letter was written (5:12–14).

The sacred writer uses in his greeting the name conferred on him by Jesus: Peter (v. 1) comes from the Greek translation of the Aramaic word *cephas*, meaning a stone (see Jn 1:35–51 and note). He introduces himself as "an apostle of Jesus Christ", that is, someone qualified to bear witness to the life and work of our Lord (see Gal 2:9). The "Dispersion" or diaspora originally referred to Jews outside Palestine, but here it has a deeper meaning: St Peter is addressing the chosen, the elect, exiles in the Dispersion, that is, Christians who are living in this world like wayfarers journeying towards their eternal homeland, heaven (see 1:17; 2:11; and, for

example, Gen 47:9; the entire book of Exodus; Ps 39:12; 119:19; Heb 11:13). The areas mentioned in v. 1 were in Asia Minor (present-day Turkey). Perhaps the first news they had received of Christianity came from Jews in those regions who had been converted to Christianity in Jerusalem on the day of Pentecost, or on some other occasion.

Verse 2 amounts to a profession of faith in the Blessed Trinity: to the Father is attributed election from all eternity; to the Son, redemption; to the Holy Spirit, sanctification.

1:3–12 The original recipients of the letter lived in a world hostile to Christian believers, and suffered as a consequence. St Peter develops what he said in v. 2, pointing out why they should feel consoled and should persevere in the faith: they have been saved by God in Christ. Christians have been reborn (cf. Jn 3:3–8; Gal 6:15) and endowed with a great dignity. By choosing them, God the Father has destined them to a wonderful inheritance in heaven (vv. 3–5); to lay hold of this, they must believe in Christ and love him, despite suffering trials (vv. 6–9); the Holy Spirit, who in the Old Testament announced the salvation that would result from Christ's sufferings,

Eph 1:19

Rom 2:7, 10
Jas 1:3
Mal 3:3
1 Cor 3:13
1 Jn 4:20

Jn 20:29

ready to be revealed in the last time. [6]In this you rejoice,[a] though now for a little while you may have to suffer various trials, [7]so that the genuineness of your faith, more precious than gold which though perishable is tested by fire, may redound to praise and glory and honour at the revelation of Jesus Christ. [8]Without having seen[b] him you[c] love him; though you do not now see him you[c] believe in him and rejoice with unutterable and exalted joy. [9]As the outcome of your faith you obtain the salvation of your souls.

Is 52:13-53:12
Lk 18:37
Acts 1:7
Rom 16:25

Eph 3:10

[10]The prophets who prophesied of the grace that was to be yours searched and inquired about this salvation; [11]they inquired what person or time was indicated by the Spirit of Christ* within them when predicting the sufferings of Christ and the subsequent glory. [12]It was revealed to them that they were serving not themselves but you, in the things which have now been announced to you by those who preached the good news to you through the Holy Spirit sent from heaven, things into which angels long to look.

1. A CALL TO HOLINESS*

Christians are called to be saints

Lk 12:35

Rom 12:2
Eph 4:17
Rom 6:19

[13]Therefore gird up your minds, be sober, set your hope fully upon the grace that is coming to you at the revelation of Jesus Christ. [14]As obedient children, do not be conformed to the passions of your former ignorance, [15]but as he who called you is

[7]ut probatio vestrae fidei multo pretiosior auro, quod perit, per ignem quidem probato, inveniatur in laudem et gloriam et honorem in revelatione Iesu Christi. [8]Quem cum non videritis, diligitis; in quem nunc non videntes, credentes autem, exsultatis laetitia inenarrabili et glorificata, [9]reportantes finem fidei vestrae salutem animarum. [10]De qua salute exquisierunt atque scrutati sunt prophetae, qui de futura in vos gratia prophetaverunt, [11]scrutantes in quod vel quale tempus significaret, qui erat in eis Spiritus Christi, praenuntians eas, quae in Christo sunt, passiones et posteriores glorias; [12]quibus revelatum est quia non sibi ipsis, vobis autem ministrabant ea, quae nunc nuntiata sunt vobis per eos, qui evangelizaverunt vos, Spiritu Sancto misso de caelo, in quae desiderant angeli prospicere. [13]Propter quod succincti lumbos mentis vestrae, sobrii, perfecte sperate in

now proclaims that salvation has come, and his message is preached by those who spread the good news (vv. 10–12). These verses help us see the role of the Holy Spirit as the source and guide of the Church's evangelizing work.

Hope of obtaining the inheritance of heaven gives Christians joy in the midst of trials that test their faith: "St Peter says that it is good to suffer trials because eternal joys cannot be obtained except through the afflictions and sorrows of this passing world. 'For a little while', he says, however, because when one receives the eternal reward, the afflictions of this world—which appeared so heavy and bitter—seem then to have been very short-lived and slight" (St Bede, *In I Epistolam Sancti Petri*, ad loc.). "If I experience pain," St Augustine teaches, "relief will come in due course. If I am offered tribulation, it will serve for my purification. Does gold shine in the craftsman's furnace? It will shine later, when it forms part of the necklace, when it is part of the

jewellery. But, for the time being, it must pass through the fire because when it sheds its impurities it will acquire its brilliant shine" (*Enarrationes in Psalmos*, 61, 11).

*1:13–2:10 The body of the letter begins here. As a consequence of the new life that Baptism confers, Christians are called to holiness. The writer stresses two points—the holiness of God who calls them (vv. 13–16) and the blood of Christ, which was the price paid for their salvation (vv. 17–21). Holiness should express itself in love (1:22–25) and in the constant effort to grow in the Christian life (2:1–3), aware that, as living stones, Christians form part of the spiritual house of the Church (2:4–10). This section includes many features of a baptismal catechesis.

1:13–16 With the Exodus theme and the Covenant of Sinai as a background, St Peter explains that Christians are the new Chosen

a Or *Rejoice in this*   b Other ancient authorities read *known*   c Or omit *you*

holy, be holy yourselves in all your conduct; [16]since it is written, "You shall be holy, for I am holy."

Mt 5:48
1 Jn 3:3
Is 43:1
Lev 11:44; 19:2

The blood of Christ has ransomed us

[17]And if you invoke as Father him who judges each one impartially according to his deeds, conduct yourselves with fear throughout the time of your exile. [18]You know that you were ransomed from the futile ways inherited from your fathers, not with perishable things such as silver or gold, [19]but with the precious blood of Christ, like that of a lamb without blemish or spot. [20]He was destined before the foundation of the world but was made manifest at the end of the times for your sake. [21]Through him you have confidence in God, who raised him from the dead and gave him glory, so that your faith and hope are in God.[d]

Rom 2:11
2 Cor 5:6
Deut 10:17
Is 52:3
1 Cor 6:20; 7:23

Eph 4:17
Jn 1:29; 17:24
Rev 5:9
Rom 3:24-25

Rom 4:24; 8:11
Gal 4:4
Heb 1:2

Brotherly love

[22]Having purified your souls by your obedience to the truth for a sincere love of the brethren, love one another earnestly from the heart. [23]You have been born anew, not of perishable seed but of imperishable, through the living and abiding word of God; [24]for

Jn 17:17
1 Pet 1:3

1 Jn 3:9
Jas 1:18

> "All flesh is like grass
> and all its glory like the flower of grass.

Is 40:6–8
Jas 1:10
Dan 6:27

eam, quae offertur vobis, gratiam in revelatione Iesu Christi. [14]Quasi filii oboedientiae, non configurati prioribus in ignorantia vestra desideriis, [15]sed secundum eum, qui vocavit vos, sanctum, et ipsi sancti in omni conversatione sitis, [16]quoniam scriptum est: «Sancti eritis, quia ego sanctus sum». [17]Et si Patrem invocatis eum, qui sine acceptione personarum iudicat secundum uniuscuiusque opus, in timore incolatus vestri tempore conversamini, [18]scientes quod non corruptibilibus argento vel auro redempti estis de vana vestra conversatione a patribus tradita, [19]sed pretioso sanguine quasi Agni incontaminati et immaculati Christi, [20]praecogniti quidem ante constitutionem mundi, manifestati autem novissimis temporibus propter vos, [21]qui per ipsum fideles estis in Deum, qui suscitavit eum a mortuis et dedit ei gloriam, ut fides vestra et spes esset in Deum. [22]Animas vestras castificantes in oboedientia veritatis ad fraternitatis amorem non fictum, ex corde invicem diligite attentius, [23]renati non ex semine cor-

People, delivered from the power of sin and called to lead holy lives, with God himself as their model.

"Gird up your minds" (v. 13) and "passions of your former ignorance" (v. 14) are phrases that echo the Exodus account. In Exodus 12:11 we are told that God established that, when the Israelites celebrated the Passover, they should do so with their loins girt, their sandals on and a staff in their hands; and Numbers 11:5 tells us that the Israelites began to miss the food they had in Egypt.

On the universal call to holiness, see the notes on Mt 5:17–48 and Lk 12:22–34.

1:17–21 Freedom from sin, and holiness, derive from the sacrifice of Christ. St Peter uses the imagery of slave redemption to explain what Christ's sacrifice means. The passage is also evocative of the Exodus: after offering the Passover lamb, the Israelites were delivered by God from slavery in Egypt (see Ex 12:5); but the price for this redemption "was not reckoned in terms of money but in terms of blood, for Christ died for us; he has set us free with his precious blood, as St Peter also reminds us in his letter (...); precious because it is the blood of a spotless Lamb, the blood of the Son of God, who has ransomed us not only from the curse of the Law, but also from that never-ending death which impiety implies" (St Ambrose, *Expositio Evangelii secundum Lucam*, 12, 6–7). The comparison of Jesus to the lamb is a way of referring to the atoning sacrifice of the cross and the spotless innocence of the Redeemer (cf. Jn 1:29).

1:22–25 Fraternal love is one of the signs of holiness. The word of God is the foundation and guarantor of the new life a person receives in Baptism (v. 23). The writer backs up this point by using the image of the flower of grass, taken from Isaiah 40:6–8 (cf. Jas 1:10), which underlines the difference between the transitory nature of earthly things and the permanence of the word of God.

d Or *so that your faith is hope in God*

The grass withers, and the flower falls,
²⁵ but the word of the Lord abides for ever."
That word is the good news which was preached to you.

Like newborn babies

Eph 4:22
Jas 1:21

Mt 18:3
1 Cor 3:2
Heb 5:12f
Ps 34:8

2 ¹So put away all malice and all guile and insincerity and envy and all slander. ²Like newborn babes, long for the pure spiritual milk, that by it you may grow up to salvation; ³for you have tasted the kindness of the Lord.

The priesthood that all believers share

Acts 4:11
Mt 21:42
Eph 2:21
Rom 12:1
Ex 19:6

Rom 9:33; 10:1

Is 28:16

⁴Come to him, to that living stone, rejected by men but in God's sight chosen and precious; ⁵and like living stones be yourselves built into a spiritual house, to be a holy priesthood, to offer spiritual sacrifices acceptable to God through Jesus Christ. ⁶For it stands in scripture:

"Behold, I am laying in Zion a stone, a cornerstone chosen and precious,
and he who believes in him will not be put to shame."
⁷To you therefore who believe, he is precious, but for those who do not believe,

ruptibili sed incorruptibili per verbum Dei vivum et permanens; ²⁴quia *omnis caro ut fenum, / et omnis gloria eius tamquam flos feni. / Exaruit fenum, et flos decidit; /* ²⁵*verbum autem Domini manet in aeternum.* Hoc est autem verbum, quod evangelizatum est in vos.   [2]¹Deponentes igitur omnem malitiam et omnem dolum et simulationes et invidias et omnes detractiones, ²sicut modo geniti infantes, rationale sine dolo lac concupiscite, ut in eo crescatis in salutem, ³si *gustastis quoniam dulcis Dominus.* ⁴Ad quem accedentes, lapidem vivum, ab hominibus quidem reprobatum, coram Deo autem electum, pretiosum, ⁵et ipsi tamquam lapides vivi aedificamini domus spiritalis in sacerdotium sanctum offerre spiritales hostias acceptabiles Deo per Iesum Christum. ⁶Propter quod continet Scriptura: «*Ecce pono in Sion lapidem angularem, electum, pretiosum; / et,*

2:1–3 The liturgy applies this passage to the newly baptized; they are like babies recently born to the new life of grace; it prays: "You wash away our sins with water, you give us new birth in the Spirit, and redeem us in the blood of Christ. As we celebrate Christ's resurrection increase our awareness of these blessings, and renew your gift of life within us" (*Roman Missal,* 2nd Sunday of Easter, Opening Prayer).

"Spiritual milk" (v. 2): this may be an allusion to the promises God made to the Chosen People to bring them into "a land flowing with milk and honey" (Ex 3:8). The phrase means, in effect, all the graces that God gives a person in Baptism to help him or her attain salvation.

2:4–10. This passage (composed of quotations from the Old Testament woven together—possibly a collection used in early apostolic catechesis) hinges on the idea of building. Baptism makes a person a member of the spiritual building of the Church, whose cornerstone is Jesus Christ (vv. 4–8). Christians are living stones that must be united to Christ by faith and grace; this unity will ensure that the building is solid, a suitable place to offer "spiritual sacrifices acceptable

to God" (v. 5). The closer their union with Christ, the stronger the building will be: "All of us who believe in Christ Jesus", Origen explains, "are called 'living stones' […]. For if you, who are listening to me, want to prepare yourself better for the construction of this building, and be one of the stones closest to the foundation, you need to realize that Christ himself is the foundation of the building we are describing. As the Apostle Paul tells us, 'no other foundation can anyone lay than that which is laid, which is Jesus Christ' (1 Cor 3:11)" (Origen, *In Iesu Nave,* 9, 1).

"As they were destined to do" (v. 8). No one is rejected out of hand. When the Bible speaks in terms of predestination it means the free actions of men, known in advance to an all-knowing, eternal God.

In contrast to those who do not believe, believers form the true Israel, the new People of God (vv. 9–10). Israel's privileges now apply to Christians. The Old Testament prophecies find fulfilment in the Church.

In this holy people, there is only one priest, Jesus Christ, and one sacrifice, that which he offered on the cross and which is renewed in the

> "The very stone which the builders rejected
> has become the head of the corner,"

Mt 21:42
Ps 118:22

[8]and

> "A stone that will make men stumble,
> a rock that will make them fall";

Is 8:14

for they stumble because they disobey the word, as they were destined to do.

[9]But you are a chosen race, a royal priesthood, a holy nation, God's own people,[e] that you may declare the wonderful deeds of him who called you out of darkness into his marvellous light. [10]Once you were no people but now you are God's people; once you had not received mercy but now you have received mercy.

Ex 19:6
Deut 7:6
Eph 5:8; 1:14
Phil 2:15
Is 43:20–21
Col 1:12–13
Hos 1:6; 9
Rom 9:25

2. THE OBLIGATIONS OF CHRISTIANS*

Setting an example for pagans

[11]Beloved, I beseech you as aliens and exiles to abstain from the passions of the flesh that wage war against your soul. [12]Maintain good conduct among the Gentiles, so that in case they speak against you as wrongdoers, they may see your good deeds and glorify God on the day of visitation.

Ps 39:12
Gal 5:17, 24
Gen 23:4
Heb 11:13
Jas 4:1
Jas 3:13
Mt 5:16
Is 10:3
1 Tim 5:10
Ex 3:16

qui credit in eo, non confundetur». [7]Vobis igitur honor credentibus; non credentibus autem *«Lapis, quem reprobaverunt aedificantes, / hic factus est in caput anguli»* [8]et *«lapis offensionis et petra scandali»*; qui offendunt verbo non credentes, in quod et positi sunt. / [9]Vos autem *genus electum, regale sacerdotium, gens sancta, populus in acquisitionem, ut virtutes annuntietis* eius, qui de tenebris vos vocavit in admirabile lumen suum; [10]qui aliquando *non populus*, nunc autem *populus Dei; qui non consecuti misericordiam*, nunc autem *misericordiam consecuti.* [11]Carissimi, obsecro tamquam advenas et peregrinos abstinere vos a carnalibus desideriis, quae militant adversus animam; [12]conversationem vestram inter gentes habentes bonam, ut in eo, quod detrectant de vobis tamquam de malefactoribus, ex bonis operibus considerantes glorificent Deum in die visita-

Mass. But all Christians, through the sacraments of Baptism and Confirmation, share in Christ's priesthood and are thereby enabled to mediate in a priestly way between God and man, and to take an active part in divine worship. This is what is called the "priesthood of all the faithful" as distinct from ministerial priesthood. "All their works, prayers and apostolic undertakings, family and married life, daily work, relaxation of mind and body, if they are accomplished in the Spirit—indeed even the hardships of life if patiently borne—all these become spiritual sacrifices acceptable to God through Jesus Christ. In the celebration of the Eucharist these may most fittingly be offered to the Father along with the body of the Lord. And so, worshipping everywhere by their holy actions, the laity consecrate the world itself to God" (Vatican II, *Lumen gentium*, 34).

*2:11—3:12 The sacred writer goes on to describe the effects of Christians' good example in a hostile world. He mentions various duties of a Christian to the society around him—in public

life (2:11–17) and private life (2:18—3:12). Love for his brethren should rank high in his priorities (3:8–12). Christ has set an example for us to follow (2:21–25).

2:11–12 Baptism gives Christians a dignity that is incompatible with leading a worldly life. Therefore, it cannot come as a surprise that worldly people criticize them for being different, for their upright lives. Even so, their exemplary lives will have an impact, and will draw some people to God: "Let your light so shine before men, that they may see your good works and give glory to your Father who is in heaven (Mt 5:16)." St John Chrysostom exhorted his flock in this way: "There would be no need for preaching if our life were a beacon of virtues— no call for words if we had deeds to show. There would be no pagans if we were truly Christians—if we kept Jesus Christ's commandments, if we put up with unjust treatment and deception, if we blessed those who cursed us, if we returned good for evil. No one would be such a monster as not to embrace

e Greek *a people for his possession*

Obedience to civil authority

[13]Be subject for the Lord's sake to every human institution,[f] whether it be to the emperor as supreme, [14]or to governors as sent by him to punish those who do wrong and to praise those who do right. [15]For it is God's will that by doing right you should put to silence the ignorance of foolish men. [16]Live as free men, yet without using your freedom as a pretext for evil; but live as servants of God. [17]Honour all men. Love the brotherhood. Fear God. Honour the emperor.

Duties towards masters. Christ's example

[18]Servants, be submissive to your masters with all respect, not only to the kind and gentle but also to the overbearing. [19]For one is approved if, mindful of God, he endures pain while suffering unjustly. [20]For what credit is it, if when you do wrong and are beaten for it you take it patiently? But if when you do right and suffer for it you take it patiently, you have God's approval. [21]For to this you have been called, because Christ also suffered for you, leaving you an example, that you should follow in his steps. [22]He committed no sin; no guile was found on his lips. [23]When he was reviled, he did not revile in return; when he suffered, he did not threaten; but he trusted to him who judges justly. [24]He himself bore our sins in his body on the tree,[g] that we might die to sin and live to righteousness. By his wounds you have been healed. [25]For you were straying like sheep, but have now returned to the Shepherd and Guardian of your souls.

tionis. [13]Subiecti estote omni humanae creaturae propter Dominum: sive regi quasi praecellenti [14]sive ducibus tamquam ab eo missis ad vindictam malefactorum, laudem vero bonorum; [15]quia sic est voluntas Dei, ut benefacientes obmutescere faciatis imprudentium hominum ignorantiam, [16]quasi liberi, et non quasi velamen habentes malitiae libertatem, sed sicut servi Dei. [17]Omnes honorate, fraternitatem diligite, Deum timete, regem honorificate. [18]Servi, subditi estote in omni timore dominis, non tantum bonis et modestis sed etiam pravis. [19]Haec est enim gratia, si propter conscientiam Dei sustinet quis tristitias, patiens iniuste. [20]Quae enim gloria est, si peccantes et colaphizati sustinetis? Sed si benefacientes et patientes sustinetis, haec est gratia apud Deum. [21]In hoc enim vocati estis, quia / et Christus passus est pro vobis, / vobis relinquens exemplum, / ut sequamini vestigia eius: / [22]qui *peccatum non fecit, / nec inventus est dolus in ore ipsius;* / [23]qui cum malediceretur, non remaledicebat; / cum pateretur, non comminabatur; / commendabat autem iuste iudicanti; / [24]qui *peccata* nostra *ipse pertulit* / in corpore suo super lignum, / ut peccatis mortui iustitiae viveremus; / cuius *livore sanati estis.* / [25]Eratis enim *sicut oves errantes,* sed conversi estis nunc ad pastorem et episcopum ani-

the true religion immediately if we really lived like that" (*In 1 Timotheum*, 10).

2:13–17. Filial fear of the Lord is the basis of respect for authority. Jesus told people about their duties as citizens (see Mt 22:21–22; 17:24–27), and St Paul, echoing that teaching, reminded us that all authority comes from God (see Rom 13:1–7 and note; cf. Jn 19:11). "The duty of obedience requires all to give due honour to authority and to treat those who are charged to exercise it with respect, and, insofar as it is deserved, with gratitude and good-will" (*Catechism of the Catholic Church*, 1900).

2:18–25 Being a good Christian also means that there should be harmony in the home. If one is a servant or slave, this means putting up with unjust treatment, as Jesus himself did. Verses 21–25 are a beautiful hymn to Christ on the

cross, in whom were fulfilled the ancient prophecies about the suffering Servant found in the book of Isaiah (see 52:13—53:12). However severe the trials we may experience, they can never compare to, or be as undeserved as, those of our Lord. Reflecting on Christ's passion led St Bernard to comment: "I have come to see that true wisdom lies in meditating on these things [...]. Some have provided me with wholesome, if bitter, drink, and I have used others as gentle and soothing unction. This gives me strength in adversity and helps me to be humble in prosperity; it allows me to walk with a sure step on the royal road of salvation, through the good things and the evil things of this present life, free from the dangers which threaten on right and left" (*In Cantica Canticorum*, 43, 4).

"Shepherd and Guardian of your souls" (v. 25). The messianic prophecies about the suffering Servant include the image of the scattered

f Or *every institution ordained for men*   g Or *carried up ... to the tree*

Exemplary family life

3 ¹Likewise you wives,* be submissive to your husbands, so that some, though they do not obey the word, may be won without a word by the behaviour of their wives, ²when they see your reverent and chaste behaviour. ³Let not yours be the outward adorning with braiding of hair, decoration of gold, and wearing of fine clothing, ⁴but let it be the hidden person of the heart with the imperishable jewel of a gentle and quiet spirit, which in God's sight is very precious. ⁵So once the holy women who hoped in God used to adorn themselves and were submissive to their husbands, ⁶as Sarah obeyed Abraham, calling him lord. And you are now her children if you do right and let nothing terrify you.

⁷Likewise you husbands, live considerately with your wives, bestowing honour on the woman as the weaker sex, since you are joint heirs of the grace of life, in order that your prayers may not be hindered.

Eph 5:22
Col 3:18
1 Cor 7:16
1 Pet 1:25

1 Pet 2:12

Is 3:18, 24
1 Tim 2:9
Rev 17:4

Gen 18:12
Prov 3:25
Gal 4:28

Eph 5:25–33
Col 3:19

Love of the brethren

⁸Finally, all of you, have unity of spirit, sympathy, love of the brethren, a tender heart and a humble mind. ⁹Do not return evil for evil or reviling for reviling; but on the contrary bless, for to this you have been called, that you may obtain a blessing. ¹⁰For

> "He that would love life
> and see good days,
> let him keep his tongue from evil
> and his lips from speaking guile;
> ¹¹ let him turn away from evil and do right;
> let him seek peace and pursue it.
> ¹² For the eyes of the Lord are upon the righteous,
> and his ears are open to their prayer.
> But the face of the Lord is against those that do evil."

Rom 12:16

Mt 5:39, 44
1 Thess 5:15
Lk 6:28

Jas 1:26

Ps 34:14–16

marum vestrarum.   [3] ¹Similiter mulieres subditae sint suis viris, ut et si qui non credunt verbo, per mulierum conversationem sine verbo lucrifiant, ²considerantes castam in timore conversationem vestram; ³quarum sit non extrinsecus capillaturae aut circumdationis auri aut indumenti vestimentorum cultus, ⁴sed qui absconditus cordis est homo in incorruptibilitate mitis et quieti spiritus, qui est in conspectu Dei locuples. ⁵Sic enim aliquando et sanctae mulieres sperantes in Deo ornabant se subiectae propriis viris, ⁶sicut Sara oboediebat Abrahae dominum eum vocans; cuius estis filiae benefacientes et non timentes ullam perturbationem. ⁷Viri similiter cohabitantes secundum scientiam quasi infirmiori vaso muliebri impertientes honorem, tamquam et coheredibus gratiae vitae, uti ne impediantur orationes vestrae. ⁸In fine autem omnes unanimes, compatientes, fraternitatis amatores, misericordes, humiles, ⁹non reddentes malum pro malo vel maledictum pro maledicto, sed e contrario benedi-

flock (cf. Is 53:6), to which Jesus refers in his allegory of the Good Shepherd (see Jn 10:11–16). St Peter, to whom our Lord gave charge of his flock (see Jn 21:15–17), seems to have been particularly fond of this pastoral metaphor.

3:1–7 The counsel and appeals contained in this passage are designed to guide spouses' mutual love towards a search for each other's greater good—that is, conversion. With an eye on the lifestyle of the world around them, the writer exhorts couples to act in a Christian way; the practical advice he gives is based on the equal dignity of husband and wife (v. 7). The essential equality of men and women is not compromised

or contradicted by the fact that they may have different roles within marriage as fathers and mothers.

3:8–12 Love is the virtue that must govern Christian life; a theological virtue, it enhances all the moral virtues. The promise of the Lord's blessing is proclaimed with words from Psalm 34:12–16, a psalm from which the writer has already quoted (see 2:3 and Ps 34:8). "Peter extends his exhortation beyond the husband and wife to lay down a law of love for all, from which springs all virtue: compassion, mercy, humility and all the other virtues that he goes on to describe" (St Andrew of Crete, *Catena*, ad loc.).

3. THE CHRISTIAN'S ATTITUDE TO SUFFERING*

Undeserved suffering is a blessing

Rom 8:34

Mt 5:10
Is 8:12–13

1 Pet 1:3
Mt 10:26–31
Prov 3:25

1 Pet 2:12

1 Pet 2:21, 24
Rom 5:6; 6:10
Heb 9:28
Is 53:11

[13]Now who is there to harm you if you are zealous for what is right? [14]But even if you do suffer for righteousness' sake, you will be blessed. Have no fear of them, nor be troubled, [15]but in your hearts reverence Christ as Lord. Always be prepared to make a defence to any one who calls you to account for the hope that is in you, yet do it with gentleness and reverence; [16]and keep your conscience clear, so that, when you are abused, those who revile your good behaviour in Christ may be put to shame. [17]For it is better to suffer for doing right, if that should be God's will, than for doing wrong.

Christ's suffering and glorification

[18]For Christ also died[h] for sins once for all, the righteous for the unrighteous, that he might bring us to God, being put to death in the flesh but made alive in the spirit; [19]in

centes, quia in hoc vocati estis, ut benedictionem hereditate accipiatis. [10]«Qui enim *vult vitam diligere / et videre dies bonos, / coerceat linguam suam a malo, / et labia eius ne loquantur dolum;* / [11]*declinet autem a malo et faciat bonum, / inquirat pacem et persequatur eam.* / [12]Quia *oculi Domini super iustos, / et aures eius in preces eorum; / vultus autem Domini super facientes mala».* [13]Et quis est qui vobis noceat, si boni aemulatores fueritis? [14]Sed et si patimini propter iustitiam, beati! *Timorem autem eorum ne timueritis et non conturbemini,* [15]*Dominum* autem Christum *sanctificate* in cordibus vestris, parati semper ad defensionem omni poscenti vos rationem de ea, quae in vobis est spe, [16]sed cum mansuetudine et timore, conscientiam habentes bonam, ut in quo de vobis detrectatur, confundantur, qui calumniantur vestram bonam in Christo conversationem. [17]Melius est enim benefacientes, si velit voluntas Dei, pati quam malefacientes. [18]Quia et Christus semel pro peccatis passus est, iustus pro iniustis, ut vos adduceret ad Deum, mortificatus quidem carne, vivificatus autem Spiritu; [19]in quo et his, qui in carcere erant, spiritibus

*3:13—4:19 This section of the letter deals with how Christians, through their suffering, share in the redemptive mystery of Christ: when they suffer unjustly, they should feel blessed (3:13–17), for Christ suffered unto death prior to entering his glory (3:18–22). Christians, as members of Christ, have broken with sin (4:1–6) and should put love into everything they do (4:7–11). The passage ends with a return to the theme of suffering provoked by undeserved persecution (4:12–19).

3:13–17 These verses introduce a new theme which takes us up to the end of the letter. They seem to be directed to people who are surprised to encounter persecution even though they are doing good (v. 13). If we act in a way consistent with our faith, those who criticize us unjustly may come to see their mistake and mend their ways (v. 16). Using words from Isaiah, the author tells Christians, in the midst of their trials, to "reverence" (literally, "sanctify", "hallow") Christ as Lord (v. 15), that is, to render him the type of worship that is due to God alone: "Impossible though it may be to understand, what does it mean to glorify Christ if not to feel his holiness in the depth of our hearts? The

flames of holiness give those who have hope the strength to triumph over sin" (St Bede, *In 1 Epistolam Sancti Petri*, ad loc.).

3:18–22 This passage may include parts of a Creed used in early Christian catechetical instruction. It clearly states the essentials of belief in Jesus Christ, as preached by the apostles from the very beginning and as found later in the Apostles' Creed: he died, descended into hell, rose from the dead and ascended into heaven.

Verse 19 is informed by the Church's belief in the descent of Christ into hell, a manifestation of the fact that salvation extends to all, irrespective of the age in which they lived: "In his human soul united to his divine person, the dead Christ went down to the realm of the dead. He opened heaven's gates for the just who had gone before him" (*Catechism of the Catholic Church*, 637; see also 633). The expression "spirits in prison" has been interpreted in a number of ways: these spirits may be the souls of the just of the Old Testament, who were held in the bosom of Abraham. That is the interpretation given by some Fathers of the Church. But the words may also refer to the fallen angels who were confined in the darkest depths—

h Other ancient authorities read *suffered*

which he went and preached to the spirits in prison, ²⁰who formerly did not obey, when God's patience waited in the days of Noah, during the building of the ark, in which a few, that is, eight persons, were saved through water. ²¹Baptism, which corresponds to this, now saves you, not as a removal of dirt from the body but as an appeal to God for a clear conscience, through the resurrection of Jesus Christ, ²²who has gone into heaven and is at the right hand of God, with angels, authorities, and powers subject to him.

1 Pet 4:6

2 Pet 2:5; 3:9
Gen 7:7, 17

Heb 10:22
Col 2:12–13
Rom 6:4

Eph 1:21
Ps 110:1

The Christian has broken with sin

4 ¹Since therefore Christ suffered in the flesh,ⁱ arm yourselves with the same thought, for whoever has suffered in the fleshⁱ has ceased from sin,* ²so as to live for the rest of the time in the flesh no longer by human passions but by the will of God. ³Let the time that is past suffice for doing what the Gentiles like to do, living in licentiousness, passions, drunkenness, revels, carousing, and lawless idolatry. ⁴They are surprised that you do not now join them in the same wild profligacy, and they abuse you; ⁵but they will give account to him who is ready to judge the living and the dead. ⁶For this is why the gospel was preached even to the dead, that though judged in the flesh like men, they might live in the spirit like God.

Rom 6:2, 7

1 Jn 2:16f
Rom 7:14f

Tit 3:3
Rom 1:28
Eph 4:17–18

Acts 10:42
2 Tim 4:1
1 Pet 3:19
Rom 8:10
1 Cor 5:5
2 Cor 5:5

A call for charity

⁷The end of all things is at hand; therefore keep sane and sober for your prayers. ⁸Above all hold unfailing your love for one another, since love covers a multitude of sins. ⁹Practise hospitality ungrudgingly to one another. ¹⁰As each has received a gift,

1 Cor 10:11
2 Cor 6:2
Prov 10:12
Jas 5:20
1 Pet 1:22

adveniens praedicavit, ²⁰qui increduli fuerant aliquando, quando exspectabat Dei patientia in diebus Noe, cum fabricaretur arca, in qua pauci, id est octo animae, salvae factae sunt per aquam. ²¹Cuius antitypum, baptisma, et vos nunc salvos facit, non carnis depositio sordium sed conscientiae bonae rogatio in Deum, per resurrectionem Iesu Christi, ²²qui est in dextera Dei, profectus in caelum, subiectis sibi angelis et potestatibus et virtutibus. [4] ¹Christo igitur passo in carne, et vos eadem cogitatione armamini, quia, qui passus est carne, desiit a peccato, ²ut iam non hominum concupiscentiis sed voluntate Dei quod reliquum est in carne vivat temporis. ³Sufficit enim praeteritum tempus ad voluntatem gentium consummandam, vobis, qui ambulastis in luxuriis, concupiscentiis, vinolentiis, comissationibus, potationibus et illicitis idolorum cultibus. ⁴In quo mirantur non concurrentibus vobis in eandem luxuriae effusionem, blasphemantes; ⁵qui reddent rationem ei, qui paratus est iudicare vivos et mortuos. ⁶Propter hoc enim et mortuis evangelizatum est, ut iudicentur quidem secundum homines carne, vivant autem secundum Deum Spiritu. ⁷Omnium autem finis appropinquavit. Estote itaque prudentes et vigilate in orationibus. ⁸Ante omnia mutuam in vosmetipsos caritatem continuam habentes, quia caritas operit multitudinem peccatorum; ⁹hospitales invicem sine murmuratione; ¹⁰unusquisque, sicut accepit donationem, in

in which case the letter is underlining Christ's victory over the devil. The waters of the flood are a figure of those of Baptism: just as Noah and his family were saved in the ark from the destruction wrought by the flood, now people are saved through Baptism, by which they become members of Christ's Church (vv. 20–22).

4:1–6 Christians should act differently from the way they did before they were baptized, and differently from the unbaptized, even if that leads to misunderstanding and unjust criticism. By dying mystically with Christ in Baptism (v. 1), they have been absolved of sin, and it would make no sense for them to continue to live in sin (cf. Rom 6:1ff; 1 Jn 3:9; 5:18). We should remember that we must all appear before the Judge of the living and the dead, Jesus Christ (vv. 5–6).

It is not easy to interpret what v. 6 means. It may be an allusion to Christ's descent into the bosom of Abraham or to Christians who die before witnessing the final victory of Christ. In any event, the sacred writer is speaking about those who have stayed true to God; for people without a supernatural outlook, the lives that Christians lead make no sense at all. The message is reminiscent of Wisdom 3:1–4.

4:7–11 The incarnation of Jesus Christ marked the beginning of the last days, a period that extends to the end of the world and the Last Judgment. That is why the writer says that "the end of all things is at hand" (v. 7), and why he urges Christians to practise prayer and charity, and also hospitality.

"Love covers a multitude of sins" (v. 8). This, an allusion to Proverbs 10:12 (cf. Jas 5:20),

i Other ancient authorities add *for us*; some *for you*

Lk 12:42
1 Cor 12:4–11
Rom 3:2; 12:7; 16:7
1 Cor 10:31

employ it for one another, as good stewards of God's varied grace: [11]whoever speaks, as one who utters oracles of God; whoever renders service, as one who renders it by the strength which God supplies; in order that in everything God may be glorified through Jesus Christ. To him belong glory and dominion for ever and ever. Amen.

The Christian meaning of suffering

1 Pet 1:6f; 3:14
Mt 5:11–12
Acts 5:41
Rom 3:3–5
Acts 5:41
Rom 8:17
Jas 1:2
Col 3:4

Is 11:2
Ps 89:50f
Lk 10:6
Acts 5:41
1 Pet 2:20

Acts 11:26; 26:28
Phil 1:20

Ezek 9:6
Jer 25:29
Lk 23:31
Prov 11:31
1 Cor 11:32
2 Thess 1:8

Lk 23:46

[12]Beloved, do not be surprised at the fiery ordeal which comes upon you to prove you, as though something strange were happening to you. [13]But rejoice in so far as you share Christ's sufferings, that you may also rejoice and be glad when his glory is revealed. [14]If you are reproached for the name of Christ, you are blessed, because the spirit of glory[j] and of God rests upon you. [15]But let none of you suffer as a murderer, or a thief, or a wrongdoer, or a mischief-maker; [16]yet if one suffers as a Christian, let him not be ashamed, but under that name let him glorify God. [17]For the time has come for judgment to begin with the household of God; and if it begins with us, what will be the end of those who do not obey the gospel of God? [18]And

> "If the righteous man is scarcely saved,
> where will the impious and sinner appear?"

[19]Therefore let those who suffer according to God's will do right and entrust their souls to a faithful Creator.

4. FINAL EXHORTATIONS*

To priests

Mt 17:5
Rom 8:17
Acts 11:30
Col 3:4

5 [1]So I exhort the elders among you, as a fellow elder and a witness of the sufferings of Christ as well as a partaker in the glory that is to be revealed. [2]Tend the

---

alterutrum illam administrantes sicut boni dispensatores multiformis gratiae Dei. [11]Si quis loquitur, quasi sermones Dei; si quis ministrat, tamquam ex virtute, quam largitur Deus, ut in omnibus glorificetur Deus per Iesum Christum: cui est gloria et imperium in saecula saeculorum. Amen. [12]Carissimi, nolite mirari in fervore, qui ad tentationem vobis fit, quasi novi aliquid vobis contingat, [13]sed, quemadmodum communicatis Christi passionibus, gaudete, ut et in revelatione gloriae eius gaudeatis exsultantes. [14]Si exprobramini in nomine Christi, beati, quoniam Spiritus gloriae et Dei super vos requiescit. [15]Nemo enim vestrum patiatur quasi homicida aut fur aut maleficus aut alienorum speculator; [16]si autem ut christianus, non erubescat, glorificet autem Deum in isto nomine. [17]Quoniam tempus est, ut incipiat iudicium a domo Dei; si autem primum a nobis, qui finis eorum, qui non credunt Dei evangelio? [18]«Et si *iustus vix salvatur, / impius et peccator ubi parebit?*». [19]Itaque et hi, qui patiuntur secundum voluntatem Dei, fideli Creatori commendent animas suas in benefacto.   [5] [1]Seniores ergo, qui in vobis sunt, obsecro, consenior et testis Christi pas-

---

can be read as meaning both the sins of others (which love understands, forgives and excuses) and also one's own sins. "Love unites us to God; love covers a multitude of sins; love bears all; love is patient. In love, nothing is base or proud. Love does not cause disunity, nor inspire rebellion; love does all things in harmony. All His chosen ones will reach God through love; without love, nothing is pleasing to Him" (St Clement of Rome, *Ad Corinthios*, 49, 5).

4:12–19 This passage harks back to the main theme of this section. Christians who share in Christ's sufferings (see 1:6–7; 2:18–25; 3:13–17) will also share in his exaltation. "God wants to open our eyes to all the mercy he shows us

through what the world calls dishonour, and how greatly honoured we are in being dishonoured when we seek to give honour to God" (St John of Avila, *Epístola*, 58). Given the imminence of divine judgment (another recurring theme in the letter), no one should be complacent (vv. 17–18). The apostle's stern warnings are reminiscent of what Jesus said to the women of Jerusalem on the road to Calvary: "if they do this when the wood is green, what will happen when it is dry?" (Lk 23:31). If a Christian has suffered for Christ in this life, he or she can face God's judgment with greater confidence (cf. Mt 5:11–12; 10:32).

*5:1–14 The final part of the letter consists of exhortations to priests (5:1–4) and to the faithful

---

j Other ancient authorities insert *and of power*

flock of God that is your charge,[k] not by constraint but willingly,[l] not for shameful gain but eagerly, [3]not as domineering over those in your charge but being examples to the flock. [4]And when the chief Shepherd is manifested you will obtain the unfading crown of glory.

Jn 21:16
Acts 20:28
Philem 14
Tit 1:7
1 Cor 4:16
1 Cor 9:25
Heb 13:20
Tit 2:7
1 Pet 2 :25
Is 40:10-11

To all the faithful

[5]Likewise you that are younger be subject to the elders. Clothe yourselves, all of you, with humility toward one another, for "God opposes the proud, but gives grace to the humble."

Jn 13:4, 14
Eph 5:21
Jas 4:6–10

Prov 3:34

[6]Humble yourselves therefore under the mighty hand of God, that in due time he may exalt you. [7]Cast all your anxieties on him, for he cares about you. [8]Be sober, be watchful. Your adversary the devil prowls around like a roaring lion, seeking some one to devour. [9]Resist him, firm in your faith, knowing that the same experience of suffering is required of your brotherhood throughout the world. [10]And after you have suffered a little while, the God of all grace, who has called you to his eternal glory in Christ, will himself restore, establish, and strengthen[m] you. [11]To him be the dominion for ever and ever. Amen.

Job 22:29
Ps 55:22
Phil 2:8–9
Mt 6:25
1 Thess 5:6

Eph 6:11, 13
1 Thess 2:14

1 Thess 2:12; 5:24
Rom 8:18
2 Cor 4:17
1 Pet 4:1

Rev 1:8

sionum, qui et eius, quae in futuro revelanda est, gloriae communicator: [2]Pascite, qui est in vobis, gregem Dei, providentes non coacto sed spontanee secundum Deum, neque turpis lucri gratia sed voluntarie, [3]neque ut dominantes in cleris sed formae facti gregis. [4]Et cum apparuerit Princeps pastorum, percipietis immarcescibilem gloriae coronam. [5]Similiter, adulescentes, subditi estote senioribus. Omnes autem invicem humilitatem induite, quia *Deus superbis resistit, / humilibus autem dat gratiam.* [6]Humiliamini igitur sub potenti manu Dei, ut vos exaltet in tempore, [7]omnem sollicitudinem vestram proicientes in eum, quoniam ipsi cura est de vobis. [8]Sobrii estote, vigilate. Adversarius vester Diabolus tamquam leo rugiens circuit quaerens quem devoret. [9]Cui resistite fortes fide, scientes eadem passionum ei, quae in mundo est, vestrae fraternitati fieri. [10]Deus autem omnis gratiae, qui vocavit vos in aeternam suam gloriam in Christo Iesu, modicum passos ipse perficiet, confirmabit, solidabit, fundabit.

(5:5–11), in which the theme of Christ's sufferings is still present. The epilogue (5:12–14), as in other New Testament letters, carries greetings from the church where the writer is based and ends with a few words of blessing.

5:1–4 These exhortations are reminiscent of our Lord's words when he spoke about the Good Shepherd (Jn 10:11), and when he told Peter after the resurrection: "Feed my lambs ... Feed my sheep" (Jn 21:15–17). Pastors should preach by example (see v. 3): "The word more easily gains access to the hearts of hearers when it carries with it the endorsement of the life of him who when giving instructions assists in their fulfilment by his own example" (St Gregory the Great, *Regula pastoralis*, 2, 3).

"Elder" (v. 1). In many New Testament passages, the Greek words *presbýteros* and *epískopos* seem to have the same meaning, and are used indiscriminately to designate the pastors of local communities (see, e.g. Acts 11:30; 20:28). From the second century onwards, the terminology became fixed: *epískopoi* (bishops) have the fullness of the sacrament of Holy Orders and

rule local churches; *presbýteroi* (priests) minister as co-workers of their bishops.

5:5–11 Referring to the trials that God permits, the apostle calls for a solidarity among the faithful that is based on humility and docility (vv. 5–6). "Humility is the source and foundation of every kind of virtue; it is the door by which all God-given grace may enter; it is what seasons all our actions, making them so valuable and so pleasing to God. Finally, it makes us masters of God's heart, to the point, so to speak, of making him our servant; for God has never been able to resist a humble heart" (St John Vianney, *Sermon on the 10th Sunday after Pentecost*).

The ascetical effort to resist temptation is strengthened by trust in the Lord (vv. 7–11). If they stay "firm in the faith" (v. 9), Christians will be able to resist the attacks of the enemy. Any trials they experience serve to purify them and are a pledge of the glory that awaits them in heaven: "For this momentary affliction is preparing for us an eternal weight of glory beyond all comparison" (2 Cor 4:17). "So great is the good that I hope for, that any pain is for

k Other ancient authorities add *exercising the oversight* l Other ancient authorities add *as God would have you* m Other ancient authorities read *restore, establish, strengthen and settle*

Words of farewell

Acts 15:22–27
Heb 13:22

Acts 12:12

2 Cor 13:12

[12]By Silvanus, a faithful brother as I regard him, I have written briefly to you, exhorting and declaring that this is the true grace of God; stand fast in it. [13]She who is at Babylon,* who is likewise chosen, sends you greetings; and so does my son Mark. [14]Greet one another with the kiss of love.

Peace to all of you that are in Christ.

[11]Ipsi imperium in saecula saeculorum. Amen. [12]Per Silvanum vobis fidelem fratrem, ut arbitror, breviter scripsi, obsecrans et contestans hanc esse veram gratiam Dei; in qua state. [13]Salutat vos, quae est in Babylone, coelecta et Marcus filius meus. [14]Salutate invicem in osculo caritatis. Pax vobis omnibus, qui estis in Christo.

me a pleasure" (St Francis of Assisi, *Reflections on Christ's Wounds*, 1).

5:12–14 As do the writers of other New Testament letters, St Peter in his words of farewell sends greetings from the church where he is based, and ends with a few words of blessing. Silvanus, called Silas in Acts 15:22, was with St Paul on his second apostolic journey through Asia Minor and Greece (see Acts 15:36—18:5).

He may have been the bearer of the letter, or the secretary who took down Peter's dictation, or even the editor of ideas given him by the apostle.

"Babylon" (v. 13) is a figurative way of referring to Rome, the archetypal idolatrous and worldly city of the time (see also Rev 16:19; 17:5).

The Mark referred to here is the author of the second Gospel. Tradition says that he acted as St Peter's interpreter in Rome. The apostle calls him "son", using the word in a spiritual sense.

THE SECOND LETTER OF

PETER

Introduction

The First Letter of Peter (addressed to Christians in Asia Minor) is followed by another attributed to the same apostle, but addressed to all Christians, evidencing a fact which reflects the catholic scope of Peter's authority. In this letter we see the efforts made by the first Christians to practise and pass on the faith handed down by the apostles, in an environment that was implacably hostile to their perseverance. The entire letter is imbued with hope in the second, definitive, coming of Christ.

Of all the New Testament books, this is the one whose authenticity (and therefore canonicity) has been most debated. The earliest evidence of its attribution to St Peter comes from the third century and from the Eastern Church. Origen, who was aware of doubts about the letter's authenticity, cites 2 Peter 1:4 as words of St Peter;[1] and he says elsewhere that "Peter proclaims with the trumpets of his two epistles".[2] From this period also comes the testimony of Firmilian, bishop of Caesara in Cappadocia (d. 269), in his Letter to Cyprian.[3] The Bodmer VIII papyrus (P[72]) shows that the letter was copied down in Egypt in the third century, when it was also translated into Coptic. In the fourth century, Eusebius of Caesarea includes this letter among the New Testament texts that are "disputed", that is, not unanimously accepted, but accepted by most.[4] St Athanasius, St Basil, St Gregory Nazianzen and Didymus of Alexandria use it in their works. In the Western Church there are no references to its authority until the second half of the fourth century. St Jerome mentions that there are doubts as to its Petrine authorship, and gives the reasons for these, but he accepts it as canonical.[5] From the fourth century on, these doubts gradually disappear, and in the sixth and seventh centuries the letter earned universal acceptance. It is to be found in the earliest official lists of canonical books, such as those of the councils of Hippo (393), Carthage III (397) and Carthage IV (419), and the letter of Pope Innocent I (405). The Council of Trent solemnly defined the canonicity and inspiration of this letter and all the other books of the Bible.

1. STRUCTURE AND CONTENT

The letter has a clear structure. It begins with a greeting similar to those found in other New Testament writings (1:1–2), and ends with an exhortation to perseverance (3:17–18). The body of the letter is made up of three distinct sections:

1. The first (1:3–21) is an appeal for fidelity to authoritative teaching.

2. The second (2:1–22) is a long denunciation of false teachers, immoral people who try to corrupt others.

3. The third (3:1–16) deals with the Second Coming, refuting false speculation and expounding sound teaching.

---

1 See *In Leviticum homiliae*, 4, 4. **2** *In Iesu Nave*, 7, 1. **3** See *Epistula ad Cyprianum*, 75, 6. **4** See *Historia ecclesiastica*, 3, 25, 3. **5** *De vivis illustribus*, 1; *Epistula ad Hedibiam*, 120, 11.

2. CONTEXT

In the heading to the letter, the author introduces himself as "Simon Peter, a servant and apostle of Jesus Christ" (1:1). Over the course of the letter, which reads as a kind of spiritual testament, a number of references to Peter's life are made: he was an eyewitness to the transfiguration of Jesus (cf. 1:16–18); this is his "second letter" to his addressees (3:1), 1 Peter being the earlier letter; he calls St Paul "our beloved brother" (3:15), and implies that he has a degree of authority over him in terms of the interpretation of the Scriptures; and he speaks about his own death, an allusion perhaps to Jesus' prophecy about his martyrdom (1:14; cf. Jn 21:18–19).

Despite these details, however, internal analysis of the text makes it somewhat difficult to attribute this letter to the leader of the apostles: the vocabulary and the style (which is sophisticated and rather baroque) are markedly different from that of the First Letter of Peter; some of the expressions used here seem to belong to a later period. In many ways the style and content are similar to those of the Letter of Jude, which the author probably drew on and develops (compare, for example, 2 Pet 2:1–3:3 with Jude 4–18). None of the theories advanced to solve these difficulties adequately explains who the author was, or when and to whom he was writing. Whether the author was St Peter, via an editor or secretary, or whether he was an anonymous disciple of Peter who, inspired by the Holy Spirit, sought to pass on teaching in line with that of Peter, the Second Letter of St Peter has been associated by church tradition with the figure of the leader of the apostles.

The letter is addressed to "those who have obtained a faith of equal standing with ours" (1:1), that is, to Christians in general, although it is true that some remarks (indicating that the audience may be the same as that for 1 Peter and for some of Paul's letters: see 3:1, 15–16) lead one to suppose that the immediate addressees were the Christian communities of Asia Minor or Greece, whom the writer wants to warn against false teachers.

As regards the date of composition, opinions range from the year 60 to the first decades of the second century, with Rome the most likely place of writing.

3. MESSAGE

Besides refuting erroneous theories about the second coming of Christ that have been proposed by false teachers, and exhorting people to be vigilant, the author of the letter comments on the question of the inspiration of the Scriptures (1:19–21) and on the value and interpretation of St Paul's writings (3:15–16). Its teaching is very important because it provides criteria for assessing whether a text is canonical or not: it must have apostolic authority and it must be inspired.

Among the verses most commented on by the Fathers of the Church is 2 Peter 1:4, which speaks of how Christians have the good fortune to become "partakers of the divine nature". Still, the main doctrine in the letter is eschatological—concerning the second coming of Christ. That event will indeed come to pass, because our Lord himself revealed it, and it is attested to by Scripture (see 1:16–19). Against those who maintain that the second coming is being delayed, the letter states that time is relative when compared with the eternity of God (3:8), and that if God delays the end of time it is on account of his mercy, his not "wishing that any should perish" (3:9). As regards the specific form the glorious coming of Christ will take, the letter contains expressions that are difficult to interpret. It is possible that the sacred writer uses obscure language (as our Lord himself did: cf. Mt 24:36ff and par.) in order to encourage the faithful to be vigilant, and also to underline the sublimity of God's mysterious design. That Jesus will come in glory to judge the living and the dead has formed part of the Church's teaching from the very beginning, as can be seen from the early Creeds, and it is a teaching that was defined as a dogma of faith by Benedict XII in the Constitution *Benedictus Deus* in 1336.[6]

---

6 See also *Catechism of the Catholic Church*, 1020–1060.

2 Peter

Greeting*

1 ¹Simon Peter, a servant and apostle of Jesus Christ,
To those who have obtained a faith of equal standing with ours in the righteousness of our God and Saviour Jesus Christ:ᵃ

²May grace and peace be multiplied to you in the knowledge of God and of Jesus our Lord.

Acts 15:14
Rom 1:17

Jude 2
Phil 3:8–10

1. A CALL TO FIDELITY*

Divine largesse

³His divine power has granted to us all things that pertain to life and godliness, through the knowledge of him who called us toᵇ his own glory and excellence, ⁴by which he has granted to us his precious and very great promises, that through these you may escape from the corruption that is in the world because of passion, and become partakers of the divine nature.*

1 Pet 2:9
2 Cor 4:4, 6
Jn 1:10, 12, 14
Eph 3:16–19
Acts 17:28
2 Cor 3:18
1 Jn 2:15f; 5:19

[1] ¹Simon Petrus servus et apostolus Iesu Christi his, qui coaequalem nobis sortiti sunt fidem in iustitia Dei nostri et salvatoris Iesus Christi: ²gratia vobis et pax multiplicetur in cognitione Dei et Iesu Domini nostri. ³Quomodo omnia nobis divinae virtutis suae ad vitam et pietatem donatae per cognitionem eius, qui vocavit nos propria gloria et virtute, ⁴per quae pretiosa et maxima nobis promissa donata sunt, ut per haec effi-

*1:1–2 This letter, which is similar in some ways to the Letter of Jude, is aimed at strengthening peoples' hope in the second coming of our Lord. Christians need to grow in the faith they have received, and they should rely on apostolic teaching (1:3–21), and guard against false teachers who, because they do not believe in a second coming, give themselves over to licentious living and encourage others to do the same; this will earn them divine condemnation (2:1–22). Even though the Parousia may seem to have been delayed, it will come about (3:1–16), so one must always be vigilant (3:17–18).

"Knowledge" of God and of Jesus Christ (v. 2) is obtained through a sound faith and conduct consistent with that belief (see 1:5–11). The writer emphasizes this point from the very start, because he wants to prepare people to reject the false ideas that can undermine their belief.

This is one of the most explicit passages in the New Testament about the divinity of Jesus Christ, for it calls him "our God and Saviour" (v. 1; cf. 1:11, 2:20; 3:2, 18).

The greeting contains two words frequently found in this context—"grace" and "peace" (cf. 1 Pet 1:2)—which sum up the gifts that Christians have received.

*1:3–21 Against those who say that there will be no Second Coming, the sacred writer exhorts the faithful to abide by the teaching they have received from the apostles. He encourages them to strive for steadfastness in virtue, using a simple yet profound argument (vv. 3–11). Then (vv. 12–21) he reminds them that hope in the second coming of Christ is well-founded and forms part of the deposit of faith.

1:3–4 Almighty God chose his apostles and endowed them with abundant graces so that all could become "partakers of the divine nature" (v. 4). This succinct phrase, which has played a key role in the history of theological thought, particularly in connexion with the doctrine of grace, sums up the great good that grace works for Christians. Man becomes God-like through the

Christian virtues

Gal 5:6
1 Thess 4:9

Gal 6:10
2 Pet 1:2

1 Jn 2:9, 11

1 Thess 1:4
2 Thess 1:11
1 Jn 3:6

Jn 3:5f
Lk 1:33

Jude 5

2 Cor 5:1
Is 38:12

⁵For this very reason make every effort to supplement your faith with virtue, and virtue with knowledge, ⁶and knowledge with self-control, and self-control with steadfastness, and steadfastness with godliness, ⁷and godliness with brotherly affection, and brotherly affection with love. ⁸For if these things are yours and abound, they keep you from being ineffective or unfruitful in the knowledge of our Lord Jesus Christ. ⁹For whoever lacks these things is blind and shortsighted and has forgotten that he was cleansed from his old sins. ¹⁰Therefore, brethren, be the more zealous to confirm your call and election, for if you do this you will never fall; ¹¹so there will be richly provided for you an entrance into the eternal kingdom of our Lord and Saviour Jesus Christ.

Spiritual testimony

¹²Therefore I intend always to remind you of these things, though you know them and are established in the truth that you have. ¹³I think it right, as long as I am in this

ciamini divinae consortes naturae, fugientes eam, quae in mundo est in concupiscentia, corruptionem; ⁵et propter hoc ipsum curam omnem subinferentes ministrate in fide vestra virtutem, in virtute autem scientiam, ⁶in scientia autem continentiam, in continentia autem patientiam, in patientia autem pietatem, ⁷in pietate autem amorem fraternitatis, in amore autem fraternitatis caritatem. ⁸Haec enim vobis, cum adsint et abundent, non vacuos nec sine fructu vos constituunt in Domini nostri Iesu Christi cognitionem; ⁹cui enim non praesto sunt haec, caecus est et nihil procul cernens, oblivionem accipiens purgationis veterum suorum delictorum. ¹⁰Quapropter, fratres, magis satagite, ut firmam vestram vocationem et electionem faciatis. Haec enim facientes non offendetis aliquando; ¹¹sic enim abundanter ministrabitur vobis introitus in aeternum regnum Domini nostri et salvatoris Iesu Christi. ¹²Propter quod incipiam vos semper commonere de his, et quidem scientes et confirmatos in praesenti veritate.

union of human nature and divine nature in the Person of the Word: "The Son of God became man so that we might become God" (St Athanasius, *De Incarnatione*, 54, 3; cf. *Catechism of the Catholic Church*, 460). This "divinization" is both the origin and the final goal of Christian life. It is the beginning insofar as it means incorporation into Christ through Baptism, and brings with it (through grace and adoptive divine filiation) participation in the very life of God. It is the final goal insofar as that participation will reach its fullness and perfection in heaven, with the contemplation of God "as he is" (1 Jn 3:2). At the same time, the Holy Trinity already dwells in the soul that is in a state of grace (see e.g. Jn 14:17–23; 1 Cor 3:16; 6:19). "Our faith teaches us that man, in the state of grace, is divinized—filled with God" (St Josemaría Escrivá, *Christ Is Passing By*, 103).

1:5–11 Christians must respond to God's initiative with faith and the practice of virtue if they are to reach the goal and the fullness to which they are called. For Christians, virtues are not an end in themselves, but a means

necessary for attaining knowledge of Christ (v. 8); if they fail to practise virtue, they will not be able to see God (v. 9). "If we practise them, God shows himself to us through these virtues; but if we do not practise them, we cannot see God" (Pseudo-Hilary of Arles, *In 2 Petrum*, ad loc.). That is why St Teresa of Avila stressed the need to combine contemplation with the effort to grow in virtue: "I repeat that if you have this in view you must not build upon foundations of prayer and contemplation alone, for, unless you strive after the virtues and practise them, you will never grow to be more than dwarfs. God grant that nothing worse than this may happen—for, as you know, anyone who fails to go forward begins to go back" (*Interior Castle*, 7, 4, 9). The virtues of faith (v. 5) and love (v. 7) are "the origin and end of our lives. Faith is the beginning; love, the end. Both, bonded together, bring us to God, and everything else related to perfection and holiness flows from them" (St Ignatius of Antioch, *Ad Ephesios*, 14, 1–2).

1:12–15 This passage sums up the purpose of the letter (which is a kind of spiritual will and

body,[c] to arouse you by way of reminder, [14]since I know that the putting off of my   Jn 21:18, 19
body[c] will be soon, as our Lord Jesus Christ showed me. [15]And I will see to it that   Wis 9:15
after my departure you may be able at any time to recall these things.

The Transfiguration, an earnest of the Second Coming

[16]For we did not follow cleverly devised myths when we made known to you the   Mt 17:1–8
power and coming of our Lord Jesus Christ, but we were eyewitnesses of his   Mk 9:2–8
Lk 9:28–35
Jn 1:14
majesty.* [17]For when he received honour and glory from God the Father and the
voice was borne to him by the Majestic Glory, "This is my beloved Son,[d] with   Mt 17:5 and par.
whom I am well pleased," [18]we heard this voice borne from heaven, for we were   Rev 2:28
Lk 1:78
with him on the holy mountain.

Prophecy and the Second Coming

[19]And we have the prophetic word made more sure. You will do well to pay attention to this as to a lamp shining in a dark place, until the day dawns and the morning star rises in your hearts. [20]First of all you must understand this, that no prophecy
of scripture is a matter of one's own interpretation, [21]because no prophecy ever came   2 Tim 3:16
Acts 3:21
1 Pet 1:10–12
by the impulse of man, but men moved by the Holy Spirit spoke from God.[e]

---

[13]Iustum autem arbitror, quamdiu sum in hoc tabernaculo, suscitare vos in commonitione, [14]certus quod velox est depositio tabernaculi mei, secundum quod et Dominus noster Iesus Christus significavit mihi; [15]dabo autem operam et frequenter habere vos post obitum meum, ut horum memoriam faciatis. [16]Non enim captiosas fabulas secuti notam fecimus vobis Domini nostri Iesu Christi virtutem et adventum, sed speculatores facti
illius magnitudinis. [17]Accipiens enim a Deo Patre honorem et gloriam, voce prolata ad eum huiuscemodi a magnifica gloria: «Filius meus, dilectus meus hic est, in quo ego mihi complacui»; [18]et hanc vocem nos audivimus de caelo prolatam, cum essemus cum ipso in monte sancto. [19]Et
habemus firmiorem propheticum sermonem, cui bene facitis attendentes quasi lucernae lucenti in caliginoso loco, donec dies illucescat, et lucifer
oriatur in cordibus vestries, [20]hoc primum intellegentes quod omnis prophetia Scripturae propria interpretatione non fit; [21]non enim voluntate

---

testament)—namely, to remind people of the
Christian truths and to encourage them to
practise virtue. The image of the tent (v. 13; cf.
Is 38:12; 2 Cor 5:1) forcefully conveys the
ephemeral nature of human life on earth: "At
the end of his life in this world, man is like a
pilgrim who leaves behind his tent and returns
home when the pilgrimage is ended; or like a
soldier who returns to his homeland after a
military campaign, when he has defeated his
enemy or been routed by him. Man's true home
and city and homeland is heaven" (St Bede, *In
2 Epistolam Sancti Petri*, ad loc.).

1:16–18 The apostles' authority for saying that
Jesus is divine does not come from "cleverly
devised myths" (v. 16), but from the fact that
three apostles were eyewitnesses to a divine revelation. Jesus' transfiguration guarantees the
truth of the Parousia or second coming of Christ,
which some people tried to deny. If our Lord
allowed them to have a momentary glimpse of
his divinity on that occasion, at the end of time

Christians will be able to see him as he truly is,
clearly and for ever.

1:19–21 The prophets' testimony is another
guarantee of the truth of the Second Coming,
because it too is the Word of God. The word of
the prophets (the Scriptures) should not be
reduced to "private", arbitrary interpretation, on
the basis of personal feelings or vague, mythical
speculation (cf. 1:16).

Verse 21 makes it clear what biblical
inspiration is, and its purpose. Holy Scripture was
written under the inspiration of the Holy Spirit. In
the writing of it God took an active part, as did the
human author, in such a way that the resultant text
is, at one and the same time, entirely of God's
making and entirely of man's. Therefore, as the
sacred writer points out (v. 20), Scripture must not
be subjected to arbitrary interpretation.

The Church has received the commission and
the duty of conserving and interpreting the word
of God, as Vatican II, *Dei Verbum*, 10 makes
clear.

---

c Greek *tent*   d Or *my son, my* (or *the*) *Beloved*   e Other authorities read *moved by the Holy Spirit holy men of God spoke*

2. FALSE TEACHERS DENOUNCED*

The harm done by false teachers

Deut 13:2–6
Mt 24:24
Jude 4
2 Pet 3:3
Rom 2:24
Is 52;5

2 ¹But false prophets also arose among the people, just as there will be false teach-ers among you, who will secretly bring in destructive heresies, even denying the Master who bought them, bringing upon themselves swift destruction. ²And many will follow their licentiousness, and because of them the way of truth will be reviled.

Rom 16:18
1 Thess 2:5

³And in their greed they will exploit you with false words; from of old their con-demnation has not been idle, and their destruction has not been asleep.*

The punishment that awaits them

Mt 8:29
Jude 6

Gen 8:18
1 Pet 3:6
Wis 10:4

⁴For if God did not spare the angels when they sinned, but cast them into hell^f and committed them to pits of nether gloom to be kept until the judgment; ⁵if he did not spare the ancient world, but preserved Noah, a herald of righteousness, with seven

humana prolata est prophetia aliquando, sed a Spiritu Sancto ducti locuti sunt a Deo homines.   [2] ¹Fuerunt vero et pseudoprophetae in populo, sicut et in vobis erunt magistri mendaces, qui introducent sectas perditionis et eum, qui emit eos, Dominatorem negantes superducent sibi cel-erem perditionem. ²Et multi sequentur eorum luxurias, propter quos via veritatis blasphemabitur; ³et in avaritia fictis verbis de vobis negotiabun-tur. Quibus iudicium iam olim non cessat, et perditio eorum non dormitat. ⁴Si enim Deus angelis peccantibus non pepercit, sed rudentibus inferni detractos in tartarum tradidit in iudicium reservatos; ⁵et originali mundo non pepercit, sed octavum Noe iustitiae praeconem custodivit diluvium mundo impiorum inducens; ⁶et civitates Sodomae et Gomorrae in cinerem redigens eversione damnavit, exemplum ponens eorum, quae sunt

---

*2:1–22 Before refuting the basic error of the false teachers (their denial of the Second Coming), the sacred writer denounces their moral misconduct—their greed and sexual immorality. The corresponding passage in the Letter of St Jude (vv. 4–16), from which the writer of 2 Peter seems to have taken his inspira-tion (see the Introduction to this letter), rounds off and illustrates the teachings found in this chapter.

2:1–3. Holy Scripture contains many warnings about false teachers who try to sow confusion. Christians, therefore, should not be surprised to encounter such people. The writer of the letter bemoans the harm they do. The tone of these verses suggests that these false teachers were still to be found in the ranks of the Christian communities.

2:4–10. Eternal punishment awaits false teach-ers, as is illustrated by three well-known exam-ples from the Bible—God's casting the rebellious angels into hell; the great flood; and the destruction of Sodom and Gomorrah. In the parallel passage in Jude (vv. 5–10), instead of speaking about the flood, the author mentions the punishment that befell rebellious Israelites in

the wilderness. In contrast to the condemnation that awaits the unrighteous is the salvation that God grants to those who remain faithful, just as in their days he saved Noah and Lot. All this serves as encouragement to persevere in virtue, even if the environment is hostile.

Verse 4 speaks about the sin of the angels. "The devil and the other demons were created good by God, but they turned against Him and became evil" (Lateran Council IV, *De fide catholica*). "This 'fall' consists in the free choice of these created spirits, who radically and irrev-ocably *rejected* God and his reign" (*Catechism of the Catholic Church*, 392). Holy Scripture does not say what the angels' sin was. Many saints (Augustine and Thomas Aquinas, for example) believed that it was a sin of pride. The fact that angels were condemned should serve as a stern warning: even though they were privi-leged, they did not escape punishment. The nature of their punishment indicates how evil sin is.

Apparently, the main sin of the false teachers and the one that most perverted the faithful was that of lust (v. 10), as was the case with Sodom and Gomorrah (cf. the note on Jude 5–7). That vice so clouds the mind that a person who becomes steeped in it ends up despising the "authority" of

f Greek *Tartarus*

other persons, when he brought a flood upon the world of the ungodly; [6]if by turning the cities of Sodom and Gomorrah to ashes he condemned them to extinction and made them an example to those who were to be ungodly; [7]and if he rescued righteous Lot, greatly distressed by the licentiousness of the wicked [8](for by what that righteous man saw and heard as he lived among them, he was vexed in his righteous soul day after day with their lawless deeds), [9]then the Lord knows how to rescue the godly from trial, and to keep the unrighteous under punishment until the day of judgment, [10]and especially those who indulge in the lust of defiling passion and despise authority.

Gen 19:24f
Jude 7
Wis 10:6–8
Sir 16:7-8
Mt 10:15
Gen 19:6f

Ezek 9:4

1 Cor 10:13
Jude 6
Rev 3:10
2 Thess 1:5–10

Jude 7, 8, 16
Rom 2:6

Their arrogance and immorality

Bold and wilful, they are not afraid to revile the glorious ones, [11]whereas angels, though greater in might and power, do not pronounce a reviling judgment upon them before the Lord. [12]But these, like irrational animals, creatures of instinct, born to be caught and killed, reviling in matters of which they are ignorant, will be destroyed in the same destruction with them, [13]suffering wrong for their wrongdoing. They count it pleasure to revel in the daytime. They are blots and blemishes, revelling in their dissipation,[g] carousing with you. [14]They have eyes full of adultery, insatiable

Jude 8–10
Ps 49:12
Jude 10

Jude 12

impiis futura; [7]et iustum Lot oppressum a nefandorum luxuria conversationis eruit: [8]aspectu enim et auditu iustus habitans apud eos, de die in diem animam iustam iniquis operibus cruciabat. [9]Novit Dominus pios de tentatione eripere, iniquos vero in diem iudicii puniendos reservare, [10]maxime autem eos, qui post carnem in concupiscentia immunditiae ambulant dominationemque contemnunt. Audaces, superbi, glorias non metuunt blasphemantes, [11]ubi angeli fortitudine et virtute cum sint maiores, non portant adversum illas coram Domino iudicium blasphemiae. [12]Hi vero velut irrationabilia animalia naturaliter genita in captionem et in corruptionem, in his, quae ignorant, blasphemantes, in corruptione sua et corrumpentur [13]inviti percipientes mercedem iniustitiae; voluptatem existimantes diei delicias, coinquinationes et maculae deliciis affluentes, in voluptatibus suis luxuriantes vobiscum, [14]oculos habentes plenos adulterae et incessabiles delicti, pellicientes animas instabiles, cor exercitatum avaritiae

God (cf. Jude 8–10). By contrast, chastity "is a virtue that dignifies the human person and enables him or her to express and appreciate a love that is true and not self-seeking, generous, and respectful of others" (Congregation for the Doctrine of the Faith, *Persona humana*, 12).

2:10–19 The section in the Letter of St Jude that runs parallel to this passage (vv. 8–16) helps to explain some of the phrases used here to describe the immoral conduct of false teachers.

"The glorious ones" (v. 10) may refer to all the angels, or only to the fallen angels who rule the world and whose dignity is seen as lower than that of the angels who minister in the presence of the Lord (cf. Jude 8–10). This passage might be interpreted to mean, therefore, that false teachers, blinded by their own pride, have blasphemed against beings superior to themselves, a blasphemy whose gravity is reflected in the fact that not even the angels themselves presume to pass judgment on their fallen brethren, the demons. Or perhaps the false teachers have dismissed the power of demons altogether, denying that it can hold any sway over them, and thus justifying the

depravity of their lives. The passage may even mean that the angels have been called as witnesses or patrons of the false teachers' vices.

Balaam was seen as the epitome of the evil and avaricious person because he led the Israelites into idolatry and fornication (see Num 31:16; Rev 2:14), whereas he had previously blessed them (Num 22:1—24:25).

The terrible consequence of the ideas spread by false teachers was the corruption of the faith of new believers: they were returned to the life of sin they had left behind. They were returned to it through a false promise of freedom, as though freedom consisted in yielding to instincts and passions and temptations (vv. 18–19). "Christ, our Liberator, has freed us from sin and from slavery to the Law and to the flesh, which is the mark of the condition of sinful mankind. Thus it is the new life of grace, fruit of justification, which makes us free. This means that the most radical form of slavery is slavery to sin. Other forms of slavery find their deepest root in slavery to sin. That is why freedom in the full Christian sense, characterized by the life of the Spirit, cannot be confused with a licence to give

g Other ancient authorities read *love feasts*

Num 22:5
Jude 11
Rev 2:14
Jude 12, 13
for sin. They entice unsteady souls. They have hearts trained in greed. Accursed children! [15]Forsaking the right way they have gone astray; they have followed the way of Balaam, the son of Beor, who loved gain from wrongdoing, [16]but was rebuked for his own transgression; a dumb ass spoke with human voice and restrained the prophet's madness.

Jude 16
[17]These are waterless springs and mists driven by a storm; for them the nether gloom of darkness has been reserved. [18]For, uttering loud boasts of folly, they entice with licentious passions of the flesh men who have barely escaped from those who live in error.
Jn 8:34
Rom 6:16
[19]They promise them freedom, but they themselves are slaves of corruption; for whatever overcomes a man, to that he is enslaved.

Apostasy, a grave sin

Mt 12–45
Lk 11:24

Lk 12:47, 48

Prov 26:11
Mt 7:6
[20]For if, after they have escaped the defilements of the world through the knowledge of our Lord and Saviour Jesus Christ, they are again entangled in them and overpowered, the last state has become worse for them than the first. [21]For it would have been better for them never to have known the way of righteousness than after knowing it to turn back from the holy commandment delivered to them. [22]It has happened to them according to the true proverb, The dog turns back to his own vomit, and the sow is washed only to wallow in the mire.

3. THE SECOND COMING OF CHRIST*

The teaching of Tradition

2 Pet 1:13
3 [1]This is now the second letter that I have written to you, beloved, and in both of them I have aroused your sincere mind by way of reminder; [2]that you should

habentes, maledictionis filii, [15]derelinquentes rectam viam erraverunt, secuti viam Balaam ex Bosor, qui mercedem iniquitatis amavit, [16]correptionem vero habuit suae praevaricationis; subiugale mutum in hominis voce loquens prohibuit prophetae insipientiam. [17]Hi sunt fontes sine aqua et nebulae turbine exagitatae, quibus caligo tenebrarum reservatur. [18]Superba enim vanitatis loquentes pelliciunt in concupiscentiis carnis luxuriis illos, qui paululum effugiunt eos, qui in errore conversantur, [19]libertatem illis promittentes, cum ipsi servi sint corruptionis; a quo enim quis superatus est, huius servus est. [20]Si enim refugientes coinquinationes mundi in cognitione Domini nostri et Salvatoris Iesu Christi his rursus implicati superantur, facta sunt eis posteriora deteriora prioribus. [21]Melius enim erat illis non cognoscere viam iustitiae quam post agnitionem retrorsum converti ab eo, quod illis traditum est, sancto mandato. [22]Contigit enim eis illud veri proverbii: «Canis reversus ad suum vomitum, / et sus lota in volutabro luti». [3] [1]Hanc vobis, carissimi, iam secundam scribo epistulam, in quibus excito vestram in commonitione sinceram mentem, [2]ut memores sitis eorum, quae praedicta sunt verborum a sanctis prophetis, et ab apostolis traditi vobis praecepti Domini et Salvatoris; [3]hoc

in to the desires of the flesh. Freedom is a new life in love" (Congregation for the Doctrine of the Faith, *Libertatis nuntius*, 4, 2).

2:20–22 The sacred writer uses two popular proverbs (v. 22)—the first taken from Proverbs 26:11, the other commonly found in Semitic and Greek tradition—to show the gravity involved when someone returns to a life of sin after having come to know the sacred teaching of Christ. To the ungodly and to those who lead others astray the writer applies what our Lord said about a person who, after a devil has been cast out of him, falls under his sway once more: "The last state of that man becomes worse than the first" (Mt 12:45). St Gregory the Great com-

ments: "A person who weeps for his sin and yet does not give it up becomes guilty of a greater fault; because he scorns the forgiveness which he could obtain by weeping, and then wallows in the mire. When, despite his tears, he prevents his life being cleansed, then in the sight of God he causes those very tears to be stained" (*Regula pastoralis*, 3, 30).

3:1–10 The truth of faith most directly denied by the false teachers was the second coming of the Lord; by rejecting it, they wrote off the moral demands of Christianity. The sacred writer now sets about refuting their arguments and outlining correct teaching on the subject of the End. One reason why it is difficult to understand certain

remember the predictions of the holy prophets and the commandment of the Lord and Saviour through your apostles.

Jude 17
2 Pet 1:18–20

Mistaken notions

[3]First of all you must understand this, that scoffers will come in the last days with scoffing, following their own passions [4]and saying, "Where is the promise of his coming? For ever since the fathers fell asleep, all things have continued as they were from the beginning of creation."

1 Tim 4:1
Jude 18
2 Pet 1:16, 2:1

Is 5:19
Ezek 12:22
Mt 24:48

True teaching about the End

[5]They deliberately ignore this fact, that by the word of God heavens existed long ago, and an earth formed out of water and by means of water, [6]through which the world that then existed was deluged with water and perished. [7]But by the same word the heavens and earth that now exist have been stored up for fire, being kept until the day of judgment and destruction of ungodly men.

Gen 1:2, 6, 9

Gen 7:21
2 Pet 2:5
Mt 24:38–39

2 Pet 3:10
Mt 3:12
Rom 2:6

[8]But do not ignore this one fact, beloved, that with the Lord one day is as a thousand years, and a thousand years as one day. [9]The Lord is not slow about his promise as some count slowness, but is forbearing toward you,[h] not wishing that any should perish, but that all should reach repentance. [10]But the day of the Lord will come like a thief, and then the heavens will pass away with a loud noise, and the elements will be dissolved with fire, and the earth and the works that are upon it will be burned up.

Ps 90:4

Hab 2:3
1 Tim 2:4
Rom 2:4
Sir 35:19
Lk 18:7

Mt 24:29, 43
1 Thess 5:2
Rev 20:11

primum scientes quod venient in novissimis diebus in illusione illudentes, iuxta proprias concupiscentias suas ambulantes, [4]dicentes: «Ubi est promissio adventus eius?». Ex quo enim patres dormierunt, omnia sic perseverant ab initio creaturae. [5]Latet enim eos hoc volentes quod caeli erant prius et terra de aqua et per aquam consistens Dei verbo, [6]per quae ille tunc mundus aqua inundatus periit; [7]caeli autem, qui nunc sunt, et terra eodem verbo repositi sunt igni, servati in diem iudicii et perditionis impiorum hominum. [8]Unum vero hoc non lateat vos, carissimi, quia unus dies apud Dominum sicut mille anni, et mille anni sicut dies unus. [9]Non tardat Dominus promissionem, sicut quidam tarditatem existimant, sed patienter agit in vos nolens aliquos perire, sed omnes ad paenitentiam reverti. [10]Adveniet autem dies Domini ut fur, in qua caeli magno impetu transient, elementa vero calore solventur, et terra et opera, quae in ea invenientur. [11]Cum haec omnia ita dissolvenda sint, quales oportet esse vos

expressions he uses is that we just do not know the positions held by the false teachers he confronts here. See also Jude 16–18.

3:1–2 The author calls on Christians to lead lives based on the sound criteria (v. 1) that derive from our Lord's words as passed on by the apostles (v. 2). The fact that the apostles are mentioned alongside the prophets shows that, from the start, they have had a role similar to that of the Old Testament prophets, insofar as they have been given special authority to pass on Revelation. "What was handed on by the apostles comprises everything that serves to make the People of God live their lives in holiness and increase their faith" (Vatican II, *Dei Verbum*, 8).

3:3–4 The false leaders referred to in the letter denied the Second Coming on the grounds that nothing really has changed: none of the catastrophes they expected have come about.

"The fathers" (v. 4) may mean the first generation of Christians, and may also mean Old Testament forebears. The false teachers argued that if no great change had taken place up to now, then that was a sign that no such change would ever occur in the future.

3:5–10 The sacred writer reproaches the false teachers for their lack of faith and reminds them that things have not remained the same from the beginning: God, by his word, brought the universe into being, and by that same word sent the flood to punish men: that event involved a huge transformation (vv. 5–6). Therefore, we must believe that the word of God will cause the entire cosmos to undergo such a profound transformation that "new heavens and a new earth" will come into being (cf. vv. 7, 10; 3:12–13). Moreover, time is relative when compared with the eternity of God (v. 8), and if God puts off the final moment, that is due to his mercy; it is

h Other ancient authorities read *on your account*

Moral lessons to be drawn

Acts 3:19–20
Is 34:4
Is 60:21; 65:17;
66:22
Rev 21:1, 27
Rom 8:19
Jude 24
Rom 2:4
1 Tim 1:15, 16

¹¹Since all these things are thus to be dissolved, what sort of persons ought you to be in lives of holiness and godliness, ¹²waiting for and hastening[i] the coming of the day of God, because of which the heavens will be kindled and dissolved, and the elements will melt with fire! ¹³But according to his promise we wait for new heavens and a new earth in which righteousness dwells.

¹⁴Therefore, beloved, since you wait for these, be zealous to be found by him without spot or blemish, and at peace. ¹⁵And count the forbearance of our Lord as salvation. So also our beloved brother Paul wrote to you according to the wisdom given him, ¹⁶speaking of this* as he does in all his letters. There are some things in them hard to understand, which the ignorant and unstable twist to their own destruction, as they do the other scriptures.

Final exhortation and doxology

Mk 13:5
Heb 2:1
Rom 16:27
Jude 25

¹⁷You therefore, beloved, knowing this beforehand, beware lest you be carried away with the error of lawless men and lose your own stability. ¹⁸But grow in the grace and knowledge of our Lord and Saviour Jesus Christ. To him be the glory both now and to the day of eternity. Amen.

in sanctis conversationibus et pietatibus ¹²exspectantes et properantes adventum diei Dei, propter quam caeli ardentes solventur, et elementa ignis ardore tabescent. ¹³*Novos* vero *caelos et terram novam* secundum promissum ipsius exspectamus, in quibus iustitia habitat. ¹⁴Propter quod, carissimi, haec exspectantes satagite immaculati et inviolati ei inveniri in pace ¹⁵et Domini nostri longanimitatem salutem arbitramini, sicut et carissimus frater noster Paulus secundum datam sibi sapientiam scripsit vobis, ¹⁶sicut et in omnibus epistulis loquens in eis de his, in quibus sunt quaedam difficilia intellectu, quae indocti et instabiles depravant sicut et ceteras Scripturas ad suam ipsorum perditionem. ¹⁷Vos igitur, dilecti, praescientes custodite, ne iniquorum errore simul abducti excidatis a propria firmitate; ¹⁸crescite vero in gratia et in cognitione Domini nostri et Salvatoris Iesu Christi. Ipsi gloria et nunc et in diem aeternitatis. Amen.

because he wants all mankind to be saved (v. 9; cf. 1 Tim 2:4; Rom 11:23). One thing is certain—the need to be vigilant, because the day of the Lord will come without advance warning (v. 10; cf. Mk 13:32–37). "Since we know neither the day nor the hour, we should follow the advice of the Lord and watch constantly so that, when the single course of our earthly life is completed (cf. Heb 9:27), we may merit to enter with him into the marriage feast and be numbered among the blessed (cf. Mt 25:31–46) and not, like the wicked and slothful servants (cf. Mt 25:26), be ordered to depart into the eternal fire (cf. Mt 25:41)" (Vatican II, *Lumen gentium*, 48).

3:11–16 The moral lessons drawn here stem from the belief that the world will end and the Lord will come a second time. "At the end of time, the Kingdom of God will come in its fullness. After the universal judgment, the righteous will reign for ever with Christ, glorified in body and soul. The universe itself will be renewed. […] Sacred Scripture calls this mysterious renewal, which will transform humanity and the world, 'new heavens and a new earth'" (*Cate-chism of the Catholic Church*, 1042–1043). These beliefs should not make Christians afraid; in fact, it should bolster their hope (vv. 12–14). At the same time, expectation of these events should not cause them to neglect temporal affairs: "The expectation of a new earth must not weaken but rather stimulate our concern for cultivating this one. For here grows the body of a new human family, a body which even now is able to give some kind of foreshadowing of the new age" (Vatican II, *Gaudium et spes*, 39).

The reference to St Paul's writings (vv. 15–16) is clear evidence of the fact that, from the very earliest days of Christianity, unity in faith was seen as essential to the life of the Church.

3:17–18 The letter ends with a succinct summary of some of its main points—pastoral concern, ways of guarding against false teachers, and faith in the divinity of Christ.

New Testament doxologies usually praise directly God the Father (see Jude 25; Rom 16:27); this one is addressed to Christ, whose divinity is explicitly acknowledged here, as it is elsewhere in the letter.

i Or *earnestly desiring*

THE FIRST LETTER OF

JOHN

Introduction

According to a tradition that dates back to the second century, the apostle St John wrote his three letters in Ephesus, on his return from exile on Patmos, in the years 95–96. An echo of 1 John is to be found in a text by St Polycarp from the year 150 when he says, "Anyone who does not confess that Jesus Christ has come in the flesh …".[1] Around the year 180 St Irenaeus takes it that the letter was written by the apostle St John, for he quotes passages from it, attributing them to the "disciple of the Lord".[2] Clement of Alexandria, around the year 200, as well as writing a commentary on 1 John, fragments of which have come down to us, frequently quotes the letter in his writings, explicitly attributing it to the apostle St John.[3] Tertullian (d. *c*.222)[4] makes the same attribution, as does Origen (d. *c*.253),[5] who highlights the close relationship between the fourth Gospel and 1 John. The letter appears in all the early lists and canons of inspired books, giving St John as the author.

1. STRUCTURE AND CONTENT

A prologue (1:1–4) and a short epilogue (5:13), followed by an appendix (5:14–21), gives the letter its shape. The prologue, which is very like that of the fourth Gospel, conveys the basic idea of the letter—the communion or union of the Christian with God, which expresses itself in faith in Jesus Christ and in the practice of brotherly love. This idea is summed up in the epilogue: "I write this to you who believe in the name of the Son of God, that you may know that you have eternal life" (5:13). However, it is not easy to find any clear breaks in the body of the letter, because its thought does not develop linearly but, rather, in a spiral way: again and again the same basic ideas recur, addressed from different angles. Even so, the letter can be said to have three parts: The first (1:5—2:29) begins with the message "God is light", and goes on to outline the holiness that a Christian life should produce: Christian life is depicted as walking in the light (see 1:7). In the second part (3:1–24), which begins with a statement about the Christian's divine filiation, the author lays further stress on holiness as a call and a command that follow from the status of divine sonship. In the third part (4:1—5:12) he further develops the central themes of the letter, arranging them in the form of a literary triptych—faith in Jesus Christ (4:1–6), love (4:7–21) and, again, faith in our Lord (5:1–12).

2. CONTEXT

The letter contains no mention by name of who wrote it or to whom it is addressed; nor does it carry the usual greetings at the opening or close. This suggests that it may be a circular letter sent to the Christian communities in an entire region. According to a tradition passed down by St Ire-

1 Cf. 1 Jn 4:2–3; cf. St Polycarp, *Ad Philippenses*, 7, 1, 2. 2 E.g., 1 Jn 2:18, 19, 21; 4:1–3; 5:1; see St Irenaeus, *Adversus haereses*, 3, 16, 5 and 8. 3 Cf. *Stromata* 2, 15, 66; 3, 4, 32; 3, 5, 44; 3, 6, 45. 4 See *Adversus Praxeam*, 15; *Scorpiace*, 12; *Adversus Marcionem*, 5, 16. 5 According to Eusebius of Caesarea, *Historia ecclesiastica*, 6, 25, 8.

naeus,[6] the apostle St John, on his return from exile on the island of Patmos, spent the last years of his life in Ephesus, the capital, at that time, of the Roman province of Asia. From that city he ruled over the various churches in Asia Minor, whose names are given in the book of Revelation (see Rev 2—3).

According to that tradition, the letter must have been written after the year 95/96, when, in the reign of Nerva, St John returned from Patmos. Although the question is still unresolved, most scholars are inclined to the view that this letter is later than the fourth Gospel, since it seems to presuppose the teachings contained therein. Of the three New Testament letters attributed to St John, this one appears to be the latest in chronological terms, written towards the end of the first century of the Christian era.

As we learn from the letter itself, some false teachers (antichrists, deceivers, children of the devil, false prophets as St John calls them: see 2:18, 26; 3:7, 10; 4:1) had troubled the life and development of these young churches and, although they probably no longer had any links with them (see 2:19), their ideas still posed a threat to purity of faith and Christian morality. The apostle writes to denounce their errors and to bolster the faith of believers. These errors, concerning the Person and salvific work of Christ, denied that Jesus was the Messiah, the Son of God (see 2:22; 4:3, 14–15). John's insistence on acknowledgment of the fact that Jesus Christ "has come in the flesh" (4:2) suggests that they did not accept that the Word of God became man (see also the prologue: 1:1–4). Besides these Christological errors, the false teachers spread an erroneous view of the moral demands of Christian life: they asserted that they were without sin (see 1:8); they claimed to have special knowledge of God that exempted them from obedience to his commandments (see 2:4–6); they said they loved God and lived in union with him, but they did not love their brethren (see 2:9–11). Against these and other errors, the apostle makes his own teaching clear.

3. MESSAGE

Communion with God

St John gives a detailed outline of the doctrine of the communion or union of the Christian with God. His reason for doing so was (at least in part) the claims of false teachers who made out that they had a higher understanding of God, a *gnosis*, unconnected with traditional Christian teaching; they had, they said, an abiding union with God, such that they felt no obligation to keep the commandments, particularly that of fraternal charity. To counter these errors, St John stresses that only those who remain in communion with the apostles and accept their message can attain union with the Father and the Son (see 1:3). To describe that communion, he uses clear, bold language: true union is knowing God (see 2:3, 13, 14; 3:1, 6; 4:6–8; 5:20), being in God (see 2:5; 5:20) or in the light (see 2:9), having the Father (see 2:23) or the Son (see 5:12) and therefore eternal life (see 3:15; 5:12); and, above all, it is to "abide" in God (see 2:6, 24, 27; 3:6, 24). This abiding reaches its climax in a mutual indwelling: "All who keep his commandments abide in him, and he in them" (3:24).

True knowledge and love of God are shown by obedience to his commandments (see 2:3–6): "All who keep his commandments abide in him, and he in them" (3:24). The greatest command-

---

6 *Adversus haereses,* 3, 1, 1.

ment of all is the commandment of love (see 2:9–11; 3:14–17; 4:12): "He who abides in love abides in God, and God abides in him" (4:16).

Faith in Jesus Christ

From start (see 1:1–3) to finish (see 5:13, 20), the letter stresses faith in the Person and redemptive work of the Son of God, Jesus Christ. Both to expose errors and to fortify Christians in the faith they had from the beginning, the apostle emphasizes the divinity of Jesus Christ, his redemptive Incarnation, and his role as the only Mediator between God and man. The prologue itself summarizes key dogmatic truths about Christ:[7] he is the Word (1:1), that is, the second Person of the Blessed Trinity, the Son of God (1:3); he exists eternally alongside the Father (see 1:1–2); he took on a true human nature in time (ibid.). He is Life itself, imperishable, and through him life is given to all believers. These ideas are developed throughout the letter.

Love

Love, charity, is the central theme of the letter. St John uses both the noun "love"[8] and the verb "to love".[9] Twice he says that "God is love" (4:8, 16). As St Augustine observes, in this letter the apostle "said many things, practically all of them about charity".[10] God is love because in himself, in the life of the Trinity, he is a living community of love. Inspired by the Holy Spirit, St John arrives at this understanding through deep meditation on the manner in which God works in the history of salvation and, in a special way, in the redemptive Incarnation: "In this the love of God was made manifest among us, that God sent his only Son into the world, so that we might live through him" (4:9).

Divine filiation

Communion with God, and the life of grace received from Jesus Christ, make a Christian a child of God: "See what love the Father has given us, that we should be called children of God; and so we are" (3:1). Although different from Christ's natural filiation to God,[11] a Christian's divine filiation is a marvellous, supernatural reality. God, through Christ, gives people his Life, making them partakers of his own divine nature (see 2 Pet 1:4), and so St John often refers to Christians as "born of God" (see 3:9; 4:7; cf. 5:4; 2:29, 5:1). It is not, then, just an extrinsic relationship (like a title of honour, or human-style adoption): we truly are children of God (see 3:1).

---

7 1 Jn 1:1–4. See also the prologue to the Gospel of St John (Jn 1:1ff), which it echoes.   **8** Eighteen times. In the original Greek the word is always the same (*agápe*); in translations, it is sometimes rendered as "love" and sometimes as "charity".   **9** Twenty-eight times.   **10** *In Epistulam Ioannis ad Parthos*, prologue.   **11** St John even uses different words in Greek to refer to the Son of God (*hyiós*) and to Christians (*tekna*). When addressing his disciples, affectionately calling them "little children", John uses other terms (*teknia*, *paidía*).

1 John

Prologue*

Jn 1:1–18; 20:20
1 Jn 2:13
Lk 24:39

Jn 1:4, 14; 14:6;
15:27

Mt 13:17
Acts 4:20; 26:16;
2:42f
1 Cor 1:9

Jn 15:11; 16:22–24
2 Jn 12

1 [1]*That which was from the beginning, which we have heard, which we have seen with our eyes, which we have looked upon and touched with our hands, concerning the word of life—[2]the life was made manifest, and we saw it, and testify to it, and proclaim to you the eternal life which was with the Father and was made manifest to us—[3]that which we have seen and heard we proclaim also to you, so that you may have fellowship* with us; and our fellowship is with the Father and with his Son Jesus Christ. [4]And we are writing this that our joy[a] may be complete.

[1] [1]Quod fuit ab initio, quod audivimus, quod vidimus oculis nostris, quod perspeximus, et manus nostrae contrectaverunt de verbo vitae [2]—et vita apparuit, et vidimus et testamur et annuntiamus vobis vitam aeternam, quae erat coram Patre et apparuit nobis—[3]quod vidimus et audivimus, annuntiamus et vobis, ut et vos communionem habeatis nobiscum. Communio autem nostra est cum Patre et cum Filio eius Iesu Christo. [4]Et haec scribimus nos, ut gaudium nostrum sit plenum. [5]Et haec est annuntiatio, quam audivimus ab eo et annuntiamus vobis, quoniam Deus lux est, et tenebrae in eo non sunt ullae. [6]Si dixerimus quoniam communionem habemus cum eo et in tenebris ambulamus, mentimur et non facimus veri-

*1:1–4 Although this letter carries no greeting or words of farewell, the writer and his addressees were obviously very close. The main subject is communion with God, with Christ and with our brethren. To encourage this communion, St John lets his thoughts run on a number of themes structured in concentric circles, each examined in greater depth as the letter progresses. They read like key points in a baptismal catechesis whereby Christians are enabled to discern the difference between true communion and false. One attains true communion with God by walking in the light, in sincerity, by keeping the commandments and abiding in the truth of Christ and in Christ himself (1:5—2:29). Communion with God is a form of sonship and it requires a person to break with sin and to practise the commandment of brotherly love with deeds (3:1–24). Communion with God means we must profess the truth concerning Christ, love as God loves, and believe in the goodness of God who has given us his Son (4:1—5:12). The letter ends with a reaffirming of the power of prayer and of the sense of confidence that faith confers (5:14–21).

The prologue (vv. 1–4), which states the basic theme of the letter, has many similarities to that of the fourth Gospel (Jn 1:1–18): Jesus is the Word of life revealed to mankind. Commenting on this passage, the *Catechism of the Catholic Church*, 425, points out: "The transmission of the Christian faith consists primarily in proclaiming Jesus Christ in order to lead others to faith in him. From the beginning, the first disciples burned with the desire to proclaim Christ: 'We cannot but speak of what we have seen and heard' (Acts 4:20). And they invite people of every era to enter into the joy of their communion with Christ."

The apostle bears witness to Christ (vv. 3–4) for two purposes—to encourage fellowship (communion) and to make Christians' joy complete. Fellowship with the apostles (the author uses the technical term *koinonía*) implies, firstly, having the same faith as those who lived with Jesus: "They saw our Lord in the body," St Augustine reminds us, "and they heard words from his lips and have proclaimed them to us; we also have heard them, but we have not seen him [...]. They saw him, we do not see him, and yet we have fellowship with them, because we have the same faith" (*In Epistolam Ioannis ad Parthos*, 1, 3).

Complete joy is the fruit of communion with God (v. 4). Most manuscripts say "our joy"; some translations, including the Vulgate, say "your joy" (cf. RSV note **a**). The difference is unimportant, because the use of "our" includes the apostles and the faithful, and fits well with the view of the mutual fellowship already alluded to (cf. Jn 15:11; 17:13).

a Other ancient authorities read *your*

1. UNION WITH GOD*

God is light

⁵This is the message we have heard from him and proclaim to you, that God is light and in him is no darkness* at all.

Walking in the light. Rejecting sin

⁶If we say we have fellowship with him while we walk in darkness, we lie and do not live according to the truth; ⁷but if we walk in the light, as he is in the light, we have fellowship with one another, and the blood of Jesus his Son cleanses us from all sin. ⁸If we say we have no sin, we deceive ourselves, and the truth is not in us. ⁹If we confess our sins, he is faithful and just, and will forgive our sins and cleanse us from all unrighteousness. ¹⁰If we say we have not sinned, we make him a liar, and his word is not in us.

tatem; ⁷si autem in luce ambulemus, sicut ipse est in luce, communionem habemus ad invicem, et sanguis Iesu Filii eius mundat nos ab omni peccato. ⁸Si dixerimus quoniam peccatum non habemus, nosmetipsos seducimus, et veritas in nobis non est. ⁹Si confiteamur peccata nostra, fidelis est et iustus, ut remittat nobis peccata et emundet nos ab omni iniustitia. ¹⁰Si dixerimus quoniam non peccavimus, mendacem facimus eum, et

*1:5—2:29 This section explains the nature of union with God and the demands it brings.

1:5 The metaphor of light helps to show what revelation involves: God is light, Jesus Christ has made him known to us, and Christian revelation is the splendour, the shining, of that light. St John uses the statement "God is light" to encourage Christians to lead upright lives. St Augustine comments that we must be united to God and that "darkness should be cast away from us so as to allow light to enter, because darkness is incompatible with light" (*In Epistolam Ioannis ad Parthos*, 1, 5).

1:6—2:2 The wording "If we say …" introduces three suppositions—probably claims made by some early heretics, especially Gnostics, who boasted that they had attained fullness of knowledge and were on that account incapable of committing sin.

To lead a life of union with God, Christians must acknowledge that they are sinners and strive to avoid sin. Christ, who is our advocate before the Father (2:1), cleanses us from all sin with his blood (v. 7). Because God has shown us his mercy, we each need to confess our faults. The penance imposed in the sacrament of Reconciliation helps us to become more like Christ who atoned for our sins once and for all (see *Catechism of the Catholic Church*, 1460).

Walking in darkness, walking in the light are graphic ways of describing sinful behaviour and upright behaviour. St John stresses that one cannot justify a life of sin by claiming to be in communion with God: "Mere confession of faith is in no sense sufficient", St Bede declares, "if that faith is not confirmed by good works" (*In 1 Epistolam Sancti Ioannis*, ad loc.).

John Paul II points out how relevant v. 8 is to the present day: "Deceived by the loss of the sense of sin and at times tempted by an illusion of sinlessness which is not at all Christian, the people of today also need to listen again to St John's admonition, as addressed to each one of them personally: 'If we say we have no sin, we deceive ourselves, and the truth is not in us' (1 Jn 1:8), and indeed 'the whole world is in the power of the evil one' (1 Jn 5:19). Every individual therefore is invited by the voice of divine truth to examine realistically his or her conscience, and to confess that he or she has been brought forth in iniquity, as we say in the *Miserere* Psalm (cf. Ps 51:5)" (*Reconciliatio et paenitentia*, 22).

St Augustine explains v. 9 in this way: "If you confess yourself to be a sinner, the truth is in you: the truth is light. Your life does not yet shine as brightly as it might, because there are sins in you; but now you are beginning to be enlightened, because you confess your iniquities" (*In Epistolam Ioannis ad Parthos*, 1, 6).

"The apostle St John", St Alphonsus com-

2 [1]My little children, I am writing this to you so that you may not sin; but if any one does sin, we have an advocate with the Father, Jesus Christ the righteous; [2]and he is the expiation for our sins, and not for ours only but also for the sins of the whole world.

Jn 14:16
Rom 8:34
Heb 7:25; 8:6
Acts 3:14
1 Jn 3:6
Jn 14:16
Jn 11:5iff; 4:42
1 Jn 4:10
Rom 3:25

Keeping the commandments

[3]And by this we may be sure that we know him, if we keep his commandments.* [4]He who says "I know him" but disobeys his commandments is a liar, and the truth is not in him; [5]but whoever keeps his word, in him truly love for God is perfected. By this we may be sure that we are in him: [6]he who says he abides in him ought to walk in the same way in which he walked.

Jn 10:14

1 Jn 3:19; 4:20

1 Jn 5:3
Jn 8:32; 14:21, 23

Jn 13:15, 34
2 Thess 3:7
Eph 5:2

[7]Beloved, I am writing you no new commandment, but an old commandment which you had from the beginning; the old commandment is the word which you have heard. [8]Yet I am writing you a new commandment, which is true in him and in you, because[b] the darkness is passing away and the true light is already shining. [9]He who says he is in the light and hates his brother is in the darkness still. [10]He who loves his brother abides in the light, and in it[c] there is no cause for stumbling. [11]But he who hates his brother is in the darkness and walks in the darkness, and does not know where he is going, because the darkness has blinded his eyes.

Deut 6:5
Mt 22:37–40

Jn 13:34; 1:5
Rom 13:12

Jn 8:12

Jn 11:10
Prov 4:19

Jn 12:35–36
Mt 15:14

The apostle's confidence in the faithful

[12]I am writing to you, little children, because your sins are forgiven for his sake. [13]I am writing to you, fathers, because you know him who is from the beginning. I am

1 Jn 1:7; 2:2
1 Cor 6:11
Acts 3:16

1 Jn 1:1
Jn 1:1
Eph 6:16

verbum eius non est in nobis. [2] [1]Filioli mei, haec scribo vobis, ut non peccetis. Sed si quis peccaverit, advocatum habemus ad Patrem, Iesum Christum iustum; [2]et ipse est propitiatio pro peccatis nostris, non pro nostris autem tantum sed etiam pro totius mundi. [3]Et in hoc cognoscimus quoniam novimus eum: si mandata eius servemus. [4]Qui dicit: «Novi eum», et mandata eius non servat, mendax est, et in isto veritas non est; [5]qui autem servat verbum eius, vere in hoc caritas Dei consummata est. In hoc cognoscimus quoniam in ipso sumus. [6]Qui dicit se in ipso manere, debet, sicut ille ambulavit, et ipse ambulare. [7]Carissimi, non mandatum novum scribo vobis, sed mandatum vetus, quod habuistis ab initio: mandatum vetus est verbum, quod audistis. [8]Verumtamen mandatum novum scribo vobis, quod est verum in ipso et in vobis, quoniam tenebrae transeunt, et lumen verum iam lucet. [9]Qui dicit se in luce esse et fratrem suum odit, in tenebris est usque adhuc. [10]Qui diligit fratrem suum, in lumine manet, et scandalum ei non est; [11]qui autem odit fratrem suum, in tenebris est et in tenebris ambulat et nescit quo vadat, quoniam tenebrae obcaecaverunt

ments, "exhorts us to avoid sin, but because he is afraid we will lose heart when we remember our past faults, he encourages us to hope for forgiveness provided we are firmly resolved not to fall again; he tells us that we have to put our affairs in order with Christ, who died not only to forgive us but also (after dying) to become our advocate with the heavenly Father" (*Reflections on the Passion*, 9, 2).

2:3–11 Throughout the letter, "knowing God" means not theoretical knowledge but, rather, union with him through faith and love and a life of grace.

The novelty of the new commandment lies not in the basic precept (which is to be found in the Old Testament: see Lev 19:18) but in the standard that Jesus sets — "even as I have loved

you" (Jn 13:34) — and in the fact that this love encompasses everyone: we must love friends and enemies, without distinction of race or culture or social status. "What is perfection in love?" St Augustine asks. "Loving our enemies and loving them so that they may be converted into brothers" (*In Epistolam Ioannis ad Parthos*, 1, 9). "The principal apostolate we Christians must carry out in the world, and the best witness we can give of our faith, is to help bring about a climate of genuine charity within the Church" (St Josemaría Escrivá, *Friends of God*, 226).

2:12–14 These verses can be read as an appeal to all Christians, whatever the situation or circumstances they find themselves in. "Children", "little children", may refer to those recently baptized, whereas "fathers" and "young men" may

b Or *that*   c Or *him*

Jn 5:38; 3:11

writing to you, young men, because you have overcome the evil one. I write to you, children, because you know the Father. [14]I write to you, fathers, because you know him who is from the beginning. I write to you, young men, because you are strong, and the word of God abides in you, and you have overcome the evil one.

Jn 5:42; 1:10
Jas 4:4
Prov 27:20
Tit 2:12
Jas 4:16
Mt 6:24

Mt 7:21
1 Pet 4:2
1 Cor 7:31
Is 40:8
Prov 10:25

Detachment from the world

[15]Do not love the world or the things in the world. If any one loves the world, love for the Father is not in him. [16]For all that is in the world, the lust of the flesh and the lust of the eyes and the pride of life, is not of the Father but is of the world. [17]And the world passes away, and the lust of it; but he who does the will of God abides for ever.

oculos eius. [12]Scribo vobis, filioli: Remissa sunt vobis peccata propter nomen eius. [13]Scribo vobis, patres: Nostis eum, qui ab initio est. Scribo vobis, adulescentes: Vicistis Malignum. [14]Scripsi vobis, parvuli: Nostis Patrem. Scripsi vobis, patres: Nostis eum, qui ab initio est. Scripsi vobis, adulescentes: Fortes estis, et verbum Dei in vobis manet, et vicistis Malignum. [15]Nolite diligere mundum neque ea, quae in mundo sunt. Si quis diligit mundum, non est caritas Patris in eo; [16]quoniam omne, quod est in mundo, concupiscentia carnis et concupiscentia oculorum et iactantia divitiarum, non est ex Patre, sed ex mundo est. [17]Et mundus transit et concupiscentia eius; qui autem facit voluntatem Dei, manet in aeternum.

refer to people whose faith is deeper and more mature; they are able to draw others to the Church and are people who struggle against and, with the help of grace, overcome the temptations the world presents: "Remember that you are fathers; if you forget Him who is from the beginning, you will have lost your paternity. Also see yourselves over and over again as young men: strive to win; win so as to be crowned; be humble in order not to succumb in the struggle" (St Augustine, *In Epistolam Ioannis ad Parthos*, 2, 7).

Commenting on the phrase "you have overcome the evil one" (v. 13), John Paul II taught: "It is necessary to keep going back to *the origin of evil and of sin* in the history of mankind and the universe, just as Christ went back to these same roots in the Paschal Mystery of his Cross and Resurrection. There is no need to be afraid to call *the first agent of evil* by his name—*the Evil One*" (*Letter to Young People*, 15).

2:15–17 Here "world" is used in a pejorative sense, to mean an enemy of God and man and includes everything that stands against God—in other words, the whole kingdom of sin.

"The pride of life" (v. 16) is pride in possessions. "St John distinguishes three kinds of covetousness or concupiscence. (...) In the Catholic catechetical tradition, the ninth commandment forbids carnal concupiscence; the tenth forbids coveting another's goods" (*Catechism of the Catholic Church*, 2514).

The list St John gives here of the signs of a worldly life comprises all the things opposed to fidelity to the love of God. "Lust of the flesh is not limited to disordered sensuality. It also means softness, laziness bent on the easiest, most pleasurable way, any apparent shortcut, even at the expense of fidelity to God. [...] The other enemy is the lust of the eyes, a deep-seated avariciousness that leads us to appreciate only what we can touch. Such eyes are glued to earthly things and, consequently, they are blind to supernatural realities. We can, then, use this expression of sacred Scripture to indicate that disordered desire for material things, as well as that deformation which views everything around us—other people, the circumstances of our life and of our age—with just human vision. Then the eyes of our soul grow dull. Reason proclaims itself sufficient to understand everything, without the aid of God. This is a subtle temptation, which hides behind the power of our intellect, given by our Father God to man so that he might know and love him freely. Seduced by this temptation, the human mind appoints itself the centre of the universe, being thrilled with the prospect that 'you shall be like gods' (Gen 3:5). So filled with love for itself, it turns its back on the love of God. In this way does our existence fall prey unconditionally to the third enemy: pride of life. It's not merely a question of passing thoughts of vanity or self-love, it's a state of general conceit. Let's not deceive ourselves, for this is the worst of all evils, the root of every false step. The fight

Not listening to heretics

¹⁸Children, it is the last hour;* and as you have heard that antichrist is coming, so now many antichrists have come; therefore we know that it is the last hour. ¹⁹They went out from us, but they were not of us; for if they had been of us, they would have continued with us; but they went out, that it might be plain that they all are not of us. ²⁰But you have been anointed by the Holy One, and you all know.^d ²¹I write to you, not because you do not know the truth, but because you know it, and know that no lie is of the truth. ²²Who is the liar but he who denies that Jesus is the Christ? This is the antichrist, he who denies the Father and the Son. ²³No one who denies the Son has the Father. He who confesses the Son has the Father also. ²⁴Let what you heard from the beginning abide in you. If what you heard from the beginning abides in

1 Jn 2:22
2 Jn 7
1 Tim 4:1
2 Thess 2:4
Acts 20:30
1 Cor 11:19
2 Cor 6:14–18
1 Jn 1:3
Jn 5:22
1 Jn 2:27
2 Cor 1:21
Jn 14:26
2 Pet 1:12
2 Jn 1–2
1 Jn 3:19
1 Jn 4:3
2 Thess 2:4
1 Jn 4:15
Jn 5:23; 14:7–9; 17:6
1 Jn 1:3; 2:7

¹⁸Filioli, novissima hora est; et sicut audistis quia antichristus venit, ita nunc antichristi multi adsunt, unde cognoscimus quoniam novissima hora est. ¹⁹Ex nobis prodierunt, sed non erant ex nobis, nam si fuissent ex nobis, permansissent nobiscum; sed ut manifestaretur quoniam illi omnes non sunt ex nobis. ²⁰Sed vos unctionem habetis a Sancto et scitis omnes. ²¹Non scripsi vobis quasi nescientibus veritatem sed quasi scientibus eam, et quoniam omne mendacium ex veritate non est. ²²Quis est mendax, nisi is qui negat quoniam Iesus est Christus? Hic est antichristus, qui negat Patrem et Filium. ²³Omnis, qui negat Filium, nec Patrem habet; qui confitetur Filium, et Patrem habet. ²⁴Vos, quod audistis ab initio, in vobis permaneat; si in vobis permanserit, quod ab initio audistis, et vos in Filio et in Patre manebitis. ²⁵Et haec est repromissio, quam ipse pollicitus est

against pride has to be a constant battle, to such an extent that someone once said that pride only disappears twenty-four hours after each of us has died. It is the arrogance of the Pharisee whom God cannot transform because he finds in him the obstacle of self-sufficiency. It is the haughtiness which leads to despising others, to lording it over them, to mistreating them. For 'when pride comes, then comes disgrace' (Prov 11:2)" (St Josemaría Escrivá, *Christ Is Passing By*, 5–6).

2:18–29 The fact that there are heretics to the true faith suggests that our Lord's prediction about the coming of the antichrist (see Mt 24:15–28 and par.) is nearing fulfilment and that the "last hour" has begun (v. 18). It is evidence, too, in support of the early Christians' keen desire to see the second coming of Christ; in this age, everything that happens is a preparation for the Second Coming.

"Antichrist" is a term found only in the letters of St John (2:18, 22; 4:3; 2 Jn 7), although the figure it denotes shares some features with the "son of perdition" and the "man of lawlessness" described by St Paul (see 2 Thess 2:1–12), and with the "beast" in the book of Revelation (see e.g. Rev 11:7; 13:1ff): the distinctive feature of all is their brutal opposition to Christ, his teaching and his followers. It is not easy to say whether the antichrist is a person or a group. The letters of St John suggest the latter—meaning all

those who oppose Jesus Christ (the "many antichrists": v. 18), who have been active ever since the start of Christianity, and who will continue to oppose him until the end of time. See the notes on 2 Thess 2:1–12 and Rev 20:1–6.

"Anointed by the Holy One" (v. 20; cf. v. 27) refers to the action of the Father and of the Son through the Holy Spirit on the soul of the Christian at Baptism. Christians have no need to listen to the teachings of those outside the Church, for, guided by the Holy Spirit, they have the certainty of faith "when, 'from the bishops to the last of the faithful' (see St Augustine, *De Praed. Sanct.* 14, 27), they manifest a universal consent in matters of faith and morals" (Vatican II, *Lumen gentium*, 12). This is what is termed "supernatural appreciation of the faith" (*sensus fidei*).

Verse 22 contains a basic tenet of faith: to be a Christian, a person must believe that Jesus, who lived among us, is the Messiah, the Son of God: "Clearly opposed to this belief are those opinions according to which it would not be revealed and known that the Son of God subsists from eternity in the mystery of God, distinct from the Father and from the Holy Spirit; and, equally, the opinions that argue for the jettisoning of the idea of the unique person of Jesus Christ, born of the Father before time began in respect of his divine nature, and born in time of the Virgin Mary in respect of his human nature; and, finally, the idea that the human nature of Jesus Christ would exist, not as something

d Other ancient authorities read *you know everything*

Jn 5:24; 6:40, 68;
17:2

you, then you will abide in the Son and in the Father. ²⁵And this is what he has promised us,ᵉ eternal life.

1 Jn 2:20
Jn 14:26
Jer 31:34
Jn 6:45

²⁶I write this to you about those who would deceive you; ²⁷but the anointing which you received from him abides in you, and you have no need that any one should teach you; as his anointing teaches you about everything, and is true, and is no lie, just as it has taught you, abide in him.

1 Jn 4:17
2 Thess 1:9
Mt 24:3
1 Cor 15:23
1 Jn 3:7, 10

²⁸And now, little children, abide in him, so that when he appears we may have confidence and not shrink from him in shame at his coming. ²⁹If you know that he is righteous, you may be sure that every one who does right is born of him.

2. LIVING AS GOD'S CHILDREN*

We are children of God

Rom 8:14–17, 37–39
Eph 1:5
Jn 15:21; 17:25; 1:12
Col 3:4
Rom 8:29
Phil 3:21
1 Cor 13:12

3 ¹See what love the Father has given us, that we should be called children of God; and so we are. The reason why the world does not know us is that it did not know him. ²Beloved, we are God's children now; it does not yet appear what we shall be, but we know that when he appears we shall be like him, for we shall see him as he is.

Mt 5:48
Lev 19:2
1 Jn 2:6

A child of God does not sin

Jn 1:29; 8:46
Is 53:5
1 Pet 2:24
Heb 7:26; 9:26
1 Jn 1:3; 2:14
Mt 2:18

³And every one who thus hopes in him purifies himself as he is pure.

⁴Every one who commits sin is guilty of lawlessness; sin is lawlessness. ⁵You know that he appeared to take away sins, and in him there is no sin. ⁶No one who

---

nobis: vitam aeternam. ²⁶Haec scripsi vobis de eis, qui seducunt vos. ²⁷Et vos unctionem, quam accepistis ab eo, manet in vobis, et non necesse habetis, ut aliquis doceat vos; sed sicut unctio ipsius docet vos de omnibus, et verum est et non est mendacium, et, sicut docuit vos, manetis in eo. ²⁸Et nunc, filioli, manete in eo, ut, cum apparuerit, habeamus fiduciam et non confundamur ab eo in adventu eius. ²⁹Si scitis quoniam iustus est, scitote quoniam et omnis, qui facit iustitiam, ex ipso natus est. [3] ¹Videte qualem caritatem dedit nobis Pater, ut filii Dei nominemur, et sumus! Propter hoc mundus non cognoscit nos, quia non cognovit eum. ²Carissimi, nunc filii Dei sumus, et nondum manifestatum est quid erimus; scimus quoniam, cum ipse apparuerit, similes ei erimus, quoniam videbimus eum, sicuti est. ³Et omnis, qui habet spem hanc in eo, purificat se,

---

assumed into the eternal person of the Son of God but rather as being itself a human person, in which case the mystery of Jesus Christ would consist in the fact that God, in revealing himself, becomes most eminently present in the human person of Jesus" (Congregation for the Doctrine of the Faith, *Mysterium Filii Dei*, 3).

The "anointing" (v. 27) refers to the Holy Spirit, who acts in the faithful by instructing them "about everything".

*3:1–24 In this second section, St John in his exhortations draws on the fact that the Christian is a child of God.

3:1–2 Divine filiation is a wonderful gift whereby God gratuitously grants us supernatural status, an intimacy with him that makes us *domestici Dei*, "members of the household of God" (Eph 2:19). "This is the great boldness of the Christian

faith—to proclaim the value and dignity of human nature and to affirm that we have been created to obtain the dignity of children of God" (St Josemaría Escrivá, *Christ Is Passing By*, 133).

3:3–10 The prospect of seeing God (see 3:2) is the hope that sustains Christians and encourages them to keep on the road to holiness and to struggle against sin. "Sin is lawlessness" (v. 4) "This expression," Pope John Paul II explains, "which echoes what St Paul writes concerning the *mystery of evil* (cf. 2 Thess 2:7), helps us to grasp the obscure and intangible element hidden in sin. Clearly, sin is a product of man's freedom. But deep within its human reality there are factors at work which place it beyond the merely human, in the border-area where man's conscience, will and sensitivity are in contact with the dark forces which, according to St Paul, are active in the world almost to the point of ruling

---

ᵉ Other ancient authorities read *you*

abides in him sins;* no one who sins has either seen him or known him. ⁷Little chil- 1 Jn 2:29
dren, let no one deceive you. He who does right is righteous, as he is righteous. ⁸He Jn 8:44; 12:31–32
Gen 3:15
1 Jn 3:5
who commits sin is of the devil; for the devil has sinned from the beginning. The
reason the Son of God appeared was to destroy the works of the devil. ⁹No one born 1 Jn 2:14; 3:6; 5:18
of God commits sin; for God'sᶠ nature abides in him, and he cannot sin because he
isᵍ born of God. ¹⁰By this it may be seen who are the children of God, and who are 1 Jn 1:7; 3:8; 3:38
Mt 4:1
the children of the devil: whoever does not do right is not of God, nor he who does
not love his brother.

Loving one another

¹¹For this is the message which you have heard from the beginning, that we should 1 Jn 2:7
Jn 13:34
love one another, ¹²and not be like Cain who was of the evil one and murdered his Gen 4:8
Jn 8:44
brother. And why did he murder him? Because his own deeds were evil and his 1 Jn 3:8
brother's righteous. ¹³Do not wonder, brethren, that the world hates you. ¹⁴We know Jn 15:18–21
Mt 24:9
that we have passed out of death into life, because we love the brethren. He who Jn 5:24
Heb 6:1
does not love abides in death. ¹⁵Any one who hates his brother is a murderer, and Mt 5:21f
you know that no murderer has eternal life abiding in him. ¹⁶By this we know love,

sicut ille purus est. ⁴Omnis, qui facit peccatum, et iniquitatem facit, quia peccatum est iniquitas. ⁵Et scitis quoniam ille apparuit, ut peccata tolleret, et peccatum in eo non est. ⁶Omnis, qui in eo manet, non peccat; omnis, qui peccat, non vidit eum nec novit eum. ⁷Filioli, nemo vos seducat. Qui facit iustitiam, iustus est, sicut ille iustus est; ⁸qui facit peccatum, ex Diabolo est, quoniam a principio Diabolus peccat. Propter hoc apparuit Filius Dei, ut dissolvat opera Diaboli. ⁹Omnis, qui natus est ex Deo, peccatum non facit, quoniam semen ipsius in eo manet; et non potest peccare, quoniam ex Deo natus est. ¹⁰In hoc manifesti sunt filii Dei et filii Diaboli: omnis, qui non facit iustitiam, non est ex Deo, et qui non diligit fratrem suum. ¹¹Quoniam haec est annuntiatio, quam audistis ab initio, ut diligamus alterutrum. ¹²Non sicut Cain: ex Maligno erat et occidit fratrem suum. Et propter quid occidit eum? Quoniam opera eius maligna erant, fratris autem eius iusta. ¹³Nolite mirari, fratres, si odit vos mundus. ¹⁴Nos scimus

it (cf. Rom 7:7–25; Eph 2:2; 6:12)" (*Reconciliatio et paenitentia*, 14).

The false teachers with whom St John had to contend claimed to have special knowledge of God (*gnosis*) that put them beyond good and evil so that they gave no importance to sin. St John answers them by echoing our Lord's words, "The tree is known by its fruit" (Mt 12:33). The criteria for identifying children of God are: the practice of righteousness, that is, striving for holiness and struggling against sin, and a life of brotherly love (v. 10).

The expression "children of the devil" (v. 10) is not used in the literal sense; it stems from a Semitic turn of phrase and means "supporters of the devil".

3:11–24 Those who do not practise brotherly love are as murderous as Cain (v. 12). By contrast, the model of love is Christ, who gave his life for us (vv. 13–16). Brotherly love should express itself in deed and in truth (vv. 17–18) and it leads a person to have serene confidence in God, who knows all things (vv. 19–22). "This is the pearl sought by the merchant described in

the Gospel, who, when he found it, sold all that he had and bought it (cf. Mt 13:46). This is the precious pearl—charity. Without it, anything else you have does you no good; and if you do possess it, you have all that you need [...]. You may tell me, 'I have not seen God'; but can you say, 'I have not seen man'? Love your brother. If you love your brother whom you see, you will also see God, because you will see charity and God dwells within charity" (St Augustine, *In Epistolam Ioannis ad Parthos*, 5, 7).

Using an example very like that found in James 2:15–16, St John shows in vv. 17–18 that genuine love expresses itself in actions. "What the Lord desires is works. If you see a sick woman to whom you can give some help, never be affected by the fear that your devotion will suffer, but take pity on her: if she is in pain, you should feel pain too; if necessary, fast so that she may have your food, not so much for her sake as because you know it to be your Lord's will. That is true union with his will. Again, if you hear someone being highly praised, be much more pleased than if they were praising you" (St Teresa of Avila, *Interior Castle*, 5, 3, 11).

f Greek *his*   g Or *for the offspring of God abide in him, and they cannot sin because they are*

Jn 15:13
Eph 5:2
Mt 20:28
1 Jn 2:6
Jas 2:16
Deut 15:7–11
Jn 5:42
1 Jn 2:5; 4:12
Mt 7:21
Jas 1:22; 2:15f
2 Jn 4
3 Jn 3–4
1 Jn 4:4
1 Jn 4:17
Heb 4:16
Mt 7:7
Jn 14:13–15; 8:29
Jn 13:34; 15:10, 17
1 Jn 4:13
Rom 8:9
1 Jn 1:3–7
Jn 14:21–23

that he laid down his life for us; and we ought to lay down our lives for the brethren. [17]But if any one has the world's goods and sees his brother in need, yet closes his heart against him, how does God's love abide in him? [18]Little children, let us not love in word or speech but in deed and in truth.

[19]By this we shall know that we are of the truth, and reassure our hearts before him [20]whenever our hearts condemn us; for God is greater than our hearts, and he knows everything. [21]Beloved, if our hearts do not condemn us, we have confidence before God; [22]and we receive from him whatever we ask, because we keep his commandments and do what pleases him. [23]And this is his commandment, that we should believe in the name of his Son Jesus Christ and love one another, just as he has commanded us. [24]All who keep his commandments abide in him, and he in them. And by this we know that he abides in us, by the Spirit which he has given us.

3. FAITH IN CHRIST. BROTHERLY LOVE*

1 Jn 2:18
2 Jn 7
Mt 24:24
Deut 13:1–6;
18:20–22
1 Cor 12:3
1 Thess 5:21

1 Jn 2:22
2 Thess 2:4

Faith in Christ, not in false prophets

4 [1]Beloved, do not believe every spirit, but test the spirits* to see whether they are of God; for many false prophets have gone out into the world. [2]By this you know the Spirit of God: every spirit which confesses that Jesus Christ has come in the flesh is of God, [3]and every spirit which does not confess Jesus is not of God. This is

quoniam transivimus de morte in vitam, quoniam diligimus fratres; qui non diligit, manet in morte. [15]Omnis, qui odit fratrem suum, homicida est, et scitis quoniam omnis homicida non habet vitam aeternam in semetipso manentem. [16]In hoc novimus caritatem quoniam ille pro nobis animam suam posuit; et nos debemus pro fratribus animas ponere. [17]Qui habuerit substantiam mundi et viderit fratrem suum necesse habere et clauserit viscera sua ab eo, quomodo caritas Dei manet in eo? [18]Filioli, non diligamus verbo nec lingua sed in opere et veritate. [19]In hoc cognoscemus quoniam ex veritate sumus, et in conspectu eius placabimus corda nostra, [20]quoniam si reprehenderit nos cor, maior est Deus corde nostro et cognoscit omnia. [21]Carissimi, si cor nostrum non reprehenderit nos, fiduciam habemus ad Deum [22]et, quodcumque petierimus, accipimus ab eo, quoniam mandata eius custodimus et ea, quae sunt placita coram eo, facimus. [23]Et hoc est mandatum eius, ut credamus nomini Filii eius Iesu Christi et diligamus alterutrum, sicut dedit mandatum nobis. [24]Et, qui servat mandata eius, in ipso manet, et ipse in eo; et in hoc cognoscimus quoniam manet in nobis, ex Spiritu, quem nobis dedit. [4] [1]Carissimi, nolite omni spiritui credere, sed probate spiritus si ex Deo sint, quoniam multi pseudoprophetae prodierunt in mundum. [2]In hoc cognoscitis Spiritum Dei: omnis spiritus, qui confitetur Iesum Christum in carne venisse, ex Deo est. [3]Et omnis spiritus, qui non confitetur Iesum, ex Deo non est; et hoc est antichristi, quod audistis quoniam venit, et nunc iam in mundo est. [4]Vos

God's commandments can be summed up in two virtues that are the two sides of the same coin (see vv. 22–24)—faith in Jesus Christ and love for the brethren. "We cannot truly love one another without faith in Christ, nor can we truly believe in the name of Jesus Christ without fraternal charity" (St Bede, *In 1 Epistolam Sancti Ioannis*, ad loc.).

*4:1–5:12 In this section the central themes of the letter are developed further in a literary triptych in which belief in Jesus Christ (4:1–6; 5:1–12) forms the framework in which the commandment of love (4:7–21) is set.

4:1–6 Belief that the Son of God truly became man is the distinguishing mark of the Christian faith. "The first heresies denied not so much

Christ's divinity as his true humanity (Gnostic Docetism). From apostolic times the Christian faith has insisted on the true incarnation of God's Son 'come in the flesh' (cf. 1 Jn 4:2–3; 2 Jn 7)" (*Catechism of the Catholic Church*, 465).

Victory over sin leads to humility: "Do not become proud; recognize who has conquered in you. Why did you win? 'Because he who is in you is more powerful than he who is in the world.' Be humble; carry your Lord; be a little donkey for your rider. It is in your best interest to have him guide and direct you; because if you do not have him as your rider, you will be inclined to toss your head and kick out; but woe to you if you have no guide! That freedom would mean your ending up as prey for wild beasts" (St Augustine, *In Epistolam Ioannis ad Parthos*, 7, 2).

the spirit of antichrist, of which you heard that it was coming, and now it is in the world already. [4]Little children, you are of God, and have overcome them; for he who is in you is greater than he who is in the world. [5]They are of the world, therefore what they say is of the world, and the world listens to them. [6]We are of God. Whoever knows God listens to us, and he who is not of God does not listen to us. By this we know the spirit of truth and the spirit of error.

1 Jn 2:13–14; 3:20
Jn 3:31; 10:29; 15:19
1 Jn 3:8
Jn 8:47; 10:26; 14:17
1 Jn 1:3; 3:10

God is love. Brotherly love, the mark of Christians

[7]Beloved, let us love one another; for love is of God, and he who loves is born of God and knows God. [8]He who does not love does not know God; for God is love. [9]In this the love of God was made manifest among us, that God sent his only Son into the world, so that we might live through him. [10]In this is love, not that we loved God but that he loved us and sent his Son to be the expiation for our sins. [11]Beloved, if God so loved us, we also ought to love one another. [12]No man has ever seen God; if we love one another, God abides in us and his love is perfected in us.

1 Thess 4:9
1 Jn 1:7
1 Jn 4:16
Jn 3:16
1 Jn 2:2
Rom 3:25; 5:8; 8:51
Mt 18:33
Jn 1:18; 6:46
Ex 33:20
1 Jn 1:3

ex Deo estis, filioli, et vicistis eos, quoniam maior est, qui in vobis est quam qui in mundo. [5]Ipsi ex mundo sunt; ideo ex mundo loquuntur, et mundus eos audit. [6]Nos ex Deo sumus. Qui cognoscit Deum, audit nos; qui non est ex Deo, non audit nos. Ex hoc cognoscimus Spiritum veritatis et spiritum erroris. [7]Carissimi, diligamus invicem, quoniam caritas ex Deo est, et omnis, qui diligit, ex Deo natus est et cognoscit Deum. [8]Qui non diligit, non cognovit Deum, quoniam Deus caritas est. [9]In hoc apparuit caritas Dei in nobis, quoniam Filium suum unigenitum misit Deus in mundum, ut vivamus per eum. [10]In hoc est caritas, non quasi nos dilexerimus Deum, sed quoniam ipse dilexit nos et misit Filium suum propitiationem pro peccatis nostris. [11]Carissimi, si sic Deus dilexit nos, et nos debemus alterutrum diligere. [12]Deum nemo vidit umquam; si diligamus

4:7–21 The thread of the argument here is as follows: God is love, and he loved us before we loved him (vv. 7–10); brotherly love is the response that God's love calls for (vv. 11–16). When our love is perfect, we feel no fear (vv. 17–18); brotherly love is a sign and an expression of love for God (vv. 19–21).

The central theme of the letter is summed up in the statement "God is love" (vv. 8, 16). "Even if nothing else were said in praise of love in all the pages of this epistle, even if nothing else were said in all the pages of Holy Scripture, and the only thing we heard from the mouth of the Holy Spirit were 'God is love,' we would need to search no more" (St Augustine, *In Epistolam Ioannis ad Parthos*, 7, 4). "By sending his only Son and the Spirit of Love in the fullness of time, God has revealed his innermost secret: God himself is an eternal exchange of love, Father, Son and Holy Spirit, and he has destined us to share in that exchange" (*Catechism of the Catholic Church*, 221).

"'God is love, and he who abides in love abides in God, and God abides in him' (1 Jn 4:16). These words from the First Letter of John express with remarkable clarity the heart of the Christian faith: the Christian image of God and the resulting image of mankind and its destiny.

In the same verse, St John also offers a kind of summary of the Christian life: 'We have come to know and to believe in the love God has for us.'

"'*We have come to believe in God's love*': in these words the Christian can express the fundamental decision of his life. Being Christian is not the result of an ethical choice or lofty idea, but the encounter with an event, a person, which gives life a new horizon and decisive direction. St John's Gospel describes that event in these words: 'God so loved the world that he gave his only Son, that whoever believes in him should … have eternal life' (3:16). In acknowledging the centrality of love, Christian faith has retained the core of Israel's faith, while at the same time giving it new depth and breadth. The pious Jew prayed daily the words of the Book of Deuteronomy which expressed the heart of his existence: 'Hear, O Israel: the Lord our God is one Lord, and you shall love the Lord your God with all your heart, and with all your soul and with all your might' (6:4–5). Jesus united into a single precept this commandment of love for God and the commandment of love for neighbour found in the Book of Leviticus: 'You shall love your neighbour as yourself' (19:18; cf. Mk 12:29–31). Since God has first loved us (cf. 1 Jn 4:10), love is no longer a mere 'command'; it is the

1 Jn 1:7; 3:24
Rom 5:5

Jn 3:17; 4:42

1 Jn 5:5

1 Jn 1:3; 4:8
Jn 17:6

1 Jn 2:6, 28; 3:23
Jas 2:13

Rom 8:15
2 Thess 3:7
2 Tim 1:7

1 Jn 4:10
1 Jn 2:4
1 Pet 1:8

Mt 22:37–40
Jn 14:15, 21; 15:17

[13]By this we know that we abide in him and he in us, because he has given us of his own Spirit. [14]And we have seen and testify that the Father has sent his Son as the Saviour of the world. [15]Whoever confesses that Jesus is the Son of God, God abides in him, and he in God. [16]So we know and believe the love God has for us. God is love, and he who abides in love abides in God, and God abides in him. [17]In this is love perfected with us, that we may have confidence for the day of judgment, because as he is so are we in this world. [18]There is no fear in love, but perfect love casts out fear. For fear has to do with punishment, and he who fears is not perfected in love. [19]We love, because he first loved us. [20]If any one says, "I love God," and hates his brother, he is a liar; for he who does not love his brother whom he has seen, cannot[h] love God whom he has not seen. [21]And this commandment we have from him, that he who loves God should love his brother also.

1 Jn 1:3; 2:22
Mt 16:16

Jn 14:25
Mt 11:30
Rom 13:9
2 Jn 6
Gal 5:14
Deut 30:11

Everyone who believes in Jesus overcomes the world

5 [1]Every one who believes that Jesus is the Christ is a child of God, and every one who loves the parent loves the child. [2]By this we know that we love the children of God, when we love God and obey his commandments. [3]For this is the love of God, that we keep his commandments. And his commandments are not burdensome.

invicem, Deus in nobis manet, et caritas eius in nobis consummata est. [13]In hoc cognoscimus quoniam in ipso manemus, et ipse in nobis, quoniam de Spiritu suo dedit nobis. [14]Et nos vidimus et testificamur quoniam Pater misit Filium salvatorem mundi. [15]Quisque confessus fuerit: «Iesus est Filius Dei», Deus in ipso manet, et ipse in Deo. [16]Et nos, qui credidimus, novimus caritatem, quam habet Deus in nobis. Deus caritas est, et, qui manet in caritate, in Deo manet, et Deus in eo manet. [17]In hoc consummata est caritas nobiscum, ut fiduciam habeamus in die iudicii, quia sicut ille est, et nos sumus in hoc mundo. [18]Timor non est in caritate, sed perfecta caritas foras mittit timorem, quoniam timor poenam habet; qui autem timet, non est consummatus in caritate. [19]Nos diligimus, quoniam ipse prior dilexit nos. [20]Si quis dixerit: «Diligo Deum», et fratrem suum oderit, mendax est; qui enim non diligit fratrem suum, quem videt, Deum, quem non videt, non potest diligere. [21]Et hoc mandatum habemus ab eo, ut, qui diligit Deum, diligat et fratrem suum. [5] [1]Omnis, qui credit quoniam Iesus est Christus, ex Deo natus est; et omnis, qui diligit Deum qui genuit, diligit et eum qui natus est ex eo. [2]In hoc cognoscimus quoniam diligimus natos Dei, cum Deum diligamus et mandata eius faciamus. [3]Haec est enim caritas Dei, ut mandata eius servemus; et mandata eius gravia non sunt, [4]quoniam omne, quod natum est ex Deo, vincit mundum;

response to the gift of love with which God draws near to us" (Benedict XVI, *Deus caritas est*, 1).

It is not possible to love God and not love one's neighbour. Clement of Alexandria summarizes Christian tradition in a beautiful phrase: "Seeing your brother is seeing God" (*Stromata*, 1, 19; 2, 15). And St John Climacus says: "Love of God cannot be understood if there is no love for one's neighbour. It would be as though I dreamt that I was walking; it would only be a dream: I would not really be walking. Anyone who does not love his neighbour does not love God" (*Scala paradisi*, 33).

5:1–5 Through faith in Jesus Christ, and by their Baptism, people become children of God. This leads them to love others, who are their brothers and sisters (it is axiomatic that someone who loves his parents should love his siblings); it also means that they keep the commandments and share in Christ's victory over the world. Chris-

tians, as members of Christ through faith, have access to all the grace necessary to overcome temptation and share in Christ's own glory. In this passage "world" has a pejorative sense, meaning everything opposed to Christ's work of redemption and therefore to man's salvation.

5:6–12 It appears that some Gnostics argued that Jesus of Nazareth became the Son of God at his baptism and ceased to have that status prior to his passion. St John addresses these errors head on and, by reference ("water and blood") to the baptism of Jesus and his death on the cross, he asserts that these events are inseparable from the testimony borne by the Spirit: if one denied them, one would be calling God a liar (cf. v. 10).

The Fathers of the Church, who interpreted the words of v. 8 as referring to the sacraments, comment that in the sacraments the grace of God is communicated interiorly and is signalled externally. St Bede follows this interpretation when he says: "The Holy Spirit makes us adop-

h Other ancient authorities read *how can he*

[4]For whatever is born of God overcomes the world; and this is the victory that overcomes the world, our faith. [5]Who is it that overcomes the world but he who believes
that Jesus is the Son of God?

1 Jn 3:23
Jn 16:33
1 Jn 2:13, 14

1 Jn 4:4

Testimony borne to Christ

[6]This is he who came by water and blood, Jesus Christ, not with the water only but
with the water and the blood. [7]And the Spirit is the witness, because the Spirit is the
truth. [8]There are three witnesses,* the Spirit, the water, and the blood; and these
three agree. [9]If we receive the testimony of men, the testimony of God is greater; for
this is the testimony of God that he has borne witness to his Son. [10]He who believes
in the Son of God has the testimony in himself. He who does not believe God has
made him a liar, because he has not believed in the testimony that God has borne to
his Son. [11]And this is the testimony, that God gave us eternal life, and this life is in
his Son. [12]He who has the Son has life; he who has not the Son of God has not life.

Jn 1:33; 14:26; 19:34
1 Jn 2:20, 27

Jn 5:32, 37; 8:18

Jn 3:33
Rom 8:16

1 Jn 1;2; 5:20
Jn 1:4; 3:11; 5:21–26

Jn 3:36

4. CONCLUSION*

[13]I write this to you who believe in the name of the Son of God, that you may know
that you have eternal life.

Jn 1:12; 20:31

Prayer for sinners

[14]And this is the confidence which we have in him, that if we ask anything according to his will he hears us. [15]And if we know that he hears us in whatever we ask, we

1 Jn 3:21f
Mt 7:7
Jn 14:13

et haec est victoria, quae vicit mundum: fides nostra. [5]Quis est qui vincit mundum, nisi qui credit quoniam Iesus est Filius Dei? [6]Hic est qui venit
per aquam et sanguinem, Iesus Christus; non in aqua solum sed in aqua et in sanguine. Et Spiritus est, qui testificatur, quoniam Spiritus est veritas. [7]Quia tres sunt qui testificantur: [8]Spiritus et aqua et sanguis; et hi tres in unum sunt. [9]Si testimonium hominum accipimus, testimonium Dei
maius est, quoniam hoc est testimonium Dei, quia testificatus est de Filio suo. [10]Qui credit in Filium Dei, habet testimonium in se. Qui non credit
Deo, mendacem facit eum, quoniam non credidit in testimonium, quod testificatus est Deus de Filio suo. [11]Et hoc est testimonium, quoniam vitam
aeternam dedit nobis Deus, et haec vita in Filio eius est. [12]Qui habet Filium, habet vitam; qui non habet Filium Dei, vitam non habet. [13]Haec scripsi
vobis, ut sciatis quoniam vitam habetis aeternam, qui creditis in nomen Filii Dei. [14]Et haec est fiducia, quam habemus ad eum, quia si quid petier-

tive sons of God; the water of the sacred fount
cleanses us; the blood of the Lord redeems us:
the spiritual sacrament bears dual witness, one
visible, one invisible" (*In Epistolam Sancti Ioannis*, ad loc.).

*5:13–21 After his final conclusion to the letter
(v. 13), St John offers a brief summary of the
letter's central theme, which is followed by a
kind of appendix that contains a few last recommendations and exhortations to the letter's readers.

5:13–17 The sacred writer here bolsters peoples'
confidence in prayer and urges the need to pray
for sinners. "Mortal" sin (v. 16), literally, "sin
that leads to death", reminds us of the sin against
the Holy Spirit (see Mt 12:31–32) and that of
apostasy (see Heb 6:4–8). "John seems to wish

to emphasize the incalculable seriousness of
what constitutes the very essence of sin, namely
the rejection of God. This is manifested above all
in *apostasy* and *idolatry*: repudiating faith in
revealed truth and making certain created realities equal to God, raising them to the status of
idols or false gods" (John Paul II, *Reconciliatio
et paenitentia*, 17).

   Although St John makes a point of not
saying that these sinners should be prayed for, he
does not deny that there is hope for them, given
the power and mercy of God. Pope St Gelasius I
taught: "There is a sin of death for those who
persist in that same sin; there is a sin not of death
for those who desist from sin. There is, certainly,
no sin for the pardon of which the Church does
not pray or from which, by the power which was
divinely granted to it, it cannot absolve those
who desist from it" (*Ne forte*).

Mt 12:31
Jn 15:22–24
Jas 5:19
know that we have obtained the requests made of him. ¹⁶If any one sees his brother committing what is not a mortal sin, he will ask, and God[i] will give him life for those whose sin is not mortal. There is sin which is mortal; I do not say that one is to pray for that. ¹⁷All wrongdoing is sin, but there is sin which is not mortal.

The Christian's confidence as a child of God

1 Jn 1:3; 2:13; 3:6, 9
Jn 17:15
¹⁸We know that any one born of God does not sin, but He who was born of God keeps him, and the evil one does not touch him.

Jn 17:3
Jn 24:7
¹⁹We know that we are of God, and the whole world is in the power of the evil one.

²⁰And we know that the Son of God has come and has given us understanding, to know him who is true; and we are in him who is true, in his Son Jesus Christ. This 1 Cor 10:14 is the true God and eternal life. ²¹Little children, keep yourselves from idols.

imus secundum voluntatem eius, audit nos. ¹⁵Et si scimus quoniam audit nos, quidquid petierimus, scimus quoniam habemus petitiones, quas postulavimus ab eo. ¹⁶Si quis videt fratrem suum peccare peccatum non ad mortem, petet, et dabit ei Deus vitam, peccantibus non ad mortem. Est peccatum ad mortem; non pro illo dico, ut roget. ¹⁷Omnis iniustitia peccatum est, et est peccatum non ad mortem. ¹⁸Scimus quoniam omnis, qui natus est ex Deo, non peccat, sed ille qui genitus est ex Deo, conservat eum, et Malignus non tangit eum. ¹⁹Scimus quoniam ex Deo sumus, et mundus totus in Maligno positus est. ²⁰Et scimus quoniam Filius Dei venit et dedit nobis sensum, ut cognoscamus eum, qui verus est; et sumus in eo, qui verus est, in Filio eius Iesu Christo. Hic est qui verus est, Deus et vita aeterna. ²¹Filioli, custodite vos a simulacris!

5:18–21 Jesus Christ, true God and true man, is also eternal life, because only in him can we attain that life. "In this Johannine affirmation there is an indication of hope, based on the divine promises: the Christian has received the guarantee and the necessary strength not to sin" (John Paul II, *Reconciliatio et paentitentia*, 20). In his closing words, St John appeals to Christians to realize what a great gift it is to be a child of God. As St Leo the Great says, reminding the Christian of his or her dignity, "Think about the head and body of which you now form part. Never forget that you were freed from the power of darkness and led into the light and the Kingdom of God" (*Sermo 1 in Nativitate*, 13).

i Greek *he*

THE SECOND AND THIRD LETTERS OF

JOHN

Introduction

These two letters, which because of their brevity are also known as the "lesser epistles of St John", reflect the style of letters of the period in the Greco-Roman world: they begin in the usual formal way—with the sender's name, then that of the addressees, and a greeting—and end with a salutation. The writer introduces himself in both as "the elder" (see 2 Jn 1; 3 Jn 1).

The Second Letter is addressed "to the elect lady and her children" (2 Jn 1), a symbolic way of referring to a local church, probably one in Asia Minor. The Third is addressed to a Christian named Gaius (2 Jn 1) and through him, perhaps, to a group of faithful. The wide circulation these letters received from the very beginning (despite their brevity) is an implicit testimony to the authority of the writer. There is considerable evidence from very early on that the author is St John the apostle. For example, St Polycarp (d. *c*.156), a disciple of John, in his *Letter to the Philippians*, appears to quote words from 2 John 7.[1] St Irenaeus (d. *c*.202), in turn a disciple of Polycarp, quotes 2 John 7 and 11, attributing the letter to the apostle John.[2] Tertullian (d. *c*.222), a witness to tradition in North Africa, makes reference to 2 John 7.[3] An indirect testimony to it is to be found in Clement of Alexandria (d. *c*.214), who, to introduce a quotation from 1 John, uses these words: "John in his longer epistle ...", implying that he knew of at least one, shorter letter by the same writer.[4] Explicit quotations from the two letters are to be found in a number of third- to fifth-century writers, including St Denys of Alexandria,[5] St Athanasius,[6] St Cyril of Jerusalem,[7] St Gregory Nazianzen[8] and St Augustine.[9] Both letters figure along with 1 John as works of St John the apostle in the earliest lists or canons of inspired books. Alongside this very wide consensus (found in so many testimonies from many different places where the Church was established), there were also some in the early centuries who expressed doubts about the Johannine authorship of these letters. Origen (d. *c*.253) mentions that these doubts were current in his time.[10] Eusebius puts both letters in the category of "disputed" New Testament books, that is, books that were not unanimously accepted as canonical,[11] though he himself did accept them as such.[12] The same may be said of St Jerome, who thought them to be authentic, but still mentioned that in his own time not all were agreed on this point. The doubts are traceable to a text by Papias of Hierapolis (written around 130) which mentions a John "the elder", a different person, seemingly, from John "the apostle".[13]

1. CONTENT

In 2 John the addressees are "the elect lady and her children" (v. 1). More likely than not, this addressee is not a particular Christian noblewoman and her family, but a local church. In the farewell at the end of the letter, in fact, the Christian community from where the apostle is writing (Ephesus, probably) is referred to as "your elect sister" (v. 13). The counsels found in the

---

1 See *Epistola ad Philippenses*, 7, 1. **2** See *Adversus haereses*, 1, 16, 3; 3, 16, 8. **3** See *De carne Christi*, 24. **4** See *Stromata*, 2, 16, 76. **5** See Eusebius, *Historia ecclesiastica*, 7, 25, 11. **6** See *Epistulae*, 39. **7** See *Catecheses*, 4, 36. **8** See *Carmina*, 1, 12, 37. **9** See *De doctrina christiana*, 2, 8, 12. **10** See *In Ioannem* 5, 3 and Eusebius, *Historia ecclesiastica*, 6, 25, 7–10. **11** See *Historia ecclesiastica*, 3, 25, 3. **12** See *Demonstratio Evangelica*, 3, 5, 88. **13** See Eusebius, *Historia ecclesiastica*, 3, 39, 4.

letter deal with themes considered at greater length in 1 John—brotherly love and keeping the commandments (vv. 4–6), and the need to be vigilant against the threat of deceivers (vv. 7–11). Because those deceivers "will not acknowledge the coming of Jesus Christ in the flesh" (v. 7), St John tells the faithful to abide in the doctrine of Christ (v. 9), who is the Son of the Father (v. 3), and thus enter into communion with the Father and the Son (v. 9).

The Third Letter of John is addressed to a Christian named Gaius (v. 1), about whom we know nothing more. John praises him for being a true Christian (vv. 3–4), as was shown by the welcome he gave to envoys of the apostle (vv. 5–8), itself a sign of his respect for John himself. Gaius' behaviour is in marked contrast to that of Diotrephes, who appears to have been the person in charge of that community (v. 9): he did not acknowledge the apostle's authority, or receive his envoys, and even sought to excommunicate those who wanted to welcome them (vv. 9–10). That explains why an earlier letter from the apostle (v. 9) failed to produce the intended effect. John also mentions a man named Demetrius, probably the bearer of the letter, a person who "has testimony from every one" (v. 12). Demetrius is generally thought to have been charged with the task either of replacing Diotrephes as head of the community or of installing Gaius in that office.

2. CONTEXT AND MESSAGE

In addition to the testimonies from Tradition, there are also similarities of language and content between these letters and the First Letter and the Gospel of St John which show the hand of that apostle at work as the author of all. There is certainly no doubt about both the Second and the Third letters being by the same author: it is enough to compare the initial greetings and endings, which are almost identical in wording.[14] Moreover, both letters, and particularly the Second, contain a number of expressions and ideas characteristic of St John. There are typically Johannine turns of phrase—"love in the truth" (2 Jn 1; 3 Jn 1; cf. 1 Jn 3:18); "know the truth" (1 Jn 2:21; 2 Jn 1); "abide in [Christ]" or "in the doctrine of Christ" (1 Jn 2:28; 2 Jn 9); "has both the Father and the Son" (1 Jn 2:23; 2 Jn 9); reference to traditional Christian teaching in the phrase "[what/which/as] you have heard from the beginning" (1 Jn 2:24; 3:11; 2 Jn 6); insistence on brotherly love ("[that] we [should] love one another": 1 Jn 3:11, 23; 4:7; 2 Jn 5), a commandment which is not new but which we have heard from the beginning (see 1 Jn 2:7; 2 Jn 5); love for God consists in keeping the commandments (see 1 Jn 5:3; 2 Jn 6); he who does right is "of God" (1 Jn 3:10; 3 Jn 11), whereas he who does evil has not "seen" God (1 Jn 3:6; 3 Jn 11). The first two letters speak of "many antichrists", "false prophets" or "deceivers [who] have gone out into the world" (1 Jn 2:18; 4:1; 2 Jn 7); these are people who do not confess "that Jesus Christ has come in the flesh" (1 Jn 4:2; 2 Jn 7). Also, in 1 and 2 John, the apostle expresses the wish that "our joy may be complete" (1 Jn 1:4; 2 Jn 12). There is scarcely a verse of 2 John that does not have its parallel in 1 John; in fact, the Second Letter is often regarded as a first draft (or as a summary) of the First.

In the absence of any further information from Tradition, it is reasonable to suppose that these letters were written in the last years of the first century, words of warning at a time when the dangers posed by heretics and false teachers was not as serious as it was when 1 John was written.

---

14 Compare, e.g., 2 Jn 1 with 3 Jn 1; 2 Jn 4 with 3 Jn 3 and 4; 2 Jn 12 with 3 Jn 13 and 14.

2 John

Greeting

[1]The elder* to the elect lady* and her children, whom I love in the truth, and not only I but also all who know the truth, [2]because of the truth which abides in us and will be with us for ever:

[3]Grace, mercy, and peace will be with us, from God the Father and from Jesus Christ the Father's Son, in truth and love.

3 Jn 1
1 Pet 5:13
Jn 8:32; 14:17

1 Tim 1:2
2 Tim 1:2

The law of love

[4]I rejoiced greatly to find some of your children following the truth, just as we have been commanded by the Father. [5]And now I beg you, lady, not as though I were writing you a new commandment, but the one we have had from the beginning, that we love one another. [6]And this is love, that we follow his commandments; this is the commandment, as you have heard from the beginning, that you follow love.

3 Jn 3
Philem 7
1 Jn 3:19

1 Jn 2:7

1 Jn 5:3

---

[1]Presbyter electae dominae et filiis eius, quos ego diligo in veritate, et non ego solus, sed et omnes, qui noverunt veritatem, [2]propter veritatem, quae permanet in nobis et nobiscum erit in sempiternum. [3]Erit nobiscum gratia, misericordia, pax a Deo Patre et a Iesu Christo, Filio Patris, in veritate et caritate. [4]Gavisus sum valde quoniam inveni de filiis tuis ambulantes in veritate, sicut mandatum accepimus a Patre. [5]Et nunc rogo te, domina, non tamquam mandatum novum scribens tibi, sed quod habuimus ab initio, ut diligamus alterutrum. [6]Et haec est caritas, ut ambulemus secundum mandata eius; hoc mandatum est, quemadmodum audistis ab initio, ut in eo ambuletis. [7]Quoniam multi seductores prodierunt in

---

*1–3 The text reflects the style of letter in its time (greeting, body of the letter, farewell); it contains advice to a Christian community on matters dealt with more extensively in 1 John—brotherly love, keeping the commandments (vv. 4–6), and vigilance against the threat of deceivers (vv. 7–11).

"The elder" (v. 1). In the New Testament and during the early stage of Christianity the titles of "priest" (elder) and "bishop" were used indiscriminately to refer to pastors of local communities, pastors appointed by apostles (see Acts 20:28 and note on Titus 1:5–9). Here the definite article ("*the* elder") indicates that the writer is someone who is well known to those he is addressing, and who has authority over them. That elder or priest is none other than St John himself. The "elect lady" or "Electa" is probably a metaphorical name for a particular church in Asia Minor.

The word "truth" appears four times in this passage. It means the revelation of God that reaches its climax in Jesus Christ, and includes all the truths in which we are to believe. But it is also, and above all, an inner principle of life and of supernatural action: to "love in the truth" is to "love in Christ".

According to St Bede, in v. 3 St John bears witness to the fact that "the grace, mercy and peace that are given to the faithful also come from Christ, as well as from God the Father; and in order to show that he is equal to the Father and coeternal with him he says that the gifts of the Son are the same as those of the Father" (*In 2 Epistolam Sancti Ioannis*, ad loc.).

4–6 All the commandments can be summed up in one—to love God and one's neighbour. "Listen carefully to a brief precept: love and do as you like. If you stay silent, stay silent out of love; if you cry out, cry out with love; if you correct, correct out of love; if you forgive, forgive with love" (St Augustine, *In Epistolam Ioannis ad Parthos*, 7, 8). Tradition is categorical on this point: anyone who teaches otherwise is a liar and a deceiver. The false teachers caused harm in two ways—by corrupting the faith and by destroying fellowship and brotherly love.

Precautions against heretics

1 Jn 2:18; 4:2–3
7For many deceivers have gone out into the world, men who will not acknowledge the coming of Jesus Christ in the flesh; such a one is the deceiver and the antichrist. 1 Jn 2:22
Gal 4:11 **8**Look to yourselves, that you may not lose what you[a] have worked for, but may win a full reward. 1 Jn 2:23 **9**Any one who goes ahead and does not abide in the doctrine of Christ does not have God; he who abides in the doctrine has both the Father and the Son. **10**If any one comes to you and does not bring this doctrine, do not receive him into the house or give him any greeting; **11**for he who greets him shares his wicked work.

Conclusion and greetings

3 Jn 13f
1 Jn 1:4
12Though I have much to write to you, I would rather not use paper and ink, but I hope to come to see you and talk with you face to face, so that our joy may be complete.

13The children* of your elect sister greet you.

mundum, qui non confitentur Iesum Christum venientem in carne; hic est seductor et antichristus. ⁸Videte vosmetipsos, ne perdatis, quae operati estis, sed ut mercedem plenam accipiatis. ⁹Omnis, qui ultra procedit et non manet in doctrina Christi, Deum non habet; qui permanet in doctrina, hic et Patrem et Filium habet. ¹⁰Si quis venit ad vos et hanc doctrinam non affert, nolite accipere eum in domum nec «Ave» ei dixeritis; ¹¹qui enim dicit illi: «Ave», communicat operibus illius malignis. ¹²Plura habens vobis scribere nolui per chartam et atramentum, spero enim me futurum apud vos et os ad os loqui, ut gaudium nostrum plenum sit. ¹³Salutant te filii sororis tuae electae.

7–11 These verses are in effect a summary of what is said in 1 John. The sacred writer provides criteria to identify heretics of the time: they do not acknowledge the divinity of Jesus Christ incarnate; and he warns that anyone who parts company with sound teaching abandons the Father and the Son.

In the Middle East, hospitality and greetings were not mere marks of courtesy or good manners: they involved a real sense of solidarity and close affinity. Hence the warning that the reception of the kind of people specified in vv. 10–11 might imply complicity in their evil actions and thereby cause scandal to other members of the Christian community.

The duty to safeguard the faith (and to try to get those who undermine it to change their ways) explains why the Church, in exceptional cases, can have recourse to strict disciplinary measures if she finds that "neither by fraternal correction or reproof, nor by any methods of pastoral care, can the scandal be sufficiently repaired, justice restored and the offender reformed" (*Code of Canon Law*, can. 1341).

On the "antichrist" (v. 7), see 1 Jn 2:18–29.

12–13 The greeting sent in v. 13 comes from the members of the church in the city where the writer is based, probably Ephesus.

a Other ancient authorities read *we*

3 John

Greeting*

[2 Jn 1]

¹The elder to the beloved Gaius, whom I love in the truth.

²Beloved, I pray that all may go well with you and that you may be in health; I know that it is well with your soul.

Praise of Gaius

[2 Jn 4]
[1 Jn 3:19]
[Jn 8:2]

³For I greatly rejoiced when some of the brethren arrived and testified to the truth of your life, as indeed you do follow the truth. ⁴No greater joy can I have than this, to hear that my children follow the truth.

⁵Beloved, it is a loyal thing you do when you render any service to the brethren, especially to strangers, ⁶who have testified to your love before the church. You will do well to send them on their journey as befits God's service. ⁷For they have set out for his sake and have accepted nothing from the heathen. ⁸So we ought to support such men, that we may be fellow workers in the truth.

[Mt 10:40; 18:5]
[Heb 13:2]
[1 Tim 5:18]

¹Presbyter Gaio carissimo, quem ego diligo in veritate. ²Carissime, in omnibus exopto prospere te agere et valere, sicut prospere agit anima tua. ³Nam gavisus sum valde venientibus fratribus et testimonium perhibentibus veritati tuae, quomodo tu in veritate ambules. ⁴Maius horum non habeo gaudium, quam ut audiam filios meos in veritate ambulare. ⁵Carissime, fideliter facis, quidquid operaris in fratres et hoc in peregrinos, ⁶qui testimonium reddiderunt caritati tuae in conspectu ecclesiae. Bene facies subveniens illis in via digne Deo; ⁷pro nomine enim profecti sunt, nihil accipientes a gentilibus. ⁸Nos ergo debemus sublevare huiusmodi, ut cooperatores simus veritatis. ⁹Scripsi aliquid ecclesiae; sed is qui amat pri-

*1–2 This letter is very similar in form to the previous one. It was written in response to disagreements that had arisen in a Christian community. St John praises Gaius, the addressee, for his hospitable reception of the apostle's envoys (vv. 3–8), and he condemns Diotrephes' behaviour (vv. 9–10), and commends a man named Demetrius (vv. 11–12) to the community.

An ancient Christian text (*Constitutiones Apostolicae*, 7, 46) mentions a Gaius as bishop of Pergamum, and a Demetrius (v. 12) as bishop of Philadelphia; but the reliability of this information is doubtful. From what this letter says, Gaius does not seem (at least not yet) to hold any hierarchical office; he appears to have been simply a prominent Christian faithful to his responsibilities in the church.

On four occasions St John calls Gaius "beloved" (vv. 1, 2, 5, 11). This is clearly a sign of special affection, a good example of the deep fellowship the early Christians practised, which could not be further from cold formality. Gaius' soul "is well" but John's concern also extends to his physical health. "How well the early Christians practised this ardent charity which went far beyond the limits of mere human solidarity or natural kindness. They loved one another, through the heart of Christ, with a love both tender and strong. Tertullian, writing in the second century, tells us how impressed the pagans were by the behaviour of the faithful at that time. So attractive was it both supernaturally and humanly that they often remarked: 'See how they love one another' (*Apologeticum*, 39)" (St Josemaría Escrivá, *Friends of God*, 225).

3–8. With great simplicity, St John explains why his paternal heart feels so happy—because Gaius, as his charity shows (vv. 5–8), is a good man (vv. 3–4). John uses a typically Semitic turn of phrase to describe Gaius' upright life: "You do follow the truth." To "live in Christ" (see Col 2:6), to "walk in the light" (1 Jn 1:7), "following the truth" (2 Jn 4) all mean the same thing—having such a close fellowship with Christ as to be a genuine Christian in everything one thinks and does.

"They have set out for his sake" (v. 7), literally "for his name", means "for Christ" (cf. Acts 5:41; Phil 2:9–10; Jas 2:7).

Diotrephes' misconduct

[9]I have written something to the church; but Diotrephes, who likes to put himself first, does not acknowledge my authority. [10]So if I come, I will bring up what he is doing, prating against me with evil words. And not content with that, he refuses himself to welcome the brethren, and also stops those who want to welcome them and puts them out of the church.

Commendation of Demetrius

[11]Beloved, do not imitate evil but imitate good. He who does good is of God; he who does evil has not seen God. [12]Demetrius* has testimony from every one, and from the truth itself; I testify to him too, and you know my testimony is true.

Conclusion and farewell

[13]I had much to write to you, but I would rather not write with pen and ink; [14]I hope to see you soon, and we will talk together face to face.

[15]Peace be to you. The friends greet you. Greet the friends, every one of them.

matum gerere in eis, Diotrephes, non recipit nos. [10]Propter hoc, si venero, commonebo eius opera, quae facit verbis malignis garriens in nos; et quasi non ei ista sufficiant, nec ipse suscipit fratres et eos, qui cupiunt, prohibet et de ecclesia eicit. [11]Carissime, noli imitari malum, sed quod bonum est. Qui benefacit, ex Deo est; qui malefacit, non vidit Deum. [12]Demetrio testimonium redditur ab omnibus et ab ipsa veritate; sed et nos testimonium perhibemus, et scis quoniam testimonium nostrum verum est. [13]Multa habui scribere tibi, sed nolo per atramentum et calamum scribere tibi; [14]spero autem protinus te videre, et os ad os loquemur. [15]Pax tibi. Salutant te amici. Saluta amicos nominatim.

"Fellow workers in the truth" (v. 8). The Second Vatican Council applies these words to laypeople in order to explain how their apostolate and the ministry proper to the clergy complement each other: "The apostolate of the Church [...] and of each of its members, aims primarily at announcing to the world by word and action the message of Christ and communicating to it the grace of Christ. The principal means of bringing this about is the ministry of the word and of the sacraments. Committed in a special way to the clergy, it leaves room however for a highly important part for the laity, the part namely of 'helping on the cause of truth' (3 Jn 8)" (*Apostolicam actuositatem*, 6).

9–12 These verses contrast the behaviour of Diotrephes with that of Demetrius. We know no more about Diotrephes than what is said here. All the indications are that he held a position of authority, somewhat similar to a bishop's. His ambition has led him astray: he does not recognize St John's authority and has been bad-mouthing him; he has refused to receive the brethren sent by the apostle (itinerant missionaries), and even tries to prevent others

from doing so. Of Demetrius, too, we know nothing more than what is written here. He may have been one of the missionaries sent by St John, and possibly the bearer of this letter. The passage is a further example of how and why the Church must always be attentive to the intentions and behaviour of her pastors: "In exercising his office of father and pastor, the bishop should be with his people as one who serves (cf. Lk 22:26–27), as a good shepherd who knows his sheep and whose sheep know him, as a true father who excels in his love and solicitude for all" (Vatican II, *Christus Dominus*, 16).

In v. 11, the apostle sums up the teaching found in a more developed form in his First Letter (cf. e.g. 1 Jn 2:18–29; 3:3–10; 5:18–20): he who does right shows he is of God, a child of God, someone who has fellowship with him and abides in him; whereas anyone who sins is no longer one with God and has become an ally of the devil.

13–15 "Peace be to you". This is the typical Hebrew greeting, "*Shalom*", which the apostles continued to use in their letters, giving it a Christian meaning.

THE LETTER OF

JUDE

Introduction

After the letters associated with the pillars of the Church, James, Peter and John, comes the Letter of Jude. A letter that deals with matters concerning the End and that contains features found in Jewish apocalyptic writing, it acts as a bridge between the apostolic letters and the Apocalypse of John, which follows it. This short letter takes issue with false teachers who held that because a Christian was not bound by the Mosaic Law he was also free of moral obligations; it calls on Christians to be steadfast in the faith, and outlines the moral implications of the Gospel.

Along with apparent allusions to this letter in the *Didache* and in St Polycarp's *Letter to the Philippians*, the Letter of St Jude appears in the Muratorian Canon (second century), which lists it among the canonical books of the New Testament. To the testimony of Origen[1] and Tertullian[2] should be added that of Clement of Alexandria, who not only quoted from the letter in his writings[3] but also wrote a commentary on it.[4] Two papyri also, P[72] and P[78], imply that the letter was read as part of Holy Scripture in the third–fourth century. In the fourth century, St Athanasius[5] and St Cyril of Jerusalem,[6] among others, attest to its canonicity. Eusebius of Caesarea notes that most people accepted it as canonical, though some did question its authority; for that reason he includes it among the "disputed" texts.[7] St Jerome explains the origin of the doubts about the letter's canonicity: "Jude has left us a short epistle, which is one of the catholic epistles; but since he quotes the apocryphal book of Enoch it is rejected by many; however, its authority merits it a place among the Holy Scriptures, as does the use that has been made of it".[8] The canonicity of this letter, like that of the other works of the Old and New Testaments, was solemnly defined by the Council of Trent.

1. STRUCTURE AND CONTENT

The structure of the letter is clear. In addition to the opening greeting (vv. 1–2), followed by verses explaining why it was written (vv. 3–4), and a solemn doxology at the end (vv. 24–25), the body of the letter is composed of two main sections—one exposing false teachers (vv. 5–16) and the other exhorting the faithful to persevere (vv. 17–23). In the first section, after the showing (with some biblical examples) of the punishment that awaits the ungodly (vv. 5–7), blasphemy and other evil conduct is denounced (vv. 8–13) and the coming of divine justice and retribution is recalled (vv. 14–16). In the exhortation St Jude reminds readers that, even in their early preaching, the apostles warned that false teachers would trouble the Church (vv. 17–19); he encourages them to ground their life on faith, prayer, charity and hope (vv. 20–21). Finally, he tells them how they should behave towards those who fall under the influence of ungodly teaching (vv. 22–23).

---

1 See *Commentarii in Romanos*, 5, 1. **2** See *De cultu feminarum*, 1, 3. **3** See *Paedagogus*, 3, 8; *Stromata*, 3, 2. **4** See Eusebius of Caesarea, *Historia ecclesiastica*, 6, 14. **5** See *Epistula*, 39. **6** See *Catecheses ad illuminandos*, 4, 35. **7** See *Historia ecclesiastica*, 3, 25, 3; 6, 13, 6. **8** *De viris illustribus*, 4.

2. CONTEXT

The author introduces himself as "Jude, a servant of Jesus Christ and brother of James" (v. 1). The reference to "James" adds authority to the letter, since James had been the leader of the church of Jerusalem (cf. the Introduction to the Letter of St James, above). The name "Jude" (not Jude/Judas Iscariot) is included with that of James and other "brothers" of Jesus, that is, relatives of our Lord, in Matthew 13:55 and Mark 6:3; this may be the Jude to whom the letter is attributed. Some Fathers of the Church identify him with one of the Twelve, the one called "Judas the son of James" or Judas Thaddaeus.[9]

It is not clear who the original addressees of the letter were, for the opening greeting is not specific and extends to all Christians: "To those who are called" (v. 1). It is possible that it was written to (for the most part) Christian converts from Judaism. This would explain the references to extrabiblical Jewish traditions and to apocryphal writings. The fact that no specific addressees are mentioned may explain why this letter is included among the "catholic letters", from the time of Origen on.[10] The explicit reference to James could indicate that the letter was addressed to the same group of believers as the Letter of James, among whom James enjoyed special authority.

Some scholars are of the view that the letter must have been written before the year 70, given that it makes no reference to the destruction of Jerusalem; but others think that this silence proves nothing. The dates proposed for the letter range from the year 50 to the end of the first century, and even to the early second century. It was probably written in Palestine, where relatives of Jesus were held in high regard and held positions of authority in local churches.

3. MESSAGE

The author's intention is to exhort the faithful to safeguard the faith they have been given (see v. 3); he reminds them that the apostles predicted that ungodly men would come, who follow only their own passions (vv. 17–18). News that such people had intruded into Christian communities may in fact have occasioned the letter (see v. 4).

According to the letter, their errors were more of morals than of faith; these are people who "pervert the grace of our God into licentiousness" (v. 4) and spread a false interpretation of Christian freedom (an error that St Paul, too, exposed).[11] Sexual immorality and greed are the main vices mentioned (see vv. 4, 8, 11, 13, 16, 23). Nevertheless, this heretical movement seems to have been in its early stages: these people create divisions (see v. 19), but they still take part in the life of the community (see v. 12) and there appears to be some hope that many of them might be won back to the faith (see vv. 22–23).

The problem of false teachers and their evil influence is also dealt with in the Second Letter of St Peter; there are great similarities of thought and language between the two letters, especially between Jude 4–18 and 2 Peter 2:1—3:3. A comparative reading of both passages suggests that

9 See Lk 6:16; Acts 1:13; Mt 10:3; Mk 3:18. The difficulty arises from the fact that Jude 17–18 seems to indicate that the author was not one of the apostles. **10** See the Introduction to the Catholic Letters, above. **12** See, e.g., Rom 6:1–15; 1 Cor 6:12ff; Gal 5:13ff.

the Letter of St Jude influenced 2 Peter, where some of the ideas expressed by Jude are developed further and slightly modified—or it may be that both passages draw on a (third) common source. The author of Jude uses arguments drawn from biblical and extrabiblical tradition and quotes passages from apocryphal writings such as the Assumption of Moses (see v. 9) and the Book of Enoch (see vv. 14–15).

The Book of Enoch was a very highly regarded text among the Jews, but that does not mean they considered it to be inspired. Even the fact that this letter says that "Enoch […] prophesied" (v. 14) should not be read to mean that the Book of Enoch is inspired: it simply reflects the custom of the time to call important biblical personages "prophets". For a book to be accepted as inspired—in Israel or, later, in the Church—it had to be recognized as canonical by the appropriate authority. In any case, the fact that the Letter of Jude draws on Jewish and Christian traditions that are not in themselves recognized as canonical or inspired in no way undermines the letter's own authority.

Jude

Mt 13:55
Acts 12:17

2 Pet 1:2

2 Pet 2:1
Acts 9:13

Gal 2:4; 5:13
1 Pet 2:16
1 Jn 4:1
2 Jn 10

Greeting and blessing*

¹Jude, a servant of Jesus Christ and brother of James,

To those who are called, beloved in God the Father and kept for Jesus Christ:

²May mercy, peace, and love be multiplied to you.

His reason for writing

³Beloved, being very eager to write to you of our common salvation, I found it necessary to write appealing to you to contend for the faith which was once for all delivered to the saints. ⁴For admission has been secretly gained by some who long ago were designated for this condemnation, ungodly persons who pervert the grace of our God into licentiousness and deny our only Master and Lord, Jesus Christ.ᵃ

¹Iudas Iesu Christi servus, frater autem Iacobi, his qui sunt vocati, in Deo Patre dilecti et Christo Iesu conservati: ²misericordia vobis et pax et caritas adimpleatur. ³Carissimi, omnem sollicitudinem faciens scribendi vobis de communi nostra salute necesse habui scribere vobis, deprecans certare pro semel tradita sanctis fide. ⁴Subintroierunt enim quidam homines, qui olim praescripti sunt in hoc iudicium, impii, Dei nostri gratiam transferentes in luxuriam et solum Dominatorem et Dominum nostrum Iesum Christum negantes. ⁵Commonere autem vos volo, scientes vos omnia, quoniam Dominus semel populum de terra Aegypti salvans, secundo eos, qui non crediderunt, perdidit; ⁶angelos vero, qui non servaverunt

*1–2 In this letter we find themes similar to those in 2 Peter, but dealt with more briefly. After explaining why he feels obliged to write (vv. 3–4), the author reminds his readers that God punished people whose blasphemies and licentious behaviour are now being imitated by some among them (vv. 5–16); consequently, he encourages the faithful to be steadfast in faith and love (vv. 17–23). He concludes with solemn praise of God through Jesus Christ our Lord (vv. 24–25).

By the way that he refers to his addressees, the writer provides a description of what a Christian is: his or her life starts with a call from God, develops thanks to the grace of God, and reaches its proper end and glory in Jesus Christ.

"Those who are called" (v. 1): literally, "the called" (cf. Rom 1:6; 1 Cor 1:24). The word "church" comes from the same Greek root; the Church is the community of those whom God has "called [...] out of darkness into his marvellous light" (1 Pet 2:9), the new People of God, chosen freely by him without any merit on their part.

3–4 These verses explain the reason for the letter. The faith "delivered to the saints" implies an already formed deposit of truths, which the author seeks to defend (see e.g. Gal 1:6–9; 1 Cor 11:23ff; 15:1ff). It is the responsibility of the Church to carry on that work: "She guards the memory of Christ's words; it is she who from generation to generation hands on the apostles' confession of faith. As a mother who teaches her children to speak and so to understand and communicate, the Church our Mother teaches us the language of faith in order to introduce us to the understanding and the life of faith" (*Catechism of the Catholic Church*, 171).

"Admission has been secretly gained" (v. 4). The Greek verb, which means "to enter from outside", conveys very well the way the false teachers worked; they were probably itinerant preachers who moved from one community to the next. St Jude accuses them of two faults—one moral and practical (that of perverting grace into licentiousness) and the other doctrinal (that of denying Jesus Christ). Using the pretext of the freedom that Christ has won for us, they tried to tone down the need to conform to moral norms—whereas in fact we need to learn from Jesus if we are to understand the true nature of our freedom. "Freedom finds its true meaning when it is put to the service of the truth which redeems, when it is spent in seeking God's infinite Love which liberates us from all forms of

a Or *the only Master and our Lord Jesus Christ*

1. FALSE TEACHERS DENOUNCED*

The punishment that awaits them

2 Pet 1:12
Num 14:35
1 Cor 10:5

Gen 6:1–2
2 Pet 2:4–9

Gen 19:4–25
Mt 10:15
2 Pet 2:6–10

[5]Now I desire to remind you, though you were once for all fully informed, that he[b] who saved a people out of the land of Egypt, afterward destroyed those who did not believe. [6]And the angels that did not keep their own position but left their proper dwelling have been kept by him in eternal chains in the nether gloom until the judgment of the great day;* [7]just as Sodom and Gomorrah and the surrounding cities, which likewise acted immorally and indulged in unnatural lust, serve as an example by undergoing a punishment of eternal fire.

Their immorality

2 Pet 2:10

Dan 10:13
Zech 3:2
2 Pet 2:11

[8]Yet in like manner these men in their dreamings defile the flesh, reject authority, and revile the glorious ones.[c] [9]But when the archangel Michael, contending with the devil, disputed about the body of Moses, he did not presume to pronounce a reviling judgment upon him, but said, "The Lord rebuke you."* [10]But these men revile

suum principatum, sed dereliquerunt suum domicilium, in iudicium magni diei vinculis aeternis sub caligine reservavit. [7]Sicut Sodoma et Gomorra et finitimae civitates, simili modo exfornicatae et abeuntes post carnem alteram, factae sunt exemplum, ignis aeterni poenam sustinentes. [8]Similiter vero et hi somniantes carnem quidem maculant, dominationem autem spernunt, glorias autem blasphemant. [9]Cum Michael archangelus cum Diabolo disputans altercaretur de Moysis corpore, non est ausus iudicium inferre blasphemiae, sed dixit: *«Increpet te Dominus!»*. [10]Hi autem, quaecumque quidem ignorant, blasphemant, quaecumque autem naturaliter tamquam muta animalia norunt, in his corrumpuntur. [11]Vae illis, quia via

slavery" (St Josemaría Escrivá, *Friends of God*, 27).

*5–16. This section of the letter exposes who the "ungodly persons" are (see v. 4) and spells out their fate.

5–7 The three biblical examples refer to three basic vices (see v. 8): the unbelieving and complaining Israelites who perished in the wilderness (see Num 14:26–38) are a paradigmatic example of unbelief; according to Jewish tradition, the angels who rebelled against God were cast into hell by God (Gen 6:1–2; Book of Enoch, chaps. 10, 12 and 13): they are an example of disobedience and pride; the perversions of Sodom and Gomorrah (Gen 18:16ff) are proverbial instances of lust. See also 2 Pet 2:4–10.

Verse 7 is an explicit condemnation of homosexual immorality (cf. Rom 1:24–27; 1 Cor 6:9; 1 Tim 1:10). "Basing itself on Sacred Scripture [...] tradition has always declared that 'homosexual acts are intrinsically disordered' (*Persona humana*, 8). They are contrary to the natural law. They close the sexual act to the gift of life. They do not proceed from a genuine affective and sexual complementarity. Under no circumstances

can they be approved" (*Catechism of the Catholic Church*, 2357). See the note on Rom 1:18–32.

"The Lord" [RSV alternate reading for the "he" in v. 5]. In other Greek manuscripts the text says "Jesus", thereby expressly attributing to Christ the liberation of Israel from Egypt, and interpreting the Old Testament in the light of the New, which brings the former to its fullness.

"Undergoing a punishment of eternal fire" (v. 7) shows that divine judgment is irrevocable. The Church's faith echoes this expression to describe the suffering of the damned in hell (cf. the note on Rev 20:7–10). However, the existence of hell as a place of eternal punishment, as one of the "last things", is part of Christian teaching, revealed not in order to strike terror into us but to encourage us to have a change of heart and to persevere in faith and the good life: "Only in this eschatological vision can one realize the exact nature of sin and feel decisively moved to penance and reconciliation" (John Paul II, *Reconciliatio et paenitentia*, 26).

8–13 To illustrate the sinfulness of these offences (see v. 4), the sacred writer uses a popular legend recorded in the apocryphal *Assumption of Moses*:

whatever they do not understand, and by those things that they know by instinct as irrational animals do, they are destroyed. ¹¹Woe to them! For they walk in the way of Cain, and abandon themselves for the sake of gain to Balaam's error, and perish in Korah's rebellion. ¹²These are blemishes[d] on your love feasts, as they boldly carouse together, looking after themselves; waterless clouds, carried along by winds; fruitless trees in late autumn, twice dead, uprooted; ¹³wild waves of the sea, casting up the foam of their own shame; wandering stars for whom the nether gloom of darkness has been reserved for ever.

2 Pet 2:12
Gen 4:8
2 Pet 2:15
Num 16:22; 22:2
1 Jn 3:12
Rev 2:14
Prov 25:14
2 Pet 3:13, 17

Is 57:20

The judgment of God

¹⁴It was of these also that Enoch in the seventh generation from Adam prophesied, saying, "Behold, the Lord came with his holy myriads, ¹⁵to execute judgment on all, and to convict all the ungodly of all their deeds of ungodliness which they have committed in such an ungodly way, and of all the harsh things which ungodly sinners have spoken against him." ¹⁶These are grumblers, malcontents, following their own passions, loud-mouthed boasters, flattering people to gain advantage.

Gen 5:18–24

Mt 25:31
Dan 7:10

2 Pet 2:10, 18
Lev 19:15
Dan 7:8, 20

Cain abierunt et errore Balaam mercede effusi sunt et contradictione Core perierunt! ¹²Hi sunt in agapis vestris maculae convivantes sine timore, semetipsos pascentes, nubes sine aqua, quae a ventis circumferuntur, arbores autumnales infructuosae bis mortuae, eradicatae, ¹³fluctus feri maris despumantes suas confusiones, sidera errantia, quibus procella tenebrarum in aeternum servata est. ¹⁴Prophetavit autem et his septimus ab Adam Henoch dicens: «Ecce venit Dominus in sanctis milibus suis ¹⁵facere iudicium contra omnes et arguere omnem animam de omnibus operibus impietatis eorum, quibus impie egerunt, et de omnibus duris, quae locuti sunt contra eum peccatores impii». ¹⁶Hi sunt murmuratores, querelosi, secundum concupiscentias suas ambulantes, et os illorum loquitur superba, mirantes personas quaestus causa. ¹⁷Vos autem, carissimi, memores estote verborum, quae praedicta sunt ab apostolis Domini nostri Iesu Christi, ¹⁸quoniam dicebant vobis: «In novissimo tempore venient illusores, secun-

as St Michael prepared to bury Moses' body, the devil tried to wrest it from him. St Michael prevented him from doing so, but he did the devil no harm; he simply appealed to the judgment of God. See also the note on 2 Pet 2:10–19.

Three biblical examples (v. 11) are also given to show the evildoing of false teachers—Cain (Gen 4:4), Balaam (Num 31:16; Rev 2:14; 2 Pet 2:15), and Korah and his followers who rebelled against Moses (Num 16).

The false teachers are happy to attend Christian assemblies, but they lead immoral lives and cause scandal. They take part in the Christians' fraternal meals (cf. the note on 1 Cor 11:17–22), where they freely indulge their greed and spread false ideas. They are "blemishes" (v. 12): the Greek word used here means scandal; it originally meant a "reef", that is, a rock lying just under the surface of the water and therefore a danger to navigation; but it can also be translated as "blemish" in the proper or moral sense (as it is in the New Vulgate). "He who sins is stained: sin stains the sinner" (St Bede, *In Epistolam Iudae*, ad loc.).

The false teachers are "waterless clouds" (v.

12) because "they do not have within themselves the fruitfulness of the divine word" (Clement of Alexandria, *Exegesis in Iudam*, ad loc.).

"Twice dead" (v. 12): this may mean that their apostasy puts them in a worse position than they were in prior to Baptism (cf. 2 Pet 2:20–22).

14–16 The sacred writer quotes here from the Book of Enoch, an apocryphal text written some years before the time when Jesus lived and which contains legends that have some connexions with the more obscure passages in the Old Testament. Enoch was a mysterious figure much respected in Jewish tradition. He preached on the ways of God and was taken up into heaven before his death. He was praised for his goodness (see Gen 5:18, 22–24; cf. Sir 44:16; 49:14; Heb 11:5). There are other allusions to the Book of Enoch in the letter (vv. 6–7). In the apocalyptic language of this type of literature, future events are spoken of as if they had already taken place. St Jude uses the Book of Enoch to illustrate church teaching about the punishment of the ungodly.

b Ancient authorities read *Jesus* or *the Lord* or *God*   c Greek *glories*

2. EXHORTATION*

False teachers were predicted

¹⁷But you must remember, beloved, the predictions of the apostles of our Lord Jesus Christ; ¹⁸they said to you, "In the last time there will be scoffers, following their own ungodly passions." ¹⁹It is these who set up divisions, worldly people, devoid of the Spirit.

2 Pet 3:2

1 Tim 4:1
2 Pet 3:3

1 Cor 2:14; 15:44

Faith, hope and charity

Col 2:7
1 Thess 5:11

2 Cor 13:13

²⁰But you, beloved, build yourselves up on your most holy faith; pray in the Holy Spirit; ²¹keep yourselves in the love of God; wait for the mercy of our Lord Jesus Christ unto eternal life.

Attitude towards waverers

Amos 4:11
Rev 3:4

²²And convince some, who doubt; ²³save some, by snatching them out of the fire; on some have mercy with fear, hating even the garment spotted by the flesh.^e

Final doxology

1 Thess 5:23
Phil 1:10
2 Pet 3:14

²⁴Now to him who is able to keep you from falling and to present you without blem-

dum suas concupiscentias ambulantes impietatum». ¹⁹Hi sunt qui segregant, animales, Spiritum non habentes. ²⁰Vos autem, carissimi, superaedificantes vosmetipsos sanctissimae vestrae fidei, in Spiritu Sancto orantes, ²¹ipsos vos in dilectione Dei servate, exspectantes misericordiam Domini nostri Iesu Christi in vitam aeternam. ²²Et his quidem miseremini disputantibus, ²³illos vero salvate de igne, rapientes, aliis autem mis-

*17–25 To counter the errors of the false teachers, the writer gives in this part of the letter an exhortation to protect one's faith, practise virtue and set good example.

17–19 These warnings can be traced back to what Jesus himself said: "False Christs and false prophets will arise and show great signs and wonders, so as to lead astray, if possible, even the elect" (Mt 24:24).

"The last time" (v. 18): this refers to the messianic age, which began with the coming of Christ (cf. Gal 4:4).

"Worldly people" (v. 19): literally, "animal" or "natural" people. As in some passages in St Paul (see 1 Cor 2:14; 15:44–46), these are the opposite of "spiritual" people, that is, Christians who have the Holy Spirit and are true to him (see Rom 5:5; 8:14). Those "devoid of the Spirit", who is the source of supernatural life, form judgments and make decisions guided only by human nature wounded by sin. Their wisdom is merely worldly (cf. Jas 3:15), "of the flesh" (1 Cor 3:3). Such people sow division among believers. "No enemy of unity can partake of divine charity. Those outside the Church do not share in the Holy

Spirit" (St Augustine, *Epistolae*, 185, 11, 50).

20–21 As elsewhere in the New Testament, an invocation of the Blessed Trinity is here combined with an exhortation to practise the three theological virtues (faith, hope and charity): "The theological virtues relate directly to God. They dispose Christians to live in a relationship with the Holy Trinity. They have the One and Triune God for their origin, motive, and object" (*Catechism of the Catholic Church*, 1812).

22–23 Christians should always be kind to those who break with sound teaching, but should be careful not to put their own souls at risk. "It is a feature of those who are perfect that they hate in sinners only their sins; and that they love these same persons" (St Augustine, *Contra Adimantum*, 17, 5).

24–25 The doxology or praise addressed to God the Father through Jesus Christ shows that Jesus is the Mediator both of our salvation and of our praise of the Father. From the very beginning, the Church has had the custom of addressing liturgical prayer to the Father through Jesus

d Or *reefs*

ish before the presence of his glory with rejoicing, [25]to the only God, our Saviour through Jesus Christ our Lord, be glory, majesty, dominion, and authority, before all time and now and for ever. Amen.

Rom 16:27
2 Pet 3:18
Rev 5:13

eremini in timore, odientes et eam, quae carnalis est, maculatam tunicam. [24]Ei autem, qui potest vos conservare sine peccato et constituere ante conspectum gloriae suae immaculatos in exsultatione, [25]soli Deo salvatori nostro per Iesum Christum Dominum nostrum gloria, magnificentia, imperium et potestas ante omne saeculum et nunc et in omnia saecula. Amen.

Christ. Commenting on v. 25, St Bede says: "This verse attributes to the Father and the Son equal and co-eternal glory and power forever and ever. The verse makes clear that those who believe that the Son is inferior and posterior to the Father are in error when it says that the Father's glory, majesty, dominion and authority are 'through Jesus Christ, our Lord'. This is true from before all time, and now, and forever. Amen" (*In Epistolam Iudae*, ad loc.).

e The Greek text in this sentence is uncertain at several points

THE

REVELATION TO JOHN

(THE APOCALYPSE)

Introduction

The Apocalypse or book of Revelation comes last in the collection of books that make up Holy Scripture, and parallels in some ways the book of Genesis, the first book in the Bible. The last chapters of the Revelation to John mention the river that watered Paradise (see Gen 2:6; Rev 22:1) and the tree of life (see Gen 2:9; Rev 22:14).

The oldest testimonies to the authority of the book, which date to the second century, are unanimous in attributing it to the apostle St John. Around the year 150, St Justin refers to "a man named John, one of the apostles of Christ", who received the revelations contained in the Apocalypse.[1] At around the same time, according to Eusebius of Caesarea,[2] St Miletus, bishop of Sardis, wrote a commentary on this book. Other second-century authors attest to the authenticity of the book—for example, Papias,[3] bishop of Hierapolis, and St Irenaeus, who frequently quotes from it.[4] In the third century, Origen of Alexandria says that the author of the Apocalypse also wrote the Gospel (of John) and had the good fortune to rest his head on Jesus' breast.[5] Tertullian, in the West, also attributes the book of Revelation to St John.[6] However, alternative views were also expressed at the time by, for example, a priest of Rome named Caius (who was of the view that the book was written by a Gnostic, a contemporary of John)[7] and other writers from a slightly later period, who were called *alogoi* because they denied that Christ was the Logos.[8] Denys of Alexandria, around the mid-fourth century, did not accept that the Apocalypse was canonical because millenarians had used it to defend their heretical stance.[9] St Athanasius, bishop of Alexandria, recognized it as canonical and used it in his controversy against Arians.[10] St Basil and St Gregory of Nyssa also accepted the tradition in favour of authenticity. However, the school of Antioch had its reservations, and St Cyril of Jerusalem, St John Chrysostom, Theodoret and others avoided making any reference to it. Eusebius of Caesarea did not express a definitive opinion in either direction.[11] This lack of conviction among some writers of the Eastern Church must be set against the unanimity of the Latin Church, which always accepted the book as canonical and written by St John. Once the danger from millenarianism disappeared, the book was accepted by the whole Church until the time of Luther, who initially argued against its authenticity and canonicity, but later changed his view.[12]

1. STRUCTURE AND CONTENT

The book contains two clearly distinct parts—one consisting of the letters to the seven churches of Asia (1:4—3:22), and another comprised of eschatological visions (4:1—22:15). These parts are preceded by a prologue that introduces the author and the book (1:1–3), and are followed by a conclusion or epilogue that contains a dialogue between Jews and the Church, and some words of warning to the reader along with words of farewell (22:16–21).

---

1 *Dialogus cum Tryphone*, 81, 3. **2** See *Historia ecclesiastica*, 4, 26, 2. **3** See Andrew of Caesarea, *Commentarium in Apocalypsim*, prologue. **4** See *Adversus haereses*, 4, 20. **5** See *In Ioannem*, 1, 14. **6** See *Adversus Marcionem*, 3, 14; *De resurrectione carnis*, 25. **7** See Eusebius, *Historia ecclesiastica*, 3, 28, 2. **8** See St Epiphanius, *Adversus haereses* (Panarion), 51, 1–35. **9** See Denys of Alexandria, *Ex libro de promissione*, 3–7. **10** See *Oratio II, contra Arianos*, 23. **11** See *Historia ecclesiastica*, 3, 25, 2. **12** See M. Luther, *Praefatio in Apocalypsim*.

The part made up of letters begins with a formal epistolatory greeting (1:4–8); this is followed by an introductory passage which tells how Christ in glory instructed John to write (1:9–20); then come the letters—to the churches of Ephesus (2:1–7), Smyrna (2:8–11), Pergamum (2:12–17), Thyatira (2:18–29), Sardis (3:1–6), Philadelphia (3:7–13) and Laodicea (3:14–22).

The part of the book dealing with the visions begins with an introductory vision in which the author sees God in his glory, from where he shapes the destinies of the world and the Church. These are mysteries that only Christ can disclose, for only he is able to open the seven seals (chaps. 4–5). Then comes a first section, covering the events prior to the final outcome; these are described through a series of visions that culminates with that of the seventh trumpet (6:1—11:14). The sounding of that trumpet marks the start of a second section, which recounts (a) Christ's triumph over the powers of evil and (b) the glorification of the Church (11:15–22:5). First, the opposing forces are introduced—the Church and the Lamb, on the one hand; the serpent and the beasts, on the other (12:1—16:21). Then the punishments that will be meted out to the latter prior to their defeat are announced (17:1—18:24), and we read of the joy that this defeat will cause in heaven (19:1–10). This is followed by an account of the battles that result in the victory of Christ, the Last Judgment and the coming of the new creation and the messianic Jerusalem (21:1—22:5). Finally, the seer is charged with making the visions known (22:6–15).

Several themes recur throughout the second part, such as the punishments prior to the End (cf. 6:1–15; 8:6–9, 21; 16:1–21), the triumph of the elect (cf. 7:9–17; 14:1–5; 19:1–10), and the fall of Babylon (cf. 14:6–11; 18:1–3). Sometimes the account of one vision is suddenly interrupted to give way to another (see 8:2; 10:1; 12:1). Occasionally, themes are introduced in a way that seems to break the rhythm of the narrative, such as those having to do with the two witnesses (see 11:1–14) and the woman who appears in heaven (see 12:1–18). The author seems determined to expound the full meaning of his message in each of the visions, feeling under no obligation to defer to any thematic or chronological order of the type normally reflected in writings of most other genres. He uses various literary devices to hold the reader's attention until the very end. For example, his use of the number seven; after the seven letters to the seven churches, we are told of a book sealed with seven seals (see 5:1—8:1); there are seven trumpet blasts (see 8:2—11:15); and seven bowls pour out seven plagues over the earth (see 15:5—16:17).

2. CONTEXT

At the beginning of the book, in 1:9–10, we are told about its background: "I John, your brother, who share with you in Jesus the tribulation […], was on the island called Patmos on the Lord's day." Patmos is a small island in the Aegean Sea; it is part of a group of islands known as the Dodecanese. It was a Sunday, he says, "the Lord's day", the day that, from the very start of the Church, Christians had dedicated to divine worship, soon observing it in place of the Jewish sabbath. St Irenaeus speculates that the book was written at the end of Domitian's reign, around the year 96,[13] a view that is confirmed by information in the text itself. It was after the 70s, in fact, that the first day of the Christian week began to be called *Dies Domini*, the day of the Lord; besides, the life of the Christian communities of Asia Minor as reflected in the book clearly indicates that they had reached quite a mature stage of development. The book is addressed to the

---

13 See *Adversus haereses*, 5, 30.

"seven churches that are in Asia" (1:4); scholars read this number as symbolic and conclude that the text is addressed to the whole Church.

The book seeks to alert Christians to the grave dangers that threaten faith, while consoling and encouraging those who are suffering tribulation, and in particular the fierce and long-drawn-out persecution mounted by Domitian. Some early heresies were already making inroads among the Christian communities: the Nicolaitans, for example, argued for some degree of compromise with idolatry and pagan lifestyles (see 2:6, 15); there was evidence of a loss of earlier fervour (see 2:4), and a weakening of charity (see 3:2). Persecution came from both Jews and pagans. Jewish opponents are called false Jews, a "synagogue of Satan" (see 2:9–10). The first major pagan persecution started in the time of Nero, and it was still fresh in people's memory thirty years later. St John seeks to console Christians who experience such cruel injustice and harassment, and strives to keep alive their hope in the ultimate victory of Christ and of all who stay true to him, even in the face of death (see 2:10).

The genre used by the author of the Apocalypse is similar to that of other works that date to the same period, Jewish and Christian; it has two basic features: (a) it deals with the subject of the last age of the world, when good will triumph and evil will be annihilated; (b) it makes a great deal of use of symbolism taken from the animal kingdom, astrology, numbers etc., to depict past and present history and to prophesy about the future. The very phrase "apocalyptic writing" used now to describe these works comes from the title of John's Apocalypse. The content and form of all these works are a later development of or derivation from prophetical literature, for the prophets in their time spoke of "the day of the Lord"[14] and used symbolic images to convey their message. In apocalyptic writing, visions are interwoven with moral exhortations, invitations to reflection, and promises of future beatitude or retribution. The Apocalypse of John defines itself, in fact, as a "prophecy" (1:3; cf. 22:7, 9, 10, 18, 19), and although for the most part John uses language and symbolism similar to what is found in Jewish apocalyptic writings, his historical perspective is quite different: human history acquires new meaning under the aegis of Christ, whose lordship is acknowledged and celebrated in the Church, the new People of God, who like their Lord suffer persecution at the hands of the forces of evil. For the author of the Apocalypse, the final outcome has already been revealed by the resurrection and ascension of Christ, and the ground for it is laid over the course of history by the holiness, good works and suffering of the just. Christ's definitive victory will come at the End, and the Church will be raised on high in a new world where there will be no more mourning or pain (see 21:4).

3. MESSAGE

The central teaching of the book of Revelation concerns the second coming of the Lord (the Parousia) and the definitive establishment of his Kingdom at the end of time. Around this key belief, John builds his teaching about God, Jesus Christ, the Holy Spirit, the angels and the Church.

God is described as "the Alpha and the Omega", "the beginning and the end" (1:8; 22:13), and as he "who is and who was and who is to come" (1:4). These expressions spell out the name of *Yhwh*, "I am who I am", revealed to Moses (Ex 3:14). God is he who existed in the past (he is

14 See Amos 5:18–20; Is 2:6–21; Jer 30:5–7; Joel 2:1–17.

eternal); he who is (he is active in the world ever since its creation); and he who is to come (that is, his dynamic and saving presence will never cease). Nothing falls outside the range of his providence; he is the just and truthful Father who will reveal himself to the victor as he promised: "I will be his God and he shall be my son" (21:7). At the End, God's creative power and unbounded love will lead him to restore all things and create a new world (see 21:5). He is also the Judge of all, against whose verdict there is no appeal; none can escape his judgment (see 20:12).

Jesus Christ is portrayed repeatedly as being the Redeemer, through his death on the cross (see 1:7; 7:14; 11:8; 12:11). Much emphasis is given to the stately, yet humble, figure of the Lamb who was "slain" (see 5:12; 13:8), the victim of the greatest of all sacrifices. However, the predominant image of our Lord depicts him in the glory of heaven, in the symbol of the Lamb enthroned on Mount Zion, the river of the water of life flowing from his throne (see 5:6; 14:1; 22:1, 3). He will shepherd and guide his people (7:17).

His enemies will make war on him, but he will emerge victorious (see 17:14). He is worthy to receive power and glory and to be worshipped by all creation (see 5:12). Jesus is also given the title of "Son of man", that figure destined to have power and dominion over all peoples, nations and languages (see Dan 7:13–14; Rev 1:13–16). He is "Lord of lords and King of kings" (see 17:14; cf. 19:16); he is above the angels, who are his emissaries, and unlike them he receives the worship that is due to God alone.

The Holy Spirit is referred to on a number of occasions in the book, when we are told that it is he who is speaking to the churches (see 2:7, 11, 17). At the end of the book the voice of the Spirit joins that of the Bride to entreat the coming of Christ. The Holy Spirit is linked to the Church, which he nourishes by his word and moves interiorly to plead for the Lord's coming.

In a more or less explicit way the Church is present throughout the book of Revelation. It teaches that the Church is one and universal, she is the Bride of Christ, who prays without ceasing for the Lord's coming (see 22:17, 20). She is portrayed through the use of imagery whose symbolism helps us see her beauty and grandeur. We are told of the Church, the Holy City, the new Jerusalem, the place of dwelling with God; she is also called the "beloved city" (see 20:9), and her glory and splendour are described in a wealth of detail (see 21:16–27; 22:1–2). She is the "temple of God", whose pillars are those who have won victory; in that temple stands the ark of the Covenant, where the countless multitudes of the elect worship God (see 3:12; 7:15; 11:19). The woman whom the seer sees in the heavens (see chap. 12), though she can also be interpreted as being the Blessed Virgin or ancient Israel, stands primarily for the Church, afflicted with great tribulation.

But the Church is also described as the Christian communities found in various cities of proconsular Asia (see chaps. 2–3). These communities do not constitute a church distinct from the Church as such; rather, the idea is stated here that the Church universal becomes present in these believing communities, which are "parts" of the one Church of Christ.[15]

Angels and their work are very much in evidence throughout the book. They are in heaven, in the presence of God, forever rendering praise to him and to the Lamb (see 5:11; 7:11) and interceding for mankind (see 8:3–4). They are bearers of divine revelation,[16] and are charged with the protection of man (see 7:1; 21:12), and have responsibility for the churches (see 1:20; 2:1, 8, 12, 18; 3:1, 7, 14). (It is possible that the "angels of the churches" may be a symbolic reference to the bishops of these churches, whose office it was to watch over them.) Angels are on occasion

15 See Vatican II, *Christus Dominus*, 6.   **16** See Rev 1:1; 7:2; 8:2; 11:15; 14:6–19; 16:17; 19:17; 22:6, 16.

deputed to carry out God's punishment (see 9:15; 14:18–20). With the archangel Michael at their head, they fight the great battle that takes place in heaven between Good and Evil (see 12:7ff), against the dragon, "that ancient serpent, who is called the Devil and Satan, the deceiver of the whole world" (12:9). This war continues throughout history. We are told that the demons, temporarily released to roam the earth, cause war and confusion among mankind (see 20:7–8), but that in the end they will be cast down into hell, where they will suffer everlasting torment (see 12:9; 20:10).

4. INTERPRETATION OF THE APOCALYPSE

Because the style and language of this book are so symbolic, many different interpretations of it have been offered over the centuries.

In early times, it was read mainly as a prophetic description of the history of the Church, an overview that takes in important events of past and future, leading up to the period of a thousand years when Christ and his followers will reign prior to the End of the world, that is, if Revelation 20:1–7 is to be taken literally. This interpretation dominated in the early centuries and throughout the Middle Ages. Beginning in the eighteenth century, the dominant idea was that the book is primarily concerned with the End times, a view that is still held by some scholars. Another, different, interpretation is that the book is the be read in the light of events in St John's own time— that it provides an account of the persecutions and trials that the Church was then undergoing. This interpretation began to emerge in the sixteenth century, and it is still favoured by those influenced by Rationalist criticism.

Nowadays, the most widely held interpretation, and the one most in line with the text and with Tradition, reads the book of Revelation as providing a theological perspective on all history, with a clear emphasis on the transcendental and religious dimension of history. St John shows the position and situation of the Church at the time when he was writing, and he also gives a panoramic view of the End times, even as he makes clear that the final Age has already been inaugurated by the coming of Jesus Christ, the Son of God made man.

Revelation

Prologue*

1 ¹The revelation of Jesus Christ, which God gave him to show to his servants what must soon take place; and he made it known by sending his angel to his servant John, ²who bore witness to the word of God and to the testimony of Jesus Christ, even to all that he saw. ³Blessed is he who reads aloud the words of the prophecy, and blessed are those who hear, and who keep what is written therein; for the time is near.

Dan 2:28
Rev 1:9; 22:6, 16

Rev 6:9
1 Jn 1:1–3
Rev 16:15; 19:9;
20:6; 22:7, 18

PART ONE

Letters to the seven churches*

Address and greeting

⁴John to the seven churches that are in Asia:*

Grace to you and peace from him who is and who was and who is to come, and from the seven spirits who are before his throne, ⁵and from Jesus Christ the faithful witness, the first-born of the dead, and the ruler of kings on earth.

Ex 3:14
Rev 1:8; 11:17
Is 11:2ff

Ps 89:27, 37
Is 55:4
Col 1:18

[1] ¹Apocalypsis Iesu Christi, quam dedit illi Deus palam facere servis suis, quae oportet fieri cito, et significavit mittens per angelum suum servo suo Ioanni, ²qui testificatus est verbum Dei et testimonium Iesu Christi, quaecumque vidit. ³Beatus, qui legit et qui audiunt verba prophetiae et servant ea, quae in ea scripta sunt; tempus enim prope est. ⁴Ioannes septem ecclesiis, quae sunt in Asia: Gratia vobis et pax ab eo, qui est et qui

*1:1–3 This book contains the revelation which Jesus Christ, risen and now in glory, is speaking to his Church through the apostle St John. After an introduction which gives the book its title, names the addressees and identifies God as the source of its message (1:1–20), there come the letters to the seven churches (2:1—3:22) and an explanation of God's plan for the future of the world and the Church (4:1—22:21).

"Revelation" in Greek is "*apokalypsis*", hence the name often given to this book of Holy Scripture. Revelation always implies the unveiling of something previously hidden—in this case, future events. The future is known to God the Father (the Greek text uses the definitive article, "*the* God", which is how the New Testament normally refers to God the Father), and to Jesus Christ, who, being the Son, shares in the knowledge that is communicated to the author of the book. The text speaks of the "revelation of Jesus Christ", not only because it reaches John through Christ but also because our Lord is the main subject, the beginning and the end of this revelation;

he occupies the central position in all these great visions, in which the veils concealing the future are torn and darkness is dispelled, yielding to the Light, Jesus Christ himself (see 21:23; 22:5).

Jesus continues to speak to his Church through the apostles—in this instance, St John (vv. 1–2). When the author says that these events will take place "soon", he does not mean to indicate an early date but to strengthen Christians' faith and their conviction that Christ will definitively overcome evil; his victory has in fact begun. Happy are those who believe this and stay loyal. The circumstances at the time in which St John was writing called for just the sort of exhortations and warnings found in this book. Its words call for a prompt, committed response that yields no ground for doubt or hesitation. They are also a dire warning to those who try to hinder the progress of the Kingdom of God, a Kingdom that will inevitably come and that is in some way already with us.

*1:4—3:22 The book is written for the whole Church, as symbolized by the seven churches of

Rev 3:4
1 Cor 15:20
Ex 19:6
1 Pet 2:9
Rom 16:27
Is 61:6
Rev 5:10; 20:6
Dan 7:13
Zech 12:10, 14
Jn 19:37
Mt 24:30
Rev 1:4; 21:6; 22:13

To him who loves us and has freed us from our sins by his blood ⁶and made us a kingdom, priests to his God and Father, to him be glory and dominion for ever and ever. Amen. ⁷Behold, he is coming with the clouds, and every eye will see him, every one who pierced him; and all tribes of the earth will wail on account of him. Even so. Amen.

⁸"I am the Alpha and the Omega," says the Lord God, who is and who was and who is to come, the Almighty.

erat et qui venturus est, et a septem spiritibus, qui in conspectu throni eius sunt, ⁵et ab Iesu Christo, qui est testis fidelis, primogenitus mortuorum et princeps regum terrae. Ei, qui diligit nos et solvit nos a peccatis nostris in sanguine suo ⁶et fecit nos regnum, sacerdotes Deo et Patri suo, ipsi gloria et imperium in saecula saeculorum. Amen. ⁷*Ecce venit cum nubibus,* et *videbit* eum omnis oculus et qui eum *pupugerunt, et plangent se super eum omnes tribus terrae.* Etiam, amen. ⁸Ego sum Alpha et Omega, dicit Dominus Deus, qui est et qui erat et qui venturus est, Omnipotens. ⁹Ego Ioannes, frater vester et particeps in tribulatione et regno et patientia in Iesu, fui in insula, quae appellatur Patmos, propter verbum Dei et testimonium Iesu. ¹⁰Fui in spiritu in dominica die et audivi post me vocem magnam tamquam tubae ¹¹dicentis: «Quod vides, scribe in libro et mitte

Asia Minor. The author first explains how he was given the divine revelation and told to make it known (1:4–20); then he reports what the Lord says to each church in its particular circumstances—about faults that must be corrected and the reward promised to those who overcome evil.

1:4–8 The revelation comes from God, who is almighty and all-knowing (as can be seen from the references to the divine name ("he who is and who was and who is to come") and to the spirits who serve him (v. 4); and it comes from Jesus Christ, who died and rose again, the ruler of history, the Redeemer of man and the Lord of his Church.

Verse 5 applies three messianic titles to Jesus Christ, all from Psalm 89 but which take on a new meaning in the light of the Christian faith. (1) Jesus is "the faithful witness" to the fulfilment of God's Old Testament promises of a Saviour, a Son of David (see 2 Sam 7:12–14; Rev 5:5), for it is through Christ that salvation reaches us. That is why, later in the book, St John calls Jesus Christ "the Amen" (see 3:14)— which means that through the life and work of Christ, God has ratified and kept his word; John also says that Jesus "is called Faithful and True" (19:11), because in him God's fidelity and the truth of his promises have been made plain for all to see. (2) Jesus is then proclaimed the "first-born of the dead" because his resurrection is a victory in which those who abide in him will share (cf. Col 1:18). (3) Jesus is the "ruler of kings on earth", for he is Lord of the world; this

truth will be revealed in all its glory when he comes a second time, but his dominion is already making itself felt, because his reign has begun with the breaking of the power of sin and death.

Not content with setting us free from our sins, our Lord gave us a share in his kingship and priesthood; for this he deserves praise for ever and ever. "The baptized, by regeneration and the anointing of the Holy Spirit, are consecrated to be a spiritual house and a holy priesthood, that through all the works of Christian men and women they may offer spiritual sacrifices and proclaim the perfection of him who has called them out of darkness into his marvellous light (cf. 1 Pet 2:4–10)" (Vatican II, *Lumen gentium*, 10).

Although the text speaks in the present tense ("he is coming with the clouds": v. 7), it should be read as referring to the future: the prophet saw future events as if they were actually happening (cf. Dan 7:13). This will be the day of final victory, when those who crucified Jesus, "every one who pierced him" (cf. Zech 12:10; Jn 19:37) and those who have rejected him over the course of history, will be astonished by the majesty and glory of the crucified One.

Commenting on this passage, St Bede says: "He who at his first coming came in a hidden way and in order to be judged (by men) will then come in a manifest way. [John] recalls these truths in order to help the Church bear its suffering: now it is being persecuted by its enemies, later it will reign at Christ's side" (*Explanatio Apocalypsis*, 1, 1).

Reason for writing

[9]I John, your brother, who share with you in Jesus the tribulation and the kingdom and the patient endurance, was on the island called Patmos on account of the word of God and the testimony of Jesus. [10]I was in the Spirit on the Lord's day, and I heard behind me a loud voice like a trumpet [11]saying, "Write what you see in a book and send it to the seven churches, to Ephesus and to Smyrna and to Pergamum and to Thyatira and to Sardis and to Philadelphia and to Laodicea."

[12]Then I turned to see the voice that was speaking to me, and on turning I saw seven golden lampstands, [13]and in the midst of the lampstands one like a son of man,* clothed with a long robe and with a golden girdle round his breast; [14]his head and his hair were white as white wool, white as snow; his eyes were like a flame of fire, [15]his feet were like burnished bronze, refined as in a furnace, and his voice was like the sound of many waters; [16]in his right hand he held seven stars, from his mouth issued a sharp two-edged sword, and his face was like the sun shining in full strength.

[17]When I saw him, I fell at his feet as though dead. But he laid his right hand upon me, saying, "Fear not, I am the first and the last, [18]and the living one; I died, and behold I am alive for evermore, and I have the keys of Death and Hades. [19]Now write what you see, what is and what is to take place hereafter. [20]As for the mystery of the seven stars which you saw in my right hand, and the seven golden lampstands,

Rom 5:6

Rev 4:1–2

Rev 1:4, 20; 19:9

Ex 25:31–37

Dan 7:13; 10:5
Rev 14:14; 15:6
Dan 7:9; 10:5
Rev 2:18; 19:12

Ezek 1:24; 43:2
Dan 10:6
Mt 17:2
Is 49:2
Rev 2:12

Ezek 1:28
Dan 8:18; 10:5–19
Is 44:6; 48:12
Rev 2:8; 22:13
Heb 7:25
Rev 4:9
Rev 1:1
Rev 1:11-16

septem ecclesiis: Ephesum et Smyrnam et Pergamum et Thyatiram et Sardis et Philadelphiam et Laodiciam». [12]Et conversus sum, ut viderem vocem, quae loquebatur mecum; et conversus vidi septem candelabra aurea [13]et in medio candelabrorum *quasi Filium hominis, vestitum podere* et *praecinctum* ad mamillas zonam *auream*; [14]*caput* autem *eius* et *capilli erant candidi tamquam lana alba, tamquam nix, et oculi eius velut* flamma *ignis*, [15]*et pedes eius similes orichalco* sicut in camino ardenti, *et vox illius tamquam vox aquarum multarum*, [16]et habebat in dextera manu sua stellas septem, et de ore eius gladius anceps acutus exibat, et facies eius sicut sol lucet in virtute sua. [17]Et cum vidissem eum, cecidi ad pedes eius tamquam mortuus; et posuit dexteram suam super me dicens: «Noli timere! Ego sum primus et novissimus, [18]et vivens et fui mortuus et ecce sum vivens in saecula saeculorum et habeo claves mortis et inferni». [19]Scribe ergo, quae vidisti et quae sunt et quae oportet fieri post haec. [20]Mys-

1:9–20 The island of Patmos was a penitentiary. Ever since the apostolic age, the Lord's day (v. 10), Sunday, is the day which the Church has kept as its holy day in place of the Jewish sabbath (Saturday), for it was the day on which Jesus rose from the dead. The scene painted in the vision has a liturgical quality to it: we are given to understand that the writer received the vision during the celebration of a Sunday liturgy: the liturgy on earth is raised and joined to that of heaven.

The seven churches listed stand for the entire Church, and therefore what is said in the seven letters is addressed to all Christians, who in one way or another may find themselves in situations like those of these churches in proconsular Asia.

The lampstands (v. 12) in the vision symbolize the churches at prayer; they are reminiscent of the *menoráh*, the seven-branched candlestick that burned in the temple of Jerusalem. Jesus Christ, as Son of man (cf. Dan 7:13), is the Judge at the end of time, and the features mentioned here symbolize his priesthood ("long

robe": cf. Ex 28:4; Zech 3:4); his kingship ("golden girdle": cf. 1 Mac 10:89); his eternity (hair "white as snow": cf. Dan 7:9); his divine wisdom (eyes "like a flame of fire": cf. 2:18); and his power (feet "like burnished bronze": cf. Dan 10:6; voice "like the sound of many waters": cf. Ezek 43:2). The Lord holds the churches in his hand; he protects them.

The risen Christ is depicted as reassuring the Christian (vv. 17–18), who sees him as having absolute dominion over all things (he is the first and the last) even though he shares man's mortal nature. By his death and resurrection Christ has overcome death and he has dominion over the mysterious world beyond the grave—Hades (v. 18), that is, the place of the dead (cf. Num 16:33). "Christ is alive. This is the great truth which fills our faith with meaning. Jesus, who died on the cross, has risen. He has triumphed over death; he has overcome sorrow, anguish and the power of darkness" (St Josemaría Escrivá, *Christ Is Passing By*, 102).

the seven stars are the angels of the seven churches and the seven lampstands are the seven churches.

Letter to the church of Ephesus

Acts 19
Rev 1:16, 20

2 ¹To the angel of the church in Ephesus write: 'The words of him who holds the seven stars in his right hand, who walks among the seven golden lampstands.

2 Cor 11:13
1 Jn 4:1
1 Thess 1:3

²'I know your works, your toil and your patient endurance, and how you cannot bear evil men but have tested those who call themselves apostles but are not, and found them to be false; ³I know you are enduring patiently and bearing up for my name's sake, and you have not grown weary. ⁴But I have this against you, that you have abandoned the love you had at first. ⁵Remember then from what you have fallen, repent and do the works you did at first. If not, I will come to you and remove your lampstand from its place, unless you repent. ⁶Yet this you have, you hate the works of the Nicolaitans, which I also hate. ⁷He who has an ear, let him hear what the Spirit says to the churches. To him who conquers I will grant to eat of the tree of life, which is in the paradise of God.'

Rev 2:16, 22;
3:3, 19

Rev 2:15
Ps 139:21

Gen 2:9
Rev 2:11, 17, 29;
22:2, 14, 19

terium septem stellarum, quas vidisti ad dexteram meam, et septem candelabra aurea: septem stellae angeli sunt septem ecclesiarum, et candelabra septem septem ecclesiae sunt. [2] ¹Angelo ecclesiae, quae est Ephesi, scribe: Haec dicit, qui tenet septem stellas in dextera sua, qui ambulat in medio septem candelabrorum aureorum: ²Scio opera tua et laborem et patientiam tuam, et quia non potes sustinere malos et tentasti eos, qui se dicunt apostolos et non sunt, et invenisti eos mendaces; ³et patientiam habes et sustinuisti propter nomen meum et non defecisti. ⁴Sed habeo adversus te quod caritatem tuam primam reliquisti. ⁵Memor esto itaque unde excideris, et age paenitentiam et prima opera fac; sin autem, venio tibi et movebo candelabrum tuum de loco suo, nisi paenitentiam egeris. ⁶Sed hoc habes, quia odisti facta Nicolaitarum, quae et ego odi. ⁷Qui habet aurem, audiat quid Spiritus dicat ecclesiis. Vincenti dabo ei edere de ligno vitae, quod est in paradiso Dei. ⁸Et angelo ecclesiae, quae est Smyr-

2:1–7 The seven stars in the Lord's right hand indicate that he has dominion over the whole Church, for he has the power to instruct the angels who rule over the fate of each of the communities. Christ's walking among the lampstands shows his loving care and vigilance for the churches (the lampstand symbolizes their prayer and liturgical life). Because the church at Ephesus was the foremost church of the seven, Christ is portrayed to it as the Lord of all the churches. Ephesus was the largest city in Asia Minor and therefore its church took precedence. Christ praises that church's patience and endurance in staying loyal to the true faith, but he criticizes it for its lack of fervour; if Ephesus does not pay heed, it will lose its pre-eminent position: "He did not accuse them of lacking in love, rather that they were no longer as fervent, open or fruitful as they had been in the beginning; in the same way as we would describe a man who was strong, cheerful and brave, as being sad and timid if he became defeated" (St Francis de Sales, *Treatise on the Love of God*, 4, 22).

Verse 5 is a call to conversion, to a change of heart that moves through three stages. The first is recognizing that one is at fault—having the humility to admit one is a poor sinner. "*To acknowledge one's sin*, indeed—penetrating still more deeply into the consideration of one's own personhood—*to recognize oneself as being a sinner*, capable of sin and inclined to commit sin, is the essential first step in returning to God" (John Paul II, *Reconciliatio et paenitentia*, 13). Then comes "love-sorrow" or contrition, which leads us to mend our ways. This is followed by acts of penance that lead us to draw closer to God and have greater intimacy with him.

The Nicolaitans (v. 6), it seems, held that it was possible to be a Christian and yet worship idols.

The image of the tree of life (v. 7; see also 22:2) recalls Genesis 2:9 and 3:22, where we find that tree in the middle of Paradise, beyond the reach of man; it is a symbol of immortality. The fruit of that tree is now Christ's to give, and he promises it to those who are victorious. "We cannot take it easy. Our Lord wants us to fight more, on a broader front, more intensely each day. We have an obligation to outdo ourselves, for in this competition the only goal is to arrive at the glory of heaven. And if we did not reach heaven,

Letter to the church of Smyrna

8"And to the angel of the church in Smyrna write: 'The words of the first and the last, who died and came to life.

Is 44;6; 48:12
Rom 14:9
Rev 1:17, 18

9"'I know your tribulation and your poverty (but you are rich) and the slander of those who say that they are Jews and are not, but are a synagogue of Satan. 10Do not fear what you are about to suffer. Behold, the devil is about to throw some of you into prison, that you may be tested, and for ten days* you will have tribulation. Be faithful unto death, and I will give you the crown of life. 11He who has an ear, let him hear what the Spirit says to the churches. He who conquers shall not be hurt by the second death.'

Rev 3:9

Mt 10:28
Jn 8:44
Dan 1:12, 14
1 Cor 9:25

Letter to the church of Pergamum

12"And to the angel of the church in Pergamum write: 'The words of him who has the sharp two-edged sword.

Rev 1:16; 19:15
Heb 4:12

13"'I know where you dwell, where Satan's throne is; you hold fast my name and you did not deny my faith even in the days of Antipas my witness, my faithful one, who was killed among you, where Satan dwells. 14But I have a few things against

Num 25:1, 2; 31:16
2 Pet 2:15
Jude 11

nae, scribe: Haec dicit Primus et Novissimus, qui fuit mortuus et vixit: 9Scio tribulationem tuam et paupertatem tuam —sed dives es— et blasphemiam ab his, qui se dicunt Iudaeos esse et non sunt, sed sunt synagoga Satanae. 10Nihil horum timeas, quae passurus es. Ecce missurus est Diabolus ex vobis in carcerem, ut tentemini, et habebitis tribulationem diebus decem. Esto fidelis usque ad mortem, et dabo tibi coronam vitae. 11Qui habet aurem, audiat quid Spiritus dicat ecclesiis. Qui vicerit, non laedetur a morte secunda. 12Et angelo ecclesiae, quae est Pergami, scribe: Haec dicit, qui habet romphaeam ancipitem acutam: 13Scio, ubi habitas, ubi thronus est Satanae, et tenes nomen meum et non negasti fidem meam et in diebus Antipas, testis meus fidelis, qui occisus est apud vos, ubi Satanas habitat. 14Sed habeo adversus te pauca, quia habes illic tenentes doc-

the whole thing would have been useless" (St Josemaría Escrivá, *Christ Is Passing By*, 77).

2:8–11 Smyrna was renowned for its ritual worship of the emperor; appropriately, therefore, Christ portrays himself to the church of this city as true God, the First and the Last (see v. 8; cf. 1:8); he urges the Christians to be steadfast in the face of the persecution provoked by some Jews.

The severe reproach in v. 9 refers to Jews who at that time were spreading lies about the Christians and thereby collaborating with idolatry, instead of defending the worshippers of the true God; that is why they do not deserve the honourable title of "Jews", but followers of Satan, God's adversary.

To attain salvation, each person must persevere to the very end (v. 10), as St Teresa of Avila puts it, "by making an earnest and most determined resolve not to halt until the goal [eternal life] is reached, whatever may come, whatever may happen, however much effort one needs to make, whoever may complain, whether one dies on the road or has no heart to face the trials one meets, even if the ground gives away under one's feet" (*Way of Perfection*, 21, 2).

"Second death" (v. 11). This is a reference to final damnation. Later, the book is more specific about what this means, and who will suffer it (see 20:6, 14; 21:8).

2:12–17 Among its many temples, Pergamum had a huge altar dedicated to Zeus. Christians of the city were tempted to take part in pagan religious celebrations. Some of them even encouraged this, rather as Balaam did in ancient times when he encouraged Moabite women to marry Israelites and lead them to worship the god of Moab (see Num 31:16). As regards the Nicolaitans, some early authors held that this was a heresy started by Nicolaus, one of the first seven deacons (cf. Acts 6:5); however, there is no solid evidence to support that view.

Christians are reminded that Christ is the Judge and carries a sword of punishment. The promise of hidden manna to the victors is counterposed to the sin of attending idolatrous meals. The "white stone" is a reference to the custom of showing a little stone, with some appropriate mark on it, to gain entrance to a festival or banquet. The name inscribed on the stone shows that the Christian has a right to partake of the good

you: you have some there who hold the teaching of Balaam, who taught Balak to put a stumbling block before the sons of Israel, that they might eat food sacrificed to idols and practise immorality. [15]So you also have some who hold the teaching of the Nicolaitans. [16]Repent then. If not, I will come to you soon and war against them with the sword of my mouth. [17]He who has an ear, let him hear what the Spirit says to the churches. To him who conquers I will give some of the hidden manna, and I will give him a white stone, with a new name written on the stone which no one knows except him who receives it.'

Rev 2:6

Rev 1:16
Jn 21:5

Ex 16:32
Is 62:2; 65:15
Rev 3:12; 19:12
Ps 78:24

Letter to the church of Thyatira

Rev 1:14, 15

[18]"And to the angel of the church in Thyatira write: 'The words of the Son of God, who has eyes like a flame of fire, and whose feet are like burnished bronze.

[19]"'I know your works, your love and faith and service and patient endurance, and that your latter works exceed the first. [20]But I have this against you, that you tolerate the woman Jezebel, who calls herself a prophetess and is teaching and beguiling my servants to practise immorality* and to eat food sacrificed to idols. [21]I gave her time to repent, but she refuses to repent of her immorality.* [22]Behold, I will throw her on a sickbed, and those who commit adultery with her I will throw into great tribulation, unless they repent of her doings; [23]and I will strike her children dead. And all the churches shall know that I am he who searches mind and heart, and I

Rev 2:14
1 Kings 16:31
2 Kings 9:22

Rom 8:27
Jer 11:20; 17:10
Ezek 33:27
Prov 24:12

trinam Balaam, qui docebat Balac mittere scandalum coram filiis Israel, edere idolothyta et fornicari; [15]ita habes et tu tenentes doctrinam Nicolaitarum similiter. [16]Ergo paenitentiam age; si quo minus, venio tibi cito et pugnabo cum illis in gladio oris mei. [17]Qui habet aurem, audiat quid Spiritus dicat ecclesiis. Vincenti dabo ei de manna abscondito et dabo illi calculum candidum, et in calculo nomen novum scriptum, quod nemo scit, nisi qui accipit. [18]Et angelo ecclesiae, quae est Thyatirae, scribe: Haec dicit Filius Dei, qui habet oculos ut flammam ignis, et pedes eius similes orichalco: [19]Novi opera tua et caritatem et fidem et ministerium et patientiam tuam et opera tua novissima plura prioribus. [20]Sed habeo adversus te, quia permittis mulierem Iezabel, quae se dicit prophetissam, et docet et seducit servos meos fornicari et manducare idolothyta. [21]Et dedi illi tempus, ut paenitentiam ageret, et non vult paeniteri a fornicatione sua. [22]Ecce mitto eam in lectum et, qui moechantur cum ea, in tribulationem magnam, nisi paenitentiam egerint ab operibus eius. [23]Et filios eius interficiam in morte, et scient omnes ecclesiae quia ego sum scrutans renes et

things the Lord reserves for those who win victory.

2:18–29 Thyatira was a small city noted for its industries of smelting, weaving and dyeing. Lydia came from there (see Acts 16:13–15). Christ is depicted to this church as the mighty Son of God, and they are exhorted not to engage in idolatrous practices.

Our Lord again inveighs against those Christians who tolerate some of their number taking part in pagan worship, because it involved idolatry and immoral practices. The reference to Jezebel, the wife of King Ahab, who led many of the people of Israel into the sin of idolatry (see 1 Kings 16:31; 2 Kings 9:22), serves to show how evil such behaviour must be regarded. The text may refer to a real person (described here symbolically by this biblical name) who alleged that she was a prophetess and led many people astray by encouraging them to take part in idolatrous

rites and banquets. Faced with a situation like this one, silence can never be an option, because if one fails to point out an error when one should, silence involves a degree of complicity.

The passage reveals how patient God is: he has waited for the people to mend their ways, and it is only at a later stage that he condemns them for not doing so (v. 21). This is a warning which those who persist in doing wrong need to bear in mind for "the more we postpone getting out of sin and turning to God", the Curé of Ars warns us, "the greater the danger we run of dying with our sins on us, for the simple reason that bad habits become more and more difficult to shed. Every time we despise a grace, our Lord is going further away from us, and we are growing weaker, and the devil gets more control of us. So, my conclusion is that the longer we remain in sin, the greater the risk we run of never being converted" (*Sermon on the 4th Sunday in Lent*).

will give to each of you as your works deserve. ²⁴But to the rest of you in Thyatira, who do not hold this teaching, who have not learned what some call the deep things of Satan,* to you I say, I do not lay upon you any other burden; ²⁵only hold fast what you have, until I come. ²⁶He who conquers and who keeps my works until the end, I will give him power over the nations, ²⁷and he shall rule them with a rod of iron, as when earthen pots are broken in pieces, even as I myself have received power from my Father; ²⁸and I will give him the morning star.* ²⁹He who has an ear, let him hear what the Spirit says to the churches.'

Rev 3:11

Ps 2:7
Rev 12:5; 19:15

Is 14:12
2 Pet 1:19
Rev 22:16

Letter to the church of Sardis

3 ¹"And to the angel of the church in Sardis write: 'The words of him who has the seven spirits of God and the seven stars.

Rev 1:16; 2:2

"'I know your works; you have the name of being alive, and you are dead. ²Awake, and strengthen what remains and is on the point of death, for I have not found your works perfect in the sight of my God. ³Remember then what you received and heard; keep that, and repent. If you will not awake, I will come like a thief, and you will not know at what hour I will come upon you. ⁴Yet you have still a few names in Sardis, people who have not soiled their garments; and they shall walk with me in white, for they are worthy. ⁵He who conquers shall be clad thus in white garments, and I will not blot his name out of the book of life; I will confess

Mt 24:43
Mk 13:33

Lk 12:39
2 Pet 3:10

1 Thess 5:2
Rev 13 :8; 17:8;
20:12

Dan 12:1
Lk 10:20; 12:8
Ps 69:28
Mt 10:32–34
Ex 32:32

corda, et dabo unicuique vestrum secundum opera vestra. ²⁴Vobis autem dico ceteris, qui Thyatirae estis, quicumque non habent doctrinam hanc, qui non cognoverunt altitudines Satanae, quemadmodum dicunt, non mittam super vos aliud pondus; ²⁵tamen id quod habetis, tenete, donec veniam. ²⁶Et, qui vicerit et qui custodierit usque in finem opera mea, / *dabo illi* potestatem super *gentes,* / ²⁷et *reget illas in virga ferrea,* / *tamquam vasa fictilia confringentur,* / ²⁸sicut et ego accepi a Patre meo, et dabo illi stellam matutinam. ²⁹Qui habet aurem, audiat quid Spiritus dicat ecclesiis. [3] ¹Et angelo ecclesiae, quae est Sardis, scribe: Haec dicit, qui habet septem spiritus Dei et septem stellas: Scio opera tua, quia nomen habes quod vivas, et mortuus es. ²Esto vigilans et confirma cetera, quae moritura erant, non enim invenio opera tua plena coram Deo meo; ³in mente ergo habe qualiter acceperis et audieris, et serva et paenitentiam age. Si ergo non vigilaveris, veniam tamquam fur, et nescies qua hora veniam ad te. ⁴Sed habes pauca nomina in Sardis, qui non inquinaverunt vestimenta sua et ambulabunt mecum in albis, quia digni sunt. ⁵Qui vicerit, sic vesti-

3:1–6 Sardis was an important hub in the road and communication network and was noted for the notorious licentious lifestyle of its inhabitants. Christ is portrayed to this Christian community as the one who sends the Spirit who can change their hearts. The church is accused of only giving the impression of being Christian, whereas many of its members are living in sin and have no spiritual life.

Our Lord himself described the situation of the prodigal son as a kind of death: "my son was dead, and is alive again", the father explains in the parable (Lk 15:24), and St Paul invites Christians to offer themselves to God "as men who have been brought from death to life" (Rom 6:13). In this passage of Revelation, we are told that the cause of this spiritual, but real, death is the fact that the works of this church were imperfect in the sight of God (v. 2); they were works that lead to spiritual death, that is, what are known as "mortal sins". "With the whole tradi-

tion of the Church", John Paul II says, "we call *mortal sin* the act by which man freely and consciously rejects God, his law, the covenant of love that God offers, preferring to turn in on himself or to some created and finite reality, something contrary to the divine will (*conversio ad creaturam*) [...]. Man perceives that this disobedience to God destroys the bond that unites him with his life-principle: it is a *mortal sin*, that is, an act which gravely offends God and ends in turning against man himself with a dark and powerful force of destruction" (*Reconciliatio et paenitentia*, 17).

The phrase "I will come like a thief" (v. 3) occurs elsewhere in the New Testament (cf. Mt 24:42–51, Mk 13:36; Lk 12:39ff; 1 Thess 5:2; 2 Pet 3:10). It does not mean that our Lord lies in wait for man, ready to pounce when he is unaware—as the hunter stalks his prey. It is simply a warning to us to live in the grace of God and be ready to render our account to him.

his name before my Father and before his angels. ⁶He who has an ear, let him hear what the Spirit says to the churches.'

Letter to the church of Philadelphia

Rev 1:18; 19:11
Job 12:14
Is 6:3; 22:22

⁷"And to the angel of the church in Philadelphia write: 'The words of the holy one, the true one, who has the key of David, who opens and no one shall shut, who shuts and no one opens.

1 Cor 16:9
2 Cor 2:12
Col 4:3

Rev 2:9
Is 43:4; 49:23; 60:14
Ps 86:9

2 Pet 2:9
2 Thess 2:12

⁸"'I know your works. Behold, I have set before you an open door, which no one is able to shut; I know that you have but little power, and yet you have kept my word and have not denied my name. ⁹Behold, I will make those of the synagogue of Satan who say that they are Jews and are not, but lie—behold, I will make them come and bow down before your feet, and learn that I have loved you. ¹⁰Because you have kept my word of patient endurance, I will keep you from the hour of trial which is coming

Rev 2:25; 22:7, 12
1 Cor 9:25
Zech 2:14
Rev 21:2
Gal 2:9
Ezek 48:3

on the whole world, to try those who dwell upon the earth. ¹¹I am coming soon; hold fast what you have, so that no one may seize your crown. ¹²He who conquers, I will make him a pillar in the temple of my God; never shall he go out of it, and I will write on him the name of my God, and the name of the city of my God, the new Jerusalem which comes down from my God out of heaven, and my own new name.*
¹³He who has an ear, let him hear what the Spirit says to the churches.'

etur vestimentis albis, et non delebo nomen eius de libro vitae et confitebor nomen eius coram Patre meo et coram angelis eius. ⁶Qui habet aurem, audiat quid Spiritus dicat ecclesiis. ⁷Et angelo ecclesiae, quae est Philadelphiae, scribe: Haec dicit Sanctus, Verus, qui habet *clavem David, qui aperit, et nemo claudet; et claudit, et nemo aperit:* ⁸Scio opera tua —ecce dedi coram te ostium apertum, quod nemo potest claudere— quia modicam habes virtutem, et servasti verbum meum et non negasti nomen meum. ⁹Ecce dabo de synagoga Satanae, qui dicunt se Iudaeos esse et non sunt, sed mentiuntur; ecce faciam illos, ut veniant et adorent ante pedes tuos et scient quia ego dilexi te. ¹⁰Quoniam servasti verbum patientiae meae, et ego te servabo ab hora tentationis, quae ventura est super orbem universum tentare habitantes in terra. ¹¹Venio cito; tene quod habes, ut nemo accipiat coronam tuam. ¹²Qui vicerit, faciam illum columnam in templo Dei mei, et foras non egredietur amplius, et scribam super eum nomen Dei mei et nomen civitatis Dei mei, novae Ierusalem, quae descendit de caelo a Deo meo, et nomen meum novum. ¹³Qui habet aurem, audiat quid Spiritus dicat ecclesiis. ¹⁴Et angelo ecclesiae, quae est Laodiciae, scribe: Haec dicit Amen, testis fidelis et verus, principium creaturae

If we do that, we will not run the risk of being found unprepared at the moment of death. "That day will come for us. It will be our last day, but we are not afraid of it. Trusting firmly in God's grace, we are ready from this very moment to be generous and courageous, and take loving care of little things: we are ready to go and meet our Lord, with our lamps burning brightly. For the feast of feasts awaits us in heaven" (St Josemaría Escrivá, *Friends of God*, 40).

3:7–13 Philadelphia was a port that gave access to the whole province of Phrygia. It had suffered an earthquake in the year 17 BC, and when it was rebuilt it took the new name of Neocaesarea, but that name soon fell into disuse. Here, however, it is promised another new name (see v. 12), one that will endure forever. The metaphor of the "open door" (v. 8) assures Christians that their work of evangelization will bear fruit, despite the difficulties caused by their enemies (cf. 1 Cor

16:9; 2 Cor 2:12; Col 4:3). These words can also be interpreted as a promise to hold open the entrance to the Kingdom.

On the "synagogue of Satan", see 2:9. The promise that their enemies will admit defeat and do obeisance to the victor is reminiscent of Isaiah 49:23 and 60:14, which prophesy that the nations will do homage to the Chosen People. Before that happens, however, the entire world will undergo tribulation, as described later on in this book (cf. chaps. 8, 9 and 16); but those who stay faithful will be protected. As regards the imminence of these predicted events, see what is said in the note on Revelation 1:1–3 which deals with the question of timing (see also 22:12, 20). When all comes to a close, the strife and the victory, "he who conquers" (3:12) will be a pillar of the temple, that is, will have a place of honour (cf. Gal 2:9). The faithful of that city are reminded that Christ holds the keys to the Kingdom of God, and they are assured that many Jews will be converted.

Letter to the church of Laodicea

¹⁴"And to the angel of the church in Laodicea write: 'The words of the Amen, the faithful and true witness, the beginning of God's creation.

¹⁵"I know your works: you are neither cold nor hot. Would that you were cold or hot! ¹⁶So, because you are lukewarm, and neither cold nor hot, I will spew you out of my mouth. ¹⁷For you say, I am rich, I have prospered, and I need nothing; not knowing that you are wretched, pitiable, poor, blind, and naked. ¹⁸Therefore I counsel you to buy from me gold refined by fire, that you may be rich, and white garments to clothe you and to keep the shame of your nakedness from being seen, and salve to anoint your eyes, that you may see. ¹⁹Those whom I love, I reprove and chasten; so be zealous and repent. ²⁰Behold, I stand at the door and knock; if any one hears my voice and opens the door, I will come in to him and eat with him, and he with me. ²¹He who conquers, I will grant him to sit with me on my throne, as I myself conquered and sat down with my Father on his throne. ²²He who has an ear, let him hear what the Spirit says to the churches.'"

Rev 1:5
Prov 8:22
Is 35:16
Col 1:15
Jn 1:3

Hos 12:9
Zech 11:5
1 Cor 4:8
2 Pet 1:9
1 Pet 1:7
Is 55:1
Rev 6:11; 16:15

Prov 3:12
1 Cor 11:32
Heb 12:6
Jn 10:3; 14:23
Lk 12:36; 22:30
Song 5:2
Mt 19:28
Rev 20:4

PART TWO

Eschatological visions*

1. INTRODUCTORY VISION*

God in majesty

4 ¹After this I looked, and lo, in heaven an open door! And the first voice, which I had heard speaking to me like a trumpet, said, "Come up hither, and I will show

Ex 19:16
Rev 1:1

Dei: ¹⁵Scio opera tua, quia neque frigidus es neque calidus. Utinam frigidus esses aut calidus! ¹⁶Sic quia tepidus es et nec calidus nec frigidus, incipiam te evomere ex ore meo. ¹⁷Quia dicis: "Dives sum et locupletatus et nullius egeo", et nescis quia tu es miser et miserabilis et pauper et caecus et nudus, ¹⁸suadeo tibi emere a me aurum igne probatum, ut locuples fias et vestimentis albis induaris, et non appareat confusio nuditatis tuae, et collyrium ad inunguendum oculos tuos ut videas. ¹⁹Ego, quos amo, arguo et castigo. Aemulare ergo et paenitentiam age. ²⁰Ecce sto ad ostium et pulso. Si quis audierit vocem meam et aperuerit ianuam, introibo ad illum et cenabo cum illo, et ipse mecum. ²¹Qui vicerit, dabo ei sedere mecum in throno meo, sicut et ego vici et sedi cum Patre meo in throno eius. ²²Qui habet aurem, audiat quid Spiritus dicat ecclesiis». [4] ¹Post haec vidi: et ecce ostium apertum in caelo, et vox prima, quam audivi, tamquam tubae loquentis mecum dicens: «Ascende huc, et ostendam

3:14–22 The prosperity that Laodicea enjoyed may have contributed to the laxity and lukewarmness that some Christians there are accused of. Christ is depicted as eternal with God; he is faithful to his promises, and demands that people love him ardently. The presence of hot springs close to the city explains the language used in this passage (vv. 15–16), which makes plain God's repugnance for mediocrity and bourgeois living.

Christ knocking on the door is one of the most touching images in the Bible. It is reminiscent of the Song of Songs, where the bridegroom says: "Open to me, my sister, my love, my dove,

my perfect one; for my head is wet with dew, my locks with the drops of the night" (Song 5:2). This is a way of describing God's love for us, inviting us to greater intimacy, as happens at countless times in the course of our life. "Little by little the love of God makes itself felt like a rustle in the soul. It is Christ who pursues us lovingly: 'Behold, I stand at the door and knock' (Rev 3:20)" (St Josemaría Escrivá, *Christ Is Passing By*, 8).

Jesus promises that those who win victory will sit beside him on his throne. He gave a similar promise to St Peter: the apostles will sit on twelve thrones to judge the twelve tribes of

Ps 11:4
Rev 1:10
Ezek 1:26
Is 6:1
Rev 10:1
Is 24:23
Rev 10:1
Zech 6:11

Zech 4:2
Ex 19:16
Ezek 1:13
Rev 8:5; 16:18
Ex 24:10

Ezek 10:14

Ezek 1:18; 10:12
Ex 3:14

you what must take place after this." ²At once I was in the Spirit, and lo, a throne stood in heaven, with one seated on the throne! ³And he who sat there appeared like jasper and carnelian, and round the throne was a rainbow that looked like an emerald.* ⁴Round the throne were twenty-four thrones, and seated on the thrones were twenty-four elders,* clad in white garments, with golden crowns upon their heads. ⁵From the throne issue flashes of lightning, and voices and peals of thunder, and before the throne burn seven torches of fire, which are the seven spirits of God; ⁶and before the throne there is as it were a sea of glass, like crystal.

And round the throne, on each side of the throne, are four living creatures,* full of eyes in front and behind: ⁷the first living creature like a lion, the second living creature like an ox, the third living creature with the face of a man, and the fourth living creature like a flying eagle. ⁸And the four living creatures, each of them with six wings, are full of eyes all round and within, and day and night they never cease to sing,

tibi, quae oportet fieri post haec». ²Statim fui in spiritu: et ecce thronus positus erat in caelo; et supra thronum sedens; ³et, qui sedebat, similis erat aspectu lapidi iaspidi et sardino; et iris erat in circuitu throni, aspectu similis smaragdo. ⁴Et in circuitu throni, viginti quattuor thronos et super thronos viginti quattuor seniores sedentes circumamictos vestimentis albis et super capita eorum coronas aureas. ⁵Et de throno procedunt fulgura et voces et tonitrua; et septem lampades ignis ardentes ante thronum, quae sunt septem spiritus Dei, ⁶et in conspectu throni tamquam mare vitreum simile crystallo. Et in medio throni et in circuitu throni quattuor animalia, plena oculis ante et retro: ⁷et animal *primum* simile *leoni et secundum* animal simile *vitulo et tertium* animal habens *faciem* quasi *hominis et quartum* animal simile *aquilae* volanti. ⁸Et quattuor animalia *singula*

Israel (see Mt 19:28; 20:20ff). The "throne" is a reference to the sovereign authority that Christ has received from the Father. Therefore, the promise of a seat next to him is a way of saying that those who stay true to Christ will share in his victory and kingship (cf. 1 Cor 6:2–3).

*4:1—22:21. After Christ's messages to the seven churches, we are now shown God's plan for mankind and the Church as manifested to the author of the book in a series of visions. An elaborate vision of heaven (4:1—5:14) acts as an introduction to the visions that follow. Other visions depict events that will take place in the time prior to the last battle (6:1—11:14). This is followed by visions of the battle, in which evil is defeated forever and the Kingdom of God and the heavenly Jerusalem are manifested in all their splendour (11:15—22:15). The book concludes with an epilogue that swears to the truth of its contents (22:16–21).

*4:1—5:14. This great vision of heaven shows God in all his majesty (4:1–11) and the risen Christ, who reveals to man God's mysterious plans (5:1–14).

4:1–8 "I looked", "I was in the Spirit": these mean the same thing—that God is making a rev-

elation to the author. In this passage we find imagery taken from the Old Testament: the throne reminds us of the visions in Isaiah 6 and Ezekiel 1:26–28; the rainbow is the sign of God's covenant in Genesis 9:8–17; the thunder and lightning appear in the theophany on Sinai (see Ex 19:16); the sea of glass is part of the description of the temple of Jerusalem in 1 Kings 7:23–26 and Ezekiel 10:14. The four living creatures are very like those in the prophet Ezekiel's vision of the chariot of the Lord drawn by four angels, who represent intelligence, nobility, strength and agility (see Ezek 1:10; 10:12; Is 6:2). Christian Tradition going back as far as St Irenaeus has interpreted these creatures as standing for the four evangelists, for they "carry" Jesus Christ to mankind. The one with the face of a man is St Matthew, who starts his book with the human genealogy of Jesus; the lion stands for St Mark: his Gospel begins with the voice crying in the wilderness (which is where the lion's roar can be heard); the ox is a reference to the sacrifices in the temple of Jerusalem, which is where St Luke begins his account of Christ's life; and the eagle represents St John, who soars to the heights to contemplate the divinity of the Word.

This imagery and other symbolism, such as that of colours, are used to depict the majesty of God and the praise that he receives in heaven.

"Holy, holy, holy,* is the Lord God Almighty,
   who was and is and is to come!"

Is 6:2, 3

[9]And whenever the living creatures give glory and honour and thanks to him who is seated on the throne, who lives for ever and ever, [10]the twenty-four elders fall down before him who is seated on the throne and worship him who lives for ever and ever; they cast their crowns before the throne, singing,

Ps 47:8
Dan 4:31
Rev 5:14

   [11]"Worthy art thou, our Lord and God,
   to receive glory and honour and power,
   for thou didst create all things,
   and by thy will they existed and were created."

1 Chron 29:11
Rom 4:17
Sir 18:1
Wis 1:14
Rev 14:7

The sealed scroll and the Lamb

5 [1]And I saw in the right hand of him who was seated on the throne a scroll* written within and on the back, sealed with seven seals; [2]and I saw a strong angel proclaiming with a loud voice, "Who is worthy to open the scroll and break its

Is 29:11
Ezek 2:9, 10

eorum habebant *alas senas*, in circuitu et intus plenae sunt oculis; et requiem non habent die et nocte dicentis: «*Sanctus, sanctus, sanctus Dominus, Deus omnipotens*, qui erat et qui est et qui venturus est!». [9]Et cum darent illa animalia gloriam et honorem et gratiarum actionem sedenti super thronum, viventi in saecula saeculorum, [10]procidebant viginti quattuor seniores ante sedentem in throno et adorabant viventem in saecula saeculorum et mittebant coronas suas ante thronum dicentes: [11]«Dignus es, Domine et Deus noster, / accipere gloriam et honorem et virtutem, / quia tu creasti omnia, / et propter voluntatem tuam erant et creata sunt». [5] [1]Et vidi in dextera sedentis super thronum librum scriptum intus et foris, signatum sigillis septem. [2]Et vidi angelum fortem praedicantem voce magna: «Quis est dignus aperire librum et solvere signacula eius?».

The twenty-four elders (v. 4) may stand for the heavenly Church, which includes the old and the new Israel (the twelve tribes and the twelve apostles), and which in heaven renders God perfect praise and intercedes for the Church on earth. Sometimes it is not easy to work out what the symbolism means—for example, the sea of glass and the four living creatures in front of and behind the throne. The whole scene might be a heavenly replica of the way that Solomon's temple was laid out; in front of the Holy of Holies, the place of God's presence, stood a huge water container used for purifications and called the "molten sea", supported by figures of oxen, twelve in number (cf. 1 Kings 7:23–26; 2 Chron 4:2–5). This parallel between Heaven and Temple would convey the connexion between liturgy on earth and the worship of God in heaven.

4:9–11 To the praise offered by the four creatures is joined that of the entire People of God as represented by the twenty-four elders, that is, the Church triumphant in heaven. The casting down of the crowns shows that the elders acknowledge their victory is due to God, and that all power belongs to him. The main reason for the praise offered here is God's work of creation. In narrat-

ing this vision, the author invites the pilgrim Church on earth to join in the worship and praise offered in heaven to the Creator. The Church uses this praise in the Eucharistic liturgy when, at the end of the Preface, she chants the angelic *Sanctus* ("Holy, holy, holy") in preparation for the canon of the Mass. But all the Church's liturgy, in fact, seeks to link up with the constant praise offered in heaven: "It is especially in the sacred liturgy that our union with the heavenly Church is best realized; in the liturgy, through the sacramental signs, the power of the Holy Spirit acts on us, and with community rejoicing we celebrate together the praise of the divine majesty, when all those of every tribe and tongue and people and nation who have been redeemed by the blood of Christ and gathered together into one Church glorify, in one common song of praise, the one and triune God" (Vatican II, *Lumen gentium*, 50).

5:1–5 The sealed scroll symbolizes God's plan for each person and for all mankind. If a person does not strive to know this plan, he or she is steeped in ignorance and anguish. But Christ, because he redeemed man by his death on the cross and has won victory over death, has revealed God's plans to him. "Christ the Lord, Christ the new Adam, in

seals?" ³And no one in heaven or on earth or under the earth was able to open the scroll or to look into it, ⁴and I wept much that no one was found worthy to open the scroll or to look into it. ⁵Then one of the elders said to me, "Weep not; lo, the Lion of the tribe of Judah, the Root of David, has conquered, so that he can open the scroll and its seven seals."

⁶And between the throne and the four living creatures and among the elders, I saw a Lamb standing, as though it had been slain, with seven horns and with seven eyes,* which are the seven spirits of God sent out into all the earth; ⁷and he went and took the scroll from the right hand of him who was seated on the throne. ⁸And when he had taken the scroll, the four living creatures and the twenty-four elders fell down before the Lamb, each holding a harp, and with golden bowls full of incense, which are the prayers of the saints; ⁹and they sang a new song, saying,

"Worthy art thou to take the scroll and to open its seals,
for thou wast slain and by thy blood didst ransom men for God
from every tribe and tongue and people and nation,
¹⁰and hast made them a kingdom and priests to our God,
and they shall reign on earth."

¹¹Then I looked, and I heard around the throne and the living creatures and the elders the voice of many angels, numbering myriads of myriads and thousands of thousands, ¹²saying with a loud voice, "Worthy is the Lamb who was slain, to receive power and wealth and wisdom and might and honour and glory and blessing!" ¹³And I heard every creature in heaven and on earth and under the earth and in the sea, and all therein, saying, "To him who sits upon the throne and to the Lamb be blessing and honour and glory and might for ever and ever!" ¹⁴And the four living creatures said, "Amen!" and the elders fell down and worshipped.

Marginal references:
Gen 49:9f
Is 11:1, 10
Rom 15:12
Heb 7:14
Rev 22:16

Ex 12:1–27
Is 53:7; 11:2
Jer 11:19
Jn 1:29
Jn 1:29
Rev 5:12; 7:17; 13:8
Zech 3:9; 4:10

1 Kings 22:19
Is 6:1
Ps 47:9
Ps 141:2; 144:9

Rev 4:11; 5:12; 7:9; 14:3–4
Is 53:7
1 Pet 1:19
Rom 3:24

Ex 19:6
Is 61:6
Rev 1:6; 20:6

Dan 7:10
Heb 12:22
Jude 14

Is 53:7
1 Chron 29:11
Rev 4:11

Phil 2:10
1 Tim 1:17
Ps 146:6
Rev 5:3

³Et nemo poterat in caelo neque in terra neque subtus terram aperire librum neque respicere illum. ⁴Et ego flebam multum, quoniam nemo dignus inventus est aperire librum nec respicere eum. ⁵Et unus de senioribus dicit mihi: «Ne fleveris; ecce vicit leo de tribu Iudae, radix David, aperire librum et septem signacula eius». ⁶Et vidi in medio throni et quattuor animalium et in medio seniorum Agnum stantem tamquam occisum, habentem cornua septem et oculos septem, qui sunt septem spiritus Dei missi in omnem terram. ⁷Et venit et accepit de dextera sedentis in throno. ⁸Et cum accepisset librum, quattuor animalia et viginti quattuor seniores ceciderunt coram Agno, habentes singuli citharas et phialas aureas plenas incensorum, quae sunt orationes sanctorum. ⁹Et cantant novum canticum dicentes: «Dignus es accipere librum / et aperire signacula eius, / quoniam occisus es et redemisti Deo in sanguine tuo / ex omni tribu et lingua et populo et natione / ¹⁰et fecisti eos Deo nostro regnum et sacerdotes, / et regnabunt super terram». ¹¹Et vidi et audivi vocem angelorum multorum in circuitu throni et animalium et seniorum, et erat numerus eorum myriades myriadum et milia milium ¹²dicentium voce magna: «Dignus est Agnus, qui occisus est, / accipere virtutem et divitias et sapientiam / et

the very revelation of the mystery of the Father and of his love, fully reveals man to himself and brings to light his most high calling" (Vatican II, *Gaudium et spes*, 22).

5:6–14 Christ in glory deserves the same worship as the Father. The majesty of Christ the Lamb is acknowledged by the worship given him, in the first instance, by the four living creatures and the twenty-four elders, by all the angels, and finally by all creation (vv. 11–13). St John records these three moments to highlight the praise rendered by the heavenly Church, to which the pilgrim Church on earth is linked, through the prayer symbolized by the golden bowls of incense (v. 8).

The myriad angels assembled around the throne in the form of a guard of honour (v. 11) proclaim the fullness of divine perfection that belongs to Christ the Lamb. Their prayer lists out seven attributes to show that Christ has everything that belongs to the Godhead (v. 12).

After the chant of the spiritual, invisible, creation comes the hymn of the material, visible, world. This hymn (v. 13) differs from the previous one in that it is also addressed to him who sits on the throne. It thereby puts on the same level God and the Lamb, whose Godhead is proclaimed. This marks the climax of the universal, cosmic praise rendered to the Lamb. The emphatic "Amen!" of the four living creatures and the worship given by the twenty-

2. EVENTS PRIOR TO THE FINAL OUTCOME*

Christ opens the first six seals. Vision of the four horsemen

6 *[1]Now I saw when the Lamb opened one of the seven seals, and I heard one of the four living creatures say, as with a voice of thunder, "Come!" [2]And I saw, and behold, a white horse, and its rider had a bow; and a crown was given to him, and he went out conquering and to conquer.

[3]When he opened the second seal, I heard the second living creature say, "Come!" [4]And out came another horse, bright red; its rider was permitted to take peace from the earth, so that men should slay one another; and he was given a great sword.

[5]When he opened the third seal, I heard the third living creature say, "Come!" And I saw, and behold, a black horse, and its rider had a balance* in his hand; [6]and I heard what seemed to be a voice in the midst of the four living creatures saying, "A quart of wheat for a denarius,[a] and three quarts of barley for a denarius;[a] but do not harm oil and wine!"

[7]When he opened the fourth seal, I heard the voice of the fourth living creature say, "Come!" [8]And I saw, and behold, a pale horse, and its rider's name was Death, and Hades followed him; and they were given power over a fourth of the earth, to kill with sword and with famine and with pestilence and by wild beasts of the earth.

[9]When he opened the fifth seal, I saw under the altar the souls of those who had been slain for the word of God and for the witness they had borne; [10]they cried out

Margin references:
Rev 5:1–2
Zech 1:8–10; 6:1–3
Ezek 21:14–16
Ezek 4:16f
2 Kings 7:1
Hos 13:14
Ezek 5:12; 14:21
Jer 14:12; 15:2–3
Rev 1:2, 9
Rev 3:7; 8:13; 18:24
Zech 1:12

fortitudinem et honorem et gloriam et benedictionem». [13]Et omnem creaturam, quae in caelo est et super terram et sub terra et super mare et quae in eis omnia, audivi dicentes: «Sedenti super thronum et Agno benedictio et honor et gloria et potestas in saecula saeculorum». [14]Et quattuor animalia dicebant: «Amen»; et seniores ceciderunt et adoraverunt.   [6] [1]Et vidi, cum aperuisset Agnus unum de septem sigillis, et audivi unum de quattuor animalibus dicens tamquam vox tonitrui: «Veni». [2]Et vidi: et ecce equus albus; et, qui sedebat super illum, habebat arcum, et data est ei corona, et exivit vincens et ut vinceret. [3]Et cum aperuisset sigillum secundum, audivi secundum animal dicens: «Veni». [4]Et exivit alius equus rufus; et, qui sedebat super illum, datum est ei, ut sumeret pacem de terra, et ut invicem se interficiant, et datus est illi gladius magnus. [5]Et cum aperuisset sigillum tertium, audivi tertium animal dicens: «Veni». Et vidi: et ecce equus niger; et, qui sedebat super eum, habebat stateram in manu sua. [6]Et audivi tamquam vocem in medio quattuor animalium dicentem: «Bilibris tritici denario, et tres bilibres hordei denario; et oleum et vinum ne laeseris». [7]Et cum aperuisset sigillum quartum, audivi vocem quarti animalis dicentis: «Veni». [8]Et vidi: et ecce equus pallidus; et, qui sedebat desuper, nomen illi Mors, et Infernus sequebatur eum, et data est illis potestas super quartam partem terrae, interficere gladio et fame et morte et a bestiis terrae. [9]Et cum aperuisset quintum sigillum, vidi subtus altare animas interfectorum propter verbum Dei et propter testimonium, quod

four elders bring this introductory vision to a close.

As in other passages in the book, reference is made to the role of the angels in heaven (v. 11), with special emphasis on their worship and praise before the throne of God (cf. 7:11), their role in putting God's plans into effect (cf. 11:15; 16:17; 22:6), and their intercession on behalf of mankind (cf. 8:4). "Have confidence in your guardian Angel. Treat him as a lifelong friend— that is what he is—and he will render you a thousand services in the ordinary affairs of each day" (St Josemaría Escrivá, *The Way*, 562).

*6:1–11:14 In the image of the Lamb opening the seven seals one by one (6:1–7:17), the author shows the deep meaning that history has under the aegis of Christ, and why so many misfortunes

afflict mankind. Our sense of expectation increases the nearer the narrative draws to the opening of the seventh seal (cf. 8:1). When that moment comes, seven trumpets begin to sound, one by one, symbolizing the voice of God (8:2–11, 13). Only at the seventh trumpet blast will the mystery of the End be revealed (see 10:7; 11:15); meanwhile the reader is kept in suspense, while he gradually comes to see the hand and power of God at work over the course of history.

6:1–17 When each of the first four seals is opened (vv. 1–8), a horse and rider appear. The first rider stands for Jesus Christ and the others symbolize war, famine and pestilence. When the fifth seal is broken (v. 9), the glory of the martyrs is revealed, and, at the opening of the sixth, the tribulations that Jesus said would mark the end of

a The denarius was a day's wage for a labourer

Ps 79:5, 10
Deut 32:43
Gen 4:10
Lk 18:7

Rev 3:4, 18; 4:4; 7:9,
13; 19:14

Is 13:10
Ezek 32:7, 8; 38:19
Joel 2:10; 3:3, 4
Mt 24:29
Is 34:4; 50:3

Rev 16:20; 20:11
Ezek 26:15

Ps 2:2
Is 2:10, 19, 21;
24:21; 34:12
Jer 4:29

Hos 10:8
Lk 23:30
Ps 47:8

Joel 2:11; 3:4
Rom 2:5
Mal 3:2
Nahum 1:6
Zeph 1:14–15

Jer 49:36
Ezek 7:2; 37:9
Dan 7:2
Zech 6:5
Mt 24:31
Rev 9:14–15

Rev 18:2
Is 41:25

Ezek 9:4, 6
Rev 9:6

Rev 9:6; 14:1, 3;
21:12
Rom 4:11
Is 49:6
Num 1:21–43
Gen 35:22–26

with a loud voice, "O Sovereign Lord, holy and true, how long before thou wilt judge and avenge our blood on those who dwell upon the earth?" ¹¹Then they were each given a white robe and told to rest a little longer, until the number of their fellow servants and their brethren should be complete, who were to be killed as they themselves had been.

¹²When he opened the sixth seal, I looked, and behold, there was a great earthquake; and the sun became black as sackcloth, the full moon became like blood, ¹³and the stars of the sky fell to the earth as the fig tree sheds its winter fruit when shaken by a gale; ¹⁴the sky vanished like a scroll that is rolled up, and every mountain and island was removed from its place. ¹⁵Then the kings of the earth and the great men and the generals and the rich and the strong, and every one, slave and free, hid in the caves and among the rocks of the mountains, ¹⁶calling to the mountains and rocks, "Fall on us and hide us from the face of him who is seated on the throne, and from the wrath of the Lamb; ¹⁷for the great day of their wrath has come, and who can stand before it?"

The great multitude of the saved

7 ¹After this I saw four angels standing at the four corners of the earth, holding back the four winds of the earth, that no wind might blow on earth or sea or against any tree. ²Then I saw another angel ascend from the rising of the sun, with the seal of the living God, and he called with a loud voice to the four angels who had been given power to harm earth and sea, ³saying, "Do not harm the earth or the sea or the trees, till we have sealed the servants of our God upon their foreheads." ⁴And I heard the number of the sealed, a hundred and forty-four thousand* sealed, out of every tribe of the sons of Israel, ⁵twelve thousand sealed out of the tribe of Judah, twelve thousand of the tribe of Reuben, twelve thousand of the tribe of Gad, ⁶twelve thousand of the tribe of Asher, twelve thousand of the tribe of Naphtali, twelve thousand of the tribe of Manasseh, ⁷twelve thousand of the tribe of Simeon, twelve thousand of the tribe of Levi, twelve thousand of the tribe of Issachar, ⁸twelve thousand

habebant. ¹⁰Et clamaverunt voce magna dicentes: «Usquequo, Domine, sanctus et verus, non iudicas et vindicas sanguinem nostrum de his, qui habitant in terra?». ¹¹Et datae sunt illis singulae stolae albae, et dictum est illis, ut requiescant tempus adhuc modicum, donec impleantur et conservi eorum et fratres eorum, qui interficiendi sunt sicut et illi. ¹²Et vidi, cum aperuisset sigillum sextum, et terraemotus factus est magnus, et sol factus est niger tamquam saccus cilicinus, et luna tota facta est sicut sanguis, ¹³et stellae caeli ceciderunt in terram, sicut ficus mittit grossos suos, cum vento magno movetur, ¹⁴et caelum recessit sicut liber involutus, et omnis mons et insula de locis suis motae sunt. ¹⁵Et reges terrae et magnates et tribuni et divites et fortes et omnis servus et liber absconderunt se in speluncis et in petris montium; ¹⁶et dicunt montibus et petris: «Cadite super nos et abscondite nos a facie sedentis super thronum et ab ira Agni, ¹⁷quoniam venit dies magnus irae ipsorum, et quis poterit stare?». [7] ¹Post haec vidi quattuor angelos stantes super quattuor angulos terrae tenentes quattuor ventos terrae, ne flaret ventus super terram neque super mare neque in ullam arborem. ²Et vidi alterum angelum ascendentem ab ortu solis, habentem sigillum Dei vivi, et clamavit voce magna quattuor

the world. "The inspired evangelist not only saw the devastation brought about by sin, war, starvation and death; he saw, before all other things, the victory of Christ. There can be no doubt but that the journey of the Church through the centuries is a *via crucis*, but it has also been, at the same time, a triumphant procession. The Church of Christ, the people of Christian faith and love, are always those who bring light, salvation and peace to a humanity without hope. Jesus Christ, yesterday and today, one and the same forever" (Pius XII, *Address*, 15 November 1946).

In verse 15 there is a reference to seven social groups, from the highest to the lowest, which encompass all mankind. No one escapes God's judgment, against which there is no appeal. The *Dies Irae* has come (v. 17), the day of the Lamb's wrath.

7:1–17 The suspense is heightened by the insertion of two visions prior to the opening of the seventh seal. The first (vv. 1–8) shows God's protection of Christians—a great number, 144,000—who are the new People of God. The

of the tribe of Zebulun, twelve thousand of the tribe of Joseph, twelve thousand sealed out of the tribe of Benjamin.

⁹After this I looked, and behold, a great multitude which no man could number, from every nation, from all tribes and peoples and tongues, standing before the throne and before the Lamb, clothed in white robes, with palm branches in their hands, ¹⁰and crying out with a loud voice, "Salvation belongs to our God who sits upon the throne, and to the Lamb!" ¹¹And all the angels stood round the throne and round the elders and the four living creatures, and they fell on their faces before the throne and worshipped God, ¹²saying, "Amen! Blessing and glory and wisdom and thanksgiving and honour and power and might be to our God for ever and ever! Amen."

¹³Then one of the elders addressed me, saying, "Who are these, clothed in white robes, and whence have they come?" ¹⁴I said to him, "Sir, you know." And he said to me, "These are they who have come out of the great tribulation;* they have washed their robes and made them white in the blood of the Lamb.

¹⁵ Therefore are they before the throne of God,
    and serve him day and night within his temple;
    and he who sits upon the throne will shelter them with his presence.
¹⁶ They shall hunger no more, neither thirst any more;
    the sun shall not strike them, nor any scorching heat.
¹⁷ For the Lamb in the midst of the throne will be their shepherd,
    and he will guide them to springs of living water;
    and God will wipe away every tear from their eyes."

Margin references:
Rev 5:9; 6:11; 15:2–5
Gen 15:5
Rev 19:1
Ps 47:8
Rev 5:11; 11:16
Rev 22:14
1 Jn 1:7
Ex 19:10, 14
Mt 24:21
Is 49:10
Ps 121:6
Ps 23:2, 3
Is 25:8; 49:10
Ezek 34:23
Jer 31:16
Rev 21:4, 6

The opening of the seventh seal

8 ¹When the Lamb opened the seventh seal, there was silence in heaven for about half an hour. ²Then I saw the seven angels who stand before God, and seven

Margin references: Zech 2:17 / Hab 2:20 / Zeph 1:7 / Wis 18:14

angelis, quibus datum est nocere terrae et mari, ³dicens: «Nolite nocere terrae neque mari neque arboribus, quoadusque signemus servos Dei nostri in frontibus eorum». ⁴Et audivi numerum signatorum, centum quadraginta quattuor milia signati ex omni tribu filiorum Israel: ⁵ex tribu Iudae duodecim milia signati, ex tribu Ruben duodecim milia, ex tribu Gad duodecim milia, ⁶ex tribu Aser duodecim milia, ex tribu Nephthali duodecim milia, ex tribu Manasse duodecim milia, ⁷ex tribu Simeon duodecim milia, ex tribu Levi duodecim milia, ex tribu Issachar duodecim milia, ⁸ex tribu Zabulon duodecim milia, ex tribu Ioseph duodecim milia, ex tribu Beniamin duodecim milia signati. ⁹Post haec vidi: et ecce turba magna, quam dinumerare nemo poterat, ex omnibus gentibus et tribubus et populis et linguis stantes ante thronum et in conspectu Agni, amicti stolis albis, et palmae in manibus eorum; ¹⁰et clamant voce magna dicentes: «Salus Deo nostro, qui sedet super thronum, et Agno». ¹¹Et omnes angeli stabant in circuitu throni et seniorum et quattuor animalium, et ceciderunt in conspectu throni in facies suas et adoraverunt Deum ¹²dicentes: «Amen! Benedictio et gloria et sapientia et gratiarum actio et honor et virtus et fortitudo Deo nostro in saecula saeculorum. Amen». ¹³Et respondit unus de senioribus dicens mihi: «Hi qui amicti sunt stolis albis, qui sunt et unde venerunt?». ¹⁴Et dixi illi: «Domine mi, tu scis». Et dixit mihi: «Hi sunt qui veniunt de tribulatione magna et laverunt stolas suas et dealbaverunt eas in sanguine Agni. ¹⁵Ideo sunt ante thronum Dei et serviunt ei die ac nocte in templo eius; et, qui sedet in throno, habitabit super illos. ¹⁶*Non esurient* amplius *neque sitient* amplius, *neque cadet super illos sol neque ullus aestus,* ¹⁷quoniam Agnus, qui in medio throni est, *pascet illos et deducet eos ad vitae fontes aquarum, et absterget Deus omnem lacrimam ex oculis eorum».*   [8] ¹Et cum aperuisset sigillum septimum, factum est silentium in caelo quasi media hora. ²Et vidi septem angelos, qui stant

second vision (vv. 9–17) shows the glory enjoyed after death by those whom Christ has redeemed. "The blood of the Lamb, offered in sacrifice for all, has worked its saving power in every corner of the world, bringing grace and salvation to this 'great crowd'. Having undergone trials and been purified by the blood of Christ, the redeemed are safe in the Kingdom of God, where they praise and worship him for all time" (John Paul II, *Homily*, 1 November 1981).

The revelation of these consoling scenes is intended to encourage us to imitate those Christians, who were once like us and now have won victory and are in heaven. To this end, the Church invites us to pray: "Father, you sanctified the Church of Rome with the blood of its first martyrs. May we find strength from their courage and rejoice in their triumph" (*Roman Missal*, Feast of the First Martyrs of the Church of Rome, Opening Prayer).

8:1–6 The silence that results when the seventh seal is opened is a signal that the long-awaited

Mt 24:31
Tob 12:15
Rev 5:8
Ex 39:38

Ps 141:2

Lev 16:12
Ezek 10:2
Rev 4:5; 11:19
Ex 19:16

Joel 2:1

Joel 3:3
Ex 9:23–26
Ezek 5:12; 38:22
Sir 39:29
Wis 16:22

Jer 51:25
Ex 7:20f
Rev 16:2, 3

Is 14:12
Rev 9:1; 16:4

Jer 9:14; 23:15
Ex 15:23

Ex 10:21
Amos 8:9
Rev 6:12

trumpets were given to them. [3]And another angel came and stood at the altar with a golden censer; and he was given much incense to mingle with the prayers of all the saints upon the golden altar before the throne; [4]and the smoke of the incense rose with the prayers of the saints from the hand of the angel before God. [5]Then the angel took the censer and filled it with fire from the altar and threw it on the earth;* and there were peals of thunder, voices, flashes of lightning, and an earthquake.

[6]Now the seven angels who had the seven trumpets made ready to blow them.

The first six trumpet calls. The three woes

[7]The first angel blew his trumpet, and there followed hail and fire, mixed with blood, which fell on the earth; and a third of the earth was burnt up, and a third of the trees were burnt up, and all green grass was burnt up.

[8]The second angel blew his trumpet, and something like a great mountain, burning with fire, was thrown into the sea; [9]and a third of the sea became blood, a third of the living creatures in the sea died, and a third of the ships were destroyed.

[10]The third angel blew his trumpet, and a great star fell from heaven, blazing like a torch, and it fell on a third of the rivers and on the fountains of water. [11]The name of the star is Wormwood. A third of the waters became wormwood, and many men died of the water, because it was made bitter.

[12]The fourth angel blew his trumpet, and a third of the sun was struck, and a third of the moon, and a third of the stars, so that a third of their light was darkened; a third of the day was kept from shining, and likewise a third of the night.

in conspectu Dei, et datae sunt illis septem tubae. [3]Et alius angelus venit et stetit ante altare habens turibulum aureum, et data sunt illi incensa multa, ut daret orationum sanctorum omnium super altare aureum, quod est ante thronum. [4]Et ascendit fumus incensorum de orationibus sanctorum de manu angeli coram Deo. [5]Et accepit angelus turibulum et implevit illud de igne altaris et misit in terram; et facta sunt tonitrua et voces et fulgura et terraemotus. [6]Et septem angeli, qui habebant septem tubas, paraverunt se, ut tuba canerent. [7]Et primus tuba cecinit. Et facta est grando et ignis mixta in sanguine, et missum est in terram: et tertia pars terrae combusta est, et tertia pars arborum combusta est, et omne fenum viride combustum est. [8]Et secundus angelus tuba cecinit. Et tamquam mons magnus igne ardens missus est in mare: et facta est tertia pars maris sanguis, [9]et mortua est tertia pars creaturarum, quae in mari sunt, quae habent animas, et tertia pars navium interiit. [10]Et tertius angelus tuba cecinit. Et cecidit de caelo stella magna ardens tamquam facula et cecidit super tertiam partem fluminum et super fontes aquarum. [11]Et nomen stellae dicitur Absinthius. Et facta est tertia pars aquarum in absinthium, et multi hominum mortui sunt de aquis, quia amarae factae sunt. [12]Et quartus angelus tuba cecinit. Et percussa est tertia pars solis et tertia pars lunae et tertia pars stellarum, ut obscuraretur tertia pars eorum, et diei non luceret

end has come. It is the preface to the prayer of the saints, symbolized by the odour of incense: "Contemplative prayer is *silence*, the 'symbol of the world to come' (St Isaac of Nineveh, *Tract. Myst.*, 66) or 'silent love' (St John of the Cross, *Maxims and Counsels* 53). Words in this kind of prayer are not speeches; they are like kindling that feeds the fire of love. In this silence, unbearable to the 'outer' man, the Father speaks to us his incarnate Word, who suffered, died, and rose; in this silence the Spirit of adoption enables us to share in the prayer of Jesus" (*Catechism of the Catholic Church*, 2717).

The seven seals are followed by seven trumpets, and the last of these, in turn, leads to the seven bowls. But before that, we are told what happens when the first six trumpets are blown (chaps. 8–9) and God's judgments are visited on

the world. There is a certain parallel here with the plagues of Egypt (see Ex 7:14—12:34). Before the seventh trumpet is sounded, there is a sort of interlude (see 10:1—11:14).

8:7–13 The trumpet blasts stand for the will of God heralding and inflicting punishment for the sins of mankind. The first four blasts (8:7–12) announce calamities similar to those caused by the plagues of Egypt, though much worse: now these misfortunes affect the elements created by God—land, sea, the waters of the earth, and the firmament.

The motif of the eagle (v. 13), a symbol perhaps of an angel, creates a sense of suspense and anxiety as to what the three remaining trumpet blasts will bring. (They are imminent.) The eagle's "woe, woe, woe" betokens horror and

¹³Then I looked, and I heard an eagle crying with a loud voice, as it flew in mid-heaven, "Woe, woe, woe to those who dwell on the earth, at the blasts of the other trumpets which the three angels are about to blow!"

Rev 9:12; 11:14; 12:12
Hos 4:1
Is 24:17; 26:21

9 ¹And the fifth angel blew his trumpet, and I saw a star* fallen from heaven to earth, and he was given the key of the shaft of the bottomless pit; ²he opened the shaft of the bottomless pit, and from the shaft rose smoke like the smoke of a great furnace, and the sun and the air were darkened with the smoke from the shaft. ³Then from the smoke came locusts on the earth, and they were given power like the power of scorpions of the earth; ⁴they were told not to harm the grass of the earth or any green growth or any tree, but only those of mankind who have not the seal of God upon their foreheads; ⁵they were allowed to torture them for five months, but not to kill them, and their torture was like the torture of a scorpion, when it stings a man. ⁶And in those days men will seek death and will not find it; they will long to die, and death will fly from them.

⁷In appearance the locusts were like horses arrayed for battle; on their heads were what looked like crowns of gold; their faces were like human faces, ⁸their hair like women's hair, and their teeth like lions' teeth; ⁹they had scales like iron breastplates, and the noise of their wings was like the noise of many chariots with horses rushing into battle. ¹⁰They have tails like scorpions, and stings, and their power of hurting

Rev 8:10; 20:1
Lk 10:18

Gen 19:28
Ex 19:18
Joel 2:10

Ex 10:12, 15
Wis 16:9

Rev 7:3
Ezek 9:4, 6

Job 3:21
Jer 8:3
Hos 10:8
Lk 23:30

Joel 2:4–5
Job 39:19–20

Joel 1:6

Joel 2:5

Rev 9:19

pars tertia, et nox similiter. ¹³Et vidi et audivi unam aquilam volantem per medium caelum dicentem voce magna: «Vae, vae, vae habitantibus in terra de ceteris vocibus tubae trium angelorum, qui tuba canituri sunt!». [9] ¹Et quintus angelus tuba cecinit. Et vidi stellam de caelo cecidisse in terram, et data est illi clavis putei abyssi. ²Et aperuit puteum abyssi, et ascendit fumus ex puteo sicut fumus fornacis magnae, et obscuratus est sol et aer de fumo putei. ³Et de fumo exierunt locustae in terram, et data est illis potestas, sicut habent potestatem scorpiones terrae. ⁴Et dictum est illis, ne laederent fenum terrae neque omne viride neque omnem arborem, nisi tantum homines, qui non habent signum Dei in frontibus. ⁵Et datum est illis, ne occiderent eos, sed ut cruciarentur mensibus quinque; et cruciatus eorum ut cruciatus scorpii, cum percutit hominem. ⁶Et in diebus illis quaerent homines mortem et non invenient eam; et desiderabunt mori, et fugit mors ab ipsis. ⁷Et similitudines locustarum similes equis paratis in proelium, et super capita earum tamquam coronae similes auro, et facies earum sicut facies hominum, ⁸et habebant capillos sicut capillos mulierum, et dentes earum sicut leonum erant, ⁹et habebant loricas sicut loricas ferreas, et vox alarum earum sicut vox curruum equorum multorum currentium in bellum. ¹⁰Et habent caudas similes scorpionibus et aculeos, et in caudis earum potestas earum nocere hominibus mensibus quinque. ¹¹Habent super se regem angelum abyssi, cui nomen Hebraice Abaddon et Graece nomen habet Apollyon. ¹²Vae unum abiit. Ecce veni-

compassion at the events that are to follow. "Those who dwell on the earth" is a reference to idolaters who persecute Christians. They do not, therefore, include the faithful, but only those who have allowed themselves be led astray by Christ's enemies.

9:1–12 The fifth and sixth trumpet blasts directly impact on mankind, producing effects more horrific than all the previous ones (9:1–21). The fallen stars symbolize Satan (cf. Lk 10:18), whom God allows to release for a time the demons incarcerated in the bowels of the earth (where they were, according to the thinking of the time), in order to wreak havoc on those who refuse to acknowledge God.

To describe the demons and the harm they do, the author evokes the eighth plague of Egypt, the plague of locusts (see Ex 10:14ff), making it clear,

however, that this new plague is of a different order and much more terrible. It will do such grievous harm to man that he will wish to die, but he will have to endure it for the established length of time. The "five months" (v. 5), the lifetime of the locust, conveys the idea that the afflictions will be temporary. The crowns of gold (v. 7) identify the locusts as conquerors; their faces, as creatures with intelligence; their hairiness and lions' teeth symbolize ferocity; their iron breastplates show them to be fully armed warriors; and the noise they create and their scorpion tails show their extreme cruelty. They obey a leader, Satan, whose name (Abaddon, Apollyon: v. 11) means destruction and extermination. His name contrasts with that of Jesus, which means "Yhwh saves". At the end of the book, after Christ's victory, the author sees Satan and his followers once again entombed in the abyss (see 20:1–3).

Job 26:6
Prov 15:11

Rev 8:13; 11:14

Ex 27:2; 30:1–3;
40:5
Gen 15:18
Deut 1:7
Josh 1:4
Rev 16:12
Rev 7:1

Rev 9:10

Is 2:8, 20; 17:8
Dan 5:4, 23
Ps 115:4–7;
135:15–17
Mic 5:12
Rev 16:9, 11
1 Cor 10:20
Ex 20:13–15

Rev 4:3; 5:2; 18:1;
20:1

men for five months lies in their tails. [11]They have as king over them the angel of the bottomless pit; his name in Hebrew is Abaddon, and in Greek he is called Apollyon.[b]

[12]The first woe has passed; behold, two woes are still to come.

[13]Then the sixth angel blew his trumpet, and I heard a voice from the four horns of the golden altar before God, [14]saying to the sixth angel who had the trumpet, "Release the four angels who are bound at the great river Euphrates."* [15]So the four angels were released, who had been held ready for the hour, the day, the month, and the year, to kill a third of mankind. [16]The number of the troops of cavalry was twice ten thousand times ten thousand; I heard their number. [17]And this was how I saw the horses in my vision: the riders wore breastplates the colour of fire and of sapphire[c] and of sulphur, and the heads of the horses were like lions' heads, and fire and smoke and sulphur issued from their mouths. [18]By these three plagues a third of mankind was killed, by the fire and smoke and sulphur issuing from their mouths. [19]For the power of the horses is in their mouths and in their tails; their tails are like serpents, with heads, and by means of them they wound.

[20]The rest of mankind, who were not killed by these plagues, did not repent of the works of their hands nor give up worshipping demons and idols of gold and silver and bronze and stone and wood, which cannot either see or hear or walk; [21]nor did they repent of their murders or their sorceries or their immorality* or their thefts.

The seer is given a little scroll to eat

10 [1]Then I saw another mighty angel coming down from heaven, wrapped in a cloud, with a rainbow over his head, and his face was like the sun, and his

unt adhuc duo vae post haec. [13]Et sextus angelus tuba cecinit. Et audivi vocem unam ex cornibus altaris aurei, quod est ante Deum, [14]dicentem sexto angelo, qui habebat tubam: «Solve quattuor angelos, qui alligati sunt super flumen magnum Euphraten». [15]Et soluti sunt quattuor angeli, qui parati erant in horam et diem et mensem et annum, ut occiderent tertiam partem hominum. [16]Et numerus equestris exercitus vicies milies dena milia; audivi numerum eorum. [17]Et ita vidi equos in visione et, qui sedebant super eos, habentes loricas igneas et hyacinthinas et sulphureas; et capita equorum erant tamquam capita leonum, et de ore ipsorum procedit ignis et fumus et sulphur. [18]Ab his tribus plagis occisa est tertia pars hominum, de igne et fumo et sulphure, qui procedebat ex ore ipsorum. [19]Potestas enim equorum in ore eorum est et in caudis eorum, nam caudae illorum similes serpentibus habentes capita, et in his nocent. [20]Et ceteri homines, qui non sunt occisi in his plagis neque paenitentiam egerunt de operibus manuum suarum, ut non adorarent daemonia et *simulacra aurea et argentea et aerea et lapidea et lignea, quae neque videre* possunt *neque audire neque ambulare*, [21]et non egerunt paenitentiam ab homicidiis suis neque a veneficiis suis neque a fornicatione sua neque a furtis suis. [10] [1]Et vidi alium angelum fortem descendentem de caelo amictum nube, et iris super caput, et facies eius erat ut sol, et pedes eius

9:13–21. The angels bound at the river Euphrates are the terrifying angels of death (9:15). God alone can command them. In the last analysis, all the punishments described here are designed (like the calls to penance addressed to the churches of Asia Minor: see 2:5, 16, 21; 3:3; etc.) to move people to repentance. And still they do not listen: they turn away from God and worship idols—scarecrows, compared to the majesty of the living God (cf. Ps 115; Jer 10:3–5).

In the last analysis, idolatry is the root of all other sins, for, by turning his back on God, man comes under the control of the power of evil (forces within himself as well as outside him), which pushes him to commit all kinds of sins and perversions. The same idea is found in St Paul's Letter to the Romans, where he says that,

by cutting themselves off from God, men are given over to their own passions and commit most abominable sins (cf. Rom 1:18–32). Sometimes the effect of punishment is to make people even more obdurate. That was what happened in the case of Pharaoh, when he refused to allow the Israelites to leave Egypt.

10:1–11 Before the seventh trumpet blast, the sacred writer inserts a further vision (the seer is once again returned to earth). This insertion helps to heighten the sense of expectation and prepares the reader to face what will happen when the third woe comes and the events of the End are announced (cf. 11:14–15).

Although the angel is not named, he may be Gabriel: he is described as "mighty" (*geber* in

b Or *Destroyer*   c Greek *hyacinth*

legs like pillars of fire. [2]He had a little scroll open in his hand. And he set his right foot on the sea, and his left foot on the land, [3]and called out with a loud voice, like a lion roaring; when he called out, the seven thunders sounded. [4]And when the seven thunders had sounded, I was about to write, but I heard a voice from heaven saying, "Seal up what the seven thunders have said, and do not write it down." [5]And the angel whom I saw standing on sea and land lifted up his right hand to heaven [6]and swore by him who lives for ever and ever, who created heaven and what is in it, the earth and what is in it, and the sea and what is in it, that there should be no more delay, [7]but that in the days of the trumpet call to be sounded by the seventh angel, the mystery of God,* as he announced to his servants the prophets, should be fulfilled.

[8]Then the voice which I had heard from heaven spoke to me again, saying, "Go, take the scroll which is open in the hand of the angel who is standing on the sea and on the land." [9]So I went to the angel and told him to give me the little scroll; and he said to me, "Take it and eat; it will be bitter to your stomach, but sweet* as honey in your mouth." [10]And I took the little scroll from the hand of the angel and ate it; it was sweet as honey in my mouth, but when I had eaten it my stomach was made bitter. [11]And I was told, "You must again prophesy about many peoples and nations and tongues and kings."

Ezek 2:9

Hos 11:10
Amos 3:8
Ps 29:3–9
Jer 25:30

Dan 12:4, 9
Rev 22:10

Deut 32:40
Dan 12:7

Neh 9:6
Ex 20:11
Acts 4:24

Acts 3:21
Amos 3:7
Jer 7:25
Zech 1:6
Dan 9:10
Rev 11:15; 17:17
1 Cor 15:51–52
Rom 16:25

Ezek 3:3
Ps 119:103

Ezek 3:3

Dan 3:4
Jer 1:10; 25:30
Ezek 25:2

tamquam columnae ignis, [2]et habebat in manu sua libellum apertum. Et posuit pedem suum dexterum supra mare, sinistrum autem super terram, [3]et clamavit voce magna, quemadmodum cum leo rugit. Et cum clamasset, locuta sunt septem tonitrua voces suas. [4]Et cum locuta fuissent septem tonitrua, scripturus eram; et audivi vocem de caelo dicentem: «Signa, quae locuta sunt septem tonitrua, et noli ea scribere». [5]Et angelus, quem vidi stantem supra mare et supra terram, *levavit manum suam dexteram ad caelum* [6]*et iuravit per Viventem in saecula* saeculorum, qui creavit caelum et ea, quae in illo sunt, et terram et ea, quae in ea sunt, et mare et ea, quae in eo sunt: «Tempus amplius non erit, [7]sed in diebus vocis septimi angeli, cum coeperit tuba canere, et consummatum est mysterium Dei, sicut evangelizavit servis suis prophetis». [8]Et vox, quam audivi de caelo, iterum loquentem mecum et dicentem: «Vade, accipe librum apertum de manu angeli stantis supra mare et supra terram». [9]Et abii ad angelum dicens ei, ut daret mihi libellum. Et dicit mihi: «Accipe et devora illum; et faciet amaricare ventrem tuum, sed in ore tuo erit dulcis tamquam mel». [10]Et accepi libellum de manu angeli et devoravi eum, et erat in ore meo tamquam mel dulcis; et cum devorassem eum, amaricatus est venter meus. [11]Et dicunt mihi: «Oportet te iterum prophetare super populis et gentibus et linguis et regibus multis».   [11] [1]Et datus est

Hebrew), and Gabriel (*gabri'el* in Hebrew) means "strength of God" or "man of God" or "God shows his strength". Be that as it may, Gabriel is the name given to the angel charged with explaining the messianic prophecies to Daniel and with communicating divine messages to Zechariah (see Lk 1:19) and to the Blessed Virgin (see Lk 1:26). He performed a function parallel to that of the angel who appears in 8:3–5 and who is usually identified as St Michael. The way he is described highlights his heavenly character and his strength.

Man can never know God's plans in their totality, the plans proclaimed by the seven trumpet calls (v. 4), but God does make them known to John the seer. That revelation is symbolized by the small, open scroll, which is different from the scroll we read about in 5:1–5. This open scroll symbolizes the divine revelation made to the prophets. The scroll is open, that is, its content can be known. But we are not told what is in

it—a silence that the writer uses to highlight his authority as a prophet. He wants people to be in no doubt about the fact that his prophecies apply to all creation—earth and sea (see v. 6). The scroll is like that described in Ezekiel 2:9—3:1, designed to be eaten by the seer (vv. 9–10). The symbol means that God speaks through Holy Scripture, and promises blessing and chastisement. The reader must accept as true everything he reads in the scroll.

With a gesture and a solemn oath the angel assures the seer that the definitive establishment of the Kingdom of God will come about: when that moment comes, time will have run out for this present world (vv. 6–7). However, as to the timing, all that is said is that it will happen when the mystery of God, his plan of salvation, has reached its culmination; when the harvest time has come (cf. Mt 13:24–30), good and evil—wheat and weeds—will be wholly exposed (cf. 2 Thess 2:6ff).

Death and resurrection of the two witnesses

Ezek 40:3
Zech 2:5
Rev 21:15

11 *¹Then I was given a measuring rod like a staff, and I was told: "Rise and measure the temple of God and the altar and those who worship there, ²but do

Is 63:18
Ps 79:1
Dan 8:14
Lk 21:24
Rev 13:5

not measure the court outside the temple; leave that out, for it is given over to the nations, and they will trample over the holy city for forty-two months.* ³And I will grant my two witnesses* power to prophesy for one thousand two hundred and sixty days, clothed in sackcloth."

Zech 4:3, 11–14

⁴These are the two olive trees and the two lampstands which stand before the

2 Kings 1:10
Jer 5:14
Ps 97:3
2 Sam 22:9

Lord of the earth. ⁵And if any one would harm them, fire pours out from their mouth and consumes their foes; if any one would harm them, thus he is doomed to be

1 Kings 17:1
Ex 7:17, 19
Judg 5:17

killed. ⁶They have power to shut the sky, that no rain may fall during the days of their prophesying, and they have power over the waters to turn them into blood, and

Dan 7:3, 7, 21
Rev 13:1, 7

to smite the earth with every plague, as often as they desire. ⁷And when they have finished their testimony, the beast that ascends from the bottomless pit will make

Ezek 11:6; 16:46
Is 1:9-10

war upon them and conquer them and kill them, ⁸and their dead bodies will lie in the

mihi calamus similis virgae dicens: «Surge et metire templum Dei et altare et adorantes in eo. ²Atrium autem, quod est foris templum, eice foras et ne metiaris illud, quoniam datum est gentibus, et civitatem sanctam calcabunt mensibus quadraginta duobus. ³Et dabo duobus testibus meis, et prophetabunt diebus mille ducentis sexaginta amicti saccis». ⁴*Hi sunt duae olivae et duo candelabra in conspectu Domini terrae stantes.* ⁵Et si quis eis vult nocere, ignis exit de ore illorum et devorat inimicos eorum; et si quis voluerit eos laedere, sic oportet eum occidi. ⁶Hi habent potestatem claudendi caelum, ne pluat pluvia diebus prophetiae ipsorum, et potestatem habent super aquas convertendi eas in sanguinem et percutere terram omni plaga, quotienscumque voluerint. ⁷Et cum finierint testimonium suum, bestia, quae ascendit de abysso, faciet adversus illos bellum et vincet eos et occidet illos. ⁸Et corpus eorum in platea civitatis magnae, quae vocatur spiritaliter Sodoma et Aegyptus, ubi et Dominus eorum

11:1–14 These verses contain the prophecy of the seer who has eaten the scroll, a prophecy about the tribulation the Church will undergo as a prelude to the events at the End that follow the seventh and final trumpet blast (11:15ff). The Church is symbolized by the temple and the altar of Jerusalem, which God protects. The rest of the city is that part of mankind that does not belong to the Church and before whom the Church bears witness to the point of martyrdom.

Jerusalem was overrun by the Gentiles in the times of Antiochus IV Epiphanes, who profaned the temple and installed a statue of Zeus (cf. 1 Mac 1:54); much worse destruction was done by the Romans who razed temple and city, leaving not a stone upon a stone (see Mt 24:21; Mk 13:14–23; Lk 21:20–24). Taking his cue from all these events, St John prophesies that the Church will never suffer the same fate, for God protects her from the power of her enemies (see Mt 16:16–18). Christians may suffer persecution in one way or another, but physical or moral violence cannot overpower the Church because God protects her. "The Church, 'like a stranger in a foreign land, presses forward amid the persecutions of the world and the consolations of God' (St Augustine, *The City of God*, 18, 51),

announcing the cross and death of the Lord until he comes (cf. 1 Cor 11:26). But by the power of the risen Lord it is given strength to overcome, in patience and in love, its sorrows and its difficulties, both those that are from within and those that are from without, so that it may reveal in the world, faithfully, however darkly, the mystery of its Lord until, in the consummation, it shall be manifested in full light" (Vatican II, *Lumen gentium*, 8).

The "two witnesses" (v. 3) symbolize the witness borne by the Church. These witnesses are not identified. They are called "olive trees" (v. 4), the same expression as is used in reference to Zerubbabel, a prince of the line of David and Joshua, a high priest (cf. Zech 3:3—4:14); but they are given features associated with Elijah, who brought about a drought (see 1 Kings 17:1–3; 18:1), and with Moses, who turned the Nile to blood (see Ex 7:14–16). The enemies of Elijah and Moses were also devoured by fire from heaven (see 2 Kings 1:10; Num 16:35). However, because the two witnesses testify to Jesus Christ and die martyrs, Tradition identifies them with St Peter and St Paul, who suffered martyrdom in Rome, the city which the book of Revelation later mentions symbolically. Some

street of the great city* which is allegorically[d] called Sodom and Egypt, where their Lord was crucified. [9]For three days and a half men from the peoples and tribes and tongues and nations gaze at their dead bodies and refuse to let them be placed in a tomb, [10]and those who dwell on the earth will rejoice over them and make merry and exchange presents, because these two prophets had been a torment to those who dwell on the earth. [11]But after the three and a half days a breath of life from God entered them, and they stood up on their feet, and great fear fell on those who saw them. [12]Then they heard a loud voice from heaven saying to them, "Come up hither!" And in the sight of their foes they went up to heaven in a cloud. [13]And at that hour there was a great earthquake, and a tenth of the city fell; seven thousand people were killed in the earthquake, and the rest were terrified and gave glory to the God of heaven.

[14]The second woe has passed; behold, the third woe is soon to come.

Ps 79:2

Jn 16:20

Ezek 35:5, 10
Ex 15:16
Ps 105:38

2 Kings 2:11

Ezek 38:19, 20
Mt 27:51–53

Rev 8:13; 9:12

crucifixus est; [9]et vident de populis et tribubus et linguis et gentibus corpus eorum per tres dies et dimidium, et corpora eorum non sinunt poni in monumento. [10]Et inhabitantes terram gaudent super illis et iucundantur et munera mittent invicem, quoniam hi duo prophetae cruciaverunt eos, qui inhabitant super terram. [11]Et post dies tres et dimidium spiritus vitae a Deo intravit in eos, et steterunt super pedes suos; et timor magnus cecidit super eos, qui videbant eos. [12]Et audierunt vocem magnam de caelo dicentem illis: «Ascendite huc»; et ascenderunt in caelum in nube, et viderunt illos inimici eorum. [13]Et in illa hora factus est terraemotus magnus, et decima pars civitatis cecidit, et occisi sunt in terraemotu nomina hominum septem milia, et reliqui in timorem sunt missi et dederunt gloriam Deo caeli. [14]Vae secundum abiit; ecce vae tertium venit cito. [15]Et septimus angelus tuba cecinit, et factae sunt voces magnae in caelo dicentes: «Factum est regnum huius mundi Domini nostri et Christi eius, et regnabit in

early commentators (e.g., Ticonius and St Bede) saw the two witnesses as standing for the Old and New Testaments, but this interpretation has had little following. St Jerome (*Epistulae*, 59) says that the witnesses are Elijah and Enoch—an interpretation followed by St Augustine (*De civitate Dei*, 39) and St Gregory the Great (*Moralia*, 9, 4).

In the last analysis, the tribulation is caused by the powers of evil, that is, the beast, who symbolizes the antichrist, and makes his appearance in the Holy City (vv. 7–8). For a limited period of time (that is, the period of history symbolized by the forty-two months, the one thousand two hundred and sixty days or the three days and a half), there are moments when the forces of evil appear among men, causing many people to waver. Simultaneously, the witnesses of the true God come on the scene, preaching penance (vv. 3–6), and for this they suffer martyrdom, to the great delight of their foes (vv. 7–10). But God steps in on the martyrs' side and sweeps them up to heaven; he decimates their foes, and in their terror those who survive praise God (vv. 11–13). "From the earliest times, then, some Christians have been called upon—and some will always be called

upon—to give the supreme testimony of this love to all men, but especially to persecutors. The Church, then, considers martyrdom as an exceptional gift and as the fullest proof of love. By martyrdom a disciple is transformed into an image of his Master by freely accepting death for the salvation of the world—as well as his conformity to Christ in the shedding of his blood. Though few are presented such an opportunity, nevertheless all must be prepared to confess Christ before men. They must be prepared to make this profession of faith even in the midst of persecutions, which will never be lacking to the Church, in following the way of the cross" (Vatican II, *Lumen gentium*, 42).

The tribulations connected with the blowing of the last three trumpets are thrown into sharp and terrifying relief by the three "woes" announced from heaven (see 8:13), which are a kind of loud lamentation. Now the second woe is described as "passed" (v. 14), and the third is heralded. Thus, after the parenthesis of 10:1—11:13, the thread of the narrative (which follows the successive trumpet blasts) is taken up again, and our attention is drawn to the importance of what is to follow.

d Greek *spiritually*

3. CHRIST'S VICTORY OVER THE POWERS OF EVIL.
THE CHURCH IN GLORY*

The seventh trumpet call

Rev 10:7
Dan 2:44; 7:14, 27;
Zech 14:9
Ps 2:2; 22:28
1 Cor 15:25
Lk 1:33

Rev 4:10; 7:11

Ex 3:14
Rev 1:4; 4:8; 19:6

Ps 2:1, 5; 46:6
Acts 4:25, 28
1 Thess 1:10
Amos 3:7
Rom 1:18
Rev 10:7; 15:1; 19:5;
20:12

Ex 19:16; 25:8–10
2 Mac 2:5–8
Is 29:6
Rev 4:5; 8:5; 15:5
16:18, 21

¹⁵Then the seventh angel blew his trumpet, and there were loud voices in heaven, saying, "The kingdom of the world has become the kingdom of our Lord and of his Christ, and he shall reign for ever and ever." ¹⁶And the twenty-four elders who sit on their thrones before God fell on their faces and worshipped God, ¹⁷saying,

"We give thanks to thee, Lord God Almighty, who art and who wast,
that thou hast taken thy great power and begun to reign.
¹⁸The nations raged, but thy wrath came,
and the time for the dead to be judged,
for rewarding thy servants, the prophets and saints,
and those who fear thy name, both small and great,
and for destroying the destroyers of the earth."

¹⁹Then God's temple in heaven was opened, and the ark of his covenant was seen within his temple; and there were flashes of lightning, voices, peals of thunder, an earthquake, and heavy hail.

saecula saeculorum». ¹⁶Et viginti quattuor seniores, qui in conspectu Dei sedent in thronis suis, ceciderunt super facies suas et adoraverunt Deum ¹⁷dicentes: «Gratias agimus tibi, / Domine, Deus omnipotens, / qui es et qui eras, / quia accepisti virtutem tuam magnam et regnasti. / ¹⁸Et iratae sunt gentes, / et advenit ira tua, et tempus mortuorum iudicari / et reddere mercedem servis tuis prophetis et sanctis / et timentibus nomen tuum, pusillis et magnis, / et exterminare eos, qui exterminant terram». ¹⁹Et apertum est templum Dei in caelo, et visa est arca testamenti eius in templo

*11:15—22:15 The sounding of the last trumpet opens a new section which will describe the triumph of Christ (proclaimed at the very start: 11:15–19). First, the adversaries are introduced—Christ and his followers, on one side, and the dragon and the beast on the other (12:1—14:5). Then the judgment is announced (14:6–20), and the tribulations of the End times, symbolized by the pouring out of the seven bowls (15:1—16:21). The text goes on to describe the beast and to herald his fall after the victory of the Lamb (17:1—19:10), and it tells of the eschatological battles leading to the eventual and total defeat of Satan (19:11—20:10) and the execution of the sentence (20:11–15). This is followed by the vision of the new world in the new Jerusalem descended from heaven (21:1—22:5), and, finally, the commission to the seer to make known what has been revealed to him (22:6–15).

11:15–19 These verses, which proclaim the definitive coming of the Kingdom of Christ, act as an introduction to the whole section. The voices in heaven, symbolizing divine revelation, announce that God's plan has come to fruition— his plan that Christ should reign over the cosmos for ever and ever. The words of Psalm 2 are thereby fulfilled. In effect, the Church "is, on earth, the seed and the beginning of that kingdom. While she slowly grows to maturity, the Church longs for the completed kingdom and, with all her strength, hopes and desires to be united in glory with her king" (Vatican II, *Lumen gentium*, 5). The final victory of Christ is revealed as an already existing reality—and this causes the entire People of God (represented by the twenty-four elders: cf. 4:4) to worship God and give him thanks. The vision shows God's dwelling-place in heaven and that he has been faithful to his Covenant.

The promise in v. 18, "which surpasses all human possibilities, directly concerns our life in this world. For true justice must include everyone; it must explain the immense load of suffering borne by all generations. In fact, without the resurrection of the dead and the Lord's judgment, there is no justice in the full sense of the term. The promise of the resurrection is freely made to meet the desire for true justice dwelling in the human heart" (Congregation for the Doctrine of the Faith, *Libertatis conscientia*, 60).

The woman pursued by the dragon*

12 *[1]And a great portent appeared in heaven, a woman clothed with the sun, with the moon under her feet, and on her head a crown of twelve stars; [2]she was with child and she cried out in her pangs of birth, in anguish for delivery. [3]And another portent appeared in heaven; behold, a great red dragon, with seven heads and ten horns, and seven diadems upon his heads. [4]His tail swept down a third of the stars of heaven, and cast them to the earth. And the dragon stood before the woman who was about to bear a child, that he might devour her child when she brought it forth; [5]she brought forth a male child, one who is to rule all the nations with a rod of iron, but her child was caught up to God and to his throne, [6]and the woman fled into the wilderness, where she has a place prepared by God, in which to be nourished for one thousand two hundred and sixty days.

Rev 15:1
Gen 37:9

Gen 3:15, 16
Is 7:14; 26:17
Mic 4:10
Dan 7:7, 24
Is 27:1

Dan 8:10
Wis 2:24

Is 66:7
Ps 2:9
Rev 2:27

Hos 2:16
1 Kings 17:1–7

eius; et facta sunt fulgura et voces et terraemotus et grando magna. [12] [1]Et signum magnum apparuit in caelo: mulier amicta sole, et luna sub pedibus eius, et super caput eius corona stellarum duodecim; [2]et in utero habens, et clamat parturiens et cruciatur, ut pariat. [3]Et visum est aliud signum in caelo: et ecce draco rufus magnus, habens capita septem et cornua decem, et super capita sua septem diademata; [4]et cauda eius trahit tertiam partem stellarum caeli et misit eas in terram. Et draco stetit ante mulierem, quae erat paritura, ut, cum peperisset, filium eius devoraret. [5]Et peperit filium, masculum, qui *recturus est* omnes *gentes in virga ferrea*; et raptus est filius eius ad Deum et ad thronum eius. [6]Et mulier fugit in desertum, ubi habet locum paratum a Deo, ut ibi pascant illam diebus mille ducentis sexaginta. [7]Et factum est proelium in caelo, Michael et

The thunder and lightning that accompany the appearance of the ark are reminiscent of the way God made his presence felt on Sinai; they show the power of his intervention (cf. 4:5; 8:5), now accompanied by the chastisement of the wicked, symbolized by the earthquake and the hailstones (cf. Ex 9:13–35). Early commentators often interpreted the ark here as a reference to Christ's holy human nature, and St Bede says that just as the manna was kept in the original ark, so Christ's divinity lies hidden in his sacred body (see *Explanatio Apocalypsis*, 11, 19).

*12:1—14:5 God's faithfulness to his Covenant, symbolized by the display of the ark (11:19), will now be seen in the victory of Christ and the Church over the powers of evil. The confrontation between these adversaries takes place in heaven when the dragon or devil attacks the Woman and her Son, the Messiah, and in the battle between Michael and the devil (12:1–12). It then moves down to earth and takes place in human time when the beast and the false prophet attack the Woman's children (12:13—13:18), but Christ will appear, and victory will be his and for his followers (14:1–5).

12:1–6 The fact that the dragon's onslaught takes place in heaven means that the birth of Christ and the devil's powerlessness against him were pre-ordained by God from all eternity.

The Woman is depicted by features that can apply to Israel, the Blessed Virgin and the Church. This passage becomes clearer and more meaningful in the light of Revelation as a whole. For example, St Luke, in his account of the Annunciation, sees Mary as representing the faithful remnant of Israel: the angel salutes her with the greeting given in Zephaniah 3:14–15 to the daughter of Zion (cf. the note on Lk 1:26–38). But the sacred text of the Apocalypse is open to an interpretation of this Woman as a direct reference to the Blessed Virgin who, as mother, shares in the pain of Calvary (see Lk 2:35) and who was earlier prophesied in Isaiah 7:14 as a "sign" (cf. Mt 1:22–23). St Paul in Galatians 4:26 already sees in a woman, Sarah, an allegory of the Church our Mother; and, in non-canonical Jewish writings of the same period as this book, the community is not infrequently personified as a woman. Reading the Woman of the Apocalypse as the Church, St Gregory the Great wrote: "The sun stands for the light of truth, and the moon for the transitoriness of temporal things; the holy Church is clothed like the sun because she is protected by the splendour of supernatural truth, and she has the moon under her feet because she is above all earthly things" (*Moralia*, 34, 12).

Interpreting the Woman as the Blessed Virgin, St Bernard said: "The sun contains permanent colour and splendour; whereas the moon's

Dan 10:31, 21; 12:1
Jude 9
⁷Now war arose in heaven, Michael and his angels fighting against the dragon; and the dragon and his angels fought, ⁸but they were defeated and there was no Lk 10:18
Gen 3:1, 14
Zech 3:1–2
Rev 20:2
Job 1:9, 11; 2:4
Lk 22:31
Rev 11:15 longer any place for them in heaven. ⁹And the great dragon was thrown down, that ancient serpent, who is called the Devil and Satan, the deceiver of the whole world—he was thrown down to the earth, and his angels were thrown down with him. ¹⁰And I heard a loud voice in heaven, saying, "Now the salvation and the power and the kingdom of our God and the authority of his Christ have come, for the accuser of our brethren has been thrown down, who accuses them day and night before our Rev 7:14
Mt 16:25
Rom 8:37
Jn 12:25
1 Jn 2:14 God. ¹¹And they have conquered him by the blood of the Lamb and by the word of their testimony, for they loved not their lives even unto death. ¹²Rejoice then, O heaven and you that dwell therein! But woe to you, O earth and sea, for the devil has come down Is 44:23; 49:13
Deut 32:43
Ps 96:11 to you in great wrath, because he knows that his time is short!"

angeli eius, ut proeliarentur cum dracone. Et draco pugnavit et angeli eius, ⁸et non valuit, neque locus inventus est eorum amplius in caelo. ⁹Et proiectus est draco ille magnus, serpens antiquus, qui vocatur Diabolus et Satanas, qui seducit universum orbem; proiectus est in terram, et angeli eius cum illo proiecti sunt. ¹⁰Et audivi vocem magnam in caelo dicentem: «Nunc facta est salus et virtus et regnum Dei nostri / et potestas Christi eius, / quia proiectus est accusator fratrum nostrorum, / qui accusabat illos ante conspectum Dei nostri die ac nocte. / ¹¹Et ipsi vicerunt illum propter sanguinem Agni / et propter verbum testimonii sui; / et non dilexerunt animam suam / usque ad mortem. / ¹²Propterea laetamini, caeli / et qui habitatis in eis. Vae terrae et mari, quia descendit Diabolus ad vos habens iram magnam, sciens quod modicum tempus habet!». ¹³Et postquam

brightness is unpredictable and changeable, for it never stays the same. It is quite right, then, for Mary to be depicted as clothed with the sun, for she entered the profundity of divine wisdom much further than one can possibly conceive" (*Dominica infra octavam Assumptionis*, 3).

Even while the Church makes her pilgrim way on earth, "the Mother of Jesus in the glory which she possesses in body and soul in heaven is the image and beginning of the Church as it is to be perfected in the world to come. Likewise she shines forth on earth, until the day of the Lord shall come (cf. 2 Pet 3:10), a sign of certain hope and comfort to the pilgrim People of God" (Vatican II, *Lumen gentium*, 68).

12:7–12 The war between the dragon, with his angels, and Michael and his, and the defeat of the former, are depicted here as closely connected with the death and glorification of Christ (see v. 11, 12:5). The reference to Michael and the "ancient" serpent (v. 9) and the outcome of the battle (the devil cast down from heaven) prompt the question of the origin of the devil. Once a most exalted creature, according to some Jewish traditions (see *Latin Life of Adam and Eve*, 12–16), he became the devil because he refused to acknowledge the dignity bestowed on man when God made man in his image and likeness (see Gen 1:26; 2:7). The devil refused to bow before this image of God. Michael, on the

other hand, obeyed. Then the devil and his angels, regarding man as their inferior, rebelled against God; on that account they were cast into hell and down to earth, and ceaselessly tempt man, tempting him to sin so as to see him deprived of the glory that God gave him.

In Daniel 10:13 and 12:1 we are told that it is the archangel Michael who defends the Chosen People on God's behalf. His name means "Who is like God?", and his mission is to guard the rights of God against those who would usurp them, be they human tyrants or Satan himself, who, according to the Letter of St Jude, tried to steal the body of Moses (Jude 9). This explains why Michael appears in the book of Revelation as the one who confronts Satan, the ancient serpent, although victory and punishment are decided by God or Christ. The Church therefore invokes St Michael as her guardian in adversity and as her protection against the snares of the devil (see *Divine Office*, 29 September, office of readings).

The Fathers of the Church interpret these verses of Revelation as a testimony to the battle between Michael and the devil at the dawn of history, a battle that stemmed from the test that angelic spirits had to undergo. In the light of the Apocalypse, they interpret the words uttered by the prophet Isaiah against the king of Babylon as referring to that climactic moment: "How you are fallen from heaven, O Day Star, son of Dawn! How you are cut down to the ground, you who laid

¹³And when the dragon saw that he had been thrown down to the earth, he pursued the woman who had borne the male child. ¹⁴But the woman was given the two wings of the great eagle that she might fly from the serpent into the wilderness, to the place where she is to be nourished for a time, and times, and half a time.* ¹⁵The serpent poured water like a river out of his mouth after the woman, to sweep her away with the flood. ¹⁶But the earth came to the help of the woman, and the earth opened its mouth and swallowed the river which the dragon had poured from his mouth. ¹⁷Then the dragon was angry with the woman,* and went off to make war on the rest of her offspring, on those who keep the commandments of God and bear testimony to Jesus. And he stood^e on the sand of the sea.

Gen 3:15

Ex 19:4
Is 40:31
Dan 7:25; 11:6

Num 16:32
Ex 15:12

1 Jn 5:10

The beasts given authority by the dragon

13 ¹And I saw a beast* rising out of the sea, with ten horns and seven heads, with ten diadems upon its horns and a blasphemous name upon its heads. ²And the

Rev 11:7; 17:3, 9, 12
Dan 7:3, 7, 24

vidit draco quod proiectus est in terram, persecutus est mulierem, quae peperit masculum. ¹⁴Et datae sunt mulieri duae alae aquilae magnae, ut volaret in desertum in locum suum, ubi alitur per tempus et tempora et dimidium temporis a facie serpentis. ¹⁵Et misit serpens ex ore suo post mulierem aquam tamquam flumen, ut eam faceret trahi a flumine. ¹⁶Et adiuvit terra mulierem, et aperuit terra os suum et absorbuit flumen, quod misit draco de ore suo. ¹⁷Et iratus est draco in mulierem et abiit facere proelium cum reliquis de semine eius, qui custodiunt mandata Dei et habent testimonium Iesu. ¹⁸Et stetit super arenam maris.   [13] ¹Et vidi de mari bestiam ascendentem habentem cornua decem et capita septem, et super

the nations low!" (Is 14:12). They also see this passage in the Apocalypse as referring to the war that Satan wages against the Church down the ages, a war that will take its most dreadful form at the end of time: "Heaven is the Church," St Gregory writes, "which in the night of this present life, the while it possesses in itself the countless virtues of the saints, shines like the radiant heavenly stars; but the dragon's tail sweeps the stars down to the earth [...]. The stars which fall from heaven are those who have lost hope in heavenly things and covet, under the devil's guidance, the sphere of earthly glory" (*Moralia*, 32, 12).

12:13–18 Here the dragon's onslaught is presented in terms of the Church in her suffering. The woman who gives birth to a male child is an image of the Mother of the Messiah, the Blessed Virgin Mary, and of the Church who "faithfully fulfilling the Father's will, by receiving the word of God in faith, becomes herself a mother" (Vatican II, *Lumen gentium*, 64). By means of the Church, a person becomes a member of Christ and contributes to the growth of his Body (cf. the notes on Eph 4:1–16). It is in this sense that we can say the Church is the Woman who gives birth to Christ.

The struggle the Church maintains against the powers of evil is described here using imagery taken from the Exodus (a time of great peril for the people of Israel). God brought the Israelites into

the wilderness "on eagles' wings" (Ex 19:4), that is, by ways man could not devise. When the prophet Isaiah announces the liberation from captivity in Babylon, he says that "they shall mount up with wings like eagles" (Is 40:31). Over the course of history, the Church enjoys this same divine protection that enables her to have the intimacy with God symbolized by the wilderness. The period of "a time, and times, and half a time" (v. 14), that is, three and a half years, was regarded, conventionally, as the duration of any persecution (at least from Daniel 7:25 onwards).

The river of water (v. 15) symbolizes the destructive forces of evil unleashed by the devil. Just as in the wilderness of Sinai the earth swallowed up those who rebelled against God (see Num 16:30–34), so will these forces be frustrated in their attack on the Church, for, as our Lord promised, "the powers of death [hell] shall not prevail against it" (Mt 16:18). "This is nothing new. Since Jesus Christ our Lord founded the Church, this Mother of ours has suffered constant persecution. In times past, perhaps, the attacks were delivered openly. Now, in many cases, persecution is disguised" (St Josemaría Escrivá, *In Love with the Church*, 18).

13:1–10 Satan, the serpent of old, launches his attack through the beasts on whom he has bestowed his power (see v. 1; 13:11). Most

e Other ancient authorities read *And I stood*, connecting the sentence with 13.1

Dan 7:4–6
Lk 4:6

Rev 17:8

Rev 12:7
Ex 15:11
Ps 89:6

Dan 7:8, 11, 25
Rev 11:2

Dan 11:11, 38

Rev 11:7
Dan 7:21, 25

Ps 69:28
Dan 12:1
Rev 3:5

Mt 13:9

Jer 15:2; 43:11

Rev 14:12

Mt 7:15
Dan 8:3
Rev 16:13

Rev 13:3

beast that I saw was like a leopard, its feet were like a bear's, and its mouth was like a lion's mouth. And to it the dragon gave his power and his throne and great authority. ³One of its heads seemed to have a mortal wound, but its mortal wound was healed, and the whole earth followed the beast with wonder. ⁴Men worshipped the dragon, for he had given his authority to the beast, and they worshipped the beast, saying, "Who is like the beast, and who can fight against it?"

⁵And the beast was given a mouth uttering haughty and blasphemous words, and it was allowed to exercise authority for forty-two months; ⁶it opened its mouth to utter blasphemies against God, blaspheming his name and his dwelling, that is, those who dwell in heaven. ⁷Also it was allowed to make war on the saints and to conquer them.ᶠ And authority was given it over every tribe and people and tongue and nation, ⁸and all who dwell on earth will worship it, every one whose name has not been written before the foundation of the world in the book of life of the Lamb that was slain. ⁹If any one has an ear, let him hear:

¹⁰ If any one is to be taken captive,
to captivity he goes;
if any one slays with the sword,
with the sword must he be slain.

Here is a call for the endurance and faith of the saints.

The beast rising from out of the earth

¹¹Then I saw another beast* which rose out of the earth; it had two horns like a lamb and it spoke like a dragon. ¹²It exercises all the authority of the first beast in its pres-

cornua eius decem diademata, et super capita eius nomina blasphemiae. ²Et bestia, quam vidi, similis erat pardo, et pedes eius sicut ursi, et os eius sicut os leonis. Et dedit illi draco virtutem suam et thronum suum et potestatem magnam. ³Et unum de capitibus suis quasi occisum in mortem, et plaga mortis eius curata est. Et admirata est universa terra post bestiam, ⁴et adoraverunt draconem, quia dedit potestatem bestiae, et adoraverunt bestiam dicentes: «Quis similis bestiae, et quis potest pugnare cum ea?». ⁵Et datum est ei os loquens magna et blasphemias, et data est illi potestas facere menses quadraginta duos. ⁶Et aperuit os suum in blasphemias ad Deum, blasphemare nomen eius et tabernaculum eius, eos, qui in caelo habitant. ⁷Et datum est illi bellum facere cum sanctis et vincere illos, et data est ei potestas super omnem tribum et populum et linguam et gentem. ⁸Et adorabunt eum omnes, qui inhabitant terram, cuiuscumque non est scriptum nomen in libro vitae Agni, qui occisus est, ab origine mundi. ⁹Si quis habet aurem, audiat: ¹⁰Si quis in captivitatem, / in captivitatem vadit; / si quis in gladio debet occidi, / oportet eum in gladio occidi. Hic est patientia et fides sanctorum. ¹¹Et vidi aliam bestiam ascendentem de terra, et habebat cornua duo similia agni, et loquebatur sicut draco. ¹²Et potestatem prioris bestiae omnem facit in conspectu eius. Et facit terram et inhabitantes in ea adorare bestiam primam, cuius curata est plaga mortis.

Fathers of the Church see the antichrist in the beast of v. 1; thus, St Irenaeus says: "The beast that rises up is the epitome of evil and falsehood, so that the full force of apostasy which it embodies can be cast into the fiery furnace" (*Adversus haereses*, 5, 29). The beasts symbolize those who over the course of history have embodied the powers of evil in one way or another.

The first beast (vv. 1–10) symbolizes political power taken to such an extreme that it supplants God; the second (see 13:11–18), those who defend and propagate that deification of power by giving it an acceptable face.

The beasts are depicted with the features found in the prophets' descriptions of the enemies of Israel, and they can be read as meaning (at the time of the book's writing) the Roman

empire; that empire is also seen as the symbolic tool of a diabolical power that ceaselessly hovers over mankind and will become more virulent as the End approaches: "Idolatry is an extreme form of the disorder produced by sin. The substitution of the worship of creatures for the adoration of the living God deforms relationships between people and leads to various forms of oppression" (Congregation for the Doctrine of the Faith, *Libertatis conscientia*, 39).

13:11–18 Further on (cf. 16:13; 19:20), this second beast is identified with false prophets because his role consists in leading people astray and convincing them to worship the first beast. Because he has real (but evil) power, he is able to work prodigies similar to those

f Other ancient authorities omit this sentence

ence, and makes the earth and its inhabitants worship the first beast, whose mortal wound was healed. [13]It works great signs, even making fire come down from heaven to earth in the sight of men; [14]and by the signs which it is allowed to work in the presence of the beast, it deceives those who dwell on earth, bidding them make an image for the beast which was wounded by the sword and yet lived; [15]and it was allowed to give breath to the image of the beast so that the image of the beast should even speak, and to cause those who would not worship the image of the beast to be slain. [16]Also it causes all, both small and great, both rich and poor, both free and slave, to be marked on the right hand or the forehead, [17]so that no one can buy or sell unless he has the mark, that is, the name of the beast or the number of its name. [18]This calls for wisdom: let him who has understanding reckon the number of the beast, for it is a human number, its number is six hundred and sixty-six.g*

Mt 24:24
2 Thess 2:9–10
Lk 9:54
Mk 13:22
Deut 13:2–4
Rev 19:20

Dan 3:5f

Rev 14:9, 11; 16:2;
19:20; 20:4
Is 44:5

Rev 17:9

The Lamb and his entourage

14 [1]Then I looked, and lo, on Mount Zion stood the Lamb, and with him a hundred and forty-four thousand who had his name and his Father's name written on their foreheads. [2]And I heard a voice from heaven like the sound of many waters and like the sound of loud thunder; the voice I heard was like the sound of harpers playing on their harps, [3]and they sing a new song before the throne and before the four living creatures and before the elders. No one could learn that song

Ezek 9:4
Joel 3:5
Rev 7:4–5
Is 4:5

Ezek 1:24; 43:2
Rev 1:15

Is 42:10
Ps 33:3; 40:3; 98:1;
144:9; 149:1
Rev 5:9

[13]Et facit signa magna, ut etiam ignem faciat de caelo descendere in terram in conspectu hominum. [14]Et seducit habitantes terram propter signa, quae data sunt illi facere in conspectu bestiae, dicens habitantibus in terra, ut faciant imaginem bestiae, quae habet plagam gladii et vixit. [15]Et datum est illi, ut daret spiritum imagini bestiae, ut loquatur imago bestiae et faciat, ut quicumque non adoraverint imaginem bestiae, occidantur. [16]Et facit omnes pusillos et magnos et divites et pauperes et liberos et servos accipere characterem in dextera manu sua aut in frontibus suis, [17]et ne quis possit emere aut vendere, nisi qui habet characterem, nomen bestiae aut numerum nominis eius. [18]Hic sapientia est: qui habet intellectum, computet numerum bestiae; numerus enim hominis est: et numerus eius est sescenti sexaginta sex.   [14] [1]Et vidi: et ecce Agnus stans supra montem Sion, et cum illo centum quadraginta quattuor milia, habentes nomen eius et nomen Patris eius scriptum in frontibus suis. [2]Et audivi vocem de caelo tamquam vocem aquarum multarum et tamquam vocem tonitrui magni; et vox, quam audivi, sicut citharoedorum citharizantium in citharis suis. [3]Et cantant quasi canticum novum ante thronum et ante quattuor animalia et seniores. Et nemo poterat discere canticum nisi illa centum quadraginta quattuor milia, qui empti sunt de terra. [4]Hi sunt qui cum mulieribus non sunt coinquinati, virgines enim sunt. Hi qui sequun-

performed by the prophets (for example, Elijah, who brought fire down from heaven: cf. 1 Kings 18:38) and even appears to vie with the power of the life-giving Spirit by breathing life into the images of the beasts. He symbolizes regimes and ideologies that reject God and put man on a pedestal. Materialism, "understood as a theory which explains reality and accepted as the key principle of personal and social action", works in the same deceptive way, for "though it sometimes also speaks of the 'spirit' and of 'questions of the spirit', as for example in the fields of culture or morality, it does so only insofar as it considers certain facts as derived from matter (*epiphenomena*), since according to this system matter is the one and only form of being. It follows, according to this interpretation, that religion can only be understood as a kind of 'idealistic illusion', to be fought with the most suitable means and

methods according to circumstances of time and place, in order to eliminate it from society and from man's very heart" (John Paul II, *Dominum et Vivificantem*, 56).

14:1–5 Against the powers of this world, who have been led astray by Satan and oppose God and the Church, stands the Lamb, the risen Christ, with his followers, who sing in praise of his glory and triumph. Mount Zion symbolizes the Church, protected by Christ and gathered around him. This assembly includes all who belong to Christ and to the Father and who therefore bear the mark that identifies them as children of God. They are so numerous that it is impossible to count them, but their number is fixed and God has it in his mind: this People of God is represented by a number that is the result of multiplying 12 (tribes) by 12 (apostles) by 1,000 (that is, a huge number): cf. 7:3–8. They

g Other ancient authorities read *six hundred and sixteen*

Jn 10:8
Jas 1:18

Ps 32:2
Zeph 3:13
Col 1:22
Eph 5:27

Rev 8:13

Mt 10:28
Jer 13:16
Ex 20:11

Dan 4:27
Jer 51:7, 8
Is 21:9
Rev 16:19; 18:2–3

Rev 13:15–17, 22

Is 51:17
Ps 75:9
Gen 19:24
Ezek 38:22
Jer 25:15
Rev 16:19; 19:20
Is 34:9–10

except the hundred and forty-four thousand who had been redeemed from the earth. [4]It is these who have not defiled themselves with women, for they are chaste;[h]* it is these who follow the Lamb wherever he goes; these have been redeemed from mankind as first fruits for God and the Lamb, [5]and in their mouth no lie was found, for they are spotless.

Proclamation and symbols of the Judgment*

[6]Then I saw another angel flying in midheaven, with an eternal gospel to proclaim to those who dwell on earth, to every nation and tribe and tongue and people; [7]and he said with a loud voice, "Fear God and give him glory, for the hour of his judgment has come; and worship him who made heaven and earth, the sea and the fountains of water."

[8]Another angel, a second, followed, saying, "Fallen, fallen is Babylon* the great, she who made all nations drink the wine of her impure passion."

[9]And another angel, a third, followed them, saying with a loud voice, "If any one worships the beast and its image, and receives a mark on his forehead or on his hand, [10]he also shall drink the wine of God's wrath, poured unmixed into the cup of his anger, and he shall be tormented with fire and sulphur in the presence of the holy angels and in the presence of the Lamb. [11]And the smoke of their torment goes up

tur Agnum, quocumque abierit. Hi empti sunt ex hominibus primitiae Deo et Agno; [5]et in ore ipsorum non est inventum mendacium: sine macula sunt. [6]Et vidi alterum angelum volantem per medium caelum, habentem evangelium aeternum ut evangelizaret super sedentes in terra et super omnem gentem et tribum et linguam et populum, [7]dicens magna voce: «Timete Deum et date illi gloriam, quia venit hora iudicii eius, et adorate eum, qui fecit caelum et terram et mare et fontes aquarum». [8]Et alius angelus secutus est dicens: «Cecidit, cecidit Babylon illa magna, quae a vino irae fornicationis suae potionavit omnes gentes!». [9]Et alius angelus tertius secutus est illos dicens voce magna: «Si quis adoraverit bestiam et imaginem eius et acceperit characterem in fronte sua aut in manu sua, [10]et hic bibet de vino irae Dei, quod mixtum est mero in calice irae ipsius, et cruciabitur igne et sulphure in conspectu angelorum sanctorum et ante conspectum Agni. [11]Et fumus tormentorum eorum in saecula saeculo-

are not yet in heaven; they are on earth, where they praise God, uniting their voices to the praise offered in the heavenly liturgy.

The author is referring to all the members of the Church, saints in the sense that they are called to holiness; but the symbolism he uses draws attention to the fact that virginity and celibacy for the sake of the Kingdom of heaven is a special expression and clear sign of the Church as the Bride of Christ. "Celibacy, lifelong virginity 'for the sake of the kingdom of heaven', in the life of the disciples and followers of Christ has come to be understood as a particular response to the love of the Divine Spouse, and thus has come to mean an act of betrothal — that is, a betrothing of the self, to respond in a special way to the betrothing love of the Redeemer, a gift of self seen as an act of self-sacrifice, but inspired by love" (Pope John Paul II, *General Audience*, 25 April 1982).

*14:6–20 The appearance of the Lamb here (14:1–5) anticipates his final victory—which

explains how the beast's defeat can already be announced (14:6–13) as can the judgment that is imminent (14:14–20).

14:6–13 Three angels announce the Judgment (vv. 6, 8, 9); Christ, the Son of man, will pronounce it (14:14); and three more angels will carry it out (14:15–20). All are capable of acknowledging and loving their Creator; those who do so will be rewarded on the day of Judgment. This is the "eternal Gospel" (v. 6).

God's blessing (v. 13) proclaims the joy felt by those who stay loyal to Christ unto death. Jewish rabbis taught that "when a man dies, neither silver nor gold, neither precious stones nor pearls, follow him, but rather the law and good works" (*Pirqué Abot*, 6, 9). It is not simply that the righteous are rewarded for their works but that those works (in some way) stay with them, remain theirs; as the Church teaches, "When we have spread on earth the fruits of our nature and our enterprise – human dignity, brotherly communion, and freedom – according

h Greek *virgins*

for ever and ever; and they have no rest, day or night, these worshippers of the beast Rev 19:3; 13:16
and its image, and whoever receives the mark of its name."

¹²Here is a call for the endurance of the saints, those who keep the command-Rev 12:17
ments of God and the faith of Jesus.

¹³And I heard a voice from heaven saying, "Write this: Blessed are the dead who Is 57:2
die in the Lord henceforth." "Blessed indeed," says the Spirit, "that they may rest Heb 4:10
Mt 11:28–29
from their labours, for their deeds follow them!"

The harvest and the vintage

¹⁴Then I looked, and lo, a white cloud, and seated on the cloud one like a son of Dan 7:13; 10:16
Mt 13:39, 41; 24:30
man, with a golden crown on his head, and a sharp sickle in his hand. ¹⁵And another Joel 4:13
angel came out of the temple, calling with a loud voice to him who sat upon the Mt 13:36–43
Mk 4:29
cloud, "Put in your sickle, and reap, for the hour to reap has come, for the harvest of Jn 4:35
Jer 51:53
the earth is fully ripe." ¹⁶So he who sat upon the cloud swung his sickle on the earth, Zech 5:2-3
and the earth was reaped.

¹⁷And another angel came out of the temple in heaven, and he too had a sharp Rev 6:9; 8:3–5
Joel 4:13
Jer 25:30
sickle. ¹⁸Then another angel came out from the altar, the angel who has power over Rev 19:15
fire, and he called with a loud voice to him who had the sharp sickle, "Put in your Lam 1:15
Mt 21:39
sickle, and gather the clusters of the vine of the earth, for its grapes are ripe." ¹⁹So Heb 13:12–13
the angel swung his sickle on the earth and gathered the vintage of the earth, and
threw it into the great wine press of the wrath of God; ²⁰and the wine press was trodden outside the city, and blood flowed from the wine press, as high as a horse's
bridle, for one thousand six hundred stadia.ⁱ

rum ascendit, nec habent requiem die ac nocte, qui adoraverunt bestiam et imaginem eius, et si quis acceperit characterem nominis eius». ¹²Hic
patientia sanctorum est, qui custodiunt mandata Dei et fidem Iesu. ¹³Et audivi vocem de caelo dicentem: «Scribe: Beati mortui, qui in Domino
moriuntur amodo. Etiam, dicit Spiritus, ut requiescant a laboribus suis; opera enim illorum sequuntur illos». ¹⁴Et vidi: et ecce nubem candidam,
et supra nubem sedentem quasi Filium hominis, habentem super caput suum coronam auream et in manu sua falcem acutam. ¹⁵Et alter angelus
exivit de templo clamans voce magna ad sedentem super nubem: «Mitte falcem tuam et mete, quia venit hora, ut metatur, quoniam aruit messis
terrae». ¹⁶Et misit, qui sedebat supra nubem, falcem suam in terram, et messa est terra. ¹⁷Et alius angelus exivit de templo, quod est in caelo,
habens et ipse falcem acutam. ¹⁸Et alius angelus de altari, habens potestatem supra ignem, et clamavit voce magna ad eum, qui habebat falcem
acutam, dicens: «Mitte falcem tuam acutam et vindemia botros vineae terrae, quoniam maturae sunt uvae eius». ¹⁹Et misit angelus falcem suam
in terram et vindemiavit vineam terrae et misit in lacum irae Dei magnum. ²⁰Et calcatus est lacus extra civitatem, et exivit sanguis de lacu usque
ad frenos equorum per stadia mille sescenta. [15] ¹Et vidi aliud signum in caelo magnum et mirabile: angelos septem habentes plagas septem

to the command of the Lord and in his Spirit,
we will find them once again, cleansed this time
from the stain of sin, illuminated and transfigured, when Christ presents to his Father an eternal and universal kingdom 'of truth and life, a
kingdom of holiness and grace, a kingdom of
justice, love and peace'" (Vatican II, *Gaudium
et spes*, 39).

14:14–20 This preview of the Last Judgment is
presented in two scenes—the harvest (vv. 14–16)
and the vintage (vv. 17–20)—in line with Joel's
prophecy about how God will judge nations hostile to Israel: "Put in the sickle, for the harvest is
ripe. Go in, tread, for the winepress is full. The

vats overflow, for their wickedness is great"
(Joel 3:12–13).

In both scenes, an angel has the prominent role
of giving the order (see vv. 15, 18). The fact that
angels emerge from the altar and the temple shows
that the outcome is linked to the prayers of the
saints and martyrs, which stir Christ to action (cf.
8:3–4). So it is that, when Christ is made present
on the altar through the consecration of the bread
and wine, the Church calls for him to come
again—calls for his second coming, the Parousia,
which will make his victory complete: "When we
eat this bread and drink this cup, we proclaim your
death, Lord Jesus, until you come in glory"
(*Roman Missal*, Eucharistic Acclamation).

i About two hundred miles

The hymn of the saved*

Lev 26:21
Rev 16:17

Rev 13:15, 18

Ex 15:1, 11
Ps 92:5; 111:2;
135:14; 145:17
Rev 14:3
Ex 34:10
Deut 32:4

15 ¹Then I saw another portent in heaven, great and wonderful, seven angels with seven plagues, which are the last, for with them the wrath of God is ended.
²And I saw what appeared to be a sea of glass mingled with fire, and those who had conquered the beast and its image and the number of its name, standing beside the sea of glass with harps of God in their hands. ³And they sing the song of Moses,* the servant of God, and the song of the Lamb, saying,

> "Great and wonderful are thy deeds,
> O Lord God the Almighty!
> Just and true are thy ways,
> O King of the ages!ʲ

Jer 10:6, 7; 16:19
Ps 86:9; 98:2
Mic 1:11
Rev 14:17

> ⁴ Who shall not fear and glorify thy name, O Lord?
> For thou alone art holy.
> All nations shall come and worship thee,
> for thy judgments have been revealed."

The seven bowls of plagues

Ex 25:21; 40:24

Dan 10:5–6
Rev 19:8

⁵After this I looked, and the temple of the tent of witness in heaven was opened, ⁶and out of the temple came the seven angels with the seven plagues, robed in pure bright

novissimas, quoniam in illis consummata est ira Dei. ²Et vidi tamquam mare vitreum mixtum igne et eos, qui vicerunt bestiam et imaginem illius et numerum nominis eius, stantes supra mare vitreum, habentes citharas Dei. ³Et cantant canticum Moysis servi Dei et canticum Agni dicentes: «Magna et mirabilia opera tua, / Domine, Deus omnipotens; / iustae et verae viae tuae, / Rex gentium! ⁴Quis non timebit, Domine, / et glorificabit nomen tuum? / Quia solus Sanctus, / quoniam omnes gentes venient / et adorabunt in conspectu tuo, / quoniam iudicia tua manifestata sunt». ⁵Et post haec vidi: et apertum est templum tabernaculi testimonii in caelo, ⁶et exierunt septem angeli habentes septem plagas de templo, vestiti lino mundo candido et praecincti circa pectora zonis aureis. ⁷Et unum ex quattuor animalibus dedit septem angelis septem phialas aureas plenas

***15:1—16:21** With the appearance of the Lamb (14:1–5), the End approaches, which is why God's praise is chanted in heaven (15:1–4) and earth sees the arrival of the tribulations that mark the End; these are symbolized by the outpouring from the seven bowls (15:5—16:21).

15:1–4 The third portent (see the two others in 12:1, 3) heralds the final outcome of the contention between the powers of evil and the Church of Jesus Christ. This is depicted by the symbolic number seven repeated now for a third time, after the seven seals (see 5:1) and the seven trumpets (see 8:2). The sea of glass is somewhat reminiscent of the crossing through the Red Sea during the Exodus (see Wis 19:6–7), and of the molten bronze container used for purifications in the temple of Jerusalem (see the note on 4:1–8). Whatever the interpretation, the Church's prayer of praise precedes God's intervention. "Praise is the form of prayer which recognizes most immediately that God is God. It lauds God for his own sake and gives him glory, quite beyond what he does, but simply because HE IS. It shares in the

blessed happiness of the pure of heart who love God in faith before seeing him in glory" (*Catechism of the Catholic Church*, 2639).

15:5—16:21 The tent (15:5), like the ark in 11:19, symbolizes the presence of God, who takes decisive action through his angels. The seven golden bowls are the devices used to pour out plagues over the world; that is why they are said to be full of the wrath of God—full of the divine justice that will now be made plain for all to see. The golden bowls are also a symbol of the prayers of the saints (which motivate God to intervene: see 5:8) and of their fruits—the victory of good and the punishment of the powers of evil. The content of the bowls is not strictly speaking the plagues but the effects of prayers—action on God's part that serves to console the righteous (the perfume of incense) and punish the devil's followers, those who work iniquity (the wrath of God).

The imagery used to describe the punishment inflicted by God derives from the plagues of Egypt. The first four come from the elements of

j Other ancient authorities read *the nations*

linen, and their breasts girded with golden girdles. ⁷And one of the four living creatures gave the seven angels seven golden bowls full of the wrath of God who lives for ever and ever; ⁸and the temple was filled with smoke from the glory of God and from his power, and no one could enter the temple until the seven plagues of the seven angels were ended.

16 ¹Then I heard a loud voice from the temple telling the seven angels, "Go and pour out on the earth the seven bowls of the wrath of God."

²So the first angel went and poured his bowl on the earth, and foul and evil sores came upon the men who bore the mark of the beast and worshipped its image.

³The second angel poured his bowl into the sea, and it became like the blood of a dead man, and every living thing died that was in the sea.

⁴The third angel poured his bowl into the rivers and the fountains of water, and they became blood. ⁵And I heard the angel of water say,

"Just art thou in these thy judgments,
thou who art and wast, O Holy One.

iracundiae Dei viventis in saecula saeculorum. ⁸Et impletum est templum fumo de gloria Dei et de virtute eius, et nemo poterat introire in templum, donec consummarentur septem plagae septem angelorum. [16] ¹Et audivi vocem magnam de templo dicentem septem angelis: «Ite et effundite septem phialas irae Dei in terram». ²Et abiit primus et effudit phialam suam in terram; et factum est vulnus saevum ac pessimum in homines, qui habebant characterem bestiae, et eos, qui adorabant imaginem eius. ³Et secundus effudit phialam suam in mare; et factus est san-

Rev 14:10; 16:1; 17:1; 21:9
Ex 40:34–35; 1 Kings 8:10; 2 Chron 5:13–14; Is 6:4; Ezek 44:4
Is 66:6; Ezek 14:19; 23:31; Jer 10:25; Zech 3:8
Rev 8:6–12; Ex 9:10–11; Deut 28:35; Rev 13:15–17
Ex 7:19–24; Rev 8:8–9
Rev 8:10; Ps 78:44
Deut 32:4; Ps 119:137; 145:17; Ex 3:14

nature (see 16:2–9 and 8:7–13), the fifth and sixth from forces at work in history (cf. 16:10–16 and 9:1–21). The Hebrew name Armageddon means "the mountain of Megiddo", the place where King Josiah suffered defeat (cf. 2 Kings 23:29–30) and which now symbolizes defeat for the assembled armies of the enemy (cf. 12:11).

In the middle of the prophecy the author breaks into an exhortation to vigilance and faithfulness (v. 15), rather as he did in 3:1–3, 18, for God, although he can use his powers to overcome all obstacles, prefers to win people over by persuasion, as can be seen from what Psalm 2:10 says: "Therefore, O kings, be wise; be warned, O rulers of the earth ..."

Evils are the product of sin, and the wrath of God manifests itself by giving people over to the desires of their idolatrous hearts (cf. Rom 1:18–32). As time advances, the signs are that sin, too, is on the increase; sin is the ultimate cause of the new plagues that threaten the world. "It must be added that on the horizon of contemporary civilization—especially in the form that is most developed in the technical and scientific sense—*the signs and symptoms of death* have become particularly present and frequent. One has only to think of the arms race and of its inherent danger of nuclear self-destruction. Moreover,

everyone has become more and more aware of the grave situation of vast areas of our planet marked by death-dealing poverty and famine. It is a question of problems that are not only economic but also and above all ethical. But on the horizon of our era there are gathering ever darker 'signs of death': a custom has become widely established—in some places it threatens to become almost an institution—of taking the lives of human beings even before they are born, or before they reach the natural point of death" (John Paul II, *Dominum et Vivificantem*, 57).

The symbolic action of pouring the seventh and last bowl out into the air (16:17) means that the entire world is affected. What happens now is final and irreversible: this is proclaimed by the heavenly voice which comes from the temple, from the centre of heaven, and makes plain that God, Lord of all, is answering the prayers of the saints.

The episode of the seventh bowl introduces the final scene of the book, in which are described the last battles, the victory of Christ and the definitive establishment of his royal power. The scene is a triptych: first we see the harlot (*porné*) or "Babylon" (cf. 16:19; 17:5; 18:7, 10, 21), already mentioned (see 14:8), and her trial, condemnation and destruction by fire

Ps 79:3
Mt 23:35, 37
Acts 7:52
Lk 11:49–50
Rev 17–16; 18:24
⁶For men have shed the blood of saints and prophets,
and thou hast given them blood to drink.
It is their due!"

Ps 19:9; 119:137
Rev 19:2
Dan 3:27–28
⁷And I heard the altar cry,
"Yea, Lord God the Almighty,
true and just are thy judgments!"

Rev 8:12
⁸The fourth angel poured his bowl on the sun, and it was allowed to scorch men
Rev 9:20–21
Amos 4:11
with fire; ⁹men were scorched by the fierce heat, and they cursed the name of God who had power over these plagues, and they did not repent and give him glory.

Rev 9:1–2
Ex 10:21
Is 8:21–22
¹⁰The fifth angel poured his bowl on the throne of the beast, and its kingdom was in darkness; men gnawed their tongues in anguish ¹¹and cursed the God of heaven for their pain and sores, and did not repent of their deeds.

Rev 9:14
Gen 15:18
Deut 1:7
Josh 1:4
Is 44:27

Ex 8:3
Rev 12:9; 13:1, 13;
19:19
Ps 105:30
Rev 13:13; 19:19

1 Thess 5:2
Rev 3:3–18
Mt 24:43
Lk 12:39

2 Kings 9:27; 23:29
Zech 12:11
2 Pet 3:10
¹²The sixth angel poured his bowl on the great river Euphrates, and its water was dried up, to prepare the way for the kings from the east. ¹³And I saw, issuing from the mouth of the dragon and from the mouth of the beast and from the mouth of the false prophet, three foul spirits like frogs; ¹⁴for they are demonic spirits, performing signs, who go abroad to the kings of the whole world, to assemble them for battle on the great day* of God the Almighty. ¹⁵("Lo, I am coming like a thief! Blessed is he who is awake, keeping his garments that he may not go naked and be seen exposed!") ¹⁶And they assembled them at the place which is called in Hebrew Armageddon.*

Is 66:6
Rev 21:6

Ex 19:16
Rev 4:5; 8:5
Dan 12:1
Mk 13:19

Rev 6:14
¹⁷The seventh angel poured his bowl into the air, and a loud voice came out of the temple, from the throne, saying, "It is done!" ¹⁸And there were flashes of lightning, voices, peals of thunder, and a great earthquake such as had never been since men were on the earth, so great was that earthquake. ¹⁹The great city was split into three parts, and the cities of the nations fell, and God remembered great Babylon, to make

guis tamquam mortui, et omnis anima vivens mortua est, quae est in mari. ⁴Et tertius effudit phialam suam in flumina et in fontes aquarum; et factus est sanguis. ⁵Et audivi angelum aquarum dicentem: «Iustus es, qui es et qui eras, Sanctus, quia haec iudicasti, ⁶quia sanguinem sanctorum et prophetarum fuderunt, et sanguinem eis dedisti bibere: digni sunt!». ⁷Et audivi altare dicens: «Etiam, Domine, Deus omnipotens, vera et iusta iudicia tua!». ⁸Et quartus effudit phialam suam in solem; et datum est illi aestu afficere homines in igne. ⁹Et aestuaverunt homines aestu magno et blasphemaverunt nomen Dei habentis potestatem super has plagas et non egerunt paenitentiam, ut darent illi gloriam. ¹⁰Et quintus effudit phialam suam super thronum bestiae; et factum est regnum eius tenebrosum, et commanducaverunt linguas suas prae dolore ¹¹et blasphemaverunt Deum caeli prae doloribus suis et vulneribus suis et non egerunt paenitentiam ex operibus suis. ¹²Et sextus effudit phialam suam super flumen illud magnum Euphraten; et exsiccata est aqua eius, ut praepararetur via regibus, qui sunt ab ortu solis. ¹³Et vidi de ore draconis et de ore bestiae et de ore pseudoprophetae spiritus tres immundos velut ranas: ¹⁴sunt enim spiritus daemoniorum facientes signa, qui procedunt ad reges universi orbis congregare illos in proelium diei magni Dei omnipotentis. ¹⁵Ecce venio sicut fur. Beatus, qui vigilat et custodit vestimenta sua, ne nudus ambulet, et videant turpitudinem eius. ¹⁶Et congregavit illos in locum, qui vocatur Hebraice Harmagedon. ¹⁷Et septimus effudit phialam suam in aerem; et exivit vox magna de templo a throno dicens: «Factum est!». ¹⁸Et facta sunt fulgura et voces et tonitrua, et terraemotus factus est magnus, qualis numquam fuit, ex quo homo fuit super terram, talis terraemotus sic magnus. ¹⁹Et facta est civitas magna in tres partes, et civitates gentium ceciderunt. Et Babylon magna venit in memoriam ante Deum dare ei calicem vini indignationis irae eius. ²⁰Et omnis insula fugit, et montes non

(see chaps. 17–18). Then, in the centre of the triptych is the victory of Christ, the Lamb, "Lord of lords and King of kings" (17:14). The third part of the triptych shows the exaltation of the Bride (*nymphé*) and Spouse of the Lamb (see 19:7), the Church or heavenly Jerusalem (see chaps. 21–22).

God's intervention is described in terms of a great storm, as in the theophany on Sinai (see Ex 19:16) and earlier passages in the Apocalypse (see 4:5; 8:5; 11:19). In this instance the storm is

compounded by an earthquake, its unique character underlined by words of the prophet Daniel to the effect that the like has never been seen before (16:18; see Dan 12:1). The storm shows that God's intervention has reached its climax; sea as well as land suffers upheaval. The enormous hailstones recall the seventh plague of Egypt (see Ex 9:24) and show how drastic the punishment is. The great city, Rome, whose ruin has already been decreed (16:19), is singled out for special punishment.

her drain the cup of the fury of his wrath. ²⁰And every island fled away, and no mountains were to be found; ²¹and great hailstones, heavy as a hundred-weight, dropped on men from heaven, till men cursed God for the plague of the hail, so fearful was that plague.

Ex 9:23
Num 11:33

The great harlot and the beast*

17 ¹Then one of the seven angels who had the seven bowls came and said to me, "Come, I will show you the judgment of the great harlot* who is seated upon many waters, ²with whom the kings of the earth have committed fornication, and with the wine of whose fornication* the dwellers on earth have become drunk." ³And he carried me away in the Spirit into a wilderness, and I saw a woman sitting on a scarlet beast which was full of blasphemous names, and it had seven heads and ten horns. ⁴The woman was arrayed in purple and scarlet, and bedecked with gold and jewels and pearls, holding in her hand a golden cup full of abominations and the impurities of her fornication; ⁵and on her forehead was written a name of mystery: "Babylon the great, mother of harlots and of earth's abominations." ⁶And I saw the woman, drunk with the blood of the saints and the blood of the martyrs of Jesus.

When I saw her I marveled greatly. ⁷But the angel said to me, "Why marvel? I will tell you the mystery of the woman, and of the beast with seven heads and ten horns that carries her. ⁸The beast that you saw was, and is not, and is to ascend from the bottomless pit and go to perdition; and the dwellers on earth whose names have not

Rev 21:9
Jer 51:13
Ezek 16

Is 23:27
Nahum 3:4
Jer 25:15; 51:7

Dan 7:7
Is 21:1f
Rev 13:1; 21:10
Ezek 28:13
Jer 51:7

2 Thess 2:7
Rev 14:8

Rev 16:1; 18:24
Mt 23:35, 37
Lk 11:49–50; 13:34
Rev 13:1–5

Rev 13:1–5

sunt inventi. ²¹Et grando magna sicut talentum descendit de caelo in homines; et blasphemaverunt homines Deum propter plagam grandinis, quoniam magna est plaga eius nimis. [17] ¹Et venit unus de septem angelis, qui habebant septem phialas, et locutus est mecum dicens: «Veni, ostendam tibi damnationem meretricis magnae, quae sedet super aquas multas, ²cum qua fornicati sunt reges terrae, et inebriati sunt, qui inhabitant terram, de vino prostitutionis eius». ³Et abstulit me in desertum in spiritu. Et vidi mulierem sedentem super bestiam coccineam, plenam nominibus blasphemiae, habentem capita septem et cornua decem. ⁴Et mulier erat circumdata purpura et coccino et inaurata auro et lapide pretioso et margaritis, habens poculum aureum in manu sua plenum abominationibus et immunditiis fornicationis eius, ⁵et in fronte eius nomen scriptum, mysterium: «Babylon magna, mater fornicationum et abominationum terrae». ⁶Et vidi mulierem ebriam de sanguine sanctorum et de sanguine martyrum Iesu. Et miratus sum, cum vidissem illam admiratione magna. ⁷Et dixit mihi angelus: «Quare miraris? Ego tibi dicam mysterium

These events are the last call to conversion—all in vain, for, instead of turning to God, men in their fury curse his name.

*17:1–19:10 Before moving on to recount its defeat, the text describes the beast in greater detail (17:1–18), and also the lamentation that his fall will occasion on earth (18:1–24) and the rejoicing that will resound in heaven (19:1–10).

17:1–18 The great harlot is the city of Rome, described enigmatically (v. 9) in imagery that the book of Isaiah applied to Tyre and Nineveh (see Is 23:16–17; Nahum 3:4). The "many waters", as explained in v. 15, stand for the peoples over whom the great harlot holds sway. The city is also called Babylon because that city is the symbol of all cities hostile to God (see 17:5; Is 21:9; Jer 51:1–14) and a byword for licentious living. The beast, with its seven heads and horns,

stands for the antichrist as embodied in the emperors who persecute the Church. Of these, the sixth (see v. 10), the one in power when St John was writing, was Domitian (ruled 81–96), and the previous five: Caligula (37–41), Claudius (41–54), Nero (54–68), Vespasian (69–79) and Titus (79–81); the seventh would be Nerva (96–98). The beast is number eight, although the writer identifies it with one of the seven (see v. 11)—probably with Nero, who, according to a contemporary legend, would be reborn and return to power. The ten kings (v. 12) symbolize those whom Rome set up as kings in the nations it conquered, and who were subject to the emperor.

The figure of the "great harlot" (v. 1) and the influence she wields are also interpreted as referring to licentious living. St John of the Cross, for example, explains the passage as follows: "This phrase 'have become drunk' should be noted.

been written in the book of life from the foundation of the world, will marvel to behold the beast, because it was and is not and is to come. ⁹This calls for a mind with wisdom: the seven heads are seven hills on which the woman is seated; ¹⁰they are also seven kings, five of whom have fallen, one is, the other has not yet come, and when he comes he must remain only a little while. ¹¹As for the beast that was and is not, it is an eighth but it belongs to the seven, and it goes to perdition. ¹²And the ten horns that you saw are ten kings who have not yet received royal power, but they are to receive authority as kings for one hour, together with the beast. ¹³These are of one mind and give over their power and authority to the beast; ¹⁴they will make war on the Lamb, and the Lamb will conquer them, for he is Lord of lords and King of kings, and those with him are called and chosen and faithful."

¹⁵And he said to me, "The waters that you saw, where the harlot is seated, are peoples and multitudes and nations and tongues. ¹⁶And the ten horns that you saw, they and the beast will hate the harlot; they will make her desolate and naked, and devour her flesh and burn her up with fire, ¹⁷for God has put it into their hearts to carry out his purpose by being of one mind and giving over their royal power to the beast, until the words of God shall be fulfilled. ¹⁸And the woman that you saw is the great city which has dominion over the kings of the earth."

The fall of Babylon announced

18 ¹After this I saw another angel coming down from heaven, having great authority; and the earth was made bright with his splendour. ²And he called out with a mighty voice,

"Fallen, fallen is Babylon the great!
It has become a dwelling place of demons,
a haunt of every foul spirit,
a haunt of every foul and hateful bird;
³ for all nations have drunk^k the wine of her impure passion,
and the kings of the earth have committed fornication with her,
and the merchants of the earth have grown rich with the wealth of her wantonness."

Marginal references (left column):

Rev 13:18

Rev 17:8; 19:20

Dan 7:20, 24
Rev 13:1

Rev 19:11-21

Deut 10:17
Dan 2:47
Ps 136:3
2 Mac 13:4
1 Tim 6:15

Rev 18:8
Ps 27:2
Mic 3:3
Ezek 16:39–41;
23:29
Ezek 26:19
Jer 34:22

Ps 2:2; 89:27
Is 24:21
Rev 11:8

Ezek 43:2

Rev 14:8
Is 13:21; 21:9; 34:11, 14
Jer 9:10; 50:39; 51:8
Bar 4:35

Is 23:8, 17
Jer 25:15; 51:7
Ezek 27:12, 18, 33
Nahum 3:4
Rev 17:2

mulieris et bestiae, quae portat eam, quae habet capita septem et decem cornua: ⁸bestia, quam vidisti, fuit et non est, et ascensura est de abysso et in interitum ibit. Et mirabuntur inhabitantes terram, quorum non sunt scripta nomina in libro vitae a constitutione mundi, videntes bestiam, quia erat et non est et aderit. ⁹Hic est sensus, qui habet sapientiam. Septem capita septem montes sunt, super quos mulier sedet. Et reges septem sunt: ¹⁰quinque ceciderunt, unus est, alius nondum venit et, cum venerit, oportet illum breve tempus manere. ¹¹Et bestia, quae erat et non est, et is octavus est et de septem est et in interitum vadit. ¹²Et decem cornua, quae vidisti, decem reges sunt, qui regnum nondum acceperunt, sed potestatem tamquam reges una hora accipiunt cum bestia. ¹³Hi unum consilium habent et virtutem et potestatem suam bestiae tradunt. ¹⁴Hi cum Agno pugnabunt; et Agnus vincet illos, quoniam Dominus dominorum est et Rex regum, et qui cum illo sunt vocati et electi et fideles». ¹⁵Et dicit mihi: «Aquae, quas vidisti, ubi meretrix sedet, populi et turbae sunt et gentes et linguae. ¹⁶Et decem cornua, quae vidisti, et bestia, hi odient fornicariam et desolatam facient illam et nudam, et carnes eius manducabunt et ipsam igne concremabunt; ¹⁷Deus enim dedit in corda eorum, ut faciant, quod illi placitum est, et faciant unum consilium et dent regnum suum bestiae, donec consummentur verba Dei. ¹⁸Et mulier, quam vidisti, est civitas magna, quae habet regnum super reges terrae». [18] ¹Post haec vidi alium angelum descendentem de caelo, habentem potestatem magnam, et terra illuminata est a claritate eius. ²Et clamavit in forti voce dicens: «Cecidit, cecidit Babylon magna et facta est habitatio daemoniorum et custodia omnis spiritus immundi et custodia omnis bestiae immundae et odibilis, ³quia de vino irae fornicationis eius biberunt omnes gentes, et reges

For, however little a man may drink of the wine of this rejoicing, it at once takes hold of the heart, as wine does to those who have been corrupted by it. So, if some antidote is not at once taken against this poison, to expel it quickly, the life of the soul is put in jeopardy" (*Ascent of Mount Carmel*, 3, 22).

18:1–24 These verses describe the downfall of Rome and follow the prophetical style of foretelling an event by reporting it as if it had already taken place: the fall of the city is proclaimed (vv. 1–3); the People of God are exhorted to leave behind the city and its depravities, which are the reason for its chastisement

k Other ancient authorities read *fallen by*

[4]Then I heard another voice from heaven saying,

"Come out of her, my people,

lest you take part in her sins,

lest you share in her plagues;

[5]for her sins are heaped high as heaven,

and God has remembered her iniquities.

[6]Render to her as she herself has rendered,

and repay her double for her deeds;

mix a double draught for her in the cup she mixed.

[7]As she glorified herself and played the wanton,

so give her a like measure of torment and mourning.

Since in her heart she says, 'A queen I sit,

I am no widow, mourning I shall never see,'

[8]so shall her plagues come in a single day,

pestilence and mourning and famine,

and she shall be burned with fire;

for mighty is the Lord God who judges her."

[9]And the kings of the earth, who committed fornication and were wanton with her, will weep and wail over her when they see the smoke of her burning; [10]they will stand far off, in fear of her torment, and say,

"Alas! alas! thou great city,

thou mighty city, Babylon!

In one hour has thy judgment come."

[11]*And the merchants of the earth weep and mourn for her, since no one buys their cargo any more, [12]cargo of gold, silver, jewels and pearls, fine linen, purple, silk and scarlet, all kinds of scented wood, all articles of ivory, all articles of costly wood, bronze, iron and marble, [13]cinnamon, spice, incense, myrrh, frankincense, wine, oil, fine flour and wheat, cattle and sheep, horses and chariots, and slaves, that is, human souls.

[14]"The fruit for which thy soul longed has gone from thee,

and all thy dainties and thy splendour are lost to thee,

never to be found again!"

Margin references:
Is 48:20; 52:11
Jer 51:6
2 Cor 6:17
Gen 18:20–21
Jer 51:9

Ps 137:8
Is 40:2
Jer 50:15, 29
2 Thess 1:6

Is 47:8

Jer 50:31, 34
Is 47:9, 14
Rev 17:16

Ezek 26:16–17;
27:30, 33, 35
Is 23:17
Rev 18:17, 19

Ezek 37:36

Ezek 27:12, 13, 22

terrae cum illa fornicati sunt, et mercatores terrae de virtute deliciarum eius divites facti sunt!». [4]Et audivi aliam vocem de caelo dicentem: «Exite de illa, populus meus, ut ne comparticipes sitis peccatorum eius et de plagis eius non accipiatis, [5]quoniam pervenerunt peccata eius usque ad caelum, et recordatus est Deus iniquitatum eius. [6]Reddite illi, sicut et ipsa reddidit, et duplicate duplicia secundum opera eius; in poculo, quo miscuit, miscete illi duplum. [7]Quantum glorificavit se et in deliciis fuit, tantum date illi tormentum et luctum. Quia in corde suo dicit: "Sedeo regina et vidua non sum et luctum non videbo", [8]ideo in una die venient plagae eius, mors et luctus et fames, et igne comburetur, quia fortis est Dominus Deus, qui iudicavit illam». [9]Et flebunt et plangent se super illam reges terrae, qui cum illa fornicati sunt et in deliciis vixerunt, cum viderint fumum incendii eius, [10]longe stantes propter timorem tormentorum eius, dicentes: «Vae, vae, civitas illa magna, Babylon, civitas illa fortis, quoniam una hora venit iudicium tuum!». [11]Et negotiatores terrae flent et lugent super illam, quoniam mercem eorum nemo emit amplius: [12]mercem auri et argenti et lapidis pretiosi et margaritarum, et byssi et purpurae et serici et cocci, et omne lignum thyinum et omnia vasa eboris et omnia vasa de ligno pretiosissimo et aeramento et ferro et marmore, [13]et cinnamomum et amomum et odoramenta et unguenta et tus, et vinum et oleum et similam et triticum, et iumenta et oves et equorum et raedarum, et mancipiorum et animas hominum. [14]Et fructus tui, desiderium animae,

(vv. 4–8); and the lamentation of those in league with the doomed city is described (vv. 9–19). Finally, we are shown the joy of those who have suffered under her yoke and now see God's judgment implemented (v. 20). Among the sins imputed to the city and which cause its ruin is unbridled sexual indulgence (see vv. 7, 12–14).

That sort of lifestyle degrades a society and leads to its destruction, as can be seen from history and in our own time. It was already denounced by Pius XI when he said that "the greatest disease of the modern age, the source of all the evils we condemn, is the lack of reflection, the effusive attachment to and the feverish demand for

Rev 18:3

¹⁵The merchants of these wares, who gained wealth from her, will stand far off, in fear of her torment, weeping and mourning aloud,

Rev 17:4; 18:10, 19

¹⁶ "Alas, alas, for the great city

that was clothed in fine linen, in purple and scarlet,

bedecked with gold, with jewels, and with pearls!

Ezek 27:27–29
Mt 23:29
Lk 13:35

¹⁷ In one hour all this wealth has been laid waste."

And all shipmasters and seafaring men, sailors and all whose trade is on the sea,

Ezek 27:32
Jer 22:8
Is 34:10

stood far off ¹⁸and cried out as they saw the smoke of her burning,

"What city was like the great city?"

Ezek 26:19;
27:30–34
Mt 24:15
Lk 21:20
Rev 18:10, 16

¹⁹And they threw dust on their heads, as they wept and mourned, crying out,

"Alas, alas, for the great city

where all who had ships at sea grew rich by her wealth!

In one hour she has been laid waste.

Rev 19:1–2
Deut 32:43
Is 44:23
Jer 51:58

²⁰ Rejoice over her, O heaven,

O saints and apostles and prophets,

for God has given judgment for you against her!"

Jer 51:63–64
Ezek 26:21
Mt 18:6
Mk 9:43
Lk 17:2
Is 24:8
Ezek 26:13
Jer 25:10

²¹Then a mighty angel took up a stone like a great millstone and threw it into the sea, saying,

"So shall Babylon the great city be thrown down with violence,

and shall be found no more;

²² and the sound of harpers and minstrels, of flute players and trumpeters,

shall be heard in thee no more;

and a craftsman of any craft

shall be found in thee no more;

and the sound of the millstone

shall be heard in thee no more;

Jer 25:10
Is 23:8; 47:9
Nahum 3:4

²³ and the light of a lamp

shall shine in thee no more;

and the voice of bridegroom and bride

shall be heard in thee no more;

for thy merchants were the great men of the earth,

and all nations were deceived by thy sorcery.

discesserunt a te, et omnia pinguia et clara perierunt a te, et amplius illa iam non invenient. ¹⁵Mercatores horum, qui divites facti sunt ab ea, longe stabunt propter timorem tormentorum eius flentes ac lugentes, ¹⁶dicentes: «Vae, vae, civitas illa magna, quae amicta erat byssino et purpura et cocco, et deaurata auro et lapide pretioso et margarita, ¹⁷quoniam una hora desolatae sunt tantae divitiae!». Et omnis gubernator et omnis, qui in locum navigat, et nautae et, quotquot maria operantur, longe steterunt ¹⁸et clamabant, videntes fumum incendii eius, dicentes: «Quae similis civitati huic magnae?». ¹⁹Et miserunt pulverem super capita sua et clamabant, flentes et lugentes, dicentes: «Vae, vae, civitas illa magna, in qua divites facti sunt omnes, qui habent naves in mari, de opibus eius, quoniam una hora desolata est! ²⁰Exsulta super eam, caelum, et sancti et apostoli et prophetae, quoniam iudicavit Deus iudicium vestrum de illa!». ²¹Et sustulit unus angelus fortis lapidem quasi molarem magnum et misit in mare dicens: «Impetu sic mittetur Babylon magna illa civitas et ultra iam non invenietur. ²²Et vox citharoedorum et musicorum et tibia canentium et tuba non audietur in te amplius, et omnis artifex omnis artis non invenietur in te amplius, et vox molae non audietur in te amplius, ²³et lux lucernae non lucebit tibi amplius, et vox sponsi et sponsae non audietur in te amplius, quia mercatores tui erant magnates terrae, quia in veneficiis tuis

external things, the immoderate desire for riches and pleasures, which bit by bit deprives the soul of its most noble ideals, submerges it in the most base and transitory things, and renders it incapable of contemplating the eternal realities" (*Mens nostra*, 5).

In sharp contrast to the lamentation just mentioned (vv. 10, 16, 19) comes a call to rejoice (v.

20) and the response to it, which comes in 19:1–8, where we are told that the elect joyfully intone songs in praise of the Almighty. The throwing of the millstone into the sea (v. 21), an instance of "prophetic action" (cf., e.g., Jer 51:60–64), is used to prophesy the total ruin of Babylon. The millstone also appears in Luke 17:2 (and par.) as a symbol of disgrace and shame.

²⁴ And in her was found the blood of prophets and of saints,
    and of all who have been slain on earth.”

Mt 23:35–37
Jer 51–49
Lk 11:49ff
Rev 16:6

Songs of victory in heaven

19 ¹After this I heard what seemed to be the mighty voice of a great multitude in heaven, crying,

Rev 7:10
Dan 10:6
Tob 13:18

    “Hallelujah! Salvation and glory and power belong to our God,
    ²for his judgments are true and just;

Ps 19:9
Rev 16:7
Deut 32–43
2 Kings 9:7

    he has judged the great harlot who corrupted the earth with her fornication,
    and he has avenged on her the blood of his servants.”

³Once more they cried,

Is 34:10
Rev 14:11

    “Hallelujah! The smoke from her goes up for ever and ever.”

⁴And the twenty-four elders and the four living creatures fell down and worshipped God who is seated on the throne, saying, “Amen. Hallelujah!” ⁵And from the throne came a voice crying,

Rev 4:6, 10

Ps 22:23; 115:13;
134:1; 135:1, 20

    “Praise our God, all you his servants,
    you who fear him, small and great.”

⁶Then I heard what seemed to be the voice of a great multitude, like the sound of many waters and like the sound of mighty thunderpeals, crying,

Ezek 1:24; 43:2
Rev 11:17
Ps 93:1; 97:1; 99:1
Zech 14:9

    “Hallelujah! For the Lord our God the Almighty reigns.
    ⁷Let us rejoice and exult and give him the glory,

Ps 118:24
1 Chron 16:28
Rev 19:9; 21:2, 9

    for the marriage of the Lamb* has come,
    and his Bride has made herself ready;
    ⁸it was granted her to be clothed with fine linen, bright and pure”—

Is 61:10
Ps 45:13–14

    for the fine linen is the righteous deeds of the saints.

⁹And the angel said[l] to me, “Write this: Blessed are those who are invited to the marriage supper of the Lamb.” And he said to me, “These are true words of God.”

Rev 1:3
Mt 22:1–14
Lk 14:15–16

¹⁰Then I fell down at his feet to worship him, but he said to me, “You must not do that! I am a fellow servant with you and your brethren who hold the testimony of Jesus. Worship God.” For the testimony of Jesus is the spirit of prophecy.

Acts 10:25–26
Jn 1:19; 5:33, 39, 45
Rev 22:8–9

The first battle—the beast is destroyed*

¹¹Then I saw heaven opened, and behold, a white horse! He who sat upon it is called Faithful and True, and in righteousness he judges and makes war. ¹²His eyes

Jn 1:51
Acts 10:11
Ezek 1:1
Is 11:4–5
2 Mac 3:25; 11:8
Rev 1:5; 3:7, 14; 4:1

erraverunt omnes gentes, ²⁴et in ea sanguis prophetarum et sanctorum inventus est et omnium, qui interfecti sunt in terra!». [19] ¹Post haec audivi quasi vocem magnam turbae multae in caelo dicentium: «Alleluia! / Salus et gloria et virtus Deo nostro, / ²quia vera et iusta iudicia eius; / quia iudicavit de meretrice magna, quae corrupit terram in prostitutione sua, et vindicavit sanguinem servorum suorum de manibus eius!». ³Et iterum dixerunt: «Alleluia! Et fumus eius ascendit in saecula saeculorum!». ⁴Et ceciderunt seniores viginti quattuor et quattuor animalia et adoraverunt Deum sedentem super thronum dicentes: «Amen. Alleluia». ⁵Et vox de throno exivit dicens: «Laudem dicite Deo nostro, omnes servi eius / et qui timetis eum, pusilli et magni!». ⁶Et audivi quasi vocem turbae magnae et sicut vocem aquarum multarum et sicut vocem tonitruum magnorum dicentium: «Alleluia, / quoniam regnavit Dominus, Deus noster omnipotens. / ⁷Gaudeamus et exsultemus et demus gloriam ei, / quia venerunt nuptiae Agni, / et uxor eius praeparavit se. ⁸Et datum est illi, ut cooperiat se byssino splendenti mundo: byssinum enim iustificationes sunt sanc-

19:1–10 The righteous rejoice to see their enemy's downfall; their song celebrates not only the destruction and defeat of evil, but also the definitive installation of the Kingdom of God, a kingdom of love which is depicted as a wedding feast celebrating the imminent nuptials of the Lamb. This marriage, viewed from the vantage point of the end of time, depicts the Church in all ages, as well as the goal and daily mission of all Christians—to prepare their wedding garment (through good works, praise of God, and a holy life), so as to gain access to the wedding feast.

*19:11—20:15 The prophetical account of the fall of Rome, given in the form of a proclamation, is followed by a description of Christ as he

l Greek *he said*

Rev 1:14; 2:18;
19:16
Is 49:2; 63:1f
Jn 1:1

Rev 17:14

Is 49:2; 63:3
Ps 2:9
Rev 1:16; 2:27;
14:19
Deut 10:7
1 Tim 6:15
Rev 17:14

Ezek 39:17–20

Ps 2:2
Rev 17:12–14; 16:14,
16

Dan 7:11, 26
Rev 13:1, 13–17;
20:10, 14–15
Is 30:33
Ps 55:16

Ezek 39:17, 20
Is 11:4

are like a flame of fire, and on his head are many diadems; and he has a name inscribed which no one knows but himself. [13]He is clad in a robe dipped in[m] blood, and the name by which he is called is The Word of God. [14]And the armies of heaven, arrayed in fine linen, white and pure, followed him on white horses. [15]From his mouth issues a sharp sword with which to smite the nations, and he will rule them with a rod of iron; he will tread the wine press of the fury of the wrath of God the Almighty. [16]On his robe and on his thigh he has a name inscribed, King of kings and Lord of lords.

[17]Then I saw an angel standing in the sun, and with a loud voice he called to all the birds that fly in midheaven, "Come, gather for the great supper of God, [18]to eat the flesh of kings, the flesh of captains, the flesh of mighty men, the flesh of horses and their riders, and the flesh of all men, both free and slave, both small and great." [19]And I saw the beast and the kings of the earth with their armies gathered to make war against him who sits upon the horse and against his army. [20]And the beast was captured, and with it the false prophet who in its presence had worked the signs by which he deceived those who had received the mark of the beast and those who worshipped its image. These two were thrown alive into the lake of fire that burns with sulphur. [21]And the rest were slain by the sword of him who sits upon the horse, the sword that issues from his mouth; and all the birds were gorged with their flesh.

torum». [9]Et dicit mihi: «Scribe: Beati, qui ad cenam nuptiarum Agni vocati sunt!». Et dicit mihi: «Haec verba Dei vera sunt». [10]Et cecidi ante pedes eius, ut adorarem eum. Et dicit mihi: «Vide, ne feceris! Conservus tuus sum et fratrum tuorum habentium testimonium Iesu. Deum adora. Testimonium enim Iesu est spiritus prophetiae». [11]Et vidi caelum apertum: et ecce equus albus; et, qui sedebat super eum, vocabatur Fidelis et Verax, et in iustitia iudicat et pugnat. [12]Oculi autem eius sicut flamma ignis, et in capite eius diademata multa, habens nomen scriptum, quod nemo novit nisi ipse, [13]et vestitus veste aspersa sanguine, et vocatur nomen eius Verbum Dei. [14]Et exercitus, qui sunt in caelo, sequebantur eum in equis albis, vestiti byssino albo mundo. [15]Et de ore ipsius procedit gladius acutus, ut in ipso percutiat gentes, et ipse *reget eos in virga ferrea*; et ipse calcat torcular vini furoris irae Dei omnipotentis. [16]Et habet super vestimentum et super femur suum nomen scriptum: Rex regum et Dominus dominorum. [17]Et vidi unum angelum stantem in sole, et clamavit voce magna dicens omnibus avibus, quae volabant per medium caeli: «Venite, congregamini ad cenam magnam Dei, [18]ut manducetis carnes regum et carnes tribunorum et carnes fortium et carnes equorum et sedentium in ipsis et carnes omnium liberorum ac servorum et pusillorum ac magnorum». [19]Et vidi bestiam et reges terrae et exercitus eorum congregatos ad faciendum proelium cum illo, qui sedebat super equum, et cum exercitu eius. [20]Et apprehensa est bestia et cum illa pseudopropheta, qui fecit signa coram ipsa, quibus seduxit eos, qui acceperunt characterem bestiae et qui adorant imaginem eius; vivi missi sunt hi duo in stagnum ignis ardentis sulphure. [21]Et ceteri occisi sunt in gladio sedentis super equum, qui procedit de ore ipsius, et omnes aves saturatae sunt carnibus eorum.   [20] [1]Et vidi angelum descendentem de caelo habentem clavem abyssi et catenam magnam in manu sua. [2]Et apprehendit draconem, serpentem

appears in all his power and wins victory in two battles; in the first he defeats the beasts and the earthly powers who are their allies (19:11–21) and undoes the power of the devil (20:1–6); in the second, the devil is cast into hell for ever and ever (20:7–10). After this happens, the Last Judgment will take place (20:11–15).

19:11–21 The vision of the glorious and conquering Christ (vv. 11–16) is similar to the way he is portrayed at the start of the book: attention is focused on parts of his body (although not in any systematic way; cf. 1:5, 12–16), so that we can see he is the same person as the rider on the white horse mentioned when the first seal was broken (see 6:2). "The whole of man's history has been the story of dour combat with the powers of

evil, stretching, so our Lord tells us, from the very dawn of history until the last day. Finding himself in the midst of the battlefield, man has to struggle to do what is right, and it is at great cost to himself, and aided by God's grace, that he succeeds in achieving his own inner integrity" (Vatican II, *Gaudium et spes*, 37).

The fact that the beast and the false prophet are thrown alive into the fire (v. 20) emphasizes how horrific their punishment is. Eternal frustration and emptiness accompany their being cut off from God. As St John Chrysostom puts it, "The pain of hell is indeed unbearable. Even if one were to imagine ten thousand hells, this suffering would be nothing compared to the pain caused by the loss of heaven and by being rejected by Christ" (*In Matthaeum*, 28).

m Other ancient authorities read *sprinkled with*

The thousand-year reign of Christ and his people

20 ¹Then I saw an angel coming down from heaven, holding in his hand the key of the bottomless pit and a great chain. ²And he seized the dragon, that ancient serpent, who is the Devil and Satan, and bound him for a thousand years, ³and threw him into the pit, and shut it and sealed it over him, that he should deceive the nations no more, till the thousand years were ended. *After that he must be loosed for a little while.

⁴Then I saw thrones, and seated on them were those to whom judgment was committed. Also I saw the souls of those who had been beheaded for their testimony to Jesus and for the word of God, and who had not worshipped the beast or its image and had not received its mark on their foreheads or their hands. They came to life, and reigned with Christ a thousand years. ⁵The rest of the dead did not come to life until the thousand years were ended. This is the first resurrection. ⁶Blessed and holy is he who shares in the first resurrection! Over such the second death has no power, but they shall be priests of God and of Christ, and they shall reign with him a thousand years.

The second battle—Satan is overthrown

⁷And when the thousand years are ended, Satan will be loosed from his prison ⁸and will come out to deceive the nations which are at the four corners of the earth, that

Marginal references:
Rev 9:1
Jude 6
Gen 3:1
Ps 90:4
2 Pet 3:8
2 Thess 2:8–9
Is 24:21–22
Dan 7:9, 22, 27
Mt 19:28
Lk 22:30
1 Cor 6:9
Rev 5:10; 13:16
Ezek 37:10
1 Cor 15:21–27
Rev 1:3, 6; 2:11;
5:10; 21:8
Rev 16:14, 16
Ezek 7:2; 38:2, 9, 15

antiquum, qui est Diabolus et Satanas, et ligavit eum per annos mille ³et misit eum in abyssum et clausit et signavit super illum, ut non seducat amplius gentes, donec consummentur mille anni; post haec oportet illum solvi modico tempore. ⁴Et vidi thronos, et sederunt super eos, et iudicium datum est illis; et animas decollatorum propter testimonium Iesu et propter verbum Dei, et qui non adoraverunt bestiam neque imaginem eius nec acceperunt characterem in frontibus et in manibus suis; et vixerunt et regnaverunt cum Christo mille annis. ⁵Ceteri mortuorum non vixerunt, donec consummentur mille anni. Haec est resurrectio prima. ⁶Beatus et sanctus, qui habet partem in resurrectione prima! In his secunda

20:1–6 The harlot (Rome) has been defeated (18:1–24), and the beast and his false prophet likewise—the forces of persecution (19:1–21); there remains the dragon (Satan), of whom we were told in chapter 12; his defeat marks the final outcome of the war that began there. The battle between Satan and God is described in two scenes: the first tells how Satan is brought under control for a time only (vv. 1–3); the second covers his last assault on the Church, and what happens to him in the end (20:7–10). Between these two scenes comes the reign of Christ and his followers, which lasts a thousand years (vv. 4–6). In ancient times, some Christian writers, interpreting this passage literally, thought that this reign of Christ would take place on earth prior to the end of the world. Others, notably St Augustine, interpreted the thousand years as referring to the period between the Incarnation of the Son of God and his second coming at the end of time—a period during which the activity of the devil is to some degree restricted, as if he were on a leash; so, although "he desires to do us harm, he cannot do so because his power is subject to another's power [...]. He who gives him the ability to tempt, also gives his mercy to the one who is tempted. He has put limits on the devil's ability to tempt people" (*De Sermone Domini in monte*, 2, 9, 34). "The kingdom will be fulfilled, then, not by a historic triumph of the Church through a progressive ascendancy, but only by God's victory over the final unleashing of evil, which will cause his Bride to come down from heaven. God's triumph over the revolt of evil will take the form of the Last Judgment after the final cosmic upheaval of this passing world" (*Catechism of the Catholic Church*, 677).

The first resurrection (v. 6) should be understood in a spiritual sense, meaning Baptism, which regenerates man and gives him new life by freeing him from sin and making him a son of God. The second resurrection is the one that will take place at the end of time, when the body is brought back to life and the human being, body and soul, enters into everlasting joy. The "rest of the dead" (v. 5) are those who have not received Baptism; they, too, will be raised up on the last day, to be judged according to their deeds.

20:7–10 God will allow the devil to be very active during the last days, "when the thousand

is, Gog and Magog, to gather them for battle; their number is like the sand of the

2 Kings 1:10
Gen 19:24
Lk 21:24
Ezek 38:22; 39:6
sea. ⁹And they marched up over the broad earth and surrounded the camp of the
saints and the beloved city; but fire came down from heaven[n] and consumed them,

Rev 12:9; 14:10;
16:13; 19:20
¹⁰and the devil who had deceived them was thrown into the lake of fire and sulphur
where the beast and the false prophet were, and they will be tormented day and night
for ever and ever.

The Last Judgment of the living and the dead

Dan 7:9
Mt 25:31–46
¹¹Then I saw a great white throne and him who sat upon it; from his presence earth

2 Pet 3:7, 10, 12
Rev 5:7; 6:14; 16:20;
21:1
and sky fled away, and no place was found for them. ¹²And I saw the dead, great and
small, standing before the throne, and books were opened. Also another book was
opened, which is the book of life. And the dead were judged by what was written in

Jn 5:28–29
the books, by what they had done. ¹³And the sea gave up the dead in it, Death and

1 Cor 15:26, 54
Is 25:8
Rev 14:10; 2:11
Hades gave up the dead in them, and all were judged by what they had done. ¹⁴Then
Death and Hades were thrown into the lake of fire. This is the second death, the lake

Ps 69:28
of fire; ¹⁵and if any one's name was not found written in the book of life, he was
thrown into the lake of fire.

mors non habet potestatem, sed erunt sacerdotes Dei et Christi et regnabunt cum illo mille annis. ⁷Et cum consummati fuerint mille anni, solvetur Satanas de carcere suo ⁸et exibit seducere gentes, quae sunt in quattuor angulis terrae, Gog et Magog, congregare eos in proelium, quorum numerus est sicut arena maris. ⁹Et ascenderunt super latitudinem terrae et circumierunt castra sanctorum et civitatem dilectam. Et descendit ignis de caelo et devoravit eos; ¹⁰et Diabolus, qui seducebat eos, missus est in stagnum ignis et sulphuris, ubi et bestia et pseudopropheta, et cruciabuntur die ac nocte in saecula saeculorum. ¹¹Et vidi thronum magnum candidum et sedentem super eum, a cuius aspectu fugit terra et caelum, et locus non est inventus eis. ¹²Et vidi mortuos, magnos et pusillos, stantes in conspectu throni; et libri aperti sunt. Et alius liber apertus est, qui est vitae; et iudicati sunt mortui ex his, quae scripta erant in libris secundum opera ipsorum. ¹³Et dedit mare mortuos, qui in eo erant, et mors et infernus dederunt mortuos, qui in ipsis erant; et iudicati sunt singuli secundum opera ipsorum. ¹⁴Et mors et infernus missi sunt in stagnum ignis. Haec mors secunda est, stagnum ignis. ¹⁵Et si quis non est inventus in libro vitae scriptus, missus est in stagnum ignis.   [21] ¹Et vidi caelum novum et

years are ended" (v. 7). Our Lord also said that those times would be marked by tribulation, the like of which had never been seen before (see Mt 24:21–22); and St Paul refers to the "man of lawlessness" who will take his seat in the temple and proclaim himself God (see 2 Thess 2:3–8). Gog and Magog (v. 8) symbolize forces that will create vast destruction (see Ezek 38—39). The casting of the devil into the fiery lake is his final defeat; never again will evil afflict the world. In that fire, along with the beast and the false prophet, the ungodly will suffer for ever—a further instance of Scripture's teaching of the everlasting duration of this punishment (see Mt 18:8; 25:41, 46; Mk 9:43, 47–48). "The teaching of the Church affirms the existence of hell and its eternity. Immediately after death the souls of those who die in a state of mortal sin descend into hell, where they suffer the punishments of hell, 'eternal fire'. The chief punishment of hell is eternal separation from God, in whom alone man can possess the life and happiness for which he was created and for which he longs" (*Catechism of the Catholic Church*, 1035).

20:11–15 After the defeat of evil and the disappearance of its source, the devil, comes the resurrection and the General Judgment. The Judgment is described in the metaphor of two books—one for recording the actions of men (cf. Dan 7:10); the other, a special book, for the names of those predestined to eternal life (cf. Dan 12:1). In this way the Apocalypse teaches us two truths (the link between which is shrouded in mystery)—the fact that we are free, and that there is a grace of predestination. The "second death" (v. 14) is eternal damnation.

The Last Judgment is a truth of faith of which Paul VI wrote: "Christ ascended into heaven, and will come again, in glory, to judge the living and the dead, each according to his merits: those who responded to the Love and Piety of God will enter eternal life; those who rejected him to the very end, into unquenchable fire [...]. We believe in eternal life. We believe that souls who die in the grace of Christ, those who must be purified in Purgatory, as well as those carried directly by Jesus to heaven like the Good Thief, make up the People of God beyond

n Other ancient authorities read *from God, out of heaven*, or *out of heaven from God*

A new world comes into being. The new Jerusalem

21 ¹Then I saw a new heaven and a new earth; for the first heaven and the first earth had passed away, and the sea was no more.* ²And I saw the holy city, new Jerusalem, coming down out of heaven from God, prepared as a bride adorned for her husband; ³and I heard a loud voice from the throne saying, "Behold, the dwelling of God is with men. He will dwell with them, and they shall be his people,^o and God himself will be with them;^p ⁴he will wipe away every tear from their eyes, and death shall be no more, neither shall there be mourning nor crying nor pain any more, for the former things have passed away."

⁵And he who sat upon the throne said, "Behold, I make all things new." Also he said, "Write this, for these words are trustworthy and true." ⁶And he said to me, "It is done! I am the Alpha and the Omega, the beginning and the end. To the thirsty I will give from the fountain of the water of life without payment. ⁷He who conquers shall have this heritage, and I will be his God and he shall be my son. ⁸But as for the cowardly, the faithless, the polluted, as for murderers, fornicators, sorcerers, idolaters, and all liars, their lot shall be in the lake that burns with fire and sulphur, which is the second death."*

⁹Then came one of the seven angels who had the seven bowls full of the seven last plagues, and spoke to me, saying, "Come, I will show you the Bride, the wife of the

Is 65:17; 66:22
2 Pet 3:13
Rom 8:19–23
Rev 20:11

Is 52:1; 61:10
Gal 4:26
Rev 3:12

Is 7:14; 8:8
Ezek 37:27
Ps 95:7
2 Chron 6:18

Jn 1:14
Zech 2:14–15; 8:8

Rev 7:17
Is 25:8; 35:10;
43:18; 51:11;
65:17, 19

2 Cor 5:17
Is 43:19
Gal 6:15
Rev 5:1, 7; 16:17

Is 55:1
Zech 14:8
Jer 2:3
Rev 1:8; 22:17
Jn 7:37

2 Sam 7:14
Rev 2:7
Rom 1:29
Eph 5:5–6
Tit 1:16
Rev 20:6; 22:15

Rev 15:1, 6, 7; 17:1;
19:7

terram novam; primum enim caelum et prima terra abierunt, et mare iam non est. ²Et civitatem sanctam Ierusalem novam vidi descendentem de caelo a Deo, paratam sicut sponsam ornatam viro suo. ³Et audivi vocem magnam de throno dicentem: «*Ecce tabernaculum* Dei cum hominibus! *Et habitabit cum eis, et ipsi populi eius erunt, et* ipse Deus cum eis erit eorum Deus, ⁴*et absterget omnem lacrimam* ab oculis eorum, et mors ultra non erit, neque luctus neque clamor neque dolor erit ultra, quia prima abierunt». ⁵Et dixit, qui sedebat super throno: «Ecce nova facio omnia». Et dicit: «Scribe: Haec verba fidelia sunt et vera». ⁶Et dixit mihi: «Facta sunt! Ego sum Alpha et Omega, principium et finis. Ego sitienti dabo de fonte aquae vivae gratis. ⁷Qui vicerit, hereditabit haec, et *ero illi Deus, et ille erit mihi filius*. ⁸Timidis autem et incredulis et exsecratis et homicidis et fornicatoribus et veneficis et idololatris et omnibus mendacibus, pars illorum erit in stagno ardenti igne et sulphure, quod est mors

death, who will triumph fully on the day of the Resurrection when their souls will be united once more with their bodies" (*Creed of the People of God*).

21:1—22:5 Now that the forces of evil, including death, have been vanquished, the author turns his attention to contemplate the establishment of the Kingdom of God in all its fullness. Thus, the climax of the book shows a new world, where a renewed mankind will dwell—the new Jerusalem (21:1–4; cf. Is 65:17–25); its arrival is vouched for by the Word of God, eternal and almighty (21:5–8). Mankind—the new People of God—is portrayed as the Bride of the Lamb; a detailed description shows a city of wondrous beauty in which God the Father and Christ reign (21:9—22:5). The vision is similar to that of the prophet Ezekiel when he saw Jerusalem's future temple (see Ezek 40:1—42:20). But here the city comes down from heaven—meaning that the complete establishment of the messianic Kingdom, an event so long desired, is brought about

by the power of God and in fulfilment of his will.

In 21:5–8, for the first and only time in this book, we hear God the Father speak, confirming with his absolute authority what has been said. He says that he is making (present tense) all things new. Thus, even though the new world will emerge in its complete form only on the last day, the whole process of its renewal has already begun; it began with Jesus Christ, who died and has risen. "The kingdom of life has begun," St Gregory of Nyssa teaches, "and the empire of death has been undone. Another generation, another life, another way of loving has made its appearance: our very nature is transformed. What type of generation am I referring to? A generation which comes not from blood or carnal love or human love, but from God. Are you wondering how that can be? I shall explain it in a few words. This new creature is begotten by faith; the regeneration of Baptism brings it to birth; the Church, its nurse, weans it by her teaching and institutions and nourishes it with

o Other ancient authorities read *peoples* p Other ancient authorities add *and be their God*

Mt 4:8
Ezek 40:2
Rev 17:3; 21:2

Rev 21:23
Ezek 43:2–4
Is 58:8
Ezek 48:31–35

Ex 28:21; 39:14
Rev 7:1–8

Heb 11:10
Ezek 40:3, 5
Rev 11:1

Ezek 43:16;
48:16f
Zech 2:6

Deut 3:11

Is 54:11–12
Ex 28:17–20
Ezek 28:13
Tob 13:17

Lamb." ¹⁰And in the Spirit he carried me away to a great, high mountain, and showed me the holy city Jerusalem coming down out of heaven from God, ¹¹having the glory of God, its radiance like a most rare jewel, like a jasper, clear as crystal. ¹²It had a great, high wall, with twelve gates, and at the gates twelve angels, and on the gates the names of the twelve tribes of the sons of Israel were inscribed; ¹³on the east three gates, on the north three gates, on the south three gates, and on the west three gates. ¹⁴And the wall of the city had twelve foundations, and on them the twelve names of the twelve apostles of the Lamb.

¹⁵And he who talked to me had a measuring rod of gold to measure the city and its gates and walls. ¹⁶The city lies foursquare, its length the same as its breadth; and he measured the city with his rod, twelve thousand stadia;�q its length and breadth and height are equal. ¹⁷He also measured its wall, a hundred and forty-four cubits by a man's measure, that is, an angel's. ¹⁸The wall was built of jasper, while the city was pure gold, clear as glass. ¹⁹The foundations of the wall of the city were adorned with every jewel; the first was jasper, the second sapphire, the third agate, the fourth emerald, ²⁰the fifth onyx, the sixth carnelian, the seventh chrysolite, the eighth beryl, the ninth topaz, the tenth chrysoprase, the eleventh jacinth, the twelfth amethyst. ²¹And the twelve gates were twelve pearls, each of the gates made of a single pearl, and the street of the city was pure gold, transparent as glass.

secunda». ⁹Et venit unus de septem angelis habentibus septem phialas plenas septem plagis novissimis et locutus est mecum dicens: «Veni, ostendam tibi sponsam uxorem Agni». ¹⁰Et sustulit me in spiritu super montem magnum et altum et ostendit mihi civitatem sanctam Ierusalem descendentem de caelo a Deo, ¹¹habentem claritatem Dei; lumen eius simile lapidi pretiosissimo, tamquam lapidi iaspidi, in modum crystalli; ¹²et habebat murum magnum et altum et habebat *portas* duodecim et super portas angelos duodecim et *nomina* inscripta, quae sunt duodecim *tribuum filiorum Israel*. ¹³Ab oriente portae tres et ab aquilone portae tres et ab austro portae tres et ab occasu portae tres; ¹⁴et murus civitatis habens fundamenta duodecim, et super ipsis duodecim nomina duodecim apostolorum Agni. ¹⁵Et, qui loquebatur mecum, habebat mensuram arundinem auream, ut metiretur civitatem et portas eius et murum eius. ¹⁶Et civitas in quadro posita est, et longitudo eius tanta est quanta et latitudo. Et mensus est civitatem arundine per stadia duodecim milia; longitudo et latitudo et altitudo eius aequales sunt. ¹⁷Et mensus est murum eius centum quadraginta quattuor cubitorum, mensura hominis, quae est angeli. ¹⁸Et erat structura muri eius ex iaspide, ipsa vero civitas aurum mundum simile vitro mundo. ¹⁹Fundamenta muri civitatis omni lapide pretioso ornata: fundamentum primum iaspis, secundus sapphirus, tertius chalcedonius, quartus smaragdus, ²⁰quintus sardonyx, sextus sardinus, septimus chrysolithus, octavus beryllus, nonus topazius, decimus chrysoprasus, undecimus hyacinthus, duodecimus amethystus. ²¹Et duodecim portae duodecim margaritae sunt, et singulae portae erant ex singulis margaritis. Et platea civitatis aurum mundum tamquam vitrum perlucidum. ²²Et templum non vidi in ea: Dominus enim, Deus omnipotens, templum illius est, et

her heavenly bread. This new creature matures through holiness of life; its marriage is marriage with Wisdom; its children, hope; its home, the Kingdom; its inheritance and its riches, the delights of paradise; its final destiny is not death, but eternal and joyful life in the dwelling-place of the saints (Rev 21:5–8)" (*Oratio 1 in Christi resurrectionem*). As the Second Vatican Council teaches, we should remember that "the Kingdom is mysteriously present here on earth; when the Lord comes it will enter into its perfection" (*Gaudium et spes*, 39).

The names of the tribes of Israel and of the apostles are given (vv. 12, 14), to convey the continuity between the ancient chosen people and the Church of Christ, and at the same time to show that the Church is new, founded on the twelve apostles of the Lord (cf. Eph 2:20). The positioning of the gates shows the universality of

the Church; they give access to salvation to people from all points of the compass; this is what St Augustine means when he says that "outside the Catholic Church one can find everything except salvation" (*Sermo ad Caesariensis ecclesiae plebem*, 6). Surprisingly, there is no temple in the City (21:22), whereas there was one in Ezekiel's vision; the reason is that there is no longer any need for there to be a sign of where God dwells, since the blessed contemplate the Father and the Lamb directly. If the water of life symbolizes the Holy Spirit (see 21:6), we can see why some Fathers of the Church and modern commentators have noted a Trinitarian meaning in this passage: the Holy Spirit, who proceeds from the Father and the Son, is represented by the power that flows out from the throne of God and the Lamb.

This passage in the book of Revelation

q About fifteen hundred miles

²²And I saw no temple in the city, for its temple is the Lord God the Almighty and the Lamb. ²³And the city has no need of sun or moon to shine upon it, for the glory of God is its light, and its lamp is the Lamb. ²⁴By its light shall the nations walk; and the kings of the earth shall bring their glory into it, ²⁵and its gates shall never be shut by day—and there shall be no night there; ²⁶they shall bring into it the glory and the honour of the nations. ²⁷But nothing unclean shall enter it, nor any one who practises abomination or falsehood, but only those who are written in the Lamb's book of life.

Is 24:23; 60:1, 19
Rev 22:5
Is 60:3, 5

Ps 68:30
Rev 22:5
Is 60:11
Ps 72:10–11

Is 35:8; 52:1
2 Pet 3:13

22 ¹Then he showed me the river of the water of life, bright as crystal, flowing from the throne of God and of the Lamb ²through the middle of the street of the city; also, on either side of the river, the tree of life^r with its twelve kinds of fruit, yielding its fruit each month; and the leaves of the tree were for the healing of the nations. ³There shall no more be anything accursed, but the throne of God and of the Lamb shall be in it, and his servants shall worship him; ⁴they shall see his face, and his name shall be on their foreheads. ⁵And night shall be no more; they need no light of lamp or sun, for the Lord God will be their light, and they shall reign for ever and ever.

Ezek 47:1, 7
Gen 2:9
Jn 7:38
Rev 21:6
Ezek 47:12
Ps 46:4

Zech 14:11
Rev 7:15

1 Jn 3:2
1 Cor 13:12
Ps 17:15

Rev 21:25; 5:10
Is 60:19
Dan 7:18, 27

The visions come to an end

⁶And he said to me, "These words are trustworthy and true. And the Lord, the God of the spirits of the prophets, has sent his angel to show his servants what must soon take place. ⁷And behold, I am coming soon."

Dan 2:28–29, 45
1 Cor 14:32
Rev 1:1; 19:21, 5

Rev 2:6; 3:11; 1:3;
22:12, 20

Agnus. ²³Et civitas non eget sole neque luna, ut luceant ei, nam claritas Dei illuminavit eam, et lucerna eius est Agnus. ²⁴Et ambulabunt gentes per lumen eius, et reges terrae afferunt gloriam suam in illam; ²⁵et portae eius non claudentur per diem, nox enim non erit illic; ²⁶et afferent gloriam et divitias gentium in illam. ²⁷Nec intrabit in ea aliquid coinquinatum et faciens abominationem et mendacium, nisi qui scripti sunt in libro vitae Agni. [22] ¹Et ostendit mihi fluvium aquae vitae splendidum tamquam crystallum, procedentem de throno Dei et Agni. ²*In medio* plateae eius et *fluminis ex utraque parte lignum vitae* afferens fructus duodecim, *per menses* singulos reddens *fructum suum, et folia* ligni *ad sanitatem* gentium. ³Et omne maledictum non erit amplius. Et thronus Dei et Agni in illa erit; et servi eius servient illi ⁴et videbunt faciem eius, et nomen eius in frontibus eorum. ⁵Et nox ultra non erit, et non egent lumine lucernae neque lumine solis, quoniam Dominus Deus illuminabit super illos, et regnabunt in saecula saeculorum. ⁶Et dixit mihi: «Haec verba fidelissima et vera sunt, et Dominus, Deus spirituum prophetarum, misit angelum

continues to nourish the Church with faith and hope, as she journeys on her pilgrim way. As the Second Vatican Council put it, "We know neither the moment of the consummation of the earth and of man nor the way the universe will be transformed. The form of this world, distorted by sin, is passing away and we are taught that God is preparing a new dwelling and a new earth in which righteousness dwells, whose happiness will fill and surpass all the desires of peace arising in the hearts of men. Then with death conquered the sons of God will be raised in Christ, and what was sown in weakness and dishonour will put on the imperishable: charity and its works will remain and all of creation, which God made for man, will be set free from its bondage to decay" (*Gaudium et spes*, 39).

22:6–15 The Church in all her glory stands in

such marked contrast to her present position on earth that we can only glimpse that glory if we trust in those who speak on God's behalf (vv. 6–9). St John is conscious of having put down his text in the way that the prophets spoke their message; they were inspired by "the God of the spirits of the prophets" (v. 6). That is why the angel describes the book as "prophecy" (v. 10). It is a prophecy pronounced not as an esoteric secret but as something for all to hear (that is why the book must be left open), and it can lead readers to a change of heart, for with the redemption won by Christ the final stage of salvation has begun. That is what is meant by the words "what must soon take place" (v. 6). This passage is, then, an appeal for continuous growth in holiness. "No one deserves to be called good who does not strive to be better; and when you begin not to want to be better, you cease to be good" (St Bernard, *Epistolae*, 91).

r Or *the Lamb. In the midst of the street of the city, and on either side of the river, was the tree of life*, etc.

Blessed is he who keeps the words of the prophecy of this book.

Rev 1:9; 19:10
Jn 1:1–3
Dan 8:26; 12:4
Rev 10:4; 1:3

[8]I John am he who heard and saw these things. And when I heard and saw them, I fell down to worship at the feet of the angel who showed them to me; [9]but he said to me, "You must not do that! I am a fellow servant with you and your brethren the prophets, and with those who keep the words of this book. Worship God."

Dan 12:10
Ezek 3:27
Is 56:1

[10]And he said to me, "Do not seal up the words of the prophecy of this book, for the time is near. [11]Let the evildoer still do evil, and the filthy still be filthy, and the righteous still do right, and the holy still be holy."

Ps 62:12
Jer 17:10
Is 40:10
Is 41:4; 44:6;
48:12
Heb 13:8
Rev 1:17, 8

[12]"Behold, I am coming soon, bringing my recompense, to repay every one for what he has done. [13]I am the Alpha and the Omega, the first and the last, the beginning and the end."

Gen 2:9; 3:22
Rev 7:14; 22:2
Rev 21:8, 27
Phil 3:2
Eph 5:5
Rom 1:29

[14]Blessed are those who wash their robes,[s] that they may have the right to the tree of life and that they may enter the city by the gates. [15]Outside are the dogs and sorcerers and fornicators and murderers and idolaters, and every one who loves and practises falsehood.

4. EPILOGUE*

Rev 1:1; 2:28
Rom 1:3
Mal 3:1
Num 24:17
Is 11:1, 10; Lk 1:78

[16]"I Jesus have sent my angel to you with this testimony for the churches. I am the root and the offspring of David, the bright morning star."

Prayer of the Spirit and the Bride. Words of warning and farewell

Zech 14:8
Jn 7:37
Is 55:1
Rev 2:7; 21:6, 9

[17]The Spirit and the Bride say, "Come." And let him who hears say, "Come." And let him who is thirsty come, let him who desires take the water of life without price.

suum ostendere servis suis, quae oportet fieri cito. [7]Et ecce venio velociter. Beatus, qui servat verba prophetiae libri huius». [8]Et ego Ioannes, qui audivi et vidi haec. Et postquam audissem et vidissem, cecidi, ut adorarem ante pedes angeli, qui mihi haec ostendebat. [9]Et dicit mihi: «Vide, ne feceris. Conservus tuus sum et fratrum tuorum prophetarum et eorum, qui servant verba libri huius; Deum adora!». [10]Et dicit mihi: «Ne signaveris verba prophetiae libri huius; tempus enim prope est! [11]Qui nocet, noceat adhuc, et, qui sordibus est, sordescat adhuc, et iustus iustitiam faciat adhuc, et sanctus sanctificetur adhuc. [12]Ecce venio cito, et merces mea mecum est, reddere unicuique sicut opus eius est. [13]Ego Alpha et Omega, primus et novissimus, principium et finis. [14]Beati, qui lavant stolas suas, ut sit potestas eorum super lignum vitae, et per portas intrent in civitatem. [15]Foris canes et venefici et impudici et homicidae et idolis servientes et omnis, qui amat et facit mendacium! [16]Ego Iesus misi angelum meum testificari vobis haec super ecclesiis. Ego sum radix et genus David, stella splendida matutina». [17]Et Spiritus et sponsa dicunt: «Veni!». Et, qui audit, dicat: «Veni!». Et, qui sitit, veniat; qui vult, accipiat aquam vitae gratis. [18]Contestor ego omni audienti verba prophetiae libri huius: Si quis appo-

*22:16–21 Jesus Christ solemnly confirms the authenticity of the prophetical content of the book. Then it is ratified by the Church at prayer (v. 17), and by the author of the written text (vv. 18–19); and, before the words of farewell, Christ once more confirms its authority (v. 20).

22:17–21 The Bride is the Church, who, in reply to Christ's promise (see 22:12), ardently desires and prays for his coming. She is moved by the Holy Spirit, the voices of both Church and Spirit joined in a single appeal. Every Christian is invited to join in this prayer and to discover in the Church the gift of the Spirit, symbolized by the water of life (21:6); this gift allows Christians a foretaste of the good things of the Kingdom.

Christ himself replies to the supplication of the Church and the Spirit: "I am coming soon" (v. 20). This assertion appears seven times in the book (see 2:16; 3:11; 16:15; 22:7, 12, 20), showing that this is a promise that will certainly be kept. "Strengthened by this certainty, let us set out again along the ways of the earth, feeling greater unity and solidarity with one another, and at the same time bearing in our heart the desire that has become more eager to make known to our brothers and sisters, still enveloped by the clouds of doubt and depression, the 'joyful proclamation' that there has risen over the horizon of their lives 'the bright morning star' (Rev 22:16), the Redeemer of man, Christ the Lord" (John Paul II, *Homily*, 18 May 1980).

s Other ancient authorities read *do his commandments*

¹⁸I warn every one who hears the words of the prophecy of this book: if any one adds to them, God will add to him the plagues described in this book, ¹⁹and if any one takes away from the words of the book of this prophecy, God will take away his share in the tree of life and in the holy city, which are described in this book. Deut 4:2; 13:1; 29:19

²⁰He who testifies to these things says, "Surely I am coming soon." Amen. Come, Lord Jesus! 1 Cor 16:22

²¹The grace of the Lord Jesus be with all the saints.^t Amen. 1 Cor 16:23

suerit ad haec, apponet Deus super illum plagas scriptas in libro isto; ¹⁹et si quis abstulerit de verbis libri prophetiae, huius, auferet Deus partem eius de ligno vitae et de civitate sancta, de his, quae scripta sunt in libro isto. ²⁰Dicit, qui testimonium perhibet istorum: «Etiam, venio cito». «Amen. Veni, Domine Iesu!». ²¹Gratia Domini Iesu cum omnibus.

Christian hope is not in vain, for it is founded on Christ's victory and prefigured in that of the Woman. "Victory over the 'prince of this world' (Jn 14:30) was won once for all at the Hour when Jesus freely gave himself up to death to give us his life. This is the judgment of this world, and the prince of this world is 'cast out' (Jn 12:31; Rev 12:10). 'He pursued the woman' (Rev 12:13–16) but had no hold on her: the new Eve, 'full of grace' of the Holy Spirit, is pre-served from sin and the corruption of death (the Immaculate Conception and the Assumption of the Most Holy Mother of God, Mary, ever virgin). 'Then the dragon was angry with the woman, and went off to make war on the rest of her offspring' (Rev 12:17). Therefore the Spirit and the Church pray: 'Come, Lord Jesus' (Rev 22:17, 20) since his coming will deliver us from the Evil One" (*Catechism of the Catholic Church*, 2853).

t Other ancient authorities omit *all*; others omit *the saints*

Explanatory Notes

Asterisks in the text of the New Testament refer to these RSVCE "Explanatory Notes".

MATTHEW

1:1: The genealogy is given to show that Jesus had the descent required for Messiahship, i.e. from Abraham and, in particular, from David the king.

1:16: Joseph's, not Mary's, descent is given here, as the Jews did not usually reckon descent through the mother. Joseph was the legal and presumed father, and it was this fact that conferred rights of inheritance, in this case, the fulfilment of the Messianic promises.

1:25: This means only that Joseph had nothing to do with the conception of Jesus. It implies nothing as to what happened afterwards.

3:2: *Repent* implies an internal change of heart.

3:6: Not a Christian baptism but a preparation for it.

3:15: Though without sin, Jesus wished to be baptized by John, as this was the final preparation for his Messianic mission.

5:17: Jesus came to bring the old law to its natural fulfilment in the new while discarding what had become obsolete; cf. Jn 4:21.

5:29: An exaggeration to emphasize the need to avoid occasions of sin.

5:32: *unchastity*: The Greek word used here appears to refer to marriages which were not legally marriages, because they were either within the forbidden degrees of consanguinity (Lev 18:6–16) or contracted with a Gentile. The phrase *except on the ground of unchastity* does not occur in the parallel passage in Lk 16:18. See also Mt 19:9 (Mk 10:11–12), and especially 1 Cor 7:10–11, which shows that the prohibition is unconditional.

6:6: This does not, of course, exclude public worship but ostentatious prayer.

6:24: *mammon*: i.e., riches.

8:3: The miracles of Jesus were never performed to amaze people and shock them into belief. They were worked with a view to a real strengthening of faith in the recipient or beholder, from whom the proper dispositions were required.

8:29: *before the time*: Before the day of judgment the demons are permitted by God to tempt men and even to possess them.

10:5: The gospel, the Messianic salvation, had first to be preached and offered to the chosen people, Israel. Later it would be offered to the Gentiles.

11:3: The Baptist expected more obvious signs of the Messiah. By quoting the prophet Isaiah, Jesus showed that he was indeed inaugurating the Messianic kingdom — but by doing good rather than by glorious manifestations or sudden punishments.

11:27: This shows a profound relationship between the Son and the Father, far superior to adoptive sonship.

12:14: The Pharisees regarded healing as work and so forbade it on the sabbath.

12:24: *Beel-zebul*: Name of a Canaanite god meaning "the Prince-god". The Jews interpreted this name as "Prince of demons", because for them all false gods were demons.

12:31: To attribute to the devil the works of the Holy Spirit seems to imply a hardness of heart which precludes repentance.

12:46: *brethren*: The Greek word or its Semitic equivalent was used for varying degrees of blood relationship; cf. Gen 14:14; 29:12; Lev 10:4.

12:48: Jesus puts the work of salvation before family relationships. It is not said, however, that he refused to see them.

13:12: To those well-disposed Jews who have made good use of the old covenant will now be given the perfection of the new. On the other hand, from those who have rejected God's advances will now be taken away even that which they have, because the old covenant is passing away.

13:52: This is Matthew's ideal: that the learned Jew should become the disciple of Jesus and so add the riches of the new covenant to those of the old, which he already possesses; cf. verse 12.

13:55: See note on Mt 12:46.

14:33: Their realization of his Godhead was the prelude to Peter's confession of faith at Caesarea Philippi (Mt 16:16).

15:5: By dedicating his property to God, i.e., to the temple, a man could avoid having to help his parents, without actually giving up what he had. The scribes held such a vow to be valid without necessarily approving it.

15:24: See note on 10:5.

16:14: The title of prophet had a Messianic significance because the gift of prophecy, which had been extinct since Malachi, was expected to return at the beginning of the Messianic era, especially by an outpouring of the Spirit as foretold by the prophet Joel and as realized in Acts 2:16.

16:16: The context shows that Peter recognizes the sonship of Jesus as divine and not adoptive like ours. Mark and Luke in the parallel passages mention only the confession of the Messiahship.

16:18: The name "Peter" comes from the Greek word for "rock". Jesus makes him the foundation on which the Church is to be built. The word "church" means "assembly" or "society" of believers. The Hebrew equivalent is used in the Old Testament to indicate the chosen people. In applying it to the church Jesus shows it to be the Messianic community foretold by the prophets. See note on Mt 18:18.

16:19: *the kingdom of heaven*: Peter has the key to the gates of the city of God. This power is exercised through the church. "Binding" and "loosing" are rabbinic terms referring to excommunication, then later to forbidding or allowing something. Not only can Peter admit to the kingdom; he also has power to make authoritative decisions in matters of faith or morals.

16:25: *life* (both times): A play on the word "life" — natural and supernatural; cf. Mk 8:35–36.

17:4: Peter thought the glorious Messianic kingdom had come. In fact, Jesus allowed this glimpse of his glory to strengthen them for the coming passion.

18:9: *Gehenna* (see footnote **b**) was the name of a valley south of Jerusalem where human sacrifice had once been practised; cf. 2 Chron 33:6. Later it became a cursed place and refuse dump, and the name came to symbolize the Christian place of punishment.

18:18: To the other apostles is given a share in the authority given to Peter.

19:9: This appears to refer to the case in Mt 5:32, though the Greek word for "except" is different.

19:11–12: Jesus means that a life of continence is to be chosen only by those who are called to it for the sake of the kingdom of God.

21:9: The crowd openly recognize Jesus as the Messiah and he allows it for the first time.

21:23: They object to the assumption of authority implicit in the manner of his entry into the city and in his expulsion of the sellers from the temple.

21:33–44: This parable really is an allegory in which almost every detail represents something in God's dealings with Israel.

22:11: The wedding garment represents the dispositions necessary for admission to the kingdom.

23:5: *phylacteries*: Little leather boxes containing, on a very small scroll, the principal words of the law; cf. Deut 6:4–9. Taking the command literally, they fastened these to their arms and their foreheads.

23:9: i.e., "Do not use the title without reference to God's universal fatherhood." He cannot mean that the title is never to be used by a son to his father.

24:1—25:46: The "eschatological discourse", as it is called, deals with the fall of Jerusalem and the end of the world. The two themes seem to be inextricably intermingled in the Gospel as we now have it, but it is possible that originally they were in separate discourses. However, the fusion of the two does bring out their connection. The one prefigures the other. Moreover, in the reverse direction, so to speak, the language used to describe the day of the Lord in Joel and elsewhere is here applied to the fall of Jerusalem, the details of which must therefore not be taken too literally (24:29).

25:29: See note on 13:12.

26:17: The passover was celebrated this year on the Friday evening (Jn 18:28). Jesus must have anticipated the passover meal because he would be dead the following day and because the meal prefigured his death.

26:26: The details of the Eucharist are superimposed on the ritual of the passover.

26:51: It was Peter, as John in his later Gospel tells us (Jn 18:10), though Matthew is reluctant to say so.

26:59: They sought evidence against him and this was necessarily false.

26:64–65: For the first time Jesus speaks clearly of his own identity. Caiaphas evidently understands him to claim divinity.

27:46: Jesus applies Psalm 22 to himself.

27:66: The sealing and guarding only helped to make the subsequent resurrection more obvious.

28:1–20: The resurrection appearances. There are divergent traditions in the Gospels, Galilean and Judean. Paul adds his own record (1 Cor 15). The accounts do not easily fit together, but this is surely evidence of their genuineness. There is no attempt to produce an artificial conformity.

MARK

1:34: Throughout his ministry Jesus forbade the demons and those he healed of their infirmities to reveal his identity as Messiah, because the people, with their ideas of a national leader to come, were only too prone to mistake his true mission.

2:14: *Levi*: Mark does not identify him with Matthew the apostle; cf. Mt 9:9.

3:31: *brethren*: See note on Mt 12:46.

4:12: *so that . . .*: One might rephrase this: "so that the scripture might be fulfilled"; cf. Jn 18:32; 19:24, 28. It was not God's intention to prevent their understanding. Matthew avoids this difficulty by writing, "I speak to them in parables, *because* seeing they do not see" (Mt 13:13).

5:43: Knowing their nationalistic views about the Messiah to come, Jesus wished to avoid a tumult.

7:3: Mark, writing for Gentiles, explains these Jewish customs.

8:36: *life*: See note on Mt 16:25.

9:13: *Elijah has come*: i.e., in the person of the Baptist (Mt 11:14).

10:24: *amazed at his words*: The Old Testament often records God's offers of material rewards for observance of his laws. This was because the future life was not yet revealed. It was therefore taken for granted, in spite of contrary evidence, that riches were a sign of God's favour.

10:30: Some of the reward will be given in this life.

14:13: It was unusual for a man to carry water; it was a woman's task.

14:51–52: This young man is usually supposed to have been the evangelist himself.

15:1: The Jews could not execute Jesus without the Roman governor's permission.

15:40: *the younger*, or "the Less".

16:1: There had been no time on the Friday to anoint him before the sabbath rest.

16:9–20: This passage is regarded as inspired and canonical scripture even if not written by Mark. As it is missing from some important manuscripts, it is possible that Mark did not write it. On the other hand, he would hardly have left his Gospel unfinished at verse 8. Many think that the original ending was lost at a very early date and this ending was composed at the end of the apostolic period to take its place

LUKE

1:3: *Theophilus* is again referred to in Acts 1:1, but nothing is known of him.

1:5—2:52: The "Infancy Gospel", as it is called, is written in a markedly Semitic style, which differs from that of the rest of the Gospel. It appears to be based on the reminiscences of Mary.

1:30: The words of the angel are drawn from Messianic passages in the Old Testament.

1:46–55: The *Magnificat* is based on the Song of Hannah (1 Sam 2:1–10), and other Old Testament passages which describe God's favour towards Israel and especially towards the poor and lowly.

1:69: *a horn of salvation*: i.e., a mighty saviour.

2:7: *first-born*: The term connotes possession of certain rights, privileges and obligations; cf. Ex 13:1–2, 11–16. The word is used even in modern times without necessarily implying subsequent births.

2:34: *for the fall*: i.e., in the sense that by rejecting his claims many would sin grievously.

2:49: Jesus stresses the priority of his duty to his Father, which involves a high degree of independence of earthly ties.

3:2: See note on Jn 18:13.

3:7: *brood of vipers*: This epithet seems to have been directed mainly at the Pharisees; cf. Mt 3:7.

3:23: This genealogy, more universalist than that of Matthew, goes back to Adam, the ancestor of all men, and then to God, his Maker. Like Matthew, however, it gives the genealogy of Joseph, though Mary may well have been of the family of David.

4:16–30: This account of the visit to the synagogue seems to be composed of the details of more than one visit. Luke is trying here to underline the contrast between Christ's offer of salvation and the people's refusal of it.

6:20–49: Luke's discourse is shorter than that of Matthew because it does not contain Matthew's additional material collected from other occasions, or his details which would interest only Jews.

7:28: John, by virtue of his office, belonged to the old dispensation, the time of preparation for the kingdom. In terms of spiritual status, even the humbler members of the kingdom were superior to him.

7:47: The preceding parable suggests that she loved much because she had been forgiven much. Jesus now implies that her love is a sign rather than a cause of forgiveness, thus confirming the point of the parable.

8:19: *brethren*: See note on Mt 12:46.

8:39: There was no reason for secrecy (to avoid popular disturbance) in a non-Jewish area.

9:51: Here begins the "Travel Narrative" of Luke, which continues up to the passion.

received up: i.e. into heaven; cf. 2 Kings 2:9–11; Acts 1:2, 11. The term here includes his passion, death, resurrection and ascension.

9:53: The Samaritans worshipped on Mount Gerizim, while orthodox Jews, of course, went to Jerusalem, and to Jerusalem only, for sacrifice.

10:18: Jesus refers to the fall of the angels (cf. Rev 12:9), while he speaks of his conquest of the forces of evil.

14:26: Christ's disciples must be prepared to part from anyone who prevents them from serving him.

16:8: The master commended his foresight without approving what he actually did.

17:20: At that time many people were expecting to see the kingdom inaugurated with striking manifestations; cf. 19:11.

19:41–44: These moving words spoken over the city are full of scriptural allusions. Moreover, the details given could apply as well to the siege of 587 BC as to that of AD 70. It is not safe, therefore, to argue from this passage that the fall of the city had already taken place when Luke wrote his Gospel.

20:37: As elsewhere (1 Cor 15:13–19), survival after death is linked with the resurrection of the body.

21:24: *the times of the Gentiles*: i.e., those during which the Gentiles will take the place of the unbelieving people of Israel. Evidently, therefore, the end of the world does not coincide with the fall of Jerusalem. St Paul says that the Jews will be converted before the end (Rom 11:26).

22:52: Matthew and Mark describe the arrest first, before Christ's words. Luke and John both put his address to the soldiers and officials before the arrest, doubtless to stress his command over events.

23:2: They purposely produce political charges, as these alone would interest Pilate.

23:14: Luke, writing for Gentiles, makes it clear that Pilate wanted to release Jesus.

23:31: One does not burn green wood. The meaning is that, if an innocent man is thus punished, what must the guilty (dry wood) expect?

24:38: Luke stresses this episode for the benefit of his Greek readers, for whom the resurrection of the body was both impossible and absurd; cf. Acts 17:32.

JOHN

1:1: John begins by giving his Gospel a theological background. By speaking at once of "the Word" he implies that his readers are familiar with the term. To Gentiles it indicated some form of divine revelation or self-expression. Jews would equate it with the divine Wisdom described in Proverbs, which already appears as something more than a divine quality and has some relationship with the visible world. In Sirach and Wisdom the idea is further developed. In the last-named book, Wisdom appears as a pre-existing person, taking part in the creation of the world and having a mission to reveal God to his creatures; cf. Wisdom 7:22—8:1.

1:5: *light . . . darkness*: One of the familiar themes of the Gospel.

1:29: John applies to Jesus the Messianic prophecy of Is 53:6–7, perhaps worded more explicitly by the evangelist in later years.

2:4: *what have you to do with me?* While the expression always implies a divergence of view, the precise meaning is to be determined by the context, which here shows that it is not an unqualified refusal, still less a rebuke.

2:12: *brethren*: See note on Mt 12:46.

3:22: *baptized*: A baptism like that of John. The time for baptism "in the Spirit" had not yet come.

3:24: From the other Gospels we learn that, after John was arrested, Jesus withdrew from Judea.

4:20: *this mountain*: Gerizim, on which the Samaritans worshipped.

5:18: *broke the sabbath*: i.e., broke the sabbath as interpreted by them; see note on Mt 12:14.

6:51: Jesus is the "living bread", both as Word of God (verses 32ff) and as sacrificial victim for the salvation of man.

6:52: A natural question to ask. Jesus answers, not by explaining it away, but by re-emphasizing the reality, though not, of course, in the crude sense implied in their question.

6:62: When Jesus ascends into heaven they will know that he spoke the truth.

7:3: *brethren*: See note on Mt 12:46.

7:53—8:11: This passage, though absent from some of the most ancient manuscripts, is regarded as inspired and canonical by the church. The style suggests that it is not by St John, and that it belongs to the Synoptic Tradition.

8:21: *die in your sin*: Theirs is that sin against the truth which is the sin against the Holy Spirit; cf. Mt 12:31.

8:41: They mean, "We are not idolaters", and protest their fidelity to God their Father; see notes on Rev 14:4 and 17:2.

8:56: *he saw it* either in prophetic vision while on earth or by some special privilege after death.

8:58: The present tense indicates Christ's eternal existence as God.

9:4: Jesus explains in advance the purpose of the miracle.

10:14: *the good shepherd*: The name has Messianic significance; cf. Ezek 34.

10:18: Throughout the Gospel, Jesus insists that he is master of his own life and no one takes it from him; cf. 18:6 (at his arrest); 19:11 (before Pilate); 19:30 (on the cross).

11:6: *stayed two days longer*: This is explained in verse 15.

11:50: Caiaphas agreed that, as Jesus was not (in their opinion) the Messiah, any popular insurrection now could only end in disaster; so it was better, he argued, to do away with him. He was unconscious of the deeper meaning of his words, namely that Jesus must die for the salvation of man.

12:1: Here begins the last week of Jesus' public life. This is described in great detail, as was the first week in chapter 1.

12:32: *lifted up*: i.e., on the cross; but the words also contain a reference to his going up into heaven. The two mysteries are inseparable.

13:1: John begins here to unfold the mystery of the love of Jesus for "his own". Note the solemn introduction to the "hour" of his passion and death.

13:34: *new commandment*: Jesus gives a new depth to the familiar commandment of the Old Testament. The standard now is, "as I have loved you".

14:26: *all things*: After Jesus has gone to his Father, the Holy Spirit will complete his revelation to the world.

15:18: Jesus contrasts the love his disciples have with the hatred the world bears them.

16:10: Jesus is taken from them because they did not receive him.

17:1–26: The priestly prayer of Jesus, before his sacrifice.

17:5: Declares his pre-existence.

18:13: According to Jewish law the high-priesthood was for life. The Romans had deposed Annas, the legal holder, in AD 15, and appointed another in his place, but many Jews continued to recognize Annas.

18:28: They would have contracted a legal impurity by entering the house of a pagan.

18:29: See note on Lk 23:2.

18:31: Crucifixion was a Roman not a Jewish punishment.

19:7: At last, because of Pilate's reluctance, they produce the real charge.

19:8–9: Pilate is afraid and asks Jesus where he comes from—not his country but his mysterious origins, as implied in the charge.

19:27: *took her to his own home*: Joseph must now have been dead.

20:17: The death and resurrection of Jesus had put an end to the ordinary familiar relationships of human life, and the time of lasting companionship had not yet come.

21:1–25: This chapter was added later, either by the evangelist or by a disciple; cf. 20:30–31 and 21:24.

21:7: John remembered a similar miracle before; cf. Lk 5:6.

21:15–17: The threefold question addressed to Peter alone corresponds to the threefold denial. Jesus gives Peter charge over his flock.

THE ACTS OF THE APOSTLES

1:1: *the first book*: i.e., St Luke's Gospel.

1:14: *brethren*: See note on Mt 12:46.

1:22: An apostle must be a witness to Christ's resurrection.

2:14: Peter assumes the leadership in public. In this discourse we have the earliest form of the apostolic preaching.

3:1: In the early days, the first Christians observed the prescriptions of the Jewish law.

4:2: The Sadducees did not believe in the resurrection of the dead.

4:32: *everything in common*: They freely shared what was theirs individually; cf. Acts 5:4.

5:11: *church*: i.e., the Christian and Messianic community, a term borrowed from the Old Testament.

5:20: *Life*: cf. Acts 9:2, "the Way". These terms recall the words of Jesus, "I am the way, and the truth, and the life" (Jn 14:6).

5:34: *Gamaliel*: teacher of St Paul; cf. Acts 22:3.

6:1: *Hellenists*: Greek-speaking Jews of the Dispersion, who had their own synagogues in Jerusalem and read the scriptures in Greek.

8:20: Hence the word "simony", meaning "buying and selling spiritual powers and privileges".

9:5: Jesus identifies himself with his followers.

9:13: *saints*: i.e., Christians, made holy by baptism.

10:16: The vision was to prepare Peter for his reception of Cornelius

the Gentile and his household into the church; cf. also Acts 15.

12:1: The second wave of persecution; cf. Acts 8:1.

13:16–41: This first recorded sermon of Paul is similar to that of Peter in Acts 2:14–36.

16:10: This is the first of the passages in Acts in which the story is told in the first person plural, indicating that Luke, the author, was there. The manuscript Codex Bezae, however, has a "we" passage in 11:28.

16:13: Being a Roman colony, Philippi had no synagogue within its walls.

19:35: *the sacred stone* or statue of the goddess which, according to legend, came down from heaven. Possibly a meteorite.

20:7: Celebration of the Eucharist on the Lord's day, i.e. Saturday evening, according to the Jewish way of reckoning a day from sunset to sunset.

20:34: Paul insisted on working for his living, though recognizing the apostle's right to support by the faithful; cf. 1 Cor 9:4–7.

21:4: *told Paul not to go*: This was not a command. The Holy Spirit enlightened them about what lay before Paul and they naturally wished to spare him; cf. verse 11.

22:20: *thy witness*: Greek, "martyr". Witnessing by one's death (i.e., martyrdom) is the supreme example.

ROMANS

1:1–7: The opening address and salutation are very much in the style of contemporary letter-writing, giving the name of the sender and recipient, and following this with greetings.

1:10: Paul did not found the church at Rome.

1:13, *harvest*: Perhaps those who founded the church at Rome had confined themselves largely to Jews and had not made much headway with Gentiles.

3:27: Above all it is faith, not works alone, that will justify both Jew and Gentile, and (as is made clear later) faith in Jesus.

5:12: Physical death is a sign of spiritual death; though physical death remains after justification.

5:15: The *felix culpa* praised in the *Exsultet* at the Easter Vigil.

6:4, *buried*: Immersed in the water of Baptism.

6:15: As before in the case of the Law (Rom 2:17–29), so now in the case of grace, Paul says it is not a licence to sin.

7:13–25: Man under the law of Moses and perhaps man under the

natural law too.

8:19: Material creation too shares man's destiny, made as it was for him. Many ancient philosophers thought matter to be evil, and that the spirit should be freed from it.

9:19–24: Paul's words here, taken by themselves, seem to leave no room for moral responsibility; but they must be taken in conjunction with other passages; see chapters 1–2.

10:1: Paul is afraid he has spoken too strongly of their sins, so he declares his love for Israel.

14:1—15:13: Paul is tolerant of the Jewish Christians' reluctance to abandon the ritual prescriptions of the law of Moses, while being equally insistent that they shall not be forced on Gentile Christians.

14:14: Conscience is the ultimate guide.

15:15–16: Paul again justifies his writing to a church he did not found.

16:16, *all the churches of Christ greet you*: A remarkable salutation, not used elsewhere.

1 CORINTHIANS

1:2, *saints*: A word commonly used for Christians in Paul's letters and in Acts.

1:12, *Cephas*: i.e., Peter. It does not follow from this that he had ever been to Corinth, but it does indicate his authority there.

2:1–2: Paul's failure at Athens convinced him that lofty words and worldly wisdom were less effective than Jesus crucified.

3:13, *the Day*: i.e., the day of the Lord, God's searching judgments.

3:16, *God's temple*: The dignity of the Christian.

5:1, *father's wife*: Evidently his stepmother.

5:5, *to Satan*: not only excommunicated, but in some sense given over to suffering, for his own good.

5:9–10, *immoral*: Literally, "fornicators".

5:11, *guilty of immorality*: Literally, "a fornicator".

6:1, *the unrighteous*: i.e., civil courts in which the judges were, of course, pagans.

6:9, *the immoral*: Literally, "fornicators". *homosexuals*: Greek has, "effeminate or sodomites." The apostle condemns not the inherent tendencies of such, but the indulgence of them.

6:12: This saying is possibly an exaggeration of the freedom from the Mosaic law which Christians enjoyed. The saying had been applied to sinful practices, as is clear from the following verses.

6:13, 18, *immorality*: i.e., sexual immorality.

7:2: Note Paul's insistence on equality of man and woman in certain aspects of christian marriage, and his recognition that the unmarried state is also a gift from God.

8:1–13: Animals sacrificed to pagan gods were often sold as meat in the market. Could Christians buy such meat? Paul allows it so long as scandal is avoided.

9:3: Paul sets great store by the fact that he has earned his living and waived his right to support by the faithful. He uses this as an authentication of his apostolate.

9:5, *a wife*: Greek, "a woman, or a sister". This could mean either a woman who is a Christian, or a wife who is a Christian. There were pious women who ministered to the apostles (Lk 8:3). As many of the apostles must have been married, they may have been ministered to by their wives; though it is possible they had left their wives in answer to the Lord's command to leave all (Lk 18:28–29). *brethren*: See note on Mt 12:46.

10:20: Paul appears to forbid partaking in sacrificial meals. In verse 27 he says they may eat meat offered to idols if it is at an ordinary meal, unless it would cause scandal to any one present.

11:20: There was apparently a common meal before the Eucharist at which food and drink were to be shared. Paul condemns the abuses that had crept in.

12:1: The spiritual gifts here referred to were common in the first age of the church and helped to establish it on a firm basis.

12:31: Love, however, is far superior to these gifts.

15:13: Again, the resurrection of the dead is linked with Christ's resurrection; cf. Rom 8:11.

15:29: Apparently a custom of vicarious baptism for those who had died without it. Paul mentions it without approving it.

16:1: The collection to be made everywhere for the poor Christians in Jerusalem.

2 CORINTHIANS

1:8, *affliction*: Possibly the disturbance at Ephesus (Acts 19:23–41), or perhaps a serious illness.

3:18: Cleansed in baptism through the power of the Holy Spirit, our soul shines with the reflected glory of God.

4:7, *this treasure*: i.e., the apostolate.

4:12: i.e., we suffer, if necessary, even unto death, that you may have (spiritual) life.

5:19: Or, "God was reconciling the world to himself through Christ."

5:21, *made him to be sin*: i.e., "Sending his own Son in the likeness of

sinful flesh and for sin, he condemned sin in the flesh" (Rom 8:3).

9:1, *superfluous*: Yet Paul goes on to do so at some length, exhorting them to be generous.

10:1: Paul is referring ironically to what some people are saying about him; see verse 10.

12:7, *a thorn*: Perhaps some form of sickness or disability, or the opposition of Israel to his teaching.

12:13: Paul ironically asks forgiveness for not being a charge on them as the other apostles were.

GALATIANS

1:6: After the greeting there is no commendation, as was usual, but rather strong rebuke.

1:10: No doubt Paul was accused of exempting Gentile converts from the law of Moses in order to curry favour.

2:16, *works of the Law*: Paul is contrasting not faith with good works but faith in Jesus Christ with observance of the law of Moses.

3:2, *Spirit*: He probably refers to the outward manifestations of the Spirit, such as the gift of the tongues.

5:11, *stumbling block of the cross*: So far as the Jews were concerned, this would consist largely in the exemption of converts from the obligations of the law of Moses

EPHESIANS

1:1, *To the saints who are*: The addition "at Ephesus" is doubtful. The letter may have been a form of encyclical.

1:10, *to unite*: Or, "to sum up." This is one of the chief themes of the letter. Men are to be under Christ as head of the Mystical Body, and even irrational creatures must be in some way under him as the cornerstone of creation.

2:14, *dividing wall*: A metaphor taken from the wall that divided the court of the Gentiles from the court of the Israelites in the temple.

3:3, *the mystery*: i.e., that the Gentiles were to be admitted to the church on a basis of equality.

5:14: Apparently a fragment of an early Christian hymn; cf. 1 Tim 3:16.

PHILIPPIANS

1:14, *because of my imprisonment*: i.e., because I continue to preach in their midst, though in prison.

1:20, *honoured in my body*: i.e., through my sufferings.

2:6, *in the form of God*: The Greek shows that divine attributes, and therefore nature, are implied here. It is not the divine nature he set

no store by, but equality of treatment and recognition of his divinity.

2:7, *emptied himself* of this external recognition which was his right.

3:12, *made me his own*: On the road to Damascus.

3:19: These Judaizers made holiness a question of distinction of foods and set great store by circumcision.

COLOSSIANS

1:15, *first-born*: Born of the Father before all ages. The reference here is to the divine person of the Word; see verse 16.

1:18: His human nature.

1:24, *what is lacking*: Christ's sufferings were, of course, sufficient for our redemption, but we may all add ours to his, in order that the

fruits of his redemption may be applied to the souls of men.

3:18–4:5: The whole passage corresponds closely to Eph 5:22—6:9.

4:10: Mark, the evangelist, and, probably, the John Mark of Acts 12:12, 25.

4:14: Luke, the evangelist.

1 THESSALONIANS

1:1: Paul joins with himself two who had evangelized Thessalonica with him.

2:18, *I, Paul*: He distinguishes himself from Silvanus and Timothy.

4:3, *sanctification*: with special reference to the practice of purity which was specially difficult to those newly converted from paganism.

immorality: i.e., sexual immorality.

4:11: The Thessalonians thought that the Second Coming of Christ was at hand and tended to neglect their daily duties. He corrects this misconception.

4:13: Paul tells them that those who died before Christ's Second Coming are no worse off than those who will still be alive at his coming.

4:17: i.e., we who are alive shall go out to meet him and accompany him back on his return to this earth.

2 THESSALONIANS

2:2: Paul warns against over eagerness to expect the Second Coming, and specifies various signs to be looked for first.

2:3, *the man of lawlessness*: i.e., Antichrist.

2:7: Evil will operate secretly till the final unmasking.

1 TIMOTHY

1:2: Timothy, son of a Greek father and a Jewish mother, was already a Christian when Paul met him (Acts 16:1). A close association ensued.

1:4, *myths and endless genealogies*: A reference to the Jewish legends and spurious pedigrees added by false Judaizers to the Biblical narratives; cf. the Book of Jubilees.

1:20, *delivered to Satan*: A form of excommunication; see note on 1 Cor 5:5

2:6, *ransom for all*: This is why Paul wants prayers for all (verse 1).

3:1, *bishop*: At this time an office probably not distinct from that of priest.

3:11, *women*: i.e., deaconesses.

4:3, *forbid marriage*: As some Gnostics did.
   abstinence from foods: As practised by Judaizers.

5:3, *real widows*: i.e., with no one to help and support them.

5:12: Paul had no objection to widows marrying again; cf. 1 Cor 7:8–9. But the widows here had clearly made some sort of vow or promise to serve the Church in singleness. Paul recommended that younger widows should marry again (verse 14).

2 TIMOTHY

1:15, *Asia*: The Roman province of that name, now in western Turkey.

2:18: They explained the resurrection by saying it was the rising to newness of life in Baptism, thus ignoring a bodily resurrection, a doctrine the Greeks found very hard to accept; cf. Acts 17:32.

3:16: Paul refers to the Old Testament scriptures.

4:6, *on the point of being sacrificed*: Literally, "poured out in sacrifice" as a drink offering or libation.

4:21, *Linus*: According to tradition, the successor of Peter in the see of Rome.

TITUS

1:5, *elders*: Each Christian community was ruled by a body of elders.

2:13, *God and Saviour*: Both terms appear to refer to Jesus Christ.

3:5–7: A brief and clear statement of the doctrine of justification.

HEBREWS

1:1–4: A contrast between the progressive and piecemeal revelation of the old dispensation and the complete revelation of the new given by a single representative—no mere prophet but the Son of God himself.

2:2, *angels*: The Covenant of Sinai was thought to have been given through the angels.

2:10, *suffering*: The divinely appointed means of progress towards God; cf. verse 18.

3:11: Those who murmured against God in the desert were excluded from the promised land (the "rest"). Christians should be aware lest, by offending God, they be excluded from heaven, the true rest, of which the promised land was a type.

5:1–5: If Jesus was to be mediator, he had to have a human nature like ours and, moreover, he could not appoint himself, but had to be appointed by God.

6:4, *impossible*: The apostasy referred to in verse 6 is clearly thought of as so deliberate as to preclude any real possibility of repentance; or there may be a reference here to the impossibility of being baptized a second time.

7:3, *without father*: i.e., the father is not mentioned in scripture.

neither beginning of days nor end of life: So too here, they are not mentioned in scripture either. Thus his priesthood can be taken to foreshadow or symbolize the Christian priesthood. "You are a priest for ever after the order of Melchizedek" (Ps 110:4; cf. Heb 7:17).

8:11: This verse merely means that knowledge of God will be commonly shared, and is not literally intended to exclude the ministry of teaching in the Messianic times.

10:1ff.: The sacrifices of the old law, being imperfect, were repeated, and did at least keep alive a sense of sin. Contrast with Christ's sacrifice (verse 14).

11:6: Here is stated the minimum necessary for salvation.

12:1ff: After explaining in the preceding chapters how we are redeemed through faith in Jesus Christ, the author now exhorts his readers to run the race with perseverance.

13:1ff: Moral exhortation.

13:9: Again the warning against false doctrine, especially the Judaizers' teachings; cf. Phil 3:19; 1 Tim 1:4; 4:3.

13:13: i.e., "Let us leave the observances of Judaism behind us."

JAMES

1:1, *twelve tribes*: i.e., Jewish Christians outside Palestine.

1:22: This is the main theme of the letter.

2:1–7: These are hard words, but no harder than those of Jesus.

2:10: In keeping the Law, we must keep *the whole Law*. We cannot pick and choose.

2:14: Good works are necessary besides faith.

5:3: The "treasure" they have laid up is described in the following verses.

5:13–15: This passage is the scriptural basis for the sacrament of Anointing of the Sick.

1 PETER

1:1: See note on Jas 1:1. Baptism is the main theme of this letter, which may, in fact, have been a baptismal address.

1:11, *Spirit of Christ*: Christ, as the eternally existing Word, is envisaged as inspiring the prophets of old.

3:1–6: Peter's teaching on the behaviour and status of women corresponds to that of Paul, though without Paul's forthrightness.

4:1, *ceased from sin*: Peter means that a continual acceptance of suffering is incompatible with a proneness to sin.

5:13, *Babylon*: Rome was as full of iniquity as ancient Babylon; cf. Rev 17:9.

2 PETER

1:4, *partakers of the divine nature*: A strong expression to describe the transformation of human nature by divine grace.

1:16–18: A reference to the transfiguration.

2:3: Much of the material of this chapter appears to be from the Letter of Jude.

3:16: *this* seems to refer to the theme of the end of the world and the Second Coming of Christ, about which Paul had written in his letters to the Thessalonians.

1 JOHN

1:1–7: Note the likeness with John's Gospel 1:1–18.

1:3, *fellowship*: A Johannine theme.

1:5, *light . . . darkness*: Another familiar theme in John's Gospel.

2:3: cf. the words of Jesus, "If you love me, you will keep my commandments" (Jn 14:15).

2:18, *the last hour*: John exhorts his readers to hold fast, as though the end were at hand.

3:6, *sins*: i.e., remains in sin, or has a habit of sin.

4:1, *test the spirits*: i.e., examine those who claim to have special gifts

from the Holy Spirit; cf.1 Cor 14:32.

5:8, *There are three witnesses*: After these words, the Vulgate adds the following: "in heaven, the Father, the Word, and the Holy Ghost. And these three are one. And these are three that give testimony on earth." This passage, known as the Comma Johanneum or "The Three Heavenly Witnesses," is first found in the Latin (fourth century), and does not appear in any Greek New Testament manuscript before the sixteenth century. It is probably a marginal gloss which found its way into the text.

2 JOHN

1, *The elder*: Perhaps the head of the group or "college" of elders that presided over each Christian community. John was head not only of the Ephesus community but of all the communities in the province of Asia.

the elect lady: Probably not an individual lady but a particular church or community in Asia.

13, *children*: i.e., the Christians of Ephesus.

3 JOHN

12, *Demetrius*: Evidently a leading Christian, recommended to Gaius.

JUDE

6: It is not clear to what Jude refers. Perhaps Gen 6:2 or the apocryphal Enoch, chapters 6–15.

9: Apparently a reference to another apocryphal work, the Assumption of Moses.

REVELATION

1:4–8: Describes the glorious coming and reign of the Messiah.

1:13, *son of man* refers to Dan 7:13. The Messiah is described in symbolic terms.

2:10, *ten days*: Not literally. It means the persecution will be short.

2:20–21, *immorality* here seems to mean idolatry rather than sexual excess.

2:24, *deep things of Satan*: The doctrine of the Nicolaitans. *They* called them the "deep things of God".

2:28, *morning star*: Probably Christ himself.

3:12, *new name*: cf. Is 62:2. Perhaps it was "the Word", or perhaps it is not to be revealed till the last day.

4:3: John describes God in symbolic terms.

4:4, *elders*: They perform a priestly and royal task, since they praise God and share in the government of the world.

4:6, *four living creatures*: cf. Ezek 1:4–25: the four angels who preside over the government of the world. But in Christian tradition these

symbols are used for the four evangelists.

4:8, *Holy, holy, holy*: Quoted in the *Sanctus* at Mass.

5:1, *a scroll*: This contained God's designs, kept secret till now; being written on both sides, nothing could be added.

5:6: The seven horns and seven eyes symbolize Christ's full power and knowledge.

6:1: Begins the account of the destruction of the Roman Empire, chapters 6–9.

6:5, *balance*: Symbol of famine. The balance was to measure rations.

7:4, *a hundred and forty-four thousand*: A symbolic number, i.e., 12 (the sacred number) squared and multiplied by 1,000 to denote a multitude. It is the church, the spiritual Israel, that is meant.

7:14, *the great tribulation*: The Neronian persecution?

8:5: Coals from the altar of burnt offering were brought to the altar of incense.

9:1, *star*: A fallen angel.

9:14, *Euphrates*: The region of the Parthians.
9:21, *immorality*: See note on 2:20–21.
10:7, *mystery of God*: i.e., the establishment of the kingdom of God following on the destruction of Israel's enemies.
10:9, *bitter ... sweet*: The scroll related both the sufferings and the victories of Christ's church.
11:1–19: The Jerusalem here described stands for the church, which is to be persecuted by the Romans.
11:2: The three and a half years' persecution of the Jews by Antiochus Epiphanes, 168–165 BC, had become the standard time of a persecution.
Three and a half years = 42 months = 1,260 days (verse 3).
11:3, *two witnesses*: As they have yet to die, possibly they are Elijah and Enoch.
11:8, *the great city*: i.e., Rome.
12:1–6: The *child* brought forth is the Messiah; the *dragon* is the devil; the *woman* who gave birth to the Messiah is Israel, and then becomes the Christian church, which continually gives birth to the faithful.
12:14, *a time, and times, and half a time*: This is the three and a half years of 11:2.
12:17: Mary; the mother of the Messiah, must also be included in the meaning.
13:1, *a beast*: This symbolizes the material forces of evil, arrayed against the church.
13:11, *another beast*: i.e., the false prophets.
13:18, *six hundred and sixty-six*: The letters of Nero's name plus the title of Caesar, given their numerical meaning in Hebrew and added together, make 666.
14:4: Although tradition tends to take this literally, the context and Old Testament metaphor suggest that it means they have kept free from idolatry.
14:8, *Babylon*: i.e., Rome.
15:3–4: The song of Moses in Ex 15:1–18 celebrated victory over Pharaoh. This is seen as foreshadowing the triumph of the Lamb.
16:14, *the great day*: On which all the Gentile armies shall be gathered to give battle.
16:16, *Armageddon*: i.e., Megiddo, where Josiah was defeated by the king of Egypt; cf. 2 Kings 23:29.
17:1, *great harlot*: i.e., Rome.
17:2, *fornication*: i.e., idolatry.
18:11–20: The description abruptly assumes the language of Ezekiel's prophecy of the destruction of Tyre, another city notorious for its sins (Ezek 27:1—28:19).
19:7, *marriage of the Lamb*: i.e., final establishment of the kingdom of God. The spouse is the church.
20:3: The destruction of the dragon must coincide in time with that of the beast (19:20), so that the first resurrection with the reign of the martyrs refers to the revival and expansion of the church after the years of persecution.
21:1: Creation will be renewed one day, freed from corruption and illumined by God's glory.
21:8, *second death*: i.e., eternal damnation.

CHANGES IN THE RSV FOR THE CATHOLIC EDITION

	TEXT		FOOTNOTES	
	RSV	RSVCE	RSV	RSVCE
Mt 1:19	divorce her	send her away		
Mt 12:46, 47 (note), 48, 49	brothers	brethren		
Mt 13:55	brothers	brethren		
Mt 18:24			[f]Delete existing note and substitute:	[f]A talent was more than fifteen years' wages of a labourer
Mt 18:28			[g]Delete existing note and substitute:	[g]The denarius was a day's wage for a labourer
Mt 19:9		... commits adultery; and he who marries a divorced woman commits adultery."[k]		[k]Other ancient authorities omit *and he ... adultery*
Mt 20:2			[m]Delete existing note and substitute:	[m]The denarius was a day's wage for a labourer
Mt 21:44		[q]+44 And he who falls on this stone will be broken to pieces; but when it falls on any one, it will crush him		[q]Other ancient authorities omit verse 44

	TEXT		FOOTNOTES	
	RSV	RSVCE	RSV	RSVCE
Mt 25:15			ᵈDelete existing note and substitute:	ᵈA talent was more than fifteen years' wages of a labourer
Mt 27:24		ᶦthis righteous man's blood		ᶦOther ancient authorities omit *righteous* or *man's*
Mk 6:37			ᵘDelete existing note and substitute:	ᵘThe denarius was a day's wage for a labourer
Mk 9:29		ʲ+ and fasting		ʲOther ancient authorities omit *and fasting*
Mk 3:31, 32, 33, 34 brothers		brethren		
Mk 10:24		ʳ+ for those who trust in riches		ʳOther ancient authorities omit *for those . . . in riches*
Mk 13:33		ᵃ+ and pray		ᵃOther ancient authorities omit *and pray*
Mk 14:5			ᵇDelete existing note and substitute:	ᵇThe denarius was a day's wage for a labourer
Mk 16:9–20		ᵏ(Insert into the text after verse 8) ⁹Now when he rose early on the first day of the week, he appeared first to Mary Magdalene, from whom he had cast out seven demons. ¹⁰She went and told those who had been with him, as they mourned and wept. ¹¹But when they heard that he was alive and had been seen by her, they would not believe it. ¹²After this he appeared in another form to two of them, as they were walking into the country. ¹³And they went back and told the rest, but they did not believe them. ¹⁴Afterwards he appeared to the eleven themselves as they sat at table; and he upbraided them for their unbelief and hardness of heart, because they had not believed those who saw him after he had risen. ¹⁵And he said to them, "Go into all the world and preach the gospel to the whole creation. ¹⁶He who believes and is baptized will be saved; but he who does		ᵏOther ancient authorities omit verses 9–20. Some ancient authorities conclude Mark instead with the following: *But they reported briefly to Peter and those with him all that they had been told. And after this, Jesus himself sent out by means of them, from east to west, the sacred and imperishable proclamation of eternal salvation.*

	TEXT		FOOTNOTES	
	RSV	RSVCE	RSV	RSVCE
		not believe will be condemned. [17]And these signs will accompany those who believe: in my name they will cast out demons; they will speak in new tongues; [18] they will pick up serpents, and if they drink any deadly thing, it will not hurt them; they will lay their hands on the sick, and they will recover." [19]So then the Lord Jesus, after he had spoken to them, was taken up into heaven, and sat down at the right hand of God. [20]And they went forth and preached everywhere, while the Lord worked with them and confirmed the message by the signs that attended it. Amen.		
Lk 1:28	O favoured one	full of grace[b2]		[b2]Or *O favoured one*
Lk 8:19, 20, 21	brothers	brethren		
Lk 8:43		[b]+ and had spent all her living upon physicians		[b]Other ancient authorities omit *and had spent . . . physicians*
Lk 10:35			[i]Delete existing note and substitute:	[i]The denarius was a day's wage for a labourer
Lk 15:8			[t]Delete existing note and substitute:	[t]The dracma, rendered here by *silver coin*, was about a day's wage for a labourer
Lk 19:13			[e]Delete existing note and substitute:	[e]The mina, rendered here by *pound*, was about three months' wages for a labourer
Lk 22:19–20		[j]+ which is given for you. Do this in remembrance of me." [20]And likewise the cup after supper, saying, "This cup which is poured out for you is the new covenant in my blood.		[j]Some ancient authorities omit *which is given . . . blood*
Lk 24:5		[u]+ He is not here, but has risen.		[u]Other ancient authorities omit *He is . . . has risen*
Lk 24:12		[v]+[12] But Peter rose and ran to the tomb; stooping and looking in, he saw the linen cloths by themselves; and he went home wondering at what had happened.		[v]Other ancient authorities omit verse 12

	TEXT		FOOTNOTES	
	RSV	RSVCE	RSV	RSVCE
Lk 24:36		ˣ + and said to them, "Peace to you!"		ˣOther ancient authorities omit *and said ... to you*
Lk 24:40		ʸ+⁴⁰And when he had said this, he showed them his hands and feet.		ʸOther ancient authorities omit verse 40
Lk 24:51		ᵃ+ and was carried up into heaven.		ᵃOther ancient authorities omit *and was . . . heaven*
Lk 24:52		ᵇ + worshipped him, and		ᵇOther ancient authorities omit *worshipped him, and*
Jn 2:12	brothers	brethren		
Jn 6:7			ˡDelete existing note and substitute: for a labourer	ʳThe denarius was a day's wage
Jn 7:3, 5, 10	brothers	brethren		
Jn 7:52		ʳ(Insert into the text here) ⁵³They went each to his **8** own house, ˡ but Jesus went to the Mount of Olives. ²Early in the morning he came again to the temple; and he sat down and taught them. ³The scribes and the Pharisees brought a woman who had been caught in adultery, and placing her in the midst ⁴they said to him, "Teacher, this woman has been caught in the act of adultery. ⁵Now in the law Moses commanded us to stone such. What do you say about her?" ⁶ This they said to test him, that they might have some charge to bring against him. Jesus bent down and wrote with his finger on the ground. ⁷And as they continued to ask him, he stood up and said to them, "Let him who is without sin among you be the first to throw a stone at her." ⁸And once more he bent down and wrote with his finger on the ground. ⁹But when they heard it, they went away, one by one, beginning with the eldest, and Jesus was left alone with the woman standing before him. ¹⁰Jesus looked up and said to her, "Woman,		ʳSome ancient authorities insert 7:53–8:11 either at the end of this gospel or after Lk 21:38, with variations of the text. Others omit it altogether

TEXT		FOOTNOTES	
RSV	RSVCE	RSV	RSVCE
	where are they? Has no one condemned you?" [11]She said, "No one, Lord." And Jesus said, "Neither do I condemn you: go, and do not sin again."		
Jn 12:5		[b]Delete existing note and substitute:	[b]The denarius was a day's wage for a labourer
Acts 1:14	brothers	brethren		
Rom 1:4		designated[a2]		[a2]Or *constituted*
Rom 5:5	which	who		
Rom 8:11	which	who		
Rom 9:5	… Christ. God who is over all be blessed for ever.[n]	… Christ, who is God over all, blessed for ever.[n]	[n]Or *Christ, who is God over all, blessed for ever*	[n]Or *Christ. God who is God over all be blessed for ever*
1 Cor 3:9	fellow workers for God[f]	God's fellow workers[f]	[f]Or *God's fellow workers*	[f]Or *fellow workers for God*
1 Cor 4:6	to live according to Scripture	·not to go beyond what is written		
1 Cor 7:25		the unmarried[x2]		[x2]Greek *virgins*
1 Cor 7:28		a girl[m2]		[m2]Greek *virgi*
1 Cor 7:34		girl[m2]		
1 Cor 7:36		betrothed[m2]		
1 Cor 7:37		betrothed[m2]		
1 Cor 7:38		betrothed[m2]		
1 Cor 9:5			[n]Delete existing note and substitute:	[n]Greek a *woman,* a *sister*
1 Cor 9:5	brothers	brethren		
Eph 1:14	which	who		
Eph 5:32	I take it to mean	I mean in reference to		
Phil 2:5	you have	was		
1 Thess 4:4	how to take a wife for himself	how to control his own body		
1 Thess 5:13	among yourselves[c2]		[c2]Or *with them*	
Heb 11:19	hence, figuratively speaking, he did receive him back	hence he did receive him back, and this was a symbol		
Rev (Title)	THE REVELATION TO JOHN	THE REVELATION TO JOHN (THE APOCALYPSE)		
Rev 6:6			[a]Delete existing note and substitute:	[a]The denarius was a day's wage for a labourer

Headings Added to the Biblical Text

MATTHEW

JOHN

THE ACTS OF THE APOSTLES

ROMANS

1 CORINTHIANS

2 CORINTHIANS

GALATIANS

EPHESIANS

PHILIPPIANS

COLOSSIANS

JAMES

1 PETER

2 PETER

1 JOHN

2 JOHN

Greeting 1
The law of love 4

Precautions against heretics 7
Conclusion and greetings 12

3 JOHN

Greeting 1
Praise of Gaius 3

Diotrephes' misconduct 9
Commendation of Demetrius 11

Conclusion and farewell 13

JUDE

Greeting and blessing 1
His reason for writing 3

1. FALSE TEACHERS DENOUNCED
The punishment that awaits them 5

Their immorality 8
The judgment of God 14

2. EXHORTATION
False teachers were predicted 17

Faith, hope and charity 20
Attitude towards waverers 22
Final doxology 24

REVELATION

Prologue 1:1

Part One: Letters to the seven churches
Address and greeting 1:4
Reason for writing 1:9
Letter to the church of Ephesus 2:1
Letter to the church of Smyrna 2:8
Letter to the church of Pergamum 2:12
Letter to the church of Thyatira 2:18
Letter to the church of Sardis 3:1
Letter to the church of Philadelphia 3:7
Letter to the church of Laodicea 3:14

Part Two: Eschatological visions
1. INTRODUCTORY VISION
God in majesty 4:1
The sealed scroll and the Lamb 5:1

2. EVENTS PRIOR TO THE FINAL
   OUTCOME

Christ opens the first six seals. Vision of the
   four horsemen 6:1
The great multitude of the saved 7:1
The opening of the seventh seal 8:1
The first six trumpet calls. The three woes
   8:7
The seer is given a little scroll to eat 10:1
Death and resurrection of the two witnesses
   11:1

3. CHRIST'S VICTORY OVER THE POWERS OF
   EVIL. THE CHURCH IN GLORY
The seventh trumpet call 11:15
The woman pursued by the dragon 12:1
The beasts given authority by the dragon 13:1
The beast rising from out of the earth 13:11
The Lamb and his entourage 14:1
Proclamation and symbols of the Judgment
   14:6
The harvest and the vintage 14:14

The hymn of the saved 15:1
The seven bowls of plagues 15:5
The great harlot and the beast 17:1
The fall of Babylon announced 18:1
Songs of victory in heaven 19:1
The first battle—the beast is destroyed
   19:11
The thousand-year reign of Christ and his
   people 20:1
The second battle—Satan is overthrown
   20:7
The Last Judgment of the living and the dead
   20:11
A new world comes into being. The new
   Jerusalem 21:1
The visions come to an end 22:6

4. EPILOGUE
Prayer of the Spirit and the Bride. Words of
   warning and farewell 22:17

Sources Quoted in This Volume

CCL   Corpus Christianorum, Series Latinae (Turnhout, 1947–)
CSCO   Corpus Scriptorum Christianorum Orientalium (Leuven, 1930—)
CSEL   Corpus Scriptorum Ecclesiasticorum Latinorum (Vienna, 1866—)
PG   Patrologiae cursus completes. Series Graecae, ed. J.P. Migne (Paris, 1856–1866)
PL   Patrologiae cursus completes. Series Latinae, ed. J.P. Migne (Paris, 1841–1864)
SC   Sources Chrétiennes (Paris, 1942—)

DOCUMENTS OF THE CHURCH AND OF POPES IN ORDER OF DATE; WITH ABBREVIATIONS

Second Council of Orange, *De gratia* *De gratia*, coeptum 3 July 529, DS 373–395.

Fourth Lateran Council, *De fide catholica* *Capitulum I: De fide catholica. Definitio contra Albigenses et Catharos*, 11–30 November 1215, DS 800–802.

Council of Trent

    De peccato originali *Sessio V: Decretum de peccato originali*, 17 June 1546, DS 1510–1516.

    De iustificatio *Sessio VI: Decretum de iustificatio*, 13 January 1547, DS 1520–1583.

    De Paenitentia *Sessio XIV: Doctrina de Sacramento Paenitentiae*, 25 November 1551, DS 1667–1719.

    De Extrema Unctione *Sessio XIV: Doctrina de Sacramento Extremae Unctionis*, 25 November 1551, DS 1667–1719.

    De SS. Missae sacrificio *Sessio XXII: Doctrina de SS. Missae sacrificio*, 17 November 1562, DS 1738–1760.

Roman Catechism *Catechism of the Council of Trent for parish priests*, issued by Pius V (1566; English ed. 1829).

Pius IX, *Ineffabilis Deus* Apostolic constitution *Ineffabilis Deus*, 8 December 1854, DS 2803–2804.

First Vatican Council

    Dei Filius Dogmatic constitution *Dei Filius,* on the Catholic faith, 24 April 1870, ASS 5 (1869) 481–493.

    Pastor aeternus Dogmatic constitution *Pastor aeternus*, on the Church of Christ, 18 July 1870, ASS 6 (1870/71) 40–47.

Leo XIII

    Libertas praestantissimum Encyclical *Libertas praestantissimum*, 20 June 1888, ASS 20 (1887) 593–613.

    Divinum illud munus Encyclical *Divinum illud munus*, 9 May 1897, ASS 29 (1897) 644–658.

St Pius X

    Haerent animo Apostolic exhortation *Haerent animo*, 4 August 1908, ASS 41 (1908) 555–577.

    Sacra Tridentina Synodus Decree *Sacra Tridentina Synodus*, 20 December 1905, ASS 38 (1905) 401–405.2.

Pius XI

    Mens nostra Encyclical letter *Mens nostra*, 20 December 1929, AAS 21 (1929) 689–706.

    Ad catholici sacerdotii, Encyclical letter *Ad catholici sacerdotii*, 20 December 1935, AAS 28 (1936) 5–53.

Pius XII

    Mystici Corporis Encyclical letter *Mystici Corporis*, on the mystical body of Christ, 29 June 1943, AAS 35 (1943) 193–248.

    Address 15 November 1946, AAS 38 (1846) 432–437.

    Mediator Dei Encyclical letter *Mediator Dei*, on the Sacred Liturgy, 20 November 1947, AAS 39 (1947) 521–595.

    Menti nostrae Apostolic exhortation *Menti nostrae*, on the holiness of priestly life, 23 September 1950, AAS 42 (1950) 657–702.

Second Vatican Council

    Sacrosanctum Concilium Constitution *Sacrosanctum Concilium*, on the Sacred Liturgy, 4 December 1963, AAS 56 (1964) 97–138.

Lumen gentium Dogmatic constitution *Lumen gentium*, on the Church, 21 November 1964, AAS 57 (1965) 5–71.

Unitatis redintegratio Decree *Unitatis redintegratio*, on ecumenism, 21 November 1964, AAS 57 (1965) 90–111.

Christus Dominus Decree *Christus Dominus*, on the pastoral office of bishops in the Church, 28 October 1965, AAS 58 (1966) 673–701.

Nostra aetate Declaration *Nostra aetate*, on the relation of the Church to non-Christian religions, 28 October 1965, AAS 58 (1966) 740–744.

Dei Verbum Dogmatic constitution *Dei Verbum*, on divine Revelation, 18 November 1965, AAS 58 (1966) 817–835.

Apostolicam actuositatem Decree *Apostolicam actuositatem*, on the apostolate of lay people, 18 November 1965, AAS 58 (1966) 837–864.

Dignitatis humanae Declaration *Dignitatis humanae*, on religious liberty, 7 December 1965, AAS 58 (1966) 929–946.

Ad gentes Decree *Ad gentes*, on the Church's missionary activity, 7 December 1965, AAS 58 (1966) 947–990.

Presbyterorum ordinis Decree *Presbyterorum ordinis*, on the ministry and life of priests, 7 December 1965, AAS 58 (1966) 991–1024.

Gaudium et spes Pastoral constitution *Gaudium et spes*, on the Church in the modern world, 7 December 1965, AAS, 58 (1966) 1025–1120.

Paul VI

Mysterium fidei Encyclical letter *Mysterium fidei*, on the doctrine and worship of the Holy Eucharist, 3 September 1965, AAS 57 (1965) 753–774.

Populorum progressio Encyclical letter *Populorum progressio*, on the need to promote the development of peoples, 26 March 1967, AAS 59 (1967) 257–299.

Sacerdotalis caelibatus, Encyclical letter *Sacerdotalis caelibatus*, 24 June 1967, AAS 59 (1967) 657–697.

Creed of the People of God Sollemnis professio fidei, 30 June 1968, AAS 60 (1968) 433–445.

General audience, 20 February 1974, *Insegnamenti di Paolo VI*, 12 (1974) 183–188.

Holy Thursday homily, 27 March 1975, *Insegnamenti di Paolo VI*, 12 (1975) 252–255.

Evangelium nuntiandi Apostolic exhortation *Evangelium nuntiandi*, 8 December 1975, AAS 68 (1976) 9–26.

John Paul II

Address to Latin-American bishops Address to the third general conference of the Latin-American bishops (Puebla, Mexico), 28 January 1979, AAS 71 (1979) 187–205.

Redemptor hominis Encyclical letter *Redemptor hominis*, on the Redeemer of man, 4 March 1979, AAS 71 (1979) 257–324.

Letter to all priests Letter to all priests on the occasion of Holy Thursday, 8 April 1979, AAS 71 (1979) 393–417.

Catechesi tradendae Apostolic exhortation *Catechesi tradendae*, on catechesis in our time, 16 October 1979, AAS 71 (1979) 1277–1340.

General audience, 14 November 1979, *Insegnamenti di Giovanni Paolo II*, II, 2 (1979) 1155–1157.

Homily, 18 May 1980, *Insegnamenti di Giovanni Paolo II*, III, 1 (1980) 1396–1402.

Dives in misericordia Encyclical letter *Dives in misericordia*, on the mercy of God, 30 November 1980, AAS 72 (1980) 1177–1232.

General audience, 25 March 1981, *Insegnamenti di Giovanni Paolo II*, IV, 1 (1981) 760–771.

Laborem exercens Encyclical letter *Laborem exercens*, on human work, 14 September 1981, AAS 73 (1981) 577–647.

Homily, 1 November 1981, *Insegnamenti di Giovanni Paolo II*, IV, 2 (1981) 531–535.

Familiaris consortio Apostolic exhortation *Familiaris consortio*, on the duties of Christian families, 22 November 1981, AAS 73 (1981) 81–191.

Salvifici doloris Apostolic letter *Salvifici doloris*, on the Christian meaning of human suffering, 1 February 1984, AAS 76 (1984) 201–250.

Reconciliatio et paenitentia Apostolic exhortation *Reconciliatio et paenitentia*, on reconciliation and penance, 2 December 1984, AAS 77 (1985) 185–275.

Letter to young people Apostolic letter to young people of the world on the occasion of the International Youth Year, 31 March 1985, AAS 77 (1985) 579–628.

Dominum et Vivificantum Encyclical letter *Dominum et Vivificantum*, on the Holy Spirit in the life of the Church and the world, 18 May 1986, AAS 78 (1986) 809–900.

Redemptoris Mater Encyclical letter, on the Mother of the Redeemer, 25 March 1987, AAS 79 (1987) 361–433.

Sollicitudo rei socialis Encyclical letter, on the twentieth anniversary of *Populorum progressio*, 30 December 1987, AAS 80 (1988) 515–586.

Mulieris dignitatem Apostolic letter *Mulieris dignitatem*, on the dignity and vocation of women, 15 April 1988, AAS 80 (1988) 1635–1729.

Christi fideles laici Post-synodal apostolic exhortation *Christi fides laici*, on the vocation and mission of lay people in the Church and in the world, 30 December 1988, AAS 81 (1989) 393–531.

Redemptoris Custos Apostolic exhortation *Redemptoris Custos*, on the person and mission of St Joseph in the life of Christ and in the Church, 15 April 1984, AAS 82 (1990) 5–34.

Veritas splendor Encyclical letter *Veritatis splendor*, on some basic aspects of the moral teaching of the Church, 6 April 1993, AAS 85 (1993) 1133–1228.

Tertio millenio adveniente Apostolic letter *Tertio millenio adveniente* in preparation of the jubilee in the year 2000, 10 November 1994, AAS 87 (1995) 5–41.

Address at the Symposium on "The roots of anti-Semitism in Christian settings", 31 October 1997, *Insegnamenti di Giovanni Paolo II*, XX, 2 (1997) 723–726.

Dies Domini Apostolic letter *Dies Domini*, on the sanctification of Sunday, 31 May 1998, AAS 90 (1998) 713–766.

Letter proclaiming three women saints as co-patrons of Europe Apostolic letter *"motu proprio,"* proclaiming St Brigit of Sweden, St Catherine of Siena and St Teresa Benedicta of the Cross co-patrons of Europe, 1 October 1999, AAS 92 (2000) 220–229.

Novo millenio ineunte Apostolic letter, *Novo millenio ineunte*, to bishops, clergy and the faithful, to mark the end of the great jubilee of the year 2000, 6 January 2001, AAS 93 (2001) 266–309.

Address, 12 January 2002, Address to participants at a congress on "The greatness of ordinary life", *L'Osservatore Romano* (Spanish ed.), 3 February (no. 1725).

Misericordia Dei Apostolic letter "motu proprio" *Misericordia Dei*, on aspects of the celebration of the Sacrament of Penance, 7 June 2002, AAS 94 (2002) 452–459.

Catechism of the Catholic Church (Dublin, 1994).

Code of Canon Law *Codex Iuris Canonici* (Vatican City, 1983).

Benedict XVI

Deus caritas est Encyclical letter *Deus caritas est*, 25 December 2005, AAS 98 (2006) 217–252.

Spe salvi Encyclical letter *Spe salvi*, 30 November 2007

Congregation for the Doctrine of the Faith

Mysterium Filii Dei Declaration *Mysterium Filii Dei* to protect the faith from some recent errors regarding the mysteries of the Incarnation and of the Trinity, 21 February 1972, AAS 64 (1972) 237–241.

Persona humana Declaration *Persona humana* on some aspects of sexual ethics, 29 December 1975, AAS 68 (1976) 77–96.

Inter insigniores Declaration *Inter insigniores* on the subject of the admission of women to the priestly ministry, 15 October 1976, AAS 69 (1977) 98–116.

Libertatis nuntius Instruction *Libertatis nuntius* on some aspects of "Liberation Theology", 6 April 1984, AAS 76 (1984) 876–909.

Libertatis conscientia Instruction *Libertatis conscientiae* on Christian freedom and liberation, 22 March 1986, AAS 79 (1987) 554–599.

Dominus Iesus Declaration *Dominus Iesus* on the unicity and salvific universality of Jesus Christ and of the Church, 6 April 2000, AAS 92 (2000) 742–765.

LITURGICAL TEXTS

Roman Missal *Missale Romano*, edition typica altera (Vatican City, 1975).
The Divine Office *Liturgia Horarum iuxta Ritum Romanum*, editio typica altera (Vatican City, 1987).

FATHERS, ECCLESIASTICAL WRITERS AND OTHER AUTHORS

Alcuin of York
Interrogationes in Genesium [*Interrogationes et responsiones in Genesim*], PL 100, 515–566

Alphonsus Liguori, St
Meditations for Advent
The Love of Our Lord Jesus Christ reduced to practice
Thoughts on the Passion
Sermons

Álvaro del Portillo
On Priesthood (Chicago, 1974).

Amadeus of Lausanne, St
Homiliae de Maria [*Homiliae octo de Maria Virginea Matre*, PL 188, 1303–1346.]

Ambrose, St
De excessu fratris sui Satyri, CSEL 73
De fuga mundi [*De fuga saeculi*] , CSEL 32/2
De mysteriis [*De mysteriis liber unus*], PL 405–426
De officiis [*De officiis ministrorum libri*], PL 16, 23–184
De Sacramentis [*De Sacramentis libri IV*], PL 16, 435–482
De Spiritu Sancto, CSEL 79
De virginitate [*De virginitate liber unus*], PL 16, 279–316
Epistulae, CSEL 81/1–3
Expositio Evangelii secundum Lucam [*Exposition Evangelii secundum Lucam libris X comprehensa*], CCL 14
Expositio psalmi CXVIII [*In Psalmi CXVIII expositionem*], CSEL 62

Ambrosiaster
Ad Corinthios, CSEL 81/3
Ad Ephesios, CSEL 81/3
Ad Philemonem, CSEL 81/3
Ad Philippenses, CSEL 81/3
Ad Romanos, CSEL 81/3

Aphraates
Demonstratio, SC 349 and 359

Asterius of Amasea, St
Homiliae, PG 40, 355–362

Athanasian Creed, PG 28, 1581–1584

Athanasius, St
De Incarnatione [*Oratio de Incarnatione Verbi*], PG 25, 95–198
De Incarnatione contra Apollinarium [*De Incarnatione Domini Nostri Jesu Christi, contra Apollinarium*], PG 26, 1093–1166
Epistula ad episcopos Aegypti et Libyae [*Epistola encyclical ad episcopos Aegypti et Libyae*], PG 25, 535–594
Epistulae festales [*Epistolae heortasicae*], PG 26, 1339–1450
Historia Arianorum [*Historia Arianorum ad monachos*], PG 25, 695–796
Homilia de semente, PG 28, 143–168
Orationes adversus Arianos, PG 26, 12–524
Sermones [*Fragmenta et sermones*], PG 26, 1293–1326; PG 28
Vita Antonii [*Vita et conversation S.P.N. Antonii*], PG 26, 835–978

Augustine, St
Ad Probam [*Epistola CXXX (alias 121) Ad Probam*], PL 33, 493–507
Confessiones, PL 32, 659–868
Contra Adimantum [*Contra Adimantum Manichaei discipulum liber I*], PL 42, 129–172
Contra Faustum [*Contra Faustum manichaeum libri XXXIII*], PL 42, 207–518
De civitate Dei, PL 41, 13–804
De consensus Evangelistarum [*libri quatuor*], PL 34, 1041–1230
De doctrina christiana [*De doctrina christiana libri IV*], PL 34, 16–122
De fide et symbolo [*De fide et symbolo liber I*], PL 40, 181–196
De moribus Ecclesiae [*De moribus Ecclesiae Catholicae et de moribus Manichaeorum*], PL 32, 1309–1378
De nuptiis et concupiscentia, CSEL 42
De Sermone Domini in monte [*De Sermone Domini in monte libri II*], PL 34, 1229–1308
De sancta virginitate, CSEL 60
De Trinitate, CCL 50–60a

Cyril of Jerusalem, St
Catecheses [*Catecheses ad illuminandos*], PG 33, 331–1180
Homilia in paralyticum [*Homilia in paralyticum piscinam iacentem*], PG 33, 1131–1154

Ephrem, St
Catena Armenia super Acta [*The Commentary of Ephrem on Acts*, ed. F.C. Conybeare, in F.J. Foakes Jackson & K. Lake, *The Beginnings of Christianity, I, 3: The Acts of the Apostles. The text of Acts*, London 1926, pp 373–453]
Commentarii in Acta [ibid.]
Commentarii in Diatessaron, CSCO 137 and 145
Hymnus de Nativitate, CSCO 186

Francis of Assisi, St
Admonitiones
Letter to all the faithful
Little Flowers
On Christ's wounds

Francis de Sales, St
Introduction to the Devout Life
Treatise on the Love of God

Fulgentius of Ruspe, St
De fide ad Petrum, CCL 91
De remissione peccatorum [*De remissione peccatorum ad Euthymium libri II*], PL 65, 527–574
Epistulae, CCL 91
Sermones, PL 85, 729–739

Gelasius I, St
Ne forte [*Tomus de anathematis vinculo*], PL 59, 102–110

Gregory the Great, St
Homiliae in Evangelia [*XL homiliarum in Evangelia libri II*], PL 76, 1075–1312
Homiliae in Ezechielem [*Homiliarum in Ezechielem prophetam libri II*], PL 76, 785–1072
Moralia [*Moralium libri sive exposition in librum beati Iob*], PL 75, 509; 76, 782
Regula pastoralis [*Liber regulae pastoralis*], PL 77, 9–149

Gregory Nazianzen, St
De pauperum amore [*Oratio XIV de pauperum amore*], PG 35, 857–910
De theologia [*Oratio XXX theologica IV*], PG 36, 104–133
In Sanctum Pascha, PG 36, 624–664

Gregory of Nyssa, St
Contra Eunomium [*Contra Eunomium libri duodecim*], PG 45, 243–1122
De beatitudinibus, PG 44, 1193–1302
De instituto christiano, PG 46, 287–306
De vita Moysis, PG 44, 297–430
In Cantica Canticorum commentaries, PG 44, 755–1120
Oratio 1 de beatitudinibus [*De beatitudinibus oratio I*], PG 44, 1193–1208
Oratio 1 in Christi resurrectionem [*In Christi resurrectionem oratio I*], 46, 599–628
Oratio catechetica [*Oratio catechetica magna*], PG 45, 9–106

Hilary of Poitiers, St
Commentarius in Mattheum [*In Evangelium Matthaei commentarius*], PL 9, 914–1078
De Trinitate, CCL 62a

Hippolytus, St
Contra haeresin Noeti [*Contra haeresin Noeti cuiusdam*], PG 10, 803–830
De theophania [*Sermo in sancta theophania*], PG 10, 851–862

Ignatius of Antioch, St
Ad Ephesios
Ad Magnesios
Ad Polycarpum
Ad Romanos
Ad Smyrnaeos
Ad Traianos

Ignatius Loyola, St
Spiritual exercises
Letters

Irenaeus, St
Adversus haereses
Demonstratio praedicationis apostolicae

Jerome, St
Adversus Helvidium [*De perpetua virginitate B. Mariae adversus Helvidium*], PL 23, 193–216
Commentarii in Ephesios [*Commentariorum in epistolam ad Ephesios libri tres*], PL 26, 467–590
Commentarii in Galatas [*Commentariorum in epistolam ad Galatas libri tres*], PL 26, 331–468
Commentarii in Isaiam, PL 24, 9–678
Commentarii in Matthaeum [*Commentariorum in Evangelium S. Matthaei libri quatuor*], PL 26, 15–218

Leo the Great, St (contd.)

Sermones, PL 54, 141–468

Tractatus [*Sermo XCVI sive tractatus contra haeresin Eutychis*], PL 54, 466–468

Maximus the Confessor, St

Centuria [*Capita de charitate centuria: de charitate centena prima capita*], PG 90, 961–984

Mistagogia, PG 91, 657–718

Patrick, St

Confessio [*Confessio in epistola ad Hibernos explicata*], PL 53, 801–814

Peter Chrysologus, St

Sermones, PL 52, 183–680

Polycarp, St

Ad Philippenses [*Epistola ad Philippenses*], PG 1005–1024

Quodvultdeus, St

Sermo 2 de Symbolo, CCL 60

Robert Bellarmine, St

De ascensione mentis in Deum

Severiano of Gábala

Fragmenta in Colossenses

Fragmenta in Titum

Teresa of Avila, St

Book of Foundations

Exclamations of the soul to God

Interior Castle

Life

Poems

Way of Perfection

Teresa Benedicta of the Cross, St

The Science of the Cross

Tertullian

Apologeticum [*Apologeticus adversus gentes pro christianis*], PL 1, 305–604

De oratione, CSEL 20

De praescriptione haereticorum [*De praescriptionibus adversus haereticus*], PL 2, 12–74

De resurrectione mortuorum [*De resurrectione carnis*], PL 2, 791–886

De virginibus velandis, PL 2, 887–914

Liber ad Scapulum, CSEL 76

Theodore the Studite, St

Oratio in adoratione cruces, PG 99, 691–699

Theodoret of Cyrrhus

De incarnatione Domini, PG 75, 1419–1478

Interpretatio in Romanos [*Interpretatio epistolae ad Romanos*], PG 82, 43–226

Interpretatio in Colossenses [*Interpretatio epistolae ad Colossenses*], PG 82, 591–628

Interpretatio ad Hebraeos [*Interpretatio epistolae ad Hebraeos*], PG 82, 673–786

Theophilact of Bulgaria

Enarratio in Evangelium Marci, PG 123, 487–682

Enarratio in Evangelium Ioannis, PG 123, 1133–1348

Theophilus of Antioch, St

Ad Autolycum [*Libri tres ad Autolycum*], PG 6, 1023–1168

Thérèse of Lisieux, St

The Story of a Soul

Autobiographical Writings

Thomas Aquinas, St

On the Lord's Prayer

Catena aurea

Expositio in Credum

Summa theologiae

Super Evangelium Matthaei

Super Evangelium Ioannis

Super Epistolam ad Romanos

Super Epistolam primam ad Corinthios

Super Epistolam secundam ad Corinthios

Super Epistolam primam ad Thessalonicenses

Super Epistolam ad Hebraeos

Super 1 Timotheum

Super 2 Timotheum

Super Galatas

Thomas à Becket, St

Epistulae 74, PL 190, 533–536

Thomas à Kempis

Imitation of Christ

Thomas More, St

Letters written in prison to his daughter Margaret

De tristitia Christi

Vincent Ferrer, St

Treatise on the Spiritual Life

Vincent of Lerins, St

Commonitorium, PL 50, 637–686

William Abbot, St

Speculum fidei, PL 180, 365–398

Subject Index

abandonment to divine providence: Lk 12:22–34

Abraham: justified by faith: Rom 4:1–25; Gal 3:6–9; the promises given to him are irrevocable: Heb 6:13–20; 11:8–19

adoration: by the wise men: Mt 2:3–11; by the shepherds: Lk 2:8–20; of God: Jn 4:1–45

adultery: Mt 5:27–30; the woman caught in adultery: Jn 8:1–11

almsgiving: upright intention needed: Mt 6:2–4; generosity in: 2 Cor 9:6–15; the cheerful giver: Phil 4:10–20; the poor widow in the temple: Mk 12:41–44; Lk 21:1–3

Ananias: a Christian who baptizes Saul: Acts 9:10–19; high priest who strikes Paul: Acts 23:1–11; Ananias and Sapphira: Acts 5:1–11

Andrew, St: his calling: Mt 4:18–25; Mk 1:16–20; Lk 5:1–11; Jn 1:35–51; one of the Twelve: Mt 10:1–4; Mk 3:13–19; Lk 6:12–16; Acts 1:12–13; at Jesus' side: Jn 6:8; 12:22

angels: Christ's servants: Mt 4:1–11; Mk 1:12–13; Lk 4:1–13; 22:39–46; are lower than Christ: Heb 1: 5–14; 2:5–18; their relations with us: Mt 18:10; Acts 12:1–9. See St Gabriel, St Michael.

Anointing the Sick, sacrament: Mk 6:6–13; Jas 5:13–18

Antioch, church of: its beginnings: Acts 11: 19–26; it sends help to the Jerusalem church: Acts: 27–30; its difficulties with Judaizers: Acts 15:1–2; Gal 1:11–21

apostasy: gravity: 2 Pet 2:20–22; danger: Heb 6:4–12

apostles: their election, their features: Mt 10:1–4; Lk 6:12–16; Mk 3:13–19; their mission and preaching: Mt 10:5–15; Mk 6:6–13; Lk 9:1–6; they are sent to the whole world: Mt 28:16–20; Mk 16: 14–18; 16:20; the apostolic college: Acts 1:12–26; their self-denial: 1 Cor 4:8–13; their upkeep: 1 Cor 9:1–14

apostolate: Jas 5:19–20; 3 Jn 3–8. See apostles; evangelization.

appearances of Jesus after the Resurrection: to the women: Mt 28:1–10; to Mary Magdalen: Mk 16: 9-11; Jn 20:11-18; in Galilee: Mt 28:16–20; Mk 16: 14–18; on the road to Emmaus: Lk 24: 13-135; in the upper room: Lk 24:36–49; Jn 20:19–31; on the Sea of Tiberias: Jn 21:1–14; to many disciples: 1 Cor 15:1–11

Aquila and Priscilla: Acts 18:1–4

Ascension of Christ: Mk 16:19; Lk 24:50–53; Acts 1:6–11

asceticism: Rom 7:14–24; 1 Cor 9:24–27; Eph 5:8–20; 6:10–20; Phil 1:27–30; 3:12–16; 1 Pet 5:5–11; Rev 19:11–21

authorities: obedience and respect due to: Mk 12:13–17; Rom 13:1–7; 1 Pet 2: 13–17; Tit 3:1–2

authority: of Jesus' teachings: Mt 7:28–29

Baptism: of Jesus: Mt 3:13–17; Mk 1:19–11; Lk 3:21–22;

of many at Pentecost: Acts 2:37–41; of the Ethiopian official: Acts 8:26–40; of Paul: Acts 9:10–11; of Cornelius and his household: Acts 10:44–48; of Peter's gaoler, of children: Acts 16:25–34; a rebirth; Jn 3:1–21; 1 Pet 2:1–10; it confers a share in Christ's death and resurrection: Rom 6:1–11

Barnabas, St: Acts 4:32–37; 9:26–30; 11:19–30; 12:24–25; 13:1–15:41

Bartholomew, St: Mt 10:1–4; Mk 3:13–19; Lk 6: 12–16; Jn 1:35–51; 21:2; Acts 1:12–14

Beatitudes: Mt 5:1–12; Lk 6:20–26

Bethany: Mt 26:6–13; Mk 14:3–11; Jn 11:1–44

Bethlehem: Mt 2:1–18; Lk 2:1–20; Jn 7:42

bishops: qualities needed in: 1 Tim 3:1–7

body, the: dignity of; 1 Cor 6:12–20. See purity.

burial of Jesus: Mt 27:57–66; Mk 15:42–47; Lk 23:50–56

Caesar: tribute to: Mt 22:15–22; Mk 12:13–17; Lk 20:20–26. See authorities.

Caiaphas: Mt 26: 3, 57–68; Lk 3:2; Jn 11: 45–57; 18:13–27; Acts 4:6

calling: that of the first disciples: Mt 4:18–25; Mk 1:16–20; Lk 5:1–11; Jn 1:35–51; that of Matthew: Mt 9:9–13; Mk 2:13–17; Lk 5:27–32; the frustrated calling of the rich young man: Mt 19:16–30; Mk 10:17–29; Lk 18:18–30; that of St Paul: Acts 9:1–19; 22:1–21; 26:9–18; Gal 1:11–12; 1 Tim 1:12–13; response to: 1 Cor 7:17–24; Col 1:24–29

Cana: Jn 2:1–12; 4:46–54

celibacy: see virginity.

charisms: Rom 12:1–8; 1 Cor 12:1–31; 14:1–40

charity: of first importance: 1 Cor 13:1–13; the fullness of the Law: Rom 13: 8–14; fraternal: Gal 6:1–10; 1 Thess 4:9–12; 1 Pet 1:22–25; 4:7–11; 1 Jn 311–24; 1 Jn 4:7–21; towards one's neighbour: Rom 12:9–21; is due to everyone: Jas 2:1–13; passim are the source of discord: Jas 4:1–12. See love.

chastity: see purity.

childhood, life of: Mt 18:1–14; 19:13–15; Mk 10:13–16; Lk 9:46–50; 10:21–24; 18:15–17

children: their duties: Eph 6:1–4

Christian, the: is free of the Law: Rom 7:1–6; a son or daughter of God: Rom 8:14–30; is called to be holy: 1 Pet 1:13–16; is redeemed by Christ's blood: 1 Pet 1:17–21; is the light of the world: Phil 2:12–18; duties depending on one's position in life: Tit 2:1–10

Christians, the early: daily life: Acts 2:42–47; Acts 4:32–37; Rom 16:1–24; prayer: Acts 4:23–31; fraternal spirit: Acts 28:11–16. *Behaviour*: towards sinners: 1 Cor 5:9–13; towards one's fellow Christians in disputes: 1 Cor 6:1–11; towards waverers: Jude 22–23

son of the royal official: Jn 4:46–54; the man with the withered hand: Mt 12: 9–14; Mk 3:1–6; Lk 5:12–16; the epileptic boy: Mt 17:14–20; Mk 9:14–29; Lk 9:37–43; a woman on the sabbath: Lk 13:10–17; a paralyzed man: Mt 9:1–7; Mk 2:1–12; Lk 5:17–26; the cripple at the pool: Jn 5:1–18; the servant of a centurion: Mt 8:5–13; Lk 7:1–10; Peter's mother-in-law: Mt 8:14–15; Mk 1:29–31; Lk 4:38–39; a man deaf and dumb: Mk 7:31–36; many people at the Sea of Galilee: Mk 3:7–12; many sick people: Mt 8:16–17; Mk 1:32–34; Lk 4:40–41; many people at Gennesaret: Mt 14:34–36; Mk 53–56; many rich people: Mt 15:29–31. *To do with the elements of nature*: walking on water: Mt 14:22–32; Mk 6:45–52; Jn 6:16–21; multiplication of the loaves: Mt 14:13–21; 15:32–39; Lk 6:30–44; 8:1–10; Lk 9:10–17; Jn 6:1–15; miraculous catch of fish: Lk 5:1–11; Jn 21:1–14; calming of the storm: Mt 8:23–27; Mk 4:35–41; Lk 8:22–25. *Their meaning*: Mt 8:14–17; 15:29–16:12; Mk 2:1–12; Jn 2:1–12; 11:1–44; Acts 5:12–16

(b) *worked by apostles*: Peter and John cure a man lame from bith: Acts 3:1–11; Peter cures a lame man in Lydda: Acts 9:32–35; Peter raises Tabitha to life in Joppa: Acts 9:36–43; Paul cures a lame man in Lystra: Acts 14:8–18; Paul revives Euctyches in Troas: Acts 20:7–11

mission, apostolic: instructions given to the Twelve: Mt 10:16–42; Mk 6:6–13; Lk 9:1–6; of the seventy(-two): Lk 10:1–12; of St Paul: Eph 3:1–13

Moses: his ministry and that of Christ: Heb 3:1–6; the yoke of the Mosaic Law and that of Jesus: Mt 11:25–30; Jesus, the new Moses: Mt 2:13–18; 4:1–11; 5:17–48

neighbour: love of one's neighbour: Mt 5:17–43; 22:34–40; 25:31–46; Mk 12:28–34; Lk 10:25–37; Rom 12:9–21; we should not judge our neighbour: Mt 7:1–5 but should show him/her understanding: Rom 14:1–12

Nicodemus: Jn 3:1–36; 7:50; 19:31–42

obedience: Christ's example: Phil 2:5–11; to authorities: Rom 13:1–7; 1 Pet 2:13–17; to church pastors: Heb 13:7–19

Our Father prayer: Mt 6:5–15; Lk 11:1–4

parables: the faithful and wise steward: Lk 12:35–48; the unjust steward: Lk 16:1–15; the good Samaritan: Lk 10:25–37; the Pharisee and the tax collector: Lk 18:9–14; the mustard seed: Mt 13:31–32; Lk 13:18–19; Mk 4:30–32; the prodigal son: Lk 15:11–32; the unjust judge: Lk 18:1–8; Lazarus and the rich man: Lk 16:19–31; the rich fool: Lk 12:13–21; the sower: Mt 13:1–23; Mk 4:1–20; Lk 8:1–15; the unforgiving servant: Mt 18:21–35; the hidden treasure: Mt 13:44; the weeds: Mt 13:24–30, 36–43; the lost coin: Lk 15:8–10; the barren big-tree: Lk 13:6–9; the lamp: Mk 4:21–23; Lk 8:16–18; the leaven: Mt 13:33; Lk 13:20–21; the meas- ure: Mk 4:24–25; the lost sheep: Mt 18:12–14; Lk 15:1–7; the pearl: Mt 13:45; the net: Mt 13:47–50; the seed: Mk 4:26–29; the sheep and the goats: Mt 25:31–46;

the wise and foolish virgins: Mt 25:1–13; the two sons: Mt 21:18–32; the people invited to the marriage feast: Mt 22:1–14; Lk 14:15–24; the guests who chose the places of honour: Lk 14:7–11; the workers in the vineyard: Mt 20:1–16; the talents: Mt 25:14–30; Lk 19:11–27; the wicked tenants: Mt 21:33–46; Mk 12:1–12; Lk 20:9–19. *Meaning of the parables*: Mt 13:1–23; Mk 4:1–20; Lk 8:1–15

parents: their duties: Eph 6:1–4

patience: God's: Mt 18:21–35; Lk 13:6–9; that of the Christian; Lk 217–19; towards those who stray: 2 Tim 2:22–26

Paul, St: *Life*: calling: Heb 9:1–9; 22:1–21; 26:9–18; Gal 1:11–12; 1 Tim 1:12–13; his baptism and his early work as evangelizer: Acts 9:10–30; apostolic journeys: Acts 13:1–14: 28; 15:35–18:22; 18:23–21:16; 27:1–28; addresses: Acts 13:16–11; 17:22–31; 20: 17–35; 22:1–21; 24:10–21; 26:2–23. *Apostolic ministry*: he glories in Christ: Rom 15:22–33; 1 Cor 2: –15; why he does so: 2 Cor 11:16–12:18; visions and revelations: 2 Cor 12:1–10; severity of his life as an apostle: 1 Cor 4:8–13; he renounces everything for the sake of the apostolate: 1 Cor 9:15–23; trials: 2 Cor 4:1–12; 2 Cor 11, 21–33; his response to his calling: Col 1:24–29; the sincerity with which he acts: 2 Cor 4:1–6; his solicitude for others: Col 2:1–3; 1 Thess 2:17–20; his apostolic zeal: Acts 26:24–32. *See* Introduction to the Letters of St Paul.

peace: a gift from Jesus: Lk 24:36; Jn 14:27; 20:19–31; seeking peace: Heb 12:14–29; not losing peace in the midst of trials: Phil 4:10–20

Penance, sacrament of: Jn 20:19–31. *See* fasting; conversion; binding and loosing.

persecutions: on account of the Gospel: Mt 24:3–13; they should be faced up to bravely: Lk 12:1–12; wisdom given by God to those persecuted: Acts 4:1–12; the benefits that derive from persecutions: Acts 8:1–8; 16:19–29

perseverance: in the Christian life: Lk 8:15; 21:7–19; in prayer: Lk 18:1–7; in the faith: Heb 6:4–12; 10:19–39; 1 Jn 2:18–29; fixing one's gaze on Christ: Heb 12:1–3; despite trials: Heb 12:1–3; reasons for perseverance: 1 Pet 1:3–12; perseverance in preaching: 2 Tim 4:1–5. *See* constancy.

Peter, St: *His life at Jesus' side*: calling: Mt 4:18–25; Mk 1:16–20; Lk 5:1–11; Jn 1:35–51; he sinks in the sea due to his lack of faith: Mt 14:22–34; he acknowledges Jesus as the Messiah: Mt 16:13–20; Mk 8:27–30; Lk 9:18–21; he is made leader of the apostles: Mt 16:13–20; Jn 21:15–23; Jesus associates him in the payment of temple dues: Mt 17:22–26; Jesus foretells that Peter will deny him, and he charges him to strengthen his brethren: Lk 22:31–34; Peter denies Jesus: Mt 26:69–75; Mk 14:66–72; Jn 18:13–27; Lk 22:54–61. *His apostolic work in the early Church*: Acts 1–6; 8:1–25; 9:32–12:19; 15:1–35. *Addresses*: Acts 2:14–36; 3:11–26; 4:5–22; 10:34–43; 11:4–17; 15:7–11. *See* Introduction to the Letters of St Peter.